W9-CTW-417

Contemporary Authors

Contemporary Authors

A BIO-BIBLIOGRAPHICAL GUIDE TO
CURRENT AUTHORS AND THEIR WORKS

CLARE D. KINSMAN
Editor

volumes 53-56

GALE RESEARCH COMPANY • THE BOOK TOWER • DETROIT, MICHIGAN 48226

CONTEMPORARY AUTHORS

Published by
Gale Research Company, Book Tower, Detroit, Michigan 48226
Each Year's Volumes Are Cumulated and Revised About Five Years Later

Frederick G. Ruffner, *Publisher* James M. Ethridge, *Editorial Director*

Clare D. Kinsman, *Editor*
Cynthia R. Fadool and Alexander James Roman, *Associate Editors*
Adele C. Sarkissian, *Assistant Editor*
Anne Commire, *Consultant*
Eunice Bergin, *Copy Editor*
Laura Bryant, *Operations Supervisor*
Daphne Cox, *Production Manager*

WRITERS

Linda Cairo, Laurelyn Niebuhr,
Mary Reif Stevenson, Benjamin True

EDITORIAL ASSISTANTS

Frances Locher, Norma Sawaya, Shirley Seip

ISBN 0-8103-0022-2

CONTEMPORARY AUTHORS

**Indicates that a listing has been compiled from secondary sources believed to be reliable, but has not been personally verified for this edition by the author sketched.*

ABBOTT, Rowland A(ubrey) S(amuel) 1909-

PERSONAL: Born November 17, 1909, in Oxford, England; son of George Samuel and Fanny E. (Smith) Abbott; married Nancy Mary Bashforth (a secretary), July 4, 1938. *Education:* Attended high school in Oxford, England. *Home:* 8 Springfield Rd., Old Botley, Oxford OX2 9HJ, England.

CAREER: Oxford Electric Co., Oxford, England, electrical engineer, 1926-32; City of Oxford Electricity Supply Department, Oxford, England, electrical engineer, 1932-48; Southern Electricity Board, Oxford, England, electrical engineer, 1948-74. *Member:* Newcomen Society, Talyllyn Railway Preservation Society.

WRITINGS: The Fairlie Locomotive, David & Charles, 1970; *Crane Locomotives*, Goose & Son, 1974. Contributor to proceedings and to *Engineer, Engineering, Model Engineer, Locomotive*, and *Country Life*.

AVOCATIONAL INTERESTS: Travel, archaeology, architecture, ships.

* * *

ABDELSAMAD, Moustafa H(assan) 1941-

PERSONAL: Born March 12, 1941, in Cairo, Egypt; son of Hassan S. and Fatmah (Abou-Awad) Abdelsamad; married Margaret Dinneen, December 26, 1968. *Education:* Cairo University, B.Commerce, 1961; George Washington University, M.B.A., 1965, D.B.A., 1970. *Home:* 1101 J North Hamilton St., Richmond, Va. 23221. *Office:* Department of Business Administration, Virginia Commonwealth University, Richmond, Va. 23284.

CAREER: Virginia Commonwealth University, Richmond, Va., assistant professor, 1968-72, associate professor of business administration, 1972—. *Member:* Academy of Management, American Accounting Association, American Finance Association, Financial Management Association, Society for Advancement of Management (chapter president, 1974-75), Eastern Finance Association, Southern Finance Association, Virginia Social Science Association, Alpha Kappa Psi.

WRITINGS: A Guide to Capital Expenditure Analysis, American Management Association, 1973. Contributor to business and management journals, including *Accounting Review, Administrative Management, Management Adviser, Training and Development Journal*, and *Virginia Social Science Journal*.

WORK IN PROGRESS: Research on financial management, especially budgeting, and on publication of forecasted financial statements.

* * *

ABERNATHY, David M(yles) 1933-

PERSONAL: Born June 27, 1933, in Connelly Springs, N.C.; son of James William and Lorena (Alexander) Abernathy; married Kathryn Lynn Fordham, October 16, 1971; *Education:* High Point College, A.B., 1955; University of Maryland, Tokyo Campus, graduate study, 1956-57; Emory University, M.Div., 1962; Union Theological Seminary, New York, N.Y., S.T.M., 1964; RCA Institutes, diplomate, 1964; graduate study at Columbia University and New School for Social Research, 1964-65.

CAREER: University of Maryland, Tokyo Campus, Tokyo, Japan, instructor in English, 1957-59; Atlanta University, Atlanta, Ga., visiting instructor in communications, 1961-63; Emory University, Atlanta, Ga., visiting adjunct professor of communications, 1965-72, visiting instructor in speech, 1969-70; Sandpiper Productions (producer of films and radio and television productions), Atlanta, Ga., president, 1967—. Instructor in advertising and marketing, Massey College, 1969-70; Beall Memorial Humanities Lecturer, Lon Morris College, 1974. Producer, director, and writer for radio, television, and motion pictures, 1955—; producer and director, "The Protestant Hour," nationally syndicated radio program, 1959—; producer of television commercials, 1960—. Lieutenant colonel and aide-de-camp, staff of governor of Georgia, 1971-74. Member of board of trustees, CRISIS, Inc.; member of advisory board, Protestant Radio and Television Center. *Military service:* U.S. Air Force, 1956-59; served in Japan.

Member: American Society of Composers, Authors and Publishers, National Education Association, National Academy of Recording Arts and Sciences. *Awards, honors:* Far East Network Gold Mike Award, 1959, for exceptional performance; LL.D., Institute of Communicative Arts, Atlanta, Ga., 1970; Litt.D., Rust College, 1974.

WRITINGS: (Editor with Theodore H. Runyon) *Theology for the Layman*, SLP Publishing Co., 1962; (editor with

Norman H. Perrin) *The Teaching of Jesus*, CRS Publishing, 1963; *A Child's Guidebook to Rome*, Guiseppe Publishing (Rome), 1964; (editor) *Reflections*, Massey College Press, 1969; (with Wayne Knipe) *Ideas, Inventions and Patents*, Pioneer Press (Atlanta), 1973, 2nd edition, 1974; *The Plight of the Independent Inventor in America Today* (pamphlet), Pioneer Press, 1974.

Author of plays, "J.W.," 1963, "Never Look Up," 1964, and "The Bridge," 1972. Author of radio documentary on Methodism, "Methodism on the Move," broadcast by NBC, 1963. Contributor to *Junction* (of Emory University).

WORK IN PROGRESS: Copyright Procedure; Fundamentals of Communication.

* * *

ABLER, Ronald 1939-

PERSONAL: Born May 30, 1939, in Milwaukee, Wis.; son of Ambrose F. (an executive) and Lucille (a secretary; maiden name, Chartraw) Abler; married Rosella Lanz, February 27, 1960; children: Frederick, Kenneth. *Education:* University of Minnesota, B.A., 1963, M.A., 1966, Ph.D., 1968. *Politics:* Independent. *Religion:* Independent. *Home:* 721 Holmes Ave., State College, Pa. 16801. *Office:* Department of Geography, Pennsylvania State University, 403 Deike Bldg., University Park, Pa. 16802.

CAREER: Pennsylvania State University, University Park, assistant professor, 1967-71, associate professor of geography, 1971—. Visiting professor at University of British Columbia, 1971, and University of Minnesota, 1972-74. *Member:* International Communications Association, Association of American Geographers, Canadian Association of Geographers, American Association for the Advancement of Science, World Future Society, Postal History Society, American Geographical Society of New York.

WRITINGS: (With John S. Adams and Peter R. Gould) *Spatial Organization: The Geographer's View of the World*, Prentice-Hall, 1971; (editor with others) *Human Geography in a Shrinking World*, Duxbury Press, 1975.

WORK IN PROGRESS: A Geography of Communications.

* * *

ABSE, Dannie 1923-

PERSONAL: Born September 22, 1923, in Cardiff, Wales; son of Rudy (a cinema theatre owner) and Kate (Shepherd) Abse; married Joan Mercer (an art historian), August 4, 1951; children: Keren, Susanna, David. *Education:* Studied at University of Wales, 1941-42, and at Kings College, London, and Westminster Hospital; Royal College of Surgeons, M.R.C.S., 1949; Royal College of Physicians, L.R.C.P., 1950. *Home:* 85 Hodford Rd., London NW. 11, England; and Green Hollows, Craig-yr-Eos Rd., Ogmore-by-Sea, Glamorgan, Wales. *Agent:* Anthony Sheil, 52 Floral St., London WC 2, England.

CAREER: Physician, part-time, at chest clinic in Soho, London, England, 1955—; free-lance writer, 1955—. Writer-in-residence, Princeton University, 1973-74. *Military service:* Royal Air Force, 1951-55; became Squadron Leader. *Awards, honors:* Charles Henry Foyle award, 1960, for "House of Cowards"; Welsh Arts Council Literature award, and Jewish Chronicle book award, both 1970, for *Selected Poems*.

WRITINGS—Poetry: *After Every Green Thing*, Hutchinson, 1949; *Walking Under Water*, Hutchinson, 1952; *Tenants of the House*, Hutchinson, 1957; *Poems, Golders Green*, Hutchinson, 1962; *Dannie Abse: A Selection*, Studio Vista, 1963; *A Small Desperation*, Hutchinson, 1968; *Selected Poems*, Oxford University Press, 1970; *Funland, and Other Poems*, Oxford University Press, 1973.

Novels: *Ash on a Young Man's Sleeve*, Hutchinson, 1954; *Some Corner of an English Field*, Hutchinson, 1956; *O.Jones, O.Jones*, Hutchinson, 1970.

Plays: *Fire in Heaven* (three-act; verse; first produced in London, England, by Group 28, 1948), Hutchinson, 1956, revised prose version produced as "Is the House Shut?" by Questors Company in West London, 1964, and published as "In the Cage" (see below); "Hands Around the Wall" (three-act), first produced in London at Embassy Theatre, 1950; *The Eccentric* (one-act; first produced in London at Mountview Theatre, 1961), Evans Brothers, 1961; "The Joker" (two-act), first produced by Questors Company in West London, 1962; *Three Questor Plays* (includes "In the Cage," "House of Cowards" [three-act] first produced by Questors Company in West London, 1960, and "Gone" [one-act], first produced by Questors Company in West London, 1962), Scorpion Press, 1967; *The Dogs of Pavlov* (three-act; first produced in London by Questors Company, 1969), Vallentine, Mitchell, 1973.

Radio plays: "Conform or Die," 1957; "No Telegrams, No Thunder," 1962; "You Can't Say Hello to Anybody," 1964; "A Small Explosion," 1964; "The Courting of Essie Glass," 1975.

Other: (Editor with Howard Sergeant) *Mavericks*, Editions Poetry and Poverty, 1957; (editor) *European Verse*, Studio Vista, 1964; *Medicine on Trial*, Aldus Books, 1967, Crown, 1969; (editor) *Modern Poets in Focus*, Corgi Books, numbers 1, 3, 5, 1970—; *A Poet in the Family*, Hutchinson, 1974.

Poems represented in anthologies, including: *Faber Book of Twentieth Century Verse*, edited by J.F.A. Heath-Stubbs and D. H. Wright, Faber, 1953; *Presenting Welsh Poetry*, edited by Gwyn Williams, Dufour, 1959; *An Anthology of Modern Verse*, edited by Elizabeth Jennings, Methuen, 1961; *Mid-Century: English Poetry, 1940-60*, edited by Wright, Dent, 1967; *Lilting House*, edited by John S. Williams and Meic Stephens, Dent, 1969. Plays anthologized in *Best One-Act Plays, 1960-1961*, edited by Hugh Miller, Harrap, 1963; *Twelve Great Plays*, edited by L. F. Dean, Harcourt, 1970. Contributor to *New Yorker*, *Encounter*, and *Times Literary Supplement*.

WORK IN PROGRESS: Editing *Poetry Dimension—The Best of the Poetry Year*, for Robson Books.

SIDELIGHTS: Of *Funland, and Other Poems*, Alan Brownjohn wrote in the *New Statesman:* "Mystery and disquiet, while never entirely absent from the work of this informal, highly approachable poet, have indeed stayed mainly, until now, on the far side of a wall of geniality and reticence. The difference in this new book is that quite a lot of the unease, the genuine alarm, behind Abse's invariably honest yet frequently calm and relaxed writing has now been let out into the open. The new atmosphere isn't an unqualified success. 'Funland' itself . . . is desperately uneven; by turns, ingeniously lurid and peculiarly heavy in the achievement of its effects, a freewheeling fantasy that runs out of control. But in the substantial batch of shorter poems preceding it, the increasing range of theme, the new openness of approach, is impressive."

BIOGRAPHICAL/CRITICAL SOURCES: Anglo-Welsh Review, winter, 1967; Jeremy Robsen, editor, *Modern Poets in Focus, No. 4*, Corgi, 1972; *Nassau Literary Review*, spring, 1974.

* * *

ACKERMAN, Bruce A. 1943-

PERSONAL: Born August 19, 1943, in New York, N.Y.; son of Nathan and Jean (Rosenberg) Ackerman; married Susan Rose (an economist), May, 1967; children: Sybil, John. *Education:* Harvard University, B.A., 1964; Yale University, LL.B., 1967. *Office:* School of Law, Yale University, New Haven, Conn. 06520.

CAREER: University of Pennsylvania, Philadelphia, 1969-74, began as assistant professor, became professor of law and public policy analysis; Yale University, New Haven, Conn., professor of law, 1974—.

WRITINGS: (With wife, Susan Rose-Ackerman, Dale Henderson, and James Sawyer) *Uncertain Search for Environmental Quality*, Free Press, 1974; (editor) *Economic Foundations of Property Law*, Little, Brown, 1975.

WORK IN PROGRESS: A book on political philosophy, *Social Justice in the Liberal State*, completion expected in 1977.

* * *

ACKERMAN, J. Mark 1939-

PERSONAL: Born February 14, 1939, in Azusa, Calif.; son of Charles DeWitt and Genevieve (Chapman) Ackerman; married Cyrena Parker (an elementary school teacher), June 25, 1960; children: Alan, George. *Education:* Pomona College, B.A., 1964; University of Colorado, M.A., 1967, Ph.D., 1968. *Religion:* Christian. *Home:* 145 Peach Tree Lane, Albany, Ore. 97321. *Office:* Professional Plaza, 2825 Willeta, Suite B, Albany, Ore. 97321.

CAREER: Clinical psychologist in private practice in Albany, Ore., 1968—. Linn County Clinic, Albany, Ore., consulting psychologist, 1968-74; Vocational Rehabilitation Division, Albany, Ore., psychological consultant, 1970—. Adjunct professor at University of Oregon, 1970—. *Military service:* U.S. Air Force, 1956-60. *Member:* American Psychological Association, American Association for the Advancement of Behavior Therapy, American Society of Clinical Hypnosis, Council for the Advancement of Professional Psychology, Oregon Psychological Association (treasurer, 1974—).

WRITINGS: Operant Conditioning Techniques for the Classroom Teacher, Scott, Foresman, 1972; (with John L. Shelton) *Homework in Counseling and Psychotherapy*, C. C Thomas, 1974.

WORK IN PROGRESS: Research on biofeedback in treating muscle spasms and pain; studies in self-control of affects, behavior, cognitions, and sensations through systematic home practice.

AVOCATIONAL INTERESTS: Long-distance running, cross-country skiing, radio-controlled power and sail planes.

* * *

ACKLEY, Randall William 1931-

PERSONAL: Born August 9, 1931, in Minneapolis, Minn.; son of Randall Carol (a taxicab driver) and Katherine (Klym) Ackley; married Rosamartha Morales, May 21, 1956 (divorced); married Brenda Williams, October 30, 1970 (divorced); children: (first marriage) Linda M., Randall A., Holly E.; (second marriage) Katherine-Caritas R. *Education:* University of Minnesota, B.A. (magna cum laude), 1962; Union Graduate School, Yellow Springs, Ohio, Ph.D., 1974. *Politics:* Democrat. *Religion:* Roman Catholic. *Home:* 412 Northeast Fifth St., Minneapolis, Minn. 55413. *Office:* Navajo Community College, Tsaile Lake, Navajo, N.M. 87328.

CAREER: National Defense Education Act fellow at Rice University, 1962-65; University of Texas, Austin, instructor in English, 1965-66; University of Utah, Salt Lake City, assistant professor of English, 1966-67; University of the Americas, Mexico City, Mexico, assistant professor of English, 1967; University of Texas, El Paso, assistant professor of English, 1967-68; associate professor of English at St. Mary's College, 1968-69; McMurry College, Abilene, Tex., associate professor of English and chairman of department, 1969-70; Pembroke State University, Pembroke, N.C., associate professor of English, 1970-72; Navajo Community College, Navajo, N.M., coordinator of English program, 1973—. *Military service:* U.S. Marine Corps, 1948-50. U.S. Navy, 1950. U.S. Air Force, 1951-52. U.S. Army, 1952-54, 56-60; served in Korea; became first lieutenant.

MEMBER: Modern Language Association of America, Association for Studies in American Indian Literature (chairman, 1971—), American Association of University Professors, Coordinating Council of Literary Magazines, Southwest Poets Conference (director, 1969—), Phi Beta Kappa, Sigma Tau Delta. *Awards, honors:* Litt.D. from Rockdale College, 1971; fellow of International Poetry Society, 1972; grants from North Carolina Arts Council, 1970-72, and Coordinating Council of Literary Magazines, 1971-74.

WRITINGS—Poems: *Troll Songs,* Tribal Press, 1970; *Sea Troll Songs,* Solo Press, 1974; *Listen to the Wind,* Gypsy Press, in press. Contributor to about forty journals, including *Last Journal of the Tibetan Kite Society.* Poetry editor of *Conradiana,* 1969-74; editor of *Quetzal,* 1970—; associate editor of *Pembroke,* 1970-72; consulting editor for *St. Andrews Review,* 1971-72; organizer and editorial writer for *Carolina Indian Voice,* 1972—; guest editor of *Out of Sight,* 1972, and *Cafe Solo,* 1974.

WORK IN PROGRESS: Editing and writing material for *The River,* a book on the cultures of the Southwest following the Rio Grande; expanding *Listen to the Wind;* a book from American Indian literature.

SIDELIGHTS: Ackley has traveled in Mexico for more than twenty years, most recently visiting ancient sites at Puerto Angel and Tulum. He writes that he has been "influenced by the land and rivers now, before this by contemporary Indians, before that by medieval allegory, T. S. Eliot, Yeats, Shakespeare; before that by dreams."

* * *

ADAM, Michael 1919-

PERSONAL: Born February 27, 1919, in India; married, wife's name, Eya; children: Noah Michael, Shane Maya. *Education:* "Does not seem very relevant—learned to read and write at some schools and college but not very much else that matters." *Politics:* None. *Home:* Sullys, Brushford, Dulverton, Somerset, England. *Agent:* Laurence Pollinger Ltd., 18 Maddox St., London W.1, England.

CAREER: Art in Industry, Calcutta, India, editor, 1946-49; Dartington Hall, Devon, England, teacher, 1954-55; *Graphis Magazine*, Zurich, Switzerland, associate editor, 1955-59; University of Texas, Austin, 1960-69, became professor of art.

WRITINGS: A Matter of Death and Life, Ark Press, 1959; *The Labour of Love*, Ark Press, 1962; *Man Is a Little World*, Ark Press, 1969; *The Wild Strange Place*, Ark Press, 1971.

Editor: D. H. Lawrence, *The Body of God*, Ark Press, 1970. Also editor of *The Cry of a Gull: Journals of Alyse Gregory*. Associate editor, Texas Quarterly.

WORK IN PROGRESS: Four books, *Wandering in Eden: Three Ways to the East of Ourselves; Man Is a Sun and a Moon*, autobiographical journals; *Alive, Alive-O: A Paean for Pia Malone; A Fool in a Garden: The Contemplations of a Retired Clown.*

SIDELIGHTS: Of *The Wild Strange Place*, Trevor Allen has written: "How much of his story is authentic I don't know—or care. He is vague about his war service, his job in India, presumably because he is writing 'notes,'' not a full autobiography. At times he achieves rhetoric, yet also that deeply-felt fervour we associate with genius. Genius? I shy at the word, it is like shouting in a temple, outsinging everyone else in church. But I think he comes near it, and anyone acquiring this unusual book will cherish it as something personal to re-read, talk of and show to friends—indeed, a discovery."

* * *

ADAMS, Arthur Merrihew 1908-

PERSONAL: Born September 28, 1908, in Philadelphia, Pa.; son of Alexander Mackie (an architect) and Laura (a writer and speaker; maiden name, Merrihew) Adams; married Margaret Baker, October 23, 1934; children: Robert Merrihew, Janet Dickinson (Mrs. Henry Dana Fearon III). *Education:* University of Pennsylvania, A.B., 1931; Princeton Theological Seminary, Th.B., 1934. *Home:* 58 Mercer St., Princeton, N.J. 08540. *Office:* Princeton Theological Seminary, Princeton, N.J. 08540.

CAREER: Ordained minister of United Presbyterian Church, 1934; pastor in Philadelphia, Pa., 1934-44, Albany, N.Y., 1945-50, and Rochester, N.Y., 1950-62; Princeton Theological Seminary, Princeton, N.J., professor of practical theology, 1962—, dean, 1967—. Visiting professor at Pacific School of Religion, summer, 1966. Member of board of directors, Presbyterian Ministers' Fund, 1952—; trustee of Princeton Theological Seminary, 1955-62; member of United Presbyterian Council on Theological Education, 1957-62, 1965—; member of County Commission on Human Relations, Monroe County, N.Y., 1959-62; trustee of Princeton United Fund; member of board of United Presbyterian Vocation Agency, 1973—. *Member:* Society for Continuing Education of Ministers. *Awards, honors:* D.D., Beaver College, 1951.

WRITINGS: Pastoral Administration, Westminster, 1964; (editor) *Administration in the Church*, Office of General Assembly, United Presbyterian Church in U.S.A., 1970.

* * *

ADAMS, Laura 1943-

PERSONAL: Born March 6, 1943, in Detroit, Mich.; daughter of Herbert E. (an engineer) and Sophia (a teacher; maiden name, Lees) Clark; married Robert Ernest Adams (a corporaton executive), September 8, 1962; children: Thomas Clark. *Education:* Purdue University, B.A., 1963; Montclair State College, M.A., 1966; McMaster University, Ph.D., 1972. *Home:* 646 Banbury Rd., Dayton, Ohio 45459. *Office:* Department of English, Wright State University, Dayton, Ohio 45431.

CAREER: High school English and social studies teacher in Dayton, Ohio, 1963-64, Passaic, N.J., 1964-66, and Montclair, N.J., 1966-67; Montclair State College, Montclair, N.J., assistant professor II of English, 1966-67; Sinclair Community College, Dayton, Ohio, instructor in English, 1972; Wright State University, Dayton, Ohio, assistant professor of English, 1972—, director of freshman English, 1974—. *Member:* Modern Language Association of America, College English Association, Canadian Association for American Studies, Midwest Modern Language Association, College English Association of Ohio.

WRITINGS: (Editor) *Will the Real Norman Mailer Please Stand Up?*, Kennikat, 1974; *Norman Mailer: A Comprehensive Bibliography*, Scarecrow, 1974; *Norman Mailer's Aesthetics of Growth*, Ohio University Press, in press. Contributor of articles and reviews to *Victorian Poetry, Modern Fiction Studies*, and to newspapers.

WORK IN PROGRESS: Women's studies.

* * *

ADAMS, Laurie 1941-
(Laurie Schneider)

PERSONAL: Born September 29, 1941, in New York, N.Y.; daughter of Daniel E. (a physician) and Helen (a nurse; maiden name, Nelson) Schneider; married John Adams (an investment banker), July, 1970; children: Alexa. *Education:* Sophie Newcomb College, B.A., 1962; Columbia University, M.A. (art history), 1963, M.A. (psychology), 1964, Ph.D., 1967. *Office:* Department of Art History, John Jay College of Criminal Justice, City University of New York, 444 West 56th St., New York, N.Y.

CAREER: City University of New York, John Jay College of Criminal Justice, New York, N.Y., assistant professor, 1967-73, associate professor of art history, 1973—.

WRITINGS: Art Cop, Dodd, 1974; (under name Laurie Schneider) *Giotto in Perspective*, Prentice-Hall, 1974. Contributor to scholarly journals.

* * *

ADAMS, Russell L. 1930-

PERSONAL: Born August 13, 1930, in Baltimore, Md.; son of James Russell and Lilly B. (Ponder) Adams; married Eleanor P. McCurine, August 3, 1963; children: Sabrina, Russell Lowell. *Education:* Morehouse College, B.A., 1952; University of Chicago, M.A., 1954, Ph.D., 1971. *Home:* 2414 Fairhill Dr., Suitland, Md. 20023. *Office:* Afro-American Studies Department, 319 Founder Library, Howard University, Washington, D.C. 20059.

CAREER: North Carolina Central University, Durham, assistant professor of political science, 1965-69, chairman of department, 1967-69; Federal City College, Washington, D.C., associate professor of political science and assistant chairman of Division of Humanities, 1969-71; Howard University, Washington, D.C., professor of Afro-American studies, 1971—, chairman of department, 1971—. *Member:* American Political Science Association (chairman of committee on status of Blacks, 1974-76), National Conference of Black Political Scientists, National Association for the

Study of Afro-American Life and History, National Association for the Advancement of Colored People (NAACP). *Awards, honors:* George Washington Honor Medal, 1966, for "Leading American Negroes."

WRITINGS: Great Negroes Past and Present, Afro-American Publishing, 1963, 3rd revised edition, 1972. Author of "Leading American Negroes," a series of film strips, 1966.

WORK IN PROGRESS: Black Voluntary Association in the Nineteenth Century; Racial Foundations of Modern American Social Science.

* * *

ADAMSON, Donald 1939-

PERSONAL: Born March 30, 1939, in Culcheth, Cheshire, England; son of Donald (a farmer) and Hannah (Booth) Adamson; married Helen Griffiths, September 24, 1966; children: Richard, John. *Education:* Magdalen College, Oxford, B.A., 1959, B.Litt., 1962, M.A., 1963, D.Phil., 1971; also studied at Sorbonne, University of Paris, 1960-61. *Politics:* Conservative. *Religion:* Church of England. *Home:* Dodmore House, The Street, Meopham, Kent DA13 OAJ, England. *Agent:* Curtis Brown, Ltd., 1 Craven Hill, London W2 3EP, England. *Office:* Goldsmiths' College, London SE14 6NW, England.

CAREER: Lycee Louis-le-Grand, Paris, France, lecturer in English, 1964-65; J. Walter Thompson Co., London, England, account executive, 1965-67; head of department of modern languages in school in Gravesend, England, 1968; Goldsmiths' College, London, England, lecturer, 1969-70, senior lecturer in French, 1970—. Recognized teacher of University of London, 1971—, and University of London's Institute of Education, 1972—. Freeman of City of London, 1969. *Member:* Society for French Studies, Royal Automobile Club, Carlton Club, Bow Group (convenor, 1969-71; member of research council, 1971-73).

WRITINGS: The Genesis of "Le Cousin Pons," Oxford University Press, 1966; *Dusty Heritage: A National Policy for Museums and Libraries,* Bow Publications, 1971; (editor) *T. S. Eliot: A Memoir by the Late Robert Sencourt*, Dodd, 1971; (with Peter Beauclerk Dewar) *The House of Nell Gwyn: The Fortunes of the Beauclerk Family, 1670-1974*, William Kimber, 1974.

Translator: Honore de Balzac, *The Black Sheep*, Penguin, 1970; Balzac, *Ursule Mirouet*, Penguin, in press. Contributor to language journals, including *Modern Language Review, Nineteenth-Century French Studies*, and *Symposium.*

WORK IN PROGRESS: The Savage Impulse, a novel; a history of the Cavendish family, dukes of Devonshire; criticism of Balzac; a critical and biographical study of T. S. Eliot, with reference to his religious, sociological and philosophical views, completion expected in 1978.

SIDELIGHTS: Adamson writes: "I am fairly fluent in three languages—French, German, and Italian—and in learning them have travelled quite extensively. For two years I enjoyed Paris. . . . In the narrow 'professional' sense I am a literary critic and historian. . . . However, I do not think of myself as an academic so much as a writer. For the writer belongs to the world. . . . Involvement with the world's action is what I most admire in Balzac's novels; involvement with its logical structures is matchlessly present in Flaubert's works. . . . As novelists, Balzac and Flaubert seem to me incomparable. And from this concern with involvement stem, I suppose, my own political activities, more or less continuous now for eighteen years. The world has to be run, and the more the writer is involved in running the world—even if at one remove—the better. Much of the best modern literature is journalism.

"In all my books, apart from the one on Balzac, I have tried to relate in the way poetry basically relates: aiming, in other words, at a 'criticism of life.' The Balzac book was the study in depth of the evolution of one novel, but there are too many studies in depth in the world, too few in breadth. Heaven may be discernible in a wild flower, but rarely if ever in a doctoral dissertation! The words Matthew Arnold applied to criticism I would apply equally to the whole of literature: that its function is 'the creating a current of true and fresh ideas'—not merely ideas in relation to books, but principally ideas in relation to life.

"This concern both with transmitted experience (as a critic) and with personal experience (as a sentient human being) has led me to embark on a novel, in which the hero's and others' impulse to action, never entirely assuaged, endlessly cramped by the rootless contingencies of the modern world, is seen from various standpoints as a life-enhancing challenge, an inevitable moral compromise, a tragicomic adventure. . . . But the sense of a life—and even that of communal existence—is nowadays more intensely hard to convey than it was in Balzac's time. The contemporary novel has nearly reached the borderlines of expression. We are almost back to Novalis, which is no bad thing except that Novalis did not complete his masterpiece.

"If man is to have a sense not only of his own life but of a meaningful destiny, he must remain, or become, vividly aware of the past. Hence (I suppose) my involvement with history in many of its forms, and the joy I feel in the surroundings of my own home in England, whose walls date from the fourteenth century and where a manor-house has stood for seven hundred years. I'm starting to write the history of some of its early owners, the Cavendish family. Only through a sense of the past can a man find his true identity: this is the profound message of conservatism. . . .

"So, hardly surprisingly, my recreations include genealogy and local history—just as my working day includes politics."

AVOCATIONAL INTERESTS: Motoring, swimming, gastronomy.

* * *

ADAMSON, Wendy Wriston 1942-

PERSONAL: Born June 25, 1942, in Glens Falls, N.Y.; daughter of George W. (a stockbroker) and Gladys (Micks) Wriston; married William De Lancey Adamson (a teacher), 1965; children: Edward De Lancey. *Education:* Syracuse University, B.A., 1964; Simmons College, M.L.S., 1971. *Home:* 3616 40th Ave. S., Minneapolis, Minn. 55406. *Office:* Environmental Library of Minnesota, Minneapolis, Minn.

CAREER: Brown University, Providence, R.I., government documents assistant in library, 1967-68; Macalester College, St. Paul, Minn., assistant reference librarian, 1969-71; Minneapolis Public Library, Minneapolis, Minn., librarian in Environmental Conservation Library, 1971-72; Environmental Library of Minnesota, Minneapolis, librarian, 1972—.

WRITINGS: Saving Lake Superior: A Story of Environmental Action, Dillon, 1974.

ADAS, Michael 1943-

PERSONAL: Born February 4, 1943, in Detroit, Mich.; son of Harold A. (a sales representative) and Elizabeth (Rivard) Adas; married Jane Hampton, June 18, 1967; children: Joel, Claire. *Education:* Western Michigan University, B.A. (summa cum laude), 1965; University of Wisconsin, M.A. (history), 1968, M.A. (Indian studies), 1967, Ph.D., 1971. *Politics:* Democrat. *Home:* 232 Blake Ave., Somerset, N.J. 08873. *Office:* Department of History, Rutgers University, New Brunswick, N.J. 08903.

CAREER: Rutgers University, New Brunswick, N.J., assistant professor, 1971-74, associate professor of history, 1974—. *Member:* Association for Asian Studies, American Association of University Professors. *Awards, honors:* Woodrow Wilson fellowship, 1965-66; Fulbright fellowship to England, 1969-70.

WRITINGS: The Burma Delta: Economic Development and Social Change on an Asian Rice Frontier, 1852-1941, University of Wisconsin Press, 1974. Contributor of articles and reviews to *Journal of Southeast Asian Studies, Journal of Asian Studies, Journal of Asian History, Journal of Economic History*, and *Journal of Social History*.

WORK IN PROGRESS: A book, *Peasant Protest and 'Revitalization' Movements under European Colonial Regimes: A Comparative Analysis*, completion expected in 1975; a study of U.S. foreign policy and the peasant movements in Asia.

AVOCATIONAL INTERESTS: Travel, photography.

* * *

ADE, Walter Frank Charles 1910-

PERSONAL: Born October 24, 1910, in Ottawa, Ontario, Canada; son of Leonard (a sales manager) and Bertha Pauline (Rhode) Ade; married Eleanor Anne Schroeder, June 28, 1941; children: Virginia Anne (Mrs. Robert H. Miller, Jr.), George Leonard. *Education:* Queen's University at Kingston, B.A. (honors), 1933; University of Toronto, M.A., 1939, B.Paed. and M.Ed., 1943; Northwestern University, Ph.D., 1949; Indiana University, M.Sc., 1955, Ed.D., 1960; postdoctoral study at University of Erlangen, University of Munich, and University of Heidelberg, 1955-56. *Religion:* Protestant. *Home:* 8021 Schreiber Dr., Munster, Ind. 46321. *Office:* C & O Building 212A, Purdue University, Hammond, Ind. 46323.

CAREER: University of Toronto, Ontario Agricultural College, Toronto, lecturer in German, French, and English, 1933-37; Lisgar Collegiate Institute, Ottawa, Ontario, modern language specialist, 1939-49; Valparaiso University, Valparaiso, Ind., assistant professor, 1949-51, associate professor of modern languages, 1951-58; Arizona State University, Tempe, associate professor of German language and literature, 1958-59; Purdue University, Hammond Center, Hammond, Ind., professor of modern languages and education, 1959—. Examiner in German, Canada Civil Service, 1940-45; Fulbright professor, Humanistic Gymnasium, 1955-56. *Military service:* Royal Canadian Air Force, 1943-45; became flying officer.

MEMBER: Mediaeval Academy of America, Modern Language Association of America, American Association of University Professors, American Association of Teachers of French, Renaissance Society of America, American Association of Teachers of German, Indiana Foreign Language Teachers' Association, Sigma Phi Epsilon (life member), Kappa Phi Tau (life member), Munster (Indiana) Chamber of Commerce, Canadian Club of Chicago. *Awards, honors:* Purdue University Research Foundation grant, summer, 1964.

WRITINGS—Translator and author of introduction; all published by Barron's: Moliere, *The Physician in Spite of Himself*, 1967; Moliere, *The School for Husbands*, 1967; Gotthold Lessing, *Nathan the Wise*, 1972; Prosper Merimee, *Carmen*, 1973. Also author of monographs and of poetry collections, including "Siren Song," "Mermaid Magic," and "Swan Song." Contributor of thirty-six articles to scholarly journals in United States, Canada, Germany, and Belgium.

SIDELIGHTS: Ade has traveled extensively throughout North America and Europe, and spent 101 days at sea on an around-the-world voyage in 1967.

* * *

ADENEY, David Howard 1911-

PERSONAL: Born November 3, 1911, in Bedford, England; son of John Howard (an Anglican minister) and Florence (Woods) Adeney; married Ruth Temple, March 31, 1938; children: Rosemary Joy (Mrs. Kenneth Chandler), John Arthur, Michael David, Bernard Temple. *Education:* Queens' College, Cambridge, M.A., 1933. *Home:* 33H Gilstead Rd., Singapore 11. *Office:* Discipleship Training Centre, 33A Chancery La., Singapore 11.

CAREER: Missionary with China Inland Mission in Fangcheng, Honan, China, 1934-41, and in Nanking, China, 1946-50; Inter-Varsity Christian Fellowship, Chicago, Ill., missionary director, 1952-56; International Fellowship of Evangelical Students, Hongkong, associate general secretary for the Far East, 1956-68; Discipleship Training Centre, Asian Centre for Theological Studies, Singapore, founder and dean, 1968—. Vice-president of International Fellowship of Evangelical Students, 1969—.

WRITINGS: Unchanging Commission, Inter-Varsity Press, 1955; *Before Missionary Service*, Tyndale Press, 1967; *China-Christian Students Face the Revolution*, Inter-Varsity Press, 1973. Contributor to *His* and *Christianity Today*. Consulting editor of *Way*, 1956-68.

SIDELIGHTS: Adeney told *CA:* "My book, *China-Christian Students Face the Revolution* contains the story of my work with students in China, 1946-50. We spent fifteen months under the communist regime. We were also in China during part of the war with Japan and passed through a number of difficult experiences when the Japanese army occupied the city in which we were living. I speak Chinese (Mandarin). For twelve years I travelled in Asian countries lecturing and visiting Christian student university groups from Korea to India."

Adeney's books have been published in Chinese, Portuguese, and Finnish editions.

* * *

ADLER, Jacob 1873(?)-1974
(B. Kovner)

1873(?)—December 31, 1974; Austrian-born American Yiddish humorist and writer. Obituaries: *New York Times*, January 1, 1975; *Washington Post*, January 2, 1975; *Publishers Weekly*, February 10, 1975.

* * *

AGBODEKA, Francis 1931-

PERSONAL: Born December 31, 1931, in Anloga, Ghana;

son of Simon Amuzu (a farmer) and Vicentia (a trader; maiden name, Agudu) Agbodeka; married Margaret Nyomi (a teacher), September 15, 1956; children: Kobla, Adjoa, Awo. *Education:* Attended University College of Gold Coast, 1953-56; University of London, B.A., 1956; University of Ghana, Ph.D., 1968. *Home:* 5 Ferguson Rd., University of Cape Coast, Cape Coast, Ghana. *Office:* Department of History, University of Cape Coast, Cape Coast, Ghana.

CAREER: Adisadel College, Cape Coast, Ghana, teacher of history, 1956-60; University of Cape Coast, Cape Coast, Ghana, lecturer, 1962-64, senior lecturer, 1965-70, associate professor of history, 1971—, head of department, 1971—, dean of Faculty of Arts, 1974—, pro-vice chancellor of university, 1974—. Visiting associate professor at Northwestern University, 1972-73. Honorary keeper of West African Historical Museum. *Member:* Historical Society of Ghana (fellow), African Studies Association.

WRITINGS: The Rise of the Nation States, Thomas Nelson, 1965; *African Politics and British Policy in the Gold Coast: 1868-1900*, Northwestern University Press, 1971; *Ghana in the Twentieth Century*, Ghana Universities Press, 1972. Contributor to *Journal of the University of Cape Coast* and *Transactions of the Historical Society of Ghana*.

WORK IN PROGRESS: Achimota.

* * *

AGUILAR, Rodolfo J(esus) 1936-

PERSONAL: Born September 28, 1936, in San Jose, Costa Rica; naturalized U.S. citizen in 1966; son of Hector Jesus (a physician) and Nora (Espinosa) Aguilar; married Nellyn Carias, October 5, 1956; children: Rudy, Richard, Robert, Noryn. *Education:* Attended University of Santo Domingo, 1953-55; Louisiana State University, B.S., 1958, M.S., 1960, B. Arch., 1961; Illinois Institute of Technology, graduate study, 1962; North Carolina State University, Ph.D., 1964. *Home:* 4866 Whitehaven St., Baton Rouge, La. 70808. *Office:* 5551 Corporate Blvd., Baton Rouge, La. 70808.

CAREER: Louisiana State University, Baton Rouge, assistant professor, 1964-66, associate professor, 1966-69, professor of civil engineering, 1969—; Corporate Development Group, Baton Rouge, La., president, 1970—. Chairman of board of Community Bank of Lafourche, 1974—, and of Ter-Am Corp.; chairman of executive committee of board of American Bank of Houma, 1975—. Member of Baton Rouge Chamber of Commerce. *Member:* American Society of Civil Engineers (president of Baton Rouge chapter, 1974—), Operations Research Society of America, American Institute of Architects, Louisiana Engineering Society, Louisiana Architects Association. *Awards, honors:* American Institute of Architects design award, 1958; Halliburton award, 1967.

WRITINGS: Systems Analysis and Design in Engineering, Architecture, Construction, and Planning, Prentice-Hall, 1973. Contributor to journals.

WORK IN PROGRESS: Real Estate and Urban and Community Planning, Finance, and Banking.

* * *

AHMAD, Ishtiaq 1937-

PERSONAL: Born July 6, 1937, in Azamgarh, Uttar Pradesh, India; son of Sultan (a farmer) and Rogayya (Khatoon) Ahmad; married Noorus Sabah, June, 1955; children: Ghayas Alam (son), Nuzhat Ishtiaq (daughter), Razia, Asifa, Nazima. *Education:* Agra University, B.Sc., 1956; Aligarh Muslim University, M.A., 1958, Ph.D., 1964. *Religion:* Islam. *Home:* Vill + P. O., Bamhur, Azamgarh, Uttar Pradesh, India. *Office:* Department of Political Science, Aligarh Muslim University, Aligarh, Uttar Pradesh, India.

CAREER: Aligarh Muslim University, Aligarh, Uttar Pradesh, India, lecturer in political science, 1965—.

WRITINGS: Anglo-Iranian Relations: 1905-1919, Asia Publishing House, 1974. Contributor to *Indian Journal of Politics*.

WORK IN PROGRESS; A book on international law.

* * *

AKSENOV, Vassily (Pavlovich) 1932-

PERSONAL: Given name is spelled Vasilii in some bibliographic sources; born August 20, 1932, in Kazan, U.S.S.R.; son of Pavel Vassilievich and Evgenia Semenovna (Ginzburg) Aksenov; married Kira Mendeleva, March 11, 1957; children: Alexey. *Education:* First Leningrad Medical Institute, medical degree, 1956. *Politics:* Nonparty. *Religion:* Christian. *Home:* Krasnoarmeiskay 21, Apt. 20, Moscow 125319, U.S.S.R.

CAREER: Physician, Leningrad Hospital, 1956-60; full-time writer, 1960—. *Member:* Writer's Union of the U.S.S.R. *Awards, honors:* Golden Prize in International Competition of Satirical Authors, Bulgaria, 1967.

WRITINGS—Novels, except as indicated: *Kollegi*, Soviet Writer Publishing House, 1961, translation by Margaret Wettlin published as *Colleagues*, Foreign Languages Publishing House (Moscow), 1961, translation by Alec Brown published under same title, Putnam, 1962; *Zvezdnyi bilet*, Youth Magazine, 1961, translation by Brown published as *A Starry Ticket*, Putnam, 1962, translation by Andrew R. MacAndrew published as *A Ticket to the Stars*, New American Library, 1963; *Apel'siny iz Marokko* (title means "The Oranges from Maroc"), Youth Magazine, 1963; *Katapul'ta* (title means "Catapult"), Soviet Writer Publishing House, 1964; *Pora, moi drug, pora*, Young Guard Publishing House, 1965, translation by Olive Stevens published as *It's Time, My Friend, It's Time*, Macmillan, 1969, published as *It's Time, My Love, It's Time*, Aurora Publishers, 1970; *Na polputi k lune* (title means "Halfway to the Moon"; collected short stories), Soviet Russia Publishing House, 1966; *Zatovarennaia bochkotara* (title means "The Empty Barrels"), Youth Magazine, 1968; *Zhal', chto vas ne bylo s nami* (title means "I Wish You Were With Us"; collected short stories), Soviet Writer Publishing House, 1969; *Moy dedushka pamjatnik* (title means "My Grandfather Is a Monument"), Children's Literature Publishing House, 1969; *Liubov'k elektrichestvu* (title means "Love to the Electricity"), Youth Magazine, 1971. Author of play, "Always on Sale," and of five motion picture scripts.

WORK IN PROGRESS: Several works, including a long novel.

* * *

ALBAUM, Melvin 1936-

PERSONAL: Born July 13, 1936, in New York, N.Y.; son of Harry H. (a printer) and Sophie (Brendler) Albaum; married Anita E. Roberg, June 9, 1963 (divorced April, 1969); children: Jennifer Jill. *Education:* Hunter College (now Hunter College of the City University of New York), B.A., 1960; University of Wisconsin-Madison, M.S., 1964; Ohio State University, Ph.D., 1969. *Office:* Department of Geography, University of Colorado, Boulder, Colo. 80302.

CAREER: Ohio State University, Columbus, instructor in geography, 1964-69; University of Kentucky, Lexington, assistant professor of geography, 1969-71; University of Colorado, Boulder, associate professor of geography, 1971—, director of Population Dynamics Program, 1972—. Visiting professor at University of Texas, summer, 1971. Consultant to National Science Foundation and U.S. Forest Service. *Military service:* U.S. Army, 1955-56. *Member:* Association of American Geographers, Population Association of America, Regional Science Association. *Awards, honors:* National Institutes of Health grant, 1973.

WRITINGS: Geography and Contemporary Issues, Wiley, 1973. Contributor to *Professional Geographer, International Journal of Middle East Studies, Perspectives in Geography*, and *Population Index*.

WORK IN PROGRESS: Population: A Spatial Perspective; Demography and Mental Health.

AVOCATIONAL INTERESTS: Travel.

* * *

ALEXANDER, Boyd 1913-
(John Lacey)

PERSONAL: Born November 4, 1913, in Cranbrook, Kent, England; son of Robert (an army officer and landowner) and Katharine (Shaw-Stewart) Alexander; married Frederica Emma Brown Graham (an artist), 1941. *Education:* Magdalen College, Oxford, B.A. (first-class honors), 1935; Wycliffe Hall Theological College, Oxford, theology diploma, 1937. *Politics:* Conservative. *Religion:* Church of England. *Home:* Prospect House, Upton, Didcot, Oxford OX11 9HU, England. *Agent:* E.P.S. Lewin, 1 Grosvenor Ct., Sloane St., London S.W.1, England.

CAREER: Anglican clergyman, 1937-40; civil servant with British Home Office, 1941-45; curator of the Beckford Papers for the Duke of Hamilton, 1949-65. Trumbull Lecturer, Yale University, 1960; has also lectured at universities and other institutions in Canada, Jamaica, Egypt, Rhodesia, England, and United States. Representative for Council for Protection of Rural England. *Member:* Royal Insititute of International Affairs, P.E.N., Society of Authors, Anglo-Portuguese Society, British-Caribbean Society, Victorian Society, National Trust, National Art-Collections Fund.

WRITINGS: (Editor) *The Journal of William Beckford in Portugal and Spain*, Hart-Davis, 1954, John Day, 1955; (editor and translator) *Life at Fonthill* (based on the correspondence of William Beckford), Hart-Davis, 1957; (contributor under pseudonym John Lacey) Philip Toynbee, editor, *Underdogs: Eighteen Victims of Society*, Weidenfeld & Nicholson, 1961, Horizon Press, 1962; *England's Wealthiest Son: A Study of William Beckford*, Centaur Press, 1962; (editor) *Beckford's Excursion to Monasteries of Alcobaca and Batalha*, Centaur Press, 1972. Contributor to "Mendelssohn Studien," published by Duncker & Humbolt for Mendelssohn Institute, 1972-75. Contributor to *Encyclopaedia Britannica*; contributor of articles on Beckford and on foreign affairs to periodicals, including *Country Life, History Today, Quarterly Review, Cornhill*, and *Apollo*.

WORK IN PROGRESS: An edition of family manuscripts; poems.

AVOCATIONAL INTERESTS: Broadcasting, travel, picture exhibitions, music, politics, particularly foreign affairs.

* * *

ALEXANDER, I. J. 1905(?)-1974

1905(?)—October 16, 1974; American advertising executive and author. Obituaries: *New York Times*, October 17, 1974.

* * *

ALEXANDER, Marthann 1907-

PERSONAL: Born April 8, 1907, in Winchester, Ind.; married Gerald Alexander (a professor of chemistry), June 22, 1930; children: one son. *Education:* Ball State University, M.A., 1928. *Religion:* Methodist. *Home:* 701 Alden Rd., Muncie, Ind. 47304.

CAREER: Muncie Community Schools, Muncie, Ind., teacher of crafts, 1929-71; writer, 1971—.

WRITINGS: Weaving Handcraft, McKnight, 1954; *Simple Weaving*, Taplinger, 1960; *Weaving on Cardboard*, Taplinger, 1972.

* * *

ALEXANDER, Sue 1933-

PERSONAL: Born August 20, 1933, in Tucson, Ariz.; daughter of Jack M. (an electronic component manufacturer) and Edith (Pollock) Ratner; married second husband, Joel Alexander (a car agency sales manager), November 29, 1959; children: (first marriage) Glenn David; (second marriage) Marc Jeffry, Stacey Joy. *Education:* Attended Drake University, 1950-52, and Northwestern University, 1952-53. *Religion:* Jewish. *Home and office:* 6846 McLaren, Canoga Park, Calif. 91307. *Agent:* Marilyn Marlow, c/o Curtis Brown Ltd., 60 East 56th St., New York, N.Y. 10022.

CAREER: Writer, 1969—. *Member:* American Civil Liberties Union, Society of Children's Book Writers (member of board of directors, 1972—), Southern California Council on Literature for Children and Young People.

WRITINGS—Juvenile: *Small Plays for You and a Friend*, Scholastic Book Services, 1973, hardcover edition, Seabury, 1974; *Nadir of the Streets*, Macmillan, 1975; *Peacocks Are Very Special*, Doubleday, in press. Contributor of short stories to *Children's Playmate, Weekly Reader*, and Walt Disney Studios; contributor of book reviews to *Los Angeles Times*.

WORK IN PROGRESS: A holiday play book, *Small Plays for Special Days*; a book of five tales on amber.

SIDELIGHTS: Mrs. Alexander told *CA*: "I write for young people because they have imaginations that soar, touched off by a word, a phrase, an image . . . a condition I share. To be able to provide the spark for this process gives me the greatest personal joy."

* * *

ALKEMA, Chester Jay 1932-

PERSONAL: Surname is accented on first syllable; born July 17, 1932, in Martin, Mich.; son of William (a clergyman) and Jennie (Vander Meer) Alkema. *Education:* Calvin College, A.B., 1954; Michigan State University,

M.A., 1959, M.F.A., 1961. *Politics:* Republican. *Religion:* Christian Reformed. *Home:* 3365 Wildridge Dr. N.E., Grand Rapids, Mich. 49505. *Office:* College of Arts and Science, Grand Valley State Colleges, College Landing, Allendale, Mich. 49401.

CAREER: Elementary school teacher in Grand Rapids, Mich., 1954-59; art teacher in public schools in Wyoming, Mich., 1959-65; Grand Valley State Colleges, Allendale, Mich., lecturer, 1965, assistant professor, 1966-72, associate professor of art, 1972—. *Member:* National Art Education Association, Michigan Art Education Association, Michigan Education Association.

WRITINGS—Self-illustrated with photographs: *Creative Paper Crafts in Color*, Sterling, 1967; *The Complete Crayon Book in Color*, Sterling, 1969; *Alkema's Complete Guide to Creative Art for Young People*, Sterling, 1971; *Art for the Exceptional*, Pruett Press, 1971; *Masks*, Sterling, 1971; *Puppet Making*, Sterling, 1972; *Crafting with Nature's Materials*, Sterling, 1973; *Monster Masks*, Sterling, 1973; *Tissue Paper Creations*, Sterling, 1973; *Greeting Cards You Can Make*, Sterling, 1973; *Aluminum and Copper Tooling*, Sterling, 1974; *Beginning with Papier Mache*, Sterling, 1974.

Contributor to *Practical Encyclopedia of Crafts, Family Book of Crafts*, and *Family Book of Hobbies*, all published by Sterling. Contributor of more than sixty articles to art and education journals, including *Design, Instructor, Children's House, School Arts, Arts and Activities, Grade Teacher*, and *Journal of Exceptional Children*.

WORK IN PROGRESS: Create Your Own Papier Mache Jewelry; *Art from Scrap*.

* * *

**ALLBEURY, Theodore Edward le Bouthillier 1917-
(Ted Allbeury)**

PERSONAL: Born October 24, 1917, in Stockport, England; son of Theo and Florence (Bailey) Allbeury; married third wife, Grazyna Felinska, May 13, 1971; children: (first marriage) David; (second marriage) Kerry; (third marriage) Lisa, Sally. *Education:* Attended schools in Birmingham, England. *Home:* Cheriton House, Lamberhurst, Kent, England. *Agent:* John Cushman, 25 West 43rd St., New York, N.Y. 10036; and Curtis Brown Ltd., 1 Craven Hill, London W.2, England.

CAREER: E. Walter George Ltd. (advertising agency), London, England, creative director, 1950-57; W. J. Southcombe Ltd. (advertising agency), London, England, managing director, 1957-62; Allbeury Coombs & Partners (public relations and marketing consultants), Tunbridge Wells, Kent, England, co-founder and senior partner, 1964—. Managing director of Radio 390 ("pirate" radio station), 1964-67; also broadcaster for B.B.C. Network 4 and B.B.C. Radio Medway. *Military service:* British Intelligence Corps, 1939-47; became lieutenant colonel. *Member:* Society of Authors, Crime Writers Association, Special Forces Club, Institute of Directors, The Samaritans.

WRITINGS—Novels; under name Ted Allbeury: *A Choice of Enemies*, St. Martin's, 1972; *Snowball*, Lippincott, 1974; *Omega Minus*, Viking, in press. Contributor to journals and newspapers.

WORK IN PROGRESS: Three novels, *The Special Collection, Where All the Girls Are Sweeter*, and *The Only Good German*.

SIDELIGHTS: Allbeury told *CA* that he began writing novels in 1970 after the kidnapping of his four-year-old daughter whose whereabouts are still unknown to him. With his first book, the author said, "I wanted my daughter to know that I cared and tried to find her."

Allbeury has traveled widely in Europe, the Middle East, Africa, and the United States.

* * *

ALLEN, Garland E(dward) 1936-

PERSONAL: Born February 13, 1936, in Louisville, Ky.; son of Garland Edward (a lawyer) and Virginia (Blandford) Allen; married Susan J. Taylor (an artist), August 6, 1966; children: Tania Leigh, Carin Tove. *Education:* University of Louisville, B.A., 1957; Harvard University, M.A.T., 1958, M.A., 1962, Ph.D., 1966. *Address:* Box 74, Gray Summit, Mo. 63039. *Office:* Department of Biology, Washington University, St. Louis, Mo. 63130.

CAREER: Public school teacher of science in Mount Hermon, Mass., 1958-61; Harvard University, Cambridge, Mass., instructor in history of science, 1965-67; Washington University, St. Louis, Mo., assistant professor, 1967-72, associate professor of biology, 1972—. *Member:* American Association for the Advancement of Science, History of Science Society, American Association for the History of Medicine, Sigma Xi. *Awards, honors:* Sigma Xi national lecturer, 1973-74, bicentennial lecturer, 1974-75.

WRITINGS: (With J.J.W. Baker) *Matter, Energy, and Life*, Addison-Wesley, 1965, 3rd edition, 1974; (with Baker) *Study of Biology*, Addison-Wesley, 1966, 2nd edition, 1972; (with Baker) *Study of Botany*, Addison-Wesley, 1968; (editor) *Process of Biology: Primary Sources*, Addison-Wesley, 1970; (with Baker) *Course in Biology*, Addison-Wesley, 1969, 2nd edition, 1972; (with Baker) *Hypothesis, Prediction, and Implication*, Addison-Wesley, 1969; *Life Sciences in the Twentieth Century*, Wiley, in press. Contributor to *Journal of the History of Biology, Biological Science, Isis, Journal of the History of Medicine and Allied Sciences*, and *American Biology Teacher*.

WORK IN PROGRESS: A biography of Thomas Hunt Morgan, an American geneticist and embryologist who lived from 1866-1945; a volume on twentieth-century biology for "Album of Science" series, for Scribner.

AVOCATIONAL INTERESTS: Music, hiking, mountain-climbing, political organizing.

* * *

ALLSEN, Philip E(dmond) 1932-

PERSONAL: Born June 10, 1932, in Milford, Utah; son of John and Alverta (Parkinson) Allsen; married Patricia Randall, June 4, 1954; children: Kathy, John. *Education:* Ricks College, B.S., 1954; Brigham Young University, M.S., 1960; University of Utah, Ed.D., 1966. *Religion:* Latter-Day Saints (Mormon). *Home:* 284 East 3450 N., Provo, Utah 84601. *Office:* Department of Physical Education, Brigham Young University, Provo, Utah 84602.

CAREER: Brigham Young University, Provo, Utah, associate professor, 1966-69, professor of physical education, 1969—. *Military service:* U.S. Navy, 1955-60; became lieutenant commander. *Member:* National Education Association, American Association for Health, Physical Education and Recreation, American College of Sports Medicine, Nutrition Today Society, National College Physical Education Association for Men, Phi Kappa Phi, Phi Delta Kappa, Sigma Delta Psi.

WRITINGS: Scorecard for the Evaluation of Physical Education Programs in Junior Colleges, N. P. Nielson, 1966; *Paddleball*, W. C. Brown, 1970; *Fitness for Life*, Brigham Young University Press, 1974. Contributor to *Athletic Journal, Christian Athlete, MIA Explorer's Handbook, Scholastic Coach, Coach and Athlete, Swimming Techniques, Sports Illustrated*, and *Courier-Tribune*.

WORK IN PROGRESS: Research on the construction of a data bank for athletic profiles.

* * *

ALMOND, Richard 1938-

PERSONAL: Born January 19, 1938, in Chicago, Ill.; married, wife's name, Barbara (a physician); children: David, Michael, Steven. *Education:* Harvard University, A.B. (with honors), 1959; Yale University, M.D., 1963. *Office:* Collective Psychotherapy Center, Palo Alto, Calif.

CAREER: State University of New York, Upstate Medical Center, Syracuse, intern, 1963-64; West Haven Veterans Administration Hospital, West Haven, Conn., resident in psychiatry, 1964-65; Yale-New Haven Hospital, New Haven, Conn., resident in psychiatry at Psychiatric Outpatient Clinic, 1965-66; Connecticut Mental Health Center, chief resident in psychiatry, 1966-67; U.S. Public Health Service, clinical associate of National Institute of Mental Health intramural research adult psychiatry branch (in fulfillment of military obligation), 1967-69; Stanford University, Stanford, Calif., assistant professor of psychiatry and psychiatrist at Cowell Student Health Service, 1969-73; Collective Psychotherapy Center, Palo Alto, Calif., psychiatrist in private practice, 1973—. Diplomate of American Board of Psychiatry and Neurology, 1971. Member of professional advisory group of Miramonte Mental Health Services, 1970—; clinical professor at Stanford University, 1973—.

MEMBER: American Psychiatric Association, Northern California Psychiatric Society.

WRITINGS: (Contributor) F. C. Redlich, editor, *Social Psychiatry*, Williams & Wilkins, 1970; *The Healing Community: Dynamics of the Therapeutic Milieu*, Aronson, 1974. Contributor to *The Leading Edge of Mental Health*, edited by Herbert Otto. Contributor of about a dozen articles to medical journals, including *Journal of Nervous and Mental Disease, Psychiatry, Journal of Psychiatric Research, Scientific American, Archives of General Psychiatry*, and *Pharos*.

WORK IN PROGRESS: Alternative Organizations.

AVOCATIONAL INTERESTS: Nineteenth-century lieder.

* * *

ALPERN, Gerald D(avid) 1932-

PERSONAL: Born August 2, 1932, in Pittsburgh, Pa.; son of Herman R. and Goldie C. (Landy) Alpern; married Carol Bagan (a registered nurse), April, 1964; children: Tyler Jon, Thomas Eric. *Education:* University of Pittsburgh, B.Sc., 1954; University of Iowa, M.A., 1959, Ph.D., 1960. *Home:* 7150 Lakeside Dr., Indianapolis, Ind. 46278. *Office:* Medical School, Indiana University, 1100 West Michigan, Indianapolis, Ind. 46202.

CAREER: Western Psychiatric Institute and Clinics, Pittsburgh, Pa., psychiatric aide, 1951-53, child care worker, 1953-54; University of Iowa, Iowa City, research psychologist at Child Guidance Clinic, University Hospital, 1958-59, clinical psychologist, Student Counseling Service, 1959-60; Indiana University, Medical School, Indianapolis, instructor, 1960-63, assistant professor, 1963-68, associate professor, 1968-73, professor of psychology in department of psychiatry, 1973—, senior staff psychologist, Riley Child Guidance Clinic, 1960-65, director of research, Child Psychiatry Services, 1965—. Private practice as clinical psychologist, Indianapolis, 1961—. Consulting psychologist to Indiana Girls School, 1961-62, Richmond State Hospital, 1961-65, and LaRue Carter Hospital, 1963-65; director of research, Marion County Association for Retarded Children, 1971—. *Military service:* U.S. Army, 1954-56.

MEMBER: American Psychological Association, Society for Research in Child Development, Society for Clinical and Experimental Hypnosis, Indiana Psychological Association (member of executive committee, 1962-65, 1969-70; president, Division of School Psychology, 1969-70).

WRITINGS: (Contributor) Doris Hasler, *The Practical-Vocational Nurse and Today's Family*, Macmillan, 1964, 2nd edition, 1972; (editor with Don W. Churchill and Marian K. DeMyer) *Infantile Autism*, C. C Thomas, 1971; (editor with Thomas J. Boll) *Education and Care of Moderately and Severely Retarded Children*, Special Child, 1971; (contributor) James E. Simmons, *Psychiatric Examination of Children*, 2nd edition (Alpern did not contribute to first edition), Lea & Febiger, 1974. Author of *Developmental Profile Manual*, Psychological Development Publications, 1972, and contributor to medical, dental, and other journals. Bulletin editor, Indiana Psychological Association, 1962-64.

* * *

ALTABE, Joan B. 1935-

PERSONAL: Born April 27, 1935, in New York, N.Y.; daughter of Harold (a printer) and Evelyn (an executive secretary; maiden name, Cooperman) Berg; married David F. Altabe (a Spanish professor), September 28, 1958; children: Richard, Madeline. *Education:* Hunter College (now Hunter College of the City University of New York), 1952-57, B.A. and graduate study. *Studio:* 421 West Olive St., Long Beach, N.Y. 11561. *Office:* National Society of Mural Painters, 41 East 65th St., New York, N.Y. 10021.

CAREER: New York City Board of Education, New York, N.Y., art teacher in secondary schools, 1957-72; free-lance illustrator, 1970—; free-lance muralist, 1972—; free-lance writer, 1974—. Art editor and art director, Regina Publishing House, 1973-75. Director, New York City Bicentennial Committee for the Mural Painters. *Member:* National Society of Mural Painters (finance director, 1974-75), Artists Equity Association of New York. *Awards, honors:* Certificate of merit, New York International Art Show, 1970.

WRITINGS: (Editor) *National Drawing Anthology*, new edition, Regina Publishing House, 1974. Also author of *Achieving Three Dimensions with Dark and Light*, 1974, and *Painting Story-Telling Abstractions*, 1975. Artist of cartoon series, "Women's Lib," for White Heat Publishing, 1975.

AVOCATIONAL INTERESTS: Playing and arranging music for the piano.

BIOGRAPHICAL/CRITICAL SOURCES: Fine Arts Discovery, summer, 1970.

ALVEY, Edward, Jr. 1902-

PERSONAL: Born June 13, 1902, in Richmond, Va.; son of Edward (a wholesale merchant) and Ida Floyd (Huffman) Alvey; married Frances Ellen McClintic, June 16, 1927; children: Ellen (Mrs. Joseph J. Montllor). *Education:* University of Virginia, B.A., 1923, M.A., 1928, Ph.D., 1931. *Religion:* Presbyterian. *Home:* 1104 College Ave., Fredericksburg, Va. 22401.

CAREER: High school principal in Hot Springs, Va., 1924-28; University of Virginia, Charlottesville, instructor in education, 1928-34; Mary Washington College, Fredericksburg, Va., dean of the college, 1934-67, professor of education, 1967-71, professor emeritus, 1971—. President of Historic Fredericksburg, Inc., 1971; secretary and member of the board of governors, Jamestowne Society, 1974. *Member:* Southern Association of Academic Deans, Association of Virginia Colleges, Virginia Academy of Science, Phi Beta Kappa, Alpha Psi Omega, Raven Society. *Awards, honors:* Phi Delta Kappa Key Award, 1935, for outstanding service to education in Virginia; Treasury Department Silver Minuteman Award, 1966, for patriotic service.

WRITINGS: History of Mary Washington College, 1908-1972, University Press of Virginia, 1974. Contributor to *Americana Annual*, 1934-75, and to *Encyclopedia Americana* and *Reader's Digest Almanac and Yearbook*; contributor to *Free Lance-Star* (Fredericksburg, Va.).

WORK IN PROGRESS: History of Fredericksburg Presbyterian Church, 1808-1974.

AVOCATIONAL INTERESTS: Travel.

* * *

AMMAR, Abbas 1907(?)-1974

1907(?)—December, 1974; Egyptian anthropologist, government official, and international labor leader. Obituaries: *New York Times*, December 16, 1974.

* * *

ANCONA, George 1929-

PERSONAL: Born December 4, 1929, in New York; son of Efraim Jose Ancona and Emma Ancona Diaz; married Patricia Apatow (divorced); married Helga Von Sydow (a translator), June 20, 1968; children: (first marriage) Lisa, Gina, Tom; (second marriage) Isabel, Marina. *Education:* Attended Academia San Carlos, 1949-50, and School of Visual Arts, Cooper Union, and Art Students League (all New York, N.Y.). *Home address:* Crickettown Rd., Stony Point, N.Y. 10980.

CAREER: Esquire (magazine), New York, N.Y., art director, 1951-54; Grey Advertising, New York, N.Y., art director, 1954-57; Daniel & Charles, New York, N.Y., art director, 1957-61; George Ancona, Inc., New York, N.Y., photographer and film maker, 1961—. Instructor at Rockland Community College and School of Visual Arts, New York; lecturer on film, design, photography, and books.

AWARDS, HONORS: Art Director's Show awards, 1959, 1960, 1967; Cine Golden Eagle Awards from Council on Non-Theatrical Events, 1967, for film, "Reflections," and 1972, for film, "Cities of the Web"; awards from American Institute of Graphic Arts, 1967, 1968, 1974; Cindy Award from Industry Film Producers Association, 1967.

WRITINGS: Monsters on Wheels, Dutton, 1974; (with Remy Charlip and Mary Beth; also illustrator) *Handtalk*, Parents Press, 1974; *On the Job*, Dutton, 1975.

Illustrator: Barbara Brenner, *A Snake-Lover's Diary* (juvenile), Scott Young Books, 1970; Brenner, *Faces* (juvenile), Dutton, 1970; Brenner, *Bodies*, Dutton, 1973.

Filmscripts: "Doctor" and "Dentist," two short films for "Sesame Street"; "Faces" and "The River," for children; "Getting It Together," a documentary film about the Children's Television Workshop and Neighborhood Youth Corps; "Cities of the Web," for Macmillan; "Looking for Pictures," "Looking for Color," "Seeing Rhythm," a series; "Reflections," for American Crafts Council.

SIDELIGHTS: Filmmaking, to Ancona, is something like a dam breaking. "You have an idea, and then—words, concept, images, movement, rhythm—all rush together. I take all these things and relate them to what I want to say.... Some ideas burst forth, others are best expressed in gentle strolls."

BIOGRAPHICAL/CRITICAL SOURCES: Journal-News, Rockland County, N.Y., July 23, 1972.

* * *

ANDERSON, Bernard Eric 1936-

PERSONAL: Born November 1, 1936, in Modesto, Calif.; son of Henry George and Arline (Alexander) Anderson; married Phyllis Brooksby (a teacher), January 28, 1961; children: Eric, Kristen, Ross. *Education:* Attended Sacramento State College (now California State University, Sacramento), 1957-59; Arizona State College, B.S., 1960; University of Arizona, M.A., 1961; Ohio State University, Ph.D., 1964. *Politics:* Democratic. *Religion:* Methodist. *Address:* Route 1, Box 301-F, Durango, Colo. 81301. *Office:* Department of Economics, Fort Lewis College, Durango, Colo. 81301.

CAREER: Northern Arizona University, Flagstaff, assistant professor, 1964-67, associate professor of economics, 1967-70; New Mexico State University, Las Cruces, director of Center for Business Services, 1970-71; Fort Lewis College, Durango, Colo., associate professor of economics, 1971—. Partner, Anderson & Zoller (consultants); member of board of directors, Southwest Colorado Mental Health Center, 1974—, and Sheltered Workshop, 1974—. *Military service:* U.S. Navy, 1955-57. *Member:* American Economic Association, American Association for the Advancement of Science, Western Economic Association, Beta Gamma Sigma, Omicron Delta Epsilon, Blue Key.

WRITINGS: Navajo Urban Migration: The Bicultural Man, U.S. Department of Labor, 1972.

WORK IN PROGRESS: Labor Mobility among the Disadvantaged.

* * *

ANDERSON, Donald F(rancis) 1938-

PERSONAL: Born July 10, 1938, in Windsor, Ontario, Canada; naturalized U.S. citizen; married Margaret Marie Sedlock, August 14, 1964; children: Stephen, Rebecca. *Education:* University of Detroit, Ph.B., 1959, M.A., 1961; Cornell University, Ph.D., 1968. *Religion:* Roman Catholic. *Home:* 8161 Riverview, Dearborn Heights, Mich. 48127. *Office:* Department of Political Science, University of Michigan—Dearborn, 4901 Evergreen, Dearborn, Mich. 48128.

CAREER: Hampton Institute, Hampton, Va., assistant professor of political science, 1965-66; University of Detroit, Detroit, Mich., assistant professor of political science, 1966-69; University of Michigan, Dearborn, 1969—, began as assistant professor, now associate professor of political science. *Member:* American Political Science Association. *Awards, honors:* Martha Kinney Cooper Ohioana Library Association prize, 1973, for "Ohio Scene."

WRITINGS: William Howard Taft: A Conservative's Conception of the Presidency, Cornell University Press, 1973.

WORK IN PROGRESS: Political Thought of William Howard Taft; Presidential Availability.

* * *

ANDERSON, Eloise Adell 1927-

PERSONAL: Born May 13, 1927, in Warren, Minn.; daughter of Adam John and Marie (Hage) Rutkowski; married Samuel Anderson, December, 1953 (divorced, 1973); children: Suzanne, John. *Education:* Moorhead State College, B.S., 1948; University of Wyoming, M.Ed, 1968. *Politics:* Independent. *Religion:* Christian. *Home:* 24 Club Lane, Littleton, Colo. 80123. *Office:* Centennial School, 3306 West Berry Ave., Littleton, Colo. 80120.

CAREER: Elementary school teacher in Littleton Public Schools, Littleton, Colo., 1972—. *Awards, honors:* Scholarship to Colorado Women's College, 1971, for creative writing for children.

WRITINGS: Carlos Goes to School, Warne, 1973. Contributor of stories and poems to *Wee Wisdom, Quest*, and *Child Life*.

AVOCATIONAL INTERESTS: Collecting old children's books, golf, swimming.

* * *

ANDERSON, John F(reeman) 1945-

PERSONAL: Born July 15, 1945, in St. Paul, Minn.; son of William F. (a dentist) and Mildred (Knudson) Anderson. *Education:* University of Minnesota, B.S. (with distinction), 1967, M.A., 1969, Ph.D., 1974. *Home:* 860 Dodd Rd., West St. Paul, Minn. 55107. *Office:* Measurement Services Center, University of Minnesota, 9 Clarence Ave. S.E., Minneapolis, Minn. 55455.

CAREER: Anderson & Berdie Associates (survey research firm), St. Paul, Minn., partner, 1974—. Research associate at Measurement Services Center of University of Minnesota, 1971—. *Member:* World Association for Public Opinion Research, American Educational Research Association, Music Educators National Conference, Phi Mu Alpha, Phi Delta Kappa, Phi Kappa Phi, Pi Kappa Lambda.

WRITINGS: (With Douglas R. Berdie) *Graduate Assistants at the University of Minnesota,* Measurement Services Center, University of Minnesota, 1972; (with Berdie) *Questionnaires: Design and Use,* Scarecrow, 1974. Contributor to psychology and education journals, including *Journal of Applied Psychology, Improving College and University Teaching,* and *Research in Higher Education.*

WORK IN PROGRESS: Editing an anthology about questionnaires, with Douglas R. Berdie; research on the methodology of questionnaire use and on undergraduate music education.

ANDERSSON, Ingvar 1899(?)-1974

Swedish historian and author. Obituaries: *AB Bookman's Weekly*, December 2, 1974.

* * *

ANDREWS, James David 1924-

PERSONAL: Born August 7, 1924, in Fayetteville, N.C.; son of Melvin Brainerd (an educator and insurance executive) and Cara (a secretary and office manager; maiden name, Daniels) Andrews; married Ruth Elliott (a librarian), June 4, 1949; children: David Graham, Elizabeth, Richard, Harriett, Ruth. *Education:* University of North Carolina, M.S. in med., 1946, B.S., 1947; Duke University, B.D., 1952. *Politics:* "Reformist, rather than upheaval, and with strong emphasis on economics of Henry George." *Religion:* "Protestant in origin, but with interfaith inclusiveness and universalist-scientific outlook." *Home address:* P.O. Box 4641, Baltimore, Md. 21212.

CAREER: United World Federalists of Virginia, state field secretary, 1947-48; American Friends Service Committee, Greensboro, N.C. and High Point, N.C., world affairs educator, 1952-57; Friends Boarding School, Barnesville, Ohio, teacher, 1958-60; Appalachian State University, Boone, N.C., director of Wesley Foundation, 1960-62; Morgan State College, Baltimore, Md., director of Wesley Foundation, 1962-64; Johns Hopkins University, Baltimore, Md., medical editor in School of Medicine and Hospital, 1964—. President of Wesley Foundation at University of North Carolina, 1944-46, president of Interfaith Council, 1945. *Military service:* U.S. Navy, medical cadet, 1943-45. *Member:* American Medical Writers Association.

WRITINGS: (Editor with Stephen J. Ryan, Jr.) *A Survey of Ophthalmology: Manual for Medical Students*, intramural publication, Johns Hopkins University, 1970; *Five-Seven-Five: Contemporary Verse in the Classic Haiku Form*, Golden Quill Press, 1974.

WORK IN PROGRESS: Six Hundred Ships and Other Sonnets; *"Lost Haiku" of Matsuo Basho: 1644-1694*; *Travel Haiku of Matsuo Basho: A New Rendering*; editing *Carolina Adventures: Brief Sketches of Boyhood Days in Eastern North Carolina at the Turn of the Century (1889-1915)*, a book written by his father, Melvin B. Andrews.

SIDELIGHTS: Andrews writes: "I have a deep interest in nature and in human events. Although active in the world peace, civil rights, and civil liberties movements during about 1943-1963 (with nonviolent groups such as the Methodists and Quakers), since about 1964 I have been more an observer of the political scene than a direct participant, although I consistently opposed U.S. military intervention in Vietnam or elsewhere. I believe world peace and security can be achieved only through a strengthened United Nations, under world law. My concern about the present and future of the human race is still strong." *Avocational interests:* Athletic events, music, old things (especially automobiles), organic vegetable gardening, wild foods (Andrews notes: "At the Pendle Hills study center, Wallingford, Pa., we lived in the same house for a year with the Euell Gibbons family, but we ate no pine trees").

* * *

ANDREWS, William R(obert) 1937-

PERSONAL: Born October 10, 1937, in Spartanburg, S.C.; son of Robert Walton and MaeBelle (Fowler) Andrews; married Elizabeth Calvert (a teacher), June 21,

1958; children: Elizabeth, Julia, Robert. *Education:* University of Florida, B.S., 1960; Northeast Missouri State University, M.A., 1972. *Home:* 4712 Tara Dr., Fairfax, Va. 22030.

CAREER: U.S. Army, 1960—; commissioned second lieutenant, 1960; served in Viet-Nam, 1964-65, 1968-69, currently serving in Washington, D.C. at Pentagon; present rank, major; Northeast Missouri State University, Kirksville, instructor in Asian history, 1972.

WRITINGS: The Village War: Vietnamese Communist Revolutionary Activities in Dinh Tuong Province, 1960-64, University of Missouri Press, 1973. Contributor to *Military Review*.

WORK IN PROGRESS: A novel centered on the early American involvement in South Viet-Nam; a monograph on the use of mass organizations for political modernization in developing nations.

SIDELIGHTS: Andrews told *CA:* "*The Village War* is an attempt to organize the results of personal experiences and observations in the villages of South Viet-Nam. As an officer 'on loan' to the United States Information Agency, I was fortunate to see Viet-Nam in a way not afforded most foreigners. I was the only Western member of a seven-man team that traveled on foot through the reaches of the upper Mekong Delta ricelands. Living in rural villages that were the objects of contention by both the Saigon and Communist sides, we ate, worked, and talked with thousands of Vietnamese peasants who were caught up in the political and military crossfires of those turbulent days.

We learned of their aspirations, fears, and of their attitudes toward the struggle that ultimately shattered domestic unity in the United States. We learned, too, of the consummate organization ability of the Vietnamese Communist cadre."

* * *

ANGELL, Tony 1940-

PERSONAL: Born November 15, 1940, in Los Angeles, Calif.; son of H. Frank (a private investigator) and Florence (Brown) Angell; married Noel Gordon Gabie, June 18, 1966; children: Gilis Noel and Bryony Megan (twin girls). *Education:* University of Washington, Seattle, B.A., 1966. *Politics:* Independent. *Home:* 18237 40th St. N.E., Seattle, Wash. 98155. *Office:* Intermediate School District Offices, 100 Crockett St., #110, Seattle, Wash. 98109.

CAREER: High school English teacher in Seattle, Wash., 1966-69, supervisor of environmental education programs, 1969-71; State Office of Education, Olympia, Wash., state supervisor of environmental education programs, 1971—. Member of Town Park board of commissioners; member of Cornell University Laboratory of Ornithology. *Member:* American Ornithologists Union, Society of Animal Artists, Seattle Audubon Society (vice-president). *Awards, honors:* Ford Foundation national design award, 1955; Washington Governor's Award, 1973, for *Birds of Prey of the Pacific Northwest Slope*.

WRITINGS: Birds of Prey of the Pacific Northwest Slope, Pacific Search, 1972, 3rd edition, 1974; *Owls*, University of Washington Press, 1974. Regular contributor to *Living Bird* (publication of Ornithology, Cornell University); contributor of articles and illustrations to *Pacific Search*.

WORK IN PROGRESS: The Family of the Raven, a book on the family of North American jays, magpies, crows, and ravens; paintings and illustrations for *Four and Twenty Blackbirds*, by Gordon Orians.

SIDELIGHTS; Angell writes: "As an artist natural forms have been my wellspring. I have had the good fortune to associate closely with nature for most of my life . . . My books are born from long associations with the subjects in a multitude of circumstances in both my home and in their homes in nature. I travel to the fields where these life forms exist and in the case of a particular family of birds this may take me to the deep rain forests of Washington, the desert canyons of Northern Mexico, diving in the coastal waters of Northwestern Canada, or the great hardwood forests of Northern Michigan and the Lake Country of Northern Minnesota. I reach into nature by hiking, climbing, and skin diving. The birds and mammals I study will often be in the water as much as they are in the air. To understand them I study them as they are—hunting, courting, chasing, etc. It is difficult to separate avocations from vocations as the professions of writing, painting and sculpting as well as teaching are dependent on my experiences in nature as a hiker, climber, and skin diver."

BIOGRAPHICAL/CRITICAL SOURCES: "The Angells and Their Lifestyle" (film), produced by King Television (affiliate of National Broadcasting Corp. in Seattle, Wash.), 1971; "Tony Angell: Writer, Painter and Sculptor" (film), King Television, 1974.

* * *

ANGELO, Frank 1914-

PERSONAL: Born September 6, 1914, in Detroit, Mich.; son of Nicolo (a laborer) and Ida (Carini) Angelo; married Elizabeth Paton Stoll, February 25, 1950; children: Frank, Jr., Andrew Nicholas. *Education:* Wayne State University, B.A., 1934. *Politics:* Independent. *Religion:* Presbyterian. *Home:* 14424 Rutland, Detroit, Mich. 48227. *Office: Detroit Free Press*, Detroit, Mich. 48226.

CAREER: Detroit Free Press, Detroit, Mich., columnist and editor.

WRITINGS: Yesterday's Detroit, Seemann, 1974.

* * *

ANGUS-BUTTERWORTH, Lionel Milner 1900-

PERSONAL: Surname originally Butterworth, and so listed in some sources; changed by deed poll; born June 29, 1900, in Altrincham, Cheshire, England; son of Walter Butterworth; married Lilian Reay, August 16, 1937; children: Jennifer (Mrs. Kevin Fitzgerald), Alexander Walter, Elspeth Margaret. *Education:* University of Manchester, M.A.; studied at University of Sheffield and University of Toulouse. *Home:* Ashton New Hall, Ashton-on-Mersey, Cheshire, England.

CAREER: Director until 1960, of engineering and glass manufacturing companies; Abercorn Publishing Co., Ltd., London and Manchester, governing director, 1960-67. Institution of Factory Managers, organizer, secretary, editor, honorary fellow, 1945—. Chairman of trustees, Butterworth & Bayley Charity; managing governor, Royal Scottish Corporation; life governor, Royal Hospital and Home for Incurables. *Military Service:* Served in first World War, and in World War II; colonel. *Member:* Royal Geographic Society (fellow), Society of Antiquaries (Scotland; fellow), Chartered Institute of Secretaries (fellow), Ancient Monuments Society (founding member; past honorary secretary, treasurer, trustee, chairman, vice-president; honorary director), Societe de Geographie (Paris; life member), Lancashire Authors' Association (president), 1972—), Manchester Literary Club (president, 1961-62), Manchester Poetical Society (president, 1969—). *Awards, honors:* Named Freeman of the city of London, 1957.

WRITINGS: Old Cheshire Families and Their Seats, Sherratt & Hughes, 1932, reprinted, E. J. Morten, 1970; (reviser) Percival Marson, *Glass and Glass Manufacture*, 2nd edition, Pitman, 1932, 4th edition, 1949; *The Manufacture of Glass*, Pitman, 1948; *British Table and Ornamental Glass*, Leonard Hill, 1956; *The Angus Poetical Tradition*, Burns & Harris, c.1965; *Ten Master Historians*, Aberdeen University Press, 1961, 2nd edition, 1962, Books for Libraries, 1968; *Pottery and Porcelain*, Collins, 1964; *The Chinese Kitchen: Tales of the Occult and Macabre*, privately printed, 1967; *Robert Burns and the 18th-Century-Revival in Scottish Vernacular Poetry*, Aberdeen University Press, 1969, Books for Libraries, 1973; *Scottish Folk-Song*, Burns & Harris, 1971; *Selected Poems*, Shetland Times, 1973.

Contributor to *Oxford History of Technology*, Volumes III and IV. Contributor to periodicals, including *Homes & Garden, New York Story, South Atlantic Quarterly, Mirror* (New Zealand), *Newfoundland Quarterly*, and *American Machinist*.

WORK IN PROGRESS: Lancashire Literary Worthies, an account of the lives of a hundred Lancashire authors, 1550-1950.

SIDELIGHTS: Angus-Butterworth's home, an eighteenth-century Georgian Hall, has been designated a site of historic and architectural interest by the British government. Upon first occupying the hall, he and his wife had to rely on masses of candles for several weeks until electricity could be installed.

* * *

ANOBILE, Richard J(oseph) 1947-

PERSONAL: Surname is pronounced Ah-no-bee-lay; born February 6, 1947, in New York, N.Y.; son of Joseph (a printer) and Isabella (Lanzella) Anobile; married Ulla Kaekoenen (a journalist and novelist), August 15, 1972. *Education:* Institute of Film Technique of City University of New York, student, 1964-69. *Home:* 315 West 102nd St., New York, N.Y. 10025. *Office:* Darien House, Inc., 37 Riverside Dr., New York, N.Y. 10024.

CAREER: Gallery of Modern Art, New York, N.Y., assistant to film curator, 1967-68; Darien House, Inc., vice-president, 1970—; *Argosy* (magazine), New York, N.Y., film critic, 1968—.

WRITINGS: (Editor) *Drat!* (humor), World Publishing, 1968; (editor) *Why a Duck?* (humor), New York Graphic Society, 1970; (editor) *A Flask of Fields!* (humor), Norton, 1972; (editor) *Who's On First?* (humor), Norton, 1972; (with Groucho Marx) *Marx Brothers Scrapbook*, Norton, 1973; *Hooray for Captain Spaulding*, Crown, 1974; *Godfrey Daniels* (humor), Crown, in press. Editor of "The Film Classics Library," twenty-four volumes, Avon, 1974—.

WORK IN PROGRESS: The Crazy World of Laurel and Hardy.

* * *

ANSCHEL, Eugene 1907-
(Egon Polcher)

PERSONAL: Born November 27, 1907, in Germany; son of Moses (a businessman) and Rosa (Hirsch) Anschel; married Ada Heilbrunn, October 10, 1933 (divorced, 1944); married Eva Mamlock (an assistant librarian), March 4, 1944; children: (first marriage) Kurt R.; (second marriage) Barbara R. *Education:* Attended University of Bonn, 1927, University of Munich, 1927-28, University of Berlin, 1928-29; University of Cologne, LL.D., 1933. *Home:* 11 Riverside Dr., New York, N.Y. 10023.

CAREER: Schering Corp. (pharmaceuticals), Bloomfield, N.J., assistant foreign sales manager, 1940-50; Nepera Chemical Co., International Department (pharmaceuticals), manager, Yonkers, N.Y., 1951-56; Chemway Corp., International Operations (pharmaceuticals), vice-president, Wayne, N.J., 1956-67; Boy Machines, Inc., Plainview, N.Y., president, 1974—.

WRITINGS: (Editor) *The American Image of Russia, 1775-1917*, Ungar, 1974. Contributor of articles and book reviews, sometimes under pseudonym Egon Polcher to American and German publications, including *American Political Science Review*.

WORK IN PROGRESS: The American Image of Soviet Russia, 1917-1974; research on American-Chinese relations.

AVOCATIONAL INTERESTS: Travel.

* * *

ANTELL, Gerson 1926-

PERSONAL: Born February 16, 1926, in Brooklyn, N.Y.; son of Abraham and Rebecca (Levine) Antell; married Diane Darvas, March 29, 1953; children: Rachel Amy. *Education:* Brooklyn College (now Brooklyn College of the City University of New York), A.B., 1948; University of California, Los Angeles, M.B.A., 1949; Columbia University, M.A., 1951. *Home:* 80 Baker Hill Rd., Great Neck, N.Y. 11023. *Office:* Hillcrest High School, 160-05 Highland Ave., Jamaica, N.Y. 11432.

CAREER: Loew's Theatres, New York, N.Y., assistant theatre manager, 1950-51; Board of Education, New York, N.Y., high school teacher of social studies, 1951-61, assistant principal, 1961—. Assistant professor of education at Hunter College, City University of New York, and at Pace University; director of New York City Council on Economic Education, 1966-68. *Military service:* U.S. Army, Infantry and Corps of Engineers, 1944-46; became first lieutenant. *Member:* National Council for the Social Studies, Social Studies Supervisors Association, National Education Association.

WRITINGS: Economics: Institutions and Analysis, Amsco School Publications, 1970; *Economics for Everybody*, Amsco School Publications, 1973; *Current Issues in American Democracy*, Amsco School Publications, 1975. Contributor to professional journals.

WORK IN PROGRESS: History of Western Civilization.

AVOCATIONAL INTERESTS: Travel, photography, sailing, marine life.

* * *

ANTONIUTTI, Ildebrando 1898-1974

August 3, 1898—August 1, 1974; Italian Roman Catholic Cardinal and prefect of the Sacred Congregation for the Religious and Secular Institution. Obituaries: *New York Times*, August 2, 1974.

APGAR, Virginia 1909-1974

June 7, 1909—August 7, 1974; American physician and medical researcher. Obituaries: *Current Biography*, October, 1974.

* * *

APPLEBY, John T. 1909(?)-1974

1909(?)—December 17, 1974; American historian, author, and associate editor of the *American Historical Review*. Obituaries: *Washington Post*, December 21, 1974.

* * *

APT, (Jerome) Leon 1929-

PERSONAL: Born November 18, 1929, in Troy, N.Y.; son of Max Samuel (a merchant) and Bertha (Kushlan) Apt; married Patricia Harper (an adult education teacher), December 31, 1956; children: Mark Adam, Bryan Andrew. *Education:* University of Arkansas, B.A., 1956, M.A., 1957; University of Chicago, Ph.D., 1965. *Religion:* Jewish. *Home:* 1017 Burnett Ave., Ames, Iowa 50010. *Office:* Department of History, Iowa State University, Ames, Iowa 50010.

CAREER: Stanford University, Stanford, Calif., instructor in history, 1960-64; Colorado State University, Fort Collins, assistant professor of history, 1964-65; Wellesley College, Wellesley, Mass., assistant professor of history, 1966-69; Iowa State University, Ames, associate professor, 1969-74, professor of history, 1974—. Visiting professor at University of Arkansas, 1965-66. *Member:* American Historical Association, French Historical Society, American Association of University Professors, Phi Beta Kappa, Phi Alpha Theta.

WRITINGS: Louis-Philippe de Segur: An Intellectual in a Revolutionary Age, Nijhoff, 1969; (editor with Robert Herzstein) *Evolution of Western Society*, three volumes, Dryden, 1973-74; (editor) *Issues in Western Civilization*, two volumes, Holbrook, 1974. Contributor to *Journal of Modern History* and *American Historical Review*. Editorial assistant, *Journal of Modern History*; associate history editor, *Intellect*.

WORK IN PROGRESS—Three books: *Man and Politics: Europe Since 1500*, a two-volume text, completion expected in 1975; *Anti-Semitism in France Between the Wars*, 1976; *The Jews in France: A History*.

SIDELIGHTS: Leon Apt is competent in French, German, Hebrew, and Yiddish.

* * *

ARCHER, Fred C. 1916(?)-1974

1916(?)—October 27, 1974; American educator and author of textbooks on business and accounting. Obituaries: *AB Bookman's Weekly*, November 18, 1974.

* * *

ARGENZIO, Victor 1902-

PERSONAL: Surname is pronounced Ar-*gen*-zio, with "g" hard; born July 8, 1902, in New York, N.Y.; son of Andrew (a musician) and Nancy (Giliberti) Argenzio; married Margaret Henderson, January 7, 1947; children: Robert, Judith (Mrs. Steven Richards), Victor James. *Education:* Attended public schools in Brooklyn, N.Y. *Home and office:* 520 Clermont St., Denver, Colo. 80220.

CAREER: Argenzio Brothers Jewelers, Denver, Colo., vice-president until 1966, chairman of board, 1966—. Diamond consultant to Zale Corp. *Member:* Authors Guild, Colorado Author's League. *Awards, honors:* National Writers Club award, 1958, for article, "Buying Your First Diamond?"

WRITINGS: The Fascination of Diamonds, McKay, 1965; *Diamonds Eternal*, McKay, 1974. Contributor to *Lions International* and *Jewelers' Circular-Keystone*.

WORK IN PROGRESS: A book on diamonds for youth.

SIDELIGHTS: Argenzio played the cello in the Denver Civic Symphony for twenty years. *Avocational interests:* Travel.

* * *

ARKIN, Marcus 1926-

PERSONAL: Born May 13, 1926, in Cape Town, South Africa; son of Julius (a businessman) and Anne (a teacher; maiden name, Purcell) Arkin; married Susanne Mirvish, December 4, 1948; children: Antony, Glenda-Ruth. *Education:* University of Cape Town, B.Com. (with distinction), 1946, B.A. (with distinction), 1947, Ph.D., 1959. *Home:* 16 Sussex Rd., Parkwood, Johannesburg 2001, South Africa.

CAREER: University of Cape Town, Cape Town, South Africa, lecturer, 1949-62, senior lecturer in economics, 1963-66; Rhodes University, Grahamstown, Cape Province, South Africa, professor of economics, 1967-73, dean of Faculty of Social Science, 1970-73; South African Zionist Federation, Johannesburg, director-general, 1973—. *Member:* Economic Society of South Africa, Economic History Society, South African Institute of International Affairs (fellow). *Awards, honors:* Founders' medal and prize from Economic Society of South Africa, 1962, for outstanding original research on aspects of South African economic history.

WRITINGS: John Company at the Cape, South Africa Government Printer, 1962; *Supplies for Napoleon's Gaolers*, South Africa Government Printer, 1964; *Agency and Island*, South Africa Government Printer, 1965; *Economists and Economic Historians*, Rhodes University Press, 1968; *The Economist at the Breakfast Table*, College Tutorial Press (Cape Town, South Africa), 1971; *Storm in a Teacup*, Struik, 1973, Verry, 1974.

WORK IN PROGRESS: Jewish Economic History: An Introductory Survey, for Jewish Publication Society of America.

* * *

ARLOW, Jacob A. 1912-

PERSONAL: Born September 3, 1912, in New York, N.Y.; son of Adolph and Ida Arlow; married Alice Diamond, October 31, 1936; children: Michael Saul, Allan Joseph, Seth Martin, Jonathan Bruce. *Education:* New York University, B.S., 1932, M.D., 1936; New York Psychoanalytic Institute, graduate, 1947. *Home:* 94 Wildwood Rd., Kings Point, N.Y. 11024. *Office:* 120 Central Park S., New York, N.Y. 10019.

CAREER: Harlem Hosptial, New York, N.Y., intern, 1936-38; resident at Kings County Hospital, New York, N.Y., 1939-40, and at Montefiore Hospital, Bronx, N.Y., and New York State Psychiatric Institute, New York, N.Y., 1940-41; Presbyterian Hospital, New York, N.Y., associate psychiatrist, 1944-52; New York Psychoanalytic

Institute, New York, N.Y., instructor, 1950—; State University of New York, Downstate Medical Center, Brooklyn, associate professor, 1950-62, clinical professor of psychiatry, 1962—. Private practice as psychiatrist, 1942—. Visiting professor at Albert Einstein College of Medicine, 1971, and Mount Sinai College of Medicine, 1972; previously visiting professor at Columbia University and Louisiana State University. Member of professional advisory board, Pride of Judea Children's Services, 1960—.

MEMBER: American Psychiatric Association, American Psychoanalytic Association (president, 1959-60), International Psychoanalytic Association, New York Academy of Sciences, New York Psychoanalytic Institute and Society (president, 1966). *Awards, honors:* Clinical Essay Prize of British Psychoanalytical Society, 1956, for paper, "On Smugness"; Brill Award of New York Psychoanalytic Society, 1963, for paper, "Phantasy, Reality and Memory."

WRITINGS: The Legacy of Sigmund Freud, International Universities Press, 1956; (with Charles Brenner) *Psychoanalytic Concepts and the Structural Theory* (monograph), International Universities Press, 1964; (editor and author of introducation) *Selected Writings of Bertram D. Lewin, M.D.*, Psychoanalytic Quarterly, Inc., 1973.

Contributor: Flanders Dunbar and others, *Synopsis of Psychosomatic Diagnosis and Treatment*, Mosby, 1948; Sidney Hook, editor, *Psychoanalysis, Scientific Method and Philosophy*, International Universities Press, 1959; Morton Levitt, editor, *Readings in Psychoanalytic Psychology*, Appleton, 1959; R. M. Loewenstein and others, editors, *Psychoanalysis–A General Psychology: Essays in Honor of Heinz Hartmann*, International Universitites Press, 1966; Robert Litman, editor, *Psychoanalysis in the Americas*, International Universities Press, 1966; Silvano Arieti, editor, *The World Biennial of Psychiatry and Psychotherapy*, Volume I, Basic Books, 1970; John B. McDevitt and Calvin F. Settlage, editors, *Separation-Individuation: Essays in Honor of Margaret S. Mahler*, International Universities Press, 1971; H.Z. Winnik, Raphael Moses, and Mortimer Ostow, editors, *Psychological Bases for War*, Quadrangle, 1973. Contributor to *Encyclopedia of Mental Health, International Encyclopedia of the Social Sciences*, and to *Annual Survey of Psychoanalysis*. Contributor of about eighty articles and reviews to scientific journals in United States, Jerusalem, Spain, France, and other countries, and to *Saturday Review*.

WORK IN PROGRESS: Books on the methodology of psychoanalysis, on the psychology of time, and on Yukio Mishima.

* * *

ARMINGTON, John Calvin 1923-

PERSONAL: Born September 5, 1923, in Chelsea, Mass.; son of Everett Allan and Sarah Catherine Armington; married Jean Mollet, December 28, 1946; children: Stephen, Bryan, Susan (Mrs. William Holloway). *Education:* Tufts University, B.S. in E.E., 1947, M.S., 1949, Ph.D., 1952. *Home:* 35 Larch Row, Wenham, Mass. 01984. *Office:* Department of Psychology, Northeastern University, Boston, Mass. 02115.

CAREER: Brown University, Providence, R.I., research associate, 1949-52; Walter Reed Army Medical Center, Institute of Research, Washington, D.C., research psychologist, 1952-66, chief of department of sensory psychology, 1962-66; Northeastern University, Boston, Mass., professor of psychology, 1967—. Advisory member of vision committee, National Research Council. *Military service:* U.S. Navy, 1943-46; became lieutenant; received Presidential Unit Citation. *Member:* Optical Society of America (fellow), American Association for the Advancement of Science (fellow), Psychonomic Association, International Society of Clinical Electroretinography, Association for Research in Vision and Ophthalmology, Eastern Psychological Association, Sigma Xi, Tau Beta Pi.

WRITINGS: (Contributor) Eugene E. Bernard and Morley R. Kane, editors, *Biological Prototypes and Synthetic Systems,* Volume I, Plenum, 1961; *The Physiological Basis of Psychology; The Self-Selection Textbook of Psychology*, W. C. Brown, 1966, 2nd edition, 1973; (contributor) Benjamin B. Wolman, editor, *Handbook of General Psychology*, Prentice-Hall, 1973; *The Electroretinogram*, Academic Press, in press. Publications include research reports for Walter Reed Army Medical Center and National Research Council. Contributor to proceedings of international symposium on clinical electroretinography, and about sixty articles to optical and psychology journals. Member of editorial board, *Journal of General Psychology*, 1970—; member of honorary advisory board, *Vision Research*.

WORK IN PROGRESS: Research on relations between eye movements and visual potentials from the retina and from the brain.

* * *

ARMISTEAD, Samuel (Gordon) 1927-

PERSONAL: Born August 21, 1927, in Philadelphia, Pa.; son of George A. and Elizabeth R. (Tucker) Armistead; married Pilar Valcarcel, September 3, 1953. *Education:* Princeton University, A.B., 1950, M.A., 1952, Ph.D., 1955. *Home:* 4524 Spruce St., Philadelphia, Pa. 19139. *Office:* Department of Romance Languages, University of Pennsylvania, Philadelphia, Pa. 19174.

CAREER: Princeton University, Princeton, N.J., instructor in Spanish literature, 1953-55; University of California, Los Angeles, instructor, 1956-58, assistant professor, 1958-62, associate professor of Spanish literature, 1962-67; Purdue University, Lafayette, Ind., professor of Spanish literature, 1967-68; University of Pennsylvania, Philadelphia, professor of Spanish literature, 1968—. Visiting professor at California State College (now University), Los Angeles, 1969, Rutgers University, 1969-70, Columbia University, 1970-71, and State University of New York at Stony Brook, 1972-73.

MEMBER: International Society of Ethnology and Folklore, Modern Language Association of America, American Association of Teachers of Spanish and Portuguese, American Folklore Society, Mediaeval Society of America (fellow), Societe Rencesvals, Phi Beta Kappa. *Awards, honors:* Del Amo fellowship from Del Amo Foundation (Los Angeles), 1962-63; American Council of Learned Societies fellowship, 1962-63; Guggenheim fellowship, 1971-72.

WRITINGS: (With J. H. Silverman) *Diez romances hispanicos en un manuscrito sefardi de la Isla de Rodas* (monograph; title means "Ten Hispanic Ballads in a Sephardic Manuscript from the Island of Rhodes"), Instituto di Letteratura Spagnola e Ispano-americana dell 'Universita di Pisa, 1962; (with Silverman) *The Judeo-Spanish Ballad Chapbooks of Yacob Abraham Yona*, University of California Press, 1971; (with Silverman and Biljana Sljivic-Simsic) *Judeo-Spanish Ballads from Bosnia*, University of Pennsylvania Press, 1971; (with Diego Catalan and A. Sanchez Romeralo) *El romancero en la tradicion oral moderna: Ler coloquio internacional* (title means "The Hispanic Ballad in Modern Oral Tradition: First International Colloquium"), Catedra-Seminario Menendez Pidal and Rectorado, Universidad de Madrid, 1972.

Contributor of about sixty articles to language journals, including *Hispanic Review, Kentucky Romance Quarterly, Romance Philology, Romania, Sefarad*, and *University of California Publications in Modern Philology*. Member of editorial board of *Hispanic Review* and *Romance Philology*.

WORK IN PROGRESS: Research on medieval Spanish epic and lyric poetry and historiography, and on modern Hispanic and Judeo-Spanish traditional literature.

SIDELIGHTS: Armistead has conducted research on medieval Hispanic historiography in European libraries (in Spain, France, and Great Britain); has conducted field research among Sephardic Jews in the United States and in Morocco, and has collected oral literature in Spain.

* * *

ARQUETTE, Cliff(ord) 1905-1974 (Charley Weaver)

December 28, 1905—September 23, 1974; American comedian and television performer. Obituaries: *New York Times*, September 24, 1974; *Washington Post*, September 24, 1974; *Time*, October 7, 1974; *Newsweek*, October 7, 1974; *Current Biography*, November, 1974.

* * *

ARTIS, Vicki Kimmel 1945-

PERSONAL: Born December 14, 1945, in Milwaukee, Wis.; daughter of Robert Alden and Clara (Manes) Kimmel; married Paul Gregory Artis (a medical student), May 17, 1965; children: Tad Barrett, Shane Gregory. *Education:* University of Wisconsin, B.A., 1970. *Home:* 4710 C.T.B., Oregon, Wis. 53575.

CAREER: Writer and artist. *Member:* Wisconsin Council for the Gifted and Talented, Council for Wisconsin Writers.

WRITINGS—Juvenile: *Gray Duck Catches a Friend*, Putnam, 1974; *Brown Mouse and Vole*, Putnam, 1975.

SIDELIGHTS: In 1970 Vicki Artis moved with her husband and two children to an island off the coast of British Columbia; North Pender was home to about three hundred people. Vicki Artis exhibited sculpture in Vancouver, and, with her husband, ran a small ocean shipping business. Later the Artis family moved to Pym, a private five-acre island off Vancouver Island. Here "bald eagles perched in the firs, seals pulled up on the rocks off shore, and killer whales swam in the channels. I conducted school for my children, helped with the shipping business, and exhibited my art in Vancouver." Vicki Artis now lives in a small farmhouse, writing full time, attending school part-time, and teaching a course in writing children's literature, while her husband studies at University of Wisconsin Medical School.

* * *

ASCHEIM, Skip 1943-

PERSONAL: Born August 22, 1943, in Cincinnati, Ohio; son of Burton L. and Esther (Faust) Ascheim; children: Karen. *Education:* Harvard University, A.B., 1966. *Religion:* "Holism." *Home:* 111 Chestnut St., Cambridge, Mass. 02139.

CAREER: Education Development Center, Newton, Mass., materials developer, 1966-71.

WRITINGS: (Editor) *Materials for the Open Classroom*, Seymour Lawrence, 1973.

WORK IN PROGRESS: Poetry.

SIDELIGHTS: Ascheim told *CA* that he is "peculiarly influenced by black holes."

* * *

ASSAGIOLI, Roberto 1893(?)-1974

1893(?)—August 23, 1974; Italian psychiatrist, author, and associate of Carl Jung. Obituaries: *New York Times*, August 24, 1974; *AB Bookman's Weekly*, October 7, 1974.

* * *

ASTILL, Kenneth N. 1923-

PERSONAL: Surname is pronounced *As*-till; born July 16, 1923, in Westerly, R.I.; son of John H. and Mabel (Robotham) Astill; married Patricia Lamb, April 10, 1948; children: Kenneth John, Robert M. *Education:* University of Rhode Island, B.S., 1944; Harvard University, M.S., 1953; Massachusetts Institute of Technology, Ph.D., 1961. *Religion:* Episcopalian. *Home:* 72 Yale St., Winchester, Mass. 01890. *Office:* Department of Mechanical Engineering, Tufts University, Anderson Hall, Medford, Mass. 02155.

CAREER: Chrysler Corp., Detroit, Mich., engineer, 1944-47; Tufts University, Medford, Mass., assistant professor, 1947-54, associate professor, 1954-67, professor of mechanical engineering, 1967—. Consultant to Kaye Instruments, Natick Laboratories, United Shoe Machinery, Draper Laboratories, and Sylvania Electric Corp. *Member:* American Association of University Professors, American Society of Mechanical Engineers, American Society for Engineering Education, Phi Kappa Phi, Tau Beta Pi, Sigma Xi. *Awards, honors:* National Science Foundation faculty fellow, 1968.

WRITINGS: (With B. W. Arden) *Numerical Algorithms: Origins and Applications*, Addison-Wesley, 1970; *Elementary Experiments in Mechanical Engineering*, New York University Press, 1971.

WORK IN PROGRESS: Numerical Solutions of Partial Differential Equations; Viscous Flow and Secondary Flow.

AVOCATIONAL INTERESTS: Community and professional theatre.

* * *

ATTEBERRY, William L(ouis) 1939-

PERSONAL: Born August 5, 1939, in Houston, Tex.; son of William L. (a paint contractor) and Una (a contract officer; maiden name, Varney) Atteberry; married Judith Lou Reiman, January 30, 1965; children: Alexander Linwood, Julie Louise, Hunter Llwelyn. *Education:* University of Maryland, B.S., 1962; University of Baltimore, J.D., 1965. *Politics:* Conservative. *Religion:* Christian Scientist. *Home:* 421 Belle Isle, Indian Rocks Beach, Fla. 33535. *Office:* Mortgage Investment Securities, Clearwater, Fla. 33515.

CAREER: Admitted to the Bar of Maryland, 1966; General Services Administration, Washington, D.C., realty specialist, 1962-66; Carl M. Freeman Associates, Inc. (builder-developer), Silver Spring, Md., general counsel, 1966-68; Kissell Co. (mortgage company), Springfield, Ohio, senior vice-president, 1968-74; Mortgage Investment Securities,

Clearwater, Fla., president, 1974—. Instructor in real estate finance at Wittenberg University, 1970-74. Director of U.S. Jaycees, 1967-68. *Member:* Maryland Bar Association, Maryland Jaycees (vice-president; executive vice-president, 1966-68).

WRITINGS: Modern Real Estate Finance, Grid, 1972; (with Mike Litka and Karl Pearson) *Real Estate Law*, Grid, 1974. Contributor to *American Banker* and *Ohio Realtor*.

WORK IN PROGRESS: Revising *Modern Real Estate Finance*; *Real Estate Investments*, completion expected in 1976.

* * *

AUERBACH, Sylvia 1921-

PERSONAL: Born March 6, 1921, in Philadelphia, Pa.; married Albert Auerbach (a corporation president), February 28, 1942; children: Carl, Steven. *Education:* University of Pennsylvania, B.A., 1941; Columbia University, M.S., 1960; also studied at London School of Economics and Political Science. *Home and office:* 111 East 85th St., New York, N.Y. 10028. *Agent:* Paul R. Reynolds, Inc., 599 Fifth Ave., New York, N.Y. 10017.

CAREER: Editor in business publication division, Prentice-Hall, Englewood, N.J., associate editor for *Publishers Weekly*, New York, N.Y., and supervisor, writer and editor for Federal Reserve Bank of New York, New York, N.Y.; New School for Social Research, New York, N.Y., faculty member, teaching nonfiction writing, 1966—. Teacher at workshops. *Member:* Authors Guild of Authors League of America, Society of Magazine Writers.

WRITINGS: Your Money and How to Make It S-T-R-E-T-C-H, Doubleday, 1974. Editor, *How to Live on Your Income*, published by Reader's Digest. Contributor to magazines and newspapers, including *Atlantic, Denver Post, Real Estate Review, New York Times, Chicago Tribune, Mademoiselle, and Junior Scholastic*.

WORK IN PROGRESS: A book on women and money.

SIDELIGHTS: Sylvia Auerbach's goal is to help women achieve knowledge about financial matters so that they can become independent. *Avocational interests:* Writing humor.

* * *

AULETTA, Richard P(aul) 1942-

PERSONAL: Born January 4, 1942, in New York, N.Y.; son of Victor Frank (an airline supervisor) and Martha (a legal secretary; maiden name, Osherowitz) Auletta; married Ingrid Monika Laube, December 24, 1968; children: Michelle. *Education:* Long Island University, B.A. (summa cum laude), 1963; State University of New York at Buffalo, M.A., 1967, at Stony Brook, working toward doctoral degree. *Home:* 11 Harvard Lane, Commack, N.Y. 11725. *Office:* Department of Foreign Languages and Linguistics, C.W. Post College of Long Island University, Greenvale, N.Y. 11548.

CAREER: Long Island University, C.W. Post College, Greenvale, N.Y., assistant professor of foreign languages and linguistics and academic assistant to dean, 1968—. *Member:* International Linguistic Association, American Association of Teachers of German, American Association of Teachers of French, American Association of Teachers of Spanish and Portuguese, American Association of Teachers of Italian, American Council on the Teaching of Foreign Languages, American Dialect Society, New York State Association of Foreign Language Teachers. *Awards, honors:* Fulbright fellowship to University of Marburg, 1964-65.

WRITINGS: 201 Swedish Verbs Fully Conjugated in All the Tenses, Barron's, 1974. Editor of *Bulletin of the National Association of Self-Instructional Language Programs*, 1974—.

WORK IN PROGRESS: Grammatical Terminology; Outline of European Linguistic Geography; International Etymological Glossary of the Names of the Chemical Elements.

SIDELIGHTS: Auletta has studied Latin, French, Russian, German, Spanish, Italian, Portuguese, Dutch, Romanian, Swedish, Icelandic, and other languages.

* * *

AURAND, L(eonard) W(illiam) 1920-

PERSONAL: Born February 5, 1920, in Shamokin Dam, Pa.; son of J. Wilson and Ester (Weissinger) Aurand; married Eleanor May Nichols (a dietitian), February 22, 1943; children: Rebecca Louise (Mrs. George Wallace Newton), Thomas James, Sarah Jane. *Education:* Pennsylvania State University, B.S., 1941, Ph.D., 1949; University of New Hampshire, M.S., 1947. *Religion:* Methodist. *Home and office:* 921 Trailwood Dr., Raleigh, N.C. 27606.

CAREER: North Carolina State University, Raleigh, assistant professor, 1949-54, associate professor, 1954-60, professor of food science, 1960—. Consultant to U.S. Agency for International Development. *Military service:* U.S. Navy, 1942-46. U.S. Naval Reserve, Medical Service Corps, 1946-69; retired as commander. *Member:* American Chemical Society, American Dairy Science Association, American Institute of Nutrition, Institute of Food Technologists, Sigma Xi, Phi Lambda Upsilon, Phi Kappa Phi, Alpha Zeta, Gamma Sigma Delta.

WRITINGS: (With H. O. Triebold) *Food Composition and Analysis*, Van Nostrand, 1963; (contributor) Frank Welcher, editor, *Standard Methods of Chemical Analysis*, Van Nostrand, Volume III-b, 1966; (with A. E. Woods) *Food Chemistry*, Avi, 1973.

WORK IN PROGRESS: Experimental Food Chemistry, with A. E. Woods, for Avi.

AVOCATIONAL INTERESTS: Stamp collecting, gardening.

* * *

AUSTIN, (Mildred) Aurelia

PERSONAL: Born in Decatur, Ga.; daughter of Herbert O. (a minister) and Virgil Mary (Wells) Austin; married Glen O. Finch, October 8, 1938 (died January, 1965). *Education:* Attended Southern Business University, 1931, 1933, and Emory University, 1964-65 and at earlier periods. *Politics:* "Usually vote split ticket: for the man not the party." *Religion:* Baptist. *Home:* Houston House, Apt. 1516, 1617 Fannin, Houston, Tex. 77002; and 526 Hardendorf Ave., Atlanta, Ga. 30307. *Office:* Duval Sales Corp., 300 The Main Bldg., Houston, Tex. 77002.

CAREER: Duval Sales Corp. (formerly Ashcraft-Wilkinson Co.), secretary to president-chairman of the board, Atlanta, Ga., 1952-71, secretary in export department, Houston, Tex., 1972—. *Member:* National League of

American Pen Women (first vice-president of Atlanta branch, 1967-68; secretary of Houston branch, 1972-73), Georgia Writers Association (vice-president and member of board of trustees, 1955-57), Atlanta Writers Club (president, 1967-68). *Awards, honors:* Best Book of Poems award from Atlanta Writers Club, 1958, for *Bright Feathers;* Georgia Writers Association literary achievement scroll, 1968, for *Georgia Boys with "Stonewall" Jackson;* Kate Speake Penney award, 1970, for *The Ferris Wheel;* National League of American Pen Women award, 1970, for *Portraits and Penscapes;* Thelma Thompson Sladen award, 1971, for *No Larks at Sunset.*

WRITINGS: Bright Feathers (poems), privately printed, 1958; (editor) *Leaves of Life* (poems), Atlanta Writers Club, 1964; *Georgia Boys with "Stonewall" Jackson,* University of Georgia Press, 1967; (editor) *Treasures for the Heart* (poems), National League of American Pen Women, 1974. Author of two weekly columns for Georgia newspapers, 1949-52. Contributor to periodicals, including *Georgia Review* and *Seydell Quarterly.*

WORK IN PROGRESS: A biography of Georgia's colonial president, *Archibald Bulloch;* a mystery novel, *Tall Timber; The Ferris Wheel.*

AVOCATIONAL INTERESTS: Music, art.

* * *

AVERILL, E(dgar) W(aite) 1906-

PERSONAL: Born September 2, 1906, in Syracuse, N.Y.; son of Earl A. (an engineer) and Bertha (Waite) Averill; married Barbara Briggs (a teacher), July 9, 1932; children: Ann (Mrs. Joseph Bohmer), E.W., Jr., Jeffrey Briggs. *Education:* Cornell University, A.B., 1928; Harvard University, M.B.A. (with distinction), 1931; University of Michigan. Ph.D. 1963. *Politics:* Republican. *Religion:* Presbyterian. *Home:* 3253-P San Amadeo, Laguna Hills, Calif. 92653.

CAREER: Irving Trust Co., New York, N.Y., statistician, 1931-36; Investment Counsel, Detroit, Mich., statistician, 1936-42; General Motors Corp., Truck and Coach Division, Pontiac, Mich., accounting supervisor, 1944-49; public high school teacher of mathematics in Birmingham, Mich., 1957-59; Parsons College, Fairfield, Iowa, assistant professor, 1960-61, associate professor, 1961-62, professor of mathematics, 1962-64; Clarion State College, Clarion Pa., associate professor, 1964-65, professor of mathematics, 1965-72. *Wartime service:* Air Materiel Command, 1952-53. *Member:* American Mathematical Society, Mathematical Association of America, American Statistical Association, National Council of Teachers of Mathematics, Society for Industrial and Applied Mathematics, American Association of University Professors, Phi Delta Kappa, Pi Kappa Alpha, Rod and Gun, Rotary.

WRITING: Elements of Statistics, Wiley, 1972.

AVOCATIONAL INTERESTS: Golf, fishing, hunting, travel, playing bridge.

* * *

BACHMAN, Fred 1949-

PERSONAL: Born January 24, 1949, in Niles, Mich.; son of Edmund Leroy and June (Waldorf) Bachman; married Nina Jones (a substitute teacher), June 27, 1970; children: Angela, Troy. *Education:* Michigan State University, B.A., 1971. *Home:* 1214 Walsh, Lansing, Mich. 48912. *Office:* Willow Street School, Lansing, Mich. 48906.

CAREER: Willow Street School, Lansing, Mich., first grade teacher, 1972—. *Member:* National Education Association, Michigan Education Association, Lansing Schools Education Association, Conservation Club (Lansing).

WRITINGS: Hang in at the Plate (juvenile), Walck, 1974.

WORK IN PROGRESS: The Making of an Elementary Teacher: One Man's Experience, an autobiography; *Bittersweet Basketball*, for young people; *Rock Singer*, for young people.

AVOCATIONAL INTERESTS: Music (composing).

* * *

BACON, John 1940-

PERSONAL: Born May 15, 1940, in Toledo, Ohio; son of Frank R. (a chemist) and Eleanor (Bennett) Bacon; married Gertrud Elsaesser, December 26, 1961; children: David, Sarah. *Education:* Wabash College, B.A., 1962; University of Tuebingen, graduate study, 1959-60; Yale University, M.A., 1965, Ph.D., 1966. *Home:* 50 Marble Hill Ave., Bronx, N.Y. 10463. *Office:* Department of Philosophy, York College of the City University of New York, 150-14 Jamaica Ave., Jamaica, N.Y. 11451.

CAREER: University of Texas, Austin, assistant professor of philosophy, 1966-69; Hebrew University, Jerusalem, Israel, adjunct teacher of philosophy, 1969-70; Fordham University, Bronx, N.Y., assistant professor of philosophy, 1970-74; York College of the City University of New York, Jamaica, N.Y., assistant professor of philosophy, 1974—. *Member:* American Philosophical Association, American Catholic Philosophical Association, Association for Symbolic Logic, Society for Ancient Greek Philosophy. *Awards, honors:* Council for Philosophical Studies summer fellowship, 1972.

WRITINGS: (Translator) Paul Lorenzen, *Differential and Integral: A Constructive Introduction to Classical Analysis*, University of Texas Press, 1972; (contributor) Alan Ross Anderson, Ruth Barcan Marcus, and Richard M. Martin, editors, *The Logical Enterprise: Essays in Honor of Frederic B. Fitch*, Yale University Press, 1975. Contributor of articles, reviews, and abstracts to philosophy and logic journals.

WORK IN PROGRESS: A textbook, *Basic Logic: Extensional and Modal*; a contribution to *Festschrift for Henry Margenau*, for Plenum.

* * *

BAGLEY, Edward R(osecrans) 1926-

PERSONAL: Born January 11, 1926, in Cleveland, Ohio; son of Edward Harbridge (a regional officer for U.S. Department of Agriculture) and Nina (Martin) Bagley; married Lucile Cummings (a concert artist and voice teacher), December 26, 1953. *Education:* Ohio State University, B.Sc., 1947, M.B.A., 1948. *Home and office address:* Boot Rd., Box 229-A, R. D. #2, Malvern, Pa. 19355.

CAREER: McKesson & Robbins, Inc., New York, N.Y., assistant to vice-president of merchandising, 1948-51; Coty, Inc., New York, N.Y., assistant to supervisor of sales agents, 1951-52; Cresap, McCormick & Paget (general management consultants), New York, N.Y., associate, 1953-61, partner, 1961-62; Premier Industrial Corp., Cleveland, Ohio, vice-president of corporate development, 1962-64; Bagley and Co. (corporate growth consultants), New Canaan, Conn., and New York, N.Y., owner and president, 1965-70; Towers, Perrin, Forster & Crosby, Inc. (consultants), Philadelphia, Pa., vice-president, 1970-72; Bagley and Co., Malvern, Pa., owner and president, 1972—. Member of government operations committee of Chamber of Commerce of the United States, 1967-69. *Military service:* U.S. Army Air Corps, 1944-46; became sergeant. *Member:* Association for Corporate Growth, World Futurist Society, Sierra Club (life member), Union League Club of New York, Beta Gamma Sigma, Delta Sigma Rho, Tau Kappa Epsilon.

WRITINGS: Beyond the Conglomerates, Amacom, 1975. Contributor to *Management Review* and *Dun's Review.*

WORK IN PROGRESS: Bagley's Select System for Acquisitions (tentative title), completion expected in 1976; *Fantasy Growth—Real Growth* (tentative title); *The Party's Not Over Yet* (tentative title); a book about freedom of the press.

AVOCATIONAL INTERESTS: Music; antiques; collecting English copper lustre, old Bibles, and other items; travel; politics.

* * *

BAILEY, James R(ichard) A(be) 1919-

PERSONAL: Born October 23, 1919, in London, England; son of Abe (a financier) and Mary (a pilot; maiden name, Wastenra) Bailey; married Barbara Louise Epstein (a musician); children: five. *Education:* Attended Winchester College and Christ Church, Oxford. *Home:* Wardington Lodge, Banbury, England. *Office:* Drum Publications, 40-43 Fleet St., London E.C.4, England.

CAREER: Publisher, Drum Publications, London, England.

WRITINGS: National Ambitions: Being a Critical Study of the European Desire for Progress, Basil Blackwell, 1958; *F as in Flight*, Shakespeare Head Press, 1962; *Eskimo Nel* (foreword by Peter Townsend), Howard Timmins (Cape Town), 1964; *The Sky Suspended* (autobiography; foreword by Townsend), Hodder & Stoughton, 1965; *God-Kings and the Titans: The New World Ascendancy in Ancient Times*, St. Martin's, 1973.

* * *

BAILEY, Jane H(orton) 1916-

PERSONAL: Born May 14, 1916, in Chicago, Ill.; daughter of Ralph (a businessman) and Frances (Chadwick) Horton; married Donald W. Bailey, September 29, 1941; children: David Alan, Phyllis (Mrs. Michael Fisher), Christopher. *Education:* University of California, Berkeley, A.B., 1938. *Home:* 545 Bernardo Ave., Morro Bay, Calif. 93442. *Agent:* Lenniger Literary Agency, Inc., 11 West 42nd St., New York, N.Y. 10036.

CAREER: California State Relief Administration, caseworker in San Luis Obispo and Riverside counties, 1938-39; Padua Hills Institute, Claremont, Calif., enployed in public relations, 1940-41; Sacramento Country Day School, Sacramento, Calif., teacher of Spanish, 1964-66. *Member:* International House Association, American Association of University Women, Sierra Club, Audubon Society, Common Cause, Morro Bay Tomorrow, Morro Bay Environmental Association.

WRITINGS: The Sea Otter's Struggle, Follett, 1973.

WORK IN PROGRESS: A juvenile novel on the sea otter; plays, skits, monologs, and dialogs in Spanish for students; research on our violent language, on war, and on peace.

BAILEY, Kenneth P. 1912-

PERSONAL: Born February 17, 1912, in Benton Harbor, Mich.; married Irene Marie Passarini; children: Kenneth J., Darlene Marie. *Education:* University of California, Los Angeles, A.B., 1934, M.A., 1936, Ph.D., 1938. *Politics:* Democrat. *Home:* 18751 Via Siena, Irvine, Calif. 92664. *Office:* Department of Education, University of California, Irvine, Calif. 92664.

CAREER: University of California, Los Angeles, instructor in history, 1938-39; Oceanside-Carlsbad College, Oceanside, Calif., associate dean of the college and chairman of department of social science, 1939-44; Humboldt State College, Arcata, Calif., professor of history, 1945-47, chairman of department of social sciences and dean of students, 1945-48; high school and junior college superintendent in Oceanside, Calif., and director of Oceanside-Carlsbad College, 1948-50; Long Beach City College, Long Beach, Calif., coordinator of community services, 1950-53; high school principal in San Bernardino, Calif., 1953-67; University of California, Irvine, senior lecturer in history and director of teacher education, 1967—. Instructor in education at University of Redlands, 1954—, and University of California, Riverside, 1955—. Member of California State Curriculum Commission, 1955-70; chairman of California Statewide Social Science Framework Committee, 1973—.

MEMBER: International Reading Association (member of Orange County council), American Association for Higher Education, American Historical Association, Association for Supervision and Curriculum Development, National Association for Humanities Education, National Association of Secondary School Principals, Association of California School Administrators, California Council on the Education of Teachers. *Awards, honors:* American Historical Association award, 1939, for *The Ohio Company of Virginia.*

WRITINGS: The Ohio Company of Virginia and the Westward Movement, 1748-1792: A Chapter in the History of the Colonial Frontier, Arthur Clark, 1939; *Thomas Cresap: Maryland Frontiersman,* Christopher Publishing, 1944; *The Ohio Company Papers, 1753-1817: Being Primarily Papers of the "Suffering Traders" of Pennsylvania,* California Society of the Sons of the Revolution, 1947; *American Political Institutions,* Edwards Brothers, 1948, 6th edition, 1965; *Survey of American History,* Edwards Brothers, 1951; *American and California Government Background Institutions, Functions, and Popular Control,* Edwards Brothers, 1965; *The American Adventure,* Field Educational Publications, 1970; (with S. E. Frost, Jr.) *Historical and Philosophical Foundations of Western Education,* C. E. Merrill, 1973; (contributor) *Handbook of the North American Indian,* Smithsonian Institution, 1973. Contributor to *Western Pennsylvania Magazine of History, Pacific Historical Review,* and *William and Mary Quarterly Historical Magazine.*

WORK IN PROGRESS: Christopher Gist: Explorer, Guide, and Frontiersman; The Marin Journal, a translation.

* * *

BAILEY, Maralyn Collins (Harrison) 1941-

PERSONAL: Born April 24, 1941, in Nottingham, England; married Maurice Charles Bailey (a printer's clerk), December 21, 1963. *Education:* Educated in Derby, England. *Politics:* None. *Religion:* None. *Home:* 18 La Petite

Rue, St. Annes, Ile d'Aurigny, Channel Islands. *Agent:* John Farquharson Ltd., 15 Red Lion Sq., London W.C.1, England.

CAREER: Government tax officer. Director of Maulyn Ltd. of Jersey. *Awards, honors:* Named Southern Yachtsman of the Year, 1973; Uffa Fox trophy from Southern Newspapers, 1973, for outstanding seamanship.

WRITINGS: (With husband, Maurice Charles Bailey) *Staying Alive,* McKay, 1974. Contributor to *Bookseller.*

WORK IN PROGRESS: A voyage to Patagonia.

SIDELIGHTS: In 1973, the Bailey's twin-keel sloop was shipwrecked about four hundred fifty miles from the Galapagos Islands, enroute from England to New Zealand. They spent a hundred seventeen days adrift on a covered rubber raft, sometimes passing near large ships which failed to see them. They were rescued by a Korean fishing boat about fifteen hundred miles from the spot where they had been shipwrecked, and their book is one result of their misadventure.

AVOCATIONAL INTERESTS: Wildlife, conservation, travel (especially under sail), needlework, medieval history.

BIOGRAPHICAL/CRITICAL SOURCES: Time, June 3, 1974.

* * *

BAILEY, Maurice Charles 1932-

PERSONAL: Born December 27, 1932, in Derby England; married Maralyn Collins Harrison, December 21, 1963. *Education:* Educated in Derby, England. *Politics:* Socialist. *Religion:* None. *Home:* 18 La Petite Rue, St. Annes, Ile d'Aurigny, Channel Islands. *Agent:* John Farquharson Ltd., 15 Red Lion Sq., London W.C.1, England.

CAREER: Printer's clerk. Managing director of Maulyn Ltd. of Jersey. *Military service:* British Army, 1951-54. *Member:* Ocean Cruising Club. *Awards, honors:* Named Southern Yachtsman of the Year, 1973; Uffa Fox trophy from Southern Newspapers, 1973, for outstanding seamanship.

WRITINGS: (With wife, Maralyn Collins Bailey) *Staying Alive,* McKay, 1974. Contributor to *Sail, Yachting Monthly.*

WORK IN PROGRESS: A voyage to Patagonia.

SIDELIGHTS: In 1973, the Baileys' twin-keel sloop was shipwrecked about four hundred fifty miles from the Galapagos Islands, enroute from England to New Zealand. They spent a hundred seventeen days adrift on a covered rubber raft, sometimes passing near large ships which failed to see them. They were rescued by a Korean fishing boat about fifteen hundred miles from the spot where they had been shipwrecked, and their book is one result of their misadventure.

AVOCATIONAL INTERESTS: Wildlife, conservation, travel, yachting, gliding, walking, navigation.

BIOGRAPHICAL/CRITICAL SOURCES: Time, June 3, 1974.

* * *

BAIRD, Robert D(ahlen) 1933-

PERSONAL: Born June 29, 1933, in Philadelphia, Pa.; son of Jesse Dahlen (an accountant) and Clara (a teacher; maiden name, Sonntag) Baird; married Patty Jo Lutz (a teacher), December 20, 1954; children: Linda Sue, Stephen Robert, David Bryan, Janna Ann. *Education:* Houghton College, B.A., 1954; Fuller Theological Seminary, B.D., 1957; Southern Methodist University, S.T.M., 1959; University of Iowa, Ph.D., 1964. *Home:* 315 Kimball Rd., Iowa City, Iowa 52240. *Office:* School of Religion, University of Iowa, Iowa City, Iowa 52242.

CAREER: Ordained Presbyterian minister, 1971; University of Omaha, Omaha, Neb., instructor, 1962-64, assistant professor of philosophy of religion, 1964-65; University of Iowa, Iowa City, assistant professor, 1966-69, associate professor, 1969-74, professor of history of religions, 1974—. *Member:* Institute of Constitutional and Parliamentary Studies, American Academy of Religion, Association of Asian Studies, American Association of University Professors. *Awards, honors:* Ford Foundation faculty fellow at University of Wisconsin, summer, 1965, at University of Chicago, summer, 1966; Society for Religion in Higher Education postdoctoral fellowship, 1965-66; American Institute of Indian Studies faculty fellowship, 1972, for research in India.

WRITINGS: Category Formation and the History of Religions, Mouton & Co., 1971; (with others) *Religion and Man: An Introduction,* Harper, 1971; (with Alfred Bloom) *Indian and Far Eastern Religious Traditions,* Harper, 1972. Contributor to journals in his field.

WORK IN PROGRESS: A book on the categories of religion and the secular, and their role in religious change in modern India.

* * *

BAIRD, Ronald J(ames) 1929-

PERSONAL: Born June 20, 1929, in Lakewood, Ohio; son of James Lepage (a tool designer) and Ava (Rainey) Baird; married Marjorie Ann Johns, September 1, 1951; children: David, Linda. *Education:* Attended Purdue University, 1948-50; Bowling Green State University, B.S., 1952; University of Missouri, M.Ed., 1953; Michigan State University, Ed.D., 1960. *Religion:* Methodist. *Home:* 5544 Pine View Dr., Ypsilanti, Mich. 48197. *Office:* Department of Industrial Education, Eastern Michigan University, Ypsilanti, Mich. 48197.

CAREER: Murray State University, Murray, Ky., assistant professor of industrial education, 1955-57; Michigan State University, East Lansing, instructor in industrial education, 1957-60; Ohio University, Athens, assistant professor of industrial education, 1960-65; State University of New York at Buffalo, professor of industrial education, 1965-66; Eastern Michigan University, Ypsilanti, professor of industrial education, 1966-72; Goodheart-Willcox Co. (book publishers), South Holland, Ill., editor, 1972-73; Eastern Michigan University, professor of industrial education, 1973—. *Member:* American Industrial Arts Association, American Council on Industrial Arts Teacher Education, American Association of University Professors, Michigan Industrial Education Society.

WRITINGS: Industrial Plastics, Goodheart, 1971; *Contemporary Industrial Teaching,* Goodheart, 1972; (with Clois E. Kicklighter) *Architecture, Residential Drawing, and Design,* Goodheart, 1973; (with Alfred Roth) *Small Gasoline Engines,* Goodheart, 1975; *Oxyacetylene Welding,* Goodheart, 1975; (with Kicklighter) *Exploring Crafts,* Goodheart, in press.

AVOCATIONAL INTERESTS: Wood turning, camping, golf, most sports.

BAIRD, Thomas 1923-

PERSONAL: Born April 22, 1923, in Omaha, Neb.; son of Edgar A. and Alice (Kennard) Baird. *Education:* Princeton University, B.A., 1945, M.F.A., 1950. *Politics:* None. *Religion:* None. *Home:* 70 Lorraine St., Hartford, Conn. 06105. *Agent:* Harold Ober Associates, Inc., 40 East 49th St., New York, N.Y. 10017. *Office:* Trinity College, Hartford, Conn. 06105.

CAREER: Princeton University, Princeton, N.J., instructor in art history, 1949-51, 1952-53; Frick Collection, New York, N.Y., lecturer in art history, 1954-57; National Gallery of Art, Washington, D.C., member of curatorial staff, 1957-60; Dumbarton Oaks, Washington, D.C., associate director, 1967-70; Trinity College, Hartford, Conn., associate professor of history of art, 1970—; writer. *Military service:* U.S. Naval Reserve, 1943-46.

WRITINGS—Novels; all published by Harcourt: *Triumphal Entry*, 1962; *The Old Masters*, 1963; *Sheba's Landing*, 1964; *Nice Try*, 1965; *Finding Out*, 1967; *People Who Pull You Down*, 1970; *Loving People*, 1974.

WORK IN PROGRESS: A novel.

* * *

BAKER, Adolph 1917-

PERSONAL: Born November 15, 1917, in Russia; came to United States, 1929; son of Isaac I. and Anna (Kornfield) Baker; married Dora E. Krugman (a teacher), November 7, 1942; children: Linda J., Daniel R., Ellen J. *Education:* City College of New York (now City College of the City University of New York), B.A., 1938, M.S. in Ed., 1939; Polytechnic Institute of Brooklyn, B.M.E., 1946; New York University, M.S., 1949; Brandeis University, Ph.D., 1964. *Home:* 7 Gage Rd., Wayland, Mass. 01778. *Office:* Department of Physics, University of Lowell, Lowell, Mass. 01854.

CAREER: Republic Aviation Corp., Farmingdale, N.Y., engineer, 1946-47; Ranger Aircraft Engines, Farmingdale, N.Y., senior engineer, 1947-48; International Business Machines Corp. (IBM), New York, N.Y., senior staff member, 1948-49; Raytheon Co., Waltham, Mass., senior engineer, 1949-54; Radio Corporation of America (RCA), Burlington, Mass., manager of systems analysis, 1954-55, manager of computer development, 1955-59; University of Lowell (formerly Lowell Technological Institute), Lowell, Mass., professor of physics, 1963—. Consultant to Radio Corporation of America, 1959-65. *Military service:* U.S. Army, 1942-46; became first lieutenant; received Bronze Star and Purple Heart with cluster. *Member:* American Physical Society, Sigma Xi. *Awards, honors:* Senior Fulbright-Hays scholar, 1974-75, at University of Tbilisi, U.S.S.R.

WRITINGS: Modern Physics and Antiphysics, Addison-Wesley, 1970; (with others) *Physical Sciences Today: Concepts in Physics*, CRM Books, 1973. Contributor to *Physical Review, Applied Optics*, and *Physics Today*.

WORK IN PROGRESS: Research on scattering theory.

* * *

BAKER, James Lawrence 1941-

PERSONAL: Born October 25, 1941, in Buffalo, N.Y.; son of Harold A. (a personnel representative) and Catherine (Sheehan) Baker; married Barbara Buscher (a teacher), January 20, 1968; children: Kathleen, Lee Ann, Thomas. *Education:* State University of New York at Buffalo, B.A., 1963. *Home:* 131 Brentwood Dr., North Tonawanda, N.Y. 14120. *Agent:* Janet Robinson, 4511 Harlem Rd., Buffalo, N.Y. 14226. *Office: Courier-Express*, 785 Main St., Buffalo, N.Y. 14240.

CAREER: Courier-Express, Buffalo, N.Y., sports writer, 1963—. *Military service:* U.S. Army National Guard, 1964-70. *Member:* Pro Football Writers of America, American Newspaper Guild. *Awards, honors:* Page One Award from American Newspaper Guild, 1973, for feature story on O. J. Simpson.

WRITINGS: O. J. Simpson: January, 1974, Grosset, 1974; *Buffalo Bills*, Prentice-Hall, 1974; *Billie Jean King*, Grosset, 1975. Contributor to *Football Digest, Sports Digest, Buffalo Spree*, and *Buffalo Fan*.

WORK IN PROGRESS: Research on Buffalo Bills' coach Lou Saban, and on Bob McAdoo and the Buffalo Braves.

* * *

BAKER, Robert B(ernard) 1937-

PERSONAL: Born December 5, 1937, in New York, N.Y.; stepson of Hal Murray (a podiatrist) and Freda (a puppeteer; maiden name, Ginsburg) Baker; married Arlene S. Bernstein (an artist), November 28, 1958; children: Nathaniel, Meredith. *Education:* City College (now City College of the City University of New York), B.A., 1959; University of Minnesota, Ph.D., 1967; postdoctoral study at Haverford College, summer, 1974. *Politics:* "Anarchist and Feminist." *Religion:* Agnostic. *Residence:* London, England. *Office:* Department of Philosophy, Humanities Center, Union College, Schenectady, N.Y. 12308.

CAREER: University of Minnesota, Minneapolis, instructor in philosophy, 1964-65; University of Iowa, Iowa City, instructor, 1965-67, assistant professor of philosophy, 1967-69; Wayne State University, Detroit, Mich., visiting professor, 1969-70, assistant professor of philosophy, 1970-73; Union College, Schenectady, N.Y., assistant professor of philosophy, 1973—. Coordinator of medical ethics and philosophy of medicine at Albany Medical College, 1974—. Member of Michigan governor's task force on victimless crime; consultant to Michigan Institute for the Study of Non-Violence and Medical Behavioral Research Group.

MEMBER: American Philosophical Association, Hastings Institute of Society, Ethics, and the Life Sciences, Iowa Philosophical Society (president, 1969-70), Michigan Academy of Arts and Sciences. *Awards, honors:* Old Gold research fellowship, 1969; junior research fellowship from National Endowment for the Humanities, 1969, Fields fellow, 1975; summer grant from Council of Philosophical Studies, 1974; faculty development grant from Ford Foundation, autumn, 1974.

WRITINGS: (With D. B. Terrell) *A Workbook in Logic*, Holt, 1967; (editor with others and contributor) *The Report of the Governor's Task Force on Victimless Crime*, Office of Substance Abuse (Lansing, Mich.), 1973; (contributor) Richard Wasserstrom, editor, *Today's Moral Problems*, Macmillan, 1974; (editor and contributor with Frederick Elliston) *Sex from a Philosophical Point of View*, Prometheus, 1975. Contributor to *Moving Out*.

WORK IN PROGRESS: The Psychosurgery of John Doe; Illness and Deviancy; research on deviancy and medicine.

SIDELIGHTS: Prior to the social ferment of the sixties, Baker's primary interests were logic and metaphysics. During the 1960's, he wrote for the underground press, and worked closely with the "resistance" and later with various feminist groups. Since 1970, his work has been in social and political philosophy and the philosophy of medicine.

* * *

BAKJIAN, Andy 1915-

PERSONAL: Born August 20, 1915, in Union City, N.J.; son of John and Annie (Fourounjian) Bakjian; married Mary Vartanian, December 20, 1947; children: Deborah Eloise (Mrs. William J. Backstrom), Cynthia Ann. *Education:* Chapman College, A.B., 1942; University of Southern California, graduate study, 1945-53; California State University, Los Angeles, M.A., 1961. *Home:* 7812 Via Amorita, Downey, Calif. 90241. *Office:* Jefferson High School, Los Angeles, Calif. 90011.

CAREER: Santa Monica College, Santa Monica, Calif., wrestling coach, 1935-37; Los Angeles City Schools, Los Angeles, Calif., recreation director, 1938-42, physical education teacher and coach, 1945-75. Wrestling coach at Chapman College, 1937-42; member of special Olympics committee of Kennedy Foundation. *Military service:* U.S. Army Air Force, physical training instructor and director, 1942-45; became technical sergeant. *Member:* National High School Coaches Association, Olympic Trials Officials, Amateur Athletic Union (member of Southern Pacific Association), California Coaches Association, Los Angeles Coaches Association, Los Angeles Police Revolver and Athletic Club, Masons, Shriners. *Awards, honors:* Los Angeles Police Department, two service awards, 1974.

WRITINGS: *Track Management*, Jefferson Press, 1970; *Hitch in Hell*, Oliver Co., 1974. Contributor to sports magazines, including *Athletic Journal, Coach and Athlete, Scholastic Coach*, and *California Association for Health, Physical Education and Recreation Journal*.

WORK IN PROGRESS: *Till Dawn's Early Light*.

* * *

BALDREE, J(asper) Martin, Jr. 1927-

PERSONAL: Born February 4, 1927, in Williston, Fla.; son of J.M. (a minister) and Lassie (Chesser) Baldree; married Betty Ann Whaley (a receptionist), January 30, 1960; children: Tanya Elizabeth, Jon Martin. *Education:* Lee College, Cleveland, Tenn., A.A., 1947; Asbury College, A.B., 1954; Southwestern Baptist Theological Seminary, M.R.E., 1957; Southern Baptist Theological Seminary, graduate study, 1970-72. *Politics:* Republican. *Religion:* Protestant. *Home:* 3803 Crestwood Dr. N.W., Cleveland, Tenn. 37311. *Office:* Department of Christian Education, Lee College, Cleveland, Tenn. 37311.

CAREER: Lee College, Cleveland, Tenn., registrar, 1946-48; Church of God, Cleveland, Tenn., curriculum writer of Sunday school literature, 1954-55; Milford Church of God, Milford, Del., director of Christian education, 1957-60; Church of God, Cleveland, Tenn., editorial assistant in Christian education department, 1960-62; Lee College, assistant professor, 1961-67, associate professor of Christian education, 1967—. *Military service:* U.S. Navy, 1949-52. *Member:* National Education Association, Religious Education Association, National Association of Professors of Christian Education (corresponding secretary, 1966-67), East Tennessee Education Association.

WRITINGS: *How to Enlarge Your Sunday School*, Church of God Youth and Christian Education Department, 1962; *Sunday School Growth*, Pathway Press, 1971.

AVOCATIONAL INTERESTS: Gardening.

BALFOUR, Conrad George 1928-

PERSONAL: Born October 20, 1928, in Providence, R.I.; son of Garth Robert and Ruby (a social worker; maiden name, Beckair) Balfour; married Rose Strasser, 1958 (divorced, 1972); married Mary Jean Skalet (a high school counselor), July 6, 1973; children: (first marriage) Sharon Linda, Robert Kevin, Jeannine Michelle. *Education:* Attended Drake University, 1949, Boston University, 1954-55, and University of Minnesota, 1970. *Politics:* "Suspicious." *Home:* 4312 Linden Hills Blvd. #101, Minneapolis, Minn. 55410.

CAREER: Dayton-Hudson Co., Minneapolis, Minn., director of minority hiring, 1969-70; Commission of Human Rights, Minneapolis, Minn., commissioner, 1970-71; Urban Coalition, Minneapolis, Minn., director, 1971-73; full-time writer in Minneapolis, Minn., 1973—. Consultant to U.S. Navy. *Military service:* U.S. Air Force, 1950-54. *Awards, honors:* Bush fellowship award for photography, 1974.

WRITINGS: *Sack Full of Sun* (semi-autobiography), Dillon, 1974.

WORK IN PROGRESS: *Dakotah Indian Hanging: 1862*; a bicentennial trip to photograph native Americans and interview them on thoughts of America.

* * *

BALIAN, Lorna 1929-

PERSONAL: Surname rhymes with "stallion"; born December 14, 1929, in Milwaukee, Wis.; daughter of Henry W. (with the telephone company) and Molly (Pope) Kohl; married John J. Balian (an artist), March 4, 1950; children: Heather, Japheth, Ivy, Aram, Lecia, Poppy. *Education:* Attended Layton School of Art, 1948-49. *Home and office address:* Route 2, Box 84, Hartford, Wis. 53207.

CAREER: American Lace Co., Milwaukee, Wis., artist, 1949-51; free-lance artist, 1948—. Teacher of crafts in adult vocational school. *Member:* Authors Guild of Authors League of America.

WRITINGS—Juvenile; all self-illustrated: *Humbug Witch* (Junior Literary Guild selection), Abingdon, 1965; *I Love You, Mary Jane* (Junior Literary Guild selection), Abingdon, 1967; *The Aminal*, Abingdon, 1972; *Sometimes It's Turkey-Sometimes It's Feathers*, Abingdon, 1973; *Where in the World Is Henry?*, Bradbury, 1973; *Humbug Rabbit*, (Junior Literary Guild selection), Abingdon, 1974.

WORK IN PROGRESS: Writing and illustrating *The Sweet Touch*.

AVOCATIONAL INTERESTS: Gardening, cooking, sewing, painting.

* * *

BALLANTINE, John (Winthrop) 1920-

PERSONAL: Born October 1, 1920, in New York, N.Y.; son of Arthur A. (a lawyer) and Helen (Graves) Ballantine; married Lucia Heffelfinger, August 7, 1948 (divorced February, 1969); married Rosina Carone, October 3, 1970; children: (first marriage) John W., Jr., Lucia P. *Education:* Harvard University, B.A., 1942, M.S., 1948, Ph.D., 1955. *Politics:* Independent. *Religion:* Congregational. *Home:* 156 East 79th St., New York, N.Y. 10021. *Office:* Stevens Institute, Hoboken, N.J. 07030.

CAREER: New Jersey State Mediation Board, Newark, mediator, 1949-55; Baldwin-Ehret Hall, Trenton, N.J., director of industrial relations, 1955-63; Stevens Institute,

Hoboken, N.J., professor of management and head of department of management science, 1963—. *Military service:* U.S. Naval Reserve, 1942-46; became lieutenant. *Member:* American Economic Association, Industrial Relations Research Association.

WRITINGS: Transmitting Information, Industrial Relations Section, Princeton University, 1950; *The Human Side of Economics,* Mimir Publishers, 1973.

WORK IN PROGRESS: Competition or Community: Our Economic Dilemma, a collection of essays.

* * *

BALTHAZAR, Earl E(dward) 1918-

PERSONAL: Surname is pronounced Bal-tha-zar, no one syllable accented; born October 15, 1918, in Waterbury, Conn.; son of Edward Joseph (a lawyer) and Madeline Dorothea (Ritchie) Balthazar; married Gerti Amler, January 11, 1947. *Education:* University of Kansas, B.A., 1941; University of Connecticut, M.A., 1949; University of Illinois, Ph.D., 1954. *Politics:* Independent. *Religion:* Roman Catholic. *Home:* 1518 Wyldewood Dr., Madison, Wis. 53704. *Office:* Central Wisconsin Colony and Training School, 317 Knutson Dr., Madison, Wis. 53704.

CAREER: Drake University, Des Moines, Iowa, assistant professor of psychology, 1954-56; Flint Community College, Flint, Mich., Ballenger Chair in Psychology, 1956-58; Caro State Hospital, Caro, Mich., director of psychology, 1958-64; Central Wisconsin Colony and Training School, Madison, director of psychological services, 1964-68, research scientist, 1968—. Lecturer in psychology, University of Wisconsin, Madison, 1965-68. Consultant on mental retardation, Wisconsin Division of Mental Hygiene, 1964-66. *Military service:* U.S. Army, 1942-46; served in Europe; became staff sergeant; received five battle stars.

MEMBER: American Psychological Association, American Association on Mental Deficiency (fellow), International Congress on the Scientific Study of Mental Deficiency; and related state and county societies. *Awards, honors:* Rosemary F. Dybwad International Award of National Association for Retarded Children, 1970.

WRITINGS: (With G. E. English) *A System for Classifying the Social Behavior of the Severely Retarded* (monograph), Central Wisconsin Colony and Training School, 1969; (with Harvey A. Stevens) *The Emotionally Disturbed Mental Retarded: A Historical and Contemporary Perspective,* Prentice-Hall, 1974; *How to Train the Retarded Child or Adult: A Manual for Parents, Home Trainers, Teachers and Others,* Consulting Psychologists Press, in press. Publications include *The Balthazar Scales of Adaptive Behavior,* Consulting Psychologists Press, Section I, 1972, Section II, 1973; an independent series of ten monographs, "Programs for the Developmentally Disabled: A Multidisciplinary Approach," Wisconsin State Printing Division, 1975-76; and a film report, "The Balthazar Scales." Contributor to professional journals in United States, Netherlands, England, and Belgium.

WORK IN PROGRESS: With Ronald M. Sindberg, *The Psychology of the Severely Retarded*; a new film, "The Balthazar Scales: Application to Program Development."

SIDELIGHTS: Balthazar says that he was never able to fully decide in his college years whether to major in English or French literature, medieval European history, psychology, or philosophy, but has through his travels "continued my interest in European history and have secret dreams of writing fiction with a European background." He adds: "My wife, who was formerly an Austrian citizen, and I have a house in Vienna and we plan our retirement there. . . . Being the perfect dilettante, I have loved almost every minute of my ten trips to Europe, Austria particularly, and the food, the good wine, and the mountains are not the least of it."

AVOCATIONAL INTERESTS: Music, art.

* * *

BANDINELLI, Ranuccio Bianchi 1901(?)-1975

1901(?)—January 17, 1975; Italian classicist, archeologist, and political (communist) activist. Obituaries: *New York Times*, January 18, 1975.

* * *

BANNER, Melvin Edward 1914-

PERSONAL: Born July 16, 1914, in McDonald, Pa.; son of Franklin Clyde (a musician) and Carrie (Taylor) Banner; married Arline Hawkins, March 19, 1937 (died February 9, 1972); married Patricia Duignan (a teacher), June 17, 1972; children: (first marriage) Melvina (Mrs. Jon Ford). *Education:* University of Michigan, B.A., 1948, M.A., 1950; Michigan State University, graduate study, 1964-68. *Home:* 1913 Barks St., Flint, Mich. 48503.

CAREER: Flint Board of Education, Flint, Mich., teacher of humanities, 1950—. President, United Teachers of Flint, 1970-72; vice-president, Flint Human Relations Commission, 1971-72. *Member:* National Education Association, American Academy of Social and Political Science, Michigan Education Association, Michigan Archaeological and Historical Society, Phi Delta Kappa. *Awards, honors:* Law Day Liberty Bell award from Bar Association of Flint, Mich., 1972; Michigan Education Association distinguished service award, 1972.

WRITINGS: A Short Negro History, privately printed, 1964; *The Black Pioneer in Michigan,* Pendell, Volume I: *Flint and Genesee County,* 1973. Contributor to *Telescope.*

WORK IN PROGRESS: Volume II of *The Black Pioneer in Michigan.*

* * *

BARDENS, Amey E. 1894(?)-1974

1894(?)—November 21, 1974; American public health nurse and author of book on child care. Obituaries: *New York Times*, November 23, 1974; *AB Bookman's Weekly*, December 16, 1974.

* * *

BARKOW, Al 1932-

PERSONAL: Born July 13, 1932, in Chicago, Ill.; son of Harry Isidore (employed in general services) and Gertrude (Strinel) Barkow; married Shami Levine (a consultant), October 1, 1967; children: Deborah. *Education:* Roosevelt University, B.A., 1960. *Politics:* Liberal Democrat. *Religion:* "Jewish-Unitarian." *Home and office:* 9 Glenridge Pkwy., Montclair, N.J. 07042. *Agent:* Tim Seldes, 551 Fifth Ave., New York, N.Y. 10017.

CAREER: Assistant editor with R. H. Donnelley Corp. and McGraw-Hill Co., 1960-63; "Shell's Wonderful World of Golf" (television series), New York, N.Y., chief writer, 1962-69; free-lance writer, 1969-71; *Golf* (magazine), New York, N.Y., editor-in-chief, 1971-72; free-lance writer,

1972—. Writer and consultant for World Golf Hall of Fame. *Military service:* U.S. Air Force, 1952-56; became staff sergeant. *Member:* Golf Writers Association of America, U.S. Tennis Writers Association.

WRITINGS: Golf's Golden Grind, Harcourt, 1974. Contributor to *Golf Digest*, *Golf*, and *Sport*.

WORK IN PROGRESS: A history of tennis.

AVOCATIONAL INTERESTS: Music, visual arts.

* * *

BARNA, Yon 1927-

PERSONAL: Born May 31, 1927, in Oradea, Romania; son of Nicolae (a pharmacist) and Elisabeth (Rona) Barna; married Maria Kardas (a pianist); children: Julia Orit (Mrs. Itzhak Nachman). *Education:* University of Bucharest, M.A., 1949. *Religion:* Jewish. *Home:* 8 Giladi St., Talpiot, Jerusalem, Israel; and 400 Maynard St., Apt. #905, Ann Arbor, Mich. 48108 (until April, 1975). *Agent:* John Cushman Associates, 25 West 43rd St., New York, N.Y. 10036.

CAREER: Film and television director and producer in Romania, 1954-72; Beit-Zwi (The Art School for Film and Drama), Ramat-Gan, Israel, teacher of film-making, 1972-73. Visiting professor at Nova Scotia College of Art and Design, 1973, New York University, 1974, and University of Michigan, 1974-75; has lectured extensively on film at universities in Israel and the United States.

WRITINGS: Behind the Screen: An Introduction to Film Aesthetics, Editura Meridiane, 1963; *Erich von Stroheim*, Austrian Filmmuseum, 1966; *Eisenstein: A Critical Biography*, Editura Tineretului, 1967, Indiana University Press, 1974; *The World of Cinema: A Survey and Critical Analysis of the History of Cinema, Aesthetics, and Acting, with an Analysis of Film Genre*, two volumes, Editura Meridiane, 1971; *Stroheim: A Character Study*, Allen Lane, 1975.

WORK IN PROGRESS: A biography of Luis Bunuel.

SIDELIGHTS: Barna is proficient in English, Hebrew, French, German, Hungarian, and Rumanian, and reads Italian.

* * *

BARNEY, Laura D(reyfus) 1880(?)-1974

1880(?)—August 18, 1974; American philanthropist. Obituaries: *Washington Post*, August 23, 1974.

* * *

BARRETT, Henry Charles 1923-

PERSONAL: Born March 2, 1923, in Birmingham, Ala.; son of Henry Clifford (in shipping) and Marcia (a tax accountant; maiden name, White) Barrett; married Betsy Mason (a private piano teacher), July 23, 1955; children: John Mason, Marcia Helen, Mildred White. *Education:* University of Alabama, B.S., 1948, M.A., 1949; Columbia University, further graduate study, 1950—. *Religion:* Presbyterian. *Home:* 6 Fairmont Dr., Tuscaloosa, Ala. 35401. *Office:* Department of Music, University of Alabama, P.O. Box 2876, University, Ala. 35486.

CAREER: University of Alabama, Tuscaloosa, 1950—, began as instructor, now associate professor of music. Violist with Cadek Quartet, 1950—; principal violist of symphony orchestras in Birmingham and Huntsville, Ala., and Meridian, Miss.; concert master of Mobile Symphony; director of West Alabama Youth String Project; member of faculty at Sewanee Music Center and Brevard Music Center; viola soloist with ten symphony orchestras of U.S. Southeast; member, Aspen Festival Orchestra, 1961-62. *Military service:* U.S. Navy, radarman, 1943-45. *Member:* Music Teachers National Association, Music Educators National Conference, Pi Kappa Lambda (president of Alpha Phi chapter, 1972-74). *Awards, honors:* Three research grants, 1966-74.

WRITINGS: The Viola: Complete Guide for Teachers and Students, University of Alabama Press, 1972. Contributor to "Rilm Abstracts of Music Literature," 1973. Contributor to *Psychological Reports* and *Perceptual and Motor Skills*.

WORK IN PROGRESS: Editing for publication several unpublished compositions for viola, now in Library of Congress and in foreign libraries and museums; research on physical factors and musical ability, and on memory factors and musical ability.

* * *

BARRIER, Norman G(erald) 1940-

PERSONAL: Born August 22, 1940, in Statesville, N.C.; son of Frank P. (an accountant) and Frances (a teacher; maiden name, Sherrill) Barrier; married second wife, Evalyn Weedon (a social worker), December 23, 1969. *Education:* Duke University, A.B. (magna cum laude), 1962, M.A., 1964, Ph.D., 1966. *Office:* Department of History, University of Missouri, Columbia, Mo. 65201.

CAREER: Northern Illinois University, De Kalb, assistant professor of history, 1966-67; University of Missouri, Columbia, assistant professor, 1967-69, associate professor, 1969-74, professor of South Asian history, 1974—, director of South Asia Center, 1969-74. *Member:* American Historical Association (member of Watamull Prize committee), Association for Asian Studies (chairman of committee on South Asia library and documentation, 1972—), American Institute of Indian Studies (member of executive committee, 1970-72; trustee, 1972—). *Awards, honors:* American Council of Learned Societies-Social Science Research Council grant for study in London, 1967; research grants from National Endowment for the Humanities and American Institute of Indian Studies for work in India and Pakistan, 1968-69; American Council of Learned Societies grant for study in London, summer, 1973; American Philosophical Society travel grant for study in London, 1974.

WRITINGS: Punjab History in Printed British Documents: A Bibliographic Guide to Parliamentary Papers and Select, Nonserial Publications, University of Missouri Press, 1969; *The Punjab in Nineteenth-Century Tracts* (monograph), Asian Center, Michigan State University, 1969; (with Paul Wallace) *The Punjab Press, 1880-1905* (monograph), Asian Center, Michigan State University, 1970; (contributor) Ikram Ali Malik, editor, *A Book of Readings on the History of the Punjab*, West Pakistan Research Society (Lahore), 1970; *Banned: Controversial Literature and Political Control in British India*, University of Missouri Press, 1974; (contributor) Kenneth Jones, editor, *Perspectives on Punjab History,* Manohar, (in press); (editor with Harbans Singh, author of critical introduction, and contributor) *Punjab Past and Present*, Punjab University Press, in press. Contributor of articles and reviews to *Journal of Asian Studies, Indian Archives,* and other journals.

WORK IN PROGRESS: Land Records and Political Control in British India; monographs on Sikh social and political history; research on agrarian society in India.

BART, Pauline B(ernice) 1930-

PERSONAL: Born February 18, 1930, in Brooklyn, N.Y.; daughter of Mildred (Prozan) Lackow; married Max Bart, June 19, 1949 (divorced, 1961); children: William Laurence, Melinda Susan. *Education:* Attended Hunter College (now Hunter College of the City University of New York), 1946-48, and University of California, Santa Barbara, 1948-49; University of California, Los Angeles, B.A., 1950, M.A., 1952, Ph.D., 1967. *Politics:* "Feminist left." *Religion:* None. *Home:* 1745 Orrington, Evanston, Ill. 60201. *Agent:* Shirley Fisher, McIntosh & Otis, Inc., 18 East 41st St., New York, N.Y. 10017. *Office:* Department of Psychiatry, Abraham Lincoln School of Medicine, University of Illinois, Chicago, Ill. 60680.

CAREER: University of California, Berkeley, lecturer in sociology, 1968-70; University of Illinois, Abraham Lincoln School of Medicine, Chicago, assistant professor, 1970-73, associate professor of sociology in psychiatry, 1973—, and associate professor of sociology at Chicago Circle, 1973—. Visiting professor at University of Southern California, 1967-68. Consultant to Wynn Associates. Member of subcommittee on research and needs of Chicago Mayor's Commission on Child Care, 1970-73. *Member:* American Sociological Association, Society for Study of Sociological Problems, Sociologists for Women in Society (founder, 1970), Association for Behavioral Science in Medicine, Jewish Women for Affirmative Action (chairwoman, 1973—).

WRITINGS: (With Linda Frankel) *The Student Sociologist's Handbook*, Schenkman, 1971; (contributor) Vivian Gornick and Barbara K. Moran, editors, *Woman in Sexist Society: Studies in Power and Powerlessness*, Basic Books, 1971; (contributor) Rae Siporin, editor, *Female Studies V*, KNOW, 1972; (contributor) Wendell Bell and James Mau, editors, *The Sociology of the Future*, Russell Sage Foundation, 1972; (contributor) Paul M. Roman and Harrison Trice, editors, *Therapeutic Sociology*, Society for the Study of Social Problems, 1973; (with son, William Bart) *Study Guide to Free and Female*, Fawcett, 1973; (contributor) Alvin Toffler, editor, *Learning for Tomorrow*, Random House, 1974; (contributor) Jo Freeman, editor, *New Thoughts on Women: An Anthology*, National Press Books, in press; (contributor) Eleanor Zuckerman, editor, *The Seven Ages of Women*, Behavioral Publications, in press.

Contributor to professional journals. Special issue editor of *Journal of Marriage and the Family*, 1971; associate editor of *Journal of Health and Social Behavior*, 1973-74.

WORK IN PROGRESS: *Portnoy's Mother's Complaint*; research on a group of women in Chicago called Jane or The Service who learned to do illegal abortions and did eleven thousand in four years with no specified fee required.

* * *

BAS, Joe 1932-

PERSONAL: Born October 21, 1932; married Donna F. Brannan; children: Jerry Joseph, James Mitchell, Carolyn Marie. *Education:* California State University, Long Beach, A.B.; University of Southern California, A.M., 1964, Ph.D., 1966. *Politics:* "Sad Republican." *Religion:* Humanitarian. *Home:* 1519 North Eucalyptus Ave., Rialto, Calif. 92376. *Office:* California State College, 5500 State College Parkway, San Bernardino, Calif. 92407.

CAREER: California State College, San Bernardino, 1968—, now professor of Spanish. *Military service:* U.S. Army, 1954-56. *Member:* American Association of Teachers of Spanish and Portuguese, California College and University Faculty Association (president of local chapter), Modern and Classical Language Association of Southern California (treasurer).

WRITINGS: (With Carter) *Cuentos argentinos de misterio*, Appleton, 1967; (with Rymer) *El mejor alcalde: el Rey*, Cajica, 1974; *El principe don Carlos*, Cajica, in press. Also co-author of *Diccionario de terminos literarios*. Contributor to *Usted y yo*, *Nuestro mundo*, and *Vuelo*. Consultant to Macmillan Co. for high school series.

WORK IN PROGRESS: Editing a seventeenth-century Spanish drama, *El condenado por desconfiado*.

* * *

BASILE, Robert M(anlius) 1916-

PERSONAL: Born March 12, 1916, in Youngstown, Ohio; son of Justin G. and Minnie H. Basile; married Anne J. Webb, April 23, 1945; children: Lorraine, Karen. *Education:* Washington and Lee University, B.S., 1938; Michigan State Uinversity, M.S., 1940; Ohio State Uinversity, Ph.D., 1953. *Home:* 5929 Angleview Ct., Sylvania, Ohio 43560.

CAREER: Northwestern State College, Alva, Okla., instructor in soil science, 1946-47; Ohio State University, Columbus, instructor, 1950-53, assistant professor, 1953-59, associate professor, 1959-65, professor of geography, 1965-69; University of Toledo, Toledo, Ohio, professor of geography, 1969—. Visiting professor at California State University, San Jose, summer, 1966, and University of North Carolina, summer, 1967. Consultant to Kroger Co. *Military service:* U.S. Navy, 1942-45; became lieutenant senior grade; served in Pacific. *Member:* American Association for the Advancement of Science, American Society of Agronomy, Association of American Geographers, Wilderness Society, American Geographical Society of New York, Gamma Theta Upsilon. *Awards, honors:* National Science Foundation grant, 1962; Ohio State University Natural Resources Institute grant, 1964, and development fund grant, 1965.

WRITINGS: (Contributor) W. R. Collins, editor, *Ohio: The Buckeye State*, Prentice-Hall, 1956; *Physical Geogrraphy 401 Laboratory Manual*, W. C. Brown, 1959, revised edition, 1966; (contributor) Guy-Harold Smith, editor, *Conservation of Natural Resources*, Wiley, 4th edition (Basile was not associated with earlier editions), 1971; *A Geography of Soils*, W. C. Brown, 1971. Author of pamphlets. Contributor to *Agronomy Journal, Crops and Soils, Professional Geographer, Journal of Geography*, and *Geographical Abstracts*.

WORK IN PROGRESS: Research on urban climates, especially the effects of climates of cities and their industries, and on water balance in Ohio.

* * *

BATES, Timothy M(ason) 1946-

PERSONAL: Born August 3, 1946, in Sarasota, Fla.; son of Harry K. and Henrietta H. Bates; married Beth Tompkins, 1973. *Education:* University of Illinois, B.A., 1968; University of Wisconsin, M.S., 1970, Ph.D., 1972. *Politics:* "People's control of the means of production." *Religion:* "Universal Life Church." *Home:* 139 Maple St., Burlington, Vt. 05401. *Office:* Department of Economics, University of Vermont, Burlington, Vt. 05401.

CAREER: Kenyon College, Gambier, Ohio, assistant professor of economics, 1972-73; University of Wisconsin, Madison, lecturer in economics, 1973-74; University of Vermont, Burlington, assistant professor of economics, 1974—. Fellow of Joint Center for Community Studies (Los Angeles, Calif.). *Member:* Union of Radical Political Economics, American Economic Association, Monthly Review Associates. *Awards, honors:* Genevieve Gorst Herfurth Award from University of Wisconsin, 1974, for *Black Capitalism: A Quantitative Analysis*.

WRITINGS: Black Capitalism: A Quantitative Analysis, Praeger, 1973; *Black Capitalism in America: Historical Foundations, Present Orientation, and Future Prospects*, Warner Modular Publications, 1974; *Economic Man as Politician*, General Learning Press, in press. Contributor to *Review of Economics and Statistics*, *Public Policy*, *Journal of Finance*, *Review of Black Political Economy*, and *Journal of Business*.

SIDELIGHTS: Bates writes: "My writings on Black economic development are motivated by my desire to illustrate the impact of institutional racism on Black economic development, and to trace the impact of government's feeble, half-hearted efforts to promote same. My forthcoming writings attempt to reveal important interrelationships between government decision-making and the efforts of business interests to manipulate and control government."

* * *

BAUM, David William 1940-

PERSONAL: Born August 26, 1940, in Grand Island, Neb.; son of Henry Herman (a barber) and Anna (Augustyn) Baum; married Frances Dale Hunter (a teacher), June 20, 1968. *Education:* University of Nebraska, B.A., 1962, graduate study, 1962-64; further graduate study at School of Visual Arts and Art Students League, both 1973, and Pratt Institute, 1973—. *Politics:* Democrat. *Religion:* Roman Catholic. *Home:* 517 East 77th St., Apt. 4-B, New York, N.Y. 10021.

CAREER: Peace Corps volunteer in Honduras, Central America, 1964-66; Mid-City Community Congress, St. Louis, Mo., community organizer, 1966-67; Pratt Institute, Brooklyn, N.Y., assistant to the chairman of the department of foundation art, 1967-68; Parsons School of Design, New York, N.Y., assistant to the dean, 1968-69; Pratt Institute; assistant to the chairman of the department of industrial design, 1969-71, co-director of the Art School's Office of Art Programming and Counseling, 1971-72; Mind Dimensions & Controls, Inc., New York, N.Y., executive administrator, 1972-73; Margaret Gate Institute, Huntington, N.Y., art and design administrator, 1973—. Administrator and designer for New York State Council on the Arts project at Bronx State Children's Psychiatric Hospital, 1973—. *Member:* Industrial Designers Society of America (student member).

WRITINGS: (Editor with Mary L. Buckley) *Color Theory*, Gale, 1975.

SIDELIGHTS: Baum has traveled through Central America and Mexico.

* * *

BAYBARS, Taner 1936- (Timothy Bayliss)

PERSONAL: Born June 18, 1936, in Cyprus; son of Halil Fikret (a headmaster) and Shazie (a headmistress; maiden name, Rustem) Baybars; married Kristin Hughes-Stanton (a designer), March 21, 1959; children: Susila Jane. *Education:* Educated in Cyprus. *Home:* 69 Onslow Gardens, Muswell Hill, London N10 3JY, England. *Agent:* David Higham Associates, Golden Sq., Soho, London W.1, England. *Office:* British Council, 65 Davies St., London W1Y 2AA, England.

CAREER: Royal Air Force, Nicosia, Cyprus, technical librarian, 1954-55; British Council, London, England, books assistant, 1956-66, book exhibitions assistant, 1966-67, periodicals assistant, 1967-72, head of overseas reviews scheme, 1972—. Has given poetry readings on British Broadcasting Corp. Radio. Judge for Commonwealth Institute poetry prize. *Member:* Poetry Society (London; member of advisory panel for National Poetry Centre).

WRITINGS: Mendilin Ucundakiler (poems; title means "Corners of a Handkerchief"), Chardak, 1954; *To Catch a Falling Man* (poems), Scorpion Press, 1963; *A Trap for the Burglar* (novel), P. Owen, 1965; (translator) *Selected Poems of Nazim Hikmet*, J. Cape, 1967; *Plucked in a Far-Off Land* (autobiography), Gollancz, 1970; (translator) Nazim Hikmet, *The Moscow Symphony*, Deutsch, 1970; (translator) Hikmet, *The Day Before Tomorrow*, Carcanet Press, 1972; *Susila in the Autumn Woods* (poems), Sceptre Press, 1974.

Work is represented in anthologies, including: *A Group Anthology*, edited by E. Lucie-Smith and P. Hobsbaum, Oxford University Press, 1963; *A Parade of Poems*, edited by P. W. Diebel and R. McBurney, Macmillan, 1965; *P.E.N. New Poems*, edited by Harold Pinter and Peter Redgrove, Hutchinson, 1967; *Gallery*, edited by M. Greaves, Methuen, 1968; *The New York Times Book of Verse*, edited by Thomas Lask, Macmillan, 1970; *Penguin Book of Socialist Verse*, edited by A. Bold, Penguin, 1970; *In a Seashell*, edited by C. G. Stokes, Collins, 1973.

Contributor to British journals, including *Times Literary Supplement, Listener, Critical Quarterly,* and *Delos*, and to newspapers, usually under pseudonym Timothy Bayliss. Co-editor of Turkish number, *Modern Poetry in Translation*, 1971.

WORK IN PROGRESS: A novel; a collection of poems; research on the origins of Norman French in the English verbs ending in -ise.

SIDELIGHTS: Baybars writes: "I write poetry because I must. I write prose to discipline my poetry. I make translations in order not to forget that other languages exist with their own variety of nuances." *Avocational interests:* Book publishing and printing, natural history, Hasidism, baroque music, cinema.

BIOGRAPHICAL/CRITICAL SOURCES: Peter Orr, editor, *The Poet Speaks*, Routledge & Kegan Paul, 1966; *Guardian*, May 5, 1970.

* * *

BAYERLE, Gustav 1931-

PERSONAL: Born May 19, 1931, in Budapest, Hungary; naturalized U.S. citizen in 1962; son of Gyozo and Lujza (Stolzenwald) Bayerle; married Telle Ravila (an educator), October 24, 1963; children: Paul, Henry. *Education:* Attended Eotvos Lorand University, Budapest, 1955-56; University of Rochester, B.A., 1960; Columbia University, Ph.D., 1966. *Home:* 2210 Rock Creek Dr., Bloomington, Ind. 47401. *Office:* Department of Uralic and Altaic Studies, Indiana University, Goodbody Hall, Bloomington, Ind. 47401.

CAREER: Indiana University, Bloomington, assistant professor, 1966-73, associate professor of Uralic and Altaic studies, 1973—. Consultant to Columbia University, 1973—. *Member:* Middle East Studies Association of North America, American Oriental Society, American Historical Association, Middle East Institute, Permanent International Altaic Conference.

WRITINGS: Ottoman Diplomacy in Hungary: Letters from the Pashas of Buda, 1590-1593, Indiana University Press, 1972; *Ottoman Tributes in Hungary: According to Sixteenth Century Tapu Registers of Novigrad*, Mouton & Co., 1973. Contributor to *Archivum Ottomanicum* and *Acta Orientalia*.

* * *

BEASLEY, W(illiam) Conger, Jr. 1940-

PERSONAL: Born August 21, 1940, in Missouri; son of W. Conger (a businessman) and Ardus (Albrecht) Beasley; married Marian Elizabeth McCoy, June 18, 1966; children: Ardus Elizabeth, W. Conger III. *Education:* Columbia College, B.A., 1962; New York University, M.A., 1965. *Politics:* Anarchist.

CAREER: Park College, Parkville, Mo., assistant professor of literature, 1965-67. Political speech writer, 1968.

WRITINGS: Tiger Tale (novel), Sheed, 1975. Contributor of stories and poems to magazines. Book reviewer for *National Catholic Reporter*, 1968; assistant editor, Universal Press syndicate, 1971.

WORK IN PROGRESS: A second novel.

AVOCATIONAL INTERESTS: Travel, sex, liquor, reading, music, conversation ("not necessarily in that order").

* * *

BEASLEY, W(illiam) G(erald) 1919-

PERSONAL: Born December 22, 1919, in England; son of William (an actor) and Helena Beasley; married Hazel Polwin, 1955; children: John. *Education:* University College, University of London, B.A., 1940, Ph.D., 1950. *Home:* 172 Hampton Rd., Twickenham TW2 5NJ, England. *Office:* School of Oriental and African Studies, University of London, Malet St., London WC1E 7HP, England.

CAREER: University of London, School of Oriental and African Studies, London, England, lecturer, 1947-54, professor of history of the Far East, 1954—. *Military service:* Royal Naval (Volunteer) Service, 1940-46. *Member:* British Academy (fellow), Royal Historical Society (fellow). *Awards, honors:* John K. Fairbank Prize from American Historical Association, 1973, for *The Meiji Restoration*.

WRITINGS: Great Britain and the Opening of Japan, Luzac, 1951; *Select Documents on Japanese Foreign Policy: 1853-1868*, Oxford University Press, 1955; (editor with E. G. Pulleyblank) *Historians of China and Japan*, Oxford University Press, 1961; *The Modern History of Japan*, Praeger, 1963, revised edition, 1973; *The Meiji Restoration*, Stanford University Press, 1972. Contributor to history journals, including *Journal of Asian Studies, Bulletin of the School of Oriental and African Studies,* and *Transactions of the Asiatic Society of Japan*.

WORK IN PROGRESS: Research on the early development of modern Japanese society, with reference to nationalism and origins of imperialism.

SIDELIGHTS: Beasley has made several long visits to Japan since 1945.

* * *

BECK, John Jacob, Jr. 1941-

PERSONAL: Born November 10, 1941, in Monroe, Mich.; son of John Jacob (an attorney) and Eleanor (Brieschke) Beck. *Education:* Adrian College, B.A., 1963; University of Toledo, M.A., 1967. *Home:* 4313 South Detroit Ave., Toledo, Ohio 43614.

CAREER: Junior high school teacher of English and social studies in the public schools of Toledo, Ohio, 1964—. *Member:* Toledo YMCA Athletic Club.

WRITINGS: MacArthur and Wainwright: Sacrifice of the Philippines, University of New Mexico Press, 1974.

WORK IN PROGRESS: A narrative account of the Bataan Death March.

* * *

BECKER, Peter 1921-

PERSONAL: Born March 27, 1921, in Rivonia, South Africa; son of Harold (a mining engineer) and Anna (Lowe) Becker; married Connie Van Den Berg, December 13, 1946; children: Harold, Peter (adopted), Nandi (adopted), Lindi. *Education:* University of the Witwatersrand, B.A., 1944, T.T.D., 1945, D.N.A., 1948, Ph.D., 1965. *Home:* Kwavulindlela, P.O. Box 68095, Bryanston, Sandton, South Africa. *Office:* Batten, Barton, Durstine & Osborne (Proprietary) Ltd., P.O. Box 2983, Johannesburg, South Africa.

CAREER: Institute of South African Languages, Johannesburg, South Africa, director, 1950-58; Bona Magazines, Johannesburg, chief editor, 1958-60; Cloran, Heeger, and Partners (advertising and marketing), Johnnesburg, director, 1960-72; Becker, Dissel, and Partners (advertising and market research), Johannesburg, director, 1972-74; Batten, Barton, Durstine & Osborne (Proprietary) Ltd., Johannesburg, director and deputy chairman, 1974—. Principal of Franklin D. Roosevelt School, Johannesburg, 1952-58; director of Charta World Productions, 1963—, African Safaris, 1968—, and Executive Tours, 1968—; president of African Foundation of Wild Life Conservation, 1972—; consultant to Ecological Board of Southern Africa, 1971.

MEMBER: International P.E.N., Wilderness Leadership School, West Rand Bird Club, Rotary International. *Awards, honors:* Named Vulindlela, or Opener of the Road, by Prince Makhungu Dlamini of the Swazi Royal House, 1955.

WRITINGS: Eureka, Impala Press, 1949; *Sandy Tracks to the Kraals*, Dagbreek, 1956; *Crumbling Walls*, Goldfields Press, 1958; *The Peoples of South Africa*, three volumes, Dagbreek, 1958-60; *Path of Blood: The Rise and Conquests of Mzilikazi, Founder of the Matabele*, Longmans, Green, 1962; *Rule of Fear: The Life and Times of Dingane, King of the Zulu*, Longmans, Green, 1964; *Dingane: King of the Zulu, 1828-1840*, Crowell, 1965; *Hill of Destiny: The Life and Times of Moshesh, Founder of the Basotho*, Longmans, Green, 1969; *L'Atilla Noir* (title means "The Black Atilla"), Plon, 1970; *Peoples of Southern Africa: Their Customs and Beliefs*, Argus, 1971; *Tribe to Township*, Granada, 1973; *Trails and Tribes in Southern Africa*, Hart-Davis, 1974; *Mauritius '62*, Supreme Publishers, 1974.

WORK IN PROGRESS: Research among the inland tribes of Southern Africa, for a sequel to *Trails and Tribes in Southern Africa*; research on Hindu cults in South Africa, with a book expected to result; research on the Bedouins of the Middle East and on the Indians of the United States.

SIDELIGHTS: Born on a South African farm when his parents were advanced in years, Becker's playmates were tribal age-mates; hence his early acquisition of vernacular languages and exposure to African ritual.

His understanding of tribal custom and etiquette has led to close associations and friendships with princes, chieftains, and other dignitaries, and four of the most influential kings of South Africa. These leaders in turn have opened his way to witnessing and taking part in ancient rituals and ceremonies.

As a tribute to his long association with the Royal House of the Zulu nation, he was made guardian to the twenty-year-old heir-apparent to the Zulu throne in 1969. From this, Becker became known as Baba Yamazulu (father of the Zulus).

He has conducted field research among all peoples of the Southern Subcontinent of Africa, from the Cape to the Zambezi and from the Indian Ocean across to the Atlantic. More recently his researches have taken him beyond the shores of Africa—to the inhabitants of the Indian Ocean islands, the Bedouins of the Middle East, and the American Indians. He owns a research museum in which are housed hundreds of historically priceless relics.

* * *

BECKMAN, Gail McKnight 1938-

PERSONAL: Born April 8, 1938, in New York, N.Y.; daughter of Irland McKnight (a businessman) and Elizabeth (a psychologist; maiden name, Hurlock) Beckman. *Education:* Bryn Mawr College, B.A., 1959; University of Tuebingen, graduate study, 1960; Yale University, J.D., 1963; University of Pennsylvania, M.A., 1966. *Religion:* Presbyterian. *Home:* 1270 West Peachtree St., Atlanta, Ga. 30309. *Office:* Georgia State University, University Plaza, Atlanta, Ga. 30303.

CAREER: Admitted to practice before Bar of Commonwealth of Pennsylvania, District of Columbia, State of Georgia, and U.S. Supreme Court; Legal Aid Society of Philadelphia, Philadelphia, Pa., counsellor, 1960; Morgan, Lewis & Bockius, Philadelphia, lawyer, 1963-66; University of Glasgow, Glasgow, Scotland, lecturer in law, 1967-71; Georgia State University, Atlanta, associate professor of law, 1971—. Research assistant for Oliver Wendell Holmes Devise for a History of the U.S. Supreme Court, 1963; research associate of American Philosophical Association's Library, 1966-70.

MEMBER: American Bar Association, American Association of University Women, State Bar of Georgia, Georgia Association of Women Lawyers, Juristic Society (Philadelphia), Atlanta Bar Association, Colonial Dames, Soroptimist Club of Atlanta (president, 1973-74), Saint Andrew's Society of Atlanta (founder), Legal Aid Society of Atlanta, Mortar Board, Beta Gamma Sigma. *Awards, honors:* Fulbright scholarship, 1960; Colonial Williamsburg grant, 1964.

WRITINGS: Estate Planning Considerations for U.S. Citizens Abroad, Prentice-Hall, 1974; *Law for Business and Management*, McGraw, 1975. Author of videotape film "The Car Salesman: A Study in the Law of Contract and Sales," 1975. Contributor of articles and reviews to law journals. Book review editor of *American Business Law Journal*.

WORK IN PROGRESS: Statutes at Large of Pennsylvania, completion expected in 1976; videotapes on law.

SIDELIGHTS: Gail Beckman writes: "My travels abroad have caused me to become interested in other legal systems and their significance to Americans. I have traveled extensively in Europe, Asia, North Africa, and North America. I read about nine foreign languages including German, French, Greek, Russian, and Japanese . . ., and do research in them."

* * *

BEFU, Harumi 1930-

PERSONAL: Born March 20, 1930, in Los Angeles, Calif.; son of Juma (a gardener) and Komaki Befu; married Kei Tomita (a librarian), August 23, 1959; children: Marina, Justin. *Education:* University of California, Los Angeles, B.A., 1954; University of Michigan, M.A., 1956; University of Wisconsin–Madison, Ph.D., 1962. *Residence:* Stanford, Calif. *Office:* Department of Anthropology, Stanford University, Stanford, Calif. 94305.

CAREER: University of Nevada, Reno, assistant professor of anthropology, 1961-62; University of Missouri, Columbia, assistant professor of anthropology, 1962-64; University of Michigan, Ann Arbor, visiting associate professor of anthropology, 1964-65; Stanford University, Stanford, Calif., assistant professor, 1965-69, associate professor of anthropology, 1969—. *Member:* American Anthropological Association, Association for Asian Studies, Japanese Society of Ethnology, Phi Beta Kappa. *Awards, honors:* Guggenheim fellowship, 1972-73.

WRITINGS: Japan: An Anthropological Introduction, Chandler Publishing, 1971.

WORK IN PROGRESS: Gift and Exchange in Japan (tentative title), a book on the extent and forms of gift-giving in Japan and the exchange relationships which bind Japanese to each other.

SIDELIGHTS: Befu writes: "I was born in Los Angeles. At the age of six, I went to Japan and stayed there with my uncle until [the age of] seventeen, living there throughout the second World War. After the war, I returned to the U.S. Personally experiencing cultural differences, I took interest in anthropology as a way of understanding my own experiences. I have continued to maintain my interest in anthropology and in trying to understand my experiences in [the] U.S. and Japan."

* * *

BEHN, Harry 1898-1973

September 24, 1898—September 4, 1973; American scenarist and author of children's books. Obituaries: *New York Times*, September 10, 1973. (*CA*-7/8).

* * *

BEIRNE, Joseph Anthony 1911-1974

February 16, 1911—September 2, 1974; American labor leader. Obituaries: *New York Times*, September 3, 1974. (*CA*-45/48).

* * *

BELING, Willard A(dolf) 1919-

PERSONAL: Born March 16, 1919, in Great Bend, N.D.;

married, 1947; children: two. *Education:* University of California, Los Angeles, B.A., 1943; Princeton University, M.A. and Ph.D., both 1947; postdoctoral study at University of Grenoble, 1947-48, University of Basel, 1947-48, 1951-52, and American University of Beirut, 1955-56. *Office:* Middle East-North African Program, University of Southern California, Los Angeles, Calif. 90007.

CAREER: Director of socio-economic research and planning for Arabian American Oil Co., 1949-58; Harvard University, Cambridge, Mass., fellow of Middle East Institutes and research associate, 1958-60; University of Southern California, Los Angeles, professor of international relations, 1960—, regional coordinator and director of Middle East-North Africa Program, 1960—. Associate of International Institute of Social Studies, 1966—. *Member:* Rotary International, Phi Beta Kappa. *Awards, honors:* American Council of Learned Societies fellowship, 1947-48; Social Science Research Council grants, 1948-49, 1958, 1963-64; American Anthropological Association grants, 1967—; fellow of American Philosophical Association.

WRITINGS: Pan-Arabism and Labor, Harvard University Press, 1960; *Modernization and African Labor: A Tunisian Case Study*, Praeger, 1965; (editor and contributor) *The Role of Labor in African Nation-Building*, Praeger, 1968; (editor with George O. Totten III, and contributor) *Developing Nations: Quest for a Model*, Van Nostrand, 1970; *Arabism: A Study in Political Ecology*, Mid-East Forum, 1972; (editor and contributor) *The Middle East: Quest for an American Policy*, State University of New York Press, 1973. Contributor to journals on Middle East studies, economics, and development.

WORK IN PROGRESS: Transnationalism: A Tunisian Case Study; The American National Image and the Arab-Israel Conflict; articles for *Americana Annual Encyclopedia* and for Hoover Institution's *Yearbook*.

* * *

BELL, Oliver (Sydney) 1913-

PERSONAL: Born December 19, 1913, in London, England; son of Kenneth Norman (a professor) and Esther (Bell) Bell; married Eleanor Weinstein (a painter), October 8, 1941; children: Olivia (Mrs. Ronald Buehl), Kenneth, Venetia (Mrs. Gerard Fauveau), Nicholas, Victoria. *Education:* Balliol College, Oxford, M.A., 1935. *Home address:* P.O. Box 52, Hillsboro, Va. 22132.

CAREER: New York Times, New York, N.Y., editor of educational material, 1949-57; *Challenge* (magazine), New York, N.Y., senior editor, 1960-62; Greystone Press, New York, N.Y., encyclopedia editor, 1962-64; Educational Research Council of America, Cleveland, Ohio, research associate in the social sciences, 1969-71. *Awards, honors:* Filmstrip awards from *Scholastic* (magazine), 1952-57.

WRITINGS: The Two Chinas, Scholastic Book Services, 1962, revised edition, 1970; (editor and contributor) *Ohio: From Settlement to 1910*, Educational Research Council of America, 1970; (editor) *America's Changing Population*, Wilson, 1974.

WORK IN PROGRESS: Acculturation with a view to the establishment of a world state.

AVOCATIONAL INTERESTS: Travel (Western Europe, Egypt).

* * *

BELL, Sarah Fore 1920-

PERSONAL: Born August 21, 1920, in Roxobel, N.C.; daughter of Stonewall Jackson (a bank clerk) and Ethel (Gattis) Fore; married C. Ritchie Bell, January 14, 1943 (divorced August 8, 1974). *Education:* Attended Greensboro College, 1937-39; University of North Carolina, B.A., 1941, M.A., 1945, Ph.D., 1968. *Home:* 1122 Sourwood Dr., Chapel Hill, N.C. 27514. *Office:* Department of Romance Languages, University of North Carolina at Greensboro, Greensboro, N.C. 27412.

CAREER: University of North Carolina Law Library, Chapel Hill, cataloguer, 1963-64; University of North Carolina at Greensboro, instructor, 1967-69, assistant professor of Romance languages, 1969—. *Member:* Modern Language Association of America, American Association of Teachers of French, Dante Society of America, South Atlantic Modern Language Association.

WRITINGS: Charles Nodier: His Life and Works; A Critical Bibliography, 1923-1967, Studies in the Romance Languages and Literatures, University of North Carolina Press, 1971. Contributor to *Romance Notes* and *Nineteenth-Century French Studies*.

WORK IN PROGRESS: A critical edition of selected articles of literary criticism of Charles Nodier; an article updating book on Charles Nodier.

* * *

BENETAR, Judith 1941-

PERSONAL: Born June 21, 1941, in New York. *Education:* New York University, B.A. (cum laude), 1963; Trinity College, Dublin, M.B., B.Ch., and B.A.O., all 1970. *Agent:* Mary Yost Associates, 141 East 55th St., New York, N.Y. 10017

CAREER: Resident in psychiatry at a hospital in New York, N.Y., 1971-74, chief resident, 1973-74, supervising psychiatrist, 1974—. *Member:* Phi Beta Kappa.

WRITINGS: Admissions: Notes from a Woman Psychiatrist, Charterhouse Books, 1974.

WORK IN PROGRESS: A novel about a schizophrenic, completion expected in 1976.

* * *

BENNETT, Adrian A(rthur) 1941-

PERSONAL: Born November 13, 1941, in Minneapolis, Minn.; son of Adrian Arthur, Jr. (a businessman) and Betsy (Bruce) Bennett; married Cynthia Bliss (a nurse), July 6, 1963; children: Christopher Alan, Alyssa. *Education:* Antioch College, B.A., 1964; University of California, Davis, M.A., 1966, Ph.D., 1970. *Religion:* Society of Friends (Quakers). *Home:* 2227 Storm St., Ames, Iowa 50010. *Office:* Department of History, Iowa State University, 603 Ross Hall, Ames, Iowa 50010.

CAREER: Iowa State University, Ames, assistant professor, 1970-74, associate professor of history, 1974—. *Member:* Association of Asian Studies, Concerned Asian Scholars, Ch'ing Society, United States-China People's Friendship Association.

WRITINGS: John Fryer: The Introduction of Western Science and Technology into Nineteenth Century China, East Asian Research Center, Harvard University, 1967; (contributor) John K. Fairbank, editor, *The Missionary Enterprise in China and America*, Harvard University Press, 1974.

WORK IN PROGRESS: Missionary Journalism in Nineteenth Century China: Young J. Allen and the "Wan-kuo kung-pao," 1868-1874; A Research Guide to the "Chiao-hui hsin-pao": 1868-1874; A Research Guide to the "Wan-kuo kung-pao": 1874-1883, completion expected in 1977.

* * *

BENNETT, Gertrude Ryder

PERSONAL: Born in Brooklyn, N.Y.; daughter of Edward (a businessman) and Nellie May (a poet; maiden name, Ryder) Bennett; married Frank Curtis Williams (a clergyman), June 21, 1942. *Education:* New York University, B.S. 1925; Columbia University, M.A., 1927. *Home:* 1669 East 22nd St., Brooklyn, N.Y. 11229.

MEMBER: Poetry Society of America (member of governing board, 1973-74), National League of American Pen Women (president of New York branch, 1974—), New York Women Poets, Pennsylvania Poetry Society, West Virginia Poetry Society, Long Island Historical Society, Brooklyn Poetry Circle.

AWARDS, HONORS: First prizes, New York Women Poets Contest, 1936, 1948, 1961, 1968, 1971; Norfolk Prize of Poetry Society of Virginia, second prize, 1951, first prize, 1952; Arthur Davison Ficke award from Poetry Society of America, 1960, 1963; National Federation of State Poetry Societies Evans Spencer Wall Memorial Award, 1966, Lubbe award, 1972, Walter R. Lovel Memorial Award, 1973, Illinois State Poetry Society award, 1974; Poetry Fellowship of Maine, 1966; Pennsylvania Poetry Society Blanche Whiting Keysner Memorial Award, 1967, Henry W. Shoemaker Memorial Award, 1970, Edna Groff Diehl award, 1971, Kate Heanue award, 1974; Carl Sandburg award from North Carolina Poetry Society, 1968; National League of American Pen Women National Biennial Contest first prize book award, 1968, for *The Harvesters*, Ruth Mason Rice Memorial Contest, 1973; and other awards for writing.

WRITINGS: Etched in Words (lyrics), Putnam, 1938; *The Harvesters* (lyrics), Golden Quill, 1967; *Ballads of Colonial Days*, Golden Quill, 1972; *Fugitive* (ballads and narrative poem), Golden Quill, in press.

WORK IN PROGRESS: Research on M. Bach, a lieutenant in the Hessian Hanau Artillery and on Georg Ernst Toepfer, a captain of Regiment Von Ditfurth in the Revolutionary War.

AVOCATIONAL INTERESTS: Art, especially ceramics; travel.

* * *

BENNING, (Barbara) Lee Edwards 1934-

PERSONAL: Born July 13, 1934, in Chicago, Ill.; daughter of Albert I. (an engineer and dog-breeder) and Edna S. (a teacher; maiden name, Johnson) Edwards; married Arthur E. Benning (a writer); children: Arthur E., Jr. *Education:* Pennsylvania State University, B.S., 1956. *Religion:* Episcopalian. *Home:* Wingover Farm, Bethlehem Pike, R.D. #1, Ambler, Pa. 19002. *Agent:* Ann Elmo, 52 Vanderbilt Ave., New York, N.Y. 10017.

CAREER: Aitkin-Kynett Advertising Agency, Philadelphia, Pa., senior food writer, 1960-64; N. W. Ayer & Sons Inc. (advertising agency), Philadelphia, senior food writer, 1964-67; high school teacher of English in Rosemont, Pa., 1967-69, and in Upper Moreland, Pa., 1970-72; Bird Mail Advertising Services Co., Philadelphia, Pa., president, 1974—. *Member:* National Home Fashions League (corresponding secretary of Philadelphia chapter, 1960-63), Home Fashion League, Keystone English Springer Spaniel Club.

WRITINGS: How to Bring Up a Child without Spending a Fortune, McKay, 1975; *What Every Mother Should Know About Allergies*, McKay, in press; *How to Avoid the Great Pet Rip-Off*, Quadrangle, in press.

WORK IN PROGRESS: Research for several cookbooks; a book on women and advertising, on women in sports, and on brides; a contemporary novel about Philadelphia's Main Line; two historical novels; three projects of an educational nature for mothers of young children.

SIDELIGHTS: Lee Edwards Benning told *CA*: "I brought to the field of child care books something unique: I am one of the few non-doctors in this area . . . and I am the only mother. What I had to say was not important because I was a writer, but because I was a bottle-washer, diaper-changer, budget-stretcher, household manager . . . in sum, because I was a practicing mother."

* * *

BENNIS, Warren G. 1925-

PERSONAL: Born March 8, 1925, in New York, N.Y.; son of Philip and Rachel (Landau) Bennis; married Clurie Williams, March 30, 1962; children: Katharine, John Leslie, Will Martin. *Education:* Antioch College, A.B., 1951; London School of Economics and Political Science, honors certificate, 1952; Massachusetts Institute of Technology, Ph.D., 1955. *Home:* 750 Ludlow Ave., Cincinnati, Ohio 45220. *Office:* Office of President, University of Cincinnati, Cincinnati, Ohio 45221.

CAREER: Massachusetts Institute of Technology, Cambridge, instructor, 1953-55, assistant professor of social psychology, 1955-56; Boston University, Boston, Mass., assistant professor of psychology, 1956-59, senior research associate at Human Relations Center, 1956-59; Massachusetts Institute of Technology, associate professor of industrial management, 1959-63, professor of organizational and management psychology, 1963-67; State University of New York at Buffalo, provost of faculty of social sciences and administration, 1967-68, vice-president for academic development, 1968-70, acting executive vice-president and provost of natural sciences, 1969-70; University of Cincinnati, Cincinnati, Ohio, university professor and president, 1971—. Visiting lecturer at Harvard University, 1958-59; visiting professor at University of California, 1960, University of Lausanne, 1961-62, Indian Institute of Management, 1964-65, and University of Southern California, 1966. Diplomate of American Board of Professional Psychology. Member of White House task force on foreign policy, 1969, and conference on youth, 1970-71. Member of advisory board of U.S. Federal Judicial Center, U.S. Federal Executive Institute, Center for Human Development, Center for Policy Research, and National Institute of Child Health and Human Development. Member of scientific advisory board of National Institute of Mental Health, 1966—; advisor to Division of Social Systems and Human Resources of National Science Foundation; member of board of trustees of National Committee for Cooperative Education; member of advisory board of New York State Joint Legislative Committee of Higher Education. Member of Ohio governor's business and employment council, 1972, and task force on higher education, 1973. Member of panel on alternative approaches to graduate education of Council of Graduate Schools and Graduate Record Examination. Member of board of trustees of Antioch College, 1969-70, Pitzer College, and Park School (Buffalo). Member of board of directors of Cincinnati's Institute of Fine Arts and

Playhouse in the Park. Host of monthly program on local WLW-Television. Consultant to government and business, including U.S. Department of State, United Nations, and Polaroid Co. *Military service:* U.S. Army, 1943-47; became first lieutenant; received Bronze Star Medal and Purple Heart.

MEMBER: American Psychological Association (fellow), American Sociological Association (fellow), Association of American Colleges, Society for Applied Anthropology, Church Society for College Work (member of board of directors), American Management Association, American Association for the Advancement of Science (fellow), New York Academy of Sciences (fellow). *Awards, honors:* Edgar D. Hayhow Award, 1961, for article on administration; McKinsey Foundation awards for "Organizational Revitalization," 1967, for editing *The Professional Manager*, and 1969, for *The Temporary Society*; named to Wisdon Hall of Fame, 1970; LL.D. from Xavier University, 1972, and L.H.D. from Hebrew Union College, 1974; executive order of Ohio Commodore Award, 1973.

WRITINGS: (Editor with K. D. Beene and R. Chin, and contributor) *The Planning of Change: Readings in the Behavioral Sciences*, Holt, 1961, 2nd edition, 1969; *The Role of the Nurse in the Outpatient Department*, American Nurses Foundation, 1961; *The Marked Deck: A Non-Objective Playlet for Four Characters*, National Training Laboratories, 1963; (editor with others, and contributor) *Interpersonal Dynamics: Essays and Readings on Human Interaction*, Dorsey, 1964, 3rd edition, 1973; (contributor) Bradford, Gibb, and Benne, editors, *T-Group Theory and Laboratory Method*, Wiley, 1964; (editor with E. H. Schein, and contributor) *Personal and Organizational Change Through Group Methods: The Laboratory Approach*, Wiley, 1965; (editor and contributor) *Changing Organizations: Essays on the Development and Evolution of Human Organizations*, McGraw, 1966; (editor with Schein and C. McGregor) Douglas McGregor, *Leadership and Motivation: Essays*, M.I.T. Press, 1966; (contributor) H. W. Peter, editor, *Comparative Theories of Social Change*, Foundation for Research in Human Development, 1966; (editor with C. McGregor) Douglas McGregor, *The Professional Manager*, McGraw, 1967; (editor with H. Baumgartel and N. R. De) *Readings in Group Development for Managers and Trainers*, Asia Publishing House, 1967; (with P. E. Slater) *The Temporary Society*, Harper, 1968; *Organization Development: Its Nature, Origins, and Prospects*, Addison-Wesley, 1969.

American Bureaucracy, Aldine, 1970; (editor and contributor) *Today, Tomorrow, and the Day After*, University of Cincinnati, 1972; (with John Thomas) *Management of Change and Conflict*, Penguin, 1973; *The Leaning Ivory Tower*, Jossey-Bass, 1973.

Contributor of about seventy-five articles to magazines and scholarly journals, including *Newsweek, Saturday Review of Education, Journal of Higher Education, Psychology Today, Esquire,* and *Environment Planning and Design*. Associate editor of *Administrative Science Quarterly, Journal of Applied Behavioral Sciences, Trans-Action, Business and Public Administration Review,* and *Journal of Humanistic Psychology*. Member of editorial board of *Community Psychology* and *Journal of Trans-Personal Psychology*. Consulting editor for *Journal of Creative Behavior*, and social sciences and administration section of Addison-Wesley.

SIDELIGHTS: Bennis' books have been published in German, Dutch, Japanese, Portuguese, Spanish, and Italian.

* * *

BENTON, Thomas Hart 1889-1975

April 15, 1889—January 19, 1975; American artist. Obituaries: *New York Times*, January 20, 1975; *Washington Post*, January 21, 1975; *Time*, February 3, 1975; *Newsweek*, February 3, 1975.

* * *

BENTZ, William F(rederick) 1940-

PERSONAL: Born June 14, 1940, in Dayton, Ohio; son of Norman A. and Ruth (Bryant) Bentz; married Janet Mills, October 13, 1962; children: Jennifer, Michael. *Education:* University of Cincinnati, B.A., 1962; Ohio State University, M.Acc., 1965, Ph.D., 1969. *Home:* 2618 Missouri St., Lawrence, Kan. 66044. *Office:* School of Business, 210 Summerfield Hall, University of Kansas, Lawrence, Kan. 66044.

CAREER: University of Kansas, Lawrence, assistant professor of business, 1968—.

WRITINGS: (Editor with Robert R. Sterling) *Accounting in Perspective*, South-Western, 1971; (contributor) Frederic E. Mints and Lawrence B. Sawyer, editors, *Review Course for the Certified Internal Auditor Examination: Digest for Part IV, Disciplines Related to Internal Auditing*, Institute of Internal Auditors, 1974. Contributor of articles and reviews to proceedings, and to *Accounting Review* and *Management Services*.

WORK IN PROGRESS: Research on financial decision models and their related information needs, especially the development of operational input-output models, the study of sensitivity analysis in various contexts, and the study of computer processing methods.

* * *

BERDIE, Douglas R(alph) 1946-

PERSONAL: Born May 11, 1946, in Tennessee; son of Ralph F. (a professor) and Frances (a social researcher; maiden name, Strong) Berdie; married Dulce Maria Caba, June 12, 1969; children: Raymond Ralph. *Education:* University of Minnesota, B.A. (summa cum laude), 1971, graduate student, 1972—. *Home:* 2208 Folwell St., St. Paul, Minn. 55108. *Office:* Measurement Services Center, University of Minnesota, 9 Clarence Ave. S.E., Minneapolis, Minn. 55455.

CAREER: Anderson & Berdie Associates (survey research firm), St. Paul, Minn., partner, 1974—. Research fellow at Measurement Services Center of University of Minnesota, 1971-74. *Military service:* U.S. Coast Guard, 1964-68; served in Antarctic. *Member:* World Association for Public Opinion Research, American Philosophical Association, Phi Beta Kappa, Phi Kappa Phi.

WRITINGS: (With John F. Anderson) *Graduate Assistants at the University of Minnesota*, Measurement Services Center, University of Minnesota, 1972; (with Anderson) *Questionnaires: Design and Use*, Scarecrow, 1974. Contributor to *Journal of Applied Psychology*, *Improving College and University Teaching*, and *Research in Higher Education*.

WORK IN PROGRESS: Editing an anthology about questionnaires, with John F. Anderson; research on methodology of questionnaire design and use.

BERESFORD-HOWE, Constance 1922-

PERSONAL: Born November 10, 1922, in Montreal, Quebec; daughter of Russell and Marjory (Moore) Beresford-Howe; married Christopher W. Pressnell (a teacher), December 31, 1960; children: Jeremy. *Education:* McGill University, B.A., 1945, M.A., 1946; Brown University, Ph.D., 1950. *Home:* 16 Cameron Cres., Toronto, Ontario, Canada.

CAREER: McGill University, Montreal, Quebec, lecturer, 1948-49, assistant professor, 1949-61, associate professor of English, 1961-69; Ryerson Polytechnical Institute, Toronto, Ontario, professor of English, 1970—. *Member:* International P.E.N. *Awards, honors:* Dodd, Mead intercollegiate literary fellowship, 1945, for *The Unreasoning Heart*; Canadian booksellers annual award, 1974, for *The Book of Eve.*

WRITINGS—Novels: *The Unreasoning Heart*, Dodd, 1946; *Of This Day's Journey*, Dodd, 1948; *The Invisible Gate*, Dodd, 1949; *My Lady Greensleeves*, Ballantine, 1955; *The Book of Eve*, Little, Brown, 1974.

* * *

BERG, Frederick S(ven) 1928-

PERSONAL: Born October 13, 1928, in Butte, Mont.; son of Nils (a grocer) and Maurina Josephine (a seamstress; maiden name, Berggren) Berg; married Edna Clawson, May 18, 1959; children: Sven, Louis, Glenn, Leonard, Karen, Nathan. *Education:* Attended University of Washington, Seattle, 1948-50; Washington University, St. Louis, Mo., B.S., 1952; Southern Illinois University, M.A., 1956, Ph.D., 1960. *Politics:* Independent. *Religion:* Church of Jesus Christ of Latter-Day Saints. *Home:* 100 Summit Creek Dr., Smithfield, Utah 84335. *Office:* Department of Communicative Disorders, Utah State University, Logan, Utah 84322.

CAREER: Oregon College of Education, Monmouth, assistant professor of education, 1960-61; Wayne State University, Detroit, Mich., associate professor of audiology, 1961-65; Utah State University, Logan, professor of communicative disorders, 1965—. Consultant to U.S. Office of Education. *Military service:* U.S. Navy, electronic technician, 1946-48. *Member:* American Speech and Hearing Association, Alexander Graham Bell Association for the Deaf, American Organization for the Education of the Hearing Impaired (charter member, 1969), Academy of Rehabilitative Audiology, Utah Speech and Hearing Association.

WRITINGS: (Edtior with S. G. Fletcher) *The Hard of Hearing Child*, Grune, 1970; *Breakthrough for the Hard of Hearing*, privately printed, 1971; *Educational Audiology: Hard of Hearing*, Utah State University Press, 1973. Contributor to *Hearing and Speech News* and *Volta Review.*

WORK IN PROGRESS: Writing home study courses in phonetics, in speech for the hearing impaired, in listening training and auditory trainers, in educational audiology, in language for the hearing impaired, and in advanced phonetics.

* * *

BERG, Jean Horton 1913-

PERSONAL: Born May 30, 1913, in Clairton, Pa.; daughter of Harry Heber (a manufacturer) and Daisy (Horton) Lutz; married John Joseph Berg (a dentist), July 2, 1938; children: Jean Horton, Julie Joanne Berg Tapp, John Joel. *Education:* University of Pennsylvania, B.S. in Ed., 1935, A.M., 1937. *Religion:* Christian Scientist. *Residence:* Wayne, Pa. *Agent:* McIntosh & Otis, Inc., 18 East 41st St., New York, N.Y. 10017.

CAREER: Teacher of English and Latin in Bridgeville, Del., 1936-38; teacher of creative writing in adult education classes, Radnor Township, Pa., 1966—. Private tutor in Latin. *Member:* Authors Guild, National League of American Pen Women (president of Chester County branch, 1966-68), American Society of Composers, Authors and Publishers, League of Women Voters. *Awards, honors:* Follett Beginning-to-Read Award, 1961; Medallion of Philadelphia, 1963; Alumni Award of Merit, University of Pennsylvania, 1969; *What Harry Found When He Lost Archie* was named on Child Study Association Book List, 1970.

WRITINGS—Juvenile books: *Three Mice and a Cat*, Grosset, 1950; *The Jolly Jumping Man*, Grosset, 1950; *The Noisy Clock Shop*, Grosset, 1950; *Baby Susan's Chicken*, Grosset, 1951; *The Playful Little Dog*, Grosset, 1951; *The Big Jump-Up Farm Animal Book*, Grosset, 1952; *Christmas in Song and Story*, Grosset, 1953; *The Traveling Twins*, Grosset, 1953; *It's Fun to Peek*, Grosset, 1955; *The Big Jump-Up Book of Trains, Trucks and Planes*, Grosset, 1955; *Tuggy the Tugboat*, Grosset, 1958.

Pierre, the Young Watchmaker, Bobbs-Merrill, 1961; *The O'Leary's and Friends*, Follett, 1961; *The Little Red Hen* (retold), Follett, 1963; *Baby Raccoon*, Grosset, 1963; *The Wee Little Man*, Follett, 1963; *Big Bug, Little Bug*, Follett, 1964; *There's Nothing to Do, So Let Me Be You*, Westminster, 1966; *Miss Kirby's Room*, Westminster, 1966; *Miss Tessie Tate* (Junior Literary Guild selection), Westminster, 1967; *Nobody Scares a Porcupine*, Westminster, 1969.

What Harry Found When He Lost Archie, Westminster, 1970; *Mr. Koonan's Bargain*, Nautilus Press, 1971; *Next Best*, Harper, 1972; *Was She Lost?*, Harper, 1972; *The Green Lady*, Harper, 1972; *Saturday's Friends*, Harper, 1972; *The Cap and the Lamb*, Harper, 1972; *The Right Thing to Do*, Harper, 1972; *One or Many*, Harper, 1972; *All Because of Snow*, Harper, 1972; *Nothing Ever Happens*, Harper, 1972; *The Big Problem*, Harper, 1972.

Other books: *Bright Candle Light* (songs), Pro Art, 1966; (with Russell Stauffer) *Rapid Comprehension through Effective Reading*, Learn, Inc., 1969; (with Stauffer) *Communications through Effective Reading*, Learn, Inc., 1971.

Contributor of stories, articles, and poems to *Christian Science Monitor, Highlights for Children, Jack and Jill, Ranger Rick, Today's Girl, Humpty-Dumpty*, and other magazines and newspapers.

WORK IN PROGRESS: A biography of Herman Wrice; an untitled book for teen-agers.

AVOCATIONAL INTERESTS: Tennis (plays several times a week throughout the year), traveling (particularly on cruise ships).

* * *

BERG, Viola Jacobson 1918-

PERSONAL: Born September 29, 1918, in Franksville, Wis.; daughter of Edward C. (a farmer) and Mary (Anderson) Jacobson; married Howard A. Berg (vice-president of a cement company), November 27, 1943; children: Donna, Eric, Marianne, Roy. *Education:* Attended Nassau

Community College of the State University of New York, 1968-69. *Politics:* Republican. *Religion:* Baptist. *Home:* 5 Roosevelt Ave., Malverne, N.Y. 11565. *Office:* South Shore Christian School, 34 Smith St., Merrick, N.Y. 11566.

CAREER: Marshall Field & Co., Zion, Ill., secretary to business manager, 1937-41; Hamilton-Beach Co., Racine, Wis., bookkeeper, 1941-42; Rainfair, Racine, Wis., secretary to president and treasurer, 1942-44; private school secretary, assistant librarian, poetry teacher in Brookville, N.Y., 1969-73; Long Island Christian Schools, Flushing, N.Y., secretary to principal of South Shore Christian School, 1973—. Poetry judge for County Parks Recreation Commission, 1970; has conducted poetry seminars in schools of Levittown and Merrick, Long Island, 1974. *Member:* Long Island Writers (vice-president, 1970-71). *Awards, honors:* Named "Poet of the Year" by Long Island Writers, 1969; first prize in short story contest of *Author-Poet* (Birmingham, Ala.), 1970; diploma of excellence from Centro Studi e Scambi Internazionali (Rome), 1972; and numerous other awards and citations for poems.

WRITINGS—Poems: *The Heart of Things*, Prairie Press, 1969; *Wings of Good Tidings*, Good Tidings Fellowship, 1969; *Harvest of the Heart*, Verdure Publications, 1970; *Move That Mountain*, KC Publications, 1970.

Work is represented in about thirty anthologies, including: *The New Poetry Anthology*, edited by Florence Beck Unangst, Prairie Press, 1967; *American Poets Anthology*, edited by Stella Craft Tremble, American Poets Fellowship Society, 1968; *From Sea to Sea in Song*, edited by Tremble, American Poetry League, 1968; *Poetry Pageant*, edited by Jean Wood, Magnetic Publishing, 1969; *The Soul and the Singer*, Young Publications, 1969; *Friendship Trail Anthology*, edited by Pearl Kirk, Inky Trail Publications, 1970; *God I Like You*, edited by Sherwood E. Wirt and Charlene Anderson, Zondervan, 1970; *The Forever Bear Anthology*, edited by Jack Jernigan, Kentucky State Poetry Society, 1971; *Bouquets of Poems*, Centro Studi e Scambi Internazionali, 1972. Contributor of fiction, articles, and over twelve hundred poems to various publications.

WORK IN PROGRESS: A book of previously published poems, *For Kindred Hearts*; a textbook for creative writing teachers and aspiring poets, *Pathways for the Poet*.

SIDELIGHTS: Mrs. Berg's poem, "Puff, Puff, Puff," is to be included in a Columbine Records album tentatively titled, "The Now Sounds of Today."

* * *

BERGSTEIN, Eleanor 1938-

PERSONAL: Born April 17, 1938, in New York, N.Y.; daughter of Joseph (a physician) and Sarah (Rein) Bergstein; married Michael Goldman (a poet and critic), January 17, 1965. *Education:* University of Pennsylvania, B.A., 1958. *Politics:* Liberal Democrat. *Religion:* Jewish. *Home:* 425 Riverside Dr., New York, N.Y. 10025. *Agent:* Phoebe Larmore, 44 Greenwich Ave., New York, N.Y. 10011.

CAREER: Has worked in the theater, in publishing, and in documentary films. *Member:* Authors Guild of Authors League of America.

WRITINGS: *Advancing Paul Newman*, Viking, 1973. Contributor of stories to *Transatlantic Review, Redbook, Cosmopolitan,* and *Carleton Miscellany*.

WORK IN PROGRESS: A novel about obsession.

BIOGRAPHICAL/CRITICAL SOURCES: *New Republic*, February 23, 1974; *Women's Studies*, Volume II, number 1, 1974; *Partisan Review*, Volume XLI, number 3; Carolyn Riley, editor, *Contemporary Literary Criticism*, Volume IV, Gale, 1975.

* * *

BERKMAN, Harold W(illiam) 1926-

PERSONAL: Born February 22, 1926, in Brooklyn, N.Y.; son of Abel A. and Rose (Garfinkel) Berkman; married Muriel Siegel, February 3, 1950; children: Gary Keith, Karen Ann. *Education:* University of Georgia, B.B.A., 1949; St. John's University, Jamaica, N.Y., M.B.A., 1969, Ph.D., 1971. *Home:* 2715 Healy Ave., Far Rockaway, N.Y. 11691. *Office:* School of Business, C. W. Post Center, Long Island University, Greenvale, N.Y. 11548.

CAREER: Long Island University, C. W. Post Center, Greenvale, N.Y., adjunct assistant professor of business administration, 1969-70, adjunct associate professor of sociology, 1970, associate professor of business administration, 1970—. Visiting associate professor at St. John's University, 1971. President and member of board of directors of Valencia Liquor Shops, Inc., Hastings & Berwick Ltd. (importers and exporters of French wines), Halmor Management Co., Jarub Realty Corp., and Berkman Associates (marketing and management consultants). Moderator of Long Island Environmental Conference; member of board of trustees of Gustave Hartman YM-YWHA. *Military service:* U.S. Army, Infantry, 1944-46; served in European theater.

MEMBER: Academy of Marketing Science (member of board of directors), American Marketing Association, American Management Association, Money Management Institute, American Academy of Political Science, American Sociological Association, National Council on Family Relations, American Cancer Society (member of board of trustees of Nassau Division), New York State Sociological Association, Delta Mu Delta, Delta Sigma Pi. *Awards, honors:* Award for meritorious service from Federation of Jewish Philanthropies, 1963-64; certificate de merite from Le Comite des Vins de France, 1967; award for distinguished service from Academy of Marketing Science, 1972; confrerie Saint-Etienne of Alsace-France, 1973.

WRITINGS: *The Human Relations of Management*, Dickenson, 1974; (with J. M. Young) *Cases and Issues: The Human Relations of Management*, Dickenson, 1975; (editor with B. R. Armandi and J. J. Barbera, and contributor) *Contemporary and Classical Readings in Human Relations*, Kendall-Hunt, 1975; (with C. C. Gilson) *Consumer Behavior: A Life Style Approach*, Dickenson, in press.

Contributor to *Business Critique, Journal of the Academy of Marketing Science*, and *Journal of Marketing*. Member of advisory board of *Liquor Store*.

* * *

BERKOWITZ, Morris Ira 1931-

PERSONAL: Born March 6, 1931, in New York, N.Y.; son of Benjamin B. (a dentist) and Charlotte (Goldner) Berkowitz; married Janice Malsman (a social worker), August 28, 1954; children: Seth Nathan, Charlotte Rebeccah. *Education:* Purdue University, B.S., 1952, M.S., 1954; Yale University, M.A., 1956, Ph.D., 1958. *Religion:* Jewish. *Home:* 51 Yates St., St. Catharines, Ontario,

Canada. *Office:* Department of Sociology, Brock University, St. Catharines, Ontario L2S 3A1, Canada.

CAREER: Rand Corp., Santa Monica, Calif., human factors scientist, 1957-59; Systems Development Corp., Paramus, N.J., group head of systems research, 1959-62; University of Pittsburgh, Pittsburgh, Pa., assistant professor, 1962-63, associate professor of sociology, 1963-67; Chinese University of Hong Kong, Shatin, Hong Kong, visiting professor of sociology and chairman of department, 1967-69; University of Pittsburgh, associate professor of sociology, 1969-70; Brock University, St. Catharines, Ontario, professor of sociology, 1970—. Visiting lecturer, Columbia University, 1961-62. Consultant to Institute of International Education, 1962-71, American Institutes of Research, 1965-68, Committee Coordinating Regional Community Service, 1970—, Social Planning Council of Greater Niagara, 1971—, and Addiction Research Foundation, 1973—. *Member:* American Sociological Society, Canadian Society for Asian Studies, Society for the Scientific Study of Religion, Society for the Study of Social Problems, Royal Asiatic Society.

WRITINGS: (With J. E. Johnson) *Social Scientific Studies of Religion: A Bibliography*, University of Pittsburgh Press, 1967; (with Frederich Brandauer and John H. Reed) *Folk Religion in an Urban Setting*, Christian Study Centre (Hong Kong), 1970; (with Eddie K. K. Poon) *A Hong Kong Bibliography*, Chinese University Press, 1970. Contributor of articles and monographs to journals in his field.

WORK IN PROGRESS: Research in Chinese religion and change in Chinese villages; a monograph on research on aging for Ontario Ministry of Community and Social Services, completion expected in 1975.

* * *

BERNSTEIN, David 1915(?)-1974

1915(?)—August 21, 1974; American newspaper editor, publisher, and author. Obituaries: *New York Times*, August 22, 1974.

* * *

BERRETT, LaMar C(ecil) 1926-

PERSONAL: Born March 28, 1926, in Riverton, Utah; son of Harold and Stella (Wright) Berrett; married Darlene Hamilton, August 3, 1950; children: Marla, Kim, Michael, Susan, LeAnn, Nathan, Evan, Ellen, Jared. *Education:* University of Utah, B.S., 1952; Brigham Young University, M.S., 1960, Ed.D., 1963. *Religion:* Church of Jesus Christ of Latter-Day Saints. *Home:* 1032 East 400 South, Orem, Utah 84057. *Office:* Department of Church History and Doctrine, 123 JSB, Brigham Young University, Provo, Utah 84602.

CAREER: Private school teacher and principal in Heber, Utah, 1952-54, in Bingham, Utah, 1954-60, and in Orem, Utah, 1960-61; Brigham Young University, Provo, Utah, assistant professor, 1963-65, associate professor, 1966-70, professor of church history and doctrine, 1971—, chairman of department, 1964—, director of one-semester study tour of the Middle East, spring, 1972. *Military Service:* U.S. Army, 1944-46. *Member:* Mormon History Association, Sons of the Utah Pioneers, Utah State Historical Society (secretary, 1959-60; president, 1971-72).

WRITINGS: A Catalogue of Theses and Dissertations concerning the Church of Jesus Christ of Latter-Day Saints: Mormonism and Utah, Brigham Young University Press, 1971; *The Wilford C. Wood Collection*, Volume I, Brigham Young University Press, 1972; *Discovering the World of the Bible*, Brigham Young University Press, 1973.

WORK IN PROGRESS: A History of Mormon Interest in Israel; *Discovering the World of Mormonism*; a photographic essay on the Holy Land and Jesus.

SIDELIGHTS: Berrett has made nine trips to Israel since 1968. *Discovering the World of the Bible* sold more than 35,000 copies in its first year of printing.

* * *

BERSANI, Leo 1931-

PERSONAL: Born April 16, 1931, in New York, N.Y.; son of Guido and Harriet (Wischer) Bersani. *Education:* Harvard University, B.A. (summa cum laude), 1952, Ph.D., 1958. *Office:* Department of French, University of California, Berkeley, Calif. 94720.

CAREER: Wellesley College, Wellesley, Mass., instructor, 1957-60, assistant professor, 1960-66, associate professor of French, 1966-67; Rutgers University, New Brunswick, N.J., associate professor, 1967-69, professor of French, 1969-73; University of California, Berkeley, professor of French and chairman of department, 1973—. *Awards, honors:* Guggenheim fellowship, 1967-68; National Endowment for the Humanities award, 1967, for essay on French criticism.

WRITINGS: Marcel Proust: The Fictions of Life and of Art, Oxford University Press, 1965; *Balzac to Beckett: Center and Circumference in French Fiction*, Oxford University Press, 1970. Contributor of articles and reviews to *Partisan Review, New York Times Book Review, New Republic*, and *Yale Review*.

WORK IN PROGRESS: A book on desire and character in literature.

* * *

BERTHOLD, Mary Paddock 1909-

PERSONAL: Born November 24, 1909, in Wisdom, Mont.; daughter of James Francis (a rancher) and Margery (Jardine) Paddock; married John Berthold, November 4, 1939 (died, 1943). *Education:* Attended Butte Business College, 1927-28, Oregon State University, 1930-31, and Kinman Business College, 1936. *Religion:* Presbyterian. *Home and office:* 524 West Silver St., Butte, Mont. 59701.

CAREER: Montana Standard, Butte, Mont., secretary, 1928-30; WTOL (radio), Toledo, Ohio, scripts traffic manager, 1941-43; KGVO (radio), Missoula, Mont., copywriter and copy chief, 1944-48; Rathbone, King & Seeley (insurance company), Los Angeles, Calif., secretary and underwriter, 1948-64; writer, 1965—. *Member:* Copper Village Museum and Arts Center.

WRITINGS: A Local Call (mystery novel), Vantage, 1969; *Turn Here For the Big Hole*, Harlo, 1970; *Big Hole Journal: Notes and Excerpts*, Harlo, 1973; *A Later Look*, Harlo, in press.

WORK IN PROGRESS: A book on notable people of the Northwest, *Including Two Captains*.

BIOGRAPHICAL/CRITICAL SOURCES: Montana Standard, December 27, 1970; *Anaconda Leader*, January 19, 1971, April 20, 1971, July 22, 1971, June 11, 1972; *Anaconda Standard*, April 20, 1971; *Ravalli Republican* (Mont.), March 13, 1973; *Great Falls Tribune* (Mont.), April 22, 1973; *Books for Montanans*, June 7, 1974.

BERTRAND, Lewis 1897(?)-1974

1897(?)—September 29, 1974; American translator and interpreter. Obituaries: *New York Times*, October 1, 1974.

* * *

BESTUL, Thomas H(oward) 1942-

PERSONAL: Born October 30, 1942, in Evanston, Ill.; son of Howard M. (a musician) and Arvada (a secretary; maiden name, Swenson) Bestul; married Karen Christenson, June 19, 1965; children: Mark, Nicholas. *Education:* University of Wisconsin, B.A., 1964; Harvard University, M.A., 1966, Ph.D., 1970. *Residence:* Lincoln, Neb. *Office:* Department of English, University of Nebraska-Lincoln, Lincoln, Neb. 68508.

CAREER: University of Nebraska-Lincoln, assistant professor, 1968-73, associate professor of English, 1973—. *Member:* National Council of Teachers of English, Modern Language Association of America, Mediaeval Academy of America, American Federation of Teachers.

WRITINGS: Satire and Allegory in Wynnere and Wastoure, University of Nebraska Press, 1974.

WORK IN PROGRESS: Studies in Mediaeval English literature.

* * *

BETTS, Donni 1948-

PERSONAL: Born November 10, 1948, in Wichita, Kan.; daughter of Donald I. and Jean (a nurse; maiden name, Wise) Lawless; married George Betts (a teacher and writer), May 28, 1972. *Education:* University of Northern Colorado, B.A., 1971.

CAREER: Student and writer. Worked as European tour director for high school students.

WRITINGS: (With husband George Betts) *Growing Together*, Celestial Arts, 1974.

WORK IN PROGRESS: A book on healthy, productive couple relationships.

AVOCATIONAL INTERESTS: Travel.

* * *

BETZ, Hans Dieter 1931-

PERSONAL: Born May 21, 1931, in Lemgo, Germany; naturalized U.S. citizen in 1973; son of Ludwig (an educator) and Gertrude (Vietor) Betz; married Christel H. Wagner, November, 1958; children: Martin, Ludwig, Arnold. *Education:* Attended School of Theology, Bethel, Germany, 1951-52; Westminster College, Cambridge, graduate study, 1954-55; University of Mainz, Dr. Theol. habil, 1957, 1966. *Home:* 329 West Seventh St., Claremont, Calif. 91711. *Office:* Claremont Graduate School, 831 Dartmouth Ave., Claremont, Calif. 91711.

CAREER: Ordained minister of United Presbyterian Church in the U.S.A., 1961; School of Theology and Claremont Graduate School, both Claremont, Calif., assistant professor, 1963-65, associate professor, 1965-67, professor of theology, 1967—. Director of research project, Institute for Antiquity and Christianity, Claremont, Calif., 1966—. Visiting professor at University of Mainz, 1967, and University of Uppsala, 1973-74. *Member:* Studiorum Novi Testamenti Societas, Society of Biblical Literature, New Testament Colloquium.

WRITINGS: Lukian von Samosata und das Neue Testament (title means "Lucian of Samosata and the New Testament"), Akademie-Verlag, 1961; *Nachfolge und Nachahmung Jesu Christi im Neuen Testament* (title means "Discipleship and Imitation of Jesus Christ in the New Testament"), Siebeck, 1967; *Der Apostel Paulus und die sokratische Tradition* (title means "The Apostle Paul and the Socratic Tradition"), Siebeck, 1972; (editor with Luise Schottroff) *Neues Testament und Christliche Existenz: Festschrift fuer Herbert Braun* (title means "New Testament and Christian Existence: Essays in Honor of Herbert Braun"), Siebeck, 1973; (editor) *Plutarch's Theological Writings and Early Christian Literature*, E. J. Brill, 1974. Also editor of *Christology and Modern Pilgrimage*, 1971, 2nd edition, 1974. Contributor of more than forty articles and reviews to journals.

WORK IN PROGRESS: A commentary on *Paul's Letter to the Galatians*, for Fortress; directing research project with fifteen international scholars on the writings of Plutarch of Chaeronea, a first century A.D. Greek philosopher.

* * *

BHATIA, Hans Raj 1904-

PERSONAL: Born June 1, 1904, in Sialkot, Pakistan; son of Mukand Lal (a librarian) and Bhagwanti Bhatia; married Sushila Devi, October 24, 1926; children: Rajendra Nath, Bhupendra Nath, Surendra Nath, Narendra Nath, Premanjali (Mrs. Rajendra Mohan Soni), Jitendra, Rashmi. *Education:* Government College, Lahore, Pakistan, B.A. (honors), 1924, M.A., 1926. *Politics:* Conservative Democrat. *Religion:* Hindu. *Home:* 286 Adarsh Nagar, Jaipur 302004, India.

CAREER: Daganand Malthuradas College, Moga, India, vice-principal, 1926-29; Birla College (now Birla Institute of Technology and Science), Pilani, Rajasthan, India, held various posts, including professor of philosophy, 1929-44, head of department, 1944-52, education officer for Birla Education Trust, 1942-52; Government of India, Ministry of Education, New Delhi, education officer, 1952-57; Nopany Vidyalaya, Calcutta, India, principal, 1957-60; Kedarnath Gudharilal Khatry Post-Graduate College, Moradabad, India, principal, 1960-65. General secretary of All India Montessori Conference, 1946; has broadcast lectures on All India Radio. *Awards, honors:* Prize from Panjab Government, 1938, for a book on educational psychology.

WRITINGS: The Teaching of English Spelling, Oxford University Press, 1936; *Elements of Educational Psychology*, Orient Longmans, 1949; *What Basic Education Means*, Orient Longmans, 1954; *A New Deal in Secondary Education*, Orient Longmans, 1959; *Craft in Education*, Asia Publishing House, 1962; *A Textbook of Educational Psychology*, Asia Publishing House, 1965, 2nd edition, in press; *Elements of Social Psychology*, Somaiya, 1966; *General Psychology*, Oxford & IBH Publishing (Calcutta), 1969, 2nd edition, 1971; *Abnormal Psychology*, Oxford & IBH Publishing, 1969, 2nd edition, 1972; *Making the Most of Your Mind*, India Book House, 1969.

Author of ten books in Hindi on psychology and education. General editor of "Basic Education Series," Orient Longmans, 1954-60. Contributor of more than two hundred education articles to Indian journals, including *Statesman, Leader, Teaching, Calcutta Review, Indian Review,* and *Panjab Educational Journal*.

WORK IN PROGRESS: A comprehensive book on educational psychology, in Hindi.

SIDELIGHTS: As a rural education officer, Bhatia organized and directed one of the largest drives in rural education in India on behalf of the Birla Education Trust with four hundred fifty primary and secondary schools in some of the remote villages of Rajasthan and surrounding areas. He writes: "Educational practice in India is too cramped by tradition, mechanical routine, and dead wood, and while there is a great popular demand for reform and change in education very little is being done in actual day to day working. . . . I have made strong pleas for urgent reform and indicated specific areas of work in which changes should be made and how they should be made. But it is a long long road and politics is playing havoc with education in India. . . . Similarly in the field of social and inter-personal relations larger spread of psychological knowledge of human motivations will bring about greater understanding and sympathy at personal and social levels. And a greater effort at self-understanding through a study of psychology will help and promote mental health."

* * *

BHATIA, Krishan 1926(?)-1974

1926(?)—December 11, 1974; Indian journalist and author. Obituaries: *New York Times*, December 11, 1974; *Washington Post*, December 12, 1974; *AB Bookman's Weekly*, January 20, 1975.

* * *

BHUTTO, Zulfikar Ali 1928-

PERSONAL: Born January 5, 1928, in Larkana, Pakistan; son of Shahnawaz Khan and Khurshid Bhutto; married, wife's name, Nusrat; children: Benazir, Sanam Seema (daughters); Murtaza, Shahnawaz (sons). *Education:* University of California, Berkeley, B.A. (with honors), 1950; Christ Church, Oxford, M.A. (with honors), 1952. *Religion:* Islam. *Home:* Al-Murtaza, Bhutto Colony, Larkana, Pakistan. *Office:* Prime Minister's Secretariat, Prime Minister's House, Rawalpindi, Pakistan.

CAREER: Called to Bar, Lincoln's Inn, London, 1953; private practice of law, 1953-58; University of Southampton, Highfield, Southampton, England, lecturer in international law, 1952-53; West Pakistan High Court, Karachi, attorney, 1953-58; Sind Muslim Law College, Karachi, teacher of constitutional law, 1956-58; Islamic Republic of Pakistan, Rawalpindi, Pakistan, Minister for Commerce, 1958-60, Minister of Minority Affairs, and of National Reconstruction and Information, Minister of Fuel, Power, and Natural Resources, and of Kashmir Affairs, 1960-62, Minister of Industries and Natural Resources, 1962-63, Minister for Foreign Affairs and Atomic Energy, 1963-66; founder and chairman, Pakistan People's Party, 1967—; Prime Minister and Foreign Minister of Pakistan, 1971—, chief martial law administrator, 1971-72. Member or leader of numerous Pakistani delegations to United Nations. *Awards, honors:* Hilal-i-Pakistan, 1964; LL.D., University of Sind, 1966; foreign decorations.

WRITINGS: Peace-Keeping by the United Nations, Pakistan Publishing House (Karachi), 1967; *Political Situation in Pakistan*, Veshasher Prakashan, 1968, 2nd edition, Pakistan People's Party, 1969; *Pakistan and the Alliances*, Pakistan People's Party, 1969; *The Myth of Independence*, Oxford University Press, 1969; *Let the People Judge*, Pakistan People's Party, 1969; *The Great Tragedy*, Pakistan People's Party, 1971.

Speeches and writings published in collections, including *A South Asian View*, Embassy of Pakistan (Washington, D.C.), 1964, and *The Quest for Peace*, Pakistan Institute of International Affairs, 1966.

AVOCATIONAL INTERESTS: Big game hunting.

* * *

BICKEL, Alexander M(ordecai) 1924-1974

December 17, 1924—November 7, 1974; Rumanian-born American educator and Constitutional law expert. Obituaries: *New York Times*, November 8, 1974; *Washington Post*, November 9, 1974; *Time*, November 18, 1974; *Newsweek*, November 18, 1974; *AB Bookman's Weekly*, December 9, 1974. (*CA*-4).

* * *

BIDDISS, Michael Denis 1942-

PERSONAL: Born April 15, 1942, in Farnborough, Kent, England; son of Daniel and Eileen (Jones) Biddiss; married Ruth Margaret Cartwright, 1967; children: Clare, Katherine, Sarah. *Education:* Queen's College, Cambridge, B.A. (double first class honors), 1964, M.A. and Ph.D., 1968; University of Strasbourg, graduate study, 1965-66. *Agent:* Curtis Brown Ltd., 1 Craven Hill, London W2 3EW, England. *Office:* Department of History, University of Leicester LE1 7RH, England.

CAREER: Cambridge University, Downing College, Cambridge, England, fellow and director of studies in history, 1966-73; University of Leicester, Leicester, England, lecturer in history, 1973—. Visiting professor of history at University of Victoria (British Columbia), 1973; Lister Lecturer, British Association for the Advancement of Science, 1975. *Member:* Royal Historical Society (fellow), Institute of Race Relations.

WRITINGS: Father of Racist Ideology: The Social and Political Thought of Count Gobineau, Weybright, 1970; (editor) *Gobineau: Selected Political Writings*, Harper, 1970; (with F. F. Cartwright) *Disease and History*, Crowell, 1972. Contributor to academic journals.

WORK IN PROGRESS: Ideas and Mass Society: European Thought since 1870, publication expected in 1976; *European Racism: Aspects of History and Ideology*.

* * *

BIEN, Joseph Julius 1936-

PERSONAL: Born May 22, 1936, in Cincinnati, Ohio; son of Julius Joseph and Mary (Adams) Bien; married Francoise Neve (a professor), April, 1968. *Education:* Xavier University, Cincinnati, Ohio, B.S., 1957, M.A., 1958. *Residence:* Columbia, Mo. *Office:* Department of Philosophy, University of Missouri, Columbia, Mo. 65201.

CAREER: University of Texas at Austin, assistant professor of philosophy, 1968-73; University of Missouri, Columbia, associate professor of philosophy, 1973—. Associate editor for Gruner. *Member:* Societe International de Philosophie, American Philosophical Association, American Association for the Advancement of Slavic Studies, Society for Phenomenology and Existential Philosophy.

WRITINGS: (Translator) Maurice Merleau-Ponty, *Adventures of the Dialectic*, Northwestern University Press, 1973; (contributor) Garth Gillan, editor, *Horizons of the Flesh: Critical Reinterpretations of Merleau-Ponty's Thought*, Southern Illinois University Press, 1973. Contributor to *Southwestern Journal of Philosophy*, *Journal of*

Thought, and *Studies in Phenomenology and Existential Philosophy*. Series editor, "Contemporary Political and Social Philosophy," University of Texas Press, 1972—.

WORK IN PROGRESS: Co-authoring a book on Georg Lukac's social philosophy; a manuscript concerning Maurice Merleau-Ponty's political thought.

* * *

BIENVENU, Bernard J(efferson) 1925-

PERSONAL: Born April 8, 1925, in St. Martinville, La.; son of Louis Jefferson and Beatrice (Durand) Bienvenu. *Education:* University of Southwestern Louisiana, B.S., 1947; Harvard University, M.B.A., 1947, D.B.A., 1956; postdoctoral study at University of Paris and University of Lyon, 1959. *Home:* 211 North Main St., St. Martinville, La. 70582. *Office:* University of Southwestern Louisiana, P.O. Box 598, Lafayette, La. 70501.

CAREER: Worked in stock brokerage business, 1947-48; Pan American Life Insurance Co., New Orleans, La., associate general agent, 1948-50; University of Southwestern Louisiana, Lafayette, professor of business administration, 1952-55; head of department of marketing, 1955-56, head of department of management, 1956-59, head of department of managment and administrative studies, 1969—, director of alumni relations, 1952-53. Management consultant to private industry, institutions, and government; Ford Foundation fellow at Harvard University Graduate School of Business, 1954-55; member of board of directors, Louisiana State Department of Commerce and Industry, 1960-64; vice-chairman of board of directors, Evangeline Pepper & Foods, Inc., 1963-65; member and vice-chairman, Louisiana Labor Mediation Board, 1966—; visiting professor, Centre d'Enseignement Superieur des Affaires, 1970-71; visiting lecturer University of Tunis, 1971; guest lecturer to various African universities and businesses, 1974. *Military service:* U.S. Naval Reserve, active duty, 1943-46, 1950-52; became captain. *Member:* Academy of Management (member of board of governors, 1963-66), Southern Management Association (member of board of governors, 1963-66; vice-president, 1966-67; president, 1968-69), Southwest Management Association (vice-president, 1961-62; president, 1962-63), Southwest Social Science Association, John Henry Cardinal Newman Honor Society, Phi Kappa Theta, Phi Kappa Phi.

WRITINGS: (Contributor) Huxley Madeheim, Edward M. Mazze, and Charles S. Stein, editors, *Readings in Organization and Management*, Holt, 1963; (contributor) Harold Koontz and Cyril O'Donnell, editors, *Management: A Book of Readings*, McGraw, 1964; (contributor) Elizabeth Marting and Dorothy MacDonald, editors, *Management and Its People*, American Management Association, 1965; *New Priorities in Training: A Guide for Industry*, American Management Association, 1969; (contributor) Richard H. Buskirk, *Business and Administrative Policies*, Wiley, 1971; (contributor) John Champion and John James, editors, *Incidents in Management*, Irwin, 1975. Contributor to journals in his field.

WORK IN PROGRESS: Research on organizational policy and strategy.

* * *

BIKKIE, James A(ndrew) 1929-

PERSONAL: Born April 30, 1929, in Brainerd, Minn.; son of Elmer A. and Edna Irene (Thompson) Bikkie; married Shirley A. Grant, June 20, 1952; children: Ann Irene, Patty Sue. *Education:* St. Cloud State College, B.S., 1956; University of Minnesota, M.A., 1957, Ph.D., 1973. *Politics:* Democrat. *Religion:* Lutheran. *Home:* 842 North Grant, Moscow, Idaho 83843. *Office:* Division of Vocational Teacher Education, University of Idaho, Moscow, Idaho 83843.

CAREER: Kansas State Teachers College, Emporia, assistant professor of business education, 1959-63; University of Nebraska, Lincoln, assistant professor of distributive education, 1965-73; University of Idaho, Moscow, associate professor of education, 1973—, director of Division of Vocational Teacher Education, 1973—. Associate professor at University of Alberta, summer, 1972. *Military service:* U.S. Navy, 1951-54. *Member:* American Vocational Association, American Educational Research Association, Council for Distributive Teacher Education, Idaho Vocational Association, Phi Delta Kappa. *Awards, honors:* Danforth fellowship, 1961; outstanding service award from Distributive Education Clubs of America, 1962.

WRITINGS: *Careers in Marketing,* Gregg, 1971. Service editor of *Business Education Forum,* 1966-68.

* * *

BILAS, Richard A(llen) 1935-

PERSONAL: Born February 3, 1935, in Passaic, N.J.; son of Nestor J. (a businessman) and Helen E. (Smith) Bilas; married Janet Harris (a registered nurse), June 23, 1956; children: Cathy Ann, David Allen, Ami Lianne. *Education:* Duke University, A.B., 1956; University of Virginia, Ph.D., 1963. *Politics:* Republican. *Religion:* Episcopalian. *Home:* 4404 LaMirada Dr., Bakersfield, Calif. 93309. *Office:* Department of Economics, California State College, Bakersfield, Calif. 93309.

CAREER: University of Southern California, Los Angeles, assistant professor, 1962-66, associate professor of economics, 1966-67; Georgia State University, Atlanta, associate professor, 1967-68, professor of economics, 1968-70; California State College, Bakersfield, professor of economics, 1970-74, Gene Reid Professor of Economics, 1974—. *Member:* American Economic Association, Western Business and Economic Association, Southern Economic Association. *Awards, honors:* Fulbright research grant, 1966-67.

WRITINGS: *Microeconomic Theory*, McGraw, 1967, 2nd edition, 1971; (with Richard S. Wallace) *Problems in Microeconomics*, McGraw, 1972; (with Frank Alessio) *The Essentials of Macroeconomic Analysis*, Business Publications, 1974. Contributor to journals.

WORK IN PROGRESS: *The Mathematics of Price Theory; Perspectives in Economics; The Essentials of Freedom.*

* * *

BINDER, Otto O. 1911-1974

August 26, 1911—October 14, 1974; American science writer. Obituaries: *New York Times*, October 19, 1974; *AB Bookman's Weekly*, November 18, 1974. (*CA*-4).

* * *

BINGHAM, David A(ndrew) 1926-

PERSONAL: Born September 28, 1926, in Filbert, W.Va.; son of Hubert A. and Mary (Bowling) Bingham; married Patricia Crowson, April 21, 1951 (divorced, 1971); married

Kathleen Green, August 3, 1972; children: (first marriage) Jean E., Thomas S., David Andrew, Jr., Robert L. *Education:* Asbury College, student, 1949-50; Concord College, B.A. (magna cum laude), 1953; University of Iowa, M.A., 1955, Ph.D., 1957. *Home:* 426 Med. Center Dr., A-202, Morgantown, W.Va. 26505. *Office:* Bureau for Government Research, West Virginia University, Morgantown, W.Va. 26506.

CAREER: U.S. Army Air Forces, 1943-47, U.S. Air Force, 1947-48, leaving service as sergeant; administrative assistant to city manager, Iowa City, Iowa, 1953-55; Arizona State University, Tempe, instructor, 1957-58, assistant professor of public administration, 1958-59; University of Arizona, Tucson, research associate in Bureau of Business and Public Research, 1959-63, associate professor of government and public administration, 1960-63, associate professor of government, 1963-65, professor, 1965-74, associate director, Institute of Government Research, 1964-69; West Virginia University, Bureau for Government Research, Morgantown, director, 1975—. First project director of Arizona's federal urban planning assistance program, 1960; member of Arizona State Commission on the Legislature and Education, 1967-68. Radio commentator and analyst on Tucson stations in 1964 and 1966 general elections.

MEMBER: American Political Science Association, American Association for the Advancement of Science, American Society for Public Administration (secretary-treasurer, Arizona chapter, 1960-67), American Institute of Urban and Regional Affairs (state representative, 1968), Western Political Science Association, Western Governmental Research Association (president, 1964-65; state representative, 1967-74), Pi Sigma Alpha.

WRITINGS: (Contributor) Marshall Townsend, editor, *Arizona: Its People and Resources,* University of Arizona Press, 1960, revised edition, 1972; *Constitutional Municipal Home Rule in Arizona* (monograph), Bureau of Business and Public Research, University of Arizona, 1960; (principal author) *Public Land Use, Transfer and Ownership in Arizona* (monograph), Arizona Academy, 1965; (contributor) Clyde J. Wingfield, editor, *Urbanization in the Southwest,* Texas Western Press, 1968; *Some Alternative Conceptual Patterns of Governmental Organization for the Tucson S.M.S.A.,* Institute of Government Research, University of Arizona, 1974. Contributor to *Cadillac Modern Encyclopedia* and journals.

* * *

BINNS, J(ames) W(allace) 1940-

PERSONAL: Born September 1, 1940, in Harrogate, England; son of Wallace William and Madge (Ewbank) Binns. *Education:* University of Birmingham, B.A., 1964, M.A., 1965, Ph.D., 1969. *Home:* 98 St. Denis Rd., Selly Oak, Birmingham B29 4LU, England.

CAREER: British War Office, London, England, public servant, 1958-61; University of Birmingham, Birmingham, England, lecturer in Medieval and Renaissance Latin, 1965—. *Member:* Renaissance Society of America, Society for Promotion of Roman Studies, British Film Institute.

WRITINGS: (Editor) *Ovid*, Routledge & Kegan Paul, 1973; (editor) *Latin Literature of the Fourth Century*, Routledge & Kegan Paul, 1974; (editor) *The Latin Poetry of English Poets*, Routledge & Kegan Paul, 1974. Contributor to *Studies in the Renaissance, Sixteenth Century Journal, Music and Letters, Humanistica Lovaniensia,* and *Library.*

WORK IN PROGRESS: Researching Latin writings in England, 1520-1640.

AVOCATIONAL INTERESTS: Horror films, travel.

* * *

BIRCH, William G(arry) 1909-

PERSONAL: Born July 8, 1909, in Janesville, Wis.; son of Frank E. (an executive) and Lois (Hill) Birch; married Vera Anderson, June 6, 1936; children: Jae A., Dawn B. (Mrs. Oldrick K. Sebek), William G. II, James D. *Education:* Attended University of Iowa, 1926-28; Northwestern University, M.B., 1932, M.D., 1933. *Politics:* Republican. *Religion:* Episcopalian. *Home address:* Palm Hills Country Club, 62 Sabol Palm, Largo, Fla. 33540. *Office:* Medical Center, 402 Bronson, Kalamazoo, Mich. 49006.

CAREER: University of Chicago, Medical School, Chicago, Ill., assisant in department of obstetrics and gynecology, 1933-37; Chicago Lying In Hospital, Chicago, Ill., resident, 1934-37; Sault Polyclinic, Sault Ste. Marie, Mich., founder and member, 1937-42; Birch, Pearce, & Gerstner, Kalamazoo, Mich., partner, 1945-71; Bronson Methodist Hospital, Kalamazoo, Mich., gynecologyist, 1945-66, senior gynecologist, 1966-74; Obstetrics & Gynecology of Kalamazoo, Kalamazoo, Mich., president, 1971-74. Adjunct professor of biology, Western Michigan University, 1970—, and clinical director of Physician's Assistant Program, 1971-74. *Military service:* U.S. Army Reserve, 1935-69; active duty, 1942-45; retired as colonel; received Bronze Star and French Freedom Medal. *Member:* American College of Surgeons (fellow), American College of Obstetricians and Gynecologists (fellow), American Medical Association, Michigan State Medical Society, South Central Michigan Health Planning Council (founding trustee; president, 1971—), Kalamazoo Executive Club (president, 1969), Kalamazoo Symphony Society (president, 1952), Kalamazoo Rotary Club (president, 1958). *Awards, honors:* Michigan State Medical Society distinguished service award, 1973.

WRITINGS: (With Dona Z. Meilach) *A Doctor Discusses Pregnancy*, Budlong, 1965, 5th edition, 1974. Contributor to *Redbook, Cosmopolitan, Ladies Home Journal*, and others.

WORK IN PROGRESS: Memoirs, *Call Your OB Anytime.*

* * *

BIRDSALL, Steve 1944-

PERSONAL: Born October 19, 1944, in Sydney, Australia; married Sandra Telford. *Education:* Attended schools in Sydney, Australia. *Religion:* Church of England. *Home:* 20 Royal St., Chatswood 2067, Sydney, Australia.

CAREER: Has worked as advertising copywriter, as mail carrier, and in various temporary jobs. *Member:* Air Force Association, Spooky Association, 91st Bomb Group Memorial Association, 90th Bomb Group Association.

WRITINGS: *Famous Aircraft: The B-17 Flying Fortress*, Arco Publishing, 1965; *Famous Aircraft: The B-24 Liberator*, Arco Publishing, 1968; *The A-1 Skyraider*, Arco Publishing, 1970; *Hell's Angels: B-17 Aircraft*, Grenadier Books, 1970; *Log of the Liberators: An Illustrated History of the B-24*, Doubleday, 1973; *Flying Buccaneers*, Doubleday, 1975. Contributor to aviation periodicals.

SIDELIGHTS: Birdsall told *CA*: "My work involves recording the true story of men at war: their experiences and feelings, rather than the oversimplified or often intentionally false picture given of the military."

* * *

BIRNBAUM, Norman 1926-

PERSONAL: Born July 21, 1926, in New York, N.Y.; son of Silas Jacob (a teacher) and Jean (Bermen) Birnbaum; married Gudrun Apel, August 21, 1955 (divorced, July, 1970); children: Anna, Antonia. *Education:* Williams College, A.B., 1947; Harvard University, M.A., 1951, Ph.D., 1958. *Home:* 249 South Pleasant St., Amherst, Mass. 01002. *Office:* Department of Anthropology and Sociology, Amherst College, Amherst, Mass. 01002.

CAREER: Harvard University, Cambridge, Mass., tutor at Adams House, 1948-52; University of London, London School of Economics and Political Science, London, England, assistant lecturer, 1953-55, lecturer in sociology, 1955-59; Oxford University, Oxford, England, fellow at Nuffield College, 1959-66; New School for Social Research, New York, N.Y., professor of sociology, 1966-68; Amherst College, Amherst, Mass., professor of sociology, 1968—. Editor, U.S. Office of War Information, 1943-45; fellow, Social Science Research Council, 1952-53; visiting professor at University of Strasbourg, 1964-66; Giovanni Agnelli Foundation, visiting scholar, 1971-72, consultant, 1973—; visiting member, Institute of Advanced Study, 1975-76; member of executive committee of Democratic Socialist Organizing Committee.

MEMBER: International Sociological Association, Conference Internationale de Sociologie Religieuse, American Sociological Association, Society for the Scientific Study of Religion, British Sociological Association, Deutsche Gesellschaft fuer Soziologie. *Awards, honors:* Guggenheim fellowhip, 1971-72.

WRITINGS: (Editor with Gertrude Lenzer) *Sociology and Religion*, Prentice-Hall, 1968; *The Crisis of Industrial Society*, Oxford University Press, 1969; *Toward a Critical Sociology*, Oxford University Press, 1971. Contributor to sociology journals. Contributing editor of *Change in Higher Education*; member of founding editorial board of *New Left Review*, 1959; member of editorial board of *Praxis*, 1966—; consultant to *Partisan Review*.

WORK IN PROGRESS: The Universities and the End of Culture.

* * *

BISH, Robert L(ee) 1942-

PERSONAL: Born September 29, 1942, in Seattle, Wash.; son of Elmer L. and Mae (Wright) Bish; married Frances Pennell, August 15, 1970. *Education:* University of Southern California, A.B. (magna cum laude), 1964; Indiana University, A.M., 1966, Ph.D., 1968. *Home:* 26 Packet Rd., Palos Verdes Peninsula, Calif. 90274. *Office:* Department of Economics, University of Southern California, Los Angeles, Calif. 90007.

CAREER: University of Washington, Seattle, assistant professor of economics and public affairs, 1968-72; University of Southern California, Los Angeles, associate professor of economics and urban studies, 1972—. *Member:* American Economic Association, American Political Science Association, American Society for Public Administration, Public Choice Society, National Tax Association, Regional Science Association, Phi Beta Kappa.

WRITINGS: (With James A. Crutchfield) *Socioeconomic, Institutional, and Legal Considerations in the Management of Puget Sound,* Federal Water Pollution Control Board, 1969; (editor) *Papers on Local Government Finance in Washington State,* Institute of Economic Research, University of Washington, 1970; (with wife, Frances Pennell Bish) *Mobile Home Taxation in Washington State,* Institute of Governmental Research, University of Washington, 1970; (with David A. Dorfman) *The Impact of General Revenue Sharing on Washington State*, Institute of Governmental Research, University of Washington, 1971; *The Public Ecomomy of Metropolitan Areas,* Rand McNally, 1971; (with Dorfman) *An Alternative for Financing Higher Education in Washington*, Institute of Governmental Research, University of Washington, 1972; (contributor) Bostwick Ketchum, editor, *The Water's Edge: Critical Problems of the Coastal Zone*, M.I.T. Press, 1972; (with Harold M. Groves) *Financing Government,* Holt, 1973; (contributor) Selma J. Mushkin, editor, *Services to People: State and National Urban Strategies*, Public Services Laboratory, Georgetown University, 1973; (with Vincent Ostrom) *Understanding Urban Government: Metropolitan Reform Reconsidered*, American Enterprise Institute for Public Research, 1973; (with Robert J. Kirk) *Economic Principles and Urban Problems*, Prentice-Hall, 1974; (contributor) Mushkin, editor, *Services to People: Federal Aids in State Urban Strategies*, Public Services Laboratory, Georgetown University, 1974; (with Robert Warren, Louis F. Weschler, Peter Harrison and Crutchfield) *Coastal Resource Use: Decisions on Puget Sound*, University of Washington Press, 1975; (with Hugh O. Nourse) *Urban Economics and Policy Analysis*, McGraw, 1975. Contributor of articles and reviews to *Pacific Northwest Quarterly*, and to economics and planning journals.

WORK IN PROGRESS: Research for *Fiscal Reform in Urban Areas* and *Views of Man in Policy Analysis.*

* * *

BITTLE, William E(lmer) 1926-

PERSONAL: Born May 11, 1926, in Mansfield, Ohio; son of Frank Buhrman (an accountant) and Thelma (Scott) Bittle; married Christine McNab (a librarian), April 8, 1949; children: Ian Robert, Cass Elizabeth, Helen Abra. *Education:* University of California, Los Angeles, B.A., 1949, M.A., 1951, Ph.D. 1956; also studied at University of Michigan, 1951-52. *Politics:* Democrat. *Home:* 734 Jenkins, Norman, Okla. 73069. *Office:* Department of Anthropology, 505 West Lindsey, Room 505, University of Oklahoma, Norman, Okla. 73069.

CAREER: University of Oklahoma, Norman, instructor, 1952-57, assistant professor, 1957-63, associate professor, 1963-68, professor of anthropology, 1968—, curator of ethnology at Stovall Museum, 1970—. Member of board of directors of American Indian Dance Ensemble. Consultant to Peace Corps, 1962-65. *Military Service:* U.S. Navy, 1943-45. *Member:* National Association for the Advancement of Colored People. *Awards, honors:* Rockefeller Foundation grant, 1951-52.

WRITINGS: (Contributor) Harry Hoijer, editor, *Studies in the Athapaskan Languages*, University of California Press, 1963; (with Gilbert Geis) *The Longest Way Home*, Wayne State University Press, 1964; (editor with Dell Hymes) *Ethnolinguistics in the Southwest*, Mouton & Co., 1967; (editor and contributor) *Handbook of North American Indians: Plains Volume*, Smithsonian Institution, in press. Contributor to *Papers in Anthropology, Philosophy of Science, Southwestern Journal of Anthropology*, and *Plains Anthropologist*.

WORK IN PROGRESS: Ethnobotany of the Kiowa Apache; The Kiowa Apache.

AVOCATIONAL INTERESTS: Sailing, gardening, playing the bagpipes.

* * *

BIZZARRO, Salvatore 1939-

PERSONAL: Born April 15, 1939, in Tunis, Tunisia; son of Fioravante (an actor) and Albina (a teacher; maiden name, Riccio) Bizzarro. *Education:* Fordham University, B.A., 1964; Stanford University, M.A., 1965, Ph.D., 1969. *Politics:* "I favor socialism and the elimination of the free enterprise system." *Home:* 18 West Buena Ventura, Colorado Springs, Colo. 80907. *Office address:* Box 72, Colorado College, Colorado Springs, Colo. 80903.

CAREER: Colorado College, Colorado Springs, assistant professor of Spanish, 1968—. Volunteer teacher at Colorado State Penitentiary, 1970—. Regional coordinator of Colorado, Wyoming, Utah, Idaho, and Montana for Emergency Committee to Aid Latin American Scholars. *Member:* Modern Language Association of America, Latin American Studies Association, Latin American Scholarship Program of American Universities, Phi Beta Kappa. *Awards, honors:* Fulbright scholar to Chile, 1962; Woodrow Wilson fellow, 1964; National Endowment for the Humanities fellow, 1968; Ford Foundation grant to Italy, 1970.

WRITINGS: Historical Dictionary of Chile, Scarecrow, 1972. Author of one-act play, "The Kleptomaniac," first produced at Stanford University, 1967. Contributor to *Hispanic American Report, Current History, Latin American Yearly Review, Humanitas*, and *Hispania*. Associate editor of *Latin American Yearly Review*, 1973—.

WORK IN PROGRESS: A second edition of *Historical Dictionary of Chile;* a monograph, *Pablo Neruda: An Introduction to His Social and Political Poetry*.

SIDELIGHTS: Bizzarro told *CA*, "I came to America when I was sixteen years old from Italy. I was born in Tunisia of Italian parents but was taken to Italy after the breakout of World War II, where I spent the next fifteen years. I worked as a grocery clerk, cheese salesman, fruit vendor, in factories, before I decided to continue my education and teach. I traveled widely in Europe and South America and speak fluently Italian, Spanish, Portuguese, French, besides English."

* * *

BLACKBURNE, Neville Alfred Edmund 1913-

PERSONAL: Born November 20, 1913, in Portsmouth, England; son of Lionel Edward (a clergyman and dean) and Eleanor (Warren) Blackburne. *Education:* Clare College, Cambridge, B.A., 1936, M.A., 1951. *Home:* Nowton Court, Bury St., Edmunds, Suffolk, England.

CAREER: Co-founder and co-headmaster of boys preparatory boarding school, Nowton Court, Bury St. Edmonds, Suffolk, England, 1946—. *Military service:* British Army, King's Royal Rifle Corps, 1940-46; became major. *Awards, honors:* Co-winner of Sanditon (Jane Austen) Competition, British Broadcasting Corp., 1948.

WRITINGS: Ladies' Chain (short biographies), Falcon Press, 1952; *The Restless Ocean: A Life of George Crabbe, 1754-1832*, Terence Dalton, 1972.

WORK IN PROGRESS: The Tyrant's Stroke: A Life of Princess Charlotte of England; Duke or Darling?, a book on Frederick, Duke of York and Mrs. Mary Anne Clarke; a life of Jane Austen.

* * *

BLACKETT, Veronica Heath 1927-
(Veronica Heath)

PERSONAL: Born October 20, 1927, in London, England; daughter of Henry Tegner; married J. H. B. Blackett (a solicitor), April 20, 1953; children: Simon, Rupert, Rose, Juliet. *Education:* West Heath School, Kent. *Politics:* Conservative. *Religion:* Anglican. *Home:* West House, Whalton, Morpeth, Northumberland, England.

CAREER: Writer.

WRITINGS—All under name Veronica Heath: *Your Pony*, Cassell, 1954, revised and enlarged edition published as *Ponies*, 1969; *Come Riding With Me*, Muller, 1955, Sportshelf, 1956; *Susan's Riding School*, Chatto & Windus, 1956; *So You Want to Be a Show Jumper*, Colin Venton, 1957; *Ponies in the Heather*, Lutterworth, 1959; *Come Show Jumping with Me*, Muller, 1961; *Come Pony-Trekking with Me*, Muller, 1964; *Ponies and Pony Management*, Arco, 1966; *Beginner's Guide to Riding*, Pelham Books, 1970, Transatlantic Arts, 1971; *The Family Dog*, Transatlantic Arts, 1972; *Let's Own a Pony*, Colin Venton, 1974.

WORK IN PROGRESS: Books on sporting events.

SIDELIGHTS: Mrs. Blackett is an active assistant in a local riding group for the disabled.

* * *

BLACKEY, Robert 1941-

PERSONAL: Born December 17, 1941, in New York, N.Y.; son of Joseph (a salesman) and Ruth (Kalb) Blackey; married Phyllis Trachman, November 26, 1964; children: Richard Marc, Jeffrey Gordon. *Education:* City College of the City University of New York, B.A., 1963; New York University, M.A., 1964, Ph.D., 1968. *Politics:* "A conservative-radical with humanist leanings." *Religion:* Jewish-Deist. *Residence:* Rialto, Calif. *Office:* Department of History, California State College, San Bernardino, Calif. 92407.

CAREER: Hunter College of the City University of New York, New York, N.Y., lecturer in English history, 1968; California State College, San Bernardino, assistant professor, 1968-71, associate professor of history, 1971—. Blackey and his wife regularly direct Temple Emanu El Summer Day Camp in San Bernardino. *Member:* American Historical Association, Conference on British Studies, Anglo-American Associates. *Awards, honors:* Postdoctoral fellow at William Andrews Clark Memorial Library of University of California at Los Angeles, 1968.

WRITINGS: (Editor with Clifford T. Paynton, and contributor) *Why Revolution?: Theories and Analyses*, Schenkman, 1971. Contributor to *Catholic Historical Review* and *Journal of Modern African Studies*.

WORK IN PROGRESS: Revolution and the Revolutionary Ideal, with Paynton, for Schenkman; research for a political biography of George Montagu Dunk, second Earl of Halifax; *Modern Revolutions and Revolutionists: A Bibliography*, for ABC-Clio.

BLAGDEN, David 1944-

PERSONAL: Born February 8, 1944, in Biloxi, Miss.; son of Claude M. (an artist and author) and Sue (Blagden) Marks; married Sandra Cotter (an art historian), January 1, 1965. *Education:* Attended Webber Douglas School of Drama, 1964-65, and Courtauld Institute, University of London, 1965-66. *Home:* 137 Biddulph Mansions, Elgin Ave., London W.9, England.

CAREER: British Merchant Naval Service, cadet, 1960-61, junior officer of Cunard Line, 1961-63, and Furness Withy & Co., 1963-64; actor in theaters, films, and television industry in the United States, England, France, Germany, and Sweden, 1964-72; Quaesitor (largest group therapy training center in Europe), London, England, director, 1972—.

WRITINGS: Very Willing Griffin, Norton, 1974. Contributor to British and American yachting magazines.

WORK IN PROGRESS: A short novel on the sea for slow teenaged readers; a compendium of unusual designs and articles from British and American yachting magazines of the past fifty years.

AVOCATIONAL INTERESTS: Painting.

* * *

BLAIR, Paxton 1892-1974

September 30, 1892—December 25, 1974; American lawyer, legal scholar, and justice of the New York State Supreme Court. Obituaries: *New York Times*, December 27, 1974.

* * *

BLAIR, Sam 1932-

PERSONAL: Born September 26, 1932, in Dallas, Tex.; son of James Everette (a postman) and Edna (Miller) Blair; married Karen Klinefelter, October 1, 1970; children: Jason Everette, Collin Miller. *Education:* University of Texas, B. Journalism, 1954. *Home:* 6843 North Ridge Dr., Dallas, Tex. 75214. *Office:* Communications Center, *Dallas Morning News*, Dallas, Tex. 75222.

CAREER: Dallas Morning News, Dallas, Tex., sports writer and columnist, and assistant sports editor, 1954-68, author of daily sports column, and sports editor, 1968—. *Military service:* U.S. Air Force, 1955-57; became captain. *Member:* Football Writers Association of America, Professional Football Writers of America, Golf Writers Association of America, Baseball Writers Association of America, Texas Sports Writers Association. *Awards, honors:* First prizes from Texas Sports Writer Association, 1963, 1966, and 1971, all for feature stories; first prizes from Golf Writers Association of America, 1966 and 1970, both for articles.

WRITINGS: Dallas Cowboys: Pro or Con?, Doubleday, 1970; (with Roger Staubach and Bob St. John) *Staubach: First Down, Lifetime to Go*, Word Books, 1974. Contributor to sports publications, including *Golf Digest, Sporting News*, and *Pro Quarterback.*

* * *

BLAISE, Clark 1940-

PERSONAL: Surname is pronounced "blezz"; born April 10, 1940, in Fargo, N.D.; Canadian citizen; son of Leo Romeo Pierre (a furniture salesman) and Anne (a school teacher; maiden name, Vanstone) Blaise; married Bharati Mukherjee (a novelist and professor), September 19, 1963; children: Bart Anand, Bernard Sudhir. *Education:* Denison University, B.A., 1961; University of Iowa, M.F.A., 1964. *Home:* 4297 Boulevard de Maisonneuve W., Montreal, Quebec, Canada. *Agent:* Tim Seldes, Russell & Volkening, Inc., 551 Fifth Ave., New York, N.Y. 10017. *Office:* Department of English, Concordia University, 1445 Boulevard de Maisonneuve W., Montreal, Quebec, Canada.

CAREER: University of Wisconsin, Milwaukee, acting instructor in English, 1964-65; Concordia University, Montreal, Quebec, assistant professor, 1968-73, associate professor of English, 1973—. *Awards, honors:* President's Medal from University of Western Ontario, 1967, for best short story in a Canadian publication; Great Lakes College Association prize, 1973, for best first book of fiction.

WRITINGS: (With Dave Godfrey and David Lewis Stein) *New Canadian Writing: 1968*, Clark Irwin, 1968; *A North American Education*, Doubleday, 1973; *Tribal Justice*, Doubleday, 1974. Contributor of more than thirty stories to magazines, including *Shenandoah, Tri-Quarterly, American Review, Tamarack Review*, and *Journal of Canadian Fiction.*

WORK IN PROGRESS: The Bengal Journals, nonfiction travel account, with wife, Bharati Mukherjee Blaise, for Doubleday; *In the Trade* (tentative title), a novel.

SIDELIGHTS: Blaise writes: "As a native-born American with foreign parents, and as a child who attended an average of two schools a year in twenty-five different cities, I grew up with an outsider's view of America and a romanticized exile's view of French-Canada. In 1965, for personal reasons having to do with a crisis of purpose and identity I 'returned' to Montreal and claimed this area of the continent for my writings. I am a Canadian citizen. My interest is in 'tribalism' on the American continent, and in all groups who refuse amalgamation and prefer codes and taboos of their own. In addition, through marriage, I have developed a great fondness for, and modest knowledge of, India."

BIOGRAPHICAL/CRITICAL SOURCES: Journal of Canadian Fiction, fall, 1973; *Imperial Oil Review*, Volume 58, number 6, 1974.

* * *

BLAKE, Fay M(ontaug) 1920-

PERSONAL: Born September 15, 1920, in New York, N.Y.; daughter of Irving F. and Sylvia (Feiler) Montaug; married Saul W. Blakesberg, August 28, 1938 (divorced, 1949); children: Sylvia (Mrs. Andrew S. Rogers). *Education:* Hunter College (now Hunter College of the City University of New York), B.A., 1940; University of Southern California, M.S. in L.S., 1961; University of California, Los Angeles, M.A., 1963, Ph.D., 1970; graduate study at University of Vienna, 1963, University of Leningrad, 1965, Hebrew University of Jerusalem, 1967, and Hokkaido University, 1973. *Politics:* Independent. *Home:* 2450 Warring St., Berkeley, Calif. 94704. *Office:* School of Librarianship, University of California, Berkeley, Calif. 94720.

CAREER: University of California, Los Angeles, librarian, 1961-69; University of California, Berkeley, lecturer in library science, 1971—. Consultant, New York State Department of Education, 1969-70. *Member:* American Association of University Professors, American Federation of Teachers, American Civil Liberties Union, California Library Association, Phi Beta Kappa, Beta Phi Mu.

WRITINGS: The Strike in the American Novel, Scarecrow, 1972. Contributor of more than twenty articles to library journals.

WORK IN PROGRESS: Research on popular culture.

AVOCATIONAL INTERESTS: Travel, political action.

* * *

BLANCHETTE, Oliva 1929-

PERSONAL: Born May 6, 1929, in Berlin, N.H.; son of Delphis (a garagist) and Odelia (Morneau) Blanchette; married Dorothy Kennedy (an office manager), May 17, 1975. *Education:* Boston College, A.B., 1953, M.A., 1958; College of St. Albert de Louvain, Ph.L., 1954; Weston College, S.T.L., 1961; Universite Laval, Ph.D., 1966. *Residence:* Boston, Mass. *Office:* School of Philosophy, Boston College, Chestnut Hill, Mass. 02167.

CAREER: Entered Society of Jesus (Jesuits), 1947; ordained Roman Catholic priest, 1960, left priesthood, 1975. High school teacher in Boston, Mass., 1954-57; Boston College, Chestnut Hill, Mass., instructor, 1964-65, assistant professor, 1965-67, associate professor, 1967-74, professor of philosophy, 1974—, dean of School of Philosophy, 1968-73, director of Institute in Marxist Thought, 1972—. *Member:* American Philosophical Association, Society for Phenomenology and Existential Philosophy, Hegel Society of America.

WRITINGS: (Editor and author of introduction) *Initiative in History: A Christian-Marxist Exchange*, Church Society for College Work, 1967; (contributor of translation) Frederick Adelmann, editor, *Demythologizing Marxism*, Boston College, 1969; *For a Fundamental Social Ethic: A Philosophy of Social Change*, Philosophical Library, 1973; (contributor) Richard J. Clifford and George W. MacRae, editors, *The Word in the World: Essays in Honor of Frederick L. Moriarty, S.J.*, Weston College Press, 1973.

Contributor of about twenty articles and reviews to philosophy, education, and theology journals in the United States, Canada, and France, including *Studies in Soviet Thought, Journal of General Education, Philosopher's Index, Philosophical Forum, Cross Currents, Journal of Philosophy, Laval Theologique et Philosophique*, and *Projet*.

WORK IN PROGRESS: The Crisis in Christian Consciousness; research on social philosophy.

SIDELIGHTS: Blanchette writes: "My book in social ethics grew out of a concern to help students develop a social dimension in their moral or practical judgment. A better appreciation of how modern society actually works has led to an intensification of this concern, so that philosophy does not remain a purely academic discipline or merely a head-trip. It is concerned with understanding the real world and changing it, hopefully, for the better."

* * *

BLANCK, Jacob Nathaniel 1906-1974

November 10, 1906—December 23, 1974; American author and bibliographer. Obituaries: *New York Times*, December 26, 1974; *AB Bookman's Weekly*, January 6, 1975; *Publishers Weekly*, January 15, 1975. (*CA*-11/12).

* * *

BLAND, Randall Walton 1942-

PERSONAL: Born January 10, 1942, in Galveston, Tex.; son of Walter Leslie and Doris Evelyn (Reinli) Bland; married Barbara Jean Baca, November 27, 1965; children: Robert Walter. *Education:* Texas A&M University, B.A., 1964; University of Notre Dame, M.A., 1966, Ph.D., 1971. *Politics:* Democrat. *Religion:* Roman Catholic. *Home address:* Valley View, P.O. Box 291P, San Marcos, Tex. 78666. *Office:* Department of Political Science, Southwest Texas State University, San Marcos, Tex. 78666.

CAREER: Southwest Texas State University, San Marcos, instructor, 1967-70, assistant professor, 1971-73, associate professor of government, 1973—. Consultant, Texas Justice of the Peace Training Center, 1974-75. *Member:* American Political Science Association, Southwestern Social Science Association, Pi Gamma Mu.

WRITINGS: (Editor with Robert D. Wrinkle and Elmer A. DeShazo, and contributor) *Documents and Readings in American and Texas Government*, Kendall/Hunt, 1969; *Private Pressure on Public Law: The Legal Career of Justice Thurgood Marshall*, Kennikat, 1973; (with Beryl Pettus) *Government in Texas: The Politics of Modernization*, Dorsey, in press. Associate editor in public law and Texas government, *Rocky Mountain Social Science Journal*; reviewer in constitutional law and judicial process, *Journal of American History*, 1974—.

WORK IN PROGRESS: Editing an undergraduate text, *American Constitutional Law: Its Sources and Its Applications*; writing *Of Governments and Men: A Manual of Social Science Research*; compiling *An Encyclopedia of American Constitutional Law*.

AVOCATIONAL INTERESTS: Gardening.

* * *

BLAYNEY, Margaret S(tatler) 1926-

PERSONAL: Born June 11, 1926, in Pennsylvania; daughter of John Arthur and Agnes (Conway) Statler; married Glenn H. Blayney, Jr., August 24, 1951 (divorced, 1960); children: Kathleen G. *Education:* Western Maryland College, B.A. (summa cum laude), 1947; University of Pennsylvania, M.A. (honors), 1949; Lady Margaret Hall, Oxford, D.Phil., 1966. *Politics:* Independent. *Religion:* Congregationalist. *Home:* 2531 North Washington Ave., Royal Oak, Mich. 48073. *Office:* Department of English, Highland Park College, Highland Park, Mich. 48203.

CAREER: University of Colorado, Boulder, instructor in English, 1949-51; Oberlin College, Oberlin, Ohio, part-time instructor in English, 1954-56; Wayne State University, Detroit, Mich., part-time instructor in English, 1956-57; Highland Park College, Highland Park, Mich., member of faculty, department of English, 1957—. *Member:* National Society of Literature and the Arts. *Awards, honors:* Fulbright fellowship, 1951-53; American Association of University Women fellowship, 1963-64.

WRITINGS: (Editor) *Fifteenth-Century English Translations of Alain Chartier's Le Traite de l'Esperance and Le Quadrilogue Invectif*, Volume I, Oxford University Press for Early English Text Society, 1974. Contributor to *PMLA, Modern Language Review, Modern Language Notes, Review of English Studies,* and *Studies in Philology*.

WORK IN PROGRESS: Volume II of *Fifteenth-Century English Translations of Alain Chartier's Le Traite de l'Esperance and Le Quadrilogue Invectif*.

* * *

BLESSING, Richard Allen 1939-

PERSONAL: Born September 11, 1939, in Bradford, Pa.;

son of Edward John (a mechanic) and Eva Lou (a teacher; maiden name, Morrison) Blessing; married Lisa Boepple, July 4, 1964; children: Craig Edward. *Education:* Hamilton College, A.B., 1961; Tulane University, M.A., 1963, Ph.D., 1967. *Home:* 4810 88th Pl. S.E., Mercer Island, Wash. 98040. *Office:* Department of English, University of Washington, Seattle, Wash. 98195.

CAREER: Louisiana State University, New Orleans, instructor in English, 1964-68; Heidelberg College, Tiffin, Ohio, assistant professor of English, 1968-70; University of Washington, Seattle, assistant professor, 1970-73, associate professor of English, 1973—. *Awards, honors:* Guggenheim fellow, 1972.

WRITINGS: *Wallace Stevens' 'Whole Harmonium,'* Syracuse University Press, 1970; *Theodore Roethke's Dynamic Vision*, Indiana University Press, 1974. Contributor of more than fifty poems to *Prairie Schooner, Poetry Northwest, Southern Review, Denver Quarterly*, and others.

WORK IN PROGRESS: A volume of poems; research on modern prose techniques.

* * *

BLINDERMAN, Abraham 1916-

PERSONAL: Born August 8, 1916, in Brooklyn, N.Y.; son of Samuel (a laundryman) and Fannie (Rochester) Blinderman; married Rita Tublin (a musician), September 29, 1940; children: Mark Elliot, Bonnie. *Education:* Brooklyn College (now of the City University of New York), B.A., 1948; New York University, M.A., 1950, Ph.D., 1963. *Politics:* Independent. *Religion:* Jewish. *Home:* 47 Tanager Lane, Levittown, N.Y. 11756. *Office:* Department of English, State University of New York, Melville Rd., Farmingdale, N.Y. 11735.

CAREER: U.S. Post Office, New York, N.Y., 1937-48; public school teacher of English in New York, N.Y., 1948-54, Levittown, N.Y., 1954-63, and Syosset, N.Y., 1963-65; State University of New York, Farmingdale, member of faculty in department of English, 1965—. *Military service:* U.S. Navy, 1942-45. *Member:* National Council of English, History of Education Society, New York State United Teachers, Friends of Hofstra University Library. *Awards, honors:* State University of New York research fellowship, 1971; National Endowment for the Humanities fellowship, 1972-73.

WRITINGS: (Contributor) Jack Leedy, editor, *Poetry the Healer*, Lippincott, 1973; (editor) *Critics on Upton Sinclair*, University of Miami Press, 1975; *American Writers on Education before 1865*, Twayne, 1975; (editor) *Critics on Mark Twain*, University of Miami Press, 1975. Contributor of articles and reviews to *Newsday, Christian Century*, and more than thirty other periodicals.

WORK IN PROGRESS: *American Writers on Education after 1865*, publication by Twayne expected in 1975; writing a chapter on poetry therapy for a book edited by Arthur Lerner, and a chapter on community law for a textbook edited by James Friel.

SIDELIGHTS: Blinderman told *CA:* "A lifelong inferiority complex aggravated by an intense desire for recognition finally triggered me into mediocre authorship. My adolescent messianic flame has dwindled into a barely perceptible flicker, sustained by the heroic life-giving blasts of compassionate editors. My first published article appeared eight years ago when I was fifty. I hope that I'll write one appreciated book before retiring."

BIOGRAPHICAL/CRITICAL SOURCES: *Newsday*, March 5, 1973.

* * *

BLISS, Ronald G(ene) 1942-

PERSONAL: Born August 12, 1942, in Atwood, Kan.; son of Wilbur Cyril (a farmer and mechanic) and Mary (Makings) Bliss; married Margaret Jane Keeler (a high school teacher), July 25, 1965; children: Eric Dean, Kirk Ronald. *Education:* Fort Hays Kansas State College, student, 1960-62; Kansas State University, B.A., 1964; University of Missouri, M.A., 1969. *Religion:* Christian Church. *Home:* 620 James, Maize, Kan. 67101. *Agent:* Dorothy Markinko, 18 East 41st St., New York, N.Y. 10017. *Office:* KARD-Television, 833 North Main, Wichita, Kan. 67201.

CAREER: *Findlay Republican-Courier*, Findlay, Ohio, city hall reporter, 1964; *Colby Free Press-Tribune*, Colby, Kan., news editor, 1964-66; University of Missouri, Columbia, radio and television specialist, 1966-69; Kansas State Network, Wichita, 1969—, began as television investigative reporter, now director of public affairs. *Member:* Kansas Authors Club (vice president, 1973; president, 1974). *Awards, honors:* Citation for best television documentary film, from Kansas Association of Broadcasters, 1972, for "A Look at Child Abuse."

WRITINGS: *Indian Softball Summer* (juvenile novel), Dodd, 1974. Author of scripts for KSN television network. Contributor to *TV Guide, V.F.W., Sign of the Times*, and regional publications.

WORK IN PROGRESS: A juvenile novel; a novel about the life of migrant workers in western Kansas, based on factual information.

SIDELIGHTS: Bliss writes: "My writing reflects growing up with many fascinating characters in a small town in northwest Kansas. They have become key personalities in my books of fiction. Jesse Stuart and his tales of the people in the backwoods of Kentucky greatly impressed me as a youth and I think that admiration has made me want to write about common people."

* * *

BLOCHMAN, Lawrence G(oldtree) 1900-1975

February 17, 1900—January 22, 1975; American author of mystery novels and journalist. Obituaries: *New York Times*, January 23, 1975; *AB Bookman's Weekly*, February 17, 1975. (*CA*-19/20).

* * *

BLOCK, Jack 1931-

PERSONAL: Born October 3, 1931, in New York, N.Y.; son of Louis and Frances (Seligman) Block; married Eleanor Welz (a craftswoman), April 13, 1958; children: Elisabeth Fay. *Education:* Queens College (now of the City University of New York), B.A., 1954; Columbia University, M.A., 1962; Yeshiva University, doctoral studies, 1969—. *Home:* 26-23 Warren Rd., Fair Lawn, N.J. 07410. *Office:* Fair Lawn Board of Education, Fair Lawn, N.J.

CAREER: High school social studies teacher in Fair Lawn, N.J., 1957—. Member of adjunct faculty at Bergen Community College, 1968—. *Military service:* U.S. Army, 1954-56. *Member:* National Council for the Social Studies, National Education Association, New Jersey Education Association, Bergen County Historical Society (member of board of trustees).

WRITINGS: Understanding Historial Research: A Search for Truth (secondary and college textbook), Research Publications, 1971.

WORK IN PROGRESS: Historical Research for the Middle Grades.

* * *

BLOFELD, John (Eaton Calthorpe) 1913-
(Chu Ch'an)

PERSONAL; Born April 2, 1913, in London, England; son of Ernest Eaton (a businessman) and Rita (Lovel) Blofeld; married Meifang Chang (a teacher), 1947; children: James, Susan (Mrs. Andrew Molle), Suwimol. *Education:* Downing College, Cambridge, student, 1931-33, 1945-46; Cambridge University, M.A., 1947; School of Oriental Studies, London, student, 1939-40. *Religion:* Buddhist. *Home:* 80 Soi Sansabai, Rama IV Rd., Prakanong, Bangkok, Thailand. *Office:* Department of Languages, Kasetsart University, Bangkok, Thailand.

CAREER: British Embassy, Chungking, China, cultural attache, 1942-46; Chulalongkorn University, Bangkok, Thailand, lecturer in English literature, 1951-61; United Nations Economic Commission for Asia and the Far East (UNECAFE), Bangkok, chief of editorial services, 1961-73; Kasetsart University, Bangkok, lecturer in English, 1974—. *Wartime service:* British War Office, 1940-42; became captain. *Member:* China Society (United Kingdom), Buddhist Society (London).

WRITINGS: The Jewel in the Lotus: An Outline of Present Day Buddhism in China, Sidgwick & Jackson, 1948, reprinted, Hyperion Press, 1974; *Red China in Perspective*, Wingate, 1951; *The Wheel of Life* (autobiographical), Rider, 1959, 2nd edition, Shambala, 1972; *People of the Sun: Encounters in Siam*, Hutchinson, 1960; *The City of Lingering Splendour: A Frank Account of Old Peking's Exotic Pleasures*, Hutchinson, 1961; *Tantric Mysticism of Tibet: A Practical Guide*, Dutton, 1970 (published in England as *The Way of Power: A Practical Guide to the Tantric Mysticism of Tibet*, Allen & Unwin, 1970); *Mahayana Buddhism in Southeast Asia*, Donald Moore, for Asia Pacific Press, 1971; *King Maha Mongkut of Siam*, Asia Pacific Press, 1972; *The Secret and Sublime*, Dutton, 1973; *Beyond the Gods*, Dutton, 1974; *The Meaning of Mantras*, Allen & Unwin, in press.

Translator: *The Huang Po Doctrine of Universal Mind*, Buddhist Society (London), 1947; *The Zen Teaching of Huang Po on the Transmission of Mind*, Rider, 1958, Grove, 1959; *The Zen Teaching of Hui Hai*, Rider, 1962; *The Book of Change*, Allen & Unwin, 1965, Dutton, 1966, 2nd edition, Allen & Unwin, 1968.

Has written for British Broadcasting Corp. productions. Some translations published under pseudonym, Chu Ch'an. Contributor to journals, including *Tien Hsia, Economist, Eastern Horizon*, and *Central Asian Society Journal.*

WORK IN PROGRESS: Continuing studies in Buddhism, particulary in China and Tibet, Taoism, and East Asian religions, philosophy, and culture; also studying "serious" mysticism.

SIDELIGHTS: Blofeld told *CA:* "From childhood I have been fascinated by traditional Chinese civilization and, latterly, by Tibetan culture. I spent many years wandering about China, often staying in Buddhist or Taoist temples, but taking teaching jobs when short of funds. Between 1933 and 1939 I was, so to speak, a 'prototype hippy.'" Blofeld has visited nearly every Asian country, including the Mongolian People's Republic. He speaks Chinese and Thai.

* * *

BLOOMBERG, Morton 1936-

PERSONAL: Born October 26, 1936, in Winthrop, Mass.; son of Abe Sumner (an investment counselor) and Mildred (Cohen) Bloomberg; married Carolyn Cohen, August 6, 1961; children: Jeffrey, Mark. *Education:* Boston University, A.A., 1956; Clark University, A.B. (magna cum laude), 1958; State University of New York at Buffalo, Ph.D., 1963. *Politics:* Independent. *Religion:* Jewish. *Address:* R.F.D. #1, Lyrical Lane, Sandy Hook, Conn. 06482. *Office:* Department of Psychology, Western Connecticut State College, Danbury, Conn. 06810.

CAREER: State University of New York at Buffalo, lecturer in psychology, 1963; Skidmore College, Saratoga Springs, N.Y., assistant professor of psychology, 1963-66; Adelphi University, Garden City, N.Y., assistant professor of psychology, 1966-70; Western Connecticut State College, Danbury, associate professor of psychology, 1970—. *Member:* International Society for the Study of Behavioral Development, American Psychological Association, Society for Research in Child Development, Eastern Psychological Association, Psi Chi, Zeta Beta Tau. *Awards, honors:* National Science Foundation grants, summers, 1965, 1966-68; Ludwig Vogelstein Foundation grant, 1973.

WRITINGS: (Editor) *Creativity Theory and Research*, College & University Press, 1973. Contributor to professional journals.

WORK IN PROGRESS: Research on the relationship between creativity and morality.

AVOCATIONAL INTERESTS: Softball.

BIOGRAPHICAL/CRITICAL SOURCES: Human Behavior, December, 1972.

* * *

BLOSS, F(red) Donald 1920-

PERSONAL: Born May 30, 1920, in Chicago, Ill.; son of Fred Martin (an electrician) and Adele (Ludwig) Bloss; married Louise Land (a teacher), March 2, 1946; children: Terry (Mrs. Robert Kensler), Janet, Jill. *Education:* University of Chicago, B.S., 1947, M.S., 1949, Ph.D., 1951. *Politics:* Independent. *Religion:* Presbyterian. *Home:* 505 Forest Hill Dr., Blacksburg, Va. 24060. *Office:* Department of Geological Sciences, Virginia Polytechnic Institute and University, Blacksburg, Va. 24601.

CAREER: University of Tennessee, Knoxville, assistant professor, 1951-55, associate professor of geology, 1955-57; Southern Illinois University, Carbondale, associate professor, 1957-61, professor of geology, 1961-67; Virginia Polytechnic Institute and University, Blacksburg, professor of mineralogy, 1967-72, Alumni Distinguished Professor, 1972—. Consultant to Tennessee Copper Co., 1954-57, Tennessee Valley Authority, 1955-58, and U.S. Bureau of Mines, summers, 1957-66. *Military service:* U.S. Army, 1942-46. *Member:* Mineralogical Society of America (fellow; councillor, 1968-70), Geological Society of America (fellow), Mineralogical Society (London), Phi Beta Kappa, Sigma Xi. *Awards, honors:* National Science Foundation postdoctoral fellow, 1962-63.

WRITINGS: Introduction to the Methods of Optical Crys-

tallography, Holt, 1961; (with J. H. Fang) *X-Ray Diffraction Tables,* Southern Illinois University Press, 1966; *Chess at a Glance,* Van Nostrand, 1967; *Crystallography and Crystal Chemistry,* Holt, 1971; *Rate Your Own Chess,* Van Nostrand, 1972. Editor of *American Mineralogist,* 1972—.

WORK IN PROGRESS: The Spindle Stage, completion expected in 1975; *Mineralogy,* 1977.

AVOCATIONAL INTERESTS: Chess, drawing.

* * *

BLOUNT, Roy (Alton), Jr. 1941-
(Noah Sanders, C. R. Ways)

PERSONAL: Surname rhymes with "punt"; born October 4, 1941, in Indianapolis, Ind.; son of Roy Alton (a savings and loan executive) and Louise (Floyd) Blount; married Ellen Pearson, September 6, 1964 (divorced March, 1973); children: Ennis Caldwell, John Kirven. *Education:* Vanderbilt University, B.A. (magna cum laude), 1963; Harvard University, M.A., 1964. *Politics:* "Dated white Southern liberalism, with healthy undertones of redneckery and anarchism; nostalgia for Earl Long." *Religion:* "Lapsed Methodist." *Residence:* New York, N.Y. *Agent:* Liz Darhansoff, International Famous Agency, 1301 Avenue of the Americas, New York, N.Y. 10019. *Office: Sports Illustrated,* Time and Life Building, New York, N.Y. 10020.

CAREER: Decatur-Dekalb News, Decatur, Ga., reporter and sports columnist, 1958-59; *Morning Telegraph,* New York, N.Y., reporter, summer, 1961; *New Orleans Times-Picayune,* New Orleans, La., reporter, summer, 1963; *Atlanta Journal,* Atlanta, Ga., reporter, editorial writer, and columnist, 1966-68; *Sports Illustrated,* New York, N.Y., staff writer, 1968-74, associate editor, 1974—. Instructor at Georgia State College, 1967-68. *Military service:* U.S. Army, 1964-66; became first lieutenant. *Member:* Phi Beta Kappa.

WRITINGS: About Three Bricks Shy of a Load (nonfiction), Little, Brown, 1974. Author of a column in *Atlanta Journal,* 1967-70. Contributor of more than a hundred articles, short stories, poems, and drawings, sometimes under pseudonyms Noah Sanders and C. R. Ways, to *Sports Illustrated, New Yorker, Atlantic, New York Times Magazine,* and *Women-Sports.*

WORK IN PROGRESS: A novel, tentatively titled *If You Can't Wave, Stop.*

SIDELIGHTS: Blount writes: "... Raised in South by Southern parents. Couldn't play third base well enough so became college journalist. Ridiculed cultural enemies. Boosted integration. Decided to write, teach. Went to Harvard Graduate School. Didn't like it. Went back to journalism. . . . Liked it. Got a column. Ridiculed cultural enemies. Wrote limericks. Boosted integration. Wanted to write for magazines. Took writing job at *Sports Illustrated.* Have seen country, met all kinds of people, heard all different kinds of talk. Like it. Spent year with 'Pittsburgh Steelers' to write 'Bricks' book." Now Blount wants to try fiction, combining into one prose style the influences of Flannery O'Connor, Samuel Johnson, Robert Benchley, Flann O'Brien, Donald Barthelme, Dylan Thomas, Billy Joe Shaver, E. B. White, Brer Rabbit, Raymond Chandler, Roger Miller, Richard Pryor, Graham Greene, Jimmie Rodgers, Hunter Thompson, George Orwell, Peter Taylor, Max Beerbohm, A. J. Liebling.

BIOGRAPHICAL/CRITICAL SOURCES: Sports Illustrated, February 10, 1969, June 18, 1973, April 15, 1974, August 5, 1974.

* * *

BLUE, Frederick Judd 1937-

PERSONAL: Born April 18, 1937, in Staten Island, N.Y.; son of Leonard Anderson (an attorney) and Helen (Judd) Blue; married Judith Hertwig (an occupational therapist), 1962; children: Karen, Eric. *Education:* Yale University, B.A., 1958; University of Wisconsin, M.S., 1962, Ph.D., 1966. *Politics:* Democratic. *Religion:* United Church of Christ. *Home:* 3884 Edinburg Dr., Youngstown, Ohio 44511. *Office:* Department of History, Youngstown State University, Youngstown, Ohio 44503.

CAREER: Youngstown State University, Youngstown, Ohio, assistant professor, 1964-69, associate professor of history, 1969—, director of graduate program in history, 1973—. *Military service:* U.S. Army, 1958-60. *Member:* American Historical Association, Organization of American Historians.

WRITINGS: The Free Soilers: Third Party Politics, 1848-1854, University of Illinois Press, 1973.

WORK IN PROGRESS: Research on American Indian policy in the Jackson period and on third-party movements before the Civil War.

* * *

BLUMROSEN, Alfred W(illiam) 1928-

PERSONAL: Born December 14, 1928, in Detroit, Mi.; son of Sol and Frances (Netzorg) Blumrosen; married Ruth Gerber, 1952; children: Steven, Alexander. *Education:* University of Michigan, B.A., 1950, J.D., 1953. *Home:* R.D. 4, Box 225b, Wantage Township, N.J. *Office:* Rutgers University School of Law, 180 University Ave., Newark, N.J. 07102.

CAREER: Admitted to Bars of Michigan State, 1953, New Jersey State, 1962, and U.S. Supreme Court, 1967. Private practice of law in Detroit, Mich., 1953-55; Rutgers University, School of Law, Newark, N.J., assistant professor, 1955-58, associate professor, 1958-61, professor of law, 1961—. Visiting professor, Louisiana State University, 1961, and Howard Law School, 1965. First chief of conciliation and first chief of Federal-State Relations for U.S. Equal Employment Opportunity Commission, 1965-67. Arbitrator, New Jersey Mediation Board, 1957—, Federal Mediation and Conciliation Service, 1961—, and American Arbitration Association, 1965—. Consultant to U.S. Department of Labor, Department of Housing and Urban Development, state human rights and civil rights commissions, and other agencies and organizations. Lecturer on equal opportunity at universities and lawyers' seminars. *Member:* International Society for Labor Law and Social Legislation U.S. National Committee, American Bar Association, Michigan Bar Association, Order of the Coif.

WRITINGS: (Co-editor) *Labor Relations and the Law,* 2nd edition (Blumrosen was not associated with earlier edition), Little, Brown, 1960, supplement (co-author), 1962, 3rd edition, 1965; (contributor) Ralph Slovenko, editor, *Symposium on the Labor-Management Reporting and Disclosure Act of 1959,* Claitor's Book Store, 1961; *Materials and Cases on the Law of the Employment Relation,* two volumes, Rutgers University, 1962; (contributor) W. M. Evan, editor, *Law and Sociology,* Free Press, 1962; (with Leonard Zeitz) *Securing Equality: The Operation of the*

Laws of New Jersey concerning Racial Discrimination, School of Law, Rutgers University, 1964.

(With Frank Askin, Richard Chused, and others) *Enforcing Fair Housing Laws: Apartments in White Suburbia*, School of Law, Rutgers University, 1970; *Black Employment and the Law*, Rutgers University Press, 1971; (editor) *Foundations of Equal Employment Opportunity*, two volumes, Equal Employment Opportunity Commission, 1972; (with James Blair and others) *Enforcing Equality in Housing and Employment through State Civil Rights Laws*, privately printed, 1972.

Monographs: *The Settlement of Disputes concerning the Exercise of Disciplinary Power by the Employer, including Dismissal, in the United States*, International Society for Labor Law and Social Legislation, 1963; *Worker Safety and Technological Change in the United States*, International Society for Labor Law and Social Legislation, 1970. Contributor to professional journals and reviews.

* * *

BOADELLA, David 1931-

PERSONAL: Born July 6, 1931, in London, England; son of Harold (a Port of London transport officer) and Jessie (a secretary; maiden name, Marsh) Boadella; married Elsa Corbluth (a writer), September 29, 1952; children: Adam, Eilidh. *Education:* University of London, B.A. (with honors), 1953; University of Nottingham, M.Ed., 1960. *Politics:* "Libertarian." *Religion:* "Sympathetic to Taoism, but no official adherence." *Home address:* Abbotsbury, Dorsetshire, England. *Agent:* Francis Greenburger, Sanford J. Greenburger Associates, Inc., 757 Third Ave., New York, N.Y. 10017. *Office:* Abbotsbury School, Abbotsbury, Dorset, England.

CAREER: Teacher at various schools in Nottingham, England, 1960-63; Abbotsbury School, Abbotsbury, Dorset, England, headmaster, 1963—. Bioenergetic therapist at Churchill Centre, 1968—. Lecturer at University of Bristol, 1968-71, and Weymouth College of Education, 1973-75. Director of Abbotsbury Publications, 1970—; founding member of Chesil Poets, a community project in creative writing for adults, 1973—. *Military service:* British Army, Intelligence Corps, 1948-50. *Member:* Centre for Bioenergy (trustee, 1972-73), Institute of Bio-energetic Analysis (associate).

WRITINGS: *The Spiral Flame*, Ritter Press, 1956; *Maladjusted Children,* University of Nottingham Press, 1960; *Coming of Age* (poems), Outpost Publications, 1972; *Wilhelm Reich: The Evolution of His Work*, Vision Press, 1973, Regnery, 1974. Contributor of articles and poems to journals, including *Man and Woman, Granta, Orgonomic Functionalism, Poetry Workshop, Phoenix,* and *Voice*. Editor of *Energy and Character*, 1970—, and *Handfuls of Light*, 1971—.

WORK IN PROGRESS: Editing *Life-Streams*, a book about bio-energetics; *Born Unborn*, a book of poems; *New Bio-energetic Papers*, articles from *Energy and Character*.

SIDELIGHTS: Boadella reads French, German, Italian, Spanish, Danish, and Norwegian; he has traveled in Cyprus, Mexico, and Iceland. *Avocational interests:* Chess, judo, mountaineering, poetry, sculpture, music, psychic research.

BIOGRAPHICAL/CRITICAL SOURCES: *Times Educational Supplement*, October 9, 1970.

BOATWRIGHT, Howard (Leake, Jr.) 1918-

PERSONAL: Born March 16, 1918, in Newport News, Va.; son of Howard Leake (a dentist) and Inez (Alexander) Boatwright; married Helen Strassburger (a concert singer), June 25, 1943; children: Howard Leake III, Alice Karth Boatwright Bennett, David Alexander. *Education:* Early training in piano and violin; Yale University, Mus.B., 1947, Mus.M., 1948. *Home:* 7153 West Genesee, Fayetteville, N.Y. 13066. *Office:* School of Music, Syracuse University, Syracuse, N.Y. 13210.

CAREER: University of Texas, Austin, associate professor of violin, 1943; toured as concert violinist, 1944; Yale University, New Haven, Conn., assistant professor, 1948-55, associate professor of theory of music, 1955-64; Syracuse University, Syracuse, N.Y., dean of School of Music, 1964-71, professor of music, 1971—. Concertmaster, New Haven Symphony, 1950-62; conductor, Yale University Orchestra, 1952-60. Director of music, St. Thomas's Church, New Haven, 1949-64. Undertook U.S. Department of State recital tour of Germany, 1961, and concert tour of France and Germany, 1969; has performed in White House concert, and others. Member of board of directors, Syracuse Symphony, 1964—, vice-president, 1967-68. Consultant to various councils, church and government agencies, and foundations.

MEMBER: International Webern Society (charter member), Society for Asian Music (charter member; member of board of directors, 1960—), College Music Society (member of council, 1960-62, 1967-69), American Society of Composers, Authors and Publishers, National Association of Schools of Music. *Awards, honors:* Grand Prix du Disque for liturgical music, 1958, for conducting recording of Scarlatti's "Passion According to St. John"; Fulbright lectureship in India, 1959-60, research grant to Romania, 1971-72; Rockefeller Foundation grant, 1959-60; award from Society for the Publication of American Music, 1962, for "Quartet for Clarinet and Strings."

WRITINGS: *Introduction to the Theory of Music*, Norton, 1956; *Indian Classical Music and the Western Listener* (booklet), Bharatiya Vidya Bhavan (Bombay), 1960, published with new musical illustrations in *The New Music Lovers Handbook*, compiled by Elie Siegmeister, Harvey House, 1973; *A Handbook on Staff Notation for Indian Music*, Bharatiya Vidya Bhavan, 1960; (editor) Charles Ives, *Essays Before a Sonata and Other Writings*, Norton, 1962, abridged edition, 1964; (contributor) Benjamin Boretz and Edward T. Cone, editors, *Perspectives on American Composers*, Norton, 1971.

Composer of over sixty musical pieces (including five masses, a setting of "The Passion According to St. Matthew," and chamber music), all performed, and about thirty published by Oxford University Press, E. C. Schirmer, and other houses. Author of radio script for "Songs of Charles Ives," broadcast by BBC, 1970. Contributor to *Groves Dictionary*, Knopf's *Encyclopedia of Music and Musicians*, and Dutton's *Dictionary of Twentieth Century Music*. Contributor to music journals.

* * *

BOBKER, Lee R. 1925-

PERSONAL: Born July 19, 1925, in Belle Harbor, N.Y.; son of Harry and Theora (Katz) Bobker; married Kate Gene (a businesswoman), April 5, 1950; children: Gene Ellen, Laurie Beth, Daniel Harry. *Education:* New York University, B.A., 1949. *Politics:* Liberal Democrat. *Reli-

gion: Jewish. *Home:* 61 Sara Lane, New Rochelle, N.Y. *Office:* Vision Associates, 680 Fifth Ave., New York, N.Y.

CAREER: President of Vision Associates, New York, N.Y.; teacher at New York University. *Military service:* U.S. Army, Infantry; received Bronze Star Medal. *Member:* Screen Directors Guild. *Awards, honors:* Three Nominations for Academy Award from Motion Picture Academy of Arts and Sciences; has won about two hundred fifty awards at national and international film festivals.

WRITINGS: Elements of Film, Harcourt, 1971, 2nd edition, 1974; *Making Movies*, Harcourt, 1973.

Author of more than five hundred film scripts. Contributor to professional and popular periodicals.

WORK IN PROGRESS: A suspense novel, tentatively titled *The Drummer* or *Tigers Night*.

AVOCATIONAL INTERESTS: Tennis, skiing, travel abroad, gourmet cooking (has rated restaurants for travel publications).

* * *

BOCK, Paul J(ohn) 1922-

PERSONAL: Born March 30, 1922, in Beulah, N.D.; son of Albert F. (a clergyman) and Lydia (a teacher; maiden name, Buehrer) Bock; married Eva Chybova (a professor), January 29, 1949; children: Benjamin, Timothy, Jane. *Education:* Heidelberg College, B.A., 1944; graduate study at Eden Theological Seminary, 1944-45, and John Huss Theological Seminary (Prague), 1949-50; Yale University, B.D., 1950, S.T.M., 1951; Western Reserve University (now Case Western Reserve University), Ph.D., 1965. *Home:* 60 Clay St., Tiffin, Ohio 44883. *Agent:* Tapp Associates, Inc., 1051 Niel's Lane, West Chester, Pa. 19380. *Office:* Department of Religion, Heidelberg College, Tiffin, Ohio 44883.

CAREER: Minister of the United Church of Christ; Oregon State College, Corvallis, director of Young Men's and Young Women's Christian Association and instructor in religion, 1950-53; Bowling Green State University, Bowling Green, Ohio, campus minister of United Christian Fellowship, 1953-59; Heidelberg College, Tiffin, Ohio, assistant professor, 1959-65, associate professor, 1965-69, professor of religion, 1969—. Member of staff of World Council of Churches in Geneva, 1946-48.

MEMBER: American Society of Christian Ethics, American Society of Church History, American Academy of Religion, American Association of University Professors (president of local chapter, 1973-74), Kiwanis (president of Tiffin club, 1968). *Awards, honors:* Danforth teacher study grant, 1962.

WRITINGS: In Search of a Responsible World Society: The Social Teachings of the World Council of Churches, Westminster, 1974. Associate editor for religion of *Intellect*.

WORK IN PROGRESS: A book on patterns of Christian influence, using biographical studies to show the influence upon American society of religious groups and movements, such as Puritans and Quakers.

AVOCATIONAL INTERESTS: Travel in Europe.

* * *

BOCKUS, H(erman) William 1915-

PERSONAL: Born February 21, 1915, in Frazee, Minn.; son of Herman W. (an accountant) and Emma (Kimmerle) Bockus; married Janet Fisher, January 15, 1944; children: Genevieve, Kimmerle, William, Heidi, Jill. *Education:* University of Minnesota, B.B.A., 1937, B.S., 1947, M.Ed., 1948; also studied at University of California, Los Angeles and University of Southern California, both 1950-55. *Home:* 2843 Tanoble Dr., Altadena, Calif. 91001. *Office:* Department of Art, Pasadena City College, Pasadena, Calif. 91106.

CAREER: New Ulm Wholesale Grocery Co., New Ulm, Minn., office clerk, 1937-39; interpreter in Panama Canal Zone, 1941-42, 1948-49; Highlands University, Las Vegas, N.M., instructor in art, 1949-50; Pasadena City College, Pasadena, Calif., instructor, 1950-60, associate professor, 1960-68, professor of art, 1968—. Advertising artist for Wiancko Engine Co., summers, 1951-58; artist and technical writer for Ranger program, at Jet Propulsion Laboratory of California Institute of Technology, summers, 1961-64; wrought iron furniture designer for Inca Products, 1973-75. *Military service:* U.S. Marine Air Corps, 1942-45; became captain; served in Pacific theater.

MEMBER: National Education Association, California Teachers Association. *Awards, honors:* Award for best print at Veterans Art Exhibit, New York, N.Y., 1962; award of merit from Los Angeles Art Directors Show, 1964.

WRITINGS: Advertising Graphics, Macmillan, 1969, 2nd edition, 1974; *Checklist for Better Tennis*, Doubleday, 1973. Contributor to *California Teachers Association Journal*.

WORK IN PROGRESS: Designers Notebook, a textbook for the product designer.

AVOCATIONAL INTERESTS: Tennis, chess, building hydroplanes and sailboats, striping cars, building and designing furniture, travel (Pacific, Japan, coast of Asia, Africa, up the Amazon River, toured Europe on a bicycle).

* * *

BODINGTON, Nancy H(ermione) 1912- (Shelly Smith)

PERSONAL: Born July 12, 1912, in Richmond, Surrey, England; daughter of Leonard Henry and Maud Eve (Phillips) Courlander; married Stephen Bodington, 1933 (divorced, 1938). *Education:* Attended Cours Maintenon, Cannes, France, 1926, and College Feminin, Paris, 1928. *Home:* Old Orchard, Steyning, Sussex, England. *Agent:* McIntosh & Otis, Inc., 18 East 41st St., New York, N.Y. 10017.

CAREER: Novelist. *Member:* Society of Authors. *Awards, honors:* French Crime Writers award and Edgar Allan Poe Diploma, 1961, for *The Ballad of the Running Man*.

WRITINGS: How Many Miles to Babylon? (novel), Wingate, 1950.

Novels; under pseudonym Shelley Smith: *Background for Murder*, G. G. Swan, 1942; *Death Stalks a Lady*, G. G. Swan, 1945; *This Is the House*, Collins, 1945; *Come and Be Killed*, Harper, 1946; *He Died of Murder*, Harper, 1947; *The Woman in the Sea*, Harper, 1948; *Man with a Calico Face*, Harper, 1950; *Crooked Man*, Harper, 1952 (published in England as *Man Alone*, Collins, 1952); *An Afternoon to Kill*, Collins, 1953, Harper, 1954; *Cellar at No. 5*, Harper, 1954 (published in England as *Party at No. 5*, Collins, 1954); *The Lord Have Mercy*, Harper, 1956;

Rachel Weeping: A Triptych, Harper, 1957; *The Ballad of the Running Man*, Hamish Hamilton, 1961, Harper, 1962; *A Grave Affair*, Hamish Hamilton, 1971, Doubleday, 1973.

Filmscripts: "Tiger Boy," 1958; "The Running Man," 1961. Also author of radio and television plays in England.

WORK IN PROGRESS: A novel of suspense, tentatively entitled *Prosper House*.

SIDELIGHTS: Nancy Bodington writes: "I have aspirations to write works of more lasting value, but meanwhile I continue to write for a living."

* * *

BOEHLOW, Robert H(enry) 1925-

PERSONAL: Born March 12, 1925, in St. Louis, Mo.; son of Robert William (an engineer) and Alice (Asher) Boehlow; married Marjorie Selindh, June 10, 1957; children: Christopher Scott, Jeffrey Craig, Todd Robert, Jason Asher. *Education:* Attended Agricultural and Mechanical College of Texas (now Texas A & M University), 1943-44, and Arkansas Agricultural and Mechanical College (now University of Arkansas at Monticello), 1944; University of Missouri, B.S. in Ed., 1949; graduate study, Central Missouri State University, 1968. *Politics:* Democrat. *Religion:* Protestant. *Home:* 3140 Kingsley Dr., Florissant, Mo. 63033.

CAREER: Riverview Gardens School District, St. Louis, Mo., teacher of driver education, 1955-64; University City School District, St. Louis, Mo., teacher of driver education, 1964—. *Military service:* U.S. Marine Corps, 1943-46. *Member:* American Driver Education Association, Missouri State Driver Education Association (president, 1965). *Awards, honors:* Driver Education Teacher of the Year Award, 1965.

WRITINGS: *Teach Yourself to Drive: It's Easy*, Safety Consultants, 1974.

* * *

BOEHRINGER, Robert 1885(?)-1974

German-born poet, author, and scholar. Obituaries: *AB Bookman's Weekly*, October 7, 1974.

* * *

BOLITHO, (Henry) Hector 1897-1974 (Patrick Ney)

May 28, 1897—1974; New Zealand-born biographer. Obituaries: *AB Bookman's Weekly*, November 18, 1974. (*CA*-9/10).

* * *

BONI, Margaret Bradford 1893(?)-1974

1893(?)—December 1, 1974; American author of books on songs and music teacher. Obituaries: *New York Times*, November 27, 1974; *AB Bookman's Weekly*, December 16, 1974.

* * *

BONNER, William H(omer) 1924-

PERSONAL: Born June 5, 1924, in Nauvoo, Ala.; son of Lee H. and Willie Ann (Baughn) Bonner; married Martha Sue Wilson, December 20, 1969; children: Andrew William, Kent Wilson. *Education:* Livingston University, B.S., 1948; University of Tennessee, M.S., 1953; Ohio State University, Ph.D., 1961. *Religion:* Christian. *Home:* 1151 Mt. Vernon Rd., Cookeville, Tenn. 38501. *Office:* Department of Business Education, Tennessee Technological University, Cookeville, Tenn. 38501.

CAREER: U.S. Civil Service, Aberdeen, Miss., clerk, 1942-45; Livingston University, Livingston, Ala., assistant treasurer, 1948-54; University of Tennessee, Knoxville, assistant professor of business, 1954-62; Tennessee Technological University, Cookeville, professor of business education and office management and chairman of department, 1962—. Consultant in business communications; visiting professor at Capital University, 1960-61, and University of North Dakota, 1967. *Member:* American Business Communication Association (vice-president, 1974—), National Business Education Association, Southern Business Education Association (president, 1971), Tennessee Business Education Association (president, 1965), Beta Gamma Sigma, Kappa Delta Pi, Delta Pi Epsilon, Pi Omega Pi, Phi Delta Kappa, Lions International.

WRITINGS: *Better Business Writing*, Irwin, 1974. Contributor to *National Business Education Association Yearbook* and professional journals.

WORK IN PROGRESS: A chapter for a handbook.

AVOCATIONAL INTERESTS: Travel.

* * *

BONNIE, Richard J(effrey) 1945-

PERSONAL: Born August 22, 1945, in Richmond, Va.; son of Herbert H. (a dentist) and Helene (Berz) Bonnie; married Kathleen Ford (a teacher), June 15, 1967; children: Joshua Ford, Zachary Andrew. *Education:* Johns Hopkins University, B.A., 1966; University of Virginia, LL.B., 1969. *Home:* 917 Rugby Rd., Charlottesville, Va. 22903. *Office:* School of Law, University of Virginia, Charlottesville, Va. 22901.

CAREER: Admitted to Bar of Supreme Court of Appeals of Virginia, U.S. District Court, and U.S. Court of Appeals. University of Virginia, Charlottesville, assistant professor of law, 1969-70; National Commission on Marihuana and Drug Abuse, Washington, D.C., associate director, 1971-73; University of Virginia, Charlottesville, associate professor of law, 1974—. Research chairman of Bill of Rights subcommittee of Virginia Commission for Constitutional Revision; consultant to Executive Office of the President and to Medicine in the Public Interest. *Military service:* U.S. Air Force Reserve, 1969-70, active duty with Office of the General Counsel, 1970-71; became captain.

MEMBER: American Bar Association, Virginia State Bar Association, Order of the Coif.

WRITINGS: (With Charles H. Whitebread II) *The Marihuana Conviction: The History of Marihuana Prohibition in the United States,* University Press of Virginia, 1974; (with Michael R. Sonnenreich) *Legal Aspects of Drug Dependence,* Chemical Research Corporation Press, 1974. Contributor of reports to the U.S. President. Contributor to *Virginia Law Review* and *Science*. Notes and decisions editor of *Virginia Law Review,* 1968-69.

WORK IN PROGRESS: *Selective Justice.*

* * *

BOOKSTEIN, Abraham 1940-

PERSONAL: Born March 22, 1940, in New York, N.Y.; son of Alex (a laborer) and Dora (Cohen) Bookstein; married Marguerite Vickers, June 20, 1968. *Education:* City

College of the City University of New York, B.S., 1961; University of California, Berkeley, M.S., 1966; Yeshiva University, Ph.D., 1969; University of Chicago, M.A., 1971. *Office:* Graduate Library School, University of Chicago, Chicago, Ill. 60637.

CAREER: University of Chicago, Chicago, Ill., assistant professor of library science, and of behavioral science, 1971—. *Member:* American Society of Information Science, Association of Computing Machinists.

WRITINGS: (Editor with Don R. Swanson) *Operations Research: Implications for Libraries*, University of Chicago Press, 1972. Contributor to *Library Quarterly, Journal of the American Society for Information Science, Journal of Library Automation, Communications of the Association of Computing Machinists, Journal of Documentation*, and *Library Resources and Technical Services*. Member of editorial board, *Library Quarterly*, 1971—.

WORK IN PROGRESS: Research on application of mathematical techniques to information sciences.

* * *

BOOTH, Ernest Sheldon 1915-

PERSONAL: Born October 8, 1915, in Lehman, Pa.; son of Sherman (a teacher) and Mary (Henkes) Booth; married Dorothy Cushman, September 5, 1938; children: Lowell Sheldon, Laurel Ann. *Education:* Pacific Union College, B.A., 1938; University of Washington, Seattle, M.S., 1940; State College of Washington (now Washington State University), Ph.D., 1947. *Home:* 1438 Rosario Rd., Anacortes, Wash. 98221. *Office address:* Outdoor Pictures, Box 277, Anacortes, Wash. 98221.

CAREER: Walla Walla College, College Place, Wash., instructor, 1938-44, assistant professor, 1944-66, associate professor, 1946-47, professor of biology and director of biological station, 1947-58; Loma Linda University, Loma Linda, Calif., professor of biology, 1962-68; Outdoor Pictures (publishers), Anacortes, Wash., president, 1968—. Conducted eight scientific expeditions for students to Mexico and Central America, 1946-58. *Member:* American Society of Mammalogists, American Ornithologists' Union, Kiwanis International (past chapter president).

WRITINGS: Laboratory Anatomy of the Cat, [College Place, Wash.], 1943, 5th edition, W. C. Brown, 1973; *Birds of the West*, [College Place, Wash.], 1948, 4th edition, Outdoor Pictures, 1971, published as *Birds of North America: West of the Rockies*, Country Beautiful, 1974; *Biology: The Story of Life*, Pacific Press, 1950, revised edition, 1954; *How to Know the Mammals*, W. C. Brown, 1950, 3rd edition, 1972; *Field Record for Birds*, Outdoor Pictures, 1960; *Birds of the East*, Outdoor Pictures, 1962, revised edition published as *Birds of North America: East of the Rockies*, Country Beautiful, 1974; *Western Bird Guide for Youth*, Outdoor Pictures, 1963; *Eastern Bird Guide for Youth*, Outdoor Pictures, 1963; *Mammals of Southern California*, University of California Press, 1968; *Life List for Birds*, Outdoor Pictures, 1969.

Author of works published by Department of Biological Sciences, Walla Walla College, including *Field Key to the Mammals of Washington*, 1941; *Ecological Distribution of the Birds of the Blue Mountains Region of Southeastern Washington and Northeastern Oregon*, 1952; (with Chester E. Horner) *Spring Flowers of Southeastern Washington and Northeastern Oregon*, 1953. Editor or co-editor of fifteen laboratory anatomy guides for W. C. Brown. Contributor of about seventy-five articles to scientific journals, 1940-60. Editor, *Outdoor World*, 1969-72.

SIDELIGHTS: Booth has traveled throughout Central and South America, North America, the West Indies, Europe, Africa, and southern Asia.

* * *

BOOTH, Rosemary Frances 1928-
(Frances Murray)

PERSONAL: Born February 10, 1928, in Glasgow, Scotland; daughter of Donald (an author, playwright, and journalist) and Frances (an artist; maiden name, Wotherspoon) Sutherland; married Robert Edward Booth (a manager), August 28, 1950; children: Lesley (Mrs. Alan Milligan), Judith, Frances. *Education:* Attended University of Glasgow, 1945-47; University of St. Andrews, M.A. (honors), 1965, Ed. Diploma, 1966; Dundee College of Education, teaching certificate, 1966. *Politics:* "Liberal fence-sitter (a plague o' both their houses)." *Religion:* Agnostic. *Residence:* Perthshire, Scotland.

CAREER: History teacher at Perth Academy, Perthshire, Scotland, 1966-72; Linlathen High School, Dundee, Scotland, principal teacher of history, 1972—. *Member:* Educational Institute of Scotland. *Awards, honors:* Principal award of Romantic Novelists Association and Mary Elgin Award, both 1974, both for *The Burning Lamp*; elected a "Daughter of Mark Twain" by *Mark Twain Journal*, 1974.

WRITINGS—Under pseudnym Frances Murray: *Ponies on the Heather* (juvenile), Collins, 1966, revised edition, 1973; *The Dear Colleague* (novel), Hodder & Stoughton, 1972, St. Martins, 1973; *The Burning Lamp* (novel), Hodder & Stoughton, 1973; *The Heroine's Sister* (novel), Hodder & Stoughton, in press; *Ponies and Parachutes* (juvenile), Hodder & Stoughton, in press. Author of history scripts for BBC radio school programs. Contributor to magazines.

WORK IN PROGRESS: Red Rowan Berry, a novel set in Scotland.

AVOCATIONAL INTERESTS: Sailing, the sea, cooking, good food and wine, beer.

* * *

BOOTH, Taylor L(ockwood) 1933-

PERSONAL: Born September 22, 1933, in Middletown, Conn.; son of George R. (a salesman) and Della (Bell) Booth; married Aline Loyzim, January 1, 1955; children: Laurine, Michael, Shari. *Education:* University of Connecticut, B.S., 1955, M.S., 1956, Ph.D., 1962. *Home:* 451 Wormwood Hill Rd., Mansfield Center, Conn. 06250. *Office:* U-157 Department of Electrical Engineering and Computer Science, University of Connecticut, Storrs, Conn. 06268.

CAREER: Westinghouse Electric Corp., Baltimore, Md., analytical engineer, 1956-59; University of Connecticut, Storrs, instructor, 1959-63, assistant professor, 1963-67, associate professor, 1967-69, professor of electrical engineering and computer science, 1969—. *Member:* Institute of Electrical and Electronic Engineers (fellow), Association of Computing Machinery, American Society of Engineering Education. *Awards, honors:* Frederick Emmons Terman Award, 1972.

WRITINGS: Sequential Machines and Automata Theory, Wiley, 1967; *Digital Networks and Computer Systems*,

Wiley, 1971; (with Y. T. Chien) *Computing: Fundamentals and Applications*, Hamilton-Hall, 1974. Associate editor of *IEEE Transactions Computer*, 1971—.

AVOCATIONAL INTERESTS: Amateur radio, skiing, swimming.

* * *

BORGHESE, Junio Valerio 1906(?)-1974

1906(?)—August 26, 1974; Italian prince, war hero, and neo-fascist leader. Obituaries: *New York Times*, August 28, 1974; *Washington Post*, August 30, 1974.

* * *

BORLAND, Kathryn Kilby 1916-
(Alice Abbott, Jane Land and Ross Land, joint pseudonyms)

PERSONAL: Born August 14, 1916, in Pullman, Mich.; daughter of Paul M. (a diamond broker) and Vinnie (Bensinger) Kilby; married James Borland (a chemist), May 16, 1942; children: James, Susan. *Education:* Butler University, B.S., 1937. *Religion:* Christian Disciple. *Home:* R.R. 3, South Maish Rd., Frankfort, Ind. 46041. *Agent:* Jay Garon-Brooke Associates, Inc., 415 Central Park W., 17D, New York, N.Y. 10025.

CAREER: North Side Topics (weekly newspaper), Indianapolis, Ind., editor, 1939-42; free-lance writer. *Member:* Theta Sigma Phi, Kappa Alpha Theta. *Awards, honors:* Co-recipient of Indiana University award for most distinguished children's book by an Indiana author, 1970.

WRITINGS—All with Helen Speicher: *Southern Yankees*, Bobbs-Merrill, 1960; *Allan Pinkerton: Young Detective*, Bobbs-Merrill, 1962; *Eugene Field: Young Poet*, Bobbs-Merrill, 1964; *Phyllis Wheatley: Young Colonial Poet*, Bobbs-Merrill, 1968; *Harry Houdini: Boy Magician*, Bobbs-Merrill, 1969; *Clocks: From Shadow to Atom*, Follett, 1969; *Goodbye to Stony Crick*, McGraw, 1975.

With Speicher, under pseudonym Jane Land and Ross Land, except as indicated: *Miles and the Big Black Hat*, E. C. Seale, 1963; *Everybody Laughed and Laughed*, E. C. Seale, 1964; (with Speicher, under pseudonym Jane Land) *Stranger in the Mirror*, edited by Sharon Jarvis, Ballantine, 1974.

With Speicher, under pseudonym Alice Abbott: *The Third Tower*, Ace Books, 1974; *Goodbye Julie Scott*, Ace Books, 1975.

SIDELIGHTS: Kathryn Borland commented to *CA* on her association with Helen Speicher: "We are often asked how two people can write together, and it probably does require special circumstances—in our case friendship since childhood, similar viewpoints, and insatiable curiosity about people, events, and places. It is our hope that whatever we write will reinforce the positive values of integrity, love, and responsibility for one another.

* * *

BOSE, Irene Mott 1899(?)-1974

1899(?)—December 22, 1974; American social worker in India. Obituaries: *New York Times*, December 27, 1974.

* * *

BOSLEY, Harold A(ugustus) 1907-1975

February 19, 1907—January 20, 1975; American Protestant minister, educator, author, and lecturer. Obituaries: *New York Times*, January 22, 1975, January 23, 1975; *AB Bookman's Weekly*, February 17, 1975. (*CA*-49-52).

* * *

BOTTRALL, (Francis James) Ronald 1906-

PERSONAL: Born September 2, 1906, in Camborne, Cornwall, England; son of Francis John and Clara Jane (Rowe) Bottrall; married Margaret Florence Saumarez Smith, October 5, 1934 (divorced, 1954); married Margot Pamela Samuel (a personnel assistant), July 10, 1954; children: (first marriage) Anthony Francis. *Education:* Pembroke College, Cambridge, B.A., 1929, M.A., 1933. *Home:* Via della Quattro Fontane 16, 00184 Rome, Italy.

CAREER: University of Helsinki, Helsinki, Finland, lecturer in English, 1929-31; Princeton University, Princeton, N.J., Commonwealth Fund Fellow, 1931-33; University of Singapore, Singapore, Johore Professor of English, and head of department, 1933-37; British Institute of Florence, Florence, Italy, acting director, 1937-38; University of London, London, England, secretary of School of Oriental and African Studies, 1939-45; seconded to British Air Ministry, serving as priority officer, 1940-41; British Council, London, England, representative in Sweden, 1941-44, in Italy, 1945-50, controller of education in London office, 1950-54, representative in Brazil, 1954-56, Greece, 1957-59, and Japan, 1959-61; United Nations, chief of fellowships and training branch of Food and Agriculture Organization in Rome, 1963-65. Trustee, Kinsman Trust, 1953-54.

MEMBER: International Poetry Society (vice-president, 1973), Royal Society of Literature (fellow), Athenaeum Club. *Awards, honors:* Officer of Order of the British Empire, 1949; Coronation Medal, 1953; Theocritus International Poetry Prize from city of Syracuse, in Sicily, 1954; Knight of the Order of St. John, 1972; Grand Officer of the Order of Merit of the Republic of Italy, 1973.

WRITINGS—Books of poems: *The Loosening and Other Poems*, Minority Press (Cambridge, England), 1931; *Festivals of Fire*, Faber, 1934; *The Turning Path*, Arthur Barker, 1939; *Farewell and Welcome*, Editions Poetry (London), 1945; *Selected Poems*, Editions Poetry, 1946; *The Palisades of Fear*, Editions Poetry, 1949; *Adam Unparadised*, D. Verschoyle (London), 1954; *Collected Poems*, Sidgwick & Jackson, 1961; *Day and Night*, London Magazine Editions, 1974; *Poems: 1955-1973*, Routledge & Kegan Paul, 1974.

Editor of anthologies: (With Gunnar Ekeloef) *T. S. Eliot's "Dikter i Urval,"* Bonniers (Stockholm), 1942; (with Margaret Bottrall) *The Zephyr Book of English Verse*, Bonniers, 1945; (with Margaret Bottrall) *Collected English Verse*, Sidgwick & Jackson, 1946; *Rome: Art Centres of the World*, World Publishing, 1968.

WORK IN PROGRESS: Poems; work on contemporary Italian writers; memoirs.

SIDELIGHTS: Bottrall has traveled in much of Europe, North Africa, North America, Brazil, South-East Asia, China, and Japan. He knows Swedish, Italian, French, Portuguese, Spanish, German, modern and ancient Greek, and Latin.

* * *

BOUCHER, Wayne I(rving) 1934-

PERSONAL: Born December 12, 1934, in Bay City, Mich.; son of Harold O. and Mildred (Born) Boucher; divorced; children: Michele Annette, Robert Alain. *Education:* University of Michigan, B.A., 1956, M.A., 1960; graduate study, University of Missouri, 1958-61. *Home address:* P.O. Box 454, Glastonbury, Conn. 06033. *Office:* The Futures Group, 124 Hebron Ave., Glastonbury, Conn. 06033.

CAREER: University of Missouri, Columbia, instructor in English, 1958-63; RAND Corp., Santa Monica, Calif., editor and administrator in reports department, 1963-65, deputy assistant to president, 1965-69; Institute for the Future, Middletown, Conn., research associate, 1969-71; The Futures Group, Glastonbury, Conn., co-founder, secretary, and senior project manager, 1971—. Evening instructor at University of California, Los Angeles, University of Missouri Extension Division in St. Louis, and University of Connecticut Graduate School of Business. Program adviser, Campus-Free College. *Military service:* U.S. Army Reserve, Corps of Engineers, 1957-63; received outstanding achievement award. *Member:* National Association of Science Writers, Policy Studies Organization.

WRITINGS: (Editor with E. S. Quade) *Systems Analysis and Policy Planning: Applications in Defense*, American Elsevier, 1968; (with Selwyn Enzer and F. D. Lazar) *Futures Research as an Aid to Government Planning in Canada: Four Workshop Demonstrations*, Institute for the Future, 1971; (with T. J. Gordon and T. R. Mullaney) *A Backdrop for Planning in the Electronics Industry*, Electronics Industries Association, 1971; *The Future Environment for Technology Assessment*, Futures Group (Glastonbury, Conn.), 1971; *Report on a Hypothetical Focused Planning Effort (FPE)*, Futures Group, 1972; *Quantifiable Goal Statements for the U.S. Criminal Justice System: A Preliminary Assessment*, Futures Group, 1972; *Description of a System for Identifying and Evaluating Important Social Trends*, Futures Group, 1972, revised edition, 1973; (with Gordon and J. E. Lamson) *Priorities for Technology Assessment: A Survey of Candidate Technologies*, Futures Group, 1973, published as *A Survey of Candidate Technologies*, U.S. Government Printing Office, for National Science Foundation, 1974; *Nongovernmental Institutions for Forecasting the Impact of Change*, Futures Group, 1974.

Contributor: M. J. Cetron and Bodo Bartocha, editors, *Technology Assessment in a Dynamic Environment*, Gordon & Breach, 1973; Henry Cohen, editor, *Administrative Arrangements in the United States for Forecasting the Impact of Social and Economic Change*, New School for Social Research, 1974. Contributor to *New Priorities, Technology Assessment*, and other publications.

WORK IN PROGRESS: The Study of the Future: An Agenda for Research, a book on the possibility of making forecasting more scientific; projects on barriers to technological innovation, and on the future of the scientific journal.

AVOCATIONAL INTERESTS: "Post-Parker" jazz, German history between World War I and II, philosophy of the seventeenth century, contemporary Russian politics, book collecting, motorcycling.

* * *

BOURNE, Aleck William 1886(?)-1974

1886(?)—December 27, 1974; British gynecologist and author. Obituaries: *AB Bookman's Weekly*, February 3, 1975.

BOURNE, Lyle E(ugene), Jr. 1932-

PERSONAL: Born April 12, 1932, in Boston, Mass.; son of Lyle Eugene and Blanche (White) Bourne; children: Barbara, Elizabeth, Andrew. *Education:* Brown University, B.A. (with distinction), 1953; University of Wisconsin, M.Sc., 1955, Ph.D., 1956. *Residence:* Denver, Colo. *Office:* Department of Psychology, University of Colorado, Boulder, Colo. 80302.

CAREER: University of Utah, Salt Lake City, assistant professor, 1956-61, associate professor of psychology, 1961-63; University of Colorado, Boulder, associate professor, 1963-65, professor of psychology, 1965—. Visiting associate professor at University of California, Berkeley, 1961-62, visiting professor, 1968-69; clinical professor of psychiatry at University of Kansas Medical Center, 1967—. Visiting summer professor at University of Alberta, 1961, University of Wisconsin, 1966, University of Montana, 1967, and University of Hawaii, 1969. Consultant in experimental psychology to U.S. Veterans Administration, 1965—; member of psycholobiology panel, National Science Foundation, 1970-73.

MEMBER: American Psychological Association (member of executive committee, Division 3, 1968-71; division representative to council, 1972-74), Society of Experimental Psychologists, Psychonomic Society, Midwestern Psychological Association, Sigma Xi. *Awards, honors:* National Institute of Mental Health grant for research on logico-conceptual skills and rules, 1972-76; National Science Foundation grant for research on cognitive factors in learning and memory, 1972-77.

WRITINGS: Human Conceptual Behavior, Allyn & Bacon, 1966; (with Bruce R. Ekstrand) *Psychology: Its Principles and Meanings*, Dryden, 1973; (editor with Ekstrand) *Readings in the Principles and Meanings of Psychology*, Dryden, 1973.

Contributor: Joseph B. Sidowski, editor, *Experimental Methods and Instrumentation in Psychology*, McGraw, 1966; Benjamin Kleinmuntz, editor, *Concepts and the Structure of Memory*, Wiley, 1967; Theodore R. Dixon and D. L. Horton, editors, *Verbal Behavior and General Behavior Theory*, Prentice-Hall, 1968; James F. Voss, editor, *Approaches to Thought*, C. E. Merrill, 1969; Benjamin B. Wolman, editor, *Handbook of General Psychology*, Prentice-Hall, 1973; Robert L. Solso, editor, *Contemporary Issues in Cognitive Psychology*, Halstead, 1973; P.C. Wason and P. N. Johnson-Laird, editors, *Readings in the Psychology of Reasoning*, Penguin, in press. Contributor to other symposia and of about sixty articles to psychology journals.

Academic editor, "Learning-Cognition" series, Scott, Foresman; academic co-editor, "Basic Psychological Concepts" series, Scott, Foresman. Associate editor, *Journal of Experimental Psychology*, 1973-74, editor, 1974—; editor for experimental psychology section, *Journal Supplement Abstract Service*, American Psychological Association, 1971; consulting editor, *Psychological Reports*, 1960—, *Journal of Experimental Psychology*, 1963-72, *Psychological Monographs*, 1965-66, *Psychonomic Science*, 1968-70, *Journal of Verbal Learning and Verbal Behavior*, 1968-73, and *Journal of Experimental Child Psychology*, 1969-73.

BOWDEN, Jean 1925-
(Jocelyn Barry, Jennifer Bland, Avon Curry, Belinda Dell)

PERSONAL: Born October 16, 1925, in Edinburgh, Scotland; daughter of Harold Mackenzie (a printer) and Jeanie (Dick) Hill; married George Bowden (a civil servant), October 23, 1943; children: Julian, Adrian. *Education:* Educated in Scotland. *Politics:* None. *Religion:* None. *Home and office:* Laurel Cottage, 138 Himley Rd., London S.W. 17, England. *Agent:* Laurence Pollinger Ltd., 18 Maddox St., London W.1, England.

CAREER: Panther Books, London, England, editorial assistant, 1957-59; Four Square Books, London, editorial assistant, 1959-61; Armada Books, London, editorial assistant, 1961-62; *Woman's Mirror* (magazine), London, feature writer, 1962-64; *Woman's Own* (magazine), London, assistant fiction editor, 1964-71; novelist. Editorial consultant to Mills & Boon (book publishers). *Member:* International P.E.N., Crime Writers Association (vice-chairman, 1974—), Society of Women Writers and Journalists, Society of Authors (chairman, 1974—), Detection Club, Press Club (London), National Union of Journalists, Institute of Journalists, Royal Horticultural Society (fellow).

WRITINGS: Grey Touched with Scarlet: The Experiences of the Army Nursing Sisters, R. Hale, 1959; *Call an Ambulance! The Story of the London Ambulance Crews,* R. Hale, 1960; *In a Winged World,* Central Office of Information, 1962; *The Ceaseless Challenge,* Red Cross, 1964; *Your Welcome,* Government of Northern Ireland, 1965; *Come Dancing,* W. H. Allen, 1966; *The Dancing Years of Bill and Bobby Irvine,* W. H. Allen, 1968.

Under pseudonym Jocelyn Barry: *Summer in the City,* Hurst & Blackett, 1968.

Under pseudonym Jennifer Bland: *Accomplice,* Arthur Barker, 1974; *Death in Waiting,* St. Martin's, 1974.

Under pseudonym Avon Curry: *Derry Down Death,* W. H. Allen, 1960; *Dying High,* W. H. Allen, 1961; *A Place of Execution,* John Long, 1969; *Shack-Up,* John Long, 1971; *The Girl in the Killer's Bed,* Ace Books, 1972; *Fetish Murders,* Ace Books, 1973; *Hunt for Danger,* Milton House Books, 1974.

Under pseudonym Belinda Dell: *Island of Love,* Ward, Lock, 1958; *Heights of Love,* Ward, Lock, 1959; *Who Claims My Heart,* Ward, Lock, 1959; *Happiness Has Wings,* Ward, Lock, 1960; *See if I Care,* Ward, Lock, 1960; *Dearest Enemy,* Ward, Lock, 1961; *Fateful Enchantress,* Ward, Lock, 1961; *There's No Turning Back,* Ward, Lock, 1962; *Where the Rata Blossoms,* Mills & Boon, 1968; *The Cruise to Curacao,* Mills & Boon, 1968; *Dancing on My Heart,* Mills & Boon, 1969; *Vermillion Gateway,* Mills & Boon, 1970; *Next Stop Gretna,* Mills & Boon, 1970; *Change Partners,* Mills & Boon, 1971; *Flowers for the Festival,* Harlequin Books, 1972.

Also author, under pseudonym Belinda Dell: "Lovely Is the Rose," "The Darling Pirate," and "Lake of Silver."

Contributor to *Times* (London), *Telegraph* (London), *London Evening News, Woman's Own, Woman's Realm,* and others.

WORK IN PROGRESS: A biography of a "battered baby" victim, a human interest plus sociological work; research on William Paterson, a 17th-18th century financier.

SIDELIGHTS: Mrs. Bowden told *CA:* "I write to earn my living but have definite fields of interest besides the fiction which is my 'bread and butter.' I prefer sociology and history as non-fiction themes. I travel as much as I can—recently went to Singapore, Bangkok and Hong Kong but usually remain in Europe because I speak the main European languages—French, German and Italian."

* * *

BOWER, Fay Louise 1929-

PERSONAL: Born September 10, 1929, in San Francisco, Calif.; daughter of James Joseph (a restaurant owner) and Emily (Andrews) Saitta; married Robert Davis Bower (a business manager), July 2, 1949; children: Robert D., Carol (Mrs. John Raymond Tomei), Dennis James, Thomas John. *Education:* St. Mary's Hospital School of Nursing, San Francisco, Calif., diploma, 1949; attended Foothill Community College, 1960-62; San Jose State College (now San Jose State University), B.S. (with distinguished honors), 1965; University of California, San Francisco, M.S.N., 1966. *Politics:* Democrat. *Religion:* Roman Catholic. *Home:* 874 Miranda Green, Palo Alto, Calif. 94306. *Office:* Department of Nursing, San Jose State University, San Jose, Calif. 95192.

CAREER: Office nurse in Palo Alto, Calif., 1950-55; Stanford University Medical Center, Stanford Hospital, Stanford, Calif., part-time positions as staff nurse, 1964-66, charge nurse in newborn nursery, 1966-67, staff nurse in Premature Research Center, 1967-73; San Jose State University, San Jose, Calif., assistant professor, 1965-70, associate professor of nursing, 1970—. *Awards, honors:* Grant from National Institutes of Health, 1972-73, 1974, 1975.

WRITINGS: Nursing Skills I, Unit III, Department of Nursing, San Jose State University, 1971; *The Process of Planning Nursing Care,* Mosby, 1972; *Theoretical Foundations of Nursing,* three volumes, Faculty Publications Association, Department of Nursing, San Jose State University, 1972; *Communication Theory* (module), Faculty Publications Association, Department of Nursing, San Jose State University, 1973; *Changes in Perception* (module), Faculty Publications Association, Department of Nursing, San Jose State University, 1973; *Changes in Behavior* (module), Faculty Publications Association, Department of Nursing, San Jose State University, 1973. Contributor to *Nursing Outlook.*

WORK IN PROGRESS: Fundamentals of Nursing Practice: Roles and Functions of Holistic Nursing, for Mosby; a sabbatical research project on the relationship of the learning environment to ethnic minority achievement in a nursing curriculum.

* * *

BOYCE, George A(rthur) 1898-

PERSONAL: Born January 20, 1898, in Scranton, Pa.; son of Arthur Jay (a printer) and Marietta (Royce) Boyce; married Elizabeth A. Coleman, May 20, 1933 (died January 22, 1962); married Oleta Merry (a home economist), January 31, 1964; children: (first marriage) George A., Jr., Robert A. *Education:* Trinity College, Hartford, Conn., B.S., 1921; Cornell University, M.A., 1926; Columbia University, Ed.D., 1941. *Religion:* Protestant. *Home:* 1203 Calle Luna, Santa Fe, N.M. 87501. *Agent:* Jody Ellis, P.O. Box 2321, Santa Fe, N.M. 87501.

CAREER: Science and mathematics teacher in schools in Concord, N.H., 1921, Lake Placid, N.Y., 1921-23, Philadelphia, Pa., 1923-27 (head of science department and dean, 1923-27), Hudson, Ohio, 1927-31, and Bronxville, N.Y., 1931-38; U.S. Bureau of Indian Affairs, Washington, D.C., curriculum specialist, 1938-66. Director of Navajo schools; superintendent of Intermountain Indian School; member of board of directors of Verde Valley School. Chairman of long-range social-economic planning on Navajo Reservation, for U.S. Navajo Service, 1944; developed and served as superintendent of a program for Institute of American Indian Arts, 1961. *Military services:* U.S. Naval Reserve, 1918.

MEMBER: Santa Fe Westerners (vice-president), Santa Fe Council on International Relations (president). *Awards, honors:* Distinguished service gold medal from U.S. Secretary of the Interior, 1952, for social-economic survey and for Intermountain Indian School; certificate of appreciation from Navajo Tribe, 1966; certificate of appreciation from Indian Arts and Crafts Board of U.S. Department of the Interior, 1967; D.H.L. from Trinity College (Hartford, Conn.), 1968.

WRITINGS: (With Willard W. Beatty) *Mathematics of Everyday Life*, five volumes, I.N.O.R. (New York), 1936; *When Navajoes Had Too Many Sheep*, Indian Historian Press, 1974; *Some People Are Indians*, Vanguard, 1974. Editor of pamphlets for U.S. Bureau of Indian Affairs, including "Dormitory Life: Is It Living?" and "Alcohol and American Indian Students."

WORK IN PROGRESS: Neither Red Nor White.

SIDELIGHTS: Boyce writes that "Cultural differences are 'good.' To form a democratic, multi-cultural nation calls for nurturing rather than destroying cultural differences. The 'cement' is the common denominator of all sharing problems requiring mutual assistance. But cultural differences require different education insights and techniques."

* * *

BOYD, E(lizabeth) 1904(?)-1974

1904(?)—September 30, 1974; American author and museum curator. Obituaries: *New York Times*, October 4, 1974.

* * *

BOYD, Robert H. 1912-

PERSONAL: Born April 25, 1912, in Roland, Iowa; son of Otis S. and Olive (Hegland) Boyd; married Annetta Marcella Johnson, August 16, 1938; children: Anne Marie (Mrs. Kenneth S. Prestegard), Paul Nathan. *Education:* St. Olaf College, A.B., 1934; Luther Theological Seminary, St. Paul, Minn., B.D., 1938; Princeton University, M.Th., 1939, Ph.D., 1942. *Home:* 2103 Doswell Ave., St. Paul, Minn. 55108. *Office:* 2375 Como Ave., St. Paul, Minn. 55108.

CAREER: Ordained Lutheran clergyman; pastor of Lutheran churches, 1942-46; Luther Theological Seminary, St. Paul, Minn., professor of Old Testament, 1946—. Lecturer in religion, McAlester College, 1970. Tour director for Near Eastern travel groups, 1971, 1972, 1974; member of staff of American expedition to Hebron, summer, 1964. *Member:* Society of Biblical Literature, American Schools of Oriental Research, National Association of Professors of Hebrew. *Awards, honors:* American Association of Theological Schools faculty research fellowship, 1959-60; Aid Association for Lutherans grant, 1974-75.

WRITINGS: Inspiration from the Psalms, Augsburg, 1963; (translator and editor) Claus Westermann, *Handbook to the Old Testament*, Augsburg, 1967; *Exile and Restoration*, Augsburg, 1968; (translator and editor) Westermann, *Handbook to the New Testament*, Augsburg, 1969; *Learning Biblical Hebrew*, Luther Theological Seminary, 1974. Contributor of articles and reviews to theology journals, including *Lutheran Teacher, Lutheran Standard, Friend of Zion,* and *Augsburg Book News*.

WORK IN PROGRESS: Biblical Teaching Concerning Prayer and Its Significance for Today.

SIDELIGHTS: Boyd is competent in German, Norwegian, French, Swedish, Hebrew, Arabic, and Aramaic.

* * *

BOYERS, Robert 1942-

PERSONAL: Born November 9, 1942, in Brooklyn, N.Y.; son of Paul (a clothing buyer) and Selma (a computer programmer; maiden name, Busell) Boyers; married Madeleine Dolan (an elementary school teacher); children: Lowell, Zachary Meyer. *Education:* Queens College of the City University of New York, B.A., 1963; New York University, M.A., 1965. *Politics:* Left. *Religion:* Jewish. *Home:* 33 East North St., Ballston Spa, N.Y. *Office:* Department of English, Skidmore College, Saratoga Springs, N.Y. 12866.

CAREER: Member of faculty, Bernard Baruch College of the City University of New York, New York, N.Y., 1967-68, and Sullivan County Community College, South Fallsburg, N.Y., 1968-69; Skidmore College, Saratoga Springs, N.Y., assistant professor, 1969-73, associate professor of English, 1973—. Lecturer, New School for Social Research, fall, 1967; writer-in-residence, Philander Smith College, fall, 1967; co-chairman of cultural affairs programs, Fordham University at Lincoln Center, 1971-72; has lectured at Bennington College, and at annual conferences. *Member:* Association of Existential Psychology and Psychiatry (member of governing council, 1972—). *Awards, honors:* National Arts Council grants, 1967, 1969.

WRITINGS—Editor and author of preface: (With M. London; sole author of preface) *Robert Lowell: A Portrait of the Artist in His Time*, David Lewis, 1970; (with R. Orrill, and contributor; sole author of preface) *R.D. Laing and Anti-Psychiatry*, Harper, 1971; *The Legacy of the German Refugee Intellectuals*, Schocken, 1972; (and contributor) *Psychological Man: Approaches to an Emergent Social Type*, Harper, 1974; (and contributor) *Contemporary Poetry in America*, Schocken, 1974.

Critical essays represented in collections, including: *The Young American Writers*, edited by Richard Kostelanetz, Funk, 1968; *The Perverse Imagination*, edited by I. Buchen, New York University Press, 1970; *Modern American Poetry: Essays in Criticism*, edited by J. Mazzaro, McKay, 1970; *Profile of Robert Lowell*, edited by Mazzaro, C. E. Merrill, 1970; *One Flew over the Cuckoo's Nest: A Casebook*, Viking, 1973. Work has also been included in *American Literary Culture*, compiled by U.S. Information Agency and distributed abroad in ten languages.

Contributor to *Contemporary Poets of the English Language*; contributor to periodicals, including *New Leader, Salmagundi, Dissent, Kenyon Review, Denver Quarterly, Georgia Review, Partisan Review, Sewanee Review, Modern Occasions, Review of Existential Psychology and Psychiatry, New Republic, Film Heritage, Critical Quar-*

terly, and to *Annals of the American Academy of Political and Social Science*. Founder and editor-in-chief, *Salmagundi*, 1965—; associate editor, *Review of Existential Psychology and Psychiatry*, 1973—.

WORK IN PROGRESS: A study of the lie.

* * *

BOYLE, Mary 1882(?)-1975

Author of books on archeology. Obituaries: *AB Bookman's Weekly*, February 3, 1975.

* * *

BRANDER, Michael 1924-

PERSONAL: Born May 8, 1924, in Edinburgh, Scotland; married Evelyn Balfour, 1949. *Education:* St. John's College, Cambridge, M.A., 1948. *Agent:* Peter Janson-Smith Ltd., 31 Newington Green, London N16 9PU, England.

MEMBER: Authors Society.

WRITINGS: The Roughshooter's Dog, MacGibbon & Kee, 1957, revised edition, Gentry Books, 1972, St. Martin's, 1975; *Roughshooter's Sport*, MacGibbon & Kee, 1958.

Soho for the Colonel, MacGibbon & Kee, 1961, revised edition published as *A Hunt around the Highlands: Following Colonel Thornton's Tour of the Highlands of 1784*, Standfast Press, 1973; *Gundogs: Their Care and Training*, A. & C. Black, 1963; *Soho for East Anglia: Following de la Rochefoucald's Tour of East Anglia of 1784*, Bles, 1963; *Groundgame*, Percival Marshall, 1963; *The Hunting Instinct: A History of British Field Sports*, Oliver & Boyd, 1964; *Ho for the Borders*, Bles, 1964; *Over the Lowlands*, Bles, 1965; *The Game Shot's Vade Mecum*, A. & C. Black, 1965, revised edition, 1969; *Around the Highlands*, Bles, 1967; *A Dictionary of Sporting Terms*, A. & C. Black, 1968; *The 10th Royal Hussars*, Leo Cooper, 1969.

The Scottish Highlanders and Their Regiments, Leo Cooper, 1971; *The Horseman's Vade Mecum*, A. & C. Black, 1971, published as *The Complete Guide to Horsemanship*, Scribner, 1972; *Hunting and Shooting, from Earliest Times to the Present Day*, Putnam, 1971; (editor) *An International Encyclopedia of Shooting*, Pelham, 1972; *The Georgian Gentleman*, Heath, 1973; *The Life and Sport of the Inn: The Drinking Habits of the British*, Gentry Books, 1973, St. Martin's, 1975; *The Original Scotch: A History of Scotch Whisky*, Hutchinson, 1974; *Scottish Crafts and Craftsmen*, Johnston & Bacon, 1974; *A Guide to Scotch Whisky*, Johnston & Bacon, 1975; *Scottish and Border Battles and Ballads*, Scribner, 1975; *The Victorian Gentleman*, Heath, 1975; *A Brace of Sporting Colonels*, Standfast Press, in press; *The Country Divine*, Gentry Books, in press; *The Newmarket and Thurlow Hunt*, Hutchinson, in press.

AVOCATIONAL INTERESTS: Fishing, hunting, shooting.

* * *

BRANSTON, (Ronald Victor) Brian 1914-

PERSONAL: Born February 2, 1914, in Deepcar, England; son of George (an electrician) and Ellen (Marshall) Branston; married Nellie Doreen Davies, February 5, 1946; children: Shirley, John, Peter, Timothy, Philip, Katherine. *Education:* University of Sheffield, B.A. (first class honors), 1935, M.A., 1936. *Home:* Rhandir Isaf, Croesaubach, Oswestry, England. *Agent:* John Farquharson, 15 Red Lion Sq., London W.C.1, England. *Office:* British Broadcasting Corp., London, England.

CAREER: Ballymena Academy, Northern Ireland, senior English master, 1937-40; British Broadcasting Corp., London, England, radio producer, 1946-57, television producer, 1957-72, consultant, 1974—. *Military service:* British Army, 1940-41. Indian Army, 1941-45; became captain; received Burma Star. *Member:* Hakluyt Society.

WRITINGS: Breeding for Production, Faber, 1951; *Time and Motion on the Farm*, Faber, 1953; *Gods of the North*, Viking, 1955; *Lost Gods of England*, Thames & Hudson, 1957, Oxford University Press, 1974; *A Film Maker's Guide*, Allen & Unwin, 1965; *The Last Great Journey on Earth*, Weybright, 1970; *Beyond Belief*, Walker & Co., 1974.

Television documentary films, all for British Broadcasting Corp.: "Balloons Over the Alps," 1964; "Bird's Eye View of Great Britain," 1967; "Last Great Journey on Earth," 1968; "A Dream of Two Cities," 1968; "River of Death," 1969; "Some Very Gallant Gentlemen," 1972; "The Old Lady and the Sea," produced jointly with Time-Life, Inc., 1972; Riddle of the Runestone," produced jointly with Time-Life, Inc., 1972; Contributor to *Collier's Encyclopedia*.

WORK IN PROGRESS: Mysteries of Travel and Exploration; researching the Kensington, Minn. runestone hoax.

SIDELIGHTS: Branston writes: "My lifelong interests have been out-of-the-way travel and ESP. I have paddled the Burmese River Kalapanzin in a sampan, sought the source of the Orinoco in an Indian dugout canoe and shot the forty-five mile long Maipures and Atures rapids (Orinoco) in a hovercraft, traversed the Cotswolds in a hydrogen balloon and flown for three weeks in a helicopter round the British Isles. In an effort to understand ESP I have been fortunate enough to bring myself into situations where I have seen a ghost, seen ectoplasm, taken spirit photographs and watched a medium in trance produce stigmata on different parts of his body."

* * *

BRAUTIGAN, Richard 1935-

PERSONAL: In 1961, stated he "was married, and had an infant daughter." *Home:* San Francisco, Calif. *Agent:* Helen Brann, 14 Sutton Pl.S., New York, N.Y. 10022.

WRITINGS—Novels: *A Confederate General from Big Sur*, Grove Press, 1965; *Trout Fishing in America*, Four Seasons Foundation, 1967; *In Watermelon Sugar*, Four Seasons Foundation, 1967; *Revenge of the Lawn: Stories, 1962-1970*, Simon & Schuster, 1971; *The Abortion: An Historical Romance, 1966*, Simon & Schuster, 1971.

Poetry: *The Return of the Rivers*, Inferno Press, c. 1957; *The Galilee Hitch-Hiker*, White Rabbit Press, 1958, reprinted, Cranium Press, 1966, reprinted, Or Press, 1968; *Lay the Marble Tea: Twenty-Four Poems*, Carp Press, 1959; *The Octopus Frontier*, Carp Press, 1960; *All Watched Over by Machines of Loving Grace*, Communications Company, 1967; *The Pill Versus the Springhill Mine Disaster*, Four Seasons Foundation, 1968; *Please Plant This Book* (eight poems printed on separate seed packet envelopes), printed by Graham Mackintosh, 1968; *Rommel Drives On Deep Into Egypt*, Delacorte, 1970.

Collections: *Trout Fishing in America, The Pill Versus the Springhill Mine Disaster, and In Watermelon Sugar*, Delacorte Press, 1969. Co-editor, *Change* (single issue magazine), 1963.

SIDELIGHTS: "Like all true humorists," writes Stephen Schneck, "Richard Brautigan eschews the label. Spies and humorists can only function under cover. So rather than think of Brautigan as a comic writer, imagine a six-foot country boy, with wire-rim glasses and a homemade haircut and a shaggy Wild West moustache that doesn't quite hide a perpetual grin. . . . Inside this hulking innocent, this country bumpkin, is a special (very special) correspondent from a terribly literate sort of Field & Stream magazine."

Some of Brautigan's works have been recorded by Columbia Records.

BIOGRAPHICAL/CRITICAL SOURCES: Tony Tanner, *City of Words*, Harper, 1971; Carolyn Riley, editor, *Contemporary Literary Criticism*, Gale, Volume I, 1973, Volume III, 1974.†

* * *

BRAVERMAN, Harry 1920-

PERSONAL: Born December 9, 1920, in New York, N.Y.; son of Morris (a shoe worker) and Sarah (Wolf) Braverman; married Miriam Ruth Gutman, December 25, 1941 (separated, 1964); children: Thomas Raymond. *Education:* New School for Social Research, B.A., 1963. *Home:* 201 West 11th St., New York, N.Y. 10014. *Office:* Monthly Review Press, 62 West 14th St., New York, N.Y. 10011.

CAREER: New York Naval Shipyard, Brooklyn, N.Y., coppersmith, 1938-45; William B. Pollock Co., Youngstown, Ohio, in steel layout, 1947-50; Owen Structural Steel, Youngstown, in steel layout and fitting, 1951-53; *American Socialist*, New York, N.Y., editor, 1953-60; Grove Press, New York, editor, 1960-67, vice-president and general manager, 1963-67; Monthly Review Press, New York, director, 1967—. *Military service:* U.S. Army, 1945-47.

WRITINGS: The Future of Russia, Macmillan, 1963; *Labor and Monopoly Capital: The Degradation of Work in the Twentieth Century*, Monthly Review Press, 1975. Contributor to *Monthly Review, Nation,* and *American Socialist*.

* * *

BRAWLEY, Ernest 1937-

PERSONAL: Born October 8, 1937, in Los Angeles, Calif.; son of Ernest Calvin (a prison guard) and Helen Bee (a waitress; maiden name, Wasson) Brawley; married Clare Coletti (a writer), June 8, 1969. *Education:* Modesto Junior College, A.A., 1957; University of California, Santa Barbara, student, 1958-59; San Francisco State College (now University), B.A., 1962, M.A., 1969. *Residence:* Montparnasse, Paris, France. *Agent:* John Hawkins, Paul R. Reynolds, Inc., 12 East 41st St., New York, N.Y. 10017.

CAREER: Railroad switchman for Southern Pacific Railroad, 1956-59; janitor for Greyhound Bus Lines, Mill Valley, Calif., 1960; guard at San Quentin State Prison, 1962; activist for Catholic Action groups in Cochabamba, Bolivia, and Porto Corumba, Brazil, 1963; *Buenos Aires Herald,* Buenos Aires, Argentina, translator, 1963; Berlitz School, Paris, France, English teacher, 1964; English teacher in Shimokitazawa, Japan, 1965; truck driver for United Parcel Co., San Francisco, 1965-66; hop picker in Kent, England, 1966; bartender in Spain, 1967; shipping clerk for American Heart Association, San Francisco, 1968; University of Hawaii, Honolulu, instructor in English, 1969; teacher of world literature, 1969-70. *Military service:* U.S. Army Reserve, 1960-66, active duty, 1961.

AWARDS, HONORS: American Music Corp. award in creative writing, 1966, for *Samsara,* an unpublished book of short stories; Joseph Henry Jackson award from San Francisco Foundation, 1970, for *In the Shadow of Thy Wings,* an unpublished novel.

WRITINGS: The Rap (novel), Atheneum, 1974. Contributor of short stories and travel articles to magazines, including *Contact, Story, Oui, Mediterranean Review,* and *Lifestyle*.

WORK IN PROGRESS: The Scam, a novel; *The Dressing of the Dead,* a book of short stories.

AVOCATIONAL INTERESTS: Travel (has hitch-hiked to almost every country of the world, to every continent except Australia and Antarctica), surfing, swimming, skiing, skin diving, mountaineering, walking tours.

* * *

BRAZILL, William J., Jr. 1935-

PERSONAL: Surname rhymes with "dazzle"; born December 19, 1935, in Pittsfield, Mass.; son of William J. and Gertrude (Johnson) Brazill; married Elizabeth L. Morrissey (a teacher), June 19, 1965; children: Elizabeth, Maura. *Education:* Williams College, B.A., 1957; University of Minnesota, M.A., 1959; Yale University, A.M., 1960, Ph.D., 1966. *Home:* 935 Berkshire, Grosse Pointe Park, Mich. 48230. *Office:* Department of History, Wayne State University, Detroit, Mich. 48202.

CAREER: Amherst College, Amherst, Mass., instructor in history, 1962-64; Williams College, Williamstown, Mass., assistant professor of history, 1964-69; Michigan State University, East Lansing, associate professor of history, 1969-74, associate chairman of department, 1969-74; Wayne State University, Detroit, Mich., professor of history, 1974—, head of department, 1974—. *Member:* American Historical Association. *Awards, honors:* Grant-in-aid from American Philosophical Society, 1969.

WRITINGS: The Young Hegelians, Yale University Press, 1970. Contributor of articles and reviews to *Central European History, Dalhousie Review,* and *American Historical Review*.

WORK IN PROGRESS: A study of Austrian intellectual history, 1890-1937.

* * *

BREALEY, Richard A. 1936-

PERSONAL: Born June 9, 1936, in Barnet, England; son of Albert E. (a teacher) and Irene (a teacher; maiden name, Dolling) Brealey; married Diana Brown Kelly, February 10, 1967; children: David, Charles. *Education:* Exeter College, Oxford, B.A., 1959, M.A., 1963. *Home:* Haydens Cottage, The Pound, Cookham, Berkshire, England. *Office:* London Business School, Sussex Pl., Regents Park, London, N.W.1, England.

CAREER: Sun Life Assurance Company of Canada, Montreal, Quebec, member of investment staff, 1959-66; Keystone Custodian Funds, Boston, Mass., member of investment staff, 1966-68; London Business School, London, England, Barclay Trust Professor of Portfolio Investment, 1968—.

WRITINGS: Introduction to Risk and Return from

Common Stocks, M.I.T. Press, 1969; *Security Prices in a Competitive Market*, M.I.T. Press, 1971; (editor with J. H. Lorie) *Modern Developments in Finance*, Praeger, 1972; (editor with Connie Pyle) *A Bibliography of Finance and Investment*, M.I.T. Press, 1973. Contributor to journals in his field.

* * *

BRECHER, Charles Martin 1945-

PERSONAL: Born October 9, 1945, in New York, N.Y.; son of Bernard and Sylvia (Klausner) Brecher; married Madeline Agatstein (a teacher), June 18, 1970. *Education:* University of Florida, B.A. (with honors), 1965; City University of New York, Ph.D., 1972. *Home:* 98-05 67th Ave., Forest Hills, N.Y. 11374. *Office:* Department of Conservation of Human Resources, Columbia University, New York, N.Y. 10027.

CAREER: Department of Welfare, New York, N.Y., caseworker, 1965; U.S. Department of Labor, Washington, D.C., investigator for Wage and Hour Division, 1966; Columbia University, New York, N.Y., faculty member in Conservation of Human Resources, 1968—, adjunct lecturer in social policy, 1974; Fordham University, Lincoln Center, New York, N.Y., adjunct assistant professor of social sciences, 1972—. Adjunct lecturer at State University of New York College at Purchase, 1973; lecturer at New School for Social Research, 1973—. Consultant for Human Designs Corp., 1974.

MEMBER: American Political Science Association, American Society for Public Administration, American Academy of Political Science, American Academy of Political and Social Scientists, Policy Studies Organization, Committee on Health Politics, Community Council of Greater New York, Phi Kappa Phi, Pi Sigma Alpha.

WRITINGS: (With Eli Ginzberg and others) *Urban Health Services: The Case of New York*, Columbia University Press, 1971; *Upgrading Blue Collar and Service Workers*, Johns Hopkins Press, 1972; *The Impact of Federal Antipoverty Policies*, Praeger, 1973; (with Ginzberg and others) *New York Is Very Much Alive: A Manpower View*, McGraw, 1973; *Where Have All the Dollars Gone?: Public Expenditures for Human Resource Development in New York City, 1961-1971*, Paeger, 1974; (with David Lewin and others) *The Urban Labor Market: Information, Institutions, Linkages*, Praeger, 1974; (contributor) Ginzberg and Alice Yohalem, editors, *The University Medical Center and the Metropolis*, Josiah Macy, Jr. Foundation, 1974.

Contributor of articles and reviews to *City Almanac and Monthly Labor Review*.

* * *

BREINBURG, Petronella 1927-
(Bella Ashey)

PERSONAL: Born April 16, 1927, in Paramaribo, Suriname, South America; daughter of Charles and Emma (Telg) Van Rhemen; married Emiel Charles Breinburg (an engineer), December 12, 1945; children: Lloyd Kenneth, Aubrey Deryck. *Education:* City of London College, diploma in English, 1965; attended Avery Mill Teachers College, 1969-72, and Goldsmith College, London, 1972-74. *Politics and religion:* None. *Home:* 7 Tuam Rd., Plumstead, London SE182CX, England. *Office:* Hurstmere Secondary School for Boys, Sidcup, Kent, England.

CAREER: School teacher in Paramaribo, Suriname, 1945-61; has worked variously in a factory, as a post office clerk, nursesassistant,andteacherinLVONDON,England,1961-74; full-time writer, 1974—. Has done volunteer work for the Red Cross and Girls' Life Brigade in Suriname, South America, 1942-61; lecturer in creative writing and outdoor storyteller at various libraries in London, 1972-74; part time teacher in English and creative writing, Hurstmere Secondary School for Boys, 1974—. *Member:* Royal Society of Health. *Awards, honors:* Royal Society of Health award, 1962; Suriname Linguistic Bureau "honorary place" award, 1972, for *Legend of Surinam*; Library Association of London Kate Greenaway Medal "runner-up," 1974, for *My Brother Sean*.

WRITINGS—Children's books: *Legend of Surinam*, Panther House, 1971; *My Brother Sean*, Bodley Head, 1973; *Shawn Goes to School*, Crowell, 1973; *Doctor Shawn*, Crowell, 1974 (published in England as *Doctor Sean*, Bodley Head, 1974); *Tiger, Tinker and Me*, Macmillan, 1974; *Sean's Red Bike*, Bodley Head, in press; *What Happened at Rita's Party*, Longman, in press; *Sally-Ann*, Bodley Head, in press.

Plays: "A Streak of Gold" (for children; one-act), first produced in London, England, 1972; "Some Creation" (for older children; one-act), first produced in London, 1972; "Requiem" (adult play; one-act), first produced in London at Greenwich Youth Theatre, 1973; "Velvet Curtains" (adult play; three-act), first produced at Greenwich Youth Theatre, 1974.

Work represented in anthologies, including *Tell Me a Story*, edited by Dorothy Edwards, Metheun, 1974; (under pseudonym Bella Ashey) *Plum in Common*, edited by Dulan Barber, David Poynter, 1974. Contributor of poems, short stories, and articles, sometimes under pseudonym Bella Ashey, to British publications.

WORK IN PROGRESS: Hail Bwana, a novel for young adults; a collection of ghost stories set in Suriname; *Teaching in London*.

SIDELIGHTS: Mrs. Breinburg told *CA* that she has no politics "except to support individual 'freedom of choice' providing that freedom does not harm anyone else, i.e., the bright child has as much right as the dull one and must not be held back to suit the latter, no more than the latter should be neglected to suit the former. Writers must be free to write what *they* want to write and get it published too, i.e., a writer who is black (there is a big difference between a 'black writer' and 'a writer who is black') should not be forced to write only about racial discrimination because it is the only thing she/he can get published. Such a writer should be free to write, say, love stories, murder, the lot, without having to put across 'a racial message.'"

* * *

BREISKY, William J(ohn) 1928-

PERSONAL: Surname is pronounced *Bry*-ski; born October 27, 1928, in Pittsburgh, Pa.; son of John V. and Laura (Baer) Breisky; married Barbara Bohl, July 4, 1960; children: John, Karen, Gretchen. *Education:* Attended University of Illinois, 1946-47; Syracuse University, B.A. (cum laude), 1950. *Religion:* Presbyterian. *Home and office:* Eastleigh, Somerset 9-15, Bermuda. *Agent:* Curtis Brown Ltd., 60 East 56th St., New York, N.Y. 10022.

CAREER: Saturday Evening Post, Philadelphia, Pa., associate editor, 1953-62; Enfield Press, Enfield, Conn., editor and publisher, 1962-67; Bermuda News Bureau, Hamilton, manager, 1968-74. Has served with organizations concerned with youth, mental health, brain-injured children, and redevelopment. *Military service:* U.S. Army, 1950-52; became captain.

WRITINGS: I Think I Can (nonfiction), Doubleday, 1974. Contributor to popular magazines, including *Smithsonian, Saturday Evening Post*, and *Good Housekeeping*.

WORK IN PROGRESS: A book on the human brain for Holt.

* * *

BRENNER, Anita 1905-1974

August 13, 1905—December 1, 1974; American journalist and author. Obituaries: *New York Times*, December 3, 1974; *AB Bookman's Weekly*, December 16, 1974. (*CA*-49/52).

* * *

BRESKY, Dushan

EDUCATION: Charles University, J.U.Dr., 1948; University of Washington, Seattle, Ph.D., 1962. *Office:* Department of Romance Studies, University of Calgary, Calgary, Alberta T2N 1N4, Canada.

CAREER: University of Calgary, Calgary, Alberta, associate professor, 1968-75, professor of Romance studies, 1975—. *Member:* L'Association des Professeurs de francais des universites canadiennes. *Awards, honors:* Grants from Canada Council, and Humanities Research Council of Canada.

WRITINGS: Bez konce jsou lesy (title means "Endless Are the Forests"), Vaclac Petr (Prague), 1943; *Hory, lyze, snih* (title means "Mountains, Ski, and Snow"), Jaromir Velat (Prague), 1946; *The Art of Anatole France*, Mouton & Co., 1969; *Cathedral or Symphony: Essays on Jean-Christophe*, Herbert Lang, 1973; *Nova Flipila proti mizo muzum* (title means "In Defense of the Czech Language"), Orbis, in press. Contributor to language journals, including *French Review, Comparative Literature, French Series*, and *L'Espril Createur*.

WORK IN PROGRESS: Research on literary metier in France.

SIDELIGHTS: Bresky was a member of the Czechoslovakian national ski team from 1946 to 1948; he participated in the World Ski Championship in Alpine competition in 1946. He also held a one-man show of sculpture in Calgary in 1971.

* * *

BRESLIN, Herbert H. 1924-

PERSONAL: Born October 1, 1924, in New York, N.Y.; son of Frank (an insurance underwriter) and Rose (Chipman) Breslin; married Carol Gluck (an editor), January 28, 1954; children: Eric, Andrea. *Education:* Columbia University, M.A., 1951. *Home:* 863 Park Ave., New York, N.Y., 10021. *Agent:* Helen Merrill, 337 West 22nd St., New York, N.Y. 10011. *Office:* 119 West 57th St., New York, N.Y. 10019.

CAREER: National Association of Manufacturers, New York, N.Y., writer, 1953-55; Chrysler Corporation, Detroit, Mich., writer, 1955-57; manager of own public relations, promotion, and concert management agency in New York, N.Y,, 1959—.

WRITINGS: (Editor) *The Tenors*, Macmillan, 1974.

BREWER, William C. 1897(?)-1974

1897(?)—December 29, 1974; American army officer and author on international affairs. Obituaries: *Washington Post*, December 31, 1974.

* * *

BREWINGTON, Marion Vernon 1902-1974

June 23, 1902—December 8, 1974; American museum curator and author of books on maritime history. Obituaries: *New York Times*, December 10, 1974; *AB Bookman's Weekly*, January 13, 1975. (*CA*-5/6).

* * *

BRICKER, Victoria Reifler 1940-

PERSONAL: Born June 15, 1940, in Hong Kong; daughter of Erwin (a professor) and Henrietta (a librarian; maiden name, Brown) Reifler; married Harvey M. Bricker (a professor of anthropology), December 27, 1964. *Education:* Stanford University, A.B., 1962; Harvard University, A.M., 1963, Ph.D., 1968. *Office:* Department of Anthropology, Tulane University, New Orleans, La. 70118.

CAREER: Tulane University, New Orleans, La., visiting lecturer, 1969-70, assistant professor, 1970-73, associate professor of anthropology, 1973—. Has made field expeditions to Zinacantan, Chiapas, Mexico, 1963-1964 (summers), 1965-66, 1968-69; Chamula, Chiapas, Mexico, 1968-69; Yucatan, Mexico, summers, 1971, 1972. *Member:* American Anthropological Association, American Ethnological Society, Royal Anthropological Institute (fellow).

WRITINGS: (Contributor) Evon Z. Vogt, editor, *Los Zinacantecos: Un Pueblo Tzotzil de los Altos de Chiapas* (title means "The Zinacantecos: A Tzotzil Town in the Highlands of Chiapas"), Instituto Nacional Indigenista, 1966; *Ritual Humor in Highland Chiapas*, University of Texas Press, 1973; (contributor), Muro S. Edmonson, editor, *Meaning in Mayan Languages*, Mouton & Co., 1973; (contributor) Richard Bauman and Joel Sherzer, editors, *Explorations in the Ethnography of Speaking*, Cambridge University Press, 1974; (contributor) Barbara Kirshenblatt Gimblett, editor, *Speech Play on Display*, University of Pennsylvania Press, in press. Contributor to papers; contributor of articles and book reviews to journals in her field. Book review editor of *American Anthropologist*, 1971-73; editor of *American Ethnologist*, 1973—.

WORK IN PROGRESS: The Indian Christ, The Indian King; Indian Correspondence from the Caste War of Yucatan (1847-1901).

* * *

BRINEY, Robert E(dward) 1933-

PERSONAL: Born December 2, 1933, in Benton Harbor, Mich.; son of Robert Edward (an electrician) and Catherine (Duncan) Briney. *Education:* Northwestern University, A.B., 1955; Massachusetts Institute of Technology, Ph.D., 1961. *Residence:* Salem, Mass. *Office:* Department of Mathematics, Salem State College, Salem, Mass. 01970.

CAREER: Massachusetts Institute of Technology, Cambridge, instructor in mathematics, 1961-62; Purdue University, Lafayette, Ind., assistant professor of mathematics, 1962-68; Salem State College, Salem, Mass., associate professor, 1968-70, professor of mathematics, 1970—, chairman of department, 1970—. *Member:* American Mathematical Society, Mathematical Association of America, Mystery Writers of America.

WRITINGS: (Editor and contributor) *Shanadu* (fiction), SSR Publications, 1953; (editor with Cay Van Ash and Elizabeth Sax Rohmer, and contributor) *Master of Villainy: A Biography of Sax Rohmer,* Bowling Green University Popular Press, 1972; (with Edward Wood) *SF Bibliographies,* Advent, 1973, revised edition, in press; (editor with F. M. Nevins, Jr.) Anthony Boucher, *Multiplying Villainies,* Bouchercon IV, 1973; (author of introduction) Sax Rohmer, *The Wrath of Fu Manchu and Other Stories,* Tom Stacey, 1973.

Work is anthologized in *The Mystery Writer's Art,* edited by Nevins, Bowling Green State University, 1971; *The Conan Grimoire,* edited by L. Sprague deCamp and George Scithers, Mirage Press, 1972. Author of "SF in Review," a column in *Views and Reviews,* 1972-74. Contributor of articles and reviews to *American Book Collector, Journal of Popular Culture, Views and Reviews, Armchair Detective,* and *Mystery Reader's Newsletter.* Editor of *Rohmer Review,* 1970—.

AVOCATIONAL INTERESTS: Linguistics, philately, music, ballet, genre fiction, popular culture.

* * *

BRINITZER, Carl 1907-1974
(Usikota)

January 30, 1907—October, 1974; German-born British author, translator, and broadcaster. Obituaries: *Washington Post,* October 31, 1974. (*CA*-7/8).

* * *

BRINKMAN, George L(oris) 1942-

PERSONAL: Born October 3, 1942, in Minneapolis, Minn.; son of Loris B. (an engineer) and Aline (a school teacher; maiden name, Slyfield) Brinkman; married Elizabeth Neal, January 30, 1965; children: Lori, Diane, Deborah. *Education:* Washington State University, B.S., 1964, Ex.M., 1965; Michigan State University, Ph.D., 1969. *Home:* 14 Hickory St., Guelph, Ontario N1G 241, Canada. *Office:* School of Agricultural Economics and Extension Education, University of Guelph, Guelph, Ontario N1G 2W1, Canada.

CAREER: Kansas State University, Manhattan, assistant professor of agricultural economics, 1969-73; University of Guelph, Guelph, Ontario, associate professor of rural development and agricultural policy, 1973—.

WRITINGS: (Editor and contributor) *The Development of Rural America,* University Press of Kansas, 1974. Contributor to *Journal of the Community Development Society* and *American Journal of Agricultural Economics.*

WORK IN PROGRESS: With Luther Tweeten, *Micropolitan Development,* completion expected in 1975; research on rural industrialization, on employment, on rural settlement patterns, and on agricultural and rural development policy.

SIDELIGHTS: Brinkman was an exchange student in Germany from 1960-61. He did research in agricultural planning and development in Nigeria in 1968 and in Mali and Senegal in 1970.

* * *

BRISSENDEN, Paul F(rederick) 1885-1974

September 21, 1885—November 28, 1974; American economist, labor mediator, and author. Obituaries: *New York Times,* December 1, 1974. (*CA*-17/18).

BROCK, D(ewey) Heyward 1941-

PERSONAL: Born June 2, 1941, in Greenville, S.C.; son of Dewey Calhoun (a carpenter) and Sarah Edith (Moose) Brock; married Patricia Lee Farmer (an accountant), August 25, 1963; children: Sarah Michelle, Paul Heyward, David Patrick. *Education:* Newberry College, A.B., 1963; University of Kansas, M.A., 1965, Ph.D., 1969. *Politics:* Democrat. *Religion:* Lutheran. *Home:* 10 Anita Dr., Yorkshire, Newark, Del. 19713. *Office:* Department of English, University of Delaware, Newark, Del. 19711.

CAREER: University of Kansas, Lawrence, assistant instructor in English, 1963-68; University of Delaware, Newark, instructor, 1968, assistant professor of English, 1969—, assistant to dean of College of Arts and Science, 1969. *Member:* Modern Language Association of America, Renaissance Society of America, Blue Key. *Awards, honors:* Fellow of Institute for Humanistic Computation, 1970; research grant from American Council of Learned Societies and National Science Foundation, 1971.

WRITINGS: (With James M. Welsh) *Ben Jonson: A Quadricentennial Bibliography, 1947-1972,* Scarecrow, 1974; *A Facsimile Edition of the First Folio of Ben Jonson,* Scolar Press, in press; *A Ben Jonson Campanion: 1573(?)-1973,* Indiana University Press, in press. Contributor to literature journals, including *Comparative Drama, English Miscellany,* and *Renascence.*

WORK IN PROGRESS: Poet and Society: A Critical Study of Ben Jonson's Concept of Society in the Light of Classical and Renaissance Ideals; Percy MacKaye: The Poet of Democracy, completion expected in 1978.

SIDELIGHTS: Brock writes: "Like many young boys who grew up in America, I wanted to be a professional baseball player, but when I got to high school I realized I couldn't be outstanding with both the bat and the books, so I chose to concentrate on the books although I have never abandoned my interest in sports. Disenchanted with high school after my junior year, I entered college (I still don't have a high school diploma) to major in English with the primary intention of preparing for the ministry. Inspired by several of my college professors, I found myself more attracted to the classroom than the pulpit."

Brock states that "if modern man is to survive and prosper, he must be guided by the humanistic principles which have evolved over the centuries and which have inspired the most enlightened societies and cultures in the civilized world."

* * *

BRODE, Wallace R. 1900(?)-1974

1900(?)—August 10, 1974; American chemist, educator, government official, and author. Obituaries: *New York Times,* August 13, 1974; *Washington Post,* August 14, 1974.

* * *

BRODWIN, Leonora Leet 1929-

PERSONAL: Born March 24, 1929, in New York, N.Y.; daughter of Cecil Robert (an engineer) and Tania (Neznir) Leet; married Stanley Brodwin (a professor of English), July 31, 1960; children: Tamar Elizabeth, Susannah Rachel. *Education:* University of Michigan, B.A. (with distinction), 1950; Yale University, M.A., 1952, Ph.D., 1960. *Home:* 110 Irving Ave., Freeport, N.Y. 11520. *Office:* Department of English, St. John's University, Jamaica, N.Y. 11439.

CAREER: Hofstra University, Hempstead, N.Y., instructor in English, 1957-60; Queens College of the City University of New York, New York, N.Y., instructor in English, 1960-63; St. John's University, Jamaica, N.Y., assistant professor, 1965-66, associate professor, 1966-71, professor of English, 1971—. *Member:* Modern Language Association of America, Milton Society of America.

WRITINGS: Elizabethan Love Tragedy: 1587-1625, New York University Press, 1971; (contributor) James D. Simmonds, editor, *Milton Studies*, University of Pittsburgh Press, Volume VI, 1974, Volume VII, in press. Contributor to *Journal of English Literary History, Modern Philology, Studies in Philology, Studies in English Literature*, and *Journal of English and Germanic Philology*.

WORK IN PROGRESS: A book on Milton's *Paradise Lost*.

* * *

BRODY, Saul Nathaniel 1938-

PERSONAL: Born March 6, 1938, in Bronx, N.Y.; son of Irving Bernard and Ethel (Spiegel) Brody; married Frohma-Esther Besner (a biologist), January 24, 1960; children: Audrey Rachel, Ruth Elizabeth. *Education:* Columbia University, A.B., 1959, M.A., 1960, Ph.D., 1968. *Home:* 20 Glenwood Ave., Demarest, N.J. 07627. *Office:* Department of English, City College of the City University of New York, New York, N.Y. 10031.

CAREER: City University of New York, New York, N.Y., lecturer in English at Hunter College, 1962-65, lecturer at City College, 1961-62, 1965-68, instructor, 1968, assistant professor, 1968-73, associate professor of English, 1974—. Researcher and teacher at University of Paris-Vincennes, 1974-75. *Member:* International Arthurian Society, Modern Language Association of America, Mediaeval Academy of America.

WRITINGS: The Disease of the Soul: Leprosy in Medieval Literature, Cornell University Press, 1974.

WORK IN PROGRESS: Research on Chaucer, medieval medicine, and melodrama; editor of a series of booklets on Chaucer, for Harper.

* * *

BROMELL, Henry 1947-

PERSONAL: Born September 19, 1947, in New York, N.Y.; son of W. B. and Mary M. (MacGaffin) Bromell. *Education:* Amherst College, B.A., 1970. *Agent:* Robert S. Nathan, 110 West 80th St., New York, N.Y. 10024.

CAREER: Writer, Lecturer at Iowa Writer's Workshop, 1975. *Member:* Phi Beta Kappa. *Awards, honors:* Houghton Mifflin Literary Fellowship Award, 1974, for *The Slightest Distance*.

WRITINGS: The Slightest Distance (short stories), Houghton, 1974. Contributor of short stories to *New Yorker* and *Atlantic Monthly*.

* * *

BRONOWSKI, Jacob 1908-1974

January 18, 1908—August 22, 1974; Polish-born British scientist and author. Obituaries: *New York Times*, August 23, 1974; *Washington Post*, August 23, 1974; *Time*, September 2, 1974; *Newsweek*, September 2, 1974; *Publishers Weekly*, September 2, 1974; *Current Biography*, October, 1974. (*CA*-2).

BROOKS, Charles E(dward) 1921-

PERSONAL: Born February 28, 1921, in Venice, Ill.; son of John E. (a gunsmith) and Martha (Clements) Brooks; married Maxine Webb, October, 1942 (divorced, 1944); married Grace Swanson, July 17, 1946. *Education:* Attended public schools in Milan, Mo. *Politics:* Independent. *Religion:* Independent. *Home:* Lazy Acres, West Yellowstone, Mont. 59758.

CAREER: U.S. Army Air Forces, 1942-48; U.S. Air Force, 1948-64, counter-intelligence agent, 1948-52, squadron commander and atomic defense officer, 1955-58, retiring as major. *Member:* Pi Phi Epsilon. *Awards, honors*—Military: Air Medal with six oak-leaf clusters, Distinguished Flying Cross, European Theater of Operations medal with six battle stars, Presidential Unit Citation with two oak-leaf clusters.

WRITINGS: Larger Trout for the Western Fly Fisherman, A. S. Barnes, 1970; *The Trout and the Stream,* Crown, 1974. Contributor to *Tiger Talk*.

WORK IN PROGRESS: Researching and writing a book on nymph fishing tentatively titled *Fishing the Nymph for Larger Trout,* completion expected in 1975.

* * *

BROPHY, Robert J(oseph) 1928-

PERSONAL: Born February 6, 1928, in San Francisco, Calif.; son of John Emmet (a civil engineer) and Marie Gertrude (Vizzard) Brophy; married Mary Louise Burg, September 13, 1968; children: Charise Marie (deceased), Christopher Louis, Rachel Patrice, Matthew Emmet. *Education:* Gonzaga University, B.A., 1952, Ph.L., 1953; Loyola University, Los Angeles, Calif., M.A. (literature), 1956; University of Santa Clara, M.A. (theology), 1960; University of North Carolina, Ph.D., 1966. *Politics:* Democrat. *Home:* 4182 Loma St., Irvine, Calif. 92705. *Office:* Department of English, California State University, Long Beach, Calif. 90840.

CAREER: Teacher of mathematics and English at Roman Catholic high school in San Francisco, Calif., 1953-55; Roman Catholic priest of the Jesuit order, 1959-68; California State University, Long Beach, assistant professor, 1968-72, associate professor of English, 1972—. Hospital and prison chaplain in Grafton, Ohio, 1960-61; assistant Newman chaplain at University of North Carolina, 1961-65; instructor at University of San Francisco, 1965-66, assistant professor of English, 1966-68. Member of board of directors of Encounter Theater Group, 1967-68; coordinator and host of Jeffers Summer Poetry Festival, 1969-71; curator of Robinson Jeffers Special Collection at Gleeson Library, 1966-68.

MEMBER: Conference on Christianity and Literature, Western Literature Association. *Awards, honors:* State College Foundation fellowships, summers, 1972, 1974.

WRITINGS: Robinson Jeffers: A Checklist, privately printed, 1967; *Robinson Jeffers: Myth, Ritual, and Symbol in His Narrative Poems*, Press of Case Western Reserve University, 1973. Contributor of more than forty articles and reviews to periodicals, including *Christianity and Literature, Robinson Jeffers Newsletter, Western American Literature, American Literature, American Transcendental Quarterly*, and *Clinical Toxology*. Editor of *Robinson Jeffers Newsletter*, 1968—; member of bibliography staff of *Western American Literature*, 1972—.

WORK IN PROGRESS: Robinson Jeffers: An Evaluative

Critical Bibliography, for American Library Association; *Robinson Jeffers: Man and Poet of the West*, a pamphlet, for Boise; "Strategies of Salvation: Narratives of Robinson Jeffers," a chapter to be included in a book on western American literature, edited by John S. Bullen and Gerald Haslam, publication by Everett-Edwards expected in 1976.

SIDELIGHTS: Brophy tape recorded "On Robinson Jeffers" for Big Sur Recordings, in 1969, and "Robinson Jeffers," for Cassette Curriculum, Everett-Edwards, 1975. He writes: "I have a sort of messianic attitude toward literature: to be able to interpret poetry is a kind of human salvation. I teach to sensitize my students to life, to human suffering, to religious questions. I write from a parallel involvemet: to pull my reader into the 'holy of holies,' the human heart, to have him break down his 'doors of perception' to allow divinity to rush in. Jeffers has been my special focus because his vision is cosmic, his time is astronomic history, his context is religious, his questions are all ultimate ones: is there a god and if so what is his nature? is there life after death? how should men live? I am deeply interested in the primitive insight, the aboriginal sense of a sacramental universe, the universal need for religious ritual."

* * *

BROWDER, Walter Everett 1939-

PERSONAL: Born September 6, 1939, in Kansas City, Mo.; son of Montford Johnson (a carpenter) and Ruth Marie (Hipps) Browder; married Sue Ellen Hurdle (a writer), June 17, 1967; children: Dustin Scott, Erin Kimberly. *Education:* University of Missouri, A.B., 1969. *Address:* R.F.D. #1, Storrs, Conn. 06268. *Agent:* Julian Bach Literary Agency, 3 East 48th St., New York, N.Y. 10017.

CAREER: Private school teacher of mathematics and science in Pomona, Calif., 1969-70, and in Brooklyn, N.Y., fall, 1970. *Military service:* U.S. Navy, 1958-62; became petty officer second class.

WRITINGS: The Sand Castle (novel), Dial, 1973.

WORK IN PROGRESS: A suspense novel about a lost nuclear weapon, *The Accident*; a volume of poetry.

* * *

BROWN, Elizabeth Louise 1924-

PERSONAL: Born October 12, 1924, in Grand Rapids, Mich.; daughter of Charles William and M. Fern (Whitney) Brown. *Education:* Grand Rapids Junior College, A.A., 1948; Baptist Bible Institute, graduate, 1960. *Politics:* Republican. *Religion:* Baptist. *Home:* 0-9161 Kenowa S.W., Grand Rapids, Mich. 49504. *Office:* 1415 Lake Dr. S.E., Grand Rapids, Mich. 49506.

CAREER: Michigan Crippled Children Commission, Grand Rapids, clerk-typist, 1949-56; Zondervan Publishing House, Grand Rapids, Mich., executive secretary, 1960-67; Kregel Publications, Grand Rapids, Mich., executive secretary, 1967-69; Zondervan Publishing House, Grand Rapids, Mich., executive secretary, 1969—. *Member:* National Audubon Society.

WRITINGS: The Message of the Bells (a Christmas program), Moody, 1960; *The Candle of the Wicked* (novel), Zondervan, 1972.

WORK IN PROGRESS: A second suspense novel; a nonfiction work on national political attitudes.

BROWN, Emily Clara 1911-

PERSONAL: Born January 1, 1911, in the Philippines; daughter of Orville Graham (a colonel in the Medical Corps of the U.S. Army) and Clara (Topping) Brown. *Education:* Student at Wayne State University, 1926-27, and Oberlin College, 1927-28; Ohio State University, A.B., 1930; Arizona State University, M.A.Ed., 1955; University of Arizona, Ph.D., 1967. *Politics:* Democrat. *Religion:* Episcopalian. *Home:* 215 Tremont, Cedar Falls, Iowa 50613. *Office:* Department of History, University of Northern Iowa, Cedar Falls, Iowa 50613.

CAREER: Panama American, Panama City, Panama, general assignment reporter, 1934-36; *Arizona Daily Star*, Tucson, reporter, 1937-42, 1946; United Press International, staff correspondent from Southeast Asia, 1947-50; American Institute of International Management, Phoenix, Ariz., assistant professor of Asian studies and director of public relations, 1950-60; University of Arizona, Tucson, instructor in history, 1960-66; University of Northern Iowa, Cedar Falls, associate professor, 1966-69, professor of history, 1969—. Fulbright professor in India, 1961-62; coordinator of travel seminar in India, 1960. *Military service:* U.S. Army, Women's Army Corps, 1942-46. U.S. Army Reserve, 1945-65; became major. *Member:* Association for Asian Studies, Phi Alpha Theta, Delta Zeta.

WRITINGS: Har Dayal: Hindu Revolutionary and Rationalist, University of Arizona Press, 1975.

* * *

BROWN, Gwilym Slater 1928-1974

February 17, 1928—August 12, 1974; American author and magazine editor. Obituaries: *New York Times*, August 13, 1974. (*CA*-11/12).

* * *

BROWN, Joseph E(dward) 1929-

PERSONAL: Born December 14, 1929, in San Francisco, Calif.; son of LeRoy D. and Ora E. (Ackley) Brown; married Christa Brigitte, August 12, 1967; children: Joseph, Mark, Teri, Erik. *Education:* Attended University of Wisconsin, 1952, and University of Hawaii, 1953. *Residence:* San Diego, Calif.

CAREER: San Diego Union, San Diego, Calif., reporter, 1959-69; *Oceans*, San Diego, Calif., editor, 1969-71; free-lance writer, 1971—. *Military service:* U.S. Navy, 1948-52. *Member:* Society of Magazine Writers, Authors Guild, Sigma Delta Chi.

WRITINGS: The Golden Sea (nonfiction), Playboy Press, 1974; *Wonders of a Kelp Forest* (juvenile), Dodd, 1974; *Farming the Sea* (juvenile), Dodd, in press.

WORK IN PROGRESS: Ghost-writing a book; research for books on Micronesia, on brown pelicans, and on Columbus' colony at Haiti.

AVOCATIONAL INTERESTS: Oceanography, marine science, marine resources.

* * *

BROWN, Marvin L., Jr. 1920-

PERSONAL: Born September 1, 1920, in Philadelphia, Pa.; son of Marvin L. and Helen (DePue) Brown; married Elizabeth Dodge, July 16, 1943; children: Elizabeth F. (Mrs. Walter R. Tucker), Helen D. *Education:* Haverford College, A.B., 1943; University of Pennsylvania, A.M.,

1947, Ph.D., 1951. *Religion:* Episcopalian. *Address:* P.O. Box 607, Garner, N.C. 27529. *Office:* Department of History, North Carolina State University, Raleigh, N.C. 27607.

CAREER: Haverford College, Haverford, Pa., instructor in history, 1949; North Carolina State University, Raleigh, instructor, 1949-51, assistant professor, 1951-57, associate professor, 1957-59, professor of history, 1959—. Fulbright research professor at University of Vienna, 1955-56; visiting professor at Duke University, 1961, 1968. *Military service:* U.S. Marine Corps, 1942-46. U.S. Marine Corps Reserve, 1942-63; retired as major. *Member:* American Historical Association, Society for French Historical Studies.

WRITINGS: *American Independence through Prussian Eyes,* Duke University Press, 1959; *French Society and Culture Since the Old Regime,* Holt, 1964; *The Baroness von Riedesel and the American Revolution,* University of North Carolina Press, 1965; *The Comte de Chambord,* Duke University Press, 1967; *Diplomacy in an Age of Nationalism,* Nijhoff, 1972; *Heinrich von Haymerle,* University of South Carolina, 1973; *Major Themes in Modern History,* three volumes, Moore Publishing, 1974-75. Editor of *French Historical Studies,* 1958-63.

WORK IN PROGRESS: A biography of Louis Veuillot.

* * *

BROWN, Norman D(onald) 1935-

PERSONAL: Born June 28, 1935, in Pittsburgh, Pa.; son of Donald M. (an insurance executive) and Regina (a teacher; maiden name, Koehler) Brown; married Betty Aldrich, April 2, 1966; children: David Lawrence, Tracy Lynn. *Education:* Indiana University, B.A., 1957; University of North Carolina, M.A., 1959, Ph.D., 1963. *Politics:* Democrat (Liberal). *Religion:* Methodist. *Home:* 2607 Barton Skyway, Austin, Tex. 78704. *Office:* Department of History, University of Texas, Austin, Tex. 78712.

CAREER: University of Texas, Austin, instructor, 1962-65, assistant professor, 1965-69, associate professor of history, 1969—. *Member:* Organization of American Historians, Southern Historical Association, Texas State Historical Association, Red River Valley Historical Association, Phi Beta Kappa, Phi Kappa Phi, Phi Alpha Theta.

WRITINGS: *Daniel Webster and the Politics of Availability*, University of Georgia Press, 1969; *Edward Stanly: Whiggery's Tarheel "Conqueror,"* University of Alabama Press, 1974. Contributor of articles and book reviews to historical journals.

WORK IN PROGRESS: *Hood, Bonnet, and Little Brown Jug: Texas Politics, 1921-1933.*

AVOCATIONAL INTERESTS: Collecting books on Southern politics and literature.

* * *

BROWN, Parker B(oyd) 1928-

PERSONAL: Born June 5, 1928, in Shaker Heights, Ohio; son of Edson Jacob (a surgeon) and Lillian (Boyd) Brown; married Rosalie May Bovey, August 30, 1952; children: Karen Susan. *Education:* Heidelberg College, A.B., 1950; Colgate Rochester Divinity School, M.Div., 1953; graduate study at University of Chicago, 1958, Union Theological Seminary, New York, N.Y., 1958-59, Upsala College, 1959-62, Institute for Advanced Pastoral Studies, 1967, and Center for the Ministry, 1971; Andover Newton Theological School, certificate, 1966; Princeton Theological Seminary, M.R.E., 1971. *Residence:* New Carrollton, Md. 20784. *Office:* Protestant Chaplain's Activities, St. Elizabeth's Hospital, Washington, D.C. 20013.

CAREER: Ordained minister of the American Baptist Church, 1953; minister in Pittsburgh, Pa., 1953-57, East Orange, N.J., 1957-66, and Margate, N.J., 1966-73; St. Elizabeth's Hospital, Washington, D.C., Protestant chaplain, 1973—. *Member:* American Baptist Ministers Council, Academy of Parish Clergy. *Awards, honors:* D.D., Heidelberg College, 1969.

WRITINGS: *He Came from Galilee*, Hawthorn, 1974. Contributor of articles, reviews, and devotional selections to religious denominational periodicals.

AVOCATIONAL INTERESTS: Jogging, model ship building, history and political biography, tandem kite-flying.

* * *

BROWN, Peter Lancaster 1927-

PERSONAL: Born April 13, 1927, in Leeds, England; married Johanne Nyreroed (a teacher), August 15, 1953.

CAREER: Has worked as a civil engineer, surveyor, construction engineer, astronomer, and mining engineer. *Military service:* Royal Air Force, navigator. British Army Intelligence. *Member:* International Astronomical Union, Royal Astronomical Society, Royal Geographical Society, Society of Authors, British Science Writers.

WRITINGS: *Twelve Came Back*, R. Hale, 1957; *Call of the Outback*, R. Hale, 1970; *What Star Is That?*, Viking, 1971; *Astronomy in Colour*, Macmillan, 1972; *Coast of Coral and Pearl*, R. Hale, 1972; (with C. F. Hickling) *The Seas and Oceans in Colour*, Blandford, 1973, Macmillan, 1974; *Comets, Meteorites, and Men*, R. Hale, 1973, Taplinger, 1974; *Australia's Coast of Coral and Pearl*, Rigby (Adelaide), 1974; *Star and Planet Spotting*, Blandford, 1974; *The Earth as a Planet in Colour*, Macmillan, 1975.

WORK IN PROGRESS: *Megalithic Astronomy*, a popular-level astro-archaeology book; *Travellers in the Outback*, an Australian travel history *Fjord of Silent Men*, a novel set in Norway.

SIDELIGHTS: Brown was a member of the Australian expedition to Heard Island in the Antarctic, 1952-53. He has lived as a gold prospector in Australia, and has been a member of an expedition to Siberia and a whaling expedition. He now resides in England and Norway.

* * *

BROWN, Rex V(andesteene) 1933-

PERSONAL: Born September 25, 1933, in London, England; son of Leonard A. (a journalist) and Diane M. Brown; married Dalia Levy (an interior designer), November 5, 1965; children: Karen, Leora, Tamara. *Education:* Queens' College, Cambridge, B.A., 1957, M.A., 1960; London School of Economics and Political Science, University of London, graduate study, 1957-58; Institute of Statisticians, A.I.S., 1964; Harvard University, D.B.A., 1968. *Religion:* Jewish. *Residence:* Reston, Va. *Office:* Decisions and Designs, Inc., 7900 Westpark Dr., McLean, Va. 22101.

CAREER: Wallace Atwood Co., London, England, market researcher, 1958-59; Metra International (consultants),

London, England, head of business research section, 1959-64; Harvard University, Graduate School of Business Administration, Boston, Mass., lecturer in managerial economics and marketing, 1964-68; University of Michigan, Ann Arbor, associate professor of business administration, 1969-73; Decisions and Designs, Inc. (consultants and researchers), McLean, Va., senior analyst, 1973—. Visiting scholar at Cambridge University, 1962, 1972; principal of Management Analysis Center, 1969-73. *Military service:* Royal Navy, Russian coder, 1952-54.

MEMBER: Royal Statistical Society (fellow), Institute of Statisticians (fellow), Institute of Management Science. *Awards, honors:* C. Oswald George prize in applied statistics from British Institute of Statisticians, 1967; Ford Foundation grant to Cambridge University, summer, 1972; Social Science Research Council senior fellowship, 1973.

WRITINGS: (Contributor) Alex Inkeles and Kent Geiger, editors, *Soviet Society,* Houghton, 1961; (with R. D. Buzzell and D. F. Cox) *Marketing Research and Information Systems,* McGraw, 1969; *Research and the Credibility of Estimates,* Graduate School of Business Administration, Harvard University, 1969; (contributor) Thomas Schriber and Laurence Madeo, editors, *Fortran Applications in Business Administration,* Volume I, Graduate School of Business Administration, University of Michigan, 1970; (with A. S. Kahr and C. R. Peterson) *Decision Analysis for the Manager,* Holt, 1974; (with Kahr and Peterson) *Decision Analysis: An Overview,* Holt, 1974.

Author of technical reports. Contributor of about twenty articles to professional journals, including *Harvard Business Review, Journal of Marketing, Journal of Marketing Research, Journal of Management Studies,* and *Operational Research Quarterly.*

WORK IN PROGRESS: Handbook of Decision Analysis, with C. R. Peterson and others, for Defense Documentation Center; research on technology of decision analysis as applied to business and government decisions.

* * *

BROWN, Richard D(avid) 1939-

PERSONAL: Born October 31, 1939, in New York, N.Y.; son of Alvyn A. and Dorothy (a teacher in special education; maiden name, Kruskal) Brown; married Irene Quenzler (a teacher of history), June 10, 1962; children: Josiah Henry, Nicholas Alvyn. *Education:* Oberlin College, B.A., 1961; Harvard University, M.A., 1962, Ph.D., 1966. *Office:* Department of History, University of Connecticut, Storrs, Conn. 06268.

CAREER: University of Toulouse, Toulouse, France, Fulbright fellow in history, 1965-66; Oberlin College, Oberlin, Ohio, assistant professor of history, 1966-71; University of Connecticut, Storrs, associate professor of history, 1971—, chairman of department, 1974—. Research fellow, Charles Warren Center for Studies in American History, Harvard University, 1970-71. Clerk, Early Massachusetts Records, Inc.

MEMBER: Organization of American Historians, American Historical Association, American Association of University Professors, Essex Institute, Association for the Study of Connecticut History (founding member). *Awards, honors:* Woodrow Wilson dissertation fellow, 1961-62; Social Science Research Council faculty fellow, 1970-71; National Endowment for the Humanities grant as principal investigator for early Massachusetts records, 1974-75.

WRITINGS: Urbanization in Springfield, Massachusetts, 1790-1830, Connecticut Valley Historical Museum, 1962; *Slavery in American Society,* Heath, 1969; *Revolutionary Politics in Massachusetts: The Boston Committee of Correspondence and the Towns, 1772-1774,* Harvard University Press, 1970. Contributor to *New England Quarterly, Journal of American History, Journal of Interdisciplinary History, William and Mary Quarterly,* and other journals.

* * *

BROWN, Sheldon S. 1937-

PERSONAL: Born December 12, 1937, in Sioux City, Iowa; son of Jacob M. (a rabbi) and Tillie (Silverstein) Brown. *Education:* Wayne State University, B.A., 1959. *Religion:* Jewish. *Home and office:* 24660 Gardner, Oak Park, Mich. 48237.

CAREER: Free-lance writer and photographer, preparing illustrated articles for national publications, 1960—. *Member:* Authors League of America, Associated Business Writers of America, National Trust for Historic Preservation.

WRITINGS: Remade in America: The Grand Tour of Europe and Asia within the U.S.A., Old Time Bottle Publishing Co., 1972.

WORK IN PROGRESS: A legal guide to treasure hunting, completion expected in 1975; further writing and photography for magazines.

* * *

BRUBAKER, Dale L(ee) 1937-

PERSONAL: Born July 16, 1937, in Michigan; son of Herbert C. (a clergyman) and Helen (a teacher; maiden name, Miller) Brubaker; married Barbara S. Stewart, June 11, 1974; children: John, Michael, Carol. *Education:* Albion College, B.A., 1959; Michigan State University, M.A., 1960, Ph.D., 1965. *Religion:* Methodist. *Home:* 4 Covent Garden Ct., Greensboro, N.C. 27412. *Office:* 103 Curry, University of North Carolina–Greensboro, Greensboro, N.C. 27412.

CAREER: University of California, Santa Barbara, assistant professor of education, 1965-69; University of Wisconsin, Milwaukee, associate professor of education, 1969-71; University of North Carolina, Greensboro, professor of education, 1971—.

WRITINGS: Alternative Directions for the Social Studies, International Textbook Co., 1967; *The Teacher as a Decision-Maker,* W. C. Brown, 1970; (with R. Murray Thomas) *Decisions in Teaching Elementary Social Studies,* Wadsworth, 1971; (with Thomas) *Curriculum Patterns in Elementary Social Studies,* Wadsworth, 1971; (with Roland H. Nelson) *Creative Survival in Educational Bureaucracies,* McCutchan, 1974.

* * *

BRUCE, Dickson D., Jr. 1946-

PERSONAL: Born April 11, 1946, in Dallas, Tex.; son of Dickson D. (in insurance business) and Helen (Woodcock) Bruce; married Mary M. Watson, September 28, 1967; children: Emily Sarah. *Education:* Texas Technological College (now Texas Tech University), student, 1964-65; University of Texas, B.A. (with honors), 1967; University of Pennsylvania, M.A., 1968, Ph.D., 1971. *Residence:* Tustin, Calif. *Office:* Program in Comparative Culture, University of California, Irvine, Calif. 92664.

CAREER: University of California, Irvine, assistant professor of comparative culture, 1971—. *Member:* American Anthropological Association, American Folklore Society, Organization of American Historians, American Association of University Professors, Southern Anthropological Society, Southern Historical Association. *Awards, honors:* James Mooney Award from Southern Anthropological Society, 1973, for *And They All Sang Hallelujah.*

WRITINGS: And They All Sang Hallelujah: Plain-Folk Camp-Meeting Religion, 1800-1845, University of Tennessee Press, 1974. Contributor to *Phylon* and *American Quarterly.*

WORK IN PROGRESS: Research on social and recreational life in the ante-bellum American South, and on antebellum social values as related to politics and social life.

* * *

BRUCE, Robert V(ance) 1923-

PERSONAL: Born December 19, 1923, in Malden, Mass.; son of Robert G. (an auto mechanic) and Bernice (a pianist; maiden name, May) Bruce. *Education:* University of New Hampshire, B.S., 1945; Boston University, A.M., 1947, Ph.D., 1953. *Politics:* Democrat. *Religion:* None. *Home:* 482 Franklin St., Reading, Mass. 01867. *Office:* Department of History, Boston University, 226 Bay State Rd., Boston, Mass. 02215.

CAREER: University of Bridgeport, Bridgeport, Conn., instructor in history, 1947-48; Lawrence Academy, Groton, Mass., history master, 1948-51; Boston University, Boston, Mass., instructor, 1955-58, assistant professor, 1958-60, associate professor, 1960-66, professor of history, 1966—. President of Lincoln Group of Boston, 1969-74. *Military service:* U.S. Army, combat engineers, 1943-46. *Member:* Society for the History of Technology (member of advisory council, 1974—), Society of American Historians (fellow), American Association for the Advancement of Science, American Historical Association, Organization of American Historians (life member). *Awards, honors:* Guggenheim fellowship, 1956; Huntington fellowship, 1966; National Book Award finalist, 1974, for *Bell: Alexander Graham Bell and the Conquest of Solitude.*

WRITINGS: Lincoln and the Tools of War, Bobbs-Merrill, 1956; *1877: Year of Violence*, Bobbs-Merrill, 1959; *Bell: Alexander Graham Bell and the Conquest of Solitude*, Little, Brown, 1973.

WORK IN PROGRESS: The Scientific Enterprise in America: 1846-1876, completion expected in 1975.

* * *

BRUCH, Hilde

PERSONAL: Born in Germany; came to United States in 1934, naturalized in 1940; daughter of Hirsch and Adele (Rath) Bruch. *Education:* University of Freiburg, M.D., 1929; psychiatric training at Johns Hopkins University, 1941-43; psychoanalytic training at Washington Baltimore Institute, 1941-45. *Office:* Baylor College of Medicine, Houston, Tex.

CAREER: Diplomate of American Board of Pediatrics, 1937, and American Board of Child Psychiatry, 1962; University Clinic, Kiel, Germany, trainee in physiological research, 1929-30; University Clinic, Leipzig, Germany, trainee in pediatrics, 1930-33; with East End Child Guidance Clinic, London, England, 1933-34; Columbia University, College of Physicians and Surgeons, New York, N.Y., instructor in pediatrics, 1934-43, associate in psychiatry, 1943-53, clinical associate professor, 1954-59, clinical professor of psychiatry, 1959-64, associate psychoanalyst at Psychoanalytic Clinic, 1947-64; private practice in psychoanalysis, 1943-64; Baylor College of Medicine, Houston, Tex., professor of psychiatry, 1964—. New York State Psychiatric Institute, director of Children's Service, 1954-56, psychotherapeutic supervisor, 1956-64.

MEMBER: International Psychoanalytic Association, American Psychiatric Association, American Association for the Advancement of Science (fellow), American Psychoanalytic Association, American Psychosomatic Society. *Awards, honors:* Rockefeller Foundation fellowship, Johns Hopkins University, 1941-43.

WRITINGS: Don't Be Afraid of Your Child, Farrar, Straus, 1952; *The Importance of Overweight*, Norton, 1957; *Schizophrenia*, Munksgaard (Copenhagen), 1959; *Eating Disorders: Obesity, Anorexia Nervosa, and the Person Within*, Basic Books, 1973; *Learning Psychotherapy: Rationale and Ground Rules*, Harvard University Press, 1974. Contributor of articles on anorexia nervosa, diabetes, schizophrenia, and child development to scientific journals.

WORK IN PROGRESS: Too Fat and Too Thin; continuing research on underlying conceptual and perceptual problems in body awareness, verbal self-representation, and effective self-differentiation in psychosomatic disorders, schizophrenia, and anorexia nervosa.

* * *

BRUINS, Elton J(ohn) 1927-

PERSONAL: Born July 29, 1927, in Fairwater, Wis.; son of Clarence Raymond (a farmer) and Angeline Theodora (Kemink) Bruins; married Elaine Ann Redeker (an elementary school teacher), June 24, 1954; children: Mary Elaine, David Lewis. *Education:* Hope College, B.A. (magna cum laude), 1950; Western Theological Seminary, B.D., 1953; Union Theological Seminary, New York, N.Y., S.T.M., 1954; New York University, Ph.D., 1962. *Politics:* Democrat. *Home:* 191 West 15th St., Holland, Mich. 49423. *Office:* Department of Religion, Hope College, Holland, Mich. 49423.

CAREER: Ordained minister of the Reformed Church in America, 1954; minister in Elmsford, N.Y., 1955-61, and Flushing, N.Y., 1961-66; Hope College, Holland, Mich., assistant professor, 1966-70, associate professor, 1970-73, professor of religion, 1973—. Archivist for Western Theological Seminary, 1967-71, 1974—, and Netherlands Museum, 1968—. *Military service:* U.S. Navy, 1945-46. *Member:* American Society of Church History, Society of American Archivists, Wisconsin State Historical Society, Michigan Historical Society, Michigan Archival Association.

WRITINGS: The Manuscript and Archival Holdings of Beardslee Library, Western Theological Seminary, 1967, 2nd edition, 1970; *A Guide to the Archives of the Netherlands Museum*, Netherlands Museum, 1968, 2nd edition, 1971; *The Americanization of a Congregation*, Eerdmans, 1970. Contributor to *Westminister Dictionary of Church History*; contributor to *Reformed Review, Michigan History, Reformed Journal*, and *Church Herald.*

WORK IN PROGRESS: Collecting and editing the papers of Albertus C. Van Raalte, leader of the Dutch emigrants to Michigan in the nineteenth century.

AVOCATIONAL INTERESTS: Gardening, raising roses.

BRUN, Henri 1939-

PERSONAL: Born April 11, 1939, in Quebec, Quebec, Canada. *Education:* Laval University, B.A., 1958, B.Ph., 1959, LL.L., 1963; University of Paris, D.E.S., 1965, Doctorat d'Etat, 1967; Cambridge University, postdoctoral study, 1973-74. *Office:* School of Law, Laval University, Quebec, Quebec 10, Canada.

CAREER: Called to the Bar, Quebec, Canada, 1963; Laval University, Quebec, Quebec, professor of law, 1967—.

WRITINGS: La formation des institutions parlementaires quebecoises (title means "The Making of Quebec Parliamentary Institutions"), Laval University Press, 1970; *Droit public fondamental* (title means "Basic Public Law"), Laval University Press, 1972; *Le territoire du Quebec: six etudes juridiques* (title means "The Territory of Quebec: Six Law Studies"), Laval University Press, 1974. Contributor to law journals and periodicals.

WORK IN PROGRESS: Research on public law.

* * *

BRUNEAU, Thomas C. 1939-

PERSONAL: Born July 15, 1939, in Los Angeles, Calif.; son of Paul L. (a clerk) and Mary E. (a nurse; maiden name, Ryan) Bruneau; married Celia Crawford, December 27, 1966; children: Bruce, Jennifer, Christopher, Michael, Roger. *Education:* San Jose State College (now University), B.A., 1962; University of California, Berkeley, M.A., 1964, Ph.D., 1970. *Politics:* "Voted Democratic in a certain era; now between countries." *Religion:* Roman Catholic. *Home:* 463 Mount Pleasant, Westmount, Quebec, Canada. *Office:* Department of Political Science, McGill University, Montreal, Quebec, Canada.

CAREER: McGill University, Montreal, Quebec, associate professor of political science, 1969—. *Awards, honors:* Fulbright fellow in India, 1962-63; Canada Council grant, to Brazil, to study the church, popular religiosity, and political involvement.

WRITINGS: The Political Transformation of the Brazilian Catholic Church, Cambridge University Press, 1974. Contributor of articles and reviews to political science journals, including *America, Commonweal, World Today, Latin American Research Review, Journal of Inter-American Studies and World Affairs,* and *Europa-Archiv*.

WORK IN PROGRESS: A book dealing with the church, popular religiosity, and political involvement.

SIDELIGHTS: Bruneau writes: 'I wrote a book about the Church in Brazil because it appeared to be the only institution with enough independence to do some good in changing many pernicious characteristics in the society. The book is available in Portuguese and it may or may not convince the bishops about their responsibilities. I am here again doing another study which will indicate whether the Church, as institution, really can have an impact on society. I will continue to also work on Portugal and as I was there at the time of the coup feel a certain responsibility to follow events closely and interpret them outside the country." *Avocational interests:* Riding his motorcycle, riding waves in Brazil, boxing.

* * *

BRUNER, Herbert B. 1894(?)-1974

1894(?)—August 2, 1974; American educator and author. Obituaries: *New York Times*, August 4, 1974.

BRYAN, John E. 1931-

PERSONAL: Born October 1, 1931, in Plymouth, England; naturalized U.S. citizen; son of John E., Sr. and Marian (Dowrick) Bryan; children: Daphne D., Jasmine B. *Education:* Attended Somerset Agricultural College, 1949-50; Royal Botanic Garden, Edinburgh, graduate, 1955; studied at Royal Horticultural Society Gardens, 1955, at the Hague, 1956, and in Paris, 1957. *Office:* Strybing Arboretum and Botanic Garden, Golden Gate Park, Ninth & Lincoln Way, San Francisco, Calif. 94122.

CAREER: R. T. May Nurseryman, Devon, England, apprentice, 1946-48; Bourmouth Parks Department, England, studied plant care and park work, 1949-52; landscape architect for French Government, 1957; Vilmorin, Paris, France, manager of nursery, 1958-61; Oregon Bulb Farms, sales manager of Jan de Graaff Lilies, 1961-70; Golden Gate Park, San Francisco, Calif., director of Strybing Arboretum and Botanic Garden, 1971—. Public lecturer and teacher of courses in horticulture. Chairman of Gresham, Ore., Park Commission, 1962-70; member of Oregon Agricultural Board, 1971; member of San Rafael Open Space Committee; director of Marin Heritage, 1972—. Has appeared on television and radio in Oregon, California, Washington, and Canada; director of European tours. *Member:* Royal Horticultural Society, American Association of Arboreta and Botanic Gardens, American Horticultural Society, North American Lily Society (national director, 1967-70), Oregon Association of Nurserymen (chapter president, 1966-68; state director, 1967-69), Bay Area Lily Society (president, 1971-76), Rotary International. *Awards, honors:* Gardeners scholarship of Royal Horticultural Society of England, 1955-58.

WRITINGS: (With Coralie Castle) *Edible Ornamental Garden*, One Hundred One Productions, 1974. Contributor to *Time-Life Encyclopedia of Gardening*. Contributor of papers to horticultural conferences; also contributor to periodicals, including *California Horticultural Journal* and *American Horticulturist*.

WORK IN PROGRESS: A book on vegetables.

AVOCATIONAL INTERESTS: Photography, woodworking, writing, civic activities, conservation, travel, golf, tennis, cross country skiing, rugby.

* * *

BRYAN, Julien (Hequembourg) 1899-1974

May 23, 1899—October 20, 1974; American photographer and documentary film-maker. Obituaries: *Current Biography*, January, 1975.

* * *

BRYAN, Marian K(nighton) 1900(?)-1974

1900(?)—December 9, 1974; American dance instructor and author. Obituaries: *New York Times*, December 11, 1974.

* * *

BRYANT, Dorothy 1930-

PERSONAL: Born February 8, 1930, in San Francisco, Calif.; daughter of Joseph (a mechanic) and Judith (a bookkeeper; maiden name, Chiarle) Calvetti; married Louis Ungaretti, June 11, 1949 (divorced, 1963); married Robert K. Bryant (a contractor), October 18, 1968; children: (first marriage) John, Lorri; (stepchildren) Evan, Victoria. *Education:* San Francisco State College (now University),

B.A., 1950, M.A., 1964. *Politics and Religion:* "My politics and religion are identical: I would like people to stop eating each other and start becoming what we truly are." *Home:* 1920 Stuart St., Berkeley, Calif. 94703. *Agent:* James Seligmann, Seligmann & Collier, 280 Madison Ave., New York, N.Y. 10016. *Office:* Contra Costa College, San Pablo, Calif.

CAREER: High school English teacher in public schools of San Francisco, Calif., 1953-56, and at Lick-Wilmerding High School, San Francisco, 1956-61; San Francisco State College (now University), San Francisco, instructor in English, 1962; Golden Gate College, San Francisco, instructor in English, 1963; Contra Costa College, San Pablo, Calif., instructor in English and creative writing, 1964—. Alto singer with California Bach Society.

WRITINGS—Novels: *Ella Price's Journal*, Lippincott, 1972; *The Comforter*, Evan Press, 1973. Contributor to *Freedom News, Nation*, and *Redbook*.

WORK IN PROGRESS: A novel about a retired teacher; a novel about woman who aids a prisoner; a novel about a child custody suit.

* * *

BRYANT, Henry A(llen), Jr. 1943-

PERSONAL: Born March 14, 1943, in Shongaloo, La.; son of Henry and Loreen (a teacher; maiden name, Wortham) Bryant; married Peggy Knox, December 16, 1967; children: Rehema Kamaria, Moturi Roy. *Education:* College of San Mateo, A.A., 1965; San Jose State University, B.A., 1967, M.A., 1969. *Politics:* Democrat. *Religion:* Pentecostal Holiness. *Residence:* Richmond, Calif. *Office:* Laney College, 900 Fallon St., Oakland, Calif. 94804.

CAREER: Veterans Administration Hospital, Menlo Park, Calif., psychiatric social worker and general medical and surgical technician, 1962-69; San Jose State University, San Jose, Calif., assistant professor of social science, 1969-70; Laney College, Oakland, Calif., professor of ethnic studies, 1970—, chairman of department of ethnic studies, 1970-72. Instructor at Foothills College, 1969-70. *Member:* National Association of Political and Social Scientists.

WRITINGS: The Streets of Oakland, Leswing Press, 1973. Contributor to *Community College Social Quarterly* and *Laney Tower*.

* * *

BUCKLEY, Mary L(orraine)

PERSONAL: Born in New Haven, Conn.; daughter of R. Riordan and Mary (Thompson) Buckley; married Joseph M. Parriott, February 14, 1970. *Education:* Attended Keuka College, 1944-47, Yale University, 1947-49, Brooklyn Museum Art School, 1949-51, and New School for Social Research, 1951; also studied art privately. *Home address:* Bay Crest, Huntington, N.Y. 11743. *Office:* School of Art, Pratt Institute, Brooklyn, N.Y. 11205.

CAREER: Look (magazine), New York, N.Y., assistant to fashion editor, 1954; Popular Science Publishing Co., New York, N.Y., book editor, 1954-55; Pratt Institute, Brooklyn, N.Y., assistant professor, 1958-67, associate professor, 1967-71, professor of art, color, and design, 1971—. Member of faculty of People's Art Center of Museum of Modern Art, 1961-62; art teacher in Wisconsin and New York, 1960—. Partner and designer for Mary Buckley Associates (designers of British Pavilion for New York World's Fair), 1962—; director of Margaret Gate Institute; designer of White Horse Museum and murals in Seagram Building. Painter of murals for public buildings and private homes; sculptures are represented in four private collections, paintings in several hundred collections. Designer of public buildings in the New York area. Interior designer for Alex Macdonald Associates; adviser to Mertz Art Foundation; lecturer at Heckscher Museum and University of Pennsylvania.

MEMBER: International Platform Association, Industrial Designers' Association of America, National Association of Women Artists, American Association of University Professors, Eastern Arts Association, Huntington Township Art League (past vice-president). *Awards, honors:* MacDowell Foundation fellowship, 1957; New York State Council on the Arts grant, 1974, for work on Bronx State Children's Psychiatric Hospital, and in 1975 for Queens County and Downstate Hospitals.

WRITINGS: (Co-author) *How to Repair Your Own Automobile*, Popular Science Publishing, 1952; (illustrator with others) Oscar Williams, editor, *Silver Anthology of Light Verse*, New American Library, 1957; (contributor) Ralph Mayer, editor, *Technical Dictionary of Art Terms and Techniques*, Crowell, 1969, 3rd edition, 1970; (editor with David W. Baum) *Color Theory*, Gale, 1975.

* * *

BUDBERG, Moura 1892(?)-1974

1892(?)—November 1, 1974; Russian-born British literary figure and translator. Obituaries: *New York Times*, November 2, 1974.

* * *

BUETOW, Harold A(ndrew) 1919-

PERSONAL: Born September 27, 1919, in Brooklyn, N.Y.; son of Elmer Roy and Anna (Navrot) Buetow. *Education:* Catholic University of America, M.A., 1963, Ph.D., 1964. *Home address:* Curley Hall, Box 48, Catholic University of America, Washington, D.C. 20017. *Office:* O'Boyle Hall, Catholic University of America, Washington, D.C. 20017.

CAREER: Catholic University of America, Washington, D.C., assistant professor, 1965-67, associate professor, 1967-70, professor of education, 1971—. Visiting professor at St. John's University, Jamaica, N.Y., 1959-60, and St. Joseph's College, Emmetsbury, Md., 1967-68. Teacher of adult education courses in New York and Washington, D.C. *Member:* Philosophy of Education Society (fellow), History of Education Society, American Association of University Professors, American Educational Studies Association, National Catholic Educational Association. *Awards, honors:* National Catholic Book Award, 1971, for *Of Singular Benefit: The Story of Catholic Education in the United States.*

WRITINGS: What Every Bride and Groom Should Know, Bruce, 1958; *To Calvary With Christ*, Bruce, 1960; *Joy To My Youth*, Dutton, 1961; *Of Singular Benefit: The Story of Catholic Education in the United States*, Macmillan, 1970. Contributor to education and Catholic journals. *New Catholic Encyclopedia*, senior staff editor, 1961-64, and content editor of supplement, 1972-74.

WORK IN PROGRESS: A documentary history of private education in the United States.

SIDELIGHTS: Buetow has made several study trips to Europe, including in 1973 an in-depth tour of the educational systems of Russia, France, and England; he has made study trips to educational situations in Africa, Hawaii, Central America, and the Middle East, along with several throughout the United States.

* * *

BUFFALOE, Neal D(ollison) 1924-

PERSONAL: Born November 15, 1924, in Leachville, Ark.; son of William Thomas (a teacher) and Maude (a teacher; maiden name, Etherley) Buffaloe; married Inez Owens, July 3, 1947; children: Bonnie Gail, Robert Neal, Anne (Mrs. Gary Shelton Lynn), Laurie Glenn, Donald Ray. *Education:* David Lipscomb College, B.S., 1949; Vanderbilt University, M.S., 1952, Ph.D., 1957. *Politics:* Independent. *Religion:* Church of Christ. *Address:* Box 136, Route 5, Conway, Ark. 72032. *Office:* Department of Biology, State College of Arkansas, Conway, Ark. 72032.

CAREER: State College of Arkansas, Conway, professor of biology, 1957—. Lay minister of Church of Christ. *Military service:* U.S. Navy, 1943-45. *Member:* American Institute of Biological Sciences, American Association for the Advancement of Science (fellow), Arkansas Academy of Science (president, 1959-60), Sigma Xi (fellow). *Awards, honors:* American Institute of Graphic Arts best book selection, 1968, for 2nd edition of *Principles of Biology*.

WRITINGS: Principles of Biology, Prentice-Hall, 1962, 2nd edition (with J. B. Throneberry), 1967; (with R. A. Collins) *Laboratory Manual for Principles of Biology,* Prentice-Hall, 1963, 2nd edition (with Collins and Throneberry), 1968; *Animal and Plant Diversity,* Prentice-Hall, 1968; (with Throneberry) *Concepts of Biology,* Prentice-Hall, 1973.

WORK IN PROGRESS: With Dale V. Ferguson, *Principles of Microbiology,* publication by Houghton expected in 1976.

SIDELIGHTS: Buffaloe is a "gentleman farmer" who lives on a farm of one hundred and forty acres.

* * *

BUKER, George E(dward) 1923-

PERSONAL: Born September 13, 1923, in Bangor, Me.; son of Gilbert T. and Catherine (Gallagher) Buker; married Dorothy Arnold, November 22, 1945; children: Gilbert T., Gary E. *Education:* Attended University of Maine, 1941-42, and Columbia University, 1956-57; Jacksonville University, B.A., 1964; University of Florida, M.A., 1965, Ph.D., 1969. *Religion:* Roman Catholic. *Home:* 5130 Santa Cruz Lane, Jacksonville, Fla. 32210. *Office:* Department of History, Jacksonville University, Jacksonville, Fla. 32211.

CAREER: U.S. Navy, career officer, 1942-63, retiring as commander; St. John's River Junior College, Palatka, Fla., instructor in history, 1965-66; Jacksonville University, Jacksonville, Fla., instructor, 1968-69, assistant professor, 1969-74, associate professor of history, 1974—, head of Social Sciences Division, 1973—. *Member:* Retired Officers Association, Naval Historical Foundation, Conference of Latin American History, South Eastern Latin Americanists, Florida Historical Society.

WRITINGS: (Author of introduction and index) William H. Simmons, *Notices of East Florida,* University of Florida Press, 1973; *Swamp Sailors,* University of Florida Press, 1975. Contributor of articles and book reviews to *Florida Historical Quarterly, American Neptune,* and *Community College Social Sciences Quarterly.*

WORK IN PROGRESS: Research on the U.S. Naval blockade of Florida during the Civil War.

* * *

BUNCH, Clarence

PERSONAL: Born in Gray Ridge, Mo.; son of C. B. (a farmer) and Sadie (Moore) Bunch. *Education:* University of Missouri, B.S. and M.A., 1955; Columbia University, Ed.D., 1970. *Home:* 356 The Bowery, New York, N.Y. 10012. *Office:* Department of Education, Queens College of the City University of New York, Flushing, N.Y. 11367.

CAREER: Teacher in rural school in Stoddard County, Mo., 1946-50; University of Missouri, Columbia, Mo., art supervisor, 1954-55; Radford College, Radford, Va., assistant professor of art, 1955-62; Appalachian State University, Boone, N.C., associate professor of art and chairman of department, 1962-65; Queens College of the City University of New York, Flushing, N.Y., associate professor of art education, 1967—. Visiting professor of graduate art education, Pratt Institute, 1971—; consulting editor, Harcourt, Brace, Jovanovich, 1973—. *Awards, honors:* MacDowell fellowship.

WRITINGS: Acrylic for Sculpture and Design, Van Nostrand, 1972; (with John Lidstone) *Working Big,* Van Nostrand, 1974; (with Lidstone) *The Space Book,* Van Nostrand, in press.

WORK IN PROGRESS: Art Education, for "Art and Architecture Information Guide Series," Gale.

* * *

BUNTING, Anne Evelyn 1928-
(Evelyn Bolton, A. E. Bunting, Eve Bunting)

PERSONAL: Born December 19, 1928, in Maghera, Ireland; daughter of Sloan Edmund (a merchant) and Mary (Canning) Bolton; married Edward Davison Bunting (a medical administrator), April 26, 1951; children: Christine, Sloan, Glenn. *Education:* Methodist College, Belfast, graduate, 1945. *Politics:* Democrat. *Religion:* Protestant. *Home:* 1512 Rose Villa St., Pasadena, Calif. 91106. *Agent:* Larry Sternig, 2407 North 44th St., Milwaukee, Wis. 53210.

CAREER: Free-lance writer, mainly for young people. *Member:* P.E.N. International, California Writer's Guild, Southern California Council on Writing for Children and Young People.

WRITINGS—Under name Eve Bunting, except as noted: *The Two Giants,* Ginn, 1972; *A Gift for Lonny,* Ginn, 1973; *Box, Fox, Ox and the Peacock,* Ginn, 1974; *Say It Fast,* Ginn, 1974; *The Wild One,* Scholastic Book Services, 1974; *Pitcher to Center Field,* Elk Grove, 1974; *We Need a Bigger Zoo,* Ginn, 1974; (under name A. E. Bunting) *Surfing Country,* Elk Grove, 1974; *The Once-A-Year Day,* Golden Gate, 1974; *Barney the Beard,* Parents' Magazine Press, 1975; *The Haunting of Kildoran Abbey,* Macrae Smith, 1975; (under name A. E. Bunting) *High Tide for Labrador,* Golden Gate, in press; *The Mystery of the Red House,* Oddo, in press; *Josefina and the Prince,* Garrard, in press; *Winter's Coming,* Harcourt, in press.

Under name Evelyn Bolton; all published by Creative Educational Society, 1974: *Stable of Fear, Lady's Girl, Goodbye Charlie, Ride When You're Ready, The Wild Horses, Dream Dancer.*

Author of about fifteen stories for basal readers published by Heath, Lyons & Carnahan, and other educational houses. Contributor to children's magazines in United States and Canada, including *Jack and Jill* and *Cricket*. Adult articles and stories have been published in United States and Australia.

WORK IN PROGRESS: The Big Cheese; researching springboard diving for a commissioned book, *Spring-board to Summer;* a book on Ireland (many of her stories have Irish backgrounds).

* * *

BUNTING, Basil 1900-

PERSONAL: Born March 1, 1900, in Scotswood, Northumberland, England; son of T. L. (a physician) and Annie (Cheesman) Bunting; married Marian Culver, 1930 (divorced); married Sima Alladadian, 1948; children: (first marriage) two daughters; (second marriage) one son, one daughter. *Education:* Attended London School of Economics and Political Science, 1919-22. *Religion:* Quaker. *Home:* Shadingfield, Wylam, Northumberland, England.

CAREER: Poet. Has held a variety of positions, including assistant editor, with Ford Madox Ford, of *Transatlantic Review,* Paris, 1923; newspaper music critic in London, England, 1925-28; lived in Italy, 1929-33, in Canary Islands, 1933-36, and in Iran, 1943-51; *Evening Chronicle,* Newcastle, England, financial sub-editor, 1953-66; teacher of poetry at several English, American, and Canadian universities, 1966-73. *Military service:* Served in Royal Air Force during World War II. *Member:* Poetry Society (London; president, 1972—); Northern Arts Association (Newcastle-upon-Tyne; president, 1973—). *Awards, honors:* D.Litt. from University of Newcastle-upon-Tyne, 1971.

WRITINGS—Poems: *Redimiculum Matellarum,* privately printed, 1930; *Poems: 1950,* Cleaners' Press, 1950, revised edition published as *Loquitur,* Fulcrum Press, 1965; *The Spoils,* Morden Tower Book Room (Newcastle-upon-Tyne), 1965; *First Book of Odes,* Fulcrum Press, 1965; *Ode II/2,* Fulcrum Press, 1965; *Briggflatts: An Autobiography,* Fulcrum Press, 1966; *Two Poems,* Unicorn Press, 1967; *What the Chairman Told Tom,* Pym-Randall Press, 1967; (author of preface) Tom Pickard, *High on the Walls,* Fulcrum Press, 1967; *Collected Poems,* Fulcrum Press, 1968, Horizon Press, 1969; (editor and author of preface) *Selected Poems of Ford Madox Ford,* Pym-Randall Press, 1971.

SIDELIGHTS: Bunting is acknowledged as one of the direct, albeit one of the most neglected, successors of Ezra Pound. Pound, who admired and edited Bunting's early work, included thirty-three pages of the younger poet's writings in his 1933 *Active Anthology*. After a decade of silence, Bunting came to be regarded in the 1960's as one of the leaders of the new British avant-garde.

Reviewing Bunting's *Collected Poems,* Thomas Lask commented on the demand that the poet makes on his readers: "His work is compact and tight, with frequent cryptic allusions not easily grasped the first time round, and with a mind-jumping imagination that makes unusual associations between ages, people and events. These are more obvious to him than to the reader at least on first meeting. In a long and dense poem, they are qualities that act as a brake on the understanding. But they can also be explosively illuminating."

Hugh Kenner's critique of *Briggflatts* offers a contemporary perspective of Bunting's work: "It is Bunting's unique distinction that he has opened, in his seventh decade, a new career, after being in his forties the more accomplished school-of-Pound poet alive. It's ultimately Pound's lesson that he is now rethinking in local conditions, the speech of the places of his boyhood, the here-and-now he spent a lifetime leaving behind him: the lesson of the exact, the local, the word that names, the thing that is what it is. There is more to be learned about poetry from *Briggflatts* than from most anthologies."

BIOGRAPHICAL/CRITICAL SOURCES: Roger Guedalla, *Basil Bunting: A Bibliography,* Norwood Editions (Norwood, Pa.), 1973.

* * *

BURCHARD, Sue 1937-

PERSONAL: Born November 23, 1937, in Oak Park, Ill.; daughter of Louis A. (an accountant) and Candace (Mills) Huston; married Marshall Gaines Burchard (a writer), May 9, 1959; children: Marshall Gaines, Jr., Wendy Mills. *Education:* Vassar College, B.A., 1959. *Home:* 425 East 86th St., New York, N.Y. 10028. *Office:* Trinity School, 139 West 91st St., New York, N.Y. 10024.

CAREER: J. Walter Thompson (advertising agency), New York, N.Y., copywriting trainee and secretary, 1959-61; assistant teacher in private school in New York, N.Y., 1966-68; Trinity School, New York, N.Y., science teacher, 1968-71, librarian, 1971—.

WRITINGS—All juvenile books, all with husband, Marshall Burchard: *Sports Hero: Joe Namath*, Putnam, 1971; *Sports Hero: Brooks Robinson*, Putnam, 1972; *Sports Hero: Kareem Abdul Jabbar*, Putnam, 1972; *Sports Hero: Johnny Bench*, Putnam, 1973; *Sports Hero: Roger Staubach*, Putnam, 1973; *Sports Hero: Bobby Orr*, Putnam, 1973; *Sports Hero: Henry Aaron*, Putnam, 1974; *Sports Hero: Richard Petty*, Putnam, 1974; *Sports Star: Tom Seaver*, Harcourt, 1974.

WORK IN PROGRESS: Juvenile biographies of Billie Jean King, Larry Csonka, O. J. Simpson, Phil Esposito, Peggie Jackson, and Mohammed Ali, all for Putnam; juvenile biographies of Bob Griese, Walt Frazier, Brad Park, Franco Harris, Jim Hunter, and Chris Evert for Harcourt.

AVOCATIONAL INTERESTS: Travel to south of Spain, cruising aboard her ketch, sitting in the sun.

* * *

BURDICK, Donald W(alter) 1917-

PERSONAL: Born July 28, 1917, in Akron, N.Y.; son of Walter Lyman (a farmer) and Florence (Strickland) Burdick; married Violet Gamin, August 16, 1940; children: Sharon (Mrs. Gregory Sincock), Douglas. *Education:* Attended Moody Bible Institute, 1937-40; Wheaton College, Wheaton, Ill., A.B., 1945; Northern Baptist Theological Seminary, B.D., 1946, Th.M., 1952, Th.D., 1954. *Politics:* Republican. *Home:* 2738 South Xavier St., Denver, Colo. 80236. *Office:* Conservative Baptist Theological Seminary, Box 10,000, University Park Station, Denver, Colo. 80210.

CAREER: Ordained minister of the Baptist Church, 1947; pastor in Chicago, Ill., 1945-50; Northern Baptist Theological Seminary, Chicago, Ill., instructor in New Testament, 1947-50; Conservative Baptist Theological Seminary, Denver, Colo., associate professor, 1950-54, professor of New Testament, 1954—. *Member:* Society of Biblical Literature, Evangelical Theological Society, Near East Archaeological Society (board member, 1973—).

WRITINGS: (Contributor) C. F. Pfeiffer and E. F. Harrison, editors, *Wycliffe Bible Commentary,* Moody, 1962; *Tongues: To Speak Or Not To Speak,* Moody, 1969; *The Epistles of John,* Moody, 1970; (contributor) Bruce L. Shelley, editor, *A Call To Christian Character,* Zondervan, 1970; (translator and editor with others) *New International Version of the New Testament.* Zondervan, 1973; (contributor) Richard N. Longenecker and Merrill C. Tenney, editors, *New Dimensions in New Testament Study,* Zondervan, 1974.

WORK IN PROGRESS: Contributing to *Expositor's Bible Commentary,* for Zondervan.

AVOCATIONAL INTERESTS: Gardening.

* * *

BURKE, Richard C(ullen) 1932-

PERSONAL: Born August 3, 1932, in Buffalo, N.Y.; son of Paul Francis and Carolyn (Sexton) Burke; married Mary Ann Fausnaugh, August 22, 1959; children: Elizabeth, Paul, Catherine. *Education:* University of Buffalo, B.A., 1953; Catholic University of America, M.A., 1959; University of Michigan, Ph.D., 1963. *Office:* Department of Telecommunication, Indiana University, Bloomington, Ind. 47401.

CAREER: Central Michigan University, Mount Pleasant, assistant professor of telecommunication, 1962-64; Indiana University, Bloomington, assistant professor, 1964-71, associate professor of telecommunication, 1971—. Educational television advisor to Ministry of Education, El Salvador, 1968-69; consultant for World Education, Bogota, Colombia, 1973-74. *Military service:* U.S. Army, 1953-56. *Member:* Society for International Development, Latin American Studies Association.

WRITINGS: (Editor) *Instructional Television: Bold New Venture,* Indiana University Press, 1971.

WORK IN PROGRESS: Radio and the Teaching of Literacy.

* * *

**BURKE, Velma Whitgrove 1921-
(Vee Burke)**

PERSONAL: Born December 13, 1921, in Joliet, Ill.; daughter of Charles and Amanda (Holz) Whitgrove; married Vincent J. Burke (a senior member of *Los Angeles Times* Washington Bureau), December 5, 1942 (died May 7, 1973); children: Douglas, Barbara (Mrs. John H. Hubbard), Judith, Patricia. *Education:* University of Chicago, B.A., 1943. *Home:* 3336 Quesada St. N.W., Washington, D.C. 20015. *Office:* Congressional Research Service, Library of Congress, Washington, D.C. 20540.

CAREER: Member of staff of Joint Economic Subcommittee on Fiscal Policy of the U.S. Congress, Washington, D.C., 1973—. *Member:* Phi Beta Kappa.

WRITINGS: (Under name Vee Burke, with late husband, Vincent J. Burke) *Nixon's Good Deed: Welfare Reform,* Columbia University Press, 1974.

* * *

BURKETT, Molly 1932-

PERSONAL: Born April 3, 1932, in England; daughter of John and Mary Preece; married John Burkett (an engineer); children: St. Joan, Sophie. *Education:* Goldsmiths College, London, teacher's diploma. *Home and office:* Animal Rehabilitation Centre, Hough-on-the-Hill, Grantham, Lincolnshire, England.

CAREER: Teacher, youth worker, and athletics coach, 1952—. Animal Rehabilitation Centre, Grantham, England, owner and operator, 1954—. Presently establishing National Wildlife Rescue Service.

WRITINGS: High Fly, Pelham, 1968; *The Year of the Badger*, Lippincott, 1974; *Foxes Three*, Lippincott, 1975. Contributor of more than a hundred articles and stories to magazines.

WORK IN PROGRESS: Boy and Bird.

* * *

BURNET, Mary E(dith) 1911-

PERSONAL: Born November 20, 1911, in Lockland, Ohio; daughter of Norman Lot (an attorney) and Mary (Babbitt) Burnet. *Education:* University of Cincinnati, Commercial Engineer (now granted as B.S.), 1934; Xavier University, Cincinnati, Ohio, M.B.A., 1958; New York University, graduate study, 1962-70. *Politics:* Republican. *Religion:* Presbyterian. *Home:* 132 Delray Rd., Rochester, N.Y. 14610. *Office:* College of Business, Rochester Institute of Technology, Rochester, N.Y. 14623.

CAREER: Certified Public Accountant in Ohio. Kroger Co., Cincinnati, Ohio, secretary and accountant, 1934-42; Colter Corp., Palacios, Tex., resident accountant, 1942-47; Nightingale Hosp., El Campo. Tex., business manager, 1948; Cincinnati Transit Co., Cincinnati, Ohio, accountant, 1949-52; Trailmobile, Inc., Cincinnati, Ohio, accountant, 1952-55; South-Western Publishing Co., Cincinnati, Ohio, editorial assistant, 1955-61; Rochester Institute of Technology, Rochester, N.Y., assistant professor, 1961-67, associate professor, 1967-74, professor of accounting, 1974—. Accountant at Shaw's Office Service, New Zealand, fall, 1972, and at Peat, Marwick, Mitchell & Co., Rochester, N.Y., winter, 1973. Member of American Host Program.

MEMBER: American Institute of Certified Public Accountants, American Women's Society of Certified Public Accountants, American Accounting Association, American Society of Women Accountants (president of Rochester chapter, 1966-67), Ohio Society of Certified Public Accountants, New York State Society of Certified Public Accountants (associate member), Beta Gamma Sigma.

WRITINGS: (Reviser) A.B. Carson and Arthur E. Carlson, *Accounting Essentials for Career Secretaries*, 3rd edition (Burnet was not associated with earlier editions), South-Western, 1972; *Working Papers to Accompany Financial Accounting by Bierman and Drebin*, Macmillan, 1972. Contributor to *Woman C.P.A.*, *Collegiate News and Views, Accountant's Digest, Echo*, and *Accounting Review.*

WORK IN PROGRESS: An analysis of the continuing education requirements for accountants in various states.

SIDELIGHTS: Mary Burnet worked as a volunteer in Vienna, Austria, for the United Presbyterian Church in the summer of 1973. She attended the Ninth International Congress of Accountants in Paris, France, in 1967, and the Tenth International Congress of Accountants in Sydney, Australia, in 1972. *Avocational interests:* Travel, photography, cooking, gardening.

* * *

BURRELL, Evelyn Patterson

EDUCATION: Morgan State College, B.A. (magna cum

laude), 1959; Howard University, M.A., 1966, further graduate study 1970-73.

CAREER: Assistant professor of English at Bowie State College, Bowie, Md., and at Coppin State College, Baltimore, Md. Lecturer at Howard University and at Hood College. *Member:* National Association for Humanities Education, College Language Association, Association for the Study of Afro-American Life and History, Alpha Kappa Mu, Lambda Iota Tau, Kappa Delta Pi. *Awards, honors:* Ford Foundation travel and study grant.

WRITINGS: Weep No More (narrative poem), Burton-Johns, 1973, enlarged edition, 1975. Poems anthologized in *The Soul and the Singer*, Young Publications, 1969; *Anthology of American Poetry*, Books X and XI, Wright Publishing, 1970, 1971; *Yearbook of Modern Poetry*, Young Publications, 1972. Also contributor to *A Borrower Be: An Interchange of Culture in the Classroom*. Contributor to *Negro History Bulletin*.

WORK IN PROGRESS: A collection of speeches and lectures.

* * *

BURTON, Lloyd E. 1922-

PERSONAL: Born May 13, 1922, in Phoenix, Ariz.; son of John S. (an auditor) and Olive (Aaron) Burton; married Penelope J. Stodghill, April 28, 1945 (divorced, 1964); married Nellie V. Ramsey, June, 1968; children: Lloyd, Jr., Scott C., Barbara J. *Education:* University of Arizona, B.S., 1954, M.S., 1956, Ph.D., 1964. *Politics:* "Democrat (formerly Republican)." *Religion:* Christian Church. *Home:* 2802 East First St., Tucson, Ariz. 85716. *Office:* College of Pharmacy, University of Arizona, Tucson, Ariz. 85721.

CAREER: University of Arizona, Tucson, instructor, 1954-64, assistant professor, 1964-66, associate professor, 1966-69, professor of pharmaceutical education, 1969—. Chairman of board of American Red Cross, Tucson; member of City Planning Council, and Health Planning Council. *Military service:* U.S. Navy, pilot; became lieutenant; received two Air Medals. *Member:* American Association of Colleges of Pharmacy, American Public Health Association (fellow; member of council), Arizona Public Health Association (president).

WRITINGS: (With Hugh H. Smith) *Public Health and Community Medicine*, Williams & Wilkins, 1970, 2nd edition, in press.

WORK IN PROGRESS: Research on pharmaceutical education and on public health.

* * *

BUSH, Vannevar 1890-1974

March 11, 1890—June 28, 1974; American engineer, educator, inventor, and author. Obituaries: *Current Biography*, September, 1974.

* * *

BUSHA, Charles Henry 1931-

PERSONAL: Surname is pronounced Boo-*shay*; born December 14, 1931, in Liberty, S.C.; son of James Henry (an electrician) and Rosa Anna (Anderson) Busha. *Education:* Furman University, B.A., 1958; Rutgers University, M.L.S., 1961; Indiana University, Ph.D., 1971. *Politics:* Democrat. *Religion:* Unitarian-Universalist. *Home:* 8708 North 50th St., Tampa. Fla. 33617; and 175 Summit Dr., Liberty, S.C. 29657. *Office:* University of South Florida, FAO 176, Tampa, Fla. 33620.

CAREER: High school teacher of history and civics in the public schools of Greenville, S.C., 1958; Greenville County Library, Greenville, S.C., head of technical services, 1961-62, reference librarian, 1962-63; South Carolina State Library Board, Columbia, reference consultant, 1963-67; Indiana University, Bloomington, lecturer, 1970-71, assistant professor of library science, 1971-73; University of South Florida, Tampa, associate professor of library science, 1973—. *Military service:* U.S. Army, 1951-54; became second lieutenant. South Carolina National Guard, 1954-67; became captain. *Member:* American Library Association, Bibliographical Society of America, Southeastern Library Association, Florida Library Association, Tau Kappa Epsilon, Beta Phi Mu, Friends of the Tampa Public Library.

WRITINGS: Business, Technical, and Scientific Books, South Carolina State Library Board, 1967; *Freedom Versus Suppression and Censorship*, Libraries Unlimited, 1972; (contributor) Bruce Shuman, *New Approaches to Selection of Library Materials for Adults*, Libraries Unlimited, 1975. Contributor to *Library Quarterly, Journal of Education for Librarianship, Southeastern Librarian, Newsletter on Intellectual Freedom*, and *South Carolina Librarian*.

WORK IN PROGRESS: Editing and contributing to *An Intellectual Freedom Primer for Libraries Unlimited; The Scientific Investigation of Library Problems*, a research methods handbook for librarianship.

BIOGRAPHICAL/CRITICAL SOURCES: Library Quarterly, July, 1972.

* * *

BUSSIERES, Simone 1918-

PERSONAL: Born June 8, 1918, in Quebec, Quebec, Canada; daughter of Edouard (a barber) and Rachel (Veilleux) Gagnon; married Rosaire Bussieres (an accountant), July 28, 1945, (died February, 1948). *Education:* Bureau centrale, Province de Quebec, Diplome superieur d'enseignement, 1935. *Home:* 1645 Notre Dame, Notre-Dame-des-Laurentides, Quebec GOA 2SO, Canada. *Office:* Les Presses Laurentiennes, Notre-Dame-des-Laurentides, Quebec GOA 2SO, Canada.

CAREER: Elementary and junior high school teacher in Val d'Espoir, Quebec, 1941-43, and in Quebec, Quebec, 1944-45, 1948-55; Commission des Ecoles Catholiques de Quebec, Quebec, director of instruction for grades 1-3, 1955-60, assistant director of instruction for elementary schools, 1960-68; Les Presses Laurentides (formerly Les Publications Didac), Notre-Dame-des-Laurentides, Quebec, owner and publisher, 1968—. Radio station CHNC, New Carlisle, Quebec, announcer, writer, and producer, 1943-44; radio station CHRC, Quebec, Quebec, variously hostess, producer, and/or editor of programs, "Tante Colette," 1948-53, "Que Desirez-vous?," 1950-54, "Le Pere Noel," 1951-53, "Les Jeunes Savants," 1954-55, "Comment Parlez-vous?," 1959-61, and "Chansons vecues," 1960; television station CFCM, Quebec, Quebec, hostess and editor of programs, "Les Jeunes Savants," 1955, and "Les Jeunes Talents," 1956-59. Department de l'-Instruction Publique, member of subcommittee on elementary schools, 1961-63, member of committee for kindergarten level, 1961-65.

MEMBER: Association des Directeurs Generaux des Ecoles (member of board of directors, 1965-68), Syndicat des Institurices Catholiques de Quebec (vice-president, 1954-55), Societe des Ecrivains Canadiens (secretary of Quebec section, 1961-62), Club Feminin Altrusa (secretary, 1955-56). *Awards, honors:* Outstanding children's book of the year award, from Association Canadienne des Bibliothecaires pour Enfants, 1973, for *Le Petit Sapin qui a pousse sur une etoile.*

WRITINGS: *L'Heritier* (novel; title means "The Heir"), Quartier Latin (Quebec), 1951; (editor) *Joies de lire* (selected reading for grades 4-7; title means "The Joys of Reading"), four volumes, Hachette, 1961; *Le Plaisir d'apprendre* (language and science textbook for grades K-1; title means "Learning with Pleasure"), Gage (Toronto), 1962; *Les Fables des trois commeres* (juvenile; title means "The Three Wives' Tales"), Garneau (Quebec), 1962; *Je veux lire: Methode de lecture spontanee* (reading textbook, with teacher's manual and workbooks; title means "I Want to Read"), Pedagogia, 1963, supplement, *Je compose mon dictionnaire* (title means "I Make Up My Dictionary"), 1965; *Le Plaisir de connaitre* (language and science textbook for grade 2, with teacher's manual; title means "Knowing with Pleasure"), Gage, 1965; *Je sais lire: Methode de lecture spontanee* (reading textbook, with teacher's manual and workbooks; title means "I Know How to Read: Reading System"), and supplement, *Je compose mon dictionnaire*, Pedagogia, 1965; *J'aime lire: Methode de lecture spontanee* (reading textbook, with teacher's manual and workbooks; title means "I Love Reading"), and supplement, *Je compose mon dictionnaire*, Pedagogia, 1966; (editor) Maurice Careme, *Du Soleil sur ton chemin* (poems), Presses Laurentiennes, 1970; *Le Petit Sapin qui a pousse sur une etoile* (juvenile; title means "The Little Fir That Grew on a Star"), Presses Laurentiennes, 1972.

Author of a series of six elementary school level workbooks, *Mon Cahier de vacances*, Centre de Psychologie et de Pedagogie (Montreal), 1960. Contributor to newspaper *L'Action Catholique.* Founder and editor of *Detente*, a bulletin for lay teachers, 1953-54; also founder and editor of *Ecole-Education*, official review of the Commission des Ecoles Catholique de Quebec, 1962-67.

AVOCATIONAL INTERESTS: Gardening (has 300 rose bushes and a vegetable garden), raising chickens, photography, travel.

* * *

BUTLER, Natalie Sturges 1908-

PERSONAL: Born July 13, 1908, in Melrose, Mass.; daughter of Dwight Case (a newspaper artist and etcher) and Clare Blanche (Vaughan) Sturges; married Benjamin Butler (an attorney), May 23, 1932; children: Diane-Clare (Mrs. Carl A. Brinkman), Benjamin Sturges. *Education:* Attended Vesper George Art School, 1926-28. *Politics:* Republican. *Religion:* Congregationalist. *Home:* 93 Main St., Farmington, Me. 04938.

CAREER: Irving & Casson, Davenport Co., Boston, Mass., librarian and interior decorator, 1928-32; free-lance writer, 1950—. Member of board of trustees, Franklin Memorial Hospital, 1963-70; secretary, Little Red Schoolhouse Museum, 1970—; Franklin County chairman of Maine Sesquicentennial Committee, 1970; member of Maine State Museum Commission, 1974—. *Member:* Audubon Society, New England Historic Genealogical Society, New England Wildflower Society, Maine Historical Society, Maine Old Cemetery Association, John Howland Society, Maine League Historical Societies and Museums (member of board of trustees, 1973—), Maine Society of Mayflower Descendants, Citizens for Historic Preservation (secretary, 1971), Farmington Public Library Association (treasurer, 1958-74; secretary, 1958—), Delta Kappa Gamma Society (honorary member). *Awards, honors:* Award from American Association for State and Local History, 1970, for "Pilgrimage Book" series; M.A. from University of Maine at Farmington, 1972; citation from Maine State Preservation Commission, 1973.

WRITINGS: *Dwight C. Sturges: Etcher of an Era*, with photographs by brother, Richard Sturges, Wheelwright, 1974.

With husband, Benjamin Butler, "Pilgrimage Book" series, published by Farmington Historical Society: *William Allen's New World*, 1965; *Father Sewall & His Zion's Hill Neighborhood*, 1966; *Thomas Wendell Moves to Fairbanks*, 1967; *Porter and Russell Lived on a Hill*, 1969; *The Red Schoolhouse Neighborhood*, 1973.

Also author of "History of Old South Church," 1966. Contributor to *Down East, Pioneer America, Christian Science Monitor, Lewiston (Me.) Evening Journal Magazine.*

WORK IN PROGRESS: *Zephaniah Builds a Schoolhouse*, based on an 1854 diary; *From Center Meeting House to Courthouse*, with Benjamin Butler.

SIDELIGHTS: Mrs. Butler began doing local historical research with her husband in 1964. She writes: "Our greatest problem today, one which is common to most busy people, is having too many ideas and too little time to accomplish them. With the Bicentennial observance already begun, we're working on programs for our local celebration and hoping to still squeeze out enough hours to produce at least two books before 1977. Our courage is tremendous, but sometimes we're acutely aware the old flesh is weak!"

* * *

BUULTJENS, (Edward) Ralph 1936-

PERSONAL: Born December 12, 1936, in Ceylon; son of Alfred Ernest (a lawyer and judge) and Vivienne (Schokman) Buultjens. *Education:* Attended St. Peter's College and Sussex College; University of London, Ph.D.; International Council for Buddhist Studies, postdoctoral study. *Home and office:* 307 East 44th St., New York, N.Y. 10017.

CAREER: Lever Brothers Co., New York, N.Y., manager, corporate development and planning, 1963-73. Professor of international affairs at New York Theological Seminary, 1968-72; professor at Rogers College, 1970-73; professor at Marymount Manhattan College, 1971. Visiting professor and consultant, International Study and Research Institute, 1969-75. Lecturer at National Institute for Higher Studies, 1959-60; visiting lecturer at University of Bridgeport, 1967-68; lecturer at Columbia University, Pratt Institute, Hunter College of the City University of New York, Massachusetts Institute of Technology, New York University, Marknoll Seminary, and American Buddhist Academy. Member of New York City Mayor's Youth Board, 1963-65; consultant to international organizations and United Nations agencies; has appeared on television and radio programs concerning international politics and Asian philosophy.

MEMBER: World Fellowship Organization (member of

board of trustees, 1967-74), Society for Asian Affairs (chairman, 1973—), Asia Society (chairman of Srilanka Council, 1963—), New York Buddhist Council (chairman, 1965-74), New York Society for International Development (president, 1972-74). *Awards, honors:* Nominated for Nehru Literary Prize, 1974, for writing on Asia.

WRITINGS: Buddhist Doctrine and Dogma: The Challenge of Change, Orbis Books, 1969; *Traditional Faiths and Asian Development*, Asia Society, 1971; *Rebuilding the Temple: Tradition and Change in Modern Asia*, Orbis Books, 1974.

WORK IN PROGRESS: Books on the political processes and philosophy in modern Asia; collection of speeches on developmental economics and politics in third world nations.

SIDELIGHTS: Buultjens writes: "I see my work as an extension of my life. Having lived for long periods in Asia and the Third World, and also in the West, I have sought to analyze and interpret the relationship between these parts of the world. It is only through interaction and an understanding between each other that we can have progress by both—spiritual tranquility in modern industrial nations and modernization in ancient cultural areas."

* * *

BUXBAUM, Melvin H. 1934-

PERSONAL: Born May 6, 1934, in Chicago, Ill.; son of Herbert L. (a tailor) and Evelyn (Schulman) Buxbaum; married Maxine Schlesinger (a teacher), June 8, 1958; children: Julie Elizabeth, Laurel Jessica. *Education:* Roosevelt University, B.A., 1956, M.A., 1960; University of Chicago, Ph.D., 1968. *Religion:* Jewish. *Home:* 218 West End Ave., Apt. 2G, Freeport, N.Y. 11520. *Office:* Department of English, Bernard M. Baruch College of the City University of New York, 17 Lexington Ave., New York, N.Y. 10017.

CAREER: English teacher in public schools in Chicago, Ill., 1957-60, chairman of English department, John Marshall High School, 1959-60; Chicago City Junior College, Chicago, Ill., teacher of English, 1960-65, chairman of department, Amundsen-Mayfair branches, 1963-65; University of Illinois, Chicago Circle, member of faculty of department of English, 1965-72; Bernard M. Baruch College of the City University of New York, New York, N.Y., member of English faculty, 1972—. Director of Illinois Foundation for Home Health Services, 1971-72; member of board of directors of Baldwin Jewish Center. *Member:* Modern Language Association of America, Presbyterian Historical Society, National Association for the Advancement of Colored People, American Civil Liberties Union, Historical Society of Pennsylvania. *Awards, honors:* Grant from National Endowment for the Humanities, 1969.

WRITINGS: Benjamin Franklin and the Zealous Presbyterians, Pennsylvania State University Press, 1974. Contributor of about fifteen articles and reviews to journals, including *Journal of Presbyterian History, William and Mary Quarterly, Enlightenment Essays*, and *Nation*.

WORK IN PROGRESS: A Guide to Benjamin Franklin Studies, a bibliography, for G. K. Hall, completion expected in 1977; editing diaries of two Princeton University students during the period of the Confederation; research on Anglo-American literary relations between 1765 and 1799.

BYE, Ranulph (deBayeux) 1916-

PERSONAL: Born June 17, 1916, in Princeton, N.J.; son of Arthur Edwin and Mary C. (Heldring) Bye; married Mary McCarty (staff member of Friends Peace Committee), May 24, 1941; children: Dennus L., Barbara D., Stephen G., Catherine M. *Education:* Philadelphia College of Art, diploma, 1938; studied at Art Students League, New York, N.Y., 1940-41, and also studied art privately. *Religion:* Society of Friends. *Home and office address:* R.D. 4, Doylestown, Pa. 18901.

CAREER: Moore College of Art, Philadelphia, Pa., associate professor of art, 1949—. Guest instructor at workshops of Springfield Art Museum, Springfield, Mo., 1966, and Foothills Art Center, Golden, Colo., 1969. Has had one-man shows or been included in exhibitions at National Academy of Design, Audubon Artists, Smithsonian Institution, Art Institute of Mexico, and other galleries and museums; work is represented in collections of Boston Museum of Fine Arts, Smithsonian Institution, Moore College of Art, and others. Commissioned work includes Christmas card designs for American Artists Group, calendar paintings for New York Life and other insurance companies, and designs for U.S. Navy Mine Force. Member of Woodmere Art Gallery and Grand Central Art Galleries, Inc. *Military service:* U.S. Army, 1942-45.

MEMBER: American Watercolor Society, Allied Artists of America, Salmagundi Club, National Trust for Historic Preservation, Society of Industrial Archeology, Garden State Watercolor Society, Philadelphia Water Color Club. *Awards, honors:* Seventeen Salmagundi Club prizes, 1958—, including first prize in watercolor, 1972; National Arts Club Gold Medal, 1963, and prize, 1966; American Watercolor Society Grumbacher Purchase Prize, 1964, John L. Ernst Award, 1966, William Church Osborne Memorial Prize, 1971, and Emily Goldsmith Award, 1973; K & E Hirshberg Award from Baltimore Watercolor Club, 1965; Woodmere Art Gallery Van Sciver Prize, 1969, Harrison Morris Prize, 1971; RCA Prize from Garden State Watercolor Society, 1971; Muriel Alvord Award from Hudson Valley Art Association, 1972; and other art prizes.

WRITINGS: (Self-illustrated) *The Vanishing Depot*, Livingston, 1973. Illustrations appear in publications, including *Seascapes and Landscapes in Watercolor*, edited by Norman Kent, Watson, 1956. Contributor of articles or illustrations to *American Artist, American Heritage, Philadelphia Inquirer*, and *Ford Times*.

WORK IN PROGRESS: Assembling a pictorial record of nineteenth century architecture, to include town houses, country houses, and commercial buildings.

* * *

BYERLY, Henry Clement 1935-

PERSONAL: Born August 7, 1935, in St. Paul, Minn.; son of Harry Woodward and Marie Elizabeth (Clement) Byerly; married Rosemarie Schulga, April 7, 1962; children: Sonya, Tanya. *Education:* University of Minnesota, B.A., 1957, M.A., 1964, Ph.D., 1967. *Politics:* Democrat. *Home:* 2802 West Calle Carapan, Tucson, Ariz. 85705. *Office:* Department of Philosophy, University of Arizona, Tucson, 85721.

CAREER: University of Arizona, Tucson, assistant professor, 1967-70, associate professor of philosophy, 1970—. *Military service:* U.S. Army, 1957-60. *Member:* American Philosophical Association, American Association of University Professors, Phi Beta Kappa.

WRITINGS: A Primer of Logic, Harper, 1973. Contributor to *Philosophy of Science, British Journal for the Philosophy of Science*, and *Notre Dame Journal of Formal Logic*.

WORK IN PROGRESS: A monograph on philosophy of science, *Theoretical Entities*.

* * *

BYERS, David (Milner) 1941-

PERSONAL: Born October 28, 1941, in Hasbrouck Heights, N.J.; son of Irvin M. and Eleanor Byers; married Patricia A. Harper (an administrator), August 30, 1969; children: Sarah. *Education:* Assumption College, B.A., 1963; Seton Hall University, M.A., 1966; University of Minnesota, Ph.D., 1973. *Politics:* Democrat. *Religion:* Roman Catholic. *Home:* 5420 Connecticut Ave. N.W., Washington, D.C. 20015. *Office:* Glenmary Research Center, 4606 East-West Highway, Washington, D.C. 20014.

CAREER: Loras College, Dubuque, Iowa, instructor in English, 1972-73; Glenmary Research Center, Washington, D.C., religious writer, 1973—. *Member:* Religious Research Association.

WRITINGS: (With Bernard Quinn) *Readings for Town and Country Workers*, Glenmary Research Center, 1974; *Between Parish and Diocese*, Glenmary Research Center, 1974; (with Quinn) *Evangelists to the Poor*, Glenmary Research Center, 1975.

WORK IN PROGRESS: A book on Roman Catholic and ecumenical area ministry organizations in the United States, *The Middle Ground*.

* * *

BYRNE, Frank Loyola 1928-

PERSONAL: Born May 12, 1928, in Hackensack, N.J.; son of Francis L. (a banker) and Bertha (Widman) Byrne; married Marilyn L. Sobraske, June 9, 1962; children: Anne Louise, Frank Joseph. *Education:* State Teachers College, Trenton, N.J., B.S., 1950; University of Wisconsin, M.S., 1951, Ph.D., 1957. *Religion:* Roman Catholic. *Home:* 5800 Horning Rd., Kent, Ohio 44240. *Office:* Department of History, Kent State University, Kent, Ohio 44242.

CAREER: Louisiana State University, Baton Rouge, instructor in history, 1957-58; Creighton University, Omaha, Neb., assistant professor, 1958-63, associate professor of history, 1963-66; Kent State University, Kent, Ohio, associate professor, 1966-68, professor of history, 1968—. *Military service:* U.S. Army, 1954-56. *Member:* American Historical Association, Organization of American Historians, Southern Historical Association, Ohio Academy of History, Ohio Historical Society, Nebraska Historical Society, State Historical Society of Wisconsin. *Awards, honors:* Research grant from Wisconsin Civil War Centennial Commission, 1962-63; American Philosophical Society research grant, 1965.

WRITINGS: Prophet of Prohibition: Neal Dow and His Crusade, State Historical Society of Wisconsin, 1961; (editor) *The View from Headquarters: Civil War Letters of Harvey Reid,* State Historical Society of Wisconsin, 1965; (editor with Andrew T. Weaver) *Haskell of Gettysburg: His Life and Civil War Papers,* State Historical Society of Wisconsin, 1970. Contributor to *Journal of Southern History, Wisconsin Magazine of History,* and *Civil War History.*

WORK IN PROGRESS: A general history of Civil War military and political prisons.

* * *

BYRNES, Edward T(homas) 1929-

PERSONAL: Born December 4, 1929, in Elizabeth, N.J.; son of Joseph E. and Elizabeth S. (Dion) Byrnes; married Elaine R. Meixner (an elementary teacher), November 17, 1962; children: Richard J. *Education:* Seton Hall University, B.A., 1955; New York University, M.A., 1957, Ph.D., 1967. *Politics:* Independent. *Home:* 734 Colts Neck Rd., Freehold, N.J. 07728. *Office:* Department of English, Seton Hall University, South Orange, N.J. 07079.

CAREER: Seton Hall University, South Orange, N.J., assistant professor, 1960-68, associate professor, 1968-74, professor of English, 1974—, chairman of department, 1968—. *Military service:* U.S. Army, 1951-53; became sergeant. *Member:* Modern Language Association of America, American Association of University Professors, National Council of Teachers of English, College English Association, Mediaeval Academy of America, Early English Text Society.

WRITINGS: (With Charles W. Dunn) *Middle English Literature*, Harcourt, 1973.

WORK IN PROGRESS: A monograph, *English Burletta: 1750-1800*.

* * *

CABBELL, Paul 1942-

PERSONAL: Born December 3, 1942, in Pensacola, Fla.; son of Stanley Vernon (a railroad employee) and Mary (Hite) Cabbell; married Catlin Mues (a speech therapist), June 17, 1967. *Education:* Attended Yale University, 1960-61; Pomona College, B.A., 1968. *Home:* 2978 Chillon Way, Laguna Beach, Calif. 92651. *Office:* KOCE-TV, Huntington Beach, Calif. 92647.

CAREER: Free-lance writer in Laguna Beach, Calif., 1969-73; KOCE-TV (Public Broadcasting Service), Huntington Beach, Calif., television producer and reporter, 1973—.

WRITINGS: God Bless Our Second Mortgage, Federal Legal Publications, 1973. Contributor to *Harper's, New Times, Christian Science Monitor*, and *Los Angeles Free Press*. Contributor to Public Broadcasting Service documentaries.

WORK IN PROGRESS: Editing a text accompanying a twenty-part television course for college credit, *California Contemporary Issues*; producing and writing a film series.

SIDELIGHTS: Cabbell is interested in going to mainland China to produce documentary films.

* * *

CABIBI, John F(rank) J(oseph) 1912-

PERSONAL: Born April 18, 1912, in New Orleans, La.; son of Frank and Alice Ellen (Driscoll) Cabibi; married Virginia Serio, June 1, 1933; children: Anthony, Alice Cabibi Schmidt, Roxanne Cabibi Gerber, John, Virginia, Wayne. *Education:* Delgado Junior College, A.A., 1964; Louisiana State University, Baton Rouge, B.S., 1969. *Religion:* Roman Catholic. *Home:* 903 Haring Rd., Metairie, La. 70009. *Office:* Department of Visual Communications, Delgado College, 615 City Park Ave., New Orleans, La. 70114.

CAREER: Free-lance printer and linotype operator in New

Orleans, La., 1924-45; Cabibi Printing Co., New Orleans, La., owner and manager, 1947-56; Delgado College, New Orleans, La., assistant professor, 1964-74, associate professor of visual communications, 1974—, and chairman of department, 1964—. Director of Delgado Press, 1960—. *Military service:* U.S. Navy, 1945-47. *Member:* International Graphic Arts Educational Association (secretary, 1973-75), In-Plant Printing Managers Association.

WRITINGS: Elementary Printing, Delgado College, 1958, 4th edition, 1966; *Copy Preparation for Printing,* McGraw, 1973.

* * *

CABOT, Blake 1905(?)-1974

1905(?)—September 1, 1974; American medical writer and publisher. Obituaries: *New York Times*, September 2, 1974; *AB Bookman's Weekly*, November 18, 1974.

* * *

CADBURY, Henry J(oel) 1883-1974

December 1, 1883—October 7, 1974; American Quaker educator, author, and recipient of Nobel Peace Prize. Obituaries: *New York Times*, October 9, 1974; *Washington Post*, October 10, 1974. (*CA*-15/16).

* * *

CAIRNS, Huntington 1904- (Ralph Utley)

PERSONAL: Born September 1, 1904, Baltimore, Md.; son of James Duncanson (a businessman) and Helen Huntington (Heath) Cairns; married Florence Faison Butler, May 29, 1929. *Education:* Attended Baltimore City College, 1920-22; University of Maryland, LL.B., 1925. *Home and office:* 2219 California St., N.W., Washington, D.C. 20008.

CAREER: Admitted to Bar of State of Maryland, 1926, and to Bar of District of Columbia, 1943; Piper, Carey & Hall (law firm), Baltimore, Md., associate, 1926-33, partner, 1933-37; U.S. Treasury, Washington, D.C., senior assistant general counsel, 1937-43; National Gallery of Art, Washington, D.C., secretary, treasurer, and general counsel, 1943-65; full-time writer, 1965—. Special legal adviser, U.S. Treasury, 1934-37, 1943-65, and member of committee on practice, 1944-52; member of State of Maryland Tax Revision Commission, 1938-41; chairman of radio program, "Invitation to Learning," 1940-41; secretary, American Commission for the Protection and Salvage of Artistic and Historic Monuments in War Areas, 1943-46; trustee of Bollingen Foundation; president and trustee, Textile Museum, Washington, D.C.; member of Dumbarton Oaks administrative committee of Harvard University; lecturer on taxation, University of Maryland, 1935-37; Johns Hopkins University James Schouler Lecturer in political science, 1947, in criticism, 1949-59; Association of the Bar of the City of New York Benjamin Cardozo Lecturer, 1962; George Randolph Tucker Lecturer at Washington and Lee University, 1970. *Member:* American Law Institute, American Philosophical Association, Maryland Bar Association, District of Columbia Bar Association, Phi Beta Kappa, F Street Club, Maryland Club, Hamilton Street Club, Cosmos Club, Wranglers Club. *Awards, honors:* City of Baltimore Civic Medallion, 1935; Rockefeller Public Service Award; LL.D. from New York University, St. Andrews University, Johns Hopkins University, and University of Maryland; L.H.D. from Tulane University, Kenyon College.

WRITINGS: Law and the Social Sciences, Harcourt, 1935, reprinted, Rothman, 1970; (editor) *Tax Laws of Maryland*, 2nd edition (Cairns was not associated with first edition), State Tax Commission of Maryland, 1937; *The Theory of Legal Science*, University of North Carolina Press, 1941, reprinted, Rothman, 1969; (with Allen Tate and Mark Van Doran) *Invitation to Learning*, Random House, 1941; (editor with John Walker) *Masterpieces of Painting from the National Gallery of Art*, Random House, 1944; (editor) Bronislaw Malinowski, *A Scientific Theory of Culture*, University of North Carolina Press, 1944; (editor) George E. Saintsbury, *French Literature and Its Masters*, Knopf, 1945; (editor) *The Limits of Art*, three volumes, Princeton University Press, 1948, Volume I reprinted, 1969, Volume II and Volume III reprinted, 1970; *Legal Philosophy from Plato to Hegel*, Johns Hopkins Press, 1949; (editor with Walker) *Great Paintings from the National Gallery of Art*, Macmillan, 1952; (editor with Edith Hamilton) *The Collected Dialogues of Plato*, Princeton University Press, 1961; (editor with Walker) *Treasures from the National Gallery of Art*, Macmillan, 1962; *Law and Its Premises*, Association of the Bar of the City of New York, 1962; (editor) H. L. Mencken, *The American Scene: A Reader*, Knopf, 1965; (editor with Walker) *A Pageant of Painting*, Macmillan, 1966; (editor) *The Two-Story World: Selected Writings of James K. Feibleman*, Holt, 1966; *What is Law?*, Washington and Lee University, 1970; *This Other Eden*, Times Printing Co., 1973, 2nd edition, 1974.

Contributor to newspapers, sometimes under pseudonym Ralph Utley. Member of board of directors, *Journal of the History of Ideas*.

WORK IN PROGRESS: A book on Shakespeare.

BIOGRAPHICAL/CRITICAL SOURCES: Coastlander (Manteo, N.C.), August, 1974.

* * *

CALHOON, Robert M. 1935-

PERSONAL: Born October 3, 1935, in Pittsburgh, Pa.; son of Forrest O. (an engineer) and Elizabeth (McCluen) Calhoon; married Doris Abernethy, June 18, 1966; children: Claudia Marie. *Education:* College of Wooster, B.A., 1958; Western Reserve University (now Case Western Reserve University), M.A., 1959, Ph.D., 1964. *Residence:* Greensboro, N.C. *Office:* Department of History, University of North Carolina, Greensboro, N.C. 27412.

CAREER: University of North Carolina, Greensboro, member of faculty in department of history. *Member:* American Historical Association, Organization of American Historians, Southern Historical Association. *Awards, honors:* Honorable mention from Society of Colonial Wars, 1974.

WRITINGS: The Loyalist in Revolutionary America: 1760-1781, Harcourt, 1973.

WORK IN PROGRESS: Research on religion in the South during the eighteenth century.

* * *

CALIA, Vincent F(rank) 1926-

PERSONAL: Born June 25, 1926, in Somerville, Mass.; son of Frank and Annie (Blunda) Calia; married Mary Patricia Buckley, June 12, 1954; children: Paul T., Moira Jeanne. *Education:* Northeastern University, A.B., 1949; Boston University, Ed.M., 1952, Ed.D., 1959. *Office:* Department of Education, Rhode Island College, 600 Mt. Pleasant Ave., Providence, R.I. 02908.

CAREER: Boston University, Boston, Mass., instructor, 1952-57, assistant professor, 1957-61, associate professor of counselor education, 1961-64; Rhode Island College, Providence, professor of counselor education, 1964—, head of department, 1966-72. Consulting psychologist to Raytheon Manufacturing Co., 1960-62, and Espousal Center, Waltham, Mass., 1972—. *Military service:* U.S. Army, Infantry, 1944-46; became sergeant. *Member:* International Transactional Analysis Association, American Psychological Association, American Personnel and Guidance Association, Association for Counselor Educators and Supervisors, Rhode Island Personnel and Guidance Association (president, 1970-72), Massachussetts Psychological Association.

WRITINGS: *Pupil Personnel Administration,* C.C Thomas, 1968; *Critical Incidents in School Counseling,* Prentice-Hall, 1973. Contributor to *Journal of Counseling Psychology, Personnel and Guidance Journal, Counseling and Values,* and *Journal of the Association for Counselor Educators and Supervisors.* Consulting editor, *Journal of Individual Psychology,* 1974.

* * *

CALLAN, Richard J(erome) 1932-

PERSONAL: Born January 4, 1932, in New York; son of Frank (a businessman) and Marietta (Kelly) Callan; married Eleanore Gage, 1954. *Education:* Iona College, B.A. (cum laude), 1957; Fordham University, M.A., 1959; summer graduate study at Middlebury Language School, 1960, 1961; St. Louis University, Ph.D., 1965. *Home address:* RFD 1, Newmarket, N.H. 03857.

CAREER: Marquette University, Milwaukee, Wis., instructor in Spanish, 1960 (spring); St. Michael's College, Winooski, Vt., assistant professor of Spanish, 1960-63; St. Louis University, St. Louis, Mo., associate professor of Spanish, 1965-69; University of New Hampshire, Durham, associate professor of Spanish, 1969—. *Member:* Instituto International de Literatura Iberoamericana, Modern Language Association of America, Hispania, Midwest Modern Language Association.

WRITINGS: *Miguel Angel Asturias,* Twayne, 1970; (editor and author of prologue) *America: Fabula de Fabulas y otros Ensayos de Miguel Angel Asturias* (title means "America: 'Fable among Fables' and Other Essays of Miguel Angel Asturias"), Monte Avila Editores (Caracas), 1972. Contributor to journals in his field.

WORK IN PROGRESS: A study of contemporary Latin American prose writers; a second collection of the essays of Miguel Angel Asturias.

* * *

CALLIS, Helmut G(unther) 1906-

PERSONAL: Born April 6, 1906, in Breslau, Germany; son of Michael (an architect) and Margaret (Sacher) Callis; married Maud Krotosehin (a professor of history), October 18, 1934; children: Stephen Michael, Peter Christopher. *Education:* University of Leipzig, diploma, 1930, Ph.D. (with highest honors), 1932; Graduate Institute of International Studies, Geneva, Switzerland, certificate, 1939. *Politics:* Independent. *Religion:* Elective. *Home:* 2525 East 1300th St. S., Salt Lake City, Utah 84108. *Office:* Department of History, University of Utah, Salt Lake City, Utah 84112.

CAREER: University of Michigan, Ann Arbor, research associate, 1940-45, lecturer in economics, 1942-45, director of East Asia Area Program, Army Specialized Training Program, 1942-45; Yale University, New haven, Conn., associate professor of economics, 1945-47; University of Utah, Salt Lake City, professor of Oriental history, 1947—. Ramakrishna Institute of Culture, School of Intercultural Studies, Calcutta, India, academic director, 1961-62. *Member:* Asian Studies Association, Foreign Policy Association, American Association of University Professors, United Nations Association of America, American Historical Association, American Political Science Association. *Awards, honors:* Rockefeller research fellowship, 1939; Ford Faculty fellowship, Harvard University, 1953-54; Fulbright research fellowship to India, 1960-62.

WRITINGS: *Fixed Assets and the Trade Cycle,* [Leipzig], 1933; *Neutralite et le Pacte de la Societe Des Nations* [Geneva], 1938; *Foreign Capital in Southeast Asia,* Institute of Pacific Relations (New York), 1942; (contributor) Snyder and Wilson, editors, *Roots of Political Behavior,* [New York], 1949; (contributor) *Great Issues,* University of Utah Press, 1957; *China: Confucian and Communist,* Holt, 1959; *China, Asia, and the West,* University of Utah Press, 1960; (contributor) *Mankind and History,* University of New Mexico Press, 1970; *Why Not Admit Red China to the U.N.?,* McCutchan, 1970. Also author of *China, Asia, and American Policy,* 1973. Contributor to annals, proceedings, and journals in his field.

WORK IN PROGRESS: A series of six volumes concerning Asia's international relations and policies; a revision of *China: Confucian and Communist;* a book, *Eastern Civilization.*

SIDELIGHTS: Callis spent eleven years in India, China, and other Asian countries. In addition to English and German, he is competent in French, Chinese, Greek, and Latin, and speaks some Chinese. *Avocational interests:* Travel, collecting Oriental art, especially painting and sculpture.

* * *

CAMPANELLA, Francis B. 1936-

PERSONAL: Born June 6, 1936, in Boston, Mass.; son of Francis Joseph (a businessman) and Margaret (Foley) Campanella; married Janice Patricia Leary (a counselor), July 11, 1959; children: Kathleen, Patricia, Maureen. *Education:* Rensselaer Polytechnic Institute, B.S., 1958; Babson College, M.B.A. (with highest distinction), 1966; Harvard University, D.B.A., 1970. *Religion:* Roman Catholic. *Home:* 41 Wethersfield Rd., Natick, Mass. 01760. *Office:* Office of the Vice-President, Boston College, Chestnut Hill, Mass. 02167.

CAREER: Acoustical Contractors, Inc., Waltham, Mass., sales engineer and treasurer, 1961-66; Boston College, Chestnut Hill, Mass., associate professor of education, 1970-73, executive vice-president, 1973—. Trinity Mental Health Association and Clinic, member of board of trustees, chairman, and treasurer, 1968-73; founder, director, and vice-president, N.A.H.E., Inc., 1971—. *Military service:* U.S. Marine Corps, 1958-61; became captain. *Member:* American Institute for Decision Sciences, Financial Management Association, American Finance Association, Eastern Finance Association, Harvard Business School Association.

WRITINGS: (With A. J. Kelley and J. McKiernan) *Venture Capital: A Guidebook for New Enterprises*, Management Institute, Boston College, 1971; *The Measurement of Portfolio Risk Exposure: The Use of the Beta Coefficient*, Heath, 1972. Contributor to *Financial Review*.

WORK IN PROGRESS: Research on probabilistic planning models.

* * *

CAMPBELL, Ian 1899-

PERSONAL: Born October 17, 1899, in Bismarck, N.D.; son of Dugald (a rancher) and Agnes (Gilkison) Campbell; married Catherine Chase (a technical editor), September 16, 1930; children: Dugald R. *Education:* University of Oregon, A.B., 1922, A.M., 1923; Northwestern University, graduate study, 1923-24; Harvard University, Ph.D., 1931. *Politics:* Democrat. *Religion:* Unitarian Universalist. *Home:* 1333 Jones St., Apt. 906, San Francisco, Calif. 94109. *Office:* California Academy of Sciences, Golden Gate Park, San Francisco, Calif. 94118.

CAREER: Louisiana State University, Baton Rouge, assistant professor of geology, 1925-28; Harvard University, Cambridge, Mass., instructor in mineralogy, 1928-31; California Institute of Technology, Pasadena, assistant professor, 1931-34, associate professor, 1934-46, professor of petrology, 1946-59, professor emeritus, 1970—, executive officer of Division of Geological Sciences, 1952-59; State of California, chief, and state geologist in Division of Mines and Geology, 1959-69, director of department of conservation, 1966-67; California Academy of Sciences, San Francisco, Calif., president, 1971—. Chairman of California Selective Service Board, 1948-59; president of California State Board of Registration for Geologists and Geophysicists, 1972-74. *Military service:* U.S. Army, Ambulance Corps, 1917-19; served in American Expeditionary Forces.

MEMBER: American Association for the Advancement of Science (president of Pacific Division, 1958), American Geological Institute (president, 1961), Mineralogical Society of America (president, 1962), American Association of State Geologists (president, 1965-66), Geological Society of America (fellow; president, 1968), Society of Mining Engineers (western reginal vice-president, 1966-69), Society of Economic Geologists, American Geophysical Union, National Association of Geology Teachers, American Association of Petroleum Geologists, American Institute of Mining, Metallurgical and Petroleum Engineers, American Institute of Professional Geologists, Association of Engineering Geologists.

AWARDS, HONORS: Hardinge Medal from American Institute of Mining Engineers, 1964; Ben Parker Memorial Award from American Institute of Professional Geologists, 1969; Federated Mineral Society scholarship, 1969; Public Service Award from American Association of Petroleum Geologists, 1973.

WRITINGS: (With others) *The Earth and Human Affairs*, Canfield Press, 1972; (with Arthur Court) *Minerals: Nature's Fabulous Jewels*, Abrams, 1974. Contributor to U.S. Geological Survey and scientific journals. Associate editor of *Journal of the Mineralogical Society*, during late 1950's and *Bulletin of the Geological Society of America*, 1963-67; editor, *Journal of the Association of American State Geologists*, 1960-63.

CAMPBELL, J(ames) Arthur 1916-

PERSONAL: Born October 1, 1916, in Elyria, Ohio; son of James Allen (a plantation manager) and Helen I. (a nurse; maiden name, Metcalf) Campbell; married Dorothy E. Carnell, November 12, 1938; children: Kathleen Annette Fischer, Christine Edmundson. *Education:* Oberlin College, A.B. (magna cum laude), 1938; Purdue University, M.S., 1939; University of California, Berkeley, Ph.D., 1942. *Home:* 754 West 10th St., Claremont, Calif. 91711. *Office:* Department of Chemistry, Harvey Mudd College, Claremont, Calif. 91711.

CAREER: University of California, Berkeley, instructor and researcher for Manhattan Project, 1942-45; Oberlin College, Oberlin, Ohio, assistant professor, 1945-49, associate professor, 1949-53, professor of chemistry, 1953-57; National Science Foundation, Washington, D.C., program director for institutes, 1956-57; Harvey Mudd College, Claremont, Calif., professor, 1957-67, Seeley W. Mudd Professor of Chemistry, 1967—, chairman of department, 1957—, dean of faculty, 1974—. Visiting professor at Ohio State University, 1947, Michigan State University, 1948, University of Wisconsin, 1954, and University of California, Berkeley, summers, 1958-59, 1965-67, 1971. Resident scholar at Rockefeller Center, Lake Como, Italy, 1972. Director of National Science Foundation's Chemical Education Material Study, 1960-63.

MEMBER: Chemical Society (England), American Chemical Society, American Association for the Advancement of Science, American Association of University Professors, Phi Beta Kappa, Sigma Xi. *Awards, honors:* Research Corporation grant, 1951; Fund for the Advancement of Education fellowship at Cambridge University, 1952-53; Manufacturing Chemists' award for excellence in the teaching of chemistry, 1962; Guggenheim fellowship, 1963-64, for study at Kyoto University and Cambridge University; J. F. Norris award from American Chemical Society, 1964, for contribution to chemical education; Atomic Energy Commission grant, 1964-69; National Science Foundation research grant, 1964-69; faculty fellow at Harvard University, 1970-71; Scientific Apparatus Makers-American Chemical Society award in chemical education, 1972; D.Sc., Beaver College, 1972.

WRITINGS: (With Luke E. Steiner) *General Chemistry,* Macmillan, 1955; (with Steiner) *Laboratory Experiments in General Chemistry,* Macmillan, 1955; *Why Do Chemical Reactions Occur?,* Prentice-Hall, 1963; *Chemical Systems: Energetics, Dynamics and Structures,* W. H. Freeman, 1969. Contributor of monthly column, "ECO-CHEM," to *Journal of Chemical Education,* 1972—. Contributor to professional journals.

* * *

CAMPBELL, John R(oy) 1933-

PERSONAL: Born June 14, 1933, in Missouri; son of Carl J. and Helen (Nicoletti) Campbell; married Eunice J. Vieten, August 7, 1954; children: Karen L., Kathy L., Keith L. *Education:* University of Missouri, B.S., 1955, M.S., 1956, Ph.D., 1960; postdoctoral study, University of Colorado, 1968. *Politics:* Independent. *Religion:* Protestant. *Home:* 357 Crown Point, Columbia, Mo. 65201. *Office:* 209 Eckles Hall, University of Missouri, Columbia, Mo. 65201.

CAREER: University of Missouri, Columbia, assistant professor, 1960-65, associate professor, 1965-68, professor of agriculture, 1968—. *Military service:* U.S. Army, 1956-58; became lieutenant. Missouri National Guard, 1958—;

became lieutenant colonel. *Member:* American Society of Animal Science, American Dairy Science Association, American Association for the Advancement of Science, National Association of College Teachers of Agriculture, Gamma Sigma Delta (president, 1971-72), Alpha Zeta (vice-president, 1954-55), Omicron Delta Kappa. *Awards, honors:* Danforth Foundation associate, 1970; distinguished teaching award from American Dairy Science Association, 1973; distinguished teaching award from National Association of College Teachers of Agriculture, 1973.

WRITINGS: (With J. F. Lasley) *The Science of Animals that Serve Mankind*, McGraw, 1969, 2nd edition, 1975; *In Touch with Students: A Philosophy for Teachers*, Educational Affairs Publishers, 1972; (with R. T. Marshall) *The Science of Providing Milk for Man*, McGraw, 1975. Contributor to *Journal of Dairy Science*, *Journal of Animal Science*, *Journal of the American Veterinary Medicine Association*, and popular agricultural magazines.

WORK IN PROGRESS: Research on recycling various papers, cheese whey, and other nonconventional feedstuffs through ruminants; research on the chemical preservation of colostrum milk for feeding neonatal farm animals.

* * *

CAMPBELL, Karlyn Kohrs 1937-

PERSONAL: Born April 16, 1937, in Blomkest, Minn.; daughter of Meinhard and Dorothy (Siegers) Kohrs; married Paul Newell Campbell (a college professor), September 16, 1967. *Education:* Macalester College, B.A., 1958; University of Minnesota, M.A., 1959, Ph.D., 1968. *Home:* 2610 University Dr., Lawrence, Kan. 66044. *Office:* Department of Speech, University of Kansas, Lawrence, Kan. 66045.

CAREER: Macalester College, St. Paul, Minn., instructor, 1958-59, assistant professor of speech, 1964-65; State University of New York, assistant professor at Brockport campus, 1959-63, associate professor of speech at Binghamton, 1971-73; California State University, Los Angeles, assistant professor of speech, 1966-71; City College of the City University of New York, New York, N.Y., associate professor of speech, 1973-74; University of Kansas, Lawrence, professor of speech, 1974—. Editorial commentator on KPFK-FM, Los Angeles, 1970. *Member:* Speech Communication Association of America, Eastern Communication Association.

WRITINGS: Critiques of Contemporary Rhetoric, Wadsworth, 1972. Contributor to *Philosophy and Rhetoric, Western Speech, Quarterly Journal of Speech,* and *Speech Teacher*. Member of editorial board of *Today's Speech,* 1971-74, and *Speech Teacher,* 1972-75.

WORK IN PROGRESS: Power, Perspective, and Participation: The Political, Sociological, and Literary Dimensions of Rhetoric.

* * *

CAMPBELL, Robert 1922-

PERSONAL: Born January 20, 1922, in Hagerstown, Md.; son of Robert L. (a shoe manufacturer) and Adelaide (McBride) Campbell; married third wife, Nancy Van Arsdel, October 9, 1959; children: (third marriage) Thomas Scott, Stephen McBride. *Education:* St. John's College, Annapolis, Md., B.A., 1944. *Politics:* Independent. *Religion:* "Nonspecific." *Address:* R.D. 2, Box 212, Boonton, N.J. 07005.

CAREER: Life, New York, N.Y., reporter and writer, 1945-57; free-lance writer, industrial and documentary film maker, composer, assistant producer, 1957—. *Military service:* U.S. Army, 1941-42. *Member:* American Society of Composers, Authors and Publishers, American Bugatti Club. *Awards, honors:* American Medical Association citation, 1966, for *Life* article on viruses; recipient of numerous film awards.

WRITINGS: (Editor) *Skeet Shooting with D. Lee Braun*, Rutledge Books, 1967; (editor) *Trapshooting with D. Lee Braun*, Rutledge Books, 1969; (contributor) Joseph Comprone, editor, *From Experience to Expression* (college textbook), W.C. Brown, 1974; *The Chasm* (nonfiction; introduction by James Baldwin), Houghton, 1974. Contributor to *Sports Illustrated*.

WORK IN PROGRESS: An environmental picture for National Film Board of Canada; an American opera.

SIDELIGHTS: Campbell wrote *The Chasm* after a film assignment on ghetto schools.

* * *

CANCIAN, Francis Alexander 1934- (Frank Cancian)

PERSONAL: Born August 14, 1934, in Stafford Springs, Conn.; son of Frank (a mason) and Emma (a mill worker; maiden name, Lazzarin) Cancian; married Francesca M. Wendel (a professor of sociology), 1959; children: Maria Michelle, Steven Alexander. *Education:* Wesleyan University, A.B., 1956; Harvard University, Ph.D., 1963. *Home:* 1055 Vernier Pl., Stanford, Calif. 94305. *Office:* Department of Anthropology, Stanford University, Stanford, Calif. 94305.

CAREER: Reporter-photographer on *Providence Journal*, Providence, R.I., 1957-58; Harvard University, Cambridge, Mass., instructor in social anthropology, 1963-64; Stanford University, Stanford, Calif., assistant professor of anthropology, 1964-66; Cornell University, Ithaca, N.Y., associate professor of anthropology, 1966-69; Stanford University, Stanford, Calif., professor of anthropology, 1969—, chairman of department, 1974—. *Awards, honors:* Fulbright grant in Italy, 1956-57; National Institutes of Mental Health grants, 1963-64, 1970-71; Wenner-Gren Foundation grants-in-aid, summer, 1971; postdoctoral fellowship in Latin American studies from Foreign Area Fellowship Program, 1966-67, summer, 1968.

WRITINGS—Under name Frank Cancian: *Economics and Prestige in a Maya Community: The Religious Cargo System in Zinacantan*, Stanford University Press, 1965; (contributor) Robert Wauchope and Manning Nash, editors, *The Handbook of Middle American Indians*, Volume VI, University of Texas Press, 1967; (contributor) E.E. LeClair and H.K. Schneider, editors, *Economic Anthropology: Readings in Theory and Analysis*, Holt, 1968; *Change and Uncertainty in a Peasant Economy: The Maya Corn Farmers of Zinacantan*, Stanford University Press, 1972; *Another Place: Photographs of a Maya Community*, Scrimshaw Press, 1974; (contributor) John Poggie, Jr., and Robert N. Lynch, editors, *Rethinking Modernization*, Greenwood Press, 1974. Contributor of about twenty articles and reviews to professional journals.

* * *

CANNON, James P. 1890(?)-1974

1890(?)—August 21, 1974; American socialist author and organizer. Obituaries: *New York Times*, August 23, 1974.

CANTIN, Eileen 1931-

PERSONAL: Born August 31, 1931, in Waterbury, Conn.; daughter of Romeo Wilfred and Eva (Ovimet) Cantin. *Education:* Lorretto Heights College, B.A., 1962; Marquette University, M.A., 1967, Ph.D., 1972. *Home:* 4038 Mallway Dr., Indianapolis, Ind. 46234. *Office:* Center for the Exploration of Values and Meaning, 8463 Castlewood Dr., Indianapolis, Ind. 46250.

CAREER: Roman Catholic Sister of the Congregation of St. Joseph of Tipton, Ind. (C.S.J). Teacher in elementary schools and junior high schools in Marion, Kokomo, and Elwood, Ind., 1957-64; Marquette University, Milwaukee, Wis., instructor in philosophy, 1969-70; Diocesan Office of Religious Education, Kokomo, Ind., assistant director, 1970-72; Center for the Exploration of Values and Meaning, Indianapolis, Ind., vice-president, 1973—. Member of associate faculty of Indiana University at Indianapolis and Kokomo; member of board of directors of Project Omega (ecumenical program in spiritual development), 1974; member of United Nations Population Tribune, 1974; member of International Educational Development (United Nations consultant agency).

MEMBER: American Catholic Philosophical Association, National Catholic Education Association, Societe des Amis d'Emmanuel Mounier, Pi Lambda Theta. *Awards, honors:* International scholarship from Societe des Amis d'Emmanuel Mounier, 1973, for study in France and England.

WRITINGS: Mounier: A Personalist View of History, Paulist-Newman, 1973.

WORK IN PROGRESS: Editing *On Property and Possession*, a translation from the writings of Emmanuel Mounier.

SIDELIGHTS: Eileen Cantin is a personalist philosopher, interested in values and meaning questions and in relating philosophy to life issues. *Avocational interests:* Swimming, tennis.

* * *

CARDEN, Maren Lockwood

PERSONAL: Born in Stretford, England; married in 1968. *Education:* University of London, B.Sc. (honors), 1955; University of Maryland, M.A., 1957; Harvard University, Ph.D., 1963. *Home:* 193 Lawrence St., New Haven, Conn. 06511. *Office:* Department of American Studies, Yale University, New Haven, Conn. 06520.

CAREER: University of Maryland, College Park, part-time instructor in sociology, 1957-58; Harvard University, Cambridge, Mass., lecturer in social relations, spring, 1963; State University of New York at Buffalo, assistant professor of sociology, 1963-66; Boston University, Boston, Mass., associate professor of sociology, 1966-71; Yale University, New Haven, Conn., visiting associate professor, 1971-72, visiting lecturer in sociology, 1973, lecturer in American studies, spring, 1975. Visiting associate professor at Massachusetts Institute of Technology, summer, 1967.

MEMBER: American Sociological Association, Society for the Scientific Study of Religion, Eastern Sociological Society. *Awards, honors:* American Philosophical Society grant, 1963; Russell Sage Foundation fellowship, 1970-72; Radcliffe Institute fellowship, 1970-72.

WRITINGS: (Contributor) Frank E. Manuel, editor, *Utopias and Utopian Thought*, Houghton, 1966; *Oneida: Utopian Community to Modern Corporation*, Johns Hopkins Press, 1969; (contributor) Joseph R. Gusfield, editor, *Reader in Social Movements*, Wiley, 1969; *The New Feminist Movement*, Russell Sage Foundation, 1974, abridged edition published as *Why Do American Women Want "Liberation"?*, U.S. Information Service, 1974. Contributor to *Daedalus*.

* * *

CAREY, Richard John 1925-

PERSONAL: Born March 30, 1925, in San Francisco, Calif.; son of John Francis (an accountant) and Anne D. (Volosing) Carey. *Education:* University of California, Berkeley, B.A., 1947, M.A., 1949; B.L.S., 1954; graduate study at Sorbonne, University of Paris, and Ecole des Chartes, 1949-52; Columbia University, Ph.D., 1965. *Politics:* Conservative. *Home:* West 3211 Grandview Ave., Spokane, Wash. 99204. *Office:* Department of French, Eastern Washington State College, Cheney, Wash. 99004.

CAREER: San Jose State College (now University), San Jose, Calif., professional librarian, 1954-59; Columbia University, New York, N.Y., instructor in French, 1959-66; Hunter College of the City University of New York, New York, assistant professor of French, 1967-69; Eastern Washington State College, Cheney, professor of French, 1969—. Member of board of directors, Spokane Community Concerts, 1975—. *Military service:* U.S. Navy, 1942-45. *Member:* American Association of Teachers of French, American Federation of Teachers, Mediaeval Academy of America, Medievalists of the Pacific, Washington Association of Teachers of Foreign Languages. *Awards, honors:* Awarded Concours Oratoire by the French Government, 1947.

WRITINGS: (Editor) Jean Le Court, *Le Restor du paon* (title means "The Restoration of the Peacock"), Droz, 1964; (editor) Jean de Le Mote, *Le Parfait du paon* (title means "The Completion of the Peacock"), University of North Carolina Press, 1972. Contributor to *Reader's Encyclopedia*, and to *Journal of Library History*. Editor and contributor, *Bulletin des professeurs de Francais*, 1969-72.

WORK IN PROGRESS: Editing Jean Le Court's *L'Escole de foy* (title means "School of Faith").

SIDELIGHTS: Carey has varying competence in French, German, Spanish, Provencal, Latin, and Greek. *Avocational interests:* Travel, piano, gardening.

* * *

CARL, Beverly May 1932-

PERSONAL: Born November 13, 1932, in Richmond, Va.; daughter of John W., Sr. (an engineer) and Laura (a secretary; maiden name, Payne) Carl. *Education:* University of Southern California, B.L., 1955, J.D., 1956; Yale University, LL.M., 1957; attended The Hague Academy of International Law, 1957, University of Madrid, 1957, and University of Chile Law School, 1958-59. *Politics:* Democrat. *Home:* 7510 West Northwest Highway, Apt. 2, Dallas, Tex. 75225. *Office:* School of Law, Southern Methodist University, Dallas, Tex. 75222.

CAREER: Quinnipiac College, Hamden, Conn., instructor, 1959-60; U.S. Treasury Dept., Office of International Finance, Washington, D.C., attorney, 1959-60; U.S. Dept. of Commerce, Washington, D.C., special assistant to Assistant Secretary for Trade Policy, 1961-62; U.S. State Dept., Washington, D.C., special assistant to Assistant Administrator for Private Enterprise and Developmental Finance, 1963-64, investment insurance officer, 1964-65, chief of Private Investment Division, Rio de Janeiro, Brazil, 1965-67, assistant chief of Nigeria-Biafra Relief Program for Agency for International Development, 1968-70; Southern Methodist University, Dallas, Tex., associate professor of law, 1970—. *Member:* American Bar Association (member of council, 1974-76), State Bar of Texas, Dallas International Law Association (president, 1974-75). *Awards, honors:* Meritorious honor award from U.S. Department of State, 1970, for work on Nigeria-Biafra Relief Program.

WRITINGS: A Guide to Incentives for Investing in Brazil, Southern Methodist University Press, 1972; *Clinic in Transnational Legal Communications*, Association of American Law Schools, 1973. Contributor to *Harvard Journal of International Law* and other journals.

WORK IN PROGRESS: Private International Law; *Economic Development Law*.

* * *

CARLISLE, E(rvin) Fred 1935-

PERSONAL: Born March 20, 1935, in Ohio; son of Ervin Frederick and Winnifred (Lucas) Carlisle; married second wife Barbara Saenger Rutledge (an art historian), September 28, 1973; children: (first marriage) Linda, Rebecca, Ginna, Jana. *Education:* Ohio Wesleyan University, B.A., 1956; Ohio State University, M.A., 1957; Indiana University, Ph.D., 1963. *Office:* Department of English, Michigan State University, East Lansing, Mich. 48823.

CAREER: Ohio University, Athens, instructor in English, 1962-63; DePauw University, Greencastle, Ind., assistant professor of English, 1963-66; Michigan State University, East Lansing, assistant professor, 1966-68, associate professor, 1968-72, professor of English, 1972—, associate chairman of department, 1968-72. Has performed with Michigan State University's University Theater and Department of Music. *Military service:* U.S. Air Force, 1957-60; became first lieutenant. *Member:* Modern Language Association of America, National Council of Teachers of English, Philosophy of Science Association, Midwest Modern Language Association, Phi Beta Kappa. *Awards, honors:* National Endowment for the Humanities fellowship, 1972-73.

WRITINGS: (With Norman Foerster and others) *American Poetry and Prose*, Houghton, 1970; (editor with James H. Pickering) *The Harper Reader*, Harper, 1971; *The Uncertain Self: Whitman's Drama of Identity*, Michigan State University Press, 1973. Contributor of articles and reviews to *Criticism*, *Modern Fiction Studies*, *American Quarterly*, *Centennial Review*, and *American Literature*. Book selection adviser for "Annual Review of Books" in *American Quarterly*, 1967-70; manuscript reader for *American Quarterly*, Harper, Houghton, Scott, Foresman, Xerox Educational Publishing, and Canada Council.

WORK IN PROGRESS: A critical biography of Loren Eiseley; research on language forms in literature and science.

* * *

CARLISLE, Lilian (Matarose) Baker 1912-

PERSONAL: Born January 1, 1912, in Meridian, Miss.; daughter of Joseph (a lumber salesman) and Lilian (Flournoy) Baker; married E. Grafton Carlisle, Jr. (a banker), January 9, 1933; children: Lilian Diana (Mrs. Edward S. Schwerdtle), Penelope Susan (formerly Mrs. Leroy Meshel). *Education:* Attended Dickinson College, 1929-30; Peirce College of Business Administration, Philadelphia, Pa., secretarial diploma, 1931. *Politics:* Democrat. *Religion:* Congregationalist. *Home and office:* 117 Lakeview Ter., Burlington, Vt. 05401.

CAREER: Secretary, A. W. Sanson (attorney-at-law), Philadelphia, Pa., 1931-35, Royal Air Force Ferry Command, Montreal, Quebec, 1942-43, Red Cross Missing Persons Enquiring Bureau, Montreal, 1944-45, McGill University School of Social Work, Montreal, 1945-46, and Frederick P. Smith (attorney-at-law), Burlington, Vt., 1948-50; Shelburne Museum, Shelburne, Vt., member of executive staff, in charge of collections and research, 1951-61; coordinator of Burlington Area Community Health Study for National Commission on Community Health Services, 1963-64; assistant coordinator, State of Vermont Mental Retardation Planning Project, Montpelier, 1965; Office of Economic Opportunity, project director, Champlain Valley Medicare Alert, Burlington, 1966; Vermont State House of Representatives, Burlington, representative for Districts 1-5, 1969-70; New York Historical Association, Cooperstown, N.Y., member of faculty, Seminars on American Culture, 1971. Publicity and public relations agent, Champlain Valley Exposition, 1968—; member of Vermont State Bicentennial Commission, 1974-77. Has conducted seminars in nineteenth-century crafts at Champlain College. Treasurer, Community Council of Greater Burlington, 1951, vice-president, 1956-58, president, 1959-61, 1972-74. Editorial consultant, City of Burlington, 1967.

MEMBER: National League of American Pen Women, Order of Women Legislators (president of Vermont chapter, 1972-74), Vermont Historical Society (past trustee), Vermont Folklore Society, Old Cemetery Association, League of Vermont Writers (director, 1962; vice-president, 1965-66; president, 1967-68), Green Mountain Folklore Society (founding member), Chittenden County Historical Society (president, 1969-72), Chi Omega, Zonta International (president of Burlington chapter, 1964-65).

WRITINGS: (With Ralph Nading Hill) *The Story of the Shelburne Museum*, Lane Press (Burlington, Vt.), 1955, enlarged edition, 1960; *The Carriages at Shelburne Museum*, Lane Press, 1956; *Pieced Work and Applique Quilts at Shelburne Museum*, Lane Press, 1957; *Hat Boxes and Bandboxes at Shelburne Museum*, Lane Press, 1960; *Inaugural Selection of Eighteenth and Nineteenth Century American Art*, Lane Press, 1960; (contributor of biographical sketches) Henry N. Flynt and Martha Gandy Fales, *Heritage Foundation Collection of Silver, with Biographical Sketches of New England Silversmiths, 1625-1825*, (Old Deerfield, Mass.), 1968; *Vermont Clock and Watchmakers, Silversmiths and Jewelers, 1778-1878*, Stinehour Press (Lunenburg, Vt.), 1970; (contributor) Albert C. Revi, editor, *The Spinning Wheel's Complete Book of Antiques*, Grosset, 1972.

Editor of pamphlets in "Look Around" Heritage Series of Chittenden County Historical Society; all published by George Little Press (Burlington, Vt.); *Look Around Burlington*, 1972; *. . . Jericho, Underhill and Westford*, 1972; *. . . Winooski*, 1972; *. . . Essex and Williston, Vermont*, 1973; *. . . Hinesburg and Charlotte, Vermont*, 1973; *. . . Richmond, Bolton and Huntington, Vermont*, 1974; *. . . Shelburne, St. George and South Burlington, Vermont*, 1975.

Monographs: (With M. Alfred Haynes) *Profile of the Community*, National Commission on Community Health

Services, 1964; (with Frank L. Babbott, Jr.) *Environmental and Personal Health of the Community*, National Commission on Community Health Services, 1964; *Mental Retardation in Vermont: A Chronology of Changing Attitudes*, State of Vermont (Montpelier), 1965; *Vocational Opportunities for the Retarded*, State of Vermont, 1965; *Day Care, Nursery Schools and Kindergartens in Vermont*, State of Vermont, 1965; *Evaluation: "Medicare Alert" OEO Project in Four Vermont Counties*, Office of Economic Opportunity (Champlain Valley), 1966.

Columnist, *Vermont Women's Fellowship Newsletter*, 1971-74. Contributor of over one hundred articles to newspapers, journals, and magazines, including *Connecticut Antiquarian Bulletin, American Heritage, Antiques, Antiques Journal, Spinning Wheel, Canadian Antiques Collector, Antique Trader, Chittenden County Historical Society Bulletin, Burlington Free Press*, and *New England Homestead.*

WORK IN PROGRESS: Editing additional pamphlets in the Chittenden County Historical Society "Look Around" Heritage Series, with the aim of publishing one for each city in the county, and eventually expanding to cover the entire state of Vermont; contributing to bi-centennial publications; writing a historical show for Vermont educational television.

AVOCATIONAL INTERESTS: Gourmet cooking, antique collecting, Middle Eastern dancing.

* * *

CARLISLE, Thomas (Fiske) 1944-
(Balthazar Kahn)

PERSONAL: Born October 15, 1944, in Baltimore, Md.; son of Jay C. (a businessman) and Opal (a scientist; maiden name, Fiske) Carlisle; married Kathleen McKie (a graphic artist), February 28, 1970. *Education:* University of California, Santa Barbara, student, 1962-64; University of California, Los Angeles, B.A., 1970. *Politics:* "Somewhere between fascism and communism." *Religion:* "Free thinker." *Office:* c/o Angst World Library, 2307 22nd Ave. E., Seattle, Wash. 98112.

CAREER: Out of the Ashes Press, Seattle, Wash., vice-president, 1974—. Associate editor of *D.N.A. Stereo*, 1971; founder of Camelot Press, 1975; editor for Angst World Library, 1974—. *Member:* Committee of Small Magazine Editors and Publishers.

WRITINGS: Bonstonofavitch!: A Novel of Madness, Angst World Library, 1974. Contributor to underground journals, under pseudonym Balthazar Kahn.

WORK IN PROGRESS: The Innocent Wasp, a novel; *Ceremony of Innocence*, a novel; studying the impact of social science fiction upon American thought.

SIDELIGHTS: Carlisle writes: "I am impressed with the psychological ramifications of the human mind and the degree to which heredity and environment mold it. Currently very much involved with editing and publishing young and unknown writers. Have traveled throughout the world, in all continents except South America. . . . Semi-fluent in Spanish, and functional in French. My English is developing slowly. Have been arrested by the F.B.I. for unpopular draft opinions and unpopular public statements. Walk two miles every morning before a 7:00 a.m. breakfast. Am somewhat of a recluse of late and don't like to mess around with social engagements and boring people unless properly remunerated."

CARLTON, Charles 1941-

PERSONAL: Born August 5, 1941, in Epsom, Surrey, England; came to United States, 1963; son of Charles (a surgeon and Valmai (a nurse; maiden name, Davies) Carlton; married Caroline Shaw, August 20, 1966; children: Abigail, Victoria. *Education:* Attended Epsom College; University College, Cardiff, B.A. (honors), 1962; University of California, Los Angeles, M.A., 1966, Ph.D., 1970. *Home:* 3448 Bradley Pl., Raleigh, N.C. 27607. *Office:* Department of History, North Carolina State University, Raleigh, N.C. 27607.

CAREER: Ford Motor Co., Dagenham, England, management trainee, 1962-63; Pasadena Children's Training Society, Pasadena, Calif., social worker, 1963-64; RAND Corp., Systems Development Corp., Santa Monica, Calif., part-time research assistant, 1964-65; research in England, 1967-69; North Carolina State University at Raleigh, instructor, 1969-70, assistant professor of British history, 1970—. *Military service:* British Army, Territorial Army Volunteer Reserve.

MEMBER: American Historical Association, Conference on British Studies, Anglo-American Associates, American Association of University Professors, Past and Present Society, Urban History Group. *Awards, honors:* Folger Shakespeare Library fellow to work on biography of Charles I, 1974-75; American Philosophical Society grant, 1974.

WRITINGS: The Court of Orphans, Humanities, 1974. Contributor of articles and reviews to *Huntington Library Quarterly*, *Guildhall Miscellany*, and other journals.

WORK IN PROGRESS: A book of readings on the present crisis in Ulster and its historical background; a biography of Charles I.

* * *

CARMICHAEL, Calum M. 1938-

PERSONAL: Born April 1, 1938, in Scotland; son of Donald MacNeill and Euphemia (MacLellan) Carmichael; married Norma MacDonald, June 25, 1959; children: Lachlan, Roderick, John-Allan. *Education:* University of Glasgow, B.Sc., 1959; graduate study at University of Edinburgh, 1959-62, and Oxford University, 1962-64. *Home:* 109 McIntyre Pl., Ithaca, N.Y. 14850. *Office:* Department of Semitics, Cornell University, Ithaca, N.Y. 14850.

CAREER: University of Southampton, Highfield, England, senior research fellow, 1966-67; Cornell University, Ithaca, N.Y., assistant professor, 1967-70, associate professor of Semitic and Biblical studies, 1970—.

WRITINGS: The Laws of Deuteronomy, Cornell University Press, 1974.

WORK IN PROGRESS: The Role of Women in the Development of the Genesis Traditions, completion expected in 1976.

* * *

CAROZZI, Albert V(ictor) 1925-

PERSONAL: Born April 26, 1925, in Geneva, Switzerland; naturalized American citizen; son of Luigi (a physician) and Anna-Maria (Ferrario) Carozzi; married Marguerite Peier, July 23, 1949; children: Viviane (Mrs. Onoratino Marrocco), Nadine. *Education:* University of Geneva, M.S., 1947, Dr.Sc. (summa cum laude), 1948. *Home:* 709 West Delaware, Urbana, Ill. 61801. *Office:* Department of Geology, University of Illinois, Urbana, Ill. 61801.

CAREER: University of Geneva, Geneva, Switzerland, lecturer in sedimentary petrology and micropaleontology, 1953-57; University of Illinois, Urbana, assistant visiting professor, 1955-56, associate professor, 1957-59, professor of geology, 1959—, associate member of Center for Advanced Study, 1969-70. Adviser on mineral development to Republic of the Ivory Coast Government, 1960—; presently consultant to petroleum societies and companies in France, Philippines, Peru, Brazil, and United States.

MEMBER: Geological Society of America (fellow), American Association of Petroleum Geologists, Society of Economic Paleontologists and Mineralogists, International Association of Sedimentology, American Institute of Mining, Metallurgical and Petroleum Engineers, International Committee on the History of the Geological Sciences (corresponding member), U.S. Committee on the History of Geology, American Association for the Advancement of Science, Illinois State Academy of Science, Natural History Society of Geneva (life member), Sigma Xi, Phi Kappa Phi. *Awards, honors:* Davy Award in Geology, University of Geneva, 1949, 1954; Plantamour-Prevost Award in Geology, University of Geneva, 1955.

WRITINGS: Petrographie des Roches Sedimentaires (textbook), Rouge & Cie, 1953; *Microscopic Sedimentary Petrography,* Wiley, 1960, reprint with corrections, Krieger, 1972; (with Jacqueline Bouroullec, Raoul Deloffre, and Jean-Louis Rumeau) *Microfacies du Jurassique d'Aquitaine, Petrographie, Diagenese, Geochimie et Petrophysique* (English-French bilingual edition), Centre de Recherches, Societe Nationale Petroles Aquitaine, 1972; (author of introduction) Louis Agassiz, *Lake Superior: Its Physical Character, Vegetation and Animals* (reprint of original edition of 1850), Krieger, 1974; *Sedimentary Rocks: Concepts and History,* Dowden, Hutchinson & Ross, in press.

Translator (of geology classics in French, German, and Latin) and annotator: A. G. Werner, *On the External Characters of Minerals,* University of Illinois Press, 1962; J. B. Lamarck, *Hydrogeology,* University of Illinois Press, 1964; Louis Agassiz, *Studies on Glaciers,* Hafner, 1967; Benoit de Maillet, *Telliamed,* University of Illinois Press, 1968; Lucien Cayeux, *Carbonate Rocks: Limestones and Dolomites,* Hafner, 1970; (with A. N. Iversen) R. E. Raspe, *An Introduction to the Natural History of the Terrestrial Sphere,* Hafner, 1970; Cayeux, *Past and Present Causes in Geology,* Hafner, 1971. Contributor of almost two hundred papers on the petrology and petrography of sedimentary rocks to professional journals in United States and Europe; also has written reviews and abstracts.

WORK IN PROGRESS: An annotated translation of Emile Argand's *Tectonics of Asia,* a forerunner of plate tectonics, originally written in 1922.

SIDELIGHTS: Carozzi's interest in developing relationships between geology and history has resulted in his annotated translations of classical works "in order to trace the evolution of scientific concepts, particularly those pertaining to 'theories of the earth.'"

*   *   *

CARR, John C(harles) 1929-

PERSONAL: Born November 18, 1929, in Washington, D.C. *Education:* Wilson Teachers College, B.S., 1952; Catholic University of America, M.F.A., 1953, Ph.D., 1965. *Home:* 2501 Calvert St. N.W., Washington, D.C. 20008. *Office:* College of Education, University of Maryland, College Park, Md. 20742.

CAREER: Public school teacher in Prince George's County, Md., 1956-67; University of Maryland, College Park, assistant professor, 1967-71, associate professor of education, 1971—. Instructor at Prince George's County Community College, 1964-67, and Trinity College (Washington, D.C.), 1966-67; visiting member of faculty at Catholic University of America, summers, 1965—. *Member:* National Council of Teachers of English, Conference on English Education, American Film Institute, American Theatre Association, Maryland Conference on English Education (president, 1973-74), Phi Delta Kappa. *Awards, honors:* Classroom teacher's medal from Freedoms Foundation, 1963; Excellence in Teaching award from University of Maryland, 1969.

WRITINGS: (With Jean D. Grambs and Robert Fitch) *Modern Methods in Secondary Education,* 3rd edition (Carr was not associated with earlier editions), Holt, 1970; (editor with Grambs) *Black Image: Education Copes with Color,* W. C. Brown, 1972; (editor with Grambs and E. G. Campbell) *Education in the World Today,* Addison-Wesley, 1972. Contributor to *School Press Review, Grade Teacher, American Foreign Language Teacher, Virginia English Bulletin,* and *Clearing House.*

WORK IN PROGRESS: A Handbook of Theatre; An Introduction to Teaching.

*   *   *

CARR, William G(eorge) 1901-

PERSONAL: Born June 1, 1901, in Northampton, England; came to United States, 1915; son of Alfred Sutton (a cabinetmaker) and Alice Ellen (Bailey) Carr; married Elizabeth Vaughan, August 20, 1924; children: Wilfred James. *Education:* Attended University of California, Los Angeles, 1920-23; Stanford University, A.B., 1924, A.M., 1926, Ph.D., 1929. *Home:* 3601 Connecticut, Washington, D.C. 20008.

CAREER: Roosevelt Junior High School, Glendale, Calif., teacher of English and mathematics, 1924-25; Pacific University, Forest Grove, Ore., professor of education, 1926-27; California Teachers Association, San Francisco, director of research, 1927-28; National Education Association, Washington, D.C., assistant director of research, 1929-31, director of research, 1931-41, secretary of Educational Policies Commission, 1937-52, associate secretary of National Education Association, 1940-52, executive secretary, 1952-67. Participant in White House Conferences on Children and Education, 1930, 1940, 1950, 1955, 1960, and 1970; consultant, National Survey of School Finance, 1931, and to National Conference on Financing Education, 1933; participant in International Education Seminar, 1943-45; member of board of directors, C.A.R.E., 1950—, and Educational Testing Service, 1959-63; member of U.S. Department of Defense Advisory Committee on Education, 1953-65; member of board of trustees, People to People, 1962-74; visiting lecturer or professor at Stanford University, 1929, 1931, 1942, University of Michigan, 1930, 1933, 1937, 1938, University of California, Los Angeles, 1935, University of California, Berkeley, 1937, University of Denver, 1942, University of Pennsylvania, 1942, Columbia University, 1943, Western Maryland College, 1970, and Trinity College, 1972; fellow of College of Preceptors, London, England, 1967.

MEMBER: World Confederation of Organizations of the Teaching Profession (founder and secretary general, 1946-70; president, 1970-72), Council on International Non-theatrical Events (president, 1970-74), Sino-American Cultural Society (vice-president, 1936-69; president, 1969—), American Association of School Administrators, American Educational Research Association (honorary life member, secretary, 1937-52), National Congress of Parents and Teachers (honorary life member), Educational Institute of Scotland (fellow), National Union of Teachers of England and Wales (honorary life member), Kappa Delta Pi, Cosmos Club (Washington, D.C.).

AWARDS, HONORS: LL.D., Miami University, 1953, University of Tennessee, 1960; L.H.D., Columbia University, 1954, Boston University, 1957; Honorary Citizen of Jaffna, Ceylon, 1956; American Association for Health, Physical Education and Recreation presidential citation, 1965; Government of Korea Order of Cultural Merit Medal, 1966; William F. Russell Medal, 1972; Italian Federation of Cinema Clubs award, 1973.

WRITINGS: *Education for World Citizenship*, Stanford University Press, 1928; (editor) *County Unit of School Administration*, H. W. Wilson, 1931; (with John Waage) *The Lesson Assignment*, Stanford University Press, 1931; *John Swett: Biography of an Educational Pioneer*, Fine Arts Press, 1933; *School Finance*, Stanford University, 1933; (with Harley Lutz) *Essentials of Taxation*, National Education Association, 1935; (with Charles A. Beard) *Schools in the Story of Culture*, National Education Association, 1937; *The Purposes of Education in American Democracy*, Educational Policies Commission, 1938; (with others) *Learning the Ways of Democracy*, Educational Policies Commission, 1940; *Educational Leadership in This Emergency*, Stanford University Press, 1942; *Education and the People's Peace*, Educational Policies Commission, 1943; (editor) *International Frontiers in Education*, American Academy of Political and Social Science, 1944; *Only by Understanding*, Foreign Policy Association, 1945; *One World in the Making*, Ginn, 1946, 2nd edition, 1947; *On the Waging of Peace*, National Education Association, 1946; *Discovery of the Citizen*, Columbia University Press, 1955; *The Words of William G. Carr*, National Education Association, 1967; (editor) *Values and the Curriculum*, National Education Association, 1970; *White Revolution in Iranian Education*, World Confederation of Organizations of the Teaching Profession, 1970.

WORK IN PROGRESS: His memoirs.

SIDELIGHTS: Carr was present at the foundation of the United Nations and the United Nations Educational, Scientific, and Cultural Organization in 1945, and helped to write the preamble and statement of purposes of the UNESCO constitution. In 1967, the National Education Association established the William G. Carr Annual Scholarship.

* * *

CARRICK, Donald 1929-

PERSONAL: Born April 7, 1929, in Dearborn, Mich.; son of Fay and Blanche (Soper) Carrick; married Carol Hatfield (a writer), March 26, 1965; children: Christopher, Paul. *Education:* Attended Colorado Springs Fine Art Center, 1948-49, Arts Student League, 1950, and Vienna Academy of Fine Arts, 1953-54. *Address:* High St., Edgartown, Mass. 02539.

CAREER: Artist, author. *Military service:* U.S. Army, 1950-51; became corporal. *Awards, honors: The Tree* was named on the Child Study Association book list, 1971; Bank Street College of Education Irma Simonton Black Award, 1973; *Bear Mouse* was a Children's Book Showcase Title, 1974.

WRITINGS: The Tree, Macmillan, 1971; *Drip Drop*, Macmillan, 1973.

With wife, Carol Carrick: *The Old Barn*, Bobbs-Merrill, 1966; *The Brook*, Macmillan, 1967; *A Clearing in the Forest*, Dial, 1970; *The Dirt Road*, Macmillan, 1970; *Sleep Out*, Seabury, 1973.

Illustrator—All written by Carol Carrick: *Swamp Spring*, Macmillan, 1969; *The Pond*, Macmillan, 1970; *The Dragon of Santa Lalia*, Bobbs-Merril 1971; *Beach Bird*, Dial, 1973; *Lost in the Storm*, Seabury, 1974.

Illustrator: Robert Goldston, *The Civil War in Spain*, Bobbs-Merrill, 1966; Goldston, *The Russian Revolution*, Bobbs-Merrill, 1966; Goldston, *The Rise of Red China*, Bobbs-Merrill, 1967; Goldston, *The Life and Death of Nazi Germany*, Bobbs-Merrill, 1967; Goldston, *The Great Depression*, Bobbs-Merrill, 1968; *London: The Civic Spirit*, Macmillan, 1969; *Barcelona: The Civic Stage*, Macmillan, 1969; Ernestine Byrd, *Tor: Wyoming Bighorn*, Scribner, 1969; Arnold Adoff, editor, *City in All Directions*, Macmillan, 1969; Goldston, *The Cuban Revolution*, Bobbs-Merrill, 1970; *New York: Civic Exploitation*, Macmillan, 1970; *Suburbia: Civic Denial*, Macmillan, 1970; Lee McGiffin, *Yankee Doodle Dandies*, Dutton, 1970; Nancy Veglahn, *The Buffalo King*, Scribner, 1971; Yoshiko Uchida, *Journey to Topaz*, Scribner, 1971; Berniece Freschet, *Turtle Pond*, Scribner, 1971; Freschet, *Bear Mouse*, Scribner, 1973; Eleanor Schick, *Peter and Mr. Brandon*, Macmillan, 1973; David Budbill, *The Christmas Tree Farm*, Macmillan, 1974.

WORK IN PROGRESS: The Lobster Tale, The Deer in the Pasture, and *Grizzly Bear.*

SIDELIGHTS: Carrick lived and painted for several years in Spain.

* * *

CARROLL, B(illy) D(an) 1940-

PERSONAL: Born October 28, 1940, in Gatesville, Tex.; son of Cleo Herston (a farmer and politician) and Etta (a teacher; maiden name, Tharp) Carroll; married Deirdre Christenberry (a professor), June 10, 1972. *Education:* Tarleton State College, student, 1959-61; University of Texas, B.S.E.E., 1964, M.S.E.E., 1966, Ph.D., 1969. *Politics:* Democrat. *Religion:* Presbyterian. *Home:* 316 Cherry, Auburn, Ala. 36830. *Office:* Department of Electrical Engineering, Auburn University, Auburn, Ala. 36830.

CAREER: Registered professional engineer; Texas Instruments, Inc., Dallas, Tex., engineer, 1964; General Dynamics Corp., Fort Worth, Tex., project engineer, 1968-70; Auburn University, Auburn, Ala., assistant professor of electrical engineering, 1970—. *Member:* Institute of Electrical and Electronic Engineers, Association for Computing Machinery, American Society for Engineering Education, Sigma Xi, Tau Beta Pi, Eta Kappa Nu.

WRITINGS: (With H. T. Nagle and J. D. Irwin) *An Introduction to Computer Logic*, Prentice-Hall, 1975. Contributor to *Institute of Electrical and Electronic Engineers Transactions on Computers* and *Association for Computing Machinery Computing Reviews.*

WORK IN PROGRESS: Research on fault tolerant computing, on fault diagnosis of computer systems, and on innovative teaching approaches.

CARROLL, Charles Francis 1936-

PERSONAL: Born October 5, 1936, in Cambridge, Mass.; son of Patrick J. and Margaret R. (Gleason) Carroll; married Pauline Cognac, July 4, 1970. *Education:* Boston College, A.B., 1959, M.A., 1961; Brown University, Ph.D., 1970. *Home address:* Box 172, Harvard, Mass. 01451. *Office:* Department of History, Lowell State College Campus, University of Lowell, Lowell, Mass. 01854.

CAREER: University of Lowell, Lowell, Mass., instructor in history, 1962-63; University of Rhode Island, Providence, instructor in history, 1965-66; University of Lowell, instructor, 1966-68, assistant professor, 1968-70, associate professor, 1970-74, professor of history, 1974—. *Military service:* U.S. Army Reserve, 1960-66. *Member:* American Historical Association (life member), Organization of American Historians (life member), Society for the History of Technology, New England Historical Association, Plimoth Plantation, Forest History Society.

WRITINGS: The Timber Economy of Puritan New England, Brown University Press, 1973; (contributor) Brooke Hindle, editor, *America's Wooden Age: Aspects of Its Early Technology*, Sleepy Hollow Restorations, 1975.

WORK IN PROGRESS: Research in the colonial history of New England.

* * *

CARROLL, Tom M. 1950-
(St. Thomas Marion Carroll)

PERSONAL: Born September 26, 1950, in Excelsior Springs, Mo.; son of Glen O. (a pharmacist) and Mary Frances (a bookkeeper; maiden name, Payne) Carroll; married Tina Lynn Hutcheson (employed in newspaper circulation), June 15, 1975. *Education:* Attended William Jewell College, 1971-72, spring, 1973. *Politics:* Independent liberal. *Religion:* "God." *Home:* 524 Regent, Excelsior Springs, Mo. 64024.

CAREER: Operator of an old-fashioned soda fountain in Excelsior Springs, Mo.

WRITINGS: (Under pseudonym St. Thomas Marion Carroll) *Aliens*, Mojave Books, 1974. Author of a daily column, and contributor of articles, to a local newspaper; also contributor to *Kansas City Star*.

WORK IN PROGRESS: Anti-Earth, "testimony (autobiography), psychic visions, dreams, and experiences, revolutionary spiritual philosophy, new movement in God."

SIDELIGHTS: Carroll told *CA*: "My motivation is centered around God and Jesus Christ, around being in harmony with the truth and all that is true: true life, true love, true peace, true freedom, true happiness. In other words, outside of the world experience, for the world of man is Anti-God." *Avocational interests:* Sports, nature and the outdoors, physical fitness.

* * *

CARTER, Angela 1940-

PERSONAL: Born May 7, 1940, in London, England; daughter of Hugh Alexander (a journalist) and Olive (Farthing) Stalker; married Paul Carter, September 10, 1960 (divorced, 1972). *Education:* University of Bristol, B.A., 1965. *Politics:* Left. *Religion:* None. *Home:* 5 Hay Hill, Bath BA1 5LZ, England. *Agent:* Deborah Rogers, 29 Goodge St., London, England.

CAREER: Journalist for newspapers in Croyden, Surrey, England, 1958-61; novelist and short story writer. *Awards, honors:* John Llewllyn Rhys Prize, 1968, for *The Magic Toyshop*; Somerset Maugham Award, 1969, for *Several Perceptions*.

WRITINGS: Shadow Dance, Heinemann, 1966, published as *Honeybuzzard*, Simon & Schuster, 1967; *The Magic Toyshop* (children's book), Heinemann, 1967, Simon & Schuster, 1968; *Several Perceptions*, Heinemann, 1968, Simon & Schuster, 1969; *Heroes and Villains*, Heinemann, 1969, Simon & Schuster, 1970; *Miss Z, the Dark Young Lady* (children's book), Simon & Schuster, 1970; *The Donkey Prince* (children's book), Simon & Schuster, 1970; *Love*, Hart-Davis, 1971; *The Infernal Desire Machines of Doctor Hoffman*, Hart-Davis, 1972, published as *The War of Dreams*, Harcourt, 1974; *Fireworks: Nine Profane Pieces*, Quartet Books, 1974, Harcourt, in press.

WORK IN PROGRESS: A feminist study of the Marquis de Sade, for Virago and Harcourt.

SIDELIGHTS: Angela Carter has traveled in Japan and the U.S.S.R. She claims "witch blood on her father's side; solid radical trade-unionists on mother's."

* * *

CARTER, Barbara (Ellen) 1925-

PERSONAL: Born August 7, 1925, in Detroit, Mich; daughter of John M. (a physician) and Nell Luise (Dougan) Carter. *Education:* University of Michigan, B.A., 1948; Oxford University, graduate study, 1948. *Home:* 8 Garmany Pl., Yonkers, N.Y. 10710. *Office:* Free Lance Associates, 8 Garmany Pl., Yonkers, N.Y. 10710.

CAREER: Reporter (magazine), New York, N.Y., staff writer, 1958-65; free-lance writer and editor for education organizations, government, and civil rights groups. *Member:* Society of Magazine Writers. *Awards, honors:* Avery Hopwood award from University of Michigan, 1943, for short stories; National School Bell Award, 1961, for article on integration.

WRITINGS: (With Gloria Dapper) *A Guide for School Board Members*, Follett, 1966; *The Road to City Hall: How John V. Lindsay Became Mayor*, Prentice-Hall, 1967; *Pickets, Parents, and Power: The Story Behind the New York Teachers' Strike*, Citation Press, 1971; (with Dapper) *School Volunteers: What They Do, How They Do It*, Citation Press, 1972; (with Dapper) *Organizing School Volunteer Programs*, Citation Press, 1974. Contributor to *Saturday Review* and *News and Views*.

AVOCATIONAL INTERESTS: Literature, music (organ), foreign travel.

* * *

CARTY, James William, Jr. 1925-

PERSONAL: Born February 20, 1925, in Shelbyville, Mo.; son of James William (a mechanic) and Pauline Doris E. (Boyd) Carty; married Majorie Warren Tufts (a teacher of Spanish), March 21, 1948; children: Cynthia Tufts Carty Cornelius, James William III, Paul Dickinson. *Education:* Culver-Stockton College, A.B., 1945; University of Chicago, B.D., 1948; Northwestern University, M.S., 1951; further graduate study at University of Oklahoma, 1948-56, Scarritt College, George Peabody College for Teachers, State Teachers College of Seattle, Bethany College, Bethany, W.Va.; Ohio University, 1971, and University of Denver, 1973. *Politics:* Democrat. *Religion:* Christian Church (Disciples of Christ). *Home:* 207 Richardson St.,

Bethany, W.Va. 26032. *Office:* Department of Communications, Bethany College, P.O. Box 327, Bethany, W.Va. 26032.

CAREER: Ordained clergyman of Christian Church (Disciples of Christ), 1948; pastor of churches in Oklahoma City, Okla., 1948-49, Moundsville, W.Va., 1960-61; *Daily Oklahoman*, Oklahoma City, Okla., reporter, 1949; *Quincy Herald-Whig*, Quincy, Ill., reporter, 1949; *Yukon Sun*, Yukon, Okla., news editor, 1949-50; *Nashville Tennessean*, Nashville, Tenn., education and religion editor, 1953-59; Bethany College, Bethany, W.Va., professor of communications, 1959—, chairman of department, 1959—, director of public relations and publications, 1959-68. Visiting professor at Scarritt College, 1955-57, Ohio University (Belmont Branch), 1964-66, and Evangelical Seminary of Puerto Rico, 1974; lecturer at University of Tennessee (Nashville Center), 1958-59, Central American University, 1963-64, and West Virginia University, 1967—; Fulbright-Hays lecturer at University of Nicaragua, 1963-64; lecturer for Organization of American States and Inter-American Federation of Working Newspapermens' Organization in Bolivia, 1967; lecturer in El Salvador, Dominican Republic, Guatemala, and Tanzania. *Military service:* U.S. Air Force, 1951-53; became first lieutenant.

MEMBER: Inter-American Press Association, Regional Council of International Education, Association of Industrial Advertisers, National Council of College Publications Advisers, National Religious Public Relations Council (fellow), Pi Delta Epsilon, Sigma Delta Chi, Danforth Associates, Bethany Kiwanis Club (past president). *Awards, honors:* Brotherhood citation from National Conference of Christians and Jews, 1956; George Washington Honors Medal from Freedoms Foundation, 1958, 1959.

WRITINGS: Working with the Latin American Press, Algonquin Press, 1966; *Advertising the Local Church*, Augsburg, 1966; *An Educator's Guide for Preparing Articles for Periodicals*, Bethany College, 1960; *Communicating with God*, The Upper Room (Nashville, Tenn.), 1964; *Relaciones Publicas* (title means "Public Relations"), Bethany College, 1970; *The Gresham Years*, Bethany College, 1970.

Author of "International Communications," a column in *Public Relations Digest*, 1967. Contributor of more than three thousand articles and reviews to journals.

WORK IN PROGRESS: Research on international communications, and on the student press of Africa, Asia, and Latin America.

AVOCATIONAL INTERESTS: International travel.

BIOGRAPHICAL/CRITICAL SOURCES: R. E. Wolseley, *Careers in Religious Journalism*, Association Press, 1955, 2nd edition, Herald Press, 1966.

* * *

CARVALHO-NETO, Paulo de 1923-

PERSONAL: Born September 10, 1923, in Simao Dias, Sergipe, Brazil; came to United States, 1968; son of Antonio Manuel de Carvalho-Neto (a criminologist, politician, and labor law historian) and Veturia Prata Carvalho; married Ivolina Rosa de Souza, 1949; children: Luiz, Jose, Lucy, Paulo Antonio, Arthur. *Education:* University of Brazil, Bacharel em Ciencias Sociais, 1947, Licenciado em Ciencias Sociais, 1949; University of Sao Paulo, Doutor em Letras, 1971. *Home:* 1307 Federal Ave., Apt. 2, Los Angeles, Calif. 90025. *Agent:* Bertha Klausner International Literary Agency, Inc., 71 Park Ave., New York, N.Y. 10016.

CAREER: University of Paraguay, Asuncion, professor of ethnology, 1949-51; Universidad de la Republica, Montevideo, Uruguay, director of sociology seminar, 1952-59; Universidad Central del Ecuador, Quito, professor of Brazilian studies, 1960-67; Instituto Chileno-Brasilero de Cultura, Santiago, Chile, director, 1967; University of California, Los Angeles, lecturer in Brazilian literature, Portuguese language, and in folklore, 1968-72; Indiana University, Bloomington, research associate and visiting professor of folklore, 1973-74; University of West Florida, Pensacola, visiting professor of anthropology, 1974; University of the Pacific, Elbert Covell College, Stockton, Calif., visiting professor of social institutions, 1974—. Cultural attache for Brazilian Foreign Ministry in Ecuador, 1960-67, and in Chile, 1967-68; participant in international conferences. Member of editorial advisory board, *Gran Enciclopedia de la Educacion* (Buenos Aires). *Military service:* Brazilian Army, 1940-45; became lieutenant.

MEMBER: International Society for Folk-Narrative Research and Societe des Americanistes (both Paris); Sociedad Folklorica de Bolivia (Sucre); Asociacion Tucumana de Folklore, Asociacion Folklorica Argentina, Sociedad "Amigos del Arte Popular," and Asociacion Latino-Americana de Sociologia (all Argentina); Sociedad Brasileira de Folklore, Sociedad Luso-Brasileira de Etnologia, Academia Sergipana de Letras, Instituto Historico e Geografico de Santos, and Associacao Brasileira de Folklore (all Brazil); Sociedad Peruana de Folklore (Lima); Grupo America, Sociedad Amigos de la Arqueologia, and Casa de la Cultura Ecuatoriana (all Quito, Ecuador); Sociedad de Antropologia del Uruguay (Montevideo); Sociedad Chilena de Antropologia (Santiago); Sociedad Folklorica de Mexico (Mexico City); Asociacion Espanola de Etnologia y Folklore (Madrid), Afro-Hispanic Studies Group (Kisangani, Congo).

AWARDS, HONORS: Guiseppe Pitre International Folklore Prize (Italy), 1969, for *History of Iberoamerican Folklore*; University of Chicago Folklore Prize, 1971, for *The Concept of Folklore*; Casa de las Americas Prize honorable mention (Cuba), 1973, for *El folklore de las luchas sociales*, and 1974, for *Los ilustres maestros*.

WRITINGS: Vila do Principe (novella), Edicoes Elzio Dolabella, 1950; *La obra afro-uruguaya de Ildefonso Pereda Valdes* (title means "The Afro-Uruguayan Works of I. Pereda Valdes"), Centro de Estudios Folkloricos del Uruguay, 1955; *Concepto de Folklore*, Editorial Livraria Monteiro Lobato, 1956, 2nd edition, Editorial Pormaca, 1965, translation by Jacques M. Wilson published as *The Concept of Folklore*, University of Miami Press, 1971; *Folklore y psicoanalisis*, Editorial Psique, 1956, 2nd edition, Editorial Joaquin Mortiz, 1968, translation by Wilson published as *Folklore and Psychoanalysis*, University of Miami Press, 1972.

Folklore del Paraguay (title means "Folklore of Paraguay"), Editorial Universitaria, 1961; *Folklore y educacion* (title means "Folklore and Education"), Casa de la Cultura Ecuatoriana, 1961, 2nd edition, Editorial Omeba, 1969; *Diccionario del folklore ecuatoriano* (title means "Dictionary of Ecuadorian Folklore"), Humanities, 1964; *Antologia del folklore ecuatoriano* (title means "Anthology of Ecuadorian Folklore"), Volume I, Editorial Universitaria, 1964, Volume II, Casa de la Cultura Ecuatoriana, 1970; *Um precursor do direito trabalhista brasileiro* (title means

"A Pioneer of Brazilian Labor Law"), Edicao da Revista Brasileira de Estudos Politicos, 1964; *El Negro uruguayo* (title means "Uruguayan Blacks"), Editorial Universitaria, 1965; (editor) *Arte Popular del Ecuador* (title means "Ecuadorian Folk Arts"), Volume I, Alianza para el Progreso, 1965, Volume II, Universidad Central del Ecuador, 1970.

Cuentos folkloricos del Ecuador (title means "Ecuadorian Folktales"), Editorial Universitaria, 1966; *Folklore poetico* (title means "Poetic Folklore"), Editorial Universitaria, 1966; *Geografia del folklore ecuatoriano* (title means "Geography of Ecuadorian Folklore"), Casa de la Cultura Ecuatoriana, 1967; *El carnaval de Montevideo* (title means "The Carnival of Montevideo"), Universidad de Sevilla, 1967; *Estudios de Folklore* (title means "Studies on Folklore"), Editorial Universitaria, Volumes I and II, 1968, Volume III, 1973; *Historia del folklore iberoamericano*, Editorial Universitaria, 1969, translation by Pollack Neutzer published as *History of Iberoamerican Folklore*, Humanities, 1969.

Folklore Sergipano (title means "Folklore of Sergipe, Brazil"), Junta Distrital do Porto, Museu de Etnografia e Historia, 1970; *Estudios Afros* (title means "Afro Studies"), Instituto de Antropologia e Historia, Universidad Central de Venezuela, 1971; *Mi tio Atahualpa* (novel; title means "My Uncle Atahualpa"), Siglo Veintiuno, 1972; *El folklore de las luchas sociales* (title means "Folklore of Social Struggles"), Siglo Veintiuno, 1973; *Los Ilustres Maestros* (title means "Great Teachers"), Editorial Monte Avila, 1974; *Decameron Ecuatoriano* (title means "Ecuadorian Decameron"), Editorial V Siglos, 1974.

Contributor of over 100 articles to journals, including *Cuadernos americanos, Estudios Brasileiros, Revista de Folklore*, and *Revista de la Universidad Catolica "Andres Bello."* Founder and director, *Revista del folklore ecuatoriano* (Quito), 1965—; founder and member of editorial advisory board, *Revista del Instituto Azuayo de Folklore* (Ecuador), 1968—; member of editorial advisory boards, *Revista de Sociologia* (Montevideo), 1970—, *Estudios filologicos* (Chile), 1971—, *Boletin de antropologia* (of the University of Antioquia, Colombia), 1971—, *Studies in Folklore* (Bloomington, Ind.), 1973—, and *Studies in Third World Societies* (Va.), 1973—.

WORK IN PROGRESS: A novel on sexual problems tentatively titled, *Una flor para Julieta* (title means "A Flower to Juliet").

SIDELIGHTS: "[The] belief that the individual dignity reigns supreme over all considerations in life continues as a theme in Carvalho-Neto's writing," notes *Pensacola Journal* writer Sharon Demarko, citing Jacques Wilson's reference to *Mi tio Atahualpa* as exhibiting a "John Steinbeck-style overview of the human parade." A *Hispania* reviewer refers to Carvalho-Neto's "gift [in *Mi tio Atahualpa*] of blending myth and reality . . .," and continues: "It takes an unusual talent to combine harmoniously the rich Hispanic tradition of epic, ballad, and picaresque novel with the *indigenista* theme of social injustice, up-dated and modernized without sacrificing the essence of the classics to the creative impulse. But the author has managed to accomplish just that. . . ."

Carvalho-Neto left Brazil as a voluntary expatriate in 1968, retaining his Brazilian citizenship although he now resides in the United States. "A writer can live in geographic exile," he commented, "but this does not mean spiritual exile. Many of those who remain, those who allow suppression of their inner thoughts, are the spiritually exiled, the castrated. . . . To write, for a real writer, is an act of liberation. To read a good book is to try to liberate ourselves."

BIOGRAPHICAL/CRITICAL SOURCES: La Patria (Colombia), September 3, 1973; *Pensacola Journal*, June 13, 1974.

* * *

CARVIC, Heron

PERSONAL: Born in London, England; married Phyllis Neilson-Terry (an actress). *Education:* Attended Eton College. *Residence:* Kent, England. *Agent:* Curtis Brown Ltd., 1 Craven Hill, London W2 3EW, England.

CAREER: Dancer, actor, designer, builder, decorator, and market gardener; novelist. *Member:* Writers Guild of Great Britain, Crime Writers Association. *Awards, honors:* Special award from Mystery Writers of America, 1969.

WRITINGS—All crime novels: *Picture Miss Seeton*, Harper, 1968; *Miss Seeton Draws the Line*, Harper, 1970; *Witch Miss Seeton*, Harper, 1971; *Miss Seeton Sings*, Harper, 1973; *Odds on Miss Seeton*, Harper, 1975.

* * *

CASPER, Jonathan D(avid) 1942-

PERSONAL: Born June 2, 1942, in Tacoma Park, Md.; son of Barry (a civil servant) and Florence (a teacher; maiden name, Becker) Casper. *Education:* Swarthmore College, B.A., 1964; Yale University, M.A., 1965, Ph.D., 1968. *Home:* 928 Addision Ave., Palo Alto, Calif. 94301. *Office:* Department of Political Science, Stanford University, Stanford, Calif. 94305.

CAREER: Brookings Institution, Washington, D.C., research fellow, 1967-68; Yale University, New Haven, Conn., assistant professor of political science, 1968-72; Stanford University, Stanford, Calif., assistant professor of political science, 1972—. *Member:* American Political Science Association, Law and Society Association, Phi Beta Kappa. *Awards, honors:* Grant from Law Enforcement Assistance Administration, 1974-76.

WRITINGS: American Criminal Justice: The Defendant's Perspective, Prentice-Hall, 1972; *Lawyers before the Warren Court*, University of Illinois Press, 1972; *The Politics of Civil Liberties*, Harper, 1972.

WORK IN PROGRESS: A study of defendant attitudes toward criminal courts.

AVOCATIONAL INTERESTS: Playing tennis, reading mysteries, watching television.

* * *

CASTELLANOS, Rosario 1915-1974

1915—1974; Mexican novelist and diplomat. Obituaries: *AB Bookman's Weekly*, October 7, 1974.

* * *

CASTRO, Antonio 1946- (Tony Castro)

PERSONAL: Born December 2, 1946, in Waco, Tex.; son of Antonio, Sr. and Mary (Veracruz) Castro; married Mary Nell Walker (a secretary), July 22, 1968 (separated). *Education:* Baylor University, B.A., 1970; Washington Journalism Center, graduate study, spring, 1971. *Religion:* Roman Catholic. *Home:* 1420 Hawthorne, Houston, Tex. 77006. *Office: Houston Post,* 4747 Southwest Freeway, Houston, Tex. 77001.

CAREER: Dallas Times Herald, Dallas, Tex., reporter, 1970-71; *Dallas Morning News,* Dallas, Tex., political reporter, 1971-73; KERA-Television (of Public Broadcasting System), Dallas, Tex., producer and reporter, 1973-74; *Houston Post,* Houston, Tex., political reporter, 1974—. Produced documentary film on the Farah labor organizing struggle for KERA-Television, 1973. *Awards, honors:* Dallas Press Club news reporting award, 1971, and feature writing award, 1972; political reporting award from Headliners Club of AVUSTIN, Tex., 1973; nominated for Pulitzer Prize, 1973, for series of stories on Chicano political development.

WRITINGS: Chicago Power: The Emergence of Mexican-America, Saturday Review Press, 1974; *True Sentences of My Mind,* Dutton, in press. Contributor to magazines and newspapers, including *Saturday Review, Race Relations Reporter, Boston Globe,* and *Washington Post.* Contributing editor of *Race Relations Reporter.*

WORK IN PROGRESS: Grace, Glory and Graft: The Rise and Fall of John Connally.

SIDELIGHTS: It was not until the second grade that Castro learned to speak English. The early problems with the language were probably the underlying motivation for his desire to go into journalism and write seriously. When he was ten, a school teacher gave him a paperback copy of *The Old Man and the Sea* to read when he "grew older." He read it that same year and became an instant Hemingway buff. Today, he considers Hemingway, Mailer, Faulkner, Gay Talese, and Steinbeck the cornerstones of his literary interests.

While Chicano Power has been a personal catharsis for Castro, he himself has remained detached from the Chicano movement. He writes: "As a journalist, you're suspect enough without endangering your credibility. For a black or Chicano journalist to become involved in movements would be professionally suicidal. As a writer, I would hope that my work transcends my personal outrage and bitterness to achieve some semblance of literary meaning."

AVOCATIONAL INTERESTS: Tennis (tournament player), sailing, bullfighting, professional football, sports cars.

* * *

CASTRO, Jose Maria Ferreira de 1898-1974

Portuguese journalist and novelist. Obituaries: *AB Bookman's Weekly*, October 7, 1974.

* * *

CATE, Curtis 1924-

PERSONAL: Born May 22, 1924, in Paris, France; son of Karl Springer (a businessman) and Josephine Savilla (Wilson) Cate; married Helena Bajanova, October, 1965. *Education:* Harvard University, graduate (magna cum laude), 1947; Ecole des Langues Orientales, diploma in Russian, 1949; Magdalen College, Oxford, graduate study, 1949-52. *Agent:* Harold Matson Co., Inc., 22 East 40th St., New York, N.Y. 10016.

CAREER: Atlantic Monthly, Boston, Mass., European editor, 1958-65; author. *Military service:* U.S. Army, 1943-46. *Awards, honors:* Grand Prix Litteraire from l'Aero-Club de France, 1974, for *Antoine de Saint-Exupery: His Life and Times.*

WRITINGS: Antoine de Saint-Exupery: His Life and Times, Putnam, 1970; *George Sand*, Houghton, 1975. Contributor to popular magazines, including *Horizon, National Review, Tour d'Horizon, Cornhill*, and *New York Times Book Review.*

SIDELIGHTS: Cate considers himself a biographer and historian first, and only incidentally a journalist. He has a strong interest in philosophy and hopes to write a major life of Leibniz, calling this "the work of my old age."

* * *

CATON, Hiram 1936-

PERSONAL: Born August 16, 1936, in Concord, N.C.; son of Hiram Pendleton (a cotton broker) and Dorothy Virginia (Corl) Caton; married Sophia Margarete Richter, July 19, 1959; children: Sonia Luise, Claudia Ingeborg. *Education:* University of Chicago, B.A., 1960, M.A., 1962; University of Freiburg, graduate study, 1962-63; Yale University, Ph.D., 1966. *Home:* 65 David St., O'Connor, Canberra 2601, Australia. *Office:* Research School of Social Sciences, Australian National University, Canberra 2601, Australia.

CAREER: Bucknell University, Lewisburg, Pa., assistant professor of philosophy, 1966-67; Pennsylvania State University, University Park, assistant professor of philosophy, 1967-71; Australian National University, Research School of Social Sciences, Canberra, senior research fellow, 1971—. *Military service:* U.S. Army, 1955-58. *Member:* American Philosophical Association.

WRITINGS: The Origin of Subjectivity: An Essay on Descartes, Yale University Press, 1973. Contributor to journals.

WORK IN PROGRESS: An essay in political philosophy, *The Politics of Progress.*

* * *

CAYLEY, Michael (Forde) 1950-

PERSONAL: Born February 26, 1950, in London, England; son of Forde E. (a physician) and Eileen (Dalton) Cayley. *Education:* St. John's College, Oxford, B.A., 1971. *Religion:* Agnostic. *Home:* 44 Earl's Court Sq., London S.W.5, England.

CAREER: Board of Inland Revenue, London, England, administrative trainee, 1971-73; Price Commission, London, private secretary to chairman, 1973-75; Board of Inland Revenue, London, member of staff, 1975—.

WRITINGS: Moorings (poems), Carcanet Press, 1971; (editor) *Selected Poems of Crashaw*, Carcanet Press, 1972; *The Spider's Touch* (poems), Carcanet Press, 1973. Contributor of poems to *Carcanet, Tribune, Southern Arts Review*, and *Poetry Nation.*

WORK IN PROGRESS: A novel and a book of poems.

AVOCATIONAL INTERESTS: Art, classical music.

* * *

CAZEAUX, Isabelle 1926-

PERSONAL: Surname rhymes with "chateau"; born February 24, 1926, in New York, N.Y.; daughter of Francois and Marie-Anne (Fort) Cazeaux. *Education:* Attended Manhattan School of Music, 1940-41, 1947-48, Sorbonne, University of Paris, 1948-53, Ecole nationale des Chartes, Paris, 1950, and Ecole pratique des hautes etudes, Paris, 1950-53; Hunter College (now Hunter College of the City University of New York), B.A. (magna cum laude), 1945;

Smith College, M.A., 1946; Ecole normale de musique, Paris, Licence d'Enseignement, 1950; Conservatoire national de musique, Paris, Premiere medaille, 1950; Columbia University, M.S., 1959, Ph.D., 1961. *Religion:* Roman Catholic. *Home:* 415 East 72nd St., New York, N.Y. 10021. *Office:* Department of Music, Bryn Mawr College, Bryn Mawr, Pa. 19010.

CAREER: New York Public Library, New York, N.Y., head of music and phonorecords cataloging section in circulation department, 1957-62, music cataloger in reference department, 1962-63; Bryn Mawr College, Bryn Mawr, Pa., lecturer, 1963-66, assistant professor, 1966-69, associate professor of music and musicology, 1969—. Teacher of musicology and music history at Manhattan School of Music, 1969—. Guest lecturer on French Renaissance music before various groups and on television; has given violin recitals in Paris, France, and Trondheim, Norway. *Member:* International Musicological Society, American Musicological Society (member of council, 1968-70), Societe francaise de musicologie, International Association of Music Libraries, Music Library Association (assistant chairman of New York chapter, 1964-65), American Library Association, American Association of University Professors, Phi Beta Kappa. *Awards, honors:* Martha Baird Rockefeller Fund grant, 1971-72.

WRITINGS: (Editor with Francois Lesure and others) *Anthologie de la chanson parisienne au XVIe siecle*, L'Oiseau-lyre (Monaco), 1953; (contributor) Carol J. Bradley, editor, *Manual of Music Librarianship*, Music Library Association, 1966; (translator) Hans Tischler, *A Structural Analysis of Mozart's Piano Concertos*, Institute of Mediaeval Music, 1966; (editor) Claudin de Sermisy, *Chansons*, A. Broude, 1967; (translator) Samuel Kinser, editor, *The Memoirs of Philippe de Commynes*, University of South Carolina Press, Volume I, 1969, Volume II, 1973; (contributor, and contributor of translations) Bradley, editor, *Reader in Music Librarianship*, IHS-Microcard Editions Books, 1973; (editor with Gaston Allaire) Sermisy, *Opera Omnia*, Volumes III and IV (*Corpus Mensurabilis Musicae*, 52), American Musicological Society, 1974; *French Music in the Fifteenth and Sixteenth Centuries*, Basil Blackwell, in press. Contributor to *New Catholic Encyclopedia* and *Dictionaire de la musique* (Paris).

WORK IN PROGRESS: Several articles for *Grove's Dictionary of Music and Musicians*, 6th edition, and for *Dictionnaire de la musique* (Paris); research in the history of musical criticism.

AVOCATIONAL INTERESTS: French history and literature, concerts, opera, travel (has visited most of the countries of Europe), and cats.

* * *

CECIL, Robert 1913-

PERSONAL: Born March 25, 1913, in England; son of Charles and Marjorie (Porteous) Cecil; married Kathleen Marindin, September 17, 1938; children: Veronica, Brigid, Robert. *Education:* Caius College, Cambridge, B.A., 1935, M.A., 1961. *Home:* Barb Ridge, Hambledon, Portsmouth, England. *Office:* Department of German, University of Reading, Reading, Berkshire, England.

CAREER: Entered British Foreign Service, 1936, served in the Foreign Office, London, 1939-45; British Embassy, Washington, D.C., first secretary, 1945-48; Foreign Office, 1948-52, counsellor and head of American Department, 1951; British Embassy, Copenhagen, Denmark, counsellor, 1952-55; consul-general in Hanover, West Germany, 1955-57; British Embassy, Bonn, West Germany, counsellor, 1957-59; British Information Services, New York, N.Y., director-general, 1959-61; Foreign Office, head of Cultural Relations Department, 1962-67; Reading University, Reading, England, reader in contemporary German history, 1968—. *Member:* Institute for Cultural Research (chairman, 1972—), Royal Institute of International Affairs. *Awards, honors:* Companion of Order of St. Michael and St. George.

WRITINGS: *Levant and Other Poems,* Fortune Press, 1940; *Time and Other Poems,* Putnam (London), 1955; *Life in Edwardian England,* Batsford, 1969; *The Myth of the Master Race: Alfred Rosenberg and Nazi Ideology,* Batsford, 1972. Contributor to *American Heritage, Poetry, Atlantic Monthly,* and *History Today.*

WORK IN PROGRESS: *Hitler's Decision to Invade Russia,* publication expected in 1975.

AVOCATIONAL INTERESTS: Sufism, gardening, chess.

* * *

CERF, Jay H(enry) 1923-1974

May 17, 1923—August 15, 1974; American government official and author. Obituaries: *Washington Post*, August 18, 1974. (*CA*-19/20).

* * *

CERMAK, Laird S(cott) 1942-

PERSONAL: Born June 24, 1942, in Cleveland, Ohio; son of George Frank (a teacher) and Rhita (a real estate broker; maiden name, Benjamin) Cermak; married Sharon Herzog (an occupational therapist), August 16, 1969. *Education:* Ohio Wesleyan University, B.A., 1964; Ohio State University, M.A., 1965, Ph.D., 1968. *Religion:* Jewish. *Residence:* Watertown, Mass. *Office:* Boston Veterans Administration Hospital, 150 South Huntington Ave., Boston, Mass. 02130.

CAREER: Ohio Wesleyan University, Delaware, visiting instructor in psychology, 1966-68; Tufts University, Medford, Mass., assistant professor of psychology, 1968-72; Boston Veterans Administration Hospital, Boston, Mass., clinical investigator, 1972—. Lecturer at Northeastern University, 1970—; assistant professor at Boston University, 1972—; adjunct professor at Tufts University, 1972—; assistant professor at Clark University, 1973; director of research at Landmark School, 1975—.

MEMBER: International Neuropsychology Society, American Psychological Association, Psychonomic Society, American Association for the Advancement of Science, American Association of University Professors, Midwestern Psychological Association, Eastern Psychological Association. *Awards, honors:* National Institute of Mental Health grants, 1972-74, to study memory impairments of alcoholic Korsakoff patients, 1972-75, to study cognitive deficits related to chronic alcoholism, and 1975-78, to study developmental deficits in information processing.

WRITINGS: *Human Memory: Research and Theory*, Ronald, 1972; (contributor) K. H. Pribram and R. L. Isaacson, editors, *The Hippocampus*, Plenum, 1974; *Psychology of Learning: Research and Theory*, Ronald, 1975; (contributor) M. G. Gross, editor, *Experimental Studies of Alcohol Intoxication and Withdrawal*, Plenum, in press. Contributor to *International Encyclopedia of Neurology, Psychiatry, Psychoanalysis, and Psychology*. Contributor of about thirty articles to psychology journals, including *Neuropsychologia, Cortex, Developmental Psychology, Brain and Language, Annals of the New York Academy of Science*, and *Journal of Experimental Psychology*.

WORK IN PROGRESS: Improving Your Memory.

AVOCATIONAL INTERESTS: Travel (Europe, Israel, Soviet Union), skiing, motorcycling, photography, plants.

* * *

CETTA, Lewis T(homas) 1933-

PERSONAL: Born June 21, 1933, in Connecticut; son of John A. and Kate (DiNatoli) Cetta. *Education:* University of Connecticut, B.A., 1953; Wesleyan University, M.A., 1962; Syracuse University, Ph.D., 1970. *Politics:* "Liberal Pacifist." *Home:* 105 Bennett Ave., Waterbury, Conn. 06708. *Office:* Division of Humanities, Eisenhower College, Seneca Falls, N.Y. 13148.

CAREER: U.S. Civil Service, Washington, D.C., teacher in France, 1957-60, education specialist in Italy, 1960-66; Rochester Institute of Technology, Rochester, N.Y., assistant professor of English, 1968-71; Eisenhower College, Seneca Falls, N.Y., associate professor of literature, 1971—. Member of board of advisers of American Leadership Study Groups. *Member:* Modern Language Association of America, American Association of University Professors, Northeast Modern Language Association (conference chairman, 1975). *Awards, honors:* Outstanding performance award from U.S. Civil Service, 1965.

WRITINGS: Profane Play, Ritual, and Jean Genet: A Study of His Drama, University of Alabama Press, 1974. Contributor to *Theater Annual, Connecticut Review, Notes on Contemporary Literature*, and *Contemporary Literature*.

WORK IN PROGRESS: The Reincarnation Motif in the Works of William Butler Yeats (tentative title), with Uma Bhowani-Sethi, a book on Hindu influences in the work of Yeats, completion expected in 1976.

SIDELIGHTS: Cetta writes: "After nine years residence in Europe, I have developed a life-long interest in European ways." Fluent in Italian, Spanish, and French, his major recent interests include comparative Western theater, film, and myth in modern life.

* * *

CHABE, Alexander M(ichael) 1923-

PERSONAL: Surname is pronounced *Chay*-bee; born January 12, 1923, in Gary, Ind.; son of Michael John (a steelworker) and Barbara (Lysak) Chabe; married Mary Janice Gilbert (a teacher for the hard-of-hearing), April 7, 1951; children: Daniel Stafford, David Gilbert. *Education:* Michigan State University, A.B., 1943, A.B., 1948; Indiana University, M.S. in Ed., 1950, Ed.D., 1959. *Politics:* Independent. *Religion:* Episcopalian. *Home:* 126 Central Ave., Fredonia, N.Y. 14063. *Office:* State University of New York, College at Fredonia, Fredonia, N.Y. 14063.

CAREER: Elementary school supervisor in Grand Haven, Mich., 1954-56; Park College, Parkville, Mo., assistant professor of education, 1956-58; State University of New York, College at Fredonia, associate professor, 1959-62, professor of education, 1962—. *Military service:* U.S. Army, 1943-46; served in Asiatic Pacific theater; became first lieutenant. *Member:* Comparative and International Education Society, American Association for the Advancement of Slavic Studies, National Council for the Social Studies, National Education Association, Delta Tau Kappa.

WRITINGS: How People Live in the U.S.S.R., Benefic, 1969, revised edition, 1971; *Democracy and Communism*, Benefic, 1973. Author of filmstrips, "The Soviet Union Today," "Russia and Communism," and "How Nations Are Governed," all for Filmstrip House. Also author of sound-slide sets, "Soviet State and Society," "Soviet Economy," "Soviet Education and Recreation," and "Soviet Cultural Values," for the Society for Visual Education.

WORK IN PROGRESS: "Focus on the Russian Language," a series of four film strips, with personal photographs of the Soviet Union, and with text and script in Russian, for Encore Visual Education, Inc.

AVOCATIONAL INTERESTS: World-wide travel (including eleven trips to the Soviet Union), photography, skiing.

* * *

CHADEAYNE, Lee 1933-

PERSONAL: Born December 22, 1933, in White Plains, N.Y.; son of Leander Fisher and Marie Elizabeth (an attorney; maiden name, Jessen) Chadeayne; married Evelyn Anna Schumann (a teacher), June 23, 1962; children: Marie Elizabeth, Theodore Leander. *Education:* Attended Hamilton College, 1951-53; Columbia University, B.S., 1959, M.A. (education), 1961; Syracuse University, graduate study, 1961-62; Ohio State University, M.A. (German), 1966; attended Middlebury College, summer, 1970. *Politics:* Independent. *Religion:* Presbyterian. *Home:* 45 Gunwhale Way, Yarmouthport, Mass. 02675.

CAREER: Columbia Artists Management, New York, N.Y., tour director and traveling company representative, 1953-56; Hobart and William Smith Colleges, Geneva, N.Y., instructor in German, 1960-63; Ohio State University, Columbus, instructor in German, 1966-71; Gymnasium an der Max-Planck-Strasse, Delmenhorst, West Germany, instructor in English, 1971-72; Ohio State University, instructor in German, 1972-73; high school teacher of French and German in South Yarmouth, Mass., 1973—. Member of advisory board, "Deutsche Welle" ("The Voice of Germany"). Taught a pilot first-year German class in a Columbus, Ohio high school, 1970-71. *Member:* American Association of Teachers of German, Massachusetts Teachers Association, National Education Association. *Awards, honors:* American Translation Association grant, 1970.

WRITINGS: (Contributor of translation) Paul Lauter, editor, *Theories of Comedy*, Doubleday, 1966; (translator with Paul Gottwald) Wolfgang Seiferth, *Synagogue and Church in the Middle Ages: Two Symbols in Art and Literature*, Ungar, 1970; (translator with Gottwald) Max Luethi, *Once Upon a Time: On the Nature of Fairy Tales*, Ungar, 1970; (editor with Gottwald) Hans Fallada (pseudonym for Rudolph Ditzen), *Damals bei uns daheim* (textbook version), Scott, Foresman, 1972. Contributor to *German Quarterly*. Regional editor, *Massachusetts Foreign Language Bulletin*, 1974—.

WORK IN PROGRESS: Translating Max Luethi's major study, *Shakespeares Dramen*.

AVOCATIONAL INTERESTS: Music (twelve years of piano study), travel, family and church activities (organist and choir director in local church).

CHADOURNE, Marc 1896(?)-1975

1896(?)—January 30, 1975; French author and educator. Obituaries: *New York Times*, February 1, 1975; *AB Bookman's Weekly*, February 17, 1975.

* * *

CHAFIN, Andrew 1937-

PERSONAL: Born January 14, 1937, in Matewan, W.Va.; son of Tom C. and Hazel (Isaac) Chafin; married Vickie Griffith, January 12, 1962; children: Andrew, Lorrain, Adrienne. *Education:* Morris Harvey College, B.A., 1967; University of Northern Colorado, M.A., 1972. *Religion:* Baptist. *Home:* Pruner Division, Lebanon, Va. 24266. *Office:* Cumberland Plateau Planning District, Lebanon, Va. 24266.

CAREER: West Virginia Road Commission, Planning Division, Charleston, technician, 1963-67; Tug Valley Chamber of Commerce, Williamson, W.Va., managing director, 1967-68; Cumberland Plateau Planning District, Lebanon, Va., executive director, 1968—. *Military service:* U.S. Army, 1959-65. *Member:* American Society for Public Administration, American Society for Planning Officials.

WRITINGS: So You're the New Planning Commissioner, Sharon Books, 1972; *So You're the New City Councilman*, Sharon Books, 1973; *Public Relations for Planning Agencies*, Sharon Books, 1973; *The Super Fans*, Sharon Books, 1974.

WORK IN PROGRESS: Research for a book on regional planning in rural America.

* * *

CHAMBERLAIN, Samuel 1895-1975 (Phineas Beck)

October 10, 1895—January 10, 1975; American photographer, artist, and author. Obituaries: *New York Times*, January 11, 1975; *AB Bookman's Weekly*, February 3, 1975, February 17, 1975; *Publishers Weekly*, February 10, 1975. (*CA*-23/24).

* * *

CHAMBERLIN, Leslie J(oseph) 1926-

PERSONAL: Born August 16, 1926, in St. Louis, Mo.; son of George Albert (a businessman) and Margaret Mary (Cassidy) Chamberlin; married Virginia Rose Schauer, April 19, 1947; children: Veronica, Barbara, Linda, Mark, Theresa, Matthew. *Education:* Harris Teachers College, A.A., 1948; Washington University, St. Louis, Mo., B.S., 1951, M.A., 1953; University of Missouri, Ed.D., 1960. *Religion:* Roman Catholic. *Home:* 11934 Sugar Ridge Rd., Bowling Green, Ohio 43402. *Office:* Department of Educational Administration and Supervision, Bowling Green State University, Bowling Green, Ohio 43402.

CAREER: St. Louis Public Schools, St. Louis, Mo., elementary school teacher, 1951-56, administrator, 1956-63; Bowling Green State University, Bowling Green, Ohio, associate professor, 1967-70, professor of educational administration and supervision, 1970—. Visiting professor at University of Nevada at Las Vegas, Southwest Missouri State University, and University of Akron. *Military service:* U.S. Army, Infantry, 1945-46.

MEMBER: National Higher Education Association (life member), American Association for Higher Education (life member), National Education Association (life member), American Association of School Administrators, National Association of Elementary Principals, Association for Supervision and Curriculum Development, Ohio Association of Elementary Principals, Ohio School Supervisor's Association.

WRITINGS: (Contributor) Robert E. Chasnoff, editor, *Elementary Curriculum*, Pitman, 1964; *Team Teaching; Organization and Administration*, C. E. Merrill, 1969; (contributor) Jean Spealman Kujoth, editor, *The Teacher and School Discipline*, Scarecrow, 1970; *Effective Instruction through Dynamic Discipline*, C. E. Merrill, 1971; (contributor) Hal D. Funk and Robert T. Olber, editors, *Learning to Teach in the Elementary School*, Dodd, 1971; (with Ron Cotee) *Administration, Education, and Change*, Kendall/Hunt, 1972; (with Joseph B. Carnot) *Improving School Discipline*, C. C Thomas, 1974. Contributor of about thirty-five articles to professional journals.

WORK IN PROGRESS: The Innovative School: Organization and Administration; research on Project SEE (Successful Educational Environment) concerned with improved direction through environmental awareness, and on the importance and relationship of various factors to the educational environment.

* * *

CHANDLER, Alice 1931-

PERSONAL: Born May 29, 1931, in Brooklyn, N.Y.; married Horace W. Chandler; children: Seth, Donald. *Education:* Barnard College, A.B. (magna cum laude), 1951; Columbia University, M.A., 1953, Ph.D., 1960. *Office:* Office of Institutional Advancement, City College of the City University of New York, Convent Ave. at 138th St., New York, N.Y. 10031.

CAREER: Challenge (magazine), New York, N.Y., associate editor, 1952-53; Skidmore College, Saratoga Springs, N.Y., instructor in English, 1953-54; Barnard College, New York, N.Y., lecturer in English, 1954-55; Hunter College of the City University of New York, New York, N.Y., lecturer in English, 1956-57; City College of the City University of New York, New York, N.Y., instructor, 1961-65, assistant professor, 1965-69, associate professor, 1970-72, professor of English, 1973—, assistant vice-president for institutional advancement, 1974—. *Member:* Modern Language Association of America, Phi Beta Kappa, Andiron Club.

WRITINGS: The Prose Spectrum: A Rhetoric and Reader, Allyn & Bacon, 1968; *The Theme of War*, W. C. Brown, 1969; *The Rationale of Rhetoric: A Developmental Text in Composition*, Holt, 1970; *A Dream of Order: The Medieval Ideal in Nineteenth-Century English Literature*, University of Nebraska Press, 1970; (editor with Marlene Fisher) *The Rationale of the Essay: A Reader for Writers*, Holt, 1971. Editor of "Form and Content" series for W. C. Brown.

* * *

CHAPIN, Kim 1942-

PERSONAL: Born July 18, 1942, in Bay City, Mich.; son of Wendell Phillips (a printer) and Roberta (a realtor; maiden name, Cameron) Chapin. *Education:* Attended Vanderbilt University, 1960-64. *Home and office:* 65 West 95th St., New York, N.Y., 10025.

CAREER: Atlanta Journal, Atlanta, Ga., reporter, 1964-66; *Sports Illustrated*, New York, N.Y., member of staff, 1966-68, staff writer, 1968-69; free-lance writer, 1969—;

Santa Fe Reporter, Santa Fe, N.M., sports editor, 1974. *Military service:* U.S. Army Reserve, 1965-69.

WRITINGS: (With Billie Jean King) *Tennis to Win*, Harper, 1970; (with King) *Billie Jean*, Harper, 1974. Co-author of "The Speed Merchants," a documentary filmscript, 1972. Contributor to *True, Car and Driver, World Tennis*, and *American Home*.

WORK IN PROGRESS: A non-fiction book on stock-car racing.

AVOCATIONAL INTERESTS: Travel.

* * *

CHAPMAN, Loren J(ames) 1927-

PERSONAL: Born January 5, 1927, in Muncie, Ind.; son of Herbert Lee (a farmer) and Lurana (Treff) Chapman; married Jean Paulsen (a psychologist), 1953; children: Nancy, Laurence. *Education:* Harvard University, B.A. (cum laude), 1948; Northwestern University, M.A., 1952, Ph.D., 1954. *Home:* 129 Richland Lane, Madison, Wis. 53705. *Office:* Department of Psychology, University of Wisconsin, Charter at Johnson, Madison, Wis. 53706.

CAREER: University of Chicago, Chicago, Ill., instructor, 1956-58, assistant professor of psychology, 1958-59; University of Kentucky, Lexington, associate professor of psychology, 1959-62; Southern Illinois University, Carbondale, associate professor, 1962-64, professor of psychology, 1964-66; University of Wisconsin, Madison, professor of psychology, 1966--. National Institute of Mental Health, consultant on intramural research, 1960-64, study section member of Clinical Projects Research Review Committee, 1966-72. *Member:* American Psychological Association, Psychonomic Society, American Psychopathology Association. *Awards, honors:* U.S. Public Health Service fellow, University of Chicago, 1954-56; National Institute of Mental Health Research Scientist Award, 1970-75.

WRITINGS: (With wife, Jean Paulsen Chapman) *Disordered Thought in Schizophrenia,* Appleton, 1973. Associate editor of *Journal of Abnormal Psychology,* 1971-74.

WORK IN PROGRESS: Research on schizophrenic cognition and on the genetics of conditioned avoidance responses in rats.

* * *

CHAPPELOW, Allan (Gordon)

PERSONAL: Born in Copenhagen, Denmark; son of Archibald Cecil (a fine art consultant) and Karen (Ragnhild) Chappelow. *Education:* Attended University College, Birkbeck College, and Slade School of Fine Art of University of London, 1944-46; Trinity College, Cambridge, B.A. (honors), 1948, M.A., 1953; London School of Economics and Political Science, graduate study, 1949-51. *Politics:* Independent liberal. *Religion:* Agnostic. *Home:* The Manor House, 9, Downshire Hill, Hampstead, London N.W.3, England.

CAREER: Free-lance writer, researcher, photographer, and sculptor. *Member:* British Psychological Society (graduate member), Royal Society of Arts (fellow), Society of Authors, Shaw Society, Vincent Owner's Club. *Awards, honors: Shaw—"The Chucker-Out"* selected by *Choice* for "Outstanding Academic Books of the Year" list, 1973.

WRITINGS: Russian Holiday, Harrap, 1955; *Shaw the Villager, and Human Being*, Skilton, 1961, Macmillan, 1962; *Shaw—"The Chucker-Out,"* Allen & Unwin, 1969, AMS Press, 1971. Contributor to *Daily Mail* (London), *Daily Express* (London), *Times* (London), *Listener, Illustrated London News, Vogue, Times Literary Supplement, Journal of Hellenic Studies*, and others.

SIDELIGHTS: Chappelow's first book, *Russian Holiday*, is an account of his experiences as a member of the first party of ordinary tourists to visit the Soviet Union after Stalin's death. As a photographer, he took portraits of many famous British figures, including George Bernard Shaw, H. G. Wells, Hilaire Belloc, Walter de la Mare, Bertrand Russell, Augustus Johns, Ralph Vaughan Williams, and Sean O'Casey. He writes: "Aims as a writer are, as far as possible, to combine scholarship with entertainment value, i.e., to have dual appeal to both the academic world and the general public." *Avocational interests:* Ballet, music, foreign travel, motor-cycling.

* * *

CHARLESWORTH, Arthur Riggs 1911-

PERSONAL: Born September 23, 1911, in South Fork, Pa.; married Martha Jean Hamilton (a head librarian), July 11, 1935; children: Lois Jean Charlesworth Jones, James Hamilton, Arthur Thomas. *Education:* University of Pittsburgh, B.A., 1933; Drew University, B.D. (with honors), 1936, M.Div., Ph.D.; summer postdoctoral study at Princeton Theological Seminary, Oxford University, University of Edinburgh, and at universities in North Africa. *Home:* 1231 Florence Ct., Holly Hill, Fla. 32017. *Office address:* Box 303, Bethune-Cookman College, Daytona Beach, Fla. 32015.

CAREER: Ordained minister of the United Methodist Church; formerly minister of University Methodist Church, and director of Wesley Foundation at University of Florida, Gainesville, and senior minister in Miami, Fla.; Bethune-Cookman College, Daytona Beach, Fla., professor of religion, 1963—, head of department, 1963—. Director of Methodist Student Movement of the State of Florida. *Member:* American Schools of Oriental Research, Society of Biblical Literature, American Academy of Religion, American Association of University Professors.

WRITINGS: Paradise Found, Philosophical Library, 1973.

BIOGRAPHICAL/CRITICAL SOURCES: Miami Herald, April 13, 1974.

* * *

CHASE, Cleveland B(ruce) 1904(?)-1975

1904(?)—January 17, 1975; American editor, author, and film-maker. Obituaries: *New York Times*, January 19, 1975; *AB Bookman's Weekly*, February 3, 1975.

* * *

CHASE, Donald 1943-

PERSONAL: Born August 25, 1943, in New Britain, Conn.; son of A. D. and Helen (a businesswoman; maiden name, Chudzik) Cieszynski. *Education:* Boston University, B.A. (magna cum laude), 1965. *Home:* 121 East 90th St., New York, N.Y. 10028.

CAREER: Dun & Bradstreet, Inc., New York, N.Y., municipal bond analyst, 1966-69; free-lance editor in New York, 1969—. *Member:* Phi Beta Kappa.

WRITINGS: Filmmaking: The Collaborative Art, Little, Brown, 1975. Author of "Gloria at Large," an original feature-length screenplay. Contributor to *Interview, Show,* and *Coast.*

SIDELIGHTS: Chase writes: "I began writing about film to make sense of my experience of film art; I turned to writing film scripts to make sense of my experience of life." He has traveled in the United States and Europe, often to film location sites.

* * *

CHATT, Orville K(eith) 1924-

PERSONAL: Born December 12, 1924, in Tekamah, Neb.; son of Mr. & Mrs. Steve Chatt; married Pat Horner (a registered nurse), January 14, 1951; children: Beth (Mrs. Larry Crye), Julie, Mark, Scott, David, Jay. *Education:* Art Institute of Chicago, B.F.A., 1951; Drake University, M.F.A., 1963. *Religion:* Church of Jesus Christ of Latter Day Saints (Mormon). *Home:* 903 Jameson, Sedro Woolley, Wash. 98284. *Office:* Department of Fine Arts, Skagit Valley College, Mount Vernon, Wash. 98273.

CAREER: Iowa State University, Ames, instructor, 1961-64, craft coordinator, 1961-64; Skagit Valley College, Mount Vernon, Wash., professor of craft design, 1964—. *Military service:* U.S. Army Air Forces, pilot, 1947; served in South Pacific theater; became second lieutenant. *Member:* American Craft Council, Northwest Designer Craftsmen. *Awards, honors:* Local, National, and international awards in jewelry and design.

WRITINGS: Design Is Where You Find It, Iowa State University Press, 1972.

WORK IN PROGRESS: A textbook for making jewelry, completion expected in 1975.

AVOCATIONAL INTERESTS: Interior decorating.

* * *

CHEIFETZ, Philip M(orris) 1944-

PERSONAL: Born October 8, 1944, in Brooklyn, N.Y.; son of Bernard (a stock broker) and Adele (Speilman) Cheifetz; married Pauline Gutman, June 24, 1967; children: Melissa, Robin. *Education:* Wilkes College, B.A., 1966; Hofstra University, M.S., 1969; University of Sarasota, Ph.D., 1973. *Home:* 2 Morning Glory Rd., Levittown, N.Y. 11756. *Office:* Department of Mathematics, Nassau College, Stewart Ave., Garden City, N.Y. 11530.

CAREER: Nassau College, Garden City, N.Y., assistant professor, 1967-74, associate professor of mathematics and computer science, 1974—. Adjunct professor at State University of New York at Stony Brook, 1971-73. *Member:* Mathematics Association of America, Mathematics Association of Two Year Colleges (member of board of directors, 1971—).

WRITINGS: (With Frank Avenoso) *Logic and Set Theory*, Wadsworth, 1970; (with Louis Auslander and others) *Mathematics through Statistics*, Williams & Wilkens, 1973; (editor) *Statistics through Problem Solving*, Mathematical Alternatives, 1973; (with Avenoso) *Elementary Statistics through Problem Solving*, Williams & Wilkens, 1974. Contributor to *Mathematics Association of Two Year Colleges Journal*. Mathematics editor for Mathematical Alternatives, Inc., 1972—.

WORK IN PROGRESS: Editing *Calculus through Problem Solving*, completion expected in 1976; research on aircraft noise pollution and its annoying effects on airport communities.

AVOCATIONAL INTERESTS: Bridge, collegiate wrestling, karate, reading.

* * *

CHEN, King C(hing) 1926-

PERSONAL: Born October 24, 1926, in China; naturalized U.S. citizen; son of Teh-ching (an educator) and Chu-ying Chen; married Grace Ho (a librarian), 1963; children: David W., Donald D. *Education:* National Chengchi University, B.A., 1948; University of Virginia, M.A., 1957; Pennsylvania State University, Ph.D., 1962; also studied at Columbia University, 1959-61. *Home:* 25 Rynda Rd., Maplewood, N.J. 07040. *Office:* Department of Political Science, Rutgers University, Newark, N.J. 07102.

CAREER: Brooklyn College of the City University of New York, Brooklyn, N.Y., instructor in Far Eastern affairs, 1962-63; State University of New York, assistant professor, 1963-64, associate professor of political science, 1964-65; Brown University, Providence, R.I., assistant professor of political science, 1965-69; Rutgers University, Newark, N.J., associate professor of political science, 1969—. Interpreter for U.S. State Department, summer, 1960; trustee of National Federation for Chinese Culture and Heritage. *Member:* American Political Science Association, Association for Asian Studies, New Jersey Chinese Culture Association (vice-chairman). *Awards, honors:* Senior fellowship from Research Institute for Communist Affairs at Columbia University, and faculty research fellowship from Rutgers University, both 1972-73.

WRITINGS: Vietnam and China: 1938-1954, Princeton University Press, 1969; (editor and contributor) *The Foreign Policy of China,* East & West, 1972; (contributor) Wu Yuan-li, editor, *China: A Handbook,* Praeger, 1973; (contributor) Gene Hsiao, editor, *The Role of External Powers in the Indochina Crisis,* Southern Illinois University, 1973. Contributor of more than a dozen articles to professional journals, including *Asian Survey, Yale Review, Asie-France,* and *Pacific Affairs.*

WORK IN PROGRESS: China and the Vietnam War; China's Relations with the Third World; contributing to *Dimensions of China's Foreign Relations,* edited by Chun-tu Hseuh.

AVOCATIONAL INTERESTS: Music, Chinese painting, art.

* * *

CHENERY, William L(udlow) 1884(?)-1974

1884(?)—August 18, 1974; American journalist and magazine editor. Obituaries: *Washington Post*, August 22, 1974.

* * *

CHERASKIN, Emanuel 1916-

PERSONAL: Born June 9, 1916, in Philadelphia, Pa.; son of Herman and Celia (Homes) Cheraskin; married Caroline Elwood, September 23, 1944; children: Lisa. *Education:* Studied at St. Joseph's College, Philadelphia, and Georgetown University; University of Alabama, A.B., 1939, M.A., 1941, D.M.D., 1952; University of Cincinnati, M.D., 1943. *Home:* 2435 Monte Vista Dr., Vestavia Hills, Ala. 35216. *Office:* Medical Center, University of Alabama, 1919 Seventh Ave. S., University Station, Birmingham, Ala. 35294.

CAREER: Hartford Municipal Hospital, Hartford, Conn.,

intern, 1943-44; St. Mary's Hospital, Evansville, Ind., resident in medicine, 1946-47; private practice of medicine in Moundville, Ala., 1947-48; University of Alabama Medical Center, Birmingham, instructor in anatomy, Medical College of Alabama, 1948-50, assistant professor of physiology, Medical College of Alabama, 1950-52, associate professor of oral medicine, School of Dentistry, 1953-56, professor of oral medicine, 1956—, chairman of department of oral medicine, 1952-56, 1962—, chairman of Division of Oral Surgery and Oral Medicine, 1956-62. Staff member of University Hospital and Hillman clinic, Medical Center, 1957—; assistant professor of medicine, Medical Center, 1959—. Visiting lecturer at College of Dental Medicine, Medical University of South Carolina. Consultant to Southern Academy of Clinical Nutrition, 1965—, Southern California Academy of Nutritional Research, 1967—, and Northeast Academy of Clinical Nutrition, 1970—. Diplomate, American Board of Oral Medicine, 1956. *Military service:* U.S. Army, Medical Corps, 1944-46; became captain.

MEMBER: American College of Dentists (fellow, 1959-64), American Medical Association, American Dental Association, American Public Health Association (fellow), American Academy of Oral Medicine, American Geriatrics Society (fellow), American College of Pharmacology and Chemotherapy (fellow), International College of Angiology (fellow), International Academy of Preventive Medicine (fellow; honorary president, 1974-75), Royal Society of Health (London; life member), American College of Sports Medicine, Society of Prospective Medicine, Society for Nutritional Education, New York Academy of Sciences, Southern Medical Association (life member); honorary member of International Academy of Metabology, and of medical and dental societies in Paraguay, Italy, China, and other countries; Omicron Kappa Upsilon. *Awards, honors:* Doctor honoris causa, University of Sao Paulo, 1961; Honors Achievement Award of Angiology Research Foundation, 1968.

WRITINGS: (With L. L. Langley) *The Physiological Foundation of Dental Practice*, Mosby, 1951, 2nd edition, 1956; (with Langley) *The Physiology of Man*, Reinhold, 1954, 3rd edition, 1956; (with Langley) *Dynamics of Oral Diagnosis*, Year Book Publishers, 1956; (contributor) Sidney B. Finn, *Clinical Pedodontics*, Saunders, 1957, 3rd edition, 1967; (with Langley and Ruth Sleeper) *Dynamic Anatomy and Physiology*, McGraw, 1958; *Diagnostic Stomatology*, McGraw, 1961; (contributor) John J. Sharry, *Complete Denture Prosthodontics*, McGraw, 1962, 2nd edition, 1968; (with W. M. Ringsdorf, Jr. and J. W. Clark) *Diet and Disease*, Rodale Books, 1968; (with Ringsdorf and Clark) *Diet and the Periodontal Patient*, C. C Thomas, 1970; (with Ringsdorf) *New Hope for Incurable Diseases*, Exposition, 1971; (with Ringsdorf) *Predictive Medicine*, Pacific Press Publishing Association, 1973; (with Ringsdorf and Arline Brecher, *Psychodietetics*, Stein & Day, 1974.

Contributor of more than 350 articles to dental, medical, nutrition, and education journals. Chairman of editorial board, *Practical Dental Monographs*, 1955-62; editorial consultant, *Stedman's Medical Dictionary*, 1962; member of editorial staff, *Exerpta Medica*, 1964—; member of editorial board, *Nutrition Reports International*, 1969, and *Journal of Orthomolecular Medicine*, 1973.

* * *

CHERIM, Stanley M(arshall) 1929-

PERSONAL: Born September 13, 1929, in Philadelphia, Pa.; son of Herman and Betty (Kaufman) Cherim; married Solveig Gregersen, July 16, 1955; children: Jan Gregersen, Lise Maynard. *Education:* University of Pennsylvania, B.A., 1951, M.S., 1965; Vanderbilt University, graduate study, 1951-53. *Politics:* Democrat. *Religion:* Quaker. *Home:* 213 Wallingford Ave., Wallingford, Pa. 19086. *Office:* Department of Chemistry, Delaware County Community College, Media, Pa. 19063.

CAREER: Tarsus American College, Tarsus, Turkey, instructor in science and methematics, 1954-57; private high school teacher of science in Philadelphia, Pa., 1957-69; Delaware County Community College, Media, Pa., assistant professor, 1969-71, associate professor, 1971-75, professor of chemistry, 1975—. Member of board of trustees of Providence Friends School, 1974. *Member:* American Chemical Society, National Science Teachers Association, Danish Brotherhood.

WRITINGS: *Chemistry for Laboratory Technicians*, Saunders, 1971; *Laboratory Manual for Technicians*, Saunders, 1971; *Preliminary College Chemistry*, Saunders, 1973.

WORK IN PROGRESS: A philosophical book, *For All Times and All Seasons*, completion expected in 1975.

AVOCATIONAL INTERESTS: Travel, carpentry, sketching, choral singing, sports.

* * *

CHERINGTON, Paul Whiton 1918-1974

June 16, 1918—August 11, 1974; American educator, transportation expert, and government official. Obituaries: *New York Times*, August 13, 1974; *Washington Post*, August 13, 1974. (*CA*-4).

* * *

CHIARA, Piero 1913-

PERSONAL: Born March 23, 1913, in Luino, Varese, Italy; son of Eugenio and Virginia (Maffei) Chiara; married Jula Scherb (divorced, 1972); children: Marco. *Education:* Attended Scuole Medie Superiori. *Religion:* Roman Catholic. *Home:* Via Metastasio 19, Varese, Italy. *Agent:* Avv. Giorgio Moscon, Viale Giulio Cesare 7, Rome, Italy.

CAREER: Author, editor, novelist. Began publishing a literary journal independently in 1942; after an order was issued for his capture for anti-fascist activities, sought refuge in Switzerland, escaping a fifteen-year sentence; held position of professor of letters, history, and philosophy at an Italian school in Zug, Switzerland, and was affiliated with Istituto Montana. *Member:* Rotary (Varese). *Awards, honors:* "Silver-Caffe" prize, 1962, for *Il piatto piange;* Accademia del Ceppo di Pistoia prize for best story of the year, 1964; Alpi-Apuane-Pea Prize and Campiello Prize, both 1964, for *La spartizione;* Veillon Prize (Switzerland), 1965, for *Con la faccia per terra;* Officiel des Palmes Academiques (Paris), 1967; Bagutta Prize, 1968, for *Il balordo;* Knight Commander of Republic of Italy, 1971; Ambrogino d'oro and citation as "Cittadino benemerito" from city of Milan, both 1973; "Nastro d'argento" for best screenplay of the year, for collaboration on "Venga a prendere il caffe da noi."

WRITINGS: *Incantavi* (poetry), Poschiavo, 1945; *Itinerario svizzero* (travelog), Edicioni "Giornale del Popolo," 1950.

Dolore del tempo (short stories), Rebellato, 1960; (author of preface and notes) Giovan Pietro Olina, *L'uccelliera,*

Ferriani, 1960; *L'opera grafica di Giuseppe Viviani,* Rebellato, 1960; *Il paitto piange* (novel), Mondadori, 1962; *Mi focoragio da me,* Scheiwiller, 1963; *La spartizione* (novel), Mondadori, 1964, translation by Julia Martinez published as *A Man of Parts,* Little, Brown, 1968; (with C. Colombo) *Le Prealpi Varesine,* Editore L. E. A., 1964.

Con la faccia per terra, Vallecchi, 1965; *Ti sento Giuditta* (short fiction), Scheiwiller, 1965; *Il povero Turati* (short fiction), Renzo Sommaruga, 1966; *I ladri* (short fiction), Scheiwiller, 1967; *Il balordo* (novel), Mondadori, 1967; *Disegni di Giovanni Carnovali,* Scheiwiller, 1968; *Nuovi disegni di Giovanni Carnovali,* Scheiwiller, 1969; *L'uovo al cianuro e altre storie* (short stories), Mondadori, 1969.

I giovedi della signora giulia (television script), Mondadori, 1970; *Un turco tra di noi* (short fiction), Scheiwiller, 1970; *Ella, signor giudice . . .* (short fiction), Scheiwiller, 1971; (author of introductory essay and notes) *Quaranta sonetti di Giorgio Baffo,* Luigi Maestri, 1972; *Con la faccia per terra e altre storie* (novel), Mondadori, 1972; *Il pretore di Cuvio* (novel), Mondadori, 1973; *Sotto la sua mano* (short stories), Mondadori, 1974; (author of preface and notes) Giorgio Baffo, *Poesie*, Mondadori, 1974.

Editor: (With Luciano Erba) *Quarta generazione* (poetry anthology), Magenta, 1954; Giacomo Casanova, *Lettere a un maggiordomo*, Ferriani, 1960; Casanova, *Storia della mia vita*, seven volumes, Mondadori, 1964-65; Casanova, *Saggi libelli e satire*, Longanesi, 1968; Casanova, *Epistolario*, Longanesi, 1969; Lamberto Vitali, *Dodici acquarelli o disengni di Alberto Duerer*, Scheiwiller, 1970; *Dodici disegni di Giuseppe Viviani*, Scheiwiller, 1971; Stefano Franscini, *La Svizzera Italiana*, Luigi Maestri, 1973.

Translator: (And author of note) Luis de Gongora y Argote, *I sonetti funebri*, Scheiwiller, 1955; (and author of preface and notes) Marianna Alcoforado, *Lettere portoghesi*, Ferriani, 1960; Gongora, *I sonetti funebri e altre composizioni*, Einaudi, 1970; (and author of introduction) Johann Jacob Weitzel, *Viaggio pittoresco al Lago Maggiore e al Lago di Lugano*, "Il Polifilio," 1973.

Author of television scripts, "I gioved della signora Giulia" and "Un curioso uomo," both for RAI-TV Itàlia, and "I capitani forse," for Televisione della Svizzera Italiana. Co-author of screenplay for film "Venga a prendere il caffe da noi" (based on his novel, *La spartizione*), 1970. Contributor to *Il corriere della Sera*, *Epoca* (a weekly), and to journals and daily newspapers.

SIDELIGHTS: Il paitto piange was filmed and released under same title in 1974. Chiara's works have been published in Germany, France, England, Romania, Yugoslavia, Hungary, Poland, Czechoslovakia, and Argentina.

* * *

CHIELENS, Edward E(rnest) 1943-

PERSONAL: Surname is pronounced *Shil*-luns; born February 12, 1943, in Detroit, Mich.; son of Ernest C. (an automobile worker) and Lucy (Davies) Chielens; married Carole Youngblood (a legal secretary), September 12, 1970. *Education:* Wayne State University, B.A., 1965, Ph.D., 1971; University of Michigan, M.A., 1966. *Politics:* Democrat. *Home:* 17323 Wildemere, Detroit, Mich. 48221. *Office:* Detroit College of Business, Dearborn, Mich. 48216.

CAREER: Wayne State University, Detroit, Mich., instructor in English, 1969-71; Detroit College of Business, Detroit, Mich., 1971—, began as instructor, now associate professor of English. *Member:* Modern Language Association of America, Michigan College English Association, Phi Beta Kappa, Omicron Delta Kappa.

WRITINGS: (Editor) *The Literary Journal in America to 1900*, Gale, 1975.

WORK IN PROGRESS: Research on the American familiar essay, with publication expected to result; *The Literary Journal in America, 1900-1950*, for Gale.

AVOCATIONAL INTERESTS: European travel.

* * *

CHIROVSKY, Nicholas L. 1919-

PERSONAL: Born August 5, 1919, in West Ukraine; came to United States in 1949, naturalized in 1955; son of Nicholas and Zenbia (Zarycky) Chirovsky; married Iwanna Smishkevich (a library employee), September 21, 1947; children: Leo, George, Andrew, John. *Education:* Attended University of Lublin; University of Graz, J.S.D., M.A.; Free University of Munich, D.Pol. Econ. *Politics:* Republican. *Religion:* Roman Catholic. *Home:* 7 Madison Ave., Maplewood, N.J. 07040. *Office:* Department of Economics, Seton Hall University, South Orange, N.Y. 07079.

CAREER: Ukranian Graduate School of Economics, Munich, Germany, instructor in economics, 1947-49; Seton Hall University, South Orange, N.J., professor of economics, 1955—, head of department, 1963—. *Member:* American Economic Association, Shevcheko Scientific Society, Catholic Economics Association.

WRITINGS: The Economic Factors in the Growth of Russia, Philosophical Library, 1957; *The Old Ukraine*, Florham, 1963; *The Ukrainian Economy*, Shevcheko Society, 1965; *An Introduction to Russian History*, Philosophical Library, 1967; (co-author) *Philosophy in Economic Thought*, Florham, 1972; *A History of the Russian Empire*, Volume I, Philosophical Library, 1973; *Ukraine and the European Turmoil: 1917-1920*, Shevcheko Society, 1973. Also author of *Ukraine on the European Crossroads*, 1971. Contributor to professional journals.

WORK IN PROGRESS: A History of the Russian Empire, Volume II.

* * *

CHITTENDEN, Margaret 1935-

PERSONAL: Born January 31, 1935, in London, England; naturalized U.S. citizen in 1962; daughter of James F. (a production supervisor) and Jenny (an accountant; maiden name, Huthert) Barrass; married James C. Chittenden (a research technician), October 4, 1958; children: Stephen John, Sharon Lynne. *Education:* Educated in England. *Religion:* "Relaxed Presbyterian." *Home:* 6101 Nyanza Park Dr., Tacoma, Wash. 98499. *Agent:* Lenniger Literary Agency, Inc., 437 Fifth Ave., New York, N.Y. 10016.

CAREER: Ministry of Works, London, England, clerical officer, 1951-53; J. Arthur Rank Productions, Denham, Buckinghamshire, England, accountant for Pinewood Studios, 1953-54, and Denham Film Laboratories, 1954-59; doctor's secretary in Sacramento, Calif., 1959-60; freelance writer, 1968—. *Member:* National League of American Penwomen (past historian of local branch), Pacific Northwest Writers Conference (vice-president, 1974-75), Seattle Freelances.

WRITINGS: When the Wild Ducks Come (children's reader), Follett, 1972; *Merrymaking in Great Britain* (children's non-fiction), Garrard, 1974; *Findlay's Landing* (mystery-romance novel), Ace Books, 1975. Contributor of short stories and articles to children's and women's magazines, including *Good Housekeeping* and *Girl Talk*.

WORK IN PROGRESS: House of the Twilight Moon, a mystery-romance novel set in Japan.

SIDELIGHTS: "Whenever I am asked why I write, I wish I could give an intellectual reply," Margaret Chittenden told *CA*. "But the truth is, when I write I am happy, when I don't write I am miserable—ergo, I write. I just want to be a storyteller." *Avocational interests:* Fishing, dressmaking, music.

* * *

CHITTY, Arthur Benjamin 1914-

PERSONAL: Born June 15, 1914, in Jacksonville, Fla; son of Arthur Benjamin and Hazel Talitha (Brown) Chitty; married Mary Elizabeth Nickinson, 1966; children: Arthur Benjamin III, John A. M., Em Turner, Nathan H. B. *Education:* University of the South, B.A., 1935; Tulane University, M.A., 1952. *Office:* 815 Second Ave., New York, N.Y. 10017.

CAREER: Chitty & Co., Jacksonville, Fla., sales manager, 1935-45, vice-president, 1935-45, chairman of board of directors, 1962-67; University of the South, Sewanee, Tenn., director of public relations, 1946-65, 1970-73. First historian of Franklin County, Tenn., 1963-68; American coordinator of Episcopal scholarships at Keble College, Oxford University, 1969—; consultant to schools and colleges, 1969—; member of board of trustees, St. Andrew's School, Sewanee, Tenn., 1970—, St. Augustine's College, 1971—, and St. Paul's College, Lawrenceville, Va., 1974—. *Member:* American College Public Relations Association (director of Southeast Division, 1947-48), Association of Episcopal Colleges (president, 1965-70, 1974—), Church Historical Society (member of board of directors, 1969—), English Speaking Union (president of Hudson Stuck Chapter, 1972-73; member of national board of directors, 1974—), Brotherhood of St. Andrew's (vice-president, 1968—), Phi Beta Kappa, Sigma Nu (president of educational foundation, 1971—). *Awards, honors:* L.H.D. from Canaan College, 1970; LL.D. from Cuttington College, 1974; elected to Sigma Nu Hall of Honor, 1974.

WRITINGS: Reconstruction at Sewanee: The Founding of the University of the South and Its First Administration, 1857-1872, Sewanee University Press, 1954, reprinted, Lemoyne College Press, 1970; (editor with wife, Mary Elizabeth Chitty, and author of introduction) Ely Green, *Ely: Too Black, Too White*, University of Massachusetts Press, 1970, abridged edition, New American Library, 1971. Contributor to periodicals in his field. Editor, *Sewanee News*, 1946-65, *Historiographical Newsletter*, 1962-70.

WORK IN PROGRESS: Histories of Episcopal colleges in the United States, and of University of the South; *Sewanee Now and Then*, a collection of anecdotal sketches.

SIDELIGHTS: Chitty was made an honorary paramount chief of the Kpelle Tribe in the West African country of Liberia in 1974.

* * *

CHIU, Hong-Yee 1932-

PERSONAL: Born October 4, 1932, in Shanghai, China; son of Hanping (a legislator) and Min-non (Yang) Chiu; married Bella C. Chao, June 25, 1960 (divorced May 2, 1966); married Celia C. H. Chen (a teacher), July 2, 1966; children: (first marriage) Mason L.; (second marriage) Tien-seng (son), Tien-Yee (daughter). *Education:* National Taiwan University, student, 1951-54; Oklahoma State University, B.Sc., 1956; Cornell University, Ph.D., 1959. *Home:* 71 Chestnut St., Englewood, N.J. 07631. *Office:* Institute for Space Studies, 2880 Broadway, New York, N.Y. 10025.

CAREER: Institute for Advanced Study, Princeton, N.J., member, 1959-61; Goddard Space Flight Center, Greenbelt, Md., National Academy of Sciences-National Research Council research associate, 1960-61; Yale University, New Haven, Conn., assistant professor of physics, 1961-62; National Aeronautics and Space Administration, Institute for Space Studies, New York, N.Y., staff scientist, 1962—. Adjunct assistant professor at Columbia University, 1962-65, adjunct associate professor, 1965-67; adjunct associate professor at State University of New York at Stony Brook, 1965-68, adjunct professor, 1968-73, director of Summer Institute for Astronomy and Astrophysics, 1968-73; adjunct professor at City College of the City University of New York, 1969—. Visiting scientist at Goddard Space Flight Center, 1970-71; visiting professor at National Tsing Hwa University, 1971; visiting summer professor at Brandeis University and University of Colorado, 1963, National Tsing Hwa University, 1964, 1973, and Les Houches Summer Institute, France, 1966.

MEMBER: American Physical Society, American Astronomical Society, Royal Astronomical Society (England), Institute of Electrical and Electronics Engineers, Sigma Pi Sigma. *Awards, honors:* National Aeronautics and Space Administration Exceptional Scientific Achievement Medal, 1970.

WRITINGS: (Editor with W. F. Hoffmann) *Gravitation and Relativity*, Benjamin (New York), 1964; *Neutrino Astrophysics*, Gordon & Breach, 1965; (editor) *English-Chinese, Chinese-English Astronomical Nomenclature Dictionary*, Consultants Bureau Enterprises, 1966; *Stellar Physics*, Blaisdell, 1968.

Contributor: *Lectures in Theoretical Physics*, Volume VI, University of Colorado Press, 1964; Ivor Robinson and others, editors, *Quasi-Stellar Sources and Gravitational Collapse*, University of Chicago Press, 1965; R. F. Stein and A. G. W. Cameron, editors, *Stellar Evolution*, Plenum, 1966; *High Energy Astrophysics*, Volume II, Gordon & Breach, 1967; R. D. Davies and F. G. Smith, editors, *The Crab Nebula*, Springer Verlag, 1971; Allen M. Lenchek, editor, *The Physics of Pulsars*, Gordon & Breach, 1972.

Co-editor, Proceedings of Summer Institute for Astronomy and Astrophysics, State University of New York at Stony Brook, published by Gordon & Breach: *Stellar Astronomy*, two volumes, 1969; *Galactic Astronomy*, two volumes, 1970; *Stellar Evolution*, 1972. Contributor to *Annual Review of Nuclear Science, Encyclopedia of Atmospheric Sciences and Astrogeology, Encyclopaedic Dictionary of Physics*, and about fifty scientific papers to proceedings and journals. Translation editor, *Acta Astronomica Sinica*, 1974—.

SIDELIGHTS: Chiu coined the word "quasar" for the recently discovered astronomical objects "believed to be located at the most distant parts of our universe."

* * *

CHRISTENSEN, Clyde M. 1905-

PERSONAL: Born August 8, 1905, in Sturgeon Bay, Wis.;

son of Peter K. (a farmer) and Christine (Christensen) Christensen; married Katherine Barry, September 27, 1935; children: Sarah Ellen (Mrs. William R. Nelson), Melanie Barry, Jane Martin (Mrs. Gary T. Vance). *Education:* University of Minnesota, B.S., 1929, M.S., 1930, Ph.D., 1937; University of Halle, graduate study, 1932-33. *Home:* 2350 Carter Ave., St. Paul, Minn. 55108. *Office:* Department of Plant Pathology, University of Minnesota, St. Paul, Minn. 55101.

CAREER: University of Minnesota, St. Paul, instructor, 1930-32, 1934-39, assistant professor, 1939-46, associate professor, 1946-48, professor of plant pathology, 1948—, Regents Professor, 1973, professor emeritus, 1974—. Scientific aide, Rockefeller Foundation Latin American Agricultural Program, 1959-60, 1963, 1968. *Member:* American Phytopathological Society (fellow). *Awards, honors:* National Institutes of Health and Massachusetts Institute of Technology grant, Bangkok, Thailand, 1967.

WRITINGS: Common Edible Mushrooms, University of Minnesota Press, 1943; *The Molds and Man*, University of Minnesota Press, 1951; *Common Fleshy Fungi*, Burgess, 1965; *Grain Storage: The Role of Fungi in Quality Loss*, University of Minnesota Press, 1969; (editor) *Storage of Cereal Grains and Their Products*, American Association of Cereal Chemists, 1974; *Mushrooms, Molds, and Mycotoxins*, University of Minnesota Press, in press. Contributor of more than two hundred articles to professional journals.

* * *

CHRISTENSEN, Eleanor Ingalls 1913-

PERSONAL: Born January 29, 1913, in Brooklyn, N.Y.; daughter of Orlando DuBois (a physician) and Jane (a secretary; maiden name, Myer) Ingalls; married Conrad Lincoln Christensen (an army officer and management engineer), November 29, 1946; children: Jan Peter, Jane Elizabeth, Jeffrey Scott. *Education:* Wheaton College, Norton, Mass., A.B., 1935; graduate study at Radcliffe College, 1936-37, and State University of New York College at New Paltz, 1973—. *Home address:* Hurley, N.Y. 12443. *Office:* Fair Street School, 209 Fair St., Kingston, N.Y.

CAREER: Tutor in Taxco, Mexico, 1938-39; elementary school teacher in Washington, D.C., 1939-43, New York, N.Y., 1943-46, 1953-55, and Hurley, N.Y., 1960; Fair Street School, Kingston, N.Y., pre-school teacher, 1960—. Organizing Ulster County Council for the Arts; president of Ulster Council, 1973-75. *Member:* Association for the Education of Young Children (co-founder and past secretary of mid-Hudson chapter), American Federation of Arts, Hudson Valley Philharmonic Society, Hurley Heritage Society, BenMarl Societe des Vignerons, Wiltwyck Golf Club.

WRITINGS: (Contributor) *Fun and Fancy*, Ginn, 1956; *The Art of Haiti*, A. S. Barnes, 1975. Contributor to *Golf Magazine Annual* and *Albany Times Union*.

WORK IN PROGRESS: A children's story; research on Louis C. Tiffany and his times; an article about sailing on the Hudson River.

SIDELIGHTS: Eleanor Christensen writes: "The work of the young untaught painters of Haiti caught my attention because of my interest in children's art. I was told they had appeared as if from a void—that Haiti had no artistic heritage upon which they drew. This seemed so unlikely in a country that had been France's richest colony, that I determined to find out. The result is *The Art of Haiti* . . . a carefully researched reference work, and a recreational book to be read for its human interest appeal. . . .

"I have no causes, but take pleasure in enriching the part of life lived through the eyes, pointing out aspects of the creative process not widely recognized."

AVOCATIONAL INTERESTS: Golf, sailing, skiing, gardening, photography.

* * *

CHRISTENSEN, J(ack) A(rden) 1927-

PERSONAL: Born September 14, 1927, in Gunnison, Utah; son of Angus Arden (a farmer) and Affalone (Madsen) Christensen. *Education:* Brigham Young University, B.A., 1950; University of Utah, M.S., 1956; University of Nevada, graduate study, 1963. *Politics:* Democrat. *Religion:* "Strong leaning toward Buddhism." *Home:* 967 South 13th E., Salt Lake City, Utah 84105. *Office:* Salt Lake City School District, 840 South 13th E., Salt Lake City, Utah 84102.

CAREER: Public school teacher of English in Hyrum, Utah, 1950-51, in Gooding, Idaho, 1951-52, in Layton, Utah, 1954-56, and of history in Clearfield, Utah, 1953-54; Veterans Administration Hospital, Salt Lake City, Utah, psychiatric aide, 1952, Los Angeles, Calif., medical aide, 1953; Lund Machinery Co., Salt Lake City, Utah, office manager, 1953; Salt Lake School District, Salt Lake City, Utah, teacher of English, 1956—. *Member:* National Writer's Club, Idaho Writer's Guild, Utah Poetry Society, Utah Council of Teachers of English (president, 1970-71). *Awards, honors:* Marie Louise D'Esternaux Memorial Award in Poetry, 1956; Marie Schroeder Devrient Award for Dramatic Poetry, 1957; Morgan-Pehrson Book Publication Award from Utah State Poetry Society, 1969.

WRITINGS: Impressions and Aftermaths (poems), Creative Arts Studio, 1960; *Whispers in the Wind* (poems), Creative Art Studio, 1963; *The Deep Song* (poems), Utah Poetry Society, 1969; *The Young Writer* (textbook), Pacific Books, 1970. Author of teacher's manuals for McDougal-Littell. Associate editor of *Media and Methods*, 1970—.

WORK IN PROGRESS: A textbook on mass media, completion expected in 1975; two books of poems, *Children of the Sun*, 1975, and *Garden of the Moon's Embrace*, 1975.

SIDELIGHTS: Christensen grew up on a sheep ranch and a farm. He developed a love for the scenery, the history, and the people of the West. His grandparents were early Utah settlers and entertained him with stories of the "early days," which he has used as the basis for much of his writing. Recently he has become interested in Asian studies, particularly in the culture of China and Japan. He is now a student of the Japanese tea ceremony and language.

* * *

CHRISTIAN, Carol (Cathay) 1923-

PERSONAL: Born November 15, 1923, in Peking, China; daughter of Melsom Sabinas (a secretary of the Young Men's Christian Association) and Ruth (a social worker; maiden name, Dietrich) Tuttle; married John Christian (a civil servant), June 23, 1945; children: David, Diana, Robin, Russell. *Education:* Smith College, B.A., (magna cum laude), 1944. *Politics:* Liberal. *Religion:* Christian ("with special concern for pastoral counselling"). *Home:*

22 Pitfold Ave., Shottermill, Haslemere, Surrey GU 21 1PN, England.

MEMBER: Society of Authors.

WRITINGS: Into Strange Country (novel), Allen & Unwin, 1958; (with Gladys Plummer) *God and One Redhead: Mary Slessor of Calabar*, Hodder & Stoughton, 1970, Zondervan, 1971; *Tales of the Cross River* (reader), Macmillan Education, 1972; *Great People of Our Time* (reader), Macmillan Education, 1973; *Proverbs and Rhymes* (reader), Evans, 1974; *The Girl Who Laughed* (reader), Evans, 1975; *Johnny Ring* (reader), Macmillan Education, 1975. Editor for Macmillan Education, 1973—.

SIDELIGHTS: Carol Christian became interested in writing readers for teaching English as a foreign language when she spent eleven years in Nigeria.

* * *

CHRISTIANSEN, Harley Duane 1930-

PERSONAL: Born September 10, 1930, in Isle, Minn.; son of Harley Edward (a pharmacist) and Sophie (a saleslady; maiden name, Seamann) Christiansen. *Education:* University of Minnesota, B.S., 1952, Ph.D., 1959. *Mailing address:* Box 4261, Tucson, Ariz. 85717. *Office:* Counseling and Guidance Department, College of Education, University of Arizona, Tucson, Ariz. 85721.

CAREER: University of Arizona, Tucson, assistant professor, 1960-66, associate professor of counseling and guidance, 1966—; co-director of Counseling and Consulting Center (private practice counseling agency), 1973—. *Member:* American Psychological Association, American Personnel and Guidance Association, American Society of Clinical Hypnosis, Arizona State Psychological Association, Arizona Society of Clinical Hypnosis (president, 1970—).

WRITINGS: Ethics in Counseling: Problem Situation, University of Arizona Press, 1972; (with Marie Vergata) *Study Power, Better Study Skills: Greater Success in College*, Peter Juul Press, 1975.

WORK IN PROGRESS: Three books dealing with relaxation, using hypnosis, and sexual adjustment, respectively.

AVOCATIONAL INTERESTS: Yoga.

* * *

CHRISTIE-MURRAY, David (Hugh Arthur) 1913- (Hugh Arthur, Hugh Christie)

PERSONAL: Born July 12, 1913, in London, England; son of Dudley (an automobile engineer) and Miriam Violet (Hume) Christie-Murray; married Ena Louise Elisabeth Mumford, July 11, 1942 (died January 13, 1967); married Sheila Mary Watson (an author's agent), April 10, 1972; children: Anne Elisabeth (Mrs. Anthony Hall-Williams), Martin Ross (adopted), Alison Jean, Susan Hilary; stepdaughters: Karen Anne, Laura. *Education:* University College, London, Diploma in Journalism, 1934; St. Peter's Hall (now College), Oxford, M.A., 1942; graduate study at Wycliffe Hall, Anglican Theological College, 1939-42. *Politics:* "A plague on all their houses!" *Religion:* Christian. *Home:* Imber Court Cottage, Orchard Lane, East Molesey, Surrey KT8 OBN, England. *Agent:* Sheila Watson (wife), Bolt & Watson Ltd., 8 Storey's Gate, London S.W.1, England.

CAREER: Positions in journalism, publishing, and advertising, 1934-37; St. Lawrence College, Ramsgate, Kent, England, teacher of English, Latin, and scripture, and assistant master, 1937-38; youth organizer in Gravesend, Kent, England, 1942-46; Harrow School, Harrow-on-the-Hill, Middlesex, England, teacher of English, Latin, and divinity, 1946-73. *Member:* Royal Archaeological Institute, Heraldry Society, College of Psychic Studies, Society for Psychical Research.

WRITINGS: Heraldry in the Churches of Beckenham, privately printed, 1954; *The Hamlyn Bible for Children*, Hamlyn, 1974. Author of religious and heraldic subjects for British Broadcasting Corp. (BBC). Contributor, sometimes under pseudonym Hugh Christie, to professional journals and popular magazines, including *Photography, Heiress*, and *Philatelic Magazine*.

WORK IN PROGRESS: Voices from the Gods, a survey of glossolalia in history, anthropology, Christianity, abnormal psychology, and spiritualism; *A History of Heresy*, for New English Library; *Astrology*, under pseudonym Hugh Arthur, for Hamlyn.

* * *

CHRISTOPHER, Joe R(andell) 1935-

PERSONAL: Born June 27, 1935, in Bartlesville, Okla.; son of Ernest Randell (a postmaster) and Blanche (an elementary school teacher; maiden name, Woods) Christopher; married Mary Lynn Hayes, June 9, 1958; children: Saralinda Michelle, Vandy Maria, Randell Llewellyn-Hayes. *Education:* University of Oklahoma, B.A., 1957, M.A., 1959, Ph.D., 1969. *Politics:* Usually Democratic. *Religion:* Episcopal. *Home:* 820 Charlotte, Stephenville, Tex. 76401. *Office:* Department of English, Tarleton State University, Stephenville, Tex. 76402.

CAREER: Tarleton State University, Stephenville, Tex., instructor, 1963-67, assistant professor, 1967-68, associate professor of English, 1968—. Visiting professor at Western New Mexico University, 1970. Member of board of directors of Mythopoeic Press, 1973—. *Member:* Modern Language Associaton of America, Mythopoeic Society, Fantasy Association, NeoPreRaphaelite Guild, South Central Modern Language Association, New York C.S. Lewis Society, Portland C.S. Lewis Society.

WRITINGS: (With Dean W. Dickensheet and Robert E. Briney) *A. Boucher Bibliography*, Allen J. Hubin, 1969; (with Joan K. Ostling) *C. S. Lewis: An Annotated Checklist of Writings About Him and His Works*, Kent State University Press, 1974; *Priestesses in the Church* (poems), privately printed, 1974; *abSURD! and, The World Reform Act* (poems), Outworlds Productions, in press. "A Foretaste of Blood to Come" (three-act play), produced at Tarleton State University, 1973. Author of column in Mythprint, 1973—. Contributor of essays and poems to *Armchair Detective*, *Cimarron Review*, *CLS*, *Mythlore*, *No*, *Orcrist*, *Riverside Quarterly*, *Parma Eldalamberon*, *Shaw Review*, *Unicorn*, *Yandro*, *Fantasiae*, *Mythril*, and *Outworlds*.

WORK IN PROGRESS: Perceptions of Lyndia, a poem sequence, completion expected in 1975; a Dorothy L. Sayers bibliography, 1977; *The Sun Quest of Los*, a narrative poem, 1977.

* * *

CICOUREL, Aaron V. 1928-

PERSONAL: Born August 29, 1928, in Atlanta, Ga.; son of Victor Aaron and Julia (Mezrah) Cicourel; married Merryl Berner (a ceramicist), June 24, 1951; children:

Gregg, Denise, Eric. *Education:* University of California, Los Angeles, B.A., 1951, M.A., 1955; Cornell University, Ph.D., 1957. *Office:* Department of Sociology, University of California, San Diego, La Jolla, Calif. 92037.

CAREER: Northwestern University, Evanston, Ill., visiting assistant professor of sociology, 1958-60; University of California, Riverside, 1960-65, began as assistant professor, became associate professor of sociology; University of California, Berkeley, lecturer in sociology and associate research sociologist at Center for the Study of Law and Society, 1965-66; University of California, Santa Barbara, professor of sociology, 1966-70; University of California at San Diego, La Jolla, professor of sociology, 1970—. Visiting professor at University of Buenos Aires, 1963-64, and National Autonomous University of Mexico, summers, 1967, 1973. *Military service:* U.S. Army, 1951-53.

MEMBER: American Sociological Association, American Anthropological Association, American Association for the Advancement of Science, Latin American Studies Association, Pacific Sociological Association. *Awards, honors:* Russell Sage Foundation fellowship to Medical Center of University of California, Los Angeles, 1957-58; Social Science Research Council fellowship to Center for Social Research in Buenos Aires, summer, 1968; National Science Foundation postdoctoral fellowship to Institute of Education at University of London, 1970-71.

WRITINGS: (With John I. Kitsuse) *The Educational Decision-Makers*, Bobbs-Merrill, 1963; (contributor) M. Weinberg and E. Rubington, editors, *Deviance: The Interactionistic Perspective*, Macmillan, 1968; *The Social Organization of Juvenile Justice*, Wiley, 1968.

Method and Measurement in Sociology, Free Press, 1964; (contributor) J. Douglas, editor, *Understanding Everyday Life*, Aldine, 1970; (contributor) H. P. Dreitzel, editor, *Recent Sociology*, Volume II, Macmillan, 1970; (contributor) D. Sudnow, editor, *Studies in Interaction*, Free Press, 1972; (contributor) Douglas and R. Scott, editors, *Theoretical Perspectives on Deviance*, Basic Books, 1972; (contributor) C. Cazden, D. Hymes, and V. John, editors, *The Functions of Language*, Teachers College Press, 1972; *Cross-Modal Communication: The Representational Context of Sociolinguistic Information Processing* (monograph), Georgetown University, 1973; *Theory and Method in a Study of Argentine Fertility*, Wiley, 1974; *Cognitive Sociology: Language and Meaning in Social Interaction*, Penguin (London), 1973, Free Press, 1974; (with K. Jennings, S. Jennings, and others) *Language Use and Classroom Performance*, Academic Press, 1974; (contributor) T. A. Sebeok, A. S. Abramson, and other editors, *Current Trends in Linguistics*, Volume XII, Mouton & Co., 1974; (contributor) Colin Cherry, editor, *Theory and Decision*, Reidel, 1974; (contributor) I. Schlesinger and L. Namir, editors, *Current Trends in Studies of the Sign Language of the Deaf*, Mouton & Co., in press; (contributor) *The Mentally Retarded and Society: A Social Science Perspective*, University Park Press, in press; (contributor) R. Harre, editor, *The Psychology of Everyday Language*, Wiley in press.

Contributor of about fifteen articles to professional journals, including *Sign Language Studies, Semiotica, Communications, American Annals of the Deaf, Sociological Focus,* and *Economic Development and Culture Change.*

* * *

CID PEREZ, Jose (Diego) 1906-

PERSONAL: Born November 12, 1906, in Guanabacoa, Havana, Cuba; came to United States in 1960; son of Ramon (a businessman) and Marcedes (Perez) Cid; married Dolores Marti (a professor), June 15, 1939; children: Isabel (Mrs. Miguel Angel Sirgado). *Education:* Instituto de la Habana, B.A., 1925; Universidad de la Habana, M.A., 1936, Ph.D., 1938. *Religion:* Roman Catholic. *Home:* 929 Windsor Dr., West Lafayette, Ind. 47906. *Office:* Department of Modern Languages, Purdue University, West Lafayette, Ind. 47906.

CAREER: Teacher or principal in high schools in Cuba, 1927-36; Instituto Escuela Rockefeller, Havana, Cuba, teacher, 1940-42; Compania Cinemato-grafica Cubana, Havana, director, 1943-46; Universidad Nacional, Havana, professor of literature, 1955-57; Washburn University, Topeka, Kan., visiting professor of Spanish, 1962-63; Purdue University, West Lafayette, Ind., assistant professor, 1964-66, associate professor, 1966-71, professor, 1971-72, professor emeritus, 1972—. Theatre director for radio stations in Cuba, 1932-34, 1935-41; director of newsreel filming, radio, and newspaper, E Crisol, 1941-45; commentator on Cuban radio, 1951-52. Professor of Spanish-American theatre, University of Havana summer school, 1946-60; visiting professor at a dramatic arts seminary in Buenos Aires, 1947-48; University of Kansas, consultant to NDEA Spanish Institute, 1962, chairman of advanced language study, 1963; guest lecturer at universities and institutes in United States, Central America, and South America.

MEMBER: Asociacion de Concordia Americana (Buenos Aires; honorary member), Sociedad Colombista Panamericana (Cuba), Club Amigos del teatro (Buenos Aires: honorary member), Sigma Delta Pi (honorary member of Beta Pi chapter). *Awards, honors:* "Silver Anniversary" Grand National Prize from Republic of Cuba, 1927, for play "Cadenas de amor"; first prize in literature from *Mi Novela semanal* (Madrid), 1927; National Theatre Prizes (Cuba), 1931, 1932, 1934; first prize in literature from Institute of Cultura Dante Alighieri (Havana), 1956; commander, Order of Honneur et Merite, from government of Haiti; Order of Centenario de la Bandera Cubana, from government of Cuba.

WRITINGS: Secreto de confesion (novel), [Madrid], 1926; *Pensando*, La Milagrosa, 1926; *Serafin Sanchez: Visionario, creyente, mambi*, Imprenta Almendares, 1929; *Rebeca la rusa* (novel), La Mujer, 1933; (with wife, Dolores Marti de Cid) *Teatro Indio precolombino* (criticism; title means "Pre-Colombian Indian Theatre"), Aguilar (Madrid), 1964; (with Marti de Cid and James McKinney) *Paginas de un diario* (reader), McGraw, 1966; (with Marti de Cid) *Teatro Indoamericano colonial* (criticism), Aguilar, 1973.

Plays: *La Duda* (dramatic comedy; title means "The Doubt"), La Mujer, 1923; *Altares de sacrificio* (title means "Sacrificial Altars"), Siboney, 1932; *Azucena* (for children; title means "Honey-suckle"), La Veronica, 1943; *Hombres de dos mundos* (three-act comedy), Aguilar, 1959, 2nd edition, 1962, translation by Mary H. Jackson published as *Men of Two Worlds*, Northwest Missouri State College, 1966; *La Comedia de los muertos*, translation by John P. Dyson published as *The Comedy of the Dead*, Purdue University, 1967; *Un Triptico y dos comedias* (title means "A Triptych and Two Comedies"), El Carro de Tespis (Buenos Aires), 1972.

Contributor: Dolores Marti de Cid, editor, *Teatre cubano contemporaneo* (title means "Contemporary Cuban Theatre"), Aguilar, 2nd edition, 1962; Agnes Marie Brady and Harley D. Oberhelman, *Espanol Moderno II*, C. E.

Merrill, 1965; Brady, *Historia de la cultura hispanoamericana*, Macmillan, 1966.

Translator: Pedro Bloch, *As Maos de Euridice*; Percival Wilde, *The Finger of God*; Sem Benelli, *L'Orchidea*; Luigi Pirandello, *L'Amica della moglie*.

Contributor to *Enciclopedia dello spettacolo* (Rome) and *Encyclopaedia Britannica;* contributor to magazines and journals, including *Carteles* and *Nosotros*. Director of Latin American theatre section, *Enciclopedia dello spettacolo*, 1957-61.

WORK IN PROGRESS: Contemporary Indian Theater; An Anthology of Contemporary Latin American Plays.

SIDELIGHTS: Cid Perez's plays have been produced in Cuba, South America, Spain, and the United States. He has traveled in South and North America, Central America, the West Indies, and Europe, is fluent in Italian and English, and has reading knowledge of French, Portuguese, Latin, and Greek.

* * *

CITATI, Pietro 1930-

PERSONAL: Born February 20, 1930, in Florence, Italy; son of Antonio and Andreina (Amadeo) Citati; married Elena Londini, March 21, 1953; children: Stefano. *Education:* University of Pisa, laurea in lettere, 1951. *Religion:* Roman Catholic. *Home:* Via Lutezia 10, Rome, Italy. *Office:* Fondazione Lorenzo Valla, via Monzambano 9, Rome, Italy.

CAREER: le Giorno, Mailand, Italy, literary critic, 1960-73; *le Corriere della Sera*, Mailand, Italy, literary critic, 1973—. Lecturer in Italian, University of Munich, 1952-54. *Awards, honors:* Premio Viareggio, 1970, for *Goethe*.

WRITINGS: (Compiler with Attilio Bertolucci) *Gli umoristi moderni* (title means "Modern Humorists"), Garzanti, 1956; (editor and translator) Leo Spitzer, *Marcel Proust e altri saggi di letteratura francese moderna* (title means "Marcel Proust and Other Essays of Modern French Literature"), Einaudi, 1960; *Goethe*, Mondadori, 1970, translation by Raymond Rosenthal published under same title, Dial, 1974; *Il te del cappellaio matto* (title means "The Mad Hatter's Tea-party"), Mondadori, 1972; (editor) Emilio Cecchi, *La Letteratura italiana del Novecento* (title means "Italian Twentieth Century Literature"), Mondadori, 1972; *Immagini di Alessandro Manzoni* (title means "An Idea of Alessandro Manzoni"), Mondadori, 1973; *Alessandro Magno* (title means "Alexander the Great"), Rizzoli, 1974; (translator) Athanasius, *Vita Antonii*, Fondazione Lorenzo Valla and Mondadori, 1974. Also editor, with others, of series, "Scrittori greci e latini," published for Fondazione Lorenzo Valla by Mondadori, 1974—.

WORK IN PROGRESS: Two books, one on the nineteenth century European novel and another on the *Odyssey*.

* * *

CLARK, Admont Gulick 1919-

PERSONAL: Born November 19, 1919, in Schenectady, N.Y.; son of Edward Leeds and Eleanor (Fowle) Clark; married Ruth Francis (a medical assistant), October 4, 1941; children: Susan (Mrs. Jerome J. McDonald), David Leeds. *Education:* Amherst College, A.B., 1941, Bridgewater State College, M.Ed., 1961. *Residence:* Dennis, Mass. *Office:* Department of English, Cape Cod Community College, West Barnstable, Mass. 02668.

CAREER: Massachusetts Maritime Academy, Buzzards Bay, watch officer, 1946-60, instructor in English, 1946-60; McMillan Industrial Corp., Ipswich, Mass., assistant to president, 1960-61; Cape Cod Community College, West Barnstable, Mass., instructor, 1961-64, assistant professor, 1964-67, associate professor, 1967-71, professor of English, 1971—. Founding president, trustee, and chairman of the board, Cape Cod Museum of Natural History, Brewster, Mass., 1953-73. *Military service:* U.S. Coast Guard Reserve, 1943-74; became captain. *Member:* College English Associaton, National Council of Teachers of English, American Association of University Professors.

WRITINGS: They Built Clipper Ships, Parnassus, 1965; *The Real Imagination*, Science Research Associates, 1972. Contributor to *Cosmopolitan*, *Rotarian*, *Yankee*, and other publications.

WORK IN PROGRESS: Three Americas, an anthology of American literature presenting Endo-, Afro-, and Euro-American contributions to our literature.

* * *

CLARK, Ben T. 1928-

PERSONAL: Born May 8, 1928, in Gilroy, Calif.; son of Ben W. (a farmer) and Marie (White) Clark; married Lorna Zbitnoff, November 22, 1959; children: Jeffry, Larissa, Thomas. *Education:* University of California, Berkeley, B.A., 1957; Indiana University, M.A.T., 1966. *Home:* 250 Ocean View Ave., Santa Cruz, Calif. 95062. *Office:* Department of Slavic Languages, University of California, College 8, Santa Cruz, Calif. 95064.

CAREER: High school teacher of Russian in the public schools of Minneapolis, Minn., 1958-59, and Salinas, Calif., 1959-60; Cabrillo College, Aptos, Calif., teacher of German and Russian, 1960-68; University of California, Santa Cruz, lecturer in Russian, 1968—, coordinator of language studies, 1968—. *Military service:* U.S. Army, 1952-55. *Member:* American Association of Teachers of Slavic and East European Languages.

WRITINGS: Russian for Americans, Harper, 1967, 2nd edition, 1973.

* * *

CLARK, David Gillis 1933-

PERSONAL: Born May 14, 1933, in Lubbock, Tex.; son of James Cuthbert (a construction executive) and Lena Drucilla Clark; married Margaret Jean Dvorak, June 13, 1959 (divorced December 6, 1973); married Alice Anne Cappon, December 21, 1974; children: (first marriage) Andrew Gillis. *Education:* Texas Technological College, B.A., 1955; State University of Iowa, M.A., 1956; University of Wisconsin, Ph.D., 1965. *Politics:* Liberal Democrat. *Home address:* P.O. Box 87, Bellvue, Colo. 80512. *Office:* Department of Technical Journalism, Colorado State University, Fort Collins, Colo. 80523.

CAREER: KCBD-AM Radio and Television, Lubbock, Tex., news editor, 1952-54; *Lubbock Avalanche-Journal*, Lubbock, Tex., reporter, 1956; *Lincoln Star*, Lincoln, Neb., reporter, 1958-59; University of Cincinnati, Cincinnati, Ohio, instructor in English, 1959-64; Stanford University, Palo Alto, Calif., assistant professor of communication, 1965-67; University of Wisconsin-Madison, assistant professor, 1967-69, associate professor of journalism and mass communications, 1969-73; Colorado State University, Fort Collins, professor of technical journalism and chairman of department, 1973—. Instructor at University of Nebraska, 1958-59. *Military service:* U.S. Army, 1956-58. *Member:* American Association of University Professors, Association for Education in Journalism.

WRITINGS: (With Clifford F. Weigle) *The American Newspaper*, Iowa State University Press, 1969; (with E. R. Hutchison) *Mass Media and the Law*, Wiley, 1970; (with W. B. Blankenburg) *You and Media: Mass Communications and Society*, Canfield, 1973. Contributor to magazines, including *Journalism Quarterly* and *Journal of Broadcasting*, and to newspapers.

WORK IN PROGRESS: A history of the ways in which communications media have shaped society.

AVOCATIONAL INTERESTS: Tennis, hiking, camping in the wilds.

* * *

CLARK, Leonard H(ill) 1915-

PERSONAL: Born November 18, 1915, in Guilford, Conn.; son of Ridgley C. (a school administrator) and Idella (Hill) Clark; married Maria Aleksandra Langowska, August 30, 1947. *Education:* Wesleyan University, B.A., 1937; Boston University, Ed.M., 1948, Ed.D., 1953. *Religion:* United Church of Christ. *Home:* 193 Watchung Ave., Chatham, N.J. 07928. *Office:* Department of Education, Jersey City State College, Jersey City, N.J. 07305.

CAREER: High school teacher of English and social studies in Windsor, Conn., 1938-42; Lyndon Teachers College (now Lyndon State College), Lyndon Center, Vt., dean, 1949-54; University of Hartford, West Hartford, Conn., associate professor of secondary education and chairman of department, 1955-59; Jersey City State College, Jersey City, N.J., professor of education, 1959—. *Military service:* U.S. Army, 1942-47. U.S. Army Reserve, 1947-70; retired as lieutenant colonel. *Member:* National Association of Secondary School Principals, Association for Supervision and Curriculum Development, Association of Teacher Educators, National Council for the Social Studies, World Education Fellowship, American Educational Research Association, New Jersey Council on Education, Phi Delta Kappa.

WRITINGS: (With Irving Starr) *Secondary School Teaching Methods*, Macmillan, 1958, 2nd edition, 1967; (with Ray Klein and John Burks) *American Secondary School Curriculum*, Macmillan, 1965, 2nd edition, 1972; (editor) *Strategies and Tactics in Secondary School Teaching*, Macmillan, 1968; *Teaching Social Studies in Secondary Schools*, Macmillan, 1973.

WORK IN PROGRESS: Third edition of *Secondary School Teaching Methods*; editing a series on teacher education for Macmillan.

* * *

CLARKE, John Henrik 1915-

PERSONAL: Born January 1, 1915, in Union Springs, Ala.; son of John (a farmer) and Willella (Mays) Clarke; married Eugenia Evans (a teacher), December 24, 1961; children: Nzingha Marie, Sonni Kojo. *Education:* Attended New York University, 1948-52, New School for Social Research, 1956-58. *Politics:* Socialism. *Religion:* Nondenominational. *Home:* 223 West 137th St., New York, N.Y. 10030. *Office:* Hunter College, City University of New York, 695 Park Ave., New York, N.Y. 10021. *Agent:* Ronald Hobbs, 211 East 43rd St., New York, N.Y. 10017.

CAREER: *Pittsburgh Courier*, Pittsburgh, Pa., feature writer, 1957-58; *Ghana Evening News*, Accra, Ghana, feature writer, 1958; African Study Center, New York, N.Y., developer, 1957-59, assistant to director, 1958-60; Hunter College of the City University of New York, New York, N.Y., professor, 1958—; African Heritage Exposition, New York, N.Y., research director, 1959; *Freedomways* (magazine), New York, N.Y., associate editor, 1962—. Director, Haryou-Act (teaching program), 1964-69; coordinator and special consultant to C.B.S. television series, "Black Heritage," 1968; consultant to American Heritage Press and John Wiley & Sons (publishers); director of training program in Black history, Columbia University, summer, 1969; adjunct professor in Department of Black and Puerto Rican Studies, 1969—; Carter G. Woodson Visiting Professor in African History, Cornell University, 1969—; visiting lecturer, New York University; member of board of directors of Langston Hughes Center for Child Development, 1967—; member of advisory board of Martin Luther King Library Center, 1969. Teacher (by special license) at Malverne High School (People's College), Malverne, N.Y. *Military service:* U.S. Army Air Forces, 1941-45; became master sergeant. *Member:* International Society of African Culture, African Studies Association, American Society of African Culture, Black Academy of Arts and Letters (founding member), Association for Study of Negro Life & History (vice-president, 1949-55), American Historical Society, American Academy of Political and Social Science, African Heritage Studies Association (president, 1969-73), African Scholars Council (member of board of directors), Harlem Writers Guild (founding member). *Awards, honors:* Carter G. Woodson Award for excellence in teaching, 1958, 1971; National Association for Television and Radio Announcers citation for meritorious achievement in educational television, 1969; L.H.D. from University of Denver, 1970.

WRITINGS: *Rebellion in Rhyme* (poems), Dicker Press, 1948; (editor) *Harlem U.S.A.*, Seven Seas Books (Berlin), 1964, revised edition, Collier, 1970; (editor) *Harlem: A Community in Transition*, Citadel, 1965; (editor) *American Negro Short Stories*, Hill & Wang, 1966; (editor) *William Styron's Nat Turner: Ten Black Writers Respond*, Beacon Press, 1968; (editor and author of introduction) *Malcolm X: The Man and His Time*, Macmillan, 1969; (editor with Vincent Harding) *Slave Trade and Slavery*, Holt, 1970; (editor) *Harlem* (short stories), New American Library, 1970; (editor with others) *Black Titan: W.E.B. Du Bois*, Beacon Press, 1970; (editor with Amy Jacques Garvey) *Marcus Garvey and the Vision of Africa*, Random House, 1974.

Also author of "The Lives of Great African Chiefs" published serially in *Pittsburgh Courier*, 1957-58. Contributor to *Negro History Bulletin, Chicago Defender, Journal of Negro Education, Phylon, Presence Africaine*, and others. Book review editor, *Negro History Bulletin*, 1947-49; cofounder and associate editor, *Harlem Quarterly*, 1949-51; editor, *African Heritage*, 1959. Also author of syndicated column, "African World Bookshelf."

WORK IN PROGRESS: *The Black Woman in History*; an African curriculum for elementary school teachers.

* * *

CLARKE, Thomas E(mmet) 1918-

PERSONAL: Born August 4, 1918, in New York, N.Y.; son of James and Mary (Mahon) Clarke. *Education:* St.

Peter's College, A.B., 1941; Woodstock College, Ph.L., 1946, Th.L., 1951; Gregorian University, S.T.D., 1954. *Home and office:* Gonzaga Retreat Center, Monroe, N.Y. 10950.

CAREER: Entered Society of Jesus (Jesuits), 1941, ordained Roman Catholic priest, 1950; Woodstock College, Woodstock, Md., assistant professor, 1954-57, associate professor, 1957-60, professor of systematic theology, 1960-70; Woodstock College, New York, N.Y., professor of systematic theology, 1970-74; Gonzaga Retreat Center, staff member, 1974—. *Member:* Catholic Theological Society of America.

WRITINGS: (With James M. Carmody) *Christ and His Mission*, Newman, 1966; (with Carmody) *Word and Redeemer*, Paulist-Newman, 1966; *New Pentecost or New Passion?*, Paulist-Newman, 1973. Contributor to *New Catholic Encyclopedia*. Contributor to popular and theology journals, including *Theological Studies*, *Thought*, *America*, and *Commonweal*.

WORK IN PROGRESS: Studying Christian spirituality related to society and culture.

* * *

CLAYDON, Leslie Francis 1923-

PERSONAL: Born October 19, 1923, in Somerset, England; son of Francis Edward (a shipwright) and Mabel (Marler) Claydon; married Patricia Whitehouse, January 10, 1969; children: Matthew, Benedict, Cressida. *Education:* University of Bristol, diploma in education, 1954, M.A. (educational psychology), 1958; University of London, M.A. (philosophy of education), 1966. *Office:* School of Education, La Trobe University, Bundoora, Melbourne, Australia.

CAREER: School teacher in England, 1948-54; Coventry College of Education, Coventry, England, lecturer, 1954-59, senior lecturer in education, 1959-68; principal lecturer in education at Edge Hill College of Education, 1968-71; La Trobe University, Bundoora, Melbourne, Australia, founding member of School of Education, 1971—, director of City Educational Task Force program. *Military service:* Royal Navy, served on minesweeper,1942-45. *Member:* Philosophy of Education Society of Great Britain (member of national committee, 1967-69), Philosophy of Education Society of Australia (vice-president).

WRITINGS: (Editor, translator, and author of introduction) *Rousseau on Education*, Collier, 1969; (editor) *Renewing Urban Teaching*, Cambridge University Press, 1974; (editor) *The Urban School*, Pitman (Australia), 1974. Contributor to *Journal of Curriculum Studies* and *Educational Philosophy and Theory*.

WORK IN PROGRESS: Research on epistemological issues in education as they are related to social ideals; studying education of migrant communities; research on the development of the City Educational Task Force as an instrument of innovation in schools, using teams of specially selected teachers.

SIDELIGHTS: Claydon writes: "I lost my adolescence in a war and later tried to find out how that happened. I believe with Kant that we have yet to learn to live with uncertainty. I've taught people in Europe and Australia and in most kinds of institutions given to education. In a world replete with answers but no solutions I look for questions. I see the educator's job to be one of exciting ideas which can inform action. In a crowd the one you don't notice is me."

CLEMENT, Evelyn Geer 1926-

PERSONAL: Born September 1, 1926, in Springfield, Mass.; daughter of Elihu (a civil engineer and educator) and Helen (Schenck) Geer; married J. Randall Clement, September 9, 1946 (divorced, April, 1971); children: James Randall, Timothy Bruce, Susan (Mrs. Robin Henson), Marc Weldon, Audrey Hart. *Education:* Oklahoma College for Women, student, 1946-47; University of Tulsa, B.A., 1965; University of Oklahoma, M.L.S., 1966; Indiana University, doctoral study, 1968—. *Home:* 585 South Goodlett, Memphis, Tenn. 38111. *Office:* Department of Library Services, Memphis State University, Memphis, Tenn. 38152.

CAREER: Tulsa City-County Library, Tulsa, Okla., bookmobile librarian, 1960-63, reference librarian, 1963-65, readers' adviser, 1965-66; Oral Roberts University Library, Tulsa, Okla., learning resources librarian, 1966-68; Memphis State University, Memphis, Tenn., associate professor of library service, 1972—, chairman of department, 1972—. Special instructor at University of Oklahoma, 1966-70.

MEMBER: American Library Association, Association for Education Communications and Technology, Association of American Library Schools, American Society for Information Science, American Association of University Professors, South Eastern Library Association, Tennessee Library Association, West Tennessee Education Association, West Tennessee Library Association, Memphis Library Council (chairman, 1974-75), Pi Gamma Mu, Phi Alpha Theta, Beta Phi Mu, Pi Lambda Theta.

WRITINGS: (With Pearce S. Grove) *Bibliographic Control of Nonprint Media,* American Library Association, 1972. Contributor to *Oklahoma Librarian, Focus on Indiana Libraries, Wilson Library Bulletin,* and *Southeastern Librarian.*

WORK IN PROGRESS: Research on the activities of the American Library Association related to audiovisual materials and services, from 1918 to 1970; biographical sketches of librarians Frederick M. Crunden and Adam Strohm.

* * *

CLEMENTS, Bruce 1931-

PERSONAL: Born November 25, 1931, in New York, N.Y.; son of Paul Eugene (a salesman) and Ruth (an editor; maiden name, Hall) Clements; married Hanna Charlotte Margarete Kiep (a community worker), January 30, 1954; children: Mark, Ruth, Martha, Hanna. *Education:* Columbia University, A.B., 1954; Union Theological Seminary, New York, N.Y., B.D., 1956; State University of New York at Albany, M.A., 1962. *Politics:* Democrat. *Home:* Fernwood Dr., Willimantic, Conn. 06226.

CAREER: Ordained minister of United Church of Christ; pastor in Schenectady, N.Y., 1957-64; Union College, Schenectady, N.Y., teacher, 1964-67; Eastern Connecticut State College, Willimantic, Conn., teacher, 1967-74.

WRITINGS: *Two Against the Tide* (novel), Farrar, Straus, 1967; *The Face of Abraham Candle* (novel), Farrar, Straus, 1969; *From Ice Set Free: The Story of Otto Kiep*, Farrar, Straus, 1972; *I Tell a Lie Every So Often*, Farrar, Straus, 1974. Also author of plays for radio and theatre.

WORK IN PROGRESS: A report from a therapeutic community, *Going through Changes*; a novel, *4 + 2*.

CLEPPER, Irene E(lizabeth)

PERSONAL: Born in Dewar, Iowa; daughter of Irving J. (a teacher) and Helen M. (a teacher; maiden name, Kildow) French; married P. M. Clepper (a newspaper columnist), July 22, 1950; children: Candace, Vickora, Lorianne, Patrice. *Education:* Simpson College, B.A.; graduate study at University of Minnesota. *Politics:* Democrat. *Religion:* Methodist. *Home:* 3244 Sandeen Rd., St. Paul, Minn. 55112. *Office:* 100 East 14th St., Minneapolis, Minn, 55403.

CAREER: Free-lance magazine writer. *Member:* Associated Business Writers of America.

WRITINGS: Growing Up with Toys, Augsburg, 1974. Also author of mystery novelettes for children, all published by Better Reading Foundation: *Dive into Danger,* 1967; *The Skeleton's Secret,* 1969; *The Mile-High Detectives,* 1969; *The Disappearing Diamonds,* 1969. Contributor of articles on business and science to periodicals.

* * *

CLIFFORD, John Garry 1942-

PERSONAL: Born March 3, 1942, in Haverhill, Mass.; son of John (a businessman) and Doris (a hair stylist; maiden name, Champagne) Clifford; married Dale Lothrop, December 22, 1969 (divorced December 22, 1972). *Education:* Williams College, B.A., 1964; Indiana University, M.A., 1965, Ph.D., 1969. *Politics:* Democrat. *Home address:* Old Colony Rd., Eastford, Conn. 06242. *Office:* Department of Political Science, University of Connecticut, Storrs, Conn. 06268.

CAREER: University of Tennessee, Knoxville, instructor in history, 1968-69; University of Connecticut, Storrs, assistant professor, 1969-72, associate professor of political science, 1973—. Visiting associate professor at Dartmouth College, 1972-73. *Member:* American Historical Association, Organization of American Historians, Phi Beta Kappa. *Awards, honors:* Frederick Jackson Turner Award from Organization of American Historians, 1971.

WRITINGS: The Citizen Soldiers: The Plattesburg Training Camp Movement, 1913-1920, University Press of Kentucky, 1972; (editor with Norman Cousins) *Memoirs of a Man: Grenville Clark*, Norton, in press.

WORK IN PROGRESS: A History of the Selective Service Act of 1940, with Samuel R. Spencer, Jr., completion expected in 1976; *Biography of Grenville Clark*, 1977.

* * *

CLOR, Harry M(ortimer) 1929-

PERSONAL: Born July 20, 1929, in Springfield, Ill.; married Margaret Hyink, June 26, 1966; children: Katherine. *Education:* Lawrence College, B.A., 1951; University of Chicago, Ph.D., 1967. *Politics:* Independent. *Religion:* Jewish. *Home address:* P.O. Box 597, Gambier, Ohio 43022. *Office:* Department of Political Science, Kenyon College, Gambier, Ohio 43022.

CAREER: Kenyon College, Gambier, Ohio, 1965—, began as assistant professor, now professor of political science, head of department, 1973—. Director of Public Affairs Conference Center, 1969-72. *Military service:* U.S. Army, 1952-54. *Member:* National Association for the Advancement of Colored People, Phi Beta Kappa.

WRITINGS: Obscenity and Public Morality: Censorship in a Liberal Society, University of Chicago Press, 1969; (editor) *Censorship and Freedom of Expression*, Rand McNally, 1971; (editor) *Violence and Civil Disorder*, Rand McNally, 1972; (editor) *Mass Media and Modern Democracy*, Rand McNally, 1974. Contributor to *Minnesota Law Review*.

WORK IN PROGRESS: Research in legal philosophy.

* * *

CLOTFELTER, Beryl E(dward) 1926-

PERSONAL: Born March 23, 1926, in Prague, Okla.; son of Cecil F. (a minister) and Velma Z. (Stringer) Clotfelter; married Mary Lou Hixson (a college instructor), August 16, 1951; children: Anne E., David B., Susan K. *Education:* Oklahoma Baptist University, B.S., 1948; University of Oklahoma, M.S., 1949, Ph.D., 1953; graduate study at Ohio State University, 1950-51. *Politics:* Democrat. *Religion:* Congregationalist. *Home:* 1421 Sixth Ave., Grinnell, Iowa 50112. *Office:* Department of Physics, Grinnell College, Grinnell, Iowa 50112.

CAREER: Phillips Petroleum Co., Bartlesville, Okla., research physicist, 1953-55; University of Idaho, Moscow, assistant professor of physics, 1955-56; Oklahoma Baptist University, Shawnee, assistant professor, 1956-58, associate professor, 1958-61, professor of physics, 1961-63; Grinnell College, Grinnell, Iowa, professor of physics, 1963—. *Member:* American Physical Society, American Association of Physics Teachers, American Association for the Advancement of Science, American Association of University Professors, Sigma Xi.

WRITINGS: Reference Systems and Inertia, Iowa State University Press, 1970. Contributor to journals in his field.

WORK IN PROGRESS: The Universe and Its Structure, publication expected in 1975.

* * *

CLOTFELTER, Cecil F. 1929-

PERSONAL: Born April 3, 1929, in Anthony, Kan.; son of Cecil F. (a minister and teacher) and Velma (a teacher; maiden name, Stringer) Clotfelter; married Mary Long (a librarian and teacher), September 20, 1957. *Education:* Summer study at University of Havana, 1950; Oklahoma Baptist University, B.A., 1951; attended Trinidad State Junior College, 1955-56; Oklahoma State University, M.A., 1958; University of Oklahoma, M.L.S., 1959. *Home address:* Route 2, Box 43A, Portales, N.M. 88130. *Office:* Eastern New Mexico University Library, Portales, N.M. 88130.

CAREER: New Mexico Highlands University Library, Las Vegas, assistant librarian of public services, 1959-67; Texas A & M University Library, College Station, assistant director for technical preparation, 1967-69; Eastern New Mexico University Library, Portales, technical services librarian, 1969—. Member of board of directors of Portales (N.M.) Lions Club, 1972, 1973. *Member:* American Library Association, National Rifle Association (life member), Izaak Walton League (president, local chapter, 1961), Southwest Library Association, New Mexico Library Association (treasurer, 1965-66), Las Vegas Rifle and Revolver Club (president, 1965), La Escalera Art Guild, Lions Club (Portales; member of board, 1972, 1973), Portales Gem and Mineral Society (president, 1970).

WRITINGS: (Compiler with Laura McGuire) *A Selected List of Materials Relating to Mexican-Americans*, Eastern New Mexico University Library, 1972; *Hunting and Fishing*, Libraries Unlimited, 1974. Contributor of book reviews to *Library Journal* and *American Reference Books Annual*.

WORK IN PROGRESS: Research on the histories of libraries in New Mexico.

SIDELIGHTS: Clotfelter has been an avid hunter and fisherman since childhood. During high school he ran traplines during the winter. He attended Trinidad State Junior College to learn gunsmithing, and states he "may very well be the only professional librarian in the U.S. who is also a trained, experienced gunsmith." His special interest is in custom rifle building. *Avocational interests:* Leather work, lapidary, silversmithing, jewelry-making, genealogy, farming, gardening, oil painting, rare books.

* * *

CLUNIES ROSS, Anthony (Ian) 1932-

PERSONAL: Born March 9, 1932, in Sydney, New South Wales, Australia; son of Ian (a scientist) and Janet (a criminologist; maiden name, Carter) Clunies Ross; married Morag McVey, July 1, 1961; children: James, David, Sarah, Brigit. *Education:* University of Melbourne, B.A., 1958; Cambridge University, B.A., 1961, M.A., 1966. *Politics:* Democratic Socialist. *Religion:* Anglican. *Home address:* Kinbuck by Dunblane, Perthshire FK15 ONL, Scotland. *Office:* Department of Economics, University of Strathclyde, 173 Cathedral St., Glasgow GH ORQ, Scotland.

CAREER: University of Melbourne, Melbourne, Australia, tutor in history, 1958-59; Monash University, Melbourne, Australia, lecturer, 1961-65, senior lecturer in economics, 1966-67; University of Papua New Guinea, Port Moresby, senior lecturer, 1967-69, professor of economics, 1969-74; University of Strathclyde, Glasgow, Scotland, lecturer in economics, 1975—. Chairman of Australian Student Christian Movement, 1963-66. *Member:* Royal Economic Society, Papua New Guinea Economic Society.

WRITINGS: (With R. I. Downing and others) *One Per Cent: The Case for Greater Australian Foreign Aid*, Melbourne University Press, 1963; (with Peter King) *Australia and Nuclear Weapons*, University of Sydney Press, 1966; (editor with John Langmore) *Alternative Strategies for Papua New Guinea*, Oxford University Press (Melbourne), 1973. Contributor to *Philippine Economic Journal, New Guinea Research Bulletin, Economic Record, Australia's Neighbours, Dissent*, and *New Guinea Quarterly*. Editor of *Papua New Guinea Journal of the Social Sciences and Humanities*, 1974.

* * *

COATS, Alice M(argaret) 1905-

PERSONAL: Born June 15, 1905, in Birmingham, England; daughter of Robert Hay (a Baptist minister) and Margaret (MacConnachie) Coats. *Education:* Attended Birmingham College of Art, 1922-27, Slade School of Art, University of London, 1927-28, and Academie Andre Lhote, Paris, 1932. *Home:* 32 Radnor Rd., Handsworth, Birmingham B20 3SR, England.

CAREER: Landscape artist and designer. *Wartime service:* Women's Land Army, 1939-45. *Member:* Royal Horticultural Society, Garden History Society, Hardy Plant Society, Alpine Garden Society.

WRITING: The Story of Horace (juvenile), Faber, 1938; *The Travels of Maurice* (juvenile), Faber, 1939; *Flowers and Their Histories*, Hulton, 1956, 2nd edition, McGraw, 1968; *Garden Shrubs and Their Histories*, Vista Books, 1963; *The Quest for Plants*, McGraw, 1969; *The Book of Flowers*, McGraw, 1973. Contributor to gardening and horticulture journals, including *Journal of the Royal Horticultural Society, Gardener's Chronicle, Popular Gardening*, and *Garden History*.

WORK IN PROGRESS: The Earl of Bute, a biography, for Shire Publications; *A Treasury of Flowers*, with historical botanical illustrations, for Phaidon.

* * *

COBURN, Andrew 1932-

PERSONAL: Born May 1, 1932, in Exeter, N.H. *Politics:* Liberal Democrat. *Religion:* None. *Home:* 7 Tobey Lane, Andover, Mass. 01810. *Agent:* Sanford J. Greenburger Associates, Inc., 757 Third Ave., New York, N.Y. 10017.

CAREER: Writer and editor for newspapers in Lawrence, Mass., and for *Boston Globe*, Boston, Mass. *Military service:* U.S. Army, 1951-54; became staff sergeant.

WRITINGS: The Trespasser, Houghton, 1974. Contributor of short stories to *Transatlantic Review*.

WORK IN PROGRESS: A novel about a trial lawyer.

* * *

COCHRANE, Glynn 1940-

PERSONAL: First syllable of surname is pronounced "cough"; born March 25, 1940, in Northern Ireland; son of Norman Moore and Jean D. (Anderson) Cochrane; married second wife, Mary Ann Keenan; children: (first marriage) Brendan, Siobhan, Rory. *Education:* Trinity College, Dublin, M.A., 1961; Oxford University, D.Phil., 1967. *Politics:* "No party affiliations." *Religion:* "Lowest Anglicanism." *Home:* 1301 Euclid Ave., Syracuse, N.Y. 13224. *Office:* Syracuse University, Syracuse, N.Y. 13210.

CAREER: British Overseas Civil Service and Diplomatic Services, district officer in West Pacific islands, 1961-64, assistant secretary, 1964-66, district commissioner, H.M. O.C.S., 1966-67, second secretary in diplomatic service, London, 1967-68; Syracuse University, Syracuse, N.Y., assistant professor, 1968-69, associate professor, 1969-73, professor of public administration and anthropology, 1973—. Consultant to U.S. State Department and World Bank Group.

WRITINGS: Big Men and Cargo Cults, Clarendon Press, (of Oxford University), 1970; *Development Anthropology*, Oxford University Press, 1971.

WORK IN PROGRESS: Research on manpower requirements and behavioral science utilization in international development; design and implementation of measures to alleviate distress in third world countries.

SIDELIGHTS: Cochrane writes: "I think anthropology will survive as a discipline for about five to ten years. Given the response by anthropologists to the pressing problems of the day, no other outcome now seems likely."

* * *

COCKING, J(ohn) M(artin) 1914-

PERSONAL: Born November 9, 1914, in St. Ives, Cornwall, England; son of Matthew Maddern Bottrell (a shopkeeper) and Annie (Tucker) Cocking; married May Parsons Wallis (a teacher of adult education), September 4, 1941; children: Romilly John. *Education:* King's College, University of London, B.A. (first class honors), 1935, M.A.

(with distinction), 1939; Sorbonne, University of Paris, Diplome, 1937; attended British Institute in Paris, 1937-38. *Politics:* Liberal. *Religion:* "Agnostic with a sense of mystery." *Home:* 12 Clorane Gardens, London NW3 7PR, England. *Office:* King's College, University of London, Strand, London WC2R 2LS, England.

CAREER: British Institute in Paris, Paris, France, lecturer in English, 1937-39, assistant to director, 1938-39; King's College, University of London, London, England, lecturer, 1939-52, professor of French, 1952—, fellow, 1965—. Visiting professor at University of Ghana, 1960-61, University of Western Australia, 1965, University of Illinois, 1971, University of Wisconsin at Madison, 1971. *Military service:* British Army, 1940-45; became major. *Member:* Association Internationale des Etudes Francaises, Modern Humanities Research Association, Society for French Studies, Societe des Amis de Marcel Proust et des Amis de Combray. *Awards, honors:* Officier de L'Ordre National du Merite from French Government, 1973.

WRITINGS: Marcel Proust, Yale University Press, 1956; (contributor) Ulrich Finke, editor, *French Nineteenth-Century Painting and Literature*, Manchester University Press, 1972; (contributor) L. B. Price, editor, *Marcel Proust: A Critical Panorama*, University of Illinois Press, 1973; (editor with Ernest Beaumont and John Cruickshank, and contributor) *Order and Adventure in Post-Romantic French Poetry*, Blackwell, 1973. Contributor to *Times Literary Supplement*, *Listener*, *London Magazine*, and others.

WORK IN PROGRESS: A study of the concept of imagination, its role in philosophy, aesthetics, art criticism, and contemporary assumptions about art.

AVOCATIONAL INTERESTS: Music, walking.

* * *

CODY, Martin L(eonard) 1941-

PERSONAL: Born July 8, 1941, in England; son of Thomas (a huntsman) and Florence (Leonard) Cody; married Jane Merriam (a professor of classics), July 25, 1964; children: Erin Elizabeth, Thomas Edan. *Education:* University of Edinburgh, M.A., 1963; University of Pennsylvania, Ph.D., 1966. *Home:* 20965 Waveview Dr., Topanga, Calif. 90200. *Office:* Department of Biology, University of California, Los Angeles, Calif. 90024.

CAREER: University of California at Los Angeles, assistant professor, 1966-72, professor of biology, 1972—. *Member:* Ecological Society of America, Society for the Study of Evolution, American Society of Naturalists, Cooper Ornithological Society. *Awards, honors:* Research grants from National Science Foundation.

WRITINGS: Competition and the Structure of Bird Communities, Princeton University Press, 1974; (editor with Jared M. Diamond) *The Ecology and Evolution of Communities*, Harvard University Press, 1975. Contributor to journals in his field. Associate editor of *Evolution*, 1972—, and *Theoretical Population Biology*, 1972—.

WORK IN PROGRESS: Research in ecological biogeography, bird communities, and behavioral ecology.

* * *

COHEN, Barbara 1932-

PERSONAL: Born March 15, 1932, in New Jersey; daughter of Leo Kauder and Florence (an innkeeper; maiden name, Marshall) Kauder Nash; married Eugene Cohen (an innkeeper), September 14, 1954; children: Leah, Sara, Rebecca. *Education:* Barnard College, B.A., 1954; Rutgers University, M.A., 1957. *Religion:* Jewish. *Home:* 540 Foothill Rd., Somerville, N.J. 08876.

CAREER: High school teacher of English in the public schools of Tenafly, N.J., 1955-57, Somerville, N.J., 1958-60, and Hillsborough, N.J., 1970—. *Member:* National Education Association, Authors Guild, League of Women Voters, Hadassah, New Jersey Education Association, Phi Beta Kappa.

WRITINGS—Juveniles: *The Carp in the Bathtub*, Lothrop, 1972; *Thank You Jackie Robinson*, Lothrop, 1974. Contributor to *New Jersey Education Association Review*. Author of column, "Books and Things," in *Somerset Messenger-Gazette*, 1967—.

WORK IN PROGRESS: Another juvenile book.

* * *

COHEN, David Steven 1943-

PERSONAL: Born July 12, 1943, in Hackensack, N.J.; son of Lewis (a real estate broker) and Molly (Gottlieb) Cohen; married Linda Prentice (an editor), September 21, 1974. *Education:* Rutgers University, B.A., 1965; Claremont Graduate School, M.A. (history), 1967; University of Pennsylvania, M.A. (American civilization), 1968, Ph.D., 1971. *Home:* 123 South Adelaide Ave., Apt. 5-P, Highland Park, N.J. 08904. *Office:* Department of History, Rutgers University, Newark, N.J. 07102.

CAREER: Rutgers University, Newark, N.J., instructor, 1970-71, assistant professor of history, 1971—. *Member:* American Historical Association, American Studies Association, American Folklore Society, New Jersey Historical Society.

WRITINGS: The Ramapo Mountain People, Rutgers University Press, 1974. Contributor to *Journal of American Folklore*.

WORK IN PROGRESS: Research in culture areas in American history.

* * *

COHEN, Elie Aron 1909-

PERSONAL: Born July 16, 1909, in Groningen, Netherlands; son of Aron Elie (a waiter) and Jetje (Behr) Cohen; married Aaltje van der Wonde, 1936 (died September 16, 1943); married second wife Marguerite Herrmann, April 16, 1947; children: (first marriage) Aron Elie (deceased); (second marriage) Naomi, Dan. *Education:* University of Groningen, M.D., 1935; University of Utrecht, D.Med. Science, 1952; University of Leiden, specialist youth doctor. *Politics:* Progressive. *Religion:* Jewish. *Home:* Wagnerlaan 67, Arnhem, Netherlands. *Agent:* Julian Bach, Jr., 3 East 48th St., New York, N.Y.

CAREER: Physician in general practice in Aduard, Netherlands, 1936-41; physician in general practice, 1947-66, medical adviser, 1947—, youth doctor, 1966-74, and psychotherapist, 1974—, all in Arnhem, Netherlands. *Member:* Netherlands Society of Literature. *Awards, honors:* Officier in Orde van Oranje Nassau, 1974.

WRITINGS: Human Behavior in Concentration Camps, Norton, 1952; *The Abyss,* Norton, 1973. Contributor to professional journals.

SIDELIGHTS: Cohen was not permitted to practice medicine in the German-occupied Netherlands. His attempt to escape from the Netherlands to Sweden in 1942 was betrayed, and he spent the next three years in concentration camps, including Auschwitz. He lost his first wife and their four-year-old child to the gas chambers at Auschwitz.

* * *

COHEN, Kathleen Rogers 1933-

PERSONAL: Born April 21, 1933, in Fresno, Calif.; daughter of Harold Edward and Mary (Graham) Rogers; married William I. Cohen (an attorney), August 13, 1955; children; Roger, Stuart. *Education:* Stanford University, B.A. (cum laude), 1954, graduate study, 1956-57; University of California, Berkeley, M.A., 1955, Ph.D., 1968; also studied at University of Ebinburg, 1952-53, and Ecole du Louvre, 1958-59. *Home:* 3639 Ross Rd., Palo Alto, Calif. 94303. *Office:* Department of Art, San Jose State University, San Jose, Calif. 95192.

CAREER: San Jose State University, San Jose, Calif., assistant professor, 1962-68, associate professor, 1968-72, professor of art, 1972—, chairman of department, 1972—. *Member:* College Art Association, American Federation of the Arts, National Association of Arts Administrators, State College Art History Association, Phi Beta Lambda. *Awards, honors:* Soroptomist fellowship, 1958-59; American Association of University Women fellowship, 1964-65; American Council on Education administrative intern fellowship, 1970-71.

WRITINGS: Metamorphosis of a Death Symbol, University of California Press, 1973; (with Karen Shellhammer) *Study Guide for Audio Tutorial in Art History*, Spartan Books (San Jose), 1973; *Evaluation of Audio Tutorial in Art History*, California State University and Colleges System, 1974.

WORK IN PROGRESS: Continuing audio-tutorial course in art history, from the prehistoric period to the Renaissance.

* * *

COHEN, Susan 1938-
(Elizabeth St. Clair)

PERSONAL: Born March 27, 1938, in Chicago, Ill.; daughter of Michael Mark (a salesman) and Ida (a nursery school teacher; maiden name, Goldman) Handler; married Daniel E. Cohen (a writer), February 2, 1958; children: Theodora Eugenia. *Education:* Attended University of Illinois, 1957-59; New School for Social Research, B.A., 1962; Adelphi University, M.S.W., 1966. *Politics:* Democrat. *Religion:* None. *Home and office:* 49 Canal St., Pt. Jervis, N.Y. 12771. *Agent:* Henry Morrison, 58 West Tenth St. New York, N.Y. 10011.

CAREER: Foster Care Riverdale Children's Association, New York, N.Y., social worker, 1962-64; Travelers Aid Society, New York, N.Y., social worker, 1966-67.

WRITINGS: The Liberated Couple, Lancer Books, 1971, reissued as *Liberated Marriage,* 1973; (under pseudonym Elizabeth St. Clair) *Stonehaven* (gothic novel), Signet, 1974; (under pseudonym Elizabeth St. Clair) *The Singing Harp,* Signet, 1975.

BIOGRAPHICAL/CRITICAL SOURCES: Publishers Weekly, August 30, 1971; *Chicago Tribune Book World,* October 10, 1971; *Sun-Sentinal* (Tampa, Fla.), November 5, 1971; *Albany Times-Union* (Albany, N.Y.), December 2, 1971; *Times-Herald Record* (Middletown, N.Y.), December 19, 1971; *Pt. Jervis Union Gazette* (Pt. Jervis, N.J.), July 15, 1974.

COLBERT, Roman 1921-

PERSONAL: Born June 11, 1921, in Brussels, Belgium; married, wife's name, Manuela. *Education:* Attended University of Brussels; University of California, Los Angeles, B.A., 1966, M.A., 1967, Ph.D., 1970. *Home:* 10620 Esther Ave., Los Angeles, Calif. 90064. *Office:* Department of Foreign Languages, Santa Monica College, 1815 Pearl St., Santa Monica, Calif. 90405.

CAREER: Teacher of French and English in Bogota, Columbia, and in Mexico City, Mexico; Occidental College, Los Angeles, Calif., teacher of French, 1966-69; teacher of French at University of California at Los Angeles, and of French and Spanish at Valley College, 1969-70; Santa Monica College, Santa Monica, Calif., professor of foreign languages, 1971—. Official interpreter of French and Spanish at Municipal and Superior Courts of Los Angeles County, 1967—. *Member:* Superior and Municipal Court Interpreters Association for the County of Los Angeles, University of California at Los Angeles Alumni Association (life member).

WRITINGS: Brief French Reference Grammar, Van Nostrand, 1972; *Brief Spanish Reference Grammar*, Van Nostrand, in press.

AVOCATIONAL INTEREST: Travel.

* * *

COLBY, Robert A(lan) 1920-

PERSONAL: Born April 15, 1920, in Chicago, Ill.; son of Meyer (a realtor) and Ida (Lewis) Colby; married Vineta Blumoff (a professor of English and writer), May 8, 1947. *Education:* University of Chicago, B.A., 1941, M.A., 1942, Ph.D., 1949; Columbia University, M.S., 1953; also studied at New York University, 1942-43. *Home:* 33-24 86th St., Jackson Heights, N.Y. 11372. *Office:* Department of Library Science, Queens College of the City University of New York, Flushing, N.Y. 11367.

CAREER: Lake Forest College, Lake Forest, Ill., assistant professor of English, 1949-51; Hunter College of the City University of New York, New York, N.Y., lecturer in English, 1951-53; Queens College of the City University of New York, Flushing, N.Y., language, literature, and arts librarian, 1953-64; Southern Connecticut State College, New Haven, associate professor of library science, 1964-66; Queens College of the City University of New York, associate professor, 1966-69, professor of library science, 1969—. Visiting member of faculty at University of Washington (Seattle), summer, 1961. *Military service:* U.S. Army, Medical Corps, engaged in personnel work and newscasting, 1943-46. *Member:* American Library Association, Bibliographical Society of America, American Printing History Association, Modern Language Association of America, Research Society for Victorian Periodicals (member of board of directors), American Association of University Professors, New York Library Association.

WRITINGS: (With wife, Vineta Colby) *The Equivocal Virtue: Mrs. Oliphant and the Victorian Literary Market Place*, Archon, 1966; *Fiction with a Purpose: Major and Minor Nineteenth Century Novels*, Indiana University Press, 1967; (editor with Morris A. Gelfand) *Access to the Literature of the Social Sciences and the Humanities*, Queens College Press, 1974. Contributor to literature journals and other periodicals, including *PMLA, Nineteenth Century Fiction, Modern Philology, Victorian Newsletter, Journal of Religion, Dublin Review,* and *Wilson Library Bulletin.*

WORK IN PROGRESS: A book on Thackeray as a representative Victorian man of letters; research on the uses of the novel or the decline of didactic fiction after the Victorian period.

SIDELIGHTS: Colby writes: "My interest in novels as educational media and as indicators of literary tastes and trends has meant a certain preoccupation with the unread—which is not necessarily the unreadable."

* * *

COLDWELL, M(ichael) J. 1888-1974

December 2, 1888—August 25, 1974; Canadian socialist politician and writer. Obituaries: *Current Biography*, October, 1974.

* * *

COLE, E(ugene) R(oger) 1930-

PERSONAL: Born November 14, 1930, in Cleveland, Ohio; son of Bernard James (an engineer) and Mary Louise (Rogers) Cole. *Education:* Sulpician Seminary of the Northwest, B.A., 1954, M.Div., 1958; Central Washington State College, A.B., 1960; Seattle University, M.A., 1970. *Politics:* Independent. *Religion:* "Christotheism." *Home:* 26301 Shirley Ave., Euclid, Ohio 44132.

CAREER: Ordained Roman Catholic priest, 1958; Central Washington State College, Ellenburg, Newman moderator, 1958-59; high school English teacher and chairman of department in parochial schools in Yakima, Wash., 1959-69; National Writers Club, Denver, Colo., poetry critic, 1969-72; writer, 1972—. *Member:* International Platform Association, Western World Haiku Society, Authors Guild of Authors League of America, Poetry Society of America, National Writers Club, Academy of American Poets (founder), National Federation of State Poetry Societies, Poetry Society (London), American Contract Bridge League, Kappa Delta Pi.

WRITINGS: What Did St. Luke Mean by "Kecharitomene"? (monograph), Catholic University of America Press, 1958; *April Is the Cruelest Month* (one-act play), Literary Publications Foundation, 1970; (editor with James Edwards) *Grand Slam: Thirteen Great Short Stories about Bridge*, Putnam, 1975.

Work in represented in anthologies, including *Experiment Theatre*, edited by C. E. Harper, Experiment Press, 1959; *The Golden Year*, edited by Melville Cane and others, Fine Editions Press, 1960; *La Poesie Contemporaine aux Etats-Unis* (title means "Contemporary Poetry of the United States"), edited by Jacques Cardonnet, Editions de La Revue Moderne, 1962; *Adam among the Television Trees*, edited by Virginia R. Mollenkott, Word Books, 1971; *The Diamond Anthology*, edited by Charles Angoff and others, A. S. Barnes, 1971.

Contributor to literary journals and popular magazines, including *Saturday Review, Western Humanities Review, Dalhousie Review, Literary Cavalcade, New Mexico Quarterly*, and *Northwest Review*. Guest editor of *Experiment: An International Review*, 1961.

WORK IN PROGRESS: Uneasy Camber, a book of poems; *Shrines of American Authors: A Geo-Literary Journal*; *Pensees II: Jottings of a Christian Parvulist*; *Chicago's Outdoor Art*; a collection of literary quizzes.

AVOCATIONAL INTERESTS: Bridge, astronomy, deltiology, piano, chess, Mexican archaeology, logistics, Latin, Greek, French, horseback riding, travel, attending concerts, cinema, art history, ballet, Assyriology, Egyptology.

* * *

COLE, Jonathan R(ichard) 1942-

PERSONAL: Born August 27, 1942, in New York, N.Y.; son of Richard and Sylvia (Dym) Cole; married Joanna Lewis (a professor), June 5, 1968; children: Daniel Lewis. *Education:* Columbia University, B.A., 1964, Ph.D., 1969. *Residence:* New York, N.Y. *Office:* Department of Sociology, Columbia University, New York, N.Y. 10027.

CAREER: Columbia University, New York, N.Y., instructor, 1968-69, assistant professor, 1969-73, associate professor of sociology, 1973—. Associate project director of Bureau of Applied Social Research, 1968-72. *Member:* American Sociological Association, American Association for the Advancement of Science, Sociological Research Association. *Awards, honors:* National Science Foundation grant, 1968; Center for Advanced Study in the Behavioral Sciences fellowship, 1975.

WRITINGS: (With brother, Stephen Cole) *Social Stratification in Science*, University of Chicago Press, 1973; *Women's Place in the Scientific Community*, Interscience, 1975. Contributor to sociological journals.

WORK IN PROGRESS: Research on the sociology of science and knowledge, the determinant of scientific revolutions.

* * *

COLE, Sheila R(otenberg) 1939-

PERSONAL: Born January 5, 1939, in Toronto, Ontario, Canada; daughter of Ben (a grocer) and Helen (Wise) Rotenberg; married Michael Cole (a research psychologist), December 18, 1957; children: Jennifer, Alexander. *Education:* Attended University of California at Los Angeles, 1957-59; Indiana University, B.A., 1961; Columbia University, M.S., 1965. *Home:* 450 East 63rd St., New York, N.Y. 10021. *Agent:* Donald Cutler, Sterling Lord Agency, 660 Madison Ave., New York, N.Y. 10021.

CAREER: Sunnyvale Daily Standard, Sunnyvale, Calif., reporter, 1963-64; *Newport Beach Pilot,* Newport Beach, Calif., reporter, 1966-67; University of California, Irvine, research associate, 1968-69. *Member:* Authors Guild, Society of Children's Bookwriters. *Awards, honors:* Golden Kite Honor Book award from Society of Children's Bookwriters, 1974, for *Meaning Well.*

WRITINGS: Meaning Well (children's book), F. Watts, 1974. Contributor of articles and book reviews to *Psychology Today, Ms., New York Times Sunday Magazine,* and *New York Times Book Review.*

WORK IN PROGRESS: Sing for the Rain Gods, a children's novel about the Maya; a children's novel about a pioneer paleontologist.

* * *

COLEGROVE, Kenneth 1886-1975

October 8, 1886—January 3, 1975; American political scientist and author. Obituaries: *New York Times*, January 4, 1975; *AB Bookman's Weekly*, January 20, 1975. (*CA*-5/6).

* * *

COLLINS, Fletcher, Jr. 1906-

PERSONAL: Born November 19, 1906, in Pittsburgh, Pa.;

son of Fletcher, Sr. (a manager) and Elizabeth (Sellers) Collins; married Margaret James (a playwright), April 23, 1932; children: Christopher, Brandon, Fletcher III, Francis Sellers. *Education:* Yale University, Ph.B., 1928, Ph.D., 1934. *Home:* 437 East Beverley St., Staunton, Va. 24401. *Office:* Department of Dramatic Arts, Mary Baldwin College, Staunton, Va. 24401.

CAREER: Montclair State Teachers College (now Montclair State College), Upper Montclair, N.J., assistant professor of English, 1932-34; Arthurdale (W.Va.) Community School, director of drama and music, 1934-36; Elon College, Elon College, N.C., professor of English and head of English and drama, 1936-42; Fairchild Aircraft, Burlington, N.C., assistant to general manager, 1942-44; Republic Aviation Corp., Farmingdale, Long Island, N.Y., manager of Organization Division, 1944-46; Mary Baldwin College, Staunton, Va., assistant professor, 1947-49, associate professor, 1949-50, professor of dramatic arts, 1950—. Founder and executive director of Oak Grove Theater, 1954—; co-producer of Theater Wagon, Inc., 1969—. *Member:* Medieval Academy of America, American Theatre Association, Southeastern Theatre Conference, Virginia Theater Conference.

WRITINGS: (Contributor) Elsie Ripley Clapp, *Community Schools in Action*, Viking, 1939; *Alamance Play-Party Songs and Singing Games*, [Graham, N.C.], 1940, reprinted, Norwood Editions, 1973; *The Production of Medieval Church Music-Drama*, University Press of Virginia, 1972; (editor with wife, Margaret Collins) *Theater Wagon: Plays of Place and Any Place*, University Press of Virginia, 1973. Also author of transcriptions of medieval playscripts and editor of folksong collections. Contributor to journals and periodicals, including *Speculum*, *Southern Folklore Quarterly*, *Philological Quarterly*, *PMLA*, and *Design*.

WORK IN PROGRESS: A practical edition of sixteen medieval music-dramas, completion expected in 1975.

SIDELIGHTS: Collins writes that his "most exalted theatrical experience was the organization and production in 1974 of 'The Raising of Lazarus' in the Abbey of St. Benoit de Fleury, where the play was first produced 800 years ago." He hopes to produce all sixteen Fleury plays in the same abbey.

* * *

COLLINS, Joseph B. 1898(?)-1975

1898(?)—January 23, 1975; American Roman Catholic priest, educator, and author. Obituaries: *Washington Post*, January 24, 1975.

* * *

COLLINS, Marie (Margaret) 1935-

PERSONAL: Born October 8, 1935, in New York, N.Y.; daughter of James F. and Marie M. (Hebron) Collins. *Education:* Trinity College, Washington, D.C., A.B., 1956; graduate study, University of Paris and University of Besancon, 1956-58; Middlebury College, A.M., 1957; New York University, Ph.D., 1969. *Residence:* New York, N.Y. *Office:* Department of Foreign Languages and Literatures, Rutgers University, Newark, N.J. 07102.

CAREER: College of St. Elizabeth, Convent Station, N.J., instructor in French, 1958-60; Trinity College, Washington, D.C., instructor in French, 1960-61; Rutgers University, Newark, N.J., instructor, 1963-70, assistant professor, 1970-74, associate professor of French, 1974—, coordinator of Women's Studies Program, 1972-74. Fulbright teaching fellow at University of Besancon, 1957-58. *Member:* Modern Language Association of America, American Association of Teachers of French, National Organization for Women, New York University Colloquium on Comparative Literature. *Awards, honors:* Fulbright travel grant, 1956-58; French government fellowship at University of Paris, 1956-57; Danforth teaching grant, 1961-64.

WRITINGS: (Translator from the French) Guy Michaud, *Mallarme*, New York University Press, 1965; (editor and translator from the French) *Black Poets in French* (bi-lingual anthology and instructor's manual), Scribner, 1972; (editor with S. W. Sayre) *Les Femmes en France* (title means "Women in France"; anthology of French feminist writings), Scribner, 1974; *Ghelderode*, Twayne, 1975. Contributor to *Nineteenth Century French Studies*.

WORK IN PROGRESS: Critical biographies of French feminists.

* * *

COLLINS, Michael 1930-

PERSONAL: Born October 31, 1930, in Rome, Italy; son of James L. (a U.S. Army officer) and Virginia (Stewart) Collins; married Patricia Mary Finnegan (a real estate agent), April 28, 1957; children: Kathleen, Ann Stewart, Michael Lawton. *Education:* U.S. Military Academy, B.S., 1952. *Agent:* George Scheer, Box 87, Chapel Hill, N.C. 27514. *Office:* National Air and Space Museum, Smithsonian Institution, Washington, D.C. 20560.

CAREER: U.S. Air Force, 1952-70, became colonel; U.S. Air Force Reserve, 1970—, now brigadier general. Served as experimental test officer at Edwards Air Force Base, Calif., 1960-63, and as an astronaut with the National Aeronautics and Space Administration (NASA), 1963-70. While serving as an astronaut, piloted Gemini X, 1966, and became the third American to "walk in space"; in 1969, piloted the command module of man's first moon landing mission, Apollo II. U.S. Department of State, Washington, D.C., assistant secretary for public affairs, 1970-71; Smithsonian Institution, Washington, D.C., director of National Air and Space Museum, 1971—. *Member:* National Aeronautics Association ((member of board of directors), National Space Club (member of board of governors), American Institute of Aeronautics and Astronautics, Society of Experimental Test Pilots, Royal Aeronautical Society (fellow). *Awards, honors*—Military: Air Force Distinguished Service Medal; Distinguished Flying Cross; General Thomas D. White Space Trophy. Civilian: Hubbard Medal; Collier Trophy; Harmon Trophy; Presidential Medal of Freedom; D.Sc. from Northeastern University, and from Stonehill College; LL.D. from St. Michael's College.

WRITINGS: (With others) *First on the Moon: The Astronauts' Own Story*, Little, Brown, 1970; *Carrying the Fire*, Farrar, Straus, 1974.

SIDELIGHTS: Of *Carrying the Fire*, Edward Weeks wrote in the *Atlantic*: "[Collins'] account of the five years that went into the testing of the men for Apollo, the designing of the spaceship and equipment, the apprehension of what might go wrong is a magnificent piece of exposition alive with humor, candid in its anxiety, very sensitive in its appreciation of the men involved. . .This is a splendid and affirmative book which tells the nation of the amazingly precise training these men went through and of what they endured."

COLLINS, Ruth Philpott 1890-1975

March 17, 1890—January 10, 1975; American author of children's books and magazine writer. Obituaries: *New York Times*, January 18, 1975; *AB Bookman's Weekly*, February 3, 1975. (*CA*-2).

* * *

COLLISON, Koder M(acklin) 1910-

PERSONAL: Born January 25, 1910, in Philadelphia, Pa.; son of Harry Benjamin and Lulu Mae (Macklin) Collison; married Sibyl Joan Rhoades, September 24, 1943; children: Judith Dunning (Mrs. William C. Holliday), Kathryn Macklin (Mrs. Thomas A. Solomon). *Education:* Attended University of Virginia, 1929-30, University of Pennsylvania, 1945-46, and Rutgers University, 1945. *Religion:* Protestant. *Home and office:* 3440 Olentangy River Rd., Columbus, Ohio 43202.

CAREER: Pennsylvania Railroad, Philadelphia, industrial representative, 1941-48, industrial agent in Indianapolis, Ind., 1949-52; Springfield Development Council, Springfield, Ohio, director, 1953-57; Dayton Chamber of Commerce, Dayton, Ohio, director of business and industrial expansion, 1957-59; State of Ohio, Department of Economic Development, Columbus, director, and cabinet officer in industrial and economic development, 1959-62; West Virginia Department of Commerce, deputy commissioner, 1963, commissioner, 1963-65; Appalachian Regional Commission of the U.S. Government, director of industrial development, 1965-74; president of Unlimited Consultant Services. Past member of industrial steering committee of Ohio Chamber of Commerce and Great Lakes State Industrial Development Council.

MEMBER: American Industrial Development Council (fellow; honorary life member; past member of executive committee), Southern Industrial Development Council (past member of executive committee), Northeastern Industrial Developers Association (past member of executive committee), West Virginia Industrial Development Association, Ohio Planning Conference.

WRITINGS: The Developers' Dictionary and Handbook, Lexington Books, 1974.

WORK IN PROGRESS: Humor in Development, a collection of anecdotes from several developers.

* * *

COLQUITT, Betsy Feagan 1926-

PERSONAL; Born March 5, 1926, in Fort Worth, Tex.; daughter of Belton Dial (a newspaper worker) and Eddie (Young) Feagan; married Landon A. Colquitt (a professor of mathematics), May 29, 1954; children: Clare Elizabeth, Catherine Amanda. *Education:* Texas Christian University, B.A., 1947; University of Denver, graduate study, 1947; Vanderbilt University, M.A., 1948; University of Wisconsin, graduate study, 1953. *Politics:* Democrat. *Home:* 2601 McPherson, Fort Worth, Tex. 76109. *Office:* Department of English, Texas Christian University, Fort Worth, Tex. 76129.

CAREER: Alabama College (now University of Montevallo), Montevallo, instructor in English, 1948-49; University of Kansas, Lawrence, instructor in English, 1949-52; Texas Christian University, Fort Worth, instructor, 1954-57, assistant professor, 1957-71, associate professor of English, 1971—. *Member:* National Council of Teachers of English, Conference of College Teachers of English, American Association of University Professors, South Central Modern Language Association, Texas Association of Teachers of Creative Writing, Ampersand, Mortar Board, Phi Beta Kappa, Alpha Lambda Delta, Alpha Chi.

WRITINGS: (Editor) *A Part of Space: Ten Texas Writers*, Texas Christian University Press, 1969; (contributor) John J. McAleer, editor, *Artist and Citizen Thoreau*, Transcendental Books, 1971; (editor) *Studies in Medieval, Renaissance, and American Literature: A Festschrift*, Texas Christian University Press, 1971; (editor) M. K. Spears, *Space Against Time in Modern Poetry*, Texas Christian University Press, 1972; (editor) Joseph Addison Clark and James M. Moudy, *A Hope of Wisdom*, Texas Christian University Press, 1973; (editor) Jerome Moore, *Texas Christian University: A Hundred Years of History*, Texas Christian University Press, 1974. Poems included in *Christian Century Reader*, editor by Harold E. Fey and Margaret Frakes, Association Press, 1962. Editor, *Descant*, 1963—.

* * *

COLSON, Elizabeth 1917-

PERSONAL: Born June 15, 1917, in Hewitt, Minn.; daughter of Louis Henry and Metta (Damon) Colson. *Education:* University of Minnesota, B.A., 1938, M.A., 1940; Radcliffe College, M.A., 1941, Ph.D., 1945. *Office:* Department of Anthropology, University of California, Berkeley, Calif. 94720.

CAREER: War Relocation Authority, Poston, Ariz., assistant social science analyst, 1942-43; Harvard University, Cambridge, Mass., research assistant, 1944-45; Rhodes-Livingstone Institute, Livingstone, Northern Rhodesia, senior research officer, 1946-47, director, 1948-51; Manchester University, Manchester, England, senior Simon fellow, 1951, senior lecturer, 1951-53; Goucher College, Towson, Md., associate professor of anthropology, 1954-55; Boston University, Boston, Mass., associate professor and research associate in African studies program, 1955-59; Brandeis University, Waltham, Mass., professor, 1959-63; University of California, Berkeley, professor of anthropology, 1964—. Fellow of Center for Advanced Study in the Behavioral Sciences (Stanford), 1967-68; Morgan Lecturer at University of Rochester, 1973.

MEMBER: American Anthropological Association, American Ethnological Society, Association of Social Anthropologists, American Association of African Studies, Society for the Scientific Study of Religion, Royal Anthropological Institute, Phi Beta Kappa. *Awards, honors:* Simon senior fellowship at University of Manchester, 1951.

WRITINGS: The Makah, Manchester University Press, 1953; *Marriage and the Family among the Plateau Tonga,* Manchester University Press, 1958; *The Social Organization of the Gwembe Tonga,* Manchester University Press, 1960; *The Plateau Tonga,* Manchester University Press, 1962; *The Social Consequences of Resettlement,* Manchester University Press, 1971; *Three Pomo Life Histories,* Archaeological Facility, University of California, Berkeley, 1974; *Tradition and Contract,* Aldine, 1974. Contributor to *Africa, Current Anthropology,* and *Southwestern Journal of Anthropology.*

* * *

COLSTON, Lowell G(wen) 1919-

PERSONAL: Born April 14, 1919, in Des Moines, Iowa;

son of Garold Viron (a school superintendent) and Ethel (Bliss) Colston; married Frances Peterson, September 5, 1943; children: Barbara Colston Young, Jeffrey, Cheryl. *Education:* Attended Bloomfield Junior College, 1939-41; Drake University, A.B., 1943; Union Theological Seminary, New York, N.Y., M.Div., 1947; University of Chicago, Ph.D., 1961. *Politics:* Democrat. *Home:* 4701 North Rookwood Ave., Indianapolis, Ind. 46208. *Office:* Department of Pastoral Care, Christian Theological Seminary, 1000 West 42nd St., Indianapolis, Ind. 46208.

CAREER: Ordained Disciples of Christ minister, 1943. Licensed psychologist in Indiana; certified by Indiana State Board of Examiners in Psychology, 1970; private practice in psychology, part-time, 1971-75; Christian Theological Seminary, Indianapolis, Ind., assistant professor, 1958-61, associate professor, 1961-64, professor of pastoral care, 1964—. President of Indianapolis Institute of Transactional Analysis, 1973—. Member of Committee on Alcohol Safety Action, Indianapolis, Ind., 1973-75. *Member:* International Association for Transactional Analysis, American Association of Pastoral Counselors (diplomate), Association for Clinical Pastoral Education, American Psychological Association, Torch Club International.

WRITINGS: (With Seward Hiltner) *Context of Pastoral Counseling*, Abingdon, 1961; *Wake Up Self*, Christian Board of Publication, 1969; *Judgment in Pastoral Counseling*, Abingdon, 1969; (with Paul Johnson) *Personality and Christian Faith*, Abingdon, 1973.

WORK IN PROGRESS: Cinch of the Corn Belt, an autobiographical study of adolescent years on an Iowa farm; *Sheep in the Meadow*, a pastoral theological challenge to laymen.

* * *

COLWELL, Ernest Cadman 1901-1974

January 19, 1901—September 13, 1974; American biblical scholar and educator. Obituaries: *New York Times*, September 14, 1974; *AB Bookman's Weekly*, October 7, 1974. (*CA*-5/6).

* * *

COMPRONE, Joseph J(ohn) 1943-

PERSONAL: Surname is pronounced Com-*pron*-e; born March 11, 1943, in Darby, Pa.; son of John Joseph (a skilled laborer) and Anne (a hospital receptionist; maiden name, Lombardo) Comprone; married Pamela Jane Gay (an English teacher), June 5, 1965; children: Raphael John. *Education:* Springfield College, B.A., 1965; University of Massachusetts, M.A., 1967, Ph.D., 1970. *Politics:* Democrat. *Religion:* Roman Catholic. *Home:* 320 Oregon St., Cincinnati, Ohio 45202. *Office:* Department of English, University of Cincinnati, McMicken Hall, Cincinnati, Ohio 45221.

CAREER: University of Minnesota, Morris, assistant professor of English, 1969-72; University of Cincinnati, Cincinnati, Ohio, associate professor of English, 1972—. Democratic campaign coordinator at University of Massachusetts, 1968. Consultant and reviewer for Holt, W. C. Brown, Houghton, Prentice-Hall, Winthrop, and Scott, Foresman. *Member:* National Council of Teachers of English, College English Association, Modern Language Association of America, American Association of University Professors, Conference on College Composition and Communication.

WRITINGS: (Editor with James Holte) *The Modern Essay: Writing from Experience*, Collegiate Publishing, 1973; *From Experience to Expression: A Collegiate Rhetoric*, W. C. Brown, 1974. Contributor to professional journals.

WORK IN PROGRESS: An anthology of essays, rhetorically and thematically organized, *Substance and Form: The Modern Essay*, for W. C. Brown; poems; a textbook, *Writing about Film*.

* * *

CONANT, Eaton H. 1930-

PERSONAL: Born May 7, 1930, in Boston, Mass; son of Ronald (a businessman) and Catherine (Clarke) Conant; married Mary E. Frost, June 25, 1957; children: James Eaton, Katherine Irene, Clarke Robert, Keith David. *Education:* University of Wisconsin, B.S., 1957, M.S., 1958, Ph.D., 1960. *Home:* 2251 Columbia St., Eugene, Ore. 97403. *Office:* Industrial and Labor Relations Institute, University of Oregon, Eugene, Ore. 97403.

CAREER: University of Chicago, Chicago, Ill., assistant professor of industrial relations, 1961-66; University of Oregon, Eugene, associate professor, 1966-71, professor of economics and industrial relations, 1971—, research associate at Industrial and Labor Relations Institute, 1966-69, director of institute, 1969—. Consultant to federal government, corporations, and labor unions. *Military service:* U.S. Army, Security Agency, 1952-55; became sergeant. *Member:* American Economic Association, American Arbitration Association, Industrial Relations Research Association.

WRITINGS: (Contributor) *The Measurement and Interpretation of Job Vacancies*, National Bureau of Economic Research, 1966; (contributor) Max S. Wortman, editor, *Critical Issues in Labor*, Macmillan, 1969; *A Cost-Effectiveness Study of Employment of Nonprofessional Teaching Aides in Public Schools*, U.S. Department of Health, Education, and Welfare, 1971; *Teacher and Paraprofessional Work Productivity*, Heath, 1973; (with Raymond Mikesell) *Vocational Training and Retraining in the World Mining Industries*, International Labor Organization, for United Nations, 1974. Contributor of about twenty articles and reviews to scholarly journals, including *Industrial and Labor Relations Review, Monthly Labor Review, Employment Service Review, Oregon Business Review, Proceedings of the American Educational Research Association New York Meetings*, and *Saturday Review World*.

WORK IN PROGRESS: A study of training activities of multinational corporations in "Third World" nations; a study of public employee collective bargaining; research on work productivity of public employees.

* * *

CONNOLLY, Cyril (Vernon) 1903-1974

September 10, 1903—November 26, 1974; British literary critic, author, and magazine editor. Obituaries: *New York Times*, November 27, 1974; *Washington Post*, November 28, 1974; *Time*, December 9, 1974; *Newsweek*, December 9, 1974; *AB Bookman's Weekly*, December 16, 1974; *Publishers Weekly*, December 16, 1974. (*CA*-21/22).

* * *

CONNOR, Seymour V(aughan) 1923-

PERSONAL: Born March 4, 1923, in Paris, Tex.; son of

Aikin Beard (an engineer) and Gladys (Vaughn) Connor; married Ann Smith, January, 1946 (divorced, June, 1964); children: Charles Seymour. *Education:* University of Texas at Austin, B.A., 1946, M.A., 1948, Ph.D., 1952. *Politics:* Independent. *Home:* 3503 45th St., Lubbock, Tex. 79413. *Office:* Department of History, Texas Tech University, Lubbock, Tex. 79409.

CAREER: West Texas State University, Canyon, archivist, 1952-53; Texas State Archives, Austin, archivist, 1953-55; Texas Tech University, Lubbock, associate professor, 1955-56, professor of history, 1956—. Visiting professor at Angelo State University, 1964-65. *Military service:* U.S. Army, Paratroops, 1943-45; became first lieutenant. *Member:* Society of American Archaeologists, Organization of American Historians, Oral History Association, Society for Historical Archaeology, Western Historical Association, Texas State Historical Association (fellow; past president), West Texas Museum Association, West Texas Historical Association, Phi Kappa Tau, Phi Alpha Theta, Phi Kappa Phi. *Awards, honors:* American Association for State and Local History award of merit, 1955; Texas State Historical Association fellow, 1956; Huntington Library research grants, 1970, 1971; National Park Service research grants, 1971-72, 1972-73, 1974-75.

WRITINGS: (Contributor) Walter P. Webb and H. Bailey Carroll, editors, *Handbook of Texas*, two volumes, Texas State Historical Association, 1953; (editor) *Texas Treasury Papers*, three volumes, Texas State Library, 1955; *Preliminary Guide to the Archives of Texas*, Texas State Library, 1956; (editor) *The West Is for Us: The Reminiscences of Mary A. Blankenship*, West Texas Museum Association, 1958; (editor and contributor) *Builders of the Southwest*, Texas Tech University, 1959; *The Peters Colony of Texas*, Texas State Historical Association, 1959.

A Biggers Chronicle, Texas Tech University, 1961; *Adventure in Glory: The Saga of Texas, 1836-1848*, Steck, 1965; (editor) *The Saga of Texas*, six volumes, Steck, 1965; (contributor) *Battles of Texas*, Texian Press, 1967; (author of introduction) Eugene C. Barker, *Life of Stephen F. Austin*, DaCapo Press, 1968.

(Contributor) *The Capitols of Texas*, Texian Press, 1970; *Texas: A History*, Crowell, 1971; (with Odie B. Faulk) *A History of the Mexican War*, Oxford University Press, 1971; (editor) *Dear America: Some Letters of Orange Cicero and Mary America Connor*, Pemberton Press, 1971; (with William C. Pool) *Texas: The 28th Star*, Graphic Ideas, 1971; (contributor) Faulk, editor, *The Mexican War: Changing Interpretations*, Swallow Press, 1973; (with others) *Water for the Southwest*, American Society of Civil Engineers, 1974; (editor with Faulk) *Politics and the American West*, Swallow Press, 1975; (with Skaggs) *The Santa Fe Trail*, Oxford University Press, in press. Author of monographs. Contributor of more than four hundred articles and reviews to encyclopedias and journals. Editor, *Panhandle-Plains Historical Review*, 1955-60.

* * *

CONRAD, John W(ilfred) 1935-

PERSONAL: Born August 3, 1935, in Cresson, Pa.; son of W. L. and Elizabeth (Bouch) Conrad; married Barbara Jean Daugherty (a part-time teacher), June 5, 1963; children: William T., Khristan E. *Education:* Indiana University of Pennsylvania, B.S., 1958; Carnegie-Mellon University, M.F.A., 1963; University of Pittsburgh, Ed.D., 1970. *Home:* 3675 Syracuse Ave., San Diego, Calif. 92122. *Office:* Department of Fine Arts, Mesa College, Mesa College Dr., San Diego, Calif. 92111.

CAREER: Public school teacher of arts and crafts in Pittsburgh, Pa., 1958-64; Mesa College, San Diego, Calif., associate professor, 1966-70, professor of fine arts, 1970—. Has exhibited ceramics at local, regional, and national exhibits. *Member:* College Art Association of America, National Council on Education for the Ceramic Arts.

WRITINGS: *Ceramic Formulas: The Complete Compendium*, Macmillan, 1973.

WORK IN PROGRESS: *Contemporary Ceramics*, publication by Prentice-Hall expected in 1976.

AVOCATIONAL INTERESTS: Photography, collecting German antique beer steins, skiing, scuba diving.

* * *

CONROY, Michael R(alph) 1945-

PERSONAL: Born April 20, 1945, in Gallipolis, Ohio; son of Joseph Ralph (a deputy sheriff in Dallas, Tex.) and Fayma Beatrice (a secretary; maiden name Cowan) Conroy; married Jerrie Lee Payne (a journalist), September 6, 1969 (divorced December 4, 1973); children: Janie Faye. *Education:* Attended South Texas Junior College, 1966, Corpus Christi Junior College, 1969, Los Angeles Valley College, 1970, and Lee College, Baytown, Tex, 1973—. *Politics:* Non-partisan. *Religion:* Agnostic. *Home:* 15031 Nuwood Lane, Houston, Tex. 77045. *Agent:* Mary Travers, 9806 Cedardale Lane, Houston, Tex. 77055. *Office:* Mike Conroy & Associates, Architects and Engineers, 601 Westbury Square, Houston, Tex.

CAREER: United States Marine Corps., 1963-69, served in South Vietnam; owner, Contract Drafting Service, 1969—, Mike Conroy & Associates, Architects and Engineers, 1970—, and Mike Conroy Drafting Service, 1970—, all Houston, Tex.; author. *Member:* Veterans of Foreign Wars. *Awards, honors*—Military: Vietnam Service Medal with one star, Purple Heart with star, Vietnamese Cross of Gallantry with device.

WRITINGS: *Truong Oi Mai*, Mandala, Inc., 1968; *The Green Ghosts of Vietnam*, Yellow Jacket Press, 1974; *The Mission at San Y Sydro*, Yellow Jacket Press, 1974.

WORK IN PROGRESS: *The Crusaders*, a historical novel; *Khe Sahn Stands*; *Death in Hue*; *Tham Biet Tri*; *Operation Taylor Common*; *People's Soldier*; *Canvasback*; *The Girl He Left Behind*; *The Isle of Palms*; *The Priapist*; *Fourth Down and Bedroom to Go*; and a detective story, as yet untitled.

SIDELIGHTS: Conroy speaks, reads, and writes Vietnamese and speaks Japanese. *Avocational interests:* Distance-running, boxing, games of chance, theatre (designs sets).

BIOGRAPHICAL/CRITICAL SOURCES: *Houston Post*, November 1, 1970.

* * *

CONROY, Peter V(incent), Jr. 1944-

PERSONAL: Born April 9, 1944, in New York, N.Y.; son of Peter V. (a policeman) and Winifred (Raftery) Conroy; married Beverly Ann Kruk (a reading skills teacher), June 10, 1967. *Education:* Queens College of the City University of New York, B.A., 1965, M.A., 1967; graduate study at University of Nancy, 1965-66; University of Wisconsin, Ph.D., 1970. *Religion:* Roman Catholic. *Home:* 739 South

Elmwood, Oak Park, Ill. 60302. *Office address:* University of Illinois, Box 4348, Chicago, Ill. 60680.

CAREER: University of Illinois, Chicago, assistant professor, 1970-74, associate professor of French language and literature, 1974—. Resident director, Illinois Junior Year Abroad, Rouen, France, 1972-73, and Paris, France, 1973-74. *Member:* Modern Language Association of America, American Association of Teachers of French.

WRITINGS: Crebillon fils: Techniques of the Novel, Oxford University Press, 1972; (contributor) L. Price, editor, *Marcel Proust: A Critical Panorama*, University of Illinois Press, 1973; (contributor) Roger Johnson, editor, *Moliere and the Commonwealth of Letters*, University of Southern Mississippi Press, 1974. Contributor of articles and reviews to professional journals.

WORK IN PROGRESS: Research on detective fiction, both novels and short stories.

AVOCATIONAL INTERESTS: Playing flute, sports.

* * *

CONYNGHAM, William Joseph 1924-

PERSONAL: Born August 13, 1924, in Wilkes-Barre, Pa.; son of William J. and Margaret (Jordan) Conyngham; married Margaret Hennessy (a librarian), September 5, 1955; children: William J., Jr., Monica, Michael, Maura. *Education:* Catholic University of America, B.A., 1950; University of Notre Dame, M.A., 1952; Columbia University, Ph.D., 1969. *Religion:* Roman Catholic. *Home:* 12907 Goodhill Rd., Wheaton, Md. 20096. *Office:* Department of Politics, Catholic University of America, Washington, D.C. 20017.

CAREER: United States Government, Washington, D.C., analyst, 1952-57; Manhattanville College, Purchase, N.Y., assistant professor of politics, 1957-65; Catholic University of America, Washington, D.C., associate professor of politics, 1965—. *Military service:* U.S. Army, Infantry, 1943-46; served in European theater. *Member:* American Political Science Association, American Association for the Advancement of Slavic Studies, Phi Beta Kappa.

WRITINGS: Industrial Management in the Soviet Union: The Role of the CPSU in Industrial Decision-Making, 1917-1970, Hoover Institution Press, 1973.

WORK IN PROGRESS: Contemporary Soviet Management Theory: A Search for Relevance; *Soviet Management: Structures and Functions*, completion expected in 1975.

* * *

COOK, Blanche Wiesen 1941-

PERSONAL: Maiden name is pronounced *Wee*-zen; born April 20, 1941, in New York, N.Y.; daughter of David Theodore and Sadonia (Ecker) Wiesen. *Education:* Hunter College (now Hunter College of the City University of New York), B.A., 1962; Johns Hopkins University, M.A., 1964, Ph.D., 1969. *Home:* 240 West 98th St., New York, N.Y. 10025. *Agent:* Betty Anne Clarke, International Famous Agency, 1301 Avenue of the Americas, New York, N.Y. 10019. *Office:* John Jay College of Criminal Justice of the City University of New York, 445 West 59th St., New York, N.Y. 10019.

CAREER: Hampton Institute, Hampton, Va., instructor in American history, 1963; Yeshiva University, Stern College for Women, instructor in history, 1964-68; John Jay College of Criminal Justice of the City University of New York, New York, N.Y., instructor, 1969-70, assistant professor, 1970-74, associate professor of history, 1974—. Instructor at Hunter College of the City University of New York, 1965, 1966; consultant to Institute for World Order.

MEMBER: International Peace Research Association, Women's International League for Peace and Freedom (member of executive committee of New York metropolitan area branch, 1966—; member of national board of directors, 1971-73), American Historical Association, Organization of American Historians, American Studies Association, Union for Radical Political Economy, American Association for the Advancement of Science, Coordinating Committee of Women in the Historical Profession (cochairwoman of New York metropolitan area branch, 1972-73), Conference on Peace Research in History (member of executive council, 1968—; executive secretary, 1969-73), Consortium on Peace, Research, Education, and Development, Columbia University Seminar on American Civilization, Inter-University Seminar on the Armed Forces and Society.

WRITINGS: (Editor) *Bibliography on Peace Research in History,* Clio Press, 1969; (editor with Alice Harris and Ronald Radosh, and contributor) *Past-Imperfect: Alternative Readings in U.S. History,* Knopf, 1973; (contributor) Charles Chatfield, editor, *American Peace Movements,* Schocken, 1973; *Dwight David Eisenhower: Antimilitarist in the White House* (monograph), Forum, 1974.

Contributor to "One Woman's Voice," a weekly syndicated column distributed by Anderson-Moberg Syndicates, 1974—. Contributor to professional publications, including *American Studies Journal*. Senior editor of "The Garland Library on War and Peace," a 360 volume reprint series, Garland Publishers, 1972-74. Member of board of editors of *Journal of Voluntary Action Research,* 1972—, and *Journal of Peace and Change,* 1972—.

WORK IN PROGRESS: Then Conquer We Must: Violence and Change in the United States, for Institute for World Order; *Dwight David Eisenhower and Richard Nixon: The Presidential Impact on War and Peace,* for Doubleday, completion expected in 1976; *Democracy in Wartime,* an investigation of the impact of antimilitarism and wartime dissent on the political process from World War I to the war in Indochina.

* * *

COOK, Daniel J(oseph) 1938-

PERSONAL: Born June 27, 1938, in Philadelphia, Pa.; son of Theodore H. (an executive) and Leah (a travel agent; maiden name, Porush) Cook; married Lucille A. Roussin, June 21, 1970. *Education:* Haverford College, B.A. (honors), 1960; Columbia University, M.A., 1963, Ph.D., 1968; Hebrew Union College, B.Heb.Lit., 1964. *Politics:* Left-liberal. *Religion:* Jewish. *Home:* 230 Riverside Dr., 9-H, New York, N.Y. 10025. *Office:* New School of Liberal Arts, Brooklyn College of the City University of New York, 210 Livingston St., Brooklyn, N.Y. 11201.

CAREER: Hunter College of the City University of New York, Bronx, N.Y., lecturer in philosophy, 1967-68; Lehman College of the City University of New York, Bronx, N.Y., instructor, 1968-69, assistant professor of philosophy, 1969-71; Brooklyn College of the City University of New York, assistant professor of philosophy, 1972—. *Member:* American Philosophical Association, American Professors for Peace in the Middle East, Hegel

Society of America (charter member). *Awards, honors:* Woodrow Wilson fellowship, 1960-61; research grant from Heinrich Hertz Stiftung, 1971-72, for study at University of Bonn; American Philosophical Society travel grant, 1971-72; American Council of Learned Societies travel grant, 1973.

WRITINGS: Language in the Philosophy of Hegel, Mouton & Co., 1973. Contributor of articles and reviews to *Journal of the History of Philosophy, Dimensions of American Judaism, Germanic Review,* and *Philosophy East and West.*

WORK IN PROGRESS: Research on William James on Hegel, Drugs and Mysticism, and Marx on Language; translation of Leibniz's Letter on Chinese Philosophy.

AVOCATIONAL INTERESTS: Travel.

* * *

COOLING, Benjamin Franklin 1938-

PERSONAL: Born December 8, 1938, in New Brunswick, N.J.; son of Benjamin Franklin, Sr. (a chemist) and Helene Emma (Weisshaar) Cooling. *Education:* Rutgers University, B.A., 1961; University of Pennsylvania, M.A., 1962, Ph.D., 1969. *Politics:* Independent Republican. *Religion:* Episcopalian. *Home:* 3729 Jenifer St. N.W., Washington, D.C. 20015. *Office:* U.S. Army Military History Research Collection, Carlisle Barracks, Pa. 17013.

CAREER: U.S. Department of the Interior, Fort Donelson National Military Park, Tenn., park historian, 1962-63; U.S. Department of the Army, Washington, D.C., research historian in office of chief of military history, 1963-68; PMC Colleges, Chester, Pa., began as instructor, later assistant professor of history, 1968-70, chief of research studies, 1970-74; U.S. Army Military History Research Collection, Carlisle Barracks, Pa., assistant director of historical services, 1974—. Faculty instructor at U.S. Army War College, 1971—. *Military service:* U.S. Army Reserve, 1956-63.

MEMBER: American Historical Association, American Military Institute (trustee), Company of Military Historians (fellow), Omar N. Bradley Foundation (member of board of governors), Army Military History Research Collection Fund Council, Cruiser Olympia Association (curator and historian, 1965—), Phi Alpha Theta. *Awards, honors:* Associate for advanced research at Naval War College, 1973-74, to study U.S. Navy's search for armor and armament from 1881-1917.

WRITINGS: (Contributor) Robert McBride, editor, *More Highlights of Tennessee History*, Tennessee Historical Commission, 1968; (contributor) Maurice Matloff, editor, *American Military History*, U.S. Government Printing Office, 1969; (editor) *Soldiering in Sioux Country*, Frontier Heritage Press, 1971; *Historical Highlights of Bull Run Regional Park*, Northern Virginia Park Authority, 1971; (editor with Allan Millett) *Doctoral Dissertations in Military Affairs*, Library, Kansas State University, 1972; (editor with Don Rickey, Jr.) *Essays in Some Dimensions of Military History*, U.S. Army Military History Research Collection, Volume I, 1973, Volume II, 1974; *Benjamin Franklin Tracy: Father of the Modern American Fighting Navy*, Archon, 1973; *Curricular Archives of the U.S. Army War College: 1907-1941*, U.S. Army Military History Research Collection, 1973; *The Era of Civil War and Reconstruction: 1820-1876*, U.S. Army Military History Research Collection, 1975; *Symbol, Sword, and Shield: Defending Washington during the Civil War*, Archon, 1975; (contributor) Robin Higham, editor, *Sources in American Military History*, Archon, in press; (contributor) Higham, editor, *U.S. Army in Peacetime: Its Impact on American Life*, Kansas State University Press, in press.

Contributor to *Encyclopedia Americana*. Contributor of more than forty articles and reviews to military and history journals, including *American Historical Review, Journal of American History, Journal of Southern History, Conflict, Naval War College Review, National Defense, Aerospace Historian, Parameters: Journal of the Army War College*, and *Military Affairs*. Member of editorial board and book review editor of *Military Affairs*.

WORK IN PROGRESS: Gray Steel and Blue Water Navy: Foundation of the Military-Industrial Complex; editing *Marx, Business, and American Society: Historical Perspectives on the Military-Industrial Complex*; *Key to the Western Gateway: The Henry-Donelson Campaign.*

AVOCATIONAL INTERESTS: Historical preservation and interpretation, collecting, displaying, and preserving material culture from the period of the Civil War (military and non-military), raising collie dogs, travel in Europe, sports and physical fitness (running, team sports).

* * *

COOMBES, B. L. 1894(?)-1974

British author. Obituaries: *AB Bookman's Weekly*, October 7, 1974.

* * *

COONEY, Seamus (Anthony) 1933-

PERSONAL: Given name is pronounced *Shay*-muss; born June 5, 1933, in Dublin, Ireland; son of Eamonn (a politician) and Gertrude (Kennedy) Cooney; married Kay Teru Takahashi (a potter), March 24, 1960; children: Hugh Eamonn, Michael Shiyogo, Tamar Brigid. *Education:* National University of Ireland, B.A. (honors), 1954; Indiana University, M.A., 1959; University of California, Berkeley, Ph.D., 1964. *Home:* 2003 Stearns Ave., Kalamazoo, Mich. 49008. *Office:* Department of English, Western Michigan University, Kalamazoo, Mich. 49008.

CAREER: St. Patrick's College, Armagh, Northern Ireland, French master, 1954-56; supply teacher in London, England, 1956-57; University of California, Berkeley, acting instructor, 1962-64; Indiana University, Bloomington, lecturer in English, 1964-68; Loyola University, Los Angeles, Calif., assistant professor of English, 1968-71; Western Michigan University, Kalamazoo, assistant professor, 1971-74, associate professor of English, 1974—. *Member:* American Association of University Professors.

WRITINGS: Introduction to Poetry, Correspondence Study Division, Indiana University, 1967; *A Checklist of the First One Hundred Publications of the Black Sparrow Press,* Black Sparrow, 1971; (editor and author of introduction) Charles Reznikoff, *By the Well of Living and Seeing: New and Selected Poems, 1918-1973,* Black Sparrow, 1974. Contributor of critical essays to *Contemporary Poets,* edited by James Vinson, St. Martin's, 1974. Contributor of about fifty articles and reviews to literature journals, including *Studies in Short Fiction, Explicator, Studies in Scottish Literature, Eire-Ireland, Victorian Newsletter,* and *Modern Language Notes.*

COOPER, James L(ouis) 1934-

PERSONAL: Born December 24, 1934, in Merchantville, N.J.; son of James H. (a tree surgeon) and Gladys M. (a secretary; maiden name, Wambaugh) Cooper; married Sheila R. McIsaac, June 10, 1957; children: James L., Jr., Mairi. *Education:* College of Wooster, B.A., 1956; University of Wisconsin–Madison, M.A., 1959, Ph.D., 1964. *Home:* 629 East Seminary St., Greencastle, Ind. 46135. *Office:* Department of History, DePauw University, #5-FOB, Greencastle, Ind. 46135.

CAREER: Junior high school history teacher in Sterling, Ohio, 1956-57; Oakland University, Rochester, Mich., instructor in history, 1962-64; DePauw University, Greencastle, Ind., assistant professor, 1964-68, associate professor of history, 1968—. *Member:* American Historical Association, Organization of American Historians, American Association of University Professors, Phi Beta Kappa, Pi Sigma Alpha, Phi Alpha Theta. *Awards, honors:* Humanities award from Great Lakes Colleges Association and Carnegie Foundation, 1968-69; bicentennial grant from National Endowment for the Humanities, 1971-72; Great Lakes Colleges Association teaching fellowship, 1974—.

WRITINGS: (With wife, Sheila M. Cooper) *Roots of American Feminist Thought*, Allyn & Bacon, 1973.

WORK IN PROGRESS: A monograph on the social structure of thirty New Hampshire towns from 1750 to 1800; studying the relationship between political theory, political economy, and foreign policy in the era of the American Revolution.

* * *

COOPER, Phyllis 1939-

PERSONAL: Born August 2, 1939, in Washington, D.C.; daughter of Harry L. (a builder) and Bertha (a community health worker; maiden name, Willis) Stevens; married Kenneth Cooper (a teacher), July 24, 1959; children: Scott, Kevin. *Education:* University of Maryland, B.S., 1962; Temple University, M.Ed., 1969; Pennsylvania State University, graduate study, 1970-73. *Home:* 39 Frog Hollow Rd., Churchville, Pa. 18966. *Office:* Department of Physical Education, Trenton State College, Trenton, N.J. 08625.

CAREER: Public high school teacher of physical education in Gaithersburg, Md., 1962-64; West Chester State College, West Chester, Pa., instructor in physical education, 1964-68; Trenton State College, Trenton, N.J., assistant professor of physical education, 1969—. Coach of United States gymnastics team at 1966 North American Championships. *Member:* United States Gymnastics Federation, National Gymnastics Association, Middle Atlantic Gymnastics Directors Association.

WRITINGS: *Feminine Gymnastics*, Burgess, 1968, 2nd edition, 1974.

WORK IN PROGRESS: *Mental Rehearsal in Athletics; Gymnastics for the Elementary School.*

* * *

COOPER, Signe Skott 1921-

PERSONAL: First name is pronounced *Sig*-na; born January 29, 1921, in Iowa; daughter of Hans Edward (a soils conservationist) and Clara (a teacher and writer; maiden name, Steen) Skott; married Clois Cooper, July 20, 1944 (divorced April, 1946). *Education:* University of Wisconsin, B.S., 1948; summer graduate study at Columbia University, 1948, 1950, 1951; University of Minnesota, M.Ed., 1955. *Home:* 7207 University Ave., Middleton, Wis. 53562. *Office:* University Extension, 610 Langdon St., Madison, Wis. 53706.

CAREER: Registered nurse; University of Wisconsin-Madison, instructor, 1948-51, assistant professor, 1951-57, associate professor, 1957-62, professor of nursing, 1962—, holding joint appointment at Extension branch, Madison, as assistant professor, 1955-57, associate professor, 1957-62, professor of nursing, 1962—. Consultant on nursing books to McGraw-Hill Book Co. *Military service:* U.S. Army Nurse Corps, 1943-46; served in China-Burma-India theater; became first lieutenant. *Member:* American Nurses' Association, National League for Nursing, American Heart Association, Adult Education Association of the United States, Wisconsin Nurses' Association (president, 1958-60), Wisconsin League for Nursing, State Historical Society of Wisconsin. *Awards, honors:* Linda Richards Award from National League for Nursing, 1967, for pioneering efforts in continuing education in nursing.

WRITINGS: *Wisconsin Nursing Pioneers* (monograph), University of Wisconsin Extension, 1968; *Contemporary Nursing Practice: A Guide for the Returning Nurse,* McGraw, 1970; (with May Hornback) *Continuing Nursing Education,* McGraw, 1973. Contributor to nursing publications. Member of editorial board of *R. N.,* 1959-69; coeditor of *Cardiovascular Nursing,* 1967-70; member of editorial board of *Nursing Forum,* 1969—; contributing editor of *Journal of Continuing Education in Nursing,* 1970—.

WORK IN PROGRESS: A photo history of the University of Wisconsin-Madison School of Nursing; research on the history of nursing in Wisconsin.

AVOCATIONAL INTERESTS: Travel, stamp collecting.

* * *

COPPER, Marcia S(nyder) 1934-

PERSONAL: Born March 30, 1934, in New York; daughter of Daniel H. (a realtor) and Dorothea (Kirkman) Snyder; married Craig M. Copper (an architect), August 28, 1954; children: Deborah, Daniel, Scott. *Education:* Attended Mary Washington College, 1951-54; University of Virginia, B.S. in Ed., 1955. *Home:* 1910 Tenth St. Pl. N.W., Hickory, N.C. 28601. *Agent:* Perry Knowlton, c/o Curtis Brown Ltd., 60 East 56th St., New York, N.Y.

CAREER: Lake Erie College, Painesville, Ohio, assistant director of equestrian center, 1973; Visiting Nurse Association, Cleveland, Ohio, secretary to associate director, 1973-74.

WRITINGS: *Take Care of Your Horse,* Scribner, 1974. Contributor of a short story to *Chronicle of the Horse*.

WORK IN PROGRESS: A book on horses dealing with tradition, attire, and riding etiquette, for Scribner.

AVOCATIONAL INTERESTS: Skiing, tennis, reading, amateur theater, riding, foxhunting.

* * *

CORDER, Brice W(ood) 1936-

PERSONAL: Born January 28, 1936, in Washington, D.C.; son of William Elmer and Irene (Wood) Corder; married Maryanne Claire (an instructor); children: Brett, Vanessa. *Education:* Lynchburg College, B.A., 1960; Temple University, M.Ed., 1961, Ed.D., 1967. *Home:* 2172 East

Broadmor Dr., Tempe, Ariz. 85282. *Office:* Department of Health Science, Arizona State University MPE266, Tempe, Ariz. 85281.

CAREER: Pennsylvania State University, State College, Pa., assistant professor of health science and coordinator of Health Science area, 1965-71; Arizona State University, Tempe, associate professor of health science, 1971—. *Military service:* U.S. Marine Corps, 1956-58. *Member:* American School Health Association, American Public Health Association, Arizona Public Health Association (member of executive committee).

WRITINGS: (With Ronda K. Showalter) *It's Your Life*, W. C. Brown, 1971; (with Showalter) *Health Science and College Life*, W. C. Brown, 1972, 2nd edition, in press; *Drug Abuse Prevention: Perspectives and Approaches for Educators*, W. C. Brown, 1974.

WORK IN PROGRESS: Modification of Destructive Health Behavior.

* * *

CORLISS, Charlotte N(uzum) 1932-

PERSONAL: Born June 14, 1932, in Charleston, W.Va.; daughter of Karl J. and Louise (Shroeder) Nuzum; married Robert J. Corliss, June, 1956 (divorced, 1960). *Education:* University of Pittsburg, B.S., 1956, M.N., 1973, working toward doctoral degree; University of Minnesota, M.Ed., 1963. *Politics:* Republican. *Religion:* Episcopalian. *Home:* 516 North Sheridan Ave., Pittsburgh, Pa. 15206.

CAREER: Pennsylvania Hospital School of Nursing, Philadelphia, Pa., clinical instructor in obstetrics and gynecology, 1956-59; University of Cincinnati, College of Nursing and Health, Cincinnati, Ohio, instructor in obstetrics, 1960-62; Arizona State University, College of Nursing, Tempe, assistant professor of maternity nursing, 1963-71. *Member:* American Nurses Association, Arizona Nurses Association (district vice-president, 1970-71), Pittsburgh Ski Club, Kappa Kappa Gamma, Sigma Theta Tau.

WRITINGS: (With Violet Broadribb) *Maternal-Child Nursing*, Lippincott, 1973.

WORK IN PROGRESS: Research on psychological responses of women to elective abortions.

AVOCATIONAL INTERESTS: Travel, skiing, horseback riding, music, spectator sports.

* * *

CORMIER, Raymond J(oseph) 1938-

PERSONAL: Born November 23, 1938; son of Alphonse J. (a restaurateur) and Mary H. (Wilinich) Cormier; married Patricia Picard (a health educator), June 9, 1960; children: Jean-Louis, Madelaine. *Education:* University of Bridgeport, A.B., 1960; Stanford University, A.M., 1962; Harvard University, Ph.D., 1967. *Home:* 2427 Sunset Rd., Charlottesville, Va. 22903. *Office:* Department of French, University of Virginia, Charlottesville, Va. 22903.

CAREER: Tufts University, Medford, Mass., instructor in French, 1965-67; University of Virginia, Charlottesville, assistant professor of French, 1967—, founder and director of Medieval Circle, 1968—. *Military service:* U.S. Navy, 1957. *Member:* International Arthurian Society, Modern Language Association of America, Mediaeval Academy of America, American Association of University Professors, Modern Humanities Research Association, American Association of Teachers of French, Irish Texts Society, South Atlantic Modern Language Association, Harvard Lodge. *Awards, honors:* Sesquicentennial associateship, University of Virginia, 1972-73.

WRITINGS: (Editor with Urban T. Holmes) *Essays in Honor of Louis F. Solano*, University of North Carolina Press, 1970; (translator) Jean Frappier, *Chretien de Troyes*, University of Alabama Press, 1973; (editor with Holmes, G. Daniel, J. Keller, and others) *One Heart One Mind: The Rebirth of Virgil's Hero in Medieval French Romance*, Romance Monographs, in press. Contributor of about forty articles and reviews to academic journals, including *Quartet, Modern Language Journal, Music Journal, Moyen Age, Studia Hibernica,* and *Eire-Ireland.*

WORK IN PROGRESS: Cu Chulainn: Saga Hero of Ireland and Early Irish Mythology, a monograph; several volumes of translations of Old French and Old Irish literary texts; editing a single manuscript of *Roman d'Eneas*, with a prose translation and complete glossary; research on the medieval hero.

* * *

CORNETT, Joe D(elayne) 1935-

PERSONAL: Born February 28, 1935, in Tulsa, Okla.; son of Arron Leo and Rose (McClain) Cornett; married Elayne Sutherlin, June 2, 1960; children: Jeffery, Cara. *Education:* Northwestern State University, Natchitoches, La., B.A., 1960, M.Ed., 1963; University of Arkansas, Ed.D., 1965. *Politics:* Democrat. *Religion:* Baptist. *Home:* 1604 Bangor, Lubbock, Tex. 79416. *Office:* Department of Education, Texas Technological University, Lubbock, Tex. 79409.

CAREER: Teacher of history in the public schools of Bossier, La., 1960-63; Southeastern Louisiana University, Hammond, assistant professor of education, 1965-68; Texas Technological University, Lubbock, professor of education, 1968—. *Military service:* U.S. Army, 1955-58; became staff sergeant. *Member:* American Educational Research Association, Phi Delta Kappa.

WRITINGS: Secondary School Curriculum, Intext, 1972; *Introductory Statistics*, C. E. Merrill, 1975. Contributor to *Improving College and University Teaching, Peabody Journal of Education*, and *Journal of Educational Research.*

WORK IN PROGRESS: A book on computer use.

* * *

COSTAS, Procope 1900(?)-1974

1900(?)—August 26, 1974; American classicist and author. Obituaries: *New York Times*, August 27, 1974.

* * *

COTT, Jonathan 1942-

PERSONAL: Born December 24, 1942, in New York, N.Y.; son of Ted (a television executive) and Jean (an artist; maiden name, Cahan) Cott. *Education:* Columbia University, B.A., 1964; University of California, Berkeley, M.A., 1966. *Home:* 247 East 33rd St., New York, N.Y. 10016. *Office:* Stonehill Publishing Co., 38 East 57th St., New York, N.Y. 10022.

CAREER: Fulbright fellow at University of Essex, England, 1967-69; Granada Television, London, England, production deviser, 1969-70; *Rolling Stone*, San Francisco, Calif., associate editor, 1970-71, contributing editor, 1971-

75; Stonehill Publishing Co., New York, N.Y., executive editor, 1974—. Producer of contemporary music programs, WNYC-Radio, New York, 1960-62, and KPFA-Radio, Berkeley, 1965-67. *Awards, honors:* Woodrow Wilson fellowship, 1964; Ingram Merrill Foundation grant, 1972.

WRITINGS: He Dreams What Is Going On inside His Head: Ten Years of Writing (film reviews, poems, essays), Straight Arrow, 1973; *Stockhausen: Conversations with the Composer*, Simon & Schuster, 1973; (editor and author of introduction) *Beyond the Looking Glass: An Anthology of Victorian Fairy Tales, Novels, Stories, and Poems*, Stonehill and Bowker, 1974; (editor) *The Roses Race around Her Name: Poems from Fathers to Daughters*, Stonehill, 1975; *City of Earthly Love* (poems), Stonehill, 1975; (general editor) *Masterworks of English Children's Literature: 1550-1900*, three volumes, Stonehill and Chelsea House, 1975.

Contributor: Richard Kostelanetz, editor, *On Contemporary Literature*, Avon, 1964; Kostelanetz, editor, *New American Arts*, Horizon Press, 1965; *Young American Writing*, Funk, 1967; Burton J. Fishman, editor, *Viewpoints*, St. Martin's, 1972.

Poetry represented in anthologies: *Young American Poets*, edited by Paul Carroll, Follett, 1968; *A Cinch: Amazing Works from the Columbia Review*, edited by Leslie Gottesman and others, Columbia University Press, 1969; *The World Anthology*, edited by Anne Waldman, Bobbs-Merrill, 1969; *Another World*, edited by Waldman, Bobbs-Merrill, 1971; *In Youth*, edited by Kostelanetz, Ballantine, 1972.

Contributor of poetry to magazines, including *American Poetry Review, Paris Review*, and *World*, and articles to *New York Times, Ramparts, Sunday Ramparts, Rolling Stone, American Review*, and *Radio Times* (London).

* * *

COTTRELL, Robert D(uane) 1930-

PERSONAL: Born February 20, 1930, in Farmersburg, Iowa; married Jane E. Wetton, July 31, 1965; children: Amelia Anne. *Education:* Columbia University, B.S., 1957; Yale University, Ph.D., 1961. *Office:* Department of Romance Languages, Ohio State University, Columbus, Ohio 43210.

CAREER: Northwestern University, Evanston, Ill., instructor, 1960-62, assistant professor of French, 1962-65; Amherst College, Amherst, Mass., assistant professor of French, 1965-68; Ohio State University, Columbus, associate professor, 1968-71, professor of French, 1971—, chairman of department, 1974. Visiting professor at Trinity College, Hartford, Conn., summer, 1966, and at University of Pittsburgh, 1972. *Military service:* U.S. Army, 1951-53. *Member:* Modern Language Association of America, American Association of Teachers of French, Modern Humanities Research Association, Societe des Amis de Montaigne, Association Humanisme et Renaissance.

WRITINGS: Brantome: The Writer as Portraitist of His Age, Droz, 1970; (with wife, Jane E. Cottrell) *Repondez-Moi! Pratique orale des verbes irreguliers francais* (title means "Answer Me! Oral Practice in Irregular French Verbs"), Prentice-Hall, 1971; (translator with Jane E. Cottrell) *Alain on Happiness*, Ungar, 1973; *Colette*, Ungar, 1974; *Simone de Beauvoir*, Ungar, in press. Contributor to scholarly journals.

WORK IN PROGRESS: Robert Garnier, completion expected in 1976.

COUGER, J. Daniel 1929-

PERSONAL: Born October 20, 1929, in Olney, Tex.; son of James Larry Rogers (an engineer) and Faye Schly (Saylors) Couger; married Shirley Anne Thomas, March 4, 1951; children: Daniel Ray, Todd David, Timothy Lee, Julie Anne. *Education:* Phillips University, B.A., 1951; University of Missouri, M.A., 1958; University of Colorado, D.B.A., 1964. *Politics:* Republican. *Religion:* Disciples of Christ. *Home:* 2611 Northridge Dr., Colorado Springs, Colo. 80907. *Office:* Department of Management, University of Colorado, Colorado Springs, Colo. 80907.

CAREER: Hallmark Cards, Kansas City, Mo., supervisor, 1954-58; Martin Marietta Corp., Littleton, Colo., chief, 1958-65; University of Colorado, Colorado Springs, member of faculty, department of management, 1965—. Has lectured in twenty-three countries. *Military service:* U.S. Air Force, 1951-53; became lieutenant. *Member:* Operations Research Society of America, Institute of Management Sciences, Society for Management Information Systems (secretary; member of executive council). *Awards, honors:* National award from American Association for Collegiate Schools of Business, for curriculum innovation; distinguished service award from Association for Systems Management.

WRITINGS: Computers and the Schools of Business, Business Research Division, 1967; (with Loren Shannon) *Fortran IV*, Irwin, 1968; (with Shannon) *Fortran: A Beginner's Approach*, Irwin, 1971; (with Robert Knapp) *System Analysis Techniques*, Wiley, 1974; *Acts of the Holy Spirit*, Full Gospel Business Men's Fellowship, 1974. Co-editor, Wiley series on "Business Data Processing." Editor, *Computive Newsletter*; columnist, *Computerworld*. Contributor of over thirty articles to professional journals.

WORK IN PROGRESS: Research on the design of computer-based information systems; works of the Holy Spirit.

* * *

COULET du GARD, Rene 1919-
(Andre Algery, Raphael Anduze-Dufy)

PERSONAL: Born December 29, 1919, in Saint-Denis-du-Sig, Algeria; came to United States, 1952; naturalized citizen, 1958; son of Jean Marius (a military officer) and Josephine (Courbin) Coulet du Gard. *Education:* University of Pennsylvania, M.Ed., 1963; Universite de Besancon, Ph.D., 1966. *Home address:* R.D. 6, Elkton, Md. 21221. *Agent:* Raoul Cadenet, P.O. Box 56, Newark, Del. 19711. *Office:* Department of Language & Literature, University of Delaware, Newark, Del.

CAREER: Maroc Press, Casablanca, Morocco, reporter, 1945-51; *Les Echos du Monde*, Casablanca, reporter, 1951-57; free-lance writer in Francfort, N.Y., 1957-66; University of Delaware, Newark, associate professor of French language and literature, 1966—. Alliance Francaise, president of Chester County branch, 1957-69, of Southern Delaware branch, 1969-71. Fulbright campus adviser, 1967-72; consultant in French, *New College Dictionary*. *Military service:* French Army, 1940-45; became first lieutenant. *Member:* Association des Amis de l'Ile de Re, Societe Culturelle et Philanthropique de France, Internationale des Arts et des Lettres (Nice, France), Societe des Gens de Lettres de France. *Awards, honors:* First prize in adventure novels from Societe des Arts et Lettres of Algeria, 1952, for *Une Etrange Odyssee*; decorated Chevalier des

Palmes Academiques, 1967; Gold Medal award from Academie Internationale Lutece, 1974.

WRITINGS: Sous la cendre (collected short stories; title means "Beneath the Ashes"), Librairie du Centre (Casablanca), 1947; *Anacreon cherche un emploi* (play; title means "Anacreon in Search of a Job"), Librairie du Centre, 1950; *Une Affaire de stupefiants* (detective novel; title means "An Affair of Drug Smuggling"), Librairie du Centre, 1950; *Gregor, gentleman-cambioleur* (detective novel; title means "Gregor, Gentleman-Smuggler"), Librairie du Centre, 1951; *Une Etrange Odyssee* (adventure novel; title means "A Strange Odyssey"), Editions R.I.P. (Morocco), 1952.

Petit Mememto d'histoire de France (textbook), Editions Renaissance (Kimberton, Pa.), 1960; *Pas a pas* (textbook; title means "Step by Step"), *Livre premier* (Book I), West Chester State College, 1963, *Deuxieme livre* (Book II), Editions Renaissance, 1963, Spanish-language edition published in one volume as *Paso a paso*, Editions Renaissance, 1963; *Poemes pour dire* (title means "Poems to Say . . ."), Grassin (Paris), 1964; *L'Epopee algerienne* (poems; title means "The Algerian Epic"), Editions Renaissance, Volume I, 1964, Volume II, 1965; *Les Poemes du boeux* (title means "The Poems of the Street Cleaner"), Editions du Sphinx (France), 1968; *Feux Follets* (poems; title means "Will-o'-the-Wisp"), Editions du Sphinx, 1969.

(Editor) *Anthologie des poetes et prosateurs francophones de l'Amerique septentrionale* (title means "Anthology of French-Speaking Poets and Prose Writers of North America"), Edition des Deux Mondes, Volume I, 1970, Volume II, 1971; *L'Arithmosophie de Gerard de Nerval* (essays; title means "Arithmosophy of Gerard de Nerval"), Adams Press, 1972; *Reine* (novel; title means "Queen"), Edition de la Revue Moderne, 1973; *The Handbook of French Place Names in the U.S.A.*, Edition des Deux Mondes, 1974.

Contributor, sometimes under the pseudonyms Andre Algery and Raphael Anduze-Dufy, to bulletins and to *French Review* and *Les Echos du Monde*.

WORK IN PROGRESS: A novel, *Hier. . .Aujourd'hui. . . Demain et l'Eternite* (title means "Yesterday. . . Today. . .Tomorrow and Eternity"); *Les Fruits Verts* (title means "The Green Fruits"), a collection of short stories; *Peter Stephen Duponceau, Man of Knowledge*.

SIDELIGHTS: Coulet du Gard has traveled throughout Europe, Africa, the Middle East, and the United States, and is fluent in French, Spanish, and English.

* * *

COUNTS, George S(ylvester) 1889-1974

December 9, 1889—November 10, 1974; American educator and author. Obituaries: *New York Times*, November 11, 1974; *Washington Post*, November 13, 1974; *AB Bookman's Weekly*, December 2, 1974; *Current Biography*, January, 1975. (*CA*-5/6).

* * *

COURSEN, Herbert R(andolph), Jr. 1932-

PERSONAL: Born March 28, 1932, in Newark, N.J.; son of Herbert R. (in life insurance) and Mildred (Huntoon) Coursen; married Susan Kirkconnell (a teacher), February 15, 1957 (divorced); children: Elizabeth, Susan Leigh, Virginia. *Education:* Amherst College, B.A., 1954; Wesleyan University, M.A., 1962; University of Connecticut, Ph.D., 1965. *Politics:* Liberal. *Religion:* Episcopalian. *Home:* 16 Thompson St., Brunswick, Me. 04011. *Agent:* Lester Lewis Associates, Inc., 15 East 48th St., New York, N.Y. 10017. *Office:* Department of English, Bowdoin College, Brunswick, Me. 04011.

CAREER: Choate School, Wallingford, Conn., English teacher, 1958-62; Bowdoin College, Brunswick, Me., instructor, 1964-65, assistant professor, 1965-69, associate professor, 1969-74, professor of creative writing and Shakespeare, 1974—. *Military service:* U.S. Air Force, fighter pilot, 1954-58; became captain. *Awards, honors:* Ford Foundation fellowship, 1969-71; Folger Library fellowship, 1970-71.

WRITINGS: "The Rarer Action": Hamlet and Revenge, University of Wisconsin Press, 1969; *As Up They Grew: The Autobiographical Essay*, Scott, Foresman, 1970; *Storm in April* (poems), Arco Multi-Media, 1973; *Survivor* (poems), Ktaadn Poetry Press, 1974; *Lookout Point* (poems), Samisdat, 1974; *Christian Ritual and the World of Shakespeare's Tragedies*, Bucknell University Press, in press; *Shaping the Self: Style and Technique in the Narrative*, Harper, in press.

WORK IN PROGRESS: The Lost One, poems; *Shakespearean Films*, criticism.

SIDELIGHTS: Coursen writes: "I can only say that if I am a poet at all it is because I moved to Maine a decade ago, and that Maine bit the poetry in me. The combination of living in Maine, teaching Shakespeare, and writing poetry seems to have been what I was destined and fortunate to find."

* * *

COVATTA, Anthony Gallo 1944-

PERSONAL: Born July 11, 1944, in Louisville, Ky.; son of Anthony and Rosemary (Danenburg) Covatta; children: Christopher. *Education:* Bellarmine College, Louisville, Ky., B.A., 1966; Columbia University, M.A. (high honors), 1967, Ph.D., 1971. *Home:* 38 Circular St., Saratoga Springs, N.Y. 12866. *Office:* Department of English, Skidmore College, Saratoga Springs, N.Y. 12866.

CAREER: Skidmore College, Saratoga Springs, N.Y., instructor, 1970-71, assistant professor of English, 1971—. *Member:* Renaissance Society of America, Modern Language Association of America, Shakespeare Association of America, Northeastern Modern Language Association. *Awards, honors:* Woodrow Wilson fellow, 1966-67; Folger Library fellow, 1973 (summer).

WRITINGS: Thomas Middleton's City Comedies, Bucknell University Press, 1973; *The Renaissance: A Handbook for Study, Writing, and Research*, St. Martin's, in press. Contributor to *Notes and Queries, Renaissance Quarterly, New Republic*, and *Shakespeare Quarterly*.

* * *

COWAN, Henry J(acob) 1919-

PERSONAL: Born August 21, 1919, in Glogow, Poland, son of Arthur (a physician) and Erna (Salisch) Cowan; married Renate Proskauer; children: Judith Anne, Esther Katherine. *Education:* University of Manchester, B.Sc. (first class honors), 1939, M.Sc., 1940; University of Sheffield, Ph.D., 1952, D.Eng., 1963. *Home:* 93 Kings Rd., Vaucluse, New South Wales 2030, Australia. *Office:* Department of Architectural Science, University of Sydney, Sydney, New South Wales 2006, Australia.

CAREER: Employed in building industry in England, 1945-46; assistant lecturer at University of Wales, University College, Cardiff, 1946-48, and lecturer at University of Sheffield, Sheffield, England, 1948-53; University of Sydney, Sydney, Australia, professor of architectural science, 1953—, head of department, 1953—, dean of Faculty of Architecture, 1966-67. Visiting professor at Cornell University, 1962; president of Building Science Forum of Australia, 1970-71. *Military service:* British Army, Royal Engineers, 1941-45.

MEMBER: International Association for Bridge and Structural Engineering (chairman of Australian group), Institution of Engineers of Australia (fellow), Royal Society of Arts (fellow), Institution of Structural Engineers (fellow), American Society of Civil Engineers (fellow). *Awards, honors:* Chapman Medal from Institution of Engineers of Australia, 1956.

WRITINGS: Theory of Prestressed Concrete Design, Macmillan (London), 1956; *Design of Reinforced Concrete*, Angus & Robertson, 1963, 3rd edition, Sydney University Press, 1975; *Concrete in Torsion*, Arnold, 1965; *An Historical Outline of Architectural Science*, Elsevier (Amsterdam), 1966; *Design of Prestressed Concrete*, Angus & Robertson, 1966; *Models in Architecture*, Elsevier (London), 1968; *Architectural Structures*, American Elsevier, 1971, 2nd edition, 1975; *Dictionary of Architectural Science*, Halsted Press, 1973; *Design of Building Frames*, Applied Science Publishers, 1975; *History of Building Science*, Applied Science Publishers, in press; *Building Science Laboratory Manual*, Applied Science Publishers, in press.

Contributor of about two hundred articles and a thousand reviews to magazines. Editor of *Architectural Science Review*, 1958—, and *Vestes: Magazine of Federation of Australian University Staff Associations*, 1966-75.

SIDELIGHTS: Cowan writes: "My most successful books have been concerned with interpreting architecture to the engineers, and engineering to the architects, and both to the general public."

* * *

COWAN, Richard O(lsen) 1934-

PERSONAL: Born January 24, 1934, in Los Angeles, Calif.; son of Lee R. (a credit representative) and Edith (an accountant; maiden name, Olsen) Cowan; married Dawn Houghton, August 14, 1958; children: Sandra, Linda, Reed, Lee, Patricia. *Education:* Occidental College, B.A., 1958; Stanford University, M.A., 1959, Ph.D., 1961. *Religion:* Church of Jesus Christ of Latter-day Saints (Mormon). *Office:* Department of Church History and Doctrine, Brigham Young University, 138 JSB, Provo, Utah 84602.

CAREER: Brigham Young University, Provo, Utah, assistant professor, 1961-65, associate professor, 1965-71, professor of church history and doctrine, 1971—. *Member:* Utah State Historical Society, Mormon History Association, Phi Beta Kappa. *Awards, honors:* Danforth Foundation fellowship, 1958-61; White House recognition, 1959, for recordings for the blind.

WRITINGS: (With James B. Allen) *Mormonism in the Twentieth Century*, Brigham Young University Press, 1964, revised edition, 1967; *The Doctrine and Covenants: Our Modern Scripture*, Brigham Young University Press, 1966, revised edition, 1969; *Temple Building gancient and Modern*, Brigham Young University Press, 1971; (with Wilson K. Anderson) *The Living Church*, Brigham Young University Press, 1974.

WORK IN PROGRESS: A history of the Church of Jesus Christ of Latter-day Saints, 1930-1950.

SIDELIGHTS: Cowan is legally blind.

* * *

COWDEN, Joanna Dunlap 1933-

PERSONAL: Born February 9, 1933, in Woburn, Mass.; daughter of Chesley M. and Helen (Cummings) Dunlap; married George Robert Cowden, January 15, 1955 (divorced, 1972); children: Jean, Sandra, Rebecca, Jennifer. *Education:* Radcliffe College, A.B., 1955; Trinity College, Hartford, Conn., M.A., 1965; University of Connecticut, Ph.D., 1974. *Politics:* Democratic. *Home:* 1158 Lawton Dr., Chico, Calif. 95926. *Office:* Department of History, California State University, Chico, Calif. 95926.

CAREER: California State University, Chico, assistant professor of American history, 1973—. *Member:* American Historical Association, Organization of American Historians, Association for the Study of Connecticut History.

WRITINGS: (Editor with Richard O. Curry) *Slavery in America: Theodore Weld's American Slavery as It Is*, F. E. Peacock, 1972.

WORK IN PROGRESS: Dissertation, "Politics in Connecticut During the Civil War and Reconstruction Era."

* * *

COWELL, (Frank) Richard 1897-

PERSONAL: Born November 16, 1897, in London, England; son of William Frank (a manager) and Emma (Pearce) Cowell; married Lilian Margaret Palin (an artist), September 1, 1937 (died, 1970); children: John Richard, Robert Adrian. *Education:* University of London, King's College, B.A., 1921, London School of Economics and Political Science, B.Sc., 1927, Ph.D., 1938. *Politics:* "Aristotelian." *Address:* c/o Athenaeum Club, London SW1Y 5ER, England.

CAREER: H.M. Government, London, England, civil servant with Admiralty, 1917-19, H.M. Stationery Office, 1921-39, Foreign Office, 1939-46, United Kingdom National Commission, 1946-58. *Military service:* British Army, 1916. *Member:* Society for the Promotion of Roman Studies (member of council, 1950), British Society for Aesthetics, Mind Association, Classical Association, Garden History Society, Royal Horticultural Society, Private Libraries Association, Athenaeum Club. *Awards, honors:* Named Companion of the Most Noble Order of St. Michael and St. George, 1952; Rockefeller Foundation research fellowship in the social sciences, 1929-31.

WRITINGS: Cicero and the Roman Empire, Pitman, 1948, 6th edition, Penguin, 1972; *History, Civilization, and Culture,* A. & C. Black, 1952; *Culture in Public and Private Life,* Thames & Hudson, 1959; *Everyday Life in Ancient Rome,* Putnam, 1961, 7th edition, 1973; *Revolutions of Ancient Rome,* Thames & Hudson, 1962; *Dominance of Rome,* Paul Hamlyn, 1969; *Values in Human Society,* Porter Sargent, 1970; *The Athenaeum in Club and Social Life of London: 1824-1974,* Heinemann, in press.

Contributor: *Les Ecrivains Celebres* (title means "Renowned Writers"), Mazerod, 1951; *Weltgeschichte des Abenlandischen Kultur,* Westermann Verlag, 1963; Michael Grant, editor, *The Birth of Western Civilization,* Thames &

Hudson, 1965; Philip J. Allen, editor, *Pitirim A. Sorokin in Review,* Duke University Press, 1965; Timothy Raison, editor, *Founding Fathers of Social Science,* Penguin, 1969; Harold Osborne, editor, *Oxford Companion to Art,* Oxford University Press, 1970.

Contributor to *Collier's Encyclopedia.* Contributor of articles and reviews to magazines, including *Economist, Journal of Public Administration, Times Literary Supplement, History Today,* and *British Journal of Aesthetics.*

WORK IN PROGRESS: Gardens and Civilizations, for David & Charles; *Leibniz,* for Rowohlt Verlag.

* * *

COX, Albert W(esley) 1921-

PERSONAL: Born January 16, 1921, in Peoria, Ill.; son of John Wesley (a machinist) and Berenice (a secretary; maiden name, Rigg) Cox; married Lillian Burnley, August 8, 1942; children: Anne (Mrs. Robert B. Stenhouse), Barbara (Mrs. Timothy H. Bahti). *Education:* U.S. Naval Academy, B.S., 1942; graduate study at George Washington University, 1957-59, and at Catholic University of America, 1969. *Politics:* Republican (independent). *Religion:* Protestant. *Home:* 167 Taylor Rd., Portsmouth, R.I. 02871. *Address:* Raytheon Co., P.O. Box 360, Portsmouth, R.I. 02871.

CAREER: U.S. Navy, career officer, 1942-69, retiring as captain; served as fire control officer, navigator, and executive officer aboard ships in the Pacific theatre, 1942-48, assistant professor of naval science at Duke University, 1948-50, aide to the Joint U.S. Military Aid Group to Greece, 1950-53, commanding officer of USS F. M. Robinson, 1954-56, staff officer with Office of the Joint Chiefs of Staff, 1956-59, commanding officer of USS Willis A. Lee, 1960-62, commander of Destroyer Division 202, 1962-63, commanding officer of Fleet Training Center, Newport R.I., 1963-66, test director and later technical director with Antisubmarine Warfare Systems Project, 1966-69; Raytheon Co., Portsmouth, R.I., engineer, 1969—. Consultant to U.S. Naval War College in antisubmarine warfare matters, 1973—. *Member:* U.S. Naval Institute, American Defense Preparedness Association, National Security Industrial Association, Rotary Club, Ida Lewis Yacht Club. *Awards, honors:* Citation from Rhode Island legislature, 1966, for assistance provided for training of southern New England fire fighting companies; numerous commendations for naval service, including Philippine Presidential Unit Citation, and certificate of recognition, 1972, for contributions to Antisubmarine Warfare Systems Project; authors awards from Raytheon Co., 1973, 1974

WRITINGS: Sonar and Underwater Sound, Heath, 1974, revised edition, in press.

WORK IN PROGRESS: A science-fiction book dealing with undersea technology, completion expected in 1977.

AVOCATIONAL INTERESTS: Travel, sailing, organic gardening, woodworking, stamp collecting, reading.

* * *

COX, Thomas R(ichard) 1933-

PERSONAL: Born January 16, 1933, in Portland, Ore.; son of James Louis and Helen Melissa (a bookkeeper; maiden name, Case) Cox; married Mary Margaret MacGillivray (a teacher), November 24, 1954; children: Dianne Lynne, James Kimberly, Cynthia Ann, Michael William. *Education:* Attended Whitman College, 1951-52; Oregon State College, B.S., 1955; University of Oregon, M.S., 1959; University of Hawaii, Ph.D., 1969. *Politics:* Liberal Republican. *Religion:* Presbyterian. *Home:* 8615 Hudson Dr., San Diego, Calif. 92119. *Office:* Department of History, San Diego State University, San Diego, Calif. 92115.

CAREER: High school teacher of biology and social studies in Sisters, Ore., 1956-59, in Tulelake, Calif., 1959-63; San Diego State University, San Diego, Calif., assistant professor, 1967-70, associate professor, 1970-74, professor of history, 1974—. City councilman in Sisters, Ore., 1958-59. *Member:* Organization of American Historians, Forest History Society, Agricultural History Society, American Association of University Professors, United Professors of California.

WRITINGS: (Contributor) J. A. Carroll, editor, *Reflections of Western Historians*, University of Arizona Press, 1969; *Mills and Markets: A History of the Pacific Coast Lumber Industry to 1900*, University of Washington Press, 1974. Contributor to *Oregon Historical Quarterly, Pacific Historical Review, Pacific Northwest Quarterly*, and *Forest History*. Editor of *Tropical Breeze*, 1973—; member of board of editors of *Journal of Forest History*, 1972—.

WORK IN PROGRESS: The History of the Conservation Movement, completion expected in 1976; *The World's Great Historians: Their Work and Their Legacy*, 1977; *The Far West as Colony; The Intellectual Milieu at the Beginning of the Twentieth Century.*

AVOCATIONAL INTERESTS: Aquarist.

* * *

COZE, Paul 1903(?)-1974

1903(?)—December 2, 1974; French-born American artist and writer. Obituaries: *New York Times*, December 4, 1974.

* * *

CRACRAFT, James (Edward) 1939-

PERSONAL: Born February 16, 1939, in Minneapolis, Minn.; son of John J. and M. Carol (Welch) Cracraft; married Caroline Pinder, July 9, 1966; children: Elizabeth A. W. *Education:* Georgetown University, B.S.A., 1961, M.A., 1963; Oxford University, D.Phil., 1968. *Home:* 606 West Belden Ave., Chicago, Ill. 60614. *Office:* Department of History, University of Illinois, Chicago, Ill. 60680.

CAREER: University of Illinois, Chicago, assistant professor, 1969-70, associate professor of history, 1970—. *Awards, honors:* Outstanding academic book of the year from *Choice*, 1971, for *The Church Reform of Peter the Great.*

WRITINGS: The Church Reform of Peter the Great, Stanford University Press, 1971; (contributor) J. G. Garrard, editor, *The Eighteenth Century in Russia*, Clarendon Press, 1973. Contributor of articles and reviews to *English Historical Review, Russian Review, Slavic Review, Historian, Canadian-American Slavic Studies, Slavonic and East European Review, Oxford Slavonic Papers*, and *Cahiers du monde russe et sovietique.*

WORK IN PROGRESS: A Portrait of Petrine Russia, completion expected in 1976.

* * *

CRACROFT, Richard Holton 1936-

PERSONAL: Born June 28, 1936, in Salt Lake City, Utah;

son of Ralph (a businessman) and Grace (White) Cracroft; married Janice Marie Alger, September 17, 1959; children: Richard Alger, Jeffrey Ralph, Jennifer. *Education:* University of Utah, B.A., 1961, M.A., 1963; University of Wisconsin, Ph.D., 1969. *Politics:* Liberal Republican. *Religion:* Church of Jesus Christ of Latter-day Saints (Mormons). *Home:* 814 East Center St., Provo, Utah 84601. *Office:* Department of English, Brigham Young University, Provo, Utah 84602.

CAREER: Missionary of the Church of Jesus Christ of Latter-day Saints in Switzerland and Austria, 1956-59; Business Enterprises for the Blind, director, 1960-61; Brigham Young University, Provo, Utah, 1963—, became associate professor of English, 1969—, chairman of department. *Military service:* Utah National Guard, eight years. *Member:* Mormon History Association, Western Literature Association, Rocky Mountain Modern Language Association, Phi Kappa Phi.

WRITINGS: A Believing People: Literature of the Latter-day Saints, Brigham Young University Press, 1974. Contributor of more than thirty-five articles and reviews to literature journals, including *New Era, American Quarterly Dialogue, Brigham Young University Studies, Mark Twain Journal, Western American Literature, Utah Historical Quarterly*, and *Utah Libraries*.

WORK IN PROGRESS: A history of Mormon literature; research on Mark Twain; research on Washington Irving and the West; studying the Mormon image in nineteenth-century literature.

* * *

CRADDOCK, Patricia (Bland) 1938-

PERSONAL: Born October 28, 1938, in New Orleans, La.; daughter of French Hood, Jr. (a physician) and Jane (a writer; maiden name, Bland) Craddock. *Education:* Stephens College, A.A., 1957; Indiana University, B.A. (summa cum laude), 1959; Stanford University, M.A., 1960; Yale University, Ph.D., 1964. *Politics:* Democrat. *Religion:* Roman Catholic. *Home:* 106 Hillside Dr., Sylacauga, Ala. 35150. *Office:* Department of English, Boston University, 236 Bay State Rd., Boston, Mass. 02215.

CAREER: Alabama College (now University of Montevallo), Montevallo, instructor in English, 1960-61; Connecticut College, New London, instructor in English, 1963-66; Goucher College, Baltimore, Md., assistant professor of English, 1966-72; Boston University, Boston, Mass., associate professor of English, 1972—. *Member:* Modern Language Association of America, English Institute, American Association of University Professors, Phi Beta Kappa. *Awards, honors:* Woodrow Wilson fellowship, 1959-60; Goucher College and Ford Foundation humanities faculty development grant, summer, 1969; Guggenheim fellowship, 1971-72.

WRITINGS: The English Essays of Edward Gibbon, Clarendon Press (of Oxford University), 1973. Contributor of articles and reviews to language and literature journals, including *Studies in Bibliography, Style, Modern Philology*, and *Studies in Burke and His Time*.

WORK IN PROGRESS: Edward Gibbon's First Book, completion expected in 1976; a biography of Edward Gibbon, 1980.

* * *

CRAGHAN, John Francis 1936-

PERSONAL: Born July 21, 1936, in Brooklyn, N.Y.; son of John Francis (an office worker) and Margaret (Shannon) Craghan. *Education:* Mount St. Alphonsus Seminary, A.B., 1959, M.R.E., 1963; University of Munich, Th.D., 1965; Pontifical Biblical Institute, S.S.L., 1967; Columbia University, M.A., 1973. *Home and office address:* Mount St. Alphonsus Seminary, Esopus, N.Y. 12429.

CAREER: Ordained Roman Catholic priest of Redemptorists Order (C.SS.R.), 1962; Mount St. Alphonsus Seminary, Esopus, N.Y., professor of Old Testament, 1968—. *Member:* Catholic Biblical Association, Mariological Society of America. *Awards, honors:* Cardinal Wright Award, 1971.

WRITINGS: Mary: The Virginal Wife and the Married Virgin, privately printed, 1967; *This Is the Word of the Lord*, Liguori Publications, 1972. Contributor to *Catholic Biblical Quarterly, American Ecclesiastical Review, Marian Studies*, and *Homiletic and Pastoral Review*. Associate editor of *Biblical Theology Bulletin*, 1971—.

* * *

CRAIG, Richard B(lythe) 1935-

PERSONAL: Born January 28, 1935, in Blytheville, Ark.; son of Joel H. (a farmer) and Zelma (a teacher; maiden name, Goad) Craig; married Christel Manderbach, October 24, 1960 (divorced); children: Stefan. *Education:* University of Missouri, B.A., 1958, M.A., 1963, Ph.D., 1969. *Politics:* Independent. *Office:* Department of Political Science, Kent State University, Kent, Ohio 44242.

CAREER: Public school teacher in Salisbury, Mo., 1963-65; University of Missouri, Columbia, instructor in political science, 1965-69; Kent State University, Kent, Ohio, assistant professor, 1969-72, associate professor of political science, 1972—, director of quarter-in-Mexico program, 1973—. *Military service:* U.S. Army, 1958-60. *Member:* American Political Science Association, Latin American Studies Association. *Awards, honors:* Quarter research fellow of Kent State University for visit to American-Mexican border, summer, 1971, spring, 1975.

WRITINGS: The Bracero Program: Interest Groups and Foreign Policy, University of Texas Press, 1972. Contributor to *Latin American Research Review*.

WORK IN PROGRESS: Operation Intercept: The International Politics of Narcotics; Mexico's Anti-Drug Campaign.

* * *

CRANDELL, Richard F. 1901-1974

October 20, 1901—August 30, 1974; American journalist and author. Obituaries: *New York Times*, September 1, 1974.

* * *

CRANSTON, Mechthild (Michele Delorme)

PERSONAL: Born in Berlin, Germany; daughter of Gerhard and Charlotte (Fuerst) Grieser; married Philip Edward Cranston (a professor), June 10, 1962. *Education:* Attended Sorbonne, University of Paris, 1962-64; University of California, Berkeley, Ph.D., 1966. *Religion:* Protestant. *Home:* 510 North Griffing Blvd., Asheville, N.C. 28804. *Office:* Department of Foreign Languages, University of North Carolina, Asheville, N.C. 28801.

CAREER: University of San Francisco, San Francisco, Calif., assistant professor of French, 1966-68; University of

North Carolina, Asheville, associate professor of French and German, 1971—, head of department of foreign languages, 1971-72. Visiting professor at University of Marburg, 1970. *Member:* Modern Language Association of America, American Association of Teachers of French, Societe des Amis de Guillaume Apollinaire, Les Amis de Rimbaud, Societe de Poesie Contemporaine, Societe d'Etudes du Vingtieme Siecle, South Atlantic Modern Language Association, California National Scholarship Federation, Phi Beta Kappa, Pi Delta Phi. *Awards, honors:* Woodrow Wilson fellowship, 1958; grants from French and Belgian Governments 1962, 1963, 1967; American Council of Learned Societies fellow, 1973-74.

WRITINGS: Enfance, mon amour: La Reverie vers l'enfance dans l'oeuvre de Guillaume Apollinaire, Saint-John Perse et Rene Char (title means "Childhood, My Love: The Reverie of Childhood in the Poetry of Guillaume Apollinaire, Saint-John Perse, and Rene Char"), Debresse, 1970; (under pseudonym Michele Delorme) *Mains Serrees* (title means "Hands Held"; poems), Debresse, 1971. Contributor to professional journals.

WORK IN PROGRESS: A study of the poetry of Rene Char.

SIDELIGHTS: Dr. Cranston is competent in French, German, Italian, and Spanish. *Avocational interests:* Music, travel.

* * *

CRAPANZANO, Vincent (Bernard) 1939-

PERSONAL: Born April 15, 1939, in Glen Ridge, N.J.; son of Domenico (a psychiatrist) and Florence (Matz) Crapanzano; married Jane Kramer (a staff writer for *New Yorker*), April 30, 1967; children: Aleksandra Dominique. *Education:* Harvard University, A.B., 1960; Columbia University, Ph.D., 1970. *Politics:* "Disgusted concern or concerned indifference." *Home:* 333 Central Park W., New York, N.Y. 10025. *Office:* Queens College of City University of New York, Flushing, N.Y. 11367.

CAREER: Princeton University, Princeton, N.J., assistant professor of anthropology, 1970-74; Queens College of the City University of New York, Flushing, N.Y., associate professor of comparative literature, 1974—. Member of faculty of New Jersey State Residency Training Program in Psychiatry, 1972. *Military service:* U.S. Army, 1961-64. *Member:* American Anthropological Association (fellow), Royal Anthropological Institute (fellow). *Awards, honors:* Postdoctoral research grant to France, from Princeton University, 1971.

WRITINGS: The Fifth World of Forster Bennett, Viking, 1972; (contributor) Nikki R. Keddie, editor, *Saints, Scholars, and Sufis: Muslim Religious Institutions in the Middle East since 1500*, University of California Press, 1972; *The Hamadsha: A Study in Moroccan Ethnopsychiatry*, University of California Press, 1973. Contributor to *Partisan Review, Harper's, Psychiatry, New Yorker, International Journal of Middle Eastern Studies, Political Science Quarterly*, and *American Anthropologist*, and to newspapers, including the *New York Times Magazine* and *Village Voice*. Editor of *Harvard Advocate*, 1958-60.

WORK IN PROGRESS: Tuhami, a biography of a demon-afflicted Moroccan.

SIDELIGHTS: Crapanzano writes: "I am concerned with two major fields: anthropological approaches to literature and psychiatric anthropology. I am specifically interested in the articulation of personal history. I fell into anthropology and academia, and I have rebelled against the denigration of the human in both my field and my institutional affiliations."

* * *

CRAPPS, Robert W. 1925-

PERSONAL: Born November 30, 1925, in North Carolina; married Dovie Wright, June 6, 1949; children: Robert Stephen, John Maury, Philip Andrew. *Education:* Gardner-Webb College, A.A., 1944; Wake Forest University, A.B., 1946; Southern Baptist Theological Seminary, B.D., 1951, Th.D., 1955. *Home address:* Route 3, Zelma Dr., Greenville, S.C. 29609. *Office:* Department of Religion, Furman University, Greenville, S.C. 29613.

CAREER: Kentucky State Hospital, Danville, chaplain, 1951-55; pastor of Baptist church in Hickory, N.C., 1955-57; Furman University, Greenville, S.C., professor of religion, 1957—. Consultant to Commonwealth of Kentucky, 1954-55. *Member:* American Academy of Religion, Association of Baptist Professors of Religion, Association of Mental Hospital Chaplains, Phi Beta Kappa (president of Piedmont area branch).

WRITINGS: (With H. S. Flanders and D. A. Smith) *People of the Covenant*, Ronald, 1963, revised edition, 1973; (with Smith and E. V. McKnight) *Introduction to the New Testament*, Ronald, 1969.

WORK IN PROGRESS: Popular Folk Religion of South Carolina-Appalachia.

SIDELIGHTS: Crapps participated in excavations at Biblical Ai and Khirbet Khudryeh, 1966. He has traveled in Europe, Turkey, and Greece.

* * *

CRAWFORD, John W(illiam) 1936-

PERSONAL: Born September 2, 1936, in Ashdown, Ark.; son of John C. and Allie B. (Phillips) Crawford; married Kathryn Bizzell, June 17, 1962; children: Jeffry Wayne, Sonja Rene. *Education:* Ouachita Baptist University, B.S.E. (with honor), 1959; Drake University, M.S.E., 1962; Oklahoma State University, Ed.D. (with honor), 1968. *Politics:* Independent. *Religion:* Baptist. *Home:* 1813 Walnut, Arkadelphia, Ark. 71923. *Office:* Henderson State College, Arkadelphia, Ark. 71923.

CAREER: English teacher in public schools in Iowa, 1959-62; Clinton Community College, Clinton, Iowa, instructor in English, 1962-66; Henderson State College, Arkadelphia, Ark., assistant professor, 1967-68, associate professor, 1968-73, professor of English, 1973—.

MEMBER: National Education Association, College English Association, South Central Modern Language Association, South Central College English Association, Ozark Writers and Artists Guild, Poets' Roundtable of Arkansas, Arkansas Philological Association, Arkansas Teachers of College English, Phi Delta Kappa, Kappa Delta Pi. *Awards, honors:* Poetry awards from *Mentor* (magazine) summer contests, 1964, 1965, 1966; Iowa Poetry Association contest, 1965, 1966; Southwest Literary Festival, 1969; Kentucky Poetry Society, 1970; South and West Literary Arts Festival, 1970; Arkansas Writers Conference, 1971, 1972, 1973, 1974; Arkansas Poetry Day, 1971, 1972, 1973, 1974; Mississippi Poetry Society, 1971; New Mexico Poetry Society, 1972.

WRITINGS: Shakespeare's Comedies: A Guide, privately printed, 1968; *Shakespeare's Tragedies: A Guide*, privately printed, 1968; *What's Up Doc?: Or How to Succeed in College by Really Trying*, Kendall-Hunt, 1974.

Work is anthologized in *American Poetry*, edited by Jeanne Holleyfield, 1965; *Lyrical Iowa*, edited by Ruth Peterson, 1965, 2nd edition, 1966; *Counterpoint*, edited by H. M. Rosenberg, 1966; *America Sings*, edited by Dennis Hartmann, 1967; *Poems by Arkansas Poets' Roundtable*, edited by Arkansas Poets' Roundtable, 1969; *Contemporary Poets of Arkansas*, edited by Sue Abbot Boyd, 1969, 2nd edition, 1971; *American Poets*, edited by Stella Croft Tremble, 1969.

Contributor of poems and articles to magazines, including *Bardic Echoes, Encore, Modern Images, Mississippi Poetry Journal, Victorian Poetry, Research Studies, Seventeenth Century News, CEA Critic, The Roundtable, The Clearing House, University of Dayton Review, Dekalb Literary Arts Journal, Missouri English Bulletin, Statement*, and *Montclair Journal of Social Sciences and Humanities*.

WORK IN PROGRESS: Shakespeare's Spirit: The Age of Elizabeth, a compilation of selections from the plays that illustrate Elizabethan society, with editorial comment; research on comparative literature, motifs, themes; a volume of verse titled *Blow Out Your Candles*; a play on a bicentennial theme titled *A Cause of Honor*, about John Andre's dilemma; a collection of private essays on literature titled *New Perspectives in Literature*.

* * *

CRISPIN, John 1936-

PERSONAL: Born May 3, 1936, in Tienen, Belgium; naturalized U.S. citizen in 1959; son of Albert and Marie Aline (Piron) Crispin; married Ruth Katz (a children's librarian and college teacher of Spanish), June 9, 1966; children: Melissa, Leah. *Education:* University of St. Thomas, B.A., 1960; University of Wisconsin, M.A., 1962, Ph.D., 1967. *Home:* 3305 Orleans Dr., Nashville, Tenn. 37212. *Office:* Department of Spanish, Vanderbilt University, Nashville, Tenn. 37235.

CAREER: Vanderbilt University, Nashville, Tenn., instructor, 1965-67, assistant professor, 1967-70, associate professor of Spanish, 1970—. *Member:* American Association of Teachers of Spanish and Portuguese, Modern Language Association of America, South Atlantic Modern Language Association.

WRITINGS: (With wife, Ruth K. Crispin) *Progress in Spanish: Grammar and Composition for the Second Year*, Scott, Foresman, 1972; (editor with Ramon Buckley) *Los vanguardistas espanoles: estudio y antologia* (title means "Spanish Avant-Garde Writers, 1925-1935"), Alianza, 1973; *Pedro Salinas*, Twayne, 1974. Contributor of articles and reviews to *Books Abroad, Archivum, Insula*, and *Hispania*.

WORK IN PROGRESS: Translating M. de Unamuno's *Niebla* (title means "Mist"); editing and translating *Spanish Contemporary Poetry;* research on Spanish literature of the 1920-1936 era, especially poetry.

AVOCATIONAL INTERESTS: Classical music, art history, philosophy, travel, camping, hiking.

* * *

CRIST, Lyle M(artin) 1924-

PERSONAL: Born May 1, 1924, in Alliance, Ohio; son of Dillon and Gertrude (Martin) Crist; married Marilyn Turner, June 15, 1946; children: Rachel Lee, Jennifer Lynn. *Education:* Purdue University, B.S., 1946; Indiana University, M.S., 1947. *Religion:* Christian Science. *Home:* 2550 Belleflower, Alliance, Ohio 44601. *Office:* Department of English, Mount Union College, Alliance, Ohio 44601.

CAREER: Iowa State College, Ames, instructor in English and journalism, 1947-48; high school teacher of English and journalism in the public schools of Alliance, Ohio, 1948-53; Mount Union College, Alliance, Ohio, assistant professor, 1953-59, associate professor, 1960-68, professor of English and journalism, 1969—. Member of Alliance City Board of Education, 1966-73, president, 1970, 1971. *Member:* International Platform Association, National Council of Teachers of English, Sigma Delta Chi, Rotary Club.

WRITINGS: Man Expressed: The Realm of Writing, Glencoe Press, 1971; *Through the Rain and Rainbow: The Remarkable Life of Richard Kinney*, Abingdon, 1974.

* * *

CRITCHFIELD, Howard J(ohn) 1920-

PERSONAL: Born September 24, 1920, near Vernon, Colo.; son of Owen I. (a farmer) and Mabel Luella (a teacher; maiden name, McCutchan) Critchfield; married Rose Doreen Caygill, February 17, 1950 (died July 27, 1969); children: David Owen, Anne Louise. *Education:* Attended Lewiston State Normal School, 1938-40, and University of North Carolina, 1943; University of Washington, B.A., 1946, M.A., 1947, Ph.D., 1952. *Home:* 156 Forest Lane, Bellingham, Wash. 98225. *Office:* Department of Geography, Western Washington State College, Bellingham, Wash. 98225.

CAREER: Elementary teacher in the public schools of Boundary County, Idaho, 1940-42; Washington State University, Pullman, instructor in geography, 1947-48; Western Washington State College, Bellingham, assistant professor, 1951-54, associate professor, 1954-57, professor of geography, 1957—, head of department, 1960-74. Visiting lecturer at University of Canterbury, 1948-50, 1959, University of Virginia, summer, 1953, and University of Colorado, summer, 1956; visiting professor at University of Waikato, 1966, and University of Stellenbosch, 1972; research professor at University of Canterbury, 1971. Bellingham (Wash.) City Planning Commission, member, 1957-62, chairman, 1961-62; member of Interdisciplinary Advisory Committee, Washington State Department of Ecology, 1972-74. *Military service:* U.S. Army Air Forces, Weather Service, 1942-46.

MEMBER: American Association for the Advancement of Science (life member), American Geographical Society (life fellow), American Meteorological Society, Association of American Geographers (life member), Canadian Association of Geographers (life member), National Council for Geographic Education (life member), New Zealand Geographic Society, Sigma Xi. *Awards, honors:* Carnegie grant, 1948; Fulbright award, 1950; honorary research associate of University College, London, 1964.

WRITINGS: General Climatology, Prentice-Hall, 1960, 3rd edition, 1974; (contributor) John W. Morris, editor, *Methods of Geographic Instruction*, Blaisdell, 1968. Contributor to *Economic Geography, Economic Botany, New Zealand Geographer, Geographical Review of India*, and *Ochanomizu University Studies in Arts and Culture*. Editorial consultant, Field Enterprises Education Corp., 1956-64, and Grolier Inc., 1958-72.

WORK IN PROGRESS: Research on climatic maritimity and water budgets of the Southern Hemisphere.

* * *

CROMWELL, Richard Sidney 1925-

PERSONAL: Born June 15, 1925, in Los Angeles, Calif.; son of Edmund C. and Mildred Clara Cromwell; married Shirley Foster Dunn, September 11, 1962; children: Adelaide Courtney. *Education:* University of Southern California, B.A., 1949; Stanford University, M.A., 1955, Ph.D., 1961. *Religion:* Episcopalian. *Home:* 5350 Selton Ave., Jacksonville, Fla. 32211. *Office:* Department of History, Jacksonville University, Jacksonville, Fla. 32211.

CAREER: University of North Carolina, Chapel Hill, instructor in history, 1958-61; Randolph-Macon College, Ashland, Va., 1961-67, began as assistant professor, became professor of history; Jacksonville University, Jacksonville, Fla., professor of history, 1967—. *Military service:* U.S. Army, Medical Corps, 1950-52. *Member:* American Historical Association, American Association of University Professors, Southern Historical Association, Florida College Teachers of History. *Awards, honors:* Fulbright fellowship for study in Germany, 1956-58; fellow of Cooperative Program in the Humanities at Duke University and University of North Carolina, 1966-67; fellow in Asian studies at Florida State University, 1965.

WRITINGS: David Friedrich Strauss and His Place in Modern Thought, Burdick, 1974. Contributor *Western Political Quarterly* and *East European Quarterly*.

WORK IN PROGRESS: A History of the French Army, 1789-1793; *The Protestant Church in Germany: 1933-1945.*

* * *

CROSBY, Donald A(llen) 1932-

PERSONAL: Born April 7, 1932, in Mansfield, Ohio; son of Edmund Bevington (an accountant) and Mary Lou (Bogan) Crosby; married Charlotte Mae Robinson (a visiting nurse), September 15, 1956; children: Colleen Judith, Kathleen Bridgett. *Education:* Davidson College, A.B., 1953; Princeton Theological Seminary, B.D., 1956, Th.M., 1959; Columbia University, Ph.D., 1963. *Home:* 1108 East Lake Pl., Fort Collins, Colo. 80521. *Office:* Department of Philosophy, Colorado State University, Fort Collins, Colo. 80521.

CAREER: Ordained minister of Presbyterian Church, 1956; minister in Christiana, Del., 1956-59, and Norwalk, Conn., 1959-61; left ministry, 1967. Centre College of Kentucky, Danville, assistant professor of philosophy and religion, 1962-65; Colorado State University, Fort Collins, assistant professor, 1965-69, associate professor, 1969-73, professor of philosophy, 1973—. *Member:* American Philosophical Association, American Academy of Religion, American Federation of Teachers.

WRITINGS: Horace Bushnell's Theory of Language, Mouton & Co., 1974. Contributor to *Christian Scholar, Process Studies,* and *Journal of the American Academy of Religion.*

WORK IN PROGRESS: Interpretive Theories of Religion, completion expected in 1976; other writing on philosophy of religion and metaphysics.

* * *

CROSLAND, Andrew T(ate) 1944-

PERSONAL: Born August 17, 1944, in San Francisco, Calif.; son of Herbert Henry (a postmaster) and Dolores (von Raesfeld) Crosland; married Phebe Hebb (a social worker), November 27, 1968; children: Matthew Edward. *Education:* Belmont Abbey College, A.B., 1966; George Peabody College for Teachers, M.A., 1968; University of South Carolina, Ph.D., 1975. *Home:* 245 West Hampton Ave., Spartanburg, S.C. 29301. *Office:* Department of English, University of South Carolina, Spartanburg, S.C. 29303.

CAREER: University of South Carolina, Spartanburg, instructor, 1968-72, assistant professor of English and computer science, 1973—. *Member:* Modern Language Association of America, South Atlantic Modern Language Association.

WRITINGS: A Concordance to F. Scott Fitzgerald's "The Great Gatsby," Gale, 1975; *A Concordance to the Complete Poetry of Stephen Crane*, Gale, 1975. Contributor to *Fitzgerald-Hemingway Annual*.

WORK IN PROGRESS: A Concordance to Thoreau's "Walden"; source study for *Gone with the Wind*; research on the uses and importance of the prose concordance.

* * *

CROSS, Milton (John) 1897-1975

April 16, 1897—January 3, 1975; American radio announcer, musicologist, and author. Obituaries: *Time*, January 13, 1975; *Newsweek*, January 13, 1975; *AB Bookman's Weekly*, January 20, 1975.

* * *

CROUCH, Steve 1915-

PERSONAL: Born February 25, 1915, in Anson, Tex.; son of Stephen Dallas (a clergyman) and Esther (Poindexter) Crouch; married Mary Mayginnes, March 3, 1937 (divorced, 1937); married Ethlyn Douglas (a painter), June 6, 1939; children: (second marriage) Stephen D. III. *Education:* University of Oklahoma, B.A., 1938; graduate study at University of Chicago, 1943-44. *Home and office address:* Box 2085, Carmel, Calif. 93921.

CAREER: U.S. Army, Artillery, 1938-47, leaving service as a major. Member of board of trustees, Monterey Peninsula Museum of Art, 1965—, Friends of Photography, 1973—. *Awards, honors*—Military: Bronze Star Medal. Civilian: Silver Medal from Commonwealth Club of California, 1974, for *Steinbeck Country*.

WRITINGS: Peninsula Pictorial, G. C. Beaman, 1950; *Steinbeck Country*, American West, 1973. Contributor to *American West*, *Audubon*, *Place*.

WORK IN PROGRESS: A book on the southwestern desert, including personal photographs.

AVOCATIONAL INTERESTS: Travel.

* * *

CROWLEY, John Edward 1943-

PERSONAL: Born June 5, 1943, in Grass Valley, Calif.; son of John Denis (an army officer) and Mary Elizabeth (Foley) Crowley; married Mary Lora Noffsinger (a teacher), 1966; children: Amy Elizabeth. *Education:* Princeton University, A.B., 1965; University of Michigan, M.A., 1966; Johns Hopkins University, Ph.D., 1970. *Address:* Box 35, Rose Bay, Nova Scotia, Canada. *Office:* Department of History, Dalhousie University, Halifax, Nova Scotia, Canada.

CAREER: Dalhousie University, Halifax, Nova Scotia, assistant professor of history, 1970—.

WRITINGS: This Sheba, Self: The Conceptualization of Economic Life in Eighteenth-Century America, Johns Hopkins University Press, 1974.

* * *

CROWSON, P(aul) S(piller) 1913-

PERSONAL: Born November 3, 1913, in Taunton, Somerset, England; son of Robert (a merchant) and Florence (a pianist; maiden name, Spiller) Crowson; married Joan Ormiston, December 30, 1955; children: Culain Morris, Deigan Morris, Sean Morris (stepsons). *Education:* Exeter College, Oxford, M.A., 1937. *Religion:* Church of England. *Home:* Tarvers, Crofts Lane, Adderbury, Banbury, Oxfordshire OX17 3NB, England.

CAREER: Chillon College, Montreux, Switzerland, schoolmaster, 1937-39; Watford Grammar School, Watford, England, schoolmaster, 1939-45; Radley College, Abingdon, England, schoolmaster, 1945-74; writer. *Member:* English Speaking Union, Historical Association, Assistant Masters' Association.

WRITINGS: A History of the Russian People, Longmans, Green, 1948; *Tudor Foreign Policy*, St. Martin's, 1973.

WORK IN PROGRESS: The Oxford Scientific Film Company Limited, for Edward Arnold.

* * *

CRUICKSHANK, Allan D(udley) 1907-1974

August 29, 1907—October 11, 1974; American ornithologist and author. Obituaries: *New York Times*, October 12, 1974.

* * *

CULLEN, Charles T(homas) 1940-

PERSONAL: Born October 11, 1940, in Gainesville, Fla.; son of Spencer L., Sr. and Blanche (Johnson) Cullen; married Shirley Harrington, June 13, 1964; children: Leslie Lanier, Charles Spencer Harrington. *Education:* University of the South, B.A., 1962; Florida State University, Tallahassee, M.A., 1963; University of Virginia, Ph.D., 1971. *Home:* 145 Winston Dr., Williamsburg, Va. 23185. *Address:* Institute of Early American History and Culture, P.O. Box 220, Williamsburg, Va. 23185.

CAREER: Averett College, Danville, Va., assistant professor of history, 1963-66; Institute of Early American History and Culture, Williamsburg, Va., associate editor, 1971-73, co-editor of *Papers of John Marshall*, 1973—. *Member:* Organization of American Historians, American Society for Legal History.

WRITINGS: (Editor with Herbert A. Johnson) *The Papers of John Marshall*, Volume I, University of North Carolina Press, 1974. Contributor to *Virginia Magazine of History and Biography, New York History, New England Quarterly, William and Mary Quarterly, American Historical Review*, and *Historian*. Editor of *American Society for Legal History Newsletter*, 1974—.

WORK IN PROGRESS: Editing with Herbert A. Johnson, volume two of *The Papers of John Marshall*; *St. George Tucker: A Biography.*

* * *

CUMBERLAND, Kenneth Brailey 1913-

PERSONAL: Born October 1, 1913, in Bradford, Yorkshire, England; son of Ernest (a company manager) and Lucy (Hodgson) Cumberland; married Marjorie Denham, November 30, 1940 (died June 6, 1963); children: Garth, Sheevaun, Tanya. *Education:* University of London, B.A. (first class honors), 1935, M.A., 1938; University of New Zealand, D.Sc., 1946. *Home:* Kettlewelldale Farm, Arakotinga, Brookby, Manurewa, R.D., New Zealand. *Office:* Department of Geography, University of Auckland, Private Bag, Auckland, New Zealand.

CAREER: University of London, University College, London, England, assistant lecturer in geography, 1937-38; University of Canterbury, Canterbury, England, lecturer in geography, 1938-45; University of Auckland, Auckland, New Zealand, senior lecturer in charge, 1946-49, professor of geography, 1949—. Owner and operator of farms in Brookby, 1964, Clevedon, 1968, and Te Kuiti, 1974 (all New Zealand). Member of Auckland City Council, 1953-62; member of Auckland Metropolitan Drainage Board, 1953-62; member of Auckland Regional Planning Authority, 1953-62, chairman, 1956-59; member of board of directors, Pouto Forest Farms Ltd., 1972—; visiting professor, University of Wisconsin, 1951, Universitat des Saarlandes, 1966. *Member:* International Geographical Union (vice-president representing the United Kingdom, Dominions, and Colonies, 1960-69), New Zealand Geographical Society (first honorary life member), Royal Society of New Zealand (fellow), American Geographical Society (fellow), Royal Geographical Society (honorary corresponding member), Royal Scottish Geographical Society (corresponding member). *Awards, honors:* Fulbright travel grant, 1951; Carnegie travel grant, 1958; Deutscher Foreschungsgemeinschaft travel grant, 1966.

WRITINGS: Whitcombe's Atlas of Geography for New Zealand and Australian Schools, 3rd revised edition (Cumberland was not associated with earlier editions), Whitcombe & Tombs, 1943, 12th revised edition, 1961; *Soil Erosion in New Zealand*, Soil Conservation and Rivers Control Council (Wellington), 1943, 2nd edition, Whitcombe & Tombs, 1947; *A Regional Geography of New Zealand*, Common Grounds Ltd. (London), 1948; *New Zealand in Outline*, Whitcombe & Tombs, 1949, all subsequent editions published as *This Is New Zealand*, 5th edition, 1960; *Southwest Pacific: A Geography of Australia, New Zealand and Their Pacific Island Neighbourhoods*, Whitcombe & Tombs, 1954, McGraw, 1956, 2nd edition, Methuen, 1958, 4th revised edition, Praeger, 1968; (with James W. Fox) *New Zealand: A Regional View*, Whitcombe & Tombs, 1959, 2nd edition, 1964, Aldine, 1970; (editor with Fox and contributor) *Land, Life and Agriculture in Western Samoa*, Whitcombe & Tombs, 1962; (with J. S. Whitelaw) *New Zealand*, Aldine, 1970; (editor) *New Zealand: Pacific Land Down Under*, Kuemmerly and Frey (Berne), 1973. Also author of booklets published under title *New Zealand: Topical Geographies*, Whitcombe & Tombs, 1965-67. First editor, *New Zealand Geographer*, 1945-55.

WORK IN PROGRESS: Animal breeding and development of new breeds of sheep.

* * *

CUMMINGS, Larry L(ee) 1937-

PERSONAL: Born October 28, 1937, in Indianapolis, Ind.; son of Garland R. and Lillian P. (Smith) Cummings; married Suzanne Jay, June 21, 1959; children: Lee Anne, Glenn Nelson. *Education:* Wabash College, A.B. (summa cum laude), 1959; University of California, Berkeley, graduate study, 1959-60; Indiana University, M.B.A., 1961, D.B.A., 1964. *Home:* 4145 Iroquois Dr., Madison, Wis. 53711. *Office:* Graduate School of Business, University of Wisconsin, 1155 Observatory Dr., Madison, Wis. 53706.

CAREER: Indiana University, Bloomington, assistant professor, 1964-67, associate professor of organizational behavior, 1967; University of Wisconsin, Madison, associate professor, 1968-70, professor of organizational behavior in Graduate School of Business and in Industrial Relations Research Institute, 1970—, lecturer in department of psychology, 1970—, director of Center for the Study of Organizational Performance, 1973—. Visiting associate professor at Columbia University, 1967-68; visiting professor at University of British Columbia, 1971-72. Consultant to Dow Chemical Co., Eli Lilly & Co., Prudential Insurance Co., of America, and other firms. Lecturer in Europe, 1969-70, at universities in Africa, 1972, and in Japan and Thailand.

MEMBER: American Psychological Association, Academy of Management (fellow), Industrial Relations Research Association, American Sociological Association, Society for Personnel Administration, American Society for Personnel Administration, Phi Beta Kappa, Sigma Xi, Beta Gamma Sigma, Tau Kappa Alpha. *Awards, honors:* Ford Foundation research fellow at Carnegie-Mellon University, 1965; McKinsey Foundation Management Research Design Award (shared with D. L. Hartnett), 1967; research grants from Richardson Foundation, 1967—, and Ford Foundation, 1968-70.

WRITINGS: (Editor with William E. Scott and contributor) *Readings in Organizational Behavior and Human Performance*, Irwin, 1969, revised edition, 1973; (with Fremont A. Shull and A. L. Delbecq) *Organizational Decision Making*, McGraw, 1970; (with Donald P. Schwab) *Performance in Organizations: Determinants and Appraisal*, Scott, Foresman, 1973.

Contributor: Joe Kelley, *Organizational Behavior*, Irwin, 1969; Bernhardt Lieberman, editor, *Social Choice*, Gordon & Breach, 1972; Paul Pigors and others, editors, *Readings in Personnel Administration*, revised edition (Cummings did not contribute to earlier edition), McGraw, 1972; W. T. Stanbury and Mark Thompson, editors, *People, Productivity, and Technological Change*, Versatile Publishing, 1973. Contributor of about forty-five articles and occasional reviews to journals. Consulting editor, "Irwin Series in Management and the Behavioral Sciences," 1972—. Member of board of editors, *Academy of Management Journal*, 1970—; associate editor, *Decision Sciences*, 1972—; member of review board, *Journal of Business Research*, 1972—.

AVOCATIONAL INTERESTS: Fishing, billiards.

* * *

CUNEO, John R(obert) 1911-

PERSONAL: Born July 16, 1911, in Norwalk, Conn.; son of John Joseph (a lawyer) and Anna (Heidt) Cuneo; married Myrtle Wood; children: Robert J., Sara J. *Education:* Yale University, B.A., 1933, LL.B., 1936. *Home:* 11 Pine Tree Dr., Westport, Conn. 06880. *Office:* Lovejoy, Cuneo & Curtis, 168 East Ave., Norwalk, Conn. 06854.

CAREER: Lovejoy, Cuneo & Curtis, Norwalk, Conn., partner in law firm, 1937—. Assistant prosecutor in Norwalk City Court, 1939, 1943-45. Chairman of Norwalk mayor's Historical Sites Committee; past member of Norwalk Planning Commission. *Member:* Company of Military Historians (fellow), Connecticut Bar Association (member of council, 1951-56), Norwalk Bar Association (president, 1945-46), Norwalk Historical Society (past president), Westport Historical Society (past president).

WRITINGS: *Winged Mars*, Military Service Publishing, Volume I: *The German Air Weapon, 1870-1914*, 1942, Volume II: *The Air Weapon, 1914-1916*, 1947; *Robert Rogers of the Rangers*, Oxford University Press, 1959; *The Battles of Saratoga*, Macmillan, 1967; *Benjamin Franklin: Ingenious Diplomat*, McGraw, 1969; *John Marshall: Judicial Statesman*, McGraw, 1975. Contributor to military magazines, including *Military Affairs, Field Artillery Journal, Marine Corps Gazette*, and *Sportsman Pilot*.

AVOCATIONAL INTERESTS: Archaeology of the Americas, travel (South America, Mexico, Central America).

* * *

CUNLIFFE, Barrington Windsor 1939-
(Barry Cunliffe)

PERSONAL: Born December 10, 1939, in Portsmouth, England; son of George (a naval officer) and Beatrice (Mersh) Cunliffe. *Education:* St. John's College, Cambridge, B.A., 1961, M.A., 1963, Ph.D., 1966. *Residence:* Oxford, England. *Agent:* Curtis Brown Ltd., 1 Craven Hill, London W2 3EP, England. *Office:* Institute of Archaeology, Oxford University, 35 Beaumont St., Oxford, England.

CAREER: University of Bristol, Bristol, England, lecturer in classics, 1963-66; University of Southampton, Southampton, England, professor of archaeology, 1966-72; Oxford University, Institute of Archaeology, Oxford, England, professor of European archaeology and fellow of Keble College, 1972—. *Member:* Society of Antiquaries (fellow), Royal Archaeological Institute, Prehistoric Society, Medieval Society, Society for the Promotion of Roman Studies, *Antiquity* Trust, *Vindolanda* Trust.

WRITINGS—Under name Barry Cunliffe: *Excavations at Richborough*, Volume V, Society of Antiquaries, 1968; (editor and contributor) *Roman Bath*, Society of Antiquaries, 1969; *Excavations at Fishbourne: 1961-1969*, Society of Antiquaries, 1971; *Fishbourne: A Roman Palace and Its Gardens*, Johns Hopkins Press, 1971; *Roman Bath Discovered*, Routledge & Kegan Paul, 1971; *The Cradle of England*, British Broadcasting Corp., 1972; *The Making of the English*, British Broadcasting Corp., 1973; *The Regni*, Duckworth, 1974; *Iron Age Communities in Britain*, Routledge & Kegan Paul, 1974. Author of television scripts for British Broadcasting Corp., "Cradle of England" (six programs), 1972, "Making of the English" (six), 1973, "Pompeii," 1974, and "Throne of Kings" (six), 1975. Contributor to archaeological journals, and contributor of reviews to *Times Literary Supplement*, *Nature*, and *New Scientist*. Executive editor of *World Archaeology*.

WORK IN PROGRESS: Results of archaeological excavations in Great Britain; research on Europe during the thousand years before the Romans invaded it.

AVOCATIONAL INTERESTS: Travel (East Europe, Mediterranean), Tunisian sun and life style, food, Chinese pottery.

* * *

CUNNINGHAM, Robert Stanley 1907-

PERSONAL: Born January 31, 1907, in Wheeling, W.Va.;

son of Harry Sanford (a contractor) and Florence Ivy Cunningham; married Violette Amelia Marker, January 28, 1929 (divorced September, 1952); married Dora Irene Pomeroy, November 8, 1952 (deceased); children: (first marriage) Robin Gay (Mrs. H. D. Shinn); (second marriage) Kathy (Mrs. C. A. Wahl; stepdaughter). *Education:* West Virginia University, A.B., 1930, B.Sc., 1932; University of Chicago, M.D., 1937. *Politics:* Conservative Republican. *Religion:* Presbyterian. *Home:* 4013 South 262nd Pl., Kent, Wash. 98031. *Agent:* Kathy Wahl, 1308 28th S.E., Auburn, Wash. 98002.

CAREER: Physician specializing in internal medicine, 1937—, interned at Tacoma (Washington) General Hospital, served with the Civilian Conservation Corps in Chelan, Wash., prior to World War II, and until 1967, was in continuous government service, particularly with the Veterans Administration. Before entering medicine, held a variety of jobs, including hospital switchboard operator and social worker. *Military service:* Served two years in U.S. Army during World War II; served thirty-three years in U.S. Army Reserve, retiring as lieutenant colonel, 1967. *Member:* International Platform Association, American Medical Association, Royal Society of Health (fellow), Masons, Elks.

WRITINGS: Rationale (poems), Mojave Books, 1974; *Love Poems*, Mojave Books, 1975. Contributor of articles and poems to *Veterans Administration Bulletin, American Heart Journal*, and *Northwest Medicine*.

WORK IN PROGRESS: Rippling Rhymes and Fairy Tales, for Mojave Books; Science Fiction; *The Hippy Messiah*, a novelette; *Sacrifice*, a novel; *Twice Told Tales*, poems.

AVOCATIONAL INTERESTS: Painting.

* * *

CUNNINGTON, Phillis 1887-1974

1887—October 24, 1974; British physician and author of books on the history of costume. Obituaries: *AB Bookman's Weekly*, December 2, 1974.

* * *

CURLEY, Walter J(oseph) P(atrick) 1922-

PERSONAL: Born September 17, 1922, in Pittsburgh, Pa.; son of Walter Joseph Patrick (an industrialist) and Marguerite (Cowan) Curley; married Mary Taylor Walton, December 8, 1948; children: Margaret Cowan, Walter III, John Walton, James Mellon. *Education:* Yale University B.A., 1943; Harvard University, M.B.A., 1948. *Politics:* Independent. *Religion:* Roman Catholic. *Home:* 791 Park Ave., New York, N.Y. 10021. *Agent:* James Oliver Brown, 22 East 60th St., New York, N.Y. 10022. *Office:* J. H. Whitney & Co., 630 Fifth Ave., New York, N.Y. 10020.

CAREER: J. H. Whitney & Co. (private investment banking firm), New York, N.Y., partner, 1961—. Director of several related business firms. Trustee of Barnard College, Buckley School, Miss Porter's School, and Brooks School; Commissioner of Public Events and Chief of Protocol for New York City, 1973-74. *Military service:* U.S. Marine Corps, 1942-46; became captain; received Bronze Star, Presidential unit citation, and Cloud and Banner (Nationalist Government of China).

WRITINGS: Bantam Traveller, privately printed, 1938; *Letters from the Pacific*, privately printed, 1960; *Monarchs-in-Waiting*, Dodd, 1973. Contributor to *Town and Country* and *New York Times*.

* * *

CURTAYNE, Alice 1898-

PERSONAL: Born November 6, 1898, in Tralee, County Kerry, Ireland; daughter of John and Bridget (O'Dwyer) Curtayne; married Stephen Rynne (a writer and farmer), February 14, 1935; children: Brigid, Catherine, Davoc, Andrew. *Education:* Attended St. Anne's School, Southampton, Hampshire, England, 1913-17. *Politics:* Irish Nationalist ("but never belonged to a party"). *Religion:* Roman Catholic. *Home:* Macalla, Downings, Prosperous, Naas, County Kildare, Ireland.

CAREER: Teacher in a primary school in Birmingham, England, 1917-18; secretarial work in Milan, Italy, 1923-27, and in Liverpool, England, 1927-32. Author and translator. Lecturer at Anna Maria College, Paxton, Mass., and Cardinal Cushing College, Boston, 1959; also undertook lecture tours in United States, beginning 1951. *Awards, honors:* Dr. of Humane Letters, Anna Maria College, 1959; given key to city of Worcester, Mass., 1959.

WRITINGS: Saint Catherine of Siena, Macmillan, 1929; (translator) Giovanni Papini, *Labourers in the Vineyard*, Sheed & Ward, 1930; *St. Anthony of Padua*, Father Mathew Record Office (Dublin), 1931, Franciscan Herald Press (Chicago), 1952; (contributor) *The Irish Way*, Sheed & Ward, 1932; *A Recall to Dante*, Macmillan, 1932; *Borne on the Wind* (essays), Browne & Nolan (Dublin), 1933; *Saint Brigid of Ireland*, Browne & Nolan, 1933, Sheed & Ward, 1954, revised edition, Browne & Nolan, 1955; (translator) Maria Montessori, *The Mass Explained to Children*, Sheed & Ward, 1934; *Patrick Sarsfield*, Talbot Press (Dublin), 1934; *The Servant of God: Mother Mary Aikenhead, Foundress of the Irish Sisters of Charity, 1787-1858*, Anthonian Press (Dublin), 1935; *Jean-Baptiste Debrabant*, St. Anthony Guild Press (Paterson, N.J.), 1936.

House of Cards (novel), Bruce (Milwaukee), 1940; *Lough Derg: St. Patrick's Purgatory*, Burns, Oates & Washbourne, 1944, revised edition, 1945; *The Trial of Oliver Plunkett*, Sheed & Ward, 1953; *Twenty Tales of Irish Saints* (juvenile), Sheed & Ward, 1955 (published in Ireland as *Irish Saints for Boys and Girls*, Talbot Press, 1955); *More Tales of Irish Saints*, Sheed & Ward, 1957.

The Irish Story: A Survey of Irish History and Culture, Kenedy, 1960; (contributor) *An Irish Tribute to Dante on the Seventeenth Century of His Birth*, Istuto Italiano de Cultura (Dublin), 1965; *Francis Ledwidge: A Life of the Poet, 1887-1917*, Martin Brian & O'Keefe, 1972; (editor) *The Complete Poems of Francis Ledwidge*, Martin Brian & O'Keefe, in press.

Author of radio play, "Mary Aikenhead," broadcast during late 1930's in Dublin. Contributor to periodicals, including *Spectator, Universe,* and *Clergy Review* (all London); *Standard, Hibernia, Irish Press,* and *Kerryman* (all Ireland); and *Missionary* (Washington, D.C.).

* * *

CURTIN, William M(artin) 1927-

PERSONAL: Born March 19, 1927, in Brooklyn, N.Y.; son of Martin A. and Bridget (Walsh) Curtin; married Mary E. Beckman, January, 1955; children: Maryellen, Martin. *Education:* St. John's University, Brooklyn, N.Y., B.A., 1950; Columbia University, M.A., 1952; University of

Wisconsin, Ph.D., 1959. *Politics:* Democrat. *Religion:* Roman Catholic. *Home:* 15 Farmstead Rd., Storrs, Conn. 06268. *Office:* Department of English, University of Connecticut, U-25, Storrs, Conn. 06268.

CAREER: Georgetown University, Washington, D.C., instructor in English, 1952-53; University of Illinois, Urbana, instructor, 1958-61, assistant professor, 1961-67, associate professor of English, 1967-69; University of Connecticut, Storrs, associate professor of English, 1969—. Fulbright lecturer at University of Dijon, 1968-69. Consultant to Appleton, 1968. *Military service:* U.S. Marine Corps, 1945-46. *Member:* Modern Language Association of America, National Council of Teachers of English. *Awards, honors:* Penrose Award from American Philosophical Society, 1963.

WRITINGS: (Editor) *The World and the Parish: Willa Cather's Articles and Reviews, 1893-1902*, two volumes, University of Nebraska Press, 1970. Contributor of articles and reviews to *Colby Library Quarterly, Cross Currents*, and *Commonweal.*

WORK IN PROGRESS: Research on the emotions of character, in William James and Willa Cather; a study of psychology in the novels of Crane, Norris, London, Cather, Stein, Dreiser, and Anderson.

* * *

CUSHING, Barry E(dwin) 1945-

PERSONAL: Born July 6, 1945, in Lansing, Mich.; son of William Eldon (an automobile factory worker) and Abigail Frances (an elementary school teacher; maiden name, Stevens) Cushing; married Cherry Lee Barker, June 25, 1966; children: Dennis Earl, Rebecca Lynn. *Education:* Michigan State University, B.A. (with high honors), 1966, Ph.D., 1969. *Residence:* Austin, Tex. *Office:* Department of Accounting, University of Texas, BEB 300, Austin, Tex. 78712.

CAREER: FMC Corp., John Bean Division, Lansing, Mich., accountant, 1966-67; Michigan State University, East Lansing, assistant instructor in accounting, 1967; University of Texas, Austin, assistant professor, 1969-71, associate professor of accounting, 1971—. Staff accountant for Ernst & Ernst, 1969; certified public accountant by State of Texas, 1970; visiting associate professor at University of Illinois, 1972-73. *Member:* American Accounting Association, American Institute of Certified Public Accountants, American Institute for Decision Sciences, National Association of Accountants (past vice-president), Texas Society of Certified Public Accountants, Beta Alpha Psi, Phi Kappa Phi.

WRITINGS: Accounting Information Systems and Business Organizations, Addison-Wesley, 1974. Contributor of about a dozen articles to accounting journals, including *Accounting Review*, *Journal of Accountancy*, *Management Advisor*, *Tax Executive*, *Abacus*, and *Journal of Business*.

WORK IN PROGRESS: Research on real-time information processing in marketing, on earnings manipulation and management motives, on discretionary expenses as a source of earnings manipulation, and on basic issues in internal pricing of computer services.

* * *

CUSHING, Mary W(atkins) 189(?)-1974

189(?)—October 4, 1974; American journalist and author. Obituaries: *New York Times*, October 5, 1974.

DAENZER, Bernard John 1916-

PERSONAL: Born January 15, 1916, in New York, N.Y.; son of Bernard C. and Amelia (Heinze) Daenzer; married Valerie A. Lee, June 8, 1941; children: Peter B., Jean (Mrs. Edward Alken), John, Richard. *Education:* Fordham University, A.B. (magna cum laude), 1937, LL.B., 1942. *Religion:* Roman Catholic. *Home:* 265 Forest Rd., South Orange, N.J. 07079. *Office:* Wohlreich & Anderson Ltd., 55 John St., New York, N.Y. 10038.

CAREER: Admitted to New York State Bar, 1942. Firemen's Insurance Co., New York, N.Y., underwriter and special agent, 1937-42; Security-Connecticut Companies, New Haven, executive vice-president and member of board of directors, 1943-57; Wohlreich & Anderson Ltd., New York, N.Y., president and member of board of directors, 1957—. President and member of board of directors of Howden Reinsurance Corp., 1971—; member of board of directors of Alexander Howden Group (London), R.L.I. Corp., Lincoln Insurance Co., and Countrywide Managers; underwriting member of Lloyds of London, 1969—; member of education committee on College Insurance, 1969—, trustee, 1974—. *Military service:* U.S. Naval Reserve, active duty, 1943-47; became lieutenant junior grade.

MEMBER: American Bar Association, American Institute for Property and Casualty Underwriters (member of examining committee in Bryn Mawr, Pa., 1964—), American Management Association (member of insurance advisory council, 1963—), Society of Chartered Property and Casualty Underwriters (past president of Media, Pa. chapter), Bankers Club (New York, N.Y.), Orange Lawn Tennis Club, Ocean Reef Club (Key Largo, Fla.), Lavallette Yacht Club (New Jersey).

WRITINGS: Ethics and Insurance, Prentice-Hall, 1953; *Cover Notes*, Underwriter Printing & Publishing, 1964; (editor and contributor) *Excess and Surplus Lines Manual*, Merritt Co. (Santa Monica, Calif.), 1970; *Fact-Finding Techniques in Risk Analysis*, American Management Association, 1970. Contributor to professional journals. Editor of *Weekly Underwriter*, 1961—.

* * *

DALEY, Joseph A(ndrew) 1927-

PERSONAL: Born September 18, 1927, in Rome, N.Y.; son of Joseph A. (an executive) and Catherine (Murphy) Daley; married Loraine M. Hagemann (a court reporter), October 5, 1955; children: Debora Lynn Daley Edelstein. *Education:* Villanova University, A.B., 1951. *Home:* 4525 Hayvenhurst Ave., Encino, Calif. 91316. *Office:* Department of Public Relations, Continental Airlines, Los Angeles, Calif.

CAREER: Rowe-Doherty Associates (public relations firm), New York, N.Y., director of television and radio, 1953-55; Edward Gottlieb & Associates (public relations firm), New York, N.Y., director of radio and television, 1955-58, account executive, 1958-63, vice-president, 1963-66, senior vice-president, 1966-68; Continental Airlines, Los Angeles, Calif., vice-president for public relations, 1968—. Arbitrator for American Arbitration Association. Past chairman of Nassau County Manpower Utilization Council. Democratic candidate for U.S. House of Representatives from the Fourth District in New York, 1962. *Military service:* U.S. Navy, 1946-47. *Member:* Public Relations Society of America, Society of American Travel Writers, Mystery Writers Association, Authors League of America, Society of Aviation and Space Writers.

WRITINGS—Novels: *Exit with Drums*, St. Martin's, 1970; *Spicy Lady*, St. Martin's, 1973.

* * *

DAMERON, J(ohn) Lasley 1925-

PERSONAL: Born July 29, 1925, in Burlington, N.C,; son of Edgar S. W., Sr. (a lawyer) and Lola (Lasley) Dameron; married Elizabeth Eaddy, December 29, 1949; children: George W., John E. *Education:* University of North Carolina, B.S., 1950, M.A., 1952; University of Tennessee, Ph.D., 1962. *Religion:* Methodist. *Home:* 5491 Walnut Grove Rd., Memphis, Tenn. 38117. *Office:* Department of English, Memphis State University, Memphis, Tenn. 38152.

CAREER: Emory and Henry College, Emory, Va., instructor in English, 1953-55; University of Tennessee, Knoxville, instructor in English, 1960-61; Memphis State University, Memphis, Tenn., assistant professor, 1962-66, associate professor, 1966-71, professor of English, 1972—. *Military service:* U.S. Navy, pharmacist's mate, 1943-46. *Member:* Modern Language Association of America, American Association of University Professors, Bibliographical Association of America, Poe Studies Association (vice-president, 1974), South Atlantic Modern Language Association, Tennessee Philological Association. *Awards, honors:* National Endowment for the Humanities grant, 1966-67, 1972, for research on a bibliography of criticism on Edgar Allan Poe.

WRITINGS: Edgar Allan Poe in the Mid-Twentieth Century: His Literary Reputation in England and America, 1928-1960, and a Bibliography of the Criticism of Edgar Allan Poe, 1942-1960, University of Tennessee, 1962; (with Charles Stagg) *An Index to Poe's Critical Vocabulary*, Transcendental, 1966; *Edgar Allan Poe: A Checklist of Criticism, 1942-1960*, Bibliographical Society of Virginia, 1966; (editor) *Southern Write-In*, University of Tennessee, 1969; (editor with Eric W. Carlson) *Emerson's Relevance Today*, Transcendental, 1971; (with Irby B. Cauthen, Jr.) *Edgar Allan Poe: A Bibliography of Criticism, 1827-1967*, University Press of Virginia, 1974. Contributor of about twenty-five articles to education and literature journals, including *American Transcendental Quarterly*, *Education Quest*, *American Literature Abstracts*, *Interpretations*, *Poe Newsletter*, and *English Studies*. Member of editorial board of *Poe Studies*.

WORK IN PROGRESS: Index to Critical Vocabulary of Early Nineteenth Century Periodicals; editing reprints on Edgar Allan Poe; further research on Poe and Nathaniel Hawthorne.

AVOCATIONAL INTERESTS: Travel (especially Europe), tennis, fishing.

* * *

D'ANCONA, Mirella Levi 1919-

PERSONAL: Surname sometimes appears as Levi D'Ancona; born June 7, 1919, in Florence, Italy; naturalized American citizen, 1952; daughter of Ezio and Flora (Aghib) D'Ancona. *Education:* University of Florence, Dottore in Lettere e Filosofia, 1941, further study, 1945-46; New York University, graduate study at Institute of Fine Arts, 1946-48, 1949-51; Bryn Mawr College, M.A., 1949. *Home:* 300 East 71st St., Apt. 11B, New York, N.Y. 10021. *Office:* Hunter College, 695 Park Ave., New York, N.Y. 10021.

CAREER: Research assistant at Wildenstein & Co., New York, N.Y., 1948, 1950-51, and Frick Art Reference Library, New York, 1952-54; Wildenstein & Co., researcher, 1954-60, working on catalogue of Italian illuminations; State University of New York College on Long Island, Oyster Bay, assistant professor of art, 1959-60; City University of New York, Hunter College, New York, N.Y., lecturer, 1960-61, assistant professor, 1961-66, associate professor, 1967-72, professor of art, 1972—. Adjunct professor at Institute of Fine Arts, New York, 1967. Consultant (collaboratrice) of Vatican Library, 1968—. *Member:* College Art Association of America, Istituto d'Arte Lombarda. *Awards, honors:* Grants from American Philosophical Society, 1955, 1956, Bollingen Foundation, 1960, and American Council of Learned Societies, 1960, 1964, 1965, 1966.

WRITINGS: (With others) *The Frick Collection: An Illustrated Catalogue*, Thistle Press, Volume V: *Sculpture*, 1953, Volume VI: *Sculpture*, 1954, Volume XII: *Italian Paintings*, 1955; *The Iconography of the Immaculate Conception in the Middle Ages and the Early Renaissance* (monograph), New York University Press, for Archaeological Institute of America and College Art Association of America, 1957; *Miniatura e Miniatori a Firenze dal XIV al XVI secola*, Olschki (Florence), 1962; *The Wildenstein Collection of Illuminations: The Lombard School*, Olschki, 1970; *The Garden of the Renaissance*, Olschki, 1975.

Contributor: *Studi di Bibliografia e di Storia in Onore di Tammaro de Marinis*, Giovannia Mardersteig (Verona), 1964; L. F. Sandler, editor, *Essays in Memory of Karl Lehmann*, J. J. Augustin, 1964; *Contributi alla Storia del libro italiano: Miscellanea in Onore di Lamberto Donati*, Olschki, 1969; *Miscellanea di Studi in Onore di Roberto Ridolfi*, Olschki, for British Museum, 1973. Contributor to *Dizionario Biografico degli Italian, Victoria and Albert Museum Yearbook*, and about sixty articles and reviews to journals, including *Commentari, Art Bulletin, Gazette des Beaux-Arts*, and *Bibliofilia*.

WORK IN PROGRESS: Venetian Illuminations in the Vatican, a monograph; *Essays in Honor of Millard Meiss*; *History of Venetian Book-illumination*; *History of Italian Illumination*, with Angela Daneo Laetanzi; *Florentine Book Illumination of the Renaissance*.

* * *

DANIEL, Ralph T(homas) 1921-

PERSONAL: Born April 10, 1921, in Kerens, Tex.; son of Robert S. (a businessman) and Edith (Watson) Daniel; married Genevieve Barr (a teacher), November 14, 1943. *Education:* North Texas State University, B.M., 1940, M.M., 1942, B.A., 1947; Harvard University, M.A., 1949, Ph.D., 1955. *Religion:* Episcopalian. *Home:* 1700 Longwood W., Bloomington, Ind. 47401. *Office:* School of Music, Indiana University, Bloomington, Ind. 47401.

CAREER: North Texas State University, Denton, instructor in music, 1946-47; Indiana University, Bloomington, assistant professor, 1949-51, associate professor, 1951-55, professor of music history, 1955—. *Military service:* U.S. Army, 1942-46. *Member:* International Musicological Society, American Musicological Society, College Music Society, Music Teachers National Association, Phi Mu Alpha, Phi Delta Kappa. *Awards, honors:* Guggenheim fellowship, 1961-62.

WRITINGS: (With Willi Apel) *The Harvard Brief Dictionary of Music*, Harvard University Press, 1960: *The Anthem in New England Before 1800*, Northwestern University Press, 1966; (with Peter le Huray) *The Sources of*

English Church Music: 1549-1660, Stainer & Bell, 1972. Contributor to *Encyclopaedia Britannica, Collier's Encyclopedia, Grove's Dictionary of Music and Musicians*, and to *Journal of the American Musicological Society*, and *Musical Quarterly*.

WORK IN PROGRESS: Editing the earliest source of English church music.

* * *

DANIELS, David 1933-

PERSONAL: Born December 20, 1933, in Penn Yan, N.Y.; son of Carroll C. (a contractor) and Ursula (Wilder) Daniels; married Jimmie Sue Evans (a teacher), August 11, 1956; children: Michael, Abigail, Andrew. *Education:* Oberlin College, A.B., 1955; Boston University, M.A., 1956; University of Iowa, M.F.A. and Ph.D., 1963. *Home:* 1215 Gettysburg, Rochester, Mich. 48063. *Office:* Department of Music, Oakland University, Rochester, Mich. 48063.

CAREER: Culver-Stockton College, Canton, Mo., instructor in music, 1956-58; Berkshire Athenaeum, Pittsfield, Mass., music librarian, 1958-61; University of Redlands, Redlands, Calif., assistant professor of music, 1963-64; Knox College, Galesburg, Ill., assistant professor of music, 1964-69; Oakland University, Rochester, Mich., associate professor of music, 1969—. Conductor of Central Illinois Youth Symphonh, 1966-68, and Warren Symphony, Warren, Mich., 1974—. *Member:* American Symphony Orchestra League, American Association of University Professors, Michigan Orchestra Association.

WRITINGS: Orchestral Music: A Source Book, Scarecrow, 1972.

WORK IN PROGRESS: Handbook of Musical Form, with Clifford Pfeil.

* * *

DANIELS, Draper 1913-

PERSONAL: Born August 12, 1913, in Morris, N.Y.; son of John Albert (a civil engineer) and Fanny (a teacher; maiden name, Draper) Daniels; married Louise Parker Lux Cort, October 9, 1937 (divorced, 1967); married Myra Janco (an advertising executive), August 19, 1967; children: (first marriage) John, Bruce, Marie and Curtis (twins). *Education:* Syracuse University, B.S., 1934. *Residence:* Chicago, Ill. *Office:* Draper Daniels, Inc., 875 North Michigan, Chicago, Ill. 60611.

CAREER: Vick Chemical Co., New York, N.Y., in sales and advertising departments, 1935-40; Young and Rubicam (advertising agency), New York, N.Y., copywriter, 1940-44; McCann-Erickson, Kenyon & Eckhardt (advertising agency), New York, N.Y., copy supervisor, 1944-46; Young and Rubicam, New York, N.Y., copywriter, 1946-47, copy chief in Chicago, 1947, vice-president, 1948, chairman of plans board, 1949-54; Leo Burnett Co., Inc. (advertising agency), Chicago, Ill., copy supervisor, 1954, vice-president, 1954-56, vice-president in charge of copy and member of plans board, 1956-57, director and vice-president in charge of creative departments, 1957-58, executive vice-president of creative services, 1958-61, member of executive committee, 1958-61, director, 1961-62, chairman of executive committee, 1961-62; U.S. Government, Washington, D.C., national export expansion coordinator, 1962-63; McCann-Erickson, Inc., Chicago, Ill., executive vice-president, 1963-64; Compton Advertising, Inc., Chicago, Ill., executive vice-president, 1964-65; Draper Daniels, Inc. (advertising agency), Chicago, Ill., chairman of the board and chief executive officer, 1965—. Member of advisory board, College of Business Administration, Roosevelt University, 1956—, and School of Journalism, Syracuse University, 1962-73; chairman of Democratic Central Committee, Lake County, Ill., 1954-56; delegate to Democratic National Convention, 1956; member of Lake Forest (Ill.) Board of Education, 1966, 1967; member of Manufacturing Export Advisory Committee of Illinois, 1967, 1970.

WRITINGS: (Contributor) Elbrun French, *The Copywriter's Guide*, Harper, 1958; *Giants, Pigmies, and Other Advertising People*, Crain Books, 1974. Contributor to periodicals in his field.

WORK IN PROGRESS: A collection of near verse, *The Jaded Doggerel; Back Where I Came From*, memoirs of upstate New York.

BIOGRAPHICAL/CRITICAL SOURCES: Julian Watkins, *The One Hundred Greatest Advertisements*, Dover, 1959.

* * *

DANTO, Bruce L. 1927-

PERSONAL: Born April 27, 1927, in Detroit, Mich.; son of Samuel B. (a dentist) and Sylvia (a newspaper writer; maiden name, Gittleman) Danto; married Joan Fried (a teacher), June 25, 1953; children: Jeffrey, Susan, Lisa, Steven. *Education:* Wayne State University, B.A., 1951, M.S.W., 1953, M.D., 1961. *Politics:* Democrat. *Religion:* Jewish. *Home:* 944 Stuyvessant Rd., Birmingham, Mich. 48010. *Office:* 466 Fisher Building, Detroit, Mich. 48202.

CAREER: Northville State Hospital, Northville, Mich., founder of family home care program and psychiatric social worker, 1953-57; Detroit Memorial Hospital, Detroit, Mich., intern, 1961-62; Detroit Receiving Hospital, Detroit, Mich., psychiatric resident, 1962-65; psychiatrist in private practice in Detroit, Mich., 1965—. Assistant professor at Wayne State University, 1968-73, associate professor, 1973—, field work instructor and special guest lecturer in social work, 1969—; instructor at Detroit Police Academy; instructor at Macomb County Community College and Law Enforcement Officers Training Council, both 1972—. Director of community psychiatry and co-director of in-patient department of Herman Kiefer Hospital, 1967-68; founder and director of Suicide Prevention Center at Detroit Psychiatric Institute, 1968—; founding member of Crisis Center Council, 1972—; member of professional board of advisers of Foundation of Thanatology, 1969—. Member of Detroit mayor's skid row committee, 1964-72, chairman, 1968-72, member of committee on crime and violence, 1971. *Military service:* U.S. Army Air Forces, 1945-47.

MEMBER: International Association for Suicide Prevention, World Medical Association, American Psychiatric Association (fellow), American Medical Association, National Association of Social Workers, American Association of Suicidology, American Academy of Psychiatry and Law, American Medical Writers Association, Michigan Psychiatric Society, Michigan Association for Psychoanalysis, Michigan Association for Neuropsychiatric Hospital and Clinic Physicians, Michigan Medical Society, Wayne County Medical Society. *Awards, honors:* David Clark scientific research award from Detroit Receiving Hospital, 1964, 1965; research award from Michigan Association of

Neuropsychiatric Hospital and Clinic Physicians, 1964; Chaves Rega humanitarian award, 1970; Pawolski Peace Prize from Pawolski Peace Foundation, 1971; Detroit mayor's community service award, 1972; human relations award from city of Detroit, 1973.

WRITINGS: (Contributor) Henry Krystal, editor, *Massive Psychic Trauma,* International Universities Press, 1968; (editor) *Jail House Blues,* Epic Publications, 1973; (contributor) A. Kutscher, editor, *Psychopharmacologic Agents for the Terminally Ill and Bereaved,* Columbia University Press, 1973; (contributor) J. H. Masserman, editor, *Current Psychiatric Therapies,* Grune, 1973; (co-author) *Preparation to See a Psychiatrist,* Health Science, Inc., in press.

Contributor of more than thirty articles to medical and corrections journals, including *Focus, Police Law Quarterly, Life-Threatening Behavior, Police Chief, Society of Humanistic Judaism,* and *International Journal of Offender Therapy.* Editor-in-chief of Police Education Audio Library Service, 1973—. Editor of *VITA* of International Association for Suicide Prevention, 1973—; member of editorial board of *Crises Intervention* and *Michigan Police Officer,* both 1974—; consulting editor of *Bulletin of Suicidology,* 1969—.

WORK IN PROGRESS: Co-author of *Suicide and Violence; Suicide and Bereavement,* with Kutscher.

AVOCATIONAL INTERESTS: Camping, photography.

* * *

DARLING, Edward 1907-1974

June 19, 1907—December 12, 1974; American author and publisher. Obituaries: *New York Times,* December 18, 1974; *Washington Post,* December 21, 1974; *AB Bookman's Weekly,* January 13, 1975; *Publishers Weekly,* January 15, 1975. (*CA*-49/52).

* * *

DARLING, Mary Kathleen 1943-
(Kathy Darling)

PERSONAL: Born September 8, 1943, in Hudson, N.Y.; daughter of Andrew J. (a major in the U.S. Army) and Helen C. (McCourt) Sipos; married Joseph Darling; children: Tara Ann. *Education:* Attended Russell Sage College. *Home:* 46 Cooper Lane, Larchmont, N.Y. 10538. *Office:* Garrard Publishing Co., 2 Overhill Rd., Scarsdale, N.Y. 10583.

CAREER: Garrard Publishing Co., Scarsdale, N.Y., children's book editor and promotion director, 1968—.

WRITINGS—For children; under name Kathy Darling: *The Jelly Bean Contest,* Garrard, 1972; (with Leland B. Jacobs) *April Fool!,* Garrard, 1973; *Little Bat's Secret,* Garrard, 1974. Contributor to magazines about dogs.

AVOCATIONAL INTERESTS: Raising Irish wolfhounds.

* * *

DAS GUPTA, Jyotirindra 1933-

PERSONAL: Born in 1933, in Calcutta, India; married Rupasree Dutta-Mazumdar (a researcher), 1964; children: Modhurima (daughter). *Education:* University of Calcutta, B.A., 1953, M.A., 1955; University of California, Berkeley, Ph.D., 1966. *Religion:* Hindu. *Residence:* Berkeley, Calif. *Office:* Department of Political Science, University of California, Berkeley, Calif. 94720.

CAREER: Lecturer in political science at City College and St. Xavier's College, Calcutta, India, 1956-61; University of California, Berkeley, assistant professor, 1965-69, associate professor of political science, 1970—. *Member:* American Political Science Association.

WRITINGS: (With J. A. Fishman and C. A. Ferguson) *Language Problems of Developing Nations,* Wiley, 1968; *Language Conflict and National Development,* University of California Press, 1970. Contributor to journals. Member of board of editors of *Asian Survey.*

WORK IN PROGRESS: Contributing to and editing a book with C. A. Ferguson, on language planning in India, Israel, Indonesia, and Sweden.

* * *

DAUSTER, Frank (Nicholas) 1925-

PERSONAL: Surname is pronounced Daw-ster; born February 5, 1925, in Irvington, N.J.; son of Frank Nicholas and Wilma (Johnson) Dauster; married Helen Thode (a librarian), June 21, 1949; children: Robert, Nicholas. *Education:* Rutgers University, B.A., 1949, M.A., 1950; Yale University, Ph.D., 1953. *Religion:* Unitarian. *Home:* 159 Lakeside Dr. N., Piscataway, N.J. 08854. *Office:* Department of Spanish and Portuguese, Rutgers University, New Brunswick, N.J. 08903.

CAREER: Wesleyan University, Middletown, Conn., instructor, 1950-54, assistant professor of Spanish, 1954-55; Rutgers University, New Brunswick, N.J., assistant professor, 1955-58, associate professor, 1958-62, professor of Spanish, 1962—. *Military service:* U.S. Army, Ordnance, 1943-46; became technical sergeant. *Member:* American Association of Teachers of Spanish and Portuguese, Modern Language Association of America, Latin American Studies Association, Instituto Internacional de Literatura Iberoamericana, American Association of University Professors, Phi Beta Kappa.

WRITINGS: Breve historia de la poesia mexicana, Ediciones de Andrea, 1956; *Ensayos sobre poesia mexicana,* Studium, 1963; (editor) *Teatro hispanoamericano,* Harcourt, 1965; *Historia del teatro hispanoamericano,* Studium, 1966, 2nd edition, 1973; (compiler and author of prologue and notes) *Poesia mejicana* (anthology), Editorial Ebro, 1970; (editor with Luis Leal) *Literatura de Hispanoamerica,* Harcourt, 1970; *Xavier Villaurrutia,* Twayne, 1971; (editor with Leon F. Lyday) *En un Acto,* Van Nostrand, 1973.

WORK IN PROGRESS: Ensayos sobre teatro hispanoamericano; research in contemporary Spanish theater and in twentieth-century Spanish-American poetry.

AVOCATIONAL INTERESTS: Music (classical and Dixieland).

* * *

DAUW, Dean C(harles) 1933-

PERSONAL: Surname is pronounced Dow; born July 31, 1933, in Rock Island, Ill. *Education:* Spring Hill College, B.S., 1960; St. Thomas College, M.A., 1961; University of Minnesota, Ph.D., 1965. *Home:* 1212 Lake Shore Dr., Chicago, Ill. 60610. *Office:* 112 West Oak St., Chicago, Ill. 60610.

CAREER: Human Resource Developers, Inc., Chicago, Ill., president, 1968—; DePaul University, Chicago, Ill., professor of management, 1969—. Director of Three C's

Medical Center. *Member:* American Psychological Association, Association for Humanistic Psychology, American Personnel and Guidance Association, National Vocational Guidance Association.

WRITINGS: (With A. J. Fredian) *Dynamics of Black Employee Relations*, Simon & Schuster, 1971; *Creativity and Innovation in Organizations*, Kendall-Hunt, 1971, 2nd edition, 1974. Contributor to journals and periodicals, including *Washington Post*, *Gifted Child Quarterly*, *Insight*, *Religious Education*, *Personnel*, *Hospital Topics*, *Management Review*, *Business World*, and *Journal of Creative Behavior*.

WORK IN PROGRESS: Up Your Career: How to Salve the Pain in Your Career.

* * *

DAVES, Jessica 1898(?)-1974

1898(?)—September 22, 1974; American magazine editor and writer. Obituaries: *Washington Post*, September 25, 1974.

* * *

DAVID, Michael Robert 1932-

PERSONAL: Born September 12, 1932. *Education:* Attended City College (now City College of the City University of New York), 1949-53; studied acting privately, and with American Theatre Wing. *Address:* c/o Writers Guild of America, West, 8955 Beverly Blvd., Los Angeles, Calif. 90048.

CAREER: Actor, director, producer, writer for theatre, film, television, and radio. Newscaster and host of television interview program for WNYC-Radio and Television, New York, N.Y., 1960-66; actor on dramatic programs for television, beginning in 1950's; has acted in about ten Off-Broadway productions, and in summer stock. Conducted apprentice acting program at Ivoryton Playhouse, Connecticut, two years; guest lecturer at New York University School of Continuing Education, New School for Social Research, Florida State University, and University of Texas at Austin; has also coached actors privately. *Military service:* U.S. Army, 1953-54. *Member:* Writers Guild of America, American Federation of Television and Radio Artists, Screen Actors Guild, Actors Equity, O'Neill Playwrights, Actors Studio Playwrights' Unit.

WRITINGS—Plays: "Entre Nous," first produced Off-Off-Broadway at The Playbox, 1968; "A Couple o' Charleys," first produced in Waterford, Conn., at O'Neill Theatre Center Playwrights Conference, 1970; "The Justice Box," first produced Off-Broadway at Theatre de Lys, 1971, published in *Drama & Theatre*, fall, 1972; "Out of Gas," first produced at University of Texas at Austin, 1974.

Writer (and producer) of human relations films for Anti-Defamation League, and writer of public affairs spots for television, sponsored by Department of the Interior, National Tuberculosis Association, VISTA, and others; also writer for industrial and educational films. Author of scripts for television series, "One Life to Live," ABC, 1972-73, and "Love of Life," CBS, 1973-74.

* * *

DAVIDSON, Abraham A. 1935-

PERSONAL: Born June 27, 1935, in Dorchester, Mass.; son of Isaac (a postal clerk) and Ruth (Feinsilver) Davidson. *Education:* Harvard University, A.B. (cum laude), 1957; Boston University, A.M., 1960; Hebrew Teachers College, Boston, Mass., B.J.Ed., 1960; Columbia University, Ph.D., 1965. *Religion:* Jewish. *Office:* Department of Art History, Temple University, Philadelphia, Pa. 19122.

CAREER: Oakland University, Rochester, Mich., assistant professor of art history, 1965-68; Temple University, Tyler School of Art, Philadelphia, Pa., assistant professor, 1968-70, associate professor of art history, 1970—. *Awards, honors:* Group 17 prize for photography, 1969, from Detroit Institute of Arts annual exhibition for Michigan artists.

WRITINGS: The Story of American Painting, Abrams, 1974. Contributor to *American Quarterly*, and to art journals, including *Artforum, Art News, Art Quarterly*, and *Art Journal*.

AVOCATIONAL INTERESTS: Photography (has had group and solo shows), trumpet, travel (Europe, Israel, the Caribbean).

* * *

DAVIDSON, Eva Rucker 1894(?)-1974

1894(?)—August 4, 1974; American author and historian. Obituaries: *Washington Post*, August 5, 1974.

* * *

DAVIES, Ivor K(evin) 1930-

PERSONAL: Born December 19, 1930, in Birmingham, England; son of Howard (an executive) and Selina (a nurse; maiden name, Stockton) Davies; married Shirley D. Winyard, February 24, 1966; children: Simon Winyard, Michelle Winyard. *Education:* University of Birmingham, B.A. (special honors), 1952, M.A., 1953, certificate in education, 1955; University of Illinois, M.S., 1954; University of Nottingham, Ph.D., 1967. *Home:* 2447 Rock Creek Dr., Bloomington, Ind. 47401; and 27 Broughton Rd., Wollescote, Stourbridge, Worcestershire 0XP DY9, England. *Office:* School of Education, Indiana University, Bloomington, Ind. 47401.

CAREER: Royal Air Force, career officer, 1955-71, retiring as lieutenant colonel; Ministry of Defence, Royal Air Force Training Command, Brampton, England, senior research officer, 1955-66; Royal Air Force College, Cranwell, England, senior lecturer and head of behavioral science, 1966-71; Indiana University, Bloomington, professor of education, and executive director of Audio-Visual Center, 1972—. *Member:* English-Speaking Union, British Psychological Society, American Psychological Association, American Educational Research Association, Royal Air Force Club. *Awards, honors*—Military: General Service Medal, 1957. Civilian: Fulbright fellowship, 1953.

WRITINGS: (With C. A. Thomas) *Programmed Learning in Perspective*, Educational Methods, 1963; *Management of Learning*, McGraw, 1971; *Competency Based Learning*, McGraw, 1972; (with J. A. Hartley) *Organization of Training*, McGraw, 1972; (with Hartley) *Aspects of Educational Technology*, Butterworth, 1973; *Objectives in Education*, McGraw, in press. Contributor to *Instructional Science, Journal of Programmed Learning and Educational Technology*, and *AV Communication Review*.

AVOCATIONAL INTERESTS: Foreign travel, design, photography, music, theatre.

DAVIES, Peter 1937-

PERSONAL: Born February 22, 1937, in London, England; emigrated to Canada, 1957; son of Tony (a timber merchant) and Joan (Howell) Davies; married Lan Rayside (a teacher), April 28, 1967; children: Wendy. *Education:* Attended schools in Croydon, Surrey, England. *Politics:* "Hard to say! Both liberal and socialist, depending on how I feel on a particular day." *Religion:* Christian. *Home:* 60 Underhill Dr., Apt. 210, Don Mills, Ontario M3A 2J7, Canada.

CAREER: Held a variety of jobs, including microfilming concentration camp records in West Germany for the Israeli government, working for a lumber company in New Zealand, and as a telephone salesman, clerk, swimming instructor, and lifeguard, 1957-58; supervisor of a home for boys in Montreal, Quebec, 1958-60; Royal Trust Co., Montreal, Quebec, member of staff, 1963-67; full-time writer, 1967—.

WRITINGS: Fly Away Paul (novel), Crown, 1974. Contributor to *Chatelaine*.

WORK IN PROGRESS: The second and third novels of a trilogy, with *Fly Away Paul* as the first, based on the effects of broken marriages on young people, for publication by Crown; a play; magazine articles.

SIDELIGHTS: Davies told *CA* that his experience as a supervisor in a Montreal boys' home was the catalyst for his writing. "I sympathized with these young people," Davis writes. "My parents were divorced while I was still a middle teenager. Though I did not spend any time as a boy in a home, I knew how they felt. The boys in the home were not criminal though they were often treated as such." *Fly Away Paul*, which Davies describes as a "short bitter novel" that nevertheless contains hope, is about such a boy who ultimately gains freedom. Davies speaks "some French, more German."

AVOCATIONAL INTERESTS: Travel, photography (Davies has a 4,000-slide collection), music ("mostly serious, my current favorite composer being Gustave Mahler"), the supernatural, a "lifelong hobby to gain greater control over my physical body, thus allowing my spirit to develop to its ultimate point" (Davies noted here, however, his belief in reincarnation), swimming, ping-pong, tennis, long walks, reading.

* * *

DAVIS, David Howard 1941-

PERSONAL: Born September 14, 1941, in Washington, D.C.; son of Dorland J. (a physician) and Caroline (a teacher; maiden name, Baker) Davis. *Education:* Cornell University, A.B., 1963; Johns Hopkins University, M.A., 1969, Ph.D., 1971. *Politics:* Democrat. *Religion:* Episcopalian. *Home:* 20-K Franklin Greens, Somerset, N.J. 08873. *Office:* Department of Political Science, Rutgers University, New Brunswick, N.J. 08903.

CAREER: Democratic National Committee, Washington, D.C., member of staff, 1964; Rutgers University, New Brunswick, N.J., assistant professor of political science, 1971—. Member of Office of Legislation of U.S. Environmental Protection Agency, 1973-74. *Military service:* U.S. Army, artillery, forward observer, 1964-67; served in Vietnam; became captain; received Air Medal. *Member:* American Political Science Association, American Society for Public Administration, American Economic Association. *Awards, honors:* Woodrow Wilson fellowship, 1970-71; National Association of Schools of Public Affairs and Administration fellowship, 1973-74.

WRITINGS: How the Bureaucracy Makes Foreign Policy: An Exchange Analysis, Heath, 1972; *Energy Politics*, St. Martin's, 1974.

SIDELIGHTS: Davis writes: "I am a sworn enemy of the dull introduction, the poor transition, and the editorial 'we.' I am not too fond of the passive voice, either."

* * *

DAVIS, Donald Gordon, Jr. 1939-

PERSONAL: Born August 15, 1939, in San Marcos, Tex.; son of Donald Gordon (a clergyman) and Ethel (Henning) Davis; married Avis Jane Higdon, December 6, 1969; children: Lucinda Ellen, Samuel Higdon. *Education:* University of California, Los Angeles, B.A., 1961; University of California, Berkeley, M.A., 1963, M.L.S., 1964; University of Illinois, Ph.D., 1972. *Politics:* "Reform, regardless of party." *Religion:* Presbyterian. *Home:* 2702 Geraghty Ave., Austin, Tex. 78757. *Office:* Graduate School of Library Science, University of Texas, P.O. Box 7576, Austin, Tex. 78712.

CAREER: Fresno State College (now California State University at Fresno), Library, senior reference librarian, 1964-68, head of department of special collections, 1966-68, instructor in library resources, 1967-68; University of Texas, Graduate School of Library Science, Austin, assistant professor of library science, 1971—. Part-time senior library assistant, University of California, Berkeley, 1961-64; member of board, Fresno Community Chorus, 1966-68. *Member:* American Library Association, American Historical Association, American Scientific Affiliation, Association of American Library Schools, Christian Library Fellowship, Conference on Faith and History, Organization of American Historians, Southwestern Library Association, Texas Library Association, Texas Association of College Teachers, Beta Phi Mu. *Awards, honors:* Newberry Library fellowship, 1974.

WRITINGS: The American Medical Association and the American Library Association: A Study of Developing Organizational Structure, Graduate School of Library Science, University of Illinois, 1972; *The Association of American Library Schools, 1915-1968: An Analytical History* (revision of Part I of doctoral thesis), Scarecrow, 1974; *Comparative Historical Analysis of Three Associations of Professional Schools*, Graduate School of Library Science, University of Illinois, 1974. Abstractor, *Historical Abstracts* and *America: History and Life*, 1965—; regular reviewer, *American Reference Books Annual*, *Booklist*, *Choice*, and *HIS*; referee, *Journal of Library History*.

WORK IN PROGRESS: With others, *The Social Sciences: A Selective Guide to Information Sources*; a volume on William Frederick Poole, for "Heritage of Librarianship" series, publication expected in 1976; with Roland E. Stevens, a 4th edition of *Reference Books in the Social Sciences and Humanities*, 1976; articles for *Dictionary of American Library Biography*, 1976; research on the rise of the public library in Texas.

AVOCATIONAL INTERESTS: Working with Inter-Varsity Christian Fellowship, serious choral music, collecting private press fine printing, visiting local historical and landmark sites, handball, backpacking, bicycling.

DAVIS, Elizabeth G. 1910(?)-1974

1910(?)—July 31, 1974; American author. Obituaries: *New York Times*, August 2, 1974; *AB Bookman's Weekly*, October 7, 1974.

* * *

DAVIS, Gordon B(itter) 1930-

PERSONAL: Born August 9, 1930, in Idaho Falls, Idaho; son of Orson P. (a grocer) amd Olive (Bitter) Davis; married LaNay Marie Flint, August 19, 1954; children: Alison, Jennifer, Clark, Flint. *Education:* Idaho State University, B.A., 1955, B.S., 1955; Stanford University, M.B.A., 1957, Ph.D., 1959. *Religion:* Church of Jesus Christ of Latter-day Saints (Mormon). *HKOME:* 2148 Folwell, St. Paul, Minn. 55108. *Office:* College of Business Administration, University of Minnesota, Minneapolis, Minn. 55455.

CAREER: Touche, Ross & Co. (certified public accountants), San Francisco, Calif., auditor, 1958-59, consultant in New York, N.Y., 1959-61; University of Minnesota, College of Business Administration, Minneapolis, assistant professor, 1961-63, associate professor, 1963-67, professor of business administration, 1967—. Visiting professor at European Institute for Advanced Study in Management, Brussels, 1971-72. Consultant to American Institute of Certified Public Accountants, 1966-67. *Member:* American Institute of Certified Public Accountants, American Accounting Association, Institute of Management Science, Association for Computing Machinery, American Institute for Decision Sciences.

WRITINGS: Introduction to Electronic Computers, McGraw, 1965, 2nd edition, 1971; *Auditing and EDP*, American Institute of Certified Public Accountants, 1968; *Computer Data Processing*, McGraw, 1969, 2nd edition, 1973; *Elementary Cobol Programming*, McGraw, 1971; *Management Information Systems: Conceptual Foundations, Structure, and Development*, McGraw, 1974. Contributor to journals.

* * *

DAVIS, Johanna 1937-1974

October 2, 1937—July 25, 1974; American journalist and author. Obituaries: *Time*, August 5, 1974; *AB Bookman's Weekly*, October 7, 1974. (*CA*-41/44).

* * *

DAVIS, Julian 1902(?)-1974

1902(?)—September 13, 1974; American gold miner and poet. Obituaries: *New York Times*, September 14, 1974; *AB Bookman's Weekly*, October 7, 1974.

* * *

DAVIS, Lance E(dwin) 1928-

PERSONAL: Born November 3, 1928, in Seattle, Wash.; son of Maurice L. (a logger) and Marjorie (a teacher; maiden name, Seibert) Davis; divorced; children: Maili (daughter). *Education:* University of Washington, Seattle, B.A. (magna cum laude), 1950; Johns Hopkins University, Ph.D. (with distinction), 1956. *Home:* 1746 Grevelia, Apt. E, South Pasadena, Calif. 91030. *Office:* Division of Humanities and Social Sciences, California Institute of Technology, Pasadena, Calif. 91125.

CAREER: Johns Hopkins University, Baltimore, Md., instructor in economics, 1954-55; Purdue University, Lafayette, Ind., instructor, 1955-56, assistant professor, 1956-59, associate professor, 1959-62, professor of economic history, 1962-68; California Institute of Technology, Pasadena, professor of economics, 1968—. Visiting fellow at Nuffield College, Oxford University, 1964-65. *Military service:* U.S. Naval Reserve, 1945-52; active duty, 1945-48. *Member:* American Economic Association, Economic History Association, Council on Research in Economic History (chairman, 1973-74), Phi Beta Kappa. *Awards, honors:* Ford Foundation faculty fellowship, 1959-60; Guggenheim fellow, 1964-65; Arthur Cole Prize of Economic History Association, 1966.

WRITINGS: (With Peter L. Payne) *The Savings Bank of Baltimore, 1818-1866: A History and Analytical Study*, Johns Hopkins Press, 1956; (with J. R. T. Hughes and Duncan McDougall) *American Economic History: The Development of a National Economy*, Irwin, 1961, 3rd edition, 1969; *The Growth of Industrial Enterprise*, Scott, Foresman, 1964; (with Douglass North) *Institutional Change and American Economic Growth*, Cambridge University Press, 1971; (contributor) G. R. Taylor and L. F. Ellsworth, editors, *Approaches to American Economic History*, University Press of Virginia, 1971; (editor with R. E. Easterlin and William Parker) *American Economic Growth: An Economist's History of the United States*, Harper, 1972; (contributor) Roger G. Noll, editor, *Government and the Sports Business*, Brookings Institution, 1974. Contributor to *Cambridge Economic History of Europe* and to economic, history, and statistical journals. Member of board of editors, *Journal of Economic History*, 1965-73.

WORK IN PROGRESS: Research on the impact of imperialism on economic growth and welfare, 1850-1914, with particular reference to the British Empire; other research on the process of institutional adaptation to the pressures generated by economic development, on the relationship between capital, financial intermediaries, money markets, and economic growth, and on economic aspects of professional sports.

* * *

DAVIS, Louis E(lkin) 1918-

PERSONAL: Born September 10, 1918, in New York; son of David G. (a broker) and Anna (Elkin) Davis; married Edith Kaufmann, March 26, 1944; children: Jonathan F., Carol V. *Education:* Georgia Institute of Technology, B.S.M.E., 1940; University of Iowa, M.S., 1942; Columbia University, further graduate study, 1944-46. *Residence:* Beverly Hills, Calif. *Office:* Graduate School of Management, University of California, Los Angeles, Calif. 90024.

CAREER: University of California, Berkeley, assistant professor, 1947-53, associate professor, 1953-59, professor of industrial engineering, 1959-66; University of California, Los Angeles, professor of organizational sciences, 1966—. Lucas Professor at University of Birmingham, 1962-63; research fellow at Tavistock Institute, 1966. Manpower commissioner for State of California, 1957-63. Consultant to governments, business, and unions in the United States and abroad; senior advisor, Organization for European Economic Cooperation, 1957-58. *Member:* International Council for Quality of Working Life. *Awards, honors:* Awards from Maritime Transportation Research Board of the National Academy of Sciences, 1968-74; Hayhow Award from American College of Hospital Administrators, 1971.

WRITINGS: (With James C. Taylor) *Design of Jobs*, Penguin, 1972; (with Albert B. Cherns) *Quality of Working Life*, Free Press, 1975, Volume I: *Problems, Prospects, State of the Art*, Volume II: *Cases*; (contributor) R. Dubin, editor, *Society, Organizations and Work*, Rand McNally, 1975; (contributor) A. W. Clark, editor, *Experiences in Action Research*, Malaby Press (London), 1975. Contributor of chapters to about a dozen other books. Contributor of about a hundred technical articles to professional journals.

WORK IN PROGRESS: Organization Design with Human Values, two volumes, completion expected in 1976; continuing research on the quality of working life.

* * *

DAVIS, Murray S(tuart) 1940-

PERSONAL: Born February 10, 1940, in Pittsburgh, Pa.; son of William W. (a pharmacist) and Reva (Lippard) Davis. *Education:* University of Chicago, B.A., 1961, M.A., 1962; University of California, Berkeley, further graduate study, 1962-65; Brandeis University, Ph.D., 1969. *Residence:* La Jolla, Calif. *Office:* Department of Sociology, University of California at San Diego, La Jolla, Calif. 92037.

CAREER: Northern Illinois University, DeKalb, assistant professor of sociology, 1969-73; University of California at San Diego, La Jolla, visiting associate professor of sociology, 1973—. *Member:* American Sociological Association.

WRITINGS: Intimate Relations, Free Press, 1973. Contributor to *Philosophy of the Social Sciences* and *Social Forces*.

WORK IN PROGRESS: A small study of the obnoxious; a middle-sized study of the obscene, completion expected in 1976; a large scale study of laughter and comedy, 1980.

SIDELIGHTS: "I do not write my books," Davis told *CA*. "My books write themselves. I am merely the often unwilling conduit between ideas and words, between thought and print."

* * *

DAVIS, Natalie Zemon 1928-

PERSONAL: Born November 8, 1928, in Detroit, Mich.; daughter of Julian Leon (a businessman) and Helen (Lamport) Zemon; married Chandler Davis (a professor of mathematics), August 16, 1948; children: Aaron Bancroft, Hannah Penrose, Simone Weil. *Education:* Smith College, B.A., 1949; Radcliffe College, M.A., 1950; University of Michigan, Ph.D., 1959. *Residence:* Berkeley, Calif. *Office:* Department of History, University of California, Berkeley, Calif. 94720.

CAREER: Brown University, Providence, R.I., 1959-63, began as lecturer, became assistant professor of history, 1961; University of Toronto, Toronto, Ontario, 1963-71, began as lecturer, became associate professor of history, 1967; University of California, Berkeley, professor of history, 1971—. *Member:* American Historical Association (member of council, 1972-75), Society for French Historical Studies, Society for Reformation Research, Renaissance Society of America. *Awards, honors:* William Koran, Jr. Prize from Society for French Historical Studies, 1968, 1971, honorable mention, 1973.

WRITINGS: Society and Culture in Early Modern France: Eight Essays, Stanford University Press, 1975.

Contributor: G. Berthoud and others, editors, *Aspects de la propagande religieuse*, Librairie Droz (Geneva), 1957; R. J. Shoeck, editor, *Editing Sixteenth-Century Texts*, University of Toronto Press, 1966; Dorothy McGuigan, editor, *A Sampler of Women's Studies*, University of Michigan Center for Continuing Education of Women, 1973; Charles Trinkaus and H. Oberman, editors, *The Pursuit of Holiness*, E. J. Brill, 1974; Michel Mollat, editor, *Etudes sur l'histoire de la pauvrete (Moyen Age-XVIe siecle)*, Publications de la Sorbonne, 1974; Alfred Soman, editor, *The Massacre of St. Bartholomew: Reappraisals and Documents*, M. Nijhoff, 1974.

Contributor of about forty articles to history journals, including *Past and Present*.

WORK IN PROGRESS: Research on religion and society in sixteenth-century French cities and on sex roles in early modern Europe.

SIDELIGHTS: Natalie Davis writes: "I'm especially interested in the 'people,' the artisans and poor of sixteenth-century French cities, and also in the culture of peasants. When I study sex roles and sexual symbolism, I'll look more closely at the city street than at the royal court, at the proverb and street riot than at the Latin sermon or court masque. I'm interested in the ways in which anthropology can help historians who are working on populations which are only partly literate."

* * *

DAVIS, Richard

PERSONAL: Born in London, England. *Education:* Educated in England. *Home:* 77 Quintin Ave., London W.10, England. *Agent:* Michael Bakewell, Associates Ltd., 118 Tottenham Court Rd., London W.1, England.

CAREER: Writer, film producer, and editor.

WRITINGS—Editor: (And contributor) *Tandem Horror 2*, Tandem Press, 1968; (and contributor) *Tandem Horror 3*, Tandem Press, 1969; *Years Best Horror Stories*, Sphere Books, 1971; *Years Best Horror Stories 2*, Sphere Books, 1972, Daw Books, 1974; *Years Best Horror Stories 3*, Sphere Books, 1973, Daw Books, 1975; *Space One*, Abelard, 1973; *Spectre One*, Abelard, 1973; *Space Two*, Abelard, 1974; *Spectre Two*, Abelard, 1974; *Space Three*, Abelard, 1974; *Spectre Three*, Abelard, 1974; *Armada SF One*, Fontana, 1975; *Armada SF Two*, Fontana, 1975.

Work represented in anthologies, including *4th Pan Book of Horror Stories*, edited by Herbert Van Thal, Pan Books, 1963; *Graves Give Up Their Dead*, edited by Frederick Pickersgill, Corgi Books, 1964; *No Such Thing as a Vampire*, edited by Pickersgill, Corgi Books, 1965; *Horror 7*, edited by Pickersgill, Corgi Books, 1965; *6th Pan Book of Horror Stories*, edited by Van Thal, Pan Books, 1965; *5th Ghost Book*, edited by Rosemary Timperley, Barrie & Jenkins, 1969; *6th Ghost Book*, edited by Timperley, Barrie & Jenkins, 1970; *New Writing in Horror and Fantasy*, edited by David Sutton, Sphere Books, 1971.

Author and producer of film, "Viola," 1968; story editor of BBC-TV dramas, "13 Against Fate" and "Late Night Horror"; contributor to BBC-Radio series, "Price of Fear." Critic and columnist, *Films and Filming*, 1964-71.

WORK IN PROGRESS: Two feature film scripts; *Rags to Riches*, for Abelard; *You Always Remember the First Time*, for Alison & Busby.

* * *

DAVIS, Thomas J(oseph) 1946-

PERSONAL: Born January 6, 1946, in New York, N.Y.;

son of Otto Joseph and Alice (McKenzie) Davis; married Lula Johnson (a cinema manager), April 1, 1969. *Education:* Fordham University, A.B. (cum laude), 1967; Columbia University, M.A., 1968, Ph.D., 1973; further study at Cornell University and University of New Delhi. *Home:* 1003 Gurney Dr., Richmond, Ind. 47374. *Office:* Department of History, Earlham College, National Rd. W., Richmond, Ind. 47374.

CAREER: Columbia University, New York, N.Y., instructor in history, summer, 1968; Southern University, Baton Rouge, La., instructor in history, 1968-69; Fordham University, New York, N.Y., instructor in history, 1969-71; Manhattanville College, Purchase, N.Y., instructor in history, 1970-71; Earlham College, Richmond, Ind., assistant professor, 1971-74, associate professor of history, 1974—. Member of New York City Anti-Poverty Council, 1964-65, and Council Against Poverty, New York, N.Y., 1965-68. *Member:* Association of Afro-American Life and History, African Studies Association, Phi Beta Kappa, Alpha Mu Gamma. *Awards, honors:* National teaching fellow, 1968; Herbert H. Lehman fellow, 1969; Ford Foundation Advanced Study fellow, 1972.

WRITINGS: (Editor) *The New York Conspiracy*, Beacon Press, 1971. Member of editorial board of *Journal of Negro History*, 1973—.

WORK IN PROGRESS: Analysis of the New York Conspiracy; a fictional trilogy set in eighteenth-century New York.

* * *

DAWDY, Doris Ostrander

PERSONAL: Born in the United States; married David R. Dawdy (a research hydrologist and consultant). *Education:* Attended MacPhail School of Music and Los Angeles City College. *Politics:* Democrat. *Home:* 1315 James Ave., Redwood City, Calif. 94062.

CAREER: Writer; researcher. *Member:* California Historical Society.

WRITINGS: Annotated Bibliography of American Indian Painting, Heye Foundation, 1968; *Artists of the American West*, Swallow Press, 1974. Contributor to journals.

WORK IN PROGRESS: Two books.

* * *

DAY, Robert Adams 1924-

PERSONAL: Born October 3, 1924, in Providence, R.I.; son of Irving Woodman (a catalogue editor) and Mabel (Adams) Day. *Education:* Brown University, A.B., 1948; Harvard University, M.A., 1949, Ph.D., 1952. *Politics:* "Improvised." *Religion:* "Comparative." *Home:* 336 West 12th St., New York, N.Y. 10014. *Office:* Department of English, Queens College of the City University of New York, Flushing, N.Y. 11367.

CAREER: Dartmouth College, Hanover, N.H., instructor in English, 1952-54; Queens College of the City University of New York, Flushing, N.Y., instructor, 1954-62, assistant professor, 1963-65, associate professor, 1965-69, professor of English, 1970—. City University of New York, Graduate Center, New York, N.Y., professor in doctoral faculty in English, 1970—, professor in doctoral faculty in comparative literature, 1973—. *Military service:* U.S. Army, Medical Corps, 1943-45; received European Theater ribbon with five battle stars. *Member:* Modern Language Association of America, English Association (England), English Institute, American Society for Eighteenth-Century Studies, Modern Humanities Research Association, Phi Beta Kappa. *Awards, honors:* Dexter traveling fellowship, Harvard University, 1952; Newberry Library fellowship, 1965.

WRITINGS: (Author of introduction and bibliography of epistolary fiction, 1660-1740) Mary Davys, *Familiar Letters Betwixt a Gentleman and a Lady*, William Andrews Clark Memorial Library, University of California, 1955; *Told in Letters: Epistolary Fiction Before Richardson*, University of Michigan Press, 1966; (editor) Catherine Trotter, *Olinda's Adventures*, Augustan Reprint Society, 1969; *Joyce's "Waste Land" and Eliot's "Unknown God"* (monograph), University of Wisconsin Press, 1971; (editor) Francis Coventry, *Pompey the Little*, Oxford University Press, 1974. Contributor to *New Cambridge Bibliography of English Literature* and to literature journals.

WORK IN PROGRESS: An edition of seven short novels for the Oxford University Press "English Novels" series; other editions of works by Tobias Smollett, for University of Iowa Bicentennial edition of Smollett, and by Daniel Defoe, for Southern Illinois University edition of Defoe; book-length studies of the English comic novel and modernist creativity; articles on Smollett, Eliot, and Joyce.

AVOCATIONAL INTERESTS: The theater, ballet, collecting classical records.

* * *

DEAK, Edward Joseph, Jr. 1943-

PERSONAL: Born March 17, 1943, in New Haven, Conn.; son of Edward Joseph (a manager) and Anne (a salesperson; maiden name, Coleman) Deak; married Alice Rockwell (a teacher), August 20, 1966; children: Patrick Joseph, Bryan Michael. *Education:* University of Connecticut, B.A., 1965, M.A., 1966, Ph.D., 1974. *Politics:* Democrat. *Religion:* Roman Catholic. *Home:* 85 Sanford Pl., Stratford, Conn. 06497. *Office:* Department of Economics, Fairfield University, Fairfield, Conn. 06430.

CAREER: Fairfield University, Fairfield, Conn., assistant professor, 1970-74, associate professor of economics, 1974—. Candidate for Connecticut State Senate, autumn, 1974. *Member:* American Economic Association, Eastern Economic Association, Eastern Finance Association, Omicron Delta Epsilon.

WRITINGS: Environmental Factors in Transportation Planning, Heath, 1972. Contributor to *Highway Research Record, Rhode Island Business Quarterly*, and *New England Journal of Business and Economics*.

WORK IN PROGRESS: The Economics of Transportation Subsidies; Monopoly Power in America.

SIDELIGHTS: Deak writes: "The role of the economist is to portray the consequences of choice. As an actor in the policy process it is important that he know the kinds of statements the science will allow and vital that he be aware of the conclusions which are beyond his reach."

* * *

DEAN, John A(urie) 1921-

PERSONAL: Born May 9, 1921, in Sault Sainte Marie, Mich.; son of Aurie Jerome (a teacher) and Gertrude (a teacher; maiden name, Saw) Dean; married Elizabeth Louise Cousins, June 20, 1943; children: Nancy Elizabeth

(Mrs. Stephen G. Fischer), Thomas Alfred, John Randolph, Laurie Alice, Clarissa Elaine. *Education:* University of Michigan, B.S., 1942, M.S., 1944, Ph.D., 1949. *Politics:* Independent. *Religion:* Presbyterian. *Home:* 1112 West Nokomis, Knoxville, Tenn. 37919. *Office:* Department of Chemistry, University of Tennessee, Knoxville, Tenn. 37916.

CAREER: Chrysler Corp., Detroit, Mich., chemist in Manhattan Project, 1944-45; University of Michigan, Ann Arbor, lecturer in chemistry, 1946-48; University of Alabama, Tuscaloosa, associate professor of chemistry, 1948-50; University of Tennessee, Knoxville, assistant professor, 1950-53, associate professor, 1953-58, professor of chemistry, 1958—. Consultant to Nuclear Division of Union Carbide Corp., 1953-74, and Stewart Laboratories, 1968—. *Member:* American Chemical Society (secretary of East Tennessee section, 1953), Society for Applied Spectroscopy (chairman of southeastern section, 1971-73), Archaeological Institute of America, U.S. Naval Institute, Sigma Xi (treasurer of University of Tennessee chapter, 1954). *Awards, honors:* Charles H. Stone Award from Carolina section of American Chemical Society, 1974, for outstanding achievements in chemistry for resident of southeastern section of United States.

WRITINGS: (With H. H. Willard and L. L. Merritt, Jr.) *Instrumental Methods of Analysis*, Van Nostrand, 1948, 5th edition, 1974; *Flame Photometry*, McGraw, 1960; (contributor) G. L. Clark, editor, *Encyclopedia of Spectroscopy*, Van Nostrand, 1960; (contributor) *Developments in Applied Spectroscopy*, Plenum, Volume III, edited by J. E. Forrette and E. Lanterman, 1964, Volume IV, edited by E. Davis, 1965, Volume V, edited by L. R. Pearson and E. L. Grove, 1966; (contributor) F. J. Welcher, editor, *Standard Methods of Chemical Analysis*, 6th edition (Dean was not associated with earlier editions), Volume III, Part A, Van Nostrand, 1966; *Chemical Separation Methods*, Van Nostrand, 1969; (editor with T. C. Rains and contributor) *Flame Emission and Atomic Absorption Spectrometry*, Dekker, Volume I, 1969, Volume II, 1971, Volume III, 1975; (editor and contributor) *Lange's Handbook of Chemistry*, 11th edition (Dean was not associated with earlier editions), McGraw, 1973.

Contributor to *Encyclopaedic Dictionary of Physics* and of almost one hundred articles to scientific journals.

WORK IN PROGRESS: Research on flame photometric methods, particularly as applied to archaeology; twelfth edition of *Lange's Handbook of Chemistry*; a short version of *Instrumental Methods of Analysis*; *Nonflame and Semiflame Atomic Absorption and Emission Spectrometry*, with T. C. Rains.

SIDELIGHTS: Instrumental Methods of Analysis leads its field with more than 100,000 copies in English, plus translations into Japanese, Spanish, French, and Portuguese.

* * *

DE BLASIS, Celeste 1946-

PERSONAL: Born May 8, 1946, in California; daughter of Raymond (a realtor) and Jean (a manager of a family owned guest ranch; maiden name, Campbell) De Blasis. *Education:* Attended Wellesley College, 1964-65, and Oregon State University, 1965-66; Pomona College, B.A. (cum laude), 1968. *Politics:* "Democrat but basically disenchanted with the whole game." *Religion:* "Pantheist." *Home and office:* Kemper Campbell Ranch, Victorville, Calif. 92392. *Agent:* Jane Rotrosen, 212 East 48th St., New York, N.Y. 10017.

CAREER: Writer and poet. *Awards, honors:* Award in letters from Southern California Division of National League of American Pen Women, 1969.

WRITINGS: The Night Child (mystery novel), Coward, 1975. Contributor of poems to small literary magazines.

WORK IN PROGRESS: A mystery novel, tentatively titled *Suffer a Sea Change*; a saga based in California between 1840 and 1900; television scripts.

SIDELIGHTS: Celeste De Blasis was raised and still lives in the Mojave Desert, at an elevation of three thousand feet. Her home has been a cattle ranch, an Arabian horse ranch, a sugar beet farm, and at the same time, since the 1930's, a guest ranch. She has a love for living creatures and wide open spaces unhampered by trees, buildings, and people. She has found some of this in parts of New England and in Scotland, but the desert remains her home.

AVOCATIONAL INTERESTS: Travel, reading on stormy days, tennis, bird watching, hand crafts, painting.

* * *

de CASTRO, Fernando J(ose) 1937-

PERSONAL: Born November 11, 1937, in Havana, Cuba; son of Fernando R. (an architect) and Maria A. (Freyre de Andrade) de Castro; married Catalina Alvarez, June 9, 1962; children: Maria, Ana, Fernando, Ramon, Teresa, Pablo, Jose Manuel. *Education:* Attended Havana University, 1955-58; Tulane University, M.D., 1962; University of Michigan, M.P.H., 1966. *Religion:* Roman Catholic. *Home:* 7210 Maryland, St. Louis, Mo. 63130. *Office:* 1465 South Grand, St. Louis, Mo. 63104.

CAREER: University of Michigan, Ann Arbor, instructor, 1966-69, assistant professor of pediatrics, 1969-70; St. Louis University, St. Louis, Mo., associate professor of pediatrics and community medicine, 1970—. Director of Ambulatory Service at Cardinal Glennon Hospital, St. Louis, Mo., 1970—; director of Poison Control Center, St. Louis, Mo., 1970—. *Member:* Ambulatory Pediatric Association, American Academy of Pediatrics, American Public Health Association, American Association of University Professors, Midwestern Society for Pediatric Research, Alpha Omega Alpha.

WRITINGS: The Pediatric Nurse Practitioner, Mosby, 1972.

* * *

DeCHANT, John A(loysius) 1917-1974

June 21, 1917—October 9, 1974; American public relations expert and author. Obituaries: *Washington Post*, October 12, 1974. (*CA*-23/24).

* * *

DECI, Edward L(ewis) 1942-

PERSONAL: Surname is pronounced like D.C.; born October 14, 1942, in New York, N.Y.; son of Charles H. (an engineer) and Janice (an administrator; maiden name, Upchurch) Deci. *Education:* Hamilton College, A.B., 1964; University of London, graduate study, 1965; University of Pennsylvania, M.B.A., 1967; Carnegie-Mellon University, M.S., 1969, Ph.D., 1970. *Home:* 129 Dartmouth St., Rochester, N.Y. 14607. *Office:* Department of Psychology, University of Rochester, Rochester, N.Y. 14627.

CAREER: University of Rochester, Rochester, N.Y., assistant professor of psychology, 1970—. *Member:* American Psychological Association, Association for Humanistic Psychology.

WRITINGS: (Editor with V. H. Vroom) *Management and Motivation*, Penguin, 1970; (editor with B. V. H. Gilmer and H. W. Karn) *Readings in Industrial and Organizational Psychology*, McGraw, 1972; *Intrinsic Motivation*, Plenum, in press. Contributor to *Journal of Personality and Social Psychology* and *Psychology Today*.

WORK IN PROGRESS: Industrial and Organizational Psychology, with B. V. H. Gilmer, publication expected in 1976; research on human motivation; operating therapy groups and growth groups.

* * *

DEELEY, Roger 1944-

PERSONAL: Born January 1, 1944, in Rugby, Warwickshire, England; son of Cyril and Brenda (Adams) Deeley. *Education:* Attended University of Bristol, 1962-64. *Politics:* "Liberal (with capital L as in British political system, small L as in humanity)." *Religion:* "Nothing formal, but there has to be something." *Home:* 50 Uphill Way, Uphill, Weston-super-Mare, Avon BS23 4TN, England. *Agent:* Tessa Sayle, Leresche, Hope & Steele, 11 Jubilee Pl., Chelsea, London SW3 3TE, England.

CAREER: Librarian, 1964-69; writer, 1969—. Has lectured at educational institutions. *Member:* Society of Authors.

WRITINGS—Novels: *King's Man*, R. Hale, 1968; *By Courtesy of the Cardinal*, R. Hale, 1970; *Three Crowns for the Queen*, R. Hale, 1972; *The Byzantine Eagle*, R. Hale, 1974.

Work is anthologized in *Protostars*, edited by David Gerrold, Ballantine, 1971; *Generation*, Volume I, edited by Gerrold, Dell, 1972. Author of "Rameses," a cartoon strip syndicated in England, Europe, and South America, by Central Press Features, 1971—. Author of material for British Independent Television and British Broadcasting Corp. Contributor to British and American magazines, including *Galaxy*.

WORK IN PROGRESS: A novel; a musical play; a film or television script.

SIDELIGHTS: Deeley writes: "In the past six years I have written historical novels, science fiction, television scripts, work for children's magazines (very good discipline, that; you have to change your whole style); one of my main loves and interests is my adult cartoon strip, 'Rameses,' which is syndicated reasonably widely, but nowhere near as widely as I would like. All of these things are different, catering for different tastes, and also preventing me from getting in a rut. But I hope they also entertain. There is always room for writers who take themselves desperately seriously, and pour out streams of dedicated prose, all to make some supposedly vital point, but for God's sake, let's not forget that one of the writer's tasks is to entertain. . . .

"It's no coincidence that I live in an old cottage and sleep in a four-poster bed, and collect vintage cars; my chief recreational interest is, in fact, motor sport, which started with rallying older cars, and has eventually overlapped into modern motor sport. Also there is an old French title (that of the Duke de Tourmalin) which has come down in our family, which is quite useless nowadays, as all lands, money, etc. were lost in the French Revolution nearly two centuries ago, but I like to retain it out of interest and respect for the past, rather than let it disappear into limbo like so many old things just because no one can see any immediate profitable use for them. . . .

"I believe that life is here to be lived. I don't want just to exist. I don't know the reason we're here on this planet, I'm not even sure there is one, but while we're around let's try and enjoy things. Don't take life too seriously, I've got a sneaky feeling that the whole thing is really one vast cosmic joke, and we're the fall guys. I wouldn't want my tombstone to read: 'Here lies Roger Deeley, who missed the bus of life without ever making any really serious effort to catch it.' I try to run after the bus. One day I may end up having a ride."

* * *

DEI-ANANG, Michael 1909-

PERSONAL: Born October 16, 1909, in Mampong-Akwapim, Ghana, West Africa; son of Gustav and Sarah Delphina Dei-Anang; married Cecilia Ozilind Epton; children: six. *Education:* Achimata College, Intermediate B.A., 1933; University of London, B.A., 1936, Diploma in Education, 1938. *Home:* Awonkae Fie, Mampong-Akwapim, Ghana, West Africa. *Agent:* William McTighe, New York, N.Y. *Office:* Department of African and Afro-American Studies, State University of New York at Brockport, Brockport, N.Y. 14420.

CAREER: Mfantsipim School, Cape Coast, Ghana, Latin master, 1934-43; Government of the Gold Coast (now Ghana), Accra, inspector of schools, 1944-50, senior education officer and acting director of education, 1951, senior assistant secretary in Ministry of Defence and External Affairs, 1952-53, deputy director of recruitment and training, 1953-55, and director, 1955-57, secretary to governor-general, 1957-59, permanent secretary in Ministry of Foreign Affairs, 1959-61, secretary in office of the president and Ambassador Extraordinary and Plenipotentiary, 1960-66; University of London, Institute of Commonwealth Studies, London, England, senior research fellow, 1970; State University of New York at Brockport, visiting professor, 1970-71, professor of history and African and Afro-American Studies, 1971—, chairman of department of African and Afro-American Studies, 1973—. Special lecturer, Michigan State University and at Victoria University, 1973. *Awards, honors:* D.Litt. from London Institute of Applied Research, 1974.

WRITINGS: Wayward Lines from Africa: Collection of Poems (also see below), United Society for Christian Literature (London), 1946; *Cocoa Comes to Mampong: A One-Act Play* (also see below), Methodist Book Depot (Accra, Ghana), 1949; *Africa Speaks: Collection of Poems*, Guinea Press (Accra), 1959, 2nd edition, 1960; *Okomfo Anokye's Golden Stool: A Play in Three Acts*, A. A. Stockwell, 1959, 2nd edition, Waterville Publishing House (Accra), 1963; *Ghana Semi-Stones: Collection of Poems*, Presbyterian Book Depot (Accra), 1962; *Ghana Resurgent: A Historical Sketch of Ghana*, Waterville Publishing House, 1964; (with Yaw Warren) *Ghana Glory: Collection of Poems*, foreword by Kwame Nkrumah, Thomas Nelson, 1965; (with Dennis Chukude Osadebay) *Wayward Lines from Africa, Cocoa Comes to Mampong and Occasional Verse* [*and*] *Africa Sings* [*by*] *Dennis Chukude Osadebay*, Kraus Reprint, 1970; (contributor) Evelyn Jones Rich and Immanuel Wallerstein, *Africa: Tradition and Change*, Random House, 1972; (contributor) Basil Davidson, *Black Star*, Allen Lane, 1973; (with son, Kofi Dei-Anang) *Two Faces of Africa: A Collection of Poems*, Black Academy

Press, 1974; *The Administration of Ghana's Foreign Policy, 1957-1966*, University of London Press, 1975; *Man's Inhumanity to Man*, Exposition Press, 1975.

Work represented in anthologies, including *Which Way Africa?*, edited by Basil Davidson, Penguin, 1960; *Africa: The Politics of Independence*, edited by Immanuel Wallerstein, Vintage Books, 1961; *Poems from Black Africa*, edited by Langston Hughes, Indiana University Press, 1963; *West African Verse*, edited by Donatus I. Nwoga, Longman, 1967; *Learning Through English*, edited by S. Nagarajan, M. G. Desai, M. V. Ghaskadbi, and S. K. Mukherjee, University of Poona Press (India), 1967; *Britain, Europe and the Modern World (1918-1968)*, edited by Paul Richardson, Cambridge University Press, 1970; *Henry: An Anthology by World Poets*, edited by Margaret E. Porter, Bern Porter, 1970. Contributor to *Encyclopedia of Black Peoples*.

WORK IN PROGRESS: Little Fishes in Big Ponds, novel on the theme of African Unity; "Yaa Asantewa," a one-act play on a Ghanaian historical theme; *The Gods Come from Ghana*, memoirs.

* * *

de JONGE, Alex 1938-

PERSONAL: Born September 26, 1938, in London, England; son of Henry Robert Alexander and Alexandra (Skwarskaya) de Jonge; married Judith Twynam, August 20, 1962; children: Edward, James. *Education:* New College, Oxford, B.A., 1962, M.A., 1966, Ph.D., 1969. *Religion:* Anglican. *Office:* New College, University of Oxford, Oxford, England.

CAREER: University of Oxford, New College, Oxford, England, tutorial fellow in French and Russian, 1964—. *Member:* Piscatorial Society, Newbury Race Club.

WRITINGS: Nightmare Culture, St. Martin's, 1973; (contributor) J.L.I. Fennell, editor, *Nineteenth Century Russian Literature: Studies of Ten Russian Writers*, University of California Press, 1973.

WORK IN PROGRESS: The Real Life of Vladimir Nabokov; Dostoevsky and the Age of Intensity; Baudelaire: A Life, completion expected in 1976; *Solzhenitsyn: A Reader's Handbook*, 1976.

AVOCATIONAL INTERESTS: Horse-racing, fishing.

* * *

DEJU, Raul A(ntonio) 1946-

PERSONAL: Surname sounds like Day-*you*; born March 14, 1946, in Havana, Cuba; son of Jose M. (a manager) and Olga (a painter; maiden name, Nunez) Deju; married Leticia E. Perez, December 19, 1968 (divorced, 1974); children: Raul, Jr. *Education:* New Mexico Institute of Mining and Technology, B.S. (summa cum laude), 1966, Ph.D., 1969. *Politics:* "A little moderation." *Religion:* "Always thankful for what I have." *Home:* 1754-D Arlin Pl., Fairborn, Ohio 45324. *Office:* Department of Geology, Wright State University, Dayton, Ohio 45431.

CAREER: University of Mexico, Mexico City, visiting associate professor of hydrology and chairman of department of geohydrology and geochemistry, 1969-70; University of Pittsburgh, Pittsburgh, Pa., adjunct professor of geology, 1970-72; Wright State University, Dayton, Ohio, associate professor of geology, 1972—. Research chemist for Gulf Research & Development Co., 1970-72; founder of New Mexico conferences on pure and applied mathematics, 1965; counsel on hydrology to Atlantic Richfield Hanford Co., 1972—. Consultant on disposal of nuclear wastes.

MEMBER: American Association of Petroleum Geologists, American Institute of Mining, Metallurgical, and Petroleum Engineers, Pi Mu Epsilon (founder and president, 1966). *Awards, honors:* National Aeronautics and Space Administration fellowship, Columbia University, summer, 1965; fellowship from Institute on Pollution Economics of University of Pittsburgh, 1973.

WRITINGS: (Contributor) David L. Black, editor, *Materials Technology: An Interamerican Approach*, American Society of Mechanical Engineers, 1968; (contributor) Black, editor, *An Interamerican Approach to the Seventies*, American Society of Mechanical Engineers, 1970; *Regional Hydrology Fundamentals*, Gordon & Breach, 1971; *The Environment and Its Resources*, Gordon & Breach, 1972; (contributor) Jon A. Berger, editor, *Flow: Its Measurement and Control in Science and Industry*, American Institute of Physics and Instrument Society of America, 1973; *Extraction of Minerals and Energy: Today's Dilemmas*, Ann Arbor Science Publishers, 1974.

Author of technical reports. Contributor of more than eighty articles and short stories to professional journals in the United States and abroad, including *Southeastern Geology*, *Geophysics*, *Geological Society of America Bulletin*, *Transactions of the Society of Mining Engineers*, and *Water and Sewage Works*.

WORK IN PROGRESS: A book tracing the theory of evolution through the evolution of the reproductive system; *The Zeta Conspiracy*, a novel; *Glimpses in the Life of a Young Man*, a novel; *Water and Conservation*, a book for laymen, for Ann Arbor Science Publishers; continuing research on hydrology.

AVOCATIONAL INTERESTS: Social work (local and national programs to help the handicapped and disadvantaged), tennis, golf, singing and dancing (has worked as a nightclub entertainer), mountain climbing, glaciology, fishing, plain living.

* * *

DELANEY, Mary Murray 1913-
(Mary D. Lane)

PERSONAL: Born January 1, 1913, in New Richmond, Wis.; daughter of Christopher James and Rachel Agnes (Newell) Murray; married Thomas J. Delaney, Jr. (a travel agent), June 1, 1932; children: Thomas J. III, Joan Mary (Mrs. Thomas Patrick O'Connell). *Education:* Graduated from Twin City Business College, 1930; attended Macalester College, 1955, 1956, 1958. *Politics:* Independent. *Religion:* Roman Catholic. *Home:* 1606 Highland Pkwy., St. Paul, Minn. 55116. *Office:* Delaney, Joyce & O'Dell, Inc., 249 South Snelling, St. Paul, Minn. 55105.

CAREER: Montgomery Ward & Co., St. Paul, Minn., secretary, 1930-32; E. I. Dupont de Nemours, St. Paul, Minn., auditor, 1942; Delaney, Joyce & O'Dell, Inc. (travel agency), St. Paul, Minn., vice-president and escort for European tours, 1962—; writer. *Member:* Irish American Cultural Institute, National League of American Pen Women, Sons and Daughters of Ireland, Twin Cities Irish American Club, St. Gregory's Guild.

WRITINGS: Of Irish Ways, Dillon, 1973. Contributor of short stories and articles under pseudonym Mary D. Lane to *Writer, Redbook, Woman's Own, My Weekly, Mathilda*

Zeigler Magazine for the Blind, and magazines in England, Norway, Sweden, Denmark, Australia, and Italy.

WORK IN PROGRESS: A novel, *The Hollow Places*; research on a semi-autobiographical novel.

* * *

de LAUBENFELS, David J(ohn) 1925-

PERSONAL: Born December 5, 1925, in Pasadena, Calif.; son of Max W. (a professor) and Beth (Jones) de Laubenfels; married Gudrun J. Erickson, December 21, 1954 (divorced January 3, 1973); married Linda E. Price, December 27, 1973; children: (first marriage) Eric A., Lucia B., Evelyn J., Marion J. *Education:* Pasadena Junior College (now Pasadena City College), A.A., 1946; Colgate University, A.B., 1949; University of Illinois, A.M., 1950, Ph.D., 1953. *Home:* 201 Butternut Dr., DeWitt, N.Y., 13214. *Office:* Department of Geography, Syracuse University, Syracuse, N.Y. 13210.

CAREER: University of Georgia, Athens, assistant professor, 1953-58, associate professor of geography, 1958-59; Syracuse University, Syracuse, N.Y., associate professor, 1959-71, professor of geography, 1971—. *Military service:* U.S. Army, 1944-46; served in Pacific Theater. *Member:* International Society of Plant Morphologists, International Society for Plant Geography and Ecology, Association of American Geographers, American Geographical Society, Ecological Society of America, Botanical Society of America, American Society of Plant Taxonomists, National Council for Geographic Education, American Association of University Professors, Sigma Xi.

WRITINGS: (Contributor) John H. Garland, editor, *The North American Midwest*, Wiley, 1955; (contributor) John H. Thompson, editor, *Geography of New York State*, Syracuse University Press, 1966; (contributor) F. E. Dohrs and L. M. Sommers, editors, *Cultural Geography: Selected Readings*, Crowell, 1967; *A Geography of Plants and Animals*, W. C. Brown, 1970; *Gymnospermes*, Museum of Natural History (Paris), 1972. Contributor of articles to professional journals, including *Science, Annals of the Association of American Geographers, Geographical Review, Professional Geographer, Journal of Geography, Blumea*, and *Phytomorphology*.

WORK IN PROGRESS: World Patterns of Vegetation: An Examination of the Major Regionalizations of Vegetation and Flora, for Syracuse Geographical Series; a study of conifers in the *Flora Malesiana*.

SIDELIGHTS: De Laubenfels told *CA*: "... I am a specialist in the geography of vegetation but on the side I have become a botanist and the only expert on worldwide conifers and their taxonomy. This has led to various trips to the tropics to collect specimens and observe vegetation. As a result I am conversant in Spanish and French and can get along in German, Portuguese, and Italian."

* * *

DELAY-BAILLEN, Claude 1934-
(Claude Baillen)

PERSONAL: Born December 22, 1934, in Paris, France; daughter of Jean (a psychiatrist and professor) and Marie-Madeline (Carrez) Delay; married Norbert Baillen; children: Isabelle, Maria. *Education:* Received Diploma in Political Science, Ph.D. in psychology. *Home:* 47 Quai des Grand Augustins, Paris 75006, France.

CAREER: Psychoanalyst and writer.

WRITINGS: (Under name Claude Baillen) *Chanel Solitaire*, Gallimard, 1971, translation by Barbara Bray published under same title, Quadrangle, 1974.

* * *

DELDERFIELD, Eric R(aymond) 1909-

PERSONAL: Born May 4, 1909, in London, England; married Dora Hedgethorn; married Dena Ward; children: (first marriage) one daughter; (second marriage) two daughters. *Education:* Attended schools in Selhurst, London, England. *Home:* 10 Sarlsdown Rd., Exmouth, Devonshire, England. *Office:* Erd Publications Ltd., 53 Strand, Exmouth, Devonshire, England.

CAREER: Manager of printing, stationery, and photography, Rotol Airscrew Co., 1940-45; managing director, *Exmouth Chronicle* (newspaper), 1945-60; Erd Publications Ltd., Exmouth, England, managing director, 1964—. Member of board of directors of David & Charles (publishers), 1964-70. *Member:* Rotary International (president of Exmouth branch, 1935, 1946, 1955, 1971).

WRITINGS: Cavalcade by Candlelight, Raleigh, 1950; *Exmouth Yesterdays*, Raleigh, 1952; *North Devon Story*, Erd Publications, 1952; *Lynmouth Flood Disaster*, Erd Publications, 1953; *Exmoor Wanderings*, Erd Publications, 1956.

The Cotswolds: Its Villages and Churches, Erd Publications, 1961; *British Inn Signs and Their Stories*, David & Charles, 1965; *Yorkshire Sketches*, Erd Publications, 1966; *Cotswold Sketches*, Erd Publications, 1966; *Kings and Queens of England and Great Britain*, Stein & Day, 1966; *Church Treasure*, David & Charles, 1966; *Cotswold Countyside and Its Characters*, David & Charles, 1967; *Fascinating Facts and Figures of the Bible*, Erd Publications, 1967; *West Country Historic Houses and Their Families*, David & Charles, Volume I, 1968, Volume II, 1970, Volume III, 1970; *Introduction to Inn Signs*, David & Charles, 1969.

Eric Delderfield's True Animal Stories, Volume I, Taplinger, 1970, Volume II, Taplinger, 1972, Volume III, Pan Books, 1975; *Stories of Inns and Their Signs*, David & Charles, 1974; *Alphabetical Guide to Inns and Their Signs*, David & Charles, 1975.

Contributor: G. Frere Cook, editor, *England after the Reformation*, Cassell, 1972; *New Book of the Road*, Reader's Digest, 1974. Author of a series of twenty topographical brief guides for Erd Publications, 1956-73. Contributor to magazines and newspapers.

AVOCATIONAL INTERESTS: Walking, history.

* * *

de LIMA, Agnes 1887(?)-1974

1887(?)—November 27, 1974; American educator and author. Obituaries: *New York Times*, November 28, 1974; *AB Bookman's Weekly*, December 16, 1974.

* * *

DELISLE, Francoise 1886(?)-1974

1886(?)—December 5, 1974; author. Obituaries: *AB Bookman's Weekly*, January 20, 1975.

* * *

DE LORA, Joann S(chepers) 1935-

PERSONAL: Born March 6, 1935, in Texas; daughter of

Joseph W. and Ella (Bruce) Schepers; married Jack R. De Lora (a university professor); children: Elinor Kathryn De Lora Hayes, Mary Annette. *Education:* University of Texas, B.A., 1957, M.A., 1958, Ph.D., 1969. *Office:* Department of Sociology, San Diego State University, San Diego, Calif. 92115.

CAREER: San Diego State University, San Diego, Calif., assistant professor, 1967-69, associate professor of sociology, 1969—.

WRITINGS: (With husband, Jack R. De Lora) *Intimate Life Styles: Marriage and Its Alternatives*, Goodyear Publishing, 1972.

WORK IN PROGRESS: Understanding Sexual Interaction, for Houghton; a statistics textbook, for Wadsworth.

* * *

DELORIA, Vine (Victor), Jr. 1933-

PERSONAL: Born March 26, 1933, in Martin, S.D.; son of Vine (a clergyman) and Barbara (Eastburn) Deloria; married Barbara Jeanne Nystrom, June, 1958; children: Philip, Daniel, Jeanne. *Education:* Iowa State University, B.S., 1958; Lutheran School of Theology, Rock Island, Ill., M.Th., 1963; University of Colorado, J.D., 1970. *Politics:* Democrat. *Religion:* "Seven Day Absentist." *Home and office:* 14675 West 30th Pl., Golden, Colo. 80401. *Agent:* Elaine Markson, 44 Greenwich Ave., New York, N.Y.

CAREER: United Scholarship Service, Denver, Colo., staff associate, 1963-64; National Congress of American Indians, Washington, D.C., executive director, 1964-67. Lecturer, Western Washington State College, 1970-72, and University of California, Los Angeles, 1972-74. Chairman, Institute for the Development of Indian Law, 1970—. *Military service:* U.S. Marine Corps Reserve, 1954-56. *Member:* American Bar Association, American Judicature Society, Authors Guild, Amnesty International, Colorado Authors League. *Awards, honors:* Anisfield-Wolf Award, 1970, for *Custer Died for Your Sins*; D.H.Litt., Augustana College, 1971; Indian Achievement Award from Indian Council Lire, 1972.

WRITINGS: Custer Died for Your Sins: An Indian Manifesto, Macmillan, 1969; *We Talk, You Listen: New Tribes, New Turf*, Macmillan, 1970; (editor and author of introduction) Jennings Cooper Wise, *The Red Man in the New World Drama*, Macmillan, 1971; (compiler) *Of Utmost Good Faith*, Straight Arrow Books, 1971; *God Is Red*, Grosset, 1973; *Behind the Trail of Broken Treaties*, Delacorte, 1974; *The Indian Affair*, Friendship, 1974.

WORK IN PROGRESS: Research on Indian legends concerning the creation of mountains, rivers, and other natural phenomena; research on Indian treaties, social problems, and political history.

SIDELIGHTS: Of *Custer Died for Your Sins*, J. A. Phillips notes: "If this book is indicative of Deloria's methods, he's more interested in results than in being tactful. Nauseated by the traditional Indian image, he asserts the worth if not the dignity of the redman and blasts the political, social, and religious forces that perpetuate the Little Big Horn and wigwam stereotyping of his people." Reading Deloria's books, writes Thomas Lask, "is challenging, heady and invigorating stuff. The very extremity of his stance, the cold logic of his arguments hone the mind. And though part of the spirit rages to come to grips with his charges, the other is buoyed up by the level of the discourse."

DELPAR, Helen 1936-

PERSONAL: Born May 10, 1936, in New York, N.Y.; daughter of Nicholas and Dolores (Ricaurte) Delpar. *Education:* Rutgers University, B.A., 1957; New York University, M.A., 1961; Columbia University, Ph.D., 1967. *Home address:* P.O. Box 5004, University, Ala. 35486. *Office:* Department of History, University of Alabama, University, Ala. 35486.

CAREER: Indiana State University, Terre Haute, assistant professor of history, 1967-69; Florida State University, Canal Zone Branch at Albrook Air Force Base, assistant professor of history, 1969-73; Ohio Wesleyan University, Delaware, visiting assistant professor of history, 1973-74; University of Alabama, University, assistant professor of history, 1974—. *Member:* American Historical Association, Conference on Latin American History.

WRITINGS: (Editor) *Borzoi Reader in Latin American History*, Knopf, 1972; (editor) *Encyclopedia of Latin America*, McGraw, 1974. Contributor to scholarly journals.

* * *

DE MONFRIED, Henri 1879(?)-1974

1879(?)—December 12, 1974; French author and adventurer. Obituaries: *New York Times*, December 14, 1974; *Washington Post*, December 14, 1974.

* * *

de NEUFVILLE, Richard 1939-

PERSONAL: Born May 6, 1939, in Jamaica, N.Y.; son of Lawrence (a stockbroker) and Adeline (McCreary) de Neufville; married Judith Innes (a professor), May 23, 1964; children: Robert. *Education:* Massachusetts Institute of Technology, S.B., 1961, S.M., 1961, Ph.D., 1965. *Home:* 10 Acacia St., Cambridge, Mass. 02138. *Agent:* John Cushman Associates, 23 West 43rd St., New York, N.Y. 10036. *Office:* Room 1-153, Massachusetts Institute of Technology, Cambridge, Mass. 02139.

CAREER: White House Fellow in Washington, D.C., 1965-66; Massachusetts Institute of Technology, Cambridge, director of Civil Engineering Systems Laboratory, 1970-73, associate professor of engineering, 1970—. Visiting professor at Imperial College of Science and Technology, London, 1973-74, Graduate School of Business, London, 1973-74, and University of California, Berkeley, 1974-75. Director of Urban Data Processing, Inc., 1969—; owner of Systems Analysis, 1969—. *Awards, honors:* Guggenheim fellow, 1973-74.

WRITINGS: Systems Analysis for Engineers and Managers, McGraw, 1971; *Systems Planning and Design: Case Studies in Modeling, Optimization and Evaluation*, Prentice-Hall, 1974.

WORK IN PROGRESS: A book, *Airport Systems Planning: New Myths and Old Realities*, for Macmillan, London.

AVOCATIONAL INTERESTS: Travel.

* * *

DENHAM, Robert D(ayton) 1938-

PERSONAL: Born October 20, 1938, in Mooresville, N.C.; son of Chester Dayton (a minister) and Louise (Lowrance) Denham; married Rachel Kanipe, August 26, 1961; children: Scott Dayton, Kristin Elizabeth. *Education:* Davidson College, A.B., 1961; University of Chicago,

M.A., 1964, Ph.D., 1972. *Politics:* Independent. *Religion:* Methodist. *Home address:* Box 28, Emory, Va. 24327. *Office:* Department of English, Emory and Henry College, Emory, Va. 24327.

CAREER: Emory and Henry College, Emory, Va., assistant professor, 1969-73, associate professor of English, 1973—. *Military service:* U.S. Army, 1964-66; became captain. *Member:* Modern Language Association of America, National Council of Teachers of English, South Atlantic Modern Language Association, Northeast Modern Language Association. *Awards, honors:* National Endowment for the Humanities, summer stipend, 1973, and summer seminar fellow, 1974.

WRITINGS: *Northrop Frye: An Enumerative Bibliography*, Scarecrow, 1974. Contributor to *Explicator*, *Canadian Literature*, *Modern Philology*, and other journals in his field.

WORK IN PROGRESS: *Northrop Frye's Criticism.*

* * *

DENKLER, Horst 1935-

PERSONAL: Born September 18, 1935, in Thale, Germany; son of Otto Martin (a teacher) and Anneliese (Bertram) Denkler; married Irmgard Gertrud Steilen, March 12, 1964; children: Tilman Christian, Verena Katarina. *Education:* Attended Free University of Berlin, 1956-57; University of Muenster, Ph.D., 1963. *Home:* 8 Strasse zum Loewen, Berlin, Germany. *Office:* Fachbereich 16, Free University, Berlin, Germany.

CAREER: University of Frankfurt, Frankfurt, Germany, assistant professor of German literature, 1964-65; University of Mannheim, Mannheim, Germany, assistant professor of German literature, 1965-67; University of Massachusetts, Amherst, associate professor, 1967-69, professor of German literature, 1969-73; Free University of Berlin, Berlin, Germany, professor of German literature, 1973—. *Member:* Modern Language Association of America, American Association of Teachers of German.

WRITINGS: (Contributor) Gerhard G. Muras, editor, *Jahrbuch der Evangelischen Akademie Tutzing XV 1965/66*, Evangelische Akademie Tutzing, 1966; *Drama des Expressionismus* (title means "Expressionist Drama"), Wilhelm Fink, 1967; *Georg Kaisers 'Buerger von Calais'* (title means "Georg Kaiser's 'Buerger von Calais'"), R. Oldenbourg, 1967; (editor) *Einakter und kleine Dramen des Expressionismus* (title means "Expressionist One-Act Plays"), Reclam, 1968, 2nd edition, 1972; (contributor) Wolfgang Rothe, editor, *Expressionismus als Literatur*, Francke Verlag (Berne), 1969; (contributor) Kaete Hamburger and Helmut Kreuzer, editors, *Gestaltungsgeschichte und Gesellschaftgeschichte*, J. B. Metzler (Stuttgart), 1969; (contributor) Renate von Heydebrand and Klaus Guenther Just, editors, *Wissenschaft als Dialog*, J. B. Metzler, 1969; (contributor) Wolfgang Paulsen, editor, *Das Nachleben der Romantik in der modernen deutschen Literatur*, Lothar Stiehm Verlag (Heidelberg), 1969.

(Contributor) Paulsen, editor, *Der Dichter und seine Zeit*, Lothar Stiehm Verlag, 1970; (contributor) Bernhard Poll, editor, *Rheinische Lebensbilder IV*, Rhineland Verlag (Duesseldorf), 1970; (contributor) Manfred Brauneck, editor, *Das deutsche Drama vom Expressionismus bis zur Gegenwart*, C. C. Buchner (Bamberg, Germany), 1970; (contributor) Reinhold Grimm and Jost Hermand, editors, *Die sogenannten zwanziger Jahre*, Verlag Gehlen (Bad Homburg, Germany), 1970; (editor) *Der deutsche Michel: Revolutionskomoedien, 1848-1850* (title means "The German 'Michel' Comedies, 1848-1850"), Reclam, 1971; (editor) *Alfred Brust: Dramen, 1917-1924* (title means "Alfred Brust: Plays, 1917-1924"), Wilhelm Fink, 1971; (contributor) Grimm, editor, *Deutsche Dramentheorien*, Athenaeum Verlag (Frankfurt), 1971; (editor) *Gedichte der 'Menschheitsdaemmerung'* (title means "Expressionist Poems"), Wilhelm Fink, 1971; (contributor) Wolfgang Paulsen, editor, *Revolte und Experiment*, Lothar Stiehm Verlag, 1972; *Restauration und Revolution: Drama zwischen 1815 und 1850* (title means "Restauration and Revolution: German Drama, 1815-1850"), Wilhelm Fink, 1972; (contributor) Wolfgang Rothe, editor, *Die deutsche Literatur der Weimarer Republik*, Philipp Reclam (Stuttgart), 1974; (contributor) Jost Hermand and Reinhold Grimm, editors, *Popularitaet und Trivialitaet in der deutschen Literatur*, Athenaeum Verlag, 1974.

Contributor of twenty-seven articles to *Deutsche Vierteljahrsschrift*, *Der Deutschunterricht*, *Wirkendes Wort*, *Monatshefte fur deutschen Unterricht*, *Zeitschrift fur Deutsche Philologie*, *Basis*, and *New German Critique*.

WORK IN PROGRESS: *Conservatism, Nationalism, Fascism, Nationalsocialism in German Literature*; editing works of Niebergall and Platen; editing two anthologies.

AVOCATIONAL INTERESTS: Theatre, visual arts, first editions.

* * *

DENNISON, George M(arshel) 1935-

PERSONAL: Born August 11, 1935, in Buffalo, Ill.; son of Earl Frederick (a businessman) and Irene (McWhorter) Dennison; married Jane I. Schroeder (a clerk typist), December 26, 1954; children: Robert Gene, Rick Steven. *Education:* University of Montana, B.A., 1962, M.A., 1963; University of Washington, Seattle, Ph.D., 1967. *Home:* 229 Annabel La., Ft. Collins, Colo. 80521. *Office:* Department of History, Colorado State University, Ft. Collins, Colo. 80523.

CAREER: University of Arkansas, Fayetteville, assistant professor of history, 1967-68; Colorado State University, Ft. Collins, assistant professor, 1969-73, associate professor of history, 1973—. *Military service;* U.S. Navy, 1953-57. *Member:* American Society for Legal History, Organization of American Historians, American Historical Association, Rocky Mountain Social Science Association.

WRITINGS: *Popular Sovereignty and Peaceable Revolution in the American Republic: 1830-1861*, University Press of Kentucky, in press. Contributor to *Rocky Mountain Social Science Journal*, *American Journal for Legal History*, *St. Louis University Law Journal*, *Social Studies*, *Journal of American History*, and *Reviews in American History*.

WORK IN PROGRESS: Research for a book tentatively titled, *Consolidating Jim Crow: State Action and Equal Protection in Civil Rights Jurisprudence, 1866-1896*.

* * *

DENOEU, Francois 1898-1975

PERSONAL: Born July 22, 1898, in Estree-Blanche, Pasde-Calais, France; son of Sosthene Henri (a farmer) and Henriette (Pauchet) Denoeu; married Suzanne Julie Chaise, 1923 (died May, 1974); children: Genevieve (Mrs. Beuford N. Willes), Monique (Mrs. John C. Cone). *Education:* Ecole normale d'Arras, Brevet superieur, 1917; Sorbonne, University of Paris, Agregation d'anglais, 1928. *Home:* 8 Parkway, Hanover, N.H. 03755.

CAREER: High school teacher in Scotland, 1921-22; College de Poligny, Poligny, France, professor of French and English, 1924-25; teacher of English at lycees in France, 1925-29; Dartmouth College, Hanover, N.H., assistant professor, 1929-38, professor of French, 1938-63, professor emeritus, 1963—. *Military service:* French Army, Infantry, 1917-20, 1939-40; became captain; received Legion of Honor, 1952, and Croix de Guerre. *Member:* American Association of Teachers of French (president of New Hampshire chapter, 1950-52), Academie des Palmes Academiques. *Awards, honors:* A.M., Dartmouth College, 1938; Richelieu Medal of French Academy.

WRITINGS: La Vierge aux yeux de feu (novel), Gamber, 1933; *French comme il faut* (grammar and reader), Gamber, 1933; *Petit miroir de la civilisation francaise*, Heath, 1938, revised edition, 1949; *Peches de jeunesse* (poems), printed in France for Dartmouth Bookstore, 1939; (with Robert A. Hall, Jr.) *Spoken French: Basic Course*, two volumes, editions for U.S. Armed Forces Institute and for colleges, Heath, 1943; *Military French*, Heath, 1943; (with Hall) *Spoken and Written French: A First-Year Course for Colleges*, Heath, 1947; *Getting Around in French*, with three records, Holt, 1949; *Lectures litteraires pour commencants*, Macmillan, 1950; *Beginning French: A Grammar and Reader*, Ronald, 1950; *L'Amour en bouton* (novel), Editions de Minuit, 1950; *Fluent French: A Practical Course for the Second Year*, Heath, 1951; *La Guerre d'un bleu* (novel; sequel to *L'Amour en bouton*), Mordacq, 1954; *Image de la France: Reflets de la civilisation francaise des origines a nos jours* (outgrowth of *Petit miroir de la civilisation francaise*, supra), Heath, 1963, revised edition published as *French Cultural Reader: Petit miroir, images et reflets de la civilisation francaise des origines a nos jours*, 1971; *France-Nord*, Mordacq, Volume I: *Artois, Picardie, Flandre, Hainaut, Ardennes*, 1970, Volume II: *Les Hauts de France*, 1975; (compiler) *Dictionary of French and English Idioms*, Barron's, 1973.

Editor: *Contes et recits des grands ecrivains francais*, Holt, 1947; *L'Heritage francais: Lectures de civilisation francaise*, Holt, 1953, revised and augmented edition, 1966; *Sommets litteraires francais: Anthologie-histoire de la litterature francaise des origines a nos jours*, Heath, 1957, revised and updated edition, 1967; *Parmi les meilleurs contes* (short stories for second-year students of French), Holt, 1958.

WORK IN PROGRESS: Comprehensive French-American, American-French Dictionary.

(Died January 8, 1975)

* * *

DENZEL, Justin F(rancis) 1917-

PERSONAL: Born January 15, 1917, in Clifton, N.J.; son of George and Alvina (Munzell) Denzel; married Josephine Ogazaly, 1947. *Education:* Attended Paterson State College (now William Paterson College of New Jersey), 1939, and University of California, Los Angeles, 1940. *Politics:* Independent. *Religion:* Roman Catholic. *Home:* 73 Livingston St., Clifton, N.J. 07013. *Office:* Hoffman La Roche, Nutley, N.J.

CAREER: Has worked as a field naturalist for American Museum of Natural History, New York, N.Y., sailed on oceanographic vessel, *Atlantis*, collected marine life in Alaska, and is currently a scientific librarian with Hoffman La Roche in Nutley, N.J. *Military service:* U.S. Army, 1941-45; became sergeant; received Purple Heart. *Awards, honors:* New Jersey Association of Teachers of English award, 1972, for *Genius with a Scalpel*, and 1973 for *Jumbo: Giant Circus Elephant.*

WRITINGS: Adventure North (biography), Abelard, 1968; *Champion of Liberty* (biography), Messner, 1969; *Genius with a Scalpel* (biography), Messner, 1971; *Jumbo: Giant Circus Elephant* (juvenile), Garrard, 1973; *Black Kettle: King of the Wild Horses* (juvenile), Garrard, 1974; *Wild Wing: Eagle of the Canyons* (juvenile), Garrard, 1975. Contributor of more than one hundred short stories and articles to *Coronet, American Mercury, Frontiers, Twelve/Fifteen, Upward, Catholic Boy, Venture, Snowy Egret*, and other publications.

WORK IN PROGRESS: A book of personal nature essays, *My Patch of Earth; Snowfoot: White Reindeer of the Arctic.*

AVOCATIONAL INTERESTS: Natural history.

* * *

De RISI, William J(oseph) 1938-

PERSONAL: Born January 24, 1938, in Jersey City, N.J.; son of Joseph Aloysius (an accountant) and Susan V. (Cummings) De Risi; married Ruth Robertson (a registered nurse), August 25, 1963; children: Joseph L., Maria D. *Education:* Fairleigh Dickinson University, B.A., 1963; New Mexico Highlands University, M.S., 1966; University of Utah, Ph.D., 1969. *Politics:* Democrat. *Home:* 2630 El Segundo Dr., Rancho Cordova, Calif. 95670. *Office:* State of California Department of Health, 714 P St., Sacramento, Calif. 95817.

CAREER: Psychology extern in Division of Mental Health, New Mexico Department of Public Health, 1964-65; psychology intern at Veterans Administration Hospital, Salt Lake City, Utah, 1965-66, at Southern Utah Guidance Clinic, 1966-67, and at Veterans Administration Hospital, Phoenix, Ariz., 1967-68; Veterans Administration Hospital, Salt Lake City, psychologist, 1968; Behavior Systems Corp., research psychologist and consultant to Nelles School for Boys, Whittier, Calif., 1969-70; American Justice Institute, research psychologist and consultant to Karl Holton School for Boys, Stockton, Calif., 1970-72; University of California at Los Angeles, Camarillo-Neuropsychiatric Institute, research psychologist and project coordinator, 1972; Oxnard Community Mental Health Center, Oxnard, Calif., senior clinical psychologist, 1973-74; State of California Department of Health, research specialist, 1974—. Instructor at Chapman College, summer, 1972. *Military service:* U.S. Air Force, cryptographic specialist, 1956-60; served in Germany. *Member:* American Psychological Association, Western Psychological Association.

WRITINGS: (Contributor) Jerome Stumphauzer, editor, *Behavior Modification with Delinquents*, C. C Thomas, 1973; (contributor) Jules Masserman, editor, *Current Psychiatric Therapies*, Volume XIII, Grune, 1973; (contributor) Park O. Davidson, Frank W. Clark, and Leo A. Hamerlynck, editors, *Evaluation of Behavioral Programs*, Research Press, 1974; (with George Butz) *Contract: A Simulation Game for Field Workers*, Research Press, 1974; *How to Write Contingency Contracts*, Research Press, 1974. Contributor to *Hospital and Community Psychiatry* and *Journal of Applied Behavior Analysis.*

WORK IN PROGRESS: The Clinician's Guide to Personal Effectiveness Training, a manual for training clinicians in assertive training, with R. P. Liberman and L. W. King, for Research Press.

* * *

De ROSSI, Claude J(oseph) 1942-

PERSONAL: Born October 3, 1942, in Amsterdam, N.Y.; son of Rolando R. and Angelina (Bombardatore) De Rossi; married Cynthia M. Slusarz (a medical secretary), October 3, 1964; children: Marialana, David. *Education:* Attended Albany Business College, 1961-63; College of Saint Rose, B.S., 1972. *Residence:* Amsterdam, N.Y.

CAREER: General Electric Co., Schenectady, N.Y., financial systems analyst, 1963—, instructor in data processing and technical writer and editor, 1970-72. Lecturer at College of Saint Rose, 1972. *Member:* Big Brother Organization, Knights of Columbus.

WRITINGS: Computers: Tools for Today, Childrens Press, 1972; *Learning BASIC Fast*, Reston Publishing, 1974; *Exploring the World of Data Processing*, Reston Publishing, 1975. Reviewer for Reston Publishing Co., 1974—.

* * *

DERR, Richard L(uther) 1930-

PERSONAL: Surname sounds like "durr"; born December 27, 1930, in Hughesville, Pa.; son of Luther and Nora (Hanlon) Derr; married Evelyn Musielak, April 11, 1953; children: Stephanie, Christopher. *Education:* State University of New York College at Brockport, B.S., 1951; University of Illinois, M.Ed., 1955, Ed.D., 1959. *Home:* 4280 Lander Rd., Orange Village, Ohio 44022. *Office:* Department of Education, Case Western Reserve University, Cleveland, Ohio 44106.

CAREER: Elementary school teacher in Niagara Falls, N.Y., 1951, and St. Louis, Mo., 1957-59; Case Western Reserve University, Cleveland, Ohio, assistant professor, 1959-65, associate professor of education, 1966—. Assistant professor at Washington University (St. Louis, Mo.), 1957-59. *Military service:* U.S. Army, 1951-53. *Member:* American Educational Research Association, Philosophy of Education Society, American Educational Studies Association, Ohio Valley Philosophy of Education Society, Phi Delta Kappa. *Awards, honors:* Award for outstanding book in education from *American School Board Journal*, 1973, for *A Taxonomy of Social Purposes of Public Schools: A Handbook.*

WRITINGS: (Contributor) Marilyn Gittell, editor, *Educating an Urban Population*, Sage Publications, 1967; *A Taxonomy of Social Purposes of Public Schools: A Handbook*, McKay, 1973. Contributor to educational reports and to proceedings. Contributor of about thirty articles and reviews to education journals, including *Elementary School Journal, Intellect, Education Forum, School and Society, Phi Delta Kappan*, and *Educational Theory*.

WORK IN PROGRESS: An analysis of the class oppression model of schooling; research on the systematization and critique of two models of schooling.

* * *

DERR, Thomas Sieger 1931-

PERSONAL: Born June 18, 1931, in Boston, Mass.; son of Thomas S. (an engineer) and Mary (Sebring) Derr; married Virginia Anne Bush (a program director for Young Women's Christian Association), June 9, 1956; children: Peter Bulkeley, Laura Seely, Mary Williams. *Education:* Harvard University, A.B. (magna cum laude), 1953; Union Theological Seminary, New York, N.Y., M.Div., 1956; Columbia University, Ph.D., 1972. *Office:* Department of Religion, Smith College, Northampton, Mass. 01060.

CAREER: Ordained minister of United Church of Christ, 1956; Stanford University, Stanford, Calif., assistant chaplain, 1956-59; World Council of Churches, Geneva, Switzerland, researcher, 1961-62; Smith College, Northampton, Mass., assistant chaplain, 1963-65, assistant professor, 1965-70, associate professor of religion, 1970—, chairman of department, 1971-74. *Member:* American Society of Christian Ethics, American Association of University Professors. *Awards, honors:* Fellowship from Danforth Foundation, 1959, 1965.

WRITINGS: (Contributor) Z. K. Matthews, editor, *Responsible Government in a Revolutionary Age*, Association Press, 1966; (contributor) Jacob Needleman, A. K. Bierman, and J. A. Gould, editors, *Religion for a New Generation*, Macmillan, 1973; *Ecology and Human Liberation*, World Council of Churches, 1973, revised edition published as *Ecology and Human Need*, Westminister, 1975. Contributor of about fifteen articles and reviews to periodicals, including *Study Encounter, Anticipation, This Month, Worldview, Smith Alumnae Quarterly*, and *Cross Currents*.

WORK IN PROGRESS: Continuing research on social ethics.

* * *

DE SEVERSKY, Alexander P(rocofieff) 1894-1974

June 7, 1894—August 24, 1974; Russian-born American aviation pioneer and inventor. Obituaries: *New York Times*, August 26, 1974; *Time*, September 9, 1974; *Newsweek*, September 9, 1974; *Current Biography*, October, 1974.

* * *

DESHLER, G(eorge) Byron 1903-

PERSONAL: Born September 9, 1903, in Columbus, Ohio; son of George A. (a clergyman) and Mary Helen (Mead) Deshler; married M. Irene Marshburn (a teacher); children: J. David, James, Thomas, Patricia (Mrs. Charles L. Johnson). *Education:* Whittier College, A.B., 1926; graduate study at University of Southern California, 1927; University of California, Berkeley, M.A., 1929; graduate study at Union Theological Seminary, New York, N.Y., 1940. *Politics:* Independent. *Home address:* P.O. Box 836, Idyllwild, Calif. 92349.

CAREER: Ordained minister of Methodist Church, 1938; pastor in Fresno, Bell, Pasadena, Santa Ana, and San Gabriel, all Calif., and in Ajo and Yuma, Ariz. Director of evangelism, Los Angeles Council of Churches, 1944-47; director of Prayer Life Movement, 1961-67.

WRITINGS: Power of the Personal Group, Tidings, 1963; *Finding the Truth about God*, Tidings, 1964; *Finding the Truth about Man*, Tidings, 1966; *For Preachers Only*, Zondervan, 1973.

AVOCATIONAL INTERESTS: Botany, ornithology, music.

De SOLA, Ralph 1908-

PERSONAL: Born July 26, 1908, in New York, N.Y.; son of Solomon (a dental surgeon) and Grace (a historical researcher; maiden name, von Geist) De Sola; married Dorothy Clair, December 24, 1946. *Education:* Attended Columbia University, 1927, 1929, 1931, and Swarthmore College, 1928. *Politics:* "Conservative liberal." *Home:* 1819 Puterbaugh St., San Diego, Calif. 92103.

CAREER: Ran away to sea at age thirteen; collector and field naturalist for New York Zoological Society, New York, N.Y., 1928-32; curator of reptiles, Tropical Biological Society, Miami, Fla., 1933-34; Federal Writers Project, New York, N.Y., zoological editor, 1935-38; Microstat and U.S. Microfilm Corp., New York, N.Y., technical director, 1939-50; Travel U.S. 90 and Mexican Border Trails Association, Del Rio, Tex., historical director, 1951-54; Convair, San Diego, Calif., publications editor, 1954-67; San Diego Community Colleges, San Diego, Calif., instructor in technical English, 1956—. Consultant to U.S. Navy during World War II and to U.S. Department of Defense, 1963.

WRITINGS: (With Fredrica De Sola) *Strange Animals and Their Ways* (juvenile), Scribner, 1933; *Microstat Technicians Handbook*, Microstat, 1943; *Microfilming*, Essential Books, 1944; *Abbreviations Dictionary*, Duell, Sloan & Pearce, 1958, 4th edition, American Elsevier, 1974; (editor) Stephen Naft, *International Conversion Tables* (based on Naft's *Conversation Equivalents in International Trade*, published in 1931), Duell, Sloan & Pearce, 1961; (compiler) *Great Americans Discuss Religion* (booklet), Freethinkers of America, 1963; (compiler with wife, Dorothy De Sola) *A Dictionary of Cooking* (introduction by Peg Bracken), Meredith, 1969; *Worldwide What & Where*, ABC-Clio, in press; (translator) Hector Berlioz, *Beethoven-by-Berlioz*, Crescendo, in press.

Editor—Most books juveniles, with material compiled under Federal Writers Project: *Birds of the World*, Albert Whitman, 1937; *Reptiles and Amphibians*, Albert Whitman, 1937; *Who's Who in the Zoo: Natural History of Animals*, Albert Whitman, 1938; *American Wildlife Illustrated*, Grosset, 1940; *Maritime History of New York*, Doubleday, 1941; *The Zoo Book*, Albert Whitman, 1941; *The Bird Book*, Albert Whitman, 1941; *The Reptile Book*, Albert Whitman, 1941.

Writer of scientific papers published by American Society of Ichthyologists and Herpetologists in *Copeia*, 1928-32, and of reviews of classical records and concerts published in *Freeman, Del Rio News-Herald*, and *San Diego Engineer*.

WORK IN PROGRESS: Music and Music Makers, a reference book on music and musicians; *Technical Writing Tips*; a compilation of terms for next edition of *Abbreviations Dictionary*.

* * *

DESSAUER, John P(aul) 1924-

PERSONAL: Surname is accented on first syllable; born October 22, 1924, in Vienna, Austria; naturalized U.S. citizen; son of Wilhelm (an art critic and painter) and Augusta (a draftswoman; maiden name, Hatschek) Dessauer; married Elaine Rafter (a poet), June 28, 1947; children: Antonia (Mrs. Ronald R. Hamilton). *Education:* Attended Don Bosco College, 1942. *Politics:* Independent. *Religion:* Roman Catholic. *Residence:* Darien, Conn. *Office:* John P. Dessauer, Inc., 25 Dubois St., Darien, Conn. 06820.

CAREER: Manager, Concord Books, 1943-48; Harlem Book Co., New York, N.Y., promotion manager, 1948-54; Ballantine Books, New York, N.Y., manager of special sales, 1954; Barnes & Noble, New York, N.Y., field representative, 1954-55, manager in Cambridge, Mass., 1955-56; British Book Centre, New York, N.Y., vice-president and general manager, 1956-58; editor and manager, Marboro Book Club, 1958-60; Indiana University Press, Bloomington, Ind., sales manager, 1960-63, assistant director, 1963-65, associate director, 1965-67; University Press of Kansas, Lawrence, Kan., director, 1967-69; Grolier Educational Corp., New York, N.Y., consultant and project director, 1969-70; consultant to Communication Services Division of J. K. Lasser & Co., 1970-71; vice-president, James B. Kobak, Inc., 1971-72; John P. Dessauer, Inc. (consultant and statistical survey firm), Darien, Conn., president, 1972—. Consultant to National Science Foundation; lecturer at Harvard University, summer, 1974.

WRITINGS: (Contributor) *Marketing Handbook for Scholarly Publishers*, American University Press Services, 1971; (contributor) Charles B. Anderson and G. Royce Smith, editors, *A Manual on Bookselling*, Crown, 1974; *Book Publishing: What It Is, What It Does*, Bowker, 1974. Contributing editor of *Publishers Weekly*.

WORK IN PROGRESS: Research on the book industry.

* * *

de SYLVA, Donald Perrin 1928-

PERSONAL: Born July 20, 1928, in Rochester, N.Y.; son of Richard Ortega (a musician) and Elizabeth (an author and editor; maiden name, English) de Sylva; married Doris Drexel (a teacher), August 26, 1950; children: Lisa, Marsha. *Education:* Attended Northwestern University, 1948-50; Cornell University, B.S., 1950, Ph.D., 1958; University of Miami, Coral Gables, Fla., M.S., 1953; University of California, Los Angeles, graduate study, 1953-54. *Politics:* Democrat. *Religion:* Protestant. *Home:* 12601 Southwest 80th Ave., Miami, Fla. 33156. *Office:* School of Marine and Atmospheric Science, University of Miami, Miami, Fla. 33149.

CAREER: University of Delaware, Newark, assistant research professor, 1958-61; University of Miami, Coral Gables, Fla., assistant professor, 1961-66, associate professor of marine science, 1966—. Consultant to Atomic Energy Commission and National Academy of Science. *Military service:* U.S. Army, 1946-48. *Member:* American Society of Ichthyologists and Herpetologists (member of board of governors, 1966-68), American Fisheries Society, Ecological Society of America, American Association for the Advancement of Science, American Institute of Fisheries Research Biologists, Tropical Audubon Society (member of advisory board of Florida), Phi Kappa Phi, Sigma Xi.

WRITINGS: Life History of the Great Barracuda, University of Miami Press, 1963; *Argosy Expedition to Ecuador*, University of Miami Press, 1973. Contributor of about eighty articles to professional journals. Editor of *Bulletin of Marine Science*; senior translations editor of English edition of *Gidrobiologicheskii Zhurnal*.

WORK IN PROGRESS: Research on the ecological effects of the war in Viet Nam, on ecology and systematics of marine fishes, and on marine ecology and pollution; a popular book on fish ecology.

SIDELIGHTS: de Sylva has traveled and been a diver all over the world, and has led several underwater expeditions.

He reads eight foreign languages. *Avocational interests:* Eating oriental food and smelling oriental fragrances.

* * *

DETER, Dean (Allen) 1945-

PERSONAL: Born April 23, 1945, in Findlay, Ohio; son of Cloyce Eugene (a merchandiser) and Fern Mae (a teacher) Deter; married Ellen Roscher (an associate editor), June 8, 1968; children: Daniel Joseph. *Education:* University of Southern Mississippi, student, 1963-65; Wittenberg University, B.A., 1967; Ohio University, M.A., 1968; Northern Illinois University, graduate study, 1971. *Politics:* Southern Democrat. *Religion:* Lutheran. *Home address:* Nelson Heights Rd., Cazenovia, N.Y. 13035. *Office:* Blackbird Press, Inc., P.O. Box 218, Cazenovia, N.Y. 13035.

CAREER: Storkline, Inc., Jackson, Miss., employed in production control, 1963; Northern Illinois University, DeKalb, instructor in English, 1968-71; Cazenovia College, Cazenovia, N.Y., assistant professor of English, 1971-74, poet-in-residence, 1971-74. Editor and publisher of Blackbird Press, Inc., 1970—. Partner, Deter, Deter & Swan (conference and workshop consultants). *Member:* Committee of Small Magazine Editors and Publishers, Coordinating Council of Literary Magazines. *Awards, honors:* George Bower Poetry Award.

WRITINGS: Eight Poems, Chantry Press, 1966; *Poems from Sleepless Summer Nights: 1967-1969*, Chantry Press, 1969. Author of "The Corner," a column in *Blackbird Circle*. Contributor of poems to literary magazines. Editor, *Blackbird Circle*.

WORK IN PROGRESS: The True Story of the New Fulton County Scalpings, a novel; a second novel; *Stone Wall Day*, a book of poems.

AVOCATIONAL INTERESTS: Fishing, woodcarving, farming, carpentry, watching professional football on television, "being generally disagreeable and anti-intellectual."

* * *

DE VALERA, Sinead 1879(?)-1975

1879(?)—January 7, 1975; Irish children's author and wife of the former president of the Republic of Ireland. Obituaries: *New York Times*, January 8, 1975; *Washington Post*, January 9, 1975.

* * *

de VINCK, Antoine 1924-

PERSONAL: Born April 24, 1924, in Kortenaken, Belgium; son of Marcel de Vinck; married Alice Damville (a naturalist); children: Pascale, Ande, Agnes. *Education:* Attended Ecole Nationale Superieure d'Architecture et Arts Decoratifs, Brussels, 1952-53. *Religion:* Roman Catholic. *Home:* 2 Dreve des Melezes, 1950, Kraainem, Belgium. *Agent:* Stella Seidenman, 16 Av. Calas, Geneva, 1206, Switzerland.

CAREER: Artist, specializing in pottery, sculpture, industrial design; author of children's books. *Member:* Union Professionnelle des Industrial Designers de Belgique.

WRITINGS: Wim of the Wind (juvenile), Doubleday, 1974.

WORK IN PROGRESS: Books for children, including *Big Black Bill* and *Little Joe and the Magpie*.

AVOCATIONAL INTERESTS: Nature, archaeology, toys.

DE VRIES, Carrow 1906-

PERSONAL: Born July 6, 1906, in Overisel, Mich.; son of Igear Rinke (a physician) and Maggie (a school teacher; maiden name, Hoeksema) De Vries; married Billie Schulz, April 17, 1936; children: Carrol (daughter), Robert Barton. *Education:* University of Michigan, student, 1926-27. *Politics:* None. *Religion:* None. *Home address:* R.R. 3, Holland, Mich. 49423.

CAREER: Held a variety of jobs, including linoleum installer, blueprint boy, house painter, bank boy in a newspaper print shop, "grunter" on a power gang, and night clerk in a hotel ("bummed" his way across country), 1927-30; state police trooper, 1930-35; Great Lakes Steel Corp., Ecorse, Mich., industrial policeman, 1936-46; farmer near Ligonier, Ind., 1946-56; Weatherhead Corp., Syracuse, Ind., chief of plant protection, 1956-68; writer, 1968—. *Wartime service:* Auxiliary Military Police, Great Lakes Steel Corp., during World War II. *Member:* National Society of Literature and the Arts, Alpha Tau Omega. *Awards, honors:* Certificate of appreciation from Hayden Library, Arizona State University, 1970, for contribution to American Mosaic Collection.

WRITINGS: Passing Butterflies: Haiku, S. Nishiguchi Art Publishers, 1957; *Moment of Flower and Leaf: Tanka,* S. Nishiguchi Art Publishers, 1957; *Hawthorn* (poems), Prairie Press, 1967; *An Alphabet Book of Haiku and Tanka,* Cartwright's Oldtime Print Shop, 1973.

* * *

DEZA, Ernest C. 1923-

PERSONAL: Born August 6, 1923, in Iloilo City, Republic of Philippines; son of Honorio D. (a teacher and principal) and Ursula (Cabangal) Deza; married Mary Brillantes, November 12, 1949; children: Alfonso, Edmundo, Zenaida (Mrs. Federico Pastelero). *Education:* University of San Agustin, A.A., 1946; University of Santo Tomas, M.D., 1951. *Religion:* Roman Catholic. *Home:* 31 Park Dr., Richmond, Ind. 47374. *Agent:* Robert Olmsted, Box 24, Big Fork, Minn. 56628. *Office:* Richmond State Hospital, Richmond, Ind. 47374.

CAREER: Licensed to practice medicine in Kentucky, Idaho, and Indiana; certified by American Board of Psychiatry and Neurology; Central State Hospital, Louisville, Ky., supervising psychiatrist, 1957-58; State Hospital South, Blackfoot, Idaho, clinical director, 1958-60; Western State Hospital, Hopkinsville, Ky., clinical director, 1970-72; Richmond State Hospital, Richmond, Ind., director, 1972—. Psychiatric consultant to St. Mary's Hospital. *Military service:* U.S. Army Forces, Far East, guerilla in Philippines. *Member:* American Psychiatric Association, American Group Therapists, Guild of Catholic Psychiatrists, Indiana Philippine Medical Association, Lyrical Guild of Iowa, Vox Populi Club (president), Lions Club, St. Joseph's Society. *Awards, honors:* Received award for abstract painting.

WRITINGS: Laugh Poems, Star Publishing, 1969; *New Laugh Poems*, Northwood Institute Press, 1974. Contributor of column to *Visayan Tribune*, and to *Western Star*. Guest editor of *Team Talk* and *News & Views*.

WORK IN PROGRESS: A novel, *The Psychiatrists*, completion expected in 1975; a nonfiction book, *Stop Feeling Depressed*, 1975.

AVOCATIONAL INTERESTS: Sculpture, oil painting, cartoons, music, poetry.

DIAZ, Janet W(inecoff) 1935-

PERSONAL: Born January 29, 1935, in Chicago, Ill.; daughter of Paul H. and Bertie (a postmaster; maiden name, McFadden) Coon; married Larry Winecoff, February 20, 1961 (divorced May, 1967); married David S. Diaz (an assistant professor of Spanish), July 8, 1967; children: (second marriage) Julia, Paul. *Education:* University of Kansas City (now University of Missouri at Kansas City), B.A., 1955; Duke University, M.A., 1957, Ph.D., 1961. *Residence:* Chapel Hill, N.C. *Office:* Department of Romance Languages, University of North Carolina, Chapel Hill, N.C. 27514.

CAREER: Duke University, Durham, N.C., instructor in Spanish literature, 1962-64; Queens College of the City University of New York, Flushing, N.Y., assistant professor of Spanish literature, 1964-66; University of North Carolina, Chapel Hill, associate professor of Spanish literature, 1967—. *Member:* Modern Language Association of America, American Association of Teachers of Spanish and Portuguese, American Association of University Professors, South Atlantic Modern Language Association, South Central Modern Language Association. *Awards, honors:* Fulbright grant for post-doctoral study in Spain, 1961-62; American Philosophical Society grant; first *Hispania* award, 1968, for best article on peninsular literature in a three-year period, 1965-68.

WRITINGS: The Major Themes of Existentialism in the Works of Ortega, University of North Carolina Press, 1969; *Ana Maria Matute*, Twayne, 1970; *Miguel Delibes*, Twayne, 1971; *The Theater of Garcia Lorca*, Ungar, in press. Contributor to professional journals. Associate editor of *Estudios de Hispanofila*; member of editorial board, *Romance Notes*, and *Hispanofila*; collaborator, *Hispanic World*, 1970—; reviewer for *Hispanofila*.

WORK IN PROGRESS: A. Saavedra: Duque de Rivas, publication by Twayne expected in 1976; *Jose Zorrilla*, for Twayne, 1977.

SIDELIGHTS: Janet Diaz lived in Spain, 1961-62 and 1965-66, and in Venezuela and Colombia, 1966-67. *Avocational interests:* Cooking, particularly foreign and exotic dishes, collecting cookbooks, crafts, foreign folk music, photography of children.

* * *

DICKE, Robert H(enry) 1916-

PERSONAL: Surname is pronounced *Dick*-ee; born May 6, 1916, in St. Louis, Mo.; son of Oscar H. (a patent attorney and electrical engineer) and Flora (Peterson) Dicke; married Annie Currie, June 6, 1942; children: Nancy Jean (Mrs. John Rapoport), John Robert, James Howard. *Education:* Princeton University, A.B., 1939; University of Rochester, Ph.D., 1941. *Home:* 321 Prospect Ave., Princeton, N.J. 08540. *Office:* Joseph Henry Laboratories, Princeton University, Princeton, N.J. 08540.

CAREER: Massachusetts Institute of Technology, Radiation Laboratory, Cambridge, staff member, 1941-46; Princeton University, Princeton, N.J., assistant professor, 1946-47, associate professor, 1947-55, professor of physics, 1955—, Cyrus Fogg Brackett Professor of Physics, 1957-75, Albert Einstein Professor of Science, 1975—, head of department, 1967-70. National Bureau of Standards, chairman of advisory committee on atomic physics, 1961-63, member of advisory panel, 1973-76, and member of visiting committee, 1974—; member of National Science Board, 1970—; member of President's Commission on National Medal of Science, 1974-75.

MEMBER: National Academy of Sciences, American Academy of Arts and Sciences, American Physical Society (member of council and executive committee, 1970-73), American Astronomical Society, Royal Astronomical Society, American Geophysical Union, American Association of Physics Teachers. *Awards, honors:* Rumford Medal from American Academy of Arts and Sciences, 1967; National Medal of Science, 1970; D.Sci., University of Edinburgh, 1972; Comstock Prize from National Academy of Sciences, 1973; Elliot Cresson Medal, Franklin Institute, 1974.

WRITINGS: (With Purcell Montgomery) *Principles of Micro-wave Circuits*, McGraw, 1948; (with J. P. Wittke) *An Introduction to Quantum Mechanics*, Addison-Wesley, 1960; *The Theoretical Significance of Experimental Relativity*, Gordon & Breach, 1964; *Gravitation and the Universe*, American Philosophical Society, 1970.

* * *

DICKENS, A(rthur) G(eoffrey) 1910-

PERSONAL: Born July 6, 1910, in Hull, England; son of Arthur James (a railway official) and Gertrude (Grasby) Dickens; married Molly Bygott, August 1, 1936; children: Peter Geoffrey, Paul Jonathan. *Education:* Magdalen College, Oxford, B.A., 1932, M.A., 1936. *Religion:* Church of England. *Residence:* London, England. *Office:* Institute of Historical Research, University of London, Senate House, London WCIE 7HU, England.

CAREER: Oxford University, Keble College, Oxford, England, fellow, 1933-49; University of Hull, Hull, England, professor of history, 1949-62; University of London, King's College, London, England, professor of history, 1962-67, director of Institute of Historical Research, 1967—. Chairman and general secretary of British National Committee of Historians, 1972—. *Military service:* British Army, Royal Artillery, 1940-45; became captain. *Member:* British Academy (fellow; foreign secretary, 1969—), Society of Antiquaries (fellow), Royal Historical Society (fellow), Athenaeum Club. *Awards, honors:* D.Lit., University of London, 1965; Companion of the Order of St. Michael and St. George, 1974.

WRITINGS: Luebeck Diary, Gollancz, 1947; *The Register of Butley Priory*, Warren, 1951; *The East Riding of Yorkshire*, A. Brown, 1954; *Lollards and Protestants*, Oxford University Press, 1959; *Thomas Cromwell*, English Universities Press, 1959; *Tudor Treatises*, Yorkshire Archaeological Society, 1960; *Clifford Letters*, Surtees Society, 1962; *The English Reformation*, Schocken, 1964, revised edition, Fontana, Collins, 1973; *Reformation and Society in Sixteenth Century Europe*, Thames & Hudson, 1966; *Martin Luther and the Reformation*, English Universities Press, 1967; *The Counter-Reformation*, Thames & Hudson, 1968; *The Age of Humanism and Reformation*, Prentice-Hall, 1972; *The German Nation and Martin Luther*, Harper, 1974. Editor of *Bulletin of the Institute of Historical Research*, 1967—.

WORK IN PROGRESS: A general history of the Renaissance and the Reformation; research on the life, works, and influence of Erasmus, and the life of Cardinal Wolsey.

SIDELIGHTS: Reformation and Society in Sixteenth Century Europe has been issued in Dutch, Portuguese, Spanish, and French translations; *The Counter-Reformation* has been issued in Dutch, Portuguese, and French. *Avocational interests:* Travel.

BIOGRAPHICAL/CRITICAL SOURCES: American Historical Review, April, 1972.

* * *

DICKEY, Glenn 1936-

PERSONAL: Born February 16, 1936, in Virginia, Minn.; son of Glenn Ernest and Madlyn (Emmert) Dickey; married Nancy McDaniel, February 25, 1967; children: Kevin Scott. *Education:* University of California, Berkeley, B.A., 1958. *Politics:* Democrat. *Religion:* Presbyterian. *Home:* 120 Florence Ave., Oakland, Calif. 94618. *Agent:* Charles Neighbors, 240 Waverly Pl., New York, N.Y. 10014. *Office: San Francisco Chronicle*, 501 Mission St., San Francisco, Calif. 94119.

CAREER: Watsonville Register-Pajaronian, Watsonville, Calif., sports editor, 1958-63; *San Francisco Chronicle*, San Francisco, Calif., sports writer, 1963-71, sports columnist, 1971—. *Member:* Newspaper Guild, Baseball Writers Association of America. *Awards, honors:* "Best Sports Stories" award, 1963, 1968, and 1971.

WRITINGS: The Jock Empire, Chilton, 1974. Author of a television script for a pilot children's sports program. Contributor to magazines, including *TV Guide, Argosy, Sport, Women Sports*, and *Pro Quarterback*.

WORK IN PROGRESS: The Twelfth Man, a novel on professional football; *The Great No-Hitters*, nonfiction.

* * *

DICKSON, Franklyn 1941-

PERSONAL: Born July 26, 1941; married Pauline Marshall, July 21, 1967; children: Laura, Rex. *Education:* Fairleigh Dickinson University, B.S., 1963; New York University, M.B.A., 1963. *Home:* 586 Kipp St., Teaneck, N.J. 07666. *Office:* 1657 Broadway, New York, N.Y. 10019.

CAREER: Fairleigh Dickinson University, Teaneck, N.J., assistant professor of business administration, 1963—. President of Ray Bloch Enterprises, Inc., New York, N.Y., 1968—. *Member:* American Marketing Association, American Management Association, Rotary Club.

WRITINGS: Successful Management of the Small and Medium-Sized Business, Prentice-Hall, 1971. Contributor to *Sales Meetings Magazine, Meetings and Conventions Magazine*, and *Journal of Public Relations*.

* * *

DICKSON, Stanley 1927-

PERSONAL: Born September 3, 1927, in New York, N.Y.; son of Irving Richard and Beatrice (Weinshank) Dickson; married Marion Ruth Ernstorff (an administrative assistant), November 22, 1950; children: Johanna Miriam (Mrs. Arnold Sohinki), Fran Celia, Neil Howard. *Education:* Brooklyn College (now Brooklyn College of the City University of New York), B.A., 1950, M.A., 1954; University of Buffalo, Ed.D., 1960. *Home:* 49 Louraine Dr., Kenmore, N.Y. 14223. *Office:* Department of Communication Disorder, State University of New York College at Buffalo, 1300 Elmwood Ave., Buffalo, N.Y. 14222.

CAREER: State University of New York College at Buffalo, associate professor, 1956-60, professor of speech, 1961—. Chairman of the board of directors of Industrial Hearing Conservation, Inc. *Military service:* U.S. Coast Guard, 1945-46. *Member:* American Speech and Hearing Association (fellow), New York State Speech and Hearing Association (past president). *Awards, honors:* Commendation for service from New York State Speech and Hearing Association, 1968-69.

WRITINGS: (Editor) *Communication Disorders: Remedial Principles and Practices*, Scott, Foresman, 1974. Contributor to *Journal of Speech and Hearing Research, Journal of Communication Disorders, Exceptional Children*, and *New York State Speech and Hearing Review*. Consulting editor of *Journal of Speech and Hearing Disorders*.

* * *

DIEBOLD, John (Theurer) 1926-

PERSONAL: Born June 8, 1926, in Weehawken, N.J.; son of William and Rose (Theurer) Diebold; married Doris Hackett, November 22, 1951; children: Joan. *Education:* U.S. Merchant Marine Academy, B.S., 1946; Swarthmore College, B.A. (with high honors), 1949; Harvard University, M.B.A. (with distinction), 1951. *Home:* 1 East End Ave., New York, N.Y. 10021. *Office:* 430 Park Ave., New York, N.Y. 10022.

CAREER: Griffenhagen & Associates (later Griffenhagen-Kroeger, Inc.; management consultants), New York, N.Y., and Chicago, Ill., associate, 1951-57, owner 1957—; Diebold Group, Inc. (management consultants), New York, founder, president, and chairman of the board, 1954—; founder of Diebold Europe S.A. and of Management Science Training Institute, 1958; founder and chairman of the board of John Diebold, Inc., 1967—; chairman of the boards of Diebold Venture Capital Corp., 1968, of D.C.L., Inc. (holding company of Diebold Computer Leasing, Inc.), 1967—, of Gemini Computer Systems, Inc., 1968—, and of Intermodal Transportation Systems, Inc., 1969—. Member of board of Genesco.

Member of national advisory council of the Peace Corps, 1965—; member of U.S. advisory committee for European Institute of Business Administration, 1965—; vice-chairman of National Committee on U.S.-China Relations, 1969—; member of International Institute for Strategic Studies, 1971—, public member, Hudson Institute; member, often in an advisory capacity, of numerous other committees and councils in business, education, and government. Member of board of directors of American Council on Germany, 1970—, Business Council for International Understanding, 1970—, and Academy for Educational Development. Member of boards of trustees of Freedom House, 1969—, Committee for Economic Development, 1970—, Council of Americans, 1971—, and National Planning Association, 1971—. *Military service:* Served in U.S. Naval Reserve during World War II.

MEMBER: International Cybernetics Association (member of board of directors, 1965—), Society for the History of Technology (member of executive council), Council on Foreign Relations, Young Presidents Organization, Center for Inter-American Relations Institute of Directors (London), International Chamber of Commerce, U.S. Chamber of Commerce, Author's Guild, Harvard Business School Club, Economic Club, Union League, Harvard Club (New York City), Metropolitan Club (Washington, D.C.), Chicago Club, Bohemian Club (San Francisco), Reform Club, Burkes Club (London). *Awards, honors:* LL.D., Rollins College, 1965; Sc.D., Clarkson College, 1965; D.Eng., Newark College of Engineering,

1970, fellow of Pierpont Morgan Library, 1971; D.Comml.Sc., Manhattan College, 1973; decorated grand officer, Order of Istiqlal (Jordan); grand cross, Eloy Alfaro Foundation (Panama); grand cross, Order of St. Martin (Vienna); commendatore, Order of Merit (Italy); Order of Merit (Germany).

WRITINGS: Automation: The advent of the Automatic Factory, Van Nostrand, 1952; *Beyond Automation: Managerial Problems of an Exploding Technology*, McGraw, 1964; *Man and the Computer: Technology as an Agent of Social Change*, Praeger, 1969; *Business Decisions and Technological Change*, Praeger, 1970; (editor) *World of the Computer*, Random House, 1973. Contributor of articles to magazines and journals.

BIOGRAPHICAL/CRITICAL SOURCES: Wilbur Cross, *John Diebold: Breaking the Confines of the Possible*, Heinemann, 1966; Carl Heyel, *John Diebold on Management*, Prentice-Hall, 1972.

* * *

DIEHL, (Robert) Digby 1940-

PERSONAL: Surname is pronounced "deal"; born November 14, 1940, in Boonton, N.J.; son of Edwin Samuel (a writer) and Mary Jane (a professor; maiden name, Ellsworth) Diehl; married Emilie Robertson, June 7, 1967 (divorced August, 1970). *Education:* Rutgers University, A.B., 1962; University of California, Los Angeles, M.A., 1967. *Home:* 9507 Santa Monica Blvd., #219, Beverly Hills, Calif. 90210. *Office: Los Angeles Times*, Los Angeles, Calif. 90053.

CAREER: Learning Center (for educational research), Princeton, N.J., editor, 1962-65; *Coast* (magazine), Los Angeles, Calif., editor, 1965-68; *Show* (magazine), New York, N.Y., editor, 1968-69; *Los Angeles Times*, Los Angeles, Calif., book editor and author of weekly column "Book Talk," 1969—. Lecturer at University of California (Los Angeles), 1968—. *Member:* Society of Magazine Writers, National Book Critics' Circle (vice-president, 1974—), American Association of University Professors, Phi Beta Kappa, Sigma Delta Chi.

WRITINGS: (Editor) *The Dissonant Eye*, University of California Press, 1968; *Supertalk* (nonfiction), Doubleday, 1974; *Drug-Related American Fiction*, National Institute of Mental Health, 1974.

WORK IN PROGRESS: All by Myself on a Bicycle Built for Two, a novel; *El Marlino!*, a nonfiction study of marlin fishing.

AVOCATIONAL INTERESTS: Travel (South America, Europe), boating, fishing, jazz musicology, playing bridge, California history.

* * *

DIETRICH, Richard V(incent) 1924-
(R. Dirk)

PERSONAL: Born February 7, 1924, in LaFargeville, N.Y.; son of Roy Eugene (a businessman) and Mida (Vincent) Dietrich; married Frances Smith, December 28, 1946; children: Richard S., Kurt, Krista. *Education:* Colgate University, A.B., 1947; Yale University, M.S., 1950, Ph.D., 1951. *Politics:* Independent. *Religion:* "Unorthodox." *Home:* 2499 East Broomfield Rd., Mount Pleasant, Mich. 48858. *Office:* Department of Geology, Central Michigan University, Mount Pleasant, Mich. 48859.

CAREER: Has worked as ditchdigger, cabinetmaker's helper, farm laborer, store clerk and manager, insurance agent, and professional musician; Virginia Polytechnic Institute, Blacksburg, Va., assistant professor, 1951-52, associate professor, 1952-56, professor of geology, 1956-69, associate dean, 1966-69; Central Michigan University, Mount Pleasant, professor of geology and dean of arts and sciences, 1969—. Fulbright research professor, University of Oslo, 1958-59. *Military service:* U.S. Army Air Forces, 1943-46; served in South Pacific Theatre; became sergeant. *Member:* Geological Society of America (fellow), Society of Economic Geologists, Mineralogical Society of America (fellow), Geological Society of Finland, Norwegian Geological Society, Association of Earth Science Editors (president, 1972-73), American Geological Institute (member of board of governors, 1972-74), Phi Beta Kappa, Sigma Xi, Phi Kappa Phi.

WRITINGS: Virginia Minerals and Rocks, Virginia Polytechnic Institute, 1954, 3rd edition, 1960; *Precambrian Geology and Mineral Resources of the Brier Hill Quadrangle, New York*, University of the State of New York, 1957; *Geology and Mineral Resources of Floyd County of the Blue Ridge Upland, Southwestern Virginia*, Virginia Engineering Experiment Station, 1959; *Southern Field Excursion Guidebook*, International Mineralogical Association, 1962; (editor) *Geological Excursions in Southwest Virginia*, Department of Geological Science, Virginia Polytechnic Institute, 1963; *Mineral Tables: Hard Specimen Properties of Fifteen-Hundred Minerals*, McGraw, 1969; *Geology and Virginia*, University Press of Virginia, 1970.

Contributor of poems, sometimes under pseudonym R. Dirk, to *Snowy Egret*, *Green's Magazine*, *Dragonfly*, *Small Pond*, *Speakeasy Culture*, *Humorama*, *Phi Kappa Phi Journal*. Editor of *Virginia Engineering Experiment Bulletin*, 1952-58, and *Mineral Industries Journal*, 1954-58, 1964; business editor, *Economic Geology*, 1966-71; member of editorial board, *Mineralogical Record*, 1969-74.

WORK IN PROGRESS: An anthology of his poetry and haiku.

* * *

DIETZ, Howard 1896-

PERSONAL: Born September 8, 1896, in New York, N.Y.; son of Herman (a merchant) and Julia (Bloomgarten) Dietz; married Elizabeth Hall, 1918; married Tanis Guinness Montagu, January, 1937 (divorced, 1951); married Lucinda Goldsborough Ballard, July 31, 1951; children: Liza Buckley (Mrs. Christopher Shaw); stepchildren: Robert F. R. Ballard, Jenifer Ballard (Mrs. Walter Ramberg). *Education:* Attended Columbia University, 1913-17. *Politics:* "Independent verging on Democrat." *Religion:* None. *Home:* 1 Lincoln Plaza, New York, N.Y. 10023. *Agent:* Arnold Weissberger, 120 East 56th St., New York, N.Y.

CAREER: Lyricist, librettist. Began as journalist while attending college, serving as Columbia correspondent for the *New York American*, and writing for the *Bronx Home News*, *New York Sun*, and *New York World*; worked briefly as copywriter for Philip Goodman Advertising Agency, creating the "Leo the Lion" trademark that continues to appear on all Metro-Goldwyn-Mayer films; Goldwyn Pictures Corp., New York, N.Y., director of public relations and advertising, 1918-24; Metro-Goldwyn-Mayer Corp., New York, N.Y., director of promotions, 1924-57, vice-president, 1940-57, consultant, 1957—.

Member of board of directors and vice-president in charge of advertising and publicity, Loew's, Inc., 1941-57. Publicity director for U.S. Treasury Department, 1940-41, screen and radio chairman for war bond program, 1941-48. *Military service:* U.S. Navy, 1917-18; edited publication *Navy Life.*

MEMBER: American Society of Composers, Authors and Publishers (member of board of directors, 1959-64), American Federation of Television and Radio Artists, Actors' Equity Association, American Guild of Variety Artists, Dramatists Guild, Authors and Composers Illustrator's League, Regency Club.

WRITINGS: June Goes Down Town: A Story for City Children, A. & C. Boni, 1925; *Dancing in the Dark: Words by Howard Dietz* (autobiography), Quadrangle, 1974.

Musicals; author of book and lyrics: (Book co-authored with Morrie Ryskind) "Merry-Go-Round," first produced in New York, N.Y., at Klaw Theatre, May 31, 1927; (book co-authored with George S. Kaufman) "The Band Wagon," first produced in New York at New Amsterdam Theatre, June 3, 1931; "Revenge with Music," first produced at New Amsterdam Theatre, November 28, 1934; "Between the Devil," first produced in New York at Imperial Theatre, December 22, 1937.

Author of lyrics: "Dear Sir," first produced in New York at Times Square Theatre, September 23, 1924; "The Second Little Show," first produced on Broadway at Royale Theatre, September 2, 1930; "Three's a Crowd," first produced in New York at Selwyn Theatre, October 15, 1930; (and author of sketches with Ryskind and others) "Flying Colors," first produced on Broadway at Imperial Theatre, September 15, 1932; (and author of sketches) "At Home Abroad," first produced on Broadway at Winter Garden Theatre, September 19, 1935; (and author of sketches) "Follow the Sun," first produced in London at Adelphi Theatre, February 4, 1936.

(With Al Dubin) "Keep off the Grass," first produced on Broadway at Broadhurst Theatre, May 23, 1940; "Dancing in the Streets" (pre-Broadway tryout), first produced in Boston at Shubert Theatre, 1943; "Jackpot," first produced on Broadway at Alvin Theatre, January 13, 1944; "Inside U.S.A.," first produced in New York at Century Theatre, April 30, 1948.

"The Gay Life," first produced on Broadway at Shubert Theatre, November 18, 1961; "Jennie," first produced on Broadway at Majestic Theatre, October 17, 1963; "That's Entertainment," first produced in New York at Edison Theatre, April, 1972.

Contributor of lyrics: "Alibi Baby," 1923; (and contributor of sketches) "The Little Show," first produced on Broadway at The Music Box, April 30, 1929; "Grand Street Follies of 1929," first produced on Broadway at Booth Theatre, May 1, 1929; "Garrick Gaieties," first produced in New York at Guild Theatre, October 16, 1930; "The Show Is On," first produced on Broadway at Winter Garden Theatre, December 25, 1936; "Ziegfield Follies," first produced at Winter Garden Theatre, March 1, 1957.

Adaptations: (With Rouben Mamoulian) "Sadie Thompson" (based on W. Somerset Maugham's story, "Rain"), first produced on Broadway at Alvin Theatre, November 16, 1944; (with Garson Kanin) Johann Strauss, *Die Fledermaus* (in English; first performed in New York by Metropolitan Opera Co., December 20, 1950), Boosey & Hawkes, 1950, Metropolitan Opera version, 1951; Giacomo Puccini, *La Boheme* (in English; first produced by Metropolitan Opera Co., December 27, 1952), Ricordi, 1952.

Author of lyrics for films, including "Hollywood Party" (also co-scenarist), MGM, 1934, "Under Your Spell," Fox, 1936, and "The Band Wagon," MGM, 1953. Lyricist for radio musical serial, "The Gibson Family," 1934, and for television programs, "Surprise for Santa," CBS, 1948, and "A Bell for Adano," CBS, 1956. Author of lyrics and sketches for Coast Guard revue, "Tars and Spars," 1943-44.

Author of introductions to books on bridge by Goren, Jacoby, and others. Contributor of articles, book reviews, and poems to *New York Times, New York Sun, Saturday Review, Life, New Republic*, and other periodicals.

WORK IN PROGRESS: How to Write a Song, with Maurice Levine; planning a songwriting program and a lyricists' evening for a Young Men's Hebrew Association series; writing television commercials in verse.

SIDELIGHTS: Despite his genuine versatility, Dietz insists that his calling is that of an advertising and publicity man. During the years spent pursuing his prolific "sideline," he has written several hundred songs, including "Something to Remember You By," "Dancing in the Dark," "You and the Night and the Music," "I Guess I'll Have to Change My Plan," "I See Your Face before Me," "Under Your Spell," and "Louisiana Hayride." He began his long association with composer Arthur Schwartz about 1924, and has collaborated with him on numerous occasions; he has also collaborated with Vernon Duke, Jerome Kern, Jimmy McHugh, Ralph Rainger, Sammy Fain, and others.

Dietz produced and directed "Flying Colors," which opened on Broadway in 1932; he co-produced "Hollywood Party" for MGM in 1934, and produced the Coast Guard revue, "Tars and Spars," 1943-44.

AVOCATIONAL INTERESTS: Golf, bridge, painting, spectator sports.

* * *

DIGENNARO, Joseph 1939-

PERSONAL: Born February 16, 1939, in New York, N.Y.; son of Phillip J. and Rose (Cavalin) DiGennaro; married Jo-Tina Colicchio (a physical education teacher), December 16, 1968; children: Joann, Joe, Jr. *Education:* Hunter College of the City University of New York, B.A., 1961; University of Illinois, M.S., 1962; Columbia University, Ed.D., 1968. *Religion:* Roman Catholic. *Home:* 272 Coachlight Sq., Montrose, N.Y. 10548. *Office:* Department of Physical Education, Lehman College, Bedford Park Blvd., New York, N.Y. 10468.

CAREER: Lehman College of the City University of New York, New York, N.Y., assistant professor, 1968-73, associate professor of physical education, 1973—, freshman basketball coach, 1962-65, varsity track and field coach, 1963-64, varsity basketball coach, 1965-69, head of service program, 1965-69. *Member:* National College Physical Education Association for Men, American Association for Health, Physical Education and Recreation, United States Professional Tennis Association, New York State Association for Health, Physical Education and Recreation.

WRITINGS: Individualized Exercise and Optimal Physical Fitness: A Review Workbook for Men and Women, Lea & Febiger, 1974. Contributor to *Research Quarterly, Physical Educator*, and *New York State Journal for Health, Physical Education, and Recreation.*

DILLINGHAM, Beth 1927-

PERSONAL: Born March 9, 1927, in Ann Arbor, Mich.; daughter of Raymond L. (a mathematician) and Una (Greene) Wilder; married Harry C. Dillingham (a sociologist), September 1, 1947; children: Daniel Clay, Raymond Giles, Harry Brett, Helen Eve. *Education:* University of Michigan, B.A., 1949, M.A., 1950, Ph.D., 1963. *Politics:* None. *Religion:* None. *Home:* 3876 Dakota, Cincinnati, Ohio 45229. *Office:* Department of Anthropology, University of Cincinnati, Cincinnati, Ohio 45221.

CAREER: Still Oesteopathic Medical College, Des Moines, Iowa, lecturer in anthropology, 1960; Meharry Medical School, Nashville, Tenn., lecturer in anthropology, 1961-62; Central Michigan University, Mt. Pleasant, assistant professor of anthropology, 1962-65; University of Cincinnati, Cincinnati, Ohio, assistant professor, 1965-73, associate professor of anthropology, 1973—. *Member:* American Anthropological Association (fellow), American Association for the Advancement of Science, Phi Kappa Phi, Phi Sigma. *Awards, honors:* American Association of University Women fellow, 1954-55.

WRITINGS: (With Leslie A. White) *The Concept of Culture*, Burgess, 1973. Contributor to *World Anthropology*; contributor to American College Testing program.

WORK IN PROGRESS: Research on the changing role of women and on American Indian ethnohistory.

* * *

DINERMAN, Helen Schneider 1921(?)-1974

1921(?)—August 14, 1974; American sociologist, public-opinion analyst, and author. Obituaries: *New York Times*, August 17, 1974.

* * *

DINTIMAN, George B(lough) 1936-

PERSONAL: Born October 4, 1936, in Hershey, Pa.; son of George B. (a professor) and Gladys (Blough) Dintiman; married Elda Cabrera-Chico (a college professor), July 31, 1958; children: Brenda, Lynne, Brian. *Education:* Lock Haven State College, B.S., 1958; New York University, M.A., 1961; Columbia University, Ed.D., 1964. *Religion:* Protestant. *Home:* 14150 Netherfield Dr., Midlothian, Va. 23113. *Office:* Department of Physical Education, Virginia Commonwealth University, Richmond, Va. 23220.

CAREER: High school teacher and coach in South Williamsport, Pa., 1958-59; Inter-American University, San German, Puerto Rico, instructor, 1959-61, associate professor of physical education, 1961-65; Southern Connecticut State College, New Haven, associate professor of physical education, 1965-68; Virginia Commonwealth University, Richmond, associate professor, 1968-70, professor of physical education and chairman of department, 1968-75. *Member:* American Association for Health, Physical Education and Recreation; College Physical Education Association for Men; Virginia Association for Health, Physical Education and Recreation.

WRITINGS: A Comprehensive Manual of Physical Education Activities, Appleton, 1970; *Evaluation Manual in Physical Education*, Appleton, 1970; *Sprinting Speed: Its Improvement for Major Sports Competition*, C.C Thomas, 1971; *What Research Tells the Coach About Sprinting*, American Association for Health, Physical Education and Recreation, 1974; (with others) *The Art and Science of Coaching*, F. L. Productions, in press.

Co-author of "Champion Athlete," a syndicated column of Centurion Press International, 1972—. Contributor of about a dozen articles to physical education journals, including *Scholastic Coach, United States Track Coaches Association Quarterly Review, Journal of the American Association for Health, Physical Education and Recreation*, and *Coach and Athlete.*

WORK IN PROGRESS: Introduction to Measurement and Research in Physical Education, for Macmillan.

* * *

DIOLE, Philippe V. 1908-

PERSONAL: Born August 24, 1908, in Saint Maur, France; son of Marcel (a jurist) and Elizabeth (Legrand) Diole; married Marguerite Monsenergue, July 6, 1953. *Education:* University of Paris, Licencie en Droit, 1928. *Religion:* Roman Catholic. *Home:* 80 rue de l'Universite Paris, Paris, France 75007.

CAREER: Journalist and archeologist. *Member:* Club des Explorateurs francais. *Awards, honors:* Grand Prix Walter de l'Academie francaise, 1965.

WRITINGS: (With Raymond Manevy) *Sous les plis du drapeau noir* (title means "Under the Black Flag"), Domat (Paris), 1949; *L'Aventure sous-marine*, Michel (Paris), 1951, translation by Alan Ross published as *The Undersea Adventure*, Messner, 1953; *Promenades d'archeologie sous-marine*, Michel, 1952, translation by Gerard Hopkins published as *4,000 Years Under the Sea*, Messner, 1954; *Les Portes de la mer*, Michel, 1953, translation by Ross published as *The Gates of the Sea*, Messner, 1955; *Au bord de la terre: Fragments de la vie d'un plongeur* (title means "A Diver's Life"), Michel, 1954; *Underwater Exploration: A History*, translated from the French by A. M. Burton, Elek, 1954; *Le plus beau desert du monde*, Michel, 1955, translation by Katherine Woods published as *Sahara Adventure*, Messner, 1956 (published in England as *The Most Beautiful Desert of All*, J. Cape, 1959); *Dans le Fezzan inconnu* (title means "In the Unknown Fezzan"), Michel, 1956; *Le Tresor du banc d'argent* (title means "The Treasure of the Silver Bank"), Andre Bonne editeur, 1956; *Du ciel a la stratosphere* (title means "From the Sky to the Stratosphere"), Andre Bonne editeur, 1958; *L'Eau profonde: Roman* (title means "Deep Water"), Gallimard, 1959; *L'Okapi: Roman*, Gallimard, 1963, translation by Peter Green published as *Okapi Fever: A Novel*, Viking, 1965; *Chasse d'Afrique* (title means "Big Game in Africa"), Librairie Marguerat, 1965; *Les Animaux malades de l'homme*, [France], 1974, translation by J. F. Bernard published as *The Errant Ark: Man's Relationship with Animals*, Putnam, 1974.

With Jacques Yves Cousteau; all translated by J. F. Bernard: *Diving for Sunken Treasure*, Doubleday, 1971; *Life and Death in a Coral Sea*, Doubleday, 1971; *The Whale: Mighty Monarch of the Sea*, Doubleday, 1972; *Three Adventures: Galapagos, Titicaca, the Blue Holes*, Doubleday, 1973; *Octopus and Squid: The Soft Intelligence*, Doubleday, 1973; *Diving Companions: Sea-Lions, Elephant Seal, Walrus*, Doubleday, 1974; *Dolphins*, Doubleday, 1975.

WORK IN PROGRESS: Le mysterie animal, for Dargaud.

* * *

DiRENZO, Gordon J(ames) 1934-

PERSONAL: Born July 19, 1934, in North Attleboro,

Mass.; son of Santo and Guilia (Petti) DiRenzo; married Mary Kathleen Ryan (a social service administrator), July 6, 1968; children: Maria Guilia, Chiara Veronica. *Education:* University of Notre Dame, B.A. (cum laude), 1956, A.M., 1957, Ph.D., 1960; Harvard University, graduate study, 1959; postdoctoral study at Columbia University, 1963-65, and University of Colorado, 1964. *Home address:* Little Baltimore Farms, R.R.3, Newark, Del. 19711. *Office:* Department of Sociology, University of Delaware, Newark, Del. 19711.

CAREER: Certified social psychologist. College of St. Rose, Albany, N.Y., instructor in sociology, 1957-59; University of Notre Dame, Notre Dame, Ind., research associate in sociology, 1960-61; University of Portland, Portland, Ore., instructor in sociology, 1961-62; Fairfield University, Fairfield, Conn., assistant professor, 1962-66; Indiana University, South Bend, associate professor of sociology, 1966-70; University of Delaware, Newark, professor of sociology, 1970—. Lecturer at Albany Medical Center and Siena College, both 1958-59; research sociologist at University of Rome, 1960-61, senior Fulbright-Hays Professor, 1968-69; lecturer at Fairfield University, 1963-65, Western Connecticut State College, 1964, and Brooklyn College of the City University of New York, 1965; visiting professor at University of Notre Dame, summer, 1965, and State University of New York College at Cortland, summer, 1966. Private practice in social psychology, 1963—. Executive director of Sociological Consultants Group, 1963—. Research associate at Social Science Training and Research Laboratory at University of Notre Dame, 1966—.

MEMBER: International Sociological Association, International Political Science Association, American Sociological Association (fellow), American Psychological Association, American Political Science Association, American Association for the Advancement of Science, American Association of University Professors, Society for the Psychological Study of Social Issues, World Future Society, Italian-American Historical Association, Society for the Study of Social Problems, Eastern Sociological Society, Notre Dame Alumni Association of Delaware (member of board of directors, 1973—), Alpha Kappa Delta. *Awards, honors:* Grant from Italian Government, 1960; Ford Foundation grant, 1960; grant from National Science Foundation and University of Colorado, 1964; grant from Ford Foundation and Indiana University, 1967; grant from National Science Foundation and American Political Science Association, 1967; Fulbright-Hays grant, 1968; National Science Foundation postdoctoral grant, 1973; National Endowment for the Humanities grant, 1975.

WRITINGS: (Editor with Talcott Parsons, Muzafer Sherif, Paul F. Lazarsfeld, and others, and contributor) *Concepts, Theory, and Explanation in the Behavioral Sciences*, Random House, 1966; *Personality, Power, and Politics*, University of Notre Dame Press, 1967; (contributor) Thomas W. Milburn and Margaret G. Hermann, editors, *A Psychological Examination of Political Man*, Free Press, 1974; (contributor) Raj P. Mohan and Don Martindale, editors, *Handbook of Contemporary Developments in World Sociology*, Greenwood Press, 1974; (editor and contributor) *Personality and Politics*, Doubleday, 1974. Contributor of more than twenty articles and reviews to journals of the social sciences.

WORK IN PROGRESS: Social Change and Social Character; Personality and Social Systems, completion expected in 1977.

AVOCATIONAL INTERESTS: International travel, aviation (private pilot), photography, gourmet cooking, making wine.

* * *

DISON, Norma 1928-

PERSONAL: Born February 7, 1928, in Ohio; daughter of Carl Ludwig (a farmer) and Nellie (Casteel) Greenler; married Harold Dison, Jr. (employed by International Business Machines), August 15, 1953; children: Larry Alan, Val Ludwig. *Education:* Valparaiso University, B.A., 1952; Methodist-Kahler School of Nursing, diploma, 1952; Winona State College, graduate study; University of Minnesota, M.A., 1974. *Religion:* Lutheran. *Residence:* Rochester, Minn. *Office:* Nursing Department, Rochester Community College, Rochester, Minn. 55901.

CAREER: Methodist-Kahler School of Nursing, Rochester, Minn., instructor in nursing, 1952-62; Saint Marys School of Nursing, Rochester, Minn., instructor in nursing, 1962-68; College of Saint Teresa, Winona, Minn., assistant professor of nursing, 1968-73; Rochester Community College, Rochester, Minn., instructor in nursing, 1973—. Registered nurse. *Member:* National League for Nursing, National Education Association, Minnesota Association for Learning Disabilities.

WRITINGS: (Contributor) *Mosby's Comprehensive Review of Nursing*, Mosby, 6th edition (Dison was not associated with earlier editions), 1965, 8th edition, 1973; *An Atlas of Nursing Techniques*, Mosby, 1967, 2nd edition, 1971; *Clinical Nursing Techniques*, Mosby, 1975, 3rd edition, 1975; (with Minette Nast) *Simplified Drugs and Solutions for Nurses, Including Arithmetic*, Mosby, 4th edition (Dison was not associated with earlier editions), 6th edition, in press. Contributor to *American Journal of Nursing*. Abstractor for *Nursing Research*.

WORK IN PROGRESS: A new nursing book, with others.

AVOCATIONAL INTERESTS: Quilting, needlepoint, sewing, crocheting, creative handwork, gardening, camping.

* * *

DIXON, Roger 1930-
(John Christian, Charles Lewis)

PERSONAL: Born January 6, 1930, in Portsmouth, England; son of Robert George (a sales director) and Gladys (an opera singer; maiden name, Florence) Dixon; married Carolyn Anne Shepheard (a ballet dancer), June 28, 1966; children: two boys and four girls. *Education:* Attended Ffouks-Lynch Business School, 1950-55; *Politics:* Liberal. *Religion:* Christian. *Home and office:* 1 St. Annes Crescent, Lewes, Sussex, England. *Agent:* Basil Bova, 1619 Broadway, New York, N.Y. 10019.

CAREER: Self-employed chartered accountant in London, England, 1955-64; full-time writer, 1964—. *Military service:* British Army, 1949-50; became captain. *Member:* Institute of Chartered Accountants, Screen Writers Guild of Great Britain, British Astronomical Society, Sussex County Cricket Club (life member).

WRITINGS: Noah II, Ace Books, 1968; *Christ on Trial*, Pinnacle Books, 1974; *The Messiah*, Collins, 1975; (under pseudonym John Christian) *Five Gates to Armageddon*, Harwood Smart Publishers, 1975; (under pseudonym Charles Lewis) *The Cain Factor*, Harwood Smart Publishers, 1975; *The Patriarch*, Harwood Smith Publishers, in press; *Kings*, Harwood Smith Publishers, in press; *Jerusalem Agogo*, Collins, in press.

WORK IN PROGRESS: The Mars Project.

AVOCATIONAL INTERESTS: Middle East, with particular reference to current Israeli/Arab problems, religion (comparative), travel, and science, particularly astronomy.

* * *

DOBBYN, John F(rancis) 1937-

PERSONAL: Born August 21, 1937, in Boston, Mass.; son of John F. (a teacher) and Madolyn (a nurse; maiden name, Ashford) Dobbyn; married wife, Lois, June 28, 1969; children: John George. *Education:* Harvard University, B.A., 1959, LL.M., 1969; Boston College, J.D., 1965. *Religion:* Roman Catholic. *Office:* School of Law, Villanova University, Villanova, Pa. 19085.

CAREER: Admitted to Bar of State of Massachusetts, 1965; law clerk of federal district court judge in Boston, Mass., 1965-67; Burns & Levinson (law firm), Boston, Mass.; attorney, 1967-68; Villanova University, School of Law, Villanova, Pa., assistant professor, 1969-70, associate professor, 1970-71, professor of law, 1971—. *Military service:* U.S. Air Force, 1959-62; became captain. *Member:* Valley Forge Mountain Association (president, 1973—).

WRITINGS: Injunctions in a Nutshell, West Publishing, 1974; *So You Want to Go to Law School*, West Publishing, 1975.

* * *

DOBIE, Bertha McKee 1890(?)-1974

1890(?)—December 18, 1974; American editor and author. Obituaries: *AB Bookman's Weekly*, January 6, 1975.

* * *

DOBIN, Abraham 1907-

PERSONAl: Born September 23, 1907, in Dayton, N.J.; son of Elias Hirsch (a farmer) and Celia (Freiman) Dobin; married Esther Kogelman, August 29, 1930; children: Barbara Rachel (Mrs. Ivan Saiff), Betty Ann (Mrs. Martin Siegel). *Education:* Rutgers University, B.S., 1927. *Politics:* Republican. *Religion:* Jewish. *Home address:* Box 2134, Monmouth Junction, N.J. 08852.

CAREER: Jewish Agricultural Society, Inc., New York, N.Y., instructor in extension education, 1927-45; Central Jersey Farmers Cooperative Association, Highstown, N.J., superintendent, 1945-46; Holland & McChesney, Freehold, N.J., manager of Feeds Division, 1946-58; Stoller Brothers, Inc. (restaurant and bar supplies), Monmouth Junction, N.J., co-owner and secretary, 1958-72. President, Jewish Community Center of South Brunswick, N.J., 1942-62; South Brunswick Township, N.J., member of township committee, 1960-66, member of planning board, 1960-72, mayor of township, 1961-65, and chairman of planning board, 1968-72; member of advisory board of directors, First Charter National Bank, South Brunswick Branch, 1972—. *Member:* Pioneer Grange, Lions Club. *Awards, honors:* Bronze plaques from Israel Bonds, Histadrut, and United Jewish Appeal, 1958.

WRITINGS: Fertile Fields: Recollections and Reflections of a Busy Life, A. S. Barnes, 1974.

DOBLER, Bruce 1939-

PERSONAL: Born June 30, 1939, in Chicago, Ill.; son of John Martin (a bookkeeper) and Doris (Chilton) Dobler; married Patricia Averdick (a research secretary), December 30, 1961; children: Stephanie, Lisa. *Education:* University of Illinois, student, 1957-60; Roosevelt University, B.A., 1963; University of Iowa, M.F.A., 1968. *Residence:* Putney, Vt. *Agent:* John Hawkins, Paul R. Reynolds, Inc., 12 East 41st St., New York, N.Y. 10017.

CAREER: Illinois Central Railroad, Chicago, Ill., flagman and collector, 1957-65; Central States Exhibitors, Iowa City, Iowa, movie projectionist, 1967-68; Windham College, Putney, Vt., assistant professor of English, 1969-71, director of public relations, 1971-73; Alyeska Pipeline Project, Valdez to Prudhoe, Alaska, pipeline worker, 1974—. Writer-in-residence at Phillips Exeter Academy; member of Putney Volunteer Fire Department. *Awards, honors:* George Bennett Memorial Fellowship from Phillips Exeter Academy, 1968-69.

WRITINGS: (With M. M. Landress) *I Made It Myself*, Grosset, 1973; *Icepick* (novel), Little, Brown, 1974.

WORK IN PROGRESS: Terminal Camp (tentative title), a novel about the Alaska pipeline, for Little, Brown, completion expected in 1976; a novel about Vermont.

SIDELIGHTS: Dobler writes: "I am a son of working class parents. I grew up on the south side of Chicago and hope to write a novel about the vacant lot near where I lived and where I return in all dreams about being at 'home!'"

* * *

DOBNEY, Fredrick J(ohn) 1943-

PERSONAL: Born December 4, 1943, in Phoenix, Ariz.; son of Fredrick John Dobney (a teacher) and Flossie Shofner (an inspector; maiden name, Melton); married Elaine Voss, April 16, 1965; children: Matthew Fredrick. *Education:* Attended Texas Christian University, 1962-63; Baylor University, B.A. (cum laude), 1966; Rice University, Ph.D., 1970. *Home:* 7748 Burr Oak, St. Louis, Mo. 63130. *Office:* Department of History, St. Louis University, 221 North Grand, St. Louis, Mo. 63103.

CAREER: St. Louis University, St. Louis, Mo., assistant professor, 1970-74, associate professor of history, 1974—, director of Man, Technology, and Society Program, 1973—. *Member:* American Historical Association, Organization of American Historians, Society for Historians of American Foreign Relations, Southern Historical Association, Phi Alpha Theta, Pi Gamma Mu, Alpha Chi. *Awards, honors:* Harry S. Truman Library Institute research grant, 1971; American Philosophical Society research grant, 1972.

WRITINGS: (Editor) *Selected Papers of Will Clayton*, Johns Hopkins Press, 1971. Contributor of articles and reviews to *Historian, Texana, Great Events in History, St. Louis Post-Dispatch, Journal of Southern History, Review of Politics, Journal of Economic History, American Political Science Review, Wisconsin Magazine of History, Annals of American Academy of Political and Social Science, Pacific Historical Review, Western Political Quarterly*, and *Technology and Culture*.

WORK IN PROGRESS: A biography of Will Clayton; a book on the history of the corps of engineers of the St. Louis district; a study of government agencies in World War II.

DOBREE, Bonamy 1891-1974

1891—September 3, 1974; British author and educator. Obituaries: *AB Bookman's Weekly*, October 7, 1974. (*CA*-5/6).

* * *

DOBSON, Margaret J(une) 1931-

PERSONAL: Born June 20, 1931, in Seattle, Wash.; daughter of Walter James and France (Howard) Dobson. *Education:* University of Oregon, B.S., 1954, M.S., 1959, Ed.D., 1965; graduate study at University of Wisconsin, 1961-63. *Office:* Department of Health and Physical Education, Portland State University, Portland, Ore. 97207.

CAREER: High school teacher of health and physical education in the public schools of Portland, Ore., 1954-55; Portland State University, Portland, Ore., instructor, 1955-60, assistant professor, 1960-65, associate professor, 1965-68, professor of health and physical education, 1968—, assistant chairman of department, 1972—, acting dean, 1975. Instructor at Portland Continuing Education Center, 1959—; instructor at Oregon State University, summer workshops, 1963, 1965; visiting professor at Mt. Hood Community College, 1969-70; instructor, Portland Bureau of Parks and Recreation Softball Youth Program, 1971; visiting lecturer at Lewis and Clark College, fall, 1973; instructor, Military Special Services in Japan, Okinawa, Philippine Islands, Hawaiian Islands, and Formosa. Member of Oregon State Committee on Physical Education for the Mentally Retarded, 1970—.

MEMBER: International Association for Physical Education and Sports for Girls and Women, American Association for Health, Physical Education and Recreation (fellow; state softball chairman, 1957-58), American School Health Association (fellow), Royal Society for the Promotion of Health (fellow), National Association for the Physical Education of College Women, National Physical Education Foundation (charter member), American Association of University Professors, American College of Sports Medicine, Amateur Softball Association of America, Northwest District Association for Health, Physical Education and Recreation, Western Society for the Physical Education of College Women, Oregon Association for Health, Physical Education and Recreation (secretary-treasurer, 1958-59; member of executive committee, 1968), Oregon Northern Board of Officials, Pi Lambda Theta. *Awards, honors:* Miss Softball award and World Tournament most outstanding player award, 1952, from National Softball Congress; Bill Hayward Award, 1952, for most outstanding Oregon woman athlete; World Tournament leading hitter award, 1954; elected to Amateur Softball Association's National Hall of Fame, 1962, and Northwest Hall of Fame, 1965; President Kennedy Award from Portland Junior Chamber of Commerce, 1966, for physical fitness leadership; ten times U.S. all-American softball third baseman.

WRITINGS: (With Becky Sisley) *Softball for Girls and Women*, Ronald, 1971. Contributor to *Amateur Softball Association Rule Book, AAHPER Division of Girl's and Women's Sports Basketball Guide, OAHPER Newsletter, Physical Educator*, and *Balls and Strikes*.

* * *

DOCTORS, Samuel I(saac) 1936-

PERSONAL: Born July 1, 1936, in Philadelphia, Pa.; son of Abraham and Celia (Lakoff) Doctors; married Veta T. Appel (a researcher in community development), May 26, 1974; children: Eric H., Rachel L.; Sindy R., Elizabeth F., Judith K. (stepchildren). *Education:* University of Miami, B.S. (magna cum laude), 1956, graduate study, 1958-59; Harvard University, J.D., 1967, D.B.A., 1969. *Politics:* Independent. *Home:* 505 South Linden, Pittsburgh, Pa. 15208. *Office:* Department of Business Administration, University of Pittsburgh, 2112 C.L., Pittsburgh, Pa. 15260.

CAREER: Westinghouse Electric Corp., Baltimore, Md., associate engineer, 1956-58; General Motors, AC Sparkplug Division, El Segundo, Calif., senior mathematical analyst, 1958-59; Honeywell Corp., Aero Division, St. Petersburg, Fla., senior development engineer and work director, 1961-64; University of Connecticut, New England Research Applications Center, Storrs, associate director and technology transfer consultant, 1968-69; Northwestern University, Evanston, Ill., associate professor of management and urban affairs in Graduate School of Management, 1969-73, faculty adviser and director of Management Assistance Clinic, 1969-73; University of Pittsburgh, Graduate School of Business, Pittsburgh, Pa., professor of business administration, 1974—. Consultant to U.S. Government and to private industry and institutions; developer of special courses for Legal Aid Foundation of Chicago and De Paul University, 1971-74; member of U.S. Office of Education Task Force on Minority Business Education and Training, 1972-73; member of board of directors, Senior Citizen Service Corp., 1974—; visiting lecturer, Harvard Business School, 1968-69.

MEMBER: American Bar Association, American Political Science Association, American Economic Association, National Association for Community Development, American Association for the Advancement of Science, Chicago Urban League, Chicago Community Venture Corporation (member of advisory committee, 1970-71), Phi Beta Kappa, Delta Theta Mu.

WRITINGS: The Role of Federal Agencies in Technology Transfer, M.I.T. Press, 1969; *The Management of Technological Change*, American Management Association, 1970; *The NASA Technology Transfer Program: An Evaluation*, Praeger, 1971; (editor and contributor) *Report of the President's Council on Minority Business Enterprise*, two volumes, U.S. Government Printing Office, 1971; (with F. Cassell and S. Director) *A Study of Internal Labor Markets: A Micro Study of Three Companies' Internal Mobility Systems for Blue Collar and Lower Level White Collar Workers*, U.S. Government Printing Office, 1973; (with Anne S. Huff) *Minority Business Enterprise and the President's Council*, Ballinger Press, 1973; (editor and co-author) *Whatever Happened to Minority Business Enterprise*, Dryden Press, 1974; (editor and principal author) *Final Report of the HEW/OMBE Task Force for Minority Business Education and Training*, two volumes, U.S. Government Printing Office, 1974; (with D. Banner and A. Gordon) *The Politics of Social Science Evaluation*, Ballinger Press, 1975.

WORK IN PROGRESS: Research on minority banks and their impact on their communities, the impact of education on minority small business success, and the use and scope of social action programs in graduate schools of business management.

* * *

DODSON, James L. 1910-

PERSONAL: Born March 28, 1910, in Clinton, Mo.; son of James G. (a merchant) and Grace Anna (a music teacher; maiden name, Lingle) Dodson; married Ann Mary Hjelt (a registered nurse), July 26, 1941; children: Katherine (Mrs. Donald Tuttle), Jane Mary (Mrs. Kenneth Smith). *Education:* Colorado College, A.B., 1933; Princeton University, A.M., 1935; University of Colorado, Ph.D., 1937. *Address:* Box 8221, La Crescenta, Calif. 91214. *Office:* Department of History, Los Angeles Valley College, Van Nuys, Calif. 91401.

CAREER: Texas A. & M. College, College Station, assistant professor of history, 1938-45; Los Angeles Valley College, Van Nuys, Calif., professor of history, 1949—. *Member:* Classical Society of American Academy in Rome, Vergilian Society, American Classical League, District Senate of Los Angeles Community Colleges (chairman, 1967-68), Los Angeles Valley College Faculty Association (president, 1966-67), Phi Beta Kappa. *Awards, honors:* Fulbright scholar at American Academy in Rome, summer, 1956.

WRITINGS: Readings in Western Civilization, Dryden, 1972; *Student Guide for Mark Naidis' The Western Tradition*, and instructor's manual, Dryden, 1972. Contributor of reviews to *Journal of the West*.

WORK IN PROGRESS: A Brief History of Los Angeles Valley College, completion expected in 1975.

SIDELIGHTS: Dodson has conducted student groups to Europe to visit the principal archaeological sites in Italy and Greece.

* * *

DOHERTY, William Thomas, Jr. 1923-

PERSONAL: Born March 30, 1923, in Cape Girardeau, Mo.; son of William T. (a teacher) and Kittie (Baird) Doherty; married Dorothy Ashley Huff, August 13, 1947; children: Victor, Ashley (Mrs. Joseph E. Fortenberry), Catherine, Julia, William Thomas III. *Education:* Southeast Missouri State College, A.B. and B.S., 1943; American University, M.A., 1950; University of Missouri, Ph.D., 1951. *Home:* 140 Waitman St., Morgantown, West Va. 26505. *Office:* Department of History, West Virginia University, Morgantown, W.Va. 26506.

CAREER: Westminster College, Fulton, Mo., instructor in history, 1947-48; University of Missouri, Columbia, instructor in history, 1948-49; Christian College, Columbia, Mo., instructor in history, 1949-50; University of Missouri, instructor in history, 1950-51; University of Mississippi, Oxford, assistant professor of history, 1951-53; University of Arkansas, Fayetteville, assistant professor, 1953-55, associate professor of history, 1955-56; University of Mississippi, Oxford, associate professor, 1956-58, professor of history, 1958-61, head of department, 1958-61; Kansas State University, Manhattan, professor of history, 1961-63, director of Ford Foundation three-year master's program, 1961-63; West Virginia University, Morgantown, professor of history, 1963—, head of department, 1963—. Member of Mississippi Historical Commission, 1958-61. *Military service:* U.S. Army, 1943-46; served in Pacific Theater; received Bronze Star.

MEMBER: American Academy of Political and Social Sciences, American Association of University Professors, American Historical Association, Organization of American Historians, Southern Historical Association, Phi Alpha Theta, Alpha Pi Zeta, Sigma Tau Delta, Kappa Delta Pi.

WRITINGS: Louis Houck: Missouri Historian and Entrepreneur, University of Missouri Press, 1960; (editor) *Minerals*, Van Nostrand, 1971; *Berkeley County, U.S.A.: A Bicentennial History of a Virginia and West Virginia County, 1772-1972*, McClain Printing, 1972; *West Virginia History*, Education Foundation, 1974.

* * *

DONAGHY, Henry J(ames) 1930-

PERSONAL: Born April 11, 1930, in New York, N.Y.; son of Joseph P. and Catherine (McQuaid) Donaghy; married Joyce Aasen, December 7, 1968; children: Nora, Martin. *Education:* Stonehill College, A.B., 1954; Fordham University, M.A., 1960; New York University, Ph.D., 1966. *Religion:* Roman Catholic. *Address:* Route 3, Box 260A, Pocatello, Idaho 83201. *Office:* Department of English, Idaho State University, Pocatello, Idaho 83209.

CAREER: High school teacher of English, 1958-62, and chairman of department in Bridgeport, Conn., 1960-62; Georgia State University, Atlanta, assistant professor of English, 1966-69; State University of New York at Oswego, associate professor of English, 1969-71, and director of graduate studies in English, 1970-71; California State University, Fresno, associate professor of English, 1971-73; Idaho State University, Pocatello, associate professor of English, 1973—.

WRITINGS: James Clarence Mangan, Twayne, 1974. Contributor to *Shaw Review, Studies in Literary Imagination, Worship*, and *Victorian Studies*.

WORK IN PROGRESS: Editing works of Byron.

* * *

DONAGHY, William A. 1910(?)-1975

1910(?)—January 24, 1975; American Roman Catholic priest, author, and educator. Obituaries: *Washington Post*, January 26, 1975.

* * *

DONNELL, John D(ouglas) 1920-

PERSONAL: Born December 2, 1920, in Waterloo, Iowa; son of Alan Douglas (a business executive) and Anita (Rath) Donnell; married Florence Bentz, August 3, 1942; children: Alan D., Cathlin, Linnet (Mrs. Robert E. Spangler), Brian K., Duane L. *Education:* Northwestern University, student, 1941; Princeton University, A.B., 1943; State University of Iowa, J.D., 1948; Harvard University, D.B.A., 1966. *Politics:* Independent. *Religion:* Presbyterian. *Home address:* Route 1, Unionville, Ind. 47468. *Office:* Graduate School of Business, Indiana University, Bloomington, Ind. 47401.

CAREER: State University of Iowa, Iowa City, instructor in sociology, 1946-47; Rath Packing Co., Waterloo, Iowa, corporate counsel to vice-president in administration, 1948-62; Indiana University, Bloomington, assistant professor, 1965-68, associate professor, 1968-71, professor of business administration, 1971—, chairman of department of business law, 1969—. Director of Rath Packing Co., 1959—; chairman of personnel relations committee of American Meat Institute, 1958-61; member of board of directors of National Food Conference, 1960-62. *Military service:* U.S. Army, Field Artillery, 1942-45; received Purple Heart and Air Medal. *Member:* American Bar Association, American Business Law Association, Phi Beta Kappa, Order of the Coif.

WRITINGS: Corporate Counsel: A Role Study, Division of Research, Graduate School of Business, Indiana University, 1970; (with Harold F. Lusk, Charles M. Hewitt, and A. James Barnes) *Business Law: Principles and Cases*, Irwin, 1970, 3rd edition, 1974. Co-editor of *American Business Law Journal*, 1969-74, editor-in-chief, 1974—.

WORK IN PROGRESS: Research on the liability of outside corporate directors.

* * *

DONOHOE, Thomas 1917-

PERSONAL: Born February 5, 1917, in Williamsburg, Iowa; son of Joseph (an artisan) and Ellen (a teacher; maiden name, McEachran) Donohoe; married Lillian Doerr (a physician), February 22, 1954; children: Ellen, Kevin, Robert, John. *Education:* Attended St. John's University, Collegeville, Minn.; St. Ambrose College, A.B., 1941; University of California, Berkeley, graduate study, 1953-54; Arizona State University, M.A., 1954, Ph.D., 1965. *Home:* 4980 Oakmont Dr., Flagstaff, Ariz. 86001. *Office address:* Northern Arizona University, Box 6032, Flagstaff, Ariz. 86001.

CAREER: High school teacher of English in the public schools of Phoenix, Ariz., 1954-63; Phoenix College, Phoenix, Ariz., assistant professor of English, 1963-65; Northern Arizona University, Flagstaff, associate professor, 1965-73, professor of English, 1973—. *Military service:* U.S. Army, 1943. *Member:* Phi Kappa Phi.

WRITINGS: Rhetoric for Survival, Allyn & Bacon, 1973.

WORK IN PROGRESS: Sabbatical study in Ireland.

SIDELIGHTS: "I suspect," Donohoe observed, "that were we able to see the parallel rise of Romantic subjectivism and the rise of the 'middle class,' we might well be able to get a better focus on our own pretensions." *Avocational interests:* Playing organ.

* * *

DONOVAN, Timothy Paul 1927-

PERSONAL: Born December 25, 1927, in Terre Haute, Ind.; son of Harry T. (a chemist) and Gretchen (Stakeman) Donovan; married Eugenia Trapp (a librarian), June 1, 1950; children: Kevin Andrew, Rebecca (Mrs. John P. Adkins), David Michael, Richard Timothy. *Education:* University of Oklahoma, B.A., 1949, M.A., 1950, Ph.D., 1960. *Religion:* Roman Catholic. *Home:* 1503 Cedar, Fayetteville, Ark. 72701. *Office:* Department of History, University of Arkansas, Fayetteville, Ark. 72701.

CAREER: Texas Tech University, Lubbock, assistant professor, 1960-63, associate professor, 1963-68, professor of history, 1968-69; University of Arkansas, Fayetteville, professor of history, 1969—. *Member:* Organization of American Historians, American Historical Association, Popular Culture Association, Southern Historical Association, Arkansas Historical Society. *Awards, honors:* Excellence in teaching award from Standard Oil Co., 1968.

WRITINGS: Henry Adams and Brooks Adams: The Education of Two American Historians, University of Oklahoma Press, 1961; *American Historical Thought: Postwar Patterns*, University of Oklahoma Press, 1973.

WORK IN PROGRESS: A history of the popular arts in the United States, 1940-1945.

DOOB, Penelope Billings Reed 1943-

PERSONAL: Born August 16, 1943, in Hanover, N.H.; daughter of Thomas Lloyd (a professor of art history) and Betsy (a teacher of apparel design; maiden name, Mook) Reed; married Anthony Newcomb Doob, June 18, 1966 (separated, 1973). *Education:* Radcliffe College, B.A. (summa cum laude), 1965; Stanford University, M.A., 1967, Ph.D., 1970. *Residence:* London, England, and Toronto, Ontario, Canada. *Office:* Department of English, Glendon College, York University, 2275 Bayview Ave., Toronto, Ontario, Canada.

CAREER: York University, Glendon College, Toronto, Ontario, assistant professor, 1969-74, associate professor of English, 1974—. *Member:* Modern Language Association of America, Mediaeval Academy of America, Association of Canadian University Teachers of English, Dance Critics Association, Phi Beta Kappa. *Awards, honors:* Woodrow Wilson fellowship, 1965-66; Guggenheim fellowship, 1974-75; research grants from Canada Council, 1971-73, for *Nebuchadnezzar's Children: Conventions of Madness in Middle English Literature*, and 1973-74, for research on medieval labyrinths.

WRITINGS: Nebuchadnezzar's Children: Conventions of Madness in Middle English Literature, Yale University Press, 1974. Contributor to *Chaucer Review*, *English Literary Renaissance*, *Renaissance and Reformation*, *York Dance Review*, *Transplantation*, and *Annals of the New York Academy of Science*.

WORK IN PROGRESS: Chaucer's Maze of Memory, a book on labyrinths in medieval culture and especially in Chaucer's *House of Fame*; *Juggling*, a novel.

AVOCATIONAL INTERESTS: Dance criticism; feminist studies, campaigns, poetry readings.

* * *

DOOLEY, Howard J(ohn) 1944-

PERSONAL: Born September 12, 1944, in Pittsburgh, Pa.; son of Edward J. and Mary E. (Donovan) Dooley; married Carol Ellen Bigelow (a teacher), August 5, 1972; children: Christopher John. *Education:* University of Notre Dame, B.A. (magna cum laude), 1966, M.A., 1970, Ph.D., 1975. *Politics:* Moderate liberal. *Religion:* "Cultural Catholic." *Home:* 5286 Rolling Hills Dr., Kalamazoo, Mich. 49007. *Agent:* C. M. Vandeburg, Vandeburg-Linkletter Associates, 8530 Wilshire Blvd., Suite 403, Beverly Hills, Calif. 90211. *Office:* Humanities Area, College of General Studies, Western Michigan University, Kalamazoo, Mich. 49008.

CAREER: Western Michigan University, Kalamazoo, instructor in history, 1970-72, assistant professor of humanities, 1972—. *Member:* Michigan Council for the Humanities.

WRITINGS: (With Joel R. Connelly) *Hesburgh's Notre Dame: Triumph in Transition*, Hawthorn, 1972. Contributor of articles and reviews to *Nation*, *Progressive*, *History Teacher*, *Chicago Sunday Sun-Times*, *Seattle Post-Intelligencer*, *Review of Politics*, and *Choice*.

WORK IN PROGRESS: Developing his doctoral dissertation into a full-scale analysis of the Suez Crisis of 1956, and the events of that year.

* * *

DOOLEY, Patrick K(iaran) 1942-

PERSONAL: Born June 23, 1942, in Fargo, N.D.; son of

Kiaran L. (a teacher) and Katharine (a teacher; maiden name, McDonald) Dooley; married Nora Ann Householter (a teacher), December 27, 1969. *Education:* St. Paul College, St. Paul, Minn., B.A., 1964; University of Notre Dame, M.A., 1967, Ph.D., 1969. *Politics:* Democrat. *Religion:* Roman Catholic. *Home:* 128 South 17th, Olean, N.Y. 14760. *Office:* Department of Philosophy, St. Bonaventure University, St. Bonaventure, N.Y. 14778.

CAREER: Stanley Clark School, South Bend, Ind., instructor in Latin, 1966-67; University of Notre Dame, Notre Dame, Ind., instructor in philosophy, 1967-68; St. Bonaventure University, St. Bonaventure, N.Y., assistant professor, 1969-74, associate professor of philosophy, 1974—. *Member:* American Catholic Philosophical Association (president of regional unit), American Philosophical Association, Society for the Advancement of American Philosophy. *Awards, honors:* Postdoctoral grants from Finger Lakes College Consortium, 1972, Council for Philosophical Studies, 1973.

WRITINGS: Pragmatism as Humanism: The Philosophy of William James, Nelson-Hall, 1974. Contributor to *Transactions of the C. S. Peirce Society* and *New Scholasticism.*

* * *

DOOLITTLE, Jerome (Hill) 1933-

PERSONAL: Born July 15, 1933, in Pittsburgh, Pa.; married Gretchen Rath (a teacher), February 4, 1956; children: Timothy, Theodore, Jonathan, Michael, Matthew. *Education:* Middlebury College, B.A., 1955. *Residence:* West Cornwall, Conn. 06796.

CAREER: Newspaperman, holding positions at various times with *Middletown Times-Herald, Northern Virginia Sun*, and *Washington Daily News* and *Washington Post*, both Washington, D.C.; with U.S. Information Agency, in Morocco, 1966-69, and in Laos, 1969-70. *Military service:* U.S. Army, 1955-57. *Member:* Authors Guild of Authors League of America, Federal City Club. *Awards, honors:* First prize for humor from Washington Newspaper Guild, 1962.

WRITINGS: Canyons and Mesas, Time-Life, 1974; *The Southern Appalachians*, Time-Life, in press. Contributor to *Esquire, Holiday, Sports Illustrated, Saturday Evening Post, Penthouse, Oui*, and *Reader's Digest*.

AVOCATIONAL INTERESTS: Skindiving, skiing, backpacking, herpetology, photography, collecting orchids.

* * *

DORFMAN, Nancy S(chelling) 1922-

PERSONAL: Born December 5, 1922, in Rockford, Ill.; daughter of John M. (a naval officer) and Zelda (Ayers) Schelling; married Robert Dorfman (an economist at Harvard University), November 6, 1949; children: Peter John, Ann Elizabeth. *Education:* University of California, Berkeley, B.A., 1945, Ph.D., 1967. *Home:* 81 Kilburn Rd., Belmont, Mass. 02178. *Office:* Robert R. Nathan Associates, Inc., 1200 18th St. N.W., Washington, D.C. 20036.

CAREER: Federal Reserve Board of Governors, Washington, D.C., economist, 1946-47; U.S. Bureau of the Budget, Washington, D.C., fiscal analyst, 1948-49; Massachusetts Institute of Technology, Cambridge, Mass., economist at Center for International Studies, 1967-68; Northeastern University, Boston, Mass., lecturer in economics, 1971-73; Robert R. Nathan Associates, Inc., Washington, D.C., economist, 1973—. Member of Hill-Burton Advisory Committee on Hospital Construction (State of Massachusetts), 1973-74; member of postdoctoral fellowship selection committee for Resources for the Future, Inc., 1974—; consultant to Arthur D. Little, Inc., and Public Interest Economics Center, 1973-74.

WRITINGS: (Editor with Robert Dorfman) *Economics of the Environment: Selected Readings,* Norton, 1973. Contributor to proceedings and to economics journals.

* * *

DOTT, R(obert) H(enry), Jr. 1929-

PERSONAL: Born June 2, 1929, in Tulsa, Okla.; son of Robert H. (a geologist) and Esther (Reed) Dott; married Nancy Robertson (a naturalist), September 20, 1951; children: James, Karen, Eric, Cynthia, Brian. *Education:* Attended University of Oklahoma, 1946-48; University of Michigan, B.S., 1950, M.S., 1951; Columbia University, Ph.D., 1955. *Religion:* Unitarian. *Home:* 231 DuRose Terrace, Madison, Wis. 53705. *Office:* Department of Geology and Geophysics, L. G. Weeks Hall, University of Wisconsin, Madison, Wis.

CAREER: Humble Oil and Refining Co., Oregon and California, geologist, 1954-58; University of Wisconsin, Madison, assistant professor, 1958-61, associate professor, 1961-66, professor of geology, 1966—, chairman of department, 1974—. Visiting professor, University of California at Berkeley, 1969; lecturer at Tulsa University and for Exxon Research, Arco, and Phillips Petroleum Corp.; guest lecturer at many universities. Consultant to Roan Selection Trust (Zambia) and Shell Oil Co. *Military service:* U.S. Air Force, 1956-58; became first lieutenant; received Commendation Ribbon. U.S. Air Force Reserve, 1950-64; became captain. *Member:* American Association of Petroleum Geologists, Geological Society of America, International Association of Sedimentologists, American Association for the Advancement of Science, Society of Economic Mineralogists and Paleontologists (secretary-treasurer, 1970-72; vice-president, 1972-73), Sigma Xi. *Awards, honors:* President's Award from American Association of Petroleum Geologists, 1956.

WRITINGS: (With Roger L. Batten) *Evolution of the Earth*, with instructor's manual, McGraw, 1971; (editor with R. L. Shaver) *Modern and Ancient Geosynclinal Sediments*, Society of Economic Mineralogists and Paleontologists, 1974. Advisory editor for *Encyclopedia of Science and Technology* published by McGraw. Contributor of articles to geological journals.

WORK IN PROGRESS: The second edition of *Evolution of the Earth*; research on the geologic history, involving continental drift, of Tierra del Fuego, the Scotia Sea region, and Antarctica.

SIDELIGHTS: Dott told *CA:* "Love of out-of-doors, camping, hiking, backpacking, and photography, acquired as a youth, influenced my career choice. Love of mountains led me to focus my geologic research in the history and structure of mountain belts. . . . Have travelled all over North America (including Greenland and Alaska), South America, Europe, Africa, and Antarctica (sailed around and landed on Cape Horn in 1974)."

* * *

DOTY, Gladys 1908-
(Marcia Kent Douglass)

PERSONAL: Born November 7, 1908, in Shelbyville, Mo.;

daughter of Charles W. (an appraiser) and Peryl Josephine (a writer; maiden name, Wade) Parsons; married Ralph Perry Yohe, May 10, 1932 (died, 1948); married George David Doty, March 23, 1958; children: (first marriage) Ralph Vincent, Cynthia Vaughn (Mrs. Kenneth Kincheloe). *Education:* University of Colorado, B.A., 1929, M.A., 1949. *Politics:* Republican. *Religion:* Presbyterian. *Home:* 2550 University Heights, Boulder, Colo. 80302.

CAREER: Junior College of Southeastern Colorado, Lamar, instructor in English, 1942-43; University of Colorado, Boulder, instructor, 1948-64, assistant professor of English, 1964-73, professor emeritus, 1973. *Member:* National League of American Penwomen, National Association for Foreign Student Affairs, Teachers of English to Speakers of Other Languages (chairman of local region, 1958, 1968).

WRITINGS: (With Janet Ross) *Language and Life in the United States of America*, Harper, 1960, 3rd edition, 1973; (with Ross) *Writing English*, Harper, 1964, 2nd edition, 1975. Contributor to *Collier's*.

AVOCATIONAL INTERESTS: Travel, reading, music.

* * *

DOTY, Roy 1922-

PERSONAL: Born September 10, 1922, in Chicago, Ill.; son of E. Roy (a salesman) and Dorothy (Schroeder) Doty; married Louise Hall, April 10, 1949 (divorced, 1954); married Jean Slaughter (a writer), July 19, 1955; children: Debbie (Mrs. Steven Hugo), Jeffrey, Christopher, Didi. *Education:* Attended Columbus School of Art. *Politics:* Independent liberal. *Religion:* Methodist. *Home and office:* 1173 Rockrimmon Rd., Stamford, Conn. 06903.

CAREER: Free-lance writer, artist, cartoonist, and illustrator, 1946—. Wrote and illustrated comic strip "Laugh In," 1968-71. *Military service:* U.S. Army, 1942-46; became technical sergeant. *Member:* National Cartoonist Society. *Awards, honors:* Named illustrator of the year by National Cartoonist Society, twice; also received three art director awards.

WRITINGS: (With Richard Wolters) *Instant Dog*, Dutton, 1968; (with Robert Stevenson) *Illustrated Almanac for Homeowners*, Harper, 1972; (with Norma Klein) *Girls Can Be Anything*, Dutton, 1973; (with Eleanor Clymer) *Take Tarts as Tarts Is Passing*, Dutton, 1974; *Puns, Gags, Quips, and Riddles*, Doubleday, 1974; (with Stevenson) *Almanac for Home Makers*, Grosset, 1974; (with Barbara Rinkoff) *No Pushing, No Ducking*, Lothrop, 1974; *Q's Are Weird O's*, Doubleday, in press; *Where Are You Going with That Tree?*, Doubleday, in press; *Where Are You Going with That Oil?*, Doubleday, in press. Illustrator of *Wordless Workshop*, edited by Harry Walton, Taplinger, 1967, and other publications. Contributor to popular magazines, including *Popular Science, Business Week, Newsweek*, and *New York Times*.

* * *

DOTY, William G(uy) 1939-

PERSONAL: Born August 7, 1939, in Raton, N.M.; son of William H. and Marcia (Freeman) Doty; married A. Joan Thomas (a civil rights investigator), September 7, 1965. *Education:* Attended Free University of Berlin, 1958-59; University of New Mexico, A.B., 1961; San Francisco Theological Seminary, B.D., 1963; Drew University, Ph.D., 1966. *Home:* 161 Nichol Ave., New Brunswick, N.J. 08901. *Office:* Department of Religion, Douglass College, Rutgers University, New Brunswick, N.J. 08903.

CAREER: Rutgers University, New Brunswick, N.J., instructor in religion, 1965-66; Garrett Theological Seminary, Evanston, Ill., instructor in New Testament, 1966-67; Vassar College, Poughkeepsie, N.Y., lecturer in religion, 1967-68, Mellon House fellow, 1967-68; Rutgers University, Douglass College, New Brunswick, N.J., assistant professor of religion, 1968-75. *Member:* Society of Biblical Literature, American Academy of Religion, Society for the Arts, Religion, and Contemporary Culture, American Association of University Professors, Sierra Club, American Civil Liberties Union, Philadelphia Seminar on Christian Origins, Columbia University Seminar on the New Testament. *Awards, honors:* Society for Religion in Higher Education fellowship, 1971-72.

WRITINGS: Meaningful Leisure: An Interpretive Bibliographic Essay, National Council of Churches, 1963; *The Literature and Discipline of Form Criticism*, Garrett Theological Seminary Library, 1967, revised edition, 1972; *Contemporary New Testament Interpretation*, Prentice-Hall, 1972; *Letters in Primitive Christianity*, Fortress, 1973. Editorial advisory board, *Religious Book Review*, 1973—.

WORK IN PROGRESS: With W. C. Beane, *Myth, Rite, Symbol: A Mircea Eliade Reader* (tentative title), for Harper; *We Shall All Be Changed* (working title); tape-slide presentations, "Southwestern American Indians," for commercial distribution.

AVOCATIONAL INTERESTS: Photography, art, plants, travel.

* * *

DOUGHTY, Nina Beckett 1911-

PERSONAL: Born January 31, 1911, in Beaufort, S.C.; daughter of George W. (a lawyer) and Elinor Louise (Mansfield) Beckett; married Arthur W. Doughty, September 10, 1929; children: Arthur, Joyce Doughty Swallow, Lillian Doughty Masschelin, Mary Alice Doughty Martin, Louise Doughty Mathieson. *Education:* Now attending University of Georgia. *Politics:* Independent. *Religion:* Episcopal. *Home:* 2008 El Josa, Waycross, Ga. 31501.

CAREER: Poet, author; worked as newspaper reporter in Beaufort, S.C., during 1940's. *Member:* World Poetry Society, South Carolina Poetry Society.

WRITINGS: Poetically Speaking (poems), Brantley Publishing, 1974. Poetry is included in anthologies published by Young Publications, including *New Voices in the Wind*, 1969, *Yearbook of Modern Poetry*, 1971, and *Lyrics of Love*, 1972. Contributor of poems to *Poet*, and to newspapers, including *Glynn Reporter* and *Savannah Morning News*.

WORK IN PROGRESS: Research on Revolutionary War spies for a novel; *Executor's Handbook*, a book to help people handle estates.

* * *

DOWDEN, George 1932-

PERSONAL: Born September 15, 1932, in Philadelphia, Pa.; son of George Duncan (a hotel manager) and Corrine (Legault) Dowden; married Pauline Chatterton, June 11, 1969 (divorced, 1973). *Education:* Bucknell University, A.B., 1957; New York University, M.A., 1960. *Politics:* "God's Party." *Religion:* Yoga. *Home:* 11B Adelaide Crescent, Hove, Sussex BN3 2JE, England.

CAREER: Brooklyn College of the City University of New

York, Brooklyn, N.Y., lecturer in English and world literature, 1960-63, 1966. *Military service:* U.S. Navy, 1950-53.

WRITINGS: Flight from America (long poem), Mandarin Books, 1965; *Because I Am Tired of the Night* (poems), Eleventh Finger Books, 1966; *Letters to English Poets* (nonfiction), Rain Press, 1967; *He: Or Genesis* (prose poetry), Parodox Press, 1968; *Birth Vision and Green Song* (poems), Five Poets Press, 1968; *Poems from the Paintings of David Jenkins*, Second Aeon Publications, 1969; *Renew Jerusalem* (long poem), Smyrna Press, 1969; *This Is the Land of the Dead: The Island of the Blessed* (poems), Hapt Free-Print, 1970; *A Bibliography of Works by Allen Ginsberg*, City Lights, 1971; *New York: First Poems*, Unicorn Publications, 1971; (translator with Yogananda from the Hindi) Swami Muktananda Paramahansa, *Mukteshwari: The Way of Muktananda*, Shree Gurudev Ashram Publications, Volume I, 1972, Volume II, 1973. Contributor of poems and prose to journals.

WORK IN PROGRESS: A novel, *The Revealed*, completion expected in 1975; a psychedelic journal, *A Message to Isis*, 1976; *Yogic Poetry*, 1976; a Yogi study of Jesus, 1977.

SIDELIGHTS: Dowden told *CA*: "My exploration is all inward, in yogic fashion, not to the subconscious (though that had its part) but to the superconscious, the Self, the God-within consciousness. My explorations through poetry led me to Shree Gurudev Ashram in India and to my Guru, Swami Muktananda Paramahansa, who gifted me with a Kundalini initiation (Shaktipat Diksha) on 15 December 1971. All since has been a developing of consciousness."

* * *

DOWNING, John (Allen) 1922-

PERSONAL: Born May 28, 1922, in London, England; son of Harold Allen (a travel agent) and Gertrude (Langley) Downing; married Marianne Neuer, September 7, 1946; children: Andrew, Charles, Rupert. *Education:* Oakley College, Cheltenham, England, teacher's certificate, 1949; University of London, B.A. (honors), 1957, Ph.D., 1966. *Home:* 4601 Cordova Bay Rd., Victoria, British Columbia, Canada. *Office:* Faculty of Education, University of Victoria, Victoria, British Columbia, Canada.

CAREER: Teacher in public schools of Somerset and Middlesex, England, 1949-58; Uniliver Ltd., London, England, director of communications research, 1958-60; University of London, London, England, director of reading research, 1960-67, senior lecturer in educational psychology, 1968-69; University of Victoria, Victoria, British Columbia, professor of educational psychology, 1970—. Visiting lecturer at University of California, Berkeley, 1967-68. *Member:* American Psychological Association, British Psychological Association (fellow), Canadian Psychological Association, International Reading Association, World Federation for Mental Health, United Kingdom Reading Association (president, 1963-64), American Educational Research Association.

WRITINGS: To Be or Not to Be: The New Augmented Roman Alphabet Explained and Illustrated, Cassell, 1962; *The Initial Teaching Alphabet Explained and Illustrated*, Macmillan, 1964; *The Initial Teaching Alphabet Reading Experiment*, Evans Brothers, 1964, Scott, Foresman, 1965; (with others) *The i.t.a. Symposium*, National Foundation for Educational Research in England and Wales, 1967; *Evaluating the Initial Teaching Alphabet: A Study of the Effects of English Orthography on Learning to Read and Write*, Cassell, 1967; (with Amy L. Brown and John Sceats) *Words Children Want to Use*, Chambers, 1971; (with Derek V. Thackray) *Reading Readiness*, University of London Press, 1971; *Comparative Reading: Cross-National Studies of Behavior and Processes in Reading and Writing*, Macmillan (New York), 1973.

Textbooks: (With Olive Robinson) *i.t.a. Alphabet Book*, Educational Supply Association, 1961; "Downing Readers," eighteen books, Initial Teaching Publishing Co., 1963; (with Amy L. Brown and John Sceats) "Pyramid Primary Dictionaries," Pyramid Publications, Books 1-2, 1971, Book 3, 1972, Book 4, 1973 (published in United Kingdom as "Young Set Dictionaries," Chambers, Books 1-2, 1971, Book 3, 1972, Book 4, 1973).

Contributor: Arthur E. Traxler, editor, *Frontiers of Education*, American Council on Education, 1963; J. A. Figurel, editor, *Reading as an Intellectual Activity*, Scholastic Magazines, 1964; W. G. Cutts, editor, *Teaching Young Children to Read*, U.S. Office of Education, 1964; Fred Guggenheim and C. I. Guggenheim, editors, *New Frontiers in Education*, Grune, 1966; John P. De Cecco, editor, *The Psychology of Language, Thought and Instruction*, Holt, 1967; A. L. Brown, editor, *Reading: Current Research and Practice*, Chambers, 1967; Alfred R. Bintner, John J. Dlabal, and Leonard K. Kise, editors, *Readings on Reading*, International Textbook Co., 1969; O. M. Gayford, *i.t.a. in Primary Education*, Initial Teaching Publishing Co., 1970; J. E. Merritt, editor, *Reading and Curriculum*, Ward, Lock, 1971; Vera Southgate, editor, *Literacy at All Levels*, Ward, Lock, 1972; Joyce Morris, editor, *The First R*, Ward, Lock, 1972; *The Reading Curriculum*, University of London Press, 1972; T. D. Johnson and Kerry Quorn, editors, *Problems in Reading: How Can They be Corrected?*, Faculty of Education, University of Victoria, 1972; Amelia Melnik and John Merritt, editors, *Reading Today and Tomorrow*, University of London Press, 1972; Eldon E. Ekwall, editor, *Factors in the Psychology of Teaching Reading*, C. E. Merrill, 1973; Henri Adamczewski and Denis Keen, *Phonetique et Phonologie de l'Anglais Contemporain*, Armand Colin, 1973.

Contributor to a number of other symposia, including books published by International Reading Association, National Reading Conference, and United Kingdom Reading Conference. Author of pamphlets; co-author of film, "Reading Is the Key: A British Primary School Puts i.t.a. to Work," 1973. Contributor to encyclopedias and of about 150 articles to journals and newspapers in United States, Canada, England, Australia, France, Yugoslavia, and other countries.

Editor with Amy L. Brown, *International Reading Symposium*, annually, 1966-68. Member of editorial board, *Science of Reading* (Tokyo).

WORK IN PROGRESS: Physiology and Psychology of Reading, for Macmillan, completion expected in 1976; research on sex role stereotyping in education, on cerebral dominance and writing behavior, and on non-verbal communication in different cultures.

SIDELIGHTS: "Since secondary school I have been interested in international relations," Downing writes. "This interest is reflected in my book *Comparative Reading*, and in my travels to many parts of the world to work with people of other countries to improve literacy. My other strong motivation is a delight in the honesty and eagerness of young children. This has led me to focus most of my research on this level."

DOWNING, Warwick 1931-

PERSONAL: Born January 3, 1931, in Denver, Colo.; son of Richard (a lawyer) and Dorothy (Simpson) Downing; married Barbara Greene, December 21, 1954; children: Phillip Miller, Paul Herman, John Richard. *Education:* Attended University of Wyoming, 1948-50; University of Denver, B.A., 1951, LL.B., 1956; San Francisco State College (now University), graduate study, 1957-60. *Politics:* Democrat. *Religion:* "Thinking about it." *Home and office address:* P.O. Box 10535, Denver, Colo. 80210. *Agent:* Paul R. Reynolds, Inc., 12 East 41st St., New York, N.Y. 10017.

CAREER: Bancroft-Whiteny, San Francisco, Calif., legal editor, 1956; Manning's Bakery, San Francisco, employee, 1957-60; San Francisco State College (now University), assistant coordinator of evening school, 1960-62; deputy district attorney in Merced, Calif., 1962-63; Leep & Saunders (attorneys), Redding, Calif., attorney, 1963-65; deputy county counsel in Monterrey County, Calif., 1965-68; assistant U.S. attorney in Denver, Colo., 1968-70; Clanahan, Turner, Downing & Knowlton (law firm), Denver, Colo., associate, 1970—. *Military service:* U.S. Marine Corps, 1951-53; became sergeant.

WRITINGS: The Player (suspense novel), Dutton, 1974.

WORK IN PROGRESS: The Mountains West of Town, a suspense novel; *The Gambler, the Minstrel, and the Dance Hall Queen*, a novel; *Kid Curry's Last Ride*, juvenile fiction; *The Helping Hand*, juvenile fiction.

* * *

DOYLE, Brian 1930-

PERSONAL: Born November 26, 1930, in London, England; son of John and Doris (Blackmore) Doyle; married Josephine Holmes (a teacher), March 31, 1956; children: Pandora, Tarquin. *Education:* Educated in London, England. *Religion:* Church of England. *Home:* 14a Clarendon Dr., Putney, London SW15 1AA, England.

CAREER: Woolwich Public Library, London, England, assistant librarian, 1947-49, 1951-57; Rank Film Studios, Pinewood, Buckinghamshire, England, 1957-60, employed as assistant film publicist, and later film publicist; free-lance film publicity director, 1960-63, Columbia Pictures, London, press officer, 1963-67; free-lance film publicist and author, 1967—. Member of judges' panel, *Daily Mail* National Television Awards, 1952, 1953. *Military service:* Royal Air Force, 1949-51. *Member:* Association of Cinema, Television and Allied Technicians, Film Publicity Guild, Society of Authors, National Book League, Old Boys' Book Club, Sherlock Holmes Society of London, Savage Club, Middlesex County Cricket Club. *Awards, honors: The Who's Who of Children's Literature* was chosen by the American Library Association as one of the best reference books of 1969.

WRITINGS—Compiler and editor: *The Who's Who of Boys' Writers and Illustrators*, privately printed, 1964; *The Who's Who of Children's Literature*, Hugh Evelyn, 1968, Schocken, 1969. Contributor to *Boys World Annual*, *Film and TV Annual*, *Collector's Digest Annual*, and to periodicals, including *Books and Bookmen*, *Collectors Digest*, *Books* (journal of the National Book League), *London Times*, *Evening Standard* (London), *Showtime*, and *Kentish Independent*.

WORK IN PROGRESS: A revised and enlarged edition of *The Who's Who of Children's Literature*, completion expected in 1976; *The Who's Who of Crime and Detective Fiction*, 1977; *BBC Radio "Children's Hour" Scrapbook*.

SIDELIGHTS: Doyle told *CA* he prepared *The Who's Who of Boys' Writers and Illustrators* mainly for the benefit of fellow collectors of old boys' papers and magazines. His own collection includes complete runs of *Boy's Own Paper*, *Chums*, and *The Captain* stretching from the late nineteenth to mid-twentieth century, in addition to a library of about 15,000 children's and general books. Doyle writes: "I am fascinated by popular fiction and the trends it has followed over the last 100 years or so, and this interest will probably be reflected in my future books. . . . Basically, I just love books and anything to do with them, and my favourite pastime is browsing in secondhand bookshops." Doyle's favorite novelists include Charles Dickens, J. B. Priestley, Thomas Wolfe, and P. G. Wodehouse, and Sir Arthur Conan Doyle's Sherlock Holmes stories are among his favorite books. "I am also especially keen on humorous novels and stories," he continues, "and one of my ambitions is to write a successful humorous book."

AVOCATIONAL INTERESTS: The cinema, watching cricket, Sherlockiana.

* * *

DRACHLER, Rose 1911-

PERSONAL: Born February 11, 1911, in Brooklyn, N.Y.; daughter of Zachariah (a rabbi) and Sarah (Levine) Kaplowitz; married Jacob Drachler (a painter and writer), June 26, 1932; children: Nina (Mrs. Michael Riback). *Education:* Hunter College (now Hunter College of the City University of New York), B.A., 1932; graduate study at Columbia University, 1935-36, and New School for Social Research, 1944. *Politics:* Radical conservative. *Religion:* Jewish Orthodox. *Home and office:* 3814 Maple Ave., Brooklyn, N.Y. 11224.

CAREER: Public school teacher in New York, N.Y., 1933-67. Member of Consumer Cooperative, 1940. *Member:* Poets and Writers (New York, N.Y.), Rochdale Cooperative Society.

WRITINGS: Burrowing In, Digging Out (poems), Tree Books, 1974. Contributor to *New York Times*, *New York Quarterly*, *Minnesota Review*, *Montclair Journal*, *Invisible City*, and *Tree*.

WORK IN PROGRESS: Shield of Water (tentative title), a book of poems.

* * *

DRAKE, W(alter) Raymond 1913-

PERSONAL: Born January 2, 1913, in Middlebrough, England; son of Walter William (a steelworker) and Elizabeth (a dressmaker; maiden name, Hoskins) Drake; married Marjorie Cawthorne, June 24, 1944. *Education:* Attended primary and secondary school in England. *Religion:* "Methodist (now Cosmic)." *Home:* 2 Peareth Grove, Roker, Sunderland, Durham, England. *Agent:* Ernest Hecht, Euro-Features Ltd., 95 Mortimer St., London W.1, England. *Office:* H.M. Customs and Excise, West Sunniside, Sunderland, England.

CAREER: H.M. Post Office, Middlebrough, England, telegraphist, 1929-31; H.M. Inland Revenue, Middlebrough, clerk, 1931-35; H.M. Customs and Excise, customs officer in England and Scotland, 1935-50, surveyor in Sunderland, England, 1950—. *Member:* Society of Authors, Sunderland Rotary Club.

WRITINGS: Gods or Spacemen?, Amherst Press, 1964; *Gods and Spacemen in the Ancient East*, Neville Spearman, 1968, New American Library, 1974; *Gods and Spacemen in the Ancient West*, New American Library, 1974; *Gods and Spacemen in the Ancient Past*, New American Library, 1974; *Spacemen Throughout History*, Regnery, 1975; *Gods and Spacemen in Greece and Rome*, Sphere, 1975. Also author of four novels "Knight Errant," "Prima-Donna," "Hoffstein," and "Tallus-1980." Author of plays, "Miss Venus," 1960; "Boadicea," 1964; "Charles, the Martyr King," first produced in London at Little Theatre Club, October, 1967; "Man-in-the-Moon," 1971; "Eve," 1972.

WORK IN PROGRESS: Space Initiates; Man-in-the Moon, a novel based on his play; "Queen Jane," a play about ill-fated Lady Jane Grey.

SIDELIGHTS: Drake told *CA:* "I believe that literature can redeem the world by stressing the wonder of life, the beauty of the world around us, the pageantry of noble deeds."

BIOGRAPHICAL/CRITICAL SOURCES: Lynn E. Catoe, *UFOs and Related Subjects: An Annotated Bibliography*, U.S. Government Printing Office, 1969.

* * *

DRAPER, Norman R(ichard) 1931-

PERSONAL: Born March 20, 1931, in England. *Education:* Pembroke College, Cambridge, B.A., 1954, M.A., 1958; University of North Carolina, Ph.D., 1958. *Office:* 1210 West Dayton St., Madison, Wis. 53706.

CAREER: Imperial Chemical Industries, Welwyn Garden City, Hertfordshire, England, statistician, 1958-60; Mathematics Research Center, Madison, Wis., member, 1960-61; University of Wisconsin, Madison, assistant professor, 1961-62, associate professor, 1962-66, professor of statistics, 1966—, head of department, 1968-73. Lecturer, American Society for Quality Control, 1963—; visiting professor at Imperial College, London, England, fall, 1967, 1968, and Mathematics Research Center, 1973-74. *Member:* Royal Statistical Society (fellow), Institute of Mathematical Statistics (fellow), American Statistical Association (fellow), Biometric Society, American Society for Quality Control (fellow).

WRITINGS: (With Harry Smith) *Applied Regression Analysis*, Wiley, 1966; (with George E. P. Box) *Evolutionary Operation*, Wiley, 1969; (with Willard E. Lawrence) *Probability: An Introductory Course*, Markham, 1970.

* * *

DRUMHELLER, Sidney J(ohn) 1923-

PERSONAL; Born December 20, 1923, in Rochester, N.Y.; son of Sidney E. (an assembly foreman) and Olive (Thorne) Drumheller; married Katherine Braidwood (an accountant), October 31, 1953; children: Susan, Mark, Craig. *Education:* Denison University, B.A., 1948; Columbia University, M.A., 1949, Ed.D., 1961. *Home:* 7022 Sunset Ter., Des Moines, Iowa 50311. *Office:* College of Education, Drake University, Des Moines, Iowa 50311.

CAREER: High school social science teacher in Honeoye Falls, N.Y., 1949-50; guidance director in public school in Churchville, N.Y., 1953-56; State University of New York College at Brockport, assistant professor, 1956-62, associate professor of education, 1962-67; Drake University, Des Moines, Iowa, associate professor, 1967-72, professor of education, 1972—. Curriculum specialist with Basic Systems, 1965-66, and with Xerox Educational Division, 1966-67. *Military service:* U.S. Army, artillery, 1943-45. *Member:* American Educational Research Association, Comparative Education Association, Association for Supervision and Curriculum Development, American Association of University Professors.

WRITINGS: Handbook for Curriculum Design for Individualized Instruction, Educational Technology Publications, 1971; *Teacher's Handbook for Developing a Functional Behavior-Based Curriculum*, Educational Technology Publications, 1972; (with Desmond Bragg and Ruth Ann Brown) *Social Studies for Behavioral Change*, Educational Resource Information Center, 1973. Contributor to *Educational Technology*.

WORK IN PROGRESS: Resensitizing Educational Technology.

* * *

DRURY, Margaret Josephine 1937-

PERSONAL: Born April 3, 1937, in Morganfield, Ky.; daughter of George Ignatius (a lawyer) and Bertha Ann (a teacher; maiden name, Greenwell) Drury. *Education:* Barry College, student, 1955-57; Purdue University, B.S., 1960; Cornell University, M.A., 1967, Ph.D., 1968. *Politics:* Democrat. *Religion:* Roman Catholic. *Home:* 1255 New Hampshire Ave., Washington, D.C. 20036. *Office:* Urban Institute, 2100 M St. N.W., Washington, D.C. 20036.

CAREER: Urban Institute, Washington, D.C., senior research associate in housing group studies, 1969—. Peace Corps volunteer in Ethiopia, 1962-64. *Member:* National Association of Housing and Redevelopment Officials.

WRITINGS: Mobile Homes: The Unrecognized Revolution in American Housing, Praeger, 1972.

WORK IN PROGRESS: An integrated analysis of the experimental housing allowance program for the federal government; research on housing allowances in rural America.

AVOCATIONAL INTERESTS: Travel, collecting antiques, swimming, water skiing, belly dancing, cooking, sewing.

* * *

DRURY, Tresa Way 1937-

PERSONAL: Born September 27, 1937, in Highland Park, Mich.; daughter of Edward Steve (a contractor) and Frances Anna (Merrill) Sikorski; married Joseph Douglas Drury (an actor), June 27, 1959. *Education:* Attended University of Michigan, 1954-56; Will-O-Way Apprentice Theatre, graduate, 1956. *Residence:* Tujunga, Calif. 91042. *Office:* KABC Radio, 3321 South LaCienega Blvd., Los Angeles, Calif. 90016.

CAREER: Worked as a disc jockey, program director, and copywriter for radio stations in Michigan, 1958-67; KHJ-TV, Hollywood, Calif., consumer affairs director, 1970-73; KABC Radio, Los Angeles, Calif., host of talk show, 1973—. Lecturer on consumer affairs to public and private organizations; member of President's Conference on Nutrition, 1968, member of California Governor's Consumer Fraud Task Force, 1970-73; member of California Consumer Advisory Council, 1973—, chairwoman, 1974—. *Member:* International Consumers Association, American

Consumer Council, Consumer's Union, American Council on Consumer Interests, Consumer Federation of America, National Health Organization, Radio Television News Association (second vice-president, 1975), National Federation of Press Women, National Academy of Television Arts and Sciences, American Federation of Television and Radio Artists, American Women in Radio and Television, California Press Women. *Awards, honors:* American Society for Quality Control award for outstanding service, 1968; Tuberculosis and Respiratory Disease Association award "for outstanding service toward improving community health," 1971; American Women in Radio and Television merit award, 1971; California Press Women 1st & 2nd place TV news writing award, 1972; National Health Federation service award, 1972.

WRITINGS: (With William L. Roper) *Consumer Power*, Nash Publishing, 1974; *Savvy Shopper*, J. P. Tarcher, 1974. Columnist, *Consumer Newsletter* (Van Nuys, Calif.).

WORK IN PROGRESS: Oldies but Goodies, a collection of household hints; a slide film presentation on consumer education for schools.

* * *

DUCKERT, Mary 1929-
(Ann Hall)

PERSONAL: Surname is pronounced *Duke*-ert; born March 19, 1929, in Wisconsin; daughter of H. W. (an insurance executive) and Mabel (Hoveland) Duckert. *Education:* University of Wisconsin, B.S., 1950; McCormick Theological Seminary, M.A., 1953. *Politics:* "Never on Sundays." *Religion:* Presbyterian. *Home:* 125 Prospect Ave., Hackensack, N.J. 07601. *Office:* United Presbyterian Church of the U.S.A., 475 Riverside Dr., New York, N.Y. 10027.

CAREER: Board of Christian Education, Philadelphia, Pa., editor, 1957-60; director of children's work at Presbyterian church in Cleveland, Ohio, 1962-66; Board of Christian Education, Philadelphia, Pa., editor, 1966-73; Program Agency of United Presbyterian Church of the U.S.A., New York, N.Y., editor, 1973—.

WRITINGS: Help!: I'm a Sunday School Teacher, Westminster, 1969; *Help!: I Run a Sunday School*, Westminster, 1971; *Tailor-Made Teaching in the Church School*, Westminster, 1974. Contributor to church school publications. Editor of *Elementary Education in the Church*, and contributor under pseudonym Ann Hall.

WORK IN PROGRESS: Research on open education in the church school.

SIDELIGHTS: Mary Duckert writes: "I write to people who know they have clay feet, some who have the grace to laugh about them."

* * *

DUGGAN, Maurice d.1975

New Zealand author of children's books and short story writer. Obituaries: *AB Bookman's Weekly*, February 3, 1975.

* * *

DUKER, Abraham G(ordon) 1907-

PERSONAL: Born September 27, 1907, in Rypin, Poland; came to United States in 1923, naturalized in 1926; son of Asher Zelig and Feiga Haya (Gorodensky) Duker; married Lillian Miriam Sandrow (a social worker), December 1, 1940; children: Nahum Johanan, Sara Rivkah, Dvora Peninah Marmon. *Education:* City College of New York (now City College of the City University of New York), B.A., 1930; Columbia University, Ph.D., 1956. *Home:* 2015 Avenue I, Brooklyn, N.Y. 11210. *Office:* Department of Judaic Studies, Brooklyn College of the City University of New York, Brooklyn, N.Y. 11210.

CAREER: Jewish Theological Seminary, New York, N.Y., clerk and cataloger, 1927-33; Graduate School for Jewish Social Work, New York, N.Y., research librarian, instructor, 1934-38; American Jewish Committee, Research Institute on Peace and Post-War Problems, New York, N.Y., managing editor, later editor, 1938-43; *The Day* (weekly magazine), editor, 1945-49; held positions as lecturer or instructor at various institutions, 1949-52; Jewish Social Studies, New York, N.Y., managing editor, 1952-58; College of Jewish Studies, Chicago, Ill., professor and president of college, 1955-62; Yeshiva University, New York, N.Y., professor, and director of libraries, 1962-72; Brooklyn College of the City University of New York, Brooklyn, N.Y., member of faculty, department of Judaic studies. Associate, Training Bureau for Jewish Communal Service, 1947-49. Visiting professor at Wayne State University, 1955, and at Columbia University, 1966-67. *Wartime service:* Political analyst with Office of Strategic Services, 1944-45.

MEMBER: American Academy for Jewish Research (fellow), Conference on Jewish Social Studies (member of board of directors, 1952—; president, 1970-74), YIVO Institute for Jewish Research (member of board of directors, 1948—), American Jewish Historical Society (member of national council, 1958-63), Jewish Book Council of America (member of executive board), Histadruth Cultural Exchange Institute (member of national board), National Council for Jewish Education (member of executive committee). *Awards, honors:* Miller Foundation fellow, Columbia University, 1933-34; research grants from Littauer Foundation, 1956, American Council of Learned Societies, 1962, and Wurzweller Foundation, 1967.

WRITINGS: The Situation of Jews in Poland, Conference on Jewish Relations (New York), 1936; *Jewish Survival in the World Today*, Hadassah, 1939-41; (co-author) *Jews in the Post-War World*, Dryden Press, 1945; (with Mordecai Kosover) *Minha l'Yitshaq* (title means "An Offering to Isaac"), [New York], 1949; *Jewish Community Relations*, Jewish Reconstructionist Foundation, 1952; *Workshop in Jewish Community Affairs*, [New York], 1952-53; (co-author) *Joshua Starr Memorial Volume: Studies in History and Philology*, Ktav, 1953; *The Impact of Zionism on American Jewry*, Herzl Institute (New York), 1958; (editor with Meir Ben Horin) *Emancipation and Counter-Emancipation*, Ktav, 1971; *Selection of Essays on Polish-Jewish History*, Ktav, in press.

Also author of *Culture Patterns in American Jewish Life*, 1950. Contributor of articles to periodicals. Founding and managing editor, *Contemporary Jewish Record* (now *Commentary*), 1938-41; managing editor, *Jewish Social Service Quarterly*, 1942-43. Editor of English section, *Jewish Book Annual*.

WORK IN PROGRESS: Mickiewicz's "Jewish Mystique"; contributions to various festschrift volumes.

AVOCATIONAL INTERESTS: Painting.

DUNATHAN, Arni T(homas) 1936-

PERSONAL: Born May 2, 1936, in Menominee, Mich.; son of Clinton B. (a journalist) and Haldora F. (Hagen) Dunathan; married Novelle Cunningham (a college teacher), May 11, 1957; children: Clinton Arni, Dari Novelle. *Education:* Attended Northwestern University, 1954-57; Michigan State University, B.A., 1958, M.A., 1960; University of Utah, Ed.D., 1967. *Politics:* Independent. *Religion:* Methodist. *Home:* 1004 Falcon Dr., Columbia, Mo. 65201. *Office:* College of Education, University of Missouri, 225 Education Bldg., Columbia, Mo. 65201.

CAREER: University of Missouri, Columbia, assistant professor, 1967-71, associate professor, 1971-74, professor of education, 1974—. *Military service:* U.S. Navy, 1954-57. *Member:* Association of Educational Communications and Technology, Smithsonian Associates, Phi Delta Kappa, Kappa Delta Pi.

WRITINGS: The American B.B. Gun: A Collector's Guide, A. S. Barnes, 1971.

WORK IN PROGRESS: While the Iron Was Hot, a novel that mixes fact and fiction about iron smelting days at a pig iron foundry in Fayette, Michigan.

AVOCATIONAL INTERESTS: Antiquities, decoy carving.

* * *

DUNCAN, Robert F. 1890(?)-1974

1890(?)—September 13, 1974; American professional fund-raiser. Obituaries: *New York Times*, September 18, 1974.

* * *

DUNKLE, William F(rederick), Jr. 1911-

PERSONAL: Born May 16, 1911, in McAlester, Okla.; son of William F. (a clergyman) and Nell (Munn) Dunkle; married Carolyn Watson, June 12, 1936; children: Amelia Ann Dunkle Libby, William F. III, Zillan Beth. *Education:* University of Florida, A.B., 1934; Emory University, B.D., 1937; Union Theological Seminary, Th.M., 1949. *Politics:* Republican. *Office:* Trinity Church, 1024 Lake, Wilmette, Ill. 60091.

CAREER: Ordained Methodist clergyman, 1937; pastor of Methodist churches in Florida, Virginia, and Delaware, 1936-66; Trinity Church, Wilmette, Ill., senior pastor, 1966—. Lecturer at Crozer Seminary, 1960-66, and Garrett Theological Seminary, 1968—. Exchange pastor in London, England, 1950; conducted preaching mission for American military forces in Korea, 1953; retreat leader for Methodist military chaplains in Europe, 1965, and in the Pacific, 1966. Chaplain to Virginia State Senate, 1946. President of Delaware State Council of Churches, 1960-61. Member of board of directors of Methodist Foundation; member of board of trustees of American University, Drew University, and Wesley Junior College. Member of White House Conference on Youth, 1950, 1960. *Military service:* U.S. Air Force, during Korean conflict; became colonel.

MEMBER: Hymn Society of America, Societas Liturgica, English Speaking Union, Phi Delta Theta, Blue Key, Lincoln Club, Rotary International, Masons (grand chaplain, 1955), Scottish Rites, Knights Templar, Union League Club, Westmoreland Country Club, Michigan Shores Club. *Awards, honors:* D.D. from American University, 1951; LL.D. from McMurray College, 1968; also received D.H.L.

WRITINGS: Values in the Church Year, Abingdon, 1959; (editor with Joseph Quillian, Jr.) *Companion to the Book of Worship*, Abingdon, 1970. Also author of *The Office of a Steward*, 1962, and *The Lectionary of the Methodist Church*, 1964. Contributor to *Methodist Altars*, 1961, and *Best Sermons*, 1962. Contributor to *Encyclopedia of Methodism*. Contributor to church magazines, including *Christian Advocate, Together, Sermon Preparation, Upper Room Pulpit, Christian Action,* and *Methodist Recorder*.

* * *

DUNNING, Robert William 1938-

PERSONAL: Born March 16, 1938, in East Coker, England; son of William T. H. (a farmer) and Constance (Williams) Dunning; married Anne Moyle, October 1, 1968; children: Jeremy P. S. *Education:* University of Bristol, B.A., 1959, Ph.D., 1962; University of Exeter, certificate in education, 1960. *Religion:* Anglican. *Home:* 16 Comeytrowe Rise, Taunton, Somerset, England. *Office:* Somerset County Council, County Hall, Taunton, Somerset, England.

CAREER: History of Parliament Trust, London, England, researcher, 1962-64; Victoria County Histories, London, England, senior assistant to the general editor, 1964-67; *Victoria History of Somerset*, Taunton, England, county editor, 1967—. *Member:* Royal Historical Society, Ecclesiastical History Society, Society of Antiquaries (London), Somerset Archaeological Society, Somerset Record Society (honorary general editor, 1970—), Rotary International.

WRITINGS: (Editor) *Hylle Cartulary*, Somerset Record Society, 1968; (editor with T. D. Tremlett and T. B. Dilks) *Bridgwater Borough Archives: 1468-1485*, Somerset Record Society, 1971; *Local Sources for the Young Historian*, Muller, 1973; (editor) *Victoria History of Somerset*, Volume III (Dunning was not associated with earlier volumes), Oxford University Press, 1974; (author of introduction) William Hale, editor, *A Series of Precedents and Proceedings in Criminal Causes*, Bratton, 1974; (editor with David Bromwich) *Victorian and Edwardian Somerset in Photographs*, Batsford, in press; *Somerset*, David & Charles, in press. Contributor to *Bulletin of the Institute for Historical Research, Proceedings of the Somerset Archaeological Society, Studies in Church History, Archives, Bulletin of the Board of Celtic Studies*, and *Friends' Quarterly*.

WORK IN PROGRESS: Editing *Victoria History of Somerset*, Volume IV; editing *Christianity in Somerset*; writing new introduction for a reprint of *History of Taunton*; two landscape studies; a study of the office of rural dean.

AVOCATIONAL INTERESTS: Travel (especially France).

* * *

DUNOYER DE SEGONZAC, Andre 1884-1974

July 6, 1884—September 17, 1974; French naturalist painter. Obituaries: *New York Times*, September 18, 1974; *Washington Post*, September 18, 1974; *Time*, September 30, 1974.

* * *

DURAM, James C(arl) 1939-

PERSONAL: Born August 24, 1939, in Muskegon, Mich.;

son of Richard (a machinist) and Wilma (Johnston) Duram; married Eleanor Berger (a researcher), August 25, 1962; children: Leslie Aileen, Brian Nicolaas. *Education:* Muskegon Community College, A.A., 1959; Western Michigan University, B.A. (magna cum laude), 1962, M.A., 1963; Wayne State University, Ph.D., 1968. *Politics:* Democratic Socialist. *Religion:* Unaffiliated. *Home:* 2924 North Fairmount, Wichita, Kan. 67220. *Agent:* G. K. Hall, 70 Lincoln St., Boston, Mass. 02111. *Office:* Department of History, Wichita State University, Wichita, Kan. 67208.

CAREER: Public school teacher of social studies in Allegan, Mich., 1961-63; Wayne State University, Detroit, Mich., instructor in history, 1965-66; Hope College, Holland, Mich., instructor in history, 1966-68; Wichita State University, Wichita, Kan., assistant professor, 1968-71, associate professor of history, 1971—. Visiting scholar at Associated Colleges of Central Kansas, spring, 1970.

MEMBER: American Historical Association, Organization of American Historians, Kansas State Historical Society, Michigan State Historical Society, Phi Alpha Theta. *Awards, honors:* Detroit Historic Memorials Society award, 1964; Henry Rowe Schoolcraft research grant from Michigan State Historical Society, 1968, for study of the use of newspaper sources as an index to constitutional conservatism in Michigan; National Endowment for the Humanities grant, summer, 1970, for study of the impact of European social democratic thought on Norman Thomas, including research in England, the Netherlands, Austria, West Germany, and Canada; Fulbright-Hays research grant, summer, 1972, for study of the transference of reform ideas between European and American social democrats, including research in the Netherlands.

WRITINGS: *Norman Thomas*, Twayne, 1974. Contributor of more than twenty articles and reviews to history journals, including *Western Pennsylvania Historical Magazine*, *Labor History*, *Journal of Presbyterian History*, *Agricultural History*, *Michigan History*, and *Russell: The Journal of the Bertrand Russell Archives*.

WORK IN PROGRESS: *Justice William O. Douglas*, for Twayne; a book about the Brown school segregation case; a book on reform idea exchange between American and European socialists.

* * *

DURBIN, Richard Louis 1928-

PERSONAL: Born August 28, 1928, in Millersport, Ohio; son of Babe Clark and Mabel (Bushee) Durbin; married Carolyn Bohren, March 18, 1955; children: Richard Louis, Margot Jane, Melissa Bushee. *Education:* Ohio State University, B.A., 1949; University of Chicago, M.B.A., 1956; University of Arizona, M.P.A., 1969. *Home:* 148 Hunt Dr., Princeton, N.J. 08540.

CAREER: Educational administrator. *Military service:* U.S. Navy; became lieutenant. *Member:* Sigma Xi.

WRITINGS: *Statistical Methodology for Evaluating a Medical Staff*, University of Chicago, 1961; *Organization and Administration of Health Care*, Mosby, 1969, 2nd edition, 1974.

* * *

DURKIN, Henry P(aul) 1940-

PERSONAL: Born June 24, 1940, in Czechoslovakia; son of Edward James and Barbara (Wachter) Durkin; married Jane Elizabeth Lewis, April 27, 1968; children: Jennifer Marie, Peter Christopher. *Education:* Fordham University, B.A., 1962; graduate study at University of Bonn, 1962-63. *Politics:* Conservative Republican. *Religion:* Roman Catholic. *Agent:* Harold Ober Associates, 40 East 49th St., New York, N.Y. 10017.

CAREER: Walker & Co., Publishers, New York, N.Y., director of advertising, promotion, and publicity, 1969-72; World Publishing Co., New York, N.Y., subsidiary rights director, 1972-73; Hawthorn Books, Inc., New York, N.Y., associate editor and subsidiary rights director, 1973—. *Member:* Authors Guild.

WRITINGS: *Forty-Four Hours to Change Your Life: Marriage Encounter*, Pyramid Press and Paulist-Newman, 1974. Contributor to *Realist*, *Human Events*, *Rally*, *New Guard*, *Jewish Press*, *Private Practice*, and *Combat*.

WORK IN PROGRESS: *Documentary History of the Communist International*, two volumes; *Documentary History of the Communist Party, USA*.

* * *

DUTT, R(ajani) Palme 1896-1974

June 19, 1896—December 20, 1974; British marxist theoretician and author. Obituaries: *New York Times*, December 21, 1974; *AB Bookman's Weekly*, January 6, 1975. (*CA*-11/12).

* * *

DWORKIN, Gerald 1937-

PERSONAL: Born December 27, 1937, in the United States; son of Morris and Miriam (Halbfinger) Dworkin; married Joan Shapiro (a social worker), April 13, 1960; children: Lisa Nicole, Julie Michelle. *Education:* City College (now City College of the City University of New York), B.S., 1959; University of California, Berkeley, M.A. (mathematics), 1961, M.A. (philosophy), 1963, Ph.D., 1966. *Home:* 4718 35th Ave. N.E., Seattle, Wash. 98105. *Office:* Battelle Seattle Research Center, 4000 Northeast 41st St., Seattle, Wash. 98105.

CAREER: Harvard University, Cambridge, Mass., instructor in philosophy, 1965-66; Massachusetts Institute of Technology, Cambridge, Mass., assistant professor, 1966-72, associate professor of philosophy, 1972-73; University of Illinois, Chicago Circle, Chicago, associate professor of philosophy, 1973—. Visiting fellow at Battelle Seattle Research Center, Seattle, Wash., 1973-75; fellow of Institute of Society, Ethics and the Life Sciences, 1975. *Member:* Society for Philosophy and Public Affairs, Society for Ethical and Legal Philosophy, Phi Beta Kappa. *Awards, honors:* Woodrow Wilson fellow, 1959-60; Woodrow Wilson dissertation fellow, 1964-65; fellow in law and philosophy at Harvard Law School, 1967-68; National Endowment for the Humanities fellow, 1968.

WRITINGS: (Editor with Judith Thomson) *Ethics*, Harper, 1968; (editor) *Determinism, Free-Will, and Moral Responsibility*, Prentice-Hall, 1970; (with N. J. Block) *IQ, Heritability, and Inequality*, Philosophy and Public Affairs, 1974; (editor with Block) *The IQ Controversy*, Pantheon, 1975.

WORK IN PROGRESS: Co-editing *Markets and Morals*; research in social and ethical implications of behavior genetics.

DWYER-JOYCE, Alice 1913-

PERSONAL: Born September 7, 1913, in Birr, Offaly, Ireland; daughter of John Peacocke (a pharmaceutical chemist) and Mary Stuart (Purves) Myles; married Robert Dwyer-Joyce (a physician), November 21, 1936; children: Robert. *Education:* Royal College of Surgeons, Dublin, medical degree, 1936. *Home and office:* Greystones, Histon, Cambridge, England.

CAREER: In general practice of medicine in partnership with husband, Dr. Robert Dwyer-Joyce, at Histon, Cambridge, 1936—.

WRITINGS—Novels; all published by R. Hale, with further publication as noted: *Price of Inheritance*, 1963; *The Silent Lady*, 1964; *Dr. Ross of Harton*, 1966; *The Story of Dr. Esmond Ross*, 1967; *Verdict on Dr. Esmond Ross*, 1968; *Dial Emergency for Dr. Ross*, 1969; *Don't Cage Me Wild*, 1970; *For I Have Lived Today*, 1971; *Message for Dr. Ross*, 1971; *Cry the Soft Rain*, 1972, St. Martin's, 1974; *Reach for the Shadows*, 1972, St. Martin's, 1973; *The Rainbow Glass*, St. Martin's, 1973; *The Brass Islands*, 1974; *Prescription for Melissa*, 1974; *The Moonlit Way*, St. Martin's, 1974.

WORK IN PROGRESS: Four novels, *The Strolling Players, The Diamond Cage, Death of a Swan*, and *Don't Weep, Little Monkey*.

SIDELIGHTS: Dr. Dwyer-Joyce writes: "I love humanity, deplore the rat-race of modern life and yearn for the happiness that seems to have departed from many people's lives. I deplore the contamination of our generation of the loveliness of nature, deplore the all important accent on sex and pornography. I have the good luck to have a large garden with birds flying freely, wild and tame—a kind of 'Walt Disney Land.'"

* * *

DYEN, Isidore 1913-

PERSONAL: Born August 16, 1913, in Philadelphia, Pa.; son of Jacob and Dena (Bryzell) Dyen; married Edith Brenner (an educator), June 11, 1939; children: Doris Jane (Mrs. Deane L. Root), Mark Ross. *Education:* University of Pennsylvania, B.A., 1933, M.A., 1934, Ph.D., 1939. *Home:* 1955 Paradise Ave., Mt. Carmel, Conn. 06518. *Office:* 323 Hall of Graduate Studies, Yale University, New Haven, Conn. 06520.

CAREER: Yale University, New Haven, Conn., instructor, 1942-43, assistant professor, 1943-48, associate professor, 1948-57, professor of Malayopolynesian and comparative linguistics, 1957—, director of graduate studies of the department of Indic and Far Eastern languages and literature, 1960-62, director of graduate studies for South and Souteast Asia for the department of East and South Asian languages and literatures, 1962-67, director of graduate studies in linguistics, 1966-68. Pacific Science Board of National Research Council, linguist for coordinated investigation of Micronesian anthropology, 1947, and scientific investigation of Micronesia, 1949; Linguistic Institute of Linguistic Society of America, visiting associate professor at University of Chicago, summer, 1955, visiting professor at University of Michigan, summer, 1957, University of Padjadjaran, 1960-61, and University of Auckland, summer, 1969; visiting research professor at Australian National University, 1971, and University of the Philippines, 1972. Participant in international conferences.

MEMBER: Linguistic Society of America, American Oriental Society (vice-president, 1965-66), American Anthropological Association, Current Anthropology, Koninklijk Instituut voor Taal-, Land-, en Volkenkunde, Societe de Linguistique de Paris, New Haven Oriental Club. *Awards, honors:* American Council of Learned Societies grant-in-aid, 1939-40, and research fellowship, 1941-42, to Yale University; Guggenheim fellowship, 1949, 1964; Tri-Institutional Pacific Program research grants, 1956, 1957; research grant from Office of Education, U.S. Department of Health, Education, and Welfare, 1960-61; National Science Foundation research grants, 1960-66, 1967-73; American Institute of Indian Studies fellowship, 1964.

WRITINGS: Spoken Malay, two volumes, Holt, 1945; *The Proto-Malayo-Polynesian Laryngeals,* [Baltimore, Md.], 1953; (contributor) *Handbook of Indonesia,* Human wrelations Area Files, 1956; *The Lexicostatistical Classification of the Austronesian Languages,* [New Haven, Conn.], 1963; *A Sketch of Trukese Grammar,* American Oriental Society, 1965; *Beginning Indonesian,* four volumes, [New Haven], 1967; *A Descriptive Indonesian Grammar: Preliminary Edition,* [New Haven], 1967; (contributor) George Cardona, Henry M. Hoenigswald, and Alfred Senn, editors, *Indo-European and Indo Europeans: Papers Presented at the Third Indo-European Conference at the University of Pennsylvania, 1966,* University of Pennsylvania Press, 1970; (contributor) *Mathematics in the Archaeological Sciences,* [Edinburgh], 1971; (editor and contributor) *Lexicostatistics in Genetic Linguistics: Proceedings of the Yale Conference,* Yale University Press, 1973; *Linguistic Subgrouping and Lexicostatistics,* Mouton & Co., in press; (with David Aberle) *Lexical Reconstruction: The Case of the Athapaskan Kinship System,* Cambridge University Press, in press.

Co-author of *Index to Journal of the American Oriental Society* (Volumes 21-60), 1955. Associate editor of "William Dwight Whitney Linguistic Series," 1953—. Contributor to *Indo-Pacific Linguistic Studies,* 1965, and to proceedings. Contributor of articles and reviews to journals in his field.

* * *

EAGLESON, John 1941-

PERSONAL: Born July 19, 1941, in Philadelphia, Pa.; son of John R. (a mechanical engineer) and Mary Rose (a secretary; maiden name, Collins) Eagleson; married Mary Ellen Sipos, February 21, 1971; children: Ian Micah. *Education:* Providence College, B.A., 1964; University of the Americas, M.A., 1965; Maryknoll Seminary, M.Div., 1970. *Religion:* Roman Catholic. *Home:* 620 Underhill Ave., Yorktown Heights, N.Y. 10598. *Office:* Orbis Books, Maryknoll, N.Y. 10545.

CAREER: Orbis Books, Maryknoll, N.Y., editor, 1971—.

WRITINGS—All published by Orbis Books: (Editor with Philip Scharper) *The Radical Bible*, 1972; (editor with Scharper) *The Patriot's Bible*, 1975; (editor) *Christians and Socialism*, 1975.

Translator—All published by Orbis Books: (With Rockwell Gray) Vittorio di Giralamo, *Bo and the Sad King*, 1972; (with Sister Caridad Inda) Gustavo Gutierrez, *A Theology of Liberation*, 1973; Jose Miranda, *Marx and the Bible*, 1974; (with Ed Garcia) Nestor Paz, *My Life for My Friends*, 1975.

WORK IN PROGRESS: Editing and translating books from the "Third World," specializing in Latin American theology.

SIDELIGHTS: Eagleson writes: "I believe the Churches have an important part to play in bringing about a world of liberty and justice. My editorial work is dedicated to fostering greater effectiveness of the Churches in this area."

* * *

EAKIN, Frank Edwin, Jr. 1936-

PERSONAL: Born September 4, 1936, in Roanoke, Va.; son of Frank Edwin (a railwayman) and Vera (Taylor) Eakin; married Frances Crockett (a medical secretary), June 28, 1958. *Education:* University of Richmond, B.A., 1958; Southern Baptist Theological Seminary, B.D., 1961; Duke University, Ph.D., 1964. *Politics:* "Not strict party follower." *Home:* 7013 Bandy Rd., Richmond, Va. 23229. *Office:* Department of Religion, University of Richmond, Richmond, Va. 23173.

CAREER: Duke University, Durham, N.C., insturctor in religion, 1965-66; University of Richmond, Richmond, Va., assistant professor, 1966-69, associate professor of religion, 1969—. Visiting professor at Wake Forest University, 1964-65. *Member:* Society of Biblical Literature, Phi Beta Kappa, Omicron Delta Kappa.

WRITINGS: The Religion and Culture of Israel, Allyn & Bacon, 1971; (contributor) James M. Efird, editor, *The Use of the Old Testament in the New, and Other Essays: Studies in Honor of William Franklin Stinespring,* Duke University Press, 1972; (contributor) C. J. Allen, editor, *Broadman Bible Commentary,* Volume VII, Broadman, 1972. Contributor to *Journal of Biblical Literature.*

WORK IN PROGRESS: Religion and Western Culture; The Tragic Dimension of Existence.

AVOCATIONAL INTERESTS: Travel, golf.

* * *

EARNSHAW, Anthony 1924-

PERSONAL: Born October 9, 1924, in Ilkley, England; son of Ernest (a watchmaker) and Dorothy (Myers) Earnshaw; married Monica Simpson (divorced); children: Ruth, Francis. *Education:* Attended elementary school in England. *Politics:* "Disband the army—open the jails." *Religion:* "Ha ha." *Home:* 1 Regent St., Flat 2, Leeds 7, England.

CAREER: Has worked in factories, as a crane driver, and lecturer in art.

WRITINGS: (With Eric Thacker) *Musrum* (novel), J. Cape, 1968, Grove, 1970; (with Thacker) *Wintersol* (novel), J. Cape, 1971; *Seven Secret Alphabets* (drawings), J. Cape, 1972.

WORK IN PROGRESS: A book with illustrations, "to provide, I hope, ideal stretcher-side reading."

SIDELIGHTS: Earnshaw is interested in surrealism, and writes that at heart he is work-shy.

* * *

EASTMAN, Roger (Herbert) 1931-

PERSONAL: Born June 7, 1931, in New York, N.Y.; son of Herbert Henry (a business executive) and Ella (Coghlan) Eastman; married Gloria Jean Byram, December 29, 1962; children: Carolyn Eileen, Jennifer Lynn. *Education:* Pasadena City College, A.A., 1951; San Jose State University, B.A., 1954; Stanford University, M.A., 1961. *Home:* 8234 South Frankwood Ave., Reedley, Calif. 93654. *Office:* Department of Religion and Philosophy, Reedley College, Reedley, Calif. 93654.

CAREER: Reedley College, Reedley, Calif., instructor in English, 1958-62, instructor in philosophy and religion, 1962—. *Military service:* U.S. Marine Corps, 1954-57. *Awards, honors:* Fellowship from National Foundation for the Humanities, 1971-72.

WRITINGS: (Editor) *Coming of Age in Philosophy*, Canfield, 1973; (editor) *The Ways of Religion*, Canfield, in press.

WORK IN PROGRESS: A Fieldguide for Young Philosophers; editing *Meditations on Work.*

SIDELIGHTS: Eastman writes: "Western civilization has come to Kafka and *Catch-22*: ennui and absurdity abound. I admire the thought of such peoples and writers as the early Taoists, the American Indians, Wendell Berry, and Gary Snyder. My books urge the examined life."

* * *

EATON, Evelyn (Sybil Mary) 1902-

PERSONAL: Born December 22, 1902, in Montreux, Switzerland; naturalized U.S. citizen, 1944; daughter of Daniel Isaac Vernon (a colonel in the Royal Canadian Horse Artillery) and Myra (Randolph) Eaton; married Ernst Paul Richard Viedt, October 28, 1928 (died, 1942); children: Theresa Neyana (Mrs. Richard Logan Brengle). *Education:* Attended the Sorbonne, University of Paris, 1920-21. *Politics:* "Discouraged." *Religion:* Paiute. *Home and office:* 112 Rosedale, Independence, Calif. 93526. *Agent:* McIntosh & Otis, 18 East 41st St., New York, N.Y. 10017.

CAREER: Poet and novelist. War correspondent in China-Burma-India Theater, 1945. Lecturer at Columbia University, 1949-51; lecturer for the Arts Program of the Association of American Colleges, 1950-60; visiting lecturer at Sweet Briar College, 1951-60; lecturer in adult education programs at various centers in Virginia, 1955-60; visiting professor at Mary Washington College of the University of Virginia, 1957-59; lecturer on station WLVA-TV for 26-week series, "The Arts in the Age of Space," sponsored by the University of Virginia, 1960; visiting lecturer at Ohio University, 1962; visiting professor, Pershing College, 1967. Fellow of MacDowell Colony, 1948, 1949, 1950, 1956, 1957, 1960, 1967, 1968; fellow of "Wavertree," the Virginia Center for the Creative Arts, 1973. Writer-in-residence, Montalvo Association, 1960 and 1963, Deep Springs College, 1961, Hartford Foundation, 1960 and 1962. Member of board of directors of Draco Foundation of Virginia, 1958; founder of Draco Foundation of California, Inc., 1965; founder of Deepest Valley Theater, Owens Valley, Calif., 1965.

MEMBER: Authors Guild, P.E.N., Poetry Society of America, Canadian Authors Association (vice-president, 1940-41), International Platform Association, Pen and Brush Club (president, 1946-50), Poetry Society of Virginia. *Awards, honors:* John Masefield Award, 1923, for short lyrics later published in *Stolen Hours.*

WRITINGS—Novels, except as indicated: *The Encircling Mist*, Selwyn & Blount, 1925; *Desire: Spanish Version*, Chapman & Hall, 1932, Morrow, 1933; *Summer Dust*, Bles, 1936; *John: Film Star* (juvenile), Nelson, 1937; *Pray to the Earth*, Houghton, 1938; *Canadian Circus* (juvenile), Nelson, 1939; *Quietly My Captain Waits* (Literary Guild selection), Harper, 1940; *Restless Are the Sails*, Harper, 1941; *The Sea Is So Wide*, Harper, 1943; *In What Torn Ship*, Harper, 1944; *Every Month Was May* (short stories),

Harper, 1947; (with Edward Roberts Moore) *Heart in Pilgrimage* (biography), Harper, 1948, reprinted, Doubleday, 1960; *The North Star Is Nearer* (short stories), Farrar, Straus, 1949.

Give Me Your Golden Hand, Farrar, Straus, 1951; *Flight*, Bobbs-Merrill, 1954; *I Saw My Mortal Sight*, Random House, 1959; *The King Is a Witch*, Cassell, 1965, St. Martin's, 1974; *Go Ask the River*, Harcourt, 1969; *The Trees and the Fields Went the Other Way* (autobiography), Harcourt, 1974; *Snowy Earth Comes Gliding*, Draco, 1974.

Poems: *The Interpreter*, Selwyn & Blount, 1923; *Stolen Hours*, Selwyn & Blount, 1923; *Birds before Dawn*, Ryerson Press, 1943; *The Small Hour*, Golden Quill, 1955; *Love Is Recognition*, Dragon's Teeth Press, 1971.

Author of twenty-five short stories published in the *New Yorker*, 1946-60. Contributor to periodicals, including *Lyric, Yankee, The Sentinel, Different, London Tatler*, and *Connotation*.

WORK IN PROGRESS: Preparing cassette tape recordings, "An Hour with Matthew Arnold," "An Hour with Browning," and "Modern Poetry"; a second volume of autobiography.

SIDELIGHTS: Partly Indian by descent, Evelyn Eaton is particularly concerned with fostering and preserving Indian Art. She has ties with the Micmac and Malisite, or Algonquin tribes of Nova Scotia; since 1965, she has similar ties with the Paiutes of Owens Valley, California.

Quietly My Captain Waits, an historical novel, has been published in seventeen foreign editions. Five poems from *The Small Hour* were set to music by Joseph Wood and performed at Oberlin College in 1960 and at Carnegie Hall in 1965. *The Progression*, an unpublished poem set to music by Wood, was performed as a ballet-oratorio at Oberlin College in 1968. Seven other poems, set to music by Paul Earls, have also been publicly performed.

Miss Eaton has made several cassette tape recordings, including "Love Is Recognition," 1973, and "An Hour with Shelley," "An Hour with Keats," and "Stories for Pleasure," all 1974. Since 1966, her books, manuscripts, and personal papers have been housed in a permanent collection in the Mugar Memorial Library at Boston University.

* * *

EATON, Theodore H(ildreth), Jr. 1907-

PERSONAL: Born November 16, 1907, in Boston, Mass.; son of Theodore H. (a university professor) and Theodora (West) Eaton; married Grace Worthy Janlen (a physical therapist), August 25, 1934; children: George Theodore, Lois West (Mrs. William M. Bueler), Margaret Rose (Mrs. Gordon T. Stallknecht). *Education:* Cornell University, A.B., 1930; University of California, Berkeley, Ph.D., 1933. *Politics:* Independent, generally Democrat. *Home:* 1740 Indiana St., Lawrence, Kan. 66044. *Office:* Museum of Natural History, University of Kansas, Lawrence, Kan. 66044.

CAREER: National Park Service, Berkeley, Calif., naturalist technician, 1935-37; Union College, Schenectady, N.Y., instructor in biology, 1937-40; Cornell University, Ithaca, N.Y., assistant in agronomy, 1940-42; University of Buffalo, Buffalo, N.Y., assistant professor of biology, 1942-45; George Washington University, Washington, D.C., assistant professor of biology, 1945-47; Southwestern College, Winfield, Kan., professor of biology, 1947-50; East Carolina College, Greenville, N.C., professor of biology, 1950-58; University of Kansas, Lawrence, professor of zoology, 1958—, curator of lower vertebrate fossils at Museum of Natural History, 1958—. *Member:* American Society of Zoologists, American Society of Ichthyologists and Herpetologists, Society of Vertebrate Paleontology.

WRITINGS: Comparative Anatomy of the Vertebrates, Harper, 1951, 2nd edition, 1960; *Evolution*, Norton, 1970. Contributor of one hundred and eight scientific articles to professional journals.

WORK IN PROGRESS: A description of the skeleton of a new fossil pelycosaur; two books, one on fish biology and one on animal behavior.

SIDELIGHTS: Eaton has collected fossils in Rocky Mountain States, spent a year in Vietnam, a year in New Zealand, and visited East Africa three times and Borneo once.

* * *

EBEL, Henry 1938-

PERSONAL: Born July 5, 1938, in Berlin, Germany; son of Richard (an executive) Anna (an executive; maiden name, Salomon) Ebel; married Julia Gracia Sarah Sophia Hirsch, June 15, 1960 (divorced January 6, 1972); married Sheila Krinsky (a teacher), September 6, 1973; children: (first marriage) Katherine. *Education:* Columbia University, A.B. (summa cum laude), 1959, Ph.D., 1965; Clare College, Cambridge, B.A., 1961, M.A., 1964. *Politics:* "Anarchist." *Religion:* Jewish. *Home:* 6 Horizon Rd., Fort Lee, N.J. 07024. *Office:* Richmond College of the City University of New York, 130 Stuyvesant Pl., Staten Island, N.Y. 10301.

CAREER: Wesleyan University, Middletown, Conn., instructor, 1964-65, assistant professor of English, 1965-68; Fordham University, New York, N.Y., associate professor of humanities, 1968-69; Richmond College of the City University of New York, Staten Island, N.Y., assistant professor, 1969-71, associate professor of English, 1971—. Director of Argonaut Books, 1973—. Co-founder and publicity director of Riverside Parks and Playgrounds Committee, 1962-64, and Middletown Democrats for McCarthy, 1967-68.

WRITINGS: After Dionysus: An Essay on Where We Are Now, Fairleigh Dickinson University Press, 1972; *Odyssey through the Dead Land,* Argonaut Books, 1973. Contributor of articles, poems, and reviews to journals, including *Psychoanalytic Review, College English, Jerusalem Post, Studies in English Literature, Victorian Studies,* and *Victorian Newsletter*. Contributing editor of *History of Childhood Quarterly: The Journal of Psychohistory*.

WORK IN PROGRESS: In Prayse of the Lord Our God, Who Makes Us Free (tentative title), a book of meditations.

* * *

EBERSTADT, Charles F. 1914(?)-1974

1914(?)—June 29, 1974; American bibliophile and author. Obituaries: *AB Bookman's Weekly*, August 12-19, 1974.

* * *

ECCLES, David (McAdam) 1904-

PERSONAL: Born September 18, 1904 in London, England; son of William McAdam (a surgeon) and Anna Coralie (Anstie) Eccles; married Sybil Frances Dawson, October 10, 1929; children: John, Simon, Selina Polly (Marchioness of Lansdowne). *Education:* New College, Oxford, B.A., 1926. *Politics:* Conservative. *Home:* Dean Farm, Upper Chute, Andover, Hampshire, England; and 6 Barton St., Westminster, London SW 1, England.

CAREER: Central Mining & Investment Corp., London, England, 1926-39, began as clerk, became manager in 1939; chairman, Anglo-Spanish Construction Co., 1939; joined British Ministry of Economic Warfare, September, 1939; economic adviser to His Majesty's ambassadors in Madrid, Spain, and Lisbon, Portugal, 1940-42; assistant director of general programs and planning, Ministry of Production, 1942-43; elected as Conservative member to British Parliament for Chippenham, Wiltshire, in 1943, 1945, 1950, 1951, 1955, 1959; Minister of Works, 1951-54; Privy Councillor, 1951; Minister of Education, 1954-57, 1959-62; president of Board of Trade, 1957-59; paymaster general, with responsibility for the arts, 1970—. Knighted, 1953; created first baron, 1962, first viscount, 1964. British Museum, trustee, 1963—, chairman of trustees, 1968-70; chairman of the board of British Library, 1973—; president of World Crafts Council, 1974—. Director Courtaulds, Ltd., 1962-70; chairman, West Cumberland Silk Mills Ltd., 1964-70.

MEMBER: Royal Institute of British Architects (honorary fellow), Anglo-Hellenic League (chairman, 1967-70), Brook's and Roxburghe Clubs (both London). *Awards, honors:* Knight Commander of the Royal Victorian Order, 1953; Grand Cross of the Liberator (Venezuela), 1974.

WRITINGS: Wages on the Farm (booklet), Signpost Press, 1945; *Your Generation* (address), McCorquodale & Co., 1945; *Conservatism after 1945* (extracts from speeches), A. P. Tayler & Co., 1946; *Forward From the Industrial Charter*, Conservative Political Centre, 1948; *About Property-Owning Democracy: Some Facts and Ideas for Discussion Groups* (booklet), Conservative Political Centre, 1948; *The New Conservatism* (speech), Conservative & Unionist Central Office (London), 1951; *Halfway to Faith*, Westminster Press, 1966; *Life and Politics: A Moral Diagnosis*, Longmans, Green, 1967; *On Collecting*, Longmans, Green, 1968; *Politics and the Quality of Life*, Conservative Political Centre, 1970.

AVOCATIONAL INTERESTS: Collecting early English water colors and books on travel and exploration.

* * *

EDELSTEIN, J. M. 1924-

PERSONAL: Born July 31, 1924, in Baltimore, Md.; son of Joseph (a businessman) and Irene (Schwartz) Edelstein; married Eleanor Rockwell (a writer and editor), November 5, 1950; children: Paul, Nathaniel. *Education:* Johns Hopkins University, A.B., 1947, graduate study, 1947-49; University of Florence, further graduate study, 1949-50; University of Michigan, M.A. in L.S., 1953. *Politics:* Liberal Democrat. *Religion:* Jewish. *Office:* National Gallery of Art, Washington, D.C. 20565.

CAREER: Library of Congress, Washington, D.C., assistant chief of Rare Book Division, 1955-62; University of California, Los Angeles, bibliographer for medieval and Renaissance studies, 1962-64; New York University, New York, N.Y., librarian for special collections, 1964-66; University of California, Los Angeles, humanities bibliographer and lecturer in bibliography, 1966-72; National Gallery of Art, Washington, D.C., chief librarian, 1972—. President of board of directors of Crossroads School, 1970-72; member of board of directors of Santa Monica Canyon Civic Association, 1968-72. *Military service:* U.S. Army, 1943-46.

MEMBER: Bibliographical Society of America, American Library Association, Association of College and Research Libraries, Grolier Club, Bibliographical Society (London), Authors Club (London), Rounce and Coffin Club (Los Angeles), Phi Beta Kappa. *Awards, honors:* Fulbright grant, 1949-50, for study in Italy.

WRITINGS: A Bibliographical Checklist of the Writings of Thornton Wilder, Library, Yale University, 1959; *A Garland for Jake Zeitlin . . .*, Dahlstrom & Marks, 1967; *The Library of Don Cameron Allen . . .*, Library, University of California (San Diego), 1968; (contributor) *Influences on California Printing*, Clark Memorial Library, University of California (Los Angeles), 1970; *Wallace Stevens: A Descriptive Bibliography*, University of Pittsburgh Press, 1974. "News and Notes" editor of *Papers of the Bibliographical Society of America*, 1964—.

WORK IN PROGRESS: A history and bibliography of the Banyan Press; a bibliography of the works of Robert Lowell; a study of books in paintings and as parts of sculptures.

* * *

EDGERTON, Harold Eugene 1903-

PERSONAL: Born April 6, 1903, in Fremont, Neb.; son of Frank Eugene (a lawyer) and Mary (Coe) Edgerton; married Esther May Garrett (a teacher), February 25, 1927; children: MaryLou (Mrs. Charles Dixon), Robert Frank, William Eugene. *Education:* University of Nebraska, B.S., 1925; Massachusetts Institute of Technology, M.A., 1927, D.Sc., 1931. *Home:* 100 Memorial Dr., Cambridge, Mass. 02142. *Office:* Department of Electrical Engineering, Room 4-405, Massachusetts Institute of Technology, Cambridge, Mass. 02139.

CAREER: Massachusetts Institute of Technology, Cambridge, instructor, 1928-32, assistant professor, 1932-38, associate professor, 1938-48, professor of electrical measurement, 1948-66, professor emeritus, 1966—. Founding partner of E.G. & G., Inc., 1933, vice-president, 1947-66, chairman of board of directors, 1954-66. Member of Woods Hole Oceanographic Institution and Boston Museum of Science.

MEMBER: Institute of Electrical and Electronic Engineers (fellow), Photographic Society of America (fellow), Society of Motion Picture and Television Engineers (fellow), Academy of Applied Science, Academy of Underwater Arts and Sciences, American Academy of Arts and Sciences, American Philosophical Society, Marine Technology Society, National Academy of Engineering, National Academy of Sciences, Society of Photographic Engineers, Explorers Club, Royal Photographic Society of Great Britain, New England Aquarium, Photographers Association of New England, Boston Camera Club (honorary member), Boston Sea Rovers (honorary member), Fairhaven Whalers Club (honorary member), Sigma Xi, Eta Kappa Nu (eminent member), Sigma Tau.

AWARDS, HONORS: Medal from Royal Photographic Society of London, 1936; Potts Medal from Franklin Institute, 1941; Medal of Freedom from U.S. Government, 1946; D.Eng. from University of Nebraska, 1948; M.Photography from Photographers Association of America, 1949; Joseph A. Sprague Memorial Award from National Press Photographic Association, 1949; Franklin L.

Burr prize from National Geographic Society, 1953; George W. Harris achievement award from Photographers Association of America, 1959; Boston Sea Rovers award, 1961; Gordon Y. Billard Award from Massachusetts Institute of Technology, 1962; E.I. duPont gold medal from Society of Motion Picture and Television Engineers, 1962; Silver Progress Award from Royal Photographic Society of Great Britain, 1964; Morris E. Leeds award from Institute of Electrical and Electronic Engineers, 1965; Richardson Medal from Optical Society of America, 1968; John Oliver LaGorce gold medal from National Geographic Society, 1968; LL.D. from Doane College and from University of South Carolina, both 1969; Alan Gordon memorial award from Society of Photo-Optical Instrumentation Engineers, 1969; Albert A. Michelson medal from Franklin Institute, 1969; NOGI Award from Underwater Society of America, 1973; Holley medal from American Society of Mechanical Engineers, 1973; national medal of science from President of the United States, 1973; and other awards for engineering and photography.

WRITINGS: (With J. R. Killian) *Flash: Seeing the Unseen,* Branford, 1939, 2nd edition, 1954; *Electronic Flash: Strobe,* McGraw, 1970. Contributor of about one hundred twenty-five articles to technical journals.

* * *

EDGERTON, Robert B(reckenridge) 1931-

PERSONAL: Born November 28, 1931, in Maywood, Ill.; married, 1966. *Education:* University of California, Los Angeles, B.A. (with highest honors), 1956, Ph.D., 1960. *Home:* 319 Sumac Lane, Santa Monica, Calif. 90402. *Office:* Neuropsychiatric Institute, University of California, 760 Westwood Plaza, Los Angeles, Calif. 90024.

CAREER: U.S. Air Force, 1951-59; Pacific State Hospital, Pomona, Calif., research anthropologist, 1960-61; University of California, Los Angeles, Neuropsychiatric Institute, research anthropologist, 1961-62, instructor in residence, 1962-64, assistant professor in residence, 1964-68, associate professor in residence, 1968-72, professor in residence of cultural anthropology, departments of psychiatry and anthropology, 1972—, research social scientist, 1962-68, research specialist, 1968—, coordinator of socio-behavioral studies, Mental Retardation Program, 1970—. Visiting fellow at Social Science Research Institute, University of Hawaii, 1970. Consultant to National Science Foundation.

MEMBER: American Anthropological Association (fellow), Society for Applied Anthropology, American Association on Mental Deficiency, American Ethnological Society, Southwestern Anthropological Association, Sigma Xi.

WRITINGS: *The Cloak of Competence*, University of California Press, 1967; (editor with Stanley C. Plog, and contributor) *Changing Perspectives in Mental Illness*, Holt, 1969; (with Craig MacAndrew) *Drunken Comportment: A Social Explanation*, Aldine, 1969; (author of foreword) Jerry Jacobs, *The Search for Help: A Study of Careers of Mentally Retarded Children*, Brunner, 1969; *The Individual in Cultural Adaptation: A Study of Four East African Societies*, University of California Press, 1971; *Deviant Behavior and Cultural Theory*, Addison-Wesley, 1973; (with L. L. Langness) *Methods and Styles in the Study of Culture*, Chandler & Sharp, 1974.

Contributor: David Krech and others, *Individual in Society: A Textbook of Social Psychology*, McGraw, 1962; Y. A. Cohen, editor, *Man in Adaptation: The Cultural Present*, Aldine, 1968; P. K. Manning, editor, *Research and Theories in Social Deviance*, Lippincott, 1969; Philip K. Bock, editor, *Culture Shock*, Knopf, 1970; Lowell D. Holmes, editor, *Readings in General Anthropology*, Ronald, 1970; H. C. Haywood, editor, *Social-Cultural Aspects of Mental Retardation*, Appleton, 1970; Raoul Naroll and Ronald Cohen, editors, *Handbook of Method in Cultural Anthropology*, Natural History Press, 1970; Francis L. K. Hsu, editor, *Kinship and Culture*, Aldine, 1970; C. Whalen, editor, *Survey of Social Ecology Part I, Human Behavior: Development and Change*, Volume II, Associated Educational Services, 1971; James P. Spradley and David W. McCurdy, editors, *Readings in Contemporary Anthropology*, Little, Brown, 1971; Y. A. Cohen, editor, *Man in Adaptation: The Psychosocial Interface*, Aldine, 1971; Iago Galdston, editor, *The Interface Between Psychiatry and Anthropology*, Brunner, 1971; H. L. Cordova, editor, *Perspectives on Mexican-American Studies*, Holt, 1971; A. K. Romney, editor, *You and Others: An Anthropological Perspective*, Winthrop, 1972; Eliot Freidson and Judith Lorber, editors, *Medical Men and Their Work*, Aldine-Atherton, 1972; Harry C. Bredemeier and Jackson Toby, editors, *Social Problems in America*, 2nd edition (Edgerton did not contribute to earlier edition), Wiley, 1972; James F. Short, Jr. and Marvin E. Wolfgang, editors, *Collective Violence*, Aldine-Atherton, 1972; Felix de la Cruz and Gerald LaVeck, editors, *Human Sexuality and Mental Retardation*, Brunner, 1973; Laura Nader and T. Maretzki, editors, *Cultural Illness and Health: Essays in Human Adaptation*, American Anthropological Association, 1973; Robert A. LeVine, editor, *Culture and Personality*, Aldine, 1974; B. P. Hammond, editor, *Cultural and Social Anthropology: Selected Readings*, Macmillan, in press; H. Jerison, editor, *Human Intelligence*, Appleton, in press. Contributor to other symposia, *Encyclopaedia Britannica Yearbook*, and to anthropology, eugenics, medical, and nursing journals.

Member of editorial board, *Ethos*; consulting editor, *American Journal of Mental Deficiency*.

* * *

EDWARDS, George 1914-

PERSONAL: Born August 6, 1914, in Dallas, Tex.; son of George Clifton (a lawyer) and Octavia (Nichols) Edwards; married Margaret McConnell, April 10, 1939; children: George Clifton III, James McConnell. *Education:* Southern Methodist University, B.A., 1933; Harvard University, M.A., 1934; Detroit College of Law, J.D., 1944. *Politics:* Democrat. *Religion:* Episcopalian. *Home:* 4057 Egbert, Cincinnati, Ohio 45220. *Office:* U.S. Court of Appeals, 622 U.S. Courthouse, Cincinnati, Ohio 45202.

CAREER: League for Industrial Democracy, secretary, 1934-35; Kelsey-Hayes Wheel Co., Detroit, Mich., production worker, 1936; United Automobile Workers-Congress of Industrial Organizations (UAW-CIO), Detroit, representative, 1937, director of welfare department, 1938-39; Detroit Housing Commission, Detroit, director and secretary, 1940-41; member of Common Council of Detroit, 1941-49, president, 1945-49; admitted to Michigan Bar, 1944; Edwards & Bohn, Detroit, lawyer, 1946-50; Rothe, Marston, Edwards & Bohn, Detroit, lawyer, 1950-51; Wayne County Juvenile Court, Detroit, probate judge in charge, 1951-54; Third Judicial Circuit (Wayne County), Detroit, circuit judge, 1954-56; Supreme Court of Michigan, Lansing, Mich., associate justice, 1956-62; commissioner of police in Detroit, 1962-63; U.S. Court of Appeals,

Sixth Circuit, Cincinnati, Ohio, circuit judge, 1963—. Chairman of Thirteenth Congressional District Democratic Party (Wayne County), 1950-51; chairman of committee for administration of criminal laws of Judicial Conference of the United States, 1966-70; member of National Committee for Reform of Federal Criminal Laws, 1967-71. *Military service:* U.S. Army, Infantry, 1943-46; became second lieutenant.

MEMBER: Federal Bar Association, American Bar Association, American Law Institute, American Judicature Society, Institute of Judicial Administration, Council of Judges, National Council on Crime and Delinquency, State Bar of Michigan, American Legion, Veterans of Foreign Wars, Phi Beta Kappa, Kappa Sigma. *Awards, honors:* Workmen's Circle award for community work for social progress, 1949; Veterans of Foreign Wars award for outstanding achievements in juvenile rehabilitation, 1953; Jewish War Veterans Americanism award, 1953; judiciary award from Association of Federal Investigators, 1971.

WRITINGS: (With Sol Rubin, Henry Weihofen, and Simon Rosenzweig) *Law of Criminal Correction*, West Publishing, 1963; *Police on the Urban Frontier*, Institute of Human Relations Press, 1968; *Pioneer at Law*, Norton, 1974. Contributor of articles on crime and delinquency to professional journals.

* * *

EDWARDS, O(tis) C(arl), Jr. 1928-

PERSONAL: Born June 15, 1928, in Bienville, La.; son of Otis Carl (in personnel) and Margaret (Hutchinson) Edwards; married Jane Hanna Trufant (a teacher), February 19, 1957; children: Carl Lee, Samuel Adams Trufant, Louise Reynes. *Education:* Centenary College, A.B., 1949; General Theological Seminary, S.T.B., 1952; Cambridge University, graduate study, 1952-53; Southern Methodist University, S.T.M., 1962; University of Chicago, M.A., 1963, Ph.D., 1971. *Politics:* "Liberal to radical Democrat." *Office:* Seabury-Western Theological Seminary, 2122 Sheridan Rd., Evanston, Ill. 60201.

CAREER: Ordained Episcopal priest, 1954; served as minister in Morgan City, La., 1957-60, Waxahachie, Tex., 1960-61, and Chicago, Ill., 1961-63; Wabash College, Crawfordsville, Ind., instructor in religion, 1963-64; Nashotah House, Nashotah, Wis., assistant professor, 1964-69, associate professor, 1969-72, professor of New Testament, 1972-74, sub-dean, 1973-74, acting dean, 1973-74; Seabury-Western Theological Seminary, Evanston, Ill., dean and president, 1974—. *Military service:* U.S. Naval Reserve, chaplain, 1957-67; became lieutenant commander.

MEMBER: Canadian Biblical Society, Society of Biblical Literature, American Academy of Religion, Catholic Biblical Society, Chicago Society of Biblical Research, Chicago Area Patristics Seminar. *Awards, honors:* Christian Research Foundation grant, 1963, for translation of Tatian's *Oratio*; Mystery Writers of America special award, 1965, for "Gospel According to 007"; Episcopal Church Executive Council fellowship, 1971.

WRITINGS: (Editorial assistant, and contributor) *Westminster Dictionary of Church History*, Westminster Press, 1971; *How It All Began: Origins of the Christian Church*, Seabury, 1973; (with Merrill Abbey) *Proclamation, Epiphany: A Series*, Fortress, 1974; *The Living and Active Word: One Way to Preach from the Bible Today*, Seabury, 1975. Contributor to *Living Church* and *Journal of Religion*. Book review editor of *Anglican Theological Review*, 1971—.

WORK IN PROGRESS: Barbarian Philosophy: Tatian and the Greek Paideia.

AVOCATIONAL INTERESTS: Travel, camping, photography, Blue Grass music, mystery stories.

* * *

EHRE, Milton 1933-

PERSONAL: Surname is pronounced Air; born April 15, 1933, in New York, N.Y.; son of Isaac (a printer) and Sylvia (Weissberg) Ehre; married Roberta Greene, June 9, 1963; children: Joelle, Julie Anne. *Education:* City College of New York (now City College of the City University of New York), B.A., 1955; Columbia University, M.A., 1966, Ph.D., 1970. *Home:* 535 Forest Ave., Oak Park, Ill. 60302. *Office:* Department of Slavic Languages, University of Chicago, Chicago, Ill. 60637.

CAREER: New York City Board of Education, New York, N.Y., teacher of English, 1956-63; University of Chicago, Chicago, Ill., assistant professor, 1967-72, associate professor of Russian literature, 1972—. *Military service:* U.S. Army Reserve, 1957-63; active duty, 1957. *Member:* American Association of Teachers of Slavic and East European Languages.

WRITINGS: Oblomov and His Creator: The Life and Art of Ivan Gomcharov, Princeton University Press, 1973. Contributor to *Slavic Review*, *Slavonic and East European Review*, and *Chicago Review*.

WORK IN PROGRESS: A book on Shchedrin (pseudonym of Mikhail Saltykov).

* * *

EHRENPREIS, Anne Henry 1927-

PERSONAL: Born April 19, 1927, in Boston, Mass.; daughter of Richard and Dorothy (Miller) Henry; married Irvin Ehrenpreis (a professor), August 19, 1961; children: David Henry. *Education:* Bryn Mawr College, A.B., 1948; St. Hugh's College, Oxford, B.Litt., 1953. *Home:* 1830 Fendall Ave., Charlottesville, Va. 22903.

CAREER: Harvard College Library, Cambridge, Mass., bibliographer, 1953-60. *Member:* Modern Language Association of America, Bibliographical Society of University of Virginia (member of council).

WRITINGS—Editor: *The Literary Ballad*, Edward Arnold, 1966; Charlotte Smith, *The Old Manor House*, Oxford University Press, 1969; Smith, *Emmeline*, Oxford University Press, 1971; Jane Austen, *Northanger Abbey*, Penguin, 1972.

WORK IN PROGRESS: Editing *Travel Diary of Henry Arthur Bright*.

* * *

EHRLICH, Nathaniel J(oseph) 1940-

PERSONAL: Born July 26, 1940, in Boston, Mass.; son of David (a jeweler) and Rose (Brown) Ehrlich; married Elizabeth Angeline Waides, June 29, 1963 (divorced October 2, 1972); married Mary Jean Spens, December 27, 1972 (separated); children: (first marriage) Nicholas Graham, Emily Diane. *Education:* Harvard University, A.B. (cum laude), 1961; University of Michigan, Ph.D., 1964. *Politics:* "Left-conservative." *Religion:* Taoist. *Home:* 2131 Glencoe Hills Dr., Ann Arbor, Mich. 48104. *Office:* Center for Forensic Psychiatry, University of Michigan, Box 2060, Ann Arbor, Mich. 48104.

CAREER: University of Michigan, Ann Arbor, research psychologist, 1964-67; City College of the City University of New York, New York, N.Y., assistant professor of psychology, 1967-69; University of Michigan, Flint, associate professor of psychology, 1969-74; University of Michigan, Ann Arbor, associate professor of psychology and research director of Center for Forensic Psychiatry, 1974—. Director of Forensic Consultants, Inc.

WRITINGS: *Psychology and Contemporary Affairs*, Brooks-Cole, 1972. Contributor of about twenty articles to academic journals.

SIDELIGHTS: Ehrlich writes: "Perhaps I'm not qualified to comment here, since my only published book thus far has been a financial disaster. . . . I have worked as a laborer, in a hospital kitchen, and I can honestly say that, given the opportunity, I would prefer writing to laboring but I'd rather not do either. My primary vocational interest involves interpersonal relations—athletic competition, sexual interchange, and social structures—as they affect one's physical being.

"Unlike most authors, I have made my acquaintance and my peace with my own death, and I have little desire to attempt to convince others that they, too, can find their own peace, their own life, their own death."

* * *

EHRLICH, Walter 1921-

PERSONAL: Born December 20, 1921, in St. Louis, Mo.; son of Simon Joseph (a merchant) and Gertrude (Gellman) Ehrlich; married Sylvia Trattner (a teacher), February 24, 1946; children: Kenneth Ellis, Susan Dale, Steven Mark, Jerrold Richard. *Education:* Washington University, St. Louis, Mo., B.S.Ed., 1942, M.A., 1947, Ph.D., 1950. *Politics:* Liberal. *Religion:* Jewish. *Home:* 9036 Watsonia Court, St. Louis, Mo. 63132. *Office:* Department of History, University of Missouri, St. Louis, Mo. 63121.

CAREER: High school history teacher in University City, Mo., 1950-59, 1959-60; United Hebrew Temple, St. Louis, Mo., superintendent of education, 1959-60; high school history teacher in St. Louis County, Mo., 1961-69; University of Missouri-St. Louis, associate professor of history and education, 1969—. Director of American Freedoms Summer Institute at Washington University, 1962-67. *Military service:* U.S. Army, 1942-46; became first lieutenant. *Member:* American Historical Association, Organization of American Historians, American Society for Legal History, Association of History Educators, National Council for the Social Studies.

WRITINGS: *Presidential Impeachment: An American Dilemma*, Forum Press, 1974. Contributor to *Journal of American History, Missouri Historical Review, Journal of Negro History, Journal of Education*, and *Improving College and University Teaching.*

WORK IN PROGRESS: *The Dred Scott Case*; research for a biography of constitutional activist Paul W. Preisler.

* * *

EIBY, George 1918-

PERSONAL: Born September 17, 1918, in Wellington, New Zealand. *Education:* University of New Zealand, M.Sc., 1950. *Religion:* Church of England. *Home:* 2 Shortland St., Khandallah, Wellington-4, New Zealand. *Office:* Seismological Observatory, P.O. Box 8005, Wellington, New Zealand.

CAREER: New Zealand Department of Scientific and Industrial Research, Wellington, seismologist, 1939—. Has made radio and television appearances; seismological consultant on Southeast Asia to UNESCO. *Military service:* Royal New Zealand Air Force, 1942-46. *Member:* Royal Astronomical Society of New Zealand (president), New Zealand Federation of Film Societies (vice-president), Royal Astronomical Society (London), American Geophysical Union, Seismological Society of America. *Awards, honors:* Fellowship from Royal Astronomical Society of New Zealand, 1969.

WRITINGS: *Earthquakes*, Muller, 1957, 2nd edition, 1967, published in the United States as *About Earthquakes*, Harper, 1957; *This Earth of Ours*, New Zealand Education Department, 1958; *Writing in New Zealand: The Scientists*, New Zealand Education Department, 1961; *The Marlborough Earthquakes of 1848*, New Zealand Department of Scientific and Industrial Research, in press.

Author of three-act play, "Taurus Opposing," produced in Wellington at Unity Theatre, 1965. Contributor of articles and reviews to journals, including *New Zealand's Heritage, New Zealand Nature Heritage, Southern Stars, New Zealand Listener*, and *Landfall.* Editor of *Southern Stars* (journal of Royal Astronomical Society of New Zealand), 1958-73.

WORK IN PROGRESS: *The Latter Rain*, a novel.

SIDELIGHTS: Eiby has been involved in more than thirty productions in amateur theater as designer and producer, especially at Unity Theatre in Wellington. He is an authority on the history of theater architecture and stage design, and a pioneer of the film society movement. *Avocational interests:* Renaissance and baroque music, playing the recorder, travel (Europe, Russia, Southeast Asia, Japan, Southwest Pacific).

* * *

EINSTEIN, Stanley 1934-

PERSONAL: Born July 5, 1934, in New York, N.Y.; son of Abe (a millinery worker) and Rebecca (Siskind) Einstein; married Sarah Wenger (an early-childhood specialist), August 31, 1958; children: Tamar, Joshua. *Education:* City College (now City College of the City University of New York), B.A. (cum laude), 1957, M.A. (social psychology), 1958; New School for Social Research, graduate study, 1958; University of Pennsylvania, M.A. (clinical psychology), 1960; Yeshiva University, Ph.D., 1964; also studied at Institute for Research in Hypnosis, 1964. *Home:* 113-41 East Talpiot, Jerusalem, Israel. *Office:* Institute for the Study of Drug Misuse, Inc., 111 Fifth Ave., New York, N.Y. 10003.

CAREER: University of Pennsylvania, Philadelphia, psychodiagnostician in psychological clinic of University Hospital, 1960; New York Clinic for Mental Hygiene, New York, N.Y., psychology trainee, 1960-61; private practice in psychology, 1961—. Clinical and research psychologist at Riverside Hospital, 1960-63; clinical psychologist, research associate, and assistant professor of psychiatry at New York Medical College, 1963-67; executive director and founder of Institute for the Study of Drug Addiction, 1963—; executive director, Institute for the Study of Drug Misuse, 1965—; executive director and director of department of research, New York Council on Alcoholism (ACCEPT), 1967-69; lecturer at New York University, 1968; adjunct associate professor at Fordham University, 1969-70; assistant professor at College of Medicine and Dentistry of New Jersey at Newark, 1969-71, associate professor, 1971-73, associate director of Division of Drug Abuse, 1969-73, coordinator of drug abuse education, 1969-73; associate professor, Department of Criminology, Bar Illan University, Ramat Gan, Israel, 1974—. Developed and moderated "Drugs and You," WOR-Radio, and "Drug Forum," public service radio series; correspondent, "As It Happens," Canadian Broadcasting Corp., 1973—; has appeared on national and international television programs. Has participated in international conferences. Consultant to government, business, and mass media groups in the United States and abroad.

MEMBER: International Council on Alcoholism and Other Addictions (member of executive board), American Psychological Association, American Public Health Association, American Criminological Association, Institut za Proucavamje i Suzbijanje Alkoholizma (Yugoslavia; foreign member), New York Society for Clinical Psychologists.

WRITINGS: The Use and Misuse of Drugs: A Social Dilemma, Wadsworth, 1970; (editor) *Methadone Maintenance*, Dekker, 1971; (editor with Max Allan) *Student Drug Surveys*, Baywood Publishing, 1972; *Going Beyond Drugs*, Pergamon, in press; (editor with Louis Miller) *Drug Abuse and Clinical Issues*, S. Karger, in press.

Author of "Drug Forum," a weekly column for *Newark News*, 1972, and *Star Ledger*, 1972-73.

Founder and co-editor of "The Non-Medical Use of Drugs," a monograph series published annually by Institute for the Study of Drug Misuse, 1972—. Contributor to professional journals. Editor and founder of *International Journal of the Addictions*, 1966—; co-founder and co-editor of *Drug Forum*, 1971—; co-founder and executive editor of *Altered States of Consciousness*, 1973—. Addictions editor for Marcel Dekker, 1968—; abstract editor for alcohols and drug addictions for *Excerpta Criminilogica*, 1964-66; member of editorial board of *Caveat* (monthly newsletter), 1973—. Book reviewer for *Journal of the American Public Health Association*, 1970—; manuscript reviewer for *New England Journal of Medicine*, 1970—.

* * *

EISNER, Victor 1921-

PERSONAL: Born December 5, 1921, in Redbank, N.J.; son of Victor and Helene (Monsey) Eisner; married Rosemarie Lingg; children: Julie, Lorenz. *Education:* Stanford University, B.A., 1946; Harvard University, M.D., 1950; University of California, M.P.H., 1963. *Home:* 619 Corbett St., San Francisco, Calif. 94114. *Office:* School of Public Health, University of California, Berkeley, Calif. 94720.

CAREER: University Hospitals, Pittsburgh, Pa., intern, 1950-51; Johns Hopkins Hospital, Baltimore, Md., intern, 1951-52, fellow in pediatric cardiology, 1952-53, assistant resident, 1953-54, fellow pediatrician, 1954-57; Family and Children's Society, Baltimore, Md., medical director, 1957-59; Johns Hopkins University, Baltimore, Md., fellow at School of Hygiene, 1958-59; Kaiser Research Institute, Oakland, Calif., pediatrician, 1959-60; Kaiser Hospital, San Francisco, Calif., pediatrician, 1959-62; University of California, Medical School, San Francisco, clinical instructor, 1959-61, assistant clinical professor of pediatrics, 1961-67; University of California, School of Public Health, Berkeley, lecturer, 1963-64, associate clinical professor, 1964-70, clinical professor of pediatrics, 1970—. Member of consulting staff, Children's Hospital Medical Center, Oakland, 1964—; volunteer physician, Haight-Ashbury Medical Clinic, 1968-70. Member of board of directors, Youth for Service, San Francisco, 1963-71, vice-president, 1967-71; member of board of directors, Community Streetwork Center, San Francisco, 1971—, president, 1971-73. *Military service:* U.S. Army, Field Artillery, 1941-45; served in Europe; became lieutenant.

MEMBER: American Academy of Pediatrics (fellow), American Public Health Association (fellow), Society for Adolescent Medicine, Association of Teachers of Maternal and Child Health, American School Health Association, Public Health League of California, Alameda-Contra Costa Counties Medical Association, Phi Beta Kappa, Delta Omega.

WRITINGS: (Editor with Daniel Bergsma and Robert E. Sharkey) *Human Genetics*, National Foundation (New York), 1968; *The Delinquency Label: The Epidemiology of Juvenile Delinquency*, Random House, 1969; (contributor) E. J. Hart and W. C. Sechrist, editors, *Dynamics of Wellness*, Wadsworth, 1970; (with Lawrence B. Callan) *The Dimensions of School Health*, C.C Thomas, 1974; (contributor) Helen M. Wallace and others, editors, *Maternal and Child Health*, C.C Thomas, 1974. Contributor to *Advances in Pediatrics* and other symposia. Contributor of about forty articles to medical and public health journals.

* * *

EITZEN, D(avid) Stanley 1934-

PERSONAL: Born August 4, 1934, in Glendale, Calif.; son of David D. (a psychologist) and Amanda (Heidebrecht) Eitzen; married Florine Kay Voran, May 29, 1956; children: Keith, Michael, Kelly. *Education:* Bethel College, Newton, Kan., A.B., 1956; College of Emporia, M.S., 1962; University of Kansas, M.A., 1966, Ph.D., 1968. *Politics:* Democrat. *Religion:* Mennonite. *Home:* 1756 Concord, Fort Collins, Colo. 80521. *Office:* Department of Sociology, Colorado State University, Fort Collins, Colo. 80521.

CAREER: Menninger Foundation, Topeka, Kan., recreational therapist, 1956-58; public school teacher of social science in Galva, Kan., 1958-60, and in Turner, Kan., 1960-65; University of Kansas, Lawrence, instructor, 1967-68, assistant professor, 1968-72, associate professor of sociology, 1972-74; Colorado State University, Fort Collins, professor of sociology, 1974—. *Military service:* Alternative service in lieu of military, 1956-58. *Member:* International Sociological Association, International Committee for the Sociology of Sport, American Sociological Association, Society for the Study of Social Problems, Southwestern Social Science Association, Midwest Sociological Society.

WRITINGS: Social Structure and Social Problems in America, Allyn & Bacon, 1974. Contributor of more than twenty-five articles to professional journals.

WORK IN PROGRESS: Sport in America, for Free Press; *The Sociology of Political Power, Behavior, and Change*, Allyn & Bacon; *Introduction to Social Problems and Individual Deviance*.

* * *

ELISON, George 1937-

PERSONAL: Born January 6, 1937, in Kaunas, Lithuania; naturalized U.S. citizen in 1955; son of Jurgis (a professor of zoology) Elisonas and Ona (a physician; maiden name, Kunskaite) Elisoniene; married Nakabayashi Toshiko, 1961; children: William, Antony. *Education:* University of

Michigan, B.A., 1957, M.A., 1959; Harvard University, Ph.D., 1969. *Home:* 249 Church St., Oakland, Me. 04963. *Office:* East Asian Research Center, Harvard University, 1737 Cambridge St., Cambridge, Mass. 02138.

CAREER: Colby College, Waterville, Me., instructor, 1964-66, assistant professor, 1966-73, associate professor of Japanese history and literature, 1973—; Harvard University, East Asian Research Center, Cambridge, Mass., research fellow, 1970, 1972, associate in research, 1972—. Visiting assistant professor and research associate, Indiana University, 1969; research associate and visiting professor, Kyoto University, 1971-72. *Military service:* U.S. Army, Artillery, 1957-59; became lieutenant. *Awards, honors:* Woodrow Wilson fellow, 1957; Ford Foundation foreign area training fellow, 1961-64; National Endowment for the Humanities fellow, 1970-71.

WRITINGS: Deus Destroyed: The Image of Christianity in Early Modern Japan, Harvard University Press, 1973; (with Caryn Callahan) *Osome and Hisamatsu: Their Amorous History, Read All About It*, Sophia University Press, in press. Contributor to *Monumenta Nipponica, Journal of Asian History, Journal of Japanese Studies*, and *Harvard Journal of Asiatic Studies.*

WORK IN PROGRESS: Research on the history of sixteenth and seventeenth century Japan, on the history of the city of Kyoto, and on the history and literature of the Japanese popular theatre.

SIDELIGHTS: Elison is competent in Castilian, Chinese, French, German, Italian, Japanese, Latin, Lithuanian, Portuguese, and Russian. *Avocational interests:* Travel.

* * *

ELKIN, Judith Laikin 1928-

PERSONAL: Born June 7, 1928, in Baltimore, Md.; daughter of Benjamin (a manufacturer) and Anna (Golomb) Laikin; married Sol Elkin (a professor of education and labor arbitrator), August 5, 1960; children: Alissa, Susannah. *Education:* University of Michigan, B.A., 1948, further study, 1971—; Columbia University, M.A., 1950; London School of Economics and Political Science, University of London, graduate study, 1957. *Home:* 1200 Michigan Ave., Albion, Mich. 49224. *Office:* Albion College, Albion, Mich. 49224.

CAREER: Foreign Service Officer with U.S. Department of State, serving as third secretary of embassy in New Delhi, India, 1952-54, and vice-consul in London, England, 1954-56; Wayne State University, Detroit, Mich., assistant professor of political science, 1964-68; Albion College, Albion, Mich., assistant professor of history, 1969—. *Member:* Conference on Latin American History, Association for Jewish Studies, Phi Alpha Theta. *Awards, honors:* Avery Hopwood Literary Awards, 1947, 1948; Phi Alpha Theta award in history, 1974.

WRITINGS: Background: Indochina (pamphlet), U.S. Department of State, 1951; *Background: Iran* (pamphlet), U.S. Department of State, 1951; *Report on the United Nations* (pamphlet), U.S. Department of State, 1952; *The United States in the United Nations* (pamphlet), North Central Association of Colleges and Secondary Schools, 1960; *Understanding Israel*, Laidlaw Brothers, 1962; *A People-to-People School and Classroom Exchange* (pamphlet), North Central Association of Colleges and Secondary Schools, 1962; *Krishna Smiled: Assignment to Southeast Asia*, Wayne State University Press, 1972. Ghost writer for political and business people.

Author of foreign news analysis column in *Detroit Free Press*, 1958-62, and nationally distributed by Spadea Syndicate. Contributor to *Reporter*, *Travel*, and *Congress Weekly*.

WORK IN PROGRESS: Research for a book on the Jewish dimension of Latin American history in modern times.

* * *

ELLIS, B(yron) Robert 1940-

PERSONAL: Born November 7, 1940, in Hartford, Conn.; son of Byron Orville (a lithographer) and Ruth (Field) Ellis; married Carolyn Colby (a music teacher), August 24, 1963; children: Scott Colby, Margaret Ruth. *Education:* Attended Connecticut Central State College, 1958-59; University of New Hampshire, B.A., 1962. *Residence:* Dover, N.H. 03820. *Office:* University of New Hampshire, Thompson Hall, Durham, N.H. 03824.

CAREER: Public high school teacher of mathematics in Exeter, N.H., 1962-63, in Wells, Me., 1963-67, and in Durham, N.H., 1967-69; University of New Hampshire, Durham, instructor in computer science in department of mathematics, 1969-74, assistant registrar, 1974—. Programmer and consultant for Blackberry Falls Project. President of Garrison Players, Inc., 1972-74.

WRITINGS: (With James W. Estes) *Elements of Computer Science*, Canfield Press, 1973.

WORK IN PROGRESS: A "society and computers" text for the average person, for interest and background alone.

* * *

ELLIS, Joseph J(ohn) 1943-

PERSONAL: Born July 18, 1943, in Washington, D.C.; son of Joseph and Jeanette (Sigafoose) Ellis; married Antonia Woods (a teacher), June 27, 1970. *Education:* College of William and Mary, A.B., 1965; Yale University, M.A., 1967, Ph.D., 1969. *Politics:* Skeptic. *Religion:* Atheist. *Home:* 144 North Main St., South Hadley, Mass. 01075. *Office:* Department of History, Mount Holyoke College, South Hadley, Mass. 01075.

CAREER: U.S. Military Academy, West Point, N.Y., assistant professor of history, 1969-72; Mount Holyoke College, South Hadley, Mass., assistant professor of history, 1972—. *Military service:* U.S. Army Reserve, 1965-72; became captain. *Member:* American Historical Society, Institute of Early American History, Inter-Service Seminar, Phi Beta Kappa. *Awards, honors:* Woodrow Wilson fellowship, 1965-66; National Endowment for the Humanities fellowship, 1974.

WRITINGS: The New England Mind in Transition: A Life of Samuel Johnson, 1696-1772, Yale University Press, 1973; (with Robert Moore) *School for Soldiers: West Point and the Profession of Arms*, Oxford University Press, 1974.

WORK IN PROGRESS: Editing *Essays on the American Enlightenment*, publication expected in 1976.

* * *

ELSON, Lawrence M(cClellan) 1935-

PERSONAL: Born October 10, 1935, in Pasadena, Calif.; son of Eugene M. (an attorney) and Edith (Lowe) Elson; divorced; children: Christopher Lowe. *Education:* Attended University of Redlands, 1953-55; University of California, Berkeley, A.B., 1963, Ph.D., 1968. *Home and office:* 4227 Ulloa, San Francisco, Calif. 94116.

CAREER: City College of San Francisco, San Francisco, Calif., instructor in human anatomy, 1966-68; Baylor College of Medicine, Houston, Tex., assistant professor of anatomy, 1968-72; Rice University, Houston, Tex., lecturer in anatomy, 1969-72; University of California School of Medicine, San Francisco, lecturer in anatomy, 1972-74; City College of San Francisco, instructor in anatomy, 1972—. Lecturer and laboratory instructor, Texas Women's University School of Physical Therapy, 1969-70; lecturer for Anatomy for Attorneys series, Medi-Legal Institute of Southern California, 1973—; consultant in personal injury, malpractice, and workmen's compensation litigation; member of Anatomical State Board of Texas, 1969-72. *Military service:* U.S. Navy, 1955-60; helicopter pilot. U.S. Naval Air Reserve, 1962—; present rank, commander. *Member:* Naval Reserve Association, Faculty Association of California Community Colleges, Sigma Xi, Kiwanis International.

WRITINGS: It's Your Body, with laboratory manual, McGraw, 1975.

WORK IN PROGRESS: An anatomy and physiology text, completion expected in 1976; an introductory text on the human nervous system.

* * *

ELTON, Edwin J(oel) 1939-

PERSONAL: Born October 5, 1939, in Milwaukee, Wis.; son of Edwin Joel (a computer manager) and Kathryn (Davis) Elton; married Diane Ramsey, February 10, 1964; children: Annette, Edwin, Kathryn, John. *Education:* Ohio Wesleyan University, B.S., 1961; Carnegie-Mellon University, M.S., 1965, Ph.D., 1970. *Home:* 330 South Pleasant Ave., Ridgewood, N.J. 07450. *Office:* Department of Finance, New York University, 100 Trinity Pl., New York, N.Y. 10006.

CAREER: New York University, New York, N.Y., assistant professor, 1965-70, associate professor, 1970-72, professor of finance, 1972—. *Member:* American Economic Association, American Finance Association, Institute of Management Science. *Awards, honors:* Senior research fellow at International Institute of Management, 1972-74.

WRITINGS: (Editor with M. J. Gruber) *Security Evaluation and Portfolio Analysis*, Prentice-Hall, 1972; (co-author) *Finance as a Dynamic Process*, Prentice-Hall, 1974; *International Financial Markets*, North-Holland Publishing, 1975. Associate editor of *Journal of Finance*.

* * *

ELY, David 1927-

PERSONAL: Born November 19, 1927, in Chicago, Ill.; married Margaret Jenkins, August 7, 1954; children: Michael, Pamela (Mrs. Michael Black), David, Margaret. *Education:* Attended University of North Carolina, 1944-45; Harvard University, A.B., 1949; St. Antony's College, Oxford, graduate study, 1954-55. *Agent:* Roberta Pryor, International Famous Agency, 1301 Avenue of the Americas, New York, N.Y. 10019.

CAREER: Has worked as a reporter and rewrite man for a daily newspaper, 1949-56, an administrative assistant, 1956-59, part-time writer for a weekly newspaper, 1959-60, and an editorial assistant, 1961-67. *Military service:* U.S. Navy, 1945-46. U.S. Army, 1950-52; became technical sergeant.

WRITINGS: Trot (novel), Pantheon, 1963; *Seconds* (novel), Pantheon, 1963; *The Tour* (novel), Delacorte, 1967; *Time Out* (short stories), Delacorte, 1968; *Poor Devils* (novel), Houghton, 1970; *Walking Davis* (novel), Charterhouse, 1972; *Mr. Nicholas* (novel), Putnam, 1974.

* * *

ELY, Paul (Henri) 1897-1975

December 17, 1897—January 16, 1975; French Army chief of staff and author. Obituaries: *Washington Post*, January 20, 1975; *Time*, February 3, 1975.

* * *

EMANS, Robert 1934-

PERSONAL: Born June 12, 1934, in Madison, Wis.; son of Lester M. (a dean) and Anita (a teacher; maiden name, Jones) Emans; married Jeanne Faughman (a social worker), June 21, 1958; children: Charlotte, Jenifer, Rebecca. *Education:* University of Wisconsin, B.S. (honors), 1957; University of Chicago, M.A., 1958, Ph.D., 1963, postdoctoral study, 1965-66. *Home:* 7009 Kepner Ct., Lanham, Md. 20801. *Office:* College of Education, University of Maryland, College Park, Md. 20742.

CAREER: Teacher in Montreal, Quebec, 1959-60; University of Wisconsin, Milwaukee, instructor, 1963-64, assistant professor of education, 1964; Chicago Teachers College, Chicago, Ill., assistant professor, 1964-65, research associate and visiting assistant professor of education, 1965-66; Temple University, Philadelphia, Pa., associate professor of education, 1966-68; Ohio State University, Columbus, 1968-74, began as associate professor, became professor of education and head of department; University of Maryland, College Park, dean of College of Education, 1974—. *Member:* International Reading Association, National Council of Teachers of English, National Conference on Research in English, National Society for the Study of Education, American Educational Research Association, National Education Association, Phi Kappa Phi, Phi Delta Kappa, Pi Lambda Theta.

WRITINGS: (Editor with Florence V. Shankman) *Readings about Reading Instruction*, Associated Educational Services, 1968; (with Justin Fishbein) *A Question of Competence*, Science Research Associates, 1972; (editor with Martha L. King and Patricia J. Cianciolo) *The Language Arts in the Elementary School: A Forum for Focus*, National Council of Teachers of English, 1973. Contributor to education journals.

* * *

EMERICK, Kenneth F(red) 1925-

PERSONAL: Born July 19, 1925, in Brookville, Pa.; son of Fred M. (a machinist) and Minnie (Smith) Emerick; married Leona F. Rice, 1951; children: Schuyler Stevenson. *Education:* Clarion State College, B.S., 1950; Rutgers University, M.L.S., 1960. *Politics:* Democrat. *Religion:* Unitarian-Universalist. *Home address:* Box 37, Lucinda, Pa. 16235. *Office:* Carlson Library, Clarion State College, Clarion, Pa. 16214.

CAREER: Public librarian in East Liverpool, Mansfield, Massillon, and Wadsworth, Ohio, 1950-63; Denison University Library, Granville, Ohio, librarian, 1957-58; Carlson Library, Clarion State College, Clarion, Pa., assistant professor and librarian, 1963—. *Member:* American Civil Liberties Union, American Association of University

Professors, War Resisters' League, Fellowship of Reconciliation.

WRITINGS: War Resisters Canada: The World of the American Military-Political Refugees, Free Press (Knox, Pa.), 1972. Author of column, "From Over Here," *Clarion News*, 1964-65.

* * *

EMERSON, Frank C(reighton) 1936-

PERSONAL: Born August 1, 1936, in Philadelphia, Pa.; son of Hugh N. (a college teacher and oil corporation executive) and Catherine (McCurley) Emerson. *Education:* Davidson College, B.S., 1958; New York University, M.B.A., 1962; Stockholm University, certificate, 1963; University of Minnesota, Ph.D., 1969. *Home:* 421 Stanwood, Kalamazoo, Mich. 49007. *Office:* Department of Economics, Western Michigan University, Kalamazoo, Mich. 49001.

CAREER: University of Minnesota, Minneapolis, instructor in economics, 1964-68; College of St. Thomas, St. Paul, Minn., instructor in economics, 1967-68; Western Michigan University, Kalamazoo, 1968—, began as instructor, currently assistant professor of economics. Consultant to QEI, Inc., Bedford, Mass. *Military service:* U.S. Navy, Corps of Engineers, 1959-62; became lieutenant. *Member:* American Economic Association, Econometric Society, Institute of Management Sciences, American Recorder Society. *Awards, honors:* National Science Foundation fellow, Stanford University, 1970 (summer).

WRITINGS: (Editor) *The Economics of Environmental Problems*, University of Michigan Press, 1973. Contributor to *Appraisal Journal* and *Environmental Affairs*.

WORK IN PROGRESS: Research on the economics of noise pollution, especially benefits of noise control.

AVOCATIONAL INTERESTS: Music, travel.

* * *

EMSHWILLER, Carol

PERSONAL: Born in Ann Arbor, Mich.; daughter of Charles C. (a professor) and Agnes (Carswell) Fries; married Edmund Emshwiller (a film maker), August 30, 1949; children: Eve, Sue, Peter. *Education:* University of Michigan, B.A. (music) and B.Design; also studied at Ecole nationale superieure des Beaux-Arts, Paris, France. *Home:* 43 Red Maple Dr., Wantagh, N.Y. 11793. *Agent:* Virginia Kidd, P.O. Box 278, Milford, Pa. 18339.

CAREER: Writer. *Member:* Science Fiction Writers of America, Authors Guild of Authors League of America. *Awards, honors:* MacDowell fellowship, 1971.

WRITINGS: Joy in Our Cause (short stories), Harper, 1974. Author of television script, "Pilobolus and Joan," broadcast by WNET, New York, 1974. Contributor of short stories to literary and science fiction magazines.

WORK IN PROGRESS: Short stories.

* * *

ENDE, Jean 1947-

PERSONAL: Born March 29, 1947, in New York, N.Y.; daughter of Joe (a salesman) and Hilde (Auerbach) Ende. *Education:* City College of the City University of New York, B.A., 1966. *Religion:* Jewish. *Home:* 45 West 10th St., New York, N.Y. 10011. *Office:* New York City Department of Consumer Affairs, 80 Lafayette St., New York, N.Y. 10013.

CAREER: Daily Argus, Mt. Vernon, N.Y., reporter, 1967-68; *Jersey Journal*, Jersey City, N.J., reporter, 1968-69; New York City Department of Consumer Affairs, New York, N.Y., director of consumer information, 1970—.

WRITINGS: (With Clifford Earl) *Buy It Right!: An Introduction to Consumerism*, Dutton, 1974.

* * *

ENGEL, (Srul) Morris 1931-

PERSONAL: Born March 3, 1931, in Promow, Poland; son of Isaac Leib (a rabbi) and Feige Leah (Pessin) Engel; married Faegel Chisvin, 1953; children: Michael, Hartley. *Education:* University of Manitoba, B.A., 1953, M.A., 1955; University of Toronto, Ph.D., 1959. *Office:* School of Philosophy, University of Southern California, Los Angeles, Calif. 90007.

CAREER: University of New Brunswick, Fredericton, New Brunswick, assistant professor of philosophy, 1959-61; University of Southern California, Los Angeles, assistant professor, 1962-64, associate professor of philosophy, 1964—, acting director of department, spring, 1965, summers, 1966-73. *Awards, honors:* Canada Council postdoctoral fellowship, 1961-62.

WRITINGS: (Translator from the Yiddish, and author of preface and introduction) Shloyme Zanvl Ansky (pseudonym of Solomon Rappoport), *The Dybbuk*, Comet Press, 1953, revised edition, Nash Publishing, 1974; (translator from the Yiddish) Rachmil Bryks, *A Cat in the Ghetto*, Bloch Publishing, 1959; *The Problem of Tragedy*, Brunswick Press, 1960; *Language and Illumination: Studies in the History of Philosophy*, Nijhoff, 1969; *Wittgenstein's Doctrine of the Tyranny of Language: An Historical and Critical Examination*, Nijhoff, 1971; *Informal Logic: An Introduction*, St. Martin's, in press. Author of television programs, "The Art of Thinking," 1973-74.

* * *

ENGERMAN, Stanley L(ewis) 1936-

PERSONAL: Born March 14, 1936, in New York; son of Irving (a salesman) and Edith (Kaplan) Engerman; married Judith Rader, June 21, 1963; children: David, Mark, Jeffrey. *Education:* New York University, B.S., 1956, M.B.A., 1958; Johns Hopkins University, Ph.D., 1962. *Office:* Department of Economics, University of Rochester, Rochester, N.Y. 14627.

CAREER: Yale University, New Haven, Conn., assistant professor of economics, 1962-63; University of Rochester, Rochester, N.Y., assistant professor of economics, 1963-67, associate professor, 1967-71, professor of economics and history, 1971—. *Member:* American Economics Association, American Historical Association, Economic History Association.

WRITINGS: (Editor with Robert Fogel) *The Reinterpretation of American Economic History*, Harper, 1971; (with Fogel) *Time on the Cross*, two volumes, Little, Brown, 1974; (editor with Eugene Genovese) *Race and Slavery in the Western Hemisphere: Quantitative Studies*, Princeton University Press, 1974.

WORK IN PROGRESS: Research on American and British economic history.

* * *

ENGLER, Larry 1949-

PERSONAL: Born February 17, 1949, in New York,

N.Y.; son of Sidney A. (a printer) and Joan (Bloomstein) Engler. *Education:* New York University, B.A., 1971; also studied at University of Lancaster, 1969-70. *Home:* 124 Overlook Ter., Roslyn Heights, N.Y. 11577.

CAREER: Poko Puppets, Roslyn Heights, N.Y., director, 1966—. Has taught in the Roslyn school system and at the Museum of the City of New York; has conducted workshops in puppeteering. Has performed on television programs, including an Ed Sullivan Christmas special program and the New York City Board of Education's "Saturday Theater for Children," and with the Philadelphia Orchestra. *Member:* Union Internationale de la Marionnette, Puppeteers of America, Puppetry Guild of Greater New York (president, 1974-75). *Awards, honors:* Annual award from Puppeteers of America, 1974, for *Making Puppets Come Alive.*

WRITINGS: (With Carol Fijan) *Making Puppets Come Alive*, Taplinger, 1974. Author of scripts for puppet shows, including "Aesop's Fables," "Jazz Puppet Show," and "A Canterbury Tale for Children." Contributor to *Puppetry Journal*. Former theater critic for *Heights Daily News.*

SIDELIGHTS: Poko's Puppets has a well-received jazz program for five- to twelve-year-old children, as well as a large and varied repertoire for older children. Engler has been working with puppets since he was a high school student.

BIOGRAPHICAL/CRITICAL SOURCES: Newsday, November 15, 1974.

* * *

ENGLISH, Isobel 1925-

PERSONAL: Born in 1925, in London, England; married Neville Braybrooke. *Education:* Educated in a convent in Somerset, England. *Home:* 10 Gardnor Rd., London N.W.3, England.

CAREER: Writer. *Awards, honors:* Katherine Mansfield Prize from P.E.N., 1974, for *Life After All and Other Stories.*

WRITINGS: The Key That Rusts (novel), Deutsch, 1953; *Every Eye* (novel), Deutsch, 1956, Crowell, 1959; *Four Voices* (novel), Longmans, Green, 1961; *Life After All and Other Stories*, Martin Brian & O'Keeffe, 1973. Contributor to *Commonweal* and *New Statesman.*

* * *

ENKE, Stephen 1916(?)-1974

1916(?)—September 21, 1974; American economist, demographer, and author. Obituaries: *New York Times*, September 28, 1974.

* * *

ENSLIN, Theodore (Vernon) 1925-

PERSONAL: Born March 25, 1925, in Chester, Pa.; son of Morton Scott (a professor) and Ruth May (a teacher; maiden name, Tuttle) Enslin; married Mildred Marie Stout, August 1, 1945 (divorced June 6, 1961); married Alison Jane Jose, September 14, 1969; children: (first marriage) Deirdre, Jonathan Morton; (second marriage) Jacob Hezekiah. *Education:* Private study of musical composition with Nadia Boulanger and Francis Judd Cooke. *Home address:* Box 522, Temple, Me. 04984.

CAREER: Full-time writer. *Member:* American Foundation for Homeopathy. *Awards, honors:* Niemann Award, 1955, for weekly newspaper column, "Six Miles Square," in *The Cape Codder*; Hart Crane Award, 1969, for *To Come, to Have Become.*

WRITINGS—Poems: *The Work Proposed*, Origin Press, 1958; *New Sharon's Prospect*, Origin Press, 1962 (also see below); *The Place Where I am Standing*, Elizabeth Press, 1964; *This Do (& The Talents)*, El Corno Emplumado (Mexico), 1966; *New Sharon's Prospect & Journals*, Coyote's Journal, 1966; *To Come, to Have Become*, Elizabeth Press, 1966; *Characters in Certain Places*, Wine Press, 1967; *The Diabelli Variations, and Other Poems*, Matter Books, 1968; *2/30-6/31: Poems, 1967*, Vermont Stoveside Press, 1968; *Agreement & Back: Sequences*, Elizabeth Press, 1969.

Forms, Elizabeth Press, *Part I: The First Dimensions*, 1970, *Part II: The Tessaract*, 1971, *Part III: The Experiences*, 1972; *The Poems*, Elizabeth Press, 1970; *Views 1-7*, Maya, 1970; *The Country of Our Consciousness: Selected Poems*, Sand Dollar, 1971; *Etudes*, Elizabeth Press, 1972; *With Light Reflected*, Sumac Press, 1973; *Views*, Elizabeth Press, 1973; *Forms: Coda*, Elizabeth Press, 1974; *The Median Flow: Selected Poems, 1943-1973*, Black Sparrow Press, 1974; *The Mornings*, Shaman Drum Press, 1974; *Sitio*, Granite Publications, 1974.

"Barometric Pressure 29.83 and Steady" (play), first produced in New York at Hardware Poets Theatre, October, 1965. Author of weekly newspaper column, "Six Miles Square," in *The Cape Codder*, 1949-56. Also author of an extended essay on Gustav Mahler published by Black Sparrow Press. Contributor of poems to periodicals.

WORK IN PROGRESS: Ranger, a long poem; *Carmina*, short poems in sequence.

SIDELIGHTS: James L. Weil observed of *This Do (& The Talents)*: "What happens here is how love and poem are never for giving or taking, but are forever for sharing. . . . These poems aren't to 'get' any more than they are to give. They don't invite close reading, but demand the open one. I open, respond to Theodore Enslin; and that's lovely."

* * *

EPPINK, Norman R(oland) 1906-

PERSONAL: Born July 29, 1906, in Cleveland, Ohio; son of Herman (a salesman) and Catherine (Koch) Eppink; married Helen Brenan (a painter), June 15, 1931; children: Karen (Mrs. Ricardo Ferrari). *Education:* Cleveland School of Art, B.E.A., 1928; John Huntington Polytechnic Institute, graduate study, 1931-32; Western Reserve University (now Case Western Reserve University), M.A., 1936. *Home:* 2101 Canterbury Rd., Emporia, Kan. 66801. *Office:* Department of Art, Kansas State Teachers College, Emporia, Kan. 66802.

CAREER: High school teacher of art in Lakewood, Ohio, 1928-30, and in Cleveland, Ohio, 1935-37; Cleveland Clinic Foundation, Cleveland, Ohio, head of department of medical illustration, 1930-33; Kansas State Teachers College, Emporia, Kan., 1937—, began as instructor, currently professor of art history, 1967—, head of department, 1947-67. Chairman of Emporia Civic Beautification Committee; member of Kansas Cultural Arts Commission. *Member:* Kansas Art Teachers Association, Kansas Federation of Art (member of board of directors), Rotary. *Awards, honors:* Xi Phi honorary service award, 1968.

WRITINGS: *One Hundred One Prints*, privately printed, 1967, University of Oklahoma Press, 1971. Editor of *Kansas Art Teachers Association Journal*.

SIDELIGHTS: Eppink told *CA*: "The unique purpose of *101 Prints* is to provide students of the graphic arts with a single reference source for all the processes and technical variations which also includes (in the first edition) original prints to illustrate each method under discussion. The National Gallery of Art is circulating two additional sets of the prints from their collection. These are made up into four exhibits."

His prints have been exhibited at the Brooklyn Museum, Cleveland Museum of Art, Cleveland Public Library, Linda Hall Library, Walker Art Museum, Joslyn Art Museum, Denver Art Museum, Derby Museum, and Kennedy Galleries. His work was included in the International Exhibition of Color Lithographs at the Cincinnati Art Museum and at the Society of American Graphic Artists show. He was represented in the 1966 and 1968 Internation Exhibition of Miniature Prints circulated by Pratt Graphic Art Center. He has also had eight one-man shows.

* * *

ERICKSON, Edsel L(ee) 1928-

PERSONAL: Born November 18, 1928, in Muskegon, Mich.; son of Fritz John (a farmer) and Winifred (Thompson) Erickson; married Ruth Rogers (a psychologist), July 31, 1954; children: Fritz, Karl, Carol, Ingrid. *Education:* Central Michigan University, B.S., 1958; Michigan State University, M.A., 1959, Ed.D., 1965; also studied at Washington State University, 1959-60. *Home:* 2706 Heatherdowns, Kalamazoo, Mich. 49001. *Office:* Center for Sociological Research, Western Michigan University, Kalamazoo, Mich. 49001.

CAREER: Fullerton Junior College, Fullerton, Calif., instructor in sociology, 1960-62; Michigan State University, East Lansing, instructor, 1962-65; Western Michigan University, Kalamazoo, assistant professor, 1965-67, associate professor, 1967-69, professor of sociology and education, 1969—. Research associate at School of Advanced Studies of Michigan State University, 1965-66; president of Teaching and Learning Corp., 1967—; adjunct professor at Northern Colorado University, 1973-74. *Military service:* U.S. Air Force, 1950-54. *Member:* American Psychological Association, American Sociological Association, American Educational Research Association.

WRITINGS: *Schools, Society, and Learning*, Allyn & Bacon, 1969; *Social Change, Conflict, and Education*, C. E. Merrill, 1972; *Sociology of Education*, Dorsey, 1975.

WORK IN PROGRESS: *Children with Reading Problems: A Guide for Parents*.

* * *

ERVIN-TRIPP, Susan Moore 1927-
(Susan Ervin)

PERSONAL: Born June 29, 1927, in Minneapolis, Minn.; daughter of Kingsley (a salesman) and Marian (Moore) Ervin; married Robert Daniel Tripp (a physicist), September 18, 1965; children: Alexander Dushan, Catherine Ivana, Nicholas Kingsley. *Education:* Vassar College, A.B., 1949; University of Michigan, M.A., 1950, Ph.D., 1955. *Politics:* Radical Democrat. *Religion:* None. *Home:* 1636 Leroy Ave., Berkeley, Calif. 94709. *Office:* Department of Psychology, University of California, Berkeley, Calif. 94720.

CAREER: Bureau of Social Science Research, Washington, D.C., study director, 1951-54; Social Science Research Council, Washington, D.C., research assistant, 1955-57; Harvard Graduate School of Education, Cambridge, Mass., instructor in psychology, 1955-58; University of California, Berkeley, assistant professor, 1958-64, associate professor, 1964-68, professor of rhetoric, 1968—. Director of Social Science Research Council, 1972-74; fellow, Center for Advanced Study in the Behavioral Sciences, 1974-75. *Member:* Society for the Psychological Study of Social Issues, College Art Association, Linguistic Society of America. *Awards, honors:* Guggenheim fellow, 1974-75.

WRITINGS: *Language Acquisition and Communicative Choice*, Stanford University Press, 1973. Contributor to *Language in Society*, *Journal of Abnormal and Social Psychology*, and *American Journal of Psychology*. Member of editorial boards of *Child Language*, 1974—, and *Journal of Sociology of Language*, 1974—.

WORK IN PROGRESS: Research in early child language and in bilingualism and acculturation, completion expected in 1975.

* * *

ESLER, William K. 1930-

PERSONAL: Born September 25, 1930, in Akron, Ohio; son of Harrison Norris (a machinist) and Grace (Salkeld) Esler; married Mary Brown (a teacher); children: Jennifer, Susan, Loyd. *Education:* Akron State University, B.A., 1956; Kent State University, M.A., 1958, Ph.D., 1968. *Home address:* Route 1, Box 1594, Maitland, Fla. 32751. *Office:* Department of Education, Florida Technological University, Orlando, Fla. 32816.

CAREER: Teacher of mathematics and science in the public schools of Akron, Ohio, 1956-66; Kent State University, Kent, Ohio, instructor in education, 1966-68; Florida Technological University, Orlando, member of faculty in department of education, 1968—. *Military service:* U.S. Army; became staff sergeant. *Member:* Childhood Education in Science International, National Science Teachers Association, Florida Science Teachers Association, Phi Delta Kappa.

WRITINGS: *Modern Physics Experiments for the High School*, Parker Publishing, 1970; *Teaching Elementary Science*, Wadsworth, 1973; *Teaching Secondary and Middle School Science*, Wadsworth, 1975. Contributor to journals in his field.

WORK IN PROGRESS: *Classroom Questioning and Inquiry* for Florida Technological University Press.

AVOCATIONAL INTERESTS: Fishing, boating, playing tennis.

* * *

ESSICK, Robert N(ewman) 1942-

PERSONAL: Born October 19, 1942, in Los Angeles, Calif.; son of Bryant (a business executive) and Jeanette M. (a secretary; maiden name, Quinn) Essick. *Education:* Attended Williams College, 1961-64; University of California, Los Angeles, B.A. (honors), 1965, San Diego, Ph.D., 1969. *Home:* 100 South Chester Ave., Pasadena, Calif. 91106. *Office:* Department of English, California State University, Northridge, Calif. 91324.

CAREER: California State University, Northridge, assistant professor, 1970-73, associate professor of English,

1973—. Essick Investment Co., Los Angeles, Calif., vice-president and member of board of directors, 1973—; Essick Foundation, Inc., Los Angeles, treasurer, 1973—. Member of advisory board of directors of American Blake Foundation, 1971—. *Member:* Modern Language Association of America, American Association of University Professors, Renaissance Society of America, American Society for Eighteenth-Century Studies. *Awards, honors:* Woodrow Wilson fellowships, 1965, 1969; National Endowment for the Humanities grant, 1972.

WRITINGS: (With Roger R. Easson) *William Blake: Book Illustrator*, American Blake Foundation, Volume I, 1972, Volume II, in press; (editor) *The Visionary Hand*, Hennessey & Ingalls, 1973. Contributor of articles and reviews to journals. Regular contributor to *Blake Newsletter*, 1969—. Associate editor of *Blake Studies*, 1973—.

WORK IN PROGRESS: Volume III of *William Blake: Book Illustrator*; a book-length study of William Blake as an engraver; editing a commentary of Blake's designs to Blair's *Grave*; a catalogue of Huntington Library Blake collection.

AVOCATIONAL INTERESTS: Skin-diving, book and print collecting, engraving and photo-etching.

* * *

EVANS, Elizabeth 1932-

PERSONAL: Born September 25, 1932, in Colon, Panama; daughter of John Humphrey (an army officer and professor) and Sara (Pick) Evans. *Education:* Attended Stephens College and George Washington University. *Politics:* Democrat. *Religion:* Episcopalian. *Home:* 205 West 54th St., New York, N.Y. 10019. *Agent:* Dorothy Pittman, John Cushman Associates, Inc., 25 West 43rd St., New York, N.Y. 10036.

CAREER: Actress, 1954-62; *Saturday Evening Post*, Philadelphia, Pa., and New York, N.Y., member of editorial staff, 1962; Time-Life Books, New York, N.Y., member of editorial staff, 1962-70; free-lance writer on the American Revolution, for the American Revolution Bicentennial, 1970—.

WRITINGS: *Weathering the Storm: Women of the American Revolution*, Scribner, 1975; *The Shaping of the American Past*, Prentice-Hall, 1975.

WORK IN PROGRESS: Working with Helen Gahagan Douglas on her autobiography, for Doubleday.

* * *

EVANS, (Cyril) Kenneth 1917-

PERSONAL: Born June 13, 1917, in Briton Ferry, Glamorganshire, Wales; son of Willie and Beatrice (Hopes) Evans; married Irene Lilian Skinner, December 28, 1946. *Education:* Attended Newport Technical College, 1934-35, 1973; diploma in youth leadership from University College of Swansea, 1947; certificate in applied psychology from Welsh College of Advanced Technology, 1954; certificate in social work from College of Food Technology & Commerce, 1969. *Home:* 13 Kensington Place, Newport, Monmouthshire, Wales. *Office:* Boverton House, Chepstow, Monmouthshire, Wales.

CAREER: Has worked as a youth leader, careers officer, and welfare officer on local government level since 1947, now senior social services officer; part-time lecturer in social sciences at Caldicot and Chepstow Community Colleges; novelist. *Military service:* British Army, 1940-46; served in Africa, Italy, and Germany. *Member:* Crime Writers Association, National Association of Local Government Officers, Royal Anthropological Institute.

WRITINGS—Novels: *Oasis of Fear*, Roy, 1968; *No Cause for Dying*, R. Hale, 1969; *Shadows of Violence*, R. Hale, 1971; *A Rich Way to Die*, R. Hale, 1973; *Blueprint to Kill*, R. Hale, in press.

WORK IN PROGRESS: A crime novel, *The Crow's Graveyard*; research for a period novel.

* * *

EWING, John Melvin 1925-

PERSONAL: Born March 29, 1925, in Cincinnati, Iowa; son of Claude Melvin (a farmer) and Carrie (Jones) Ewing; married Roberta Boone (a teacher), April 17, 1948; children: June Ellen, Janet Lynn. *Education:* Northeast Missouri State University, B.S., 1954, M.A., 1958; University of Missouri, certificate of specialization, 1964; University of Nebraska, Ed.D., 1966. *Religion:* Methodist. *Home:* 1205 North School, Normal, Ill. 61761. *Office:* Department of Education, Illinois State University, Normal, Ill. 61761.

CAREER: Burlington School Board, Burlington, Iowa, elementary school teacher, 1955-58, principal, 1958-64; University of Nebraska, Lincoln, assistant professor of education, 1966-69; Illinois State University, Normal, associate professor, 1969-73, professor of education, 1973—. *Member:* International Reading Association, Futurist Society, Association for the Study of Perception, Illinois Reading Association, Kiwanis Club, Phi Delta Kappa. *Awards, honors:* Danforth associate, 1968—; Pilot Award from Southeast Iowa Boy Scouts of America, 1959.

WRITINGS: *Word Analysis for Teachers*, Interstate, 1973, revised edition, 1974.

WORK IN PROGRESS: *Comprehension Competencies for Teachers*, completion expected in 1975.

* * *

EZEKIEL, M(ordecai) J. B. 1899(?)-1974

1899(?)—October 31, 1974; American economist, government official, and author. Obituaries: *New York Times*, November 2, 1974.

* * *

EZEKIEL, Raphael S. 1931-

PERSONAL: Born November 24, 1931, in Bryan, Tex.; son of Walter N. (a mycologist) and Sarah (a community worker; maiden name, Ritzen) Ezekiel; children: Daniel, Margalete, Joshua. *Education:* University of Chicago, B.A. (with honors), 1950; University of California, Ph.D., 1964. *Religion:* Jewish. *Home:* 1120 Olivia, Ann Arbor, Mich. 48104. *Office:* Department of Psychology, University of Michigan, Ann Arbor, Mich. 48104.

CAREER: Georgetown University, Transportation Research Project, Washington, D.C., research analyst, 1955-60; University of Michigan, Ann Arbor, 1964—, began as assistant professor, now associate professor of psychology. *Military service:* U.S. Army, 1953-55. *Member:* Society for the Psychological Study of Social Issues.

WRITINGS: (With H. C. Kelman) *Cross-National Encounters*, Jossey-Bass, 1970. Contributor to *Journal of Personal and Social Psychology* and *Merrill-Palmer Quarterly*.

WORK IN PROGRESS: Naturalistic research on the construction of lives.

FABRICIUS, Johan (Johannes) 1899-

PERSONAL: First name is sometimes listed as Johan Wigmore; born August 24, 1899, in Bandung, Java; son of Jan (a playwright) and Minke (Dornseiffen) Fabricius; married Ruth Freudenberg, April 17, 1925 (died October 7, 1968); married Anna Bleeker (a lawyer), October 29, 1968; children: (first marriage) Jan, Jelle, Famke. *Education:* Attended Art Academies in the Hague and in Amsterdam. *Politics:* "Not interested." *Home:* 15 Meentweg, 7 Glimmen (gem. Haren, Gron.), Netherlands. *Agent:* Internationaal literatuurbureau, Hilversum, Koninginneweg 2a, Holland.

CAREER: Writer, painter. Painter on Austro-Italian front, 1918; correspondent in Indonesia for B.B.C. and *London Times*, 1945-46; free-lance broadcaster in Dutch, English, German, and Malay for the B.B.C. and A.B.S.I.E. (American Broadcasting Station in Europe) during World War II. *Member:* P.E.N., De Ploeg (society of painters; Groningen). *Awards, honors:* Vanderhoogt prize, 1932, for *Komedianten trokken voorbij*.

WRITINGS—Novels, except as indicated; all Dutch editions published by H. P. Leopold (The Hague), unless otherwise noted: *Het meisje met de blauwe hoed*, 1927, reprinted, Meulenhoff (Amsterdam), 1967, translation by Winifred Katzin published as *The Girl in the Blue Hat*, Cassell, 1932; *Charlotte's grote reis* (title means "Charlotte's Big Journey"), 1928, reprinted, 1969; *Mario Ferraro's ijdele liefde*, 1929, translation by Katzin published as *The Love of Mario Ferraro*, Little, Brown, 1931 (published in England as *Vain Love*, Gollancz, 1931).

Avontuur in Venetie (title means "Adventure in Venice"), Zsolnay (Berlin), 1932; *Komedianten trokken voorbij* (title means "Comedians Passed By"), 1932 (also see below); *Melodie der verten* (title means "Melody from Afar"), 1932 (also see below); *De dans om de galg* (title means "The Dance around the Gallows"), 1934 (also see below); *Komedianten trokken voorbij* [and] *Melodie der verten* [and] *De dans om de galg* (trilogy), 1962, translation by Irene Clephane and David Hallett published as *The Son of Marietta*, Little, Brown, 1936; *Loewen hungern in Neapel*, Zsolnay, 1934, translation by Phyllis and Trevor Blewitt published as *Lions Starve in Naples*, Gollancz, 1934, Little, Brown, 1935, new edition, Little, Brown, 1936; *Flipje*, 1936, translation published as *Flip Wonders Why*, Heinemann, 1949, published as *World at Six*, Westminster Press, 1950; *Kasteel in Karinthie*, 1938, translation by G. J. Renier and Hallett published as *Castle in Carinthia*, Random House, 1940.

Eiland der demonen, 1940, reprinted, Meulenhoff, 1963, translation by Fernand G. Renier and Anne Cliff published as *No Return from Bali*, Collins, 1941; *A Malayan Tragedy* (translation from the original manuscript by F. G. Renier and Anne Cliff Renier), Heinemann, 1942, published as *Halfbloed* (title means "Halfcaste"), 1946, reprinted, Boekenkring, Bosch & Keuning (Baarn), 1964; *Nacht over Java*, 1942, Querido (New York), 1944, translation published as *Night over Java*, Heinemann, 1944, Greenberg, 1946; *Hotel Vesuvius* (translation from the original manuscript by M. S. Stephens, with illustrations by the author), Heinemann, 1945, Rinehart, 1947, published in Dutch under same title, Leopold, 1948; *De kraton* (poem; title means "Sultan's Palace"), De Bezige (Amsterdam), 1945; *Hoe ik Indie terugvond* (nonfiction), 1947, translation by Stephens published as *Java Revisited*, Heinemann, 1947; *Brandende aarde: De Vernieling en de evacuatie van de olieterreinen in Nederlandsch-Indie* (nonfiction; title means "Scorched Earth: East Indies Episode"), 1949; *De Grote Geus*, 1949, translation published as *Beggars' Banquet*, British Book Service, 1951.

De Grote Beproeving, 1950, translation by Roy Edwards, with illustrations by the author, published as *The Great Ordeal*, British Book Service, 1951; *Mijn huis staat achter de kim: Vrijmoedige memoires*, 1951, translation by Edwards, with illustrations by the author, published as *A Dutchman at Large*, Heinemann, 1952; *De Ontvoering van Europa* (title means "The Rape of Europe"), 1952; *Langs de Leie: Twee variaties op een thema*, 1952, translation by H. Schuurbecque Boeye published as *The Pike Beelzebub [and Heartbreak in Flanders]: Two Variations on a Theme, One in Major and One in Minor*, Heinemann, 1953; *Een wereld in beroering: Verdere memoires, 1936-46* (title means "A World in Uproar"), 1952; *Gordel van smaragd* (short stories), 1953, translation by Edwards published as *Girdle of Emerald*, British Book Service, 1955; *De Nertsmantel* (title means "The Mink Coat"), 1953; *Toernooi met de dood*, 1954, translation by Edwards published as *Mortal Pageant: A Romance of the Year of the Great Plague in Florence*, British Book Service, 1956; *Nacht zonder Zegen* (title means "Night without Bliss"), 1955, reprinted, 1963; *Setoewo de tijger*, 1956, translation by Edwards published as *Setuwo, the Tiger*, Heinemann, 1957; *Johan Fabricius Omnibus*, De Arbeiderspers (Amsterdam), 1956; *Luie stoel* (title means "Easy Chair"), 1957; *De heilige paarden* (title means "The Sacred Horses"), 1959.

Ballade van de zeeman Joris Breebaert (poem; title means "Ballad of the Seaman Joris Breebaert"), 1960; *Ballade van de zilver reiger* (poem; title means "Ballad of the Silver Heron"), 1960; *Mijn Rosalie* (title means "My Rosalie"), 1961; *Dromen is ook leven* (title means "To Dream Is to Live"), 1962; *Jongensspel* (title means "Boys' Play"), 1963; *Herinneringen van eene oude pruik* (title means "Memories of an Old Wig: A Goldoni Biography"), 1963; *Wat u nodig hebt, mevrouw, is een vriend* (title means "What You Need, Lady, Is a Lover"), 1964; *Hopheisa, in regen en wind* (memoirs; title means "With hei ho, the Wind and the Rain"), 1964; *Die heiligen Pferde* (title means "The Sacred Horses"), 1964; *Dag, leidseplein* (title means "Goodbye, Leidse Plein"), 1965; *Weet je nog, Yoshi?* (title means "Remember, Yoshi?"), 1966; *Wij, Tz'e Hsi, Keizerin van China* (title means "We, Tz'e Hsi, Empress of China"), 1967; *Het water weet van niets* (title means "The Water Keeps Its Secret"), 1968; *Wittebroodsweken met mama* (title means "Honeymooning with Mama [that is, Mother-in-law]"), 1969; *Voorijden, mevrouw?* (title means "Car Is Ready, Madam"), 1969.

Onder de hete Caraibische zon (short stories; title means "Under the Hot Caribbean Sun"), 1970; *De kop van Jut* (the story of a famous murder; title not translatable), 1970; *Sentimental Journey: Een reis door het niewe Indonesie* (nonfiction; title means "A Journey through Modern Indonesia"), 1971; *Met Klein orkest* (short stories; title means "With Small Orchestra"), 1971; *Partnerruil niet uitgesloten* (title means "Change of Partners Will Be Considered"), 1971; *Carlinho mijn kleinzoon* (title means "Carlinho, My Grandson"), 1973; *Het fordijn met de ibissen* (title means "The Curtain with the Ibises"), 1973; *Het portret* (title means "The Portrait"), 1973; *De wijze goeroes van Benares* (title means "The Wise Gurus of Benares"), in press; *Barcarole*, in press.

Plays—All published by H. P. Leopold, except as noted: *Hans de klokkeluider* (title means "Hans the Bellringer"),

1922; *Idylle*, 1953; *Het duistere bloed* (title means "The Dark Blood"), 1954; *Schimmenspel* (title means "Shadow Play"), 1958; *Mas'Aniello*, 1972; *Shock Treatment*, Toneel-Centrale (Bussum), 1973.

Books for children—all Dutch editions published by H. P. Leopold: *De scheepsjonges van Bontekoe*, 1924, reprinted 1968, translation and abridgment by M. C. Darnton, with illustrations by the author, published as *Java ho! The Adventures of Four Boys amid Fire, Storm, and Shipwreck*, Coward-McCann, 1931; *Het geheim van het oude landhuis* (title means "The Secret of the Old Country House"), 1965; *De avonturen van Jantje en zyn vrieden Koko en Sebastiaan* (title means "The Adventures of Little Jan and His Friends Koko and Sebastian"), 1966; *Heintje heeft kabouters op zolder* (title means "Little Hein Has Dwarfs in the Loft"), 1967; *Heintje en het geheim van het houten paard Joris* (title means "Heintje and the Secret of the Wooden Horse Joris"), 1968; *Heintje speelt voor leeuw* (title means "Heintje Acts like a Lion"), 1969; *Heintje bouwt een huis voor Sinterklaas* (title means "Heintje Builds a Home for Santa Claus"), 1970; *De duivel in de toren*, 1971, translation by Lance Salway published as *The Devil in the Tower: Seven Diabolical Tales*, Longman, 1973; (self-illustrated) *Hanneke's bruiloft* (title means "Hanneke's Wedding"), 1972.

WORK IN PROGRESS: A book of memories as a "war painter" at the Austrian-Italian front in 1918, as yet untitled.

SIDELIGHTS: Fabricius told *CA* that the name Wigmore, which was taken from his mother's family, was used as a pseudonym. He has made recordings spoken in an almost forgotten language, "Petjuk," which he describes as "the language of the low class Eurasians in Indonesia."

Hans the Bellringer, a Christmas play, was adapted by John Wright as a puppet play and is presented each Christmas season in London.

AVOCATIONAL INTERESTS: Travel, music.

BIOGRAPHICAL/CRITICAL SOURCES: Johan W. Fabricius, *Java Revisited*, Heinemann, 1947; Fabricius, *A Dutchman at Large*, Heinemann, 1951; Rico Bulthuis, *Johan Fabricius: Een schrijver en zijn werk*, H. P. Leopold, 1959.

* * *

FAHEY, James C(harles) 1903-1974

1903—September 30, 1974; American authority on military ships and aircraft, and publisher and editor of books in the field. Obituaries: *Washington Post*, October 4, 1974.

* * *

FAIRBAIRN, Ian J(ohn) 1933-

PERSONAL: Born March 22, 1933, in Western Samoa; son of James and Moa Emily Fairbairn; married Hedy Margaret Baumwald, December 23, 1967; children: John Ian, Nari Margaret, Karene Fetu. *Education:* Attended Victoria University, Wellington, 1952-53; University of Washington, Seattle, B.A., 1956, M.A., 1958; Australian National University, Ph.D., 1963. *Office:* South Pacific Commission, Noumea, New Caledonia.

CAREER: University of Newcastle, Newcastle, New South Wales, Australia, lecturer, 1963-68, senior lecturer in economics, 1968-72; South Pacific Commission, Noumea, New Caledonia, economist, 1972—. Visiting senior lecturer at University of the South Pacific, spring, 1971; consultant to United Nations Industrial Development Organization. *Member:* Economic Society of Australia and New Zealand, South Pacific Social Sciences Association. *Awards, honors:* Research grant from Myer Foundation, 1971; grant from Social Science Research Council of Australia, 1970-71; grant from Reserve Bank of Australia, 1972.

WRITINGS: (Editor) *Namasu: New Guinea's Largest Indigenous-Owned Company*, Australian National University, 1969; (with Raul Jofre and Peter H. Kruck) *A Survey of Industry and Its Potential in Western Samoa, A Final Report*, United Nations Industrial Development Organization, 1973; *The National Income of Western Samoa*, Oxford University Press, 1973. Contributor of about twenty-five articles and reviews to economics and social science journals, including *Australian Quarterly, Journal of Pacific History, Australian External Territories, Journal of the Polynesian Society, Pacific Viewpoint*, and *South Pacific Bulletin*.

WORK IN PROGRESS: Report on Industrial Incentives in the South Pacific; research on employment creation in the South Pacific.

AVOCATIONAL INTERESTS: Poetry and literature about the Pacific and sports.

* * *

FALLER, Kevin 1920-

PERSONAL: Born July 4, 1920, in Galway, Ireland; son of John (a jeweler) and Madeleine (Quinn) Faller; married Una Cloherty, April 27, 1945; children: John, Madeleine (Mrs. Ronan O'Siochain), Carol. *Education:* University College at Galway, National University of Ireland, M.B., B.Ch., B.A.O., all 1945. *Home:* 274 Clontarf Rd., Dublin 3, Ireland. *Agent:* John Johnson, 51-54 Goschen Buildings, 12-13 Henrietta St., London WC2 8LF, England. *Office: Irish Independent*, Middle Abbey St., Dublin, Ireland.

CAREER: Free-lance writer and journalist, 1945—; *Irish Independent*, Dublin, Ireland, member of editorial staff, 1963—. *Member:* International P.E.N., Society of Irish Playwrights. *Awards, honors:* James Clarence Mangan centenary award from Book Association of Great Britain and Ireland for lyric poem, "For Mangan."

WRITINGS: Lyric and Script (poems and a radio drama), Loescher, 1947; *Genesis* (novel), T. V. Boardman, 1953; *Island Lyrics*, Three Candle Press, 1963; *Lament for the Bull Island and Other Poems*, Goldsmith Press, 1973.

Work is anthologized in *New Poets of Ireland*, edited by Donald Carroll, Alan Swallow, 1963; *The Penguin Book of Irish Verse*, edited by Brendan Kennelly, Penguin, 1970. Author of radio plays for Radio Telefis Eireann, British Broadcasting Corp., Corporation for Public Broadcasting, and University of Wisconsin.

WORK IN PROGRESS: A novel; a full-length play; poems.

BIOGRAPHICAL/CRITICAL SOURCES: Capuchin Annual (Dublin), 1972.

* * *

FANNING, Odom 1920-

PERSONAL: Born September 8, 1920, in Atlanta, Ga.; son of Odom Olin (a physician) and Susie G. (a teacher; maiden name, Sandiford) Fanning; married Elaine M. Michael, November 10, 1948; children: Carol, Kathryn. *Edu-*

cation: Emory University, A.B., 1942. *Home and office:* 9206 Bulls Run Pkwy., Bethesda, Md. 20034.

CAREER: Atlanta Journal, Atlanta, Ga., reporter and science writer, 1943-46; Center for Disease Control, Atlanta, Ga., in public information, 1949-53; Georgia Institute of Technology, Atlanta, in public information, 1953-55; Midwest Research Institute, Kansas City, Mo., in public information, 1955-60; Columbia Broadcasting System Laboratories, Inc., Stamford, Conn., in public relations and advertising, 1960-62; Baird-Atomic, Inc., Cambridge, Mass., in public relations and advertising, 1962-65; U.S. Government, Washington, D.C., writer in various programs in science, technology, environment, and energy, 1965—; free-lance writer, 1965—. Vice-chairman, Bethesda Help (ecumenical community organization), 1972—. *Military service:* U.S. Marine Corps, 1943-46; combat correspondent; became sergeant; served in Pacific theater. *Member:* National Association of Science Writers (life member), National Press Club, Marine Corps Combat Correspondents Association, American Association for the Advancement of Science, Society of Professional Journalists of Sigma Delta Chi, National Audubon Society, Nature Conservancy, Sierra Club.

WRITINGS: Opportunities in Oceanographic Careers, Vocational Guidance Manuals, 1969; *Opportunities in Environmental Careers*, Vocational Guidance Manuals, 1971, revised edition, 1975; *Man and His Environment: Citizen Action*, Harper, 1975. Editor of White House reports, "Marine Science Affairs: A Year of Plans and Progress," 1968, and "Environmental Quality: The First Annual Report," 1970. Contributor of more than twenty articles to magazines. Book review editor, *Newsletter of the National Association of Science Writers*.

WORK IN PROGRESS: A book on bioethics.

* * *

FARJEON, (Eve) Annabel 1919-
(Sarah Jefferson)

PERSONAL: Born March 19, 1919, in Berkshire, England; daughter of Herbert (an author) and Joan (an artist; maiden name, Thornycroft) Farjeon; married Hugh Adams, May 30, 1945 (deceased); married Igor Anrep (a cardiologist), July 9, 1949; children: (first marriage) Olivia; (second marriage) Benjamin. *Education:* Privately tutored by governess and father. *Home:* 42 Southwood Lane, London N.6, England. *Agent:* A. M. Heath & Co. Ltd., 40 William IV St., London W.C.2, England.

CAREER: Sadlers Wells Ballet Co., London, England, ballet dancer, 1934-42; *Time & Tide*, London, assistant literary editor, 1946-48; *New Statesman*, London, ballet critic, 1949-64; *Evening Standard*, London, ballet critic, 1959-73; writer.

WRITINGS—Books for children: *The Alphabet*, J. Cape, 1941; *Maria Lupin*, Abelard, 1967; *The Siege of Trapp's Mill*, Dent, 1972, Atheneum, 1974; *Poems*, privately printed, 1973; *The Poetry of Cats*, Batsford, 1974. Contributor to BBC broadcasts, and to *Life & Letters, New Writing, New Statesman, Evening Standard* (under pseudonym Sarah Jefferson), *Daily Telegraph, Guardian*, and *Observer*.

WORK IN PROGRESS: A children's book, *The Unicorn Drum*, for Kaye & Ward; an adult novel, *The Ivy Memorial*; an autobiography.

FARNER, Donald S(ankey) 1915-

PERSONAL: Born May 2, 1915, in Waumandee, Wis.; son of John (a mechanic) and Lillian O. (a teacher; maiden name, Sankey) Farner; married Dorothy S. Copps, December 24, 1940; children: Carla M. (Mrs. Gregory Fletcher), Donald C. *Education:* Hamline University, B.S., 1937; University of Wisconsin, M.A., 1939, Ph.D., 1941. *Home:* 4533 West Laurel Dr., Seattle, Wash. 98105. *Office:* Department of Zoology, University of Washington, Seattle, Wash. 98195.

CAREER: University of Wisconsin, Madison, instructor in zoology, 1941-43; University of Kansas, Lawrence, assistant professor of zoology and assistant curator of birds, 1946-47; University of Colorado, Boulder, assistant professor of biology, 1947; Washington State University, Pullman, associate professor, 1947-52, professor of zoophysiology, 1952-65, dean of Graduate School, 1960-64; University of Washington, Seattle, professor of zoophysiology, 1965—, chairman of department of zoology, 1966—. Chairman of Division of Biology and Agriculture and Division of Biological Sciences of National Research Council, 1969-74. *Military service:* U.S. Naval Reserve, Medical Service Corps, active duty, 1943-46. U.S. Naval Reserve, 1946-75; retired with rank of captain.

MEMBER: International Union for the Biological Sciences (president, 1967-73), American Association for the Advancement of Science (fellow), American Physiological Society, American Society of Zoology, American Institute of Biological Sciences, American Society of Naturalists, American Chemical Society, American Ornithologists Union (fellow; president, 1973-75), Society for Endocrinology, Ecological Society of America, Society for Systematic Zoology, Cooper Ornithological Society, Deutsche Ornithologen-Gesellschaft, Ornithologiska Foereningen i Finland, Phi Beta Kappa, Sigma Xi, Phi Kappa Phi, Phi Sigma, Gamma Alpha, Omicron Delta Kappa. *Awards, honors:* Fulbright research scholarship and lectureship, University of Otago, 1953-54; Guggenheim fellowship, University of Western Australia, 1958-59; D.Sc. from Hamline University, 1962; Brewster Medal from American Ornithologists Union, 1962.

WRITINGS: The Birds of Crater Lake National Park, University Press of Kansas, 1952; (editor with James R. King) *Avian Biology*, Academic Press, Volume I, 1971, Volume II, 1972, Volume III, 1973, Volume IV, 1974, Volume V, 1975; (editor) *Breeding Biology of Birds*, National Academy of Sciences, 1973; (with Andreas Oksche) *Neurohistological Studies of the Hypothalamohypophysical System of Zonotrichia leucophrys gambelii*, Springer-Verlag, 1974.

Contributor of about a hundred ninety articles to scientific journals. Co-editor of *Zeitschrift fuer Zellforschung*, 1967—; managing editor of *Zoophysiology of Comparative Physiology and Biochemistry*, 1969—; comparative physiology editor of *Journal of Experimental Zoology*, 1974—.

WORK IN PROGRESS: Research on the neuroendocrinologic basis of control of reproductive cycles.

SIDELIGHTS: Farner has been elected president of the next International Ornithological Congress, to be held in Germany in 1978. He is fluent in German, and reads seven additional foreign languages.

* * *

FARNHAM, Thomas J(avery) 1938-

PERSONAL: Born May 7, 1938, in Bennington, Vt.; son

of Harold Frederick (a telephone company executive) and Marjorie (Javery) Farnham; married Mary Davis (a professor of English), June 13, 1959; children: Jonathan, Christopher, Julia. *Education:* Ohio Wesleyan University, B.A., 1959; University of North Carolina, M.A., 1961, Ph.D., 1964. *Home:* 1703 Middletown Ave., Northford, Conn. 06472. *Office:* Department of History, Southern Connecticut State College, New Haven, Conn. 06515.

CAREER: Moorhead State College, Moorhead, Minn., assistant professor of history, 1964-66; Southern Connecticut State College, New Haven, assistant professor, 1966-68, associate professor, 1968-74, professor of history, 1974—, chairman of department, 1973—. Chairman of New Haven Bicentennial Commission history committee, 1974. *Military service:* U.S. Marine Corps Reserve, 1957-63. *Member:* Society for Historians of American Foreign Relations, Association for the Study of Connecticut History. *Awards, honors:* National Endowment for the Humanities fellow, 1969.

WRITINGS: (With William S. Powell and James K. Huhta) *The North Carolina Regulators: A Documentary History*, North Carolina State Department of Archives and History, 1971; *Guida Bibliografica a las Insurgencias Independistas de los Estados Unidos Mexicanos y Norteamericanos* (title means "Bibliographical Guide to the War for Independence in Mexico and the United States"), National Autonomous University of Mexico, 1974. Contributor to *Virginia Magazine of History and Biography*, *Louisiana History*, *Connecticut Review*, *Arizona and the West*, *New England Galaxy*, *Convivium*, and *Register of the Kentucky Historical Society*.

WORK IN PROGRESS: To Preserve the Republic: Foreign Policy Dissent in the New Nation.

AVOCATIONAL INTERESTS: Mountaineering, restoring his eighteenth-century home.

* * *

FARNSWORTH, Robert M. 1929-

PERSONAL: Born May 5, 1929, in Detroit, Mich.; son of Merle O. and Irene (Schimmel) Farnsworth; married Sylvia Binkowski (a teacher), June 25, 1950; children: Laurel, Wendy, Margaret, Christopher, Katherine. *Education:* University of Michigan, B.A., 1950; University of Connecticut, M.A., 1952; Tulane University, Ph.D., 1957. *Home:* 4520 Rockhill Terrace, Kansas City, Mo. 64110. *Office:* Department of English, University of Missouri-Kansas City, Kansas City, Mo. 64110.

CAREER: University of Missouri, Kansas City, 1960—, currently professor of American literature. Fulbright professor to India, 1966-67, and Turkey, 1973-74.

WRITINGS: (Editor) Charles Chesnutt, *The Marrow of Tradition*, University of Michigan Press, 1969; (editor) Chesnutt, *The Conjure Woman*, University of Michigan Press, 1969; (co-editor) Richard Wright, *Impressions and Perspectives*, University of Michigan Press, 1973.

WORK IN PROGRESS: A study of unpublished manuscripts of Melvin B. Tolson.

* * *

FARRAR, John C(hipman) 1896-1974

February 25, 1896—November 6, 1974; American publisher, editor, founder of Breadloaf Writer's Conference, author of poems, plays, short fiction, and criticism. Obituaries: *New York Times*, November 7, 1974; *Washington Post*, November 8, 1974; *AB Bookman's Weekly*, December 9, 1974; *Current Biography*, January, 1975.

* * *

FARRAR, Lancelot Leighton, Jr. 1932-

PERSONAL: Born November 28, 1932, in New York, N.Y.; son of L. Leighton (an accountant) and Pearl Elizabeth (Shepard) Farrar; married Marjorie Milbank (a college teacher), September 12, 1959; children: Olivia Milbank, Elizabeth Shepard. *Education:* Princeton University, A.B., 1954; graduate study at University of Heidelberg, 1956, and University of Goettingen, 1956-57; Oxford University, D.Phil., 1961. *Politics:* Liberal Democrat. *Home:* 1 Perrin Rd., Brookline, Mass. 02146. *Office:* Department of History, Boston College, Chestnut Hill, Mass. 02167.

CAREER: University of Wisconsin, Milwaukee, instructor in history, 1961-62; Stanford University, Stanford, Calif., assistant professor of history, 1962-65; University of Washington, Seattle, assistant professor of history, 1966-73; Lewis and Clark College, Portland, Ore., assistant professor of history, 1973-74; Boston College, Chestnut Hill, Mass., assistant professor of history, 1975—. *Military service:* U.S. Army, Signal Corps, 1954-56. *Member:* International Studies Association, American Historical Association, Inter-University Seminar on Armed Forces and Society.

WRITINGS: The Short-War Illusion: An Analysis of German Policy, Strategy, and Domestic Affairs, August-December, 1914, Clio Press, 1973; (translator and author of introduction) Fritz Fischer, *World Power or Decline*, Norton, 1974; (editor) *War and Society: An Interdisciplinary Study*, Clio Press, in press. Contributor to *Journal of Conflict Resolution*, *World Affairs*, *East European Quarterly*, *New Review*, *International Revue for Military History*, *Canadian Journal of History*, *International Review of History and Political Science*, and *Militaergeschichtliche Mitteilungen*.

WORK IN PROGRESS: Research on international relations and diplomatic history.

* * *

FARRINGTON, Benjamin 1891-1974

1891—November 17, 1974; Irish-born classicist and author. Obituaries: *AB Bookman's Weekly*, December 16, 1974.

* * *

FARZAN, Massud 1936-

PERSONAL: Born June 2, 1936, in Tabriz, Iran; son of Ali Akbar (an accountant) and Tahereh (Ganje) Farzan; married Jean Anne Kristinat (a teacher), April 25, 1970. *Education:* Tabriz University, Licentiate, 1958; University of Michigan, M.A., 1961, Ph.D., 1964. *Home:* 373 Troy Del Way, Williamsville, N.Y. 14221.

CAREER: High school teacher of English in Abadan, Iran, 1958-59; North Montana College, Havre, associate professor of English, 1964-65; Pahlavi University, Shiraz, Iran, head of department of English, 1965-67; California State University, Fullerton, associate professor of English and creative writing, 1969-71; Columbia University, New York, N.Y., lecturer in Persian, 1971-73; Pahlavi University, professor of English and comparative literature, 1973—. *Member:* Modern Language Association of America, Society for Iranian Studies.

WRITINGS: (Translator) *Mortad* (title means "The Apostate"), Afshari Publications, 1954; (editor with M. A. Jazayery and others) *Modern Persian Reader*, University of Michigan Press, 1963; *Another Way of Laughter*, Dutton, 1973; *The Tale of the Reed Pipe*, Dutton, 1974; *From Kashan to Kalamazoo* (poems and poems in translation), Pahlavi University Press, 1974. Author of *Figures in the Darkness*, a serialized novel in *Tehran Journal Magazine*, 1958-59. Contributor to journals in his field.

WORK IN PROGRESS: A book on Rumi and the Sufi idea of the Complete Man; poems and stories.

* * *

FAULHABER, Charles Bailey 1941-

PERSONAL: Surname is pronounced *Fall*-hay-ber; born September 18, 1941, in East Cleveland, Ohio; son of Kenneth Frederick (a teacher) and Lois Marie (Bailey) Faulhaber; married Jami Sue O'Banion (a marketing representative for IBM), June 5, 1971. *Education:* Yale University, B.A. (summa cum laude), 1963, M.Phil., 1969, Ph.D., 1969; University of Wisconsin, M.A., 1966. *Office:* Department of Spanish, University of California, Berkeley, Calif. 94720.

CAREER: University of California, Berkeley, assistant professor of Spanish, 1969—. *Member:* Modern Language Association of America, American Association of University Professors, Mediaeval Academy of America, American Association of Teachers of Spanish and Portuguese, Hispanic Society of America (corresponding member), Medieval Association of the Pacific, Phi Beta Kappa. *Awards, honors:* Fulbright-Hays fellowship to Spain, 1967-68; National Endowment for the Humanities summer grant, 1971.

WRITINGS: Latin Rhetorical Theory in Thirteenth and Fourteenth Century Castile, University of California Press, 1972; (editor) Iohannes Egidii Zamorensis, *Dictaminis Epithalamium*, Studi Mediolatini e Volgari (Pisa, Italy), in press. Contributor to Spanish journals.

WORK IN PROGRESS: The relationship between medieval Latin and Spanish literatures.

* * *

FAVRETTI, Rudy J(ohn) 1932-

PERSONAL: Born December 3, 1932, in Mystic, Conn.; son of Giovanni Sante (a carpenter) and Giovanna (Lazzaris) Favretti; married Joy Van de Vere Putnam (a researcher), July 16, 1956; children: Giovanni, Elizabeth Emily, Margaret. *Education:* University of Connecticut, B.S., 1954; Cornell University, M.S., 1955; University of Massachusetts, B.L.A., 1965, M.L.A., 1967. *Politics:* Democrat. *Religion:* Unitarian Universalist. *Home:* 1066 Middle Turnpike, Storrs, Conn. 06268. *Office:* Department of Plant Science, University of Connecticut, Storrs, Conn. 06268.

CAREER: University of Connecticut, Storrs, instructor, 1955-57, assistant professor, 1957-64, associate professor, 1964-73, professor of landscape architecture, 1973—. Consultant to Old Sturbridge Village, 1961-65. Chairman of Mansfield History Workshop, 1963-74, and of Mansfield Bicentennial Commission; member of Mansfield Historic District Commission, and Friends of Cast Iron Architecture; trustee of Storrs Cemetery Association, 1970—. *Member:* American Society of Landscape Architects, Society of Architectural Historians, American Name Society, Society for the Preservation of New England Antiquities, Connecticut Horticultural Society, Massachusetts Horticultural Society, Worcester Horticultural Society, Mansfield Historical Society, Pi Alpha Xi, Gamma Sigma Delta, Epsilon Sigma Phi. *Awards, honors:* Bronze medal from Federated Garden Clubs of Connecticut, 1961.

WRITINGS: Growing for Showing, Doubleday, 1961; *Once upon Quoketaug*, Parousia Press, 1974. Contributor of more than sixty articles to journals. Author of pamphlets on gardens.

WORK IN PROGRESS: A book on nineteenth century American gardens and grounds; research on the development of a scenic corridor model for eastern Connecticut, and on the evaluation of attitudes that must be changed for its acceptance.

SIDELIGHTS: Favretti has been granted commissions to design many projects in historic preservation in New England and throughout the Northeast.

* * *

FAY, Gordon S(haw) 1912-

PERSONAL: Born April 27, 1912, in Chicopee Falls, Mass.; son of Robert Hamilton (an engineer) and Tassel (Singleton) Fay; married Constance Bronderslev (a teacher), June 18, 1947; children: Douglas, Michael, Jeffrey. *Education:* Montana School of Mines, B.S., 1939; University of Southern California, M.S.Ed., 1954. *Home:* 19512 Winifred St., Tarzana, Calif. 91356. *Office:* Los Angeles Valley College, 5800 Fulton Ave., Van Nuys, Calif. 91401.

CAREER: Cerro de Pasco Copper Corp., Morococha, Peru, chief mine surveyor, 1940-42; Northrop Aeronautical Institute, Inglewood, Calif., 1946-48; Los Angeles City College, Los Angeles, Calif., instructor in engineering, 1948-52; Los Angeles Valley College, Van Nuys, Calif., instructor, 1952-62, assistant professor, 1962-64, associate professor of earth science and engineering, 1964—. Licensed land surveyor in California; former U.S. Mineral Surveyor. *Military service:* U.S. Marine Corps, engineering officer, 1942-46; served in the Pacific theater and in China; became first lieutenant; received one battle star. *Member:* National Education Association, California Teachers Association.

WRITINGS: Physical Geography, Doubleday, 1965; *The Rockhound's Manual*, Harper, 1972. Contributor to *Science Digest* and *Los Angeles Times*.

WORK IN PROGRESS: Research in meteorology.

AVOCATIONAL INTERESTS: Rockhounding, growing oranges, travel.

* * *

FEAR, David E. 1941-

PERSONAL: Born February 22, 1941, in Decatur, Ill.; son of John D. (an engineer) and Jean (an employment counselor) Fear; married Sharon Tripp (an instructor), March 21, 1964; children: Lynn Ellen, Stephanie Ellen. *Education:* Southern Illinois University, B.S., 1964, M.S., 1967; also studied at Northern Illinois University, 1965-70. *Home address:* R.R. 1, Box 512G, Longwood, Fla. 32750. *Office:* Department of English, Valencia Community College, Box 3028, Orlando, Fla. 32802.

CAREER: High school English teacher in Aurora, Ill., 1964-66, and Newark, N.J., 1966-67; Sauk Valley College, Dixon, Ill., instructor in technical writing, 1967-70; Valencia Community College, Orlando, Fla., instructor in technical writing, 1970—. *Member:* Conference on College Composition and Communication, American Association of University Professors.

WRITINGS: Technical Writing, Random House, 1973. Contributor to *Teaching English in the Two-Year College*, and *Technical Writing Teacher.*

WORK IN PROGRESS: A comprehensive text on technical communication.

* * *

FEIBES, Walter 1928-

PERSONAL: Born January 26, 1928, in Aachen, Germany; son of L. Erich (a physician) and Gertrude (Herz) Feibes; married Marie Molloy, July 9, 1950; children: Elizabeth, Erica Marie, Mark Henry. *Education:* Union College, Schenectady, N.Y., B.S. 1952; Western Reserve University (now Case Western Reserve University), M.S.L.S., 1953; State University of New York at Buffalo, Ph.D., 1967. *Politics:* Democrat. *Religion:* Unitarian-Universalist. *Home:* 808 Old Fort Rd., Bowling Green, Ky. 42101. *Office:* Department of Mathematics, Western Kentucky University, Bowling Green, Ky. 42101.

CAREER: U.S. Government, Washington, D.C., information officer, 1953-55; General Electric Co., Louisville, Ky., manager of technical library, 1955-63; State University of New York at Buffalo, instructor in mathematics, 1963-67; Western Kentucky University, Bowling Green, associate professor of mathematics, 1967—. Consultant to Marine Midland Bank, Buffalo, N.Y., 1965-67. Democratic councilman in Bowling Green, Ky., 1968-72. *Military service:* U.S. Navy, 1946-48. *Member:* Mathematical Association of America, Operations Research Society of America, American Statistical Association, American Institute of Decision Sciences, Sigma Xi.

WRITINGS: Introduction to Finite Mathematics, Hamilton Publishing, 1974. Contributor to *Journal of the Royal Statistical Society* and *American Statistician.*

WORK IN PROGRESS: Studies of decision theory, applied stochastic processes, and the time series.

SIDELIGHTS: Feibes told *CA*, "There are, in my estimation, too many mathematicians today who sprinkle their social science and liberal arts mathematics courses with Greek letters and seemingly have RIGOR tattooed on their foreheads. There is a time and place for everything! For the majority of social science students, mathematics is synonymous to a 'bad trip'. Hopefully, this text *(Introduction to Finite Mathematics)* will serve in some small measure to reverse this situation." *Avocational interests:* Current events, reading, chess, ping pong, swimming, music.

* * *

FEIERMAN, Steven 1940-

PERSONAL: Surname sounds like "fireman"; born December 12, 1940, in New York, N.Y.; son of Alexander (a lawyer) and Jeanette (a teacher; maiden name, Sobel) Feierman; married Elizabeth Karlin, July 25, 1964; children: Joshua, Jessica. *Education:* Columbia University, B.A., 1961; Northwestern University, M.A., 1962, Ph.D. (history), 1970; Wadham College, Oxford, diploma in social anthropology, 1965, D.Phil. (anthropology), 1972. *Home:* 2301 Rugby Row, Madison, Wis. 53705. *Office:* Department of History, University of Wisconsin, Madison, Wis. 53706.

CAREER: University of Wisconsin, Madison, instructor, 1969-70, assistant professor, 1970-72, associate professor of African history, 1972—. *Member:* International African Institute, African Studies Association, Historical Association of Tanzania, Historical Society of Kenya.

WRITINGS: The Shambaa Kingdom: A History, University of Wisconsin Press, 1974; *Symbols and Change in Shambaa Politics*, Clarendon Press, in press.

WORK IN PROGRESS: Research on conceptions of time in East Africa, and on the history and sociology of African medicine.

SIDELIGHTS: In 1966-68 Feierman lived in the villages of rural Tanzania.

* * *

FEIGERT, Frank B(rook) 1937-

PERSONAL: Born November 10, 1937, in New York, N.Y.; son of Morris Samuel (a salesman) and Anna (a bookkeeper; maiden name, Frank) Feigert; married Frances Goodside (a librarian), June 17, 1961; children: Benjamin, Daniel. *Education:* Allegheny College, B.A., 1959; University of Maryland, M.A., 1965, Ph.D., 1968. *Politics:* "Visceral Democrat." *Home:* 35 Lynnwood Dr., Brockport, N.Y. 14420. *Office:* Department of Political Science, State University of New York at Brockport, Brockport, N.Y. 14420.

CAREER: Knox College, Galesburg, Ill., instructor, 1966-68, assistant professor of political science, 1968-70; State University of New York, Brockport, assistant professor, 1970-71, associate professor, 1971-75, professor of political science, 1975—. *Military service:* U.S. Air Force, 1959-64; became captain. *Member:* American Political Science Association, American Civil Liberties Union, Sierra Club, Midwest Political Science Association, Southern Political Science Association, Northeastern Political Science Association. *Awards, honors:* State University of New York Research Foundation grants, 1971, 1974.

WRITINGS: (With M. M. Conway) *Political Analysis: An Introduction*, Allyn & Bacon, 1972, 2nd edition, in press; (with Conway) *American Political Parties*, Allyn & Bacon, in press. Contributor to *American Political Science Review, Polity, American Behavioral Scientist*, and *Western Political Quarterly.*

WORK IN PROGRESS: Research on the relationships between social stress and electoral change in America, 1860 to the present.

AVOCATIONAL INTERESTS: Amateur photography.

* * *

FELDMAN, Louis H(arry) 1926-

PERSONAL: Born October 29, 1926, Hartford, Conn.; son of Sam and Sarah (Vine) Feldman; married Miriam Blum, March 8, 1966; children: Moshe Yaakov, Sarah Rivkah, Leah Chanah. *Education:* Trinity College, Hartford, Conn., B.A., 1946, M.A., 1947; Harvard University, Ph.D., 1951. *Religion:* Jewish. *Home:* 915 West End Ave., New York, N.Y. 10025. *Office:* Yeshiva University, 500 West 185th St., New York, N.Y. 10033.

CAREER: Trinity College, Hartford, Conn., teaching fellow, 1951-52, instructor in classics, 1952-53; Hobart and William Smith Colleges, Geneva, N.Y., instructor in classics, 1953-55; Yeshiva University, New York, N.Y., instructor in humanities and history, 1955-56, assistant professor, 1956-61, associate professor, 1961-66, professor of classics, 1966—. *Member:* American Philological Association, American Classical League, American Philosophical Association, Classical Association of the Atlantic States (member of executive committee, 1957-59), Phi Beta Kappa. *Awards, honors:* Ford Foundation fellowship, 1951-52; Guggenheim fellowship, 1963; Memorial Foundation for Jewish Culture grant, 1969; American Council of Learned Societies senior fellow, 1971; American Philosophical Association grant, 1972; Littauer Foundation fellow, 1973; Wurzweiler Foundation fellow, 1974; American Academy for Jewish Research grant, 1975.

WRITINGS: Scholarship on Philo and Josephus (1937-1962), Yeshiva University Press, 1963; (editor, translator, and author of commentary) *Jewish Antiquities*, Books 18-20, Harvard University Press, 1965; (contributor) Jacob Neusner, editor, *Religions in Antiquity: Essays in Memory of Erwin Ramsdell Goodenough*, E. J. Brill (Leiden), 1968; (author of prolegomenon) M. R. James, *The Biblical Antiquities of Philo*, Ktav, 1971. Departmental editor of Hellenistic Literature of *Encyclopaedia Judaica*, 1967-71. Contributor to *Encyclopaedia Judaica* and *Encyclopaedia Britannica*. Also contributor to journals in his field. Associate editor, *Classical Weekly*, 1955-57; managing editor, *Classical World*, 1957-59.

WORK IN PROGRESS: Research on Josephus as an historian: contributing to *World History of the Jewish People*, *Cambridge History of Judaism*, and *Morton Smith Festschrift*.

SIDELIGHTS: Feldman's command of languages includes Greek, Latin, Hebrew, Aramaic, Yiddish, French, German, and Italian.

* * *

FELL, John L(ouis) 1927-

PERSONAL: Born September 19, 1927, in Westfield, N.J.; son of Shelby G. (an engineer) and Frances (Hildebrand) Fell; married Suzanne Shillington (a librarian), December 5, 1958; children: Justine Richmond, John Shillington, Eliza Marritt. *Education:* Hamilton College, A.B., 1950; New York University, M.A., 1954, Ph.D., 1958. *Home:* 1263 15th Ave., San Francisco, Calif. 94122. *Office:* Film Department, San Francisco State University, San Francisco, Calif. 94132.

CAREER: Free-lance jazz musician in New York and Montana, 1951-60; DPM Productions, New York, N.Y., film writer, 1953-58; Montana State University, Bozeman, assistant professor of film and television, 1958-60; San Francisco State University, San Francisco, Calif., assistant professor, 1960-64, associate professor, 1964-69, professor of film, 1970—. Broadcaster of film and book reviews. *Military service:* U.S. Army Air Forces, 1946-47. *Member:* Society for Cinema Studies; University Film Association; Writers Guild of America, West; American Federation of Musicians; Phi Beta Kappa; Kappa Delta Pi; Alpha Epsilon Rho.

WRITINGS: Film and the Narrative Tradition, University of Oklahoma Press, 1974; *Film: An Introduction*, Praeger, 1975. Writer of album notes for three "Jazz Panorama" recordings and for "For Discriminating Collectors." Contributor of articles and reviews on film, music, books, theater, photography, and humorous topics to *Arts in Society*, *Esquire*, *Film Quarterly*, *Film Comment*, *Gambit*, *Photo Arts*, *Show*, *Saturday Review*, *Sportsman*, *Men*, *He*, and other periodicals. Guest editor, *Cinema Journal*, fall, 1973.

WORK IN PROGRESS: Public Eyes and Private Guilt; and a study of the film genre and its literary and theatrical antecedents.

* * *

FELLMAN, Gordon 1934-

PERSONAL: Born May 10, 1934, in Omaha, Neb.; son of Charles (a grocer) and Rose (Shyken) Fellman. *Education:* Antioch College, B.A., 1957; Harvard University, Ph.D., 1964. *Home:* 1039 Massachusetts Ave., Cambridge, Mass. 02138. *Office:* Department of Sociology, Brandeis University, Waltham, Mass. 02154.

CAREER: Harvard University, Cambridge, Mass., lecturer in sociology, 1963-64; Brandeis University, Waltham, Mass., assistant professor, 1964-71, associate professor of sociology, 1971—. *Member:* American Sociological Association, American Association of University Professors, Eastern Sociological Society, Massachusetts Sociological Association, American Civil Liberties Union.

WRITINGS: (Contributor) Hans Spiegel, editor, *Citizen Participation in Urban Renewal*, National Training Laboratories, Volume I, 1969; *Implications for Planning Policy of Neighborhood Resistance to Urban Renewal and Highway Proposals* (monograph), National Technical Information Center, 1970; (with Barbara Brandt) *The Deceived Majority: Politics and Protest in Middle America*, Trans-Action Press, 1973. Contributor to journals in his field.

WORK IN PROGRESS: Research on Israel and American Jewry and the social psychology of social class.

* * *

FELLOWS, Muriel H.

EDUCATION: University of Pennsylvania, B.S. (cum laude) and M.A.

WRITINGS—Books for children: *The Land of Little Rain* (Junior Literary Guild selection), Winston, 1936; *The Magic Painter* (Junior Literary Guild selection), Winston, 1938; *Ancient Aztecs*, Franklin Publishing, 1974.

* * *

FENNELLY, John F(auntleroy) 1899-1974

July 18, 1899—December 27, 1974; American inventor, economist, stockbroker, and author of nonfiction works. Obituaries: *New York Times*, December 29, 1974.

* * *

FENTEN, Barbara D(oris) 1935-

PERSONAL: Born August 25, 1935, in New York, N.Y.; daughter of Isaac (an inspector) and Mae (Brownstein) Levy; married D. X. Fenten (a writer), April 7, 1957; children: Donna Ruth, Jeffrey Allan. *Education:* New York University, B.S., 1956; Long Island University, M.L.S., 1970. *Home:* 27 Bowdon Rd., Greenlawn, N.Y. 11740.

CAREER: Free-lance writer and editor, 1957-66; Huntington Free School District No. 3, Huntington, N.Y., library media specialist, 1966—. *Member:* Suffolk County Library Association.

WRITINGS: (With husband, D. X. Fenten) *The Organic Grow It, Cook It, Preserve It Guidebook*, Grosset, 1972; (with D. X. Fenten) *The Concise Guide to Natural Foods*, F. Watts, 1974. Contributor to *Instructor* and *K-Eight*.

WORK IN PROGRESS: Two novels for elementary school children.

* * *

FENTON, John Y(oung) 1933-

PERSONAL: Born July 12, 1933, in French Camp, Miss.; son of H. G. (a teacher) and Lil (Thompson) Fenton; married Julia A. Gray (an artist), June 10, 1958; children: John Kyle. *Education:* Millsaps College, student, 1951-53; Davidson College, A.B., 1955; graduate study at Middlebury College, summer, 1955, and Philipps Universitaet, 1955-56; Princeton University, M.A., 1960, Ph.D., 1962; postdoctoral study at University of Chicago, 1966-67, and University of Washington, Seattle, summer, 1970. *Politics:* Democrat. *Religion:* Episcopalian. *Office:* Department of Religion, Emory University, Atlanta, Ga. 30322.

CAREER: Pennsylvania State University, University Park, research associate in religious studies, 1960-68; Emory University, Atlanta, Ga., instructor, 1960-68, research associate and associate professor of religion, 1968—. *Member:* American Academy of Religion, Association for Asian Studies, Society for South Indian Studies.

WRITINGS: (Editor with C. Conrad Cherry) *Religion in the Public Domain*, Department of Continuing Liberal Education, Pennsylvania State University, 1966; (editor and contributor) *Theology and Body*, Westminster Press, 1974. Contributor to *Journal of Religion*, *Journal of Religious Thought*, *Journal of the American Academy of Religion*, *Anglican Theological Review*, and *Soundings*.

WORK IN PROGRESS: A Metaphysics of Commitment: A Study in the Epistemology of Religions, the first volume of a two-volume study.

SIDELIGHTS: Fenton's main interests are in cross-cultural studies of religious thought structures, meditation, altered states of consciousness, Hinduism, and Buddhism.

* * *

FERBER, Andrew 1935-

PERSONAL: Born July 7, 1935, in New York, N.Y.; son of William L. (a urologist) and Diana (a teacher; maiden name, Behrman) Ferber; married Jane Schwarzberg (a psychiatrist), June 11, 1961; children: Joshua, Elizabeth. *Education:* University of Wisconsin, B.S., 1955; Columbia University, College of Physicians and Surgeons, M.D., 1959. *Politics:* "Limits to growth." *Religion:* Buddhist. *Home:* 55 Wildcliff Rd., New Rochelle, N.Y. 10805. *Office:* Harlem Valley Psychiatric Center, Wingdale, N.Y.

CAREER: Yeshiva University, Albert Einstein College of Medicine, Bronx, N.Y., psychiatric resident and fellow in social psychiatry, 1959-64, associate professor of psychiatry, 1970—, director of Family Studies program, 1964-74; Bronx State Hospital, Bronx, N.Y., director of Family Studies section, 1964—; now at Harlem Valley Psychiatric Center, Wingdale, N.Y.

WRITINGS: (Editor with Marilyn Mendelsohn and Gus Napier) *The Book of Family Therapy*, Science House, 1972. Contributor to scientific journals. Member of editorial board of *Family Process*, 1969—.

WORK IN PROGRESS: Secret Teachings of Family Therapists, for Aronson; *Book for Personal Liberation.*

* * *

FEREJOHN, John A(rthur) 1944-

PERSONAL: Born June 6, 1944, in Deming, N.M.; son of George Arthur and Olga (Collazo) Ferejohn; married Sally Rhea, February 23, 1963; children: Christopher George, Sara Nicole. *Education:* San Fernando Valley State College (now California State University, Northridge), B.A., 1966; Stanford University, Ph.D., 1972. *Politics:* Democrat. *Residence:* Altadena, Calif. *Office:* Department of Political Science, California Institute of Technology, Pasadena, Calif.

CAREER: California Institute of Technology, Pasadena, associate professor of political science, 1972—. *Member:* American Political Science Association, American Economic Association, Public Choice Society. *Awards, honors:* Brookings Institute fellowship, 1970-71; fellow of the Center for Advanced Study, University of Illinois, 1971-72.

WRITINGS: Pork Barrel Politics: Rivers and Harbors Legislation, 1947-1968, Stanford University Press, 1974. Contributor of articles to *American Political Science Review, Political Science Annual, American Economic Review*, and *Journal of Economic Theory.*

WORK IN PROGRESS: Research on congressional elections, models of political campaigns, and social choice theory.

* * *

FERGUS, Patricia M(arguerita) 1918-

PERSONAL: Born October 26, 1918, in Minneapolis, Minn.; daughter of Golden M. (a salesman) and Mary (a businesswoman; maiden name, Smith) Fergus. *Education:* University of Minnesota, B.S., 1939, M.A., 1941, Ph.D., 1960. *Religion:* Roman Catholic. *Residence:* Minneapolis, Minn. *Office:* Department of English, University of Minnesota, Minneapolis, Minn. 55455.

CAREER: U.S. Government, Minneapolis-St. Paul, Minn., personnel chief, 1943-46, secretary and civilian personnel supervisor, 1946-50, administrative assistant, 1950-54, office supervisor, 1957-58, administrative assistant, 1958-59 (all for Department of Defense), secretary for Department of the Interior, 1954-57; University of Minnesota, Minneapolis, lecturer, 1961-64, instructor, 1964-72, assistant professor of English, 1972—. *Member:* National Council of Teachers of English, American Association of University Professors, American Association of University Women, Minnesota Council of Teachers of English, Pi Lambda Theta.

WRITINGS: Spelling Improvement: A Program for Self-Instruction, McGraw, 1964, 2nd edition, 1973. Contributor to *Journal of Research in Music Education* and *Minnesota Studies in Education.*

WORK IN PROGRESS: A program on critical writing and thinking; a series of personal essays; research on teaching of writing in secondary schools and colleges.

AVOCATIONAL INTERESTS: Classical music, chamber music, opera, concert pieces for viola, drama.

* * *

FERREOL, Marcel Auguste 1899-1974 (Marcel Achard)

July 5, 1899—September 4, 1974; French playwright and member of the French Academy. Obituaries: *New York Times*, September 5, 1974; *Washington Post*, September 6, 1974.

FESSENDEN, Katherine 1896(?)-1974

1896(?)—August 20, 1974; American social worker and author of children's book. Obituaries: *New York Times*, August 22, 1974.

* * *

FICHTELIUS, Karl-Erik 1924-

PERSONAL: Born March 29, 1924, in Stockholm, Sweden; son of Erik Hildor and Martha (Oestroem) Fichtelius; married Jeanette Setterquist (a language teacher), June 3, 1967. *Education:* University of Uppsala, M.D., 1953. *Address:* Box 62, Skog 87024, Sweden.

CAREER: University of Uppsala, Uppsala, Sweden, associate professor, 1953-60, assistant professor, 1960-62, professor of histology, 1962-72; in medical practice as a country physician in northern Sweden, 1972—. Research professor at University of Minnesota, 1967-68. *Member:* German Hematological Society (honorary member), Swiss Hematological Society (corresponding member), Collegium Internationale Allergologicum (corresponding member), Royal Lymphatic Society of Uppsala (honorary president).

WRITINGS: (Editor and contributor) *Maenniskans villkor* (title means "The Conditions of Man"), Wahlstroem & Wistrand, 1967; (with Sverre Sjoelander) *Maenniskan, kaskelotvalen och kunskapens traed*, Wahlstroem & Widstrand, 1971, published as *Smarter than Man*, Pantheon, 1972. Contributor to *Hematology and Immunology*.

* * *

FIFE, Austin E(dwin) 1909-

PERSONAL: Born December 18, 1909, in Lincoln, Idaho; son of Robert H. (a farmer) and Mary E. (Stocks) Fife; married Alta Stevens, March 27, 1934; children: Carolyn (Mrs. David S. Langdon), Marian (Mrs. F. W. Darks). *Education:* Attended Utah State University, 1928-29, 1931-33; Stanford University, B.A., M.A., Ph.D.; Harvard University, M.A., 1937. *Home:* 686 East 10 N., Logan, Utah 84321. *Office:* Department of Languages, Utah State University, Logan, Utah 84322.

CAREER: Santa Monica City College, Santa Monica, Calif., instructor in French, 1939-42; Occidental College, Los Angeles, Calif., 1946-58, began as associate professor, became professor of French; U.S. Office of Education, Washington, D.C., advisor in foreign languages, 1959-60; Utah State University, Logan, professor of French, and chairman of department of foreign languages, 1960—. Fulbright exchange professor at French national museums, 1949-50. *Military service:* U.S. Army Air Forces, 1942-46. U.S. Air Force, 1951-53; became lieutenant colonel. *Member:* American Folklore Society (fellow), Modern Language Association of America, Utah Heritage Foundation (fellow), Utah State Historical Society (fellow). *Awards, honors:* Guggenheim fellow, 1958-59; National Endowment for the Humanities senior scholar award, 1971-72.

WRITINGS: (With wife, Alta S. Fife) *Saints of Sage and Saddle*, Indiana University Press, 1956; (translator from the French) *The Borzoi Book of French Folk Tales*, Knopf, 1956; (editor with J. Golden Taylor) *Western Folklore Conference: Selected Papers*, Utah State University Press, 1964; (with A. S. Fife) *Songs of the Cowboys*, C. N. Potter, 1966; (editor with Ernest Bulow) *Latin American Interlude*, Utah State University Press, 1966; (with A. S. Fife) *Cowboy and Western Songs*, C. N. Potter, 1969; (editor with A. S. Fife and Henry Glassie) *Forms upon the Frontier*, Utah State University Press, 1969; (with A. S. Fife) *Ballads of the Great West*, American West, 1970; *Heaven on Horseback: Revivalist Songs and Verse in the Cowboy Idiom*, Utah State University Press, 1970. Contributor of more than one hundred articles to scholarly journals.

WORK IN PROGRESS: Transferring research files and folklore library to library of Utah State University.

* * *

FIGES, Eva 1932-

PERSONAL: Surname is pronounced *Fye*-jees; born April 15, 1932, in Berlin, Germany; daughter of Emil Eduard (a businessman) and Irma (an artist; maiden name, Cohen) Unger; married John George Figes, July 10, 1954 (divorced, 1963); children: Catherine Jane, Orlando Guy. *Education:* Queen Mary College, London, B.A. (honors), 1953. *Politics:* "Left wing (undogmatic)." *Religion:* None. *Home:* 24 Fitzjohns Ave., London N.W.3, England. *Agent:* Deborah Rogers Ltd., 29 Goodge St., London W.1, England.

CAREER: Longmans, Green & Co., Ltd., London, England, editor, 1955-57; Weidenfeld & Nicolson, Ltd., London, editor, 1962-63; Blackie & Son, Ltd., London, editor, 1964-67; writer, 1967—. *Member:* Society of Authors, Writers' Guild. *Awards, honors: Guardian* fiction prize, 1967, for *Winter Journey*.

WRITINGS: (Editor) *Classic Choice, 1* (short stories), Blackie & Son, 1965; (editor) *Modern Choice, 1-2* (short stories), two volumes, Blackie & Son, 1965-66; *Equinox* (novel), Secker & Warburg, 1966; *Winter Journey* (novel), Faber, 1967, Hill & Wang, 1968; *Konek Landing* (novel), Faber, 1969; *Patriarchal Attitudes* (nonfiction), Stein & Day, 1970 (published as *Patriarchal Attitudes: Women in Society*, Faber, 1970); *B* (novel), Faber, 1972; *Days* (novel), Faber, 1974.

Books for children: (Reteller) *The Musicians of Bremen*, Blackie & Son, 1967; *The Banger*, Lion Press, 1968; *Scribble Sam: A Story*, McKay, 1971.

Translator: Bernhard Grzimek, *He and I and the Elephants*, Hill & Wang, 1967; George Sand, pseudonym of Mme Dudevant, *Little Fadette*, Blackie & Son, 1967; Renate Rasp, *Family Failure*, Grossman, 1970.

WORK IN PROGRESS: A book on drama; a novel.

* * *

FIJAN, Carol 1918-

PERSONAL: Born February 18, 1918, in Milwaukee, Wis.; daughter of Philip Paul (a furrier) and Julia (Hauler) Fijan; married Herman Starobin (an economist and professor), September 12, 1956; children: Christina Fijan (Mrs. Mathew Leavitt). *Education:* Hunter College (now of the City University of New York), B.A., 1939. *Politics:* None. *Religion:* None. *Home:* 58 Rose Ave., Great Neck, N.Y. 11021.

CAREER: Puppet Associates, New York, N.Y., director, 1949-70; National Theatre of Puppet Arts, New York, N.Y, director, 1971—. Teacher of puppetry for Columbia Broadcasting System and Public Broadcasting Service, 1969, and National Educational Television, 1973; has performed as a television puppeteer, 1972-74. *Member:* Union Internationale de la Marionnette, Puppeteers of America (member of board, 1968-70), Actors Equity Association,

Ontario Puppetry Association (honorary member), Puppet Guild of Long Island, Great Neck Arts Council. *Awards, honors:* National citation from Puppeteers of America, 1974, for contributions to the art of puppetry.

WRITINGS: Making Puppets Come Alive, Taplinger, 1974. Contributor to *Journal of Puppeteers of America* and other puppetry journals throughout the world.

WORK IN PROGRESS: Research on acting with puppets, the change in technique throughout the ages; a book of playlets, skits, and sketches on puppet plays relating to the Bicentinnial for grade school level; a book on puppetry as an educator's tool.

* * *

FINBERG, H(erbert) P(atrick) R(eginald) 1900-1974

March 21, 1900—November 1, 1974; British publisher, historian, editor and author of books predominantly on regional English history. Obituaries: *AB Bookman's Weekly*, December 16, 1974. (*CA*-15/16).

* * *

FINCH, Donald George 1937-

PERSONAL: Born June 30, 1937, in Peoria, Ill.; son of Lloyd and Jean (Harsy) Finch. *Education:* Attended Bradley University. *Religion:* Lutheran. *Home:* 506 Northeast Monroe, Peoria, Ill. 61603.

CAREER: Has been employed as a salesman, postal clerk, and manager of apartment building; writer. *Military service:* U.S. Air Force, 1957-60. *Member:* Peoria Poetry Club (president, 1972). *Awards, honors:* Second place award from Kentucky Poetry Contest, 1972, for "Locked in an Unlocked Room."

WRITINGS—Poems: *On Strawberry Eve*, Dorrance, 1972; *She Waits for Me*, Miller Books, 1972; *A Dandelion Is Not a Rose*, Windy Row, 1973. Contributor of more than a hundred poems to magazines.

WORK IN PROGRESS—Poems: *Georgia*; *Wash'n' Wear*; *Doctor Sane*.

* * *

FINCHER, Ernest B(arksdale) 1910-

PERSONAL: Born March 21, 1910, in Mescalero, N.M.; son of Elijah B. (a clergyman) and Catherine (a teacher; maiden name, Arvin) Fincher. *Education:* Texas Technological College (now Texas Tech University), B.A., 1931; Columbia University, M.A., 1934; New York University, Ph.D., 1950. *Politics:* 'McCarthy-type Democrat." *Religion:* Society of Friends (Quakers). *Home:* Deerpath Farm, Asbury, N.J. 08802.

CAREER: Social science teacher in Amarillo, Tex., 1931-33; Columbia University Press, New York, N.Y., member of editorial staff, 1934-35; high school social science teacher in Westwood, N.J., 1935-42; New Jersey State College at Montclair, assistant professor, 1946-49, associate professor, 1949-55, professor of political science, 1955-70; free-lance writer, 1970—. *Wartime service:* Alternative service with American Friends Service Committee, 1942-46. *Member:* American Academy of Political and Social Science, New York Historical Society.

WRITINGS: (With W. G. Kimmel and Russell Fraser) *Democracy at Work*, Winston, 1939, 2nd edition, 1941; (with John Ferguson and Dean McHenry) *American Government Today*, McGraw, 1951; *The President of the United States*, Abelard, 1955; *The Government of the United States*, Prentice-Hall, 1967, 3rd edition, in press; (with Merle Prunty) *Lands of Promise*, Macmillan, 1971, 2nd edition, 1973; *In a Race with Time*, Macmillan, 1972, 2nd edition, 1974; *Spanish Americans as a Political Factor in New Mexico*, Arno, 1974.

WORK IN PROGRESS: Research for a book on the President, Congress, and the courts.

SIDELIGHTS: Fincher writes: "My outlook on the world is colored by the fact that I am a pacifist—a conscientious objector in World War Two—but a political activist who believes that the world can survive only if drastic changes are made in social, economic, and political institutions. My dissatisfaction with the present order has been heightened by extensive travel in Latin America and by taking part in seminars involving radical students in that part of the world."

* * *

FINK, Gary M. 1936-

PERSONAL: Born February 4, 1936, in Forsyth, Mont.; son of John (a farmer) and Martha (Kurtz) Fink; married Mary Balk (a teacher), March 26, 1959; children: Lisa, John, Karen, Kristen. *Education:* University of Montana, B.S., 1960; University of Missouri, M.A., 1964, Ph.D., 1968. *Politcs:* Democrat. *Religion:* None. *Home:* 611 Ridgecrest Rd., Atlanta, Ga. 30307. *Office:* Department of History, Georgia State University, Atlanta, Ga. 30303.

CAREER: Mankato State College, Mankato, Minn., assistant professor of American history, 1968-70; Georgia State University, Atlanta, associate professor of American history, 1970—. *Military service:* U.S. Army, 1954-56. *Member:* American Historical Association, Organization of American Historians, Southern Historical Association.

WRITINGS: Labor's Search for Political Order, University of Missouri Press, 1974; (editor) *Dictionary of American Labor Leaders*, Greenwood Press, 1974. Contributor to history and economics journals.

WORK IN PROGRESS: Labor Unions, one volume of a ten-volume *Encyclopedia of American Institutions*, for Greenwood Press; *A History of the Congress of Industrial Organizations*.

AVOCATIONAL INTERESTS: Baseball.

* * *

FINK, Paul Jay 1933-

PERSONAL: Born June 26, 1933, in Philadelphia, Pa.; son of John (an electrician) and Essie (Wexler) Fink; married Shirley Katz, December 23, 1956; children: David, Mark, Gary. *Education:* Temple University, B.S. (magna cum laude), 1954, M.D., 1958; Institute of Philadelphia Association for Psychoanalysis, graduate training in psychoanalysis, 1962-66. *Home:* 509 McGregor Ct., Virginia Beach, Va. 23462. *Office:* Eastern Virginia Medical School, 721 Fairfax Ave., Norfolk, Va. 23501.

CAREER: Albert Einstein Medical Center, Philadelphia, Pa., intern, 1958-59; resident in psychiatry at Philadelphia Psychiatric Center, Philadelphia, Pa., 1959-61, and Albert Einstein Medical Center, 1961-62; Hahnemann Medical College and Hospital, Philadelphia, Pa., instructor and then senior instructor in department of mental health sciences, 1962-66, assistant professor of psychiatry, 1966-67, director of psychiatric education, 1967-69, associate professor and director of education and training, 1969-71, professor of psychiatry, 1971-73; Eastern Virginia Medical School, Norfolk, professor of psychiatry and chairman of department of psychiatry and behavioral sciences, 1973—. Director of department of psychiatry, Medical Center Hospital, Norfolk, 1973—; medical director of Community Mental Health Center, Norfolk, 1973—. Certified in psychiatry, American Board of Psychiatry and Neurology, 1965; limited private practice as psychiatrist in Philadelphia, 1967-72, and Norfolk, 1973—. Adjunct professor of psychology at Old Dominion University, 1973—; visiting professor at Hershey Medical School, 1972, 1973, 1974; lectures extensively at hospitals, medical schools, and for medical groups.

MEMBER: American College of Psychiatrists (fellow), American Medical Association, American Psychiatric Association (fellow), American Psychoanalytic Association, International Psychoanalytic Association, Association of American Medical Colleges, Association of Academic Psychiatry, American College of Psychoanalysts (fellow), American Society for Adolescent Psychiatry (secretary, 1974-75), American Association of Chairman of Departments of Psychiatry, Pan American Medical Association, American Association of University Professors, Medical Society of Virginia, Neuropsychiatric Society of Virginia. *Awards, honors:* Bowman Gray Medical School fellowships, 1967, 1969; Lindbach Award for excellence in teaching, 1970.

WRITINGS: (Editor with Van Buren Hammett) *Sexual Function and Dysfunction*, F. A. Davis, 1969; (editor with Richard E. Hicks) *Psychedelic Drugs*, Grune, 1969; (editor with Wilbur W. Oaks, and contributor) *Psychiatry and the Internist*, Grune, 1970; (contributor) Stanley S. Spitzer and Wilbur W. Oaks, *Emergency Medical Care*, Grune, 1971. Contributor to psychiatry and other journals, including *Medical Aspects of Human Sexuality* and *International Journal of Psychiatry*. Contributing editor, *Pennsylvania Medicine*, 1971-73; member of editorial board, *Annals of Adolescent Psychiatry*, 1972; associate editor, *Journal of Art Psychotherapy*, 1972, editor, 1974.

* * *

FINKELSTEIN, Jacob Joel 1922-1974

March 22, 1922—November 28, 1974; American educator and author of works on early Mesopotamia and cuneiform texts. Obituaries: *New York Times*, December 1, 1974; *AB Bookman's Weekly*, December 16, 1974.

* * *

FIRST, Ruth

PERSONAL: Born in Johannesburg, South Africa; married Joe Slovo. *Education:* University of Witwatersrand, B.A. *Religion:* None. *Home:* 13 Lyme St., London N.W.1, England. *Office:* Department of Sociology, University of Durham, Durham, England.

CAREER: University of Durham, Durham, England, lecturer in sociology of underdevelopment, 1973—. Has worked as a journalist.

WRITINGS: South West Africa, Penguin, 1963; *One Hundred Seventeen Days,* Stein & Day, 1965; *The Barrel of a Gun,* Pantheon, 1970; (with Jonathan Steele and Christabel Gurney) *The South African Connection,* Temple Smith, 1972; *Libya: The Elusive Revolution,* Penguin, 1974.

WORK IN PROGRESS: A biography of South African writer, Olive Schreiner.

SIDELIGHTS: Miss First spent 1960 and 1963 in a South African prison as a result of her opposition to apartheid.

* * *

FISCHER, George 1923-

PERSONAL: Born May 5, 1923, in Berlin, Germany; U.S. citizen by birth; married, 1958; divorced, 1971; children: two. *Education:* University of Wisconsin, B.A., 1947; Harvard University, Ph.D., 1952. *Home address:* Alligerville, High Falls, N.Y. 12440. *Office:* Graduate School, City University of New York, 33 West 42nd St., New York, N.Y. 10036.

CAREER: Brandeis University, Waltham, Mass., assistant professor, 1953-58, associate professor of history, 1958-60; Cornell University, Ithaca, N.Y., professor of political science, 1961-65; Columbia University, New York, N.Y., lecturer in sociology , 1965-69; City University of New York, New York, N.Y., professor of sociology at Richmond College, 1969-73, and at Graduate School, 1969—. Fellow of Center for Advanced Study in the Behavioral Sciences (Stanford, Calif.), 1958-59. *Military service:* U.S. Army, 1942-46; became captain. *Member:* American Sociological Association, Eastern Sociological Society, Phi Beta Kappa. *Awards, honors:* Harvard University Society of Fellows junior fellowship, 1949-53; Social Science Research Council faculty research fellowship, 1959-60; Guggenheim fellowship, 1964.

WRITINGS: Russian Emigre Politics (monograph), East European Fund, Ford Foundation, 1951; *Soviet Opposition to Stalin*, Harvard University Press, 1952; *Russian Liberalism*, Harvard University Press, 1958; *The Personal Papers of Leon Trotsky* (monograph), Library, Harvard University, 1959.

Science and Politics: The New Sociology in the Soviet Union (monograph), Center for International Studies, Cornell University, 1964; *The Soviet Union, Arms Control, and Disarmament: Background Material on Soviet Attitudes* (monograph), School of International Affairs, Columbia University, 1965; *Science and Ideology in Soviet Society*, Atherton, 1967; *The Soviet System and Modern Society*, Atherton, 1968; *Ideology and Opinion Making* (monograph), Bureau of Applied Social Research, Columbia University, 1969.

The Revival of American Socialism, Oxford University Press, 1971; *What's What on Staten Island* (monograph), Richmond College of the City University of New York, 1972; *Urban Higher Education in the United States* (monograph), Central Office of the City University of New York, 1974.

* * *

FISCHER, Joel 1939-

PERSONAL: Born April 22, 1939, in Chicago, Ill.; son of Sam and Ruth Fischer; married Ursula R. (a tennis professional), June 14, 1964; children: Lisa, Nicole. *Education:* University of Illinois, B.A., 1961, M.S.W., 1964; University of California, Berkeley, D.S.W., 1970. *Home:* 965 Makaiwa St., Honolulu, Hawaii 96816. *Office:* Department of Social Work Education, University of Hawaii, Honolulu, Hawaii 96816.

CAREER: University of Hawaii, Honolulu, professor of social work education, 1970—. *Member:* National Association of Social Workers, Academy of Certified Social Workers, American Association of University Professors, Council on Social Work Education.

WRITINGS: Interpersonal Helping: Emerging Approaches for Social Work Practice, C. C Thomas, 1973; *Planned Behavior Change: Application of Behavior Modification to Social Work Practice*, Free Press, 1975. Contributor of more than thirty articles to professional journals.

WORK IN PROGRESS: Effective Casework Practice: An Eclectic Approach; *The Effectiveness of Social Casework*; *Behavior Therapy with Sexual Problems*; *Behavior Modification of Homosexuality*.

* * *

FISCHTROM, Harvey 1933-1974 (Harve Zemach)

December 5, 1933—November 2, 1974; American educator and author of children's books. Obituaries: *New York Times*, November 5, 1974; *AB Bookman's Weekly*, November 18, 1974; *Publishers Weekly*, November 25, 1974. (*CA*-25/28).

* * *

FISHER, Alan W(ashburn) 1939-

PERSONAL: Born November 23, 1939, in Columbus, Ohio; son of Sydney N. (a professor) and Elizabeth (Scipio) Fisher; married Carol Garrett (a potter), August 24, 1963; children: Elizabeth, Christy, Garrett. *Education:* DePauw University, B.A., 1961; Columbia University, M.A., 1964, Ph.D., 1967. *Home:* 830 Lantern Hill Dr., East Lansing, Mich. 48823. *Office:* Department of History, Michigan State University, East Lansing, Mich. 48824.

CAREER: Michigan State University, East Lansing, assistant professor, 1966-69, associate professor of history, 1969—. Member of board of directors, American Research Institute in Turkey, 1970—. *Member:* American Historical Association, Middle East Studies Association, American Association for the Advancement of Slavic Studies, Royal Central Asian Society (fellow).

WRITINGS: The Russian Annexation of the Crimea, Cambridge University Press, 1970. Contributor to *Slavic Review, Humaniora Islamica, Canadian American Slavic Studies, Cahiers du Monde Russe, American Historical Review*, and *Jahrbucher fur Geschichte Osteuropas*.

WORK IN PROGRESS: A book on the slave trade in the Black and Mediterranean Seas; research on the legal position of religious minorities in Russia and Turkey; editing with wife, Carol Fisher, a seventeenth-century French description of the Topkapi Palace in Istanbul.

SIDELIGHTS: Fisher is competent in Russian, Turkish, Tatar, French, and German.

* * *

FISHER, David E(limelech) 1932-

PERSONAL: Born June 22, 1932, in Philadelphia, Pa.; son of H. R. (a manufacturer) and Grace (Spicehandler) Fisher; married Leila Katz, September 4, 1954; children: Lisabeth Anne, Ronald Evan, Marshall Jon. *Education:* Trinity College, Hartford, Conn., B.S., 1954; University of Florida, Ph.D., 1958. *Politics:* Liberal. *Religion:* Jewish. *Home:* 9650 Kendale Blvd., Miami, Fla. 33176. *Agent:* Philip G. Spitzer, 111-25 76th Ave., Forest Hills, N.Y. 11375. *Office:* Department of Marine Geology, University of Miami, Rickenbacker Causeway, Miami, Fla. 33149.

CAREER: Oak Ridge National Laboratory, Oak Ridge, Tenn., physicist, 1957-58; Brookhaven National Laboratory, Upton, N.Y., chemist, 1958-60; Cornell University, Ithaca, N.Y., assistant professor of applied physics, 1960-66; University of Miami, Miami, Fla., professor of geochemistry, 1966—.

WRITINGS—Novels: *Crisis*, Doubleday, 1971; *Compartments*, W. H. Allen, 1972; *A Fearful Symmetry*, Doubleday, 1974.

Play: "A Courtesy Not to Bleed" (two act), first produced in Miami by Actors Company, 1970.

* * *

FISHER, Glenn W(illiam) 1924-

PERSONAL: Born May 23, 1924, in Lewis County, Mo.; son of Ray B. and Venus Fisher; married Marvel McFarlin, September 4, 1949; children: Paul, Gary, Rhonda. *Education:* University of Iowa, B.A., 1948; University of North Carolina, M.A., 1950; University of Wisconsin, Ph.D., 1954. *Office:* Department of Political Science, Wichita State University, Wichita, Kan.

CAREER: Lander College, Greenwood, S.C., professor of economics and head of department of commerce, 1949-51; North Dakota State University, Fargo, instructor, 1954-56, assistant professor, 1956-59, associate professor of economics, 1959-61; University of Illinois, Champaign-Urbana, associate professor, 1961-66, professor of government and public affairs, 1966-70, professor of political science, 1966-70; Wichita State University, Wichita, Kan., Regents Professor of Urban Affairs, 1970—. Visiting assistant research professor at University of Illinois, 1958-59. Research associate for Illinois Commission on Revenue, 1962; research director of Illinois Municipal Problems Commission, 1964-70. Member of Minnesota governor's tax study committee, 1956; member of Illinois governor's constitutional convention study group, 1969, committee counsel, constitutional convention, 1970. *Military service:* U.S. Army, Infantry, 1943-45; served in Germany; received Purple Heart. *Member:* American Economic Association, American Political Science Association, National Tax Association-Tax Institute of America, American Society for Public Administration.

WRITINGS: Income in North Dakota: 1929-1956 (monograph), North Dakota Institute for Regional Studies, 1958; (with William E. Koenker) *Tax Equity in North Dakota*, Bureau of Business and Economic Research, University of North Dakota, 1960; *Financing Illinois Government*, University of Illinois Press, 1960; *Financing Government in the Chicago Area: An Overview* (booklet), Center for Research in Urban Government, Loyola University (Chicago), 1966; (with Ann H. Elder) *Fiscal Management in Illinois Municipalities* (booklet), Institute of Government and Public Affairs, University of Illinois, 1967; (with Robert P. Fairbanks) *Illinois Municipal Finance*, University of Illinois Press, 1968; *Taxes and Politics: A Study of Illinois Public Finance*, University of Illinois Press, 1968.

(Contributor) Samuel K. Gove and Victoria Ranney, editors, *Con-Con: Issues of the Illinois Constitutional Convention*, University of Illinois Press, 1970; *Special Assessments and Financing Public Improvements in the City of Wichita*, Center for Urban Studies, Wichita State University, 1974; (with Joyce D. Fishbane) *Politics of the Purse: Revenue and Finance in the Sixth Illinois Constitutional Convention*, University of Illinois Press, 1974; *Financing Local Improvements by Special Assessment*, Municipal Finance Officers Association, 1974.

Contributor to *Collier's Encyclopedia*. Contributor of more than twenty-five articles and reviews to scholarly journals, including *Local Finance, Governmental Finance, Illinois Business Review, Illinois Libraries, Administrative Quarterly*, and *Delphian Quarterly*.

WORK IN PROGRESS: Financing Urban Governments, a textbook.

* * *

FISHER, Robert C(harles) 1930-

PERSONAL: Born March 3, 1930, in Burlington, Iowa; son of Ray Erwin, Sr. (a tool designer) and Blanche (a teacher; maiden name, Brolin) Fisher. *Education:* Harvard University, A.B. (cum laude), 1955; graduate study at Columbia University, 1955-56, and Tokyo University, 1957-59. *Residence:* New York, N.Y. *Office:* Fodor Guides, 750 Third Ave., New York, N.Y. 10021.

CAREER: Fodor Guides, New York, N.Y., Far Eastern representative in Tokyo, Japan, 1959-64, associate editor in Litchfield, Conn., 1964-66, executive editor in London, England, 1966-74, and New York, N.Y., 1974—. Consultant to Central Research Institute (Tokyo), 1959-64. *Military service:* U.S. Army, 1952-54; served in Korea. *Member:* Society of American Travel Writers, Japan Society, British Guild of Travel Writers, Harvard Club (New York, N.Y.).

WRITINGS: Klee, Tudor, 1967; *Picasso*, Tudor, 1967.

Editor—All published by McKay: *Japan and East Asia Fodor's*, 1962, 14th edition, in press; *Fodor's India*, 1963, 14th edition, in press; *Fodor's U.S.A.*, eight volumes, 1966; *Fodor's South America*, 1966, 11th edition, in press; *Fodor's Israel*, 1967, 10th edition, in press; *Fodor's Spain*, 1967, 10th edition, in press; *Fodor's Portugal*, 1967, 10th edition, in press; *Fodor's Great Britain*, 1968, 9th edition, in press; *Fodor's Ireland*, 1968, 9th edition, in press; *Fodor's Turkey*, 1969, 8th edition, in press.

Fodor's Czechoslovakia, 1970, 7th edition, in press; *Fodor's Hungary*, 1970, 7th edition, in press; *Fodor's Budget Europe*, 1972, 5th edition, in press; *Fodor's Europe Under Twenty-Five*, 1973, 4th edition, in press; *Fodor's Islamic Asia*, 1973, 4th edition, in press; *Fodor's Tunisia*, 1973, 4th edition, in press; *Fodor's Soviet Union*, 1974, 3rd edition, in press; *Fodor's Paris*, 1974; *Fodor's Vienna*, 1974; *Fodor's Japan*, 1975; *Fodor's South-East Asia*, 1975.

Author of column, "Letter from London," in *World Travel*.

WORK IN PROGRESS: Miki of Japan, authorized biography of Japan's prime minister; editing *Fodor's Holiday U.S.A.* and *Fodor's Canada*, publication by McKay expected in 1976 and 1977, respectively.

* * *

FITCH, Alger Morton, Jr. 1919-

PERSONAL: Born October 18, 1919, in Cornelius, Ore.; son of Alger Morton and Clara (Aune) Fitch; married Betty Chitwood, December 21, 1942; children: Luana Mason, David Fitch, Marcia McKee. *Education:* Northwest Christian College, B.Th., 1945; Phillips University, B.D., 1949; University of Southern California, M.A., 1965; Claremont Graduate School, Rel.D., 1967. *Politics:* Republican. *Home address:* Route 2, Box 250A #67, Eugene, Ore. 97401. *Office:* Department of Religion, Northwest Christian College, 11th St. and Adler, Eugene, Ore. 97401.

CAREER: Ordained minister of the Church of Christ, 1949; pastor in Milwaukie, Ore., 1942-47, 1949-59, Redrock, Okla., 1947-49, Long Beach, Calif., 1960-64, Los Angeles, Calif., 1964-67, and Portland, Ore., 1967-68; Northwest Christian College, Eugene, Ore., professor of New Testament, 1968—. *Member:* Society of Biblical Literature.

WRITINGS: Alexander Campbell: Preacher of Reform and Reformer of Preaching, R. B. Sweet, 1970; *Afterglow of Easter: The Radiance over New Testament Literature*, Standard Publishing, in press. Contributor to *Christian Standard*.

* * *

FITZHUGH, Louise 1928-1974

October 5, 1928—November 19, 1974; American author and illustrator of children's books. Obituaries: *New York Times*, November 21, 1974; *Publishers Weekly*, December 2, 1974; *AB Bookman's Weekly*, December 16, 1974. (*CA*-29/32).

* * *

FitzSIMONS, Ruth M(arie Mangan)

PERSONAL: Born in Pawtucket, R.I.; daughter of Leo A. (an estimator) and Helen (Hallis) FitzSimons. *Education:* Rhode Island College, B.Ed., 1940; Boston University, M.Ed., 1951, D.Ed., 1951. *Home:* 38 Mystic Dr., Warwick, R.I. 02886. *Office:* Department of Speech, University of Rhode Island, Kingston, R.I. 02881.

CAREER: Speech pathologist and department head in public schools in Warwick, R.I.; University of Rhode Island, Kingston, associate professor, 1969-71, professor of speech, 1971—. Consulting editor for Denison, 1969—. *Member:* American Speech and Hearing Association (fellow; past legislative councilor), American Psychological Association, Rhode Island Speech and Hearing Association (past president).

WRITINGS: (With Albert T. Murphy) *Stuttering and Personality Dynamics*, Ronald, 1960; *Christopher Listens*, Denison, 1966; *Make Believe with Me!*, Denison, 1966; *Let's Play Hide and Seek!*, revised edition, Expression Co., 1974.

AVOCATIONAL INTERESTS: Gardening, travel, cooking, painting.

* * *

FIZER, John 1925-

PERSONAL: Born June 13, 1925, in Mircha, Ukraine; son of Michael and Maria (Balazh) Fizer; married Maria Krasniv, February, 1950; children: Andrew, George, Natalie, Irene. *Education:* Columbia University, M.A., 1953, Ph.D., 1960. *Religion:* Greek Orthodox. *Home:* 26 Bedford Rd., Somerset, N.J. 08873. *Office:* Department of Slavic Language and Literature, Rutgers University, 31 Mine St., New Brunswick, N.J. 08903.

CAREER: Harvard University, Cambridge, Mass., researcher, 1952; University of Notre Dame, Notre Dame, Ind., instructor, 1954-57, assistant professor of literature, 1957-60; Rutgers University, New Brunswick, N.J., associate professor, 1960-64, professor of literature, 1964—. *Member:* Modern Language Association of America, American Association of Teachers of Slavic and East European Languages (president of New York and New Jersey chapter, 1965-69).

WRITINGS: (With Ervin Laszlo) *Philosophy and the Soviet Union*, D. Reidel, 1967; *Sumarokov: Selected Tragedies*, Northwestern University Press, 1971; (contributor) Joseph P. Strelka, editor, *The Personality of the Critic*, Pennsylvania State University Press, 1973.

WORK IN PROGRESS: Psychologism in Aesthetics and Literary Theory; *Phenomenology and Criticism*; a comparative study of Roman Ingarden's theory of literature and that of Alexander Potebura.

SIDELIGHTS: Fizer speaks eight languages, including German, French, Russian, Ukrainian, Polish, Czech, Slovak, and Hungarian.

* * *

FLEMING, Gerald 1921-

PERSONAL: Born May 11, 1921, in Mannheim, Germany; son of Arthur (a high school teacher) and Anne (Lipsky) Fleming; married Winnie Librowicz (a conservation officer at the British Museum), June 1, 1951; children: Diana, Jacqueline. *Education:* Sorbonne, University of Paris, L.es.L., 1951; Institut Francais, London, F.I.L., 1953. *Home:* 55 Golders Gardens, London N.W.11, England. *Office:* Department of Linguistics and Regional Studies, University of Surrey, Guildford, Surrey GU2 5XH, England.

CAREER: William Penn School, London, England, head of modern languages department, 1958-65; British Government, Dept. of Education and Science, research officer at University of Surrey, 1965-69; University of Surrey, Guildford, England, lecturer, 1969-73, senior lecturer in applied linguistics, 1973—. *Member:* Audio-Visual Aids Association, Association Internationale Audio-Visuelle (Brussels), Modern Language Association (England), Association of University Teachers, Society of Authors.

WRITINGS: (With Fougasse, a pseudonym of C. K. Bird) *A Book of Wall Pictures for Guided Composition*, University of London Press, 1957; *Guided Composition for Students of English*, University of London Press, 1961; (contributor) B. Libbish, editor, *Advances in the Teaching of Modern Languages*, Pergamon, 1965; (with David Langdon) *French Visual Grammar*, Macmillan, 1968, monolingual edition published as *Grammaire visuelle de francais*, 1970; (contributor) R. Schaepers and Libbish, editors, *Teaching and Learning Foreign Languages*, Piper Verlag (Munich), 1972. Author, with John Halas, of a series of twelve animated cartoon films, "Les Aventures des Carre," and two accompanying books, published by Macmillan, 1965. Contributor to *Kemdsprachen, Lehren und Lernen, Gutenburg-Jahrbuch, Wilhelm-Busch Jahrbuch*, and *Cranach Festschrift*; also contributor to periodicals, including *National Visual Aids Journal, Schoolmaster, Government of India Journal of Visual Aids, IRAL, Praxis, Times Educational Supplement*, and *Goethe Institute Publications*.

WORK IN PROGRESS: Max und Moritz: Ein Kinderbuch?; an animated cartoon film and text on "Max und Moritz"; an audio-visual teaching project, "Germany, 1933-1945"; a study of pictorial polemics during the Reformation.

BIOGRAPHICAL/CRITICAL SOURCES: Louis Kelly, *25 Centuries of Language Teaching*, Newbury House, 1969; Gilbert Jarvis, editor, *ACTFL Review of Foreign Language Education*, National Textbook Co. (Skokie, Ill.), 1974.

FOLEY, (Cedric) John 1917-1974
(John Sawyer, Ian Sinclair)

March 7, 1917—November 8, 1974; British army officer and author of novels and other works. Obituaries: *AB Bookman's Weekly*, December 16, 1974. (*CA*-9/10).

* * *

FOLKERTS, George W(illiam) 1938-

PERSONAL: Born November 26, 1938, in Beardstown, Ill.; son of George C. (a teacher) and Mathilda (Schuette) Folkerts; married Denise Millare, June 12, 1965; children: Merrill Ann, Evan William. *Education:* Southern Illinois University, B.A., 1961, M.A., 1963; Auburn University, Ph.D., 1968. *Politics:* Independent. *Religion:* Lutheran. *Home:* 638 South Dean, Auburn, Ala. 36830. *Office:* Department of Zoology and Entomology, Auburn University, Auburn, Ala. 36830.

CAREER: Auburn University, Auburn, Ala., instructor in zoology, 1963-68; Clemson University, Clemson, S.C., assistant professor of zoology, 1968-69; Auburn University, associate professor of zoology, 1969--. Consultant to environmental organizations. *Member:* Society for the Study of Organic Evolution, Society of Systematic Zoology, Herpetologist's League (secretary, 1974—), Society for the Study of Amphibians and Reptiles, American Society of Ichthyologists and Herpetologists, Coleopterists' Society, Alabama Conservancy (member of board of directors, 1970-73), Sigma Xi.

WRITINGS: (With W. H. Mason) *Environmental Problems: Principles, Readings, Comments,* W. C. Brown, 1973. Contributor of about twenty articles to journals in his field.

WORK IN PROGRESS: Research on aquatic biology; *In the Footprints of Manitou,* a book on the natural history of Reelfoot Lake, publication expected in 1976; a semi-popular book on pitcher plant bogs, 1976.

SIDELIGHTS: Folkerts has testified before a number of congressional committees. *Avocational interests:* Travel (United States, Mexico, South America, the Galapagos Islands).

* * *

FOMON, Samuel J(oseph) 1923-

PERSONAL: Born March 9, 1923, in Chicago, Ill.; son of Samuel (a physician and educator) and Isabel (Sherman) Fomon; married Betty L. Freeman, July 19, 1948; children: Elizabeth (Mrs. Richard Harrison), Kathleen Fomon Goddard, David, Christopher, Mary. *Education:* Harvard University, A.B. (cum laude), 1945; University of Pennsylvania, M.D., 1947. *Residence:* Iowa City, Iowa. *Office:* Department of Pediatrics, University Hospitals, Iowa City, Iowa 52242.

CAREER: Physician; University of Iowa, College of Medicine, Iowa City, assistant professor, 1954-57, associate professor, 1957-61, professor of pediatrics, 1961—. Medical consultant in nutrition to Bureau of Community Health Services, Health Service Administration, U.S. Department of Health, Education and Welfare, 1965—; member of advisory committee on pesticides of U.S. Food and Drug Administration, 1966-70; committee member of National Institutes of Health, 1966-70; chairman of panel, White House Conference on Food, Nutrition and Health, December, 1969; member of Inter-Society Commission for Heart Disease Resources, 1974—. *Military service:* U.S. Army, Medical Service, 1952-54; became captain.

MEMBER: American Academy of Pediatrics, American Institute of Nutrition, American Pediatric Society, American Society for Clinical Nutrition (councilor, 1971-75), Federation of American Societies for Experimental Biology, Society for Pediatric Research, Nutrition Society, Midwest Society for Pediatric Research (president, 1963-64). *Awards, honors:* U.S. Public Health Service Development Award, 1962-67; Borden Award from American Academy of Pediatrics, 1966; Rosen von Rosenstein Medal from Swedish Pediatric Association, 1974; Doctor Honoris Causa from the Catholic University of Cordoba (Argentina), 1974.

WRITINGS: Infant Nutrition, Saunders, 1967, 2nd edition, 1974; (editor with T. A. Anderson) *Practices of Low-Income Families in Feeding Infants and Small Children*, Maternal and Child Health Service, U.S. Department of Health, Education, and Welfare, 1972. Contributor to medical and nutritional journals. Member of editorial board of *Journal of Nutrition*, 1965-69.

WORK IN PROGRESS: Studying the growth and nutrition of infants and pre-school children, including possible late consequences of early nutrition, factors controlling food intake, and requirements for specific nutrients.

* * *

FONAROW, Jerry 1935-
(J. Farrow)

PERSONAL: Born October 26, 1935, in New York, N.Y.; son of Nelson (a songwriter) and Bella (Henkin) Fonarow; married Lulu Porter, 1964 (divorced, 1967). *Education:* Brooklyn College (now of the City University of New York), B.A., 1954. *Politics:* "Based on the person not party." *Home and office:* 2421 Creston Way, Los Angeles, Calif. 90068.

CAREER: Music Corporation of America, New York, N.Y., member of staff, 1957-59; Rogers & Cowan, Inc. (public relations firm), Los Angeles, Calif., account executive, 1959-61; Fonarow Associates Ltd. (public relations and management), Los Angeles, owner, 1962-68; free-lance magazine, film, and television writer in Los Angeles, 1968—. *Military service:* U.S. Marine Corps, correspondent, 1954-56. *Member:* Writers Guild of America.

WRITINGS: The Coming of a God (novel), Holloway, 1970; *Defending against the Drunk Driving Charge*, Sherbourne, 1974. Author of film script, "The Delegate." Contributor to magazines, sometimes under pseudonym J. Farrow.

WORK IN PROGRESS: The Celebrities' Diet and Exercise Book.

AVOCATIONAL INTERESTS: Law, show business, sports.

BIOGRAPHICAL/CRITICAL SOURCES: Los Angeles Herald-Examiner, June 9, 1974.

* * *

FONER, Nancy 1945-

PERSONAL: Born December 14, 1945, in New York, N.Y.; daughter of Morris (a labor union official) and Anne (a professor; maiden name, Berman) Foner. *Education:* Brandeis University, B.A., 1966; University of Chicago, M.A., 1968, Ph.D., 1971. *Office:* Department of Anthropology, State University of New York, College at Purchase, Purchase, N.Y. 10577.

CAREER: York College of the City University of New York, Jamaica, N.Y., assistant professor of anthropology, 1970-73; State University of New York, College at Purchase, assistant professor of anthropology, 1973—. *Member:* American Anthropological Association. *Awards, honors:* National Institute of Mental Health grant to London, England, 1973.

WRITINGS: Status and Power in Rural Jamaica: A Study of Educational and Political Change, Teachers College Press, 1973. Contributor to *Human Organization* and *Caribbean Studies*.

WORK IN PROGRESS: A study of Jamaican migrants in London.

* * *

FORBES, John Douglas 1910-

PERSONAL: Born April 9, 1910, in San Francisco, Calif.; son of John Franklin (an executive) and Portia (Ackerman) Forbes; married Margaret Funkhouser (a musician), February 4, 1937; children: Pamela (Mrs. Louis McLane), Peter. *Education:* University of California, Berkeley, A.B., 1931; Stanford University, M.A., 1932; Harvard University, A.M., 1936, Ph.D., 1937. *Address:* P.O. Box 3607, Charlottesville, Va. 22903. *Office:* Graduate School of Business Administration, University of Virginia, Charlottesville, Va. 22903.

CAREER: San Francisco World's Fair, San Francisco, Calif., curator of paintings, 1938-40; chairman of college art department in Kansas City, 1940-42; Bennington College, Bennington, Vt., member of faculty of history, 1943-46; Wabash College, Crawfordsville, Ind., associate professor, 1946-50, professor of history and fine arts, 1950-54; University of Virginia, Charlottesville, professor of business history, 1954—. *Military service:* U.S. Army, 1942; became second lieutenant. *Member:* Society of Architectural Historians (life member; president, 1962-64), American Institute of Architects (honorary member), College Art Association (life member), Sierra Club (life member), Wilderness Society (life member), Nature Conservancy (life member), Save-the-Redwoods League (life member), Friends of the Sea Otter, Mystery Writers of America, Pacific-Union Club, Phi Beta Kappa. *Awards, honors:* Ordre des Palmes Academiques, 1963.

WRITINGS: Victorian Architect, Indiana University Press, 1953; *Israel Thorndike,* Exposition, 1953; *Murder in Full View* (novel), Caravelle Books, 1968; *Death Warmed Over* (novel), Pageant, 1971; *Stettinius, Sr.: Portrait of a Morgan Partner,* University Press of Virginia, 1974. Editor of *Journal of the Society of Architectural Historians,* 1953-58; section editor of *Encyclopaedia Britannica,* 1956-58.

WORK IN PROGRESS: A grammar and style textbook, *The Literate Executive; The Liberal Conservative in America;* a mystery, *The Trilby Murders*.

AVOCATIONAL INTERESTS: Kite-flying, cross-country walking, listening to string quartets.

* * *

FORCHHEIMER, Paul 1913-

PERSONAL: Born July 25, 1913, in Nuremberg, Bavaria; son of Jacob (a chemist) and Dina (Neu) Forchheimer; married Regina Hirschberg, September 5, 1943; children: Jacob E., Rachel (Mrs. William Herzog). *Education:* Attended Polytechnic Aix-la-Chapelle, Federal Polytechnic, Zurich, Ecole superieure de Chimie, Chelsea Polytechnic, Johns Hopkins University, and Princeton University; Columbia University, Ph.D., 1951; New York University,

M.A., 1959. *Religion:* Jewish Orthodox. *Home:* 394 Audubon Ave., New York, N.Y. 11769. *Office:* Department of Linguistics, Dowling College, Oakdale, N.Y. 11769.

CAREER: High school teacher, 1946-63; Dowling College, Oakdale, N.Y., assistant professor, 1963-66, associate professor of linguistics, German, classics, and French, 1966—. Adjunct associate professor at Adelphi University. *Military service:* U.S. Army, Military Intelligence, 1942-45; received three campaign stars. *Member:* Linguistic Society of America, Societe de Linguistique de Paris.

WRITINGS: The Category of Person in Language, DeGruyter, 1953; (contributor) Robert C. Lugton and Milton Saltzer, editors, *Studies in Honor of J. Alexander Kerns*, Mouton & Co., 1970; *Living Judaism*, Feldheim, 1974. Contributor to *Collier's Encyclopedia*. Contributor to linguistics journals, including *Modern Language Notes, Word, Romance Philology*, and *Orbis*.

WORK IN PROGRESS: Languages of Man.

* * *

FORD, George D. 1880(?)-1974

1880(?)—July 24, 1974; American author of biographical work. Obituaries: *AB Bookman's Weekly*, October 7, 1974.

* * *

FORMHALS, Robert W(illard) Y(ates) S(arguszko) 1919-

PERSONAL: Born June 14, 1919, in Los Angeles, Calif.; son of Carl W. and Muriel (Yates) Formhals; married Elaine Mary Peters; children: Robert A.C.S. *Education:* Welch College of Law, J.D., 1943; Sacramento State College (now California State University, Sacramento), Certificate in Public Administration, 1955; Sheffield Mt. College, Doctor of Civil Law, 1965. *Residence:* Santa Clara, Calif. *Office:* West Valley College, 44 East Latimer St., Campbell, Calif. 95008.

CAREER: Worked in various capacities for the State of California in Sacramento, 1947-60; California School Boards Association, Sacramento, executive secretary-treasurer, 1960-67; Associated Management Service, Carmichael, Calif., president, 1967-70; City of San Jose (Calif.), city employee relations officer, 1970-74; West Valley College, Campbell, Calif., instructor in management and manager of Intergovernmental Management and Development Program, 1974—. Member of board of directors, Hawaiian-Pacific Lines, 1950-52; chancellor of Pacific Maritime & Engineering Academy, 1951-52; commissioner, California Commission on School District Organization, 1961-65; chairman, Governor of California's Advisory Commission on Disaster Preparedness and member of State Disaster Council, 1961-67. *Military service:* U.S. Army, 1939-40, 1942-44, 1960. U.S. Army Reserves, 1950-69; became major.

MEMBER: American Association of School Administrators, American Society of Safety Engineers (member of national executive board, 1959-60), National Labor Panel, American Arbitration Association, Commonwealth Club of California, Severance Club. *Awards, honors:* Grand Cross of the Hospitaller Order of St. John of Jerusalem, 1940; Ordo Constantini Magni of Grand Prior of North America, 1964; Knight Grand Cross of the Crown of Yugoslavia, 1969; Knight Grand Officer of the White Eagle, 1970; Knight Commander of St. Laszlo of Hungary, 1971.

WRITINGS: Handbook of the Armed Forces of the World, Delaney & Co., 1948; *Book of Precedence*, AMS Press, 1964; *History of the Order of St. John of Jerusalem*, St. John Press, 1974. Contributor to *Our Wonderful World, Encyclopedia Americana, Science Encyclopedia Supplement, 1968*, and *Groliers Encyclopedia*. Editor, *California School Boards*, 1961-67, and *School Board Policy*, 1967-70.

WORK IN PROGRESS: Compiling *Encyclopedia of World Rulers*, ten volumes, for Quaker Press.

SIDELIGHTS: Formhals holds the title of Hereditary Prince Sarguszko, and has been Grand Master, Hospitaller Order of St. John of Jerusalem since 1972.

* * *

FORTE, David F. 1941-

PERSONAL: Surname is pronounced *For*-tay; born November 2, 1941, in Somerville, Mass.; son of John Anthony (a U.S. Post Office superintendent) and Antoinette (Carboni) Forte; married Nicole Rouel (a teacher). *Education:* Harvard University, A.B. (cum laude), 1963; University of Manchester, M.A., 1965; Columbia University, further graduate study, 1964-65, 1974-75; University of Toronto, Ph.D., 1974. *Religion:* Roman Catholic. *Residence:* New York, N.Y.

CAREER: University of Toronto, Toronto, Ontario, instructor in political science, 1965-69; Skidmore College, Saratoga Springs, N.Y., instructor in political science, 1969—. Member of Saratoga Springs action plan for downtown development, 1974; alternate Republican committeeman in Saratoga Springs, 1974; member of Saratoga Springs Mass Transit Commission, 1974. Judge of Eastern Regional Championship of Judge Jessup International Law Moot Court Competition, 1971.

WRITINGS: (Editor) *The Supreme Court in American Politics: Judicial Activism versus Judicial Restraint*, Heath, 1972; (contributor) *Sourcebook of American Government*, Dushkin Publishing, 1973; (contributor) *Sourcebook of American History*, Dushkin Publishing, 1973. Contributor of articles and reviews to *Soviet Studies, Albany Law Review*, and *International Journal*.

WORK IN PROGRESS: Research on natural law as a basis of Supreme Court decision, on recent U.S. Secretaries of State, on U.S. organized crime, Vatican foreign policy, and nineteenth-century New England historians.

AVOCATIONAL INTERESTS: Photography, carpentry, philately, music, travel.

* * *

FOSTER, Alan Dean 1946-

PERSONAL: Born November 18, 1946, in New York, N.Y.; son of Maxwell (a salesman) and Helen (Smith) Foster. *Education:* University of California, Los Angeles, B.A., 1968, M.F.A., 1969. *Politics:* "Weltburger." *Residence:* Santa Monica, Calif. *Agent:* Virginia Kidd, Box 278, Milford, Pa. 18337; (for television and films) Ilse Lahn, Paul Kohmer Agency, 9169 Sunset Blvd., Los Angeles, Calif. 90069. *Office:* Los Angeles City College, Los Angeles, Calif. 90029.

CAREER: Headlines Ink Agency (public relations firm), Studio City, Calif., head copywriter, 1970-71; Los Angeles City College, Los Angeles, Calif., instructor in motion picture writing and history, 1971—. Has taught at University of California, Los Angeles. *Military service:* U.S. Army Reserve, 1969-75. *Member:* Science Fiction Writers of America (Nebula Awards chairman, 1973—).

WRITINGS—All science fiction novels published by Ballantine: *The Tar-Aiym Krang*, 1972; *Bloodhype*, 1973; *Icerigger*, 1974; *Luana*, 1974; *Star Trek Log One*, 1974; *Star Trek Log Two*, 1974; *Dark Star*, 1974; *Star Trek Log Three*, in press; *Star Trek Log Four*, in press.

Work is anthologized in *World's Best SF, 1972-73*, two volumes, edited by Donald A. Wollheim, with Arthur W. Saha, DAW Books, 1972-73; *The Alien Condition*, edited by Stephen Goldin, Ballantine, 1973; *Fellowship of the Stars*, edited by Terry Carr, Simon & Schuster, 1974; *Stellar 1*, edited by Judy-Lynn del Rey, Ballantine, 1974; *Alfred Hitchcock Presents: Thirty-Two Stories*, Random House, 1975.

Radio scripts: "Episodes in American History" series for Station KFIR, Oregon. Also author of "The Age of Ice," "Mystery of the North," "Before Watts," "Flip Wilson Did Not Discover America, but . . . ," "First into Space," "Goodyear, Cream Cheese, and Rubber," "The Monitor Was a Swede," "The Battle We Almost Lost," "The Iroquois Confederacy," and others.

Contributor of short stories to science fiction and fantasy magazines, including *Analog, Galaxy, Worlds of If, Arkham Collector, Coq, Adam*, and *Alfred Hitchcock's*. Film critic for *University of California Los Angeles Daily Bruin*, 1969—.

WORK IN PROGRESS: Midworld, Star Trek Log Five, and *Star Trek Log Six*, all novels; "Scourge of God," a play about the Spanish inquisition in South America; various short stories and film scripts.

AVOCATIONAL INTERESTS: Tang soo do (Korean karate), body-surfing, basketball, back-packing, collecting first-edition science fiction work, science fiction artwork, classical recordings, travel, chocolate chip cookies.

* * *

FOSTER, Donald (LeRoy) 1928-

PERSONAL: Born March 7, 1928, in Chicago, Ill.; son of Guy M. (a social worker) and Edna (Nelson) Foster; married Marjorie Benson, August 23, 1958; children: Scott, Todd. *Education:* DePaul University, B.Mus., 1950, M.Mus., 1953; graduate study at Northwestern University, 1955-56; University of Illinois, M.S., 1961. *Home:* 12104 Baja Dr., Albuquerque, N.M. 87111. *Office:* University of New Mexico Library, Albuquerque, N.M. 87131.

CAREER: Beatty Memorial Hospital, Westville, Ind., music therapist, 1953-54; high school teacher of music in the public schools of Chicago, Ill., and Sheffield, Ill., 1956-58; New Mexico State University, Las Cruces, instructor in music, 1958-59; University of Illinois, Urbana, librarian, 1961-64; University of New Mexico, Albuquerque, librarian, 1968—, assistant professor of librarianship, 1968—. *Military service:* U.S. Army, 1951-52. *Member:* American Association of University Professors, American Library Association.

WRITINGS: Notes Used on Music Catalog Cards, Graduate School of Library Science, University of Illinois, 1962; *The Modern Arts*, Illini Union, 1963; *Checklist of U.S. Government Publications in the Arts*, Graduate School of Library Science, University of Illinois, 1969; *Classification of Nonbook Materials*, Graduate School of Library Science, University of Illinois, 1972; *Prints in the Public Library*, Scarecrow, 1973; *Managing the Catalog Department*, Scarecrow, 1975. Contributor to library and music journals.

WORK IN PROGRESS: A textbook, *Communication for Librarians*; research in library management, and on sociological aspects of music ensembles.

* * *

FOSTER, E(lizabeth) C(onnell) 1902-

PERSONAL: Maiden name is accented on second syllable; born January 11, 1902, in Chicago, Ill.; daughter of William Perry and Anna (Ahlberg) Connell; married Robert Eugene Foster, June 19, 1937. *Education:* Attended University of Chicago, Art Institute of Chicago, and Chicago Musical College. *Politics:* "Current biased news reporting is strengthening my conservative Republican tendencies." *Religion:* "Certainly I am no materialist, far from it. But I have never been able to accept the teaching of any organized religion." *Home:* 713 Apalachicola Rd., Venice, Fla. 33595.

CAREER: Commonwealth Edison Co., Chicago, Ill., secretary, 1920-37; secretary to Ashton Stevens, columnist and drama critic for Hearst newspaper, 1922-47, did secretarial work for physician, 1928-37; writer. Volunteer worker for Institute of International Education, and North Shore Mental Health Association. *Awards, honors:* First place juvenile award from Friends of American Writers, 1974, for *The Long Hungry Night*.

WRITINGS: (With Slim Williams) *The Friend of the Singing One* (Eskimo story), Atheneum, 1967; (with Williams) *The Long Hungry Night* (Eskimo story; Junior Literary Guild selection), Atheneum, 1973.

WORK IN PROGRESS: A third Eskimo story with Slim Williams; research for a book about Shelley; revising an adventure story about the sea and the Oriental arts of self-defense, originally written with a sea-captain.

SIDELIGHTS: Elizabeth Foster writes: "Whatever I write about my life comes out a love song to Chicago." She has spent most of her life there, and speaks with great reverence of the museums and libraries, the parks, Orchestra Hall, the lake, and the Loop business district. *Avocational interests:* Reading, poetry, gardens, needlework, travel.

BIOGRAPHICAL/CRITICAL SOURCES: Sarasota Herald-Tribune/Journal, March 25, 1973; *Venice Gondolier*, April 8, 1974, May 13, 1974; *Sarasota Journal*, March 20, 1974.

* * *

FOSTER, John L(awrence) 1930-

PERSONAL: Born November 11, 1930, in Chicago, Ill.; son of Robert E. (in insurance) and Dorothy (Lockwood) Foster; married Gloria Wallace (a teacher), August 11, 1956; children: Ann Lynley, Ann Kristen, Robert Wallace. *Education:* Kalamazoo College, A.B., 1952; graduate study at Harvard University, 1953; University of Michigan, A.M., 1957, Ph.D., 1961. *Home:* 1522 Monroe St., Evanston, Ill. 60202. *Office:* Department of English, Roosevelt University, 430 South Michigan Ave., Chicago, Ill. 60605.

CAREER: University of Connecticut, Storrs, instructor in English, 1961-64; Wisconsin State University, Whitewater, associate professor of English, 1964-66; Roosevelt University, Chicago, Ill., professor of English, 1966—. *Military service:* U.S. Army, Security Agency, 1953-56; became sergeant. *Member:* Modern Language Association of America, American Research Center in Egypt, Field Museum, Oriental Institute (University of Chicago). *Awards, honors:* National Endowment for the Humanities fellowship, 1971, for translating ancient Egyptian literature.

WRITINGS: Love Songs of the New Kingdom, Scribner, 1974.

WORK IN PROGRESS: A study of the poetry and career of Ezra Pound; research on ancient Egyptian poetics; a translation of ancient Egyptian hymns.

SIDELIGHTS: Foster did research in Egypt in 1971 and 1973.

* * *

FOSTER, K(enneth) Neill 1935-

PERSONAL: Born July 27, 1935, in Grande Prairie, Alberta, Canada; son of John Neill (a businessman) and Flora Elizabeth (Hume) Foster; married Marilynne Elizabeth Klinck, July 2, 1959; children: Timothy, Donna, Jeffrey. *Education:* Attended Canadian Bible College, 1953-57, and Missionary Training Institute, Edinburg, Tex., 1967-68. *Religion:* Christian and Missionary Alliance. *Home:* 1012 Fifth Ave., Beaverlodge, Alberta TOH OCO, Canada. *Office:* Evangelistic Enterprises Society, Beaverlodge, Alberta TOH OCO, Canada.

CAREER: Pastoral ministry in Kamloops, B.C., 1957-58, in Chilliwack and Yarrow, B.C., 1959-61; itinerant evangelist, 1961—. Founder of *Communicate* (periodical), 1967, and of Horizon House (publishers), 1975.

WRITINGS: Revolution of Love, Bethany Fellowship, 1973.

* * *

FOULDS, Elfrida Vipont 1902-
(Charles Vipont, Elfrida Vipont)

PERSONAL: Born July 3, 1902, in Manchester, England; daughter of Edward Vipont (a physician) and Dorothy (Crowley) Brown; married Robinson Percy Foulds, April 21, 1926 (deceased); children: Robin, Mary, Carolyn, Dorothy, Ann. *Education:* Attended Mount School. *Religion:* Society of Friends (Quaker). *Home:* Green Garth, Yealand Conyers, nr. Carnforth, Lancashire LA5 9SG, England.

CAREER: Author of children's books; lecturer on writing children's books and on Quaker history. Head of Quaker Evacuation School for young children during World War II; member and deputy chairman of Yealand Conyers Parish Council (local government). *Member:* P.E.N., Society of Authors. *Awards, honors:* Carnegie Medal, 1950, for *Lark on the Wing*.

WRITINGS—Children's books; under name Elfrida Vipont, except as noted: *Good Adventure*, John Heywood Ltd., 1931; *Colin Writes to Friends House*, Friends Book Centre, 1934, 3rd edition, Bannisdale Press, 1957; (under pseudonym Charles Vipont) *Blow the Man Down*, Oxford University Press, 1939, Lippincott, 1951.

The Lark in the Morn, Oxford University Press, 1948, Bobbs-Merrill, 1950, 2nd edition, Holt, 1970.

Sparks Among the Stubble, Oxford University Press, 1950; *The Lark on the Wing*, Oxford University Press, 1950, Bobbs-Merrill, 1951, 2nd edition, Holt, 1970; (under name Elfrida Vipont Foulds) *The Birthplace of Quakerism* (for adults and young people), Friends Home Service Committee, 1952, 3rd edition, 1973; *The Story of Quakerism, 1652-1952* (for adults and young people), Bannisdale Press, 1954, 2nd edition published as *The Story of Quakerism Through Three Centuries*, 1960; *The Family at Dowbiggins*, Bobbs-Merrill, 1955; (under pseudonym Charles Vipont) *The Heir of Craigs*, Oxford University Press, 1955; *Arnold Rowntree: A Life* (for adults and young people), Bannisdale Press, 1955; *The Spring of the Year*, Oxford University Press, 1957; (editor) *The High Way*, Oxford University Press, 1957; (with others) *Five More*, Blackwell, 1957; *More About Dowbiggins*, Lutterworth Press, 1958, published as *A Win for Henry Conyers*, Hamish Hamilton, 1969; (editor) *Bless This Day: Anthology of Prayers for Young Children*, Harcourt, 1958; *Henry Purcell and His Times*, Lutterworth Press, 1959; *Ackworth School* (for adults and young people), Lutterworth Press, 1959; *Changes at Dowbiggins*, Lutterworth Press, 1958, published as *Boggarts and Dreams*, Hamish Hamilton, 1969.

Flowering Spring, Oxford University Press, 1960; *The Story of Christianity in Britain*, M. Joseph, 1960; *What About Religion?*, Museum Press, 1961; (editor) *The Bridge*, Oxford University Press, 1962; *Search for a Song*, Oxford University Press, 1962; *A Faith to Live By*, Friends General Conference, 1962 (published in England as *Quakerism: A Faith to Live By*, Bannisdale Press, 1965); *Some Christian Festivals* (for adults and young people), M. Joseph, 1963; *Stevie*, Hamish Hamilton, 1965; *Larry Hopkins*, Hamish Hamilton, 1965; *Rescue for Mittens*, Hamish Hamilton, 1965; *The Offcomers*, Hamish Hamilton, 1965, McGraw, 1967; *Weaver of Dreams*, Walck, 1966; *Terror by Night*, Hamish Hamilton, 1966, published as *Ghosts High Noon*, Walck, 1967; *The Secret Passage*, Hamish Hamilton, 1967; (with others) *People of the Past*, Oxford University Press, 1967; *Children of the Mayflower*, Heinemann, 1969, F. Watts, 1970; *Michael and the Dogs*, Hamish Hamilton, 1969; *The Pavillion*, Oxford University Press, 1969, Holt, 1970; *The Elephant and the Bad Baby*, Coward, 1969; *Towards a High Attic*, Hamish Hamilton, 1969, Holt, 1971.

(With others) *My England*, Heinemann, 1973; *Bed in Hell* (for adults and young people), Hamish Hamilton, 1974; *George Fox and the Valiant Sixty* (for adults and young people), Hamish Hamilton, 1975. Also author of short radio plays, for school broadcasting. Contributor to periodicals.

WORK IN PROGRESS: A book on Jane Austen for young people.

BIOGRAPHICAL/CRITICAL SOURCES: Library Association Record, May, 1951; *Junior Bookshelf*, July, 1951; *Christian Science Monitor*, January 23, 1956.

* * *

FOWLER, Gene 1931-

PERSONAL: Born October 5, 1931, in Oakland, Calif.; son of Jack (a laborer) and Janice (Campbell) Fowler. *Education:* Attended public high school in Oakland, Calif. *Home:* 463-C 61st St., Oakland, Calif. 94609.

CAREER: Worked as a night-club and specialty performer, 1949-50; served a sentence in San Quentin prison for armed robbery, 1954-59; variously employed as an appliance salesman, medical records clerk, and self-taught computer programmer and clerk at the University of California, 1959-63; poet, 1963—, working primarily in San Francisco's Haight-Ashbury district, 1963-69. Made a reading tour of college campuses, ending at the World Affairs Conference, Boulder, Colo., 1967; poet-in-residence and workshop director at University of Wisconsin—Milwaukee, 1970. *Military service:* U.S. Army, 1950-53; became corporal. *Awards, honors:* R. Buckminster Fuller's Dymaxion Award, 1969; National Endowment for the Arts achievement grant, 1970.

WRITINGS—Poems: *Field Studies,* Dustbooks, 1965; *Shaman Songs,* Dustbooks, 1967; *Her Majesty's Ship,* Grande Ronde Press, 1969; *Fires,* Thorp Springs Press, 1972; *Vivisection,* Thorp Springs Press, 1974.

Work is anthologized in *The American Literary Anthology, Number 1,* Farrar, Straus, 1968; *Thirty-One New American Poets,* edited by Ron Schreiber, Hill & Wang, 1969; *Forty Poems on Recent American History,* edited by Robert Bly, Beacon, 1970; *The Smith Poets,* edited by Harry Smith, The Smith, for Horizon Press, 1971; *New American Poetry,* edited by Richard Monaco, McGraw, 1973.

SIDELIGHTS: Commenting on San Francisco in the 1960's, Fowler wrote: "[In 1963,] I found a coffee house in what was to become (through my doings but not by my intent) the Haight-Ashbury. A place to sit. . . . I began writing poems. . . . And i began the Wednesday night readings. . . . Out of those readings and the poets' parties afterward began a wild surge. Poetry became public in S.F. again—and little mags began sprouting up. . . . For a while it looked as though i might make the H-A into Picasso's Paris or whatever. But the kids in the east got word of a 'new scene'—and it went to the wave after wave of kids into circus time and on, as the exploiters began coming, the slavers and dopers and maniacs, into a Hell, and finally, into a badly beat up tenderloin."

R. Buckminster Fuller has written of Fowler, "In all my life I have found no more brilliant, no more articulate thinker than Gene Fowler." In response, Fowler told *CA,* "Poetry is a means whereby i try to make this capability useful to members of the human community." Fowler noted that he is presently researching the potential for a poet's staying alive while holding no academic credentials and being hardcore unemployable, due to lack of education, and being an ex-convict.

BIOGRAPHICAL/CRITICAL SOURCES: Eikon, winter, 1967-68.

* * *

FOWLER, Wilton B(onham) 1936-

PERSONAL: Born July 4, 1936, in Anderson, S.C.; son of Bonham and Ellen (Branyon) Fowler. *Education:* University of South Carolina, B.A., 1960; Yale University, M.A., 1962, Ph.D., 1966. *Office:* Department of History, DP-20, University of Washington, Seattle, Wash. 98195.

CAREER: Yale University, New Haven, Conn., instructor, 1965-66, assistant professor of history, 1966-69; University of Washington, Seattle, associate professor of history, 1969—. *Military service:* U.S. Navy, 1954-57.

WRITINGS: British-American Relations, 1917-1918: The Role of Sir William Wiseman, Princeton University Press, 1969; (contributor) Lewis L. Gould, editor, *The Progressive Era,* Syracuse University Press, 1974; *American Diplomatic History Since 1890: A Bibliography,* AHM Publishing, 1975.

WORK IN PROGRESS: Research on the foreign policy of Woodrow Wilson; a biography of Secretary of State John Hay, 1838-1905.

* * *

FOX, Logan J(ordan) 1922-

PERSONAL: Born October 20, 1922, in Tokyo, Japan; son of Harry Robert (a minister) and Mary Pauline (Hickman) Fox; married Madeline Clark, 1943; children: Ramona (Mrs. Richard Gayton), Logan Lee, Violet Ann, Mary Kathryn, Matthew Clark. *Education:* Attended David Lipscomb College, 1941-43; Pepperdine College, B.A., 1946; University of Chicago, M.A., 1947; University of Southern California, Ph.D., 1967. *Politics:* Democrat. *Religion:* Protestant. *Home and office:* 2403 West 79th St., Inglewood, Calif. 90305.

CAREER: Private practice in psychology in Inglewood, Calif., 1962-73, Redondo Beach, Calif., 1974—; Ibaraki Christian College, Ibaraki, Japan, professor of psychology, 1949-60, dean, 1949-52, president, 1952-60; Pepperdine College, Los Angeles, Calif., associate professor of psychology, 1960-63; El Camino College, Torrance, Calif., associate professor, 1963-67, professor of psychology, 1967—. *Member:* California Teachers Association, California State Psychology Association. *Awards, honors:* LL.D. from Pepperdine College, 1959.

WRITINGS: (With T. Endo) *Counseling and the Problem Child,* Iwasaki, 1957; *Psychology as Philosophy, Science, and Art,* Goodyear Publishing, 1972; (consulting author) James C. Coleman and Constance L. Hammen, *Contemporary Psychology and Effective Behavior,* Scott, Foresman, 1974.

* * *

FOX, Samuel J. 1919-

PERSONAL: Born February 25, 1919, in Cleveland, Ohio; son of Joseph and Yetta (Mandel) Fox; married Edith Phyllis Muskin, February 25, 1942; children: Joseph Raphael. *Education:* Yeshiva University, B.A., 1941, rabbi, 1941; Butler University, M.A., 1944; Harvard University, Ph.D., 1959. *Home:* 145 Lynn Shore Dr., Lynn, Mass. 01902. *Office:* Congregation Chevra Tehillim, Lynn, Mass.

CAREER: Rabbi in Indianapolis, Ind., 1941-51; rabbi of Congregation Anshai Sfard, Lynn, Mass., 1951-59; rabbi of Congregation Chevra Tehillim, Lynn, Mass., 1959—. Professor at Southeastern Massachusetts University, 1969—. Chaplain at Fort Benjamin Harrison, Camp Atterbury, and Stout Field (all Indiana), 1942-51. Executive vice-president of New England Region Religious Zionists of America, 1959—; president of Massachusetts Council of Rabbis, 1959—. Served in governor's commission to study aid to private schools, and on state committee to study religion in public schools. *Member:* American Academy of Religion, College Theology Society, Rabbinical Council of America (member of executive committee), American Academy of Political and Social Science, United Rabbinic Chaplaincy Commission, Orthodox Rabbinical Council of Greater Boston (president). *Awards, honors:* National service award from Jewish Welfare Board, 1950.

WRITINGS: Hell in Rabbinic Literature, Merrimac College Press, 1972. Author of "Why? Because!," a column syndicated by Jewish Telegraphic Agency. Contributor of articles and reviews to annals and to magazines, including *Jewish Spectator, Journal of Religion,* and *Ecumenical Digest.*

WORK IN PROGRESS: A book on Jewish customs and ceremonies.

* * *

FRANCK, Phyllis 1928-

PERSONAL: Born October 11, 1928, in Winthrop, Iowa; daughter of Ed (a farmer) and Vena (Manson) Franck. *Education:* St. Luke's Hospital, Cedar Rapids, Iowa, nursing diploma, 1949; Cornell College, Mount Vernon, Iowa, further study, 1949-53; University of Iowa, B.S., 1958, M.A., 1968. *Religion:* Protestant. *Residence:* Iowa City, Iowa. *Office:* College of Nursing, University of Iowa, Iowa City, Iowa 52242.

CAREER: Cornell College, Mount Vernon, Iowa, staff nurse at Student Health Service, 1949-50, director of student health service, 1950-53; Allen Memorial Hospital, Waterloo, Iowa, staff nurse, 1953-54; nurse in doctor's office, Mount Vernon, Iowa, 1954-57; Ingham County Health Department, Mason, Mich., staff nurse, 1958-59; Oelwein Community Schools, Oelwein, Iowa, school nurse, 1959-62; Clinton Community College, Clinton, Iowa, coordinator of practical nursing education, 1962-66; University Hospitals, Iowa City, Iowa, staff nurse, summers, 1967-68; University of Iowa, College of Nursing, Iowa City, instructor, 1968-69, assistant professor of nursing, 1969—. Relief evening and night supervisor of nursing at St. Luke's Hospital, summers, 1951-52; staff nurse for Cedar Rapids Visiting Nurses Association, summer, 1960; executive director of Linn County Tuberculosis and Respiratory Disease Association, summer, 1971.

MEMBER: American Nurses Association, National League for Nursing, American Association of University Professors, American Association of University Women, American Lung Association, Easter Seal Society for Crippled Children and Adults, Sigma Theta Tau.

WRITINGS: (With Marjorie Price and Shirley Veith) *Nursing Management*, Springer Publishing, 1974. Contributor to *Journal of Nursing Education.*

* * *

FRANCOEUR, Anna K(otlarchyk) 1940-

PERSONAL: Born May 24, 1940, in New York, N.Y.; daughter of Peter and Pauline (Stadnycki) Kotlarchyk; married Robert T. Francoeur (a college professor), June 24, 1967; children: Nicole Lynn, Danielle Ann. *Education:* City College of the City University of New York, B.A., 1962; New York University, M.A., 1969. *Home:* 2 Circle Dr., Rockaway, N.J. 07866.

CAREER: Rowe International, Inc., Whippany, N.J., cost accountant, 1973-74; Van Raalte, Inc., Boonton, N.J., budgetary accountant, 1974—. Instructor at County College of Morris, spring, 1970. *Member:* Groves Conference on Marriage and the Family, American Teilhard de Chardin Association.

WRITINGS: (Contributor) Robert Whitehurst and Roger Libby, editors, *Renovating Marriage: Toward New Sexual Life Styles*, Consensus, 1973; (contributor) Maggie Tripp, editor, *Woman in the Year Two Thousand*, Arbor House, 1974; (editor with husband, Robert T. Francoeur) *The Future of Sexual Relations*, Prentice-Hall, 1974; (with Robert T. Francoeur) *Hot and Cool Sex: Cultures in Conflict*, Harcourt, 1974.

WORK IN PROGRESS: A history of American sexual customs.

* * *

FRANK, Harry Thomas 1933-

PERSONAL: Born June 7, 1933, in North Carolina; son of Dallas Merrill (a businessman) and Nancy Lee (a secretary; maiden name, Lincoln) Frank; married Elizabeth Margaret Leslie McKay (a physician), July 14, 1960; children: John Lincoln Reid, Malcolm Merrill, Ian Davidson. *Education:* Wake Forest College, B.A., 1956; graduate study at Southeastern Seminary, 1956-57; Yale University, B.D., 1959; graduate study at King's College, Aberdeen, 1959-60; Duke University, Ph.D., 1963; postdoctoral study at Leiden University, 1969-70. *Home:* 367 Reamer Pl., Oberlin, Ohio 44074. *Office:* Department of Religion, Oberlin College, Oberlin, Ohio 44074.

CAREER: Ordained Baptist minister, 1957. Randolph-Macon Women's College, Lynchburg, Va., instructor in religion, 1963-64; Oberlin College, Oberlin, Ohio, assistant professor, 1964-68, associate professor, 1968-72, professor of religion, 1972—. Supervisor of Taanach Archaeological Expedition, 1966; member of core staff, Tell el-Hesi Archaeological Expedition, 1970—, and Schechem Expedition Field Survey, 1972-74. *Member:* International Organization of Old Testament Scholars, American Schools of Oriental Research (trustee, 1970-73), American Institute of Archaeology, Society of Religion in Higher Education. *Awards, honors:* Academic awards from institutions and foundations.

WRITINGS: (With William Swain and Courtland Canby) *The Bible through the Ages*, World Publishing, 1967; (editor with William R. Reed) *Translating and Understanding the Old Testament*, Abingdon, 1970; *Bible, Archaeology, and Faith*, Abingdon, 1971; *An Archaeological Companion to the Bible*, SCM Publishing House, 1972; *Discovering the Biblical World*, Harper-Hammond, 1974.

WORK IN PROGRESS: Three books, *Herod the Great and Sectarian Judaism, Phenomenology of Biblical Religion*, and *Old Testament Characters.*

AVOCATIONAL INTERESTS: Photography (his photographs are incorporated in several books.

* * *

FRANKEL, A(rthur) Steven 1942-

PERSONAL: Born August 13, 1942, in New York, N.Y.; son of Henry Samuel and Lillian (Krasoff) Frankel; married Rita Irene Krauss (a marriage and family counselor), August 10, 1967; children: Hali Sim (daughter). *Education:* University of Vermont, B.A., 1964; Indiana University, Ph.D., 1968. *Home:* 2805 Via Rivera, Palos Verdes Estates, Calif. 90274. *Office:* Department of Psychology, University of Southern California, 734 West Adams Blvd., Los Angeles, Calif. 90007.

CAREER: Psychology intern, Columbia University Medical Center, 1967-68; University of Southern California, Los Angeles, assistant professor, 1968-72, associate professor of psychology, 1972—, director of clinical training, 1972—; private practice of clinical psychology in Rolling Hills Estates, Calif., 1974—. Research specialist at Pacific State Hospital, 1969-70; consultant to Southern California Counseling Center, 1969-71, Veterans Administration Hospitals, 1969—, and Poseidon Education Center, 1971-74. *Member:* American Psychological Association, American Association of University Professors. *Awards, honors:* U.S. Public Health Service fellow at University of Southern California, 1968-69, 1970-71.

WRITINGS: (With M. P. Duke) *Inside Psychotherapy*, Rand McNally, 1971. Contributor to *Journal of Experimental Psychology, Journal of Abnormal Psychology, Journal of Consulting and Clinical Psychology*, and *Psychotherapy: Theory, Research and Practice.*

WORK IN PROGRESS: Research on interpersonal power styles, their development, maintenance and change.

FRANKLIN, Marshall 1929-

PERSONAL: Born November 5, 1929, in Baltimore, Md.; son of Morton and Anna (Rothstein) Franklin; married; children: three. *Education:* Franklin and Marshall College, B.S., 1952; University of Maryland, M.D., 1956. *Office:* 53 Tanglewood Lane, Stamford, Conn. 06903.

CAREER: Duke Hospital, Durham, N.C., medical intern, 1956-57; Charity Hospital of Louisiana, New Orleans, resident in medicine, 1957-59, chief resident in clinical cardiology, 1959-60; Cleveland Clinic, Cleveland, Ohio, fellow, 1960-61, chief resident in department of pediatric cardiology and cardiac catheterization laboratory, 1961-62, member of assistant staff and then of associate staff, department of pediatric cardiology and cardiac catheterization laboratory, 1962-64; Norwalk Hospital, Norwalk, Conn., director of cardiac laboratory, 1964—. Diplomate, American Board of Internal Medicine, 1972. Associate attending physician at St. Joseph's Hospital and Stamford Hospital, Stamford, Conn., and White Plains Hospital, White Plains, N.Y.; lecturer in cardiology at Mount Sinai Hospital and Medical Center, New York.

WRITINGS: (With others) *The Heart Doctors' Heart Book: How to Avoid or Survive America's No. 1 Killer,* Grosset, 1974.

* * *

FRANKS, Lucinda 1946-

PERSONAL: Born July 16, 1946, in Chicago, Ill.; daughter of Thomas E. and Lorraine (a community worker; maiden name, Leavitt) Franks. *Education:* Vassar College, B.A., 1968. *Home:* 219 East 81st St., New York, N.Y. 10028. *Agent:* Karen Hitzig, William Morris Agency, 1350 Avenue of the Americas, New York, N.Y. 10019. *Office: New York Times,* Times Sq., New York, N.Y. 10036.

CAREER: United Press International, journalist in London, England, 1968-72, and New York, N.Y., 1973-74; *New York Times,* New York, N.Y., journalist, 1974—. *Awards, honors:* Pulitzer Prize for national reporting, Society of Silurians prize, New York Newspaper Writers award, and National Headliners Award, all 1971, all for UPI series on the life of Diana Oughton (member of the Weathermen).

WRITINGS: Waiting Out a War: The Exile of Private John Picciano, Coward, 1974. Contributor to *Ms.*

WORK IN PROGRESS: A novel about a suburban girl growing up in America in the 1950's.

SIDELIGHTS: Lucinda Franks writes: "I've dodged bullets in Belfast, written about beauty contestants who parade their bodies, lived among deserters in Sweden to write their story, and heard the cries of the Israeli athletes being held hostage at the Munich Olympics. I've seen a lot for my age, but I still feel the way I felt when I was twenty-one and had seen nothing but the inside of a Boston suburb. I am fascinated now, as I was then, about what goes on in the deepest recesses of people's minds—not what happens to them, but how they feel about it." *Avocational interests:* Playing the guitar, singing, weaving, vacations.

* * *

FRASER, Arthur Ronald 1888-1974
(Ronald Fraser)

1888—September 12, 1974; British diplomat and author of novels and nonfiction works. Obituaries: *New York Times,* September 13, 1974; *Washington Post*, September 14, 1974; *AB Bookman's Weekly*, November 18, 1974.

* * *

FRASER, (William Jocelyn) Ian 1897-1974

1897—December 19, 1974; British peer, politician, and businessman. Obituaries: *New York Times*, December 21, 1974; *Washington Post*, December 21, 1974.

* * *

FREDERICKS, Carlton 1910-

PERSONAL: Born October 23, 1910, in New York, N.Y.; son of David Charles (in pharmaceuticals) and Blanche (Goldsmith) Fredericks; married Betty Schacher, October, 1949; children: Alice, April, Dana, Spencer, Rhonda. *Education:* University of Alabama, B.A., 1931; New York University, M.A., 1949, Ph.D., 1955. *Politics:* Independent. *Residence:* New City, N.Y.

CAREER: Nutritionist and author; consultant to food, vitamin, and pharmaceutical companies. Lecturer or visiting professor at New York University, City University of New York, New York Institute of Technology, Rockland Community College, Fairleigh Dickinson University. *Member:* International Academy of Preventive Medicine (fellow; member of board of governors), International College of Applied Nutrition (founding fellow), American Chemical Society, American Academy of Dental Medicine, American Association for the Advancement of Science, Academy of Orthomolecular Psychiatry (associate member), Academy of Metabology, Phi Beta Kappa.

WRITINGS: Lessons in Living: A Guide to Sane Eating and Buoyant Health, privately printed, 1943, 8th edition, revised, Coyne & Co., 1944, 9th revised edition published as *Living Should Be Fun*, Institute of Nutrition Research, Inc. (New York, N.Y.), 1945; *Eat, Live and Be Merry*, Paxton Slade, 1951, revised and enlarged edition published as *Nutrition: Your Key to Good Health*, London Press (North Hollywood, Calif.), 1964.

(With Hazel Meyer) *The Carlton Fredericks Cook Book for Good Nutrition*, Lippincott, 1960; (with Herbert Bailey) *Food Facts and Fallacies: The Intelligent Person's Guide to Nutrition and Health*, Julian Press, 1965; *Great Eating for Weight Watchers*, Award Books, 1968; (with Herman Goodman) *Low Blood Sugar and You*, Grosset, 1969.

Dr. Carlton Fredericks' Low-Carbohydrate Diet, Award Books, 1970; *Eat More Lose More Diet Book*, Award Books, 1971; *Eating Right for You*, Grosset, 1972; (editor and author of foreword) Francyne Davis, *Hypoglycemia Cookbook*, Grosset, 1973.

WORK IN PROGRESS: The Vitamin Guide; a text on orthomolecular psychiatry; a physician's guide to therapeutic nutrition.

SIDELIGHTS: Fredericks told *CA* that his role in interpreting science for the layman is aimed toward "shortening the aggravated cultural lag obtaining between findings in nutrition, and their application in the marketplace, the home, the physician's office, and the hospital and clinic."

Living Should Be Fun has been translated into Braille by the Library of Congress.

* * *

FREEMAN, Donald Cary 1938-

PERSONAL: Born March 19, 1938, in Boston, Mass.; son

of Warren S. (a school headmaster) and Phyllis (Brown) Freeman; married Caroline Smith, June 30, 1962 (divorced, 1970); married Margaret Rawson (a university professor), December 19, 1970; children: (first marriage) Elizabeth Stone, Roger Cary. *Education:* Mount Hermon School, student, 1951-55; Middlebury College, A.B. (honors), 1959; Brown University, M.A., 1961; University of Connecticut, Ph.D., 1965; Massachusetts Institute of Technology, postdoctoral study, 1967-68. *Home:* R.F.D. 1, Adams Rd., Athol, Mass. 01331. *Office:* Department of Linguistics, University of Massachusetts, Amherst, Mass. 01002.

CAREER: University of California, Santa Barbara, assistant professor of English, 1965-67; University of Massachusetts, Amherst, assistant professor, 1968-69, associate professor, 1969-72, professor of linguistics, 1972—, professor of English, 1974—, head of department of linguistics, 1969-72, associate dean of Faculty of Humanities and Fine Arts, 1972-74. *Member:* Modern Language Association of America, Linguistic Society of America. *Awards, honors:* National Science Foundation postdoctoral research fellowship in linguistics, 1967-68.

WRITINGS: (Editor) *Linguistics and Literary Style,* Holt, 1970. Contributor to *College English, Journal of Linguistics, Foundations of Language, Language and Style,* and *Style.*

WORK IN PROGRESS: Research on poetic and linguistic structure.

* * *

FRENCH, Calvin L(eonard) 1934-

PERSONAL: Born June 9, 1934, in Lowell, Mass.; son of Leonard L. (a proprietor of a factory) and Gertrude (Bachmann) French. *Education:* Brown University, B.A., 1953; Columbia University, M.A., 1958, Ph.D., 1965; Waseda University, graduate study, 1961; also attended Rhode Island School of Design. *Home:* 610 Waterman Rd., Ann Arbor, Mich. 48103. *Office:* Department of History of Art, Tappan Hall, University of Michigan, Ann Arbor, Mich. 48104.

CAREER: University of Michigan, Ann Arbor, instructor, 1964-66, assistant professor, 1966-71, associate professor of history of Japanese art, 1971—. Research associate at Freer Gallery of Art at Smithsonian Institution. *Military service:* U.S. Army, microwave radio technician, 1954-56. *Member:* Asia Society, Japan Society, College Art Association. *Awards, honors:* Horace H. Rackham fellowship, 1968; National Endowment for the Humanities fellowship, 1973; Social Science Research Council fellowship, 1973.

WRITINGS: (Contributor) Shimada Shujiro, editor, *Zaigai Hiho* (title means "Treasures of Japanese Painting Abroad"), Gakken, 1969; (contributor) Donald Keene, editor, *Twenty Plays of the No Theatre*, Columbia University, 1970; *The Poet-Painters: Buson and His Followers*, Museum of Art, University of Michigan, 1974; *Shiba Kokan: Artist, Innovator, and Pioneer in the Westernization of Japan*, Weatherhill, 1974. Editor of *Occasional Papers, Number 11: Japanese Culture 11*, University of Michigan, 1969. Contributor to *Drama Survey* and *Harvard Journal of Asiatic Studies*.

WORK IN PROGRESS: Ikeno Taiga: 1723-1776.

* * *

FRETWELL, Stephen DeWitt 1942-

PERSONAL: Born January 15, 1942, in Harrisonburg, Va.; son of Jack Wilson (a beverage wholesaler) and Margaret (an elementary school teacher; maiden name, Shank) Fretwell; married Armeda Ferrarini (a health instructor in college), June 1, 1963; children: Rebecca Lynn, Jennifer Lee. *Education:* Bucknell University, B.S., 1963; North Carolina State University, Ph.D., 1968; Princeton University, postdoctoral study, 1968-69. *Politics:* Republican. *Religion:* "Full Gospel Christian." *Home:* 423 Denisen Ave., Manhattan, Kan. 66502. *Office:* Division of Biology, Kansas State University, Manhattan, Kan. 66502.

CAREER: Kansas State University, Manhattan, assistant professor of biology, 1969—. Director of Bird Populations Institute. *Member:* Wilson Ornithological Society, American Ornithologists Union, Audubon Society, Carolina Bird Club; Northeastern, Eastern, Inland, and Western Bird Banding Associations, Kansas Ornithological Society (member of board of directors), Sigma Xi.

WRITINGS: Populations in a Seasonal Environment, Princeton University Press, 1972. Contributor to *Bird Watch.*

WORK IN PROGRESS: Understanding Nature: The Extensions of God; a sacred treatment of natural history from a modernistic scientific perspective.

SIDELIGHTS: Fretwell writes: "I have, and have had, many mystical experiences, and believe firmly and literally in the Bible, as a supernaturally controlled document. My mission is to restore or generate a respect for empiricism in the personal search for truth and love."

* * *

FREY, Frederick Ward 1929-

PERSONAL: Born June 16, 1929, in Cleveland, Ohio; son of Frederick H. W. (an attorney) and Helen (Simpson) Frey; married Marcianne Herr, August 21, 1953 (divorced, 1966); married Patricia Evans, December 16, 1967; children: (second marriage) Ethan Evans, Justin Ward. *Education:* Western Reserve University, B.A., 1951; Balliol College, Oxford, B.A., 1953; Princeton University, Ph.D., 1962. *Home:* 4000 Gypsy Lane, Apt. 507, Philadelphia, Pa. 19144. *Office:* Department of Political Science, University of Pennsylvania, Philadelphia, Pa. 19174.

CAREER: Massachusetts Institute of Technology, Cambridge, assistant professor, 1960-63, associate professor, 1963-66, professor of political science, 1966-74; University of Pennsylvania, Philadelphia, professor of political science, director of Anspach Institute, and chairman of graduate program in international relations, 1974—. *Military service:* U.S. Army, 1953-55; became sergeant. *Member:* American Political Science Association, American Sociological Association. *Awards, honors:* Rhodes scholar, 1951; Pi Sigma Alpha prize from American Political Science Association, 1967; Center for Advanced Study in the Behavioral Sciences fellow, 1971-72.

WRITINGS: The Turkish Political Elite, M.I.T. Press, 1965; *Survey Research on Comparative Social Change*, M.I.T. Press, 1969; (editor) *Handbook of Communication*, Rand McNally, 1973. Contributor to journals.

WORK IN PROGRESS: Power and the Political Process, for Praeger.

* * *

FRIEDL, John 1945-

PERSONAL: Born October 7, 1945, in Cleveland, Ohio;

son of Joseph Howard and Ruth (Weiss) Friedl. *Education:* University of California, Berkeley, B.A., 1967, M.A., 1969, Ph.D., 1971. *Home:* 1348 Bronwyn Ave., Columbus, Ohio 43204. *Office:* Department of Anthropology, Ohio State University, Columbus, Ohio 43210.

CAREER: University of California, Berkeley, assistant professor of anthropology, 1971; Ohio State University, Columbus, assistant professor of anthropology, 1971—. *Member:* American Anthropological Association (fellow), Society for Applied Anthropology (fellow), American Association for the Advancement of Science (fellow), Phi Beta Kappa.

WRITINGS: (Editor and contributor) *Studies in European Society*, Mouton & Co., 1973; *Kippel: A Changing Village in the Alps*, Holt, 1974; (editor with Noel J. Chrisman, and contributor) *City Ways*, Crowell, 1975; (editor with Jeremy Boissevain) *Beyond the Community: Social Process in Europe*, Dutch Ministry for Science and Education, 1975; *Cultural Anthropology*, Harper, in press.

AVOCATIONAL INTERESTS: Baseball, hockey, piano.

* * *

FRIEDMAN, Avner 1932-

PERSONAL: Born November 19, 1932, in Israel; son of Moshe S. (a school teacher) and Hanna (Rosenthal) Friedman; married Lillia Lynn Kelley; children: Alissa, Joel, Naomi, Tamara. *Education:* Hebrew University of Jerusalem, M.Sc., 1954, Ph.D., 1956. *Religion:* Jewish. *Home:* 2669 Orrington Ave., Evanston, Ill. 60201. *Office:* Department of Mathematics, Northwestern University, Evanston, Ill. 60201.

CAREER: University of Kansas, Lawrence, research associate, 1956-57; Indiana University, Bloomington, lecturer in mathematics, 1957-58; University of California, Berkeley, assistant professor of mathematics, 1958-59; University of Minnesota, Minneapolis, associate professor of mathematics, 1959-61; Stanford University, Stanford, Calif., associate professor of mathematics, 1961-62; Northwestern University, Evanston, Ill., professor of mathematics, 1962—. *Member:* American Mathematical Society. *Awards, honors:* Sloan fellowship, 1962-65; Guggenheim fellowship, 1966-67.

WRITINGS: Generalized Functions and Partial Differential Equations, Prentice-Hall, 1963; *Partial Differential Equations of Parabolic Type*, Prentice-Hall, 1964; *Partial Differential Equations*, Holt, 1969; *Foundations of Modern Analysis*, Holt, 1970; *Advanced Calculus*, Holt, 1971; *Differential Games*, Interscience, 1972. Contributor to mathematical journals.

WORK IN PROGRESS: Two volume study of stochastic differential equations and their applications, for Academic Press.

* * *

FRIEDMAN, Ina R(osen) 1926-

PERSONAL: Born January 6, 1926, in Chester, Pa.; daughter of Jacob Sidney and Libby (Leibowitz) Rosen; married Sol Friedman, August 11, 1946 (died November 15, 1973); children: Ronne, Wendy, Lynn, Loren. *Education:* Pennsylvania State University, B.A., 1946. *Politics:* Democratic. *Religion:* Jewish. *Home:* 7515 Marbury Rd., Bethesda, Md. 20034.

CAREER: Has held positions in advertising, actress, writer. Member of advisory council of Independence Federal Savings and Loan Bank. *Member:* League of Women Voters, Urban League, Common Cause, Smithsonian Associates, Women's Auxiliary of Hebrew Home for the Aged, Jewish Social Service Agency, Hadassah, B'nai Brith Women, Women's Suburban Democratic Club.

WRITINGS: (With Ethel Dalmat) *Poetry in Prayer* (religious service), Temple Sinai, 1965; (contributor) *A Collection of Temple Sinai Religious School Poetry*, Temple Sinai, 1969; (contributor) *A Collection of Temple Sinai Religious School Poetry*, Temple Sinai, 1970; *Black Cop: A Biography of Tilmon O'Bryant*, Westminster Press, 1974.

WORK IN PROGRESS: Fantasy for fourth through sixth grades; a book on the Holocaust period for junior high school and high school level, completion expected in 1975.

AVOCATIONAL INTERESTS: Theater, gardening, cooking, travel, snorkeling, tennis.

* * *

FRIEDMAN, Isaiah 1921-

PERSONAL: Born April 28, 1921, in Luck, Poland; son of Jonah (an industrialist) and Bela Friedman; married Barbara Joan Braham, April 5, 1959; children: Jonah David. *Education:* Hebrew University of Jerusalem, M.A., 1946; London School of Economics and Political Science, University of London, Ph.D., 1964. *Religion:* Jewish. *Home:* 101 Conshohocken State Rd., Apt. D3, Bala Cynwyd, Pa. 19004. *Office:* Department of History and Political Science, Dropsie University, Broad and York Sts., Philadelphia, Pa. 19132.

CAREER: High school teacher of history in Rehovot and Tel-Aviv, Israel, and lecturer to adults, 1946-61; Hebrew University, Institute of Contemporary Jewry, Jerusalem, Israel, research fellow, 1965-68; Institute of Contemporary History, London, England, research fellow, 1968-71; Dropsie University, Philadelphia, Pa., professor of history and political science, 1971—. *Member:* American Association of University Professors, Association of Jewish Studies, Middle East Studies Association, Institute of Jewish Affairs (London, England). *Awards, honors:* Theodor Koerner Award from University of Vienna, 1965, for article "Austria and Zionism"; Morris Kaplun Award from Jewish Book Council, 1973, for *The Question of Palestine, 1914-1918: British-Jewish-Arab Relations*.

WRITINGS: The Question of Palestine, 1914-1918: British-Jewish-Arab Relations, Schocken, 1973. Contributor to *Journal of Jewish Social Studies* and *Journal of Contemporary History*.

WORK IN PROGRESS: Germany, Turkey, and Zionism: 1897-1918.

* * *

FRIEDMAN, Lawrence J. 1940-

PERSONAL: Born October 8, 1940, in Cleveland, Ohio; son of Joseph (a life insurance broker) and Lena (a life insurance agent; maiden name, Malkin) Friedman; married Sharon Bloom, April 3, 1966; children: Beth. *Education:* University of California, Riverside, B.A., 1962; University of California, Los Angeles, M.A., 1965, Ph.D., 1967. *Religion:* Agnostic. *Home:* 510 Harvest Lane, Bowling Green, Ohio 43202. *Office:* Department of History, Bowling Green University, Bowling Green, Ohio 43402.

CAREER: Arizona State University, Tempe, assistant professor of history, 1967-71; Bowling Green University, Bowling Green, Ohio, associate professor of history, 1971—. *Member:* American Historical Association, Organization of American Historians, Association for the Study of Negro Life and History. *Awards, honors:* Younger Humanist fellowship from National Endowment for the Humanities, 1971-72.

WRITINGS: The White Savage: Racial Fantasies in the Postbellum South, Prentice-Hall, 1970; *Inventors of the Promised Land: Patriotic Crusaders in the White Man's Country, 1786-1840*, Knopf, in press. Contributor to academic journals, including *Journal of Negro History, Societas, Phylon*, and *New England Quarterly*.

WORK IN PROGRESS: Abolitionist Thought in America: 1831-1859; *The Social History of American Medicine*.

SIDELIGHTS: Friedman writes: "Over the past decade I have been focusing my work on the psychological and institutional variables basic to American racial attitudes. I plan to continue in this direction enlarging my scope methodologically through technical knowledge of medical techniques and psychoanalysis."

* * *

FROMAN, Elizabeth Hull 1920-1975

April 26, 1920—January 11, 1975; American author of children's books. Obituaries: *New York Times*, January 14, 1975. (*CA*-15/16).

* * *

FROST, Robert Carlton 1926-

PERSONAL: Born August 31, 1926, in Vancouver, Wash.; son of Carl Magnus and Rose Virginia (Bullock) Frost; married Anna Ruth Tewes (a registered nurse), June 10, 1950; children: Robert Carlton, Jr., Elizabeth Ann, Alicia Julene (Mrs. Michael Glenn Rowe), Sharon Virginia. *Education:* Reed College, B.A., 1948; Rice University, M.A., 1950, Ph.D., 1952. *Religion:* Christian. *Home:* 13062 Ethelbee Way, Santa Ana, Calif. 92705. *Office:* Aglow Ministries, Inc., 13062 Ethelbee Way, Santa Ana, Calif. 92705.

CAREER: Baylor University, Houston, Tex., instructor in anatomy, 1952-56; Evangel College, Springfield, Mo., assistant professor of biology, 1956-59; Westmont College, Santa Barbara, Calif., associate professor of biology, 1959-63, chairman of Division of Natural Science, 1960-63; Oral Roberts University, Tulsa, Okla., science consultant, 1963-64; Southern California College, Costa Mesa, professor of biology and chairman of Division of Natural Science, 1964-67; Oral Roberts University, professor of biology and chairman of natural sciences, 1967-69; Aglow Ministries, Inc., Santa Ana, Calif., lay minister and teacher, 1969—. Instructor at Melodyland Christian Center School of Theology; participant in numerous international inter-faith Christian conferences. *Member:* American Scientific Affiliation, American Institute for Biological Scientists, Creation Research Society, Sigma Xi.

WRITINGS: Aglow with the Spirit, Voice Christian Publications, 1965, revised edition, Logos International, 1971; *Life's Greatest Discovery*, Voice Christian Publications, 1968, revised edition, Logos International, 1971; *Overflowing Life*, Logos International, 1971, revised edition, 1973; *Set My Spirit Free*, Logos International, 1973; *Biology of the Spirit*, Revell, 1975. Contributor to *Journal of the American Scientific Affiliation, Logos Journal, Acts, Christian Life*, and *New Covenant*. Contributing editor of *New Covenant*.

SIDELIGHTS: Frost writes: "A spiritual awakening in my own life eventually was my motivation to leave the academic profession for full-time involvement as a lay minister and teacher. Since 1969 I have been engaged in the charismatic and ecumenical ministry of the Holy Spirit worldwide." His books have been published in Spanish, Japanese, and Danish. *Avocational interests:* Camping, hiking, swimming, nature study, photography.

* * *

FRYE, Keith 1935-

PERSONAL: Born July 17, 1935, in Columbus, Ohio; son of John (a writer) and Harriet (an artist; maiden name, Bennitt) Frye; married Nancy Ferguson (a writer), July 16, 1965. *Education:* Attended University of Mexico, summer, 1954; Oberlin College, A.B., 1957; fall graduate study at California Institute of Technology, 1959; University of Minnesota, M.S., 1959; Pennsylvania State University, Ph.D., 1965. *Home:* 1042 Manchester Ave., Norfolk, Va. 23508. *Office:* Department of Geophysical Sciences, Old Dominion University, Norfolk, Va. 23508.

CAREER: U.S. Fish and Wildlife Service, Anchorage, Alaska, stream guard, summer, 1956, 1957; Hyman Laboratories, Inc., Berkeley, Calif., chemist, 1961-62; University of Georgia, Athens, assistant professor of geology, 1965-67; Old Dominion University, Norfolk, Va., associate professor of geology, 1967—. *Member:* American Association for the Advancement of Science, American Geophysical Union, American Mineralogical Society, Geological Society of America.

WRITINGS: Modern Mineralogy, Prentice-Hall, 1974. Associate editor for mineralogy, *Encyclopedia of Earth Science*, Dowden, Hutchinson & Ross.

WORK IN PROGRESS: With wife, Nancy Frye, *Habit and Habitat*, a university textbook surveying the environmental sciences with emphasis on the systemmatics of the physical and biological environment and man's interactions with it, completion expected in 1975.

AVOCATIONAL INTERESTS: Reading.

* * *

FRYSCAK, Milan 1932-

PERSONAL: Surname is pronounced *Frish*-chark; born June 27, 1932, in Dobra, Czechoslovakia; son of Josef and Otilie Fryscak; married Eva Stepanek, June 19, 1965; children: Peter, Francis. *Education:* Palacky University, promovany filolog, 1956; University of California, Berkeley, M.A., 1962; Ohio State University, Ph.D., 1969. *Politics:* Democrat. *Religion:* Roman Catholic. *Home:* 6 Round Hill Dr., Yonkers, N.Y. 10710. *Office:* Department of Slavic Languages, New York University, 19 University Pl., New York, N.Y. 10003.

CAREER: Wittenberg University, Springfield, Ohio, instructor, 1964-66, assistant professor of Russian, 1966-70; New York University, New York, N.Y., assistant professor of Slavic linguistics, 1970—. *Member:* Modern Language Association of America, Linguistic Society of America, American Association of Teachers of Slavic and East European Languages, American Association for the Advancement of Slavic Studies, Masaryk Institute, Czechoslovak Society of Arts and Sciences in America.

WRITINGS: Say It in Czech, Dover, 1973.

WORK IN PROGRESS: Josef Dobrovsky, a critical biography.

SIDELIGHTS: Fryscak lived in Italy from 1957 to 1959.

* * *

FULLER, David O(tis) 1903-

PERSONAL: Born November 20, 1903 in Brooklyn, N.Y.; son of David Jonathan (a dentist) and Olive Beatrice (an author; maiden name, Muir) Fuller; married Virginia Emery, September 9, 1931; children: Beverly, Alan, David, Mabel (deceased), Virginia. *Education:* Wheaton College, Wheaton, Ill., A.B.; Princeton Theological Seminary, Th.B. *Politics:* Republican. *Home and office:* 605 Deming St. S.E., Grand Rapids, Mich. 49507.

CAREER: Minister of the gospel. Chelsea Baptist Church, Atlantic City, N.J., pastor, 1929-34; Wealthy St. Baptist Church, Grand Rapids, Mich., pastor, 1934-74. Chairman of Children's Bible Hour (radio program); trustee of Wheaton College, Wheaton, Ill. *Military service:* U.S. Navy, chaplain, 1945-46.

WRITINGS: (Editor) *Confessions of Saint Augustine*, Zondervan, 1947; (editor) *Valiant for the Truth: A Treasury of Evangelical Writings*, Lippincott, 1961, published as *Treasury of Evangelical Writings*, Kregel, 1961; (compiler) *Which Bible?*, Grand Rapids International Publications, 1970, 4th revised edition, 1973; *Counterfeit or Genuine?*, Kregel, 1974. Also editor of *Spurgeon's Sermon Notes*, Zondervan, *True or False?*, Kregel, *Treasury of David, Calvin's Institutes*, and *Spurgeon's Autobiography*.

* * *

FULLER, Edward C. 1907-

PERSONAL: Born August 8, 1907, in Helena, Mont.; son of George Nelson (a clerk) and Claudia (a teacher; maiden name, Tinker) Fuller; married Dorothy Edsall (a librarian), June 26, 1937; children: David Edsall, Carol Margaret (Mrs. Thomas Syvertsen). *Education:* Montana State University, B.S., 1928; Columbia University, Ph.D., 1941. *Politics:* Independent. *Religion:* Episcopalian. *Home:* 2648 Riverside Dr., Beloit, Wis. 53511. *Office:* Department of Chemistry, Beloit College, Beloit, Wis. 53511.

CAREER: Bard College, Annandale-on-Hudson, N.Y., instructor, 1935-38, assistant professor, 1939-41, associate professor, 1942-44, professor of chemistry, 1944-46, president, 1946-50; State University of New York at Plattsburg, professor of chemistry, and director of Division of Natural Sciences and Mathematics, 1950-53; Beloit College, Beloit, Wis., professor of chemistry and chairman of department, 1953-73, adjunct professor, 1974—. Administrative aide at Columbia University Atomic Bomb Project, 1944-46. Visiting professor at Harvard University, summer, 1950. Member of International Congress of United Nations Educational, Scientific and Cultural Organization, Bulgaria, 1968; consultant to University of Oregon Project, 1960-65; visiting scientist for National Science Foundation, 1955.

MEMBER: American Chemical Society (chairman of Division of Chemical Education, 1963), American Association for the Advancement of Science (fellow), American Institute of Chemists (fellow), American Association of University Professors, Sigma Xi.

WRITINGS: *Discussion Guide and Laboratory Manual for Basic Natural Science*, Edwards Bros., 1951; (contributor) I. B. Cohen and F. G. Watson, editors, *General Education in Science*, Harvard University Press, 1952; (with others) *Chemical Systems: Chemical Bond Approach Project for High School Chemistry*, McGraw, 1964; *Chemistry and Man's Environment*, Houghton, 1974. Contributor of more than thirty-four articles to *Journal of Chemical Education* and *Journal of Higher Education*. Member of board of publications of *Journal of Chemical Education*, 1963-72; member of editorial advisory board of *Chemical and Engineering News*, 1968-69.

WORK IN PROGRESS: *Student Guide for Chemistry and Man's Environment*; *Laboratory Manual for Chemistry and Man's Environment*; two module texts, *Chemistry and Man's Nutrition*, and *Chemistry and the Energy Problem*.

* * *

FULLER, Hoyt (William) 1927-
(William Barrow)

PERSONAL: Born September 10, 1927, in Atlanta, Ga.; son of Thomas and Lillie Beatrice Ellafair (Thomas) Fuller; married, 1919; children: James Harold, Robert, Hoyt William. *Education:* Wayne State University, B.A., 1950, graduate study, 1950-51. *Home:* 3001 South Martin Luther King Dr., Apt. 1902, Chicago, Ill. 60616. *Agent:* Bertha Klausner, 71 Park Ave., New York, N.Y. 10016. *Office:* *Black World*, 820 South Michigan Ave., Chicago, Ill. 60605.

CAREER: *Detroit Tribune*, Detroit, Mich., reporter, 1949-51; *Michigan Chronicle*, Detroit, Mich., feature editor, 1951-54; *Ebony*, Chicago, Ill., associate editor, 1954-57; *Haagse Post*, Amsterdam, Holland, West African correspondent, 1957-60; *Collier's Encyclopedia*, New York, N.Y., assistant editor, 1960-61; *Black World* (formerly *Negro Digest*), Chicago, Ill., executive editor, 1961—. Teacher of Afro-American literature at Northwestern University, 1969-70, Indiana University, 1970-71, and Wayne State University, 1974. *Member:* Organization of Black American Culture (founder, 1967). *Awards, honors:* John Hay Whitney Opportunity Fellowship, 1965-66.

WRITINGS: *Journey to Africa*, Third World Press, 1971.

Work represented in anthologies, including *American Negro Short Stories*, edited by John Henrik Clarke, Hill & Wang, 1966; *Beyond the Angry Black*, edited by John A. Williams, Cooper Square, 1966; *Black Expression*, edited by Addison Gayle, Jr., Weybright & Talley, 1969; *The Black Aesthetic*, edited by Gayle, Doubleday, 1971; *Black Literature in America*, edited by Houston Baker, McGraw, 1971; *Points of Departure*, edited by Ernece Kelly, Wiley, 1972; *The Black American Writer*, edited by C. W. E. Bigsby, New York University Press, 1972.

Contributor to *Collier's Encyclopedia Yearbook* and to magazines and newspapers, sometimes under pseudonym William Barrow, including *New Yorker, North American Review, New Republic, Christian Science Monitor, New York Times Book Review*.

WORK IN PROGRESS: A novel, *An Hour of Breath*, and non-fiction, *History and Analysis of Black Aesthetic Movement*.

* * *

FULTON, Gere (Burke) 1939-

PERSONAL: Born January 11, 1939, in Harrisburg, Pa.; son of Graydon B. (an engineman) and Odella (Bickel) Fulton; married Marie E. Kmetz, January 4, 1960; children: Douglas, David. *Education:* East Stroudsburg State College, B.S., 1960; University of Maryland, M.A., 1962, Ph.D., 1967. *Home:* 7658 Bridgeway Rd., Temperance,

Mich. 48182. *Office:* Department of Health Education, University of Toledo, Toledo, Ohio 43606.

CAREER: Temple University, Philadelphia, Pa., assistant professor of health education, 1965-67; Trenton State College, Trenton, N.J., professor of health education, and coordinator, 1967-71; University of Toledo, Toledo, Ohio, professor of health education and chairman of department, 1971—. Visiting professor at Dalhousie University, 1971; visiting lecturer at Toledo Hospital School of Nursing, 1973—. Vice-president of Planned Parenthood League of Toledo, 1973-75; member of board of directors of Lucas County chapter of American Cancer Society, 1972. *Member:* American School Health Association, Association for Advancement of Health Education, Eta Sigma Gamma.

WRITINGS: (Editor with W. V. Fassbender) *Health Education in the Elementary School: Guidelines and Program Suggestions*, Goodyear Publishing, 1972; *Sexual Awareness*, Holbrook, 1974; (with Mary K. Beyrer, Myrna Yeakel, Rosemary Amos, and Gertrude Couch) *Completed Research in Health Education*, National Education Association, 1974.

WORK IN PROGRESS: Research on sex therapy and on sex education.

* * *

FULTS, John Lee 1932-

PERSONAL: Born March 14, 1932, in Bell Buckle, Tenn.; son of Virnie Lee (a farmer) and Mattie (Delbridge) Fults; married Anne Simmons (a teacher), August 26, 1961; children: Jeffrey Lee, Gregory John. *Education:* Middle Tennessee State College (now University), B.S., 1953, also graduate study. *Politics:* Independent. *Religion:* Church of Christ. *Home:* 11017 Rockcliff Dr., Huntsville, Ala. 35810. *Office:* Marshall Space Flight Center, Huntsville, Ala. 35810.

CAREER: Farmer, grocery clerk; junior high school and high school teacher of mathematics, physics, and science in the public schools of Christiana, Tenn., 1953, and Manchester, Tenn., 1956; ARO, Inc., Tullahoma, Tenn., engineering aide, 1957-61; State Highway Department, Nashville, Tenn., planning analyst, 1961-62; Hayes Aircraft Co., Huntsville, Ala., engineer, 1962-64; Chrysler Corp., Huntsville, Ala., engineer, 1964-66; National Aeronautics and Space Administration, Marshall Space Flight Center, Huntsville, Ala., senior engineer and mathematician, 1966—. *Military service:* U.S. Navy, 1954-56. U.S. Coast Guard Reserve, 1962—; commanding officer, Nashville, Tenn., Reserve Unit, 1973—. *Member:* Reserve Officers Association (Coast Guard chairman for Alabama, 1973—), Boy Scouts of America.

WRITINGS: *Magic Squares*, Open Court, 1974. Contributor to *Murfreesboro Daily News Journal*.

AVOCATIONAL INTERESTS: Boating, military science, history, religion, travel.

* * *

FUSSELL, Edwin 1922-

PERSONAL: Born July 4, 1922, in Pasadena, Calif.; son of Paul and Wilhma (Sill) Fussell; married Mary Everett Burton. *Education:* Pomona College, B.A., 1943; Harvard University, M.A., 1947, Ph.D., 1949. *Politics:* Marxist. *Religion:* Roman Catholic. *Home:* 5791 Soledad Rd., La Jolla, Calif. 92037. *Office:* Department of Literature, University of California at San Diego, La Jolla, Calif. 92038.

CAREER: University of California, Berkeley, instructor in English, 1949-51; Pomona College, Claremont, Calif., assistant professor of English, 1951-54; Claremont Graduate School, Claremont, Calif., assistant professor, 1955-56, associate professor, 1956-62, professor of literature, 1962-67; University of California at San Diego, La Jolla, professor of literature, 1967—. Fulbright lecturer at University of Liege, 1954-55, and Universities of Florence and Pisa, 1967-68. *Military service:* U.S. Naval Reserve, active duty, 1943-46. *Member:* Modern Language Association of America, Dante Society of America.

WRITINGS: (Editor with George R. Stewart) *San Francisco in 1866, by Bret Harte, Being Letters to the Springfield Republican,* Book Club of California, 1951; *Edwin Arlington Robinson: The Literary Background of a Traditional Poet,* University of California Press, 1954, reprinted, Russell, 1970; (editor with Charles S. Holmes and Ray Frazer) *The Major Critics: The Development of English Literary Criticism,* Knopf, 1957; *Frontier: American Literature and the American West,* Princeton University Press, 1965; (translator and author of introduction) Cesare Pavese, *American Literature: Essays and Opinions,* University of California Press, 1970; *Lucifer in Harness: American Meter, Metaphor, and Diction,* Princeton University Press, 1973.

Contributor: Sherman Paul, editor, *Thoreau: A Collection of Critical Essays,* Prentice-Hall, 1962; Arthur Mizener, editor, *Fitzgerald: A Collection of Critical Essays,* Prentice-Hall, 1963; John S. Tuckey, editor, *Mark Twain's "The Mysterious Stranger" and the Critics,* Wadsworth, 1968; Francis Murphy, editor, *Edwin Arlington Robinson: A Collection of Critical Essays,* Prentice-Hall, 1970; Gerhard Hoffman, editor, *Amerikanische Literatur des 20. Jahrhunderts: Die Erzaehlkunst,* Fischer Taschenbuch Verlag, 1972; Walter B. Rideout, editor, *Sherwood Anderson: A Collection of Critical Essays,* Prentice-Hall, 1974.

Author of "The Purgatory Poems," published in the *Little Square Review,* number 3, 1967, and "Ballad of Ash Wednesday," handprinted in a limited edition by Sun Press, 1967. Fussell's poems have appeared in *Anthology of Magazine Verse for 1958,* and in *Accent, Voices, Poetry, Prairie Schooner, kayak, Kenyon Review, Pequod,* and other literary reviews. Contributor of essays and reviews to various journals, including *American Literature, Thought* (Delhi), *American Quarterly, Kenyon Review,* and *Parnassus;* also contributor of satires and parodies, some under undisclosed pseudonyms, to *PUCRED.*

WORK IN PROGRESS: Two novels, *Gin for Breakfast* and *The Notebooks of David Winter;* a collection of poems; a selection of essays, *The Common Doom;* and *Letters to Mary; An Introduction to Dante in Extremis.*

AVOCATIONAL INTERESTS: Painting ("eclectically, but mostly in the 'abstract expressionist' mode").

* * *

GALELLA, Ron 1931-

PERSONAL: Born January 10, 1931, in Bronx, N.Y.; son of Vincenzo (a piano and casket maker) and Michelina (a croche beader; maiden name, Marinaccio) Galella. *Education:* Art Center College of Design, B.Professional Arts, 1957; studied acting and stage direction at Pasadena Playhouse, 1957. *Politics:* Independent. *Religion:* Roman Catholic. *Home and office:* 17 Glover Ave., Yonkers, N.Y. 10704.

CAREER: Ceramic artist with Associated American Artists, 1949-51; free-lance magazine and newspaper photographer, specializing in photographing celebrities in a candid, off-guard style, 1955—. Lecturer at University of Miami, Coral Gables, Fla. One man exhibits have been shown at Soho Gallery and Nikon House Gallery. *Military service:* U.S. Air Force, ground and aerial photographer and camera repairman, 1951-55.

WRITINGS: Jacqueline (with photographs), Sheed & Ward, 1974. Photographs have appeared in national magazines, and on covers of *Life, Esquire, Show, Cosmopolitan, McCall's, Tennis, Coronet,* and *Pageant*, and on national television programs.

WORK IN PROGRESS: The Gods Exposed, Confessions of an American Paparazzo, photographs and text.

SIDELIGHTS: Galella got his start in photography while in the Air Force. Before being discharged, he made a front page story in his base newspaper and the *Air Force Times* by "hopping twenty thousand miles by military aircraft to nine European countries to take photographs." He gave himself this assignment on a thirty-three day furlough. He took more than a thousand photographs. Expenses were practically nil as he used "hops" for most of his journey. Only a hundred fifty dollars was spent on travel, hotels, and meals. In 1954 he had an exhibition of some of these photographs at the Central Florida Cultural Center.

AVOCATIONAL INTERESTS: Ceramic sculpture, drawing.

BIOGRAPHICAL/CRITICAL SOURCES: Show, October, 1967; *Esquire*, March, 1972.

* * *

GALL, Meredith D(amien) 1942-

PERSONAL: Born February 18, 1942, in New Britain, Conn.; son of Theodore Albert (a procurement specialist) and Ray (Ehrlich) Gall; married Joyce Pershing (a psychologist), June 15, 1968. *Education:* Harvard University, A.B. and Ed.M., both 1963; University of California, Berkeley, Ph.D., 1968. *Residence:* Berkeley, Calif. *Office:* Far West Laboratory for Educational Research and Development, 1855 Folsom St., San Francisco, Calif. 94103.

CAREER: San Francisco Veterans Administration Hospital, San Francisco, Calif., clinical psychologist, 1965-66; University of California, Counseling Center, Berkeley, counseling psychologist, 1966-67; Far West Laboratory for Educational Research and Development, San Francisco, Calif., psychologist in Program for Effective Teacher Education, 1968—. *Member:* American Psychological Association, America Educational Research Association, Phi Delta Kappa. *Awards, honors:* Golden Eagle Award from International Film Committee for Non-Theatrical Events, 1972, for instructional films in "Higher Cognitive Questioning" training program.

WRITINGS: (With W.R. Borg) *Educational Research: An Introduction,* McKay, 2nd edition, 1971 (Gall was not associated with 1st edition); (with Borg and others) *The Minicourse: A Microteaching Approach to Teacher Education,* Macmillan Educational Services, 1970; (contributor) J. K. Hemphill and F. S. Rosenau, editors, *Educational Development,* Center for Advanced Study in Educational Administration, 1972; (contributor) Amelia Melnik and John Merritt, editors, *The Reading Curriculum,* University of London Press, 1972, General Learning Corp., 1973; (contributor) B. C. Mills and R. A. Mills, editors, *Designing Instructional Strategies for Young Children,* W. C. Brown, 1972; (contributor) Morton Bloomberg, editor, *Creativity: Theory and Research,* College & University Press, 1973; (with Borg and N. T. Bell) *Student Workbook in Educational Research,* McKay, 1974; (editor with B. A. Ward) *Critical Issues in Educational Psychology,* Little, Brown, 1974.

Training materials—Films or audio tapes with accompanying handbooks for students and manuals for teachers: (With B. B. Dunning and J. Galassi) "Individualizing Instruction in Mathematics," Macmillan, 1970; (with Dunning and R. Weathersby) "Higher Cognitive Questioning," Macmillan, 1971; (with K. A. Acheson and J. H. Hansen) "Teacher Supervision: A Brief Training Program in Observation and Conference Techniques," University of Oregon, 1973; (with Weathersby, M. K. Lai, and R. A. Elder) "Discussing Controversial Issues," Far West Laboratory for Educational Research and Development, 1973.

Contributor to journals in his field.

* * *

GALLNER, Sheldon M(ark) 1949-

PERSONAL: Born May 14, 1949, in Council Bluffs, Iowa; son of David (a grocer) and Esther (Sacks) Gallner. *Education:* American University, B.A. (cum laude), 1971; University of Iowa, J.D. (with distinction), 1974. *Politics:* Democrat. *Religion:* Jewish. *Home:* 520 Oakland Ave., Council Bluffs, Iowa 51501. *Office:* 424 Madison Ave., New York, N.Y. 10017.

CAREER: Blackman & Gallner Associates (sports consultants), New York, N.Y., partner, 1974—. Lecturer at Practicing Law Institute's Division of Sports Law. *Member:* American Bar Association, Iowa State Bar Association, Phi Kappa Phi.

WRITINGS: Pro Sports: The Contract Game, Scribner, 1974.

WORK IN PROGRESS: A book about sports and athletes' experiences in representation, with Martin Blackman; investigating the production of sports documentaries for television.

* * *

GALLWEY, W. Timothy 1938-

PERSONAL: Born January 26, 1938, in San Francisco, Calif.; son of W. Edgar (a businessman) and Irene (Grissim) Gallwey; married Sally Childs, September 22, 1974. *Education:* Harvard University, A.B., 1960. *Office:* Inner Game Resources, 527 Midvale, Westwood, Calif. 90024.

CAREER: Phillips Exeter Academy, Exeter, N.H., teacher of English, 1960-61; Mackinac College, Mackinac, Mich., director of admissions, 1965-69; Meadowbrook Swim and Tennis Club, Seaside, Calif., tennis professional, 1970-71; Inner Game Resources, Westwood, Calif., founder and president, 1974—. *Military service:* U.S. Navy, 1962-65; became lieutenant, U.S. Naval Reserve.

WRITINGS: The Inner Game of Tennis, Random House, 1974.

WORK IN PROGRESS: Playing the Inner Game, a sequel to *The Inner Game of Tennis*, emphasizing methodology more than theory; research on the relation of the state of the mind to performance.

GARA, Larry 1922-

PERSONAL: Born May 16, 1922, in San Antonio, Tex.; married Lenna Mae Goodson, December 22, 1946; children: Robin Jane, Brian David. *Education:* William Penn College, B.A., 1947; Pennsylvania State University, M.A., 1948; University of Wisconsin, Ph.D., 1953. *Religion:* Society of Friends (Quaker). *Home:* 21 Faculty Pl., Wilmington, Ohio 45177. *Office:* Wilmington College, Wilmington, Ohio 45177.

CAREER: Bluffton College, Bluffton, Ohio, instructor in history and government, 1948-49; Mexico City College, Mexico City, Federal District, Mexico, lecturer in history, 1953-54; Eureka College, Eureka, Ill., instructor, 1954-55, assistant professor of history, 1955-57; Grove City College, Grove City, Pa., professor of history, 1957-62, chairman of department of history and political science, 1958-62; Wilmington College, Wilmington, Ohio, associate professor, 1962-66, professor of history and government, 1966—, chairman of department, 1971—. Visiting professor at University of Delaware, summer, 1962. *Wartime service:* Conscientious objector; refused to register for conscription, 1942, and was jailed three times for war protests.

MEMBER: American Historical Association, Organization of American Historians, American Studies Association, Conference on Research in Peace History, Friends Historical Association, American Association of University Professors (chairman of Ohio Conference, 1966-67), War Resisters League (member of national committee, 1970—; vice-chairman, 1974—), Southern Historical Association, Ohio Academy of History (member of executive council, 1974—), Phi Alpha Theta. *Awards, honors:* American Philosophical Society research grant, 1956; W. Wistar Brown fellow at Haverford College, 1968-69.

WRITINGS: Westernized Yankee: The Story of Cyrus Woodman, State Historical Society of Wisconsin, 1956; (editor) *The Baby Dodds Story as Told to Larry Gara*, Contemporary Press, 1959; *The Liberty Line: The Legend of the Underground Railroad*, University of Kentucky Press, 1961; *A Short History of Wisconsin*, State Historical Society of Wisconsin, 1962; *War Resistance in Historical Perspective* (pamphlet), Pendle Hill, 1970.

Author of introduction: *The Narrative of Williams Wells Brown, a Fugitive Slave*, Addison-Wesley, 1969; William Joseph Chamberlain, *Fighting for Peace: The Story of the War Resistance Movement*, Garland Publishing, 1971; Adin Ballou, *Christian Non-Resistance*, Garland Publishing, 1972.

Contributor: J. Jeffrey Auer, editor, *Antislavery and Disunion, 1858-1861*, Harper, 1963; Martin Duberman, editor, *The Antislavery Vanguard*, Princeton University Press, 1965; Clifford L. Lord, editor, *Keepers of Our Past*, University of North Carolina Press, 1965; Dwight W. Hoover, editor, *Understanding Negro History*, Quadrangle, 1968; August Meier and Elliot Rudwick, editors, *The Making of Black America*, Volume I, Atheneum, 1969; Irwin Unger, editor, *Essays on the Civil War and Reconstruction*, Dryden, 1970; Tilden G. Edelstein and Seth Scheiner, editors, *The Black Americans*, Holt, 1971; Leonard Dinnerstein and Kenneth T. Jackson, editors, *American Vistas, 1607-1877*, two volumes, Oxford University Press, 1971. Contributor to other historical books and to *Notable American Women*; contributor of more than thirty articles and numerous reviews to historical journals; regular contributor to *WIN* (a war resistance magazine). Member of editorial board, *Bulletin* of Cincinnati Historical Society.

WORK IN PROGRESS: Editing the 1976 calendar of the War Resisters League; a book on the presidency of Franklin Pierce, completion expected in 1977.

SIDELIGHTS: Gara's writing has been motivated, he says, by three areas of interest—history, jazz, and the peace movement. He has been a record collector and jazz buff since high school days. He adds: "Consider war, and what it involves, to be the most serious problem facing humanity today, and am convinced that nonviolent alternatives to resolve conflicts on all levels are available and feasible. As a pacifist revolutionary, I am a radical, but this is tempered by my historical studies. Listening to jazz keeps me sane."

* * *

GARBARINO, Joseph W. 1919-

PERSONAL: Born December 7, 1919, in Medina, N.Y.; son of Joseph F. and Savina (Volpone) Garbarino; married Mary Jane Godward, September 18, 1948; children: Ann, Joan, Susan, Ellen. *Education:* Duquesne University, B.A., 1942; Harvard University, M.A., 1947, Ph.D., 1949. *Religion:* Roman Catholic. *Home:* 7708 Ricardo Ct., El Cerrito, Calif. 94530. *Office:* School of Business Administration, University of California, Berkeley, Calif. 94720.

CAREER: University of California, Berkeley, assistant professor, 1949-55, associate professor, 1955-60, professor of business administration, 1960—, director of Institute of Business and Economic Research, 1962—. Fulbright lecturer at University of Glasgow, 1969. *Military service:* U.S. Army, 1942-45, 1951-52; became captain. *Member:* American Economic Association, Industrial Relations Research Association.

WRITINGS: Health Plans and Collective Bargaining, University of California Press, 1960; *Wage Policy and Long Term Contracts*, Brookings Institution, 1962; *Faculty Bargaining: Change and Conflict*, McGraw, 1974.

* * *

GARBER, Frederick 1929-

PERSONAL: Born December 18, 1929, in Boston, Mass.; son of Barnet (a cobbler) and Ida (Levy) Garber; married Marjorie Ann Terret, August 17, 1957; children: Emily, Catherine, David. *Education:* Boston University, B.A. (magna cum laude), 1957; Yale University, Ph.D., 1963. *Residence:* Vestal, N.Y. *Office:* Department of Comparative Literature, State University of New York, Binghamton, N.Y. 13901.

CAREER: University of Washington, Seattle, instructor, 1961-64, assistant professor of English, 1964-66; State University of New York at Binghamton, assistant professor, 1966-71, associate professor, 1971-72, professor of comparative literature, 1972—, chairman of program in comparative literature, 1969-71. *Military service:* U.S. Army, 1951-53. *Member:* International Comparative Literature Association (secretary, 1971), Modern Language Association of America, American Comparative Literature Association (secretary-treasurer, 1971), Phi Beta Kappa. *Awards, honors:* Woodrow Wilson fellowship, 1957-58; American Philosophical Society grant, 1969.

WRITINGS: (Editor and author of introduction and notes) Ann Radcliffe, *The Italian*, Oxford University Press, 1968, 2nd edition, 1970; (editor with Donna Gerstenberger) *Microcosm: An Anthology of the Short Story*, Chandler Publishing, 1969; (contributor) Victor Brombert, editor, *The*

Hero in Literature, Fawcett, 1969; (contributor) Radcliffe, *The Mysteries of Udolpho*, Oxford University Press, 1970; *Wordsworth and the Poetry of Encounter*, University of Illinois Press, 1971; (contributor) Harold E. Pagliaro, editor, *Studies in Eighteenth Century Culture; Proceedings of the American Society for Eighteenth Century Studies*, Volume III, Case Western Reserve University Press, 1973; (contributor of translations) Peter Jay, editor, *The Greek Anthology*, Allen Lane, 1973; (author of foreword) Radcliffe, *The Romance of the Forest*, Arno, in press.

Contributor to *Dictionnaire international des termes litteraires*. Contributor of about thirty articles, translations, and reviews to language and literature journals, including *Literary Review, Wordsworth Circle, Etudes Anglaises, Judaism, Nineteenth Century French Studies*, and *Contemporary Literature*.

WORK IN PROGRESS: A book on Thoreau; a book on the image of the Romantic Self; editing and writing material for a book on Romantic irony; editing an anthology of essays on the literature of the Holocaust; editing an anthology of essays on Gothic fiction.

* * *

GARCIA, F(laviano) Chris 1940-

PERSONAL: Born April 15, 1940, in Albuquerque, N.M.; son of Flaviano P. and Crucita (Garcia) Garcia; married Sandra D. Galloway, September 2, 1967; children: Elaine, Tania. *Education:* University of New Mexico, B.A., 1961, M.A., 1964; graduate study at University of California at Los Angeles, 1964-65; University of California, Davis, Ph.D., 1972. *Home:* 724 La Veta N.E., Albuquerque, N.M. 87108. *Office:* Department of Political Science, University of New Mexico, Albuquerque, N.M. 87131.

CAREER: University of New Mexico, U.S. Peace Corps Training Center, Albuquerque, instructor and discussion leader, summers, 1962-65; Fullerton Junior College, Fullerton, Calif., instructor in political science, 1966-67; University of New Mexico, Albuquerque, assistant professor, 1970-74, associate professor of political science, 1974—, director of Division of Government Research, 1970-72. Visiting professor at Indiana University, 1972, and California State University, Fullerton, 1973. Lecturer and consultant, National Science Foundation Summer Institute in Political Science for Secondary and Elementary Schools, 1973; coordinator, New Mexico State Legislature Internship Program, 1971, 1972.

MEMBER: American Political Science Association, American Association of University Professors, Western Political Science Association (member of executive council, 1972-74), Southwest Social Science Association, Western Social Science Association (member of executive council, 1973—), Phi Kappa Phi, Pi Sigma Alpha, Profesores por la Raza.

WRITINGS: (Contributor) Robert D. Wrinkle, editor, *Politics in the Urban Southwest*, Division of Government Research, University of New Mexico, 1971; (contributor) Ralph Poblano, editor, *Ghosts in the Barrio: Issues in Bilingual-Bicultural Education*, Leswing Press, 1973; *The Political Socialization of Chicano Children*, Praeger, 1973; *La Causa Politica: A Chicano Politics Reader*, University of Notre Dame Press, 1974. Contributor to *National Civic Review, Aztlan: Chicano Journal of the Social Sciences, Social Science Quarterly*, and *Urban Education*.

WORK IN PROGRESS: Chicanos in U.S. Politics; a study of a high school as a political system; an investigation of the political orientation of rural Chicano school children in the Rio Grande Valley of Texas; *New Mexico Government*.

* * *

GARDINER, Robert W(orthington) 1932-

PERSONAL: Born May 3, 1932, in Newton, Mass.; son of Frederick S. (an artist) and Gertrude Mary (an artist; maiden name, Worthington) Gardiner; married Lorraine Stigbert, June 26, 1965; children: Matthew Frederick. *Education:* Amherst College, A.B., 1954; Tufts University, B.D., 1962; Andover Newton Theological School, S.T.M., 1970. *Politics:* Independent Radical (New Left). *Home address:* Main St., Pittsford, Vt. 05763. *Office:* Congregational Church, Main St., Pittsford, Vt. 05763.

CAREER: Ordained clergyman of United Church of Christ; pastor of Unitarian-Universalist church in Natick, Mass., 1963-68; Congregational Church, Pittsford, Vt., minister, 1971—. *Military service:* U.S. Air Force, 1954-58. *Member:* Audubon Society, United Nations Association, Nature Conservancy, Public Citizen, Inc., World Federalists, Wilderness Society, Defenders of Wildlife, American Civil Liberties Union, Common Cause, National Committee for a Sane Nuclear Policy, Vermonters for Amnesty, Pittsford Lions Club.

WRITINGS: The Cool Arm of Destruction: Modern Weapons and Moral Insensitivity, Westminster, 1974.

SIDELIGHTS: Gardiner writes: "... modern war, and the weapons with which it is fought, are an atrocity which cannot be justified by any political objectives, however desirable.... Any policy which seeks to preserve the values of human civilization by means of the use, or the threatened use, of such weapons as now exist is, I believe, unspeakably immoral, and, in the long run, suicidal."

* * *

GARLICK, Raymond 1926-

PERSONAL: Born September 21, 1926, in London, England; son of William (a bank official) and Elfreda (Beere) Garlick; married Elin Hughes (a translator), August 20, 1948; children: Iestyn Kevin, Angharad Mair. *Education:* University of Leeds, student, 1943-44; University College of North Wales, B.A. (honors), 1948. *Politics:* "Welsh Republican." *Religion:* Roman Catholic. *Home address:* Hen Ysgoldy, Llansteffan, Carmarthen SA33 5HA, Wales. *Office:* Department of Welsh Studies, Trinity College, University of Wales, Carmarthen, Dyfed, Wales.

CAREER: Schoolmaster in Wales, 1948-60; International School, Kasteel Eerde, Ommen, Netherlands, head of English department, 1961-67; University of Wales, Trinity College, Carmarthen, Wales, senior lecturer in English, 1967-71, principal lecturer and director of Welsh studies, 1972—. *Member:* Yr Academi Gymreig (Welsh Academy). *Awards, honors:* Welsh Arts Council literature prize, 1969, for *A Sense of Europe*, and 1973, for *A Sense of Time*.

WRITINGS: A Sense of Europe: Collected Poems, 1954-1968, Gwasg Gomer, 1968; *An Introduction to Anglo-Welsh Literature*, University of Wales Press, 1970, revised edition, 1972; *A Sense of Time: Poems and Antipoems, 1969-1972*, Gwasg Gomer, 1972; (contributor) Meic Stephens, editor, *Artists in Wales*, Volume II, Gomer Press, 1973; *Incense: Poems, 1972-1975*, Gwasg Gomer, 1975.

Contributor to magazines of contemporary poetry. Editor of *Anglo-Welsh Review*, 1949-60.

WORK IN PROGRESS: Continuing research on Anglo-Welsh literature, especially the period between 1400 and 1800.

SIDELIGHTS: Garlick writes that he is "a writer of Wales in the English language. England plays no part in my life or work." His strongest interests are in civil rights, especially Welsh language rights in courts of law, and in the Netherlands and Flanders. Selected poems from *A Sense of Europe* and *A Sense of Time*, spoken by Garlick, are recorded in the "Poets of Wales" series of Argo.

BIOGRAPHICAL/CRITICAL SOURCES: *Anglo-Welsh Review*, summer, 1972; Meic Stephens, editor, *Artists in Wales*, Volume II, Gomer Press, 1973.

* * *

GARSON, G(eorge) David 1943-

PERSONAL: Born January 10, 1943, in Newark, N.J.; son of George David (in sales) and Ruth (a secretary; maiden name, DesJardins) Garson; married Cynthia Rea (a learning disabilities specialist), June 15, 1968; children: Richard, Terry (foster children). *Education:* Princeton University, B.A., 1965; Harvard University, Ph.D., 1969. *Religion:* Christian. *Home:* 19 Hawthorne St., Somerville, Mass. 02144. *Office:* Department of Political Science, Tufts University, Medford, Mass. 02155.

CAREER: Tufts University, Medford, Mass., assistant professor, 1969-74, associate professor of political science, 1974—. Trustee of Center for the Study of Public Policy, 1970—. *Member:* American Political Science Association, American Sociological Association, American Society for Public Administration, Society for the Study of Social Problems, Union for Radical Political Economics, Caucus for a New Political Science.

WRITINGS: *Handbook of Political Science Methods*, Holbrook, 1971, 2nd edition, in press; (editor with G. Hunnius and J. Case) *Workers' Control*, Random House, 1973; *On Democratic Administration and Socialist Self-Management*, Sage Publications, 1974; *Political Science Methods*, Holbrook, 1975. Member of editorial board of *Administration and Society*, 1974—.

WORK IN PROGRESS: *Power and Politics in America*, for Heath.

* * *

GARVIN, Lawrence 1945-

PERSONAL: Born July 20, 1945, in Buenos Aires, Argentina; son of Lester (a banker) and Barbara (Nash) Garvin. *Education:* Attended Kenyon College, 1964-66; City College of the City University of New York, B.A., 1970. *Politics:* "Not definable." *Religion:* "Not definable." *Home and office:* 434 Lafayette St., New York, N.Y. 10003.

CAREER: Hatch/Billops Studio, New York, N.Y., administrative director, 1968—. Research associate, City University of New York Research Foundation, 1972—; executive director, Off-Center Space, New York, N.Y., 1974; copy editor, Media/Arts Productions, New York, 1974—.

WRITINGS—Plays: (With Aida Morales and James Hatch) "Conspiracy" (one-act), first produced in New York, N.Y., at Washington Square Methodist Church, February, 1970; (with Hatch) "If It Do Not Die," first produced in New York at Last Chance Theatre, 1971; (with Hatch) "Safe at Last," first produced in New York at New Village Theatre, 1973. Editor of performing arts section, and contributor, *Negro Almanac*, Bellwether, revised edition, 1975.

WORK IN PROGRESS: A full-length drama; a biography; a theatre anthology; research in Black and Puerto Rican theatre history; interviews with Third World artists.

* * *

GAVER, Jack 1906(?)-1974

1906(?)—December 16, 1974; American drama critic, columnist, author and editor of books predominantly on the theatre. Obituaries: *New York Times*, December 17, 1974; *Washington Post*, December 20, 1974; *AB Bookman's Weekly*, January 13, 1975.

* * *

GAVER, Jessyca (Russell) 1915-

PERSONAL: Surname rhymes with "favor"; born August 18, 1915, in New York, N.Y.; daughter of Nathan and Molly (Baron) Levine; married Kimon Patrick Russell, November 23, 1938 (divorced, 1945); married Jack Gaver (a drama critic and amusement editor with United Press International), March 24, 1945 (died December 16, 1974); children: Claudia (Mrs. James Walter Grace; an adopted daughter). *Education:* High school graduate. *Politics:* None. *Religion:* Baha'i. *Home:* 7 Peter Cooper Rd., New York, N.Y. 10010.

CAREER: Free-lance magazine and book writer for more than thirty years; publisher-editor-writer of "Writers Newsletter" and its supplement for distributors and wholesalers of magazines and paperback books.

WRITINGS: *Round Trip to Nowhere* (novel), Dell, 1963; *The Baha'i Faith*, Hawthorn, 1965; *Diamond Acres* (novel), Award Books, 1969; *A Complete Directory of Medical and Health Services*, Award Books, 1970; *Pentecostalism*, Award Books, 1971; *Vitamin C: The Protective Vitamin*, Award Books, 1971; *Birth Defects and Your Baby*, Lancer Books, 1972; *Sickle Cell Disease: Its Tragedy and Its Treatment*, Lancer Books, 1972; *You Shall Know the Truth: The Baptist Story*, Lancer Books, 1973; *How to Help Your Doctor Help You*, Pinnacle Books, 1975. More than four hundred articles have been published in magazines, some under a variety of pseudonyms.

WORK IN PROGRESS: "Always researching one or two books and working on various free-lance articles."

* * *

GAYDOS, Michael J. 1940-

PERSONAL: Born October 15, 1940; son of Michael J., Sr. and Anne Gaydos. *Education:* Robert Morris College, A.B.A.; attended Duquesne University, Holy Apostles Seminary, and St. John Vianney Seminary. *Home:* 105 Wayne Dr., Level Green, Pa. 15085.

CAREER: Roman Catholic evangelist; has held positions as elementary and secondary school teacher and counselor in parochial schools in McKeesport, Pa., Swissvale, Pa., and Harriman, N.Y., counselor and instructor at Cranwell School, Lenox, Mass., instructor in psychology at Berkeley School, Pittsburgh, Pa., and director of education at St. Perpetua's Church, McKeesport, Pa. *Member:* Western Pennsylvania Ashram, Pittsburgh Charismatic Conference.

WRITINGS: (With Russell Bixler) *Eyes to Behold Him*, Creation House, 1973.

GAYLES, Anne Richardson 1923-

PERSONAL: Born June 4, 1923, in Marshallville, Ga.; daughter of Franklin J. and Marion (Richardson) Gayles. *Education:* Fort Valley State College, B.S., 1943; Columbia University, M.A., 1949, professorial diploma, 1953; Indiana University, Ed.D., 1961; also studied at Fisk University, Oregon State University, and Harvard University. *Politics:* Republican. *Religion:* Methodist. *Home:* 609 Howard St., Tallahassee, Fla. 32304. *Office:* Area of Secondary Education Foundations, Florida Agricultural and Mechanical University, Tallahassee, Fla. 32307.

CAREER: Fort Valley State College, Fort Valley, Ga., instructor in social sciences, 1949-50; Arkansas Baptist College, Little Rock, head of department of sociology, 1950-51; Fort Valley State College, instructor in sociology, 1951-52; Stillman College, Tuscaloosa, Ala., professor of education and director of student teaching, 1952-54; Albany State College, Albany, Ga., supervisor of student teaching, 1954-57; Florida Agricultural and Mechanical University, Tallahassee, assistant professor, 1957-58, associate professor, 1958-61, professor of education, 1961—, chairman of department of secondary education, 1962-74, area chairman of Secondary Education Foundations, 1974—. Deputy director of Teachers Corps, 1967-70; member of task force on teacher education of the board of regents of University System of Florida, 1966-68; member of Florida Governor's Commission on Education, 1967; member of evaluation teams for teacher education of National Council for the Accreditation of Teacher Education; visiting member of faculty of Harvard University, 1969.

MEMBER: National Association for Teacher Educators, Association for Higher Education, National Society of Professors of Education (member of executive committee, 1969-72), National Education Association, National Council of Social Studies, Florida Association of Curriculum and Development, Florida Education Association, Florida Association for Teacher Educators, Pi Gamma Mu, Kappa Delta Pi, Delta Sigma Theta, Pi Lambda Theta, Alpha Kappa Mu.

WRITINGS: Instructional Planning on the Secondary Level, McKay, 1973; *Professional Laboratory Experiences at the Pre-Service Level* (monograph), ERIC Clearing House on Teacher Education, 1974; *Proven and Promising Innovations in Secondary Education*, C. E. Merrill, in press. Contributor of about forty-five articles to education journals, including *Journal of Secondary Education, Improving College and University Teaching, Student Teaching Topics, Negro Educational Review, Journal of the Association of Social Science Teachers*, and *Family Relations Journal*. Member of editorial staff of *Quarterly Review of Higher Education Among Negroes*. Consultant to *Choice: Books for College Libraries*; evaluator for Pi Lambda Theta's list of "Outstanding Books."

WORK IN PROGRESS: "Recent Trends in Student Teaching," "Changing a Traditional Teacher Education Program to a Competency-Based Teacher Education Program," and other articles.

* * *

GEAR, C. William 1935-

PERSONAL: Born February 1, 1935, in London, England; son of Charles J. (a painter) and Margaret (Dumbleton) Gear; married Sharon Sue Smith, January 25, 1958 (divorced October, 1970); children: Kathlyn Jo, Christopher William Gilpin. *Education:* Cambridge University, B.A., 1956, M.A., 1960; University of Illinois, M.S., 1957, Ph.D., 1960. *Home:* 1302 Eliot, Urbana, Ill. 61801. *Office:* Department of Computer Science, University of Illinois, Urbana, Ill. 61801.

CAREER: University of Illinois, Urbana, assistant professor, 1962-65, associate professor, 1965-68, professor of computer science, 1968—. Consultant to Icase, Argonne, Livermore, and Brookhaven Laboratories. *Member:* Institute of Electrical and Electronics Engineers, Association for Computing Machinery, Society for Industrial and Applied Mathematics (chairman of Special Interest Group on Numerial Mathematics, 1973-75).

WRITINGS: Computer Organization and Programming, McGraw, 1969, 2nd edition, 1974; *Numerical Initial Value Problems for Ordinary Differential Equations*, Prentice-Hall, 1971; *Introduction to Computer Science*, Science Research Associates, preliminary edition, 1971, 1st edition, 1973. Contributor to professional journals.

WORK IN PROGRESS: Revising *Introduction to Computer Science;* a book on computer graphics, completion expected in 1976; *Confidence in Computers.*

* * *

GEBHART, Benjamin 1923-

PERSONAL: Born July 2, 1923, in Cincinnati, Ohio; son of William (a plumber) and Lillian (Oettinger) Gebhart; married Francoise Paule Girardot, March 29, 1952 (divorced March 29, 1968); married Sondra Doone Raines, September 28, 1968; children: Raissa Mae, Lorna Margaretha. *Education:* University of Michigan, B.S.E., 1948, M.S.E., 1950; Cornell University, Ph.D., 1954. *Home:* 111 Blackstone, Ithaca, N.Y. 14850. *Office:* Upson Hall, Cornell University, Ithaca, N.Y. 14853.

CAREER: Cummins & Barnard, Ann Arbor, Mich., consulting engineer, 1948-50; Lehigh University, Bethelem, Pa., instructor in mechanical engineering, 1950-51; Cornell University, Ithaca, N.Y., 1951—, became professor of mechanical engineering, 1962, coordinator of College of Engineering student exchange with France, 1967—. Exchange professor in France, summer, 1963, spring, 1966; visiting professor at University of California, Berkeley, spring, 1967, and Oregon State University, 1973-74; lecturer at Heat Transfer and Fluid Mechanics Institute, June, 1972; researcher in thermal science. Consultant at various times with Esso Research and Engineering, General Electric, and IBM. *Military service:* U.S. Marine Corps, 1942-45; served in Pacific theater; received nine battle stars. *Member:* American Society of Mechanical Engineers, American Association for the Advancement of Science, Sigma Xi, Tau Beta Pi, Phi Kappa Phi, Phi Eta Sigma. *Awards, honors:* National Science Foundation research grants, 1958—; Memorial Award of American Society of Mechanical Engineers Heat Transfer Division, 1972.

WRITINGS: Heat Transfer, McGraw, 1961, 2nd edition, 1971. Contributor of seventy articles and reviews to journals in his field. Member of honorary editorial advisory board of *International Journal of Heat and Mass Transfer, 1965–.*

WORK IN PROGRESS: Articles related to fluid flows.

* * *

GEFVERT, Constance J(oanna) 1941-

PERSONAL: Born May 13, 1941, in Cleveland, Ohio; daughter of Carl Henry (a steel worker) and Florence (an executive secretary; maiden name, Youngberg) Gefvert. *Education:* Cleveland State University, B.A. (magna cum laude), 1964; University of Minnesota, M.A., 1966, Ph.D., 1971. *Politics:* Democrat. *Religion:* Episcopalian. *Home:* 850 Whitmore, Detroit, Mich. 48203. *Office:* University Studies and Weekend College Program, Wayne State University, 5229 Cass, Detroit, Mich. 48202.

CAREER: Cuyahoga County Public Library, Cleveland, Ohio, research assistant, 1962-64; Illinois State University, Normal, instructor in English, 1966-68; Wayne State University, Detroit, Mich., assistant professor of English, 1968—, director of Communications Laboratory, 1974—. Instructor at Cuyahoga Community College, summer, 1968; visiting scholar at University of Michigan, Summer Institute of Linguistics, 1973; high school teacher in Cleveland, Ohio, 1972; member of board of directors of Wayne State University Episcopal Mission, 1973—.

MEMBER: Modern Language Association of America, National Council of Teachers of English, Conference on College Composition and Communication, College English Association, Conference on Christianity and Literature, American Association of University Professors, Midwest Modern Language Association.

WRITINGS: Edward Taylor: An Annotated Bibliography, 1668-1970, Kent State University Press, 1971; (with Richard Raspa and Amy Richards) *Keys to American English*, Harcourt, 1975. Contributor to *Criticism, Research in Education*, and *Cathedral Age.* Associate editor of *Cauldron* (of Cleveland State University), 1963-64; editor of *Cathedral Digest* (of St. Paul's Cathedral, Detroit), 1973—.

* * *

GEITGEY, Doris A. 1920-

PERSONAL: Surname is pronounced *Get*-chee; born November 3, 1920, in Monroe, Mich.; daughter of Harry and Nellie (Richardson) Geitgey. *Education:* University of Toledo, B.A., 1942; Los Angeles County General Hospital School of Nursing, R.N., 1948; Immaculate Heart College, Los Angeles, M.S., 1951; University of California, Los Angeles, Ed.D., 1966. *Home:* 6255 52nd Ave. N.E., Seattle, Wash. 98115. *Office:* T314 Health Sciences Building, University of Washington, Seattle, Wash. 98195.

CAREER: High school teacher of English and history in Holland, Ohio, 1942-43; Los Angeles County General Hospital, Los Angeles, Calif., nursing and teaching posts (including instructor in obstetrics and nursing care of premature infants and chief instructor in nursing arts), 1948-57; San Diego State College (now University), San Diego, Calif., assistant professor of nursing, 1957-62; University of California, Los Angeles, specialist in in-service nursing education, 1962-64; University of Washington, Seattle, associate professor, 1966-73, professor of nursing, 1973—, associate dean of academic affairs, School of Nursing, 1970—. Director of nursing workshops in western United States and Canada. *Member:* American Nurses' Association, Washington State Nurses' Association, Sigma Theta Tau, Pi Gamma Mu.

WRITINGS: (With Ella A. Rothweiler and Jean M. White) *The Art and Science of Nursing*, 5th edition (Geitgey was not associated with earlier editions), F. A. Davis, 1954, 6th edition, 1959; *A Handbook for Head Nurses*, F. A. Davis, 1961, 2nd edition, 1971; (with others) *The Effectiveness of a Leadership Program in Nursing*, Western Interstate Commission for Higher Education, 1967; (contributor) Sandra Rasmussen, editor, *Technical Nursing: Dimensions and Dynamics*, F. A. Davis, 1972. Contributor to nursing journals.

WORK IN PROGRESS: Research on educational needs of faculty of associate degree nursing programs, on degenerative disc disease, and on sports injuries to women.

AVOCATIONAL INTERESTS: "Talking with people," reading, gardening, spectator sports, drama.

* * *

GELBER, Steven M(ichael) 1943-

PERSONAL: Born February 21, 1943, in New York, N.Y.; son of Leonard (a high school principal) and Edith (Cohen) Gelber; married Hester Goodenough, June 18, 1965; children: Gideon. *Education:* Cornell University, B.S., 1965; University of Wisconsin—Madison, M.S., 1967, Ph.D., 1972. *Home:* 489 Fenley Ave., San Jose, Calif. 95117. *Office:* Department of History, University of Santa Clara, Santa Clara, Calif. 95053.

CAREER: University of Santa Clara, Santa Clara, Calif., assistant professor of history, 1969—. Member of Santa Clara Bicentennial Committee, 1973-74. *Member:* American Historical Association, Organization of American Historians. *Awards, honors:* National Endowment for the Humanities grant, 1973-74.

WRITINGS: Business Ideology and Black Employment: A Case Study in Cultural Adaptation, Addison-Wesley, 1973; *Black Men and Businessmen: The Growing Awareness of a Social Responsibility,* Kennikat, 1974.

WORK IN PROGRESS: Research for a museum exhibit and catalog on New Deal art in California; research on late Victorian early twentieth-century architecture.

* * *

GELLMAN, Estelle Sheila 1941-

PERSONAL: Born July 27, 1941, in Brooklyn, N.Y.; daughter of Jack and Ida (Frankel) Klittnick; married Yale H. Gellman (an attorney), August 23, 1964; children: Douglas Zane, Russell Marc. *Education:* City College of the City University of New York, B.A., 1962; Columbia University, M.A., 1965, Ph.D., 1968. *Residence:* Great Neck, N.Y. *Office:* Department of Educational Psychology, Hofstra University, Hempstead, N.Y. 11550.

CAREER: Hofstra University, Hempstead, N.Y., lecturer, 1966-67, adjunct assistant professor, 1967-68, assistant professor, 1968-72, associate professor of educational psychology, 1972—. *Member:* American Psychological Association, American Educational Research Association, National Council on Measurement in Education, American Academy of Political and Social Science, American Association for the Advancement of Science, Eastern Psychological Association.

WRITINGS: Statistics for Teachers, Harper, 1972; *Descriptive Statistics for Teachers*, Harper, 1972.

* * *

GEORGE, John E(dwin) 1936-

PERSONAL: Born June 26, 1936, in Ashtabula, Ohio; son of John (an insurance executive) and Sigrid (Hakkarainen) George; married Peggy Jeffries (an artist and teacher), November 9, 1961; children: Cynthia Victoria, Stephanie Elizabeth, Mary Jennifer. *Education:* Waynesburg College, B.A., 1958; Rutgers University, M.Ed., 1962; University of South Carolina, Ph.D., 1969. *Home:* 5911 West 94th

Terrace, Overland Park, Kans. 66207. *Office:* School of Education, University of Missouri, Kansas City, Mo. 64110.

CAREER: South Plainfield (N.J.) School District, teacher of English, 1958-61; Union County (N.J.) Regional High School District, teacher of English, 1961-64; Bridgeton (N.J.) Public School District, head of English department, 1964-66; University of South Carolina, Columbia, instructor in education, 1967-69; University of Missouri-Kansas City, assistant professor, 1969-71, associate professor, 1971-75, professor of education, 1975—. President of National Tutoring Institute, 1971—; member of national research review committee of Educational Resources Information Center, 1973—; adjunct professor of English, Jersey City State College, 1965-66; part-time instructor in education, Columbia College, Columbia, S.C., 1967; visiting professor, University of Pittsburgh, 1968. *Member:* International Reading Association, American Educational Research Association, American Psychological Association, College Reading Association, National Reading Conference, National Society for the Study of Education, American Orthopsychiatric Association.

WRITINGS: (With Paul C. Berg) *Meeting the Student's Special Needs in Reading*, University of South Carolina, 1967; (editor with John A. Goodson) *Great Essays: From the 16th Century to the Present*, Dell, 1969; (contributor) Faye Branca, editor, *Reading Goals for the Disadvantaged*, International Reading Association, 1969; (contributor) Clay A. Ketcham, editor, *Reading: Today's Needs, Tomorrow's Challenges*, College Reading Association, 1969; (contributor) George B. Schick and Merrill M. May, editors, *Reading: Process and Pedagogy*, National Reading Conference, 1970; (contributor) Branca, editor, *Reading as a Basic Right*, International Reading Association, 1971; *Reading Words*, National Tutoring Institute, 1971; *Reading Sentences*, National Tutoring Institute, 1971; *Sounds in Word Phonics*, National Tutoring Institute, 1971; *Tutor-Student System in Beginning Reading*, National Tutoring Institute, 1973; (with Anne Bengfort and Linda Prugh) *Tutor-Student System in Reading Comprehension*, National Tutoring Institute, 1974.

Educational publications with Paul C. Berg; all published by International Reading Association in 1968: *Bold Action Programs for the Disadvantaged: Elementary Reading*; *Current Administrative Problems in Reading*; *Reading and Concept Attainment*; *Junior College Reading Programs*; *Interdisciplinary Approaches to Reading Disabilities*; *In-Service Programs in Reading*.

Contributor to journals in his field. Member of publication committee of College Reading Association, 1969-72.

WORK IN PROGRESS: *Teacher Reading Diagnosis Training Tapes Program* for Scholastic Books; *Methods of Teaching Elementary Reading*, a textbook for use in training elementary classroom teachers; research in studying variables related to various tutor-student arrangements in which the "Tutor-Student System" is being used; *Dennis the Menace Reading Program*, a program designed to teach basic word recognition and reading comprehension; a book, *Parents Produce the Child Who Reads*.

* * *

GEORGE, S(idney) C(harles) 1898-

PERSONAL: Born June 2, 1898, in Grimsby, England. *Education:* Educated in England. *Home:* 40 Nea Rd., Highcliffe, Christchurch, Dorset BH23 4NB, England.

CAREER: Served in the Royal Garrison Artillery of the British Army, 1917-20; career officer in Royal Air Force, 1924-53, serving in India, Palestine, Transjordan, Egypt, Sudan, Malaya, Australia, retiring as group captain. Novelist and children's writer. *Member:* Society of Authors, Institute of Chartered Accountants (fellow), Chartered Institute of Secretaries (fellow). *Awards, honors:* Member of the Order of the British Empire, 1948; member of the Royal Victorian Order, 4th class, 1953.

WRITINGS: *Cairo Card*, R. Hale, 1937; *Singapore Nights*, Jarrolds, 1942; *Wiles of Lim Quong*, Jarrolds, 1943; *Strange Courtship*, Macdonald, 1946; *Bright Moon in the Forest*, Jarrolds, 1946; *Girl in the Cabaret*, Macdonald, 1947; *Locust Years*, Jarrolds, 1947; *Devil's Delight*, Macdonald, 1948; *Bamboo Rod*, Jarrolds, 1951; *Planter's Wife*, Jarrolds, 1951; *Reluctant Infidel*, Museum Press, 1954; *Witch Doctor*, Museum Press, 1955; *Father Was a Horse*, Museum Press, 1955; *Soldier of the Line*, Museum Press, 1956; *Jutland to Junkyard* (nonfiction), Patrick Stephens, 1973.

Children's books: *Lost Empire*, Warne, 1937; *Blue Ray*, Warne, 1938; *Red Goddess*, Warne, 1939; *Secret Six*, Blackie & Son, 1940; *Eagle of the Desert*, Warne, 1944; *Escape from Singapore*, Hollis & Carter, 1946; *Pirates of the Lagoon*, Warne, 1946; *Burma Story*, Warne, 1948; *Two Spies*, Warne, 1948; *Midshipman's Luck*, Warne, 1955; *Daughters of Arabia*, Warne, 1958; *Amat's Elephant*, Macmillan, 1959; *Round the Map*, six volumes, E. J. Arnold, 1963; *Man Needs the Sun*, Hamish Hamilton, 1963; *The Happy Fisherman*, Hamish Hamilton, 1965; *The Long White March*, Hamish Hamilton, 1965; *The Shadow of the Guillotine*, E. J. Arnold, 1965; *Toko and the Bear*, Hamish Hamilton, 1965; *The Trouble Maker*, E. J. Arnold, 1965; *Fire in the Bracken*, E. J. Arnold, 1966; *Sound the Bugle*, E. J. Arnold, 1966; *Barge Boy*, Oliver & Boyd, 1968; *Chiho and Tong See: A Tale of Korea*, Chatto & Windus, 1969; *Mouse-Deer and the Swordfish*, E. J. Arnold, 1970; *Mouse-Deer's Race with Snail*, E. J. Arnold, 1970; *Sir Peace of the Forest*, E. J. Arnold, 1970; *Black Gold*, Chatto & Windus, 1970; *Hidden Treasure*, David & Charles, 1972; *The Vikings*, David & Charles, 1973.

* * *

GEORGE, W(illiam) Lloyd 1900(?)-1975

1900(?)—January 16, 1975; American C.I.A. official and author of books for boys. Obituaries: *New York Times*, January 18, 1975; *Washington Post*, January 19, 1975; *AB Bookman's Weekly*, February 3, 1975.

* * *

GERARD, Dave 1909-

PERSONAL: Born June 18, 1909, in Crawfordsville, Ind.; son of Royal Hart (a physician) and Mary B. (Bryson) Gerard; married Sarah Hunt (a library assistant), December 7, 1934; children: Barbara, Elizabeth (Mrs. Peter B. Nilsen). *Education:* Attended University of Arizona, 1928-29; Wabash College, A.B., 1931. *Politics:* Republican. *Religion:* Methodist. *Home:* 219 South Green St., Crawfordsville, Ind. 47933.

CAREER: Cartoonist for National Newspaper Syndicate, Chicago, Ill., 1949-67; creator of "Will-Yum" newspaper feature and "Will-Yum" comic books for Dell Publishing, 1953-67; author and artist of "Citizen Smith" (daily cartoon panel), Des Moines Register and Tribune Syndicate, Des Moines, Iowa, 1967—. Mayor, City of Crawfordsville,

Ind., 1972—. Member of Crawfordsville City Council, 1948-55. *Member:* Magazine Cartoonists Guild, Newspaper Comics Council, Phi Delta Theta, Pi Delta Epsilon, Kiwanis Club, Columbia Club (Indianapolis), Crawfordsville Country Club.

WRITINGS: Citizen Smith Fights Pollution, Judson, 1972.

* * *

GERAUD, Andre 1882-1974 (Pertinax)

October 18, 1882—December 11, 1974; French political reporter, editorialist, and author. Obituaries: *New York Times*, December 12, 1974; *Newsweek*, December 23, 1974; *Time*, December 23, 1974; *AB Bookman's Weekly*, January 27, 1975; *Current Biography*, January, 1975.

* * *

GERBERS, Teresa 1933-

PERSONAL: Born October 16, 1933, in Carbondale, Pa.; daughter of William (a carpenter) and Mary C. (Ford) Heines; married Olgert A. Gerbers (an accountant), January 25, 1969. *Education:* Attended Siena College. *Politics:* Democrat. *Religion:* Roman Catholic. *Home:* 28A Wiggand Dr., Glenmont, N.Y. 12077.

CAREER: WAST-TV, Albany, N.Y., continuity director, 1958-60; Goldman and Walter Advertising Co., Albany, N.Y., radio and television copywriter, 1960-67; New York State Civil Service, Albany, speechwriter and journalist, 1967-69; New York Farm Bureau, Glenmont, N.Y., editor, 1971-72.

WRITINGS: Shadow on the Snow (novel), Bouregy, 1974.

WORK IN PROGRESS: A romantic-suspense novel, *The Laughing Willows;* a suspense novel; short stories.

AVOCATIONAL INTERESTS: Skiing, horseback riding, reading, gardening.

* * *

GERMANI, Gino 1911-

PERSONAL: Born February 4, 1911, in Rome, Italy; became Argentine citizen, 1936; son of Luigi (a tailor) and Lina (Catalini) Germani; married Celia Carpi (a research associate at Harvard University), November 12, 1954; children: Luis Sergio, Ana Alejandra. *Education:* University of Rome, student, 1931-34; University of Buenos Aires, Lic. Phil. (Ph.D. equivalent), 1943. *Politics:* "No party affiliation." *Religion:* Roman Catholic. *Home:* 201 Highland St., West Newton, Mass. 02165. *Office:* Department of Sociology, 568 William James Hall, Harvard University, Cambridge, Mass. 02138.

CAREER: University of Buenos Aires, Buenos Aires, Argentina, associate research director, Institute of Sociology, 1941-46; Free College of Higher Studies, Buenos Aires, Argentina, professor of sociology, 1946-55, director of sociology seminar at Rosario, 1953-55; University of Buenos Aires, professor of sociology and director of Institute of Sociology, 1955-66, chairman of department of sociology, 1957-62; Harvard University, Cambridge, Mass., Monroe Gutman Professor of Latin American Affairs, 1966—. Visiting professor at University of Chicago, 1959, University of California, Berkeley, 1961-62, and Columbia University, 1964-65; fellow, Center for Advanced Studies in the Behavioral Sciences, 1971-72. Member of board of directors, Editorial Abril, Buenos Aires, 1948-55. Member of executive board, Latin American Faculty of Social Science, Santiago, and Latin America Center for Social Research, Rio de Janeiro, 1957-63; director of Center for Comparative Sociology, Instituto Di Tella, Buenos Aires, 1964-66.

MEMBER: International Sociological Association (member of executive committee, 1959-62; vice-president, 1962-66), International Social Sciences Council (member of executive committee, 1961-68), Asociacion Sociologica Argentina (president, 1960-65), American Sociological Association (fellow), American Academy of Arts and Sciences (foreign honorary member), Consejo Latino Americano de Ciencias Sociales (member of executive committee, 1967—). *Awards, honors:* M.A., Harvard University, 1965.

WRITINGS: Estructura social de la Argentina: Analisis estadistico, Raigal (Buenos Aires), 1955; *La Sociologia cientifica: Apuntes para su fundamentacion*, Institute of Social Investigations, National University of Mexico, 1956, revised edition, 1962; *Estudios de psicologia social*, Institute of Social Investigations, National University of Mexico, 1956.

Politica e massa: Estudo sobre a integracao das massas na vida politica dos paises em desenvolvimento, translation by Joao Claudio Dantas Campos for initial publication in Portuguese, University of Minas Gerais, 1960; *Politica y sociedad en una epoca de transicion*, Paidos (Buenos Aires), 1962, 5th edition, 1974; *La Sociologia en la America Latina: Problemas y perspectivas*, Eudeba (Buenos Aires), 1964; (with Ruth Sautu) *Regularidad y origen social en los estudiantes universitarios*, Faculty of Philosophy and Letters, University of Buenos Aires, 1965; (editor with Torcuato S. DiTella and Jorge Graciarena) *Argentina Sociedad de masas*, Eudeba, 1965; (with Alain Touraine) *America del Sur: Un proletariado nuevo*, Nova Terra (Barcelona), 1965; *Estudios sobre sociologia y psicologia social*, Paidos, 1966; *Sociologia de la modernizacion: Estudios teoricos, metodologicos, y aplicados a America Latina*, Paidos, 1969.

Social Modernization and Economic Development in Argentina (report), United Nations Research Institute for Social Development, 1970; *Sociologia della modernizzazione: L'Esperienza dell'America Latina* (Italian translation of parts of two books [supra], *Sociologia dela modernizacion* and *Politica y sociedad en un epoca de transicion*), Laterza (Bari), 1971; *Politique, Societe, et Modernisation*, Duclat, 1972; (editor) *Modernization, Urbanization and the Urban Crisis*, Little, Brown, 1973.

Contributor: Philip Hauser, editor, *Urbanisation in Latin America*, UNESCO, 1961; Egbert De Vries and Jose Medina Echavarria, editors, *Social Aspects of Economic Development in Latin America*, UNESCO, 1963; Seymour M. Lipset and Reinhard Bendix, *Movilidad social en la sociedad industrial*, Eudeba, 1963; B. F. Hoselitz and Wilbert E. Moore, editors, *Industrialization and Society*, Mouton & Co., 1963; Irving L. Horowitz, editor, *The New Sociology: Essays in Social Science and Social Values in Honor of Charles W. Mills*, Oxford University Press, 1964; Philip Hauser, editor, *Handbook of Urban Studies*, UNESCO, 1965; Neil J. Smelser and Seymour M. Lipset, editors, *Social Structure, Mobility and Economic Development*, Aldine, 1966; Shmuel N. Eisenstadt, editor, *The Protestant Ethic and Modernization*, Basic Books, 1968; Dwight Heath and Richard N. Adams, editors, *Contemporary Cultures and Societies in Latin America*, Random

House, 1968; Samuel P. Huntington, editor, *Authoritarian Politics in Modern Societies*, Basic Books, 1970. Contributor to other books and proceedings published abroad and to American, Portuguese, Spanish, French, Italian, Dutch, and Swedish journals.

WORK IN PROGRESS: A book on totalitarianism; research on national development and authoritarian regimes in Latin countries—Italy, Argentina, and Brazil.

BIOGRAPHICAL/CRITICAL SOURCES: Francisco Marsal, *La Sociologia en la Argentina*, Fabril Financiera Editora, 1962.

* * *

GERMINO, Dante (Lee) 1931-

PERSONAL: Born June 9, 1931, in Durham, N.C.; son of Dante Joseph (a newspaperman) and Nellie (Scoggins) Germino; married Virginia Lee Roseborough, June 14, 1953; children: Helen, Ruskin, Laura, Renata, Monica. *Education:* Duke University, A.B. (summa cum laude), 1952; Harvard University, A.M., 1954, Ph.D., 1956. *Politics:* Democrat. *Religion:* Anglican. *Home address:* Park Hill, Charlottesville, Va. 22901. *Office:* Department of Government, University of Virginia, 232 Cabell Hall, Charlottesville, Va. 22901.

CAREER: Wellesley College, Wellesley, Mass., instructor, 1956-58, assistant professor, 1958-64, associate professor of political science, 1964-66; Rockefeller Foundation, New York, N.Y., visiting professor of political science at University of Philippines and member of field staff, 1965-68; University of Virginia, Charlottesville, professor of government and foreign affairs, 1968—, fellow at Center for Advanced Study, 1968-70. Member of national screening committee for Fulbright Commission, 1964-65; member of Institute of International Political Philosophy, and Conference for the Study of Political Thought.

MEMBER: American Political Science Association, American Society for Political and Legal Philosophy, Guild of Scholars, Institut de Philosophie Politique. *Awards, honors:* Lilly Endowment grant, Duke University, summer, 1959; Rockefeller Foundation political and legal philosophy grant, London School of Economics and Political Science and University of Munich, 1960-61.

WRITINGS: The Italian Fascist Party in Power, University of Minnesota Press, 1959; *Beyond Ideology: The Revival of Political Theory,* Harper, 1967; (with Stefano Passigli) *The Government of Italy,* Harper, 1968; (contributor) Klaus von Beyme, editor, *Festschrift for C. J. Friedrich,* Nijhoff, 1971; *Modern Western Political Thought,* Rand McNally, 1972; (editor with Beyme) *The Open Society,* Nijhoff, 1974. Contributor to scholarly journals, including *Annals* of the American Academy of Political and Social Science, and *National Review.*

WORK IN PROGRESS: Political Theory and the Idea of the Open Society.

SIDELIGHTS: Germino writes that he is interested in the recovery of political philosophy in its pre-modern range and depth. He adds that he is a cultural conservative and a liberal on socio-economic matters.

* * *

GEROW, Edwin 1931-

PERSONAL: Born October 16, 1931, in Akron, Ohio; son of A. Denton and Corinne (Mahaffey) Gerow; married Margit Wallace (a program manager), June 18, 1957; children: Matthew Denton, Aaron Andrew. *Education:* University of Chicago, B.A., 1952, Ph.D., 1962; graduate study a University of Paris, 1954-56, 1959-60, and University of Madras, 1960-61. *Office:* Department of South Asian Languages and Civilizations, University of Chicago, 1116 East 59th St., Chicago, Ill. 60637.

CAREER: University of Rochester, Rochester, N.Y., assistant professor of Sanskrit, 1962-64; University of Washington, Seattle, 1964-73, began as assistant professor, became associate professor of Sanskrit, associate director of Far Eastern and Russian Institute, 1969-72; University of Chicago, Chicago, Ill., Frank L. Sulzberger Professor of Civilizations and professor of Sanskrit, 1973—. Lecturer at Columbia University, 1963-64. Trustee of American Institute of Indian Studies, 1968-69. *Member:* American Oriental Society, American Association of University Professors, Societe Asiatique, Philological Association of the Pacific Coast. *Awards, honors:* American Institute of Indian Studies senior fellowship, 1967-68; American Council of Learned Societies fellowship, 1968.

WRITINGS: (Editor and annotator) Sushil Kumar De, *Sanskrit Poetics as a Study of Aesthetic*, University of California Press, 1963; (contributor) D. R. Dudley and D. M. Lang, editors, *Penguin Companion to Literature* (Oriental and African), Penguin, 1968; *A Glossary of Indian Figures of Speech*, Mouton & Co., 1971; (editor with Edward C. Dimock and others, and contributor) *The Literatures of India: An Introduction*, University of Chicago Press, 1974; (editor with Margery Lang) *Studies in the Language and Culture of South Asia*, University of Washington Press, 1974.

WORK IN PROGRESS: "A History of Indian Poetics," for inclusion in *History of Indian Literature*, edited by Jan Gonda, for O. Harrassowitz (Leipzig); research on the theory and practice of Sanskrit education in India.

* * *

GERSONI, Diane 1947-
(Diane Gersoni-Stavn)

PERSONAL: Born April 16, 1947, in Brooklyn, N.Y.; daughter of James Arthur (an insurance consultant) and Edna (Krinski) Gersoni. *Education:* Vassar College, B.A. (cum laude), 1967. *Religion:* Jewish. *Home:* 104-40 Queens Blvd., Forest Hills, N.Y. 11375. *Office:* Scholastic Magazines, 50 West 44th St., New York, N.Y. 10036.

CAREER: R. R. Bowker Co. (publisher), New York, N.Y., book reviewer, 1967-70, associate editor of *School Library Journal* book review section, 1970-72; free-lance writer and editor for newspapers and magazines, 1972-74; Scholastic Magazines, Inc., New York, N.Y., writer and editor, 1974—. *Awards, honors: Sexism and Youth* was selected among nine best education books of 1974 by *American School Board Journal.*

WRITINGS: (Under name Diane Gersoni-Stavn) *Sexism and Youth*, Bowker, 1974. Author of teaching guides to accompany novels. Contributor of articles and reviews to magazines and newspapers, including *Library Journal, School Library Journal, New York Times*, and *Greensboro Daily News.*

WORK IN PROGRESS: Young Adult Literature: Anatomy of a Genre, for Bowker.

SIDELIGHTS: Diane Gersoni writes: "If labels must be used, I consider myself a humanist rather than a feminist.

Sexism and Youth is not a dogmatic feminist tract; it merely shows how rigid sexist socialization (through education, literature, films, toys, games, etc.) can prevent many girls—and boys—from becoming full, self-respecting human beings. As for myself, I plan to move on to other interests, concerns, and areas of study." *Avocational interests:* Sports, dance, opera recordings, pets.

* * *

GERSTLE, Kurt H(erman) 1923-

PERSONAL: Born November 11, 1923, in Germany; son of Siegfried and Berta (Schnell) Gerstle; married Eva Holland-Cunz, April 21, 1951; children: John H., Andrea I., Walter H., George S. *Education:* University of California, Berkeley, B.S., 1949, M.S., 1952; University of Colorado, Ph.D., 1956. *Home:* 3650 Fourth St., Boulder, Colo. 80302. *Office:* Department of Civil and Environmental Engineering, University of Colorado, Boulder, Colo. 80302.

CAREER: Structural engineer; University of Colorado, Boulder, instructor, 1952-56, assistant professor, 1956-58, associate professor, 1958-62, professor of civil and environmental engineering, 1962—. Visiting professor at SEATO Graduate School of Engineering, Bangkok, 1963-64, and Technical University (Munich), 1970-71. Consulting engineer. Member of Boulder County Planning Commission, 1968-70. *Military service:* U.S. Army, 1943-46. *Member:* American Society of Civil Engineers (fellow), American Concrete Institute. *Awards, honors:* Wason Medal from American Concrete Institute, 1964.

WRITINGS: Basic Structural Design, McGraw, 1967; *Basic Structural Analysis*, Prentice-Hall, 1974. Contributor of about thirty articles to scientific journals, including *Magazine of Concrete Research* and *Journal of the American Concrete Institute*.

WORK IN PROGRESS: Research on the behavior of concrete structures and rock structures.

* * *

GHOSH, Tapan 1928-

PERSONAL: Born November 26, 1928; son of Surendra Nath (a teacher) and Shanti (Sudha Dey) Ghosh; married Uma Dey, May 12, 1946; children: Anita (Mrs. Rathijeet Ghalak), Anup (son). *Education:* Hilkarmi City College, Jabalpur, India, B.A., 1946; Hilkarmi Law College, LL.B., 1948, M.A., 1950. *Politics:* None. *Home:* 3 South Malaka, Allahabad, Uttar Pradesh, India. *Office:* Chamber No. 14, High Court, Allahabad, India.

CAREER: Advocate. Member of the High Court of Judicature, Allahabad, India.

WRITINGS: Adventures of Shivaji, Vishwa Vijai Prakashan, 1973; *Gandhi Murder Trial*, Asia Publishing House, 1974. Contributor of seventy articles to *Caravan*.

SIDELIGHTS: Ghosh wrote *CA*: "[As a lawyer] of course, crime and criminals have been the subject [of my writing], and of how a normal person suddenly got branded for life just for a single lapse, a momentary loss of self-control, a fleeting fade-out of moral frontiers."

* * *

GIBBARD, Graham S(tewart) 1942-

PERSONAL: Born July 4, 1942, in Dallas, Tex.; son of Larry (an attorney) and Itasca (Stewart) Gibbard; married Jeanne Tetreault (a social worker), January 1, 1975. *Education:* Harvard University, A.B., 1965; University of Michigan, Ph.D., 1969. *Home:* 428 Yale Ave., New Haven, Conn. 06515. *Office:* Department of Psychiatry, Yale University, New Haven, Conn. 06510.

CAREER: Private practice as clinical psychologist in Chapel Hill, N.C., 1970-72; University of North Carolina, Chapel Hill, assistant professor of psychology, 1969-72; Yale University, New Haven, Conn., assistant professor of psychology, 1972—; U.S. Veterans Administration, West Haven, Conn., clinical psychologist, 1972—; private practice as clinical psychologist in New Haven, Conn., 1975—. *Member:* American Psychological Association.

WRITINGS: (With Richard D. Mann) *Interpersonal Styles and Group Development*, Wiley, 1967; (with John J. Hartman and Mann) *Analysis of Groups*, Jossey-Bass, 1974. Contributor to professional journals.

WORK IN PROGRESS: Research on the development of the co-therapy relationship, on the psychology of utopian communities, and on the metapsychology of group formation.

* * *

GIESBRECHT, Martin Gerhard 1933-

PERSONAL: First syllable of surname is pronounced "geese"; born August 25, 1933, in Newark, N.J.; son of Theodore Gerhard and Martha (Thurm) Giesbrecht; married Patricia Berlin (a singer and professor), July 4, 1957; children: Lisa, Martin Franz, Theodore Karl. *Education:* Rutgers University, B.A., 1955; Harvard University, graduate study, 1955-56; University of Munich, Dr.Oec.Publ. (cum laude), 1958; postdoctoral study at Indiana University, summer, 1962, University of Chicago, summer, 1966, and National Chengchi University, summer, 1967. *Home:* 20 Faculty Pl., Wilmington, Ohio 45177. *Office:* Department of Economics, Wilmington College, Wilmington, Ohio 45177.

CAREER: Wilmington College, Wilmington, Ohio, assistant professor, 1958-65, associate professor, 1965-70, professor of economics, 1970—, chairman of department, 1965—, chairman of Social Science Division, 1971—. Member of Ohio Apellate District One Judicial Nominating Council, 1972—; director of Economics Associates, 1974—. *Member:* American Association of University Professors, American Association for the Advancement of Science, American Economic Association, Peace Research Society, Midwest Economic Association, Ohio Association of Economists and Political Scientists (member of board of directors, 1973—). *Awards, honors:* Fulbright scholar at University of Munich, 1956-58; Ford Foundation postdoctoral study grant at Indiana University, summer, 1962; General Electric Foundation grant at University of Chicago, summer, 1966; Danforth Foundation associateship, 1969—.

WRITINGS: Die Bedeutung des Automobils im Amerikanischen Sozialleben (title means "The Importance of the Automobile to American Society"), Uni-Druck, 1958; *The Evolution of Economic Society*, W. H. Freeman, 1972; *Understanding Economics*, William Kaufmann, in press; *Using Economics*, William Kaufmann, in press. Editor of Economics Series published by William Kaufmann. Contributor to *Journal of Political Economy, Chinese Journal of Administration, Michigan State University Business Topics*, and *Collegiate News and Views*. Contributor to proceedings.

SIDELIGHTS: Giesbrecht attended the Regional Council for International Education in Taiwan in 1967. He has performed internationally on the piano and clarinet. *Avocational interests:* Music, nature study, gardening, mechanics, cuisine.

* * *

GIFFORD, Don (Creighton) 1919-

PERSONAL: Born February 27, 1919, in Schenectady, N.Y.; son of Henry Raoul Liddle (a title abstracter) and Edna (a Christian Science practitioner; maiden name, North) Gifford; married Ruth Cleveland, June 3, 1944 (divorced, 1961); married Honora Kammerer, October 10, 1963; children: Marin (Mrs. David O. Haythe), Nina. *Education:* Principia College, Elsah, Ill., B.A., 1940; Harvard University, graduate study, 1940-42. *Politics:* Independent. *Religion:* None. *Home address:* Bryant St., Williamstown, Mass. 01267. *Office:* Department of English, Williams College, Williamstown, Mass. 01267.

CAREER: Mills College of Education, New York, N.Y., instructor in English, 1947-51; Williams College, Williamstown, Mass., instructor, 1951-54, lecturer, 1954-55, assistant professor, 1955-58, 1959-60, associate professor, 1960-65, professor of English, 1965—. Co-chairman of Williamstown Studio for Recording for the Blind, Inc., 1971—. Consultant to Arthur D. Little, Inc., 1958-59. *Military service:* American Field Service, 1942-44; served in North Africa and Italy. U.S. Army, Infantry, 1944-46; became second lieutenant.

WRITINGS: (Editor) *The Literature of Architecture*, Dutton, 1966; *Notes for Joyce: Dubliners and A Portrait of the Artist as a Young Man*, Dutton, 1967; (with Robert J. Seidman) *Notes for Joyce: Ulysses*, Dutton, 1974. Contributor of short stories and poems to magazines.

WORK IN PROGRESS: A book of poems; research on the dependence of serious upon popular literature in nineteenth- and twentieth-century America.

SIDELIGHTS: "I write poetry," Gifford told CA, "as part of the psychological metabolism frequently (and mistakenly) called sanity."

* * *

GILBERT, Douglas 1942-

PERSONAL: Born August 14, 1942, in Muskegon, Mich.; son of Russell W. (a salesman) and Carmen (Andree) Gilbert; married Barbara E. McDonald, September 19, 1964; children: Rachel E., Robyn E. *Education:* Michigan State University, B.A., 1964; New York Theological Seminary, graduate study, 1966-69; Illinois Institute of Technology, M.S. (photography), 1972. *Religion:* Presbyterian. *Home:* 116 Travers Ave., Wheaton, Ill. 60187. *Office:* Department of Art, Wheaton College, Wheaton, Ill. 60187.

CAREER: Look (magazine), New York, N.Y., staff photographer, 1964-66; free-lance photographer in New York and Illinois, 1967—. Assistant professor of art at Wheaton College, 1972—. *Member:* Society for Photographic Education. *Awards, honors:* Page One Award for best magazine photography, from New York Newspaper Guild, 1965; Chicago Book Clinic award, 1973, for *C. S. Lewis: Images of His World*; certificate of merit from Society of Publication Designers, 1973, for photographic work in *A.D.* magazine; and other awards.

WRITINGS—With photographs by the author: (With J. Martin Bailey) *The Steps of Bonhoeffer*, Pilgrim Press, 1969; (with Clyde S. Kilby) *C. S. Lewis: Images of His World*, Eerdmans, 1973. Contributor of articles and photographs to popular and professional publications, including *Camera 35, Popular Photography, Saturday Evening Post, Life, America Illustrated*, and *Camera*.

WORK IN PROGRESS: Photographic essays on suburban landscape and on erotic sexuality in America.

SIDELIGHTS: Gilbert writes: "My current photographic work is more involved with photographs as photographs, i.e., not functioning to illuminate text. The subjects of current projects indicate working in a way which explores personal attitudes and perceptions rather than telling a story about someone or something assigned to me. In other words, photography as an art form."

BIOGRAPHICAL/CRITICAL SOURCES: Campus Life, December, 1973; *Modern Photography*, September, 1974; *Moody Monthly*, November, 1974.

* * *

GILBERT, Robert E(mile) 1939-

PERSONAL: Born October 20, 1939, in New York, N.Y.; son of Emile Paul (an insurance salesman) and Veronica (Noble) Gilbert. *Education:* Fordham University, B.A., 1961, M.A., 1963; University of Massachusetts, Ph.D., 1967. *Home:* 70 Chiswick Rd., Boston, Mass. 02135. *Office:* Department of Political Science, Northeastern University, Boston, Mass. 02115.

CAREER: Boston College, Chestnut Hill, Mass., instructor, 1965-67, assistant professor of political science, 1967-73; Northeastern University, Boston, Mass., associate professor of political science, 1973—. Visiting assistant professor at University of Wisconsin—Parkside, summer, 1968. *Member:* American Political Science Association, Policy Studies Organization, New England Political Science Association, Inter-University Seminar, Pi Sigma Alpha (president of Delta Zeta chapter, 1960-61), Delta Tau Kappa.

WRITINGS: Television and Presidential Politics, Christopher, 1972. Contributor to *International Review of History and Political Science* and *University of Missouri at Kansas City Law Review*.

WORK IN PROGRESS: Research on presidential mortality, or death and the American president; research on the media and presidential popularity.

AVOCATIONAL INTERESTS: Travel (Great Britain, Ireland, Spain, France, Italy, Germany, Switzerland, Netherlands, Denmark, Luxembourg).

* * *

GILLESPIE, James E(rnest), Jr. 1940-

PERSONAL: Born November 30, 1940, in Tazewell, Va.; son of James Ernest (with the post office) and Evelyn (with Western Union; maiden name, Ray) Gillespie; married Cheryl Kay Hopkins (a financial counselor), August 17, 1968. *Education:* Attended University of South Carolina, 1958-59; Concord College, B.S., 1962; Indiana University, M.M. (with distinction), 1963, D.M. (with distinction), 1969. *Home:* 113 Warwick Dr., Monroe, La. 71201. *Office:* School of Music, Northeast Louisiana University, Monroe, La. 71201.

CAREER: Concord College, Athens, W. Va., instructor in music, 1963- 6; University of Redlands, Redlands, Calif., assistant professor of music, 1968-69; Northeast Louisiana

University, Monroe, associate professor of music, 1969—. *Member:* International Clarinet Society, National Association of College Wind and Percussion Instructors, Phi Mu Alpha, Sinfonia, Pi Kappa Lambda, Blue Key.

WRITINGS: The Reed Trio: An Annotated Bibliography of Original Published Works, Information Coordinators, 1971; *Solos for Unaccompanied Clarinet: An Annotated Bibliography of Published Works*, Information Coordinators, 1973. Contributor of articles and reviews to *Clarinet, Instrumentalist, NACWPI Journal, School Musician*, and *Woodwind World*. Review editor of *Clarinet*, 1973—.

WORK IN PROGRESS: A Handbook of Fingerings for The Boehm System Clarinet, with Henry Gulick; researching out-of-print and manuscript works for voice and clarinet for a series of articles in *Woodwind World*; updating published bibliographies.

* * *

GILLETTE, Paul 1938-

PERSONAL: Born October 1, 1938, in Carbondale, Pa. *Residence:* Carbondale, Pa. 18407. *Agent:* Owen Laster, William Morris Agency, 1350 Avenue of the Americas, New York, N.Y. 10019.

CAREER: Author, novelist, and psychologist; has appeared on radio and television; has directed theatre, films, and television; host for "Camera Three," C.B.S.-T.V. *Awards, honors:* Pulitzer Prize in letters nomination, 1972, for *Carmela*.

WRITINGS: Ku Klux Klan: The Invisible Empire, Natlus Publications, 1964; (with Eugene Tillinger) *Inside Ku Klux Klan*, Pyramid Books, 1965; *An Uncensored History of Pornography*, Holloway, 1965; (translator and editor) Petronius Arbiter, *Satyricon: Memoirs of a Lusty Roman*, Holloway, 1965; *Psychodynamics of Unconventional Sex Behavior and Unusual Practices*, Holloway, 1966; (translator and editor) *The Complete Marquis de Sade*, Holloway, 1966; *The Lopinson Case*, Holloway, 1967; *Paul Gillette's Ribald Classics*, Orion (Japan), 1968; *The Complete Sex Dictionary*, Tandem, 1969; *Encyclopedia of Erotica*, Universal Publishing and Distributing, 1969; *Where Do I Come From*, Bantam, 1969; (editor with Marie Hornbeck) *The Complete Medical Encyclopedia*, Award Books, 1969; *What Every Woman Wants to Know About the Pill*, Bantam, 1969; (translator) Pierre Louys, *Trois Filles*, Universal Publishing and Distributing, 1969; (editor) *The Layman's Explanation of Human Sexual Inadequacy*, Award Books, 1970; (editor) *New Facts About the Pill*, Bantam, 1970; *The Big Answer Book About Sex*, Award Books, 1970; (editor) *U.S. Government Directory of Prescription Drugs and Over-the-Counter Drugs*, Universal Publishing and Distributing, 1971; (editor) *Complete Guide to Student Financial Aid*, Universal Publishing and Distributing, 1971; *Cat o' Nine Tails* (novel), Award Books, 1971; *Carmela* (novel), Arbor House, 1972; *Play Misty for Me* (novel), Award Books, 1972; *The Vasectomy Information Manual*, Outerbridge & Lazard, 1972; *Vasectomy: The Male Sterilization Operation*, Paperback Library, 1972; (with Marie Hornbeck) *Depression: A Layman's Guide*, Dutton, 1973; (with Robert L. Rowan) *Your Prostate Gland*, Doubleday, 1973; *The Single Man's Indispensable Handbook and Guide*, Playboy Press, 1973; (with Marie Hornbeck) *Psychochemistry*, Paperback Library, 1974; *Superstar* (novel), Dell, 1974; (with Peter A. Gillette) *Playboy's Book of Wine*, Playboy Press, 1974.

Contributor to *Esquire, Playboy, McCall's*, and others.

SIDELIGHTS: Cat o' Nine Tails was filmed in 1971 and *Play Misty for Me* in 1972.

* * *

GILLILAND, (Cleburne) Hap 1918-

PERSONAL: Born August 26, 1918, in Willard, Colo.; son of Samuel Smith (a realtor) and Esther (a painter on china; maiden name, Sandstedt) Gilliland; married Erma Roderick (a secretary), April 21, 1946; children: Lori (Mrs. Steve Sargent), Diane, Dwight. *Education:* Western State College, B.A., 1949, M.A., 1950; University of Northern Colorado, Ed.D., 1958. *Religion:* Disciples of Christ. *Home:* 517 Rimrock Rd., Billings, Mont. 59102. *Office:* Reading Center, Department of Education, Eastern Montana College, Billings, Mont. 59101.

CAREER: Public school teacher in Richland, Wash., 1950-53; Humboldt State University, Arcata, Calif., supervising teacher, 1953-60; Eastern Montana College, Billings, associate professor, 1960-63, professor of education, 1963—, director of Reading Center, 1960—. Director of Northern Cheyenne Remedial Reading Project, 1965-68; member of board of directors of Americans Hand in Hand. *Military service:* U.S. Army Air Forces, 1942-46. *Member:* International Reading Association, Association on American Indian Affairs, Rocky Mountain Reading Specialists Association (president, 1966-67; executive director, 1967—), Billings Art Association (vice-president, 1964), Phi Delta Kappa (foundation representative, 1974-75).

WRITINGS: Materials for Remedial Reading, Montana Reading Publications, 1965, 5th edition, 1975; *The Flood*, Montana Reading Publications, 1972; *A Practical Guide to Remedial Reading*, C. E. Merrill, 1974. Editor of "Indian Culture Series," books for children, for Montana Reading Publications, 1970—. Editor of *Montana Journal of Reading*, 1962-68; member of editorial board of *Journal of Reading*, 1972-74, *ERIC Research Materials*, 1973—, *Reading Teacher*, 1974—, and *Reading Horizons, 1974–*.

WORK IN PROGRESS: Reading Problems of the Learning Disabled; *Legends of the Yanowano Indians* (of South America); *Supervising Reading Instruction*, completion expected in 1977; *Drums of the Head Hunters* (of New Guinea), 1977.

SIDELIGHTS: Gilliland has made three trips to live with primitive Indian tribes in remote jungle areas of South America. He has also spent time with native people of Australia, New Zealand, Samoa, and New Guinea.

* * *

GILMAN, Richard 1925-

PERSONAL: Born April 30, 1925, in New York, N.Y.; son of Jacob (a lawyer) and Marion (Wolinsky) Gilman; married Esther Morgenstern, September 2, 1949; married second wife, Lynn Nesbit (a literary agent), September 17, 1966; children: (first marriage) Nicholas; (second marriage) Priscilla, Claire. *Education:* University of Wisconsin, B.A., 1947. *Politics:* Democrat. *Home:* 333 Central Park W., New York, N.Y. 10025. *Office:* School of Drama, Yale University, New Haven, Conn. 06520.

CAREER: Free-lance writer, 1950-54; *Jubilee* magazine, New York, N.Y., associate editor, 1954-57; *Commonweal*, New York, drama critic and literary editor, 1961-64; *Newsweek*, New York, associate editor and drama critic, 1964-67; *New Republic*, Washington, D.C., literary editor, 1968-70; Yale University, New Haven, Conn., professor of drama, 1967—. Visiting lecturer, Columbia University, 1964-65; visiting professor, Stanford University, summer, 1967. *Military service:* U.S. Marine Corps, 1943-46; became staff sergeant. *Awards, honors:* L.H.D., Grinnell College, 1967; George Jean Nathan Award for drama criticism, 1971-72.

WRITINGS: The Confusion of Realms, Random House, 1969; *Common and Uncommon Masks*, Random House, 1970; *The Making of Modern Drama*, Farrar, Straus, 1974. Contributor to journals; contributing editor, *Partisan Review*.

WORK IN PROGRESS: A book on decadence.

* * *

GILMAN, Sander L(awrence) 1944-

PERSONAL: Born February 21, 1944, in Buffalo, N.Y.; son of William (a traffic manager) and Rebbecca (Helfand) Gilman; married Marina von Eckardt (a singer), December 28, 1969. *Education:* Tulane University, B.A., 1963, graduate study, 1963-65, Ph.D., 1968; other graduate study in Munich, 1965, and at Free University of Berlin, 1965-66. *Religion:* Jewish. *Home:* 305 Cornell St., Ithaca, N.Y. 14850. *Office:* Department of German Literature, Cornell University, Ithaca, N.Y. 14850.

CAREER: St. Mary's Dominican College, New Orleans, La., lecturer in German, 1963-64; Dillard University, New Orleans, La., instructor in German, 1967-68; Case Western Reserve University, Cleveland, Ohio, assistant professor of German, 1968-69; Cornell University, Ithaca, N.Y., assistant professor, 1969-73, associate professor of German literature and chairman of department, 1974—. *Member:* Modern Language Association of America (president of Literature and Science Group, 1972), American Association of Teachers of German, International Association of Germanists, Linguistic Society of America, American Lessing Society, Delta Sigma Rho, Delta Phi Alpha. *Awards, honors:* American Philosophical Society grant, 1970; Guggenheim fellowship, 1972-73; International Research and Exchanges Board fellowship with Soviet Academy of Sciences, 1973.

WRITINGS: (Editor) Johannes Agricola, *Die Sprichwoertersammlungen: Eine historisch-kritische Ausgabe*, two volumes, De Gruyter, 1971; (editor) *NS-Literaturtheorie: Eine Dokumentation*, Athenaeum (Frankfurt am Main), 1971; *Forum und Funktion: Eine strukturelle Untersuchung der Romane Klabunds* (monograph), Athenaeum, 1971; *The Parodic Sermon in European Perspective: Aspects of Liturgical Parody from the Middle Ages to the Twentieth Century* (monograph), Franz Steiner, 1974; (with Wolf Von Eckardt) *Bertolt Brecht's Berlin* (monograph), Doubleday, in press. Contributor to *Jahrbuch fuer Internationale Germanistik, Encyclopedia Hebraica*, and other publications in United States and Germany.

WORK IN PROGRESS: With Von Eckardt, *Oscar Wilde's London*, for Doubleday.

* * *

GILMORE, Harold L(awrence) 1931-

PERSONAL: Born April 30, 1931, in Whitinsville, Mass.; son of Lawrence Merton and Olga (Johnson) Gilmore; married Mary Frieswyk, June 4, 1954; children: Tod Harold, Jill Mary. *Education:* Norwich University, B.S.E.E., 1953; Syracuse University, M.B.A., 1958, Ph.D., 1970. *Politics:* Republican. *Religion:* Protestant. *Home:* 1079 Beech Ave., Hershey, Pa. 17033. *Office:* Capitol Campus, Pennsylvania State University, Middletown, Pa. 17057.

CAREER: Westinghouse Electric Corp., Baltimore, Md., product reliability engineer, 1953-61; Avco Corp., Space Systems Division, Wilmington, Mass., manager of product reliability, 1961-67; Syracuse University, Syracuse, N.Y., instructor in management, 1967-70; University of North Dakota, Minot, associate professor of management, 1970-72; Pennsylvania State University, Capitol Campus, Middletown, associate professor of management, 1972—. President, H. L. Gilmore Associates (management and technical consultants), Hershey, Pa., 1967—. Adjunct professor at U.S. Army War College, 1974—. *Military service:* U.S. Army Reserve, 1953—; active duty, 1954-57; present rank, lieutenant colonel. *Member:* American Management Association, Academy of Management, American Society for Quality Control, Institute of Electrical and Electronics Engineers, Reserve Officers Association of the United States.

WRITINGS: (With Herbert C. Schwartz) *Integrated Product Testing and Evaluation*, Wiley, 1969; (editor) *Strategy and Policy: Selected Readings*, Pennsylvania State University (Middletown), 1973. Contributor of articles and reviews to professional journals.

WORK IN PROGRESS: Research in the values of contemporary society, in quality motivation in industry, and in behavioral applications in business.

* * *

GINGER, Ann Fagan 1925-

PERSONAL: Born July 11, 1925, in Lansing, Mich.; daughter of Peter (a newspaperman) and Sarah (a teacher; maiden name, Robinson) Fagan; married Ray Ginger, June 26, 1944 (divorced, 1957); married James F. Wood (an industrial designer), November 11, 1961; children: (first marriage) Thomas J., James F. *Education:* University of Michigan, B.A., 1945, LL.B., 1947; University of California, Berkeley, LL.M., 1960. *Office:* 1715 Francisco St., Berkeley, Calif. 94703.

CAREER: Admitted to the State Bars of Michigan, 1947, Ohio, 1948, California, 1972, and to the Bar of the U.S. Supreme Court, 1956; Meiklejohn Civil Liberties Institute, Berkeley, Calif., president, 1965—; practice of law in Berkeley, Calif., 1972—. Adjunct professor at University of California, San Francisco, 1972—, and Mills College, 1974. Chairperson, American Civil Liberties Union, Berkeley-Albany, 1973-74. *Member:* National Lawyers Guild, American Bar Association (Section of Individual Rights and Responsibilities), American Federation of Teachers, Society of American Law Teachers. *Awards, honors:* Avery Hopwood Minor Essay award, 1944.

WRITINGS: Civil Liberties Docket, Volumes I-XIV, Meiklejohn Civil Liberties Institute, 1955-69; *California Criminal Law Practice*, California Continuing Education of the Bar, Volume I, 1964, Volume II, 1969; *Minimizing Racism in Jury Trials*, National Lawyers Guild, 1969; *The Relevant Lawyers*, Simon & Schuster, 1972; *The Law, the Supreme Court, and the People's Rights*, Barron's, 1974. Columnist for *Union Women's Alliance to Gain Equality*, 1974—. Member of editorial board of *National Lawyers Guild Practitioner*, 1965—.

WORK IN PROGRESS: The Fagan Family Commune, completion expected in 1976.

GINGERICH, Owen (Jay) 1930-

PERSONAL: Surname rhymes with Singer-rich; born March 24, 1930, in Washington, Iowa; son of Melvin (a historian) and Verna (Roth) Gingerich; married Miriam Sensenig, June 26, 1954; children: Jonathan C., Mark P., Peter E. *Education:* Goshen College, B.A., 1951; Harvard University, M.A., 1953, Ph.D., 1962. *Religion:* Mennonite. *Home:* 100 Avon Hill St., Cambridge, Mass. 02140. *Office:* Center for Astrophysics, Harvard University, 60 Garden St., Cambridge, Mass. 02138.

CAREER: American University Observatory, Beirut, Lebanon, director, 1955-58; Harvard University, Cambridge, Mass., lecturer, 1960-68, associate professor, 1968-69, professor of astronomy and history of science, 1969—. Astrophysicist at Smithsonian Astrophysical Observatory, 1962—; member of advisory committee on the history of physics at American Institute of Physics; George Darwin Lecturer for Royal Astronomical Society, 1971; national lecturer for Sigma Xi, 1971.

MEMBER: International Academy of the History of Science, International Astronomical Union, American Association for the Advancement of Science, American Astronomical Society (councilor, 1973—), Astronomical Society of the Pacific, Bibliographical Society, History of Science Society.

WRITINGS: (Translator) Theodore Oppolzer, *Canon of Eclipses*, Dover, 1962; (with William Stahlman) *Solar and Planetary Longitudes from Minus 2500 to Plus 2000*, University of Wisconsin Press, 1963; (translator) Jean Dufay, *Introduction to Astrophysics: The Stars*, Dover, 1964; (editor) *Theory and Observation of Normal Stellar Atmospheres*, M.I.T. Press, 1969; (editor) *Frontiers in Astronomy*, Freeman, 1970, revised edition, in press; (with David Godine) *Renaissance Books of Science from the Collection of Albert E. Lownes*, Dartmouth College Press, 1970; (editor) *The Nature of Scientific Discovery*, Smithsonian Institution Press, in press; (editor with Jerzy Dobrzycki) *The Astronomy of Copernicus and Its Background*, Ossolineum, in press.

Contributor to *Encyclopaedia Britannica, Collier's Encyclopedia*, and *Encyclopedia Americana*. Contributor of more than a hundred fifty articles and reviews to scientific journals, including *Astrophysical Journal, Journal for the History of Astronomy, Scientific American, Atlantic Monthly, Science Year*, and *Sky and Telescope*. Associate editor for reviews, *Journal for the History of Astronomy*.

WORK IN PROGRESS: Translating Johannes Kepler's *Astronomia nova*; a monograph on a census of copies of Copernicus' *De revolutionibus*, completion expected in 1976; research on the Renaissance revolution in astronomy; a supplemental unit on modern astronomy for a high school physics curriculum (Project Physics).

AVOCATIONAL INTERESTS: Rare books (Gingerich assisted American designer Charles Evans with a major Copernicus exhibition and show).

* * *

GINSBURG, Ruth Bader 1933-

PERSONAL: Born March 15, 1933, in Brooklyn, N.Y.; married Martin David Ginsburg, June 23, 1954; children: Jane Carol, James Steven. *Education:* Cornell University, A.B., 1954; Harvard University, graduate study, 1956-58; Columbia University, LL.B., 1959. *Home:* 150 East 69th St., New York, N.Y. 10021. *Office:* School of Law, Columbia University, New York, N.Y. 10027.

CAREER: Member of bars of state of New York, U.S. Supreme Court, U.S. Courts of Appeals, and U.S. District Courts. Law secretary, 1959-61; Rutgers University, School of Law, Newark, N.J., assistant professor, 1963-66, associate professor, 1966-69, professor of law, 1969-72; Columbia University, New York, N.Y., professor of law, 1972—. *Member:* American Bar Association, American Law Institute, Council on Foreign Relations, American Foreign Law Association (member of board of directors, 1970—; vice-president, 1973—), Women's Law Fund (member of board of directors), Association of American Law Schools (member of executive committee, 1972), American Civil Liberties Union (general counsel, 1973—; member of national board of directors, 1974—), Association of the Bar of the City of New York (member of executive committee, 1974—), Phi Beta Kappa, Phi Kappa Phi. *Awards, honors:* LL.D. from University of Lund, 1969.

WRITINGS: (With Anders Bruzelius) *Civil Procedure in Sweden*, Nijhoff, 1965; (contributor) Hans Smit, editor, *International Cooperation in Litigation*, Nijhoff, 1965; (translator with Bruzelius) *Swedish Code of Judicial Procedure*, Rothman-Sweet & Maxwell, 1968; (editor) *Business Regulation in the Common Market Nations*, Volume I, McGraw, 1969; *A Selective Survey of English Language Studies on Scandinavian Law*, Fred B. Rothman, 1970; (with Herma Hill Kay and Kenneth M. Davidson) *Text, Cases, and Materials on Sex-Based Discrimination*, West Publishing, 1974; *Constitutional Aspects of Sex-Based Discrimination*, West Publishing, 1974. Also co-author of *The Legal Status of Women under Federal Law: Report to the United States Commission on Civil Rights*, 1974.

Contributor to law journals, including *Journal of Family Law, American Journal of Comparative Law, International and Comparative Law Quarterly, International Lawyer, American Bar Association Journal*, and *Harvard Law Review*. Member of editorial board of *American Journal of Comparative Law*, 1966-72, and *American Bar Association Journal*, 1972-75.

* * *

GINSBURGS, George 1932-

PERSONAL: Born February 13, 1932, in Shanghai, China; son of Leon A. and Rachel (Mashkovich) Ginsburgs; married Ida G. Csanyi, February 13, 1959 (divorced April 10, 1974); married Herta Getrude Schopf (a lawyer), May 13, 1974; children: (first marriage) Pauline Elizabeth; (second marriage) Boris George. *Education:* University of California, Los Angeles, B.A., 1954, M.A., 1957, Ph.D., 1960. *Home:* 438 East Sedgwick St., Philadelphia, Pa. 19119. *Office:* School of Law, Rutgers University, Fifth & Penn Sts., Camden, N.J. 08102.

CAREER: University of California, Los Angeles, instructor in political science, 1959-60; University of Iowa, Iowa City, assistant professor of political science, 1961-66; New School for Social Research, New York, N.Y., associate professor of political science, 1966-73; Rutgers University, Camden, N.J., professor of comparative law, 1973—. *Military service:* U.S. Army, 1954-56.

MEMBER: International Association for Asian Studies, International Law Association (American branch), Association for the Advancement of Slavic Studies. *Awards, honors:* Ford Foundation fellowship, 1958-59; Social Science Research Council grants, 1960-61, 1974; National Endowment for the Humanities grant, 1973-74.

WRITINGS: (With Michael Mathos) *Communist China*

and Tibet, Nijhoff, 1964; *Soviet Citizenship Law,* Sijthoff (Leiden), 1968; (with A. Z. Rubinstein) *Soviet and American Policies in the United Nations,* New York University Press, 1972; *Soviet Works on Korea: 1945-1970,* University of Southern California Press, 1973. Contributor to law and political science journals, including *American Journal of International Law, American Journal of Comparative Law, International and Comparative Law Quarterly, Soviet Studies,* and *Journal of Asian Studies.*

WORK IN PROGRESS: Dynamics of the Sino-Soviet Border Dispute.

SIDELIGHTS: Ginsburgs has traveled in the Far East, the Soviet Union, and Western Europe.

* * *

GIROD, Gerald R(alph) 1939-

PERSONAL: Born October 21, 1939, in Salem, Ore.; son of Ted R. and Ruby (Orey) Girod; married Linda Lee Hueller, March 16, 1962; children: Jeff, Chris, Mark. *Education:* Oregon College of Education, B.S., 1962, M.S., 1965; Washington State University, Ed.D., 1969. *Home:* 327 North Atwater, Monmouth, Ore. 97361. *Office:* Department of Education, Oregon College of Education, Monmouth, Ore. 97361.

CAREER: Elementary school teacher in the public schools of Salem, Ore., 1962-65; Teaching Research Division, Monmouth, Ore., research assistant, 1965-67; Oregon College of Education, Monmouth, assistant professor, 1969-73; associate professor of education, 1973—, director of Elementary Education Division, 1975—. Evaluation specialist, Northwest Region Education Laboratory, Portland, Ore., 1972. *Member:* Association for Supervision and Curriculum Development, American Educational Research Association, Phi Delta Kappa.

WRITINGS: Writing and Assessing Attitudinal Objectives, C. E. Merrill, 1973. Author of several federal research reports. Contributor to *Elementary English.*

WORK IN PROGRESS: Research in validating an affective taxonomy and in establishing predictors of teacher performance; *Techniques for Diagnosing Student Attitudes* (tentative title).

AVOCATIONAL INTERESTS: Softball, golf, tennis, travel.

* * *

GISHFORD, Anthony (Joseph) 1908-1975

1908—January 23, 1975; British musicologist, editor, translator, and author of works on music history and criticism. Obituaries: *AB Bookman's Weekly*, February 17, 1975.

* * *

GITCHOFF, G(eorge) Thomas 1938-
(Tom Gitchoff)

PERSONAL: Born April 29, 1938, in Granite City, Ill.; son of George Evan and Athena (Gounaris) Gitchoff; married Miriam Speidel, December 31, 1966; children: Gregory Thomas, Krista Lara. *Education:* Central Methodist College, B.A., 1960; University of California, Berkeley, M.Cr., 1966, D.Cr., 1968. *Home:* 7177 Keigley St., San Diego, Calif. 92120. *Office:* School of Public Administration and Urban Studies, San Diego State University, San Diego, Calif. 92182.

CAREER: Contra Costa County (Calif.) Juvenile Probation Department, street gang worker in El Cerrito-Richmond office, 1965-66; Youth Commission, Pleasant Hill, Calif., director of youth services, 1966-68; assistant professor of sociology at California State University Extension, Hayward, and assistant professor of criminology at University of California Extension, Berkeley, 1968; San Diego State University, San Diego, Calif., School of Public Administration and Urban Studies, assistant professor, 1969-71 associate professor of criminology, 1971—, director of criminal justice administration program, 1969—. Licensed marriage, family, and child counselor, State of California, 1969—; private practice as criminologist and consultant under name Tom Gitchoff, San Diego, 1969—. Vice-president and secretary, San Diego County Public Facilities Corp. (youth development center project). *Military service:* U.S. Army, Medical Corps, 1961-64; served in Germany.

MEMBER: National Council on Crime and Delinquency, American Society of Criminology (member of exeutive council, 1971-72; member of executive board, Western Division, 1974-75), American Correctional Association, Academy of Criminal Justice Sciences, International Association of Chiefs of Police, Law Enforcement Association on Professional Standards, Education and Ethical Practice (fellow; chairman of police standards committee, 1974-75), American Civil Liberties Union, National Conference of Christians and Jews, California Probation, Parole and Correctional Association (member of executive board, Southern region), California Marriage Counselors Association, California Peace Officers Association, California Council on Criminal Justice, Southern Christian Leadership Conference. *Awards, honors:* Lester J. Hayes Award of California Probation, Parole and Correctional Association for best article of 1974, "Victimless Crimes."

WRITINGS: (With others) *Middle-Class Delinquency: An Experiment in Community Control* (monograph), School of Criminology, University of California, Berkeley, 1968; *Kids, Cops and Kilos: A Study of Contemporary Suburban Youth*, Malter-Westerfield, 1969; (editor with James A. Gazell) *Youth, Crime and Society*, Holbrook, 1971; (contributor) William J. Bopp and others, editors, *Police-Community Relations* (reader), C.C Thomas, 1972; (contributor) Harry W. More, editor, *Principles and Procedures in the Administration of Justice*, Wiley, 1974.

Author of introduction or foreword: Fred Ferguson, *Creativity in Law Enforcement: The Covina Field Experiment*, Institute of Public and Urban Affairs, School of Public Administration, San Diego State University, 1970; Arthur Niederhoffer and Alexander Smith, *New Directions in Police-Community Relations*, Rinehart, 1974; Charles N. Guthrie, *The Palace Guard: A Fairytale for Policemen*, Homeland Press (San Diego), 1974.

Contributor of articles and reviews to *Criminologica*, *Police*, *Journal of Drug Issues*, and other periodicals. Editor, *Crime and Corrections* (journal of the California Probation, Parole and Correctional Association), 1972—; editorial adviser, *Journal of Crime Prevention*, 1973—.

* * *

GLADSTONE, M(yron) J. 1923-

PERSONAL: Born May 4, 1923. *Education:* Harvard University, S.B., 1944, M.A., 1946. *Home:* 310 East 75th St., New York, N.Y. 10021.

CAREER: Former managing editor, *Print* and *Print Collector's Quarterly*, Woodstock, Vt.; former art and illustrations editor, G. & C. Merriam Co., Springfield, Mass; former promotion manager and sales representative, Yale University Press, New Haven, Conn.; former advertising manager, Seven Arts Book Society, New York, N.Y.; former manager of Collector's Book Society of McGraw-Hill Book Co., New York, N.Y.; former associate director of publications, Museum of Modern Art, New York, N.Y.; former director of publications, Arno Press, New York, N.Y.; former director, Museum of American Folk Art, New York, N.Y.; Publishing Center for Cultural Resources, New York, N.Y., director, 1973—.

WRITINGS: A Carrot for a Nose: The Form of Folk Sculpture on American City Streets and Country Roads, Scribner, 1974.

* * *

GLASKIN, G(erald) M(arcus) 1923-
(Neville Jackson)

PERSONAL: Born December 16, 1923, in Perth, Western Australia; son of Gilbert Henry (a clerk) and Delia Mary (Gugeri) Glaskin. *Education:* Attended schools in Australia. *Politics:* Coalitionist ("as in the Netherlands"). *Religion:* Gnostic. *Home:* 1 "Warnham Heights," 14 Warnham Rd., Cottesloe, Western Australia 6011. *Agent:* Georges Borchardt, Inc., 145 East 52nd St., New York, N.Y. 10022; and Bolt & Watson Ltd., 8 Storey's Gate, London S.W.1, England.

CAREER: Coulton & Meagher, Perth, Western Australia, articled auditor, 1939-40; Soap Distributors Ltd., North Fremantle, Western Australia, clerk, 1940-41; J. Kitchen & Sons, Pty. Ltd., Sydney, Australia, sales clerk, 1943; Fremantle Sports Depot, Fremantle, Western Australia, acting manager, 1946; Ford Motor Co. of Australia, Fremantle, Western Australia, sales statistician, 1947-48; Wearne Brothers Ltd., Singapore, executive, 1949; McMullan & Co., Singapore, acting manager, 1949-50; Lyall & Evatt (stockbrokers), Singapore, partner, 1950-59; full-time writer, 1959—. *Military service:* Royal Australian Navy, 1941-43; Royal Australian Air Force, 1943-46, commissioned in Canada as Flying Officer. *Member:* Society of Authors (London); Australian Society of Authors; Fellowship of Australian Writers (president, 1968-69). *Awards, honors:* Commonwealth of Australia Literary Fund fellow, 1957 and 1972, for research in the Netherlands; Australian Council for the Arts (film and television board) grant, 1974; Western Australia Arts Council bursary, 1975.

WRITINGS—Novels: *A World of Our Own*, J. Barrie, 1955; *A Minor Portrait*, J. Barrie, 1957; *A Change of Mind*, Barrie & Rockliff, 1959, Doubleday, 1960; *A Lion in the Sun*, Barrie & Rockliff, 1960; *The Beach of Passionate Love*, Barrie & Rockliff, 1961; *A Waltz through the Hills* (for young readers), Barrie & Rockliff, 1961; *Flight to Landfall*, Barrie & Rockliff, 1963; *O Love, O Loneliness* (two novellas), Barrie & Rockliff, 1964; (under pseudonym Neville Jackson) *No End to the Way*, Barrie & Rockliff, 1965; Macfadden, 1969; *The Man Who Didn't Count*, Delacorte, 1965; *Two Women: Turn on the Heat* [and] *The Eaves of Night* (novella-drama/biography-memoir; *Turn on the Heat* is adapted from an earlier play, also see below), Ure Smith, 1975.

Other: *The Land That Sleeps* (travel), Doubleday, 1961; *A Small Selection* (short stories), Barrie & Rockliff, 1962; *The Road to Nowhere* (short stories), Barrie & Rockliff, 1967; *A Bird in My Hands* (memoir), Jenkins, 1967; "Turn on the Heat," (two-act play), first produced in Perth, Western Australia, at The Hole in the Wall Theatre, June, 1967; *Windows of the Mind* (nonfiction), Delacorte, 1974. Author of five screenplays based on his own books, "A Change of Mind," "A Waltz through the Hills," "No End to the Way," "The Road to Nowhere," and "O Love, O Loneliness."

Short stories appear in anthologies, including *Coast to Coast, 1946*, edited by M. Barnard Eldershaw, Angus & Robertson, 1946; *West Coast Stories, 1959*, edited by H. Drake-Brockman, Angus & Robertson, 1959; *Coast to Coast, 1963-64*, edited by Leonie Kramer, Angus & Robertson, 1964; *Coast to Coast, 1965-66*, edited by Clement Semmler, Angus & Robertson, 1966; *Summer's Tales 3, 1966*, edited by John Iggulden, St. Martin's, 1966; *Contact One, 1969*, edited by F. E. S. Finn, J. Murray, 1969; *Taste of Cockroach, 1974*, edited by John Griffin and Warwick Goodenough, Australian Association for the Teaching of English, 1974.

Contributor of articles to various periodicals, including *Fantasy and Science Fiction* (New York), *Eastern Horizon* (Hong Kong), and *Mayflower* (London).

WORK IN PROGRESS: Worlds Within, nonfiction, a second book on the "Christos Experiment" (treated earlier in *Windows of the Mind*), publication expected by Wildwood House; continuing research for a third book on the topic, tentatively titled *The Door to Eternity; At the End of It All*, a novel on the theme of the "Christos Experiment"; *One Way to Wonderland*, a memoir based on the author's "penfriendship" of almost four decades; *Small World*, a novel; *Come of Age*, short stories for young readers; *Any Girl Will Do*, short stories for adults; *The Boy Who Climbed the Sonnenberg*, a novel for young readers; research on the causes of homosexuality, for a general book on the subject.

SIDELIGHTS: Glaskin told *CA* that his earliest motivation for writing sprang from a "penfriendship," begun before World War II and still continuing, with a Dutch boy, now grown to manhood and living in Houston, Tex. Glaskin's first published works were the short stories he wrote while recuperating in a military hospital in 1942, following injury during the Battle of the Coral Sea. His career was interrupted in 1967 by a body-surfing accident at Cottesloe Beach in Western Australia. Multiple splinter-fractures of his neck and lower spine required long and painful treatment before he was able to resume writing in 1971.

Glaskins's writings have been translated into Dutch, French, German, Norwegian, Swedish, Danish, Spanish, Russian, and Japanese. His original manuscripts, correspondence, and other papers are housed in the archives of the Battye Library, Public Library Building, in Perth, Western Australia. The manuscript of *A Lion in the Sun* is at the University of Malaya, Singapore.

AVOCATIONAL INTERESTS: Music, theatre, photography, reading, study of parapsychology, walking, swimming ("but no more water-skiing, horse-riding or body-surfing"), and travel (has lived in Singapore for ten years, has visited the United States, Russia, South America, Asia from India to Japan, and has traveled around the world three times by ship).

BIOGRAPHICAL/CRITICAL SOURCES: John Hetherington, *Forty-Two Faces*, F. W. Cheshire, 1962.

* * *

GLASS, John F(ranklin) 1936-

PERSONAL: Born January 15, 1936, in Berlin, Germany;

son of Paul (an engineer) and Anni (a photographer; maiden name, Hoff) Glass; married Judith Chanin (an economist), February 27, 1966; children: Aaron Joseph. *Education:* University of Illinois, B.S., 1958, M.A., 1962; University of California at Los Angeles, Ph.D., 1968. *Home:* 4242 Wilkinson, Studio City, Calif. 91604. *Office:* California School of Professional Psychology, Los Angeles, Calif. 90004.

CAREER: California State University, Northridge, assistant professor of sociology, 1968-73; California School of Professional Psychology, Los Angeles, member of faculty and coordinator of Culture and Society Series, 1972—. *Military service:* U.S. Army, 1958-60. *Member:* American Sociological Association, Association for Humanistic Psychology, Society for Psychological Study of Social Issues, Pacific Sociological Association, California State Psychological Association.

WRITINGS: (Editor with John R. Staude) *Humanistic Society: Today's Challenge to Sociology*, Goodyear Publishing, 1972. Contributor of book reviews to *Contemporary Sociology* and *Labor and Industrial Relations Review*.

WORK IN PROGRESS: Learning in Groups.

* * *

GLASSER, Stephen A(ndrew) 1943-

PERSONAL: Born July 27, 1943, in Memphis, Tenn.; son of Melvin and Esther (Kron) Glasser; married Lynn Schreiber (vice-president of *New York Law Journal*), 1965; children: Susan, Laura, Jeffrey. *Education:* Colgate University, B.A., 1965; University of Michigan, J.D., 1968. *Home:* 86 Highland Ave., Montclair, N.J. 07042. *Office: New York Law Journal*, 258 Broadway, New York, N.Y. 10007.

CAREER: Admitted to Bar of District of Columbia, 1969. Practising Law Institute, New York, N.Y., assistant director, 1968-71; *New York Law Journal*, New York, N.Y., executive vice-president and editor, 1971—. Adjunct assistant professor at Fordham University, 1972—. *Member:* American Bar Association, District of Columbia Bar Association, Association of the Bar of the City of New York.

WRITINGS: (Associate editor) B. James George, Jr., editor, *A New Look at Confessions: Escobedo–the Second Round*, Institute of Continuing Legal Education, 1967; (editor) *Pension Plans, Deferred Compensation, and Executive Benefits*, Practising Law Institute, 1969; (editor) *Understanding Law and Psychiatry*, Practising Law Institute, 1969. Contributor to *Encyclopedia of Education*; also contributor of articles to various periodicals, including *New York Law Journal*.

* * *

GLEASON, S(arel) Everett 1905-1974

March 14, 1905—November 20, 1974; American historian, State Department official, and author of books most notably on U.S. foreign affairs. Obituaries: *New York Times*, November 22, 1974; *Washington Post*, November 23, 1974; *AB Bookman's Weekly*, December 16, 1974.

* * *

GLEAVES, Robert M(ilnor) 1938-

PERSONAL: Born March 18, 1938, in Nashville, Tenn.; son of Edwin S. (a radio announcer) and Hazel (an insurance agent; maiden name, Hunter) Gleaves; married Catherine Glosser (a tennis instructor), September 11, 1964; children: Kevin Michael, Sharon Elizabeth. *Education:* David Lipscomb College, B.A., 1960; Vanderbilt University, M.A., 1963, Ph.D., 1968. *Politics:* Democrat. *Home:* 5237 Glenbrier Dr., Charlotte, N.C. 28212. *Office:* Department of Foreign Languages, University of North Carolina, Charlotte, N.C. 28213.

CAREER: University of South Florida, Tampa, instructor, 1965-68, assistant professor of Spanish, 1968-69; University of North Carolina at Charlotte, assistant professor, 1969-72, associate professor of Spanish, 1972—, acting chairman of department of foreign languages, summers, 1972, 1973, presiding officer of College of Humanities, 1973-75. *Military service:* U.S. Air National Guard, 1956-62. *Member:* Instituto Internacional de Literatura Iberoamericana, American Association of Teachers of Spanish and Portuguese, South Atlantic Modern Language Association, Charlotte Swim and Racquet Club (member of board of directors, 1974—), Winterfield Booster Club.

WRITINGS: (Editor with Charles M. Vance) *Hispanoamerica magica y misteriosa: Once relatos* (title means "Magical and Mysterious Spanish America: Eleven Tales"), Holt, 1973. Contributor to *Language Quarterly* and to *Charlotte Observer*.

WORK IN PROGRESS: Editing and translating into English an anthology of Cuban short stories; a book-length study of magical realism in the Latin American narrative.

AVOCATIONAL INTERESTS: Travel, tennis.

* * *

GLICKMAN, Albert S(eymour) 1923-

PERSONAL: Born February 7, 1923, in Brooklyn, N.Y.; son of Irving H. (a merchandise manager) and Molly (Zuckerman) Glickman; married Blanche Buller (an educational administrator), June 14, 1945; children: Ralph, Marc, Judith, Debra. *Education:* Ohio State University, B.A. (summa cum laude), 1943, M.A., 1947, Ph.D., 1952. *Home:* 12712 Saddlebrook Dr., Silver Spring, Md. 20906. *Office:* American Institutes for Research, 3301 New Mexico Ave., N.W., Washington, D.C. 20016.

CAREER: Georgia Institute of Technology, Atlanta, assistant professor of psychology, 1947-52; American Institutes for Research, Pittsburgh, Pa., project director, 1952-55; U.S. Naval Personnel Research Activity, Washington D.C., director of department of psychological research, 1955-62; U.S. Department of Agriculture, Washington, D.C., chief of personnel research staff, 1962-67; American Institutes for Research, Silver Spring, Md., director of Institute for Research on Organizational Behavior, 1967-70, deputy director of Washington Office, 1970-74, deputy director of human performance and organizational behavior division, 1974—. Counselor at Occupational Opportunities Service of Ohio State University, 1946-47; research fellow of Boys' Apparel Buyers' Association, 1949-52. Associate professorial lecturer at George Washington University, 1960-61; lecturer for U.S. Department of Agriculture Graduate School, 1963-64; visiting professor at North Carolina State University, summer, 1966; lecturer at Montgomery College, 1971. Chief of research for Consulting Psychologists, Inc., 1948-51; partner of Joseph E. Moore & Associates (management consultants), 1951-52. *Military service:* U.S. Navy, 1943-46; became lieutenant junior grade.

MEMBER: International Association of Applied Psychology (fellow), American Psychological Association (fellow), American Association for the Advancement of Science (fellow), Eastern Psychological Association, Midwestern Psychological Association, Maryland Psychological Association, District of Columbia Psychological Association, Phi Beta Kappa. *Awards, honors:* Louis Brownlow Memorial Fund prize from International Public Personnel Association, 1965, for "Managerial Training: Reinforcement Through Evaluation"; *Training and Development Journal* author's award from American Society for Training and Development, and professional award from Eastern Public Personnel Association, both 1967, for article "What Can Critical Incidents Tell Management?"

WRITINGS: (With C. P. Hahn, E. A. Fleishman, and Brent Baxter) *Top Management Development and Succession*, Macmillan, 1968; (with R. H. Fosen and T. E. Eisenberg) *Police-Community Action: A Program for Change in Police-Community Behavior Patterns*, Praeger, 1973; (with D. I. Sheppard) *Police Careers: Constructing Career Paths for Tomorrow's Police Force*, C. C Thomas, 1973; (with Z. H. Brown) *Changing Schedules of Work: Patterns and Implications*, W. E. Upjohn Institute for Employment Research, 1974.

Contributor to *Public Personnel Review, Crime and Delinquency, Personnel Administration, Personnel Psychology,* and *Journal of Applied Psychology*. Consulting editor of *Journal of Applied Psychology*, 1970—.

WORK IN PROGRESS: Research on socialization processes and the adjustment of military personnel to army life, for the Army Research Institute in the Behavioral Sciences; research to develop a model of Reserve Officers Training Corps-Army Officer career commitment, for Army Research Institute in the Behavioral and Social Sciences; research on social security and the changing life ethos, for the Social Security Administration; a nationwide manpower survey of law enforcement and criminal justice personnel needs and training requirements, for the Law Enforcement Assistance Administration.

* * *

GLOCK, Charles Y(oung) 1919-

PERSONAL: Born October 17, 1919, in New York, N.Y.; son of Charles and Philippine (Young) Glock; married Margaret Schleef (a volunteer worker), September 12, 1950; children: Susan, James. *Education:* New York University, B.S., 1940; Boston University, M.B.A., 1941; Columbia University, Ph.D., 1952. *Politics:* Democrat. *Religion:* Lutheran. *Home:* 40 Del Mar Ave., Berkeley, Calif. 94708. *Office:* Department of Sociology, University of California, Berkeley, Calif. 94720.

CAREER: Columbia University, New York, N.Y., executive director, 1947-49, managing director, 1949-52, director of Bureau of Applied Social Research, 1952-58, lecturer, 1952-56, and professor of sociology, 1956-58; University of California, Berkeley, professor of sociology, 1958—, director of Survey Research Center, 1958-67, director of research program in religion and society, 1962—. Fellow of Center for Advanced Study in the Behavioral Sciences, 1957-58; member of board of directors of Cornerhouse Fund, Fund for the Advancement of Continuing Education, Wright Institute, and Institute for Research in Social Behavior. *Military service:* U.S. Army Air Forces, 1942-46; became captain; received Bronze Star Medal and Legion of Merit.

MEMBER: American Sociological Association, Sociological Research Association, Society for the Scientific Study of Religion (president, 1969-70), Religious Research Association, American Association for Public Opinion Research (president, 1963-64). *Awards, honors:* Fellow of Society for Religion in Higher Education, 1968-69; grants from Anti-Defamation League of B'nai B'rith, 1962—, and National Science Foundation, 1972—.

WRITINGS: (With Rodney Stark) *Religion and Society in Tension,* Rand McNally, 1965; (with Stark) *Christian Beliefs and Anti-Semitism,* Harper, 1966; (with Gertrude J. Selznick and Joe L. Spaeth) *The Apathetic Majority,* Harper, 1966; (editor) *Survey Research in the Social Sciences,* Basic Books, 1967; (with Benjamin Ringer and Earl Babbie) *To Comfort and to Challenge,* University of California Press, 1967; (with Stark) *American Piety,* University of California Press, 1968; (with Ellen Siegelman) *Prejudice, U.S.A.,* Praeger, 1969; (with Stark, Bruce Foster, and Harold Quinley) *Wayward Shepherds,* Harper, 1971; (editor) *Religion in Sociological Perspective,* Wadsworth, 1973; (with Phillip Hammond) *Beyond the Classics?*, Harper, 1973; (with Robert Withnow, Jane Piliavin, and Metta Spencer) *Adolescent Prejudice,* Harper, in press.

WORK IN PROGRESS: Editing a collection of essays on contemporary religious consciousness among youth, with Robert Bellah; *Social Indicators of Racial Prejudice,* a monograph, with Richard Apostle and Marijean Suelzli.

BIOGRAPHICAL/CRITICAL SOURCES: Journal for the Scientific Study of Religion, autumn, 1973.

* * *

GLOGAU, Art(hur H.) 1922-

PERSONAL: Born March 19, 1922, in New York; son of Otto (a physician) and Johanna (a nurse; maiden name, Blau) Glogau; married wife, Martha, January 4, 1944 (divorced April 15, 1972); children: Joanne Edith (Mrs. Royce Mosgrove), Thomas Edward, Wendy (Mrs. Fred Fischer). *Education:* Cornell University, B.S., 1945, M.S., 1946, Ph.D., 1952. *Home:* 2575 Holiday Dr. S., Salem, Ore. 97302. *Office:* Oregon College of Education, Monmouth, Ore. 97361.

CAREER: Oregon College of Education, Monmouth, assistant professor, 1953-57, associate professor, 1957-62, professor of education and psychology, 1962—, chairman of Division of Psychology, 1968-71, dean of men, 1953-57, dean of students, 1957-67, director of graduate studies, 1971. Private practice in marriage counseling. *Military service:* U.S. Army, 1941-46; became first lieutenant.

MEMBER: American Personnel and Guidance Association, Student Personnel Association for Teacher Education, American College Personnel Association, National Council on Family Relations, American Association of Marriage and Family Counselors, American Society of Group Psychotherapy and Psychodrama, American Association of Sex Educators and Counselors, American Educational Research Association, American Educational Studies Association, Association for Higher Education (of National Education Association), History of Education Society, American Association of University Professors, Association for Humanistic Psychology, National Society for the Study of Education, Northwest College Personnel Association (vice-president, 1955; president, 1956), Oregon Personnel and Guidance Association, Phi Delta Kappa.

WRITINGS: This and That, Vantage, 1971; *Longing and Belonging*, Pageant, 1972; *When I Hug You My Toes Curl*,

Pageant, 1973; *There's Time*, Pageant, 1973. Contributor of about twenty articles to professional publications, including *Phi Delta Kappan*, *Journal of Teacher Education*, *Journal of Family Welfare*, and *Oregon Education Association Journal*.

SIDELIGHTS: Glogau writes: "The areas opened by the current focus on humanistic psychology, and activities related to this, now form much of the center of my energies. Group process, encounter groups, couples' communication skills, human interaction, etc., help me find out who I am and where it's at."

* * *

GLORFELD, Louis E(arl) 1916-

PERSONAL: Born July 2, 1916, in Buffalo Center, Iowa; son of Henry Clay (a farmer) and Helen (a teacher; maiden name, Fuhlendorf) Glorfeld; married Patricia Clare Taylor (a teacher), May 4, 1943; children: Louis William. *Education:* Attended Morningside College, 1933-34, and State University of Iowa, 1934-35; University of Northern Iowa, B.A., 1948, M.A., 1956; graduate study at Claremont Graduate School, 1956-57; University of Denver, Ph.D., 1964. *Home:* 2306 Crabtree Dr., Littleton, Colo. 80121. *Office:* Department of Speech, University of Denver, University Park, Denver, Colo. 80210.

CAREER: Teacher of English and speech at secondary school level in Waterloo, Iowa, 1948-56, 1957-59, and at secondary school and junior college levels in Ontario, Calif., 1956-57; West Liberty State College, Wheeling, W.Va., assistant professor of English and speech, 1959-60; Northern Illinois University, DeKalb, Ill., assistant professor of English and director of Freshman English, 1960-67; University of Denver, Denver, Colo., professor of speech communication and linguistics, 1967—. Publications consultant for Medical Group Management Association, 1970—. *Member:* American Association of University Professors, National Council of Teachers of English, Speech Association of America, College Conference on Composition and Communication, Colorado Language Arts Society.

WRITINGS: (With Norman Stageberg and David Lauerman) *Concise Guide for Writers*, Rinehart, 1963, 3rd revised edition, 1974; (contributor) *Language Behavior*, Mouton & Co., 1970.

Editor: (With Edmund J. Thomas) *College Prep Reader*, Harper, 1965; (with Robert N. Broadus and Thomas E. Kakonis) *The Short Story: Ideas and Background*, C. E. Merrill, 1967; (with Kakonis and James C. Wilcox) *Language, Rhetoric, and Idea*, C. E. Merrill, 1967; (with Andrew MacLeish) *The Dictionary and Usage*, Holt, 1968; (with Kakonis and Wilcox) *Plays by Four Tragedians*, C. E. Merrill, 1968; *A Short Unit on General Semantics*, Glencoe Press, 1969.

* * *

GLYN, Anthony 1922-

PERSONAL: Name originally Geoffrey Leo Simon Davson; legally changed, 1957; born March 13, 1922, in London, England; son of Sir Edward, 1st baronet (a sugar planter) and Lady Margot (Glyn) Davson; married Susan Rhys-Williams (a sculptor), October 2, 1946; children: Caroline, Victoria. *Education:* Attended Eton College, 1935-40. *Home:* 6 rue Saint-Louis-en-l'Ile, Paris, France 75004. *Agent:* Brandt & Brandt, 101 Park Ave., New York, N.Y. 10017.

CAREER: Worked as a factory-hand, sugar planter, music critic, office clerk, sawmill manager, and cowboy; full-time writer. *Military service:* British Army, Welsh Guards, 1941-45; served in Europe; became captain. *Member:* P.E.N. (London and Paris centres), Savile Club, Pratt's Club. *Awards, honors:* I.T.V. Television Play Prize, 1961, for "The Travellers."

WRITINGS: *Romanza* (novel), Hutchinson, 1953; *The Jungle of Eden*, Hutchinson, 1954; *Elinor Glyn: A Biography* (Book Society choice), Doubleday, 1955, revised edition, Hutchinson, 1968; *The Ram in the Thicket* (novel), Hutchinson, 1957, expanded version published as *Pemberton, Ltd.* (Dollar Book Club choice), Dial, 1957; *I Can Take It All* (Book Society choice), Hutchinson, 1959, Harcourt, 1960; *Kick Turn*, Hutchinson, 1963; *The Terminal* (novel), Hutchinson, 1965; *The Seine* (travel book), Weidenfeld & Nicolson, 1966, Putnam, 1967; *The Dragon Variation* (novel), Simon & Schuster, 1969; *The British: A Portrait of a People*, Putnam, 1970 (published in England as *The Blood of a Britishman*, Hutchinson, 1970).

Also author of television play, "The Travellers," 1961.

Contributor to *Times* (London), *Spectator*, *Anglo-Welsh Review*, *Evening Standard* (London), *Musical Times*, *Reader's Digest*, and others.

WORK IN PROGRESS: A novel, *A Man, a Dog and a Mountain*.

SIDELIGHTS: Glyn, who succeeded his father as second baronet, is the grandson of the British novelist Elinor Glyn. He told *CA*: "Critics have said that my work has an active hedonism, but also that it is Kafkalike and nightmarish. I think it is important to explore both these aspects of human experience. Humour gives us our profoundest insights; all my books are both funny and sad. I like to say many things on different levels—a book is not a thesis."

An Anthony Glyn Collection was established at Boston University in 1970. *The Terminal* was filmed as a television play in 1971.

AVOCATIONAL INTERESTS: Travel, skiing, music, sailing, and chess.

* * *

GODOLPHIN, Francis R. B. 1903-1974

April 8, 1903—December 29, 1974; American educator, university dean, classical scholar, author and editor. Obituaries: *New York Times*, December 30, 1974; *Washington Post*, December 30, 1974; *AB Bookman's Weekly*, January 20, 1975.

* * *

GOEL, M(adan) Lal 1936-

PERSONAL: Born June 20, 1936, in Panjab, India; married Shully M. Heble (a systems analyst), July 14, 1964; children: Anu. *Education:* Panjab University, B.A., 1956; University of Oregon, M.A., 1959; State University of New York at Buffalo, Ph.D., 1969. *Office:* University of West Florida, Pensacola, Fla. 32504.

CAREER: U.S. Information Agency, Bombay, India, lecturer, 1961, consultant, 1961-63; Niagara University, Niagara University, N.Y., instructor, 1966-68, assistant professor of political science, 1968-69; University of West Florida, Pensacola, assistant professor, 1969-73, associate professor of political science, 1973—. *Member:* American Political Science Association, Southern Political Science Association, Florida Political Science Association.

WRITINGS: Political Participation in a Developing Nation, Asia Publishing House, 1974. Contributor to *Comparative Political Studies, Social Science Quarterly, Political Scientist,* and *Political Science Review.*

WORK IN PROGRESS: Political Participation, for Rand McNally.

* * *

GOERTZ, Donald C(harles) 1939-

PERSONAL: Surname rhymes with "hurts"; born October 17, 1939, in Red Rock, Tex.; son of Paul Philip (a laborer) and Margaret (Goertz) Goertz; married, wife's name, Lorraine; children: Alethea Margaret. *Education:* Summer study at Southwest Texas State University, 1960; University of Texas at Austin, B.A., 1961, M.A., 1964, Ph.D., 1972; graduate study at Free University of Berlin, 1962-63. *Politics:* "Intelligent, reflective, careful, concerned." *Religion:* "Julian—called Apostate by pagans." *Home:* 724 Beechwood Ave., Muncie, Ind. 47303. *Office:* Department of Foreign Languages, Ball State University, Muncie, Ind. 47306.

CAREER: Randolph-Macon College, Ashland, Va., assistant professor of classics and head of Greek studies, 1965-67; Hollins College, Roanoke, Va., assistant professor of classics, 1967-70; Wayne State University, Detroit, Mich., assistant professor of classics, 1970-73; Ball State University, Muncie, Ind., coordinator of classics, 1973—. *Member:* American Philological Association, American Association of University Professors, Classical Association of the Middle West and South, Indiana Classical Conference, Eta Sigma Phi, Alpha Mu Gamma.

WRITINGS: (Translator) *Select Epigrams of Martial,* University Books, 1971. Contributor of poems and translations to *Stylus* and *Roanoke Review.* Author of the television program "Women in Antiquity," Channel 7, Anderson, Ind., November, 1973. Member of editorial board of *Stylus,* 1966.

WORK IN PROGRESS: Two books, a translation of the Lesbia poems of Catullus, and a collection of primary sources on "Women in the Ancient Greek and Roman World"; research on the naturalism of death in Euripidean tragedy; a book on Orpheus and Eurydice; a mystery.

AVOCATIONAL INTERESTS: Travel, foreign languages.

* * *

GOLD, Robert S(tanley) 1924-

PERSONAL: Born June 19, 1924, in New York, N.Y.; son of Albert (a shoe salesman) and Frances (Frey) Gold; divorced; children: Eva, Joshua. *Education:* Syracuse University, B.S., 1949; New York University, M.A., 1955, Ph.D., 1962. *Home:* 62 Leroy St., New York, N.Y. 10014. *Office:* Department of English, Jersey City State College, Jersey City, N.J. 07305.

CAREER: Queens College of the City University of New York, New York, N.Y., lecturer in English, 1958-63; Jersey City State College, Jersey City, N.J., assistant professor, 1963-68, associate professor, 1968-73, professor of English, 1973—. Instructor at Hunter College of the City University of New York, 1962. *Military service:* U.S. Coast Guard, signalman, 1943-45. *Awards, honors:* Cited for outstanding reference work by *Library Journal,* 1964, for *A Jazz Lexicon.*

WRITINGS: A Jazz Lexicon, Knopf, 1964; (editor) *Point of Departure,* Dell, 1967; (contributor) Barnet Kottler and Martin Light, editors, *The World of Words,* Houghton, 1967; (with Sanford R. Radner) *Controversy* (textbook for college freshmen), Holt, 1969; (editor) *The Rebel Culture,* Dell, 1971; *Jazz Talk,* Bobbs-Merrill, 1975. Contributor of drama reviews to *Jersey Journal,* 1964-65.

WORK IN PROGRESS: Editing a sports fiction anthology; revising *Controversy.*

AVOCATIONAL INTERESTS: Jazz, sports (handball, tennis, watching football, basketball, and hockey), reading, movies.

BIOGRAPHICAL/CRITICAL SOURCES: Newark Star-Ledger, March 3, 1974; *Jersey Journal,* March 5, 1974.

* * *

GOLD, Victor Roland 1924-

PERSONAL: Born September 18, 1924, in Garden City, Kan.; son of Helmuth Hugo Carl (a minister) and Wilhelmina Johanna (Knake) Gold; married Lois Martha Stout (a hospital administrator), December 7, 1947; children: Victor Roland II, Stephen Michael, Joanne Elisabeth. *Education:* Wartburg College, B.A., 1944; Wartburg Theological Seminary, B.D., 1946; Johns Hopkins University, Ph.D., 1951; American School of Oriental Research, postdoctoral study, 1951-52. *Home:* 775 Alvarado Rd., Berkeley, Calif. 94705. *Office:* Department of Religion, Pacific Lutheran Theological Seminary, 2770 Marin Ave., Berkeley, Calif. 94708.

CAREER: Ordained Lutheran minister, 1946; Wittenberg University, Hamma Divinity School, Springfield, Ohio, assistant professor, 1952-56; Pacific Lutheran Theological Seminary, Berkeley, Calif., associate professor, 1956-61, professor of Old Testament, 1961—; Graduate Theological Union, Berkeley, Calif., professor of Old Testament, 1962—. Visiting professor of Semitic Languages at University of Calif., Berkeley, 1968—. *Member:* Deutscher Verein zur Erforschung Palaestinas, Institute for Mediterranean Studies (executive director, 1969—), Society of Biblical Literature (secretary of Pacific Coast region, 1961—; member of national council, 1961—), American Oriental Society, Archaeological Institute of America, Palestine Exploration Fund, Pacific Coast Theological Society. *Awards, honors:* Honorary associate of American Schools of Oriental Research, 1956, 1959, 1960, 1963-65; fellow of Hebrew Union College-Jewish Institute of Religion Biblical and Archaeological School, 1963.

WRITINGS: (Contributor) David N. Freedman and G. Ernest Wright, editors, *Biblical Archaeologist Reader,* Volume I, Doubleday, 1961; (editor) *Kirchenpraesident oder Bischof?* (title means "Church President or Bishop?"), Vandenhoeck & Ruprecht, 1968; (contributor) Daniel F. Martensen, editor, *Christian Hope and the Secular,* Augsburg, 1969; (editor) *Episcopacy in the Lutheran Church?,* Fortress, 1970. Contributor to *Oxford Annotated Bible* and *Interpreter's Dictionary of the Bible.*

WORK IN PROGRESS: Research on Near Eastern archaeology, and on the literature, history and intellectual movements in Judaism from about 600 B.C. to about 200 A.D.

SIDELIGHTS: Gold is fluent in German and reads French, Italian, Spanish, Swedish, Greek, and Hebrew. *Avocational interests:* Travel (Europe, Turkey, Cyprus, Lebanon, Jordan, Syria, Israel, Egypt, Libya, and Tunisia).

GOLDBARTH, Albert 1948-

PERSONAL: Born January 31, 1948, in Chicago, Ill.; son of Irving (a life underwriter) and Fannie (a secretary; maiden name, Seligman) Goldbarth. *Education:* University of Illinois, Chicago Circle, B.A., 1969; University of Iowa, M.F.A., 1971; University of Utah, further graduate study, 1973-74. *Religion:* "Non-observant Jew." *Home:* 5306 North Washtenaw, Chicago, Ill. 60625. *Office:* Department of English, Cornell University, Ithaca, N.Y. 14850.

CAREER: Elgin Community College, Elgin, Ill., instructor in English, 1971-72; University of Utah, Salt Lake City, instructor in creative writing, 1973-74; Cornell University, Ithaca, N.Y., visiting assistant professor of creative writing, 1974—. Instructor at Central Young Men's Christian Association Community College, 1971-73. Co-director of Illinois Arts Council's Travelling Writers Workshop, 1971-72. Member of advisory panel to literature committee on National Endowment for the Arts. *Awards, honors:* Theodore Roethke Prize from *Poetry Northwest*, 1972; first prize in poetry from *Northwest Review*, 1973; annual poetry award from *Ark River Review*, 1973, 1975; creative writing fellowship from National Endowment for the Arts, 1974; creative writing award from Illinois Arts Council, 1974; National Book Award in Poetry nomination, 1975.

WRITINGS—Books of poems: *Under Cover*, Best Cellar Press, 1973; *Coprolites*, New Rivers Press, 1974; *Opticks*, Seven Woods Press, 1974; *Jan. 31*, Doubleday, 1974; *Keeping*, Ithaca House, 1975.

WORK IN PROGRESS: Several long poems.

BIOGRAPHICAL/CRITICAL SOURCES: Midwest Quarterly, January, 1975; *West Coast Poetry Review*, winter-spring, 1975.

* * *

GOLDBERG, Edward M(orris) 1931-

PERSONAL: Born May 18, 1931, in New York, N.Y.; son of Harry Abraham (an upholsterer) and Pauline (Josef) Goldberg; married Dorothy Powell (an attorney), June 8, 1957; children: David Powell, Natalie Pauline. *Education:* Brooklyn College (now Brooklyn College of the City University of New York), B.A., 1953; University of New Mexico, M.A., 1956; University of Pennsylvania, Ph.D., 1965. *Home:* 1637 Mountain Ave., Claremont, Calif. 91711. *Office:* Department of Political Science, California State University—Los Angeles, Los Angeles, Calif. 90032.

CAREER: University of Pennsylvania, Philadelphia, instructor in political science, 1956-59; University of New Mexico, Albuquerque, visiting assistant professor of political science, 1959-60; San Diego State University, San Diego, Calif., visiting assistant professor of political science, 1960-61; California State University, Los Angeles, assistant professor, 1961-66, associate professor, 1966-70, professor of political science, 1970—, chairman of department, 1972—, assistant dean for graduate studies of School of Letters and Science, 1968-70. Associate research political scientist, Institute of Government Affairs of University of California, Davis, 1966-67; member of board of directors, Urban Affairs Institute, 1967-73; educational research associate, Fels Institute of Local and State Government at University of Pennsylvania, 1968-69; project coordinator, Municipal Information Systems Confidentiality Project at Claremont Graduate School, 1971-72; visiting professor, University of Southern California, spring, 1974; consultant to various governmental agencies. *Military service:* U.S. Army, Adjutant Generals Corps, 1953-55.

MEMBER: American Political Science Association, Western Political Science Association (member of executive council, 1974-76), Law and Society Association, Policy Studies Organization, Women's Caucus for Political Science, Southern California Political Science Association (member of executive council, 1970-72; vice-president, 1972-73; president, 1973-74), Phi Kappa Phi, Pi Gamma Mu, Pi Sigma Alpha.

WRITINGS: The County Commission in New Mexico (monograph), Division of Government Research, University of New Mexico, 1962; (with others) *Reapportionment in California* (monograph), Assembly of California Legislature, 1965; (with Douglas S. Hobbs) *Courts and Legislatures: A Survey of Legislative Reapportionment* (monograph), Assembly Committee on Elections and Reapportionment (Sacramento, Calif.), 1965; (contributor) Harold Sackman and Barry Boehm, editors, *Planning Community Information Utilities*, American Federation of Information Processing Societies Press, 1972; *Privacy Problems in Municipal Information Systems* (monograph), Municipal Systems Research, Claremont Graduate School, 1972; (contributor) Robert K. Yin, editor, *The City in the Seventies*, F. E. Peacock, 1972; (with O. E. Dial) *Privacy, Security, and Computers: Guidelines for Municipal and Other Public Information Systems*, Praeger, 1975. Contributor to journals in his field.

* * *

GOLDBERG, Steven 1941-

PERSONAL: Born October 14, 1941, in New York, N.Y.; son of I. J. and Claire (Brown) Goldberg. *Education:* Ricker College, B.A., 1965; graduate study at University of Toronto, 1967-68; University of New Brunswick, M.A., 1968. *Religion:* Jewish. *Home:* 205 East 78th St., New York, N.Y. 10021. *Office:* Department of Sociology, City College of the City University of New York, New York, N.Y. 10031.

CAREER: City College of the City University of New York, New York, N.Y., instructor in sociology, 1970—. *Military service:* U.S. Marine Corps, 1963-69. *Member:* American Sociological Association.

WRITINGS: The Inevitability of Patriarchy, Morrow, 1973. Contributor to *Psychiatry*, *Ethics*, *Yale Review*, *American Anthropologist*, and *Saturday Review*.

WORK IN PROGRESS: An examination of the logical connections between social values and laws.

BIOGRAPHICAL/CRITICAL SOURCES: Commentary, December, 1973.

* * *

GOLDFEDER, (Anne) Cheryl 1949-
(Zan Paz)

PERSONAL: Born January 29, 1949, in Ypsilanti, Mich.; daughter of Morris (a businessman) and Shirley (Bender) McConnell; married Kenneth James Goldfeder (a consultant for programs for the deaf), August 27, 1969. *Education:* Attended Ringling Art School; University of Tennessee, B.A., 1972. *Religion:* Jewish. *Home:* 1611 Laurel Ave., #807, Knoxville, Tenn. 37916. *Office:* Knoxville County Library, Church St., Knoxville, Tenn.

CAREER: Knoxville County Library, Knoxville, Tenn., technical assistant. Illustrator, writer, teacher. Poster designs are on display in the United States and abroad. *Member:* Society of Children's Book Writers, International

Association of Parents of the Deaf, National Association of the Deaf, National Association of the Deaf and Mute in Israel, National Congress of Jewish Deaf. *Awards, honors:* First place in design from Jewish Agency in Israel, 1974, for a poster design made for World Union of Jewish Students Institute.

WRITINGS—Self-illustrated: (With husband, Jim Goldfeder) *The Girl Who Wouldn't Talk*, National Association of the Deaf, 1975.

WORK IN PROGRESS—For children: *Robin Sees a Song*, with Jim Goldfeder; *Animals on the Move* and *Right As Can Be*, both under pseudonym Zan Paz, with Jim Goldfeder, who uses pseudonym A. Paz.

SIDELIGHTS: Cheryl Goldfeder, with her husband, Jim Goldfeder, is an advocate of the "total communication" method of educating deaf children. She writes: "Everywhere there are children . . . [who] despite all of the wishes of parents, and the expectations of teachers . . . do not develop communication skills through auditory channels. But communication . . . is the key word. It is communication . . . that makes a small world larger—and, if communication cannot be achieved auditorily, then there is still another way: the language of signs and the manual alphabet."

BIOGRAPHICAL/CRITICAL SOURCES: Tennessee Alumnus, Vol. 55, No. 2, spring, 1975; *Deaf American*, April, 1975.

* * *

GOLDFEDER, (Kenneth) James 1943- (Jim Goldfeder; A. Paz)

PERSONAL: Born September 11, 1943, in Chattanooga, Tenn.; son of Abraham (a physician) and Katherine (Suggs) Goldfeder; married Cheryl McConnel (a writer), August 27, 1969. *Education:* Ohio Wesleyan University, student, 1961-63; Tennessee Temple College, B.A., 1967; University of Tennessee, M.S., 1972, M.P.H., 1975, Ph.D. candidate, 1975. *Religion:* Jewish. *Home:* 1611 Laurel Ave., Apt. 807, Knoxville, Tenn. 37916. *Office:* School of Health, Physical Education, and Recreation, University of Tennessee, Knoxville, Tenn. 37916.

CAREER: Comprehensive Service for the Deaf, Nashville, Tenn., director, 1973-74; Tennessee School for the Deaf, Knoxville, coordinator of Title I projects, 1973-74, University of Tennessee, Knoxville, teaching assistant in public health, 1974—. Member of Tennessee Registry of Interpreters for the Deaf. *Member:* International Association of Parents of the Deaf, National Association of the Deaf, National Association of the Deaf and Mute in Israel, National Association of Hearing and Speech Agencies, Professional Rehabilitation Workers with Adult Deaf, Convention of American Instructors of the Deaf, Alexander Graham Bell Association for the Deaf, Congress of Jewish Deaf, American Public Health Association, Tennessee Registry of Interpreters for the Deaf. *Awards, honors:* Certificate of community service from Chattanooga Area Council on Alcoholism and Other Substance Abuse.

WRITINGS—Under name Jim Goldfeder: (With wife, Cheryl Goldfeder) *The Girl Who Wouldn't Talk*, National Association of the Deaf, 1975. Contributor to professional journals. Author of "Tennessee Talk," a monthly column in *Silent News*, 1975—.

WORK IN PROGRESS—For children: *Robin Sees a Song*, under name Jim Goldfeder, with Cheryl Goldfeder; *Animals on the Move* and *Right As Can Be*, under pseudonym A. Paz, with Cheryl Goldfeder, who uses pseudonym Zan Paz.

* * *

GOLDKNOPF, David 1918-

PERSONAL: Surname has silent "k" and "p"; born October 16, 1918, in Bethleham, Pa.; son of Israel (a salesman) and Lena (Widrowitz) Goldknopf; married Irma Galef (a college professor), May 30, 1941; children: Emily. *Education:* New York University, B.S., 1938; Syracuse University, M.A., 1964, Ph.D., 1969. *Politics:* "On the side of the angels." *Religion:* Jewish. *Home:* 2 Millrock Rd., New Paltz, N.Y. 12561. *Office:* Department of English, State University of New York College at New Paltz, New Paltz, N.Y. 12561.

CAREER: Technical writer for electronics firms, 1952-61; free-lance fiction writer, 1961-63; State University of New York College at New Paltz, instructor in English, 1968-69; Bennett College, Millbrook, N.Y., assistant professor of English, 1969-71; State University of New York College at New Paltz, associate professor of English, 1971—. *Military service:* U.S. Army Air Forces, 1942-46; became first lieutenant. *Member:* Modern Language Association of America. *Awards, honors:* First prize in essay contest of English Institute, 1969.

WRITINGS: Hills on the Highway (novel), Harper, 1949; *Life of the Novel*, University of Chicago Press, 1972. Contributor to literature journals.

WORK IN PROGRESS: O Lord Thou Pluckest Me Out, a novel; a collection of short stories; continuing research on D. H. Lawrence.

SIDELIGHTS: Goldknopf writes that he ". . . fled to academic life rather late in my own life and with a lingering sense of guilt, but without real regrets. As an environment, academia is dreadful—morally demeaning—for a writer, but it is possible to insulate oneself against it." *Avocational interests:* Travel (East Africa, Morocco, Bulgaria, Turkey).

* * *

GOLDMAN, Bernard 1922-

PERSONAL: Born May 30, 1922, in Toronto, Ontario, Canada; son of Benjamin and Lillian (Cohen) Goldman; married Norma Wynick, August 1, 1944; children: Mark David. *Education:* University of Michigan, Ph.D., 1959. *Home:* 6239 Eastmoor, Birmingham, Mich. 48010. *Office:* Wayne State University Press, Detroit, Mich. 48202.

CAREER: Wayne State University, Detroit, Mich., associate professor, 1960-64, professor of art history, 1964—, director of Wayne State University Press, 1974—. *Military service:* U.S. Army Air Forces, 1943-45.

WRITINGS: Sacred Portal, Wayne State University Press, 1966; *Reading and Writing in the Arts*, Wayne State University Press, 1972. Contributor to *Catholic Encyclopedia, Encyclopedia Judaica, Collier's Encyclopedia, Artibus Asiae, Natural History, Berytus, Ars Orientalis, Journal of Near Eastern Studies, American Journal of Archaeology, Ipek, Iranica Antiqua, Art Quarterly*, and *Criticism*.

* * *

GOLDMAN, Charles R(emington) 1930-

PERSONAL: Born November 9, 1930, in Urbana, Ill.; son of Marcus Seldon and Olive (Remington) Goldman; married Shirley Ann Aldous (a mathematics teacher), April 4,

1953; children: Christopher Seldon (deceased), Margaret Blanche, Olivia Remington, Anne Aldous. *Education:* University of Illinois, B.A., 1952, M.S., 1955; University of Michigan, Ph.D., 1958. *Home:* 2094 Alta Loma, Davis, Calif. 95616. *Office:* Division of Environmental Studies, University of California, Davis, Calif. 95616.

CAREER: Assistant aquatic biologist with Illinois Natural History Survey, 1954-55; fishery research biologist with U.S. Fish and Wildlife Service in Alaska, 1957-58; University of California, Davis, instructor, 1958-60, assistant professor, 1960-63, associate professor, 1964-66, professor of zoology, 1966-71, professor of limnology, 1971—, director of Institute of Ecology, 1966-69, research limnologist at Institute, 1971—. Member of California Assembly Science and Technology Advisory Council, 1970-73; member of California Solid Waste Management Board, 1973—; consultant to United Nations, Environmental Protection Agency, National Water Commission, and President's Science Advisory Council. *Military service:* U.S. Air Force, 1952-54; became captain.

MEMBER: International Society of Theoretical and Applied Limnology, American Society of Limnology and Oceanography (president, 1964-68), Ecological Society of America (vice-president, 1973-74), American Association for the Advancement of Science (fellow), California Academy of Sciences (fellow; member of water pollution delegation to the Soviet Union, 1973), Sigma Xi. *Awards, honors:* National Science Foundation senior fellowship, 1964; Guggenheim fellowship, 1965; Antarctic Service Medal, 1968. In 1967, Goldman Glacier in Antarctica was named after the author.

WRITINGS: (Editor) *Primary Productivity in Aquatic Environments*, University of California Press, 1966; (editor with James McEvoy and Peter Richerson) *Environmental Quality and Water Development*, W. H. Freeman, 1973. Contributor of more than a hundred articles to scientific journals. Member of editorial board of American Society of Limnology and Oceanography, 1964-67, and Ecological Society of America, 1966-68.

WORK IN PROGRESS: Limnology, a textbook, for McGraw; monographs on Tahoe and Castle Lake; evaluating influence of reservoirs on tropical and semi-tropical environments.

* * *

GOLDNER, Orville (Charles) 1906-

PERSONAL: Born May 18, 1906, in Toledo, Ohio; son of William Charles and Emma (Schramm) Goldner; married Dorothy Thompson (an artist), October, 1925; children: Janet, Maxine. *Education:* Attended California College of Arts and Crafts, 1924-25; Stanford University, M.A., 1954. *Home and office:* Rt. 4, Box 414D, Chico, Calif. 95926.

CAREER: Worked in Hollywood, Calif. as a technician, designer, and creator of animated films and special effects, 1928-41; worked in New York, N.Y., with International Film Foundation and Curriculum Films as a producer of educational and documentary films and filmstrips in U.S., Europe, and the Middle East, 1946-52; worked with Technical Media Section of Mutual Security Agency, Paris, France, 1952-54; director of Audio-Visual Center and instructor in educational media courses at San Francisco State University, 1954-60; worked as audio-visual director and picture editor for Columbia Broadcasting System "Panorama" program, 1960-62; professor of mass communications and director of Audio- Visual Center at California State University, Chico, 1962-70; independent film producer and researcher, 1970—. Taught special courses at Stanford University, California State University, Sacramento, University of California at Davis, University of Colorado, University of Eastern Kentucky, American University, and California State College, Sonoma. Consultant to Pacific Telephone, Polaroid Corp., and Science Research Associates. *Military service:* U.S. Navy, 1942-46; head of Training Film and Motion Picture Branch; received Navy Commendation Ribbon for film work. *Member:* Society of Motion Picture and Television Engineers, University Film Producers Association, National Education Association, California Teachers Association, International Rotary, Town Hall Club (New York), Phi Delta Kappa. *Awards, honors:* Member of Order of the British Empire, 1946.

WRITINGS: (Contributor) Godfrey Elliot, editor, *Films in Education*, Philosophical Library, 1947; (with George Turner) *The Production of King Kong*, A. S. Barnes, 1975. Contributor to *Education Leadership*, *Business Screen*, *Journal of the Society of Motion Picture and Television Engineers*, and other educational and technical journals.

WORK IN PROGRESS: Research in motion picture history, designing, and print-making.

SIDELIGHTS: Goldner states: "Probably under other circumstances I might have been a full-time rancher due to an almost overwhelming drive to raise and associate with animals and birds! I have done exactly that on a number of occasions. After World War II I carried on my film work from a large farm in New York, ninety miles from Albany. I became similarly involved on return to the west in 1954. At every opportunity over the years I have raised chickens, ducks, and geese, an obsession that tends to get out of hand."

* * *

GOLDSMITH, Barbara 1931-

PERSONAL: Born May 18, 1931, in New York, N.Y.; daughter of Joseph I. (a business executive) and Evelyn (Cronson) Lubin; married C. Gerald Goldsmith, February 14, 1954 (divorced, 1970); children: Andrew Lubin, Alice Clare, John Joseph. *Education:* Wellesley College, B.A., 1953; Columbia University, M.A., 1956. *Home:* 655 Park Ave., New York, N.Y. 10021. *Agent:* Lynn Nesbit, International Creative Management, 40 West 57th St., New York, N.Y.

CAREER: Woman's Home Companion, New York, N.Y., entertainment editor, 1954-57; *Herald Tribune*, New York, art writer for New York section, 1966-68; *New York* Magazine, New York, founding and contributing editor, and writer, 1969-72; *Harpers Bazaar*, New York, senior editor, 1970-74, editorial advisor. Founder of center for research and treatment of dyslectic children at Kennedy Center, New York. Consultant to Hearst Corp. Trustee, Parks Council; member of Junior Council, Museum of Modern Art, 1954-71, Friends of the Whitney Museum, and President's Council of Museum of the City of New York. *Awards, honors:* Penney-Missouri journalism awards, 1966, 1971; *New York Times* outstanding magazine article award, 1969.

WRITINGS: The Straw Man (novel), Farrar, Straus, 1975. Writing is included in anthology, *The New Journalists*, edited by Tom Wolfe, Farrar, Straus, 1973. Writer of Lauren Bacall special for CBS, 1968. Author of column, "Barbara Goldsmith 'On Film,'" *Harpers Bazaar*, 1969-

72. Contributor to *McCall's, Queen, Esquire*, and other periodicals. Former editor, *Town and Country*.

WORK IN PROGRESS: A novel.

* * *

GOLDSTEIN, Israel 1896-

PERSONAL: Born June 18, 1896, in Philadelphia, Pa.; son of David (a sexton) and Fanny (Silver) Goldstein; married Bertha Markowitz, July 21, 1918; children: Avram, Vivian (Mrs. Paul Olum). *Education:* University of Pennsylvania, B.A., 1914; Columbia University, M.A., 1917; Jewish Theological Seminary of America, rabbi, 1918. *Politics:* Liberal Party of New York. *Home:* 12 Pinsker St., Jerusalem, Israel.

CAREER: Ordained rabbi, 1918; Congregation B'nai Jeshurun, New York, N.Y., rabbi, 1918-61, rabbi emeritus, 1961—. President, Jewish Conciliation Board of America, 1930-68, honorary president, 1969—; delegate to World Zionist Congress, 1935-61; member, National Labor Relations Board, 1935; president, Albert Einstein Foundation of Higher Learning, Inc., 1946; founder, Brandeis University, 1946; president, World Confederation of General Zionists, 1947-56, co-chairman, 1956-72, honorary president, 1972—; United Jewish Appeal, national co-chairman, 1947-48, member of national cabinet and co-chairman of New York Campaign, 1951—; president, Jewish Restitution Successor Organization, 1950—; chairman of Western Hemisphere Executives, United Jewish Congress, 1950-59; first chairman, Amidar Israel National Housing Co., 1950; member of board of governors, Hebrew University of Jerusalem, 1950—, and Haifa University, 1970—; member of executive committee, Weizmann Institute of Science, Rehovot, Israel, 1950—; Israel Bond Drive, member of board of governors, 1951—, chairman of New York executive committee, 1951-61; council member, National Bank of Israel, 1953—; vice-president, Conference of Jewish Organizations on Material Claims against Germany and Austria, 1953-61; chairman, Israel's Tenth Anniversary Celebration in the United States, 1958; world chairman, Keren Hayesed United Israel Appeal, 1961-71; president, World Association of Hebrew Union, 1963-73; chairman, Jerusalem Artists House, 1965-70; chairman of Jerusalem Council, Israel-American Friendship League, 1969-74; chairman, World Bible Center, Jerusalem, 1973—; member of board of directors, Israel Philharmonic Orchestra, 1965-71; president, New York Board of Jewish Ministers, 1926-28; member of commission on immigration and naturalization, Department of Labor, 1921; member, Citizens Committee on Unemployment Relief, 1930-33; public representative, U.S. Department of Labor, 1935-40. Lecturer at Jewish Theological Seminary of America, 1928; professor, University of Judaism, 1954.

MEMBER: World Jewish Congress (honorary vice-president, 1959—), World Zionist Organization (former treasurer), American Jewish Congress (president, 1951-58; honorary president, 1958—), American Jewish Historical Society, Jewish Academy of Arts and Sciences, Zionist Organization of America (president, 1943-45), Synagogue Council of America (past president), Young Judea (past president), Jewish Agency of Executives (treasurer, 1949-50), Americans and Canadians in Israel (honorary president, 1961—), Israel Interfaith Commission (honorary president, 1970—), American Liberal Party (honorary vice-chairman, 1950-60), Phi Beta Kappa. *Awards, honors:* D.H.L., 1927, and D.D., 1945, Jewish Theological Seminary of America; L.H.D., Brandeis University, 1958; LL.D., New York University, 1961; D.H.L. from Chicago College of Jewish Studies, 1961, Dropsie University, 1971, and Gratz College, 1973; Ph.D., Hebrew University of Jerusalem, 1971. The following have been named in honor of Goldstein: Children's Nursing Home, by British War Relief Society, England; Children's Home, Lyon, France; Immigrant's Hostel, Tel Aviv, Israel; Youth Village, Jerusalem, 1950; tract of land in Israel, by Jewish National Fund of America; Hebrew University of Jerusalem Synagogue, 1956; chair in practical theology, Jewish Theological Seminary of America, 1958; chair in history of Zionism and modern Israel, Hebrew University of Jerusalem, 1967.

WRITINGS: A Century of Judaism in New York, 1825-1925, Congregation B'nai Jeshurun, 1930; *Toward a Solution*, Putnam, 1940; *Mourners Devotions*, Bloch, 1946; *Brandeis University: Chapter of Its Founding*, Bloch, 1951; *American Jewry Comes of Age*, Bloch, 1956; *Transition Years*, Rubin Mass (Jerusalem), 1963; *Israel at Home and Abroad*, Rubin Mass, 1972. Also author of *Shana b'Yisrael* (title means "A Year in Israel"), 1949. Contributor to *Encyclopaedia Britannica Yearbook, Universal Jewish Encyclopedia*, and *Encyclopedia Hebraica*.

WORK IN PROGRESS: Jewish Juridical Autonomy, completion expected in 1976.

BIOGRAPHICAL/CRITICAL SOURCES: H. Schneiderman, editor, *Two Generations in Perspective*, Monde Publications, 1957.

* * *

GOLDSTEIN, Philip 1910-

PERSONAL: Born May 3, 1910, in New York, N.Y.; son of Harry (in needle trades) and Sarah (Wolinsky) Goldstein; married Margaret Garber, March 26, 1939; children: Joel, Richard, Vida. *Education:* City College (now City College of the City University of New York), B.A., 1930, M.S. (education), 1937; New Mexico Highlands University, M.S. (natural science), 1961. *Politics:* Democrat. *Religion:* Jewish. *Home and office:* 3000 Marcos Dr., Miami, Fla. 33160.

CAREER: High school teacher of biology in public schools of New York, N.Y., 1931-68, and chairman of department of biology at Abraham Lincoln High School, 1949-68. Lecturer in biology, City College (now City College of the City University of New York), 1942-48; assistant examiner for New York City Board of Examiners, 1949-68; lecturer in methods of teaching science, Brooklyn College of the City University of New York, 1962-64. *Member:* National Association of Science Writers, National Association of Biology Teachers (charter member), National Association of Science Teachers, New York Association of Biology Teachers.

WRITINGS: Genetics Is Easy, Garlan, 1947, 4th edition, Lantern Press, 1967; *Practical Biology Workbook,* Van Nostrand, 1949; *How to Do an Experiment,* Harcourt, 1957; *Teacher's Manual to Accompany Exploring Biology,* Harcourt, 1961; (with others) *Biological Investigations for Secondary School Students,* Volumes I and II, Doubleday, 1963; *Triumphs of Biology,* Doubleday, 1965; (with Alvin Nason) *Biology: Introduction to Life,* and teacher's manual with Gabrielle Edwards, Addison Wesley, 1969; *Wonders of Parasites,* Lantern Press, 1969; (with Jerome Metzner) *Experiments with Microscopic Animals,* Doubleday, 1971; *Animals and Plants That Trap,* Holiday House, 1974.

Series of books: "Wonders of Life," Doubleday, Volume V: *Animal Tissues,* Volume VI: *The Skin: A Jack of All Trades,* Volume VII: *The Matter of Digestion,* Volume VIII: *Blood and Circulation,* Volume IX: *Behavior: Responding to the Environment,* Volume X: *The Nervous System: Sensation, Communication, Response,* Volume XI: *The Hormones: Chemical Control of Coordination,* Volume XII: *Respiration: The Release of Energy* (Goldstein was not associated with earlier volumes), 1963-64; "Textfolders in Biology," National Teaching Aids, Volume 67: *The Digestive System,* Volume 68: *The Circulatory System,* Volume 69: *The Central Nervous System,* Volume 70: *The Reflex Arc,* Volume 71: *The Endocrine System,* Volume 72: *The Respiratory System,* Volume 73: *Smoking and Health,* Volume 74: *Parasitism: A Way of Life,* Volume 75: *Animal Parasites of Man,* Volume 76: *The Hydra,* Volume 77: *Roots of a Flowering Plant,* Volume 78: *Stem of a Flowering Plant,* Volume 79: *Leaf of a Flowering Plant,* Volume 80: *Flower of a Flowering Plant,* Volume 81: *Non-Green Plants and Heterotrophic Nutrition,* Volume 82: *Green Plants and Autotrophic Nutrition,* Volume 83: *Chromosomes and Genes in Action,* Volume 84: *Life Cycle of the Fern,* Volume 85: *Life Cycle of Aurelia,* Volume 86: *Life Cycle of Obelia,* Volume 87: *Life Cycle of Marchantia,* Volume 88: *Life Cycle of Moss,* Volume 89: *Air Pollution and Human Health,* Volume 90: *Air Pollution and Plant Health,* Volume 91: *Measurement under the Microscope,* Volume 94: *Venereal Disease,* Volume 97: *Viruses* (Goldstein was not associated with other volumes in the series), 1964-74; "The Inquirers," National Teaching Aids, Volume I: *Anthony Van Leeuwenhoek,* Volume II: *Louis Pasteur,* Volume III: *Andreas Vesalius,* Volume IV: *Lazzaro Spallanzani,* Volume V: *Charles Darwin,* Volume VI: *Joseph Lister,* Volume VII: *William Harvey,* Volume VIII: *Edward Jenner,* Volume IX: *Robert Koch,* 1964-66.

Contributor to *World Book Encyclopedia* and *Grolier's Book of Popular Science.* Contributor to professional journals, including *Science Education, Science Perspectives, High Points, American Biology Teacher, Teaching Biologist,* and *New York State Conservationist.* Associate editor, *American Biology Teacher* and *Teaching Biologist.*

WORK IN PROGRESS: A series of folios.

* * *

GOMBRICH, E(rnst) H(ans Josef) 1909-

PERSONAL: Born March 30, 1909, in Vienna, Austria; son of Karl B. (a lawyer) and Leonie (a pianist; maiden name, Hock) Gombrich; married Ilse Heller, 1936; children: one son. *Education:* Attended Theresianum, Vienna; received M.A. from Oxford University and Cambridge University; Vienna University, Ph.D. *Home:* 19 Briardale Gardens, London N.W.3, England. *Office:* Warburg Institute, University of London, London, England.

CAREER: University of London, Warburg Institute, London, England, research assistant, 1936-39, senior research fellow, 1946-48, lecturer, 1948-54, reader, 1954-56, special lecturer, 1956-59, professor of history of classical tradition, 1959—, director of Institute, 1959—. Slade Professor of Fine Arts at Oxford University, 1950-53, and at Cambridge University, 1961-63; Durning-Lawrence Professor of the History of Art, University College, University of London, 1956-59; visiting professor, Harvard University, 1959; Lethaby Professor, Royal College of Art, 1967-68; Andrew D. White Professor-at-large, Cornell University, 1970. Served with BBC Monitoring Service, 1939-45.

MEMBER: British Academy (fellow), Society of Antiquaries (fellow), Royal Society of Literature (fellow), Royal Institute of British Architects (fellow), American Academy of Arts and Sciences, American Philosophical Society, Accademia delle Scienze de Torino (corresponding member), Royal Academy of Arts and Sciences (Uppsala; corresponding member), Royal Netherlands Academy of Arts and Sciences. *Awards, honors:* Honorary fellow, Royal College of Art, 1961, Jesus College, Cambridge University, 1963; W. H. Smith Literary Award, 1964; Commander, Order of the British Empire, 1966; New York University medal for distinguished visitors, 1970; Knighted, 1972. Honorary degrees: D.Litt., Belfast, 1963, University of Leeds, 1965, Oxford University, 1969, Cambridge University, 1970; LL.D., St. Andrews College, 1965.

WRITINGS: (With Ernst Kris) *Caricature,* Penguin Books, 1940; *The Story of Art,* Phaidon, 1950, 12th edition, revised and enlarged, 1972; *Raphael's Madonna della sedia,* Oxford University Press, 1956; *Lessing,* Oxford University Press, 1957; (editor) *Essays in Honor of Hans Tietze, 1880-1954,* Gazette des Beaux-Arts (Paris), 1958.

Art and Illusion: A Study in the Art of Pictorial Representation, Pantheon, 1960, 3rd edition, Phaidon, 1968; *The Cartoonist's Armory,* Duke University Press, 1963; *Meditation on a Hobby Horse, and Other Essays on the Theory of Art,* Phaidon, 1963, 2nd edition, 1971; *Norm and Form: Studies in the Art of the Renaissance,* Phaidon, 1966, 2nd edition, 1971; *In Search of Cultural History,* Oxford University Press, 1969.

(With others) *Perception and Reality,* Johns Hopkins Press, 1972; *Symbolic Images: Studies in the Art of the Renaissance,* Phaidon, 1972. Also author of *Weltgeschichte fuer Kinder,* 1936, and *Aby Warburg: An Intellectual Biography,* 1970. Contributor to learned journals.

SIDELIGHTS: Although opinion is divided as to whether Gombrich's writing is aimed more at the academic world than at the layman, he is generally recognized as a learned and judicious scholar of art history, having united, in Quentin Bell's estimation, "enormous erudition with fine gifts of historical imagination." Bell continues: "Professor Gombrich is not a stylist . . . but he is something better, he is a great teacher, extremely anxious to be understood and painstakingly clear; he feels and communicates a passionate interest in what he is saying. He is so much in earnest that he can lead us from historical detective work, of a kind that is guaranteed to engage the interest of any reader, to discussions of a more philosophical character, which are by no means easy, and yet he makes them easy. He is perhaps the most thoughtful of art historians. Certainly he is the most enjoyable."

A *Yale Review* writer further estimates that Gombrich, "almost single-handedly, is releasing the discipline of art history from certain grave difficulties deeply embedded, on the one hand, in the semantics of Woelfflin, and, on the other, in the increasingly hairy questions surrounding the identification of stylistic categories. Although he does not produce a needle from each haystack, he is surely on the right track in telling us which haystacks to avoid and which to search more thoroughly."

* * *

GOMEZ, Rudolph 1930-

PERSONAL: Born July 17, 1930, in Rawlins, Wyo.; son of Jesus Jose (a laborer) and Guadalupe (Navarro) Gomez; married Polly Petty (a teacher), November 11, 1956; children: Robert M., Clay P. *Education:* Utah State University, B.S., 1959; Stanford University, M.A., 1960; University of Colorado, Ph.D., 1963. *Religion:* Roman Catholic. *Office:* Graduate School, University of Texas, El Paso, Tex. 79968.

CAREER: Colorado College, Colorado Springs, instructor, 1962-64, assistant professor of political science, 1964-68; University of Denver, Denver, Colo., associate professor of political science, 1968-70; Memphis State University, Memphis, Tenn., associate professor of political science, 1970-72; University of Texas, El Paso, professor of political science, 1972—, chairman of department, 1973-74, graduate dean, 1974—. Fulbright-Hays visiting senior professor at Catholic University of Peru, 1967; member of board of directors of Southwest Ethnic Studies Center, 1972—. *Military service:* U.S. Air Force, 1950-54; served in Korea; became staff sergeant.

MEMBER: American Political Science Association, American Association of University Professors, American Civil Liberties Union (Texas unit), Western Political Science Association. *Awards, honors:* Woodrow Wilson fellowship, 1959-60.

WRITINGS: (With Curtis Martin) *Colorado Government and Politics*, Pruett, 1963, revised edition, 1972; *The Peruvian Administrative System*, University of Colorado Press, 1969; (contributor) Frank Jonas, editor, *Politics in the American West*, University of Utah Press, 1969; *State Public Finance in Tennessee*, Memphis State University Press, 1971; (editor) *The Changing Mexican American*, Pruett, 1972; (general editor with Clement Cottingham, Jr., Russell Endo, and Kathleen Jacobson) *The Social Reality of Ethnic America*, Heath, 1974. Contributor to professional journals.

WORK IN PROGRESS: Politics of the Southwest.

* * *

GOODMAN, Felicitas D(aniels) 1914-

PERSONAL: Born January 30, 1914, in Budapest, Hungary; came to United States, 1947; naturalized citizen, 1950; daughter of Nikolaus (an industrial manager) and Maria (Uhlig) Daniels; married Glenn H. Goodman (a university professor), March 27, 1937 (divorced, 1967); children: Nicolas D., Frederick K., Susan V. (Mrs. John Josephson), Beatrice Emm. *Education:* University of Heidelberg, diploma (translating and interpreting), 1936; Ohio State University, M.A., 1968, Ph.D., 1971. *Residence:* Columbus, Ohio. *Office:* Department of Sociology and Anthropology, Denison University, Granville, Ohio 43023.

CAREER: Free-lance translator, 1936—; Ohio Wesleyan University, Delaware, visiting lecturer in German, 1947-51; Battelle Memorial Institute, Columbus, Ohio, multi-lingual translator, 1951-58; American Chemical Society, Columbus, multi-lingual abstractor, 1958-64; Ohio State University, Columbus, visiting lecturer in German, 1962-68; Denison University, Granville, Ohio, assistant professor of linguistics and anthropology, 1968—. Anthropological field work in Yucatan, Mexico, 1969—. *Member:* American Anthropological Association (fellow), American Association for the Advancement of Science (fellow).

WRITINGS: Die blaue Bruecke (title means "The Blue Bridge"), Schwerdtfeger, 1947; *Speaking in Tongues: A Cross-Cultural Study of Glossolalia*, University of Chicago Press, 1972; (with Jeannette H. Henney and Esther Pressel) *Trance, Healing, and Hallucination: Three Field Studies in Religious Experience*, Wiley, 1974.

Translator from English into German: Washington Irving, *Rip Van Winkle*, Schmidt, 1948; Walter C. Reckless, *Die Kriminalitaet in den USA. and ihre Behandlung* (title means "Crime and Its Treatment in the U.S.A."), de Gruyter, 1964.

Contributor: Kurt Ruediger, editor, *Zyklische Dichtungen der Gegenwart* (title means "Modern Poetry Cycles"), Karslruher Bote, 1965; Erika Bourguignon, editor, *Religion, Altered States of Consciousness, and Social Change*, Ohio State University, 1973; Irving I. Zaretsky and Mark P. Leone, editors, *Religious Movements in Contemporary America*, Princeton University, 1975; Agenhananda Bharati, editor, *Ritual, Cults, and Shamanism*, Mouton & Co., 1975.

Contributor of about twenty articles to journals, including *Medikon, Confinia Psychiatrica, Semiotica, Journal for the Scientific Study of Religion, New Society, Psychotherapy and Psychosomatics*, and *Event*.

WORK IN PROGRESS: The Prevention of Old Age, completion expected in 1975; *Peasant Prophet of Yucatan*, 1976; *Wind in My Candle: European Women during World War II*, a collection of diaries and letters; a textbook on comparative religion, 1977.

SIDELIGHTS: Mrs. Goodman is bilingual in German and Hungarian, speaks, reads, and writes French, Spanish, Rumanian, and Maya, and translates all Germanic and Romance languages; she also knows some Russian and Navaho. She told *CA* that during the past summers she has built her own adobe home in New Mexico. *Avocational interests:* Gardening, playing the violin.

* * *

GOODMAN, Lenn Evan 1944-

PERSONAL: Born March 21, 1944, in Detroit, Mich.; son of Calvin Jerome (a consultant) and Florence (a professor of English; maiden name, Cohen) Goodman; married Madeleine Joyce Schwarzbach (a geneticist and professor of women's studies), August 29, 1965; children: Allegra, Paula. *Education:* Harvard University, B.A. (summa cum laude), 1965; Corpus Christi College, Oxford, D.Phil., 1968. *Politics:* Independent. *Religion:* Jewish. *Home:* 4138-2 Keanu St., Honolulu, Hawaii 96816. *Agent:* Gee Tee Bee, 11901 Sunset Blvd., Los Angeles, Calif. 90049. *Office:* Department of Philosophy, University of Hawaii, 2560 Campus Rd., Honolulu, Hawaii 96822.

CAREER: University of California, Los Angeles, assistant professor of philosophy and Near Eastern studies, 1968-69; University of Hawaii, Honolulu, assistant professor, 1969-74, associate professor of philosophy, 1974—. Founder and president of Congregation Sof Ma'arav, Conservative Jewish Synagogue of Honolulu, 1970-73, vice-president, 1973—. *Member:* American Philosophical Association, American Oriental Society, Middle East Studies Association. *Awards, honors:* Marshall scholar, 1965-68; Woodrow Wilson fellow, 1965; George Wise travel grant, 1974.

WRITINGS: (Translator and author of introduction and notes) *Ibn Tufayl's "Hayy Ibn Yaqzan,"* Twayne, 1972; (translator and author of introduction and notes) *Rambam: Readings in the Philosophy of Moses Maimonides,* Viking, in press; (contributor) George F. Hourani, editor, *Essays on Islamic Philosophy and Science,* State University of New York Press, in press. Contributor of about twenty-five articles and reviews to philosophy and Middle East studies journals, including *Philosophical Forum, International Journal of Middle Eastern Studies, Journal of the American Oriental Society, Studia Islamica,* and *Archiv fuer Geschichte der Philosophie.*

WORK IN PROGRESS: A philosophic reconstruction of the thought of Razi; further research on Maimonides.

* * *

GOODRICH, Norma Lorre 1917-

PERSONAL: Born May 10, 1917, in Huntington, Vt.; daughter of Charles Edmund and Edyth Annie (Riggs) Falby; married Joseph Marcel Andre Lorre, 1944; married second husband, John Hereford Howard (a businessman), 1963; children: (first marriage) Jean Joseph Lorre. *Education:* University of Vermont, B.S., 1938; University of Grenoble, Certificats, 1939; further study at University of Paris and University of Caen, 1947-53; Columbia University, Ph.D., 1965. *Religion:* Protestant. *Home:* 620 Diablo Dr., Claremont, Calif. 91711. *Office:* Scripps College, Claremont, Calif. 91711.

CAREER: High school teacher of English in Newport, Vt., 1939-43; American Villa School, Deauville-Trouville, France, director, 1947-53; Fieldston School, New York, N.Y., teacher of Latin, 1954-63; University of Southern California, Los Angeles, assistant professor, 1964-67, associate professor of French and comparative literature, 1967-71; Scripps College, Claremont, Calif., professor of French and comparative literature, 1972—, dean of faculty, 1971-72. *Member:* American Association of Teachers of French, American Association of University Professors, American Association of University Women (corporate delegate), Dante Society of America, Medieval Academy of America, Association for the Study of Dada and Surrealism, Surrealist Association, Philological Association of the Pacific Coast.

WRITINGS: The Ancient Myths, New American Library, 1960; *The Medieval Myths*, New American Library, 1961; *The Doctor and Maria Theresa* (novel), St. Martin's, 1962; *Myths of the Hero*, Orion Press, 1962; *Charles, Duke of Orleans: A Literary Biography*, Macmillan, 1963; (editor and author of introduction) Sir Thomas Malory, *Le Morte d'Arthur*, abridged edition, Washington Square Press, 1963; (compiler and translator) *The Ways of Love: Eleven Romances of Medieval France*, Beacon Press, 1964; *Charles of Orleans: A Study of Themes in His French and in His English Poetry* (doctoral thesis), Droz, 1967; *Giono: Master of Fictional Modes*, Princeton University Press, 1973. Contributor to *Grolier Encyclopedia* and *Columbia Encyclopedia*; also contributor to *Etudes Rabelaisiennes, French Review, Romanic Review*, and other journals.

WORK IN PROGRESS: A book on historical fiction, 1825-1970; a history of pastoral in world fiction; a book on Henry de Montherlant; a collection of essays on medieval paradigms; a book of lyric poetry on teaching.

SIDELIGHTS: Norma Goodrich has spent more than fifteen years in France and was, at one time, "better in French than in English."

* * *

GOODSTEIN, R(euben) L(ouis) 1912-

PERSONAL: Born December 15, 1912, in London, England; son of Alexander (a manufacturer) and Sophia (Fisher) Goodstein; married Louba Atkin, September 23, 1938; children: Peter David, Margaret Ann Sophia Goodstein Eaton. *Education:* Magdalen College, Cambridge, B.A., 1934; University of London, Ph.D., 1946, D.Lit., 1950. *Home:* 16 Clarendon Park Rd., Leicester LE2 3AD, England. *Office:* University of Leicester, Leicester, England.

CAREER: University of Reading, Reading, England, lecturer in mathematics, 1935-48; University of Leicester, Leicester, England, professor of mathematics, 1948—, dean of faculty of science, 1954-57, pro-vice-chancellor, 1966-69. *Member:* Mathematical Association (librarian, 1955—; vice-president, 1971—), Association for Symbolic Logic (member of council, 1966-69), American Mathematical Society, London Mathematical Society.

WRITINGS: Mathematical Analysis: The Uniform Calculus and Its Applications, Clarendon Press (of Oxford University), 1948; *Constructive Formalism,* University of Leicester Press, 1951, 2nd edition, 1965; *Axiomatic Projective Geometry,* University of Leicester Press, 1953, 2nd edition, 1962; *Mathematical Logic,* University of Leicester Press, 1957, 3rd edition, 1965; *Recursive Number Theory,* North-Holland Publishing Co., 1957; *Recursive Analysis,* North-Holland Publishing Co., 1961; *Fundamental Concepts of Mathematica,* Pergamon, 1962; *Boolean Algebra,* Pergamon, 1963; *Essays in the Philosophy of Mathematics,* University of Leicester Press, 1965; *Complex Functions,* McGraw, 1965; *Development of Mathematical Logic,* Logos International, 1971.

Contributor to mathematics journals in Great Britain, Germany, Scandinavia, and the United States, including *Journal of the London Mathematical Society, Journal of Symbolic Logic, American Journal of Mathematics, Transactions of the American Mathematical Society, Mathematical Gazette,* and *Fundamenta Mathematicae.* Editor of *Mathematical Gazette,* 1956-62; consulting editor for McGraw of England, 1961-70.

WORK IN PROGRESS: Mathematical Analysis; research on mathematical logic and the philosophy of mathematics.

AVOCATIONAL INTERESTS: Travel (Europe, United States, Australia, New Zealand).

* * *

GORDEN, Raymond L(owell) 1919-

PERSONAL: Born February 21, 1919, in St. Louis, Mo.; son of Zan Welby and Samma Myrtle (McCroskey) Gorden; married Olga Charlotte Gilson (a teacher), September 2, 1949; children: Gregory Alan, Karen Aileen. *Education:* Attended University of California, Los Angeles, 1939-41; University of Chicago, M.A., 1949, Ph.D., 1954. *Home:* 1302 Shawnee Dr., Yellow Springs, Ohio 45387. *Office:* Department of Sociology, Antioch College, Yellow Springs, Ohio 45387.

CAREER: Antioch College, Yellow Springs, Ohio, assistant professor, 1954-57, associate professor, 1957-63, professor of sociology, 1963—. Director of cross-cultural communication project in Bogota, Colombia, for U.S. Office of Education, 1967-69. *Member:* International Education Association, American Sociological Association, Great Lakes College Association (director of Latin America program, 1963-65).

WRITINGS: Living in Latin America, National Textbook Corp., 1974; *Interviewing: Strategy, Techniques, and Tactics*, Dorsey, 1969, revised edition, 1975. Contributor to *American Journal of Sociology, Journal of Social Psychology*, and *American Sociological Review*.

WORK IN PROGRESS: Minidramas on Cross Cultural Communication; *Scaling in the Social Sciences*, completion expected in 1976; *Poverty and Social Services*, 1977.

SIDELIGHTS: Gorden has traveled in sixteen Latin American countries, and lived there for more than three years.

* * *

GORDIN, Richard Davis 1928-

PERSONAL: Born July 16, 1928, in South Charleston, Ohio; son of Edwin R. and Mildred (Davis) Gordin; married Paula Egan, July 23, 1949; children: Richard Davis II, Robert H., Douglas P. *Education:* Ohio Wesleyan University, B.A., 1952; Ohio State University, M.A., 1954, Ph.D., 1967. *Religion:* Methodist. *Home:* 80 Hillside Dr., Delaware, Ohio 43015. *Office:* Department of Physical Education, Ohio Wesleyan University, Delaware, Ohio 43015.

CAREER: Ohio Wesleyan University, Delaware, instructor, 1954-59, assistant professor, 1959-67, associate professor, 1967-71, professor of physical education, 1971—, golf coach, 1955—, assistant athletic director, 1972—. Certified rules official by Professional Golfers' Association of America; has taught at Arnold Palmer Golf Academies and Duke University's Golf School; chairman of two divisions of National Collegiate Athletic Association's national golf tournament; consultant to National Golf Foundation. Member of Delaware City Parks and Recreation Advisory Board. *Military service:* U.S. Navy, 1946-48. *Member:* North American Society for Sport History (charter member), American Alliance for Health, Physical Education and Recreation (fellow), American Association of University Professors, National College Physical Education Association for Men, American College of Sports Medicine, Philosophic Society for the Study of Sport, Golf Coaches Association of America, Muirfield Village Golf Club (historian and archivist).

WRITINGS: (With Roderick Myers) *Golf Fundamentals*, C. E. Merrill, 1973, revised edition, 1974; *The Golf Coach* (monograph), National Golf Foundation, 1974; (editor and contributor) *Golf Coach's Guide*, National Golf Foundation, 1975. Contributor to *Golf Digest*.

WORK IN PROGRESS: A history of the Muirfield Village Golf Club.

* * *

GORDON, Esther Saranga 1935-

PERSONAL: Born March 29, 1935, in Boston, Mass.; daughter of Jacob and Fay (Barocas) Saranga; married Bernard L. Gordon (a college professor), July 19, 1959; children: Jocelyn Fay, Zimra Joy. *Education:* Boston University, A.B., 1957; Boston State College, Ed.M., 1958. *Home and office:* 20 Old Colony Rd., Chestnut Hill, Mass. 02167.

CAREER: Elementary school teacher in Ashaway, R.I., 1958-59, and Stonington, Conn., 1959-60; Boston School Department, Boston, Mass., elementary school teacher, 1961—, teacher at James A. Garfield School, 1974—. *Member:* Boston Teachers Union.

WRITINGS—For children: *There Really Was a Dodo*, Walck, 1974.

WORK IN PROGRESS: A book about passenger pigeons.

SIDELIGHTS: Esther Gordon writes to inform children about pollution, extinction, and conservation. She has traveled professionally to Paris, Moscow, and Jerusalem.

* * *

GORDON, Ethel Edison 1915-

PERSONAL: Born May 5, 1915, in New York; daughter of Abraham (a musician) and Lillian (Cohan) Edison; married Heyman Gordon (a high school principal), 1936; children: David A. *Education:* New York University, B.A. (cum laude), 1936. *Agent:* John Schaffner, 425 East 51st St., New York, N.Y. 10022.

CAREER: Writer. *Member:* Phi Beta Kappa.

WRITINGS—Novels: *Where Does the Summer Go*, Crowell Collier, 1967; *So Far from Home*, Crowell Collier, 1968; *Freer's Cove*, Coward, 1972; *The Chaperone*, Coward, 1973; *The Bird Watcher*, McKay, 1974; *The Freebody Heiress*, McKay, 1975.

Work has been anthologized in *Prize Stories of 1945*, edited by Herschel Brickell, Doubleday, Doran, 1945; *Best American Short Stories of 1951*, edited by Martha Foley, Houghton, 1951.

WORK IN PROGRESS: A Gothic novel with witchcraft for a theme.

SIDELIGHTS: Ethel Gordon's books have been published and serialized in France, England, Holland, and Germany.

* * *

GORDON, Henry Alfred 1925-
(Harry Gordon)

PERSONAL: Born November 9, 1925, in Melbourne, Australia; son of Harry and Marjorie (Keogh) Gordon; married Dorothy Mae Scott, December 7, 1951; children: Sally Anne, Michael Scott, John Matthew. *Education:* Attended University of Queensland. *Home:* 67 Mont Albert Rd., Canterbury, Victoria 3126, Australia. *Office: Herald and Weekly Times*, Melbourne, Australia.

CAREER: Reporter with *Sydney Telegraph, Brisbane Courier Mail* (both Australia), and *Straits Times* (Singapore), 1945-49; *Melbourne Sun*, Melbourne, Australia, reporter, war correspondent, and member of London bureau, 1949-68, editor, 1968-72; *Herald and Weekly Times*, Melbourne, Australia, deputy editor-in-chief, 1972—. Director of 3DB Melbourne (broadcasting station). *Military service:* Royal Air Force, member of air crew, 1943-45. *Member:* Australian Society of Authors, Fellowship of Australian Writers. *Awards, honors:* Walkley Award for journalism, 1956.

WRITINGS—Under name Harry Gordon: *Young Men in a Hurry*, Lansdowne, 1961; *The Embarrassing Australian*, Lansdowne, 1962; (with Dawn Fraser) *Below the Surface*, Morrow, 1965; *The Witnesses* (concerning the role of news reporters in Australian history), Rigby (Adelaide), 1975. Contributor to *New York Times Magazine, Reader's Digest, Bulletin,* and *National Times*.

* * *

GORDON, Leonard 1935-

PERSONAL: Born December 6, 1935, in Detroit, Mich.; son of Abraham (a businessman) and Sarah (Rosen) Gordon; married Rena Joyce Feigelman (a college academic adviser), 1955; children: Susan Melinda, Matthew Seth, Melissa Gail. *Education:* Wayne State University, B.A., 1957, jph.D., 1966; University of Michigan, M.A.,

1958. *Office:* Department of Sociology, Arizona State University, Tempe, Ariz. 85281.

CAREER: High school history teacher in Oak Park, Mich., 1957-60; Wayne State University, Detroit, Mich., instructor in sociology, 1960-62; Metropolitan Detroit Jewish Community Council, Detroit, Mich., research director, 1962-64; American Jewish Committee, New York, N.Y., Michigan area director, 1964-67; Arizona State University, Tempe, assistant professor, 1967-70, associate professor of sociology, 1970—, associate chairman of department, 1974-75. Co-secretary of Metropolitan Detroit Religion and Race Conference, 1962-67. *Member:* American Sociological Association (fellow), American Association of University Professors, Pacific Sociological Association. *Awards, honors:* National Science Foundation fellowship, 1962; Rockefeller Foundation grant, 1969-70.

WRITINGS: (Editor and contributor) *A City in Racial Crisis: Detroit Pre and Post the 1967 Riot,* W. C. Brown, 1971. Contributor of about a dozen articles and reviews to sociology journals, including *Pacific Sociological Review, American Sociological Review, Public Affairs Bulletin, Journal for the Scientific Study of Religion, Journal of Conflict Resolution,* and *Bulletin on Intergroup Relations.*

WORK IN PROGRESS: Sociology and American Social Issues.

* * *

GORDON, Sol 1923-

PERSONAL: Born June 12, 1923, in Brooklyn, N.Y.; married Judith Salzberger (a social worker); children: Josh. *Education:* University of Illinois, B.A. and M.A., both 1947; University of London, Ph.D., 1953. *Home:* 868 Ostrom Ave., Syracuse, N.Y. 13210. *Office:* Institute for Family Research and Education, 760 Ostrom Ave., Syracuse, N.Y. 13210.

CAREER: Clinical psychologist in Israel, 1948-51; Philadelphia Child Guidance Clinic, Philadelphia, Pa., chief psychologist, 1954-61; Middlesex County Mental Health Clinic, New Brunswick, N.J., chief psychologist, 1961-65; Yeshiva University, Ferkauf Graduate School of Humanities and Social Sciences, New York, N.Y., associate professor of psychology and education, and director of Project Beacon, 1965-69; high school teacher of psychology in Englewood, N.J., 1969-70; Syracuse University, Syracuse, N.Y., professor of child and family studies, director of marriage and family counseling program, and director of Institute for Family Research and Education, 1970—. Visiting lecturer at University of Pennsylvania, Newark State College, and New York University, 1961-69; visiting lecturer and consultant, Urban Studies Center and Upward Bound program, Rutgers University, 1961-69; consultant to Children's Hospital and Jewish Family Service, Philadelphia, Pa., and Headstart program in Mississippi, 1961-69. *Military service:* U.S. Army, 1942-45.

MEMBER: American Psychological Association (fellow), American Orthopsychiatric Association (fellow), American Group Psychotherapy Association, National Council on Family Relations, American Association of Sex Educators and Counselors, Sex Information and Education Council of the United States, Society for the Scientific Study of Sex, American Association of Marriage and Family Counselors. *Awards, honors:* Award from Educational Foundation for Human Sexuality, 1974.

WRITINGS: (Editor) *Pressures That Disorganize in Secondary Schools,* New Jersey Secondary Schoolteachers Association, 1966; (editor with Risa Golob) *Recreation and Socialization for the Brain-Injured Child,* New Jersey Association for Brain-Injured Children, 1966; *Facts about Sex for Today's Youth,* John Day, 1970, revised edition, 1973; *Signs: A Non-Reading Approach to Reading,* New Readers Press, 1971; *Psychology for You,* Oxford Book, 1972, 2nd edition, 1974; *Facts about VD for Today's Youth,* John Day, 1973; *Family Planning Education for Adolescents,* U.S. Government Printing Office, 1973; *The Sexual Adolescent,* Duxbury, 1973; (editor with Gertrude Williams) *Clinical Child Psychology: Current Practices and Future Perspectives,* Behavioral Publications, 1975; *Girls Are Girls and Boys Are Boys: So What's the Difference* (juvenile), John Day, 1975; *Did the Sun Shine before You Were Born?* (juvenile), Third Press, 1975; (editor) *Sexuality Today and Beyond,* Duxbury, in press; *Let's Make Sex a Household Word,* John Day, in press; *Handicapped Youth and Young Adults: A Guide to Enhancing Self-Image,* John Day, in press.

Pamphlets: *The Brain-Injured Adolescent,* New Jersey Association for Brain-Injured Children, 1964, revised edition, 1966; (with Winifred Kempton and Medora Bass) *Love, Sex, and Birth Control for the Mentally Retarded: A Guide for Parents,* Planned Parenthood Association of Southeastern Pennsylvania, 1971, revised edition, 1973; *On Being the Parent of a Handicapped Youth: A Guide to Enhance the Self-Image of Physically and Learning Disabled Adolescents and Young Adults,* New York Association for Brain-Injured Children, 1973.

Contributor: Robert Dentler and other editors, *The Urban R's,* Praeger, 1967; Paul Graubard, editor, *Children against Schools,* Follett, 1969; *The Hidden Handicap,* California Association for Neurologically Handicapped Children, 1970; B. D. Starr, editor, *The Psychology of Adjustment,* Random House, 1970; Herbert Schulberg, Frank Baker, and Sheldon Roen, editors, *Developments in Human Services,* Behavioral Publications, 1973.

Comic books—all published by Ed-U Press: "Ten Heavy Facts about Sex," 1971; "Drug Youse: A Survivor's Handbook," 1971; "VD Claptrap," 1972; "Protect Yourself from Becoming an Unwanted Parent," 1973; "Gut News," 1974; "Juice Use," 1974.

Films: "Signs," four filmstrips, with teacher's guide, Educational Activities, 1973; "Getting It Together Is Life Itself," Educational Activities, 1973. Television: "This Program Is about Sex," a series of sixty-five programs for Canadian Global Network.

Contributor of about twenty articles to education and medical journals, including *Journal of School Health, PTA, Osteopathic Physician, Changing Education, Journal of Special Education,* and *Journal of Clinical Child Psychology.*

* * *

GORHAM, J(eanne) U(rich) 1920-

PERSONAL: Born May 17, 1920, in New York, N.Y.; daughter of John F. (a businessman) and Josephine (Adams) Urich; married William A. Gorham, October 3, 1967. *Education:* Temple University, B.F.A. and B.S.Ed., 1943. *Residence:* Revere, Pa. 18953.

CAREER: Free-lance artist, 1954—.

WRITINGS: How to Hold Up the Mail (nonfiction), Greene, 1973.

WORK IN PROGRESS: A self-illustrated fantasy tentatively entitled, *Queen Zena's Farthingale.*

* * *

GORN, Janice L(eonora) 1915-

PERSONAL: Born March 23, 1915, in New York, N.Y.; daughter of Morris (an optometrist) and Emilie (an executive secretary; maiden name, Joseph) Jacoby; married Lion A. Gorn, January 18, 1940 (died November, 1943). *Education:* New York University, B.F.A., 1938, A.M., 1954, Ph.D., 1963. *Politics:* Liberal Democrat. *Religion:* Jewish. *Home:* 60 East 12th St., New York, N.Y. 10003. *Office:* School of Education, New York University, 635 East Building, Washington Sq., New York, N.Y. 10003.

CAREER: Diagnostic technician for physicians in New York, N.Y., 1939-42; Columbia University, Graduate School of Social Work, New York, N.Y., assistant registrar, 1942-55; Council on Social Work Education, New York, N.Y., chief editor and assistant to the director, 1955-58; Paterson State College, Wayne, N.J., assistant professor of history, philosophy of education, and human growth and development, 1959-61; New York University, New York, N.Y., instructor, 1961-63, assistant professor, 1963-65, associate professor, 1965-69, professor of interdisciplinary studies, 1969—. Trustee of William Hodson Community Center, 1959-60.

MEMBER: International Association of Social Workers, American Historical Association, History of Science Association, Association for Higher Education, Council on Social Work Education, American Association of University Professors, History of Education Society, Philosophy of Education Society, National Society for the Study of Education, American Association for the Advancement of Science, Smithsonian Institution, Metropolitan Museum of Art, Harry S. Truman Memorial Library, Pi Lambda Theta, Kappa Delta Pi.

WRITINGS: Style Guide for the Writing of Term Papers, Masters' Theses, and Doctoral Dissertations, Simon & Schuster, 1973. Contributor to a variety of periodicals, including *Educational Forum*, *Educational Theory*, *Saturday Review*, *Teachers College Record*, *Educational Horizons*, and *Phi Delta Kappan.*

WORK IN PROGRESS: Research on the impact of John Locke and Lord Shaftesbury on the political and philosophical bases of the U.S. Constitution and the Declaration of Independence.

* * *

GOTTSCHALK, Louis A(ugust) 1916-

PERSONAL: Born August 26, 1916, in St. Louis, Mo.; son of Max W. and Kelmie (Mutrux) Gottschalk; married Helen Reller (a dermatologist), July 24, 1944; children: Guy, Claire Gottschalk Cable, Louise, Susan. *Education:* Washington University, St. Louis, A.B., 1940, M.D., 1943; further study at Chicago Institute for Psychoanalysis, 1948-51, and Washington Psychoanalytic Institute, 1951-53. *Home:* 4607 Perham Rd., Corona Del Mar, Calif. 92625. *Office:* College of Medicine, University of California, Irvine, Calif. 92664.

CAREER: Barnes & McMillan Hospitals, St. Louis, Mo., intern, 1943-44, assistant resident, 1944-45, chief resident, 1945-46; Southwestern Medical College, Dallas, Tex., instructor in psychiatry, 1947-48; Michael Reese Hospital, Chicago, Ill., research associate at Institute of Psychosomatic Research and Training and Child Psychiatry Clinic, 1948-50, assistant chief of Child Psychiatry Clinic, 1950-51; National Institute of Mental Health, Bethesda, Md., research psychiatrist, 1951-53; University of Cincinnati, College of Medicine, Cincinnati, Ohio, associate professor, 1953-61, research professor of psychiatry, 1961-67; University of California at Irvine, professor of psychiatry and human behavior and chairman of department, College of Medicine, 1967—, professor of social science and social ecology, Division of Social Science, 1969—. Attending physician, Cincinnati General Hospital, 1953-67; training and supervising analyst, Chicago Institute for Psychoanalysis, 1957-67; supervising analyst, Southern California Psychoanalytic Institute, Los Angeles, 1974—. Director of psychiatric residency training, Orange County Medical Center and University of California at Irvine, 1967—; director of psychiatric services, Orange County Medical Center, 1971—. Member of staff, Canyon General Hospital, Anaheim; chief consultant in psychiatry, Veterans Administration Hospital, Long Beach, 1967—; committee chairman, National Institute of Drug Abuse. *Military service:* U.S. Public Health Service, 1946-53; became lieutenant commander.

MEMBER: American Psychiatric Association (fellow), American Psychosomatic Society (member of council, 1967-70), Group for the Advancement of Psychiatry, American Association for the Advancement of Science (fellow), American Psychoanalytic Association, American College of Neuropsychopharmacology (charter fellow), American College of Psychiatrists (charter fellow), American Association of Child Psychoanalysts, International College of Psychosomatic Medicine (fellow), American Association of Chairmen of Departments of Psychiatry, American Association of Directors of Psychiatric Training, Southern California Psychoanalytic Society, Southern California Psychiatric Society, Los Angeles Psychoanalytic Society, Balboa Bay Club (Newport Beach, Calif.).

AWARDS, HONORS: Honorable mention, Hofheimer Award for Research in Psychiatry, American Psychiatric Association, 1955; U.S. Public Health Service Research Career Award, National Institute of Mental Health, 1961-67; Physicians Recognition Award in continuing medical education, American Medical Association, 1969; Franz Alexander Essay Prize from Southern California Psychoanalytic Society, 1973; Distinguished Research Award, Alumni Association of University of California, Irvine, 1974.

WRITINGS: (Editor and contributor) *Comparative Psycholinguistic Analysis of Two Psychotherapeutic Interviews*, International Universities Press, 1961; (editor with Arthur H. Auerbach, and contributor) *Methods of Research in Psychotherapy*, Appleton, 1966; (with Goldine C. Gleser) *The Measurement of Psychological States Through the Content Analysis of Verbal Behavior*, University of California Press, 1969; (with Gleser and Carolyn N. Winget) *Manual of Instructions for Using the Gottschalk-Gleser Content Analysis Scales: Anxiety, Hostility, and Social Alienation-Personal Disorganization*, University of California Press, 1969; (editor with others, and contributor) *Psychosomatic Classics*, Karger, 1972; *How to Understand and Analyze Your Own Dreams*, Vantage, 1975; (author of foreword) *Emotional Crises in Children, Youth and Their Families: Emergencies in Child Psychiatry*, edited by Gilbert C. Morrison, C. C Thomas, 1975; (editor and contributor with Sidney Merlis) *Pharmacokinetics, Psychoactive*

Drug Blood Levels, and Clinical Response, Spectrum, 1975.

Contributor: *Life Stress and Bodily Disease*, Association for Research in Nervous and Mental Disease, 1950; Ruth S. Eissler and others, editors, *Psychoanalytic Study of the Child*, Volume XI, International Universities Press, 1956; Paul H. Hoch and Joseph Zubin, editors, *Psychopathology of Communication*, Grune, 1958; Leonard M. Uhr and James G. Miller, editors, *Drugs and Behavior*, Wiley, 1960; Albert D. Biderman and Herbert M. Zimmer, editors, *The Manipulation of Human Behavior*, Wiley, 1961; Charles Hofling, editor, *Textbook of Psychiatry for Medical Practice*, Lippincott, 1963, 3rd edition, 1974; *Disorders of Communication*, Williams & Wilkins, for Association for Research in Nervous and Mental Disease, 1964; J. O. Cole and J. R. Wittenborn, editors, *Pharmacotherapy of Depressions*, C. C Thomas, 1966; Kurt Salzinger and Suzanne Salzinger, editors, *Research in Verbal Behavior and Some Neurophysiological Implications*, Academic Press, 1967; Wayne Evans and N. S. Kline, editors, *Psychopharmacology of the Normal Human*, C. C Thomas, 1968; D. H. Efron and others, editors, *Psychopharmacology: A Review of Progress, 1957-1967*, U.S. Government Printing Office, 1968; Silvio Garattini and E. B. Sigg, editors, *Biology of Aggressive Behavior*, Excerpta Medica Foundation, 1968; Arnold Mandell and Mary Mandell, editors, *Methods and Theory in Psychochemical Research in Man*, Academic Press, 1969; D. V. Siva Sankar, editor, *Schizophrenic Current Concepts in Research*, PJD Publications, 1969; Robert Cancro, editor, *The Schizophrenic Syndrome*, Brunner, 1971; Harold I. Kaplan and Benjamin J. Sadock, editors, *Comparative Group Psychotherapy*, Williams & Wilkins, 1971; Robert W. Siroka, Ellen E. Siroka, and Gilbert A. Schloss, editors, *Sensitivity Training and Group Encounter*, Grosset, 1971; *Gruppendynamik und der subjektive Faktor: Repressive Entsublimierung oder politisierende Praxis*, Suhrkamp Verlag, 1972; Garattini, Emilio Mussini, and L. O. Randall, editors, *Benzodiazepenes*, Raven Press, 1973; Harvey H. Barten and Sybil S. Barten, editors, *Children and Their Families in Brief Therapy*, Behavioral Publications, 1973; Walter B. Essman and Luigi Valzelli, editors, *Current Developments in Psychopharmacology*, Spectrum, 1975; Donald Spence, editor, *Psychoanalysis and Contemporary Science*, International Universities Press, 1975.

Contributor to annual publications and yearbooks. Contributor of over one hundred articles and occasional reviews and abstracts to journals, principally medical and psychological periodicals. Member of editorial board, *Psychosomatic Medicine*, 1958-70, *Psychiatry*, 1970—, *World Journal of Psychosynthesis*, 1970—, and *American Journal of Psychotherapy*, 1975—; consulting editor, *Science*, 1960—; member of publications committee, Group for the Advancement of Psychiatry, 1966-70.

* * *

GOULD, Richard A(llan) 1939-

PERSONAL: Born October 22, 1939, in Newton, Mass.; son of Samuel Brookner (a university administrator) and Laura (Ohman) Gould; married Elizabeth Barber (an editor), December 22, 1962. *Education:* Harvard University, B.A. (cum laude), 1961; University of Chicago, graduate study, 1962; University of California, Berkeley, Ph.D., 1965. *Home:* 1548 Liholiho St., Honolulu, Hawaii 96822. *Office:* Department of Anthropology, University of Hawaii, Honolulu, Hawaii 96822.

CAREER: American Museum of Natural History, New York, N.Y., assistant curator of North American archaeology, 1965-70, associate curator, 1970-71, set up archaeological and physical anthropology laboratory; University of Hawaii, Honolulu, associate professor of anthropology, 1971—. Adjunct professor at Hunter College of the City University of New York, 1968, and New School for Social Research, 1971; has conducted field study in Utah, California, Montana, Washington, Guatemala (for Explorers Club of New York and American Broadcasting Co.), Australia, Eastern Polynesia (for American Museum of Natural History), and Hawaii; has exhibited work in American Museum of Natural History, 1965, 1968, and Idaho State University Museum, 1968. *Military service:* U.S. Army Reserve, 1962-67.

MEMBER: American Anthropological Association (fellow), Society for American Archaeology, Australian Institute of Aboriginal Studies (corresponding member), Hawaii Foundation for History and the Humanities, Explorers Club. *Awards, honors:* Social Science Research Council fellowship, 1966-67; grant from Voss Fund for Anthropological Research of American Museum of Natural History, 1969-70; National Science Foundation research grant, 1973-75.

WRITINGS: *Archaeology of the Point St. George River Site, and Tolowa Prehistory* (monograph), University of California, 1966; *Yiwara: Foragers of the Australian Desert,* Scribner, 1969; (contributor) Humphrey McQueen, editor, *Aborigines, Race, and Racism,* Penguin, 1970; (contributor) Harry L. Shapiro, editor, *Man, Culture, and Society,* Oxford University Press, 1971; (editor and author of introduction) *Man's Many Ways: A Natural History Reader in Anthropology,* Harper, 1973; (contributor) Sol Tax, editor, *Horizons of Anthropology,* Aldine-Atherton, in press; (contributor) Cynthia Irwin-Williams, editor, *Seasonality in Prehistory,* University of New Mexico Press, in press; (contributor) W. C. Sturtevant and R. F. Heizer, editors, *Handbook of North American Indians,* Volume VIII: *California,* Smithsonian Institution, in press; *Punt ut jarpa Rockshelter and the Australian Desert Culture,* American Museum of Natural History, in press.

Contributor of about fifty articles and reviews to anthropology and archaeology journals, including *Explorers Journal, Newsletter of Lithic Technology, Southwestern Journal of Anthropology, Ecologist, American Museum Novitates,* and *World Archaeology.*

SIDELIGHTS: Gould made a sound recording, with his wife, Elizabeth Barber Gould: "Songs of the Western Desert Aborigines," Asch Recording, 1969.

* * *

GOVERN, Elaine 1939-

PERSONAL: Born March 27, 1939, in Jackson Junction, Iowa; daughter of Lawrence B. (a salesman) and Lena (Langrek) Pitzenberger; married Peter J. Govern (a mathematics teacher and realtor), June 20, 1964; children: Shawn Michael. *Education:* University of Northern Iowa, B.A., 1961, M.A., 1972. *Home address:* R.R. 2, Riceville, Iowa 50466.

CAREER: High school English and speech teacher in Waterloo, Iowa, 1961-63, Independence, Iowa, 1963-64, and Riceville, Iowa, 1967-68; presently volunteer elementary school teacher in Riceville, Iowa. Licensed realtor in State of Iowa; co-founder of local recycling center; community chairman for tax aid to senior citizens. *Member:* American

Library Association, Mitchell County Historical Society, Riceville Country Club (vice-president).

WRITINGS: Ice Cream Next Summer (juvenile; with photographs by author and brother, Larry Pitzenberger), Albert Whitman, 1972.

WORK IN PROGRESS: Working on text and illustration for several picture books.

SIDELIGHTS: Elaine Govern writes: "My opinion is that children do not want everything candy-coated and unreal. They want to understand and to know about the real world that as adults, they themselves will have to confront. We do not make strong individuals when we constantly water down even the vicarious experiences in their books. With proper and sensitive treatment, even the harsh termination of a cycle that began before birth can be discussed. Dependence is not the goal of education. Each little one must make his own way and stand independently. We do them no favors by constant protection."

* * *

GOVONI, Albert P. 1914-

PERSONAL: Born January 10, 1914, in Hudson, Mass.; son of Rodolph (a merchant) and Caterina (Guidotti) Govoni; married Joanne Ellyn Cron, May 29, 1948; children: Stephen James, Catherine Margaret. *Education:* University of Washington, Seattle, B.A., 1935. *Religion:* Roman Catholic. *Home:* 39 Horton St., Rye, N.Y. 10580. *Office:* Official Detective Group, 235 Park Ave. S., New York, N.Y. 10003.

CAREER: Newspaper reporter, 1931-36; foreign correspondent in Europe, South America, and Central America, 1936-41; free-lance magazine writer, 1945-52; managing editor of *Confidential*, 1952-59; *True Detective, Master Detective*, and *Official Detective*, New York, N.Y., editor, 1959—; currently president of Official Detective Group. Member of Civilian Advisory Board of National Police Officers Association of America. *Military service:* U.S. Army Air Forces, 1941-45. *Member:* International Association of Chiefs of Police, National Police Officers Association of America, Honor Legion of Police Department of City of New York.

WRITINGS: The Beatle Book, Lancer Books, 1964; *The Lawrence Welk Story*, Pocket Books, 1967; *A Boy Named Cash: The Johnny Cash Story*, Lancer Books, 1970; *Cary Grant: An Unauthorized Biography*, Regnery, 1972.

* * *

GOWING, Peter Gordon 1930-

PERSONAL: Born May 9, 1930, in Norwood, Mass.; son of James Chick (an engineer) and Hester (a secretary; maiden name, Walls) Gowing. *Education:* Attended Oberlin College, 1948-49; University of Maine, B.A., 1954, M.A., 1955; Bangor Theological Seminary, M.Div., 1954; Boston University, Th.D., 1960; Syracuse University, Ph.D., 1968. *Home:* 357 Parkway Dr., Stratford, Conn. 06497. *Office:* Dansalan Research Center, P.O. Box 5430, Iligan City 8801, Philippines.

CAREER: Ordained Congregationalist clergyman, 1954; pastor of Congregational church in North Berwick, Maine, 1957-60; Silliman University, Dumaguete City, Philippines, assistant professor, 1960-63, associate professor, 1963-67, professor of history, 1967-71, founder and first director of Southeast Asian studies program, 1968-71; South East Asia Graduate School of Theology, Singapore, regional professor, 1971-74; Dansalan Research Center, Marawi City, Philippines, director, 1974—. Guest professor at Tainan Theological College, 1971, Trinity Theological College, 1972, St. Andrew's Theological Seminary, 1972, St. Louis Theological Consortium, 1973, Sekolah Tinggi Theologia, 1974; member of board of directors of Silliman University Hospital, 1970-71; member of board of trustees of Dansalan College, 1970-71. *Military service:* U.S. Naval Reserve, chaplain, active duty, 1955-57; became lieutenant junior grade.

MEMBER: Association for Asian Studies, American Society for Church History, Royal Asiatic Society (fellow). *Awards, honors:* Distinguished alumnus award from Bangor Theological Seminary, 1973.

WRITINGS: Mosque and Moro, Philippine Federation of Christian Churches, 1964; *Islands under the Cross*, National Council of Churches (Manila), 1967; (editor with W. H. Scott) *Acculturation in the Philippines*, New Day Publishers, 1971; (editor with R. D. McAmis) *The Muslim Filipinos*, Solidaridad Publishing, 1975; *Mandate in Moroland*, University of the Philippines Press, in press. Editor of *Silliman Journal*, 1963-65.

WORK IN PROGRESS: Filipino Muslims: Heritage and Hope; The Church in the Lands of Southeast Asia; Islam on the Island Edge of Asia.

* * *

GRACE, Helen K(ennedy) 1935-

PERSONAL: Born March 30, 1935, in South Dakota; daughter of Walter James and Ethel (Soderstrom) Kennedy; married Elliott A. Grace (a teacher), November 21, 1961; children: Elizabeth. *Education:* Loyola University, Chicago, Ill., B.S., 1963; University of Illinois, M.S., 1965; Northwestern University, Ph.D., 1969. *Home:* 406 North Fourth Ave., Maywood, Ill. 60153. *Office:* College of Nursing, University of Illinois, 845 South Damen, Chicago, Ill. 60612.

CAREER: West Suburban Hospital, Oak Park, Ill., head nurse, 1957-59; R. C. Oldfield, M.D., Oak Park, Ill., office nurse, 1959-61; Chicago State Hospital, Chicago, Ill., supervisory nurse, 1961-63; Illinois Department of Mental Health, Chicago, Ill., nursing administrator, 1965-67; University of Illinois, Chicago, assistant professor, 1968-69, associate professor, 1969-74, professor of nursing and assistant dean of College of Nursing, 1974—.

MEMBER: American Association of University Professors, American Nurses' Association, American Sociological Association, National League for Nursing, Society for the Study of Social Problems, American Academy of Nursing (fellow), Sigma Xi, Sigma Theta Tau.

WRITINGS: (Contributor) Betty Bergeson and other editors, *Current Concepts in Clinical Nursing*, Mosby, 1967; *The Development of a Child Psychiatric Treatment Program*, Schenkman, 1974; (with Janice Layton and Dorothy Camilleri) *Psychiatric Nursing: A Psychosocial Approach*, W. C. Brown, 1975; (contributor) C. R. Kneisl and H. S. Wilson, editors, *Psychiatric Nursing: Perspectives, Issues, Trends*, Mosby, in press. Contributor to *Chart, Occupational Health Nursing*, and *Nursing Clinics of North America*.

WORK IN PROGRESS: Research on socialization in adult family roles.

GRAFTON, Carl 1942-

PERSONAL: Born October 6, 1942, in Toledo, Ohio; son of Thomas Holloway (a patent attorney) and Jewell (Bricker) Grafton; married Anne Permaloff (a teacher and writer), December 28, 1974. *Education:* University of Toledo, B.S., 1963; Purdue University, M.A., 1966, Ph.D., 1970. *Home:* 5740 Gulfton, #45, Houston, Tex. 77036. *Office:* Department of Political Science, University of Houston, Houston, Tex. 77004.

CAREER: Libbey-Owens-Ford Glass Co., Toledo, Ohio, research physicist, 1963-64; University of Houston, Houston, Tex., assistant professor of political science, 1968—. *Member:* American Political Science Association, American Association of University Professors. *Awards, honors:* Realm Foundation fellowship, 1965-66; Richard Weaver fellowship, 1966-67.

WRITINGS: The Politics of Higher Education, General Learning Press, 1973; (editor with Richard D. Feld) *The Uneasy Partnership*, National Press Books, 1973. Contributor to *Administration and Society*.

WORK IN PROGRESS: The Creation and Funding of Federal Agencies; research for a book on the life and career of James E. Folsom.

* * *

GRAHAM, John Thomas 1928-

PERSONAL: Born March 28, 1928, in Brookfield, Mo.; son of Thomas Patrick (a farmer and railroader) and Zona (a teacher; maiden name, Dunnington) Graham; married Alsacia Izurietta, June 6, 1968; children: Monica Marie. *Education:* Rockhurst College, B.A. (magna cum laude), 1952; St. Louis University, Ph.D., 1957. *Politics:* Independent. *Religion:* Roman Catholic. *Home:* 2000 West 95th St., Leawood, Kan. 66206. *Office:* Department of History, University of Missouri-Kansas City, 5200 Rockhill Rd., Kansas City, Mo. 64110.

CAREER: St. Ambrose College, Davenport, Iowa, 1957-62, began as instructor, became assistant professor of history; Gonzaga University, Spokane, Wash., assistant professor of history, 1962-66; University of Missouri, Kansas City, associate professor of history, 1966—. *Military service:* U.S. Navy, 1946-48. *Member:* American Historical Association, American Association of University Professors. *Awards, honors:* Curators' Award from University of Missouri, 1973, for *Donoso Cortes: Utopian Romanticist and Political Realist*.

WRITINGS: Donoso Cortes: Utopian Romanticist and Political Realist, University of Missouri Press, 1974.

WORK IN PROGRESS: European Conservatism in the Nineteenth Century, completion expected in 1976.

SIDELIGHTS: Graham has competence in Latin, Spanish, French, German, Italian, Portuguese. *Avocational Interests:* Skiing, sailboating, tennis, golf, legitimate theater, classical music, the arts, travel.

* * *

GRAHAM, Malcolm 1923-

PERSONAL: Born November 26, 1923, in Bristol, Pa.; son of Robert Neely (a teacher) and Eva (a teacher; maiden name, Gropp) Graham; married Carolyn Leffel (a teacher), August 23, 1952; children: Joyce, John. *Education:* Attended Drexel Institute of Technology, 1941-42; Trenton State College, B.S., 1946; University of Massachusetts, M.S., 1948; graduate study at Harvard University, 1949; Columbia University, Ed.D., 1954; postdoctoral study at Michigan State University, 1959-60. *Home:* 2165 Pueblo Circle, Las Vegas, Nev. 89109. *Office:* Department of Mathematics, University of Nevada, Las Vegas, Nev. 89154.

CAREER: Marion Institute, Marion, Ala., instructor in mathematics, 1948-49; Longwood College, Farmville, Va., assistant professor, 1951-53, associate professor of mathematics, 1953-55; East Carolina College, Greenville, N.C., associate professor of mathematics, 1955-56; University of Nevada, Las Vegas, associate professor, 1956-64, professor of mathematics, 1964—, dean of College of Science and Mathematics, 1959-65, head of mathematics department, 1965-66. *Member:* American Mathematical Society, Mathematical Association of America, National Council of Teachers of Mathematics, National Education Association, Southern Nevada Mathematics Council (president, 1960-61).

WRITINGS: Modern Elementary Mathematics, Harcourt, 1970; *Mathematics: A Liberal Arts Approach*, Harcourt, 1973.

WORK IN PROGRESS: A second edition of *Modern Elementary Mathematics*, for Harcourt.

SIDELIGHTS: Graham wrote and taught the first televised mathematics course in the state of Nevada in 1965.

* * *

GRANDFIELD, Raymond J(oseph) 1931-

PERSONAL; Born August 30, 1931, in Reading, Ohio; son of Raymond Joseph and Anna Patricia (Neihaus) Grandfield; married Jennilee Vandiveer Derrick, January 9, 1957; children: Kathleen Dawn, Holly Lynne. *Education:* University of Northern Colorado, A.B., 1957; Temple University, M.Ed., 1959, Ed.D., 1972; Rutgers University, graduate study, 1959-60. *Politics:* Independent. *Religion:* Roman Catholic. *Home:* R.D. 1, Box 240, Felton, Del. 19943. *Office:* Department of Distributive Education, Delaware State College, Dover, Del. 19901.

CAREER: High school teacher and coordinator of distributive education program in Camden, N.J., 1957-60; concurrently high school teacher and coordinator of distributive education program in Carlsbad, N.M., and instructor in business, New Mexico State University, Carlsbad, 1960-64; Wyoming State Department of Education, Cheyenne, state director of business, office, and distributive education, 1964-68; Delaware State College, Dover, assistant professor, 1968-72, associate professor, 1972-73, professor of distributive education and director of program, 1973—. Member of boards of directors, Carlsbad March of Dimes, 1961-64, Cheyenne Civitan Club, 1965-68, and Wyoming State Council for Economic Education, 1965-68. Consultant in training and safety to companies. *Military service:* U.S. Marine Corps, 1951-52.

MEMBER: American Vocational Association (life member), National Education Association (life member), National Business Education Association, National Association of State Supervisors of Distributive Education (secretary, 1966-67), Distributive Education Clubs of America, Inc. (member of board of directors, 1966-68), Distributive Education Clubs of America Builders Club, National Association of Distributive Education Teachers, Council of Distributive Teacher Educators, American Association of University Professors, Eastern Business Education Association, Delaware State Education Association, Delaware Vocational Association, Phi Delta Kappa, Delta Pi Epsilon, Epsilon Delta Epsilon, Delta Mu Delta (honorary member). *Awards, honors:* Delta Pi Epsilon achievement award, 1972; Epsilon Delta Epsilon recognition award, 1972.

WRITINGS—All with Faye Gold; all published by Fairchild: *Distribution and Distributive Careers*, 1972; *Working in a Store*, 1972; *Working in a Service Industry*, 1973; *Working for a Wholesaler*, 1973; *Working in the Transportation Industry*, 1974; *Careers in Business and Office Education*, 1975. Also author of *Methods of Teaching*, Delaware State College, Volume I, 1970, Volume II, 1971, Volume III, 1974. Contributor to professional journals.

WORK IN PROGRESS: An enlarged edition of *Methods of Teaching*, with Gold, for Fairchild.

AVOCATIONAL INTERESTS: Fishing, gardening, golf, reading.

* * *

GRANOVSKY, Anatoli 1922-1974

1922—September 4, 1974; Russian-born former member of Soviet Secret Police, later author of autobiographical works and books on the Soviet government. Obituaries: *Washington Post*, October 4, 1974.

* * *

GRANT, Alexander T(homas) K(ingdom) 1906-

PERSONAL: Born in 1906, in Moscow, Russia; emigrated to England, 1913; son of Harold Allan and Marie (Hartman) Grant; married Helen Frances Newsome. *Education:* University College, Oxford, B.A., 1928, M.A. *Home:* 66 Gough Way, Cambridge CB3 9LN, England.

CAREER: Held various journalistic, secretarial, and research positions, 1928-32; Royal Institute of International Affairs, London, England, researcher on international finance, 1932-35; University of London, University College, Department of Political Economy, London, England, Leverhulme research fellow, 1935-37, lecturer, 1937-39; United Kingdom Government Service, London, member of staff of treasury department, 1939-58, and of export credits guarantee department, 1958-66, and undersecretary, 1956-66; Cambridge University, Cambridge, England, librarian-secretary of faculty of economics, 1966-71, senior research officer in department of applied economics, 1971-73, fellow of Pembroke College, 1966-73, emeritus fellow, 1973—. United Kingdom member on managing board of European Payments Union, 1952-53. *Awards, honors:* Named Companion of the Order of St. Michael and St. George, 1949, and Companion of the Bath, 1965.

WRITINGS: Society and Enterprise, Routledge & Kegan Paul, 1934; *A Study of the Capital Market in Britain*, Macmillan, 1937, revised edition, Frank Cass, 1967; *The Machinery of Finance and the Management of Sterling*, St. Martin's, 1967; *The Strategy of Financial Pressure*, Macmillan, 1972, Barnes & Noble, 1973.

WORK IN PROGRESS: Research on the changing of financial structures in the face of uncertainty.

* * *

GRANT, Barbara M(oll) 1932-

PERSONAL: Born August 20, 1932, in Paterson, N.J.; daughter of William A. (a textile manufacturer and designer) and Ethel Barbara (a textile manufacturer and singer; maiden name, Moll) Grant. *Education:* Beaver College, student, 1950-52; New Jersey State Teachers College (now William Paterson College of New Jersey), B.S., 1954; University of Virginia, M.Ed., 1959; Columbia University, Professional Diploma, 1964, Ed.D., 1970. *Politics:* Republican. *Religion:* Protestant. *Home:* 535 Concord Pl., Wyckoff, N.J. 07481. *Office:* Faculty of Language Arts and Reading, Division of Teacher Education, William Paterson College, 300 Pompton Rd., Wayne, N.J. 07470.

CAREER: Elementary teacher in Glen Rock, N.J., 1954-63; William Paterson College of New Jersey, Wayne, assistant professor of English, 1963-68, associate professor of education, 1968-72, professor, 1972—. Consultant on reading and language arts to Prentice-Hall, Inc., 1971—. *Member:* American Educational Research Association, National Council of Teachers of English (life member), Association for Supervision and Curriculum Development, International Reading Association, New Jersey Reading Association, Pi Lambda Theta (founder of Beta Chi chapter), Kappa Delta Pi.

WRITINGS: (With sister, Dorothy Hennings) *The Teacher Moves: An Analysis of Non-Verbal Activity*, Teachers College Press, 1971; (with Hennings) *Content and Craft: Written Expression in the Elementary School*, Prentice-Hall, 1973; (contributor) Ronald T. Hyman, editor, *Teaching: Vantage Points for Study*, 2nd edition (Grant did not contribute to earlier edition), Lippincott, 1974; (contributor) Arno A. Bellack, editor, *Studies in the Language of the Classroom*, Teachers College Press, in press. Contributor to education journals, including *Education, New Jersey Education Association Review, Early Years, Instructor* and *Scholastic Teacher*. Editor, *Educational Projections* (local chapter journal of Pi Lambda Theta); manuscript reviewer for *American Educational Research Journal*, 1973—.

WORK IN PROGRESS: Continuing research on directions and trends in children's literature and reading and on ways to extend literature with children.

AVOCATIONAL INTERESTS: Travel (the Far East, Europe, Canada, the Caribbean, Central America), singing, economics.

* * *

GRANT, John J. 1932-

PERSONAL: Born January 10, 1932, in Boston, Mass. *Education:* University of Florida, M.A. (with high honors), 1962. *Politics:* "Anarchist." *Home:* 1425 West North Bear Creek Dr., Merced, Calif. 95340. *Office:* Department of Social Sciences, Merced College, Merced, Calif. 95340.

CAREER: Currently instructor in social sciences at Merced College, Merced, Calif. *Military service:* U.S. Army, 1954-56.

WRITINGS: (With Wayne Pirtle) *The Social Sciences: An Integrated Approach*, Random House, 1972; *Social Problems as Human Concerns*, Consensus Press, in press.

SIDELIGHTS: Grant has spent twenty years diving for salvage and in anthropological research.

* * *

GRANT, Louis T(heodore) 1943-
(Louis Goldberg; Joseph Magister)

PERSONAL: Surname originally Goldberg; name legally

changed in 1949; born August 30, 1943, in Baltimore, Md.; son of Louis and Kathryn (a nurse; maiden name, Kirkwood) Goldberg; married Barbara Krankoski (a medical laboratory technician), July 30, 1966; children: Barth, Jason. *Education:* University of Maryland, B.A., 1967; State University of New York at Stony Brook, graduate study, 1967-68, 1970; Johns Hopkins University, M.L.A., 1972; Jagiellonian University, further study, 1974. *Politics:* "Risibilist." *Religion:* "Iconoclast." *Home:* 7104 Chamberlain Rd., Baltimore, Md. 21207. *Office:* Department of English, Catonsville Community College, Catonsville, Md. 21228.

CAREER: Catonsville Community College, Catonsville, Md., assistant professor of English, 1970—. Lecturer at University of Baltimore, 1972—. *Member:* American Association of University Professors.

WRITINGS: (Editor; also contributor, under pseudonym Joseph Magister) *Communitas: Of College and Community*, Van Nostrand, 1972. Contributor to *Nation, Saturday Review, Ramparts* (occasionally under former name, Louis Goldberg), *Columbia Forum*, and to newspapers, including *Christian Science Monitor*.

WORK IN PROGRESS: Do It Yourself, a novel; *Model Homes and Other Stories*; *Nasty Essays*; *Diary of an Ex-Shut-In*, an autobiography.

SIDELIGHTS: Grant writes: "I trace my vocation as a writer back to my discovery that everyone is ridiculous.... I admire most those writers who are in on the joke, and share in the pleasure of rubbing man's nose in his stinking soul...."

* * *

GRANT, Myrna (Lois) 1934-

PERSONAL: Born March 9, 1934, in Hamilton, Ontario, Canada; daughter of Harold and Florence Reid; married James Grant (a writer and film director), June 6, 1959; children: Christopher, Susan, Andrew, Jennifer. *Education:* Attended McMaster University, 1957; Moody Bible Institute, B.Sc., 1969; Wheaton College, Wheaton, Ill., M.A., 1971. *Religion:* Evangelical Protestant. *Home:* 1218 Greenwood, Wheaton, Ill. 60187.

CAREER: Author of books, articles, and television, radio, and film scripts. Actress on radio programs, narrator of sound recordings. Special instructor in radio and television writing at Wheaton College (Wheaton, Ill.), 1974—. *Member:* Society of Children's Book Writers.

WRITINGS: Vanya (biography), Creation House, 1974; *Let's Put on a Play*, Moody, 1974; *Ivan and the Informer* (juvenile fiction), Moody, 1974.

Films: "Bright Gem of Hope," Evangelical Alliance Mission, 1971; "Love and the Little Ones," Compassion Child Care Agency, 1972.

Television scripts: "Treehouse Club" series, 1974.

Radio scripts for series: "The Monk of Wittenburg" (Martin Luther), 1960; "Beautiful Upon the Mountains" (Madam Guyon), 1961; "Thunder on the Heather" (John Knox), 1962; "Pilgrim's Progress" (adaptation), 1962; "Ranger Bill," 1963-66; "Sailor Sam," 1965-67; "This Is My Song" (Fanny Crosby), 1965; "Ninepence in Her Pocket" (Gladys Alyward), 1966; "Hudson and Maria" (Hudson Taylor), 1969; "Anthology," 1969-70; "Harriet" (Harriet Beecher Stowe), 1970.

Author of a monthly column, "Since You Asked," for *Christian Life*, 1967-68.

Contributor to *Eternity, Moody Monthly, Christian Reader, Christian Life*, and *Spectrum*.

WORK IN PROGRESS: Ivan and the Hidden Bible, a novel for children; research on the Evangelical-Baptist dissident movement in the Soviet Union and the human rights movements in general in the Communist world, with a book expected to result.

SIDELIGHTS: Myrna Grant has traveled in Africa, South America, the Soviet Union, Southeast Asia, and Europe. She has made "Happytime Stories for Children," a sound recording, Zondervan, 1970, and "More Happy Time Stories for Children," 1970.

BIOGRAPHICAL/CRITICAL SOURCES: Christian Bookseller, May, 1974.

* * *

GRANT, Verne E(dwin) 1917-

PERSONAL: Born October 17, 1917, in San Francisco, Calif.; son of Edwin E. (an attorney) and Bessie (Swallow) Grant; married Alva Day, June, 1946 (divorced); married Karen Alt, November, 1960; children: (first marriage) Joyce, Brian, Brenda. *Education:* University of California, Berkeley, A.B., 1940, Ph.D., 1949. *Home:* 2811 Fresco Dr., Austin, Tex. 78731. *Office:* Department of Botany, University of Texas, Austin, Tex. 78712.

CAREER: Naturalist in Central and South America, 1940-42; Carnegie Institution of Washington, Stanford, Calif., visiting investigator, 1949-50; Rancho Santa Ana Botanical Garden, Claremont, Calif., geneticist and experimental taxonomist, 1950-67; Texas Agricultural & Mechanical University, College Station, professor of biology at Institute of Life Science, 1967-68; University of Arizona, Superior, professor of biological sciences and director of Boyce Thompson Southwestern Arboretum, 1968-70; University of Texas, Austin, professor of botany, 1970—. Assistant professor at Claremont Graduate School, 1951-53, associate professor, 1953-57, professor, 1957-67. *Military service:* U.S. War Department, translator, 1942-45; served in Panama.

MEMBER: International Society of Plant Taxonomists, National Academy of Sciences, American Society of Naturalists, Genetics Society of America, Society for the Study of Evolution (vice-president, 1966; president, 1968), Botanical Society of America, American Society of Plant Taxonomists, Southwestern Association of Naturalists. *Awards, honors:* National Research Council fellowship, 1949-50; Phi Beta Kappa award in science, 1964, for *The Origin of Adaptations*; certificate of merit from Botanical Society of America, 1971.

WRITINGS: The Natural History of the Phlox Family, Nijhoff, 1959; *The Origin of Adaptations*, Columbia University Press, 1963; *The Architecture of the Germplasm*, Wiley, 1964; (with wife, Karen Grant) *Flower Pollination in the Phlox Family*, Columbia University Press, 1965; (with Karen Grant) *Hummingbirds and Their Flowers*, Columbia University Press, 1968; *Plant Speciation*, Columbia University Press, 1971; *Genetics of Flowering Plants*, Columbia University Press, 1975.

Contributor of more than sixty articles to scientific journals, including *American Naturalist, Evolution, Genetics, Advances in Genetics*, and *Proceedings of the National Academy of Sciences*. Member of editorial board of *Encyclopedia Americana*, 1955-64, *Brittonia*, 1957-62, *Evolution*, 1960-62, *American Naturalist*, 1964-67, and *Biologisches Zentralblatt*, 1974—.

WORK IN PROGRESS: *Organic Evolution*, an advanced textbook.

* * *

GRAVES, Richard L(ayton) 1931-

PERSONAL: Born January 14, 1931, in Houston, Tex.; son of Andrew J. (a contractor) and Lucille (Martin) Graves; married Eloise Davis, June 10, 1955; children: Rebecca, Jeffrey, Kathryn. *Education:* Baylor University, B.A., 1956; University of Florida, M.Ed., 1960; Florida State University, Ph.D., 1967. *Religion:* Baptist. *Office:* School of Education, Auburn University, Auburn, Ala. 36830.

CAREER: High school English teacher in Tampa, Fla., 1957-63; Auburn University, Auburn, Ala., assistant professor, 1965-72, associate professor of secondary education, 1972—. *Military service:* U.S. Air Force, 1951-54. *Member:* National Council of Teachers of English, Conference on English Education, Conference on College Composition and Communication, Rhetoric Society of America, Phi Delta Kappa.

WRITINGS: (Editor) *Rhetoric and Composition: Selected Essays for Teachers*, Hayden Press, 1975.

* * *

GRAY, J(ames) M(artin) 1930-

PERSONAL: Born November 30, 1930, in Harrow, England; son of Alfred Williams (an executive) and Annie (Hughes) Gray; married Hilary Christine Parr (a child psychologist), September 1, 1961; children: Christina Anne, Emily Marion. *Education:* University of Edinburgh, M.A. (with honors), 1952, Ph.D., 1959. *Politics:* Liberal (in Britain); New Democratic Party (in Canada). *Home and office:* Orchard House, Holme Rd., Matlock Bath, Derbyshire, DE4 3NU, England.

CAREER: W. J. Gage & Co., Toronto, Ontario, assistant editor, 1952-54; school teacher in Britain and Jamaica, 1955-57, 1959-61; factory worker in Manchester, England, 1961-62; McMaster University, Hamilton, Ontario, assistant professor of English, 1962-67; independent researcher, 1967-73; Visiting professor at University of Saskatchewan, Saskatoon, 1973-74. *Member:* Modern Language Association of America, International Arthurian Society, Tennyson Society, Victorian Society, Fosse Way Exploration Group, Matlock Bath Preservation Society, Derbyshire Archaeological Association. *Awards, honors:* Canada Council research grants, 1967-70.

WRITINGS: *Man and Myth in Victorian England: Tennyson's "The Coming of Arthur"* (monograph), Tennyson Society, 1969; *Tennyson's Dopplegaenger: "Balin and Balan"* (monograph), Tennyson Society, 1971; (editor) Alfred Lord Tennyson, *Idylls of the King*, Penguin, in press. Contributor to *Renaissance and Modern Studies, Botteghe Oscure, Notes and Queries, Victorian Poetry, Victorian Studies*, and other journals. Member of publications board of Tennyson Society, 1968—.

WORK IN PROGRESS: *Thro' the Vision of the Night*, a book about Tennyson's serial and iconographic techniques, completion expected in 1975; co-authoring a book on "Balin and Balan," 1976; a monograph on "Gareth and Lynette," 1976 or 1977; a book-length study of "The Holy Grail," 1977.

GRAYSON, Janet 1934-

PERSONAL: Born June 4, 1934, in Boston, Mass.; daughter of Isador (a tailor) and Fannie (Marx) Miller; married Saul Grayson (a physical education teacher), June 7, 1958; children: Felicia, Heath, Diana. *Education:* Brooklyn College (now Brooklyn College of the City University of New York), B.A., 1958, M.A., 1962; Columbia University, Ph.D., 1968. *Home address:* Jackson Hill Rd., Chesterfield, N.H. 03443. *Office:* Department of English, Keene State College, Keene, N.H. 03431.

CAREER: Brooklyn College of the City University of New York, Brooklyn, N.Y., lecturer in English, 1962-66; Keene State College, Keene, N.H., assistant professor, 1966-71, associate professor, 1971-75, professor of English, 1975—. *Member:* International Arthurian Society, Mediaeval Academy of America.

WRITINGS: *Structure and Imagery in Ancrene Wisse*, University Press of New England, 1974.

WORK IN PROGRESS: *The Resurrection Man*, a mystery novel; research on verse of Adelaide Crapsey, on Bernardine Paranomasia in Herbert's "The Pulley," and on the apotheosis of the Virgin.

AVOCATIONAL INTERESTS: Church architecture, medieval art, classical literature, folklore, legend.

* * *

GREEN, Alan (Baer) 1906-
(Jack Alan; Glen Burne, Roger Denbie, joint pseudonyms)

PERSONAL: Born October 30, 1906, in Pittsburgh, Pa.; son of Morris (a business executive) and Josephine (Baer) Green; married Gladys E. Blun (a literary agent), June 16, 1931; children: Christopher, Stephen, Thomas. *Education:* Attended Columbia University, 1924-26. *Politics:* "Usually Democratic." *Religion:* "Non-observing Jewish." *Home:* 377 Greens Farms Rd., Westport, Conn. 06880.

CAREER: Green Brodie Co. (advertising agency), New York, N.Y., partner, 1928-54; Williams, Lewin & Saylor (advertising agency), New York, partner, 1954-59; Emil Mogul & Co. (advertising agency), New York, senior vice-president and member of board of directors, 1959-69; Griswold-Eshleman (advertising agency), New York, vice-president and member of board of directors, 1969-71. Freelance book reviewer. Publicity director for senatorial campaigns of Brien McMahon, U.S. Senator from Connecticut, 1944 and 1950; member of Writers War Board, 1942-47. *Member:* Authors League (former member of board of directors), Authors Guild (former member of board of directors), Mystery Writers of America. *Awards, honors:* Edgar Allan Poe Award for best first mystery, 1949, for *What a Body!*

WRITINGS—Novels, except as indicated: (With Julian Paul Brodie, under joint pseudonym Roger Denbie) *Death on the Limited*, Morrow, 1933 (published in England as *The Timetable Murder*, Nicholson & Watson, 1934); (under joint pseudonym Roger Denbie) *Death Cruises South*, Morrow, 1934; (with wife, Gladys Green, under joint pseudonym Glen Burne) *Murder to Music*, Dodd, 1934; (with Jack Goodman) *How to Do Practically Anything* (a collection of magazine articles originally written under pseudonym Jack Alan), Simon & Schuster, 1943; *What a Body!*, Simon & Schuster, 1949; *They Died Laughing*, Simon & Schuster, 1952; *Mother of Her Country*, Random House, 1974.

Author, with Brodie, of *Love on the Run*, published as a full-length novel in *Cosmopolitan*, 1932. Also author of regular columns, "Book Business" and "Trade Winds," in *Saturday Review*, 1971-73. Contributor of short stories to magazines, including *Colliers* and *Cosmopolitan*.

SIDELIGHTS: Green told *CA*, "I have long opposed censorship and expressed that opposition in a light novel about book publishing, *Mother of Her Country*, [and] have written for magazines on this same subject."

In 1936 *Love on the Run* was made into a motion picture of the same title, starring Joan Crawford and Clark Gable.

AVOCATIONAL INTERESTS: Travel (England, France, Ireland, Italy, Holland, and the Mediterranean), "reading new literature and re-reading favorites from the past."

* * *

GREEN, William 1926-

PERSONAL: Born July 10, 1926, in New York, N.Y.; son of Louis (a musician) and Hanna (Bernstein) Green; married Marguerite Joan Mayer, August 14, 1960; children: Jonathan, Natalie. *Education:* Queens College (now Queens College of the City University of New York), B.A., 1949; Columbia University, M.A., 1950, Ph.D., 1959. *Home:* 50-10 199th St., Fresh Meadows, N.Y. 11365. *Office:* Department of English, Queens College of the City University of New York, Flushing, N.Y. 11367.

CAREER: Upsala College, East Orange, N.J., lecturer in English, 1953-56; Queens College of the City University of New York, Flushing, N.Y., instructor, 1959-63, assistant professor, 1963-67, associate professor, 1967-72, professor of English, 1972—. Has held technical and administrative positions with various summer stock, Off-Broadway, and Broadway theatrical companies, 1951-56. *Military service:* U.S. Navy, 1944-46; became musician first class. *Member:* Modern Language Association of America, College English Association, Renaissance Society of America, International Federation for Theatre Research (corresponding secretary for the United States, 1970—), American Society for Theatre Research (secretary-treasurer, 1966-73; member of executive committee, 1973-76), Theatre Library Association (member of executive board, 1974-78), Malone Society.

WRITINGS: Shakespeare's "Merry Wives of Windsor," Princeton University Press, 1962; (editor) William Shakespeare, *The Merry Wives of Windsor*, New American Library, 1965; (editor with John Gassner) *Elizabethan Drama*, Bantam, 1967; (editor with Barbara Fass, Myron Matlaw, and Margaret Ranald) *A Style Manual for College Students*, Queens College Press, 1973, revised edition, 1974. Contributor of articles on theater to various encyclopedias, journals, and periodicals.

WORK IN PROGRESS: A book on British provincial drama of the early twentieth century; studies in American burlesque.

AVOCATIONAL INTERESTS: Music (plays the clarinet), photography, philately, and travel.

* * *

GREENBERG, Barbara L(evenson) 1932-

PERSONAL: Born August 27, 1932, in Boston, Mass.; daughter of Louis B. and Esther (Harrison) Levenson; married Harold L. Greenberg (a surgeon), February 6, 1955; children: David, Russell. *Education:* Wellesley College, B.A., 1953; Simmons College, M.A., 1973. *Home:* 47 Dolphin Rd., Newton Centre, Mass. 02159.

CAREER: Register Publications, Boston, Mass., feature editor, 1954-60. *Member:* New England Poetry Society.

WRITINGS: The Spoils of August (poems), Wesleyan University Press, 1974. Poems anthologized in *Best Poems of 1967: Borestone Mountain Poetry Awards 1968,* edited by Waddell Austin, Pacific Books, 1968; *Quickly Aging Here: Some Poets of the 1970's,* edited by Geof Hewitt, Doubleday-Anchor, 1969; *Rising Tides: Twentieth Century American Women Poets,* edited by Laura Chester and Sharon Barba, Washington Square Press, 1973. Contributor of poetry and short stories to *Atlantic, New Republic, Poetry Northwest, Yale Review,* and *Epoch.* Editorial consultant to *Newton Times,* 1972—.

WORK IN PROGRESS: "In the Death House," a two-act play derived from Camus' *The Plague;* a book-length collection of poems for children.

* * *

GREENBERG, Edward (Seymour) 1942-

PERSONAL: Born July 1, 1942, in Philadelphia, Pa.; son of Samuel (an engineer) and Yetta (Kaplan) Greenberg; married Martha Baker (a modern dance teacher), December 24, 1964; children: Joshua. *Education:* Miami University, Oxford, Ohio, B.A., 1964, M.A., 1965; University of Wisconsin, Ph.D., 1969. *Politics:* Radical. *Religion:* Jewish. *Home:* 2303 Bluff St., Boulder, Colo. 80302. *Office:* Department of Political Science, University of Colorado, Boulder, Colo.

CAREER: Stanford University, Palo Alto, Calif., assistant professor of political science, 1968-72; Indiana University, Bloomington, associate professor of political science, 1972-73; University of Colorado, Boulder, associate professor of political science, 1973—. *Member:* Phi Beta Kappa. *Awards, honors:* Russell Sage Foundation grant, 1969; Louis Rabinowitz Foundation grant, 1972.

WRITINGS: (Editor) *Political Socialization*, Lieber-Atherton, 1970; (editor and contributor) *Black Politics*, Holt, 1971; (editor with Richard Young and contributor) *American Politics Reconsidered*, Duxbury Press, 1973; *Serving the Few: Corporate Capitalism and the Bias of Government Policy*, Wiley, 1974. Contributor to *Social Science Quarterly, Public Opinion Quarterly, Politics and Society, Journal of Politics, Midwest Journal of Politics, Canadian Journal of Politics.*

WORK IN PROGRESS: Research in the potential radicalizing effects of worker participation and control experiments.

* * *

GREENBERG, Stanley Bernard 1945-

PERSONAL: Born May 10, 1945, in Philadelphia, Pa.; son of Samuel (an engineer) and Yetta (Kaplan) Greenberg; married Pamela Russell, April 16, 1967; children: Kathryn, Anna, Jonathan. *Education:* Miami University, Oxford, Ohio, B.A., 1967; Harvard University, M.A., 1968, Ph.D., 1972. *Religion:* Jewish. *Home:* 114 Linden St., New Haven, Conn. 06510. *Office:* Department of Political Science, Yale University, New Haven, Conn. 06510.

CAREER: Barss, Reitzel & Associates, Cambridge, Mass., project director, 1967-70; Yale University, New Haven, Conn., assistant professor of political science,

1971—. Visiting lecturer at University of the Witwatersrand, 1973-74. Project assistant in U.S. Office of Economic Opportunity, 1965; legislative assistant to Lee Hamilton, congressman, 1966; director of field operations for New Haven, Conn. McGovern Campaign. *Member:* American Political Science Association.

WRITINGS: Politics and Poverty: Modernization and Response in Five Poor Neighborhoods, Wiley, 1974; (with Willis Hawley and Michael Lipsky) *Theoretical Perspectives on Urban Problems,* Prentice-Hall, in press.

WORK IN PROGRESS: Research on change in multiracial societies, focusing on South Africa and the American South.

* * *

GREENE, Bette 1934-

PERSONAL: Born June 28, 1934, in Memphis, Tenn.; married Donald S. Greene (a physician), June 14, 1959; children: Carla, Jordan. *Education:* Attended University of Alabama, 1952, and Columbia University, 1955. *Home and office:* 338 Clinton Rd., Brookline, Mass. 02146. *Agent:* Sheldon Fogelman, 10 East 40th St., New York, N.Y. 10016.

CAREER: Writer. *Awards, honors: Summer of My German Soldier* was nominated for National Book Award, and received *New York Times* outstanding book award, Golden Kite Society children's book writer's award, and ALA Notable Book award, all 1973; *Philip Hall Likes Me, I Reckon Maybe* received *New York Times* outstanding book award, ALA Notable Book award, and Newberry Honor Book award, all 1974.

WRITINGS: Summer of My German Soldier (autobiographical; for young readers), Dial, 1973; *Philip Hall Likes Me, I Reckon Maybe* (for young readers), Dial, 1974. Author of a screenplay for *Summer of My German Soldier.*

WORK IN PROGRESS: A novel.

BIOGRAPHICAL/CRITICAL SOURCES: Philadelphia Inquirer, May 26, 1973.

* * *

GREENWAY, Roger S(elles) 1934-

PERSONAL: Born January 8, 1934, in Holland, Mich.; son of Leonard (a minister) and Katherine (a teacher; maiden name, Selles) Greenway; married Edna Carol Beebe (a college professor), August 20, 1954; children: Kathleen Michelle, Irma Rebeca, Wendy Ann, Jeffrey Lane, Roger Scott. *Education:* Calvin College, B.A., 1955; Calvin Theological Seminary, B.D., 1958, Th.M., 1963; graduate study, Hartford Theological Seminary, 1958-59; Southwestern Baptist Theological Seminary, Th.D., 1972. *Home:* 734 Griswold S.E., Grand Rapids, Mich. 49507. *Office:* Foreign Mission Board, Christian Reformed Church, 2850 Kalamazoo Ave. S.E., Grand Rapids, Mich. 49508.

CAREER: Ordained minister of Christian Reformed Church, 1958; missionary in Southern Asia, 1959-62, and in Latin America, 1962-70; Seminario Juan Calivno, Mexico City, Mexico, professor of church history, 1963-70; Latin American Missions of the Christian Reformed Church, Grand Rapids, Mich., director, 1972—. Director of Instituto Cristiano Mexicano, Mexico City, 1968-70.

WRITINGS: An Urban Strategy for Latin America, Baker Book, 1973; *Calling Our Cities to Christ,* Presbyterian & Reformed, 1973. Contributor to religion journals.

WORK IN PROGRESS: Editing *A World to Win: Preaching World Missions Today* and *Lengthened Cords,* Baker Book.

* * *

GREENWOOD, Walter 1903-1974

1903—September 13, 1974; British novelist, dramatist, author of filmscripts, short fiction, and an autobiography. Obituaries: *New York Times,* September 14, 1974; *Washington Post,* September 15, 1974; *AB Bookman's Weekly,* November 18, 1974.

* * *

GREER, Ann Lennarson 1944-

PERSONAL: Born December 3, 1944, in Chicago, Ill.; daughter of Vernon E. (a physician) and Dee (a teacher; maiden name, Wing) Lennarson; married Scott Greer (a professor), December 22, 1969. *Education:* Lake Forest College, B.A., 1967; Northwestern University, M.A., 1968, Ph.D., 1970. *Home:* 10 Ahwahnee Rd., Lake Forest, Ill. 60045. *Office:* Department of Urban Affairs and Sociology, University of Wisconson—Milwaukee, Milwaukee, Wis. 53201.

CAREER: Lake Forest College, Lake Forest, Ill., assistant professor of sociology, 1969-72; University of Wisconsin—Milwaukee, assistant professor of urban affairs and sociology, 1972—. Program analyst for Health Resources Administration, 1974-75. *Member:* American Sociological Association, American Political Science Association, Sociologists for Women in Society (officer), American Association of University Professors, National Association of Schools of Public Affairs and Administration, Phi Beta Kappa. *Awards, honors:* Fellowship from National Association of Schools of Public Affairs and Administration, 1974-75.

WRITINGS: The Mayor's Mandate: Municipal Statecraft and Political Trust, Schenkman, 1974; (editor with husband, Scott Greer) *Neighborhood and Ghetto: The Local Area in Large Scale Society,* Basic Books, 1974; (with Scott Greer) *Understanding Sociology,* W. C. Brown, 1974. Co-editor of "Elements of Sociology," a series, and "Brown Reprints," both for W. C. Brown.

WORK IN PROGRESS: Research on political leadership, political trust, and the politics of the American health system.

* * *

GREGORY, Paul Roderick 1941-

PERSONAL: Born February 10, 1941, in San Angelo, Tex.; son of Peter Paul (an engineer) and Elizabeth (Mundhenke) Gregory; married Annemarie I. Schultz, October 4, 1965; children: Mischa, Andrei. *Education:* University of Oklahoma, B.A., 1963, M.A., 1964; Free University of Berlin, graduate study, 1964-65; Harvard University, Ph.D., 1969. *Office:* Department of Economics, University of Houston, Houston, Tex. 77004.

CAREER: University of Oklahoma, Norman, assistant professor of economics, 1969-72; University of Houston, Houston, Tex., associate professor of economics, 1972—. *Member:* American Economic Association.

WRITINGS: Socialist and Nonsocialist Industrialization Patterns, Praeger, 1970; *Soviet Economic Structure and Performance,* Harper, 1974. Contributor to journals.

GRENANDER, M(ary) E(lizabeth) 1918-

PERSONAL: Surname rhymes with "commander"; born November 21, 1918, in Rewey, Wis.; daughter of Carl John and Mary (Whitney) Grenander; married Jean Louis Auclair, July 21, 1962 (divorced June 28, 1969); married James W. Corbett (a professor of physics), May 5, 1972. *Education:* University of Chicago, A.B., 1940, A.M., 1941, Ph.D., 1948; also studied at Sorbonne, University of Paris, summer, 1949. *Politics:* Independent. *Religion:* Humanist. *Home:* 104 Bleeker Rd., Guilderland, N.Y. 12084. *Office:* Department of English, State University of New York at Albany, Albany, N.Y. 12222.

CAREER: State University of New York at Albany, instructor, 1948-53, assistant professor, 1953-54, associate professor, 1954-61, professor of English, 1961—. Fulbright professor at University of Lille and University of Toulouse, 1960-61. *Military service:* U.S. Naval Reserve, 1942-46; became lieutenant senior grade; received citation for meritorious service from Chief of Bureau of Ships.

MEMBER: Modern Language Association of America, American Studies Association, American Association of University Professors, English Institute, Northeast Modern Language Association, New York American Studies Association (president, 1973-74), Phi Beta Kappa (Alpha Alpha and Upper Hudson Association; member of executive committee of Upper Hudson Association, 1970-71). *Awards, honors:* Fulbright fellowship, 1960-61; Huntington Library fellowship, 1957; Pforzheimer Foundation fellowship, 1958.

WRITINGS: A Record of Research and Creative Activity: State University of New York, July 1, 1948 to June 30, 1957, Research Foundation, State University of New York, 1958; *Ambrose Bierce*, Twayne, 1971. Contributor of articles to professional journals and poems and stories to little magazines.

WORK IN PROGRESS: Letters of Ambrose Bierce; a study of Thomas Szasz.

SIDELIGHTS: Grenander writes: "My approach to most subjects rests on investigation of facts and logical analysis. Although I recognize the tremendous power of bias, prejudice, emotional distortion, special interests, and plain cussedness, I like to think that most human problems are susceptible of solution through the application of reason." *Avocational interests:* Sports (Midwest women's fencing champion, 1947), music (especially string quartets), playing violin, travel (Europe, Caribbean, Brazil).

* * *

GREY, Jerry 1926-

PERSONAL: Born October 25, 1926, in New York, N.Y.; son of Abraham and Lillian (Danowitz) Grey; married Vivian Hoffman, June 27, 1948 (divorced); married Florence Maier (a fashion artist), 1974; children: (first marriage) Leslie Ann, Jacquelyn Eve (deceased). *Education:* Cornell University, B.M.E., 1947, M.S., 1949; California Institute of Technology, Ph.D., 1952. *Politics:* Registered Democrat. *Religion:* Hebrew. *Home:* Jobs Lane, Box 428, Bridgehampton, N.Y. 11932. *Office:* (Mail address) 359 West 21st St., New York, N.Y. 10011.

CAREER: Cornell University, Ithaca, N.Y., instructor in thermodynamics, 1947-49; Fairchild Corp., Engine Division, Farmingdale, N.Y., development engineer, 1949-50; California Institute of Technology, Pasadena, hypersonic aerodynamicist at Guggenheim Aerospace Laboratory, 1950-51; Marquardt Aircraft Co., Van Nuys, Calif., senior engineer, 1951-52; Princeton University, School of Engineering and Applied Science, Princeton, N.J., research associate, 1952-56, assistant professor, 1956-59, associate professor of aerospace science, 1960-67, director of Nuclear Propulsiion Research Laboratory, 1962-67; Greyrad Corp., Princeton, N.J., president, 1959-71; American Institute of Aeronautics and Astronautics, New York, N.Y., administrator for technical activities and communications, 1971—; Calprobe Corp. (high-temperature instrumentation), New York, N.Y., president, 1972—. Chairman of solar power advisory panel, Office of Technology Assessment, U.S. Congress, 1974—; presently consultant to Los Alamos Scientific Laboratory, Atomic Industry Forum, National Aeronautics and Space Administration, and Princeton University (on nuclear fusion and space power); previously consultant to Radio Corp. of America, General Electric Co., Boeing Airplane Co., and other firms and laboratories. Holds nine U.S. patents and foreign patents associated with them. *Military service:* U.S. Naval Reserve, active duty, 1943-46.

MEMBER: American Institute of Aeronautics and Astronautics (associate fellow; vice-president, 1966-71), American Astronautical Society (senior member), American Association for the Advancement of Science, American Nuclear Society, Institute of Electrical and Electronics Engineers, American Society of Mechanical Engineers, New York Academy of Sciences, Sigma Xi, Phi Kappa Phi, Tau Beta Pi, Bridgehampton Racquet and Surf Club, Midtown Tennis Club (New York), Tenafly Racquet Club.

WRITINGS: (Contributor) Angelo Miele, *Flight Mechanics: Theory of Flight Paths*, Volume I, Addison-Wesley, 1962; (technical editor with Vivian Grey) *Space Flight Report to the Nation*, Basic Books, 1962; (contributor) C. W. Watson, editor, *Nuclear Rocket Propulsion*, College of Engineering, University of Florida, 1964.

Nuclear Propulsion (audiovisual book), Educom, 1970; *The Race for Electric Power* (juvenile), Westminster, 1972; (editor with J. P. Layton) *New Space Transportation Systems: An AIAA Assessment*, American Institute of Aeronautics and Astronautics, 1973; *The Facts of Flight* (juvenile), Westminster, 1973; (editor with Arthur Henderson) *Solar System Exploration: An AIAA Review*, American Institute of Aeronautics and Astronautics, 1974; (editor) *Aircraft Fuel Conservation: An AIAA View*, American Institute of Aeronautics and Astronautics, 1974; *Noise! Noise! Noise!* (juvenile), Westminster, in press; (editor with H. Killian and G. L. Dugger) *Solar Energy for Earth: An AIAA Assessment*, American Institute of Aeronautics and Astronautics, in press.

Writer of more than thirty proprietary technical reports and collaborator on others. Contributor to *Encyclopedia of Science and Technology*. Publications include monographs, technical papers, and popular articles in periodicals, including *Journal of Spacecraft and Rockets, Astronautics and Aeronautics Times* (London), and *L'Aerotecnica*.

WORK IN PROGRESS: Urban Energy, publication by Dekker expected in 1977.

SIDELIGHTS: Grey is "highly optimistic about man's ability to ensure his own survival and, indeed, his continued movement toward maturity, despite the apparent difficulties he keeps generating." *Avocational interests:* Tennis, sailing, ice skating, and other sports.

GRIBBLE, Leonard (Reginald) 1908-

PERSONAL: Born February 1, 1908, in London, England; son of Wilfred Browning and Ada Mary (Sterry) Gribble; married Nancy Mason, June 4, 1932; children: Lois Geraldine. *Education:* Attended schools in England. *Home:* Chandons, Firsdown Close, High Salvington, Worthing, Sussex BN13 3BQ, England.

CAREER: Author, 1928—. Literary adviser to various publishers in London; writer for radio and films; judge in international novel competitions. Served in Press and Censorship Division of Ministry of Information, 1940-45.

WRITINGS—Novels, except as indicated: *The Case of the Marsden Rubies*, Harrap, 1929, Doubleday, 1930, reprinted, Withy Grove Press, 1941; *The Terrace Suicide Mystery*, Doubleday, 1929 (published as *The Gillespie Suicide Mystery*, Harrap, 1929); (editor) *A Christmas Treasury in Prose and Verse*, Macmillan, 1929.

The Grand Modena Murder, Harrap, 1930, Doubleday, 1931, abridged edition, Withy Grove Press, 1945; (editor) *The Jesus of the Poets: An Anthology*, R. R. Smith, 1930; *Is This Revenge?: Another Case for Anthony Slade and Department X2*, Harrap, 1931; *Queens of Crime*, Hurst & Blackett, 1932; *The Stolen Statesman*, Dodd, 1932 (published as *The Stolen Home Secretary*, Harrap, 1932, abridged edition, Withy Grove Press, 1941); *The Serpentine Murder*, Dodd, 1932; *Famous Feats of Detection and Deduction*, Harrap, 1933, Doubleday, 1934; *The Secret of Tangles*, Harrap, 1933, Lippincott, 1934, reprinted, W. H. Allen, 1949; *The Yellow Bungalow Mystery*, Harrap, 1933, abridged edition, Withy Grove Press, 1941; *The Death Chime*, Harrap, 1934; *The Riddle of the Ravens*, Harrap, 1934; *Mystery at Tudor Arches*, Harrap, 1935, abridged edition, Withy Grove Press, 1945; (with wife, Nancy Gribble) *All the Year Round Stories*, Hutchinson, 1935; *The Case of the Malverne Diamonds: An Anthony Slade Story*, Harrap, 1936, Greenberg, 1937; *Riley of the Special Branch*, Harrap, 1936; *The Case-Book of Anthony Slade*, Quality Press, 1937; *Who Killed Oliver Cromwell?*, Harrap, 1937, abridged edition, Withy Grove Press, 1948; *Tragedy in E Flat*, Harrap, 1938, Hillman-Curl, 1939, reprinted, W. H. Allen, 1949; *The Arsenal Stadium Mystery*, Harrap, 1939, revised edition published as *The Arsenal Stadium Mystery: A Replay*, Jenkins, 1950.

Heroes of the Fighting R.A.F., Harrap, 1941; *Epics of the Fighting R.A.F.*, Harrap, 1943; *Heroes of the Merchant Navy*, Harrap, 1944; *Battle Stories of the R.A.F.*, Burke Publishing, 1945; *Toy Folk and Nursery People* (verse), Jenkins, 1945; *Great Detective Feats*, Burke Publishing, 1946; *Murder First Class*, Burke Publishing, 1946; *On Secret Service*, Burke Publishing, 1946; (author of introduction) *The Best Children's Stories of the Year*, Burke Publishing, 1946; (editor and author of introduction) *Profiles from Notable Modern Biographies*, Sampson Low, Marston & Co., 1946; *Atomic Murder*, Ziff-Davis, 1947, reprinted, Brown, Watson, 1958; *The Secret of the Red Mill*, Burke Publishing, 1948; (editor) *Fifty Famous Stories for Boys*, Burke Publishing, 1948; (editor) *Fifty Famous Stories for Girls*, Burke Publishing, 1949.

Hangman's Moon: A West-Country Case for Anthony Slade, W. H. Allen, 1950; *The Missing Speed Ace*, Burke Publishing, 1950; *The Riddle of the Blue Moon*, Burke Publishing, 1950; (editor) *The Story Trove: A Collection of the Best Stories of To-Day for Boys and Girls*, Burke Publishing, 1950; *They Kidnapped Stanley Matthews*, Jenkins, 1950; *The Frightened Chameleon*, Jenkins, 1951, Roy, c.1957; *Mystery Manor*, Mark Goulden, 1951; *Speed Dermot, Junior Reporter*, Burke Publishing, 1951; *The Glass Alibi*, Jenkins, 1952; *Murder out of Season*, Jenkins, 1952; *The Velvet Mask, and Other Stories*, W. H. Allen, 1952; *Famous Manhunts: A Century of Crime*, John Long, 1952, Roy, 1955; *She Died Laughing*, Jenkins, 1953; (with Janet Green) *Murder Mistaken: A Suspense Novel* (adapted from the play "Murder Mistaken" by Green), W. H. Allen, 1953; *Adventures in Murder Undertaken by Some Notorious Killers in Love*, John Long, 1954, Roy, 1955; *The Inverted Crime*, Jenkins, 1954; (with Geraldine Laws) *Sally of Scotland Yard*, W. H. Allen, 1954; *Triumphs of Scotland Yard: A Century of Detection*, John Long, 1955; *Death Pays the Piper*, Jenkins, 1956, Roy, c.1958; *Superintendent Slade Investigates*, Jenkins, 1956, Roy, c.1957; *Dangerous Mission*, Brown, Watson, 1957; *Famous Judges and Their Trials: A Century of Justice*, John Long, 1957; *Stand-In for Murder*, Jenkins, 1957, Roy, c.1958; *The True Book about Scotland Yard*, Muller, 1957; *Great Detective Exploits*, John Long, 1958; *Don't Argue with Death*, Roy, 1959; *Murders Most Strange*, John Long, 1959; *The True Book about the Old Bailey*, Muller, 1959, Sportshelf (New Rochelle), 1960.

Hands of Terror: Notable Assassinations of the Twentieth Century, Muller, 1960; *The True Book about the Mounties*, Muller, 1960, Sportshelf, 1961; *Clues That Spelled Guilty*, John Long, 1961; (editor) *Stories for Boys*, Spring Books, 1961; (editor) *Stories for Girls*, Spring Books, 1961; *Wantons Die Hard*, Jenkins, 1961, Roy, 1962; (editor) *Famous Stories of High Adventure*, Arthur Barker, 1962, Hill & Wang, 1964; (editor) *Famous Stories of the Sea and Ships*, Arthur Barker, 1962, Hill & Wang, 1964; *The True Book about Great Escapes*, Muller, 1962; *When Killers Err*, John Long, 1962; *Stories of Famous Detectives*, Hill & Wang, 1963; *They Challenged the Yard*, John Long, 1963; *The True Book about Smugglers and Smuggling*, Muller, 1963; *The True Book about the Spanish Main*, Muller, 1963; *Heads You Die*, Jenkins, 1964; *Stories of Famous Spies*, Arthur Barker, 1964; *Such Women Are Deadly*, John Long, 1965, Arco, 1969; *The Violent Dark*, Jenkins, 1965; *Great Manhunters of the Yard*, Roy, 1966; (editor) *Great War Adventures*, Arthur Barker, 1966; *Stories of Famous Explorers*, Arthur Barker, 1967; *Famous Stories of the Wild West*, Arthur Barker, 1967; *Strip-Tease Macabre*, Jenkins, 1967; *They Had a Way with Women*, John Long, 1967, Roy, 1968; *Stories of Famous Conspirators*, Arthur Barker, 1968; *Famous Stories of Police and Crime*, Arthur Barker, 1968; *A Diplomat Dies*, Jenkins, 1969; *Famous Historical Mysteries*, Muller, 1969, Transatlantic, 1971; *Famous Stories of Scientific Detection*, Arthur Barker, 1969.

Stories of Famous Modern Trials, Arthur Barker, 1970, published as *Justice?: Stories of Famous Modern Trials*, Abelard, 1971; *Strange Crimes of Passion*, Sportshelf, 1970; *Alias the Victim: A Command Squad Story*, R. Hale, 1971; *Famous Detective Feats*, Arthur Barker, 1971; *They Got Away with Murder*, John Long, 1971; *More Famous Historical Mysteries*, Muller, 1972; *Sisters of Cain*, John Long, 1972; *Famous Feats of Espionage*, Arthur Barker, 1972; *Programmed for Death*, R. Hale, 1973; *Hallmark of Horror*, John Long, 1973; *Stories of Famous Master Criminals*, Arthur Barker, 1973; (editor) *Fifty Famous Animal Stories*, Burke Publishing, 1974; *Such Was Their Guilt*, John Long, 1974; *They Conspired to Kill*, John Long, 1975; *Famous Stories of The Murder Squad*, Arthur Barker, 1975.

Contributor to *Dictionary of National Biography*, and of articles on sociology to *Chambers' Encyclopedia* and to *Encyclopedia Americana*; also contributor of book reviews, feature articles, short stories, and serials to journals and newspapers throughout the world.

WORK IN PROGRESS: Research on international true-crime subjects for magazine and book publication.

SIDELIGHTS: Gribble is the author of over 200 books published under various names; his books have been translated into fifteen languages. *Avocational interests:* Motoring in Europe.

* * *

GRIEDER, Josephine 1939-

PERSONAL: Surname rhymes with "reader"; born January 24, 1939, in San Francisco, Calif.; daughter of James Elmer (a salesman) and Marie Josephine (Uhl) Booth; married Theodore Godfrey Grieder (a librarian and writer), August 20, 1958. *Education:* Stanford University, student, 1956-58; University of Nevada, B.A., 1960; University of California, Davis, M.A., 1966; New York University, Ph.D., 1969. *Politics:* Democrat. *Home:* 1236 Garden St., Hoboken, N.J. 07030. *Office:* Department of Foreign Languages, Rutgers University, Newark, N.J. 07102.

CAREER: High school French and English teacher in Reno, Nev., 1960-61, San Pablo, Calif., 1961-62, and Davis, Calif., 1963-66; Rutgers University, Newark, N.J., instructor, 1969-70, lecturer, 1970-72, assistant professor of French, 1972—. *Member:* Modern Language Association of America, American Comparative Literature Association, American Association of Teachers of French, American Society for Eighteenth-Century Studies.

WRITINGS: (With husband, Theodore Grieder) *A Student's First Aid to Writing*, Littlefield, 1972; *French Sentimental Prose Fiction in Late Eighteenth-Century England: The History of a Literary Vogue*, Duke University Press, in press. Contributor to *PMLA, French Review, French Studies, New England Quarterly, Bulletin of Bibliography*, and *Dix-Septieme Siecle*.

WORK IN PROGRESS: A study of literary, cultural, and social relations between France and England, 1740-1789.

* * *

GRIEVES, Forest L(eslie) 1938-

PERSONAL: Born September 19, 1938, in Beatty, Nev.; son of William Arthur (a truckdriver) and Alice (a teacher; maiden name, Parman) Grieves; married Irmgard Katharina Spengler, March 31, 1963; children: Kevin, Emily. *Education:* Laval University, summer study, 1958; Stanford University, B.A., 1960; University of Hamburg, graduate study, 1962-63; University of Nevada, M.A., 1964; University of Arizona, Ph.D., 1967. *Home:* 1223 Old Orchard Rd., Missoula, Mont. 59801. *Office:* Department of Political Science, University of Montana, Missoula, Mont. 59801.

CAREER: Western Illinois University, Macomb, assistant professor of political science, 1967-69; University of Montana, Missoula, assistant professor, 1969-72, associate professor of political science, 1972—. Instructor for correctional staff and inmate educational programs at Montana State Prison. *Military service:* U.S. Army, 1960-62; served in Europe; became first lieutenant. *Member:* American Society of International Law, Western Political Science Association. *Awards, honors:* Study grants from University of Montana Foundation, 1970, 1972, 1974; American Philosophical Society grant, 1972; National Endowment for the Humanities grant, 1973.

WRITINGS: Supranationalism and International Adjudication, University of Illinois Press, 1969; *International Law, Organization, and the Environment: A Bibliography and Research Guide*, University of Arizona Press, 1974.

Associate editor of "Montana Series in History," published by University of Montana Press, 1970—. Contributor of articles and reviews to academic journals, including *Western Political Quarterly, American Political Science Review, Journal of Politics, Environmental Affairs, Military Review*, and *Growth and Change*. Editorial advisor for *Western Political Quarterly* and *Growth and Change*.

WORK IN PROGRESS: Research on international law and environmental affairs and on comparative politics (Western Europe and the Soviet Union).

SIDELIGHTS: Grieves has traveled in Europe, the Soviet Union, North Africa, and Asia.

* * *

GRIFFIN, Barbara C(ook) 1945-

PERSONAL: Born December 11, 1945, in Belleville, Ill.; daughter of Charles Laster (a real estate appraiser) and Dolores (a nurse; maiden name, Sauer) Cook; divorced. *Education:* University of Arkansas, Little Rock, student, 1961-62; Washington University, St. Louis, Mo., B.A., 1964; graduate student at California State University, Long Beach, 1967-68, and University of California, Irvine, 1970-71. *Home:* 22672 Jubilo Pl., El Toro, Calif. 92630.

CAREER: Teacher in St. Louis, Mo., 1964-67, and Huntington Beach, Calif., 1968-72; small business consultant in Orange County, Calif., 1968—.

WRITINGS: A Successful Business of Your Own, Sherbourne, 1974.

WORK IN PROGRESS: Two novels, with Bett Pohnka, *A Deadly Calm* and *The Cause*.

* * *

GRIFFIN, C(harles) W(illiam) 1925-

PERSONAL: Born May 26, 1925, in Washington, D.C.; son of Charles William (a lawyer) and Lucie (Oliver) Griffin; married Jacqueline Perry (an English professor), November 23, 1949; children: Janis Bates. *Education:* George Washington University, B.C.E., 1949. *Politics:* Democrat. *Home and office:* 62 Indian Spring Trail, Denville, N.J. 07834.

CAREER: Registered professional engineer in New Jersey, 1955; United Engineers & Constructors, Philadelphia, Pa., structural designer, 1950-52; David Bloom (consulting engineers), Philadelphia, Pa., structural designer, 1952-59; *Engineering News-Record*, New York, N.Y., senior editor, 1959-67; consulting engineer in New Jersey, 1967—. Member of Denville Environmental Commission, 1972-73. *Military service:* U.S. Navy, Air Corps, 1943-46; became ensign. *Awards, honors:* American Society of Civil Engineers national award, 1953, for essay on professional ethics.

WRITINGS: Manual of Built-up Roof Systems, McGraw, 1970; *The Systems Approach to School Construction*, Educational Facilities Laboratories, 1971; *Development Building: The Team Approach*, American Institute of Architects, 1972; *Taming the Last Frontier: A Prescription for the Urban Crisis*, Pitman, 1974; *Energy Conservation in Buildings: Techniques for Economical Design*, Construction Specificaitons Institute, 1974.

WORK IN PROGRESS: A book on professional liability of architects and engineers; a book tentatively titled, *The Search for Religious Values.*

* * *

GRIFFIN, Robert 1936-

PERSONAL: Born June 20, 1936, in Riverside, Calif.; son of Hubert Stokes (a teacher) and Lettye (Wagenblast) Griffin; married Leslie Lynn Pinching, August 24, 1958; children: Laura Alexandra, Peter Stokes. *Education:* University of California, B.A. (with high honors), 1958; University of Aix-Marseilles, graduate study, 1960-61; Yale University, Ph.D., 1962. *Home:* 4008 Chapman Pl., Riverside, Calif. *Office:* Department of French and Italian, University of California, Riverside, Calif. 92502.

CAREER: Carleton College, Northfield, Minn., instructor in French, 1962-63; University of California, Riverside, assistant professor, 1963-67, associate professor, 1967-71, professor of French, 1971—, chairman of department of French and Italian, 1974—.

MEMBER: Modern Language Association of America, American Association of Teachers of French, Society for Religion in Higher Education. *Awards, honors:* Woodrow Wilson fellowship, 1958; Danforth fellowship, 1958-62; Fulbright scholarship, 1960-61; American Philosophical Association grant, 1969; Humanities Institute grant, 1969.

WRITINGS: Coronation of the Poet, University of California Press, 1969; *Ludovico Ariosto,* Twayne, 1974; *Clement Marot and the Inflections of Poetic Voice,* University of California Press, 1974. Contributor of sixteen articles to professional journals. Associate editor of *French Review;* member of editorial board of *Oeuvres et critiques.*

WORK IN PROGRESS: Charles d'Orleans, for Twayne.

* * *

GRIFFITH, Jerry 1932-

PERSONAL: Born May 28, 1932, in Findlay, Ill.; son of Earl Franklin and Hazel (Swanner) Griffith; married Nancy J. Newberry, June 18, 1955; children: Holly Ann. *Education:* Eastern Illinois University, B.S., 1954; University of Illinois, M.S., 1957, Ph.D., 1961. *Residence:* 729 Franklin, Charleston, Ill. 61920. *Office:* Department of Speech Pathology and Audiology, Eastern Illinois University, Charleston, Ill. 61920.

CAREER: Speech pathologist in Mahomet, Ill. public schools, 1957-58; Indiana State University, Terre Haute, associate professor of special education, 1961-66; Eastern Illinois University, Charleston, professor of speech pathology, 1966—. Private practice in psychology, Charleston, 1970—; partner, Griffith & Miner Associates (consultants). *Military service:* U.S. Army, 1954-56. *Member:* American Psychological Association, American Speech and Hearing Association, Conference on Visual Literacy (president, 1971-72), Illinois Speech and Hearing Association (vice-president, 1975-76). *Awards, honors:* Grants from Eastman Kodak Co., Illinois Programs for Gifted Children, and Illinois Lung Association.

WRITINGS: (Editor and contributor) *Persons with Hearing Loss*, C. C Thomas, 1969; (with L. E. Miner) *Building Basic Articulation Skills*, Bell & Howell, 1973; (with Miner) *Connected Speech Stimuli*, Bell & Howell, 1973; (with Miner and T. E. Strandberg) *Classroom Photography Projects*, Books I-II, Eastman Kodak Co., 1974. Author with Miner of other speech pathology manuals and aids published by Bell & Howell. Contributor to professional journals. Co-editor, *Proceedings* of Lincolnland Conferences on Dialectology, 1969, 1970, 1972.

* * *

GRILLO, Virgil 1938-

PERSONAL: Born January 2, 1938, in New York, N.Y.; son of Domenic (a restaurateur and film distributor) and Clara (a teacher; maiden name, Corica) Grillo; married Joanne Mudry (a potter), December 26, 1959; children: Christopher, Jennifer. *Education:* University of Southern California, B.A., 1960; University of California, Berkeley, M.A., 1962, Ph.D., 1970. *Office:* Department of English, University of Colorado, Boulder, Colo. 80302.

CAREER: University of California, Berkeley, instructor in English and speech, 1961-68; University of Colorado, Boulder, assistant professor, 1968-73, associate professor of English and film, 1973—. Director of Rocky Mountain Film Center, 1972—.

WRITINGS: Charles Dickens' Sketches of Boz: End in the Beginning, Colorado Associated Universities Press, 1974.

WORK IN PROGRESS: Further work on film and literature.

* * *

GROFF, Warren F(rederick) 1924-

PERSONAL: Born June 27, 1924, in Harleysville, Pa.; son of Reinhart and Reba Groff; married Ruth N. Davidheiser; children: David Warren. *Education:* Juniata College, B.A. (summa cum laude) 1949; Yale University, B.D., 1952, Ph.D., 1955. *Home:* 18W681 22nd St., Lombard, Ill. 60148. *Office:* Bethany Theological Seminary, Butterfield and Meyers Rds., Oak Brook, Ill. 60521.

CAREER: Ordained minister of the Congregational Church, 1947; pastor in Mapleton Depot, Pa., 1947-49, and Southington, Conn. 1951-53; Bridgewater College, Bridgewater, Va., assistant professor, 1954-56, associate professor of religion, 1956-58; Bethany Theological Seminary, Oak Brook, Ill., associate professor, 1958-62, professor of theology, 1962—, dean, 1962—. Visiting scholar at Harvard University, 1965-66. *Member:* World Council of Churches, American Theological Society (president, 1972-73), American Academy of Religion, American Association of Theological Schools. *Awards, honors:* Faculty fellowship from American Association of Theological Schools, 1965-66.

WRITINGS: The Unity of the Person of Christ in Contemporary Theology, Yale University Press, 1955; (contributor) Paul H. Bowman, editor, *The Adventurous Future*, Brethren Press, 1959; (contributor) Kendig Cully, editor, *Westminister Dictionary of Christian Education*, Westminster, 1964; (with Donald E. Miller) *The Shaping of Modern Christian Thought*, World Publishing, 1968; (contributor) Donald F. Durnbaugh, editor, *Die Kirche der Brueder: Geschichte und Gegenwart* (title means "The Church of the Brethren: Past and Present"), Evangelischen Press, 1970; *Christ the Hope of the Future: Signals of a Promised Humanity*, Eerdmans, 1971; *Story Time: God's Story and Ours*, Brethren Press, 1974. Contributor to *Christian Century, Pulpit*, and other journals.

GROIA, Phil(ip) 1941-

PERSONAL: Surname is pronounced *Groy*-a; born February 19, 1941, in New York, N.Y.; son of Nicholas F. (a physician) and Lucy (De Roberts) Groia. *Education:* Adelphi University, B.A., 1962, M.A., 1968. *Politics:* "Do away with it!" *Religion:* "Uh, none." *Home:* 800 Myrna Dr., West Hempstead, N.Y. 11552. *Office:* Three Village Central School District Number One, Setauket, N.Y. 11733.

CAREER: High school social studies teacher in West Hempstead, N.Y., 1965; Paul J. Gelinas Junior High School, Setauket, N.Y., social studies teacher, 1965—. Volunteer for Big Brothers of America, 1968-70; manager of "Harptones," a rhythm and blues vocal group. *Member:* National Council for the Social Studies, Rhythm and Blues Society (New Haven), Eta Sigma Phi.

WRITINGS: They All Sang on the Corner: New York City's Rhythm and Blues Vocal Groups of the 1950's, Edmond, 1973, revised edition, 1974. Contributor to *Black Music* and *Yesterday's Memories*. Associate editor of *Bim Bam Boom: The World's Greatest Oldies Magazine*.

WORK IN PROGRESS: A book on vocal groups of the discotheques of the 1970's; a book on the journeys of the black man in major league baseball; research on black American popular music.

SIDELIGHTS: Groia writes: "Books had been written on rock 'n' roll but none had ever given attention to the black rhythm and blues street groups of the 1950's, the true cradle of black rock.

"There would have been no rock culture of the 50's and 60's had it not been for the music culture of black neighborhoods—a theme that is sorely overlooked by today's popular news and entertainment media."

* * *

GROMACKI, Robert Glenn 1933-

PERSONAL: Surname is pronounced Gro-*mack*-ee; born September 20, 1933, in Erie, Pa.; son of Sylvester Theodore (a foreman) and Thelma (a practical nurse; maiden name, Woodell) Gromacki; married Gloria Guy Julyan (an elementary school teacher), June 4, 1954; children: Gary Robert, Gail Lynn. *Education:* Baptist Bible Seminary, Johnson City, N.Y., Th.B., 1956; Dallas Theological Seminary, Th.M., 1960; Grace Theological Seminary, Winona Lake, Ind., Th.D., 1966. *Office:* Division of Biblical Education, Cedarville College, Cedarville, Ohio 45314.

CAREER: Pastor of community church in Montrose, Pa., 1955-56; Bethany Institute, Dallas, Tex., instructor in Bible, 1958-59; Southern Bible Training School, Dallas, Tex., instructor in Bible, 1959-60; ordained Baptist clergyman, 1960; Cedarville College, Cedarville, Ohio, associate professor, 1960-66, professor of Bible and Greek, 1966—, chairman of Division of Biblical Education, 1966—. *Member:* Evangelical Theological Society, Creation Research Society, Near East Archaeological Society, Society of Biblical Literature.

WRITINGS: The Modern Tongues Movement, Presbyterian and Reformed, 1967, revised edition, 1972; *Are These the Last Days?*, Revell, 1970; *Salvation Is Forever*, Moody, 1973; *The Virgin Birth: Doctrine of Deity*, Nelson, 1974; *New Testament Survey*, Baker Book, 1974; *The Doctrine of Man and Sin*, Moody, in press; *The Corinthian Epistles*, Baker Book, in press. Contributor to *Ohio Independent Baptist, Baptist Bulletin*, and *Grace Journal*.

AVOCATIONAL INTERESTS: Golf (college coach), tennis, table tennis, swimming, travel (Israel).

* * *

GROSS, Daniel R(ussell) 1942-

PERSONAL: Born October 25, 1942, in New York, N.Y.; married; children: one. *Education:* University of Chicago, A.B., 1964; Columbia University, Ph.D., 1970. *Residence:* Brooklyn, N.Y. *Office:* Department of Anthropology, Hunter College of the City University of New York, 695 Park Ave., New York, N.Y. 10021.

CAREER: Hunter College of the City University of New York, New York, N.Y., instructor, 1969, assistant professor, 1970-74, associate professor of anthropology, 1974—. *Member:* American Anthropological Association (fellow), Columbia University Seminar on Ecological Systems and Cultural Evolution (associate; chairman, 1972-74). *Awards, honors:* Woodrow Wilson fellowship, 1964-65.

WRITINGS: (Editor) *Peoples and Cultures of Native South America*, Doubleday, 1973. Contributor of about a dozen articles and reviews to scientific journals, including *Natural History, Ethnology, American Anthropologist, Science Digest, Journal of Anthropological Research*, and *Science and Society*.

WORK IN PROGRESS: Protein Capture and Cultural Development in the Amazon Basin; *Cultural Adaptation in Central Brazil*.

SIDELIGHTS: Gross has conducted field research in Brazil, 1965, 1966, 1967-68, 1971, 1973.

* * *

GROSSINGER, Tania 1937-

PERSONAL: Born February 17, 1937, in Evanston, Ill.; daughter of Max and Karla (Seifer) Grossinger. *Education:* Brandeis University, B.A., 1956. *Politics:* Democrat. *Religion:* Jewish. *Home:* 1 Christopher St., New York, N.Y. 10017. *Agent:* Anita Diamant, 51 East 42nd St., New York, N.Y. 10017.

CAREER: Barcas & Shalit (public relations), New York, N.Y., account executive, 1961-62; *Playboy*, New York, N.Y., director of broadcast promotion, 1963-69; Stein & Day, New York, N.Y., director of publicity, 1970-72. Consultant to Sherut La'am (Israeli Peace Corps), 1969-72. *Member:* Anti-Defamation League, National Academy of Television Arts and Sciences, Publishers Publicity Association, Publicity Club of New York.

WRITINGS: The Book of Gadgets, McKay, 1974.

WORK IN PROGRESS: An autobiography, *Growing Up at Grossinger's*, completion expected in 1975; *The Success Syndrome in America*, 1976.

* * *

GROSSMAN, Julian 1931-

PERSONAL: Born September 16, 1931, in Allentown, Pa.; son of Joseph Samuel (a dealer in scrap iron and metals) and Esther B. (Einhorn) Grossman; married Carolyn F. Judus (a businesswoman), August 28, 1969. *Education:* Columbia University, B.Sc., 1953; Rutgers University, M.L.S., 1956; Lehigh University, further graduate studies, 1965-70. *Religion:* Jewish. *Home:* 211 Center Ave., Norristown, Pa. 19401.

CAREER: Muhlenberg College, Allentown, Pa., reference librarian and government documents librarian, 1964-71;

Community College of Philadelphia, Philadelphia, Pa., lecturer in history of photography, 1971-72. *Member:* American Anthropological Association, Valley Forge Historical Society, B'nai B'rith. *Awards, honors:* Muhlenberg College faculty grant, 1970, for *The Echo of a Distant Drum.*

WRITINGS: The Echo of a Distant Drum: Winslow Homer and the Civil War, Abrams, 1974. Contributor to *American Anthropologist, Special Libraries, Muhlenberg Essays,* and *RQ* (journal of American Library Association's Reference Division).

WORK IN PROGRESS: Research on art history, especially American art history.

AVOCATIONAL INTERESTS: Collecting U.S. postage stamps.

* * *

GROSSMAN, Samuel 1897-

PERSONAL: Born December 6, 1897, in Philadelphia, Pa.; son of Mayer and Goldie (Klemphner) Grossman; married Doris Boxer (an executive), August 21, 1932; children: Laurence, Judith Grossman Erber, Lucille Grossman Schwartz. *Education:* Attended American Business Institute, 1914-15, Mechanics Institute, 1916-17, and City College (now City College of the City University of New York), 1918-20. *Politics:* Independent. *Religion:* Jewish. *Home:* 10 West 16th St., New York, N.Y. 10011. *Office:* Grossman Stamp Co., Inc., 860 Broadway, New York, N.Y. 10003.

CAREER: New York Times, New York, N.Y., accountant, 1915-18, employed in advertising department, 1920, in editorial department, 1921; auditor for Fox Film Co., 1922-23; Grossman Stamp Co., Inc., New York, owner, 1929—; Longacre Publishing Co., New York, president and publisher, 1956—. *Member:* American Stamp Dealers Association (president, 1965-66), American Numismatic Association, American Philatelic Association, Grand Street Boys Association, King County Grand Jurors Association.

WRITINGS: Regent World Stamp Album, Latham, 1940, 6th edition, 1971; *Stamp Collectors Handbook*, Longacre, 1957, 15th edition, 1975; *U.S. Plate Block Album*, Latham, 1960, new edition, 1975; *Philatelic World Gazeteer*, Latham, 1970; *Postage Stamp Identifier and Guide*, Grossman Stamp Co., 1970. Contributor of articles to science, education, and philately journals.

SIDELIGHTS: Grossman writes: "If opportunity will permit, will switch writings to more of fictional, highly emotional, and perhaps semi-biographical nature."

* * *

GRUBER, Gary R. 1940-

PERSONAL: Born November 19, 1940, in New York. *Education:* City College of the City University of New York, B.S. (with honors), 1962; Columbia University, M.A., 1964; Yeshiva University, Ph.D., 1969. *Office:* Department of Physics, Hofstra University, Hempstead, Long Island, N.Y. 11550; and Educational Division, Simon & Schuster, Inc., 1 West 39th St., New York, N.Y. 10018.

CAREER: Cambridge University Press, New York, N.Y., chief editor in physics and mathematics, 1969; Hofstra University, Hempstead, Long Island, N.Y., assistant professor of physics and astronomy, and director of astronomy and mathematical physics, 1969-73, senior research scientist, 1973—. Director of public affairs and the public understanding of science, New York Academy of Sciences, 1973-74. Senior editor, Educational Division, Simon & Schuster, Inc., 1970—; consultant to Prentice-Hall, John Wiley & Sons, and Oxford University Press, 1969—. Has lectured on science on radio and television. *Member:* American Physical Society, American Association for the Advancement of Science, American Mathematical Society, American Astronomical Society, American Association of Physics Teachers, American Association of University Professors, National Association of Science Writers. *Awards, honors:* Research fellowship, University of Glasgow, 1966-68; National Science Foundation grant, 1971-72.

WRITINGS—All published by Simon & Schuster: *Physics*, 1971; *High School Equivalency Examination Test*, 1971; *General Mathematical Ability*, 1971; *Correctness and Effectiveness of Expression*, 1971; *Reading Interpretation in the Natural Sciences and Literature*, 1971; *Graduate Record Exam: Math Review*, 1971; *College Level Examination Program*, 1973; *Standard Written English Test*, 1974; *American College Testing Program*, 1974; *Professional and Administrative Career Program of the Federal Government*, 1975. Contributor to journals in his field.

* * *

GRUBER, Martin Jay 1937-

PERSONAL: Born July 15, 1937, in Brooklyn, N.Y.; son of Sam (an executive) and Betty (a teacher; maiden name, Coronell) Gruber; married Eleanor Cohen, August 13, 1961; children: Jonathan Holmes, Stacey Lynne. *Education:* Massachusetts Institute of Technology, S.B., 1959; Columbia University, M.B.A., 1961, Ph.D., 1966. *Home:* 454 George St., Ridgewood, N.J. 07450. *Office:* Graduate School of Business Administration, New York University, 90 Trinity Pl., New York, N.Y. 10006.

CAREER: New York University, New York, assistant professor, 1965-68, associate professor, 1968-72, professor of finance, 1972—. Senior research fellow at International Institute of Management, 1972-74. *Member:* European Finance Association (member of board of directors, 1973—), American Finance Association, American Economic Association, American Statistical Association, New York Society of Security Analysts.

WRITINGS: Pension Funds 1966, Investment Publishing, 1967; *The Determinants of Common Stock Prices*, Office of Research, Pennsylvania State University, 1971; *Security Evaluation and Portfolio Analysis*, Prentice-Hall, 1972; *Finance as a Dynamic Process*, Prentice-Hall, 1975. Contributor of more than twenty-five articles to professional journals. Associate editor of *Journal of Finance*, 1971-73.

WORK IN PROGRESS: International Capital of Markets, for North Holland Publishing; research on portfolio theory and the impact of regulation on the corporation.

* * *

GRUPP, Stanley E(ugene) 1927-

PERSONAL: Born May 26, 1927, in Oak Park, Ill.; son of Martin (a baker) and Mabel (a teacher; maiden name, Barron) Grupp; married Janet Hartsell, May 26, 1956; children: Denise Ann, Martin Paul, Emilee Sue. *Education:* Iowa State Teachers College (now University of Northern Iowa), B.A., 1951; University of Iowa, M.A., 1953; Indiana University, Ph.D., 1967. *Home:* 414 Bradley Lane, Normal, Ill. 61761. *Office:* Department of Sociology, Illinois State University, Normal, Ill. 61761.

CAREER: Federal Reformatory, El Reno, Okla., teaching intern, fall, 1951; high school teacher in Tama, Iowa, 1954-56, and Harvey, Ill., 1956-57; Illinois State University, Normal, instructor, 1957-61, assistant professor, 1961-67, associate professor, 1967-70, professor of sociology, 1970—. Visiting summer professor at Utah State University, 1970, and University of New Brunswick, 1972; lecturer at University of Illinois Police Training Institute, 1967, 1968, 1969. Consultant to American Justice Institute, 1971-72. *Member:* American Society of Criminology, Law and Society Association, American Sociological Association, Society for the Study of Social Problems, National Council on Crime and Delinquency. *Awards, honors:* Grants for drug research from Dope Monitors Foundation, 1962-63, and National Institute of Mental Health, 1968-69, 1969-70.

WRITINGS: (Editor) *The Positive School of Criminology: Three Lectures by Enrico Ferri*, University of Pittsburgh Press, 1968; (editor) *Marihuana*, C. E. Merrill, 1971; (author of introduction) August Drahms, *The Criminal: His Personnel and Environment* (reprint of 1900 edition), Patterson Smith, 1971; (editor) *Theories of Punishment*, Indiana University Press, 1972; *The Marihuana Muddle*, Heath, 1973.

Contributor: Frank Scarpitti and Harry Gold, editors, *Social Problems: Techniques of Intervention*, Holt, 1967; Brian Freeman, editor, *Narcotic Cases: Prosecution and Defense*, Practising Law Institute, 1970; Nick Pappas, editor, *The Jail: Its Operation and Management*, U.S. Bureau of Prisons, 1971; Ronald L. Akers and Edward Sagarin, editors, *Crime Prevention and Social Control*, Praeger, 1974. Contributor of about fifty articles to *Criminology, International Journal of the Addictions, Crime and Delinquency*, and other journals. Special reader, *American Sociological Review*.

* * *

GRUSS, Edmond C(harles) 1933-

PERSONAL: Born February 17, 1933, in Los Angeles, Calif.; son of Charles Henry and Frieda Elise (Poethe) Gruss; married Erma Geraldene Janes (a teacher), June 11, 1954; children: Susan Lynette, Mark Alan. *Education:* Los Angeles Baptist College, B.A., 1955; Los Angeles Baptist Theological Seminary, M.Div., 1958; Talbot Theological Seminary, Th.M., 1961; Drake University, M.A., 1964. *Politics:* Republican. *Religion:* Baptist *Home:* 21143 Placerita Cyn. Rd., Newhall, Calif. 91321. *Office:* Los Angeles Baptist College, 21726 West Placerita, Newhall, Calif. 91321.

CAREER: Los Angeles Baptist College, Newhall, Calif., instructor, 1960-64, assistant professor, 1965-68, associate professor, 1969-73, professor of history, 1974—, chairman of department, 1964—. Member of board of reference, Christian Apologetics Research and Information Service, 1974—. *Member:* American Historical Association, Organization of American Historians, Creation Research Society, Far West Slavic Conference.

WRITINGS: Apostles of Denial, Presbyterian and Reformed, 1970; *The Jehovah's Witnesses and Prophetic Speculation*, Presbyterian and Reformed, 1972; *Cults and the Occult in the Age of Aquarius*, Baker Book and Presbyterian and Reformed, 1974; *We Left Jehovah's Witnesses*, Baker Book and Presbyterian and Reformed, 1974; *The Ouija Board: Doorway to the Occult*, Moody Press, 1975.

WORK IN PROGRESS: Research on religion in America and on reincarnation examined in the light of Christianity (anti-reincarnation).

SIDELIGHTS: Gruss writes: "I am a conservative Bible-believing Christian and this conviction motivates me to examine and reply to that which seeks to undermine that faith. My field is also known by the term apologetics. My teaching in history is interpreted within a Christian philosophy which sees God's intervention into history as a reality."

* * *

GUBRIUM, Jaber F(andy) 1943-

PERSONAL: Born July 17, 1943, in Hull, Quebec, Canada; son of Fandy G. (a salesman) and Aline (Monette) Gubrium; married Suzanne Kish (a systems analyst), March 25, 1967; children: Aline and Erika (twins). *Education:* Wayne State University, Ph.B., 1965, Ph.D., 1970; Michigan State University, M.A., 1966. *Politics:* Democrat. *Home:* 5675 North Bay Ridge, Whitefish Bay, Wis. 53217. *Office:* Department of Sociology, Marquette University, Milwaukee, Wis. 53233.

CAREER: Marquette University, Milwaukee, Wis., assistant professor, 1970-74, associate professor of sociology, 1974—. *Member:* American Sociological Association, Gerontological Society, American Association of University Professors, Midwest Sociological Society.

WRITINGS: The Myth of the Golden Years: A Socio-Environmental Theory of Aging, C.C Thomas, 1973; (editor) *Late Life: Communities and Environmental Policy*, C.C Thomas, 1974; (editor) *Time, Roles, and Self in Old Age*, Behavioral Publications, in press; *Living and Dying at Murray Manor*, St. Martin's, in press.

* * *

GUILMARTIN, John Francis, Jr. 1940-

PERSONAL: Surname is pronounced with silent "u"; born September 18, 1940, in Chicago, Ill.; son of John Francis and Katherine (Douglas) Guilmartin; married Judith Ellen Ohr, March 9, 1966; children: Lore Ann, Eugenia Katherine. *Education:* Trinity University, San Antonio, Tex., student, 1957-58; U.S. Air Force Academy, B.S., 1962; Princeton University, M.A., 1969, Ph.D., 1971. *Home and office:* 5 Lakeshore Dr., Shalimar, Fla. 32579.

CAREER: U.S. Air Force, 1962—, rescue helicopter pilot, 1963-70, instructor at U.S. Air Force Academy, 1970-71, assistant professor, 1971-73, associate professor of history, 1973—; present rank, major. *Member:* American Aviation Historical Society, Society for Nautical Research (England), Order of Daedalians. *Awards, honors*—Military: Silver Star with oak leaf cluster; Air Medal with four oak leaf clusters.

WRITINGS: Gunpowder and Galleys: Changing Technology and Mediterranean Warfare at Sea in the Sixteenth Century, Cambridge University Press, 1974. Contributor to *Mariner's Mirror*.

WORK IN PROGRESS: Warfare and Society: 1300-1700, with T. K. Rabb, for Heath; research on dietary intake and physiological output of Spanish galley crews, 1523-1587; comparative study of piracy in the sixteenth century; research on design, manufacture, ballistics, and tactical use of cannon in the sixteenth century, especially cannon of cast bronze; research on psychological significance of serpentine and reptilian imagery of the barrel decorations of sixteenth century cannon; studying the Spanish Civil War

(1936-1939), especially socio-political factors, tactics, and relationship between tactics and the recruitment, training, and motivation of fighting organizations; a lifetime study of the relationship between military tactics and technology and relevant cultural and socio-economic factors.

AVOCATIONAL INTERESTS: Cooking (Mediterranean and non-European food), vegetable gardening, building scale models of ships and aircraft, woodcarving.

* * *

GUINEY, Mortimer 1930-

PERSONAL: Surname is pronounced *Guy*-knee; born January 27, 1930, in Boston, Mass.; son of Mortimer Martin and Frances (Quinlan) Guiney; married Louise Purves, December 21, 1953; children: Louise, Mortimer, Patrick, Elisabeth. *Education:* Attended University of Paris, 1949, 1955-56; Colby College, B.A., 1952; Middlebury College, M.A., 1956. *Home:* 206 Codfish Falls Rd., Storrs, Conn. 06268. *Office:* Department of Romance and Classical Languages, University of Connecticut, Humanities 240, Storrs, Conn. 06268.

CAREER: University of North Carolina, Greensboro, instructor, 1958-64, assistant professor of French, 1965; University of Connecticut, Storrs, assistant professor, 1965-72, associate professor of French, 1972—, director of Program in France, 1972—. Visiting professor, University of Rouen. Member of jury, Swiss Prize for Abstract Painting, 1964. *Member:* Modern Language Association of America, American Comparative Literature Association, American Association of University Professors, American Association of Teachers of French (chapter vice-president, 1960-61; chapter president, 1961-62), Council on Student Travel, Pi Delta Phi.

WRITINGS: (Editor and author of preface) *Man in Art*, University of North Carolina, Greensboro, 1965; *La Poesie de Pierre Reverdy* (title means "The Poetry of Pierre Reverdy"), Georg & Cie (Geneva), 1966; (editor) Georges Bernanos, *Un Crime* (title means "A Crime"), Prentice-Hall, 1967; *Cubisme et litteraire* (title means "Cubism and Literature"), Georg & Cie, 1972; *Poesie americaine d'aujourd'hui: Poesie I*, Librairie Saint-Germain des Pres (Paris), in press; (contributor) *A Critical Bibliography of French Literature: Twentieth Century Volumes*, Syracuse University Press, in press. Also author, with R. J. Nelson, of "A Student's Manual," 1958. Contributor of articles to *Art Actuel International, Revue des Sciences Humaines*, and reviews to *Choice, Modern Language Journal*, and *Books Abroad*.

WORK IN PROGRESS: Study of the avant-garde.

* * *

GUNDERSHEIMER, Werner L. 1937-

PERSONAL: Born April 7, 1937, in Frankfurt, Germany; son of Herman S. (a professor) and Friedl (Seigel) Gundersheimer; married Karen Rosenwald (an artist and illustrator), June 23, 1963; children: Joshua, Benjamin. *Education:* Amherst College, B.A., 1959; Harvard University, M.A., Ph.D., 1963. *Office:* Department of History, University of Pennsylvania, 208 College Hall, Philadelphia, Pa. 19174.

CAREER: Visiting assistant professor of history at University of Wisconsin, 1963-64; University of Pennsylvania, Philadelphia, assistant professor, 1966-68, associate professor, 1968-71, professor of history, 1971—. Visiting professor at Johns Hopkins University and Swarthmore College. President of board of directors of Philip H. and A. S. W. Rosenbach Foundation. *Member:* American Historical Association, Renaissance Society of America (member of council, 1972-75), Mediaeval Academy of America, Society for Italian Historical Studies, Royal Historical Society (fellow), Phi Beta Kappa. *Awards, honors:* Named Cavaliere of Order of the Star of Italian Solidarity by Republic of Italy, 1974.

WRITINGS: (Editor) *The Italian Renaissance*, Prentice-Hall, 1965; *The Life and Works of Louis LeRoy*, Droz, 1966; (editor) *French Humanism: 1470-1600*, Harper, 1971; *Ferrara: The Style of a Renaissance Despotism*, Princeton University Press, 1973; *Art and Life at the Court of Ercole I d'Este*, Droz, 1973. Contributor of articles and reviews to history journals.

WORK IN PROGRESS: Further research on the Italian Renaissance, especially its urban, cultural, and intellectual history.

* * *

GURMAN, Alan S(tephen) 1945-

PERSONAL: Born May 26, 1945, in Winthrop, Mass.; son of Joseph (a mechanical engineer) and Ethel (Frazer) Gurman; married Geraldine Kalfus (a dancer), June 9, 1968. *Education:* Boston University, B.A. (cum laude), 1967; Columbia University, M.A., 1970, Ph.D., 1971; University of Wisconsin Medical School, postdoctoral study, 1971-73. *Office:* Department of Psychiatry, Medical School, University of Wisconsin, 427 Lorch St., Madison, Wis. 53706.

CAREER: University of Wisconsin, Medical School, Madison, assistant professor of psychiatry and director of Psychiatric Intervention Clinic, 1973—. Private practice in psychotherapy, 1973—. *Member:* Society for Psychotherapy Research, Academy of Psychologists in Marital and Family Therapy, National Council on Family Relations, American Psychological Association, Association for the Advancement of Behavior Therapy, Sigma Xi, Psi Chi.

WRITINGS: (Contributor) H. H. Strupp, A. E. Bergin, P. J. Lang, and other editors, *Psychotherapy and Behavior Change 1973*, Aldine, 1974; (editor with D. G. Rice, and contributor) *Couples in Conflict: New Directions in Marital Therapy*, Aronson, 1975; (editor with A. M. Razin, and contributor) *The Therapist's Contribution to Effective Psychotherapy: An Empirical Assessment*, Pergamon, 1975. Contributor of over twenty articles to journals of the social sciences, including *Journal of Family Counseling, International Journal of Group Psychotherapy, Family Process, Journal of Nervous and Mental Diseases, Journal of Health and Social Behavior*, and *Journal of Counseling Psychology*. Member of editorial board of *Journal of Marriage and Family Counseling*.

AVOCATIONAL INTERESTS: Tennis, home gardening, guitar, dance.

* * *

GUSFIELD, Joseph R. 1923-

PERSONAL: Born September 6, 1923, in Chicago, Ill.; son of Henry I. (a butcher) and Emma (Dauber) Gusfield; married Irma Geller (a social worker), September 14, 1946; children: Julia (deceased), Daniel, Ilene. *Education:* University of Chicago, B.Ph., 1946, M.A., 1949, Ph.D., 1954. *Religion:* Jewish. *Home:* 7228 Monte Vista, La Jolla, Calif. 92037. *Office:* Department of Sociology, University of California at San Diego, La Jolla, Calif. 92037.

CAREER: University of Chicago, Chicago, Ill., instructor in social science, 1949-51; Hobart and William Smith Colleges, Geneva, N.Y., assistant professor of sociology, 1951-55; University of Illinois, Urbana, assistant professor, 1955-59, associate professor, 1959-64, professor of sociology, 1964-68, research associate in industrial relations, 1958; University of California at San Diego, La Jolla, professor of sociology, 1969—. Fulbright lecturer at Patna University, 1962-63, and American Institutes in Bangalore, 1966; exchange professor at Institute of Management and Labor of Keio University, 1967-68; visiting summer professor at University of Chicago, 1951-56. *Military service:* U.S. Army, Medical Corps, 1943-46.

MEMBER: American Sociological Association, American Association for Asian Studies, Phi Beta Kappa. *Awards, honors:* American Council of Learned Societies Asian fellowship, 1967; Guggenheim fellowship, 1973-74.

WRITINGS: Symbolic Crusade, University of Illinois Press, 1963; *Protest, Reform, and Revolt*, Wiley, 1970; (with David Riesman and Zelda Gamson) *Academic Values and Mass Education*, Doubleday, 1970; *Utopian Myths and Movements in Modern Society*, General Learning Press, 1974; *Community: A Critical Response*, Macmillan, in press; *Social Movements*, Basic Books, in press. Contributor to sociological journals. Associate editor of *American Sociological Review*, 1962-65, and *Sociology of Education*, 1972-75.

WORK IN PROGRESS: Knowledge and Public Policy: The Social Control of Drinking and Driving.

* * *

GUTHRIE, Hunter 1901-1974

January 8, 1901—November 11, 1974; American Jesuit priest, educator, university president, author and editor of works predominantly on philosophy. Obituaries: *Washington Post*, November 13, 1974.

* * *

GUTHRIE, Robert V(al) 1930-

PERSONAL: Born February 14, 1930, in Chicago, Ill.; son of Paul Lawrence (an educator) and Lerlene (Cartwright) Guthrie; married, wife's name Elodia S., September 15, 1952; children: Robert, Paul, Michael, Ricardo, Sheila, Mario. *Education:* Florida Agricultural and Mechanical University, B.S., 1955; University of Kentucky, M.A., 1960; U.S. International University, Ph.D., 1970. *Politics:* Democrat. *Religion:* African Methodist Episcopal. *Home:* 1109 Oakview Dr., Silver Spring, Md. 20903. *Office:* Psychological Sciences Division, Office of Naval Research, Arlington, Va. 22217.

CAREER: San Diego Mesa College, San Diego, Calif., instructor in psychology, 1963-70; University of Pittsburgh, Pittsburgh, Pa., assistant professor, 1970-71, associate professor of psychology, 1971-73; National Institute of Education, Washington, D.C., senior research psychologist, 1973-74; Office of Naval Research, Arlington, Va., research psychologist and associate director of psychological sciences, 1975—. Adjunct professor at George Washington University. *Military service:* U.S. Air Force, 1950-54, 1956-59.

MEMBER: American Psychological Association, Federation of American Scientists, American Academy of Social Scientists, Society for the Psychological Study of Social Issues, Eastern Psychological Association, Pennsylvania Psychological Association.

WRITINGS: Psychology in the World Today: An Interdisciplinary Approach, Addison-Wesley, 1968, 2nd edition, 1971; *Encounter: Issues on Human Concerns*, Cummings, 1970; *Being Black: Sociological and Psychological Dilemmas*, Canfield, 1970; (with E. J. Barnes) *Focus on Reality: Man and Society*, Frccl & Associates, 1972; *Even the Rat Was White: Historical Views in Psychology*, Harper, 1975. Contributor to psychology and sociology journals.

WORK IN PROGRESS: Editing and revising two books of readings in psychology; research on the history of psychology; research on basic skills acquisition for different cultural and linguistic groups.

SIDELIGHTS: Guthrie writes: "For years I have been concerned over the failure of the traditional behavioral sciences to document information pertinent to members of minority groups. In order to fulfill the gap caused by this neglect, I have directed a considerable portion of my research and writing energies to providing such information. I am much concerned over the basic research paradigms that are employed to investigate social and other human interactions and as a result, I feel confident that I will be directing my research-writing efforts into this subject area."

* * *

GUTKIND, Lee 1943-

PERSONAL: First syllable of surname is pronounced "good"; born January 3, 1943, in Pittsburgh, Pa.; son of Jack R. (a merchant) and Mollie (Osgood) Gutkind; married Pamela Johnson (a teacher), March 30, 1969 (divorced). *Education:* University of Pittsburgh, B.A., 1968. *Politics:* None. *Religion:* None. *Agent:* Curtis Brown Ltd., 60 East 56th St., New York, N.Y. 10022. *Office:* Department of English, University of Pittsburgh, Pittsburgh, Pa. 15213.

CAREER: University of Pittsburgh, Pittsburgh, Pa., instructor, 1970-71, assistant professor of English, 1972—. *Military service:* U.S. Coast Guard, 1961-69.

WRITINGS: Bike Fever, Follett, 1972; *The Best Seat in Baseball. . . . But You Have to Stand*, Dial, 1975. Contributor to more than two hundred twenty-five newspapers and magazines, including *New York Times* and *Sports Illustrated.* Contributor to Associated Press and United Feature Syndicate.

* * *

GUYOT, James F(ranklin) 1932-

PERSONAL: Born September 28, 1932, in Detroit, Mich.; son of Robert P. (a farmer) and Lucille (Fritsch) Guyot; married Dorothy Jean Hess (a professor), December 31, 1960; children: Erik Robert, Maria Khin Khin, Daniel Karl. *Education:* Michigan State College (now University), B.A., 1953; Yale University, A.M., 1954, Ph.D., 1961. *Home:* 124 Maple, Leonia, N.J. 07605. *Office:* Department of Public Administration, Baruch College of the City University of New York, New York, N.Y. 10010.

CAREER: U.S. Civil Service Commission, Boston, Mass., management intern and examiner, 1956-57; Swarthmore College, Swarthmore, Pa., instructor in political science, 1959-60; University of Connecticut, Storrs, instructor in political science, 1960-61; University of California, Los Angeles, assistant professor of political science, 1963-69; Columbia University, New York, N.Y., visiting lecturer, 1968-69, associate professor of political science, 1969-72, research associate in Southern Asian Institute, 1968—; Port

Authority of New York and New Jersey, manager of personnel research, 1972-73; Baruch College of the City University of New York, New York, N.Y., associate professor of political science and public administration, 1973—. Postdoctoral research fellow, Yale University, spring, 1963; visiting scholar, Inter-University Consortium for Political Research, University of Michigan, summer, 1965; visiting lecturer at University of Malaya, 1966-67, and University of Pennsylvania, 1970. Chairman of Political Development Seminar of Southeast Asia Development Advisory Group, U.S. Agency for International Development, 1967-70; seminar associate of University Seminar on the State, Columbia University, 1972—; fellow of Inter-University Seminar on Armed Forces and Society, 1973—. Consultant to California Office of Administrative Procedure, 1965, to *Columbia University Encyclopedia*, 1971-72, and to U.S. Department of State, 1971-72.

MEMBER: American Association for the Advancement of Science, American Political Science Association, American Society for Public Administration, Asia Society, Association for Asian Studies, International Personnel Management Association, American Civil Liberties Union, Adirondack Mountain Club, Yale Russian Chorus. *Awards, honors:* Fulbright grant, University of Rangoon, 1961-62; Human Ecology Fund grant while postdoctoral fellow, Department of Political Science of Yale University, 1962-63; Pi Sigma Alpha teaching award, 1965; Ford Foundation, International and Comparative Studies grant, 1966-67; Rockefeller Foundation grant, 1968-70.

WRITINGS: (Editor with W. Howard Wriggins) *Population, Politics, and the Future of Southern Asia*, Columbia University Press, 1974.

Contributor: Ralph Braibanti and others, *Asian Bureaucratic Systems Emergent from the British Imperial Tradition*, Duke University Press, 1966; Robert T. Deland, editor, *Comparative Urban Research*, Sage Publications, 1969; Robert O. Tilman, editor, *Man, State, and Society in Contemporary Southeast Asia*, Praeger, 1969; Joseph Fischer, editor, *The Social Sciences and the Comparative Study of Educational Systems*, International Textbook Co., 1970; Catherine M. Kelleher, editor, *Political Military Systems: Comparative Perspectives*, Sage Publications, 1974. Contributor to periodicals, including *Public Administration Review, Administrative Law Bulletin, Journal of Comparative Administration*, and *Bucknell Review*.

AVOCATIONAL INTERESTS: Hiking, music.

* * *

HAAR, Francis 1908-

PERSONAL: Born July 19, 1908, in Hungary; son of Arnold (a master craftsman) and Adel (Reiter) Haar; married Irene Papa (a dining hall manager), March 25, 1934; children: Thomas, Veronica (Mrs. Wendell Peacock), Andrew. *Education:* National Academy of Industrial Arts, Budapest, diploma, 1928. *Home and office:* 4236 Carnation Pl., Honolulu, Hawaii 96816.

CAREER: University of Hawaii, College of Continuing Education, Honolulu, lecturer in photography, 1963-74. Vice-president, Island Films, Inc., 1965; president, Honolulu Printmakers, 1969. *Member:* Hawaii Painters and Sculptors League (vice-president, 1974), Honolulu Academy of Arts. *Awards, honors:* Award from Council International of Nontheatrical Events (C.I.N.E.), 1962, for film, "Pineapple Country Hawaii"; another film, "Hawaii's Asian Heritage," was selected by C.I.N.E. in 1966 to represent the United States in international film competitions.

WRITINGS—All photographic essays: *Way to the Orient*, Ars (Tokyo), 1940; *Around Mount Fuji*, Benrido (Kyoto), 1941; *The Best of Old Japan*, Tuttle, 1951; (with Earle Ernst) *Japanese Theatre in Highlight: A Pictorial Commentary*, Tuttle, 1952, 2nd edition, revised, 1954, reprinted, Greenwood, 1971; *The Tokyo You Should See*, Tuttle, 1960; *Haar Ferenc munkassaga* (title means "The Life Work of Francis Haar"), Corvina (Budapest), 1969; (with Prithwish Neogy) *Artists of Hawaii*, Volume I: *Nineteen Painters and Sculptors*, University Press, of Hawaii, 1974. Author of script (and director) of film documentary, "Tenno-Symbol and Myth," produced in Japan, 1964.

WORK IN PROGRESS: Volume II of *Artists of Hawaii*, with Neogy.

SIDELIGHTS: In addition to Hungarian and English, Haar speaks French and Japanese.

* * *

HAAS, Kurt

EDUCATION: Pennsylvania State University, Ph.D. *Office:* Department of Psychology, State University of New York College at New Paltz, New Paltz, N.Y. 12561.

CAREER: State University of New York College at New Paltz, 1962—, became professor of psychology, 1966—.

WRITINGS: *Understanding Ourselves and Others*, Prentice-Hall, 1965; *Understanding Adjustment and Behavior*, Prentice-Hall, 1970; *Growth Encounters*, Nelson-Hall, 1975.

* * *

HAAS, Michael 1938-

PERSONAL: Born March 26, 1938, in Detroit, Mich.; son of Mark L. (a broadcaster) and Isabelle (Helm) Haas. *Education:* Stanford University, B.A., 1959, Ph.D., 1964; Yale University, M.A., 1960. *Home:* 469 Ena Rd., Apt. 2903, Honolulu, Hawaii 96815. *Office:* Department of Political Science, University of Hawaii, 2424 Maile Way, Honolulu, Hawaii 96822.

CAREER: California State University, San Jose, lecturer in political science, 1963-64; University of Hawaii, Honolulu, assistant professor, 1964-67, associate professor, 1967-71, professor of political science, 1971—. Visiting professor at Northwestern University, 1968-69, Purdue University, 1969, and University of California, Riverside, 1969. Consultant to United Nations Institute for Training and Research. *Member:* International Studies Association, Peace Science Society, American Political Science Association, Phi Beta Kappa. *Awards, honors:* Ford Foundation fellow at University of Hawaii, 1965-68; Hawaiian Electric Co. fellow, 1966-68; Carnegie Endowment for International Peace fellow.

WRITINGS: (Editor with Henry S. Kariel, and contributor) *Approaches to the Study of Political Science*, Chandler Publishing, 1970; *International Organization*, Hoover Institution, 1971; (editor and contributor) *International Systems*, Intext, 1974; *Basic Documents of Asian Regional Organizations*, Oceana, 1974; *International Conflict*, Bobbs-Merrill, 1974. Contributor to *American Political Science Review, Behavioral Science, Comparative Political Studies, Journal of Peace Research*, and *World Politics*.

WORK IN PROGRESS: The Asian Way to Peace.

HABERMANN, Helen M(argaret) 1927-

PERSONAL: Born September 13, 1927, in New York, N.Y.; daughter of Hans Otto (a cabinet maker) and Katherine (Hansen) Habermann. *Education:* State University of New York at Albany, A.B., 1949; University of Connecticut, M.S., 1951; University of Minnesota, Ph.D., 1956. *Home:* 801 Beaverbank Cir., Towson, Ind. 21204. *Office:* Department of Biological Sciences, Goucher College, Towson, Md. 21204.

CAREER: University of Chicago, Research Institutes, Chicago, research associate, 1956-57; Stanford University, Hopkins Marine Station, Pacific Grove, Calif., postdoctoral research associate, 1957-58; Goucher College, Towson, Md., assistant professor, 1958-64, associate professor, 1964-70, professor of biological sciences, 1970—, chairman of department, 1963-66, 1968. Visiting investigator at Carnegie Institution of Washington, summer, 1959, University of Goettingen, Pflanzenphysiologisches Institute, summers, 1960, 1962; National Institutes of Health research fellow at Research Institute for Advanced Study, 1966-67.

MEMBER: Japanese Society for Plant Physiology, Scandinavian Society for Plant Physiology, American Society of Plant Physiologists, Botanical Society of America, American Association for the Advancement of Science (fellow), Society for Developmental Biology, American Association of University Professors, Society for Experimental Biology and Medicine, American Society for Horticultural Science, Sigma Delta Epsilon, Sigma Xi.

WRITINGS: (Contributor) Hans Gaffron, editor, *Research in Photosynthesis,* Interscience, 1957; (contributor) M. B. Allen, editor, *Comparative Biochemistry of Photoreactive Systems,* Academic Press, 1960; (contributor) Boerge C. Christensen and B. Buchman, editors, *Progress in Photobiology,* Elsevier, 1961; (with G. B. Moment) *Biology: A Full Spectrum,* Williams & Wilkins, 1973; *Plant Physiology,* Williams & Wilkins, in press. Contributor of more than forty articles to professional journals.

WORK IN PROGRESS: A National Science Foundation project on light-dependent stomatal opening.

* * *

HAGMAN, Bette 1922-

PERSONAL: Born August 10, 1922, in Troutdale, Ore.; daughter of Carroll D. (a writer) and Daisy (in education; maiden name, Hill) Bush; married Joe L. Hagman (a certified public accountant), September 4, 1942; children: Karol Lee (Mrs. Martin Leo Mehan). *Education:* Linfield University, B.A., 1943. *Religion:* Christian. *Home:* 8752 22nd St. N.W., Seattle, Wash. 98117. *Agent:* Lenniger Literary Agency, Inc., 11 West 42nd St., New York, N.Y.

CAREER: SEA-TAC Emergency Hospital, Tacoma, Wash., receptionist, 1943-45; Bank of California, Tacoma, Wash., batch department staff member, 1945-46; Bette Hagman Home Tailoring, Seattle, Wash., proprietor, 1948-57; writer. *Member:* Pacific Northwest Writers Conference (member of board of trustees, 1974-77), Seattle Free Lance.

WRITINGS: The Death Beads (novel), Dell, 1974.

WORK IN PROGRESS: The Talking Stick; *Last Trip for Ellie Mae*.

AVOCATIONAL INTERESTS: Skiing, fishing, camping, sewing, redecorating.

HAIBLUM, Isidore 1935-

PERSONAL: Born May 23, 1935, in Brooklyn, N.Y.; son of Alex (a leather goods cutter) and Sarah (Jijmerskaia) Haiblum. *Education:* City College (now of the City University) of New York, B.A., 1958. *Religion:* Jewish. *Home and office:* 160 West 77th St., New York, N.Y. 10024. *Agent:* Henry Morrison, 58 West 10th St., New York, N.Y. 10011.

CAREER: Former door-to-door health survey interviewer, script writer, and agent for folk-singers; writer. *Military service:* U.S. Army Reserve, 1959-65. *Member:* Science Fiction Writers of America.

WRITINGS: The Tsaddik of the Seven Wonders, Ballantine, 1971; *The Return*, Dell, 1973; *Transfer to Yesterday*, Ballantine, 1973; *The Wilk Are Among Us*, Doubleday, 1975. Contributor to *Village Voice*, *National Jewish Monthly*, *Pioneer Woman*, *Congress Bi-Weekly*, *Woman's American ORT Reporter*, *Midstream*, and *Hadassah Magazine*.

WORK IN PROGRESS: Four novels, *Pull All the Stops*, *Eclectic Upheaval*, for Dell, *Through the Stasis Vault*, for Ballantine, and *Memory Masters*, for Harper (all titles tentative).

* * *

HAIMES, Norma

PERSONAL: Born in Brooklyn, N.Y.; daughter of Perry and Ida (Levine) Haimes. *Education:* Brooklyn College of the City University of New York, B.A., 1969, M.F.A. candidate; Pratt Institute, M.L.S., 1972. *Residence:* Brooklyn, N.Y. *Office:* Brooklyn College Library, City University of New York, Brooklyn, N.Y. 11210.

CAREER: Formerly staff artist with Brooklyn Public Library, Brooklyn, N.Y., and forms control supervisor with Home Life Insurance Co., New York, N.Y.; Brooklyn College Library, City University of New York, Brooklyn, N.Y., reference librarian, 1972—. *Member:* Art Libraries Society of North America, New York Library Association, Library Association of the City University of New York, Phi Beta Kappa, Beta Phi Mu.

WRITINGS: Helping Others: A Guide to Selected Social Service Agencies and Occupations, John Day, 1974. Contributor to *American Journal of Art Therapy* and *Psychologia*.

WORK IN PROGRESS: Co-editing *Directory of Art Libraries of North America*.

* * *

HAIMOWITZ, Natalie Reader 1923-

PERSONAL: Born May 27, 1923, in New York, N.Y.; daughter of Philip and Esther (a businesswoman; maiden name, Fetner) Reader; married Morris Loeb Haimowitz (a social psychologist), December 31, 1948; children: Carla, Myrna, Louise. *Education:* Attended New School for Social Research, 1943-44; Brooklyn College (now Brooklyn College of the City University of New York), B.A., 1944; Ohio State University, M.A., 1945; University of Chicago, Ph.D., 1948. *Residence:* Evanston, Ill. *Office:* 1101 Forest Ave, Evanston, Ill. 60202.

CAREER: Ohio State University, Columbus, clinical assistant at Psychological Clinic, 1944-45; research assistant, Committee on Human Development, 1945-46; University of Chicago, Chicago, Ill., externe at Counseling Center,

1946-47; Brooklyn College (now Brooklyn College of the City University of New York), Brooklyn, N.Y., lecturer in psychology, 1947-48; U.S. Veterans Administration, Mental Hygiene Clinic, Chicago, Ill., postdoctoral trainee, 1949-51; University of Chicago, Chicago, Ill., instructor in psychology, 1953-58; private practice in clinical psychology, 1955—. Chief psychologist at Women's and Children's Hospital (Chicago), 1955-59; psychologist for Milwaukee's Psychiatric Services, 1960-64; trainee at International Transactional Analysis Institute, 1967; presently member of faculty for training and supervision of practitioners, Haimowoods Institute. *Member:* International Transactional Analysis Association (trustee), American Psychological Association, American Association for the Advancement of Psychotherapy, Sigma Chi.

WRITINGS: (With husband, Morris Haimowitz) *Human Development*, Crowell, 1960, 3rd edition, 1973. Contributor to psychology journals.

* * *

HAINES, Francis D., Jr. 1923-

PERSONAL: Born June 16, 1923, in Bozeman, Mont.; son of Francis (an author) and Plesah (MacDonald) Haines; married Leslie Tiffany (a librarian), June 12, 1954; children: Mary Beth, Margaret Nan, Beverly Robin, Francis D. III. *Education:* University of California, Berkeley, A.B., 1943; Gonzaga University, M.A., 1949; Washington State University, Ph.D., 1955. *Home:* 445 Jennifer St., Ashland, Ore. 97520. *Office:* Department of History, Southern Oregon College, Ashland, Ore. 97520.

CAREER: Gonzaga University, Spokane, Wash., instructor in history, 1948-49; North Idaho College, Lewiston, instructor in history, 1950; Nez Perce Tribal Council, Lapwai, Idaho, research historian, 1955-56; Southern Oregon College, Ashland, assistant professor, 1956-59, associate professor, 1959-62, 1963-69, professor of history, 1969—. Visiting professor at Western Washington State College, 1962-63. *Military service:* U.S. Marine Corps, 1942-46. U.S. Army, Infantry, 1949-53; became first lieutenant.

WRITINGS: (With Vern S. Smith) *Gold on Sterling Creek*, Gandee Printing, 1964; *Jacksonville*, Gandee Printing, 1967; (editor) *A Bride on the Bozeman Trail*, Gandee Printing, 1970; (editor) *Snake Country Expedition: 1831-1832*, University of Oklahoma Press, 1971. Contributor to *Pacific Northwest Quarterly* and *Idaho Yesterdays*.

WORK IN PROGRESS: With Willard Leonard, *A Boyhood with Sheep on the Oregon Desert;* research on northwest Indian wars, on Oregon myths and legends, and on the history of southern Oregon.

* * *

HALDEMAN, Joe (William) 1943- (Robert Graham)

PERSONAL: Born June 9, 1943, in Oklahoma; son of Jack Carroll (a hospital administrator) and Lorena (Spivey) Haldeman; married Mary Gay Potter (a teacher), August 21, 1965. *Education:* University of Maryland, B.S., 1967; also attended American University, University of Oklahoma, and University of Iowa. *Politics:* "Skeptic." *Religion:* "Skeptic." *Home address:* P.O. Box 855, Iowa City, Iowa 52240. *Agent:* Robert P. Mills Ltd., 156 East 52nd St., New York, N.Y. 10022. *Office:* Writers Workshop, University of Iowa, Iowa City, Iowa 52241.

CAREER: Writer of speculative fiction. *Military service:* U.S. Army, 1967-69; received Purple Heart. *Member:* Science Fiction Writers of America (treasurer, 1970-72).

WRITINGS: *War Year* (novel), Holt, 1972; (editor) *Cosmic Laughter*, Holt, 1974; *The Forever War* (novel), St. Martin's, 1974.

Adventure novels, under pseudonym Robert Graham: *Attar's Revenge*, Pocket Books, in press; *War of Nerves*, Pocket Books, in press; *A Cold Place to Die*, Pocket Books, in press.

Short stories have been anthologized in *Orbit/Eleven*, edited by Damon Knight, Putnam, 1971; *The Best From Galaxy*, edited by Ejler Jakobbsen, Universal-Award, 1972; *Showcase*, edited by Roger Elwood, Harper, 1973; *Best SF:1972*, edited by Harry Harrison and Brian Aldiss, Putnam, 1973; *The Best Science Fiction of the Year—1972*, edited by Terry Carr, Ballantine, 1973; *Analog 9*, edited by Ben Bova, Doubleday, 1973; *Best SF:1973*, edited by Harrison and Aldiss, Putnam, 1974; *Combat SF*, edited by Gordon Dickson, Doubleday, 1975; *The Last Dangerous Visions*, edited by Harlan Ellison, Putnam, 1975.

Contributor of about twenty short stories to science fiction magazines, including *Analog, Galaxy, Vertex, If, Magazine of Fantasy and Science Fiction, Fantastic*, and *Amazing*.

WORK IN PROGRESS: *Peacemaker*, a novel; short stories and nonfiction.

SIDELIGHTS: Haldeman writes: "My first novel . . . was a fictionally-extended version of my own combat diary, and the main reason for writing it was to set down as accurately as possible the details of that experience. I plan to use it as a nucleus, or at least a notebook, for a large novel about the war. But I still need several years' perspective on the experience, before I start writing the novel." *Avocational interests:* Classical guitar, bicycling, woolgathering, strong drink, travel ("collect continents like scalps; lack two").

* * *

HALE, Francis Joseph 1922-

PERSONAL: Born October 24, 1922, in Manila, Philippines; son of Harold Francis (a U.S. naval officer) and Teresa (a psychologist; maiden name, Vaughan) Hale; married Frances Eugenia Keller (an interior designer), April 23, 1949; children: Francis J. III, Olin T., Margaret Anne. *Education:* U.S. Military Academy, B.S., 1944; Massachusetts Institute of Technology, S.M., 1952, Sc.D., 1963. *Religion:* Roman Catholic. *Home:* 2601 Kingsley Rd., Raleigh, N.C. 27612. *Office:* Department of Mechanical and Aerospace Engineering, North Carolina State University, Raleigh, N.C. 27607.

CAREER: U.S. Army, Corps of Engineers, 1944-48, became captain; U.S. Air Force, career officer, 1948-65, retiring as colonel; North Carolina State University, Raleigh, associate professor, 1965-70, professor of mechanical and aerospace engineering, 1970—. Visiting professor at Middle East Technical University, 1973-74. *Member:* American Institute of Aeronautics and Astronautics (associate fellow), American Society for Engineering Education, American Association for the Advancement of Science, American Society of Mechanical Engineering, Sigma Xi, Sigma Gamma Tau. *Awards, honors:* National Science Foundation fellowship, 1973-74.

WRITINGS: *Introduction to Control System Analysis and Design*, Prentice-Hall, 1973.

HALE, Nathan Cabot 1925-

PERSONAL: Born July 5, 1925, in Los Angeles, Calif.; son of N. C. (a sportsman) and Virginia Markoe (a teacher; maiden name, Ferris) Hale; married Alison Elizabeth Boothby (an occupational therapist), December 27, 1964. *Education:* Attended Chouinard Art Institute, 1945, and Art Students' League of New York, 1945-50. *Politics:* "Believe in representative government." *Religion:* "Believe in cosmic order." *Home:* Sheffield Rd., Amenia, N.Y. 12501.

CAREER: Pratt Institute, New York, N.Y., instructor in art, 1963-64; Art Students' League of New York, New York, N.Y., instructor in art, 1966-72; sculptor in New York. Member of Midtown Galleries, 1962—. Fine arts advisor to Wilson and Snibbe. *Military service:* U.S. Marine Corps, 1941-42. U.S. Merchant Marine, 1944-45.

WRITINGS: *Welded Sculpture*, Watson-Guptil, 1968; *The Embrace of Life: The Sculpture of Gustav Vigeland*, Abrams, 1969; *Abstraction in Art and Nature*, Watson-Guptil, 1972. Contributor to *American Artist*, *Environment*, and *Journal of Orgonomy*.

WORK IN PROGRESS: Research for a book on the human figure in art and nature.

* * *

HALE, Patricia Whitaker 1922-

PERSONAL: Born March 1, 1922, in Harrison, Ark.; daughter of William A. (a farmer) and Lucille (a teacher; maiden name, Tyson) Whitaker; married Robert Mead Hale (a physicist), August 13, 1955; children: Robert Patrick, Erik Alvis. *Education:* University of California at Los Angeles, B.S., 1943; Mills College, M.A., 1944; University of Southern California, Ed.D., 1955. *Residence:* Orange, Calif. *Office:* Department of Physical Education, Chapman College, 333 North Glassell, Orange, Calif. 92666.

CAREER: Mills College, Oakland, Calif., instructor in physical education, 1944-46; University of California at Santa Barbara, Goleta, assistant professor of physical education, 1946-56; Chapman College, Orange, Calif., assistant professor of physical education, 1969—. *Member:* American Association for Health, Physical Education and Recreation, National Association of Physical Education for College Women, Western Society of Physical Education for College Women.

WRITINGS: *Individual Sports: A Textbook for Teachers*, W. C. Brown, 1974. Contributor to *Tennis-Badminton Guide* and *Research Quarterly*.

AVOCATIONAL INTERESTS: Tennis, golf, cooking, wood-carving, camping.

* * *

HALKIN, Shimon 1899-

PERSONAL: Given name is listed as Simon in some bibliographical sources; born October 30, 1899, in Dovsk, Russia; son of Hillel and Hannah Halkin. *Education:* New York University, B.A., 1926, M.A., 1928; Columbia University, graduate study, 1930-32. *Home:* 5 Radak St., Jerusalem, Israel.

CAREER: Hebrew Union College, School for Teachers, New York, N.Y., instructor in Hebrew language and literature, 1924-32; Geulah High School, Tel-Aviv, Israel, teacher, 1932-39; College of Jewish Studies, Chicago, Ill., lecturer in Bible, Jewish sociology, and modern Hebrew literature, 1940-43; Jewish Institute of Religion, New York, N.Y., professor of Hebrew literature, 1943-49; Hebrew University of Jerusalem, Jerusalem, Israel, professor of Hebrew literature, 1949-68, professor emeritus, 1968—. Visiting professor, University of California at Los Angeles, 1954-55, and Jewish Theological Seminary, 1965-66. *Member:* Academy of the Hebrew Language, Israel P.E.N. (past president). *Awards, honors:* D.H.L. from Columbia University, 1947; Tchernichovsky Prize, 1953, for translation of *Leaves of Grass*; Bialik Prize for Literature, 1968.

WRITINGS: *Al Hof Santa Barbara* (poem), [Tel-Aviv], 1928; *Yehiel Ha-Hagri* (novel), [Berlin], 1928; *BenYamin Shisha Uve Leilot Shiva* (sonnets), [Tel-Aviv], 1929; *Baruch Ben-Neria* (poem), [Tel-Aviv], 1934; *Arai Va-Keva* (literary essays), [New York], 1942; *Al Ha-Iy* (poems), [Jerusalem], 1943; *Yehudim ve Yahadut Be-America* (nonfiction), [Jerusalem], 1946; *Modern Hebrew Literature: Trends and Values*, Schocken, 1950, new edition published as *Modern Hebrew Literature, from the Enlightenment to the Birth of the State of Israel: Trends and Values*, 1970; (consulting editor) *Contemporary Israeli Verse*, [Chicago], 1958. Also author of *Ad-Mashber* (novel), 1945; *Mavo La Sipporet Ha Ivrit* (lectures), 1953; *Walt Whitman* (critique), 1954; *Ma-aver Yabbok* (poems; title means "Crossing the Jabbok"), 1965; *Derakhim ve-tside-derakbim be-sifrut*, 1969; *Collected Literary Essays and Studies*, three volumes, 1971; *Nekhar* (short stories; title means "Adrift"), 1973.

Translator into Hebrew: Jack London, *Before Adam*, 1921; London, *The Sea Wolf*, 1924; Maurice Maeterlinck, *The Blue Bird*, 1928; Percy Shelley, *A Defense of Poetry*, 1928; Stefan Zweig, *Amok*, 1929; William Shakespeare, *The Merchant of Venice*, 1929; Abraham Lebensohn, *Jewish Pioneers in America*, 1933; W. W. Hudson, *Green Mansions*, 1938; Solomon Goldman, *Nations, World and Country*, 1944; Shakespeare, *King John*, 1948; Walt Whitman, *Leaves of Grass*, 1951; Giorgos Seferis, *Selected Poems*, 1973.

* * *

HALL, Halbert Weldon 1941-

PERSONAL: Born October 29, 1941, in Waco, Tex.; son of Halbert Theon (a farmer) and Edna (Faris) Hall; married Betty Gloff, December 27, 1964; children: Julia, Sarah. *Education:* University of Texas at Austin, B.A., 1964; North Texas State University, M.L.S., 1968. *Politics:* Independent. *Home:* 3608 Meadow Oaks Ln., Bryan, Tex. 77801. *Office:* Library-Serials, Texas A&M University, College Station, Tex. 77843.

CAREER: High school biology teacher in West, Tex., 1964-66; Texas A&M University, College Station, serials librarian, 1970—. *Member:* American Library Association, Texas Library Association, Science Fiction Research Association (member of board of directors, 1971-74).

WRITINGS: (Compiler) *Science Fiction Book Review Index* (annual), privately printed, 1970—; (compiler) *Science Fiction Book Review Index, 1923-1973*, Gale, 1975. Editor of *SFRA Miscellaneous Publications*, 1971—, and *SFRA Newsletter*, 1974—.

* * *

HALL, J(ames) Curtis 1926-

PERSONAL: Born February 12, 1926, in Galax, Va.; son

of Alonzo A. and Clara (Crissman) Hall; married Mary Anne Jones, March 13, 1954; children: Michael C., Suzanne K. *Education:* Duke University, A.B. (magna cum laude), 1947; Virginia Polytechnic Institute and State University, M.S., 1952; Columbia University, Ed.D., 1956. *Home:* 10408 Saxony Rd., Richmond, Va. 23235. *Office:* School of Business, Virginia Commonwealth University, Richmond, Va. 23284.

CAREER: High school teacher in Galax, Va., 1947-50; Virginia Polytechnic Institute and State University, Blacksburg, assistant professor of business education, 1951-57; Auburn University, Auburn, Ala., associate professor, 1957-60, professor of business education, 1960-62; Virginia Commonwealth University, Richmond, professor of business, 1962—, dean of School of Business, 1962—. President of Investment Enterprises, Inc., 1969—; member of board of directors of Richmond Investment Properties, Inc., 1971—. Has taught at New Jersey State College (Montclair), University of Minnesota, Columbia University, University of Colorado, Oregon State University, and University of Hawaii. *Military service:* U.S. Naval Reserve, 1943-72, active duty, 1943-46; became commander.

MEMBER: National Business Education Association (president, 1970-71), Academy of Management, Administrative Management Society (president of Richmond chapter, 1969-70), Joint Council on Economic Education (member of board of trustees), Policies Commission for Business and Economic Education (chairman), Southern Business Education Association (president, 1967), Southern Management Association, Virginia Council on Economic Education (president), Phi Beta Kappa, Phi Kappa Phi, Alpha Kappa Psi, Kappa Delta Pi, Pi Omega Pi, Delta Pi Epsilon.

WRITINGS: (With Edwin M. Robinson) *College Business Organization and Management*, McGraw, 3rd edition, 1964; (with Ray G. Price, Vernon A. Musselman, and Edwin E. Weeks) *General Business for Everyday Living*, 3rd edition, McGraw, 1966, 4th edition (with Price and Musselman), 1972; (editor) *Business Education: An Evaluative Inventory*, National Business Education Association, 1968. Contributor to business and economics journals. Office standards editor of *Business Education Forum*, 1957-58, 1962-64, basic business editor, 1964-67; editor of *National Business Education Association Yearbook*, 1968.

WORK IN PROGRESS: *General Business for Everyday Living*, 5th edition, publication by McGraw expected in 1977.

* * *

HALL, James (Herrick, Jr.) 1933-

PERSONAL: Born October 20, 1933, in Houston, Tex.; son of J. Herrick (a professor) and Loula Ben (Vining) Hall; married Bonlyn Goodwin (a music librarian), May 25, 1957; children: Christopher Vining, Jonathan Goodwin. *Education:* Johns Hopkins University, A.B., 1955; Southeastern Theological Seminary, B.D., 1958, Th.M., 1960; University of North Carolina, Ph.D., 1963; Oxford University, postdoctoral study, 1973-74. *Politics:* Democrat-Liberal. *Religion:* Baptist-Quaker. *Home:* 3810 Hawthorne Ave., Richmond, Va. 23222. *Office:* Department of Philosophy, University of Richmond, Richmond, Va. 23173.

CAREER: U.S. Government Printing Office, Washington, D.C., member of staff, 1953-56; Sears, Roebuck & Co., Raleigh and Durham, N.C., complaint clerk, 1957-62; Furman University, Greenville, S.C., assistant professor, 1963-65, associate professor of philosophy, 1965-74; University of Richmond, Richmond, Va., professor of philosophy, 1974—. Member of Richmond Symphony Chorus. *Member:* American Philosophical Association, Society for Philosophy of Religion, National Education Association, American Association of University Professors, American Civil Liberties Union (member of board of directors of Virginia-Capitol area, 1967), Southern Society for Philosophy and Psychology, Virginia Philosophical Association, Virginia Humanities Conference. *Awards, honors:* Summer grant from Council for Philosophic Studies, 1973; grant from Mednick Foundation, 1973-74.

WRITINGS: *Knowledge, Belief, and Transcendence: Philosophical Problems in Religion*, Houghton, 1974. Contributor to *Analysis, Social Forces, Review of Metaphysics*, and *Richmond Times-Dispatch*. Member of reviewing staff of *Review of Metaphysics*.

WORK IN PROGRESS: *Man and Man's World*, completion expected in 1976; *The Nature of Explanation*, 1977.

SIDELIGHTS: Hall writes: "While I have great concern for the problems that confront man today, I have little (if any) patience for the vast parade of nonsense, jargon, and 'profundity' foisted on us by those who confuse obscurity and wisdom. We best meet ourselves and our problems on everyday ground. We best solve our riddles if we intolerantly reject double talk. How can we keep the jungle back if our knives are dull?" *Avocational interests:* Chess, birdwatching, guitar, choral music, England, Wales, Switzerland.

* * *

HALL, William N(orman) 1915-1974

1915—December 3, 1974; American editor and author of books for children. Obituaries: *Publishers Weekly*, January 6, 1975.

* * *

HALLBERG, Peter 1916-

PERSONAL: Born January 25, 1916, in Gothenburg, Sweden; son of Magnus (a secondary school teacher) and Maerta (Johansson) Hallberg; married Rannveig Kristjansdottir, January 6, 1945 (died, 1952); married Kristin Kristjansdottir (a chemist), January 30, 1955; children: (first marriage) Kristjan, Maria. *Education:* University of Gothenburg, fil mag, 1939, fil lic, 1943, fil dr, 1951. *Home:* Iskaellareliden 5A, 416 55, Gothenburg, Sweden. *Office:* Department of Comparative Literature, University of Gothenburg, Vasaparken, 411 24, Gothenburg, Sweden.

CAREER: University of Iceland, Reykjavik, lecturer in Swedish, 1944-47; University of Gothenburg, Gothenburg, Sweden, lecturer, 1951-61, senior lecturer, 1962-75, professor of Scandinavian literature, 1975—. Visiting professor, University of Aabo, spring, 1955; Thord-Gray Lecturer, University of Wisconsin, 1970-71. *Member:* Societe Europeenne de Culture, Kungliga Vetenskaps and Vitterhetssamhaellet (both Gothenburg), Visindafelag Islendinga (Reykjavik; corresponding member). *Awards, honors:* Falcon Order of Iceland, 1955; Doctor Philosophiae Honoris Causa, University of Iceland, 1974; Order of the Pole Star (Sweden), 1974.

WRITINGS: *Studier i Harry Martinsons spraak* (title means "Nature Symbols in the Language of H. Martinson"), Hugo Geber (Stockholm), 1941; *Natursymboler i svensk lyrik fraan nyromantiken till Karlfeldt* (title means

"Nature Symbols in Swedish Lyric Poetry from the Romantic Movement to Karlfeldt"), Wettergren & Kerber (Gothenburg), 1951; *Halldor Kiljan Laxness*, Albert Bonnier (Stockholm), 1952; *Den store vaevaren. En studie i Laxness' ungdomsdiktning* (title means "The Great Weaver: A Study in Laxness's Early Writings"), Raben & Sjoegren (Stockholm), 1954; *Skaldens hus. Laxness' diktning fraan Salka Valka till Gerpla* (title means "The Poet's House: Laxness's Writings from Salka Valka to Gerpla"), Raben & Sjoegren, 1956; *Den islaendska sagan*, Svenska Bokfoerlaget (Stockholm), 1956, new edition, 1964, translation of first edition by Paul Schach published as *The Icelandic Saga*, University of Nebraska Press, 1962.

Snorri Sturluson och Egils saga Skallagrimssonar. Ett foersoek till spraaklig foerfattarbestaemning (title means "Snorri Sturluson and Egill Skallagrimsson's Saga: An Attempt at Philological Establishment of Authorship"), Bokautgafa Menningarsjods and University of Iceland, 1962; *Den fornislaendska poesien*, Svenska Bokfoerlaget, 1962, translation by Schach, University of Nebraska Press, in press; *Harmonisk realism. En studie i Hans Aanruds bondeberaettelser* (title means "Harmonious Realism: A Study in Hans Aanrud's Country Stories"), Universitetsforlaget (Oslo), 1963; *Olafr Thordarson hvitaskald, Knytlinga saga och Laxdaela saga. Ett foersoek till spraaklig foerfattarbestaemning* (subtitle means "An Attempt at Philological Establishment of Authorship"), Bokautgafa Menningarsjods and University of Iceland, 1963; *Stilsignalement och foerfattarskap i norroen sagalitteratur. Synpunkter och exempel* (title means "Stylistic Characteristics and Authorship in Old Norse Saga Literature: Viewpoints and Examples"), Almqvist & Wiksell (Stockholm), 1968; *Litteraer teori och stilistik* (title means "Literary Theory and Stylistics"), Akademifoerlaget (Goeteborg, Sweden), 1970, new edition, 1972; *Halldor Laxness*, Twayne, 1971.

Translator, from Icelandic to Swedish, of works by Halldor Laxness, all titles given in Swedish: *Islands klocka* (title means "Iceland's Bell"), Kooperativa Foerbundets Bokfoerlag (Stockholm), 1948; *Vaarldens ljus* (title means "The Light of the World"), Kooperativa Foerbundets Bokfoerlag, 1950; *Himlens skoenhet* (title means "The Beauty of the Skies"), Kooperativa Foerbundets Bokfoerlag, 1951; *Atomstationen* (title means "The Atom Station"), Raben & Sjoegren, 1952; *Den goda froeken och Huset* (title means "The Honor of the House"), Raben & Sjoegren, 1954; *Utsaga* (title means "Statements"; selections from Laxness's writings, 1927-59), Raben & Sjoegren, 1959; *Det aatervunna paradiset* (title means "Paradise Regained"), Raben & Sjoegren, 1960; *Stickateljen Solen* (play; title means "The Knitting Workshop Called 'The Sun'"), Zindermans (Goeteborg), 1964; *Skaldetid* (memoirs; title means "A Writer's Schooling"), Raben & Sjoegren, 1964; *Sju tecken* (short stories; title means "The Book of Seven Signs"), Raben & Sjoegren, 1966.

WORK IN PROGRESS: Research on medieval Icelandic literature, especially the family sagas; a book on poetic imagery in various periods of Scandinavian literature.

* * *

HALLIDAY, Fred 1937-

PERSONAL: Born June 19, 1937, in New York, N.Y.; son of David Graham and Louise (Gimiglano) Halliday. *Education:* University of Maryland, B.A., 1961. *Politics:* "Monarchist." *Religion:* "Druid." *Home:* 240 Central Park S., New York, N.Y. 10019. *Agent:* Henry Morrison, 58 West 10th St., New York, N.Y.

CAREER: CBS News (television), New York, N.Y., staff writer, 1961-63; free-lance writer for television, 1963-67, for films, 1968-73; novelist, 1973—. *Member:* Writers Guild of America, East.

WRITINGS—Novels: *The Chocolate Mousse Murders*, Pinnacle Books, 1974; *The Raspberry Tart Affair*, Pinnacle Books, 1975. Author of film script, "The Nine Lives of Fritz the Cat"; scriptwriter for television series "Batman," "Spiderman," "Journey to the Center of the Earth," and others. Contributor of articles on food and wine to *Holiday* and *Vintage*.

WORK IN PROGRESS: The German General Staff through Hitler's Regime.

* * *

HALLOWAY, Vance 1916-
(Alpheus Van Woeart)

PERSONAL: Born April 16, 1916, in London, England; son of Alpheus and Olive (Baker) Halloway; married Josephine Cianciulli, 1940. *Education:* Attended Fishburne Military School and Jersey Prep School. *Home:* 1444 Laura St., Wrightwood, Calif. 92397; and 1343 South Calle Rolph, Palm Springs, Calif. 92262. *Office:* Vance Halloway Agency, Box 518, Pearblossom, Calif. 93443.

CAREER: Vance Halloway Agency, Pearblossom, Calif., owner, 1958—. Conducted own poetry programs over radio stations WYNC, WAAT, WOV, WHN, and WHOM (all New York, N.Y.), 1937-39. *Awards, honors:* Ph.D. from University of Eastern Florida; Gold Medal from International Poets, 1974, for sonnets.

WRITINGS—Plays: (Under pseudonym Alpheus Van Woeart) *Johnny in a Jam* (one-act), Baker's Plays, 1946; (under pseudonym Alpheus Van Woeart; with Joseph Carl McMullen) *This Day and Age* (three-act), Baker's Plays, 1947; *Anything for the Asking* (three-act), Baker's Plays, 1947; (under pseudonym Alpheus Van Woeart; with McMullen) *Al Haddon and His Lamp* (three-act fantasy), Baker's Plays, 1947; (under pseudonym Alpheus Van Woeart; with McMullen) *Air Express* (three-act comedy-fantasy), Baker's Plays, 1948; (under pseudonym Alpheus Van Woeart; with McMullen) *Apartment 13* (three-act mystery-comedy), Baker's Plays, 1948; *Summer Fancy* (three-act comedy), Drama Guild Publishers, 1949; *Ghost Town* (three-act comedy), Drama Guild Publishers, 1949; *Johnny and the Phantom* (one-act mystery-comedy), Baker's Plays, 1950; *Flying High* (three-act comedy), Baker's Plays, 1951; *Mother Named Him Percy* (three-act comedy), Baker's Plays, 1951; *Johnny and the Atomic Bomb* (one-act comedy), Eldridge Publishing, 1951.

Novels: *China Girl,* Publisher's Export Co., 1968; *The Horn Blower,* Publisher's Export Co., 1968; *Black Boy,* Publisher's Export Co., 1968; *Hollywood, My Hollywood,* Classic Book, 1968; *The Troubadour,* Publisher's Export Co., 1969; *Leather Pushers,* Golden State News, 1969; *The Sin Makers,* United Graphics, 1969; *Bella,* United Graphics, 1969; *Bartered Black Girl,* Greenleaf Classics, 1972; *Hell in Om's Eden,* Manor Books, in press; (with Evelyn Pierce Nace) *Eat Them Alive,* Manor Books, in press.

Poetry: *Hours of Dreams,* Richard Badger, 1935; (under pseudonym Alpheus Van Woeart) *Paradise Aflame,* Chapman & Grimes, 1936.

Poetry is represented in anthologies, including *New Jersey*

Poets, H. Harrison, 1936. Author of poetry column, "The Poet Speaks," in *Bayonne Facts,* 1934-36. Contributor of articles and short stories to various publications, and poetry to *Jean's Journal, International Poetry Review,* and other journals.

* * *

HALLOWELL, A(lfred) Irving 1892-1974

December 28, 1892—October 10, 1974; American anthropologist, educator, editor, and author. Obituaries: *New York Times,* October 15, 1974. (*CA*-7/8).

* * *

HALMAN, Talat Sait 1931-

PERSONAL: Born July 7, 1931, in Istanbul, Turkey; son of Sait Talat (an admiral) and F. Iclal (Nemlizade) Halman; married Barbara Teitz, 1954 (divorced, December, 1957); married Seniha Taskiranel (a United Nations information officer), July 23, 1960; children: (first marriage) Hugh; (second marriage) Defne I., Sait S. *Education:* Robert College, B.A. (honors), 1951; Columbia University, M.A., 1954, further graduate study, 1954-55. *Religion:* Islam. *Home:* 333 East 30th St., New York, N.Y. 10016. *Office:* Department of Near East Studies, Princeton University, Jones Hall, Princeton, N.J. 08540.

CAREER: Columbia University, New York, N.Y., lecturer in Turkish language and literature, 1953-60; Record Hunter, Inc., New York, N.Y., vice-president and general manager, 1956-60; Atlantic Recording Corp., New York, N.Y., director of album production, 1965-67; Princeton University, Princeton, N.J., assistant professor, 1966-69, associate professor, 1969-71, professor of Turkish language and literature, 1972—. Adjunct professor at New York University, 1967-71; minister of culture, Turkish Republic, 1971. Member of executive board of Council on National Literatures; member of Council of Translators. *Military service:* Turkish Navy, reserve officer, 1961-62; worked with Turkish State Planning Organization; became lieutenant.

MEMBER: P.E.N. American Center (member of executive board), Modern Language Association of America, American Academy of Political Science, Middle East Studies Association, Turkish-American University Association (honorary member), Alumni Association of the American Colleges of Istanbul (president, 1964-65), Alumni Association of Columbia University. *Awards, honors:* Knight Grand Cross of the Order of the British Empire, 1971.

WRITINGS: William Faulkner, Varlik Yayinevi, 1963; *Can Kulagi* (title means "The Heart's Ear"), Yeditepe Yayinevi, 1968; (translator) *Selected Poems of F. H. Daglarca,* University of Pittsburgh Press, 1969; (translator) *I Am Listening to Istanbul: Selected Poems of Orhan Voli Kanik,* Corinth Books, 1971; *The Humanist Poetry of Yunus Emre,* Regional Cooperation for Development Culture Institute, 1972; (editor with Nermin Menemencioglu, and translator) *On the Nomad Sea: Selected Poems of Melih Gevdet Anday,* Geronimo Books, 1974.

Translator into Turkish: William Faulkner, *Knight's Gambit,* Varlik Yayinevi, 1952; *Shakespeare's Sonnets,* Yeditepe Yayinevi, 1964; *Eskimo Poems,* Yeditepe Yayinevi, 1969; *Selected Poems of Wallace Stevens,* Yeditepe Yayinevi, 1970; *Selected Poems of Langston Hughes,* Yeditepe Yayinevi, 1971; *Ancient Egyptian Poetry,* Isbankasi Yayinlari, 1972.

Columnist for *Milliyet* and *Aksam* (Istanbul daily newspapers), 1969-73. Contributor to *Encyclopedia of World Literature in the Twentieth Century, Encyclopedia of Islam, International Yearbook of Comparative Literature, Encyclopedia of Poetry and Poetics,* and *Reader's Encyclopedia of Shakespeare.* Contributor of several hundred articles to Turkish, British, and American journals and newspapers, including *Nation, Literary Review, Middle East Journal, Literature East and West, Visions,* and *American P.E.N.* Member of editorial board of *Books Abroad* and *Journal of International Literature.* Guest editor of *Literature, Books Abroad, Review of National Literatures,* and *Literature East and West.*

WORK IN PROGRESS: Modern Turkish Drama; Contemporary Turkish Literature; Eski Uygarliklarin Siirleri (title means "The Poetry of Ancient Civilizations"); *Bir'ler* (title means "One-Line Poems"); *Dogrusu* (title means "Truth of the Matter"); *Kultur Cumhuriyeti* (title means "Republic of Culture: Articles on Culture and Literature"); editing *Anthology of Modern Turkish Short Stories; Big Town Blues: The Psychological Effects of Urbanization on the Turkish Peasant as Reflected in Literature,* to be published in Turkish and English; *History of Turkish Literature,* completion expected in 1976; *Modern Turkish Poetry: A Critical Anthology,* 1976.

* * *

HALPERIN, John 1941-

PERSONAL: Born September 15, 1941, in Chicago, Ill.; son of S. William (a historian) and Elaine (a translator; maiden name, Philipsborn) Halperin. *Education:* Bowdoin College, A.B., 1963; University of New Hampshire, M.A., 1966; Johns Hopkins University, M.A., 1968, Ph.D., 1969. *Home:* 221 12th Pl., Manhattan Beach, Calif. 90266. *Office:* Department of English, University of Southern California, Los Angeles, Calif. 90007.

CAREER: Wall Street Journal, New York, N.Y., reporter, 1963; Associated Press, Albany, N.Y., editor, 1963-64; State University of New York at Stony Brook, assistant professor of English, dean of Summer School, and assistant to academic vice-president, all 1969-72; University of Southern California, Los Angeles, associate professor of English and director of graduate studies, 1972—. *Military service:* U.S. Army Reserve, 1963-69; became staff sergeant. *Member:* Modern Language Association of America, American Philosophical Society.

WRITINGS: The Language of Meditation, Stockwell, 1973; (editor) Henry James, *The Golden Bowl,* Popular Library, 1973; *The Theory of the Novel,* Oxford University Press, 1974; *Egoism and Self-Discovery in the Victorian Novel,* B. Franklin, 1974; *Jane Austen,* Cambridge University Press, 1975. Contributor of articles about Jane Austen and Trollope to academic journals.

WORK IN PROGRESS: The Political Novels of Anthony Trollope.

* * *

HAMBLIN, W. K. 1928-

PERSONAL: Born May 22, 1928, in Lyman, Wyo.; son of William and Verona Hamblin; married wife, Sarah Ann, August 29, 1952; children: William James, Lisa Ann, Laura Jane, Kimberly Kay. *Education:* Brigham Young University, B.A., M.S.; University of Michigan, Ph.D., 1957. *Religion:* Church of Jesus Christ of Latter-Day Saints.

Home: 2924 Chippewa, Provo, Utah 84601. *Office:* Department of Geology, Brigham Young University, Provo, Utah 84602.

CAREER: Brigham Young University, Provo, Utah, 1962—, now professor of geology.

WRITINGS: Physical Geology Laboratory Manual, Burgess, 1964; *Guidebook to the Colorado River*, Brigham Young University Press, 1968; *Grand Canyon Perspectives*, Brigham Young University Press, 1969; *The Earth's Dynamic Systems*, Burgess, 1975.

* * *

HAMILTON, Alfred Starr 1914-

PERSONAL: Born June 14, 1914, in Montclair, N.J.; son of Alfred Starr and Virginia (Gildersleeve) Hamilton. *Education:* Attended high school in Montclair, N.J. *Politics:* Socialist. *Religion:* "Immune." *Home and office:* 41 South Willow St., Montclair, N.J. 07042.

CAREER: Poet. *Military service:* U.S. Army, 1942-43.

WRITINGS: Poems of Alfred Starr Hamilton, Jargon Press, 1970. Contributor to *Epoch*, *New Directions*, *Foxfire*, *New Letters*, *Archive*, and *Greenfield Review*.

SIDELIGHTS: Hamilton has hitchhiked through forty-three states.

* * *

HAMILTON, Carl 1914-

PERSONAL: Born May 14, 1914, in Carroll, Iowa; son of Burton Arthur and Imogene (Heaton) Hamilton; married Ruth Farnham, August 23, 1938; children: Ann, Blair, Bruce, Mark. *Education:* Iowa State University, B.S., 1936. *Politics:* Democrat. *Religion:* Presbyterian. *Address:* R.R. 4, Ames, Iowa 50010. *Office:* Morrill Hall, Iowa State University, Ames, Iowa 50010.

CAREER: Iowa Falls Citizen, Iowa Falls, advertising manager, 1937, editor, 1948-62; U.S. Department of Agriculture, Agricultural Adjustment Administration, Washington, D.C., member of information staff, assistant to Secretary of Agriculture, and assistant administrator, Rural Electrification Administration, during years 1938-48; *Hardin County Times*, Hardin County, Iowa, editor, 1948-62; Iowa State University, Ames, head of department of technical journalism, 1962-67, vice-president for information and development, 1967—. Chairman of Iowa Governor's Advisory Committee on Governmental Reorganization, 1966-67. *Awards, honors:* Bent Cane Award from Des Moines Press and Radio Club, 1955, for contribution to Iowa journalism; Master Editor-Publisher Award from Iowa Press Association, 1961.

WRITINGS: In No Time at All, Iowa State University Press, 1974.

* * *

HAMILTON, William, Jr. 1924-

PERSONAL: Born March 9, 1924, in Evanston, Ill.; son of William (an electrical engineer) and Helen (Anderson) Hamilton; married Mary Jean Golden (a former dancer with New York City Ballet Co.), June 11, 1949; children: Ross, Donald, Katie, Patrick, Jean. *Education:* Oberlin College, B.A., 1943; Union Theological Seminary, New York, N.Y., B.D., 1949; University of St. Andrews, Ph.D., 1952. *Politics:* "Conventionally left, though tempted to a post-political irony." *Religion:* "Protestant: death of God variety." *Home:* 2221 Southwest 1st Ave., Portland, Ore. 97201. *Office:* Dean of the College of Arts and Letters, Portland State University, Portland, Ore. 97207.

CAREER: Ordained American Baptist minister, 1948; Hamilton College, Clinton, N.Y., assistant professor of religion and dean of chapel, 1951-53; Colgate Rochester Divinity School, Rochester, N.Y., assistant professor, 1953-55, associate professor, 1955-59, professor of theology, 1959-67; New College, Sarasota, Fla., professor of religion, 1967-70; Portland State University, Portland, Ore., professor of religion and dean of College of Arts and Letters, 1970—. Adjunct professor at University of Rochester, 1955-67; visiting professor and acting provost at Empire State College of State University of New York, 1973-74. Writer, host, and actor for C.B.S. television program, "Look Up and Live"; producer of WQED radio program, "Introducing Theology," 1963, and WTTG television documentary, 1965. *Military service:* U.S. Navy, 1943-46; became ensign. *Member:* American Academy of Religion, Society for Religion in Higher Education. *Awards, honors:* D.H.L., Ripon College, 1968.

WRITINGS: The Christian Man, Westminster, 1956; *The Modern Reader's Guide to the Gospels*, Association Press, 1959; *The New Essence of Christianity*, Association Press, 1961; (contributor) Chalmers Dale, editor, *In the Presence of Death*, Bethany Press, 1964; (contributor) Nathan Scott, editor, *Forms of Extremity in the Modern Novel*, John Knox, 1965; (with Thomas J. Altizer) *Radical Theology and the Death of God*, Bobbs-Merrill, 1966; (contributor) James Robinson and John Cobb, editors, *Theology as History*, Harper, 1967; (contributor) Ronald Gregor Smith, editor, *World Come of Age*, Fortress Press, 1967; (contributor) Jackson Ice and John Carey, editors, *The Death of God Debate*, Westminster, 1968; (contributor) John Cooper and Carl Skrade, editors, *Celluloid and Symbols*, Fortress, 1970; *On Taking God Out of the Dictionary*, McGraw, 1974. Contributor of articles to more than fourteen journals. Author of television scripts.

WORK IN PROGRESS: A book about Herman Melville; a novel.

SIDELIGHTS: Hamilton was an original signer of the "Call to Resist Illegitimate Authority," and he was active in the anti-war movement of the 1960's.

* * *

HAMM, Glenn B(ruce) 1936-

PERSONAL: Born May 30, 1936, in Dayton, Ohio; son of Glenn B. (an electrical engineer) and Merry Helen (a credit bureau investigator) Hamm; married Monica Margaret Scanlon (co-ordinator of publications at Virginia Museum), February 17, 1968; children: Jennifer Lorraine. *Education:* Carnegie-Mellon University, B.F.A., 1958, M.F.A., 1964; Purdue University, doctoral studies, 1973-75; also studied at University of Pittsburgh, 1958-59, and Carnegie-Mellon University, 1959. *Politics:* Independent. *Religion:* Christian. *Home:* 1704 Peachtree Blvd., Richmond, Va. 23226. *Office:* Department of Creative Arts, Purdue University, West Lafayette, Ind. 47907.

CAREER: Elementary school art teacher in Pittsburgh, Pa., 1958-62; high school arts and crafts teacher in Imperial, Pa., 1962-63; Carlow College, instructor in art, 1963-64; West Virginia University, Morgantown, instructor in art, 1965-69; Virginia Commonwealth University, Richmond, instructor in art, 1969—. Teacher of adult painting classes at Pittsburgh's Arts and Crafts Center, summers, 1958-60, 1964-65; instructor at Carlow College, summer, 1960, and at Ivy School of Professional Art, summer, 1963; co-director of summer fine arts camp at West Virginia University, 1966; art instructor and adviser in federal "Follow-Through" program in Monongalia County, W. Va., 1967-68; advisor to ro-ordinator of federal programs for West Virginia Arts and Humanities Council, summers, 1968 and 1969. Instructor at Norfolk Museum School of Art and at University of Virginia (Hampton Roads Extension), both, summer, 1969. Has worked as artist for *Pittsburgh Catholic,* KDKA-FM Radio, Carnegie Museum, Johnston-Sabatino, Stanley Greetings, Inc., Goldstone Studios (as darkroom technician), and Dayton Public Library. Juror in art shows, participant in workshops and art exhibitions in Virginia and Pennsylvania; work is in private collections throughout the United States.

MEMBER: National Art Education Association, American Association of University Professors, Virginia Art Education Association, Phi Kappa Phi. *Awards, honors:* Art prize for work in permanent collection in Latrobe, Pa., 1960.

WRITINGS: Painting the Nude, Van Nostrand, 1972; (contributor) Jerry Bowles, editor, *Art Work: No Commercial Value,* Grossman, 1972. Contributor of articles and reviews to *Leonardo: International Journal of the Contemporary Artist.*

WORK IN PROGRESS: Archetypes of Design, Volume I: *Mass and Space,* Volume II: *Line and Visual Mixtures,* Volume III: *Shape and Color Magnetism;* several monographs, *Studies on the Origins of European Playing Cards, with Emphasis on the Tarocchi, or Tarot; Giotto and His Relationship with Other Artists in the Controversial Attributions at the Chiesa di San Francesco: Assisi; Studies on the Book of Kells; Origins of the Unicorn; Fragments from the Tomb of the Haterii;* and *Problems in Mechanical Construction and Interpretation.*

SIDELIGHTS: Hamm wrote to *CA:* "The art educator often finds himself between two stereotypes—that of the artist and the scholar. . . . I have found that it is increasingly more uncomfortable to agree with those who say, 'I am first of all an artist; this is my unique response to the life force. Teaching is a vocation,' or the corollary, 'teaching is my most important contribution to life and to mankind; my art is a form of benign self-indulgence in an age already surfeited with self-expression.' Both of these goals should be compatible.

". . . In an effort to arrive at some integral self-concept in this potentially schizophrenic gestalt, in addition to my own studio involvement I have attempted to research the area of analytical design in relation to visual perception—a somewhat flexible amalgam, logically pertinent to both parties in the artist-educator dichotomy, yet ironically often regarded with varying degrees of circumspection by both. . . . I may have a difficult decision to make one day in the future if the chasm becomes too wide to bridge. For now, in my art, writing, and educational pursuits, I am still attempting a creative compromise: to develop the faculties of thinking and feeling.

"Along the way I have taught five years in a Pittsburgh ghetto; later in a coal-mining and farming district in Moon Run, Pa.; in the "backwoods" of West Virginia; then, the former capitol of the Confederacy, and in the flat plains of the Midwest. In all of these settings, the attempt to function in two often-divergent stereotypes has met with many problems and many advantages as well—the chief among these being the tendency never to fall completely under the regimen of either, while attempting to profit from the wisdom of both."

* * *

HAMMEN, Carl Schlee 1923-

PERSONAL: Born August 26, 1923, in Newark, N.J.; son of Roy Merrill (a pattern-maker) and Bertha (a teacher; maiden name, Schlee) Hammen; married Ruth Graham, 1949 (divorced, 1962); married Susan Lum, October 13, 1962; children: (first marriage) Scott, Carol (Mrs. Nick Carson); (second marriage) Ralph, John, Elizabeth. *Education:* St. John's College, Annapolis, Md., B.A., 1947; University of Chicago, S.M., 1952; Duke University, Ph.D., 1958. *Home:* 18 North Rd., Kingston, R.I. 02881. *Office:* Department of Zoology, University of Rhode Island, Kingston, R.I. 02881.

CAREER: University of Rhode Island, Kingston, assistant professor, 1963-65, associate professor, 1965-71, professor of zoology, 1971—. *Military service:* U.S. Navy, 1943-46; served in Pacific theater; became lieutenant junior grade; received Purple Heart. *Member:* American Physiological Society, American Society of Zoologists, Sigma Xi.

WRITINGS: (Contributor) M. Florkin and B. T. Scheer, editors, *Chemical Zoology,* Academic Press, 1968; *Elementary Quantitative Biology,* Wiley, 1972.

WORK IN PROGRESS: A book on the physiology of marine invertebrates.

SIDELIGHTS: A long distance runner, Hammen won the New England Amateur Athletic Union championship of over-fifty age group at marathon (twenty-six plus miles) in 1973, and at ten miles in 1974. *Avocational interests:* Racing sailor.

* * *

HAMMER, Carl, Jr. 1910-

PERSONAL: Born November 26, 1910, in Salisbury, N.C.; son of Carl (a newspaper editor and farmer) and Carrie (a painter; maiden name, McCanless) Hammer; married Mae Armes, November 25, 1939; children: Carl III, William Andrew. *Education:* Catawba College, B.A., 1934; University of North Carolina, graduate study, 1934-35; Vanderbilt University, M.A., 1936; University of Jena, graduate study, 1938; University of Illinois, Ph.D., 1939. *Politics:* Independent. *Religion:* Lutheran. *Residence:* Lubbock, Tex. *Office:* Department of Germanic and Slavonic Languages, Texas Tech University, Box 4579, Lubbock, Tex. 79409.

CAREER: Vanderbilt University, Nashville, Tenn., instructor, 1939-45, assistant professor of German, 1945-47; Louisiana State University, Baton Rouge, associate professor, 1947-55, professor of German, 1955-64; Texas Tech University, Lubbock, professor, 1964-67, Horn Professor of German and chairman of department, both 1967—. Visiting summer professor at Southern Illinois University, 1961, 1966, and Montana State University, 1962, 1967.

MEMBER: Modern Language Association of America, American Association of Teachers of German (president of Texas chapter, 1965-67), South-Central Modern Language Association, Texas Foreign Language Association, Texas Association of College Teachers. *Awards, honors:* Ford Foundation fellowship, 1953-54; visited Germany as guest of German Government, 1964; Kentucky Foreign Language Conference award, 1972, for *Goethe and Rousseau.*

WRITINGS: (Editor with John G. Frank) *Deutsch fuer Mediziner* (title means "German for Students of Medicine"), Harper, 1941; *Rhinelanders on the Yadkin* (about Pennsylvania Germans in North Carolina), privately printed, 1943, 2nd edition, 1965; (with Frank and C. M. Lancaster) *Two Moods of Minnesong,* Vanderbilt University Press, 1944; *Goethes "Dichtung und Wahrheit," 7. Buch: Literaturgeschichte oder Bildungserlebnis?* (title means "Goethe's 'Poetry and Truth,' Book Seven: Literary History or Cultural Experience?"), University of Illinois Press, 1945; (editor) *Goethe after Two Centuries,* Louisiana State University Press, 1952; (editor) *Studies in German Literature,* Louisiana State University Press, 1963; *Goethe and Rousseau: Resonances of the Mind,* University Press of Kentucky, 1973. Contributor of more than sixty articles and reviews to scholarly journals. Associate editor for German of *South Central Bulletin,* 1959-61.

WORK IN PROGRESS: The Sisterhood of German and English: A Survey of Cognates, a monograph; research on the records of Montaigne's and Goethe's Italian journeys and on Goethe's affinity with French Renaissance writers.

AVOCATIONAL INTERESTS: Travel, astronomy, gardening.

* * *

HAMPTON, Christopher 1929-

PERSONAL: Born May 3, 1929, in London, England; son of Harold Victor (a director) and Gladys Victoria Hampton; married Kathleen Boyle (an administrative officer), February 18, 1956; children: Rebecca. *Education:* Attended Guildhall School of Music, 1948-53. *Politics:* Socialist. *Home:* 161 Southwood Lane, London N6 5TA, England. *Agent:* Seligman & Collier, 280 Madison Ave., New York, N.Y. 10016. *Office:* City Literary Institute, London, England.

CAREER: Pianist, conductor, writer, and other positions, at various times, 1953-62; Shenker Institute, Rome, Italy, director of studies, 1962-66; Davies School of English, London, England, teacher, 1966-67; Polytechnic of Central London, London, England, lecturer in English, 1968—. Lecturer at City Literary Institute, 1973—. *Member:* Society of Authors, Poetry Society (member of executive council of National Poetry Centre), Association of Teachers in Technical Institutes.

WRITINGS: (Translator from the French) Rene Guillot, *The Fantastic Brother*, Methuen, 1961; *Island of the Southern Sun* (juvenile), Chatto & Windus, 1962; *A Group Anthology* (poems), Oxford University Press, 1963; *The Etruscans and the Survival of Etruria*, Gollancz, 1969, published as *The Etruscan Survival*, Doubleday, 1970; (editor) *Poems for Shakespeare*, Globe Playhouse, 1972; *An Exile's Italy* (poems), Thonnesen, 1972. Contributor of poems to magazines, including *P.E.N.*, *New Statesman*, *London*, *Critical Quarterly*, *Twentieth Century*, and *Transatlantic Review*.

WORK IN PROGRESS: A Cornered Freedom, a book of poems; *Awareness and Apathy*, nonfiction; a story set in Venice; an autobiography.

SIDELIGHTS: Hampton writes: "Four years spent in Italy have provided the context for three books so far, and the influence of Italian culture and civilisation is likely to continue to be a major source of material. But my latest book, *Awareness and Apathy*, is concerned with more fundamental issues. It is a dialectic study of crisis, of the malaise of Europe, and the antagonistic conditions that challenge and threaten the individual in the modern world in his struggle for solvency and equilibrium. The problematic nature of this struggle and of its outcome (the nature of man's place in his world) hinges around such crucial conditions as 'awareness' and 'apathy' as they appear in all their subtle manifestations, political and social. And it has seemed to me that these must be clearly differentiated and defined if there is to be any chance of establishing conditions that will enable the individual to build out of his own self independence, recognition and responsibility. . . ."

* * *

HAN, Sungjoo 1940-

PERSONAL Born September 13, 1940, in Seoul, Korea; son of Chung-ho and Chung-sook (Kim) Han; married Sungmii Lee (a college instructor), June 17, 1963; children: Charles Sungwon. *Education:* Seoul National University, B.A., 1962; University of New Hampshire, M.A., 1964; University of California, Berkeley, Ph.D., 1970. *Home:* 193-15 Nero Ave., Hollis, N.Y. 11423. *Office:* Department of Political Science, Brooklyn College, City University of New York, Brooklyn, N.Y. 11210.

CAREER: Brooklyn College of the City University of New York, Brooklyn, N.Y., assistant professor of political science, 1970—. *Member:* American Political Science Association, Association for Asian Studies. *Awards, honors:* Fulbright grant, 1962; Peter H. Odegard award, 1968; Social Science Research Council award, 1974.

WRITINGS: The Failure of Democracy in South Korea, University of California Press, 1974; (co-editor) *East Asia: From Confrontation to Accommodation*, Kyung Nam University Press, 1975.

WORK IN PROGRESS: South Korea under Authoritarian Rule: 1961-1975.

* * *

HANCOCK, Harold B(ell) 1913-

PERSONAL: Born December 5, 1913, in Dover, Del.; son of Harry R. (a hardware merchant) and Hazel (a teacher; maiden name, Cariss) Hancock. *Education:* Wesleyan University, B.A., 1936; Harvard University, M.A., 1938; Ohio State University, Ph.D., 1954. *Politics:* Democrat. *Religion:* United Methodist. *Home:* 111 West Park St., Westerville, Ohio 43081. *Office:* Department of History and Government, Otterbein College, Westerville, Ohio 43081.

CAREER: Caesar Rodney High School, Wyoming, Del., teacher of English, 1938-41; Louisburg Junior College, Louisburg, N.C., instructor in history, 1941-42; Brevard Junior College, Brevard, N.C., instructor in history, 1942-44; Otterbein College, Westerville, Ohio, assistant professor, 1944-48, associate professor, 1948-50, professor of history and government, 1950—, chairman of department, 1950—. *Member:* American Historical Society, Society of American Historians, American Philosophical Society (fellow), Pennsylvania Historical Society, Delaware Historical Society, Westerville Historical Society (president, 1971—), Phi Beta Kappa. *Awards, honors:* American Philosophical Society research grant to England, 1957-58.

WRITINGS: The Delaware Loyalists, Delaware Historical Society, 1940, revised edition, 1975; *Delaware During the Civil War: A Political History*, Delaware Historical Society, 1961; *The History of Otterbein College*, American

Yearbook Press, 1971; *The History of Westerville, Ohio*, privately printed, 1973; *Delaware in the American Revolution*, Brandywine Press, 1974.

WORK IN PROGRESS: Readings in Black Delaware History, with J. E. Newton.

* * *

HANDLER, Jerome S(idney) 1933-

PERSONAL: Born September 3, 1933, in New York, N.Y.; son of Sam and Sara (Wieder) Handler; married Eugenia de Rosales (a social worker), April 12, 1959; children: Joshua Martin, Lisa Frances. *Education:* University of California at Los Angeles, B.A., 1956, M.A., 1959; Brandeis University, Ph.D., 1965. *Home:* 201 South Maple, Carbondale, Ill. 62901. *Office:* Department of Anthropology, Southern Illinois University, Carbondale, Ill. 62901.

CAREER: New World Archaeological Foundation, Chiapas, Mexico, staff archaeologist, 1957; Southern Illinois University, Carbondale, instructor, 1962-64, assistant professor, 1964-68, associate professor, 1968-74, professor of anthropology, 1974—. Honorary research assistant at University College, University of London, 1966-67; visiting research fellow at University of the West Indies, 1969-70; O'Connor visiting professor at Colgate University, 1971-72. Consultant to Peace Corps Training Program, 1969. *Member:* American Anthropological Association (fellow). *Awards, honors:* National Institutes of Health research grant, 1965; National Science Foundation research grants, 1966-67, 1971-73; American Philosophical Society research grant, 1968; National Endowment for the Humanities fellowship, 1969-70; Wenner-Gren Foundation grant, 1971-72.

WRITINGS: A Guide to Source Materials for the Study of Barbados History, 1627-1834, Southern Illinois University Press, 1971; *The Unappropriated People: Freedmen in the Slave Society of Barbados,* Johns Hopkins Press, 1974. Contributor to *Southwestern Journal of Anthropology, Ethnology,* and other journals in his field.

WORK IN PROGRESS: African Immigrants and Their Descendants: The Social and Cultural Life of a West Indian Slave Population, 1840-1834, completion expected in 1976.

SIDELIGHTS: Handler has done field work in many islands of the Caribbean, particularly Jamaica and Barbados, since 1960; he has done archaeological research in Mexico, 1955, 1957, and Barbados, 1972, 1973; he traveled and did research in West Africa, 1964, and in western Europe, 1964, 1966-67, 1968, 1974.

* * *

HANDOVER, P(hyllis) M(argaret) 1923(?)-1974

1923(?)—July 4, 1974; British journalist, author of historical and biographical works. Obituaries: *AB Bookman's Weekly*, October 7, 1974. (*CA*-9/10).

* * *

HANER, F(rederick) T(heodore) 1929-

PERSONAL: First syllable of surname is pronounced "hay"; born September 29, 1929, in Detroit, Mich.; son of Fred L. (a manager) and Viola Mary Haner; married Margaret J. Swagler, January 30, 1954 (divorced, 1975); children: M. Lynn, Mark F. *Education:* University of Michigan, B.S., 1951; University of Pittsburgh, M.B.A., 1955, Ph.D., 1959. *Politics:* Republican. *Home:* 120 Wilbur St., E6, Newark, Del. 19711. *Office:* Department of Management, University of Delaware, Newark, Del. 19711.

CAREER: U.S. Steel Corp., New York, N.Y., commercial researcher, 1955-58; Stanford Research Institute, Menlo Park, Calif., economist, 1958-61; employed with International American Cement Corp., 1961-66; INVEST (business consultants), Newark, Del., president, 1966—; University of Delaware, Newark, professor of management, 1971—; BERI Ltd. (business information service), Newark, Del., president, 1972—. President and member of board of directors, Hansen Elektronik, 1968—, and Collins and Ryan, Inc., 1973—; consultant to U.S. Department of State. *Military service:* U.S. Army, 1951-53. *Member:* Academy of International Business, Academy of Management. *Awards, honors:* American Management Association award, 1968.

WRITINGS: Contemporary Management, C. E. Merrill, 1973; *Multinational Management,* C. E. Merrill, 1973; *Business Policy: Planning and Strategy,* Winthrop, 1975; (with S. K. Keiser and D. J. Puglisi) *Introduction to Business,* Winthrop, in press.

WORK IN PROGRESS: Co-author with William W. Boyer of *The Multinational Corporation as a Resource.*

BIOGRAPHICAL/CRITICAL SOURCES: Business International, February 26, 1971; *International Management,* August, 1974.

* * *

HANSEN, Rodney Thor 1940-

PERSONAL: Born March 27, 1940, in Spokane, Wash.; son of Thor John (a painter) and Gertrude (a teacher; maiden name, Michel) Hansen; married Karen Anderson, August 22, 1964; children: Derrick Rodney, Heather Dawn, Ty Thane. *Education:* Whitworth College, B.S., 1962; University of Washington, Seattle, M.A., 1964; Washington State University, Ph.D., 1967; University of Oregon, postdoctoral study, 1971. *Religion:* Presbyterian. *Home address:* Route 2, Box 45, Bozeman, Mont. 59715. *Office:* Department of Mathematics, Montana State University, Bozeman, Mont. 59715.

CAREER: Montana State University, Bozeman, assistant professor, 1967-72, associate professor of mathematics, 1972—. *Member:* American Mathematical Society, Mathematical Association of America, Fibonacci Association, Montana Academy of Science (vice-president, 1973-74), Montana Teachers of Mathematics. *Awards, honors:* National Science Foundation postdoctoral grant, 1971.

WRITINGS: Calculus: It's the Limit!, Wadsworth, 1972; *Solutions Manual*, Wadsworth, 1972. Contributor to *Duke Mathematical Journal, Fibonacci Quarterly, Mathematics Magazine*, and *Journal of the Australian Mathematical Society.*

WORK IN PROGRESS: Research on combinational number theory, on mathematical education, and on algebraic number theory.

AVOCATIONAL INTERESTS: Travel, photography, collecting and appreciating western art, gardening, fishing, hunting, water safety, music, especially banjo-ukulele.

* * *

HANSON, Kenneth O. 1922-

PERSONAL: Born February 24, 1922, in Shelley, Idaho.

Education: University of Idaho, B.A., 1942; University of Washington, Seattle, graduate study, 1946-54. *Home:* 3646 Southeast Carlton, Portland, Ore. 97202. *Office:* Reed College, Portland, Ore. 97202.

CAREER: Reed College, Portland, Ore., 1954—, began as instructor, now professor of literature and the humanities. *Military service:* U.S. Army, 1942-46; became staff sergeant. *Awards, honors:* Fulbright grant to attend First Institute in Chinese Civilization, 1962; Lamont Award from Academy of American Poets, 1966, for *The Distance Anywhere;* Amy Lowell Traveling Poetry Scholarship, 1973-74.

WRITINGS: Eight Poems, Graphic Arts Workshop, Reed College, 1958; *The Distance Anywhere* (poems), University of Washington Press, 1967; *Saronikos and Other Poems,* Press-22, 1970; (editor) *Clear Days: Poems by Palamas and Elytis,* Press-22, 1972; *The Uncorrected World* (poems), Wesleyan University Press, 1973.

* * *

HAO, Yen-ping 1934-

PERSONAL: Surname is pronounced "how"; born December 22, 1934, in Nanking, China; son of Pei-yun and Yu-fu (Yang) Hao; married Pin-han Tu (a teacher), June 4, 1960; children: James Ping-yi, Andrew Ping-chung. *Education:* National Taiwan University, B.A., 1958; Harvard University, M.A., 1961, Ph.D., 1966. *Home:* 7408 Bennington Dr., Knoxville, Tenn. 37919. *Office:* Department of History, University of Tennessee, Knoxville, Tenn. 37916.

CAREER: University of Tennessee, Knoxville, assistant professor, 1965-68, associate professor, 1968-71, professor of history, 1971—. *Member:* Association for Asian Studies, Society for Ching Studies, American Historical Association. *Awards, honors:* Newcomen Award, 1971, for "A New Class in China's Treaty Ports."

WRITINGS: The Comprador in Nineteenth Century China: Bridge between East and West, Harvard University Press, 1970; *Ya-chou chin-tai hua* (title means "The Modernization of Asia"), National Taiwan University Press, 1971. Contributor to proceedings; contributor to *Journal of Asian Studies*, *Bulletin of the National Palace Museum*, *Shih-ho Monthly*, and *Business History Review*.

WORK IN PROGRESS: A book, *Commercial Capitalism in Modern China.*

* * *

HARDER, Geraldine Gross 1926-

PERSONAL: Born March 14, 1926, in Doylestown, Pa.; daughter of Titus Lapp (a meat merchant) and Olive (Moyer) Gross; married Milton J. Harder (a minister), June 29, 1952; children: Robert Gross, James Milton. *Education:* Goshen College, Goshen, Ind., B.S. in Ed., 1948, B.A., 1948. *Religion:* Mennonite. *Home:* 20355 34th Ave. S., Seattle, Wash. 98188.

CAREER: Teacher in Pennsylvania elementary schools, 1948-50; Herald Press, Scottdale, Pa., editor and writer of primary Sunday school materials, 1950-53; free-lance writer in Kaiserslautern, Germany, 1956-59, Newton, Kan., 1959-67, and Seattle, Wash., 1967—; piano teacher, 1963—; operator of child care center, Seattle, Wash., 1971—. *Awards, honors:* First prize for two hymns, Hymn Society of America, 1965.

WRITINGS: When Apples Are Ripe, Herald Press, 1972. Contributor to *Bible Lessons for Primary Children,* "Herald Omnibus Bible" series, and to about twenty religious and other periodicals.

WORK IN PROGRESS: Cheyenne Dream (proposed title), the story of Rodolpe Petter, a Swiss orphan who became a missionary to the Cheyenne Indians.

* * *

HARDING, Donald Edward 1916-
(Donald Day, Donald Earl Edwards, Eugene Parrish)

PERSONAL: Born February 7, 1916, in East Liberty, Ohio. *Education:* Attended Marion Business College, Marion, Ohio, 1934-36; Kenyon College, B.A., 1950; Northwestern University, M.A., 1952. *Religion:* Episcopalian. *Home:* Ye Olde Western Inn, 19 North State St., Elgin, Ill. 60120.

CAREER: Hobby Book Store, Chicago, Ill., owner, 1950-68; full-time writer, 1968—. Poet, dramatist, author of short fiction and essays. *Military service:* U.S. Army, 1940-45; received Asiatic-Pacific Theatre Ribbon with three bronze stars, Philippine Liberation Ribbon with two bronze stars, and Bronze Star Medal.

WRITINGS: Who Walks with Dreams, Kaleidograph Press, 1947; *A Sign to Solace*, American Weave Press, 1948; *The Cycle of the Seasons*, American Weave Press, 1949; *Straw Hat*, J. & C. Transcript, 1971; *The Shepherd's Boy*, J. & C. Transcript, 1972; *Applebough*, Edwin Lee, 1972; *Pandora's Box*, Thom Henderson Press, 1972; *Little Acorns*, Thom Henderson Press, 1972; (editor) *Footprints of the Future* (anthology), J. & C. Transcript, Volume I, 1972, Volume II, 1973, Volume III, in press; *Little Twigs*, Red Cloud Press, 1973; *Acres of Gold*, Peacock Press, 1974.

Work is represented in anthologies, including: *Christ in Poetry*, edited by Thomas Curtis Clark, Association Press, 1952; *Where Is Christmas*, edited by Jean Calkins, J. & C. Transcript, 1971; *These Are My Jewels*, edited by Calkins, J. & C. Transcript, 1973.

Contributor of poetry, under pseudonyms Donald Earl Edwards and Eugene Parrish, and essays, under pseudonym Donald Day, to periodicals, including *New York Times*, *New York Herald Tribune*, *Different*, *Kaleidograph*, *Jean's Journal*, *Encore*, *Hartford Courant*, *Bardic Echoes*, *American Bard*, *Prairie Wings*, *Silk Screen*, *North Carolina Folklore*, and *Haiku Highlights*.

WORK IN PROGRESS: Several poetry books and other selected writings.

* * *

HARDY, C. Colburn 1910-
(Jonas Blake, Hart Munn, Leonard Peck)

PERSONAL: Born January 13, 1910, in Boston, Mass.; son of Charles A. (a corporate executive) and Gladys M. (an engineer; maiden name, Blake) Hardy; married Ruth E. Hart (a public relations director), June 27, 1942; children: Dorcas Ruth. *Education:* Yale University, A.B., 1931; graduate study, Columbia University, 1934. *Religion:* Unitarian-Universalist. *Home:* 120 Washington St., East Orange, N.J. 07017. *Office:* C. Colburn Hardy & Associates, 120 Washington St., East Orange, N.J.

CAREER: Republican representative in New Jersey Assembly, 1943; Carl Byoir & Associates (public relations firm), New York, N.Y., 1948-59, began as staffer, became vice-president; Jones Brakeley & Rockwell (public relations firm), New York, N.Y., executive vice-president, 1960-64; Federal Pacific Electric Co., Newark, N.J., director of public relations, 1965-67; General Dynamics Co., New York, N.Y., director of public relations, 1967-72; C. Colburn Hardy & Associates (public relations firm), East Orange, N.J., president, 1972—. President of Social Welfare Council and Community Service Council (both N.J.), 1967-69; member of board of directors, United Way, 1967-70, JET Corp., 1971—; president of board of directors, H.A.Y., 1969-72. *Military service:* U.S. Naval Reserve, 1943-46; became lieutenant commander; received seven battle stars. *Member:* Public Relations Society of America, Phi Beta Kappa.

WRITINGS: (With John Winthrop Wright) *Q-V-T: The Three Keys to Stock Market Profits*, Prentice-Hall, 1970; (editor) *Your Investments*, 19th edition (Hardy was not associated with earlier editions), Dun & Bradstreet, 1974, 20th edition published as *Dun & Bradstreet Guide to Your Investments*, 1975; *Personal Money Management*, Funk, in press. Contributor, sometimes under pseudonyms, to *Physician's Management, Dental Management, Physician's World, Banking, Chronicle, Exchange, Money*, and others.

WORK IN PROGRESS: The Art of Leverage.

* * *

HARKNESS, Georgia (Elma) 1891-1974

1891—August 21, 1974; American Methodist minister, theologian, educator, author of books on religious topics. Obituaries: *New York Times*, August 22, 1974; *Washington Post*, August 23, 1974; *Publishers Weekly*, September 2, 1974. (*CA*-1).

* * *

HARMS, Leroy Stanley 1928-

PERSONAL: Born December 3, 1928, in Spink County, S.D.; son of Henry (a rancher) and Mollie Kristina (Barness) Harms; married Joan Yuhas (an evaluation specialist for Hawaii Open Program), April 11, 1966; children: John, William, Kathleen, Kristina. *Education:* Sorbonne, University of Paris, diploma in French and phonetic science, 1954; University of Florida, B.A., 1955; Ohio State University, M.A., 1957, Ph.D., 1959. *Home:* 165 Nawiliwili St., Honolulu, Hawaii 96825. *Office:* Communication Program, University of Hawaii–Manoa, Honolulu, Hawaii 96822.

CAREER: Louisiana State University, Baton Rouge, assistant professor of speech, 1959-62; University of Kansas, Lawrence, associate professor of speech and communication, 1962-65; University of Hawaii–Manoa, Honolulu, associate professor, 1965-74, professor of communication, 1974—, senior specialist at East-West Center, 1965-66. Member of board of directors of United Nations Association–Hawaii; conference chairman of Major Issues in World Communication; organizer and chairman of Speech Communication Association of Communication Rights Commission. *Military service:* U.S. Army, 1947-50.

MEMBER: International Communication Association, International Broadcast Institute, World Future Society, Speech Communication Association of America, Asian Mass Communication Research and Information Center.

WRITINGS: Phonetic Transcription, Scott, Foresman, 1964; (with Paul Heinberg and June Yamada) *Speech Communication Learning Systems*, International Learning Systems, 1970; *International Studies of National Speech-Education Systems*, Burgess, 1970; *Intercultural Communication*, Harper, 1973; (contributor) Kgzuo Nakano, editor, *Phonetic Papers for Masao Onishi*, Phonetic Society of Japan, 1974; *Human Communication*, Harper, 1974.

WORK IN PROGRESS: Futures of Human Communication, for Prentice-Hall; editing, with Jim Richstad, *Right to Communicate: Perspectives on an Expanding Human Right*.

* * *

HARRIS, Alf(red) 1928-
(Gwen Addison, Harris Moore)

PERSONAL: Born February 2, 1928, in Toronto, Ontario, Canada; son of Samuel Henry (a vaudevillian, later a chef) and Annabelle (Golden) Harris; married Maria Justina Wittig (a high school teacher of German), May 30, 1967; stepchildren: Peter B. Ruehl, Bettina E. Ruehl. *Education:* Attended Academy of Radio Arts, Toronto, Ontario, Canada. *Home:* 29377 Quail Run Dr., Agoura, Calif. 91301.

CAREER: Kingston Whig-Standard, Kingston, Ontario, reporter, 1948; Kesten Enterprises (advertising and public relations), Toronto, Ontario, 1949-52; CKEY-Radio, Toronto, Ontario, news editor, 1952-57; full-time free-lance writer, 1957—.

WRITINGS: (Under pseudonym Harris Moore, with Arthur Moore) *Slater's Planet*, Pinnacle Books, 1971; (under pseudonym Gwen Addison, with Arthur Moore) *Storm over Fox Hill*, Pocket Books, 1973; *The Joseph File—Destroy*, Putnam, 1974. Writer of film scripts for the National Film Board of Canada and the Canadian Broadcasting Corp. Writer of dramatic, documentary, religious, and educational scripts for CBC Radio and Television and for American television series, including "Studio One," "Daktari," "Dragnet," "Space Command," "Adam-12," "Voyage under the Sea," "The Man Who Never Was," "Mission Impossible," "Bonanza," and "Lost in Space." Contributor of articles and short stories to magazines.

WORK IN PROGRESS: A novel, tentatively titled *A Bribe for Baroni*; a gothic novel.

SIDELIGHTS: Harris writes: "When writing the *Joseph File*, I set out to accomplish one thing—to entertain. True, an author's attitudes can't help intrude—but my main objective was simply to provide the reader with enjoyment. This has been the purpose in much of my work—an attitude that has been with me ever since I sold my first radio drama to the Canadian Broadcasting Corporation at the age of seventeen."

AVOCATIONAL INTERESTS: Photography (holds a one-star rating, prints, in the Photographic Society of America, indicating that more than thirty of his prints have been accepted for showing in various international salons).

* * *

HARRIS, Charles B(urt) 1940-

PERSONAL: Born November 2, 1940, in LaGrange, Tex.; son of Gus B. (a railroad conductor) and Ruth (Hess) Harris; married Victoria Frenkel (a university professor), March 16, 1968; children: Kimberly Lynne, Gregory Paul. *Education:* Texas Lutheran College, B.S., 1963; Southern Illinois University, M.A., 1965, Ph.D., 1970. *Politics:* Liberal Independent. *Religion:* Liberal Independent. *Home:* 1610 Bradford Lane, Normal, Ill. 61761. *Office:* Department of English, Illinois State University, Normal, Ill. 61761.

CAREER: Peninsula Playhouse, New Braunfels, Tex., actor, 1963-64; Southern Illinois University, Carbondale, instructor in English, 1966-68; Illinois State University, Normal, assistant professor, 1968-71, associate professor of English, 1971—. Founder, operator of, and actor in community theaters. *Member:* Modern Language Association of America, College English Association, American Association of University Professors, Midwest Modern Language Association, Independent Voters of Illinois.

WRITINGS: (Contributor) Earl A. French, editor, *Creative Approaches to Reading Literature,* Number II, American Education Publication, 1969; (contributor) French and Robert P. Burns, editors, *Creative Approaches to Reading Literature,* Number IV, American Education Publication, 1970; *Contemporary American Novelists of the Absurd,* College & University Press, 1971. Contributor of articles, cartoons, and reviews to magazines, including *College English Association Critic, Fitzgerald-Hemingway Annual,* and *American Education Publication Teacher's Guide.*

WORK IN PROGRESS: A study of the fiction of John Barth; a study of the problem of perception and perspective in the American novel, with books on both subjects expected to result.

SIDELIGHTS: Harris writes: "I went to Texas Lutheran College because they gave me a football scholarship. Was a laundry freak for four years, but wrecked my knee during my second year, which led to a loss of interest in athletics and a new interest in drama and literature. Graduated, acted professionally for two years, then, when the theater folded, got my graduate degrees specializing in modern American literature, particularly the literature of the absurd. One need only study the history of the last seventy years of our world to understand what motivated my interest in absurdity."

BIOGRAPHICAL/CRITICAL SOURCES: Atlanta Journal and Constitution, April 3, 1972; *American Literature,* November, 1972; *Novel,* spring, 1973.

* * *

HARRIS, Curtis C(lark), Jr. 1930-

PERSONAL: Born August 6, 1930, in Cape May, N.J.; son of Curtis C. (a mailman) and Jennie (Reeves) Harris; married Mary Herberta Will, September 9, 1955; children: Curtis Clark, Geoffrey Allen, Jan Suzette. *Education:* Goldey Business School, A.A., 1950; University of Florida, B.S., 1956; Harvard University, M.A., 1959, Ph.D., 1960. *Home:* 7008 Wells Pkwy., Hyattsville, Md. 20782. *Office:* Bureau of Business and Economic Research, University of Maryland, College Park, Md. 20742.

CAREER: University of California, Davis, assistant professor of economics, 1959-64; U.S. Department of Commerce, Washington, D.C., supervisory economist, 1964-67; University of Maryland, College Park, associate professor, 1967-73, professor of economics, 1973—. Consultant to Ministry of Urban Affairs of Canada, U.S. Office of Management and Budget, and Economic Development Administration. *Military service:* U.S. Coast Guard, 1951-53. *Member:* American Economic Association, Regional Science Association, Phi Kappa Phi, Beta Gamma Sigma. *Awards, honors:* Economic Development Administration grant, 1967, for work on regional forecasting; National Science Foundation grant, 1970.

WRITINGS: (With David J. Allee) *Urbanization and Its Effects on Agriculture in Sacramento County, California* (report), California Agricultural Experiment Station, Part I: *Urban Growth and Agricultural Land Use,* 1963, Part II: *Prices and Taxes of Agricultural Land,* 1963; *A Stochastic Process of Suburban Development* (technical report), Center for Real Estate and Urban Economics, Institute of Urban and Regional Development, University of California, 1966; *State and County Projections: A Progress Report of the Regional Forecasting Project,* Bureau of Business and Economic Research, University of Maryland, 1969; *A 1970 Interindustry Study of the State of Maryland,* Bureau of Business and Economic Research, University of Maryland, 1971; (with Frank E. Hopkins) *Locational Analysis: An Interregional Econometric Model of Agriculture, Mining, Manufacturing, and Services,* Lexington Books, 1972; *The Urban Economies, 1985: A Multiregional, Multi-Industry Forecasting Model,* Lexington Books, 1973; *Regional Economic Effects of Alternative Highway Systems,* Ballinger Publishing, 1974. Contributor to economic journals.

WORK IN PROGRESS: Research concerning improvements in the multiregional, multi-industry forecasting model.

* * *

HARRIS, Mary B(ierman) 1943-

PERSONAL: Born February 9, 1943, in St. Louis, Mo.; daughter of Norman (an attorney) and Margaret (a nursery school teacher; maiden name, Loeb) Bierman; married Richard J. Harris (a psychologist), June 14, 1965; children: Jennifer M., Christopher R. *Education:* Radcliffe College, B.A. (magna cum laude), 1964; Stanford University, M.A., 1965, Ph.D., 1968. *Home:* 1719 Rita N.E., Albuquerque, N.M. 87106. *Office:* Department of Educational Foundations, University of New Mexico, Albuquerque, N.M. 87131.

CAREER: Talladega College, Talladega, Ala., instructor in psychology, 1965-66; University of New Mexico, Albuquerque, N.M., assistant professor, 1968-72, associate professor of educational foundations, 1972—. Lecturer at University of Veracruz, 1973; visiting associate professor at Ohio State University, 1974-75. Consultant to Charles E. Merrill Publishing Co., Brooks-Cole Publishing Co., and several other publishers. *Member:* American Psychological Association, International Society for Research in Aggression, American Association for the Advancement of Science, American Association of University Professors, Southwestern Psychological Association, Phi Beta Kappa.

WRITINGS: (Contributor) Harold Munsinger, editor, *Readings in Child Development,* Holt, 1971; (editor and contributor) *Classroom Uses of Behavior Modification,* C. E. Merrill, 1972. Contributor of articles on child behavior norms and weight control programs to other books. More than forty articles have been published, mostly in psychology journals.

WORK IN PROGRESS: Research on altruism, aggression, social learning, and behavior modification.

* * *

HARRIS, Seymour E(dwin) 1897-1974

September 8, 1897—October 27, 1974; American educator, Keynesian economist, governmental advisor, editor, author. Obituaries: *Washington Post,* October 29, 1974; *New*

York Times, October 29, 1974; *Newsweek*, November 11, 1974; *Time*, November 11, 1974; *AB Bookman's Weekly*, November 18, 1974; *Current Biography*, December, 1974.

* * *

HARRIS, William J(oseph) 1942-

PERSONAL: Born March 12, 1942, in Fairborn, Ohio; son of William Lee (an electrician) and Camilla (Hunter) Harris; married Susan Kumin, August 25, 1968. Education: Ohio State University, student, 1961-62; Central State University, Wilberforce, Ohio, B.A., 1968; Stanford University, M.A., 1971, Ph.D., 1974. *Home:* 111 Treva Ave., Ithaca, N.Y. 14850. *Office:* Department of English, Cornell University, Ithaca, N.Y. 14850.

CAREER: Stanford University, Stanford, Calif., acting instructor in English, summer, 1969; Cornell University, Ithaca, N.Y., assistant professor of English, 1972—.

WRITINGS: Hey Fella Would You Mind Holding This Piano a Moment (poems), Ithaca House, 1974.

Work is anthologized in *Nine Black Poets*, edited by R. Baird Shuman, Moore Publishing, 1968; *Intro Two*, edited by R. V. Cassill, Bantam, 1969; *A Galaxy of Black Writing*, edited by Shuman, Moore Publishing, 1970; *Black Out Loud*, edited by Arnold Adoff, Macmillan, 1970; *Natural Process*, edited by Ted Wilentz, Hill & Wang, 1970; *Cavalcade*, edited by A. P. Davis, Houghton, 1971; *New Black Voices*, edited by Abraham Chapman, New American Library, 1972; *The Yardbird Reader*, edited by Ishmael Reed, Yardbird Press, 1972; *The Poetry of Black America*, edited by Adoff, Harper, 1972; *Starting with Poetry*, edited by Ann C. Colley, Harcourt, 1973; *Lyric Poetry*, edited by Robert Pierce, Houghton, 1973; *My Black Me*, edited by Adoff, Dutton, 1974; *Eating the Menu*, edited by Bruce Edward Taylor, Kendall-Hunt, 1974.

Contributor of poems and articles to literary magazines, including *Antioch Review, American Scholar, Beloit Poetry Review, Chicago Review*, and *Lillabulero*. Editor of *Epoch*.

WORK IN PROGRESS: A book on the poetry of Amiri Baraka (LeRoi Jones).

SIDELIGHTS: Harris writes: "Poetry is a way of clarifying my sense of the world and a way of turning failure into success: all those bad times turned into works of art. The greatest influences on me were the early ones—the poeple I read in high school: Patchen, Ginsberg, and Pound. I still read them. Of course other writers have been added . . . ."

* * *

HARRISON, Bennett 1942-

PERSONAL: Born June 27, 1942, in Jersey City, N.J.; son of Leo (a salesman) and Eve (a teacher; maiden name, Davis) Harrison; married Barbara Greenberg (a horse trainer), May 28, 1963. *Education:* Brandeis University, A.B. (with honors), 1965; University of Pennsylvania, M.A., 1966, Ph.D., 1970. *Politics:* Democrat. *Religion:* Jewish. *Residence:* Stow, Mass. *Office:* Department of Urban Studies and Planning, Massachusetts Institute of Technology, Cambridge, Mass. 02139.

CAREER: New School for Social Research, New York, N.Y., lecturer in economics, 1967-68; University of Maryland, College Park, lecturer, 1968-70, assistant professor of economics, 1970-72; Massachusetts Institute of Technology, Cambridge, Mass., associate professor of economics and urban studies, 1973—. Visiting professor, University of Pennsylvania, 1972; consultant to U.S. Government departments, Massachusetts Legislature, and National Urban Coalition.

MEMBER: American Economic Association, Union for Radical Political Economics. *Awards, honors:* Research grants from U.S. Office of Economic Opportunity, 1967-68, 1971-72, U.S. Department of Labor, 1970-72, and National Institutes of Mental Health, 1973-75; Carey Prize in Economics from University of Pennsylvania, 1970, for thesis, *Education, Training, and the Urban Ghetto.*

WRITINGS: (With Thomas Vietorisz) *The Economic Development of Harlem,* Praeger, 1970; (editor with Harold Sheppard and William Spring) *Political Economy of Public Service Employment,* Heath, 1972; *Education, Training, and the Urban Ghetto,* Johns Hopkins Press, 1972; (editor with G. M. von Furstenberg and Ann Horowitz) *Patterns of Racial Discrimination,* Heath, 1974; *Urban Economic Development,* Urban Institute, 1974. Contributor of more than twenty articles to scholarly journals, including *American Economic Review, Journal of the American Institute of Planners, New Republic,* and *Journal of Political Economy.*

WORK IN PROGRESS: A monograph, *Manpower and Economic Development in the City;* research on the relationship between work and welfare income, with Martin Rein.

SIDELIGHTS: Harrison has been a professional musician for twenty years, playing saxophone and keyboard instruments, and arranging music for jazz, rock, and "pop" dance bands. He is currently studying music theory and classical piano. *Avocational interests:* Attending concerts, horses.

* * *

HARRISON, Frank R(ussell) III 1935-

PERSONAL: Born March 11, 1935, in Jacksonville, Fla.; son of Frank Russell, Jr. and Annie Mae Harrison; married Dorothy Louise Gurdy (a systems analyst), September 10, 1966. *Education:* Summer study at Duke University, 1954, and Loyola University of the South, 1955; University of the South, B.A. (optimen merens with honors), 1957; University of Virginia, M.A., 1959, Ph.D., 1961. *Religion:* Episcopalian. *Home:* 310 Cedar Creek Dr., Athens, Ga. 30601. *Office:* Department of Philosophy, University of Georgia, Athens, Ga. 30602.

CAREER: Roanoke College, Salem, Va., instructor in philosophy, 1961-62; University of Georgia, Athens, assistant professor, 1962-66, associate professor, 1966-72, professor of philosophy, 1972—, member of graduate faculty, 1966—, member of honors program faculty, 1968—, co-ordinator of graduate studies, department of philosophy, 1971—. Summer visiting professor at University of North Carolina, 1963, and Emory University, 1965; visiting professor at Georgia Institute of Technology, 1965-66. *Member:* American Association for the Advancement of Science, American Guild of Scholars (president, 1968-69), Metaphysical Society of America, American Philosophical Association, Society for Philosophy of Religion (secretary-treasurer, 1965—), Southern Society for Philosophy and Psychology, Georgia Academy of Science, Georgia Philosophical Association, Virginia Philosophical Association, Phi Kappa Phi, Phi Sigma Tau, University of Virginia Philosophy Club.

WRITINGS: Introduction to Contemporary Logic (monograph), University of Georgia, 1965, revised edition, 1969; *Deductive Logic and Descriptive Language*, with teacher's guide, Prentice-Hall, 1969; (contributor) Robert H. Ayers and William T. Blackstone, editors, *Religious Language and Knowledge*, University of Georgia Press, 1972; (contributor) Eddy J. Van Meter, editor, *Theory Development and Educational Administration*, MSS Information Corp., 1973; (compiler and editor) *University of Georgia Fact Book*, University of Georgia, 1973. Contributor to professional journals. Managing editor, *International Journal for Philosophy of Religion*, 1972—; member of editorial advisory board, *Symposium Humanities*, 1972—.

WORK IN PROGRESS: Research on robots and sensation language, on technology and the concept of privacy, and on Wallace Matson on bodily resurrection; *Philosophy of Mind: An Appraisal*; *The Tractatus: In Defense of Value*.

* * *

HARRISON, Jay S(molens) 1927-1974

January 25, 1927—September 12, 1974; American music editor, author of play. Obituaries: *New York Times*, September 13, 1974.

* * *

HARRISON, M(ichael) John 1945-
(Joyce Churchill)

PERSONAL: Born July 26, 1945, in Great Britain; son of Alan Spencer (an engineer) and Dorothy (a clerk; maiden name, Lee) Harrison. *Education:* Educated in England. *Politics:* None. *Religion:* Atheist. *Home:* 10 Stratford Villas, London N.W.1, England. *Agent:* Kirby McCauley, 220 East 26th St., New York, N.Y. 10010. *Office:* Critical Department, *New Worlds*, 221 Camden High St., London N.W.1, England.

CAREER: Atherstone Hunt, Atherstone, Warwickshire, England, groom, 1963; student teacher in Warwickshire, England, 1963-65; Royal Masonic Charity Institute, London, England, clerk, 1966; writer, 1966—.

WRITINGS: The Committed Men (novel), Doubleday, 1971; *The Pastel City* (novel), New English Library, 1971, Doubleday, 1972; *The Centauri Device* (novel), Doubleday, 1974; *The Machine in Shaft Ten and Other Stories*, Panther, 1975. Contributor of articles, short stories, and reviews, sometimes under pseudonym Joyce Churchill, to *Transatlantic Review, New Worlds, New Worlds Quarterly, Fantasy and Science Fiction, New Writings in Science Fiction, Science Fantasy, It*, and *Frendz*. Literary editor of *New Worlds*, 1968—.

WORK IN PROGRESS: Editing *The Human Factor: Sympathy for the Devil*; research for a book on mountain rescue in Great Britain.

SIDELIGHTS: Harrison writes: "I became a professional writer in 1966, living frugally in the bleak 'bedsitter' belt of London's Tufnell Park and Camden Town—an area of one-roomed cold water apartments full of Irish expatriots, junkies and broken gas meters. I still find the area fascinating. I believe, with the Hardy of *The Return of the Native*, that the landscape *is* the fiction; all else devolves from it. I use the science fiction and fantasy forms because they allow greatest latitude of image. . . .

"I am antipolitical, and particularly opposed to 'ideological' politics as a rationale or substitute for administrative or economic (i.e., practical) politics. At the moment, two hemiglobal, implacably opposed, and totally outdated ideological systems are, in the person of various 'limited' wars, killing thousands of people who have never heard of the principles involved; and, in bolstering their own economic situations, starving millions more to death. I see no logical or humanistic reason why this state of affairs should exist, especially since it is based on precepts a hundred or more years old."

AVOCATIONAL INTERESTS: Mountaineering, fell-walking in Scotland and in England's Lake District, playing guitar, riding horses.

* * *

HARRISON, Paul M. 1923-

PERSONAL: Born May 7, 1923, in Philadelphia, Pa.; son of Robert Louis (an accountant) and Ruth (Boyd) Harrison; married Nancy Romig, September 11, 1948; children: Cynthia Lee, John Robert. *Education:* Pennsylvania State University, B.A., 1949; Colgate-Rochester Divinity School, B.D., 1952; Yale University, Ph.D., 1958. *Religion:* American Baptist. *Home:* 740 West Fairmount Ave., State College, Pa. 16801. *Office:* Department of Religion, Pennsylvania State University, Liberal Arts Tower, University Park, Pa. 16802.

CAREER: Princeton University, Princeton, N.J., Melancthon W. Jacobus Instructor in Religion, 1959-60, assistant professor of religion, 1960-63; Pennsylvania State University, University Park, associate professor, 1963-69, professor of religion, 1969—, graduate director of department, 1973—. *Military service:* U.S. Army Air Forces, 1942-45; became second lieutenant. *Member:* American Sociological Association, Society for the Scientific Study of Religion, American Society of Christian Ethics Professors.

WRITINGS: Authority and Power in the Free Church Tradition, Princeton University Press, 1959, 3rd edition, Southern Illinois University Press, 1971; *Introduction to the Memoir of John Mason Peck,* Southern Illinois University Press, 1965; (contributor) Donald R. Cutler, editor, *The Religious Situation,* Beacon Press, 1969. Contributor to *American Sociological Review, Annals of the Academy of Political and Social Science, Theology Today,* and *Theological Education.*

WORK IN PROGRESS: Religion as Dramatic Experience: A Study in Myth Symbolism and Dramatic Enactment through Role Play.

* * *

HARSHBARGER, David Dwight 1938-

PERSONAL: Born February 1, 1938, in Huntington, W.Va.; married; children: two. *Education:* West Virginia University, A.B., 1959, M.A., 1961; University of California, Berkeley, further graduate study, 1961-62; University of North Dakota, Ph.D., 1969; Harvard University, post-doctoral study, 1969-70. *Office:* Department of Psychology, West Virginia University, Morgantown, W.Va. 26506.

CAREER: Licensed psychologist in West Virginia; certified psychologist in Minnesota; Ventura College, Ventura, Calif., instructor in psychology, 1964-65; Moorhead State College, Moorhead, Minn., assistant professor of psychology, 1965-67; West Virginia University, Morgantown, assistant professor, 1970, associate professor of psychology, 1970—, research associate at Appalachian Center, 1971, acting director of clinical training, 1973-74. Member of disaster intervention task force of National Council of Community Mental Health Centers. *Military service:* U.S. Army, personnel psychologist, 1962-64.

MEMBER: American Psychological Association, Society for General Systems Research, West Virginia Psychological Association (president, 1975-76), Sigma Xi, Psi Chi. *Awards, honors:* U.S. Department of Health, Education and Welfare grant from Bureau of Community Environmental Management, 1971-73, to study human ecosystems and human service systems in Appalachia; U.S. Office of Education grant, 1972, to establish "Summerthing," an adolescent treatment program; National Institute of Mental Health clinical psychology grant, 1974-75.

WRITINGS: (With H. W. Demone, Jr.) *The Planning and Administration of Human Services*, Behavioral Publications, 1973; (contributor) H. C. Schulberg, Frank Baker, and S. R. Roen, editors, *Developments in Human Services*, Behavioral Publications, 1973; (contributor) K. W. Schaie and P. B. Baltes, editors, *Life-Span Developmental Psychology: Personality and Socialization*, Academic Press, 1973; (editor with Demone, and contributor) *A Handbook of Human Service Organizations*, Behavioral Publications, 1974; (editor with Roger Maley, and contributor) *Behavior Analysis and Systems Analysis: An Integrative Approach to Mental Health Problems*, Behaviordelia, 1974; (with W. J. Smith, R. W. Miller, and F. E. Zeller) *Human Ecosystems and Human Service Systems in Appalachia*, Appalachian Center, West Virginia University, 1974; (contributor) Nancy Datan and Leon Ginsberg, editors, *Normative Life Crises: Academic and Applied Perspectives*, Academic Press, in press.

Contributor of about fifteen articles to health and psychology journals, including *Proceedings of the West Virginia Academy of Science, Hospital and Community Psychiatry, Mental Hygiene, Human Relations, Journal of Environmental Health*, and *Omega*.

* * *

HART, Edward J(ack) 1941-

PERSONAL: Born July 31, 1941, in Yoe, Pa.; son of Edwin J. and Virginia (Moser) Hart; married Margaret Mary Kauffman (a registered nurse), August 28, 1965; children: Peter Edward. *Education:* West Chester State College, B.S., 1963; West Virginia University, M.S., 1965; University of Maryland, Ph.D., 1970. *Home:* 31 Glenn St., Cortland, N.Y. 13045. *Office:* Department of Health Education, State University of New York, Cortland, N.Y. 13045.

CAREER: State University of New York at Cortland, assistant professor, 1970-72, associate professor of health education, 1973—. Member of board of Cortland County American Cancer Society, 1973-75. *Member:* Society of Public Health Educators, American School Health Association (fellow), New York State Federation of Professional Health Educators, Phi Kappa Phi, Eta Sigma Gamma.

WRITINGS: (Editor with William Sechrist) *Dynamics of Wellness,* Wadsworth, 1970; (with Michael Haro) *Death Education,* American School Health Association, 1974; (with others) *Health Science,* Houghton, in press. Contributor to *Journal of American School Health Association* and *Journal of New York State College Health Association.*

HART, Patrick 1925-

PERSONAL: Born June 14, 1925, in Green Bay, Wis.; son of Michael (a farmer) and Frances (Fox) Hart. *Education:* University of Notre Dame, B.A., 1951. *Home and office:* Abbey of Gethsemani, Trappist, Ky. 40073.

CAREER: Roman Catholic Trappist monk and teacher, 1951—.

WRITINGS: (Editor with Naomi Burton Stone and James Laughlin) *The Asian Journal of Thomas Merton,* New Directions, 1973; (editor) *Thomas Merton, Monk: A Monastic Tribute,* Sheed, 1974.

WORK IN PROGRESS: Editing writings and correspondence of Thomas Merton.

* * *

HARTE, Thomas Joseph 1914-1974

June 27, 1914—August 15, 1974; American Redemptorist priest, educator, author of books on religious topics. Obituaries: *Washington Post*, August 18, 1974.

* * *

HARTHOORN, A(ntonie) M(arinus) 1923-

PERSONAL: Born August 26, 1923, in Rotterdam, Netherlands; married; children: one son, two daughters. *Education:* Attended Royal Veterinary College, London, 1940-50; University of Utrecht, D.V.Sc., 1952; Pharmacological Institute, D.M.V., 1953; F.R.C.V.S., 1956; University of London, Ph.D., 1965. *Home:* Dayal Bagh, 53 Ringwood Rd., Lynnwood Manor, Pretoria, South Africa. *Office:* Nature Conservation Division, Private Bag X209, Pretoria, South Africa.

CAREER: University of East Africa, Nairobi, Kenya, formerly professor of physiology and pharmacology, and head of department of physiology and biochemistry; Nature Conservation Division, Pretoria, South Africa, chief professional officer of research. Member of board of trustees of Mlilwane Wildlife Sanctuary, Swaziland. *Military service:* British Army, 1942-46. *Member:* British Veterinary Association (president of Uganda Branch), British Physiological Society, Uganda Veterinary Society (president). *Awards, honors:* Gold medal and fellowship award from Veterinary Medical Association of Great Britain and Ireland, 1949.

WRITINGS: Application of Pharmacological and Physiological Principles in Restraint of Wild Animals (monograph), Wildlife Society, 1965; (contributor) F. B. Golley and H. K. Buechner, editors, *A Practical Guide to the Study of the Productivity of Large Herbivores*, Blackwell Scientific Publications, 1969; *The Flying Syringe: Ten Years of Immobilising Wild Animals in Africa*, Bles, 1970; (contributor) L. R. Soma, editor, *Textbook of Veterinary Anesthesia*, Williams & Wilkins, 1971; (contributor) E. Young, editor, *The Capture and Care of Wild Animals*, Human & Rousseau, 1973; *Chemical Capture: A Guide to the Chemical Restraint of Wild and Captive Animals*, Bailliere, Tindall & Cassell, 1975; (contributor) Meyer Jones, editor, *Veterinary Pharmacology and Therapeutics*, 4th edition (Harthoorn was not associated with earlier editions), Iowa State University Press, in press. Contributor of more than eighty scientific articles to journals.

WORK IN PROGRESS: Research on the treatment and prevention of capture myopathy in wild animals, and on the current states of orthodox and fringe medicine.

HARTMAN, Nancy Carol 1942-

PERSONAL: Born November 22, 1942, in Pennsylvania; daughter of G. Ellwood (a grocer) and Irene (Hall) Farmer; married Robert K. Hartman, June 15, 1964 (divorced, May, 1973). *Education:* Attended Mount Union College; Pennsylvania State University, B.S., 1964; University of Connecticut, M.A., 1969, further graduate study, 1969—. *Home:* 20 Lasky Rd., Beacon Falls, Conn. 06403. *Office:* Department of Education, Sacred Heart University, 5229 Park Ave., Bridgeport, Conn. 06604.

CAREER: Elementary school teacher in Newton, Iowa, 1964-65, and Manchester, Conn., 1965-69; reading consultant in Ellington, Conn., 1969-70; Sacred Heart University, Bridgeport, Conn., assistant professor of education and student teacher supervisor, 1970—. *Member:* International Reading Association (member of executive board of Fairfield County Council), College Reading Association, Council for Exceptional Children, National Council of Teachers of English, National Reading Association, American Educational Research Association, Orton Society, New England Reading Association, Connecticut Association of Learning Disabilities.

WRITINGS: (Editor with Robert K. Hartman) *Perspectives in Reading*, MSS Educational Publishing, 1971; (editor with Robert K. Hartman) *Psychology in the Classroom*, MSS Educational Publishing, 1971. Contributor to *Reading Teacher, Learning Disabilities Newsletter*, and *Journal of Reading Behavior*.

WORK IN PROGRESS: The Efficacy of Training Mothers as Summer Tutors of Reading.

* * *

HARVEY, Maria Luisa Alvarez 1938-

PERSONAL: Born January 20, 1938, in Torreon, Mexico; daughter of Luis R. (a newspaper editor) and Juana (Mireles) Alvarez; married James C. Harvey, August 10, 1965 (divorced July, 1974); children: Rogelio Vicente Solis. *Education:* Texas Western College, B.A., 1965; University of Texas at El Paso, M.A., 1966; University of Arizona, Ph.D., 1969; Jackson State University, M.S.Ed., 1972; Harvard University, postdoctoral study, summers, 1972-73. *Politics:* Independent. *Religion:* Roman Catholic. *Home:* 1062 Robinson St., Jackson, Miss. 39203. *Office:* Department of Foreign Languages, Jackson State University, Jackson, Miss. 39217.

CAREER: College of Artesia, Artesia, N.M., assistant professor of Spanish and head of department of languages, 1969-70; Jackson State University, Jackson, Miss., associate professor of Spanish, 1970-73, professor of modern foreign languages, 1974—. Chairman of the executive committee of the Minorities Advisory Council of the Mississippi Authority for Educational Television; member of Greater Jackson Area Committee for Criminal Justice; member of Jackson Bicentennial Committee and Jackson Council on Human Relations.

MEMBER: International Reading Association, Modern Language Association of America, College Language Association, American Association of Teachers of Spanish and Portuguese (president of Mississippi chapter), National Education Association, American Association of University Women, League of Women Voters, Young Women's Christian Association Committee for Administration (Marino branch), South Central Modern Language Association, Mississippi Teachers Association, Mississippi Modern Language Association, Jackson State University National Alumni Association (member of board of directors, 1974-77), Phi Beta Kappa.

WRITINGS: Cielo y tierra en la poesia lirica de Manuel Altolaguirre (title means "Heaven and Earth in the Lyric Poetry of Manuel Altolaguirre"), University and College Press of Mississippi, 1972. Contributor of more than a dozen articles to language and education journals, including *Mexico en la Cultura, Jackson State College Review, Illinois Schools Journal, Journal of Negro Education, Elementary English,* and *Mississippi Education Journal,* and to newspapers.

WORK IN PROGRESS: Pasos Negros: Black Footsteps, a second year Spanish reader; *But Here You Would Have Your Black Children; Spanish Is Like Football,* a grammar review.

SIDELIGHTS: Maria Harvey writes: "As a member of a minority group who can be considered 'to have made it to the top' (not that I share that opinion completely . . .) I have much to offer. I am a living example of what one can achieve regardless of ethnic background, color of skin, lack of money, and obstacles placed on the way by prejudice and ignorance. I am totally and irrevocably student-oriented. I am a crusader for education. The two go together in my case. Students are very precious and dear to me, and minority group students are extra precious and extra dear. I hope to be a motivating force in their lives. They are in turn, in a very real sense, the main reason for my existence."

* * *

HASTINGS, Macdonald 1909-
(Lemuel Gulliver)

PERSONAL: Born October 6, 1909, in London, England; son of Basil Macdonald (a playwright, author, and essayist) and Wilhelmina Harriet (White) Hastings; married Anne Scott-James (an author, editor and journalist), 1944 (marriage dissolved); married Anthea Hodson Joseph (deputy chairman of Michael Joseph Ltd., publishers), 1963; children: (first marriage) Max Hugh Macdonald, Clare Selina; (second marriage) Susan Harriet Selina. *Education:* Attended Stonyhurst College, 1917-27. *Home:* Brown's Farm, Old Basing, Hampshire RG24 ODE, England. *Agent:* John Cushman Associates, Inc., 25 West 43rd St., New York, N.Y. 10036; and Curtis Brown Ltd., 1 Craven Hill, London W2 3EW, England.

CAREER: Picture Post, London, England, war correspondent and feature writer, 1939-45; *Strand Magazine*, London, editor, 1946-49; *Country Fair*, London, founder and editor, 1951-58. Broadcaster, beginning in early 1940's; television commentator for the B.B.C., beginning in 1950's. Free-lance writer. *Member:* Detection Club, Savage Club (member of board of trustees), Beefsteak Club, Saintsbury Club, Thursday Club (all London).

WRITINGS—Mystery novels, except as indicated: *Cork on the Water*, Random House, 1951, Tom Stacey Reprints, 1971; *Cork in Bottle*, M. Joseph, 1953, Knopf, 1954, new edition, M. Joseph, 1956, Tom Stacey Reprints, 1972; *Cork in the Doghoase*, M. Joseph, 1957, Knopf, 1958, Tom Stacey Reprints, 1972; *Cork and the Serpent*, M. Joseph, 1955; *A Glimpse of Arcadia* (historical novel), M. Joseph, 1960, Coward-McCann, 1961, new edition, M. Joseph, 1974; *Cork on the Telly*, M. Joseph, 1966, published as *Cork on Location*, Walker & Co., 1967.

Nonfiction: *Passed as Censored* (war reminiscences), Harrap, 1941; *Rolls Royce: The Story of a Name* (monograph), Rolls Royce Ltd., 1950; *Macdonald Hastings' Country Book: A Personal Anthology*, Newnes, 1961; *The Other Mr. Churchill: A Lifetime of Shooting and Murder* (biography), Harrap, 1963, Dodd, 1965; (editor) Robert Churchill, *Game Shooting: A Textbook on the Successful Use of the Modern Shotgun*, M. Joseph, 1963, Stackpole Books, 1967, new revised edition published as *Robert Churchill's Game Shooting*, M. Joseph, 1970, and as *Churchill's Game Shooting*, Stackpole Books, 1972; (author of commentary) John Gay, *London Observed*, John Day, 1964; *How to Shoot Straight*, Pelham, 1967, A. S. Barnes, 1970; *English Sporting Guns and Accessories*, Ward, Lock, 1969; *Jesuit Child* (autobiography), M. Joseph, 1971, St. Martin's, 1972; *Mary Celeste: The Story of an Abandoned Ship*, M. Joseph, 1972; (with Carole Walsh) *Wheeler's Fish Cookery Book*, M. Joseph, 1974; *After You, Robinson Crusoe* (autobiography), Pelham, in press.

Books for young readers: *Eagle Special Investigator*, M. Joseph, 1953; *Adventure Calling*, Hulton Press, 1955; *The Search for the Little Yellow Men*, Knopf, 1956; *Men of Glory*, Hulton Press, 1958; *More Men of Glory*, Hulton Press, 1959; *Sydney the Sparrow*, Ward, Lock, 1973.

Writer of television series, "Call the Gun Expert," "Riverbeat," "Voyage into England," and "In Deepest Britain"; also writer of television program, "The Hated Society: The Jesuits," and of a feature film commissioned by the Iranian Government, "Flame of Persia," 1973. Contributor to *Lilliput* magazine under pseudonym Lemuel Gulliver, 1940-45; regular contributor to various British periodicals and newspapers.

SIDELIGHTS: Hastings writes: "Mine is a coat of many colours. Successful authors write the same book again and again. From book to book my own taste is to write something different. It seems to me that is what life is about. I am consistent in my love of the open air. Most of my work is about green places in Britain. . . . I shoot, I fish. I hunt, I garden."

Hastings' books have been translated into Italian, German, French, Dutch, and Japanese.

* * *

HASTY, Ronald W. 1941-

PERSONAL: Born March 30, 1941, in Kermit, Tex.; son of M. F. (a plant manager) and Mildred (a teacher; maiden name, Stroup) Hasty; married Sharlott Houston, July 27, 1963; children: Shanna, Raymond. *Education:* Eastern New Mexico University, B.B.A. and M.B.A.; University of Colorado, D.B.A., 1969. *Politics:* Republican. *Religion:* Church of Christ. *Home:* 3800 Capitol Dr., Fort Collins, Colo. 80521. *Office:* Department of Marketing, Colorado State University, Fort Collins, Colo. 80521.

CAREER: Colorado State University, Fort Collins, associate professor of marketing, 1967-74; visiting professor and researcher at Middle East Technical University, 1974-75. Consultant to business, industry, and Organization for Economic Cooperation and Development. *Member:* American Marketing Association, Silver Key, Sigma Iota Epsilon, Beta Gamma Sigma.

WRITINGS: (With R. Ted Will) *Retailing: A Mid-Management Approach*, Harper, 1973; (with Will) *Marketing*, Harper, 1975. Contributor to trade and professional journals. Member of editorial staff of *Journal of Marketing*; member of book review staff of *Choice*.

WORK IN PROGRESS: Research on the Turkish economy, with books on business and marketing expected to result.

* * *

HATFIELD, Dorothy B(lackmon) 1921-

PERSONAL: Born July 28, 1921, in Clayton, Ala.; daughter of William B. and Lily Edna (Miller) Blackmon; married B. Glenn Hatfield (a building official), March 2, 1941. *Education:* Auburn University, B.S., 1951, M.A., 1960, doctoral study, 1963—. *Home:* 3103 College Ave., Columbus, Ga. 31907. *Office:* Department of Special Studies, Columbus College, Columbus, Ga. 31907.

CAREER: Columbus College, Columbus, Ga., assistant professor of English, 1959—, director of department of special studies, 1969—. *Member:* Georgia Education Association (past president of Columbus College chapter), Delta Kappa Gamma (charter member; past president).

WRITINGS: (Editor with Eugene Current-Garcia) *Shem, Ham, and Japheth*, University of Georgia Press, 1973. Contributor to *Southern Folklore Quarterly*.

* * *

HATVARY, George Egon

PERSONAL: Born in Budapest, Hungary; son of Carlo (an opera singer) and Magda (Kovacs) Hatvary; married Laurel Trencher (a college instructor), September 30, 1961; children: Maura Eve. *Education:* Attended Northwestern University and University of Chicago; New School for Social Research, B.A., 1947; New York University, M.A., 1948, Ph.D., 1957. *Residence:* New York, N.Y. *Office:* Department of English, St. John's University, Jamaica, N.Y. 11439.

CAREER: Boston University, Boston, Mass., instructor in English, 1948-49; New York University, New York, N.Y., instructor in English, 1953-59; Queens College of the City University of New York, Flushing, N.Y., instructor in English, 1959-63; St. John's University, Jamaica, N.Y., assistant professor, 1963-65, associate professor of English, 1965—. *Military service:* U.S. Army, military intelligence, 1943-46; became sergeant. *Member:* Modern Language Association of America, Poe Studies Association.

WRITINGS: (Editor with T. O. Mabbott) *Poe's Prose Romances*, St. John's University Press, 1968; *Horace Binney Wallace*, Twayne, in press. Contributor of articles and stories to literature journals, including *Hudson Review*, *American Literature*, *Irish Writing*, *Princeton University Library Chronicle*, and *University of Kansas City Review*.

WORK IN PROGRESS: Two novels.

* * *

HAUCK, Richard Boyd 1936-

PERSONAL: Born September 12, 1936, in Cincinnati, Ohio; son of Roy C. (a corporation manager) and Helen M. (a registered nurse; maiden name, Murphy) Hauck; married Dean Margaret Malmstrom (a research consultant), September 10, 1960; children: Margaret, Sarah. *Education:* Western Michigan University, B.A., 1959; Ohio University, M.A., 1960; University of Illinois, Ph.D., 1965. *Politics:* Thoreauvian. *Religion:* Puritan. *Office:* Department of English, University of West Florida, Pensacola, Fla. 32504.

CAREER: University of Washington, Seattle, assistant professor, 1965-70, associate professor of English, 1970-71;

University of West Florida, Pensacola, associate professor of English, 1971—. Liaison officer to Danforth Foundation, 1972—. *Military service:* U.S. Army Reserve, 1959-67; became captain. *Member:* American Association of University Professors, American Studies Association, National Council of Teachers of English, College English Association, Modern Language Association of America.

WRITINGS: A Cheerful Nihilism: Confidence and "The Absurd" in Humorous American Fiction, Indiana University Press, 1971. Contributor to journals.

WORK IN PROGRESS: A book tentatively titled, *A Mere and Arbitrary Grace: Reflections on a Puritan Paradox in American Literature.*

AVOCATIONAL INTERESTS: Family, fishing, and fabrication.

* * *

HAVERSTOCK, Nathan Alfred 1931-
(Richard Alfred, joint pseudonym)

PERSONAL: Born May 18, 1931, in Minneapolis, Minn.; son of Henry W. (a lawyer) and Catherine B. Haverstock; married Mary Sayre (a writer), May 22, 1954; children: Rosamond, Daniel, Julia, Jonathan, Gwendolyn. *Education:* Harvard University, A.B., 1953. *Home:* 1122 South 22nd St., Arlington, Va. 22202. *Office:* Latin American Service, 304 Colorado Building, Washington, D.C. 20005.

CAREER: Library of Congress, Hispanic Foundation, Washington, D.C., writer and consultant, 1955-61; *Saturday Evening Post*, New York, N.Y., assistant editor, 1961-62; Organization of American States, Washington, D.C., press officer, 1962-63, 1965-68; free-lance writer, 1964; Latin American Service, Washington, D.C., director, 1968—; International Development Foundation, New York, N.Y., Washington representative, 1973—. Consultant to American Chambers of Commerce in Latin America, 1973—, Environmental Fund, 1974—, and U.S.-Mexico Chamber of Commerce, 1974—. *Military service:* U.S. Army, 1953-55; became second lieutenant. *Member:* National Press Club.

WRITINGS: (Editor) *Handbook of Latin American Studies*, Volumes XXI, XXII, XXIII, University of Florida Press, 1959-61; *Give Us This Day: The Sister of Sister Dulce, the Angel of Bahia*, Appleton, 1965; *Organization of American States: The Challenge of the Americas*, Coward, 1966; (with J. Warren Nystrom) *The Alliance for Progress*, Van Nostrand, 1966; (with John P. Hoover) *Cuba in Pictures*, Sterling, 1974; (with Hoover) *El Salvador in Pictures*, Sterling, 1974; (with Hoover) *Nicaragua in Pictures*, Sterling, 1974; (with Hoover) *Uruguay in Pictures*, Sterling, 1975. Author of syndicated newspaper column on Latin American affairs with Richard C. Schroeder under joint pseudonym Richard Alfred, 1968-70, joint byline with Schroeder, 1971-72, single byline of Nathan A. Haverstock, 1973-74. Editor of *Alliance for Progress Weekly Newsletter*, 1965-68.

* * *

HAVRILESKY, Thomas M(ichael) 1939-

PERSONAL: Born March 18, 1939, in Johnstown, Pa.; son of Michael and Pauline (Duranko) Havrilesky; married Susan Newberry, September 25, 1964; children: Eric, Laura, Heather. *Education:* Attended University of Pittsburgh, 1956-58; Pennsylvania State University, B.S., 1960, M.A., 1963; University of Illinois, Ph.D., 1966. *Home:* 1508 Alabama Ave., Durham, N.C. 27705. *Office:* Department of Economics, Duke University, Durham, N.C. 27706.

CAREER: University of Maryland, College Park, assistant professor of economics, 1966-69; Duke University, Durham, N.C., associate professor of economics, 1969—. Visiting associate professor at Rice University and Simon Fraser University, both 1971. *Member:* American Economic Association, American Finance Association, Association for Evolutionary Economics, Phi Kappa Phi.

WRITINGS: (With John T. Boorman) *Money Supply, Money Demand, and Macroeconomics*, Allyn & Bacon, 1972; *Money in the Economy*, Wiley, 1972.

WORK IN PROGRESS: Non-Price Competition in Banking; *The Economics of Voluntary Activity.*

* * *

HAWES, Joseph M(ilton) 1938-

PERSONAL: Born May 9, 1938, in Fort Davis, Tex.; son of Milton Doe and Jessie (a teacher; maiden name, Weatherby) Hawes; married Kathryn Schnell, December 22, 1963; children: Lyda Kathryn. *Education:* Rice University, A.B., 1960; Oklahoma State University, M.A., 1962; University of Texas, Ph.D., 1969. *Home:* 3132 Ella Lane, Manhattan, Kan. 66502. *Office:* Department of History, Kansas State University, Manhattan, Kan. 66506.

CAREER: Teacher in Nashville, Tenn., 1962-64; Indiana University—Southeast, Jeffersonville, assistant professor of history, 1969-71; Kansas State University, Manahttan, associate professor of history, 1971—, chairman of department, 1973—. Field humanist for Kansas Committee for the Humanities, 1974-75. *Military service:* U.S. Naval Reserve, 1955-63. *Member:* American Historical Association, Organization of American Historians, American Association of University Professors, Southern Historical Association.

WRITINGS: Children in Urban Society, Oxford University Press, 1971. Contributor to *Journal of World History*, *Military Affairs*, and *Paisana.*

WORK IN PROGRESS: History of Child Psychology; *Kansas and the Coming of the Civil War*; *A Social History of the American People.*

* * *

HAY, David M(cKechnie) 1935-

PERSONAL: Born September 19, 1935; son of Donald Gordon (a sociologist) and Lillian (McKechnie) Hay; married Mary Cam Carmichael (a pre-school teacher), June 30, 1961; children: Mary Cameron, Michael David. *Education:* Duke University, B.A., 1957; Yale University, B.D., 1960, Ph.D., 1965; University of Tuebingen, graduate study, 1963-64. *Home:* 2231 Brookland Dr. N.E., Cedar Rapids, Iowa 52402. *Office:* Department of Religion, Coe College, Cedar Rapids, Iowa 52402.

CAREER: Ordained Presbyterian minister, 1966; Princeton Theological Seminary, Princeton, N.J., assistant professor of New Testament, 1964-68, 1969-71; Coe College, Cedar Rapids, Iowa, assistant professor of religion and chaplain, 1971—. Visiting lecturer at Kwangnaru Presbyterian Seminary, Seoul, Korea, 1968-69. *Member:* Society of Biblical Literature, American Academy of Religion, Presbytery of Northeast Iowa.

WRITINGS: Glory at the Right Hand: Psalm 110 in Early

Christianity, Abingdon, 1973. Contributor to *Encyclopedia Americana*, and to *Journal of Biblical Literature, Interpretation*, and *Theology Today*.

WORK IN PROGRESS: Research on concepts of faith in Hellenistic Judaism and early Christianity; translating Hellenistic Jewish fragments.

AVOCATIONAL INTERESTS: Travel, classical music for piano.

* * *

HAY, James G(ordon) 1936-

PERSONAL: Born November 5, 1936, in Waipukarau, New Zealand; son of Franklin George (a railwayman) and Irene (Smith) Hay; married Hilary Williamson, May 17, 1958; children: Linda Irene, Karen June. *Education:* University of Otago, Dip.Phys.Ed., 1956; graduate study at Christchurch Teachers' College, 1957; University of Iowa, M.A., 1956, Ph.D., 1967. *Home:* 3056 American Legion Rd., Iowa City, Iowa 52240. *Office:* Department of Physical Education, University of Iowa, Iowa City, Iowa 52242.

CAREER: High school teacher of physical education and mathematics in Hawera, New Zealand, 1957-64; University of Otago, Otago, New Zealand, lecturer, 1967-68, senior lecturer in physical education, 1968-71; University of Iowa, Iowa City, assistant professor, 1971-73, associate professor of physical education, 1973—. Scientific consultant to New Zealand Amateur Rowing Association in selection of national squads, 1968-71; coach of New Zealand track and field team, 1969; consultant to Nissen Corp., 1973—. *Member:* International Society of Biomechanics, International Society of Electrophysiological Kinesiologists, International Track and Field Coaches' Association, American Alliance of Health, Physical Education and Recreation, New Zealand Association of Health, Physical Education and Recreation, New Zealand Athletic Coaches' Association (president, 1970-71).

WRITINGS: The Biomechanics of Sports Techniques, Prentice-Hall, 1973; (with Tom Ecker and Fred Wilt) *Olympic Track and Field Techniques*, Parker Publishing, 1974. Contributor to physical education journals. Editor of *New Zealand Journal of Health, Physical Education and Recreation*, 1968-70.

WORK IN PROGRESS: An Annotated Bibliography of Biomechanics Literature, with Peter R. Francis, and a 2nd edition, *A Bibliography of Biomechanics Literature*; research in dual-media cinematography, evaluation of lifesaving techniques, and the development of a general method for evaluating human movements.

* * *

HAYMAN, Carol Bessent 1927-

PERSONAL: Born June 9, 1927, in Southport, N.C.; daughter of George Howard and Minnie (Guthrie) Bessent; married Louis DeMaro Hayman, Jr. (a cardiologist), August 30, 1945; children: Richard Louis, Susan Carol. *Education:* Louisburg College, A.A., 1946; attended East Carolina University, 1945, 1965, and Black Mountain College, 1952. *Religion:* Methodist. *Home and office:* 406 Carmen Ave., Jacksonville, N.C. 28540.

CAREER: Writer, poet. Trustee of Louisburg College, 1964-71. *Member:* World Poetry Society, International Platform Association, National League of American Pen Women (member of executive board), Academy of American Poets, Smithsonian Institution, Early American Society, North Carolina Poetry Society, North Carolina Congressional Club, Carteret Historical Research Association, Onslow County (N.C.) Medical Auxiliary, Onslow Community Concert Association, St. John's Art Gallery, Louisburg College One Hundred Club. *Awards, honors:* Award of Merit from North Carolina Poetry Contest, 1967.

WRITINGS: Keepsake (poems), Piedmont Press, 1962; *These Lovely Days* (autobiography), Piedmont Press, 1971; *A Collection of Writings Published in the North Carolina Christian Advocate*, Piedmont Press, 1972; *What Is Christmas?* (prose and poetry), Methodist Publishing House, 1974. Poems represented in anthologies, including *Award-Winning Poems of the North Carolina Poetry Society, Inc.*, North Carolina Poetry Society, 1967, 1969-72. Contributor to *Christian Advocate, Pen Woman, Tidings*, and other magazines. Author of weekly column, "These Lovely Days," in Jacksonville, N.C. *Daily News*, 1974, and *Onslow Herald*, 1974—. Southeast regional editor of *Pen Woman*, 1972-74.

WORK IN PROGRESS: Three books, one on seasonal meditations and programs for special occasions, one consisting of love poems for the married, and a novel in a medical setting.

AVOCATIONAL INTERESTS: Music, art, education, travel, interior decoration.

* * *

HAYS, Robert Glenn 1935-

PERSONAL: Born May 23, 1935, in Carmi, Ill.; son of Earl and Margaret (White) Hays; married Mary Corley, December 21, 1957; children: Alan, David. *Education:* Southern Illinois University, B.S., 1961, M.S., 1972, Ph.D., 1975. *Home:* 2724 Cedar Dr., Huntsville, Tex. 77340. *Office:* Department of Journalism, Sam Houston State University, Huntsville, Tex. 77341.

CAREER: Granite City Press-Record, Granite City, Ill., reporter and photographer, 1961-63; Southern Illinois University, Information Service, Carbondale, staff writer, 1963-66; Southern Illinois University, Carbondale, editor of *Alumnus*, 1966-71, researcher, 1971-74; campaign manager for Paul Simon, Democratic candidate from Illinois for U.S. Congress, 1974; Sam Houston State University, Huntsville, Tex., assistant professor of journalism, 1974—. Researcher for Illinois Board of Natural Resources and Conservation, 1971-74. *Military service:* U.S. Army, Adjutant General's Corps, 1955-57. *Member:* Society of Professional Journalists, Sigma Delta Chi, Kappa Tau Alpha.

WRITINGS: (With B. G. Oscar W. Koch) *G-2: Intelligence for Patton*, Whitmore, 1971; *Country Editor: The Influence of a Weekly Newspaper*, Interstate, 1974. Contributor of articles and reviews to magazines and newspapers, including *Small World* and *Electronics Illustrated*.

WORK IN PROGRESS: State Science in Illinois; "The Primary Campaign," a chapter in *Congressman: An Interdisciplinary Case Study*, edited by Keith R. Sanders for Southern Illinois University Press; *The Girls of New Haven*, with wifc, Mary Corley Hays.

* * *

HEAD, Richard G(lenn) 1938-

PERSONAL: Born January 6, 1938, in Mason City, Iowa; son of Walter Glenn (in real estate) and Margaret (Nason) Head; married Elaine Estes, December 27, 1966; children: Mark, Laura, Kathy, Timothy. *Education:* U.S. Air Force

Academy, B.S., 1960; Syracuse University, M.P.A., 1969, Ph.D., 1970. *Religion:* Episcopal. *Home:* PSC 1, Box 6773, APO SF 96286. *Office:* Third Tactical Fighter Wing, Clark Air Base, Philippines 96274.

CAREER: U.S. Air Force, career officer, 1960—; present rank, lieutenant colonel. Pilot, 1961-65; instructor pilot, 1966-68; graduate student, 1968-70; U.S. Air Force Academy, Colorado Springs, Colo., assistant professor of political science, 1970-73. *Awards, honors*—Military: Silver Star; Distinguished Flying Cross; Meritorious Service Medal; Air Medal with twelve oak leaf clusters; Air Force Commendation Medal; Presidential Unit Citation.

WRITINGS: (Editor with Ervin J. Rokke) *American Defense Policy III*, Johns Hopkins Press, 1972; (section editor with others) *Comparative Defense Policy*, Johns Hopkins Press, 1974. Contributor to journals.

WORK IN PROGRESS: Research on leadership and management in large organizations.

* * *

HEADY, Harold F(ranklin) 1916-

PERSONAL: Born March 29, 1916, in Buhl, Idaho; son of Orah Everett (a farmer) and Edith (Philbrick) Heady; married Eleanor Butler (a writer), June 12, 1940; children: Carol Marie (Mrs. Don De Maria), Kent Arthur. *Education:* University of Idaho, B.S., 1938; New York State University College of Forestry, M.S., 1940; graduate study at University of Minnesota, 1940-41; University of Nebraska, Ph.D., 1947. *Politics:* Republican. *Religion:* Congregational. *Home:* 1864 Capistrano Ave., Berkeley, Calif. 94707. *Agent:* Marilyn Marlow, 60 East 56th St., New York, N.Y. 10022. *Office:* 27 Mulford Hall, University of California, Berkeley, Calif. 94720.

CAREER: U.S. Soil Conservation Service, White Salmon, Wash., range conservationist, 1941; New York State College of Forestry, Syracuse, assistant professor, 1942; Montana State University, Bozeman, assistant professor of range management and plant ecology, 1942-47; Texas A & M University, College Station, associate professor of range management, 1947-51; University of California, Berkeley, assistant professor and assistant plant ecologist at Experimental Station, 1951-56, associate professor and associate plant ecologist, 1956-62, professor of forestry and plant ecologist, 1962—, associate dean of College of Natural Resources, 1974—. Fulbright professor at University of Queensland, 1966. Member of board of directors of Concerned Berkeley Citizens, 1971—; U.S. chairman of Australian American Rangeland Workshops, 1974-75. *Member:* Society for Range Management (founding member; first secretary-treasurer, 1947), Ecological Society of America, California Writers Club. *Awards, honors:* Fulbright and Guggenheim scholar, East Africa, 1959-60; certificate of merit from Society for Range Management, 1969.

WRITINGS: (Illustrator) wife, Eleanor B. Heady, *Coat of the Earth*, Norton, 1968; (with Eleanor B. Heady, and illustrator) *High Meadow: The Ecology of a Mountain Meadow*, Grosset, 1970; (illustrator) Eleanor B. Heady, *Make Your Own Dolls*, Lothrop, 1974; *Rangeland Management*, McGraw, 1975.

* * *

HEALEY, James 1936-

PERSONAL: Born November 5, 1936, in San Jose, Calif.; son of James Thomas (a lawyer, certified public accountant, and automobile dealer) and Grace (Barron) Healey; married Colleen LaVerne Meyer, April 8, 1961; children: Erin Colleen. *Education:* University of Santa Clara, B.S.C., 1958; University of California at Los Angeles, M.B.A., 1961. *Religion:* Roman Catholic. *Home:* 3070 Horseshoe Ct., Hayward, Calif. 94541. *Office:* Department of Business, Chabot Junior College, 25555 Hesperian Blvd., Hayward, Calif. 94545.

CAREER: Salesman and sales manager for outdoor advertising, encyclopedias, and pharmaceuticals in San Jose, Calif., 1960-62; high school teacher of retailing and salesmanship in public schools of San Francisco, Calif., 1962-65; Chabot Junior College, Hayward, Calif., instructor in marketing, 1965—. Independent consultant on direct mail advertising. *Member:* Sales and Marketing Executives Association, California Teachers Association, California Association of Work Experience Educators, California Marketing Club. *Awards, honors:* Muscular Dystrophy Association award, 1972; outstanding service award from Distributive Education Clubs of America, 1973; merit award from Sales and Marketing Executives of San Francisco, 1974.

WRITINGS: (With Mark Jones) *Mathematics for Profit*, Prentice-Hall, 1972; (with Jones) *Miracle Sales Guide: College Edition*, Prentice-Hall, 1973. Author of three radio commercials for the Council of California Growers. Contributor to *DE Today*.

WORK IN PROGRESS: *Classroom Comedy*, Volume I, gags, jokes, and bits of business for the college teacher; researching a pictorial history of the films of Abbott and Costello.

AVOCATIONAL INTERESTS: Legerdemain.

BIOGRAPHICAL/CRITICAL SOURCES: *Hayward Daily Review*, October 10, 1974.

* * *

HEARD, Nathan C(liff) 1936-

PERSONAL: Born November 7, 1936, in Newark, N.J.; son of Nathan E. (a laborer) and Gladys (a blues singer; maiden name, Pruitt) Heard; children: Melvin, Cliff, Natalie. *Education:* Educated in public schools in Newark, N.J. *Politics:* None. *Religion:* None. *Home:* 94 North 16th St., East Orange, N.J. 07017. *Agent:* Dan O'Shea, 251 East 30th St., New York, N.Y. 10016.

CAREER: Fresno State College, Fresno, Calif., guest lecturer in creative writing, 1969-70; Rutgers University, New Brunswick, N.J., assistant professor of English, 1970-72; writer, 1970—. *Military service:* U.S. Air Force, 1952-53. *Awards, honors:* Author's awards from New Jersey Association of Teachers of English, 1969, and Newark College of Engineering, 1973.

WRITINGS—Novels: *Howard Street*, Dial, 1968; *To Reach a Dream*, Dial, 1972; *A Cold Fire Burning*, Simon & Schuster, 1974; *The House of Slammers*, Simon & Schuster, in press.

WORK IN PROGRESS: *A Time of Desperation*, a novel.

SIDELIGHTS: Heard spent nearly half of his life in prison, serving terms for armed robbery and violation of parole. He began writing in prison, and his first novel was published before his parole in 1968. He was an athlete, whose trophies were awarded him in prison, and a musician, singing, playing drums, and serving as band leader.

BIOGRAPHICAL/CRITICAL SOURCES: *New York Times*, January 19, 1969.

HECK, Peter M. 1937-

PERSONAL: Born June 15, 1937, in Baton Rouge, La.; son of Harold J. (an economist) and Suzanne (Holt) Heck; married Suzanne Wright (a writer), April 11, 1957; children: Peter, Jr., Samuel, William, Elizabeth, Marie. *Education:* Louisiana State University, B.A., 1961. *Home:* 601 Avenue D, Redondo Beach, Calif. 90277.

CAREER: Copywriter, copy editor, and creative director in advertising agencies in Dallas, Tex., and Oklahoma City, Okla., 1964-71; *Swing* (magazine), Los Angeles, Calif., editor and publisher, 1971-73; writer, 1973—. *Military service:* U.S. Army, 1956-59.

WRITINGS: (With wife, Suzanne W. Heck) *Joys of Open Marriage*, Books for Better Living, 1974; (with S. W. Heck) *Sex on a Shoestring*, Books for Better Living, 1974. Columnist. Contributor of articles and reviews to magazines. Associate editor of trade publication.

WORK IN PROGRESS: Gunboat Number Five, a historical novel; "Sniper," a screenplay; a non-fiction book for Books for Better Living.

AVOCATIONAL INTERESTS: Ocean racing, sailing, flying, motorcycle racing, cooking, quiet contemplation.

* * *

HECK, Suzanne Wright 1939-

PERSONAL: Born February 19, 1939, in Dallas, Tex.; daughter of Samuel L. (a railroad executive) and Grace (Cunningham) Wright; married Peter M. Heck (a writer), April 11, 1957; children: Peter, Jr., Samuel, William, Elizabeth, Marie. *Education:* Attended University of Colorado and Louisiana State University. *Home:* 601 Avenue D, Redondo Beach, Calif. 90277.

CAREER: Librarian in Paris, France, 1958-59; editor, 1971-73; writer, 1973—.

WRITINGS: (With husband, Peter M. Heck) *Joys of Open Marriage*, Books for Better Living, 1974; (with P. M. Heck) *Sex on a Shoestring*, Books for Better Living, 1974. Columnist. Contributor to magazines.

WORK IN PROGRESS: Sorry, Charlie, a humorous mystery; *Sheila, Dark Sheila*, historical fiction.

* * *

HEICHBERGER, Robert Lee 1930-

PERSONAL: Born January 19, 1930, in Boston, N.Y.; son of Norman A. (a farmer) and Louise (Gross) Heichberger; married Elaine Boldt (a teacher), April 14, 1956; children: Lisa Elaine, Mark Robert. *Education:* State University of New York College for Teachers at Buffalo (now State University of New York at Buffalo), B.S., 1951, Ed.M., 1963, S.E.A., 1965, Ed.D., 1970. *Religion:* Christian. *Home:* 11 James Pl., Fredonia, N.Y. 14063. *Office:* School of Education, State University of New York at Fredonia, Central Ave., Fredonia, N.Y. 14063.

CAREER: East Aurora (N.Y.) Public Schools, teacher, 1951-53, principal, 1953-64; State University of New York at Fredonia, assistant professor, 1964-68, associate professor, 1968-71, professor of educational administration, 1971—, assistant dean, 1964-70, dean for teacher education, 1970-71, administrator, 1971—. Member of board of directors of Fredonia Chamber of Commerce. *Military service:* U.S. Marine Corps, 1951-53.

MEMBER: American Association of School Administrators, National Elementary Principals Association, American Association for Higher Education, American Educational Research Association, National Conference of Professors of Educational Administration, Phi Delta Kappa (past president), Kiwanis (member of local board of directors). *Awards, honors:* Distinguished service award from Phi Delta Kappa—International, 1974.

WRITINGS: Toward Humanizing the Change Process in Schools (monograph), Project Innovation, 1972; (with William Schall) *The Changing Role of the Elementary School Principal*, Project Innovation, 1973; (editor with Russell N. Cassel) *Leadership Development: Theory and Practice*, Christopher, 1975. Contributor to education journals, including *College Student Journal, Journal of Research and Development in Education, Journal of Educational Leadership*, and *Education*. Member of editorial board of *College Student Journal*.

WORK IN PROGRESS: The Principal-Supervisor: Crisis of Middle Management; editing *Toward Cracking the Code in Educational Change: A Book of Readings*, with Ronald Hull and Modan Mohan.

AVOCATIONAL INTERESTS: Outdoor sports (especially skiing and other winter sports), camping, boating.

* * *

HEILBRON, J(ohn) L(ewis) 1934-

PERSONAL: Born March 17, 1934, in San Francisco, Calif. *Education:* University of California, Berkeley, A.B., 1955, M.A., 1958, Ph.D., 1964. *Office:* Department of History, University of California, Berkeley, Calif. 94720.

CAREER: Sources for History of Quantum Physics, Berkeley, Calif., and Copenhagen, Denmark, assistant director, 1961-64; University of Pennsylvania, Philadelphia, assistant professor of history of science, 1964-67; University of California, Berkeley, assistant professor, 1967-71, associate professor, 1971-73, professor of history, 1973—, director of Center for the History of Science, 1973—. *Member:* History of Science Society, British Society for the History of Science.

WRITINGS: (With Lini Allen, Paul Forman, and T. S. Kuhn) *Sources for the History of Quantum Physics*, American Philosophical Society, 1967; *H. G. J. Mosely: The Life and Letters of an English Physicist, 1887-1914*, University of California Press, 1974; (with Forman and Spencer Weart) *Physics circa 1900: Personnel, Funding, and Productivity of the Academic Establishments*, Princeton University Press, 1975. Contributor to *Proceedings of the LII Varenna School "Enrico Fermi,"* and to various journals in history of science.

WORK IN PROGRESS: A History of Electricity in the Seventeenth and Eighteenth Centuries, completion expected in 1975; *The Institutionalization of Physics, 1600-1900*, completion expected in 1977; *Physics in the Twentieth Century*, 1977.

* * *

HEILMAN, Grant 1919-

PERSONAL: Born September 29, 1919, in Tarentum, Pa.; son of Marlin W. (a surgeon) and Martha (Grant) Heilman; married Marjorie Mapel (a sculptor), May 21, 1946 (died, March 21, 1961); married Barbara Whipple (an artist, writer, and teacher), August 14, 1961; children: (first marriage) Hans. *Education:* Swarthmore College, B.A., 1941. *Address:* Box 328, Lititz, Pa. 17543.

CAREER: Grant Heilman Photography, Lititz, Pa., owner, 1946—. Director of SGL Industries, 1968—. *Military service:* U.S. Army, Counter Intelligence, 1941-45; became captain; received Bronze Star, Croix de Guerre.

WRITINGS: The Psalms Around Us, Doubleday, 1970; *Farm Town,* Greene, 1974. Contributor of articles and photographs to encyclopedias and farm journals.

WORK IN PROGRESS: Assembling photographic books on agricultural areas of the United States, and on bees.

* * *

HEIMAN, Ernest J(ean) 1930-

PERSONAL: Born November 18, 1930, in Dubuque, Iowa; son of Ernest J. (an automotive service manager) and Edna (Wetter) Heiman; married M. Joan McCray (an educational paraprofessional), April 26, 1952; children: Beth, Julie, Kathleen, Joel Willis. *Education:* University of Wisconsin, B.S., 1958, M.S., 1961. *Religion:* Lutheran. *Home:* 5133 Spaanem Ave., Madison, Wis. 53716. *Office:* Monona Grove High School, 4400 Monona Dr., Madison, Wis. 53716.

CAREER: Monona Grove High School, Madison, Wis., drama and English coordinator, 1964—. Consultant to U.S. Office of Education, Project English, 1966. *Military service:* U.S. Air Force, 1951-55. *Member:* National Education Association (life member), National Council of Teachers of English, Wisconsin Council of Teachers of English (president, 1971-72), Wisconsin Conference of English Department Chairmen (president, 1973-74), Wisconsin Education Association.

WRITINGS: (With Allan A. Glatthorn and Charles W. Kreidler) *The Dynamics of Language*, six volumes, Heath, 1971. Also author of plays, "A Christmas Pageant" and "Number Please" (libretto and music). Contributor to *National Council of Teachers of English Journal*.

WORK IN PROGRESS: Three volumes on composition, with Clarence Brown, for American Book Co.; a manuscript on nonverbal communication, for Bantam.

AVOCATIONAL INTERESTS: Music, photography.

* * *

HEIN, Leonard William 1916-

PERSONAL: Born February 17, 1916, in Forest Park, Ill.; son of Harry Christian (a banker) and Clara Antoinette (Klein) Hein; married Mildred Lucille Wlochall, August 20, 1941. *Education:* Loyola University, Chicago, Ill., B.Sc. (magna cum laude), 1952; University of Chicago, M.B.A., 1954; University of California, Los Angeles, Ph.D., 1962. *Home:* 1225 North Granada Ave., Alhambra, Calif. 91801. *Office:* School of Business and Economics, California State University, 5151 State University Dr., Los Angeles, Calif. 90032.

CAREER: Certified public accountant in State of Illinois, 1955, certified in data processing by Data Processing Management Association, 1963. DePaul University, Chicago, Ill., instructor in business administration, 1956; California State University, Los Angeles, assistant professor, 1956-59, associate professor, 1959-64, professor of business administration, 1964—, assistant dean for graduate studies in the School of Business and Economics, 1964-72. Member of information systems advisory committees for Compton College, East Los Angeles College, Los Angeles Trade Technical College, College of the Desert, and Los Angeles Southwest College. Editorial consultant to publishers, 1967—. *Military service:* U.S. Navy, instructor, 1942-45.

MEMBER: American Arbitration Association, Operations Research Society of America, Institute of Management Sciences, American Institute of Certified Public Accountants, American Accounting Association (life member), Data Processing Management Association, California Society of Certified Public Accountants, Alpha Kappa Psi, Beta Alpha Psi, Beta Gamma Sigma (past chapter president), Phi Kappa Phi.

WRITINGS: Introduction to Electronic Data Processing for Business, Van Nostrand, 1961; *The Quantitative Approach to Managerial Decisions*, Prentice-Hall, 1967; (editor and contributor) *Contemporary Accounting and the Computer*, Dickenson, 1969; (contributor) Kenneth B. Berg, Gerhard G. Miller, and Lauren M. Walker, editors, *Readings in International Accounting*, Houghton, 1969; (with Donald G. Malcolm and Robert D. Cohn) *Report of the Task Group on Information Systems*, three volumes, California State University Press, 1973.

Contributor of more than a dozen articles and reviews to academic journals, including *Management Accounting, Journal of Accountancy, Journal of Data Management, Accounting Review*, and *University of Toronto Law Journal.*

WORK IN PROGRESS: Management Information and Control Systems, for Dickenson.

* * *

HEINKE, Clarence H. 1912-

PERSONAL: Surname is pronounced *Hine*-kee; born July 13, 1912, in Wisconsin; son of Alvin E. (a farmer) and Ida (Scholz) Heinke; married Jean F. Wilson, May 1, 1944; children: Sally Jean (Mrs. Fred M. Rosin), Linda Ann, Karl L. *Education:* Capital University, B.Sc., 1938; Ohio State University, M.A., 1942, Ph.D., 1953. *Religion:* Lutheran. *Home:* 688 South Remington Rd., Columbus, Ohio 43209. *Office:* Department of Mathematics, Capital University, Columbus, Ohio 43209.

CAREER: High school teacher of science and mathematics in the public schools of Kings Mills and Ashtabula, Ohio, 1938-41; Eau Claire State College, Eau Claire, Wis., instructor in mathematics, 1945-46; Capital University, Columbus, Ohio, 1946—, began as instructor, now professor of mathematics. Member, Entebbe Mathematics writing team, Mombassa, Kenya, 1967. *Military service:* U.S. Naval Reserve, 1942-72; became captain. Active duty, U.S. Navy, 1942-45; received two presidential unit citations, Distinguished Flying Cross, Bronze Star, and combat area ribbons. *Member:* National Council of Teachers of Mathematics (director, 1966-69), Mathematical Association of America, Ohio Academy of Science (fellow), Ohio Council of Teachers of Mathematics (president, 1958-60).

WRITINGS: How to Use a Slide Rule, privately printed, 1956; *Fundamental Concepts of Elementary Mathematics*, Dickenson, 1970. Contributor to *Yearbook* of the National Council of Teachers of Mathematics; contributor to mathematics journals.

WORK IN PROGRESS: Mathematics for Elementary Teachers; Teaching of Elementary Mathematics.

AVOCATIONAL INTERESTS: Photography, tree farming, travel.

HELLERMAN, Herbert 1927-

PERSONAL: Born July 8, 1927, in New York, N.Y.; son of Nathan and Sarah (Tobias) Hellerman; married Elaine Magid (a teacher), June 20, 1948; children: Steven, Nancy, Paul. *Education:* Purdue University, B.S.E.E., 1949; Syracuse University, Ph.D., 1955. *Home:* 501 Murray Hill Rd., Binghamton, N.Y. 13903. *Office:* School of Advanced Technology, State University of New York at Binghamton, Binghamton, N.Y. 13901.

CAREER: Syracuse University, Syracuse, N.Y., began as instructor, became assistant professor; University of Delaware, Newark, associate professor of engineering, 1957-59; International Business Machines Corp. (IBM), Yorktown Heights, N.Y., senior staff member, 1959-69; State University of New York, Binghamton, professor of engineering, 1969—. Adjunct professor, New York University, 1963-69; national lecturer for Association for Computing Machinery, 1971-73. *Military service:* U.S. Navy, 1945-46. *Member:* Institute of Electrical and Electronic Engineers, Association for Computing Machinery, Eta Kappa Nu, Sigma Xi, Pi Mu Epsilon.

WRITINGS: Digital Computer System Principles, McGraw, 1967, 2nd edition, 1973; (with T. C. Conroy) *Computer System Performance*, McGraw, 1975; (with I. A. Smith) *APL/360 and Applications*, McGraw, 1975.

WORK IN PROGRESS: Analysis and design of socioeconomic systems.

* * *

HELLISON, Donald R(aymond) 1938-

PERSONAL: Born February 25, 1938, in Chicago, Ill.; son of Raymond A. (a production operator) and Mildred (Nilsen) Hellison; married Patricia McClinton (a teacher), September 1, 1962. *Education:* Monmouth College, Monmouth, Ill., B.A., 1960; Kent State University, M.A., 1964; Ohio State University, Ph.D., 1969. *Politics:* "Democrat (loosely)." *Religion:* Unitarian. *Home:* 2546 Southwest St. Helen's Court, Portland, Ore. 97201. *Office address:* HPE, P.O. Box 751, Portland, Ore. 97207.

CAREER: Monmouth College, Monmouth, Ill., admissions counselor, 1960-61; Portland State University, Portland, Ore., assistant professor, 1969-73, associate professor of health and physical education, 1973—. Part-time assistant to dean of men, Kent State University, 1961-62; part-time instructor in sociology, East Carolina College, 1965-66; part-time assistant soccer coach, Ohio State University, 1967-69; consultant on physical education to state and local community organizations; lecturer and director of seminars. *Military service:* U.S. Marine Corps, 1962-66; became captain. *Member:* National Association of Sport and Physical Education, Association for Humanistic Psychology, National College PE Association for Men, North American Society for the Psychology of Sport and Physical Activity. *Awards, honors:* Distinguished Alumnus Award from Monmouth College, 1974.

WRITINGS: Humanistic Physical Education, Prentice-Hall, 1973; (contributor) Brian Fahey and Dorothy Allen, editors, *Being Human in Sport*, Lea & Febiger, 1975; (contributor) Joe Henderson, editor, *The Young Runner*, Mountain View/World Publications, 1973. Contributor to journals in his field. Chairman of special publication committee of American Association for Health, Physical Education and Recreation, 1974-75.

WORK IN PROGRESS: A novel concerning physical education.

SIDELIGHTS: Hellison told *CA*: "I don't consider myself primarily a writer. Instead, I view myself as about half physical education theoretician (that is too sophisticated a term for what I really do which is generate ideas) and about half physical education practitioner, trying to put my ideas into practice. I have more than a passing interest in delinquency-prone kids, so I spend some of my time trying to connect the theory and practice to these kids. The major thrust of my work, then, is to come up with ideas and then, by teaching, consulting, and performing to 'field test' these ideas."

* * *

HELMREICH, Paul C(hristian) 1933-

PERSONAL: Born July 13, 1933, in Brunswick, Maine; son of Ernst C. (a professor) and Louise (Roberts) Helmreich; married Dorothy Heise; children: James E., Alan A., Kristen L. *Education:* Amherst College, B.A. (cum laude), 1955; Harvard University, M.A., 1957, Ph.D., 1964. *Politics:* Democrat. *Religion:* United Church of Christ. *Home:* 232 Old Taunton Ave., Norton, Mass. 02766. *Office:* Department of History, Wheaton College, Norton, Mass. 02766.

CAREER: Wheaton College, Norton, Mass., instructor, 1957-63, assistant professor, 1963-67, associate professor, 1967-74, professor of history, 1974—, chairman of department, 1968—. Lecturer at Bridgewater State College, 1965, and Katharine Gibbs School, 1965—; associate professor at Rhode Island College, summer, 1969; visiting professor at Brown University, spring, 1970. Member of finance committee for Town of Norton, 1970—. *Member:* American Historical Association, American Association of University Professors (member of executive committee of Wheaton College chapter, 1965-68; president, 1973-74), New England Historical Association, Norton Historical Association. *Awards, honors:* National Endowment for the Humanities fellowship, summer, 1967.

WRITINGS: From Paris to Sevres: The Partition of the Ottoman Empire at the Peace Conference of 1919-1920, Ohio State University Press, 1974. Contributor to *Encyclopedia Americana*. Contributor to *Middle East Forum*, *Perspective*, *Annals of the American Academy of Political and Social Science*, and *Boston Globe*.

WORK IN PROGRESS: A diplomatic history of Europe between the wars.

AVOCATIONAL INTERESTS: Baseball (umpire, 1972—), swimming (won award at Amherst College), tennis, badminton, gardening.

* * *

HEMPHILL, John K(nox) 1919-

PERSONAL: Born March 9, 1919, in Aurora, Mo.; son of William H. (a farmer) and Audry (Cline) Hemphill; married Stella Crawford, July 29, 1941; children: John, Margarete, Robert, Christopher. *Education:* Fort Hays Kansas State College, A.B., 1941; Clark University, M.A., 1946; University of Maryland, Ph.D., 1948. *Home:* 1824 Jackson #F, San Francisco, Calif. 94109. *Office:* Far West Laboratory for Educational Research and Development, 1855 Folsom St., San Francisco, Calif. 94103.

CAREER: Ohio State University, Columbus, assistant professor of psychology, 1948-55, research supervisor, 1948-55; Educational Testing Service, Trenton, N.J., director of research and development, 1955-66, chairman of Social

Behavior Research Group, 1955-62, director of executive study, 1955-62; Far West Laboratory for Educational Research and Development, San Francisco, Calif., laboratory director, 1966—. Member of board of directors, Family Services Agency of San Francisco, 1972—, and Council for Educational Development and Research, 1970-71 and 1974—. *Military service:* U.S. Army Air Forces, 1942-44; became second lieutenant. *Member:* American Psychological Association, American Sociological Association, American Educational Research Association, Psychometric Society.

WRITINGS: Situational Factors in Leadership, Bureau of Educational Research, Ohio State University, 1949; (with Daniel Griffiths and Norman Frederiksen) *Administrative Performance and Personality*, Teachers College Press, 1962; (editor with Fred Rosenau) *Educational Development*, Center for the Advancement of Educational Administration, 1973. Consulting editor, *Sociometry*, 1964-68, *Journal of Applied Psychology*, 1966-72; editor, *Journal Supplement Abstract Service*, 1971-73.

* * *

HENDERSON, Archibald 1916-

PERSONAL: Born December 20, 1916, in Chapel Hill, N.C.; son of Archibald (a professor) and Barbara (Bynum) Henderson; married Helen White (a systems analyst), June 17, 1954; children: Archibald III, Russell Van. *Education:* University of North Carolina, A.B., 1937, M.A., 1941; Louisiana State University, further graduate study, 1941-42; Columbia University, Ph.D., 1954. *Religion:* Protestant. *Home:* 2711 Briarhurst, #6, Houston, Tex. 77027. *Office:* Department of English, University of Houston, Cullen Blvd., Houston, Tex. 77004.

CAREER: Auburn University, Auburn, Ala., instructor in English, 1948-49; Tulane University, Newcomb College, New Orleans, La., instructor in English, 1949-54; University of Houston, Houston, Tex., became professor of English, 1962. *Military service:* U.S. Army, Signal Corps, 1941-42. U.S. Army Air Forces, navigator, 1942-45; became captain. *Member:* Modern Language Association of America, Poetry Society of America, Poetry Society of Texas (member of board of directors, 1962—), Phi Kappa Phi, Phi Eta Sigma. *Awards, honors:* Prizes from Poetry Society of Texas, 1961—.

WRITINGS: (Translator, with Will McLendon) Charles Mauron, *Introduction to the Psychoanalysis of Mallarme*, University of California Press, 1963; William Shakespeare, *Much Ado About Nothing* (study guide), Study Master, 1966; *Omphale's Wheel* (poems), Golden Quill, 1966; *The Puzzled Picture* (poems), Pierre St. Le Macs, 1971. Contributor of poems, articles, and reviews to small literary magazines. Poetry editor of University of Houston's *Forum*.

WORK IN PROGRESS: Psychoanalytic Studies of Shakespeare.

AVOCATIONAL INTERESTS: Collecting verse translations.

* * *

HENDERSON, Harold G(ould) 1889-1974

July 25, 1889—July 11, 1974; American educator, authority on Japanese language and arts, translator, author. Obituaries: *AB Bookman's Weekly*, October 28, 1974.

HENDERSON, Laurence 1928-

PERSONAL: Born December 29, 1928, in London, England; son of William (a mechanic) and Susan (Baldock) Henderson; married Joy Knibbs, January, 1954 (divorced, 1969); married Audrey Stanton (an artist), 1972; children: (first marriage) Susan, Vanessa, Adele. *Education:* Attended primary and secondary school in England; "I regard myself as self-educated." *Politics:* "Mistrust." *Religion:* Humanist. *Home:* 57 Crown Hill, Rayleigh, Essex, England. *Agent:* Gordon Harbord, Parkside, 32 Knightsbridge, London, England.

CAREER: Has worked as a barrister's clerk, insurance salesman, and claims investigator; novelist and free-lance writer. *Military service:* Royal Air Force, 1947-49.

WRITINGS—Novels: *With Intent*, Harrap, 1968, Pyramid Publications, 1974; *Sitting Target*, Harrap, 1970, St. Martin's, 1972; *Cage Until Tame*, St. Martin's, 1972.

WORK IN PROGRESS: A novel exploring the effects that a sex murder has on the family of the victim.

SIDELIGHTS: Henderson told *CA*: "I am skeptical of writers being able to much influence the attitudes of their adult readers. What I believe can happen is that a writer can hit a nerve if he accidentally expresses that which his reader has already subconsciously felt but is unable to express. People act for concrete motives like fear, greed and lust; it is afterwards that they rationalise. Or, put it this way, plenty of girls have been seduced by fur coats: I doubt if even one has by a book."

Sitting Target was filmed by Metro-Goldwyn-Mayer in 1972.

* * *

HENKE, Dan (Ferdinand) 1924-

PERSONAL: Born February 18, 1924, in San Antonio, Tex.; son of Ferdinand (a librarian) and Frances (a librarian; maiden name, Sawyer) Henke; married Shirley Ruth Lynn (a criminal justice planner), June 10, 1950; children: Danferd William, Holly Lynn. *Education:* Georgetown University, B.S., 1943, J.D., 1951; University of Washington, Seattle, M.LL., 1956. *Home:* 258 La Espiral, Orinda, Calif. 94563. *Office:* 316 Hastings College of the Law, University of California, 198 McAllister St., San Francisco, Calif. 94102.

CAREER: U.S. Office of Business Economics, Washington, D.C., business economist, 1948-51; attorney in San Antonio, Tex., 1952-55; University of Washington, Seattle, assistant to law librarian, 1955-56; New Jersey Bureau of Law and Legislative Reference, Trenton, head of bureau, 1956-59; University of California, Berkeley, lecturer, 1959-64, professor of law, 1965-70, law librarian, 1959-70, director of Department of Health, Education and Welfare Summer Institutes in Law Librarianship, 1968-70; University of California, Hastings College of the Law, San Francisco, professor of law and law librarian, 1970—. *Military service:* U.S. Army, 1943-46; received Bronze Star Medal and Purple Heart.

MEMBER: American Bar Association, American Library Association, American Association of Law Libraries, American Association of Law Schools, American Society of Information Science, Special Libraries Association, National Microfilm Association, U.S. Supreme Court Bar, California Bar, Texas Bar, District of Columbia Bar, Beta Phi Mu, Delta Chi, Delta Theta Phi, Coif.

WRITINGS: (With Mortimer D. Schwartz) *Anglo-American Law Collections*, Fred B. Rothman, 1970; *California Legal Research Handbook: State and Federal*, Lex-Cal-Tex Press, 1971; (contributor) Morris Cohen, editor, *How to Find the Law*, 7th edition (Henke was not associated with earlier editions), West Publishing, 1975. Contributor to law journals and library publications. Chairman of *Law Library Journal*, 1964-66.

* * *

HENNINGS, Dorothy Grant 1935-

PERSONAL: Born March 15, 1935, in Paterson, N.J.; daughter of William Albert (a businessman) and Ethel (a businesswoman; maiden name, Moll) Grant; married George Hennings (a professor of biology), June 15, 1968. *Education:* Barnard College, A.B. (cum laude), 1956; University of Virginia, M.Ed., 1959; Columbia University, Ed.D., 1965. *Home:* 21 Flintlock Dr., Warren, N.J. 07060. *Office:* Department of Education, Kean College of New Jersey, Union, N.J. 07083.

CAREER: Elementary school teacher in Rutherford, N.J., 1956-58; junior high school teacher in Fairlawn, N.J., 1958-64; Kean College of New Jersey, Union, associate professor, 1965-68, professor of education, 1968—. *Member:* National Council of Teachers of English, New Jersey Council of Teachers of English, Phi Beta Kappa, Kappa Delta Pi.

WRITINGS: (With sister, Barbara Grant) *The Teacher Moves: An Analysis of Nonverbal Activities*, Teachers College Press, 1971; (with Grant) *Content and Craft: Written Expression in the Elementary School*, Prentice-Hall, 1973; *Smiles, Nods, and Pauses: Activities to Enrich Children's Communications Skills*, Citation, 1974; *Mastering Classroom Communication: What Interaction Analysis Tells the Teacher*, Goodyear Publishing, 1975; (with husband, George Hennings) *Keep Earth Blue and Green*, Citation, in press. Contributor of more than fifteen articles and reviews to education journals, including *Education*, *New Jersey Education Association Review*, *Scholastic Teacher*, *Early Years*, *Elementary English*, *Instructor*, and *Science Teacher*.

WORK IN PROGRESS: A sequel to *Smiles, Nods, and Pauses: Activities to Enrich Children's Communications Skills*.

AVOCATIONAL INTERESTS: Travel (Japan, Taiwan, Philippines, Thailand, Malaysia, Indonesia, India, Hongkong, Hungary, Turkey, Greece, Poland, Czechoslovakia, Yugoslavia, Switzerland, Germany, Norway, Denmark, the Netherlands, Italy, France, England, Scotland, Portugal, Spain, the Caribbean, Panama, Mexico, and Cuba).

* * *

HERBERT, Frank (Patrick) 1920-

PERSONAL: Born October 8, 1920, in Tacoma, Wash.; son of Frank and Eileen (McCarthy) Herbert; married Beverly Ann Stuart, June 23, 1946; children: Penny (Mrs. D. R. Merritt), Brian, Bruce. *Education:* Attended University of Washington, 1946-47. *Residence:* Port Townsend, Wash. *Agent:* Lurton Blassingame, 60 East 42nd St., New York, N.Y. 10017; and Ned Brown, P.O. Box 5020, Beverly Hills, Calif. 90210.

CAREER: Novelist. Lecturer in general and interdisciplinary studies, University of Washington, Seattle, 1970-72; consultant in social and ecological studies, Lincoln Foundation and to countries of Vietnam and Pakistan, 1971; director and photographer of television show, "The Tillers," 1973. *Member:* World Without War Council (member of national council, 1970-73; member of Seattle council, 1972—).

WRITINGS—Science fiction: *Under Pressure*, Doubleday, 1956; *Dune*, Chilton, 1965; *Green Brain*, Berkley, 1966; *Destination Void*, Berkley, 1966; *Eyes of Heisenberg*, Berkley, 1966; *Heaven Makers*, Avon, 1968; *Santaroga Barrier*, Berkley, 1968; (with others) *Five Fates* (stories), Doubleday, 1970; *Dune Messiah*, Putnam, 1970; *Whipping Star*, Putnam, 1970; (editor) *New World or No World*, Ace Books, 1970; *Worlds of Frank Herbert*, Ace Books, 1970; *Soul Catcher*, Putnam, 1971; *God Makers*, Berkley, 1971; *Book of Frank Herbert*, Daw Books, 1972; *Project 40*, Bantam, 1973; *Threshold*, Ballantine, 1973; *Best of Frank Herbert*, Sphere Books, 1974. Novels and portions of novels have first appeared in science fiction magazines.

WORK IN PROGRESS: "Dune III," a filmscript based on novel, *Soul Catcher*.

* * *

HERBERT, (Edward) Ivor (Montgomery) 1925-

PERSONAL: Born August 20, 1925, in Johannesburg, South Africa; son of Edward and Sybil Herbert; married second wife, Gillian Steele-Perkins, September 2, 1969; children: (first marriage) Nicholas; (second marriage) Kate, Jane. *Education:* Trinity College, Cambridge, M.A., 1949. *Home and office:* The Old Rectory, Bradenham near High Wycombe, Buckinghamshire, England.

CAREER: Charterhouse Finance Corp., London, executive, 1949-54; *London Evening News*, staff writer, 1954-66; Portman Bloodstock Agency, Corbridge, Northumberland, England, partner, 1974—. Racehorse trainer, 1953-68. *Military service:* British Army, Coldstream Guards, 1943-47; served in Germany; became captain. *Member:* Writers Guild, Society of Authors, National Union of Journalists.

WRITINGS: Eastern Windows (novel), Methuen, 1953; *Point-to-Point*, Brockhampton, 1964; *Arkle*, Pelham, 1966; *The Queen Mother's Horses*, Pelham, 1967; (with Patricia Smyly) *The Winter Kings*, Pelham, 1968; *The Way to the Top*, R. Maxwell, 1969; (with Jack Cusack) *Scarlet Fever*, Cassell, 1972; *Over Our Dead Bodies* (novel), Cassell, 1972; *Winter's Tale: A Study of a Stable*, Pelham, 1974; *Red Rum*, W. Luscombe, 1974; *Come Riding*, W. H. Smith, 1975. Author of film script, "The Great St. Trinian's Train Robbery," 1966; co-author, with Frank Launder, of play, "The Night of the Blue Demands," first produced in Guildford, England, at the Yvonne Arnaud Theatre, 1971. Columnist for *Sunday Express, Horse and Hound*, and *Evening News* (London); contributor of articles on travel to *Daily Express*, and of feature series to *Sunday Mirror*.

* * *

HERDECK, Donald E. 1924-

PERSONAL: Born November 19, 1924, in Chicago, Ill.; son of Elmer and Violet (Cotter) Herdeck; married wife, Margaret, April, 1971. *Education:* University of Chicago, B.A., 1947, M.A., 1948; University of Pennsylvania, Ph.D., 1968. *Office:* School of Foreign Service, Georgetown University, Washington, D.C. 20037.

CAREER: Foreign Service Officer with U.S. Department of State, in Washington, D.C., 1955-57, Palermo, Naples, and Rome, Italy, 1957-62, and Conakry, Guinea, 1962-64;

Georgetown University, School of Foreign Service, Washington, D.C., instructor, 1965-68, assistant professor, 1968-74, associate professor of English and foreign service, 1974—. President and editor of Three Continents Press, 1973. *Military service:* U.S. Army, Infantry, 1944-45. U.S. Army Air Forces, 1945-46. *Member:* Modern Language Association of America, African Studies Association. *Awards, honors:* National Endowment for the Humanities study grant, 1974.

WRITINGS: African Authors, 1300-1973, Black Orpheus Press, 1973, revised edition, 1974; (author of introduction) Rene Maran, *Batouala,* Black Orpheus Press, 1973; (author of introduction) I. O. Eligwe, *Beside the Fire,* Three Continents Press, 1974; (editor and translator with S. M. Mutswairo) *Zimbabwe: Prose and Poetry,* Three Continents Press, 1974.

WORK IN PROGRESS: Caribbean Authors: Cuba to Guyane; African Authors, Volume II, completion expected in 1976; editing a critical anthology, *Cuba South.*

SIDELIGHTS: Herdeck has travelled widely in Africa, the Caribbean, and Europe.

* * *

HERMAN, Donald L. 1928-

PERSONAL: Born October 13, 1928, in New York. *Education:* University of Michigan, B.A., 1950, Ph.D., 1964; Wayne State University, M.A., 1958. *Office:* Latin American Studies Program, Grand Valley State Colleges, Allendale, Mich. 49401.

CAREER: Grand Valley State Colleges, Allendale, Mich., professor of political science, and director of Latin American Studies Program.

WRITINGS: (Editor) *The Communist Tide in Latin America,* University of Texas Press, 1973; *The Comintern in Mexico,* Public Affairs Press, 1974. Contributor to *Hoover Institution's 1975 Yearbook on International Communist Affairs.*

WORK IN PROGRESS: The Christian Democrats of Venezuela.

* * *

HERMAN, Louis Jay 1925-

PERSONAL: Born March 2, 1925, in New York, N.Y.; son of Irving (a businessman) and Hannah (Levy) Herman. *Education:* Cornell University, student, 1941-43; New York University, B.A., 1947; Columbia University, M.A., 1949. *Religion:* Jewish. *Home:* 120 East 90th St., New York, N.Y. 10028. *Office:* English Translation Service, United Nations, New York, N.Y. 10017.

CAREER: Free-lance writer, editor, and translator, 1949-58; United Nations, New York, N.Y., translator into English from all the Romance, Germanic and Slavic languages as well as Greek, Hungarian, Turkish, and Finnish, 1958—. *Military service:* U.S. Army, 1943-46. *Member:* Mensa.

WRITINGS: (Translator from German, and editor of abridgement) Erwin Rosenberger, *Herzl As I Remember Him,* Herzl Press, 1959; *A Dictionary of Slavic Word Families,* Columbia University Press, 1975.

* * *

HERSHEY, Gerald L. 1931-

PERSONAL: Born March 7, 1931, in Detroit, Mich.; son of Von Waitz (a machinist) and Clementine Hershey; married Shirley Barbara Gauld, October 2, 1954; children: Bruce, Dale, James. *Education:* University of California, Los Angeles, A.A., 1952; Michigan State University, B.A. (with honors), 1957, M.A., 1959, Ph.D., 1961. *Politics:* Democrat. *Home:* 1526 Fisher Circle, Placentia, Calif. 92670. *Office:* Department of Psychology, Fullerton College, 321 East Chapman Ave., Fullerton, Calif. 92634.

CAREER: Michigan State University, East Lansing, assistant instructor in psychology, 1958-61; Fullerton College, Fullerton, Calif., member of faculty, head of psychology department, 1962—. Visiting professor at Chapman College, 1961-67. *Military service:* U.S. Army, served in psychological warfare, 1954-56; became first lieutenant. *Member:* American Psychological Association, Association for Humanistic Psychology, Western Psychological Association.

WRITINGS: (With J. Lugo) *Living Psychology,* Macmillan, 1971; (with Lugo) *Human Development,* Macmillan, 1974.

* * *

HERSHFIELD, Harry 1885-1974

1885—December 15, 1974; American humorist, cartoonist, columnist, author. Obituaries: *New York Times,* December 16, 1974; *AB Bookman's Weekly,* January 27, 1975.

* * *

HERSHMAN, Morris 1920-
(Evelyn Bond, Arnold English, Lionel Webb, Jess Wilcox)

PERSONAL: Born January 31, 1920; son of Benjamin (a pharmacist) and Ida (Macinski) Hershman; married Florence Verbell (a writer and editor), September 6, 1969; children: Janet Brown (stepdaughter). *Education:* Attended New York University. *Politics:* Democrat. *Religion:* Jewish. *Address:* c/o Walker & Co., 720 Fifth Ave., New York, N.Y. 10019.

CAREER: Topics Publications, New York, N.Y., editorial assistant, 1955-58; also editorial assistant with HMH Publications, New York, N.Y. Lecturer at New York University and at writers' conferences. *Member:* Mystery Writers of America (past member of board of directors).

WRITINGS—Under name Morris Hershman: *Guilty Witness,* Belmont Books, 1964; *Target for Terror,* Belmont Books, 1967; *Glory in Hell,* Lancer Books, 1967; *Mission to Hell,* Pyramid Publications, 1968; *Shareworld,* Walker & Co., 1972.

Under pseudonyms, as indicated: (Under pseudonym Evelyn Bond) *Evil in the House,* Lancer Books, 1965; (under pseudonym Lionel Webb) *Violator,* Pyramid Publications, 1970; (under pseudonym Jess Wilcox) *Vanity, My Beloved,* Avon, 1970; (under pseudonym Evelyn Bond) *The Doomway,* Beagle Books, 1971; (under pseudonym Evelyn Bond) *Raven's Eye,* Avon, 1972; (under pseudonym Evelyn Bond) *Hornet's Nest,* Avon, 1972. Author of over twenty-five additional novels, under pseudonyms listed above, as well as Arnold English.

Author of one-act play, "Love and Hisses," as yet neither published nor produced. Work is represented in anthologies. Contributor of over one hundred short stories and novelettes to magazines, including *Columbia, Greenleaf, Mercury, Vortex, Volitant, Argosy, Fiction House, Modern Woman, Crestwood, Flying Eagle, Pontiac, Popular, Standard, Weight Watchers,* and *Private Investigator.* Assistant editor, *Third Degree* (of Mystery Writers of America).

WORK IN PROGRESS: Research on the U.S. Food and Drug Administration and pharmaceutical marketing procedures for *The Savage Season,* to be published under pseudonym Jess Wilcox by Avon.

AVOCATIONAL INTERESTS: Travel to the tropics.

* * *

HESKY, Olga ?-1974

British novelist and script writer. Obituaries: *AB Bookman's Weekly*, October 7, 1974. (*CA*-25/28).

* * *

HESS, Hans 1908-1975

1908—January 21, 1975; British educator, art gallery director, author of books on art. Obituaries: *AB Bookman's Weekly*, February 17, 1975.

* * *

HETHERINGTON, John (Aikman) 1907-1974

1907—September 17, 1974; Australian author of novels and other works. Obituaries: *AB Bookman's Weekly*, November 18, 1974.

* * *

HEWARD, William L(ee) 1949-

PERSONAL: Born November 22, 1949, in Michigan City, Ind.; son of Joe William and Helen Mae Heward. *Education:* Western Michigan University, B.A. (magna cum laude), 1971; University of Massachusetts, Ed.D., 1974. *Home and address:* R. R. 1, Box 77, Three Oaks, Mich. 49128.

CAREER: Full-time writer, 1974—. Research assistant, Northeast Regional Media Center for the Deaf, University of Massachusetts, Amherst, 1972-74; director of Project Change in Greenfield, Mass., 1973.

WRITINGS: (With Dimitri V. Gat) *Some Are Called Clowns,* Crowell, 1974; *Teacher's Handbook for Use with the Visual Response System,* Northeast Regional Media Center for the Deaf, University of Massachusetts, 1974. Contributor to *Popular Sports Grand Slam.*

WORK IN PROGRESS: A college text on the principles of behavior and their application to college success; a biography of Prince Jo Henry, baseball player; research on applied behavior analysis, language acquisition by the deaf, and on little-known but historically-significant sports figures.

AVOCATIONAL INTERESTS: Baseball (player and manager).

* * *

HEWITT, John P(aul) 1941-

PERSONAL: Born November 8, 1941, in Morris Township, Pa.; son of John Henry and Anna (Davidson) Hewitt; married Myrna Livingston, December 23, 1962; children: Elizabeth, Gary. *Education:* State University of New York at Buffalo, B.A. (summa cum laude), 1963; Princeton University, A.M., 1965, Ph.D., 1966. *Home:* 181 Pondview Dr., Amherst, Mass. 01002. *Office:* Department of Sociology, University of Massachusetts, Amherst, Mass. 01002.

CAREER: State University of New York at Buffalo, instructor in sociology, summer, 1963; Oberlin College, Oberlin, Ohio, assistant professor of sociology, 1966-68; York University, Downsview, Ontario, assistant professor of sociology, 1968-70; University of Massachusetts, Amherst, assistant professor, 1970-72, associate professor of sociology, 1972—. Member of Amherst Town Meeting and local Citizens' Advisory Committee; consultant for Everglades National Park, 1974. *Member:* American Sociological Association, Society for the Study of Social Problems, National Audubon Society, National Wildlife Federation, National Parks and Conservation Association, Massachusetts Audubon Society, Phi Beta Kappa.

WRITINGS: Social Stratification and Deviant Behavior, Random House, 1970; (contributor) Michael H. Prosser, editor, *Intercommunication among Nations and Peoples*, Harper, 1972; (with Ely Chinoy) *Sociological Perspective*, Random House, 3rd edition (Hewitt was not associated with earlier editions), 1975. Contributor of articles and reviews to *American Journal of Sociology, American Sociological Review, International Journal of Comparative Sociology*, and *Social Problems*. Reader for Random House, 1970-72, University of Massachusetts Press, 1970-74, Xerox Educational Publishing, 1972, *Sociological Quarterly*, 1973-74, and *Social Problems*, 1974.

WORK IN PROGRESS: The Park Ranger: A Study in the Sociology of Environment; *Self-Construction in Mass Society*.

* * *

HEYWORTH-DUNNE, James ?-1974

?—June 9, 1974; British authority on Arabic language, author of books on Egypt. Obituaries: *AB Bookman's Weekly*, October 7, 1974.

* * *

HIBBARD, Howard 1928-

PERSONAL: Born May 23, 1928, in Madison, Wis.; son of Benjamin Horace (a professor) and Margaret (a home economist; maiden name, Baker) Hibbard; married Shirley Irene Griffith, September 14, 1951; children: Claire Alexandra, Susan Giulia, Carla Costanza. *Education:* University of Wisconsin, B.A., 1949, M.A., 1952; Columbia University, graduate study, 1952-53, postdoctoral study, 1967-70; Harvard University, Ph.D., 1958. *Politics:* Democrat. *Religion:* Atheist. *Home:* 176 Brewer Rd., Scarsdale, N.Y. 10583. *Office:* Department of Art History and Archeology, Columbia University, 815 Schermerhorn Hall, New York, N.Y. 10027.

CAREER: Columbia University, New York, N.Y., assistant professor, 1959-62, associate professor, 1962-66, professor of art history, 1966—. *Member:* College Art Association of America, Society of Architectural Historians (member of board of directors, 1963-65), American Academy in Rome (fellow), Renaissance Society of America, American Academy of Arts and Sciences (fellow), American Association of University Professors. *Awards, honors:* American Council of Learned Societies fellowship, 1962-63; Guggenheim fellowships, 1965-66, 1972-73; National Foundation for the Humanities senior fellowship, 1967.

WRITINGS: The Architecture of the Palazzo Borghese, American Academy in Rome, 1962; *Bernini*, Penguin, 1965, 4th edition, 1974; *Bernini e il barocco* (title means "Bernini and Baroque Sculpture"), Fratelli Fabbri, 1968; (with Joan Nissman) *Florentine Baroque Art from American Collections*, Metropolitan Museum of Art, 1969; *Carlo Maderno and Roman Architecture: 1580-1630*, A. Zwemmer, 1971, Pennsylvania State University Press, 1972; *Poussin: The Holy Family on the Steps*, Viking, 1974; *Michelangelo*, Harper, 1974. Co-editor of "Studies in Architecture" series, A. Zwemmer, 1971—; member of board of advisors, "Princeton Essays in the Arts" series, Princeton University Press, 1974—. Contributor of articles and reviews to scholarly journals. Book review editor of *Art Bulletin* (of College Art Association of America), 1961-65, associate editor, 1963-64, editor-in-chief, 1974—.

WORK IN PROGRESS: Research on Italian sculpture of the later sixteenth centruy, completion expected in 1980.

SIDELIGHTS: Since 1955, Hibbard has spent about half his time in Italy, especially in Rome, where he works in the libraries and archives. *Avocational interests:* Chinese cooking.

* * *

HICKFORD, Jessie 1911-

PERSONAL: Born January 17, 1911, in Chelsea, London, England; daughter of Samuel (a London metropolitan policeman) and Isabel (Snelling) Hickford. *Education:* Homerton College of Education, teacher's certificate, 1931; British Drama League, certificate, 1948. *Religion:* Christian. *Home:* 2 Plume Ave., Colchester, Essex CO3 4PG, England.

CAREER: Teacher of English and drama in Colchester, Essex, England, 1931-64. Lecturer for Guide Dogs for the Blind Association, 1965—. *Member:* National Union of Teachers (president of Colchester branch, 1938-39), Society of Women Writers and Journalists, Townswomen's Guild.

WRITINGS: Eyes at My Feet, M. Joseph, 1973; *Fire! Fire!* (one-act play) English Theatre Guild, 1974. Contributor to *New Beacon, Home and Country, Essex Countryside,* and *Woman and Home.*

WORK IN PROGRESS: Stories for children; verse.

SIDELIGHTS: Jessie Hickford wrote *Eyes at My Feet* to inform a wide public of the value of a guide dog to a blind person and as a tribute to her own dog, Prudence, and her trainer. The book has been issued in Braille and Talking Book editions.

BIOGRAPHICAL/CRITICAL SOURCES: New Beacon, November, 1973.

* * *

HIERS, Richard H(yde) 1932-

PERSONAL: Surname sounds like "myers"; born April 8, 1932, in Philadelphia, Pa.; son of Glen Sefton (a chemist) and Mildred (an educator; maiden name, Douthitt) Hiers; married Jane Leslie Gale (a social worker), January 30, 1954; children: Peter Leslie, Rebecca Hathaway. *Education:* Yale University, B.A. (magna cum laude), 1954, B.D., 1957, M.A., 1959, Ph.D., 1961. *Office:* Department of Religion, University of Florida, Reitz Union, Gainesville, Fla. 32607.

CAREER: University of Florida, Gainesville, assistant professor, 1961-67, associate professor, 1967-72, professor of religion, 1972—. Chairman of citizens' advisory committee for a workable program for Gainesville, 1969-71. *Member:* American Academy of Religion (president of Southeast region, 1969-70), American Society of Christian Ethics, Society of Biblical Literature, American Association of University Professors (president of University of Florida chapter, 1972-74), Danforth Associates in Teaching, Aurelian Honor Society, Phi Beta Kappa.

WRITINGS: Jesus and Ethics: Four Interpretations, Westminster, 1968; *The Kingdom of God in the Synoptic Tradition*, University of Florida Press, 1970; (translator, editor, and author of introduction, with D. Larrimore Holland) Johannes Weiss, *Jesus' Proclamation of the Kingdom of God*, Fortress, 1971; *The Historical Jesus and the Kingdom of God*, University of Florida Press, 1973.

WORK IN PROGRESS: Interpreting the Historical Jesus; *The Bread and Fish Symbols in Early Christian Jewish and Christian Art*, completion expected in 1977.

* * *

HIGGINS, Alice 1924(?)-1974

1924(?)—September 18, 1974; American sports journalist and author. Obituaries: *New York Times*, September 19, 1974.

* * *

HILL, Douglas (Arthur) 1935-
(Martin Hillman)

PERSONAL: Born April 6, 1935, in Brandon, Manitoba, Canada; son of William (a locomotive engineer) and Cora (a nurse; maiden name, Smith); married Gail Robinson (a poet and author), April 8, 1958; children: Michael Julian. *Education:* University of Saskatchewan, B.A. (with honors), 1957; University of Toronto, graduate study, 1957-59. *Home:* Flat 2, 16 Haslemere Rd., London N8 9QX, England. *Agent:* Bolt & Watson, 8 Storeys Gate, London S.W. 1, England.

CAREER: Free-lance writer, 1959—; Aldus Books Ltd., London, England, editor, 1962-64. Science fiction adviser to Rupert Hart-Davis, 1966-68, Mayflower Books, 1969-71, and to Pan Books, 1974—. *Member:* National Union of Journalists, Folklore Society, Writers Guild.

WRITINGS: (With Pat Williams) *The Supernatural*, Hawthorn, 1965; *The Peasants' Revolt*, Jackdaw, 1966; (editor, and contributor under pseudonym Martin Hillman) *Window on the Future* (anthology), Hart-Davis, 1966; *The Opening of the Canadian West*, John Day, 1967; (editor, and contributor under pseudonym Martin Hillman) *The Devil His Due* (anthology), Hart-Davis, 1967; *John Keats*, Morgan-Grampion, 1968; *Magic and Superstition*, Hamlyn, 1968; *Regency London*, Macdonald, 1969; *Georgian London*, Macdonald, 1970; *Return from the Dead*, Macdonald, 1970; (under pseudonym Martin Hillman) *Bridging a Continent*, Aldus, 1971; (editor, and contributor under pseudonym Martin Hillman) *Warlocks and Warriors* (anthology), Mayflower, 1971; *Fortune Telling*, Hamlyn, 1972; *The Scots to Canada*, Gentry, 1972; *The Comet*, Wildwood House, 1973; (with wife, Gail Robinson Hill) *Coyote the Trickster*, Chatto & Windus, 1975; *The English to New England*, Gentry, in press; *Dreams*, Hamlyn, in press.

Poems represented in anthologies, including *Poetmeat Anthology of British Poetry*, edited by Dave Cunliffe, Screeches Publications, 1965; *Young British Poets*, edited by Jeremy Robson, Poesie Vivante (Geneva), 1967; *Poems from Poetry and Jazz in Concert*, edited by Robson, Souvenir Press, 1969.

Contributor of poems, book reviews, and articles to *Ambit*, *Akros*, *Adam International Review*, *Canadian Forum*, *Encounter*, *Poetry Review*, *New Statesman*, *New Worlds*, *Guardian*, *Books and Bookmen*, *Mayfair*, and others. Regular columnist and literary editor of *Tribune* (London, 1971—.

WORK IN PROGRESS: Poems; a children's fantasy novel; editing three more anthologies of science fiction; research on Canadian literary history.

SIDELIGHTS: Discussing the pressures of his work, Hill told *CA*: "Diversity seems the keynote—and now extending it into children's fiction, etc. Poetry remains first love, obsession, whatever. Literary journalism new-ish central vocation. Otherwise life is filled with games, relaxation, family. Avid TV watcher, voracious and catholic reader."

* * *

HILL, Ernest 1915-

PERSONAL: Born July 14, 1915, in Stourbridge, England; son of Ernest (a farmer) and Agnes (a teacher; maiden name, Edgeler) Hill; married Marjorie Alice Potter (a craft teacher), April 1, 1950. *Education:* Studied at private schools in England. *Politics:* Socialist. *Religion:* None. *Home:* 66b Court Rd., London SE9 5NP, England. *Agent:* E. J. Carnell, 17 Burwash Rd., London SE18 7QY, England. *Office:* Benn Bros. Ltd., 25 New Street Sq., London EC4A 3JA, England.

CAREER: Royal Air Force, 1931-34. British Army, career officer, 1942-55; served in Royal Signals, 1942-45; intelligence officer with War Department, 1945-55. Thomson & Co., London, England, advertisement manager, 1965-72; Benn Bros., London, England, advertisement manager, 1972—.

WRITINGS: *Pity About Earth* (science fiction novel), Ace Books, 1968; *The GC Radiation* (science fiction novel), R. Hale, 1970.

Contributor of more than thirty short stories to journals.

WORK IN PROGRESS: Research into British constitution for a science fiction novel on a military take-over and on the relationship between royalty and the army.

* * *

HILLMAN, Ruth Estelyn 1925-

PERSONAL: Born May 31, 1925, in Winslow, Ind.; daughter of M. T. and Olive (Casey) Ryder; married Victor H. Hillman; children: Victor, Jr., Daniel, Douglas. *Education:* Ball State University, B.S., 1965, M.A., 1968. *Religion:* Christian Church. *Home address:* Route 4, Box 395, Muncie, Ind. 47302.

CAREER: English teacher in Muncie, Ind., 1966—. *Member:* National Education Association, Business and Professional Women, Indiana State Teachers Association, Delta Kappa Gamma, Order of the Eastern Star.

WRITINGS: *Four Letter Words That Are Good*, Standard Publishing (Cincinnati), 1974; *Life along the Fencerow*, Herald Press, 1974; *Pieces of Christmas*, Bethany Press (St. Louis, Mo.), 1975. Contributor of poems, short stories, and articles to small literary magazines.

WORK IN PROGRESS: Three books.

* * *

HILLOCKS, George, Jr. 1934-

PERSONAL: Born June 15, 1934, in Cleveland, Ohio; son of George, Sr. (a machinist) and Ina (a secretary; maiden name, Murray) Hillocks; married Jo Bruce (a teacher), June 15, 1957; children: Marjorie Anne, George McInnes. *Education:* College of Wooster, B.A., 1956; Western Reserve University (now Case Western Reserve University), M.A., 1958, Ph.D., 1970; University of Edinburgh, diploma in English studies, 1959. *Home:* 5461 South Dorchester, Chicago, Ill. 60615. *Office:* Graduate School of Education, University of Chicago, 5835 South Kimbark, Chicago, Ill. 60637.

CAREER: High school English teacher in Euclid, Ohio, 1956-65, chairman of department, 1959-65; University of Nebraska, Lincoln, instructor in education at Curriculum Development Center, summers, 1962-63; Western Reserve University (now Case Western Reserve University), Cleveland, Ohio, lecturer in education and director of Project English Demonstration Center, 1963-65; San Fernando Valley State College (now California State University at Northridge), Los Angeles, Calif., associate director of National Defense Education Act English Institute, summers, 1965-66; Bowling Green State University, Bowling Green, Ohio, 1965-71, began as instructor, became assistant professor of English, director of National Defense Education Act English Institute, summers, 1967-68; University of Chicago, Chicago, Ill., assistant professor, 1971-74, associate professor of education, 1974—.

MEMBER: Modern Language Association of America, National Society for the Study of Education, National Council of Teachers of English, Conference on College Composition and Communication, Conference on English Education.

WRITINGS: (Editor with Michael Shugrue, and contributor) *Patterns and Models for Teaching English*, National Council of Teachers of English, 1964; (with James F. McCampbell and others) *An Introduction to a Curriculum*, Project English Demonstration Center (Euclid, Ohio), 1964; (editor with McCampbell) *Talks on the Teaching of English*, Project English Demonstration Center, 1965; (editor with Shugrue) *Classroom Practices in Teaching of English*, National Council of Teachers of English, 1965; *Cooperative Research Project Number D-067: A Comprehensive Program in English for the Seventh, Eighth, and Ninth Grades*, U.S. Office of Education, 1965; (contributor) B. Jo Kinnick, editor, *The School Literary Magazine*, National Council of Teachers of English, 1966.

(Contributor) Lois Josephs and Erwin R. Steinberg, editors, *English Education Today*, Noble, 1970; (with Bernard J. McCabe and McCampbell) *The Dynamics of English Instruction*, Random House, 1971; *Alternatives in English: A Critical Analysis of Elective Programs*, National Council of Teachers of English, 1972; *Satire: A Scholastic Literature Unit*, Scholastic Book Services, 1974; *Observing and Writing*, National Council of Teachers of English, 1975.

Contributor of about ten articles to education and English journals, including *English Education, Arizona English Bulletin, English Journal, Bulletin of the Association of Departments of English, Bulletin of the National Association of Secondary School Principals*, and *Journal of Educational Research.*

WORK IN PROGRESS: *Response to Poetry; Responses of College Freshmen to Three Modes of Teaching; Making It Happen in English* (tentative title), with Bernard McCabe.

* * *

HILTON, John Buxton 1921- (Warwick Stanley)

PERSONAL: Born June 8, 1921, in Buxton, England; son

of John (an outfitter) and F. M. (Buxton) Hilton; married Mary Skitmore, July, 1943 (died, 1968); married Rebecca Adams, May, 1969. *Education:* Pembroke College, Cambridge, B.A., 1942, M.A., 1946. *Religion:* Christian. *Home:* White House, Kenninghall, Norwich NR16 2EN, England. *Agent:* Curtis Brown Ltd., 1 Craven Hill, London W1 3EW, England.

CAREER: Teacher of modern languages in England, 1946-57; Chorley Grammar School, Lancashire, England, headmaster, 1957-64; Department of Education and Science, London, England, inspector of schools, 1964-70; Open University, Bletchley, Buckinghamshire, England, part-time tutor in humanities, 1970—. *Military service:* British Army, Intelligence Corps, 1941-46; mentioned in dispatches. *Member:* Society of Authors, Crime Writers Association. *Awards, honors:* Robert Scarth Award, 1952, for children's story "Potter's About."

WRITINGS: The Language Laboratory in School, Methuen, 1964; *Death of an Alderman* (crime novel), Walker & Co., 1968; *Death in Midwinter* (crime novel), Walker & Co., 1969; *Language Teaching: A Systems Approach,* Methuen, 1974; *Hangman's Tide* (crime novel), St. Martin's, in press. Contributor of children's stories, under pseudonym Warwick Stanley, and other stories and articles to magazines.

WORK IN PROGRESS: Gamekeeper's Gallows, a suspense novel; *Playground,* a suspense novel; *Angevin Summer,* a children's novel.

AVOCATIONAL INTERESTS: Fishing, amateur theatricals, folksongs.

* * *

HILTON SMITH, Robert D(ennis) ?-1974

?—May 12, 1974; Canadian antiquarian bookseller, founder and president of Adelphi Book Shop Ltd. (Victoria, B.C.), publisher, librarian, scholar, university lecturer, and author. Obituaries: *AB Bookman's Weekly*, October 21, 1974.

* * *

HIMLER, Ann 1946-

PERSONAL: Born May 1, 1946, in Camden, N.J.; daughter of Chester John (an engineer) and Anna (Barrington) Danowitz; married Ronald Norbert Himler (an illustrator of children's books), June 18, 1972; children: Daniel Damien (stepson), Anna Grace. *Education:* Immaculata College, student, 1964-66; Dickinson College, B.A., 1968; University of Pennsylvania, M.A., 1971. *Religion:* Russian Orthodox. *Home and office:* 680 West End Ave., Apt. 4-D, New York, N.Y. 10025.

CAREER: Library Company of Philadelphia, Philadelphia, Pa., cataloguer, 1970; University of Pennsylvania, Philadelphia, instructor in Russian, 1971.

WRITINGS: (With husband, Ronald Himler) *Little Owl: Keeper of the Trees* (juvenile), Harper, 1974.

WORK IN PROGRESS: A novel for children, about an itinerant tinker in eighteenth-century Ireland.

* * *

HIMLER, Ronald (Norbert) 1937-

PERSONAL: Born October 16, 1937, in Cleveland, Ohio; son of Norbert (a tool designer) and Grace (Manning) Himler; married Patricia Vaughan, 1960 (divorced, 1970); married Ann Katherine Danowitz (a writer), June 18, 1972; children: (first marriage) Daniel Damien; (second marriage) Anna Grace. *Education:* Cleveland Institute of Art, Diploma, 1960; also studied at Cranbrook Academy of Art, 1960-61, and New York University, 1968-70. *Home:* 680 West End Ave., Apt. 4-D, New York, N.Y. 10025.

CAREER: General Motors Technical Center, Warren, Mich., technical sculptor (styling), 1961-63; artist and illustrator, 1963—. Toy designer and sculptor for Transogram Co., New York, N.Y., 1968, and Remco Industries, Newark, N.J., 1969. *Awards, honors:* Citation from American Institute of Graphic Arts for graphic excellence of *Baby*, and from Society of Illustrators for art work in *Baby*, both 1972; citation from Printing Industries of America, 1972, for *Rocket in My Pocket*.

WRITINGS—For children; all self-illustrated: *Run, Gabriella, Run* (poem), Holt, 1972; (compiler) *Glad Day* (classical poems), Putnam, 1972; (with wife, Ann Himler) *Little Owl: Keeper of the Trees*, Harper, 1974.

Illustrator: Robert Burgess, *Exploring a Coral Reef*, Macmillan, 1972; Oscar Wilde, *The Selfish Giant*, Holt, 1972; Fran Manushkin, *Baby*, Harper, 1972; Elizabeth Winthrop, *Bunk Beds*, Harper, 1972; Millicent Brower, *I Am Going Nowhere*, Putnam, 1972; Carl Withers, compiler, *Rocket in My Pocket* (poems), Western Publishing, 1972; Charlotte Zolotow, *Janey*, Harper, 1973; Marjorie Weinman Sharmat, *Morris Brookside: A Dog* (Junior Literary Guild selection), Holiday House, 1973; Dorothy Kunhardt, *Lucky Mrs. Ticklefeather and Other Funny Stories*, Golden Press, 1973; Tom Glazer, *Eye Winker, Tom Tinker, Chin Chopper*, Doubleday, 1973; William C. Grimm, *Indian Harvests*, McGraw, 1974; Robert Burch, *Hut School and the Wartime Home-Front Heroes*, Viking, 1974; Manushkin, *Bubblebath*, Harper, 1974; Sharmat, *Morris Brookside Is Missing*, Holiday House, 1974; Betsy Byars, *After the Goat Man*, Viking, 1974; Polly Curran, *A Patch of Peas*, Golden Press, 1975; Arnold Adoff, *Make a Circle, Keep Us In* (poems), Delacorte, 1975.

* * *

HINES, Thomas S(pight) 1936-

PERSONAL: Born October 28, 1936, in Oxford, Miss.; son of Thomas S. (a college administrator and teacher) and Polly (a teacher; maiden name, Moore) Hines; married Dorothy Taylor (a teacher), June 9, 1967; children: Tracy Odessa. *Education:* University of Mississippi, B.A., 1958, M.A., 1960; University of Wisconsin, Ph.D., 1971. *Politics:* Democrat. *Home:* 11005 Strathmore Dr., Los Angeles, Calif. 90024. *Office:* Department of History, 7272 Bunche Hall, University of California, Los Angeles, Calif. 90024.

CAREER: University of California, Los Angeles, assistant professor, 1968-74, associate professor of history, 1974—. Visiting professor at University of Texas, 1974-75. *Military service:* U.S. Army, 1960-63; became first lieutenant. *Member:* American Historical Association, American Studies Association, Society of Architectural Historians.

WRITINGS: Burnham of Chicago: Architect and Planner, Oxford University Press, 1974. Contributor of articles to *American Quarterly, Pacific Historical Review, Journal of the Society of Architectural Historians*, and of reviews to *American History, American Historical Review*, and *Architecture Plus*.

WORK IN PROGRESS: The City Beautiful Movement: The History of a Vision, for "Cities and Planning" series,

Braziller; *Richard Neutra and the Quest for Modern Architecture: A Biography and History*.

* * *

HIRST, Stephen M(ichael) 1939-

PERSONAL: Born December 20, 1939, in Dayton, Ohio; son of David Livingstone (a physician) and Charlotte Chapin (Chalker) Hirst; married Lois Ann Loesch (a preschool director), March 16, 1962. *Education:* Miami University, Oxford, Ohio, B.A., 1962; Johns Hopkins School of Advanced International Studies, Bologna, Italy, M.A., 1966. *Politics:* "Halfheartedly radical (when I think about it)." *Religion:* "Pagan." *Home and office address:* Supai, Ariz. 86435.

CAREER: Peace Corps, Washington, D.C., volunteer junior high school teacher in Tappita, Liberia, 1962-64; U.S. Department of Commerce, Washington, D.C., Soviet desk officer, 1966; European Common Market Information Service, Washington, D.C., chief of publications, 1967; *Business Abroad* (magazine), New York, N.Y., associate editor, 1968-70; Head Start director for Havasupai Tribe in Supai, Ariz., 1967-68, 1970-73, acting tribal secretary, 1970—.

WRITINGS: Life in a Narrow Place, McKay, 1975.

WORK IN PROGRESS: Establishing a Havasupai historical and photographic archive.

SIDELIGHTS: Hirst has lived or traveled in Europe and West Africa. He speaks Russian, German, French, Italian, and some Havasupai.

* * *

HISCOCKS, C(harles) Richard 1907-

PERSONAL: Born June 1, 1907, in London, England; son of Frederick William (a businessman) and Annette (Paine) Hiscocks. *Education:* St. Edmund Hall, Oxford, M.A., 1929; University of Berlin, D.Phil., 1935. *Religion:* Church of England. *Home:* Dickers, Hunworth, Melton Constable, Norfolk, England. *Agent:* Curtis Brown Ltd., 1 Craven Hill, London W2 3EW, England.

CAREER: Trinity College School, Port Hope, Ontario, assistant master, 1929-32; Bradfield College, Bradfield, Berkshire, England, teacher of history and English literature, 1936-39; Marlborough College, Marlborough, Wiltshire, England, teacher of history and social sciences, 1939-40; British Council, London, England, representative in Austria, 1946-49, and South India, 1949-50; University of Manitoba, Winnipeg, professor of political science and international relations, 1950-64; University of Sussex, Brighton, England, professor of international relations, 1964-72, professor emeritus, 1972—. Visiting fellow at Princeton University, 1970-71; fellow of Adlai Stevenson Institute of International Affairs, 1971-72. United Kingdom member of United Nations Subcommittee for prevention of discrimination and protection of minorities, 1953-62. Member of board of governors of Winnipeg Symphony Orchestra; director of Winnipeg Art Gallery (president, 1959-60). *Military service:* Royal Marines, 1940-45; served in Middle East, Ceylon, and Germany; became lieutenant colonel.

MEMBER: International Institute of Strategic Studies, Royal Institute of International Affairs, Royal Philharmonic Society (fellow), United Nations Association of the United Kingdom (member of national executive committee, 1973-74), Garrick Club. *Awards, honors:* Named honorary member of University of Vienna, 1948.

WRITINGS: The Rebirth of Austria, Oxford University Press, 1953; *Democracy in Western Germany,* Oxford University Press, 1957; *Poland: Bridge for the Abyss?,* Oxford University Press, 1963; *Germany Revived,* Gollancz, 1966, published as *The Adenauer Era,* Lippincott, 1967; (contributor) K. D. Bracher, Christopher Dawson, Will Geiger, and Rudolph Smend, editors, *Die moderne Demokratie und ihr Recht* (title means "Modern Constitutionalism and Democracy"), J. C. B. Mohr (Tuebingen), 1966; *The Security Council: A Study in Adolescence,* Free Press, 1974.

WORK IN PROGRESS: Idealism and Materialism in the Victorian Age.

AVOCATIONAL INTERESTS: Music, art, riding.

* * *

HITE, James (Cleveland) 1941-

PERSONAL: Born April 21, 1941, in Kingsport, Tenn.; son of Guy Clifford (a farmer) and Wanna (Bales) Hite. *Education:* Clemson University, B.S., 1963, Ph.D., 1966; Emory University, M.A., 1964; Harvard University, postdoctoral study, 1969-70. *Religion:* Methodist. *Home:* 102 Berry St., Clemson, S.C. 29631. *Office:* Department of Agricultural Economics, Barre Hall, Clemson University, Clemson, S.C. 29631.

CAREER: Tennessee Technological University, Cookesville, assistant professor of agricultural economics, 1967; Clemson University, Clemson, S.C., assistant professor, 1967-71, associate professor of agricultural economics, 1971—. Marine scientist affiliated with South Carolina Marine Resources Center, 1972—. *Member:* American Economic Association, American Agricultural Economic Association, Southern Regional Science Association (secretary-treasurer, 1972—), Southern Economic Association.

WRITINGS: (Editor with J. M. Stepp) *Coastal Zone Resource Management*, Praeger, 1971; (with E. A. Laurent) *Environmental Planning: An Economic Analysis*, Praeger, 1972; (with Stepp, H. H. Macauley, and Bruce Yandle, Jr.) *Economics of Environmental Quality*, American Enterprises Institute, 1972. Contributor to *Land Economics, Water Resources Journal*, and *Southern Journal of Agricultural Economics*.

WORK IN PROGRESS: The Political Economy of Land-Use Policy.

AVOCATIONAL INTERESTS: Collecting antiques, hiking.

* * *

HOBBS, Peter V(ictor) 1936-

PERSONAL: Born May 31, 1936, in London, England; son of Victor G. (a civil servant) and Daisy (Kincaid) Hobbs; married Sylvia Helen Wood, January 18, 1963; children: Stephen, Julian, Rowland. *Education:* Attended Kingston Technical College, 1952-55; Royal College of Science, A.R.C.S. (Associate of the Royal College of Science), 1960; Imperial College of Science and Technology, University of London, B.Sc. (honors), 1960, Ph.D. and D.I.C. (Diploma of the Imperial College), both 1963. *Home:* 2815 105th S.E., Bellevue, Wash. 98004. *Office:* Department of Atmospheric Sciences, University of Washington, Seattle, Wash. 98195.

CAREER: University of Washington, Seattle, assistant

professor, 1963-66, associate professor, 1966-70, professor of atmospheric sciences, 1970—. North Atlantic Treaty Organization (NATO) visiting lecturer in meteorology at Cambridge University, 1970-71. Consultant to federal and state agencies. *Military service:* Royal Air Force, 1955-57. *Member:* American Meteorological Society (fellow), American Geophysical Union, American Association for the Advancement of Science, Glaciological Society, Royal Meteorological Society. *Awards, honors:* Editor's award from American Meteorological Society, 1970.

WRITINGS: Ice Physics, Oxford University Press, 1974. Contributor of more than a hundred articles to scientific publications. Associate editor of *Journal of Atmospheric Science* and *Journal of Glaciology*; former associate editor of *Journal of Applied Meteorology*.

WORK IN PROGRESS: Fundamentals of Meteorology, with J. M. Wallace; research on cloud physics, weather modification, and atmospheric effects of pollutants.

SIDELIGHTS: Hobbs told *CA* that he was "a participator in the 'brain drain' from Europe to the United States in the early 1960's [who] survived and thrived in the American scientific scene." *Avocational interests:* Exhaustive biographical books, English country houses, coaching junior soccer players.

* * *

HOBSON, Fred Colby, Jr. 1943-

PERSONAL: Born April 23, 1943, in Winston-Salem, N.C.; son of Fred Colby (a public school superintendent) and Miriam (Tuttle) Hobson; married Linda Whitney (a teacher), June 17, 1967; children: Jane Gregory. *Education:* University of North Carolina, A.B., 1965, Ph.D., 1972; Duke University, M.A., 1967. *Home:* 12113 Northwood Lake, Northport, Ala. 35476. *Office:* Department of English, University of Alabama, Tuscaloosa, Ala. 35486.

CAREER: Associated Press, Charlotte, N.C., editor, 1966; *Winston-Salem Journal and Sentinel*, Winston-Salem, N.C., editorial writer, 1969-70; Virginia Western College, Roanoke, assistant professor of English, 1971-72; University of Alabama, Tuscaloosa, assistant professor of English, 1972—. *Member:* Modern Language Association of America, English Institute. *Awards, honors:* Co-receiver of Pulitzer Prize, 1970, for journalism as editorial writer for the *Winston-Salem Journal and Sentinel*.

WRITINGS: Serpent in Eden: H. L. Mencken and the South, University of North Carolina Press, 1974. Contributor to *Commonweal* and *Mississippi Quarterly*.

WORK IN PROGRESS: A long work, an interpretative study of Southerners from colonial days through the mid-twentieth century who have written books attempting to "explain" the South; research on Southern literature of the 1920's, and on several American writers of prose fiction of the late nineteenth century.

AVOCATIONAL INTERESTS: Sports.

* * *

HODGES, Donald Clark 1923-

PERSONAL: Born October 22, 1923, in Fort Worth, Tex.; son of Count Hal and Elinor (Clark) Hodges; married Gabrielle Baptiste, November 14, 1949 (divorced, 1963); married Margaret Helen Deutsch, January 3, 1963; children: (first marriage) Justin Blake, Peter Robin; (second marriage) MacIntyre Hardy, John Oliver, Ernest Van Every. *Education:* Attended Swarthmore College, 1942-43; New York University, B.A. (summa cum laude), 1947; Columbia University, M.A., 1948, Ph.D., 1954. *Home:* 707 Lothian Dr., Tallahassee, Fla. 32303. *Office:* Department of Philosophy, Florida State University, Tallahassee, Fla. 32306.

CAREER: Hobart College, Geneva, N.Y., instructor in philosophy, 1949-52; University of Missouri, Columbia, instructor, 1952-54, assistant professor, 1954-57, associate professor of philosophy, 1957-63; University of South Florida, Tampa, professor of philosophy, 1963-64; Florida State University, Tallahassee, professor of philosophy, 1964—, head of department, 1964-69, director of Center for Graduate and Postgraduate Studies in Social Philosophy, 1967-71. Visiting professor at University of Nebraska, 1963, and University of Hawaii, 1965-66. *Member:* American Philosophical Association, Society for the Philosophical Study of Dialectical Materialism (secretary-treasurer, 1963-73), Society for the Philosophical Study of Marxism (secretary-treasurer, 1973—), Institute for Social Philosophy of Pennsylvania State University (associate member).

WRITINGS: (Editor with Kuang T. Fann) *Readings in U.S. Imperialism*, Sargent, 1971; (editor with Abu Shanab) *National Liberation Fronts*, Morrow, 1972; (editor and translator) *Philosophy of the Urban Guerrilla: The Revolutionary Writings of Abraham Guillen*, Morrow, 1973; *Socialist Humanism: The Outcome of Classical European Morality*, Warren H. Green, 1974; *The Latin American Revolution*, Morrow, 1974; (editor) *The Legacy of Che Guevara*, Cornell University Press, in press. Consulting editor, *Indian Sociological Bulletin*, 1963—; member of editorial board, *Philosophy and Phenomenological Research*, 1969—; co-editor, *Social Theory and Practice*, 1971—; associate editor, *Philosophical Currents*, 1974—.

WORK IN PROGRESS: Guerrilla Warfare in the United States, with Paul Shang.

* * *

HODGES, Luther (Hartwell) 1898-1974

March 9, 1898—October 6, 1974; American politician, businessman, author of books on business topics. Obituaries: *New York Times*, October 7, 1974; *Washington Post*, October 7, 1974.

* * *

HOEL, Robert F(loyd) 1942-

PERSONAL: Surname is pronounced like "Hoyle"; born December 2, 1942, in Litchfield, Minn.; son of Floyd M. (a businessman) and Mae (Norgaard) Hoel; married Lois Sandra Kroc (an elementary school teacher), August 28, 1965; children: Kristen, Jeanne. *Education:* Hamline University, B.A., 1964; Indiana University, M.B.A., 1966; University of Minnesota, Ph.D., 1972. *Home:* 740 Duke Sq., Fort Collins, Colo. 80521. *Office:* College of Business, Colorado State University, Fort Collins, Colo. 80523.

CAREER: Indiana University, Bloomington, administrative assistant to director of Bureau of Business Research, 1964-66; worked for Jewell Companies Inc. and OSCO Drug Co., both Chicago, Ill., 1966-69; Colorado State University, Fort Collins, assistant professor of business, 1971—. *Member:* American Marketing Association, Southwestern Marketing Association.

WRITINGS: Marketing Now!, Scott, Foresman, 1973. Contributor of articles and reviews to *Journal of Retailing*, *Indiana Business Review*, and *Choice*.

WORK IN PROGRESS: Research on the marketing of stolen goods, for Law Enforcement Assistance Administration of U.S. Department of Justice.

SIDELIGHTS: Hoel's interest is in the use of business and marketing research and management techniques in areas outside the field of business.

* * *

HOFFMAN, Joseph G(ilbert) 1909-1974

August 19, 1909—December 9, 1974; American physicist, educator, author. Obituaries: *New York Times*, December 11, 1974; *AB Bookman's Weekly*, January 27, 1975; *Current Biography*, January, 1975.

* * *

HOFFMEISTER, Donald F(rederick) 1916-

PERSONAL: Born March 21, 1916, in San Bernardino, Calif.; son of Percival George and Julia (Hillgartner) Hoffmeister; married Helen E. Kaatz, August 11, 1938; children: James Ronald, Robert George. *Education:* University of California, Berkeley, A.B., 1938, M.A., 1940, Ph.D., 1944. *Home:* 1505 West Charles St., Champaign, Ill. 61820. *Office:* Museum of Natural History, University of Illinois, Urbana, Ill. 61801.

CAREER: University of Kansas, Lawrence, assistant curator and assistant professor of zoology, 1944-46; University of Illinois, Urbana, assistant professor, 1946-53, associate professor, 1953-59, professor of zoology, 1959—, Museum of Natural History, curator, 1946-64, director, 1964—. *Member:* American Association of Museums (member of executive council, 1973—), Association of Science Museum Directors, Midwest Museums Conference (president, 1963-64).

WRITINGS: (With W. W. Goodpaster) *Mammals of the Huachuca Mountains, Southeastern Arizona* (monograph), University of Illinois Press, 1954; (with H. S. Zim) *Mammals: A Guide to Familiar American Species,* Simon & Schuster, 1955; *Fieldbook of Illinois Mammals,* Illinois Natural History Survey, 1957, new edition, Dover, 1972; *Mammals,* Golden Press, 1963; *Zoo Animals,* Golden Press, 1967; *Mammals of Grand Canyon,* University of Illinois Press, 1971. Associate editor of *American Midland Naturalist,* 1967-70; member of editorial committee of *American Society of Mammalogists,* 1952-57, and *Illinois Biological Monographs,* 1970—.

WORK IN PROGRESS: Mammals of Arizona.

* * *

HOGE, Dean Richard 1937-

PERSONAL: Surname rhymes with "stogie"; born May 27, 1937, in Ohio; son of Arthur F. (a lumber dealer) and Meta (Meckstroth) Hoge; married Josephine Jacobson, June 27, 1965; children: Christopher, Elizabeth. *Education:* Ohio State University, B.S. (summa cum laude), 1960; University of Bonn, graduate study, 1960-61; Harvard University, B.D. (cum laude), 1964, M.A., 1966, Ph.D., 1978. *Religion:* Presbyterian. *Home:* 7314 Holly Ave., Takoma Park, Md. 20012. *Office:* Department of Sociology, Catholic University of America, Washington, D. C. 20017.

CAREER: Princeton Theological Seminary, Princeton, N.J., assistant professor of sociology, 1969-74; Catholic University of America, Washington, D.C., associate professor of sociology, 1974—. *Member:* American Sociological Association, Society for the Scientific Study of Religion, Religious Research Association (secretary, 1973-75), Association for the Sociology of Religion, Common Cause, Zero Population Growth, American Association of University Professors.

WRITINGS: Commitment on Campus: Changes in Religion and Values over Five Decades, Westminster, 1974. Contributor to religion and sociology journals.

WORK IN PROGRESS: A manuscript on tensions in the mainline Protestant church; research on religion, youth, and values.

* * *

HOGG, Robert (Lawrence) 1942-

PERSONAL: Born March 26, 1942, in Edmonton, Alberta, Canada. *Education:* University of British Columbia, B.A., 1964; State University of New York, Buffalo, graduate study, 1965-68. *Office:* Department of English, Carleton University, Ottawa, Ontario, Canada.

CAREER: Carleton University, Ottawa, Ontario, lecturer, 1968-69, assistant professor of English, 1969—. Has given poetry readings throughout Canada, at libraries, coffeehouses, schools, and art galleries. Conducted Canadian Poetry Seminar, 1972-73. *Member:* League of Canadian Poets, Canadian Association of University Teachers. *Awards, honors:* Carleton University research grant, 1970; Canada Council fellowship, 1971-72.

WRITINGS—All poetry: *The Connexions,* Oyez, 1966; *Standing Back,* Coach House Press (Toronto), 1972; *Of Light,* Coach House Press, 1974. Work is represented in anthologies, as follows: *New Wave Canada,* edited by R. Souster, Contact Press, 1966; *To Everything There Is a Season,* edited by R. Benny, Longmans, 1967; *The Book of Modern Canadian Verse,* edited by A. J. M. Smith, Oxford University Press, 1967; *The Wind Has Wings,* edited by Mary A. Downie and Barbara Robertson, Oxford University Press, 1968; *Poets of the Capital,* edited by F. Tierney, [Ottawa], 1974; *Northern Comfort,* edited by N. Whitman, [Ottawa], 1974. Contributor to *Ant's Forefoot, Cotinneh, Georgin Straight Writing Supplement, Imago, Is, Island, Motion, Open Letter, Tish,* and *Tuatara.*

* * *

HOGINS, James Burl 1936-

PERSONAL: Born January 26, 1936, in Dover, Ark.; son of Reece Buel (a farmer) and Daisie (Powers) Hogins; married Flora Ann Rutherford, April 5, 1957; children: Aenea Ann, Jonathan Buel. *Education:* University of Kentucky, B.A. and M.A., 1957. *Politics:* Democrat. *Religion:* United Church of Christ. *Home:* 6415 Crystalaire Dr., San Diego, Calif. 92120. *Office:* Department of English, San Diego Mesa College, 7250 College Dr., San Diego, Calif. 92111.

CAREER: Southeastern Christian College, Winchester, Ky., assistant professor of English and chairman of department, 1957-60; San Diego City College, San Diego, Calif., professor of English, 1960-63; San Diego Mesa College, San Diego, Calif., professor of English, 1963—, chairman of department, 1966-69. Consultant to Glencoe Press and Reader's Digest Educational Division.

WRITINGS: (Editor with Robert E. Yarber) *Reading, Writing, and Rhetoric,* Science Research Associates, 1967, revised edition, 1972; (with Yarber) *College Reading and Writing,* Macmillan, 1968; (editor with Yarber) *Language: An Introductory Reader,* Harper, 1969.

(Editor with Yarber) *Phase Blue: A Systems Approach to College English*, Science Research Associates, 1970, revised edition, 1974; (with Gerald A. Bryant, Jr.) *PACE (A Perceptual Approach to College English): Experiments in Composition*, Glencoe Press, 1970; (editor with Bryant) *Reading for Insight: A Perceptual Approach to College English*, Glencoe Press, 1970, 2nd edition, 1974; (editor with Bryant) *Juxtaposition*, Science Research Associates, 1971, revised edition, 1975; *People and Words: A Visual Rhetoric and Resource Book for Writing*, Science Research Associates, 1972; (with Thomas S. Lillard) *The Structure of Writing*, Heath, 1972; (editor) *Literature: A Collection of Mythology and Folklore, Short Stories, Poetry, Drama, and Literary Criticism*, Science Research Associates, 1973; (editor) *Cycle Seven: Essays, Short Stories, Poems for Freshman English*, Science Research Associates, 1973; *Probing Common Ground: Sources for Writing*, Prentice-Hall, 1974; *Literature: Fiction*, Science Research Associates, 1974; *Literature: Poetry*, Science Research Associates, 1974; *Literature: Mythology*, Science Research Associates, 1975.

WORK IN PROGRESS: A television script for an educational series titled "Project Literature," scheduled for 1976; a middle-school level English series, 1977.

AVOCATIONAL INTERESTS: Photography (has had many photographs published), travel (has visited Europe, Asia, and the South Pacific area), gardening, and novel writing ("always unsuccessful . . . frustrated poet").

* * *

HOHENSTEIN, Henry J(ohn) 1931-

PERSONAL: Born September 28, 1931, in Cohoes, N.Y.; son of Charles H. (a civil engineer) and Mildred (a bacteriologist; maiden name, Eldon) Hohenstein; married Mary Arline Kennedy (a nurse), August 29, 1953 (separated); children: Anne, Henry, Ellen, Elizabeth, Fredrick. *Education:* Attended Russell Sage College, 1948-50; Rutgers University, B.S., 1953. *Politics:* "To vote is to sanction the state." *Religion:* Atheist. *Home:* 2009 Manhattan Ave., Hermosa Beach, Calif. 90254. *Agent:* Jan Robinson, 4511 Harlem Rd., Buffalo, N.Y. 14226. *Office:* 1208 Artesia Blvd., Hermosa Beach, Calif. 90254.

CAREER: Upjohn Co., Schenectady, N.Y., detailman, 1956-61; Webb Laboratories, Schenectady, N.Y., president, 1961-65; Stiefel Laboratories, Oak Hill, N.Y., director of administrative services, 1965-69; Creative Equity Corp., Redondo Beach, Calif., vice-president, 1970-73; involved in several real estate projects, 1974—. Member of board of directors of National Justice Foundation, 1974—. *Military service:* U.S. Marine Corps Reserve, 1953-71, active duty, 1953-56; became major. *Member:* Delta Phi.

WRITINGS: I. R. S. Conspiracy, Nash Publishing, 1974. Contributor to *Reason*.

WORK IN PROGRESS: Three poetry manuscripts; a book on taxation in the United States, and a novel dealing with achieving personal freedom.

BIOGRAPHICAL/CRITICAL SOURCES: Time, March 19, 1973.

* * *

HOLDEN, Inez 1906-1974

Journalist and novelist. Obituaries: *AB Bookman's Weekly*, October 7, 1974.

HOLLADAY, William L(ee) 1926-

PERSONAL: Born June 23, 1926, in Dallas, Tex.; son of William L. (an electrical engineer) and Louise H. (an instructor in braiding and hooking rugs; maiden name, Cook); married Jean M. Grosbach (a teacher), August 28, 1948; children: Catherine L., David F., Martin J., Peter W. *Education:* University of California, Berkeley, B.A. (with highest honors), 1948; Pacific School of Religion, B.D. (summa cum laude), 1951; University of Leiden, Th.D., 1958. *Office:* Andover Newton Theological School, 210 Herrick Rd., Newton Centre, Mass. 02159.

CAREER: Pastor of United Churches of Christ in California, 1951-55; campus minister for United Church of Christ and Disciples of Christ in Boulder, Colo., 1958-60; Elmhurst College, Elmhurst, Ill., assistant professor of religion, 1960-63; Near East School of Theology, Beirut, Lebanon, professor of Old Testament, 1963-70; Andover Newton Theological School, Newton Centre, Mass., professor, 1970-71, Lowry Professor of Old Testament, 1971—. *Military service:* U.S. Army, 1946-47.

MEMBER: International Society for the Study of the Old Testament, Society for Biblical Literature (president of New England Region chapter, 1973-74), Phi Beta Kappa. *Awards, honors:* Hendrik Willem van Loon fellowship for study in the Netherlands, 1955-56, 1956-57.

WRITINGS: The Root Subh in the Old Testament, E. J. Brill, 1958; *A Concise Hebrew and Aramaic Lexicon of the Old Testament*, E. J. Brill, 1971; *Jeremiah: Spokesman Out of Time*, United Church Press, 1974; *The Architecture of Jeremiah 1-20*, Bucknell University Press, 1975. Contributor of articles and reviews to *Journal of Biblical Literature, Vetus Testamentum*, and *Interpretation*. Associate editor of *Journal of Biblical Literature*, 1975—. Member of editorial board of *Vetus Testamentum*, 1973—.

WORK IN PROGRESS: An exegetical commentary on the book of Jeremiah.

AVOCATIONAL INTERESTS: Camping and knapsacking (in the Middle East), bicycling long distances, working on his summer home.

* * *

HOLLAND, Thomas E(dward) 1934-

PERSONAL: Born January 10, 1934, in Esto, Fla.; son of Delmas Preston (a farmer) and Mertice Mae (Armstrong) Holland; married Doris June Hall, December 17, 1952; children: Thomas E., Jr., Deborah Lynne, Catherine Ann, Stephen Eudon. *Education:* University of Tennessee, B.S., 1957, M.S., 1958; Duke University, Ph.D., 1963. *Politics:* Moderate. *Religion:* Protestant. *Home:* 1805 Bois d'Arc, Arlington, Tex. 76013. *Office:* Department of Economics, University of Texas at Arlington, Arlington, Tex. 76019.

CAREER: Tennessee Valley Authority, Chattanooga, economist, 1958-60, 1961-63; University of Alabama, Tuscaloosa, assistant professor, 1963-64, associate professor of economics, 1964-66; Texas A&M University, Bryan, associate professor of economics, 1966-70; University of Texas at Arlington, professor of economics, 1970—. *Military service:* U.S. Air Force, 1949-52. *Member:* American Economic Association, Southern Economic Association, Beta Gamma Sigma, Phi Kappa Phi. *Awards, honors:* Ford Foundation grant, University of Chicago, summer, 1968.

WRITINGS: Microeconomic Theory and Functions, Appleton, 1973. Contributor of articles and reviews to *Proceedings of the Southern Finance Association, Journal of*

Business, International Economic Review, and *Journal of Economic Literature*.

WORK IN PROGRESS: Macroeconomic Theory and Functions; Primer of Economics, completion expected in 1977.

* * *

HOLLENWEGER, Walter J(acob) 1927-

PERSONAL: Born June 1, 1927, in Antwerp, Belgium; son of Walter O. (a book-seller) and Anna (Spoerri) Hollenweger; married Erica Busslinger, 1951. *Education:* Studied at commercial school in Zurich, Switzerland; attended International Bible Training Institute, Leamington Spa, England, 1947-58; also attended University of Basel, 1957-58; University of Zurich, propodeuticum (B.D. equivalent), 1958, Staatsexamen (M.A. equivalent), 1961, D.Th., 1966. *Home:* 61 Chadbrook Crest, Richmond Hill Rd., Birmingham, England. *Office:* Department of Theology, University of Birmingham, Birmingham, England.

CAREER: Zurich Stock Exchange, Zurich, Switzerland, apprentice and bank clerk, 1943-46; Union Bank of Switzerland, La Chaux-de-Fonds, Switzerland, bank clerk, 1946-47; Pentecostal minister of Swiss Pentecostal Mission, 1948-58; ordained minister of Swiss Reformed Church, 1961; Evangelical Academy, Zurich, Switzerland, study director, 1964-65; World Council of Churches, Geneva, Switzerland, executive secretary, 1965-71; University of Birmingham, Birmingham, England, professor of theology, 1971—.

WRITINGS: Enthusiastisches Christentum. Die Pfingstbewegung in Geschichte und Gegenwart, Zwingli Verlag (Zurich), 1969, translation by R. A. Wilson published as *The Pentecostals: The Charismatic Movement in the Churches,* Augsburg, 1972; (editor) *Die Pfingstkirchen. Selbstdarstellungen, Dokumente, Komentare* (title means "The Pentecostal Churches: Autopresentations, Documents, Comments"), Evangelisches Verlagswerk (Stuttgart), 1971; (editor) *Kirche, Benzin und Bohnensuppe. Auf den Spuren dynamischer Gemeinden* (title means "Church, Petrol and Bean Soup: In Search of Dynamic Congregations"), Theologischer Verlag (Zurich), 1971; *New Wine in Old Skins: Protestant and Catholic Neo-Pentecostalism,* Fellowship Press, 1973; *Marxist and Kimbanguist Mission: A Comparison,* University of Birmingham, 1973; *Evangelisation gestern und heute,* J. F. Steinkopf Verlag (Stuttgart), 1973, translation by the author to be published as *Evangelism,* Christian Journals Ltd. (Belfast), in press; *Pentecost between Black and White: Five Case Studies on Pentecost and Politics,* Christian Journals Ltd., 1974.

WORK IN PROGRESS: Theologie in der Tagesordnung der Welt; research on new types of theological education, and on theology in television and radio, with the ecclesiological implications of both.

SIDELIGHTS: Hollenweger writes that the book he is now preparing, *Theologie in der Tagesordnung der Welt,* involves "research on the implications of the 'ecumenical area' (based on my experiences in Geneva [with] the World Council of Churches) for evangelism and mission; in particular I want to know how to express the common witness across such different cultural borders as exist between the Kimbanguists and the Lutherans, the Latin American Pentecostals and North American Protestants, between the 'oral' and the 'written theology.' What are its implications for theological education."

In addition to English, foreign editions of Hollenweger's work have been published in German, Spanish, and French.

* * *

HOLLER, Ronald F. 1938-

PERSONAL: Born March 30, 1938, in Illinois; son of Burl C. and Stella (Lori) Holler; married Lois Goudy (a counselor), November 22, 1961; children: Lori Lee. *Education:* Millikin University, B.S., 1961; University of Miami, Coral Gables, Fla., graduate study, 1962-63; University of Illinois, M.Ed., 1964, Ed.D., 1967. *Home:* 5048 North 82nd St., Scottsdale, Ariz. 85253. *Office:* Arizona State Hospital, 2500 East Van Buren St., Phoenix, Ariz. 85008.

CAREER: Certified school psychologist in Arizona, Illinois, and Florida. Teacher of English in public schools, 1961-63; intern in school and clinical psychology at Devereux Foundation, 1965-66; school psychologist in Champaign, Ill., 1966-67; University of Illinois, Champaign-Urbana, visiting professor of psychology, summer, 1967; Western Illinois University, Macomb, assistant professor of psychology, 1967-69, and staff psychologist at Psychological Clinic; Arizona State Hospital, Phoenix, staff psychologist, 1969-70, director of education and mental health technology, 1970—, director of psychology, 1974—. Private practice in psychology, 1969—. Director of education and mental health technology at Maricopa Technical College, 1970—. Member of research and training committee of Phoenix Community Organization for Drug Abuse Control, 1970-71; member of committee for teachers in health occupations education of Arizona Department of Vocational Education, 1970—.

MEMBER: American Psychological Association, Council for Exceptional Children, Western Psychological Association, Arizona State Psychological Association, Maricopa County Society of Clinical Psychologists. *Awards, honors:* National Institute of Mental Health grants, 1971-74, for hospital staff development, 1971-75, to train mental health workers.

WRITINGS: (With G. M. DeLong) *Human Services Technology*, Mosby, 1973. Contributor to *Esprit*, *Journal of Mental Health Technology*, and *Journal of Professional Psychology*. Member of consulting board of *Journal of Mental Health Technology*, 1972—; editorial consultant for Mosby.

WORK IN PROGRESS: A book, *Transacting for Behavior Change*.

* * *

HOLLINGSWORTH, Harold M(arvin) 1932-

PERSONAL: Born October 30, 1932, in Dallas, Tex.; son of Marvin Searcy (a clerk) and Lena Mae (Cates) Hollingsworth; married Shirley Jean Patterson, September 2, 1971. *Education:* University of Texas, Arlington, A.S., 1951; North Texas State University, B.S.Ed., 1953; University of Tennessee, M.A., 1956, Ph.D., 1966. *Religion:* Unitarian-Universalist. *Home:* 6513 Alter, Dayton, Ohio 45424. *Office:* Department of History, Wright State University, Dayton, Ohio 45431.

CAREER: Mary Hardin-Baylor College, Belton, Tex., assistant professor of history, 1956-60; University of Texas, Arlington, instructor, 1963-66, assistant professor of history, 1966-70; Wright State University, Dayton, Ohio, associate professor of history, 1970—. *Military service:* U.S.

Air Force, 1953-55; became first lieutenant. *Member:* American Historical Association, Organization of American Historians.

WRITINGS: (Editor with William F. Holmes) *Essays on the American Civil War*, University of Texas Press, 1968; (editor with Holmes) *Essays on the New Deal*, University of Texas Press, 1969; (editor with Sandra Myres) *Essays on the American West*, University of Texas Press, 1969; (editor) *Essays on Recent Southern Politics*, University of Texas Press, 1970.

* * *

HOLLOWAY, James Y(oung) 1927-

PERSONAL: Born August 28, 1927, in Pensacola, Fla.; son of James L. (a railroad agent) and Amy (Young) Holloway; married Nancy Attaway, June 12, 1959; children: Kay Louisa, James William, Joseph Patrick. *Education:* Howard College, student, 1947-49; Vanderbilt University, B.A., 1951, M.A., 1952, B.D., 1954; Yale University, Ph.D., 1961; also studied at University of Basel, 1957-58. *Home address:* Davis Hollow, Berea, Ky. 40403. *Office address:* Box 936, College Station, Berea, Ky. 40403.

CAREER: University of Manitoba, United College, Winnipeg, assistant professor of political science, 1959-60; Mercer University, Macon, Ga., assistant professor of philosophy and religion, 1961-64; St. Andrews College, Laurinburg, N.C., assistant professor of history and political science, 1964-65; Berea College, Berea, Ky., professor of philosophy and religion, 1965—. *Military service:* U.S. Army, 1946-47; became sergeant. *Member:* American Political Science Association.

WRITINGS: (With Will D. Campbell) *Up to Our Steeples in Politics*, Paulist-Newman, 1970; (editor) *Introducing Jacques Ellul*, Eerdmans, 1970; (editor with Campbell) *The Failure and the Hope*, Eerdmans, 1972; (editor with Campbell) *"And the Prisoners with Him,"* Paulist-Newman, 1973; (editor with Campbell) *Callings!*, Paulist-Newman, 1974. Editor of *Katallagete: Be Reconciled* (journal of the Committee of Southern Churchmen), 1965—.

* * *

HOLMQUIST, Eve 1921-

PERSONAL: Born January 29, 1921, in Minnesota; daughter of Fred J. (a musician) and Olive (a teacher; maiden name, Seager) Holmquist; married Russell W. Smith, March, 1944 (divorced January, 1968); children: Heidi (Mrs. Alan C. Sweeney), Gene, Joel, Robin. *Education:* University of Minnesota, B.A., 1947, graduate study, 1954; Fresno State University, M.S.W., 1973. *Politics:* Independent. *Religion:* Protestant. *Home:* 13408 Christie Dr., Saratoga, Calif. 95070. *Agent:* Ruth Cantor, 156 Fifth Ave., New York, N.Y. 10010. *Office:* Santa Clara County Department of Social Services, 55 West Younger, San Jose, Calif.

CAREER: Bruce Publishing Co., St. Paul, Minn., clerical work, 1956; University of Minnesota Press, Minneapolis, proofreader, 1956-58; Santa Clara County Department of Social Services, San Jose, Calif., social worker, 1966—. *Member:* National Association of Social Workers, National Writers Club.

WRITINGS: *The Giant Giraffe* (juvenile), Carolrhoda Books, 1973. Contributor to *Poetry Digest* and *Velvet Glove*.

WORK IN PROGRESS: *No Certain Time* and another novel; short stories.

AVOCATIONAL INTERESTS: Travel (made camping trip through twelve European countries, 1973), music.

* * *

HOLROYD, Michael (de Courcy Fraser) 1935-

PERSONAL: Born August 27, 1935, in London, England; son of Basil and Ulla (Hall) Holroyd. *Education:* Attended Eton College. *Politics:* Apolitical. *Agent:* Robert Lescher, 155 East 71st St., New York, N.Y. 10021; and A. P. Watt, 26/28 Bedford Row, London WC1R 4HL, England.

CAREER: Author. *Military service:* British Army, Royal Fusiliers. *Member:* Royal Society of Literature (fellow), Society of Authors (chairman, 1973-74), National Book League (deputy chairman, 1974—). *Awards, honors:* Saxton Memorial fellowship, 1964; Bollingen fellowship, 1966; Book of the Year award from *Yorkshire Post*, 1968, for *Lytton Strachey*; Winston Churchill fellowship, 1971.

WRITINGS: *Hugh Kingsmill: A Critical Biography*, Unicorn Press, 1964, revised edition, Heinemann, 1971; *Lytton Strachey: A Critical Biography* (Book-of-the-Month Club and Literary Guild selections), Volume I: *The Unknown Years, 1880-1910*, Volume II: *The Years of Achievement, 1910-1932*, Heinemann, 1967-68, Holt, 1968, revised edition published in two volumes as *Lytton Strachey: A Biography* and *Lytton Strachey and the Bloomsbury Group: His Work, Their Influence*, Penguin, 1971; *A Dog's Life* (novel), Holt, 1969; (editor) *The Best of Hugh Kingsmill*, Gollancz, 1970, Herder & Herder, 1971; (editor) *Lytton Strachey by Himself: A Self-Portrait*, Holt, 1971; *Unreceived Opinions* (essays), Heinemann, 1973, Holt, 1974; *Augustus John* (biography), two volumes, Heinemann, 1974-75, Holt, 1975; (with Malcolm Easton) *The Art of Augustus John*, Secker & Warburg, 1974, Godine, 1975.

Contributor to periodicals, including *Times* (London), *New York Times Book Review*, *Encounter*, *Spectator*, *American Scholar*, *Harper's*, *Punch*, and *Book World*.

WORK IN PROGRESS: An official biography of George Bernard Shaw.

SIDELIGHTS: With the publication of *Lytton Strachey*, a *South Atlantic Quarterly* reviewer wrote that Holroyd "has been able to assemble a work resembling Boswell's life of Johnson and thereby to add much to our understanding of English literature in the first thirty years of the present century." John Rothenstein calls the Strachey biography "the best literary biography to appear for many years. It may well prove revolutionary in its effects by quickening the reading public's impatience with biographies that lack detailed treatment of the most intimate aspects of the subjects' lives."

Commenting on his interests, Holroyd told *CA*: "I endeavour to restrict my interest as far as I possibly can. I have been unable to quell my response to music; I have a weakness for stories and an active passion for sleep (writing all my books in bed). Being vulnerable, I avoid tame animals. Unless I close my eyes, I am greatly taken by the appearance of things—and people."

* * *

HOLSAERT, Eunice ?-1974

?—May 6, 1974; American editor and author of children's books. Obituaries: *Library Journal*, September 15, 1974.

HOLT, L. Emmett, Jr. 1895-1974

March 20, 1985—November 30, 1974; American pediatrician, researcher, author of books on baby and child care. Obituaries: *New York Times*, December 2, 1974.

* * *

HOLT, Michael (Paul) 1929-

PERSONAL: Born January 7, 1929, in Richmond, Surrey, England; son of Paul (a journalist) and Feydoris (Mayo) Holt; married Gillian Hall, May, 1962; children: Miranda, Paul. *Education:* Sheffield University, B.Sc. (with honors), 1949; Birkbeck College, London, B.Sc. (special), 1959; graduate study in electronics, 1959-60. *Home:* The Old Parsonage, Eye nr. Leominster, Herefordshire, England. *Agent:* A. P. Watt & Sons Ltd., 26128 Bedford Row, London WC1 R4HL, England.

CAREER: Worked as a journalist, actor, radio announcer, and teacher in various schools in England, 1950-56; Gas Council, London, England, research physicist in industrial laboratory, 1956-59, head of electronics laboratory, 1959-62; *World Book Encyclopedia*, Chicago, Ill., senior science and mathematics editor, 1962-64; Ginn & Co., London, England, senior science and mathematics editor, 1965-67; University of London, Goldsmiths' College, lecturer, 1967-68, senior lecturer in mathematics, 1968-70; free-lance educational writer, 1970—. Lecturer in adult education, Richmond Institute, 1967-69; lecturer in mathematics to Association of Science Education and Oxford Mathematical Association; science project adjudicator of Guinness Award Trust in Mathematics and Science, 1968; conducted experimental math program at an infant school in London, 1968-69; conducted lectures in mathematics on BBC radio and television, including one year course, "Maths Workshop," 1969-70. *Member:* Society of Authors, Association of British Science Writers (associate member), Association of Teachers of Mathematics, Mathematics Association.

WRITINGS—Children's books: (With D.T.E. Marjoran) *Mathematics Through Experience* (textbook), six volumes, Blond Educational, 1966-69, revised edition, Holt, 1971, includes four exercise books, 1971-72; *What Is the New Math?*, Blond Educational, 1967; *Decimals Through Experience*, Blond Educational, 1969; *Science Happenings*, six volumes, Ginn, 1969-70; *Mathematics in Art*, Holt, 1971; (with Ronald Ridout) *Joe's Trip to the Moon*, Bancroft, 1971; (with Ridout) *The Train Thief*, Bancroft, 1971; (with Ridout) *Joe Walks on the Moon*, Bancroft, 1971; (with Zoltan P. Dienes) *Let's Play Maths*, Penguin, 1972, Walker & Co., 1973; (with Marjoran) *Mathematics in a Changing World*, Heinemann, 1972, Walker & Co., 1973; (with Ridout) *The Big Book of Puzzles*, Longman, 1972; *Monkey Puzzle Books*, six books, Bancroft, 1972, published in two books, Scholastic Book Service, 1974; *Maths*, 12 book course, Macmillan, 1973; (with Ridout) *The Second Big Book of Puzzles*, Longman, 1973, Knopf, 1974; *Young Science Books*, six books, Mills & Boon, 1974; (with Ridout) *All Round English*, Longman, 1974; (with Ridout) "Life Cycle" series, BBC and Bancroft, *Butterfly, Frog, Cat, Kangaroo, Human Being*, all 1974; *Zero*, Hart-Davis, 1975. Also author of *Zoo*, eight non-verbal workbooks and teacher's guide, Longman, 1972.

Physical science consultant for "Natural Science," a textbook course, Pergamon; devisor and consulting editor, "Science Topic Series," Ginn.

WORK IN PROGRESS: An English language course for Kenya; research on mathematical education in high schools, with Surrey University.

* * *

HOLTZMAN, Jerome 1926-

PERSONAL: Born July 12, 1926, in Chicago, Ill.; son of Samuel and Dorothy (Sloan) Holtzman; married Marilyn Ryan, 1949; children: Arlene, Alice, Catherine, Janet, Merrill. *Education:* Attended University of Chicago, 1954-55. *Residence:* Evanston, Ill. *Agent:* Gerard McCauley Agency Inc., Suite 27A, 159 West 53rd St., New York, N.Y. 10019.

CAREER: Chicago Sun-Times, Chicago, Ill., baseball writer and columnist, 1957—. *Awards, honors:* Stick o' Type Award from Chicago Newspaper Guild, 1961, 1969.

WRITINGS: No Cheering in the Press Box, Holt, 1974. Sports editor and adviser for *Encyclopaedia Britannica;* correspondent and columnist for *Sporting News.*

* * *

HOLZ, Robert K(enneth) 1930-

PERSONAL: Surname rhymes with "bolts"; born November 3, 1930, in Kankakee, Ill.; son of Harry H. (a city fireman) and Margaret Holz; married Joyce F. Harpin (a registered nurse), May 19, 1951; children: Eric Robert. *Education:* Southern Illinois University, B.A., 1958, M.A., 1959; Michigan State University, Ph.D., 1963. *Home:* 2610 Fiset Dr., Austin, Texas 78731. *Office:* Department of Geography, University of Texas, Austin, Tex. 78712.

CAREER: University of Texas, Austin, assistant professor, 1962-66, associate professor, 1966-71, professor of geography, 1971—, chairman of department, 1971—. Member of National Aeronautics and Space Administration visual observation scientific team for Skylab IV; member of Texas Governor's Task Force on Remote Sensing. *Military service:* U.S. Army Air Forces, 1951-54. *Member:* Association of American Geographers, American Geographical Society, American Society of Photogrammetry, Canadian Institute of Chartered Cartographers, American Association of University Professors. *Awards, honors:* Fulbright U.A.R.-U.S. educational exchange grant for seminar in Cairo, Egypt, 1965; National Science Foundation grant to research in North Africa, 1965; National Aeronautics and Space Administration grants, 1973-74, 1975.

WRITINGS: (With Michael E. Bonine and others) *Atlas of Mexico*, Bureau of Business Research, University of Texas, 1970; (with M. Mayhall and S. Newman) *Texas and Its History*, Graphic Ideas, 1971; (with Charles T. Clark) *Economic and Population Growth in the Guadalupe-Blanco River Area*, Bureau of Business Research, University of Texas, 1971; (editor) *The Surveillant Science: Remote Sensing of the Environment*, Houghton, 1973. Cartographic work has been included in books and journals. Cartographic consultant for University of Texas Press and for Praeger. Contributor of articles and reviews to geographical journals and *Photogrammetric Engineering.*

WORK IN PROGRESS: Continuing studies in remote sensing of the environment.

* * *

HOLZBERGER, William George 1932-

PERSONAL: Born January 6, 1932, in Chicago, Ill.; son of William Alexander and Mary Frances (Ward) Holzberger;

married Annegret Christel Meseke, April 24, 1965; children: Stefan, Rebecca. *Education:* Wright Junior College, A.A., 1957; Northwestern University, Ph.B., 1960, M.A. (philosophy), 1965, M.A. (English), 1966, Ph.D., 1969. *Religion:* None. *Home:* 25 South 16th St., Lewisburg, Pa. 17837. *Office:* Department of English, Bucknell University, Lewisburg, Pa. 17837.

CAREER: High school English teacher in Chicago, Ill., 1961-65; Bucknell University, Lewisburg, Pa., assistant professor, 1969-74, professor of English, 1974—. *Member:* Modern Language Association of America, American Association of University Professors, Pennsylvania College English Association. *Awards, honors:* Grant from American Philosophical Society, 1970; grants from American Council of Learned Societies, 1972, 1973.

WRITINGS: (Editor) *The Complete Poems of George Santayana: A Critical Edition*, Bucknell University Press, 1975; (editor with Peter B. Waldeck) *Perspectives on Hamlet: Collected Papers of the Bucknell-Susquehanna Colloquium on Hamlet*, Bucknell University Press, 1975.

WORK IN PROGRESS: Editing *The Complete Letters of George Santayana*, (worked in part with the late Daniel Cory), for University of Illinois Press, completion expected in 1977.

AVOCATIONAL INTERESTS: Travel (Europe), reading, music (especially opera).

* * *

HOOK, Andrew 1932-

PERSONAL: Born December 21, 1932, in Wick, Caithness, Scotland; son of Wilfred Thomas (a post office radioman) and Jessie (Dunnett) Hook; married Judith Ann Hibberd (a lecturer in history), July 18, 1966; children: Sarah York, Caspar Alexander. *Education:* University of Edinburgh, M.A. (first class honors), 1954; University of Manchester, graduate study, 1956-57; Princeton University, Ph.D., 1960. *Home:* 24 Champerdown Rd., Aberdeen AB2 4NU, Scotland. *Agent:* Elaine Greene, 31 Newington Green, London NI6 9PU, England. *Office:* Taylor Building, King's College, University of Aberdeen, Old Aberdeen, Scotland.

CAREER: Duke University, Durham, N.C., instructor in English, 1959-60; University of Edinburgh, Edinburgh, Scotland, assistant lecturer in English, 1961-63, lecturer in American literature, 1963-71; University of Aberdeen, Old Aberdeen, Scotland, senior lecturer in English, 1971—. *Military service:* British Army, Intelligence Corps, 1954-56. *Member:* British Association for American Studies, Association for Scottish Literary Studies.

WRITINGS: (Editor and author of introduction and notes) *Sir Walter Scott's "Waverley,"* Penguin, 1972; (editor with wife, Judith Hook) *Charlotte Bronte's "Shirley,"* Penguin, 1974; (editor) *John Dos Passos: A Collection of Critical Essays*, Prentice-Hall, 1974; *Scotland and America: A Study of Cultural Relations, 1750-1835*, Blackie & Son, 1975.

WORK IN PROGRESS: Scotland and Romanticism.

SIDELIGHTS: Hook writes that "... graduate study at Princeton [was] a crucial experience for me. I remain fascinated by the vitality of American life and culture." He adds that he has come to share his wife's love of Italy.

HOOK, Donald D(wight) 1928-

PERSONAL: Born December 16, 1928, in Charlotte, N.C.; son of Dwight C. and Eunice (Fowler) Hook; married Harriett Blackwell (a librarian), August 18, 1954; children: Karen Fowler, Terence Blackwell. *Education:* Washington and Lee University, student, 1946-48; Emory University, B.A., 1950; University of North Carolina, graduate study, 1957-58; Duke University, M.A., 1958; Brown University, Ph.D., 1961. *Religion:* Episcopalian. *Home:* 1936 Asylum Ave., West Hartford, Conn. 06117. *Agent:* Ann Elmo Agency, Inc., 52 Vanderbilt Ave., New York, N.Y. 10017. *Office:* Department of Modern Languages and Literature, Trinity College, Hartford, Conn. 06106.

CAREER: Trinity College, Hartford, Conn., assistant professor, 1961-69, associate professor, 1969-75, professor of modern languages and literature, 1975—. Visiting professor at University of Rhode Island, University of Hartford, St. Joseph College (West Hartford, Conn.), Central Connecticut State College, and Chadron State College. *Military service:* U.S. Air Force, 1950-55; served in Germany; became first lieutenant. *Member:* American Association of Teachers of German, Linguistic Society of America, American Association of University Professors, Connecticut Council on Language Teaching.

WRITINGS: (With Lothar Kahn) *Intermediate Conversational German*, Van Nostrand, 1963, 3rd edition, 1973; (with Kahn) *Conversational German One*, Van Nostrand, 1970; (with Gerhard Strasser) *Fahrt ins Weiss-Blaue* (title means "Trip into the Blue-White"), Harrap, 1970; (with Kahn) *Stimmen aus deutschen Landen* (title means "Voices from German Lands"), Van Nostrand, 1972; (with Harold von Hofe and others) *Kultur und Alltag* (title means "Culture and Everyday Life"), Scribner, 1973. Contributor to language journals, including *Modern Language Journal, General Linguistics, Association of American Colleges Bulletin, Deutsch als Fromdsprache*, and *American Speech.*

WORK IN PROGRESS: A book about madmen in history, for Jonathan David; editing an anthology of language and feminine liberation; a technical treatise on Gothic conjugation.

SIDELIGHTS: Hook has lived in Europe, has a good knowledge of major European languages, and fluency in German and Czech. *Avocational interests:* Christian history and liturgy.

* * *

HOOVER, John P. 1910-

PERSONAL: Born November 7, 1910, in Burlingame, Calif.; son of Howard Lynn (a railroad official) and Cora Belle (a poet; maiden name, Page) Hoover; married Virginia Lee Froman (a psychotherapist), October 31, 1942; children: John, James, Virginia Lynn, Beverly. *Education:* Attended San Mateo Junior College, 1927-29; Stanford University, A.B., 1931, M.A., 1932; graduate study at Yale University, 1933-34, and Universidad de la Habana, 1938-40; American University, Ph.D., 1967. *Politics:* Republican. *Religion:* Quaker. *Home:* 6622 Braeburn Parkway, Bethesda, Md. 22034. *Office:* 304 Colorado Building, Washington, D.C. 20005.

CAREER: U.S. Department of Commerce, Washington, D.C., tariffs expert, 1934-36, assistant trade commissioner in Guatemala, 1936, and in Havana, Cuba, 1936-39; U.S.

Department of State, vice consul in Havana, Cuba, 1939-42, assistant commercial attache in Caracas, Venezuala, 1942-48, commercial attache in Montevideo, Uruguay, 1948-50, economist in Washington, D.C., 1950-52, consul general in Rhodesia and Nyasaland, 1952-54, consul general in Havana, Cuba, 1954-56, director of U.S. operations mission to Haiti, 1956-58, professor at Foreign Service Institute, 1958-60, policy planning officer in Washington, D.C., 1960-62; Organization of American States, Washington, D.C., acting director of Department of Public Information, 1962-64, special adviser to Secretary General, 1964-68, programs officer, 1968-70, representative in Jamaica, 1970-71, associate editor of *Latin American Service*, 1971—. Adjunct associate professor at Catholic University of America, 1964-70; collaborator with American Friends Service Committee. *Member:* International Club (Washington, D.C.).

WRITINGS: Sucre, Soldado y Revolucionario (title means "Sucre, Soldier, and Revolutionary"), Universidad de Oriente, 1975.

Booklet—All published by Sterling: *Cuba*, 1974; *Nicaragua*, 1974; *El Salvador*, 1974; *Uruguay*, 1975; *Paraguay*, 1975; *French Guiana*, 1975. Contributor to *Boletin de la Academia Nacional de la Historia* and *Americas*.

WORK IN PROGRESS: Newspaper writing.

* * *

HORDON, Harris E(ugene) 1942-

PERSONAL: Born December 31, 1942, in New York, N.Y.; son of Sidney (a certified public accountant) and Betty (Flacks) Hordon; married Carole Schulman (a teacher), July 27, 1969; children: Elana Sue, Robert Jason. *Education:* Brooklyn College of the City University of New York, B.A., 1963; New York University, M.A., 1965, Ph.D., 1968. *Home:* 457 FDR Dr., New York, N.Y. 10002. *Office:* Department of Economics, Jersey City State College, Jersey City, N.J. 07305.

CAREER: New York University, New York, N.Y., lecturer in economics, 1964-66; Northeastern University, Boston, Mass., instructor in economics, 1966-69; U.S. Department of Transportation, Washington, D.C., economist, 1970-71; Jersey City State College, Jersey City, N.J., associate professor of economics, 1969—. Member of Environmental Protection Committee of Citizens Advisory Board of Jersey City, 1972-73. *Member:* American Economic Association. *Awards, honors:* Brookings Institution economic policy fellowship, 1970-71.

WRITINGS: Benefit-Cost Evaluation of Exterior Protection Standard (monograph), U.S. Department of Transportation, 1971; *Economic Evaluation of Occupant Crash Protection Standard* (monograph), U.S. Department of Transportation, 1971; *A Guide to Benefit-Cost Evaluation of Federal Motor-Vehicle Safety Standards* (monograph), U.S. Department of Transportation, 1971; *Introduction to Urban Economics: Analysis and Policy*, Prentice-Hall, 1973.

WORK IN PROGRESS: Research for *New York City: Fiscal Problems and Future Prospects*.

* * *

HORN, Francis H(enry) 1908-

PERSONAL: Born November 18, 1908, in Toledo, Ohio; son of Henry Frederick (a merchant) and Orpha Ford (Bennett) Horn; married Xenia Beliavsky, June 8, 1935; children: Michael Serge, Barbara Ann (Mrs. Helmut Schaefer), Stephanie. *Education:* Dartmouth College, A.B., 1930; University of Virginia, M.A., 1934; Yale University, M.S., 1942, Ph.D., 1949. *Home:* 772 Pelton Ave., Staten Island, N.Y. 10301. *Office:* Wagner College, Staten Island, N.Y. 10301.

CAREER: American University in Cairo, Cairo, Egypt, instructor in English and history, 1930-33; Junior College of Commerce (now Quinnipiac College), New Haven, Conn., assistant dean, 1936-37, acting dean, 1937-38, dean, 1938-42; Cooperative Study of the Lincoln Schools, Lincoln, Neb., editor of reports, 1946-47; Johns Hopkins University, Baltimore, Md., associate professor of education, dean of Evening College, and director of summer session, 1947-51, part-time visiting professor, 1952-53; American Association for Higher Education, Washington, D.C., executive secretary, 1951-53; Pratt Institute, Brooklyn, N.Y., president, 1953-57; Southern Illinois University, Carbondale, distinguished visiting professor of higher education, 1957-58; University of Rhode Island, Kingston, president and professor of higher education, 1958-67; president of Commission on Independent Colleges and Universities, 1967-71; Albertus Magnus College, New Haven, Conn., president, 1971-74, president emeritus, 1974—; Wagner College, Staten Island, N.Y., executive vice-president, 1974—. Co-founder and director, Center for the Study of Liberal Education for Adults (Ford Foundation), 1951-57; member of Commission on the Plans and Objectives for Higher Education, American Council on Education, 1966-69, U.S. National Committee for UNESCO, 1967-70, and Commission for the Advancement of Christian Higher Education in Asia, 1970—; member of board of directors, National Council of Independent Colleges and Universities, 1970-71. Trustee of United Board for Christian Higher Education in Asia, 1959—, Center for the Study of the Presidency, 1969—, and Harvard-Yenching Institute, 1971—. Member of national council, Boy Scouts of America, 1965—, and a director of Near East Foundation and Futures for Children. *Military service:* U.S. Army, 1942-46; assistant dean of Biarritz American University in France, 1945-46; became lieutenant colonel; received Legion of Merit and Army Commendation Medal with oak-leaf cluster. U.S. Army Reserve, 1946-56.

MEMBER: National Education Association (life member), American Association of Junior Colleges, American Alumni Council, United World Federalists (vice-president, New England region, 1965-67), Phi Beta Kappa, Phi Kappa Phi, Phi Delta Kappa, Kappa Delta Pi, Theta Delta Chi, Omicron Delta Kappa, Delta Sigma Pi, Alpha Phi Omega, Alpha Delta Sigma, Pi Sigma Alpha; and numerous other organizations and clubs.

AWARDS, HONORS: More than twenty-five degrees from universities and colleges, including LL.D. from University of Hartford, 1955, Dickinson College, 1961, Brown University, 1963, University of New Hampshire, 1964, University of Maine, 1967, and University of Rhode Island, 1969; L.H.D. from Southern Illinois University, 1958, University of Nevada, 1969, Albertus Magnus College, 1974, and Pratt Institute, 1974; Litt.D., Kon-Kuk University (Korea), 1973. Theta Delta Chi Achievement Award, 1964; Distinguished Public Service Medal, U.S. Navy, 1967; Outstanding Civilian Service Award, U.S. Army, 1967; University of Rhode Island Alumni Award, 1967; Francis E. Horn Marine Science Laboratory at University of Rhode Island was dedicated in his name, 1969, in recognition of his having established the nation's first graduate school of oceanography; associate fellow of Timothy Dwight College, Yale University, 1972.

WRITINGS: (Editor) *Literary Masterpieces of the Western World*, Johns Hopkins Press, 1953; *Challenge and Perspective in Higher Education* (collection of addresses), Southern Illinois University Press, 1971.

Contributor: *Selection and Guidance of Gifted Students for National Survival*, American Council on Education, 1956; Gerald P. Burns, editor, *Administrators in Higher Education*, Harper, 1962; Samuel Baskin, editor, *Higher Education: Some Newer Developments*, McGraw, 1965; Arthur J. Dibden, editor, *The Academic Deanship in American Colleges and Universities*, Southern Illinois University Press, 1968. Contributor to *Representative American Speeches, Inaugural Addresses*, reports of educational conferences, and other symposia.

Editor: General Report of the Cooperative Study of Schools in Lincoln, Neb., 1947; *Current Issues in Higher Education*, 1952, 1953; and *Twenty-Five Years in the Wide, Wide World* (quarter-century report of Dartmouth Class of 1930), 1955. Contributor of more than one hundred articles to journals and about twenty reviews to *New York Times*. Editor, *College and University Bulletin*, 1951-53, and *Newsletter* of the Dartmouth Class of 1930, 1965-67.

SIDELIGHTS: Horn was in Saudi Arabia in 1966 as head of an international commission advising on the establishment of the King Abdulaziz University in Jeddah, and again in 1971 evaluating progress of the university. He went to Sikkim in 1972 as consultant to the King on the establishment of that nation's first institution of higher education. He has made other trips to the Far East as adviser to colleges and universities, traveled in all countries of Europe except Albania, in Africa, the Near and Middle East, and Australasia.

* * *

HORNBEIN, Thomas Frederic 1930-

PERSONAL: Born November 6, 1930, in St. Louis, Mo.; son of Leonard and Rosalie (Bernstein) Hornbein; married Kathryn Mikesell (a pediatrician), December 24, 1971; children: Lia, Lynn, Cari, Andrea, Robert. *Education:* University of Colorado, B.A., 1952; Washington University, St. Louis, Mo., M.D., 1956. *Home:* 366 West Lake Sammamish N.E., Bellevue, Wash. 98008. *Office:* Department of Anesthesiology RN-10, University of Washington School of Medicine, Seattle, Wash. 98195.

CAREER: Anesthesiologist; diplomate of American Board of Anesthesiology. Washington University, St. Louis, Mo., instructor in anesthesiology, 1960-61; University of Washington, School of Medicine, Seattle, assistant professor, 1963-67, associate professor, 1967-70, professor of anesthesiology, physiology, and biophysics, 1970—, vice-chairman of department of anesthesiology, 1972-74, assistant chairman for research of department of anesthesiology, 1974—. *Military service:* U.S. Navy, 1961-63; became lieutenant commander. *Member:* Society of Critical Care Medicine, American Physiological Society, American Society of Anesthesiologists, Association of University Anesthetists (president, 1975-76), King County Medical Society, Phi Beta Kappa. *Awards, honors:* Hubbard Medal from National Geographic Society; George Norlin Award, University of Colorado, 1970.

WRITINGS: *Everest: The West Ridge*, Sierra Club and Ballantine, 1966. Contributor: T. C. Ruch and H. D. Patton, editors, *Physiology and Biophysics*, Saunders, 19th edition, 1965, 20th edition, 1974. Editor of *American Physiological Society Bulletin*, 1967-73.

WORK IN PROGRESS: Physiological studies on regulation of breathing and brain ion regulation.

SIDELIGHTS: In 1963, as members of the American Mount Everest Expedition, Dr. Hornbein and Willie Unsoeld completed the first ascent of Mount Everest by the West Ridge. This event motivated Hornbein to write *Everest: The West Ridge*.

* * *

HORNE, Frank S. 1899-1974

1899(?)—September 7, 1974; American race relations administrator, poet. Obituaries: *New York Times*, September 8, 1974.

* * *

HORNSTEIN, Harvey A. 1938-

PERSONAL: Born November 16, 1938, in Brooklyn, N.Y.; son of Joseph and Florence (Schneider) Hornstein; married second wife, Madeline Heilman (an assistant professor at Yale University). *Education:* City College (now of the City University of New York), B.B.A., 1960; Columbia University, M.A., 1962, Ph.D., 1964. *Office:* Department of Psychology, Teachers College, Columbia University, New York, N.Y. 10027.

CAREER: Yeshiva University, New York, N.Y., visiting lecturer in psychology, 1963-64; Columbia University, Teachers College, New York, N.Y., research assistant to Morton Deutsch, 1963-66, research associate, Horace Mann-Lincoln Institute, 1964-66, assistant professor, 1966-68, associate professor, 1968-74, professor of psychology and education, 1974—, research associate, Institute for Policy Research. National Training Laboratories Institute for the Applied Behavioral Sciences, associate, 1966-69, fellow, 1969, adjunct project director, 1970, director of Center for Professional Development, 1971. *Member:* American Psychological Association, Society for the Psychological Study of Social Issues, Eastern Psychological Association, New York State Psychological Association (division president, 1972-73; member of board of directors, 1972-75).

WRITINGS: (Editor, author of introduction, and contributor) *Social Intervention: A Behavioral Science Approach*, Free Press, 1971; (with W. W. Burke) *The Social Technology of Organization Development*, Learning Resources Corp., 1972. Contributor to other books and to journals.

WORK IN PROGRESS: *The Human Side: A Psychological Analysis of Helping*; experimental investigations on we-group boundaries, promotive tension, and helping.

SIDELIGHTS: Hornstein regularly travels to Europe to train organization development specialists for various companies including Procter & Gamble, Imperial Chemical Industries, Shell Oil, Irish Airlines, Mobil Europe, and Irish Management Institute.

* * *

HORTON, Lowell 1936-

PERSONAL: Born October 22, 1936, in Oak Hill, Ohio; son of Wayne (a county clerk) and Francic (Jones) Horton; married Phyllis Bauer (a teacher), 1957; children: David. *Education:* Rio Grande College, B.S., 1960; Ohio University, M.Ed., 1962; Ohio State University, Ph.D., 1969. *Home:* 1203 Elizabeth, DeKalb, Ill. 60115. *Office:* Department of Education, 333 Williston Hall, Northern Illinois University, DeKalb, Ill. 60115.

CAREER: Elementary school teacher in Circleville, Ohio, 1959-60, in Xenia, Ohio, 1960-62, and principal, 1962-66; Central State University, Wilberforce, Ohio, assistant professor of education and assistant to the president, 1966-68; Wittenberg University, Springfield, Ohio, assistant professor of education, 1968-69; Northern Illinois University, DeKalb, 1969—, began as associate professor, now professor of education. *Member:* American Federation of Teachers, Association for Supervision and Curriculum Development, Phi Delta Kappa.

WRITINGS: Learning Centers: Heart of the School, Denison, 1973; *Teacher Education: Trends, Issues, Innovations*, Interstate, 1974. Contributor of more than one hundred articles to professional journals.

WORK IN PROGRESS: The Self Renewing Teacher.

* * *

HORVAT, Branko 1928-

PERSONAL: Born July 24, 1928, in Petrinja, Yugoslavia; son of Artur (a surgeon) and Dolores (a music teacher; maiden name, Stoehr) Horvat; married Ranka Peasinovic (a research worker), 1952; children: Branka, Olga. *Education:* Zagreb University, diploma in economics, 1952, D.Sc., 1955; Manchester University, Ph.D., 1959. *Politics:* Socialist. *Home:* 101 V. Rolovica, Belgrade, Yugoslavia. *Office:* Institute of Economic Studies, Zmaj Jovina 12, Belgrade, Yugoslavia; and Department of International Economy, Zagreb University, Zagreb, Yugoslavia.

CAREER: Institute of Economics, Zagreb, Yugoslavia, research associate, 1953-55; head of research department of Federal Planning Bureau and member of Federal Planning Board, 1958-62; University of Belgrade, Belgrade, Yugoslavia, associate professor of economics, 1962-63; Institute of Economic Studies, Belgrade, professor of economics, 1963—, director of Institute, 1963-70. Titular docent, Zagreb University, 1959; Ford Foundation fellow at Harvard University and Massachusetts Institute of Technology, 1964-65; visiting professor at University of Ljubljana, University of Stockholm, University of Chile, University of Michigan, and American University, Washington, D.C.; has lectured at about fifty universities in Europe, Africa, and United States. Government of Yugoslavia, member of economic council, 1963-65, member of committee for market and prices, 1967-71, economic advisor to prime minister, 1972. Has advised governments of Peru, Brazil, and Bangladesh. *Military service:* Served in Partisan War of Liberation, 1944-45; received medal of merit. *Member:* International Association for Research in Income and Wealth, Econometric Society, Yugoslav Economic Association, Yugoslav Statistical Society.

WRITINGS: Industrija nafte u Jugoslaviji (title means "History of the Yugoslav Oil Industry"), three volumes, Yugoslav Institute of Economic Research (Belgrade), 1956-65; *Ekonomska teorija planske privrede*, Kultura, 1961, revised translation published as *Towards a Theory of Planned Economy*, Yugoslav Institute of Economic Research, 1964; *Ekonomski modeli* (title means "Economic Models"), Economic Institute (Zagreb), 1962; *Ekonomika jugoslovenske naftne privrede* (title means "Economics of Yugoslav Oil Industry"), Tehnicka Knjiga, 1962; *Medusektorska analiza* (titel means "Interindustry Analysis"), Narodne Novine, 1962; *Ekonomska nauka i narodna privreda* (title means "Economic Science and National Ecomomy"), Kultura, 1967; *Privredni ciklusi u Jugoslaviji*, Institute of Economic Studies (Belgrade), 1969, translation by Helen M. Kramer published as *Business Cycle in Yugoslavia*, International Arts and Sciences Press, 1971; *Ogled o jugoslavenskom drustvu*, Mladost, 1969, translation by Henry F. Mins published as *An Essay on Yugoslav Society*, International Arts and Sciences Press, 1969.

Ekonomska politika stabilizacije (title means "Economics of Stabilization"), Oeconomica, 1975; (with Mihailo Markovic and Rudi Supek) *Self-Governing Socialism*, International Arts and Sciences Press, 1975. Author of about twelve monographs published by Institute of Economic Studies, Belgrade, 1963-74. Contributor to *Yugoslav Encyclopedia*, and to professional journals. Editor, *Economic Analysis*, 1967—; member of editorial boards, *European Economic Review*, 1970—, *Review of Income and Wealth*, 1972—, and *World Development*, 1973—.

WORK IN PROGRESS: The Theory of Socialism, completion expected in 1975.

SIDELIGHTS: Various of Horvat's books and articles have been translated into nine languages, including French, German, Hungarian, Italian, Russian, and Swedish. Horvat has reading knowledge of Bulgarian, Macedonian, Slovenian, English, French, German, Italian, Polish, Russian, Spanish, and Swedish.

BIOGRAPHICAL/CRITICAL SOURCES: American Economic Review, Number 3, 1967.

* * *

HOUSE, Robert W(illiam) 1920-

PERSONAL: Born November 28, 1920, in Bristow, Okla.; son of Richard Morton (a teacher) and Elizabeth (Swartz) House; married Esther Hawkins, June 5, 1943; children: Edmund, Richard, Russell, Kathryn. *Education:* Oklahoma State University, B.F.A., 1941; Eastman School of Music, M.Mus., 1942; summer graduate study at Northwestern University, 1951; University of Illinois, Ed.D., 1954. *Home address:* R.R. 8, Carbondale, Ill. 62901. *Office:* Director, School of Music, Southern Illinois University, Carbondale, Ill. 62901.

CAREER: Murray State College (now University), Murray, Ky., instructor in music theory, 1942; Nebraska State College, Kearney, assistant professor of band and cello, 1946-55; University of Minnesota, Duluth, associate professor, 1955-59, professor of music, 1959-67, head of department, 1955-67; Southern Illinois University, Carbondale, professor of music, 1967—, director of School of Music, 1967—. Principal cellist for Kearney (Neb.) Symphony, 1946-55, and Duluth (Minn.) Symphony, 1955-67; cellist with University String Quartet, University of Minnesota, 1955-67; composer. *Military service:* U.S. Army, 1942-46; served in Europe. *Member:* Music Education Research Council (chairman, 1958-60), Music Educators National Conference (president-elect of North Central Division, 1974-76), National Association of Schools of Music, American String Teachers Association, Minnesota Music Educators Association (vice-president, 1965-67), Phi Delta Kappa, Phi Mu Alpha, Pi Kappa Lambda.

WRITINGS: (With Charles Leonhard) *Foundations and Principles of Music Education*, McGraw, 1959, revised edition, 1972; *Instrumental Music for Today's Schools*, Prentice-Hall, 1965; *Administration in Music Education*,

Prentice-Hall, 1973. Contributor to music education journals. Member of editorial board of *Journal of Research in Music Education*, 1958-70.

* * *

HOWARD, Barbara 1930-

PERSONAL: Born April 7, 1930, in Mobile, Ala.; daughter of Charles Brock (a bus driver) and Alma (a civil servant; maiden name, Jernigan) Peavy; married Richard Perry Howard (a church historian), June 7, 1953; children: Les, Jim, Joy, Kipley. *Education:* Graceland College, A.A., 1949, B.A., 1974; also studied at University of Missouri at Kansas City, 1967-68, Central Missouri State College, 1968-69, and St. Paul's School of Theology, 1973—. *Religion:* Reorganized Church of Jesus Christ of Latter-Day Saints. *Residence:* Independence, Mo.

CAREER: Secretary in California, 1954-58; substitute teacher in public schools in Independence, Mo., 1967-70; magazine editor, 1970—. *Member:* Common Cause, League of Women Voters, Women's Political Caucus, Another Mother for Peace.

WRITINGS: The Scriptures Speak to Women Today, Herald House, 1964; *The Church in Mission* (for young people), Herald House, 1973; *Be Swift to Love*, Herald House, 1974. Author of "Parable," a column in *Saints Herald*, 1973. Editor of *Stride* and of children's magazines, *Daily Bread*, *Steps*, *Hopes*, *Vistas*, and assistant editor of *Saints' Herald*, 1970—.

WORK IN PROGRESS: Research for a book about the history of the missions of the Reorganized Church of Jesus Christ of Latter-Day Saints.

* * *

HOWARD, Clive ?-1974

?—November 28, 1974; American public relations man, author. Obituaries: *New York Times*, December 1, 1974; *AB Bookman's Weekly*, December 16, 1974.

* * *

HOWARD, John R(obert) 1933-

PERSONAL: Born January 24, 1933, in Boston, Mass.; son of John Robert (a laborer) and Louise (Harris) Howard; married Mary Doris Adams (a professor), June 22, 1968. *Education:* Boston University, A.A., 1953; Brandeis University, B.A., 1955; University of California, Berkeley, graduate study, 1955-56; New York University, M.A., 1961; Stanford University, Ph.D., 1965. *Office:* Division of Social Sciences, State University of New York College at Purchase, Purchase, N.Y. 10552.

CAREER: San Francisco State College (now University), San Francisco, Calif., instructor in social welfare, 1964; University of Oregon, Eugene, assistant professor of sociology, 1964-68, associate director of Institute for the Study of School Desegregation, 1966-67; City College of the City University of New York, New York, N.Y., assistant professor of sociology, 1968-69; Rutgers University, New Brunswick, N.J., associate professor of sociology, 1969-71, director of Black studies program of Livingston College, 1969-70; State University of New York College at Purchase, professor of sociology and dean of Division of Social Sciences, 1971—. Research assistant at Institute for the Study of Human Problems (Stanford, Calif.), 1963-64; research associate at Rice University, 1966. *Awards, honors:* Woodrow Wilson Fellowship, 1955-56.

WRITINGS: (With William McCord, Bernard Friedberg, and Edwin Harwood) *Life Styles in the Black Ghetto*, Norton, 1969; *The Hippie College Dropout* (monograph), U.S. Office of Education, 1969; (editor with Steven E. Deutsch) *Where It's At: Radical Perspectives in Sociology*, Harper, 1970; (editor) *The Awakening Minorities: American Indians, Mexican Americans, Puerto Ricans*, Aldine, 1970; *The Cutting Edge: Social Movements and Social Change in America*, Lippincott, 1974.

Contributor: Raymond Mack, editor, *Race, Class, and Power*, American Book Co., 2nd edition, 1968; Don Bower and Louis Massotti, editors, *Riots and Rebellion: Civil Violence in the Urban Community*, Sage Publications, 1968; R. Friedman, editor, *Compulsory Service System*, Artcraft, 1969.

Roberta Segal, editor, *Learning about Politics*, Random House, 1970; Lee Rainwater, editor, *The Black Experience: Soul*, Aldine, 1970; I. L. Horowitz and Mary Strong, editors, *Sociological Realities*, Harper, 1971; Robert T. Golembiewski, Charles S. Bullock III, and Harrell R. Rodgers, Jr., editors, *The New Politics: Polarization or Utopia*, McGraw, 1971; Nils I. Bateman and David M. Peterson, editors, *Targets for Change: Perspectives on an Active Sociology*, Xerox Corp., 1971; Horowitz, editor, *The Use and Abuse of Sociology*, Aldine, 1971; Edward Sagarin, editor, *The Other Minorities*, Blaisdell, 1971; Morris Medley and James E. Conyers, editors and publishers, *Sociology for the Seventies*, 1972; Lewis M. Killian and Ralph Turner, editors, *Crowd and Mass Behavior*, Prentice-Hall, 1972; Ruth Shonle Cavan, editor, *Readings in Juvenile Delinquency*, Lippincott, 1972; Elliott Aronson and Robert Helmreich, editors, *Social Psychology in the World Today*, Van Nostrand, 1973; Robert R. Evans, editor, *Social Movements*, Rand McNally, 1973; Kenneth M. Dolbeare and Murray J. Edelman, editors, *Institutions, Politics, and Goals: A Reader in American Politics*, Heath, 1973; Patricia Keith-Spiegel and Don Spiegel, editors, *The Outsiders USA*, Rinehart Press, 1973; Harold Hodges, editor, *Conflict and Consensus: Readings Toward a Sociological Perspective*, Harper, 1973; T. Ford Hoult, editor, *Sociology for a New Day*, Random House, 1974; Sawyer Sylvester and Sagarin, editors, *Politics and Crime*, Praeger, 1974; Richard T. Schaeffer, editor, *People and Prejudice: Minorities in the United States*, Xerox College Publishing, in press; Joseph Boskin and Robert Rosenstone, editors, *Seasons of Rebellion*, Holt, in press.

Contributor to *Trans-Action, American Behavioral Scientist, Forensic Quarterly*, and *Annals of the American Academy of Political and Social Science*. Associate editor of *Trans-Action*, 1969-73; consulting editor for Lippincott, 1971-74.

WORK IN PROGRESS: A Murder to Remember, a novel.

* * *

HOWARD, Maureen 1930-

PERSONAL: Born June 28, 1930, in Bridgeport, Conn.; daughter of William L. (a county detective) and Loretta (Burns) Keans; married Daniel F. Howard, August 28, 1954 (divorced, 1967); married David J. Gordon (a professor), April 2, 1968; children: (first marriage) Loretta Howard. *Education:* Smith College, B.A., 1952. *Agent:* Betty Ann Clarke, International Creative Management, 1301 Avenue of the Americas, New York, N.Y. 10019.

CAREER: Employed in publishing and advertising, 1952-

54; University of California, Santa Barbara, lecturer in English, drama, 1968-69; New School for Social Research, New York, N.Y., lecturer in English, creative writing, 1967-68, 1970-71, 1974—. *Awards, honors:* Guggenheim fellowship, 1967-68; fellow of Radcliffe Institute, 1967-68.

WRITINGS: Not a Word about Nightingale, Atheneum, 1961; *Bridgeport Bus*, Harcourt, 1966; *Before My Time*, Little, Brown, 1975.

WORK IN PROGRESS: A play; an autobiography.

AVOCATIONAL INTERESTS: Gardening, cooking.

BIOGRAPHICAL/CRITICAL SOURCES: Sewanee Review, winter, 1974-75; *New York Times Book Review*, January 19, 1975.

* * *

HOWARD, Michael S. 1922-1974

1922—December 10, 1974; British publishing executive, editor, author. Obituaries: *AB Bookman's Weekly*, January 27, 1975.

* * *

HOWARD, Richard C. 1929-

PERSONAL: Born May 13, 1929, in New York, N.Y.; son of Charles Stanley and Edna (Deehan) Howard; married Anna Marie Janes (a nurse), September 22, 1959; children: Wendy, Stanley, Ian. *Education:* State University of New York College at Oneonta, B.S., 1953; San Francisco State College (now University), M.A., 1964; University of Arizona, C.A.G.S., 1965; Syracuse University, doctoral student, 1967—. *Home:* 23 Juniper Trail, Narragansett, R.I. 02882. *Office:* Department of Educational Media, University of Rhode Island, Kingston, R.I. 02881.

CAREER: Elementary school teacher in New Jersey, 1953-54, New York, 1954-57, and California, 1957-63; Eastern Oregon College, La Grande, assistant professor of education, 1963-65; Syracuse University, Syracuse, N.Y., lecturer in library science, 1968-69; University of Rhode Island, Kingston, assistant professor of educational media, 1969—, associate director of media, 1969-73, acting director, 1973-74. *Military service:* U.S. Navy, 1946-48; served in European theater. *Member:* Association for Education, Communications, and Technology, Rhode Island Educational Media Association (vice-president).

WRITINGS: (With Bruce Dewey) *Media and Instructional Technology in the Library*, Oxhandler Memorial Library, Syracuse University, 1968; *Educational Technology, Teaching, and Learning*, Simon & Schuster, 1974. Contributor to *Rhode Island Audio Visual Education Association Newsletters*.

WORK IN PROGRESS: A textbook on film usage in the classroom; two educational films dealing with instructional modes and theory of learning.

AVOCATIONAL INTERESTS: Oil painting, films, music, sailing and sailboats (built his own sailboat and plans to sail around the world).

* * *

HOWE, Charles H(orace) 1912-
(Carleton Howard)

PERSONAL: Born April 25, 1912, in Whiteside, Ill.; son of Abner R. and Clara Belle (Sherwood) Howe. *Education:* University of Illinois, A.B., 1941; University of California, Los Angeles, graduate study, 1945-48; University of Southern California, M.A., 1951. *Religion:* Methodist. *Home:* 1412 East Fourth St., Sterling, Ill. 61081. *Office:* Department of English, Danville Junior College, 2000 East Main St., Danville, Ill. 61832.

CAREER: Grammar school teacher in Carroll County, Ill., 1934-40; high school teacher in Somers, Ia., 1940-41, Powell, Wyo., 1946-47, Las Vegas, Nev., 1948-49, in California and Michigan, 1951-54, and in Chicago, Ill., 1955-61; Danville Junior College, Danville, Ill., instructor in English, 1961—. *Military service:* U.S. Army, 1942-45; served in Europe and in D-Day invasion on Utah Beach. *Member:* World Poetry Society International, American Poetry League, American Mosaic, National Education Association, American Poets Fellowship Society, Avalon, Illinois Poetry Society, Illinois Education Association, California Federation of Chaparral Poets, Poetry Society of Southern California (first vice-president, 1951), Pasadena Chaparral Poets (president, 1950), Powell Classroom Teachers Association (president, 1947), Santa Monica Writers Club (historian, 1948; recording secretary, 1949).

WRITINGS: Black-Panther-Search (poetry), Wagon & Star, 1951; *Uranium and Kneeling Elephants* (poetry), Dorrance, 1974. Contributor of more than 150 short stories under pseudonym Carleton Howard, and articles and poems to periodicals on six continents. Free verse editor of *Swordsman Review*, 1971-73; poetry critic of *Tejas*, 1974—.

WORK IN PROGRESS: Prairie Plumes and Purple Peacocks, for Westburg; a book tentatively titled *Curled Foxes in an Orange Sun*, Mitre Press.

* * *

HOYLE, Geoffrey 1942-

PERSONAL: Born January 12, 1942, in Scunthorpe, Lancashire, England; son of Fred (a scientist and author) and Barbara (Clark) Hoyle; married Valerie Jane Coope (an accountant), April 21, 1971. *Education:* Attended St. John's College, Cambridge, 1961-62. *Home:* 11 Carlyle Rd., Cambridge CB4 3DN, England.

CAREER: Worked in documentary film production, 1963-67; novelist, 1967—.

WRITINGS—Novels, with father, Fred Hoyle: *Fifth Planet*, Harper, 1963; *Rockets in Ursa Major*, Harper, 1969; *Seven Steps to the Sun*, Harper, 1970; *The Molecule Men*, Harper, 1971; *Inferno*, Harper, 1973; *Into Deepest Space*, Harper, 1974.

For children: *2010: Living in the Future*, Parents Magazine Press, 1972; *Disaster*, Heinemann, 1975.

AVOCATIONAL INTERESTS: Motor racing, skiing, target-shooting.

* * *

HUEBNER, Anna (Ismelda Mathews) 1877(?)-1974

1877(?)—August 2, 1974; American educator and author of textbooks on English grammar. Obituaries: *New York Times*, August 6, 1974; *Washington Post*, August 6, 1974.

* * *

HUGGETT, Richard 1929-

PERSONAL: Born April 25, 1929, in London, England; son of Arthur St. George (a professor of physiology) and Marguerite Mary (Head) Huggett. *Education:* Attended Ampleforth College, Central School of Dramatic Arts, and

St. Paul's, London. *Address:* New Arts Theatre Club, Great Newport St., London W.C.2, England.

CAREER: Actor, 1950—; author. *Military service:* British Army, 1948-49. *Member:* British Actors' Equity Association.

WRITINGS: The Truth about "Pygmalion" (theatrical history), Heinemann, 1969, Random House, 1970; *The First Night of "Pygmalion"* (play; produced at Edinburgh Festival, 1968), Faber, 1970; (compiler) *The Wit of the Catholics*, Frewin, 1971; (compiler) *The Wit and Humor of Sex*, Quartet, 1975; *Supernatural on Stage*, Taplinger, 1975. Also author, with others, of plays, "Oh Calcutta," and "Weekend with Willie." Contributor to periodicals, including *Saturday Book*, *Theatre 74*, *Punch*, *Harper's Bazaar*, *Penthouse*, *Mayfair*, and *Spectator*.

SIDELIGHTS: It is reported that George Bernard Shaw once suggested to Mrs. Patrick Campbell that she write the "true story of 'Pygmalion,'" that it "would make all England and North America laugh uproariously." Mrs. Campbell, who starred in the first production of that play, did not write the story, but, according to Raymond A. Sokolov, Richard Huggett's version is "every bit as funny as Shaw had predicted." In Claire Cresswell's words, "[Huggett] does not get stuck in the marshmallow of shallow showbiz nostalgia; nor slobber in adulation of the Beautiful People; nor ape the wit of the protagonists. [He] records the boom of temperaments clashing, the temperments of George Bernard Shaw, Mrs. Patrick Campbell, and Sir Herbert Beerbohm Tree . . . with brisk wit." *Avocational interests:* Bicycling, boxing, tennis, cooking, photography.

* * *

HUGGETT, William Turner

PERSONAL: Born in Minneapolis, Min. *Education.* Emory University, A.B.; University of Florida, J.D. *Residence:* Miami, Fla.

CAREER: Former High school teacher of American history in Atlanta, Ga.; served as legal aide to U.S. District Court Judge William O. Mehrtens, to Florida State Senator, Ted Cabot, and to Florida State Legislature's Dade County senate delegation to Talahassee, 1967; formerly associated with law firm of Beckham and McAliley; private practice of law in Miami, Fla., 1973—. Florida agent for a New York-based advertising and film promotion firm. *Military service:* U.S. Marine Corps, infantry combat officer and pacification adviser, 1967-69; served in Vietnam. *Member:* Dade County Bar Young Lawyers Association (president). *Awards, honors: Body Count* won the 1973 Putnam Award for special excellence.

WRITINGS: Body Count (novel), Putnam, 1973. War correspondent in Israel for *Miami Herald,* 1973. Contributor to *Tropic* (magazine of *Miami Herald*).

WORK IN PROGRESS: Revising Arab-Israeli war correspondence from *Miami Herald,* for publication in book form.

SIDELIGHTS: In addition to a routine trial practice, Huggett is deeply involved in environmental litigation and First Amendment rights lawsuits. *Avocational interests:* Photography, sailing, skin diving, international travel (has lived in Greece).

* * *

HUGHES, John Paul 1920-1974

June 22, 1920—October 26, 1974; American educator, editor, author of books on language. Obituaries: *New York Times*, October 28, 1974; *AB Bookman's Weekly*, November 18, 1974. (*CA*-1).

* * *

HULET, Claude Lyle 1920-

PERSONAL: Born December 22, 1920, in Pontiac, Mich.; son of Arno Lincoln (a teacher) and Grace (a teacher; maiden name, Johnson) Hulet; married Norma Christine Bennett, May 30, 1942; children: Claude, Roger, Richard. *Education:* Attended Universidad Autonoma de Mexico, 1941, and English Language Institute, 1942; University of Michigan, B.A., 1942, M.A., 1947, Ph.D., 1954. *Religion:* Protestant. *Home:* 9511 Jumilla Ave., Chatsworth, Calif. 91311. *Office:* Department of Spanish and Portuguese, University of California at Los Angeles, Los Angeles, Calif. 90024.

CAREER: Washington University, St. Louis, Mo., instructor, 1951-54, assistant professor of Spanish and Portuguese, 1954-58; University of California at Los Angeles, assistant professor, 1958-64, associate professor, 1964-70, professor of Spanish and Portuguese, 1970—, assistant coordinator of Brazil Student Leader Seminar, 1963-66, coordinator, 1966-73, chairman of Romance Linguistics and Literature program, 1974—. Director of Instituto Guatemalteco Americano, 1946. *Military service:* U.S. Army Air Forces, 1942-45; became technical sergeant. *Member:* Modern Language Association of America, American Association of Teachers of Spanish and Portuguese, Instituto Internacional de Literatura Iberoamericana, Philological Association of Pacific Coast, Pacific Coast Council on Latin American Studies, Modern and Classical Language Association of Southern California, Phi Kappa Phi. *Awards, honors:* Organization of American States fellowship to Brazil, 1960; Fulbright-Hays fellowship to Brazil, 1964; Machado de Assis Medal from Brazilian Academy of Letters, 1968; Order of Rio Branco, rank of cavaleiro, from Brazilian Government, 1969; Instituto de Alta Cultura fellowship to Portugal, 1972; Fulbright-Hays travel grant to Portugal, 1972.

WRITINGS: Latin American Prose in English Translation: A Bibliography, Pan American Union, 1964; *Latin American Poetry in English Translation: A Bibliography,* Pan American Union, 1965; *Brazilian Literature,* four volumes, Georgetown University Press, 1974. Associate editor of *Hispania,* 1963—.

WORK IN PROGRESS: Anthologies of Spanish-American literature and of Brazilian literature in English translation; studies on Spanish-American and Brazilian culture; a study of popular ballads in Northeast Brazil.

* * *

HULL, George F. 1909(?)-1974

1909(?)—November, 1974; American editor, photographer, author. Obituaries: *New York Times*, November 21, 1974.

* * *

HULL, R(ichard F(rancis) C(arrington) 1913(?)-1974

1913(?)—December 16, 1974; British translator. Obituaries: *New York Times*, December 20, 1974; *AB Bookman's Weekly*, January 27, 1975; *Publishers Weekly*, January 27, 1975.

HUMPHRIES, Mary 1905-
(Mary Forrester)

PERSONAL: Born June 15, 1905, in London, England; daughter of Sidney (a barrister) and Eliza (Whittaker) Humphries. *Education:* University of London, Westfield College, B.A. (honors), 1928, King's College, teacher's diploma, 1929. *Religion:* Church of England.

CAREER: Civil servant in London, England, 1940-47; Methuen & Co. Ltd., London, England, publisher's assistant, 1947-63. Remedial teacher and coach of foreign students, 1967-73. *Member:* Society of Authors.

WRITERS: (Under pseudonym Mary Forrester) *Introduction to Great Artists,* Blandford Press, 1965, Barnes & Noble, 1967; *A World That Sings: The Story of Llangollen International Musical Eisteddfod,* John Jones (Cardiff), 1972. Composer of children's opera.

WORK IN PROGRESS: Research on history of Llangollen where the International Musical Eisteddfod takes place; a second book on great artists.

AVOCATIONAL INTERESTS: Travel.

* * *

HUNT, J. William, Jr. 1930-

PERSONAL: Born August 26, 1930, in Boston, Mass.; son of J. William (a post office inspector) and Mary (a teacher; maiden name, Canniff) Hunt. *Education:* Fordham University, B.A., 1954, Ph.L., 1955; Georgetown University, M.A., 1957; Yale University, Ph.D., 1963. *Politics:* "Democrat (independently)." *Religion:* Roman Catholic. *Home:* 1623 Turtle Creek West Dr., South Bend, Ind. 46637. *Office:* Department of Modern and Classical Languages, University of Notre Dame, Notre Dame, Ind. 46556.

CAREER: Georgetown University, Washington, D.C., instructor in classics, 1955-59, director of debate, 1955-58; Brown University, Providence, R.I., assistant professor of English and comparative literature, 1963-67; University of Massachusetts, Amherst, assistant professor of English and comparative literature, 1967-71; University of Notre Dame, Notre Dame, Ind., associate professor of classics and comparative literature, 1971—. Director of drama at Marymount College, Arlington, Va., 1958-59; reader for Princeton University Press, 1966—. *Member:* Modern Language Association of America, American Comparative Literature Association, American Philological Association, Dante Society of America, Renaissance Society of America, Indiana Classical Conference, Eta Sigma Chi. *Awards, honors:* Woodrow Wilson fellowship, 1962-63; Danforth Foundation associate fellow, 1974—.

WRITINGS: Forms of Glory: Structure and Sense in Virgil's Aeneid, Southern Illinois University Press, 1973. Associate editor of *American Comparative Literature Association Journal,* 1964-67.

SIDELIGHTS: Hunt is committed to student counseling, and has been a resident fellow for fourteen years at four universities. *Avocational interests:* Viennese classical music, nineteenth-century painting.

* * *

HURLEY, Mark J(oseph, Jr.) 1919-

PERSONAL: Born December 13, 1919, in San Francisco, Calif.; son of Mark J. and Josephine (Keohane) Hurley. *Education:* St. Joseph's College, Mountain View, Calif., student, 1937-39; St. Patrick's Seminary, Menlo Park, Calif., B.A., 1944; University of California, Berkeley, M.A., 1945; Catholic University of America, Ph.D., 1947; Lateran University, J.C.B., 1963. *Office:* Diocese of Santa Rosa, P.O. Box 1297, Santa Rosa, Calif. 95403.

CAREER: Ordained Roman Catholic priest, 1944; high school teacher in San Mateo, Calif., 1944; assistant superintendent of Roman Catholic schools in San Francisco, Calif., 1944-51; principal of Roman Catholic high school in Oakland, Calif., 1951-58, and in Marin County, Calif., 1959-61; superintendent of Roman Catholic schools in Stockton, Calif., 1962-65; assistant chancellor of Archdiocese of San Francisco, Calif., 1965-69; bishop of Santa Rosa, Calif., 1969—. Named domestic prelate by Pope John XXIII, 1962; appointed titular bishop of Thunusuda and Auxiliary of San Francisco, 1967, consecrated, 1968; administrator of churches in Santa Rosa, 1959, and San Francisco, 1961; peritus to Vatican Council, 1962-65; chancellor of Diocese of Stockton, 1962-65; auxiliary bishop of San Francisco, 1967-69; member of three committees of Vatican Council. Has taught at Loyola University (Baltimore), University of San Francisco, San Francisco College for Women, Dominican College, and Catholic University of America; member of board of trustees of North American College (Rome), 1970. Regular speaker on "Faith of Our Fathers," weekly television program, 1956-58, and panelist on "Problems Please," 1961-69. Member of board of directors of State of California Committee for the Study of Education, 1955-60; delegate to White House Conference on Youth, 1960. *Awards, honors:* LL.D. From University of Portland, 1971.

WRITINGS: Church-State Relationships in Education in California, Catholic University of America, 1948; *Course of Studies for Elementary Schools Social Studies*, San Francisco Archdiocesan Schools, 1949; *Report on Education in Peru*, National Catholic Education Association, 1965; *Commentary on Declaration of Christian Education of Vatican II*, Paulist-Newman, 1966; *Privacy: An Inalienable Right?*, U.S. Catholic Conference Publications Office, 1974. Author of a syndicated column, "The Question Mark," appearing in *San Francisco Monitor, Sacramento Herald, Oakland Voice, Yakima Our Times*, and *Guam Diocesan Press*, 1949-66.

* * *

HURST, Norman 1944-

PERSONAL: Born July 23, 1944, in Albany, Ore.; son of A. Jefferson (a laborer) and Elaine (Harader) Hurst; married Nadine Kraman (a potter), September 5, 1967. *Education:* Harvard University, A.B., 1967. *Home:* 7 Sumner Rd., Cambridge, Mass. 02138.

CAREER: Photographer in Cambridge, Mass.

WRITINGS: (With Roswell Angier) *The Patriot Game*, Godine, 1975.

* * *

HURSTFIELD, Joel 1911-

PERSONAL: Born November 4, 1911, in London, England; married Elizabeth Valmai Walters; children: one daughter, one son. *Education:* University College, London, B.A. (first class honors), 1934. *Office:* Department of History, University College, Gower St., London WC1E 6BT, England.

CAREER: University of Southampton, University College, Southampton, England, lecturer in history, 1937-40; National Savings Committee, London, England, assistant commissioner, 1940-42; Offices of War Cabinet, London, official historian, 1942-46; University of London, London, England, lecturer in history at Queen Mary College, 1946-51, University College, lecturer, 1951-53, reader, 1953-59, professor of history, 1959-62, Astor Professor of English History, 1962—, fellow, 1967—, Public Orator, 1967-71. Visiting professor at Northwestern University, 1967; Shakespeare Birthday lecturer, Washington, D.C., 1969; first Leverton Lecturer, Fairleigh Dickinson University, 1971; James Ford Special Lecturer in History, Oxford University, 1972; senior research fellow at Folger Shakespeare Library, 1973. *Member:* Royal Historical Society, Athenaeum Club. *Awards, honors:* Pollard and Gladstone Prizeman; D.Lit. from University of London, 1964.

WRITINGS: Control of Raw Materials, H.M.S.O., 1953; *The Queen's Wards: Wardship and Marriage under Elizabeth I*, Harvard University Press, 1958, 2nd edition, International School Book Service, 1973; *Elizabeth I and the Unity of England*, Macmillan, 1960, reprinted, Harper, 1969; *The Elizabethan Nation*, British Broadcasting Corp., 1964, Harper, 1967; *Freedom, Corruption and Government in Elizabethan England*, Harvard University Press, 1973.

Editor: (With S. T. Bindoff and C. H. Williams) *Elizabethan Government and Society: Essays Presented to Sir John Neale*, Oxford University Press, 1961; *Tudor Times*, Routledge & Kegan Paul, 1964; (with James R. Sutherland) *Shakespeare's World*, St. Martin's, 1964; *The Reformation Crisis*, Edward Arnold, 1965, Barnes & Noble, 1966; (with Alan G. R. Smith) *Elizabethan People: State and Society*, St. Martin's, 1972; *The Historical Association Book of the Tudors*, St. Martin's, 1973.

Contributor to *Transactions of the Royal Historical Society*; also contributor of articles and reviews to journals and periodicals, including *American Historical Review, English History Review, Economic History Review, London Times, Telegraph, Guardian,* and *Spectator.*

WORK IN PROGRESS: Research on politics and society in the sixteenth century.

* * *

HUTCHINGS, Patrick A(elfred) 1929-

PERSONAL: Born October 26, 1929, in Wellington, New Zealand; son of Alfred Robert (a civil servant) and Helen Mary (FitzGerald) Hutchings; married Susan Josephine Harding, December 22, 1955. *Education:* University of New Zealand, B.A., 1950, M.A., 1951, certificate of proficiency in philosophy, 1954; University College, Oxford, B.Litt., 1959. *Home:* 51 Kimberly St., West Leederville, Perth, Western Australia 6007. *Office:* Department of Philosophy, University of Western Australia, Crawley, Western Australia 6009.

CAREER: English master in private school in Wellington, New Zealand, 1952-53; University of New Zealand, Victoria College (now Victoria University of Wellington), Wellington, junior lecturer in philosophy, 1954-55; University of Western Australia, Crawley, lecturer, 1955-57, senior lecturer, 1961-68, associate professor of philosophy, 1969—. Honorary fellow at Birkbeck College of University of London, 1964; visiting lecturer at University of Edinburgh, 1969-70; John Power Lecturer in Fine Arts at University of Sydney, 1971. Occasional art critic for Australian Broadcasting Commission.

MEMBER: L'Association Internationale des Critiques d'Art (societaire: vice-president of Australian section, 1973—), Australian Philosophical Association, Royal Society of Arts (fellow), British Society for Aesthetics, Mind Association, American Society for Aesthetics, Society for Education through Art, Critical Quarterly Society, Western Australia Art Gallery Society (president, 1974).

WRITINGS: Kant on Absolute Value (monograph), Wayne State University Press, 1972; (contributor) Donald Brook, editor, *The Visual Arts Now,* Angus & Robertson (Sydney) and Studio Vista (London), in press; (contributor) Bernard Smith, editor, *Concerning Contemporary Art,* Clarendon Press, in press. Author of exhibition catalogs. Contributor of about sixty articles and reviews to magazines and newspapers, including *Mind, Philosophy, Art International, Arts and Community, Journal of Aesthetics and Art Criticism, Ascent,* and *Westerly.* Former member, board of directors of *Westerly.*

WORK IN PROGRESS: Subjects and Subjectivity: Persons as Limits to Actions; Simultaneity and the Aesthetic Idea; Phenomenology, Criticism, and Explication.

* * *

HUTTIG, Jack W(ilfred) 1919-

PERSONAL: Born March 13, 1919, in Kansas City, Mo.; son of Alfred (a grain broker) and Inez (Fessler) Huttig; married Amelia Goodman, July 3, 1941; children: Diana F. (Mrs. Dennis Prouty), Philip E., Pamela J. (Mrs. Vincent Lombardi), Jack, Jr. *Education:* Wichita State University, B.A., 1970, M.S., 1973. *Home:* 16 Green Mountain Dr., Iowa City, Iowa 52240. *Office:* Center for Conferences and Institutes, University of Iowa, Iowa City, Iowa 52242.

CAREER: Beech Aircraft Corp., Wichita, Kan., manager of marketing manpower development, 1951-73; University of Iowa, Center for Conferences and Institutes, Iowa City, director, 1973—. *Military service:* U.S. Air Force, 1939-45; became lieutenant colonel. *Member:* National University Extension Association, Phi Kappa Psi, Delta Sigma Pi. *Awards, honors:* Freedoms Foundation award, 1950; Sales Executives International award, 1951; *Writer's Digest* award, 1966.

WRITINGS: Psycho-Sales-Analysis, Nelson-Hall, 1971; *Fifteen Ways to Increase Sales,* Bill Publications, 1973. Contributor of more than one hundred articles to journals. Contributing editor of *Professional Salesman,* 1968—.

WORK IN PROGRESS: Research on marketing communications and on the impact of modern psychology on marketing training; developing adult education programs and promoting acceptance of the continuing education unit as a measure of adult participation in these programs.

SIDELIGHTS: Huttig has conducted sales and marketing training programs throughout the United States, Canada, England, Germany, and Switzerland.

* * *

HYMAN, Ann 1936-

PERSONAL: Born March 8, 1936, in Bradenton, Fla.; daughter of Dewey Albert (a lawyer) and Lucy (Edmonson) Dye; married Henry Hyman (an import-export executive), June 4, 1960; children: Joseph Robert, Elizabeth Dye. *Education:* Florida State University, B.A., 1958; Jacksonville University, graduate study, 1969-70. *Politics:* Democrat. *Religion:* Episcopalian. *Home:* 5355 Della Robbia Way, Jacksonville, Fla. 32210. *Agent:* Curtis Brown Ltd., 60 East 56th St., New York, N.Y. 10022.

CAREER: Bradenton Herald, Bradenton, Fla., reporter, 1958-59; *Florida Times-Union,* Jacksonville, reporter, 1959-60, feature writer for Sunday magazine, 1960—. Former member of board of directors of Episcopal Day Care Centers, Inc. *Member:* National League of American Pen Women.

WRITINGS: The Lansing Legacy, McKay, 1974. Contributor of articles and short stories to magazines.

WORK IN PROGRESS: A novel.

* * *

IANNONE, Ron(ald Vincent) 1940-

PERSONAL: Surname is pronounced *Ya*-known-*e*; born May 31, 1940, in Auburn, N.Y.; son of Emilio (a barber) and Mary (Del Santo) Iannone; married Mary Lyon, February 1, 1964; children: Patrick, Mary Beth, Jeffrey. *Education:* St. Bonaventure University, B.S., 1962; University of Rochester, M.A., 1964; Syracuse University, Ed.D., 1969; Harvard University, postdoctoral study, 1971-72. *Home:* 1013 Village Dr., Morgantown, W.Va. 26505. *Office:* West Virginia University, Morgantown, W.Va. 26506.

CAREER: Teacher of mathematics at schools in Manlius, N.Y., 1962-63, and Liverpool, N.Y., 1965-66; Hobart and William Smith Colleges, Geneva, N.Y., assistant professor of education, 1968-69; West Virginia University, Morgantown, associate professor of education, 1969-71, 1972—. *Military service:* U.S. Army, 1964-66; became first lieutenant. *Member:* National Education Association, Association for Supervision and Curriculum Development, Association of Teacher Educators, American Educational Research Association, American Association of University Professors.

WRITINGS: Alternatives to the Coming Death of Schooling, McClain Printing Co., 1971; *School Ain't No Way: Appalachian Consciousness,* McClain Printing Co., 1972; *An Ethnic Condition and Goals Beyond: Reflections of an Italian American Poet,* McClain Printing Co., 1974. Contributor to education journals.

WORK IN PROGRESS: Research studies on effects of humanistic in-service training programs and workshops, on the teaching of black literature as a method of modifying racial attitudes, and on factors related to teachers' and principals' job attitudes.

* * *

IFFT, James B(rown) 1935-

PERSONAL: Born November 8, 1935, in Stroudsburg, Pa.; son of Arthur E. and Frances (Brown) Ifft; married Evelyn D. Parth (an artist and instructor in weaving), December 28, 1957; children: Daniel, Joanna, Stephen. *Education:* Pennsylvania State University, B.S., 1957; California Institute of Technology, Ph.D., 1962. *Religion:* Presbyterian. *Home:* 506 Lytle St., Redlands, Calif. 92373. *Office:* Division of Natural Sciences, University of Redlands, 1200 East Colton, Redlands, Calif. 92373.

CAREER: University of Redlands, Redlands, Calif., assistant professor, 1963-67, associate professor, 1967-73, professor of chemistry, 1973—, dean of Division of Natural Sciences, 1973—. Visiting professor, University of California, Berkeley, 1970-71. *Member:* American Chemical Society, American Association of University Professors, American Association for the Advancement of Science, Sigma Xi.

WRITINGS: (Contributor) Alexander P. Lundgren and H. P. Lundgren, editors, *A Laboratory Manual of Analytical Methods of Protein Chemistry,* Pergamon, 1969; (contributor), C. H. W. Hirs and S. N. Timasheff, editors, *Methods in Enzymology,* Volume XXV, Academic Press, 1973; (editor and author of introduction with John E. Hearst) *General Chemistry: Readings from Scientific American,* W. H. Freeman, 1974; (with Julian L. Roberts) *Frantz/Malm's Essentials of Chemistry in the Laboratory,* 3rd edition (Ifft was not associated with earlier editions), W. H. Freeman, 1975; (with Hearst) *Contemporary Chemistry,* W. H. Freeman, 1975. Contributor to proceedings and professional journals.

SIDELIGHTS: Ifft told *CA:* "I am an avid angler to the point of teaching an interim course at the University of Redlands entitled 'Angling for a Liberal Education.' I am an avid enough backpacker that I teach a course in the physical education department in advanced hiking. I have some competence in reading and speaking Danish. I have spent a sabbatical year at the Carlsberg Laboratorium in Copehagen, Denmark in 1969-70 and ten weeks at this same laboratory during the summer of 1973."

* * *

IKENBERRY, Oliver Samuel 1908-

PERSONAL: Born January 6, 1908, in Roanoke, Va.; son of Jacob (a railroader) and Edith (Stauffer) Ikenberry; married Margaret Ruth Moulton, June 11, 1933; children: Stanley O., Dorothea Jane, Betty (Mrs. Richard Wade). *Education:* McPherson College, B.A., 1929; Colorado State College of Education (now University of Northern Colorado), M.A., 1932, Ed.D., 1941; graduate study at Columbia University, 1935-36. *Politics:* Democrat. *Religion:* Presbyterian. *Home:* 120 Acklen Park Dr., Nashville, Tenn. 37203. *Office:* George Peabody College, 108 Payne Hall, Nashville, Tenn. 37203.

CAREER: Superintendent of schools in Haswell, Colo., 1930-33; principal of high school in Lamar, Colo., 1933-37, and of schools in Delta, Colo., 1937-41; Western State College of Colorado, Gunnison, professor of education in Extension Division, 1937-41; Salem College, Salem, W.Va., professor of education, 1941-47; Shepherd State College, Shepherd, W.Va., president, 1947-68, president emeritus, 1968—; Oxford University, Institute of Education, Oxford, England, postdoctoral research, 1968-69; George Peabody College, Nashville, Tenn., professor of education, 1969—. Extension instructor, Colorado State College of Education (now University of Northern Colorado), 1933-36; visiting professor of education at West Virginia University, summers, 1946 and 1947. Representative of American Association of Colleges for Teacher Education to the American Council on Education, 1956-59; member of White House Conference on Education, 1956-59, 1966-69; member of Governor's Advisory Committee on Mental Health, 1964-68; consultant on higher education, U.S. Office of Education, 1966-70; representative to World Conference on Organizations of the Teaching Profession and International Council on Teaching, 1971.

MEMBER: American Association for Higher Education, National Education Association, American Association of State Colleges and Universities (state representative, 1966-68), West Virginia Education Association, West Virginia Council of State College and University Presidents (president, 1954-56), West Virginia Academy of Sciences, West Virginia Association of College Presidents (secretary, 1950-

51), West Virginia Intercollegiate Athletic Association (secretary-treasurer, 1952-55), Phi Delta Kappa (vice-president, 1971), Kappa Delta Pi, Rotary, University Club and Freolac Discussion Club (both Nashville). *Awards, honors:* Citations of merit for distinguished service from Kentucky College, 1967, and McPherson College, 1969.

WRITINGS: American Education Foundations: An Introduction, C. E. Merrill, 1974. Also author of *Comparative Inequalities in Educational Finance*, 1932; *Economic Factors Affecting Education*, 1934; *Health, Government, Education, and Religion in a Community*, 1941; *Leisure Activities in a Community*, 1941. Contributor of numerous articles to educational journals.

WORK IN PROGRESS: The Education of American Teachers; *The Historical and Philosophical Contributions of Western Education*; *The World's Greatest Teacher.*

* * *

ILLICH, Ivan D. 1926-

PERSONAL: Born September 4, 1926, in Vienna, Austria; son of Ivan Peter (a landowner and civil engineer) and Ellen (Regenstreif-Ortlieb) Illich. *Education:* Attended University of Florence, University of Rome, and University of Munich; Gregorian University, licentiate in theology, 1951; University of Salzburg, Ph.D., 1951. *Home and office:* Centro Intercultural de Documentacion, Rancho Tetela, Apdo 479, Cuernavaca, Mexico.

CAREER: Ordained Roman Catholic priest, 1951; Incarnation Church, New York, N.Y., assistant pastor, 1951-56; resigned priestly functions, 1969. Catholic University of Puerto Rico, Ponce, vice-rector, 1956-60; Centro Intercultural de Documentacion, Cuernavaca, Mexico, co-founder and director, 1961—. Visiting lecturer, Fordham University.

WRITINGS: Metamorfosi del clero, La locusta (Vicenza, Italy), 1968; (editor) *Spiritual Care of Puerto Rican Migrants,* Centro Intercultural de Documentacion, 1970; *Celebration of Awareness: A Call for Institutional Awareness,* introduction by Erich Fromm, Doubleday, 1970; *De-Schooling Society,* Harper, 1971; (contributor) Lionel Rubinoff, editor, *Tradition and Revolution,* St. Martin's, 1972; (contributor) Peter Bruckman, editor, *Education Without Schools,* Souvenir Press, 1973; *Retooling Society 111,* Centro Intercultural de Documentacion, 1973; *En America Latina para que sirve le escuela?,* Ediciones Busqueda (Buenos Aires), 1973; (with others) *After De-Schooling, What?,* Harper, 1973; *Tools for Conviviality,* Harper, 1973; *Energy and Equity,* J. Calder, 1973, Harper, 1974; *Medical Nemesis,* J. Calder, 1974.

WORK IN PROGRESS: A major study on the institutional impact of medical organizations on the myths, rituals, laws and customs of industrial society.

SIDELIGHTS: Of *De-Schooling Society,* Anatole Broyard wrote in the *New York Times:* "It is not difficult to pick holes in some of Mr. Illich's propositions, because in leaping from peak to peak he sometimes stumbles. Schools aren't as bad as he maintains; most learning isn't acquired casually, as he says; the 'street education' that he advocates entered schools a long time ago; schools are not entirely self-perpetuating, because even the scholarship students are clamoring for change. Instruction does not invariably 'smother the horizons of the imagination': Sometimes it enlarges them. But this is like criticizing the grammer of someone who has just delivered a speech that gave us goose-pimples. Flaws and all, 'De-Schooling Society' ought to be read by everybody."

* * *

INGRAM, Forrest L(eo) 1938-
(Ignatius van Rijn)

PERSONAL: Born October 18, 1938, in Dallas, Tex.; son of M. Herschel and Vivian (Eidt) Ingram; married Barbara Steinberg (a college teacher), January 6, 1973. *Education:* Spring Hill College, A.B. (English and education), 1962, M.A. (philosophy), 1963; University of Southern California, M.A. (comparative literature), 1965, Ph.D., 1967; Catholic Theological School of Amsterdam and City University of Amsterdam, B.A. (theology) and S.T.L., 1970. *Politics:* Independent liberal. *Religion:* Catholic. *Home:* 1615 15th Ave. S., Fargo, N.D. 58102. *Office:* Department of English, Moorhead State College, Moorhead, Minn. 56560.

CAREER: Entered Society of Jesus in Grand Coteau, La., 1956, ordained deacon in Amsterdam, Netherlands, 1969 (left Jesuit Order, 1972); Loyola University, New Orleans, La., associate professor of English, 1969-73, editor-in-chief of *New Orleans Review*, 1971-73; Open Court Publishing Co., La Salle, Ill., associate editor, 1973-74; Moorhead State College, Moorhead, Minn., associate professor of English and chairman of department, 1974—. Catholic chaplain at University of Leeds, 1970. *Member:* Modern Language Association of America, International Comparative Literature Association, American Comparative Literature Association, American Association of University Professors, Dobro Slovo, Kappa Delta Phi. *Awards, honors:* Woodrow Wilson fellowship, 1963.

WRITINGS: (Editor with Lucien Roy, and contributor) *Step Beyond Impasse* (nonfiction), Newman, 1969; (editor and contributor) *Enjoying American Short Stories* (critical anthology), Tjeenk Willink-Noorduijn, 1970, 2nd edition, 1973; *The Thin Blue Line* (short fiction), Tjeenk Willink-Noorduijn, 1970; *Representative Short Story Cycles of the Twentieth Century: Studies in a Literary Genre*, Mouton & Co., 1971, Humanities, 1972; *Sugar Sadface and the Windmills* (short fiction), Tjeenk Willink-Noorduijn, 1972; *Stinkweed in America* (short fiction), Tjeenk Willink-Noorduijn, 1974; (editor) Ring Lardner, *Champion*, Tjeenk Willink-Noorduijn, 1974.

Translator: (With others) Huub Oosterhuis and others, *Fifty Psalms*, Herder & Herder, 1968; Jan de Fraine, *Women of the Old Testament*, Norbert Abbey Press, 1969; (with others) Bernard Huijbers, *The Performing Audience*, North American Liturgy Resources (Cincinnatti, Ohio), 1974; (with others) Oosterhuis and Huijbers, *Of God and Men*, North American Liturgy Resources, 1974.

Contributor: Huub Oosterhuis, *Prayers, Poems, and Songs*, Herder & Herder, 1970; Oosterhuis, *Open Your Hearts*, Herder & Herder, 1971; Robert Bonazzi, editor, *Toward Winter: Poems for the Last Decade*, New Rivers, 2nd edition, 1972; Warren French, editor, *The Twenties*, Everett-Edwards, 1974.

Coordinator and editor of "Open Court Bilingual Foundation Program," and contributor to "Open Court Correlated Language Arts Program," both published by Open Court. Poems, articles, and reviews have been published in *America* (under pseudonym Ignatius van Rijn), *Mundus Artium, Mississippi Review, Tablet, New Orleans Review, Educastem, Latitudes*, and other periodicals.

WORK IN PROGRESS: Editing *The Winesburg Form*, a collection of critical essays on the American short story cycle of the twentieth century; three volumes of essays on the short story cycle—one on the cycle in Europe during the twentieth century, one on the cycle in Europe and America during the nineteenth century, and the third on the cycle in the world before the nineteenth century; a novel, *The Pending Case*, based on the futures and fortunes of those involved in an academic freedom case.

SIDELIGHTS: Ingram says that his writing began "in humor and in religious awe." His first book, *Step Beyond Impasse*, dealt with the issues involved in the crisis of the Dutch Catholic Church over the celibacy issue. His views on priestly celibacy eventually were a factor in his decision to leave the Jesuit order.

Enjoying American Short Stories, the Ring Lardner edition, and Ingram's short fiction published in the Netherlands are texts for English classes in Dutch schools.

AVOCATIONAL INTERESTS: Politics, painting, tennis.

* * *

INTRILIGATOR, Michael D(avid) 1938-

PERSONAL: Born February 5, 1938, in New York, N.Y.; son of Allan (a business executive) and Sarah (Jacobs) Intriligator; married Devrie Shapiro (a physicist), March 24, 1963; children: Kenneth, James, William, Robert. *Education:* Massachusetts Institute of Technology, S.B., 1959, Ph.D., 1963; Yale University, M.A., 1960. *Residence:* Santa Monica, Calif. *Office:* Department of Economics, University of California, Los Angeles, Calif. 90024.

CAREER: Boston College, Boston, Mass., lecturer in econometrics, 1962-63; University of California, Los Angeles, assistant professor, 1963-66, associate professor, 1966-72, professor of economics, 1972—. California Institute of Technology, lecturer in Division of Humanities and Social Sciences, 1969-71; University of Southern California, research associate, Human Resources Research Center, 1969—, visiting professor, 1972-73. Consultant to U.S. Arms Control and Disarmament Agency, 1968, Rockwell International Corp., 1969-74, and Institute for Defense Analyses, 1974—.

MEMBER: American Economic Association, Econometric Society (program chairman, 1969), Western Economic Association. *Awards, honors:* Woodrow Wilson fellow at Yale University, 1959-60; Distinguished Teaching Award, University of California, Los Angeles, 1966; Ford Foundation faculty research fellow at Stanford University and London School of Economics and Political Science, University of London, 1967-68.

WRITINGS: Strategy in a Missile War (monograph), Security Studies Project, University of California, Los Angeles, 1967; *Mathematical Optimization and Economic Theory*, Prentice-Hall, 1971; (editor) *Frontiers of Quantitative Economics*, North-Holland Publishing Co., Volume I, 1971, Volume II (with David A. Kendrik), 1974; (with Donald E. Yett, Leonard Drabek, and Larry J. Kimball) *A Forecasting and Policy Simulation Model of the Health Care Sector: The HRRC Prototype Microeconometric Model*, Lexington, in press.

Contributor: J. Morley English, editor, *The Economics of Engineering and Social Systems*, Wiley, 1971; J. F. Weston and S. I. Ornstein, editors, *The Impact of Large Firms on the U.S. Economy*, Heath, 1973; Mark Perlman, editor, *Economics of Health and Medical Care*, Macmillan, 1974. Contributor of articles and reviews to economic and statistical journals. Editor with Christopher Bliss, "Advanced Textbooks in Economics" series, North-Holland Publishing, 1972—. Editor, *Journal of Statistical Physics*, 1969—; referee for National Science Foundation and five economic journals.

WORK IN PROGRESS: Editing Volume III of *Frontiers of Quantitative Economics*, for North-Holland Publishing; preparing *Econometric Models, Techniques, and Applications.*

* * *

IRVING, Brian William 1932-

PERSONAL: Born July 2, 1932, in Los Angeles, Calif.; son of Edward Victor and Petra (Bemister) Irving; married Joyce Knapp (a writer), October 25, 1974; children: Kevin, Bruce. *Education:* University of California, Los Angeles, B.A., 1956; Wesleyan University, M.A.T., 1958; University of Connecticut, M.A., 1974. *Politics:* Republican. *Religion:* Roman Catholic. *Home and office:* Inter-American University, San German, P.R. 00753.

CAREER: Junior high school teacher in San Pedro, Calif., 1958-59; high school teacher at Fort Buchanan, in San Juan, P.R., 1959-60; University of Connecticut, Waterbury Branch, registrar and instructor in history, 1960-64; Inter-American University, at Ramey Air Force Base, San German, P.R., assistant professor of history, 1968—, chairman of department of history and political science and director of Caribbean Institute and Study Center for Latin America, 1970-71, dean of academic affairs, 1971-72, dean of military programs, 1972, vice-president of university, 1972—. *Military service:* Served in U.S. Air Force; became staff sergeant.

WRITINGS: Guyana, Inter-American University Press, 1972.

WORK IN PROGRESS: British Foreign Policy in the Far East: 1898-1907.

SIDELIGHTS: Irving has traveled in Japan, Panama, Germany, United Kingdom, the Caribbean, France, Spain, and Austria.

* * *

IRWIN, David 1933-

PERSONAL: Born June 24, 1933, in London, England; son of George and Doris (Tetlow) Irwin; married Francina Sorabji (an author and weaver), 1960; children: Saskia, Dickon. *Education:* Queen's College, Oxford, M.A., 1960; Courtauld Institute of Art, London, Ph.D., 1960. *Office:* Department of History of Art, King's College, University of Aberdeen, Old Aberdeen, Scotland.

CAREER: Glasgow University, Glasgow, Scotland, lecturer in department of fine arts, 1959-70; University of Aberdeen, King's College, Old Aberdeen, Scotland, associate professor of history of art, 1970—, chairman of department, 1970—. *Member:* Association Internationale des Critiques d'Art, Society of Antiquaries of London (fellow), Royal Society of Arts (fellow), British Society for Eighteenth Century Studies (vice-president, 1973—), Walpole Society (member of council, 1970—).

WRITINGS: English Neoclassical Art, New York Graphic Society, 1966; *Paul Klee*, Knowledge, 1968; *Visual Arts, Taste, and Criticism*, Blackie & Son, 1969; *Winckelmann: Writings on Art*, Praeger, 1972; *Beunat: Designs and Ornaments of Empire Style*, Dover, 1974; (with wife, Francina Sorabji) *Scottish Painters*, Faber, 1975. Contributor to *Encyclopaedia Britannica*, and to *Apollo, Burlington Magazine, Art Bulletin*, and *Connoisseur*.

WORK IN PROGRESS: John Flaxman; research on industrial design.

* * *

IRWIN, John T(homas) 1940-
(John Bricuth)

PERSONAL: Born April 24, 1940, in Houston, Tex.; son of William Henry (a business executive) and Marguerite (Hunsaker) Irwin. *Education:* University of St. Thomas, Houston, Tex., B.A., 1962; Yale University, graduate study, 1962-63; Rice University, M.A. and Ph.D., 1970. *Residence:* Athens, Ga. *Office: Georgia Review*, University of Georgia, Athens, Ga. 30602.

CAREER: National Aeronautics and Space Administration Manned Spacecraft Center, Houston, Tex., supervisor of public affairs library, 1966-67; Johns Hopkins University, Baltimore, Md., assistant professor of English, 1970-74; *Georgia Review*, Athens, Ga., editor, 1974—. *Military service:* U.S. Naval Reserve, member of staff of commander-in-chief of U.S. Pacific Fleet in Pearl Harbor, active duty, 1963-66; became lieutenant senior grade. *Awards, honors:* Emily Clark Balch Prize from *Virginia Quarterly Review*, 1970, for poem "The Musical Emblem."

WRITINGS: (Under Pseudonym John Bricuth) *The Heisenberg Variations* (poems), University of Georgia Press, 1975; *Doubling and Incest: Repetition and Revenge* (speculative reading of William Faulkner), Johns Hopkins Press, 1975.

Contributor of articles, poems, and reviews to literary journals, including *Southern Review, Sewanee Review, Poetry, Virginia Quarterly Review, Shenandoah*, and *Perspective*. Editor of *Strivers' Row*, 1973-74.

WORK IN PROGRESS: A book on the symbol of the hieroglyphics in American literature.

* * *

ISICHEI, Elizabeth 1939-

PERSONAL: Born March 22, 1939, in New Zealand; daughter of Albert V. (an agricultural scientist) and Lorna Allo; married Uche Peter Isichei (a senior lecturer in chemical pathology and consultant chemical pathologist), July 23, 1964; children: Uche Daniel, Emeka Benedict, Nkem Katherine, Chinye Caroline Mary. *Education:* University of Canterbury, New Zealand, B.A., 1959; Victoria University of Wellington, New Zealand, M.A. (first class honors), 1961; Oxford University, Ph.D., 1967. *Politics:* "I am not a member of any political party but strongly believe Christians must strive for social justice." *Religion:* Roman Catholic. *Agent:* Andrew Best, Curtis Brown Ltd., 1 Craven Hill, London W2 3EW, England. *Office:* Department of History, University of Nigeria, Enugu Campus, Enugu, Nigeria.

CAREER: University of Canterbury, Christchurch, New Zealand, assistant lecturer in history, 1962; Oxford University, Nuffield College, Oxford, England, research fellow, 1966-69; University of Dar es Salaam, Dar es Salaam, Tanzania, senior lecturer in history, 1969-71; Ahmadu Bello University, Zaria, Nigeria, senior lecturer in history, 1971-72; University of Nigeria, Nsukka, senior lecturer in history, 1972—. *Member:* Historical Society of Nigeria.

WRITINGS: Political Thinking and Social Experience: Some Christian Interpretations of the Roman Empire, University of Canterbury Publications, 1964; (contributor) B. R. Wilson, editor, *Patterns of Sectarianism*, Heinemann, 1965; *Victorian Quakers*, Oxford University Press, 1970; *The Ibo People and the Europeans: The Genesis of a Relationship, to 1906*, Faber, 1973; *A History of the Igbo People*, Macmillan, in press. Contributor to numerous learned journals.

WORK IN PROGRESS: Igbo Worlds: An Anthology of Oral Histories and Historical Descriptions; *A Life of Father Cyprian Tansi, O.C.S.O.*; *A History of West Africa since 1800*.

* * *

ISRAEL, Elaine 1945-

PERSONAL: Born January 24, 1945, in New York, N.Y.; daughter of Otto (in electrical devices business) and Kate (Mendle) Israel. *Education:* Bronx Community College, A.A., 1964; University of Rhode Island, B.A., 1966. *Home:* 42-25 80th St., New York, N.Y. 11373. *Office:* Scholastic Magazines, 50 West 44th St., New York, N.Y. 10036.

CAREER: Long Island Star Journal, Long Island, N.Y., reporter, 1966-68; Scholastic Magazines, New York, N.Y., writer and associate editor of *Newstime*, 1968—.

WRITINGS: The Great Energy Search (juvenile), Messner, 1974.

AVOCATIONAL INTERESTS: Travel, photography.

* * *

ISSER, Natalie 1927-

PERSONAL: Born July 12, 1927; daughter of David P. and Frances (Saltzman) Kleinman; married Leonard Isser (a certified public accountant), June 15, 1947; children: Raymond, Miriam, Steven, Edward. *Education:* University of Pennsylvania, B.A., 1947, M.A., 1948, Ph.D., 1962. *Home:* 8123 Cadwalader Ave., Elkins Park, Pa. 19117. *Office:* Department of History, Pennsylvania State University, Ogontz Campus, Abington, Pa. 19001.

CAREER: Pennsylvania State University, Abington, assistant professor of history, 1962—. *Member:* American Historical Association, American Association of University Professors, French Historical Society.

WRITINGS: Second Empire and the Press, Nijhoff, 1974.

WORK IN PROGRESS: Co-editing with Claire Hirsfield, *Student Revolution in History*, and with Lita Schwartz, *Oral History of Students' Study and Work Abroad Programs*.

* * *

IVERSEN, Gudmund R(agnvaldsson) 1934-

PERSONAL: Born September 14, 1934, in Trondheim, Norway; naturalized U.S. citizen in 1969; son of Ragnvald (a professor) and Torborg (Tjernstroem) Iversen; married Catherine Sharp, October 13, 1962 (died February, 1973); married Roberta Rehner (a writer), June 19, 1974; children: (first marriage) Kirsten, Eric. *Education:* Attended University of Oslo, 1954-58; University of Michigan, M.A., 1960, M.A., 1961; Harvard University, Ph.D., 1969. *Residence:* Swarthmore, Pa. 19081. *Office:* Department of Mathematics, Swarthmore College, Swarthmore, Pa. 19081.

CAREER: University of Michigan, Ann Arbor, assistant

professor of sociology, 1969-72; Swarthmore College, Swarthmore, Pa., associate professor of statistics, 1972—. *Member:* American Statistical Association, American Sociological Association, Biometric Society.

WRITINGS: Applied Statistics: Problem Sets for Instruction in Statistics in the Social Sciences, Inter-University Consortium for Political Research, University of Michigan, 1971; *Sociology and Statistics*, Bobbs-Merrill, 1972. Contributor to *Public Opinion Quarterly*, *Law and Society Review*, *Psychometrika*, *World Politics*, and *American Journal of Sociology*.

WORK IN PROGRESS: With Lawrence Boyd, a book on concepts and techniques of multi-level analysis.

* * *

JACKENDOFF, Ray S. 1945-

PERSONAL: Born January 23, 1945, in Chicago, Ill.; son of Nathaniel (a professor) and Elaine (a guidance counselor; maiden name, Flanders) Jackendoff. *Education:* Swarthmore College, B.A., 1965; Massachusetts Institute of Technology, Ph.D., 1969. *Politics:* Anarchist. *Religion:* Jewish. *Office:* Department of English, Brandeis University, Waltham, Mass. 02154.

CAREER: University of California at Los Angeles, lecturer in English, 1969-70; Brandeis University, Waltham, Mass., assistant professor, 1971-73, associate professor of English, 1973—. *Member:* Linguistic Society of America, North East Linguistic Society, Boston Musicians Association. *Awards, honors:* Gustave O. Arlt Award from Council of Graduate Schools, 1974, for *Semantic Interpretation in Generative Grammar*.

WRITINGS: Semantic Interpretation in Generative Grammar, M.I.T. Press, 1972. Contributor to journals in his field.

WORK IN PROGRESS: Lexicalist Syntax; research on the relationship of linguistics and music theory.

* * *

JACOB, Philip E(rnest) 1914-

PERSONAL: Born July 12, 1914, in Istanbul, Turkey; son of U.S. citizens, Ernest Otto (a Young Men's Christian Associations executive) and Sarah (Conrad) Jacob; married Betty Muther (a research administrator), 1935; children: Sarah Elizabeth Jacob Vogel, Albert Kirk, Stephen Philip. *Education:* Yale University, B.A., 1935; University of Pennsylvania, M.A., 1939; Princeton University, Ph.D., 1941. *Politics:* Independent. *Religion:* Society of Friends (Quaker). *Home:* 735-D Aalapapa Dr., Kailua, Hawaii 96734. *Office:* Department of Political Science, University of Hawaii, Honolulu, Hawaii 96822.

CAREER: American Friends Service Committee, Philadelphia, Pa., field secretary, 1936-38; Princeton University, Princeton, N.J., instructor in politics, 1939-40, researcher on Nazi Propaganda at Listening Center, 1940-41; American Friends Service Committee, associate secretary (civilian public service in lieu of military duty), 1941-45; University of Pennsylvania, Philadelphia, assistant professor, 1945-48, associate professor, 1948-54, professor of political science, 1955-71; University of Hawaii, Honolulu, professor of political science, 1970—. Senior specialist at East-West Center, Honolulu, 1969. Visiting lecturer at Swarthmore College, 1948-55, and Haverford College. Member of board of directors, American Friends Service Committee, 1950-54, member of international programs executive committee, 1963-69.

MEMBER: American Political Science Association (chairman of academic freedom committee, 1969-71), International Studies Association, National Council on Religion in Higher Education (fellow), American Society of International Law, Commission to Study the Organization of Peace, Phi Beta Kappa. *Awards, honors:* Franklin D. Roosevelt Award of American Political Science Association (shared with Mulford Q. Sibley), 1952, for *Conscription of Conscience* as best book of the year in field of government and public welfare; Rockefeller Foundation international relations fellow, 1962; grants from National Science Foundation, U.S. Department of State, U.S. Agency for International Development, Agnelli Foundation, Barra Foundation, UNESCO, Ford Foundation, Robert McNeil, Jr. Foundation, and Hazen Foundation.

WRITINGS: (Contributor) Harwood L. Childs and J. B. Whitton, editors, *Propaganda by Shortwave*, Princeton University Press, 1941; (with Mulford Q. Sibley) *Conscription of Conscience: The American State and the Conscientious Objector 1940-1947*, Cornell University Press, 1952; *Changing Values in College: An Exploratory Study of the Impact on Student Values of General Education*, Harper, 1957; (editor with J. V. Toscano and contributor) *The Integration of Political Communities*, Lippincott, 1964; (with A. L. Atherton) *The Dynamics of International Organization: The Making of World Order*, Dorsey, 1965, revised edition, 1972; (with others) *Values and the Active Community: A Cross-National Study of the Influence of Local Leadership* (study sponsored by International Social Science Council), Free Press, 1971; (contributor) Charles M. Bonjean and others, editors, *Community Politics: A Behavioral Approach*, Free Press, 1971. Co-author of *Values and Their Function in Decision-Making*, special issue of *American Behavioral Scientist*, May, 1962. Contributor to *Politico* (Italy), *Social Research, Orbis, International Organization*, and other journals.

WORK IN PROGRESS: Principal investigator in fifteen-nation study of the impact of automation on the motivation of workers, a project proposed by Soviet Academy of Sciences.

SIDELIGHTS: Jacob sees an emerging consciousness "of the tools that people have available to better their lives and control their hostilities—and some understanding of the factors that may enter into the decisions people make whether and how to use these tools." "This clearly implies," he says, "a continued belief that people *can* shape their destinies—that individuals *do* count—and that social scientists have a profound obligation to apply knowledge to further the social good."

* * *

JACOBS, Laurence Wile 1939-

PERSONAL: Born May 26, 1939, in Cincinnati, Ohio; son of Arthur L. (an owner of a furniture store) and Josephine (Yuster) Jacobs; married Susan Stone, August 1, 1966; children: Andrew, Julie. *Education:* University of Pennsylvania, B.S., 1961; Ohio State University, M.B.A., 1963, Ph.D., 1966. *Home:* 1474 Kamole St., Honolulu, Hawaii 96821. *Office:* Department of Marketing, University of Hawaii, 2404 Maile Way, Honolulu, Hawaii 96822.

CAREER: F. & R. Lazarus Co. (department store), Columbus, Ohio, executive trainee, 1961; Marketing Science Institute, Philadelphia, Pa., research fellow, 1965-66; University of Hawaii, Honolulu, assistant professor, 1964-68, associate professor, 1968-72, professor of marketing,

1972—. Chairman of board of directors of Family Education Centers of Hawaii. *Member:* American Marketing Association (founder of Honolulu chapter; past president), Institute of Management Science, Academy of Marketing Science, American Institute of Decision Sciences, Sales and Marketing Executives International.

WRITINGS: Timsim: A Computerized Management Game, Mid-Pacific Press (Honolulu), 1969; *Advertising and Promotion for Retailing*, Scott, Foresman, 1972. Contributor of more than twenty articles to business journals.

Editor of *Marketing Information Service for the Pacific*.

WORK IN PROGRESS: Retailing Strategies; *The Store*.

* * *

JACOBSON, Daniel 1923-

PERSONAL: Born November 6, 1923, in Newark, N.J.; son of Samuel and Mary (Siegel) Jacobson; married Iris Blachman (a counselor), August 18, 1957; children: Lisa, Darryl, Jerrold. *Education:* New Jersey State Teachers College, Montclair, B.A., 1947; Clark University, graduate study, 1947-48; Columbia University, M.A., 1950; Louisiana State University, Ph.D., 1954. *Politics:* Democrat. *Religion:* Jewish. *Home:* 1827 Mirabeau Dr., Okemos, Mich. 48864. *Office:* Social Science Teaching Institute, Erickson Hall, Michigan State University, East Lansing, Mich. 48824.

CAREER: University of Kentucky, Lexington, instructor in geography, 1952-55; Brooklyn College (now of the City University of New York), Brooklyn, N.Y., instructor in geology, 1955-57; New Jersey State College, Upper Montclair, associate professor of geography, 1957-66; Michigan State University, East Lansing, visiting professor, 1966-67, professor of geography and education, 1967—, adjunct professor of anthropology, 1974—. *Military service:* U.S. Army Air Forces, 1943-46. *Member:* Association of American Geographers, American Geographical Society, National Council for Geographic Education (president, 1968), American Anthropological Association, American Society for Ethnohistory, Society for American Archaeology, Historical Society of Michigan, New Jersey Historical Society. *Awards, honors:* Award from National Council for Geographic Education, 1965, for "The Role of Historical Geography in the American School."

WRITINGS: The Story of Man, Home Library Press, 1963; (with Stanley N. Worton and others) *New Jersey: Past and Present*, Hayden, 1964; (contributor) John Morris, editor, *Methods of Geographic Instruction*, Ginn, 1968; *Teaching the American Indian in the American School: An Adventure in Cultural Geography*, National Council for Geographic Education, 1969; *The First Americans*, Ginn, 1969.

(With Wilbur E. Apgar and Abraham Resnick) *Great Indian Tribes*, Hammond, Inc., 1970; (with Ralph H. Marsh and Howard N. Martin) *Alabama-Coushatta (Creek) Indians*, Garland Publishing, 1974; *The Hunters*, F. Watts, 1974; *The Fishermen*, F. Watts, 1975; *The Gatherers*, F. Watts, in press. Contributor to *New Book of Knowledge*, and to *Journal of Geography*. Editor of *Peninsular* (of Michigan Council for Geographic Education).

WORK IN PROGRESS: The Farmers, publication by F. Watts expected in 1977; *The Most Neglected Minority*, publication by F. Watts expected in 1978; research on the Jewish community of Lansing, Michigan.

JACOBSON, David B(ernard) 1928-

PERSONAL: Born August 13, 1928, in New York, N.Y.; son of Manes (an electrician) and Ida L. (Einson) Jacobson; married Patricia Elaine Holcomb (an artist), November 3, 1961; children: Valerie Diane (Mrs. Randall L. Davidson), Melinda Helene, Tamara Eden. *Education:* Queens College (now Queens College of the City University of New York), A.B., 1949; Stanford University, A.M., 1957; University of California, Berkeley, further graduate study, 1956-59. *Home:* 363 Calle La Montana, Moraga, Calif. 94556. *Office:* Department of English, Contra Costa College, 2600 Mission Bell Dr., San Pablo, Calif. 94806.

CAREER: University of Puget Sound, Tacoma, Wash., instructor in English, 1959-61; Lane Book Co., Menlo Park, Calif., editor, 1961-62; Contra Costa College, San Pablo, Calif., teacher, 1962—. *Military service:* U.S. Army, 1951-53. *Member:* National Council of Teachers of English, National Society for Performance and Instruction, California Federation of Teachers (past president). *Awards, honors:* Danforth fellowship, 1959.

WRITINGS: Program for Revision, Prentice-Hall, 1974. Contributor of poems to *Stonecloud* and *Outsider*.

WORK IN PROGRESS: Developing a pilot program in basic grammar, using computer-assisted instruction.

AVOCATIONAL INTERESTS: Chess, bridge, tennis, travel (Europe, Japan, Mexico).

* * *

JACOBSTEIN, J(oseph) Myron 1920-

PERSONAL: Born January 27, 1920, in Detroit, Mich.; son of Benjamin and Etta (Roberts) Jacobstein; married Belle Lottman, September 29, 1949; children: Ellen Rebecca, Bennett Mark. *Education:* Wayne State University, B.A., 1946; Columbia University, M.S.L.S., 1950; Illinois Institute of Technology, J.D., 1953. *Home:* 882 Cedro Way, Stanford, Calif. 94305. *Office:* Law Library, Stanford University, Stanford, Calif. 94305.

CAREER: University of Chicago Library, Chicago, Ill., cataloger, 1950-51, librarian, 1951-53; University of Illinois, Urbana, assistant law librarian, 1953-55; Columbia University, New York, N.Y., assistant law librarian, 1955-59; University of Colorado, Boulder, professor of law, 1959-63, law librarian, 1959-63; Stanford University, Stanford, Calif., professor of law, 1963—, law librarian, 1963—. Librarian for Cowles Commission for Research in Economics, 1951-53. *Military service:* U.S. Army Air Forces, 1942-46. *Member:* American Association of Law Libraries (member of executive board, 1973-75), American Bar Association, American Library Association, American Society for Information Sciences, American Society for International Law, California Library Association, Scribes.

WRITINGS: Water Law Bibliography: Economical and Political, W. H. Anderson, 1970; (editor with Meira G. Pimsleur) *Law Books in Print,* Glanville, three volumes, 1957-60, two volumes, 1966; (with Roy M. Mersky) *Fundamentals of Legal Research,* Foundation Press, 1973.

* * *

JAMES, Charles J(oseph) 1944-

PERSONAL: Born April 27, 1944, in St. Joseph, Mo.; son of Olin M. (a musician) and Mary Eleanor (Muller-Thym) James; married Carol Lee Plyley, June 7, 1970. *Education:* Rockhurst College, A.B., 1965; Indiana University, M.A.,

1968; University of Minnesota, Ph.D., 1973. *Home:* 53 Sieglitzhoferstrasse, Erlangen D8520, West Germany. *Office:* Institut fuer Angewandte Linguistik, Universitaet Erlangen-Nuernberg, 1 Bismarckstrasse, Erlangen D8520, West Germany.

CAREER: Linda Hall Library of Science and Technology, Kansas City, Mo., 1961-65; high school teacher of German in Minneapolis, Minn., 1970-71; Universitaet Erlangen-Nuernberg, Institut fuer Angewandte Linguistik, Erlangen, West Germany, "Wissenschaftlicher" assistant in applied linguistics and foreign language education, 1973—. *Member:* American Council on the Teaching of Foreign Languages, American Association of Teachers of German, American Educational Research Association, Gesellschaft fuer Angewandte Linguistik, Phi Delta Kappa.

WRITINGS: A Selective Bibliography of Doctoral Dissertations in Modern Language Education, Modern Language Association of America, 1972; (editor with Dale L. Lange) *Foreign Language Education: A Reappraisal*, National Textbook Co., 1972; (with Lange) *The Use of Newspapers and Magazines in the Foreign-Language Classroom*, Modern Language Association of America, 1974. Research associate for *Britannica Review of Foreign Language Education*, edited by Emma M. Birkmaier, Encyclopaedia Britannica, 1969. Editorial assistant for *American Council on the Teaching of Foreign Languages Annual Bibliography*, 1971-73.

WORK IN PROGRESS: A linguistic educational project to determine the most frequent structures in given communication situations in spoken American English and German, with some publications expected to result.

SIDELIGHTS: James regards himself as "a frustrated musician, who never learned to play the piano, guitar, and bass, became interested in foreign languages, . . . as a result got involved in language teaching and educational research, the latter being helped by a phlegmatic skill in mathematics."

* * *

JANDT, Fred E(dmund) 1944-

PERSONAL: Born July 19, 1944, in Seguin, Tex.; son of Eugene F. and Agnes (Naumann) Jandt. *Education:* Texas Lutheran College, B.A., 1966; Stephen F. Austin State University, M.A., 1967; Bowling Green State University, Ph.D., 1970. *Office:* Department of Speech Communication, State University of New York College at Brockport, Brockport, N.Y. 14420.

CAREER: State University of New York College at Brockport, assistant professor, 1970-73, associate professor of speech communication, 1973—. Staff member, Michigan State University-U.S. Agency for International Development's communication workshops, 1970—; instructor in industrial and labor relations programs at Cornell University, 1972—. *Member:* International Communication Association, Speech Communication Association, American Psychological Association, Communication Association of the Pacific, Eastern Communication Association, New York State Speech Association, State University of New York Communication Faculties Association (member of executive committee).

WRITINGS: (Editor) *Conflict Resolution through Communication*, Harper, 1973; (contributor) Gerald R. Miller and Herbert W. Simons, editors, *Perspectives on Communication in Social Conflict*, Prentice-Hall, 1974; (with Gerald E. Fisher and P. M. Joseph) *Human Relations in Administration*, Xerox College Publishing, 1974. Contributor to *Today's Speech*, *Speech Teacher*, *Journal of Communication*, *Educational Broadcasting*, and *Journal of Applied Communications Research*. Member of advisory staff for special issue of *Speech Monographs*, March, 1974; guest editor of *The Guide to Simulations/Games for Education and Training*, 3rd edition.

WORK IN PROGRESS: The Process of Interpersonal Communication, for Canfield; *Speech Communication Skills in the Organization*.

* * *

JANIK, Allan (Stanley Peter) 1941-

PERSONAL: Born September 18, 1941, in Chicopee, Mass.; son of Stanley Anthony (a college maintenance worker) and Delia (Peterson-Sales) Janik; married Linda K. Gardiner (a teacher), April 11, 1970. *Education:* St. Anselm's College, A.B., 1963; Villanova University, M.A., 1965; Brandeis University, Ph.D., 1971. *Politics:* Democrat. *Religion:* Roman Catholic. *Home:* 218 Wayne Ave., Narberth, Pa. 19072. *Agent:* Gerard McCauley Agency, 551 Fifth Ave., New York, N.Y. *Office:* Department of Philosophy, La Salle College, 20th St. and Olney Ave., Philadelphia, Pa. 19141.

CAREER: La Salle College, Philadelphia, Pa., assistant professor of philosophy, 1965-67, 1970—. *Member:* American Philosophical Association, Schopenhauer Gesellschaft, Phi Sigma Tau, Delta Epsilon Sigma.

WRITINGS: (With Stephen Toulmin) *Wittgenstein's Vienna*, Simon & Schuster, 1973. Contributor to proceedings; contributor of articles and reviews to philosophy journals, including *Philosophical Studies* and *Modern Austrian Literature*.

WORK IN PROGRESS: A book on the Austrian periodical *Der Brenner*, and its role in the development of twentieth-century philosophy; research on the foundations of Marxism (dialectics, irony, and Marx's literary style); research on the Marxist interpretation of ancient Greek thought.

SIDELIGHTS: Janik writes: "Travel, music, and good conversation are things I prize. I am happiest sipping a drink at a sidewalk cafe on the Zattere in Venice or listening to Monteverdi on Richard Strauss at the State Opera in Vienna. I have a smattering of French and Italian which I am always threatening to take up seriously, and more or less functional German. When visiting a city for the first time my first question is always 'Where's the zoo?' Like E. A. Poe's Bon-Bon and Brillat-Savarin I believe that there is an essential relationship between philosophy and cooking."

* * *

JANOWSKI, Tadeus M(arian) 1923-

PERSONAL: Born August 16, 1923, in Cracow, Poland; naturalized U.S. citizen in 1972; son of Stanley F. (a jurist) and Maria J. (Kijak) Janowski; married Zofia K. Owinski (an architect), April 19, 1949 (divorced, 1968); children: Barbara Margaret. *Education:* Polytechnic Academy, Cracow, B.Arch., 1948, M.Tech. Sci. & Arch., 1949; University of Illinois, M.Arch., 1962, working toward doctoral degree. *Religion:* Roman Catholic. *Home:* 224 Pine Grove St., Syracuse, N.Y. 13210. *Office:* Department of Architecture, Syracuse University, 417 Slocum Hall, Syracuse, N.Y. 13210.

CAREER: Chief architect of State Office of Design "Mastoprojekt" in Cracow, Poland, 1949-59; chief consulting architect of Committee for Urban Planning in Warsaw, Poland, 1959-60; University of Illinois, Urbana, instructor in architecture, 1960-62; University of Manitoba, Winnipeg, associate professor of architecture, 1962-65; Iowa State University, Ames, associate professor of architecture, 1965-70; Syracuse University, Syracuse, N.Y., professor of architecture, 1971—. Adjunct assistant professor at Polytechnic Academy, Cracow, 1946-50, 1958-60. *Member:* Institute of Polish Architects (member of senior council, 1956-58), Association of Polish Artists, Association of Polish Astronomers (honorary member), Tau Sigma Delta. *Awards, honors:* Pour le Merite medal, 1953.

WRITINGS: (With others) *Sacred Art in Poland,* Ars Christiana, 1956; *The Urban Scale,* Iowa State University Press, 1969; *3D Perception in Architecture,* Syracuse University Press, in press.

WORK IN PROGRESS: Humor in Architecture, completion expected in 1976.

SIDELIGHTS: Janowski has won more than fifty prizes in national and international architectural competitions.

* * *

JANSSENS, Paul Mary

PERSONAL: Born in Rock Island, Ill.; daughter of Elmer and Irene Janssens. *Education:* Marycrest College, B.A.; University of Illinois, M.A.; Mundelein College, M.A. *Office:* Holy Rosary School, Duluth, Minn.

CAREER: Teacher in public schools of Rock Island, Ill., 1957-64; Roman Catholic nun of order of Dominican Sisters of Springfield, Ill., 1964—; Holy Rosary School, Duluth, Minn., principal, 1974—. Religious education coordinator, St. Mary's Parish, East Moline, Ill., 1970-74. Member of advisory board to Office of Education for Dominican Sisters (Springfield, Ill.). *Member:* National Catholic Education Association.

WRITINGS: (With Pauletta Overbeck) *Things Go Better with Peace*, Fides, 1974.

* * *

JANTA, Alexander 1908-1974

1908—August 19, 1974; Polish poet, journalist, translator, author. Obituaries: *New York Times*, August 20, 1974; *AB Bookman's Weekly*, January 6, 1975.

* * *

JARNOW, Jeannette 1909-

PERSONAL: Born August 6, 1909, in Brooklyn, N.Y.; daughter of Joshua (a manufacturer) Ida (Krieger) Abelow; married Alfred A. Jarnow (a manufacturer), December 24, 1933; children: Betsy (Mrs. George R. Potter), Alfred, Jr. *Education:* Barnard College, B.A., 1930; Long Island University, M.S., 1958. *Politics:* Liberal. *Religion:* Jewish. *Home:* 552 East 17th St., Brooklyn, N.Y. 11226. *Office:* Department of Fashion Merchandising, Fashion Institute of Technology, 227 West 27th St., New York, N.Y. 10003.

CAREER: Abraham and Straus, Brooklyn, N.Y., buyer, 1930-44; Namn-Loeser's, Brooklyn, N.Y., merchandise manager, 1949-56; Fashion Institute of Technology, New York, N.Y., chairman of department of fashion merchandising, 1956-70, Edwin Goodman Professor of Fashion, 1956—, instructor in fashion marketing, 1970—. Consultant to Israeli College of Fashion and Textiles. *Member:* Phi Beta Kappa.

WRITINGS: (With Beatrice Judelle) *Inside the Fashion Business*, Wiley, 1965, 2nd edition, 1974; (editor) *Fashion Industry Curriculum Guides*, U.S. Superintendent of Documents, 1973.

AVOCATIONAL INTERESTS: Travel, tennis.

* * *

JARRETT, James Louis 1917-

PERSONAL: Born October 7, 1917, in Little Rock, Ark.; son of James Louis and Pauline (Williams) Jarrett; married Marjorie Ellen Clegg, January 4, 1956; children: Devin, Timothy, Gregory, Malcolm; (from previous marriage) Dennis, Julie (Mrs. Kenneth Pompei), Brent. *Education:* University of California, Los Angeles, student, 1934-37; University of Utah, B.S., 1939, M.S., 1940; University of Michigan, Ph.D., 1948. *Home:* 534 Arlington, Berkeley, Calif. 94707. *Office:* Department of Education, University of California, 5501 Tolman Hall, Berkeley, Calif. 94720.

CAREER: High school teacher in Murray, Utah, 1939-40; University of Utah, Salt Lake City, instructor, 1940-44, assistant professor, 1946-48, associate professor, 1948-52, professor of philosophy, 1952-55; Great Books Foundation, Chicago, Ill., regional director, 1955-57, president, 1958-59; Western Washington State College, Bellingham, president, 1959-64; University of California, Berkeley, professor of education, 1964—, associate director of Education Abroad Program (London, England), 1972-74. Member of board of directors of Athenian School; consultant to National Endowment for the Humanities. *Military service:* U.S. Army, 1944-46. *Member:* American Philosophical Association (president of Pacific Division, 1967).

WRITINGS: (With S. M. McMurrin) *Contemporary Philosophy*, Holt, 1954; (with R. T. Harris) *Language and Informal Logic*, Longmans, Green, 1956; *Quest for Beauty*, Prentice-Hall, 1957; *The Educational Theories of the Sophists*, Teachers College Press, 1969; *Philosophy for the Study of Education*, Houghton, 1969; *The Humanities and Humanistic Education*, Addison-Wesley, 1973. Contributor to professional journals.

WORK IN PROGRESS: Self and Selfhood.

* * *

JARVIE, I(an) C(harles) 1937-

PERSONAL: Born July 8, 1937, in South Shields, England; emigrated to Canada in 1966, naturalized, 1972; son of Charles Purves (a master mariner) and Eleanor (Carver) Jarvie; married May Friedman (a teacher), May 25, 1962; children: Suzanne, Max. *Education:* London School of Economics and Political Science, B.Sc., 1958, Ph.D., 1961. *Politics:* "Anti-Socialist." *Religion:* "Against it." *Home:* 132 Huron St., Toronto, Ontario, Canada. *Office:* Department of Philosophy, York University, Downsview, Ontario, Canada.

CAREER: University of Hong Kong, Hong Kong, lecturer in philosophy, 1962-66; York University, Toronto, Ontario, associate professor, 1966-69, professor of philosophy, 1969—. *Member:* American Philosophical Association, Mind Association, British Society for the Philosophy of Science, Philosophy of Science Association, Royal Institute of Philosophy, Royal Anthropological Institute (fellow). *Awards, honors:* Canada Council research grants, 1968 and 1972.

WRITINGS: The Revolution in Anthropology, Humanities, 1966; *Hong Kong: A Society in Transition*, Humanities, 1969; *Movies and Society*, Basic Books, 1970; *The Story of Social Anthropology*, McGraw, 1972; *Concepts and Society*, Routledge & Kegan Paul, 1972; *Functionalism*, Burgess, 1973. Contributor to a variety of journals, including *Philosophy*, *Ratio*, *British Journal of Sociology*, *Film Quarterly*, *American Anthropologist*, *Current Anthropology*, *Listener*, and *Encounter*.

WORK IN PROGRESS: Movies as Social Criticism; *The Hong Kong Movie Industry*; *Rationality and Relativism*.

SIDELIGHTS: Jarvie writes: "Even academic writing can be an act of self-discovery. I once thought of myself as a movie-crazy teenager who enjoyed reading Bertrand Russell and by accident went to the London School of Economics and married a philosopher's daughter who was studying anthropology. Since that time I have come to see the strong and illuminating connexions that can be forged between movies, anthropology, and the philosophy of science."

* * *

JAWORSKA, Wladyslawa Jadwiga 1910-

PERSONAL: Born July 14, 1910, in Rzeszow, Poland; daughter of Alfred and Maria (Peszkowska) Kober; married Wlodzimierz Jaworski (a former officer in the Polish Cavalry). *Education:* Jagellonian University, Magister Phil. (B.A.), 1934; Warsaw University, Ph.D., 1960. *Religion:* Roman Catholic. *Home:* Langiewicza 12 m. 4, 02-071 Warsaw, Poland. *Office:* Instytut Sztuki P.A.N., Dluga 28, 00-238 Warsaw, Poland.

CAREER: Art Institute of Polish Academy of Sciences, Warsaw, Poland, research associate, 1951-60, research instructor, 1960-65, head of department of fine arts, history, and theory, 1965—; Warsaw University, Warsaw, Poland, assistant professor, 1965-74, professor of history of art, 1974—. *Member:* Association Internationale des Critiques d'Art (Polish section, secretary, 1959; member of board of directors, 1969), P.E.N., Association of Historians of Art, Accademia Raffaello (Urbino; socio ordinario). *Awards, honors:* Brueckner Prize from the Polish Academy of Sciences, 1970, for *W kregu Gauguina: Malarze Skoly Pont-Aven;* Knight of the Cross of Polonia Restituta, 1974.

WRITINGS: Stasow i Riepin o Matejce (title means "Stasow and Riepin on Matejko"), Sztuka (Warsaw), 1953; (editor) Tadeusz Makowski, *Pamietnik* (title means "Diary"), Panstwowy Instytut Wydawniczy (Warsaw), 1961; *Tadeusz Makowski: Zycie i tworczosc, 1882-1932* (title means "Tadeusz Makowski: Life and Work, 1882-1932"), Ossolineum (Wroclaw), 1964, new edition, in press, German edition for Verlag der Kunst (Dresden), in press; (contributor) Hans Helmut Hofstaetter, *Jugendstil: Druckkunst* (title means "Modern Style Book Prints"), Holle-Verlag (Baden-Baden), 1968; *W kregu Gauguina: Malarze Szkoly Pont-Aven,* Panstwowy Instytut Wydawniczy, 1969, French translation by Simon Laks published as *Gauguin et l'Ecole de Pont-Aven*, Ides et Calendes (Neuchatel, Switzerland), 1971, translation from the French by Patrick Evans published as *Gauguin and the School of Pont-Aven,* New York Graphic Society, 1972; (editor) *Camille Pissarro, Listy do Syna Lucjana* (title means "Camille Pissarro: Letters to His Son"), Ossolineum, 1971; (contributor) *Edvard Munch: Probleme-Forschungen-Thesen* (title means "Edward Munch: Problems, Research, Theses"), Prestel Verlag (Munich), 1973. Contributor to *Larousse Dictionnaire de la Peinture*. Vice-director of revue *Sztuka i Krytyka* (title means "Art and Critic"), 1951-58; vice-director and director of a series of art texts, "Teksty Zrodlowe do Dziejow Teorii Sztuki," published by the Art Institute of the Polish Academy of Sciences and Ossolineum, 1962—.

WORK IN PROGRESS: A monograph on the Polish painter, Wladyslaw Slewinski; a history of Polish art from the nineteenth to the beginning of the twentieth century (the Polish Symbolist period); research for a comparative study of European art at the turn of the century.

* * *

JAY, James M(onroe) 1927-

PERSONAL: Born September 12, 1927, in Georgia; son of John B., Sr. (a clergyman) and Lizzie (Wells) Jay; married Patsie Phelps (an art teacher), June 6, 1959; children: Mark, Alicia, Byron. *Education:* Paine College, A.B., 1950; Western Reserve University (now Case Western Reserve University), graduate study, 1950-51; Ohio State University, M.Sc., 1953, Ph.D., 1956. *Religion:* Methodist. *Home:* 4205 Fullerton, Detroit, Mich. 48238. *Office:* Department of Biology, Wayne State University, Detroit, Mich. 48202.

CAREER: Southern University, Baton Rouge, La., assistant professor, 1957-58, associate professor, 1958-60, professor of biology, 1960-61; Wayne State University, Detroit, Mich., assistant professor, 1961-64, associate professor, 1964-68, professor of biology, 1969—. Member of Detroit Council for Political Education; member of board of directors of Metropolitan Hospital. *Military service:* U.S. Army, 1946-47; became sergeant.

MEMBER: American Chemical Society, American Society for Microbiology, American Public Health Association (fellow), Institute of Food Technologists, American Association for the Advancement of Science, American Association of University Professors, New York Academy of Sciences, Sigma Xi, Beta Beta Beta. *Awards, honors:* Probus Club award for achievement in sciences from Wayne State University, 1969; distinguished alumni award from Paine College, 1969.

WRITINGS: Modern Food Microbiology, Van Nostrand, 1970; *Negroes in Science: Natural Science Doctorates, 1876-1969*, Balamp, 1971. Contributor to *Journal of Bacteriology, Applied Microbiology, Journal of Food Science*, and *Canadian Journal of Microbiology*.

WORK IN PROGRESS: A work that will acquaint consumers with what actually goes on behind food production lines.

* * *

JAY, Martin (Evan) 1944-

PERSONAL: Born May 4, 1944, in New York, N.Y.; son of Edward (an advertising executive) and Sari (a teacher; maiden name, Sidel) Jay; married Mary Catherine Sullivan Gallagher, July 6, 1974; children: Maragret Shana Gallagher (stepdaughter). *Education:* Attended London School of Economics and Political Science, 1963-64; Union College, Schenectady, N.Y., B.A., 1965; Harvard University, Ph.D., 1971. *Residence:* Berkeley, Calif. *Office:* Department of History, University of California, Berkeley, Calif. 94720.

CAREER: University of California, Berkeley, assistant professor of history, 1971—. Senior associate at St. Antony's College, Oxford, England, 1974-75. *Member:* American Historical Association. *Awards, honors:* Danforth Foundation fellowship, 1965-71; Herbert Baxter Adams Award from American Historical Association, 1973, for best first book in European history; Guggenheim fellowship, 1974-75.

WRITINGS: The Dialectical Imagination: A History of the Frankfurt School and the Institute of Social Research, 1923-1950, Little, Brown, 1973. Contributor to history and sociology journals.

WORK IN PROGRESS: Research on the concept of totality in twentieth-century Marxist thought, and on the life and work of Siegfried Kracauer.

* * *

JELAVICH, Barbara 1923-

PERSONAL: Born April 12, 1923, in Belleville, Ill.; married Charles Jelavich (a professor of history), September 27, 1944; children: Mark, Peter. *Education:* University of California, Berkeley, A.B., 1943, M.A., 1944, Ph.D., 1948. *Office:* Department of History, Indiana University, Bloomington, Ind. 47401.

CAREER: Mills College, Oakland, Calif., instructor in history, spring, 1950; University of California, Berkeley, junior research historian at Institute of Slavic Studies, fall, 1953, lecturer in history, Extension Division, 1959-60; Indiana University, Bloomington, lecturer, 1961, assistant professor, 1962-64, associate professor, 1964-67, professor of East European history, 1967—. *Member:* Phi Beta Kappa. *Awards, honors:* Alice Freeman Palmer fellowship of American Association of University Women, 1960-61; grants from American Philosophical Society, 1962, American Council of Learned Societies, 1962, 1969-70, Rockefeller Foundation, 1963-64, and National Endowment for the Humanities, 1969-70.

WRITINGS: Russia and the Rumanian National Cause, 1858-1859, Slavic and East European Series, Indiana University, 1959, reprinted, Archon, 1974; (with husband, Charles Jelavich) *Russia in the East, 1876-1880: The Russo-Turkish War and the Kuldja Crisis as Seen Through the Letters of A. G. Jomini to N. K. Giers,* E. J. Brill, 1959; (editor with Charles Jelavich) *The Education of a Russian Statesman: The Memoirs of Nicholas Karlovich Giers,* University of California Press, 1962; *Russia and Greece During the Regency of King Othon, 1832-1835: Russian Documents on the First Years of Greek Independence,* Institute of Balkan Studies, 1962; *Russland 1852-1871: Aus den Berichten der bayerischen Gesandtschaft in St. Petersburg,* Harrassowitz, 1963; (editor with Charles Jelavich) *The Balkans in Transition,* University of California Press, 1963; *A Century of Russian Foreign Policy,* Lippincott, 1964, revised edition published as *St. Petersburg and Moscow: Tsarist and Soviet Foreign Policy, 1814-1974,* Indiana University Press, in press; (with Charles Jelavich) *The Balkans,* Prentice-Hall, 1965; *Russia and the Greek Revolution of 1843,* Oldenbourg, 1966; *The Hapsburg Empire in European Affairs,* Rand McNally, 1969; *The Ottoman Empire, the Great Powers, and the Straits Question, 1870-1887,* Indiana University Press, 1973.

Contributor: Charles Jelavich, editor, *Language and Area Studies: East Central and Southeastern Europe,* University of Chicago Press, 1969; Paul L. Horecky, editor, *Southeastern Europe: A Guide to Basic Publications,* University of Chicago Press, 1969. Contributor to yearbooks and journals. Member of editorial board, *Suedost-Forschungen (Munich).*

JENKINS, Kenneth V(incent) 1930-

PERSONAL: Born June 11, 1930, in Elizabeth, N.J.; son of Thomas A. and Rebecca M. (Williams) Jenkins; married, October 16, 1954; children: Roland, Roderick, Howard, Rebecca, Leah. *Education:* Columbia University, A.B., 1952, A.M., 1953, currently Ph.D. candidate. *Home:* 50 Holloway St., Freeport, N.Y. 11520. *Office:* Department of Afro-American Studies, Nassau Community College, Garden City, N.Y.

CAREER: Junior and senior high school teacher of English in Rockville Centre, N.Y., 1953-71, chairman of high school department of English, 1966-71; Nassau Community College, Garden City, N.Y., lecturer in English, 1966-71, acting chairman of Afro-American studies department, 1972-73, now assistant professor. Consultant to New York State Department of Education, Bureau of English, 1965-72; member of Afro-American Institute, 1970—; chairman of board of directors, Target Youth Centers, Inc., 1972—. *Member:* Afro-American Heritage Association, Association for the Study of Afro-American Life and History, Mensa, International Platform Association, Pacifica Foundation (member of national board of directors, 1974—), Unitarian Black Caucus, Rockville Centre Teachers Association (president, 1965-67). *Awards, honors:* Columbia University Baker Award, 1953; B'nai Sholem Brotherhood Award, 1956; Pendleton fellowship, Columbia Teachers College, 1968; Little Mecca Youth Centre Award, 1973.

WRITINGS: Last Day in Church (novelette), Lyle Stuart, 1966; *History of Ethiopian Women*, Organization of Ethiopian Women, 1970. Author of film, "Scandalize My Name," 1974. Contributor of articles and reviews to *Conch.*

WORK IN PROGRESS: A play, "Chaka"; research on Afro-American writers of the 1930's; an English textbook series for Heath.

* * *

JENKINS, Louis 1942-

PERSONAL: Born October 28, 1942, in Oklahoma City, Okla.; son of Burke (a painter) and Genevieve (Webring) Jenkins; married Sandra Brashear, December 7, 1963 (divorced, 1968): married Ann Jacobson (a librarian), December 26, 1970. *Education:* Wichita State University, student, 1967-69. *Home address:* P.O. Box 3082, Duluth, Minn. 55803.

CAREER: Oklahoma Natural Gas Co., Enid, laborer, 1964-66; clerk, Wichita Public Library, Wichita, Kan., 1967-69, and Jefferson County Library, Golden, Colo., 1970; Knife River Press, Duluth, Minn., owner and editor, 1971—.

WRITINGS: The Well Digger's Wife (poems), Minnesota Writers Publishing House, 1973. Editor of *Steelhead*, 1971—.

* * *

JENNINGS, Dana Close 1923-

PERSONAL: Born January 24, 1923, in Topeka, Kans.; son of Dana Thorp (a farmer) and Mary (Close) Jennings; married Mary Kay Reecy (an editor), May 13, 1972; children: Elizabeth Jane. *Education:* Kansas State University, B.S., 1949. *Politics:* "I vote the candidate, not the party." *Religion:* "Yes." *Home and office address:* Rt. 3, Box 177, Madison, S.D. 57042.

CAREER: Has worked as a janitor, farmhand, truck driver, oilfield roughneck, private secretary, employment broker, hospital orderly, shipping clerk, laboratory technician, dishwasher, cowboy, gold miner, woodcutter, advertising copywriter and account executive, farmer, farm organizer, and lecturer; free-lance writer and photographer, 1947—; *Daily Leader*, Madison, S.D., reporter, photographer, and feature writer, 1963-67; Dakota State College, Madison, S.D., instructor in journalism and photography and director of news service and publications, 1970-73; University of South Dakota, School of Medicine, Vermillion, news director and medical photographer, 1973—. *Military service:* U.S. Navy, 1942-44. *Member:* Garden Writers of America.

WRITINGS—All published by North Plains Press, except as noted: *World's Window on Your College*, General Beadle State College, 1967; *Cattle on a Thousand Hills*, 1968; *Days of Steam & Glory*, 1968; *Greatest Steam Show on Earth*, 1969; *Free Ice Water*, 1969; *Where the Buffalo Roam Again*, 1969; *Slick Trick*, 1969; *Blood on the Killdeer*, 1969; *Old Threshers*, Midwest Old Threshers & Settlers, 1971; *Farm Steam Shows*, 1972. Contributor of numerous articles to *Dakota Farmer* and other periodicals. Also author of filmscript, "This Land We Call Ours," 1964. Founding editor, *Catholic Rural Life*, 1958-61, *People!*, 1972-73, and *Buffalo!*, 1972—.

WORK IN PROGRESS: Buffalo Ranching; research on steam power on the farm, cancer therapy and vaccine, solar energy applications, and self-sufficient living.

SIDELIGHTS: Jennings told *CA* that, among other experiences, he was "sent to prison without being permitted to know the charges or his accusers; founded own [advertising] agency, failed; worked on various small newspapers and magazines, mostly rural oriented; was reprimanded while teaching journalism and photography for doing such a good job that students left college to take jobs." His books are illustrated—mostly with his own photographs. *Avocational interests:* Vegetable gardening, camping, woodcraft, horsemanship, alternative energy sources, and conservation.

* * *

JENNINGS, Jerry (Edward) 1935-

PERSONAL: Born May 12, 1935, in Kalamazoo, Mich.; son of Edward James (a school superintendent) and Marie (Hayner) Jennings; married Mary Jean McManus, September 6, 1958; children: Kathryn, James, Holly. *Education:* Michigan State University, B.A., 1957, M.A., 1974; Columbia University, graduate study, 1959-60. *Religion:* Congregationalist. *Home:* 533 Worcester N.E., Grand Rapids, Mich. 49503. *Office:* The Fideler Co., 31 Ottawa N.W., Grand Rapids, Mich. 49502.

CAREER: United Press International, Detroit, Mich., news writer, 1958-59; Scholastic Magazines, Inc., New York, N.Y., assistant editor, 1960-62; Fideler Co. (textbook publishers), Grand Rapids, Mich., editor, 1962-69; Scott, Foresman and Co. (book publishers), Glenview, Ill., developmental editor, 1969-71; Fideler Co., senior editor, 1971—. Precinct delegate for Democratic Party in Michigan, 1964-68; member of board of directors, Grand Rapids Youth Ministry, 1967-69; chairman of land use committee of West Michigan Environmental Action Council, 1973—. *Member:* American Educational Research Association, American Civil Liberties Union.

WRITINGS—All published by Fideler: (With Marion H. Smith) *The South*, 1965; (editor) *The Northeast*, 1967; (editor) *The West*, 1972; (with William D. Allen, Raymond E. Fideler, and Carol Kvande) *Africa and South America*, 1972; (with Benjamin E. Thomas and Allen) *Africa*, 1972; (with Margaret Fisher Hertel and Mary Jane Fowler) *Colonial America*, 1974; (with Hertel) *Inquiring About Freedom*, 1974.

WORK IN PROGRESS: A high school text in American government.

AVOCATIONAL INTERESTS: Reading in history and the behavioral sciences, playing piano, skiing, canoeing, camping.

* * *

JENNISON, Christopher 1938-

PERSONAL: Born July 27, 1938, in New York, N.Y.; son of Keith Warren (a writer) and Emily (a teacher; maiden name, Slocum) Jennison; married Annice Theobald, October 21, 1961; children: Clark Nicholas, Edmund Bruce. *Education:* Rutgers University, A.B., 1960. *Politics:* Democrat. *Home:* One Sylvan Way, Wayland, Mass. 01778.

CAREER: Harper & Row Publishers, Inc., New York, N.Y., employed in college sales and acquisition, 1961-68; Xerox College Publishing, Lexington, Mass., senior editor, 1968-74. *Military service:* U.S. Army Reserve, 1960-66.

WRITINGS: Wait 'Til Next Year, Norton, 1974. Contributor of articles and reviews to *OPT* and *Los Angeles Times*.

WORK IN PROGRESS: Research on sports areas for a book.

AVOCATIONAL INTERESTS: Music, collecting 1950's sports memorabilia.

* * *

JENSEN, Alan F(rederick) 1938-

PERSONAL: Born May 12, 1938, in Sioux Falls, S.D.; son of Paul C. and Mildred (a secretary; maiden name, Christensen) Jensen; married Dianne Anderson, May 28, 1959 (divorced, 1967); married Sandra Naumchik (a secretary), May 31, 1969; children: (first marriage) Gayle Lynne, Todd Alan; (second marriage) Christina Louise. *Education:* Sioux Falls College, B.A., 1961; University of South Dakota, M.A., 1962; Washington State University, Ph.D., 1967. *Politics:* Democrat. *Residence:* Chico, Calif. *Office:* Department of Sociology, California State University, First and Normal, Chico, Calif. 95926.

CAREER: California State University, Chico, assistant professor, 1965-69, associate professor, 1969-74, professor of sociology, 1974—. *Military service:* U.S. Marine Corps Reserve, 1955-61. *Member:* United Professors of California.

WRITINGS: Sociology: Concepts and Concerns, Rand McNally, 1970. Contributor to academic journals.

WORK IN PROGRESS: The History and Evolution of Human Consciousness.

* * *

JENSEN, Paul M(orris) 1944-

PERSONAL: Born January 11, 1944, in Greenport, N.Y.; son of Christian Jensen (a mariner) and Emily (a teacher; maiden name, Morris) Jensen. *Education:* State University of New York at Albany, B.A., 1965; Columbia University,

M.F.A., 1966; further graduate study at State University of New York at Buffalo, 1969, and New York University, 1973, 1974. *Home:* 114 Chestnut St., Oneonta, N.Y. 13820. *Office:* Department of Speech and Theatre, State University of New York College, Oneonta, N.Y. 13820.

CAREER: High school teacher of English, 1966-67; State University of New York College at Oneonta, instructor, 1967-70, assistant professor of film, 1970—. *Member:* Society for Cinema Studies, University Film Association. *Awards, honors:* State University of New York Research Foundation grants, 1968-70, 1970-72.

WRITINGS: The Cinema of Fritz Lang, A. S. Barnes, 1969; *Boris Karloff and His Films*, A. S. Barnes, 1975.

Contributor: Arthur Lennig, editor, *Classics of the Film*, Wisconsin Film Society Press, 1965; Arthur Lennig, editor, *The Sound Film*, Walter Snyder (Troy, N.Y.), 1969; Richard Corliss, editor, *The Hollywood Screenwriter*, Avon, 1972; Fritz Lang, *Metropolis* (film script in print), Simon & Schuster, 1973; Stanley J. Solomon, editor, *The Classic Cinema: Essays in Criticism*, Harcourt, 1973; *Masterworks of the German Cinema*, Harper, 1974. Contributor to *Films in Review*, *Film Heritage*, *Film Comment*, and other film journals; stringer for *Variety*, 1967-68.

WORK IN PROGRESS: A book analyzing the work of certain directors of horror films; articles for a book on sound film, edited by Arthur Lennig, for publication by Hopkinson & Blake; research for a book covering the range of popular genres in film.

SIDELIGHTS: Jensen did research in England the summers of 1971 and 1974, particularly at British Film Institute and London's Leighton House Theatre Museum.

* * *

JEWETT, Paul King 1919-

PERSONAL: Born October 6, 1919, in Johnson City, N.Y.; son of Paul Smith (a builder) and Lucetta (King) Jewett; married Christine Coleman (a librarian), May 10, 1945; children: Fern, Victoria. *Education:* Wheaton College, Wheaton, Ill., B.A., 1941; Westminster Theological Seminary, Philadelphia, Pa., Th.B. and Th.M., both 1945; Harvard University, Ph.D., 1951. *Religion:* Presbyterian. *Home:* 1120 Madre Vista Rd., Altadena, Calif. 91001. *Office:* Fuller Theological Seminary, 135 North Oakland, Pasadena, Calif. 91101.

CAREER: Ordained Presbyterian clergyman, 1956; Gordon Divinity School, Boston, Mass., professor of philosophy of religion, 1950-55; Fuller Theological Seminary, Pasadena, Calif., associate professor, 1955-64, professor of systematic theology, 1964—. Dean of Young Life Institute, summers, 1955—.

WRITINGS: Emil Brunner's Concept of Revelation, Evangelical Theological Society, 1954; *Emil Brunner*, Inter-Varsity Press, 1961; *The Lord's Day*, Eerdmans, 1971. Contributor to religious publications.

WORK IN PROGRESS: Man as Male and Female, for Eerdmans.

* * *

JOHNSON, B(ryan) S(tanley William) 1933-1973

February 5, 1933—November, 1973; British novelist, poet, playwright, editor, film and television director/producer. Obituaries: *AB Bookman's Weekly*, July 15, 1974; *Transatlantic Review*, summer, 1974. (*CA*-9/10).

JOHNSON, Dorothy Biddle 1887(?)-1974

1887(?)—October 18, 1974; American lecturer and author of books on flower arrangement and home crafts. Obituaries: *New York Times*, October 19, 1974; *AB Bookman's Weekly*, November 18, 1974.

* * *

JOHNSON, Dorothy E(thel) 1920-

PERSONAL: Born December 29, 1920, in Brooklyn, N.Y. *Education:* Queens College (now Queens College of the City University of New York), B.A., 1941; New York University, M.A., 1947; Purdue University, M.S., 1962, Ph.D., 1964. *Home:* 9500 Chestnut Lane, Munster, Ind. 46321. *Office:* Department of Education, Purdue University, Calumet Campus, Hammond, Ind. 46323.

CAREER: Harper & Row Publishers, Inc., New York, N.Y., production editor, 1947-58; Houghton Mifflin Co., Boston, Mass., production editor, 1958-60; high school guidance director in Delphi, Ind., 1960-62; Ball State University, Muncie, Ind., assistant professor, 1964-68, associate professor of psychology, 1968-69; Purdue University, Calumet Campus, Hammond, Ind., associate professor, 1969-74, professor of education, 1974—. *Military service:* U.S. Navy, Waves, communications officer, 1944-46. *Member:* American Personnel and Guidance Association, Association for Supervision and Curriculum Development, Association for Counselor Education and Supervision, National Vocational Guidance Association, Indiana Personnel and Guidance Association, Indiana Association for Supervision and Curriculum Development, Altrusa Club (Hammond, Ind.; member of board of directors, 1972-75).

WRITINGS: (With Harry Shaw) *Workbook to Accompany Complete Course in Freshman English*, Harper, 1959; *Expanding and Modifying Guidance Programs*, Houghton, 1968; (with Mary Vestermark) *Barriers and Hazards in Counseling*, Houghton, 1970. Contributor to *School Counselor* and *Counseling Education and Supervision*.

WORK IN PROGRESS: Self-Evaluation Guide to Professional Development for School Counselors, and manual, with Sam Paravonian.

* * *

JOHNSON, Greer 1920(?)-1974

1920(?)—October 30, 1974; American playwright, music and dance critic. Obituaries: *New York Times*, November 3, 1974.

* * *

JOHNSON, James Craig 1944-

PERSONAL: Born in 1944, in Minneapolis, Minn.; married; children: two. *Education:* University of Arizona, B.S., 1966, M.A., 1967; University of Minnesota, Ph.D., 1970. *Office:* Department of Marketing, College of Business Administration, University of Tulsa, 600 South College, Tulsa, Okla. 74104.

CAREER: University of Tulsa, Tulsa, Okla., assistant professor of marketing and transportation, 1971—. *Military service:* U.S. Army, Transportation Corps, 1967-70; became captain. *Member:* American Economic Association, American Marketing Association, American Society of Traffic and Transportation, Association of Interstate Commerce Commission Practitioners, National Council of Physical Distribution Management, Delta Nu Alpha, Delta

Sigma Pi, Beta Gamma Sigma, Omicron Delta Epsilon, Pi Sigma Epsilon.

WRITINGS: (Editor with Louis E. Boone) *Marketing Channels,* General Learning Press, 1973; *Trucking Mergers: A Regulatory Viewpoint,* Heath, 1973; (editor) *Readings in Physical Distribution,* Commerce Press, 1974. Contributor to journals in his field.

WORK IN PROGRESS: An introductory textbook on physical distribution, with Don Wood.

* * *

JOHNSON, James William 1927-

PERSONAL: Born March 1, 1927, in Birmingham, Ala.; son of J. Terry (a lawyer) and Maude Belle (Brown) Johnson; married Nan Heffelfinger, October 5, 1957; children: Miranda, Reed. *Education:* Birmingham-Southern College, A.B. (cum laude), 1950; Harvard University, M.A., 1950; Vanderbilt University, Ph.D., 1954; University College, London, postdoctoral work, 1954-55. *Politics:* Democrat. *Religion:* Agnostic. *Residence:* Rochester, N.Y. *Office:* English Department, University of Rochester, Rochester, N.Y. 14627.

CAREER: Vanderbilt University, Nashville, Tenn., instructor in English, 1952-54; University of Rochester, Rochester, N.Y., instructor, 1955-58, assistant professor, 1959-61, associate professor, 1961-65, professor of English, 1965—. *Military service:* U.S. Navy, 1945-46. *Member:* Modern Language Association of America, English Institute, American Association of University Professors, Crabtree Foundation, Phi Beta Kappa, Friends of University Libraries, Landmark Society, Memorial Art Gallery, Rochester Museum, Civic Music Association, University Club of Rochester. *Awards, honors:* American Council of Learned Societies fellowship, 1949-50, 1966-67; Fulbright fellowship, 1954-55; Folger Library fellowship, 1963; Guggenheim fellowship, 1970-71.

WRITINGS: Logic and Rhetoric, Macmillan, 1962; *The Formation of English Neo-Classical Thought*, Princeton University Press, 1967; (editor and author of introduction) *Utopian Literature: A Selection*, Modern Library, 1968; (compiler) *Concepts of Literature*, Prentice-Hall, 1970; (compiler) *Prose in Practice: A Rhetorical Reader*, Harcourt, 1971.

WORK IN PROGRESS: A critical biography of John Wilmot, Earl of Rochester; editing a critical edition of Rochester's dramatic writings; *Premises in Literary Study*, an anthology of critical essays; editing a three-volume anthology of British literature from 1650 to 1800.

SIDELIGHTS: Johnson reads Latin, Greek, Anglo-Saxon, French, German, and some Russian, Portuguese, Spanish, and Gothic.

* * *

JOHNSON, Jerry Mack 1927-
(Jerry Mack)

PERSONAL: Born October 23, 1927, in San Angelo, Tex.; son of Earnest L. and Jewell Gill (Brazier) Johnson; married Billie Alexander, May 25, 1956; children: Nancy. *Education:* San Angelo College, A.A., 1947; Sul Ross State University, B.S., 1949, M.S., 1951. *Politics:* Independent. *Religion:* Methodist. *Home and office:* 3222 North Oakes St., San Angelo, Tex. 76901.

CAREER: Has worked as miner, prospector, merchant seaman, ranch hand, rodeo clown, professional bull rider, worker in an oilfield, salesman, school teacher, naturalist, and agriculturist; Supreme Feed Mills, Inc., sales representative, 1960, vice-president, 1966—. *Military service:* U.S. Navy, Seabees, 1945-46; served in Pacific theater.

WRITINGS: Country Wisdom, Doubleday, 1974.

Under pseudonym Jerry Mack: *What's It Worth? and Where You Can Sell It!: The Collector's Marketplace*, Educator Books, 1970; *Catfish Farming Handbook*, Educator Books, 1971.

Author of "The Signs and Seasons of Mother Nature," a column distributed to country weekly newspapers, 1974—. Contributor of articles on marketing, crop, and livestock production to agricultural journals.

WORK IN PROGRESS: Country Wisdom, Volume II, *Cowboy Wisdom*; *Sea Wisdom*; *How You Can Be a Catfish Farmer: Backyard or Commercial.*

* * *

JOHNSON, Lemuel A. 1941-

PERSONAL: Born December 15, 1941, in Nigeria; son of Thomas Ishelu and Daisy (a teacher; maiden name, Williams) Johnson; married Marian Yankson (a dental hygienist), August 28, 1965; children: Yma, Yshely. *Education:* Oberlin College, B.A., 1965; Pennsylvania State University, M.A., 1966; University of Michigan, Ph.D., 1969; also studied at Middlebury College, Universite d'Aix-Marseille II, and University of Paris. *Home:* 415 Ventura Court, Ann Arbor, Mich. 48103. *Office:* Department of English, University of Michigan, Ann Arbor, Mich. 48104.

CAREER: Training program instructor, Peace Corps, Bloomington, Ind., 1964; Pennsylvania State University, University Park, member of faculty in department of Spanish, Italian, and Portuguese, 1966; University of Michigan, Ann Arbor, member of faculty of department of Romance languages and literatures, 1967-68, of English department, 1968-70; University of Sierra Leone, Fourah Bay College, Freetown, member of English faculty, 1970-72; University of Michigan, associate professor of English, 1972—. Examiner in English oral literature for West Africa Examinations Council, 1970-72; host of "Radio Forum Series," for Sierra Leone Broadcasting Service, 1971-72; has given poetry readings at University of Michigan, 1973, 1974.

MEMBER: African Studies Association, Midwest Modern Language Association. *Awards, honors:* Avery Hopwood Awards from University of Michigan, 1967, for essay "Piano and Drum" and short story collection *The Voice of the Turtle*; Bredvold-Thorpe prize for scholarly publication from University of Michigan, 1972, for *The Devil, the Gargoyle, and the Buffoon*.

WRITINGS: (Contributor of translation) *Modern Spanish Theatre*, Dutton, 1968; (contributor) *African Writing Today*, Manyland Books, 1970; (contributor) Joseph Okpaku, editor, *New African Literature and the Arts*, Crowell, 1970; *The Devil, the Gargoyle, and the Buffoon: The Negro as Metaphor in Western Literature*, Kennikat, 1971; *Highlife for Caliban: Poems*, Ardis, 1973. Also contributor to *Blacks in Hispanic Literature*, edited by Miriam DeCosta. Contributor to *Literary Review* and *Journal of New African Literature and the Arts*.

WORK IN PROGRESS: Hottentots, Coolies, and Messiahs: Nationalism in Chinese and African Literature, 1890-1960; *The Book of Coporal Bundu*, a book of poems; research toward a theory of esthetics in African literature.

SIDELIGHTS: Johnson is fluent in French, Spanish, Portuguese, Italian, and German. He has traveled in Europe and Africa.

* * *

JOHNSON, Lyndon Baines 1908-1973

PERSONAL: Born August 27, 1908, on farm near Stonewall, Tex.; son of Samuel Ealy, Jr. (a farmer and state legislator) and Rebekah (a teacher of elocution; maiden name, Baines) Johnson; married Claudia Alta (better known as Lady Bird) Taylor, November 17, 1934; children: Lynda Bird (Mrs. Charles S. Robb), Luci Baines (Mrs. Patrick J. Nugent). *Education:* Southwest Texas State Teachers College (now Southwest Texas State College), B.S., 1930; Georgetown University, law studies, 1935-36. *Home:* LBJ Ranch, Stonewall, Tex.

CAREER: Thirty-sixth President of the United States. Spent several years between high school and college doing odd jobs in California and working on road crew in Texas; teacher in public schools of Cotulla, Tex., 1928-29, and Houston, Tex., 1930-31; went to Washington, D.C., as secretary to Congressman Richard Kleberg, 1931-35; Texas state director of National Youth Administration (appointed by President Franklin D. Roosevelt), 1935-37; ran on New Deal platform to win election to U.S. House of Representatives, 1937-38, filling unexpired term of Congressman James B. Buchanan; re-elected to House of Representatives every congressional term, 1938-48, but lost race for vacant Senate seat in special election, 1941; U.S. Senator, 1949-61, serving as Democratic floor leader, 1953-61; made bid for Democratic presidential nomination, 1960, and was picked for vice-presidential post by the successful candidate, John F. Kennedy; as vice-president, 1961-63, headed National Aeronautics and Space Council, President's Committee on Equal Employment Opportunity, and Peace Corps Advisory Council; succeeded the assassinated Kennedy to presidency, November 22, 1963; elected President (486 electoral votes to 52), 1964, and sworn in January 20, 1965; declined to run again in 1968; retired to his Texas ranch and oversaw construction of Johnson Library housing his papers on University of Texas campus; a heart attack ended his life. *Military service:* U.S. Naval Reserve, active duty, 1941-42; served as special presidential emissary in Australia and New Zealand; became commander; received Silver Star; resigned commission, 1964.

AWARDS, HONORS: Forty honorary degrees from American and several foreign colleges and universities, 1943-66, including Brown University, University of Hawaii, University of the Philippines, University of Maryland, Tufts University, Southwest Texas State College, University of California, Georgetown University, University of Texas, Princeton University, Texas Christian University, Catholic University of America, University of Michigan, Yeshiva University, and Chulalongkorn University.

WRITINGS: (With Robert C. Weaver, Joseph P. Lyford, and John Cogley) *The Negro as an American*, Center for the Study of Democratic Institutions, 1963; *My Hope for America*, Random House, 1964; *The President Speaks: On Prosperity and Poverty, Civil Rights, Nuclear War, Communism, Your Future*, Dell, 1964; *A Time for Action: A Selection from the Speeches and Writings of Lyndon B. Johnson, 1953-64* (introduction by Adlai E. Stevenson), Atheneum, 1964; *President Johnson's Design for a "Great Society"* (speeches), Congressional Quarterly, 1965; *Lyndon B. Johnson on Conservation*, five volumes (looseleaf), U.S. Department of the Interior, 1965; *Public Papers of the President of the United States, Lyndon B. Johnson, Containing the Public Messages, Speeches, and Statements of the President, 1963/64-1967*, eight volumes, U.S. Government Printing Office, 1965-68; *The Promise of the New Asia: United States Policy in the Far East as Stated by President Johnson on His Pacific Journey*, U.S. Government Printing Office, 1966; *This America*, Random House, 1966; *To Heal and to Build: The Programs of Lyndon B. Johnson*, edited by James MacGregor Burns, McGraw, 1968; (author of introductory message; essays by others) Robert A. Goldwin, editor, *A Nation of Cities: Essays on American Urban Problems*, Rand McNally, 1968; *The Choices We Face*, Bantam, 1969; (author of foreword) Eugene R. Black, *Alternative in Southeast Asia*, Praeger, 1969; *The Vantage Point: Perspectives of the Presidency, 1963-1969*, Holt, 1971.

Books of quotations: Frances Spatz Leighton, editor, *The Johnson Wit*, Citadel, 1965; Bill Adler, editor, *The Johnson Humor*, Simon & Schuster, 1965; *Quotations from Chairman LBJ*, Simon & Schuster, 1968; Sarah H. Hayes and the staff of *Quote*, compilers and editors, *The Quotable Lyndon B. Johnson*, Droke, 1968.

Speeches and addresses published by U.S. Government Printing Office and other government agencies, except as noted: *Freedom, Peace and Progress for America*, Pan American Union, 1963; *The Hand and Heart of This Country*, 1964; *America as a Great Power*, 1964; *Pattern for Peace in Southeast Asia*, 1965; *We Will Stand in Viet-Nam*, 1965; *The Road to Justice: Three Major Statements on Civil Rights*, 1965; *A More Beautiful America*, American Conservation Association, 1965; *Government and the Critical Intelligence*, Brookings Institution, 1966; *Making Europe Whole: An Unfinished Task*, 1966; *Learning and Liberty*, 1967; *Protocol Relating to the Status of Refugees*, 1968; *A New Step Toward Peace*, 1968; and many other papers.

BIOGRAPHICAL/CRITICAL SOURCES: Booth Mooney, *The Lyndon Johnson Story*, Bodley Head, 1964; Harry Provence, *Lyndon B. Johnson*, Fleet, 1964; Howard B. Furer, editor, *Lyndon B. Johnson, 1908—; Chronology—Documents—Bibliographical Aids*, Oceana, 1971; Hanes Johnson and Richard Harwood, editors, *Lyndon: A Washington Post Pictorial Biography*, Praeger, 1973.

(Died January 23, 1973)

* * *

JOHNSON, Mary Anne 1943-

PERSONAL: Born January 26, 1943, in Brooklyn, N.Y.; daughter of David W. and Maria (Esteve) Sheehan; divorced; children: Mary Kathleen, Jacqueline Ann. *Education:* St. Mary's School of Nursing, Rochester, N.Y., student, 1960-61. *Politics:* Democrat. *Residence:* New York, N.Y. *Office:* Educreative Systems, Inc., 230 West 78th St., New York, N.Y. 10024.

CAREER: Worked as editor and project manager on print and audio-visual school projects; Educreative Systems (educational materials), Inc., New York, N.Y., executive vice-president and treasurer. Democratic county committeewoman for New York County.

WRITINGS: (With James Olsen) *Exiles from the American Dream*, Walker & Co., 1974; (with Olsen) *Runaways*, Harper, in press. Author of educational filmstrip scripts.

WORK IN PROGRESS: Alternatives; The Why of PSI Phenomena; Welfare Hotel; Island.

AVOCATIONAL INTERESTS: Photography, travel (Bermuda, Bahamas, Lebanon, Afghanistan, Mexico), needlepoint, weaving, cooking, baking, reading.

* * *

JOHNSON, Michael L(illard) 1943-

PERSONAL: Born June 29, 1943, in Springfield, Mo.; son of I. H. (a businessman) and Margaret Joan (Vernon) Johnson; married Lee Ann Smith, June 7, 1965. *Education:* Rice University, B.A., 1965, Ph.D., 1968; Stanford University, M.A., 1967. *Home:* 3016 Sagebrush, Lawrence, Kan. 66045. *Office:* Department of English, University of Kansas, Lawrence, Kan. 66045.

CAREER: Rice University, Houston, Tex., lecturer in English, 1968-69; University of Kansas, Lawrence, assistant professor, 1969-72, associate professor of English, 1972—. *Awards, honors:* Woodrow Wilson fellowship, 1965-66.

WRITINGS: The New Journalism: The Underground Press, the Artists of Nonfiction, and Changes in the Established Media, University Press of Kansas, 1972. Contributor of articles and poems to little magazines and professional journals.

WORK IN PROGRESS: Prometheus Reborn, a book on technology and contemporary culture; *Holistic Technology*; *Poetry of the Self*, a book on the major world lyric traditions.

SIDELIGHTS: Johnson is interested in oenology and cancer research. *Avocational interests:* Tennis, Mozart, Herbie Hancock, good poetry (in eight languages), beautiful women, a decorum of elegance in any activity.

* * *

JOHNSON, Richard Tanner 1938-

PERSONAL: Born June 14, 1938, in the United States; son of George P. (a businessman) and Marian (Tanner) Johnson. *Education:* University of California, Berkeley, B.S., 1961; Harvard University, M.B.A., 1967, D.B.A., 1971. *Office:* Graduate School of Business, Room 281, Stanford University, Stanford, Calif. 94305.

CAREER: Stanford University, Stanford, Calif., assistant professor, 1971-73, associate professor of business, 1974—. White House fellow and special assistant to Secretaries of Labor, Willard Wirtz and George Shultz, 1968-69; senior staff member of White House committee on organizing the Office of Management and Budget, 1969-70; consultant to National Commission on Productivity, 1972-73. *Member:* Tau Beta Phi.

WRITINGS: Managing the White House: An Intimate Study of the Presidency, Harper, 1974.

* * *

JOHNSON, Robert I(var) 1933-

PERSONAL: Born August 18, 1933, in Chicago, Ill.; son of Ivar Carl and Anna E. (Wirkula) Johnson; married Patricia Anne Horgan, June 30, 1962; children: Christine Anne, Selenie Anne. *Education:* Art Institute of Chicago, student, 1947-51; Wright Junior College, Diploma, 1952; Northwestern University, A.B., 1957; University of Michigan, graduate student, 1958-59. *Religion:* Lutheran. *Home:* 3 Overlook Dr., Golf, Ill. 60029. *Office:* W. C. McCrone Associates, 2820 South Michigan Ave., Chicago, Ill. 60616.

CAREER: Adler Planetarium and Astronomical Museum, Chicago, Ill., planetarium technician, 1953-55, assistant director and acting director, 1959, director, 1960-66; Kansas City Museum Association, Kansas City, Mo., director of Kansas City Museum of History and Science, 1966-70; Envirco, Inc., Northbrook, Ill., executive vice-president and director, 1970-72; W. C. McCrone Associates, Chicago, Ill., director of marketing, 1971—; Tomorrow's Products, Crystal Lake, Ill., partner and vice-president, 1972-74. Self-employed marketing consultant on scientific and educational services and materials, 1970—. Director of National Science Foundation Summer Institute in Astronomy, Chicago, 1963, 1964, 1966; lecturer at Chicago Academy of Sciences, 1959-66, Gary Campus of Indiana University, 1960-65, and Chicago Teacher's College (now Chicago State University), 1960-66; lecturer at other schools and to scientific and nonscientific organizations. Consultant author or editor at various times to Coronet Instructional Films, Encyclopaedia Britannica Educational Corp., Field Enterprises Educational Corp., National Science Foundation, Museum of Science and Technology (Tel Aviv), U.S. Army, Science Research Associates, and to industry and publishers. Representative of American Association of Museums to International Council of Museums, 1961-70; member of Midwest Museums Conference, 1964-70. *Military service:* U.S. Army, 1955-56; became sergeant.

MEMBER: American Association for the Advancement of Science (fellow); former member (until 1970) of American and Canadian astronomical and education associations; Phi Tau Epsilon, Mu Beta Phi (honorary member). *Awards, honors:* Named one of Chicago's ten outstanding young men by Chicago Junior Chamber of Commerce and Industry, 1961, and nominated for national award; and other awards.

WRITINGS: Teacher's Guide for the Celestial Globe, A. J. Nystrom, 1961; *Astronomy: Our Solar System and Beyond* (juvenile), Whitman Publishing, 1963; *The Story of the Moon* (juvenile), Replogle Globe Co., 1963, revised edition, 1969; *Galaxy Model Study Guide*, Hubbard Scientific Co., 1963; *Celestial Planetarium Guide Book*, Hubbard Scientific Co., 1964; (editor) *Techniques, Instruments and Accessories for Microanalysts: A User's Manual*, W. C. McCrone Associates, 1974. Has written parts of about two hundred television, radio, and motion picture scripts, and scripts for Radio Free Europe. Contributor to encyclopedias, science yearbooks, *Astronomical Journal*, *Science and Mechanics*, *Museum News*, and other journals and newspapers. Former member of editorial board, *Space Frontiers*; editor, *Insight* (quarterly publication on microscopy and pollution control).

WORK IN PROGRESS: A second edition of *Techniques, Instruments and Accessories for Microanalysts: A User's Manual*; continuing research on the ultramicroscopical world of atoms and the forces within them.

AVOCATIONAL INTERESTS: Archery, tennis.

* * *

JOHNSON, Roger N(ylund) 1939-

PERSONAL: Born April 22, 1939, in Dayton, Ohio; son of Earl G. and Merlie (Dameran) Johnson; married Loraine Dyson (a teacher), 1967; children: Allison, Erika. *Education:* Attended public schools in Japan and Egypt as well as in United States; Swarthmore College, B.A., 1961; University of Connecticut, M.A., 1962, Ph.D., 1966. *Home:* 100 Deerhaven Rd., Mahwah, N.J. 07430. *Office:* School of

Theoretical and Applied Science, Ramapo College of New Jersey, Mahwah, N.J. 07430.

CAREER: U.S. Veterans Administration Hospital, Northampton, Mass., research trainee in Neuropsychiatric Research Laboratory, 1963-65; Amherst College, Amherst, Mass., instructor, 1965-66, assistant professor of psychology, 1966-68; Tufts University, Medford, Mass., assistant professor of psychology, 1968-71; Ramapo College of New Jersey, Mahwah, associate professor of psychology and coordinator of behavioral sciences, School of Theoretical and Applied Science, 1971—. Instructor at University of Massachusetts, summer, 1965. Consultant to National Institute of Mental Health; consultant to Addison-Wesley, Inc., W .B. Saunders, and John Wiley, Inc. on academic manuscripts.

MEMBER: American Psychological Association, American Society of Criminology, International Society for Research on Aggression (fellow), Psychonomic Society, Animal Behaviour Society, American Association for the Advancement of Science, American Association of University Professors, Eastern Psychological Association, New Jersey Psychological Association, Sigma Xi. *Awards, honors:* Research grants from National Institute of Mental Health, 1967-68, 1968-69, 1970-71; National Science Foundation grant, 1970-72.

WRITINGS: Aggression in Man and Animals, Saunders, 1972. Contributor of about twenty articles to psychology journals. Editorial consultant and referee, *Journal of Learning and Motivation*.

WORK IN PROGRESS: Inquiry into Behavior: An Introduction to Psychology; revising *Aggression in Man and Animals*.

* * *

JOHNSON, Sherman E(lbridge) 1908-

PERSONAL: Born March 7, 1908, in Hutchinson, Kans.; son of Walter A. (a newspaperman) and Josie A. (Enderton) Johnson; married Jean Henkel (a professor), June 10, 1935; children: Carol Julia, Marcia Jean (stepdaughters); David E. *Education:* Attended George Washington University, 1923-29; Northwestern University, A.B., 1933; Western Theological Seminary, B.D., 1933; Seabury-Western Theological Seminary, S.T.M., 1934; University of Chicago, Ph.D., 1936. *Politics:* Independent. *Home and office:* 569 Forest Hill Rd., Mansfield, Ohio 44907.

CAREER: Ordained Episcopal priest, 1933; Nashotah House, Nashotah, Wis., instructor, 1936-38, professor of New Testament, 1938-40; Episcopal Theological School, Cambridge, Mass., assistant professor, 1940-46, professor of New Testament, 1946-51; Church Divinity School of the Pacific, Berkeley, Calif., dean and professor of New Testament, 1951-72. Archaeologist, expedition to el-Jib, Jordan, 1956; archaeologist and epigrapher, expedition to Sardis, Turkey, 1958; lecturer in New Testament, Union Theological Seminary, New York, N.Y., 1945; Annual Professor, American School of Oriental Research, Jerusalem, 1947-48; Yale Divinity School, lecturer in New Testament, 1950, Luther A. Weigle Visiting Professor, 1967-68; Fulbright Lecturer, University of Utrecht, 1962; scholar-in-residence, Ecumenical Institute, Jerusalem, 1971-72; visiting professor of New Testament, Seminario Episcopal del Caribe, Carolina, P.R., 1972-73.

MEMBER: Society of Biblical Literature and Exegesis (president, 1957), Studiorum Novi Testamenti Societas. *Awards, honors:* S.T.D., Nashotah House, 1940, Seabury-Western Theological Seminary, 1952, Church Divinity School of the Pacific, 1971; D.D., Occidental College, 1959, Episcopal Theological School, 1967, Pacific School of Religion, 1971.

WRITINGS: Introduction and Exegesis of Matthew, Abingdon, 1951; *Jesus in His Homeland*, Scribner, 1957 (published in England as *Jesus in His Own Times*, A. & C. Black, 1958); *A Commentary on the Gospel According to St. Mark*, Harper, 1966, 2nd edition, A. & C. Black, 1972; *The Theology of the Gospels*, Duckworth, 1966. Editor, *Anglican Theological Review*, 1955-59.

WORK IN PROGRESS: Current research in New Testament, especially Gospel of Mark and relations of N. T. to Coptic Gnostic writings.

SIDELIGHTS: Johnson has traveled throughout Europe, the Middle and Far East, Central and South America.

BIOGRAPHICAL/CRITICAL SOURCES: Anglican Theological Review, supplementary series No. 3, March, 1974.

* * *

JOHNSTON, Francis E. 1931-

PERSONAL: Born October 9, 1931, in Paris, Ky.; son of Francis C. (a machinist) and Harriet C. (Phillips) Johnston; married Patricia L. Honshul, September 3, 1955; children: Jeffry Ward, Susan Ann, Todd Clement. *Education:* University of Kentucky, B.A., 1959, M.A., 1960; University of Pennsylvania, Ph.D., 1962. *Religion:* Protestant. *Home:* 130 Parkview Dr., Springfield, Pa. 19064. *Office:* Department of Anthropology, University of Pennsylvania, Philadelphia, Pa. 19174.

CAREER: University of Pennsylvania, Philadelphia, member of faculty of department of anthropology, 1960-66, professor of anthropology, 1973—. *Military service:* U.S. Marine Corps, 1953-58; became first lieutenant. *Member:* American Association of Physical Anthropologists (vice-president, 1969-70), Society for the Study of Human Biology (member of council, 1966-70), Human Biology Council (member of executive committee, 1974—), Society for Research in Child Development, Royal Society of Medicine. *Awards, honors:* National Institutes of Health postdoctoral fellowship, 1966-68.

WRITINGS: Microevolution of Human Populations, Prentice-Hall, 1973; (with R. M. Malina) *Human Physical Growth and Development*, Lea & Febiger, 1975; (editor with E. S. Watts and G. W. Lasker) *Biosocial Interrelations in Population Adaptation*, Mouton & Co., 1975. Book review editor of *Human Biology*.

WORK IN PROGRESS: Physical Growth and Development of Guatemalan Children; *Obesity in Adolescence*; *Physical Growth of Malnourished Children*.

* * *

JOHNSTON, Jill 1929-
(F. J. Crowe)

PERSONAL: Born May 17, 1929, in London, England; daughter of Cyril Frederick (a bell founder) and Olive Margaret (Crowe) Johnston; married Richard John Lanham, 1958 (divorced, 1964); children: Richard Renault, Winifred Brook. *Politics:* "Lesbian-feminist." *Religion:* "Cosmic." *Agent:* Georges Borchardt, Inc., 145 East 52nd St., New York, N.Y. 10022.

CAREER: Village Voice (newspaper), New York, N.Y., author of column "Dance Journal," 1959—.

WRITINGS: Marmalade Me (selections from "Dance Journal"), Dutton, 1971; *Lesbian Nation: The Feminist Solution*, Simon & Schuster, 1973; *Gullibles Travels*, Links Books, 1974. Contributor to *Art News*; writes occasionally under pseudonym F. J. Crowe.

WORK IN PROGRESS: My Father in America: A Tour de Farce; *A Critique of Pure Madness*, publication by Pantheon expected about 1976.

SIDELIGHTS: Jill Johnston writes: "From 1958-1965 I wrote rather academic art and dance criticism about avant-garde art and dance events-happenings. Between 1965 and 1968 I turned inward to create myself as the subject-object of my work and invented a style that seemed appropriate to both the subject and the context of journalism. This style crystallized in several forms, both intelligible and inaccessible, by about 1969-1970. In 1972 I explored the longer form for my first book ... for a more accessible yet intimate style."

BIOGRAPHICAL/CRITICAL SOURCES: New York, May 24, 1971.

* * *

JOHNSTON-SAINT, Peter 1889-1974

British soldier, author of books on France and Spain. Obituaries: *AB Bookman's Weekly*, October 7, 1974.

* * *

JOLLY, W(illiam) P(ercy) 1922-

PERSONAL: Born December 2, 1922, in Plymouth, England; son of Percy Alec (a shipwright) and Minnie (Gargett) Jolly; married Maureen Parish (a research assistant), March 9, 1946; children: Anne Gabrielle. *Education:* University of Exeter, B.Sc. (honors), 1949. *Politics:* Radical constitutionalist. *Home:* 31 The Plantation, Blackheath, London S.E. 3, England. *Agent:* Curtis Brown Ltd., Craven Hill, London, England; John Cushman Associates, Inc., 25 West 43rd St., New York, N.Y. 10036.

CAREER: Royal Naval College, Greenwich, England, lecturer, 1949-62, professor of physics and electrical engineering, 1962-69. Tutor at National Extension College, Cambridge, 1964—; visiting professor at King's College, London, 1969—, special lecturer, 1974-75. *Military service:* Royal Naval Volunteer Reserve, radar officer, 1942-46; became lieutenant. *Member:* Royal Institution, Institution of Electrical Engineers (fellow), Institution of Electronic and Radio Engineers (fellow), Society of Authors.

WRITINGS: Physics for Electrical Engineers, Hodder & Stoughton, 1961, 2nd edition, 1970; (with K. Pennycuick and others) *Operational Research in Management*, Hodder & Stoughton, 1962; (with J. F. W. Bell and others) *Examples in Advanced Electrical Engineering*, Hodder & Stoughton, 1962; *Low Noise Electronics*, Elsevier, 1967; *Cryoelectronics*, Wiley, 1972; *Marconi: A Biography*, Stein & Day, 1972; *Teach Yourself Electronics*, Dover, 1973, 2nd edition, in press; *Oliver Lodge: Psychical Researcher and Scientist*, Constable, 1974, Associated Universities Press, in press; *William Lever, First Viscount Leverhulme*, Constable, in press. Contributor to scientific journals.

AVOCATIONAL INTERESTS: Squash rackets, amateur painting.

JONES, Alan Moore, Jr. 1942-

PERSONAL: Born September 2, 1942, in New York, N.Y.; son of Alan Moore (a business executive) and Mary (a nurse; maiden name, Affleck) Jones; married Wendy Foan (a professor), August 24, 1968; children: Mary Lynn Foan. *Education:* Brown University, A.B., 1964; University of Wisconsin, M.A., 1966; Massachusetts Institute of Technology, Ph.D., 1970. *Home:* 2370 North Taylor St., Arlington, Va. 22207. *Office:* Department of Political Science, University of California, Davis, Calif. 95616.

CAREER: Arms Control and Disarmament Agency, Washington, D.C., researcher, 1967; Massachusetts Institute of Technology, Cambridge, Mass., researcher, 1969-70; University of California, Davis, assistant professor of political science, 1970—. Analyst for Central Intelligence Agency (CIA), 1973-74. *Member:* Phi Beta Kappa.

WRITINGS: U.S. Foreign Policy in a Changing World, McKay, 1973.

* * *

JONES, David 1895-1974

November 1, 1895—October 28, 1974; British painter, engraver, poet, illustrator, and author. Obituaries: *New York Times*, October 30, 1974; *Washington Post*, October 31, 1974; *AB Bookman's Weekly*, November 18, 1974. (*CA*-9/10).

* * *

JONES, Franklin Ross 1921-

PERSONAL: Born January 3, 1921, in Charlotte, N.C.; son of William Morton (a contractor) and Ruth (an owner of a tourist home; maiden name, Moser) Jones; married Jane White (a legal stenographer), December 19, 1949 (divorced, 1972); children: Franklin Ross, Jr., Clarence Morton, Susan Noel. *Education:* Lenoir Rhyne College, A.B., 1941; University of North Carolina, A.M., 1951; Duke University, D.Ed., 1960. *Politics:* Independent. *Religion:* Baptist. *Home:* 1026 Manchester Ave., Norfolk, Va. 23508. *Office:* 161 School of Education, Old Dominion University, Hampton Blvd., Norfolk, Va. 23508.

CAREER: Science teacher in public schools in North Carolina, 1945-48, principal, 1948-56, district superintendent, 1956-58; Randolph-Macon College, Ashland, Va., professor of education and chairman of department, 1959-64; Old Dominion University, Norfolk, Va., professor of education, 1964-69, Distinguished Professor of Human Development, 1969—, dean of School of Education, 1964-69. Visiting research scholar at Duke University, 1967; lecturer at numerous colleges and universities, 1969—; regular contributor of editorial feature on "The Weekender Show," WTAR-Radio, 1974—. Member of White House Conference on Children and Youth, 1971-73; chairman of Governor's Regional Implementation Commission on Children and Youth, 1971-73; member of advisory board of Tidewater Rehabilitation Center, 1968-70; member of board of directors of North Carolina State Symphony Society, 1952-58.

MEMBER: American Educational Research Association, American Association of University Professors (president of Randolph-Macon chapter, 1961-64; member of executive committee of Virginia chapter), North Central Teachers Association (president, 1952), North Central Principals Association (president, 1956), South Atlantic Philosophy of Education Society (president, 1966-68), Tidewater Association for the Retarded, Kappa Delta Pi, Phi Delta Pi, Pi Gamma Mu, Alpha Tau Kappa, Duke University Virginia Alumni (president, 1962). *Awards, honors:* Named distinguished researcher in education by Virginia Educational Research Association, 1972, 1973; named eminent scholar by Old Dominion University Board of Visitors, 1973.

WRITINGS: (With Karl Garrison) *Psychology of Human Development*, International Textbook Co., 1969; (with Alan Mandel) *Testing and Grading College Instructors*, Old Dominion University Press, 1972. Has given talks on human development on several radio stations in Virginia, North Carolina, and other states, 1973—. Author of numerous research articles; contributor to newspapers in Virginia and North Carolina. Editorialist for Old Dominion University Informational Service Office.

WORK IN PROGRESS: Psychology of Middlescence; revising *Psychology of Human Development*.

* * *

JONES, George Thaddeus 1917-

PERSONAL: Born November 6, 1917, in Asheville, N.C.; son of William Henry (a teacher) and Edna (Lynch) Jones; married Mary Peres, January 13, 1945; children: Mary Gwenyth, Carol Ann (Mrs. Julian Sales Cox). *Education:* University of North Carolina, A.B., 1938; University of Rochester, M.A., 1942, Ph.D., 1950. *Home:* 6012 84th Ave., New Carrollton, Md. 20784. *Office:* School of Music, Catholic University of America, Washington, D.C. 20017.

CAREER: Catholic University of America, Washington, D.C., assistant professor, 1950-55, associate professor, 1955-61, professor of music, 1961—. *Military service:* U.S. Navy, instructor at School of Music, 1942-48. *Member:* American Musicological Society, American Association of University Professors, American Society of Composers, Authors, and Publishers. *Awards, honors:* Fulbright research grant, Italy, 1953-54; U.S. State Department cultural exchange grant, Romania, 1967-68.

WRITINGS: Music Composition, Summy-Birchard, 1963; *Music Theory*, Barnes & Noble, 1974.

WORK IN PROGRESS: A book on music analysis.

* * *

JONES, K(enneth) Westcott 1921-
(Eric Taunton)

PERSONAL: Born November 11, 1921, in London, England; son of George Albert and Selina G. (Westcott) Jones. *Education:* Studied at a private school in England. *Politics:* Conservative. *Religion:* Protestant. *Home:* Hillswick, Michael Rd., London SE25 6RN, England.

CAREER: Employed with Rail Passengers Assurance Co., London, 1939; Marconi Marine Co., Chelmsford, England, radio officer, 1945-51; free-lance author and travel writer, 1951—. Travel consultant to government of Uganda, 1959-65. *Military service:* Royal Naval Reserve, 1940-45; became lieutenant. *Member:* Guild of British Travel Writers (vice-chairman, 1973-75; chairman, 1975—), Sherlock Holmes Society, Institute of Journalists. *Awards, honors:* Lord Thomson travel award, 1971-72.

WRITINGS: Great Railway Journeys of the World, Greene, 1965; *By Rail to the Ends of the Earth*, A. S. Barnes, 1969; *Romantic Railways*, Arlington Books, 1971; *Business Air Travellers Guide*, Ian Allan, 1971; *Steam in the Landscape*, Blandford, 1972. Focus correspondent for *Business Travel World*, 1960—; group travel correspondent for United Newspapers, 1960—. Contributor to periodicals, sometimes under pseudonym Eric Taunton. Travel editor, *East Anglican Daily Times*, 1951—.

WORK IN PROGRESS: Post Haste.

SIDELIGHTS: Jones has visited one hundred twelve countries, and he has been to the United States fifty-nine times. He is an authority on United States railroads, especially AMTRAK.

* * *

JONES, Kenneth LaMar 1931-

PERSONAL: Born May 31, 1931, in Ogden, Utah; son of Kenneth P. (a refrigeration engineer) and Lucille (McEntire) Jones; married Cora Lee Dent (a registered nurse), July 9, 1959; children: Allison, Kathryn. *Education:* Weber College, A.A., 1956; Utah State University, B.A., 1958, M.A., 1960. *Politics:* Democrat. *Religion:* Church of Jesus Christ of Latter-Day Saints (Mormon). *Home:* 22448 Ridge Line Rd., Diamond Bar, Calif. 91765. *Office:* Department of Biology, Mount San Antonio College, Walnut, Calif. 91789.

CAREER: Science teacher in public schools in Los Angeles, Calif., 1960-62; Mount San Antonio College, Walnut, Calif., professor of biology, 1960—. National Science Foundation instructor in high school science project at Los Angeles State University, summer, 1962; member of Pomona Area Health Council (past president); member of board of directors of San Gabriel Valley Alcoholic Council. *Military service:* U.S. Navy, dental corpsman, 1950-54; served in Korea. *Member:* American Association for the Advancement of Science, American Health Association, International Council on Health, Physical Education and Recreation, Kiwanis International, Sigma Nu.

WRITINGS—All with Louis W. Shainberg and Curtis O. Byer: *Health Science*, Harper, 1968, 3rd edition, 1974; *Sex*, Harper, 1969, 2nd edition, 1973; *Drugs and Alcohol*, Harper, 1969, 2nd edition, 1973; *Marriage and Reproduction*, Canfield, 1970, 2nd edition published as *Human Sexuality*, 1974; *Drugs, Alcohol, and Tobacco*, Canfield, 1970, 2nd edition, in press; *Foods, Diet, and Nutrition*, Canfield, 1970, 2nd edition, in press; *Emotional and Neurological Health*, Canfield, 1970, 2nd edition, 1974; *Communicable and Noncommunicable Diseases*, Canfield, 1970, 2nd edition, in press; (editor) *Age of Aquarius: Contemporary Bio-Social Issues*, Goodyear Publishing, 1971; *The Human Body*, Canfield, 1971; *Environmental Health*, Canfield, 1971; *Consumer Health*, Canfield, 1971; *Dimensions: A Changing Concept of Health*, Canfield, 1972, 2nd edition, 1974; *Total Fitness*, Canfield, 1972; *V.D.*, Harper, 1974.

WORK IN PROGRESS: General Biology, a book on aging and dying.

* * *

JONES, Paul J. 1897(?)-1974

1897(?)—October 9, 1974; American newspaper columnist, author. Obituaries: *New York Times*, October 11, 1974.

* * *

JONES, Peter (Austin) 1929-

PERSONAL: Born April 25, 1929, in Walsall, England; son of Austin and Elsie (McFarlane) Jones. *Education:* Keble

College, Oxford, M.A. (honors), 1954. *Home:* 266 Councillor Lane, Cheadle Hulme, Cheadle, Cheshire SK8 5PN, England. *Office:* Carcanet Press Ltd., Cheadle Hulme, Cheadle, Cheshire SK8 5PN, England.

CAREER: Christ's Hospital, Horsham, Sussex, England, English master, 1954-69, librarian, 1964-69, housemaster, 1958-66; Carcanet Press, Cheadle, Cheshire, England, director, 1969—.

WRITINGS: Rain (poems), Carcanet, 1969; *Seagarden for Julius* (poems), Carcanet, 1970; (author of introduction) Hilda Doolittle, *Tribute to Freud, by H.D.*, reprinted, Carcanet, 1970; *The Peace and the Hook* (poems), Carcanet, 1971; (editor and author of introduction) *Imagist Poetry,* Penguin, 1972; (editor) *Reader's Guide to Fifty American Poets,* Pan Books, in press.

WORK IN PROGRESS: A contribution to *Comparative History of Literatures in European Languages,* for International Comparative Literature Association.

* * *

JONES, Thomas W(arren) 1947-
(Zulie Butck)

PERSONAL: Born May 31, 1947, in Bayonne, N.J.; son of Albert Joseph (a seaman) and Muriel (Sutton) Jones. *Education:* Attended schools in New Jersey. *Religion:* Roman Catholic. *Home:* 1779-A Belmar Blvd., Belmar, N.J. 07719. *Office:* 1300 F Street Post Office, Belmar, N.J. 07719.

CAREER: U.S. postal worker. *Military service:* U.S. Navy, 1964-68.

WRITINGS: (Under pseudonym Zulie Butck) *Some Kind of a Book,* Pageant-Poseidon, 1973.

WORK IN PROGRESS: A book of poetry, *Unexpectations.*

* * *

JONES, Tom 1928-

PERSONAL: Born February 17, 1928, in Littlefield, Tex.; son of William T. (a hatcheryman) and Jessie (Bellomy) Jones; married Elinor Wright (a writer), June 1, 1963. *Education:* University of Texas, B.F.A., 1949, M.F.A., 1951. *Residence:* West Cornwall, Conn. *Office:* 7 West 96th St., New York, N.Y. 10025.

CAREER: Playwright, lyricist. Began writing for theatre while in college, in collaboration with Harvey Schmidt; came to New York in 1955, writing material for supper club revues, for entertainers, and other free-lance material; began writing musicals in late 1950's, first production being "The Fantasticks," 1960; established, with Schmidt, Portfolio (a studio-workshop), New York, N.Y. *Military service:* U.S. Army, Counter-Intelligence Corps, 1951-53. *Member:* American Society of Composers, Authors and Publishers. *Awards, honors:* First prize in San Francisco Film Festival, for "A Texas Romance, 1909"; Vernon Rice Drama Desk Award, 1961, and Swedish Theatre Award of Merit, 1963, both for "The Fantasticks."

WRITINGS—Musical comedies; book and lyrics by Jones, unless otherwise noted; music by Harvey Schmidt: *The Fantasticks* (two-act; based on Edmond Rostand's "Les Romanesques"; first produced Off-Broadway at Sullivan Street Playhouse, May 3, 1960), Drama Book Shop, 1964; "110 in the Shade" (book by Richard Nash, based on his play, "The Rainmaker"; lyrics by Jones), first produced on Broadway at Broadhurst Theatre, October 24, 1963; "I Do! I Do!" (two-act; based on Jan de Hartog's "The Fourposter"), first produced on Broadway at 46th Street Theatre, December 5, 1966; *Celebration* (first produced on Broadway at Ambassador Theatre, January 22, 1969), published in *The Fantasticks and Celebration*, Drama Book Shop, 1973; "Colette," 1970.

Author of filmscript for "A Texas Romance, 1909," privately produced. Contributor of lyrics to Off-Broadway revues, including "Shoestring '57," 1956, and "Kaleidoscope," 1957.

WORK IN PROGRESS: Research for "Philemon," a musical play set in Antioch in the third century, A.D.

SIDELIGHTS: Although it opened to lukewarm reviews in 1960, "The Fantasticks" became the longest-running New York stage production in American theatre history in 1968 as it passed its 3,224th performance. It continued to play to capacity houses ten years after its opening, and had gone into over a thousand other productions in the United States and abroad. In accounting for the play's wide popularity, Jones once remarked that "the simpler you do something, the better off it's going to be. . . . The proper words and music can evoke a spectacle in the mind that's so much more satisfying than anything the most skillful designer could possibly devise. . . . The thing to do is to take something that is around us every day, that we see and touch, and put it in terms that are poetic."

"I have written only for the musical theatre," Jones told *CA*. "I will write only for the musical theatre. Within this form, there lies the possibility of re-establishing the greatness of the theatre. (Besides, it is all I know.) My partner and I hope someday to have a theatre of our own."

Jones played a role, incognito, in the original production of "The Fantasticks," and directed "Celebration." "The Fantasticks" was produced for television by Hallmark Hall of Fame and broadcast by NBC in 1964. Chappel Music has published the scores of "The Fantasticks," "110 in the Shade," "I Do! I Do!," and "Celebration."

BIOGRAPHICAL/CRITICAL SOURCES: New York, December 5, 1966; Martin Gottfried, *A Theatre Divided: The Post-War American Stage*, Little, Brown, 1968; *Life*, March 14, 1969; Stanley Green, *The World of Musical Comedy*, revised edition, A. S. Barnes, 1969; David Ewen, *New Complete Book of the American Musical Theatre*, Holt, 1970.

* * *

JONES, Vernon 1897-

PERSONAL: Born October 13, 1897, in Portsmouth, Va.; son of Frank A. (a farmer) and Pattie A. (McLemore) Jones; married Harriet Marble, November 2, 1929; children: Patricia (Mrs. Hugh C. Lovell), Nancy Clement (Mrs. Roy A. Pearson). *Education:* University of Virginia, B.A. and M.A., 1920; Columbia University, M.A., 1924, Ph.D., 1926. *Politics:* Republican. *Religion:* Protestant. *Home:* 267 Salisbury St., Worcester, Mass. 01609. *Office:* Department of Education, Clark University, Worcester, Mass. 01610.

CAREER: High school principal and teacher of mathematics and chemistry in the public schools of Appalachia, Va., 1917-18; Richmond Public Schools, Richmond, Va., principal, 1921-23, director of research, 1923-24; Clark University, Worcester, Mass., associate professor, 1926-38, professor of educational psychology, 1938-68, professor emeritus, 1968—, head of department of psychology and education, 1938-49, organizer and head of department of education, 1949-66, director of Veterans Administration Guidance Center for Central Mass., 1945-59. Visiting professor at University of Virginia, Columbia University, Ohio State University, University of California, and University of Indiana. Member of governing board of Worcester Junior College, 1935-47; member of planning committee of National Conference on Citizenship, 1950-67. *Member:* American Psychological Association (fellow), American Educational Research Association, American Personnel and Guidance Association, National Education Association, Phi Beta Kappa. *Awards, honors:* Award from American Educational Research Association, 1940, for outstanding research.

WRITINGS: What Would You Have Done?, Ginn, 1931; (contributor) Carl Murchison, editor, *Handbook of Child Psychology,* Clark University Press, 1931; *Character and Citizenship Training in the Public Schools,* University of Chicago Press, 1936; (contributor) Leonard Carmichael, editor, *Manual of Child Psychology,* Wiley, 1946, revised edition, 1954; *Character and Citizenship Education* (monograph), National Education Association, 1950; *Youth Decides: Group Guidance in Everyday Citizenship,* Row, Peterson, & Co., 1952; *Attitudes of College Students and Their Changes* (monograph), Journal Press, 1970. Contributor to *Collier's Encyclopedia* and *Encyclopedia of Educational Research;* contributor of over forty articles to professional journals.

* * *

JORGENSEN, Neil 1934-

PERSONAL: Born March 19, 1934, in New Jersey; son of William (an engineer) and Leonora (a political scientist; maiden name, Dow) Jorgensen; married Susan Clark (a college teacher), June 23, 1962; children: Erik, Laurie. *Education:* Tufts University, B.S., 1955; Columbia University, M.A., 1961; Harvard University, Ed.D., 1972. *Politics:* Independent. *Home address:* Cleaves Hill Rd., Harvard, Mass. 01451. *Office:* Department of Early Childhood Education, Wheelock College, 200 Riverway, Boston, Mass. 02215.

CAREER: Science teacher in public schools in Lincoln, Mass., 1962-66; Wheelock College, Boston, Mass., assistant professor, 1970-73, associate professor of education and director of Curriculum Resource Center, 1973—. Visiting professor at Lowell State College and Webster College. *Military service:* U.S. Navy, 1955-58; served in England; became lieutenant junior grade. *Member:* American Association of University Professors, New England Botanical Club, New England Wildflower Society (trustee), Phi Delta Kappa, Kappa Delta Pi.

WRITINGS: A Guide to New England's Landscape, Barre, 1971. Author of scripts for television series "Land and Sea."

WORK IN PROGRESS: New England Natural History, two volumes, for Sierra Club.

* * *

JOURARD, Sidney M(arshall) 1926-1974

January 21, 1926—December 2, 1974; Canadian-born American psychologist, educator, author. Obituaries: *New York Times,* December 4, 1974. (*CA*-7/8).

JOURDAIN, Alice M. 1923-

PERSONAL: Born March 11, 1923, in Brussels, Belgium; daughter of Henri and Marthe (van de Vorst) Jourdain; married Dietrich von Hildebrand (a writer and lecturer), July 16, 1959. *Education:* Manhattanville College, B.A., 1944; Fordham University, M.A., 1946, Ph.D., 1949. *Home:* 43 Calton Rd., New Rochelle, N.Y. 10804. *Office:* Department of Philosophy, Hunter College of the City University of New York, 685 Park Ave., New York, N.Y. 10021.

CAREER: Hunter College of the City University of New York, New York, N.Y., lecturer, 1947-57, instructor, 1957-60, assistant professor, 1960-64, associate professor, 1965-71, professor of philosophy, 1971—. Visiting summer professor at University of the Andes, 1965.

WRITINGS: (With husband, Dietrich von Hildebrand) *Graven Images: Substitutes for True Morality,* McKay, 1957; (with von Hildebrand) *The Art of Living,* Franciscan Herald, 1965; (with von Hildebrand) *Morality and Situation Ethics,* Franciscan Herald, 1966; *Greek Culture: The Adventure of the Human Spirit,* Braziller, 1966; *Introduction to a Philosophy of Religion,* Franciscan Herald, 1971.

WORK IN PROGRESS: Comparing German and Anglo-Saxon ethics.

AVOCATIONAL INTERESTS: Classical and fine arts.

* * *

JUHASZ, Anne McCreary 1922-

PERSONAL: Surname is pronounced You-haz; born January 19, 1922, in Stratford, Ontario, Canada; daughter of John Harold and Edythe Selina (Staines) Phillips; married Garnet E. McCreary, August 9, 1946 (died, 1955); married Stephen Euguene Juhasz (a physician), June 29, 1965. *Education:* State University of New York College at Cortland, B.Sc., 1958; Cornell University, M.Ed., 1959, Ph.D., 1961. *Home:* 831 Belleforte Ave., Oak Park, Ill. 60302. *Office:* Loyola University, 820 North Michigan Ave., Chicago, Ill. 60611.

CAREER: Canadian-Scandinavian research fellow in Stockholm, Sweden, 1961-62; University of British Columbia, Vancouver, assistant professor, 1962-65, associate professor of education, 1965-67; Loyola University, Chicago, Ill., associate professor, 1967-70, professor of educational foundations, 1970—. *Member:* American Educational Research Association, American Psychological Association, American School Health Association (fellow), National Council on Family Relations, American Association for the Advancement of Science, Illinois Psychological Association, Phi Kappa Phi.

WRITINGS: (With Elizabeth A. Thorn, A. C. Smith, and K. D. Munroe) "Gage Language Experience Reading Program," including readers, *For Me, Just For Me, Follow Me, Out and Away,* and *Flying Free,* four other books of stories, five teacher's source books, and eight pupil's practice books, all published by Gage, 1966, revised edition, 1970; *Effective Study,* Gage, 1966; (with George M. Szasz) *Adolescents in Society,* McClelland & Stewart, 1969; (editor) *Sexual Development and Behavior: Selected Readings,* Dorsey, 1973.

Contributor: Jerome M. Seidman, editor, *The Adolescent: A Book of Readings,* 2nd edition (Juhasz did not contribute to earlier edition), Holt, 1960; Robert E. Grinder, editor, *Studies in Adolescence,* 2nd edition (Juhasz did not contribute to earlier edition), Macmillan, 1969, 3rd edition,

1974; Gere B. Fulton and William V. Fassbender, editors, *Health Education in the Elementary School: Guidelines and Program Suggestions,* Goodyear Publishing, 1972; James F. Adams, editor, *Understanding Adolescence,* 2nd edition (Juhasz did not contribute to earlier edition), Allyn & Bacon, 1973, 3rd edition, in press. Contributor to professional journals in Sweden, Canada, Israel, and United States.

WORK IN PROGRESS: With Allan C. Ornstein and Harriet M. Talmage, *A Handbook for Paraprofessionals;* sole author, *A Liberated Woman Is. . .*; research on values and sexual decision-making, with measurements prediction and teaching materials as the goal.

AVOCATIONAL INTERESTS: Travel, nature, music, reading.

* * *

JUN, Jong S(up) 1936-

PERSONAL: Born July 28, 1936, in Sunsan, Korea; naturalized U.S. citizen in 1975; son of Myungduck and Jumsoon (Pai) Jun; married Soon Y. Kwon, September 16, 1964; children: Eugene, Amy. *Education:* Taegu Universiy, LL.B., 1960; University of Oregon, M.A., 1964; University of Southern California, Ph.D., 1969. *Home:* 5600 Trail Side Court, Castro Valley, Calif. 94546. *Office:* Department of Public Administration, California State University, Hayward, Calif. 94542.

CAREER: University of Southern California, Los Angeles, instructor in administration, 1968; California State University, Hayward, assistant professor, 1968-71, associate professor of public administration, 1971—, chairman of department, 1973—. Project specialist of Social and Rehabilitation Service of U.S. Department of Health, Education and Welfare, 1972-73. *Member:* International Studies Association, American Society for Public Administration, American Society for Political Science. *Awards, honors:* National Association of Schools of Public Affairs and Administration faculty fellowship, 1972-73.

WRITINGS: (With William B. Storm) *Tomorrow's Organizations: Challenges and Possibilities*, Scott, Foresman, 1973; (with Gary Posz and Storm) *Administrative Alternatives in Development Assistance*, Ballinger, 1973; *Management by Objectives in Government: The Theory and Practice*, Sage Publications, 1975. Member of editorial board of *Administration and Society*.

WORK IN PROGRESS: With William B. Storm, a basic text in public administration, completion expected in 1975.

* * *

JURIS, Hervey A(sher) 1938-

PERSONAL: Born September 5, 1938, in Lawrenceville, N.J.; son of Edward and Justa (Novik) Juris; married Antoinette Ruth Ulan, August 6, 1961; children: Steven Jerome, Robin Lynn. *Education:* Princeton University, A.B., 1960; University of Chicago, M.B.A., 1962, Ph.D., 1967. *Home:* 1234 Isabella St., Wilmette, Ill. 60091. *Office:* Graduate School of Management, Northwestern University, Evanston, Ill. 60201.

CAREER: University of Chicago, Graduate School of Business, Chicago, Ill., assistant dean of students, 1962-64; University of Wisconsin, School for Workers, Madison, assistant professor, 1965-70, associate professor of labor education, 1970; Northwestern University, Graduate School of Management, Evanston, Ill., associate professor, 1970-75, professor of industrial relations and urban affairs, 1975—. Consultant to President's National Advisory Council on Minority Business Enterprise, 1970-71, International Association of Chiefs of Police, 1972-74, and U.S. Bureau of Labor Statistics, 1974. Member of Illinois Governor's Labor Grievance Panel. *Member:* American Economic Association, Industrial Relations Research Association (vice-president of Chicago chapter, 1973-74; president, 1974—), Chicago Council on Foreign Relations.

WRITINGS: (With Peter Feuille) *Police Unionism: Power and Impact in Public-Sector Bargaining*, Heath, 1973; (contributor) Robert R. Sterling, editor, *Institutional Issues in Public Accounting*, Scholars Book Co., 1974; (contributor) Jerome Skolnik and Thomas Gray, editors, *Police in America*, Little, Brown, 1974. Contributor of articles and reviews to *Industrial Relations, Industrial and Labor Relations Review, Law and Society Review*, and other journals. Associate editor, *Urban Affairs Quarterly*, 1974—.

WORK IN PROGRESS: Continuing research on the manpower problems inherent in the urban police function; analysis of labor-management contracts and a broad study of the impact of unionized professionals on management in the health services industry; a study of physician unionism in the United States.

* * *

JUSTICE, William G(ross), Jr. 1930-

PERSONAL: Born August 22, 1930, in Memphis, Tenn.; son of William Gross (a machinist) and Mary (Furchak) Justice; married Annie Ruth Fowler, January 8, 1953; children: Lisa Ann, William David. *Education:* Attended Clemson University, 1948-49; Furman University, B.A., 1958; New Orleans Baptist Theological Seminary, B.D., 1961, M.Div., 1973. *Address:* Route 29, Highland View Dr., Knoxville, Tenn. 37920. *Office:* East Tennessee Baptist Hospital, Blount Ave., Knoxville, Tenn. 37901.

CAREER: Ordained Southern Baptist minister, 1959; East Tennessee Baptist Hospital, Knoxville, chaplain, 1962—. Member of board of directors of Knox Area Pastoral Counseling Service, 1973-75. *Military service:* U.S. Air Force, 1949-50, 1951-52, pilot, 1952-55; became first lieutenant. *Member:* American Protestant Hospital Association, Association of Baptist Chaplains (president, 1973-74), Lions International (vice-president of local chapter, 1972-73), Rotary.

WRITINGS: Don't Sit on the Bed: A Handbook for Visiting the Sick, Broadman, 1973. Regular columnist for *Baptist Banner*, 1964—. Contributor to *Church Administration*.

WORK IN PROGRESS: A book on guilt from the theological and psychological perspective, especially unhealthy versus healthy ways of dealing with it, publication expected in 1976; a book of "sermons in magic."

AVOCATIONAL INTERESTS: Magic, woodcrafts.

* * *

KABDEBO, Thomas 1934-
(Tamas Kabdebo)

PERSONAL: First name is sometimes listed as Tamas; born February 5, 1934, in Budapest, Hungary; naturalized British citizen, 1963; son of Bela and Klara (Kelen) Kabdebo; married Agnes Wohl (an architect), July 27, 1959; children: Lilian Claire, Andrea Mary. *Education:* Attended University of Budapest, 1952-56; University of Wales, B.A., 1960; University of London, Dip. Lib., 1962,

M.Phil., 1969. *Religion:* Roman Catholic. *Home:* 61 Gowan Ave., London S.W.6, England. *Office:* Main Library, University of Manchester, Manchester, England.

CAREER: University of London, University College, London, England, assistant librarian, 1961-69; University of Guyana, Georgetown, Guyana, university librarian, 1969-72; City of London Polytechnic, London, England, librarian, 1973-74; University of Manchester, Manchester, England, Social Sciences librarian, 1974—. *Member:* P.E.N., Library Association (London). *Awards, honors:* World Poetry Society Award, 1968, for *Hungarian Love Poems of the Twentieth Century*.

WRITINGS: (With Glynn Mills Ashton) *Gemau Hwngaria* (Hungarian short stories in Welsh; title means "Treasures of Hungary"), Gee & Sons (Denbigh, N. Wales), 1962; *Fortified Princecriptions on Poetry* (poetry satires), privately printed, 1965; *Erettsegi* (novel; title means "Maturity"), Feher Hollo (London), 1971; *Two-hearted* (poems in English and Hungarian), Poetry Seminar Workshop, University College, London, 1973; *Magyar Odisszeuszok* (short stories in Hungarian; title means "Odysseus Patronius"), Dario Detti (Rome), 1974.

Editor: (And translator) Attila Jozsef, *Poems*, Danubia, 1966; (and contributor) *University College Poetry,* Poetry Seminar Workshop, University College, London, 1967, 1969, 1973; (with Paul Tabori, and translator) *A Tribute to Gyula Illyes: Poems*, Occidental Press, 1968; (and translator) *Selected Poems of Gyula Illyes*, Chatto & Windus, 1971. Also editor of anthologies, *Hungarian Love Poems of the Twentieth Century*, 1967, and *British Poets*, 1969, published as special issues of *Poet* magazine (Madras).

Translator of books for children: Eva Janikovsky, *Basil and Barnabas*, Chatto & Windus, 1971; Ferenc Mora, *The Chimney-Sweep Giraffes*, Chatto & Windus, 1971. Contributor of articles or translations to periodicals, including *justforallthat, New Hungarian Quarterly, Image, Poetry Singapore,* and *Resurgence*. Editor of *justforallthat*, 1969-72.

WORK IN PROGRESS: A guide to the literature of the Amerindians of Guyana, completion expected in 1975.

SIDELIGHTS: Because he tried to cross the Hungarian-Czech frontier, Kabdebo was imprisoned for six months on political charges in 1955. Upon his release from prison, he worked for six months in a coal mine. A member of the National Guard and a newspaper reporter during the 1956 Hungarian Revolution, he finally emigrated to England when the revolution was crushed.

Kabdebo told *CA*: "My travels have taken me around Europe, North and South America, Australia, and a good many islands where I have tried to fish above and under the water. In some capacity or another—refugee, research worker, conference delegate, reporter, interpreter, guide, tourist or fisherman—I have been to thirty-eight countries. My urban relaxation is trying out as many swimming pools as I can (I used to be a swimming international) and looking at as many good pictures as I can find. Apart from my native language Hungarian, and my adopted tongue English, I used to be able to cope with Russian and still can do Italian."

* * *

KAGAN, Richard C(lark) 1938-

PERSONAL: Born June 24, 1938, in Los Angeles, Calif.; son of Jacob (a jeweler) and Rose (a jeweler; maiden name, Newman) Kagan; married Leigh (a professor), January 31, 1962; children: Rachel Mei, Jacob Ben. *Education:* University of California, B.A., 1960, M.A., 1963; University of Pennsylvania, Ph.D., 1969. *Religion:* Jewish. *Office:* Department of History, Hamline University, St. Paul, Minn. 55104.

CAREER: Boston State College, Boston, Mass., instructor in history, 1970-71; instructor in history at Cambridge-Goddard Graduate School for Social Change, 1971-72; University of Michigan, Ann Arbor, research associate at Center for Chinese Studies, 1972-73; assistant professor of history, jointly, at Hamline University, St. Paul, Minn. and Grinell College, Grinell, Iowa, 1973—. *Member:* Committee of Concerned Asian Scholars, National Committee on U.S.-China Relations.

WRITINGS: (Contributor with wife, Leigh Kagan) Mark Seldon and Edward Friedman, editors, *America's Asia*, Pantheon, 1971; (editor) Ross Y. Koen, *The China Lobby in American Politics*, Harper, 1973; (contributor) Gilbert Ch'an and Thomas Etzold, editors, *Nationalism and Revolution in China*, New Viewpoints Press, 1974.

WORK IN PROGRESS: A book on Ch'en Tu-hsiu, founder of the Chinese Communist Party.

* * *

KAISER, Ward L(ouis) 1923-

PERSONAL: Born July 1, 1923, in Kitchener, Ontario, Canada; son of Lorne H. (a chauffeur) and Frieda (Reuber) Kaiser; married Lorraine E. Macke (a nurse and teacher), June 25, 1949; children: Margaret Susan, Gary, K. Christopher, Jacqueline. *Education:* University of Western Ontario, B.A., 1945; graduate study at University of Toronto, 1945-46, Rutgers University, and Columbia University; Union Theological Seminary, New York, N.Y., M.Div., 1949. *Politics:* Independent-Liberal. *Home:* 251 Diane Pl., Paramus, N.J. 07652. *Office:* Friendship Press, 475 Riverside Dr., New York, N.Y. 10027.

CAREER: Ordained minister of United Church of Canada, 1969; CIMADE (relief and community organization), Paris, France, field worker, 1947-48; United Church of Canada, Toronto, Ontario, minister, 1949-57; National Council of Churches, Friendship Press, New York, N.Y., senior editor and director, 1957—. President of Fair Housing Council, Bergen County, N.J., 1962-63; member of National Council of Boy Scouts of America, 1974—. *Awards, honors:* University citation-of-the-year from Wilfred Laurier University, 1968.

WRITINGS: *Focus: The Changing City*, Friendship, 1966; *The Challenge of a Closer Moon*, National Council of Churches, 1969; *Intersection: Where School and Faith Meet* (with teacher's manual), Abingdon, 1969; (with Charles P. Lutz) *You and the Nation's Priorities*, Friendship, 1971. Contributor of over one thousand articles to magazines in the United States and Canada. Author of weekly Bible lesson commentaries for Evangelical Press, 1950-55; author of syndicated column "It's Your World," 1962-67.

WORK IN PROGRESS: General editor of *People and Systems*, a cross-cultural study of social systems in China, Cuba, Tanzania, Canada, and the United States; contribution to *Forum: Religious Faith Speaks to American Issues*.

* * *

KALB, Jonah 1926-

PERSONAL: Born September 17, 1926, in New York,

N.Y.; son of Herman and Helen (Busch) Kalb; married Mary Jeannie Astier, July 23, 1950; children: Laura Margaret, Eugene Herman. *Education:* Oberlin College, B.A., 1949. *Home:* 17 North St., Lexington, Mass. 02173. *Office:* Witan Corp., 27 Montvale Ave., Woburn, Mass. 01801.

CAREER: Kalb & Schneider, Inc. (advertising agency), Boston, Mass., president, 1963-70; Sensitivity Games, Inc., Boston, Mass., chairman, 1970-73; Witan Corp. (consulting firm), Woburn, Mass., president, 1973—. Vice-president of Longwood Management, 1973-74; member of board of directors of Lythorn Corp., 1965-70, and Visual Learning Corp., 1968-70. *Military service:* U.S. Army, 1952-54.

WRITINGS: (With D. S. Viscott) *Language of Sensitivity*, six volumes, Peter H. Wyden, 1973; (with Viscott) *What Every Kid Should Know*, twelve volumes, American Greetings, 1974; *How to Play Baseball Better Than You Did Last Year*, Macmillan, 1974; *The Politics of Barnaby Brome* (novel), Houghton, in press.

WORK IN PROGRESS: Sports fiction for children, publication expected in 1976; sports instruction books for young people, 1976.

* * *

KALIN, Martin (Gregory) 1943-

PERSONAL: Born March 21, 1943, in Chicago, Ill.; son of Paul P. (a criminologist) and Rosemary (a teacher; maiden name, Nelson) Kalin; married Janet Chessare (a teacher), December 30, 1967. *Education:* Loyola University, Chicago, Ill., B.S. (summa cum laude), 1965; University of Heidelberg, graduate study, 1968-69; Northwestern University, M.A., 1967, Ph.D., 1970. *Home:* 6538 North Ashland, Chicago, Ill. 60626. *Office:* Department of Philosophy, DePaul University, 2323 North Seminary, Chicago, Ill. 60614.

CAREER: DePaul University, Chicago, Ill., assistant professor, 1969-72, associate professor of philosophy, 1973—. *Member:* Philosophy of Science Association. *Awards, honors:* Fulbright-Hays research fellowship, 1968-69; Carnegie Foundation grant, 1971.

WRITINGS: *The Utopian Flight from Unhappiness: Freud against Marx on Social Progress*, Nelson-Hall, 1974. Contributor to *Kantstudien, Journal of Value Inquiry, Man and World, Idealistic Studies, Intellect*, and *Philosophy Today*.

WORK IN PROGRESS: *The Method of Critical Theory*; a study of neo-Marxists like Marcuse, Harermas, and Adorno.

SIDELIGHTS: Kalin is interested in appraising the method by which Marxists support their claims, particularly their utopian predictions. He has lived in Europe.

* * *

KALLMAN, Chester (Simon) 1921-1975

January 7, 1921—January 18, 1975; American poet, librettist, translator, editor. Obituaries: *New York Times*, January 19, 1975; *AB Bookman's Weekly*, February 3, 1975. (*CA*-45/48).

* * *

KALVEN, Harry, Jr. 1914-1974

September 11, 1914—November 29, 1974; American lawyer, educator, author of books on the judicial process. Obituaries: *New York Times*, October 30, 1974; *Time*, November 11, 1974; *AB Bookman's Weekly*, November 18, 1974.

* * *

KAMERSCHEN, David R(oy) 1937-

PERSONAl: Born December 8, 1937, in Chicago, Ill.; son of Robert R. (a chemical salesman) and Elsie D. (an English teacher; maiden name, Barsanti) Kamerschen; married Patricia B. Wait, December 26, 1959; children: Christine, Steven, Laura, Robert. *Education:* Attended Indiana University, 1955-56; Miami University, Oxford, Ohio, B.S., 1959, M.A., 1960; Michigan State University, Ph.D., 1964. *Religion:* Roman Catholic. *Home:* 420 Kings Rd., Athens, Ga. 30601. *Office:* Department of Economics, College of Business Administration, University of Georgia, Athens, Ga. 30602.

CAREER: Miami University, Oxford, Ohio, instructor in economics, 1960; Washington University, St. Louis, Mo., assistant professor of economics, 1964-66; University of Missouri, Columbia, associate professor, 1966-68, professor of economics, 1968-74; University of Georgia, Athens, professor of economics and chairman of department, 1974—. Expert witness in antitrust and utility regulation cases on behalf of private firms and public bodies, including Antitrust Division of Department of Justice. *Member:* American Economic Association, Econometric Society, American Statistical Association, Southern Economic Association (member of executive committee), Phi Kappa Phi, Delta Sigma Pi, Beta Gamma Sigma, Sigma Alpha Epsilon, Omicron Delta Epsilon.

WRITINGS: (Editor) *Readings in Microeconomics*, World Publishing, 1967, text edition, Wiley, 1969; (editor with Walter L. Johnson) *Macroeconomics: Selected Readings*, Houghton, 1970; (contributor) John C. Narver and Ronald Savitt, editors, *Conceptual Readings in the Market Economy*, Holt, 1971; (editor with Johnson) *Readings in Economic Development*, South-Western, 1972; (with George Vredeveld) *Economics*, Cliffs, 1975; (editor with Eugene S. Klise) *Money and Banking*, 6th edition (Kamerschen was not associated with earlier editions), South-Western, in press. Co-author of study guide on economics. Contributor of about ninety articles to journals in United States, Pakistan, Italy, Germany, India, and other countries. Member of board of editors or consulting editor, *Business and Government Review*, 1966-68, *Mississippi Valley Journal of Business and Economics*, 1969—, *Industrial Organization Review*, 1972—, *International Behavioral Scientist*, 1972—, *International Review of History and Political Science*, 1972—; editor, *Review of Social Theory*, 1972-74; reader for nine other economic journals.

* * *

KAMINSKY, Marc 1943-

PERSONAL: Born October 8, 1943, in Bronx, N.Y.; son of Peretz (a poet and graphic designer) and Mintzie (a rehabilitation counselor; maiden name, Schwartzman) Kaminsky; married Carol Talesnick (a social worker), November 30, 1974. *Education:* Columbia University, B.A. (summa cum laude), 1964, M.A., 1967. *Religion:* Jewish. *Home:* 145 Seaman Ave., New York, N.Y. 10034. *Agent:* Art Strimling, 222 West 20th St., New York, N.Y. *Office:* Jewish Association for Services for the Aged, 131 West 86th St., New York, N.Y. 10024.

CAREER: Hunter College of the City University of New

York, New York, N.Y., lecturer in composition of dramatic literature, 1967-69; East Harlem Youth Employment Service, New York, N.Y., teacher, 1969-71; City University of New York, New York, N.Y., teacher in English as a second language program, 1971-72; Jewish Association for Services for the Aged, New York, N.Y., group worker, 1972-74, project director at West Side Senior Center, 1974—. Poet and teacher for Teachers and Writers Collaborative, 1971—. *Member:* Association for Poetry Therapy, Inwood Press Collective, Phi Beta Kappa. *Awards, honors:* First prize in Boar's Head Contest from *Columbia Review*, 1963, for "Two Pigs & a Centaur"; second prize in American Scholar's Contest on Youth, 1967, for "Radical Affirmatives."

WRITINGS: Birthday Poems, Horizon Press, 1972; *What's Inside You It Shines Out of You* (prose), Horizon Press, 1974; *A New House* (poems), Inwood-Horizon, 1975. Contributor to literary magazines, including *Sun*, *Little Magazine*, *First Issue*, *Newsletter of the Teachers and Writers Collaborative*, and poetry magazine of *New York Times*.

WORK IN PROGRESS: Die Junge, a book of translations of poems by Yiddish poets Zisha Landau, Leivick, Moishe Leib Halpern, and Mani Leib; *Daily Bread*, a collection of poems.

* * *

KANZA, Thomas R(nsenga) 1933-

PERSONAL: Born October 14, 1933, in Boende, Zaire; son of Daniel Kinsona and Elisabeth (Mansangaza) Kanza; married Eugenie Maloumbi, 1968; children: Ginette (stepdaughter), Claudie (stepdaughter), Daniel, Elisabeth, Fabrice. *Education:* University of Louvain, B.A., 1954, M.A., 1956; College of Europe, Bruges, Belgium, Ph.D., 1958; University of London, M.Phil., 1969. *Religion:* Roman Catholic. *Home:* St. Antony's College, Oxford University, Oxford, England. *Office:* Department of Politics, University of Massachusetts, Boston, Mass. 02125.

CAREER: College of St. Joseph, Kinshasa (formerly Leopoldville), Republic of Congo, lecturer in psychology and education, 1956-57; European Common Market, Brussels, Belgium, international civil servant, 1958-60; ambassador from Zaire to the United Nations and cabinet minister in Zaire, 1960-62; head of diplomatic mission from Zaire to the United Kingdom, London, England, 1962-64; roving ambassador and cabinet minister in Zaire, 1964-66; Oxford University, St. Anthony's College, Oxford, England, research fellow, 1970-72; Harvard University, Center for International Affairs, Cambridge, Mass., fellow, 1972-74; University of Massachusetts, Boston, associate professor of politics, 1974—.

WRITINGS: Congo: Pays de Deux Evolues (title means "Congo: Country of Two Evolutions"), Editions Actualites Africaines, 1956; *Congo 196?*, Editions Remarques congolaises, 1962; *Sans rancune* (title means "Without Bitterness"; novel), Editions Remarques congolaises, 1964; *Eloge de la Revolution* (title means "Praise for Revolution"), Editions Remarques congolaises, 1965; *Conflict in the Congo*, Penguin, 1972; *Evolution and Revolution in Africa*, Rex Collings, 1972, revised edition, Schenkman, 1974. Joint editor of *Congo*, 1957-60.

WORK IN PROGRESS: Political Leadership and Democracy in Africa, for Schenkman; *From Congo to Zaire: Facts and Opinions, 1955-1975*, completion expected in 1976; *The Belgian Conception of Native Administration: 1884-1947*, 1976.

SIDELIGHTS: Kanza writes: "During my stay in Europe, I have visited many countries. My present writings are based on my experiences as teacher, diplomat, and politician."

* * *

KARPATKIN, Marvin M. 1926-1975

December 23, 1926—January 14, 1975; American lawyer, civil rights advocate, author. Obituaries: *New York Times*, January 14, 1975.

* * *

KARRIS, Robert J(oseph) 1938-

PERSONAL: Born January 25, 1938, in Chicago, Ill.; son of Henry (a printer) and Hannah (Altmann) Karris. *Education:* Quincy College, Quincy, Ill., A.B., 1961; Pontificium Athenaeum Antonianum, Rome, S.T.B., 1965; Catholic University of America, S.T.L., 1966; Harvard University, Th.D., 1971. *Home and office:* Catholic Theological Union at Chicago, 5401 South Cornell Ave., Chicago, Ill. 60615.

CAREER: Ordained Roman Catholic priest in Order of Friars Minor (Franciscans), 1965; Pope John XXIII National Seminary, Weston, Mass., instructor in New Testament, 1969-70; Catholic Theological Union at Chicago, Chicago, Ill., assistant professor of New Testament studies, 1970—, chairman of department of biblical literature and languages, 1974—. Instructor at St. Mary of the Lake Seminary, Winter, 1972-73. Lecturer; conductor of workshops for priests, ministers, and adult Catholics. *Member:* Society of Biblical Literature, Catholic Biblical Association of America, Chicago Society of Biblical Research.

WRITINGS: (Translator with William R. Poehlmann) Eduard Lohse, *Colossians and Philemon: A Commentary on the Epistles to the Colossians and to Philemon*, Fortress, 1971; *Following Jesus: A Guide to the Gospels* (booklet), Franciscan Herald, 1973; *Gospel of St. Luke* (booklet), Franciscan Herald, 1974. General editor, "Herald Biblical Booklets," Franciscan Herald, 1972—, and "Read and Pray Booklets," Franciscan Herald, 1974—. Contributor to journals, including *Catholic Biblical Quarterly* and *Journal of Biblical Literature*; abstractor for *New Testament Abstracts*, 1969—. Associate editor, *Catholic Biblical Quarterly*, 1973—.

WORK IN PROGRESS: An index of articles on the New Testament and the early church published in festschriften (1951-1972), in collaboration with David M. Scholer; and *A Commentary on the Gospel of St. Luke*, completion expected in 1977.

SIDELIGHTS: Father Karris is competent in Latin, Greek, Hebrew, German, French, and Spanish. He says: "When I have time, I love to bake and cook. My roots are in the back-of-the-yards area of Chicago."

* * *

KATEN, Thomas Ellis 1931-

PERSONAL: Born April 23, 1931, in Philadelphia, Pa.; son of Henry (in textile business) and Ella (an artist; maiden name, Sykes) Katen. *Education:* Temple University, B.S. (with distinction), 1954; graduate study, New School for Social Research, 1956, New York University, 1957-59; University of Pennsylvania, M.A., 1958. *Politics:* Conservative. *Religion:* Mysticism. *Home:* 7612 Lexington Ave., Philadelphia, Pa. 19152. *Office:* Philadelphia Community College, 34 South 11th St., Philadelphia, Pa. 19107.

CAREER: New York University, New York, N.Y., instructor in philosophy, 1958-59; Allegheny College, Meadville, Pa., instructor in philosophy and religion, 1959-60; Lincoln University, Lincoln University, Pa., acting chairman of department of philosophy, 1960-61; University of Delaware, Newark, instructor in philosophy, 1960-63; Monmouth College, West Long Branch, N.J., assistant professor of philosophy, 1963-65; Community College of Philadelphia, Philadelphia, Pa., assistant professor of history, 1965-68, associate professor of philosophy, 1968—. *Member:* American Philosophical Association, American Association of University Professors, Animal Protection Institute of America, Fund for Animals, New England Anti-Vivisection Society.

WRITINGS: Doing Philosophy, introduction by Steve Allen, Prentice-Hall, 1973; (author of introduction and notes) Steve Allen, *Schmock-Schmock*, Doubleday, in press. Also author of *The Funny Philosophers: A History of Human Thought from Primitive Man to the Atomic Age*, 1962. Contributor and columnist while in high school, *Wrestler* (Binghamton, N.Y.); contributor of articles and book reviews to *Midlothian Times* (Dallas), *Liberation*, and *Truth Letter*.

WORK IN PROGRESS: A Funny Thing Happened on the Way to Wisdom, a history of thought, completion expected in 1975; *Phootm*, a satirical novel, 1976; *The Philosophy of the Fantastic*, exploring the fantastic in the political, physical, psychical, and spiritual worlds, 1976.

SIDELIGHTS: Katen told *CA*: "My intellectual approach is more imaginative than descriptive, more existential than positivist, more romantic than realistic, and more symbolical than literal. I do not believe the essence of life can be grasped in dry intellectual formulas nor in laboratory experiments. Thus I am convinced that philosophy must be dialogue and human drama, as it was with Socrates and Plato. . . . I have come to the conclusion that there is a play element at the core of reality, and in coming to truth one must have a sense of play. Ultimately this leads to the realization that reality is not just a matter of fact, and to a sense of an absolute beyond the limited world of brute material fact." *Avocational interests:* Collecting books (Katen has a collection of 20,000), yoga, judo, swimming, raising German shepherds.

* * *

KATZ, Josef 1918-

PERSONAL: Born April 1, 1918, in Luebeck, Germany; came to United States, 1946; naturalized citizen, 1953; son of Max and Emma (Cohn) Katz; married Irene Laermer, June 8, 1946; children: Jean (Mrs. Richard Musicer). *Education:* Attended high school in Luebeck, Germany. *Religion:* Jewish. *Home and office:* 2806 Federal Ave., Los Angeles, Calif. 90064.

CAREER: Irene Pearls (manufacturer of ladies accessories), Los Angeles, Calif., owner, 1951-65; Irene & Josef Katz (rental property company), Los Angeles, Calif., manager, 1965—; writer, 1965—.

WRITINGS: One Who Came Back: The Diary of a Jewish Survivor, translated from the German by Hilda Reach, Herzl Press, 1973.

WORK IN PROGRESS: Ghetto stories.

BIOGRAPHICAL/CRITICAL SOURCES: National Jewish Monthly, June, 1973; *World*, July 24, 1973; *Bnai Brith Messenger* (Los Angeles), December 21, 1973; *Jewish Bookland*, October 16, 1974.

KATZMAN, David Manners 1941-

PERSONAL: Born October 25, 1941, in New York, N.Y.; son of Henry Manners (a composer and business executive) and Berdie (Miller) Katzman; married Sharyn Amelia Brooks (an artist), January 24, 1965; children: Andrea Rachel, Eric Michael. *Education:* Queens College of the City University of New York, B.A., 1963; University of Michigan, Ph.D., 1969. *Politics:* "On the left." *Religion:* Jewish. *Home:* 1642 Tennessee St., Lawrence, Kan. 66044. *Office:* Department of History, University of Kansas, Lawrence, Kan. 66045.

CAREER: University of Kansas, Lawrence, assistant professor, 1969-72, associate professor of history, 1972—. *Member:* Yidisher Visnshaftlekher Institut, American Historical Association, Organization of American Historians, Association for the Study of Afro-American Life and History, American Jewish Historical Society, Immigrant History Group. *Awards, honors:* Senior research fellow, Institute of Southern History, Johns Hopkins University, 1971-72; National Endowment for the Humanities Afro-American Studies fellow, 1972-73; American Council of Learned Societies grant-in-aid, 1973-74.

WRITINGS: (Contributor) Bernard Sternsher, editor, *Hitting Home: The Great Depression in Town and Country*, Quadrangle, 1970; (contributor) Harold M. Rose, editor, *Perspectives in Geography 2: Geography of the Ghetto*, Northern Illinois University Press, 1972; *Before the Ghetto: Black Detroit in the Nineteenth Century*, University of Illinois Press, 1973. Contributor to *Dictionary of American Biography*, *Michigan History*, *Michigan Challenge*, and *American Studies*.

WORK IN PROGRESS: With photographs by sister, Louise E. Katzman, a photo-essay on a middle-class urban community, completion expected in 1975; a book on American work patterns and the black working class, 1978.

* * *

KAUFMAN, Roger (Alexander) 1932-

PERSONAL: Born June 4, 1932, in Washington, D.C.; son of Joseph (an engineer) and Naomi (Greenhouse) Kaufman; married Janice E. Carron (a puppeteer), October 13, 1963; children: Richard J., Nancy Joy, Jac Damon. *Education:* George Washington University, B.A., 1950; Johns Hopkins University, M.A., 1956; University of California, Berkeley, graduate study, 1956-59; New York University, Ph.D., 1963. *Home:* 8011 Prospect Way, La Mesa, Calif. 92041. *Office:* Graduate School of Human Behavior, U.S. International University, San Diego, Calif. 92124.

CAREER: Diplomate of American Board of Professional Psychology, 1970; Martin Co., Baltimore, Md., head of personnel and training, 1960-61; U.S. Industries, New York, N.Y., manager, training system analyst, 1961-62; Bolt Beranek & Newman, Inc., New York, N.Y., senior consultant in education and training, 1962-64; Douglas Aircraft Co., Long Beach, Calif., assistant to vice-president for engineering and assistant to the vice-president for research and development, 1964-66; Chapman College, Orange, Calif., professor of education, 1966-70; U.S. International University, Elliott Campus, San Diego, Calif., professor of psychology and human behavior at Graduate School of Human Behavior, 1970—. Adjunct professor at University of Southern California, 1967-70; consultant to secretary of U.S. Department of Health, Education, and Welfare, 1969-70; chairman of planning, management, and educational evaluation panel, National Center for Educational Research and Development of National Institute of Education, 1972—; member, Secretary of the U.S. Navy's Advisory Board on Education and Training (SABET), 1972-76; consultant to numerous state and local education agencies, to industrial organizations, and military agencies.

MEMBER: American Psychological Association, American Educational Research Association, National Society for Performance and Instruction (secretary, 1962-63; vice-president, 1963-64; president, 1974-75), Human Factors Society, Phi Delta Kappa. *Awards, honors:* Presidential citation, National Society for Programmed Instruction.

WRITINGS: System Approach to Education: Derivation and Definition, University of Oregon, 1970; (with Leon Lessinger and Dale Parnell) *Accountability: Policies & Procedures*, Croft Educational Service, 1971; *Educational System Planning*, Prentice-Hall, 1972. Contributor to journals in his field.

WORK IN PROGRESS: Research in organizational development models—"transactional life cycle theory"; needs assessment and system planning models and procedures.

* * *

KAYE, Marvin (Nathan) 1938-
(Eugene D. Goodwin, Joseph Lavinson)

PERSONAL: Born March 10, 1938, in Philadelphia, Pa.; son of Morris (a television and radio repairman) and Theresa (Baroski) Kaye; married Saralee Bransdorf, August 4, 1963; children: Terry Ellen. *Education:* Pennsylvania State University, B.A., 1960, M.A., 1962; University of Denver, graduate study, 1960. *Politics:* Liberal. *Religion:* None. *Residence:* New York, N.Y. *Agent:* Paul R. Reynolds, Inc., 12 East 41st St., New York, N.Y. 10017.

CAREER: Grit (newspaper), Williamsport, Pa., reporter, 1963-65; Harcourt, Brace, & Jovanovich (publisher), New York, N.Y., senior editor, 1966-70; writer, 1970—. Public relations director for Light Opera of Manhattan, 1973. *Member:* Authors Guild, Authors League of America, Mystery Writers of America, Sons of the Desert, Illustrious Order of Dragon Killers.

WRITINGS: The Histrionic Holmes, Luther Norris, 1971; *A Lively Game of Death,* Saturday Review Press, 1972; *A Toy Is Born,* Stein & Day, 1973; *The Stein and Day Handbook of Magic,* Stein & Day, 1973; *The Grand Ole Opry Murders,* Saturday Review Press, 1974; (editor) *Fiends and Creatures* (anthology), Popular Library, in press; (editor) *Brother Theodore's Midnight Snack* (anthology), Pinnacle Books, in press.

Author of "Bertrand Russell's Guided Tour of Intellectual Rubbish," a play. New York correspondent for *Grit* (newspaper). Contributor of short stories, under pseudonyms Eugene D. Goodwin and Joseph Lavinson, to *Playthings*. Contributing editor of *Mass Retailing Merchandiser*.

WORK IN PROGRESS: Bullets for Macbeth; The Stein and Day Handbook of Mental Magic.

SIDELIGHTS: Kaye writes: "A thorough training in theatre as an actor, director, and playwright is my principal background and passion. My chief interests in writing are drama and philosophy."

* * *

KAZARIAN, Edward A(rshak) 1931-

PERSONAL: Born April 2, 1931, in Hamburg, Mich.; son of Hagop and Lucy (Tarbasian) Kazarian; married Margaret H. Krause, September 12, 1953; children: Steven Edward. *Education:* Michigan State University, B.S., 1954, M.S., 1956, Ph.D., 1962. *Home:* 963 Daisy Lane, East Lansing, Mich. 48823. *Office:* Department of Hotel Management, Michigan State University, 421 Eppley Center, East Lansing, Mich. 48824.

CAREER: Michigan State University, East Lansing, instructor, 1955-62, assistant professor, 1962-67, associate professor, 1967-70, professor of hotel management, 1970—. *Member:* Sigma Xi, Sigma Pi Eta.

WRITINGS: Work Analysis and Design for Hotels, Restaurants, and Institutions, Avi, 1969; *Food Service Facilities Planning*, Avi, 1975.

AVOCATIONAL INTERESTS: Gardening, golf, fishing.

* * *

KEAVENEY, Sydney Starr 1939-

PERSONAL: Surname is pronounced *Key*-venay; born November 12, 1939, in Grand Rapids, Mich.; daughter of Ben and Joan (Closterhouse) Starr; married Liam Keaveney (a photographer), April 12, 1969. *Education:* Wellesley College, B.A., 1961; Simmons College, M.S. in L.S., 1964. *Home:* 49 Grove St., New York, N.Y. 10014. *Office:* Pratt Institute, Library, Brooklyn, N.Y. 11205.

CAREER: Boston Public Library, Boston, Mass., art reference librarian, 1962-66; Pratt Institute, Brooklyn, N.Y., assistant professor, 1966-73, associate professor of art and architecture, 1973—, lecturer with Graduate School of Library and Information Science, 1968—. *Member:* Special Libraries Association (first vice-president of New York chapter, 1972-73; president of New York chapter, 1973—), Art Libraries Society of North America, College Art Association, American Contract Bridge League, Wellesley College Friends of Art.

WRITINGS: (Contributor) Ralph Mayer, editor, *Dictionary of Art Terms and Techniques*, Crowell, 1969; (editor) *American Painting*, Gale, 1975. Also editor of "Art and Architecture" series of *Gale Information Guides*, Gale, 1974—. Former columnist for *Wilson Library Bulletin*.

* * *

KEEDY, Mervin L(averne) 1920-

PERSONAL: Born August 2, 1920, in Bushnell, Neb.; son of Albert L. and Iva (Barney) Keedy; children: Michael, Nathan. *Education:* University of Chicago, B.S., 1946; University of Nebraska, M.A., 1949, Ph.D., 1957. *Home address:* Box 2416, West Lafayette, Ind. 47906. *Office:* Department of Mathematics, Purdue University, Lafayette, Ind.

CAREER: Teacher in public schools in Idaho, 1947-49; University of Nebraska, Lincoln, teaching assistant in mathematics, 1949-50; Nebraska State Teachers College at Peru (now Peru State College), supervisor of laboratory school, 1950; North Dakota State College (now University), Fargo, assistant professor of physics, 1951-53; University of Nebraska, instructor in mathematics, 1953-55, instructor in physics, 1955-56, counselor with Science Teaching Improvement Program, 1956-57; University of Maryland, College Park, associate director of mathematics project, 1957-60; supervisor of junior high school mathematics and science, Baltimore County (Md.) Public Schools, 1960-61; Purdue University, Lafayette, Ind., professor of mathematics, 1961—. Ground and flight instructor, Rodman Aircraft Co., 1948-49. *Military service:* U.S. Army Air Forces, 1940-45. *Member:* American Mathematical Society, Mathematical Association of America, National Council of Teachers of Mathematics.

WRITINGS: Laboratory Physics, Edwards Brothers, 1953; (with Alice L. Griswold and John F. Schacht) *Contemporary Algebra and Trigonometry*, Holt, 1961, 2nd edition, 1966; (with Vincent Brant) *Elementary Logic for Secondary Schools*, Holt, 1962; (with Richard E. Jameson and Patricia L. Johnson) *Exploring Modern Mathematics*, Holt, *Books I & II*, 1963, 3rd editions, 1971, *Book III*, 1964; (with Griswold and Schacht) *Contemporary Second Year Algebra*, Holt, 1963; *A Modern Introduction to Basic Mathematics*, Addison-Wesley, 1963, 2nd edition, 1968; *Number Systems: A Modern Introduction*, Addison-Wesley, 1965, 2nd edition, 1968; (with Charles W. Nelson) *Geometry: A Modern Introduction*, Addison-Wesley, 1965, 2nd edition, 1973; (with Jameson, Johnson, and Joseph Ciechon) *Exploring Elementary Algebra*, Holt, 1967; (with Jameson, Stanley Smith, and Eugene Mould) *Exploring Geometry*, Holt, 1967; (with others) *Algebra and Trigonometry*, Holt, 1967; (with Brant) *Relations Functions and Graphs*, Holt, 1967; (with Marvin L. Bittinger) *Trigonometry: A Programmed Text*, Holt, 1969.

(With others) *Exploring Elementary Mathematics*, Books I-VI, Holt, 1970; (with Bittinger) *Mathematics: A Modern Introduction*, Addison-Wesley, 1970; (with Bittinger) *Arithmetic: A Modern Approach*, Addison-Wesley, 1971, 2nd edition, 1975; (with Bittinger) *Introductory Algebra: A Modern Approach*, Addison-Wesley, 1971, 2nd edition, 1975; (with Bittinger) *Intermediate Algebra: A Modern Approach*, Addison-Wesley, 1971, 2nd edition, 1975; (with Bittinger) *Essential Mathematics: A Modern Approach*, Addison-Wesley, 1972; (with Bittinger) *College Algebra: A Functions Approach*, Addison-Wesley, 1974; (with Bittinger) *Trigonometry: A Functions Approach*, Addison-Wesley, 1974; (with Bittinger) *Algebra and Trigonometry: A Functions Approach*, Addison-Wesley, 1974. Contributor to journals in his field.

WORK IN PROGRESS: Revisions of college texts; audio-tutorial tapes.

SIDELIGHTS: Keedy teaches flying and flies his own airplane.

* * *

KEENER, Frederick M(ichael) 1937-

PERSONAL: Born December 28, 1937, in New York, N.Y.; son of Frederick J. (an accountant) and Anne (Doran) Keener; married Ann R. Monahan (a teacher), September 2, 1961; children: Thomas, David. *Education:* St. John's University, Jamaica, N.Y., B.A., 1959; Columbia University, M.A., 1960, Ph.D., 1965. *Home:* 89-32 118th St., Richmond Hill, N.Y. 11418. *Office:* Department of English, Hofstra University, Hempstead, N.Y. 11550.

CAREER: St. John's University, Jamaica, N.Y., assistant professor of English, 1961-65; Columbia University, New York, N.Y., assistant professor, 1966-72, associate professor of English and dean of summer session, 1972-74; Hofstra University, Hempstead, N.Y., associate professor of English, 1974—. *Member:* Modern Language Association of America, American Society for Eighteenth-Century Studies, Conference on British Studies, Columbia University Seminar in Eighteenth-Century European Culture.

WRITINGS: English Dialogues of the Dead, Columbia University Press, 1973; *An Essay on Pope*, Columbia University Press, 1974.

WORK IN PROGRESS: Comparative literature of the eighteenth century.

* * *

KEEVER, Jack 1938-

PERSONAL: Born May 16, 1938, in Port Arthur, Tex.; son of Robert Eldon (a refinery worker) and Annie Agnes (Honeycutt) Keever; married Cynthia Lee Pendergrass, December 23, 1961; children: Graham Lee, Erin Elizabeth. *Education:* University of Texas at Austin, B.J., 1961, M.J., 1965. *Politics:* Democrat. *Religion:* Episcopal. *Home:* 206 West 32nd St., Austin, Tex. 78705. *Office address:* Associated Press, Box 12247, Capitol Station, Austin, Tex. 78711.

CAREER: Associated Press, reporter in Dallas, Tex., 1961, and Austin, Tex., 1962—. Member of Horizons Committee of Bicentennial Commission of Austin, Tex. *Military service:* U.S. Marine Corps Reserve, 1961-65, active duty, 1962. *Member:* Texas Historical Association. *Awards, honors:* Texas Headliner awards, 1968, 1969, 1972, and 1974 (two awards), for daily newspaper stories.

WRITINGS: (With Ann Fears Crawford) *John B. Connally: Portrait in Power,* Jenkins Publishing, 1973. Contributor to *APT, Texas Monthly,* and *Texas Parade*. Contributing editor of *APT*, 1971-72, 1974.

WORK IN PROGRESS: Research on several topics, including blacks in the Texas legislature.

* * *

KEKKONEN, Sylvi 1900(?)-1974

1900(?)—December 2, 1974; Finnish author of novels and other works. Obituaries: *New York Times*, December 3, 1974; *Washington Post*, December 3, 1974; *AB Bookman's Weekly*, December 16, 1974.

* * *

KELLER, Clair W(ayne) 1932-

PERSONAL: Born January 29, 1932, in Fargo, N.D.; son of Emmet Reason (a stereotyper) and Martha (a beautician; maiden name, Aljoe) Keller; married Marilyn Foord, March 21, 1959; children: Jennifer Lynn, Robert Clair. *Education:* University of Washington, Seattle, B.A., 1957, M.A., 1962, Ph.D., 1967. *Religion:* Unitarian-Universalist. *Home:* 304 Oneil Dr., Ames, Iowa 50010. *Office:* Department of History and Education, Iowa State University, Ames, Iowa 50010.

CAREER: High school social science teacher in Kirkland, Wash., 1957-59, and Bellevue, Wash., 1960-69; Iowa State University, Ames, assistant professor, 1969-73, associate professor of history and education, 1973—. *Military service:* U.S. Navy, 1951-54. *Member:* American Historical Association, Organization of American Historians, National Council for the Social Studies, Iowa Council for the Social Studies, Phi Beta Kappa, Phi Alpha Theta. *Awards, honors:* Research grant from American Philosophical Society, 1974.

WRITINGS: Involving Students in New Social Studies, Little, Brown, 1974. Contributor to *Social Studies, History Teacher*, and *Pennsylvania Magazine of History and Biography*.

WORK IN PROGRESS: A book, *Officeholding and Poli-*

cymaking in Pennsylvania before 1750; research in using quantification techniques for analysis of data.

AVOCATIONAL INTERESTS: Golf, tennis, squash.

* * *

KELLER, Dean H(oward) 1933-

PERSONAL: Born May 20, 1933, in Ashtabula, Ohio; son of Howard Dean (a carpenter) and Fern (a teacher; maiden name, Hahn) Keller; married Patricia Scheid, June 9, 1962; children: Jonathan Howard, Jennifer Nancy. *Education:* Kent State University, B.A., 1955, M.A., 1958. *Religion:* Lutheran. *Home:* 5887 Roc Marie Ave., Kent, Ohio 44240. *Office:* Library, Kent State University, Kent, Ohio 44242.

CAREER: Kent State University, Kent, Ohio, assistant humanities librarian, 1958-63, humanities librarian, 1963-66, associate librarian for Readers Services, 1967-69, curator of special collections, 1967—, assistant professor, 1969-73, professor of library administration, 1973—. *Military service:* U.S. Army, 1955-57. *Member:* Bibliographical Society of America, Manuscripts Society, Society of Ohio Archivists, Bibliographical Society of the University of Virginia, Kent State University School of Library Science Alumni Association (president, 1968-69), Rowfant Club, Beta Phi Mu (president of Kent State University chapter, 1974-75). *Awards, honors:* Lilly Foundation fellowship in rare books librarianship, Indiana University, 1966-67.

WRITINGS: An Index to the Albion W. Tourgee Papers in the Chatauqua County Historical Society, Westfield, New York, Kent State University, 1964; *An Index to the Colophon, New Series, The Colophon, New Graphic Series, and The New Colophon*, Scarecrow, 1968; (editor) Steele MacKaye and Albion W. Tourgee, *A Fool's Errand*, Scarecrow, 1969; *Index to Plays in Periodicals*, Scarecrow, 1971, supplementary volume, 1973.

General editor of "Serif Series of Bibliographies and Checklists," Kent State University Press, 1974—. Contributor to professional journals of articles on rare book librarianship, bibliography, and book collecting. Editor of *Serif*, 1964-74.

AVOCATIONAL INTERESTS: Music (opera), travel, book collecting.

* * *

KELLEY, Robert E(mmett) 1938-

PERSONAL: Born March 1, 1938, in Waterloo, Iowa; son of Robert Emmett (a hotel manager) and Vivian (Langley) Kelley; married Judith Ann Stoltzman (a librarian), June 13, 1959; children: Mark, Brian, David. *Education:* Creighton University, B.A., 1960; Indiana University, Ph.D., 1968. *Politics:* Democrat. *Home:* 321 Windsor Dr., Iowa City, Iowa 52240. *Office:* Department of English, University of Iowa, Iowa City, Iowa 52242.

CAREER: University of Iowa, Iowa City, instructor, 1966-67, assistant professor, 1967-71, associate professor of English, 1971—. *Member:* American Society for Eighteenth-Century Studies, Augustan Reprint Society, Midwest Modern Language Association.

WRITINGS: (Contributor) Philip B. Daghlian, editor, *Essays in Eighteenth-Century Biography*, Indiana University Press, 1968; (author of introduction) John Courtenay, *A Poetical Review of the Literary and Moral Character of the Late Samuel Johnson, L.L.D.* (originally published in 1786), Augustan Reprint Society, 1969; (author of introduction) William Hayley, *Two Dialogues: Containing a Comparative View of the Lives, Characters, and Writings of Philip, the Late Earl of Chesterfield and Dr. Samuel Johnson* (originally published in 1787), Scholars' Facsimiles and Reprints, 1970; (with O. M. Brack, Jr.) *The Early Biographers of Samuel Johnson*, University of Iowa Press, 1971; (with Brack) *The Early Biographies of Samuel Johnson*, University of Iowa Press, 1974. Contributor to *University Review*.

WORK IN PROGRESS: A definitive edition of *Travels through France and Italy*, by Tobias Smollett.

* * *

KELLISON, Stephen G. 1942-

PERSONAL: Born March 20, 1942, in Ord, Neb.; son of Orin A. and Sarah V. (Crouch) Kellison; married Chery L. Sides, June 14, 1963 (divorced, 1970). *Education:* University of Nebraska, B.A., 1963, M.S., 1967. *Home:* 6100 Vine St., #K-62, Lincoln, Neb. 68505. *Office:* Department of Actuarial Service, University of Nebraska, Lincoln, Neb. 68508.

CAREER: University of Nebraska, Lincoln, associate professor, 1966—. Consultant to Retirement Systems Committee of Nebraska Legislature. *Member:* Phi Beta Kappa, Pi Mu Epsilon (vice-president, 1972-73), Phi Eta Sigma (president, 1973-74).

WRITINGS: The Theory of Interest, Irwin, 1970; *Fundamentals of Numerical Analysis*, Irwin, 1974.

* * *

KELLOUGH, Richard Dean 1935-

PERSONAL: Surname is pronounced *Kell*-o; born October 31, 1935, in Ohio; son of Stanley Eugene (a teacher) and Mayme Elizabeth (Stephens) Kellough; married Connie K. Trainer, February 17, 1956 (divorced, 1969); married Noreen G. Whyte (a foreign language teacher), March 25, 1972; children: (first marriage) Robyn Siobhan, Meribeth. *Education:* Wilmington College, Wilmington, Ohio, B.S., 1956; Miami University, Oxford, Ohio, M.A., 1959; Oregon State University, Ed.D., 1967; also attended Ohio State University, Antioch College, California State University, Sacramento, and University of California, Davis. *Home:* 2763 13th St., Sacramento, Calif. 95818. *Office:* School of Education, California State University, 6000 Jay St., Sacramento, Calif. 95819.

CAREER: High school science-math teacher and principal in Ohio, 1956-59, and California, 1961-69; California State University, Sacramento, assistant professor, 1969-73, associate professor of education, 1973—. Member of accreditation team of Western Association of Schools and Colleges, 1973-75; consultant to Nepal Peace Corps projects and American Institute of Biological Sciences film series. *Member:* National Association for Research in Science Teaching, United Professors of California, Phi Sigma.

WRITINGS: (Contributor) Jerome Metzner, editor, *Research Problems in Biology*, Series III, Doubleday, 1964; (editor and contributor) *Developing Priorities and a Style: Selected Readings in Education for Parents and Teachers*, MSS Information Corp., 1971; (contributor) *Institute of Environmental Sciences 1972 Tutorial Proceedings*, Institute of Environmental Sciences, 1972; (with E. C. Kim) *A Resource Guide for Secondary School Teaching: Planning for Competence*, Macmillan, 1974.

Contributor to *Ohio Journal of Science, Bryologist, Science Teacher*, and *Science Education*.

AVOCATIONAL INTERESTS: Bridge, chess, camping, music (playing and writing), art (batiks).

* * *

KELLY, Frederic Joseph 1922-

PERSONAL: Born June 23, 1922, in Albany, N.Y.; son of John Francis (an engineer) and Mary Loretto (Kean) Kelly. *Education:* Sacred Heart College, Manila, A.B., 1948, M.A. (philosophy), 1949; Woodstock College, S.T.B., 1956; Catholic University of America, M.A. (religious studies), 1970, Ph.D., 1972. *Politics:* "Democratic (what else in these days)." *Home and office:* Canisius College, 2001 Main St., Buffalo, N.Y. 14208.

CAREER: Ateneo de Manila University, Manila, Philippines, assistant professor, 1960-64; Canisius College, Buffalo, N.Y., assistant professor of religious studies, 1964-68, 1972—. *Member:* American Academy of Religion, College Theology Society, Catholic Theological Society of America, Catholic Biblical Association.

WRITINGS: Man Before God: Thomas Merton on Social Responsibility, Doubleday, 1974.

* * *

KELLY, James Plunkett 1920-
(James Plunkett)

PERSONAL: Born May 21, 1920, in Dublin, Ireland; son of Patrick and Cecilia (Cannon) Kelly; married Valerie Koblitz, September, 1945; children: Valerie Cecilia (Mrs. Michael Murdoch), Ross, James, Vadim. *Education:* Attended Dublin College of Music and Municipal College of Music. *Religion:* Roman Catholic. *Residence:* County Wicklow, Ireland. *Agent:* A. D. Peters, 10 Buckingham St., London WC2 N6BU, England. *Office:* Radio Telefis Eireann, Donnybrook, Dublin 4, Ireland.

CAREER: Worked as clerk and as trade union secretary; assistant head of drama for Radio Eireann, 1955-60; programme head (features) for Telefis Eireann, 1960-71; with Radio-Telefis Eireann, 1971—. Governor of Royal Irish Academy of Music, 1950-55. *Member:* Irish Academy of Letters, Music Association of Ireland. *Awards, honors:* Jacobs television award, 1964, 1966; *Yorkshire Post* award for literature, 1970.

WRITINGS—Under pseudonym James Plunkett: *The Trusting and the Maimed and Other Irish Stories*, Hutchinson, 1959, revised edition, 1969; *Strumpet City*, Delacorte, 1969; *The Gems She Wore*, Hutchinson, 1972, Holt, 1973. Author of "The Risen People," a three-act play, first performed in Abbey Theatre, Dublin, Ireland, 1958.

WORK IN PROGRESS: A novel on Irish life between 1920 and 1950; material for educational television.

AVOCATIONAL INTERESTS: Listening to and performing on the violin and viola, walking in the country, learning about Ireland, especially its writers, literature, and legends.

* * *

KELLY, Mahlon (George) 1939-

PERSONAL: Given name is pronounced May-lun; born March 24, 1939, in Plymouth, N.H.; son of Mahlon George (a manufacturer) and Emma (Mehren) Kelly; married Gretchen Wagner Leigh (a child psychiatric nurse), January 23, 1970. *Education:* Harvard University, A.B., 1960, Ph.D., 1968; University of New Hampshire, M.S., 1962. *Home:* Route 1, Box 197, Charlottesville, Va. 22901. *Office:* Department of Environmental Sciences, University of Virginia, Charlottesville, Va. 22903.

CAREER: Staff scientist, International Indian Ocean Expedition, 1962-63; Massachusetts Institute of Technology, Cambridge, staff oceanographer, 1968; University of Miami, Coral Gables, Fla., visiting assistant professor of biology, 1968-69, adjunct professor, 1969-72; New York University, New York, N.Y., assistant professor of biology, 1969-70; University of Virginia, Charlottesville, assistant professor of environmental sciences, 1970—. Associate scientist, New York Ocean Science Laboratory, and associate of Seminar on Pollution and Water Resources, Columbia University, 1970-73. Principal investigator, National Aeronautics and Space Administration Earth Resources Aircraft Program, 1968-72; consultant to Bendix Aerospace Corp., 1971-73, and U.S. Army Corps of Engineers, 1973—.

MEMBER: American Institute of Biological Sciences, American Association for the Advancement of Science, American Society of Limnology and Oceanography, Ecological Society of America, Sigma Xi, Phi Sigma. *Awards, honors:* Research grants from U.S. Naval Oceanographic Office, 1968-71, 1972, American Museum of Natural History, 1968, National Science Foundation, 1971-72, U.S. Office of Water Resources, 1972-73, 1973-75, and U.S. Corps of Engineers, 1973-74.

WRITINGS: (Contributor) Philip L. Johnson, editor, *Remote Sensing in Ecology*, University of Georgia Press, 1969; (with John C. McGrath) *Biology: Evolution and Adaptation to the Environment*, Houghton, 1975. Contributor to oceanography, biology, and water resources journals.

WORK IN PROGRESS: Research in photosynthesis and metabolism in rivers and lakes and in methods of monitoring non-point-source water pollution.

* * *

KELLY, Maurice Anthony 1931-
(Springfield)

PERSONAL: Born July 29, 1931, in Gibentley, Essex, England. *Education:* Attended Preston Technical Institute, 1956-59. *Home:* MTB 456, "Ceallaigh," Riverbank, Shoreham, Sussex, England.

CAREER: Marine engineer, 1959-69. *Member:* Merchant Navy Officers Association, Airline Officers Association, Institute of Patentees and Inventors.

WRITINGS: The Overtype Steam Road Waggon, Goose & Son, 1971; *The Undertype Steam Road Waggon*, Goose & Son, 1974. Contributor, under pseudonym Springfield, to *Old Motor*.

WORK IN PROGRESS: The Russian Motor Industry with Notes on Chinese Vehicles, for Goose & Son.

AVOCATIONAL INTERESTS: Travel (Ethiopia, Siam, China, Soviet Union).

* * *

KEMENY, Peter 1938-

PERSONAL: Accent is on first syllable of surname; born December 24, 1938, in Chicago, Ill.; son of Nicholas (a merchant) and Rose (Berry) Kemeny. *Education:* Harvard University, B.A. (cum laude), 1962. *Politics:* Liberal. *Home:* 28 West 76th St., New York, N.Y. 10023.

CAREER: Free-lance writer.

WRITINGS: The Way It Was: 1950-1960, Random House, 1962; *The Quest*, Random House, 1965; *Bully for Them*, Viking, 1968; *Joshua and Kate*, Knopf, 1971. Author of three scripts for "Police Story," 1973-74.

WORK IN PROGRESS: A biography of Sherman Billingsley.

* * *

KEMP, Patrick S(amuel) 1932-

PERSONAL: Born August 2, 1932, in Galveston, Tex.; son of Samuel H. and Florence (Moor) Kemp; married Carol Boren, August 22, 1959; children: Robert W., Cathleen A. *Education:* Rice University, B.A., 1953; University of Texas at Austin, M.P.A., 1956; University of Illinois, Ph.D., 1959. *Home:* 4170 Northwest Dale Dr., Corvallis, Ore. 97330. *Office:* School of Business, Oregon State University, Corvallis, Ore. 97331.

CAREER: Certified Public Accountant in Texas, 1956; Arthur Young & Co., Houston, Tex., staff accountant, 1954-55; University of Illinois, Urbana, instructor in accounting, 1956-59; Emory University, Atlanta, Ga., assistant professor, 1959-61, associate professor of business administration, 1961-62; University of Richmond, Richmond, Va., associate professor, 1962-65, professor of accounting, 1965-68, chairman of department, 1962-68; Virginia Polytechnic Institute and State University, Blacksburg, professor of accounting, 1968-74; Oregon State University, Corvallis, professor of business administration, 1974—. *Member:* American Accounting Association, American Institute of Certified Public Accountants, National Association of Accountants, Virginia Society of Certified Public Accountants, Alpha Kappa Psi, Beta Alpha Psi, Beta Gamma Sigma, Omicron Delta Kappa.

WRITINGS: Accounting for the Manager, Dow Jones-Irwin, 1970. Contributor of more than thirty articles to professional journals.

WORK IN PROGRESS: A textbook, *Principles of Managerial Accounting*, for Wiley.

* * *

KENNEBECK, Paul 1943-

PERSONAL: Born January 10, 1943, in Denver, Colo.; son of Eugene and Ruth Kennebeck. *Education:* Marquette University, B.A. *Agent:* Candida Donadio & Associates, 111 West 57th St., New York, N.Y. 10019.

CAREER: Writer. *Military service:* U.S. Army, 1969-71. *Awards, honors:* National Endowment for the Arts creative writing fellowship grant, 1974-75.

WRITINGS: Last Night's Farm, Nash Publishing, 1974. Contributor to *Harper's*.

WORK IN PROGRESS: A novel, completion expected in 1975.

* * *

KENNEDY, Rose (Fitzgerald) 1890-

PERSONAL: Born July 22, 1890, in Boston, Mass.; daughter of John Francis (a politician) and Mary Josephine (Hannon) Fitzgerald; married Joseph Patrick Kennedy (a financier and diplomat), October 7, 1914; children: Joseph (deceased), John Fitzgerald (deceased), Rosemary, Kathleen (deceased), Eunice (Mrs. Robert Sargent Shriver), Patricia, Robert Francis (deceased), Jean (Mrs. Stephen Smith), Edward M. *Education:* Attended Convent of the Sacred Heart, Boston, 1906-08, Blumenthal Academy, 1908-09, and Manhattanville College of the Sacred Heart, 1909-10; also attended a Sacred Heart Convent in Aachen, Germany. *Politics:* Democrat. *Religion:* Roman Catholic. *Home:* Hyannis Port, Mass. 02647; and North Ocean Blvd., Palm Beach, Fla. 33480.

CAREER: Served as hostess for her father, a U.S. Congressman and Mayor of Boston, and also for her husband; active in charities, especially involving mental retardation, and also in the political campaigns of her sons. *Awards, honors:* Recipient of title Papal Countess, 1951; L.H.D. from Manhattanville College.

WRITINGS: Times to Remember (autobiography), Doubleday, 1974.

SIDELIGHTS: "Times to Remember," writes Martin F. Nolan in the *New York Times Book Review*, "is conversational, unpretentious and above all, authentic. It is prose with all the proprietary tenderness and determination only an Irish mother can give. The timbre is as true as the rustle of lace curtains, the tinkle of cut glass. The book sounds as if it were written by a turn-of-the-century graduate of Dorchester High who went to finishing school in Europe and who still swims and says the rosary every day. And as a political document, of course, it is the most revealing tract on the Kennedys in all the shelves of Kennedy literature."

AVOCATIONAL INTERESTS: French language and literature.

* * *

KENNEDY, Sighle Aileen 1919-

PERSONAL: Given name is pronounced like "Sheila"; born July 27, 1919, in New York, N.Y.; daughter of Thomas J. (an editor) and Moira (an editor; maiden name, Coyle) Kennedy. *Education:* Manhattanville College, student, 1936-40; Columbia University, M.A., 1964, Ph.D., 1969. *Residence:* New York, N.Y. *Office:* Department of English, Hunter College of the City University of New York, 695 Park Ave., New York, N.Y. 10021.

CAREER: Architectural Forum, New York, N.Y., researcher and writer, 1943-51; Catholic Relief Services, New York, N.Y., supervisor of aid programs for Korea, 1951-63; Hunter College of the City University of New York, New York, N.Y., assistant professor of English, 1968—.

WRITINGS: Murphy's Bed: A Study of Real Sources and Sur-real Associations in Samuel Beckett's First Novel, Bucknell University Press, 1971; (contributor) James Brophy and Raymond Porter, editors, *Modern Irish Literature*, Twayne, 1972; (contributor) John Unterecker and Kathleen McGrory, editors, *Yeats, Joyce, Beckett: A Modern Critical Spectrum*, Bucknell University Press, 1975.

WORK IN PROGRESS: Examining the art of Samuel Beckett.

SIDELIGHTS: Sighle Kennedy writes: "New York City, where I have always lived, has continually involved me in work and study, which has greatly interested me: first, in research among architects and artists; next in efforts to help refugees from many countries renew their lives."

* * *

KENNEDY, T(homas) F(illans) 1921-

PERSONAL: Born January 12, 1921, in London, England;

son of Thomas (a farmer) and Sarah (Shearer) Kennedy; married Dorothy Mavis McKay (a teacher, librarian, and writer), June 24, 1968; children: Julie Fillans (Mrs. Murray Clayton), Paul Thomas Fillans. *Education:* Christchurch Teachers College, Diploma in Teaching, 1947; University of Canterbury, B.A., 1948, M.A., 1950; University of Auckland, Diploma in Education, 1968. *Religion:* "Presbyterian (brought up)." *Residence:* Wellington, New Zealand. *Office:* New Zealand Department of Education, Wellington, New Zealand.

CAREER: Teacher of agriculture, biology, and geography in secondary schools of New Zealand and the United Kingdom, 1947-54; Tonga College, Nukualofa, Tonga, principal, 1955-57; Ardmore Teachers College, Auckland, New Zealand, lecturer in social sciences, 1958-65; New Zealand Department of Education, Wellington, senior inspector of island schools, 1966-74, senior education officer in overseas division, 1975—, regular departmental representative to Pacific Education Conferences, 1969—. Chairman of Papakura Intermediate School Committee, 1962-65; senior consultant to South Pacific Commission, 1969; UNESCO lecturer, Makerere University, 1963-64. *Member:* New Zealand Geographical Society, New Zealand Volunteer Service Abroad Council, Tonga Rugby Union (president, 1956-57), Khandallah Tennis Club, Downstage Theatre (Wellington).

WRITINGS: *Farmers of the Pacific Islands* (booklet), A. H. & A. W. Reed, 1961, 2nd edition, 1968; *Ranchers and Planters of the Pacific Islands* (booklet), A. H. & A. W. Reed, 1962; *Fishermen of the Pacific Islands* (booklet), A. H. & A. W. Reed, 1962, 2nd edition, 1972; *Pacific Islands* (booklet), Longmans, 1964, New Zealand edition, 1964; *Afghanistan Village* (booklet), Longmans, 1966; (with T. O. Newnham) *Asia: The Monsoon Lands*, Whitcombe & Tombs, 1966, 3rd edition, 1973; *A Descriptive Atlas of the Pacific Islands*, A. H. & A. W. Reed, 1966, Praeger, 1968, 3rd edition, A. H. & A. W. Reed, 1968. Author of column on Rugby for *Auckland Star*, 1960-65. Contributor to journals in his field. Editor, *Pacific Islands Education*, 1966—.

WORK IN PROGRESS: Revisions of his books.

AVOCATIONAL INTERESTS: Travel, tennis, art (paintings), farming, conservation of native forest and fauna, wines, people.

* * *

KENNEY, Edwin James, Jr. 1942-

PERSONAL: Born January 9, 1942, in Hoboken, N.J.; son of Edwin James (in quality control) and Virginia (Saulina) Kenney; married Susan McIlvaine (a college teacher), November 28, 1964; children: James, Anne. *Education:* Hamilton College, B.A., 1963; Cornell University, M.A., 1964, Ph.D., 1968. *Residence:* China Village, Me. *Office:* Department of English, Colby College, Waterville, Me. 04901.

CAREER: Hamilton College, Clinton, N.Y., instructor in English, 1966-68; Colby College, Waterville, Me., assistant professor, 1968-74, associate professor of nineteenth- and twentieth-century literature, 1974—.

WRITINGS: *Elizabeth Bowen*, Bucknell University Press, 1974; (contributor of critical essay) George Eliot, pseudonym of Mary Ann Evans, *Middlemarch* (critical edition), edited by Bert G. Hornback, Norton, in press. Contributor of articles and reviews to *Nation*, *New Leader*, and *New Republic*.

WORK IN PROGRESS: Research on the novel at the turn of the century, from 1880 to 1920.

* * *

KENT, Sherman 1903-

PERSONAL: Born December 1, 1903, in Chicago, Ill.; son of William and Elizabeth (Thacher) Kent; married Elizabeth Gregory, December 20, 1934; children: Serafina Kent Bathrick, Sherman Tecumseh. *Education:* Yale University, Ph.B., 1926, Ph.D., 1933. *Home:* 2824 Chain Bridge Rd. N.W., Washington, D.C. 20016.

CAREER: Yale University, New Haven, Conn., instructor, 1928-30, 1933-36, assistant professor, 1936-44, associate professor, 1944-47, professor of history, 1947-53; U.S. Office of Strategic Services, Washington, D.C., chief of African section, 1941-43, chief of Europe-Africa division, 1943-45; U.S. Department of State, Washington, D.C., director of Office of Research and Intelligence, 1946; National War College, Washington, D.C., member of resident civilian staff, 1946; Yale University, professor of history, 1947-53; Central Intelligence Agency (CIA), Washington, D.C., director of Office of National Estimates, 1952-68. *Awards, honors:* Guggenheim fellowship, 1947; National Civil Service Award, 1961; President's Award for Distinguished Civilian Federal Service, 1967.

WRITINGS: *Electoral Procedure under Louis Philippe*, Yale University Press, 1937; *Writing History*, Appleton, 1942, revised edition, 1967; *Strategic Intelligence for American World Policy*, Princeton University Press, 1948, new edition, Shoe String, 1966; *A Boy and a Pig, but Mostly Horses* (children's book), Dodd, 1974; *The French Election of 1827*, Harvard University Press, 1975.

WORK IN PROGRESS: An edition of the 1827 diary of Comte Joseph de Villele; and a boys' adventure story, as yet untitled.

* * *

KERBY, Joe Kent 1933-

PERSONAL: Born March 22, 1933, in Provo, Utah; son of Joe M. (a painting contractor) and Zillah (Brown) Kerby; married Bonnie Kae Andrus, December 2, 1955; children: Joe Kent, Jr., Stacey, Kim, Shawn Howard, Julie, Bryce Kelly. *Education:* Brigham Young University, B.S., 1959; Northwestern University, M.B.A., 1960; Columbia University, Ph.D., 1966. *Politics:* Republican. *Religion:* Church of Jesus Christ of Latter-Day Saints (Mormon). *Home:* 616 Brule Rd., Marquette, Mich. 49855. *Office:* Management & Marketing Department, Northern Michigan University, Marquette, Mich. 49855.

CAREER: Oregon State University, Corvallis, assistant professor of business administration, 1962-65; Seton Hall University, South Orange, N.J., assistant professor of marketing, 1965-67; Miami University, Oxford, Ohio, associate professor, 1967-69, professor of marketing management, 1970-71; Northern Michigan University, Marquette, professor of management and head of management and marketing department, 1971—, acting head of accounting and marketing department, 1974—. Research assistant, Lake Shore Oil Co., 1960; consultant, Grand Union Co., 1966. *Member:* American Marketing Association, Beta Gamma Sigma.

WRITINGS: *Essentials of Marketing Management*, South-Western, 1970; (contributor) 1970; Stuart Henderson Britt, editor, *Handbook of Marketing*, Dartnell, 1973; *Con-*

sumer Behavior: Conceptual Foundations, Dum-Donnelley, 1975. Also author of monograph, "An Exploratory Inquiry Into the Use of Various Decision Aids as a Guide to Purchase When Product Quality Is Difficult to Assess." Contributor to journals in his field.

* * *

KERENSKY, V(asil) M(ichael) 1930-

PERSONAL: Born December 29, 1930, in Pontiac, Mich.; son of Michael V. and Traica Thomas (Vengeloff) Kerensky; divorced; children: Michael, Richard, John. *Education:* Central Michigan University, B.S., 1953; University of Michigan, M.A., 1960; Wayne State University, Ed.D., 1965. *Home:* 68 Southwest 10th Ter., Boca Raton, Fla. 33432. *Office:* Center for Community Education, College of Education, Florida Atlantic University, Boca Raton, Fla. 33432.

CAREER: Assistant superintendent of public schools in Waterford Township, Mich., 1966; Florida Atlantic University, Boca Raton, associate professor, 1966-70, professor of education, 1970-72, Charles Stewart Mott Professor, 1972—, director of Center for Community Education (of Charles Stewart Mott Foundation), 1966—. Adviser for Miami, Fla.'s bicentennial celebration. *Member:* National Community Educational Association, Phi Delta Kappa.

WRITINGS: (With Ernest O. Melby) *Education II*, Pendell, 1971. Contributor to *Phi Delta Kappan*, *Community Education Journal*, and *Elementary School Principal*. Associate editor of *National Community Education Association Journal*.

WORK IN PROGRESS: *Education II Revisited*, with E. O. Melby.

* * *

KERWOOD, John R. 1942-

PERSONAL: Born November 7, 1942, in Ripley, W.Va.; son of John Kenna, Jr. (a salesman) and Delcia (Hall) Kerwood; married Lynne Nelson, August 15, 1964; children: John Glenn, Jeffrey Nelson. *Education:* West Virginia Wesleyan College, B.A., 1964; Pennsylvania State University, M.A., 1967. *Religion:* Methodist. *Home:* 1120 Clintshire Dr., Centerville, Ohio 45459. *Office:* Montgomery County Historical Society, 7 North Main St., Dayton, Ohio 45402.

CAREER: U.S. Capitol Historical Society, Washington, D.C., editor and historian, 1967-71; American Association for State and Local History, Nashville, Tenn., regional workshop director, 1971-72; Montgomery County Historical Society, Dayton, Ohio, director, 1973—. *Member:* American Association for State and Local History, Society of Ohio Archivists (member of council, 1974—), U.S. Capitol Historical Society. *Awards, honors:* George Washington honor medal award from Freedoms Foundation, 1970; National Historical Publications Commission fellowship in advanced editing of documentary sources for American history, 1970-71, for *The Papers of Joseph Henry*, at Smithsonian Institution.

WRITINGS: (Editor with others) *The Papers of Joseph Henry*, Volume I: *The Albany Years: 1797-1832*, Smithsonian Press, 1972; (editor) *The United States Capitol: An Annotated Bibliography*, University of Oklahoma Press, 1973. Contributor to *American History Illustrated*, and *Civil War Times Illustrated*. Editor, *Capitol Dome*, 1967-71.

BIOGRAPHICAL/CRITICAL SOURCES: *History News*, July, 1971.

* * *

KETTERER, David (Anthony Theodor) 1942-

PERSONAL: Born June 13, 1942, in Leigh-on-Sea, Essex, England; son of Joseph Theodor (a chartered accountant) and Eileen (Philp) Ketterer; married Jacqueline Ruth Langsner (a librarian), March 17, 1972. *Education:* University of Wales, B.A. (honors), 1964; Carleton University, Ottawa, Ontario, M.A., 1965; University of Sussex, D.Phil., 1969. *Religion:* Roman Catholic. *Home:* 4231 Wilson Ave., Montreal, Quebec H4A 2V1, Canada. *Office:* Department of English, Sir George Williams Campus, Concordia University, Montreal, Quebec, Canada.

CAREER: McGill University, Montreal, Quebec, lecturer in English, 1965-66; Concordia University, Sir George Williams Campus, Montreal, Quebec, 1967—, now associate professor of English. *Awards, honors:* Canada Council fellowship, 1973-74.

WRITINGS: *New Worlds for Old: The Apocalyptic Imagination, Science Fiction, and American Literature*, Indiana University Press, 1974. Contributor to literature journals, including *P.M.L.A.*, *Journal of American Studies*, *American Transcendental Quarterly*, *Extrapolation*, *Foundation*, *Science Fiction Studies*, *Mosaic*, and *Criticism*.

WORK IN PROGRESS: *The Rationale of Deception in Poe*; an anthology of Canadian science fiction; a book on Mary Shelley's *Frankenstein*.

AVOCATIONAL INTERESTS: Art, theater, cinema.

* * *

KHATCHADOURIAN, Haig 1925-

PERSONAL: Surname is accented on last syllable; born July 22, 1925, in Jerusalem, Palestine; son of Abraham (an auto dealer) and Elizabeth (Sahakian) Khatchadourian; married Arpine Yaghlian, September 10, 1950; children: Abie Ara, Vicken, Sonia Nora. *Education:* American University of Beirut, B.A. (honors), 1948, M.A., 1950; Duke University, Ph.D., 1956. *Home:* 3250 North Downer Ave., Milwaukee, Wis. 53211. *Office:* Department of Philosophy, University of Wisconsin-Milwaukee, Milwaukee, Wis. 53201.

CAREER: Melkonian Education Institute, Nicosia, Cyprus, instructor in English, 1950-51; Haigazian College, Beirut, Lebanon, instructor in English, 1956-57; American University of Beirut, Beirut, Lebanon, assistant professor, 1956-60, associate professor, 1960-67, professor of philosophy, 1967-68; University of Southern California, Los Angeles, professor of philosophy, 1968-69; University of Wisconsin-Milwaukee, visiting professor, 1967-68, professor of philosophy, 1969—. Member of Harvard International Seminar, summer, 1962. *Member:* American Philosophical Association, American Society for Aesthetics, Phi Beta Kappa. *Awards, honors:* J. Walker Tomb prize from Princeton University, 1958; World Essay Contest second prize from International Humanist and Ethical Union, 1959; Andrew Mellon postdoctoral fellowship from University of Pittsburgh, 1963-64.

WRITINGS: *The Coherence Theory of Truth: A Critical Evaluation*, American University of Beirut Press, 1961; (with Tim Andrews, Elias Awad, George Khairallah and Christopher H. O. Scaife) *Traffic with Time* (poems), Khayats, 1963; *A Critical Study in Method*, Nijhoff, 1967;

The Concept of Art, New York University Press, 1971. Contributor of more than fifty-five philosophical papers to American and European journals; also contributor of a considerable number of poems to various magazines, including *Ararat*, the *Visvabharati Quarterly*, and *Quest*.

WORK IN PROGRESS: Philosophical Essays on Art; a book tentatively titled, *A Theory of Normative Ethics*, completion expected in 1976; *Reflections on the Palestine Tragedy*, 1976; a book concerning a general theory of language, 1978; a book on the aesthetics of literature and film.

SIDELIGHTS: Khatchadourian told *CA*: "As a Palestinian who has gone through the agonies and deprivations of the Palestine Tragedy since 1948, and who has become *heimatlos* as a result, I identify strongly with the just cause of the Palestinian people in seeking redress for the grevious wrong done to them as a result of the partition of Palestine. As a man of peace, who abhors violence and destruction in any form or manner, and from any and all quarters, I long for a peaceful settlement of the conflict. I support wholeheartedly the idea of an independent Palestinian state on the West Bank of the Jordan River and the Gaza Strip, peacefully co-existing with all its neighbors.

"My humanistic as well as humanitarian values and ideals have also been nourished and sustained by the centuries-long tribulations of the Armenian people. I believe in the dignity of man and the brotherhood and sisterhood of all men and women as human beings. I believe that all men and women have a right to enjoy equal liberties and rights; and my future writings will increasingly reflect these and similar convictions."

* * *

KIDNEY, Walter C(urtis) 1932-

PERSONAL: Born January 24, 1932, in Johnstown, Pa.; son of Walter Curtis (a teacher) and Monna (Jeannerat) Kidney. *Education:* Haverford College, A.B., 1954. *Politics:* None. *Religion:* None. *Home and office:* 1219 Buena Vista St., Pittsburgh, Pa. 15212.

CAREER: Employed in libraries and editorial offices, 1954-60; Random House, New York, N.Y., editor, 1961-67; *Progressive Architecture* (magazine), New York, N.Y., associate editor, 1967-68; Press of Case Western Reserve University, Cleveland, Ohio, editor, 1968-73; writer, 1973—. *Member:* Society of Architectural Historians, Society for Industrial Archeology, Victorian Society in America, Steamship Historical Society of America, National Trust for Historic Preservation.

WRITINGS: Historic Buildings of Ohio, Ober Park Associates, 1973; *The Architecture of Choice: Eclecticism in America, 1880-1930,* Braziller, 1974; (with Authur P. Ziegler and Leopold Adler II) *Revolving Funds for Historic Preservation,* Ober Park Associates, in press; *The Society for Industrial Archeology Guide to the Adaptive Use of Industrial Structures,* Ober Park Associates, in press; (with Lawrence G. Zimmerman) *Yesterday's Tomorrows,* Braziller, in press.

WORK IN PROGRESS: A history of composition and visual devices in American architecture; further research on eclecticism; research on the role of truth in architecture.

* * *

KILEY, Margaret A(nn)

PERSONAL: Born in Buffalo, N.Y.; daughter of James A. and Margaret (Valentine) Kiley. *Education:* State University of New York at Buffalo, B.S. (with honors), 1951; George Washington University, M.A., 1953, Ed.D., 1965. *Home:* 8415 Bellona Lane, Apt. 913, Baltimore, Md. 21204. *Office:* Department of Secondary Education, Towson State College, Baltimore, Md. 21204.

CAREER: Public school teacher and chairman of department of business education at Falls Church, Va., 1954-64; George Washington University, Washington, D.C., assistant professor of education and chairman of business education, 1964-69; Towson State College, Baltimore, Md., associate professor, 1969-72, professor of education, 1972—. Administrative assistant to Science Service of U.S. Secret Service, 1954-64. *Member:* American Personnel and Guidance Association, Association of Teacher Educators, Association for Higher Education, American Association of University Professors, National Council for the Social Studies, Phi Delta Kappa.

WRITINGS: (With M. H. Jessup) *Discipline: Positive Attitudes for Learning*, Prentice-Hall, 1971; *Personal and Interpersonal Appraisal Techniques: For Counselors, Teachers, Students*, C. C Thomas, 1975. Contributor to education journals.

WORK IN PROGRESS: Research on school success for slow learners and on a re-examination of drives and expectations of parents and students in college.

* * *

KILROY, Thomas 1934-

PERSONAL: Born September 23, 1934, in Callan, Ireland; son of Thomas and Mary (Devine) Kilroy; married Patricia Cobey; children: Hugh Benjamin, Lorcan Thomas, Desmond Patrick. *Education:* University College, Dublin, B.A., 1955, M.A., 1957. *Residence:* Portumna, Galway County, Ireland. *Agent:* Anthony Sheil, 52 Floral Street, London WC2 9DE, England.

CAREER: University of Dublin, University College, Dublin, Ireland, university lecturer in English; writer. *Member:* Irish Academy of Letters, Royal Society of Literature (fellow). *Awards, honors: Guardian* Fiction Prize, 1971, and Heinemann Award for Literature, 1972, both for *The Big Chapel*; creative writing award from American Irish Foundation, 1974.

WRITINGS: Death and Resurrection of Mr. Roche, Faber, 1969, Grove, 1970; *The Big Chapel*, Faber, 1971; (editor) *Sean O'Casey*, Prentice-Hall, 1974.

WORK IN PROGRESS: "Talbot's Box," a play; *Angela*, a novel.

* * *

KIM, Ilpyong J(ohn) 1931-

PERSONAL: Born August 15, 1931, in Seoul, Korea; married Hyunyong Chung (a librarian), June 22, 1963; children: Irene, Katherene. *Education:* Columbia University, M.A., 1961, Ph.D., 1968. *Home:* 61 Hillyndale Rd., Storrs, Conn. 06268. *Office:* Department of Political Science, University of Connecticut, Storrs, Conn. 06268.

CAREER: Indiana University, Bloomington, lecturer, 1965-68, assistant professor of government, 1968-70; University of Connecticut, Storrs, associate professor of political science, 1970—. *Military service:* Korean Army, 1950-53; became captain; received Bronze Star. *Member:* International Studies Association, American Political Science Association, Association for Asian Studies.

WRITINGS: The Politics of Chinese Communism: Kiangsi under the Soviets, University of California Press, 1974; *Communist Politics in North Korea*, Praeger, 1974. Contributor to political science journals.

WORK IN PROGRESS: China and the Question of Korea (monograph); editing *China and the Balance of Power in Asia*; *China and North Korea: A Comparative Analysis* (monograph).

SIDELIGHTS: Kim reads Chinese, Japanese, and Russian, as well as his native Korean, and practices their calligraphy regularly; he collects rare books in these languages. *Avocational interests:* Tennis, swimming.

* * *

KIM, Jung-Gun 1933-

PERSONAL: Born July 19, 1933, in Korea; naturalized U.S. citizen; son of Jae-Kyoung and Sung-Kyu (Han) Kim; married Kyoung-Hi Park (a pediatrician), December 21, 1958; children: Kyoung-Soon, Chul-Soon. *Education:* University of Missouri at Kansas City, B.A., 1958; George Washington University, M.A., 1961; University of Maryland, Ph.D., 1965. *Religion:* Presbyterian. *Home:* 400 Oxford Rd., Greenville, N.C. 27834. *Office address:* Department of Political Science, East Carolina University, P.O. Box 2752, Greenville, N.C. 27834.

CAREER: University of Maryland, College Park, instructor in government, 1963-65; East Carolina University, Greenville, N.C., assistant professor, 1965-67, associate professor, 1967-71, professor of political science, 1972—, director of graduate studies, 1967-72. Visiting professor at Yonsei University, 1972-73.

WRITINGS: (Editor with James C. Dixon, and contributor) *Readings in American National Government*, McCutchan, 1969; (editor and contributor) *Essays on the Vietnam War*, East Carolina University Publications, 1970; (with John M. Howell) *International Obligations and State Interests*, Nijhoff, 1972. Contributor of more than a dozen articles to political science journals, including *Journal of Inter-American Studies*, *Journal of Asiatic Studies*, *Revue General de Droit International Public*, *Indian Journal of International Law*, *India Quarterly*, *Korean Journal of International Law*, and *Caribbean Quarterly*.

* * *

KIM, Se-Jin 1933-

PERSONAL: Born January 16, 1933, in Pyongyang, Korea; naturalized United States citizen, 1970; son of Hang-Bok (a businessman and educator) and Chan-young Kim; married Heasun, April 13, 1963; children: Sean Jungee, Steven Junhee. *Education:* Southwestern at Memphis College, B.A. (honors), 1959; University of Massachusetts, M.A., 1962, Ph.D., 1966. *Religion:* Presbyterian. *Home:* 1925 Fountain Ridge, Chapel Hill, N.C., 27514. *Office:* Department of Political Science, North Carolina Central University, Durham, N.C. 27707.

CAREER: Eastern Kentucky University, Richmond, instructor, 1962-65, assistant professor, 1965-67, associate professor of political science, 1967-68; North Carolina Central University, Durham, professor of political science, 1969—, chairman of department, 1969—. University of North Carolina, Ford Foundation faculty fellow, 1968-69, visiting professor, summer, 1969. *Member:* American Political Science Association, Association for Asian Studies. *Awards, honors:* National Science Foundation summer award, 1971; Fulbright-Hayes award, 1975.

WRITINGS: Politics of Military Revolution in Korea, University of North Carolina Press, 1971; *Government of Politics in Korea*, Research Institute of Korean Affairs, 1972; *Afro-Asian World in Transition*, North Carolina Central University, 1974. Contributor to *Asian Survey, Asian Forum, Labor Review, Korea Journal*, and *Asian Profile*.

WORK IN PROGRESS: Concepts of Political Development.

* * *

KIMBALL, George 1943-

PERSONAL: Born December 20, 1943, in Grass Valley, Calif.; son of George E. (a colonel in the U.S. Army) and Sue (a teacher at University of Alabama; maiden name, Laslie) Kimball; married Susan Hodges, November, 1966 (divorced, 1969); married Mary Ann Stewart, September, 1970 (divorced June, 1973). *Education:* Attended University of Kansas, 1961-65, University of Iowa, 1968-69, Massachusetts Bay Community College, and Harvard University. *Religion:* "Lapsed." *Home:* 37 Catherine St., Newport, R.I. 02840. *Agent:* David Otte, 9 Park Ave., Boston, Mass. 02107. *Office: Boston Phoenix*, 100 Massachusetts Ave., Boston, Mass. 02115.

CAREER: Scott Meredith Literary Agency, New York, N.Y., editor, 1966-68; *Boston Phoenix*, Boston, Mass., sports editor, 1970—. Member of advisory board of Boston Repertory Theatre Co. Democratic candidate for sheriff of Douglas County, Kan., 1970. *Military service:* U.S. Naval Reserve, 1961-67. *Member:* American Contract Bridge League, U.S. Darting Association, Professional Basketball Writers Association of America, Kaw Valley Hemp Pickers.

WRITINGS: Only Skin Deep (novel), Olympia, 1968; (with Tom Beer) *Sunday's Fools* (nonfiction), Houghton, 1974. Work is anthologized in *The World Anthology*, edited by Anne Waldman, Bobbs-Merrill, 1969; *The New Olympia Reader*, edited by Maurice Girodias, Olympia, 1970; *The Rolling Stone Record Review*, edited by Jann Wenner, Straight Arrow, 1974. Contributing editor of *Boston* (magazine), 1974—.

WORK IN PROGRESS: A book on the Boston Red Sox; a book on the National Football League in Europe.

AVOCATIONAL INTERESTS: Travel (especially Dublin, Ireland), sailing, cooking.

BIOGRAPHICAL/CRITICAL SOURCES: Phoenix, December, 1972; Joe Flaherty, *Chez Joey*, Coward, 1974.

* * *

KIMBALL, Richard Laurance 1939-

PERSONAL: Born November 9, 1939, in San Jose, Calif.; son of Willard W. and Pauline (a nurse; maiden name, Jacob) Kimball; married Jane Frances Glass (a teacher), June 17, 1961; children: Liesel Jan: Francisco Kayanja, Robert Mkandawire (adopted). *Education:* Attended College of Idaho, 1957-59; Stanford University, B.S.E.E., 1961, M.A. (anthropology), 1970, Ph.D., 1971; Makerere University, Kampala, Uganda, diploma of education, 1962; Northeastern University, M.A. (math and science education), 1968; University of Pittsburgh, graduate study, 1969; postdoctoral study, Psychodrama Institute, San Francisco, and Center for Human Communication, Los Gatos, Calif., 1972. *Home:* 18669 Withey Rd., Monte Sereno, Calif. 95030. *Office:* Department of Teacher Education, California State University, 25800 Hillary St., Hayward, Calif.

CAREER: Participant, Entebbe Math Conference, Entebbe, Uganda, 1962-63; Uganda Technical College, Kampala, lecturer in electrical engineering, 1962-64; Education Development Center, Newton, Mass., developer of elementary science curriculum, 1964-66; science educator and director of Science Center in Domasi, Malawi, 1966-68; San Jose State University Extension, San Jose, Calif., guest lecturer, 1969; Makerere University, Kampala, Uganda, supervisor of secondary teacher training, 1970; California State University, Hayward, associate professor of education, 1970—. California State licence in marriage, family, and child guidance counseling, 1973. Lecturer and Peace Corps trainer for School Mathematics Study Group, Bogota, 1965; teacher of summer workshops and extension courses, California State University and University of California, 1970-72.

MEMBER: Institute of Electrical and Electronic Engineers, National Science Teachers Association, Elementary School Science Association, National Council for Teachers of Mathematics, American Society of Group Psychotherapy and Psychodrama, African Studies Association, Jean Piaget Society, East African Institute of Engineers, California Council for Teachers of Mathematics, Malawi Teachers Association, Malawi Biological Association, Kappa Delta Pi.

WRITINGS: (Contributor) *Entebbe Mathematics for African Schools*, Science Research Associates, 1964; (with Lynn Sagan) *Peas and Particles* (juvenile science), McGraw, 1968; *Batteries and Bulbs* (juvenile science), McGraw, 1969; *Making Small Things Look Bigger* (juvenile science), Educational Science Consultants, 1971; *Ekyetagisa Ekikulu: An Inquiry into the Relationships between a New Science Curriculum and Creative Growth*, Stanford International Development Education Center, 1971; *Substances and Mixtures and Powders and Liquids* (juvenile science), Educational Science Consultants, 1971; *San Luis, Teoloxolco: Ahorita* (title means "In Just a Bit of Time in a Mexican Village"), Educational Science Consultants, 1971; (with others) *Summary of Research on Education and Rural-Urban Transformation*, Stanford University, 1971; *You and Me* (juvenile science), Educational Science Consultants, 1972; (editor) *The Animal Book of Coloring and Feeling*, Educational Science Consultants, 1974; *A Search for the Great White Also* (fantasy), Educational Science Consultants, 1974; *NEW: Love, Life, Hope, Understanding, Trust, Responsibility*, Educational Science Consultants, 1975.

Author of science books for young people, published by Education Development Center, Newton, Mass., 1966: *Dipping Birds*, *Euglena* (with Lynn Sagan), and *Kucheza Blocks*; and books published by Science Center and Education Development Center in Domasi, Malawi, 1968: *Substances, Mixtures and Powders*; *The Fly Cycle*; *More Microscopes*; *Seeds, Soils and Plants*; *Systems I*; *Systems II*; *Buds and Twigs*; *What Is a Science Unit?*; *Ant Lions*; *Chickens I* (with Quentin Woomeb). Also author of book of photographs for teachers, *What Is Science in Malawi?*, Science Center, Malawi, 1968.

Contributor to *Nature and Science*, *This Is Malawi*, and *Chameleon* (magazine of Science Center, Domasi, Malawi). Editor, *Chameleon*, 1966-68.

WORK IN PROGRESS: A travel story for children and adults; work on Piagetian tests.

SIDELIGHTS: Kimball has traveled widely in Africa, Europe, and parts of the Middle East, South and Central America, and Japan. He reads and speaks Spanish, German, Swahili, Cewa, and Japanese.

* * *

KIMMEL, Douglas C(harles) 1943-

PERSONAL: Born June 8, 1943, in Denver, Colo.; son of Rudolph Charles (a businessman) and Mary (a writer; maiden name, Embury) Kimmel. *Education:* University of Colorado, B.A. (cum laude), 1965; University of Chicago, A.M., 1969, Ph.D., 1970. *Religion:* Presbyterian. *Home:* 30 West 88th St., New York, N.Y. 10024. *Office:* Department of Psychology, City College of the City University of New York, New York, N.Y. 10031.

CAREER: City College of the City University of New York, New York, N.Y., assistant professor of psychology, 1970—. *Member:* American Psychological Association, Gerontological Society, National Council on Family Relations.

WRITINGS: *Adulthood and Aging: An Interdisciplinary Developmental View*, Wiley, 1974; (contributor) J. O. Lugo and G. L. Hershey, editors, *Human Development*, Macmillan, 1974; (contributor) Lugo and Hershey, editors, *Living Psychology*, 2nd edition, Macmillan, in press.

WORK IN PROGRESS: Research on middle age and life span case history.

AVOCATIONAL INTERESTS: Travel.

* * *

KIMMEL, Jo 1931-

PERSONAL: Born February 11, 1931, in Mountain View, Okla.; daughter of Fred F. (a produceman) and Myrtle V. (Stone) Stuckey; married Theodore E. Kimmel, January 16, 1954 (died, 1965); children: Fran, Kay, Susan. *Education:* Oklahoma College for Women, student, 1949-51; Oklahoma City University, B.A., 1953; Columbia University, M.A., 1964. *Religion:* Christian. *Residence:* Nashville, Tenn. *Office: Upper Room*, 1908 Grand Ave., Nashville, Tenn. 37203.

CAREER: Manchester College, North Manchester, Ind., instructor in speech and drama, 1965-69; prayer laboratory leader in Phoenix, Ariz., 1968-73; *Upper Room*, Nashville, Tenn., director of family devotional life department, 1973—. *Member:* International Union of Family Organizations, National Council on Family Relations, Southeastern Council on Family Relations.

WRITINGS: *Steps to Prayer Power*, Abingdon, 1972; *Stop Playing Pious Games*, Abingdon, 1974. Contributor of devotions to *Upper Room Disciplines*, 1974. Contributor to *Catalyst*.

WORK IN PROGRESS: A devotional book for the widowed or divorced woman; a devotional book based on scripture; a mystery novel.

SIDELIGHTS: Jo Kimmel spent sixteen months in Iraq as a missionary, and one year in Madagascar. She has studied healing in England, France, and India, and led a workshop on the family in Tanzania in 1974. She writes that she is ". . . deeply interested in helping relate faith to action."

* * *

KING, Billie Jean 1943-

PERSONAL: Born November 22, 1943, in Long Beach, Calif.; daughter of Willis B. (a fireman) and Betty (Jerman) Moffitt; married Larry W. King (a lawyer, promoter, and publisher), September 17, 1965. *Education:* Attended California State College (now University), Los Angeles, 1961-66. *Religion:* Protestant. *Office:* King Enterprises, 1660 South Amphlett, San Mateo, Calif. 94402.

CAREER: Professional tennis player, 1968—. Publisher, *WomenSports* magazine, San Mateo, Calif., 1974—. Player-coach, Philadelphia Freedoms of the World Team Tennis League, 1973—. *Member:* Women's Tennis Association (president, 1973—). *Awards, honors:* Named "Sportsperson of the Year" by *Sports Illustrated*, 1972.

WRITINGS: (With Kim Chapin) *Tennis to Win*, Harper, 1970; (with Chapin) *Billie Jean*, Harper, 1974.

SIDELIGHTS: Mrs. King began playing tennis at the age of eleven, and by the time she was eighteen had upset top-ranking Margaret Smith Court at Wimbledon. By 1974 she had won five Wimbledon singles championships and two at Forest Hills. She holds the distinction of being the first woman in tennis history to win $100,000 prize money in one year (1971), a figure exceeding the amount won by any American tennis player, male or female, at that time. "Money is everything in sports," Mrs. King once commented. "Big money is the common denominator. The guy in the factory can relate to me. He says, 'If she makes all that much, she *must* be good.'" Long active in improving the lot of women in tennis, she was one of nine women founding the Virginia Slims pro tour in 1971.

BIOGRAPHICAL/CRITICAL SOURCES: Owen Davidson and C. M. Jones, *Great Women Tennis Players*, Pelham Books, 1971; Phyllis Hollander, *American Women in Sports*, Grosset, 1972; Barbaralee Diamonstein, *Open Secrets*, Viking, 1972; *Ladies' Home Journal*, April, 1974.

* * *

KING, Bruce A. 1933-

PERSONAL: Born January 1, 1933, in Philadelphia, Pa.; son of Joseph and Lillian (Gilbert) King; married Adele Cockshoot (a professor of French), December 28, 1955; children: Nicole. *Education:* Columbia University, B.A., 1954; University of Leeds, Ph.D., 1960. *Home:* c/o S-1023 Cooper River Plaza, Pennsauken, N.J. *Office:* Department of English, Ahmadu Bello University, Zaria, Nigeria.

CAREER: University of Ibadan, Ibadan, Nigeria, lecturer in English, 1962-65; University of Bristol, Bristol, England, lecturer in English, 1965-67; University of Lagos, Lagos, Nigeria, professor of English and head of department, 1967-69; University of Windsor, Windsor, Ontario, professor of English, 1970-73; Ahmadu Bello University, Zaria, Nigeria, professor of English and head of department, 1973—.

WRITINGS: *Dryden's Major Plays*, Barnes & Noble, 1966; (editor) *Twentieth Century Interpretations of All for Love: A Collection of Critical Essays*, Prentice-Hall, 1968; (editor and contributor) *Dryden's Mind and Art*, Oliver & Boyd, 1969; (editor) *Introduction to Nigerian Literature*, Africana Publishing, 1971; (editor and contributor) *Literatures of the World in English*, Routledge & Kegan Paul, 1974. Contributor of more than fifty articles, poems, and reviews to literature journals, including *Concerning Poetry, Sewanee Review, Southern Review, English Studies, College English*, and *Modern Language Review*.

SIDELIGHTS: An American by birth, King has lived mostly in the British Commonwealth, with summers spent in Spain. *Avocational interests:* Jazz music, ballet, African music.

KING, Clarence 1884(?)-1974

1884(?)—September 27, 1974; American social work educator, author of books on community organization. Obituaries: *New York Times*, September 29, 1974; *Washington Post*, October 2, 1974; *AB Bookman's Weekly*, November 25, 1974.

* * *

KING, Daniel P(atrick) 1942-

PERSONAL: Born February 23, 1942, in Milwaukee, Wis.; son of Daniel Joseph (a printer) and Margaret R. (McGowan) King; married Guadalupe Vasquez (a university professor), December 11, 1971. *Education:* Institute of Applied Science, diploma, 1961; University of Wisconsin, B.Sc., 1965; Marquette University, graduate study, 1966-68. *Home:* 5125 North Cumberland Blvd., Whitefish Bay, Wis. 53217.

CAREER: High school teacher of sociology in Milwaukee, Wis., 1965; probation officer for State of Wisconsin, 1967-74; Milwaukee Area Technical College, Milwaukee, Wis., lecturer in police science, 1974—. *Member:* Institute of Public Administration of the Republic of Ireland (fellow), Crime Writers' Association (England), Sherlock Holmes Society of London, National Rifle Association of America.

WRITINGS: *The Right of Counsel in State Courts*, Canada Law Book, 1965; *The United States Drug Problem*, Forensic Publishing, 1968; *An Alternative to the United States Bail System*, Forensic Publishing, 1971; *Firearms and Crime*, Forensic Publishing, 1973; *Conan Doyle and Holmes: In Pursuit of Justice*, Forensic Publishing, 1974. Contributor of articles and reviews to *Police Journal, Journal of Criminal Law, Criminology and Police Science, Criminologist, Criminal Law Quarterly, Criminal Law Review*, and *Baker Street Journal*.

WORK IN PROGRESS: Editing a book of essays on criminology and forensic science.

AVOCATIONAL INTERESTS: Travel, shooting, bibliophily.

* * *

KINGRY, Philip L. 1942-

PERSONAL: Born December 6, 1942, in Bellefountain, Ohio; son of W. W. (a naval officer) and Mamie (a teacher; maiden name, Rose) Kingry; married Susan Helen (a librarian); children: Indira (adopted in Bombay, India). *Education:* Attended St. Mary's Seminary, 1960-62; University of Maryland, B.A., 1967; George Washington University, graduate study, 1968-69. *Home:* 5908 Johnson Avenue, Bethesda, Md. 20034.

CAREER: Free-lance writer. *Military service:* U.S. Navy and U.S. Marine Corp. medical corpsman.

WRITINGS: (Editor) *Walker Series of Genealogical History*, sixty volumes, Heritage, 1973; *The Monk and the Marines*, Bantam, 1974. Also author of *The Cauldron of Light*.

SIDELIGHTS: Kingry told *CA*: "I grew up in Asia and the Pacific after the war and am knowledgeable of several languages. I am an associate of the Cisterian Order of The Strict Observance. Discipline, self-sacrifice, owning as little as necessary and silence, are the ideals of this contemplative enclosed order. I spend my time thinking and writing and traveling. For the next two years I will be in India and southern Asia."

KININMONTH, Christopher 1917-
(Christopher Brennan, a joint pseudonym)

PERSONAL: Born September 24, 1917, in Cheshire, England; son of Colin Peter (an engineer) and Irene Harriet Jane (Simmons) Kininmonth. *Education:* Attended Ruskin School of Drawing, 1934-36, Slade School of Art, 1936, and Chelsea Polytechnic, 1937. *Home:* 34 Foster Rd., London W4 4NY, England; and 101 Derb el Boumba, Marrakech-Medina, Morocco. *Agent:* J. Wolfers, 3 Regent Square, London W.C.1, England.

CAREER: Public Relations Associates Ltd., London, England, account executive, 1961-63; writer. *Military service:* British Army Intelligence Corps, 1941-46; became sergeant.

WRITINGS: *The Children of Thetis*, Lehmann, 1949; *Rome Alive*, Lehmann, 1951; *The Brass Dolphins*, Secker & Warburg, 1957; *Sicily*, J. Cape, 1965, revised edition, Bobbs-Merrill, 1972; *Malta and Gozo*, J. Cape, 1967, revised edition, 1968, Bobbs-Merrill, 1970; (with Roland Baird under joint pseudonym Christopher Brennan) *A Massacre of Innocents*, Hart-Davis, 1967, Panther Books, 1970; *Frontiers*, Davis-Poynter, 1971; *Morocco*, J. Cape, 1971, Bobbs-Merrill, 1972; *Maze*, Davis-Poynter, 1974. Contributor to *Sunday Times* (London), *Guardian*, *Evening Standard* (London), and others.

SIDELIGHTS: Kininmonth is competent in French, Italian, and some Greek and Arabic.

* * *

KINZER, Donald Louis 1914-

PERSONAL: Born November 9, 1914, in Kent, Wash.; son of Addison Louis and Lois M. (Fay) Kinzer; married Jane Tipton, August 20, 1955; children: William T. *Education:* Western Washington State College, B.A., 1942; University of Washington, Seattle, B.A., 1947, M.A., 1948, Ph.D., 1954. *Office:* Department of History, Indiana University-Purdue University, 925 West Michigan, Indianapolis, Ind. 46202.

CAREER: University of Washington, Seattle, instructor in history, 1954-55; University of Delaware, Newark, instructor in history, 1955-58; Trenton State College, Trenton, N.J., associate professor of history, 1958-66; Indiana University-Purdue University, Indianapolis, Ind., associate professor, 1966-70, professor of history, 1970—, chairman of department, 1970—. President of Mercer County (N.J.) Cerebral Palsy Association, 1962-66, and Princeton United Fund Board, 1962-66; secretary of New Hope Foundation, 1971. *Military service:* U.S. Army, 1942-46. *Member:* American Historical Association, Organization of American Historians, American Association of University Professors.

WRITINGS: *An Episode in Anti-Catholicism: The American Protective Association*, University of Washington Press, 1964. Contributor of articles and reviews to journals.

* * *

KIRBY, David K(irk) 1944-

PERSONAL: Born November 29, 1944, in Baton Rouge, La.; son of Thomas Austin (a professor) and Josie (a school teacher; maiden name, Dyson) Kirby; married Judy Kates (a high school French teacher), March 21, 1969; children: William. *Education:* Louisiana State University, B.A., 1966; Johns Hopkins University, Ph.D., 1969. *Home:* 1100 Carissa Dr., Tallahassee, Fla. 32303. *Office:* Department of English, Florida State University, Tallahassee, Fla. 32306.

CAREER: Florida State University, Tallahassee, assistant professor, 1969-74, associate professor of English and director of writing programs, 1974—, member of faculty at F.S.U. Study Center in Florence, Italy, 1973. Has conducted workshops and seminars for groups including elementary school children and prison inmates. *Member:* Modern Language Association of America, National Council of Teachers of English, College English Association, South Atlantic Modern Language Association.

WRITINGS: (Editor with Kenneth H. Baldwin) *Individual and Community: Variations on a Theme in American Fiction*, Duke University Press, 1975; *American Fiction to 1900: Guide to Information Sources*, Gale, 1975; *Grace King*, Twayne, in press. Contributor to journals.

WORK IN PROGRESS: Poems and reviews ("my favorite forms"); research on the writings of Henry James ("my favorite author").

SIDELIGHTS: Kirby writes: "As a writer and a teacher of writing I have two principles: (1) reverence toward language and (2) irreverence toward everything else, including myself and my own writing. I'm addicted to poetry readings, workshops, professional meetings, conferences, lectures—any situation which is likely to result in wit, brilliance, animated conversation, and perhaps a congenial glass or two among friends. I appreciate anyone who writes anything that interests me, no matter how they do it or what form it takes."

* * *

KIRK, Elizabeth D(oan) 1937-

PERSONAL: Born September 5, 1937, in Philadelphia, Pa.; daughter of Allen David (a college professor) and Helen (a college professor; maiden name, Bell) Hole; married John T. Kirk (a writer and teacher), June 14, 1959. *Education:* Earlham College, B.A., 1959; Yale University, Ph.D., 1964. *Religion:* Quaker. *Home:* 36 John St., Providence, R.I. 02906. *Office:* Department of English, Brown University, Providence, R.I. 02912.

CAREER: Yale University, New Haven, Conn., instructor in English, 1964-67; Brown University, Providence, R.I., assistant professor, 1967-72, associate professor of English, 1972—. *Member:* Modern Language Association of America, Medieval Academy of America, Society for Religion in Higher Education. *Awards, honors:* American Council of Learned Societies grant, 1974-75; *Explicator* honorable mention award, 1972, for *The Dream Thought of Piers Plowman*.

WRITINGS: *The Dream Thought of Piers Plowman*, Yale University Press, 1972. Contributor to journals.

WORK IN PROGRESS: *Julian of Norwich and Late Medieval Modes of Knowing*.

* * *

KIRKPATRICK, Diane 1933-

PERSONAL: Born June 28, 1933, in Grand Rapids, Mich.; daughter of Myron S. (in insurance business) and Alice Elizabeth (McBlain) Kirkpatrick; married Edward Charles Witke (a writer and educator), July 29, 1972. *Education:* Vassar College, B.A., 1955; Cranbrook Academy of Art, M.F.A., 1957; University of Michigan, M.A., 1965, Ph.D., 1969. *Office:* Department of History of Art, Tappan Hall, University of Michigan, Ann Arbor, Mich. 48104.

CAREER: Fideler Co. (publishers), Grand Rapids, Mich.,

manuscript editor, and in charge of pictures and layout, 1957-58; U.S. Army, Wuerzburg and Baumholder, Germany, director of service club, 1958-60; Grand Rapids Art Museum, Grand Rapids, Mich., director of children's education, 1961-63; University of Michigan Ann Arbor, lecturer, 1967 and 1968-69, instructor, 1969-70, assistant professor, 1972-74, associate professor of history of art, 1974—. Interviewer for visiting artists at University of Michigan's Television Center and for WUOM-Radio. *Member:* College Art Association of America, Phi Kappa Phi. *Awards, honors:* Senior fellow, University of Michigan Society of Fellows; Innovative Teaching Funds awards of University of Michigan, 1972-73, 1973-74.

WRITINGS: Eduardo Paolozzi, Studio Vista, 1970. Contributor to art catalogues. Author of "The Creation of Art," a series of programs for University of Michigan's Television Center. Contributor to *University of Michigan Museum of Art Bulletin* and *Studio International*.

WORK IN PROGRESS: Aesthetics of Animation; research on aesthetics of video, machine in art, man-machine interaction, American "Grotesque," and interaction of technology and society's values and aesthetics.

SIDELIGHTS: Diane Kirkpatrick's interest is the use of visual language systems for communication in the modern world. *Avocational interests:* Photography, cinematography.

* * *

KIRKPATRICK, Jeane D(uane) J(ordan) 1926-

PERSONAL: Born November 19, 1926, in Duncan, Okla.; daughter of Welcher E. (an oilman) and Leona B. (Kile) Jordan; married Evron M. Kirkpatrick (executive director of the American Political Science Association), February 20, 1955; children: Douglas Jordan, John Evron, Stuart Alan. *Education:* Barnard College, A.B., 1948; Columbia University, M.A., 1950, Ph.D., 1967; graduate study at Institut de Science Politique, University of Paris, 1952-53. *Politics:* Democrat. *Religion:* Protestant. *Home:* 6812 Granby St., Bethesda, Md. 20034. *Office:* Department of Government, Georgetown University, Washington, D.C. 20007.

CAREER: U.S. State Department, Washington, D.C., research analyst, 1951-52; George Washington University, Washington, D.C., research associate, 1954-56; Fund for the Republic, Washington, D.C., research associate, 1956-57; Trinity College, Washington, D.C., assistant professor of political science, 1962-67; Georgetown University, Washington, D.C., associate professor of government, 1967—. Vice-chairman of Democratic National Commission on Vice-Presidential Selection; member of board of directors and member of executive committee, Coalition for a Democratic Majority; consultant to American Council of Learned Societies, U.S. Department of State, Department of Defense, and Department of Health, Education, and Welfare, at various times, 1955-72. *Member:* American Political Science Association. *Awards, honors:* French Government fellowship, 1952-53; Earhart fellowship, 1956-57; National Endowment for the Humanities grant, 1970.

WRITINGS: (Editor with husband, Evron M. Kirkpatrick, and contributor) *Elections—U.S.A.: A Selection of Articles*, Holt, 1956; (editor and contributor) *Strategy of Deception: A Study in World-Wide Communist Tactics*, Farrar, Straus, 1963; (contributor) S. M. Meyers and A. D. Biderman, editors, *Mass Behavior in Battle and Captivity*, University of Chicago Press, 1968; *Leader and Vanguard in Mass Society: A Study of Peronist Argentina*, M.I.T. Press, 1971; *Political Woman*, Basic Books, 1974. Contributor to journals and periodicals, including *Commentary*, *Saturday Review World*, and *British Journal of Political Science*.

WORK IN PROGRESS: Two books, *Presidential Politics: A Study of the American Political Elite in Transition*, and *Psychological Bases of the New Utopia*.

* * *

KISHIDA, Eriko 1929-

PERSONAL: Born January 5, 1929; daughter of Kunio (a writer) and Tokiko Kishida; married; children: Micki, Koto. *Education:* Attended Tokyo Art Academy. *Home:* Daito-Ky, 5,9,4, Yanake, Tokyo, Japan. *Agent:* Fukuin-Kan Shoten, 9,1,1, Misaki-cho Chiyoda-ku, Tokyo, Japan.

CAREER: Poet and author of children's books.

WRITINGS: Hippopotamus, translated from the Japanese by Masako Matsuno, Prentice-Hall, 1963; *Wake Up Hippopotamus,* Bodley Head, 1967; *The Hippo Boat,* Bodley Head, 1967, World Publishing, 1968; (adapter) *P. I. Tchaikovsky's Swan Lake,* translated from the Japanese by Ann King Herring, Gakken (Tokyo), 1970; *The Lion and the Bird's Nest,* Crowell, 1973. Also author of "Jiojio no tanjobi," 1970.

* * *

KISSANE, John M(ichael) 1928-

PERSONAL: Surname is pronounced Kiss-*aine*; born March 30, 1928, in Oxford, Ohio; son of Donald Persefor (a violinist, conductor, and teacher) and Leedice (a professor of American studies; maiden name, McAnelly) Kissane; married Barbara Swisher, August 19, 1951; children; Michael, James, Mary, Joseph, Stephen. *Education:* University of Rochester, A.B. (with high distinction), 1948; Washington University, St. Louis, Mo., M.D. (cum laude), 1952. *Politics:* Democrat. *Religion:* None. *Home:* 6926 Kingsbury Blvd., St. Louis, Mo. 63130. *Office:* Department of Pathology, School of Medicine, Washington University, St. Louis, Mo. 63110.

CAREER: Washington University, School of Medicine, St. Louis, Mo., 1958—, began as instructor, now professor of pathology and pediatrics. Associate pathologist at Barnes and Affiliated Hospitals; associate pathologist and director of pathologic anatomy at St. Louis Children's Hospital; consultant in pathology to Jewish Hospital of St. Louis. Member, Task Force on Cancer of the Pancreas. *Military service:* U.S. Army, Medical Corps, chief of laboratory service in La Chapelle, France, 1955-57; became captain.

MEMBER: International Academy of Pathology, American Medical Association, American Association of Pathologists and Bacteriologists, Histochemical Society, Society for Experimental Pathology, Missouri Medical Society, St. Louis Medical Society, Pediatric Pathology Club of St. Louis (president), St. Louis Heart Association (member of board of directors), Phi Beta Kappa, Gamma Sigma, Alpha Omega Alpha.

WRITINGS: (With M. G. Smith) *Pathology of Infancy and Childhood*, Mosby, 1966, 2nd edition, 1975. Contributor of about sixty articles to professional journals.

WORK IN PROGRESS: Editing sixth edition of *Pathology*, by W. A. D. Anderson, with Anderson; chapters for inclusion in two books on renal disease.

SIDELIGHTS: Kissane was a professional baseball player, a catcher, in 1949. *Avocational interests:* Sports, Victorian novels (especially Hardy), Sherlock Holmes, music (the Romantics, especially Brahms; opera, especially Verdi), travel, photography, gourmet food, wines, old movies, history (especially Western Americana).

* * *

KLAPPER, M(olly) Roxana 1937-

PERSONAL: Born November 17, 1937, in Germany; daughter of Elias (a businessman) and Cipora (a businesswoman; maiden name, Weber) Teicher; married Jacob Klapper (a university professor), August 27, 1958; children: Rachelle Hannah, Robert David. *Education:* City College of the City University of New York, B.A., 1959, M.A., 1964; New York University, Ph.D., 1974. *Residence:* New York, N.Y. *Office:* Department of English, Bronx Community College, 181st St. and University Ave., Bronx, N.Y. 10453.

CAREER: Bronx Community College, Bronx, N.Y., adjunct lecturer in English, 1974—. *Member:* Modern Language Association of America. *Awards, honors:* Award from American Philosophical Society, 1974, to study Shelley's manuscripts at Bodleian Library of Oxford University.

WRITINGS: The German Literary Influence on Byron, Institut fuer Englische Sprache und Literatur, University of Salzburg, 1974; *The German Literary Influence on Shelley*, Institut fuer Englische Sprache und Literatur, University of Salzburg, 1975.

WORK IN PROGRESS: The German Literary Influence on the English Romantic Writers: Scott, Coleridge, Wordsworth, Keats.

* * *

KLAUDER, Francis John 1918-

PERSONAL: Born December 1, 1918, in Philadelphia, Pa.; son of Frank C. (a broker) and Agnes G. (Quinlan) Klauder. *Education:* Gregorian University of Rome, Ph.B., 1939, Ph.L., 1940; Fordham University, Ph.D., 1953. *Office:* Don Bosco College, Newton, N.J. 07680.

CAREER: Ordained Roman Catholic priest of Salesian Society of St. John Bosco (S.D.B.), 1947; member of faculty, Salesian High School, New Rochelle, N.Y., 1947-50; Don Bosco College, Newton, N.J., instructor in philosophy, 1953—, dean, 1953-65, dean of philosophy, 1965-74, president of college, 1974—. Weekend parish work in Wayne, N.J., 1959—. *Member:* American Philosophical Association, American Catholic Philosophical Association.

WRITINGS: Aspects of the Thought of Teilhard de Chardin, Christopher, 1971; *The Wonder of Intelligence*, Christopher, 1973; *The Wonder of the Real*, Christopher, 1973; *The Wonder of Philosophy*, Philosophical Library, 1973. Associate editor of *Salesian Bulletin*.

WORK IN PROGRESS: The Power of Goodness, a comparative study of Teilhard de Chardin and the Scholastics St. Bonaventure and St. Thomas.

* * *

KLEMPNER, Irving M(ax) 1924-

PERSONAL: Born November 28, 1924, in Poland; married Miriam Stern (a teacher), November 23, 1949; children: Yon Diane, Mark. *Education:* Brooklyn College of the City University of New York, B.A., 1951; Columbia University, M.S., 1952, D.L.S., 1967. *Home:* 864 Whitney Dr., Schenectady, N.Y. 12309. *Office:* School of Library and Information Science, State University of New York at Albany, Albany, N.Y. 12222.

CAREER: Department of State Library, Washington, D.C., intern librarian, 1952-53; Library of Congress, Washington, D.C., librarian, 1953-54, 1956; catalog librarian, National Library of Medicine, 1955; supervisory librarian, Naval Intelligence School, 1956-57, and Naval Applied Science Laboratory, 1957-58; manager of information services, United Nuclear Corp., 1958-67; State University of New York at Albany, associate professor, 1967-68, professor of library and information science, 1969—.

MEMBER: Special Libraries Association (member of executive board of upstate New York chapter, 1969-70), American Library Association, American Management Association, American Society for Information Science (chairman, Upstate New York chapter, 1972-73), Association of American Library Schools, New York Library Association. *Awards, honors:* Award from American Society for Information Science, 1971, for best chapter or special interest group publication; certificate of distinction from North Atlantic Treaty Organization (NATO) Advanced Study Institute in Information Science, 1973; Special Libraries Association award for best paper published in *Special Libraries*, 1974.

WRITINGS: Diffusion of Abstracting and Indexing Services for Government-Sponsored Research (monograph), Scarecrow, 1968; *Resource Library for Instructional Development: A Feasibility Study* (monograph), Educational Communications Center, State University of New York at Albany, 1970; *Audiovisual Materials in Support of Information Science Curricula* (monograph), Educational Resources Information Center, State University of New York at Albany, 1972; revised edition published as *Information: Part Two, Reports-Bibliographies*, Science Associates International, 1972.

Contributor of about thirty-five articles and reviews to library journals, including *Special Libraries*, *College and Research Libraries*, *American Documentation*, *Library Resources and Technical Services*, and *Proceedings of the NATO Advanced Study Institute in Information Science*. Consultant to Greenwood Press, 1973.

WORK IN PROGRESS: Research on access to information and on federal and state freedom of information legislation.

* * *

KLIN, George 1931-

PERSONAL: Born June 26, 1931, in Brussels, Belgium; son of Lou (a tailor) and Mariem (Tepper) Klin; married Paulette Schwitzer (a teacher), August 16, 1959; children: Richard, Celia. *Education:* Brooklyn College (now Brooklyn College of the City University of New York), B.A., 1953; University of Nebraska, M.A., 1955; University of Oregon, further graduate study, 1956-57; Wayne State University, Ph.D., 1963. *Politics:* Liberal Democrat. *Religion:* Jewish. *Home:* 222 Forest Dr., Linwood, N.J. 08221. *Office:* Department of Foreign Languages, Atlantic Community College, Mays Landing, N.J. 08330.

CAREER: State University of New York at Binghamton, assistant professor of Romance languages, 1963-69; Atlantic Community College, Mays Landing, N.J., professor of Romance languages, 1969—. *Member:* Modern Language Association of America, American Translator Association.

WRITINGS: (With Amy Marsland) *Victor Hugo's "Les Miserables"* (study guide), Cliffs, 1968; (with Marsland) *Racine's "Phaedra and Andromache"* (study guide), Cliffs, 1969; (translator) Charles Lehrmann, *The Jewish Element in French Literature*, Fairleigh Dickinson University Press, 1971. Contributor of articles and reviews to literature magazines, including *French Review*, *Junior College Journal*, *Books Abroad*, *Jewish Social Studies*, *Foreign Language Journal*, and *Romanic Review*.

WORK IN PROGRESS: Translating *The Jewish Element in European Thought*, by Lehrmann, for Fairleigh Dickinson University Press, *World History of Art*, for Cliff's Notes.

SIDELIGHTS: Klin writes: "As a Jew who suffered from the ordeal of German persecutions, I take a painful interest in anti-Semitism, and particularly its literary manifestation. I am contemplating an article or even a book refuting the rampant ill-will of French writers toward Jews." *Avocational interests:* Art history, cartooning, painting.

* * *

KLINGSTEDT, Joe Lars 1938-

PERSONAL: Born January 30, 1938, in Chicago, Ill.; married; children: two. *Education:* University of Oklahoma, B.M.Ed., 1962; graduate study at Oklahoma State University and University of Colorado; Texas Tech University, M.M.Ed., 1969, Ed.D., 1970. *Home:* 6441 Dawn Dr., El Paso, Tex. 79912. *Office:* College of Education, University of Texas, El Paso, Tex. 79968.

CAREER: High school music teacher and director of vocal music in Sand Springs, Okla., 1962-65, and Lubbock, Tex., 1965-68; Texas Tech University, Lubbock, instructor in secondary education, 1969-70; University of Texas, El Paso, assistant professor, 1970-73, associate professor of education, 1973—, assistant dean of College of Education, 1973—. Director of summer swimming program for American Red Cross, 1963; superintendent of boys' dormitory at Sand Springs Home, 1964-65; member of interim steering committee of Texas Council for the Improvement of Educational Systems project, 1973, director of project, 1973-74; has directed church choirs. *Military service:* U.S. Naval Reserve, air control tower operator, active duty, 1955-57.

MEMBER: National Education Association, American Choral Directors Association, National Society for the Study of Education, American Educational Research Association, Association for Supervision and Curriculum Development, American Association of University Professors, Oklahoma Education Association, Oklahoma Music Educators Association, Texas State Teachers Association, Texas Music Educators Association (regional vice-chairman), Texas Choral Directors Association (vice-chairman), Lubbock Classroom Teachers Association, Phi Delta Kappa, Phi Mu Alpha (past vice-president), Kappa Sigma. *Awards, honors:* Grant from Research Institute of University of Texas, El Paso, 1971, to study effectiveness of three feedback procedures in developing set establishing skill; grant from Texas Center for Improvement of Educational Systems, 1973, to prepare student information systems package.

WRITINGS: Methods for Performance-Based Education, W. C. Brown, 1972; *Teachers of Middle School Mexican Children: Indicators of Effectiveness and Implications for Teacher Education* (monograph), Educational Resources Information Center, 1972; (with Richard W. Burns) *Program Design for Performance-Based Teacher Education* (monograph), Educational Resources Information Center, 1972; (editor with Burns) *Competency-Based Education: An Introduction*, Educational Technology Publications, 1973. Contributor of more than a dozen articles to education journals, including *Creative Teacher*, *Clearing House*, *Man, Society, Technology*, *Improving College and University Teaching*, *Research in Education*, and *Texas Study of Secondary Education Research Journal*. Editor of *Educational Technology*, autumn, 1972.

SIDELIGHTS: Klingstedt has made audio tapes, including "A Modularized Design for Individualizing Instruction," series of six tapes, Educational Technology Publications, 1972; (with Richard W. Burns) "Individualized Learning Using Instructional Modules," a series of three tapes, Educational Technology Publications, 1973.

* * *

KLOSE, Kevin 1940-

PERSONAL: Born September 1, 1940, in Toronto, Ontario, Canada; son of Willard (an advertising representative) and Virginia (a writer; maiden name, Taylor) Klose; married Eliza Darcy Kellogg, September 5, 1964; children: Cornelia Kellogg, Brennan, Chandler Robbins. *Education:* Harvard University, B.A. (cum laude), 1962. *Residence:* Washington, D.C. *Agent:* Sterling Lord Agency, 660 Madison Ave., New York, N.Y. 10021. *Office: Washington Post*, 1150 15th St. N.W., Washington, D.C. 20071.

CAREER: Washington Post, Washington, D.C., reporter, 1967-73, District of Columbia editor, 1973—. *Military service:* U.S. Navy, 1962-64; became lieutenant junior grade.

WRITINGS: (With Sala Pawlowicz) *I Will Survive*, Norton, 1962; (with Philip A. McCombs) *The Typhoon Shipments*, Norton, 1974.

* * *

KLOTMAN, Robert Howard 1918-

PERSONAL: Born November 22, 1918, in Cleveland, Ohio; son of Louis (a manufacturer) and Pearl (Warshawsky) Klotman; married Phyllis Rauch (a professor), April 4, 1943; children: Janet (Mrs. Roger Cutler), Paul. *Education:* Ohio Northern University, B.S., 1940; Case Western Reserve University, M.A., 1951; Columbia University, D.Ed. in Music, 1956. *Home:* 3811 Morningside Dr., Apt. 36, Bloomington, Ind. 47401. *Office:* School of Music, Indiana University, Bloomington, Ind. 47401.

CAREER: Scherl & Roth (string instrument importers), Cleveland, Ohio, educational director, 1956-69; Indiana University, Bloomington, professor of music and music education, 1969—. Consultant to Summy-Birchard Co., 1973—; secretary, Indiana University Credit Union, 1974-75. *Military service:* U.S. Army, 1941-45; became technical sergeant. *Member:* Music Educators National Conference (North Central Division, president, 1972-74; national president-elect, 1974-76), American String Teachers Association (president, 1962-64), Phi Delta Kappa, Phi Mu Alpha Sinfonia. *Awards, honors:* Certificate of award from National Association of Negro Musicians, 1966; Music Educators National Conference citation, 1972, 1974.

WRITINGS: (Editor) *Scheduling School Music Programs*, Music Educators Conference, Department of National

Education Association, 1968; (with Ernest Harris) *Learning to Teach Through Playing: String Techniques and Pedagogy*, Addison-Wesley, 1971; (with Laurence Burkhalter) *String Literature for Expanding Technique*, Crescendo, 1972; *The School Music Administrator and Supervisor: Catalysts for Change in Music Education*, Prentice-Hall, 1973. Contributor to *Encyclopedia of Education* and to journals in his field. Member of editorial board, *Instrumentalist*, 1974—.

WORK IN PROGRESS: Philosophy and Foundations in Music Education.

AVOCATIONAL INTERESTS: Travel and tennis.

* * *

KLUGH, Henry E(licker, III) 1927-

PERSONAL: Born March 23, 1927, in Harrisburg, Pa; son of Henry E. (an engineer) and Florentine (Schilling) Klugh; married Barbara Jones, January 30, 1952 (divorced February 16, 1972); children: Henry, Thomas. *Education:* Attended Carnegie Institute of Technology, 1947-49; Geneva College, B.A., 1951; University of Pittsburgh, M.S., 1952, Ph.D., 1955. *Office:* Department of Psychology, Alma College, Alma, Mich. 48801.

CAREER: Alma College, Alma, Mich., professor of psychology and head of department, 1955—. *Military service:* U.S. Army Air Forces, 1944-47. *Member:* American Psychological Association (fellow), Psychonomic Society, Phi Beta Kappa, Sigma Xi.

WRITINGS: Statistics: The Essentials for Research, Wiley, 1970, 2nd edition, 1974. Contributor to *Psychological Record, American Journal of Mental Deficiency*, and other psychology journals.

* * *

KNAPP, J(ohn) Merrill 1914-

PERSONAL: Born May 9, 1914, in New York, N.Y.; son of John Harold (a broker) and Lillian (Merrill) Knapp; married Elizabeth-Ann Campbell (a farm executive), February 21, 1944; children: Joan, Phoebe. *Education:* Yale University, A.B., 1936; Columbia University, M.A., 1941. *Home address:* Rosedale Lane, Princeton, N.J. 08540. *Office:* Department of Music, Princeton University, Princeton, N.J. 08540.

CAREER: History teacher in Ojai, Calif., 1936-38; Yale University, New Haven, Conn., assistant director of Glee Club, 1938-39; Princeton University, Princeton, N.J., instructor, 1947-48, assistant professor, 1948-53, associate professor, 1953-60, professor of music, 1960—, assistant dean of college, 1955-58, dean, 1961-66, director of Glee Club, 1941-42, 1946-52. Trustee of Hun School, Westminster Choir College, and Hotchkiss School. *Military service:* U.S. Naval Reserve, active duty, 1942-46; became lieutenant commander. *Member:* American Musicological Society, College Music Association, American Association of University Professors, Century Association. *Awards, honors:* American Council of Learned Societies grant, 1968; Mus.D. from Westminster Choir College, 1970; Rockefeller Foundation grant, 1971.

WRITINGS: (Editor) *Selected List of Music for Men's Voices*, Princeton University Press, 1951; *The Magic of Opera*, Harper, 1972; (editor) G. F. Handel, "Amadigi" (opera), Barejreiter Verlag (Kassel), 1971.

WORK IN PROGRESS: The Operas of George Frederic Handel.

KNAPP, Robert Hampden 1915-1974

April 16, 1915—September 8, 1974; American educator and author. Obituaries: *New York Times*, September 9, 1974; *AB Bookman's Weekly*, November 25, 1974. (*CA*-15/16).

* * *

KNIGHT, Arthur Winfield 1937-

PERSONAL: Born December 29, 1937, in San Francisco, Calif.; son of Walter Arthur (a park supervisor) and Irja (Bloomquist) Knight; married Veronica Joyce, 1960 (annulled, 1961); married Carole Gail Smith, August 10, 1963 (divorced September 26, 1966); married Glee Marquardt (a writer and publisher), September 27, 1966. *Education:* Santa Rosa Junior College, A.A., 1958; California State University at San Francisco, B.A., 1960, M.A. (with honors), 1962. *Residence:* California, Pa. *Agent:* Ray Peekner, 2625 North 36th St., Milwaukee, Wis. 53210. *Office address:* TUVOTI, P.O. Box 439, California, Pa. 15419.

CAREER: Free-lance writer, 1962—; California State College, California, Pa., director of creative writing program, 1966—. Free-lance photographer, 1953—. European correspondent, *Redwood Rancher*, 1962-63, columnist, 1963. *Member:* Committee of Small Magazine Editors and Publishers, Associated Writing Program, Coordinating Council of Literary Magazines, Pennsylvania Council on the Arts.

WRITINGS: All Together, Shift, Horizon Press, 1972; *Extracts*, Sceptre Press, 1974; *Who Moved among the Others as They Walked*, Hilltop Press, 1974; *Our Summer Made Her Light Escape* (fiction), Realit, 1974; (with Glee Knight) *Until the Lights in Us Come On* (poems), Cider Press, 1975. Editor, with Glee Knight, *The Beat Book*, 1974.

Work is represented in textbook, *Writing: Fact and Imagination*, edited by Eleanore C. Hibbs, Prentice-Hall, 1971, and in anthologies, including *Man, the Poet*, edited by James B. Romnes, Northwoods Press, 1974, and *Quality American Poetry*, edited by William Lloyd Griffin, Valley Publications, 1974. Contributor of fiction, poetry, and articles to journals, including *Massachusetts Review*, *South Carolina Review*, *Win*, *Wisconsin Review*, *New York Culture Review*, *Great Speckled Bird*, *Global Tapestry Journal*, *Maine Review*, and *Poetry View*. Editor, with Glee Knight, *the unspeakable visions of the individual* (TUVOTI), 1971—.

WORK IN PROGRESS: Editing, with Glee Knight, *The Beat Book II*; an explication of Ginsberg's "Howl."

SIDELIGHTS: Knight has traveled in Europe, Mexico, Canada, and the United States and resided in Sussex, England in 1962. Among his published writings are an interview with Stan Laurel in 1963, and an account of a whaling expedition he made.

* * *

KNIPE, Wayne Bishop III 1946-

PERSONAL: Born May 12, 1946, in Fort Worth, Tex.; son of Wayne Bishop, Jr. (a U.S. Army career officer) and Jean (Schmidt) Knipe; married Sharyn Yalch (an airline stewardess), November 1, 1973. *Education:* Texas A & M University, student, 1965-67; University of Houston, B.B.A., 1969. *Home and office:* 34C Plum Tree Parkway, Smyrna, Ga. 30080.

CAREER: Central Adjustment Bureau, Houston, Tex., salesman, 1969-70; Estes Industries, Penrose, Colo., salesman, 1970-72; self-employed marketing consultant in Atlanta, Ga., 1972—. Member of Small Business Administration's Active Corps of Executives.

WRITINGS: Ideas, Inventions, and Patents: An Introduction to Patent Information, Pioneer Press (Atlanta, Ga.), 1973.

WORK IN PROGRESS: Research for a book on copyright laws for the layman.

SIDELIGHTS: Knipe writes: "I continue to want to provide information needed by the middle class of America. This group, of which I am a member, pays the bills and keeps this country on a firm footing. I want to express . . . readable rights of law that the majority could and should exercise."

* * *

KNIST, F(rances) Emma 1948-
(Felicia Fallere)

PERSONAL: Born September 20, 1948, in East Jeffries, Mich.; daughter of Schoenherr P. (inventor of the circular file) and Joy (a file clerk; maiden name, Delray) Merriman; married Warren Knist (a data analysis and retrieval technician), February 29, 1967; children: Cass, John R.; Chloe, Floe, Zoe (triplets). *Education:* Mt. Elliott Community College, A.A.H., 1968. *Politics:* "The less the better." *Religion:* Humanist. *Home:* 9692 Rosedale, Allen Park, Mich. 48101.

CAREER: Free-lance secretary, 1968-69; part-time clerk, Healthy Helen's Foods for Life, 1970-72; full-time writer, 1972—. Founder and editor, "Dial-a-Recipe" ("To help combat those ever-present 4:30 p.m. dinner-fixing blues," explains Mrs. Knist), 1969-70. *Member:* Hybrid Society, Friends of Ginseng (chairman of Michigan chapter, 1972-73), Daughters of World War II, Sigma Alpha Pi. *Awards, honors:* Golden Stem award from Hybrid Society, 1975, for one of the ten best ginseng recipes of the year.

WRITINGS: The Acquaintance (novel), Books for Readers, 1969; *Growing Up in the Dark, or, The Secret Life of Sprouts*, Earth Books, 1972; *It Happened Last Spring* [and] *Then Came the Rains* [and] *It Was the Fall of My Life* (autobiographical trilogy), with introduction and notes by Elizabeth Tarpey, Cedomage Press, 1972-73; *Everything's Coming Up Roses (Even Where I Planted the Asparagus)*, Earth Books, 1974; *Ginseng for Everyone: Your Key to a Long, Happy, and Honorable Life*, P. D. Leon, 1975; (self-illustrated) *One Hundred and One Ginseng Recipes*, P. D. Leon, in press. Contributor of articles, sometimes under pseudonym Felicia Fallere, to numerous magazines and newspapers. Editorial consultant, *Sprouts Afield*, 1973-75.

WORK IN PROGRESS: Getting High with Ginseng, Naturally, completion expected in 1976.

AVOCATIONAL INTERESTS: Breeding guppies, refinishing old filing cabinets.

* * *

KNOWLES, (Michael Clive) David 1896-1974

September 29, 1896—November 21, 1974; British historian, educator, author. Obituaries: *AB Bookman's Weekly*, January 13, 1975. (*CA*-7/8).

* * *

KNUTH, Helen 1912-

PERSONAL: Born March 19, 1912, in Hopkinton, Iowa; daughter of Paul William (a professor) and Sara (a teacher; maiden name, Walker) Knuth. *Education:* University of Dubuque, B.A., 1933; Northwestern University, M.A., 1939, Ph.D., 1958. *Politics:* Democrat. *Home:* 832 Main St., Clarion, Pa. 16214. *Office:* History Department, Clarion State College, Clarion, Pa. 16214.

CAREER: Junior high school librarian in Dubuque, Iowa, 1934-36; high school English and history teacher in Hopkinton, Iowa, 1936-38; *Metropolitan News Index*, Chicago, Ill., research editor, 1939-42; high school history teacher in Sturgis, Mich., 1942-44; U.S. Maritime Commission, Washington, D.C., research analyst, 1946-47; Roosevelt University, Chicago, Ill., lecturer in history, 1949-51; Milwaukee-Downer College, Milwaukee, Wis., academic dean, 1951-55; University of Wisconsin—Milwaukee, lecturer in history, 1956-57; Clarion State College, Clarion, Pa., associate professor, 1958-59, professor of American history, 1959—. *Military service:* U.S. Navy Women's Reserve (Women Accepted for Volunteer Emergency—WAVES), 1944-46; became lieutenant junior grade. *Member:* American Historical Association, Organization of American Historians, American Association of University Professors, American Association of University Women, League of Women Voters.

WRITINGS: (Contributor) David A. Horr, editor, *American Indian Ethnohistory: Chippewa Indians III*, Garland, 1973, contribution published separately as *Economic and Historical Background of Northeastern Minnesota Lands: Chippewa Indians of Lake Superior*, Clearwater, 1974; *Economic and Historical Background for Valuation of Ottawa-Potawatomi Lands in Michigan and Indiana as of August 29, 1821*, Clearwater, 1974.

WORK IN PROGRESS: Research on Michigan history in the early nineteenth century.

* * *

KOBAYASHI, Noritake 1932-

PERSONAL: Born February 23, 1932, in Tokyo, Japan; son of Daijyo (a surgeon) and Makiko (Tadokoro) Kobayashi; married Mieko Nishino, May 21, 1960; children: Norikazu (son), Sumiko and Kumiko (daughters). *Education:* Harvard University, A.B. (cum laude), 1953, graduate study, 1953-54, 1960-61; Keio University, LLB., 1954, Ph.D., 1973. *Religion:* Buddhism. *Home:* 9-13-4 Shirokane Minato-ku, Tokyo, Japan 108. *Office:* Graduate School of Business Administration, Keio University, 1960 Hiyoshi Honcho Kohoku-ku, Yokohama, Japan 223.

CAREER: Keio University, Tokyo, Japan, assistant professor, 1956-62, associate professor, 1962-73, professor of international business and comparative law, 1973—. Consultant to numerous international business organizations; head of expert group to study problems of multinational enterprise of Ministry of International Trade and Industry of Japanese Government, 1972—; visiting professor, Indiana University, 1968, Asian Institute of Management, Makati, Philippines, 1970, and Centre d'etudes industrielles, Geneva, 1974. *Member:* Academy of International Business (regional chairman for Japan, 1972), International Law Association (Japanese Branch), Academy of Management, American Academy of Political and Social Science, Comparative Law Association of Japan, Japanese American Society for Legal Studies.

WRITINGS: Eikoku junkeiyakuho (title means "The English Law of Quasi-Contract"), Chikura-shobo, 1960; *Nihon no goben gaisha* (title means "Joint Ventures in

Japan''), Toyo Keizai, 1967; (editor) *Kokusai Keiei* (title means ''International Management''), Kawade Shobo, 1968; (with Thomas F. Adams) *The World of Japanese Business*, Kodansha, 1969; *Shichijunendai no keieisha* (title means ''Requirement for Managers in the 1970's''), Takeuchi-shoten, 1970; *Sekai kigyoe no senryaku* (title means ''How to Meet the Challenge of Global Business''), Kogaku-sha, 1971; *International Business*, Chikura-shoho, 1972; (with Adams) *Geschaftspartner Japan: Wegweiser zum Vertehen und praktische Hinweise* (title means ''Business Partner Japan''), Societats-Verlag, 1973.

Contributor: Masami Itoh, editor, *Eibei-ho gairon* (title means ''An Introduction to Anglo-American Private Law''), Seirin-shoin, 1961; Teruo Minemura, editor, *Kakkoku no Komuinseido to Rodokihonken* (title means ''Comparative Studies of the Labor Rights among Public Workers''), Nihou Rodo Kyokai, 1966; Robert Ballon, editor, *Joint Ventures and Japan*, Sophia University (Tokyo), 1968; Isaiah A. Litvak and C. J. Maule, editors, *Foreign Investment: The Experience of Host Countries*, Praeger, 1971; Kernial Singh Sandhu, editor, *Southeast Asia Today: Problems and Prospects*, Institute of Southeast Asian Studies (Singapore), 1973; Virginia Shook Cameron, editor, *Private Investments and International Transactions in Asia and South Pacific Countries*, Mathew Bender, 1974.

Translator into Japanese: Theodore F. Plucknett, *A Concise History of the Common Law*, Tokyo University Press, 1959; Richard Hellman, *The Challenge to U.S. Dominance of the International Corporation*, Japan Productivity Center, 1971; William A. Dymsza, *Multinational Business Strategy*, Japan Productivity Center, 1974.

WORK IN PROGRESS: Several works in the areas of multinational business, comparative management styles, etc.

SIDELIGHTS: Kobayashi told *CA*: ''For many Japanese, there are only two worlds, one is Japanese and the other is non-Japanese. The latter is colored by American influence. After discovering European and Asian differences, I wish to promote among Japanese a more realistic appreciation of the world outside Japan.''

* * *

KOCHENBURGER, Ralph J. 1919-

PERSONAL: Born November 2, 1919, in Jersey City, N.J.; son of Jack F. (a bank clerk) and Margaret (Georgi) Kochenburger; married Elinor Mohr, September 10, 1944; children: Steven, Barbara, Peter. *Education:* Massachusetts Institute of Technology, B.S., 1940, M.S., 1941, Sc.D., 1949. *Politics:* Liberal Democrat. *Home:* 26 Southwood Rd., Storrs, Conn. 06268. *Office:* U157, University of Connecticut, Storrs, Conn. 06268.

CAREER: University of Connecticut, Storrs, 1951—, now professor of electrical engineering and computer science. Visiting professor at Technical University of Denmark, 1966. Member of board of directors of Eastern Connecticut Drug Action Program, 1970-73. *Member:* Institute of Electrical and Electronic Engineers (fellow), Sigma Xi, Tau Beta Pi, Eta Kappa Nu, Phi Kappa Phi. *Awards, honors:* Alfred Noble Award, from joint engineering societies, 1950, for a technical paper.

WRITINGS: Computer Simulation of Dynamic Systems, Prentice-Hall, 1972; (with C. Turcio) *Introduction to PL/I and PL/C Programming*, Hamilton Publishing, 1974; (with Turcio) *Computers in Modern Society*, Hamilton Publishing, 1974.

WORK IN PROGRESS: Computer Simulation in the Social Sciences, publication expected in 1977.

SIDELIGHTS: Kochenburger writes that his ''... professional interest is the problem of insuring a more moral use of technology and ... the avoidance, in the future, of the many ways technology has been abused and perverted toward anti-social ends.'' *Avocational interests:* Tennis, Denmark, sketching and painting in pastels.

* * *

KOEHLER, Ludmila 1917-

PERSONAL: Born March 30, 1917, in Troitzk, Russia; naturalized U.S. citizen, 1955; daughter of Herbert G. (an engineer) and Raisa (Bashkiroff) Soemmering; married Nicholas A. Koehler (a translator), April 27, 1952. *Education:* University of Washington, Seattle, Ph.D., 1963. *Religion:* Greek-Orthodox. *Home:* 5252 Beeler St., Pittsburgh, Pa. 15217. *Office:* Department of Slavic Languages, 114 Loeffler Bldg., University of Pittsburgh, Pittsburgh, Pa. 15260.

CAREER: Pacific University, Forest Grove, Ore., assistant professor of Slavic languages, 1963-64; University of Iowa, Iowa City, assistant professor of Slavic languages, 1964-66; Michigan State University, East Lansing, assistant professor of Slavic languages, 1966-67; University of Pittsburgh, Pittsburgh, Pa., associate professor of Slavic languages, 1967—. *Member:* American Association of Teachers of Slavic and East European Languages (chairman of Pennsylvania chapter, 1974—). *Awards, honors:* International Research and Exchanges Board research fellowship to Moscow, 1973.

WRITINGS: A. A. Del'vig: A Classicist in the Time of Romanticism, Mouton & Co., 1970. Contributor to *Slavic and East European Journal* and *Slavonic and East European Review*.

WORK IN PROGRESS: The Poetry of E. Barayntsky, completion expected in 1976.

SIDELIGHTS: Ludmila Koehler has been the organizer and director of several student tours of the Union of Soviet Socialist Republics in 1967, 1969, 1970, and 1972.

* * *

KOENIG, Fritz H(ans) 1940-

PERSONAL: Born April 27, 1940, in Ludwigshafen, Germany; married Elisabeth Jansbo; children: Morten, Ulf. *Education:* University of Heidelberg, student, 1959-60; University of Kiel, student, 1960-62; University of Oslo, cand. mag., 1966; University of Iowa, M.A., 1969, Ph.D., 1972. *Home:* 1125 West 12th St., Cedar Falls, Iowa 50613. *Office:* Department of Foreign Language and Literature, University of Northern Iowa, Cedar Falls, Iowa 50613.

CAREER: High school teacher of German in Weston-super-Mare, England, 1961-62; University of Oslo, Extension Service, Oslo, Norway, instructor, 1963-65; Wang's College of Commerce, Oslo, instructor in German business correspondence, 1965-67; American Embassy, Oslo, instructor in Norwegian, 1965-66; Japanese Embassy, Oslo, instructor in German, 1965-66; University of Northern Iowa, Cedar Falls, instructor, 1967-70, assistant professor, 1970-73, associate professor, 1973-75, professor of Germanic language and literature and Scandinavian language and literature, 1975—, director of Teacher's Summer Institute in Austria and Germany, 1973-75.

MEMBER: American Association of Teachers of German, Society for the Advancement of Scandinavian Studies, American-Scandinavian Foundation, Midwest Modern Language Association.

WRITINGS: *Tysk for bankfolk* (title means "German for Bankers"), Kreditkassen (Oslo, Norway), 1967; *Guide i tysk handelskorrespondanse* (title means "Guide to German Business Correspondence"), Wangs undervisningssenter, 1967; *Tysk grammatikk og merkantile uttrykk* (title means "German Grammar and Commercial Expressions"), Wangs undervisningssenter, 1967; *A Psycho-Generative Approach to the Teaching of German*, with slides and workbooks, Psycho-Generative, Inc., 1970; (contributor of translations) Seip-Saltveit, editor, *Geschichte der Norwegischen Sprache* (title means "History of the Norwegian Language"), deGruyter, 1971; (translator with Jerry Crisp) Tarjei Vesas, *Land of Hidden Fires*, Wayne State University Press, 1973; (translator, editor, and author of introduction) *Poetry of the German Democratic Republic*, University of Illinois Press, in press. Contributor to *Micromegas*, *North American Review*, and *Scandinavian Review*.

* * *

KOGOS, Frederick 1907-1974

January 4, 1907—October 11, 1974; Russian-born American publisher, editor, author. Obituaries: *New York Times*, October 14, 1974. (*CA*-29/32).

* * *

KOLB, John F. 1916(?)-1974

1916(?)—September 11, 1974; American editor and author. Obituaries: *New York Times*, September 20, 1974.

* * *

KOLB, Philip 1907-

PERSONAL: Born August 29, 1907, in Chicago, Ill.; son of Isidor (a business executive) and Dorothy (Friedman) Kolb; married Dorothy Dietrich (a teacher), September 2, 1941; children: Katherine (Mrs. Basil Reeve), Richard Edward, Jocelyne Townsend. *Education:* University of Chicago, Ph.B., 1931, A.M., 1932; University of Paris, graduate study, 1935-36; Harvard University, Ph.D., 1938. *Home:* 711 West Nevada St., Urbana, Ill. 61801. *Office:* Department of French, University of Illinois, Urbana, Ill. 61801.

CAREER: Williams College, Williamstown, Mass., instructor in French and Spanish, 1938-39; Cumberland University, Lebanon, Tenn., instructor in French and Spanish, 1940-41; University of Illinois, Urbana, instructor in Spanish, 1945-46, instructor in French, 1946-47, assistant professor, 1947-51, associate professor, 1951-56, professor of French, 1956—, associate fellow at Center for Advanced Study, 1960, 1962, established research center for Proust studies. Lecturer at Oxford University, Cambridge University, University of London, University of Utrecht, University of Leiden, University of Groningen, and University of Amsterdam. Panelist for National Endowment on the Arts and Humanities; co-director of Decade on Proust, 1962; has appeared on French television and radio programs. *Military service:* U.S. Naval Reserve, active duty, 1942-45; served in European theater; became lieutenant commander; received Croix de Guerre with Palm from Government of Belgium; named chevalier of Order of Leopold I.

MEMBER: Association Internationale des Etudes Francaises, Modern Language Association of America, American Association of Teachers of French, Societe des amis de Marcel Proust. *Awards, honors:* French Government fellowship, 1935-36; award from French Academy, 1951, for *La Correspondance de Marcel Proust*; Fulbright research fellowship, France, 1951-52, 1965-66; American Philosophical Society grants, 1953, 1955, 1958; American Council of Learned Societies fellowship, 1965-66; National Endowment for the Humanities senior fellowship, 1972-73.

WRITINGS: *La Correspondance de Marcel Proust: Chronologie et commentaire critique* (title means "Chronology and Critical Commentary of Marcel Proust's Correspondence"), University of Illinois Press, 1949; (editor and author of preface and notes) Marcel Proust, *Correspondance avec sa mere (1887-1905): Lettres inedites* (title means "Correspondence with His Mother, 1887-1905: Unpublished Letters"), Librairie Plon, 1953; (editor and author of notes) *Marcel Proust et Jacques Riviere: Correspondance (1914-1922)*, Librairie Plon, 1955; (editor and author of preface and notes) Proust, *Lettres a Reynaldo Hahn* (title means "Letters to Reynaldo Hahn"), Gallimard, 1956.

(Editor) Proust, *Choix de Lettres* (title means "Selected Letters"), Librairie Plon, 1965; (editor with Georges Cattaui) *Entretiens sur Marcel Proust* (title means "Symposium on Marcel Proust"), Mouton & Co., 1966; (editor and author of notes) Proust, *Lettres retrouvees* (title means "Letters Recovered"), Librairie Plon, 1966; (editor with Larkin B. Price) *Textes retrouves recueillis* (title means "Rediscovered Texts Collected"), University of Illinois Press, 1968; (editor and author of notes) Proust, *Correspondance: Texte etabli*, Volume I: *1880-1895*, Librairie Plon, 1970; *La Genese du Temps Perdu*, Gallimard, in press.

Contributor: Peter Quennell, editor, *Proust Centennial Essays*, Weidenfeld & Nicolson, 1971; *Etudes proustiennes I*, Gallimard, 1973; Larkin B. Price, editor, *Marcel Proust: A Critical Panorama*, University of Illinois Press, 1973; Monique Chefdor, editor, *In Search of Marcel Proust*, Ward Ritchie Press, 1973.

Contributor to *Encyclopaedia Universalis*. Contributor of about a dozen articles to language journals, including *L'Esprit critique*, *Revue d'histoire litteraire de la France*, *Europe*, *Romanic Review*, *French Studies*, and *PMLA*.

WORK IN PROGRESS: Editing Marcel Proust's correspondence in seventeen volumes, two volumes of which have been published.

BIOGRAPHICAL/CRITICAL SOURCES: *Europe*, February-March, 1971.

* * *

KOLOSIMO, Peter 1922-

PERSONAL: Born December 15, 1922, in Modena, Italy; son of Joseph and Josephine Mary (Mosca) Kolosimo; married Caterina Serafin (a journalist). *Education:* Received a degree in modern philology, 1946, and a degree in sexology, 1961. *Politics:* Radical. *Home and office:* Viale Corsica 59, Milan, Italy.

CAREER: Journalist and author. *Military service:* German Army, 1940; became second lieutenant. Fought with Partisans, 1944-45.

WRITINGS: *Il pianeta sconosciuto* (title means "The Unknown Planet"), Societa editrice internazionale (Turin), 1959; *Terra senza tempo*, Sugar editore (Milan), 1964, translation published as *Timeless Earth*, University Books, 1974; *Ombre sulle stelle* (title means "Shadows on the Stars"), Sugar editore, 1966; *Psicologia dell'eros* (title means "Psychology of Eroticism"), Rizzoli (Milan), 1967; *Non e terrestre*, Sugar editore, 1968, translation by A. D. Hills published as *Not of This World*, Souvenir, 1970; *Guida al mondo dei sogni* (title means "The World of Dreams"), Mediterranee (Rome), 1968; *Il comportamento erotico degli Europei* (title means "The Erotic Behavior of the European Peoples"), MEB (Turin), 1970; *Cittadini delle tenebre* (title means "Citizens of the Dark"), MEB, 1971; *Astronavi sulla preistoria* (title means "Prehistoric Space-ships"), Sugar editore, 1971; *Odissea stellare* (title means "Stellar Odyssey"), Sugar editore, 1974.

WORK IN PROGRESS: Research on Italy and Europe and cosmic mysteries.

* * *

KOMROFF, Manuel 1890-1974

September 7, 1890—December 10, 1974; American novelist, editor, author of children's books and nonfiction works. Obituaries: *New York Times*, December 11, 1974; *AB Bookman's Weekly*, January 20, 1975. (*CA*-4).

* * *

KONVITZ, Jeffrey 1944-

PERSONAL: Born July 22, 1944, in Brooklyn, N.Y.; son of Arthur Harry (a public relations executive) and Florence (Karp) Konvitz. *Education:* Cornell University, A.B. (with honors), 1966; Columbia University, J.D., 1969. *Religion:* Jewish. *Home and office:* 251 North Almont Dr., Beverly Hills, Calif. 90211. *Agent:* Peter Lampack, William Morris Agency, 1350 Avenue of the Americas, New York, N.Y. 10019.

CAREER: Admitted to Bar of New York, 1969; Creative Management Associates, New York, N.Y., attorney and agent, 1969-70; private practice of law in New York, 1970-72; Metro-Goldwyn-Mayer, Culver City, Calif., motion picture executive, 1972-73; full-time writer and producer, 1973—. General counsel, Jerry Lewis Theatre Chain, 1971-72. Co-producer, "Silent Night, Bloody Night" (motion picture), 1971; producer, "The Sentinel," Universal, 1975.

WRITINGS: The Sentinel (suspense novel), Simon & Schuster, 1974. Author of screenplays, "Silent Night, Bloody Night" (co-author), 1971, and "The Sentinel," Universal, 1975.

WORK IN PROGRESS: "Balls," a screenplay about a pool hustler during the Jewish-Irish gambling wars in New York in 1912; and a suspense novel set during a college reunion.

* * *

KORMAN, A. Gerd 1928-

PERSONAL: Born July 24, 1928. *Education:* Brooklyn College (now of the City University of New York), B.A., 1951; University of Wisconsin, M.A., 1953, Ph.D., 1959. *Home:* 103 Ithaca Rd., Ithaca, N.Y. 14850. *Office:* Cornell University, Ithaca, N.Y. 14853.

CAREER: Elmira College, Elmira, N.Y., instructor, 1956-57, assistant professor of history, 1957-62; Cornell University, Ithaca, N.Y., assistant professor, 1962-65, associate professor of history, 1965—. Visiting professor at University of Rochester, 1964-65, and Tel Aviv University, 1968-69, 1971-72. *Member:* American Historical Association, Organization of American Historians, Labor Historians (member of executive committee, 1968-71), Organization of Southern Historians. *Awards, honors:* Everest Award in Wisconsin Economic History, 1962.

WRITINGS: Industrialization, Immigrants, and Americanizers: The View from Milwaukee, State Historical Society of Wisconsin, 1967; *Hunter and Hunted: Years of the Holocaust*, Viking, 1973.

* * *

KOROTKIN, Judith 1931-

PERSONAL: Surname is pronounced Ko-*rot*-kin; born June 14, 1931, in New York, N.Y.; daughter of Bernard (a painter) and Ida (Cooper) Korotkin; married Robert Mende (a writer), 1951 (divorced, 1970); children: Nina, Beth. *Education:* Attended City College of the City University of New York, 1950, New School for Social Research, 1970-71, and Strasberg Institute, 1972. *Residence:* New York, N.Y. *Agent:* Lois Berman, 156 East 52nd St., New York, N.Y. *Office:* Suite 801, 645 Madison Ave., New York, N.Y. 10022.

CAREER: J. L. Sicari (public relations counselors), New York, N.Y., editorial assistant and account executive, 1971-72; Lobsenz Public Relations Co., Inc., New York, N.Y., account executive, 1972—. *Member:* Authors League of America (associate member of Dramatists Guild).

WRITINGS: The Spotlight (novel), Popular Library, 1974.

WORK IN PROGRESS: "Half Share," a three-act play; "Ex," a three-act play on the problems of divorced people in America; writing film and television dramas.

* * *

KOSTER, Donald N(elson) 1910-

PERSONAL: Born August 4, 1910, in New York, N.Y.; son of Albert C. (a marine decorator) and Anna (Nelson) Koster; married Rosemary Lawson (a school principal), February 24, 1930; children: Donald N., Jr., Harold A. *Education:* University of Pennsylvania, A.B., 1931, M.S., 1932, Ph.D., 1942. *Home:* 830 Shore Rd., Long Beach, N.Y. 11561. *Office:* Department of English, Adelphi University, Garden City, N.Y. 11530.

CAREER: University of Pennsylvania, Philadelphia, assistant instructor, 1933-36, instructor in English, 1936-46; Adelphi University, Garden City, N.Y., assistant professor, 1946-54, associate professor, 1954-59, professor of English, 1959—. *Member:* Modern Language Association of America, College English Association, American Studies Association (bibliographer, 1962-73), American Association of University Professors (member of national council, 1968-71).

WRITINGS: The Theme of Divorce in American Drama, University of Pennsylvania Press, 1942; (with others) *Modern Journalism*, Pitman, 1962; *Transcendentalism in America*, Twayne, in press. Editor of "American Studies Information Guide," a series published by Gale, 1974—. Contributor to literature journals, including *American Transcendental Quarterly, American Year Book, American Studies*, and *Adelphi Quarterly*. Editor of annual bibliographies for *American Quarterly*.

AVOCATIONAL INTERESTS: Travel, boating, fishing, golf.

KOSTER, John (Peter, Jr.) 1945-

PERSONAL: Born June 5, 1945, in Baltimore, Md.; son of John Peter and Mathilde (Strunck) Koster; married Shizuko Obo, December 5, 1971. *Education:* Montclair State College, B.A., 1967. *Politics:* Independent. *Religion:* Christian. *Residence:* Glen Rock, N.J. *Agent:* Bill Wassmann, 27 Sullivan Dr., Emerson, N.J. *Office: The Record*, 150 River St., Hackensack, N.J.

CAREER: The Record, Hackensack, N.J., general assignments reporter, 1967—. Historian-adviser to American Indian militants. *Military service:* U.S. Army, 1967. *Member:* National Geographic Society, American Society for Psychical Research. *Awards, honors:* Sigma Delta Chi special award for distinguished public service, 1975, for *The Road to Wounded Knee.*

WRITINGS: (With Robert Burnette) *The Road to Wounded Knee*, Bantam, 1974; *Land of Broken Dreams* (in Japanese), Sanichi Shobo, in press. Contributor to *Root, War Monthly* (England), and North American Newspaper Alliance.

WORK IN PROGRESS: A "grimly humorous" novel of teen-age life in the 1950's.

SIDELIGHTS: Koster writes: "After I got out of the service, I worked at a lot of crummy jobs, mostly rubbing shoulders with black and Spanish people and seeing a little bit of their perspective on life.

"I write because I enjoy it, to bring out the truth, and hopefully to make a living; besides serious works, I enjoy writing humor, which may also have a serious intent. I also like to cover hard-news stories—murders and so forth—becuase there's a certain legendary fascination about being a reporter and a challenge in breaking difficult stories."

Koster is presently collecting available data on the King's German Legion, a multi-national auxiliary (mostly German and Polish) which served with the British Army through the Napoleonic Wars.

AVOCATIONAL INTERESTS: Photography, scientific parapsychology, collecting old military junk and modern Indian artifacts, crafts.

* * *

KOZINTSEV, Grigori (Mikhailovich) 1905-1973

PERSONAL: Given name is variously spelled Grigorii in some bibliographic sources; born March 22, 1905, in Kiev, Russia (now U.S.S.R.); son of Mikhail (a physician) and Anna (Lurie) Kozintsev; married Valentine Graebner, May, 1944; children: Alexander. *Education:* Academy of Arts, graduate, 1922. *Home:* Bratiev Vasilievykh, 4a, KV.2, Leningrad, U.S.S.R. *Office:* Lenfilm Studio, Kirovsky 10, Leningrad, U.S.S.R.

CAREER: Film and stage director; co-founder of a traveling studio theatre prior to 1921; co-founder of Factory of the Eccentric Actor (FEX), Petrograd, 1921, and professor, 1922-26; made films for Sevzapkino, Leningradkino, Sovkino, and Soyuzkino, 1924-29, directing first film in 1924; director at Lenfilm Studio, Leningrad, 1924-73. Professor at State Cinema Institute (UGIK). Collaborated on films with Leonid Trauberg until 1947; filmed adaptations from Western literature beginning in 1957, including "Don Quixote," 1957, "Hamlet," 1964, and "King Lear," 1971; also directed stage productions, including versions of "Othello" and "Hamlet," produced in Leningrad theatres. *Member:* Cinema Workers Union, Writers Union. *Awards, honors:* U.S.S.R. state prizes, 1941, for "Trilogy of Maxim," and 1948, for "Pirogov"; Lenin Prize, 1965, for "Hamlet"; named People's Artist of U.S.S.R.; received two Lenin Orders, Order of October Revolution, Order of Red Banner of Labor, and others; also received prizes at international film festivals.

WRITINGS: (With Leonid Trauberg) *Trilogiia o Maksime* (trilogy of screenplays, filmed 1935-39), Goskinonzdat, 1939; *Nash sovremennik Vil'iam Shekspir*, Iskusstvo, 1962, 2nd edition, 1966, translation by Joyce Vining published as *Shakespeare: Time and Conscience*, Hill & Wang, 1966; *Glubokii ekran* (title means "The Deep Screen"), Iskusstvo, 1971; *Prostranstvo tragedii* (title means "The Space of Tragedy"), Iskusstvo, 1973.

Screenplays: "Pokhozhdeniya Oktyabriny" (title means "The Adventures of Oktyabrina"), 1924; (co-author) "Mishki protiv Yudenicha" (title means "Mishka against Yudenich"), 1925; "Bratishka," 1927; "Novyi Vavilon" (title means "The New Babylon"), 1929; "Odna" (title means "Alone"), 1931; "Yunost Maksima" (title means "The Youth of Maxim"), 1935; (co-author) "Vozvrashchenie Maksima" (title means "The Return of Maxim"), 1937; "Vyborgskaya Storona" (title means "The Vyborg Side"), 1939; "Prostye Lyudi" (title means "Plain People"), filmed in 1945, banned by Central Committee in 1946, released, 1956; (co-author) "Bielinsky," 1953; (co-author) "Don Quixote," 1957; "Gamlet" (based on Boris Pasternak's translation of Shakespeare's "Hamlet"), 1964.

Also author of screenplays based on the lives of Pushkin, Tolstoy, and Gogol, all published posthumously in *Novy Mir* and *Iskusstvo Kino.* Author of articles on film, the theatre, and on Shakespeare.

WORK IN PROGRESS: A book on Gogol.

AVOCATIONAL INTERESTS: Literature, painting.

BIOGRAPHICAL/CRITICAL SOURCES: Jay Leyda, *Kino: A History of the Russian and Soviet Film*, Hillary, 1960; Mario Verdone and Barthelemy Amengual, *La FEKS*, Societe d'etudes, recherches et documentation cinematographiques (Lyon, France), 1970; Marvin Rosenberg, *Masks of King Lear*, University of California Press, 1972; Luda Schnitzer and others, *Cinema in Revolution*, translated by David Robinson, Hill & Wang, 1973.

(Died May 11, 1973)

* * *

KRAEMER, Richard H(oward) 1920-

PERSONAL: Born February 24, 1920, in New York, N.Y.; married, 1971; children: five. *Education:* University of Houston, B.S., 1956; University of Pittsburgh, M.Lit., 1957; University of Texas, Ph.D., 1970. *Home:* 311 Laurel Valley Rd., Austin, Tex. 78746. *Office:* Department of Government, University of Texas, Austin, Tex. 78712.

CAREER: U.S. Air Force, career officer, 1942-62, retiring as lieutenant colonel; University of Texas, Austin, assistant professor, 1965-71, associate professor of government, 1971—. Instructor at University of Maryland, 1960-62; consultant to the Peace Corps, 1965. *Member:* International Studies Association, American Political Science Association. *Awards, honors*—Military: Distinguished Flying Cross with two oak leaf clusters; Air Medal with eight oak leaf clusters.

WRITINGS: (Editor with P. W. Barnes) *Texas: Readings*

in Politics, Government, and Public Policy, Chandler Publishing, 1971; *The American Way of War and Peace* (monograph), General Learning Press, 1974; (with Ernest Crane and Earl Maxwell) *Understanding Texas Politics*, West Publishing, 1975.

WORK IN PROGRESS: The Politics of National Defense; a book on American politics.

* * *

KRAMER, Dale 1936-

PERSONAL: Born July 13, 1936, in South Dakota; son of Dwight L. Kramer (a farmer) and Frances (Corbin) Kramer Coulthard; married Cheris Gamble, December 21, 1960; children: Brinlee, Jana. *Education:* South Dakota State College, B.S., 1958; Western Reserve University (now Case Western Reserve University), M.A., 1960, Ph.D., 1963. *Office:* Department of English, University of Illinois, Urbana, Ill. 61801.

CAREER: Ohio University, Athens, instructor, 1962-63, assistant professor of English, 1963-65; University of Illinois, Urbana, assistant professor, 1965-67, associate professor of English, 1971—.

WRITINGS: Charles Maturin, Twayne, 1973; *Thomas Hardy: The Forms of Tragedy*, Wayne State University Press, 1974. Editor of *Journal of English and German Philology*.

* * *

KRAMER, Daniel C(aleb) 1934-

PERSONAL: Born September 23, 1934, in Chicago, Ill.; son of Samuel (a professor) and Mildred (a teacher; maiden name, Tokarsky) Kramer; married Richenda Lee (a teacher), August 20, 1960; children: Tamsyn, Bruce, Elspeth. *Education:* Kenyon College, B.A., 1955; Harvard University, LL.B., 1959; University of Pennsylvania, Ph.D., 1963, M.A., 1964. *Politics:* Democrat. *Home:* 54 Rokeby Pl., Staten Island, N.Y. 10310. *Office:* Department of Political Science, Richmond College of the City University of New York, 130 Stuyvesant Pl., Staten Island, N.Y. 10301.

CAREER: University of Illinois, Urbana, assistant professor of political science, 1964-67; Richmond College of the City University of New York, Staten Island, N.Y., associate professor of political science, 1967—. Democratic county committeeman in Richmond County; member of Staten Island Citizens Planning Commission; member of City University of New York Seminar on American Politics and Constitutional Law. *Member:* American Political Science Association, Law and Society Association, Northeast Political Science Association, Staten Island Democratic Association.

WRITINGS: Participatory Democracy, Schenkman, 1972.

WORK IN PROGRESS: Comparative Civil Rights and Liberties.

AVOCATIONAL INTERESTS: Practical politics, reading novels.

* * *

KRAR, Stephen Frank 1924-

PERSONAL: Born July 20, 1924, in Mor, Hungary; son of John and Mary (Horack) Krar; married Elsie Helen Demko (a secretary), June 26, 1948; children: Judith Anne, Allan Michael. *Education:* Attended University of Toronto, 1954-55. *Religion:* Roman Catholic. *Home and office:* 420 Fitch St., Welland, Ontario L3C 4W8, Canada.

CAREER: Tool and die maker in Welland, Ontario, 1940-54; machine shop instructor in Niagara Falls, Ontario, 1955-56, and Guelph, Ontario, 1956-62; Eastdale Secondary School, Welland, Ontario, technical director and machine shop instructor, 1962—. Lecturer and head of teacher training department at University of Toronto, summers, 1961-71. President of Kostel Enterprises Ltd., 1971—, and Niagara Publishers, 1974—. *Member:* American Technical Education Association, Society of Manufacturing Engineers, Ontario Vocational Education Association (president, 1964), Ontario Machine Shop Roundtable (chairman, 1959-60), Ontario Technical Directors' Association, Welland Curling Club (president, 1973-74). *Awards, honors:* A leather-bound gold imprinted copy of *Machine Shop Training* from McGraw, 1972, for sale of one hundred thousand copies.

WRITINGS: (With J. E. St. Amand) *Machine Shop Training*, McGraw, 1962, 3rd edition, 1975; (with St. Amand and J. W. Oswald) *Machine Tools: Transparency Book #1*, McGraw, 1968; (with St. Amand and Oswald) *Technology of Machine Tools*, McGraw, 1969, 2nd edition published with two workbooks, 1975; (with E. Gudaitis) *Technical Drawing and Design: Transparency Book*, two volumes, Scott Graphics, 1969-70; (with St. Amand and Oswald) *Measurement and Layout: Transparency Book #2*, McGraw, 1970; (with Oswald) *Turning Technology*, Delmar, 1971; (with St. Amand and Oswald) *Threads and Testing Instruments: Transparency Book #3*, McGraw, 1972; (with Oswald) *Grinding Technology*, Delmar, 1973; (with St. Amand and Oswald) *Cutting Tools: Transparency Book #4*, McGraw, 1973; (with St. Amand and Oswald) *Machine Shop Operations*, McGraw, 1974; (with St. Amand, Oswald, and I. M. McGregor) *Metallurgy: Transparency Book #5*, McGraw, 1974.

WORK IN PROGRESS: How Your Car Works, 1975; *Know Your Motorcycle*, 1975; *Drilling Technology*, 1975; a remedial mathematics program for secondary schools, *Mathlab*, 1976.

AVOCATIONAL INTERESTS: Golfing, curling.

* * *

KRAUS, Joseph 1925-

PERSONAL: Born February 10, 1925, in Frankfurt-am-Main, Germany; came to United States in 1947, naturalized U.S. citizen; son of Siegfried (a sociologist) and Ida (an actress; maiden name, Moeller) Kraus; married Nana Heilbronner (a painter), June 15, 1946; children: Tania (Mrs. Claude Santa). *Education:* University of California, Los Angeles, B.A., 1960, M.A., 1962, Ph.D., 1968. *Politics:* "Registered Democrat, independent voter." *Religion:* "No formal." *Home:* 14355 Mulholland Dr., Los Angeles, Calif. 90024. *Office:* Department of Foreign Languages, Los Angeles Valley College, Van Nuys, Calif. 91401.

CAREER: Zoological Gardens, Dresden, Germany, animal keeper and trainer, 1941-44; Zirkus Krone, Munich, Germany, bear trainer, 1945-46; Rudolf Steiner School, Munich, Germany, teacher of German literature, 1962-63; Los Angeles Valley College, Van Nuys, Calif., assistant professor, 1968-72, associate professor, 1972-74, professor of German, 1974—. Translator of legal material. *Member:* American Association of Teachers of German, American Association of University Professors (president of local chapter, 1970-71), American Federation of Teachers, Alpha

Mu Gamma, Delta Phi Alpha. *Awards, honors:* Fellowship for junior college instruction from National Endowment for the Humanities, 1972-73.

WRITINGS: Wilhelm Busch (monograph in German), Rowohlt, 1970, new edition, 1973. Contributor to *Jahrbuch der Wilhelm Busch* (*Yearbook of the Wilhelm Busch Society*), 1971.

WORK IN PROGRESS: The Missing Link or the Quiet Rebellion of Hans Erich Nossack; "Billy Wilder" and "Felix Jackson," both in German, for inclusion in *Deutsche Literatur im Exil* (title means "German Literature in Exile"), to be edited by John Spalek and Joseph Strelka, for Francke Verlag; poetry and short stories in German and English.

SIDELIGHTS: Kraus writes: "The fundamental experience in my life was Nazi Germany (culminated in my experience as an inmate in Slave Labor Camp Osterode, Germany, 1944-45). My primary concern is to find meaning in life, a type of transcendent meaning that can survive conformist pressures. From afar, I admire the positive nihilism of Nietzsche, I feel close to the intellectual rebel Hans Erich Nossack, I believe in the spiritual and moral challenges presented by Rudolf Steiner's Anthroposophy and Viktor E. Frankl's Logotherapy. They counterbalance my own inclination towards flippancy and cynicism."

* * *

KRAUSZ, Michael 1942-

PERSONAL: Born September 13, 1942, in Geneva, Switzerland; came to United States, 1947; naturalized citizen, 1953; son of Laszlo (a musician and artist) and Susan (a musician; maiden name, Strauss) Krausz; married Ann Baron Shteir, July, 1966 (divorced December, 1974). *Education:* Attended London School of Economics and Political Science, 1963-64; Rutgers University, B.A., 1965; Indiana University, M.A., 1967; Linacre College, Oxford, graduate fellow, 1968-69; University of Toronto, Ph.D., 1969; also studied art at Haystack Mountain School of Crafts, Deer Isle, Me., 1972, 1973, and Philadelphia College of Art, 1974-75. *Home:* 320 North Roberts Rd., Bryn Mawr, Pa. 19010. *Office:* Department of Philosophy, Bryn Mawr College, Bryn Mawr, Pa. 19010.

CAREER: University of Toronto, Victoria College, Toronto, Ontario, assistant professor of philosophy, 1969-70; Bryn Mawr College, Bryn Mawr, Pa., assistant professor of philosophy, 1970—. Part-time instructor at York University, 1966-67, and Trent University, 1969-70; visiting assistant professor of philosophy, American University, Washington, D.C., 1973-74. *Member:* American Philosophical Association, American Association of University Professors (chapter secretary, 1971-72; chapter president, 1972-73), Royal Society of Arts (fellow). *Awards, honors:* Ford Foundation research grant, summer, 1971.

WRITINGS: (Editor and contributor) *Critical Essays on the Philosophy of R. G. Collingwood*, Clarendon Press (of Oxford University), 1972; (editor and author of introduction with Jack Meiland) *Relativism*, Princeton University Press, in press; (editor, contributor, and author of introduction) *Creative Processes*, Clarendon Press, in press; *Dialogues Concerning Creativity and the Ontology of Love*, American University (Washington, D.C.), in press. Contributor to journals, including *Philosophy of Science*, *Dialogue*, *American Philosophical Quarterly*, and *Symposia*.

SIDELIGHTS: Krausz's painting, drawing, serigraphy, and work in shaped and sculpted canvas have been exhibited in one-man shows at the University of Kent (England), Talbot Rice Arts Centre (Edinburgh), Annenberg Center for Communication Arts and Sciences (Philadelphia), and other locations; his work has also been represented in museum and gallery group shows and in public and private collections in the United States, Canada, England, Scotland, and Japan.

* * *

KRUESS, James 1926-
(Markus Polder, Felix Ritter)

PERSONAL: Born May 31, 1926, in Helgoland, Germany; son of Ludwig (an electrician) and Margarethe (Friederichs) Kruess. *Education:* Attended schools in Braunschweig and Lueneburg, both Germany. *Home:* Casa la Montaneta, La Calzada, Las Palmas de Gran Canaria, Spain. *Agent:* Hein Kohn, Koninginneweg 2A, Hilversum, Netherlands. *Office:* Roemerstrasse 96, Gilching, Germany 8031.

CAREER: Has worked as a teacher, radio reporter, and journalist; children's author. *Military service:* German Air Force, 1944-45. *Member:* P.E.N., Deutscher-Schriftsteller-Verband, Institutum Canarium. *Awards, honors:* Deutscher Jugendbuchpreis, 1960, for *Mein Urgrossvater und ich*, and 1964, for *3 X 3 an einem Tag*; Hans Christian Andersen Award, 1968, for complete works.

WRITINGS—Children's books: *Hanselmann reist um die Welt* (title means "Hanselmann Travels around the World"), G. Stalling, 1953; (under pseudonym Markus Polder) *Die Hundefarm von Pudelslust* (title means "The Dog's Farm of Poodles Joy"), G. Stalling, 1954; *Hanselmann hat grosse Plaene* (title means "Hanselmann Has Great Plans"), G. Stalling, 1954; *Christoffel und sein Schimmelchen* (title means "Christoffel and His Little White Horse"), G. Stalling, 1956; *Der Leuchtturm auf den Hummerklippen*, F. Oetinger, 1956, translation by Edelgard von Heydekampf Bruehl published as *The Lighthouse on the Lobster Cliffs*, Atheneum, 1964; *Ladislaus und Annabella*, G. Leutz, 1957; *Schimmel angespauntfahren wir aufs Land!*, G. Stalling, 1957; *Susebilles grosse Reise* (title means "Susebille's Big Voyage"), G. Stalling, 1957; (with Katharina Maillard) *Kinder, heut' ist Wochenmarkt!* (title means "Kids, Today is Weekly Market!"), G. Stalling, 1957; *Das verzauberte Dorf* (title means "The Bewitched Village"), G. Stalling, 1958; (with Maillard) *Zirkuszelt Wunderwelt* (title means "Circus Magic"), G. Stalling, 1958; *ABC, ABC, Arche Noah sticht in See!* (title means "ABC, ABC, Noah's Ark Goes into Sea!"), Obpacher Buch und Kunstverlag, 1959; (editor) *So viele Tage wie das Jahr hat: 365 Gedichte fuer Kinder und Kenner* (title means "So Many Days as Has the Year"), Mohn, 1959.

Eine lustige Froschreise (title means "A Frog's Voyage"), Boje-Verlag, 1960; *Henrietta Bimmelbahn*, translation by Marion Koenig published as *Henrietta Chuffertrain: Verses*, World's Work Ltd., 1960; *Die Gluecklichen Inseln hinter dem Winde*, two volumes, F. Oetinger, 1961, translation of Volume I by Bruehl published as *The Happy Islands Behind the Winds*, Atheneum, 1966, Volume II as *Return to the Happy Islands*, 1967; *Mein Urgrossvater und ich*, F. Oetinger, 1961, translation by Edelgard von Heydekampf Bruehl published as *My Great-Grandfather and I*, Atheneum, 1964; *Der wohltemperierte Leierkasten: 12 und 12 Gedichte fuer Kinder, Eltern und andere Leute* (title means "The Well-Tempered Barrel Organ"), Mohn, 1961; (under pseudonym Markus Polder) *Es war einmal ein*

Mann (title means "There Was Once a Man"), Obpacher Buch und Kunstverlag, 1961; *Ich moechte einmal Koenig sein: eine Geschichte* (title means "If I Were King"), O. Maier, 1961; *Michele Guck-Dich-Um* (title means "Michele Look-Around"), Obpacher Buch und Kunstverlag, 1961; *Florentine und die Tauben*, Obpacher Buch und Kunstverlag, 1961, translation by Marion Koenig published as *Florentine: A Story*, Chatto & Windus, 1967; *Florentine und die Kramerin: eine Geschichte fuer Maedchen, Buben, Eltern und Gemischtwarenhaendler* (title means "Florentine and the Groceress"), Obpacher Buch und Kunstverlag, 1962; *Die kleinen Pferde heissen Fohlen* (title means "The Little Horses Are Called Foals"), F. Oetinger, 1962; *Zehnkleine Negerlein* (title means "Ten Little Negro Boys"), Mohn, 1963; *Adler und Taube*, F. Oetinger, 1963, translation by Bruehl published as *Eagle and Dove*, Atheneum, 1965; *Die Kinderuhr* (title means "Children's Clock"), A. Betz, 1963; *3 X 3 an einem Tag*, A. Betz, 1963, translation by Geoffrey Strachen published as *Three by Three: A Picturebook for all Children Who Can Count to Three*, Macmillan, 1965; *Pauline und der Prinz im Wind*, F. Oetinger, 1964, translation by Bruehl published as *Pauline and the Prince in the Wind*, Atheneum, 1966; *ABC und phantasie* (title means "ABC and Fantasy"), O. Maier, 1964; *Hendrikje mit den Scharpen*, Boje-Verlag, 1964, translation published as *Sally's Red Sash*, Wheaton, 1967; *Auf sieben geschliffenen Kieseln* (title means "On Seven Polished Pebbles"), F. Oetinger, 1965; *Fahre mit durchs ABC: ein Bilderbuch fuer reiselustige Kinder* (title means "Travel with Me through the ABC"), Mohn, 1965; *Heimkehr aus dem Kriegs: eine Idylle*, Biederstein Verlag, 1965, translation by Bruehl published as *Coming Home From the War: An Idyll*, Doubleday, 1970; *Das Hemd des Gluecklichen und andere Spiele fuer Kinder zum Lesen und Auffuehren* (title means "The Shirt of the Happy"), Domino Verlag, 1965; *James Tierleben*, A. Betz, 1965; (compiler) *Die Hirtenfloete* (title means "The Shepherd's Flute"), Biederstein Verlag, 1965; *The Talking Machine*, Universe Books, 1965.

Lirum larum Leierkasten (title means "Lirum, Larum, Barrel Organ"), F. Oetinger, 1966; *Der Trommler und die Puppe: Oder, Wozu ein Trommler nuetze ist*, A. Betz, 1966, translation by Jack Prelutsky published as *The Proud Wooden Drummer*, Doubleday, 1969; *Was sagt die Glucke zu den Kueken?* (title means "What Says the Hen to the Little Chickens?"), Boje-Verlag, 1966; *Das rote Auto und der Peter* (title means "Peter and the Red Car"), Boje-Verlag, 1966; *Busy, Busy Bettina*, Milliken Publishing, 1966; *Was kocht die Maus im ihren Haus?* (title means "What Cooks the Mouse in Her House?"), A. Betz, 1966; *Weiches Tier hat sieben Meter Halsweh?*, A. Betz, 1966, translation by Margaret Fishback published as *The Animal Parade*, Platt & Munk, 1968.

Polunangrische Lieder (title means "Polulangnic Songs"), Damokles-Verlag, 1968; *Der verwirrte Grosspapa* (title means "The Bewildered Grandfather"), A. Holz Verlag, 1968; *Was kleine Kinder gerne Moegen*, Boje-Verlag, 1968, English adaptation by Rowen Carr published as *Our Favorite Things*, Platt & Munk, 1970; (author of text) *Jugoslawien*, Freiburg Atlantis-Verlag, 1968; *Bienchen, Trinchen, Karolinchen* (title means "Little Bee, Little She, Little Caroline"), Boje-Verlag, 1968; *Briefe an Pauline*, F. Oetinger, 1968, translation by Edelgard von Heydekampfe Bruehl published as *Letters to Pauline*, Atheneum, 1971; *Ein-, Eich & Mondhorn: Gereimte Unwahrscheinlichkeiten* (title means "Unicorn, Squirrel and Moon's Horn"), A. Betz, 1968; *Hoppla und Hue*, Ullstein, 1968; *In Tante Julies Haus* (title means "In Aunt Julie's House"), F. Oetinger, 1969; *Naivitaet und Kunstverstand* (title means "Naivete and Art's Know-How"), J. Beltz, 1969; *Das Puppenfest* (title means "The Doll's Party"), Boje-Verlag, 1969; *Zirkus auf dem Fussballplatz une andere Abenteuer von Hoppla und Hue* (title means "Circus on the Football Field"), Ullstein, 1969; *Gongo und seine Freunde* (title means "Gongo and His Friends"), A. Betz, 1969.

Gongo geht in die Luft (title means "Gongo Arises"), A. Betz, 1970; *Ich waer so gerne Zoodirektor*, English adaptation by Sarah Keyser published as *The Zoo That Grew*, Platt & Munk, 1970; (editor) *Die kleine Windsbraut Edeltraut 20 Schriftsteller aus 14 Laendern erzaehlen ein Geschichte* (title means "The Little Whirlwind Edeltraut"), K. Thienemann, 1971; (compiler) *Seifenblasen zuverkaufen: Das grosse Nonsens-Buch fuer jung und alt* (title means "Soap Bubbles to Sell: A Nonsense Anthology"), Verlagsgruppe Bertelsmann, 1972; *Der Saengerkrieg der Heidehasen, Kindern erzaehlt in zehn Gesaengen* (title means "The Singer's Match in the Hare's Heath"), F. Oetinger, 1972.

WORK IN PROGRESS: Der Kleine Flax (title means "The Little Flax"), an adaptation of the Winnebago-Trickshev cycle.

AVOCATIONAL INTERESTS: Old languages, and things related to the Canary Islands.

BIOGRAPHICAL/CRITICAL SOURCES: Bruno Horst Bull, *Von und ueber James Kruess*, Relief-Verlag, 1966; Theo Joerg, *Sprechen lernen mit James Kruess*, University Press of Saarbruecken, 1972; Joerg, *Lingua-Motorik der Verssprachen*, University Press of Saarbruecken, 1972.

* * *

KRUGLAK, Haym 1909-

PERSONAL: Surname is accented on first syllable; born March 24, 1909, in Dneprodzerzinsk, Ukraine; came to United States in 1927, naturalized U.S. citizen, 1934; son of Abram and Frada (Schuster) Kruglak; married Mary Lee Stewart, May 2, 1941; children: Joyce Doyle, David Doyle. *Education:* University of Wisconsin, B.A., 1934, M.A., 1936; University of Minnesota, Ph.D., 1951; University of Chicago, graduate study, 1942, postdoctoral study, 1963-64. *Home:* 2127 Frederick Ave., Kalamazoo, Mich. 49008. *Office:* Department of Physics, Western Michigan University, Kalamazoo, Mich. 49008.

CAREER: High school science teacher in Sheboygan, Wis., 1936-38; Milwaukee Technical College, Milwaukee, Wis., instructor in physics and mathematics, 1938-44; Princeton University, Princeton, N.J., visiting assistant professor of physics, 1944-46; University of Minnesota, Minneapolis, instructor, 1946-51, assistant professor of physics, 1951-54; Western Michigan University, Kalamazoo, associate professor, 1954-57, professor of physics, 1957—, director of National Science Foundation Summer Institute, 1961, 1967-69. Curriculum supervisor of U.S. Army Signal Corps Repairman School, 1942-44; director of research project for Office of Naval Research, 1951-54.

MEMBER: American Association of Physics Teachers, American Association of University Professors, American Association for the Advancement of Science (fellow), Phi Beta Kappa.

WRITINGS: Laboratory Performance Tests in General Physics, Western Michigan University, 1959; *Basic Mathe-*

matics for the Physical Sciences, McGraw, 1963; *Basic Mathematics with Applications to Science and Technology*, McGraw, 1973. Contributor to *Physics Teacher*, *American Journal of Physics*, *Science Teacher*, and *Mathematics Teacher*.

* * *

KUENG, Hans 1928-

PERSONAL: Born March 19,1928, in Lucerne, Switzerland; son of Hans and Emma (Gut) Kueng. *Education:* Pontifical Gregorian University, Rome, Licentiate in philosophy, 1951, Licentiate in theology, 1955; Institut Catholique, Sorbonne, University of Paris, Dr.theol., 1957; also studied in Berlin, London, Amsterdam, and Madrid. *Home:* Waldhaeuserstrasse 23, D-74 Tuebingen, Germany. *Office:* Faculty of Catholic Theology, Institute of Ecumenical Research, University of Tuebingen, Tuebingen, Germany.

CAREER: Ordained Roman Catholic priest, 1954; St. Leodegar, Lucerne, Switzerland, pastoral work, 1957-59; University of Muenster, Muenster, Germany, assistant in dogmatic theology, 1959-60; University of Tuebingen, Tuebingen, Germany, ordinary (full) professor of dogmatic theology, 1960-63, ordinary professor of dogmatic and ecumenical theology and director of Institute for Ecumenical Research, 1963—. Peritus (official theological consultant) at Second Vatican Council, appointed by Pope John XXIII, 1962. Guest professor at Union Theological Seminary, New York, 1968, and Protestant Theological Faculty, University of Basel, 1969; lecturer at numerous universities in Europe, America, Asia, and Australia.

MEMBER: Arbeitsgemeinschaft Deutschspachige Dogmatiker. *Awards, honors:* LL.D., University of St. Louis, 1963; D.D., Pacific School of Religion, 1966; HH.D., Loyola University (Chicago), 1970; D.D., University of Glasgow, 1971.

WRITINGS: Rechtfertigung: Die Lehre Karl Barths und eine katholische Besinnung (doctoral thesis; with letter by Karl Barth), Johannes Verlag, 1957, 4th enlarged edition, 1964, translation by Thomas Collins, Edmund E. Tolk, and David Granskou published as *Justification: The Doctrine of Karl Barth and a Catholic Reflection*, Thomas Nelson, 1964.

Konzil und Wiedervereinigung: Erneuerung als Ruf in die Einheit, Herder, 1960, translation by Cecily Hastings published in England as *The Council and Reunion*, Sheed, 1961, published in America as *The Council, Reform, and Reunion*, Sheed, 1962, new American edition, Doubleday, 1965; *Damit die Welt glaube*, Pfeiffer, 1962, 5th edition, 1968, translation by Hastings published as *That The World May Believe: Letters to Young People*, Sheed, 1963; *Strukturen der Kirche*, Herder, 1962, translation by Salvator Attanasio published as *Structures of the Church* (preface by Cardinal Richard Cushing), Thomas Nelson, 1964; *Kirche im Konzil*, Herder, 1963, 2nd edition, 1964, translation by Hastings published in America as *The Council in Action: Theological Reflections on the Second Vatican Council*, Sheed, 1963 (translation by Hastings and N. D. Smith published in England as *The Living Church*, Sheed, 1963, translation by Hastings, William Glen-Doepel, and H. R. Bronk published in England as *The Changing Church*, Sheed, 1965); (editor with Yves Congar and Daniel O'Hanlon) *Konzilsreden*, Benziger, 1964, translation published as *Council Speeches of Vatican II*, Paulist Press, 1964; *Die Kirche*, Herder, 1967, translation by Ray and Rosaleen Ockenden published as *The Church*, Sheed, 1967, abridged German edition published as *Was ist Kirche?*, Herder, 1970; *Wahrhaftigkeit: Zur Zukunft der Kirche*, Herder, 1968, translation by Edward Quinn published as *Truthfulness: The Future of the Church*, Sheed, 1968.

Menschwerdung Gottes: Eine Einfuehrung in Hegels theologisches Denken als Prolegomena zu einer kuenftigen Christologie, Herder, 1970; *Unfehlbar? Eine Anfrage*, Benziger, 1970, translation by Edward Quinn published as *Infallible? An Inquiry*, Doubleday, 1971; *Wozu Priester? Ein Hilfa*, Benziger, 1971, translation by Robert C. Collins published as *Why Priests? A Proposal for a New Church Ministry*, Doubleday, 1972; *Fehlbar? Eine Bilanz* (with contribution by Anton Antweiler), Benziger, 1973; *Christ sein?* Piper, 1974, translation by Edward Quinn published as *On Being Christian*, Doubleday, 1975.

Theological Meditations"—Editor of series published in German by Benziger, in English by Sheed with Cecily Hastings as translator, and author of following titles: *Freiheit in der Welt: Sir Thomas More*, 1964, translation published as *Freedom in the World: Sir Thomas More*, 1965; *Theologe und Kirche*, 1964, translation published as *The Theologian and the Church*, 1965; *Kirche in Freiheit*, 1964, translation published as *The Church and Freedom*, 1965; *Christenheit als Minderheit: Die Kirche unter den Weltreligionen*, 1965, translation included in Josef Neuner, editor, *Christian Revelation and World Religions*, Burns & Oates, 1967; *Freedom Today*, translation of various works of Kueng, 1966 (German edition, *Freiheit des Christen*, was published later); *Gott und das Leid*, 1967; *Was in der Kirche bleiben muss*, 1973.

Other volumes of "Theological Meditations" with prefaces by Kueng include: Karl Rahner, *Belief Today*, Sheed, 1967; *The Unknown God*, translation of volumes by Joseph Moeller, Herbert Haag, and Gotthold Hasenhuettl originally published separately in German, Sheed, 1967; *Life in the Spirit*, translation of volumes by Karl H. Schelkle, Thomas A. Sartory, and Michael Pfliegler originally published separately in German, Sheed, 1968.

"Concilium" series—Editor of following volumes: *The Church and Ecumenism*, Paulist Press, 1965; *Do We Know the Others?*, Paulist/Newman, 1966; *The Sacraments: An Ecumenical Dilemma*, Paulist Press, 1967; (and author of introduction and contributor) *Apostolic Succession: Rethinking a Barrier to Unity*, fourteen essays by world theologians, Paulist Press, 1968; *The Future of Ecumenism*, Paulist Press, 1969; *Post-ecumenical Christianity*, Herder & Herder, 1970; *Papal Ministry in the Church*, Herder & Herder, 1971; *The Plurality of Ministries*, Herder & Herder, 1972; (with Walter Kasper) *Polarization in the Church*, Seabury, 1973. Co-editor of related German series, "Oekumenische Forschungan" (Ecumenical Investigations), Herder, 1967—.

Contributor: Maxmilian Roesle and Oscar Cullmann, editors, *Begegnung der Christen: Festschrift O. Karrer*, Evangelisches Verlagswerk (Stuttgart), 1959, translation edited by D. J. Callahan, Heiko A. Oberman, and Daniel O'Hanlon published as *Christianity Divided: Protestant and Catholic Theological Issues*, Sheed, 1961; Joseph Ratzinger and Heinrich Fries, editors, *Einsicht und Glaube: Festschrift G. Soehngen*, Herder, 1962; *Looking Toward the Council: An Inquiry Among Christians*, Herder & Herder, 1962; John Courtney Murray, editor, *Freedom and Man*, Kenedy, 1965.

Contributor to *Lexikon fuer Theologie und Kirche II*, *Handbuch theologischer Grundbegriffe*, and *Theologisches Jahrbuch*. Contributor of more than 400 articles to theological and other journals in Germany, Switzerland, Netherlands, England, and United States, including *Cross Currents, Sign, Catholic Digest, Sunday Visitor, New York Times, Commonweal,* and *Christian Century, Critic*. Co-editor, *Tuebingen Theologische Quartalschrift,* 1960-64; associate editor, *Journal of Ecumenical Studies,* 1964—; co-editor, *Revue Internationale de Theologie Concilium,* 1965—.

SIDELIGHTS: A proponent of church reform, Kueng's views on reconciling Catholic and Protestant theology drew the Vatican's official declaration, "Mysterium Ecclesiae," in 1973. According to *Newsweek,* "The Vatican's Sacred Congregation for the Doctrine of the Faith issued an extraordinary declaration ordering the world's Catholics to reject Kueng's theories—and in the bargain underscored once again the obstacles posed by Roman doctrine to any major ecumenical movement."

At the time, Kueng's books had appeared in about a hundred foreign-language editions outside of Germany, excluding books he has edited. His first book was translated into four languages, the next into seven, the next into nine. These translations include Korean, Malay, Czech, Polish, and Japanese. Kueng himself is able to speak or read in English, French, Italian, Spanish, Dutch, Latin, Greek, and Hebrew.

AVOCATIONAL INTERESTS: Classical music, water sports, and skiing.

BIOGRAPHICAL/CRITICAL SOURCES: Time, July 8, 1962, July 16, 1973; G. H. Duggan, *Hans Kueng and Reunion,* Newman, 1965; *Newsweek,* July 16, 1973.

* * *

KUESTER, David 1938-

PERSONAL: Born January 20, 1938, in St. Louis, Mo.; son of Raymond Edwin and Olga Helen (Seybold) Kuester; married Louise Angela Harris (a teacher), June 30, 1973. *Education:* Oberlin College, B.A., 1960; Harvard University, LL.B., 1963; Stanford University, M.A., 1964. *Politics:* Democrat. *Home:* 4601 Maryland, St. Louis, Mo. 63108. *Office:* Department of English, Forest Park Community College, 5600 Oakland, St. Louis, Mo. 63110.

CAREER: Forest Park Community College, St. Louis, Mo., assistant professor of English, 1967—. *Member:* American Association of University Professors, American Civil Liberties Union, Phi Beta Kappa.

WRITINGS: (With Richard Friedrich) *It's Mine and I'll Write It That Way*, Random House, 1970. Contributor to *Harper's*.

WORK IN PROGRESS: The Partnership, a novel.

* * *

KUNZLE, David Mark 1936-

PERSONAL: Born April 17, 1936, in Birmingham, England. *Education:* Gonville and Caius College, Cambrige, B.A. (honors), 1957; University of London, Ph.D., 1964. *Politics:* Left. *Home:* 4230 Bellingham Ave., Studio City, Calif. 91604.

CAREER: University of California, Santa Barbara, assistant professor of history of art, 1965-73; California Institute of the Arts, Valencia, lecturer, 1972, 1975. *Awards, honors:* Grant from National Endowment for the Arts, 1967.

WRITINGS: Posters of Protest, Art Galleries, University of California, 1971, compact edition, New School for Social Research, 1971; *Early Comic Strip*, University of California Press, 1974; (author of introduction and translator) Ariel Dorfman and Armand Mattelart, *How to Read Donald Duck: The Ideology of Imperialism in the Disney Comic*, International General, 1975.

WORK IN PROGRESS: Fashion and Fetishism; *Revolutionary Art in Cuba and in Chile, 1970-73*; studies of the nineteenth-century comic strip, and of the caricatural work of Rodolphe Topffer.

SIDELIGHTS: Kunzle told *CA:* "Art is used as a tool for political and social action as well as a means of promoting radical and socialist changes in a world dominated by capitalism. Art should be used to oppose fascism. It should illuminate and integrate, not alienate." He believes the Disney comic, as used by Fascists in Chile and elsewhere, points up "the horrors of cultural imperialism." Kunzle speaks and writes most West European languages. *Avocational interests:* Gymnastics, ancient and modern.

* * *

KURMAN, George 1942-

PERSONAL: Born June 10, 1942, in Tallinn, Estonia; came to United States, 1947; son of U.S. citizens Hugo (an electrical engineer) and Juta (a teacher; maiden name, Tomberg) Kurman; married Tiina Abel, June 12, 1965; children: Ursula, Melba, Iris, Lulu. *Education:* Cornell University, B.A. (with honors), 1962; graduate study, Turku University, 1962-63, and Helsinki University, 1965-66, 1968; Columbia University, M.A., 1966; Indiana University, Ph.D., 1969. *Politics:* "Power to the wealthy, wealth to the powerful." *Religion:* "Faith." *Home:* 209 North Ward St., Macomb, Ill. 61455. *Office:* Department of English, Western Illinois University, Macomb, Ill. 61455.

CAREER: Teacher of English as a foreign language in Helsinki, Finland, and Duesseldorf, Germany, 1965-66; commissioned by UNESCO to translate Estonian national epic, *Kalevipoeg*, while residing in Spain and Finland, 1969-70; Western Illinois University, Macomb, assistant professor, 1970-75, associate professor of English, 1975—. Visiting summer professor, Carleton University, 1972; postdoctoral fellow of International Research and Exchanges Board, in Spain and Finland, 1972-73. Member of advisory council, Ethnic Heritage Project in Baltic Drama, Southern Illinois University at Carbondale. *Member:* Modern Language Association of America, American Comparative Literature Association, Association for the Advancement of Baltic Studies.

WRITINGS: The Development of Written Estonian, Indiana University at Bloomington, 1968; *Literatures in Contact: Finland and Estonia*, Estonian Learned Society in America (New York), 1972. Contributor to *MLA International Bibliography*; contributor of articles, translations, and reviews to periodicals, including *Canadian Slavic Studies*, *Comparative Literature*, *Mana*, *Journal of Baltic Studies*, *Mississippi Valley Review*, *Verbum Habet Sakala* (Sweden), and *Books Abroad*.

WORK IN PROGRESS: English translation of the Estonian epic, *Kalevipoeg*, and of two modern Soviet Estonian dramas; short fiction; articles and book reviews.

* * *

KUSCHE, Lawrence David 1940-

PERSONAL: Surname rhymes with "bush"; born November 1, 1940, in Racine, Wis.; son of Russell David (a truck driver) and Margaret (Riemann) Kusche; married Sally Rhodes (a teacher), August 22, 1964; children: Rebecca, Andrew. *Education:* Arizona State University, B.A., 1964, M.A., 1966; University of Denver, M.L.S., 1968. *Home:* 724 East Wesleyan Dr., Tempe, Ariz. 85282. *Office:* University Library, Arizona State University, Tempe, Ariz. 85281.

CAREER: Field laboratory technician and non-military flight instructor in Arizona, 1961-63; trained as flight engineer with Trans World Airlines (TWA), 1964; high school mathematics teacher in Peoria, Ariz., 1965-66, librarian, 1966-68; Arizona State University, Tempe, research librarian, 1969—. *Member:* Arizona State Library Association (president of College and University Division, 1973).

WRITINGS: (Editor) *Intermountain Union List of Serials*, Arizona State Library Association, 1972; (editor) *Southwestern Environment Index*, Arizona State University, 1973; *The Bermuda Triangle Mystery—Solved*, Harper, 1975.

WORK IN PROGRESS: The Fiction Best Sellers, 1895-1974; a follow-up book on the Bermuda triangle; a book on Flight 19 (the Lost Patrol); a book on the Navy ship "Cyclops"; a book on UFO's; a book on ancient astronauts; several history-cookbooks; *The Non-Fiction Best Sellers, 1895-1974*.

SIDELIGHTS: Kusche writes: "I might be called a skeptic. It's not that I disbelieve anything and everything, but I *especially* question much of the present-day written and televised information that passes for 'fact.' Much of it is nothing more than a half-fact attempt to earn as much money as possible with as little regard for truth as necessary. I have developed what might be called a 'philosophy of alternative possibilities,' and accept practically nothing as fact unless there is overwhelming evidence . . . in its favor. . . . [In writing on the Bermuda Triangle,] I did not accept what had been said earlier [by other writers], but began an independent, massive research project to locate original sources of information (the alternative possibilities)."

Kusche has about eighteen hundred hours of flying time, most of it as an instructor, none of it military. His ratings include commercial, instrument, flight instructor, instrument flight instructor, advanced ground instructor, and flight engineer. He now flies only rarely.

AVOCATIONAL INTERESTS: Hiking, camping, motorcycling, running, research on interesting topics.

* * *

KUSHNER, David Z(akeri) 1935-

PERSONAL: Born December 22, 1935, in Ellenville, N.Y.; son of Nathan (a businessman) and Rita (Forgatsh) Kushner; married Rebecca Ann Stefan (a voice teacher), December 20, 1964; children: Jonathan Moses, Joshua Sanford, Jeremy Avram, Jason Daniel. *Education:* Boston University, B.Mus., 1957; University of Cincinnati, M.Mus., 1958; University of Michigan, Ph.D., 1966. *Politics:* Independent Democrat. *Religion:* Jewish. *Home:* 2215 Northwest 21st Ave., Gainesville, Fla. 32605. *Office:* Department of Music, University of Florida, Gainesville, Fla. 32611.

CAREER: Mississippi State College for Women (now Mississippi University for Women), Columbus, assistant professor of music, 1964-66; Radford College, Radford, Va., associate professor, 1966-68, professor of music, 1968-69; University of Florida, Gainesville, professor of music and chairman of musicology faculty, 1969—, coordinator of graduate studies, 1974—. Host and commentator on "Music from Florida," a weekly radio program on WRUF-FM Radio. Vice-chairman of Gainesville Cultural Commission; charter member and program annotator of Pro Arte Musica of Gainesville.

MEMBER: American Musicological Society (chairman of Southern chapter, 1972-74), Music Teachers National Association (life member), American Liszt Society (chairman of board of directors, 1967—), Ernest Bloch Society, Florida State Music Teachers Association, Phi Mu Alpha (life member), Pi Kappa Lambda (president of Gamma Zeta chapter, 1970—).

WRITINGS: Ernest Bloch and His Music, William MacLellan, 1973. Contributor to *Grove's Dictionary of Music and Musicians* and *Dictionary of Contemporary Music*. Contributor of more than twenty articles and reviews to music and education journals, including *Florida Music Director*, *Music Journal*, *Opera Journal*, *School Musician*, *American Music Teacher*, and *Radford Review*.

WORK IN PROGRESS: Research on colonial American music and musicians, and on music in the colonial South.

BIOGRAPHICAL/CRITICAL SOURCES: Piano Guild Notes, May-June, 1971.

* * *

KUSNICK, Barry A. 1910-

PERSONAL: Born October 3, 1910, in New York, N.Y.; son of Isaac (a rabbi) and Fanny (Block) Kusnick; married June D. Lee, 1949 (divorced); married Lilyan McNeely (an administrative assistant), July 2, 1966; children: Judith Landy, Janet. *Education:* Attended University of California at Los Angeles. *Politics:* Democrat. *Religion:* None. *Home:* 1638 Waterloo St., Los Angeles, Calif. 90026.

CAREER: ITT Gilfillan, Los Angeles, Calif., senior development engineer, 1947-50; Librascope Inc. Singer, Glendale, Calif., senior engineer, 1950-63; Bell & Howell, Pasadena, Calif., senior member of technical staff, 1963-64; Houston Fearless Corp., Los Angeles, Calif., chief design engineer, 1964; Bell & Howell, Pasedena, Calif., senior member of technical staff, 1965-67; ITT Aerospace, San Fernando, Calif., senior development engineer, 1967-71; Litton Industries, Beverly Hills, Calif., engineer group leader, 1969-71. *Member:* Buccaneer Yacht Club, Griffith Park Tennis Club.

WRITINGS: The Complete Boatman, Dial, 1975.

WORK IN PROGRESS: The Yacht Inventory.

AVOCATIONAL INTERESTS: Piano playing, photography, tennis, music, sailboat racing.

* * *

LA CLAUSTRA, Vera Berneicia (Derrick) 1903-

PERSONAL: Born April 11, 1903, in Baker, Ore.; daughter of Edmond Treseia and Nellie Ann (Vessey) Derrick; married Gunnar Benson (a physician), October 15, 1920; married second husband, Seraphin Arguis La Claustra (a property manager), April 15, 1933; children: (first marriage) William Hugh. *Education:* San Jose Graduate School of Cosmetology, license, 1934. *Religion:* "Belief in the Divinity of the Lord." *Home:* 400 Perkins St., Apt. 209, Oakland, Calif. 94610.

CAREER: Owner and operator of La Vera's Beauty Shop, Oakland, Calif. for 11 years; poet. *Member:* Avalon World Arts Academy, World Poetry Society Intercontinental, American Poetry League, Centro Studi e Scambi Internazionale, California Federation of Chaparral Poets, Ladies Auxiliary of Veterans of Foreign Wars. *Awards, honors:* Accademia "Leonardo Da Vinci" Di Scienze Lettere Arti certificates of merit for poems: "Immortality," 1962, "Deceptive Arabesque," 1968, "Renewal," 1971, and "Pheasant," 1972; World Poetry Society Intercontinental certificate of merit, 1970, for poem, "Not I," and other poetry awards.

WRITINGS—Poetry: *By the Cool Waters*, Story Book Press, 1953; *The Purple Wheel*, Berkeley Mimeographing Co., 1954; *Gongs of Light*, Swordsman, 1971.

Poems represented in anthologies, including *Poetry Parade*, edited by Jeanne Hollyfield, Young Publications, 1963; *Rhyme Time*, edited by Lincoln B. Young, Young Publications, 1964; *Versatility in Verse*, edited by Young and Hollyfield, Young Publications, 1965; *A Burst of Trumpets*, edited by Young and Hollyfield, Young Publications, 1966; *Sixty Seven Poets*, edited by Jerry McCarty, Prairie Press, 1967; *Badge of Promise*, edited by Jaye Giammarino, Prairie Press, 1968, and others.

Contributor of poems to *American Bard*, *Bitterroot*, *Westminster*, *Wisconsin Poetry Magazine*, *Oakland Tribune*, *San Francisco Examiner*, *Washington Evening Star*, *Denver Post*, *Dial*, and others.

WORK IN PROGRESS: *Flints of Jade*, a book of Haiku with illustrations.

SIDELIGHTS: Mrs. La Claustra told *CA*: "Poetry is to me a realm of beauty I enter, and close the door to all else; it is not an escapement—but an entering into—the wholeness of life, the muses inspire, and time elapses into eternity; for we have always been, and shall always be. . . ."

* * *

LACY, Gene M(elvin) 1934-

PERSONAL: Born March 20, 1934, in Audubon, Iowa; son of Howard M. and Martha (Booten) Lacy; married Shirley R. Gorham (a medical technologist), November 25, 1958; children: Scott, Blair, Blake. *Education:* North Texas State University, B.S., 1960, M.M.E., 1961, doctoral study, 1968-70, and summer, 1974. *Politics:* Conservative Republican. *Religion:* Assembly of God. *Home:* 132 Cornelius Rd., Spartanburg, S.C. 29301. *Office:* School of Music, Converse College, Spartanburg, S.C. 29301.

CAREER: Converse College, Spartanburg, S.C., assistant professor of music theory and education, 1970—. *Military service:* U.S. Air Force, 1954-57. *Member:* Music Educators National Conference, South Carolina String Teachers, Pi Kappa Lambda.

WRITINGS: *Organizing and Developing the High School Orchestra*, Parker Publishing, 1971. Contributor to *American Music Teacher, Instrumentalist, American String Teacher*, and *Music Educators Journal.*

* * *

LADAS, Gerasimos 1937-

PERSONAL: Born April 25, 1937, in Greece; son of Efthimios I. (a farmer) and Aggeliki (Kaminari) Ladas; married Theodora Stamatatos, September 5, 1964; children: Homer, Andreas. *Education:* University of Athens, B.S., 1961; New York University, M.S., 1966, Ph.D., 1968. *Religion:* Greek Orthodox. *Home:* 80 Greenwood Dr., Peacedale, R.I. 02879. *Office:* Department of Mathematics, University of Rhode Island, Kingston, R.I. 02881.

CAREER: Fairfield University, Fairfield, Conn., assistant professor of mathematics, 1968-69; University of Rhode Island, Kingston, assistant professor, 1969-72, associate professor of mathematics, 1972—, chairman of department, 1972—. *Military service:* Greek Army, 1961-63; became second lieutenant. *Member:* American Mathematical Society, American Association of University Professors, Greek Mathematical Society.

WRITINGS: (With Vangipuram Lakshmikantham) *Abstract Differential Equations*, Academic Press, 1972; (with E. A. Grove) *Introduction to Complex Variables*, Houghton, 1974. Contributor to mathematical journals.

WORK IN PROGRESS: Research in differential and functional differential equations.

AVOCATIONAL INTERESTS: Chess, vegetable gardening, fishing.

* * *

LAFFIN, John (Alfred Charles) 1922-
(Carl Dekker, Mark Napier, Dirk Sabre)

PERSONAL: Born September 21, 1922, in Sydney, Australia; son of Charles George and Nellie (a nursing sister; maiden name, Pike) Laffin; married Hazelle Gloria Stonham (now her husband's assistant), October 6, 1943; children: Bronwen Diane (Mrs. Erian Katsha), Craig Antony, Pirenne Debra. *Education:* University of London, M.A., 1961. *Politics:* "Completely uncommitted." *Religion:* "Convince me." *Home:* Oxford House, Brampton Bryan, Bucknell, Shropshire SY7 0DH, England.

CAREER: Associated Newspapers, Sydney, Australia, associate editor, 1945-51; York Editing Service, Sydney, managing director, 1951-56; International Corresponding Schools, Sydney, chief instructor and examiner in creative journalism and short story writing, 1951-56; Mayfield College, Sussex, England, head of the departments of English, geography, and sociology, 1959-69; full-time writer, 1969—. Chairman of Sussex branch of British Legion, 1967-69. *Military service:* Australian Army, Infantry, 1940-45; served in New Guinea. *Member:* Royal Geographical Society (fellow), Royal Historical Society (fellow), Society for Army Historical Research, Society of Authors, Military History Society of Ireland, Society for Nautical Research, Society of Antiquaries of Scotland, Royal United Service Institution. *Awards, honors:* Brantridge College, Sussex, D.Litt., 1972.

WRITINGS—Nonfiction: *Return to Glory*, Angus & Robertson, 1956; *Middle East Journey*, Angus & Robertson, 1958; *One Man's War*, Angus & Robertson, 1957; *Digger: The Story of the Australian Soldier*, Cassell, 1959.

Scotland the Brave: The Story of the Scottish Soldier, Cassell, 1963, reprinted, White Lion, 1974; *The Face of War: The Evolution of Weapons and Tactics and Their Use in Ten Famous Battles*, Abelard, 1963; *Swifter than Eagles: The Biography of Marshal of the Royal Air Force Sir John Maitland Salmond*, W. Blackwood, 1964; *Codes and Ciphers: Secret Writing through the Ages* (Literary Guild selection), Abelard, 1964; *British Campaign Medals*, Abelard, 1964; *Anzacs at War: The Story of Australian and New Zealand Battles*, Abelard, 1965; *Jackboot: The Story *of the German Soldier*, Cassell, 1965, 2nd edition, 1966; *Links of Leadership: Thirty Centuries of Command*, Harrapp, 1966, Abelard, 1970; *Tommy Atkins: The Story of the English Soldier*, Cassell, 1966; *The Hunger to Come*, Abelard, 1966, revised and enlarged edition, 1971; *Boys in Battle*, Abelard, 1967; *Women in Battle*, Abelard, 1967; *The Anatomy of Captivity*, Abelard, 1968; *Jack Tar: The Story of the British Sailor*, Cassell, 1969.

Surgeons in the Field, Dent, 1970; (editor) *Letters from the Front, 1914-1918*, Dent, 1973; *Fedayeen: The Arab-Israeli Dilemma*, Cassell, 1973, revised edition, Free Press, 1973; *Americans in Battle*, Crown, 1973; *The French Foreign Legion*, Crown, 1974; *The Arab Mind: A Need for Understanding*, Cassell, 1975, Taplinger, in press.

Fiction—All published by Horwitz, except as noted: *Death by Ballot*, King Books, 1954; *Jungle Manhunt*, 1955, 2nd edition, 1958; *Murder on Flight 354*, King Books, 1956; *Death Has My Number*, 1957; *I'll Die Tonight*, 1957; *My Brother's Executioner*, 1957; *They Voted Me to Die*, 1957; *Crime on My Hands*, 1958; *The Dancer of San Jose*, 1958; *The Devil's Emissary*, 1958; *Murder in Paradise*, 1958; *Temptress on Trial*, 1958; *The Walking Wounded*, Amalgamated Press, 1963; *Devil's Goad*, Dent, 1970.

Under pseudonym Carl Dekker: *Silence So Deadly*, Calvert, 1953; *Don't Bother to Knock*, Calvert, 1954.

Under pseudonym Mark Napier: *Doorways to Danger*, Abelard, 1966.

Under pseudonym Dirk Sabre: *Murder by Bamboo*, Hammond, Hammond, 1958.

Author of *New Geography*, 1966-67, 1968-69, and 1970-71, published by Abelard. Regular contributor to *Spectator*, *British Army Review*, *Daily Telegraph* (London) and *International Herald-Tribune* (Paris). Contributor of short stories to *Argosy*, *Collier's*, and *Saturday Evening Post*; also contributor of articles to various newspapers and magazines in the United States, Great Britain, and Australia.

WORK IN PROGRESS: A book on how propaganda works, covering approximately 1914 to the present, and a novel on mankind's search for security, completion of both expected in 1975.

SIDELIGHTS: When Laffin was only 15 his first adult short story was published and his work was included in an Australian national anthology (*Tales by Australians*, British Authors Press, 1937). Although much of his work since then has been in the field of war and military history, Laffin told *CA* that he "refuses to glorify war but recognises that men 'find themselves' in war." His military interests include problems of leadership and command, the psychology of combat, and the development of war, as well as visiting battlefields with his wife as companion and assistant. He wrote that he has "explored thousands of years of fields of combat and is a pioneer in battlefield archaeology."

Despite his many books on war topics, Laffin regards himself more as a novelist and poet and has plans for drama. He continues to write on war, he said, "only because I am trapped by my reputation." He wants to write to warn people of great dangers—their own apathy, refusal to think for themselves, willingness to follow the loudest voice or the brightest flag. He is "appalled by the physical and intellectual flabbiness of modern man. I like them physically hard but mentally flexible—like the blade of a foil." (He is an accomplished fencer with foil, sabre, and epee.)

Angry about the treatment of authors in Britain, Laffin contends that "free public libraries rob all but a handful of writers of the opportunity to earn a living by their typewriter. It is the price we are forced to pay for being nonconformists. We are the last independents."

* * *

LAING, Lloyd (Robert) 1944-

PERSONAL: Born December 6, 1944, in Lanark, Scotland; son of George Fortune (an engineer) and Mary Irene (a teacher; maiden name, Davies) Laing; married Jennifer Clare Johnson (a writer and lecturer), January 5, 1972. *Education:* University of Edinburgh, M.A. (honors), 1966; University of Liverpool, Ph.D., 1974. *Home:* Wentworth, 47 Belle Vale Rd., Gateacre, Liverpool L25 2PA, England. *Agent:* Curtis Brown Ltd., 1 Craven Hill, London W2 3EW, England. *Office address:* School of Archaeology, University of Liverpool, P.O. Box 147, Liverpool L69 3BX, England.

CAREER: Government of Scotland, Edinburgh, assistant inspector of ancient monuments, 1966-69; University of Liverpool, Liverpool, England, lecturer in medieval archaeology, 1969—. Has directed archaeological excavations in Great Britain, especially in Scotland. *Member:* Royal Numismatic Society (fellow), Society of Antiquaries of Scotland (fellow), Prehistoric Society, Medieval Society, Royal Archaeological Institute. *Awards, honors:* Parkes-Weber Medal from Royal Numismatic Society, 1961, for work on Iron Age coin flan molds.

WRITINGS: (With George Rogers) *Gallo-Roman Pottery from Southampton* (monograph), Southampton Museum, 1966; *Coins and Archaeology*, Schocken, 1969; *Orkney and Shetland: An Archaeological Guide*, David & Charles, 1974; (with Peter Harbison) *Some Iron Age Mediterranean Imports in England* (monograph), British Archaeological Reports, 1974; *The Archaeology of Late Celtic Britain and Ireland, circa 400 to 1200 A.D.*, Barnes & Noble, in press; (with wife, Jennifer Laing) *The Archaeologist's Handbook* (juvenile), Pan Books, in press; *Scotland: An Archaeological Guide*, David & Charles, in press. Contributor of more than a hundred articles on archaeology and numismatics and of poems to journals, including *Archaeological Journal*, *Current Archaeology*, *Antiquity*, *Coins and Medals*, *North American Journal of Numismatics*, and *Scotland's Magazine*.

SIDELIGHTS: Laing writes: "My present concern is with barbarism in society, and how it manifests itself in similar guises in all countries." *Avocational interests:* Numismatics, travel, reading (especially thrillers).

* * *

LAIR, Robert L(eland) 1932-

PERSONAL: Born June 21, 1932, in Gloversville, N.Y.; son of Frank Albert and Georgia Anne (Morrison) Lair; married Zovinar Najarian (a college professor), August 16, 1956; children: Marian Patrice, Michael Paul. *Education:* Bob Jones University, B.A. (religion), 1954, M.A., 1956; Middlebury College, B.A. (English), 1961; graduate study at Miami University, Oxford, Ohio, 1962-63; Ohio State University, Ph.D., 1966. *Home:* 3413 27th St. N.W., Canton, Ohio 44708. *Office:* 525 25th St. N.W., Canton, Ohio 44709.

CAREER: Ordained minister of Church of Christ, 1954; served as interim pastor of churches in Greenville, S.C., 1954-59, Columbus, Ohio, 1963-64, and Canton, Ohio, 1973—. Bob Jones University, Greenville, S.C., instructor in English, 1956-62, 1965-68; Ohio State University, Mansfield Campus, associate professor of English, 1968-69; Malone College, Canton, Ohio, professor of English, 1969—. *Member:* Modern Language Association of America, Conference on Christianity and Literature, Northeast Ohio College English Group.

WRITINGS: *T. S. Eliot,* Barron's, 1968; *Emily Dickinson,* Barron's, 1971; *Gerard Manley Hopkins,* Barron's, in press. Contributor of one hundred articles to religion and English journals.

WORK IN PROGRESS: Work on Emily Dickinson's emotional life.

AVOCATIONAL INTERESTS: Piano playing, gemology.

* * *

LAKE, Kenneth R(obert) 1931-
(Arthur King, K. Roberts, Fred Soutter)

PERSONAL: Born July 3, 1931, in Cornwall, England; son of Sidney E. (a horticulturalist) and Eena (Cole) Lake; married Susan Elizabeth Bowyer, December 5, 1958 (divorced April 19, 1973); married Janet Oriel Else (a teacher), April 26, 1973; children: (first marriage) Susan Margaret, Andrew John, Aron Peter. *Education:* Attended schools in England. *Residence:* London, England. *Agent:* Nicholas Thompson, 23 Pont St., London S.W.1, England. *Office:* David Field Ltd., 42 Berkeley St., London W1X 5FP, England.

CAREER: Held positions as proofreader, encyclopedia salesman, clerical worker, and executive, later entering British Civil Service, including work at National Lending Library for Science and Technology, 1953-67; *Stamp Collecting Weekly*, London, England, advertisement manager, 1967-70; Stanley Gibbons Ltd., London, England, public relations officer, 1970; David Field Ltd., London, England, managing director, 1971—. Philatelic consultant to Republic of Nauru, Central Pacific, 1971—.

WRITINGS: *Stamps for Investment*, W. H. Allen, 1970, Stein & Day, 1971; *Investing in Paper Money*, Pelham Books, 1972; *Discovering Banknotes*, Shire Publications, 1973; *David Field All-World Miniature Sheet Catalogue*, David Field, 1973, supplement, 1974. Contributor of several thousand articles (under pseudonyms Arthur King, K. Roberts, Fred Soutter, and others) to philatelic publications in the United States, England, France, and Australia. Former editor of *Philately*.

WORK IN PROGRESS: Further editions of *David Field All-World Miniature Sheet Catalogue*; a book on picture postcards.

SIDELIGHTS: Lake writes: "My lifelong interest in languages stimulated my interest in stamps, and this led to my learning a smattering of some twenty languages to help with philatelic studies. My first book was motivated by reading three other books on philatelic investment which were misleading, inaccurate, and dangerous."

* * *

LAMB, G(eoffrey) F(rederick)
(Balaam)

PERSONAL: Born in London, England; son of Frederick William (an accountant) and Elizabeth (Kendall) Lamb; married Olga Heckman, July 10, 1943; children: Christopher John, Anthony Stuart. *Education:* Kings College, London, B.A., 1932, M.A., 1939. *Home:* Penfold, Legion Lane, Kingsworthy, Winchester, Hampshire, England.

CAREER: Teacher of English in schools in England, 1933-45; Camden Training College, London, England, lecturer in English, 1946-50; author, 1950—. *Member:* Society of Authors, Children's Writer's Group (honorary secretary, 1963-68), National Book League, Magic Circle (London).

WRITINGS: (Editor) *Valiant Deeds in Life and Literature*, Harrap, 1942; (editor) *United States and United Kingdom*, Harrap, 1944; *Tales of Human Endeavour*, Harrap, 1946; *Six Good Samaritans*, Oxford University Press, 1947; (with C. C. Fitz-Hugh) *Precis and Comprehension*, Harrap, 1947; *Commentaries on Galsworthy's Plays*, Pitman, 1948; *Questions Answered About Teaching*, Jordan, 1949.

(Editor) *The English at School*, Allen & Unwin, 1950; (editor) *Other People's Lives*, Harrap, 1951; (editor) *All Over the World*, Harrap, 1951; *Modern Action and Adventure*, Harrap, 1952; (with Fitz-Hugh) *Introductory Precis and Comprehension*, Harrap, 1952; (editor) *All Kinds of Adventure*, Harrap, 1952; *Your Child at School*, F. Watts, 1953; (editor) *Essays of Action*, Macmillan, 1953; (under pseudonym Balaam) *Chalk in My Hair* (autobiography), Benn, 1953; *English for General Certificate*, Harrap, 1954; *The Spirit of Modern Adventure*, Harrap, 1955; (editor) *Short Stories of Action*, Allen & Unwin, 1955; (under pseudonym Balaam) *Chalk Gets in Your Eyes*, Benn, 1955; *English for Middle Forms*, Harrap, Volume I, 1956, Volume II, 1963; *Franklin—Happy Voyager*, Benn, 1956; *English for Lower Forms*, Harrap, Volume I, 1957, Volume II, 1960, both volumes revised with D. R. Hughes and published as *English for Secondary Schools*, 1962; *Thrilling Exploits of Modern Adventure*, Harrap, 1957; *The South Pole*, Muller, 1957; (under pseudonym Balaam) *Come Out to Play*, M. Joseph, 1958; (editor) *Living Dangerously*, Allen & Unwin, 1958; (editor) *Stirring Deeds*, Harrap, 1958; *The Happiest Days*, M. Joseph, 1959; *Great Exploits of World War II*, Harrap, 1959.

Thrilling Journeys of Modern Times, Harrap, 1962; *Punctuation for Schools*, Harrap, 1962; *Modern Adventures in Air and Space*, Harrap, 1964; *Look at Schools*, Hamish Hamilton, 1964; (editor) *Story and Rhythm*, Harrap, 1966; *Composition and Comprehension for CSE*, Harrap, 1968; *The Pegasus Book of Magicians*, Dobson, 1968; *Practical Precis and Comprehension*, Harrap, 1969; *One Hundred Good Stories*, Wheaton, Books 1-4, 1969, Book 6, 1970.

Modern Adventures at Sea, Harrap, 1970; *Wonder Book of the Seashore*, Harrap, 1970; *Your Book of Card Tricks*, Faber, 1972; *Your Book of Mental Magic*, Faber, 1973; *Your Book of Table Tricks*, Faber, 1974; *Discovering Magic Charms and Talismans*, Shire Publications, 1974.

WORK IN PROGRESS: *Magic, Exorcism, and Witchcraft* for Riverwood; *War Stories* for Studio Vista; *More Good Stories* for Wheaton; *Your Book of Secret Writing* for Faber.

* * *

LAMPPA, William R(ussell) 1928-

PERSONAL: Born April 11, 1928, in Embarrass, Minn.; son of William E. (a welder) and Helen A. (a school teacher; maiden name, Sipola) Lamppa; married Shirley Ann Stafford, March 27, 1956; children: Jason Almon, Clayton Norman. *Education:* University of Minnesota, B.S., 1951. *Politics:* "Dialectical materialist." *Religion:* "Unitarian (definitely not Christian)." *Home:* 5119 Red Oak Dr., New Brighton, Minn. 55112. *Office:* Hennepin County Welfare Department, Minneapolis, Minn.

CAREER: Reserve Mine, Babbitt, Minn., truck driver, shovel oiler and caterpillar operator, 1956-57; St. Louis County Welfare Department, St. Louis, Mo., social worker, 1958-64; Hennepin County Welfare Department, Minneapolis, Minn., social worker, 1964—. *Military service:* U.S. Air Force, control tower operator, 1951-55. *Member:* Midwest Federation of Chaparral Poets, League of Minnesota Poets, New Hampshire Poetry Society, Minneapolis Writers Workshop, St. Paul Poets.

WRITINGS—Poems: *The Crucial Point and Other Poems*, Windfall Press, 1971; *In Familiar Fields with Old Friends*, Branden Press, 1972; *The Ancient Chariot and Other Poems*, Mitre Press, 1973.

Poetry is represented in anthologies, including: *Variety in Verse*, edited by C. D. Stephens, Fantasia Publications, 1966; *Timeless Treasures*, edited by Jeanne Hollyfield, Young Publications, 1966; *Golden Harvest*, edited by Lincoln B. Young, Young Publications, 1967; *Grains of Sand*, edited by C. D. Stephens, C. D. Stephens, 1971; *The Shore Poetry Anthology*, edited by Kenneth F. Kwint, Shore Publishing, 1971.

Contributor of over seven hundred poems to journals, magazines, and newspapers.

WORK IN PROGRESS: A book of poems.

* * *

LANCASTER, F(rederick) Wilfrid 1933-

PERSONAL: Born September 4, 1933, in Durham, England; son of Frederick (a coal miner) and Violet (Blackburn) Lancaster; married Maria Cesaria Volpe, June 24, 1961; children: Miriam, Owen Frederick, Jude Joseph, Aaron Ralph. *Education:* Studied at Newcastle upon Tyne School of Librarianship, 1950-54; Library Association of Great Britian, fellow (by thesis), 1969. *Religion:* Roman Catholic. *Home:* 1807 Cindy Lynn, R.R.2, Urbana, Ill. 61801. *Office:* Graduate School of Library Science, University of Illinois, Urbana, Ill. 61801.

CAREER: Newcastle upon Tyne Public Libraries, Newcastle upon Tyne, England, senior assistant, 1953-57; Tube Investments Ltd., Birmingham, England, assistant information officer, 1957-59; Akron Public Library, Akron, Ohio, senior librarian, science and technology, 1959-60; Babcock & Wilcox Co., Barberton, Ohio, technical librarian, 1960-62; ASLIB, London, England, senior research assistant, 1962; Herner & Co., Washington, D.C., resident consultant and head of systems evaluation group, 1964-65; National Library of Medicine, Bethesda, Md., information systems specialist, 1965-68; Westat Research, Inc., Bethesda, Md., director of information retrieval services, 1969-70; University of Illinois, Graduate School of Library Science, Urbana, associate professor, 1970-72, professor of library sciences, 1972—, director of program in biomedical librarianship, 1970—. Adjunct lecturer at School of Library and Information Services, University of Maryland, 1968-70; lecturer at NATO International Advanced Study Institutes in 1965, 1972, and 1975, at the Graduate School, U.S. Department of Agriculture, 1967-69, Defense Intelligence School, U.S. Department of Defense, 1970, at seminars in Europe, and at University of Chicago, University of Texas, University of Pittsburgh, and other universities in the United States, Europe, and Australia. Member of panel on information sciences technology of Federal Council for Science and Technology, 1966-67; consultant to Association for Computing Machinery, 1969-70, Center for Applied Linguistics, 1970-71, National Institutes of Health, 1970-73, and several other government agencies, professional societies, and commercial organizations.

MEMBER: American Society for Information Science, Library Association (England), Medical Library Association, Phi Kappa Phi. *Awards, honors:* American Society for Information Science Award for best paper of 1969 for "Medlars: Report on the Evaluation of its Operating Efficiency," published in *American Documentation*; American Society for Information Science Award for best book on information science, 1970, for *Information Retrieval Systems*.

WRITINGS: Information Retrieval Systems: Characteristics, Testing and Evaluation, Wiley, 1968; *Evaluation of the MEDLARS Demand Search Service* (monograph), National Library of Medicine, 1968; (contributor) Tefko Saracevic, editor, *Introduction to Information Science*, Bowker, 1970; *Vocabulary Control for Information Retrieval*, Information Resources Press, 1972; (with Emily Gallup Fayen) *Information Retrieval On-Line* (monograph), Wiley, 1973.

Author of research reports. Editor, "Specialized Information Source Guides" series, Herner & Co., 1970-73, and *Proceedings* of Annual Clinic on Library Applications of Data Processing, University of Illinois, 1971-73. Contributor to *Encyclopedia of Library and Information Sciences*; contributor of about thirty articles and reviews to library and documentation journals, and to *Journal of the American Medical Association*, *New Scientist* and *Machine Design*. Editorial adviser, *Advanced Technology/Libraries Newsletter*, 1973—; referee, *Science* and *Special Libraries*.

WORK IN PROGRESS: The Measurement and Evaluation of Library Services, for Information Resources Press; and *Towards a Paperless Information System*.

SIDELIGHTS: Information Retrieval Systems has been published in Japanese and Russian editions. *Avocational interests:* Music (especially opera).

* * *

LAND, George T(homas) Lock 1933-

PERSONAL: Born February 27, 1933, in Hot Springs, Ark.; son of George Thomas Lock (a rancher) and Mary Elizabeth Lock (an author and poet) Land; married third wife, Catherine Zanthos (a television executive producer), June 24, 1967; children: (previous marriage) Patrick A., Thomas G., Robert E. *Education:* Attended Millsaps College, 1952-54, and University of Veracruz, 1955-57. *Home:* 405 East 54th St., New York, N.Y. 10022. *Agent:* Jay Garon, Jay Garon-Brookes Associates, Inc., 415 Central Park W., #17D, New York, N.Y. 10025. *Office:* 72 Pine St., Southampton, Long Island, N.Y. 11968.

CAREER: Anthropological research in Mexico, 1954-60; Television del Norte, Mexico City and Monterrey, Mexico, director general, 1960-62; Roman Corp., St. Louis, Mo., vice-president, 1962-64; Transolve, Inc., Cambridge, Mass., chairman, 1964-67; Innotek Corp., New York, N.Y., chief executive and chairman, 1967-71; Turtle Bay Institute, New York, N.Y., chairman and partner, 1971—. President, Hal Roach Studios, 1967-71; visiting professor at Mankato State College; lecturer at Menninger Foundation, St. Louis University, Southern Illinois University, St. John's University (Jamaica, N.Y.), Harvard University, Massachusetts Institute of Technology, North Carolina Governor's School and others. Director of Motivation Sciences, Inc.; colleague of Creative Education Foundation and Committee for the Future. Member of National Action Committee on Drug Education; co-chairman of Syncon Conference, 1972, 1974. Consultant to government, industry, and educational institutions.

MEMBER: International Platform Association, American Association for the Advancement of Science, American Cybernetics Society, Society for General Systems Research, Oceanic Society, Academy of Parapsychology and Medicine, Authors Guild, Authors League of America, New York Academy of Sciences, Lambs Club.

WRITINGS: Innovation Systems, Transolve, 1967; *Innovation Techniques*, Transolve, 1967; *Grow or Die: The Unifying Principle of Transformation*, Random House, 1973; *Creative Alternatives and Decision Making*, Mankato State College Press, 1974.

Author and director of over 60 plays for Latin American and European television, 1957-60.

Contributor to magazines, including *Futurist* and *Journal of Creative Education*.

WORK IN PROGRESS: Books on personal and family growth, on joy and anguish of creative living, and on transformation therapy; research on creative and growth behavior.

AVOCATIONAL INTERESTS: Boating, archaeology, gemology, orchidry, broadening cultural experience (has lived with primitive tribes in South America).

* * *

LANDAU, Elaine 1948-

PERSONAL: Born February 15, 1948, in Lakewood, N.J.; daughter of James and May (a department store manager; maiden name, Tudor) Garmiza; married Edward William Landau (an electrical engineer), December 16, 1968. *Education:* New York University, B.A., 1970. *Religion:* Jewish. *Home:* 46-01 39th Ave., Queens, N.Y. 11104.

CAREER: Reporter on community newspaper in New York, N.Y., 1970-72; Simon & Schuster, New York, N.Y., editor, 1972-73. *Member:* National Organization for Women, Women's Equity Action League, American Library Association.

WRITINGS: (With Jesse Jackson) *Black in America: A Fight for Freedom*, Messner, 1973; *Woman, Woman! Feminism in America*, Messner, 1974.

WORK IN PROGRESS: A children's book about pioneer women, completion expected in 1975.

AVOCATIONAL INTERESTS: Botany.

* * *

LANDER, Mamie Stubbs 1891(?)-1975

1891(?)—January 11, 1975; American officer of Order of the Eastern Star, author. Obituaries: *Washington Post*, January 17, 1975.

* * *

LANDOW, George P(aul) 1940-

PERSONAL: Born August 25, 1940, in White Plains, N.Y.; son of Herman Irving (a psychiatrist) and Elizabeth Lilian (Driver) Landow (died, 1941); reared by Florence Strasmich Landow; married Ruth Macktez (a college teacher), May 22, 1966; children: Shoshona Macktez, Noah Macktez. *Education:* Princeton University, A.B., 1961, M.A., 1963, Ph.D., 1966; Brandeis University, M.A., 1962; University of London, further graduate study, 1964-65. *Religion:* Jewish. *Home:* 9 University Ave., Providence, R.I. 02906. *Office:* Department of English, Brown University, Providence, R.I. 02912.

CAREER: Columbia University, New York, N.Y., instructor in English, 1965-68; Cornell University, Ithaca, N.Y., fellow of Society for the Humanities, 1968-69; Columbia University, assistant professor of English, 1969-70, visiting associate professor, summer, 1971; University of Chicago, Chicago, Ill., visiting associate professor of English, 1970-71; Brown University, Providence, R.I., associate professor of English, 1971—.

MEMBER: Modern Language Association of America, American Society for Aesthetics, Ruskin Association, Tennyson Society, Northeast Modern Language Association, Phi Beta Kappa (honorary member). *Awards, honors:* Woodrow Wilson fellowship, 1961-62; Fulbright scholar at Birkbeck College, University of London, 1964-65; Society for the Humanities fellowship, 1968-69; M.A., Brown University, 1972; Gustave O. Aridt Award of Council of Graduate Schools in the United States, 1972, for *The Aesthetic and Critical Theories of John Ruskin*; Guggenheim fellowships, 1973, 1974; fellow of Huntington Library, 1974.

WRITINGS: The Aesthetic and Critical Theories of John Ruskin, Princeton University Press, 1971; (contributor) Joseph P. Altholtz, editor, *The Mind and Art of Victorian England*, University of Minnesota Press, in press. Contributor of about forty articles and reviews to literature and library journals, including *Revue de Litterature Comparee*, *Bulletin of the John Rylands Library*, *University of Toronto Quarterly*, *Victorian Studies*, and *Modern Philology*.

WORK IN PROGRESS: William Holman Hunt and Pre-Raphaelite Symbolism (tentative title), for Yale University Press; a study of Holman Hunt, John Ruskin, and their art and art theory; an edition of the writings—political, artistic, and polemical—of Holman Hunt; further preparatory study for a book, *Sages and Satirists: A Theory of American and English Nonfiction*, from Carlyle to Mailer and beyond; contributing to *Typology and Literature: Aspects of Figuralism from Medieval to Modern Times*, edited by Earl Miner, for Princeton University Press; contributing to *Nature and Victorian Imagination*, edited by U. C. Knoepflmacher and G. B. Tennyson, for University of California Press; editing *Approaches to Victorian Autobiography*.

SIDELIGHTS: Landow finds the Victorians especially fascinating to study, he says, "because they confronted many of the same problems we face, and they did so with some grace and dignity, a lot of brash vulgarity, much ingenuity, and an abundance of excitement and energy. We have just barely begun to understand our own roots in the Victorian age—the reputations and understanding of the great moderns Eliot, Yeats, Pound, and others will change radically in these next few decades—and I would like to answer some rather basic questions for myself about this ever relevant Victorian literature and art."

Landow "enjoys many frivolities," such as "writing letters to newspapers and taking pictures, building toys and building furniture." His "maddest enterprise" is the Albion, Pawtuxet and Galilee Railroad, a model railroad built with his daughter and based on a mythical Rhode Island line of the past century. He has written about and photographed the AP&G for hobby magazines.

LANE, Irving M(ark) 1944-

PERSONAL: Born September 18, 1944, in Brooklyn, N.Y.; son of Aaron (an accountant) and Lucy (Gold) Lane. *Education:* Brooklyn College of the City University of New York, B.A., 1965; Michigan State University, M.A., 1968, Ph.D., 1970. *Home:* 2364 Woodland Ridge Blvd., Baton Rouge, La. 70815. *Office:* Department of Psychology, Louisiana State University, Baton Rouge, La. 70803.

CAREER: Louisiana State University, Baton Rouge, assistant professor, 1970-73, associate professor of psychology, 1974—, research director of Institute of Insurance Marketing, 1972—. *Member:* American Psychological Association, Midwestern Psychological Association, Phi Kappa Phi.

WRITINGS: (With Laurence Siegel) *Psychology in Industrial Organizations,* Irwin, 1974. Contributor to *Journal of Personality and Social Psychology, Child Development, Human Development,* and *Psychonomic Science.*

WORK IN PROGRESS: Research on the development and understanding of justice and equity.

* * *

LANE, Jack C(onstant) 1932-

PERSONAL: Born April 19, 1932, in Elgin, Tex.; married Janne Jolley (a teacher), December 17, 1957; children: Alan, Anne. *Education:* Oglethorpe University, B.A., 1958; Emory University, M.A., 1959; University of Georgia, Ph.D., 1963. *Politics:* Democrat. *Home:* 1200 Lakeview Dr., Winter Park, Fla. 32789. *Office:* Department of History, Rollins College, Winter Park, Fla. 32791.

CAREER: Rollins College, Winter Park, Fla., assistant professor, 1963-64, associate professor, 1964-68, professor of history, 1968—. *Military service:* U.S. Army, Airborne Division, 1951-54; became sergeant. *Member:* Organization of American Historians, Southern Historical Association.

WRITINGS: Chasing Geronimo, University of New Mexico Press, 1970. Contributor to *Science and Society, Journal of Southern History,* and *Florida Historical Quarterly.*

WORK IN PROGRESS: Armed Progressive: A Biography of Leonard Wood, for possible publication by Macmillan.

* * *

LANE, Raymond A. 1894(?)-1974

1894(?)—July 31, 1974; American Maryknoll bishop and author. Obituaries: *New York Times*, August 3, 1974.

* * *

LANGEVIN, Sister Jean Marie 1917-

PERSONAL: Born October 10, 1917, in Ellenburg, N.Y.; daughter of Paul George and Augusta (Patenaude) Langevin. *Education:* Plattsburg Business Institute, secretarial diploma, 1937; Villanova University, B.S., 1957; Newspaper Institute of America, certificate, 1964; Famous Writers School, certificate, 1968; St. Francis College, Loretto, Pa., certification in L.S., 1970. *Home:* 303 Church St., St. Marys, Pa. 15857.

CAREER: Entered Roman Catholic Order of St. Benedict, 1937; has been principal, teacher, and librarian at diocesan schools since 1940; currently teacher and librarian at Queen of the World School, St. Marys, Pa.

WRITINGS: The Help of His Grace, Grail Publications, 1955; *Years of Sunshine, Days of Rain*, Newman, 1966; *A Pale But Splendid Morning*, Our Sunday Visitor, 1974. Contributor to *Call of India, Catholic School Journal, Benedictine Review, Lake Shore Visitor, Our Sunday Visitor.*

WORK IN PROGRESS: "I would like to write, if time permits, an autobiography of a humorous nature—similar to "The Waltons.""

SIDELIGHTS: Sister Jean Marie Langevin writes: "In the fall of 1937 I entered St. Joseph Convent, St. Marys, Pa. Here I learned many skills as well as scholastic learning. And so life went on, and when Vatican II emerged, my well-ordered life became somewhat different. However, I survived, and hope to continue doing so in my religious life. It seems to me that if I no longer pray, I will become, as St. Paul said, 'Sounding brass and tinkling cymbals.' Since I am conservative by nature I do not, to use the old cliche, 'Jump on the band wagon' when some of the changes that are advocated come into my life. Some I like, others I dislike. This has caused me much distress, since it naturally creeps into my writing. My life is a very busy one, and my writing has to be done during any leisure moments that I may have."

AVOCATIONAL INTERESTS: Decorating, art, crocheting, making rosaries for the missions, walking in the woods, reading, "and especially people—all types."

* * *

LANGFORD, George 1939-

PERSONAL: Born May 24, 1939, in Johnson City, Tenn.; son of Norris McCormick (a retailer) and Sarah (Lacy) Langford; married Anne Roberta Mirgain, June 13, 1964; children: Jennie Anne, Julie Beth. *Education:* Vanderbilt University, B.A., 1961. *Religion:* Roman Catholic. *Residence:* Deerfield, Ill. *Office: Chicago Tribune*, 435 North Michigan, Chicago, Ill. 60611.

CAREER: United Press International, reporter in St. Louis, Chicago, and New York Bureaus, 1961-66; *Chicago Tribune*, Chicago, Ill., sportswriter, 1966—, assistant sports features editor, 1974—. *Military service:* Air National Guard, 1961-67. *Member:* Baseball Writers Association, Pro Football Writers Association, Hockey Writers Association, Chicago Pro Football Writers Association (secretary-treasurer, 1970—), Chicago Baseball Writers Association (vice-chairman, 1974—), Horseshoe Club. *Awards, honors:* Associated Press story of the year award in Illinois, 1970; Baseball writer of the year award from Horseshoe Club of Chicago, 1971.

WRITINGS: The Crimson Tide: Alabama Football, Regnery, 1974. Contributor to numerous periodicals.

AVOCATIONAL INTERESTS: Family.

* * *

LANGFORD, James R(ouleau) 1937-
(Jerome J. Langford)

PERSONAL: Born June 12, 1937, in South Bend, Ind.; son of Walter McCarty (an educator) and Alice (Joubert) Langford; married Margaret Hammerot, August 30, 1968; children: Jeremy William, Joshua McCarty. *Education:* Aquinas Institute of Philosophy, Ph.B., 1961; Aquinas Institute of Theology, M.A., 1962, Ph.Lic., 1964. *Politics:* Democrat. *Religion:* Roman Catholic. *Home:* 109 Napoleon, South Bend, Ind. 46617. *Office:* University of Notre Dame Press, Notre Dame, Ind. 46556.

CAREER: St. Thomas College, St. Paul, Minn., instructor in philosophy and theology, 1965-67; Doubleday & Co., Inc. (publishers), New York, N.Y., editor, 1967-69; University of Michigan Press, Ann Arbor, executive editor, 1969-74; University of Notre Dame Press, South Bend, Ind., director, 1974—.

WRITINGS: (Under pseudonym Jerome J. Langford) *Galileo, Science, and the Church,* Desclee, 1966, revised edition, University of Michigan Press, 1971.

WORK IN PROGRESS: A history of the relationship between science and religion; translating *Apologia Pro Galileo,* by Tommasso Campanella; developing principles for a set of values applicable to life in contemporary society.

* * *

LANGIULLI, Nino 1932-

PERSONAL: Surname is pronounced Lon-*ju*-lee; born October 9, 1932, in Brooklyn, N.Y.; son of Francis Paul (a wood finisher) and Claire (a seamstress; maiden name, Pastanella) Langiulli; married Elizabeth Felleman (a teacher), October 10, 1959; children: Miriam, David, Ruth. *Education:* Maryknoll Seminary (now College), Glen Ellyn, Ill., B.A., 1955; Hunter College (now Hunter College of the City University of New York), M.A. (English), 1960; University of Turin, graduate study, 1960-61; New York University, M.A. (philosophy), 1965, Ph.D., 1973. *Politics:* "Aristotelian, but sometimes Machiavellian." *Religion:* Roman Catholic. *Home:* 32 Farnum St., Lynbrook, N.Y. 11563. *Office:* Department of Philosophy, St. Francis College, Brooklyn, N.Y. 11201.

CAREER: St. Mary's School, Pinehurst, Mass., teacher of religion, 1955-56; St. Augustine's High School, Brooklyn, N.Y., teacher of English and social studies, 1957-60; St. Francis College, Brooklyn, N.Y., instructor, 1961-65, assistant professor, 1966-72, associate professor of philosophy, 1972—. Assistant director, then director, 1960-68, of a summer day camp in Queens Village, N.Y. *Member:* American Philosophical Association, University Centers for Rational Alternatives, Danforth Associates, American Association of University Professors. *Awards, honors:* Fulbright and Italian Government grant to study in Italy, 1960-61.

WRITINGS: (Editor and translator) Nicola Abbagnano, *Critical Existentialism*, Doubleday, 1969; (editor) *The Existentialist Tradition*, Doubleday, 1971. Contributor to *Shakespeare Encyclopedia*, Crowell, 1966. Contributor of translations to *Encyclopaedia Britannica* and *Encyclopedia of Philosophy*, Macmillan, 1967.

WORK IN PROGRESS: Possibility and Existence; editing an anthology of writings on Machiavelli; translating Pseudo-Boethius' *De Diffinitione*; editing an introductory anthology of philosophic writings for high school students.

SIDELIGHTS: Langiulli told *CA*: "Three major influences on my life have been (a) the Italian immigrant experience of my parents and relatives; (b) Roman Catholicism; (c) the study of philosophy. I would like to make a lasting contribution, however small, to philosophical literature." *Avocational interests:* Touch football, carpentry.

* * *

LANGSLEY, Donald G(ene) 1925-

PERSONAL: Born October 5, 1925, in Topeka, Kan.; son of Morris J. (in clothing business) and Ruth (Pressman) Langsley; married Pauline Royal (a psychiatrist), September 9, 1955; children: Karen Jean, Dorothy Ruth, Susan Louise. *Education:* State University of New York at Albany, student, 1943-44, 1946-49, A.B. (summa cum laude), 1949; University of Rochester, M.D., 1953; further training at San Francisco Psychoanalytic Institute, 1958-61, and Chicago Institute for Psychoanalysis, 1961-67. *Home:* 524 Antioch Dr., Davis, Calif., 95616. *Office:* Division of Mental Health, University of California, Davis-Sacramento Medical Center, 2315 Stockton Blvd., Sacramento, Calif. 95817.

CAREER: U.S. Public Health Service Hospital, San Francisco, Calif., intern, 1953-54; University of California, School of Medicine, San Francisco, resident, 1954-59 (also resident in same period at Langley Porter Neuropsychiatric Institute), U.S. Public Health Service career teacher, 1959-61; University of Colorado, School of Medicine, Denver, assistant professor, 1961-65, associate professor of psychiatry, 1965-68, director of inpatient service, Colorado Psychopathic Hospital, 1961-68; University of California, Davis, School of Medicine, professor of psychiatry, chairman of department, and chairman of Division of Mental Health, 1968—. Director of Sacramento County Mental Health Services, 1968-73. Consultant in psychiatry, U.S. Department of Defense, 1966—; member of psychiatry training committee, National Institute of Mental Health, 1971-73; member of psychiatry test committee, National Board of Medical Examiners, 1973—. Diplomate in psychiatry, American Board of Psychiatry and Neurology, 1960. *Military service:* U.S. Army, 1943-46. U.S. Public Health Service, 1953-54. U.S. Public Health Service Inactive Reserve, 1954—; present rank, senior surgeon.

MEMBER: American Psychiatric Association (fellow), American Psychoanalytic Association, American Medical Association, American Association of Chairmen of Departments of Psychiatry, Association of American Medical Colleges, California Medical Association, California Association for Mental Health, Central California Psychiatric Society (president, 1973-74). *Awards, honors:* Special Award, Colorado Association for Mental Health, 1968; honorable mention, Hofheimer Prize of American Psychiatric Association, 1971; Sacramento Mental Health Association Award, 1973.

WRITINGS: (With David M. Kaplan, Frank S. Pittman, and others) *The Treatment of Families in Crisis,* Grune, 1968; (with J. F. McDermott and A. J. Enelow) *Mental Health Education in the New Medical Schools,* Jossey-Bass, 1973.

Contributor: S. M. Farber and R. H. L. Wilson, editors, *Man and Civilization: Control of the Mind,* McGraw, 1961; Bernard Bloom and Dorothy Buck, editors, *Preventive Services in Mental Health Programs,* Wiche, 1967; Jay Haley and Lynn Hoffman, *Techniques of Family Therapy,* Basic Books, 1967; Haley, editor, *Changing Families: A Family Therapy Reader,* Grune, 1971; Nathan W. Ackerman, editor, *Family Process,* Basic Books, 1971; H. H. Barten, editor, *Brief Therapies,* Behavioral Publications, 1971; Howard F. Conn, R. E. Rakel, and T. W. Johnson, *A Textbook of Family Practice,* Saunders, 1972; V. O. Hammett and Norris Hansell, editors, *Psychiatric Residency in Service Settings,* Town House Press, 1973; Howard J. Parad, editor, *Crisis Intervention,* Brady Medical Publishers, in press.

Contributor to *Current Psychiatric Therapies,* 1966, 1974. Contributor of about fifty articles, more than thirty abstracts, and reviews to medical, hospital, and mental hygiene journals. Member of abstracting and review staff, *American Journal of Psychiatry* and *American Journal of Psychotherapy*.

WORK IN PROGRESS: A contribution to *Clinical Practice in Community Mental Health*.

* * *

LANING, Edward 1906-

PERSONAL: Surname is pronounced *Lann*-ing; born April 26, 1906, in Petersburg, Ill.; son of John Lane (a lawyer) and Mabel Irene (Smoot) Laning; married Mary Elizabeth Fife (an artist), August 26, 1933. *Education:* Studied at Art Institute of Chicago, summers, 1923-24, University of Chicago, 1925-27, and Art Students League of New York, 1927-30; studied in Europe, 1929, 1931. *Office:* Art Students League of New York, 215 West 57th St., New York, N.Y. 10003.

CAREER: Art Students League of New York, New York, N.Y., instructor in painting and drawing, 1932-33; Cooper Union, New York, N.Y., instructor in painting and drawing, 1940-42; artist and correspondent for *Life*, in Aleutian Islands and Italy, 1943-44; Kansas City Art Institute, Kansas City, Mo., instructor in painting and drawing and head of department, 1945-50; Art Students League of New York, instructor in painting and drawing, 1952—. Director of mural decoration at Beaux Arts Institute of Design, 1941-44; instructor at Pratt Institute, 1952-54; painter of murals for public buildings, including Mayflower Hotel (Washington, D.C.), and several Sheraton Hotels; work is in permanent collections in prominent museums, including Whitney Museum of American Art, National Academy of Design, and Metropolitan Museum of Art (New York, N.Y.).

MEMBER: National Society of Mural Painters (president, 1969-74), National Academy of Design, Art Students League of New York (life member). *Awards, honors:* Honorary mention from Art Institute of Chicago, 1932; Pauline Palmer Memorial Popular Award from Virginia Museum of Fine Arts, 1944; grant from American Academy of Arts and Letters, 1945; Kohnstamm Prize from Art Institute of Chicago, 1945; Purple Heart Medal for work as war correspondent; Guggenheim fellowship, 1945; Fulbright fellowship, Italy, 1950-52.

WRITINGS: Perspective for Artists, Pitman, 1967, new edition, 1968; *The Act of Drawing*, McGraw, 1971; *The Sketchbooks of Reginald Marsh*, New York Graphic Society, 1973. Contributor to *American Heritage*.

WORK IN PROGRESS: Autobiographical material.

SIDELIGHTS: Laning writes: "In my youth I was uncertain whether I wanted to paint or write. Painting won, and I have made my principal career as an artist. But in recent years I have begun to write and this work is a liberation. Writing is a delayed but welcome fulfillment."

BIOGRAPHICAL/CRITICAL SOURCES: Peyton Boswell, Jr., *Modern American Painting*, Dodd, 1939.

* * *

LAPONCE, Jean Antoine 1925-

PERSONAL: Born November 4, 1925, in Decize, France; son of Fernand Nicolas (a banker) and Fernande (Ramond) Laponce; married Joyce Price, August 15, 1950 (divorced); married Iza G. M. Fiszhaut (a librarian), April 7, 1968; children: (first marriage) Jean-Antoine, Marc, Patrice; (second marriage) Danielle. *Education:* Institut d'Etudes Politiques, diploma, 1947; University of California, Los Angeles, Ph.D., 1956. *Home:* 3989 Marguerite St., Vancouver, British Columbia, Canada. *Office:* Department of Political Science, University of British Columbia, Vancouver, British Columbia, Canada.

CAREER: University of Santa Clara, Santa Clara, Calif., instructor in political science, 1956; University of British Columbia, Vancouver, assistant professor, 1956-61, associate professor, 1961-66, professor of political science, 1966—. *Member:* International Political Science Association (president, 1973-76), American Political Science Association, Canadian Political Science Association (president, 1972-73), French Political Science Association. *Awards, honors:* Canada Council senior fellowship, 1960, 1967; Guggenheim fellowship, 1974.

WRITINGS: The Protection of Minorities, University of California Press, 1961; *The Government of France under the Fifth Republic*, University of California Press, 1962; *People versus Politics*, University of Toronto Press, 1970; (editor with Paul Smoker) *Experimentation and Simulation in Political Science*, University of Toronto Press, 1971.

WORK IN PROGRESS: Space and Politics, a study of the spacial archetypes of political perceptions, completion expected in 1976.

* * *

LaPRAY, (Margaret) Helen 1919-

PERSONAL: Born August 29, 1919, in Minneapolis, Minn.; daughter of George A. (a manager) and Laura (Normandin) LaPray. *Education:* University of Minnesota, B.S. and M.A.; Cornell University, Ph.D., 1958. *Home:* 2314 Tampa, El Cajon, Calif. 92020. *Office:* Department of Education, San Diego State University, San Diego, Calif. 92115.

CAREER: San Diego State University, San Diego, Calif., 1957—, now professor of education. Director of Learning Difficulties Clinic.

WRITINGS: Teaching Children to Become Independent Readers, Center of Applied Research in Education, 1972.

* * *

LAROCK, Bruce Edward 1940-

PERSONAL: Born December 24, 1940, in Berkeley, Calif.; son of Ralph W. (a diamond setter) and Hazel Marie (Lambert) Larock; married Susan Gardner, June 17, 1968; children: Lynne Marie. *Education:* Stanford University, B.S., 1962, M.S., 1963, Ph.D., 1966. *Residence:* Davis, Calif. 95616. *Office:* Department of Civil Engineering, University of California, Davis, Calif. 95616.

CAREER: University of California, Davis, assistant professor, 1966-72, associate professor of civil engineering, 1972—. Sabbatical year at University of Wales, Swansea, 1972-73.

WRITINGS: (With Donald Newnan) *Engineering Fundamentals*, Wiley, 1970.

WORK IN PROGRESS: Research on the hydrodynamics of free surface flows, and the mechanics and applications of stratified flows.

AVOCATIONAL INTERESTS: Building ship models and hiking in Sierra Nevada.

LARSEN, Knud S(onderhede) 1938-

PERSONAL: Born May 19, 1938, in Silkeborg, Denmark; married; children: three. *Education:* Brigham Young University, student, 1957-58, Ph.D., 1969; East Los Angeles College, student, 1959-61; California State University, Los Angeles, B.A., 1964, M.A., 1966. *Office:* Department of Psychology, Oregon State University, Corvallis, Ore. 97331.

CAREER: County of Los Angeles, Los Angeles, Calif., probation counselor, 1965-66; International Peace Research Institute, Oslo, Norway, researcher, 1968-69; University of Oslo, Oslo, Norway, lecturer in social psychology, spring, 1969; Oregon State University, Corvallis, assistant professor, 1969-74, associate professor of social psychology, 1974—. Research associate of International Peace Research Institute, 1969—. Instructor at Oregon State Penitentiary; lecturer at Annual Summer School in Peace Research, 1974. Chairman of Utah New Politics Coalition, 1967-68. Delegate to World Congress of Psychology, 1972.

MEMBER: Peace Science Society (International), American Psychological Association, Society for the Psychological Study of Social Issues, American Association of University Professors, Western Psychological Association, Rocky Mountain Psychological Association, Oregon Psychological Association, Benton Humane Society (president). *Awards, honors:* Norwegian Research Council for Science and the Humanities grant, 1970; Oregon Psychological Association research grant, 1971; National Science Foundation travel grant, 1971.

WRITINGS: *Social Cost and Aggression* (monograph), Peace Research Reviews, 1973; (contributor) Johan Galtung, editor, *Images of the Year Two Thousand: A Twelve Nation Study,* Mouton & Co., 1973; *The Nature of Aggression: A Social Cost Interpretation,* Nelson-Hall, in press. Contributor of about fifty articles to psychology and peace journals, including *Psychological Reports, Journal of Social Psychology, Social Behavior and Personality, Journal of Peace Research, Journal of Marriage and the Family,* and *Journal of Personality Assessment.* Member of editorial committee of *Bulletin of Peace Proposals,* 1970—; consulting reader for *Psychological Reports* and *Perceptual and Motor Skills,* 1974—.

WORK IN PROGRESS: Research on social cost, belief congruence, and race.

* * *

LARSON, Bob 1944-

PERSONAL: Born May 28, 1944, in Westwood, Calif.; son of Earl and Viola (Baum) Larson; married Kathryn Potter, June 24, 1968. *Education:* Attended McCook Junior College, 1962-63, and University of Nebraska, 1963-64. *Religion:* Protestant. *Office:* 275 South Jay, Denver, Colo. 80226.

CAREER: Rock entertainer in the Midwest and on the East coast, 1958-64; Radio station KICK, McCook, Neb., disc jockey, 1962-63; now an evangelist with Bob Larson Crusades, Denver, Colo. *Member:* International Platform Association, National Honors Society.

WRITINGS: *Rock and Roll: The Devil's Diversion*, Bob Larson Books, 1970; *Rock and the Church*, Creation House, 1971; *Hippies, Hindus, and Rock and Roll*, Creation House, 1972; *The Day Music Died*, Creation House, 1973; *Hell on Earth*, Creation House, 1974; *The Guru*, Bob Larson Ministries, 1974.

SIDELIGHTS: Bob Larson has twice circled the world in missionary evangelism campaigns. He has lectured at more than two thousand colleges. Presently he is involved in a one-half hour television series.

BIOGRAPHICAL/CRITICAL SOURCES: Newsweek, March 9, 1970.

* * *

LARSON, Charles R(aymond) 1938-

PERSONAL: Born January 14, 1938, in Sioux City, Iowa; son of Ray Olaf and Miriam (Kamphoefner) Larson; married Roberta Rubenstein, May 2, 1971. *Education:* University of Colorado, B.A., 1959, M.A., 1961; Indiana University, Ph.D., 1970. *Home:* 3600 Underwood St., Chevy Chase, Md. 20015. *Agent:* John Cushman Associates, Inc., 25 West 43rd St., New York, N.Y. 10036. *Office:* Department of Literature, American University, Washington, D.C. 20016.

CAREER: High school teacher in Burlington, Iowa, 1959-60, and Englewood, Colo., 1961-62; grammar school teacher (as Peace Corps volunteer) in Oraukwu, Eastern Nigeria, 1962-64; University of Colorado, Boulder, instructor in English, spring, 1965; American University, Washington, D.C., instructor in English, 1965-67; Indiana University, Bloomington, lecturer in comparative literature, 1967-70; American University, associate professor, 1970-73, professor of literature, 1974—. Lecturer at universities and colleges in eleven African countries, 1973. Principal juror for annual *Books Abroad*-English Speaking Union Literary Award for English as a second language, 1972—.

MEMBER: Modern Language Association of America, American Comparative Literature Association, African Studies Association. *Awards, honors:* U.S. Department of State grantee for Africa, 1973; Younger Humanist fellowship of National Endowment for the Humanities, 1974, to complete *The Novel in the Third World.*

WRITINGS: (Author of introduction) Joyce Cary, *Mr. Johnson,* Harper, 1969; (editor and author of introduction) *African Short Stories,* Collier Books, 1970 (published in England as *Modern African Stories,* Fontana, 1971); (editor and author of introduction) *Prejudice: Twenty Tales of Oppression and Liberation,* New American Library, 1971; *The Emergence of African Fiction,* Indiana University Press, 1972.

General editor of Collier Books "African-American Library," 1968—, with titles including: Ayi Kwei Armah, *The Beautyful Ones Are Not Yet Born,* 1968; Langston Hughes, *Not Without Laughter,* 1969; Cheikh Hamidou Kane, *Ambiguous Adventure,* 1969; James Ngugi, *Weep Not, Child,* 1969; Melvin B. Tolson, *Harlem Gallery,* 1969, and *Libretto for the Republic of Liberia,* 1970; William Attaway, *Blood on the Forge,* 1970; William Wells Brown, *Clotel: Or, the President's Daughter,* 1970; George Lamming, *In the Castle of My Skin,* 1970; Ferdinand Oyono, *Boy* (original title, *Houseboy*), 1970; Richard Rive, *Emergency,* 1970; Wole Soyinka, *The Interpreters,* 1970; Wallace Thurman, *The Blacker the Berry,* 1970; Peter Abrahams, *Mine Boy,* 1970; John Bayliss, editor, *Black Slave Narratives,* 1970; Mongo Beti, *King Lazarus,* 1970; Paul Laurence Dunbar, *The Sport of the Gods,* 1970; Legson Kayira, *The Looming Shadow,* 1970; Camara Laye, *The Radiance of the King,* 1971, and *A Dream of Africa,* 1971; Victor S. Reid, *The Leopard,* 1971; Ama Ata Aidoo, *The Dilemma of a Ghost,* 1971; Ezekiel Mphahlele, *The Wan-*

derers, 1971; Eric Walrond, *Tropic Death,* 1972; and a number of other books.

Story, "Up From Slavery," included in *Prize Stories 1971: The O. Henry Awards.* Contributor of more than thirty articles, about sixty reviews, and fiction, poetry, and satire to periodicals, including *Saturday Review, Atlantic Monthly, Nation, Kenyon Review, Books Abroad, Harper's, Negro Digest, American Scholar, Africa Today, New Republic,* and *Africana Library Journal.* Associate editor, *Pucred* (satirical literary review), 1972-74; member of editorial board, *Books Abroad,* 1972—; books editor, *English Around the World* (publication of English-Speaking Union), 1972—.

WORK IN PROGRESS: The Novel in the Third World; editing Volume II of *African Short Stories;* a novel, *The Spider Man;* a literary satire, *Academia Nuts.*

* * *

LARSON, Harold J. 1934-

PERSONAL: Born November 16, 1934, in Iowa; son of Otto L. (a telegrapher) and Hazel Larson; married Monice I. Shipman, April 8, 1953 (died September 15, 1959); married Marie J. Reilly, April 11, 1962; children: Douglas, Josef, Hugh, Rachel. *Education:* Iowa State University, B.S., 1956, M.S., 1957, Ph.D., 1960. *Home:* 402 Second St., Pacific Grove, Calif. 93950. *Office:* Code 55La, Naval Postgraduate School, Monterey, Calif. 93940.

CAREER: Naval Postgraduate School, Monterey, Calif., 1962—, now professor. Fulbright professor, University of Sao Paulo, 1970-71. Consultant to North American Aviation, Litton Industries, Stanford Research Institute, Field Research, Western Antec, and other industries, 1962-70. *Member:* American Statistical Association, Sigma Xi.

WRITINGS: Introduction to Probability Theory and Statistical Inference, Wiley, 1969, 2nd edition, 1974; *Introduction to the Theory of Statistics,* Wiley, 1973; *Statistics: An Introduction,* Wiley, in press. Contributor to *Annals of Mathematical Statistics, Biometrikan, Technometrics,* and *American Statistician.*

* * *

LASKY, Melvin J(onah) 1920-

PERSONAL: Born January 15, 1920, in New York, N.Y.; son of Samuel (a manufacturer) and Esther (Kantrowitz) Lasky; married Brigitte Newiger, 1946 (divorced, 1974); children: Vivienne, Oliver. *Education:* City College of New York (now City College of the City University of New York), B.S.S., 1939; University of Michigan, M.A., 1940; Columbia University, graduate study, 1940-43. *Home:* 37 Godfrey St., Chelsea, London S.W.3, England. *Office: Encounter* Magazine, 59 St. Martins Lane, London S.W.1, England.

CAREER: New Leader, New York, N.Y., literary editor, 1941-43; *Der Monat,* Berlin, Germany, editor, 1948-58; *Encounter,* London, England, editor and publisher, 1958—. Editor and publisher, Library Press, New York, 1970—, Alcover Press, London, 1971—. *Military service:* U.S. Army, 1943-46; became captain. *Awards, honors:* Sesquicentennial Award from University of Michigan, 1967.

WRITINGS: (Editor) *The Hungarian Revolution: A White Book,* Praeger, 1957, reprinted, Books for Libraries, 1970; *Africa for Beginners: A Traveler's Notebook,* introduction by Jacques Barzun, Lippincott, 1962; *Utopia and Revolution,* University of Chicago Press, 1975. Contributor to periodicals, including *New York Times* and *Partisan Review.* Editor, *Anchor Review,* 1956-57.

* * *

LATTA, Richard 1946-

PERSONAL: Born October 16, 1946, in East Chicago, Ind.; son of John (a welder) and Ann (Nastav) Latta; married Mary Tripodi (a teacher), August 24, 1968; children: Tena, Sara. *Education:* Illinois Benedictine College, B.S., 1968. *Home:* 2418 Nuclear Dr., Joliet, Ill. 60435. *Office:* Forest Park Public Schools, 939 Beloit, Forest Park, Ill. 60130.

CAREER: Forest Park Public Schools, Forest Park, Ill., teacher of junior high school science, 1968—. Free-lance writer of word find puzzles, 1970—. *Member:* National Education Association, Illinois Education Association.

WRITINGS: Rain (poems), Windless Orchard, 1970; *Concrete Poems,* Cycle Press, 1972; *Creative Writing of Concrete Poetry for Schools,* Mafex Publishing, 1974; *A Puzzle Book,* Price, Stern, 1974; *Science Puzzles,* Business Stimulus, 1974; *Letter Recognition,* Mafex Publishing, 1975. Contributor of poems, short stories and articles to more than fifty-five journals. Advisor to *Current Science,* 1972-73.

WORK IN PROGRESS: A mathematics puzzle book, for Instructional Fair; a series of word find puzzles for schools, Gel-Sten Supply Co.; a series of five puzzle books for various curriculums in schools, Center for Applied Research in Education; a series of five books for teachers, with supplemental materials, Gamco Co.

* * *

LAUBE, Clifford J(ames) 1891-1974

1891—August 21, 1974; American journalist, publisher, poet, editor. Obituaries: *New York Times,* August 22, 1974.

* * *

LAUER, Robert H(arold) 1933-

PERSONAL: Born June 28, 1933, in St. Louis, Mo.; son of Earl Ervin and Frances P. (Bushen) Lauer; married Jeannette C. Pentecost, July 2, 1954; children: Jon Robert, Julie Anne, Jeffrey David. *Education:* Washington University, St. Louis, Mo., B.S., 1954, Ph.D., 1970; Southern Seminary, B.D., 1958; Southern Illinois University at Edwardsville, M.A., 1969. *Home:* 2545 Guildford, Florissant, Mo. *Office:* Department of Sociology, Southern Illinois University, Edwardsville, Ill. 62025.

CAREER: Clergyman of Salem Baptist Church, Florissant, Mo., 1958-68; Southern Illinois University at Edwardsville, lecturer, 1968-69, instructor, 1969-70, assistant professor, 1970-73, associate professor of sociology, 1973—, chairman of department, 1972—. Former vice-chairman of Florissant Charter Commission. *Member:* American Sociological Association, Society for Cross-Cultural Research, Midwest Sociological Society, Illinois Sociological Association.

WRITINGS: Perspectives on Social Change, Allyn & Bacon, 1973; *Social Problems,* W. C. Brown, in press; (with Warren Handel) *The Theory and Application of Social Psychology,* Houghton, in press. Contributor of about two hundred articles to religious and children's magazines.

WORK IN PROGRESS: Temporal Man: The Social Sources and Meaning of Time; research on changing patterns of international inequality.

LAUFFER, Armand A(lbert) 1933-

PERSONAL: Born May 18, 1933, in Antwerp, Belgium; naturalized U.S. citizen in 1943; son of Georges (a businessman) and Gisele (a teacher; maiden name, Sokalska) Lauffer; married Rochelle Lupovitch (a teacher), January 24, 1960; children: Joshua, Tamar. *Education:* Roosevelt University, B.A., 1956; Wayne State University, M.S.W., 1959; Brandeis University, Ph.D., 1969. *Religion:* Jewish. *Home:* 1408 Wells St., Ann Arbor, Mich. 48104. *Office:* School of Social Work, University of Michigan, 1015 East Huron St., Ann Arbor, Mich. 48104.

CAREER: Jewish Community Center and Jewish Family Service, Long Beach, Calif., youth supervisor and project director, 1961-65; University of Michigan, School of Social Work, Ann Arbor, associate professor, 1968-73, professor of social planning, 1973—, director of Program for Continuing Education in the Human Services, 1968—. Designer of gamed social simulations. Consultant to National Institute of Mental Health, Social and Rehabilitation Service, and Administration on Aging. *Member:* National Association of Social Workers, National Conference on Social Welfare, American Sociological Association, Council on Social Work Education. *Awards, honors:* Fulbright scholar in Israel, 1974-75.

WRITINGS: (With Arnold Gurin and others) *Community Organization Curriculum Report,* Council on Social Work Education, 1971; (with Joan Levin Ecklein) *Community Organizers and Social Planners,* Wiley, 1972; *The Aim of the Game: A Primer on the Use and Design of Gamed Social Simulations,* Gamed Simulations, 1973; *Area Planning for the Aging,* Administration on Aging, U.S. Department of Health, Education and Welfare, 1974.

WORK IN PROGRESS: Transcending the Now: Practice in Mental Health Continuing Education; Locality Planning for the Human Services.

* * *

LAWSON, (Richard) Alan 1934-

PERSONAL: Born January 13, 1934, in Providence, R.I.; son of Herman Albert (a physician) and Norma (a nurse; maiden name, Flaiger) Lawson. *Education:* Brown University, A.B., 1955; University of Wisconsin, M.A., 1956; University of Michigan, Ph.D., 1966. *Politics:* Independent Democrat. *Home:* 26 Circuit Rd., Chestnut Hill, Mass. 02167. *Office:* Department of History, Boston College, Chestnut Hill, Mass. 02167.

CAREER: Deerfield Academy, Deerfield, Mass., history teacher, 1958-61; University of California, Irvine, assistant professor of history, 1965-69; Smith College, Northampton, Mass., assistant professor, 1969-70, associate professor of history, 1971-72; Boston College, Chestnut Hill, Mass., associate professor of history, 1972—. *Military service:* U.S. Army, 1956-58. *Member:* American Historical Association, Society of American Historians, Organization of American Historians.

WRITINGS: The Failure of Independent Liberalism, Putnam, 1971; *The Great Depression and the New Deal: Ideas in Crisis,* Harcourt, in press.

WORK IN PROGRESS: A Documentary History of American Ideas.

SIDELIGHTS: Lawson writes: "My interest in the cultural history of the New Deal period derived from some early investigation into the fight by Jehovah's Witnesses to gain justice and toleration during the 1930's. That examination of how a fringe group made vital contributions to the way the Constitution has come to be applied suggested to me that there was much more in the 1930's to occupy historans' attention than just the New Deal and its Marxist opposition. My plans are to build on these studies toward a general account of the relationship between ideas and power in American history."

* * *

LAWSON, E(verett) LeRoy 1938-

PERSONAL: Born May 17, 1938, in Tillamook, Ore.; son of E. LaVerne (a grocer) and Margery (Foltz) Lawson; married Joy A. Whitney, June 11, 1960; children: Kimberly Joy, Candace Annette, Lane Whitney. *Education:* Northwest Christian College, B.A., 1960; Cascade College, A.B., 1962; Reed College, M.A.T., 1965; Vanderbilt University, Ph.D., 1970. *Office:* East 38th Street Christian Church, 6190 East 38th St., Indianapolis, Ind. 46226.

CAREER: Ordained Christian Church minister, 1959; minister in Portland, Ore., 1959-65; high school English teacher in Portland, 1962-64; Milligan College, Milligan College, Tenn., assistant professor, 1965-68, associate professor of English, 1970-73, chairman of department, 1965-68, vice-president, 1970-73; East 38th Street Christian Church, Indianapolis, Ind., senior minister, 1973—.

WRITINGS: Very Sure of God: Religious Language in the Poetry of Robert Browning, Vanderbilt University Press, 1974; (with Tetsunao Yamamori) *Introducing Church Growth*, Standard Publishing, 1975.

* * *

LAWSON, F(loyd) Melvyn 1907-

PERSONAL: Born June 5, 1907, in Sacramento, Calif.; son of Gray (a railroad yardman) and Lena Belle (Dunkeson) Lawson; married Verna Margarethe Kopka, June 29, 1932. *Education:* University of the Pacific, A.B., 1928, M.A., 1936. *Politics:* Republican. *Religion:* Lutheran. *Home:* 2700 22nd St., Sacramento, Calif. 95818.

CAREER: Sacramento City Schools, Sacramento, Calif., teacher and counselor, 1929-36, high school vice-principal, 1936-40, principal, 1940-43, assistant superintendent of schools, 1946-48, deputy superintendent, 1948-60, superintendent, 1960-68; California State University, Sacramento, lecturer in administration and counseling, 1968-71. Vice-chairman of Sacramento Community Hospitals, 1953—. *Military service:* U.S. Naval Reserve, active duty, 1943-46; became lieutenant senior grade. *Member:* National Congress of Parents and Teachers (honorary life member), California Museum Association (vice-president, 1952-59), California Writers Club, Sacramento Camellia Festival Association (president, 1967-68), Theta Alpha Phi, Pi Gamma Mu, Phi Delta Kappa, Phi Kappa Phi, Rotary International (president of Sacramento chapter, 1948-49), Shrine (potentate of Ben Ali Temple, 1961), York Rite Masons, Scottish Rite Masons. *Awards, honors:* Ped.D. from University of the Pacific, 1950.

WRITINGS: (With wife, Verna Kopka Lawson) *Our America Today and Yesterday*, Heath, 1938, teacher's guidebook and student study guide, 1939; *My Gypsy Mind* (poems), Hibiscus Press, 1975. Composer of music and author of lyrics for recordings of dance band music, "Camellia Girl and Eleven Other Songs," Melwood Music, 1973, and "Ask Your Heart," Melwood Music, 1975.

LAWYER, Annabel Glenn 1906(?)-1974

1906(?)—October 12, 1974; American author of children's books, stories, poems. Obituaries: *Washington Post*, October 12, 1974.

* * *

LEACH, Maria 1892-

PERSONAL: Born April 30, 1892, in Brooklyn, N.Y.; daughter of Benjamin H. (a lawyer) and Mary Eliza (Davis) Doane; married Mac Edward Leach (a university professor), November 11, 1917; children: Macdonald Harvey. *Education:* Earlham College, B.A., 1914; University of Illinois, A.M., 1917; Johns Hopkins University, further graduate study, 1918-19. *Religion:* Society of Friends (Quakers). *Home address:* R.R. 1, Barrington, Nova Scotia BOW 7EO, Canada.

CAREER: Funk & Wagnalls Co., New York, N.Y., dictionary editor, 1936-51; editor for McGraw-Hill Book Co., Blakiston Division, 1953-58. *Member:* International Folk Music Council, American Anthropological Association, American Folklore Society, American Society for Ethnohistory, Canadian Folksong Society, Northeast Folklore Society, North Carolina Folklore Society.

WRITINGS: (Compiler and editor) *Dictionary of Folklore, Mythology, and Legend*, Funk, Volume I, 1949, Volume II, 1950; *The Turnspit Dog*, Aladdin Books, 1952; *The Soup Stone: The Magic of Familiar Things*, Funk, 1954; *The Beginning: Creation Myths Around the World*, Funk, 1956; *The Rainbow Book of American Folk Tales and Legends* (for young people), World Publishing, 1958; *The Thing at the Foot of the Bed and Other Scary Stories* (for young people), World Publishing, 1959.

Noodles, Nitwits, and Numskulls (juvenile), World Publishing, 1961; *God Had a Dog: Folklore of the Dog*, Rutgers University Press, 1961; *The Luck Book* (juvenile), World Publishing, 1964; *How the People Sang the Mountains Up: How and Why Stories*, Viking, 1967; *Riddle Me, Riddle Me*, Viking, 1970; *Whistle in the Graveyard: Folktales to Chill Your Bones*, Viking, 1974.

* * *

LEAN, E(dward) Tangye 1911-1974

February 23, 1911—October 28, 1974; British journalist, broadcast director, author of novels and nonfiction works. Obituaries: *AB Bookman's Weekly*, December 2, 1974.

* * *

LEAVITT, Ruby Rohrlich

PERSONAL: Born in Montreal, Quebec, Canada; daughter of Maurice and Elise Rohrlich; divorced; children: Michael R., Matthew R. *Education:* New York University, B.A. (cum laude), 1940, Ph.D., 1969; Adelphi University, M.S., 1962. *Home:* 61 Jane St., Apt. 6A, New York, N.Y. 10014. *Office:* Department of Social Science, Borough of Manhattan Community College of the City University of New York, 1633 Broadway, New York, N.Y. 10020.

CAREER: Borough of Manhattan Community College of the City University of New York, New York, N.Y., assistant professor, 1971-74, associate professor of antropology, 1974—. Propaganda analyst for Office of War Information, 1942-44. *Member:* American Anthropological Association (fellow), Society for Applied Anthropology (fellow), Women's Coalition of Latin Americanists, New York Women's Anthropology Caucus, Phi Beta Kappa, Sigma Delta Omicron.

WRITINGS: (Contributor) Vivian Gornick and B. K. Moran, editors, *Woman in Sexist Society*, Basic Books, 1971; *The Puerto Ricans: Culture Change and Language Deviance*, University of Arizona Press, 1974; (editor) *Women Cross-Culturally: Change and Challenge*, Mouton & Co., in press; *Anthropological Approaches to Women's Studies*, Harper, in press.

WORK IN PROGRESS: Women and Men, a teaching module with Eleanor B. Leacock.

* * *

LEE, Brother Basil Leo 1909-1974 (George Leslie Lee)

1909—September 27, 1974; American educator and author. Obituaries; *New York Times*, September 28, 1974.

* * *

LEE, Douglas A(llen) 1932-

PERSONAL: Born November 3, 1932, in Carmel, Ind.; son of Ralph Henry (an insurance underwriter) and Flossie (Chandler) Lee; married Beverly Haskell (a teacher and writer), September 2, 1961. *Education:* DePauw University, B.Mus., 1950; University of Michigan, M.Mus., 1958, Ph.D., 1968. *Politics:* Independent. *Religion:* Christian. *Home:* 6420 Oneida, Wichita, Kan. 67206. *Office:* College of Fine Arts, Wichita State University, Wichita, Kan. 67208.

CAREER: Mount Union College, Alliance, Ohio, instructor in musicology, 1959-61; University of Michigan, Ann Arbor, instructor in musicology, 1961-63; Wichita State University, Wichita, Kan., assistant professor, 1964-68, associate professor, 1968-74, professor of musicology, 1974—. *Military service:* U.S. Army, 1956-57; served in special services of Far East Theatre. *Member:* American Musicological Society, Music Teachers National Association, American Society for 18th Century Studies, Pi Kappa Lambda, Phi Kappa Phi. *Awards, honors:* DePauw University rector scholar, 1950-54.

WRITINGS: The Works of Christoph Nichelmann: A Thematic Index, Information Coordinators, 1971; (editor) *Christoph Nichelmann: Two Keyboard Concertos*, A-R Editions, 1975. Contributor to *Grove's Dictionary of Music and Musicians*, 6th edition, and to *Music Quarterly*, *Kansas Music Review*.

WORK IN PROGRESS: An Index of Sources: Solo Sonatas of Franz Benda (1709-1786).

SIDELIGHTS: Lee told *CA* that his overriding concern "is to bring to musical performance a high degree of musical scholarship, and to musical scholarship a sensitive awareness of musical performance and its problems."

* * *

LEE, John A(lexander) 1891-

PERSONAL: Born October 31, 1891, in Dunedin, New Zealand; son of Alfredo and Isabel (Taylor) Lee; married Mollie Guy, March 10, 1919; children: three. *Education:* Attended public schools in New Zealand. *Home:* 48 Seaview Terrace, Auckland, New Zealand. *Office address:* Vital Books Ltd., Box 8601, Auckland, New Zealand.

CAREER: Labour member of New Zealand parliament, 1922-43, undersecretary to prime minister, 1936, minister in charge of house construction, 1936-40; writer. Member of board of directors, Printing Service Ltd., and Democratic Property Ltd., 1940-46, Vital Books Ltd., 1950-75. President, Auckland Rugby League, 1935-40. *Military service:* New Zealand Army, 1915-18; served in France; became sergeant; received Distinguished Conduct Medal. *Member:* P.E.N. (honorary president of New Zealand branch, 1969). *Awards, honors:* LL.D., Dunedin University, 1965.

WRITINGS: Children of the Poor, Vanguard, 1934, reprinted, May Fair Books, 1963; *The Hunted* (novel), Laurie, 1936, reprinted, May Fair Books, 1963; *Civilian into Soldier*, Laurie, 1937, reprinted, May Fair Books, 1963; *Socialism in New Zealand*, Laurie, 1938; *The Yanks Are Coming* (novel), Laurie, 1943; *Shining with the Shiner* (stories), F. W. Mead, 1945, reprinted, May Fair Books, 1963; *Simple on the Soap-box* (autobiography), Collins, 1963, reprinted, 1975; *Shiner Slattery*, Collins, 1964, reprinted, 1975; *Rhetoric at the Red Dawn* (recollections), Collins, 1965; *The Lee Way to Public Speaking: For Candidates for Public Office, Executives, Teachers, Examinees, Mothers and Fathers (of Large Families), with Much Useful Advice for Campaigners*, Collins, 1965; *Delinquent Days*, Collins, 1967; *Political Notebooks*, Taylor, 1973. Also author of political pamphlets and narratives for educational films. Contributor to *Auckland Herald*.

WORK IN PROGRESS: Four books, *Mine Is the Kingdom, The Politician and the Fairy, A New Zealand Cavalcade,* and *Rolling Stones, Roughnecks*.

SIDELIGHTS: Lee, who was a "Borstal boy," and was further imprisoned from 1911-1912, was expelled from New Zealand's Labour Party in 1940 for writing "Psychopathology in Politics," which was alleged to have referred to the Labour Prime Minister then holding office.

* * *

LEE, Molly K(yung) S(ook) C(hang) 1934-

PERSONAL: Born November 16, 1934, in Seoul, Korea; daughter of Suk Young Chang; married Chung Sik Lee (a professor of government), June 10, 1959; children: Margaret. *Education:* College of St. Rose, B.S., 1959; New York University, M.A., 1962, Ph.D., 1971. *Home:* 48 Idle Day Dr., Centerport, N.Y. 11721. *Office:* Dean of Division of Humanities, New York Institute of Technology, Box 170, Old Westbury, N.Y. 11568.

CAREER: New York Institute of Technology, instructor, 1964-66, assistant professor, 1966-71, associate professor, 1971-73, professor of social sciences, 1973—, chairman of department of social sciences, 1966-71, dean of Division of Humanities, 1971—. *Member:* American Association of University Professors, American Economic Association, Middle States Association of Colleges and Secondary Schools, New York State Economic Association.

WRITINGS: Off-Campus Study Guide for Economics, two volumes, New York Institute of Technology Press, 1972-73.

WORK IN PROGRESS: Economic History of Asia, for Gale.

* * *

LEE, Robert E(arl) 1906-

PERSONAL: Born October 9, 1906, in Kinston, N.C.; son of Mike (a merchant) and May (Rouse) Lee; married Louise Gattis, April 16, 1932; children: Robert E., Jr., Charles F., Betty Lee Sexton. *Education:* Wake Forest University, B.S., 1928, LL.B., 1928; Columbia University, M.A., 1929; Duke University, LL.M., 1935, S.J.D., 1941. *Politics:* Democrat. *Religion:* Baptist. *Home:* 2180 Faculty Dr., Winston-Salem, N.C. 27106. *Office:* School of Law, Wake Forest University, Winston-Salem, N.C. 27109.

CAREER: Temple University, Philadelphia, Pa., instructor, 1929-38, assistant professor, 1938-42, professor of law, 1942-45; U.S. Army University, Schrivenham, England, professor of law, 1945-46; Wake Forest University, Winston-Salem, N.C., professor of law, 1946—. Regional counsel to U.S. Office of Price Stabilization, 1951-52. *Member:* American Business Law Association (secretary-treasurer, 1940-45), North Carolina Bar Association (vice-president, 1963-64), Forsyth County Bar Association.

WRITINGS: Advanced Business Law, Bernbaum-Jackson, 1934; (with S. Homer Smith) *Cases on Contracts*, Westbrook, 1937, 2nd edition, 1948; *Law of Contracts*, Westbrook, 1946, 2nd edition, 1948; *North Carolina Family Law*, three volumes, Michie Company, 1963; *Blackbeard the Pirate*, Blair, 1974. Author of legal column, "This Is the Law," for almost one hundred North Carolina newspapers, 1954—.

* * *

LEEMING, Glenda 1943-

PERSONAL: Born June 4, 1943, in Leeds, England; daughter of Frederick Albert and Lorna (Wright) Leeming; married Simon Trussler (a writer), August 23, 1966; children: Nicholas and Anna (twins). *Education:* University College, University of London, B.A. (honors), 1965, M.Phil., 1967. *Politics:* Socialist. *Home:* Great Robhurst, Woodchurch, Ashford, Kent, England. *Agent:* Donald Copeman, London W.C.1, England.

CAREER: Freelance writer. Lecturer in English literature and modern drama.

WRITINGS: (With husband, Simon Trussler) *The Plays of Arnold Wesker*, Gollancz, 1971; *Arnold Wesker* (monograph), Longmans, Green, 1972; *Who's Who in Jane Austen and the Brontes*, Hamish Hamilton, 1974; *John Arden* (monograph), Longmans, Green, 1974; *Who's Who in Thomas Hardy*, Hamish Hamilton, 1975.

* * *

LEES, John D(avid) 1936-

PERSONAL: Born August 27, 1936, in Bury, England; son of Joseph and Alice (Leeming) Lees; married Moira Euphamia Jean Benson, December 19, 1964; children: Fergus John, Fionn David, Alasdair Diarmid. *Education:* St. Edmund Hall, Oxford, B.A. (honors), 1960; University of Michigan, M.A., 1962; University of Manchester, Ph.D., 1964. *Politics:* Liberal. *Religion:* Methodist. *Home:* 25 Larchwood, Keele, Staffordshire ST5 5BG, England. *Office:* Department of American Studies, University of Keele, Keele, Staffordshire ST5 5BG, England.

CAREER: University of Keele, Keele, Staffordshire, England, lecturer, 1964-69, senior lecturer in U.S. Government, 1969—. Parliamentary candidate in British General Elections, 1964, 1966. *Military service:* Royal Air Force, 1955-57. *Member:* American Political Science Association, Political Studies Association, British Association for American Studies (member of executive committee, 1973—). *Awards, honors:* Gilbert Campion Award from Hansard Society for Parliamentary Government, 1964.

WRITINGS: The Committee System of the U.S. Con-

gress, Routledge & Kegan Paul, 1967; *The Political System of the United States*, Humanities, 1969, revised edition, 1975; (with Richard Kimber) *Political Parties in Modern Britain*, Routledge & Kegan Paul, 1972. Contributor to journals in his field.

WORK IN PROGRESS: Editing and contributing to *Committees in Legislatures: A Comparative Analysis*, and a study of Congress.

AVOCATIONAL INTERESTS: Playing soccer and cricket, travel.

* * *

LEFCO, Helene 1922-

PERSONAL: Born August 25, 1922, in New York, N.Y.; daughter of Seymour S. (a physician) and Dorothy (a pianist; maiden name, Cherurg) Wanderman; married Herman Lefco (a business executive), July 26, 1945; children: Arthur, Anthony, Deborah. *Education:* Attended Cornell University, 1939-41; New York University, B.A., 1943. *Home and office:* 1018 Serpentine Lane, Wyncote, Pa. 19095.

CAREER: Professional dance therapist, working in mental hospitals with psychotics, regressed cases, and drug addict cases; free-lance writer.

WRITINGS: Dance Therapy, Nelson-Hall, 1973. Contributor to magazines.

WORK IN PROGRESS: A film about dance therapy; two books.

SIDELIGHTS: "If I am not writing," Helene Lefco wrote, "I feel that something is missing in my life. While I am writing, I feel that I am missing too many other things in life. On balance, I prefer to be writing."

* * *

LEGAULT, Albert 1938-

PERSONAL: Born June 7, 1938, in Montreal, Quebec, Canada; son of Fortunat and Felecilda (Geoffrion) Legault; married Cosima Dittus, July 27, 1964; children: Cornelia. *Education:* College of St. Laurent, B.A., 1959; University of Chicago, M.A., 1961; Graduate School of International Studies, Geneva, Switzerland, Ph.D., 1964. *Religion:* Roman Catholic. *Home:* 2038 Laurier Blvd., Sillery, Quebec 6, Canada. *Office:* Department of Political Science, Laval University, Quebec, Quebec, Canada.

CAREER: Professor of political science and director general of Quebec Center of International Relations at Laval University, Quebec, Quebec.

WRITINGS: Le concept de la dissuasion: Ses exigences strategiques et ses incidences sur la politique, Les Presses de Savoie, 1964; *Detterrence and the Atlantic Alliance*, translation by Archibald Day, Canadian Institute of International Affairs, 1966; *Bibliography: Peace-Keeping Operations*, World Veterans Federation, 1967; (with George Lindsey) *Le feu nucleaire*, Editions du Seuil, 1973, translation published as *The Dynamics of the Nuclear Balance*, Cornell University Press, 1974.

WORK IN PROGRESS: Comparative Analysis of Dyadic Interstate Conflict.

* * *

LEGGETT, B(obby) J(oe) 1938-

PERSONAL: Born February 25, 1938, in Alamo, Tenn.; son of Garland Harris (a farmer) and Maggie (Bodkin) Leggett; married Corinne Tickle, December 26, 1960; children: Leslie Katherine, William Harris. *Education:* Lambuth College, B.A., 1960; University of Florida, M.A., 1962, Ph.D., 1965. *Home:* 7613 Navarre Dr., Knoxville, Tenn. 37919. *Office:* Department of English, University of Tennessee, Knoxville, Tenn. 37916.

CAREER: University of Tennessee, Knoxville, assistant professor, 1965-71, associate professor of English, 1971—, assistant dean for graduate studies, 1970-71. *Member:* South Atlantic Modern Language Association.

WRITINGS: Housman's Land of Lost Content, University of Tennessee Press, 1970. Contributor to *Explicator*, *English Language*, *Victorian Newsletter*, *Walt Whitman Review*, *Tennessee Studies in Literature*, and *Modern Language Quarterly*.

WORK IN PROGRESS: The Art of A. E. Housman.

* * *

LEHMANN, Irvin J(ack) 1927-

PERSONAL: Born September 19, 1927, in Winnipeg, Manitoba, Canada; son of Azary and Bessie (Juravsky) Lehmann; married Ruth Claire Slusky, June 16, 1957; children: Ilene Ann, Allan Blair. *Education:* University of Manitoba, B.Sc., and B.Paed., both 1950, B.Ed., 1952, M.Ed., 1954; University of Wisconsin, Ph.D., 1957. *Residence:* Okemos, Mich. *Office:* Evaluation Services, Michigan State University, East Lansing, Mich. 48823.

CAREER: Teacher in public schools in Winnipeg, Manitoba, 1951-54; Michigan State University, East Lansing, instructor, 1957-60, assistant professor, 1960-63, associate professor, 1963-66, professor of education, 1967—. *Member:* American Psychological Association (fellow), American Educational Research Association, American Statistical Association, National Council on Measurement in Education (executive officer, 1964—).

WRITINGS: (With W. A. Mehrens) *Standardized Tests in Education*, Holt, 1969, 2nd edition, in press; (editor with Mehrens) *Educational Research: Readings in Focus*, Holt, 1972; (with Mehrens) *Measurement and Evaluation in Education and Psychology*, Holt, 1973. Contributor to *Journal of Educational Psychology*, *Journal of Clinical Psychology*, *Journal of Educational Measurement*, and *Review of Educational Research*.

AVOCATIONAL INTERESTS: Model railroading, swimming (swims at least one-half mile every morning).

* * *

LEINFELLNER, Werner (Hubertus) 1921-

PERSONAL: Born January 17, 1921, in Graz, Austria; son of Hubertus H. (an official) and Maria (Woschner) Leinfellner; married Elisabeth Rupertsberger, October 28, 1960; children: Ruth. *Education:* University of Graz, student, 1941-42; University of Vienna, M.S. (equivalent), 1945, Ph.D., 1959. *Home:* 839 South 15th St., Lincoln, Neb. 68508. *Office:* 1036 Oldfather Hall, University of Nebraska, Lincoln, Neb. 68508.

CAREER: University of Munich, Munich, Germany, assistant in philosophy, 1960-62; University of Vienna, Vienna, Austria, lecturer in philosophy, 1964-67; Institute of Advanced Studies, Vienna, Austria, assistant professor of philosophy and Ford Foundation fellow, 1964-67; University of Nebraska, Lincoln, professor of philosophy, 1967—.

Guest professor at University of Basel, 1966, and University of Heidelberg, 1973. *Member:* Philosophy of Science Association, Association for Symbolic Logic, American Philosophical Association, Association of Philosophical Journals Editors, American Society for Value Inquiry, Kuratorium Institut fuer Kunst und Wissenschaft (Vienna). *Awards, honors:* Theodor Koerner Foundation Prizes, 1964, 1968.

WRITINGS: Struktur und Aufbau wissenschaftlicher Theorien (title means "Structure and Construction of Scientific Theories"), Physica, 1965; *Einfuehrung in die Erkenntnis- und Wissenschaftstheorie Hochschultaschenbuch* (title means "Introduction into Philosophy of Science and Knowledge Theory"), Bibliographisches Institut, 1965, 2nd edition, 1967; *Die Entstehung der Theorie: Eine Analyse des kritischen Denkens in der Antike* (title means "The Rise of Theories: An Analysis of the Critical Thinking of Antiquity"), Alber, 1966; (editor with W. Kroeber-Riel and G. Eberlein) *Forschungslogik der Sozialwissenschaften*, Bertelsmann Universitaets-Verlag, in press; (editor with E. Koehler) *Recent Developments in the Methodology of Social Sciences*, Reidel, in press; (with wife, Elisabeth Leinfellner) *Ontologie und Semantik: Strukturelle Ontologie der Sozial- und Naturwissenschaften*, Duncker & Humblot, in press. Contributor to scholarly journals. Editor-in-chief, *Theory and Decision: An International Journal for Philosophy and Methodology*, 1970.

WORK IN PROGRESS: A book on philosophy of the social sciences.

* * *

LEIPER, Henry Smith 1891-1975

1891—January 22, 1975; American church official, ecumenist, author and editor of religious works. Obituaries: *New York Times*, January 23, 1975; *AB Bookman's Weekly*, February 17, 1975.

* * *

LEITMANN, George 1925-

PERSONAL: Born May 24, 1925, in Vienna, Austria; naturalized U.S. citizen in 1944; son of Joseph L. (a certified public accountant) and Stella (Fischer) Leitmann; married Nancy Lloyd (a businesswoman), January 28, 1955; children: Josef Lloyd, Elaine Michele. *Education:* Columbia University, B.S., 1949, M.A., 1950; University of California, Berkeley, Ph.D., 1956. *Home:* 285 Fairlawn Dr., Berkeley, Calif. 94708. *Office:* Department of Mechanical Engineering, University of California, Berkeley, Calif. 94720.

CAREER: U.S. Naval Ordnance Test Station, China Lake, Calif., physicist and head of section, 1950-57; University of California, Berkeley, assistant professor, 1957-59, associate professor, 1959-63, professor of engineering science, 1963—, Miller Professor, 1966-67, chairman of division of applied mechanics, 1970-71, vice-chairman for graduate study and research in mechanical engineering, 1972-74. Member of architectural committee of Timber Cove, 1966—. *Military service:* U.S. Army, 1944-46; became second lieutenant; received Croix de Guerre. *Member:* British Interplanetary Society (fellow).

WRITINGS: Optimization Techniques, Academic Press, 1962; *Problems in Mechanics*, McGraw, 1964; *An Introduction to Optimal Control*, McGraw, 1966; *Topics in Optimization*, Academic Press, 1967; *Quantitative and Qualitative Games*, Academic Press, 1969; (translator from the German) Bela Balazs, *The Mantle of Dreams*, Kodansha, 1974; *Cooperative and Non-Cooperative Many Player Differential Games* (monograph), Springer, 1974. Associate editor of *Journal of Optimization Theory and Application*, 1967—, *Journal of Mathematical Analysis and Application*, 1970—, and *Astronautica Acta*, 1974—.

WORK IN PROGRESS: Editing lecture volume of Centre International des Sciences Mecanique seminars on decision making.

* * *

LeMON, Cal 1945-

PERSONAL: Born December 7, 1945, in Niagara Falls, N.Y.; son of Robert Ernest (a minister) and Marie (a minister; maiden name, Borsellino) LeMon; married Kathleen Zezzo, August 5, 1967; children: Daphne Rae. *Education:* Evangel College, B.A., 1968; Gordon-Conwell Theological Seminary, M.Div., 1971. *Home:* 464 West St., Reading, Mass. 01867. *Office:* Cambridge Christian Center, 1430 Massachusetts Ave., Cambridge, Mass. 02138.

CAREER: Ordained Assemblies of God minister, 1971; Evangel College, Springfield, Mo., chaplain, 1971-73; Cambridge Christian Center, Cambridge, Mass., pastor, 1974—. Member of Harvard-Radcliffe Chaplaincy, and Harvard Square Clergy. *Member:* National Association of Evangelicals, Society for Pentecostal Studies.

WRITINGS: God: You've Got to Be Kidding, Creation House, 1974. Contributor to journals.

WORK IN PROGRESS: Research for a book on the contemporary church; a book on creative worship for charismatics.

* * *

LENARD, Yvone 1921-

PERSONAL: Born March 24, 1921, in France; daughter of Henry Edmond Bernard and Marguerite (Dedieu) Delavallade; married Wayne Rowe (a photo-illustrator); children: Michele. *Education:* Faculte de Droit, Bordeaux, Licence en Droit, 1943; University of California, Los Angeles, B.A., 1955, M.A., 1956. *Home:* 23 Cove Colony, Malibu, Calif. 90265. *Office:* California State College, Dominguez Hills, Calif.

CAREER: University of California, Los Angeles, lecturer in French, 1956-68; California State College, Dominguez Hills, associate professor, 1968-72, professor of French, 1972—. *Member:* Modern Language Association of America, American Association of Teachers of French (president of Southern California branch, 1968). *Awards, honors:* Named Knight of National French Order of Academic Palms, 1971.

WRITINGS: Parole et Pensee (with photography by husband, Wayne Rowe; title means "Word and Thought"), Harper, 1965, 2nd edition, 1971; (with Ralph Hester) *L'Art de la Conversation* (title means "The Art of Conversation"), Harper, 1967; (editor with Monica Faulkner) Louis Pauwels and Jacques Bergier, *Le Matin des Magiciens* (title means "The Morning of the Magicians"), Harper, 1967; *Jeunes Voix, Jeunes Visages* (with photography by Rowe; title means "Young Voices, Young Faces"), Harper, 1969; *Fenetres sur la France* (with photography by Rowe; title means "Windows on France"), Harper, 1969; *Tresors du Temps* (with photography by Rowe; title means "Treasures of Time"), Harper, 1972. Also contributor to

The Enticing Products of France, and to *Architecture in France*, both with photography by Rowe.

WORK IN PROGRESS: A third edition of *Parole et Pensee*; second editions of *Jeunes Voix, Jeunes Visages* and *Tresors du Temps*.

* * *

LENGYEL, Melchior 1879(?)-1974

1879(?)—October 26, 1974; Hungarian playwright and filmscript writer. Obituaries: *New York Times*, October 27, 1974; *Washington Post*, October 31, 1974.

* * *

LENNEBERG, Eric H. 1921-

PERSONAL: Born September 19, 1921, in Germany; son of Robert and Gertrud Lenneberg; married Elizabeth Smith. *Education:* Harvard University, Ph.D., 1955. *Office:* Department of Psychology, Uris Hall, Cornell University, Ithaca, N.Y. 14850.

CAREER: Cornell University, Ithaca, N.Y., professor of psychology and neurobiology, 1968—.

WRITINGS: *New Directions in the Study of Language*, M.I.T. Press, 1964; *Biological Foundations of Language*, Wiley, 1967; *Foundations of Language Development*, Academic Press, 1975.

* * *

LENSKI, Lois 1893-1974

October 14, 1893—September 11, 1974; American author and illustrator of children's books. Obituaries: *New York Times*, September 14, 1974; *Time*, September 23, 1974; *Publishers Weekly*, September 30, 1974; *AB Bookman's Weekly*, October 7, 1974; *Library Journal*, November 15, 1974. (*CA*-13/14).

* * *

LEONARD, Leo D(onald) 1938-

PERSONAL: Born November 23, 1938, in Salt Lake City, Utah; son of Leo B. (a lieutenant colonel in the U.S. Army) and Florence V. (a teacher) Leonard; married Marilynn R. Hoyt (a college teacher), January 2, 1962; children: Richard C. *Education:* University of Utah, B.S. (with honors), 1961; graduate study at University of Washington, Seattle, 1961, 1962, 1965, and Lewis and Clark College, 1964; Utah State University, M.S., 1967, Ed.D., 1969. *Residence:* Toledo, Ohio. *Office:* College of Education, University of Toledo, Toledo, Ohio 43606.

CAREER: University of Toledo, Toledo, Ohio, assistant professor, 1969-72, associate professor of educational sociology, 1972—. Coordinator of Canadian Consortium for Curriculum Development and Catholic Diocese of Toledo Curriculum Development Project. Member of board of trustees of Toledo Symphony Orchestra, 1970—; chairman of Toledo Music Festival. *Military service:* U.S. Army Reserve, 1955-62.

MEMBER: International Teacher Education Consortium (member of board of directors), International Council on Education for Teaching, Studies in Federal Education Policy, Comparative Education Society, American Educational Studies Association, American Educational Research Association, Comparative Education Association of Canada, Phi Delta Kappa, Phi Alpha Theta, Phi Kappa Phi. *Awards, honors:* Fulbright scholarship to Africa, summer, 1967; Research fellowship from International Teacher Education Consortium, 1970; American Association of Colleges for Teacher Education diplomat scholarship from U.S. State Department, 1971.

WRITINGS: (With John Ahern, William Wiersma, and Sam Yarger) *Training Competency Based Instructional Personnel* (booklet), U.S. Office of Education, 1970; (contributor) Alfred P. Wilson, editor, *Social Issues to Promote Inquiry*, Simon & Schuster, 1970; (with Robert T. Utz) *A Competency Based Curriculum: A Model for Teachers*, Kendall-Hunt, 1971; (with George E. Dickson, Richard W. Saxe, and others) *Partners for Educational Reform and Renewal*, McCutchan, 1973; (with Utz) *Building Skills for Competency Based Teaching*, Harper, 1974; (with Utz) *Social Foundations and Competency Based Education*, Kendall-Hunt, in press.

Contributor of about twenty-five articles to education and social science journals, including *Educational Studies*, *Educational Comment*, *University of Quebec Newsletter*, *Journal of Social Science*, *New Directions in Teaching*, and *Education New Mexico*. Member of board of publishers of *Studies in Federal Education Policy*; co-editor of *Journal of Abstracts in International Education*.

WORK IN PROGRESS: Seven teachers' manuals for individually guided education in science, mathematics, social sciences, psychology, evaluation, and children's progress through individually guided education, with Dean L. Meinke, Robert T. Utz, and Darryl Yorke, publication by Addison-Wesley expected between 1976 and 1978; research on education in southern Africa and Canada.

AVOCATIONAL INTERESTS: Travel, classical music, golf, painting.

* * *

LEPLEY, Paul M(ichael) 1933-

PERSONAL: Born February 16, 1933, in Clinton, Ohio; son of Leo G. (an upholsterer) and Mary (Burg) Lepley; married Virginia A. Martinski (a registered nurse), October 8, 1956; children: Paul, Jr., Joseph, Mary, Thomas. *Education:* University of Michigan, B.S., 1955; Pennsylvania State University, M.Ed., 1961; Temple University, Ed.D., 1968. *Religion:* Roman Catholic. *Home:* 38 Blacksmith Rd., Wilbraham, Mass. 01095. *Office:* Division of Health, Physical Education and Recreation, Springfield College, Springfield, Mass. 01109.

CAREER: Castleton State College, Castleton, Vt., assistant professor of health, physical education and recreation, 1961-67; University of Maine, Orono, associate professor of health, physical education and recreation, and chairman of department, 1967-72; Springfield College, Springfield, Mass., professor of health, physical education and recreation, and director of division, 1972—. *Member:* American Alliance for Health, Physical Education and Recreation, National College Physical Education Association for Men, Massachusetts Association for Health, Physical Education and Recreation, Maine Association for Health, Physical Education and Recreation (president, 1971). *Awards, honors:* Maine Association for Health, Physical Education and Recreation honor award, 1972.

WRITINGS: *Contemporary Philosophies of Physical Education and Athletics*, C. E. Merrill, 1973. Contributor to *Encyclopedia of Sports Sciences & Medicine* and to journals in his field.

LEPP, Henry 1922-

PERSONAL: Born March 4, 1922, in Halbstadt, Russia; naturalized U.S. citizen in 1960; son of David Abraham (an accountant) and Marie (Willms) Lepp; married Maxine M. Foster, September 15, 1952; children: Kathleen M., Stephen, H., David F., Tamara J. *Education:* University of Saskatchewan, B.S., 1944; University of Minnesota, Ph.D., 1953. *Religion:* "Originally Mennonite; currently none." *Home:* 3042 Sandy Hook Dr., St. Paul, Minn. 55113. *Office:* Department of Geology, Macalester College, St. Paul, Minn. 55105.

CAREER: Exploration engineer for Cominco Ltd. in Yukon Territory, in British Columbia, and in Northwest Territories, 1944-46; N. W. Byrna (mining engineer consultants), Yellowknife, Northwest Territories, mining engineer, 1946-48; Alcan Aluminium, Conakry, Guinea, geologist, 1948-50; geologist with Freeport Sulphur Co., New York, 1953-54; University of Minnesota, Duluth, assistant professor, 1954-57, associate professor, 1957-61, professor of geology, 1961-64; Macalester College, St. Paul, Minn., professor of geology, 1964—, chairman of department, 1964—. Consultant to Quebec Cartier Mining Co., 1955-58, and Roberts Mining Co., 1961-64. *Member:* Geological Society of America (fellow), Society of Economic Geologists, American Association for the Advancement of Science, Sigma Xi.

WRITINGS: (Contributor) R. L. Heller, editor, *Geology of Earth Sciences Sourcebook*, Holt, 1962, 2nd edition, 1971; (contributor) *Investigating the Earth*, Houghton, 1967; *Dynamic Earth: An Introduction to Earth Science*, McGraw, 1973; (editor and contributor) *The Geochemistry of Iron*, Dowden, Hutchinson & Ross, in press. Contributor of more than twenty articles to professional journals.

* * *

LERNER, Herbert J. 1933-

PERSONAL: Born December 20, 1933, in Bronx, N.Y.; son of Nathan (a businessman) and Anna (Rothberg) Lerner; married Hadassah J. Levine, December 15, 1963; children: David, Jonathan. *Education:* Yeshiva University, B.A. (magna cum laude), 1955; Columbia University, M.A., 1957; J.D., 1961; New York University, Ph.D., 1970. *Religion:* Jewish. *Home:* 1260 Northeast 171 Terrace, North Miami Beach, Fla. 33162. *Office:* School of Business, Florida International University, Miami, Fla. 33144.

CAREER: Lawyer in private practice, New York, N.Y., 1962-63; U.S. Atomic Energy Commission, New York, N.Y., management intern, 1963-64; State University of New York Downstate Medical Center, Brooklyn, instructor, 1967-69; University of Missouri, Kansas City, assistant professor, 1969-70, associate professor, 1970-74, lecturer in medicine, 1971-74; Florida International University, Miami, Fla., professor of health care management, 1975—. Consultant to various health related organizations in Kansas City, Mo., 1970-74. *Military service:* U.S. Army Reserve; active duty during Berlin and Cuban Crises, 1961-62. *Member:* American Public Health Association (fellow).

WRITINGS: *State Association for Retarded Children and New York State Government, 1948-1968*, New York State Association for Retarded Children, 1972; *Manpower Issues and Voluntary Regulation in the Medical Specialty System*, Prodist, 1974.

WORK IN PROGRESS: Research in medical and other health professional manpower training programs, national health policy, and public and mental health.

LERNER, Joel J. 1936-

PERSONAL: Born September 18, 1936, in New York, N.Y.; son of David (a retailer) and Rose (Snyder) Lerner; married Anita Joyce Levy, August 13, 1961; children: Marc, Steven, Caren. *Education:* New York University, B.S., 1958; Columbia University, M.A., 1960, P.D., 1964. *Home:* Dillon Rd., Box 252N, Monticello, N.Y. 12701. *Office:* Sullivan County Community College, Loch Sheldrake, N.Y. 12759.

CAREER: New York City Community College, Brooklyn, N.Y., instructor in accounting, 1959-63; Sullivan County Community College, Loch Sheldrake, N.Y., assistant professor, 1963-65, associate professor, 1965-68, professor of accounting, 1968—, chairman of business division, 1968—. Examiner, Accrediting Commission for Business Schools, 1970—. *Military service:* U.S. Army, 1959-60, 1961-62. *Member:* National Education Association, Eastern Business Teachers Association, Delta Pi Epsilon.

WRITINGS: *The New York Times in Teaching Business Subjects at the Community College* (booklet), New York Times Educational Division, 1966; (editor) *Readings in Business Organization & Management*, Selected Academic Readings, 1968; (editor) *Introduction to Business: A Contemporary Reader*, Prentice-Hall, 1969; (with James Cashin) *Theory and Practice of Accounting I*, McGraw, 1973; (with Cashin) *Theory and Practice of Accounting II*, McGraw, 1974; (with Cashin) *Intermediate Accounting I*, McGraw, 1975; (with Cashin) *Intermediate Accounting II*, McGraw, in press.

* * *

LESLIE, Kenneth 1893(?)-1974

1893(?)—October 7, 1974; Canadian poet. Obituaries: *New York Times*, October 9, 1974; *AB Bookman's Weekly*, December 2, 1974.

* * *

LeTARTE, Clyde E(dward) 1938-

PERSONAL: Born August 22, 1938, in Muskegon, Mich.; son of Harold E. (a pattern maker) and Ellen L. (a nurse; maiden name, Bullman) LeTarte; married Kathleen Coutlet (a teacher), June 18, 1966; children: Richard, Rhonda. *Education:* Hope College, A.B., 1960; Michigan State University, M.A., 1964, Ed.D., 1969. *Home:* 600 Roosevelt, Ypsilanti, Mich. 48197. *Office:* Graduate School, Eastern Michigan University, 116 Pierce, Ypsilanti, Mich. 48197.

CAREER: Mt. Morris Public Schools, Mt. Morris, Mich., teacher of English and social studies, 1960-63; Muskegon Public Schools, Muskegon, Mich., director of community education, 1963-67; Michigan Department of Education, Lansing, Mich., consultant, 1967-69; Eastern Michigan University, Ypsilanti, assistant professor, 1969—, associate dean of Graduate School, 1971—. *Member:* National Community Education Association (president, 1966-67).

WRITINGS: *Community Education: From Program to Process*, Pendell, 1972.

WORK IN PROGRESS: Development of an evaluation instrument for assessing community education; revising and expanding *Community Education*.

* * *

LeTOURNEAU, Richard H(oward) 1925-

PERSONAL: Surname is pronounced "leh-*ter*-know";

born January 3, 1925, in Stockton, Calif.; son of Robert G. (a manufacturer) and Evelyn (Peterson) LeTourneau; married Louise Jensen, February 8, 1947; children: Robert Gilmour, Caleb Roy, Linda Louise, Liela Lynn. *Education:* Texas A&M University, B.S., 1958, M.S., 1961; Oklahoma State University, Ph.D., 1970. *Politics:* Republican. *Religion:* Protestant-Evangelical. *Home:* 511 Ruth Lynn Dr., Longview, Tex. 75601. *Address:* LeTourneau Foundation, P.O. Box 7333, Longview, Tex. 75601.

CAREER: LeTourneau College, Longview, Tex., president, 1962-68; R. G. LeTourneau, Inc., Longview, Tex., president, 1966-71; Marathon Manufacturing Co., Houston, Tex., senior vice-president, 1971-72; LeTourneau Foundation, Longview, Tex., vice-president, 1972—; LeTourneau College, Longview, Tex., president, 1975—. Commissioner of Texas Industrial Commission, 1961-67. Member of board of trustees of Toccoa Falls Institute, 1954—, and Simpson College, 1974; member of board of directors of Marathon Manufacturing Co., 1970, and Wycliff Bible Translators, U.S. Home Division, 1973; chairman of board of Industrial Arts Advisory Commission, Texas Department of Education, 1971—. *Military service:* U.S. Army, 1944-46; served in Pacific Theater.

MEMBER: Society of Automotive Engineers, American Institute of Industrial Engineers, American Society for Engineering Education, Tau Beta Pi, Phi Kappa Phi, Alpha Pi Mu, Sigma Xi.

WRITINGS: Management Plus, Zondervan, 1973; *Keeping Your Cool in a World of Tension*, Zondervan, 1975. Contributor to *Now*.

WORK IN PROGRESS: Research on the relationships between business, Christianity, and education; a diary on the trauma of a chief executive after a company merger; a fictional book of humor and lessons, based on fact, in an industrial missionary project.

* * *

LEUKEL, Francis 1922-

PERSONAL: First syllable of surname is pronounced "loi"; born August 29, 1922, in Decatur, Ill.; son of Walter A. and Ruth (Hostetler) Leukel; married Mary Brown, 1954 (divorced, 1955); married Deborah Griswold, 1955 (divorced, 1962); married Eleanor Taylor, 1967 (divorced, 1974). *Education:* University of Florida, B.S., 1947; Northwestern University, M.S., 1949; University of Washington, Seattle, Ph.D., 1955. *Religion:* None. *Residence:* San Diego, Calif. *Office:* Department of Psychology, San Diego State University, San Diego, Calif. 92115.

CAREER: Roosevelt College (now Roosevelt University), Chicago, Ill., instructor in psychology, 1948-49; San Diego State University, San Diego, Calif., assistant professor, 1956-60, associate professor, 1960-65, professor of psychology, 1965—. *Member:* American Association for the Advancement of Science, American Psychological Association. *Awards, honors:* U.S. Public Health Service postdoctoral fellow at University of Washington, 1955-56.

WRITINGS: Introduction to Physiological Psychology, Mosby, 1968, 2nd edition, 1972; *Physiological Psychology: A Study Guide*, Mosby, 1972; (editor) *Issues in Physiological Psychology*, Mosby, 1974.

WORK IN PROGRESS: Third edition of *Introduction to Physiological Psychology*, completion expected in 1976; third edition of *Physiological Psychology: A Study Guide*, 1976; research on brain mechanisms in learning, memory, and consciousness.

LEVACK, Brian P(aul) 1943-

PERSONAL: Born April 6, 1943, in New York, N.Y.; son of Arthur Paul (a professor) and Helen (O'Brien) Levack; married Nancy Buecker (a teacher), December 17, 1966; children: Christopher, Andrew. *Education:* Fordham University, B.A., 1965; Yale University, M.A., 1967, Ph.D., 1970. *Home:* 2209 Greenlee Dr., Austin, Tex. 78703. *Office:* Department of History, University of Texas, Austin, Tex. 78712.

CAREER: University of Texas at Austin, instructor, 1969-70, assistant professor, 1970-74, associate professor of history, 1974—. *Member:* Phi Beta Kappa. *Awards, honors:* Woodrow Wilson fellow, 1965.

WRITINGS: The Civil Lawyers in England, 1603-1641: A Political Study, Clarendon Press (of Oxford University), 1973.

WORK IN PROGRESS: A book on the union of England and Scotland in the seventeenth century.

* * *

LEVENSON, Myron H(erbert) 1926-1974

PERSONAL: Born February 9, 1926, in Pittsburgh, Pa.; son of John H. (a jeweler) and Elizabeth S. Levenson; married Beverly Lazarus (an anthropologist), December 28, 1958; children: Barton P., Elliott I. *Education:* University of Pittsburgh, B.S., 1949, M.A., 1957; University of North Carolina, Ph.D., 1966. *Residence:* Pittsburgh, Pa. *Office:* Indiana University of Pennsylvania, 113 Keith Hall, Indiana, Pa. 15701.

CAREER: State University of New York College at Oneonta, assistant professor of sociology and anthropology, 1961-64; Cornell University, Ithaca, N.Y., assistant professor of housing in the College of Home Economics, and assistant director of Center for Housing and Environmental Studies, 1964-66; Sacramento State College, Sacramento, Calif., assistant professor of sociology, 1966-68; Indiana University of Pennsylvania, Indiana, associate professor, 1968-71, professor of sociology and anthropology, 1971-74, chairman of department of sociology-anthropology, 1969-74. *Military service:* U.S. Army Air Forces, 1944-46. U.S. Army, Antiaircraft Artillery, 1951-52; served in Korea; became second lieutenant. *Member:* American Sociological Association, American Ethnological Society, Population Reference Bureau. *Awards, honors:* Ford Foundation grant, 1963.

WRITINGS: Human Relationships: An Introduction to Sociological Concepts, Prentice-Hall, 1974. Contributor to *Folkhealthways Newsletter*, *North Carolina Folklore*, and *Social Forces*.

WORK IN PROGRESS: Individuals, Groups, and Social Change (tentative title), a sociology textbook; a reader in general sociology; a monograph on community structure.

(Died November 1, 1974)

* * *

LEVI, Carlo 1902-1975

November 29, 1902—January 4, 1975; Italian artist, politician, journalist, author. Obituaries: *New York Times*, January 5, 1975; *Publishers Weekly*, January 15, 1975; *AB Bookman's Weekly*, January 20, 1975.

* * *

LEVIN, Jack 1941-

PERSONAL: Born June 28, 1941, in New Orleans, La.;

son of Max (a business executive) and Flory (Liebman) Levin; married Flora Lench, June 14, 1964; children: Michael Steven, Bonnie Lynn, Andrea Ilene. *Education:* American International College, B.A., 1963; Boston University, M.S., 1964, Ph.D., 1968. *Home:* 24 Lantern Lane, Sharon, Mass. 02067. *Office:* Department of Sociology, Northeastern University, Boston, Mass. 02115.

CAREER: Boston University, Boston, Mass., assistant professor of sociology, 1968-70; Northeastern University, Boston, Mass., assistant professor, 1970-74, associate professor of sociology, 1974—. Consultant to President's Commission on Obscenity and Pornography, 1970, and to Columbia Point Nursery School Project, 1972. *Member:* American Sociological Association, Society for the Study of Social Problems, Eastern Sociological Society, Massachusetts Sociological Association (president, 1973-74).

WRITINGS: Elementary Statistics in Social Research, Harper, 1973; (with Gerald S. Ferman) *Social Science Research: A Handbook for Students*, Schenkman, 1974; *The Functions of Prejudice*, Harper, 1975; (with James L. Spates) *Sociology from the Beginning*, Harper, in press. Contributor to professional journals.

WORK IN PROGRESS: Research on socialization functions of games, on sex role identification in young children, and on problems of the aged.

* * *

LEVINE, Donald N(athan) 1931-

PERSONAL: Born June 16, 1931, in New Castle, Pa.; son of Abe (a businessman) and Rose (Gusky) Levine; married Joanne Bull, November 6, 1955 (divorced, 1967); married Ruth Weinstein (a social worker), August 26, 1967; children: (first marriage) Theodore Berhanu, William Haskell; (second marriage) Rachel Shaindel. *Education:* University of Chicago, A.B., 1950, M.A., 1954, Ph.D., 1957; also studied at University of Frankfurt, 1952-53. *Religion:* Jewish. *Home:* 4901 South Kimbark Ave., Chicago, Ill. 60615. *Office:* Department of Sociology, University of Chicago, Chicago, Ill. 60637.

CAREER: University of Chicago, Chicago, Ill., visiting assistant professor, 1961-62, assistant professor, 1962-65, associate professor, 1965-73, professor of sociology and social science, 1973—, associate dean of the college and master of the Social Science Collegiate Division, 1965-68. *Military service:* U.S. Army Reserve, 1951-54. *Member:* American Sociological Association, American Anthropological Association. *Awards, honors:* Ford Foundation fellowships, 1958-60, 1971-72.

WRITINGS: Wax and Gold: Tradition and Innovation in Ethiopian Culture, University of Chicago Press, 1965, revised edition, 1972; (contributor) Lucien Page and Sidney Verba, editors, *Political Culture and Political Development*, Princeton University Press, 1965; *Georg Simmel on Individuality and Social Forms*, University of Chicago Press, 1971; *Greater Ethiopia: The Evolution of a Multiethnic Society*, University of Chicago Press, 1974. Contributor to *International Encyclopedia of the Social Sciences*, and to *Journal of Social Issues*.

* * *

LEVITAN, Max 1921-

PERSONAL: Born March 1, 1921, in Tverai, Lithuania; naturalized U.S. citizen in 1935; son of Solomon L. (a rabbi) and Hannah (Siev) Levitan; married Beth German, October 25, 1947; children: Eve, SaraAnne, Marjorie. *Education:* University of Chicago, A.B., 1944; University of Michigan, M.A., 1946; Columbia University, Ph.D., 1951. *Religion:* Orthodox Judaism. *Home:* 1212 Fifth Ave., New York, N.Y. 10029. *Office:* Mt. Sinai School of Medicine, City University of New York, New York, N.Y. 10029.

CAREER: U.S. Public Health Service, Chicago, Ill., statistician, 1944-45; Virginia Polytechnic Institute, Blacksburg, associate professor of genetics, 1949-55; Medical College of Pennsylvania, Philadelphia, assistant professor, 1955-60, associate professor, 1960-62, professor of anatomy and medical genetics, 1962-66, acting chairman of department of anatomy, 1964-66; George Mason University, Fairfax, Va., professor of biology and chairman of department, 1966-68; City University of New York, Mt. Sinai School of Medicine, New York, N.Y., professor of anatomy, 1968—. Lecturer at University of Pennsylvania, 1962-63.

MEMBER: American Association for the Advancement of Science, American Association of Anatomists, American Society of Human Genetics, American Society of Naturalists, Genetics Society of America, Society for the Study of Evolution, Society for the Study of Social Biology, New York Academy of Sciences, Sigma Xi.

WRITINGS: (With Ashley Montagu) *Textbook of Human Genetics*, Oxford University Press, 1971.

* * *

LEVTZION, Nehemia 1935-

PERSONAL: Born November 24, 1935, in Tel Aviv, Israel; son of Aron (an accountant) and Penina (Perlou) Levtzion; married Tirtza Gindel (a secondary school teacher), May 4, 1961; children: Moshe and Avner (sons), Osnath and Noga (daughters). *Education:* Hebrew University of Jerusalem, B.A., 1960, M.A., 1962; University of London, Ph.D., 1965. *Religion:* Jewish. *Home:* 8 Hameshorereth, Beth Hakerem, Jerusalem, Israel. *Office:* Institute of Asian and African Studies, Hebrew University, Jerusalem, Israel.

CAREER: Hebrew University, Institute of Asian and African Studies, Jerusalem, Israel, lecturer, 1966-68, senior lecturer, 1968-72, associate professor of history, 1972—, chairman of African studies departments, 1968-72. Visiting professor at Northwestern University, 1969, and University of California, Los Angeles, 1975; overseas fellow at St. John's College, Cambridge, 1972-73.

WRITINGS: Muslims and Chiefs in West Africa, Clarendon Press (of Oxford University), 1968; *Ancient Ghana and Mali*, Methuen, 1973. Contributor to *Cambridge History of Africa*, and *Journal of African History, Bulletin of the School of Asian and African Studies, Annales*, and other journals in his field.

WORK IN PROGRESS: Research on the history of West Africa, and on Islam in Africa; a comparative study of conversion to Islam.

* * *

LEWIS, Eugene 1940-

PERSONAL: Born August 21, 1940, in Philadelphia, Pa.; son of Martin (an artist) and Matilda (a teacher; maiden name, Epstein) Lewis; married Wilma Shirley, June 7, 1962 (died May 24, 1963); married Maren Donaldson, December 23, 1964; children: (second marriage) Katherine Martin, Charles Henry. *Education:* Temple University, B.A., 1962; Indiana University, M.A., 1964; Syracuse University, Ph.D., 1967. *Home:* 301 College Hill Rd., Clinton, N.Y.

13323. *Office:* Office of the Provost, Hamilton College, Clinton, N.Y. 13323.

CAREER: Hamilton College, Clinton, N.Y., assistant professor, 1967-72, associate professor of government, 1972—, provost of college, 1974—. Visiting professor at Southern Illinois University, 1969-70; administrative assistant in office of Philadelphia's Commissioner of Public Health, 1964. *Member:* American Political Science Association, American Society for Public Administration.

WRITINGS: The Urban Political System, Dryden, 1973.

* * *

LEWIS, George H(allam) 1943-

PERSONAL: Born October 18, 1943, in Houlton, Me.; son of Richard L. (a customs officer) and Ruth (Dodge) Lewis; married Cheryl M. Wilson, May 1, 1970. *Education:* Bowdoin College, B.A. (summa cum laude), 1965; University of Oregon, M.A., 1967, Ph.D., 1969. *Office:* Department of Sociology, University of the Pacific, 3601 Pacific Ave., Stockton, Calif. 95204.

CAREER: University of the Pacific, Stockton, Calif., assistant professor of sociology, 1970—. Visiting professor at Vanderbilt University, 1973; lecturer at University of Sarajevo, 1974.

WRITINGS: The STGPROC System of Data Processing, University of Oregon Press, 1970; *Side-Saddle on the Golden Calf: Social Structure and Popular Culture in America*, Goodyear Publishing, 1972; *Fistfights in the Kitchen: Manners and Methods of Social Research*, Goodyear Publishing, in press. Contributor of articles and poems to *Journal of Popular Culture*, *Popular Music and Society*, *Youth and Society*, *Radix*, and *Contact*. Associate editor of *Pacific Sociological Review*, 1972-75.

WORK IN PROGRESS: A book on country music and performers.

SIDELIGHTS: Lewis has spent time in Paris examining French popular culture.

* * *

LEWIS, Lionel Stanley 1933-

PERSONAL: Born July 29, 1933, in Ottawa, Ontario, Canada; naturalized U.S. citizen; married Ann Winifred Herman, November 9, 1962; children: Peter George, Andrew Philip. *Education:* Washington University, St. Louis, Mo., A.B., 1957; Cornell University, M.A., 1958; Yale University, Ph.D., 1961. *Home:* 17 Morningside Lane, Williamsville, N.Y. 14221. *Office:* Department of Sociology, State University of New York at Buffalo, 4224 Ridge Lea, Amherst, N.Y. 14226.

CAREER: University of Nevada, Reno, assistant professor of sociology, 1961-63; State University of New York at Buffalo, assistant professor, 1963-67, associate professor, 1967-73, professor of sociology, 1973—, adjunct professor of higher education, 1973—, director of graduate studies, 1971-72. *Military service:* U.S. Army, 1953-55. *Member:* American Sociological Association, Society for the Study of Social Problems, Popular Culture Association, Phi Beta Kappa. *Awards, honors:* Social Science Research Council research grant, 1969-70.

WRITINGS: (With William Petersen) *The Changing Population of Nevada*, Bureau of Business and Economic Research, University of Nevada, 1963; (contributor) Ailon Shiloh, editor, *Studies in Human Sexual Behavior: The American Scene*, C. C Thomas, 1970; (contributor) Arlene Skolnick and Jerome H. Skolnick, editors, *The Family in Transition*, Little, Brown, 1971; (contributor) Saul D. Feldman and Gerald W. Theilbar, editors, *Life Styles: Diversity in American Society*, Little, Brown, 1972; (contributor) Robert S. Browne and other editors, *The Social Scene*, Winthrop, 1972; (contributor) James W. Maddock and Deborah Dickman, editors, *Human Sexuality: A Resource Book*, Book III, [Minnesota], 1972; (contributor) Eliot Freidson, editor, *The Professions and Their Prospects*, Sage, 1973; (editor with Joseph Lopreato) *Social Stratification: A Reader*, Harper, 1974; (contributor) Alfred M. Mirande, editor, *The Age of Crisis: Deviance, Disorganization, and Societal Problems*, Harper, 1974; (contributor) Brad Parlin and Kooros M. Malimoudi, editors, *Sociological Inquiry: A Humanistic Perspective*, Kendall/Hunt, 1974.

Contributor of more than fifty articles and reviews to education and sociology journals, including *Journal of Popular Culture, Journal of Higher Education, Change, Education and Urban Society, Social Problems*, and *American Behavioral Scientist*. Advisory editor of *Sociological Quarterly*, 1969—.

WORK IN PROGRESS: University Faculty and the Principle of Merit: A Sociological Essay.

* * *

LIBERSAT, Henry 1934-

PERSONAL: Born July 4, 1934, in Groves, Tex.; son of Henry Pierre (a carpenter) and Elder (Zeringue) Libersat; married Margaret Peggy LeBlanc, June 4, 1951; children: David, Anthony, Karen, Mary, Suzanne, Angela, Pierre. *Education:* Attended University of Southwestern Louisiana. *Politics:* Democrat. *Religion:* Roman Catholic. *Home:* 1013 Oakhurst St., Altamonte Springs, Fla. 32701. *Agent:* William A. Holub, Holub & Associates, 432 Park Ave. S., New York, N.Y. 10016. *Office: Florida Catholic*, P.O. Box 3551, Orlando, Fla. 32802.

CAREER: Louisiana Department of Highways, Lafayette, engineering aide, 1953-59; *Southwest Louisiana Register*, Lafayette, managing editor, 1959-69; *Florida Catholic*, Orlando, managing editor, 1969—. Member of board of directors of Acadiana Neuf, 1965. *Member:* Catholic Press Association of the United States and Canada (member of board of directors, 1965—), Greater Orlando Press Club. *Awards, honors:* Catholic Press Association awards, 1961, for best food page, 1961 and 1963, for best campaign in the public interest; Cardinal Newman Award for outstanding community service and family life, 1965.

WRITINGS: Ragin' Cajun, Liguorian, 1974. Author of "A Letter from Pierre," column in *Florida Catholic* and *Southwest Louisiana Register*, 1957—. Contributor to religious publications. Associate editor of *Our Sunday Visitor*, 1969.

WORK IN PROGRESS: Marriage: Beyond the Obvious (tentative title), a book about a Christian marriage from a Roman Catholic perspective; *Gam*, a novel about the Acadians, completion expected in 1977.

* * *

LICHTY, Lawrence W(ilson) 1937-

PERSONAL: Born June 14, 1937, in Pasadena, Calif.; son of Kenneth B. (a farmer) and Juanita (Wilson) Lichty; married Sandra K. Shaw (a social worker), August 4, 1962;

children: Belinda, Laurel. *Education:* University of Southern California, A.B., 1959; Ohio State University, M.A., 1961, Ph.D., 1964. *Home:* 2124 Chamberlain Ave., Madison, Wis. 53705. *Office:* 6037 Vilas Hall, University of Wisconsin, Madison, Wis. 53706.

CAREER: University of Wisconsin, Madison, assistant professor, 1964-67, associate professor, 1967-72, professor of communication arts, 1972—. *Member:* Broadcast Education Association, Sigma Delta Chi.

WRITINGS: (Compiler) *World Broadcasting: A Bibliography*, Association for Professional Broadcasting Education, 1970; (with M. C. Topping) *American Broadcasting: A Sourcebook on the History of Radio and Television*, Hastings House, 1975.

* * *

LIEBERMAN, Fredric 1940-

PERSONAL: Born March 1, 1940, in New York, N.Y.; son of Stanley (a lawyer) and Bryna (a teacher; maiden name, Mason) Lieberman; married Nguyen Kim-Oanh, September 8, 1964; children: Kim-An. *Education:* University of Rochester, Eastman School of Music, B.Mus., 1962; University of Hawaii, M.A.Mus., 1965; University of California, Los Angeles, Ph.D candidate, 1965-68; Cleveland Institute of Electronics, Diploma (with great distinction), 1973. *Home:* 28 Memorial Rd., Providence, R.I. 02906. *Office:* Department of Music, Brown University, Providence, R.I. 02912.

CAREER: David Hochstein Memorial Music School, Rochester, N.Y., instructor in composition and piano, 1961-62; Brown University, Providence, R.I., assistant professor of music, 1968—. Choir director, Schofield Barracks Chapel Center, 1962-64; instructor in ethnomusicology at University of California, Los Angeles, summer, 1968; visiting assistant professor at University of Washington, Seattle, summer, 1971; visiting professor at Colorado College, May, 1972, May, 1974; visiting lecturer at University of Maryland, 1972-73; adjunct professor at Goddard College, 1974—.

MEMBER: Society for Ethnomusicology (member of national council, 1970—), Society for Asian Music, Conference on Chinese Oral and Performing Literature (member of executive board, 1971-74), College Music Society (member of national council, 1973-75; member of executive board, 1974—), American Anthropological Association, Society for the Anthropology of Visual Communication, American Musicological Society, International Folk Music Council, American Society of Composers, Authors and Publishers, Association for Asian Studies, Catgut Acoustical Society. *Awards, honors:* East-West Center fellowship, 1962-65; JDR 3rd Fund (a Rockefeller foundation) fellowships, 1970-71, 1974-75.

WRITINGS: (Author of preface) Liang Tsai-Ping, *Music of Cheng*, Chinese Music Association (Taiwan), 1967; *Chinese Music: An Annotated Bibliography*, Society for Asian Music, 1970, supplement published in *Asian Music 5*, 1973; (with Diane Larrabee) *A Table of Cents for Frequencies from 0 to 4000.9 Hertz*, Music Department, Brown University, 1970; (editor with Fritz A. Kuttner, and contributor) *A Birthday Offering for Laurence Picken*, Society for Asian Music, in press.

Contributor: (Of composition for piano) John Cage, editor, *Notations*, Something Else, 1969; Harry Lincoln, editor, *The Computer and Music*, Cornell University Press, 1970; David M. Y. Liang, editor, *Festschrift for Liang Tsai-Ping*, Chinese National Music Association (Taipei), in press; (of translation) Klaus Wachsmann, editor, *Hornbostel Opera Omnia*, Volume III, Nijhoff, in press.

Musical compositions: "Suite for Piano," E. C. Schirmer, 1964; "Sonatina for Piano," E. C. Schirmer, 1964; "Card Music for John Cage," Kuch Press, 1964; "Divertevents One," Fluxus Press, 1965; "Two Short String Quartets," E. C. Schirmer, 1966; "Leaves of Brass" (for brass quartet), Franco Colombo, 1967; "Psalm 137: By the Rivers of Babylon," E. C. Schirmer, 1971.

Other: (Author of notes, transcriptions, and analyses) "Chinese Music," Anthology Records, Record I: "String Instruments," 1969, Record II: "Amoy Music," 1971; (author of record notes) "China: Shantung Folk Music," Nonesuch Records, 1972; (producer, director, editor, and photographer with Michael Moore) "Traditional Music and Dance of Sikkim" (hour-long film), Parts I-II, for Government of Sikkim, 1973; "Music of Sikkim," ABC Records, 1975; "Sikkimese Music," three records, Anthology Records, in press.

Contributor to *Grove's Dictionary of Music and Musicians* and to journals and newspapers, including *Ongaku Geijutsu* (Tokyo) and *China Post*. While student contributed poetry to several journals. Series editor, Asian Music Publications of Society for Asian Music (produced in cooperation with Brown University), and member of editorial board, *Asian Music*, 1968—; member of editorial board, *Ethnomusicology*, 1969-72.

WORK IN PROGRESS: Compiling selected readings in ethnomusicology, for publication by Norton; compiling selected readings on music in the People's Republic of China, for Asian Music Publications; with his mother, Bryna Mason Lieberman, translating and annotating a dissertation on the music of the Chinese by Jean-Joseph-Marie Amiot, for Asian Music Publications and Fritz Knuf (Amsterdam); completing his doctoral dissertation, "Form and Style in the Contemporary Repertoire of the Chinese Long Zither Ch'in."

SIDELIGHTS: Lieberman did field work in Taiwan and Japan and took private lessons in Chinese musical instruments and Noh kotsuzumi drumming during 1963-64. In the winter of 1970 he directed a musical project in Sikkim for the Government of Sikkim. Along with a diploma in electronics technology, 1973, he received a first class commercial radiotelephone operator license.

* * *

LIEBHAFSKY, Herman A(lfred) 1905-

PERSONAL: Surname is accented on second syllable; born November 18, 1905, in Zwittau, Austria-Hungary; came to United States, 1912; son of Hugo (a tailor) and Aurelie (Dehmel) Liebhafsky; married Sybil Small, November 30, 1935; children: Douglas Small, Alison Bowe (Mrs. Roger Van Vranken Des Forges). *Education:* Agricultural and Mechanical College of Texas (now Texas A & M University), B.S., 1926; University of Nebraska, M.S., 1927; University of California, Berkeley, Ph.D., 1929. *Politics:* Independent. *Religion:* Lutheran. *Home:* 2610 Melba Circle, Bryan, Tex. 77801. *Office:* Department of Chemistry, Texas A & M University, College Station, Tex. 77843.

CAREER: University of California, Berkeley, instructor in chemistry, 1927-34; General Electric Co., Research Laboratory, Schenectady, N.Y., research associate, 1934-41, in charge of inorganic and analytical chemistry, 1941-45, section head of analytical chemistry and special problems, 1945-47, acting manager, later manager of physical chemistry research, 1947-65, manager of electrochemistry branch of Research and Development Center, 1965-67; Texas A & M University, College Station, professor of chemistry, 1972—. *Wartime service:* U.S. Army, Ordnance, technical observer, 1945; served in European theater, on loan from General Electric Co. with simulated rank of colonel.

MEMBER: American Chemical Society, Electrochemical Society, Society for Applied Spectroscopy (honorary member), Sigma Xi, Mohawk Golf Club. *Awards, honors:* American Chemical Society award in analytical chemistry (first industrial chemist to receive this award), 1962.

WRITINGS: (With Heinz G. Pfeiffer, Earl Holden Winslow, and Paul D. Zemany) *X-Ray Absorption and Emission in Analytical Chemistry*, Wiley, 1960; (with Elton J. Cairns) *Fuel Cells and Fuel Batteries*, Wiley, 1968; (with Pfeiffer, Winslow, and Zemany) *X-Rays, Electrons, and Analytical Chemistry*, Wiley, 1972; *William David Coolidge: A Centenarian and His Work*, Wiley, 1974. Contributor of more than a hundred-fifty articles to scientific journals.

WORK IN PROGRESS: A historical survey of silicone development, completion expected in 1976.

* * *

LIENHARD, John H(enry IV) 1930-

PERSONAL: Born August 17, 1930, in St. Paul, Minn.; son of John H. (a newspaper writer) and Catherine E. (a musician; maiden name, Henderson) Lienhard; married Carol Ann Bratton (a violinist), June 20, 1959; children: John H., Andrew J. *Education:* Multnomah Junior College, A.A., 1949; Oregon State College, B.S., 1951; University of Washington, Seattle, M.S., 1953; University of California, Berkeley, Ph.D., 1961. *Politics:* "Minimal." *Religion:* Episcopalian. *Home:* 600 Raintree Rd., Lexington, Ky. 40502. *Office:* Department of Mechanical Engineering, University of Kentucky, Lexington, Ky. 40506.

CAREER: Member of state and federal highway surveying crews, summers, 1949-50; Boeing Airplane Co., Seattle, Wash., engineer, 1951-52; University of Washington, Seattle, instructor in mechanical engineering, 1955-56; Pacific Car and Foundry Co., Renton, Wash., engineer, summer, 1956; Washington State University, Pullman, associate professor of mechanical engineering, 1961-67; University of Kentucky, Lexington, professor of mechanical engineering, 1967—, associate dean for graduate affairs, 1972-74. Lecturer, University of California, Berkeley, 1965; consultant to U.S. Gypsum Co.; visiting professor at Boris Kidric Institute and University of Exeter, 1974-75. *Military service:* U.S. Army, Signal Corps, mechanical engineer at Engineering Laboratories, 1954-55.

MEMBER: American Society for Engineering Education, American Society of Mechanical Engineering, American Association for the Advancement of Science, Society for the History of Technology, Lexington Musical Theatre Society (member of board of directors and business manager), Sigma Xi. *Awards, honors:* National Science Foundation fellowships, 1970, to study history of technology at Smithsonian Institution, and 1972, to study history, philosophy, and sociology of science at Catholic University of America.

WRITINGS: (Contributor) *The Domain of the Faculty in a Growing University*, Common Ministry, Washington State University, 1967; (with C. L. Tien) *Statistical Thermodynamics*, Holt, 1971. Author of technical reports and bulletins. Contributor of more than a hundred articles and reviews to technical and musical journals, including *International Journal of Heat and Mass Transfer, Journal of Heat Transfer, Nordic Hydrology, Journal of Basic Engineering*, and *Quarterly of Applied Mathematics*. Member of editorial board of *Iranian Journal of Science and Technology*.

WORK IN PROGRESS: Research on variable gravity influences on flames and boiling, natural convection in stratified media, bursting bubbles in relation to air pollution, and lignite gasification.

SIDELIGHTS: Lienhard is a tenor soloist, whose recordings include "Music of Bach, Josquin, and Hindemith," University of California, Berkeley, 1959; "Sixteenth Century Music," Part II, Pleiades, 1971; "Late Sixteenth Century Music," Part I, Pleiades, 1971. He has been heavily involved in liturgical and chamber vocal music since 1948. He has recently performed extensively in theatre with roles in "Amahl and the Night Visitors," "H.M.S. Pinafore," "Fantasticks," "Hedda Gabler," "Carousel," and several chamber operas.

* * *

LIGHT, Martin 1927-

PERSONAL: Born April 5, 1927, in Pittsburgh, Pa.; son of David H. (a publisher) and Evelyn (a publisher; maiden name, Finkelpearl) Light; married Dorothy Aronson (a teacher), December 23, 1951; children: Judith, Susan, Katherine, Steven. *Education:* Pennsylvania State University, B.A., 1949; University of Chicago, M.A., 1951; University of Illinois, Ph.D., 1960. *Home:* 701 North Chauncey, West Lafayette, Ind. 47906. *Office:* Department of English, Purdue University, West Lafayette, Ind. 47907.

CAREER: Pennsylvania State University, Forest School Branch, State College, instructor in English, 1949; Wayne State University, Detroit, Mich., instructor in English, 1951-52; Purdue University, West Lafayette, Ind., instructor, 1960-61, assistant professor, 1961-68, associate professor of English, 1968—. Instructor at Writers Workshop in Chautauqua, N.Y., 1963-67, and National Defense Education Act Institute for high school English department chairmen, 1968, 1969. *Military service:* U.S. Navy, 1944-45. *Member:* Modern Language Association of America, National Council of Teachers of English, Conference on College Composition and Communication, Hoosier Folklore Society.

WRITINGS: (Editor with Ray B. Browne) *Critical Approaches to American Literature*, two volumes, Crowell, 1965; (editor with Barnet Kottler) *The World of Words*, Houghton, 1967; (editor) *Studies in "Babbitt"*, C. E. Merrill, 1971; *The Quixotic Vision of Sinclair Lewis*, Purdue University Press, 1975. Contributor to *Journal of Popular Culture*, *Western Humanities Review*, and *Arizona Quarterly*.

WORK IN PROGRESS: Critical research on Faulkner, Fitzgerald, and Anderson.

* * *

LIGHTFOOT, Alfred 1936-

PERSONAL: Born July 23, 1936, in Shawano, Wis.; son of Alfred and Kordula (White) Lightfoot. *Education:* University of Wisconsin, B.S., 1958; Marquette University, M.A.,

1966, Ed.D., 1968; postdoctoral study at University of California at Los Angeles. *Politics:* Democrat. *Religion:* Lutheran. *Home:* 4312 Gentry Ave., Studio City, Calif. 91604. *Office:* Department of Education, Loyola Marymount University, Loyola Blvd. at West 80th St., Los Angeles, Calif. 90045.

CAREER: Social studies teacher in public schools in Milwaukee, Wis., 1958-66; Milwaukee Technical College, Milwaukee, Wis., instructor in sociology, 1966-68; Loyola Marymount University, Los Angeles, Calif., assistant professor of education, 1968-69; California State University, Los Angeles, assistant professor of educational foundations, 1969-71; Loyola Marymount University, associate professor of education, 1971—, director of graduate program in inner city education. Part-time teacher at Mount St. Paul College and Cardinal Stritch College, 1958-66; instructor at Marquette University, 1966-68; lecturer at Loyola Marymount University and Los Angeles City College, both 1969-71; director of Inner City Certificate Specialist Program in Urban Education at Pepperdine University, 1973-75; lecturer at Occidental College, Chapman College, California State University (Los Angeles), and Los Angeles City College; adjunct professor at Windsor University. Expert witness for Los Angeles Bar Association; consultant on minority education for the State of California. *Awards, honors:* Honorary Sc.D. from University of California at Los Angeles.

WRITINGS: (Editor) *Schools and Society: Readings in the Sociological Foundations*, Simon & Schuster, 1969; *The Culturally Disadvantaged: Perspectives in Urban Education*, Simon & Schuster, 1970; *American Urban Education: Inquiries into Changing Patterns*, MSS Educational Publishing, 1971; *Socio-Psychological Dimensions of Education*, MSS Educational Publishing, 1971; *Inquiries into the Social Foundations of Education: Schools in Their Urban Settings*, Rand McNally, 1972; (contributor) Ingeborg Assman, editor, *Socio-Cultural Aspects of Education*, Simon & Schuster, 1972. Contributor to history and education journals, including *Missouri Historical Review*, *American Education*, *Journal of Teacher Education*, and *Education Summary*.

WORK IN PROGRESS: Robert Owen and Utopian Education; *Social Foundations of Urban Education*, for Rand McNally; *The Pathology of Inner City Education*.

* * *

LILES, Bruce (Lynn) 1934-

PERSONAL: Born May 27, 1934, in Longview, Tex.; son of John F. (a lawyer) and Laura (Kuykendall) Liles. *Education:* North Texas State University, A.B., 1953, M.A., 1954; Stanford University, Ph.D., 1967. *Office:* Department of English, University of Missouri-St. Louis, St. Louis, Mo. 63121.

CAREER: San Antonio College, San Antonio, Tex., instructor in English, 1963-65; North Texas State University, Denton, assistant professor of English, 1966-70; University of Missouri, St. Louis, associate professor of English, 1970—. *Member:* Linguistic Society of America, Modern Language Association of America, Midwest Modern Language Association.

WRITINGS: An Introductory Transformational Grammar, Prentice-Hall, 1971; *Linguistics and the English Language*, Goodyear Publishing, 1972; *An Introduction to Linguistics*, Prentice-Hall, 1975.

LINDBERGH, Charles A(ugustus, Jr.) 1902-1974

February 4, 1902—August 26, 1974; American aviator, conservationist, author. Obituaries: *New York Times*, August 27, 1974; *Washington Post*, August 27, 1974; *Newsweek*, September 9, 1974; *Time*, September 9, 1974; *Current Biography*, October, 1974.

* * *

LINDBLOM, (Christian) Johannes 1882-1974

Swedish Biblical scholar and author. Obituaries: *AB Bookman's Weekly*, December 2, 1974.

* * *

LINGENFELTER, Sherwood Galen 1941-

PERSONAL: Born November 18, 1941, in Hollidaysburg, Pa.; son of Galen Miller (a minister) and Kathern Margareta (Rogers) Lingenfelter; married Judith Elaine Beaumont (a librarian), August 10, 1962; children: Jennifer Elaine, Joel Sherwood. *Education:* Wheaton College, Wheaton, Ill., B.A., 1963; University of Pittsburgh, Ph.D., 1971. *Politics:* Democrat. *Religion:* Brethren. *Home:* 3731 Lake Rd. N., Clarkson, N.Y. 14430. *Office:* Department of Anthropology, State University of New York, Brockport, N.Y. 14420.

CAREER: University of Pittsburgh, Pittsburgh, Pa., director of School of Liberal Arts underclass advising program, 1965-66; State University of New York at Brockport, instructor, 1966-67, assistant professor, 1969-74, associate professor of anthropology, 1974—. National Institutes of Mental Health research fellow at Yap, West Caroline Islands, 1967-69. Anthropology consultant to Department of Education of U.S. Trust Territory of the Pacific Islands. *Member:* Polynesian Society, American Anthropological Association, Society for Applied Anthropology, Association for Social Anthropology.

WRITINGS: (Editor with Daniel T. Hughes) *Political Development in Micronesia*, Ohio State University Press, 1974; *Yap: Political Leadership and Cultural Change in an Island Society*, University Press of Hawaii, 1975. Editor with Jack Fraenkel of Prentice-Hall's "Inquiry into World Cultures" series, 1975.

WORK IN PROGRESS: Between Two Worlds: Micronesia's Future, completion expected in 1976; *Colonialism and Political Change in Oceania*, 1976; *Port Town and Progress: Socio-Economic Change in Yap*, 1976.

* * *

LINK, Frederick M(artin) 1930-

PERSONAL: Born September 2, 1930, in Reno, Nev.; son of Harry G. and Kathleen (Martin) Link; married Peggy Lou Williamson, July 20, 1970; children: John Franklin, Sarah. *Education:* Southwestern-at-Memphis College, A.B., 1953; Boston University, A.M., 1954, Ph.D., 1958. *Office:* Department of English, University of Nebraska, Lincoln, Neb. 68508.

CAREER: Boston University, Boston, Mass., instructor, 1957-60, assistant professor of English, 1960-63; University of Nebraska, Lincoln, assistant professor, 1963-65, associate professor, 1965-68, professor of English, 1968—, executive director of University of Nebraska Press, 1973-75. *Member:* American Association of University Professors, American Civil Liberties Union, Sierra Club. *Awards, honors:* Danforth Foundation fellow, 1953-58.

WRITINGS: (Editor) Walter Scott, *The Fortunes of Nigel*, University of Nebraska Press, 1965; (editor) Aphra Behn, *The Rover*, University of Nebraska Press, 1967; *Aphra Behn*, Twayne, 1968; (editor) John Dryden, *Aureng-Zebe*, University of Nebraska Press, 1971. Author of articles, reviews, and poems.

WORK IN PROGRESS: Editing *English Drama: 1660-1800*, for Gale Information Guide Library.

* * *

LINKLATER, Eric (Robert Russell) 1899-1974

March 8, 1899—November 7, 1974; Scottish author of novels, plays, biographies, and other works. Obituaries: *New York Times*, November 8, 1974; *Newsweek*, November 18, 1974; *AB Bookman's Weekly*, December 2, 1974. (*CA*-13/14).

* * *

LINNELL, Robert H(artley) 1922-

PERSONAL: Born August 15, 1922, in Kalkaska, Mich.; son of Earl Dean (a businessman) and Constance Ruth (a town official; maiden name, Hartley) Linnell; married Myrle Talbot (a music teacher), June 17, 1950; children: Charlene LeGro, Lloyd Robert, Randa Ruth, Dean Maxfield. *Education:* University of New Hampshire, B.S. (honors), 1944, M.S., 1947; University of Rochester, Ph.D., 1950. *Politics:* Independent. *Religion:* Unitarian-Universalist. *Home:* 23212 Audrey Ave., Torrance, Calif. 90505. *Office:* Office of Institutional Studies, University of Southern California, Los Angeles, Calif. 90007.

CAREER: University of New Hampshire, Durham, instructor in chemistry, 1944-47; American University of Beirut, Beirut, Lebanon, assistant professor, 1950-52, associate professor of chemistry and chairman of department, 1952-55; Tizon Chemical Co., Flemington, N.J., director and vice-president, 1955-58; University of Vermont, Burlington, associate professor of chemistry, 1958-61; Scott Laboratories, Plumsteadville, Pa., director, 1961-62; National Science Foundation, Washington, D.C., program director of physical chemistry, 1962-65, planning associate, 1965-67, program manager of science development, 1967-69; University of Southern California, Los Angeles, professor of chemistry and dean of letter arts and science, 1969-70, director of institutional studies, 1970—. *Military service:* U.S. Naval Reserve, 1944-46.

MEMBER: American Chemical Society, Air Pollution Control Association, American Academy of Political and Social Science, American Association for the Advancement of Science, Association for Institutional Research, American Association of Higher Education.

WRITINGS: (Editor) *Directory of Agencies and Foundations*, American Chemical Society, 1966; *Graduate Student Support and Manpower Resources in Graduate Science Education*, U.S. Government Printing Office, 1968; (with S. N. Vinogradov) *Hydrogen Bonding*, Van Nostrand, 1971.

WORK IN PROGRESS: Air Pollution, a college textbook; *Energy and the Future of Industrial Society*; *The No-Growth Society*, publication expected in 1976.

* * *

LIONNI, Leo 1910-

PERSONAL: Born May 5, 1910, in Amsterdam, Holland; came to United States, 1939; naturalized citizen, 1945; son of Louis and Elisabeth (a concert soprano; maiden name, Grossouw) Lionni; married Nora Maffi, December, 1931; children: Louis, Paolo. *Education:* Attended schools in Holland, Belgium, United States, Italy, Switzerland; University of Genoa, Ph.D., 1935. *Politics:* "Sometimes on the left—sometimes beyond." *Religion:* None. *Home:* "Porcignano," Radda in Chianti (Siena), Italy. *Agent:* Agenzia Letteraria Internazionale, Corso Matteotti 3, Milano, Italy.

CAREER: Free-lance writer, designer, and painter, 1930-39; N. W. Ayer & Sons, Inc. (advertising firm), Philadelphia, Pa., art director, 1939-47; Olivetti Corp. of America, San Francisco, Calif., design director, 1949-59; author and illustrator of children's books, 1959—. Head of graphics design department, Parsons School of Design, 1952-54; art director of *Fortune*, 1949-62; has had many one-man shows of his paintings and sculpture in galleries, museums, and at universities in U.S. and Europe, including Metropolitan Museum of Modern Art, New York, N.Y. *Member:* Alliance Graphique Internationale, American Institute of Graphic Arts (president, 1956), Society of Typographic Arts (honorary member), Bund Deutscher Buchkunstler (honorary member), Authors League of America, Artists Equity. *Awards, honors:* Elected art director of the year by National Society of Art Directors, 1955; Gold Medal for Architecture from Architectural League, 1956; *Inch by Inch* was Caldecott Award runner-up, 1961, and received Lewis Carroll Shelf Award, 1962, and Children's Book Prize in Germany, 1963; *Swimmy* was Caldecott Award runner-up in 1963, as was *Frederick* in 1968; German Government Illustrated Book Award, 1965, for *Swimmy*; Golden Apple Award at Bratislava First Biennial, 1967, for *Swimmy*; five major awards at Teheran Film Festival in 1970 for two animated films; elected to Art Directors Hall of Fame, 1974.

WRITINGS—Self-illustrated children's books: *Little Blue and Little Yellow*, Obolensky, 1959; *Inch by Inch*, Obolensky, 1960; *On My Beach There Are Many Pebbles*, Obolensky, 1961; *Swimmy*, Pantheon, 1963; *Tico and the Golden Wings*, Pantheon, 1964; *Frederick*, Pantheon, 1967; *The Alphabet Tree*, Pantheon, 1968; *The Biggest House in the World*, Pantheon, 1968; *Alexander and the Wind-up Mouse*, Pantheon, 1969; *Fish Is Fish*, Pantheon, 1970; *Theodore and the Talking Mushroom*, Pantheon, 1971; *Il Taccuino di Leo Lionni* (title means "Leo Lionni's Notebook"), Electra (Milan), 1972; *The Greentail Mouse*, Pantheon, 1973; *In The Rabbitgarden*, Pantheon, 1975; *A Color of His Own*, Abelard, 1975; *Pezzettino*, Pantheon, 1975. Contributor to *Casabella, Domus, Print, Fortune, Architecture Plus*. Editor, *Print*, 1955-57, *Panorama* (Italy), 1964-65.

WORK IN PROGRESS: Essays in Parallel Botany for Adelphi.

SIDELIGHTS: Lionni writes: "When I have a story in mind I am not conscious of the average age of my potential readers. I believe, in fact, that a good children's book should appeal to all people who have not completely lost their original joy and wonder in life. When I am asked the embarassing question of what do I know about children, their psychology, and their needs, I must confess my total ignorance. I know no more about children than the average parent or grandparent. I like to watch them, and when they are exceptionally sweet I like to hold them on my knee. But often I have not much patience for them. This is childish of me, perhaps, since children have very little patience with other children. The fact is that I really don't make books for children at all. I make them for that part of us, of myself and of my friends, which has never changed, which is still a child." Lionni adds that his major regret is "Not to have learned to play a musical instrument, any instrument, well."

BIOGRAPHICAL/CRITICAL SOURCES: Lee Bennett Hopkins, *Books Are by People*, Citation Press, 1969.

* * *

LIPKIND, William 1904-1974

1904—October 2, 1974; American anthropologist, educator, author of children's books. Obituaries: *New York Times*, October 3, 1974; *Library Journal*, November 15, 1974.

* * *

LIPPMANN, Walter 1889-1974

September 23, 1889—December 14, 1974; American political analyst, journalist, author of books predominantly on political topics. Obituaries: *New York Times*, December 15, 1974; *Time*, December 23, 1974; *Newsweek*, December 23, 1974; *AB Bookman's Weekly*, January 6, 1975. *Current Biography*, January, 1975. (*CA*-9/10).

* * *

LISS, Jerome 1938-

PERSONAL: Born July 23, 1938, in Bronx, N.Y.; son of Daniel and Betty (a secretary; maiden name, Zucker) Liss; married Barbara Cohen, 1963 (divorced, 1967); children; Aaron William. *Education:* Bard College, B.A., 1960; Albert Einstein College of Medicine, Yeshiva University, M.D., 1964. *Agent:* Francis Greenburg, 757 Third Ave., New York, N.Y. 10003.

CAREER: Psychiatrist. Licensed to practice medicine in New York, Massachusetts, and California. Jewish Hospital of Brooklyn, Brooklyn, N.Y., medical intern, 1964-65; Massachusetts Mental Health Center, Boston, Mass., psychiatric resident, 1965-68. *Member:* Arbours Association.

WRITINGS: Family Talk, Ballantine, 1972; *Free to Feel*, Praeger, 1974. Contributor to *Energy and Character*, *Self and Society*, *New Society*, *Spectator*, and *Forum*.

WORK IN PROGRESS: Helpful Listening.

AVOCATIONAL INTERESTS: Studying French, drama, dancing.

* * *

LISTON, Mary Dawn 1936-

PERSONAL: Born November 30, 1936, in Salt Lake City, Utah; daughter of John Arthur (an attorney) and Ruth (Johnson) Bailey; married Paul Floyd Liston (a college professor), December 29, 1959; children: Richard Lee, Scott Arthur, Cynthia Dawn. *Education:* University of Utah, B.S., 1959; University of Maryland, Far East Division, graduate study, 1964-65; University of Michigan, M.S., 1972; also attended U.S. Army Language School, 1964-65. *Politics:* Democrat. *Home:* 205 South St., Davidson, N.C. 28036. *Office:* Institute for Urban Studies and Community Service, and Department of Geography and Earth Science, University of North Carolina, Charlotte, N.C. 28223.

CAREER: Science teacher in public schools in Salt Lake City, Utah, 1959-61; Department of Defense Overseas Schools, Okinawa, Japan, teacher of language arts, science, and mathematics, 1964-66; substitute teacher in public schools in Ann Arbor, Mich., 1969-70; University of North Carolina, Charlotte, administrative instructor in geography, 1973—, program director of National Science Foundation Environmental Studies Institute, institute associate and internship coordinator for Institute for Urban Studies and Community Service. Mathematics teacher in Honolulu, Hawaii, summer, 1959; instructor in liberal arts program for teachers at Davidson College, 1973, 1974, 1975. Special assistant to Michigan governor's task force to develop a state environmental education plan, 1971-72; regional chairperson of North Carolina Environmental Information and Education Network.

MEMBER: International Union for Conservation of Natural Resources, Conservation Education Association, North Carolina Conservation Council, Metrolina Environmental Concern Association, Mortar Board.

WRITINGS: (With James W. Clay) *Metrolina Environment*, University of North Carolina at Charlotte, 1974; (editor with William Stapp) *Environmental Education Information Guide*, Gale, 1975. Contributor to *Environmental Education Report*. Contract writer for National Television Learning System, 1972. Editor of *Mortar Board Forum*, 1970—.

* * *

LITTLEFIELD, James Edward 1932-

PERSONAL: Born February 3, 1932, in Akron, Ohio; son of Thomas O. (in own business) and Helen J. (Mayberry) Littlefield; married Shirley Joyce Gibitz, September 7, 1957; children: Jonathan E., Melissa A. *Education:* Kent State University, B.S., 1954; University of Chicago, M.B.A., 1957; University of Wisconsin—Madison, Ph.D., 1967. *Home:* 409 Ridgecrest Dr., Chapel Hill, N.C. 27514. *Office:* Graduate School of Business Administration, University of North Carolina, Chapel Hill, N.C. 27514.

CAREER: General Motors Corp., Chevrolet Motor Division, Detroit, Mich., member of product planning staff, 1958-60; B. F. Goodrich Co., Akron, Ohio, corporate marketing researcher, 1960-64; University of North Carolina, Chapel Hill, assistant professor, 1966-69, associate professor, 1969-74, professor of business administration, 1974—, coordinator in marketing, 1968—. Instructor at University of Akron, 1962-63, and Syracuse University, 1968-70; visiting associate professor at Middle East Technical University, 1971-72; instructor at University of Wisconsin—Madison, 1974. *Military service:* U.S. Army Security Agency, 1954-56; served in Europe. *Member:* American Marketing Association, Academy of Advertising, Southern Marketing Association.

WRITINGS: (With Charles A. Kirkpatrick) *Advertising: Mass Communication in Marketing*, Houghton, 1970; (with William P. Glade, Jon G. Udell, and William A. Strang) *Marketing in a Developing Nation*, Heath, 1970; (with Grady J. Burney and William V. White) *Branch Bank Location*, Bank Marketing Association, 1973; (with John R. Kerr) *Marketing: An Environmental Approach*, Prentice-Hall, 1974; (editor) *Readings in Advertising*, West Publishing, 1975. Contributor to professional journals.

WORK IN PROGRESS: Research on marketing in less-developed countries, on advertising, and on bank marketing.

* * *

LITTLETON, Harvey K(line) 1922-

PERSONAL: Born June 14, 1922, in Corning, N.Y.; son of

Jesse Talbot (a physicist) and Bessie (Cook) Littleton; married Bess Tamura, September 6, 1947; children: Carol (Mrs. Robert Shay), Thomas, Maurine, John. *Education:* University of Michigan, B.Design, 1947; Cranbrook Academy of Art, M.F.A., 1951. *Home address:* Route 1, Littleton Rd., Verona, Wis. 53593. *Office:* Department of Art, University of Wisconsin, Madison, Wis. 53706.

CAREER: Toledo Museum of Art, Toledo, Ohio, instructor in ceramics, 1949-51; University of Wisconsin, Madison, instructor, 1951-54, assistant professor, 1954-61, associate professor, 1961-65, professor of art, 1965—, chairman of department, 1964-67, 1969-71. *Military service:* U.S. Army, 1942-45; became staff sergeant. *Member:* National Council on Education in the Ceramic Arts (honorary member), American Crafts Council (trustee, 1957, 1961-64). *Awards, honors:* Louis Comfort Tiffany grant, 1971.

WRITINGS: Glassblowing: A Search for Form, Van Nostrand, 1971. Contributor to *Crafts Horizons*.

SIDELIGHTS: Littleton's work has been included in many exhibitions; work is represented in thirty-nine public collections in the United States and abroad.

* * *

LIVINGSTON, George Herbert 1916-

PERSONAL: Born July 27, 1916, in Russell, Iowa; son of George W. (a farmer) and Clara (Baker) Livingston; married Maria Saarloos, August 12, 1937; children: Burton George, Nellie (Mrs. Ralph J. Kester), David Herbert. *Education:* Kletzing College, A.B., 1945; Asbury Theological Seminary, B.D., 1948; Drew University, Ph.D., 1955. *Politics:* Republican. *Home:* 502 Bellevue St., Wilmore, Ky. 40390. *Office:* Asbury Theological Seminary, Wilmore, Ky. 40390.

CAREER: Methodist minister in Wisconsin, Iowa, South Dakota, Ohio, and New York, 1937-54; Wessington Springs College, Wessington Springs, S.D., dean, 1951-53; Asbury Theological Seminary, Wilmore, Ky., professor of Old Testament, 1953—, chairman of Division of Biblical Literature, 1970—. Lecturer on biblical subjects in Europe, Africa, and Asia. *Member:* Academy of Religion, Society of Biblical Literature, National Association of Professors of Hebrew, Evangelical Theological Society, Wesleyan Theological Society, Kentucky Archaeological Association, Theta Phi.

WRITINGS: A New Approach to Hebrew Grammar, Asbury Theological Seminary, 1968; *The Pentateuch in Its Cultural Environment*, Baker Book, 1974.

Contributor: Charles F. Pfeiffer, editor, *Wycliffe Bible Commentary*, Moody, 1962; Donald Joy, editor, *Arnold's Commentary*, Light and Life Press, 1963, 1965, 1966, 1969, 1971, 1973, 1975; Charles W. Carter, editor, *The Wesleyan Bible Commentary*, Eerdmans, Volume I, 1967, Volume II, 1968; W. T. Purkiser, editor, *Beacon Bible Commentary*, Beacon Hill Press (Kansas City), Volume I, 1969.

Also contributor to "Aldersgate Biblical Series," Light and Life Press, four volumes, 1960-64. Contributor to *Herald*, *Seminarian*, *Sermon Builder*, and *Free Methodist*.

WORK IN PROGRESS: A book on the Old Testament prophets; editorial work on the Old Testament of the New International Version; a programmed learning text for Hebrew.

AVOCATIONAL INTERESTS: Archaeology (Livingston has participated in four digs in Israel).

LLEWELLYN LLOYD, Richard Dafydd Vyvyan 1906-
(Richard Llewellyn)

PERSONAL: Born December 8, 1906, in St. David's, Pembrokeshire, Wales; son of William (a hotelier) and Sarah Anne (Thomas) Llewellyn Lloyd; married Nona Theresa Sonsteby, 1952 (divorced, 1968); married Susan Frances Heimann (an editor), March 29, 1974. *Education:* Educated in Great Britain. *Politics:* Plaid Cymru (Welsh Nationalist). *Religion:* Roman Catholic. *Residence:* Dublin, Ireland.

CAREER: Novelist, playwright, scripwriter, and journalist. *Military service:* Indian Army, 1925-31. British Army, Welsh Guards, 1940-46; became captain. *Awards, honors:* National Book Award, 1940, for *How Green Was My Valley*.

WRITINGS—All under name Richard Llewellyn: *How Green Was My Valley* (first volume of trilogy), M. Joseph, 1939, Macmillan, 1940; *None But the Lonely Heart*, Macmillan, 1943, new edition, 1969; *A Few Flowers for Shiner*, Macmillan, 1950; *A Flame for Doubting Thomas*, Macmillan, 1953; *The Witch of Merthyn*, Doubleday, 1954; *The Flame of Hercules*, Doubleday, 1955; *Mr. Hamish Gleave*, Doubleday, 1956; *Chez Pavan*, Doubleday, 1958; *Warden of the Smoke and Bells*, Doubleday, 1956.

Up, into the Singing Mountain (second volume of trilogy), Doubleday, 1960; *A Man in a Mirror*, Doubleday, 1961; *Sweet Morn of Judas' Day*, Doubleday, 1964; *Down Where the Moon is Small* (title is sometimes listed *And I Shall Sleep . . . Down Where the Moon Is Small*; third volume of trilogy), Doubleday, 1966; *The End of the Rug*, Doubleday, 1968; *But We Didn't Get the Fox*, Doubleday, 1969; *White Horse to Banbury Cross*, Doubleday, 1970; *The Night Is a Child*, Doubleday, 1972; *Bride of Israel, My Love*, Doubleday, 1973; *A Hill of Many Dreams*, Doubleday, 1974; *Green, Green My Valley Now*, Doubleday, 1975.

Also author of plays, "Poison Pen," 1938; "Noose," 1946; "The Scarlet Suit," 1962; "Ecce," 1972.

WORK IN PROGRESS: At Sunrise, the Rough Music, a novel of India.

SIDELIGHTS: The author's first novel, *How Green Was My Valley*, was filmed in 1941. It starred Walter Pidgeon and Maureen O'Hara, and was directed by John Ford.

Before leaving for military service in the Second World War, Llewellyn left the manuscript of *None But the Lonely Heart* on his desk. The unfinished novel was published in the author's absence (he first learned of its publication from a correspondent in Italy who showed him a review of the novel in *Time* magazine) and subsequently became a best-seller and was made into a movie starring Cary Grant and Ethel Barrymore. A quarter of a century later, Llewellyn completed the novel (adding 160 pages of new manuscript) for a new edition.

Llewellyn told *CA*: "Important to most of my books has been—and will ever remain—writing *in situ*. Whatever truths my characters tell me about themselves they tell me, as it were, at home. They couldn't do it—as I could not—elsewhere."

* * *

LOBEL, Anita (Kempler) 1934-

PERSONAL: Born June 3, 1934 in Cracow, Poland; married Arnold Lobel, 1955; children: Adrianne, Adam. *Education:* Pratt Institute, B.F.A.

CAREER: Author and illustrator of books for children. *Awards, honors: Under a Mushroom* was named on Child Study Association Book List, 1971; *Book World* Children's Spring Book Festival Award, 1973, for *Little John*; *A Birthday for the Princess* was a Children's Book Showcase Title, 1974.

WRITINGS—All self-illustrated; all published by Harper: *Sven's Bridge*, 1965; *The Troll Music*, 1966; *Potatoes, Potatoes*, 1967; *The Seamstress of Salzburg*, 1970; *Under a Mushroom*, 1971; *A Birthday for the Princess*, 1973.

Illustrator: Paul Kapp, *Cock-A-Doodle Doo! Cock-A-Doodle-Dandy!*, Harper, 1966; Meindert de Jong, *Puppy Summer*, Harper, 1966; F. N. Monjo, *Indian Summer*, Harper, 1968; Alice Dalgliesh, *The Little Wooden Farmer*, Macmillan, 1968; Benjamin Elkin, *The Wisest Man in the World*, Parents' Magazine Press, 1968; Barbara Borack, *Someone Small*, Harper, 1969; Doris Orgel, *Uproar*, McGraw, 1970; Mirra Ginsburg, editor, *Three Rolls and One Doughnut: Fables from Russia*, Dial, 1970; Benjamin Elkin, *How the Tsar Drinks Tea*, Parents' Magazine Press, 1971; Theodore Storm, *Little John*, retold by Doris Orgel, Farrar, Straus, 1972; John Langstaff, *Soldier, Soldier, Won't You Marry Me*, Doubleday, 1972; Cynthia Jameson, *One for the Price of Two*.

SIDELIGHTS: Ms. Lobel was born in Poland, has lived in Stockholm, and came to the United States in 1952. "Having lived close to much peasant art as a child, I have always been interested in the decorative arts. It is hard for me to leave any white surface alone. I embroider clothes whenever I can and have also designed needlepoint tapestries."

* * *

LOCHNER, Louis P(aul) 1887-1975

February 22, 1887—January 8, 1975; American journalist, foreign correspondent, governmental consultant on German affairs, author. Obituaries: *New York Times*, January 9, 1975; *Washington Post*, January 12, 1975; *AB Bookman's Weekly*, February 3, 1975; *Current Biography*, February, 1975.

* * *

LOCKE, Lucie 1904- (Lucie Locke Price)

PERSONAL: Born February 22, 1904, in Valdosta, Ga.; daughter of Stevens Thomas (a physician) and Caroline (a teacher; maiden name, Haygood) Harris; married David Roger Locke, September 9, 1926 (died January, 1960); married Armstrong Price (a geological expert on shorelines), February 27, 1962; children: (first marriage) Brent (Mrs. Carrol Laverne Riley), Elizabeth (Mrs. David Crilley Clarke), David Roger, Jr. *Education:* Attended Newcomb College Art School of Tulane University. *Politics:* Independent. *Religion:* Unitarian-Universalist. *Home:* 401 Southern St., Corpus Christi, Tex. 78404.

CAREER: Art teacher in public schools of El Paso, Tex., 1924-25; art curator for Corpus Christi (Tex.) Centennial Museum, 1937-40; artist, poet. *Member:* Southwest Sculpture Society, Poetry Society of Texas, Texas Fine Arts (member of board of directors, 1947-48), South Texas Art League (member of board of directors). *Awards, honors:* First prize in landscape painting from Eagle Pass International Exposition, 1942, for "With Head Unbowed"; Avalon presidential citation for excellence in poetry, 1969, for "The Spiral"; Diploma di Benemerenza for *Seize the Ring* and "Moon-Pulled."

WRITINGS: Naturally Yours, Texas (children's poems), Naylor, 1949; *Seize the Ring* (poems), von Boeckmann-Jones Press, 1972. Poems represented in anthologies, including *Bouquet of Poems*, 1968, and *Masters of Modern Poetry*, 1974, both published by Centro Studi e Scambi Internazionali. Art critic for *Corpus Christi Caller-Times*, 1940-70.

WORK IN PROGRESS: Poems; *Caroline and I, Or 'Summer Brook' and Other Poems*, childhood reminiscences of life in Highlands, N.C.

SIDELIGHTS: Miss Locke told *CA*: "I have taken an active part in the development of art organizations in this area since 1939. I began my active writing career in the 1940's and have been a 'pioneer' in this section in both areas. I attended the Southwest Writer's Conference every year (except two) from 1945 until its demise in 1966 (now revived in Houston, Tex.) and won awards each year, as well as in the Colony Writers (which I helped establish). I am still an active writer of poetry at age seventy, and am also doing miniature nudes in terra cotta."

* * *

LODGE, Henry Cabot 1902-

PERSONAL: Born July 5, 1902, in Nahant, Mass.; son of George Cabot (a poet and secretary to his father, Henry Cabot Lodge, Sr.) and Mathilda Elizabeth Frelinghuysen (Davis) Lodge; married Emily Esther Sears, July 1, 1926; children: George Cabot, Henry Sears. *Education:* Harvard University, A.B. (cum laude), 1924. *Politics:* Republican. *Home:* 275 Hale St., Beverly, Mass. 01915.

CAREER: Boston *Transcript*, Boston, Mass., reporter, 1923; New York *Herald Tribune*, New York, N.Y., political reporter and member of editorial staff, 1924-32; Massachusetts Legislature, Boston, member, 1933-37; U.S. Senator from Massachusetts, 1937-43, reelected in 1942 but resigned to enter U.S. Army, resuming seat, 1946-53; campaign manager for Dwight D. Eisenhower, 1952; appointed to United Nations, and member of President Eisenhower's cabinet, 1953-60; Republican vice-presidential candidate, 1960; Atlantic Institute, Paris, director general, 1961-62; U.S. ambassador to South Vietnam, 1963-64, 1965-67, amabassador-at-large, 1967-68, ambassador to Federal Republic of Germany, 1968-69; chief U.S. negotiator at Paris peace talks, 1969; special presidential envoy to the Vatican, 1970—; North Shore Community College, Beverly, Mass., lecturer in U.S. foreign relations, 1972—. Member of board of overseers, Harvard University, 1939-45. *Military service:* U.S. Army Reserve, 1925-62, active duty, 1941-42, 1944-45; served in Africa, Italy, France, Germany; retired as major general; received Bronze Star, Legion of Merit, and seven battle stars.

AWARDS, HONORS: Chevalier's Cross, Order of Polonia Restituta, 1930; Croix de Guerre with palm and Legion d'Honneur (both France), 1945; Theodore Roosevelt Association Medal, 1959; Sylvanus Thayer Medal, West Point Military Academy, 1960; Humane Order of African Redemption (Liberia), 1960; National Order of Republic of Vietnam, 1964; Distinguished Honor award from U.S. Department of State, 1968; Grand Cross of Merit (Malta). Honorary degrees: LL.B., Northeastern University, 1938; LL.D. from Clark University, 1951, Norwich University,

1951, Hamilton College, 1953, Franklin and Marshall College, 1953, Boston University, 1953, Harvard University, 1954, New York University, 1955, Fordham University, 1955, Rensselaer Polytechnic Institute, 1955, Lehigh University, 1956, University of Pennsylvania, 1956; Docteur-es-Lettres, Laval University, 1952; D.C.L., Bishop's University, 1953; also received degrees from William College, Union College, Boston College, Princeton University, Adelphi University, and Columbia University.

WRITINGS: The Cult of Weakness, Houghton, 1932; *The United Nations: A Place to Promote Peace*, U.S. Government Printing Office, 1953; (contributor) William W. Wade, editor, *The Reference Shelf: The U.N. Today*, H. W. Wilson, 1954; *You and the United Nations*, U.S. Government Printing Office, 1955, revised edition, 1956; *The Storm Has Many Eyes: A Personal Narrative*, Norton, 1973. Contributor to *Atlantic*, *Collier's*, *Life*, *Reader's Digest*, *Saturday Evening Post*, *Harper's*, *Herald Tribune* (New York), and other publications.

* * *

LOGAN, Albert Boyd 1909-

PERSONAL: Born January 27, 1909, in Colorado Springs, Colo.; son of Glen Hayes (a railroad executive) and Margaret (McGee) Logan; married Martha Elizabeth Hutchison, September 28, 1934; children: Marla Lee (Mrs. Al Hollingsworth), Glenda Sue (Mrs. Stephen Harrison). *Education:* University of Colorado, A.B., 1930, LL.B., 1932, J.D., 1968. *Politics:* Republican. *Religion:* Roman Catholic. *Home:* 2727 29th St. N.W., Washington, D.C. 20008. *Agent:* Irwin Zucker, 6565 Sunset Blvd., Hollywood, Calif. *Office:* 2607 Connecticut Ave. N.W., Washington, D.C. 20008.

CAREER: Admitted to Bar of State of Colorado, 1932; private practice of law in Colorado Springs, Colo., 1932-56; U.S. Department of Interior, Office of Solicitor, Denver, Colo., attorney-advisor, 1956-66; Indian Claims Commission, Washington, D.C., counsel, 1966-70; Veterans Administration, Office of General Counsel, Washington, D.C., trial attorney, 1970—. Executive director, American Judges Association, 1960-67; director, National Institute of Judicial Dynamics, 1968—. President of Colorado Junior Chamber of Commerce, 1937; member of board of directors of U.S. Junior Chamber of Commerce, 1938-39, and Harmony Foundation, Inc., 1969—. Consultant to National Center for Alcohol Education. *Military service:* U.S. Marine Corps, 1944-45.

MEMBER: National Press Club, National Lawyers Club, American Judicature Society, National Council on Crime and Delinquency, American Bar Association, Federal Bar Association, Colorado Bar Association, Exchange Club, El Paso Club. *Awards, honors:* National Association of Municipal Judges awards, 1960-68, including award for "Beyond Call of Duty," 1961, and award for "Amicus Curiae," 1964.

WRITINGS: The Struggle for Equal Justice, U.S. Government Printing Office, 1969; *Justice in Jeopardy*, C. C Thomas, 1974. Contributor to *American Bar Journal*, *Judicature*, *Dicta*, *Editor and Publisher*, and *Addictions*. Editor of *Municipal Court Briefs* and *Municipal Court Review*, 1960-68.

WORK IN PROGRESS: American Corrections System: Utter Failure; research on court reorganization; a national program for education on addictions for judges, and for court, law enforcement, and corrections personnel; activation of a new Advisory Council of Judges for the Alcohol and Drug Problems Association.

* * *

LOKKEN, Roy N(orman) 1917-

PERSONAL: Surname is pronounced *Lock*-in; born October 28, 1917, in Fargo, N.D.; son of Olaf K. and Olga (Hendricksen) Lokken; married Ruth Hayes, October 15, 1966. *Education:* University of Puget Sound, B.A., 1941; University of Washington, Seattle, M.A., 1951, Ph.D., 1955. *Politics:* Democrat. *Religion:* Baptist. *Home:* 418 West Fifth St., Greenville, N.C. 27834. *Office:* Department of History, East Carolina University, Greenville, N.C. 27834.

CAREER: State Historical Society of Wisconsin, Madison, assistant archivist, 1955-58; Wisconsin Legislative Council, Madison, research associate, 1958-62; University of Texas, Arlington, instructor, 1962-64, assistant professor of history, 1964-67; East Carolina University, Greenville, N.C., associate professor, 1967-74, professor of history, 1974—. *Military service:* U.S. Army, 1942-45. *Member:* American Historical Association, Organization of American Historians, American Political Science Association, Southern Historical Association. *Awards, honors:* Louis Pelzer Award from Mississippi Valley Historical Association (now Organization of American Historians), 1953, for "Has the Mystery of 'A Public Man' Been Solved?"

WRITINGS: David Lloyd: Colonial Lawmaker, University of Washington Press, 1959; (editor) *The Scientific Papers of James Logan*, American Philosophical Society, 1972.

WORK IN PROGRESS: Cadwallader Colden: Colonial Scientist and Philosopher.

* * *

LOMBARDI, John V(incent) 1942-

PERSONAL: Born August 19, 1942, in Los Angeles, Calif.; son of John and Janice (Pidduck) Lombardi; married Cathryn L. Lee, January 25, 1964; children: John Lee, Mary Ann. *Education:* National University of Mexico, student, 1960; Pomona College, B.A., 1963; Columbia University, M.A., 1964, Ph.D., 1968. *Residence:* Bloomington, Ind. *Office:* Department of History, Indiana University, Bloomington, Ind. 47401.

CAREER: Central University of Venezuela, Caracas, contract professor of history, Faculty of Humanities and Education, 1967; Indiana University, Southeast Campus, Jeffersonville, lecturer, 1967-68, assistant professor of history, 1968-69; Indiana University, Bloomington, visiting assistant professor, 1968-69, assistant professor, 1969-71, associate professor of history, 1971—, director of Latin American Studies Program, 1971-74, director of Caracas Project, 1974—. *Member:* American Historical Association, Latin American Studies Association, Conference on Latin American History. *Awards, honors:* Fulbright-Hays research fellowship in Venezuela, 1965-66; Fundacion Crele fellowship in Venezuela, 1966-67.

WRITINGS: The Political Ideology of Fray Servando Teresa de Mier: Propagandist for Independence, Centro Intercultural de Documentacion, 1968; *The Decline and Abolition of Negro Slavery in Venezuela, 1820-1854*, Greenwood Press, 1971.

Contributor: Charles C. Griffin, editor, *Latin America: A Guide to Historical Literature*, University of Texas Press, for Conference on Latin American History, 1971; Richard Graham and Peter H. Smith, editors, *Approaches to Latin American History*, University of Texas Press, 1974; Martin L. Kilson and Robert I. Rothberg, editors, *Harvard Studies on the African Diaspora*, Volume III, Harvard University Press, in press. Contributor to *Encyclopedia of Latin America*; articles and about twenty reviews and notes have been published in journals in United States, Mexico, and Venezuela.

WORK IN PROGRESS: Three volumes on Venezuela—Volume I: *The Distribution and Composition of Population in the Bishopric of Caracas, 1776-1810: An Essay in the Historical Demography of Venezuela*; Volume II: (with Trent M. Brady) *The Population of the Bishopric of Caracas, 1780-1830: A Workbook in the Historical Demography of Venezuela*; Volume III: *Household Patterns in the Bishopric of Caracas, 1750-1780*.

* * *

LONERGAN, Bernard Joseph Francis 1904-

PERSONAL: Born December 17, 1904, in Buckingham, Quebec, Canada; son of Gerald Joseph (a surveyor) and Josephine Helen (Wood) Lonergan. *Education:* Studied at Loyola College, Montreal, Quebec, 1920-22, Ignatius College, 1922-26, and Heythrop College (now of University of London), 1926-30; University of London, B.A., 1930; Gregorian University, S.T.L., 1937, S.T.D., 1945. *Office:* Regis College, Willowdale, Ontario, Canada.

CAREER: Entered Society of Jesus (Jesuits), 1922, ordained Roman Catholic priest, 1936; L'Immaculee Conception, Montreal, Quebec, extraordinary professor, 1940-42, ordinary professor of theology, 1942-47; Jesuit Seminary, Toronto, Ontario, ordinary professor of theology, 1947-53; Gregorian University, Rome, Italy, ordinary professor of theology, 1953-65; Regis College, Willowdale, Ontario, research professor of theology, 1965—. Stillman Professor at Harvard University Divinity School, 1971-72. Peritus of Second Vatican Council; member of International Theological Commission, 1969-74; consultor of Secretariat for Non-Believers, 1973—.

AWARDS, HONORS: Honorary doctorates from St. Mary's University (Halifax), 1964, Holy Cross College (Worcester, Mass.) and University of St. Michael's (Toronto), 1969; Marquette University and Boston College, 1970; Catholic University of America, University of Notre Dame, Fordham University, and University of Santa Clara, 1971; St. Joseph's College (Philadelphia), and St. Louis University, 1972; Sir Wilfred Laurier University, 1973; and University of Chicago, 1974; Spellman Award from Catholic Theological Society of America, 1949; Aquinas Medal from American Catholic Philosophical Association, 1970; Companion of the Order of Canada, 1970; John Courtney Murray Award from Catholic Theological Society of America, 1973; Aquinas Award from Aquinas College, 1974.

WRITINGS: *Insight*, Philosophical Library, 1957; *Collection*, Herder & Herder, 1967; *Verbum*, University of Notre Dame Press, 1967; *The Subject*, Marquette University Press, 1968; *Doctrinal Pluralism*, Marquette University Press, 1971; *Grace and Freedom in Aquinas*, Herder & Herder, 1971; *Method in Theology*, Herder & Herder, 1972; *Philosophy of God and Theology*, Longman, 1973, Westminster, 1974; *A Second Collection*, Longman, 1974, Westminster, 1975.

Books in Latin: *De Constitutione Christi* (title means "Systematic Theology of the Incarnation"), Gregorian Press, 1956; *De Deo Trino* (title means "On the Trinity"), Gregorian Press, Volume I, 1959, Volume II, 1961, 3rd edition, 1964; *De Verbo Incarnato* (title means "On the Incarnation"), Gregorian Press, 1961, revised edition, 1964.

WORK IN PROGRESS: Circulation Analysis.

BIOGRAPHICAL/CRITICAL SOURCES: Continuum 2, #3, 1964; David Tracy, *The Achievement of Bernard Lonergan*, Herder & Herder, 1970; Giovanni Sala, *Das Apriori in der menschlichen Erkenntnis: Eine Studie ueber Kant's KRV und Lonergan's Insight*, Anton Hain, 1971; Philip McShane, editor, *Papers from Lonergan Congress*, University of Notre Dame Press, Volume I, 1971, Volume II, 1972.

* * *

LONGACRE, Edward G(eorge) 1946-

PERSONAL: Born December 22, 1946, in Camden, N.J.; son of Edgar Thorp (a laboratory technician) and Evelyn (Weisser) Longacre. *Education:* La Salle College, B.A., 1969; University of Nebraska, M.A., 1974; Temple University, graduate study, 1974—. *Politics:* Independent. *Religion:* Roman Catholic. *Home:* 447 Chestnut St., Audubon, N.J. 08106. *Agent:* Paul R. Reynolds, Inc., 12 East 41st St., New York, N.Y. 10017. *Office:* Department of History, Temple University, Philadelphia, Pa. 19141.

CAREER: University of Nebraska, Lincoln, instructor in English and history of film, 1972-74; Temple University, Philadelphia, Pa., teaching assistant, 1974—.

WRITINGS: From Union Stars to Top Hat: A Biography of the Extraordinary General James Harrison Wilson, Stackpole, 1972; *Mounted Raids of the Civil War*, A. S. Barnes, 1975. Contributor to history journals.

WORK IN PROGRESS: Editing *From Atlanta to the Sea: The Civil War Letters of Eli S. Ricker*; *The Man behind the Guns: A Biography of General Henry J. Hunt, Commander of Artillery, Army of the Potomac*, completion expected in 1975; *The Cavalry at Gettysburg: A Comprehensive Study of Mounted Operations during the Gettysburg Campaign*, in 1975; *Hardluck Army: A History of General Benjamin F. Butler and the Army of the James, 1864-65*, in 1976; a regimental history of the Twelfth New Jersey Volunteer Infantry, 1862-65, in 1976; a novel about the New York City draft riots of July, 1863; a history of the Cavalry Corps of the Army of the Potomac; a biography of early screen comedienne Mabel Normand.

AVOCATIONAL INTERESTS: Making documentary films, playing tennis and basketball.

* * *

LONGACRE, Robert E(dmondson) 1922-

PERSONAL: Born August 22, 1922, in Akron, Ohio; son of William K. (a printer) and Sylvia (Steed) Longacre; married Gwendolyn Stratton (a teacher), June 28, 1946; children: Roberta, William, Stephen, David. *Education:* Houghton College, A.B. (magna cum laude), 1943; Faith Theological Seminary, Wilmington, Del., B.D., 1946; University of Pennsylvania, M.A., 1953, Ph.D., 1955. *Religion:* Reformed Presbyterian. *Home:* 7500 West Camp Wisdom Rd., Dallas, Tex. 75211. *Office:* Summer Institute of Linguistics, Huntingdon Beach, Calif.

CAREER: Summer Institute of Linguistics, Huntingdon Beach, Calif., field investigator in Mexico, beginning 1946, consultant for Mexican branch, 1955-70, international linguistic consultant, 1966—, visiting professor for Institute's summer sessions at University of Oklahoma and University of North Dakota. Teacher of linguistics at University of Michigan, Ann Arbor, 1960-61, and at State University of New York at Buffalo, 1966-67; University of Texas at Arlington, professor of linguistics, 1972—. Visiting professor at annual summer Institute of Linguistic Society of America, State University of New York at Buffalo, 1971.

MEMBER: Linguistic Society of America, Linguistic Society of Papua New Guinea, Linguistic Society of the Philippines. *Awards, honors:* Grants from U.S. Department of Health, Education, and Welfare, 1967 and 1969, for study in the Philippines and New Guinea; grant for writing from Institute for Advanced Christian Studies, 1973; National Science Foundation and National Endowment for the Humanities grant, 1974-75, for research in Colombia, Ecuador, and Panama.

WRITINGS: *Grammar Discovery Procedures*, Mouton & Co., 1964; *Philippine Languages: Discourse, Paragraph, and Sentence Structure*, Summer Institute of Linguistics (Santa Ana, Calif.), 1968; *Hierarchy and Universality of Discourse Constituents in New Guinea Languages*, Georgetown University Press, 1972; (editor) *Philippine Discourse and Paragraph Studies in Memory of Betty McLachlin*, Australian National University, 1973.

WORK IN PROGRESS: *An Anatomy of Speech Notions*, publication expected by Indiana University Press; a book based on the discourse structure of Indian languages of Colombia, Ecuador, and Panama.

SIDELIGHTS: Longacre lived in Mexico from 1946 to 1972. He translated the New Testament of the Bible into the Trique language of southern Mexico, under the auspices of the Wycliffe Bible Translators. He writes that he is "... interested in applying results of theoretical linguistics to translation and composition ... interested in language as an index to human nature and human life."

* * *

LONGINO, Charles F(reeman), Jr. 1938-

PERSONAL: Born March 3, 1938, in Brookhaven, Miss.; son of Charles F. (a businessman) and Alma (Harris) Longino; married Loyce White, July 11, 1964; children: Laura Elizabeth, Charles F. III. *Education:* Mississippi College, B.A., 1960; University of Colorado, M.A., 1962; University of North Carolina, Ph.D., 1967. *Politics:* Democrat. *Religion:* Baptist. *Home:* 1532 Trailridge Rd., Charlottesville, Va. 22903. *Office:* Department of Sociology, University of Virginia, Charlottesville, Va. 22903.

CAREER: University of North Carolina, Chapel Hill, assistant professor of sociology, 1967-68; University of Virginia, Charlottesville, assistant professor of sociology, 1968—, research associate at Center for Program Effectiveness Studies, 1970—. Visiting lecturer at University of Kansas, 1974-75; chairman of board of directors of Overseas Medical Fund, 1972-74; consultant to Center for Criminal Justice. *Member:* American Sociological Association, Society for the Scientific Study of Religion, Southern Sociological Society.

WRITINGS: (Editor with David G. Bromley) *White Racism and Black Americans*, Schenkman, 1972; (with Jeffrey K. Hadden) *Gideon's Gang: A Case Study of the Church in Social Action*, Pilgrim, 1974. Contributor to professional journals.

WORK IN PROGRESS: *Occupation in Transition: Black Dentists in America; Invasion of the Elderly: Case Study of a Natural Retirement Community*, completion expected in 1977.

* * *

LOPEZ, Cecilia L(uisa) 1941-

PERSONAL: Born March 13, 1941, in New York, N.Y.; daughter of Cecilio G. (a mechanic) and Luisa (a secretary; maiden name, Roman) Lopez. *Education:* Florida State University, B.A., 1964, M.A., 1967. *Politics:* Democrat. *Home:* 1631 Franrose Lane, Concord, Calif. 94519. *Office:* Department of English, Chabot College, Hesperian Blvd., Hayward, Calif. 94545.

CAREER: High school English teacher in Tallahassee, Fla., 1964-65; Florida Agricultural & Mechanical University, Tallahassee, instructor in English, 1966-68; Chabot College, Hayward, Calif., instructor in English, 1969—, director of Writing Center. *Member:* Modern Language Association of America, American Society for Eighteenth-Century Studies.

WRITINGS: *Alexander Pope: An Annotated Bibliography, 1945-1967*, University of Florida Press, 1970.

WORK IN PROGRESS: Ten programmed textbooks in remedial writing.

* * *

LORD, Graham 1943-

PERSONAL: Born February 16, 1943, in Umtali, Rhodesia; son of Harold (a businessman) and Ida (McDowell) Lord; married Jane Carruthers, 1962; children: Mandy, Kate. *Education:* Churchill College, Cambridge, B.A. (honors), 1965. *Agent:* Brandt & Brandt, 101 Park Ave., New York, N.Y. 10017. *Office: Sunday Express*, Fleet Street, London, England.

CAREER: *Cambridge News*, Cambridge, England, reporter, 1964; *Sunday Express*, London, England, reporter, 1965-69, books columnist, 1969—. *Member:* Institute of Journalists.

WRITINGS: *Marshmallow Pie* (novel), Coward, 1970; *A Roof under Your Feet* (novel), Macdonald, 1974; *The Spider and the Fly* (novel), Viking, 1975.

WORK IN PROGRESS: A novel, completion expected in 1975.

SIDELIGHTS: "Writing novels," Lord wrote, "is cheaper than booze and more effective than psychiatry, and like both should be firmly resisted as far as possible." *Avocational interests:* Travel (Western Europe and Africa).

* * *

LORD, John Vernon 1939-

PERSONAL: Born April 9, 1939, in Glossop, England; son of Herbert Vernon (a baker) and Isobel Marjorie (a hairdresser; maiden name, Smith) Lord; married Lorna Deanna Trevelyan (a nurse and artist), August 20, 1961; children: Rachel Joanna, Katie Ruhamah, Corin Derry. *Education:* Salford Art School, D.A., 1960; attended Central School of Arts and Crafts, London, England, 1960-61. *Home and office:* Upwell, 4 Orchard Lane, Ditchling, Hassocks, Sussex BN6 8TH, England.

CAREER: Has worked as a chef, sandwich-board man, postman, factory worker; free-lance book illustrator, 1960—; Brighton Polytechnic, Faculty of Art & Design,

Brighton, England, principal lecturer in drawing and illustration, 1961—. Member of graphic design panel of National Council for Diplomas in Art and Design. *Member:* Society of Illustrators.

WRITINGS—Self-illustrated children's books: *The Runaway Rollerskate*, Houghton, 1974; *Mr. Mead and His Garden*, Houghton, 1974.

Illustrator: Lena F. Hurlong, *Adventures of Jaboti on the Amazon*, Abelard-Schuman, 1968; Joseph Jacobs, *Reynard the Fox*, as retold by Roy Brown, Abelard-Schuman, 1969; Janet Burroway, *The Truck on the Track*, J. Cape, 1970, Bobbs-Merrill, 1971; Ann Coates, *Dinosaurs Don't Die*, Longman Young, 1970; Joel Chandler Harris, *The Adventures of Brer Rabbit*, British Broadcasting Company, 1972; Burroway, *The Giant Jam Sandwich*, J. Cape, 1972, Houghton, 1973; Rosemary Sutcliffe, *Sword at Sunset*, Heron Books, 1975.

WORK IN PROGRESS: Certain aspects of children's literature, a short lecture course.

SIDELIGHTS: Lord told *CA*: "A good children's book should appeal to child, uncle, Mum, Dad, Grandma, teenager alike and should not be self-consciously written with just the child in mind." *The Giant Jam Sandwich* was dramatized on BBC-TV. *Avocational interests:* Music (especially English Tudor composers, Monteverdi, Bach, Purcell), gardening, natural history (especially bird-watching), walking in the country, keeping geese and hens.

* * *

LORENZO, Carol Lee 1939-

PERSONAL: Born February 28, 1939, in Atlanta, Ga.; daughter of Henry George (a grocer) and Freddye Lee (a supervisor of beauty salons; maiden name, Williams) Newman; married Samuel Lorenzo (a lawyer and exhibiting photographer), November 21, 1964. *Education:* Attended American Theatre Wing, 1957-58, Herbert Berghof Acting Studio, 1959, and New School for Social Research, 1970—.

CAREER: Writer for children. Has worked as an actress on Off-Off Broadway.

WRITINGS—For children: *Mama's Ghosts*, Harper, 1974; *Heart-of-Snowbird*, Harper, in press. Contributor of articles and reviews to magazines.

WORK IN PROGRESS: The White Sand Road (tentative title), a third novel for children.

SIDELIGHTS: Carol Lee Lorenzo writes that she regrets that she "never learned to do anything tangible—neither writing or acting deals with known quantities. . . . At writing's most frustrating times, I dream of being a chemist and putting A and B together and making Alka Seltzer (but that's only because I don't understand what's involved in Chemistry)." *Avocational interests:* Natural history, animals (especially dogs), reading, walking, sketching with charcoal.

* * *

LORY, Robert 1936-

PERSONAL: Born December 29, 1936, in Troy, N.Y.; son of Edward Austin (a shirt-cutter) and Dorothy (Doughty) Lory; married second wife, Barbara Banner (a writer), 1968; children: (first marriage) Dominique Lynn, Robert, Jr.; (second marriage) Shana Erin, Joshua Jared. *Education:* State University of New York at Binghamton, B.A., 1961; Washington School of Art, further study, 1973. *Residence:* Houston, Tex. *Office:* Esso Eastern, Inc., Houston, Tex.

CAREER: New York State Electric and Gas Corp., Binghamton, copywriter, 1961-64; Reynolds Metal Co., Richmond, Va., manager of publications, 1964-67; Exxon Corp., New York, N.Y., communications specialist, 1967-68; Esso Libya, Tripoli, communications coordinator, 1968-70; Esso Eastern, Inc., Houston, Tex., public relations adviser, 1971—. Free-lance industrial photographer, country rock singer. Head of Lory Creative Services. *Military service:* U.S. Army, 1954-57. *Member:* Science Fiction Writers of America.

WRITINGS—Novels: *The Eyes of Bolsk*, Ace Books, 1969; *Master of the Etrax*, Dell, 1970; *Masters of the Lamp*, Ace Books, 1970; *A Harvest of Hoodwinks* (short stories), Ace Books, 1970; *The Veiled World*, Ace Books, 1972; *Dracula Returns*, Pinnacle, 1973; *The Hand of Dracula*, Pinnacle, 1973; *Dracula's Brothers*, Pinnacle, 1973; *Dracula's Gold*, Pinnacle, 1973; *Identity Seven*, D.A.W. Books, 1974; *The Drums of Dracula*, Pinnacle, 1974; *The Witching of Dracula*, Pinnacle, 1974; *The Green Flames of Aries*, Pinnacle, 1974; *The Revenge of Taurus*, Pinnacle, 1974; *The Curse of Leo*, Pinnacle, 1974; *The Thirteen Bracelets*, Ace Books, 1974.

WORK IN PROGRESS: Research on the black arts (witchcraft, demonology, and astrology), and the mythology of all people.

SIDELIGHTS: Lory writes: "I've always been interested in what I call the 'alternate explanation,' [as] in *You're a Good Man, Charlie Brown* . . . where Lucy is 'explaining' things to Linus, how snow really comes up from the ground, then comes down; how earthworms tug at the grass to make it grow. That's a perfect example of alternate explanation. . .

"I am highly opinionated, pompous and bombastic, crudely sophisticated. There's only one thing I like doing better than blowing holes in my own arguments (after my antagonists have adopted them), and that is doing what Conan Doyle reportedly said he wanted to do in his writing: 'Tell a whopping good tale.'"

* * *

LOVE, Alan C(arson) 1937-

PERSONAL: Born April 2, 1937, in Dallas, Tex.; son of Alan Cavitt (a civil engineer) and Lina (Carson) Love; married Roberta Wells, October 15, 1959 (divorced September 27, 1968); married Geraldine Rosalie Payson Stewart Yanta, August 2, 1969 (divorced December 27, 1972); children: (first marriage) Roberta Ellen; (second marriage) Alyne Christina. *Education:* Texas A&M University, B.A., 1964, M.A., 1966; graduate study at Texas Tech University, 1973—. *Home:* 204 East Elmview, San Antonio, Tex. 78209. *Office:* Department of English, San Antonio College, San Antonio, Tex. 78284.

CAREER: San Antonio College, San Antonio, Tex., instructor, 1966-69, assistant professor of English, 1969—. *Military service:* U.S. Air Force, 1955-59. *Member:* Conference of College Teachers of English, South Central Modern Language Association.

WRITINGS: (With Robert O'Neal) *English for You*, Heath, 1972.

WORK IN PROGRESS: Two novels, *Guyot* and *The Venusian Report*; a technical writing text.

SIDELIGHTS: "I take in all topics—too many at times," Love wrote, "so that the divergence of a contemporary novel . . . a science fiction novel . . . technical writing . . . teaching, my interest in electronics, music, or just plain hard work does not get in my way. My liking for the writing process leads me into paths that my critical training keeps from becoming 'yellow brick roads' or dead ends. But I work hard to keep that critical training from destroying my purpose."

* * *

LOWDEN, Desmond 1937-

PERSONAL: Born September 27, 1937, in Winchester, England; son of Patrick Alfred Thomas (a physician) and Margaret Elizabeth Lucy Lowden; married Gillian Ann Best; children: Matthew Thomas, Annabel Laura. *Education:* Attended Marlborough College, Wiltshire, England, 1951-55. *Agent:* Deborah Rogers Ltd., 20 Goodge St., London W.1, England.

CAREER: Movie assistant director and assistant editor, at Pinewood-Shepperton Studios, 1956-60; deckhand and English teacher in the Mediterranean countries, 1961-63; television and film writer in London and Hampshire, England, 1963-70; novelist, 1970—.

WRITINGS—Novels: *Bandersnatch*, Holt, 1969; *The Boondocks*, Eyre Methuen, 1972, Holt, 1973; *Bellman and True*, Holt, 1975.

Television plays: "No Baby at All," 1956; "The Newsbenders," 1968.

WORK IN PROGRESS: *Belladonna* (tentative title), a novel.

SIDELIGHTS: Lowden writes: "I was awarded a county grant to a university, but decided not to go. I got a job as a runner at Pinewood Studios, and stayed in the film industry for five years. I wrote abortive scripts for film director Clive Donner. I got on a yacht leaving for the Mediterranean and stayed two years. Married in Athens, returned from the island of Crete to the strange London of 1963. . . . Ten years now out in the country, and the score is two kids, three and a half novels, and a dog and a cat."

* * *

LOWRIE, Donald A(lexander) 1889-1974

January 29, 1889—October 12, 1974; American war relief leader, publishing executive, author. Obituaries: *New York Times*, October 15, 1974. (*CA*-5/6).

* * *

LUBOWE, Irwin I(rville) 1905-

PERSONAL: Born January 13, 1905, in New York, N.Y.; son of Harry and Fanny Lubowe; married Ruth Katz, 1945; children: Mark, Stephen. *Education:* City College (now City College of the City University of New York), B.A., 1926; New York Medical College, M.D., 1930; New York Postgraduate Medical College, postdoctoral study, 1940-41, 1945. *Home:* 45 Sutton Pl., New York, N.Y. 10022. *Office:* 667 Madison Ave., New York, N.Y. 10021.

CAREER: Diplomate, American Board of Dermatology and Syphilology, 1946. Private practice of dermatology in New York, N.Y.; Flower-Fifth Avenue Hospital, New York, N.Y., intern, 1930-31; Metropolitan Hospital, New York, N.Y., chief dermatologist in clinic, 1934—; New York Medical College, Metropolitan Hospital Center, New York, N.Y., clinical professor of dermatology, 1946—. Epidemiologist, New York City Department of Health, clinic chief physician in Bureau of Social Hygiene, assistant visiting dermatologist, New York University Skin and Cancer Unit, and Bellevue Hospital Medical Center, 1946-57; associate visiting dermatologist, Metropolitan Hospital Department of Dermatology and Syphilology, and Flower-Fifth Avenue Hospital. Consultant to cosmetic companies. *Military service:* U.S. Army, 1942-46; served as chief dermatologist with 61st Station Hospitals in Europe and North Africa; became captain; received battle stars.

MEMBER: International College of Applied Nutrition, American Academy of Dermatology and Syphilology (fellow), American College of Allergists (fellow), American Public Health Association (fellow), American Medical Association (fellow), American Pharmaceutical Association (fellow), American College of Pharmacology and Chemotherapy (fellow), American Chemical Society, American Medical Writers' Association, Argentinian Society of Dermatology (honorary fellow), Royal Society of Health, New York Academy of Sciences (fellow), New York Council of Surgeons (fellow in dermatology), Dermatology Society of New York State, New York County Medical Society, Bronx Dermatological Society.

WRITINGS: *Tell Me the Truth, Doctor*, Dorrance, c. 1960; *New Hope for Your Hair*, Dutton, 1962; *New Hope for Your Skin*, Dutton, 1963; (with F. V. Wells) *Cosmetics and the Skin*, Reinhold, 1964; (with Morris Dauer) *Dermatology Formulary and Pharmaceutical Manual*, New York Medical College, 1964; (with Barbara S. Huss) *A Teen Age Guide for Healthy Hair and Skin*, Dutton, 1965, revised edition, 1972; (with Harry Ober) *Modern Book of Skin Care*, Dutton, 1973. Author of over one hundred scientific papers. Contributor to annals and proceedings, and to professional journals. Contributing editor, *Indian Journal of Dermatology and Venereal Disease*.

WORK IN PROGRESS: Research on new clinical, pharmaceutical, and cosmetic products.

SIDELIGHTS: Lubowe holds patents on about twenty-five products. *Avocational interests:* Collecting etchings and graphics.

* * *

LUCK, David Johnston 1912-

PERSONAL: Born April 26, 1912, in Toledo, Ohio; son of Charles Arthur (a sales executive) and Cora Pearl (Johnston) Luck; married Adele Suzanne Kanter, June 14, 1941; children: Charles A., David K., Edward C. *Education:* Dartmouth College, A.B., 1934; University of Pennsylvania, M.B.A., 1940; University of Texas, Ph.D., 1947. *Politics:* Republican. *Religion:* Methodist. *Home:* 931 University Dr., Edwardsville, Ill. 62025. *Office:* Department of Marketing, Southern Illinois University, Edwardsville, Ill. 62025.

CAREER: Branch office manager for E. F. MacDonald Corp., 1934-36; assistant sales manager with an advertising agency, 1936-38; University of Pennsylvania, Philadelphia, assistant instructor in marketing, 1939-40; University of Texas, instructor in accounting and marketing, 1940-46; University of Illinois, assistant professor, 1946-49, associate professor of marketing, 1949; Michigan State University, East Lansing, associate professor, 1949-51, professor of marketing, 1951-60, director of business research; Stanford Research Institute, Menlo Park, Calif., senior industrial economist, 1960-62; Marketing Science Institute,

Philadelphia, Pa., associate director, 1962-63; Southern Illinois University, Edwardsville, professor of marketing, 1963—, chairman of department, 1969—. Lecturer, Brunel, 1968. *Military service:* U.S. Naval Reserve, active duty, 1942-46; became lieutenant. *Member:* American Marketing Association (past director), Southern Marketing Association, Rotary International.

WRITINGS: (Senior author, with H. C. Wales, and D. A. Taylor) *Marketing Research*, Prentice-Hall, 1952, 4th edition, 1974; (with P. J. Robinson) *Promotional Decision Making*, McGraw, 1965; (with A. E. Prell) *Market Strategy*, Prentice-Hall, 1968; *Product Policy and Strategy*, Prentice-Hall, 1972. Contributor to business and marketing journals, including *Journal of Marketing* and *Harvard Business Review*. Editor of *Business Topics*, 1961-67.

WORK IN PROGRESS: Product Management, a textbook and reference guide.

* * *

LUDLOW, James Minor 1917-1974

May 26, 1917—August 8, 1974; American State Department official, educator, author. Obituaries: *Washington Post*, August 10, 1974; *New York Times*, August 13, 1974.

* * *

LUDWIGSON, Kathryn Romaine 1921-

PERSONAL: Born July 30, 1921, in York, Pa.; daughter of Norman Henry (a pattern maker) and Verna (Gohn) Miller; married Carl Raymond Ludwigson, 1947; children: Carl Raymond, Jr. *Education:* Columbia University, B.A. (cum laude), 1944; Wheaton College, Wheaton, Ill., M.A., 1946; Northern Illinois University, M.S., 1957; Northwestern University, Ph.D., 1963. *Residence:* New Canaan, Conn. *Office:* Division of Humanities, King's College, Briarcliff Manor, N.Y. 10510.

CAREER: Wheaton College, Wheaton, Ill., instructor in Greek, 1945-47; Trinity College, Deerfield, Ill., assistant professor of English, 1955-56; Wheaton College, instructor in English, 1957-58, 1959-62; high school teacher in West Chicago, Ill., 1958-59; Northern Illinois University, DeKalb, assistant professor of English, 1963-65; Trinity College, professor of English, 1965-70, chairman of department, 1965-69, chairman of Division of Humanities, 1965-70; King's College, Briarcliff Manor, N.Y., professor of English, 1970-75, chairman of Division of Humanities, 1970-74, director of Learning Center for Adults, 1974-75, founder of Community Speakers Bureau, 1970. *Member:* Modern Language Association of America, College English Association, National Education Association, Conference on Christianity and Literature.

WRITINGS: (With husband C. R. Ludwigson) *A Survey of Bible Prophecy*, Zondervan, 1973; *Edward Dowden*, Twayne, 1973. Ghost writer of a book on achievement motivation for college students, 1969. Author of text for "Christianity and Literature Cassettes," produced by King's College, Briarcliff Manor, N.Y., 1973. Author of multi-media travel films, "Great Lakes Country," "Florida Fantasy," and "Of Old New England," all 1968.

WORK IN PROGRESS: Literature and Belief; *An Interpretation of the Old Testament*; *The Structure of the Revelation*; *A Study of the English Sentence*; an audio-visual presentation on Apocalyptic literature.

SIDELIGHTS: Kathryn Ludwigson has conducted a literary tour of the British Isles for college students.

LUESCHEN, Guenther R(udolf) 1930-

PERSONAL: Born January 21, 1930, in Oldenburg, Germany; son of Gustav (a master craftsman) and Elsa (Magnus) Lueschen; married Klara M. Mertens, December 20, 1958; children: Birgit, Gerhard. *Education:* University of Graz, Ph.D., 1959. *Home:* 10 Shuman Circle, Urbana, Ill. 61801. *Office:* Department of Sociology, University of Illinois, Urbana, Ill. 61801.

CAREER: University of Bremen, Bremen, Germany, professor of sociology, 1966; University of Illinois, Urbana, associate professor, 1966-71, professor of sociology, 1971—. *Member:* International Sociology Association. *Awards, honors:* Philipp Noel Baker award from International Council of Sport and Physical Education, 1974.

WRITINGS: (With R. Koenig) *Jugend in der Familie* (title means "Youth in the Family"), Juventa, 1965; (editor) *Kleingruppenforschung* (title means "Small Group Research"), Westdeutscher Verlag, 1966; (editor with E. Lupri) *Soziologie der Familie* (title means "Sociology of the Family"), Westdeutscher Verlag, 1970; (editor) *The Cross-Cultural Analysis of Sport and Games*, Stipes, 1970.

WORK IN PROGRESS: Policymaking in West European Education; a cross-national study, *Family, Kinship, and Ritual*.

* * *

LUKAS, Susan 1940-

PERSONAL: Born October 9, 1940, in Chicago, Ill.; daughter of Hugo (a businessman) and Rose (a painter; maiden name, Stern) Ries; married Christopher Lukas (a television producer), July 1, 1962; children: Megan, Gabriela. *Education:* University of California at Los Angeles, B.A., 1962, graduate study, 1963. *Agent:* Robert Lescher, 155 East 71st St., New York, N.Y. 10021.

CAREER: Political consultant.

WRITINGS: Fat Emily (novel), Stein & Day, 1974.

WORK IN PROGRESS: A novel, completion expected in 1975.

* * *

LUTZ, Harley L. 1882-1975

July 30, 1882—January 3, 1975; American economist, educator, author of books on public finance and related topics. Obituaries: *New York Times*, January 4, 1975; *AB Bookman's Weekly*, January 20, 1975.

* * *

LYMAN, Mary Ely 1887-1975

November 24, 1887—January 9, 1975; American theologian, educator, author of books on religious topics. Obituaries: *New York Times*, January 11, 1975.

* * *

LYONS, Nick 1932-

PERSONAL: Born June 5, 1932, in New York; married Mari Blumenau (a painter), September 1, 1957; children: Paul, Charles, Jennifer, Anthony. *Education:* University of Pennsylvania, B.S., 1953; Bard College, graduate study, 1956-57; University of Michigan, M.A., Ph.D., 1963. *Home:* 342 West 84th St., New York, N.Y. 10024. *Office:* Department of English, Hunter College of the City University of New York, New York, N.Y.

CAREER: Hunter College of the City University of New York, New York, N.Y., 1961—, now associate professor of English. Executive editor of Crown Publishers, 1964-74. *Military service:* U.S. Army, 1953-54.

WRITINGS: Jones Very: Selected Poems, Rutgers University Press, 1966; *Fisherman's Bounty*, Crown, 1970; *The Seasonable Angler*, Funk, 1970; *Fishing Widows*, Crown, 1974. Contributor of articles, stories, and poems to journals and popular magazines, including *Harper's, Yale Review, Field and Stream*, and *Quarterly Review of Literature*.

WORK IN PROGRESS: Bright Rivers, a philosophical angling book.

AVOCATIONAL INTERESTS: Travel, angling, literary criticism.

* * *

MACAULAY, David (Alexander) 1946-

PERSONAL: Born December 2, 1946, in Burton-on-Trent, England; son of James and Joan (Lowe) Macaulay; married Janice Elizabeth Michel (an organist and choir director), June 13, 1970; children: Elizabeth Alexandra. *Education:* Rhode Island School of Design, B.Arch., 1969. *Home:* 42 Burlington St., Providence, R.I. 02906. *Office:* Freshman Foundation Program, Rhode Island School of Design, Providence, R.I. 02903.

CAREER: Public school teacher of art in Central Falls, R.I., 1969-70, and Newton, Mass., 1973-74; Rhode Island School of Design, Providence, instructor in architecture, 1974—. Teacher of adult education, 1969-74.

WRITINGS: Cathedral: The Story of Its Construction, Houghton, 1973; *City: A Story of Roman Planning and Construction*, Houghton, 1974.

* * *

MacDONALD Simon G(avin) G(eorge) 1923-

PERSONAL: Born September 5, 1923, in Beauly, Scotland; son of Simon (a seedsman) and Jean (Thomson) MacDonald; married Eva-Leonie Austerlitz (a German teacher), October 22, 1948; children: Neil, Carolyn. *Education:* University of Edinburgh, M.A., 1948; University of St. Andrews, Ph.D., 1953. *Politics:* None. *Religion:* None. *Home:* 10 Westerton Ave., Dundee DD5 3NJ, Scotland. *Office:* University of Dundee, Perth Rd., Dundee DD1 4HN, Scotland.

CAREER: Royal Aircraft Establishment, Farnborough, England, junior scientific officer, 1943-46; University of St. Andrews, St. Andrews, Scotland, lecturer in physics, 1948-57; University College of the West Indies, Kingston, Jamaica, senior lecturer in physics, 1957-62; University of St. Andrews, senior lecturer in physics, 1962-67; University of Dundee, Dundee, Scotland, senior lecturer, 1967-73, professor of physics, 1973—, dean of faculty of science, 1970-73, vice-principal, 1974—. Visiting professor at Ohio State University. Member of Scottish Universities Council on Entrance, 1969—, deputy convenor, 1973—; member of Working Party on Transition from School to University (of Scottish Secretary of State), 1970; member of Universities Central Council on Admissions, 1971—.

MEMBER: Institute of Physics (fellow), Royal Society of Edinburgh (fellow), Society of Authors.

WRITINGS: Problems and Solutions in General Physics, Addison-Wesley, 1967; (with Desmond M. Burns) *Physics for Biology and Premedical Students*, Addison-Wesley, 1970, 2nd edition, 1975; (with Burns) *Physics for the Life and Health Sciences*, Addison-Wesley, 1975. Contributor to scientific journals and to science fiction and detective magazines.

SIDELIGHTS: MacDonald told *CA:* "Fiction writing is a relaxation (my others are bridge at which I'm pretty good and golf at which I am very bad, but what else would you do in Scotland. . .). My life is increasingly filled with committees and administration and a novel would be just the thing to soothe one after a hard day. Indeed a detective novel is planned and half written."

* * *

MACDOUGALL, Curtis D(aniel) 1903-

PERSONAL: Born February 11, 1903, in Fond du Lac, Wis.; son of Gilbert T. (a physician) and Mae Isabella (a bookkeeper; maiden name, McCollum) MacDougall; married Elizabeth Pier, June 11, 1929 (divorced, 1941); married Genevieve Rockwood (a teacher), June 20, 1942; children: (first marriage) Gordon Pier, Allan Kent, Lois Mae (Mrs. Gilbert West); (second marriage) Priscilla Ruth, Bonnie Maurine (Mrs. Stuart Cottrell). *Education:* Ripon College, B.A., 1923; Northwestern University, M.S., 1926; University of Wisconsin, Ph.D., 1933. *Politics:* Independent-Democrat. *Religion:* Humanist. *Home:* 537 Judson Ave., Evanston, Ill. 60202.

CAREER: Reporter for *Commonwealth-Reporter*, Fond du Lac, Wis., 1918-23, *Two Rivers Chronicle*, Two Rivers, Wis., 1923-25, and United Press International (UPI), Chicago, Ill., 1926-27; Lehigh University, Bethlehem, Pa., assistant professor of journalism, 1927-31; University of Wisconsin, Madison, lecturer in journalism, 1931-33; *St. Louis Star-Times*, St. Louis, Mo., reporter, 1933-34; *Evanston Daily News-Index*, Evanston, Ill., editor, 1934-37; *National Almanac and Year Book* (formerly *Chicago Daily News Almanac*), Chicago, editor, 1937-38; *News Map of the Week*, Chicago, editor, 1938-40; Work Projects Administration (WPA), Illinois Writers Project, state supervisor, 1940-42; *Chicago Sun*, Chicago, editorial writer, 1942; Northwestern University, Evanston, Ill., professor of journalism, 1942-73, professor emeritus, 1973—. Visiting professor at Universities of South Florida, Tennessee, Indiana, North Dakota, and at Carleton University (Ottawa), Bowling Green University, and Auburn University; lecturer for Centro Internacional de Estudios Superiores de Perodismo para America Latina (Latin American journalists), Quito, Ecuador, 1962; external examiner for department of journalism, University of Nigeria, 1966. Consultant for Fuller Newspapers, 1959-60, Suburban Press Foundation, 1959-63, *Chicago South End Reporter*, 1961-64, *Random House Dictionary of the English Language*, 1966, *Encyclopaedia Britannica Yearbook*, 1967, and Paddock Publications. Conductor of "Editorial Page of the Air," radio station WEAW, 1945-48; panelist on "Matters of Opinion" program, radio station WBBM (CBS), 1973—. Chairman and commissioner of Cook County Housing Authority, 1946-56; president, Evanston Human Relations Council, 1966-68; member of Advisory Committee on Academic Freedom, American Civil Liberties Union; member of Public Information Council of National Safety Council; chairman, Chicago Industrial Relations Council. Democratic candidate for Congress, 1944; Progressive candidate for U.S. Senate, 1948.

MEMBER: American Association of Teachers of Journalism (past president), Association for Education for Journalism (past second vice-president; head of newspaper division, 1965-70), American Sociological Association (fellow), American Society for the Study of Social Problems, American Society for the Study of Communication, American Association for Public Opinion Research, National Conference of Editorial Writers (life member), Authors League of America, Society of Midland Authors, Chicago Headline Club, Pi Kappa Delta, Pi Delta Epsilon, Alpha Kappa Delta, Sigma Delta Chi, Phi Beta Kappa. *Awards, honors:* Sigma Delta Chi research citation, 1946, for *Covering the Courts*, research award, 1953, for *Understanding Public Opinion*, and distinguished teaching in journalism award, 1968; Chicago Newspaper Guild award, 1947, for *Interpretative Reporting*; American Negro Museum and Historical Foundation citation, 1951; Litt.D., Columbia University, 1965; distinguished service to journalism awards from Ball State University, 1964, and from University of Wisconsin, 1971; Journalism Educator of the Year award, Southern Illinois University, 1972; Pi Delta Epsilon Medal of Merit, 1972.

WRITINGS: A College Course in Reporting for Beginners, Macmillan, 1932; *Interpretative Reporting*, with teacher's manual, Macmillan, 1938, 6th edition, 1972; *Hoaxes*, Macmillan, 1940, 2nd edition, Dover, 1958; *Newsroom Problems and Policies*, Macmillan, 1941, revised and enlarged edition, Dover, 1963; *Covering the Courts*, Prentice-Hall, 1946; *Understanding Public Opinion: A Guide for Newspapermen and Newspaper Readers*, Macmillan, 1952, revised edition, W. C. Brown, 1966.

Greater Dead than Alive, Public Affairs Press, 1963; *The Press and Its Problems*, W. C. Brown, 1964; *Gideon's Army*, Marzani & Munsell, Volume I, 1965, Volumes II and III, 1966; (editor) *Reporters Report Reporters*, Iowa State University Press, 1968; *News Pictures Fit to Print . . . Or Are They?: Decision-Making in Photojournalism*, Journalistic Services, 1971; *Principles of Editorial Writing*, W. C. Brown, 1973.

Editor of journalism series for W. C. Brown. Contributor of numerous articles to professional and general periodicals; editorial contributor to *Focus/Midwest* magazine. Associate editor of *Journal of Communication*, 1950-60; member of advisory editorial board, *International Journal of Opinion and Attitude Research*, 1947-51.

WORK IN PROGRESS: Preparing the 7th edition of *Interpretative Reporting*.

SIDELIGHTS: MacDougall told *CA* that he is motivated by "a passionate belief in Jeffersonian democracy which means the Bill of Rights, chiefly freedom of the press and absolutely no censorship or suppression of anything."

* * *

MACHOLTZ, James Donald 1926-

PERSONAL: Born August 28, 1926, in St. Joseph, Mich.; son of Adam (a die-maker) and Augusta (a seamstress; maiden name, Jesswein) Macholtz; married Phyllis Bluhm (a teacher), June 10, 1951; children: Jean, Bob. *Education:* Anderson College, B.S., 1951; University of Michigan, M.S., 1952; Indiana University, M.A., 1953, D.P.E., 1956. *Politics:* Independent. *Religion:* Protestant. *Home:* 802 Maplewood, Anderson, Ind. 46012. *Office:* Department of Physical Education, Anderson College, Anderson, Ind. 46011.

CAREER: Anderson College, Anderson, Ind., instructor, 1953-58, assistant professor, 1958-63, associate professor, 1963-68, professor of physical education, 1968—, chairman of department, 1960—. Member of board of directors of Madison County Red Cross, 1968-72. *Military service:* U.S. Maritime Service, 1944-46. U.S. Army, 1946-47. *Member:* American Association for Health, Physical Education and Recreation, National College Physical Education Association. *Awards, honors:* Fulbright grant, Philippines, 1964-65.

WRITINGS: Good Times Together, Warner Press, 1958; *How to be a Winning Loser*, Warner Press, 1973.

SIDELIGHTS: Macholtz led a student group on an eight-week tour of Japan in 1970.

* * *

MACKAY, James (Alexander) 1936- (Ian Angus, William Finlay, Bruce Garden, Peter Whittington)

PERSONAL: Born November 21, 1936, in Inverness, Scotland; son of William James (an engineer) and Minnie (Matheson) Mackay; married Mary Jackson, September 24, 1960 (divorced April 16, 1973); married Joyce Greaves (a secretary and researcher), October 8, 1973; children: (first marriage) Fiona Elizabeth, Alastair Andrew. *Education:* University of Glasgow, M.A. (honors), 1958. *Home and office:* 11 Newall Terrace, Dumfries DG1 1LN, Scotland.

CAREER: British Museum, London, England, assistant keeper, 1961-71; full-time writer, 1971—. Member of board of directors, Philatelic Publishers Ltd., 1969-72; antiques advisory editor, Ward, Lock, 1972—. *Military service:* British Army, 1958-61; became lieutenant. *Member:* Postal History Society, British Postmark Society. *Awards, honors:* Silver Medals in philatelic literature at international exhibitions in Leipzig, 1965, Vienna, 1965, Amsterdam, 1967, Sofia, 1969, Prague, 1970, and Poznan, 1973.

WRITINGS: A Guide to the Uists, British War Office, 1961, 3rd edition, revised, 1966; *St. Kilda*, Scottish Postmark Group, 1963; *The Tapling Collection*, British Museum, 1964; *The World of Stamps*, Christopher Johnson, 1964; (with George F. Crabb) *Tristan da Cunha: Its Posts and Philately*, privately printed, 1965; *One Hundred Leaves*, British Museum, 1965; *Commonwealth Stamp Design, 1840-1965*, British Museum, 1965; *Churchill on Stamps*, privately printed, 1966; *The Story of Malta and Her Stamps*, Philatelic Publishers, 1966; (under pseudonym Bruce Garden) *Make Money with Stamps*, Philatelic Publishers, 1967; *The Story of Great Britain and Her Stamps*, Philatelic Publishers, 1967; *Money in Stamps*, Lindquist, 1967; *The Story of Eire and Her Stamps*, Philatelic Publishers, 1968; *Value in Coins and Medals*, Christopher Johnson, 1968; (under pseudonym Bruce Garden) *Learn About Stamps*, Philatelic Publishers, 1968; *Cover Collecting*, Philatelic Publishers, 1968.

The Story of East Africa and Its Stamps, Philatelic Publishers, 1970; *An Introduction to Small Antiques*, Garnstone Press, 1970; *Antiques of the Future*, Universe Books, 1970; *Airmails, 1870-1970*, Batsford, 1970; *Commemorative Pottery and Porcelain*, Garnstone Press, 1970; *Commemorative Medals*, Arthur Barker, 1970; *Greek and Roman Coins*, Arthur Barker, 1971; (under pseudonym Peter Whittington) *Undiscovered Antiques*, Garnstone Press, 1971, Scribner, 1972; *Coin Collecting for Grown-Up Beginners*, Garnstone Press, 1971; (under pseudonym Ian Angus) *Collecting Antiques*, Ward, Lock, 1971; (under pseudonym Ian

Angus) *Stamps Posts and Postmarks*, Ward, Lock, 1972; *The World of Classic Stamps*, Putnam, 1972; (under pseudonym Ian Angus) *Coins and Money Tokens*, Ward, Lock, 1972; *The Dictionary of Stamps*, Macmillan, 1973; (translator under pseudonym William Finlay) Dmitri Kandaouroff, *Collecting Postal History*, Eurobook, 1973; *The Animaliers*, Dutton, 1973; (under pseudonym Ian Angus) *Medals and Decorations*, Ward, Lock, 1973; *Glass Paperweights*, Viking, 1973; *Source Book of Stamps*, Ward, Lock, 1974; *Robert Bruce, King of Scots*, R. Hale, 1974; (under pseudonym Ian Angus) *Paper Money*, Ward, Lock, 1974; *Turn of the Century Antiques: An Encyclopedia*, Dutton, 1974; (under pseudonym William Finlay) *Stamp Design*, Peter Lowe, 1974; (under pseudonym Peter Whittington) *Kitchen Antiques*, Garnstone Press, 1975; *Collecting Famous Faces*, Ward, Lock, 1975; (under pseudonym Ian Angus) *History of Pitney Bowes Ltd.*, Pitney Bowes, 1975; *Encyclopedia of Small Antiques*, Harper, 1975.

Editor-in-chief, *International Encyclopedia of Stamps*, 1969-72; English language editor, *New World Encyclopedia*, Ward, Lock, 1973. Columnist, *New Daily*, 1962-66, and *Financial Times*, 1967—; feature writer, *British Post Office*, 1970-72. Contributor to *Stamp Magazine*, *Gibbons Stamp Monthly*, *Investing Professional*, *Meccano Magazine*, and *Coins and Medals*.

WORK IN PROGRESS: Two books, *Japanese Antiques* and *Nursery Antiques*; research on post-World War II stamps of the world, Lady Grange (1680-1745), the Scottish Covenanters of 1676-1690, and the social impact of air raids and gas warfare, 1925-1940.

AVOCATIONAL INTERESTS: Offbeat aspects of social history, biography, and travel, applied and decorative arts, and languages (reads most European languages).

* * *

MACKY, Peter W(allace) 1937-

PERSONAL: Born July 22, 1937, in Auckland, New Zealand; son of Wallace Armstrong (a meteorologist) and Mary (a teacher; maiden name, Whitfield) Macky; married Nancy Ann Space, September 9, 1961; children: Cameron Wallace, Christopher Peter. *Education:* Harvard University, A.B., 1957; Oxford University, B.A., 1962, M.A., 1966, Ph.D., 1967; Princeton Theological Seminary, B.D., 1963, Th.D., 1970. *Home:* Susan Trace, New Wilmington, Pa. 16142. *Office:* Department of Religion, Westminster College, New Wilmington, Pa. 16142.

CAREER: Ordained Presbyterian minister, 1967; associate engineer with Lockheed Aircraft, 1957-59; assistant pastor in Pacific Palisades, Cal., 1967-70; Westminster College, New Wilmington, Pa., assistant professor, 1970-74, associate professor of religion, 1974—. *Member:* American Academy of Religion. *Awards, honors:* Rhodes scholar, 1960; National Endowment for the Humanities fellowship, 1975.

WRITINGS: *The Bible in Dialogue with Modern Man*, Word, Inc., 1970; *Violence: Right or Wrong?*, Word, Inc., 1973.

WORK IN PROGRESS: *The Pursuit of the Divine Snowman: Biblical Theology in Modern Parables*, completion expected in 1976.

* * *

MACLEOD, Alison 1920-

PERSONAL: Born April 12, 1920, in Hendon, Middlesex, England; daughter of Norman (a civil servant) and Winifred Alice (a teacher; maiden name, Fairfield) Macleod; married Jack Selford (a teacher), March 11, 1950; children: Catherine, Ruth Stella. *Education:* Attended Central School of Arts and Crafts, 1938. *Politics:* Labour. *Home:* 63 Muswell Hill Pl., London N10 3RP, England. *Agent:* Laurence Pollinger, 18 Maddox St., London W.1, England.

CAREER: Free-lance journalist. Visiting tutor at London College of Printing, 1970—.

WRITINGS—Novels, except as indicated: "Dear Augustine" (three-act play), first produced in London at Royal Court Theatre, 1958; *The Heretics*, Hodder & Stoughton, 1965, published as *The Heretic*, Houghton, 1966; *The Hireling*, Houghton, 1968 (published as *The Trusted Servant*, Hodder & Stoughton, 1968); *City of Light*, Houghton, 1969 (published as *No Need of the Sun*, Hodder & Stoughton, 1969); *The Muscovite*, Houghton, 1971; *The Jesuit*, Hodder & Stoughton, 1972, published as *Prisoner of the Queen*, Houghton, 1973. Contributor to various periodicals, including *Punch* and *New Statesman*. Editor of *Greater London Guardian* (a trade union journal), 1968—.

WORK IN PROGRESS: A novel, *The Portingale*.

SIDELIGHTS: Reviewer Anne Francis called *The Trusted Servant* "an excellently plotted and first-class novel ... that makes the permissive times [of the sixteenth century] come marvellously alive.... The story is a joy to read." Reviewing *City of Light*, P. Albert Duhamel wrote: "Whether she sets her scene in Venice, Geneva or Naples, the author has a strong feeling for place. With few details, she can suggest a panorama of canals during a freezing winter ... or the interior of a grandee's reception chamber.... As a vivid dramatization of the conflicts a Renaissance Everyman might contemplate, it [*City of Light*] reflects a real grasp of the issues."

Alison Macleod is competent in French, German, Italian, Russian, and Portuguese.

* * *

MACMILLAN, William Miller 1885-1974

October 1, 1885—1974; Scottish historian, educator, author of books on South African affairs and other topics. Obituaries: *AB Bookman's Weekly*, December 2, 1974. (*CA*-11/12).

* * *

MADDEN, Donald L(eo) 1937-

PERSONAL: Born April 3, 1937, in Indianapolis, Ind.; son of George W. (a public servant) and Anna A. (Delaney) Madden; married Elaine McVay, January 21, 1960; children: Kathy, Tricia, Beth, Lynn. *Education:* Indiana University, B.S., 1961, M.B.A., 1964; University of Texas, Ph.D., 1967. *Office:* Department of Accounting, University of Kentucky, Lexington, Ky. 40506.

CAREER: Kroger Co., Indianapolis, Ind., management accounting intern, summer, 1960; Alexander Grant & Co. (certified public accountants), Chicago, Ill., staff auditor, 1961-62; became certified public accountant (C.P.A.) in State of Illinois, 1962; Radio Corp. of America, Bloomington, Ind., operations auditor, 1962-64; University of Texas, Austin, lecturer in accounting, 1964-66; Michigan State University, East Lansing, assistant professor of accounting, 1966-68; University of Kentucky, Lexington, assistant professor, 1968-70, associate professor, 1970-74, professor of accounting, 1974—; received Certificate in Management

Accounting (C.M.A.), 1974. Faculty intern in financial planning with Eli Lilly & Co., 1968. *Military service:* U.S. Navy, disbursing clerk on a destroyer, 1956-58.

MEMBER: American Accounting Association, American Institute of Certified Public Accountants, Financial Executives Institute, National Association of Accountants (president of Blue Grass area chapter, 1972-73), Planning Executives Institute, Beta Alpha Psi, Beta Gamma Sigma, Phi Kappa Phi.

WRITINGS: (Contributor) Glenn A. Welsch, editor, *Cases in Profit Planning and Control*, Prentice-Hall, 1970; (editor and contributor) *Managerial Accounting for the Hospitality Service Industries*, W. C. Brown, 1971; *Accounting for the Travel Agent*, University Press of Kentucky, 1972. Contributor to *Journal of Accountancy, Accounting Review, Ohio Certified Public Accountant, Certified Public Accountants Journal, Management Accounting*, and *Journal of Accounting Research*.

* * *

MADDISON, Angela Mary 1923- (Angela Banner)

PERSONAL: Married name legally changed from Parsons to Maddison, 1968; born May 14, 1923, in Bombay, India; daughter of Sydney Howard (an engineer) and Iris Lydia (MacDiarmid) Phipps-Lincke; married Lionel Parsons (an army officer), March 24, 1941; children: John Lincke Maddison, Danne Mary Diarmid Maddison. *Education:* Attended boarding schools in England. *Politics:* Liberal. *Religion:* Roman Catholic. *Home:* 24 Cranley Mews, South Kensington, London, England. *Office:* Ant & Bee Partnership, c/o Grindlay's Bank Ltd., 13 St. James's Sq., London S.W.1, England.

CAREER: Author and illustrator of children's books. *Member:* Hurlingham Club.

WRITINGS—Children's books; all under pseudonym Angela Banner: *Mr. Fork and Curly Fork*, Edmund Ward, 1956.

"Ant and Bee" series: *Ant and Bee: An Alphabetical Story*, Edmund Ward, 1950, F. Watts, 1958; *More Ant and Bee*, Edmund Ward, 1956, F. Watts, 1958; *One, Two, Three with Ant and Bee*, Edmund Ward, 1958, F. Watts, 1959; *Around the World with Ant and Bee*, F. Watts, 1960; *More and More Ant and Bee*, Edmund Ward, 1961, F. Watts, 1962; *Ant and Bee and the Rainbow*, Edmund Ward, 1962, F. Watts, 1963; *Ant and Bee and Kind Dog*, Edmund Ward, 1963, F. Watts, 1964; *Happy Birthday with Ant and Bee*, F. Watts, 1964; *Ant and Bee and the ABC*, F. Watts, 1966; *Ant and Bee Time*, F. Watts, 1969; *Ant and Bee and the Secret*, F. Watts, 1970; *Ant and Bee and the Doctor*, F. Watts, 1971; *Ant and Bee Big Buy Bag*, Kaye & Ward, 1971; *Ant and Bee Go Shopping*, F. Watts, 1972.

"Kind Dog" series: *Kind Dog on Monday*, Ant & Bee Partnership, 1972; *Kind Dog Up and Down the Hill*, Ant & Bee Partnership, 1972.

"Which Two" series: *Fayida, Pierre, Khesoo, Carlos*, Ant & Bee Partnership, 1972.

WORK IN PROGRESS: Private study of law.

SIDELIGHTS: Angela Maddison told *CA*: "No child is too young to 'read' a few words from memory in return for praise and this leads to reading confidence (too often destroyed by educating adults). I believe that children make the best reading teachers so I make books for shared-reading between children of different ages." *Avocational interests:* Painting.

* * *

MAHAJANI, Usha 1933-

PERSONAL: Born February 6, 1933, in Poona, India; daughter of Ganesh Sakharam (president of University of Poona) and Indumati (Paranjpye) Mahajani. *Education:* University of Rajasthan, B.A., 1952; Smith College, M.A., 1954; Johns Hopkins University, Ph.D., 1957. *Religion:* Hindu. *Office:* Department of Political Science, Central Washington State College, Ellensburg, Wash. 98926.

CAREER: Government of India, External Affairs Ministry, New Delhi, associate research officer in Historical Division, 1959-61; Australian National University, Canberra, Australian Capital Territory, research fellow, 1962-67, associate professor of international relations, 1967-69; Central Washington State College, Ellensburg, professor of political science, 1969—. *Member:* International Studies Association, Association for Asian Studies, American Academy of Political and Social Science, American Judicature Society, American Civil Liberties Union.

WRITINGS: The Role of Indian Minorities in Burma and Malaya, Vora & Co., 1960, Greenwood Press, 1973; *Soviet and American Aid to Indonesia 1949-1968*, Ohio University Press, 1970; *Philippine Nationalism: External Challenge and Filipino Response*, University of Queensland Press, 1971. Contributor to *London Yearbook of World Affairs, Journal of Southeast Asian Studies, Asian Survey, World Affairs*, and other periodicals in her field.

WORK IN PROGRESS: Laos in the Web of International Intervention; New Configurations and Alignments in Southeast Asia, completion expected in 1975.

* * *

MAHONEY, Michael J(ohn) 1946-

PERSONAL: Born February 22, 1946, in Streator, Ill.; son of Daniel F. and Zita E. Mahoney; married Kathryn Herron (a psychologist), August 31, 1974; children: Benjamin. *Education:* Joliet Junior College, A.A., 1967; Arizona State University, B.A., 1969; Stanford University, Ph.D., 1972. *Religion:* Humanist. *Home:* 309 Toftrees Ave., Apt. 142, State College, Pa. 16801. *Office:* Department of Psychology, Pennsylvania State University, University Park, Pa. 16802.

CAREER: Palo Alto Veterans Hospital, Palo Alto, Calif., trainee in clinical psychology and instructor to nursing services, 1970-71; Learning House (delinquency program), Palo Alto, Calif., assistant director, 1971-73; Pennsylvania State University, University Park, assistant professor of psychology, 1972—. Consultant to Laurelton State Hospital for the Retarded, 1972-74. *Member:* Association for the Advancement of Behavior Therapy, American Psychological Association, American Humanist Association, Pennsylvania Psychological Association.

WRITINGS: (With Carl E. Thoresen) *Behavioral Self-Control*, Holt, 1974; (editor with Thoresen) *Self-Control: Power to the Person*, Brooks-Cole, 1974; *Cognition and Behavior Modification*, Ballinger, 1974; (with W. E. Craighead and A. E. Kazdin) *Behavior Modification: Principles, Issues, and Applications*, Houghton, 1976; (contributor) Harold Leitenberg, editor, *Handbook of Behavior Modification*, Appleton, in press. Contributor to *International Encyclopedia of Neurology, Psychiatry, Psychoanalysis and Psychology* and to journals, including *Behavior Therapy*.

WORK IN PROGRESS: Two books, *Belief and Behavior* and *Learning Self-Control*, completion of both expected in 1976.

* * *

MAISEL, Herbert 1930-

PERSONAL: Surname is pronounced May-*zell*; born September 22, 1930, in New York; son of Hyman (a soft drink bottler) and Dora (Goldstein) Maisel; married Millicent Kushner (a secretary), April 13, 1957; children: Scott Alan, Raymond Bruce. *Education:* City College (now City College of the City University of New York), B.S., 1951; New York University, M.S., 1952; Catholic University of America, Ph.D., 1964. *Office:* Academic Computation Center, Georgetown University, 37th and O Sts. N.W., Washington, D.C. 20007.

CAREER: Statistician with U.S. Department of Defense, 1954-63; Georgetown University, Washington, D.C., assistant professor, 1963-64, associate professor, 1964-72, professor of computer science, 1972—, director of Academic Computation Center, 1963—. Consultant to Social Security Administration, National Bureau of Standards, and Baltimore Housing Authority. *Military service:* U.S. Army, 1952-54. *Member:* Association for Computing Machinery (chairman of Washington chapter), American Statistical Association, American Association of University Professors, American Association for the Advancement of Science, Phi Beta Kappa (chairman of Georgetown chapter), Sigma Xi.

WRITINGS: (With R. R. Baldwin, W. E. Cantney, and J. P. McDermott) *Playing Blackjack to Win*, Barrows, 1957; *Introduction to Electronic Digital Computers*, McGraw, 1969; (with Giuliano Gnugnoli) *Simulation of Discrete Stochastic Systems*, Science Research Associates, 1972; *Introduction to Computers and Programming with Applications*, Science Research Associates, in press. Contributor to proceedings. Editor of *Journal of Programming Languages*.

WORK IN PROGRESS: Research on simulation, on applications to statistics of computer science, and on programming languages.

AVOCATIONAL INTERESTS: Handball.

* * *

MAKELY, William O(rson) 1932-

PERSONAL: Born December 31, 1932, in Staten Island, N.Y.; son of Ralph G. (an engineer) and Helen (Craig) Makely; married Ethel Dee (an artist), December 20, 1958; children: Jennifer, Katherine, Gordon. *Education:* University of Wisconsin, B.S., 1955; University of Chicago, M.A., 1961. *Home:* 6948 West 35th St., Berwyn, Ill. 60402. *Office:* Field Enterprises Educational Corp., Merchandise Mart, Chicago, Ill. 60654.

CAREER: Rose-Hulman Institute, Terre Haute, Ind., assistant professor of humanities, 1961-65; Roosevelt University, Chicago, Ill., instructor in English, 1965-69; Field Enterprises Education Corp., Chicago, Ill., senior index editor of *World Book Encyclopedia*, 1969—. Instructor at Indiana State University, Presbyterian-St. Luke's Hospital School of Nursing, and Loop Junior College. Free-lance indexer for Rand McNally. Member of board of directors of Lone Tree Area Girl Scout Council, 1972-75. *Military service:* U.S. Navy, photographer, 1955-57.

WRITINGS: *A Study of the Teaching Practices of Teachers with and without Formal Training in Linguistics*, U.S. Office of Education, 1969; *City Life: Writing from Experience*, St. Martin's, 1974. Contributor of poems and reviews to *World Book Encyclopedia*, *Childcraft*, *American-Scandinavian Review*, and other journals.

WORK IN PROGRESS: *Building a Paper*; translating some Danish poems.

* * *

MALCOLM, Andrew H(ogarth) 1943-

PERSONAL: Born June 22, 1943, in Cleveland, Ohio; son of Ralph M. (a plant manager) and Beatrice (Bowles) Malcolm; married June Hielscher (a photographer), June 24, 1967; children: Christopher Andrew, Spencer Duncan. *Education:* Northwestern University, B.S., 1966, M.S., 1967. *Office:* *New York Times*, 925 Grosvenor Plaza Building, San Francisco, Calif. 94102.

CAREER: *New York Times*, New York, N.Y., assistant to foreign editor, 1967-68, reporter, 1969, reporter for United Nations Bureau, 1969, reporter of education news, 1970-72, national correspondent from Chicago, 1972-74, national correspondent from San Francisco, 1974—. *Awards, honors:* George Polk Memorial Award for National Reporting, from Long Island University, 1974, for a newspaper series exposing illegal drug raids.

WRITINGS: *Unknown America*, Quadrangle, 1974.

AVOCATIONAL INTERESTS: Studying history, travel.

* * *

MALMSTROM, Jean 1908-

PERSONAL: Born June 19, 1908, in St. Louis, Mo.; married Vincent F. Malmstrom (a businessman), December 26, 1949; children: Val (Mrs. Calvin G. Covell), Dean (Mrs. Richard B. Hauck), Frederick V. *Education:* Washington University, St. Louis, Mo., B.A., 1928, M.A., 1929; University of Minnesota, Ph.D., 1958; University of Illinois, postdoctoral study, 1962. *Home:* 1324 Long Rd., Kalamazoo, Mich. 49008. *Office:* Department of English, Western Michigan University, Kalamazoo, Mich, 49001.

CAREER: Elementary school teacher in Sewell, Chile, 1929-30; high school English teacher in Manila, P.I., 1943-45; Western Michigan University, Kalamazoo, instructor, 1948-52, assistant professor, 1952-58, associate professor, 1958-63, professor of English, 1963—. Visiting professor at Kalamazoo College, summers, 1964-65.

MEMBER: International Linguistic Association, International Reading Association, Modern Language Association of America, National Council of Teachers of English (director), American Dialect Society, College English Association, Association for Machine Translation and Computational Linguistics, American Association of University Professors, American Association for Higher Education, Teachers of English to Speakers of Other Languages, Michigan Council of Teachers of English (past president), Michigan College English Association, Phi Beta Kappa, Alpha Lambda Delta, Pi Lambda Theta.

WRITINGS: (With Annabel Ashley) *Dialects: U.S.A.*, National Council of Teachers of English, 1963; *Language in Society*, Hayden, 1965; *An Introduction to Modern English Grammar*, Hayden, 1968; (editor with Theone Hughes) *Who's Afraid of Linguistics?*, Michigan Council of Teachers of English, 1968; (with Janice Lee) *Teaching En-*

glish Linguistically: Principles and Practices for High School, Appleton, 1971; (with Constance Weaver) *Transgrammar: English Structure, Style, and Dialects*, Scott, Foresman, 1973; (with Barbara Bondar) *Language Alive: Linear A and Linear B*, Harper, 1975; (with Diane McCarty) *Performance Skillskit*, Harper, in press; (with William Strong) *Language Alive: Linear C*, Harper, in press; (with Barbara Bondar) *Language Art*, St. Martin's, in press. Contributor to journals in her field.

* * *

MANCH, Joseph (Rodman) 1910-

PERSONAL: Born January 1, 1910, in Poland; son of Isaac (a rabbi) and Ida (Rodman) Manch; married Dorothy Strom, October 14, 1933; children: David Eliot, Richard Allen. *Education:* University of Buffalo, B.A., 1932, M.A., 1940, Ed.D., 1955. *Religion:* Jewish. *Home:* 259 Lincoln Pkwy., Buffalo, N.Y. 14216. *Office:* Buffalo Public Schools, 712 City Hall, Buffalo, N.Y. 14202.

CAREER: Held positions as teacher at high schools in Buffalo, N.Y., and at Millard Fillmore College, University of Buffalo; Buffalo Public Schools, Buffalo, N.Y., director of guidance, 1948-51, director of pupil personnel services, 1951-53, assistant superintendent for pupil personnel, 1953-54, associate superintendent for school-community coordination, 1954-57, superintendent of schools, 1957—. Visiting professor, State University of New York College at Buffalo, 1968-69, 1969-70. Member or officer of numerous civic, social, and professional organizations and councils. Delegate to White House conferences on youth and education.

MEMBER: American Association of School Administrators, National Education Association (life member), National Conference of Christians and Jews (member of executive council), National Schools Committee for Economic Education, American Council on Education, Anti-Defamation League of B'nai B'rith, Association for the Help of Retarded Children (Erie County Chapter), National Multiple Sclerosis Society (member of regional board of directors, 1963), United Jewish Federation (member of local board of governors), New York State Council of School District Administrators, New York State Educational Radio and Television Association (member of board of trustees), New York State Teachers Association, Old Fort Niagara Association, Buffalo Historical Society, Buffalo Society of Artists, Buffalo Fine Arts Academy Board (honorary member), Phi Delta Kappa, Rotary; and other national and local organizations. *Awards, honors:* American Educators Medal of Freedoms Foundation, 1959, 1975; President's Medal from Canisius College, Buffalo, 1964; Liberty Bell Award, from Erie County Bar Association, and from New York State Bar Association, both 1965; LL.D., D'Youville College, 1967. A Dr. Joseph Manch Scholarship fund was established by Jewish Theological Seminary of America, 1963.

WRITINGS: *Monkey in a Cage* (poems), A.M. Ricciuti (Buffalo), 1932; *Jonathan Swift and Women*, [Buffalo], 1941; *33 Ways Parents Can Help*, Croft Educational, 1971; *A City Is People*, (poems and photographs), privately printed, in conjunction with fund of National Conference of Christians and Jews, 1972. Contributor of articles to local and national magazines and journals.

* * *

MANHEIM, Werner 1915-

PERSONAL: Born February 17, 1915, in Germany; son of Martin (a pharmicist) and Else Manheim; married Eliane Housiaux (a singer and voice teacher), August 18, 1951. *Education:* University of Berlin, B.Ed., 1936; Cincinnati Conservatory of Music, B.Mus., 1940, M.Mus., 1941; University of Chicago, D.F.A., 1950. *Home:* 2906 Hazelwood Ave., Fort Wayne, Ind. 46805. *Office:* Indiana University, 266 Kettler Hall, 2101 East Coliseum Blvd., Fort Wayne, Ind. 46805.

CAREER: Indiana University, assistant professor of music, East Chicago campus, 1948-54, research associate at Institute of Sex Research, Bloomington campus, 1954-58, associate professor of French and German, Fort Wayne campus, 1958—. Part-time instructor in music and piano at St. Francis College, 1959—. Composer. *Military service:* U.S. Army, teacher in Military Intelligence, 1941-45; served in European theater; received Bronze Star Medal. *Member:* Modern Language Association of America, American Association of Teachers of German, American Association of Teachers of French, American Association of University Professors, Phi Mu Alpha (Sinfonia).

WRITINGS: *Martin Buber*, Twayne, 1974.

WORK IN PROGRESS: Eight poems in German, to be included in *Lyrik und Prose*, for State University of New York at Buffalo; further research on Martin Buber as a poet; research on the songs of Mozart.

SIDELIGHTS: "Although I started out as a musician, particularly as pianist," Manheim wrote, "...I became more and more interested in writing. The book on Martin Buber grew out of an unforgettable experience when, as a young man, I participated in a seminary in which Professor Buber was the principal educator. Already then I was hoping that some day I [would] be able to devote my efforts to an interpretation of Buber's philosophy."

* * *

MANICAS, Peter T(heodore) 1934-

PERSONAL: Born February 3, 1934, in Binghamton, N.Y.; son of Theodore and Esther (Calcagno) Manicas; married Shirley Kauanoe; children: Tantaise, Theodore. *Education:* Syracuse University, A.B., 1955; University of Buffalo, M.A., 1960; State University of New York at Buffalo, Ph.D., 1963. *Office:* Department of Philosophy, Queens College of the City University of New York, Flushing, N.Y. 11771.

CAREER: Ohio Wesleyan University, Delaware, visiting assistant professor of philosophy, 1963-64; C. W. Post College of Long Island University, Brookville, N.Y., assistant professor of philosophy, 1964-66; Queens College of the City University of New York, Flushing, N.Y., associate professor of philosophy, 1967—. *Military service:* U.S. Air Force, 1955-59; became captain.

WRITINGS: (With A. N. Kruger) *Essentials of Logic*, American Book Co., 1968; (editor) *Logic as Philosophy*, American Book Co., 1971; *Death of the State*, Putnam, 1974.

* * *

MANNIN, Ethel Edith 1900-

PERSONAL: Born October 11, 1900, in London, England; daughter of Robert (a post office sorter) and Edith (Gray) Mannin; married John A. Porteous, 1919 (deceased); married Reginald Reynolds (an author and poet), 1937 (deceased); children: (first marriage) Jean Porteous Faulks. *Education:* Self-educated after age of 14. *Politics:* "Left revolutionary." *Religion:* None. *Home:* Overhill, Brook Lane, Shaldon, Teignmouth, Devonshire, England.

CAREER: Stenographer for advertising firm, 1915, copy writer, 1916-19; author of novels, short stories, travel books, and nonfiction works.

WRITINGS—Novels, except as indicated; all published by Hutchinson, unless otherwise noted: *Martha*, Duffield, 1923; *Hunger of the Sea*, 1924; *Sounding Brass*, 1925, Duffield, 1926, reprinted, Hutchinson, 1972; *Pilgrims*, Doran, 1927; *Green Willow*, Doubleday, Doran, 1928; *Crescendo, Being the Dark Odyssey of Gilbert Stroud*, Doubleday, Doran, 1929.

Confessions and Impressions (nonfiction), 1930; *Children of the Earth*, Doubleday, Doran, 1930; *Ragged Banners*, Knopf, 1931, reprinted, Hutchinson, 1973; *Green Figs* (short stories), 1931; *Common-Sense and the Child: A Plea for Freedom* (nonfiction), introduction by A. S. Neill, 1931, Lippincott, 1932, 2nd edition, Jarrolds, 1937; *All Experience* (memoirs/travel), 1932; *Linda Shawn*, Knopf, 1932; *Dryad* [*and Other Tales*], 1933; *Venetian Blinds*, Knopf, 1933, reprinted, Hutchinson, 1972; *Men Are Unwise*, Knopf, 1934; *Forever Wandering* (travel), Jarrolds, 1934, Dutton, 1935.

Cactus, 1935, Penguin, 1941, revised edition, Jarrolds, 1944, reprinted, Hutchinson, 1973; *The Falconer's Voice* (short stories), 1935; *The Pure Flame*, 1936; *South to Samarkand* (travel), 1936, Dutton, 1937; *Women Also Dream*, Putnam, 1937; *Women and the Revolution* (nonfiction), Secker & Warburg, 1938, Dutton, 1939; *Rose and Sylvie*, 1938; *Darkness My Bride*, 1939; *Privileged Spectator: A Sequel to 'Confessions and Impressions'* (autobiographical), 1939, revised edition, 1948.

Christianity—or Chaos? A Restatement of Religion (nonfiction), 1940; *Rolling in the Dew*, 1940; *Red Rose: A Novel Based on the Life of Emma Goldman ("Red Emma")*, 1941; *The Blossoming Bough*, 1942, reprinted, Hutchinson, 1969; *Captain Moonlight*, 1942; *Commonsense and Morality* (nonfiction), preface by A. S. Neill, 1942; *No More Mimosa* (short stories), 1943; *Proud Heaven*, 1944.

Bread and Roses: An Utopian Survey and Blue-Print (nonfiction), Macdonald, 1945; *Lucifer and the Child*, 1945, reprinted, 1975; *The Dark Forest*, 1946; *Comrade O Comrade, or, Low-Down on the Left*, 1947; *Connemara Journal* (nonfiction), Westhouse, 1947; *Late Have I Loved Thee*, Putnam, 1948, reprinted, Hutchinson, 1974; *German Journey* (travel), 1948; *Every Man a Stranger*, 1949; *Bavarian Story*, 1949, Appleton, 1950, reprinted, Hutchinson, 1974.

Jungle Journey (travel; with photographs by daughter, Jean Porteous), 1950; *At Sundown the Tiger*, Putnam, 1951; *The Fields at Evening*, 1952; *The Wild Swans and Other Tales Based on the Ancient Irish*, 1952; *This Was a Man: Some Memories of Robert Mannin by His Daughter* (nonfiction), 1952; *Moroccan Mosaic* (travel), 1953; *Lover Under Another Name*, 1953, Putnam, 1954; *Two Studies in Integrity: Gerald Griffin and the Rev. Francis Mahony* (nonfiction), Putnam, 1954; *So Tiberius...*, 1954, Putnam, 1955.

Land of the Crested Lion: A Journey through Modern Burma (travel), 1955; *The Living Lotus*, Putnam, 1956; *Pity the Innocent*, Putnam, 1957, reprinted, Hutchinson, 1975; *The Country of the Sea: Some Wanderings in Brittany* (travel), 1957; *Fragrance of Hyacinths*, 1958; *Brief Voices: A Writer's Story* (autobiographical), Hutchinson, 1959; *The Blue-Eyed Boy*, 1959.

Ann and Peter in Sweden (juvenile), F. Muller, 1960; *The Flowery Sword: Travels in Japan* (nonfiction), 1960; *Ann and Peter in Japan* (juvenile), F. Muller, 1960; *Sabishisa*, 1961; *Ann and Peter in Austria* (juvenile), F. Muller, 1962; *With Will Adams through Japan* (juvenile), F. Muller, 1962; *Curfew at Dawn*, 1962; *The Road to Beersheba*, 1963, Regnery, 1964; *A Lance for the Arabs: A Middle East Journey* (nonfiction), 1963; *Aspects of Egypt: Some Travels in the United Arab Republic*, 1964; *Rebels' Ride: The Revolt of the Individual* (nonfiction), 1964.

The Lovely Land: The Hashemite Kingdom of Jordan (travel), 1965; *The Burning Bush*, 1965; *The Night and Its Homing*, 1966; *Loneliness: A Study of the Human Condition* (nonfiction), 1966; *An American Journey* (travel), 1967; *The Lady and the Mystic*, 1967; *Bitter Babylon*, 1968; *England for a Change* (travel), 1968; *Practitioners of Love: Some Aspects of the Human Phenomenon* (nonfiction), 1969, Horizon, 1970; *The Saga of Sammy-Cat*, Pergamon, 1969; *The Midnight Street*, 1969.

Free Pass to Nowhere, 1970; *England at Large*, 1970; *My Cat Sammy*, M. Joseph, 1971; *Young in the Twenties* (autobiographical), 1971; *The Curious Adventure of Major Fosdick*, 1972; *England My Adventure* (nonfiction), 1972; *Mission to Beirut*, 1973; *Stories from My Life* (autobiographical), 1973; *Kildoon*, 1974; *An Italian Journey* (travel), 1974; *The Late Miss Guthrie*, 1975; *Sunset over Dartmoor* (autobiographical), in press.

Associate editor, *Pelican*, 1917-19.

SIDELIGHTS: Certain of Ethel Mannin's works have been translated into German, Italian, French, Dutch, Swedish, Spanish, and Arabic.

* * *

MANNING, Frank E(dward) 1944-

PERSONAL: Born April 29, 1944, in Boston, Mass.; son of Frank and Ruth Manning; married Gail Devine, August, 1968; children: Carolyn. *Education:* Boston College, B.A., 1966; University of North Carolina, M.A., 1968, Ph.D., 1972. *Office:* Department of Anthropology, Memorial University, St. John's Newfoundland, Canada.

CAREER: *Boston Herald American*, Boston, Mass., staff reporter, 1965-66; Memorial University, St. John's, Newfoundland, assistant professor of anthropology, 1971—. Visiting lecturer at Centre for Multi-Racial Studies, Barbados, 1973. *Member:* American Anthropological Association (fellow), Canadian Ethnology Society, Caribbean Studies Association, Southern Anthropological Society.

WRITINGS: *Black Clubs in Bermuda*, Cornell University Press, 1973. Contributor to *Proceedings of Southern Anthropological Society*.

WORK IN PROGRESS: Research in the modernization and development in the Caribbean and the culture of Bermuda.

* * *

MANSBACH, Richard W(allace) 1943-

PERSONAL: Born January 3, 1943, in New York, N.Y.; son of Milton (an attorney) and Florence (Appel) Mansbach; married Agnes Rhoda Urie (novelist), August 8, 1967. *Education:* Swarthmore College, B.A. (with high honors), 1964; Oxford University, D.Phil., 1967. *Home:* 970 Severin Dr., Somerville, N.J. 08876. *Office:* Department of Political Science, Rutgers University, New Brunswick, N.J. 08903.

CAREER: Swarthmore College, Swarthmore, Pa., assistant professor of political science, 1967-69; Rutgers University, New Brunswick, N.J., assistant professor, 1969-73, associate professor of political science, 1973—. *Member:* International Studies Association, American Political Science Association, New Jersey Political Science Association (member of council, 1973), Phi Beta Kappa. *Awards, honors:* Marshall scholarship from British Government, 1964-67.

WRITINGS: (Editor) *Dominican Crisis: 1965*, Facts on File, 1971; (editor) *Northern Ireland: Half a Century of Partition*, Facts on File, 1973; (with Raymond Hopkins) *Structure and Process in International Politics*, Harper, 1973; (with Yale Ferguson and Donald Lampert) *Nonstate Actors in the Global System*, Prentice-Hall, 1975.

WORK IN PROGRESS: Directing Rutgers University's nonstate actor project, a data-oriented research project on the role and behaviors of actors in international relations other than nation-states.

* * *

MANZINI, Gianna 1899-1974

Italian novelist. Obituaries: *AB Bookman's Weekly*, October 7, 1974.

* * *

MAPLE, Eric William 1915-

PERSONAL: Born January 22, 1915, in London, England; son of William Alfred and Edith Anne (Baker) Maple; married Dora Savage (a teacher), December 22, 1951; children: Alan. *Education:* Attended schools in Southend, England; primarily self-educated. *Politics:* "Radical." *Religion:* "Pantheist." *Home:* 52 Buckingham Rd., London E11, England.

CAREER: Employed in gas industry as accounts supervisor in Southend-on-Sea and London, England, 1929-66; writer. Witchcraft consultant; lecturer; broadcaster, 1960—. *Military service:* British Army, 1940-46. *Member:* Folklore Society, Society for Psychical Research, Ghost Club, Savage Club.

WRITINGS: *The Dark World of Witches*, R. Hale, 1962, A.S. Barnes, 1964; *The Realm of Ghosts*, A.S. Barnes, 1964; *The Domain of Devils*, A.S. Barnes, 1966; *Magic, Medicine and Quackery*, A.S. Barnes, 1968; *Superstition and the Superstitious*, W.H. Allen, 1971, A.S. Barnes, 1972; *The Magic of Perfume: Aromatics and Their Esoteric Significance*, Samuel Weiser, 1973; *Witchcraft*, Octopus, 1974; *Incantations and Words of Power*, Samuel Weiser, 1974; *The Ancient Art of Occult Healing*, Samuel Weiser, 1974. Contributor and consultant to *Man, Myth, and Magic: Encyclopedia of the Supernatural*; contributor and consultant to *Folklore, Myths, and Legends of Britain* and to *Guide to Britain*, both published by Reader's Digest. Also contributor to British travel journals.

WORK IN PROGRESS: Research in the folklore of English witchcraft, crime and the supernatural, English gypsies, and the folklore of Shakespeare's England.

* * *

MARCUS, Aaron 1943-

PERSONAL: Born May 22, 1943, in Omaha, Neb.; son of Nate and Libbie (Burstein) Marcus; married Susan Wightman-Douglas (an art historian and graphic designer), September 10, 1968; children: Joshua. *Education:* Princeton University, B.A., 1965; Yale University, B.F.A. and M.F.A., 1968. *Politics:* Democrat. *Religion:* Jewish. *Home:* 5-Y Magie Apartments, Faculty Rd., Princeton, N.J. 08540. *Office:* School of Architecture, Princeton University, Princeton, N.J. 08540.

CAREER: Princeton University, Princeton, N.J., assistant professor of typography and printing, and graphic design, 1969—. Work has been exhibited at Princeton's Art Museum; has had one-man and group exhibits in eastern states, Michigan, Sweden, Austria, and Finland. Consultant in computergraphics to Bell Telephone Laboratories, 1969-71; member of advisory board of American Institute of Writing Research. *Member:* American Institute of Graphic Arts, Computer Arts Society.

WRITINGS: *Book*, Wittenborn, 1972; *Parables on Dropping Out*, Wittenborn, 1972; *Songs* (poems), Softwhere, 1973; *Softwhere, Inc.*, West Coast Poetry Review Press, 1974. Contributor to *Visible Language* (formerly *Journal of Typographic Research*), *Print*, *Eye*, *Penrose Annual*, *West Coast Poetry Review*, *New Republic*, and *Print Review*. Member of advisory board of *Visible Language*.

WORK IN PROGRESS: Research on concrete poetry, conceptual art, and computer graphics.

SIDELIGHTS: Concerned with making apparent the aesthetic possibilities of mass media communications, Marcus' forms conscientiously distort elements of their normal syntactic and semantic structure, emphasizing the multiple nature of sign (symbol) compositions as drawings, poems, and sculpture. He writes:

"The line between
awake/dreaming
design/art
expression/statement
order/chaos
objects/light
conscious/unconscious
left brain/right brain
poem/drawing
particle/wave
here/there
now/then
myself/others
is a dotted line."

BIOGRAPHICAL/CRITICAL SOURCES: *Publishers' Weekly*, March 5, 1973; *Print*, March-April, 1973; *Design and Environment*, spring, 1973; *West Coast Poetry Review*, fall-winter, 1974.

* * *

MARCUS, Stanley 1905-

PERSONAL: Born April 20, 1905, in Atlanta, Ga.; son of Herbert (a merchant) and Minnie (Lichtenstein) Marcus; married Mary Cantrell, November 7, 1932; children: Jerrie (Mrs. Frederick M. Smith III), Richard Cantrell, Wendy (Mrs. Henry Raymont; Richard and Wendy are twins). *Education:* Amherst College, student, 1921; Harvard University, B.A., 1925, graduate study at Business School, 1926. *Home:* 1 Nonesuch Rd., Dallas, Tex. 75214. *Office:* 4800 Republic National Bank Tower, Dallas, Tex. 75201.

CAREER: Neiman-Marcus, Dallas, Tex. (and branches in Fort Worth, Houston, and elsewhere), secretary, treasurer, and director, 1928, merchandise manager for sports shop, 1928-29, merchandise manager for all apparel, 1929-35, executive vice-president, 1935-50, president, 1950-72, chairman of the board and chief executive officer, 1973-75. Corporate executive vice-president, Carter Hawley Hale Stores; member of board of directors, New York Life Insurance Co., and Republic of Texas Corp.; former director of Slick Airways, Dallas Transit Co., and other businesses. Chief of clothing section, War Production Board, 1942; former member of national council, National Planning Association, and of National Committee for International Development; founding member, Business Committee for the Arts. Trustee of Urban Institute and Southern Methodist University; honorary trustee of Committee for Economic Development. President of Dallas Symphony Society, 1948-49; former director of Southwest Center for Advanced Studies, Dallas Council on World Affairs, and Better Business Bureau of Dallas.

MEMBER: American Retail Federation (chairman of trustees, 1949-50), Council on Foreign Relations, American Institute of Architects (honorary fellow), American Arbitration Association, Dallas Art Association, Harvard Club (Dallas and New York), Grolier Club (New York); Columbian, Dallas, Chaparral, and City Clubs (all Dallas). *Awards, honors:* Tobe Award for distinguished service to American retailing, 1945; Chevalier, French Legion of Honor, 1949, and Officier, 1958; Star of Italian Solidarity (Italy), 1956; Commandeur of Economic Merit (France), 1957; New York Fashion Designers Annual Award, 1958; Order of the British Empire, 1959; Chevalier of Order of Leopold II (Belgium), 1959; Gold Medal of National Retail Merchants Association, 1961; Commendetore al Merito della Republica Italiana, 1961; *Ambassador* Award for Achievement (London), 1963; Royal Order of Dannebrog (Denmark), 1965; Great Cross of Austria, 1965; D.Humanities, Southern Methodist University, 1965.

WRITINGS: Minding the Store, Little, Brown, 1974. Contributor of articles to *Fortune*, *Atlantic*, *Reader's Digest*, *Look*, *Pageant*, *Glamour*, *Business Horizons*, *Saturday Evening Post*, and other periodicals and newspapers.

* * *

MARGOLIS, Maxine L(uanna) 1942-

PERSONAL: Born August 2, 1942, in New York, N.Y.; daughter of Benjamin (a manufacturer) and Norma (Germain) Margolis; married Jerald T. Milanich (a professor of anthropology), December 20, 1970; children: Nara Bales. *Education:* New York University, B.A., 1964; Columbia University, Ph.D., 1970. *Politics:* Democrat. *Religion:* Jewish. *Home:* 111 Southwest 23rd Ter., Gainesville, Fla. 32607. *Office:* Department of Anthropology, University of Florida, Gainesville, Fla. 32611.

CAREER: University of Florida, Gainesville, assistant professor, 1969-73, associate professor of anthropology, 1974—. Member of Equal Rights Amendment Coalition, 1974. *Member:* American Anthropological Association (fellow), Latin American Studies Association, Southern Anthropological Association. *Awards, honors:* National Science Foundation grant, 1971; Wenner-Gren Foundation grant, 1971; University of Florida faculty grant for field research in Parana, Brazil, summer, 1971.

WRITINGS: The Moving Frontier: Social and Economic Change in a Southern Brazilian Community, University of Florida Press, 1973. Contributor to *Luso-Brazilian Review*.

WORK IN PROGRESS: Editing a book of readings on Brazilian anthropology, with William Carter; a comparison of the coffee frontier in Brazil and the cotton frontier in the United States.

SIDELIGHTS: Maxine Margolis writes: "Recently, as a feminist, I have become interested in cross-cultural variations in sex roles and eventually intend to do a book on that subject. I am active in feminist causes in the University."

* * *

MARGULIS, Lynn 1938-

PERSONAL: Born March 5, 1938, in Chicago, Ill.; daughter of Morris (a lawyer) and Leone (a travel agent; maiden name, Wise) Alexander; married Carl Sagan, June 16, 1957 (divorced, 1963); married Thomas N. Margulis (a crystallographer), January 18, 1967; children: (first marriage) Dorion, Jeremy; (second marriage) Zachary, Jenny. *Education:* University of Chicago, A.B., 1957; University of Wisconsin-Madison, M.S., 1960; University of California, Berkeley, Ph.D., 1965. *Politics:* "Closet radical." *Religion:* "Not being prejudiced, I hate all religions equally." *Home:* Gibbs St., Newton Centre, Mass. 02159. *Office:* Department of Biology, Boston University, Boston, Mass. 02215.

CAREER: Boston University, Boston, Mass., assistant professor, 1967-71, associate professor of biology, 1971—. Director of Biology, Brandeis University Peace Corps Colombia Project, summers, 1965, 1966; member of African Primary Science Project, Akosomba, Ghana, 1967. Consultant to Educational Development Center, and to Instituto Brasileiro de Educacao, Ciencia e Cultura (Brazilian Institute of Education, Science, and Culture), Sao Paulo, Brazil, summer, 1970. *Member:* Society for Study of Evolution, American Society of Microbiology, Genetics Society of America, American Institute of Biological Science, New England Aquarium, Massachusetts Audubon Society, Newton Conservators (member of board of directors, 1974), Appalachian Mountain Club, Sigma Xi. *Awards, honors:* Boston University Shell Award, 1967; George Lamb Award, University of Nebraska, for outstanding U.S. botanist, 1972; Dimond Award, 1974.

WRITINGS: Origin of Eukaryotic Cells, Yale University Press, 1970; (editor) *Origins of Life*, Gordon & Breach, Volume I, 1970, Volume II: *Cosmic Evolution, Abundance, and Distribution of Biologically Important Elements*, 1971, Springer-Verlag, Volume III: *Planetary Astronomy*, 1973, Volume IV: *Chemistry and Radioastronomy*, 1973. Contributor of more than fifty articles and reviews to scientific journals. Author of children's science booklets. An editor of journal *Origins of Life*.

WORK IN PROGRESS: A monograph, *Genetic and Evolutionary Consequences of Symbiosis*; with K. V. Schwartz and J. C. Schaadt, an illustrated catalogue of the phyla of the five kingdoms, *The Kinds of Life on Earth*; contribution to the commemoration of the 300th anniversary of Antoni van Leeuwenhoek.

SIDELIGHTS: Lynn Margulis has been invited to international conferences in Pont-a-Mousson, London, Montreal, Barcelona, Ustaoset (Norway), Bristol, Amsterdam, and Leningrad. One summer she studied curanderos (native healers) in Tepoztlan, Mexico, and has maintained contacts with the Spanish world since then. Mrs. Margulis writes, "Since my major social goal (the eradication of poverty and ignorance by population control and education) is hopeless, I spend my time deducing the early evolutionary history of life on earth."

MARIAH, Paul 1937-

PERSONAL: Born June 3, 1937, in Whittington, Ill. *Education:* Southern Illinois University, B.S., 1959; San Francisco State College (now University), M.A., 1969. *Office: ManRoot*, Box 982, South San Francisco, Calif. 94080.

CAREER: San Francisco State College (now University), San Francisco, Calif., teaching assistant in English, 1969-70; Indiana University, Bloomington, project scheduler and research assistant on Kinsey study, 1969-70; *ManRoot* (magazine), South San Francisco, Calif., founder and co-editor, 1969—; poet. Chairman of poetry and writing workshop of Society of Individual Rights, 1967; organizer of Conference of Small Magazines, 1968; personal secretary to Kay Boyle and Robert Duncan, 1968-69; has made documentary films, video tapes, and tape recordings, and tape recordings of his own poetry. *Member:* Council of Religion and the Homosexual (president, 1972), Phi Sigma Kappa (charter member of Kappa Tetarton Chapter).

WRITINGS—Poetry: *Personae Non Gratae*, Shameless Hussy Press, 1971; *The Soon Ring*, Contraband Press, 1973; *Robert Duncan: A Complete Bibliography*, Kent State University Press, 1975. Also author of poetry broadsides. Work is represented in anthologies, including *The Anthology*, edited by John Oliver Simon and Richard Krech, Noh Directions Press, 1968; *Diana*, Goliards Press, 1968; *The San Francisco Bark*, edited by Thomas Head and Paul Foreman, Thorp Springs Press, 1972; *Love Today*, edited by Herbert A. Otto, Association Press, 1972; *Madness Network News Reader*, Glide Publications, 1974; *Love Poems to an Army Deserter Who Is in Jail*, Empty Elevator Shaft Press, 1974; *The Electric Holding Company*, ManRoot Press, 1974; *Gay Sunshine Anthology*, edited by Winston Leyland, Panjundrum Press, 1975. Contributor of poems to over 200 magazines.

WORK IN PROGRESS: Essays on Jean Genet; *Crimes Against Criminals*; *Dances with Dali*; *Looking Towards Greece*; *Songs of the Wind*.

* * *

MARINACCIO, Anthony 1912-

PERSONAL: Born August 26, 1912, in Bridgeport, Conn.; son of Paul and Louisa (DeLibero) Marinaccio; married Elsie Elizabeth Kleps, September 5, 1936 (died September 14, 1964); married Mary Maxine Reynolds (an associate professor and counselor), October 15, 1965; children: (first marriage) Warren, Karen (Mrs. John Beacon), Lee; (second marriage) Linda. *Education:* Connecticut State College, B.Ed., 1937; Ohio State University, M.A., 1939; Yale University, Ph.D., 1949. *Religion:* Christian. *Home:* 13919 Turnmore Rd., Chaddsford, Md. 20906. *Office:* School of Education, George Washington University, Washington, D.C. 20006.

CAREER: Moore Printing Service, Stratford, Conn., part-time printer, 1925-31; junior high school teacher of graphic arts, social studies, civics, and drawing in Hartford, Conn., 1935-42, elementary school principal, 1942-46; Oswego State Teachers College (now State University of New York College at Oswego), professor of education and principal of Campus School, 1946-49; assistant superintendent of school in Peoria, Ill., 1949-53; superintendent of schools in Mexico, Mo., 1953-55, Kankakee, Ill., 1955-59, and Davenport, Iowa, 1959-64; Parsons College, Fairfield, Iowa, dean, 1964-65; Hiram Scott College, Scottsbluff, Neb., founding president, 1965-69; George Washington University, Washington, D.C., professor of education, 1969—. Part-time professor at Bradley University, 1949-53, in extension courses, 1956, 1957, 1958; professiorial lecturer at George Washington University, summers, 1952-69; visiting professor at Ohio State University, summers, 1953-54; consultant to the colleges and boards of trustees of Palmer Junior College and Palmer College of Chiropractics, 1973—. Engineer for Keeney Manufacturing Co., 1942-43.

MEMBER: American Association of School Administrators, American Association for Higher Education, National Education Association, American Association of College Presidents, Association of Professors of Higher Education, Phi Delta Kappa, Epsilon Pi Tau, Phi Sigma Phi. *Awards, honors:* LL.D. from Parsons College, 1961.

WRITINGS: Exploring the Graphic Arts, Van Nostrand, 1959; *Human Relations: The New Dimension in American Education*, Kendall-Hunt, 1974. Contributor to magazines and newspapers.

* * *

MARISCAL, Richard N(orth) 1935-

PERSONAL: Born October 4, 1935, in Los Angeles, Calif.; son of Joseph Francis (an engineer) and Janet (Whittemore) Mariscal; married Elaine Seales Byrd (a preschool teacher), November 30, 1974; children: Scott Byrd. *Education:* Stanford University, B.A., 1957, M.A., 1961; University of California, Berkeley, Ph.D., 1966. *Home address:* Route 3, Box 574, Tallahassee, Fla. 32303. *Office:* Department of Biological Science, Florida State University, Tallahassee, Fla. 32306.

CAREER: Stanford University, Stanford, Calif., member of expedition in biological oceanography of Hopkins Marine Station to the South Pacific, summer, 1963; University of California, Berkeley, member of Galapagos International Scientific Project in the Galapagos Islands, 1964; Stanford University, faculty assistant for expedition in biological oceanography of Hopkins Marine Station to the Indian Ocean, 1964-65; University of California, Berkeley, lecturer in invertebrate zoology, 1966; University of Hawaii, Hawaii Institute of Marine Biology, Honolulu, visiting investigator and instructor in National Science Foundation summer training program in coelenterate physiology and biochemistry, summer, 1967; University of California, Santa Barbara, visiting assistant professor of marine biology, summer, 1968; Florida State University, Tallahassee, assistant professor, 1968-72, associate professor of biological science, 1972—. Visiting assistant professor at Oregon State University, summer, 1969, University of Washington (Seattle), summer, 1970, and University of California (Berkeley), summer, 1971, visiting associate professor, summer, 1972; visiting associate professor at West Indies Laboratory (Virgin Islands), summer, 1974. Conducted field work in Hawaii, Samoa, Fiji, Santa Cruz Islands, Solomon Islands, New Guinea, Australia, Society Islands, Galapagos Islands, Costa Rica, Africa, Maldive Islands, Ceylon, Singapore, Hong Kong, Malaysia, and Thailand. Member of Second International Coral Reef Expedition to Australia's Great Barrier Reef, summer, 1974. *Military service:* U.S. Navy, 1957-59; became lieutenant senior grade.

MEMBER: International Bryozoology Association, American Association for the Advancement of Science (life member), American Society of Zoologists, Ecological Society of America, Animal Behavior Society, Association for Tropical Biology, American Institute of Biological Sciences, American Society of Ichthyologists and Herpetologists, Association of Southeastern Biologists, Sierra Club, Wilderness Society, National Audubon Society, East African Wildlife Society, Western Society of Naturalists, Florida Academy of Sciences, New York Academy of Sciences, Northern California Society for Electron Microscopy, California Academy of Sciences, Sigma Xi. *Awards, honors:* National Institutes of Health postdoctoral fellowship at Laboratory for Quantitative Biology of University of Miami (Coral Gables, Fla.), 1967-68.

WRITINGS: Marine Biology (booklet, with film slides), Harper, 1972; (editor) *Experimental Marine Biology*, Academic Press, 1974. Contributor of about thirty articles to scientific journals.

WORK IN PROGRESS: A book on electron microscopy and symbiotic associations of marine organisms; *Man and the Marine Environment*; research and writings on the behavior, ecology, and physiology of marine organisms.

* * *

MARKS, Charles 1922-

PERSONAL: Born January 28, 1922, in Kremenchug, Ukraine, Russia; naturalized U.S. citizen; son of Abe (a businessman) and Sonia (Beck) Marks; married Joyce Wernick (an artist), December 11, 1949; children: Malcolm, Peter, Ian, Anthony. *Education:* University of Cape Town, B.A., 1942, M.D., 1945; Royal College of Surgeons of England, F.R.C.S., 1952; Royal College of Physicians of Edinburgh, M.R.C.P., 1952, F.R.C.P.; Marquette University, M.S., 1966; Tulane University, Ph.D., 1973. *Religion:* Judaic. *Home:* 1680 State St., New Orleans, La. 70118. *Office:* 1542 Tulane Ave., New Orleans, La. 70112.

CAREER: Groote Schuur Hospital, Cape Town, Union of South Africa, intern, 1946, resident, 1947-49; further residencies at Royal College of Surgeons affiliated hospitals, London, England, 1949-53; private practice of surgery in Salisbury, Rhodesia, 1953-63; Marquette University, School of Medicine, Milwaukee, Wis., associate professor of surgery, 1963-67; Case Western Reserve University, School of Medicine, Cleveland, Ohio, associate clinical professor of surgery, 1967-71; Louisiana State University, School of Medicine, New Orleans, La., professor of surgery, 1971—. Hunterian Professor at Royal College of Surgeons, 1956. Chief of surgery, Mount Sinai Hospital, Cleveland, 1967-71; currently attending surgeon at Charity Hospital, Touro Infirmary, Hotel Dieu, and U.S. Veterans Administration Hospital, all New Orleans. Visiting professor or lecturer at medical schools, hospitals, and for medical societies throughout United States and in England, South Africa, Rhodesia, Canada, Israel, and Australia.

MEMBER: American College of Surgeons (fellow), American College of Chest Physicians (fellow), American College of Cardiology (fellow), American Medical Association, British Medical Association, Royal Society of Medicine, American Association of Anatomists, South African College of Surgeons, American Thoracic Society, Society for Surgery of the Alimentary Tract, British Association of Surgical Oncology, Pan-Pacific Surgical Association, New York Academy of Surgeons; and other regional, state, and local medical societies. *Awards, honors:* Fellowship in cardio-thoracic surgery at Cleveland Clinic, 1971; named clinical teacher of the year at Louisiana State University School of Medicine, 1972, 1974; Schlieder Foundation research grant.

WRITINGS: (Contributor) John P. Madden, editor, *Atlas of Technics in Surgery*, 2nd edition (Marks did not contribute to earlier edition), two volumes, Appleton, 1965; (contributor) John H. Mulholland and others, editors, *Current Surgical Management*, Saunders, 1965; *Applied Surgical Anatomy*, C.C Thomas, 1972; *The Portal Venous System*, C.C Thomas, 1972; *A Surgeon's World: The Story of a Dedicated Physician's Crusade for Excellence*, Whitmore, 1972. Contributor of about eighty articles and papers to medical journals.

WORK IN PROGRESS: A monograph on carcinoid tumors; a novel, *The Ultimate Gift*, completion expected in 1976.

* * *

MARLAND, Sidney P(ercy, Jr.) 1914-

PERSONAL: Born August 19, 1914, in Danielson, Conn.; son of Sidney P. (a merchant) and Ruth (an artist; maiden name, Johnson) Marland; married Virginia Partridge (a volunteer worker), June 29, 1940; children: Sidney Percy III, Pamela M. (Mrs. Maurice Izard), Judith. *Education:* University of Connecticut, A.B., 1936, M.A., 1950; New York University, Ph.D., 1955. *Religion:* Episcopalian. *Office:* College Entrance Examination Board, 888 Seventh Ave., New York, N.Y. 10019.

CAREER: High school English teacher in West Hartford, Conn., 1938-41; superintendent of schools in Darien, Conn., 1948-56, Winnetka, Ill., 1956-63, and Pittsburgh, Pa., 1963-68; Institute for Educational Development, New York, N.Y., president, 1968-70; U.S. Commissioner of Education in Washington, D.C., 1970-72 (created National Institute of Education and Fund for the Improvement of Postsecondary Education); assistant secretary of Department of Health, Education and Welfare in Washington, D.C., 1972-73; College Entrance Examination Board, New York, N.Y., president, 1973—. Has lectured at Harvard University, Northwestern University, National College of Education, and University of Montana; adjunct professor at Columbia University, New York University, and University of Connecticut. Vice-chairman of White House Conference on Education, 1965; member of advisory council of Office of Economic Opportunity, 1963-68, Education for Disadvantaged Children, 1964-68, Council for the Progress of Nontraditional Study, and National Chamber of Commerce's Advisory Group of Scholars; member of boards of directors of Joint Council on Economic Education of Urban League of Pittsburgh, 1963-68, National Merit Scholarship Corp., 1968-70, Educational Testing Service, American College of Life Underwriters, and Thomas A. Edison Foundation. Trustee of John F. Kennedy Center for Performing Arts, National Educational Television, 1962-70, University of Pittsburgh, 1965-68, and Allegheny Community College; president of Great Cities School Improvement Council, 1967-68; assistant director of Young Men's Christian Association (YMCA) summer camp, 1937-40. *Military service:* U.S. Army, infantry, 1941-47; became colonel; received Distinguished Service Cross, Legion of Merit, and Bronze Star Medal.

MEMBER: National Education Association, American Association of School Administrators, American Legion, Rotary International. *Awards, honors:* LL.D. from University of Pittsburgh, 1967, New York University, 1971, and Northwestern University, 1971; D.H.L. from Ripon College, 1972, Denison University, 1972, Bishop College, 1973, Rhode Island College, 1973, Fairfield University, 1973, and University of Akron, 1973; distinguished public service award from U.S. Department of Defense, 1974.

WRITINGS: (Contributor) *Religion in the Public Schools*, American Association of School Administrators, 1962; (with Carleton A. Washburn) *Winnetka: The History and Significance of an Educational Experiment*, Prentice-Hall, 1963; (contributor) *The Unfinished Journey: Issues in American Education* (preface by Lyndon B. Johnson), 2nd edition, John Day, 1968; (editor) *Essays on Career Education*, U.S. Office of Education, 1971; *Career Education: A Proposal for Reform*, McGraw, 1974.

* * *

MARPLE, Hugo D(ixon) 1920-

PERSONAL: Born August 4, 1920, in McMechen, W.Va.; son of Nile A. (a banker) and Mary O. (an elementary school teacher; maiden name, Dixon) Marple; married Annette L. Wilson (a lawyer), August 15, 1950; children: Craig Wilson, Karen Jane, Elaine Carol. *Education:* West Liberty State College, A.B., 1940; University of Michigan, M.M., 1946; University of Rochester, Ph.D., 1949; summer postdoctoral study at Harvard University, 1951, and University of Michigan, 1960. *Home:* 4417 Tenth St., Lubbock, Tex. 79416. *Office:* Department of Music, Texas Tech University, Lubbock, Tex. 79409.

CAREER: High School teacher of music in public schools of Benwood, W.Va., 1940-42; Louisville Symphony, Louisville, Ky., bassoonist, 1942-46; Indiana Central College, Indianapolis, member of faculty and head of department of music, 1949-54; Wisconsin State University, Stevens Point, professor of music, 1954-69, head of department, 1954-69; Texas Tech University, Lubbock, professor of music, 1969—, director of music education, 1969—. Visiting professor at New York University College, Fredonia, 1964, 1969. Regional chairman of Danforth Associates, 1968. *Military service:* U.S. Army, 1942-46; became sergeant. *Member:* Music Educators National Conference, Music Teachers National Association (regional president, 1966-68).

WRITINGS: The Beginning Conductor, McGraw, 1972; *The World of Music*, Allyn & Bacon, 1975; *Backgrounds and Approaches to Junior High Music*, W.C. Brown, 1975. Contributor to *Muziek en Onderwijs, Music in Education, Musart*, and *Music Educators Journal*.

WORK IN PROGRESS: Arranging for the Band, completion expected in 1977; *Music of the Twentieth Century*, 1978; *Psychology of Music*, 1980.

* * *

MARQUEZ, Robert 1942-

PERSONAL: Born July 14, 1942, in New York, N.Y.; son of Juan (a furniture polisher) and Iris Virginia (a bookbinder; maiden name, Binet) Marquez; married Madelaine Samalot (a teacher and doctoral candidate), May 31, 1970. *Education:* Aviation High School, New York, Engine and Airframe Mechanic's License, 1960; Bronx Community College, evening classes, 1960-62; Brandeis University, B.A., 1966; Harvard University, M.A., 1970, Ph.D., 1974; also studied at University of Madrid, 1964-65, and National University of San Marcos of Lima, 1966-67. *Politics:* "Anti-imperialist." *Home:* 222 Northeast St., Amherst, Mass. 01002. *Office:* Hampshire College, Amherst, Mass. 01002.

CAREER: New York Public Library, New York, N.Y., 1960-62, started as page, became clerk-photostat operator and technical assistant; Centro Cultural Peruano-Norteamericano, Lima, Peru, part-time instructor in literature, 1966-67; Commonwealth Service Corps, Boston, Mass., area coordinator of Migrant Education Project, 1967; Brandeis University, Waltham, Mass., assistant director of Transitional Year Program, 1969-70, visiting lecturer in Caribbean literature and history, 1971-72; Hampshire College, Amherst, Mass., assistant professor, 1970-74, associate professor of Hispanic American literature, 1974—. *Member:* Latin American Studies Association. *Awards, honors:* Fulbright-Hays fellowship for study in Peru, 1966-67.

WRITINGS: (With David Arthur McMurray, translator and author of introduction and notes) *Man-Making Words: Selected Poems of Nicolas Guillen*, University of Massachusetts Press, 1972; (author of foreword) Arthur Gillette, *Cuba's Educational Revolution*, Fabian Society, 1972; (translator and author of introduction and notes) *Patria o Muerte: The Great Zoo and Other Poems by Nicolas Guillen*, Monthly Review Press, 1972; (editor, major translator, and author of introduction) *Latin American Revolutionary Poetry/Poesia revolucionaria latinoamericana* (bilingual anthology), Monthly Review Press, 1974.

Contributor of poetry translations to *Folio*, *Confrontation*, *Monthly Review*, *Black Scholar*, and other literary journals; his own poems in Spanish have been published in *Romanica*. Member of poetry board, University of Massachusetts Press, 1972-73; member of editorial board, *Massachusetts Review*, 1973—, and editor of *Caliban*, a special issue devoted to Latin America and the Caribbean, winter-spring, 1974; founder and editor, *Caliban: A Journal of New World Thought and Writing*, 1974—.

WORK IN PROGRESS: The End of Blood: The Poems of Paul Rivero, a translation of Rivero's first book, *Papel de hombre*; with David Arthur McMurray, *Racism, Culture, and Revolution: The Prose Writings of Nicolas Guillen*, an annotated edition with a substantial introduction; "Zombie to Synthesis," an essay on the Negro in Spanish American literature for a collection edited by Jan Carew, *Rape the Sun*; research on literature of the French Antilles for an eventual book.

SIDELIGHTS: Marquez is a Black Puerto Rican ("in the islands, if not in the U.S., this description would suffer, historically, from a certain redundancy," he says), who was born and raised in Spanish Harlem. He adds: "As a typical Antillean offspring of immigration—forced immigration—and exile, my interests are focused precisely on those 'islands inbetween' and on the mainland continent of Latin America, its peoples and their struggles, which are my struggles, no less than on the United States' own domestic 'Third World' of which I, equally, form a part.

"As my own poems are, on the whole, written in Spanish and tend to be what I refer to as occasional pieces, I have done nothing more than accumulate them in various drawers and files. . . . But I am toying with the idea of putting together a collection of sonnets for eventual publication. Pero quien sabe?

"I am a real participant-fan of football and horseback riding and just plain loafing and get into each of them anytime I have the chance. I also enjoy going to movies—am, in fact, a flick-freak of sorts."

BIOGRAPHICAL/CRITICAL SOURCES: Casa de Las Americas (Havana), Volume 15, number 85, July-August, 1974.

MARSHALL, Roderick 1903-1975

March 29, 1903—January 29, 1975; American educator and author of books on literary topics. Obituaries: *New York Times*, January 31, 1975.

* * *

MARSHALL, Rosalind Kay 1939-

PERSONAL: Born March 23, 1939, in Dysart, Scotland; daughter of Arthur Frederick Kay Robertson (a school teacher) and Nan (Duncan) Marshall. *Education:* University of Edinburgh, M.A., 1959, Dip.Ed., 1960, M.A. (honors), 1966, Ph.D., 1970. *Home:* 11 St. Clair Terrace, Edinburgh EH10 5NW, Scotland. *Office:* Scottish National Portrait Gallery, 1 Queen St., Edinburgh, Scotland.

CAREER: High school teacher of history in the schools of Kirkcaldy, Scotland, 1960-64; *Dictionary of the Older Scottish Tongue*, Edinburgh, Scotland, assistant editor, 1970-71; Scottish Record Office, Edinburgh, Scotland, outside editor, 1971-73; Scottish National Portrait Gallery, Edinburgh, Scotland, assistant keeper, 1973—. *Member:* Scottish History Society, Royal Society of Literature (fellow), Scottish Record Society, Scottish Genealogical Society, Scottish Mediaevalists' Group, Costume Society of Scotland, Costume Society of England, Scottish Historical Conference, Old Edinburgh Club. *Awards, honors:* New Writing Award from Scottish Arts Council, 1974, for *The Days of Duchess Anne*.

WRITINGS: The Days of Duchess Anne: Life in the Household of the Duchess of Hamilton, 1656-1716, St. Martin's, 1973. Contributor of articles and reviews to *Costume*, *Bulletin of the Scottish Costume Society*, *Local Historian*, and *Scottish Historical Review*.

WORK IN PROGRESS: Biography of Mary of Guise: 1515-1560, for Collins.

AVOCATIONAL INTERESTS: Historical monuments, concerts, drawing, oil painting, weaving, embroidery, cooking, tapestry.

* * *

MARTIN, Bernard 1928-

PERSONAL: Born March 13, 1928, in Seklence, Czechoslovakia; son of Benjamin Adam and Helen (Hershkowitz) Martin; married Nancy Louise Platt, June 30, 1955; children: Rachel, Joseph Louis. *Education:* University of Chicago, B.A., 1947; Hebrew Union College, M.H.L., 1951; University of Illinois, Ph.D., 1961. *Home:* 2359 Dysart Rd., University Heights, Ohio 44118. *Office:* Department of Religion, Yost Hall, Case Western Reserve University, Cleveland, Ohio 44106.

CAREER: Rabbi of Jewish congregation in Champaign, Ill., 1951-57; associate rabbi of congregation in Chicago, Ill., 1957-61; senior rabbi of congregation in St. Paul, Minn., 1961-65; Case Western Reserve University, Cleveland, Ohio, associate professor, 1966-68, professor, 1968, Abba Hillel Silver Professor of Jewish Studies, 1968—, chairman of department of religion, 1967—. Member of board of directors of Cleveland chapter of National Conference on Christians and Jews, 1966-71; trustee of Cleveland Jewish Federation, 1967-74. *Military service:* U.S. Army, chaplain, 1953-55.

MEMBER: American Association of University Professors, American Academy for Jewish Research, American Philosophical Association, Society for Biblical Literature, American Academy of Religion, National Association of Professors of Hebrew, Association of Jewish Studies, Central Conference of American Rabbis.

WRITINGS: The Existentialist Theology of Paul Tillich, Bookman Associates, 1963; (translator) Lev Shestov, *Athens and Jerusalem*, Ohio University Press, 1966; *Prayer in Judaism*, Basic Books, 1968; (editor) *Contemporary Reform Jewish Thought*, Quadrangle, 1968; (translator) Shestov, *Potestas Clavium*, Ohio University Press, 1968; *Great Twentieth Century Jewish Philosophers*, Macmillan, 1970; (editor) *A Shestov Anthology*, Ohio University Press, 1970; (translator) Israel Zinberg, *History of Jewish Literature*, five volumes, Volumes I to III, Press of Case Western Reserve University, 1972-73, Volumes IV and V, Ktav, 1973-74; (with Daniel J. Silver) *A History of Judaism*, two volumes, Basic Books, 1974.

Contributor to religious publications, including *American Jewish Archives*, *Jewish Spectator*, *Journal of the Central Conference of American Rabbis*, *Reconstructionist*, *Judaism*, and *Theology Today*. Editor of *Journal of the Central Conference on American Rabbis*, 1975—.

WORK IN PROGRESS: Translating the remaining volumes of *History of Jewish Literature*, by Israel Zinberg.

* * *

MARTIN, Curtis 1915-

PERSONAL: Born October 29, 1915, in Raton, N.M.; son of George Lewis and Viola (Rodarmel) Martin; married Ann Federici (a literary agent), September 25, 1934; children: Brooke George, Curtis William. *Education:* University of New Mexico, B.A., 1938, M.A., 1940; Harvard University, M.A., 1949, Ph.D., 1950. *Home:* 2018 Hermosa Dr., Boulder, Colo. 80302. *Office:* Department of Political Science, University of Colorado, Boulder, Colo. 80302.

CAREER: High school teacher in Maxwell, N.M., 1938-42; University of Colorado, Boulder, instructor, 1948-50, assistant professor, 1950-55, associate professor, 1955-57, professor of political science, 1957—. Assistant director of New Mexico Merit System Council, 1940; visiting professor at University of Sydney and University of Tasmania, 1964. *Military service:* U.S. Navy, active duty, 1942-45; became lieutenant senior grade. *Member:* American Political Science Association, Western Political Science Association (president, 1955-56), Rocky Mountain Social Science Association (president, 1956-57). *Awards, honors:* Fulbright fellowship, Australia, 1964.

WRITINGS: The Hills of Home (novel), Houghton, 1943; *Reflections on Individualism*, University of Colorado Press, 1953; (with R. John Eyre) *Colorado Preprimary System*, University of Colorado Press, 1967; (with Rudolf Gomez) *Colorado Government and Politics*, Pruett, 1973; (editor) *Readings in Colorado Government and Politics*, University of Colorado Press, 1975. Contributor of about thirty-five articles and stories to journals. Fiction editor of *New Mexico Quarterly*, 1937-40; editor of *Research*, 1938.

WORK IN PROGRESS: Two novels, *Beneath Another Sky* and *The November Enemy*.

* * *

MARTIN, Ira Jay III 1911-

PERSONAL: Born September 2, 1911, in Pawtucket, R.I.; son of Ira Jay, Jr. (a delivery man) and Vivian (Kinne) Martin; married Ethel Virginia Augenstein (director of mountain social work), June 3, 1936; children: Rita Elaine Gay (adopted daughter; Mrs. Hearon Dale Prater). *Education:* Brown University, Ph.B., 1933; Andover Newton Theological School, B.D., 1936; Boston University, Th.D., 1942; postdoctoral study at University of Chicago, 1954-55, 1956, and American Schools of Oriental Research in Jerusalem, Jordan, and Baghdad, 1965-66. *Home:* 118 Van Winkle Dr., Berea, Ky. 40403. *Office:* Department of Philosophy and Religion, Berea College, Box 2311, Berea, Ky. 40403.

CAREER: Pastor of American Baptist Convention churches in Woolwich, Maine, 1934-36, Littleton, Mass., 1936-41, and Athol, Mass., 1941-44; Berea College, Berea, Ky., instructor, 1944-46, assistant professor, 1946-50, associate professor, 1950-59, professor of religion, 1959-66, Henry Mixter Penniman Professor, 1966—, director of Wesley Foundation, 1948-62.

MEMBER: Society of Biblical Literature (past president of Southern section), American Academy of Religion (first president, 1964), Society for the Scientific Study of Religion, American Association of University Professors, Archaeological Institute of America (charter member of Kentucky chapter; past president), Academy of Religion and Mental Health, American School of Oriental Research (honorary associate), Phi Kappa Phi (charter member of Berea chapter; past president).

WRITINGS: The Faith of Jesus, Exposition, 1956; *Glossolalia in the Apostolic Church*, Berea College Press, 1960; *The Faith of Paul*, Pageant, 1965; *Glossolalia: A Bibliography*, Pathway Press, 1970. Contributor to *Encyclopaedia Britannica.* Contributor of articles and reviews to learned journals.

WORK IN PROGRESS: Through the Epistles to Paul; *Bunyan's "Pilgrim's Progress,"* two volumes; *Early Christian Thought: A.D. 30-451*, Volume I: *Apostolic Age*, Volume II: *Apologetic Age*, Volume III: *Great Thinkers of the Church*, Volume IV: *The Niceaen Council*, Volume V: *The Trinitarian Quest Complete*, completion expected in 1977; *The Faith of John*; research on snake handling.

* * *

MARTIN, Marjorie 1942-

PERSONAL: Born July 18, 1942, in New York, N.Y.; daughter of Robert James (a writer) and Ellen (Hamill) Martin. *Education:* Attended high school in Prospect Heights, N.Y.; Newspaper Institute of America, certificate, 1970; Christian Writer's Institute, certificate, 1973. *Address:* P.O. Box 1035, F.D.R. Station, New York, N.Y. 10022.

CAREER: Free-lance editor in New York, N.Y., 1970—. *Member:* American Poets Fellowship Society (director of Brooklyn chapter, 1971-73), American Platform Association, Composers, Authors and Artists of America, New York Poetry Forum, Poetry Society of Texas. *Awards, honors:* Spencer Book publications third prize, 1969, for poem, "Child Prodigy."

WRITINGS—Poems: *A Friend Asked Me and Other Poems*, Windfall Press, 1969; *The Span of Dreams*, Candor Press, 1970. Editor of poetry columns of *Shore Record, Coney Island Times, Williamsburg News, Mizpah Messenger*, and *Town and Country Tabloid.*

WORK IN PROGRESS: A games and puzzles book for children, *Rainy Day Think and Do Book*; a book of poetry; education materials for children and religious training projects for youth.

MASON, Bobbie Ann 1940-

PERSONAL: Born May 1, 1940, in Mayfield, Ky.; daughter of Wilburn A. (a dairy farmer) and Christie (Lee) Mason; married Roger B. Rawlings (a college teacher), April 12, 1969. *Education:* University of Kentucky, B.A., 1962; State University of New York at Binghamton, M.A., 1966; University of Connecticut, Ph.D., 1972. *Home address:* R.D. 1, Covington, Pa. 16917. *Office:* Department of English, Mansfield College, Mansfield, Pa. 16933.

CAREER: Mayfield Messenger, Mayfield, Ky., writer, 1960; Ideal Publishing Co., New York, N.Y., writer for magazines, including *Movie Stars*, *Movie Life*, and *T.V. Star Parade*, 1962-63; Mansfield State College, Mansfield, Pa., assistant professor of English, 1972—.

WRITINGS: Nabokov's Garden: A Nature Guide to Ada, Ardis, 1974; *The Girl Sleuth: A Feminist Guide to the Bobbsey Twins, Nancy Drew, and Their Sisters*, Feminist Press, 1975.

WORK IN PROGRESS: The Clue of the Skinny Balloon, a novel.

SIDELIGHTS: Bobbie Ann Mason writes: "After graduating from the University of Kentucky I went to New York City and worked as a writer on some fan magazines. I interviewed Fabian, Annette Funicello, Ann-Margaret, and others and wrote mainly about 'Bonanza' and Pernell Roberts' hairpiece. It wasn't the writing career I had had in mind when I was an iconoclastic columnist on the University of Kentucky *Kernel*, so I went off to graduate school to study literature and that took a long time. When I finally came to my senses after finishing the dissertation (on Nabokov), I lapsed back into my childhood and started reading Nancy Drew books. Life has been steady progress since then. My interest in childhood extends all the way from Nancy Drew to Nabokov, whose magnificent childhood permeates all his works. . . . He read Pushkin as a child, whereas I read Nancy Drew. I am interested in that contrast as a literary theme, and in the culture shock one can experience because of geographical and economic isolation."

* * *

MASON, Ruth Fitch 1890-1974

1890—December 20, 1974; American literary agent, novelist, poet. Obituaries: *New York Times*, December 22, 1974; *AB Bookman's Weekly*, January 27, 1975.

* * *

MATCHETTE, Katharine E. 1941-

PERSONAL: Surname is accented on first syllable; born May 30, 1941, in Corvallis, Ore.; daughter of Jo Kenneth (a contract logger) and Harriet (a bookkeeper; maiden name, Wright) Dingus; married Dennis Matchette (a printer), April 15, 1967. *Education:* Seattle Pacific College, B.A. (cum laude), 1963; graduate study at Oregon State University, 1965—. *Politics:* "Conservative Republican (Would prefer a good new party if someone would start one)." *Religion:* Protestant ("My closest association has been with 'holiness movement' churches"). *Home address:* P.O. Box 504, Philomath, Ore. 97370. *Office:* Controller's Office, Oregon State Board of Higher Education, P.O. Box 488, Corvallis, Ore.

CAREER: Elementary school teacher in Hillsboro, Ore., 1963-64, in a Christian school in Eugene, Ore., 1964-65, and in a mission school in Tampa, Fla., 1965-66; Free Methodist Church of North America, World Headquarters, Winona Lake, Ind., promotional writer for General Missionary Board, 1966-70; Curry Public Library, Gold Beach, Ore., assistant librarian, 1971-72; Free Methodist Church of North America, World Headquarters, promotional writer for General Missionary Board, 1972; Evans Products Co., Corvallis, Ore., technical librarian, 1972-73; Oregon State Board of Higher Education, Corvallis, payroll clerk, 1974—. *Member:* Benton County Mental Health Association.

WRITINGS: Walk Safe through the Jungle, Herald Press, 1974. Author of church school material for Aldersgate Associates, 1970-73. Author of "Pitstop," a Bible column. Contributor of articles, poems, and stories to magazines, including *Today's Girl*, *Young Teen Power*, *Junior Counselor*, and *Christian Reader*, and to newspapers.

WORK IN PROGRESS: Feel with Faith's Fingers (tentative title), an adult suspense novelette about the supernatural, dealing with the realities of evil and God's power; a historical novel for young people, set in Southwestern Oregon.

SIDELIGHTS: Katharine Matchette writes: "By the middle of my third year of teaching... I had discovered that in some developing countries people actually forget how to read because they have no books or magazines or newspapers available. I began to wonder if I might fit in some kind of a mission literature program. To find out, I took a brief orientation course from Evangelical Literature Overseas. With only this background, I accepted a job as a writer. . . .

"Basically I am a 'story' person. Outside of writing I am deeply interested in kids with problems and helping them. I have taken part in volunteer work in a state girls' school, and with my husband have done what I could to promote and help a group foster home for girls in Corvallis. This theme shows up in much of my writing."

AVOCATIONAL INTERESTS: Reading historical novels, biographies, and history, music (plays piano and organ), Oregon history, camping, hiking on the beach, pets.

* * *

MATTHEW, Henry Colin Gray 1941-

PERSONAL: Born January 15, 1941, in Inverness, Scotland; son of Henry J.S. (a physician) and Joyce M. (McKendrick) Matthew; married Sue Ann Curry (an historian), December, 1966; children: David H.C., Lucy E., Oliver J.G. *Education:* Oxford University, B.A., 1963, M.A., 1968, D.Phil., 1970. *Home:* 107 Southmoor Rd., Oxford, England. *Office:* Christ Church, Oxford University, Oxford, England.

CAREER: Education officer in Tanzania, 1963-66; Oxford University, Christ Church, Oxford, England, lecturer in Gladstone studies, 1970—.

WRITINGS: The Liberal Imperialists, Clarendon Press (of Oxford University), 1973; (editor with M.R.D. Foot) *The Gladstone Diaries*, Volumes III and IV (Matthew was not associated with earlier volumes), Clarendon Press, 1975.

WORK IN PROGRESS: A biography of W.E. Gladstone.

* * *

MATTHEWS, Clayton 1918-
(Patty Brisco, a joint pseudonym)

PERSONAL: Born October 24, 1918, in Waurika, Okla.; son of Virgil and Mittie Jane Matthews; married Patricia Brisco (a secretary and writer), November 3, 1972. *Education:* Attended John Tarleton Junior College, 1937. *Politics:* Democrat. *Religion:* None. *Home and office:* 3783 Latrobe St., Los Angeles, Calif. 90031. *Agent:* Jay Garon, Jay Garon-Brooke Associates, Inc., 415 Central Park W., #17D, New York, N.Y. 10025.

CAREER: Writer. Has worked as surveyor, animal trainer in a carnival, carnival barker, and truck driver. *Member:* Mystery Writers of America (vice-president of Southern California chapter, 1968-69), Writers Guild of America (Western Division).

WRITINGS: A Rage of Desire, Monarch Books, 1960; *The Strange Ways of Love*, Monarch Books, 1961; *The Promiscuous Doll*, Monarch Books, 1962; *Faithless*, Monarch Books, 1962; *Nude Running*, Monarch Books, 1963; *The Corrupter*, Monarch Books, 1963; *Dive into Death*, Sherbourne, 1969; *The Mendoza File*, Powell Publications, 1970; *Nylon Nightmare*, Powell Publications, 1970; *Hager's Castle*, Powell Publications, 1970; (with Gary Brandner) *Saturday Night in Milwaukee*, Curtis Books, 1973; *Bounty Hunt at Ballarat*, Pinnacle Books, 1973; *141 Terrace Drive*, Berkley Publishing, 1974; *River Falls*, Berkley Publishing, 1974; (with Arthur Moore) *Las Vegas*, Pocket Books, 1974; *The Big Score*, Brandon Books, 1974; *Mardi Gras*, Pocket Books, 1975; *The Statesman*, Pyramid Publications, 1975; *The Year of the Tiger*, Pocket Books, in press; *The Wheeler-Dealers*, Pocket Books, in press.

(Under joint pseudonym Patty Brisco; with wife, Patricia Brisco) *Merry's Treasure*, Avalon Books, 1969; *Horror at Gull House*, Belmont Tower, 1972; *House of Candles*, Manor Books, 1973; *The Crystal Window*, Avon, 1973; *House of Shadows*, Manor Books, 1975.

Work is anthologized in *Best Detective Stories of the Year*, edited by Allen J. Hubin, Dutton, 24th edition, 1970, 25th edition, 1971; *Dear Dead Days*, edited by Edward D. Hoch, Walker & Co., 1972. Contributor of about thirty stories to mystery magazines and adventure publications, including *Alfred Hitchcock Mystery Magazine*, *Mike Shayne Mystery Magazine*, and *Manhunt*.

WORK IN PROGRESS: The Harvesters, a novel.

* * *

MATTHEWS, L(eonard) Harrison 1901-

PERSONAL: Born June 12, 1901, in Bristol, England; son of Harold Evan and Sarah Susannah (Harrison) Matthews; married Dorothy Helene Harris, November 4, 1924; children: Jean Dorothy (Mrs. Christopher Trewhella), John Michael. *Education:* King's College, Cambridge, B.A., 1922, M.A., 1930, Sc.D., 1939. *Politics:* "Not member of any political party." *Religion:* None. *Home:* The Old Rectory, Stansfield via Sudbury, Suffolk, England.

CAREER: Member of scientific staff of "Discovery" Expedition, 1924-28; University of Bristol, Bristol, England, special lecturer in zoology, 1931-39, research fellow, 1945-50; Zoological Society of London, London, England, scientific director, 1951-66. Has made numerous radio and television broadcasts. *Military service:* British Army, 1940-41; served with anti-aircraft command of Royal Artillery; became radio officer. Served with Telecommunications Research Establishment, 1941-45; became senior scientific officer. *Member:* Royal Society (fellow), British Association for the Advancement of Science (president of Section D, 1959), Association of British Zoologists (president, 1960),

Marine Biological Association of the United Kingdom (member of council, 1944-51), Ray Society, Natural Environment Research Council, Institute of Biology (member of council, 1954-57), British Academy of Forensic Science (president, 1962), Linnean Society of London (member of council, 1953-57), Zoological Society of London (member of council, 1943-45, 1946-49, 1950-51; vice-president, 1944-45, 1947-49, 1950-51).

WRITINGS: South Georgia: The Empire's Subantarctic Outpost, Simpkin Marshall, 1931; *Wandering Albatross: Adventures Among the Albatrosses and Petrels in the Southern Ocean*, Macmillan, 1951; *British Amphibia and Reptiles*, Methuen, 1952; *British Mammals*, Collins, 1952, 2nd edition, 1960; *Sea Elephant: The Life and Death of the Elephant Seal*, MacGibbon & Kee, 1952; *Beasts of the Field*, Collins, 1954; *Animals in Colour*, Witherby, 1959; (author of introduction) Erich Tylinek, *London Zoo*, Spring Books, 1960; (with Maxwell Knight) *Senses of Animals*, Philosophical Library, 1963; (with others) *The Whale*, Simon & Schuster, 1968; *The Life of Mammals*, Volume I, Weidenfeld & Nicolson, 1969, Universe Books, 1970, Volume II, Universe Books, 1971; (editor with Richard Carrington, and contributor) *The Living World of Animals*, Reader's Digest, 1970; (author of introduction) Charles Darwin, *Origin of Species*, Everyman Library, 1971; (editor and author of introduction and explanatory notes) Charles Waterton, *Wanderings in South America*, Oxford University Press, 1973; *Man and Wildlife*, Croom Helm, 1975.

Organizer and editor of *Sunday Times* (London) "Animals in Britain" series, 1960-64. Contributor to *Chamber's Encyclopedia*, *Encyclopaedia Britannica*, *World Book Encyclopedia*, and to proceedings and symposia. Also contributor to numerous periodicals, including *Times* (London), *Times Literary Supplement*, *Listener*, *Punch*, *Observer* (London), *Smithsonian*. Editor, *Journal of Zoology*, 1951-66; chairman, *World List of Scientific Periodicals*, 1958-66.

WORK IN PROGRESS: Four books, one on Antarctic travel, one on RADAR work during World War II, a book of essays, and a historical novel.

SIDELIGHTS: Matthews has participated in scientific expeditions to Iceland, Brazil, and East Africa and "dislikes humbug."

* * *

MAUCHLINE, Mary 1915-

PERSONAL: Surname is pronounced *Moch*-line; born May 7, 1915, in Dundee, Scotland; daughter of Alexander (a clergyman) and Janet Kerr (Neil) Mauchline. *Education:* University of St. Andrews, pass degree, 1936, M.A. (honors), 1940; Cambridge University, certificate in education, 1938; University of Glasgow, diploma in Biblical studies, 1954. *Agent:* John McLaughlin, Cambell Thomson and McLaughlin Ltd., 80 Chancery Lane, London WC2A 1DD, England.

CAREER: Teacher in Scotland, 1940-44, 1949-54, and in England, 1944-47; Ripon College of Education, Ripon, England, lecturer, 1954-55, senior lecturer, 1955-64, principal lecturer in history, 1964-75, head of department, 1954-75. *Member:* Historical Association, Furniture History Society, Chippendale Society, Yorkshire Archaeological Society, York Georgian Society.

WRITINGS: (With others) *Ripon: Some Aspects of Its History*, Dalesman, 1972; *Harewood House*, David & Charles, 1974.

WORK IN PROGRESS: Research on Cistercian abbeys of Yorkshire, on John Lewyn, fourteenth century master mason, and on history of English gentry, especially of the eighteenth century.

SIDELIGHTS: Miss Mauchline's aim is to write local historical works of general interest. She is especially interested in the history of buildings, less from an architectural than a social viewpoint, to show how they can reveal the mode of life, and social structure of their period, and reflect the economy and conditions of building and artist craftsmen. She is also interested in stimulating children's appreciation of history. She writes: "Yorkshire is very rich in historical sites and buildings and my aim is simply to write and lecture for those who visit or live in the area."

* * *

MAUGHAN, A(nne) M(argery)

PERSONAL: Surname is pronounced like "Morn"; born in Darlington, England; daughter of Thomas Bell (a director) and Dorothy C. (Coxon) Maughan. *Education:* Attended school in Harrogate, Yorkshire, England. *Religion:* Church of England. *Home:* 2 Ryton Sq., Sunderland, Durham SR2 TUF, England. *Agent:* A. M. Heath, 40 King William IV St., London WC2N 4DD, England. *Office:* Broadwood Limestone Co., West Cornforth, Ferry Hill, Durham DL17 9LF, England.

CAREER: Broadwood Limestone Co., Durham, England, company director, 1956—. *Member:* English-Speaking Union.

WRITINGS: Monmouth Harry, Morrow, 1956; *Young Pitt*, John Day, 1975. Contributor to *Holiday* and *Woman's Journal*.

WORK IN PROGRESS: Research on eighteenth-century England.

* * *

MAYE, Patricia 1940-

PERSONAL: Born May 20, 1940, in Brooklyn, N.Y.; daughter of John F. and Agnes (Burke) Maye. *Education:* Brooklyn College of the City University of New York, B.F.A., 1963; also studied with Ad Reinhardt. *Politics:* "Reactionary with a hint of anarchy." *Religion:* Roman Catholic. *Home:* 33 Bank St., New York, N.Y. 10014. *Office: Nikon World*, Ehrenreich Photo Optical, 623 Stewart Ave., Garden City, N.Y. 11530.

CAREER: Time-Life Books, New York, N.Y., picture editor, 1963-72; American Photographic Book Publishing Co., Inc., Garden City, N.Y., managing editor, 1972-74; Ehrenreich Photo Optical, Garden City, N.Y., editor of *Nikon World*, 1974—. Free-lance writer, editor, and designer.

WRITINGS: Fieldbook of Nature Photography, Sierra Club Books, 1974; (editor and designer) *Creative Color Photography of Robin Perry*, Amphoto, 1974; (editor and designer) Joseph D. Cooper, *Pentax Manual*, Amphoto, 1974.

WORK IN PROGRESS: Principles of Color Photography, with illustrations; *ABC*, a children's alphabet book, poems illustrated by photographs.

AVOCATIONAL INTERESTS: Travel.

* * *

MAYER, Gary (Richard) 1945-

PERSONAL: Born December 20, 1945, in Brooklyn,

N.Y.; son of Harry Seymour (a businessman) and Anita (Galowitz) Mayer; married Jo Ann Sockel, June 8, 1968 (divorced July 8, 1972). *Education:* Temple University, B.S., 1968. *Politics:* "Radical Populist." *Religion:* "Jewish with gnostic leanings." *Home:* 95 Christopher, New York, N.Y. 10014. *Agent:* Gary Cosay, Creative Management Associates Ltd., 8899 Beverly Blvd., Los Angeles, Calif. 90048.

CAREER: William Morris Agency, New York, N.Y., literary agent, 1968-71; free-lance writer, 1971—. *Military service:* U.S. Army, 1968. *Member:* Young Men's Christian Association.

WRITINGS: Bookie: My Life in Disorganized Crime, J. P. Tarcher, 1974.

WORK IN PROGRESS: A book on the modern-day bounty hunter, for J. P. Tarcher.

SIDELIGHTS: Mayer writes that his motivation is "... money, a love of anything or anybody who drops out of the 'system' and beats it, money, ego, money." He has appeared on the "Tonight Show," and several other talk shows. *Avocational interests:* Golf, basketball, bridge.

* * *

MAYES, Edythe Beam 1902-

PERSONAL: Born May 9, 1902, in Kingsmountain, N.C.; daughter of Charles Lemuel (a farmer) and Mary Florence (McGinnes) Beam; married Leroy Harold Mayes (president of Rio Grande College and State Department official), September, 1926 (deceased). *Education:* Attended Lenoir Rhyne College, Juilliard School of Music, Rio Grande College, and New York University; studied opera in Paris and Italy. *Home:* 358 Clark Ave., Staten Island, N.Y. 10306. *Agent:* George Glay, Inc., 663 Fifth Ave., New York, N.Y. 10022.

CAREER: New York Times, New York, N.Y., secretary, 1920-22; MacFadden Publications, New York, N.Y., in charge of foreign department, 1923-26; Rio Grande College, Rio Grande, Ohio, librarian, 1929; writer, 1962—. *Member:* World Poetry Society, International Clover Poetry Association, American Poetry League, American Poets Fellowship Society, Major Poets, Poetry Society of South Carolina, Avalon. *Awards, honors:* Recipient of numerous poetry awards.

WRITINGS: Washington: God's Workshop, Northwoods Press, 1973; *Gift: 1973*, Northwoods Press, 1973; *Our Debt to the Negro*, Northwoods Press, 1973; *Mrs. Patty's Place* (novel), Northwoods Press, 1975. Contributor of more than five hundred short stories, poems, and articles to little literary magazines.

WORK IN PROGRESS: Never Too Old, a novel; *The Night's Sweet Bird*, a novel; *Hunger Creek Road*, a novel; *Seed Time and Harvest*, a novel; *Bird of Time*, a novel; *Upon the Wings of the Morning*, a novel; *Flesh Is Grass*, a novel; a book about Washington, D.C.

SIDELIGHTS: Edythe Mayes writes that her family has played a part in the political life of North Carolina since they settled there in 1767. This family has produced two governors, two U.S. Senators, and a British Ambassador in this generation. The founders of the clan were John Teeter Beam and Rebecca Rousseau Reynold. "Through Rebecca I'm the sixth great-niece of Jean Jacques Rousseau; and through John Teeter, the sixth great-grand-daughter of Sarah Rudolph of Hapsburg, who was a direct descendant of Rudolph I, who became Emperor of Germany in 1273. This information is on an old stone monument at the original homesite of John Teeter and Rebecca."

* * *

MAZMANIAN, Daniel (Aram) 1945-

PERSONAL: Born March 27, 1945, in Oakland, Calif.; son of Vaughn (a retailer) and Zabell (Paul) Mazmanian; married Mary Catherine Becker (a primary school teacher), January 29, 1967. *Education:* San Francisco University, B.A., 1966, M.A., 1967; Washington University, St. Louis, Mo., Ph.D., 1970. *Agent:* Leo Flynn, Carnegie Towers, Claremont, Calif. 91711. *Office:* Department of Government, Pomona College, Claremont, Calif. 91711.

CAREER: Forest Park Community College, St. Louis, Mo., instructor in American national government, 1968; Southern Illinois University, East St. Louis, lecturer in American politics, 1969; Washington International Center, Washington, D.C., lecturer in American national politics, 1971-72; Pomona College, Claremont, Calif., assistant professor of government, 1974—. Research associate at Brookings Institution, 1970-74. *Member:* American Political Science Association, Western Political Science Association.

WRITINGS: Third Parties in Presidential Elections, Brookings Institution, 1974. Contributor to *Public Administration Review* and *Forensic Quarterly*.

WORK IN PROGRESS: Citizens and Bureaucracy: The Environmental Movement and the Army Corps of Engineers, for Brookings Institution.

* * *

McCABE, Bernard P(atrick), Jr. 1933-

PERSONAL: Born March 14, 1933, in Portsmouth, N.H.; son of Bernard P. and Florence (Jackson) McCabe; married Norma G. Williams, August 18, 1956; children: Brent Poe. *Education:* Emerson College, B.A., 1956, M.A., 1957; New York University, Ph.D., 1961. *Home:* 152 Blake Rd., Hamden, Conn. 06517. *Office:* Department of Speech Communication, Southern Connecticut State College, New Haven, Conn. 06515.

CAREER: Brooklyn College of the City University of New York, New York, N.Y., instructor in speech, 1957-59; teacher of English in public schools in New York, N.Y., 1959-61; St. John's University, Jamaica, N.Y., assistant professor of public address, 1961-65; Mount Holyoke College, South Hadley, Mass., assistant professor of public address and rhetoric, 1966-67; Southern Connecticut State College, New Haven, associate professor, 1967-70, professor of communication, 1970—, director of undergraduate communication studies, 1972. Lecturer at City College of the City University of New York, 1963-65. *Member:* Speech Communication Association of America, Connecticut Speech Association.

WRITINGS: (With C. C. Bender) *Speaking Is a Practical Matter*, Holbrook, 1968, 3rd edition, in press; *Communicative Voice and Articulation*, Holbrook, 1970.

WORK IN PROGRESS: Interpersonal Communication as Public Communication.

* * *

McCALLUM, John D(ennis) 1924-

PERSONAL: Born June 27, 1924, in Tacoma, Wash.; son of George A. and Mildred (Tiedeman) McCallum; married Marjie Millar (a motion picture actress), 1962 (died, 1966).

Education: Attended Washington State University, 1942-43, 1945-47, and New York University, 1943. *Home and office:* 11509 17th Ave. E., Tacoma, Wash. 98445. *Agent:* Barthold Fles, 507 Fifth Ave., New York, N.Y. 10017.

CAREER: Was member of staff of *Tacoma News Tribune*, *Tacoma Times*, *Oregonian* (Portland), and *Spokane Daily Chronicle*, prior to 1948; Newspaper Enterprise Association, New York, N.Y., assistant sports editor, 1950-54; A. S. Barnes & Co., Inc., New York, N.Y., director of premium book division, 1954-58; lecturer for Antrim Bureau, Philadelphia, Pa. and National School Assemblies, Los Angeles, Calif., 1963-71; full-time writer, 1971—. Member of sports committee, National Cerebral Palsy Foundation, 1949; member of board of directors, Tacoma Athletic Commission, 1969-75. *Military service:* U.S. Army, 1943-45. *Member:* Pacific Northwest Industrial Editors Association, Washington State University Alumni Association, Sigma Delta Chi, Q-Club of Pacific Lutheran University. *Awards, honors:* Member of Tacoma-Pierce County, Washington Sports Hall of Fame, 1969; distinguished service award from Pacific Lutheran University, 1972.

WRITINGS: (With W. W. Heffelfinger) *This Was Football*, A. S. Barnes, 1954; (with Whitney Martin) *How You Can Play Little League Baseball*, Prentice-Hall, 1954; *The Tiger Wore Spikes: An Informal Biography of Ty Cobb*, A. S. Barnes, 1956; *That Kelly Family*, A. S. Barnes, 1957; (with David Stidolph) *The Coit Fishing Pole Club Beginners Book of Fishing*, Prentice-Hall, 1958; (with Edgar Eisenhower) *Six Roads from Abilene: Some Personal Recollections of Edgar Eisenhower*, Wood & Reber, 1960; *Scooper: Authorized Story of Scoop Conlon's Motion Picture World*, Wood & Reber, 1960; (with Lorraine W. Ross) *Port Angeles, U.S.A.*, Wood & Reber, 1961; *Everest Diary*, Follett, 1966; *Going Their Way* (autobiography), Chilton, 1969; (with Charles H. Pearson) *College Football, U.S.A.*, Hall of Fame Publishing and McGraw, 1971; *The Story of Dan Lyons, S. J.*, Guild Books, 1973; *The Gladiators*, Pacific Lutheran Press, 1974; *The World Heavyweight Boxing Championship*, Chilton, 1974; *The Encyclopedia of World Boxing Champions, 1882-1975*, Chilton, 1975. Contributor to *Encyclopaedia Britannica*, and to *Sport*, *Argosy*, *Grit*, *True*. Former contributing editor of *Inside Baseball* and *Boxing & Wrestling*.

WORK IN PROGRESS: A biography of Ty Cobb; *The Crime Doctor*, with James Warner Bellah; a biography of Knute Rockne, with Paul Castner.

BIOGRAPHICAL/CRITICAL SOURCES: John D. McCallum, *Going Their Way*, Chilton, 1969.

* * *

McCALLUM, Phyllis 1911-

PERSONAL: Born April 5, 1911, in Pacific Grove, Calif.; daughter of Henry Garfield (a judge) and Mae (an artist; maiden name, Hull) Jorgensen; married George Alexander McCallum (a college professor), December 20, 1936; children: Alexsan (Mrs. Paul L. Dillon, Jr.), Michael Douglas. *Education:* Stanford University, B.A., 1936. *Politics:* Republican. *Religion:* United Methodist. *Home:* 1187 Clark Way, San Jose, Calif. 95125.

CAREER: Author, playwright. Member of advisory board of Pioneer Drama Service, 1970—; San Jose Junior Theatre, member of advisory board, 1951—, president, 1967-69; vice-president of San Jose Entertainment Commission, 1971, and Council of Arts, Greater San Jose Area, 1974-75. *Member:* National League of American Pen Women (president of Santa Clara County branch, 1972-74), Chi Omega.

AWARDS, HONORS: Seattle Junior Programs national playwriting contest first prize, 1958, for *The Pale Pink Dragon*; Community Children's Theatre, Inc., playwriting first prize, 1963, for *Kangalou*, second prize, 1967, for *The Tough and Tender Troll*; Pioneer Drama Service second prize, 1967, for *The Tough and Tender Troll*; National League of American Pen Women national letters contest first prize, 1974, for *Hansel and Gretel and the Golden Petticoat*, and third prize, 1974, for *Williamsburg Won't*; Children's Theatre of Richmond playwriting contest fourth prize, 1974, for *The Pudgy Pony of Pompeii*.

WRITINGS—Plays, all published by Pioneer Drama Service: *The Pale Pink Dragon* (three-act; first produced in 1967), 1966; *The Tough and Tender Troll* (three-act; first produced at Yuba College Theatre, December 1, 1967), 1967; *The Vanilla Viking* (three-act; first produced in Santa Clara, Calif., at Haman School, April 10, 1970), 1967; *The Gratefull Griffin* (three-act), 1968; *Hansel and Gretel and the Golden Petticoat* (one-act; first produced in Jonesboro, Ark., at Dudley Elementary School), 1973; *Crumple, Rumpelstiltskin* (one-act), 1974. Also author of *The Uniform Unicorn* (three-act; first produced in Wilmington, N.C., at City Children's Theatre, 1968), published by Pioneer Drama Service. Contributor of plays, stories, and articles to *Eleusis, Pen Woman, Lutheran, Vista, Instructor*, and *Plays*.

WORK IN PROGRESS: A children's play for San Jose's Bicentennial titled *Alberto of Almaden*, completion expected in 1975; a musical dramatization of "Pollyanna," 1975.

SIDELIGHTS: Phyllis McCallum told *CA*: "Even as a child, I wrote plays for the neighborhood and I wrote my own senior class play, 'Yes Girl'. . . .My other enthusiasms are running my church library, traveling with and studying the out-of-doors with my biologist husband, researching future plays."

* * *

McCONNELL, John Lithgow Chandos 1918- (John Chandos)

PERSONAL: Born July 27, 1918, in Glasgow, Scotland. *Residence:* Dublin, Ireland. *Agent:* A. D. Peters, 10 Buckingham St., London W.C.2, England.

CAREER: Author.

WRITINGS—All under pseudonym John Chandos: *A Guide to Seduction: Notes Towards the Study of Eros in the Western Tradition*, Muller, 1953, 2nd edition, 1957; *London Airport*, H.M.S.O., 1956; (editor) *To Deprave and Corrupt: Original Studies in the Nature and Definition of "Obscenity,"* Association Press, 1962; *Norman Birkett, Uncommon Advocate*, Mayflower Books, 1963; *In God's Name: Examples of Preaching in England from the Act of Supremacy to the Act of Uniformity, 1534-1662*, Hutchinson, 1971.

WORK IN PROGRESS: *Up in Smoke: An Independent View of the British American Tobacco Company*; *Boys Together: Early Victorian Gentleman at School*.

* * *

McCROSSEN, V(incent) A(loysius) 1918-

PERSONAL: Born November 21, 1918, in Meshoppen,

Pa.; son of Edward Henry (a federal worker) and Alice (Hope) McCrossen; married Rose Bunnell, October 25, 1940 (died, 1965); married A. S. Schmidt (a teacher), May 12, 1966; children: (second marriage) Peter, Max, Valerie, Molly. *Education:* Dickinson College, A.B., 1933; University of Pittsburgh, Ph.D., 1936; Naval Graduate School of Languages, D.M.L., 1945. *Politics:* Independent. *Religion:* Roman Catholic. *Home address:* R.D. 4, Dallas, Pa. 18612. *Office:* Penn Consortium, Pott Falls Ln., Meshoppen, Pa. 18630.

CAREER: Bucknell University, Lewisburg, Pa., instructor in German and world literature, 1933-35; Creighton University, Omaha, Neb., instructor in modern languages, 1935-36; Bucknell University, assistant professor, 1936-40, associate professor, 1940-42, professor of modern languages, 1942-46, associate dean, 1940-46; Marietta College, Marietta, Ohio, professor of modern languages and chairman of department of humanities, 1946-49; Harvard-Tech Consortium, Cambridge, Mass., professor of comparative literature and modern languages, 1949-70, academic vice-president, 1960-70; University of Hawaii, Honolulu, dean, 1970-71; Middle Atlantic Consortium, Dallas, Pa., executive vice-president, 1971—. Distinguished Lecturer, Campus Visitors Program of American Association of Colleges and Universities, 1949—; member of international committee on translations of U.N.E.S.C.O., 1966—. *Military service:* U.S. Navy, Intelligence, 1943-45.

MEMBER: Internationales Institut fuer Kunstwissenschaften, Modern Language Association of America, Zurich Academy (life fellow), Il Centro di Studii e Scambe Internazionali (life fellow), American Association of University Professors (Marietta College chapter president, 1947-49; Harvard-Tech Consortium chapter president, 1955-57), Middle Atlantic Archeological Society (member of board of directors, 1956—), Phi Beta Kappa, Delta Phi Alpha, Azilum Village Restoration Project (president, 1960—).

WRITINGS: The New Renaissance of the Spirit, Philosophical Library, 1949; *And After This Our Exile*, Madeleine Press, 1953; *And Again to See the Stars*, Madeleine Press, 1955; *The Empty Room*, Philosophical Library, 1955; *Judas Iscariot/Mary Magdalene: Two Loves*, Madeleine Press, 1958; *Confrontations in American-European Literary Relations*, Internationales Institut fuer Kunstwissenschaften (Kreuzbach, Switzerland), 1973. Contributor to *Renascence*, *Modern Language Notes*, *Comparative Literature*, and other journals in his field.

WORK IN PROGRESS: Before Memory Dims, a survey of 20th century thought; *Mace, Manacles, Misjustice*, a critique of U.S. judicial system.

* * *

McCULLY, Robert (Stephen) 1921-

PERSONAL: Born January 28, 1921, in Anderson, S.C.; son of Robert Stephen (a broker) and Sarah (Giles) McCully; married Patricia Ann Crowley, December 4, 1965; children: R. Duff, Nina Keys. *Education:* Washington University, St. Louis, Mo., A.B., 1947, M.A., 1948; Columbia University, Ph.D., 1961. *Home:* 43 Society St., Charleston, S.C. 29401. *Office:* 80 Barre St., Charleston, S.C. 29401.

CAREER: Cornell University, Medical College, Payne Whitney Psychiatric Clinic of New York Hospital, New York, N.Y., instructor, 1956-58, assistant professor, 1958-62, associate professor of psychology, 1962-69; University of South Carolina, Medical College, Charleston, professor of psychology, 1969—. Member of South Carolina State Board of Examiners in Psychology, 1971—. *Member:* International Association for Analytical Psychology, International Rorschach Society, Sigma Xi.

WRITINGS: Rorschach Theory and Symbolism, Williams & Wilkins, 1971; (contributor) M. Rickers-Ovisiankina, editor, *Rorschach Psychology*, 2nd edition (McCully was not associated with first edition) Wiley, 1975. Contributor of more than thirty-five articles to journals. Consulting editor of *Journal of Personality Assessment*, 1972—; foreign associate editor of *Rorschachiana Japonica*, 1974—.

WORK IN PROGRESS: Research on symbolism of childrens' fairy tales.

* * *

McCUTCHEON, W(illiam) A(lan) 1934-

PERSONAL: Born March 2, 1934, in Belfast, Northern Ireland; son of William John and Margaret Elizabeth (Fullerton) McCutcheon; married Margaret Craig, June 30, 1956; children: Patrick John, Conor Alan, Kevin Craig. *Education:* Queen's University, B.A. (honors), 1955, M.A., 1958, Ph.D., 1962. *Office:* Ulster Museum, Botanic Gardens, Belfast BT9 5AB, Northern Ireland.

CAREER: Royal Belfast Academical Institution, Belfast, Northern Ireland, teacher of geography, 1955-62; Government of Northern Ireland, Ministry of Finance, Belfast, director of Survey of Industrial Archaeology, 1962-68; Ulster Museum Botanic Gardens, Belfast, keeper of technology and local history, 1968—. *Member:* Royal Geographical Society (fellow), Association for Industrial Archaeology, Irish Railway Record Society, Economic History Society, Society for the Study of the History of Technology (United States), Irish Society for Industrial Archaeology, Ulster Architectural Heritage Society, Newcomen Society (London), Society of Antiquaries of London (fellow).

WRITINGS: The Canals of the North of Ireland, Taplinger, 1965; *Railway History in Pictures: Ireland*, David & Charles, Volume I, 1969, Volume II, 1971; (contributor) Kevin B. Nowlan, editor, *Travel and Transport in Ireland*, Barnes & Noble, 1973; *Technology in Ireland: Aspects of Irish Industrial History*, Blackstaff Press, in press; *The Industrial Archaeology of Northern Ireland*, H.M.S.O., in press.

Contributor to *Ulster Folklife*, *Journal of Industrial Archaeology*, *Ulster Journal of Archaeology*, *Transactions of the Newcomen Society*, *Technology and Culture*, *Economic History Review*, *Geographical Journal*, *Irish Geography*.

* * *

McDOWELL, Frank 1911-

PERSONAL: Born January 30, 1911, Marshfield, Mo.; son of Hollie Andrew and Louise (North) McDowell; married Mary Neal (an editorial assistant), June 10, 1934; children: Robert L., George E., Carole L. *Education:* Drury College, A.B. (cum laude), 1932; Washington University, St. Louis, Mo., M.D. (cum laude), 1936. *Religion:* Congregational. *Home:* 100-F North Kalaheo, Kailua, Hawaii 96734. *Office:* Alexander Young Bldg., Honolulu, Hawaii 96813.

CAREER: Washington University, St. Louis, Mo., 1941-67, began as instructor, became professor of surgery; University of Hawaii, Honolulu, professor of plastic surgery,

1967—. Vice-president of Hawaii Medical Library, 1969—. Trustee of Drury College, 1956—. Consulting surgeon to Tripler Army Hospital, 1967—. *Member:* American Surgical Association, American Association of Plastic Surgeons (president, 1963), American Society of Plastic and Reconstructive Surgeons, Israeli Association of Plastic Surgeons (honorary member), Societe francaise de chirurgie plastique et reconstructive (honorary member). *Awards, honors:* First International Dow-Corning Award in Plastic Surgery, 1971; D.Sc., Drury College, 1973.

WRITINGS: (With J. B. Brown) *Skin Grafting*, Lippincott, 1943, 3rd edition, 1958; (with Brown) *Plastic Surgery of the Nose*, Mosby, 1952; (with Brown) *Neck Dissections*, C. C Thomas, 1954; *Surgery of Face, Mouth and Jaws*, Mosby, 1954; *History of Plastic Surgical Societies*, Williams & Wilkins, 1963; (with C. D. Enna) *Surgical Rehabilitation in Leprosy*, Williams & Wilkins, 1974. Contributor of chapters to books on surgery. Contributor to *Encyclopedia Americana Yearbook* and *Lawyers Medical Cyclopedia*; contributor of about one hundred articles to scientific journals. Editor-in-chief of *Journal of Plastic and Reconstructive Surgery*, 1967—.

WORK IN PROGRESS: A student textbook in plastic surgery.

* * *

McELHANON, K(enneth) A(ndrew) 1939-
(E. Saqorewec)

PERSONAL: Born May 8, 1939, in Milwaukee, Wis.; son of Harvey Ray (a laborer) and Helen (Gould) McElhanon; married Noreen Annis Frost (a linguist), October 14, 1961; children: Cheryl Gaylene, Cynthia Louise, Geoffrey Kent. *Education:* Wheaton College, Wheaton, Ill., A.B., 1961; graduate study at University of North Dakota, summer, 1961; Australian National University, Ph.D., 1970. *Home and office address:* Summer Institute of Linguistics, Box 69, P.O. Ukarumpa via Lae, Papua, New Guinea.

CAREER: Summer Institute of Linguistics, Papua, New Guinea, chief editor, chairman of research circle, consultant on phonology and grammar, 1963—.

WRITINGS—All published by Australian National University, except as indicated: *Selepet Phonology*, 1970; (with wife, Noreen A. McElhanon) *Selepet-English Dictionary*, 1970; (with C.L. Voorhoeve) *The Trans-New Guinea Phylum: Explorations in Deep-Level Genetic Relationships*, 1970; *Selepet Grammar, Part I: From Root to Phrase*, 1972; *Towards a Typology of the Finisterre-Huon Languages*, 1973; (editor and contributor) *Legends from Papua New Guinea*, Summer Institute of Linguistics, 1974; (contributor) S.A. Wurm, editor, *Current Trends in the Study of New Guinea Area Languages*, in press.

Contributor to, and editor of, proceedings; contributor of articles and reviews, some under pseudonym E. Saqorewec, to journals, including *Oceanic Linguistics, Ethnology, Oceania, Journal of the Papua New Guinea Society, Anthropos, Kivung*, and *Oral History*. Associate editor of *Kivung*.

SIDELIGHTS: McElhanon told *CA*: "In view of the English-speaking peoples having vast quantities of literature available to them, including scores of versions of the Bible, and in view of the many minority groups in the world having no literature in their languages, I was motivated to do my part in correcting this imbalance and providing literature for the minority groups. I have lived in Papua, New Guinea for ten years and speak two of the vernacular languages."

* * *

McELLHENNEY, John Galen 1934-

PERSONAL: Born May 4, 1934, in Lewisburg, Pa.; son of J. Paul (a certified public accountant) and Katherine (Hassinger) McEllhenney; married Nancy Grace Wolf (a registered nurse), June 27, 1959; children: Anne Gray, Peter John Galen. *Education:* Franklin and Marshall College, A.B. (summa cum laude), 1956; Drew University, B.D. (magna cum laude), 1959. *Politics:* Republican. *Home:* 525 Parkview Dr., Wynnewood, Pa. 19096. *Office:* Ardmore United Methodist Church, Argyle Rd. and Linwood Ave., Ardmore, Pa. 19003.

CAREER: Ordained United Methodist minister, 1960; associate pastor in Allentown, Pa., 1959-62; pastor in Gladwyne, Pa., 1962-67, in Philadelphia, Pa., 1967-70; Ardmore United Methodist Church, Ardmore, Pa., pastor, 1970—. Member of board of Ardmore Free Library, 1971—, and Young Men's Christian Association, Main Line Branch, 1973—; member of board of trustees of University of Pennsylvania, Wesley Foundation, 1971—, and Methodist Hospital, 1973—. *Member:* Phi Beta Kappa (member of executive committee, 1970-71), Phi Alpha Clergy Club (secretary, 1972—).

WRITINGS: Cutting the Monkey-Rope, Judson, 1973. Contributor to *Together, real, Christian Studies for Late Teens*, and *Today's Ministry*.

WORK IN PROGRESS: Research on the life of the mind in America with emphasis on Herman Melville and Robert Frost.

AVOCATIONAL INTERESTS: Travel in Europe.

* * *

McGRATTY, Arthur R. 1909-1975

1909—January 2, 1975; American Jesuit priest, author. Obituaries: *New York Times*, January 3, 1975.

* * *

McINTIRE, Roger W(arren) 1935-

PERSONAL: Born September 20, 1935, in Auburn, N.Y.; son of Clifton N. (a manufacturer) and Ellen J. (Weiler) McIntire; married Caroline F. Breck (a librarian), July 13, 1957; children: Pamela, Jennifer, Donna. *Education:* Northwestern University, B.A., 1958; Louisiana State University, M.A., 1960, Ph.D., 1962. *Home:* 11065 Swansfield, Columbia, Md. 21044. *Office:* Department of Psychology, University of Maryland, College Park, Md. 20742.

CAREER: University of Maryland, College Park, assistant professor, 1962-66, associate professor, 1966-70, professor of psychology, 1970—. *Member:* American Psychological Association.

WRITINGS: For Love of Children (nonfiction), CRM Books, 1970; *Child Psychology: A Behavioral Approach*, Behaviordelia, 1975. Contributor to *Journal of Experimental Analysis of Behavior*.

WORK IN PROGRESS: Research on educational psychology, on family adjustment, and on future societal control of human behavior.

* * *

McINTURFF, Roy A(rthur) 1905-

PERSONAL: Born February 17, 1905, in Nardin, Okla.;

son of James Benjiman (a farmer) and Sarah Lucinda (McGrew) McInturff; married Verna Bell, May 25, 1928 (died, 1938); married Violet Stillwell (a teacher), May 25, 1941; children: (first marriage) Nancy Bell McInturff Ledbetter; (second marriage) Joyce Louise McInturff Biddle. *Education:* Phillips University, A.B., 1927; summer graduate study at University of Chicago, 1930-31, and University of Southern California, 1939, 1947. *Politics:* Republican. *Religion:* Presbyterian. *Home:* 5455 Eighth St., Fallbrook, Calif. 92028.

CAREER: High school teacher of science in the county school of Worland, Wyo., 1928-47, and the public schools of El Monte, Calif., 1947-67. Life insurance salesman for Sun Life of Canada, 1933. *Member:* Camera Club (Fallbrook, Calif.).

WRITINGS: Wilderness Fishing for Salmon and Steelhead, A. S. Barnes, 1974. Contributor to outdoor magazines.

WORK IN PROGRESS: The Substitute.

AVOCATIONAL INTERESTS: Nature study, conservation, fishing.

* * *

McKALE, Donald M(arshall) 1943-

PERSONAL: Born October 24, 1943, in Clay Center, Kan.; son of Donald Vincent (a motel owner) and Mildred (Wedd) McKale; married Janna Fredregill, June 4, 1966; children: Emily Anne, David Marshall. *Education:* Iowa State University, B.S., 1966; University of Missouri, M.A., 1967; Kent State University, Ph.D., 1970. *Religion:* Presbyterian. *Home:* 241 Beechwood Circle, Milledgeville, Ga. 31601. *Office:* Department of History, Georgia College, Milledgeville, Ga. 31061.

CAREER: Georgia College, Milledgeville, assistant professor, 1970-74, associate professor of history, 1974-75; University of Nebraska, Lincoln, visiting associate professor of history, 1975—. *Member:* American Historical Association, Conference Group on Central European History.

WRITINGS: The Nazi Party Courts: Hitler's Management of Conflict in His Movement, 1921-1945, University Press of Kansas, 1974. Contributor of articles and reviews to *Research Studies* (of Washington State University), *Jewish Social Studies*, *International Review of History and Political Science*, *Journal of European Studies*, and *Choice*.

WORK IN PROGRESS: The Third Reich Outside Germany: Nazi Party Groups in Foreign Countries, 1931-1945, a monograph.

AVOCATIONAL INTERESTS: Watching athletics on television, reading, spending time with the family.

* * *

McKERCHER, Berneth N(oble) 1915-

PERSONAL: Born January 18, 1915, in Michigan; daughter of Kenneth (a physician) and Berthia (Zephia) Noble; married September 19, 1937 (widow); children: Patrick L., Judith Ann. *Education:* Eastern Michigan University, B.S., 1934; Michigan State University, M.A., 1957. *Religion:* Protestant. *Home:* 4152 Naubinway Rd., Okemos, Mich. 48864. *Office:* School of Education, Michigan State University, East Lansing, Mich. 48823.

CAREER: Elementary school teacher, 1937-39; school commissioner in Monroe County, Mich., 1948-57; elementary school teacher in Nashville and Swartz Creek, Mich., 1957-60; Michigan State University, East Lansing, instructor in continuing education, 1960-64, methods instructor in reading and language arts and assistant in Elementary Intern Program, 1964—. Reading consultant, Genesee County, Mich. schools, 1957-60. *Member:* International Reading Association, National Society for the Study of Education, Association for Supervision and Curriculum Development, Michigan Reading Association.

WRITINGS: What You See Is What You Get, Michigan State University Press, 1972; *Dear Tom*, Vantage, 1973; *Along Came Tom*, Vantage, 1973; *People Shall Lead the Way*, Vantage, 1975.

* * *

McKILLOP, Alan D(ugald) 1892-1974

May 24, 1892—August 5, 1974; American educator and author of books on English literature. Obituaries: *AB Bookman's Weekly*, October 7, 1974. (*CA*-19/20).

* * *

McLAUGHLIN, Curtis P. 1932-

PERSONAL: Born January 27, 1932, in Brooklyn, N.Y.; son of Wilmer (an underwriter) and Ida J. (a textile worker; maiden name, Bryson) McLaughlin; married Tanya Meeker, June, 1954 (divorced, May, 1973); married Ann Hunter (a religious educator), June, 1973; children: (first marriage) Lianne, Craig, Gwenn, Tricia. *Education:* Wesleyan University, Middletown, Conn., B.A. (honors), 1954; Harvard University, M.B.A. (with distinction), 1956, D.B.A., 1966. *Religion:* Protestant. *Home:* 6 Briarbridge Lane, Chapel Hill, N.C. 27514. *Office:* Department of Business Administration, University of North Carolina, Carroll Hall, Chapel Hill, N.C. 27514.

CAREER: Union Carbide Corp., Linde Division, Tonawanda, N.Y., research administrator, 1956-58; Graphic Controls Corp., Buffalo, N.Y., sales manager, 1958-62; Harvard University, Cambridge, Mass., instructor, 1965-66, assistant professor of business administration, 1966-68, visiting lecturer on health systems analysis, 1968-71; University of North Carolina, Chapel Hill, associate professor, 1968-72, professor of business administration, 1972—. Consultant to RAND Corp., Ford Foundation, U.S. Department of Health, Education and Welfare, World Health Organization, United Nations Fund for Population Activities, Committee on Space, American Association for the Advancement of Science, Brookings Institution, American Public Health Association, National Institute of Health Administration and Education, and American Association of Medical Colleges.

MEMBER: Institute of Management Science, American Institute of Decision Sciences (member of council, 1968-69), Society for General Systems Research.

WRITINGS: (With Ben-Ami Lipetz) *A Guide to Case Studies of Scientific Activity*, Intermedia, 1965; (editor with A. P. Sheldon and Frank Baker, and contributor) *Systems and Medical Care*, M.I.T. Press, 1970; (with R. I. Levin, R. P. Lamone, and J. F. Kottas) *Production/Operations Management: Contemporary Policy for Managing Operating Systems*, McGraw, 1972; (with L. G. Sprague and Sheldon) *Teaching Health and Human Services Administration by the Case Method*, Behavioral Publications, 1973; (with Sheldon) *The Future and Medical Care: A Health Manager's Guide to Forecasting*, Ballinger, 1974.

Contributor: J. R. Bright, editor, *Research Development and Technological Innovation*, Irwin, 1964; A. R. Dooley, W. K. Holstein, J. R. McKenney, R. S. Rosenbloom, C. W. Skinner, and P. H. Thurston, editors, *Casebooks in Production Management: Basic Problems, Concepts, and Techniques*, revised edition (McLaughlin was not associated with earlier editions), 1968; H. C. Schulberg, Frank Baker, and S. R. Roen, editors, *Developments in Education for the Human Services*, Behavioral Publications, 1973; Bruce Waxman and R. W. Stacy, editors, *Computers in Biomedical Research*, Volume IV, Academic Press, 1974; H. Wexler, M. LaMontaigne, and John Noble, editors, *Emergency Health Care Services: Behavioral and Managerial Perspectives*, Behavioral Publications, 1974; A. P. Sheldon and W. Abernathy, editors, *The Management of Technology in Health Organizations*, Ballinger, in press.

Author of monographs. Contributor to proceedings and professional journals.

* * *

McLEMORE, Richard Aubrey 1903-

PERSONAL: Born June 6, 1903, in Perry County, Miss.; son of Hezekiah (a teacher) and Tabitha (a teacher; maiden name, Small) McLemore; married Nannie Pitts (a writer), June 2, 1927; children: Harry Kimbrell. *Education:* Mississippi College, A.B., 1923; George Peabody College for Teachers, M.A., 1926; Vanderbilt University, Ph.D., 1933. *Religion:* Southern Baptist. *Home:* 224 Kitchings Dr., Clinton, Miss. 39056. *Office address:* Mississippi Baptist Historical Commission, P. O. Box 51, Clinton, Miss. 39056.

CAREER: Principal, and later superintendent, of rural schools in Mississippi, 1923-26; Jones County Junior College, Ellisville, Miss., instructor in history and dean, 1926-30, 1933-34; Judson College, Marion, Ala., professor of history and dean, 1934-38; Mississippi Southern College (now University of Southern Mississippi), Hattiesburg, professor of history, 1938-57, dean, 1945-57, acting president, 1955; Mississippi College, Clinton, president, 1957-68; Mississippi Department of Archives and History, director, 1969-73. *Member:* American Historical Association, Southern Historical Association, Mississippi Historical Society, Southern Baptist Historical Commission. *Awards, honors:* Mississippi College, Litt.D., 1969; Outstanding Mississippian Award, 1973.

WRITINGS: Franco-American Diplomatic Relations, 1816-1836, Louisiana State University Press, 1941, reprinted, Kennikat Press, 1972; *An Outline of Mississippi History*, Mississippi Southern College, 1941 (some later editions with wife, Nannie Pitts McLemore, and John Edmond Gonzales), 5th revised edition, 1969; *The Mississippi Story*, Laidlaw Brothers, 1945, 4th revised edition, 1973; (with Everett Augspurger) *Our Nation's Story*, Laidlaw Brothers, 1954, revised edition, 1962; (with Boyd C. Shafer and Augspurger) *United States History for High Schools*, 1966, revised edition, 1969; (with Shafer and Augspurger) *1865 to the Present: A United States History for High Schools*, Laidlaw Brothers, 1966; (with Shafer and Augspurger) *A High School History of Modern America* (adapted by Milton Finkelstein), Laidlaw Brothers, 1966; *A History of Mississippi Baptists, 1780-1970*, Mississippi Baptist Convention Board, 1971; (editor) *A History of Mississippi*, two volumes, University and College Press, 1973. Contributor to encyclopedias and historical journals. History editor of Official Map of Mississippi, 1953; editor-in-chief of *Journal of Mississippi History*, 1969-73.

WORK IN PROGRESS: A History of the First Baptist Church of Jackson, Mississippi.

* * *

MEARS, Brainerd, Jr. 1921-

PERSONAL: Born June 24, 1921, in Williamstown, Mass.; son of Brainerd (a professor) and Sarah (Bliss) Mears; married Anne Carter (an illustrator), June 5, 1948; children: Alison B., Caroly C., Holly G., B. Bartlett. *Education:* Williams College, B.A., 1943; Columbia University, Ph.D., 1950. *Office:* Department of Geology, University of Wyoming, Laramie, Wyo. 82071.

CAREER: University of Wyoming, Laramie, assistant professor, 1949-57, associate professor, 1957-63, professor of geology, 1963—. *Military service:* U.S. Marine Corps, 1942-45; became sergeant. *Member:* International Society for Quaternary Research, Geological Society of America (president of Rocky Mountain section, 1972), Nakomis Club.

WRITINGS: The Changing Earth, Van Nostrand, 1970; (editor and contributor) *The Nature of Geology*, Van Nostrand, 1970. Contributor to proceedings and to professional journals.

WORK IN PROGRESS: Revising *The Changing Earth*; research on the Quaternary and on the environment.

* * *

MEDOFF, Mark 1940-

PERSONAL: Born March 18, 1940, in Mount Carmel, Ill.; son of Lawrence R. (a physician) and Thelma (a psychologist; maiden name, Butt) Medoff; married Stephanie Thorne (an editor), June 24, 1972; children: Debra Ann. *Education:* University of Miami, Coral Gables, Fla., B.A., 1962; Stanford University, M.A., 1966. *Residence:* Las Cruces, N.M. *Agent:* Gilbert Parker, 60 East 56th St., New York, N.Y. 10022. *Office:* Department of English, New Mexico State University, Box 3E, Las Cruces, N.M. 88001.

CAREER: Capitol Radio Engineering Institute, Washington, D.C., supervisor of publications, 1962-64; New Mexico State University, Las Cruces, instructor, 1966-71, assistant professor, 1971-74, associate professor of English, 1974—, writer-in-residence, 1966—. *Member:* Writers Guild of America, Actors Equity Association. *Awards, honors:* Obie Award from *Village Voice*, Outer Critics Circle John Gasner Award, and Jefferson Award from Joseph Jefferson Award Committee, all 1973-74, for *When You Comin' Back, Red Ryder?*; Guggenheim fellowship in playwrighting, 1974-75; Drama Desk Award for Distinguished Playwrighting, 1974.

WRITINGS—Plays: "The Wager," first produced in New York, N.Y. at HB Playwrights Foundation Theatre, January, 1972, produced Off-Broadway at Eastside Playhouse, October, 1974; "The Kramer," first produced in San Francisco at American Conservatory Theatre, March, 1972; *When You Comin' Back, Red Ryder?* (first produced Off-Off-Broadway at Circle Repertory Theatre, October, 1973, produced Off-Broadway at Eastside Playhouse, December, 1973), Dramatists Play Service, 1974; (with Carleene Johnson) *The Odyssey of Jeremy Jack* (first produced at New Mexico State University, December, 1974), Dramatists Play Service, 1974; *Four Short Plays*, Dramatists Play Service, 1974. A story is anthologized in *Prize College Stories: 1963*, edited by Whit and Hallie Burnett, Random House, 1962.

BIOGRAPHICAL/CRITICAL SOURCES: Detroit Free Press, November 29, 1974.

* * *

MEEKER, Mary Nacol 1928-

PERSONAL: Born April 24, 1928, in Clarksville, Tex.; daughter of William Sam (a merchant) and Hattie Mae (Bordelon) Nacol; married Norman Scott Maxwell, 1945 (divorced, 1958); married Robert John Meeker (an administrator in computer field), 1958; children: (first marriage) Jessica Maxwell, Valerie Maxwell; (second marriage) Heather. *Education:* University of Texas, B.S., 1945; University of Southern California, M.S., 1957. Ed.D., 1966. *Home:* 1800 Highland, Manhattan Beach, Calif. 90266. *Office:* Graduate School of Education, Loyola Marymount University, Los Angeles, Calif. 90045.

CAREER: Psychologist in private clinic, 1948-50; teacher in Los Angeles, Calif., and Manhattan Beach, Calif., 1952-56; RAND Corp., System Development Co., Santa Monica, Calif., problem designer, 1956-59; Manhattan Beach public schools, testing of the gifted, 1962-63; University of Southern California, Los Angeles, adjunct professor of education for exceptional children, 1966-69; Loyola Marymount University (formerly Loyola University of Los Angeles), Los Angeles, Calif., associate professor of educational psychology, 1969—. Visiting summer professor at University of British Columbia, 1967, and University of the Pacific, 1969-71. Member of advisory council for American Government Schools, American Samoa, 1970—; member of school psychology examining committee, State of California; commissioner for County of Los Angeles, 1970—. Coordinator, S.O.I. Institute, 1970—.

MEMBER: American Psychological Association, National Association of School Psychologists, National Science Teachers Association, American Association of University Professors, American Association of University Women, California Association of School Psychologists and Psychometrists, California Psychological Association, California Teachers Association, Psi Chi, Lambda Delta Epsilon, Sigma Iota Epsilon.

WRITINGS: The Structure of Intellect: Its Interpretation and Uses, C.E. Merrill, 1969; *SOI Abilities Workbook*, S.O.I. Institute, 1970; (contributor) Edward Hauck and Maurice F. Freehill, editors, *Case Studies of Gifted Children*, W.C. Brown, 1972; (contributor) Richard H. Coop and Kinnard P. White, editors, *Psychological Concepts in the Classroom*, Harper, 1974. Author of various other workbooks, and of *Master Framework for Educating the Gifted in the State of California*, California Department of Education.

WORK IN PROGRESS: Your Gifted Child: Creative or Stressed; Doubling Up the Alphabet, a book for children; a paradigm for special education.

* * *

MEGLITSCH, Paul A(llen) 1914-

PERSONAL: Born March 3, 1914, in Harvey, Illinois; son of William J. (a railway agent) and Christine (Hendricks) Meglitsch; married Alison Mitchell, December 31, 1938 (deceased); children: Gail (Mrs. Gary Reynolds), Neil, Steven. *Education:* Illinois College, student, 1931-32; University of Illinois, B.S., 1935, M.S., 1936, Ph.D., 1938. *Religion:* Unitarian-Universalist. *Home:* 4333 Ingersoll, Des Moines, Iowa 50312. *Office:* Department of Biology, 327 Olin Hall, Drake University, Des Moines, Iowa 50311.

CAREER: Instructor in biology at Wright Junior College, 1939-42, Garry College, 1943, and Herzl Junior College, 1943-49; Drake University, Des Moines, Iowa, associate professor, 1949-58, professor of biology, 1958—, coordinator of Science Division, 1971—. Visiting fellow of Cottingham Road College of Education; member of Polk County Central Democratic Committee. *Military service:* U.S. Army Air Forces, 1942-45; became first lieutenant. *Member:* Society for Protozoology, Society for Systematic Zoology, American Association for the Advancement of Science, American Institute of Biological Sciences, Wild Life Disease Association, American Association for Higher Education, American Microbiology Society, Iowa Academy of Sciences (president-elect, 1974). *Awards, honors:* Fulbright fellow in New Zealand, 1958-59.

WRITINGS: (Contributor) Ander Stauffer, editor, *Introductory Biology*, Mosby, 1940; (with J.P. Wessel and W.H. Leigh) *A Laboratory Text for General College Zoology*, Burgess, 1947; *Invertebrate Zoology*, Oxford University Press, 1967, 2nd edition, 1972. Contributor to scientific publications, including *Transactions of the American Society for Microbiology, Journal of Protozoology, Journal of Parasitology*, and *Proceedings of the Iowa Academy of Sciences*. Editor of *Proceedings of the Iowa Academy of Sciences*, 1962-71, and American Microbiology Society.

WORK IN PROGRESS: A monograph on myxosporida; a third edition of *Invertebrate Zoology*, completion expected in 1977; research on tardigrades and air pollutants, and on myxosporida.

AVOCATIONAL INTERESTS: Music, theater, philately, travel.

* * *

MEHRTENS, Susan E(mily) 1945-

PERSONAL: Born September 27, 1945, in Elmhurst, N.Y.; daughter of William F. (a contractor) and Pauline (a secretary; maiden name, Kaufman) Mehrtens. *Education:* Queens College of the City University of New York, B.A., 1967; Yale University, M.Phil., 1969, Ph.D., 1973. *Politics:* "Democrat—radical environmentalist." *Religion:* "Non-denominational Protestant." *Home:* 55 East Williston Ave., East Williston, N.Y. 11596. *Office:* Department of History, Queens College of the City University of New York, Flushing, N.Y. 11367.

CAREER: Queens College of the City University of New York, Flushing, N.Y., assistant professor of history, 1971—. Instructor in young boatman's safety for New York State Department of Marine and Recreational Vehicles. Speaker for Nassau County Zero Population Growth, Inc. *Member:* American Historical Association, Mediaeval Academy of America, Economic History Society, National Organization for Women, Zero Population Growth, American Civil Liberties Union, Medieval Club of New York, Yale Club of New York City, Phi Beta Kappa, Phi Alpha Theta. *Awards, honors:* American Council of Learned Societies grant, 1973.

WRITINGS: (Editor with Charles Juzek) *Earthkeeping: Readings in Human Ecology*, Boxwood Press, 1974.

WORK IN PROGRESS: A biography of Jacqueline de Baviere, last countess of independent Holland; a study of medieval manners and etiquette.

SIDELIGHTS: Susan Mehrtens reads Latin, French, German, Italian, Spanish, Old English, Old Norse, and Old French. *Avocational interests:* Celestial navigation (with

U.S. Power Squadron), sewing, cooking, plants, belly-dancing, people, European travel (has lived in England).

* * *

MELE, Frank Michael 1935-

PERSONAL: Born August 15, 1935, in Englewood, N.J.; son of Michael and Anna (Ettari) Mele; married June Doris Filiatrault, August 12, 1961; children: Dawn Lynn, Frank Michael, Jr. *Education:* Davis & Elkins College, B.S., 1954; Montclair State College, M.A., 1963; further graduate study at New York University, 1966-68, and Fordham University, 1973—. *Religion:* Presbyterian. *Home:* 545 Bergen Ave., Westwood, N.J. 07675. *Office:* Department of Biology, Jersey City State College, 2039 Kennedy Blvd., Jersey City, N.J. 07305.

CAREER: Jersey City State College, Jersey City, N.J., assistant professor of biology, 1964—. *Member:* American Institute of Biological Science, National Science Teachers Association, American Association of University Professors, Association of New Jersey State College Professors, Phi Delta Kappa.

WRITINGS: Professional Growth for Teachers, Croft, 1965-66; *The Atom and the Earth*, Harper, 1967; *Energy and the Atom*, Harper, 1967; *Investiguide*, Harper, Volume IV, 1967, Volumes V and VI, 1968; *From Generation to Generation: A Story about Human Reproduction*, Natural History Press, 1970; *Earth Science*, Wiley, 1971. Contributor to journals.

WORK IN PROGRESS: Research for *Human Sexual Biology*.

* * *

MELLERSH, H(arold) E(dward) L(eslie) 1897-

PERSONAL: Born May 28, 1897, in London, England; son of F. H. (an insurance secretary) and Florence (Parker) Mellersh; married Margot Sadler, August, 1921; children: Jacqueline (Mrs. Tony Nayman), Sally, Nicholas, Angela (Mrs. Robert Myers). *Education:* University of London, B.Sc., 1921. *Religion:* Church of England. *Home:* 6 Hill St., Stogumber, Taunton, England. *Agent:* Peter Janson-Smith, 31 Newington Green, London N16 9PU, England.

CAREER: Civil servant with Ministry of Supply until 1957; author. *Military service:* British Army, 1915-19; served in France; became lieutenant. *Member:* Linnean Society of London (fellow), West Country Writers' Association.

WRITINGS: Let Loose (novel), Selwyn & Blount, 1926; *Ill Wind* (novel), Chapman & Hall, 1930; *The Salt of the Earth*, Chapman & Hall, 1931; *The World and Man: A Guide to Modern Knowledge*, Hutchinson, 1952; *The Story of Life*, Hutchinson, 1957, Putnam, 1958; *The Story of Man: Human Evolution to the End of the Stone Age*, Hutchinson, 1959, published as *The Story of Early Man: Human Evolution to the End of the Stone Age*, Viking, 1960; *From Ape Man to Homer: The Story of the Beginnings of Western Civilization*, R. Hale, 1962, Taplinger, 1963; *Soldiers of Rome*, R. Hale, 1964, published as *The Roman Soldier*, Taplinger, 1965; *Archaeology: Science and Romance*, Wheaton, 1966; *Minoan Crete*, Putnam, 1967; *FitzRoy of the Beagle*, Hart-Davis, 1968, Mason & Lipscomb, 1974; *The Destruction of Knossos: The Rise and Fall of Minoan Crete*, Weybright, 1970; *Chronology of the Ancient World*, Barrie & Jenkins, 1975.

Children's books: *Finding Out About Ancient Egypt*, Muller, 1960, Lothrop, 1962; *Finding Out About Stone Age Britain*, Muller, 1961; *Saxon Britain*, Weidenfeld & Nicolson, 1961; *Finding Out About the Trojans*, Muller, 1962; *Carthage*, Weidenfeld & Nicolson, 1963; *Charles Darwin: Pioneer of the Theory of Evolution*, Arthur Barker, 1964, published as *Charles Darwin: Pioneer in the Theory of Evolution*, Praeger, 1969; *The Boys' Book of the Wonders of Man and His Achievements*, Roy, 1964; *Sumer and Babylon*, Wheaton, 1964, Crowell, 1965; *The Discoverers: The Story of the Great Seafarers*, Wheaton, 1969; *The Explorers: The Story of the Great Adventurers by Land*, Wheaton, 1969.

Contributor to *Reader's Digest Dictionary* and to *New Statesman*, *Fortnightly*, and *Contemporary Review*.

WORK IN PROGRESS: A short history of Peru.

* * *

MELVILLE, J. Keith 1921-

PERSONAL: Born September 22, 1921, in Bountiful, Utah; son of John Harvey (a teacher and farmer) and Theodocia (Shelley) Melville; married Ruth Weller (a vocal teacher), October 31, 1947; children: Shelley, Mary Margaret, Rebecca, James, John, Joan, Richard, Janet, Matthew. *Education:* University of Utah, B.A., 1947, Ph.D., 1956; University of California, Berkeley, M.A., 1949. *Religion:* Church of Jesus Christ of Latter-Day Saints. *Home:* 1748 North 1350 West, Provo, Utah 84601. *Office:* 390 Maeser Bldg., Brigham Young University, Provo, Utah 84601.

CAREER: Ricks College, Rexburg, Idaho, instructor in political science, 1950-57, dean of students, 1956-57; Brigham Young University, Provo, Utah, professor of political science, 1957—. Staff assistant to Congressman Gunn McKay, Washington, D.C., 1972. *Military service:* U.S. Army Air Forces, 1942-45; became captain; received Air Medal and Distinguished Flying Cross. *Member:* American Political Science Association, Western Political Science Association (past secretary-treasurer).

WRITINGS: Conflict and Compromise: The Mormons in Mid-Nineteenth Century American Politics, Brigham Young University Press, 1974; *The American Democratic System*, Dodd, 1974.

WORK IN PROGRESS: Political Accommodation in Utah; Corruption and Ethics in American Politics; The Constitution: A Mormon Perspective, completion expected in 1975.

* * *

MENDELSSOHN, Kurt (Alfred Georg) 1906-

PERSONAL: Born January 7, 1906, in Berlin, Germany; son of Ernst M. and Eliza (Ruprecht) Mendelssohn; married Jutta Lina Charlotte Zarniko, December 19, 1932; children: Corinna (Mrs. J. Welch), Ursula (Mrs. K. Meadows), Monica, Diana (Mrs. G. Bentley), James. *Education:* Oxford University, M.A.; University of Berlin, M.A. and D.Phil. *Home:* 235 Iffley Rd., Oxford, England. *Office:* Wolfson College, Oxford University, Oxford, England.

CAREER: Has held earlier teaching and research appointments at Berlin University and Breslau University; Oxford University, Oxford, England, reader in physics, 1955-73, emeritus reader, 1973—, professorial fellow of Wolfson College, 1971-73, emeritus professorial fellow, 1973—. Visiting professor at Rice Institute (now University), 1952, Purdue University, 1956, Tokyo University, 1960, University of Science and Technology (Ghana), 1964, and Tata

Institute (Bombay), 1969. *Member:* Royal Society (fellow), Institute of Physics (fellow), Athenaeum Club. *Awards, honors:* Hughes medal from Royal Society, 1967; Simon Memorial Prize from Institute of Physics, 1968.

WRITINGS: *What Is Atomic Energy?*, Sigma Books, 1946; *Cryophysics*, Wiley, 1960; *The Quest for Absolute Zero*, Weidenfeld & Nicolson, 1966; *In China Now*, Hamlyn, 1969; *The World of Walther Nernst*, Macmillan, 1973; *The Riddle of the Pyramids*, Thames & Hudson, 1974. Contributor to *Proceedings of the Royal Society;* also contributor to scientific and medical journals. Editor of *Cryogenics*, 1960—.

AVOCATIONAL INTERESTS: Oriental art, Egyptology.

* * *

MENDOZA, Manuel G. 1936-

PERSONAL: Born September 21, 1936, in New York, N.Y.; son of Manuel G., Sr. (a waiter) and Elvira (a seamstress; maiden name, Gonzalez) Mendoza; married twice; children: Manuel G. III, Tanya Marie. *Education:* University of South Florida, B.A., 1963; Johns Hopkins School of Advanced International Studies, M.A., 1965; further graduate study at Wayne State University, 1967-68, University of Miami, Coral Gables, Fla., 1968-69, Florida Atlantic University, 1970-71, and Florida International University, 1974-75. *Politics:* "Liberal reformer, active Democrat." *Religion:* None. *Home:* 8110 Southwest 73rd Ave., #3, Miami, Fla. 33143. *Office:* Department of Sociology, Anthropology and Social Institutions, Miami-Dade Community College (South Campus), 11011 Southwest 104th St., Miami, Fla. 33156.

CAREER: Brookings Institution, Washington, D.C., research assistant, 1964; American University, Washington, D.C., research associate in special operations research office, 1965; Miami-Dade Community College, Miami, Fla., associate professor of social science, 1965-67; Wayne State University, Detroit, Mich., assistant professor of social science, 1967-68; Miami-Dade Community College, associate professor of social science, 1968—. Research associate at University of Miami (Coral Gables, Fla.), 1968-69; adjunct professor at Florida Atlantic University, 1970-73, and at Florida International University, 1974. President and chairman of board of directors of Professional Research Institute, 1973—, and Community Action and Research, Inc., 1975—. *Military service:* U.S. Naval Reserve, hospital corpsman, 1954-62.

MEMBER: American Civil Liberties Union, Academy of Political Science, Community College Social Science Association, Spanish-American Caucus for Higher Education, Spanish-Speaking Democratic Caucus, Spanish-American League against Discrimination (member of board of directors), Urban League, Florida Education Association, Florida Higher Education Association. *Awards, honors:* Woodrow Wilson fellowship, 1963.

WRITINGS: (With Vince Napoli) *Systems of Man: An Introduction to Social Science*, Heath, 1973; (contributor) *The Cuban Minority in the U.S.: Final Report on Need Identification and Program Evaluation*, Cuban National Planning Council, 1974; *Housing Conditions of Cubans, Puerto Ricans and Mexicans in Dade County, Florida*, U.S. Department of Housing and Urban Development, 1974. Author of audio-visual tapes, including "Totalitarianism," Miami-Dade Community College, 1966; "Theories of International Relations," Miami-Dade Community College, 1966; "History of Soviet Foreign Policy," Miami-Dade Community College, 1966; "The Political Dynamics of Castro's Cuba," University of Miami, Coral Gables, Fla., 1967. Author of television special, "A Search for Freedom: The Bill of Rights," 1975. Contributor to *Anthropos.*

WORK IN PROGRESS: *Politics American Style: A Systemic Analysis*; research on world regional subsystems; preparing a political profile of Dade County.

SIDELIGHTS: Mendoza, who regards Martin Luther King, Jr. as a hero, writes: "I have spent most of my life in bilingual-bicultural neighborhoods or cities. I lived my first fourteen years in New York's Spanish Harlem, and the next thirteen in Tampa's main Latin Quarter. . . . Humor is very important in my life. If a person cannot laugh at man's foibles, I don't know how he can keep his sanity. I feel particularly compassionate toward minorities, the poor, the sick, the very young, and, especially, the very old." *Avocational interests:* Music, sports, dancing, the theater, movies.

* * *

MENENDEZ, Albert J(ohn) 1942-

PERSONAL: Born October 23, 1942, in Philadelphia, Pa.; son of Albert Joseph and Alice (Briggs) Menendez; married Shirley Ann Corbin (a librarian), June 15, 1974. *Education:* Jacksonville University, B.A. (cum laude), 1967. *Politics:* Liberal Democrat. *Religion:* Episcopalian. *Home:* 14151 Castle Blvd., Apt. 402, Silver Spring, Md. 20904. *Office:* Americans United for Separation of Church and State, 8120 Fenton St., Silver Spring, Md. 20910.

CAREER: Florida Medical Association, Jacksonville, editor, 1968-69; Georgia Department of Comprehensive Health Planning, Atlanta, editor and researcher, 1970-71; U.S. Department of Labor, Washington, D.C., program planner, 1972; Americans United for Separation of Church and State, Silver Spring, Md., director of research and assistant editor of *Church and State*, 1972—. *Member:* Authors Guild of Authors League of America.

WRITINGS: *The Bitter Harvest: Church and State in Northern Ireland*, Luce, 1974; *Sherlock Holmes Quiz Book*, Drake Publishers, 1975; *Presidential Quiz Book*, Drake Publishers, 1975. Contributor to *Churchman*, *Christian Herald*, *U.S. Catholic*, and *Baker Street Journal*.

WORK IN PROGRESS: Research on church and state in Europe and in the Vatican; Christmas folklore; a history of anti-Catholicism; research on Ireland, and on religion and politics in the United States.

* * *

MENZEL, Paul T(heodore) 1942-

PERSONAL: Born September 18, 1942, in Elmhurst, Ill.; son of Theophil W. and Annemarie (Mueller) Menzel; married Barbara Stein, 1969. *Education:* College of Wooster, B.A., 1964; Yale University, B.D., 1967; Vanderbilt University, Ph.D., 1971. *Office:* Department of Philosophy, Pacific Lutheran University, Tacoma, Wash. 98447.

CAREER: Pacific Lutheran University, Tacoma, Wash., assistant professor of philosophy, 1971—. *Member:* American Philosophical Association, Institute for Society, Ethics and the Life Sciences, Phi Beta Kappa. *Awards, honors:* Rockefeller fellowship and Woodrow Wilson fellowship, 1964-65; Danforth graduate fellow, 1964-70; Danforth associate, 1973—; National Endowment for the Humanities fellow, 1975.

WRITINGS: (Editor) *Moral Argument and the War in Vietnam*, Aurora, 1971. Contributor to *Journal of Value Inquiry* and *Personalist*.

WORK IN PROGRESS: Research on individual rights in medical relationships; *Freedom, Determinism, and Responsibility*.

* * *

MEREDITH, Joseph C(harlton) 1914-

PERSONAL: Born June 29, 1914, in Oakland, Calif.; son of John Giles (a gold miner) and Stella Marie (a teacher; maiden name, Holden) Meredith; married Edna Belle White, August 20, 1948 (divorced, 1965); children: Michael Steven, Polly, Robert John Giles. *Education:* Olivet College, B.A., 1934; University of California, Berkeley, M.L.S., 1967. *Home:* 832 Pin Oak Ln., Park Forest South, Ill. 60466. *Office:* Learning Resources Center, Governors State University, Park Forest South, Ill.

CAREER: U.S. Navy, 1942-62; held four commands and NATO staff duties; retired as lieutenant commander. Governors State University, Park Forest South, Ill., professor of library science, 1971—, systems librarian in Learning Resources Center, 1971—. Founding president, Citizens Planning Council of Park Forest South, Inc., 1972—; member, Park Forest South Police Commission, 1972—. *Member:* American Society for Information Science, Society for Nautical Research, Hakluyt Society, California Historical Society, Hawaiian Historical Society.

WRITINGS: The Tattooed Man, Andr Fred Hoest & Son (Copenhagen), 1958, Duell, Sloan & Pearce, 1959; *The CAI Author/Instructor*, Educational Technology Publications, 1971. Contributor to U.S. Naval Institute *Proceedings* and to *Journal of the American Society for Information Science*, *Government Publications Review*, *Foreign Service Quarterly*, and *Scientia Paedagocica Experimentalis*.

WORK IN PROGRESS: Research on selective dissemination of microfiche in a university setting and research in information theory; *The Court Martial of Pierre Landis, Captain, Continental Navy*; English edition of *Voyage pittoresque autour du monde* by Louis Choris; *The ALLIANCE Frigate: Biography of a Ship*; *Ponape*, the history of a Pacific island.

SIDELIGHTS: Meredith told *CA*: "My interest in maritime history comes partly from WWII naval experience, but to a much greater degree from postwar patrol duties in the Trust Territories of the Pacific Islands, as captain of the USS Hanna, a destroyer escort. The unpublished manuscript "A Handful of Emeralds" (the title comes from Conrad's *Karain: A Memory*) grew out of this experience . . . I hope eventually to roll back to a revision of "A Handful of Emeralds," predominantly as personal adventure rather than as travel or survey."

* * *

MERKEL, Miles Adair 1929-

PERSONAL: Born September 1, 1929, in Schnecksville, Pa.; son of Walter Charles (a bricklayer) and Bernice (Ridenbaugh) Merkel. *Education:* Pennsylvania State University, B.S.E.E., 1953; University of Maryland, graduate study, 1955-67. *Residence:* Sierra Vista, Ariz. *Office:* Commander, U.S.A.C.E.E.I.A., Attention: C.C.C.-C.E.D.-R.P., Ft. Huachuca, Ariz. 85613.

CAREER: U.S. Department of Defense, Washington, D.C., electronic engineer, 1955-67; Textron, Tucson, Ariz., principal engineer, 1967-68; Syracuse University Research Corp., Syracuse, N.Y., senior scientific advisor, 1969-74; United States Army Communications Command, Fort Huachuca, Ariz., supervisory electronic engineer, 1974—. *Military service:* U.S. Navy, 1947-49; became midshipman.

WRITINGS: Smooth in the Saddle (novel), Lennox Hill Press, 1973.

WORK IN PROGRESS: Myself and I, juvenile science fiction; genealogical research reaching back over six generations from Pennsylvania and Maryland into Germany, England, and France, with a book expected to result.

SIDELIGHTS: Merkel lived for years in the Orient and travelled through Australia, Hong Kong, Germany, France, and England. *Avocational interests:* Languages, karate, oil painting.

* * *

MERMIN, Samuel 1912-

PERSONAL: Born August 14, 1912, in New Haven, Conn.; son of Charles (a businessman) and Nechame (Rosenquait) Mermin; married Lora N. Nifong (a researcher and volunteer worker in child development), July 1, 1937; children: Peter N., Daniel J., Katharine M. *Education:* Yale University, B.A., 1933, LL.B., 1936. *Politics:* "Independent; usually Democrat." *Home:* 765 West Washington Ave., Madison, Wis. 53715. *Office:* School of Law, University of Wisconsin, Madison, Wis. 53706.

CAREER: U.S. Government, Washington, D.C., attorney with Department of Labor, 1936-38, Department of Agriculture, 1938-40, Department of Interior and Office of Bituminous Coal Consumers' Counsel, 1940-42, Office of Price Administration, Enforcement Department, 1942-47; University of Oklahoma, Norman, professor of law, 1947-51; University of Wisconsin, Madison, lecturer, 1951-52, associate professor, 1952-54, professor of law, 1954—. Fulbright lecturer in Japan, 1968-69; visiting researcher and lecturer in Japan for Japan Society for Promotion of Science, 1975-76. *Member:* International Association for Philosophy of Law and Social Philosophy, American Society for Political and Legal Philosophy, American Association of University Professors, Phi Beta Kappa. *Awards, honors:* Rockefeller Foundation fellowship, 1950-51; Ford Foundation fellowship, 1959-60; D. C. Everest Prize from State Historical Society of Wisconsin for manuscript, "Law and the Promotion of Enterprise," the basis of two subsequent books.

WRITINGS: (With Carl Auerbach, Willard Hurst, and Lloyd Garrison) *The Legal Process*, Chandler Publishing, 1961; *Jurisprudence and Statecraft*, University of Wisconsin Press, 1963; *The Fox-Wisconsin Rivers Improvement*, Law Extension, University of Wisconsin, 1968; (contributor) Hubert Hubien, editor, *Legal Reasoning*, Bruylant (Brussels), 1971; *Law and the Legal System*, Little, Brown, 1973; (contributor) J. R. Pennock and J. W. Chapman, editors, *Participation in Politics*, Lieber-Atherton, 1975. Contributor of about fifteen articles to law journals, including *Illinois Law Review*, *Indiana Law Review*, *Kobe University Law Review* (Japan), *Wisconsin Law Review*, *Michigan Law Review*, *Oklahoma Law Review*, and *Yale Law Journal*.

WORK IN PROGRESS: Research on the analytical side of jurisprudence: the area of law, language, and logic.

MERRILL, Frederick Thayer 1905-1974

February 5, 1905—November 30, 1974; American foreign service officer, researcher, author, lecturer, and sportsman. Obituaries: *Washington Post*, December 2, 1974.

* * *

METZ, Mary (Seawell) 1937-

PERSONAL: Born May 7, 1937, in Rock Hill, S.C.; daughter of Columbus Jackson (an accountant) and Mary (a teacher; maiden name, Dunlap) Seawell; married F. Eugene Metz (a professor of architecture), December 21, 1957; children: Mary Eugena. *Education:* Furman University, B.A. (summa cum laude), 1958; Louisiana State University, Ph.D. (magna cum laude), 1966. *Home:* 688 Castle Kirk Ave., Baton Rouge, La. 70803. *Office:* Department of Foreign Languages, Louisiana State University, Baton Rouge, La. 70803.

CAREER: High school teacher of French and English in Anderson, S.C., 1958-60; Louisiana State University, Baton Rouge, instructor, 1965-66, assistant professor, 1966-72, associate professor of French, 1972—. Visiting assistant professor at University of California at Berkeley, 1967-68; consultant to McGraw-Hill Book Co., 1967-69; speaker on educational, pedagogical, and political topics. *Member:* Modern Language Association of America, American Council on the Teaching of Foreign Languages, American Association of Teachers of French, Business and Professional Women's Foundation, American Association of University Women, American Association of University Professors, South Central Modern Language Association, Southern Conference on Language Teaching (member of board of directors), Louisiana Teachers Association, Louisiana Foreign Language Teachers Association, Phi Kappa Phi, Alpha Lambda Delta. *Awards, honors:* Fulbright fellowship in France, 1962-63; Standard Oil of Indiana award for excellence in undergraduate instruction, Louisiana State University, 1971; American Council on Education fellow in academic administration, 1974-75.

WRITINGS: Reflets du monde francais: sa langue, sa litterature, sa culture, McGraw, 1971; (with Jo Helmstrom) *Learning French the Modern Way*, Volume I: *Le Francais a decouvrir*, Volume II: *Le Francais a vivre*, with teacher's manuals and workbooks, 3rd edition, McGraw, 1972 (earlier editions by J. A. Evans and M. Baldwin, 1963 and 1967). Contributor to journals in her field, including *Foreign Language Annals*.

WORK IN PROGRESS: A study tentatively titled *Stylistic and Thematic Patterns of Contemporary French Women Novelists*.

* * *

METZGER, Norman 1924-

PERSONAL: Born December 21, 1924, in New York, N.Y.; son of Murray (a shoe designer) and Evelyn (Goldstein) Metzger; married Marcia Averack, August 25, 1946; children: Bart. *Education:* School of Business and Civic Administration of the City College (now Bernard M. Baruch College of the City University of New York), B.B.A., 1948; Columbia University, M.A., 1954. *Home:* 250 East 87th St., New York, N.Y. 10028. *Office:* Mount Sinai Medical Center, 100th St. and Fifth Ave., New York, N.Y. 10029.

CAREER: Employed as assistant to controller for Hillman Periodicals, 1948-49, production manager for Coronet Handballs, Inc., 1949-52, and personnel director for Norden-Ketay Corp., 1952-59; Bernard M. Baruch College of the City University of New York, New York, N.Y., adjunct instructor, 1957-67, adjunct associate professor of health care administration, 1967—. Vice-president for personnel at Mount Sinai Medical Center, 1960—, associate professor at Mount Sinai School of Medicine, 1966—. *Military service:* U.S. Navy, 1943-46.

MEMBER: American Society for Hospital Personnel Administration, Association of Hospital Personnel Administrators, Commerce and Industry Association, League of Voluntary Hospitals and Homes of New York (member of board of directors). *Awards, honors:* Editorial award from *Hospital Management*, 1965, for article "The Challenge Ahead: The Effects of Union Organizing Efforts on Hospital Administration"; first annual award for outstanding contribution to hospital personnel administration literature, from Association of Hospital Personnel Administrators and American Hospital Association, 1972.

WRITINGS: Labor-Management Relations in the Health Services Industry, Science & Health, 1972; *Personnel Administration in Hospitals and Homes*, Spectrum, 1975; *The National Labor Relations Act: A Guidebook for Health Care Administrators*, Spectrum, 1975; *Personnel Management and Labor Relations: A Guide for the Nursing Home Administrator*, American Nursing Home Association, 1975. Contributor of about fifty articles to hospital journals, including *Hospital Management*, *Hospitals: Journal of the American Hospital Association*, *Medical Laboratory Observer*, *Nursing Care*, *Executive Housekeeper*, and *Journal of the Association of Hospital Personnel Administrators*. Member of editorial board of *Hospital Supervision*.

* * *

METZLER, Ken 1929-

PERSONAL: Born January 2, 1929, in Portland, Ore.; son of Walter V. (a laborer) and Erna (Kneuppel) Metzler; married Betty Jane Paterson, August 30, 1952; children: Barbara, Scott, Douglas. *Education:* University of Oregon, B.S., 1956; Northwestern University, M.S., 1967. *Politics:* Democrat. *Religion:* Congregationalist. *Home:* 2051 East 26th Ave., Eugene, Ore. 97403. *Office:* School of Journalism, University of Oregon, Eugene, Ore. 97403.

CAREER: Roseburg News-Review, Roseburg, Ore., reporter, 1951-53; *Coos Bay Times*, Coos Bay, Ore., reporter, 1953-56; free-lance magazine writer in Eugene, Ore., 1956-60; University of Oregon, Eugene, director of student publications, 1960-62, managing editor of University of Oregon Books, 1962-63, editor of alumni magazine, 1963-71, assistant professor, 1971, associate professor of journalism, 1971—. Member of board of trustees of Editorial Projects for Education, the publisher of *Chronicle of Higher Education*.

WRITINGS: Confrontation: The Destruction of a College President, Nash Publishing, 1973.

WORK IN PROGRESS: Research on journalistic interviewing and information gathering methods, with a textbook expected to result.

* * *

MEWSHAW, Michael 1943-

PERSONAL: Born February 19, 1943, in Washington, D.C.; son of John Francis and Mary Helen (Murphy Dunn) Mewshaw; married Linda Kirby, June 17, 1967.

Education: University of Maryland, B.A., 1965; University of Virginia, M.A., 1966, Ph.D., 1970. *Religion:* Roman Catholic. *Home address:* Route 7, Box 932-D, Austin, Tex. 78703. *Agent:* Owen Laster, William Morris Agency, 1350 Avenue of the Americas, New York, N.Y. 10019. *Office:* Department of English, University of Texas, Austin, Tex. 78712.

CAREER: University of Virginia, Charlottesville, instructor in English, 1970; University of Massachusetts, Amherst, assistant professor of English, 1970-71; University of Texas, Austin, assistant professor of English, 1973—. *Awards, honors:* Fulbright fellowship in creative writing, 1968-69; William Rainey fellowship to Breadloaf Writers Conference, 1970; National Endowment for the Arts fellowship, 1974-75.

WRITINGS—Novels: *Man in Motion*, Random House, 1970; *Waking Slow*, Random House, 1972; *The Toll*, Random House, 1974. Contributor of short stories, poetry, articles, and reviews to literary journals and newspapers, including *Sewannee Review, London Magazine, Yale Review, Listener, New York Times Book Review*, and *Washington Post*.

WORK IN PROGRESS: Earthly Bread, a religious comedy.

SIDELIGHTS: Mewshaw writes: "In some ways *Man in Motion* is more than the title of my first novel. I've spent most of my adult life traveling, sometimes out of curiosity, sometimes out of boredom, more often a combination of both."

* * *

MEYER, Renate 1930-

PERSONAL: Born March 5, 1930, in Berlin, Germany; daughter of Peter Ferdinand (a cardiologist) and Eva (Tauber) Meyer; married Charles Keeping (a book illustrator), September 20, 1955; children: Jonathan, Vicki, Sean Frank. *Education:* Polytechnic of Central London (better known as Regent Street Polytechnic), National Diploma, 1952. *Home:* 16 Church Rd., Shortlands, Kent BR2 OHP, England. *Agent:* B. L. Kearley, 33 Chiltern St., London W.1, England.

CAREER: Writer and illustrator of books for children.

WRITINGS—Self-illustrated: *Vicki*, Bodley Head, 1968, Atheneum, 1969; *Hide and Seek*, Bodley Head, 1969, Bradbury, 1972; *Let's Play Mums and Dads*, Bodley Head, 1970; *The Story of Little Knittle and Threadle*, Bodley Head, 1971; *Mr. Knitted and the Family Tree*, Bodley Head, 1972; *Susie's Doll's Pram*, Bodley Head, in press.

Illustrator: Helen Cresswell, *The Bird Fancier*, Benn, 1970.

SIDELIGHTS: Renate Meyer writes: "I am interested in portraying the sort of situations that children really find themselves in, rather than fantasy or cartoon humour. There seem to be so many Victorian settings for children's books. I like to set them in contemporary settings, with the sort of companions they are liable to find themselves with. I agree with the argument that coloured children should be introduced there more, looking like they do, not like white kids with tinted skin. I was never able to identify with fairy princesses as a child, and I still prefer the real life situation. My husband and I discuss this endlessly as we both feel strongly about this sort of thing."

MEYERS, Walter E(arl) 1939-

PERSONAL: Born July 1, 1939, in Pittsburgh, Pa.; son of Walter F. (a truck driver) and Margaret (Bentz) Meyers; married Julia Reed (a music teacher), February 11, 1961; children: Matthew, Michael, Julia Margaret. *Education:* Duquesne University, A.B., 1964; University of Florida, Ph.D., 1967. *Politics:* Democrat. *Religion:* Roman Catholic. *Home:* 403 Carriage Lane, Cary, N.C. 27511. *Office:* Department of English, North Carolina State University, Raleigh, N.C. 27607.

CAREER: North Carolina State University, Raleigh, assistant professor, 1967-72, associate professor of medieval literature and modern linguistics, 1972—. *Military service:* U.S. Army, 1956-59. *Member:* Modern Language Association of America, National Council of Teachers of English, South Atlantic Modern Language Association, Phi Beta Kappa. *Awards, honors:* Danforth fellowship, 1964.

WRITINGS: A Figure Given: Typology in the Wakefield Plays, Duquesne University Press, 1970; *Handbook of Contemporary English*, Harcourt, 1974. Contributor to *College English, PMLA, College Composition and Communication, American Speech, North Carolina Folklore*, and *North Carolina English Teacher*.

WORK IN PROGRESS: A book on linguistics and languages in science fiction; a collection of essays on historical linguistics; a dictionary of current American usage, completion expected in 1977.

AVOCATIONAL INTERESTS: Playing the five-string banjo.

BIOGRAPHICAL/CRITICAL SOURCES: Raleigh Times, May 29, 1973.

* * *

MICALLEF, Benjamin A(nthony) 1925-

PERSONAL: Surname is pronounced Mac-*call*-lif; born March 21, 1925, in Detroit, Mich.; son of Benjamin (a building engineer) and Josephine (Scicluna) Micallef. *Education:* San Francisco State University, A.B., 1953; University of California, Berkeley, M.A., 1955. *Residence:* Oakland, Calif. *Office:* Department of Business Administration, Merritt College, 12500 Campus Dr., Oakland, Calif. 94619.

CAREER: Wells Fargo Bank, San Francisco, Calif., supervisor of data processing department, 1955-62; Merritt College, Oakland, Calif., professor of data processing, 1962—. *Military service:* U.S. Army, 1943-46. *Member:* California Teachers Association, Mechanics Institute of San Francisco, Ligure Club of Oakland.

WRITINGS: Electric Accounting Machine Fundamentals, Cummings, 1968, 2nd edition, 1972; *An Introduction to Data Processing*, Cummings, 1971; *Keypunching: A Basic Office Skill*, Cummings, 1974.

* * *

MICHEL, Henri (Jules) 1907-

PERSONAL: Born April 28, 1907, in Vidauban, Var, France; son of Stanislas (a farmer) and Anastasie (Poncet) Michel; married Suzanne Ernouf, March 26, 1934; children: Annie (Mrs. Charles Eloffe), Pierre, Jacques. *Education:* Attended University of Aix-en-Provence, 1926-28; Sorbonne, University of Paris, Agrege de l'Universite, 1932, Docteur es lettres, 1962. *Home:* 12 rue de Moscou, 75008 Paris, France. *Office:* Comite de'Histoire de la Seconde

Guerre Mondiale, 32 rue de Leningrad, 75008 Paris, France.

CAREER: Teacher of history in lycee of Toulon, France, 1934-44; inspector of schools in the department of Var, 1944-46; Comite d'Histoire de la Seconde Guerre Mondiale, Paris, France, secretary-general and liaison to the Prime Minister of France, 1946—; Centre National de la Recherche Scientifique, research director, 1966—. President of the International Committee for the History of the Second World War. Participant in numerous international conferences on the history of the Second World War, including those in London, Manchester, Brussels, Liege, Amsterdam, Moscow, Warsaw, Cracow, Belgrade, Munich, Vienna, Tel Aviv, Sofia, Prague, Budapest, Washington, Tokyo, Kyoto, Seoul, and Rio de Janeiro. *Military service:* Served in the French Resistance in World War II. *Member:* Commission Superieure des Archives, Commission des Archives militaires. *Awards, honors:* Officier of the Legion of Honor, 1958; grand prix d'histoire from the French Academy, 1969, for *La Seconde Guerre mondiale*.

WRITINGS: Quatre annees dures (title means "Four Difficult Years"), Grasset, 1945; *Histoire de la Resistance en France, 1940-1944* (title means "History of the French Resistance"), Presses Universitaires, 1952, revised edition, 1972; (with Boris Mirkine-Guetzevitch) *Les Idees politiques and sociales de la Resistance* (title means "The Political and Social Ideas of the French Resistance"), Presses Universitaires, 1954; (with Olga Wormser) *Tragedie de la deportation* (title means "Tragedy of the Deportation"), Hachette, 1954; (with Marie Granet) *Combat: Histoire d'un mouvement de Resistance* (title means "Combat: History of a French Resistance Group"), Presses Universitaires, 1955.

Les Mouvements clandestins en Europe (title means "The Underground Activities in Europe, 1940-1945"), Presses Universitaires, 1960; *Histoire de la France-Libre* (title means "History of Free-France, London, 1940-1943"), Presses Universitaires, 1962, revised edition, 1972; *Les Courants de pensee de la Resistance* (title means "Currents of Thought in the French Resistance"), Presses Universitaires, 1963; *Jean Moulin, l'unificateur* (title means "Jean Moulin: The Man Who Unified the French Resistance"), Hachette, 1964; *Bibliographie critique de la Resistance* (title means "Bibliography of the French Resistance"), Institut Pedagogique National (Paris), 1964; *Vichy annee 40* (title means "Vichy during 1940"), Laffont, 1966; *La Seconde Guerre mondiale*, two volumes, Presses Universitaires, 1968-69, translation by Douglas Parmee published as *Second World War*, Praeger, 1975, also published in France in one volume under same title, 1971, translation by Gilles Cremonesi published as *World War II: A Short History*, Saxon House, 1973, Atheneum, 1974.

La Guerre de l'ombre, Grasset, 1970, translation by Richard Barry published as *The Shadow War: European Resistance, 1939-1945*, Harper, 1972, also published as *The Shadow War: Resistance in Europe, 1939-1945*, Deutsch, 1972; *La Drole de guerre* (title means "The Phony War: September, 1939-March, 1940"), Hachette, 1972; *Petain, Laval, Darlan: Trois Politiques?* (title means "Petain, Laval, Darlan: Three Political Ways?"), Flammarion, 1972.

Editor, with Daniel Mayer, of "Esprit de la Resistance" series, 1954-65; series editor of "The Liberation of France" for Hachette, 1974-75. Editor of *Le Var Libre* (newspaper), 1944, and of *Revue d'Histoire de la Seconde Guerre Mondiale*, 1950-75.

WORK IN PROGRESS: Books on DeGaulle and the French Resistance, and on the Communist party and the French Resistance.

* * *

MIHALAS, Dmitri M(anuel) 1939-

PERSONAL: Born March 20, 1939, in Los Angeles, Calif.; son of Emmanuel Demetrious and Jean (Christo) Mihalas; married Alice Joelen Covalt, June 15, 1963 (divorced November 15, 1974); children: Michael Demetrious, Genevieve Alexandra. *Education:* University of California, Los Angeles, B.A. (with highest honors), 1959; California Institute of Technology, M.S., 1960, Ph.D., 1964. *Home:* 3225 Dover Dr., Boulder, Colo. 80303. *Office:* High Altitude Observatory, National Center for Atmospheric Research, P.O. Box 3000, Boulder, Colo. 80303.

CAREER: Member of technical staff at Space Technology Laboratories, summer, 1959; University of California, Los Angeles, acting instructor, summer, 1960; Princeton University, Princeton, N.J., Eugene Higgins visiting fellow, 1963-64, assistant professor of astrophysical sciences, 1964-67; University of Colorado, Boulder, assistant professor of astrophysics, 1967-68; University of Chicago, Chicago, Ill., associate professor, 1968-70, professor of astronomy and astrophysics, 1970-71; University of Colorado, professor adjoint of astro-geophysics, physics, and astrophysics, 1972—. Member of Joint Institute for Laboratory Astrophysics, 1967-68; senior scientist at High Altitude Observatory of National Center for Atmospheric Research, 1971—; member of astronomy advisory panel of National Science Foundation, 1972—.

MEMBER: International Astronomical Union, American Astronomical Society, American Association of University Professors, Royal Astronomical Society (fellow), Astronomical Society of the Pacific, Sigma Xi. *Awards, honors:* Alfred P. Sloan Foundation fellowship, 1969-71; Warner Prize from American Astronomical Society, 1974.

WRITINGS: (With Paul Routly) *Galactic Astronomy*, W. H. Freeman, 1968; *Stellar Atmospheres*, W. H. Freeman, 1970; (with B.E.J. Pagel and P. Souffrin) *Theorie des Atmospheres Stellaires* (title means "Theory of Stellar Atmospheres"), Observatoire de Geneve, 1971. Contributor of more than seventy articles to scientific journals, including *Astrophysical Journal, Astronomical Journal, Publications of the Astronomical Society of the Pacific, Monthly Notices of the Royal Astronomical Society, Solar Physics*, and *Astrophysics and Space Sciences*. Associate editor of *Astrophysical Journal*, 1970—.

WORK IN PROGRESS: Research on a theory of stellar atmospheres, radiative transfer, and spectral line formation, with emphasis on partial redistribution problems and extended and expanding stellar atmospheres.

AVOCATIONAL INTERESTS: Hiking, camping, skiing, American Indian history, literature, poetry, cooking, music (plays banjo).

* * *

MIKULAS, William Lee 1942-

PERSONAL: Born December 27, 1942, in Lansing, Mich.; son of William and Katherin (Voelker) Mikulas; married Benita Boehm (a teacher), August 7, 1969. *Education:* University of Michigan, B.A., 1964, M.A., 1966, Ph.D., 1969. *Office:* Department of Psychology, University of West Florida, Pensacola, Fla. 32504.

CAREER: University of West Florida, Pensacola, assistant professor, 1969-73, associate professor of psychology, 1973—.

WRITINGS: Behavior Modification: An Overview, Harper, 1972; *Concepts in Learning*, Saunders, 1974; (editor) *Psychology of Learning: Readings*, Nelson Hall, in press.

WORK IN PROGRESS: Second edition of *Behavior Modification: An Overview; Self-Control.*

* * *

MILGROM, Jacob 1923-

PERSONAL: Born February 1, 1923, in New York; married Jo Berman (a teacher), June 27, 1948; children: Shira (Mrs. David Elcott), Jeremy, Etan, Asher. *Education:* Brooklyn College (now Brooklyn College of the City University of New York), B.A., 1943; Jewish Theological Seminary, B.H.L., 1943, M.H.L., 1946, D.H.L., 1953, D.D., 1973. *Home:* 1042 Sierra St., Berkeley, Calif. 94707. *Office:* Department of Near Eastern Studies, University of California, Berkeley, Calif. 94720.

CAREER: Rabbi of Jewish congregations in Orange, N.J., 1948-51, and Richmond, Va., 1951-65; Virginia Union University, Graduate School of Religion, Richmond, instructor, 1955-56, assistant professor, 1956-59, associate professor, 1959-62, professor, 1962-65; University of California, Berkeley, associate professor, 1965-72, professor of Hebrew and Bible, 1972—, director of Study Center at Hebrew University of Jerusalem, 1969-71. *Member:* Society of Biblical Literature, Association for Jewish Studies. *Awards, honors:* Solomon Goldman Literary Creativity Award, from Anshe Emet Synagogue, Chicago, 1973, for body of work; elected fellow of Biblical Colloquium of America, 1974.

WRITINGS: Studies in Levitical Terminology, University of California Press, 1970; *Cult and Conscience*, E. J. Brill (Leiden), 1975. Contributor to *Encyclopedia Judaica*, *Interpreter's Dictionary of the Bible*, and *Encyclopedia Biblica*. Contributor to scholarly journals.

WORK IN PROGRESS: Commentary on Numbers, for Jewish Publication Society; *Understanding Leviticus*, publication by Melton Foundation expected in 1977.

* * *

MILLER, C(larence) William 1914-

PERSONAL: Born June 5, 1914, in Sunbury, Pa.; son of Clarence G. (a merchant) and Anna B. (Yeager) Miller; married Clara Josephine Williams, August 31, 1940; children: William Laubach, Douglas Wynne. *Education:* Gettysburg College, B.A., 1936; University of Virginia, M.A., 1938, Ph.D., 1940. *Home:* 119 Gladstone Rd., Lansdowne, Pa. 19050. *Office:* Department of English, Temple University, Philadelphia, Pa. 19122.

CAREER: University of Virginia, Charlottesville, instructor in English, 1940-46; Temple University, Philadelphia, Pa., assistant professor, 1946-48, associate professor, 1948-60, professor of English, 1960—. Councilman of Borough of Lansdowne, Pa., 1970-74. *Member:* American Antiquarian Society, Raven Society, Phi Beta Kappa.

WRITINGS: Benjamin Franklin's Philadelphia Printing, American Philosophical Society, 1974.

* * *

MILLER, Jon (Gordon) 1921-

PERSONAL: Born July 14, 1921, in Southend, Essex, England; son of Jack (an astronomer) and Edie (Drapkin) Miller; married Rita Mary Hallerman, March 5, 1948 (divorced, 1964); married Cecily Margaret Power (a horse dealer), January 23, 1965; children: (first marriage) Ginty, Michele, Anthony; (second marriage) Kim, Jakie. *Education:* Attended secondary school in England; Reimann School of Photography, photographic diploma, 1939. *Politics:* Liberal. *Home:* Albia House, Gillan, Manaccan, near Helston, Cornwall TR12 6HJ, England.

CAREER: John Gordon Miller Ltd., London, England, managing director, 1946-64; British Independent Television, Southampton, England, presenter and researcher for "HOW" (a children's television program), 1964—. *Military service:* Royal Air Force, photographer, 1941-46; became sergeant. *Member:* National Trust, Rationalist Press Association, Zoological Society of London (fellow), Cornwall Naturalists Trust, Helford River Sailing Club.

WRITINGS: Of Fish and Men, Jarrolds, 1958; *How to Keep Unusual Pets*, Studio Vista, in press; *How to Fool Your Brain*, Studio Vista, in press. Author of material for Southern Television, Westward Television, and British Broadcasting Corp. Contributor to *Geographical*, *Illustrated Weekly of India*, and *Tribune*.

* * *

MILLER, Nathan 1927-

PERSONAL: Born May 26, 1927, in Baltimore, Md.; son of David (a grocer) and Jennie Miller; married Jeanette Martick (a social worker), February 22, 1963. *Education:* University of Maryland, B.A., 1950, M.A., 1951. *Home:* 4916 Western Ave., Chevy Chase, Md. 20016. *Agent:* Michael Hamilburg, Mitchell J. Hamilburg Agency, 1105 Glendon Ave., Los Angeles, Calif. 90024. *Office:* Senate Committee on Appropriations, Room 1243, Dirksen Senate Office Building, Washington, D.C. 20510.

CAREER: Baltimore Sun, Baltimore, Md., 1954-69, Latin American Correspondent, 1962-66, Washington correspondent, 1966-69; *Editorial Research Reports* (division of *Congressional Quarterly*), Washington, D.C., associate editor of "Daily Service," 1969-71; *Kiplinger Washington Letters*, Washington, D.C., associate editor and editor of *Kiplinger Tax Letter*, 1971; Senate Committee on Appropriations, Washington, D.C., professional staff member (speech and editorial writer), 1971—. Consultant to National Park Service on naval aspects of the American Revolution Bicentennial. *Military service:* U.S. Navy, 1945-46. *Awards, honors:* Award from American Political Science Association, 1961, for distinguished reporting of public affairs.

WRITINGS: (Contributor) Charles Peters and Timothy Adams, editors, *Inside the System*, Praeger, 1970, 2nd edition, 1973; *Sea of Glory: The Continental Navy Fights for Independence, 1775-1783*, McKay, 1974. Contributor to *New Republic*, *Johns Hopkins Magazine*, *Reader's Digest Almanac*, *Washington Monthly*, and *Washington Post*.

WORK IN PROGRESS: The Founding Finaglers, a history of corruption in American politics, for McKay.

* * *

MILLER, Samuel Jefferson 1919-

PERSONAL: Born August 7, 1919, in Jewett, Ohio; son of Monfred Leroy (a farmer) and Grace (Amos) Miller. *Education:* Ohio State University, B.Sc. in Ed., 1941, M.A., 1948; Brown University, Ph.D., 1952. *Politics:* Independent. *Religion:* Roman Catholic. *Home:* 23 Hillside St., Roxbury, Mass. 02120. *Office:* Department of History, Boston College, Chestnut Hill, Mass. 02167.

CAREER: Boston College, Chestnut Hill, Mass., assistant professor, 1952-55, associate professor of history, 1955—. *Member:* American Historical Association, American Catholic Historical Association.

WRITINGS: (With John P. Spielman) Cristoval Rojas y Spinola: Cameralist and Irenicist (1626-1695), *American Philosophical Society, 1962;* Peter Richard Kendrick: Bishop and Archbishop of St. Louis, 1806-1896, *American Catholic Historical Society of Philadelphia, 1973. Contributor to* Speculum *and* Church History.

WORK IN PROGRESS: Portugal and the Holy See; research on political Jansenism in the Catholic Enlightenment in the eighteenth century, especially in Portugal and Italy.

SIDELIGHTS: Miller is competent in Portuguese, German, Italian, French, and Latin.

* * *

MILLHISER, Marlys (Joy) 1938-

PERSONAL: Born May 27, 1938, in Charles City, Iowa; daughter of Harold Henry and Doris (Britton) Enabnit; married David Ralph Millhiser (a mechanical engineer), June 25, 1960; children: Jay David, Joy Marie. *Education:* University of Iowa, B.A., 1960; University of Colorado, M.A., 1963. *Home:* 1743 Orchard Ave., Boulder, Colo. 80302. *Agent:* Ruth Cantor, 156 Fifth Ave., Room 1005, New York, N.Y. 10010.

CAREER: Boulder Community Hospital, Boulder, Colo., E.K.G. technician, 1961; junior high school teacher of history in the Boulder Valley School System, Boulder, Colo., 1963-65. *Member:* Authors Guild of Authors League of America, National Writers Club, Colorado Authors' League.

WRITINGS: Michael's Wife (novel), Putnam, 1972; *Nella Waits* (novel), Putnam, 1974.

WORK IN PROGRESS: A Third novel, a modern suspense story set in the high country of Colorado Rockies; research on oil shale, I.T.T., and the C.I.A.

* * *

MILLS, Alison 1951-

PERSONAL: Born March 20, 1951, in Long Island, N.Y.; daughter of Theodore H. (a chemist) and Margaret A. (an educator; maiden name, Cyrus) Mills; married Francisco Toscono Newman (a film-maker); children: Francisco Havana-Reed. *Education:* Graduated from high school in Los Angeles, Calif., 1968. *Religion:* God. *Home:* 940 Westchester Pl., Los Angeles, Calif. 90019.

CAREER: Actress (has acted in Off-Broadway productions and on television, including series "Julia" and "The Leslie Uggams Show").

WRITINGS: Francisco, Reed, Cannon & Johnson, 1974. Also contributor to *Yardbird Reader*, Volume II, 1974.

WORK IN PROGRESS: Kangaroo, a novel.

* * *

MILLS, Clarence A(lonzo) 1891-1974

December 9, 1891—September 17, 1974; American scientist, educator, environmentalist, and author. Obituaries: *New York Times*, September 20, 1974. (*CA*-15/16).

MILLWARD, Celia M(c Cullough) 1935-

PERSONAL: Born July 27, 1935, in Endicott, N.Y.; daughter of Ross W. and Ruth (Williams) McCullough; married Richard B. Millward (a professor of psychology), September 7, 1954; children: James Andrew. *Education:* Syracuse University, A.B., 1955; Brown University, A.M., 1963, Ph.D., 1966; post-doctoral study at University of Edinburgh, 1973. *Office:* Department of English, Boston University, 236 Bay State Rd., Boston, Mass. 02215.

CAREER: Boston University, Boston, Mass., assistant professor, 1966-70, associate professor of English, 1970—. *Member:* Linguistic Society of America, Modern Language Association of America, American Name Society, Early English Text Society, Phi Beta Kappa. *Awards, honors:* National Endowment for the Humanities junior fellowship, 1972-73.

WRITINGS: Imperative Constructions in Old English, Mouton & Co., 1971. Contributor to academic journals.

WORK IN PROGRESS: Research in early American dialects, Shakespearean English, history of the English language, Old and Middle English language and literature, and onomastics.

AVOCATIONAL INTERESTS: History, needlework, hiking, puzzles, bird-watching, nature, piano-playing.

* * *

MILTON, Charles R(udolph) 1925-

PERSONAL: Born July 20, 1925, in Wake Forest, N.C.; son of Carl Yeoman and Ruth (Jones) Milton; married Fay L. Walton, August 12, 1946; children: Charles R., Carl L., Pamela F. *Education:* University of North Carolina, B.A., 1949, Ph.D., 1960; North Carolina State College, M.S., 1951. *Religion:* Presbyterian. *Home address:* Route 3, Box 215, Chapin, S.C. 29036. *Office:* College of Business Administration, University of South Carolina, Columbia, S.C. 29208.

CAREER: North Carolina State College (now North Carolina State University at Raleigh), instructor in psychology, 1954-56; University of North Carolina, Chapel Hill, N.C., instructor in psychology, 1956-57, lecturer in personnel relations, 1957-58, lecturer in economics and statistics, 1958-59; University of Virginia, Charlottesville, assistant professor of human relations, statistics, industrial management, and principles of management, 1959-64; University of South Carolina, Columbia, associate professor, 1964-69, professor of organization theory, behavior, and development, 1969—, director of management program, 1964—. *Military service:* U.S. Navy, 1943-46. U.S. Naval Reserve, 1946-69.

MEMBER: Academy of Management, American Psychological Association, Southern Management Association (member of board of directors, 1963, 1968-72), Organization Development Network. *Awards, honors:* Ford Foundation grants, 1961, 1963; International Business Machines (IBM) grant, 1962; Institute for Research in Social Sciences grant, 1962.

WRITINGS: (Contributor) John M. Champion and Francis J. Bridges, editors, *Critical Incidents in Management*, Irwin, 1963; *Ethics and Expediency in Personnel Management*, University of South Carolina Press, 1970. Contributor to *American Psychologist*, *Southern Journal of Business*, *Business and Economic Review*, *Bobbin*, and *Personnel*.

MISKOVITS, Christine 1939-

PERSONAL: Born July 17, 1939, in Elizabeth, N.J.; daughter of John, Jr. (a millwright) and Stella (Smolen) Sabora; married Walter J. Miskovits (a customer service agent for Delta Airlines), February 7, 1959; children: Daniel, Ronald, Michael, Eric. *Education:* Attended Rutgers University, 1957-59; additional study in an external degree program. *Religion:* Roman Catholic. *Home:* 28 Hurden St., Hillside, N.J. 07205.

CAREER: St. Elizabeth Hospital, Elizabeth, N.J., technician, 1970—.

WRITINGS: Where Do Insects Go in Winter? (juvenile), Denison, 1973. Contributor to *Highlights*, *Weekly Reader*, *Young World*, *Accent on Youth*, *My Pleasure*, *Junior Trails*, *Friend*, *Young Miss*, *Golden*, *Child Life*, *Primary Treasure*, *Wee Wisdom*, and *Kindergartner*.

WORK IN PROGRESS: A juvenile adventure novel, tentatively titled *From the Fire and the Ashes*.

SIDELIGHTS: Mrs. Miskovits told *CA:* "Many of my stories are based on facts—real people from history, real incidents—because I feel that the history of our country is a treasure trove of exciting events." *From the Fire and the Ashes*, for example, is placed accurately during the San Francisco earthquake, although the story is fiction. "Life is full of questions," she added. "I enjoy answering them. . .in a way that young children can understand."

* * *

MISSIROLI, Mario 1886-1974

November, 1886—November, 1974; Italian journalist and author. Obituaries: *New York Times*, November 30, 1974; *Washington Post*, December 1, 1974.

* * *

MITCHELL, David (John) 1924-

PERSONAL: Born January 24, 1924, in London, England; son of James Watt (a grain broker) and Clare (Hayden) Mitchell; married twice and divorced; children: (second marriage) Jason. *Education:* Trinity College, Oxford, M.A., 1947. *Politics:* "Armchair anarchist." *Religion:* "Christian agnostic." *Residence:* London, England. *Agent:* Hope Leresche & Steele, 11 Jubilee Pl., London SW3 3TE, England.

CAREER: Hulton Press, staff writer for *Picture Post*, 1947-52; Pictorial Press (photo-journalistic agency), London, England, editor, 1953-56; Central Office of Information, London, England, picture editor, 1957-65; writer, 1965—. *Military service:* Royal Air Force, pilot, 1942-44.

WRITINGS: Monstrous Regiment: The Story of the Women of the First World War, Macmillan, 1966; *The Fighting Pankhursts*, Macmillan, 1967; *The Pankhursts*, Heron Books, 1970; *1919 Red Mirage*, Macmillan, 1970; (contributor) Stephen W. Sears, editor, *The Horizon History of the British Empire*, American Heritage Press, 1973. Contributor to journals, including *History Today*, *Times*, *Daily Telegraph*, *Horizon*, *Mankind*, and *Aspect*.

WORK IN PROGRESS: Bernardo O'Higgins: Chilean Liberator, for Verlag Plata; *The Riot: Fascism and the Crisis of Democracy, 1920-1950*; a history of piracy, for Thames & Hudson; research for a book on the simple life.

SIDELIGHTS: Mitchell writes that he decided to try to earn a living as a writer in 1965 after a lifetime of prevarication or muddled preparation. He lived in Spain from 1965 until devaluation of the pound and rising local prices in 1973 forced a return to the United Kingdom. Though he has written three books and a number of articles on suffrage-feminist themes, he is not a convinced "women's libber." His main interest is in "utopian, often fanatical characters, beautiful (or at least sympathetic) losers" and he has a keen interest in the Spanish anarchist movement and the early stages of Italian fascism. He finds it hard to believe in the brotherhood of Man but longs to get involved in a brotherhood of men. On the other hand, however, he finds full commitment to any system of belief impossible and considers the doctrine of original sin the best available working clue to human behavior and human history. Despite this, he hopes for a grand global upheaval issuing in drastic social and spiritual revolution and "half expects to live to see it." *Avocational interests:* Sweeping leaves and making bonfires, listening to traditional jazz and swing (Louis Armstrong, Benny Goodman, Hot Club de France), writing verse.

* * *

MITCHELL, Edgar D(ean) 1930-

PERSONAL: Born September 17, 1930, in Hereford, Tex.; son of Joseph T. and Ollidean (Arnold) Mitchell; married Anita K. Rettig, November 23, 1973; children: Karlyn Louise, Elizabeth Randall, Kimberly, Paul, Marybeth. *Education:* Carnegie Institute of Technology (now Carnegie-Mellon University), B.S. (Industrial Management), 1952; U.S. Naval Postgraduate School, B.S. (Aeronautics), 1961; Massachusetts Institute of Technology, Sc.D., 1964.

CAREER: U.S. Navy, 1951-72, became aviator, 1954, military test pilot, 1958, technical director of Navy Space Systems, 1964-65, served with National Aeronautics and Space Administration (NASA) and the Astronaut Corps, 1966-72, as member of support crew for Apollo 9, member of backup crews for Apollo 10 and Apollo 16, and as lunar module pilot during Apollo 14 mission, becoming the sixth man to walk on the moon, 1971, retired with rank of captain, 1972; Edgar D. Mitchell & Associates (consultants), Atherton, Calif., president, founder, and chairman of the board, 1972—; Institute of Noetic Sciences, Palo Alto, Calif., president, founder, and chairman of the board, 1973—. Public speaker, lecturer, writer, and television discussant on human potential and societal alternatives, 1971—; Albert Schmidt Lecturer, University of Notre Dame, 1972.

MEMBER: American Institute of Aeronautics and Astronautics, Society of Experimental Test Pilots, Parapsychology Association, International Platform Association, American Federation of Television and Recording Artists (life member), Adventurers Club, Sigma Xi. *Awards, honors:* Presidential Medal of Freedom; Navy Distinguished Service Medal; NASA Distinguished Service Medal; two NASA Group Achievement Awards; Sc.D. from New Mexico State University, and Eng.D. from Carnegie-Mellon University, both 1971; named outstanding man of the year by Carnegie-Mellon alumni, and by Kappa Sigma, both 1972; Engineering and Science Award, Drexel University, 1974; Medal of the City of New York and numerous honorary citizen and distinguished citizen awards from various cities in the United States and abroad.

WRITINGS: (Editor with John White) *Psychic Exploration: A Challenge for Science*, Putnam, 1974. Contributor to journals and periodicals.

MITCHELL, (Sibyl) Elyne (Keith) 1913-

PERSONAL: Born December 30, 1913, in Melbourne, Australia; daughter of Harry George (a soldier) and Sibyl (Keith-Jopp) Chauvel; married Thomas Walter Mitchell (a grazier and member of Victoria Parliament), November 4, 1935; children: Indi (Mrs. John Hill), Walter-Harry (deceased), Honor, John. *Education:* Educated in Melbourne, Australia. *Religion:* Anglican. *Home:* Towong Hill, Corryong, Victoria, Australia 3707. *Agent:* Curtis Brown Ltd., 1 Craven Hill, London, England.

CAREER: Writer of children's books. Works with her husband on their cattle ranch. *Member:* Lyceum Club, Alexandra Club, Ski Club of Australia, Ski Club Arlberg.

WRITINGS: Australia's Alps, Angus & Robertson, 1942, revised edition, 1962; *Speak to the Earth*, Angus & Robertson, 1945; *Soil and Conservation*, Angus & Robertson, 1946; *Images in Water*, Angus & Robertson, 1947; *Flow River, Blow Wind*, Harrap, 1953; *Black Cockatoos Mean Snow*, Hodder & Stoughton, 1956.

For children: *Silver Brumby*, Hutchinson, 1958, Dutton, 1959; *Silver Brumby's Daughter*, Hutchinson, 1960, published as *The Snow Filly*, Dutton, 1961; *Kingfisher Feather*, Hutchinson, 1962; *Winged Skis*, Hutchinson, 1964; *Silver Brumbies of the South*, Hutchinson, 1965; *Silver Brumby Kingdom*, Hutchinson, 1966; *Moon Filly*, Hutchinson, 1968; *Jinki: Dingo of the Snows*, Hutchinson, 1970; *Light Horse to Damascus*, Hutchinson, 1971; *Silver Brumby Whirlwind*, Hutchinson, 1973.

Contributor to *Age* (Melbourne newspaper) and *Walkabout*.

WORK IN PROGRESS: Text for *Snowy Mountains*, a book of photographs of Australia.

* * *

MIX, Katherine Lyon (Katherine Lyon)

PERSONAL: Born in Collinsville, Conn.; daughter of Stephen Joseph and Katherine (Perry) Lyon; married Arthur Jackson Mix (chairman of department of botany at University of Kansas), November 5, 1917 (died, 1956). *Education:* Cornell University, A.B., 1916; University of Kansas, graduate study, 1924-30. *Home:* 900 East Harrison Ave., #F-14, Pomona, Calif. 91767.

CAREER: University of Kansas, Lawrence, instructor in English, 1945-50, 1956-58; Baker University, Baldwin, Kan., instructor in English, 1958-66.

MEMBER: National League of American Pen Women, League of Women Voters, Common Cause, Zodiac Club, Phi Beta Kappa. *Awards, honors:* Decorated with Royal Order of St. Olav, by King Haakon VII of Norway, 1951, for writing about Norway's war efforts; grant from American Council of Learned Societies, 1962.

WRITINGS—Under name Katherine Lyon: (Contributor) Charles Neider, editor, *Men of the High Calling*, Abingdon, 1954; *A Study in Yellow*, University Press of Kansas, 1960; *Max and the Americans*, Greene, 1974. Contributor of short stories to popular magazines, including *New Yorker*, *American*, *Coronet*, *Maclean's*, and *Liberty*, and of reviews to *Kansas City Star*.

WORK IN PROGRESS: A biographical study of Laurence Housman, brother of A. E. Housman.

AVOCATIONAL INTERESTS: Antiques (collection of "Beerbohmiana"), travel (England, Norway, and other countries around the world).

MODIGLIANI, Andre 1940-

PERSONAL: In surname, "g" is silent; born May 21, 1940, in New York, N.Y.; son of Franco (an economist) and Serena (Calabi) Modigliani; married Katherine Horst (a teacher), June 15, 1963; children: Leah, Julia. *Education:* Harvard University, A.B. (summa cum laude), 1962; University of Michigan, Ph.D., 1966. *Politics:* Independent. *Religion:* None. *Home:* 1616 Lincoln Ave., Ann Arbor, Mich. 48104. *Office:* Department of Sociology, University of Michigan, Ann Arbor, Mich. 48104.

CAREER: Harvard University, Cambridge, Mass., assistant professor of social psychology, 1967-72; University of Michigan, Ann Arbor, associate professor of sociology, 1972—. Visiting professor at University of California, Los Angeles, 1970; member of social science research review committee of National Institute of Mental Health, 1971-73. *Member:* American Sociological Association, American Psychological Association, Society for the Psychological Study of Social Issues, Peace Research Society, American Association of University Professors. *Awards, honors:* National Institute of Mental Health grant, 1969-71.

WRITINGS: (With William Gamson) *Untangling the Cold War: A Strategy for Testing Rival Theories*, Little, Brown, 1971; (with Gamson) *Conceptions of Social Life*, Little, Brown, 1974. Contributor to professional journals, including *Public Opinion Quarterly*, *Sociometry*, *Journal of Personality and Social Psychology*, and *American Political Science Review*.

WORK IN PROGRESS: Research on hair styles and social change; further research in social psychology.

* * *

MOHLENBROCK, Robert H. 1931-

PERSONAL: Born September 26, 1931, in Murphysboro, Ill.; son of Robert Herman (a postmaster) and Elsie (Treece) Mohlenbrock; married Beverly Ann Kling, October 19, 1957; children: Mark William, Wendy Ann, Trent Alan. *Education:* Southern Illinois University, B.S., 1953, M.A., 1954; Washington University, St. Louis, Mo., Ph.D., 1957. *Home:* 1 Bird Song Dr., Route 1, Carbondale, Ill. 62901. *Office:* Department of Botany, Southern Illinois University, Carbondale, Ill. 62901.

CAREER: Southern Illinois University, Carbondale, assistant professor, 1957-60, associate professor, 1960-66, professor of botany and chairman of department, 1966—. Member of board of trustees of Illinois Nature Conservancy; consultant to Illinois Nature Preserves Commission. *Military service:* Illinois National Guard, 1957-63. *Member:* International Association for Plant Taxonomists, American Association for Plant Taxonomists, American Fern Society, Southern Appalachian Botanical Club, New England Botanical Club, Illinois Academy of Science, Sigma Xi.

WRITINGS: Flowering Plants and Ferns of Giant City State Park (booklet), Illinois Department of Conservation and Illinois State Museum, 1954; (with J. W. Voigt) *An Ozark Odyssey* (booklet), Southern Illinois University, 1958; *A Key to Common Woody Plants* (booklet), Southern Illinois University, 1959, 2nd edition, 1961; (with Voigt) *A Flora of Southern Illinois*, Southern Illinois University Press, 1959.

(Contributor) G. N. Jones, editor, *Flora of Illinois*, American Midland Naturalist, University of Notre Dame, 3rd edition (Mohlenbrock did not contribute to earlier editions),

1963; (with Voigt) *Plant Communities of Southern Illinois*, Southern Illinois University Press, 1964; *Habits and Habitats of Southern Illinois Ferns* (booklet), Southern Illinois University, 1965; (with others) *Wild Flowers of North America*, Volume I: *The Northeastern States*, McGraw, 1966; *Ferns*, Southern Illinois University Press, 1967.

Flowering Plants: Flowering Rush to Rushes, Southern Illinois University Press, 1970; *Flowering Plants: Lilies to Orchids*, Southern Illinois University Press, 1970; *Taxonomy of the Local Flora*, Stipes, 1970; *Grasses: Bromus to Paspalum*, Southern Illinois University Press, 1972; *Grasses: Panicum to Danthonia*, Southern Illinois University Press, 1973; *Forest Trees of Illinois*, Illinois Department of Conservation, 1973; (with Voigt) *A Flora of Southern Illinois*, Southern Illinois University Press, 1974.

Author of abstracts. Contributor of about a hundred sixty articles to scientific and locally popular journals, including *Outdoor Illinois, Rhodora, Castanea, Transactions of the Illinois Academy of Science, Sandlapper, Southern Illinois Sportsman*, and *South Carolina*. Botanical editor of *Transactions of the Illinois Academy of Science*.

* * *

MOJICA, Jose 1896-1974 (Brother Jose de Guadaloupe)

1896—September 20, 1974; Mexican-born Peruvian monk, author, former star of opera, stage, and screen in North and South America. Obituaries: *Washington Post*, September 22, 1974; *New York Times*, September 23, 1974.

* * *

MOLLAND, Einar 1908-

PERSONAL: Born March 11, 1908, in Oslo, Norway; son of Jacob and Laura (Heyerdahl) Molland; married Vera Moe, May 27, 1940; children: Inger Marie, Kristin Irene. *Education:* Attended University of Uppsala, 1928, University of Strasbourg, 1929, University of Copenhagen, 1930; University of Oslo, cand. theol., 1932, dr. theol., 1938; graduate study, University of Berlin, 1933-34, University of Strasbourg, 1936-37. *Home:* 45 B Jac. Aall's Gate, Oslo, Norway. *Office:* Institutt for Kirkehistorie, Universitetet I Oslo, Oslo, Norway.

CAREER: University of Oslo, Oslo, Norway, research fellow, 1934-38, professor of church history, 1938—. *Member:* Norwegian Academy of Science and Letters, Royal Society of Letters (Sweden), British Academy. *Awards, honors:* Received honorary degrees from University of Durham, 1953, and University of Uppsala, 1962.

WRITINGS: Das paulinische euangelion, das wort und die sache (title means "The Pauline Gospel: The Word and the Thing"), Norwegian Academy of Science and Letters, 1934; *The Conception of the Gospel in Alexandrian Theology*, Norwegian Academy of Science and Letters, 1938; *Hoemiddelalderen* (title means "The High Middle Ages"), Aschehoug (Oslo), 1943, 5th edition, 1967; *Fra Hans Nielsen Hauge til Eivind Berggrav: Hovedlinjer i Norges Kirkehistorie i de 19. og 20. aarhundre*, Gyldendal (Oslo), 1951, 3rd edition, 1972, translation of 1st edition by Harris Kaasa published as *Church Life in Norway, 1800-1950*, Augsburg, 1957; *Konfesjonskunnskap: Kristenhetens trosbekjennelser og kirkesamfunn*, Land og Kirke (Oslo), 1953, revised edition, 1961, translation of 1st edition by the author and H. E. W. Turner published as *Christendom: The Christian Churches, Their Doctrines, Constitutional Forms, and Ways of Worship*, Philosophical Library, 1959; *Statskirke og Jesu Kristi kirke* (title means "The State Church and the Church of Christ"), Land og Kirke, 1954; (with others) *Universitetene i gaar og i dag* (title means "Universities Yesterday and Today"), Universitetsforlaget (Oslo), 1961; *Latinske lesestykker for teologer* (title means "A Latin Reader for Theologians"), two volumes, Universitetsforlaget, 1963; *Opuscula patristica* (title means "Essays on Patristic Subjects"), Universitetsforlaget, 1970. Contributor to journals in his field.

WORK IN PROGRESS: A completely new edition of *Konfesjonskunnskap*.

* * *

MONROE, (Marilyn) Lynn Lee 1935-

PERSONAL: Born March 6, 1935, in Chicago, Ill.; daughter of Harry E. (a salesman) and Olive (a practical nurse; maiden name, Chamness) Lewis; married Eugene A. Monroe (a professor and dentist), June 12, 1954; children: Steven, Yvonne, Stanley. *Education:* University of Illinois, B.A., 1961; Alfred University, M.A., 1969. *Politics:* Independent. *Home and office:* 46 Pine Hill Dr., Alfred, N.Y. 14802.

CAREER: Alfred University, Alfred, N.Y., lecturer in English literature, 1967-69; Englewood Cliffs College, Englewood Cliffs, N.J., instructor in English literature, 1969-70; Bergen County Welfare Board, Hackensack, N.J., caseworker, 1971-72, supervisor, 1973—; business manager of husband's dental practice, 1974—.

WRITINGS: Boneshakers and Other Bikes, Lerner, 1973.

WORK IN PROGRESS: Two books for Lerner tentatively titled, *The Tale of Tennis*, and *Basketballs and Peachbaskets*; a children's history of bowling, and of gymnastics, completion of both expected in 1975; a fictionalized book of social work experiences for teenagers.

AVOCATIONAL INTERESTS: Bike riding, travel, needlework, tennis, indoor plants, reading.

* * *

MONTGOMERY, Brian (Frederick) 1903-

PERSONAL: Born October 18, 1903, in London, England; son of Henry Hutchinson (an Anglican bishop) and Maud (Farrar) Montgomery; married Barbara Peggy Hincks, April 1, 1944; children: Thomas (a stepson). *Education:* Attended Royal Military College, 1921-23. *Politics:* Conservative. *Religion:* Church of England. *Home:* 11a The Gateways, Chelsea, London SW3 3HX, England.

CAREER: British Army, 1923-48; retired as lieutenant colonel. Commissioned second lieutenant in Royal Warwickshire Regiment, 1923; transferred to King's African Rifles and served in Kenya, 1927-34; transferred to Baluch Regiment of Indian Army in 1935 and served in Burma, 1941-45, where he was mentioned in dispatches and personally took surrender of Japanese 33rd Army; commanded Indian regiments, 1945-47. Transferred to Diplomatic Service in 1948, and travelled extensively in the Middle East and Africa, retiring in 1970. Served as councillor of Royal Borough of Chelsea and Kensington, 1971-74. *Member:* Society of Authors, Pakistan Society, Army and Navy Club (London), London Library. *Awards, honors:* Member of Order of the British Empire, 1942.

WRITINGS: A Field-Marshal in the Family, Constable, 1973, Taplinger, 1974. Contributor to *Country Life* and *Blackwoods*.

WORK IN PROGRESS: A book, *The Story of the Jawan*, dealing with the soldier in the ranks of the Indian Army during British rule.

SIDELIGHTS: Brian Montgomery, who is a younger brother of Viscount Montgomery of Alamein, told *CA*: "In my book *A Field-Marshal in the Family*, I have tried to trace the influence of heredity and environment, together, in the moulding of the character and career of a great British soldier. To this I have added the story of my brother's life, including more or less personal and generally unknown facts which I believe can only be supplied by one of his own blood."

* * *

MOOD, Alexander M(cFarlane) 1913-

PERSONAL: Born May 31, 1913, in Amarillo, Tex.; son of Alexander M. (an attorney) and Edna (Leavell) Mood; married Harriet Harper, 1936; children: Alexander III, Carolyn (Mrs. Ronald Olsen), Margaret. *Education:* University of Texas, B.A., 1934; Princeton University, Ph.D., 1940. *Office:* Graduate School of Administration, University of California, Irvine, Calif. 92664.

CAREER: Instructor in applied mathematics, University of Texas, 1940-42; statistician with Bureau of Labor Statistics, 1942-44; research associate, Princeton University, 1945; Iowa State College (now University), Ames, 1945-48, began as associate professor, became professor of mathematics; RAND Corp., Santa Monica, Calif., deputy chief of mathematics division, 1948-55; president, General Analysis Corp., 1955-60; CEIR, Inc., Los Angeles, Calif., vice-president, 1960-64; U.S. Office of Education, Washington, D.C., U.S. commissioner of education, 1964-67; University of California, Irvine, professor of administration, 1968—. Guest lecturer at Army War College and Air War College; consultant to U.S. Department of Defense.

WRITINGS: Introduction to Theory of Statistics, McGraw, 1950, revised edition, 1974; *The Future of Higher Education*, McGraw, 1973.

* * *

MOODY, Paul Amos 1903-

PERSONAL: Born January 13, 1903, in Randolph Center, Vt.; son of Lewis Nathaniel (a clergyman) and Florence (Tower) Moody; married Judith Inlay, July 27, 1927; children: Marilyn Jean (Mrs. Wayne A. Hurlbut), Dorothy Helen (Mrs. Melton M. Miller, Jr.). *Education:* Morningside College, A.B., 1924; University of Michigan, Ph.D., 1927. *Politics:* Republican. *Religion:* Congregationalist. *Home:* 197 Howard St., Burlington, Vt. 05401.

CAREER: University of Vermont, Burlington, assistant professor, 1927-31, associate professor, 1931-45, Howard Professor of Natural History, 1945-75, professor emeritus, 1968—, director of graduate study, 1942-49. Visiting lecturer at University of Colorado, summers, 1962, 1963. *Member:* American Society of Human Genetics, Society for the Study of Evolution, American Society of Zoologists, American Society of Mammalogists, American Society of Naturalists, American Association of Physical Anthropologists, American Association for the Advancement of Science (fellow), Sigma Xi, Gamma Alpha, Phi Sigma. *Awards, honors:* Research grant from American Philosophical Society, 1941.

WRITINGS: Introduction to Evolution, preliminary edition, Edwards Bros., 1950, 3rd edition, Harper, 1970; *Genetics of Man*, Norton, 1967, 2nd edition, 1975.

MOON, Harold K(ay) 1932-

PERSONAL: Born July 24, 1932, in Mesa, Ariz.; son of Harold K. and Ellen (DeWitt) Moon; married Mayva Anne Magleby, November 25, 1959; children: Jacqueline, Kelley Anne, Todd, Leslie, Shawn, Kristen, Elaine. *Education:* Brigham Young University, B.A., 1957, M.A., 1959; Syracuse University, Ph.D., 1963. *Religion:* Church of Jesus Christ of Latter-day Saints (Mormon). *Home:* 764 West Center St., Orem, Utah 84057. *Office:* Department of Spanish, Brigham Young University, Provo, Utah 84602.

CAREER: Spanish teacher in school in American Fork, Utah, 1956-57; Syracuse University, Syracuse, N.Y., instructor in Spanish, 1962-63; Brigham Young University, Provo, Utah, assistant professor, 1963-66, associate professor, 1966-71, professor of Spanish, 1971—.

WRITINGS: (Contributor) German Bleiberg and E. Inman Fox, editors, *Spanish Thought and Letters in the Twentieth Century*, Vanderbilt University Press, 1966; *Alejandro Casona: Playwright* (monograph), Brigham Young University Press, 1970; *Spanish Literature: A Critical Approach*, Xerox College Publishing, 1972. Author of "That's the Spirit," a play, with John A. Green, first performed on KBYU-Television, September 29, 1969. Contributor of articles and reviews to *Hispania*, *Brigham Young University Studies*, *French Review*, and *Proceedings of the Pacific Northwest Conference on Foreign Languages*.

WORK IN PROGRESS: It Will Flower Again, a novel; "To See the Stars," a play; a collection of short stories.

* * *

MOORE, Barbara 1934-

PERSONAL: Born April 29, 1934, in Tulsa, Okla.; daughter of Prentiss Thomas (an oil journalist) and Edna (Swaggerty) Moore; married John Lee (a writer and professor of journalism), April 14, 1957. *Education:* University of Arizona, B.A. (magna cum laude), 1971, M.A., 1972. *Politics:* Democrat. *Religion:* None. *Agent:* Don Congdon, Harold Matson Co., Inc., 22 East 40th St., New York, N.Y. 10016.

CAREER: Reporter on newspapers in Fort Worth, Tex., 1955-57, in Denver, Colo., 1958-60, in San Antonio, Tex., 1963-65. *Member:* Phi Beta Kappa, Phi Kappa Phi.

WRITINGS: Hard on the Road (novel), Doubleday, 1974. Contributor, often under name Barbara Lee, to *Holiday*, *Signature*, *Braniff International*, and *Airfair*.

WORK IN PROGRESS: Mr. Poe, a novel about the last five years of Edgar Allan Poe's life spent in New York, completion expected in 1975.

* * *

MOORE, Samuel Taylor 1893-1974

1893—November 13, 1974; American journalist, author, and retired Air Force colonel. Obituaries: *Washington Post*, December 8, 1974.

* * *

MORAN, Gabriel 1935-

PERSONAL: Born August 11, 1935, in Manchester, N.H.; son of John Francis and Mary (Murphy) Moran. *Education:* Attended University of New Hampshire; Catholic University of America, B.A., 1958, M.A., 1962, Ph.D., 1965. *Office:* Department of Religion, New York Theological Seminary, New York, N.Y.

CAREER: Member of Roman Catholic order of Christian Brothers. High school teacher in Providence, R.I., 1958-61; college teacher of religion and philosophy in Washington, D.C., 1962-65; Manhattan College, Bronx, New York, N.Y., professor of religion, 1965, director of graduate religious studies, 1965-70; now professor of religion at New York Theological Seminary, New York, N.Y. President of Christian Brothers, Long Island-New England province, 1970-73; visiting professor at New School of Religion, Pontiac, Mich., 1971-73; secretary, The Alternative (adult education program), 1972—. Lecturer in Africa, Canada, and United States.

WRITINGS—All published by Herder & Herder except as indicated: *Scripture and Tradition*, 1963; *Theology of Revelation*, 1966; *Catechises of Revelation*, 1966; *Vision and Tactics*, 1968; *Experiences in Community*, 1968; *The New Community*, 1970; *Design for Religion*, 1970; *The Present Revelation*, 1972; *Religious Body*, Seabury, 1974. Contributor of over ninety articles to religion and education journals.

* * *

MORAUD, Marcel I(an) 1917-

PERSONAL: Born December 27, 1917, in Washington, D.C.; son of Marcel (a professor at Rice University) and May (Middleton) Moraud; married Paulette Demoiseau, January 18, 1945; children: May, Linda. *Education:* Attended Rice University, 1934-35, 1936-37; University of Texas, M.A., 1938; University of Paris, Licence es Lettres, 1947, Diplomes d'Etudes Superieures, 1940, Doctorat (highest honors), 1948; graduate study at Brown University, 1941-42. *Home:* 27 Bristol Rd., Clinton, N.Y. 13323. *Office:* Department of Romance Languages, Hamilton College, Clinton, N.Y. 13323.

CAREER: Brown University, Providence, R.I., assistant professor of French, 1949-50; Biarritz American University, Biarritz, France, instructor in French, 1945-46; Hamilton College, Clinton, N.Y., associate professor, 1950-55, professor of Romance languages, 1955—, head of department, 1950—, Burgess Professor, 1955—, director of Junior Year in France, five years, 1957—, director of French Institute, 1961, 1963-65, president of Center for Overseas Undergraduate Programs, 1965—. Summer visiting professor at Yale University, 1950, New York University, 1957, and University of Cincinnati, 1960. *Military service:* French Army, 1939-40. U.S. Army, 1942-46. U.S. Army Active Reserve, 1946-60; became major. *Member:* American Association of Teachers of French, American Association of University Professors (president of Rhode Island branch, 1949-50; president of Central New York branch, 1952-54; member of executive board, 1969-71), Modern Language Association of America, New York Federation of Foreign Language Teachers.

WRITINGS: (With Fred Shelton) *Basic French Grammar*, Banks Upshaw, 1938; *Lady Morgan*, Didier, 1950; *Une Nouvelle Revolution Francaise* (title means "A New French Revolution"), Hamilton College Press, 1958; (with L. Clark Keating) *Graded French Readers*, seven volumes, American Book Co., 1958-69; (editor with Keating) *Selections de Moliere, Voltaire, Hugo*, Van Nostrand, 1972. Contributor to *French Review*, *F. A. Magazine*, *Comparative Literature*, *Revue Pedagogique*, *Modern Language Journal*, and *Cithara*. Assistant editor of *New York Foreign Language Bulletin*, 1954-55. Consultant, *Encyclopaedia Britannica Multilanguage Dictionary*, 1956—.

MORE, Harry W(illiam), Jr. 1929-

PERSONAL: Born May 18, 1929, in Cheyenne, Wyo.; son of Harry W. and Faye (Taylor) More; married Virginia Carey (a nurse), June 10, 1951; children: Debbie, James. *Education:* University of California, Berkeley, A.B., 1952; American University, M.P.A., 1959; University of Idaho, Ph.D., 1969. *Home:* 4847 Tonino Dr., San Jose, Calif. 95123. *Office:* Department of Administration of Justice, San Jose State University, San bjose, Calif. 95143.

CAREER: Washington State University, Pullman, assistant professor of police science, 1962-66; Indiana University of Pennsylvania, Indiana, Pa., associate professor of criminology and chairman of department, 1966-69; San Jose State University, San Jose, Calif., professor of administration of justice and chairman of department, 1969. President, Justice Systems Development, Inc., 1972—. *Military service:* U.S. Army, 1952-54. U.S. Army Reserves, 1954-65; became major. *Member:* Academy of Criminal Justice Sciences (secretary, 1963-65), American Society of Criminology, California Association of Administration of Justice Educators (chairman of Northern section, 1974—).

WRITINGS: (With Vivian A. Leonard) *The General Administration of Criminal Justice*, Foundation Press, 1967; *The New Era of Public Safety*, C. C Thomas, 1970; (with Leonard) *Police Organization and Management*, 3rd edition (More was not associated with earlier editions), Foundation Press, 1971, 4th edition, 1974; (editor) *Critical Issues in Law Enforcement*, W. H. Anderson, 1972; *Principles and Procedures in the Administration of Justice*, Wiley, 1974; (with Richard Chang) *Contemporary Criminal Justice*, Justice Systems Development, Inc., 1974; *Effective Police Administration*, Justice Systems Development, Inc., 1975; *Foundations of Justice*, Justice Systems Development, Inc., in press.

* * *

MORGAN, Kay Summersby 1909-1975

1909—January 20, 1975; Irish-born American, member of British Women's Auxiliary Corps, and later American Women's Army Corps (WAC), serving on General Eisenhower's staff during World War II; model, costume and set designer, and author. Obituaries: *New York Times*, January 21, 1975; *Washington Post*, January 21, 1975; *Time*, February 3, 1975.

* * *

MORGAN, Lael 1936-

PERSONAL: Given name rhymes with "sail"; born May 12, 1936, in Rockland, Maine; daughter of Eugene D. and Hazel (Abbott) Warren; married Dodge Morgan, March, 1958 (divorced, 1970). *Education:* Emerson College, student, 1956-57; Boston University, B.S., 1959. *Religion:* Protestant. *Home and office address:* P. O. Box 4-EEE, Anchorage, Alaska. *Agent:* Paul R. Reynolds, Inc., 12 East 41st St., New York, N.Y. 10017.

CAREER: With *Fairbanks News-Miner*, Fairbanks, Alaska, 1966-67, and *Jessen's Weekly*, Fairbanks, 1967; *Los Angeles Times*, Los Angeles, Calif., writer and photographer, 1968-71; *Tundra Times*, Fairbanks, Alaska, writer and photographer, 1971; *Los Angeles Times*, writer and photographer, 1973-74; *Alaska* (magazine), Anchorage, associate editor, 1974—. *Awards, honors:* Alicia Patterson Foundation grant from Rockefeller Foundation, 1972, for research in the Alaskan bush.

WRITINGS: Woman's Guide to Boating and Cooking, Wheelwright, 1968, 2nd edition, Doubleday, 1974; *And the Land Provides: Alaskan Natives in a Year of Transition*, Doubleday, 1974.

WORK IN PROGRESS: A book on the past, present, and future of Alaskan natives; visiting every native village in Alaska.

SIDELIGHTS: Lael Morgan writes: "In the mid 1960's I became concerned with the political maturing of Alaska's Eskimo, Indian, and Aleut people, then the poorest citizens under the U.S. flag. In the time since then the Alaskan natives have grown strong. In 1971 they won the largest land claim settlement ever gained from the U.S. government but they are still in the process of transition from a subsistence to money economy."

* * *

MORLAND, Nigel 1905-
(Mary Dane, John Donavan, Norman Forrest, Roger Garnett, Neal Shepherd)

PERSONAL: Born June 24, 1905, in London, England; son of John and Gertrude Morland; married Peggy Barwell (divorced); married Pamela Hunnex (divorced); married Jill Harvey; children: Terence, John, Ruth. *Education:* Privately educated. *Politics:* Neutral. *Religion:* Christian. *Home:* Seaspray, Canning Rd., Felpham, Bognor Regis, Sussex, England. *Office:* Forensic Publishing Co., 9 Old Bailey, London E.C. 4, England.

CAREER: Began as a crime reporter at the age of 15; has since worked variously as a features editor, managing editor, or editor on a number of publications, including *News Review*, *Doctor*, *Edgar Wallace Mystery Magazine*, and *Shanghai Sports*; has been wartime foreign correspondent; when asked to supply details of his career, Morland replied: "Long forgotten; do not regard past positions of any importance at all." Adviser on crime and detection to various publications in England and the United States. *Member:* Crime Writers' Association (founder along with John Creasey, 1953), Forensic Science Society, Medico-Legal Society, Royal Photographic Society, Press Club (London).

WRITINGS: The Goofus Man: A Fantasy for Children in Three Acts, Scholartis Press, 1930, Samuel French, 1937; (with wife, Peggy Barwell) *Cachexia: A Collection of Prose Poems*, Felix Barbier, 1930, fourth edition, 1933; (with Barwell) *Dawn Was Theirs: A Play in Three Acts*, Felix Barbier, 1931; (with Barwell) *People We Have Never Met: A Book of Superficial Cameos*, Felix Barbier, 1931, fifth edition, 1931; (with Barwell) *"Mary!" A Story of the Magdalene*, Felix Barbier, 1932; (with Barwell) *Abrakadabra! Verse for Modern Children*, Felix Barbier, 1932; *The Phantom Gunman*, Cassell, 1935; *The Moon Murders*, Cassell, 1935; *The Street of the Leopard*, Cassell, 1936; *Finger Prints: An Introduction to Scientific Criminology*, Street & Massey, 1936; *How to Write Detective Novels*, Allen & Unwin, 1936; *The Clue of the Bricklayer's Aunt*, Cassell, 1936, Farrar & Rinehart, 1937; (under pseudonym Norman Forrest) *Death Took a Publisher*, Harrap, 1936, Hillman-Curl, 1938, abridged edition, Withy Grove Press, 1946; (under pseudonym Norman Forrest) *Death Took a Greek God*, Harrap, 1937, Hillman-Curl, 1938, abridged edition, Withy Grove Press, 1946; *The Clue in the Mirror*, Cassell, 1937, Farrar & Rinehart, 1938; *The Conquest of Crime*, Cassell, 1937.

(Under pseudonym John Donavan) *The Case of the Rusted Room*, R. Hale, 1937; (under pseudonym Roger Garnett) *Death in Picadilly*, Wright & Brown, 1937; (under pseudonym Roger Garnett) *Starr Bedford Dies*, Wright & Brown, 1937; (under pseudonym Mary Dane) *Death Traps the Killer*, Wright & Brown, 1938; (under pseudonym John Donavan) *The Case of the Beckoning Dead*, R. Hale, 1938; *The Case Without a Clue*, Farrar & Rinehart, 1938; (under pseudonym Neal Shepherd) *Death Flies Low*, Constable, 1938; (under pseudonym Neal Shepherd) *Death Walks Softly*, Constable, 1938; *A Rope for the Hanging*, Cassell, 1938, Farrar & Rinehart, 1939; (under pseudonym Roger Garnett) *The Killing of Paris Norton*, Wright & Brown, 1938; (under pseudonym Roger Garnett) *The Creaker*, Wright & Brown, 1938; *Crime Against Children: An Aspect of Sexual Criminology*, Cassell, 1939; (under pseudonym Roger Garnett) *Danger—Death at Work*, Wright & Brown, 1939; *Murder at Radio City*, Farrar & Rinehart, 1939 (published in England as *A Knife for the Killer*, Cassell, 1939); (under pseudonym Neal Shepherd) *Death Rides Swiftly*, Constable, 1939; (under pseudonym John Donavan) *The Case of the Coloured Wind*, Hodder & Stoughton, 1939.

Murder in Wardour Street, Farrar & Rinehart, 1940 (published in England as *A Gun for a God*, Cassell, 1940); (under pseudonym Neal Shepherd) *Exit to Music: A Problem in Detection* (also see below), Constable, 1940; *The Clue of the Careless Hangman*, Cassell, 1940, published as *The Careless Hangman*, Farrar & Rinehart, 1941; (under pseudonym John Donavan) *The Case of the Plastic Man*, Hodder & Stoughton, 1940; *The Corpse on the Flying Trapeze*, Farrar & Rinehart, 1941; *Death Takes a Star*, Todd Publishing, 1943, Vallancey Press, 1944; *The "Sooper's" Case*, Todd Publishing, 1943; (under pseudonym Roger Garnett) *A Man Died Talking*, Wright & Brown, 1943; *The Laboratory Murder, and Other Stories*, Polybooks, 1944; *Corpse in the Circus*, Vallancey Press, 1945, Polybooks, 1946; *The Big Killing*, William Foster, 1946; *Death Spoke Sweetly*, Wright & Brown, 1946.

How Many Coupons for a Shroud?, Morgan, Laird & Co., 1946; *Murder Runs Wild*, A. Halle, 1946; *Strangely She Died*, Jenkins, 1946; *Exit to Music, and Other Stories* (includes *Exit to Music: A Problem in Detection*), Arthur Bonds, 1947, abridged edition published as *Death's Sweet Music*, Century Press, 1947; *Dressed to Kill*, Cassell, 1947; *The Hatchet Murders*, Martin & Reid, 1947; (under pseudonym Roger Garnett) *Eve Finds the Killer*, Martin & Reid, 1947; *26 Three Minute Thrillers: A Collection of Ingenious Puzzle Yarns*, Martin & Reid, 1947; *The Case of the Innocent Wife*, Martin & Reid, 1947; *Dusky Death*, Wright & Brown, 1948; *Fish Are So Trusting*, Century Press, 1948; *She Didn't Like Dying*, Sampson Low, Marston & Co., 1948; *No Coupons for a Shroud*, Sampson Low, Marston & Co., 1949; *Two Dead Charwomen*, Sampson Low, Marston & Co., 1949; *Death Takes an Editor*, Aldus Publications, 1949.

The Corpse Was No Lady, Sampson Low, Marston & Co., 1950; *An Outline of Scientific Criminology*, Philosophical Library, 1950, 2nd edition, St. Martin's, 1971; *Blood on the Stars*, Sampson Low, Marston & Co., 1951; *Death When She Wakes*, Evans Brothers, 1951; *He Hanged His Mother on Monday*, Sampson Low, Marston & Co., 1951; *The Lady Had a Gun*, Cassell, 1951; *Call Him Early for the Murder*, Cassell, 1952; *A Girl Died Singing*, Evans Brothers, 1952; *The Moon Was Made for Murder*, Sampson Low, Marston & Co., 1953; *Sing a Song of Cyanide*, Cassell, 1953; *Hangman's Clutch*, Werner Laurie, 1954; *Background to Murder*, Werner Laurie, 1955; *Death for Sale*, R. Hale, 1957; *Look in Any Doorway*, Cassell, 1957; *That Nice Miss Smith*, Muller, 1957; *This Friendless Lady*, Muller, 1957; *A Bullet for Midas*, Cassell, 1958; *Death and the Golden Boy*, Cassell, 1958; *Science in Crime Detection*, R. Hale, 1958, Emerson, 1960; *Death to the Ladies*, R. Hale, 1959.

The Concrete Maze, Cassell, 1960; *So Quiet a Death*, Cassell, 1960; *The Dear Dead Girls*, Cassell, 1961; *An Outline of Sexual Criminology*, P. Tallis, 1966, Hart Publishing, 1967; *Pattern of Murder*, Elek, 1966.

(Editor) *Papers from "The Criminologist,"* Wolfe, 1971, Library Press, 1972.

Author of hundreds of stories and articles, including ghost-written works, of theatre sketches, cabaret acts, and film treatments—many of them written under pseudonyms. Editor of *Criminologist*, 1966—, *Forensic Photography*, 1972—, *International Journal of Forensic Dentistry*, 1973—, and *Current Crime*, 1973—.

WORK IN PROGRESS: A biographical memoir of Edgar Wallace; *Encyclopaedic Dictionary of Crime and Criminology*; *Forensic Medical Dictionary*.

SIDELIGHTS: Nigel Morland, who has authored over 300 books, told *CA*: "I can offer little personal material about myself. I am, and always have been, a professional writer (mainly on crime) with little time for motivations or self analysis. I have always written for a living (I began at 11) and do whatever job is required of me. For the last nine years, however, I have been almost exclusively an editor of learned and scientific journals. Frankly, in 1965, I found that writing fiction bored me to tears and I gave it up." He added: "I have been badgered for years to write 'at least one more' adventure of my durable old 'Mrs. Pym of Scotland Yard' and have reluctantly toiled towards half a new novel about her; I may finish it one day but this is a matter for the gods, as I have just agreed to edit a new journal—this time for lawyers—for publication to begin in November, 1975, so. . . ."

* * *

MORRAH, Dermot (Michael Macgregor) 1896-1974 (Yorkist)

April 16, 1896—September 30, 1974; British journalist, expert on British royalty, court historian, assistant at royal ceremonial occasions, and author of books on the royal family. Obituaries: *New York Times*, October 2, 1974; *Washington Post*, October 2, 1974. (*CA*-29/32).

* * *

MORRIS, Freda 1933-

PERSONAL: Born May 22, 1933, in Heavener, Okla.; daughter of Fred O. (a land company owner) and Grace (Fields) Addison; married George Morris, April 16, 1954 (divorced, 1961); children: Crystal, Allen. *Education:* Eastern Oklahoma A & M College, A.S., 1953; University of Oklahoma, B.A., 1958, M.S., 1959; Illinois Institute of Technology, Ph.D., 1967. *Home and office:* 2301 Stuart St., Berkeley, Calif. 94705.

CAREER: Kankakee State Hospital, Kankakee, Ill., psychologist, 1962-67; University of California at Los Angeles Medical School, Los Angeles, Calif., assistant professor of medical psychology, 1968-72; private practice as a hypnotherapist in Berkeley, Calif., 1972—. *Military service:* U.S. Air Force, 1953-54. *Member:* Society of Clinical and Experimental Hypnosis, American Society of Clinical Hypnosis, American Society for Psychical Research.

WRITINGS: Self-Hypnosis in Two Days, Intergalactic Publishing, 1974. Contributor to psychology journals. Associate editor of *Self-Publishing Writer*, 1974—.

WORK IN PROGRESS: Researching articles on self-publishing; two books, *Hitchhiking Hypnotist* (an autobiography), and *Mutual Hypnosis in Two Days*; books on self-control of the autonomic system and on freeing children.

* * *

MORRIS, Jan 1926- (James Morris)

PERSONAL: Born October 2, 1926, in Clevedon, Somerset, England. *Address:* 9 Marlborough Bldgs., Bath, Somerset, England.

CAREER: Author.

WRITINGS: Conundrum, Harcourt, 1974.

WORK IN PROGRESS: "Pax Britannica," a trilogy about the British Empire.

SIDELIGHTS: Miss Morris wrote *Conundrum* to describe her transformation from male to female.

For additional biographical/bibliographical information see sketch for James (Humphrey) Morris in *Contemporary Authors*, Volume 1-4, revised, Gale, 1967.

* * *

MORRIS, Mary (Elizabeth) 1913-

PERSONAL: Born March 2, 1913, in Ironton, Ohio; daughter of J. Boyd (a civic leader and insurance broker) and Elizabeth (a civic leader; maiden name, Jones) Davis; married William Morris (a lexicographer, editor, writer, and columnist), February 8, 1947; children: Elizabeth (Mrs. Paul Downie), Susan, John, William F., Mary, Evan. *Education:* Ohio State University, student, 1930-34. *Politics:* Democrat. *Religion:* Episcopalian. *Home:* 355 South Beach Ave., Old Greenwich, Conn. 06870. *Office:* Los Angeles Times Syndicate, Times-Mirror Sq., Los Angeles, Calif. 90053.

CAREER: Ohio Republican Woman (monthly magazine), Columbus, editor, 1930-32; *Columbus Citizen*, Columbus, Ohio, Ohio State University campus correspondent, 1931-34; *The Ohio Shoemaker* (monthly publication), Columbus, editor, 1934-35; *Akron Beacon Journal*, Akron, Ohio, book reviewer, 1936-37; free-lance writer, 1937-41; American National Red Cross, Washington, D.C., founder and chief of labor section of public relations department, 1941-45; free-lance writer and editor, 1945—. Editor of *Northern Star*, Columbus, summers, 1930, 1931. *Member:* Theta Sigma Phi.

WRITINGS—All with husband, William Morris: *The Concise Dictionary of Famous Men and Women*, revised edition (Mary Morris was not associated with original edition), Grosset, 1951; *The Word Game Book*, Harper, 1959; *Dictionary of Word and Phrase Origins*, Harper, Volume I, K⅛&¾¼, Volume II, 1967, Volume III, 1971; *It's Easy to Increase Your Vocabulary*, Harper, 1957; *Harper Dictionary of Contemporary Usage*, Harper, 1975.

Executive editor of *Xerox Intermediate Dictionary*, Xerox Education Division, 1973; *Weekly Reader Beginning Dictionary*, Xerox Education Division, 1973; *Ginn Interme-*

diate Dictionary, Ginn, 1974; *Ginn Beginning Dictionary*, Ginn, 1974. Co-author of "Words, Wit and Wisdom," a column distributed by Los Angeles Times Syndicate, 1967—. Editor of church school manuals of National Council of the Episcopal Church, for Seabury, 1955-56. Writer for Grosset's *Words: The New Dictionary*, 1947. Contributor to *New Book of Knowledge*, *Encyclopedia International*, and *Grolier Universal Encyclopedia*. News editor of *Lantern* (Ohio State University daily newspaper), 1931-32, managing editor, 1932-33.

WORK IN PROGRESS: Two books, with husband, William Morris, for Harper; continuing research on usage and origin of language.

SIDELIGHTS: Mary Morris writes: "It is extremely distressing to us that politicians and advertising agencies not only abuse but distort the language. It is not only a matter of grammar but deliberate attempts to confuse, mislead, and even lie to the American people. Language is a means of communication and words have precise meaning. When we are subjected to what is called 'double-speak' there is no true communication."

* * *

MORTON, Richard Lee 1889-1974

September 20, 1889—September 8, 1974; American educator, historian, advisor to Colonial Williamsburg, and author. Obituaries: *Washington Post*, September 12, 1974. (*CA*-2).

* * *

MUECKE, D(ouglas) C(olin) 1919-

PERSONAL: Surname rhymes with "new key"; born August 28, 1919, in Adelaide, South Australia; son of Emil Hugo Franz (a farmer) and Johanna (Stewart) Muecke; married Audrey Weiss, March 29, 1945 (died, 1972); children: Frances, Stephen. *Education:* University of Adelaide, B.A. (honors), 1948; Oxford University, B.A., 1950, M.A., 1954. *Politics:* "Skeptic." *Religion:* "Unbeliever." *Home:* 34 Waimarie Dr., Mount Waverley, Victoria 3149, Australia. *Office:* Centre for General and Comparative Literature, Monash University, Clayton, Victoria 3168, Australia.

CAREER: University of Adelaide, Adelaide, South Australia, lecturer in English literature, 1950-54; University of Newcastle, Shortland, New South Wales, senior lecturer in English literature, 1955-61; Monash University, Clayton, Victoria, senior lecturer, 1962-70, reader in English literature, 1970—, director of Centre for General and Comparative Literature, 1971-74. *Military service:* Royal Australian Air Force, 1944-46.

WRITINGS: (Editor with Barbara Wall) *Well Measur'd Song*, F. W. Cheshire, 1968; *The Compass of Irony*, Methuen, 1969; *Irony*, Methuen, 1970. Contributor to literature journals.

WORK IN PROGRESS: Folktale Patterns in the Novels of Samuel Richardson; further research on irony.

* * *

MUIR, William Ker, Jr. 1931-

PERSONAL: Born October 30, 1931, in Detroit, Mich.; son of William Ker (a business executive) and Florence (Bodman) Muir; married Paulette Wauters, January 16, 1960; children: Kerry, Harriet. *Education:* Yale University, B.A., 1954, M.A., 1962, Ph.D., 1965; University of Michigan, J.D., 1958. *Politics:* Republican. *Religion:* Episcopalian. *Home:* 68 Plaza Dr., Berkeley, Calif. 94705. *Office:* Department of Political Science, University of California, Berkeley, Calif. 94720.

CAREER: University of Michigan, Ann Arbor, instructor in law, 1958-59; Davis, Polk, & Wardwell (law firm), New York, N.Y., attorney, 1959-60; Yale University, New Haven, Conn., lecturer in political science, 1960-67; Tyler, Cooper, Grant, Bowerman, & Keefe (law firm), New Haven, Conn., attorney, 1964-68; University of California, Berkeley, associate professor of political science, 1968—. *Awards, honors:* Corwin Prize from American Political Science Association, 1966, for *Law and Attitude Change*.

WRITINGS: Defending the "Hill" against Metal Houses, University of Alabama Press, 1955; *Prayer in the Public School*, University of Chicago Press, 1967, also published as *Law and Attitude Change*, 1973.

WORK IN PROGRESS: Streetcorner Politicians, a book about the police; research on legislative politics and on taxation policy.

* * *

MULLINS, Edwin (Brandt) 1933-

PERSONAL: Born September 14, 1933, in London, England; son of Claud (a lawyer) and Gwendolen (Brandt) Mullins; married wife, Gillian (a psychologist), 1960; children: Frances, Jason, Selina. *Education:* Oxford University, M.A. (honors), 1957. *Politics:* Socialist. *Home:* 7 Lower Common S., London SW15 IBP, England.

CAREER: The Sunday Telegraph, London, England, art critic, 1962-69; British Broadcasting Corp., London, England, television art correspondent, 1973—, presenter of radio programs, "Critics Forum," 1974—, and "Kaleidoscope," 1975—. Writer and film-maker. *Military service:* British Army, 1952-54.

WRITINGS: Souza, Anthony Blond, 1962; *Alfred Wallis*, Macdonald & Co., 1967; *Josef Herman*, Cory Adams & Mackie, 1967; *Braque*, Abrams, 1969; *Elisabeth Frink*, Lund Humphries, 1973; *The Pilgrimage to Santiago*, Taplinger, 1974. Author of about thirty documentary films for British Broadcasting Corp. and other film makers. Contributor to *Daily Telegraph*, *Guardian*, and *Financial Times*.

WORK IN PROGRESS: Scripts for twelve films about the National Gallery in London; a series of television dramas; a series of articles entitled "The Art of the Invaders," for the *Daily Telegraph Magazine*.

SIDELIGHTS: Mullins writes: "Professionally I write mainly about painting and sculpture—from books to film-scripts and newspaper criticism. I am not an art historian; I am concerned with the experience of art, not its dry bones. But I interpret art very broadly, to include travel, archeology, the environment, even natural history. I like to write about anything I can see—the visual world is my oyster. Privately I write lots of other things—mainly poetry. The relationship between words and our experience of images is what excites me most in writing. I also love practising the varied skills of writing for different media, though it is a love which embodies many moments of exasperation."

* * *

MUNBY, A(lan) N(oel) L(atimer) 1913-1974

December 25, 1913—December 27, 1974; British bibliographer, librarian, historian of English book collecting, university lecturer, and author. Obituaries: *AB Bookman's Weekly*, February 3, 1975.

* * *

MURPHY, Beatrice M. 1908-
(Beatrice Murphy Campbell)

PERSONAL: Born June 25, 1908, in Monessen, Pa.; children: one son. *Education:* Attended public schools in Washington, D.C. *Politics:* Democrat. *Religion:* Roman Catholic, *Home:* 117 R St. N.E., Washington, D.C. 20002.

CAREER: Has held secretarial positions at Catholic University of American and with U.S. Office of Price Administration, both Washington, D.C.; Negro Bibliographic and Research Center, Washington, D.C., founder, 1965, managing editor, 1965-72, and director, 1965—.

WRITINGS: (Editor) *Negro Voices*, Exposition, 1938; (contributor) Arna Bontemps, editor, *Golden Slippers*, Harper, 1939; (editor) *Ebony Rhythm*, Exposition, 1948, 2nd edition, 1968; (contributor) Langston Hughes and Bontemps, editors, *Poetry of the Negro*, Doubleday, 1949; *Catching the Editor's Eye*, Hobson, 1949; *Love is a Terrible Thing*, Hobson, 1949; (with Nancy L. Arnez) *The Rocks Cry Out*, Broadside, 1969; (editor) *Today's Negro Voices*, Messner, 1970. Contributor of poems and reviews to *Afro-American, Christian Herald, Easterner, Interracial Review, New York Times, Pulse*, and *Tan Confessions*.

Author of book review column, "Bookworm," for Afro-American newspapers, and of syndicated book review and poetry columns for Associated Negro Press. Feature and children's editor of *Washington Tribune*; editor of *Bibliographic Survey: The Negro in Print*, 1965-72.

SIDELIGHTS: Miss Murphy began to lose her eyesight in 1967, and she has undergone numerous operations since 1969 in a futile effort to save her sight.

BIOGRAPHICAL/CRITICAL SOURCES: Negro Digest, August, 1969.

* * *

MURPHY, Irene L(yons) 1920-

PERSONAL: Born October 23, 1920, in New York, N.Y.; daughter of George Vincent (a businessman) and Marie Agnes (Mackey) Lyons; divorced; children: Diane (Mrs. John P. Ramo), Bennett Justin. *Education:* Barnard College, B.A., 1941; Columbia University, M.A., 1946, Ph.D., 1970. *Politics:* Democrat. *Home:* 4701 Willard Ave., Chevy Chase, Md. 20015. *Office:* Federation of Organizations for Professional Women, 828 Washington St., Wellesley, Mass. 02181.

CAREER: Postmaster in Hicksville, N.Y., 1961-65; Federal Water Quality Administration, Washington, D.C., legislative specialist, 1969-70; author, political consultant, and lecturer, 1970-74; Federation of Organizations for Professional Women, Wellesley, Mass., executive director, 1974—. Member of national staff for Muskie for President campaign; member of town council of Village of Friendship Heights (Chevy Chase, Md.), 1973-75. *Military service:* U.S. Naval Reserve, active duty, 1942-46; became lieutenant senior grade. *Member:* American Political Science Association, Women's Caucus for Political Science, Women's Equity Action League. *Awards, honors:* Policy research award from Eagleton Institute of Politics, 1972-73.

WRITINGS: Public Policy on the Status of Women: Agenda and Strategy for the Seventies, Lexington Books, 1973. Author of columns in *Oyster Bay Guardian*, 1940-41, and *Mid-Island Times*, 1959-60.

WORK IN PROGRESS: Research on the impact of citizens' groups on land use politics, and on policy goals of the women's movement.

AVOCATIONAL INTERESTS: Travel (Europe).

* * *

MURPHY, Marion Fisher 1902-

PERSONAL: Born October 7, 1902, in St. Paul, Minn.; daughter of William Richard (an engineer) and Florence Frances (a teacher; maiden name, Finch) Fisher; married Raymond Edward Murphy (a geographer), 1926; children: Patrick Alan. *Education:* University of Wisconsin, B.A., 1925, M.A., 1930; University of Kentucky, graduate study, 1926-28. *Politics:* Independent. *Religion:* None. *Home:* 1299 Briarwood Ave., Deltona, Fla. 32763.

CAREER: Pennsylvania State College (now Pennsylvania State University), University Park, instructor in geography, 1931-45; free-lance writing and research in geography, 1945-75. Instructor in geography, University of New Hampshire, Keene, 1964-65. *Member:* National League of American Pen Women (Massachusetts president, 1964-66; Worcester president, 1962-64; auditor, 1970-72).

WRITINGS: (With husband, Raymond E. Murphy) *Pennsylvania: A Regional Geography*, Pennsylvania Book Service, 1937; (with Raymond E. Murphy) *Pennsylvania Landscapes*, Penns Valley, 1938, 3rd edition, 1974; (with Stephen B. Jones) *Geography and World Affairs*, Rand McNally, 1950, 4th edition, 1975; (with Ralph C. Preston and John Tottle) *Culture Regions in the Eastern Hemisphere*, Heath, 1971.

WORK IN PROGRESS: To Choose a Capital (tentative title).

AVOCATIONAL INTERESTS: Travel (United States and Africa).

* * *

MURRAY, G(erald) E(dward, Jr.) 1945-

PERSONAL: Born December 17, 1945, in Buffalo, N.Y.; son of Gerald Edward (a salesman) and Mary (Heffron) Murray; married Joanne Burns (a consumer consultant), October 9, 1971. *Education:* Canisius College, A.B., 1968; Northeastern University, M.A., 1970; Brown University, graduate study, 1971. *Home:* 142 North Ridgeland, #1-N, Oak Park, Ill. 60302. *Office:* Amco Industries, Carol Stream, Ill.

CAREER: Northeastern University, Boston, Mass., instructor in English, 1968-71; Allstate Insurance Co., Northbrook, Ill., public relations copy writer, 1971-73; Amco Industries, Franklin Park, Ill., public relations manager, 1973—. Co-director of poetry program at Cambridge Center for Adult Education, 1971. *Member:* Public Relations Society of America, Chicago Press Club. *Awards, honors:* Bridgeman scholar at Bread Loaf Writer's Conference, 1973.

WRITINGS—Poems: *A Mile Called Timothy*, Ironwood Press, 1972; *Holding Fast*, Brown University Press, 1973. Poems are represented in anthologies, including *Hellcoal Annual*, edited by Bruce McPherson, Brown University Press, 1972; *Heartland II: Poets of the Midwest*, edited by Lucien Stryk, Northern Illinois University Press, in press.

Contributor of monthly book column to *Chicago Sun Times* and *Chicago Daily News*, 1971—. Contributing editor of *Fiction International*, 1974—.

WORK IN PROGRESS: A collection of poems, *American Gasoline Dreams*, completion expected in 1975; a novel tentatively titled, *Orphans All*, 1976.

AVOCATIONAL INTERESTS: Travel.

* * *

MURRAY, Robert Keith 1922-

PERSONAL: Born April 9, 1922, in Union City, Ind.; son of Darrell Richard and Orpha Alice (Michael) Murray; married Evelyn Fay Keller (a teacher), December 7, 1943; children: Vicki Lynn, William Michael, Constance Lane. *Education:* Ohio State University, B.A. and B.Sc., 1943, M.A., 1946, Ph.D., 1949. *Politics:* Independent. *Religion:* Presbyterian. *Home:* 1222 Old Boalsburg Rd., State College, Pa. 16801. *Office:* Department of History, Pennsylvania State University, University Park, Pa. 16802.

CAREER: Ohio State University, Columbus, instructor in history, 1948-49; Pennsylvania State University, University Park, assistant professor, 1950-54, associate professor, 1954-59, professor of American history, 1959—, head of department, 1959-69, assistant dean of Graduate School, 1965-69, professor of history and fellow of Humanities Institute, 1973—. Consultant to Bicentennial Television Commission and National Archives Commission. *Military service:* U.S. Army, 1943-46; served in European theater; received three battle stars. U.S. Army Reserve, 1946-54.

MEMBER: American Historical Association, Organization of American Historians, American Association of University Professors (president of local chapter, 1969-70), Ohio Historical Society, Pennsylvania Historical Society, Phi Beta Kappa, Phi Alpha Theta, Phi Delta Kappa, Kappa Sigma. *Awards, honors: The Harding Era* was nominated for the Pulitzer Prize in history and biography, received the Phi Alpha Theta national book award, and the McKnight distinguished book award from the University of Minnesota, all 1969; distinguised research service award from the State of Ohio, 1970.

WRITINGS: Red Scare: A Study in National Hysteria, 1919-1920, University of Minnesota Press, 1955; *The Harding Era: Warren G. Harding and His Administration*, University of Minnesota Press, 1969; *The Politics of Normalcy: Governmental Theory and Practice in the Harding-Coolidge Era*, Norton, 1973.

Contributor: Stanley Elam, editor, *New Dimensions for Education Progress*, Phi Delta Kappa, 1963; Milton Plesur, editor, *The Twenties: Problems and Paradoxes*, Allyn & Bacon, 1969; John A. Garraty, editor, *Interpreting American History: Conversations with Historians*, Volume II, Macmillan, 1970; Richard O. Curry, editor, *Conspiracy: The Fear of Subversion in American History*, Holt, 1972; Frank O. Gatell, Paul Goodman, and Allen Weinstein, editors, *The Growth of American Politics: A Modern Reader*, Oxford University Press, 1972; James Brann and Thomas A. Emmet, editors, *The Academic Department or Division Chairman: A Complex Role*, Balamp Publishing, 1972; Julius Weinberg and John Cary, editors, *American Life: A Historical Reader*, Little, Brown, 1974.

Contributor to *Encyclopaedia Britannica*; also contributor of articles and reviews to history journals, including *Civil War History*, *Negro History Bulletin*, *Current History*, *Journal of American History*, *American Heritage*, *American History Illustrated*, *Historian*, and *Mississippi Valley Historical Review*.

WORK IN PROGRESS: It Happened in the Garden, an analysis of the Democratic Party in the 1920's, especially the fight in Madison Square Garden.

SIDELIGHTS: Murray writes: "I am a blue-water sailor and yacht racer. I own a home and a sailing auxiliary in the Virgin Islands where I spend a part of each year. I have sailed extensively in the Caribbean area, visiting all the Leeward and Windward islands at one time or another. My interest in the sea, in sailing, and in yachting in general is second only to my passion for interpreting our recent national past and for making American history live."

* * *

MURRAY, William Cotter 1929-

PERSONAL: Born June 18, 1929, in Milltown Malbay, Clare, Ireland; naturalized U.S. citizen in 1952; son of David (a victualler) and Susan (Cotter) Murray; married Barbara Hayes, March 4, 1960; children: Margaret, David, Eleanor, John. *Education:* Southern Connecticut State College, B.S., 1956; University of Iowa, M.A., 1959, Ph.D., 1964; University of California, Berkeley, graduate study, 1960. *Address:* Box 227, Route 1, West Branch, Iowa. *Agent:* Tim Seldes, Russell & Volkening, 551 Fifth Ave., New York, N.Y. 10017. *Office:* Department of English, University of Iowa, Iowa City, Iowa 52240.

CAREER: University of Iowa, Iowa City, instructor in modern British and Irish fiction, 1965—, acting director of International Writing Program, spring, 1974. Lecturer at Iowa Writers' Workshop, 1965-70; managing editor of Iowa School of Letters award for short fiction, 1969—. *Military service:* U.S. Army, 1951-53; served in Japan. *Member:* Authors Guild. *Awards, honors:* Meredith fiction prize, 1965, for *Michael Joe*.

WRITINGS—Novels: *Michael Joe*, Meredith, 1965; *A Long Way from Home*, Houghton, 1974. Contributor of articles and short stories to *New York Times Magazine*, *North American Review*, *Ford Times*, *American Heritage*, *December*, and *Irish Press*.

WORK IN PROGRESS: A book with Orville E. Kelly, a man terminally ill with lymphoma.

* * *

MUSSI, Mary 1907-
(Josephine Edgar, Mary Howard)

PERSONAL: Born December 27, 1907, in London, England; daughter of George (an author) and Jenny (Howard) Edgar; married Rudolph F. Mussi, March 6, 1934; children: Max Edgar, Susan Jane (Mrs. F. Renaga Sykes). *Education:* "Private and brief." *Home:* 27 Woodfield Ave., London SW16 1LQ, England. *Agent:* Irene Josephy, 35 Craven St., London WC25 5NG, England.

CAREER: Writer. *Member:* P.E.N., Crime Writers Association (London), Society of Women Writers and Journalists (London; past chairman). *Awards, honors:* Two awards from Romantic Novelists Association, Major Award, 1960, for *More Than Friendship*, and Elinor Glynn Award, 1961, for *Surgeon's Dilemma*.

WRITINGS—Novels; under pseudonym Josephine Edgar: *My Sister Sophie*, Collins, 1964, Pocket Books, 1974; *The Dark Tower*, Collins, 1966; *The Dancer's Daughter*, Collins, 1969, Dell, 1970; *The Devil's Innocents*, Collins, 1972;

The Stranger at the Gate, Collins, 1973; *Time of Dreaming*, Collins, 1968, Pocket Books, 1974; *The Lady of Wildersley*, McDonald & Jane's, in press.

Under pseudonym Mary Howard: *Windier Skies*, John Long, 1930; *Dark Morality*, John Lane, 1932; *Partners for Playtime*, Collins, 1938; *Strangers in Love*, Collins, 1939, Doubleday, 1941; *It Was Romance*, Collins, 1939.

The Untamed Heart, Collins, 1940; *Far Blue Horizons*, Collins, 1940, Doubleday, 1942; *Uncharted Romance*, Doubleday, 1941; *Devil in My Heart*, Doubleday, 1941; *Tomorrow's Hero*, Collins, 1941, Doubleday, 1942; *Reef of Dreams*, Collins, 1942; *Gay Is Life*, Doubleday, 1943; *Have Courage, My Heart*, Collins, 1943; *Anna Heritage*, Collins, 1944, Arcadia House, 1945; *The Wise Forget*, Collins, 1944, Arcadia House, 1945; *Family Orchestra*, Arcadia House, 1945; *Return to Love*, Arcadia House, 1946; *The Man from Singapore*, Collins, 1946; *Weave Me Some Wings*, Collins, 1947; *The Clouded Moon*, Arcadia House, 1948; *Strange Paths*, Collins, 1948; *Star-Crossed*, Collins, 1949; *First Star*, Arcadia House, 1949; *There Will I Follow*, Collins, 1949, White Lion, 1973.

The Young Lady, Arcadia House, 1950 (published in England as *Bow to the Storm*, Collins, 1950); *Mist on the Hills*, Arcadia House, 1950; *Sixpence in Her Shoe*, Collins, 1950, Arcadia House, 1954; *Two Loves Have I*, Collins, 1950; *Promise of Delight*, Arcadia House, 1952; *The Gate Leads Nowhere*, Collins, 1953; *Fool's Haven*, Collins, 1954, Arcadia House, 1955; *Sew a Fine Seam*, R. Hale, 1954; *Before I Kissed*, Collins, 1955; *The Grafton Girls*, Collins, 1956; *A Lady Fell in Love*, R. Hale, 1956; *Shadows in the Sun*, Collins, 1957; *Man of Stone*, Collins, 1958; *The Intruder*, Collins, 1959, White Lion, 1973.

The House of Lies, Collins, 1960, published as *The Crystal Villa*, Lenox Hill Press, 1970; *More Than Friendship*, Collins, 1960; *Surgeon's Dilemma*, Collins, 1961; *The Pretenders*, Collins, 1962; *The Big Man*, Collins, 1965; *The Interloper*, Collins, 1967; *The Repeating Pattern*, Collins, 1968; *The Bachelor Girls*, Collins, 1968.

The Pleasure Seekers, Collins, 1970; *Home to My Country*, Collins, 1971; *A Right Grand Girl*, Collins, 1972; *The Cottager's Daughter*, Dell, 1972; *Soldiers and Lovers*, Collins, 1973. Also author of *Who Knows Sammy Halliday?*

SIDELIGHTS: Mrs. Mussi told *CA* that she considers herself purely a "popular" writer, with "no axe to grind apart from writing a 'good read' for entertainment and relaxation." Her work falls into two categories: novels with a contemporary setting written under the pseudonym Mary Howard, and novels set in the nineteenth century, under the pseudonym Josephine Edgar. The author notes that the Josephine Edgar novels have been the more popular of the two in the United States.

* * *

MYCUE, Edward

PERSONAL: Born in Niagara Falls, N.Y. *Education:* Attended schools in New York, Texas, Massachusetts, California, Washington, D.C., Ghana, and Denmark. *Home:* 1200 Masonic Ave., San Francisco, Calif. 94117.

CAREER: Poet.

WRITINGS—Poems: *Damage within the Community* (first volume of "The Assault on Summer," a trilogy), Panjandrum, 1973; *Her Children Come Home Too*, Sceptre, 1973; *Chronicle* (a section of *Muddy on the Horizon*, see below), Mother's Hen, 1974.

WORK IN PROGRESS: "The Assault on Summer," Volume II: *Muddy on the Horizon*, Volume III: *Beyond the Source*.

* * *

MYLANDER, Maureen 1937-

PERSONAL: Born July 16, 1937, in Honolulu, Hawaii; daughter of Willard George (an Army officer) and Eunice (Murray) Root; married W. Charles Mylander III (a professor), November 21, 1964. *Education:* George Washington University, B.A., 1959. *Home and Office:* 1845 Beulah Rd., Vienna, Va. 22180. *Agent:* Marcia Higgins, William Morris Agency, Inc., 1350 Avenue of the Americas, New York, N.Y. 10019.

CAREER: Office of the Army Surgeon General, Washington, D.C., information specialist, 1959-61; National Institutes of Health, Bethesda, Md., information officer, 1962-65; University of California, San Francisco, editor for Medical Center, 1965-66; *Per-Se* (magazine), Stanford, Calif., senior editor and book review editor, 1967-68; *Smith* (magazine), New York, N.Y., Washington editor, 1969-70; writer, 1970—. Reporter for World Wide Medical News Service, 1964; congressional monitor for Common Cause, 1974. *Member:* National Press Club, American Newspaper Women's Club, Armed Forces Writers League, Association of the U.S. Army, Pi Beta Phi. *Awards, honors:* Bread Loaf writer's fellowship, 1974.

WRITINGS: The Generals: Making It, Military Style, Dial, 1974. Contributor of more than thirty articles to magazines and newspapers, including *Washington Monthly*, *Washington Sunday Star Magazine*, *National Observer*, *Army Times*, *Journal of the American Medical Association*, *Medical World News*, *Maryland Magazine*, and *Per/Se*.

WORK IN PROGRESS: Research on military affairs, public interest concerns, and government and politics.

AVOCATIONAL INTERESTS: Horseback riding, swimming, hiking, ice skating, antique collecting, interior decorating, reading, music (piano, autoharp, dulcimer, banjo).

* * *

NACHBAR, Jack 1941-

PERSONAL: Surname is pronounced *Knock*-bar; born January 8, 1941, in Minneapolis, Minn.; married Lynn Stanton (an artist), September 7, 1963; children: Luke, Jennifer, Elizabeth. *Education:* College of St. Thomas, B.A., 1964; Purdue University, M.A., 1968; Bowling Green State University, Ph.D., 1974. *Home:* 200 West Main, Portage, Ohio 43451. *Office:* Bowling Green State University, 100 University Hall, Bowling Green, Ohio 43403.

CAREER: University of Minnesota, Morris, instructor in English, 1966-70; Bowling Green State University, Bowling Green, Ohio, instructor in English, 1973-74, assistant professor of popular culture, 1974—. *Member:* American Studies Association, Popular Culture Association, Western Literature Association.

WRITINGS: (Editor) *Focus on the Western*, Prentice-Hall, 1974; *Western Films: An Annotated Critical Bibliography*, Garland, 1975. Co-editor of *Journal of Popular Film*.

WORK IN PROGRESS: Research on the American Indian in film.

NADEAU, Roland 1928-

PERSONAL: Born July 9, 1928, in Rhode Island; son of Roland and Angelina (Cote) Nadeau; married M. Beverly Knapp (an antiques dealer), 1952; children: Lorraine, Jean, Nicole. *Education:* New England Conservatory of Music, B.M. (with honors), 1951, M.M., 1953. *Religion:* Protestant. *Office:* Department of Music, Northeastern University, Boston, Mass. 02115.

CAREER: New England Conservatory of Music, Boston, Mass., teacher of piano and music theory at undergraduate and graduate levels, 1953-63; Northeastern University, Boston, Mass., 1963—, currently professor of music, chairman of department, and conductor of Brockton Symphony Orchestra. Has given piano concerts and lecture recitals, including several appearances with Arthur Fiedler and the Boston Pops Orchestra; church organist and choir director; has appeared on more than eight hundred radio and television programs; host of "A Note to You," weekly program on WHDH-Radio. *Awards, honors:* National Federation of Music Clubs individual merit award, 1973; radio and television award from Sigma Alpha Iota, 1974, for "A Note to You."

WRITINGS: Notes on the Symphony, Northeastern University Press, 1966; *Music for the Listener*, Allyn & Bacon, 1968; *The Symphony: Structure and Style*, Northeastern University Press, 1970, revised edition, Crescendo, 1973; *Scores and Sketches: An Anthology for Listening*, Addison-Wesley, 1970; *Listen: A Guide to the Pleasures of Music*, Allyn & Bacon, 1971; *Form in Music: Process and Procedure*, Crescendo, 1974.

Author of educational series for *Boston Globe*. Music critic and feature writer for *Christian Science Monitor*. Contributor of articles and reviews to *Music Educators Journal, Piano Teacher, Keyboard Junior*, and *Piano Quarterly*.

WORK IN PROGRESS: Revising *Listen: A Guide to the Pleasures of Music*, completion expected in 1976; *The Harmonic Process in the Music of Debussy*, publication by Northeastern University Press expected in 1976.

AVOCATIONAL INTERESTS: Organic gardening, fishing, shop work.

* * *

NADLER, Leonard 1922-

PERSONAL: Born July 3, 1922, in New York, N.Y.; married Zeace Moret (a consultant), February 22, 1945; children: David Allen, Mark Brian, Scott Elliot. *Education:* City College (now City College of the City University of New York), B.B.A., 1948, M.S., 1950; Columbia University, Ed.D., 1962. *Home address:* Box 536 Berwyn Station, College Park, Md. 20740. *Office:* Department of Education, George Washington University, Washington, D.C. 20006.

CAREER: Board of Education, New York, N.Y., teacher of business, 1950-54; New York State Department of Civil Service, Albany, training supervisor, 1954-57; Pennsylvania Department of Public Welfare, Harrisburg, chief of training division, 1957-59; U.S. Agency for International Development, training officer in Japan and Ethiopia, 1959-64; George Washington University, Washington, D.C., associate professor, 1965-71, professor of education, 1971—. President, Nadler Associates, 1968—; consultant in individual and organizational development to public and private organizations. *Military service:* U.S. Army, 1942-45. *Member:* American Society for Training and Development, Adult Education Association, National Association for Public and Continuing Education, American Academy of Political and Social Science. *Awards, honors:* Several awards from American Society for Training and Development.

WRITINGS: Employee Training in Japan, Education and Training Consultants, Inc., 1965; *Developing Human Resources*, Gulf Publishing, 1970. Editor of "Releasing Human Potential" series, Gulf Publishing, eight books, including *People, Evaluation & Achievement*, by George Nixon, 1973, and *Human Resources Development in Europe*, by H. Eric Frank, 1974. Contributor to journals in his field.

WORK IN PROGRESS: Research on management's role in developing human resources, types of human resource developers, and human resource development practices of foreign companies operating in the United States.

* * *

NAGEL, Thomas 1937-

PERSONAL: Born July 4, 1937, in Belgrade, Yugoslavia; naturalized U.S. citizen, 1944; son of Walter and Carolyn (Baer) Nagel; married Doris G. Blum, June 19, 1954 (divorced, 1973). *Education:* Cornell University, B.A., 1958; Oxford University, B.Phil., 1960; Harvard University, Ph.D., 1963. *Office:* Department of Philosophy, Princeton University, Princeton, N.J. 08540.

CAREER: University of California, Berkeley, assistant professor of philosophy, 1963-66; Princeton University, Princeton, N.J., assistant professor, 1966-69, associate professor, 1969-72, professor of philosophy, 1972—. *Awards, honors:* Guggenheim fellowship, 1966-67; National Science Foundation fellowship, 1968-70.

WRITINGS: The Possibility of Altruism, Oxford University Press, 1970. Associate editor of *Philosophy and Public Affairs*, 1971.

* * *

NAGLEE, David Ingersoll 1930-

PERSONAL: Surname is pronounced *Nay*-glee; born September 15, 1930, in Somers Point, N.J.; son of Jacob Hann (a printer and clergyman) and Dorcas (a legal secretary; maiden name, Ingersoll) Naglee; married Elfriede Elsa Kurz (a registered nurse and supervisor in a hospital), September 6, 1952; children: David Stephen, Joanna Jane, Deborah Ruth, Miriam Louise, Joy Ann. *Education:* Houghton College, A.B., 1953; Temple University, graduate study, 1956-58, A.M., 1963, Ph.D., 1966; Crozer Theological Seminary, B.D., 1959. *Politics:* Democrat. *Home:* 804 Piney Woods Dr., LaGrange, Ga. 30240. *Office:* LaGrange College, Vernon St., LaGrange, Ga. 30240.

CAREER: Ordained minister of the Methodist church in 1959; pastor of Methodist churches in Eagle, N.Y., 1952-53, Ellicottville and West Valley, N.J., 1953-56, Bridgeton, N.J., 1956-58, 1962-64, Port Norris, N.J., 1958-62, and Milville, N.J., 1964-66; pastor of Congregational church in LaGrange, Ga., 1966—; LaGrange College, LaGrange, Ga., assistant professor, 1966-67, associate professor, 1967-71, Flora Glenn Candler Professor of Religion and Philosophy, 1971-73, professor of religion and philosophy, 1973—, director of music, 1972-74. Visiting lecturer at Young Harris College, Lake City Junior College, and South Georgia College. Director of community tutoring program for indigent black children, 1966-68; member of advisory council of Maidee Smith Nursery (for black children), 1966—; member of LaGrange Human Relations Council, 1966—. Has presented religious lecture programs on WTRP-Radio, 1968-70, and WLAG-Radio, 1973—. Cellist with Columbus Symphony Orchestra (Georgia), 1969-74. Automotive consultant, 1971-72. *Military service:* U.S. Naval Reserve, active duty, 1948-52.

MEMBER: American Church History Society, American Association of University Professors, Georgia Philosophical Society, Mutual Concert Association (member of board of directors, 1967—; stage manager, 1967-72), Pi Gamma Mu, Masons.

WRITINGS: The History of the Methodist Church at Port Norris, privately printed, 1962; *The Hauls of Holy Ivy: Pensive Parables and Horrendous Hymns from the Chapel*, Pageant, 1974.

Hymns: "Hymn of Church Renewal," Southern New Jersey Annual Conference of United Methodist Church, 1969; "We Have Come of Age," United Methodist Musicians, 1970; "Contemporary Pilates," United Methodist Musicians, 1970; "Lenten Hymn," McDaniel, 1970.

WORK IN PROGRESS: From Font to Faith; *The Fathers of the Church and Antichrist*; *More Hauls for Holy Ivy*.

SIDELIGHTS: Naglee writes: "My sense of humor overcomes me quite frequently during periods of stress and trauma. The result is generally inspiration to produce something literary on the issue and save the day for sanity." *Avocational interests:* Keeping bees, cabinet making, racing cars (mechanic and member of pit crew), camping, fishing, archery, hunting, foreign travel (Middle East, Europe, Central America).

* * *

NAKAMURA, Hajime 1912-

PERSONAL: Born November 28, 1912, in Matsue, Japan; son of Kiyoji and Tomo (Takahaski) Nakamura; married Rakuko Nozu (a physician), August 3, 1944; children: Sumiko, Yasuko. *Education:* University of Tokyo, B.A., 1936, D.Litt., 1943. *Religion:* Buddhist. *Home:* Kugayama 4-37-15, Suginami-ku, Tokyo, Japan. *Office:* Eastern Institute, Inc., Meiko Bldg., Soto-Kanda 2-12-4, Chiyoda-ku, Tokyo, Japan.

CAREER: University of Tokyo, Tokyo, Japan, assistant professor, 1943-54, professor of Indian and Buddhist philosophy, 1954-73, professor emeritus, 1973—; Eastern Institute, Inc., Tokyo, director, 1970—. Visiting professor at Stanford University, 1951-52, University of Hawaii, 1959, 1963, 1964, 1969, at University of Florida, 1961-62, Harvard University, 1963-64, Van Hanh University (Saigon), 1973, and State University of New York at Buffalo, 1974-75. *Member:* Institut International de la Philosophie (titular member), Japan-India Society (president, 1960—), Japanese Association for Indian and Buddhist Studies (member of board of directors, 1954-73), All-Japan Buddhist Association (vice-president, 1964-66), Academy of Austria (corresponding member). *Awards, honors:* Imperial Prize from Academy of Japan, 1957.

WRITINGS: History of Early Vedanta, four volumes, Iwanami Press (Tokyo), 1950-57; (contributor) K. W. Morgan, editor, *Path of the Buddha: Buddhism Interpreted by Buddhists*, Ronald, 1956; *Ways of Thinking of Eastern Peoples*, Printing Bureau, Japanese Government, 1960, revised translation edited by Philip P. Wiener, East-West Center Press, 1964; *Japan and Indian Asia: Their Cultural Relationships in the Past and Present*, K. L. Mukhopadhyay (Calcutta), 1961; *History of the Development of Japanese Thought from A.D. 592 to 1868*, two volumes, Society for International Cultural Relationships (Tokyo), 1967, William Gannon (San Francisco), 1970; *Companion to Contemporary Sanskrit*, Motilal Banarsidas (Delhi), 1972, Verry, 1973; *Selected Works of Hajime Nakamura*, sixteen volumes, Shunjusha Co. (Tokyo), 1973. Contributing editor, *Journal of the History of Ideas*, editorial adviser, *Philosophy East and West*.

WORK IN PROGRESS: Comparative History of Thought: Parallel Developments (in English), for Kodansha (Tokyo).

* * *

NAMIKAWA, Banri 1931-

PERSONAL: Born October 29, 1931, in Tokyo, Japan; son of Ryo and Hisako Namikawa. *Education:* Nihon University, graduate, 1952. *Home:* 2-14, 5-chome, Kugayama, Suginami-ku, Tokyo 168, Japan. *Agent:* Orion Press, 1-55, Jonbocho-Kanda, Chiyoda-ku, Tokyo 101, Japan.

CAREER: Tokyo Broadcasting System, Tokyo, Japan, member of television news section, 1952-55; free-lance photographer, 1955—. Director and executive photographer, Reconstructive Borobudur (Indonesia), 1969; member and executive photographer, Asian Cultural Centre for UNESCO, 1970; executive photographer, EXPO '70 and EXPO '75. *Member:* Japan Professional Photographers Society, Photographic Society of Japan, New Photographers Society, Japan Pen Club, Japan-Turkey Society (director). *Awards, honors:* Frankfurt Photographers Society award, 1966; Cultural Prize, Spanish Government, 1967; award from Guadalajara City, 1968, for photography; special prize, Turkish Journalists Association, 1969; International Prize, Photographic Society of Granada, 1970; Grand Prix, Photographic Society of Japan, 1971; Cultural Decoration, His Imperial Majesty Mohamad Reza Pahlavi Aryamehr, Shahanshah of Iran, 1972; Art Grand Prix award for 7th Asian Games in Iran, 1975.

WRITINGS: Kamigami no iseki (title means "The Lost Splendour of the Ancient Remains"), Mainichi Newspapers (Tokyo), 1966; *Chichyukai rekishi no tabi* (title means "Trip to the Mediterranean Historical Remains"), Shuei-Sha, 1967; *Maya no shinden* (title means "Palaces in Maya"), Kodan-Sha, 1968; *Isulam no sekai* (title means "The World of Islam"), Kodan-Sha, 1968; *Orient no haikyo* (title means "Dawn of the Orient"), Kodan-Sha, 1968; *Nihon bi no tenkai* (title means "Genealogy of Japanese Beauty"), Kodan-Sha, 1969; *Girisha no shinden* (title means "The Greek Temples"), Kodan-Sha, 1969.

Romanesque to Gothic no seidoo (title means "The Romanesque and Gothic Cathedral"), Kodan-Sha, 1970; *Bizantine no bijutu* (title means "The World of Byzantine Arts"), Kodan-Sha, 1970; *Aruhambura kyuden* (title means "The Alhambra Palace"), Kodan-Sha, 1970; *Dariusu no isan* (title means "Darius the Great"), Kawade-Shobo, 1970.

Mexico, Kodansha International, 1971; *Spain*, Kodansha International, 1971; (editor) Ryo Namikawa, *Borobudoru*, Heibon-Sha, 1971; *Istanbul bijutukan* (title means "Istanbul Archaeological Museum"), Kodan-Sha, 1971; *Kyuros no isan* (title means "The Legacy of Cyrus the Great"), Tokyo International Press and Kawade-Shobo, 1971.

(With father, Ryo Namikawa) *Istanbul: Tale of Three Cities*, Kodansha International, 1972; *Teioo no eikoo* (title means "The Glory of the Persian Empire"), Shuei-Sha, 1972; *Sabaku to hoshi no inori* (title means "The Cultural Inheritance in Iraq and Syria"), Shuei-Sha, 1972; *Karei na genzo* (title means "The Magnificence of Turkey"), Shuei-Sha, 1972; *Persia no shihoo* (title means "The Great Treasures of Persia"), Mainichi Newspapers, 1972; *Kodai toshi no eikoo* (title means "The Great City of Ancient Times"), Koocho-Sha, 1972; *Maboroshi no maya bunmei* (title means "Phantasmal of the Great Civilization of Maya"), Keishoo-Sha, 1972.

Islam bijutsu (title means "Islam Arts"), Gakken, 1973; *Silk Road no kenchiku to bijyutu* (title means "The Arts and Architecture of Silk Road"), Koocho-Sha, 1973; *Iran*, Kodansha International, 1973; *Turk no shihoo* (title means "The Great Treasures of Turkey"), Mainichi Newspapers, 1973; *Chugoku toojiki* (title means "Chinese Ceramics of the Topkapi Sarayi Collection"), Heibon-Sha, 1974.

* * *

NANASSY, Louis C(harles) 1913-

PERSONAL: Born December 3, 1913, in Debrecen, Hungary; son of Kalman and Elizabeth (Olah) Nanassy; married Evelyn Horner Starkey, August 21, 1941; children: Richard Louis, Jean Evelyn (Mrs. Francis D. Harris). *Education:* Indiana University of Pennsylvania, B.S., 1936; Ohio State University, M.A., 1941; Harvard University, graduate study, 1942; Columbia University, Ed.D., 1952. *Religion:* Protestant. *Home:* 930 Lincoln Ave., Pompton Lakes, N.J. 07442. *Office:* Montclair State College, Upper Montclair, N.J. 07043.

CAREER: Chairman of business education department at high schools in Rockwood, Pa., 1936-37, and Manasquan, N.J., 1937-40, and teacher in Irvington, N.J., 1940-46; Paterson State, Paterson, N.J., assistant professor, 1946-51, associate professor, 1951-55, professor of business education, 1955-57; Montclair State College, Upper Montclair, N.J., professor of business education, 1957—, chairman of department, 1963-65. Visiting professor at Teachers College, Columbia University, 1962-63; visiting summer professor at other universities most years, 1950—, including Pennsylvania State University, 1955, University of Southern California, 1958, Brigham Young University, 1961, Ohio State University, 1963, Syracuse University, 1965, and University of Wyoming, 1973. Vice-president and guidance consultant, Sherwood School of Business, Paterson, 1950-56.

MEMBER: American Vocational Association, Association of Teacher Educators, International Society for Business Education, National Association for Business Teacher Education (member of executive board, 1964-66), National Association of Supervisors of Business Education, National Business Education Association (member of executive board, 1956-59), National Education Association, Eastern Business Teachers Association, Association of New Jersey State College Faculties (member of executive board, 1949-52), New Jersey Business Education Association (president, 1956-57), New Jersey Education Association, Delta Pi Epsilon, Kappa Delta Pi, Phi Delta Kappa. *Awards, honors:* Distinguished Service Award, Ohio State University, 1970; Outstanding Service Award, Delta Pi Epsilon, 1972.

WRITINGS: Clerical Payroll Project, Pitman, 1954; *Standard Payroll Project*, Pitman, 1955, 6th edition, in press; (with Albert C. Fries) *Business Timed Writings*, Prentice-Hall, 1960, revised edition, Glencoe Press, 1974; (compiler with W. H. Selden) *Business Dictionary*, Prentice-Hall, 1960; (with others) *College Typewriting*, Pitman, 1961; (with Nathan Krevolin) *Timed Writings for Teen-Agers*, Pitman, 1963; (with Leonard J. Porter) *Managing Your Money*, American Bankers Association, 1967; (with C. M. Fancher) *General Business and Economic Understandings*, 3rd edition (earlier editions by Fancher and J. F. Gallagher published as *Business Fundamentals for Everyone*), Prentice-Hall, 1968, 4th edition, 1973; (with Krevolin and John E. Whitcraft) *Personal Typing*, Pitman, 1970, 2nd edition, revised, in press; (with Herbert A. Tonne) *Principles of Business Education*, 4th edition (Nanassy was not associated with earlier editions), Gregg, 1970; (with Selden and Jo Ann Lee) *Ready Reference Manual for Office Workers*, Glencoe Press, in press.

Contributor of more than fifty articles to business education and other professional journals. Associate editor, *American Business Education Yearbook*, 1947-48; editor, *Business Education Index* (Delta Pi Epsilon publication), 1947—; editor and business manager, *Business Education Observer*, 1954-55; business manager, *American Business Education Quarterly*, 1956-58; basic business editor, *Business Education Forum*, 1966-68; editorial associate, *Eastern Business Teachers Association Yearbook*, 1967.

WORK IN PROGRESS: A revision of *Principles of Business Education* for 5th edition, publication by Gregg expected in 1977; a revision of *General Business and Economic Understandings* for 5th edition, with C. M. Francher and Anthony G. Porreca, publication by Prentice-Hall expected in 1978.

* * *

NANGIA, Sudesh 1942-

PERSONAL: Born March 14, 1942, in Multan, Pakistan; daughter of H. K. (a physician) and Janak (Radhu) Nangia; married J. K. Gupta, June 9, 1965; children: one son. *Education:* Government College for Women, B.A., 1961; Delhi University, M.A., 1963, LL.B., 1966, Ph.D., 1972. *Home:* W4, West Wing, Godavari Hostel, Jawaharlal Nehru University, New Delhi 57, India. *Office:* Centre for the Study of Regional Development, Jawaharlal Nehru University, New Delhi 57, India.

CAREER: University of Delhi, Delhi, India, lecturer in geography, 1968-69; Jawaharlal Nehru University, New Delhi, India, associate fellow, 1972—. *Member:* Indian Regional Science Association.

WRITINGS: (With R. K. Aggerwal) *Economic and Employment Potential of Archaeological Monuments in India*, Asia Publishing House, 1974. Contributor to *Analytical Geography*, and *Journal of Regional Science*.

WORK IN PROGRESS: A project on identification of agro-industrial growth centers and a strategy of their development.

AVOCATIONAL INTERESTS: Indian, vocal, and classical music.

* * *

NARASIMHA CHAR, K. T. 1903-

PERSONAL: Surname is listed in some bibliographical references as Char and as Narasimhachar; born February 26, 1903, in Mysore, India; son of K. Tatachar (an advocate) and Ambujamma Narasimha Char; married Rajalakshmi

Ramanchandrachar, November 25, 1925; children: Ramchander, Venugopal, Suvarna. *Education:* Nizam College, B.A., 1926; Law College, Poona, LL.B., 1926. *Politics:* "Nil." *Religion:* Hindu. *Home and office:* 24A Sarojini Devi Rd., Secunderabad 25, Andhra Pradesh, India.

CAREER: In practice of law as advocate and legal adviser, Secunderabad, Andhra Pradesh, India, 1933—. Osmania University, Hyderabad, lecturer in social legislation and comparative constitutional laws in Law College, 1950-59, lecturer in journalism, 1956-62, member of University Senate, 1950-52. Member of Secunderabad Municipal Corporation, 1949-51.

WRITINGS: (Editor) *A Day Book of Thoughts from Mahatma Gandhi*, Macmillan, 1951, reprinted, 1969; *The Constitution of India*, Eastern Law House (Calcutta), 1956; (editor and author of introduction) *The Quintessence of Nehru*, Allen & Unwin, 1962; *Profile of Jawaharlal Nehru*, Book Centre (Bombay), 1965; (editor) *Sanjiva Row's "The Indian Railway Act"*, 4th edition (Narasimha Char was not associated with earlier editions), Law Book Co. (Allahabad), 1965; (editor and reviser) H. G. Basu, *Fraud and Mistake in Law*, 2nd edition (Narasimha Char was not associated with earlier edition), Allahabad Law Agency, 1965; (editor) *Sanjiva Row's "The Indian Succession Act"*, 3rd edition (Narasimha Char was not associated with earlier editions), Law Book Co., 1966; *Principles and Precedents of Estate Duty*, Asia Publishing House (Bombay), 1970, Asia Publishing House (New York), 1971.

Unpublished plays: "Hell's Highway" (on prohibition), first produced in Secunderabad, India, 1932; "Atonement" (on untouchability); "The Torchbearers" (five-act drama on Gandhi); "Shining Lights" (on title-hunters). Writings include about twenty short stories and one hundred sonnets, some of the stories and sonnets published in Indian journals.

WORK IN PROGRESS: The Vagabond, a collection of prose poems.

SIDELIGHTS: "Literature is my first love," Narasimha Char writes, "though law is my profession. Influenced by Mahatma Gandhi, Abraham Lincoln, Tagore, and Kahlil Gibran."

* * *

NAUGLE, Helen Harrold 1920-

PERSONAL: Born August 11, 1920, in West Point, Miss.; daughter of Judson N. and Helen (a school principal; maiden name, Weddle) Harrold; married Jefferson B. Naugle (an engineer for Georgia Department of State Parks), June 1, 1942; children: Helen Elizabeth (Mrs. Lynn L. Deibler). *Education:* Mississippi State College for Women (now Mississippi University for Women), A.B., 1942; University of Mississippi, M.A., 1949; University of Alabama, Ph.D., 1968. *Religion:* Methodist. *Home:* 3929 Wieuca Rd., Atlanta, Ga. 30342. *Office:* Department of English, Georgia Institute of Technology, Atlanta, Ga. 30332.

CAREER: U.S. Armed Forces Institute, Mariannas Island, Guam, civilian assistant director, 1950; Department of Health, Education, and Welfare, Fort Buchanan, Puerto Rico, teacher, 1958-60; Georgia Institute of Technology, Atlanta, instructor, 1961-65, assistant professor, 1965-70, associate professor of English, 1970—. *Member:* Modern Language Association of America, National Council of Teachers of English, Conference on College Composition and Communication, American Society for Eighteenth Century Studies, American Association of University Women, Johnsonian Society, U.S. Army Officers' Wives' Club, Southeastern Society for Eighteenth Century Studies, South Atlantic Modern Language Association.

WRITINGS: A Concordance to the Poems of Samuel Johnson, Cornell University Press, 1973. Contributor to *Round the Mountain*.

WORK IN PROGRESS: Mighty Like a Whale: Dr. Samuel Johnson's Fishes, an analysis of Johnson's poetical vocabulary; *Bildad*, a study of the character in Sherwood Anderson's *I Want to Know Why*; a study of terminal illness in comparative literature.

AVOCATIONAL INTERESTS: Travel (Guam, Okinawa, Japan, Mexico, Panama, Trinidad, Puerto Rico, Caribbean Islands).

* * *

NAUMAN, St. Elmo, Jr. 1935-

PERSONAL: First syllable of surname rhymes with "law"; born March 11, 1935, in Phoenix, Ariz.; son of St. Elmo and Frances (a poet; maiden name, Wolf) Nauman; married June Anderson (an artist), August 20, 1954; children: Constance Ann, April Diana. *Education:* University of Chicago, A.B., 1954; Berkeley Divinity School, B.D., 1957; Boston University, Ph.D., 1969. *Religion:* United Church of Christ. *Home:* 1200 Roberts Rd., Newport News, Va. 23606. *Office:* Department of Philosophy, Christopher Newport College of the College of William and Mary, Newport News, Va. 23606.

CAREER: Rutgers University, New Brunswick, N.J., member of faculty, department of philosophy, 1968-71; College of William and Mary, Christopher Newport College, Newport News, Va., associate professor of philosophy, 1971—. Member of board of directors of Inter-Church Child Care Society, 1968-71. *Military service:* U.S. Naval Reserve, 1971—; present rank, lieutenant. *Member:* American Philosophical Association, Virginia Philosophical Association, Hampton Roads Philosophical Forum (executive secretary, 1973-74), Franklin Council of Churches (president, 1965-66), Masons.

WRITINGS: The New Dictionary of Existentialism, Philosophical Library, 1971; *Dictionary of American Philosophy*, Philosophical Library, 1973; (editor) *Exorcism through the Ages*, Philosophical Library, 1974; *Logic: Reality in Search of a Form*, McGraw, 1975; *Dictionary of Asian Philosophies*, Philosophical Library, 1975.

WORK IN PROGRESS: The Social Philosophy of N.F.S. Grundtvig.

* * *

NEHRLING, Arno H. 1886-1974

July 25, 1886—November 23, 1974; American horticulturist, educator, and author. Obituaries: *Publishers Weekly*, December 16, 1974. (*CA*-11/12).

* * *

NEISSER, Hans P(hilip) 1895-1975

September 3, 1895—January 1, 1975; German-born American educator, economist, and author. Obituaries: *New York Times*, January 3, 1975; *AB Bookman's Weekly*, January 27, 1975. (*CA*-15/16).

NELSEN, Hart M(ichael) 1938-

PERSONAL: Born August 3, 1938, in Pipestone, Minn.; son of Noah I. (a teacher) and Nova (a college professor; maiden name, Ziegler) Nelsen; married Anne Kusener (a writer, researcher, and historian), June 13, 1964; children: Jennifer. *Education:* University of Northern Iowa, B.A., 1959, M.A., 1963; Princeton Theological Seminary, M.Div., 1963; Vanderbilt University, Ph.D., 1972. *Politics:* Democrat. *Religion:* United Presbyterian. *Office:* Department of Sociology, Catholic University of America, Washington, D.C. 20064.

CAREER: Western Kentucky University, Bowling Green, assistant professor, 1965-70, associate professor of sociology, 1970-73; Catholic University of America, Washington, D.C., associate professor, 1973-74, professor of sociology and chairman of department, 1974—. *Member:* American Sociological Association, Association for the Sociology of Religion (member of executive council, 1974-77), Society for the Scientific Study of Religion, Religious Research Association, British Sociological Association, Southern Sociological Society. *Awards, honors:* Presbyterian denominations grant, 1966-68, for research study in Appalachia; National Science Foundation faculty fellowship, 1969-71; National Institute of Mental Health grant, 1969-72, to study the Black church as a socializing and politicizing agency; Russell Sage Foundation grant, 1972-73, to study church involvement and voting.

WRITINGS: (Editor with Raytha L. Yokley and wife, Anne K. Nelsen) *The Black Church in America*, Basic Books, 1971; (with Anne K. Nelsen) *Black Church in the Sixties*, University Press of Kentucky, 1975. Contributor to sociology journals, including *American Sociological Review*, *American Journal of Sociology*, *Social Forces*, *Journal for the Scientific Study of Religion*, *Sociological Analysis*, and *Review of Religious Research*.

* * *

NELSON, Ethel Florence 1913-
(Nina Nelson)

PERSONAL: Born March 20, 1913, in St. Johns, Newfoundland, Canada; daughter of Claude (a director) and Florence Noonan; married Anthony D. Nelson (a colonel in the British Army), June 25, 1938. *Education:* Attended Bishop Spencer College, St. Johns, Newfoundland. *Home:* The Knowle, Crown Lane, Virginia Water, Surrey GU25 4HW, England. *Agent:* Laurence Pollinger Ltd., 18 Maddox St., London W1R 0EU, England.

CAREER: Writer. Occasional broadcaster for BBC. *Member:* Guild of Travel Writers.

WRITINGS—Under name Nina Nelson: *Shepheards Hotel*, Barrie & Rockliff, 1960, reprinted, Chivers, 1974; *Holland*, Batsford, 1970; *Mena House*, Upper Egypt Hotels, 1970; *Denmark*, Batsford, 1973; *Tunisia*, Batsford, 1974; *Belgium and Luxembourg*, Batsford, 1975; *Egypt*, Batsford, in press.

Author of "Your Guide" series, published by Redman: *Your Guide to Egypt*, 1964; *... to Lebanon*, 1965; *... to Jordan*, 1966; *... to Syria*, 1966; *... to Czechoslovakia*, 1968; *... to Malta*, 1969.

Contributor to newspapers. Belgium and Iran editor for Fodor, 1974—.

WORK IN PROGRESS: *Malta* for Batsford.

AVOCATIONAL INTERESTS: Photography (contributor of photographs to her books), singing, music, growing flowers.

* * *

NELSON, Gideon E(dmund, Jr.) 1924-

PERSONAL: Born February 21, 1924, in Jacksonville, Fla.; son of Gideon Edmund (a businessman) and Floy (Parker) Nelson; married Betty Holmes, January 17, 1947; children: Rebecca Sue, Donald Kirby, Joseph Parker. *Education:* Emory University, A.B., 1948; University of Florida, M.S., 1950, Ph.D., 1954. *Religion:* Unitarian Universalist. *Home:* 2305 Cape Bend Ave., Tampa, Fla. 33612. *Office:* Department of Biology, University of South Florida, Tampa, Fla. 33620.

CAREER: Alabama College (now University of Montevallo), Montevallo, assistant professor, 1952-54, associate professor of biology, 1954-60; University of South Florida, Tampa, associate professor, 1960-68, professor of biology, 1968—. *Military service:* U.S. Army, 1944-46; became staff sergeant. *Member:* American Association for the Advancement of Science, American Institute of Biological Sciences, Association of Southeastern Biologists.

WRITINGS: (With Gerald Robinson) *Fundamental Concepts of Biology*, Wiley, 1967, 3rd edition, 1974; (with Albert Latina) *Experiments in Fundamental Concepts of Biology*, Wiley, 1967, 3rd edition, 1974; (editor with James D. Ray) *What a Piece of Work is Man*, Little, Brown, 1971; (editor with Ray) *Biologic Readings for Today's Students*, Wiley, 1971; (editor with Ray) *Readings in Contemporary Biology*, Wiley, 1974.

WORK IN PROGRESS: A human biology and a general biology textbook.

* * *

NELSON, Lawrence E(rnest) 1928-

PERSONAL: Born October 4, 1928, in Des Moines, Iowa; son of G. Ernest (a salesman) and Martha E. (a registered nurse; maiden name, Jessen) Nelson; married Mary Jane Ostrem (a teacher), June 30, 1951; children: Christopher P., Jeffrey D., Sarah Ruth, John M. *Education:* Drake University, B.A., 1950; Lutheran Theological Seminary, Gettysburg, Pa., M.Div., 1953; University of Pennsylvania, further study, 1963, 1964. *Politics:* Independent. *Home:* 1037 Morgan Ave., Drexel Hill, Pa. 19026. *Office:* Division for Parish Services, 2900 Queen Lane, Philadelphia, Pa. 19129.

CAREER: Assistant pastor of Lutheran church in Baltimore, Md., 1953-55; pastor of Lutheran church in Bettendorf, Iowa, 1955-57; Board of Parish Education, Philadelphia, Pa., secretary for youth work, 1957-64; Commission on Youth Ministry, Philadelphia, Pa., executive director, 1965-72; Division for Parish Services, Philadelphia, Pa., director of research and planning, 1973—. Host of "The Pastor's Desk," a series of weekly broadcasts on WOC-Television, 1956. Guest professor at Lutheran Theological Seminary (Gettysburg), 1970-71, and Lutheran Theological Seminary (Philadelphia), 1971. Chairman of Drexel Hill Interfaith Council on Human Relations, 1966-71; chairman of Joint Youth Publications Council, 1967-71. Vice-president of CIStems, Inc., 1973—. Member of board of directors of Holden Village, 1965-70.

WRITINGS: *Working with Young People* (monograph), Board of Parish Education (Philadelphia, Pa.), 1959; *Planning Your Catechetical Program* (monograph), Board of Parish Education (Philadelphia, Pa.), 1959; *Ways to Teach*

Teens, with teacher's guide, Fortress, 1965; *Foundations for Youth Ministry* (monograph), Commission on Youth Ministry (Philadelphia, Pa.), 1966; *Move It*, with teacher's guide, Lutheran Church Press, 1971; *Creative Ways to Use Youth Forum Books*, Nelson, 1971.

Author of "Cross at the Crossroads," a television script for WBAL-Television, 1974. Author of "Ask Noah," a column in *Now*, a publication of the Lutheran Church in America, 1968-69. Editor of *Viewpoint*, a newspaper for youth, 1962-64.

WORK IN PROGRESS: On Meaning and Making a Difference.

SIDELIGHTS: Nelson is interested in establishing a home for first-offender youth, and in helping them to develop personal competency, self-worth, and use of communication skills. *Avocational interests:* Carpentry (especially cabinet-making).

* * *

NELSON, Ralph C(arl) 1927-

PERSONAL: Born November 20, 1927, in Evanston, Ill.; son of Ragnar C. (a purchasing agent) and Irene (Sullivan) Nelson; married Louise Vanhee (a teacher), December 16, 1967; children: Christine, Max. *Education:* DePaul University, B.A., 1953, M.A., 1955; graduate study at University of Paris, 1958-59; Notre Dame University, Ph.D., 1960. *Religion:* Roman Catholic. *Home:* 389 Askin Blvd., Windsor, Ontario, Canada. *Office:* Department of Political Science, University of Windsor, Windsor, Ontario, Canada.

CAREER: Loyola University, Chicago, Ill., lecturer in philosophy, 1959-60; DePaul University, Chicago, Ill., lecturer in philosophy, 1960-61; University of Windsor, Windsor, Ontario, instructor, 1961-62, assistant professor, 1962-65, associate professor of philosophy, 1965-66, associate professor of political science, 1966-69, professor of political science, 1969—. *Military service:* U.S. Marine Corps, 1945-49. *Member:* Canadian Philosophical Association, Canadian Political Science Association. *Awards, honors:* Fulbright scholarship to University of Paris, 1958-59; Canada Council grant to Belgium, 1964.

WRITINGS: (With Walter L. White and Ron H. Wagenberg) *Jacques Maritain: The Man and His Achievement*, Sheed, 1963; (translator with others) Jacques Maritain, *Moral Philosophy*, Scribner, 1964; *Introduction to Canadian Government and Politics*, Holt, 1972.

WORK IN PROGRESS: A study of political thought in France.

* * *

NEMIRO, Beverly Anderson 1925-

PERSONAL: Born May 29, 1925, in St. Paul, Minn.; daughter of Martin (a contractor) and Anna Mae Anderson; married Jerome Nemiro (president of a chain of stores); children: Guy; Lee, Dee (twins). *Education:* Reed College, student, 1942-44; University of Colorado, B.A., 1947. *Home:* 476 Westwood Dr., Denver, Colo. 80206. *Agent:* Malcolm Reiss, Paul R. Reynolds, Inc., 599 Fifth Ave., New York, N.Y. 10017. *Office:* Department of Continuing Education, University of Colorado, Denver Center, Denver, Colo.

CAREER: Public school teacher in Seattle, Wash., summers, 1945-46; Denver Dry Goods Co., Denver, Colo., fashion director, 1948-51; Denver Market Week Association, Denver, fashion director, 1952-53; KRMA-TV, Denver, moderator of "Your Preschool Child," 1955-56; University of Colorado, Denver Center, instructor in writing, 1970—. Fashion model, 1951-58.

MEMBER: National Woman Writers, Authors Guild of Authors League of America, Society of Magazine Writers, Colorado Authors League (member of board of directors), Denver Women's Press Club. *Awards, honors:* Best article of the year award from Colorado Authors League, 1969, for "Be Your Teenage Prettiest," and best non-fiction book of the year award, 1972, for *Busy People's Cookbook; House Beautiful* award, 1969, for *High Altitude Cookbook; New York Times* list of 100 best books of the year included *High Altitude Cookbook*, 1969, and *Busy People's Cookbook*, 1971.

WRITINGS: (With Donna Hamilton) *The Complete Book of High Altitude Baking*, Sage Books, 1961; (with Hamilton) *Colorado a la Carte*, Sage Books, 1963; (with Marie Von Allman) *The Lunch Box Cookbook*, Sage Books, 1965; (with Hamilton) *Colorado a la Carte: Series II*, Sage Books, 1966; (with Hamilton) *Where to Eat in Colorado*, Heather Enterprises, 1967; (with Hamilton) *The High Altitude Cookbook*, Random House, 1969; *The Busy People's Cookbook* (Better Homes and Gardens Book Club selection), Random House, 1971. Contributor of articles on cooking, self-improvement, fashion, and travel to magazines, including *Better Homes and Gardens, Extension, Today's Health, Sunset, Contemporary Colorado*, and *Rocky Mountain News*.

WORK IN PROGRESS: Fiction and nonfiction.

AVOCATIONAL INTERESTS: Skiing, bicycling, travel, music, tennis, yoga, entertaining, international cooking.

* * *

NETER, John 1923-

PERSONAL: Born February 8, 1923, in Germany; married Dorothy Rachman, 1951; children: Ronald, David. *Education:* University of Buffalo, B.S., 1943; University of Pennsylvania, M.B.A., 1947; Columbia University, Ph.D., 1949. *Office:* College of Business Administration, University of Minnesota, Minneapolis, Minn. 55455.

CAREER: Syracuse University, Syracuse, N.Y., assistant professor of business statistics, 1949-55; University of Minnesota, Minneapolis, associate professor, 1955-58, professor of quantitative analysis, 1958—. U.S. Bureau of the Census, supervisory mathematical statistician, 1959-60, consultant, 1960-65. Member of City of St. Louis Park Planning Commission, 1974—. *Military service:* U.S. Army, 1943-45. *Member:* American Statistical Association (fellow; member of board of directors, 1975—), Institute of Management Science, American Institute of Decision Sciences (member of council, 1973; vice-president, 1975), Institute of Mathematical Statistics, American Society for Quality Control, American Association for the Advancement of Science (fellow). *Awards, honors:* Ford Foundation faculty research fellow at University of Minnesota, 1957-58.

WRITINGS: (With L. L. Vance) *Statistical Sampling for Auditors and Accountants*, Wiley, 1956; (with G. A. Whitmore and William Wasserman) *Self-correcting Problems in Statistics*, Allyn & Bacon, 1970; (with Wasserman and Whitmore) *Fundamental Statistics for Business and Economics*, Allyn & Bacon, 1956, 4th edition, 1974; (with Wasserman) *Applied Linear Statistical Models*, Irwin, 1974. Contributor to professional journals.

NEVE, Lloyd 1923-

PERSONAL: Surname is pronounced "navy"; born October 16, 1923; son of Anders Valdemar and Dora (Larsen) Neve; married Muriel Eileen Hayward (a university teacher), August 30, 1949; children: Kaj Allan, Rachael Lee (Mrs. James Benbow), Nina Jean, Leif Jonathan, Kim Arthur, Peter Joel. *Education:* Dana College, B.A., 1945; Trinity Theological Seminary, Blair, Neb., B.D., 1947; Union Theological Seminary, New York, N.Y., S.T.M., 1955, Ph.D., 1967. *Politics:* Democrat. *Home and office:* 24-10-one chome, Kyonancho, Musashino City, Tokyo 180, Japan.

CAREER: Ordained minister of Lutheran Church, 1947; rural evangelistic missionary in Kyushu, Japan, 1949-60; Japan Lutheran Theological Seminary, Tokyo, Japan, associate professor, 1961-67, professor of Old Testament, 1967—. *Member:* Society of Biblical Literature.

WRITINGS: *The Spirit of God in the Old Testament*, Seibunsha, 1972; *Japan: God's Door to the Far East*, Augsburg, 1973; *Rekidaishi* (title means "Commentary on Chronicles I and II"), Seibunsha, 1974.

SIDELIGHTS: Neve is competent in Japanese, Hebrew, German, French, and Greek.

* * *

NEWCOMB, Duane G(raham) 1929- (Tom Firestone)

PERSONAL: Born February 12, 1929, in Oklahoma City, Okla.; son of Wilbur Kenneth (a teacher and businessman) and Grace (Graham) Newcomb; married E. Jacqueline Piazza (a bookstore owner), October, 1971; children: Katherine Ann, Ronald Alan. *Education:* University of Washington, Seattle, B.S., 1951, M.S., 1953; graduate study at University of Colorado, 1955, University of Oklahoma, 1956, California State University, San Jose, 1966, and Sierra College, 1973. *Home:* 10410 Scott Rd., Newcastle, Calif. 95658. *Agent:* Alex Jackinson, 55 West 42nd St., New York, N.Y. 10036. *Office:* 3475 Sunset Blvd., Rocklin, Calif. 95677.

CAREER: U.S. Geological Survey, Sacramento, Calif., photogrametric cartographer, 1953-56; West Valley Firestone (retail store), Los Gatos, Calif., owner, 1957-62; professional writer in Rocklin, Calif., 1962—. Teacher of writing at American River College, 1967—. *Military service:* U.S. Army, Chemical Corps, 1953-55. *Member:* Associated Business Writers of America, Phi Sigma, Phi Delta Kappa.

WRITINGS: *Mobile Home Gardening Guide: 1963*, Trail-R Club of America, 1963; *Trailering in Canada*, Trail-R Club of America, 1964; *Trailer Owner's Driving Guide*, Trail-R Club of America, 1965; *How to Make Big Money Freelance Writing*, Parker Publishing, 1970; *Spare Time Fortune Guide*, Parker Publishing, 1973; *The Wonderful World of Houseboating*, Prentice-Hall, 1974; *Word Power Makes the Difference*, Parker Publishing, 1974; *The Postage Stamp Gardening Book*, J. P. Tarcher, 1975; *The Poor Man's Guide to Great Riches*, Parker Publishing, in press. Contributor, sometimes under pseudonym Tom Firestone, of more than three thousand articles to *American Home*, *Field and Stream*, *Outdoors*, *Trailer Life*, and other magazines. Contributor of trailering column to *Trailer Life*, 1962—. Field and western editor of *Trailer Life*, 1964—, *Western Materials Handling*, 1967-69, *Family Houseboating*, 1967-69, *Recreational Vehicle Retailer*, 1973—, and other publications.

WORK IN PROGRESS: *Frustrated America*, a book that deals with frustration with work and how Americans have coped with the problem, especially the dropping out syndrome of several million middle class white collar workers in the over twenty thousand dollar income bracket.

SIDELIGHTS: Newcomb told *CA*: "My students in American River College classes have published almost a half million dollars worth of articles. Current book class puts about ten books under contract each semester." *Avocational interests:* Conservation.

BIOGRAPHICAL/CRITICAL SOURCES: *San Jose Mercurs News*, November 20, 1966; *Organic Gardening*, January, 1974.

* * *

NEWMAN, Harold 1927-

PERSONAL: Born May 18, 1927, in New York, N.Y.; married Lona Gilbert, July 1, 1962; children: Alan. *Education:* Brooklyn College of the City University of New York, B.A., 1948; Columbia University, Ed.D., 1964. *Home:* 84-39 153 Ave., Howard Beach, N.Y. 11414. *Office:* Department of Reading and Language Arts, Jersey City State College, 2039 Kennedy Blvd., Jersey City, N.J. 07305.

CAREER: Junior high school and high school teacher of English, reading, and social studies in New York, N.Y., 1948-66; Jersey City State College, Jersey City, N.J., professor of reading and language arts, 1966—. Consultant to and member of board of directors of Education Resources Information Center, 1972—. *Member:* International Reading Association, National Council of Teachers of English, College Reading Association, Phi Delta Kappa, Kappa Delta Pi.

WRITINGS: *Reading Disabilities: Identification and Treatment*, Odyssey, 1969; *Your Child's Reading and What You Can Do about It*, MSS Information, 1972; *Effective Language Arts Practices for Elementary Teachers*, Wiley, 1973. Contributor of more than twenty-five articles to journals.

WORK IN PROGRESS: Research on parent education, and on teacher training in reading and languages.

* * *

NEWMARK, Joseph 1943-

PERSONAL: Born December 26, 1943, in New York, N.Y.; son of Jack Morris (a clerk) and Sylvia (a bookkeeper; maiden name, Weinstein) Newmark; married Gertrude Hoffman (a teacher), November 24, 1968; children: Sharon Renee, Rochelle Fay. *Education:* Brooklyn College of the City University of New York, B.S. (magna cum laude), 1965, M.A., 1967; New York University, Ph.D., 1973. *Home:* 1432 58th St., Brooklyn, N.Y. 11219. *Office:* Department of Mathematics, Staten Island Community College, 715 Ocean Ter., Staten Island, N.Y. 10301.

CAREER: Private high school teacher of mathematics in Brooklyn, N.Y., 1964-68; Brooklyn College of the City University of New York, Brooklyn, N.Y., lecturer, 1966-68, part-time assistant professor, 1972-74, part-time associate professor of mathematics, 1974—; Staten Island Community College of the City University of New York, Staten Island, N.Y., associate professor of mathematics, 1968—. *Member:* American Association for the Advancement of Science, Mathematical Association of America, New York State Mathematics Association of Two Year

Colleges, Phi Beta Kappa, Pi Mu Epsilon. *Awards, honors:* National Science Foundation grant, 1974-76, for the production of educational mathematics tapes.

WRITINGS: (With Frances Lake) *Mathematics as a Second Language*, Addison-Wesley, 1974; *Statistics and Probability in Modern Life*, Holt, 1975. Contributor to *Bulletin of the Psychonomic Society*.

WORK IN PROGRESS: An elementary calculus book for social science students, for Prentice-Hall; a self-study oriented statistics project.

AVOCATIONAL INTERESTS: Traveling, vegetable gardening, photography, building things.

* * *

NEWTON, Byron Louis 1913-

PERSONAL: Born March 20, 1913, in Monticello, Ark.; son of Frederick E. (a logging contractor) and Mary E. (Stinson) Newton; married Ola May Yates, December 22, 1935; children: Richard M., Mary Carolyn, Janis M. *Education:* Northwestern State College, B.S., 1935; graduate study at University of Pittsburgh, 1939; Oklahoma State University, M.S., 1939, Ed.D., 1945. *Politics:* Democrat. *Religion:* Presbyterian preference. *Home:* 3223 Northwest Walnut Blvd., Corvallis, Ore. 97330. *Office:* Department of Accounting and Management Science, Oregon State University, Corvallis, Ore. 97331.

CAREER: North Texas State University, Denton, instructor, 1940-42; Oklahoma State University, Naval Training School, WAVES, member of faculty, 1942-45; North Texas State University, assistant professor of business administration, 1945-47; Oregon State University, Corvallis, assistant professor, 1947, associate professor, 1949-54, professor of business administration, 1954-72. Consultant, Management Information System, Bay Area Rapid Transit District, San Francisco, Calif., 1970-72. *Military service:* U.S. Naval Reserve, 1948.

WRITINGS: *Naval Correspondence*, Naval School, Oklahoma State University, 1943; *Accounting and the Analysis of Financial Data*, McGraw, 1958; *Statistics for Business*, Science Research Associates, 1973. Contributor to journals in his field.

* * *

NEWTON, William Simpson 1923- (Gilroy Mitcham, Macdonald Newton)

PERSONAL: Born December 31, 1923, in Sunderland, Durham, England; son of John Scarfe (a director) and Lilian (Simpson) Newton; married Margo Thompson, August 28, 1956; children: Anne, Graham. *Education:* Attended Sunderland Technical College and School of Accountancy, Glasgow, Scotland. *Politics:* Conservative. *Religion:* Church of England. *Home:* Dineiro, 9 Barnes Rd., Mowden Park, Darlington, Durham DL3 9BH, England.

CAREER: Formerly business representative for Vanx and Associated Breweries Ltd., and sales manager of Francose Ltd., both of Sunderland, Durham, England; writer. Member of municipal council, magistrate, and member of police authority in borough of Darlington. Interviewer for British Broadcasting Corp. program, "Radio Cleveland"; chairman of North of England Open Air Museum. *Military service:* Royal Air Force, 1940-41; became captain. *Member:* Crime Writers Association (London), Magistrates Association, Veteran Motorists Association.

WRITINGS—Novels; under pseudonym Gilroy Mitcham: *The Full Stop*, Roy, 1957; *The Man from Bar Harbour*, Roy, 1958; *The Dead Reckoning*, Roy, 1960; *Uncertain Judgement*, Dobson, 1961, Roy, 1962; *The Dark Echoes*, Dobson, 1962; *The Violent Ones*, Dobson, 1965; *If the Price Is Right*, Dobson, 1965.

Under pseudonym Macdonald Newton: *To Have and to Hold*, T. V. Boardman, 1963.

Also author of *Through Endeavour to Achievement*, 1972, *Personal Choice*, 1972, *No Way Back*, 1973, *Arno*, 1974. Author of a television play, "Thistle and Catchpole," 1974. Writer of newspaper column, "Off the Cuff," in the *Northern Despatch* (Darlington), and of a weekly column, "Newton's Law on Plain Cooking."

WORK IN PROGRESS: *History of Darlington*, completion expected in 1977.

* * *

NICHOL, B(arrie) P(hillip) 1944-

PERSONAL: Name is often cited as bpNichol; born September 30, 1944, in Vancouver, British Columbia, Canada; son of G. F. and Avis Aileen (Workman) Nichol. *Education:* University of British Columbia, elementary basic teaching certificate, 1963. *Home:* 61 Admiral Rd., Toronto, Ontario M5R 2L4, Canada. *Agent:* Linda McCartney, Box 193, Station S, Toronto, Ontario M5M 4L7, Canada. *Office:* c/o Village Bookstore, 239 Queen St. W., Toronto, Ontario, Canada.

CAREER: Worked briefly as an elementary school teacher; Therafields Environmental Centre Ltd., "theradramist," 1966—. Co-founder, Toronto Research Group, 1972. Member of The Four Horsemen (a collaborative sound poem group), 1970—. *Awards, honors:* Governor General's Award, 1970; three grants from Canada Council.

WRITINGS—All poetry: *bp* (includes recording and packet of concrete poem objects), Coach House Press, 1967; (editor) *The Cosmic Chef: An Evening of Concrete*, Oberon Press, 1970; *Still Water*, Talonbooks, 1970; *ABC: the aleph beth book*, Oberon Press, 1971; *Monotones*, Talonbooks, 1971; *The Martyrology Book I & II*, Coach House Press, 1972; *Love: a book of remembrances*, Talonbooks, 1974.

Pamphlets—All published by Ganglia Press, except as indicated: *Cycles Etc.*, 7 Flowers Press, 1965; *Scraptures: 2nd Sequence*, 1965; *Calendar*, Openings Press, 1966, 2nd edition published as *A New Calendar*, Ganglia Press, 1969; (with David Aylward) *Strange Grey Town*, 1966; *Scraptures: 3rd Sequence*, 1966; *Scraptures: 4th Sequence*, Press Today, 1966; *Fodder Folder*, 1966; *Portrait of David*, 1966; *A Vision in the U of T Stacks*, 1966; *A Little Pome for Yur Fingertips*, 1966; *Langwedge*, 1966; *Alphabit*, 1966; *Stan's Ikon*, 1966; *The Birth of O*, 1966; *Chocolate Poem*, privately printed, 1966.

Last Poem with You in Mind, 1967; *Scraptures: 10th Sequence*, 1967; *Scraptures: 11th Sequence*, Fleye Press, 1967; *Ruth*, Fleye Press, 1967; *The Year of the Frog*, 1967; *Konfessions of an Elizabethan Fan Dancer*, Writers Forum, 1967; *Ballads of the Restless Are*, Runcible Spoon, 1968; *Dada Lama*, Cavan McCarthy, 1968; *D.A. Dead* (a lament), grOnk, 1968; *Kon 66 & 67*, grOnk, 1968; *The Complete Works*, 1968; *3rd Fragment from a Poem Continually in the Process of Being Written*, 1969; *Astronomical Observations: July 69*, 1969; *Sail*, 1969.

A Condensed History of Nothing, 1970; *Lament*, 1970, 2nd

edition, Writers Forum, 1970; *Beach Head*, Runcible Spoon, 1970; *The Captain Poetry Poems*, Blew Ointment Press, 1972; (with Steve McCaffery) *Collbrations*, grOnk, 1972; *The Other Side of the Room*, Weed/Flower Press, 1972.

Prose: *Two Novels* (contains "Andy" and "For Jesus Lunatick"), Coach House Press, 1969, 2nd edition, 1971; *Nights on Prose Mountain* (short prose), grOnk, 1969.

Work is represented in anthologies as follows: *Concrete Poetry: Britain, Canada, United States*, Hansjorg Mayer (Stuttgart), 1966; *New Wave Canada*, edited by Raymond Souster, Contact Press, 1966; *Anthology of Concrete Poetry*, edited by Emmett Williams, Something Else Press, 1967; *Concrete Poetry*, edited by M. E. Solt and Willis Barnstone, Indiana University Press, 1969.

Collaborated with Barbara Caruso on volume of prints, *The Adventures of Milt the Morph in Colour*, Seripress, 1973. Author of six-episode radio serial, "Little Boy Lost Meets Mother Tongue," broadcast by Canadian Broadcasting Corp., 1969. Contributing editor, *Open Letter* (second series); editor, *Ganglia*, 1965-66, *grOnk*, 1967—, and *Synapsis*, 1969-71.

WORK IN PROGRESS: The Martyrology, book IV.

SIDELIGHTS: Nichol told *CA*: "i define language as *all* the avenues through which people are aware of themselves and others. hence the importance of my work as a theradramist as part of my commitment to this process." Nichol's poetry is recorded on his album, "Motherlove," Allied Records, 1968, and on "Canadada" (as one of The Four Horsemen), Griffin House, 1972.

BIOGRAPHICAL/CRITICAL SOURCES: Frank Davey, *From There to Here*, Press Porcepic, 1974; *Essays in Canadian Criticism*, volume I, number I, 1974.

* * *

NICHOLAS, Robert L(eon) 1937-

PERSONAL: Born December 10, 1937, in Lebanon, Ore.; son of Elmer L. Nicholas and Luella (Haberling) Nicholas Haffner; married Carole Roberts (a teacher), June 11, 1967; children: Scott Alan, Paul Elliot. *Education:* Attended Midwest Theological Seminary, Stanberry, Mo., 1955-56, and Northwest Missouri State College, 1956-57; University of Oregon, B.A., 1959, M.A., 1963, Ph.D., 1967; also studied at University of California, Los Angeles, summer, 1960, and University of Madrid, 1963-64. *Politics:* "Democrat—most of the time." *Home:* 24 North Prospect Ave., Madison, Wis. 53705. *Office:* Department of Spanish and Portuguese, University of Wisconsin, Van Hise Hall, Madison, Wis. 53706.

CAREER: University of Wisconsin, Madison, instructor, 1965-67, assistant professor, 1967-71, associate professor of Spanish and Portuguese, 1971—, director of inter-university foreign studies program in Madrid, 1972-73. *Member:* Modern Language Association of America, American Association of Teachers of Spanish and Portuguese.

WRITINGS: El mundo de hoy (title means "Today's World"), Scott, Foresman, 1971; *The Tragic Stages of Antonio Buero Vallejo*, Estudios de Hispanofila, 1972; (with Eduardo Neale-Silva) *Fundamentos del espanol* (title means "Foundations of Spanish"), Scott, Foresman, in press. Contributor to *Revista de estudios hispanicos*.

WORK IN PROGRESS: Editing *Lauro Olmo: Playwright of the People*, for Castalia.

AVOCATIONAL INTERESTS: Books, animals, farming.

NICHOLS, Charles H(arold) 1919-

PERSONAL: Born July 6, 1919, in New York; son of Charles F. (a clergyman) and Julia (King) Nichols; married Mildred Thompson (a career counselor), August 19, 1950; children: David, Keith, Brian. *Education:* Brooklyn College (now Brooklyn College of the City University of New York), B.A. (with honors), 1942; Brown University, Ph.D., 1948. *Politics:* Independent. *Religion:* Society of Friends (Quakers). *Residence:* Providence, R.I. *Office:* Department of English, Brown University, Providence, R.I. 02912.

CAREER: Morgan State College, Baltimore, Md., associate professor of English, 1948-49; Hampton Institute, Hampton, Va., professor of English, 1949-59; Free University of Berlin, Berlin, Germany, professor of North American literature, 1959-69; Brown University, Providence, R.I., professor of English, 1969—. Visiting professor at Grinnell College, 1969, and Stanford University, 1973. *Member:* Modern Language Association of America, American Studies Association, American Association of University Professors. *Awards, honors:* Fulbright lecturer at Aarhaus University, 1954-55; senior fellowship from National Endowment for the Humanities, 1973-74; Fulbright grant for research in Germany, 1973-74.

WRITINGS: Many Thousand Gone: The Ex-Slaves' Account of Their Bondage and Freedom, E. J. Brill, 1963, Indiana University Press, 1969; *Instructor's Guide to Accompany "Cavalcade: Negro American Writing from 1760 to the Present,"* Houghton, 1970; (editor) *African Nights: Black Erotic Folk Tales*, Herder & Herder, 1971; (editor) *Black Men in Chains: An Anthology of Slave Narratives*, Lawrence Hill, 1972.

Contributor of more than sixty articles and reviews to education, literature, and literary journals in the United States and abroad, including *William and Mary Quarterly*, *America in the Twentieth Century*, *Nation*, *Modern Language Journal*, *Phylon*, *American-Scandinavian Review*, *School and Society*, and *Jahrbuch fuer Amerikastudien*. Member of editorial boards of *Studies in Black Literature* and of *Novel: A Forum in Fiction*.

WORK IN PROGRESS: Biography of Theodore Parker and His Age.

BIOGRAPHICAL/CRITICAL SOURCES: Ernest Dunbar, *The Black Expatriates*, Dutton, 1968.

* * *

NICHOLSON, Robert Lawrence 1908-

PERSONAL: Born October 17, 1908, in Chicago, Ill.; son of Benjamin Franklin and Grace I. (Butters) Nicholson. *Education:* University of Chicago, A.B., 1930, A.M., 1931, Ph.D., 1938. *Home:* 7023 South Jeffery Blvd., Chicago, Ill. 60649. *Office:* Department of History, University of Illinois at Chicago Circle, Chicago, Ill. 60680.

CAREER: Culver-Stockton College, Canton, Mo., professor of political science and history, 1942-43; Bucknell University, Wilkes-Barre, Pa., assistant professor of history and political science, 1943-46; University of Illinois at Chicago Circle, Chicago, 1946—, professor of history, 1963—. *Member:* Foreign Policy Association, Council on Foreign Relations (Chicago), English-Speaking Union (Chicago), Sons of the American Revolution, Atlantic Union Committee, Phi Beta Kappa.

WRITINGS: Joscelyn I: Prince of Edessa, University of Illinois Press, 1954; (contributor) Marshall W. Baldwin, editor, *The Pennsylvania History of the Crusades*, University of Pennsylvania Press, Volume I, 1955; *Joscelyn III and the Fall of the Crusader States, 1134-1199*, E. J. Brill, 1973.

SIDELIGHTS: Nicholson writes: "I have been and still am an internationalist in political outlook for the past fifty years. Deeming the Hitlerian threat to be incompatible with the continuation of the freedom of the democratic world, I was an outspoken member of the Committee to Defend America by Aiding the Allies and Fight for Freedom in 1941." *Avocational interests:* Travel (Morocco, Egypt, Lebanon, Cyprus, Turkey, all of Europe and North America).

* * *

NICKELSBURG, George W(illiam) E(lmer), Jr. 1934-

PERSONAL: Born March 15, 1934, in San Jose, Calif.; son of G. W. E. (a clergyman) and Elsie (Schwab) Nickelsburg; married Marilyn Miertschin, August 28, 1965; children: Jeanne Marie, Michael John. *Education:* Attended Concordia College, Bronxville, N.Y., 1951-53; Valparaiso University, B.A., 1955; Washington University, St. Louis, Mo., graduate study, 1956-57, 1961; Concordia Seminary, B.D., 1960, S.T.M., 1962; Harvard University, Th.D., 1968. *Politics:* Democrat. *Home:* 1713 East Court St., Iowa City, Iowa 52230. *Office:* School of Religion, University of Iowa, Iowa City, Iowa 52242.

CAREER: Pastor of Lutheran church in Akron, Ohio, 1966-69; University of Iowa, Iowa City, assistant professor, 1969-72, associate professor of religion, 1972—. Fellow of American School of Oriental Research (Jerusalem), 1963-64. *Member:* Society of Biblical Literature, Society of New Testament Studies.

WRITINGS: *Resurrection, Immortality, and Eternal Life in Intertestamental Judaism*, Harvard University Press, 1972; (editor) *Studies in the Testament of Moses*, Society of Biblical Literature, 1973. Contributor to journals in his field.

WORK IN PROGRESS: Research on the Book of Enoch, the Jewish apocalyptic work.

* * *

NICKERSON, John Mitchell 1937-

PERSONAL: Born July 1, 1937, in Lewiston, Maine; son of Elmer Winfield (a business executive) and Marion (an accountant; maiden name, Howard) Nickerson. *Education:* University of Maine, B.A., 1959; Washington State University, M.A., 1966; University of Idaho, Ph.D., 1971. *Home:* 190 Capitol St., Augusta, Maine 04330. *Office:* Department of Political Science, University of Maine, Augusta, Maine 04330.

CAREER: University of Maine, Orono, research associate in public administration, 1967-68; University of Maine, Augusta, assistant professor, 1970-74, associate professor of political science, 1974—. Director of New England Governmental Research Institute. *Member:* American Political Science Association, American Society for Public Administration.

WRITINGS: (Editor with Roy W. Shin and Roger Teachont) *A Study of Policy Making: The Dynamics and Adaptability of the U.S. Federal System*, McCutchan, 1971. Author of technical reports. Contributor to *Maine Townsman* and *Police Chief*.

WORK IN PROGRESS: *Municipal Government*, a textbook; *Regional Government*, a textbook.

* * *

NICOL, D(onald) M(acGillivray) 1923-

PERSONAL: Born February 4, 1923, in Portsmouth, England; married Joan Mary Campbell; children: three. *Education:* Pembroke College, Cambridge, M.A., 1948, Ph.D., 1952; British School of Archaeology at Athens, graduate study, 1949-50. *Religion:* Christian. *Home:* 5 West Park, Mottingham, London SE9 4RY, England. *Office:* Department of Byzantine and Modern Greek Studies, King's College, University of London, Strand, London WC2R 2LS, England.

CAREER: National University of Ireland, Dublin, lecturer in classics, 1952-64; Dumbarton Oaks, Washington, D.C., visiting fellow, 1964-65; Indiana University, Bloomington, visiting professor of Byzantine history, 1965-66; University of Edinburgh, Edinburgh, Scotland, reader in Byzantine history, 1966-70; University of London, King's College, London, England, Koraes Professor of Modern Greek and Byzantine History, Language, and Literature, 1970—. *Member:* Royal Historical Society (fellow), Society for the Promotion of Hellenic Studies (member of council), Ecclesiastical History Society (president, 1975-76), Royal Irish Academy.

WRITINGS: *The Despotate of Epiros*, Basil Blackwell, 1957; *Meteora: The Rock Monasteries of Thessaly*, Chapman & Hall, 1963; (contributor and editorial assistant) J. M. Hussey, editor, *Cambridge Medieval History*, Cambridge University Press, Volume IV, 1967; *The Byzantine Family of Kantakouzenos (Cantacuzenus): Circa 1100-1460*, Dumbarton Oaks, 1968; *The Last Centuries of Byzantium: 1261-1453*, Hart-Davis, 1972; *Byzantium: Its Ecclesiastical History and Relations with the Western World*, Variorum, 1972. Contributor to *Encyclopaedia Britannica*. Contributor to Byzantine, classical, and historical journals. Editor of *Byzantine and Modern Greek Studies*, an Anglo-American journal.

AVOCATIONAL INTERESTS: Book binding.

* * *

NIZER, Louis 1902-

PERSONAL: Born February 6, 1902, in London, England; came to United States in 1905; son of Joseph (in real estate) and Bella (Bealestock) Nizer; married Mildred Mantel Wollins, July, 1939; children: Donald Wollins, Tony Wollins (stepsons). *Education:* Columbia University, B.A., 1922, LL.B., 1924. *Politics:* Democrat. *Religion:* Jewish. *Home:* 180 West 58th St., New York, N.Y. 10019. *Office:* Phillips, Nizer, Benjamin, Krim & Ballon, 40 West 57th St., New York, N.Y. 10019.

CAREER: Admitted to New York Bar, 1924; attorney in New York, N.Y., 1924-28; Phillips, Nizer, Benjamin, Krim & Ballon (law firm), New York, N.Y., 1928—, now senior partner. Executive secretary and attorney for New York Film Board of Trade, 1928—; general counsel, Motion Picture Association of America, Inc., 1966—; chairman of theatrical divisions of political campaigns, organizations, and charity funds and drives. *Member:* American Bar Association, American Motion Picture Academy (honorary member), New York State Bar Association, Bar Association of the City of New York, Odd Fellows, Lotos Club. *Awards, honors:* Brotherhood award from National Conference of Christians and Jews, 1970; honorary degrees from colleges and universities.

WRITINGS: New Courts of Industry, Longacre, 1935, reprinted, J. S. Ozer, 1971; *Legal Essays*, [New York], 1939; *Thinking on Your Feet*, Liveright, 1940, reissued with special foreword by Nizer, 1963; *What to Do with Germany*, Ziff Davis, 1944; *Between You and Me*, Beechurst, 1948, revised edition, Yoseloff, 1963; *My Life in Court*, Doubleday, 1961; *Commentary and Analysis of the Official Warren Commission Report*, Doubleday, 1964; *The Jury Returns*, Doubleday, 1966; *The Implosion Conspiracy*, Doubleday, 1973.

Author of legal textbooks. Author of dramatic sketch, "The New Voice," 1948. Weekly columnist for Chicago Tribune-New York News Syndicate, 1971-72. Contributor to legal journals and popular periodicals, including *New York Times Magazine*, *McCall's*, and *Reader's Digest*.

SIDELIGHTS: Nizer, writes Marcus Duffield, knows "how to write in a way to make a courtroom scene build up excitement years after you knew how the case came out.... Nizer is interested in the drama, including the human reactions of the people involved as well as the quirks in the law." Commenting on *The Jury Returns*, Pamela Marsh notes: "Louis Nizer's high sense of theater, his play on the emotions, is as effective ... on paper as in the courtroom." In *My Life in Court*, F. X. Busch finds that "the facts, the drama, the emotion in these litigations are presented with enthusiasm and eloquence, and in a literary style that holds the reader captive to the end of the book."

My Life in Court was adapted as a three-act play by Henry Denker, and produced as "A Case of Libel" in New York, N.Y., at Longacre Theatre, October 10, 1963; the play was published by Random House in 1964. *The Implosion Conspiracy* is scheduled for filming as a documentary by Otto Preminger.

* * *

NOLAN, James 1947-

PERSONAL: Born September 3, 1947, in New Orleans, La.; son of Eugene, Jr. (an accountant) and Helen (a medical secretary; maiden name, Partee) Nolan. *Education:* Florida Presbyterian College (now Eckerd College), B.A. (with honors), 1969; State University of New York at Stony Brook, M.A. (with honors), 1970. *Politics:* "Dedicated to overthrow of the American world empire." *Religion:* "Pagan." *Address:* 9021 Inez Dr., New Orleans, La. 70123.

CAREER: Upward Bound Project, St. Petersburg, Fla., teacher of creative writing, summers, 1967, 1968; New Orleans Public Library, New Orleans, La., assistant, 1968; Rising Sun (crafts store), Sebastopol, Calif., owner, 1971; *Ramparts* (magazine), Berkeley, Calif., feature writer, 1971-73; worked in Vermont Poets-in-the-Schools Program, 1975; Eckard College, St. Petersburg, Fla., writer-in-residence, 1976. Organizer for International Day of Protest Against the War, Student Activist Committee, Student Strike Against the War, 1970, and Non-Intervention in Chile, 1974. Member of Ossabaw Island Project.

WRITINGS: (Contributor) Jacob Needleman, editor, *Religion for a New Generation*, Macmillan, 1973; *Why I Live in the Forest*, Wesleyan University Press, 1974.

Work is anthologized in *New American Review*, Volume XIII, edited by Theodore Solotaroff, Simon & Schuster, 1971; *Adam among the Television Trees*, edited by Virginia Mollenkott, Word Books, 1971. Contributor to little literary magazines, and to *Florida Quarterly, Ramparts*, and *Organ*.

WORK IN PROGRESS: A second book of poems; *The Other Side*, a "meta-fairy-tale"; translating *Stones of the Sky*, by Pablo Neruda.

SIDELIGHTS: Nolan writes: "Aside from the wild visual imagery and rhythms of my writing (I always wanted to be a painter and blues singer, too) I feel my poetry as well as my first-person journalism are ways of building communicative bridges between the Dying Order, not quite dead, and the New Age, not quite born. This is the edge upon which I live, and about which I write."

AVOCATIONAL INTERESTS: Horseback riding, archaeology, painting.

* * *

NOLAN, Jeannette Covert 1897-1974 (Caroline Tucker)

March 31, 1897—October 12, 1974; American author of books for children, adult novels, and literary criticism. Obituaries: *Washington Post*, October 17, 1974; *AB Bookman's Weekly*, November 11, 1974. (*CA*-7/8).

* * *

NOLL, Roger G. 1940-

PERSONAL: Born March 13, 1940, in Monterey Park, Calif.; son of Cecil Ray (a broadcaster and realtor) and Hjordis A. (a realtor; maiden name, Westover) Noll; married Robyn R. Schreiber, August 25, 1962; children: Kimberlee Elizabeth. *Education:* California Institute of Technology, B.S. (with honors), 1962; Harvard University, A.M., 1965, Ph.D., 1967. *Office:* Division of Humanities and Social Sciences, California Institute of Technology, Pasadena, Calif. 91125.

CAREER: California Institute of Technology, Pasadena, instructor, 1965-67, assistant professor, 1967-69, associate professor, 1969-71, professor of economics, 1973—. Senior staff economist for President's Council of Economic Advisers, 1967-68; senior fellow and co-director of Studies in the Regulation of Economic Activity at Brookings Institution, 1970-73. Has testified on the financing of professional basketball before U.S. Senate; consultant to Ford Foundation, RAND Corp., National Science Foundation, and U.S. Department of Justice. *Member:* American Economic Association, Western Economic Association, Sierra Club. *Awards, honors:* Book award for work in communications from National Association of Educational Broadcasters, 1974, for *Economic Aspects of Television Regulation*.

WRITINGS: Reforming Regulation: An Evaluation of the Ash Council Report, Brookings Institution, 1971; (with Merton J. Peck and John J. McGowan) *Economic Aspects of Television Regulation*, Brookings Institution, 1973; (editor and contributor) *Government and the Sports Business*, Brookings Institution, 1974.

Contributor: *Increasing Understanding of Public Problems and Policies*, Farm Foundation, 1969; John P. Crecine, editor, *Financing the Metropolis: Public Policy in Urban Economics, the Urban Affairs Annual Reviews IV*, Sage Publications, 1970; *On the Cable: Report of the Sloan Commission on Cable Communications*, McGraw, 1971; William Capron, editor, *Technological Change in Regulated Industries*, Brookings Institution, 1971; *Compendium on Price and Wage Controls: Now and the Outlook for 1973*, Joint Economic Committee, U.S. Congress, 1972; Anthony M. Woodward, editor, *Transportation Policy: The Economic-Political Interface*, Business Research Center, Syracuse University, 1972; Rolla Edward Park, editor, *The Role of Analysis in Regulatory Decisionmaking: The Case of Cable Television*, Heath, 1973; *The Economics of Federal Subsidy Programs*, Part VIII: *Selected Subsidies*, U.S. Government Printing Office, 1974.

Contributor to proceedings; contributor of about a dozen articles and reviews to professional journals, including *Review of Social Economics*, *American Economic Review*, *Virginia Law Review*, *Bell Journal of Economics and Management Science*, *Yale Law Journal*, and *Administrative Law Review*.

WORK IN PROGRESS: Economics and Politics: Campaign Financing and Strategy; *Bureaucratic Behavior*; *Nuclear Power Regulation*; *Public Broadcasting*.

BIOGRAPHICAL/CRITICAL SOURCES: Washington Post, September 26, 1971.

* * *

NOON, William T(homas) 1912-1975

May 17, 1912—January 17, 1975; American educator, author, and Roman Catholic priest. Obituaries: *New York Times*, January 19, 1975.

* * *

NORDEN, Heinz 1905-

PERSONAL: Born December 18, 1905, in London, England; came to United States, 1924; son of Julius and Hermine (Mandel) Norden; married Helen Ovenden, 1926 (divorced); married Helen Strough Brown (a writer, often under name Helen Lawrenson), 1931 (divorced); married Claire Harper (a violinist), 1944; children: (third marriage) Barbara. *Education:* Attended University of Chicago, 1926, and New School for Social Research, 1949-50. *Politics:* "Unlabeled radical." *Religion:* "A need never felt." *Home:* 3A Greenaway Gardens, London NW3 7DJ, England. *Office:* 91-101 Oxford St., London W1R 2LU, England.

CAREER: U.S. Gypsum Co., Chicago, Ill., salesman, 1926-27; Haldeman-Julius Publications, Girard, Kan., editor, 1928-29; Myers & Golden, New York, N.Y., copywriter, 1930-31; Grolier Society, Inc., New York, editor on staff of *Book of Knowledge*, 1931-37; Modern Age Books, New York, production manager, 1937-38; *Saturday Review of Literature*, New York, assistant to publisher, 1939-40; New York City Housing Authority, New York, deputy director of Application Bureau, 1941-42; *Heute* (official U.S. German-language magazine), Munich, editor, 1946-48; Limited Editions Club, New York, editor, 1950-51; William Douglas McAdams, Inc. (advertising firm), New York, member of executive staff, 1951-58; *Spectrum*, New York, editor, 1952-53; Medimetric Institute (opinion and market research firm), New York, director, 1954-58; Intercon International (advertising firm), managing and creative director in New York, Frankfurt, and London, 1958-63; Portland Publications, London, editorial director, 1964—; consultant on medical antiques, 1968—. *Military service:* U.S. Army, Infantry, 1942-45; also served in counter-intelligence; served in Greenland, the Far East, and Europe; became major.

MEMBER: International Association of the History of Medicine, International Association of the History of Pharmacy, American Translators Association (charter member), Translators Association of the Society of Authors (London; past member of council), Medical Journalists' Association, American Medical Writers Association, Institute of Linguists (London; fellow), American Institute of the History of Pharmacy, P.E.N., British Association of Social Psychiatry (co-founder; deputy chairman, 1964—), Royal Society of Medicine, Osler Club (London; member of council, 1972—), British Unidentified Flying Objects Research Association, Parapsychology Research Unit (United Kingdom), Worshipful Company of Apothecaries (London).

WRITINGS—Editor: (With Ruth Norden) Franz Mehring, *Karl Marx*, Covici-Friede, 1935; (with Otto Nathan) Albert Einstein, *Einstein on Peace*, preface by Bertrand Russell, Simon & Schuster, 1960.

Translator from the German of about fifty volumes, including Konrad Heiden, *The New Inquisition*, Starling Press-Alliance, 1939; Erica and Klaus Mann, *The Other Germany*, Modern Age Books, 1940; (with Ruth Norden) Robert Neumann, *Twenty-three Women*, Dial, 1940; (with Ruth Norden) Heinz Pol, *Suicide of a Democracy*, Reynal & Hitchcock, 1940; (with Ruth Norden) E. W. Dobert, *Convert to Freedom*, Putnam, 1940; (with Ruth Norden) Martin Gumpert, *First Papers*, Duell, Sloan & Pearce, 1941; (with Ruth Norden) Max Werner, *Battle for the World*, Modern Age Books, 1941; (with Ruth Norden) Emil Ludwig, *The Germans*, Little, Brown, 1942; (with Ruth Norden) Bernard Aschner, *The Art of the Healer*, Dial, 1942; (with Ruth Norden) Franz Carl Weiskopf, *Dawn Breaks* (novel), Duell, Sloan & Pearce, 1942; (with Ruth Norden) Werner, *The Great Offensive*, Viking, 1943; Weiskopf, *Children of Their Time* (novel), Knopf, 1948; A. Mitscherlich and F. Mielke, *Doctors of Infamy: The Story of the Nazi Medical Crimes*, H. Schuman, 1949; Rudolf Magnus, *Goethe as a Scientist*, Schumann, 1949.

E. Kogon, *The Theory and Practice of Hell*, Farrar, Straus, 1950; (with Ruth Norden) Paul Nettl, *The Other Casanova*, Philosophical Library, 1951; R. M. Rilke, *Letters to Benvenuta*, Philosophical Library, 1951; (with Ruth Norden) Heinrich Pestalozzi, *The Education of Man*, Philosophical Library, 1951; J. A. Schumpeter, *Imperialism and Social Classes*, edited by Paul M. Sweezy, Kelley, 1951; Max Brod, *The Master* (novel), Philosophical Library, 1951; Frederick Hiebel, *Novalis*, University of North Carolina Press, 1954.

(And author of introduction) Georg Brandes, *Michelangelo: His Life, His Times, His Era*, Ungar, 1963; *Goethe's World View*, Ungar, 1963; Max Friedlander, *Early Netherlandish Painting*, fourteen volumes, Praeger, 1967-75; Hanspeter Landolt, *German Painting: The Late Middle Ages*, Skira, 1968; Horst Gerson, *Rembrandt* (Book-of-the-Month Club selection), Meulenhoff, 1968; Gerhard Ritter, *The Sword and the Scepter: The Problem of Militarism in Germany*, University of Miami Press, Volume I, 1969, Volume II, 1970, Volume III, 1972, Volume IV, 1973.

Paul Klee, *The Nature of Nature* (based on his notebooks), Lund-Humphries-Wittenborn, 1973; R. Rathscheck, *The Great Drug Debate*, Med-Pharm, 1974; Max Friedlander and Jakob Rosenberg, *The Paintings of Lucas Cranach*, Gary Schwartz, 1975.

Also author of books in "Little Blue Books" series of Haldeman-Julius; author of unpublished manuscript, "How I Overthrew the Government of the United States, or The FB & I," 1950. Translator of articles and stories from the

German. Author of column, "Intelligence about Intelligence," published in *Mensa Journal*, 1967-68, 1970-72. Contributor to periodicals, including *Saturday Review*, *Heute*, *Debunker*, *New York Times Magazine*, *Insight*, *Chemical Age*, and *New Doctor*.

SIDELIGHTS: Norden told *CA* that he was "founder and head of tenants' rights and slum clearance movement, N.Y., in the 1930's, resulting in persecution as 'red' during army service and ultimately dismissal as editor of *Heute*; successfully contested in the federal courts and resulting in turn in reinstatement and 'rehabilitation' (from what? . . .)." He founded, and headed until 1972, Group 68, Concerned Americans Abroad, in London, which spearheaded overseas anti-Vietnam and anti-Nixon campaigns.

Norden owns large collections of medical antiquities and books on medical history; he also collects "Charles Fort-type curiosities."

* * *

NORRIS, Louanne 1930-

PERSONAL: Born June 13, 1930, in Seoul, Korea; daughter of John M. (a professor) and Oma (Goodson) Norris; married Howard E. Smith, Jr. (an editor and writer), June 1, 1953; children: Carolyn L., Alexander. *Education:* Oberlin College, B.A., 1952; graduate study at Colorado College, 1952, and New School for Social Research, 1963. *Home:* 128 Willow St., Brooklyn, N.Y. 11201.

CAREER: New Mexico Department of Public Welfare, Sante Fe, intake-caseworker, 1954-55; U.S. Social Security Administration, Sante Fe, N.M., adjudicator, 1957-61.

WRITINGS: Newsmakers: The Press and the Presidents, Addison-Wesley, 1974; *What Are You Doing Today, Henry?* (novel), McGraw, 1975; *Welfare and Poverty*, McGraw, in press.

WORK IN PROGRESS: A book on the future.

AVOCATIONAL INTERESTS: Reading fiction for children.

* * *

NORRIS, Russell Bradner (Jr.) 1942-

PERSONAL: Born March 3, 1942, in New Jersey; son of Russell B. and Ann (Dubanowitz) Norris; married Dixie Krouse Battistella (a cost analyst), June 1, 1974; children: Claire Ann Battistella. *Education:* Massachusetts Institute of Technology, B.S.E.E., 1964; graduate study at University of Illinois, 1964-65; Lutheran School of Theology at Chicago, B.D., 1969; University of Strasbourg, Docteur es Sciences Religieuses, 1972. *Politics:* Liberal independent. *Home:* 110 South Jefferson St., Mount Union, Pa. 17066. *Office:* Mt. Union Lutheran Parish, Box 96, Mt. Union, Pa. 17066.

CAREER: Ordained minister of the Lutheran Church; Department of Public Aid, Cook Co., Ill., caseworker, 1969; Mount Union Lutheran Parish, Mount Union, Pa., pastor, 1972—. Editorial assistant at Institute for Ecumenical Research, Strasbourg, France, 1970-72. *Awards, honors:* Rockefeller Theological Fellowship, 1965-66; World Council of Churches Overseas Study fellowship, 1969-70.

WRITINGS: God, Marx, and the Future, Fortress, 1974. Contributor to *Journal of Ecumenical Studies*. Assistant editor of *International Ecumenical Bibliography*, 1967-68, *Gospel and Unity*, 1971, and *Gospel and Human Destiny*, 1971.

WORK IN PROGRESS: An essay, "The Rise and Fall of the Christian-Marxist Dialogue".

* * *

NORSE, Harold (George) 1916-

PERSONAL: Born July 6, 1916, in New York, N.Y.; son of Fanny Rosen. *Education:* Brooklyn College (now Brooklyn College of the City University of New York), B.A., 1938; New York University, M.A., 1951. *Politics:* "Truth." *Religion:* "Love." *Home:* 29-B Guy Pl., San Francisco, Calif. 94105. *Office:* Department of English, San Jose State University, San Jose, Calif. 95114.

CAREER: Held jobs as sheet metal worker, ballt dancer, editorial assistant, book reviewer, proofreader, beach boy, ghost writer, assistant to French publisher in New York, 1941-44; Cooper Union, New York, N.Y., instructor in English, 1949-52; Lion School of English, Rome, Italy, instructor in English, 1956-57; U.S. Information Service School, Naples, Italy, instructor in English, 1958; California State University, San Jose, lecturer in creative writing, 1973—. Has also worked as film-dubber in Italy. *Awards, honors:* Poetry grant from Rome-New York Foundation, 1962; National Endowment for the Arts fellowship for poetry, 1974; De Young Museum grant (San Francisco), 1974, for publication of literary magazine, *Bastard Angel*.

WRITINGS—All poetry: *The Undersea Mountain*, Alan Swallow, 1953; (translator and adapter) *The Roman Sonnets of G. G. Belli*, preface by William Carlos Williams and introduction by Alberto Moravia, Jargon Books, 1960, 2nd edition, Perivale Press, 1974; *The Dancing Beasts*, Macmillan, 1962; *Karma Circuit*, Nothing Doing (London), 1966, Panjandrum Press (San Francisco), 1974; (co-author) *Charles Bukowski, Philip Lamantia, Harold Norse* (Penguin Modern Poets Series), Penguin Books, 1969; *Hotel Nirvana: Selected Poems 1953-1973*, City Lights, 1974; *I See America Daily*, Mother's Hen (San Francisco), 1974.

Work is represented in anthologies, including *Best Poems of 1968: Borestone Mountain Poetry Awards*, edited by Hildegarde Flanner, Lionel Stevensen, and others, Pacific Books, 1969; *Acid Anthology*, edited by Brinkmann and Ryguela, Maerz Verlag (Darmstadt, Germany), 1969; *The Male Muse*, edited by Ian Young, Crossing Press, 1973; *185 Anthology*, edited by Alix Geluardi, Mongrel Press, 1973; *Panjandrum Anthology*, edited by Dennis Koran, [San Francisco], 1973.

Contributor to periodicals, including *Poetry* (Chicago), *Kenyon Review*, *Ole*, *Sewanee Review*, *Paris Review*, *Transatlantic Review*, *Hudson Review*, *Saturday Review*, *Evergreen Review*, *Partisan Review*, *City Lights Journal*, *Commentary*, *Accent*, *Two Cities*, (Paris), *Klactoveedsedsteen* (Heidelberg), *Isis* (Oxford), *Pali* (Athens), *Shi'r* (Lebanon), *Botteghe Oscure* (Rome), *Between Worlds* (Puerto Rico), *Cold Turkey* (Rotterdam), *Nation*, *New Republic*, *Amphora*, and *Hyperion*.

Editor and founder, *Bastard Angel* (non-profit literary magazine), 1972—.

WORK IN PROGRESS: A new book of poems, as yet untitled, completion expected in 1975; memoirs, tentatively titled *Bastard Angel*, 1975; collecting unpublished short stories and writing new ones.

SIDELIGHTS: Norse told *CA* that his work "is concerned

with the terrors of survival in a hostile universe. Search for and growth of awareness and individuation in a threatening world of collective control of consciousness. The threat of personal extinction is a dominant theme in my poetry, with awareness in the here and now as a response to destruction by time and events." William Arrowsmith, reviewing *The Undersea Mountain*, describes Norse's style as including "a sure feeling for the march forward of the poem and especially for the flat but powerful close; a gruff and jagged movement yoked together by dashes, parentheses and run-ons, but muscular throughout; tact in language everywhere visible in his respect for the meanings of words as well as their gestures; the ironic clash of formal and familiar; a rough but appropriately rough ear."

Norse became a voluntary expatriate in 1953 after the publication of his first book; he lived in Morocco, Greece, and western Europe for the next fifteen years, returning to live on the west coast of the United States in 1968. He has read his poetry at museums and universities in Europe and America, including the Museum of Modern Art in New York and the San Francisco Art Institute, and has been invited to record his work for the Library of Congress. Norse is fluent in Italian, French, and Spanish, and speaks a "smattering" of Greek and German.

BIOGRAPHICAL/CRITICAL SOURCES: *Ole 5* (Harold Norse issue), 1966; *California Living* (of San Francisco *Chronicle/Examiner*), December 30, 1973; *Amphora*, number 8, 1973; *Poetry Now*, July, 1974.

* * *

NORTH, Sterling 1906-1974

November 4, 1906—December 22, 1974; American literary editor, critic, novelist, author of books for children, naturalist, and conservationist. Obituaries: *New York Times*, December 23, 1974; *AB Bookman's Weekly*, January 6, 1975; *Time*, January 6, 1975; *Publishers Weekly*, January 13, 1975; *Current Biography*, February, 1975. (*CA*-5/6).

* * *

OAKES, Philip (Barlow) 1928-

PERSONAL: Born January 31, 1928, in Burslem, Staffordshire, England; son of Sam (a traveler) and Constance (a teacher; maiden name, Barlow) Oakes; married Stella Fleming (a librarian), September 9, 1950; children: Susan Jill, Toby Alan. *Education:* Attended school in Darwen, Lancashire, England. *Politics:* Radical. *Religion:* None. *Home:* Pinnock Farm House, Pluckley, Kent, England. *Agent:* Curtis Brown Ltd., 1 Craven Hill, London W2 3EP, England. *Office: Sunday Times*, Thomson House, 200 Grays Inn Rd., London WC1X 8EZ, England.

CAREER: Eric R. Sly's Court Reporting Service Ltd., London, England, reporter, 1945-46, 1949-55; *Daily Express*, London, England, reporter and author of column "The World I Watch," 1955-56; *Evening Standard*, London, England, film critic, 1956-58; Granada Television Film Unit, London, England, scriptwriter, 1959-61; *Sunday Times*, London, England, editor of "Coming On" (arts interview column), 1965—. *Military service:* British Army, newspaper writer, 1946-49; served in Cairo and Athens.

WRITINGS: *Unlucky Jonah* (poems), University of Reading Press, 1955; *Exactly What We Want* (novel), M. Joseph, 1962; *In the Affirmative* (poems), Deutsch, 1968; *Miracles* (novel), John Day, 1969 (published in England as *The Godbotherers*, Deutsch, 1969); *Experiment at Proto* (novel), Coward, 1973; *Married/Singular* (poems), Deutsch, 1974.

Work is anthologized in *Poetry Now*, edited by George S. Fraser, Faber, 1956; *John Bull's Schooldays*, edited by Brian Inglis, Hutchinson, 1961; *Footballers Companion*, edited by Brian Glenville, Eyre & Spottiswoode, 1962; *London Magazine Poems, 1961-66*, edited by Hugo Williams, Alan Ross, 1966; *A Taste of Living*, edited by George G. Urwin, Faber, 1967; *Alamein & the Desert War*, edited by Derek Jewell, Sphere, 1967; *I Knew Daisy Smuten*, edited by Hunter Davis, Coward, 1970; *Baker's Dozen*, Ward, Lock, 1973; *Rule Britannia*, Times Newspapers Ltd., 1974.

Author of more than a hundred fifty scripts for films on animal behavior, with Desmond Morris; author of documentary programs and plays for television. Columnist and literary editor, *Truth*, 1955-56.

WORK IN PROGRESS: Editing and writing material for "The Great Entertainers," a series for Woburn, the first volume being a biography of Tony Hancock; a novel.

SIDELIGHTS: Oakes writes: "I write mostly about the world in which I've worked—the world of media. I'm interested in how people communicate and the difficulties they have in doing so. I've been described as mordant and pessimistic. Not so; I believe I am painfully realistic. I dislike to travel—except by boat, rail, or foot. Detest flying." *Avocational interests:* Cats, fishing.

BIOGRAPHICAL/CRITICAL SOURCES: *Guardian*, December 17, 1968; *Smith's Trade News*, June, 1969; *Harper's*, June 1969.

* * *

OAKLAND, Thomas David 1939-

PERSONAL: Born November 23, 1939, in Kenosha, Wis.; son of Oscar T. (a salesman) and Nancy (Nygren) Oakland; married Judy Defferding (an editor), June 15, 1963; children: David Thomas, Christopher. *Education:* Lawrence College, B.A., 1962; Indiana University, M.S., 1965, Ph.D., 1967. *Religion:* Methodist. *Home:* 2905 Dover Pl., Austin, Tex. 78731. *Office:* Department of Educational Psychology, University of Texas, 604 West 24th St., Austin, Tex. 78705.

CAREER: Teacher in public schools of DeKalb, Ill., 1962-63, and Orland Park, Ill., 1963-64; Indiana University, Bloomington, research associate, Institute for Child Study, 1966-67; University of Texas at Austin, assistant professor, 1967-72, associate professor of educational psychology, 1972—. Licensed psychologist in Texas, 1970—. Consultant to Science Research Associates, 1969-71, U.S. Office of Education, 1971—, and Texas Education Agency, 1973—. President of Austin Child Guidance Center, 1972-73. *Member:* American Educational Research Association, American Psychological Association, National Society for the Study of Education, Texas Psychological Association, Phi Delta Kappa.

WRITINGS: (Contributor) J. L. Frost and G. T. Rowland, editors, *The Elementary School: Principles and Problems*, Houghton, 1969; (with Fern C. Williams) *Auditory Perception: Diagnosis and Development for Language and Reading Abilities*, Special Child, 1971. Contributor to psychology and special education journals. Contributing editor, *School Psychologist Newsletter*, 1969-71, associate editor, 1971—; guest editor, *Journal of School Psychology*, Number 4, 1973.

WORK IN PROGRESS: Understanding Minority Group Children, completion expected in 1976.

*   *   *

OBERHELMAN, Harley D(ean) 1928-

PERSONAL: Born June 30, 1928, in Clay Center, Kan.; son of Gideon Alfred (a farmer) and Anna (Vittetoe) Oberhelman; married Hope Constance Nansen, September 9, 1954; children: Richard, David. *Education:* University of Kansas, B.S., 1950, M.A., 1952, Ph.D., 1958. *Office:* Department of Classical and Romance Languages, Texas Technological University, Lubbock, Tex. 79409.

CAREER: Lawrence Public Schools, Lawrence, Kan., high school teacher of Spanish, 1950-55, director of foreign languages, 1956-58; University of Kansas, Lawrence, instructor in Spanish, 1955-56; Texas Technological University, Lubbock, assistant professor, 1958-61, associate professor, 1961-63, professor of foreign languages and head of department, 1963-70, chairman of Latin American studies, 1969—. Fulbright lecturer at National University of Tucuman, 1961; lecturer at University of Wisconsin, summer, 1955; visiting professor at University of New Mexico, summer, 1956, Eastern Montana College, summer, 1959, University of Kansas, summer, 1960, and Texas Technological University National Defense Education Act Institutes in Argentina, summers, 1962-64.

MEMBER: Oficina Nacional de Correspondencia Escolar (member of board of directors, 1953-65), American Association of Teachers of Spanish and Portuguese, Modern Language Association of America, Rocky Mountain Conference of Latin American Studies, Southwest Council of Latin American Studies, South Central Modern Language Association, Texas Foreign Language Association (president, 1971-72), Sigma Delta Pi, Pi Delta Phi, Omicron Delta Kappa, Phi Kappa Phi. *Awards, honors:* State of Texas research grant in Uruguay, 1962.

WRITINGS: (Contributor) Eunice J. Gates, editor, *Homage to Charles Blaise Qualia*, Texas Tech Press, 1962; (contributor) Priscilla Tyler, editor, *Writers the Other Side of the Horizon*, National Council of Teachers of English, 1964; (author of introduction) Ernesto Sabato, *Obras de ficcion*, (title means "Works of Fiction") Losada, 1967; (contributor) Harvey L. Johnson, editor, *Contemporary Latin America*, Office of International Affairs, 1968; (with Agnes M. Brady) *Espanol moderno* (title means "Modern Spanish"), C. E. Merrill, Volume I, 1964, 2nd edition, 1970, Volume II, 1965, 2nd edition, 1970; *Ernesto Sabato*, Twayne, 1970. Contributor to proceedings and to journals. Associate editor of *Hispania*, 1962-66.

WORK IN PROGRESS: Research on the contemporary Spanish American novel, especially the Colombian novelist, Gabriel Garcia Marquez.

SIDELIGHTS: Oberhelman was a Rotary International group study exchange leader to Chile in May and June of 1970. He has traveled throughout Central and South America and western Europe.

*   *   *

OBERMANN, C. Esco 1904-

PERSONAL: Born July 31, 1904, in Yarmouth, Iowa; son of Albert B. (a farmer) and Evalyne (Calloway) Obermann; married Avalon Law, June 3, 1929. *Education:* University of Iowa, B.A., 1926, M.A., 1932, Ph.D., 1938. *Politics:* Independent. *Home:* 14754 50th St. S., Afton, Minn. 55001. *Office address:* Box 241, Hudson, Wis. 54016.

CAREER: Diplomate, American Board of Professional Psychologists. Chief of vocational education for Rochester, Minn. schools, 1928-36; University of Iowa, Iowa City, research fellow, 1938-40; U.S. Veterans Administration, Minneapolis, Minn., director of rehabilitation, 1946-60; St. Paul Rehabilitation Center, St. Paul, Minn., director, 1960-63; U.S. Department of Health, Education, and Welfare, Washington, D.C., research fellow with Rehabilitation Services Administration, 1963-65; Iowa Wesleyan College, Mt. Pleasant, associate professor of psychology, 1965-66; University of Iowa, associate professor of psychology, 1966-70; rehabilitation consultant in Hudson, Wis., 1970—. Associate professor of psychology, University of Texas at Austin, 1946; member of committee for the handicapped of People-to-People Program; member of President's Committee on Employment of the Handicapped; research consultant to Goodwill Industries of America. *Military service:* U.S. Army Air Forces, 1940-46; became colonel; received commendation medal.

MEMBER: American Psychological Association (fellow), American Association for the Advancement of Science (fellow), National Rehabilitation Association (president, 1961-62; member of executive board), National Rehabilitation Counseling Association, American Personnel and Guidance Association, American Speech and Hearing Association, Iowa Rehabilitation Association (president, 1967), Minnesota Rehabilitation Association (president, 1954), Sigma Xi, Delta Upsilon.

WRITINGS: Coordination of Services for Handicapped Children (monograph), National Education Association, 1964; *A History of Vocational Rehabilitation in America*, T. S. Denison, 1965; (with others) *Continuing Education for Rehabilitation Counselors* (monograph), University of Iowa, 1969; (editor) *Basic Issues in Rehabilitation* (monograph), National Rehabilitation Association, 1972; *A Code of Ethics for Rehabilitation Counselors*, National Rehabilitation Counseling Association, 1972.

WORK IN PROGRESS: Writing the summary of a workshop on the needs of severely handicapped persons; writing a synthesis of concepts in disability and rehabilitation and concepts in sociology, anthropology, and psychology.

SIDELIGHTS: Obermann is involved in promoting multidisciplinary training of persons entering the "helping" professions. He writes: "I am impressed with the essential unity (integrity) of the individual and the need to combat the tendency of the disciplines to fractionate the individual in treatment; current organization of science tends to encourage overspecialization and failure to treat 'the whole person'."

*   *   *

O'BRIEN, Cyril C(ornelius) 1906-
(Crane Wilson)

PERSONAL: Born March 22, 1906, in Halifax, Nova Scotia, Canada; son of Arthur Michael (an accountant) and Mary Jane (a musician; maiden name, Buchanan) O'Brien; married Madeleine Agatha Jones, July 4, 1939 (died August 28, 1946); married Patricia Florence Davison (an educator), July 27, 1957; children: (first marriage) Maureen, Terry, Christopher. *Education:* St. Mary's University, Halifax, Nova Scotia, B.A., 1926; McGill University, L.Mus., 1931; Mount Allison University, M.A., 1932; University of Toronto, B.Paed., 1934; Laval University, B.Mus., 1937; University of Montreal, D.Paed., 1937, D.Mus., 1950; University of Ottawa, Ph.D., 1944. *Politics:* Independent.

Religion: Roman Catholic. *Home:* 10209 42nd St., Edmonton, Alberta, Canada. *Office:* Adan Research Co., P.O. Box 666, Edmonton, Alberta T5J 2K8, Canada.

CAREER: Teacher and principal of schools in Nova Scotia, 1927-47; Marquette University, Milwaukee, Wis., assistant professor, 1947-54, associate professor, 1954-59, professor of education, 1959-63; Alcoholism Foundation of Alberta, Edmonton, director of research, 1963-65; Province of Alberta, Department of Health, Edmonton, director of research, 1965-68; University of Alberta, Edmonton, lecturer in industrial psychology, 1968—. Head of psychology department at Maritime Academy of Music, 1935-47; lecturer at St. Mary's University, Halifax, 1942-46; lecturer at Milwaukee Institute of Technology, 1959-63, and St. Francis Monastery, Milwaukee, 1958-63. Vice-president of Interpersonal Communicators, Inc., 1961—; president of Adan Research Co., 1969—. Member of Wisconsin Governor's Commission on Youth, 1957-58; chairman of Milwaukee Commission on Alcoholism, 1960-62. Church organist and choirmaster in Toronto and Halifax, 1929-47. Consulting psychologist. *Military service:* Canadian Army, 1942-46; became lieutenant.

MEMBER: International Academy of Forensic Psychology (fellow), Royal Canadian College of Organists (vice-president, 1946-47), American Psychological Association (fellow), American Association for the Advancement of Science (fellow), American Educational Research Association, Royal Society of Arts (fellow), Royal Statistical Society (fellow), Royal Society of Teachers, Nova Scotia Music Teachers Association (president, 1941-42; honorary member), Wisconsin Academy of Sciences, Arts, and Letters (vice-president, 1958-61). *Awards, honors:* Named honorary fellow of department of physics of University of Wisconsin, 1950; named honorary associate of American Institute of Management, 1956; named knight commander of Sweden's Order of St. Bridget, 1968; silver certificate from Acoustical Society of America, 1972.

WRITINGS: (Contributor) Edward Podolsky, editor, *Management of Addictions*, Philosophical Library, 1955; *Contemporary Studies in Industrial Psychology*, Associated Educational Services, 1969; *Perception and Alcoholism* (monograph), Department of Psychology, University of Alberta, 1970. Author of musical compositions, under pseudonym Crane Wilson. Contributor of about a hundred thirty articles and poems to journals, including *America*, *School and Society*, *American Business Education*, *Journal of Educational Psychology*, *School Musician*, and *Journal of Psychology*. Guest editor of *Education*, March, 1960; founder and first editor of *Normalite* of Nova Scotia Teachers College.

WORK IN PROGRESS: Verbal Communications in Industry; research on biography, industrial psychology, university education, music, learning, mental health, and communication.

* * *

O'BRIEN, Kate 1897-1974

December 3, 1897—August 13, 1974; Irish novelist and playwright. Obituaries: *New York Times*, August 15, 1974; *Washington Post*, August 18, 1974; *Publishers Weekly*, September 16, 1974; *AB Bookman's Weekly*, October 7, 1974.

O'BRIEN, Kevin P. 1922-

PERSONAL: Born December 22, 1922, in Bronx, N.Y.; son of Patrick J. and Mary C. (Curran) O'Brien; married Kathleen A. MacBride, February, 1948; children: Kevin, Jr. (deceased), Rory, Stephen, Kathleen, Eileen. *Education:* Attended New York University, 1942-43; Manhattan College, B.S., 1948; Bernard M. Baruch School (now Bernard M. Baruch College of the City University of New York), M.P.A., 1954; also attended Boston College and Hunter College of the City University of New York. *Politics:* Conservative. *Religion:* Roman Catholic. *Home:* 14 North Wilmarth Rd., Pittsford, N.Y. 14534. *Office:* Department of Criminal Justice, Monroe Community College, 1000 East Henrietta Rd., Rochester, N.Y. 14623.

CAREER: New York City Police Department, New York, N.Y., patrolman, 1948-49, member of police laboratory, 1949-68, retiring with rank of detective, first grade; currently professor of criminal justice at Monroe Community College, Rochester, N.Y. Lecturer at Bernard M. Baruch College of the City University of New York; has also lectured at Manhattan College, Brooklyn College of the City University of New York, Mt. Saint Vincent's College, and Seton Hall University. *Military service:* U.S. Army Air Forces, 1943-45; received Air Medal and ETO Medal with three battle stars. *Member:* International Association of Criminal Justice Professors, Academy of Police Science (charter member).

WRITINGS: (With Robert C. Sullivan) *Criminalistics: Theory and Practice*, Holbrook, 1973, revised edition, in press. Contributor to *Police, Police Chief, Norelco Reporter*, United Nations *Bulletin of Narcotics*, and other publications.

* * *

O'BRIEN, Marian P(lowman) 1915- (Mavis Bryan)

PERSONAL: Born November 14, 1915, in St. Louis, Mo.; daughter of Alfred (a teacher) and Jessie (a teacher; maiden name, Leister) Plowman; married Thomas L. O'Brien (a manufacturer), December 21, 1935; children: Sheila Ann (Mrs. G. B. McClintock), Kathleen Estelle (Mrs. R. T. Muckerman). *Education:* Washington University, St. Louis, Mo., A.B., 1931. *Religion:* Episcopalian. *Home:* #3 Orchard Lane, Kirkwood, Mo. 63122. *Agent:* Lenniger Literary Agency, 437 Fifth Ave., New York, N.Y. 10016.

CAREER: St. Louis Globe Democrat, St. Louis, Mo., food editor, 1958-73. *Member:* Magazine Writers of America, Missouri Literary Guild, Theta Sigma Phi.

WRITINGS: Gay 90's Gourmet, Doubleday, 1956; *The Bible Cookbook*, Bethany Press, 1958; *The Bible Herb Book*, Bethany Press, 1960; (editor) *The Shaw House Cook Book*, St. Louis Botanical Gardens, 1963; *Time Saver Cookbook*, Tower, 1970; *Collector's Guide to Doll Houses*, Hawthorn, 1973; *Craftsman's Guide to Doll Houses*, Hawthorn, 1975; *Craftsman's Guide to Doll Houses & Doll House Miniatures*, Hawthorn, 1975. Also compiler of fifteen other cookbooks.

Contributor of over 100 fiction stories to magazines under pseudonym Mavis Bryan.

WORK IN PROGRESS: A novel, *The Guilty Ones*, under pseudonym Mavis Bryan.

SIDELIGHTS: Marian O'Brien has traveled all over the world. She has "for years taken groups to foreign countries just to eat and drink."

O'CONNOR, Patrick Joseph 1924-
(Padraic Fiacc)

PERSONAL: Born April 15, 1924, in Belfast, Northern Ireland; son of Bernard (a subway clerk) and Anne (McGarry) O'Connor; married Nancy Wayne (a teacher), August 4, 1956; children: Brigid. *Education:* Attended St. Joseph's Seminary, Calicoon, N.Y., 1942-45. *Politics:* Socialist. *Religion:* Roman Catholic. *Home and office:* 43 Farmley Park, Glengormley, Newtownabbey, Antrim, Northern Ireland.

CAREER: Poet. *Awards, honors:* A. E. (George Russell) Memorial Prize from Bank of Ireland, 1957, for collection of poems, "Woe to the Boy."

WRITINGS—All under pseudonym Padraic Fiacc: *By the Black Stream: Selected Poems, 1947-1967*, Dufour, 1969; *Odour of Blood*, Goldsmith Press, 1973; (editor) *The Wearing of the Black*, Blackstaff Press, 1974. Also author of poetry collection, "Woe to the Boy," 1957. Contributor of poems to anthologies and to *Irish Times*.

WORK IN PROGRESS: Two poetry collections, *Hurricane Deirdre* and *Nights in the Bad Place*.

* * *

O'DEA, Thomas F(rancis) 1915-1974

December 1, 1915—November 13, 1974; American educator in sociology and religion, and author of books on related subjects. Obituaries: *New York Times*, November 14, 1974. (*CA*-23/24).

* * *

O'DRISCOLL, Robert 1938-

PERSONAL: Born May 3, 1938, in Newfoundland, Canada; son of William J. and Annie Mae (Connors) O'Driscoll; married Treasa Ni Argadain (a singer), July 18, 1966; children: Brian William Butler, Michael Robert, Declan Patrick. *Education:* Memorial University of Newfoundland, B.A. (Ed.), 1958, B.A. (first class honors), 1959, M.A., 1960; University of London, Ph.D., 1963. *Home:* 50 Summerhill Gardens, Toronto, Ontario, Canada. *Office:* Department of English, St. Michael's College, University of Toronto, Toronto, Ontario, Canada.

CAREER: University of Reading, Reading, England, research fellow, 1963-64; University of Toronto, Toronto, Ontario, assistant professor, 1966-69, associate professor of English, 1969—. Visiting professor at University College, Dublin, Ireland, 1964-66. Founder and artistic director of Irish Theatre Society, and Irish Arts Canada, 1967-74. *Military service:* Royal Canadian Navy Reserve, 1956-61; became captain. *Member:* International Association for the Study of Anglo-Irish Literature (member of executive board, 1969—), Canadian Association for Irish Studies (founder, 1968; first chairman, 1968-72), National Library of Ireland Committee. *Awards, honors:* Canada Council research grants, 1967, 1968, 1970, 1971, leave fellowships, 1969, 1972.

WRITINGS: (Editor) *Theatre and Nationalism in Twentieth Century Ireland,* University of Toronto Press, 1971; (editor with Lorna Reynolds) *Yeats Studies,* Irish University Press, Volume I: *Yeats and the 1890's,* 1971, Volume II: *Theatre and the Visual Arts: Jack Yeats and John Synge,* 1972; *Intruder: A Poem,* Advent, 1972; (editor) *Yeats Studies,* Macmillan, Volume I: *Yeats and the Theatre,* 1974, Volume II: *Yeats and the Occult,* in press, Volume III: *John Butler Yeats*, in press. Contributor to *Times Literary Supplement, Eire-Ireland, Irish University Review, Studies, University of Toronto Quarterly, Globe and Mail,* and *Irish Times.*

WORK IN PROGRESS: Ferguson and the Foundations of an Irish National Literature.

SIDELIGHTS: O'Driscoll spends about four months of each year in Ireland. He has produced thirteen Irish plays in Toronto of which seven were North American premieres. He has also arranged international conferences on Irish studies in Toronto.

BIOGRAPHICAL/CRITICAL SOURCES: Toronto Star, October 15, 1971, October 16, 1971; *This Week,* October 5, 1972; *Performing Arts in Canada,* winter, 1972.

* * *

OGDEN, Dunbar H.

PERSONAL: Married wife, Annegret (a rare book cataloguer); children: Stephanie, Christopher. *Education:* Yale University, Ph.D., 1962. *Home:* 887 Indian Rock Ave., Berkeley, Calif. 94707. *Office:* Department of Dramatic Art, University of California, Berkeley, Calif. 94720.

CAREER: University of California, Berkeley, now associate professor of dramatic art and chairman of graduate studies.

WRITINGS: (General editor) James Butler, *The Greek and Roman Drama and Theatre,* Chandler Publishing, 1972; *The Italian Baroque Stage,* University of Miami Press, in press; *The Staging of Drama within the Medieval Church,* Yale University Press, in press.

* * *

O'GORMAN, James F(rancis) 1933-

PERSONAL: Born September 19, 1933, in St. Louis, Mo.; son of Paul J. and Dorothy (Hogan) O'Gorman; married Jean Baer, 1957; children: four. *Education:* Washington University, St. Louis, Mo., B.Arch., 1956; University of Illinois, M.Arch., 1961; Harvard University, Ph.D., 1966. *Home address:* Box 98, Lanesville Station, Gloucester, Mass. 01930.

CAREER: University of Pennsylvania, Philadelphia, assistant professor of fine arts, 1966-71; visiting lecturer at Boston University, Boston, Mass., Massachusetts Institute of Technology, Cambridge, Mass., and Tufts University, Medford, Mass., part-time, 1971—. *Member:* Society of Architectural Historians (director, 1967; president, 1970-72), College Art Association of America, Renaissance Society of America, Mediaeval Academy of America.

WRITINGS: (Editor and translator) Paul Frankl, *Principles of Architectural History*, M.I.T. Press, 1968; *The Architecture of the Monastic Library in Italy: 1300-1600*, New York University Press, 1972; *The Architecture of Frank Furness*, Philadelphia Museum of Art, 1973; *Portrait of a Place: Some American Landscape Painters in Gloucester*, Gloucester 350th Anniversary Committee, 1973; *H. H. Richardson and His Office: Selected Drawings*, Houghton Library, Harvard University, 1974.

* * *

O'GRADY, Anne
(E. A. Scollan)

PERSONAL: Born in Melbourne, Victoria, Australia; daughter of Edward and Eleanor Edith (Lucas) Scollan; married John Patrick O'Grady (a television comedy scriptwriter); children: Shaunna. *Education:* Attended school in Tasmania, Australia. *Politics:* "Swinging voter." *Religion:* Protestant. *Residence:* New South Wales, Australia. *Agent:* Paul R. Reynolds, Inc., 599 Fifth Ave., New York, N.Y. 10017; John Farquharson Ltd., 15 Red Lion Sq., London WC1 R 4QW, England.

CAREER: Reporter on daily newspapers in Sydney, Australia; freelance photojournalist in New South Wales, Australia. Member of Women's Electoral Lobby, and Pennant Hills Community Health Centre. *Member:* Australian Society of Authors.

WRITINGS: (Under pseudonym E. A. Scollan) *The Mud Millionaires*, Horwitz, 1969; *Operation Midas*, Harper, 1973; *The Sugar-Coated Comfortable*, Ure Smith, in press; *The Ibis Seal*, Davies, in press. Feature writer for *Pix* magazine.

WORK IN PROGRESS: Research on Australian aboriginals today, on world prehistory, and on feminism.

* * *

OLCOTT, Jack 1932-

PERSONAL: Born January 13, 1932, in New Britain, Conn.; married Suzanne Cordier (a teacher), 1967. *Education:* Denison University, B.A., 1958; Bowling Green State University, M.Ed., 1961; Central Connecticut State College, further graduate study, 1973. *Home:* 3-12 King Arthurs Way, Newington, Conn. *Office:* Department of Physical Education and Athletics, Central Connecticut State College, New Britain, Conn. 06050.

CAREER: Slippery Rock State College, Slippery Rock, Pa., assistant professor of physical education and head football coach, 1965-67; Boston College, Boston, Mass., football coach, 1967; Tufts University, Medford, Mass., football coach, 1968; Boston University, Boston, Mass., football coach, 1969; Central Connecticut State College, New Britain, assistant professor of physical education and football coach, 1970—. *Military service:* U.S. Army, 1953-55.

WRITINGS—All published by Parker Publishing: *Organizational Keys and Check Lists for Successful Football Coaching*, 1968; *Football Coach's Guide to Successful Pass Defense*, 1970; *Coaching the Quarterback*, 1972; *Football's Fabulous Forty Defense*, 1974; *Complete Book on Triple Option Football*, 1975. Work is anthologized in *The Best of Football from Scholastic Coach*, Scholastic Coach Magazine, 1970.

Contributor to *Scholastic Coach* and *Athletic Journal*.

* * *

OLDSON, William O(rville) 1940-

PERSONAL: Born January 23, 1940, at Langley Air Force Base, Va.; son of James O. (a lieutenant colonel in the U.S. Air Force) and Kathryn (Zephir) Oldson; married Judith A. Kinsinger (a microbiologist and laboratory technician), June 11, 1967; children: Scott Ryan, Darren Randall. *Education:* Attended Loyola University, New Orleans, La.; Spring Hill College, B.A. (magna cum laude), 1965; Indiana University, M.A., 1966, Ph.D., 1970. *Office:* Department of History, Florida State University, Tallahassee, Fla. 32306.

CAREER: Entered Society of Jesus (Jesuits), 1959, left order in 1965; Florida State University, Tallahassee, assistant professor, 1969-74, associate professor of history, 1974—, associate chairman of department, 1973—. Consultant to U.S. Information Agency and U.S. State Department. *Member:* American Historical Association, American Association for the Advancement of Slavic Studies, Conference on Slavic and East European History, Romanian Studies Group, Sigma Pi Sigma, Delta Tau Kappa. *Awards, honors:* Fulbright-Hays fellowship, Bucharest, 1967-68; fellowship from State of Romania, 1967-68; Russian and East European Institute grant, Bucharest, 1967-68; fellowship from American Council of Learned Societies and Social Science Research Council, Cluj, Romania, 1973.

WRITINGS: The Historical and Nationalistic Thought of Nicolae Iorga (monograph), Columbia University Press, 1973. Contributor of articles and reviews to *East European Quarterly, Slavic Review*, and *Southeastern Europe*.

WORK IN PROGRESS: Habsburg and Jesuit in Eighteenth-Century Transylvania: Impact on the Romanian Uniates.

* * *

OLIVEN, John F. 1915(?)-1975

1915(?)—January 6, 1975; German-born American psychiatrist, teacher, and author. Obituaries: *New York Times*, January 8, 1975.

* * *

OLIVER, Kenneth A(rthur) 1912-

PERSONAL: Born February 17, 1912, in Oregon; son of Harry and Iris (Tarbell) Oliver; married Madaline Schmidt, 1935; children: Michael. *Education:* Willamette University, B.A., 1935; University of Washington, M.A., 1939; University of Wisconsin, Ph.D., 1947. *Home:* 2385 Addison Way, Los Angeles, Calif. 90041. *Office:* Department of English and Comparative Literature, Occidental College, 1600 Campus Rd., Los Angeles, Calif. 90041.

CAREER: Occidental College, Los Angeles, Calif., associate professor, 1948-52, professor of English and comparative literature, 1952—, chairman of department, 1949-67, chairman of division of humanities and fine arts, 1963-69. Fulbright Lecturer at University of Salonica, 1956-57. *Military service:* U.S. Navy, 1943-46; served in Pacific; became lieutenant commander. U.S. Naval Reserve, 1942-72. *Member:* American International Associations of Comparative Literature, National Council of Teachers of English, Council for Basic Education, Reserve Officers Association.

WRITINGS: Our Living Language, privately printed, 1957, 2nd edition, 1962; (editor) Theodore Parker, *The Road & the Stars*, Wings Press, 1957; (translator) *Impromptu: The Courtship of Brunhild* (from *Nibelungenlied*), Occidental College, 1961; (contributor of translation) Angel Flores, editor, *An Anthology of Medieval Literature*, Modern Library, 1962; (contributor of translation) Angel Flores, editor, *Laurel Masterpieces of World Literature: Medieval Age*, Dell, 1963; (with others) *On Writing Well*, Odyssey, 1965; (editor) *Walk the Rugged Earth* (poetry), Multnomah Press, 1967; (contributor) Robert T. Oliver, editor, *Effective Speech*, Holt, 1970; (contributor of poem) R. T. Oliver, editor, *Making Your Meaning Effective*, Holbrook, 1971; *Words Every College Student Should Know*, privately printed, 1974. Contributor to journals in his field.

WORK IN PROGRESS: Revising *Words Every College Student Should Know; Knowledge of the English Language: Why Needed, How Learned, Basic Principles;*

translating from contemporary and medieval German; with others, revising Robert O'Neal's *Teachers Guide to World Literature*.

* * *

OLLER, John W(illiam), Jr. 1943-

PERSONAL: Born October 22, 1943, in Las Vegas, N.M.; son of John W. (an author) and Betty Evelyn (Rickard) Oller; married Lois Elaine Klotz; children: Mark Louis, Laura Lynn. *Education:* Fresno State College (now California State University, Fresno), B.A., 1966; University of Rochester, M.A., 1968, Ph.D., 1969. *Politics:* "I believe in Jesus Christ." *Religion:* "I don't believe in religion." *Residence:* Albuquerque, N.M. *Office:* Department of Linguistics, University of New Mexico, Albuquerque, N.M. 87131.

CAREER: University of California, Los Angeles, assistant professor, 1969-72, associate professor of English, 1972-73; University of New Mexico, Albuquerque, associate professor of linguistics and educational foundations and chairman of department of linguistics, 1973—. Director of communication arts program to Southwestern Cooperative Educational Laboratory, 1972. *Member:* International Linguistics Association, Linguistics Society of America, Modern Language Association of America, Organization of Teachers of English to Speakers of Other Languages, Linguistics Association of Canada.

WRITINGS: Coding Information in Natural Languages, Mouton & Co., 1971; *Basic Program Plan for Communication Arts Program II*, Southwest Cooperative Educational Laboratory, 1972; *Focus on the Learner: Pragmatic Perspectives for the Language Teacher*, Newbury House, 1973. Consulting editor for *Modern Language Journal*.

WORK IN PROGRESS: Ransom of the Self: A Personal Adventure; *The Secular Religion*; *Language Testing: A Handbook for Language Teachers and Bilingual Educators*.

SIDELIGHTS: Oller writes: "The book entitled *Ransom of the Self* expresses what I consider to be my most vital experience in life. That experience has completely revolutionized my marriage, my personal relationships, and my ability to succeed professionally. The follow up book, *The Secular Religion*, is a statement concerning the alternative of unbelief in Jesus Christ. People who have influenced me greatly include Hal Lindsey, author of *The Late Great Planet Earth*, and several of the staff at Campus Crusade for Christ headquarters in Arrowhead Springs. Professionally I have traveled to Copenhagen, Denmark, Cairo, Egypt, Cambridge, England. . ."

* * *

OLSEN, V(iggo) Norskov 1916-

PERSONAL: Born July 18, 1916, in Denmark; married Anita Lippi (a piano teacher), October 4, 1949. *Education:* Emmanuel Missionary College (now incorporated in Andrews University), B.A., 1948; Seventh-Day Adventist Theological Seminary (now incorporated in Andrews University), M.A., 1950, B.D., 1951; Princeton Theological Seminary, M.Th., 1960; University of London, Ph.D., 1966; University of Basel, D.Th., 1968. *Home:* 5281 Marengo Court, Riverside, Calif. 92505. *Office:* Loma Linda University, Loma Linda, Calif. 92354.

CAREER: Ordained Seventh-Day Adventist clergyman. Lefjord Hojere Skole, Daugaard, Denmark, dean of men, 1936-37; pastor of Seventh-Day Adventist churches in Denmark, 1937-46; Lefjord Hojere Skole, Bible teacher, 1951-54; Newbold College, Bracknell, Berkshire, England, professor of church history and chairman of Bible department, 1954-59, academic dean, 1956-59, president of college, 1960-66; Loma Linda University, Loma Linda, Calif., professor of church history, 1968—, dean of College of Arts and Sciences, 1972-74, president of university, 1974—. Distinguished faculty lecturer at Loma Linda University, 1942; member of Inland Action (for economic development) and Riverside City Manager's Group. *Member:* American Church History Society, Society for Reformation Studies, American Association of Higher Education, British Ecclesiastical History Society, Western Interstate Commission for Higher Education, Southern California Academic Deans.

WRITINGS: The New Testament Logia on Divorce, J.C.B. Mohr, 1971; *John Foxe and the Elizabethan Church*, University of California Press, 1974. Contributor to religious publications.

WORK IN PROGRESS: Editing and writing a chapter for *The Christian Hope in Scripture and History*.

AVOCATIONAL INTERESTS: Travel (Europe, Middle East), gardening.

* * *

OLSON, David John 1941-

PERSONAL: Born May 18, 1941, in Brantford, N.D.; son of Lloyd (a custodian) and Alice (Black) Olson; married Sandra Crabb, June 11, 1966; children: Maia. *Education:* Concordia College, Moorhead, Minn., B.A., 1963; Union Theological Seminary, New York, N.Y., graduate study, 1963-64; University of Wisconsin, Madison, M.A., 1966, Ph.D., 1971. *Home:* 7743 38th Ave. N.E., Seattle, Wash. 98115. *Office:* Department of Political Science, University of Washington, Seattle, Wash. 98105.

CAREER: Madison Redevelopment Authority, Madison, Wis., community planner, 1965-66; University of Wisconsin, Madison, lecturer at Institute of Governmental Affairs, 1966-67; Indiana University, Bloomington, lecturer, 1969-71, assistant professor, 1971-73, associate professor of political science, 1973—. Visiting associate professor at University of Washington, Seattle, 1974-75; member of advisory board of Institute for the Study of Ethical Issues, 1969-71.

WRITINGS: (Contributor) *Task Force Report on Organized Crime*, U.S. Government Printing Office, 1967; (contributor) Peter Rossi, editor, *Ghetto Revolts*, Transaction Books, 1970; (editor with Edward S. Greenberg and Neal Milner, and contributor) *Black Politics: The Inevitability of Conflict*, Holt, 1971; (contributor) Herbert Hirsch and David C. Perry, editors, *Violence as Politics: A Series of Original Essays*, Harper, 1973; (editor with John A. Gardiner, and author of introduction) *Theft of the City: Readings on Corruption in Urban America*, Indiana University Press, 1975; (with Michael Lipsky) *Riot Commission Politics: The Processing of Racial Crisis in America*, Transaction Books, 1975; (with Philip Meyer) *To Keep the Republic*, McGraw, 1975.

Contributor to *Dictionary of American History*. Contributor of articles and reviews to scholarly journals, including *Discourse, University of Illinois Bulletin, Trans-Action*, and *Journal of Politics*.

WORK IN PROGRESS: Politicans, Professionals, and

the Poor; contributing to *Perspectives on the Unheavenly City*, edited by Harry C. Bredemeier.

* * *

OLSON, Eric 1944-

PERSONAL: Born October 27, 1944, in Frederick, Md.; son of Frank Rudolf (a bacteriologist) and Alice (a teacher and counselor; maiden name, Wicks). *Education:* Student at Lafayette College, 1962, and New School for Social Research, 1965; Oberlin College, B.A., 1966; Harvard University, M.A.T., 1971, doctoral candidate, 1971—. *Home:* 1 Dana St., Cambridge, Mass. 02130. *Agent:* International Famous Agency, 1301 Avenue of the Americas, New York, N.Y. 10019.

CAREER: Teacher at American College and at Lady Dook College, both in South India, 1966-67; Yale University, New Haven, Conn., research associate in psychiatry, 1972—.

WRITINGS: *Living and Dying*, Praeger, 1974. Contributor to *Change*.

WORK IN PROGRESS: Editing *Explorations in Psychohistory: The Wellfleet Papers*, with Robert Jay Lifton, for Simon & Schuster; research on a new kind of psychological test based on making collages.

* * *

OLSON, Everett C. 1910-

PERSONAL: Born November 6, 1910, in Waupaca, Wis.; son of Claire Myron (a dentist) and Aimee (Hicks) Olson; married Lila Richardson Baker, July 15, 1939; children: Claire (Mrs. Thomas McAleer), George Everett, Mary Ellen (Mrs. Daniel Hansburg). *Education:* University of Chicago, B.S., 1932, M.S., 1933, Ph.D., 1935. *Home:* 13760 Bayliss Rd., Los Angeles, Calif. 90049. *Office:* Department of Zoology, University of California, Los Angeles, Calif. 90024.

CAREER: University of Chicago, Chicago, Ill., instructor, 1935-42, assistant professor, 1943-47, associate professor, 1947-53, professor of geology, 1954-69, chairman of department, 1956-60, associate dean of Division of Physical Sciences, 1948-58; University of California, Los Angeles, professor of zoology, 1969—, chairman of department, 1970-72. *Member:* Society of Vertebrate Paleontology (president, 1950), Society for Study of Evolution (president, 1965), Geological Society of America, American Society of Zoologists, Ecological Society, Society of Systematics, Paleontological Society, Society of American Naturalists.

WRITINGS: (With Agnes Whitmarsh) *Foreign Maps*, Harper, 1944; (with Robert Miller) *Morphological Integration*, University of Chicago Press, 1958; *The Evolution of Life*, New American Library, 1965; *Vertebrate Paleozoology*, Interscience, 1971; *Concepts of Evolution*, C. E. Merril, 1975; *Introduction to Zoology*, Macmillan, in press. Editor of *Evolution*, 1952-58, and of *Journal of Geology*, 1960-68.

AVOCATIONAL INTERESTS: Collecting lepidoptera, playing piano, travel.

* * *

O'MALLEY, J(ohn) Steven 1942-

PERSONAL: Born July 28, 1942, in Indiana; son of John J. (a merchant) and Mary (Scheidler) O'Malley; married Angie Gommel (a teacher), June 11, 1966; children: Sarah. *Education:* Indiana Central College, A.B., 1964; Yale University, B.D., 1967; Drew University, Ph.D., 1970. *Office:* Department of Religion, Phillips University, Enid, Okla. 73701.

CAREER: Ordained minister of the Evangelical United Brethren Church (now United Methodist Church), 1967; Indiana Central College, Indianapolis, assistant professor of philosophy and religion, 1970-72; Phillips University, Enid, Okla., assistant professor of historical theology and Methodist studies, 1972—. Member of United Methodist Commission on Archives and History, 1972-76. *Member:* American Academy of Religion.

WRITINGS: *Pilgrimage of Faith: The Legacy of the Otterbeins*, Scarecrow, 1973. Contributor to *Drew Gateway*, *Disciple*, and *Christian*.

WORK IN PROGRESS: Translating and editing the German theological writings of the Otterbeins.

* * *

O'MORRISON, Kevin

PERSONAL: Born in St. Louis, Mo.; son of Sean E. and Dori (Adams) O'Morrison; married Linda Soma (a theatrical secretary), April 30, 1966. *Education:* Tutored privately for university equivalent. *Home and office:* 239 East 18th St., New York, N.Y. 10003.

CAREER: Playwright; stage, film, television, and radio actor. Playwright-in-residence, University of Minnesota, summer, 1966, and Trinity University, 1974. *Military service:* U.S. Army Air Forces, three years. *Member:* Dramatists Guild, Writers Guild of America, Authors League of America, O'Neill Playwrights, Actors Equity, Screen Actors Guild, American Federation of Radio and Television Artists, Players Club. *Awards, honors:* *The Morgan Yard* named O'Neill Playwrights Selection by National Conference of Playwrights, 1971; Creative Artists Public Service fellowship, 1975.

WRITINGS—Plays: "Three Days Before Yesterday," first produced in New York, N.Y. at Chelsea Theatre Center, 1965, produced as "The Long War" in New York at Triangle Theatre, 1969; *The Morgan Yard* (first produced at O'Neill Playwrights' Conference, 1971, performed at Dublin Theatre Festival, 1974), Samuel French, 1975; "The Realist," first produced in San Antonio, Tex. at Trinity University, October 16, 1974.

Television plays: "The House of Paper," produced on NBC-TV, February 15, 1959; "And Not a Word More," produced on CBS-TV, July 3, 1960; "A Sign for Autumn," produced on NBC-TV, March 11, 1962.

Also author of plays "A Report to the Stockholders" and "Requiem," as yet unpublished and unproduced.

Play anthologized in *Playwrights for Tomorrow*, Volume 4, edited by A. H. Ballet, University of Minnesota Press, 1967.

WORK IN PROGRESS: A full-length play, "Ladyhouse Blues"; a screenplay, "Next Time, Dynamite, and Honey."

SIDELIGHTS: O'Morrison told *CA*: "One writes, I suppose, to attempt to impose a moment's order on chaos."

Further information on Morrison's work is on file at the Library for the Performing Arts, Lincoln Center, New York City; at the Walter Hampden Library, The Players, New York City; and at the Eugene O'Neill Memorial Library, Waterford, Conn.

BIOGRAPHICAL/CRITICAL SOURCES: Evening Herald (Dublin), October 1, 1974; *Irish Independent*, October 1, 1974; *Irish Times*, October 2, 1974; *San Antonio Express*, October 18, 1974.

* * *

O'NEILL, John 1933-

PERSONAL: Born July 17, 1933, in London, England; son of John (a roofer) and Catherine (Hayburn) O'Neill; married Maria Charlotte Doerig, November 27, 1963; children: Daniela Kathleen, Gregory Sean, Brendan Dionys. *Education:* London School of Economics and Political Science, B.Sc., 1955; University of Notre Dame, M.A., 1956; Stanford University, Ph.D., 1962. *Home:* 105 Rochester Ave., Toronto M14 1N9, Ontario, Canada. *Office:* Department of Sociology, York University, 4700 Keele St., Downsview, Toronto, Ontario, Canada.

CAREER: Woodside Priory School, Portola Valley, Calif., senior instructor in French, Greek, and Latin, 1958-63; San Jose State College (now California State University at San Jose), assistant professor of philosophy and humanities, 1963-64; Stanford University, Stanford, Calif., acting instructor in economics, 1963-64; York University, Toronto, Ontario, assistant professor, 1964-67, associate professor, 1967-69, professor of sociology, 1969—, chairman of department, 1969-71. Visiting professor at New School for Social Research, 1969-71. Member of international scientific advisory council, Centre Royaumont pour une Science de l'Homme, Paris, 1974—.

MEMBER: Canadian Sociology and Anthropology Association, Canadian Philosophical Association, American Sociological Association, Society for Phenomenology and Existential Philosophy, International Institute of Sociology, International Association for Semiotic Studies, Association Internationale des Sociologues de Langue Francaise, International Sociological Association, Conference for the Study of Political Thought (secretary-treasurer, 1972-75).

AWARDS, HONORS: Fellow of Founders College, York University, 1965; Canada Council grants for research in Paris, 1966, and Louvain, 1967; Canada Council travel grants for Vienna, 1968, Rome, 1969, and Caracas, 1972; Canada Council sabbatical leave fellowship, 1971-72; Canadian Institute of International Affairs travel grant for England, 1973.

WRITINGS: (Editor, translator, and author of introduction) Jean Hyppolite, *Studies on Marx and Hegel*, Basic Books, 1969, edition with bibliography, Torchbooks, 1973; (translator and author of notes) Maurice Merleau-Ponty, *Humanism and Terror*, Beacon Press, 1969; *Perception, Expression and History: The Social Phenomenology of Merleau-Ponty*, Northwestern University Press, 1970; (editor, translator, and author of preface) Maurice Merleau-Ponty, *Themes from the Lectures at the College de France 1952-1960*, Northwestern University Press, 1970; (editor and author of introduction) Paul A. Baran, *The Longer View: Essays Toward a Critique of Political Economy*, Monthly Review Press, 1970; *Sociology as a Skin Trade: Essays Toward a Reflective Sociology*, Harper, 1972; (editor, author of introduction, and contributor) *Modes of Individualism and Collectivism*, St. Martin's, 1973; (translator and author of introduction) Maurice Merleau-Ponty, *The Prose of the World*, Northwestern University Press, 1973; *Making Sense Together: An Introduction to Wild Sociology*, Harper, 1974.

Contributor: Abraham Rotstein, *Power Corrupted*, New Press, 1971; Paul A. Walton, editor, *Situating Marx: Evaluations and Departure*, Chaucer Press, 1972; Hans Peter Dreitzel, editor, *Sexual Revolution and Family Crisis*, Macmillan, 1972; Maurice Natanson, editor, *Phenomenology and the Social Sciences*, Northwestern University Press, 1973; Hans Peter Dreitzel, editor, *Childhood and Socialization*, Macmillan, 1973; George Psathas, editor, *Phenomenological Sociology*, Wiley, 1973; Kooros M. Mahmoudi and Bradley W. Parlin, editors, *Sociological Inquiry: A Humanistic Perspective*, Kendall/Hunt, 1973.

Contributor of about thirty articles and occasional reviews to journals in United States, Canada, and Italy. Associate editor, *Canadian Journal of Sociology*; book review editor for Canada, *International Journal of Comparative Sociology*, 1965-69, consulting editor, 1969; editor, *Philosophy of the Social Sciences*, 1970; member of editorial board, *International Journal for Contemporary Social Theory*, 1970; Canadian member of editorial board, *Human Context*, 1972—.

WORK IN PROGRESS: On Critical Theory, completion expected in 1976; *Lordship and Bondage in Hegel and Marx*, 1976; *Essaying Montaigne*, 1977; *Sociology of the Body*, 1978.

BIOGRAPHICAL/CRITICAL SOURCES: Telos, number 14, winter, 1972.

* * *

ORNSTEIN, Allan C(harles) 1941-

PERSONAL: Born March 6, 1941, in Pittsburgh, Pa.; son of Joseph and Bella Ornstein. *Education:* City College of the City University of New York, B.A., 1962; Brooklyn College of the City University of New York, M.A., 1965; New York University, M.A., 1967, Ed.D., 1970. *Office:* Department of Education, Loyola University, 820 North Michigan, Chicago, Ill. 60611.

CAREER: Public school teacher of social studies in New York, N.Y., 1962-67; Fordham University, New York, N.Y., instructor, 1967-72; Loyola University, Chicago, Ill., associate professor of education, 1972—.

WRITINGS: How to Teach Disadvantaged Youth, McKay, 1969; *Urban Education*, C. E. Merrill, 1972; *Educational Foundations*, C. E. Merrill, 1973; *Analysis of Contemporary Education*, Crowell, 1973; *Accountability for Teachers and School Administrators*, Fearon, 1973; *Metropolitan Schools: Administrative Decentralization Versus Community Control*, Scarecrow, 1974; *Race and Politics in School/Community Organizations*, Goodyear Publishing, 1974; *Reforming Metropolitan Schools*, Goodyear Publishing, 1975; *A Handbook for Teacher Aides and Paraprofessionals*, Fearon, 1975; *Interdisciplinary Analysis of American Education*, Goodyear Publishing, in press.

WORK IN PROGRESS: Public Issues and the Teaching Profession.

* * *

ORNSTEIN, Robert E. 1942-

PERSONAL: Born February 17, 1942, in New York, N.Y. *Education:* Queens College of the City University of New York, B.A., 1964; Stanford University, Ph.D., 1968. *Office:* Langley Porter Institute, University of California, San Francisco, Calif. 94143.

CAREER: University of California, San Francisco, assistant professor of medical psychology, 1969—, president of

Langley Porter Institute. *Member:* International Society for the Study of Time, American Psychological Association, Institute for the Study of Human Consciousness, Biofeedback Society. *Awards, honors:* Creative talent award from American Institute for Research, 1968; UNESCO award for best contribution to psychology, 1972; media award from American Psychological Foundation, 1973.

WRITINGS: On the Experience of Time, Penguin, 1968; (with Claudio Naranjo) *On the Psychology of Meditation*, Viking, 1971; *The Psychology of Consciousness*, Viking, 1973; (editor) *The Nature of Human Consciousness*, Viking, 1974. Contributor to *Psychonomic Science, Psychophysiology, Neuropsychologia*, and *Psychology Today*.

* * *

OSBORNE, William S(tewart) 1923-

PERSONAL: Born December 21, 1923, in Nichols, N.Y.; son of William B. (a businessman) and Mabel (Stewart) Osborne; married Ruth Corcoran, August 26, 1950. *Education:* University of North Carolina, B.A., 1947; Columbia University, M.A., 1948, Ph.D., 1960. *Home:* 23 Surrey Dr., Wallingford, Conn. 06492. *Office:* Department of English, Southern Connecticut State College, New Haven, Conn. 06515.

CAREER: Southern Connecticut State College, New Haven, instructor, 1954-59, assistant professor, 1959-62, associate professor, 1962-65, professor of American literature, 1965—. *Military service:* U.S. Army Air Forces, 1943-45. *Member:* South Atlantic Modern Language Association.

WRITINGS: (Editor) John P. Kennedy, *Swallow Barn*, Hafner, 1962; (editor) Kennedy, *Rob of the Bowl*, College & University Press, 1965; (editor) Caroline M. Kirkland, *A New Home*, College & University Press, 1965; (editor) William H. Brown, *Power of Sympathy* and Hannah Foster, *Coquette* (combined into one volume), College & University Press, 1970; *Caroline M. Kirkland*, Twayne, 1972.

WORK IN PROGRESS: Editing *Among the Isles of Shoals*, by Celia Thaxter.

* * *

OSOFSKY, Gilbert 1935(?)-1974

1935(?)—1974; American educator, historian, and author or editor of books on Afro-American history and race relations. Obituaries: *AB Bookman's Weekly*, October 7, 1974.

* * *

OST, David H(arry) 1940-

PERSONAL: Born February 1, 1940, in Parkers Prairie, Minn.; son of Harry and Adele (Ostgarrd) Ost; married Belva J. Massie, September 24, 1960; children: DeeAnn Carol, Phillip Douglas, John Mathew. *Education:* Augsburg College, B.A., 1961; University of Michigan, M.A., 1965; University of Iowa, Ph.D., 1970. *Home:* 5805 Hesketh Dr., Bakersfield, Calif. 93309. *Office:* California State College, 9001 Stockdale Hwy., Bakersfield, Calif. 93309.

CAREER: B. F. Paper Mill, Minneapolis, Minn., press operator, 1959-61; biology teacher in public schools of Owatonna, Minn., 1961-64; Wisconsin State University—Platteville, instructor in biology, 1965-66; Carthage College, Kenosha, Wis., assistant professor of biology, 1966-67; University of Iowa, Iowa City, instructor in science education, 1967-70; California State College at Bakersfield, associate professor, 1971-74, professor of education and biology, 1974—. Coordinator of teacher education program in science and mathematics, American Association for the Advancement of Science, 1970; consultant for elementary science study implementation, Webster Division, McGraw-Hill Book Co., 1973—.

MEMBER: Association for the Education of Teachers in Science (member of board of directors, 1974-76), National Association of Biology Teachers (life member; vice-president, 1975), National Education Association (life member), American Association for the Advancement of Science, National Association for Research in Science Teaching, National Science Teachers Association (life member), School Science and Mathematics Association (life member), American Association for Higher Education (life member).

WRITINGS: A Laboratory Manual for a Survey of Science, University of Iowa Press, 1968; (coordinator) *Guidelines for the Education of Secondary School Teachers of Science*, American Association for the Advancement of Science, 1971.

Programmed texts: *Evolution*, Educational Methods, 1970; *The Chemical Basis of Life*, Educational Methods, 1974; *DNA*, Silver Burdett, in press; *Energy Relationships*, Silver Burdett, in press; *Human Reproduction*, Silver Burdett, in press. Contributor of over thirty articles and reviews to educational journals. Chairman of publications committee, School Science and Mathematics Association, 1972-75; chairman of editorial board, *Yearbook* of Association for the Education of Teachers in Science, 1973—.

WORK IN PROGRESS: With Michael Abraham, *Problem-Solving and Change*; research in the role of public education in cultural evolution, with special attention to aspects of behavioral genetics.

* * *

OSTER, Ludwig (Friedrich) 1931-

PERSONAL: Born March 8, 1931, in Konstanz, Germany; came to United States in 1958, naturalized citizen, 1963; son of Ludwig Friedrich and Emma Josefine (Schwarz) Oster; married Rose-Marie Hagetorn (a university professor), May 17, 1956; children: Ulrika, Mattias. *Education:* University of Freiburg, B.S., 1951, M.S., 1954; University of Kiel, Ph.D., 1956. *Politics:* "Looking for a Republican to vote for (since 1963)." *Home:* 2145 Sixth St., Boulder, Colo. 80302. *Office:* Joint Institute for Laboratory Astrophysics, University of Colorado, Boulder, Colo. 80302.

CAREER: University of Kiel, Kiel, Germany, research associate of German Science Council, 1956-58; Yale University, New Haven, Conn., research associate, 1958-60, assistant professor, 1960-64, associate professor of physics, 1964-67; University of Colorado, Boulder, associate professor, 1967-70, professor of physics and astrophysics, 1970—, fellow of Joint Institute for Laboratory Astrophysics, 1967—. Visiting professor at University of Bonn, 1966; consultant to aviation corporations.

MEMBER: International Astronomical Union, American Physical Society, American Astronomical Society, German Astronomical Society, Sigma Xi. *Awards, honors:* Fellowship from National Bureau of Standards, 1966-67; senior U.S. scientist award from Federal Republic of Germany, 1974.

WRITINGS: (Editor and translator) G. A. Chebotarev, *Celestial Mechanics*, Elsevier, 1967; *Modern Astronomy*, Holden-Day, 1973. Contributor of about fifty articles to scientific publications, including *Astrophysical Journal, Physical Review, Astronomy and Astrophysics*, and *Zeitschrift Astrophysik*. Editor of *Scripta Technica*, 1960—.

WORK IN PROGRESS: Research on solar physics, radio astronomy, and pulsars and neutron stars.

SIDELIGHTS: Oster writes: "I'm one of those sad people who decide at age twelve what to do (professionally) with one's life and then do it. . . . I'm always telling my (young) students how they are going to see the world come apart. Now, I think, I even might have a chance myself!. . . I love lots of preferably unpolluted water, like oceans."

* * *

OSTERHOUDT, Robert G(erald) 1942-

PERSONAL: Born June 17, 1942, in Scranton, Pa.; son of Clarence Burns (a salesman) and Rita E. (Wilmarth) Osterhoudt; married Kerry Kay Kyle, March 31, 1962; children: Kris Kyle, Nicole Odette, Kirk Kyle. *Education:* Attended Monterey Peninsula College, 1962-63, University of California, 1962-63, and University of Maryland, 1963-64; Pennsylvania State University, B.Sc., 1966, M.Sc., 1969; University of Illinois, Ph.D., 1971. *Politics:* Socialist Democrat. *Religion:* Humanism. *Home:* 14550 Biscayne Way W., Rosemount, Minn. 55068. *Office:* Department of Physical Education, University of Minnesota, Minneapolis, Minn. 55455.

CAREER: While a student worked as janitor, plumber's helper, recreation leader, machine operator, and variety of other jobs; Pennsylvania State University, University Park, graduate assistant and assistant track and field coach, 1967; Lock Haven State College, Lock Haven, Pa., instructor in physical education and head cross country and track and field coach, 1967-69; State University of New York College at Brockport, assistant professor of physical education and head track and field coach, 1971-72; University of Minnesota, Minneapolis, assistant professor, 1972-74, associate professor of physical education, 1974—. *Military service:* U.S. Army, 1962-64; Rumanian-language translator. *Member:* American Association for Health, Physical Education, and Recreation, National College Physical Education Association for Men, Philosophic Society for the Study of Sport, American Association of University Professors, Phi Epsilon Kappa.

WRITINGS: (Editor and contributor) *The Philosophy of Sport: A Collection of Original Essays*, C. C Thomas, 1973; *An Introduction to the Philosophy of Physical Education and Sport*, Lea & Febiger, 1975. Contributor to journals in his field. Founding editor, *Journal of the Philosophy of Sport*, 1973—.

WORK IN PROGRESS: An Inquiry Concerning the Nature and Significance of Sport.

* * *

OSTLING, Richard N(eil) 1940-

PERSONAL: Born July 14, 1940, in Endicott, N.Y.; son of Acton Eric (a music teacher) and Christine (Cumins) Ostling; married Joan Kerns, July 8, 1967; children: Margaret Anne, Elizabeth Anne. *Education:* University of Michigan, A.B., 1962; Northwestern University, M.S.J., 1963; George Washington University, M.A., 1970. *Religion:* Protestant. *Home:* 483 Cumberland Ave., Teaneck, N.J. 07666. *Office:* Time & Life Building, Rockefeller Center, New York, N.Y. 10020.

CAREER: Reporter and copyreader on newspapers in Wilmington, Delaware, 1963-64; *Christianity Today*, Washington, D.C., assistant news editor, 1965-67, news editor, 1967-69; *Time*, New York, N.Y., religion correspondent, 1969-74, religion editor, 1975—. *Military service:* U.S. Army National Guard, 1964-70; served in band; became staff sergeant. *Member:* Religion Newswriters Association (president, 1974—), Phi Beta Kappa.

WRITINGS: Secrecy in the Church: A Reporter's Case for the Christian's Right to Know, Harper, 1974.

* * *

OUROUSSOW, Eugenie 1908-1975
(Eugenie Ouroussow Lehovich)

1908—January 7, 1975; Russian-born American educator, administrator, and author, associated with the New York City Ballet's School of American Ballet since its founding. Obituaries: *New York Times*, January 8, 1975.

* * *

OUTHWAITE, Leonard 1892-

PERSONAL: Born July 12, 1892, in Sierra Madre, Calif.; son of Joseph Husband and Annette (Boyce) Outhwaite; married second wife, Lucille Conrad, March 1, 1936; children: (first marriage) Joan; (second marriage) Ann Outhwaite Clark, Lynn (Mrs. Richard Sparrow Pulsifer). *Education:* Yale University, B.A., 1915; University of California, Berkeley, B.A., 1916; graduate study at University of California and Columbia University. *Home and office:* Beachmound, Bellevue Ave., Newport, R.I. 02840.

CAREER: Conducted archaeological expedition to Santa Cruz for University of California department of anthropology, 1916-17; industrial consultant to Bureau of Industrial Research, 1919-22; member of staff, Laura Spelman Rockefeller Memorial, 1923-28; captained schooner "Kinkajou" on 14,000 mile Atlantic cruise, 1929-30; consultant in anthropology to Rockefeller Foundation, 1932; secretary, American Institute of Persian Art and Archaeology, 1933; special investigator, Rockefeller Foundation, 1935; consultant to Academy of Natural Science, Phildelphia, Pa., 1935-36, Franklin Institute, 1936, and New York Zoological Society, New York, N.Y., 1937-38; head of Leonard Outhwaite Exhibitions (design engineering and museum consultants firm), during 1930's; U.S. Government, Washington, D.C., associate director of resettlement for Farm Security Administration, 1940, consultant to Office of Price Management and Natural Resources Planning Board, secretary of Conference of Postwar Readjustment of Civilian and Military Personnel, 1942-43, director of Federal Board of Hospitalization, 1943-45; director of research for Nature Centers, Inc., New York, N.Y.; Institute of Public Administration, New York, N.Y., director for study of cultural institutions, 1962—. *Military service:* Served in U.S. Army, World War I.

MEMBER: International Oceanographic Foundation, Society for the Advancement of Management (member of Taylor Key award committee, 1944-45), American Anthropological Association, American Geographical Society, Explorer's Club (New York City and Boston), End of the Earth Club, Mystic Seaport Club, Union Club (New York City), Reading Room (Newport, R.I.), Clambake Club.

WRITINGS: Atlantic Circle: Around the Ocean with the Winds and the Tides, Scribner, 1931; *The Atlantic: A History of the Ocean*, Coward, 1957; *Unrolling the Map: The Story of Exploration*, Reynal & Hitchcock, 1935, new edition, John Day, 1972; *Museums and the Future* (booklet), New York Institute of Public Administration, 1967. Founder and editor, *Journal of Personnel Research;* editor, *Journal of the Explorer's Club.*

AVOCATIONAL INTERESTS: Mountain climbing, sailing, exploration.

* * *

OWEN, Charles A(braham), Jr. 1914-

PERSONAL: Born June 5, 1914, in Johnstown, Pa.; son of Charles A. (a businessman) and Edith (Rosenthal) Owen; married Mabel DeGeer Welles, June 8, 1946; children: Lucy DeGeer, Sarah Ann (Mrs. Paul Tabor), Jennifer, Charles Welles. *Education:* Princeton University, A.B., 1935; New College, Oxford, B.Litt., 1939. *Politics:* Democrat. *Religion:* Episcopalian. *Home address:* Separatist Rd., Storrs, Conn. 06268. *Office:* Department of English, University of Connecticut, Storrs, Conn. 06268.

CAREER: University of Buffalo, Buffalo, N.Y., instructor in English, 1938-41; University of Connecticut, Storrs, instructor, 1946-51, assistant professor, 1951-59, associate professor, 1959-63, professor of English, 1963—. Member of Democratic Town Committee of Mansfield, Conn., 1950-64; prosecutor for Town of Mansfield, Conn., 1955-61; member of board of directors of Imperial Coal Corp., 1959-64. *Military service:* U.S. Army, 1941-46; became captain. *Member:* Modern Language Association of America, Mediaeval Academy of America, American Association of University Professors, World Federalists, English Institute (secretary, 1969—), New England College English Association (secretary-treasurer, 1957-66; president, 1968-69), Phi Beta Kappa.

WRITINGS: (Editor) *Discussions of the "Canterbury Tales,"* Heath, 1961; *From Pilgrimage to Story-Telling: The Dialectic of "Ernest" and "Game" in the "Canterbury Tales,"* University of Oklahoma Press, in press.

WORK IN PROGRESS: Serving on the advisory committee of the *Variorum Chaucer,* and co-authoring the general prologue.

SIDELIGHTS: Owen writes that he has "a commitment to the University as the most successful of our Western institutions, and find present tendencies to politicize it and to weaken its standards deplorable."

* * *

OWEN, D(enis) F(rank) 1931-

PERSONAL: Born April 4, 1931, in London, England; son of Frank and Rose (Nightingale) Owen; married Jennifer Bak (a biologist), July 12, 1958; children: Richard, Susan. *Education:* Oxford University, M.A., 1958; University of Michigan, Ph.D., 1961. *Politics:* Socialist. *Religion:* None. *Home:* 66 Scraptotf Lane, Leicester, England.

CAREER: Makerere University, Kampala, Uganda, lecturer in zoology, 1961-66; University of Sierra Leone, Freetown, professor of zoology, 1966-70; University of Lund, Lund, Sweden, professor of ecology, 1971-73; University of Massachusetts, Amherst, professor of zoology, 1974—. Consultant to UNESCO, 1967.

WRITINGS: (Editor) *Research and Development in East Africa*, East African Publishing House (Nairobi), 1966; *Animal Ecology in Tropical Africa*, Oliver & Boyd, 1966; *Tropical Butterflies*, Oxford University Press, 1971; (with others) *Ecological Biology*, Longman, 1972; *Man in Tropical Africa*, Oxford University Press, 1973; *What Is Ecology?*, Oxford University Press, 1974. Contributor of about a hundred twenty articles to scientific publications.

WORK IN PROGRESS: Research on human ecology, especially in Africa, and on population genetics.

SIDELIGHTS: Owen's belief is that Africa should solve its own problems in its own way.

* * *

OWEN, Dolores B(ullock)

PERSONAL: Born in Shreveport, La.; daughter of Andrew Jackson (a civil engineer) and Dolores (a social worker; maiden name, Nichols) Bullock; married Emery Hollier, May 30, 1955 (divorced April, 1965); married Travis Owen (a criminalist), August 14, 1965; children: (first marriage) Dolores Alexandra, Gabrielle Tointette, Ann Monique. *Education:* Louisiana State University, B.A., 1954, M.S., 1968. *Politics:* Democrat. *Home:* 218 Vermilion Dr., Lafayette, La. 70501. *Office:* University Library, University of Southwestern Louisiana, Lafayette, La. 70501.

CAREER: Louisiana State University Library, Baton Rouge, reference librarian, 1968-71; University of Southwestern Louisiana, University Library, Lafayette, assistant professor of library science and documents librarian, 1972—. Member of board of directors of Lafayette Little Theater, 1973—. *Member:* American Library Association, Society of Southwest Archivists, Southwest Library Association, Louisiana Library Association.

WRITINGS: (With Marguerite M. Hanchey) *Abstracts and Indexes in Science and Technology: A Descriptive Guide*, Scarecrow, 1974.

WORK IN PROGRESS: With Dennis Gibson, *Guide to the Literature of Home Economics;* with Herbert M. Levine, *American Guide to British Social Science Resources; Guide to the Literature of Speech; Guide to Recurring Material in Scientific Journals; Abstracts and Indexes in Social Sciences: A Descriptive Guide.*

AVOCATIONAL INTERESTS: Music, community theater.

* * *

OXNAM, Robert B(romley) 1942-

PERSONAL: Born December 14, 1942, in Los Angeles, Calif.; son of Robert Fisher (a college president) and Dalys (Houts) Oxnam; married Barbara Foehl, August 22, 1964; children: Geoffrey Fisher, Deborah Elizabeth. *Education:* Williams College, B.A., 1964; Yale University, M.A., 1966, Ph.D., 1969. *Home:* 59 Arnoldale Rd., West Hartford, Conn. 06119. *Office:* Department of History, Trinity College, Hartford, Conn. 06106.

CAREER: Trinity College, Hartford, Conn., assistant professor, 1969-74, associate professor of history, 1974—, special assistant to the president, 1971-73. *Member:* American Historical Association, Association for Asian Studies, Phi Beta Kappa, Pi Gamma Mu.

WRITINGS: *History and Simulation: The Ch'ing Game*, Foreign Area Materials Center, 1972; *Ruling from Horseback*, University of Chicago Press, 1975. Contributor to *Journal of Asian Studies.*

WORK IN PROGRESS: *The Shun-chih Emperor, 1643-1661; The Merchant Corps Uprising of 1924.*

SIDELIGHTS: Oxnam has traveled to the People's Republic of China and to Japan; he speaks Chinese.

OZ, Amos 1939-

PERSONAL: Born May 4, 1939, in Jerusalem, Israel; son of Yehuda Arieh (a writer) and Fania (Mussman) Klausner; married Nily Zuckerman, April 5, 1960; children: Fania, Gallia. *Education:* Hebrew University of Jerusalem, B.A., 1963; St. Cross College, Oxford, M.A., 1970. *Residence:* Israel. *Agent:* Mrs. D. Owen, 28 Narrow St., London E.14, England.

CAREER: Has worked as tractor driver, youth instructor, school teacher, and agricultural worker. Visiting fellow, St. Cross College, Oxford University, 1969-70. *Military service:* Israeli Army, 1957-60; also fought as reserve soldier in the tank corps in Sinai, 1967, and in the Golan, 1973. *Member:* P.E.N. International, Hebrew Writers Association. *Awards, honors:* Holon Prize for Literature, 1965; Israel-American Cultural Foundation award, 1968; B'nai B'rith annual literary award, 1973.

WRITINGS: *Artzot ha'tan* (title means "Where the Jackals Howl"; collected short stories), Massada (Tel Aviv), 1965; *Ma'kom a'her* (novel), Sifriat Poalim (Tel Aviv), 1966, translation by Nicholas De Lange published as *Elsewhere, Perhaps,* Harcourt, 1973; *Michael sheli* (novel), Am Oved (Tel Aviv), 1968, translation by De Lange in collaboration with Oz published as *My Michael,* Knopf, 1972; *Ad m'aret* (title means "Unto Death—Crusade"; novella), Sifriat Poalim, 1971, translation published in *Commentary* (New York), August, 1971; *Laguat ba'maim* (title means "Touch the Water, Touch the Wind"), Am Oved, 1973.

Co-editor of *Siach lochamium* (title means "The Seventh Day"). Contributor of articles and short stories to periodicals in more than twelve languages.

SIDELIGHTS: "Oz at 33 has clearly established himself as one of Israel's most gifted and original writers," writes Robert Alter, citing the author's "growing artistic control over the hallucinatory vision of spiritual and sexual unrest that is his hallmark as a novelist. . . . No one until Amos Oz has so strikingly realized the potential of [Jerusalem] as a correlative for isolation and alienation." He describes *My Michael,* Oz's first book to be translated into English, as "the study of a minutely felt process of psychological erosion, rendered with uncompromising consistency in an imaginatively wrought prose rich with suggestive imagery. It bespeaks a talent that should command growing attention in the years to come."

* * *

PAGE, P(atricia) K(athleen) 1916-
(Judith Cape, P. K. Irwin)

PERSONAL: Born November 23, 1916, in Swanage, Dorsetshire, England; emigrated to Canada, 1919; daughter of Lionel Frank and Rose Laura (Whitehouse) Page; married W. Arthur Irwin (a publisher), December, 1950; children: (stepchildren) Neal A., Patricia J. Irwin Morley, Shelia A. Irwin Irving. *Education:* Attended Art Students' League, New York, N.Y., and Pratt Institute; studied art privately in Brazil and New York. *Home:* 3260 Exeter Rd., Victoria, British Columbia, Canada.

CAREER: Poet, artist. Has held jobs as sales clerk and radio actress in Saint John, New Brunswick, filing clerk and historical researcher in Montreal, Quebec; script writer for National Film Board, 1946-50. Has had solo exhibitions of paintings (under name P. K. Irwin) at Picture Loan Society, Toronto, 1960, Galeria de Arte Moderna, Mexico City, 1962, and Art Gallery of Greater Victoria, 1965; participant in group exhibitions in Canada and Mexico; work is represented in collections, including National Gallery of Canada, Art Gallery of Toronto, and Vancouver Art Gallery. *Member:* Academia Brazileira de Letras (Rio de Janeiro). *Awards, honors:* Bertram Warr Award from *Contemporary Verse* (Vancouver), 1940; Oscar Blumenthal Award from *Poetry* (Chicago), 1944; Canadian Governor-General's Award in Poetry, 1954, for *The Metal and the Flower.*

WRITINGS: (Under pseudonym Judith Cape) *The Sun and the Moon* (novel), Macmillan, 1944; *As Ten as Twenty* (poems), Ryerson, 1946; *The Metal and the Flower* (poems), McClelland & Stewart, 1954; *Cry Ararat! Poems New and Selected*, McClelland & Stewart, 1967; (contributor) John R. Colombo, editor, *How Do I Love Thee: Sixty Poets of Canada (and Quebec) Select and Introduce Their Favourite Poems from Their Own Work*, Hurtig, 1970; *The Sun and the Moon and Other Fictions*, Anansi, 1973; *Poems (1942-1973): Selected and New*, Anansi, 1974.

Poetry, short fiction, and essays are represented in anthologies and collections, as follows: *Unit of 5*, edited by R. Hambleton, Ryerson, 1944; *Other Canadians*, edited by John Sutherland, First Statement Press, 1947; *Book of Canadian Poetry*, edited by A.J.M. Smith, University of Chicago Press, 1948; *A Book of Canadian Stories*, edited by D. Pacey, Ryerson, 1950; *Canadian Poems, 1850-1952*, edited by Louis Dudek and Irving Layton, Contact, 1952: *Twentieth Century Canadian Poetry*, edited by Earle Birney, Ryerson, 1954; *The Blasted Pine*, edited by F. R. Scott and Smith, MacMillan, 1957; *The Penguin Book of Canadian Verse*, edited by Ralph Gustafson, Penguin, 1958.

Canadian Short Stories, edited by Robert Weaver, Oxford University Press, 1960; *Love Where the Nights Are Long*, edited by Irving Layton, McClelland & Stewart, 1962; *Poetry Mid-Century*, edited by Milton Wilson, McClelland & Stewart, 1964; *The Oxford Book of Canadian Verse*, edited by A.J.M. Smith, Oxford University Press, 1965; *Poetry of Our Time*, edited by Louis Dudek, MacMillan, 1965; *Modern Canadian Verse*, edited by Smith, Oxford University Press, 1967; *To Everything There Is a Season*, edited by R. Beny, Longmans, Green, 1967; *The Wind Has Wings*, edited by Mary Alice Downie and Barbara Robertson, Oxford University Press, 1968.

Made in Canada, edited by Douglas Lockhead and Raymond Souster, Oberon, 1970; *Tribal Drums*, compiled by A. O. Hughes, McGraw, 1970; *Contemporary Poetry of British Columbia*, edited by J. Michael Yates, Sono Nis Press, 1970; *A Little Treasury of Modern Poetry*, 3rd edition, edited by Oscar Williams, Scribner, 1970; *The Broken Ark*, edited by Ondaatje and Urquhart, Oberon, 1971; *I Am a Sensation*, edited by Goldberg and Wright, McClelland & Stewart, 1971; *40 Women Poets of Canada*, edited by D. Livesay, Ingluvin Press, 1972; *The Oxford Anthology of Canadian Literature*, edited by Robert Weaver and William Toye, Oxford University Press, 1973; *Selections from Major Canadian Writers*, edited by Desmond Pacey, McGraw, 1974.

Contributor to periodicals and little magazines, including *Alphabet, Artscanada, Canadian Forum, Canadian Poetry, Saturday Night, Contemporary Verse, First Statement, Here and Now, Northern Review, Poetry, Preview, Reading, Tamarack Review, Voices, Ariel, Tuatara*, and *Encounter* and *Observer* (both England). Formerly, co-editor of *Preview*, and regional editor for *Northern Review*.

PAIRAULT, Pierre 1922-
(Stefan Wul)

PERSONAL: Born March 27, 1922, in Paris, France; son of Henri (a factory director) and Graziella (Le Creurer) Pairault; married Jeanne Brault (a personal secretary), January 8, 1951. *Education:* College Rocroy-Saint-Leon, Baccalaureat Philo-Lettres, 1940; Ecole dentaire de Paris, chirurgien-dentiste F.M.P., 1945. *Politics:* "Agnostic." *Religion:* Roman Catholic. *Home:* Epieds 27730, Normandy, France. *Office:* Rue Henri IV, Ivry-la-Bataille, France.

CAREER: Dentist in private practice in Ivry-la-Bataille, France, 1945—; novelist. *Awards, honors:* Grand Prix du Roman Science-Fiction, 1956, for *Retour a "o."*

WRITINGS—All under pseudonym Stefan Wul: *Retour a "o"* (novel; title means "Return to Zero"), Editions Fleuve Noir, 1956; *Niourk* (novel), Editions Fleuve Noir, 1957; *Rayons pour Sidar* (novel; title means "Rays for Planet Sidar"), Editions Fleuve Noir, 1957; *La Peur geante* (title means "The Gigantic Fear"), Editions Fleuve Noir, 1957; *Oms en Serie*, Editions Fleuve Noir, 1957; *Le Temple du passe* (also see below), Editions Fleuve Noir, 1957, translation published as *Temple of the Past*, Seabury, 1973; *L'orphelin de Perdide* title means "Orphan of the Planet Perdide"), Editions Fleuve Noir, 1958; *La Mort vivante* (also see below; title means "The Living Death"), Editions Fleuve Noir, 1958; *Piege sur Zarkass* (also see below; title means "Snare on Zarkass"), Editions Fleuve Noir, 1958; *Terminus I*, Editions Fleuve Noir, 1958; *Odyssee sous controle* (title means "Guided Odyssey"), Editions Fleuve Noir, 1959; *Oeuvres*, Volume I (includes *Le Temple du passe, Piege sur Zarkass, La Mort vivante),* R. Laffont, 1970.

Also author of novelettes, "Le Bruit," 1957; "Expertise," 1958; "Echec au Plan 3," 1958; "Il suffit d'un rien," 1958.

WORK IN PROGRESS: Hazy Waste, a novel.

BIOGRAPHICAL/CRITICAL SOURCES: Fiction, January, 1973.

* * *

PALAZZESCHI, Aldo 1885-1974
(Aldo Giurlani)

1885—August 17, 1974; Italian poet, novelist, and short story writer. Obituaries: *New York Times*, August 18, 1974; *Washington Post*, August 18, 1974, and August 19, 1974; *AB Bookman's Weekly*, October 7, 1974.

* * *

PALMEDO, Roland 1895-

PERSONAL: Born April 5, 1895, in Brooklyn, N.Y.; son of Ulric (a banker) and Emma (Sondern) Palmedo; married Elizabeth M. Franklin, October 22, 1925; children: Philip F., Elizabeth (Mrs. Gerard Thompson). *Education:* Williams College, B.A., 1917. *Politics:* Conservative Party. *Religion:* Presbyterian. *Home:* 1185 Park Ave., New York, N.Y. 10028.

CAREER: Held executive positions in investment banking with Guaranty Trust Co. and with Lehman Brothers, Harriman, Ripley & Co., 1920-67; president of Mad River Corp. (ski area company), 1940-72. Former member of boards of directors of Libby-Owens-Ford Co. and of several airlines. *Military service:* U.S. Navy, 1917-19, 1941-45; became lieutenant commander. *Awards, honors:* Member of Ski Hall of Fame, Phi Beta Kappa.

WRITINGS: Skiing: The International Sport, Derrydale Press, 1937; *Ski New Horizons*, Pan Am Publications, 1956, 3rd edition, 1968; *The New Official Austrian Ski System*, A.S. Barnes, 1958; *The New National Austrian Ski System*, A. S. Barnes, 1974. Contributor to sports journals.

AVOCATIONAL INTERESTS: Kayaking, travel, skiing, photography, stamp collecting, tennis, golf.

* * *

PALMER, Donald C. 1934-

PERSONAL: Born October 8, 1934, in Nelson, Minn.; son of Roy A. and Cora Plamer; married Dorothy M. Nordquist (a nurse), March 16, 1962; children: Jean Marie, John Eric. *Education:* University of Minnesota, student, 1952-55; Briercrest Bible Institute, diploma, 1958; Trinity Evangelical Divinity School, M.A., 1958. *Religion:* Baptist. *Home:* 1611 North Woodland, Kansas City, Mo. 64118. *Office:* Gospel Missionary Union, Smithville, Mo. 64089.

CAREER: Gospel Missionary Union, Smithville, Mo., missionary in Colombia, 1959-71, coordinator of union, 1971, area secretary for Latin America, 1971-72, vice-president for field affairs, 1972—.

WRITINGS: Explosion of People Evangelism, Moody, 1974. Contributor to *Christian Reader* and *Gospel Message*.

WORK IN PROGRESS: "Jesus Only," a chapter for a book to be edited and published by David Hesselgrave.

* * *

PALMER, Marian 1930-

PERSONAL: Born March 24, 1930, in Rossland, British Columbia, Canada; daughter of Leonard (a photographer) and Beryl Adelaide (Morgan) Postill; married Guy Stewart Palmer (a photographer), August 16, 1958; children: Elizabeth Rosemary. *Education:* Attended public schools in Rossland, British Columbia, Canada. *Home:* 2590 West 43rd Ave., Vancouver, British Columbia, Canada. *Agent:* Peter H. Matson, Harold Matson Co., Inc., 22 East 40th St., New York, N.Y. 10016.

CAREER: Barber-Ellis of Canada Ltd. (wholesale paper company), Vancouver, British Columbia, accountant and office manager, 1951-68; full-time writer, 1968—. *Member:* Canadian Authors' Association. *Awards, honors:* Canada Council grant, 1969, for travel and research.

WRITINGS: The White Boar, Doubleday, 1968; *The Wrong Plantagenet,* Doubleday, 1972.

WORK IN PROGRESS: Historical novel of Simon de Montfort and the Barons' War, tentatively titled *Lion Rampant,* for Simon & Schuster, completion expected in 1975.

* * *

PALMER, Pamela Lynn 1951-
(Lynn Palmer)

PERSONAL: Born May 29, 1951, in Shreveport, La.; daughter of Harold Arthur (a chemist) and Velma (Frazier) Palmer. *Education:* Stephen F. Austin State University, B.A., 1971, M.A., 1973; Texas A. & M. University, working toward doctoral degree. *Home:* 5235 Lymbar, Houston, Tex. 77035. *Office:* Department of English, Texas A. & M. University, College Station, Tex. 77843.

CAREER: Texas A. & M. University, College Station, teaching assistant in English, 1973—. *Member:* International Poetry Institute, American Association of University Professors, Texas Folklore Society, Poetry Society of Texas (life member). *Awards, honors:* Poetry Society of Texas award, 1968, for "Sun and Faces"; Deep South Writers and Artists Conference award, 1969, for "The Tune of Pilgrimage"; Piney Woods Writers and Artists Conference award, 1969, for "Come Softly Down the Road That Leads to Mihr"; International Poetry Institute awards, 1971, for "A Piece of the Big Thicket," 1973, for "Pension," and 1974, for "Fireflies, Cicadas. . . ."

WRITINGS: (Under name Lynn Palmer) *Rain is for Dreaming* (poems), Naylor, 1968. Contributor to *Jean's Journal of Poems, Houston Chronicle, Encore, Lifestyle,* and *American Forests.*

WORK IN PROGRESS: A collection of poems; research in Southwestern poetry.

* * *

PANASSIE, Hugues 1912-1974

February 27, 1912—December 8, 1974; French authority on American jazz, impresario, critic, lecturer, author, founder of Hot Club de France, and editor of the club's bulletin. Obituaries: *New York Times,* December 9, 1974.

* * *

PANCAKE, John S(ilas) 1920-

PERSONAL: Born July 14, 1920, in Staunton, Va.; son of William C. (an insurance executive) and Frank May (Robbins) Pancake; married Frances M. Hutcheson, October 26, 1945; children: John S., Jr. *Education:* Hampden-Sydney College, B.A., 1942; University of Virginia, M.A., 1947, Ph.D., 1949. *Politics:* Democrat. *Religion:* Presbyterian. *Home:* 14 The Downs, Tuscaloosa, Ala. 35401. *Office address:* Box 2001, University, Ala. 35486.

CAREER: University of Alabama, University, assistant professor, 1949-59, associate professor, 1959-69, professor of history, 1969—. *Military service:* U.S. Naval Reserve, 1942-63, active duty, 1942-46; became commander. *Member:* American Association of University Professors, Southern Historical Association.

WRITINGS: Samuel Smith and the Politics of Business, University of Alabama Press, 1972; (contributor) John Boles, editor, *America in the Middle Period: Essays in Honor of Bernard Mayo,* University of Virginia Press, 1973; *Thomas Jefferson and Alexander Hamilton,* Barron's, 1974. Contributor to *Journal of Southern History, Maryland Historical Magazine,* and *William and Mary Quarterly.*

WORK IN PROGRESS: 1777: Crisis of the Revolution, completion expected in 1976.

* * *

PARETTI, Sandra

PERSONAL: Born in Regensbuerg, Germany. *Education:* University of Munich, D.Phil, 1960. *Residence:* Zurich, Switzerland. *Agent:* Joan Daves, 515 Madison Ave., New York, N.Y. 10022.

CAREER: Author; music critic.

WRITINGS—Novels: *Rose und Schwert,* Krueger, 1967, translation by A. J. Pomerans published as *The Rose and the Sword,* Heinemann, 1968, Coward, 1969; *Lerche und Loewe* (title means "The Lark and the Lion"), Krueger, 1969; *Purpur und Diamant* (title means "Scarlet and Diamonds"), Krueger, 1971; *Der Winter, der ein Sommerva,* C. Bertelsmann, 1972, translation by Sophie Wilkins published as *The Drums of Winter,* M. Evans, 1974; *Geliebte Caroline* (title means "Beloved Caroline"), C. Bertelsmann, 1974; *Die paechter der Erde,* C. Bertelsmann, 1973, translation published as *The Tenants of Earth,* M. Evans, 1975; *Der Wunschbaum* (title means "The Wishing Tree"), Droemer, in press.

* * *

PARK, O'Hyun 1940-

PERSONAL: Born March 15, 1940, in Taegu, Korea; son of Heekwan and Myung-Ok (Kim) Park; married Heeshin Yoo; children: Lynn Junehee, Linda Junemee. *Education:* Yonsei University, B.Th., 1964; Knox College, New Zealand, graduate study, 1964-65; Temple University, Ph.D., 1972. *Home address:* Route 1, Box 189-C, Blowing Rock, N.C. 28605. *Office:* Department of Philosophy-Religion, Appalachian State University, Boone, N.C. 28608.

CAREER: Temple University, Philadelphia, Pa., instructor in religion and philosophy, 1970-71; Appalachian State University, Boone, N.C., assistant professor of oriental religion and philosophy, 1971—. *Member:* American Academy of Religion.

WRITINGS: Oriental Ideas in Recent Religious Thought, Christian Spiritual Alliance, 1974.

WORK IN PROGRESS: Religion and Man's Life; Korean Zen Buddhism.

* * *

PARKER, Percy Spurlark 1940-

PERSONAL: Born April 6, 1940, in Chicago, Ill.; son of Percy S. and Ponce (a high school teacher; maiden name, Jones) Parker Cooke; married Shirley Davis, August 2, 1958; children: Sheila, Sherri, Percy III. *Education:* Graduated from high school in Chicago, Ill., 1958. *Politics:* "Democrat, mostly." *Religion:* Baptist. *Home:* 11351 South Lowe, Chicago, Ill. 60628. *Agent:* Marjorie Peters-Pierre Long, 5744 South Harper, Chicago, Ill. 60637.

CAREER: Apprentice pharmacist with independent drug store in Chicago, Ill., 1958-65; Osco Drug, Chicago, Ill., store manager, 1965-72; Jewel Family Center, Chicago, Ill., general merchandise manager, 1972—. *Member:* Mystery Writers of America (director of Midwest chapter).

WRITINGS: Good Girls Don't Get Murdered (mystery novel), Scribner, 1974. Work is anthologized in *Mirror, Mirror, Fatal Mirror,* edited by Hans Stefan Santesson, Doubleday, 1973. Contributor to *Ellery Queen Mystery Magazine.*

WORK IN PROGRESS: Death Deals Dirty, a murder mystery.

* * *

PARKES, (Graham) Roger 1933-

PERSONAL: Born October 15, 1933, in Chingford, Essex, England; son of Eric William (a solicitor) and Gwyneth Anne (Roberts) Parkes; married Tessa Isabella MacLean, February 5, 1963; children: Wanda Ann, Brandon Lee. *Education:* Attended Royal Medical College, 1946-50, and Royal Agricultural College, 1953-55. *Home:* Cartlands Cottage, Kings Lane, Cookham Dean, Berkshire, England.

Agent: Richard Scott Simon, 32 College Cross, London N1, England.

CAREER: Beaverbrook Newspapers Ltd., London, England, reporter and feature writer, 1959-64; BBC-TV, London, England, story editor, 1965-72. *Military service:* Royal Air Force, 1951-53; became sergeant. *Member:* Writers Guild of Great Britain, Writers Action Group.

WRITINGS: *Deathmask*, Constable, 1970; *Line of Fire*, Constable, 1971; *The Guardians*, Constable, 1973, St. Martin's, 1974; *The Dark Number*, Constable, 1973, Walker & Co., 1974. Author of scripts for television series, including "Strange Report," "Prisoner," "Man in a Suitcase."

WORK IN PROGRESS: *Muzungo*, a novel about Frelimo terrorist activities in Mozambique; *The Fourth Monkey*, a novel about the population explosion in Africa.

SIDELIGHTS: Parkes told *CA:* "I have now lived in India, Africa, Malta and visited most countries in Europe. I consider this a vital part of my work as well as a stimulating and pleasant activity."

* * *

PARSONS, Martin 1907-

PERSONAL: Born August 4, 1907, in Swanage, Dorsetshire, England; son of William Henry (a clergyman) and Evelyn (Watton) Parsons; married Emily Evelyn Wynne, April 14, 1936; children: David, Dorothy Evelyn (Mrs. David Evans), Robert Martin. *Education:* Queens' College, Cambridge, B.A., 1928, M.A., 1932; attended London College of Divinity, 1929-30. *Home:* 61 Elm Tree Rd., Locking, Weston-Super-Mare, England.

CAREER: Ordained priest of Church of England, 1931; London College of Divinity, London, England, lecturer in church history, 1930-34; missionary and chaplain in Warsaw, Poland, 1935-39; St. Kevin's Church, Dublin, Ireland, rector, 1939-43; Hibernian Church Missionary Society, Dublin, Ireland, general secretary, 1944-48; St. John's Church, Blackheath, London, England, vicar, 1948-56; Emmanuel Church, Northwood, Middlesex, England, vicar, 1956-64; St. Andrew's Church, Oxford, England, vicar, 1964-69.

WRITINGS: *Your Marriage*, Hodder & Stoughton, 1958; *The Holy Communion*, Hodder & Stoughton, 1961; *The Ordinal: An Exposition of the Ordination Services*, Hodder & Stoughton, 1964; *A Christian's Guide to Growing Old*, Hodder & Stoughton, 1966, published as *Towards the Senior Years*, Moody, 1967; *Marriage Preparation*, S.P.C.K., 1967; *Family Life*, Falcon Press, 1972; *The Call to Holiness*, Darton Longman & Todd, 1974, Eerdmans, in press.

* * *

PATEL, Harshad C(hhotabhia) 1934-

PERSONAL: Born November 27, 1934, in Nairobi, Kenya; son of Chhotabhia R. and Surujben Patel; married Madhuben Harshadbhai; children: Smitaben, Arunaben. *Education:* College of Commerce (India), B.Comm., 1958. *Religion:* Hindu. *Home:* 24 Riddlesdown, Purley, Surrey, England.

CAREER: Sales director for City Printing Works Ltd., Nairobi, Kenya. *Member:* Mount Kenya Safari Club.

WRITINGS: *Vanishing Herds*, Macmillan, 1973.

WORK IN PROGRESS: *Wildlife Studies of India.*

PATTEMORE, Arnel W(ilfred) 1934-

PERSONAL: Born May 3, 1934, in Smiths Falls, Ontario, Canada; son of C. Wilfred (a farmer) and Jean (a teacher; maiden name, Davidson) Pattemore. *Education:* Ottawa Teachers College, student, 1950-51; McMaster University, B.A., 1974. *Religion:* United Church of Canada. *Home:* 28 Ottawa St., St. Catharines, Ontario L2R 1Y9, Canada. *Office:* Lincoln County Board of Education, 112 Oakdale Ave., St. Catharines, Ontario L2P 3J9, Canada.

CAREER: Public school teacher in Brighton, Ontario, 1951-56; art supervisor in public school in Brockville, Ontario, 1956-59; art consultant for public school in St. Catharines, Ontario, 1959-70; Lincoln County Board of Education, St. Catharines, Ontario, visual arts consultant, 1970—. *Member:* Canadian Society for Education through Art (president), National Art Education Association, Ontario Society for Education through Art.

WRITINGS: *Printmaking Activities for the Classroom*, Davis Publications (Worcester, Mass.), 1966; *Art and Crafts for Slow Learners*, Instructor Publications, 1969; (with Sarita Rainey) *Ways with Paper: Construction and Poster*, Davis Publications, 1971; *Art and Environment*, Van Nostrand, 1974. Director of publications for Canadian Society for Education through Art.

WORK IN PROGRESS: *Paper Techniques for the Art Class; Mixed Media in the Art Class,* completion expected in 1976.

SIDELIGHTS: Pattemore writes: "The objective in my writing is to provide practical help to classroom teachers and art teachers built on a philosophical base that recognizes the individuality of students and their ability to create. The emphasis is on a continuum of classroom projects that will develop desired art concepts."

* * *

PATTERSON, (James) Milton 1927-

PERSONAL: Born October 15, 1927, in De Queen, Ark.; son of Charles Edward (an orchidist) and Allene (a civil servant; maiden name, Steel) Patterson; married Harriet Frazier, November 16, 1949 (divorced, 1964); married D. Jeanne Hays (a professor), July 3, 1964; children: Robert T., Donald A., J. Marshall, Julia Marie. *Education:* U.S. Merchant Marine Academy, B.S., 1948; Cornell University, M.B.A. (with distinction), 1954, Ph.D., 1961. *Politics:* Democrat. *Religion:* None. *Home:* 2431 Norh Dunn, Bloomington, Ind. 47401. *Office:* Department of Marketing, Indiana University, Bloomington, Ind. 47401.

CAREER: Esso Shipping Co., New York, N.Y., on seagoing staff, 1948-52; Cornell University, Ithaca, N.Y., administrative assistant to dean and to director of Executive Development Program, 1954-56; Northwestern University, Evanston, Ill., instructor in business administration, 1957-60; Indiana University, Bloomington, assistant professor, 1960-63, associate professor, 1963-68, professor of marketing, 1968—, chairman of department, 1972—. Lecturer at Center for Programs in Government Administration of University of Chicago, 1959; visiting associate professor at Northwestern University, 1967. *Member:* American Marketing Association, American Economic Association, Phi Kappa Phi.

WRITINGS: (With D. R. Forbush) *Management's Relationships with Its Publics*, Northwestern University, 1959; (with S. F. Otteson and W. G. Panschar) *Marketing: The Firm's Viewpoint*, Macmillan, 1964; (with Fred C. Allvine)

Competition Ltd.: The Marketing of Gasoline, Indiana University Press, 1972; (with Allvine) *Highway Robbery: An Analysis of the Gasoline Crisis*, Indiana University Press, 1974.

Contributor: William Gomberg and Arthur B. Shostak, editors, *The Blue Collar World*, Prentice-Hall, 1964; Robert J. Lavidge and R. J. Holloway, editors, *Marketing and Society: The Challenge*, Irwin, 1969; Robin T. Peterson, editor, *Selected Readings in Marketing*, MSS Publishing, 1970; Louis E. Boone, editor, *Management Perspectives in Marketing*, Dickinson, 1970; *Economics: Government and Business*, American Institute for Property and Liability Underwriters, 1970; John W. Bonge and Bruce P. Coleman, editors, *Readings in Business Policy*, Macmillan, 1971; Stewart H. Britt, editor, *Consumer Behavior in Theory and Action,* Wiley, 1971; J. W. Koning, editor, *Readings in Marketing*, H. E. Sternfert Kroese, 1972; Allvine, editor, *Public Policy and Marketing Practices*, American Marketing Association, 1973; David Acker and George S. Day, *Consumerism: Search for the Consumer Interest*, Free Press, 2nd editon (Patterson did not contribute to original edition), 1973; Britt, editor, *The Marketing Handbook*, Dartnell Corp., 1973. Also contributor to *How Marketing Works: Practical Readings in Marketing*, edited by Henry Ang and Paul T. McElhiney, 1970.

Contributor of about fifteen articles to economics journals, including *Journal of Marketing, American Business Law Journal, Business Horizons, Indiana Business Review, Proceedings of the International Congress of the American Marketing Association*, and *Proceedings of the British Columbia Energy Conference*. Editor of "Research Clearing House" of *Business Horizons*, 1961-67.

WORK IN PROGRESS: How to Break Up Major Oil Companies.

* * *

PATTY, James S(ingleton) 1925-

PERSONAL: Surname rhymes with "katie"; born July 17, 1925, in Florence, Ala.; son of Isham Harrison (an engineer) and Clara (Singleton) Patty. *Education:* University of North Carolina, A.B., 1945, M.A., 1947, Ph.D., 1953. *Politics:* Independent Democrat. *Religion:* Episcopalian. *Home:* 1823 Cedar Lane, Nashville, Tenn. 37212. *Office:* Department of French, Vanderbilt University, Box 1630, Nashville, Tenn. 37235.

CAREER: University of Colorado, Boulder, instructor in French and Spanish, 1953-54; University of Tennessee, Knoxville, assistant professor, 1954-57, associate professor of French, 1957-60; Washington and Lee University, Lexington, Va., associate professor of French, 1960-64; Vanderbilt University, Nashville, Tenn., associate professor, 1964-69, professor of French, 1969—. *Member:* Societe Chateaubriand, American Association of University Professors, American Comparative Literature Association, Modern Language Association of America, American Association of Teachers of French (secretary-treasurer of Tennessee chapter, 1968—), Tennessee Education Association, Phi Beta Kappa. *Awards, honors:* Fulbright scholarship at University of Toulouse, 1951-52.

WRITINGS: (Editor with Merlin Thomas and Simon Lee) *Jean Giraudoux's Electre* (two-act play; school edition) Appleton, 1965; (editor with Claude Pichois) *Hommage a W. T. Bandy* (title means "Homage to W. T. Bandy"), La Baconniere, 1973. Contributor of articles to journals. Member of editorial board of *Bulletin baudelairien*, 1965-73.

WORK IN PROGRESS: Protestantism and French Romanticism; *Albrecht Duerer and the French Romantics*; a critical bibliography on Sismondi.

AVOCATIONAL INTERESTS: Travel.

* * *

PEABODY, Velton 1936-

PERSONAL: Born July 27, 1936, in Beals, Maine; son of Clyde Bertram (a captain of a sardine boat) and Arlene Aseliah (Beal) Peabody; married Marilyn Blanchard (a speech therapist), April 28, 1962. *Education:* Graceland College, A.A., 1957; University of Missouri, B.J., 1965. *Politics:* Democrat. *Religion:* Reorganized Church of Jesus Christ of Latter Day Saints. *Home:* 345-G Evans St., Williamsville, N.Y. 14221. *Office: Buffalo Evening News*, 1 News Plaza, Buffalo, N.Y. 14240.

CAREER: Maine Coast Fisherman, Camden, Me., correspondent, 1952-54; *Bangor Daily News*, Bangor, Maine, reporter and copy editor, 1955-56; *Abilene Reflector-Chronicle*, Abilene, Kan., reporter, 1957-58; *Bangor Daily News*, Washington County bureau chief, 1958-61, copy editor, 1961-63; United Press International, correspondent from Columbia, Mo., 1964-65; *Rochester Times-Union*, Rochester, N.Y., copy editor, 1965-68; *Buffalo Evening News*, Buffalo, N.Y., night wire editor, 1968—. Owner of Peabody's Book Store, 1963-65; member of board of directors of Literacy Volunteers of Buffalo, 1971.

MEMBER: Society of Professional Journalists of Sigma Delta Chi, Mormon History Association, New England Historic Genealogical Society, Cumorah Historical Society (president, 1972), Moosabec Historical Society, Genealogical Society of Western New York, Kappa Tau Alpha. *Awards, honors:* Plaque from Maine Highway Safety Committee, 1962, for a newspaper series on highway safety; award from Hearst Foundation, 1965, for newspaper writing.

WRITINGS: Tall Barney's People: A Genealogy, Periwinkle Press, 1974. Contributor to *Saints Herald* and *Buffalo Evening News Magazine*. Editor of *Mormonia: A Quarterly Bibliography of Works on Mormonism*, 1972-73. Book reviewer for *Journal of the Genealogical Society of Western New York*.

WORK IN PROGRESS: A book on folklore about Barna Beal (Tall Barney), tentatively titled *Tales of Tall Barney*, for Periwinkle Press; research on the life of Joseph Smith III, son of the Mormon Prophet, and on the attempt of George Adams to establish a Christian colony from New England in the Holy Land in the 1860's.

SIDELIGHTS: Peabody writes: "My interest in genealogy may stem from the fact that I am the oldest of my father's twenty-two children (he was married four times). The family will *require* a genealogist to keep the record straight."

* * *

PEACOCK, Ronald 1907-

PERSONAL: Born November 22, 1907, in Great Britain; son of Arthur Lorenzo and Elizabeth (Agar) Peacock; married Ilse Gertrud Eva Freiwald, 1933. *Education:* University of Leeds, B.A. (1st class French/German), 1929, M.A., (with distinction), 1930; University of Marburg, Dr. phil., 1933. *Home:* "Greenshade," Woodhill Ave., Gerrards Cross, Buckinghamshire, England. *Office:* Department of German, Bedford College, University of London, Regent's Park, London NW1 4NS, England.

CAREER: University of Leeds, Leeds, England, assistant lecturer, 1931-38, lecturer, 1938-39, professor of German, 1939-45; University of Manchester, Manchester, England, Henry Simon Professor of German, 1945-62, dean of faculty of arts, 1954-56, pro-vice-chancellor, 1958-62; University of London, Bedford College, professor of German, 1962-75; Cornell University, Society of the Humanities, Ithaca, N.Y., senior research fellow, 1975—. Visting professor at Cornell University, 1949, University of Heidelberg, 1960-61, and University of Freiburg, 1965, 1967-68. *Member:* P. E. N., Modern Languages Association, Modern Humanities Research Association, English Goethe Society. *Awards, honors:* Robertson Prize from University of London, 1942; Gold Medal of the Goethe-Institut, Munich, West Germany, 1969; D.Litt., University of Leeds, 1954.

WRITINGS: Hoelderlin, Methuen, 1938; *The Poet in the Theatre*, Harcourt, 1946, new edition, Hill & Wang, 1960; *The Art of Drama*, Routledge & Kegan Paul, 1957; *Goethe's Major Plays*, Macmillan, 1959; *Criticism and Personal Taste*, Clarendon Press, 1972. Contributor to professional journals.

AVOCATIONAL INTERESTS: Music, theater, travel.

* * *

PEARL, Joseph L. 1886(?)-1974

1886(?)—December 8, 1974; American educator, classicist, and author. Obituaries: *New York Times*, December 10, 1974; *AB Bookman's Weekly*, January 13, 1975.

* * *

PELLS, Richard Henry 1941-

PERSONAL: Born November 6, 1941, in Kansas City, Mo.; son of Alvin J. (a musician) and Helen (a saleslady; maiden name, Selley) Pells; married Betty Wismer (a psychologist), June 17, 1966; children: Jason, Joshua. *Education:* Rutgers University, B.A., 1963; Harvard University, M.A., 1964, Ph.D., 1969. *Home:* 7602 Downridge, Austin, Tex. 78731. *Office:* Department of History, University of Texas, Austin, Tex. 78712.

CAREER: Harvard University, Cambridge, Mass., lecturer in history, 1968-71; University of Texas, Austin, assistant professor, 1971-75, associate professor of history, 1975—. *Member:* Phi Beta Kappa. *Awards, honors:* Woodrow Wilson fellow, 1963-64; fellow of Charles Warren Center for Studies in American History, Harvard University, 1970-71; Rockefeller Foundation Humanities fellowship, 1976.

WRITINGS: Radical Visions and American Dreams: Culture and Social Thought in the Depression Years, Harper, 1973.

WORK IN PROGRESS: A book on American culture and social thought, 1945-1960, for Harper.

* * *

PENDERY, Rosemary (Schmitz)

PERSONAL: Born in Elgin, Ill.; daughter of Theodore William and Phyllis (Schickler) Schmitz; married John Manning Pendery (self-employed), July 11, 1965; children: Samantha Sue; foster children: nine. *Education:* University of California, Santa Barbara, B.A., 1962; University of California, Los Angeles, graduate study, 1965. *Address:* P.O. Box 149, De Funiak Springs, Fla. 32433.

CAREER: Private tutor at levels through high school in De Funiak Springs, Fla., and Santa Monica, Calif., 1962—; teacher of piano privately in De Funiak Springs, Fla., 1972—. Has done demonstration and master teaching in kindergarten and elementary grades in public and private schools of California; director of Santa Monica Head Start program, 1966, and volunteer chairman of De Funiak Springs Head Start program, 1973. *Member:* Delta Phi Upsilon, Pilot Club.

WRITINGS: A Home for Hopper (juvenile), Morrow, 1971.

SIDELIGHTS: Rosemary Pendery writes: "My husband and I love to travel, back pack, hike, and camp. We enjoy riding bicycles and motor bikes, swimming and playing tennis. I am especially interested in the special needs of the slow learner and the emotionally disturbed child."

* * *

PEPPARD, Murray B(isbee) 1917-1974

May 23, 1917—September 3, 1974; American educator, translator, and author. Obituaries: *New York Times*, September 5, 1974. (*CA*-21/22).

* * *

PEPPLER, Alice Stolper 1934-

PERSONAL: Born March 14, 1934, in Saginaw, Mich.; daughter of Lothar E. (a teacher and music director) and Hulda (a high school cafeteria manager; maiden name, Koenig) Stolper; married James Schneider, July 28, 1956 (divorced, 1962); married Gerald Pollo Peppler (a Lutheran minister), June 28, 1964; children: (first marriage) Jeanne, Jon; (second marriage) Jan. *Education:* Concordia Teachers College, River Forest, Ill., B.S., 1956; University of Illinois, graduate study, 1966-67. *Religion:* Lutheran. *Home:* 3110 South Lowe Ave., Chicago, Ill. 60616. *Office:* Rand McNally & Co., P.O. Box 7600, Chicago, Ill. 60680.

CAREER: Elementary school teacher, librarian, and music director in Lutheran school in Chicago, Ill., 1956-63; Scott, Foresman & Co., Glenview, Ill., assistant editor of language arts materials, 1963-70, associate editor, 1970-71; Lyons & Carnahan, Chicago, Ill., senior editor of language arts materials, 1972-73; Rand McNally & Co., Chicago, Ill., senior editor of language arts materials, 1973-74, marketing director of language arts and foreign language publications in school department, 1974—. Piano teacher, 1956-63. Has demonstrated reading materials on educational television programs, 1968; has directed religious education workshops and language arts workshops, 1970—; conducted divorce forums and seminars, 1974—. *Member:* International Reading Association, National Council of Teachers of English, National Education Association, Lutheran Education Association.

WRITINGS: Who Put the Finger on God?: The Diminution of the Deity in American Textbooks (monograph), Lutheran Education Association, 1974; *Divorced and Christian*, Concordia, 1974.

Books with sound recordings and workbooks: *Bible Children I Know*, Concordia, 1971; *God's Love for Everyone*, Concordia, 1971; *Why Jesus Came*, Concordia, 1972.

Contributor of articles and poems to religious periodicals, including *Lutheran Forum, Lutheran Witness, Reporter, Advance, My Devotions*, and *Bridge*. Editor of *Lutheran Education Association Yearbook*, 1972—.

WORK IN PROGRESS: A humorous history of children's literature.

AVOCATIONAL INTERESTS: Music (plays pipe organ, piano, and flute; vocal soloist), travel (leads European tours).

* * *

PERCEVAL-MAXWELL, M(ichael) 1933-

PERSONAL: Born September 8, 1933, in England; son of John R. (a barrister) and Phoebe (Cherry) Perceval-Maxwell; married Maria J. A. deHoltzer, August 20, 1960; children: Shaun, Dylan. *Education:* Sir George Williams University, B.A., 1959; McGill University, M.A., 1961, Ph.D., 1966. *Office:* Department of History, McGill University, Montreal, Quebec, Canada.

CAREER: McGill University, Montreal, Quebec, lecturer, 1963-66, assistant professor, 1966-69, associate professor of history, 1969—, chairman of department, 1972. *Awards, honors:* Woodrow Wilson fellowship, 1961; Canada Council fellowship, 1971.

WRITINGS: The Scottish Migration to Ulster in the Reign of James I, Routledge & Kegan Paul, 1973. Contributor to *Irish Historical Studies*.

WORK IN PROGRESS: Research on seventeenth century Irish and Scottish history.

* * *

PERKINS, Rollin M(orris) 1889-

PERSONAL: Born March 15, 1889, in Lawrence, Kan.; son of Lucius Hiram (a lawyer) and Clara (a music teacher; maiden name, Morris) Perkins; married Florence Mary Payne, June 28, 1913 (died April 15, 1971); children: Rollin M. II, Helen (Mrs. Charles VanEpps), Clara (Mrs. Harold B. Beck). *Education:* University of Kansas, A.B., 1910; Stanford University, J.D., 1912; Harvard University, S.J.D., 1916. *Religion:* Presbyterian. *Home:* 2360 Pacific Ave., San Francisco, Calif. 94115. *Office:* Hastings College of Law, University of California, 198 McAllister St., San Francisco, Calif. 94102.

CAREER: Private practice of law in Lawrence, Kan., 1912-15; University of Iowa, Iowa City, assistant professor, 1916-19, associate professor, 1919-20, professor of law, 1920-46, director of peace officers' short course, 1937-46, director of Bureau of Public Affairs, 1945-46; Vanderbilt University, Nashville, Tenn., Frank C. Rand Professor of Law, 1946-49, acting dean, 1949; University of California, Los Angeles, Connell Professor of Law, 1950-57; University of California, San Francisco, professor of law at Hastings College of Law, 1957—. President of Iowa City Chamber of Commerce, 1928-30. *Military service:* U.S. Army, infantry, 1918-19; became second lieutenant. *Member:* American Bar Association, American Law Institute (life member).

WRITINGS: Cases on Criminal Procedure, University of Iowa Press, 1920, 3rd edition, 1929; *Iowa Criminal Justice*, University of Iowa Press, 1932; *Elements of Police Science*, Foundation Press, 1942; *Police Examinations*, Foundation Press, 1947; *Cases on Criminal Law and Procedure*, with teacher's manual, Foundation Press, 1952, 4th edition, 1972; *Perkins on Criminal Law*, Foundation Press, 1957, 2nd edition, 1969. Contributor to law journals, including *Journal of Criminal Law and Criminology, Illinois Law Forum, Harvard Law Review, Yale Law Journal, Boston University Law Review*, and *University of Pennsylvania Law Review*, and to *Harper's*.

PERKINS, William H(ughes) 1923-

PERSONAL: Born February 21, 1923, in Kansas City, Mo.; son of William C. (an engineer) and Edna (Hughes) Perkins; married Jill Thompson (a writer), June 16, 1952; children: Christopher, Scott, Alizon, Kyle. *Education:* Southwest Missouri State College, B.S., 1943; University of Missouri, M.A., 1949, Ph. D., 1952. *Home:* 5425 Weatherford Dr., Los Angeles, Calif. 90008. *Office:* Center for Study of Communicative Disorders, University of Southern California, Los Angeles, Calif. 90007.

CAREER: University of Southern California, Los Angeles, assistant professor, 1952-56, associate profesor, 1956-60, professor of communicative disorders, 1960—. *Military service:* U.S. Naval Reserve, 1943-46; became lieutenant commander. *Member:* American Speech and Hearing Association (fellow), American Psychological Association, Acoustical Society of America, American Association for the Advancement of Science, American Association of University Professors, American Cleft Palate Association, Sigma Xi. *Awards, honors:* Dart award, 1972, for innovative teaching.

WRITINGS: Speech Pathology: An Applied Behavorial Science, Mosby, 1971. Contributor to *Journal of Speech and Hearing Disorders, Journal of Speech and Hearing Research*, and *Journal of Behavioral Research and Therapy*.

WORK IN PROGRESS: Investigating stuttering as an incoordination of phonation with articulation.

* * *

PERRETT, Geoffrey 1940-

PERSONAL: Born April 15, 1940; married Ann Margaret Davies. *Education:* Long Beach City College, A.A., 1965; University of Southern California, B.A., 1967; Harvard University, M.A., 1969. *Home:* Springstone House, Ossett, Yorkshire, England.

CAREER: Author. *Military service:* U.S. Army, 1958-61. *Member*: Authors Guild of Authors League of America, Phi Beta Kappa.

WRITINGS: Days of Happiness, Years of Triumph, Coward, 1973; *Executive Privilege*, Coward, 1974.

WORK IN PROGRESS: The Woozle War, a novel; "A.D.," a play.

* * *

PERROY, Edouard (Marie Joseph) 1901-1974

August 2, 1901—1974; French historian, authority on medieval English history, and author. Obituaries: *AB Bookman's Weekly*, October 7, 1974.

* * *

PERRY, Jim (Angelo) 1942-

PERSONAL: Born June 18, 1942, in Los Angeles, Calif.; son of Frank George (a retail sales clerk) and Dorothy V. (Postestio) Perry; married Catherine Hofman (an elementary school teacher), May 12, 1973. *Education:* University of Southern California, B.A., 1964. *Home:* 532 Midvale Ave., #4, Los Angeles, Calif. 90024. *Agent:* Mike Hamilburg, 292 South La Cienega Blvd., Beverly Hills, Calif. 90211. *Office:* Sports Information Office, University of Southern California, University Park, Los Angeles, Calif. 90007.

CAREER: United Press International, Los Angeles, Calif., sportswriter, 1964-65; University of Southern California, Los Angeles, assistant director of Sports Information Office, 1966-67; KTLA-Television (Channel 5), Hollywood, Calif., sports producer, 1967; *Los Angeles Herald-Examiner*, Los Angeles, Calif., sportswriter, 1968-74; University of Southern California, Los Angeles, director of Sports Information Office, 1974—. *Military service:* U.S. Army Reserve, 1964-70. *Member:* College Sports Information Directors of America, Football Writers Association of America, Southern California Basketball Writers Association. *Awards, honors:* First prize from Hearst Newspapers Organization, 1972, for best sports story, an in-depth look at Satchel Paige.

WRITINGS: (With John McKay) *McKay: A Coach's Story*, Atheneum, 1974.

SIDELIGHTS: Perry told *CA:* "I have always felt good sportswriting should be clear, informative and, if possible, clever. The field of sports also offers a chance to be dramatic or sad or angry in your writing, because the ups and downs seem to mirror the frustration and elation of life itself. But never should people forget—and John McKay, a very witty man, subscribes to this theory—that athletic contests are just games. A sports story may be very revealing, a sports book may be very controversial, but never should the writer lose sight of the fact it should also be entertainment. I think too often that sports are taken too seriously. And I speak here both of those who celebrate sport without reservation and those who criticize it, or spend all their time looking for the problems in it." *Avocational interests:* Reading, jogging, "sitting in dark corners of bars."

* * *

PERRY, Rosalie Sandra 1945-

PERSONAL: Born May 31, 1945, in Little Rock, Ark.; daughter of John W. (a tax consultant) and Rosalie (a painter; maiden name, Baer) Perry. *Education:* University of Arkansas at Fayetteville, B.Mus., 1967; University of Texas at Austin, M.A., 1969, Ph.D., 1971. *Politics:* Democrat. *Home:* 8112 Westwood, Little Rock, Ark. 72204. *Office:* Office of Arkansas State Arts and Humanities, Little Rock, Ark. 72204.

CAREER: University of Texas at Austin, Division of Financial Aid, information specialist, 1968-70; Office of Arkansas State Arts and Humanities, Little Rock, executive director, 1971—. *Member:* Phi Beta Kappa, Alpha Lambda Delta, Sigma Alpha Iota.

WRITINGS: *Charles Ives and the American Mind*, Kent State University Press, 1974. Contributor to *Journal of Popular Culture*. Editor of *Historical Genealogies*, 1967, and *Dimensions*, 1969—.

WORK IN PROGRESS: Research on the position of the intellectual woman in American society, on the way in which decisions are made in political realms, on psychic phenomena and the influence of the emotions, and on the coming dark ages.

* * *

PETERS, Margaret Evelyn 1936-

PERSONAL: Born March 12, 1936, in Dayton, Ohio; daughter of Joseph Andrew (a contractor) and Mary (a clerk-typist; maiden name, Smith) Peters. *Education:* University of Dayton, B.A., 1959, B.S.Ed., 1963, M.A., 1972. *Religion:* Baptist. *Home:* 1312 Princeton Dr., Dayton, Ohio 45406. *Office:* Colonel White High School, 501 Niagara, Dayton, Ohio 45405.

CAREER: Teacher of history, English, and reading in public schools in Dayton, Ohio, 1963-67, teacher of Black history resources, 1967-73; Colonel White High School, Dayton, Ohio, teacher of history, English, and reading, 1973—. Conducts "Understanding through Education," a weekly radio program, dealing with minority history. Consultant to Pflaum. *Member:* National Education Association, National Association for the Advancement of Colored People, Dayton Area Reading Council.

WRITINGS: *The Ebony Book of Black Achievement*, Johnson Publishing Co. (Chicago), 1970.

WORK IN PROGRESS: Research on the male revolt in Bahia.

* * *

PETERSON, John Eric 1933-

PERSONAL: Born February 9, 1933, in Chicago, Ill.; son of Henry Norman (a milkman) and Lillian (a nurse; maiden name, Safholm) Peterson; married Barbara Brown, August 21, 1954 (divorced, 1968); married Jeanne Tiller (a university lecturer), September 14, 1968; children: Linda Joyce, Eric Coleman, Kristin Anne, Ian Carl, Karin Abeodu. *Education:* Kalamazoo College, B.A. (cum laude), 1954; University of Colorado, M.A., 1955; Northwestern University, Ph.D., 1963. *Politics:* Democrat. *Home:* K-19, Fourah Bay College, Freetown, Sierra Leone. *Office:* Department of History, Fourah Bay College, Freetown, Sierra Leone.

CAREER: Kalamazoo College, Kalamazoo, Mich., assistant professor, 1961-66, associate professor of history, 1966-68; Fourah Bay College, Freetown, Sierra Leone, professor of history, 1968—. Acting director of Institute of African Studies at University of Sierra Leone, 1971-72, 1973—; member of public archives committee of Sierra Leone, 1974—. *Awards, honors:* Ford Foundation foreign area training fellowship, 1958-60; Great Lakes College Association faculty fellowships, 1965, 1966-67.

WRITINGS: *Province of Freedom: A History of Sierra Leone, 1787-1870*, Northwestern University Press, 1969. Contributor of articles and reviews to learned journals. Editor of *Sierra Leone Studies*, 1969—, and *Africana Research Bulletin*, 1971-72.

WORK IN PROGRESS: *The Story of Sierra Leone*, with wife, Jeanne Peterson; research on the pre-colonial history of the Sierra Leone interior, especially the Temne and the Kono.

* * *

PETERSON, John J. 1918-

PERSONAL: Born November 22, 1918, in Chester, Pa.; son of Carl (a policeman) and Ellen (Maher) Peterson; married C. Lorraine Franz (an artist), October, 1950; children: Elizabeth Susan, Michael Joseph, Patrick Glenn. *Education:* Texas Christian University, B.A., 1958; University of Houston, M.A., 1965. *Politics:* Independent. *Religion:* Roman Catholic. *Residence:* Clinton, Md. *Office address;* Clavier House, P.O. Box 326, Clinton, Md. 20735.

CAREER: Served for 22 years in U.S. Army, Military Police, leaving service as a captain; *Daily Press*, Newport News, Va., reporter, 1960-61; National Aeronautics and

Space Administration, chief of the News Bureau for Space Task Group, Langley Air Force Base, Va., and Manned Spacecraft Center, Houston, Tex., 1961-64, special assistant to the Chief of Astronauts, 1964-68; Big Brothers of the National Capital Area, Washington, D.C., executive director, 1968-69; Communications Satellite Corp. (COMSAT), Washington, D.C., information officer, 1969—. Publisher, Clavier House, Clinton, Md. *Member:* International Association of Business Communicators.

WRITINGS: Into the Cauldron, Clavier House, 1973. Editor, *COMSAT News.*

WORK IN PROGRESS: A manuscript dealing with a nonfiction account of the murder and assault of police officers.

* * *

PETTERSSEN, Sverre 1898-1974

February 19, 1898—December 31, 1974; Norwegian-born American meteorologist, educator, and author. Obituaries: *AB Bookman's Weekly*, February 3, 1975.

* * *

PETTIT, Arthur G. 1938-

PERSONAL: Born May 20, 1938, in San Diego, Calif.; son of Gordon and Elsa (Marston) Pettit; married wife, Lynn, December 20, 1960; children: Kristina, Tom. *Education:* Attended Pomona College, 1956-58; San Diego State College (now University), B.A., 1961, M.A., 1962; University of California, Berkeley, Ph.D., 1970. *Politics:* Independent. *Home:* 115 East Caramillo, Colorado Springs, Colo. 80907. *Office:* Department of History, Colorado College, Colorado Springs, Colo. 80903.

CAREER: Colorado College, Colorado Springs, associate professor of American history, 1968—. Member of board of directors of Health Association of the Pikes Peak Region; member of citizens advisory committee of Pikes Peak Area Council of Governments; member of Springs Area Beautiful Association. *Member:* Organization of American Historians, Modern Language Association of America, Organization of Southern Historians. *Awards, honors:* American Philosophical Society fellow, 1969; National Endowment for the Humanities fellow, 1971-72.

WRITINGS: Mark Twain and the South, University Press of Kentucky, 1974. Contributor to *Western Historical Quarterly, Journal of Negro History, Rocky Mountain Social Science Journal*, and *Southern Literary Journal.*

WORK IN PROGRESS: Gringo and Greaser, completion expected in 1975; *The Mexican in American Film and Fiction*, 1975.

* * *

PHILLIPS, Edwin A(llen) 1915-

PERSONAL: Born March 18, 1915, in Lowell, Fla.; son of William Henry and Jane (Goodman) Phillips; married Margaret Ellen Knight, January 16, 1942; children: Ellen Knight, Nancy Jane. *Education:* Colgate University, A.B. (magna cum laude), 1937; University of Michigan, M.A., 1941, Ph.D., 1948. *Residence:* Claremont, Calif. *Office:* Department of Botany, Pomona College, Claremont, Calif. 91711.

CAREER: High school teacher in St. Johnsville, N.Y., 1937-39; Colgate University, Hamilton, N.Y., instructor in botany, 1946-48; Pomona College, Claremont, Calif., assistant professor, 1948-53, associate professor, 1953-57, professor of botany, 1957—, Wig Distinguished Professor, 1966, chairman of department, 1973. Visiting professor of plant ecology at University of Michigan Biological Station, summers, 1955, 1956, 1958, 1970, 1971; researcher at University of Kyoto, 1968. Consultant to Government of India, summers, 1964, 1965, University of Hawaii, 1968—, and Government of Indonesia, 1973. *Military service:* U.S. Naval Reserve, 1941—; active duty on destroyers, 1941-46; present rank, commander.

MEMBER: Botanical Society of America, American Bryological and Lichenological Soriety, British Bryological Society, Ecological Society of America, American Association for the Advancement of Science (fellow), American Society of Naturalists, Phi Beta Kappa, Sigma Xi, Phi Sigma. *Awards, honors:* National Science Foundation fellow at Harvard University, summer, 1961, and Oxford University, 1961-62; research grants from National Science Foundation for studies on California chaparral, 1966-68, Atomic Energy Commission for tracer studies in mosses, 1968—, and Schenck Research Fund for Botany, 1968—.

WRITINGS: Methods of Vegetation Study, Holt, 1959; *Field Ecology,* Heath, 1964; *Basic Ideas in Biology* and (with Edwin Battley) *Basic Demonstrations in Biology* (manual to accompany text), Macmillan, 1970; (with Frank Pottenger, Sister Edna Demanche, and others) "The Environment and Organisms: An Ecosystems Approach" (junior high school textbook series), Curriculum Laboratory, University of Hawaii, 1970—. Writer or editor of other biology texts and manuals for high school use. Contributor to *Grolier International Encyclopedia* and botanical journals.

WORK IN PROGRESS: A revised edition of *Methods of Vegetation Study:* succession studies on Michigan forests; other research on factors influencing fall coloration, and on design for controlled fires in Kenya game parks.

* * *

PICKENS, Donald Kenneth 1934-

PERSONAL: Born May 28, 1934, in Foss, Okla.; son of Kenneth and Lois Pickens; married Mary Jo Freeman, June 26, 1957; children: Kenneth, Elizabeth. *Education:* University of Oklahoma, B.A., 1956, M.A., 1957; University of Texas, Ph.D., 1964. *Office:* Department of History, North Texas State University, Denton, Tex. 76203.

CAREER: North Texas State University, Denton, assistant professor, 1965-68, associate professor of history, 1968—. *Member:* Organization of American Historians, American Studies Association.

WRITINGS: Eugenics and the Progressives, Vanderbilt University Press, 1968; (with G. L. Seligmann, Jr.) *American in Process*, Winston, 1973. Contributor to scholarly journals.

WORK IN PROGRESS: A book on William Graham Sumner.

* * *

PICKERING, Ernest 1893(?)-1974

1893(?)—August 30, 1974; American architect, educator, and author of books on architecture. Obituaries: *Washington Post*, September 1, 1974; *New York Times*, September 2, 1974; *AB Bookman's Weekly*, November 25, 1974.

PICKETT, Calder M. 1921-

PERSONAL: Born July 26, 1921, in Providence, Utah; son of Leland M. and Julia (Gessel) Pickett; married Nola Agricola, March 20, 1947; children: Carolyn, Kathleen. *Education:* Utah State University, B.S., 1941; Northwestern University, M.S.J., 1948; University of Minnesota, Ph.D., 1959. *Politics:* Democrat. *Religion:* Unitarian-Universalist. *Home:* 712 Lawrence Ave., Lawrence, Kan. 66044. *Office:* School of Journalism, University of Kansas, 204 Flint, Lawrence, Kan. 66045.

CAREER: Franklin County Citizen, Preston, Idaho, printer, 1937-41; *Salt Lake Tribune*, Salt Lake City, Utah, copyreader, 1946; Utah State University, Logan, instructor in English and journalism, 1946-48; *Deseret News*, Salt Lake City, Utah, copyreader, 1948-49; University of Denver, Denver, Colo., instructor in journalism, 1949-51; University of Kansas, Lawrence, professor of journalism, 1951—, Oscar S. Stauffer Professor of Journalism, 1973—. Copyreader for *Topeka Daily Capital*, summers, 1952-55, and *Kansas City Star*, summers, 1954, 1956-60, 1962. Adviser to Douglas County Bicentennial Commission, 1974—.

MEMBER: Association for Education in Journalism, Sigma Delta Chi. *Awards, honors:* Standard Oil Foundation distinguished teaching award, 1967; Frank Luther Mott research award from Kappa Tau Alpha, 1970; George Foster Peabody broadcasting award, 1974, for radio program "The American Past."

WRITINGS: Ed Howe: Country Town Philosopher, University Press of Kansas, 1969; *An Annotated Journalism Bibliography: 1959-1968*, University of Minnesota Press, 1970. Contributor to *Journalism Quarterly*, *Public Telecommunication Review*, and *Kansas City Star*. Book review editor of *Journalism Quarterly*.

SIDELIGHTS: Pickett owns an extensive collection of geographical, historical, photographic, and motion picture material concerning American cultural history, which he uses in connection with his radio program, "The American Past," on KANU-FM, to illustrate American history.

* * *

PIERCE, Bessie Louise 1888-1974

April 20, 1888—October 3, 1974; American historian, educator, and author of books on history and education. Obituaries: *New York Times*, October 5, 1974.

* * *

PINCUS, Lily 1898-

PERSONAL: Born March 13, 1898, in Karlovivary, Czechoslovakia; married Fritz Pincus (a bank's legal adviser), June 1, 1922 (died May 2, 1963). *Education:* Educated in Berlin, Germany. *Home:* 2 St. Alban's Rd., London N.W.5, England.

CAREER: Social worker and psychotherapist; staff member of Institute for Marital Studies, Tavistock Centre, London, England, until 1973. Former teacher in Israel.

WRITINGS: (With others) *Social Case Work in Marital Problems*, Tavistock Publications, 1955; (co-editor and contributor) *Marriage: Studies in Emotional Conflict and Growth*, Methuen, 1970; *Shared Fantasy in Marital Problems*, Tavistock Publications, 1965; *Death and the Family*, Pantheon, 1975.

PIOVENE, Guido 1907-1974

July 27, 1907—November 12, 1974; Italian journalist, essayist, and novelist. Obituaries: *New York Times*, November 13, 1974; *AB Bookman's Weekly*, December 2, 1974; *Publishers Weekly*, December 16, 1974.

* * *

PIPPERT, Wesley Gerald 1934-

PERSONAL: Born May 13, 1934, in Iowa; son of Harry V. (a farmer) and Magda E. (a farmer; maiden name, Halsor) Pippert. *Education:* State University of Iowa, B.A. (with honors), 1955; Wheaton College, Wheaton, Ill., M.A., 1966. *Politics:* Republican. *Religion:* Methodist. *Home:* 1330 Massachusetts Ave. N.W., Washington, D.C. 20005. *Office:* United Press International, 315 National Press Building, Washington, D.C. 20045.

CAREER: United Press International, reporter and editor in Minneapolis, Minn., Bismarck and Sioux Falls, S.D., Pierre, N.D., Chicago, Ill., and Washington, D.C., 1955-66; press aide to U.S. Senator Charles H. Percy, Republican of Illinois, 1967-69; United Press International, Washington, D.C., reporter and editor, 1969—. *Member:* American Political Science Association, Phi Beta Kappa, Phi Eta Sigma, Sigma Delta Chi. *Awards, honors:* Congressional fellow of American Politcal Science Association, 1966-67.

WRITINGS: Missions and Reconciliations, United Methodist Board of Missions, 1969; *Faith at the Top*, David Cook, 1974; *Memo for 1976: Some Political Options*, Inter-Varsity Press, 1974; (contributor) Clifford W. Brown, Jr., editor, *Jaws of Victory*, Little, Brown, 1974. Contributor to *Dictionary of Christian Social Ethics*. Contributor to *Christianity Today, Christian Life, Eternity*, and *Moody Monthly*.

WORK IN PROGRESS: A book on the ethical implications of Watergate, tentatively titled *Misguided Loyalty*, for Creation House.

* * *

PIRSIG, Robert M(aynard) 1928-

PERSONAL: Born September 6, 1928, in Minneapolis, Minn.; son of Maynard E. (a professor) and Harriet (Sjobeck) Pirsig; married Nancy James (an administrator), May 10, 1954; children: Christopher, Theodore. *Education:* University of Minnesota, B.A., 1950, M.A., 1958. *Home:* 458 Otis Ave., St. Paul, Minn. 55104.

CAREER: Montana State College (now University), Bozeman, instructor in English composition, 1959-61; University of Illinois, Chicago, instructor in rhetoric, 1961-62; technical writer at several Minneapolis, Minn., electronic firms, 1963-67; Century Publications, Minneapolis, Minn., contract technical writer, 1967-73; writer. Minnesota Zen Meditation Center, member of board of directors, 1973—, vice-president, 1973-75. *Military service:* U.S. Army, 1946-48. *Member:* Society of Technical Communicators (past secretary and treasurer). *Awards, honors:* Guggenheim fellowship, 1974.

WRITINGS: Zen and the Art of Motorcycle Maintenance: An Inquiry into Values, Morrow, 1974.

WORK IN PROGRESS: Anthropological research, intended to relate metaphysics of quality, as defined in first book, to cultural problems of today.

SIDELIGHTS: "*Zen and the Art of Motorcycle Maintenance* is an exciting autobiography that is at the same time a serious philosophical reflection on contemporary American culture," recounts Richard L. Rubenstein. "Pirsig tells of an extraordinary motorcycle journey he took during the summer of 1968 with his 11-year-old son Chris. . . . Pirsig takes a commonplace article of technological society and teaches us to see it as a simple yet profound image of ourselves and our world."

R. Z. Sheppard writes: "*Zen and the Art of Motorcycle Maintenance* is an unforgettable trip. It accelerates from the befuddlements of transmission linkage through Pirsig's history of Western thought to the mysteries of divine madness with scarcely a wobble. The fact that much of Pirsig's torque-wrenched dissertation echoes the quandaries that some high-energy physicists have about the nature of matter is not of primary importance. What matters most is that he communicates how very much he cares about living as a whole man and how hard he has worked at it. Indeed, the special gift of the universal principle that Pirsig calls Quality is caring, even if one reaches for the heavens with grease on his hands."

George Steiner sums up his reaction to Pirsig's book: "A detailed technical treatise on the tools, on the routines, on the metaphysics of a specialized skill; the legend of a great hunt after identity, after the salvation of mind and soul out of obsession, the hunter being hunted; a fiction repeatedly interrupted by, enmeshed with, a lengthy meditation on the ironic and tragic singularities of American man—the analogies with *Moby Dick* are patent. Robert Pirsig invites the prodigious comparison."

BIOGRAPHICAL/CRITICAL SOURCES: Carolyn Riley, *Contemporary Literary Criticism*, Volume IV, Gale, 1975.

* * *

PLANZ, Allen 1937-

PERSONAL: Born January 2, 1937, in New York; son of John and Adeline Planz; married Doris Somers (a research director), 1963; children: Laurel. *Education:* New York University, M.A., 1961. *Home address:* P.O. Box 212, East Hampton, N.Y. 11937.

CAREER: Has taught in English department at Hunter College of the City University of New York, New York, N.Y., University of North Carolina at Chapel Hill, and at Queens College of the City University of New York, Flushing, N.Y.; New York University, New York, N.Y., member of faculty of School of the Arts, 1967-68; *Nation* (magazine), New York, N.Y., poetry editor, 1969-71; Chapman College, Montauk, N.Y., lecturer in poetry, 1973-74. Captain of charter fishing boat in Montauk, N.Y., 1970—. Director of St. Mark's Poetry Project, 1966-68; director of Upstairs Gallery Poetry Series; participating American poet in International Poetry Conference, 1968, and N.Y. State Poets-in-the-Schools program, 1974-75. *Military service:* U.S. Army, 1960-61.

MEMBER: International P.E.N. *Awards, honors:* Won Mid-South Literary Competition, 1963; won New York Poetry Center competition for younger poets, 1966; Hart Crane Award, 1968; National Arts Club grant, 1969; N.Y. Council on the Arts CAP award, 1975.

WRITINGS: Heir to Anger (poems), Lower East Press, 1964; *Studsong* (poems), Lower East Press, 1965; *Poor White and Other Poems*, Goosetree Press, 1966; *A Night for Rioting* (poems), Swallow, 1969; *Wild-Craft* (poems), Island Press, 1975.

Work is anthologized in *Poets of Today*, edited by Walter Lowenfels, International Publishers, 1964; *Where Is Vietnam?*, edited by Lowenfels and Nan Braymer, Doubleday, 1967; *East Side Scene*, edited by Allen DeLoach, University of Buffalo Press, 1969; *Poems from the Third World*, edited by Lowenfels, Macmillan, 1969. Contributor to *Nation, Sierra Club*, and *Saltwater Sportsman*. Contributing editor of *Street* (magazine).

WORK IN PROGRESS: A book on marine life in inshore ecosystems, with staff of Ocean Science Laboratories at Montauk; research on daily and seasonal movement of fish.

* * *

PLOWMAN, Stephanie 1922-

PERSONAL: Born December 28, 1922; daughter of Franklyn James (a power station employee) and Violet (Grainger) Plowman; married Arthur Richard Hamilton-Dee (died, 1957). *Education:* University of London, B.A. (honors), 1944, further study, 1948-50, Ph.D. *Religion:* Russian Orthodox Church. *Home:* 2 The Knell, Mathon, Malvern, Worcestershire, England.

CAREER: Teacher and lecturer at various times in England, South Africa, and Ghana; Calouste Gulbenkian research fellow at Lucy Cavendish College, Cambridge University, Cambridge, England.

WRITINGS: Nelson, Methuen, 1955; *Sixteen Sail in Aboukir Bay*, Methuen, 1956; *To Spare the Conquered*, Methuen, 1960; *The Road to Sardis*, Bodley Head, 1965, Houghton, 1966; *Three Lives for the Czar*, Bodley Head, 1969, Houghton, 1970; *My Kingdom for a Grave*, Bodley Head, 1970, Houghton, 1971.

WORK IN PROGRESS: A non-fiction historical book on Anglo-Russian relations 1914-1918, researched under auspices of the Gulbenkian Foundation; a juvenile novel centered on the daughter of Marie Antoinette.

* * *

PLUMMER, William J(oseph) 1927-

PERSONAL: Born August 20, 1927, in Eau Claire, Wis.; son of William Edmund (a truckdriver) and Agnes (Bruckner) Plummer; married Wanda Ash (a registered nurse), September 17, 1950; children: Leslie (Mrs. Tom Dorn), Christopher, Robert, (William) Michael. *Education:* University of Wisconsin, B.S., 1949, E.E., 1960; University of Nevada at Las Vegas, M.B.A., 1972. *Politics:* "No." *Religion:* "Non-denominational Christian: and sometimes Unitarian." *Home:* 4317 Woodcrest Rd., Las Vegas, Nev. 89121. *Office:* E.G.& G., Inc., 680 Sunset Rd., Las Vegas, Nev. 89101.

CAREER: Registered professional engineer in New Mexico, 1955; University of Wisconsin, College of Engineering, Madison, instructor in mechanics, 1948-50; Gisholt Machine Tool Co., Madison, Wis., design engineer, 1950-51; Los Alamos Scientific Laboratory, Los Alamos, N.M., staff member, 1952-59, assistant group leader in test instrumentation (J8), 1960-61; E.G.&G., Inc., Las Vegas, Nev., program manager and operations manager, 1962-71, manager of administration, contract group, 1972—. Has held part-time teaching positions at University of Nevada at Las Vegas and at University of New Mexico. *Military service:* U.S. Naval Reserve, 1945-46. *Member:* Tau Beta Pi, Eta Kappa Nu, Phi Kappa Phi.

WRITINGS: A Quail in the Family (nonfiction), Regnery, 1974; *Friends of the Family* (nonfiction), Regnery, 1975.

WORK IN PROGRESS: Five of a Kind, another authentic account of quail raised in a suburban back yard, completion expected in 1975; a novel set in the mountains of New Mexico, combining nature lore with socio-psychological peculiarities of secluded scientific community, tentatively titled, *Day of the Puma*; a biography of a living celebrity; studies of animal behavior, with photographs.

SIDELIGHTS: "Although always interested in communication, never seriously considered writing," Plummer told *CA*. "Wrote first book (at age forty-six) simply because the story needed telling. It was fun. There was a logical follow-on (second book), and now I am hooked. I hope to devote full-time in a few years."

* * *

POAGE, Scott T(abor) 1931-
(P. T. Scott)

PERSONAL: Surname rhymes with "vogue"; born December 5, 1931, in Waco, Tex.; son of Scott Allen (a rancher) and Robbie Lee (Tabor) Poage. *Education:* Texas Technological College (now Texas Tech University), B.S. in Ind. Engr., 1953; Agricultural and Mechanical College of Texas (now Texas A&M University), M.S., 1957; Oklahoma State University, Ph.D., 1962. *Politics:* Democrat. *Religion:* Episcopalian. *Home:* 2828 Bammel, No. 1205, Houston, Tex. 77006. *Office:* Department of Industrial Engineering, University of Houston, Houston, Tex. 77004.

CAREER: Registered professional engineer in Texas and Oklahoma. Phillips Petroleum Co., McGregor, Tex., production control engineer, 1953; Agricultural and Mechanical College of Texas (now Texas A&M University), College Station, instructor in industrial engineering, 1957-59; Oklahoma State University, Stillwater, assistant professor of industrial engineering, 1959-61; University of Texas, Arlington, associate professor, 1961-62, professor of industrial engineering, 1962-67. chairman of department, 1961-67; University of Houston, Tex., professor of industrial engineering and chairman of department, 1967—. Vice-president and member of board of directors of Brazoes Bolt Co.; member of board of trustees of Canturbury House, Arlington, Tex. Consultant, at various times, to business and government agencies, including American Manufacturing Company of Texas, Texas Instruments, Inc., American Airlines, Ling-Temco-Vought, and U.S. Agency for International Development, India. *Military service:* U.S. Air Force, 1953-55; became first lieutenant. U.S. Air Force Reserve; now captain (retired).

MEMBER: American Institute of Industrial Engineers (fellow; president of Fort Worth-Dallas chapter, 1964-65; national vice-president, 1965-67; director of Houston chapter, 1971-75), American Society of Engineering Education, Operations Research Society of America (chairman of Houston chapter, 1969-73), Houston Area Colloquium on Operations Research, Petroleum Club of Fort Worth, Houston Engineering and Scientific Society, Tau Beta Pi, Sigma Xi, Phi Kappa Phi, Alpha Pi Mu, Kappa Sigma, Rotary, Masons. *Awards, honors:* Danforth Foundation award.

WRITINGS: Quantitative Management Method, Barnes & Noble, 1970. Author of technical reports. Writes fiction under pseudonym, P. T. Scott. Contributor to proceedings; also contributor to journals and periodicals, including *Journal of Industrial Engineering, Journal of Engineering Education*, and *Library Quarterly*. Member of editorial boards of *Journal of Industrial Engineering*, 1967-69, and of *American Institute of Industrial Engineers Transactions*, 1969—.

WORK IN PROGRESS: A book tentatively titled *Production: Theoretical Foundations;* research on the theory of queues, on engineering economy, and on production theory.

SIDELIGHTS: Poage told *CA* that he and his family "operate farm and ranch properties in West Texas which have been the principal family interest for generations." *Avocational interests:* Travel, Russian antiques, reading (history, biography, Brann, "the Iconoclast," Mencken, Shaw).

* * *

POCOCK, Nick 1934-

PERSONAL: Born June 15, 1934, in London, England; son of Derrick Geoffrey (an engineer) and Mabel (Knight) Pocock; married Alvena Prause (a newspaper columnist, artist, and author of children's literature), December 7, 1963; children: Stephen Guy, Alicia Annette. *Education:* Kingston Technical College, Higher National Diploma in mechanical engineering, 1959. *Residence:* China Spring, Tex. *Mailing address:* Box 672, Hillsboro, Tex. 76645. *Office:* Certain-teed Products Corp., P.O. Box 403, Hillsboro, Tex. 76645.

CAREER: Central Electricity Generating Board, Kingston-upon-Thames, England, graduate trainee and control engineer, 1959-63; cropspraying pilot in Texas, Mississippi, and Central America, 1964-65; Certain-teed Products Corp., Hillsboro, Tex., industrial engineer, 1966—. *Military service:* Royal Air Force Volunteer Reserve, cadet pilot, 1953-56. Royal Air Force, junior technician and instrument fitter, 1956-58. *Member:* American Aviation Historical Society, Experimental Aircraft Association, Institution of Mechanical Engineers.

WRITINGS: Did W. D. Custead Fly First?, Special Aviation Publications, 1974. Contributor to *Popular Flying, Antiquer, Private Pilot, Pilot, Flying, Sport Aviation, Safe Worker*, and *National Safety News*.

WORK IN PROGRESS: A manual on flying aerobatics; research on the history of early aviation in the area of Waco, Tex.

SIDELIGHTS: Pocock has been an aviation enthusiast for most of his life. From boyhood aeromodelling, he graduated to full-size airplanes, when he learned to fly in the "Tiger Moths" of the London Aeroplane Club. Flying aerobatics with the Tiger Club air shows for several years, he also won several contests, and was the sole representative of the United Kingdom competing in the World Aerobatic Championships in Budapest.

In addition to aerobatic flying, Pocock's skills include sky-writing, soaring, glider-towing, aerial photography, motion picture filming, antique aircraft, and instruction.

BIOGRAPHICAL/CRITICAL SOURCES: Flight International, August 16, 1962; *Air Progress*, December, 1966.

* * *

PODBIELSKI, Gisele 1918-

PERSONAL: Born December 3, 1918, in Vienna, Austria; daughter of Arnold and Lusia (Landau) Schneider; married Rene Gerhard Podbielski (a writer), June 21, 1946; children: Andrew Peter. *Education:* University of Geneva, Licence es Sciences Economiques, 1939; also studied at London School of Economics and Political Science, 1939-

40, and Cambridge University, 1951-52. *Home:* 25 via della Lungara, Rome, Italy.

CAREER: University of Melbourne, Melbourne, Australia, lecturer in economics, 1941-44; Department of External Affairs, Canberra, Australia, economic affairs officer, 1944-46. Economic affairs officer for Economic Commission for Europe of the United Nations, 1947-65. Visiting professor at Johns Hopkins University in Bologna. *Awards, honors:* Rockefeller Foundation scholarship, Cambridge University, 1951-52.

WRITINGS: Italy: Development and Crisis in the Postwar Economy, Oxford University Press, 1974. Contributor to *Twenty Economic Surveys of Europe*, published by United Nations.

* * *

POLSBY, Nelson W(oolf) 1934-
(Arthur Clun)

PERSONAL: Born October 25, 1934, in Norwich, Conn.; son of Daniel II (a businessman) and Edythe (Woolf) Polsby; married Linda Dale Offenbach, August 3, 1958; children: Lisa Susan, Emily Ann, Daniel Ralph. *Education:* Brown University, student, 1955-56; Johns Hopkins University, A.B., 1956; Yale University, M.A., 1958, Ph.D., 1961. *Residence:* Berkeley, Calif. *Office:* Department of Political Science, University of California, Berkeley, Calif. 94720.

CAREER: University of Wisconsin, Madison, instructor in political science, 1960-61; Wesleyan University, Middletown, Conn., assistant professor, 1961-64, associate professor, 1964-67, professor of government, 1967-68; University of California, Berkeley, professor of political science, 1967—. Visiting member of faculty at Columbia University, 1963, Yale University, 1963, 1967, and Hebrew University of Jerusalem, 1970; fellow of Center for Advanced Studies in the Behavioral Sciences, Stanford, Calif., 1965-66. Member of committee on public engineering policy of National Academy of Engineering, 1973—. Member of commission on vice-presidential selection of Democratic National Committee, 1973-74.

MEMBER: American Political Science Association (member of council, 1971—), American Sociological Association, Phi Beta Kappa. *Awards, honors:* Social Science Research Council fellowship, 1959; Brookings Institution fellowship, 1959-60; Ford Foundation fellowship, 1970-71.

WRITINGS: Community Power and Political Theory, Yale University Press, 1963; (editor with Robert A. Dentler and Paul A. Smith) *Politics and Social Life: An Introduction to Political Behavior*, Houghton, 1963; (editor with R. L. Peabody) *New Perspectives on the House of Representatives*, Rand McNally, 1963, revised edition, 1969; *Congress and the Presidency*, Prentice-Hall, 1964, revised edition, 1971; (with Aaron Wildavsky) *Presidential Elections*, Scribner, 1964, 3rd edition, 1971; *Congress: An Introduction*, Rand McNally, 1968; (editor with Wildavsky) *American Governmental Institutions*, Rand McNally, 1968; *The Citizen's Choice: Humphrey or Nixon*, Public Affairs Press, 1968.

(Editor) *Congressional Behavior*, Random House, 1971; (editor) *Reapportionment in the 1970's*, University of California Press, 1971; (editor) *The Modern Presidency*, Random House, 1973; *Political Promises*, Oxford University Press, 1974.

Contributor, occasionally under pseudonym Arthur Clun, to political science periodicals, national magazines, including *Harper's*, and newspapers, including *Washington Post* and *Wall Street Journal*. Managing editor of *American Political Science Review*, 1971—; book review editor of *Transaction*, 1968-71; member of editorial advisory board of *Law and Society Review*, *Political Science Quarterly*, and *Journal of Political and Military Sociology*.

WORK IN PROGRESS: Further research on Congress, national politics, policy innovation in America, and comparative study of legislatures.

* * *

PONS, Maurice 1927-

PERSONAL: Born September 14, 1927, in Strasbourg, France; son of Emile (a teacher) and Jeanne (Dole) Pons. *Education:* Sorbonne, University of Paris, licencie es lettres, 1946, diplome d'etudes superieures de philosophie, 1947. *Home:* le Moulin d'Ande, Saint-Pierre-de-Vauvray, France.

CAREER: Writer. *Awards, honors:* Grand Prix de la nouvelle, 1955, for *Virginales*.

WRITINGS—Novels, except as indicated: *Metrobate*, Julliard, 1951; *La Mort d'Eros*, Julliard, 1953; *Virginales* (title means "In All Innocence"), Julliard, 1955; *Le Cordonnier Aristote* (title means "A Shoemaker Named Aristotle"), Julliard, 1958; *Le Passager de la nuit* (title means "The Passenger of the Night"), Julliard, 1960; *Les Saisons* (title means "The Seasons"), Julliard, 1965; *Rosa*, Denoel, 1967, translation by Richard Howard published under same title, Dial, 1972; *La Passion de Sebastien N.: Une Histoire d'amour* (title means "The Passion of Sebastian"), Denoel, 1968; *Chto!* (two-act play), C. Bourgois, 1970; *Mademoiselle B*, Denoel, 1973, translation by Patricia Wolf published under same title, St. Martin's, 1973.

Author of French adaptation of play, "La Danse du Sergent Musgrave," by John Arden, 1963; author of dialog for film, "La Belle Vie," 1962, and of screenplay for "La Dormeuse," 1962, and "Sam Gizanya," 1973.

* * *

PORTAL, Colette 1936-

PERSONAL: Born March 9, 1936, in Paris, France; married Jean Michel Folon, March 20, 1961 (separated); children: Francois. *Education:* Studied four years at art school in Paris. *Politics:* "Love." *Religion:* "Love." *Home:* 65 bis Boulevard Brune, Paris 75014, France. *Agent:* John Locke, 15 East 76th St., New York, N.Y. 10021.

CAREER: Artist and illustrator.

WRITINGS: Le Premier cri, Quist, 1973, adaptation by Guy Daniels published as *The Beauty of Birth*, Knopf, 1971.

Illustrator: *La Vie d'unc reine*, Hatier, 1964, translation by Marcia Nardi published as *The Life of a Queen*, Braziller, 1964; A. M. Cocagnac, *La Creation du monde*. Editions du Cerf, 1967; Franklin Russell, *The Honeybees*, Knopf, 1967.

WORK IN PROGRESS: Ten books without text, with one theme, "all beginning."

SIDELIGHTS: Colette Portal works in crayon, pastels, water color, gouache, oils, the earth ("the marble that comes from the earth"). In illustrating, she doesn't believe that it is necessary to portray children *for* children. "They love life just as it is, the truth. With each making up their own characters, their dreams, their images.

"The act of drawing, painting, modeling, sculpturing, comes from the senses. They are not a cerebral act. Between the materials and the hand an exchange, a purely sensitive flow, sensual. There is a time for each technique. It is a matter of spirit. One has a crayon, a color, one has the earth."

* * *

PORTER, Andrew 1928-

PERSONAL: Born August 26, 1928, in Cape Town, South Africa. *Education:* University College, Oxford, M.A., 1950. *Office: New Yorker*, 25 West 43rd St., New York, N.Y. 10036.

CAREER: Financial Times, London, England, music critic, 1950—. Music critic for *New Yorker*, 1972—. Visiting fellow at All Souls College, Oxford, 1973-74. Member of music panel of Arts Council of Great Britain, 1962—; member of music advisory committee of British Council, 1966—. *Member:* Royal Musical Association (member of council, 1964—), Critics Circle of Great Britain (president, 1971, 1972), Donizetti Society (vice-president).

WRITINGS: (With Desmond Shawe-Taylor, Edward Sackville-West, and William Mann) *The Record Guide*, Collins, 1955; *A Musical Season*, Viking, 1974. Has translated Wagner's "Ring of the Nibelung," Verdi's "Don Carlos" and "Rigoletto," and Richard Strauss's "Intermezzo," for performances; writer of vocal scores and libretti. Editor of *Musical Times*, 1960-67; member of editorial board of *Opera*, 1953—; member of editorial executive committee of *Grove's Dictionary of Music and Musicians*, 6th edition.

WORK IN PROGRESS: Writing on Verdi.

* * *

PORTER, J(oshua) R(oy) 1921-

PERSONAL: Born May 7, 1921, in Godley, England; son of Joshua (a solicitor's clerk) and Bessie Evelyn (Earlam) Porter. *Education:* Merton College, Oxford, B.A. (modern history), 1942; St. Stephen's House, Oxford, B.A. (theology), 1945, M.A., 1948. *Politics:* Tory. *Home address:* Jasin, Taddyforde, Exeter, Devonshire, England. *Office:* Queen's Building, University of Exeter, Exeter, Devonshire EX4 4QJ, England.

CAREER: Clerk in holy orders of Church of England; Oxford University, Oxford, England, lecturer in theology, 1949-62, tutor in theology, fellow, and chaplain of Oriel College, 1949-62; University of Exeter, Exeter, England, professor of theology and head of department, 1962—, dean of arts, 1968-71. Canon and prebendary of wightring at Chichester Cathedral, 1965—. Member of Apocrypha Panel for the New English Bible, 1956-70; visiting professor at Southeastern Seminary (North Carolina), 1967. *Member:* Anglican Association, Royal Stuart Society, Society for Old Testament Study, Society of Biblical Literature, Folklore Society, Institute of Religion and Theology (member of council), Society of British Orientalists.

WRITINGS: World in the Heart, Fortune Press, 1944; *Moses and Monarchy*, Basil Blackwell, 1963; *The Extended Family in the Old Testament*, Edutext Publications, 1967; *Proclamation and Presence*, John Knox, 1970; *The Non-Juring Bishops*, Royal Stuart Society, 1973; *The Book of Leviticus*, Cambridge University Press, 1975.

Contributor: F. F. Bruce, editor, *Promise and Fulfillment*, T. & T. Clark, 1963; M. Walton, editor, *A Source Book of the Bible for Teachers*, S.C.M. Press, 1969; G. W. Anderson, editor, *Tradition and Interpretation*, Oxford University Press, 1975.

Contributor to *Chamber's Encyclopaedia*. Contributor to theology journals, including *Journal of Theological Studies, Journal of Biblical Literature, Expository Times, Theology, Church Quarterly Review*, and *Faith and Unity*.

WORK IN PROGRESS: Books on Joshua and Judges; research on the problems of kingship in the Old Testament.

* * *

POSNER, Richard 1944-
(Iris Foster, Beatrice Murray, Paul Todd, Dick Wine)

PERSONAL: Born October 7, 1944, in Manhattan, N.Y.; son of Murray (an accountant) and Beatrice (an executive secretary; maiden name, Dorfman) Posner; married Iris Hoffman, December 4, 1971; children: Jarrod Seth. *Education:* Hofstra University, B.A., 1965; Queens College of the City University of New York, graduate study, 1965-67. *Politics:* "Independent; slightly conservative; but usually vote Democratic." *Religion:* Jewish. *Residence:* Selden, N.Y. *Agent:* Henry Morrison, Inc., 58 West 10th St., New York, N.Y. 10011.

CAREER: Scott Meredith Literary Agency, Inc., New York, N.Y., editor, 1967-72; writer, 1972—.

WRITINGS: (With Jonathan Craig) *The New York Crime Book*, Pyramid Publications, 1972; *The Mafia Man* (novel), Fawcett, 1973; *The Seven Ups* (novel from a film), Fawcett, 1973; *The Trigger Man* (novel), Fawcett, 1974; *Welcome, Sinner* (novel), Putnam, 1974; *The Image and the Flesh* (novel), Fawcett, 1975; *Lucas Tanner* (novel), Pyramid Publications, 1975.

Under pseudonym Iris Foster—Gothic novels: *The Moorwood Legacy*, Lancer Books, 1972; *Deadly Sea, Deadly Sand*, Lancer Books, 1972; *Nightshade*, Lancer Books, 1973; *The Sabath Quest*, Lancer Books, 1973; *The Crimson Moon*, Lancer Books, 1973.

Under pseudonym Beatrice Murray: *The Dark Sonata* (gothic novel), Dell, 1971.

Under pseudonym Dick Wine: *Allegro with Passion* (novel), Lancer Books, 1973.

Work is anthologized in *Living City Adventures*, edited by Mildred Freeman, Globe Book, 1970; *Infinity Three*, edited by Robert Hoskins, Lancer Books, 1971.

WORK IN PROGRESS: The Seventh Season, a novel, for Putnam; *Blood All Over* (tentative title), a novel, under pseudonym Paul Todd.

SIDELIGHTS: Posner writes: "I have no particular axe to grind in my books, and I'm suspicious of writers who do. As soon as a writer states that he is going to explore the moral tragedy of mankind or demonstrate the collapse of the ego, or whatever, I'm turned off. These themes can be used, and used well, but I firmly believe that the story must come first, and the theme out of that.

"I prefer controlled writing to overemotional writing, just as I prefer classical and baroque music to romantic music. I read Iris Murdoch, Louis Auchincloss, and others to absorb the talent of understating powerful emotion. I find a face averted and a clenched hand far more moving than flowing tears and hand-wringing. I suppose I like well-wrought suspense thrillers for the same reasons. I'm repelled when a writer becomes lavish with naked emotion."

AVOCATIONAL INTERESTS: Classical music, drawing in pencil, reading, playing sonatas on the piano.

* * *

POTTER, Jeremy 1922-

PERSONAL: Born April 25, 1922, in London, England; married Margaret Newman (a novelist under name Margaret Potter, and pseudonym Anne Betteridge), 1950; children: Jocelyn, Jonathan. *Education:* Oxford University, M.A., 1953. *Agent:* A. D. Peters & Co., 10 Buckingham St., London W.C.2, England.

CAREER: Novelist and publisher.

WRITINGS—Novels: *Hazard Chase*, Constable, 1964; *Death in the Office*, Constable, 1965; *Foul Play*, Constable, 1967; *The Dance of Death*, Constable, 1968, Walker & Co., 1969; *A Trail of Blood*, Constable, 1970, McCall Publishing, 1971; *Going West*, Constable, 1972; *Disgrace and Favour*, Constable, 1975.

(Translator with Kennedy McWhirter) Hans Becker, pseud., *Devil on My Shoulder*, Landsborough Publications, 1958.

* * *

POUSSAINT, Alvin F(rancis) 1934-

PERSONAL: Born May 15, 1934, in East Harlem, N.Y.; son of Christopher Thomas and Harriet (Johnson) Poussaint; married Ann Ashmore (a social worker), November 4, 1973. *Education:* Columbia University, B.A., 1956; Cornell University, M.D., 1960; University of California, Los Angeles, M.S., 1964. *Home:* 28 Bellingham Rd., Brookline, Mass. 02167. *Office:* School of Medicine, Harvard University, 25 Shattuck St., Boston, Mass. 02115.

CAREER: University of California, Los Angeles, intern with Center for the Health Sciences, 1960-61, psychiatric resident with Neuropsychiatric Institute, 1961-64, chief resident, 1964-65; Tufts University, Medical School, Boston, Mass., senior clinical instructor of psychiatry, 1965-66, assistant professor of psychiatry and preventive medicine, 1967-69; Harvard University, School of Medicine, Boston, Mass., associate professor of psychiatry, 1969—, associate dean for student affairs, 1969—. Director of psychiatry at Columbia Point Health Center, 1968-69; associate psychiatrist at Massachusetts Mental Health Center, 1969—; chairman of board of directors of Solomon Fuller Institute; member of board of trustees of Operation PUSH (People United to Save Humanity), 1971—. *Member:* American Psychiatric Association (fellow), National Association of Afro-American Artists (member of board of trustees, 1968—).

WRITINGS: (Contributor) Floyd Barbour, editor, *Black Power Revolt*, Sargent, 1968; (contributor) John Henrik Clarke, editor, *William Styron's Nat Turner: Ten Black Writers Respond*, Beacon Press, 1968; (contributor) *Urban Violence*, University of Chicago Press, 1969; (contributor) Robinson, Foster, and Ogilvie, editors, *Black Studies in the University: A Symposium*, Yale University Press, 1969.

(Author of introduction) *What Students Want: A National Survey Prepared by the United States Commission on Civil Rights*, Emerson Hall, 1971; *Why Blacks Kill Blacks*, Emerson Hall, 1972; (contributor) Alvin Toffler, editor, *Learning for Tomorrow*, Random House, 1974; (with James P. Comer) *Black Child Care*, Simon & Schuster, in press.

Contributor to *Grolier Encyclopedia Yearbook*. Contributor of about sixty articles to social sciences and black studies journals, and to popular magazines, including *Ebony, Black Scholar, Psychology Today, Redbook, Rehabilitation Record*, and *International Journal of Psychiatry*, and to newspapers, including *New York Times* and *Boston Globe*.

BIOGRAPHICAL/CRITICAL SOURCES: George R. Metcalf, *Up from Within*, McGraw, 1971.

* * *

POWE, Bruce 1925-
(Ellis Portal)

PERSONAL: Surname rhymes with "cow"; born June 9, 1925, in Edmonton, Alberta, Canada; son of Wilbur (an accountant) and Lillian (Barr) Powe; married Alys M. Brady, June 30, 1949; children: Bruce William, Kathleen. *Education:* University of Alberta, B.A., 1949, M.A., 1951. *Politics:* Liberal Party of Canada. *Religion:* Anglican. *Home:* 158 Ridley Blvd., Toronto, Ontario M5M 3M1, Canada. *Office:* Canadian Life Insurance Association, 44 King St. W., Toronto, Ontario, Canada.

CAREER: Government of Canada, Ottawa, Ont., special assistant to minister of Mines and Technical Surveys, 1951-57; Imperial Oil Ltd., Toronto, Ontario, editorial assistant, 1957-60; Ontario Liberal Association, Toronto, Ontario, executive director, 1960-63; Baker Advertising Ltd., Toronto, Ontario, vice-president in public relations, 1964-66; Canadian Life Insurance Association, Toronto, Ontario, director of public relations, 1966—. *Military service:* Canadian Army, 1944-45; served in United Kingdom. *Member:* Canadian Public Relations Society, Toronto Men's Press Club.

WRITINGS: *Expresso '67* (satire), Peter Martin Associates, 1966; (under pseudonym Ellis Portal) *Killing Ground: The Canadian Civil War* (novel), Peter Martin Associates, 1968, 2nd edition published under name Bruce Powe, Peter Martin Associates, 1972; *Last Days of the American Empire* (novel), St. Martin's, 1974.

WORK IN PROGRESS: A novel.

* * *

POWERS, Edward Alton 1927-

PERSONAL: Born October 26, 1927, in Jamestown, N.Y.; son of Leslie Edgar (a banker) and Mabelle (Alton) Powers; married Ella Pierson (a Congressional staff member), June 18, 1949; children: Randall Edward, Christopher Alan, Ann Lyn. *Education:* College of Wooster, B.A., 1948; Yale University, B.D., 1952; Columbia University, Ed.D., 1973. *Home:* 124 North Norwinden Dr., Springfield, Pa. 19064. *Office:* United Church Board for Homeland Ministries, 287 Park Ave. S., New York, N.Y. 10010.

CAREER: Pastor of churches in Hamden, Conn., 1949-53, and Pleasant Hill, Ohio, 1953-56; Congregational Christian Board of Home Missions, Boston, Mass., youth work executive, 1956-60; United Church Board for Homeland Ministries, New York, N.Y., general secretary, 1960—. Democratic committeeman in Springfield, Pa.; delegate to Democratic National Convention, 1972. *Member:* American Academy of Political and Social Science, Joint Strategy and Action Committee (member of board of directors), Joint Educational Development (member of executive committee).

WRITINGS: *Journey into Faith*, United Church Press,

1964; (editor) Everett Parker, *Crisis in the Church*, United Church Press, 1968; (editor) John Westerhoff, *A Colloquy on Christian Education*, Pilgrim Press, 1972; *Signs of Shalom*, United Church Press, 1973. Contributor to *Westminster Dictionary of Christian Education*.

* * *

PRASAD, S(rinivas) Benjamin 1929-

PERSONAL: Born March 2, 1929, in Bangalore, India. *Education:* Marquette University, M.B.A., 1958; University of Wisconsin—Madison, Ph.D., 1963. *Home:* 97 Wonder Hills Dr., Athens, Ohio 45701. *Office:* College of Business, Ohio University, Athens, Ohio 45701.

CAREER: University of Minnesota, Morris, assistant professor of economics and business, 1963-65; University of Nevada, Reno, associate professor of management, 1965-67; Ohio University, Athens, associate professor, 1967-69, professor of business administration, 1969—. *Member:* American Economic Association, Academy of Management, British Institute of Management.

WRITINGS: (Editor) *Management in International Perspective*, Appleton, 1967; (with Anant Negandhi) *Managerialism for Economic Development*, Martinus-Nijhoff, 1968; *Enterprise in Ireland*, Stein Publishing, 1969; (with Negandhi) *Comparative Management*, Appleton, 1971. Contributor to *Academy of Management Journal*.

WORK IN PROGRESS: Social Psychology of Managing Work; *Managing Productivity in Organizations*.

* * *

PRICE, Marjorie 1929-

PERSONAL: Born July 25, 1929, in George, Iowa; daughter of Homer M. (a teacher) and Bertha (a teacher; maiden name, Thompson) Price. *Education:* University of Iowa, nursing diploma, 1950, B.S., 1955, M.A., 1964. *Home:* 716 Greenwood Dr., Iowa City, Iowa 52240. *Office:* College of Nursing, University of Iowa, Iowa City, Iowa 52242.

CAREER: University of Iowa, Hospital, Iowa City, staff nurse, 1950-52; Stanford University Hospital, San Francisco, Calif., staff nurse, 1953-54; Michael Reese Hospital, Chicago, Ill., staff nurse, 1955-56; Veterans Administration Hospital, Iowa City, Iowa, head nurse and in-service instructor in nursing, 1956-67; Southeast Iowa Community College, Keokuk, coordinator of associate degree program in nursing, 1967-68; University of Iowa, College of Nursing, Iowa City, instructor, 1968-70, assistant professor of nursing, 1971—. *Member:* American Nurses' Association, Sigma Theta Tau.

WRITINGS: (With Phyllis Franck and Shirley Veith) *Nursing Management*, Springer Publishing, 1974. Contributor to *Journal of Nursing Education*.

* * *

PRISCO, Michele 1920-

PERSONAL: Born January 18, 1920, in Naples, Italy; son of Salvatore (a lawyer) and Annamaria Prisco; married Sarah Buonomo, October 6, 1951; children: Annella, Caterina. *Education:* University of Naples, Laurea in Giurisprudenza, 1942. *Politics:* Democratic. *Religion:* Roman Catholic. *Home:* Via Stazio n. 8, Naples, Italy 20123.

CAREER: Author and novelist; founder and director of *Le Ragioni narrative* (magazine), 1961-62. *Military service:* Scuola Allievi Ufficiali di Complemento, 1942-43. *Member:* Nazionale del Sindacato Scrittori (vice-secretary, 1959—), Lions Club di Napoli. *Awards, honors:* Prize Venezia, 1950; Prize Strega, 1966, for *A Spiral of Mist*.

WRITINGS: La provincia addormentata (novel), Mondadori (Milan), 1949; *Gli eredi del vento* (novel), Rizzoli (Milan), 1952, translation by Violet M. Macdonald published as *Heirs of the Wind*, D. Verschoyle (London), 1953; *Figli difficili* (novel), Rizzoli, 1954; *Fuochi a mare* (short stories), Rizzoli, 1957; *La dama di piazza* (novel), Rizzoli, 1961; *Punto franco* (short stories), Rizzoli, 1965; *Una spirale di nebbia* (novel), Rizzoli, 1966, translation by Isabel Quigley published as *A Spiral of Mist*, Dutton, 1969; *I cieli della sera*, Rizzoli, 1970. Also translator, Francois Mauriac, *Le Sagouin*. Work represented in anthologies. Contributor to Italian newspapers and magazines, including *Il Messaggero, Il Mattino, Mercurio, Aretusa*, and *Tempo presente*.

WORK IN PROGRESS: Inventario della memoria, an autobiography.

SIDELIGHTS: Of *A Spiral of Mist*, Michael Ricciardelli writes in *Books Abroad:* "The product of a conscientious and mature artist, [*A Spiral of Mist*] . . . augers well for the starting of an Italian cultural tradition in today's Italian milieu, too often dominated by the gossips and envies of social climbers, or aborted in cold experiments and new *isms*. Prisco is a writer who has kept himself always away from experiments and *isms*, because he writes in obedience to his intellectual, transcendental need for expressing his inner world, and of saying something worth while and dignified." *Avocational interests:* Tennis, furniture, and antiques.

* * *

PROCKTOR, Richard (Edward Christopher) 1933-

PERSONAL: Born September 7, 1933, in Dublin, Ireland; son of Eric and Barbara Procktor. *Education:* St. Catherine's College, Oxford, M.A., 1959; University of Exeter, diploma in education, 1960. *Politics:* "Gladstonian Liberal." *Religion:* Anglican. *Home:* High View, Thames Rd., Long Crendon, Buckinghamshire, England. *Office:* Lord Williams' School, Thames, Oxford, England.

CAREER: History teacher in Sevenoaks, Kent, England, 1960-66, and Bracknell, England, 1966-70 (head of history department, 1966-70); Lord Williams' School, Oxford, England, director of studies, 1970—. School teacher fellow at School of Oriental and African Studies at University of London, 1968.

WRITINGS: Nazi Germany, Bodley Head, 1970, Holt, 1973; *Akbar the Great* (booklet), P.E.B. Sevenoaks, 1974.

WORK IN PROGRESS: Gandhi and the Indian Independence Movement.

SIDELIGHTS: Procktor's books have been published in Italian and Dutch. *Avocational interests:* Cricket (Procktor is county coach), plays, collecting paintings.

* * *

PROTHRO, Edwin Terry 1919-

PERSONAL: Born December 11, 1919, in Robeline, La.; son of Edwin Thomas (an auditor) and Frances (Terry) Prothro; married Najla Salman (a teacher), July 31, 1968; children: Martha Carol, Edwin Terry, Jr., Gwendolyn. *Education:* Louisiana College, B.A., 1939; Louisiana State

University, M.A., 1940, Ph.D., 1942; also studied at Sorbonne, University of Paris, summer, 1948. *Politics:* Democrat. *Office:* Center for Behavioral Research, American University of Beirut, Beirut, Lebanon.

CAREER: Louisiana State University, Baton Rouge, assistant professor of psychology, 1946-49; University of Tennessee, Knoxville, associate professor of psychology, 1949-51; American University of Beirut, Beirut, Lebanon, associate professor, 1951-55, professor of psychology, 1955—, dean of Faculty of Arts and Sciences, 1965-73, director of Center for Behavioral Research, 1965—, university provost, 1967-70. Associate professor at Brooklyn College of the City University of New York, 1953-54; lecturer at University of Michigan, 1957-58; fellow at Middle East Center of Harvard University, 1960; senior research fellow at City University of New York, 1963. Regional director of International Union of Scientific Psychology Project, 1958-60; member of board of trustees of American Community School (Beirut), 1965-66. Consultant to UNICEF. *Military service:* U.S. Naval Reserve, aviation psychologist, active duty, 1943-46; became lieutenant.

MEMBER: American Psychological Association (fellow; foreign affiliate), American Sociological Association, American Association of University Professors, Middle East Studies Association (fellow), Society for Cross-Cultural Research, Sigma Xi. *Awards, honors:* Social Science Research Council research grants, 1958-59, 1962-63; National Institute of Mental Health special research fellowships, 1963, 1964, 1966-70; research grants from Foundations' Fund for Research in Psychiatry, 1963-64, 1964-65; decorated Order of the Cedars by Republic of Lebanon, 1969.

WRITINGS: (With P. T. Teska) *Workbook for Psychology*, Ginn, 1950; (with Teska) *Psychology: A Biosocial Study of Behavior*, Ginn, 1950; *Child Rearing in the Lebanon* (monograph), Harvard University Press, 1961; (with L. N. Diab) *Changing Family Patterns in the Arab East*, American University of Beirut Press, 1974 (distributed in United States by Syracuse University Press).

Contributor: L. H. Malikah, editor, *Readings in Social Psychology in the Arab World*, Al-Dar Al-Quamiyyah, 1965; Ailon Shiloh, editor, *Peoples and Cultures of the Middle East*, Random House, 1969; J. G. Snider and C. E. Osgood, editors, *Semantic Differential Technique*, Aldine, 1969; Ihsan Al-Issa and Wayne Dennis, editors, *Cross-Cultural Studies of Behavior*, Holt, 1970.

Contributor of about fifty articles to journals of the social sciences, including *Psychological Reports, Journal of Social Psychology, Child Development, Journal of Abnormal and Social Psychology, Journal of Psychology*, and *Educational and Psychological Measurement*. Member of editorial board of *Journal of Social Psychology*.

WORK IN PROGRESS: Serving as regional editor for *Handbook of Cross-Cultural Psychology*, edited by H. C. Triandis, for Allyn & Bacon.

* * *

PROVENSEN, Alice 1918-

PERSONAL: First syllable of surname rhymes with "grow"; born August 14, 1918, in Chicago, Ill.; daughter of Jay H. (a broker) and Kathryn (an interior decorator; maiden name, Zelanis) Twitchell; married Martin Provensen (a writer and illustrator of children's books), April 17, 1944; children: Karen Anna. *Education:* Studied at Art Institute of Chicago, University of California at Los Angeles, and Art Students League, New York. *Home address:* Rural Delivery, Staatsburg, N.Y. 12580.

CAREER: Walter Lantz Studios, Hollywood, Calif., employed in animation, 1942-43; Office of Strategic Services, Washington, D.C., graphics, 1943-45; writer and illustrator of children's books, 1946—.

WRITINGS—All self-illustrated children's books, with husband, Martin Provensen: *The Animal Fair*, Simon & Schuster, 1952, revised edition, 1974; *Karen's Curiosity*, Golden Press, 1963; *Karen's Opposites*, Golden Press, 1963; *What Is a Color?*, Golden Press, 1967; *Who's in the Egg?*, Golden Press, 1968; (editors) *Provenson Book of Fairy Tales*, Random House, 1971; *Play on Words*, Random House, 1972; *My Little Hen*, Random House, 1973; *Roses Are Red*, Random House, 1973; *Our Animal Friends*, Random House, 1974.

Illustrator, with Martin Provensen: Margaret Bradford Boni, editor, *Fireside Book of Folksongs*, Simon & Schuster, 1947; Boni, editor, *Fireside Book of Lovesongs*, Simon & Schuster, 1954; James A. Beard, *Fireside Cook Book*, Simon & Schuster, 1949.

All published by Golden Press: Dorothy Bennett, editor, *The Golden Mother Goose*, 1948; R. L. Stevenson, *A Child's Garden of Verses*, 1951; Elsa Jane Werner, adapter, *The New Testament*, 1953; Jan Werner Watson, adapter, *Iliad and Odyssey*, 1956; Anne Terry White, adapter, *Treasury of Myths and Legends*, 1959; *The First Noel*, 1959; George Wolfson, editor, *Shakespeare: Ten Great Plays*, 1962; Alfred, Lord Tennyson, *The Charge of the Light Brigade*, 1964; Louis Untermeyer, adapter, *Aesop's Fables*, 1965; Untermeyer, editor, *Fun and Nonsense*, 1967; Untermeyer, adapter, *Tales from the Ballet*, 1968.

* * *

PROVENSEN, Martin 1916-

PERSONAL: Surname is pronounced *Proh*-ven-sen; born July 10, 1916, in Chicago, Ill.; son of Marthin (a musician) and Berendina (a teacher; maiden name, Kruger) Provensen; married Alice Twitchell (a writer and illustrator of children's books), April 17, 1944; children: Karen Anna. *Education:* Studied at Art Institute of Chicago and University of California at Berkeley. *Home address:* Rural Deliver, Staatsburg, N.Y. 12580.

CAREER: Walt Disney Studios, Hollywood, Calif., member of story board, 1938-42; writer and illustrator of children's books, 1946—. *Military service:* U.S. Navy, 1942-45.

WRITINGS—All self-illustrated children's books, with wife, Alice Provensen: *The Animal Fair*, Simon & Schuster, 1952, revised edition, 1974; *Karen's Curiosity*, Golden Press, 1963; *Karen's Opposites*, Golden Press, 1963; *What Is a Color?*, Golden Press, 1967; *Who's in the Egg?*, Golden Press, 1968; *Play on Words*, Random House, 1972; *My Little Hen*, Random House, 1973; *Roses Are Red*, Random House, 1973; *Our Animal Friends*, Random House, 1974.

Illustrator, with Alice Provensen: Margaret Bradford Boni, editor, *Fireside Book of Folksongs*, Simon & Schuster, 1947; Boni, editor, *Fireside Book of Lovesongs*, Simon & Schuster, 1954; James A Beard, *Fireside Cook Book*, Simon & Schuster, 1949.

All published by Golden Press: Dorothy Bennett, editor,

The Golden Mother Goose, 1948; R. L. Stevenson, *A Child's Garden of Verses*, 1951; Elsa Jane Werner, adapter, *The New Testament*, 1953; Jan Werner Watson, adapter, *Iliad and Odyssey*, 1956; Anne Terry White, adapter, *Treasury of Myths and Legends*, 1959; *The First Noel*, 1959; George Wolfson, editor, *Shakespeare: Ten Great Plays*, 1962; Alfred, Lord Tennyson, *The Charge of the Light Brigade*, 1964; Louis Untermeyer, adapter, *Aesop's Fables*, 1965; Untermeyer, editor, *Fun and Nonsense*, 1967; Untermeyer, adapter, *Tales from the Ballet*, 1968.

* * *

PUGH, Anthony (Roy) 1931-

PERSONAL: Born August 16, 1931, in Liverpool, England; son of Walter (a local government officer) and Mary Dilys (a school teacher; maiden name, Jones) Pugh; married Mary E. Hooton, December 29, 1962; children: Elizabeth, David, Margaret. *Education:* Pembroke College, Cambridge, B.A., 1953, M.A., 1956, Ph.D., 1959. *Politics:* "Mildly left of centre." *Religion:* Anglican. *Home:* 47 Simcoe Ct., Fredericton, New Brunswick E3B 2W9, Canada. *Office:* Department of Romance Languages, University of New Brunswick, Fredericton, New Brunswick, Canada.

CAREER: University of London, King's College, London, England, assistant lecturer in French, 1956-59; Queen's University, Belfast, Northern Ireland, lecturer in French, 1959-69; University of New Brunswick, Fredericton, professor of French, 1969—, chairman of department of Romance languages, 1973—. Visiting professor at University of New Brunswick, 1968. *Member:* Canadian Society for Eighteenth Century Studies, Humanities Association of Canada, Association des professeurs de francais des universites canadiennes, Canadian Association of University Teachers, Modern Language Association of America, American Association of Teachers of French. *Awards, honors:* Canada Council research grants, 1972, 1973, 1974.

WRITINGS: From Montaigne to Chateaubriand, Macmillan, 1966; *Beaumarchais–Le Mariage de Figaro: An Interpretation*, Macmillan, 1968; (editor with D. G. Charlton, Jean Gaudon) *Studies in Balzac and the Nineteenth Century*, Leicester University Press, 1972; *Balzac's Recurring Characters*, University of Toronto Press, 1974.

WORK IN PROGRESS: A chapter on Balzac, for inclusion in *The Cabeen Bibliography of French Literature, 1800-1850*, to be published by Syracuse University Press; a collection of essays on works of French literature, using their formal unity as a key to interpretation; a study of the composition of Pascal's *Pensees*.

AVOCATIONAL INTERESTS: Music, walking (especially in the wilder parts of Great Britain), relaxing with his family.

* * *

PULKINGHAM, W(illiam) Graham 1926-

PERSONAL: Born September 14, 1926, in Alliance, Ohio; son of William Graham and Marion (Sweeney) Pulkingham; married Betty Jane Carr, September 1, 1951; children: William Graham, Mary Graham, Nathan Carr, Elizabeth Jane, Martha Louise, David Earle. *Education:* University of Western Ontario, B.A., 1948; attended University of Texas, 1950-51; Episcopal Theological Seminary of the Southwest, B.D., 1957. *Home:* Yeldall Manor, Hare Hatch, near Twyford, Berkshire, England. *Office address:* The Fishermen, Inc., P.O. Box 18648, Houston, Tex. 77023.

CAREER: Ordained priest of the Episcopal Church, 1958; priest-in-charge in Hitchcock, Tex. and Alta-Loma, Tex., 1957-58; University of Texas Medical Branch, Galveston, chaplain, 1957-60; assistant rector in Austin, Tex., 1960-63; Church of the Redeemer, Houston, Tex., rector, 1963—. Executive director of The Fishermen, Houston, Tex., 1969—; chairman of Community of Celebration Christian Trust, Berkshire, England, 1973—. *Military service:* U.S. Navy, 1953-55; became lieutenant junior grade.

WRITINGS: Gathered for Power, Morehouse, 1972; *They Left Their Nets*, Morehouse, 1973. Contributing editor to *New Convenant*, 1974—.

BIOGRAPHICAL/CRITICAL SOURCES: Michael Harper, *A New Way of Living*, Hodder & Stoughton, 1973; David and Neta Jackson, *Living Together in a World Falling Apart*, Creation House, 1974.

* * *

PULLING, Albert Van Siclen 1891- (Pierre Pulling)

PERSONAL: Born August 27, 1891, in Brooklyn, N.Y.; son of Albert Irving (a farmer) and Bertha (Van Siclen) Pulling; married Gertrude Bassett, December 21, 1916; children: Barton Sebring. *Education:* New York State College at Syracuse, B.S.; University of Michigan, M.F. *Politics:* Republican ("but very unreliable"). *Religion:* Presbyterian ("backslidden"). *Home:* 734 South Ninth Ave., Pocatello, Idaho 83201. *Office:* Department of Biology, Idaho State University, Pocatello, Idaho 83201.

CAREER: Has taught at University of New Brunswick, Fredericton, 1919-24, and New York State College at Syracuse, 1924, 1928; biologist with U.S. Forest Service and U.S. Fish and Wildlife Service, 1933-48; Idaho State University, Pocatello, 1948—, now professor emeritus of biology. Summer work includes coaching canoeing and directing mountain trips for organized camps, and serving as seasonal ranger with National Park Service in Yellowstone. *Military service:* U.S. Army, Corps of Engineers, 1917-19; became sergeant. *Member:* American Wildlife Society, National Rifle Association (life member), National Parks Association (honorary life member), Wilderness Society (honorary life member), Society of American Foresters, Idaho Wildlife Federation, Idaho Writers League, Alpha Xi Sigma, Robinhood, Phi Sigma, Alpha Psi Omega.

WRITINGS: The Elements of Canoeing, Ann Arbor Publishers, 1933; (under pseudonym Pierre Pulling) *The Principles of Canoeing*, Macmillan, 1954; (under pseudonym Pierre Pulling) *Game and the Gunner: Common Sense Observations on the Practice of Game Conservation and Sport Hunting*, Winchester Press, 1973; *Living Outdoors*, Winchester Press, in press. Also author of booklet, *Indian Canoeing*. Work is represented in anthologies. Writer of column, "Woods and Waters" (later titled "Pierre's Lookout"), for *Intermountain Observer*, Boise, Idaho. Contributor to periodicals, including *American Rifleman* and *Gun Digest*.

WORK IN PROGRESS: Sketches, for Clark Publishing.

SIDELIGHTS: Van Siclen, who took his last English course in 1912, until a summer graduate course in 1966, told *CA*: "I'm really not a writer. Simply a technician who writes some. . . .After I started teaching in 1919, I wrote casually for most of the sporting slicks. . .I got going on canoeing. . .because I learned professional woods canoeing in Quebec the summer of 1915. . . .Aboriginal canoeing has been much neglected. The gawdawful stuff published by the Red Cross is approached from swimming. The Indians did not believe in upsetting!" *Avocational interests:* Shooting (Pulling owns one hundred thirteen guns), fly-casting.

* * *

PURTON, Rowland W(illiam Crisby) 1925-

PERSONAL: Born April 14, 1925, in London, England; son of Frederick J. and Catherine Dean Purton; married Marie Ellen Pain, August 1, 1949 (died December 25, 1974); children: Colleen Ellen (Mrs. Malcolm Brown), Andrew James. *Education:* Westminster College, London, Teacher's Certificate, 1949; University of London, further study, 1959-61. *Religion:* Methodist. *Home:* 61 Windsor Rd., Forest Gate, London E7 OQY, England. *Office:* Seven Sisters Junior School, South Grove, London N15 5QE, England.

CAREER: Teacher in primary and secondary schools in London, England, 1949-61; Colegrave Junior School, London, England, deputy head, 1961-65; Seven Sisters Junior School, London, England, headmaster, 1965—. Lecturer on libraries and books at teacher's courses. Methodist lay preacher, 1947—; member of board of governors, Westminster College, Oxford. *Military service:* Royal Naval Volunteer Reserve, 1943-47; commander of minesweeper; became lieutenant; later lieutenant commander in Sea Cadet Corps. *Member:* School Library Association, Educational Development Association, World Ship Society, Westminster Club (honorary secretary-treasurer), National Trust.

WRITINGS—Mostly nonfiction for school-age children: "New View Histories," Collins, four books titled *Our Heritage*, *Our Commonwealth*, *Our People*, and *Our Democracy*, 1958.

(With others) *A Pageant of History* (encyclopedia), Collins, 1958; "Junior New View Histories," Collins, four books titled *Days of Glory*, 1961, *Days of Adventure*, 1961, *Days of Challenge*, 1962, and *Days of Discovery*, 1962; *Surrounded by Books: The Library in the Primary School* (teacher's reference), Educational Supply Association, 1962, enlarged edition, Ward, Lock Educational, 1970; *Discovering Ports and Harbours*, University of London Press, 1964; "Star Book" series, Hamish Hamilton, eight books titled *Man in Antarctica*, 1964, *Man in Australia*, 1964, *Man in Canada*, 1964, *Man in New Zealand*, 1964, *Man and Games*, 1966, *Man Tells the Time*, 1966, *Man in the West Indies*, 1967, *Man in the Bible Lands*, 1969; *English for Work and Play*, four books, Hamish Hamilton, 1966-67; *Captain Scott*, McGraw (England), 1968; *Doctor Livingstone*, McGraw (England), 1968; *Study Book of the Fire Service*, Bodley Head, 1969.

Let's Look at Maps and Mapmaking, Muller, 1971; *Farms and Farming*, Routledge & Kegan Paul, 1972; *Churches and Religions*, Blandford, 1972; *Ports and Sea Transport*, Blandford, 1972; *Rivers and Canals*, Routledge & Kegan Paul, 1972; *Day by Day* (stories and prayers for school assembly), Basil Blackwell, 1973; *Markets and Fairs*, Routledge & Kegan Paul, 1973; *Parks and Open Spaces*, Blandford, 1975.

Educational publications include teachers' guides, project folders of books and cards on forests and farming, information and work cards for local studies, and reading cards. Contributor of articles to education journals; reviewer for *School Librarian*. Editor, *Westminster Club Bulletin*.

WORK IN PROGRESS: Several ideas for books to be used as environmental study background material; a book on folklore and superstition.

SIDELIGHTS: Purton says that he came into writing almost by accident when he could not find a suitable textbook for teaching constitutional history and civics to fourteen-year olds and solved the problem by putting his lesson notes together for *Our Democracy*, which evolved into "New View Histories."

"*Day by Day* is in more than one sense the climax of my writing," he notes. "In British schools the day begins with a short religious service. This book provides enough material in stories and prayers for an assembly every school day for two years without repeating. . . .It is not only the largest of my books but the one which endeavours to highlight a set of values for life."

Purton has been making miniature scale model ships for twenty-five years. He also is a photographer and takes many of the pictures used in his books.

* * *

PUTNAM, Robert E. 1933-

PERSONAL: Born September 13, 1933, in Mt. Sterling, Ill.; son of John Harold and Florence Pauline (Curran) Putnam; married Linda Jane Wiant, August 30, 1960; children: Justine, Robbie, Dylan. *Education:* Attended University of Missouri, 1951-52, and Eastern State Teachers College, 1955-56; University of Illinois, B.A., 1959; Roosevelt University, M.A., 1969. *Home:* 84 Dogwood, Park Forest, Ill.

CAREER: Western Electric Company, Chicago, Ill., associate engineer, 1960-62; American Technical Society, Chicago, Ill., technical editor, 1964-71, managing editor, 1971-72, editor-in-chief, 1972—. *Military service:* U.S. Army Engineers, 1953-55. *Member:* Americans for Democratic Action, American Vocational Association, National Association for Trade and Industrial Education, United States Metric Association, Independent Voters of Illinois, Chicago Book Clinic.

WRITINGS: (Editor with Peter Hutchinson) *Young Poets of Illinois*, privately printed, 1959.

Reviser of indicated editions (not associated with earlier editions); all published by American Technical Society: *Fundamentals of Carpentry*, Volume I, 4th edition, 1967; *Concrete Block Construction*, 3rd edition, 1973; *Bricklaying Skill and Practice*, 3rd edition, 1974; *Architectural and Building Trades Dictionary*, 3rd edition, 1974.

Editor; all published by American Technical Society: *Architectural Drafting*, 1965; *Engineering Drafting Problems*, 1965; *The Instructor and His Job*, 1966; *Machine Trades Blueprint Reading*, 1966; *Building Trades Blueprint Reading*, Volume I, 1967; *Food Preparation for Hotels, Restaurants and Cafeterias*, 1968; *Fundamentals of Carpentry*, Volume II, 1969; *Heavy Timber Construction*, 1969; *The Performance-Demonstration Lesson*, Part I and Part II, 1969; *Printing Estimating*, 1970; *Electrical Construction Wiring*, 1970; *Plastering Skill and Practice*, 1971.

Contributor of poems to *Road Apple, Northeast, Wild Onion, Wood Ibis, Sou'wester, Tolar Creek, Back Roads*.

WORK IN PROGRESS: Revising *Fundamentals of Carpentry*, Volume I.

QUELLER, Donald E(dward) 1925-

PERSONAL: Born January 14, 1925, in St. Louis, Mo.; son of A. J. (a businessman) and Lee (Straub) Queller; married Marilyn Lucille Johnson (a nurse), June 12, 1949; children: Kurt, David, Susan, Katherine, Sarah. *Education:* University of Michigan, A.B., 1949, M.A., 1951; attended Stanford University Law School, 1949-50; University of Wisconsin, Ph.D., 1954. *Politics:* Democrat. *Religion:* Lutheran. *Home:* 2406 South Prospect, Champaign, Ill. 61820. *Office:* Department of History, University of Illinois, Urbana, Ill. 61801.

CAREER: Beloit College, Beloit, Wis., instructor in history, 1955-56; University of Southern California, Los Angeles, assistant professor, 1956-61, associate professor, 1961-67, professor of history, 1967-68, associate dean of Graduate School, 1963-68; University of Illinois, Urbana, professor of history, 1968—. Chairman, South Pasadena Human Relations Committee; member of board, Interfaith Housing, Champaign-Urbana, 1964-65; member of board and chairman, C-U Day Care Center, Champaign-Urbana, 1973—. *Military service:* U.S. Army, 1946-49; became staff sergeant. *Member:* American Historical Association, Mediaeval Academy, Phi Beta Kappa. *Awards, honors:* Fulbright fellow in Belgium, 1954-55, in Italy, 1962-63; Rockefeller Foundation fellowship and grant-in-aid, 1962-63, 1963-64; Guggenheim fellow, 1972-73; National Endowment for the Humanities grant-in-aid, 1972-73; American Council of Learned Societies grant-in-aid, 1973.

WRITINGS: Early Venetian Legislation on Ambassadors, Librairie Droz, 1966; *The Office of the Ambassador in the Middle Ages*, Princeton University Press, 1967; (editor) *The Latin Conquest of Constantinople*, Wiley, 1971; (editor with Joseph R. Strayer) *Post Scripta: Essays in Honor of Gaines Post*, Pontifical Institute for Canon Law (Rome), 1972; (with others) *One Thousand Years: Western Europe in the Middle Ages*, Houghton, 1974. Contributor to *Speculum, English Historical Review, Revue belge de philologie et d'histoire, Moyen Age, Studies in the Renaissance, Studies in Medieval and Renaissance History, Medievalia et Humanistica, Explorations in Economic History.*

WORK IN PROGRESS: Newly Discovered Early Venetian Legislation on Ambassadors; *The Fourth Crusade*, completion expected in 1976; *The Civic Virtue of the Venetian Patriciate: Myth or Reality?*, completion expected in 1978.

* * *

RABIN, A(lbert) I(srael) 1912-

PERSONAL: Surname is pronounced *Ray*-bin; born June 20, 1912, in Merkine, Lithuania; naturalized United States citizen son of David J. (a businessman) and Sarah (Syman) Rabin; married Beatrice Marceau (a laboratory assistant), May 4, 1949; children: Sarah. *Education:* Boston University, B.S., 1935, M.A., 1936, Ph.D., 1939; attended Harvard University, 1936-38. *Religion:* Jewish. *Home:* 2472 Hawthorne Lane, Okemos, Mich. 48864. *Office:* Department of Psychology, Michigan State University, 114 Olds Hall, East Lansing, Mich. 48824.

CAREER: Boston State Hospital, Boston, Mass., psychologist, 1938-39; New Hampshire State Hospitals and Clinics, Concord, N.H., chief psychologist, 1939-47; Michael Reese Hospital, Chicago, Ill., research psychologist, 1947-48; Michigan State University, East Lansing, associate professor, 1948-53, professor of psychology, 1953—, Centennial Review Lecturer, 1973. Lecturer at Boston University, 1941, and Harvard Extension of Boston University, 1944; guest professor at Hebrew University (Jerusalem) and Bar-Ilan University, both 1962; professor at City University of New York, 1964-65; Fulbright professor at Aarhus University, 1970-71. Member of Michigan governor's commission on criminally sexual deviates, 1949-53.

MEMBER: American Psychological Association, American Orthopsychiatric Association, American Association for the Advancement of Science, Society for Projective Techniques (president), Midwest Psychological Association.

WRITINGS: (Editor with M. R. Haworth) *Projective Techniques with Children*, Grune, 1960; *Growing Up in the Kibbutz*, Springer Publishing, 1965; (editor) *Projective Techniques in Personality Assessment*, Springer Publishing, 1968; *Kibbutz Studies*, Michigan State University Press, 1971; (editor with Bertha Hazan) *Collective Education in the Kibbutz*, Springer Publishing, 1973; (editor) *Clinical Psychology: Issues of the Seventies*, Michigan State University Press, 1974. Contributor of more than a hundred articles to psychology journals, including *Journal of Consulting and Clinical Psychology, Journal of Personality Assessment*, and *Journal of Psychology*. Consulting editor of *Journal of Personality Assessment* and *Journal of Consulting and Clinical Psychology*.

WORK IN PROGRESS: Research for *Twenty Years Later*, a follow-up study of kibbutz-raised children; *Temporal Experience*.

* * *

RADCLIFFE, George L. 1878(?)-1974

1878(?)—July 29, 1974; American lawyer, scholar, businessman, author, athlete, and former U.S. Senator from Maryland. Obituaries: *Washington Post*, July 31, 1974.

* * *

RAFFA, Frederick Anthony 1944-

PERSONAL: Born February 19, 1944, in Liberty, N.Y.; son of Anthony (a physician) and Julia (a nurse; maiden name, Segar) Raffa; married Jean Benedict, June 15, 1964; children: Juliette Louise, Matthew Benedict. *Education:* Florida State University, B.S., 1965, M.B.A., 1966, Ph.D., 1969. *Politics:* Democrat. *Religion:* Episcopalian. *Home:* 2901 Lolissa Lane, Maitland, Fla. 32751. *Office:* Department of Economics, Florida Technological University, P.O. Box 25000, Orlando, Fla. 32816.

CAREER: Florida State University, Tallahassee, instructor in economics, 1967-69; Florida Technological University, Orlando, assistant professor, 1969-74, associate professor of economics, 1974—. State director of Florida Clergy Economic Education Foundation; charter member of Florida Department of Commerce Input-Output technical advisory council. *Member:* American Economic Association, Southern Economic Association, Omicron Delta Epsilon, Delta Sigma Pi.

WRITINGS: (Editor with R. E. Hicks and W. J. Klages) *Economics: Myth, Method, or Madness*, McCutchan, 1971; (with Burton Wright II) *Perspectives on Man: An Introduction to the Social Sciences*, Crowell, 1975; (with others) *The Contemporary Business Enterprise*, Saunders, in press. Contributor to professional periodicals.

WORK IN PROGRESS: Labor Migration Theory in Retrospect; *On the Rationality of Soviet Aid to Underdeveloped Countries*.

RAINWATER, Lee 1928-

PERSONAL: Born January 7, 1928, in Oxford, Miss.; married wife, Carol, 1959; children: Jonathan, Katherine. *Education:* University of Chicago, M.A., 1951, Ph.D., 1954. *Home:* 26 Craigie St., Cambridge, Mass. 02138. *Office:* Department of Sociology, Harvard University, Cambridge, Mass. 02138.

CAREER: Social Research, Inc., Chicago, Ill., staff psychologist, director of special studies, and associate director of corporation, 1950-63; Washington University, St. Louis, Mo., associate professor, 1963-65, professor of sociology and anthropology, 1965-69; Harvard University, Cambridge, Mass., professor of sociology, 1969—. Member of Population Crisis Committee, 1966—, and national advisory health council of U.S. Public Health Service, 1967-71. *Military service:* U.S. Army, 1946-48. *Member:* American Sociological Association (fellow), American Anthropological Association (fellow), Society for the Study of Social Problems, Society for the Psychological Study of Social Issues, National Council on Family Relations. *Awards, honors:* Ainsfield-Wolf Award, 1973, for *Behind Ghetto Walls: Black Families in a Federal Slum.*

WRITINGS: (With R. Coleman and G. Handel) *Workingman's Wife: Her Personality, World, and Life Style*, Oceana, 1959; *And the Poor Get Children: Sex, Contraception, and Family Planning in the Working Class*, Quadrangle, 1960; (with Anselm Strauss) *Professional Scientist: A Study of American Chemists*, Aldine, 1962; *Family Design: Marital Sexuality, Family Size, and Contraception*, Aldine, 1965; (with William Yancey) *The Moynihan Report and the Politics of Controversy*, M.I.T. Press, 1967; (editor) *Black Experience: Soul*, Aldine, 1970, 2nd edition, 1973; *Behind Ghetto Walls: Black Families in a Federal Slum*, Aldine, 1970; *Social Problems and Public Policy*, Volume I: *Inequality and Justice*, Volume II: *Deviance and Liberty*, Aldine, 1974; *What Money Buys: Inequality and the Social Meaning of Income*, Basic Books, 1974.

Contributor to professional journals. Senior editor of *TransAction*, 1963-70; associate editor of *Journal of Marriage and the Family*.

* * *

RAMAMURTY, K(otamraju) Bhaskara 1924-

PERSONAL: Born June 15, 1924, in Kakinada, Andhra Pradesh, India; son of Sanyasi Raju and Meenakshi (Damaraju) Kotamraju; married Lakshmi Basavaraju, March 2, 1945; children: Meenakshi, Raju, Kameswara Rao, Anasuya, Kamala Manga. *Education:* Maharajah's College, Vizianagram, India, B.A., 1943; Andhra University, M.A., 1948, Ph.D., 1969. *Religion:* Hindu. *Home:* Kotamraju Buildings, Kaspa, Vizianagram 2, Andhra Pradesh, India 531202. *Office:* Shreeram Junior College, Shreeramnagar, Andhra Pradesh, India 532101.

CAREER: Maharajah's College, Vizianagram, Andhra Pradesh, India, lecturer, 1953-58, senior lecturer in English, 1958-71; Shreeram Junior College, Shreeramnagar, Andhra Pradesh, India, principal, 1971—.

WRITINGS: Aldous Huxley: A Study of His Novels, Asia Publishing House, 1975.

WORK IN PROGRESS: This Ismatic Age: A Study of Twentieth Century English Literary Trends; a study of D. H. Lawrence's novels.

RAMEH, Clea 1927-

PERSONAL: Born January 9, 1927, in Recife, Pernambuco, Brazil; daughter of Abdon S. (a businessman) and Josefina (Amena) Rameh. *Education:* University of Sao Paulo, B.A., 1947, Licenciate, 1948, Especialization, 1955; Georgetown University, M.S., 1962, Ph.D., 1970. *Religion:* Roman Catholic. *Home:* 5401 Westbard Ave., #1202, Bethesda, Md. 20016. *Office:* Department of Linguistics, Georgetown University, Washington, D.C. 20007.

CAREER: High school teacher of Portuguese in the public schools of Sao Paulo, Brazil, 1951-68; Georgetown University, Washington, D.C., instructor, 1969-70, assistant professor of Portuguese, 1970—, director of Summer Institute in Portuguese, 1973, 1974. Summer visiting lecturer at Ohio State University, 1968. Consultant to Spoken Brazilian Portuguese Research Project, U.S. Naval Institute, 1969-72. *Member:* Modern Language Association of America, Linguistic Society of America, American Association of Teachers of Spanish and Portuguese, Associacao de Linguistica e Filologia da America Latina, Associacao Brasileira de Linguistica, Association for Literary and Linguistic Computing, Associacao dos Professores do Ensino Secundario e Normal Oficial do Estado de Sao Paulo (former secretary), Phi Beta Kappa, Phi Lambda Beta.

WRITINGS: (With Maria Isabel Abreu) *Portugues Contemporaneo*, Georgetown University Press, Volume I, 1966, 3rd revised edition, 1972, Volume II, 1967, 3rd revised edition, 1973; (co-translator) E. R. Hilgard, *Theory of Learning*, Herder Co., 1966. Contributor to *Estudos Linguisticos*, 1966.

WORK IN PROGRESS: Syntactic Analysis of Portuguese by Computer; Linguistic Analysis of Cecilia Meireles' Poems by Computer; research on native speakers reaction to so called "errors" in the spoken language.

* * *

RAMSBOTTOM, John 1885-1974

October 25, 1885—December 14, 1974; British-born botanist, authority on fungi, and author of books on botany. Obituaries: *AB Bookman's Weekly*, January 20, 1975.

* * *

RANADIVE, Gail 1944-

PERSONAL: Surname is pronounced Ra-na-*dee*-vee; born February 16, 1944, in Boston, Mass.; daughter of Fred Leach (supervisor for Western Electric) and Audrey J. (Steeves) Collins; married Manmohan V. Ranadive (a physician in the U.S. Army), August 23, 1964; children: Nina M., Shawna M. *Education:* Laurence General Hospital School of Nursing, R.N., 1964; student at Antioch College, Baltimore, Md., 1973-74. *Politics:* Independent. *Religion:* Unitarian-Universalist. *Residence:* Edgewood Arsenal, Md.

CAREER: Free-lance writer. *Member:* Children's Literature Association, Society of Children's Book Writers, Edgewood Arsenal Army Flying Club, Aircraft Owners' and Pilots' Association.

WRITINGS: If You'd Been Born in India, Albert Whitman, 1973.

WORK IN PROGRESS: Putting her daughters' experiences as mixed-race, -religion, -nation children into a family-story form.

SIDELIGHTS: Gail Ranadive is a private pilot and a

former operations officer of the U.S. Army Edgewood Flying Club, the first woman and first student pilot to hold this position in the club's history. Photographs taken on a visit to her husband's family in Bombay were used by the artist to illustrate *If You'd Been Born in India*.

* * *

RAPPOPORT, Ken 1935-

PERSONAL: Born February 14, 1935, in Brooklyn, N.Y.; son of Jacob (a marine engineer) and Marge (a bookkeeper; maiden name, Geller) Rappoport; married Bernice Goodman, March 26, 1961; children: Felicia, Sharon, Lawrence. *Education:* Rider College, B.S., 1956. *Home:* 29 Owens Rd., Old Bridge, N.J. 08857. *Office:* Associated Press, 50 Rockefeller Plaza, New York, N.Y. 10020.

CAREER: Dorf Feature Service, Newark, N.J., feature writer and reporter, 1960-61; *Doylestown Intelligencer*, Doylestown, Pa., reporter, 1961-63; Associated Press, reporter in Philadelphia, Pa., 1963-69, sports writer in New York, N.Y., 1969—. *Military service:* U.S. Army, 1958-60. *Member:* Baseball Writers Association of America. *Awards, honors: Sports Digest* Best Story of the Month, November, 1973.

WRITINGS: (Contributor) Will Grimsley, editor, *A Century of Sports*, Associated Press, 1971; (contributor) Grimsley, editor, *The Sports Immortals*, Prentice-Hall, 1972; *The Nittany Lions: A Story of Penn State Football*, Strode, 1973; *The Trojans: A Story of Southern California Football*, Strode, 1974. Contributor to national sports journals.

WORK IN PROGRESS: A complete history of the Syracuse University football team from the 1800s to modern times, *The Syracuse Football Story*, completion expected in 1975; a definitive football history of the University of Notre Dame, *Wake Up The Echoes*, 1975.

AVOCATIONAL INTERESTS: Travel, photography.

* * *

RASMUSSEN, David (William) 1942-

PERSONAL: Born December 20, 1942, in Chicago, Ill.; son of William R. and Mabel E. (Houser) Rasmussen. *Education:* Earlham College, A.B., 1964; graduate study at University of Helsinki, 1962; Washington University, St. Louis, Mo., A.M., 1967, Ph.D., 1969. *Home:* 226 Day St., Tallahassee, Fla. 32304. *Office:* Department of Economics, Florida State University, Tallahassee, Fla. 32306.

CAREER: Washington University, St. Louis, Mo., instructor in economics, summer, 1965; Florida State University, Tallahassee, assistant professor of economics and urban and regional planning, 1968-72, associate professor of economics, 1972—. Fellow of Economic Development Administration's summer institute on regional economic development, 1966; lecturer at University of Utrecht, 1973; referee for National Sciencc Foundation, 1974. Manuscript reviewer for Harper & Row and Wadsworth Publishing. *Member:* American Economic Association, Regional Science Association, Union for Radical Political Economy.

WRITINGS: Urban Economics, Harper, 1973; (editor with C. T. Haworth, and contributor) *The Modern City: A Book of Readings*, Harper, 1973. Author of research reports. Contributor of articles and reviews to economics journals. Referee for *Journal of Human Resources*, 1971, *Review of Regional Studies*, 1971, *Growth and Change*, 1973, and *Social Science Quarterly*, 1974.

WORK IN PROGRESS: Research on the effect of national economic growth on the income distribution, on urban agglomeration economies and regional development policies, and on income redistribution effects of urban population growth.

* * *

RATHBONE, Ouida Bergere 1886(?)-1974

1886(?)—November 29, 1974; American writer for stage and screen, actress, theatrical agent, and widow of actor Basil Rathbone. Obituaries: *New York Times*, December 1, 1974.

* * *

RATHER, Dan 1931-

PERSONAL: Born October 31, 1931, in Wharton, Tex.; son of Irvin (a laborer) and Byrl (Page) Rather; married Jeannie Grace Goebel (a painter), April 21, 1957; children: Dawn Robin, Daniel Martin. *Education:* Sam Houston State Teachers College (now University), degree in journalism, 1953; attended University of Houston Law School, 1957-59, and South Texas School of Law, 1959. *Politics:* Independent. *Religion:* Protestant. *Residence:* Washington, D.C. *Office:* CBS News, 524 West 57th St., New York, N.Y., 10019.

CAREER: KSAM-Radio, Huntsville, Tex., writer, reporter, broadcaster, 1950-54; reporter for Associated Press, 1951-52, and for United Press International, 1953, both from Huntsville; Sam Houston State Teachers College (now University), Huntsville, member of faculty in department of journalism, 1953-54; journalist with *Houston Chronicle* and KTRH-Radio, both Houston, Tex., 1954-59, and with KHOU-Television, Houston, 1960-61; Columbia Broadcasting System News, reporter and journalist from Dallas, New Orleans, Washington, D.C., London, and Saigon Bureaus, 1961—. *Military service:* U.S. Marine Corps, 1954. *Member:* Sigma Delta Chi. *Awards, honors:* Received National Headliners award and Overseas Press Club award, and four Emmy Awards from National Academy of Television Arts and Sciences.

WRITINGS: (With Gary P. Gates) *The Palace Guard* (nonfiction), Harper, 1974. Occasional contributor of articles to *Newsday* and other newspapers.

WORK IN PROGRESS: A novel about a broadcaster; a play about the John F. Kennedy assassination.

SIDELIGHTS: In *The Palace Guard*, CBS newsmen Rather and Gates have produced a detailed study of the Nixon cabinet and domestic affairs staff, with particular focus on H. R. Haldeman and those close to him, and, writes a *Time* reviewer, "have sliced through conventional explanations with some offbeat conclusions about what went wrong." A *Saturday Review/World* reviewer notes that "it is one of the virtues of this work that . . . it is not too awed to be witty. Although it is by no means a lighthearted book, Mr. Rather and Mr. Gates have brought to the written history of Watergate and the Nixon presidency a recognizable human element, a quality that has been singularly lacking in the high-minded literature thus far produced on those subjects."

AVOCATIONAL INTERESTS: Rather writes: "I am a basketball fan, play tennis, like to fish, am a student of sculpture."

RAVITCH, Diane 1938-

PERSONAL: Born July 1, 1938, in Houston, Tex.; daughter of Walter and Ann Silvers; married Richard Ravitch (a construction executive), June 26, 1960; children: Joseph, Michael. *Education:* Wellesley College, B.A., 1960; Columbia University, Ph.D., 1975. *Home:* 1021 Park Ave., New York, N.Y. 10028. *Office:* Box 211, Teachers College, Columbia University, New York, N.Y. 10027.

CAREER: Columbia University, New York, N.Y., fellow of Institute of Philosophy and Politics of Education at Teachers College, 1971—.

WRITINGS: *The Great School Wars, New York City: 1805-1973*, Basic Books, 1974. Contributor to popular journals, including *Commentary, Change, Societas, New Leader*, and to *New York Historical Society Quarterly* and *New York Times*. Member of editorial board of *New York Affairs*.

WORK IN PROGRESS: A history of American education since World War II.

* * *

RAYMOND, Walter J(ohn) 1930-

PERSONAL: Born February 24, 1930, in Poland as U.S. citizen; son of John (a farmer) and Anna (a farmer) Raymond; married, wife's name Marianne; children: William, John. *Education:* Polish University Abroad, London, England, LL.M., 1959, LL.D., 1966; University of Maryland, M.A., 1961; Atlanta University, Ph.D., 1975. *Home:* 102 Park Dr., Lawrenceville, Va. 23868. *Office:* Department of Social Science, St. Paul's College, Lawrenceville, Va. 23868.

CAREER: Hampton Institute, Hampton, Va., assistant professor of political science, 1966-69; St. Paul's College, Lawrenceville, Va., associate professor of political science and chairman of department, 1969—. *Member:* American Political Science Association, American Academy of Political and Social Sciences, Society for the Advancement of Management, Polish Institute of Arts and Sciences in America, Virginia Social Science Association, Pi Sigma Alpha.

WRITINGS: *Dictionary of Politics: Selected American and Foreign Political and Legal Terms*, Hampton Institute Press, 1973; (contributor) Sulyman Nyang, editor, *Africa: Seminar Papers on African Studies*, Howard University Press, 1974. Contributor to *Virginia Social Science Association Journal*.

WORK IN PROGRESS: *Substate Regional Planning in the United States*; revising *Dictionary of Politics: Selected American and Foreign Political and Legal Terms*.

SIDELIGHTS: Raymond acquired his U.S. citizenship from his father who became naturalized while serving in the U.S. Army during World War I.

BIOGRAPHICAL/CRITICAL SOURCES: *Polish Review*, Volume XIX, numbers 3-4, 1974.

* * *

RAZZI, James 1931-

PERSONAL: Born August 20, 1931, in New York, N.Y.; son of Guido (a waiter) and Marie (Cicatelli) Razzi; married Hedi Studiger, June 1, 1963 (died May 2, 1970); married Mary Mooney, January 29, 1971; children: Signe, Christina, Jennifer. *Education:* Attended University of Florence, School of Visual Arts, and Art Students League. *Residence:* Brooklyn, N.Y.

CAREER: Commercial artist for a variety of concerns, 1956-67; free-lance commercial artist, 1967—. *Military service:* U.S. Navy, 1949-51.

WRITINGS—Juvenile: *Simply Fun!*, Parents' Magazine Press, 1968; *Easy Does It!*, Parents' Magazine Press, 1969; *Bag of Tricks!*, Parents' Magazine Press, 1971; *Don't Open This Box*, Parents' Magazine Press, 1973; *Just For Kids*, Parents' Magazine Press, 1974. Activities consultant to *Humpty-Dumpty*.

WORK IN PROGRESS: A pun and puzzle book for Scholastic Book Services; *Extra! 1*, a school magazine teaching aid, for Macmillan.

AVOCATIONAL INTERESTS: Travel.

* * *

READ, Helen Appleton 1887(?)-1974

1887(?)—December 3, 1974; American art historian, critic, gallery director, former associate art editor of *Vogue* magazine, and author of books on art history. Obituaries: *New York Times*, December 5, 1974; *AB Bookman's Weekly*, January 13, 1975.

* * *

REAGAN, Charles E(llis) 1942-

PERSONAL: Born October 24, 1942, in New York; son of Lewis Martin and Gabrielle D. (a nurse; maiden name, Perreault) Reagan; married Sharon Elaine Stephan (a speech pathologist), August 9, 1969; children: Lewis Matthew. *Education:* Holy Cross College, A.B., 1964; University of Kansas, M.A., 1966, Ph.D., 1967; also studied at Sorbonne, University of Paris, and Institut d'Etudes Europeennes, 1962-63. *Home:* 2110 Timber Creek, Manhattan, Kan. 66502. *Office:* Department of Philosophy, Kansas State University, Manhattan, Kan. 66502.

CAREER: Kansas State University Manhattan, assistant professor, 1967-72, associate professor of philosophy, 1973—, acting head of department, 1974. *Member:* American Philosophical Association, American Association of University Professors, Mountain-Plains Philosophical Association.

WRITINGS: *Ethics for Scientific Researchers*, C. C Thomas, 1972; (editor with B. R. Tilghman and J. R. Hamilton) *Readings for Introduction to Philosophy*, Macmillan, in press. Contributor of articles and reviews to *International Philosophical Quarterly, Philosophical Studies*, and *Kansas Alumni*.

WORK IN PROGRESS: Editing a collection of original essays of the philosophy of Paul Ricoeur; writing on Ricoeur and Freud.

SIDELIGHTS: Reagan is a pilot, sometimes for Capitol Airlines, with a commercial license, single and multi-engine airplane ratings, instrument rating, and instructor certificate.

* * *

REBERT, M. Charles 1920-

PERSONAL: Born May 10, 1920, in Hanover, Pa.; son of Gereon G. (a shopkeeper) and Sylvia (an organist; maiden name, Baumgardner) Rebert. *Education:* Western Maryland College, A.B., 1941; graduate study at Western Maryland College, 1961-62, Shippensburg State College, 1962-63, Pennsylvania State University, 1963-64, York College of Pennsylvania, 1973. *Religion:* Protestant. *Home:* 140 Meade Ave., Hanover, Pa. 17331.

CAREER: Mid-South Broadcasting Network, Tupelo, Miss., program director, 1944-46; Pennsylvania State Government, Harrisburg, Pa., claims agent, 1946-47; Atlantic Richfield Oil Co., Philadelphia, Pa., statistical analyst, 1947-60; high school teacher of English and journalism in public schools of Hanover, Pa., 1960-63, and Littlestown, Pa., 1963—. Poetry teacher, consultant, and speaker at St. Davids (Pa.) Writers' Conferences. *Military service:* U.S. Army Air Forces, 1941-43; became sergeant. *Member:* International Academy of Writers, International Poetry Society (fellow), Pennsylvania Press Association, Pennsylvania State Poetry Society, Pennsylvania State Teachers Association, Pennsylvania State Antique Dealers' Association, Littlestown (Pa.) Teachers' Association. *Awards, honors:* Pennsylvania State sonnet first award, 1961; C. Sterling Clifton first award for poetry, 1962; National O'Donnol Award for poetry, 1966; Medal of Honor from Rome, Italy, 1967; Vagabond International First Prize for poetry, Munich, Germany, 1968; four International Awards for poetry from *Manifold*, London, 1969.

WRITINGS—All poetry: *Shadow Prints*, Dorrance, 1958; *I Remember*, Hanover Public Library, 1964; *Waiting for the Red Light*, Verb, 1965; *Like Sudden Roses*, Young Publications, 1967; *An Armistice of Flesh*, Lucius Markus, 1967; *The Glass Scene*, Prairie Press, 1973. Contributing editor, *Time of Singing*, 1960-63.

WORK IN PROGRESS: A technical book on American and English majolica for the antique collector market.

SIDELIGHTS: Rebert told *CA*, "To write well, one must see well, not only through physical sight, but through the insight of the emotions and mind. It is not the poet's duty to solve life's problems, but to suggest, evaluate, and even to pinch upon the nerves that cause our problems. The poet must believe in truth and beauty if he is to achieve poetic stature and relate to the realities of life. Reading is as vital as writing to the poet, and involvement is his obligation if he is to share his poems with the reader. Meter, rhyme, and rhythm prepare the lines, but the poems begin where the lines leave off."

* * *

REBISCHUNG, James A. 1928-

PERSONAL: Born May 27, 1928, in Long Island City, N.Y.; son of Aime (a self-employed businessman) and Fernande (a self-employed businesswoman; maiden name Bruno) Rebischung; married May Yee, December 31, 1968; children: Danielle, Noelle, Michele. *Education:* San Francisco State College (now University), B.A., 1962, M.A., 1964. *Politics:* None. *Religion:* None. *Home:* 1336 Oddstad Blvd., Pacifica, Calif. 94044.

CAREER: High school teacher of English in the public schools of San Francisco, Calif., 1965—. *Military service:* U.S. Army, 1947-50.

WRITINGS: Japan: The Facts of Modern Business and Social Life, James May, 1973, 2nd revised edition, Tuttle (Tokyo), 1974.

WORK IN PROGRESS: The Three 'R's: Rigid, Rotten, 'Rong, a diatribe against American education as a whole.

AVOCATIONAL INTERESTS: Photography, travel.

* * *

REDDY, John F. X. 1912(?)-1975

1912(?)—January 24, 1975; American editor, writer, and radio and television producer. Obituaries: *New York Times*, January 26, 1975.

* * *

REED, H(erbert) Owen 1910-

PERSONAL: Born June 17, 1910, in Odessa, Mo.; son of Joseph M. and Della (Fine) Reed; married Esther Richard Morris (an assistant professor at Michigan State University), August 18, 1931; children: Sara Jo Reed Ferrar, Carol Ann Reed Wetters. *Education:* University of Missouri, music student, 1929-33; Louisiana State University, B.M. (with distinction), 1934, M.M., 1936, B.A., 1937; University of Rochester, Ph.D., 1939; also studied with Bohuslav Martinu at Berkshire Music Center and privately with Roy Harris. *Religion:* Protestant. *Home:* 4690 Ottawa Dr., Okemos, Mich. 48864. *Office:* Department of Music, Michigan State University, East Lansing, Mich. 48823.

CAREER: Michigan State University, East Lansing, instructor, 1939-41, assistant professor, 1941-45, associate professor, 1945-53, professor of music, 1953—, chairman of theory and composition, 1958-67, chairman of composition, 1967—. Visiting professor at Montana State University, summer, 1950, and Gettysburg College, spring, 1969. Pianist and trumpet player; composer of works for band, stage, orchestra, chorus, and of chamber music; commissions include compositions for Michigan State University Centennial, for dedication of University of Illinois Band Building, for Detroit Symphony Orchestra's 50th anniversary, and for Ohio Music Education Association. Assistant conductor and arranger for Louisiana Kings (30-piece brass ensemble), on tour, 1936; guest conductor with symphony orchestras.

MEMBER: American Society of Composers, Authors and Publishers, American Society of University Composers, Percussive Arts Society, Teatro International (past vice-president), American Music Center (associate member), Michigan Orchestra Association, Michigan School Band and Orchestra Association (honorary member), Michigan Composers Club (past president), Phi Mu Alpha, Sinfonia, Kappa Sigma, Michigan State University Club (president, 1966).

AWARDS, HONORS: Guggenheim fellowship for composition, 1948-49; Symphonic Award of Composers Press, 1949, for "Concerto for Violincello and Orchestra"; Huntington Hartford Foundation resident fellowship, 1960; Michigan State University Distinguished Faculty Award, 1962; Greater Michigan Foundation citation for distinguished contributions in the arts, 1963; Helene Wurlitzer Foundation resident fellowship, 1967; Neil A. Kjos Memorial Award for best band composition in 1974, for "For the Unfortunate"; various grants from American Society of Composers, Authors and Publishers.

WRITINGS—All books and music published by Belwin-Mills, except as noted: *A Workbook in the Fundamentals of Music*, 1947; *Basic Music* (college theory text) and *Workbook*, 1954; (with Paul Harder) *Basic Contrapuntal Technique* and *Workbook*, 1964; (with Joel T. Leach) *Scoring for Percussion and the Instruments of the Percussion Section*, Prentice-Hall, 1969.

Orchestral works published: "Symphony Number 1," 1939; "Overture," 1940; "Concerto for Violincello and Orchestra," Seesaw Music Corp., 1951; "Overture for Strings," 1961; "The Turning Mind," 1968.

Stage works: "Peter Homan's Dream" (two-act folk opera;

book and libretto by John Jennings), first performed at Michigan State University Centennial celebration, 1955, published, 1955, revised version, 1959, musical version, 1971; "Earth Trapped" (Indian spirit legend based on story by Hartley Alexander), 1960; "Living Solid Face" (Indian spirit legend based on story by Alexander; libretto by Forrest Coggan), 1974.

Band works: "Spiritual," Associated Music Publishers, 1948; "Missouri Shindig," 1952; "Theme and Variations," 1954; "La Fiesta Mexicana," 1956, transcription for orchestra, 1964, orchestra version premiered by Detroit Symphony Orchestra, 1965; "Renascence," 1959; "Cheba-kun-ah" (for band and string quartet), 1959; "Fanfares," 1962; "The Touch of the Earth" (for concert band, chorus, and soloists), 1972; "For the Unfortunate" (for concert band and chorus on tape), Neil A. Kijos Music Co., 1975.

Chamber music: "Three Nationalities," 1951; "Michigan Morn" (from "Peter Homan's Dream"), 1955; "The Ox-Driving Song," 1955; "Scherzo for Clarinet and Piano," 1959; "The Passing of John Blackfeather" (lyrics by Merrick F. McCarthy), 1959; "Mountain Meditation" (lyrics by Marian Cuthbertson), 1960; "Symphonic Dance," 1963; "El Muchacho," 1963.

Choral works: "Two Tongue Twisters," 1951; "Ripley Ferry" (text by Merrick F. McCarthy), 1958; A Psalm of Praise," Sam Fox, 1959; "A Tabernacle for the Sun" (libretto by McCarthy).

Composer of other performed but unpublished orchestral, band, choral, and chamber music. Works included in "Panorama," American Music Publishers, 1953, and "Music for the High School Chorus," Allyn & Bacon, 1967.

WORK IN PROGRESS: With Robert Sidnell, a three-book series in composition and theory at the elementary level.

SIDELIGHTS: Reed spent six months in Mexico composing and studying folk music, 1948-49, and studied folk music there again the summer of 1960. "La Fiesta Mexicana" has been recorded by the Eastman Symphonic Wind Ensemble, U.S. Air Force Band, and University of Illinois Concert Band. Selections from "La Fiesta" and from "Peter Homan's Dream" also have been recorded, as well as four other compositions by Reed.

* * *

REED, John Shelton (Jr.) 1942-

PERSONAL: Born January 8, 1942; son of J. Shelton (a surgeon) and Alice (Greene) Reed; married Dale Volberg (a musician), July 11, 1964; children: Elisabeth Marshall, Sarah Greene. *Education:* Massachusetts Institute of Technology, B.S., 1964; Columbia University, Ph.D., 1970. *Home:* 109 Oleander Rd., Chapel Hill, N.C. 27514. *Office: Social Forces*, Hamilton Hall, University of North Carolina, Chapel Hill, N.C. 27514.

CAREER: University of North Carolina, Chapel Hill, instructor, 1969-71, assistant professor of sociology, 1971-73; Hebrew University of Jerusalem, Jerusalem, Israel, Fulbright-Hays senior lecturer in American studies and sociology, 1973-74; University of North Carolina, Chapel Hill, associate professor of sociology, 1974—. *Member:* World Association for Public Opinion Research, American Sociological Association, American Association for Public Opinion Research, Southern Sociological Society, Southern Historical Association.

WRITINGS: The Enduring South: Subcultural Persistence in Mass Society, Heath, 1972; (with Herbert H. Hyman and Charles Wright) *The Enduring Effects of Education*, University of Chicago Press, in press. Contributor of articles and reviews to sociology journals, including *Phylon, Political Science Quarterly, National Review, Public Opinion Quarterly, Southern Journal, Subterranean Sociology Newsletter*, and *Baker Street Journal*. Book review editor of *Social Forces*.

WORK IN PROGRESS: A textbook on secondary analysis of survey data; research on the social psychology of sectionalism and cognitive dimensions of liturgy.

* * *

REED, Peter J. 1935-

PERSONAL: Born May 14, 1935, in London, England; son of John Reed; married, wife's name, Margaret. *Education:* University of Idaho, B.A., 1960; University of Washington, Seattle, M.A., 1962, Ph.D., 1965; also studied at Harvard University, 1962-63. *Home:* 4900 First Ave. S., Minneapolis, Minn. 55409. *Office:* Department of English, University of Minnesota, Minneapolis, Minn. 55455.

CAREER: University of Minnesota, Minneapolis, associate professor of English, 1965—. *Military service:* Royal Air Force, 1953-56.

WRITINGS: Writers for the Seventies: Kurt Vonnegut, Warner Paperback Library, 1972.

WORK IN PROGRESS: Research on violence and aggression in modern British fiction.

* * *

REED, Rex (Taylor) 1938-

PERSONAL: Born October 2, 1938, in Fort Worth, Tex.; son of J. M. (an oil company supervisor) and Jewell (Smith) Reed. *Education:* Louisiana State University, B.A., 1960. *Residence:* New York, N.Y. *Agent:* Ad Schulberg, 300 East 57th St., New York, N.Y. 10022.

CAREER: Worked variously as a jazz singer, television performer, pancake cook, record salesman, and actor, 1960-65; film critic for *Women's Wear Daily*, 1965-69, *Cosmopolitan, Status, Holiday*, 1965—, and a syndicated film critic for New York Daily News-Chicago Tribune News Syndicate, 1970—. Member of jury at Berlin, Venice, Atlanta, and U.S.A. Film Festivals; lecturer.

WRITINGS: Do You Sleep in the Nude?, New American Library, 1968; *Conversations in the Raw*, World Publishing, 1970; *Big Screen, Little Screen*, Macmillan, 1971; *People Are Crazy Here*, Delacorte, 1974. Contributor to *Esquire, Harper's Bazaar, New York Times, Playboy, Vogue*.

WORK IN PROGRESS: Two screenplays; a novel, *Love in Strawberry Weather*.

SIDELIGHTS: In 1970, Reed appeared as an actor in the film "Myra Breckinridge."

* * *

REES, Barbara 1934-

PERSONAL: Born January 9, 1934, in Worcester, England; daughter of Thomas Arthur (an engineer) and Elizabeth (Howells) Rees; married Larry Herman (a photographer), September 1, 1967; children: Melissa Mary. *Education:* Lady Margaret Hall, Oxford, B.A. (honors), 1956. *Agent:* Elaine Greene Ltd., 31 Newington Green, London N.16, England.

CAREER: Administrative assistant for Food and Agriculture Organization in Rome, Italy, 1963-65, and United Nations Development Program, New York, N.Y., 1965-67; University of London, Extra-Mural Department, London, England, teacher of literature, 1971—.

WRITINGS: *Try Another Country* (three short novels), Harcourt, 1969; *Diminishing Circles* (novel), Secker & Warburg, 1970, Harcourt, 1971; *Prophet of the Wind* (novel), Harcourt, 1973; *The Victorian Lady*, Saxon House, in press.

AVOCATIONAL INTERESTS: Italy, travel, music, the countryside.

* * *

REESE, Thomas R. 1890(?)-1974

1890(?)—December 22, 1974; American physician specializing in otolaryngology, and author of books of humor and verse. Obituaries: *Washington Post*, December 24, 1974.

* * *

REHRAUER, George 1923-

PERSONAL: Surname is pronounced *Ray*-rou-er; born February 26, 1923, in New Jersey; son of Paul (a machinist) and Anna (Zamek) Rehrauer. *Education:* Newark College of Engineering, B.S.C.E., 1943; Columbia University, M.A., 1949, Ed.D., 1959. *Office:* Graduate School of Library Service, Rutgers University, 189 College Ave., New Brunswick, N.J. 08903.

CAREER: Curtiss Wright, Buffalo, N.Y., aeronautics engineer, 1943-44; assistant borough engineer in Leonia, N.J., 1947-49; high school teacher of English, science, and Social studies in Port Jefferson, N.Y., 1949-50, assistant principal, 1960-63; junior high school assistant principal in Plainview, N.Y., 1963-65; high school principal in Mahwah, N.J., 1965-67; Prentice-Hall, Englewood Cliffs, N.J., audio visual consultant, 1967-68; Rutgers University, New Brunswick, N.J., associate professor in Graduate School of Library Service, 1968—. Visiting professor at Wagner College, 1971—. *Military service:* U.S. Navy, Seabees, 1943-46; became lieutenant junior grade.

MEMBER: National Education Association, National Association of Secondary School Principals, American Association of School Administrators, National Council of Teachers of Mathematics, American Library Association, Association for Educational Communications and Technology, School Media Association, New York State Teachers Association, New York State Educational Communication Association, Westchester County Teachers Association, Hartsdale Teachers Association (president, 1957), Phi Delta Kappa.

WRITINGS: *Cinema Booklist*, Scarecrow, 1972, Supplement I, 1974, Supplement II, in press; *The Short Film*, Macmillan, 1975; *The Film User's Handbook*, Bowker, 1975; *The Film in America*, Smithsonian Institution Press, in press.

WORK IN PROGRESS: *Cinema Booklist: Foreign Language Books*, for Scarecrow.

SIDELIGHTS: Rehrauer writes: "My interest in film has been life-long and the opportunity to write about one's enthusiasms is appreciated. Those elements which compose film history to date will become more important with the advent of new technologies such as the video disc or cassette and my writing is done in anticipation of those forms of communication."

REID, Albert Clayton 1894-

PERSONAL: Born July 26, 1894, in High Rock, N.C.; son of William Albert (a planter) and Mary (Cole) Reid; married Eleanor Frances Jones, June 30, 1923; children: Eleanor Frances (Mrs. Brian D. Forrow), Albert Clayton, Jr. *Education:* Wake Forest College, B.A., 1917, M.A., 1918; Cornell University, Ph.D., 1923. *Politics:* Democrat. *Religion:* Baptist. *Home:* 223 West Sycamore, Wake Forest, N.C. 27587.

CAREER: Anderson College, Anderson, S.C., professor of philosophy, 1918-20; Wake Forest University, Winston-Salem, N.C., associate professor, 1920-23, professor of philosophy, 1923-65; Southeastern Theological Seminary, Wake Forest, N.C., visiting professor, 1965-67. Guest chaplain at Harvard University, summer, 1936, 1946. *Member:* Phi Beta Kappa, Sigma Xi, Omicron Delta Kappa, Kappa Alpha, Masons.

WRITINGS: *Christ and the Present Crisis*, Wake Forest College Press, 1936; (editor) *Wake Forest Seminar on Christianity*, Wake Forest College Press, 1938; *Elements of Psychology*, Prentice-Hall, 1939; *Invitation to Worship*, Abingdon, 1942; *Resources for Worship*, Abingdon, 1949; *Man and Christ*, Duke University Press, 1954; *One Hundred Chapel Talks*, Abingdon, 1955; *Christ and Human Values*, Broadman, 1961; *Tales from Cabin Creek*, Edwards & Broughton, 1967; *Christ or Confusion*, Wake Forest University Press, 1973.

* * *

REID, Malcolm 1941-

PERSONAL: Born July 4, 1941, in Ottawa, Ontario, Canada; son of Ewart P. (an economist) and Charlotte (Clare) Reid; married Rejeanne Cyr (a budgeting counselor), October 15, 1966; children: Joelle. *Education:* Attended McGill University, 1948-59, 1960-61. *Politics:* Socialist. *Religion:* Atheist. *Home:* 694 Rue St-Jean, Quebec, Quebec, Canada.

CAREER: Canadian Pacific Railway, Montreal, Quebec, publicity man, 1959-60; *Daily Record*, Sherbrooke, Quebec, reporter, 1962-63; *Globe and Mail*, Toronto, Ontario, political correspondent in Quebec, 1968-71; Canadian Broadcasting Corp., Montreal, Quebec, writer and interviewer, 1972.

WRITINGS: *The Shouting Signpainters: A Literary and Political Account of Quebec Revolutionary Nationalism*, Monthly Review Press, 1972. Contributor to *Le Devoir* and *Last Post*.

WORK IN PROGRESS: *House Book*, about housework; research on Balzac; a study of English Canada's socialist traditions.

SIDELIGHTS: "I am a middle-class sixties new-leftist," Reid told *CA*. "But not quite the same as an American one. I started out as a political journalist trying to explain these differences, but felt myself drifting over to pure literature; telling a little bit of my own story with each book, whatever the subject."

* * *

REIDY, Joseph 1920-

PERSONAL: Born March 25, 1920, in Chicago, Ill. *Education:* Loyola University, Chicago, Ill., M.D., 1948. *Address:* P.O. Box 5449, Towson, Md. 21204.

CAREER: Currently in private practice of psychoanalysis

and child psychiatry in Towson, Md. Member of staff at Sheppard and Enoch Pratt Hospital, 1970—, and at St. Joseph Hospital, 1974—. Assistant professor at Johns Hopkins University, 1959—. *Member:* International Psychoanalytic Association, Association for Child Psychiatry, American Psychiatric Association (fellow), American Psychoanalytic Association, Medical and Chirurgical Society of Maryland, Baltimore County Medical Society, Baltimore-District of Columbia Society for Psychoanalysis (president, 1974-75).

WRITINGS: The Sensitivity Phenomenon, Abbey Press, 1972.

* * *

REILLY, Robin 1928-

PERSONAL: Born January 3, 1928, in England; son of Noel Edmund (a soldier) and Margaret Mary (Dearbergh) Reilly. *Education:* Attended Royal Military Academy, Sandhurst, England, 1947-48. *Agent:* Curtis Brown, 1 Craven Hill, London W2 3EW, England.

CAREER: Josiah Wedgwood & Sons Ltd. (pottery manufacturers), Barlaston, Stoke-on-Trent, England, sales manager, 1952-64; Hogarth Gallery, New Orleans, La., partner, 1970—. Member of National Trust Committee for Quebec House, Kent, 1960—, *Military service:* British Army, Royal Artillery, 1946-52.

WRITINGS: The Rest to Fortune, Cassell, 1960; *The Sixth Floor*, Frewin, 1969; *Wedgwood Jasper*, Letts, 1972; (with George Savage) *Wedgwood: The Portrait Medallions*, Barrie & Jenkins, 1973; *Wedgwood Portrait Medallions: An Introduction*, Barrie & Jenkins, 1973; *Wolfe of Quebec*, White Lion, 1973; *The British at the Gates*, Putnam, 1974; *British Watercolours*, Letts, 1974. Contributor to *Encyclopaedia Britannica* and *Collins Encyclopedia of Knowledge*.

* * *

REINES, Alvin J. 1926-

PERSONAL: Born October 12, 1926, in Paterson, N.J.; married Hermene Ginsburg, 1962; children: Jennifer, Kip, Adam. *Education:* Hebrew Union College, M.A.H.L.; Harvard University, Ph.D. *Office:* Hebrew Union College, Cincinnati, Ohio 45220.

CAREER: Hebrew Union College, Cincinnati, Ohio, 1958—, now professor of philosophy. Chairman of board of trustees of Institute of Creative Judaism.

WRITINGS: Maimonides and Abrabanel on Prophesy, Hebrew Union College Press, 1970; *Elements in a Philosophy of Reform Judaism*, Institute of Creative Judaism, 1972; *Reform Judaism as a Polydoxy*, Institute of Creative Judaism, 1973. Contributor to *Hebrew Union College Annual*.

WORK IN PROGRESS: A curriculum for the liberal religious school.

* * *

REISER, Martin 1927-

PERSONAL: Born September 25, 1927, in Philadelphia, Pa.; son of Edward E. and Rose (Bunin) Reiser; married Enid Furman, December 31, 1952; children: Mary. *Education:* Temple University, B.A., 1950, Ed.M., 1956, Ed.D., 1961. *Residence:* Los Angeles, Calif. *Office:* Los Angeles Police Department, 150 North Los Angeles St., Los Angeles, Calif. 90012.

CAREER: Pennsylvania State University, College Station, assistant professor of psychology, 1961-64; Camarillo State Hospital, Camarillo, Calif., clinical psychologist, 1964-65; San Fernando Valley Child Guidance Clinic, Van Nuys, Calif., senior clinical psychologist, 1965-68; Los Angeles Police Department, Los Angeles, Calif., department psychologist, 1968—. Staff psychologist at Woodview-Calabasas Hospital. *Military service:* U.S. Air Force, 1951-54; became first lieutenant. *Member:* American Psychological Association (fellow), Los Angeles County Psychological Association (president, 1971-72), Mental Health Association of Los Angeles County, Los Angeles Society for Psychoanalytic Psychology (president, 1968-69), Los Angeles Society of Clinical Psychologists (president, 1970). *Awards, honors:* Silver PSI Award from California State Psychological Association, 1972.

WRITINGS: The Police Department Psychologist, C. C Thomas, 1972; *Practical Psychology for Police Officers*, C. C Thomas, 1973. Author of "Psychologist's Corner," a column in *Los Angeles Police Beat*. Contributor of articles on police psychology to professional journals.

WORK IN PROGRESS: Police Psychologist, a novel.

* * *

REISSMAN, Leonard 1921-1975

June 10, 1921—January 29, 1975; American sociologist, educator, and author of books on American society and industrial urbanization. Obituaries: *New York Times*, February 1, 1975. (*CA*-5/6).

* * *

REMSON, Irwin 1923-

PERSONAL: Born January 23, 1923, in New York, N.Y.; son of Nathan (a salesman) and Julia (Gottlieb) Remson; married Edna Dian Miller (a banker), January 25, 1948; children: Cathy Jill, Kenneth Alan. *Education:* Columbia University, B.A., 1946, M.S., 1949, Ph.D., 1954. *Home:* 1016 Cathcart Way, Stanford, Calif. 94305. *Office:* Department of Geology, Stanford University, Stanford, Calif. 94305.

CAREER: U.S. Geological Survey, Seabrook, N.J., geologist, 1949-60; Drexel Institute of Technology, Philadelphia, Pa., associate professor, 1960-64, professor of civil engineering and mechanics, 1964-68; Stanford University, Stanford, Calif., professor of geology, 1968—. *Military service:* U.S. Army Air Forces, 1943-46. *Member:* International Association of Mathematical Geologists, Geological Society of America (fellow), Soil Science Society of America, American Geophysical Union, Peninsula Geological Society, Sigma Xi, Tau Beta Pi, Phi Kappa Phi. *Awards, honors:* American Geophysical Union best first paper in hydrology, 1955.

WRITINGS: (With G. M. Hornberger and F. J. Molz) *Numerical Methods in Subsurface Hydrology*, Wiley, 1971; (with A. H. Howard) *Geology in Environmental Planning*, McGraw, 1975. Contributor of more than sixty-five articles to journals.

WORK IN PROGRESS: Research on environmental geology and on subsurface water.

* * *

RESSLER, Alice 1918-
(Alice Wayne)

PERSONAL: Born July 6, 1918, in Allentown, Pa.;

daughter of Abraham (a merchant) and Rose (Denitz) Dobnoff; married Edward Weiner (a doctor), June 23, 1940 (divorced, 1962); married Frederic Ressler (a maitre d'), April 9, 1972; children: (first marriage) Jeffery R., David J., Bart I. *Education:* Temple University, B.S., 1939; graduate study at Muhlenberg College and University of Southern California. *Residence:* Miami Beach, Fla. *Agent:* Toni Mendez, Inc., 140 East 56th St., New York, N.Y. 10022.

CAREER: Has worked as a social hostess at resorts, country clubs, and on cruise ships. Kutsher's Country Club, Monticello, N.Y., social hostess, 1964—.

WRITINGS—Under pseudonym Alice Wayne: *Love, Anyone?*, Bartholomew House, 1968; (with John Harper) *Games Single People Play*, Popular Library, 1974.

WORK IN PROGRESS: A book on menopause reactions in men.

SIDELIGHTS: Alice Wayne writes: "In this country and throughout the world, wherever printed or electronic headlines imply wrongdoings, most of us have a tendency to pass sentence before hard evidence is presented. Despite my experience, I was one of those guilty of scorning the opinions that deviated from the accepted 'norms'—before I began interviewing the strangers who told me their stories for [*Games Singles Play*]. I was like others who feared the unknown. I was timid about asking exact answers to inevitable questions, but I soon lost my hesitancy when I found I was dealing with people who had the courage and stamina to do what they thought was right for them, no matter whether society approved or disapproved. The people I interviewed were sometimes hurt, humiliated, and depressed, but their arrangement was of their own choice, and they would not, because of setbacks, give up doing what they felt was right for them."

She has appeared on television and radio programs, including the "Mike Douglas Show" and "David Susskind Show."

* * *

REYNOLDS, Roger 1934-

PERSONAL: Born July 18, 1934, in Detroit, Mich.; son of George Arthur (an architect) and Katherine (a teacher; maiden name, Butler) Reynolds; married Sandra Byers (divorced); married Karen Hill (a musician), April 11, 1964; children: (second marriage) Erika Lynn. *Education:* University of Michigan, B.S.E., 1957, B.M., 1960, M.M., 1961. *Office:* Department of Music, University of California San Diego, La Jolla, Calif. 92037.

CAREER: University of California, San Diego, La Jolla, associate professor, 1969-73, professor of music, 1973—, director of Center for Music Experiment, 1972-78. Member of Institute of Current World Affairs, 1972-76; member of Broadcast Music, Inc. *Awards, honors:* Fulbright fellowship, 1962-63; Guggenheim fellowship, 1964-65; Rockefeller Foundation grant, 1965-66; Institute of Current World Af fairs fellowship, 1966-69; awards from Fromm Foundation, 1968, Ford Foundation, 1972, and National Institute of Arts and Letters, 1972.

WRITINGS: Mind Models: New Forms of Musical Experience, Praeger, 1974.

* * *

RICE, Eve (Hart) 1951-

PERSONAL: Born February 2, 1951, in New York, N.Y.; daughter of Henry Hart (a real estate broker) and Grace (Hecker) Rice. *Education:* Yale University, B.A., 1972, graduate study, 1972-73; New School for Social Research, further study, 1973-74. *Home:* 69 West 9th St., New York, N.Y. 10011; and Greenwich Rd., Bedford, N.Y. 10506.

CAREER: Free-lance writer and illustrator of children's books in New York, N.Y., 1973—.

WRITINGS—All self-illustrated: *Oh, Lewis!*, Macmillan, 1974; *New Blue Shoes*, Macmillan, 1975; *Mr. Brimble's Hobby and Other Stories*, Morrow, 1975; *Ebbie*, Morrow, 1975; *What Sadie Sang*, Morrow, in press.

Illustrator: Helen Puner, *I Am Big: You Are Little*, Young Scott Books, 1973.

WORK IN PROGRESS: Poetry for children.

AVOCATIONAL INTERESTS: Walking, bicycling, exploring New York City, hiking in country, collecting wild flowers, history, calligraphy, etching, collecting children's books.

* * *

RICE, George H(all), Jr. 1923-

PERSONAL: Born November 17, 1923, in Freeport, Tex.; son of George H. (a school teacher) and Vera (Legett) Rice; married Glorianne Wilson (a school teacher), August 18, 1951; children: Jennifer Lee, John Wilson. *Education:* Agricultural and Mechanical College of Texas (now Texas A & M University), B.S., 1950; University of Denver, M.B.A., 1958; Stanford University, Ph.D., 1964. *Religion:* Baptist. *Home address:* Route 1, Box 91, Bryan, Tex. 77801. *Office:* Department of Management, College of Business Administration, Texas A & M University, College Station, Tex. 77843.

CAREER: Registered professional engineer in Colorado. Westinghouse Electric Corp., Denver, Colo., applications engineer, 1950-58; Martin Co., Littleton, Colo., senior engineer, 1959; Stanford Research Institute, Menlo Park, Calif., industrial economist, 1961-63; California State College (now University), Hayward, associate professor of business administration, 1963-64; Texas A & M University, College Station, associate professor, 1964-67, professor of business administration, 1967—, head of management department, 1966-72. Member of consulting faculty at U.S. Army Command and General Staff College. *Military service:* U.S. Army Air Forces, 1943-46; became technical sergeant. U.S. Army Reserve, 1946—; present rank, lieutenant colonel. *Member:* Academy of Management, Academy of Management—Southwest Division (vice-president, 1969-70; president, 1970-71), Southwestern Social Sciences Association.

WRITINGS: (With Dean W. Bishoprick) *Conceptual Models of Organization*, Appleton, 1971. Contributor to professional journals, including *Experimental Publication System, Southern Journal of Business, Business Studies*, and *Personnel Journal.*

WORK IN PROGRESS: Research on decision making in small businesses; studying organization theory.

SIDELIGHTS: Rice owns and operates a small cattle ranch in Texas. He also flies his own plane.

* * *

RICHARDSON, Betty 1935-

PERSONAL: Born February 14, 1935, in Louisville, Ky.; daughter of Robert F. and Dora (Freiberg) Ritchie; married

Robert Crain (divorced); married Kermit T. Hoyenga (divorced); married John Adkins Richardson (a professor of art), October, 1971; children: (first marriage) Victor L. *Education:* University of Louisville, A.B., 1957; University of Nebraska, M.A., 1963, Ph.D., 1968. *Home:* 802 West High St., Edwardsville, Ill. 62025. *Office:* Department of English, Southern Illinois University, Edwardsville, Ill. 62025.

CAREER: Southern Illinois University, Edwardsville, associate professor of English, and assistant chairperson of department. Formerly reporter and society editor, Springfield, Ohio, *Daily News and Sun. Member:* Modern Language Association of America (member of Women's Caucus), National Organization of Women, American Association of University Professors, Popular Culture Association, Midwest Modern Language Association, University and College Women of Illinois.

WRITINGS: Sexism in Higher Education, Seabury, 1974. Contributor of articles and reviews to journals, including *Papers on Language and Literature, American Association of University Professors Bulletin, Bulletin of the Midwest Modern Language Association, Prairie Schooner*, and *Midcontinent American Studies Journal.* Formerly assistant editor of *Prairie Schooner*, and associate and acting editor of *Papers of Language and Literature*; editor of *Concerns* (of Women's Caucus of Modern Language Association of America).

WORK IN PROGRESS: Death and the Learned Ladies, a novel; a nonfiction book about women, with husband, John Adkins Richardson.

SIDELIGHTS: Betty Richardson writes: "I believe that the sad, dismal state of university education is a function, at least in part, of the traditional professorial blindness to such matters as what has been happening to better than half the human race—and more than that, when one counts in the minorities. The university has been committed to the avoidance of new knowledge, not to the discovery of it. . . . The whole narrow, rigid, radical notion of sisterhood rather chills my blood, but the rich, various abundance of human types, experiences, characters, personalities is a source of constant delight and intellectual enrichment. Higher education has hurt only itself in shunning that variety."

* * *

RICHARDSON, James Nathaniel 1942- (Nat Richards)

PERSONAL: Born January 27, 1942, in Tarheel, N.C.; son of James D. (a laborer) and Lila (a maid; maiden name, Robinson) Richardson; married Cherry Key Allen, June 29, 1968; children: Guy James, Alan Mitchell. *Education:* Livingstone College, B.A., 1963; Furman University, graduate study, summer, 1966. *Politics:* None. *Religion:* Jehovah's Witness. *Home:* 119 Middleton St., Greenville, S.C. 29601.

CAREER: High school English teacher in Charlotte, N.C., 1963-64, and Greenville, S.C., 1964-67; missionary for Jehovah's Witnesses in Greenville, S.C., 1967-71; high school English teacher in Greenville, S.C., 1972-73; writer, 1973—. Retail sales manager at Goodyear Service Store, 1963—.

WRITINGS—Under pseudonym Nat Richards: *Otis Dunn: Manhunter* (detective novel), Ashley Books, 1974.

WORK IN PROGRESS: The Midnight Shootout, and *The Doomsday Arrest*, Otis Dunn detective novels; *The Converter*, a historical romance set in the first century.

SIDELIGHTS: Richardson wrote his first detective story at the age of thirteen.

* * *

RICHEY, Margaret Fitzgerald 1883(?)-1974

1883(?)—1974; British scholar, poet and author of books on medieval German poetry. Obituaries: *AB Bookman's Weekly*, December 16, 1974.

* * *

RICHMOND, Robert W(illiam) 1927-

PERSONAL: Born July 21, 1927, in Stockton, Kan.; son of Emmett Knox (a businessman) and M. Janet (Felible) Richmond; married Mary Belle Tillotson,September 6, 1950 (died April, 1967); married Nell F. Lindner, January 19, 1968; children: (first marriage) John D., Douglas R.; (second marriage) Catherine (Mrs. Ken Wasinger), John M. Lindner, Peter F. Lindner. *Education:* Washburn University, A.B., 1950; University of Nebraska, M.A., 1951. *Politics:* Independent. *Religion:* Protestant. *Home:* 1401 College, Topeka, Kan. 66604. *Office:* Kansas State Historical Society, Topeka, Kan. 66612.

CAREER: Nebraska Historical Society, Lincoln, archivist, 1951-52; Kansas State Historical Society, Topeka, state archivist, 1952—. Adjunct professor of history at Washburn University, 1957—; visiting professor at University of Manitoba, 1972. Member of board of directors of Crawford Landmark Plaza, Inc.; member of board of directors of Topeka Civic Symphony Society; member of Kansas Committee for the Humanities. Consultant to Union Pacific Railroad. *Military service:* U.S. Army, 1945-47; became staff sergeant.

MEMBER: Organization of American Historians, American Association for State and Local History, Scottish National Trust, Western History Association, Kansas History Teachers (president, 1967-68), Kansas State Historical Society, Nebraska Historical Society, Shawnee County Historical Society (president, 1972), Fortnightly Literary Club, Topeka Press Club, Washburn Alumni Association (past member of board of directors), Kappa Sigma.

WRITINGS: (With Nyle H. Miller and Edgar Langsdorf) *Kansas: A Pictorial History*, Kansas State Historical Society, 1961; (with Miller and Langsdorf) *Kansas in Newspapers*, Kansas State Historical Society, 1963; (editor with Robert W. Mardock) *A Nation Moving West*, University of Nebraska Press, 1966; *Kansas: A Land of Contrasts*, Forum Press, 1974.

Author and moderator of "Kansas History," a series, for KTWU Television, 1971-74. Contributor to *Encyclopaedia Britannica*. Contributor of articles and reviews to history journals, including *Kansas Historical Quarterly, American History Illustrated, Journal of American History, Western History Quarterly, American Archivist*, and *Civil War History*, and to regional newspapers.

WORK IN PROGRESS: Research on American social history and on Western settlement.

AVOCATIONAL INTERESTS: British history (especially Scotland), travel in Great Britain, music (choral and symphonic; performing and listening), sports.

* * *

RICHTER, Horst-Eberhard 1923-

PERSONAL: Born April 28, 1923, in Berlin, Germany; son

of Otto and Charlotte (Domzalski) Richter; married Bergrun Luckow, July 15, 1947; children: Jutta Richter Forchmann, Elena Richter Strahlendorf, Clemens. *Education:* University of Berlin, Dr.phil., 1949, Dr.med., 1957. *Office:* Psychosomatische Universitatsklinik, Ludwigstrasse 76, 63 Giessen, West Germany.

CAREER: Director of Advisory and Research Centre for Childhood Emotional Disturbances at Berlin Wedding Children's Hospital, 1952-62, and physician at Psychiatric Clinic of Free University, Berlin, 1955-62; University of Giessen, Giessen, West Germany, chief of department of psychosomatic medicine, 1962—. Director, Berlin Psychoanalytic Institute, 1959-62. West-German representative in psychotherapy section of World Psychiatric Society, 1973—. *Member:* German Psychoanalytic Association (president, 1964-68), P.E.N. International. *Awards, honors:* Research prize of the Swiss Society for Psychosomatic Medicine, 1970.

WRITINGS: Eltern, Kind und Neurose: Psychoanalyse der kindlichen Rolle (title means "Parents, Child and Neurosis: The Psychoanalysis of the Role of the Child"), Klett, 1963; (with Dieter Beckmann) *Herzneurose* (title means "Cardiac Neurosis"), Thieme, 1969, revised edition, 1973; *Patient Familie: Entstehung, Struktur und Therapie von Konflikten in Ehe und Familie*, Rowohlt, 1970, translation by Denver Lindley published as *The Family as Patient: The Origin, Structure, and Therapy of Marital and Family Conflict*, Farrar, Straus, 1974; *Familienkonflikte und Familienberatung* (title means "Family Conflicts and Family Counseling"), Butzon & Bercker, 1970; *Die Gruppe* (title means "The Group"), Rowohlt, 1972; (with Beckmann) *Giessen-Test: Ein Test fuer Individual- und Gruppendiagnostik Handbuch* (title means "Giessen Test: A Test for Individual and Group Diagnosis"), Huber (Bern), 1972; *Lernziel Solidaritaet* (title means "How to Realize Solidarity"), Rowohlt, 1974. Author of television script, "Sidelung Eulenkopf," presented on station ARD, Germany, 1972. Co-editor, *Jahrbuch der Psychoanalyse*, published by Huber, and *Zeitschrift fuer Psychotherapie und Medizinische Psychologie*, published by Thieme.

WORK IN PROGRESS: Research on family therapy, on new types of social therapy, and on the interaction between individual, group, and institution.

*   *   *

RILING, Raymond L. J. 1896(?)-1974

1896(?)—November 26, 1974; American expert on antique firearms, publisher, founder of Ray Riling Arms Books Co., and author of books on arms and related subjects. Obituaries: *AB Bookman's Weekly*, January 6, 1975.

*   *   *

RINGROSE, David R. 1938-

PERSONAL: Born June 1, 1938, in Minneapolis, Minn.; son of Robert G. (a newspaper executive) and Leona (Krengle) Ringrose; married Kathryn Mackay, June 24, 1961; children: Daniel, Robert. *Education:* Carleton College, B.A., 1960; University of Wisconsin, Madison, M.A., 1962, Ph.D., 1966. *Office:* Department of History, University of California at San Diego, La Jolla, Calif. 92037.

CAREER: Rutgers University, New Brunswick, N.J., 1965-74, began as assistant professor, became associate professor of history; University of California at San Diego, La Jolla, associate professor of history, 1974—. *Member:* American Historical Association, Economic History Association, Society for Spanish and Portuguese Historical Studies (general secretary, 1971-73). *Awards, honors:* Fulbright fellowships, 1963-65, 1968-69; National Endowment for the Humanities fellowship, 1973-74.

WRITINGS: Transportation and Economic Stagnation in Spain, 1750-1850, Duke University Press, 1970. Contributor to *Journal of Economic History, Economic History Review, Hispanic American Historical Review, Moneda y Credito, Historia Iberica*, and *Hacienda Publica Espanola*.

WORK IN PROGRESS: Research on pre-industrial Madrid and its role in the development of the society and economy of the Spanish interior to 1850.

*   *   *

RIPLEY, Randall B(utler) 1938-

PERSONAL: Born January 24, 1938, in Des Moines, Iowa; son of Henry Dayton and Aletha (Butler) Ripley; married Grace Anne Franklin, October 15, 1974; children: Frederick Joseph, Vanessa Gail. *Education:* DePauw University, B.A., 1959; Harvard University, M.A., 1961, Ph.D., 1963. *Home:* 948 Thomas Rd., Columbus, Ohio 43212. *Office:* Department of Political Science, Ohio State University, Columbus, Ohio 43210.

CAREER: Brookings Institution, Washington, D.C., research fellow, 1962-63; U.S. House of Representatives, Office of the Democratic Whip, Washington, D.C., intern, 1963; Brookings Institution, research assistant, 1963-64, research associate, 1964-67; Ohio State University, Columbus, associate professor, 1967-69, professor of political science, 1969—, chairman of department, 1969—. Consultant to Department of Housing and Urban Development, Senate Committee on Rules and Administration, House Select Committee on Committees, Commission on Population Growth and the American Future, and Commission on the Organization of the Government for the Conduct of Foreign Policy.

MEMBER: American Political Science Association, Midwest Political Science Association, Southern Political Science Association, Phi Beta Kappa. *Awards, honors:* Woodrow Wilson fellow, 1959-60; Danforth Foundation fellow, 1959-63.

WRITINGS: (Editor) *Public Policies and Their Politics* (reader), Norton, 1966; (with Charles O. Jones) *The Role of Political Parties in Congress: A Bibliography and Research Guide*, University of Arizona Press, 1966; *Party Leaders in the House of Representatives*, Brookings Institution, 1967; *Majority Party Leadership in Congress*, Little, Brown, 1969; *Power in the Senate*, St. Martin's, 1969; (contributor) Frederick N. Cleaveland and others, editors, *Congress and Urban Problems*, Brookings Institution, 1969; *The Politics of Economic and Human Resource Development*, Bobbs-Merrill, 1972; *Kennedy and Congress*, General Learning Press, 1972; (editor with Theodore J. Lowi) *Legislative Politics, U.S.A.*, 3rd edition (Ripley was not associated with earlier editions), Little, Brown, 1973; *American National Government and Public Policy*, Free Press, 1974; *Congress*, Norton, 1975; (editor with Grace A. Franklin, and contributor) *Policy-making in the Federal Executive Branch*, Free Press, 1975. Contributor of articles and book reviews to political science journals. Editor of "Sage Professional Papers in American Politics," 1972—; member of editorial board of *Journal of Politics*, 1969—, and *American Politics Quarterly*, 1973—.

WORK IN PROGRESS: Research on policy-making in public bureaucracies, the implementation of the Comprehensive Employment and Training Act of 1973, and Congress and the bureaucracy.

* * *

RIPPA, S(ol) Alexander 1925-

PERSONAL: Born November 15, 1925, in St. Petersburg, Fla.; son of Guss and Hinda (Landfield) Rippa; married Barbara Frogel, June 27, 1954; children: Diane Carol, Joel Mark. *Education:* Attended U.S. Naval Academy, 1946; University of Miami, Coral Gables, Fla., A.B. (cum laude), 1948; Vanderbilt University, M.A., 1949; Harvard University, Ed.D., 1958. *Residence:* Burlington, Vt. *Office:* College of Educaton, University of Vermont, Waterman Building, Burlington, Vt. 05401.

CAREER: Social studies teacher in public schools in Tampa, Fla., 1949-55, and Newton, Mass., 1955-58; Northern Illinois University, DeKalb, assistant professor of education, 1958-60; University of Vermont, Burlington, associate professor, 1960-65, professor of education, 1965—. Visiting scholar at Oxford University, 1968-69. *Military service:* U.S. Navy, 1943-46. *Member:* National Education Association (life member), American Historical Association, History of Education Society (charter member), American Association of University Professors. *Awards, honors:* Ford Foundation fellowship, 1952-53.

WRITINGS: Education in a Free Society: An American History, McKay, 1967, 2nd edition, 1971; *Educational Ideas in America: A Documentary History*, McKay, 1969. Contributor to journals in his field.

WORK IN PROGRESS: Public Schooling in America: Historical Roots and New Directions; research on Maria Montessori's contributions to the mainstream of educational history; research on comparative and international education.

AVOCATIONAL INTERESTS: Creative writing, Nordic skiing, swimming, gardening.

* * *

RIPPERGER, Helmut Lothar 1897-1974

July 21, 1897—August 4, 1974; American art research librarian, former aide to Czechoslovakian President Thomas Masaryk, newspaper editor, foreign service officer, translator, and author. Obituaries: *New York Times*, August 6, 1974.

* * *

RITZER, George 1940-

PERSONAL: Born October 14, 1940, in New York, N.Y.; son of Jacob and Ruth (Davis) Ritzer; married Susan Axelrod, June 21, 1964; children: David, Jeremy. *Education:* City College of the City University of New York, B.A., 1962; University of Michigan, M.B.A., 1964; Cornell University, Ph.D., 1968. *Office:* Department of Sociology, University of Maryland, College Park, Md. 20740.

CAREER: Ford Motor Co., Detroit, Mich., personnel manager, 1964-65; Tulane University, New Orleans, La., assistant professor of sociology, 1968-70; University of Kansas, Lawrence, associate professor of sociology, 1970-74; University of Maryland, College Park, professor of sociology, 1974—. *Member:* American Sociological Association, Midwest Sociological Association, District of Columbia Sociological Association. *Awards, honors:* Fulbright-Hays fellowship, 1975.

WRITINGS: (With Harrison Trice) *An Occupation in Conflict: A Study of the Personnel Manager*, Cornell University Press, 1969; *Man and His Work: Conflict and Change*, Appleton, 1972; *Issues, Debates and Controversies: An Introduction to Sociology*, Allyn & Bacon, 1972; *Social Realities: Dynamic Perspectives*, Allyn & Bacon, 1974; *Sociology: A Multiple Paradigm Science*, Allyn & Bacon, 1975. Contributor of articles to professional journals.

WORK IN PROGRESS: Research on industrial innovations in Europe and the United States; *Social Problems: Values and Interests in Conflict*, with R. J. Antonio.

* * *

ROBACKER, Earl Francis 1904-

PERSONAL: Born April 11, 1904, in Panther, Pa.; son of Francis A. and Anna C. (Huguenin) Robacker; married Ada Fenner, March 16, 1929. *Education:* East Stroudsburg State College, B.S., 1928; New York University, M.A., 1931, Ph.D., 1941. *Residence:* White Plains, N.Y. 10605.

CAREER: Public school teacher of English in South Sterling, Pa., 1922-24, and in Easton, Pa., 1926-28; White Plains Public Schools, White Plains, N.Y., teacher of English, 1928-59, head of department, 1953-59, division director of decentralized high school, 1960-68. Lecturer at New York University, 1945-49. Historical consultant to National Park Service, 1970—. *Awards, honors:* Historic Schaefferstown citation for distinguished service, 1972; with wife, Ada Robacker, Incentive Award for distinguished service from National Park Service, 1973; with Ada Robacker, silver loving cup from Kutztown Folk Festival, 1974, for twenty-five years of service.

WRITINGS: Pennsylvania German Literature, University of Pennsylvania Press, 1942; *Pennsylvania Dutch Stuff*, University of Pennsylvania Press, 1944; (wife, Ada F. Robacker) *Pennsylvania German Cooky Cutters and Cookies* (monograph), Plymouth Meeting, 1946; *Touch of the Dutchland*, A. S. Barnes, 1965; *Old Stuff in Up-Country Pennsylvania*, A. S. Barnes, 1973. Contributor to *Antiques*, newpapers, and other journals. Antiques editor of *Pennsylvania Folklife Quarterly*, 1954—.

WORK IN PROGRESS: Research on Pennsylvania Dutch folk art and antiques, especially ceramics.

SIDELIGHTS: Robacker has a reading knowledge of Pennsylvania Dutch dialects.

* * *

ROBBINS, Richard G., Jr. 1939-

PERSONAL: Born March 6, 1939, in Buffalo, N.Y.; son of Richard G. (a salesman) and Anne (Jones) Robbins; married Catherine Codispoti (an executive secretary), April 2, 1966; children: Carla. *Education:* Williams College, B.A., 1961; Columbia University, M.A., 1965, Ph.D., 1970. *Home:* 224 12th St. N.W., Albuquerque, N.M. 87102. *Office:* Department of History, University of New Mexico, Albuquerque, N.M. 87131.

CAREER: University of New Mexico, Albuquerque, assistant professor, 1969-74, associate professor of history, 1974—, chairman of Russian Studies Program. *Member:* American Historical Association, American Association for the Advancement of Slavic Studies, Rocky Mountain

Association for Slavic Studies, Phi Beta Kappa. *Awards, honors:* Fulbright-Hays fellowship, 1967-68.

WRITINGS: Famine in Russia: 1891-1892, Columbia University Press, 1975.

WORK IN PROGRESS: Research on Russian institutional history and on the provincial governors of the late nineteenth and early twentieth centuries.

* * *

ROBBINS, Vesta O(rdelia) 1891-

PERSONAL: Born February 28, 1891, in Baxter, Iowa; daughter of William Howard (a farmer) and Etta (Wier) Simanton; married Raymond Robbins, December 2, 1913 (divorced, 1948); children: Vesta Norine (Mrs. Leonard Hjelmeland). *Education:* Attended Iowa State Teacher's College (now Iowa State University), 1908, Huron College, 1911, and Montana State College (now University), 1940. *Politics:* "I vote for the man." *Religion:* Disciples of Christ. *Home:* 390 North Winchester, #15-A, Santa Clara, Calif. 95050.

CAREER: Teacher in one and two room schools in Iowa and South Dakota, 1907-12; lightning crayon artist and soprano for American Concert Co., 1912-13; pianist for silent movies, 1913-20; feature story writer on newspapers in Great Falls, Mont., 1924-35, and in Spokane, Wash., 1959-61; Robbins Studio, Spokane, Wash., instructor in art, 1948-67. Member of Russell Commission, 1929-40, and of National Advisory Committee for New York World's Fair, 1939; Montana state chairman of National Art Week, 1937-38. *Member:* Montana Federation of Women's Clubs (president, 1925-32; member of board of directors, 1938-39), Montana American Artists Professional League, 1937-38, Spokane Realistic Art Association (life member; advisor, 1959—), Eugenia Walsh Writers, Porter Writers. *Awards, honors:* Art exhibited at New York World's Fair and at San Francisco World's Fair, both 1939.

WRITINGS: Early Community History, Montana Federation of Women's Clubs, 1923; *Basics in Art*, privately printed, 1972; *No Coward Soul*, Iowa State University Press, 1974. Contributor to *Spokesman Review*.

WORK IN PROGRESS: Three books, one on her life as a ranger's wife in Glacier National Park from 1921-22, one on homesteading in northeast Montana from 1915-20, and one on pioneer days in Iowa before it became a state.

* * *

ROBERTSON, Jennifer Sinclair 1942-

PERSONAL: Born February 21, 1942, in Datchet, Buckinghamshire, England; daughter of William and Gertrude (Ball) Brown; married Stuart Lang Robertson (a theological student), February 19, 1966; children: Neil Sinclair, Aileen Margaret. *Education:* University of Glasgow, M.A., 1963, social sciences diploma, 1964; University of Warsaw, graduate study, 1964-65. *Politics:* "On the left." *Religion:* Christian. *Home:* 11 Oban Rd., Chilwell, Nottingham, England.

CAREER: School social worker in Glasgow, Scotland, 1965-68.

WRITINGS—Children's novels: *Fior*, Scripture Union, 1974; *Circle of Shadows*, Scripture Union, 1975. Contributor to *Encyclopedia of Bible Stories*, and to newspapers and journals.

WORK IN PROGRESS: A book on an unmarried mother, *Linda*, completion expected in 1975; research on Celtic Britain in prehistory and in the Christian era as a follow-up to *Circle of Shadows*.

SIDELIGHTS: Jennifer Robertson worked in Germany with displaced persons in 1961, and told *CA* she continues to be concerned with rights of Christians in East Europe.

* * *

ROBINSON, Albert J(ohn) 1926-

PERSONAL: Born January 12, 1926, in Mildura, Australia; son of Clarence R. (a businessman) and Jessie (Skelton) Robinson; married Marjorie Dickson (a librarian), 1951; children: Colan M. *Education:* University of Melbourne, B.Com., 1949; Australian National University, B.A., 1952; Duke University, Ph.D., 1962. *Home:* 55 Fenn Ave., Willowdale, Ontario M2L IM9, Canada. *Office:* Department of Economics, York University, 4700 Keele St., Downsview, Ontario M3J IP3, Canada.

CAREER: Employee of Federal Government of Australia, Canberra, 1950-59; Queen's University, Kingston, Ontario, Canada, assistant professor of economics, 1962-64; York University, Downsview, Ontario, associate professor, 1964-72, professor of economics, 1973—. *Military service:* Royal Australian Air Force, 1944-45. *Member:* Canadian Economics Association, Canadian Tax Foundation, American Economic Association, Economic History Association, Southern Economic Association. *Awards, honors:* Canada Council grants, 1968, 1972; Fulbright award, 1969; Central Mortgage and Housing Corporation grant, 1970.

WRITINGS: (With James Cutt) *Public Finance in Canada*, Methuen, 1968, 2nd edition, 1973; *Economic Evaluation of Municipal Expenditures*, Canadian Tax Foundation, 1971; *Economics and New Towns*, Praeger, 1975. Contributor to professional journals.

WORK IN PROGRESS: Economics of New Towns; an analysis of government policies using economic tools, *Economics of Government*.

* * *

ROBINSON, Hubbell 1905-1974

October 16, 1905—September 4, 1974; American broadcasting executive, radio and television producer, chairman of the quarterly of the National Academy of Television Arts and Sciences, former advertising executive, film critic, and author. Obituaries: *New York Times*, September 6, 1974; *Washington Post*, September 8, 1974; *Newsweek*, September 16, 1974.

* * *

ROBINSON, (Frances) Olvis 1923-

PERSONAL: Born June 8, 1923, in Greenville, Tex.; daughter of Olvis Jordan (a minister and writer) and Frances Elizabeth (a deputy district clerk; maiden name, Musick) Robinson; married Henry Harper Fortenberry, June 15, 1947 (divorced, 1970); children: Elizabeth Fern (Mrs. David LeGrant), Charlotte Claire Robinson Riley. *Education:* North Texas State University, B.Mus., 1943, M.Mus., 1947, Ed.D., 1971. *Home:* 820 East Ward, Douglas, Ga. 31533. *Office:* Division of Developmental Education, South Georgia College, Douglas, Ga. 31533.

CAREER: South Georgia College, Douglas, Ga., instructor in reading and English, 1972—, acting chairman of Division of Developmental Education, 1973-74. *Member:*

Association for Humanistic Psychology, College Reading Association, Georgia Association of Educators, Douglas Music Club (treasurer, 1973-75), Sigma Alpha Iota. *Awards, honors:* Poetry Society of Texas awards, 1964-66; South & West manuscript publication award at Pineywoods Writer's Conference, 1968, for *Spindrift*.

WRITINGS—Poems: *Sashay*, Robalee Publications, 1966; *Spindrift*, South & West, 1969. Work is represented in anthologies, including *Flame Annual, Poetry Americana*, and *Avalon Anthology of Texas Poets*. Contributor of more than one hundred poems to *South & West, Poet, Encore, Cyclo-Flame, Swordsman Review, Seed, Creative Review, Other Voices, Fireflower*, and other publications.

WORK IN PROGRESS: Research on developmental education and on language arts; a compilation of previously published poems titled, *To Build a Pyramid*; a long poem, *In Life With Love*.

AVOCATIONAL INTERESTS: Music, theater, travel.

* * *

ROBINSON, Sondra Till 1931-

PERSONAL: Born November 24, 1931, in Santa Monica, Calif.; daughter of Charles Gilson (an accountant) and Gertrude (a comptometer operator; maiden name, Till) Rhoads; married David Robinson (an engineer), June 15, 1952; children: Kathleen Till, Rebecca Starr. *Education:* University of California, Los Angeles, student, 1950-53. *Politics:* "There is no name for my politics." *Religion:* "Pantheist." *Residence:* Los Angeles, Calif. *Agent:* Mary Yost Associates, 141 East 55th St., New York, N.Y. 10022; and H. N. Swanson, Inc., 8523 Sunset Blvd., Los Angeles, Calif. 90069.

CAREER: Writer. *Member:* Authors Guild of Authors League of America. *Award, honors:* Los Angeles City Council resolution for writing.

WRITINGS: Almansor, Nash Publishing, 1974. Author of text for cantata "The Serpent," composed by Nancy Webster Bloomer, first performed in Palo Alto, Calif., at Palo Alto Contemporary Arts Concert Series, May 20, 1966. Contributor of stories and poems to *Carolina Quarterly, Challenge, Integrator, Nimrod, South Dakota Review, Redbook*, and *Literary Review*.

WORK IN PROGRESS: Three novels.

AVOCATIONAL INTERESTS: Mythology, anthropology, classical music.

* * *

ROBINSON, Trevor 1929-

PERSONAL: Born February 20, 1929, in Chicopee, Mass.; son of Thomas Francis (an engineer) and Helen (Dalton) Robinson; married Laura Barme, May 30, 1952; children: June, Heather, Mark. *Education:* Harvard University, A.B., 1950, A.M., 1951; University of Massachusetts, M.S., 1953; Cornell University, Ph.D., 1956. *Politics:* Independent. *Religion:* Society of Friends. *Home:* 65 Pine St., Amherst, Mass. 01002. *Office:* Department of Biochemistry, University of Massachusetts, Amherst, Mass. 01002.

CAREER: University of Massachusetts, Amherst, assistant professor, 1961-63, associate professor of biochemistry, 1963—. *Member:* Phytochemical Society of North America, American Association for the Advancement of Science, American Society of Plant Physiologists, Early American Industries Association, Galpin Society, Sigma Xi.

WRITINGS: The Organic Constituents of Higher Plants, Burgess, 1963, 2nd edition, 1967; *The Biochemistry of Alkaloids*, Springer Publishing, 1968; *The Amateur Wind Instrument Maker*, University of Massachusetts Press, 1973.

WORK IN PROGRESS: A third edition of *Organic Constituents of Higher Plants*.

AVOCATIONAL INTERESTS: Travel.

* * *

ROCHELLE, Jay C. 1938-

PERSONAL: Born December 28, 1938, in Southampton, Pa.; son of Norman Harold and Marion Emma (an artist; maiden name, Sommer) Rochelle; married Cynthia Ann Hull, 1962; children: Leah Suzanne, Peter Christopher, Glynis Andrea, Micah Nicholas. *Education:* St. John's College, Winfield, Kan., A.A., 1959; Concordia Senior College, Fort Wayne, Ind., B.A., 1961; Lutheran Theological Seminary, Philadelphia, Pa., graduate study, 1961-63; Concordia Theological Seminary, St. Louis, Mo., M.Div., 1965; Pittsburgh Theological Seminary, Th.M., 1968. *Residence:* Bloomsburg, Pa.

CAREER: Lutheran clergyman in Pittsburgh, Pa., 1965-68, Allentown, Pa., 1968-70, and Bloomsburg, Pa., 1970—. *Member:* Association for Creative Change, Fellowship of St. Augustine.

WRITINGS: Create and Celebrate, Fortress, 1971; (with Victor I. Gruhn) *Psalms for Today*, Fortress, 1973; *The Revolutionary Year*, Fortress, 1973; *I'm Not the Same Person I Was Yesterday*, Fortress, 1974. Contributor of articles, poems, and reviews to *Dialog, Event, Pittsburgh Perspective, Quinto Lingo, People's Pulse*, and *Olympian*.

WORK IN PROGRESS: Two devotional books; a book on "finding meaning by telling your own story"; a book of poems.

AVOCATIONAL INTERESTS: Vegetable gardening, baking bread.

* * *

RODALE, Robert 1930-

PERSONAL: Born March 27, 1930; son of Jerome Irving (a playwright, publisher, and editor) and Anna A. (Andrews) Rodale; married Ardath Harter (a decorator and school counselor), June 23, 1951; children: Heather, Heidi, David, Maria, Anthony. *Education:* Lehigh University, student, 1947-52. *Home address:* R.D.2, Box 313, Allentown, Pa. 18103. *Office:* Rodale Press, Inc., 33 East Minor St., Emmaus, Pa. 18049.

CAREER: Organic Gardening and Farming and *Prevention* (magazines), Emmaus, Pa., editor and publisher, 1953—. Publisher of *Compost Science*, 1960—, and *Environment Action Bulletin* and *Executive Fitness Newsletter*, 1970—; president of Soil and Health Foundation; member of board of associates of Muhlenberg College, 1970—; president and chairman of the board of directors of Rodale Press; chairman of board of directors of Rodale Manufacturing Co.; member of board of directors of J. I. Rodale Ltd. (England). Vice-president of Lehigh Valley Land Conservancy; member of board of directors of Trexlertown Playground Association; coordinator of Trexlertown Velodrome Committee.

MEMBER: American Association for the Advancement of

Science, Society for the Advancement of Management, National Rifle Association, National Skeet Shooting Association, China-America Relations Society (member of board of directors), Sierra Club, National Audubon Society, Pennsylvania Association for the Advancement of Science. *Awards, honors:* Distinguished International Shooter Badge for clay target shooting.

WRITINGS: The Challenge of Earthworm Research, Soil and Health Foundation, 1961; *The Basic Book of Organic Gardening*, Ballantine, 1971; *Sane Living in a Mad World*, Rodale Books, 1972; *The Best Health Ideas I Know*, Rodale Books, 1974. Author of "Organic Living," a column syndicated by CT-NY News Syndicate, and "Trap and Skeet Department," a column in *Outdoor Life*.

* * *

RODGERS, Harrell R(oss), Jr. 1939-

PERSONAL: Born August 25, 1939, in Columbus, Miss.; son of Harrell Ross and Eunice Rodgers. *Education:* Sam Houston State College (now University), B.A., 1963; University of Houston, M.A., 1964; University of Iowa, Ph.D., 1968. *Home:* 8124 Cornell, University City, Mo. 63130. *Office:* Department of Political Science, University of Missouri, St. Louis, Mo. 63121.

CAREER: Sam Houston State College (now University), Huntsville, Tex., instructor in political science, 1964-65; University of Georgia, Athens, assistant professor, 1968-71, associate professor of political science, 1971; University of Missouri at St. Louis, associate professor of political science, 1971—, chairman of department, 1974—. *Member:* American Political Science Association, American Civil Liberties Union, Common Cause, Committee Against Racism, National Association for the Advancement of Colored People, Midwest Political Science Association, Southern Political Science Association, Southwestern Political Science Association, Missouri Political Science Association. *Awards, honors:* Research grants from National Science Foundation, 1967, 1973, and Meyer Foundation, 1969; Southwestern Political Science Association Award for best paper presented at 1972 meeting.

WRITINGS: Community Conflict, Public Opinion and the Law, C. E. Merrill, 1969; (editor with Robert Golembiewski and Charles S. Bullock) *The New Politics: Polarization or Utopia?*, McGraw, 1970; (with Bullock) *Law and Social Change: Civil Rights and Their Consequences*, McGraw, 1972; (editor with Bullock) *Black Political Attitudes: Implications for Political Support*, Markham, 1972; (contributor) Dan Nimmo and Charles Bonjean, editors, *Political Attitudes and Public Opinion*, McKay, 1972; (with Bullock) *Racial Equality in America: In Search of an Unfulfilled Goal*, Goodyear Publishing, 1975; (editor and contributor) *Alternatives to Racism and Racial Inequality*, W. H. Freeman, 1975. Contributor of about twenty articles to black studies, social science, education, and law journals, and reviews to political science journals.

WORK IN PROGRESS: With Charles Bullock, *School Desegration: A Policy Evaluation of the Role of Law in Effectuating Social Change* (tentative title), for University of Chicago Press; also with Bullock, a longitudinal analysis of law as an agent of social change and a study of distortion in survey analysis.

RODINSON, Maxime 1915-
(Jean Ronsin)

PERSONAL: Born January 26, 1915, in Paris, France; son of Maurice Zoundel (a worker) and Anna (Gottlibovski) Rodinson; married Genevieve Gendron, July 31, 1937; children: Daniel, Claudine, Michel. *Education:* Ecole nationale des langues orientales vivantes, eleve diplome, 1936; Sorbonne, University of Paris, licence es-lettres, 1947, docteur es-lettres, 1970; Ecole pratique des Hautes Etudes, eleve diplome, 1955. *Politics:* Independent Left. *Religion:* Agnostic. *Residence:* Paris, France. *Office:* Ecole pratique des Hautes Etudes, Sorbonne, 47 rue des Ecoles, Paris, France 75005.

CAREER: Moslem College, Sidon, Lebanon, teacher of French literature, 1940-41; Direction des Antiquites, Beirut, Lebanon, official, 1941-46; National Library, Paris, France, librarian, 1948-55; Ecole pratique des hautes etudes, Paris, France, professor of Old Ethiopic and Old South Arabian in section of historical and philologic sciences, 1955-59, lecturer in Near Eastern anthropology in section of economic and social sciences, 1959-71. Publisher, *Moyen-Orient*, 1950-51; honorary member, Centre for Yemeni Studies, 1974—. *Military service:* French Army, 1939-40; served in France and Syria. *Member:* Societe asiatique, Association des sociologues de langue francaise, Societe francaise de sociologie, Societe des etudes juives, Societe de linguistique de Paris, Societe Ernest Renan. *Awards, honors:* Chevalier des palmes academiques, 1960, officier, 1966; medaille commemorative of voluntary service in Free French administration, 1961; Isaac Deutscher Prize, 1974, for *Islam and Capitalism*.

WRITINGS: (Under pseudonym Jean Ronsin) *Tilka atharuna* (title means "These are Our Traces"), Dar al-makshuf (Beirut), 1943; *Mahomet*, Club francais du Livre (Paris), 1961, 2nd edition, Seuil (Paris), 1968, translation of 1st edition by Anne Carter published under original title, Pantheon, 1971; *Islam et capitalisme*, Seuil, 1966, translation by Brian Pearce published as *Islam and Capitalism*, Pantheon, 1974; *Magie, medecine et possession a Gondar* (title means "Magic, Medicine and Possession in Ethiopia"), Mouton & Co., 1967; *Israel, fait colonial?* (monograph), 1967, translation by D. Thorstad published as *Israel: A Colonial-Settler State?*, Monad Press, 1973; *Israel et le refus arabe, 75 ans d'histoire*, Seuil, 1968, 2nd edition, 1969, translation of 1st edition by Michael Perl published as *Israel and the Arabs*, Pantheon, 1968; *Marxisme et monde musulman* (title means "Marxism and the Modern World"; also see below), Seuil, 1972; (with Jacques Berque and others) *Les Palestiniens et la crise israelo-arabe* (title means "The Palestinians and the Israeli-Arab Crisis"), Editions Sociales (Paris), 1974.

Contributor: R. Grousset and E. G. Leonard, editors, *Encyclopedie de la Pleiade: Histoire universelle*, Volume II, Gallimard, 1957; *La Lune, mythes et rites* (title means "The Moon: Myths and Rituals"), Seuil, 1962; *L'ecriture et la psychologie des peuples* (title means "Writing and Psychology of Peoples"), Armand Colin (Paris), 1963; M. A. Cook, editor, *Studies in the Economic History of the Middle East*, Oxford University Press, 1970; P. J. Vatikiotis, editor, *Egypt Since the Revolution* (contains a portion of *Marxisme et monde musulman*), Allen & Unwin, 1972; Maurice Crouzet, editor, *Le Monde depuis 1945* (title means "The World Since 1945"), Volume II, Presses Universitaires de France, 1973; J. Schacht and C. E. Bosworth, editors, *The Legacy of Islam*, 2nd edition (Rodinson was not associated with 1st edition), Clarendon Press, 1974.

Adviser for series, "Religion and Reason," Mouton & Co. Contributor to journals in his field.

WORK IN PROGRESS: Research on the market in an anthropological perspective, the prehistory of Arab souq, the Arab conception of time, and possession rites in Egypt; a book, *Ideology and History*.

SIDELIGHTS: Rodinson, who was a member of the French Communist Party from 1937 to 1958, writes: "I have retained from my Marxist past many ideas which seem still correct to me, militant ethical orientation and a big interest for the mode of operation of ideologies and of what I have called ideological movements among which I reckon many religious movements of the past and the Communist movement of the present alike. I have alluded to many problems seen in this perspective in my books and articles published till now. I hope to develop these ideas in syntheses to come."

* * *

ROGERS, Elizabeth F(rances) 1892-1974

June 29, 1892—November 1, 1974; American historian, educator, and author. Obituaries: *New York Times*, November 3, 1974. (*CA*-5/6).

* * *

ROGERS, Kenneth Paul 1940-

PERSONAL: Born April 3, 1940, in Chicago, Ill.; son of Harry B. (a postman) and Grace (a retail manager; maiden name, Staab) Rogers; married Wilma Worthen, September 25, 1969 (died December 24, 1969); married Louan M. McGee (a teacher), December 24, 1974; children: (first marriage) Angela Worthen (step-daughter). *Education:* Attending Southern Illinois University. *Politics:* "Wishy-washy Democrat." *Religion:* "Catholic-like." *Home address:* P.O. Box 711, Menard, Ill. 62259.

CAREER: Has been employed as a manager in Walgreen Stores, Chicago, Ill., and as a chef for Conrad Hilton Hotel, Chicago, Ill.; artist and writer. *Member:* National Society for the Arts and Literature, Authors Guild of Authors League of America, Lifers Incorporated. *Awards, honors:* Purchase prize from North Shore Art League, 1973, for pencil drawing.

WRITINGS: For One Sweet Grape (autobiography of a murderer and rapist), Playboy Press, 1974.

WORK IN PROGRESS: The Journeyman, a novel; *Corky Morgan's Defunct*, a novel or screenplay; *Devoured in Peace*, a novel.

SIDELIGHTS: Rogers is now serving a life sentence in prison for the rape-murder of a teenage girl and the murders of his first wife and her best friend.

* * *

ROGERS, Max Gray 1932-

PERSONAL: Born February 19, 1932, in Richmond, Va.; son of John Max (a salesman) and Hattie (Gray) Rogers; married Hannelore Maria Simon, June 25, 1961; children: Deborah Suzanne, Stephanie Elizabeth, Stefan Gray. *Education:* Duke University, A.B. (summa cum laude), 1955; Union Theological Seminary, New York, N.Y., B.D., 1958; Columbia University, Ph.D., 1964. *Religion:* Baptist. *Home:* 1022 West Trinity Ave., Durham, N.C. 27701. *Office:* Southeastern Baptist Theological Seminary, Wake Forest, N.C. 27587.

CAREER: Ordained Baptist minister, 1958; Columbia University, New York, N.Y., lecturer in religion, 1959-60; Southeastern Baptist Theological Seminary, Wake Forest, N.C., assistant professor, 1960-63, associate professor, 1963-68, professor of Old Testament, 1968—. *Member:* Society for Religion in Higher Education, Society of Biblical Literature, American Society of Church History, American Association of University Professors, Phi Beta Kappa. *Awards, honors:* Woodrow Wilson fellowship, 1955-56; Danforth fellowship, 1955-60; Alexander von Humboldt fellowship from West German Government, 1966-67.

WRITINGS: (Contributor) George H. Shriver, editor, *American Religious Heretics*, Abingdon, 1966; (translator) Rudolf Smend, *Yahweh War and Tribal Confederation*, Abingdon, 1970.

WORK IN PROGRESS: Research on the period of the judges in the Old Testament and on nineteenth-century American religious thought.

* * *

ROHEN, Edward 1931-
(Bruton Connors)

PERSONAL: Born February 10, 1931, in Dowlais, South Wales; son of William (a steelworker) and Margaret (O'Donovan) Rohen; married Elizabeth Mary Jarrett (a nurse), April 4, 1961; children: Margaret Mary. *Education:* Cardiff College of Art, A.T.D., 1952. *Politics:* "I approve of neither capitalism nor communism." *Religion:* Agnostic. *Home:* 57 Kinfauns Rd., Goodmayes, Ilford, Essex 1G3 9QH, England. *Office:* Ilford County High School, Fremantle Rd., Ilford, Essex, England.

CAREER: Junior and senior high school teacher of art in the public schools of Ladysmith, B.C., 1956-57, and London, England, 1958-73; Ilford County High School for Boys, Ilford, Essex, England, art teacher, 1973—. *Military service:* Royal Army Ordnance Corps, 1952-54; served in Korea; received United Nations Medal. *Member:* Academician of Centro Cultural, Literario e Artistico de "O Jornal de Felgeiras."

WRITINGS—Under pseudonym Bruton Connors: *Nightpriest* (poetry), Breakthru Publications, 1965; *Old Drunk Eyes Haiku* (poetry), Spectre Press, 1974. Poems anthologized in *It's World That Makes the Love Go Round*, edited by Ken Geering, Corgi Books, 1968; *Doves for the Seventies*, edited by Peter Robins, Corgi Books, 1969. Contributor of poetry and prose to magazines in England, New Zealand, United States, Australia, Japan, and India.

WORK IN PROGRESS: A book of poems, *The Death of Seaneen*; a book of short stories.

AVOCATIONAL INTERESTS: Bullfighting.

* * *

ROHRLICH, Chester 1900(?)-1974

1900(?)—December 17, 1974; American lawyer specializing in corporate law, teacher, and legal author. Obituaries: *New York Times*, December 18, 1974.

ROOKE, Daphne (Marie) 1914-
(Robert Pointon)

PERSONAL: Born March 6, 1914, in Boksburg, Transvaal, South Africa; daughter of Robert (a soldier) and Maria (a writer; maiden name Mare) Pizzey; married Irvin Rooke, January 6, 1937; children: Rosemary Elizabeth (Mrs. John Bower Hutchinson). *Education:* Attended school in South Africa. *Home:* Bent St., Bardouroka, New South Wales 2315, Australia. *Agent:* Paul R. Reynolds, Inc., 12 East 41st St., New York, N.Y. 10017.

CAREER: Writer. *Member:* P.E.N. South Africa. *Awards, honors:* Afrikaanse Pers Beperk novel prize, 1946, for *The Sea Hath Bounds*.

WRITINGS—Novels: *The Sea Hath Bounds*, A.P.B. Bookstore (Johannesburg), 1946, published as *A Grove of Fever Trees*, Houghton, 1950; (under pseudonym Robert Pointon) *Apples in the Hold*, Museum Press, 1950; *Mittee*, Gollancz, 1951, Houghton, 1952; *Ratoons*, Houghton, 1953; *Wizards' Country*, Houghton, 1957; *Beti*, Houghton, 1959; *A Lover for Estelle*, Houghton, 1961; *The Greyling*, Gollancz, 1962, Reynal, 1963; *Diamond Jo*, Reynal, 1965; *Boy on the Mountain*, Gollancz, 1969; *Margaretha de la Porte* (first volume of a proposed trilogy), Gollancz, 1974.

Books for children: *The South African Twins*, J. Cape, 1953, published as *Twins in South Africa*, Houghton, 1955; *The Australian Twins*, J. Cape, 1954, published as *Twins in Australia*, Houghton, 1956; *New Zealand Twins*, J. Cape, 1957; *Double Ex!*, Gollancz, 1971; *A Horse of His Own*, Gollancz, in press.

Short stories appear in anthologies, including *South African Stories*, edited by D. H. Wright, British Book Service, 1960; *Over the Horizon*, Duell, 1960. Author of short stories published in periodicals, including *John Bull* (London) and *Woman* (Sydney). Contributor of articles to periodicals, including *Opima* (Johannesburg).

WORK IN PROGRESS: The second volume in the trilogy begun with *Margaretha de la Porte*.

SIDELIGHTS: Daphne Rooke's manuscript collection is housed in the Boston University Library.

BIOGRAPHICAL/CRITICAL SOURCES: Forum (Johannesburg), April, 1952.

* * *

ROOS, Charles A. 1914(?)-1974

1914(?)—October 23, 1974; American medical librarian, author of bibliographical studies for the National Library of Medicine, and of other books on medical subjects. Obituaries: *Washington Post*, October 26, 1974.

* * *

ROSE, Wendy 1948-
(Bronwen Elizabeth Edwards, Chiron Khanshendel)

PERSONAL: Born May 7, 1948, in Oakland, Calif. *Education:* Attended Cabrillo College and Contra Costa College; University of California, Berkeley, student, 1974—. *Politics:* "Yes." *Religion:* "Yes." *Home:* c/o Richard Edwards, 11 Edgecroft Rd., Kensington, Calif. 94707. *Agent:* Terry Garey, 820 Everett St., El Cerrito, Calif. 94530.

CAREER: Lowie Museum of Anthropology of University of California, Berkeley, manager of museum bookstore, 1974—. *Member:* American Anthropological Association, Society for California Archaeology, Kroeber Anthropological Society, Society for Creative Anachronism, United Native Americans, American Association for the Advancement of Science, Elves, Gnomes, and Little Mens' Marching and Chowder Society, Southwestern Anthropological Association, Native Americans of Contra Costa County (member of community council).

WRITINGS: All under name Wendy Rose, except as indicated *Hopi Roadrunner Dancing* (self-illustrated), Greenfield Review Press, 1973.

Illustrator: Duane Niatum, *Taos Pueblo* (poems), Greenfield Review Press 1974; (and contributor) Diane Niatum, editor, *Carriers of the Dream Wheel*, Harper, in press.

Work appears, under name Wendy Rose or pseudonym Chiron Khanshendel, in *Speaking for Ourselves*, edited by Lillian Faderman and Barbara Bradshaw, Scott, Foresman, 1969, revised edition, in press; *From the Belly of the Shark*, edited by Walter Lowenfels, Random House, 1974; *Time to Greez*, edited by Roberto Vargas, Glide Press, in press. Contributor, occasionally under pseudonym Chiron Khanshendel, of articles and poems to literary magazines, including *Margins*, *Alcaeus Review*, *Greenfield Review*, and *Many Smokes*.

WORK IN PROGRESS: Four Worlds and Times of Light, a self-illustrated story-picture book of the Hopi creation story for pre-adolescents; *Lost Copper*, a book of poems; poems for *The Shadow of the Savage*, edited by Robert Alan McGill; several other poems for anthologies; illustrations for childrens' books.

SIDELIGHTS: Rose writes: "Writing is just something that always has been and just is. For everything in this universe there is a song to accompany its existence; writing is another way of singing these songs. Everyone knows the words and tune; it's just that not everyone feels the confidence in themselves to keep their ears open and their senses feeling. Writing just comes from those less afraid of themselves (although possibly more afraid of other-than-themselves). Sometimes the songs are in color; then they become pictures. Sometimes the songs are audible; then they are sung. It doesn't really matter how they happen or where they go; they will be, no matter what. Some people have tried to say I sing my songs because I'm half-Hopi; that's not true. . . . I sing them because I hear them. People who think that are just looking for reasons why they don't want to hear them for themselves. I love my songs; I love my people.

"The usual practice in bookstores upon receiving books of poems by American Indians is to classify them as 'Native Americana' rather than as poetry; the poets are seen as literate fossils more than as living, working artists. I have run into this kind of thing too often. Also, there is a great deal of stereotyping of Indian poetry (and Indian art in general); we may be seen as 'nature children' tapping some great earth-nerve and producing poems like pulses. But all art is that way; not just Indian art. There is also the concrete, the abstract, the analytical, the mystical—all components and levels of human understanding and expression. And those qualities stereotypically Indian also exist. The deferential treatment accorded to Indians in artistic and academic settings is just as destructive, ultimately, as out-and-out racism. It is startling to find your book of poems in an anthropology section of a bookstore instead of in the poetry section. . . . My songs are self-conscious when they have to dance alone. You know, I really just want to make people feel good."

ROSENBERG, Samuel 1912-

PERSONAL: Born September 4, 1912, in Cleveland, Ohio; son of Jacob S. (a composer) and Fanny (Miller) Rosenberg; married Angela Nizzardini, December 23, 1938; children: Ruth A. *Education:* Attended New York Institute of Photography. *Politics:* Democrat. *Home:* 117-29 Union Turnpike, Forest Hills, N.Y. 11375. *Agent:* Robert Lantz, 114 East 55th St., New York, N.Y. 10022.

CAREER: Photographer; producer and director of documentaries; North Carolina State College (now University of North Carolina), Raleigh, associate professor of design, 1954-56.

WRITINGS: Come As You Are Masquerade Party, Prentice-Hall, 1970; *Confessions of a Trivialist*, Penguin, 1972; *Naked Is the Best Disguise*, Bobbs-Merrill, 1974.

* * *

ROSENBLATT, Milton B. 1908(?)-1975

1908(?)—January 25, 1975; American physician specializing in internal medicine and chest diseases, and author of books on medical subjects. Obituaries: *New York Times*, January 28, 1975.

* * *

ROSENBLATT, Samuel 1902-

PERSONAL: Born May 5, 1902, in Bratislava, Czechoslovakia; came to United States in 1912; son of Josef (a cantor) and Taube (Kaufman) Rosenblatt; married Claire Woloch, October 3, 1926; children: David Hirsch, Judah Isser, Josef Ellis. *Education:* City College (now City College of the City University of New York), A.B. (cum laude), 1921; Jewish Theological Seminary of America, rabbi, 1925; Universal Yeshiva of Jerusalem, rabbi, 1926; Columbia University, Ph.D., 1927. *Home:* 3310 Old Forest Rd., Baltimore, Md. 21208. *Office:* Beth Tfiloh Synagogue, 3300 Old Court Rd., Baltimore, Md. 21208.

CAREER: Rabbi of Jewish congregation in Trenton, N.J., 1926-27. Rabbi of Beth Tfiloh congregation in Baltimore, Md., 1927—. Lecturer at Columbia University, 1926-28; lecturer in Jewish literature at Johns Hopkins University, 1928-47, associate professor of Oriental languages, 1947—. *Member:* Rabbinical Assembly, Society of Biblical Literature, American Oriental Society, American Jewish Congress (president of Baltimore chapter, 1942-44), B'nai B'rith, Religious Zionists of America (president of Baltimore chapter, 1938-42, 1944-47, 1973—). *Awards, honors:* D.D. from Jewish Theological Seminary of America, 1965; Sidney Hollander Award from Baltimore branch American Jewish Congress, 1968; Simchah Award from Menorah Lodge of B'nai B'rith, 1971.

WRITINGS: The Highways to Perfection of Abraham Maimonides, Volume I, Columbia University Press, 1927, Volume II, Johns Hopkins Press, 1938; *The Interpretation of the Bible in the Mishnah*, Johns Hopkins Press, 1935; *Our Heritage*, Block Publishing, 1940; *This Is the Land*, Mizrachi, 1940; *The People of the Book*, Behrman, 1943; *The Book of Beliefs and Opinions of Saadia Gaon*, Yale University Press, 1948; *Yossele Rosenblatt*, Farrar, Straus, 1954; *The History of the Mizrachi Movement*, Mizrachi, 1957; *Hear Oh Israel*, Feldheim, 1961; *Under the Nuptial Canopy*, Feldheim, 1975. Author of memoirs "The Days of My Years," published in weekly installments in *Baltimore Jewish Times*, 1974—; also author of a weekly column in *Baltimore News-American*, 1960—. Contributor to *Jewish Quarterly Review*.

SIDELIGHTS: Rosenblatt has made a Passover Seder recording, "This Night Is Different," 1961. *Avocational interests:* Travel.

* * *

ROSENFARB, Chawa 1923-

PERSONAL: Born February 9, 1923, in Lodz, Poland; daughter of Abraham and Sima (Pinczewska) Rosenfarb. *Education:* Attended Jewish Teachers Seminary, Montreal, Quebec, Canada. *Home:* 456 Barton Ave., Montreal 304, Canada. *Agent:* Bertha Klausner, 70 Park Ave., New York, N.Y.

CAREER: Writer. *Member:* P.E.N. International. *Awards, honors:* J. J. Segal Prize (Canada), 1972, and Niger Prize (Argentina), 1973, both for *The Tree of Life*.

WRITINGS: Ghetto Poems, M. Oved, 1947; *The Song of Abraham the Waiter*, M. Oved, 1948; *Getto and Other Poems*, Hershman, 1950; *The Bird of the Ghetto* (play; first produced in Tel Aviv, Israel, at Habimah Theatre, 1967), [Montreal], 1958; *Out of Paradise* (poems), J. L. Peretz Publishing House (Tel Aviv), 1965; *The Tree of Life* (trilogy), Hamenorah Publishing (Israel), 1972. Poems and essays included in anthology, *Di Goldene Keit*, published in Tel Aviv.

SIDELIGHTS: Chawa Rosenfarb writes: "*The Tree of Life* is my most important work. It is a novel about the ghetto in Lodz, Poland during the Second World War. As a survivor of that ghetto and of the concentration camps in Auschwitz and Bergen-Belsen, I fictionalized my experiences in that work. . . ."

* * *

ROSS, Alf (Niels Christian Hansen) 1899-

PERSONAL: Born June 10, 1899, in Copenhagen, Denmark; son of Frederik C. C. Hansen-Ross (in civil service) and Johanne (Hansen) Ross; married Else Merete Helweg-Larsen (former member of Danish parliament), December 27, 1923. *Education:* University of Copenhagen, graduate of College of Law, 1922, Dr. of Law, 1934; University of Uppsala, M.Phil., 1929, D.Phil., 1929. *Politics:* None. *Religion:* None. *Home:* 22 I.H. Mundtsvei, 2830 Virum, Denmark.

CAREER: Member of staff in Office of the Kammeradvokat (counsel to the Danish Crown), 1922-23; left position to make study tour of universities and libraries in Paris, Vienna, Berlin, and London, 1923-26; returned to Denmark, 1926, and continued studies and work in law and philosophy, 1926-34; University of Copenhagen, Copenhagen, Denmark, assistant professor, 1935-38, professor of law, 1938-69. George A. Miller Visiting Professor of Law at University of Illinois, 1956. Counsel for Chamber of Commerce for the Provinces in Denmark, 1935—; member of Danish constitutional committee, 1946-53; member of European Court of Human Rights, Strasbourg, 1959-71. Made study tour of U.S. law schools, 1949-50. *Awards, honors:* Dr. of Law from University of Oslo, 1951, and University of Lund, 1969.

WRITINGS: Theorie der Rechtsquellen (in German), F. Deuticke (Leipzig), 1929; *Kritik der sogenannten praktischen Erkenntnis*, Levin & Munksgaard, 1933; *Virkelighed og gyldighed i retslaeren*, Levin & Munksgaard, 1934, translation by Annie Fausboell published as *Towards a Realistic Jurisprudence: A Criticism of the Dualism in Law*, E. Munksgaard, 1946; *Ejendomsret og ejendomsovergang*, Levin & Munksgaard, 1935.

Laerebog i folkeret, Munksgaard, 1942, 4th edition, 1961; (editor with Viking Abel) *Folkeretlig materialesamling I. Trakter og love*, E. Munksgaard, 1944, 2nd edition, 1949; *Hvorfor Demokrati?*, E. Munksgaard, 1946, 2nd edition, Nyt Nordisk, 1967, translation published as *Why Democracy?*, Harvard University Press, 1952; *A Textbook of International Law*, Longmans, 1947; (editor with Hal Koch) *Nordisk demokrati*, Westermann (Copenhagen), 1949.

Constitution of the United Nations: Analysis of Structure and Function, E. Munksgaard, 1950; *Om ret og retfaerdighed*, Nyt Nordisk, 1953, translation by Margaret Dutton published as *On Law and Justice*, Stevens, 1958, University of California Press, 1959; (editor with Isi Foighel) *Studiebog i folkeret*, Nyt Nordisk, 1954, 2nd edition (edited with Foighel and Allan Philip), 1964; (with Stig Iuul and Joergen Trolle), *Indledning til retsstudiet*, Nyt Nordisk, 1956, 3rd edition, 1963; *Statsretlige studier*, Nyt Nordisk, 1959; *Dansk statsforfatningsret*, two volumes, Nyt Nordisk, 1959-60, revised edition, 1966.

De Forenede nationer: Fred og fremskridt, Nyt Nordisk, 1963, 2nd edition, revised, 1968, translation published as *The United Nations: Peace and Progress*, Bedminster Press, 1966; *Directives and Norms*, revised by Brian Loar, Humanities Press, 1968.

Skyld, ansvar og straf, Berlingske, 1970, translation published as *Guilt, Responsibility and Punishment*, University of California Press, 1974; *Forbrydelse og straf*, Nyt Nordisk, 1974.

Author of brochures on the nature of communist doctrine. Contributor to festschrift volumes and to professional journals.

SIDELIGHTS: Various of Ross's works have been translated into German, French, Spanish, Italian, and Finnish, in addition to English.

* * *

ROSS, Martin J. 1912-

PERSONAL: Born October 7, 1912, in Russia; son of Joseph (in china and porcelain) and Rebecca (Weisman) Rusofsky; married Diane Antelle (an editor), February 27, 1949; children: Jeffrey Steven, Elizabeth Gail. *Education:* City College (now of the City University of New York), B.S., 1933; Brooklyn Law School, J.D., 1937. *Religion:* Hebrew. *Home and office:* 50 North Terrace Pl., Valley Stream, N.Y. 11580.

CAREER: Admitted to the Bar of New York State, 1937, and the Bar of Florida, 1947; New York City Magistrates Court, New York, N.Y., probation officer, 1947-49; parole officer for New York State, 1949-51; Adult Education, Valley Stream, N.Y., instructor in law, 1956-58; City College of the City University of New York, New York, N.Y., instructor in law, 1959-62; Nassau Community College, Garden City, N.Y., instructor in law, 1963-65; Adelphi University, Garden City, N.Y., adjunct assistant professor of law, 1965; Supreme Court, State of New York, Bronx County, N.Y., matrimonial clerk, 1971—. Conducted radio program "You and the Law," WEVD, New York, N.Y., 1958-59; director of Law Education Institute, 1970—. *Military service:* U.S. Army, 1941-46; became captain; received Army Commendation Ribbon. *Member:* Florida Bar Association.

WRITINGS: Handbook of Everyday Law, Harper, 1958, revised edition, 1975; *New Encyclopedic Dictionary of Business Law with Forms*, Prentice-Hall, 1975; *Matrimonial Practice*, Advanced Practice Institute, School of Law, Hofstra University, 1975. Author of column, "Con la Ley en la Mano," for *La Prensa*, 1961-62. Contributor to *New York Law Journal*.

SIDELIGHTS: Ross's *Handbook of Everyday Law* has been recorded for the blind.

* * *

ROSS, Zola Helen 1912-
(Z. H. Ross; Helen Arre, Bert Iles)

PERSONAL: Born May 9, 1912, in Dayton, Iowa; daughter of Sherman Andrew (a farmer) and Bertha (Iles) Girdey; married Frank William Ross, May 28, 1934. *Education:* MacMurray College, B.A., 1932; University of Washington, graduate study, 1943-45. *Religion:* Methodist. *Home:* 16907 72nd Ave. N.E., Bothell, Wash. 98011. *Agent:* Ann Elmo, 52 Vanderbilt Ave., New York, N.Y. 10017. *Office:* Lake Washington Schools, 6511 112th Ave. N.E., Kirkland, Wash. 98033.

CAREER: University of Washington, Seattle, associate professor of creative writing, 1948-55; Lake Washington Schools, Kirkland, Wash., teacher of adult education, 1956—. Co-founder, Pacific Northwest Writers Conference, member of board of trustees, 1956-72, president, 1962. *Member:* National League of American Penwomen, Women in Communications, Free Lances, Western Writers of America, Theta Sigma Phi. *Awards, honors:* Theta Sigma Phi award, 1948; Phi Beta Nu award, 1960; Washington State Press Women award, 1961; State of Washington Governor's award, 1966; Torchbearers Award, 1972.

WRITINGS—Published by Bobbs-Merrill: (Under name Z. H. Ross) *Three Down Vulnerable*, 1946; (under name Z. H. Ross) *Overdue for Death*, 1947; *One Corpse Missing*, 1948; *Bonanza Queen: A Novel of the Comstock Lode*, 1948; *Tonopah Lady*, 1950; *Reno Crescent*, 1951; *The Green Land*, 1952; *Cassy Scandal*, 1954; *A Land to Tame*, 1956; *The Golden Witch*, 1956; *Spokane Saga: A Novel of the Rebuilding of a City Destroyed*, 1957.

With Lucile Saunders McDonald; all published by Nelson, except as indicated: *The Mystery of Catesby Island* (Junior Literary Guild selection), 1950; *Stormy Year*, 1951; *Friday's Child* (Junior Literary Guild selection), 1954; *Mystery of the Long House* (Junior Literary Guild selection), 1956; *Pigtail Pioneer*, Holt, 1956, excerpts published in *Grandma Moses Story Book*, Random House, 1961; *Winter's Answer*, 1957; *Wing Harbor* (Junior Literary Guild selection), 1957; *The Courting of Ann Maria*, 1958; *Assignment in Ankara* (Junior Literary Guild selection), 1959, published as *Stolen Letters*, Pyramid Publications, c.1959; *The Sunken Forest*, Weybright & Talley, 1968; *For Glory and the King*, Meredith, 1969.

Mysteries, under pseudonym Helen Arre; all published by Arcadia House: *The Corpse by the River*, 1953; *No Tears at the Funeral*, 1954; *Write It Murder*, 1956; *Murder by the Book*, 1956; *The Golden Shroud*, 1958.

Under pseudonym Bert Iles: *Murder in Mink* (mystery), Arcadia House, 1956.

WORK IN PROGRESS: A mystery novel; a young adult book, with Lucile Saunders McDonald.

* * *

ROSSEL, Seymour 1945-

PERSONAL: Surname is pronounced *Ros*-sel; born August 9, 1945, in Chicago, Ill.; son of Willy O. (a master chef) and Leona (an interior decorator; maiden name, Wadler) Rossel; married Linda Hart, January, 1969 (divorced December, 1973); married Helen Karen Trager (a school registrar), November 10, 1974. *Education:* Youth Leader's Institute, Jerusalem, Machon Certificate, 1963; attended Louisiana State University, 1964-65; Southern Methodist University, B.A., 1968. *Religion:* Jewish. *Home:* 245 East 40th St., 4-B, New York, N.Y. 10016. *Agent:* Julian Bach, 3 East 48th St., New York, N.Y. 10017. *Office:* Behrman House, Inc., 1261 Broadway, New York, N.Y. 10016.

CAREER: Van Gogh Studio, Dallas, Tex., photographer, 1965-68; Temple Beth El, Chappaqua, N.Y., director of education, 1969-72; Behrman House Publishers, Inc., New York, N.Y., senior editor, 1972—; Hebrew Union College, New York, N.Y., instructor in education, 1973—. *Member:* National Association of Temple Educators, Association for Jewish Studies.

WRITINGS: (Contributor) R. A. Rosenbaum, editor, *Growing Up in America*, Doubleday, 1968; (editor and contributor) *Lessons from Our Living Past*, Behrman, 1972; (editor) *Teacher's Guide* and *Workbooks* to *Lessons from Our Living Past*, Behrman, 1972; *When a Jew Prays*, Behrman, 1973; *Workbooks to Child's Introduction to Torah*, Behrman, 1974; *When a Jew Seeks Wisdom*, Behrman, 1975.

WORK IN PROGRESS: The First Book of Judaism, for F. Watts; *A Child's Imagination Game*, illustrated by Peter Max; *A Children's Bulfinch*, in three volumes.

SIDELIGHTS: "My writings seek to reinstate mythology in an age of doubt and search," Rossel writes. "There is an attempt to connect the basic myths with the reality of the world around us. . . . Just as in Judaism, stories capture the flavor and serve to carry on the tradition, so too this was true of the stories of the Greeks, the Romans, and the Medieval balladeers. Mine is an attempt merely to recreate an ever-present reality."

* * *

ROSTON, Murray 1928-

PERSONAL: Born December 10, 1928, in London, England; son of Hyman and Matilda (Jacobs) Roston; married Faith C. Lehrman, April 8, 1956; children: Yardenna, Nina, Yonit (daughters). *Education:* Queens' College, Cambridge, M.A., 1952; Queen Mary College, London, M.A., 1954, Ph.D., 1961. *Religion:* Orthodox Jew. *Home:* 51 Katznelson St., Kiryat Ono, Israel.

CAREER: Bar-Ilan University, Ramat Gan, Israel, assistant professor, 1956-65, associate professor, 1965-69, professor of English, 1969—. Visiting professor at Stanford University, 1966-67, 1971-72. Member of academic council, Everyman's University, Israel, 1974—.

WRITINGS: Prophet and Poet: The Bible and the Growth of Romanticism, Northwestern University Press, 1965; (editor) *The Shakespearean World*, Am-Hassefer (Tel Aviv), 1965; *Biblical Drama in England from the Middle Ages to the Present Day*, Northwestern University Press, 1968; *The Soul of Wit: A Study of John Donne*, Clarendon Press (of Oxford University), 1974.

WORK IN PROGRESS: Majesty Divine: Milton and the Baroque, completion expected in 1976.

ROTH, Andrew 1919-

PERSONAL: Born April 23, 1919, in New York, N.Y.; son of Emil (a waiter) and Bertha (a seamstress; maiden name, Rosenberg) Roth; married Renee Knitel, 1942 (divorced, 1948); married Mathilda Friederich-Bouma (a teacher), June 30, 1949; children: (second marriage) Neil, Teresa. *Education:* City College (now City College of the City University of New York), B.S.S., 1939; Columbia University, M.A., 1940; Harvard University, qualification in Japanese, 1942. *Home:* 34 Somali Rd., London NW2 3RC, England. *Office: Parliamentary Profiles*, 26 Palace Chambers, Bridge St., London SW1, England.

CAREER: High school teacher in New York, N.Y., 1939-41; Institute of Pacific Relations, New York, N.Y., research associate, 1940; free-lance correspondent in Asia, contributing to *Nation, Star Weekly*, and other periodicals, 1946-50; London editor of *France Observateur, Sekai*, and *Singapore Standard*, 1950-60; *Parliamentary Profiles*, London, England, research director, 1960—; *Manchester Evening News*, Manchester, England, political correspondent, 1972—. *Military service:* U.S. Navy, Intelligence, 1941-45; became lieutenant senior grade. *Member:* Royal Institute of International Affairs, Foreign Press Association, Phi Beta Kappa.

WRITINGS: Japan Strikes South: The Story of French Indo-China Passing under Japanese Domination, Institute of Pacific Relations, 1941; (with Roger Levy and others) *French Interests and Policies in the Far East*, Institute of Pacific Relations, 1942; *Dilemma in Japan*, Little, Brown, 1945; *Enoch Powell: Tory Tribune*, Macdonald & Co., 1970; *Can Parliament Decide–about Europe, or about Anything?*, Macdonald & Co., 1971; *Heath and the Heathmen*, Routledge & Kegan Paul, 1972; (with Janice Kerbey) *Lord on the Board*, Parliamentary Profiles, 1972. Editor, with others at various times, *Business Background of Members of Parliament* and of *Members of Parliament Chart*, both published at intervals by Parliamentary Profiles. Contributor to various periodicals, including *Nation, Sekai*, and *New Statesman*. Editor of *Westminster Confidential*, 1955—, and of *World Balance of Power*, 1958—.

WORK IN PROGRESS: The Second Coming of Harold Wilson, completion expected in 1976.

* * *

ROTH, Arthur J(oseph) 1925- (Barney Mara, Slater McGurk, Pete Pomeroy)

PERSONAL: Born August 3, 1925, in New York, N.Y.; son of Joseph (a printer) and Bella (a maid; maiden name, McGurk) Roth; married Ruth E. Buchalter, June 29, 1958; children: Mark. *Education:* Arizona State University, B.A., 1954; Columbia University, M.A., 1961. *Home address:* Box A/O, Amagansett, N.Y. 11930. *Agent:* John Cushman Associates, 25 West 43rd St., New York, N.Y. 10036.

CAREER: Has worked as a bartender, carpenter, coalminer, factory worker, logger, farmer, high school teacher of Spanish, college instructor in writing, clerk-typist, and truck driver; full-time writer. *Military service:* Irish Army, 1944-46. U.S. Air Force, 1950-51.

WRITINGS: A Terrible Beauty, Farrar, Straus, 1958; *What Is the Stars?*, Farrar, Straus, 1959; *The Shame of Our Wounds*, Crowell, 1961; *The Iceberg Hermit*, Four Winds, 1974.

Juveniles, under pseudonym Barney Mara: *Forest Fire*, Scholastic Magazines, 1975.

Under pseudonym Slater McGurk: *Grand Central Murders*, Macmillan, 1964; *The Denmark Bus*, Walker & Co., 1966; *The Big Dig*, Macmillan, 1968.

Juveniles, under pseudonym Pete Pomeroy: *Wipeout!*, Four Winds, 1968; *The Mallory Burn*, Grosset, 1971; *Crash at Salty Bay*, Scholastic Magazines, 1972.

WORK IN PROGRESS: Half a dozen adult and juvenile novels in various stages of completion.

* * *

ROTSLER, William 1926-

PERSONAL: Born July 3, 1926, in Los Angeles, Calif.; son of Charles Golden (a rancher) and Sarah (Flynn) Rotsler; married Marian Abney, October 10, 1953 (divorced, 1958); children: Lisa Araminta. *Education:* Attended Ventura College, 1946, and Los Angeles County Art Institute, 1946-50. *Politics:* Democrat. *Religion:* None. *Home and office:* 1525 North Van Ness Ave., #401, Los Angeles, Calif. 90028.

CAREER: Rancher in Camarillo, Calif., 1942-44, 1946, 1953-58; sculptor in Los Angeles, Calif., 1950-59, photographer, 1959—, film-maker, 1961—, writer, 1970—. *Military service:* U.S. Army, 1944-45. *Member:* Science Fiction Writers of America. *Awards, honors:* Guest of honor at Thirty-first World Science Fiction Convention, Toronto, Canada, 1973.

WRITINGS: Contemporary Erotic Cinema, Ballantine, 1973; *Patron of the Arts*, Ballantine, 1974; *Children of Eros* (science fiction novel), Ballantine, 1975; *Ship Me Tomorrow* (science fiction short story collection), Ballantine, 1975. Work is anthologized in four science-fiction "best of the year" collections. Contributor of hundreds of short stories and articles to science-fiction and men's magazines.

SIDELIGHTS: Rotsler has written, produced, and directed twenty-six feature films. He has also directed over two hundred hours of commercials, documentaries, and industrial films.

* * *

ROUNDS, Glen H(arold) 1906-

PERSONAL: Born April 4, 1906, in Near Wall, S.D.; son of William E. (a rancher) and Janet I. (Barber) Rounds; married Margaret Olmsted, January, 1938 (died December, 1968); children: William E. II. *Education:* Attended Kansas City Art Institute, 1926-27, and Art Student's League, New York, N.Y., evenings, 1930-31. *Residence:* Southern Pines, N.C. 28387.

CAREER: Traveled throughout United States, holding a variety of jobs, including those of muleskinner, cowboy, sign painter, railroad section hand, baker, carnival medicine man, and textile designer; began experimenting with etching and painting, then wrote stories to accompany his drawings; full-time author and illustrator of adult and children's books, 1936—. *Military service:* U.S. Army, Coast Artillery and Infantry, 1942-45; became staff sergeant. *Member:* Authors Guild.

WRITINGS—All self-illustrated; all published by Holiday House, except as indicated: *Ol' Paul, the Mighty Logger*, 1936; *Lumbercamp*, 1937, reissued as *Whistle Punk*, 1959; *Paydirt*, 1938; *The Blind Colt* (Junior Literary Guild selection), 1941; *Whitey's Sunday Horse* (excerpted from *The Blind Colt*), 1943; *Whitey's First Roundup* (Junior Literary Guild selection), Grosset, 1942; *Whitey Looks for a Job*, Grosset, 1944; *Whitey and Jinglebob*, Grosset, 1946; *Stolen Pony* (sequel to *The Blind Colt*), 1948, revised edition, 1969; *Rodeo*, 1949.

Whitey and the Rustlers, 1951 (also see below); *Hunted Horses*, 1951; *Whitey and the Blizzard*, 1952 (also see below); *Buffalo Harvest*, 1952; *Lone Muskrat*, 1953; *Whitey Takes a Trip*, 1954; *Whitey Ropes and Rides*, 1956; *Swamp Life: An Almanac*, Prentice-Hall, 1957; *Whitey and the Wild Horse*, 1958; *Wildlife at Your Doorstep*, Prentice-Hall, 1958, new edition, Holiday House, 1974.

Whitey's New Saddle (contains *Whitey and the Rustlers* and *Whitey and the Blizzard*), 1960; *Beaver Business*, Prentice-Hall, 1960; *Wild Orphan*, 1961; *Whitey and the Colt Killer*, 1962; *Rain in the Woods*, World Publishing, 1964; (editor) Andy Adams, *Trail Drive* (originally published as *Log of a Cowboy*, 1903), 1965; (editor) George F. Ruxton, *Mountain Men*, 1966; *The Snake Tree*, World Publishing, 1967; (compiler) *Boll Weevil*, Golden Gate, 1967; *The Treeless Plains*, 1967; *The Prairie Schooners*, 1968; (compiler) *Casey Jones*, Golden Gate, 1968; *Wild Horses of the Red Desert*, 1969.

Strawberry Roan, Golden Gate, 1970; *The Cowboy Trade*, 1971; *Once We Had a Horse*, 1971; *Sweet Betsy from Pike*, Golden Gate, 1973; *The Day the Circus Came to Lonetree*, 1973.

Illustrator: Irma S. Black, *Flipper, a Sea Lion*, Holiday House, 1940; Walter Blair, *Tale America*, Coward, 1944; Frank O'Rourke, *"E" Company*, Simon & Schuster, 1945; Martha Hardy, *Tatoosh*, Macmillan, 1947; Wheaton P. Webb, *Uncle Swithin's Inventions*, Holiday House, 1947; *Aesop's Fables*, Lippincott, 1949.

Vance Randolph, *We Always Lie to Strangers*, Columbia University Press, 1951; Randolph, *Who Blowed Up the Church House?*, Columbia University Press, 1952; Sarah R. Riedman, *Grass, Our Greatest Crop*, Thomas Nelson, 1952; Jim Kjelgaard, *Haunt Fox*, Holiday House, 1954; Paul Hyde Bonner, *Those Glorious Mornings*, Scribner, 1954; Randolph, *The Devil's Pretty Daughter*, Columbia University Press, 1955; Paul M. Sears, *Firefly*, Holiday House, 1956; Randolph, *The Talking Turtle*, Columbia University Press, 1957; Randolph, *Sticks in the Knapsack*, Columbia University Press, 1958.

Elizabeth Seeman, *In the Arms of the Mountain*, Crown, 1961; Wilson Gage, *A Wild Goose Tale*, World Publishing, 1961; Gage, *Dan and the Miranda*, World Publishing, 1962; Gage, *Big Blue Island*, World Publishing, 1964; Adrien Stoutenburg, *The Crocodile's Mouth*, Viking, 1966; Richard Chase, *Billy Boy*, Golden Gate, 1966; Maria Leach, *How the People Sang the Mountains Up*, Viking, 1967; Rebecca Caudill and James Ayars, *Contrary Jenkins*, Holt, 1968; Gladys Conklin, *Lucky Lady Bug*, Holiday House, 1968; Stoutenburg, *American Tall Tale Animals*, Viking, 1968; John Greenway, *Folklore of the Great West*, American West, 1969.

Austin Fife and Alta Fife, *Ballads of the Great West*, American West, 1970; Wilson Gage, *Mike's Toads*, World Publishing, 1970; Alexander L. Crosby, *Go Find Hanka*, Golden Gate, 1970; Ida Chittum, *Farmer Hoo and the Baboons*, Delacorte, 1971; Alvin Schwartz, *A Twister of Twists, a Tangler of Tongues*, Lippincott, 1972; Gladys Conklin, *Tarantula, the Giant Spider*, Holiday House, 1972; Sandra S. Sivulich, *I'm Going on a Bear Hunt*, Dutton, 1973; Schwartz, *Tomfoolery*, Lippincott, 1973; Schwartz, *Witcracks*, Lippincott, 1973; Schwartz, *Cross Your Fingers, Spit in Your Hat*, Lippincott, 1974;

Schwartz, *Whoppers, Tall Tales and Other Lies*, Lippincott, 1975; Mark Taylor, *Miss Jenny Jenkins*, Little, Brown, 1975; Betty Baker, *Three Fools and a Horse*, Macmillan, 1975; Berniece Freschet, *Lizard in the Sun*, Scribner, 1975.

Author of scripts for "School of the Air," CBS, 1938-39. Work is represented in school readers and anthologies, including *Treasury of American Folklore*, edited by Benjamin Botkin, Crown, 1944, and *Subtreasury of American Humor*, edited by E. B. White and Katherine S. White, Modern Library, 1948. Contributor to *Story Parade*.

SIDELIGHTS: Reviewers have described Rounds' work as "delightful," "authentic to the last detail," and "salted with wry but realistic humor." Further, Rounds "knows what he's writing about, never writes down, never misses a telling detail." One said "he could illustrate the dictionary . . . and make it fascinating and amusing." And another wrote: "Not only animals and artifacts but people are drawn with such intelligent and humorous skill that volumes about their character, economy, culture and even nutrition are conveyed in these duotone line sketches."

Rounds' books have been published in Denmark, Spain, and Germany. *Whitey's First Round-Up* was adapted for broadcast by the BBC in 1960; several of his books have been recorded for the blind. *Avocational interests:* Woodcut print-making.

* * *

ROY, Gabrielle 1909-

PERSONAL: Born March 22, 1909, in St. Boniface, Manitoba, Canada; daughter of Leon and Melina (Landry) Roy; married Marcel Carbotte (a physician), August 30, 1947. *Education:* Educated in Canada. *Religion:* Roman Catholic. *Home:* 135 Grande Allee, Quebec City, Quebec G1R 2H1, Canada.

CAREER: Teacher in a Canadian prairie village school, 1928-29, and in St. Boniface, Manitoba, 1929-37; author and novelist. *Member:* Royal Society of Canada (fellow). *Awards, honors:* Medaille of L'Academie Francaise, 1947; Prixfemina (France), 1947, for *Bonheur d'Occasion*; Canadian Governor General's Award, 1947, for *Bonheur d'Occasion*, 1954, for *Alexandre Chenevert*; Duvernay Prix, 1955; Companion of the Order of Canada, 1967; Canadian Council of the Arts Award, 1968; Prix David, 1971; Knight of the Order of Mark Twain.

WRITINGS—Novels: *Bonheur d'Occasion*, Societe des editions Pascal (Montreal), 1945, translation by Hannah Josephson published as *The Tin Flute* (Literary Guild selection), Reynal, 1947; *La Petite Poule d'Eau* (also see below), Beauchemin (Montreal), 1950, translation by Harry L. Binsse published as *Where Nests the Water Hen: A Novel*, Harcourt, 1951, revised French language edition, Beauchemin, 1970; *Alexandre Chenevert, caissier*, Beauchemin, 1954, translation by Binsse published as *The Cashier*, Harcourt, 1955; *Rue Deschambault*, Beauchemin, 1955, translation by Binsse published as *Streets of Riches*, Harcourt, 1957; *La Montagne secrete*, Beauchemin, 1961, translation by Binsse published as *The Hidden Mountain*, Harcourt, 1962; *La Route d'Altamont*, Editions HMH (Montreal), 1966, translation by Joyce Marshall published as *The Road Past Altamont*, Harcourt, 1966; (with others) *Canada . . .* (includes *La Petite Poule d'Eau*), Editions du Burin (St. Cloud, France), 1967; *La Riviere sans repos*, Beauchemin, 1970, translation by Marshall published as *Windflower*, McClelland & Stewart, 1970; *Cet ete qui chantait*, Editions francaise, 1972.

Also author of short story anthologized in *Great Short Stories of the World*, Reader's Digest, 1972.

BIOGRAPHICAL/CRITICAL SOURCES: Monique Geniust, *La Creation romanesque chez Gabrielle Roy*, Cercle du Livre de France, 1966; *Dossiers de Documentation de la litterature canadienne-francaise*, Fides, 1967; Marc Gagne, *Visages de Gabrielle Roy*, Beauchemin, 1973; Francois Ricard, *Gabrielle Roy*, Fides, 1975.

* * *

RUBENSTEIN, Boris B. 1907(?)-1974

1907(?)—December 31, 1974; American physician specializing in endocrinology, medical researcher, and author of books on medical subjects. Obituaries: *New York Times*, January 2, 1975.

* * *

RUBIN, Mark 1946-

PERSONAL: Born May 30, 1946, in New York, N.Y.; son of Murray (a treasury agent) and Edith (an employee of Easter Seals; maiden name, Kasten) Rubin; married Barbara Messenger (a teacher), August 23, 1969. *Education:* Cooper Union, B.F.A., 1967. *Home:* 117 East 71st St., New York, N.Y. 10021. *Agent:* Ann Retta, 14 East 38th St., New York, N.Y. 10016. *Office:* Penny Tax Productions, 14 East 38th St., New York, N.Y. 10016.

CAREER: Mark Rubin Design, New York, N.Y., principal designer, 1972-74; Penny Tax Productions, New York, N.Y., principal designer, 1974—.

WRITINGS: The Boy Who Painted Wallpaper (juvenile), F. Watts, 1974. Writer of filmstrip, "Little Lou and His Strange Little Zoo," Urban Media Materials, 1972.

WORK IN PROGRESS: A magazine, *Penny Tax*.

* * *

RUDDER, Robert S(ween) 1937-

PERSONAL: Born August 9, 1937, in Long Beach, Calif.; son of George Walter and Nora (Sween) Rudder; married Karen E. Foshee, December 28, 1963; children: Elizabeth Ann, Christopher Michael. *Education:* University of Redlands, B.A., 1959; University of Minnesota, M.A., 1964, Ph.D., 1968. *Agent:* Bertha Klausner, International Literary Agency, Inc., 71 Park Ave., New York, N.Y. 10016. *Office:* Department of Spanish and Portuguese, University of California, Los Angeles, Calif. 90024.

CAREER: University of Minnesota, Minneapolis, instructor in Spanish literature, 1963-68; University of California, Los Angeles, assistant professor of Spanish literature, 1968—. *Military service:* U.S. Navy, 1960-62. *Member:* Modern Language Association of America, American Association of Teachers of Spanish and Portuguese, Center for Medieval and Renaissance Studies.

WRITINGS: (Translator) Arturo Serrano Plaja, *"Magic" Realism in Cervantes: "Don Quixote" as Seen through "Tom Sawyer" and "The Idiot"*, University of California Press, 1970; (editor and translator) *The Life of Lazarillo of Tormes: His Fortunes and Misfortunes, with a Sequel by Juan de Luna* (sequel translated with Carmen Criado de Rodriguez Puertolas), Ungar, 1973; (editor with Gerardo Luzuriaga, and translator) *The Orgy: Modern One-Act Plays from Latin America*, Latin American Center, University of California at Los Angeles, 1974. Has written English subtitles for Spanish films. Contributor of articles, poems, translations of poetry, stories, plays, and reviews to literary publications, including *Poet Lore*, *Minnesota Review*, *Greenfield Review*, and *Drama and Theatre*. Member of editorial board of *Explicacion de textos literarios*.

WORK IN PROGRESS: The Literature of Spain in English Translation: A Bibliography, for Ungar.

* * *

RUDDOCK, Ralph 1913-

PERSONAL: Born September 18, 1913, in Leicester, England; son of Frank and Margaret (Smallwood) Ruddock; married February 19, 1938; children: Benjamin. *Education:* Attended University of Leicester, 1935-38; University of Nottingham, BSC., 1948. *Politics:* "Radical." *Home:* 22 Wycke Rd., Malvern, Worcestershire, England. *Office:* Department of Adult Education, University of Manchester, Manchester, England.

CAREER: University of Manchester, Manchester, England, tutor in Holly Royde College, 1949-51, resident tutor in extra-mural department, 1951-65, senior staff tutor and director of courses in social studies, 1965-71, senior lecturer in adult education, 1971—. *Military service:* British Army, Artillery, 1939-45.

WRITINGS: Roles and Relationships, Routledge & Kegan Paul, 1969, Humanities, 1970; (editor and author of preface) *Six Approaches to the Person*, Routledge & Kegan Paul, 1972; *Sociological Perspectives on Adult Education*, Department of Adult Education, University of Manchester, 1972.

WORK IN PROGRESS: Research for a book on health education for adults.

SIDELIGHTS: Ruddock writes that he is "convinced of the need to destroy large private enterprises, or bring them into public ownership."

Roles and Relationships has been published in Italian, Dutch, and Japanese editions.

* * *

RUDY, Peter 1922-

PERSONAL: Born April 9, 1922, in Buffalo, N.Y.; son of Stephen and Tekla (Rudy) Rudy; married Hildred Ethel Thau, September 20, 1947; children: George, Elizabeth. *Education:* University of Buffalo, B.A., 1943, M.A., 1948; Columbia University, Ph.D., 1957. *Politics:* Democrat. *Home:* 635 Milburn St., Evanston, Ill. 60201. *Office:* Department of Slavic Languages, Northwestern University, Evanston, Ill. 60201.

CAREER: University of Buffalo, Buffalo, N.Y., instructor in English, 1946, 1947; Dartmouth College, Hanover, N.H., instructor in English and Russian, 1947-48; Northwestern University, Evanston, Ill., instructor in Russian, 1951-52; Pennsylvania State University, State College, assistant professor of Russian, 1952-58; Northwestern University, Evanston, Ill., associate professor, 1958-69, professor of Slavic languages, 1969—. *Military service:* U.S. Army, 1943-46. *Member:* Modern Language Association of America, American Association of Teachers of Slavic and East European Languages, Phi Beta Kappa.

WRITINGS: (Editor and author of introduction) Eugene Zamiatin, *We*, Dutton, 1959; (editor and author of introduction) *Darkness and Light: Three Short Works of Leo Tolstoy*, Holt, 1965; *Russian: A Complete Elementary Course*, Norton, 1970. Contributor to *Philological Quarterly*, *Slavic and East European Journal*, and *Modern Language Journal*.

WORK IN PROGRESS: A book on Leo Tolstoy, completion expected in 1976.

* * *

RUPLE, Wayne Douglas 1950-

PERSONAL: Born November 27, 1950, in Birmingham, Ala.; son of Amy Lucille Ruple. *Education:* Attended Jefferson State Junior College. *Politics:* "Not involved." *Religion:* "There is truth and false in all religions. I have no preference." *Home and office address:* Route 1, Box 147, Springville, Ala. 35146.

CAREER: S.S. Kresge Co., Birmingham, Ala., assistant manager of camera department, 1973-74; free-lance photographer and writer, 1974—. Has directed research on unidentified flying objects (UFO's); field investigator for Midwest Unidentified Flying Object Network (MUFON).

WRITINGS—Poems, except as indicated: (With Tommy Kuykendall) *From Hidden Corners of the Mind*, Transcend, 1970; (with Kuykendall) *Thoughts on a Daydream*, Transcend, 1970; (with Kuykendall) *Running Through the Shadows*, Transcend, 1971; (editor) *Children of the Morning* (anthology), Transcend, 1971; *You Are* (quotations), Transcend, 1973. Poems are represented in anthologies, including *Anthology of Alabama Poets*, Thomas Henricks, 1970; *The Golden Ones*, Transcend, 1972. Contributor to *Showcase, Group Three O*, and to newspapers.

WORK IN PROGRESS: A photographic book on the South; a book on unidentified flying objects; a third book, *How to Find True Happiness and Live with It*; a movie dealing with ancient civilizations in North and South America.

* * *

RUSTIN, Bayard 1910-

PERSONAL: Born March 10, 1910, in West Chester, Pa.; son of Janifer (a caterer) and Julia (a social worker; maiden name, Davis) Rustin. *Education:* Attended Wilberforce University, 1930-31, Cheyney State Normal School (now Cheyney State College), 1931-33, and City College (now City College of the City University of New York), 1933-35. *Politics:* Socialist. *Religion:* Society of Friends (Quaker). *Home:* 340 West 28th St., New York, N.Y. 10001. *Office:* A. Philip Randolph Institute, 260 Park Ave. S., New York, N.Y. 10010.

CAREER: Race relations director, Fellowship of Reconciliation, 1941-53; executive secretary, War Resisters' League, 1953-55; special assistant to Martin Luther King, Jr., 1955-60; A. Philip Randolph Institute, New York, N.Y., director, 1966—. Ratner Lecturer, Columbia University, 1974. Chairman of Leadership Conference on Civil Rights, and Recruitment and Training Program (R.T.P., Inc.). Field secretary, Congress for Racial Equality, 1941; organizer, March on Washington for Jobs and Freedom, 1963. Co-chairman, Social Democrats of the U.S.A. Member of boards of directors, Notre Dame University, Metropolitan Applied Research Center, and League for Industrial Democracy. *Awards, honors:* Eleanor Roosevelt Award from Trade Union Leadership Council, 1966; Liberty Bell Award from Howard University Law School, 1967; LL.D. from New School for Social Research, 1968, and Brown University, 1972; Litt.D. from Montclair State

College, 1968; John Dewey Award from United Federation of Teachers, 1968; Family of Man Award from National Council of Churches, 1969; John F. Kennedy Award from National Council of Jewish Women, 1971; Lyndon Johnson Award from Urban League, 1974; honorary degrees from Columbia University and from Clark College.

WRITINGS: Down the Line: The Collected Writings of Bayard Rustin, Quadrangle, 1971. Contributor to periodicals. Editor, *Liberation* (magazine).

WORK IN PROGRESS: An edition of his Ratner Lectures, to be published by Columbia University.

SIDELIGHTS: Rustin was a conscientious objector during World War II, and spent three years in jail as a result.

* * *

RUTSTEIN, Nat(han) 1930-

PERSONAL: Born December 5, 1930, in New York, N.Y.; son of Louis (a plumber) and Lillian (Wilson) Rutstein; married Carol Kelsey (a singer), June 4, 1955; children: David, Dale, Tod, Valerie. *Education:* DePauw University, B.A., 1953. *Religion:* Baha'i. *Home:* 34 High Point Dr., Amherst, Mass. 01002. *Office:* Department of Telecommunications, Springfield Technical Community College, Springfield, Mass.

CAREER: KFMJ-Radio, Tulsa, Okla., news director, 1955-56; WCCO-Television, Minneapolis-St. Paul, Minn., reporter and writer, 1956-58; WRCV-Television and Radio (now KYW), Philadelphia, Pa., producer of news and public affairs programs, 1958-61; WNEW-Television, New York, N.Y., associate news director, 1961-62; American Broadcasting Co., New York, N.Y., foreign assignment editor for news division, writing network radio and television newscasts, 1962-63; National Broadcasting Co., New York, network news editor, 1964-70; University of Massachusetts, Amherst, director of Media/Communications Center, School of Education, 1970-73; Springfield Technical Community College, Springfield, Mass., associate professor and chairman of telecommunications department, 1974—. Visiting lecturer, American International College, 1974; consultant and adjunct professor, Institute of Space Research, Brazil. Producer of ten-part television series on physical diagnosis for College of Medicine and Dentistry, New Jersey, and television productions for St. Michael's Hospital, Newark, and Massachusetts Department of Education; producer of films, "Education SOS," for White House Conference on Children, 1970, and "Up in the Valley," for Pioneer Valley Association, 1974; writer for NBC "Today" show, 1974; producer for Kiva Films, Inc. Consultant to Harlem Preparatory School, New York, and to organizations in his field. *Military service:* U.S. Army, 1953-55; served on Okinawa.

WRITINGS: "Go Watch TV", Sheed & Ward, 1974. Author of booklet, *Dealing with the Television Child: An Educational Crisis*, University of Massachusetts, 1971. Author of filmscript, "Up in the Valley," for Pioneer Valley Association, and of filmscripts for Massachusetts Bilingual Education Bureau and Springfield (Mass.) Bicentennial Committee, all 1974. Contributor of articles to *Reading Teacher, Media and Methods, Massachusetts Teacher, Trend, World Order*, and to newspapers.

WORK IN PROGRESS: A novel; a textbook on television journalism.

SIDELIGHTS: Rutstein told *CA*: "It is an exciting time to be alive! For we are beginning to notice the climax of that ancient drama: the coming together of the human family. My greatest joy is being an active participant." Rutstein has traveled in Great Britain, Israel, Japan, and parts of Central, South, and North America.

* * *

RYAN, Cornelius John 1920-1974

June 5, 1920—November 23, 1974; Irish-born American journalist, magazine editor, and author of books on a variety of subjects, including three international best-sellers about World War II. Obituaries: *New York Times*, November 25, 1974; *Washington Post*, November 25, 1974; *Publishers Weekly*, December 2, 1974; *Time*, December 9, 1974; *AB Bookman's Weekly*, December 16, 1974.

* * *

RYAN, James H(erbert) 1928-

PERSONAL: Born April 12, 1928, in Centralia, Ill.; son of Charles (a merchant) and Marie (a merchant; maiden name, Waggoner) Ryan; married Anita Joyce Gazin, July 11, 1948; children: Kathryn J., Thomas P., Colleen M. *Education:* St. Louis University, B.S., 1948, M.D., 1952. *Politics:* Republican. *Religion:* Roman Catholic. *Home address:* R.R. 2, Box 41, Kankakee, Ill. 60901. *Agent:* Porter, Gould, & Dierks, 1236 Sherman Ave., Evanston, Ill. 60201. *Office:* Pediatrics Ltd., 401 North Wall St., Kankakee, Ill. 60901.

CAREER: Certified by American Board of Pediatrics. St. Vincent's Hospital, Toledo, Ohio, intern, 1952-53; Brooke Army Medical Center, San Antonio, Tex., resident in pediatrics, 1953-56; pediatrician in Kankakee, Ill., 1958—. Chief of pediatrics at St. Mary's Hospital, 1962-63, 1970-71, president-elect of medical staff, 1973, member of executive committee, 1973-74; chief of pediatrics at Riverside Hospital and member of executive committee, 1963-66. Coroner in Kankakee, 1964—; president of Pediatrics Ltd., 1965—. Member of Illinois governor's commission to investigate hospitalization for paraplegics, 1959-60; member of governor's council on necropsy service to coroners of Illinois; member of advisory board of Manteno State Hospital. Member of local citizens committee for a new constitution; member of committee for the health needs of Kankakee County. Consultant to Family Life Achievement Center, 1973—. *Military service:* U.S. Army, 1953-58, chief of pediatrics at U.S. Army Hospital in Heidelberg, Germany, 1956-58; became captain.

MEMBER: American Medical Association, American Academy of Pediatrics (fellow), Authors Guild, Authors League of America, Illinois State Medical Society, Illinois Police Association, Illinois Pediatric Society, Kankakee County Medical Society (vice-president, 1967; president, 1968), Kankakee Country Club, Kankakee Racquet Club, One Hundred Club of Kankakee, Union League Club (Chicago), Phi Beta Pi, St. Jude League, Elks.

WRITINGS: Coroner's Plan for Mass Casualties Resulting from Localized Disasters (monograph), Phillips Press, 1965, 2nd edition, 1969; *Suffer the Little Ones*, Aurora, 1972; *Pablum, Parents, and Pandemonium*, Crowell, 1975. Contributor to *Prism, Sepia, Journal of Family Life Achievement Center*, and *Chicago Tribune*.

AVOCATIONAL INTERESTS: Tennis, scuba diving, fishing.

SABINE, William H(enry) W(aldo) 1903-

PERSONAL: Surname rhymes with "cab sign"; born April 2, 1903, in Birkenhead, England; emigrated to the U.S. in 1947; son of Henry Wilmshurst (a banker) and Mary (Goderich) Sabine; married Ellen Rosina Borcherding (an artist), July 2, 1937. *Education:* Studied at private schools in England, and under tutors. *Home:* 21-A Yorkshire Court, Lakehurst, N.J. 08733.

CAREER: Teacher of English, French, and other subjects in Middlesex County and in London, England, prior to 1947; Colburn & Tegg (publishers and booksellers), Hollis, N.Y., partner, 1954—.

WRITINGS: Second Sight in Daily Life, Coward, 1949; *Suppressed History of General Nathaniel Woodhull*, Colburn, 1954; (editor) *New York Diary of Lieutenant Jabez Fitch*, Arno, 1954; *Historical Memoirs of William Smith: 1763-1783*, Arno, 1956-1971; *Katarina Van Buskirk*, Colburn, 1957; *A Prophecy Concerning the Swedish Monarchy*, Colburn, 1968; *Murder: 1776 and Washington's Policy of Silence*, Gaus, 1973; *A Letter about Distorted History*, Colburn, 1975.

WORK IN PROGRESS: Historical Instances of Precognition; Letters and Diaries.

SIDELIGHTS: Sabine told *CA* that, since 1954, he has been "heavily engaged in historical research, especially in connection with his editing of the *Historical Memoirs* of Chief Justice William Smith which, until he [Sabine] dealt with it single-handed, was the biggest remaining unpublished record of the Revolutionary era."

* * *

SACK, Saul 1912-

PERSONAL: Born January 28, 1912, in Philadelphia, Pa.; son of I. Charles and Clara (Budinoff) Sack; married Irma E. Stein (a social work supervisor). *Education:* Temple University, B.S., 1940; University of Pennsylvania, M.S., 1947, Ph.D., 1959. *Home:* Fairfax Apartments, 43rd & Locust Sts., Philadelphia, Pa. 19104. *Office:* Graduate School of Education, University of Pennsylvania, 37th & Walnut Sts., Philadelphia, Pa. 19174.

CAREER: University of Pennsylvania, Philadelphia, lecturer, 1955-59, assistant professor, 1959-61, associate professor, 1961-64, professor of education, 1964—. *Member:* American Historical Association, American Association for the Advancement of Science, American Academy of Political and Social Science, Comparative and International Education Society, John Dewey Society. *Awards, honors:* Certificate of commendation from American Association for State and Local History, 1965, for *History of Higher Education in Pennsylvania*.

WRITINGS: (Contributor) W. W. Brickman and Stanley Lehrer, editors, *A Century of Higher Education*, Volume IV, Society for the Advancement of Education, 1962; *History of Higher Education in Pennsylvania*, two volumes, Pennsylvania Historical and Museum Commission, 1963; (contributor) Charles Coleman Sellers, editor, *The Boyd Lee Spahr Lectures in Americana*, Dickinson College, 1970. Contributor to *Pennsylvania History, Pennsylvania Magazine of History and Biography, History of Education Quarterly, Paedagogica Historica*, and *Educational Theory*.

WORK IN PROGRESS: Life and Education in the Christian Era; Education and the Natue of Man.

SIDELIGHTS: "I am assiduously attempting," Sack told *CA*, "to refrain from making too many contributions to knowledge pollution."

* * *

SACKS, Oliver W(olf) 1933-

PERSONAL: Born July 9, 1933, in London, England; son of Samuel (a physician) and Elsie (a physician; maiden name, Landau) Sacks. *Education:* Queen's College, Oxford, M.A., B.M., B.Ch., all 1958; further study at Middlesex Hospital, London, England, 1955-60, and University of California, Los Angeles, 1960-65. *Home and office:* 11 Central Parkway, Mt. Vernon, N.Y. 10552. *Agent:* John Farquharson Ltd., 15 Red Lion Sq., London W.C.1, England.

CAREER: Albert Einstein College of Medicine, New York, N.Y., instructor in neurology, 1965—. Consultant to Bronx State Hospital, 1965—. *Member:* American Academy of Neurology (fellow).

WRITINGS: Migraine: Evolution of Common Disorder, University of California Press, 1970; *Awakenings*, Duckworth, 1973, 2nd edition, Doubleday, 1974, 3rd edition, Penguin, in press. Contributor to *Listener* and to technical journals.

WORK IN PROGRESS: A book on pain; a book on tics; *Ward Twenty-Three; The Tumble.*

AVOCATIONAL INTERESTS: Mountaineering, swimming.

BIOGRAPHICAL/CRITICAL SOURCES: New York Times, May 9, 1971; *New York Review of Books*, June 3, 1971; *Listener*, October 26, 1972; *Daily Telegraph*, January 26, 1973.

* * *

SADKER, Myra Pollack 1943-

PERSONAL: Born March 5, 1943, in Portland, Me.; daughter of Louis Robert (a linotype operator) and Shirley (a secretary; maiden name, Schilling) Pollack; married David Sadker (an assistant professor), July 4, 1965; children: Robin Jennifer. *Education:* Boston University, B.A., 1964; Harvard University, M.A.T., 1965; University of Massachusetts, Ed.D., 1971. *Home:* 9 Leonard Ct., Rockville, Md. 20850. *Office:* Department of Education, American University, Washington, D.C. 20016.

CAREER: Pattaya School, Pattaya, Thailand, teaching principal, 1967; University of Wisconsin at Parkside, assistant professor of education, 1971-73; American University, Washington, D.C., assistant professor of education and director of elementary education, 1973—. Consultant to Tororo Girls School, Uganda, Africa, 1971, and Minneapolis Task Force on Racism, 1974. *Member:* American Educational Research Association, Phi Delta Kappa.

WRITINGS: (With Nancy Frazier) *Sexism in School and Society*, Harper, 1973. Contributor to *Elementary School Journal, Education Digest, National Elementary Principal*, and other education journals.

WORK IN PROGRESS: A text analyzing the presentation of various contemporary issues as they are reflected in children's literature, publication by Harper expected in 1976.

* * *

SADOFF, Ira 1945-

PERSONAL: Born March 7, 1945; married Dianne Fallon

(a college professor), July 29, 1968. *Education:* Cornell University, B.A., 1966; University of Oregon, M.F.A., 1968. *Residence:* Xenia, Ohio. *Agent:* Curtis Brown Ltd., 60 East 56th St., New York, N.Y. 10022.

CAREER: University of Oregon, Eugene, instructor in English, 1967-68; Hobart and William Smith Colleges, Geneva, N.Y., instructor in English, 1968-71; Antioch College, Yellow Springs, Ohio, visiting assistant professor of literature, 1972-73, writer-in-residence, 1974; poet and author. *Awards, honors:* Ernest Haycox Fiction Prize from University of Oregon, 1968; fellow of Squaw Valley Community of Writers, 1973, and Breadloaf Writer's Conference, 1974.

WRITINGS: Settling Down (poems), Houghton, 1975.

Work is anthologized in *Eating the Menu: Contemporary Poetry, 1963-73*, Prentice-Hall, 1974. Contributor of more than seventy-five poems, stories, translations of poetry, criticism, and reviews to literary journals, including *New American Review, American Poetry Review, Transatlantic Review, Granite, Dalhousie Review*, and *Western Humanities Review*. Co-founder and co-editor of *Seneca Review*.

WORK IN PROGRESS: A second book of poems.

* * *

SAGNIER, Thierry (Bright) 1946-

PERSONAL: Born March 1, 1946, in Paris, France; son of Octave Jean (a journalist) and Marie Therese (an artist; maiden name, Fevrier) Sagnier; married Barbara Bright (a reporter), September 29, 1973; children: Elizabeth. *Education:* Attended Georgetown University, 1968-70; George Washington University, 1970-72. *Politics:* Independent. *Home:* 1814 Belmont Rd. N.W., Washington, D.C. 20009.

CAREER: Washington Post, Washington, D.C., staff writer on national newsdesk, 1968-73; *Le Devoir*, Montreal, Quebec, correspondent, 1973—; *Washingtonian Magazine*, Washington, D.C., contributing editor, 1974—.

WRITINGS: Bike!: Motorcycles and the People Who Ride Them, Harper, 1974. Has written for National Public Radio.

WORK IN PROGRESS: Research on music.

* * *

SAHAKIAN, Lucille 1894-

PERSONAL: Born July 1, 1894, in Bloomington, Ind.; daughter of Dave (a merchant) and Alice (a teacher; maiden name, Lynch) Yeo; married Joseph Sahakian, September 21, 1921. *Education:* Attended Indiana State Normal School, 1916, Indiana University, 1917-18, St. Mary's University of San Antonio, 1956. *Politics:* Republican. *Religion:* Methodist. *Home:* 223 Hillwood Dr., San Antonio, Tex. 78213.

CAREER: Elementary school teacher, 1921, English and public speaking teacher, 1922, both in Fairmount, Ind. President of San Antonio Manuscript Club, 1954-55. *Member:* International Travel Study Club (president of Lady Aberdeen artist chapter, 1933-38), American Poetry League, Composers, Authors and Artists of America (national auditor, 1957-63; president of Texas chapter, 1959-60), Alpha Omicron Alpha. *Awards, honors:* Certificate of recognition of services rendered to nation and state of Indiana, October 16, 1940; San Antonio Poetry Club first prize winner, 1970, for "Historical Alamo"; Doctor of Arts and Letters, International Academy at Hull, England, 1968.

WRITINGS—Poems: *War and Romance*, Stallings, 1942; *A Heart Speaks*, Stallings, 1948; *Stars from a Texas Sky*, Naylor, 1956; *Faith Treasures*, Stallings, 1961; *Starlight*, Stallings, 1963; *Bonds of Friendship*, Stallings, 1964; *A Calender of Thoughts*, Stallings, 1966; *A Star's Delight*, Stallings, 1969; *The Brightest Star*, Stallings, 1972. Writer of song lyrics. Regular contributor of poetry to *Triangle* (of Alpha Omicron Alpha), 1944—.

WORK IN PROGRESS: A book of essays and poems, *A Star of Hope*; a novel, *Hearts Aflame*; a children's book, *Sunbeams*; a book of romantic poetry, *A Rainbow of Romance*.

SIDELIGHTS: Lucille Sahakian is an artist who has displayed her paintings in twenty shows.

* * *

SALES, M(illard) Vance 1929-

PERSONAL: Born March 3, 1929, in Forrest City, Ark.; son of Joseph Kennedy and Jenneye (Reames) Sales; married Dorothy Jean Johnson, December 19, 1955; children: Vance, Jr., Hugh, David, Summer-Lee. *Education:* State College of Arkansas, B.A., 1950; Florida State University, M.S., 1951; University of Mississippi, M.Ed., 1957; Duke University, Ed.D., 1960. *Politics:* Democrat. *Religion:* Methodist. *Home:* 1008 Sylvan Hill Dr., Jonesboro, Ark. 72401. *Office:* Arkansas State University, Box 839, State University, Ark. 72467.

CAREER: Forrest City Public Schools, Forrest City, Ark., teacher, 1953-58; Arkansas State University, State University, director of guidance, 1960-61, associate professor, 1961-63, professor of education, 1963—. *Military service:* U.S. Army, 1951-53. *Member:* American Association of School Administrators, National Organization of Legal Problems on Education, Arkansas Education Association, Phi Delta Kappa. *Awards, honors:* Danforth Associate, 1964-74.

WRITINGS: (With Robert Moore) *Who Went to College and Where They Went* (pamphlet), Arkansas State University Press, 1963; (contributor) E. C. Bolmeier, editor, *Legal Issues in Education*, Michie Company, 1970; (with Lee O. Garber) *The Law and the Teacher in Arkansas*, Interstate, 1971; (with Joseph C. Taylor) *The Arkansas School Superintendent*, Arkansas State University Press, 1973. Author of *Arkansas High School Graduates* (monographs). Contributor to professional journals.

WORK IN PROGRESS: Revising *The Law and the Teacher in Arkansas*.

* * *

SALTER, Elizabeth

PERSONAL: Born in Australia; daughter of Alfred Fulton and Sarah (Wilkinson) Salter. *Education:* Attended University of Adelaide, 1937-39, and Conservatorium of Adelaide, 1939-41. *Politics:* Liberal. *Religion:* Christian. *Home:* 9 Regina Court, 40 Fitzjohns Ave., London, England. *Agent:* International Famous Agency, 244 East 49th St., New York, N.Y.

CAREER: Australian Broadcasting Commission, Adelaide, programmer of music, 1941-47; Secretary to Dame Edith Sitwell in London, England, 1957-64; writer. *Military service:* Australian Women's Auxiliary Air Force, 1944-46; became entertainments officer.

MEMBER: Crime Writers Association. *Awards, honors:*

Commonwealth Literary Award, 1971, for *Daisy Bates*, and in 1973-74, for *The Lost Impressionist*.

WRITINGS: Death in a Mist (novel), Bles, 1957, Ace Books, 1958; *Will to Survive*, Bles, 1957, Ace Books, 1958; *There Was a Witness: The Voice of the Peacock* (novel), Bles, 1961, Ace Books, 1963; *Once Upon a Tombstone* (novel), Ace Books, 1965; *The Last Years of a Rebel* (biography), Houghton, 1967; *Daisy Bates* (biography), Angus & Robertson, 1971, Coward, 1972; *The Lost Impressionist* (biography), Angus & Robertson, 1975. Contributor of poems and short stories to *Woman's Own, Woman's Realm, Woman's Day, Sydney Morning Herald*, and *Woman's Weekly*.

WORK IN PROGRESS: An anthology of poems and prose by Edith Sitwell; a biography of Sir Robert Walpole.

AVOCATIONAL INTERESTS: Music, tennis, swimming, walking, reading, theatre, opera, ballet.

* * *

SALTHE, Stanley N(orman) 1930-

PERSONAL: Surname is pronounced *Saul*-thee; born October 16, 1930, in Brooklyn, N.Y.; son of Christian (a carpenter) and Ruth (Idland) Salthe; married Barbara May, May 23, 1959; children: Rebecca May, Eric Peter. *Education:* Columbia University, B.S. (cum laude), 1959, M.A., 1960, Ph.D., 1963. *Office:* Department of Biology, Brooklyn College of the City University of New York, Brooklyn, N.Y. 11210.

CAREER: Brandeis University, Waltham, Mass., research associate, 1963-65; Brooklyn College of the City University of New York, assistant professor, 1965-71, associate professor, 1971-73, professor of biology, 1973—. *Military service:* U.S. Air Force, 1951-55. *Member:* American Society of Naturalists, Society for the Study of Evolution, American Society of Zoologists, American Society of Ichthyologists and Herpetologists, Society of Systematic Zoology, Society for the Study of the Origin of Life, New York Academy of Sciences. *Awards, honors:* National Science Foundation research grants in systematic biology, 1966-70.

WRITINGS: Evolutionary Biology, Holt, 1972; (contributor) Brian Lofts, editor, *Physiology of the Amphibia*, Volume II, Academic Press, 1974. Contributor to *Encyclopedia Americana*; contributor to professional journals.

WORK IN PROGRESS: Research in applying a thermodynamic viewpoint to the evolution of living systems involving work in reproductive strategies and in ecological specialization; poems.

* * *

SANBORN, Margaret 1915-

PERSONAL: Born December 7, 1915, in Alameda, Calif.; daughter of David Warren (an author) and Angela (Desimone) Ryder; married Francis Sanborn (an accountant), July 18, 1936; children: David, Catherine. *Education:* Attended San Francisco Conservatory of Music, 1924-28, College of Marin, 1932-34, and California School of Fine Arts, 1934-36. *Residence:* Mill Valley, Calif. 94941.

CAREER: Writer. *Awards, honors:* California Literature Gold Medal Award for best non-fiction by a California author, 1968, for *Robert E. Lee: A Portrait, 1807-1861*, and *Robert E. Lee: The Complete Man, 1861-1870*.

WRITINGS: Robert E. Lee: A Portrait, 1807-1861, Lippincott, 1966; *Robert E. Lee: The Complete Man, 1861-1870*, Lippincott, 1967; *The American: River of El Dorado*, Holt, 1974. Contributor to *Assembly*.

WORK IN PROGRESS: Research for books in the field of Western Americana.

AVOCATIONAL INTERESTS: Preservation of historic sites and buildings, preservation of wilderness areas and wildlife, exploration of Sierra Nevadan foothills and wilderness of higher elevations; music, gardening, photography.

* * *

SANDBERG, Lars G(unnarsson) 1939-

PERSONAL: Born June 20, 1939, in Uppsala, Sweden; naturalized U.S. citizen in 1967; son of Gunnar A. (a United Nations official) and Laila (Dillner) Sandberg; married Joyce Bigelow, June 29, 1963; children: Per L., Kerstin M., Elisabet K. *Education:* Harvard University, A.B. (summa cum laude), 1961, A.M., 1963, Ph.D., 1964. *Home:* 1970 Upper Chelsea Rd., Columbus, Ohio 43271. *Office:* Department of Economics, Ohio State University, Columbus, Ohio 43210.

CAREER: Harvard University, Cambridge, Mass., instructor, 1964-66, assistant professor of economics, 1966-67; Dartmouth College, Hanover, N.H., associate professor of economics, 1967-70; Ohio State University, Columbus, associate professor, 1970-71, professor of economics, 1971—. Expert witness for U.S. Department of Justice, 1967—. *Member:* American Economic Association, Economic History Association, Phi Beta Kappa.

WRITINGS: Lancashire in Decline, Ohio State University Press, 1974. Contributor to *Review of Economics and Statistics, Journal of Economic History, Quarterly Journal of Economics*, and *Explorations in Economic History*.

WORK IN PROGRESS: Research on European economic history.

* * *

SANDERS, (Charles) Richard 1904-

PERSONAL: Born August 14, 1904, in Murfreesboro, Tenn.; son of William Josiah (a physician and dentist) and Fanny (Adams) Sanders; married Virginia Hightower, August 28, 1932; children: Charles Richard, Jr., Nancy Virginia (Mrs. Caufurd Goodwin), Martha Frances (Mrs. George Gilmore). *Education:* Emory University, A.B., 1926, M.A., 1927; University of Chicago, Ph.D., 1934. *Home:* 103 Pinecrest Rd., Durham, N.C. 27705. *Office:* 211 West Duke Bldg., College Station, Durham, N.C. 27708.

CAREER: Duke University, Durham, N.C., assistant professor, 1937-44, associate professor, 1944-51, professor of English, 1951-72. *Member:* Modern Language Association of America, Phi Beta Kappa. *Awards, honors:* Carnegie Foundation grant, 1947; Rockefeller Foundation grant, 1947; Guggenheim fellowships, 1960, 1972; grant from Institute of Higher Learning in the Humanities, University of Edinburgh, 1972.

WRITINGS: (Editor with C. E. Ward) Thomas Malory, *Morte D'Arthur*, Crofts, 1940; *Coleridge and the Broad Church Movement*, Duke University Press, 1942; *The Strachey Family: 1588-1932*, Duke University Press, 1953; *Lytton Strachey: His Mind and Art*, Yale University Press, 1957; (general editor) *The Collected Letters of Thomas and Jane Welsh Carlyle*, forty volumes, Duke University Press, 1970-74; *The Cameron Plantation in Central North*

Carolina (1776-1973) and Its Founder Richard Benneha, privately printed, 1974.

WORK IN PROGRESS: An edition of the Carlyle letters; *Collected Essays on Carlyle and Other Subjects*.

* * *

SANKAR, D(evarakonda) V(enkata) Siva 1927-

PERSONAL: Born April 7, 1927, in Vizianagram, India; came to United States, 1953; naturalized citizen, 1963; son of D. V. Jagannadham and D. (Neti) Pullamma; married Barbara Cosanno, June 4, 1959; children: Jason, Douglas, Priscilla. *Education:* University of Madras, M.Sc., 1949, Ph.D., 1951; attended Massachusetts Institute of Technology, 1953-55, and Johns Hopkins University, 1956. *Office:* Queens Children's Hospital, Bellerose, N.Y. 11426.

CAREER: Adelphi College (now University), Garden City, N.Y., assistant professor of biochemistry, 1956-58; Creedmoor State Hospital, Children's Unit, Queens Village, N.Y., senior research scientist and director of research laboratory, 1959-63, associate research scientist, 1963-70; diplomate, American Board of Clinical Chemistry, 1970; Queens Children's Hospital, Bellerose, N.Y., research scientist, 1970—. Adjunct professor, Fordham University, 1970—, and St. John's University, Jamaica, N.Y., 1971—. *Member:* American Association for the Advancement of Science, American Chemical Society, American Society for Microbiology, American Association of Clinical Chemists, Royal Institute of Chemistry (fellow), American Society for Pharmacology and Experimental Therapeutics, Eastern Psychiatric Research Association (president, 1974—). *Awards, honors:* London City and Guilds silver medal, 1948; Indian Chemical Society gold medal, 1953; Fulbright fellowship, 1953-55; National Science Foundation fellowship, 1956.

WRITINGS—All published by PJD Publications, except as indicated: (Editor) *Some Biological Aspects of Schizophrenic Behavior*, New York Academy of Science, 1962; *Schizophrenia: Current Concepts and Research*, 1969; *LSD: A Total Study*, 1974; *Mental Health in Children*, three volumes, 1975; *Childhood Psychopharmacology*, 1975; *Quantitative Problems in Physical and Chemical Biology: A Workbook*, 1975. Contributor of over a hundred articles to scientific and technical publications. Editor-in-chief, *Research Communications in Chemical Pathology and Pharmacology*; associate editor-in-chief, *Journal of Medicine*; editor, *Physicians Drug Manual*.

WORK IN PROGRESS: A textbook of medical biochemistry; a book on problems in biochemical sciences; books for children and philosophers.

AVOCATIONAL INTERESTS: Travel and sculpture.

* * *

SANTMIRE, H(arold) Paul 1935-

PERSONAL: Born November 28, 1935, in Buffalo, N.Y.; son of Harold Clinton (a dentist) and Elsajean (Pankow) Santmire; married Laurel Oliver, July 15, 1967; children: Heather, Matthew. *Education:* Harvard University, B.A. (cum laude), 1957, Th.D., 1966; Lutheran Theological School, Philadelphia, Pa., B.D., 1960. *Home and office address:* Department of Religion, Wellesley College, Wellesley, Mass. 02181.

CAREER: Ordained minister of the Lutheran Church, 1960; Harvard University, Harvard, Mass., chaplain, 1965-68; Wellesley College, Wellesley, Mass., chaplain, 1968—, lecturer in religion, 1968—. *Awards, honors:* Danforth fellow, 1974-75.

WRITINGS: Brother Earth: Nature, God, and Ecology in a Time of Crisis, Nelson, 1970; (with Paul Lutz) *Ecological Renewal*, Fortress, 1972; (contributor) Ian Barbour, editor, *Western Man and Environmental Ethics*, Addison-Wesley, 1972; (contributor) Franklin Jensen, editor, *The Human Crisis in Ecology*, Lutheran Church in America, 1972; (contributor) Roger A. Johnson, editor, *Critical Issues in Modern Religion*, Prentice-Hall, 1973; (contributor) Herman G. Stuempfle, Jr., editor, *Preaching in the Witnessing Community*, Fortress, 1973.

WORK IN PROGRESS: Study in feminism, ecology, and theology.

* * *

SAPHIRE, Saul 1896(?)-1974

1896(?)—August 15, 1974; Russian-born American novelist, writer of short stories, articles, and essays for the Yiddish press, and teacher. Obituaries: *New York Times*, August 17, 1974.

* * *

SARNOFF, Jane 1937-

PERSONAL: Born June 25, 1937, in Brooklyn, N.Y.; daughter of Murray (a jewelry executive) and Teresa (a teacher; maiden name, Rehr) Sarnoff. *Education:* Goucher College, B.A., 1959. *Religion:* Jewish.

CAREER: Sudler & Hennessey Advertising, New York, N.Y., copy supervisor, 1967-71; free-lance writer, 1971—.

WRITINGS—Books for young people, all with illustrator, Reynold Ruffins: *A Great Bicycle Book*, Scribner, 1973; *The Chess Book*, Scribner, 1973; *What? A Riddle Book*, Scribner, 1974; *A Riddle Calendar: 1975*, Scribner, 1974.

WORK IN PROGRESS: The Code and Cipher Book, with illustrator, Reynold Ruffins, for Scribner; free-lance pharmaceutical writing.

AVOCATIONAL INTERESTS: Travel (Japan, Hong Kong, Europe, Mexico).

* * *

SAROYAN, Arshalyus 1923-1974

1923—1974; Armenian poet, and newspaper, radio, and television editor. Obituaries: *Washington Post*, December 2, 1974.

* * *

SASNETT, Martena T(enney) 1908-

PERSONAL: Born May 2, 1908, in Patchogue, N.Y.; daughter of Henry Allen (a lawyer) and Grace (a teacher; maiden name, Kelley) Tenney; married J. Randolph Sasnett (an educator), September 23, 1943. *Education:* Bradford College, graduate, 1925; Academy of Speech Arts, graduate, 1927; further study at George Washington University, 1927-28, and Theatre Odeon, Paris, 1928-29; studied educational exchange, in Scandinavia, 1957. *Politics:* Independent. *Religion:* Protestant. *Home:* 2829 Miradero Dr., Santa Barbara, Calif. 93105. *Office:* Educational Futures International, 2829 Miradero Dr., Santa Barbara, Calif. 93105.

CAREER: Monodramatist, 1931-47; University of Southern California, Los Angeles, foreign student admissions officer, 1947-52; University of California, Los Angeles, coördinator of international education studies, 1964-66; Religion in Education Foundation, Pasadena, Calif., associate director, 1969-73; Educational Futures International, Santa Barbara, Calif., associate director, 1974—. *Member:* Comparative and International Education Society, American Association of Collegiate Registrars and Admissions Officers, National Association of Foreign Student Affairs. *Awards, honors:* Citation from Boston University, 1958, for work in international education; achievement award from Bradford College, 1961.

WRITINGS: Personalities (monologues), Baker's Plays, 1947; *Educational Systems of the World*, University of Southern California Press, 1952; *A Guide to the Admission and Placement of Foreign Students*, Institute of International Education, 1956, 2nd edition, 1962; (editor) *Foreign Students Look at the United States*, Cole-Holmquist, 1960; (with Inez Sepmeyer) *Educational Systems of Africa*, University of California Press, 1966; (with Sepmeyer) *Graduate Study in the United States: A Guide for Foreign Students*, Council of Graduate Schools and Institute of International Education, 1966; *Financial Planning for Study in the United States: A Guide for Students from Other Countries*, College Entrance Examination Board, 1967; (with Sepmeyer and T. E. Sharp) *The Country Index: Interpretations for Use in the Evaluation of Foreign Secondary Credentials*, Severy, 1971.

* * *

SATTERLUND, Donald R(obert) 1928-

PERSONAL: Born April 10, 1928, in Polk County, Wis.; son of Alvin Gustav (a stone mason) and Winifred (Bush) Satterlund; married Lily-Ann Pearson (an occupational therapist), June 6, 1955; children: Nels Eric, Ruth Ann, Lisa Louise. *Education:* University of Michigan, B.S.F., 1951, M.F., 1955, Ph.D., 1960. *Politics:* Republican. *Religion:* American Lutheran Church. *Office:* Department of Forestry and Range Management, Washington State University, Pullman, Wash. 99163.

CAREER: Syracuse University, Syracuse, N.Y., instructor, 1958-60, assistant professor of forestry, 1960-64; Washington State University, Pullman, assistant professor, 1964-66, associate professor, 1966-71, professor of forestry, 1971—. *Military service:* U.S. Navy, 1945-46, 1951-52; received presidential unit citation. *Member:* American Geophysical Union, Society of American Foresters (chairman of Snake River chapter, 1971-72). *Awards, honors:* Public service award from New York Temporary State Commission on Water Resources Planning, 1964.

WRITINGS: Wildland Watershed Management, Ronald, 1972. Contributor to *Water Resources Research, Forest Science, Journal of Forestry*, and *Journal of Hydrology*.

WORK IN PROGRESS: Research on topoclimatology, on environmental quality of forest and range management practices, on forest ecology, on watershed management, and on conservation land use.

AVOCATIONAL INTERESTS: Traveling in back country of northern Rocky Mountains, hunting birds, fishing trout and steelhead.

* * *

SAUERS, Richard James 1930-

PERSONAL: Born April 3, 1930, in Pittsburgh, Pa.; son of Stephen Francis (a fireman) and Edna (a chocolate dipper; maiden name, Sosinski) Sauers; married Elaine M. Sykes, August 22, 1964; children: Cheryl Ann, Stephen David. *Education:* Slippery Rock State College, B.S., 1951; Pennsylvania State University, M.Ed., 1955, D.Ed., 1961. *Religion:* Roman Catholic. *Home:* 22 Delee Ave., Albany, N.Y. 12203. *Office:* State University of New York at Albany, 1400 Washington Ave., Albany, N.Y. 12222.

CAREER: State University of New York at Albany, assistant professor, 1955-62, associate professor, 1962-69, professor of physical education, 1969—, basketball coach, 1955—. *Military service:* U.S. Navy, 1951-54; became lieutenant junior grade. *Member:* International Association of Approved Basketball Officials, National Association of Basketball Coaches, Wolferts Roost Country Club.

WRITINGS: Basketball's Stack Offense and "20" Defense, Parker Publishing, 1973.

* * *

SAUL, Norman E(ugene) 1932-

PERSONAL: Born November 26, 1932, in LaFontaine, Ind.; son of Ralph Odis (a farmer) and Jessie (Neff) Saul; married Mary Ann Culwell (a social worker), June 27, 1959; children: Alyssa, Kevin, Julia. *Education:* Indiana University, B.A., 1954; University of London, graduate study, 1954-55; Columbia University, M.A., 1959, Ph.D., 1965. *Home:* 1002 Crestline Dr., Lawrence, Kan. 66044. *Office:* Department of History, University of Kansas, Lawrence, Kan. 66045.

CAREER: Purdue University, West Lafayette, Ind., instructor in history, 1962-65; Brown University, Providence, R.I., assistant professor of history, 1965-68; University of Kansas, Lawrence, associate professor of history, 1970—. Visiting professor of history at Northwestern University, 1969-70. Research assistant of Council on Foreign Relations, 1961-62. *Military service:* U.S. Army, 1955-57. *Member:* American Historical Association, American Association for the Advancement of Slavic Studies, American Historical Society of Germans from Russia, Rocky Mountain Social Science Association, Kansas Historical Society. *Awards, honors:* Fulbright research scholar at University of Helsinki, 1968-69.

WRITINGS: Russia and the Mediterranean: 1797-1807, University of Chicago Press, 1970. Contributor to *William and Mary Quarterly, Slavic Review, Slavonic and East European Review, Soviet Studies, Russian Review, Kansas Historical Quarterly, Maryland Historical Magazine*, and *History Today*.

WORK IN PROGRESS: Sailors in Revolution: The Russian Baltic Fleet in 1917; Russia and America: 1830-1875; The Russian Revolution and Ireland.

* * *

SAVAGE, Charles 1918-

PERSONAL: Born September 25, 1918, in Berlin, Conn. *Education:* Yale University, B.A., 1939; University of Chicago, M.D., 1945; also attended Washington-Baltimore Psychoanalytic Institute, 1957. *Office:* Drug Treatment Center, Veterans Administration Hospital, 3900 Loch Raven Blvd., Baltimore, Md. 21218.

CAREER: University of Chicago, Chicago, Ill., intern, 1945; Yale University, New Haven, Conn., assistant resident in psychiatry, 1946; U.S. Naval Hospital, Bethesda, Md., resident psychiatrist, 1947-48; U.S. Naval Hospital, Charleston, S.C., chief psychiatrist, 1948-49; Naval Medical Research Institute and National Naval Medical Center, both Bethesda, Md., research psychiatrist, 1949-52; National Institute of Mental Health, Bethesda, Md., acting chief adult psychiatrist, 1953-58; Livermore Sanitarium, Livermore, Calif., psychiatrist, 1958-60; Cornell University, Ithaca, N.Y., research associate on Aro Project at Abeo Kuta, Nigeria, 1961; Stanford Veterans Administration Hospital, Palo Alto, Calif., psychiatrist, 1961-62; International Foundation for Advanced Study, Menlo Park, Calif., medical director, 1962-64; County of Santa Clara, San Jose, Calif., psychiatrist, 1964-65; Spring Grove State Hospital, Baltimore, Md., director of research, 1965-68; Maryland Psychiatric Research Center, Baltimore, associate director and research scientist, 1968-72; Veterans Administration Hospital, Baltimore, Md., chief of psychiatric services and chief of Drug Treatment Center, 1972—. Diplomate of American Board of Psychiatry and Neurology, 1951; fellow of Center for Advanced Study in the Behavioral Sciences, Stanford, Calif., 1957-58; assistant professor at Johns Hopkins University, 1965—; clinical assistant professor at University of Maryland, 1965-68, clinical associate professor, 1968-72, associate professor, 1972—; David C. Wilson Society lecturer at University of Virginia, 1967.

MEMBER: American Psychiatric Association (fellow), American Psychoanalytic Association, American Electroencephalogram Society, American Association for the Advancement of Science, Washington Psychoanalytic Society, Baltimore Psychoanalytic Society, San Francisco Psychoanalytic Society. *Awards, honors:* National Institute of Mental Health grant, 1972-75, to study selected narcotics agonists and antagonists.

WRITINGS: (Contributor) J. M. Murphy and A. H. Leighton, editors, *Approaches to Cross-Cultural Psychiatry*, Cornell University Press, 1965; (associate editor) *Research in Psychotherapy*, Volume III, American Psychological Association, 1968; (with Brown) *The Drug Abuse Controversy*, National Educational Consultants, 1971; (contributor) F. M. R. Walshe, editor, *Diseases of the Nervous System*, Williams & Wilkins, 1972.

Contributor of about forty articles to professional journals. Member of editorial board of *Psychiatry*.

* * *

SAWYER, W(alter) W(arwick) 1911-

PERSONAL: Born April 5, 1911, in St. Ives, Huntingdonshire, England. *Education:* St. John's College, Cambridge, B.A. (first class honors with distinction), 1933, graduate study, 1933-35. *Office:* Department of Mathematics, University of Toronto, Toronto, Ontario, Canada.

CAREER: University of Dundee, Dundee, Scotland, assistant lecturer in mathematics, 1935-37; University of Manchester, Manchester, England, assistant lecturer in mathematics, 1937-44; Leicester College of Technology, Leicester, head of department of mathematics, 1945-47; University of Ghana, Accra, head of department of mathematics, 1948-50; University of Canterbury, University College, Christchurch, New Zealand, lecturer in mathematics, 1951-56; Wesleyan University, Middletown, Conn., professor of mathematics, 1958-65; University of Toronto, Toronto, Ontario, professor of mathematics and education, 1965—. Visiting professor at University of Illinois, 1957-58, and Rockefeller Institute, 1963-64. *Member:* Institute for Mathematics and Its Applications (fellow), Edinburgh Mathematical Society, British Mathematical Association (life member), Society for Preservation of Rural England, Canadian Mathematical Congress. Cambridge Philosophical Society, Cambridgeshire and Isle of Ely Naturalists Trust.

WRITINGS: Mathematician's Delight, Penguin, 1943; *Mathematics in Theory and Practice*, Odhams, 1950; *Designing and Making*, Blackwell, 1951; *Prelude to Mathematics*, Penguin, 1955; *A Concrete Approach to Abstract Algebra*, W. H. Freeman, 1959; *What is Calculus About?*, Yale University Press, 1961; *Vision in Elementary Mathematics*, Penguin, 1964; *A Path to Modern Mathematics*, Penguin, 1966; *Search for Pattern*, Penguin, 1970; *An Engineering Approach to Linear Algebra*, Cambridge University Press, 1972. Contributor to proceedings and to journals. Editor of *Mathematics Student Journal*, 1958-61, and founder of *Student Mathematics*, 1970—.

* * *

SAYLES, George O(sborne) 1901-

PERSONAL: Born April 20, 1901, in Chesterfield, Derbyshire, England; son of Larret Pearson (a clergyman) and Margaret (a teacher; maiden name, Brown) Sayles; married Agnes Sutherland, September 2, 1936; children: Michael George Alexander, Hilary Margaret Jean. *Education:* Glasgow University, M.A. (first-class honors), 1923, D.Litt., 1932; University College, London, graduate study, 1923-24. *Home:* Warren Hill, Crowborough, Sussex, England.

CAREER: Glasgow University, Glasgow, Scotland, assistant lecturer, 1924-25, lecturer, 1925-34, senior lecturer in history, 1934-45; Queen's University, Belfast, Northern Ireland, professor of modern history, 1945-53; Aberdeen University, Aberdeen, Scotland, Burnett-Fletcher Professor of History, 1953-62; New York University, New York, N.Y., Kenan Professor of History, 1967. Leverhulme Research fellow, 1939; visiting professor, Louvain University, 1951; Woodward Lecturer, Yale University, 1952; visiting member, Institute for Advanced Study, Princeton, N.J., 1969. Managing director, Messrs. Blair and Munsie, Yarn Merchants, Glasgow, 1941-45. Vice-president, Selden Society, London, 1953; fellow, Folger Library, Washington, D.C., 1960-61. *Wartime service:* British Home Guard, 1940-44. *Member:* British Academy (fellow), Royal Irish Academy, Royal Historical Society (fellow). *Awards, honors:* James Barr Ames Medal from law faculty of Harvard University, 1958; Litt.D. from Trinity College, Dublin, 1964.

WRITINGS: (Editor) *Select Cases in the Court of King's Bench*, Quaritch, Part I: *Under Edward I*, three volumes, 1936-39, Part II: *Under Edward II*, 1956, Part III: *Under Edward III*, two volumes, 1958 and 1965, Part IV: *Under Richard II, Henry IV, Henry V*, 1971; *Medieval Foundations of England*, Methuen, 1948, revised edition, University of Pennsylvania Press, 1950; *Contemporary Sketches of Members of Irish Parliament in 1782*, Royal Irish Academy (Dublin), 1954; *The King's Parliament of England*, Norton, 1974.

With H. G. Richardson: (Editors) *The Provisions of Oxford*, Manchester University Press, 1933; *The Early Statutes*, Stevens, 1934; (editors) *Select Cases of Procedure without Writ*, Selden Society, 1941; (editors) *Parliaments and Councils of Medieval Ireland*, Stationery Office (Dublin), 1947; *The Irish Parliament in the Middle Ages*, University of Pennsylvania Press, 1952; (editors and translators) *Fleta*, Quaritch, Volume I, 1956, Volume II, 1973;

Parliaments and Great Councils in Medieval England, Stevens, 1961; *Irish Revenue, 1278-1384*, Royal Irish Academy, 1962; *The Administration of Ireland, 1172-1377*, Stationery Office, 1963; *The Governance of Medieval England from the Conquest to Magna Carta*, Edinburgh University Press, 1963, 2nd edition, 1974; *Law and Legislation from Aethelberht to Magna Carta*, Edinburgh University Press, 1966. Contributor to history and law journals.

WORK IN PROGRESS: Editing parliamentary documents and published papers, completion expected in 1976; research on common law in England and medieval parliaments.

* * *

SAYRE, John L(eslie) 1924-

PERSONAL: Born March 28, 1924, in Hannibal, Mo.; son of John L. (a lumberman) and Clara (Haden) Sayre; married Herwanna Lee Harrouff (a teacher), June 18, 1948; children: Barbara Ann, John Richard, Alan Douglas, Melody Lyn (Mrs. Roy) Hildebrand. *Education:* Phillips University, B.A., 1946; Yale University, M.Div., 1950; University of Texas, M.L.S., 1963, Ph.D., 1973. *Politics:* Democrat. *Home:* 2416 East Elm, Enid, Okla. 73701. *Office:* University Library, Phillips University, Enid, Okla. 73701.

CAREER: Ordained Disciples of Christ minister, 1946; minister in Stillwater, Okla., 1954-57, and in Austin, Tex., 1957-62; Phillips University, Enid, Okla., director of university libraries, 1962—. *Member:* American Theological Library Association (member of board of directors, 1974—), American Library Association, Oklahoma Library Association, Beta Phi Mu.

WRITINGS: History of Disciples Student Work, United Christian Missionary, 1950; *A Manual of Forms for Term Papers and Theses*, Seminary Press, 1966, fourth edition, 1973; *An Index to Festschriften in Religion*, Seminary Press, 1970; *An Illustrated Guide to the Anglo-American Cataloging*, Seminary Press, 1971; (with John Knightly) *The Personalized System of Instruction in Higher Education*, Seminary Press, 1972.

WORK IN PROGRESS: A theological bibliography.

AVOCATIONAL INTERESTS: Vegetable gardening.

* * *

SCAMMON, John H(umphrey) 1905-

PERSONAL: Born October 4, 1905, in East Rochester, N.H.; son of Thomas Harmon (a minister) and Nina (Landman) Scammon; married Margaret Morris (a registered nurse), June 6, 1931; children: Ruth Elizabeth (Mrs. Kenneth Albert Sargent), James Peter. *Education:* Bates College, A.B. (cum laude), 1927; Newton Theological Institution (now Andover Newton Theological School), B.D. (cum laude), 1930, S.T.M., 1939; Simmons College, M.S. in L.S., 1937; Harvard University, Th.D., 1949. *Politics:* Democrat. *Home:* 18 Lake St., Kingston, Mass. 02364.

CAREER: Ordained Baptist minister, 1930; pastor in Weston, Mass., 1930-36; Andover Newton Theological School, Newton Center, Mass., instructor, 1937-49, assistant professor, 1949-51, associate professor, 1951-55, professor of Hebrew and Old Testament, 1955-71, librarian, 1937-55. Visiting professor at Near East School of Theology, Beirut, 1952-53, and at Central Philippine University, 1966-67, 1971-72. *Member:* Society of Biblical Literature, National Association of Professors of Hebrew, Phi Beta Kappa.

WRITINGS: Living with the Psalms, Judson, 1967; *If I Could Find God*, Judson, 1974. Contributor to reference books and journals. Editor of *Andover Newton Bulletin*, 1939-50.

SIDELIGHTS: Scammon has studied in Israel and has travelled to Jordan and Egypt.

* * *

SCANDURA, Joseph M(ichael) 1931-

PERSONAL: Born April 29, 1931, in Bay Shore, N.Y.; son of Joseph (a barber) and Lucy (a teacher; maiden name, Stella) Scandura; married Alice Baker (a teacher), August 13, 1960; children: Jeanne, Janette, Joseph, Julie. *Education:* University of Michigan, A.B., 1953, M.A., 1955; Syracuse University, Ph.D., 1962. *Home:* 1249 Green Tree La., Narberth, Pa. 19072. *Office:* Department of Education, University of Pennsylvania, Philadelphia, Pa. 19174.

CAREER: State University of New York, Buffalo, assistant professor of education and mathematics, 1963-64; Florida State University, Tallahassee, assistant professor of mathematics education, 1964-66; University of Pennsylvania, Philadelphia, associate professor, 1966-69, professor of education, 1969—. Chairman of board of scientific advisors of MERGE Research Institute. *Member:* American Psychological Association (fellow), American Educational Research Association, National Council of Teachers of Mathematics.

WRITINGS: (Contributor) P. C. Burns and A. M. Johnson, editors, *Research on Elementary School Curriculum and Organization*, Allyn & Bacon, 1969; (contributor) R. B. Ashlock and W. L. Herman, editors, *Current Research in Elementary School Mathematics*, Macmillan, 1970; *Mathematics: Concrete Behavioral Foundations*, Harper, 1971; (with J. H. Durnin, W. Ehrenpreis, and G. Luger) *An Algorithmic Approach to Mathematics: Concrete Behavioral Foundations*, Harper, 1971; (editor) *Structural Learning*, Gordon & Breach, Volume I: *Theory and Research*, 1973, Volume II: *Issues and Approaches*, in press. Editor with others, and contributor to *1974 Proceedings: Fifth Annual Interdisciplinary Conference on Structural Learning*. Author of a series of workbooks. Contributor of more than eighty-six articles to professional journals.

WORK IN PROGRESS: Human Problem Solving: Synthesis of Content, Cognition, and Individual Differences.

* * *

SCHARF, Bertram 1931-

PERSONAL: Born March 3, 1931, in New York, N.Y.; son of Louis Gershon (a salesman) and Nettie (Fink) Scharf; married Anna-Liisa Pylvaenen, April 10, 1965; children: Riitta, Jonathan Lauri. *Education:* City College (now City College of the City University of New York), B.A. (cum laude), 1953; University of Paris, diplome, 1955; Harvard University, Ph.D., 1958. *Politics:* Radical. *Religion:* None. *Home:* 30 Griggs Rd., Brookline, Mass. 02146. *Office:* Department of Psychology, 413 Mugar, Northeastern University, Boston, Mass. 02115.

CAREER: Northeastern University, Boston, Mass., assistant professor, 1958-64, associate professor, 1964-69, professor of psychology, 1969—. Chairman of standardization working group of American National Standards Association; visiting research associate, Technische Hochschule, Stuttgart, Germany, 1962. *Member:* American Psychological Association, Acoustical Society of America (fellow),

Psychonomic Society, American Association for the Advancement of Science, Phi Beta Kappa.

WRITINGS: (Contributor) J. V. Tobias, editor, *Foundations of Modern Auditory Theory*, Volume I, Academic Press, 1970; (contributor) *Psychology Today: An Introduction*, CRM Books, 1970, revised edition, 1974; (editor with A. R. Moskowitz and J. C. Stevens) *Sensation and Measurement: Papers in Honor of S. S. Stevens II*, Reidel, 1974; (editor) *Experimental Sensory Psychology*, Scott, Foresman, 1975. Contributor of more than thirty-five articles to hearing and psychology journals, including *Journal of the Acoustical Society of America, Journal of Experimental Psychology*, and *Perception and Psychophysics*. Member of editorial board of *Sensory Processes*.

WORK IN PROGRESS: Research on human hearing, with normal and hard-of-hearing people.

AVOCATIONAL INTERESTS: Cross-country and downhill skiing, folkdancing, chess.

* * *

SCHEINGOLD, Stuart A(llen) 1931-

PERSONAL: Born December 22, 1931, in Cleveland, Ohio; son of Morton F. (a dentist) and Theresa (Phillips) Scheingold; married Ruth Nash Majdrakoff, December 25, 1955 (divorced, 1965); married Leanora Dreisinger (a therapist and author), June 3, 1968. *Education:* Ohio State University, B.S., 1953; University of California, Berkeley, M.A., 1960, Ph.D., 1962. *Religion:* Jewish. *Home:* 616 38th Ave., Seattle, Wash. 98122. *Office:* Department of Political Science, University of Washington, Seattle, Wash. 98195.

CAREER: University of California, Davis, assistant professor of political science, 1962-64; Harvard University, Center for International Affairs, Cambridge, Mass., research associate, 1964-66; University of Wisconsin, Madison, assistant professor, 1966-69, associate professor of political science, 1969-70; University of Washington, Seattle, associate professor, 1970-74, professor of political science, 1974—. *Military service:* U.S. Air Force, 1954-56; became first lieutenant. *Member:* American Political Science Association, Law and Society Association, American Civil Liberties Union. *Awards, honors:* Social Science Research Council fellowships, 1960, 1961, and 1967.

WRITINGS: The Rule of Law in European Integration: The Path of the Schuman Plan, Yale University Press, 1965; (with Leon N. Lindberg) *Europe's Would-Be Polity: Patterns of Change in the European Community*, Prentice-Hall, 1970; *The Law in Political Integration*, Center for International Affairs, Harvard University, 1971; (editor with Lindberg) *Regional Integration: Theory and Research*, Harvard University Press, 1971; *The Politics of Rights: Lawyers, Public Policy, and Political Change*, Yale University Press, 1974. Contributor to *International Organization, American Scholar, International Studies Quarterly*, and *Journal of Public Law*.

WORK IN PROGRESS: Research in the role of lawyers in American politics, the police in American politics, and the politics of criminal justice processes.

* * *

SCHERER, Jacqueline Rita 1931-

PERSONAL: Born June 29, 1931, in Oceanside, N.Y.; daughter of Louis R. (a chemist) and Agnes (a nurse; maiden name, Reilly) Hyman; married Ralph S. Scherer (an engineer), June 7, 1952; children: Susan, Judy, Kathie, Randall. *Education:* Barnard College, student, 1952; Columbia University, B.A., 1952; Wayne State University, M.A., 1956; Syracuse University, Ph.D., 1969. *Home:* 842 Westchester, Grosse Pointe Park, Mich. 48230. *Office:* Department of Sociology, Oakland University, Rochester, Mich. 48063.

CAREER: University of London, London, England, research associate in department of higher education, 1967-70; Schoolcraft College, Livonia, Mich., instructor in sociology, 1970-71; Oakland University, Rochester, Mich., assistant professor of sociology, 1971—. *Member:* American Sociological Association, American Association of University Professors.

WRITINGS: Contemporary Community: Sociological Illusion or Reality, Tavistock Publications, 1972. Contributor to professional journals.

WORK IN PROGRESS: Community research.

* * *

SCHISGAL, Oscar 1901- (Jackson Cole, Stuart Hardy)

PERSONAL: Born February 23, 1901, in Belgium; son of Nathan (a merchant) and Helen (Blumenthal) Schisgal; married Lillian Gelberg (a writer), September 19, 1926; children: Richard, James. *Education:* Attended College of the City of New York (now City College of the City University of New York), 1919-21, and New York University, 1921-23. *Politics:* Independent. *Home:* 85 East End Ave., New York, N.Y. 10028.

CAREER: Author and speechwriter. *Member:* Authors League, Authors Guild, Society of Magazine Writers, American Society of Composers, Authors, and Publishers, Overseas Press Club. *Awards, honors:* Benjamin Franklin Award for magazine writing.

WRITINGS: Barron Ixell, Crime Breaker, Longmans, Green, 1929; *The Devil's Daughter*, Fiction League, 1932; *Swastika*, Knopf, 1939; *The Big Store*, Prentice-Hall, 1955; *Laura Jane Sees Everything at Hess's* (children's book), Public Service Syndicate, 1966; *The Magic of Mergers: The Saga of Meshulam Riklis*, Little, Brown, 1968; *That Remarkable Creature, the Snail* (children's book), Messner, 1970; *My Years with Xerox*, Doubleday, 1972; *Out of One Small Chest: The History of the Bowery Savings Bank*, American Management Association, 1975.

Novels; under pseudonym Jackson Cole: *The Ramblin' Kid*, G. H. Watt, 1933; *Gun Justice*, G. H. Watt, 1933; *The Outlaws of Caja Basin*, G. H. Watt, 1934; *The Cholla Kid*, G. H. Watt, 1935; *The Outlaw Trail*, G. H. Watt, 1935; *Black Gold: A Story of the Texas Rangers*, William Caslon Co., 1936; *Six-gun Stampede*, Dodge Publishing, 1937; *The Miracle at Gopher Creek*, Green Circle Books, 1938; *Lone Star Law*, M. S. Mill, 1939; *Lone Star Silver*, M. S. Mill, 1939; *Lone Star Legion*, M. S. Mill, 1940; *Lone Star Terror*, M. S. Mill, 1940; *Lone Star Treasure*, Arcadia House, 1944; *The Valley of Revenge*, Arcadia House, 1944; *Haunted Valley*, Arcadia House, 1945; *The Frontier Legion*, Arcadia House, 1945; *The Devil's Legion*, Arcadia House, 1946.

Novels; under pseudonym Stuart Hardy: *The Man from Nowhere*, Macaulay Co., 1935; *Arizona Justice*, Green Circle Books, 1936; *Montana Bound*, Green Circle Books, 1936; *The Mountains Are My Kingdom*, Green Circle Books, 1937; *Trouble from Texas*, Macaulay Co., 1938.

Also author of five screenplays and 20 radio and television plays. Contributor to periodicals.

WORK IN PROGRESS: Several magazine articles.

* * *

SCHLESINGER, Hilde S(tephanie)

PERSONAL: Born in Vienna, Austria; daughter of Edmond Robert and Frida Schlesinger. *Education:* University of Arizona, B.A. (cum laude), 1948; University of Louisville, M.D., 1953. *Office:* Mental Health Services for the Deaf, 1474 Fifth Ave., San Francisco, Calif. 94143.

CAREER: U.S. Public Health Service Hospital, Boston, Mass., intern, 1953-54, staff member, 1954-55; U.S. Public Health Service Hospital, San Francisco, Calif., senior surgeon, 1960-62; Langley Porter Neuropsychiatric Institute, San Francisco, Calif., resident in psychiatry, 1962-64, fellow in child psychiatry, 1964-66; Mental Health Services for the Deaf, San Francisco, Calif., project director, working with University of California at San Francisco, State Department of Mental Hygiene, and Langley Porter Neuropsychiatric Institute, 1966—. Fellow of Center for Training in Community Psychiatry and Mental Health Administration, 1966-68, member of faculty, 1968-70; assistant clinical professor at University of California, San Francisco, 1969-73, associate clinical professor, 1973—. Member of guest faculty at San Francisco State College (now University), 1967, University of Rochester, 1969, San Fernando Valley State College, 1969, 1970, 1971, Western Maryland College, 1971, and University of Maryland's Institute on Services for the Hearing Handicapped. Member of board of fellows of Gallaudet College, 1974. Lecturer at workshops for parents, teachers, and vocational counselors for the deaf. *Military service:* U.S. Public Health Service, senior surgeon and medical officer in Foreign Quarantine Station of American Consulate General, 1953-60, active duty, 1955-60; served in Germany; became lieutenant commander.

MEMBER: American Psychiatric Association (fellow), Society for Research in Child Development, National Association for the Deaf, California Psychiatric Association, Alpha Omega Alpha. *Awards, honors:* Grants from Social and Rehabilitation Services, 1967-68, and 1968-71; Rosenberg Foundation grant, 1971-74; San Francisco Foundation grant, 1971-74; U.S. Office of Education grant, 1971-77; U.S. Department of Health, Education, and Welfare grant, 1971-75; fellow of American Psychiatric Association, 1973; Dan Cloud Memorial Leadership Award from California State University (Northridge), 1974.

WRITINGS: (With Kathryn P. Meadow) *Sound and Sign: Childhood Deafness and Mental Health*, University of California Press, 1972.

Contributor: David Lille, editor, *Parent Programs in Child Development Centers: First Chance for Children*, Volume I, University of North Carolina Press, 1972; D. W. Naiman, editor, *Inservice Training of Afterclass Staff in Residential Schools for Deaf Children*, Deafness Research and Training Center, New York University, 1972; R. C. Sampson, editor, *State Association Manual*, National Association of the Deaf, 1972; I. M. Schlesinger and Lila Namir, editors, *Current Trends in the Study of Sign Languages of the Deaf*, Mouton & Co., 1974; Norbert Enzer, editor, *Workbook for Pre-School Teachers*, University of North Carolina Press, 1974; *What the Deaf Child Sees and Knows* (pamphlet), Los Angeles Junior Arts Museum, in press.

Contributor to proceedings; contributor of about fifteen articles and reviews to professional journals, including *Hearing and Speech News*, *Exceptional Children*, *Community Mental Health Journal*, *American Annals of the Deaf*, *Deaf American*, and *Psychiatry Digest*. Member of editorial boards of *American Annals of the Deaf* and *Professional Rehabilitation Workers with the Adult Deaf*.

WORK IN PROGRESS: Handbook for Parents and Teachers of Deaf Children, with Kathryn P. Meadow, for University of California Press, completion expected in 1976.

BIOGRAPHICAL/CRITICAL SOURCES: American Medical News, June 17, 1974.

* * *

SCHMID, Elenore 1939-

PERSONAL: Born March 15, 1939, in Lucerne, Switzerland; daughter of Josef and Elise (Wunderli) Schmid; married Aja Iskander Schmidlin (a painter), 1969 (divorced, 1973); children: Caspar Iskander. *Education:* School of Arts and Crafts, Lucerne, Switzerland, degree in graphics, 1961. *Home:* Wasserwerkstrasse 27, 8006 Zurich, Switzerland.

CAREER: Worked in graphics in Zurich, Switzerland, 1961-64, Paris, 1965, and in New York, N.Y., 1965-68; author and illustrator of children's books. *Awards, honors:* Awards of excellence from societies of illustrators in New York, Bolognia, and Bratislava.

WRITINGS—Children's books: (Self-illustrated) *The Tree*, Quist, 1966; (self-illustrated) *Horns Everywhere*, Quist, 1967; (illustrator) Hans Baumann, *Fenny*, Pantheon, 1968; (self-illustrated) *Tonia*, Putnam, 1970; (illustrator) James Kruss, *Die Geschichte vom grossen A* (title means "The Story of Big A"), Thienemanns Verlag, 1973.

WORK IN PROGRESS: New illustrations and children's books.

* * *

SCHMITT, David (Edward) 1940-

PERSONAL: Born February 26, 1940, in East Cleveland, Ohio; son of Edward William (a sales manager) and Violet (a registered nurse; maiden name, Gilliam) Schmitt; married Gabrielle Condron (a registered nurse), October 23, 1965; children: Alana, Michael, Kara. *Education:* Miami University, Oxford, Ohio, B.A., 1961; University of Texas, Ph.D., 1971. *Religion:* Nonsectarian. *Residence:* Medfield, Mass. *Office:* Department of Political Science, Northeastern University, Boston, Mass. 02115.

CAREER: Northeastern University, Boston, Mass., assistant professor, 1970-74, associate professor of political science, 1974—. *Military service:* U.S. Navy, 1961-65; became lieutenant. *Member:* American Political Science Association, American Association for Public Administration, American Committee for Irish Studies.

WRITINGS: The Irony of Irish Democracy: The Impact of Political Culture on Administrative and Democratic Political Development in Ireland, Heath, 1973; (editor and contributor) *Dynamics of the Third World: Political and Social Change*, Winthrop, 1974; *Violence in Northern Ireland: Ethnic Conflict and Radicalization in an International Setting*, General Learning Press, 1974. Contributor to *Administration*, *Eire-Ireland* and other journals.

WORK IN PROGRESS: With James A. Medeiros, *The*

Dynamics of Responsive Bureaucracy, for Duxbury Press; research on management theory and comparative ethnic conflict.

* * *

SCHMITT, Martin (Ferdinand) 1917-

PERSONAL: Born March 25, 1917, in River Forest, Ill.; son of Ferdinand Henry (a businessman) and Clara Elizabeth (Grauer) Schmitt; married Martha Foster (a librarian), April 9, 1948; children: Sallie (Mrs. Gary Lowenthal). *Education:* University of Illinois, B.S., 1938, B.S., 1939. *Home:* 45 Sunset Dr., Eugene, Ore. 97403. *Office:* University of Oregon Library, Eugene, Ore. 97403.

CAREER: Eureka College, Eureka, Ill., librarian, 1939-40; University of Idaho, Moscow, assistant librarian, 1946-47; University of Oregon, Eugene, curator of special collections, 1947—. Editor, Champoeg Press, 1953-59. *Military service:* U.S. Army,1942-45; became sergeant. *Member:* Society of American Archivists, American Library Association, Cannon Hunters Association of Seattle. *Awards, honors:* Waldo Gifford Leland Award from Society of American Archivists, 1972, for *Catalogue of Manuscripts: University of Oregon Library*.

WRITINGS: (Editor) *General George Crook*, University of Oklahoma Press, 1946; (with Dee Brown) *Fighting Indians of the West*, Scribner, 1948; (with Brown) *Trail Driving Days*, Scribner, 1952; (editor) *Journal of Travel by E. S. McComas*, Champoeg Press, 1954; (with Brown) *Settler's West*, Scribner, 1955; (editor) *Cattle Drives of David Shirk*, Champoeg Press, 1956; *Catalogue of Manuscripts: University of Oregon Library*, University of Oregon, 1971. Editor of *Call Number*, 1957-68, and *Imprint: Oregon*, 1973—.

WORK IN PROGRESS: Cats in Art; editing pioneer diaries and letters.

* * *

SCHMULLER, Aaron 1910-

PERSONAL: Born May 27, 1910, in Lakovich-Minsk, Poland (now part of Russia); came to United States in 1923, naturalized in 1947; son of Joseph Gerson (a lawyer) and Rachel (Muraskin) Schmuller; married Sara Riba, June 29, 1940; children: David, Joseph. *Education:* Primarily self-educated; attended City College of New York (now City College of the City University of New York), 1933. *Home and office:* 9227 Kaufman Pl., Brooklyn, N.Y. 11236.

CAREER: Has held various jobs, including delivery boy, store clerk, dishwasher in a summer hotel, store manager, laundry worker, section-head in a mail-order house, and glove worker; owner and manager of food stores and laundromats in Brooklyn, N.Y., 1940-68; Parthenon Publishing Co., Brooklyn, N.Y., owner and director, 1962—. Poet and translator. *Member:* Poetry Society of America, American Poetry League.

WRITINGS: Man in the Mirror (poems), Harbinger, 1945; *Moments of Meditation: A Collection of Poems, and Translations from Yiddish* (translations are by Schmuller from the poetry of Joseph Bovshover), Humphries, 1953; (editor, translator, and author of introduction) *Treblinka Grass: Poetical Translations from the Yiddish*, Shulsinger, 1957; *Crossing the Borderland: Poems, Prose Poems, and Poetical Translations* (Schmuller's own work, and his translations), Villiers, 1959.

(With Delina Margot-Parle and Grace Gilombardo Fox) *Three Contemporary Poets: Delina Margot-Parle, Aaron Schmuller, Grace Gilombardo Fox*, Poets of America Publishing, 1960; (editor with Mildred Moon Howell) *The Muse Anthology*, Parthenon Publishing, 1962; (editor with Howell and Bonnie Parker) *The Singing Muse Anthology*, Parthenon Publishing, 1963; (contributor) Helen G. Woods, editor, *The Guild Anthology*, Guild Quarterly Press, 1966; *While Man Exists: A Collection of Poems and Translations from the Yiddish* (Part I consists of original poems by the author; Part II includes his translations from the poetry of Hersh Glick and other Jewish poets), Parthenon Publishing, 1970; *Triumphalis: Poems, and Translations* (Schmuller's own work and his translations), Parthenon Publishing, 1973; *Sixty-Five at Sixty-Five: Poems, and Translations from the Yiddish and the Russian* (Schmuller's own work and his translations), Parthenon Publishing, in press.

Poems are represented in more than twenty anthologies, including *New Orlando Anthology, Golden Year Anthology, Yearbook of American Poetry, Golden Quill Anthology*, and *Prairie Poet Anthology*. Contributor of poems and translations to more than one hundred fifty periodicals, including *Poet Lore, Humanist, Pegasus, Judaism Quarterly, Phylon, Fairleigh Dickinson Literary Review, Western Poet*, and *Bitterroot*.

WORK IN PROGRESS: Research for a biography of Professor Alexander Schmuller of Holland, a cousin.

* * *

SCHNEIDER, Ronald M(ilton) 1932-

PERSONAL: Born September 29, 1932, in Minneapolis, Minn.; son of Howard Edward (a civil servant) and Mildred (a teacher; maiden name, Davis) Schneider; married Anita Lombana (a librarian), June 15, 1954; children: Ronald Milton, Jr., Carol Jean, Diana Marie. *Education:* Northwestern University, B.S., 1954; Princeton University, M.A., 1956, Ph.D., 1958. *Politics:* Independent. *Religion:* Methodist. *Home:* 36 East Glen Ave., Ridgewood, N.J. 07450. *Office:* Department of Political Science, Queens College of the City University of New York, Kissena Blvd., Flushing, N.Y. 11367.

CAREER: Foreign Policy Research Institute, Philadelphia, Pa., research assistant, 1956-57; U.S. Department of State, Washington, D.C., intelligence research specialist, 1957-63; Columbia University, New York, N.Y., visiting associate professor, 1963-66, associate professor of political science, 1966-69; Queens College of the City University of New York, Flushing, N.Y., professor of political science, 1969—, head of department, 1973—. Consultant to U.S. Department of State, 1974—. *Member:* American Political Science Association, Latin American Studies Association, International Studies Association, Inter-American Association for Democracy and Freedom, Academy of Political Science, Center for Inter-American Relations. *Awards, honors:* Fulbright-Hays faculty research fellowship, 1966-67.

WRITINGS: Communism in Guatemala: 1944-1954, Praeger, 1959; *Brazil Election Factbook*, Institute for the Comparative Study of Political Systems, 1965; *An Atlas of Latin American Affairs*, Praeger, 1965; *Latin American Panorama*, Foreign Policy Association, 1966; *The Political System of Brazil*, Columbia University Press, 1971. Contributor to symposia and journals. Member of editorial board of *World Affairs*, 1970—; advisory editor of *Contemporary Politics*, 1972—.

WORK IN PROGRESS: Modernization and the Military

in Brazil: 1822-1964; a monograph on Brazilian foreign and defense policy-making; a comparative study of long-lived military regimes.

AVOCATIONAL INTERESTS: Traveling, watching soccer.

* * *

SCHNEIER, Edward (Vincent) 1939-

PERSONAL: Surname rhymes with "fire"; born May 25, 1939, in Bronx, N.Y.; son of Edward Vincent (a businessman) and Lillian (a secretary; maiden name, Buhr) Schneier; married Janice Bernier, June 16, 1960 (divorced, 1974); children: Andrew V., Katherine W. *Education:* Oberlin College, B.A., 1960; Claremont Graduate School, M.A., 1961, Ph.D., 1963. *Politics:* Democrat. *Religion:* None. *Home:* 1 Harrison St., New York, N.Y. 10013. *Office:* Department of Political Science, City College of the City University of New York, New York, N.Y. 10031.

CAREER: Legislative assistant to Senator Birch Bayh in Washington, D.C., 1963-64; Johns Hopkins University, Baltimore, Md., assistant professor of political science, 1964-65; Princeton University, Princeton, N.J., assistant professor of political science, 1965-68; City College of the City University of New York, New York, N.Y., associate professor of political science, 1968—, acting director of Urban Legal Studies program, 1974—. Co-founder of Movement for a New Congress, 1970; Democratic candidate for mayor in Princeton, N.J., 1971; president of Princeton Community Democratic Organization, 1970-71; member of Downtown Independent Democrats. *Member:* American Political Science Association. *Awards, honors:* Brookings Institute fellowship, 1963-64.

WRITINGS: (Editor) *Policy-Making in American Government*, Basic Books, 1969; (reviser) Julius Turner, *Party and Constituency*, revised edition (Schneier was not associated with earlier editions), Johns Hopkins Press, 1970; (with William Murphy) *Vote Power*, Prentice-Hall, 1970, revised edition, Doubleday, 1974. Contributor to *Annals of the American Academy of Political and Social Science*, *Bulletin of the Atomic Sciences*, *Nation*, and *Society*.

WORK IN PROGRESS: With Janice Bernier Schneier, *Ideals and Realities of American Democracy*, completion expected in 1975; with Bertram Gross, *The Legislative Struggle*, 1976.

* * *

SCHOENBERGER, Guido L. 1891-1974

February 26, 1891—August 20, 1974; German-born American art historian, educator, museum curator, and author of books on art. Obituaries: *New York Times*, August 23, 1974.

* * *

SCHOEP, Arthur Paul 1920-

PERSONAL: Surname rhymes with "hope"; born December 13, 1920, in Orange City, Iowa; son of Arie Anton (a baker) and Lena (DeMey) Schoep; married Donna Swainey (a musician), June 8, 1957; children: Laurence Dale. *Education:* University of South Dakota, B.F.A. (summa cum laude), 1942; Eastman School of Music, performer's certificate in voice and M.Mus., 1945; New England Conservatory of Music, artist's diploma in voice, 1948; University of Colorado, D.M.A., 1962. *Home:* 1705 Emery Dr., Denton, Tex. 76201. *Office:* School of Music, North Texas State University, Denton, Tex. 76203.

CAREER: North Texas State College (now University), Denton, instructor in music, 1948-50; Tyler Junior College, Tyler, Tex., head of voice program, 1951-53; professional singer in New York, N.Y., 1953-55; New England Conservatory of Music, Boston, Mass., instructor in opera, 1955-58; University of Tennessee, Knoxville, assistant professor of music, 1958-60; Colorado Woman's College, Denver, associate professor of music, 1962-67; North Texas State University, Denton, professor of music, 1967—. Associate director of Oglebay Institute Opera Workshop, 1954—; artistic director and general manager of Denver Lyric Theatre, 1961-67; director of voice and opera division of Summer School of Arts, Elliot Lake, Ontario, 1966—. Soloist with Boston Symphony, Denver Symphony, Rochester Civic and Philharmonic Orchestra. Guest artist with Brussels Opera, 1955. Member of national tours with Goldovsky Opera Theater, 1953, 1954, 1968. Performer in concert, oratorio, and radio in Holland and Germany. *Military service:* U.S. Army Reserve, Infantry, 1942-44; became second lieutenant. *Member:* National Opera Association (vice-president, 1968-71; president, 1972-73), National Association of Teachers of Singing, American Guild of Musical Artists, Actor's Equity.

WRITINGS: (Translator from the Italian with Boris Goldovsky) Giambattista Casti, librettist, *King Theodore in Venice* (music composed by Giovanni Paisiello), Presser, 1963; (with Daniel Harris) *Word-to-Word Translation of Songs and Arias* (Italian to English), Scarecrow, 1972; (with Goldovsky) *Bringing Soporano Arias to Life*, G. Schirmer, 1973. Contributor to *National Association of Teachers of Singing Bulletin*, *National Opera Association Journal*, and *Opera/Canada*. Contributing editor of *Opera/Canada*, 1974—.

* * *

SCHREIBER, Flora (Rheta) 1918-

PERSONAL: Born April 24, 1918, in New York, N.Y.; daughter of William Leonard (a librarian) and Esther (a librarian; maiden name, Aaronson) Schreiber. *Education:* Columbia University, B.S., 1938, M.A., 1939; Central School of Speech Training and Dramatic Art, London, certificate, 1938; attended New York University, 1941-42. *Politics:* Independent. *Religion:* "Free thinker." *Home:* 32 Gramercy Park S., New York, N.Y. 10003. *Agent:* Patricia Myrer, McIntosh & Otis, Inc., 18 East 41st St., New York, N.Y. 10017. *Office:* John Jay College of the City University of New York, 444 West 56th St., New York, N.Y. 10019.

CAREER: Instructor at Exeter College, University of the Southwest, England, 1937; Brooklyn College (now Brooklyn College of the City University of New York), Brooklyn, N.Y., instructor in speech and dramatic art, 1944-46, creator and producer of radio forum, 1944-46; Adelphi College (now University), Garden City, Long Island, N.Y., assistant professor of speech and dramatic arts, 1947-53, director of radio and television division in Center for Creative Arts, 1948-51; City University of New York, New York, N.Y., lecturer, 1952—, member of faculty of John Jay College of Criminal Justice, 1964—, professor of English and speech, 1974—, director of public relations, director of publications, and assistant to president of John Jay College, 1964—. Lecturer in writing, New School for Social Research, 1952—. Producer of community theatre forum for NBC-Radio, 1949. Consultant to National Broadcasting Company, Batten, Barton, Durstine & Osborn, Inc., and other organizations.

MEMBER: American Association of University Professors, Speech Communications Association, Speech Association of America, American National Theater and Academy, American Association of University Women, Society of Magazine Writers (secretary, 1963; vice-president, 1973-74), Authors League of America, Speech Association of Eastern States. *Awards, honors:* Family Service Association Award, 1960, for magazine article, "The Tragedy of Emotional Divorce"; certificate of merit from Dictionary of International Biology, 1969.

WRITINGS: (With Vincent Persichetti) *William Schuman* (biography), G. Schirmer, 1954; *Your Child's Speech: A Practical Guide for Parents for the First Five Years*, Putnam, 1956, revised edition published as *Your Child's Speech*, Ballantine, 1973; *A Job with a Future in Law Enforcement and Related Fields*, Grosset, 1970; *Sybil*, Regnery, 1973.

Author of three-act play, "Bending Sickle." Also author of short stories, opera libretti, and additional plays. Monthly columnist, *Science Digest*; author of syndicated articles for Belle-McClure and United Feature Syndicate, Inc., and for New York Times Special Features. Contributor of over 400 articles to magazines and journals, including *Cosmopolitan, Redbook, Ladies' Home Journal, Quarterly Journal of Speech, Poet Lore, French Forum*, and *Quarterly of Film, Radio and Television*. Drama critic, *Players' Magazine*, 1941-46; psychiatry editor, *Science Digest*.

WORK IN PROGRESS: A case history in the field of parapsychology, to be handled as a "nonfiction novel"; a "psycho-historical-biographical" book about recent U.S. presidents, particularly Kennedy, Johnson, and Nixon; *The Nazi Aftermath*, recollections of concentration camps.

SIDELIGHTS: Flora Schreiber's background in psychology and psychiatry was the point of embarkation for the writing of *Sybil*, a nonfiction novel—the biography of a real person. Ms. Schreiber says: "Sybil's condition is acting-out in its purest form—acting out what lies buried in the human unconscious. That condition, as I've tried to represent it, lays bare our unconscious, holding the mirror up to our deepest fears, frustrations, angers, tensions. Perhaps to know Sybil is to know ourselves."

Ms. Schreiber told *CA*: "I always believed that a 'woman's place is as far away from home as her talents will take her!' When I was nineteen, I published a scholarly piece, a psychograph of the poetry of Emily Dickinson, juxtaposing her dominant images to achieve a dramatic and psychological whole. This, I think, was an early precursor of the kind of talent that produced *Sybil*."

Sybil has been published in fourteen countries, including Italy, France, Denmark, Japan, Switzerland, and Turkey. The film rights have been sold to Lorimar Productions.

* * *

SCHULL, (John) Joseph 1916-

PERSONAL: Born February 6, 1916, in Watertown, S.D.; son of Charles Henry (a lawyer) and Aveline Alice (Travers) Schull; married Helene Gougeon (a journalist), January 8, 1955; children: Christiane, Joseph, Michael. *Education:* Attended Queen's University and University of Saskatchewan. *Religion:* Roman Catholic. *Home:* 180 Grande Cote Rd., Rosemere, Quebec, Canada.

CAREER: Employed in banking and advertising. *Military service:* Royal Canadian Naval Volunteer Reserve, 1941-45; became lieutenant commander.

WRITINGS: *The Legend of Ghost Lagoon* (narrative poem), Macmillan, 1937; *I, Jones, Soldier*, Macmillan, 1944; *The Far Distant Ships*, E. Cloutier, 1952; *The Salt Water Men: Canada's Deep Sea Sailors*, St. Martin's, 1957; *100 Years of Banking in Canada: A History of the Toronto-Dominion Bank*, Copp, 1958; *Battle for the Rock: The Story of Wolfe and Montcalm*, St. Martin's, 1960; *Ships of the Great Days: Canada's Navy in World War II*, St. Martin's, 1962; *Laurier: The First Canadian*, St. Martin's, 1966; *The Nation Makers*, Macmillan, 1967; *The Jinker* (novel), Macmillan (London), 1968, Dodd, 1969; *Rebellion: The Rising in French Canada–1837*, Macmillan, 1971; *The Century of the Sun*, Macmillan, 1971; *Edward Blake*, Macmillan, 1975.

Also author of over 200 radio plays and 30 television plays.

WORK IN PROGRESS: *History of Ontario since 1867*.

* * *

SCHWARTZ, Larry 1922-

PERSONAL: Born March 25, 1922, in New York, N.Y.; son of Samuel L. (an engineer) and Esther L. (a writer) Schwartz; married wife, Sheila (a professor and writer), June 30, 1949; children: Nancy, Jonathan, Elizabeth. *Education:* Union College, A.B., 1941; graduate study at Columbia University, 1941-42, 1946-49, Yale University, 1943-44, and University of Michigan, 1944-45. *Politics:* Democrat. *Religion:* Jewish. *Home:* 5 Spies Rd., New Paltz, N.Y. 12561. *Office:* Books by Phone, 717 Fifth Ave., New York, N.Y. 10022.

CAREER: President, Wexton Advertising Agency, 1947-62; Crowell Collier & Macmillan, Inc., New York, N.Y., corporate director of advertising, 1964-66; publisher, Travel Books, Inc., 1969-73; Books by Phone (of National Order Systems, Inc.), New York, N.Y., founder and president, 1974—. Consultant to Xerox Education Group, 1973. *Military service:* U.S. Army, intelligence, 1943-46; became second lieutenant. *Member:* Phi Beta Kappa.

WRITINGS: *World Travel and Vacation Almanac*, Harper, 1970. Contributing editor of *Sales Management*, 1954-58.

WORK IN PROGRESS: *The Great Retirement Robbery; How to Stay Healthy Daily and Young Forever*.

* * *

SCOTT, Herbert 1931-

PERSONAL: Born February 8, 1931, in Norman, Okla.; son of Herbert Hicks (an educator) and Betty (an educator; maiden name, Pickard) Scott; married Virginia Corbin, August 24, 1950 (divorced June 29, 1972); married Shirley Stephens (a professor), October 8, 1972; children: (first marriage) Herbert A., Megan, Rannah, Erin, Clay, Kyla; (second marriage) Wallace, Brian (stepchildren). *Education:* Fresno State College, B.A., 1964; University of Iowa, M.F.A., 1966; also studied at University of Oklahoma, Lake Forest College, College of Sequoias, and Fresno City College. *Home:* 2620 Outlook, Kalamazoo, Mich. 49001. *Office:* Department of English, Western Michigan University, Kalamazoo, Mich. 49001.

CAREER: Worked at Safeway Stores in various California cities, 1953-64, began as clerk, became produce manager; Southeast Missouri State College, Cape Girardeau, instructor in English, 1966-68; Western Michigan University, Kalamazoo, assistant professor, 1968-72, associate professor of English, 1972—. Creative writing coordinator for

Michigan Council for the Arts, 1971-74; chairman of Michigan Youth Arts Festival Creative Writing Awards; member of Michigan Cultural Activities Board. Has given poetry readings at colleges and universities. *Military service:* U.S. Naval Reserve, 1948-54. *Member:* Michigan Council of Teachers of English.

WRITINGS: Disguises (poems), University of Pittsburgh Press, 1974; *The Shoplifter's Handbook* (poems), Blue Mountain Press, 1974. Contributor of poems to literary magazines, including *Beloit Poetry Journal, Epoch, Harper's, Iowa Review, North American Review*, and *Southern Review*.

WORK IN PROGRESS: Groceries, a book of poems; another book of poems.

* * *

SCOTT, Sheila 1927-

PERSONAL: Born April 27, 1927, in Worcester, England. *Education:* Attended Alice Ottley School, Worcester, England, 1931-43. *Home:* 593 Park West, London W2 2RB, England.

CAREER: Competitive pilot, actress, lecturer, writer. *Member:* Aircraft Owners and Pilots Association, Royal Aeronautical Society, Royal Geographical Society (fellow), Institute of Journalists, Guild of Air Pilots and Air Navigators, British Balloon and Airships Club, British Women Pilots' Association, Royal Aero Club, Whirly Girls, Institute of Sports Medicine, Actors Equity, British Light Aviation Center, Seaplane Club, Ninety-Nines, Inc., Tiger Club, Zonta. *Awards, honors:* Jean Lennox Bird Award, 1961, 1971, for noteworthy achievement in aviation; Brabazon of Tara Award, 1965, 1967, 1968, for outstanding achievements in aviation by a woman pilot; Sir Alan Cobham Achievement Award, 1965, 1966, 1971; Amelia Earhart Medal, 1966; Silver Award of Merit from British Guild of Air Pilots and Air Navigators, 1966, for first round the world flight records; Isabella D'este Award from Italian government, 1966, for exceptional undertakings accomplished; diploma from Academia Romana Vel Sodalitis Quirinale, for world flight; Harmon Trophy, 1967, for World's Outstanding Aviatrix; Britannia Trophy and Silver Medal, 1968, Gold Medal, 1972, from Royal Aero Club of the United Kingdom; member of the Order of the British Empire, 1968; Lady Hay Drummond WIA Award, 1973; honorary naval aviator of Royal Navy; awarded over fifty trophies for aircraft racing events.

WRITINGS: I Must Fly, Hodder & Stoughton, 1968; (contributor) William Wordsworth, editor, *Women and Men's Daughters*, Schlesinger, 1970; (contributor) Martin Boddey, editor, *The Twelfth Man*, Cassell, 1971; *On Top of the World*, Hodder & Stoughton, 1973, published as *Barefoot in the Sky*, Macmillan, 1974.

WORK IN PROGRESS: Children's books; a novel on flying; philosophical short stories; a documentary film on personal solo world flights in small aircraft.

SIDELIGHTS: Sheila Scott, holder of 100 world-class flying records, was the first person ever to fly a light aircraft solo over the North Pole and Arctic Ocean. She has flown solo three times around the world.

BIOGRAPHICAL/CRITICAL SOURCES: J.R.L. Anderson, *Ulysses Factor*, Hodder & Stoughton, 1970.

* * *

SCURO, Vincent 1951-

PERSONAL: Born September 28, 1951, in Jersey City, N.J.; son of Joseph E. (an executive) and Phyllis (Amato) Scuro. *Education:* St. Peter's College, Jersey City, N.J., A.B., 1973; Fairleigh Dickinson University, graduate study, 1975—. *Politics:* Independent. *Religion:* Roman Catholic. *Residence:* Bergenfield, N.J.

CAREER: Writer and musician. Performs with five-piece rock music group, "Sweet Ensemble," playing trumpet, guitar, and bass guitar in night clubs and on cruise ships. *Member:* American Federation of Musicians.

WRITINGS: (With own photographs) *Presenting the Marching Band*, Dodd, 1974; (with Sigmund A. Lavine) *Wonders of the Bison World*, Dodd, 1975. Contributor to *Twin-Boro News* and *Pauw Wow* (of St. Peter's College).

WORK IN PROGRESS: A music book; research on the American Indian and on sports.

SIDELIGHTS: Scuro was a member of McDonald's All-American High School Marching Band in 1967. *Avocational interests:* Baseball (played on varsity team in college), photography.

* * *

SEATON, Mary Ethel ?-1974

?—1974; British educator, authority on the literature of the late Middle Ages and the Renaissance, and author of books on related subjects. Obituaries: *AB Bookman's Weekly*, October 21, 1974.

* * *

SEGRE, Claudio Giuseppe 1937-

PERSONAL: Born March 2, 1937, in Palermo, Italy; son of Emilio G. (a physicist) and Elfriede (Spiro) Segre; married Elisabeth Bregman (a professor of French), February 19, 1967; children: Gino, Francesca. *Education:* Reed College, B.A., 1957; Stanford University, M.A., 1961; University of California, Berkeley, M.A., 1964, Ph.D., 1970. *Residence:* Austin, Tex. *Office:* Department of History, University of Texas, Austin, Tex. 78712.

CAREER: United Press International (UPI), New York, N.Y., reporter from Los Angeles, 1960-61; *Wall Street Journal*, New York, N.Y., reporter from San Francisco, 1962-63; Stanford University, Stanford, Calif., instructor in history, 1967-70; University of Texas, Austin, assistant professor of history, 1970—. *Military service:* California Army National Guard, 1960-65. *Member:* Society for Italian Historical Studies. *Awards, honors:* American Philosophical Society grant, 1970; Younger Humanist fellowship from National Endowment for the Humanities, 1973-74; American Council of Learned Societies grant, summer, 1974.

WRITINGS: Fourth Shore: The Italian Colonization of Libya (monograph), University of Chicago Press, 1974. Contributor to *Journal of Contemporary History*.

WORK IN PROGRESS: Italo Balbo: A Fascist Life, a biography of the politician and pioneer aviator, completion expected in 1978.

AVOCATIONAL INTERESTS: Bicycling, skiing, cooking.

* * *

SEITZ, William Chapin 1914-1974

June 19, 1914—October 26, 1974; American artist, art scholar, educator, critic, former curator at New York's Museum of Modern Art, and author of books on art. Obituaries: *New York Times*, October 28, 1974: *Washington Post*, October 28, 1974. (*CA*-3).

* * *

SELZER, Joae Graham 1926-

PERSONAL: Given name sounds like "joy"; born June 14, 1926, in Boston, Mass.; daughter of Collins (an insurance executive) and Hannah (a nurse; maiden name, Benton) Graham; married Norman Leymore Selzer, December 11, 1955; children: Anne Benton, Jane Graham. *Education:* Massachusetts General Hospital, R.N., 1947; University of Rochester, A.B., 1950, M.D., 1954. *Politics:* Democrat. *Religion:* Protestant. *Home:* 90 Salisbury Rd., Brookline, Mass. 02146. *Office:* 1101 Beacon St., Brookline, Mass. 02146.

CAREER: Duke Hospital, Durham, N.C., intern, 1954-55; Boston Psychopathic Hospital (now Massachusetts Mental Health Center), Boston, Mass., resident in adult psychiatry, 1955-57; Beth Israel Hospital, Boston, Mass., resident in child psychiatry, 1957-59, member of medical staff, 1959—; private practice in child and adult psychiatry in Brookline, Mass., 1959—. Instructor at Harvard Medical School, 1964—. Consultant to New England Home for Little Wanderers and Jewish Family and Children's Service. *Member:* American Psychiatric Association, American Academy of Child Psychiatry, New England Council of Child Psychiatry, Massachusetts Psychiatric Society.

WRITINGS: No More Diapers!, Delacorte, 1971; *When Children Ask About Sex*, Beacon Press, 1975. Contributor to *Journal of the American Academy of Child Psychiatry*.

WORK IN PROGRESS: A book about childbirth, for preschool-age children.

* * *

SELZER, Michael 1940-

PERSONAL: Born October 16, 1940, in Lahore, India; son of Hermann Marcus (a physician) and Kate (Neumann) Selzer. *Education:* Balliol College, Oxford, B.A., 1963, M.A., 1967; City University of New York, Ph.D., 1973. *Office:* Department of Political Science, Brooklyn College of the City University of New York, Brooklyn, N.Y. 11210.

CAREER: Brooklyn College of the City University of New York, Brooklyn, N.Y., assistant professor of political science, 1971—.

WRITINGS: Outcasts of Israel: Ethnic Tensions in the Jewish State, Council of the Sephardi Community, 1965; *The Aryanization of the Jewish State: A Polemic,* Black Star Publishing, 1967; *The Wineskin and the Wizard,* Macmillan, 1970; (editor) *Zionism Reconsidered,* Macmillan, 1970; *Politics and Jewish Purpose,* Greenleaf Books, 1972; (editor) *Kike: A Documentary History of Anti-Semitism in America,* World Publishing, 1972. General editor of "Ethnic Prejudice in America Series," World Publishing, 1970-72. Contributor to journals.

WORK IN PROGRESS: A psychological biography of Benjamin Disraeli, for Quadrangle; a psychological study of imperialism and nationalism; a critical edition of Disraeli's private papers.

* * *

SENDY, Jean 1910-

PERSONAL: Born November 16, 1910, in St. Petersburg, Russia. *Education:* Attended Sorbonne, University of Paris. *Politics:* "Strictly non-believer." *Religion:* Rationalist. *Home:* 68 rue J.J. Rousseau, Paris 75001, France.

CAREER: Formerly a journalist and translator; author. *Military service:* Fought with French regular army and with French Underground.

WRITINGS: Les Cahiers de cours de Moiese, Julliard, 1962; *Les dieux nous sont nes,* Grasset, 1966; *La Lune cle de la Bible,* Julliard, 1968; *Nous autres, gens du Moyen Age,* Julliard, 1969; *Ces dieux qui firent le ciel et la terre, le roman de la Bible,* R. Laffont, 1969, translation published as *Those Gods Who Made Heaven and Earth,* Berkley, 1972; *L'ere du Verseau,* R. Laffont, 1970, translation published as *The Coming of the Gods,* Berkley, 1973; *Plaidoyer pour un genocide,* Julliard, 1973.

WORK IN PROGRESS: Research on Biblical authenticity.

* * *

SENIOR, Clarence (Ollson) 1903-1974

June 9, 1903—September 8, 1974; American sociologist, economist, educator, and author of books on Puerto Rican migration and Latin American land reform. Obituaries: *New York Times*, September 10, 1974; *Current Biography*, November, 1974; *AB Bookman's Weekly*, November 18, 1974.

* * *

SEXTON, Anne (Harvey) 1928-1974

November 9, 1928—October 4, 1974; American poetess, teacher, and Pulitzer Prize winner. Obituaries: *New York Times*, October 6, 1974; *Washington Post*, October 6, 1974; *Time*, October 14, 1974; *Publishers Weekly*, October 28, 1974; *AB Bookman's Weekly*, December 2, 1974. (*CA*-4; *CLC* 2, 4).

* * *

SEYBOLT, Peter J(ordan)

PERSONAL: Born August 15, 1934, in Cincinnati, Ohio; son of Crosby Jordan and Jean (Bond) Seybolt; married Cynthia Taylor, December 27, 1960; children: Taylor, Amy. *Education:* University of Cincinnati, B.A., 1956; Harvard University, M.A.T., 1960, Ph.D., 1970. *Office:* Department of History, University of Vermont, Burlington, Vt. 05401.

CAREER: University of Vermont, Burlington, assistant professor, 1969-73, associate professor of history, 1974—.

WRITINGS: (Editor) *Revolutionary Education in China*, International Arts and Sciences Press, 1973; (editor) *Through Chinese Eyes*, two volumes, Praeger, 1974. Contributor of articles and reviews to scholarly journals. Editor, *Chinese Education: A Journal of Translations*.

* * *

SEYMOUR, Alan 1927-

PERSONAL: Born June 6, 1927, in Perth, West Australia; son of Herbert Augustus (a seaman) and Louisa Mary (Warren) Seymour. *Education:* Attended secondary school in Perth, Australia. *Politics:* Left. *Religion:* Atheist. *Home and office:* 74 Upland Rd., London SE22, England. *Agent:* Film Rights Ltd., 113 Wardour St., London W1, England.

CAREER: "Worked full-time for tinpot radio station in home town, Perth, W.A., went to Sydney, worked another tinpot station, then ran School of Arts in country town, Wagga Wagga, then in Sydney free-lanced and failed, returned to Perth, was film critic for Australian Broadcasting Commission, radio announcer, returned to Sydney for full-time free-lance writing in radio, television (plays and documentaries), documentary films, stage plays, literary and theatre criticism. Directed chamber operas, founded film societies and theatre groups in spare time. To England in 1961. Recently television producer and script editor with BBC Television, London." *Member:* Society of Authors, Writers' Guild. *Awards, honors:* "Swamp Creatures" was *Observer* (London) world-wide play competition finalist, 1957; "Donny Johnson" shared Sydney Journalist Club play competition prize, 1961.

WRITINGS—Plays: *The One Day of the Year* (three-act; first produced in Sydney, Australia at Palace Theatre, April, 1961), Angus & Robertson, 1962; "Donny Johnson" (two-act), first produced in Finland, at Helsinki Theatre, 1962; "Swamp Creatures" (three-act), first produced in Canberra, Australia at Canberra Repertory Theatre, 1957; "A Break in the Music" (two-act), first produced in Perth, West Australia at Perth Playhouse, 1966; "O Grave Thy Victory" (two-act), first produced in Canberra at Childer's Hall, Playwright's Conference, 1973; "The Wind From the Plain" (two-act; adapted from novel by Yashar Kemal), first produced in Turku, Finland at Civic Theatre, 1973. Also author of two-act play, "The Shattering," neither produced or published, and of two-act play, "Wanderers," scheduled for premiere in Los Angeles in 1975.

Novels: *The One Day of the Year* (based on play of same name), Souvenir Books, 1967; *The Coming Self-Destruction of the United States of America*, Souvenir Books, 1969, Grove, 1970.

Television plays: "The Runner," 1961; "Lean Liberty," 1962; "The One Day of the Year" (adaptation of play), 1962; "Auto Stop," 1964; "Trial and Torture of Sir John Rampayne," 1965; adaptation of "Three Short Stories by Jean Rhys," 1973.

Theatre critic, *Bulletin* (Sydney), 1958-61, *Observer* (London), 1964-65, *London Magazine*, 1962-65, 1971—, and *Plays and Players*, 1972—.

WORK IN PROGRESS: A play, "Mateship"; an opera libretto, "Ned Mark 2."

SIDELIGHTS: Seymour writes: "Fascinated by balance between subjective and objective, personal and social, favourite topics sex and politics. Travelled to U.K. for stage production *The One Day of the Year*, travelled and lived in Saudi Arabia, Lebanon, and mainly Turkey. Returned to U.K. in '71 for further television drama writing, recently with BBC Television finding new writers of original plays. Never been in U.S. so far, wrote *The Coming Self-Destruction of the United States of America* out of the experience of living with American enclaves in Middle East."

* * *

SHAGAN, Steve 1927-

PERSONAL: Born October 25, 1927, in New York, N.Y.; son of Barney (an owner of a pharmacy) and Ray (Anhalt) Shagan; married Elizabeth Leslie Florance, November 18, 1956; children: Robert. *Education:* Attended New York University. *Residence:* Beverly Hills, Calif. *Agent:* Jeff Berg, Creative Management Associates Ltd., 8899 Beverly Blvd., Los Angeles, Calif. 90048.

CAREER: Writer and producer; has worked as a salesman, film-printer, assistant theatre director, electrician, and advertising copywriter. Guest lecturer in screenwriting at University of Southern California. *Military service:* U.S. Coast Guard, 1944-48; served in Europe and Africa. *Member:* Writers Guild of America. *Awards, honors:* Best drama award from Writers Guild of America, 1973, for original screenplay "Save the Tiger"; nominated for Academy Award by Motion Picture Academy of Arts and Sciences, 1973, for screenplay "Save the Tiger."

WRITINGS: Save the Tiger, Dial, 1973; *City of Angels*, Putnam, 1975. Author of screenplays "Save the Tiger" and "City of Angels."

WORK IN PROGRESS: "They Shall Not Pass," a major screenplay on the Spanish Civil War, based on novel by Bruce Dalmer.

SIDELIGHTS: Shagan writes that he tries ". . . to reflect the condition of the 'average' man in current American system—the lack of and need for sharper focus of national interest in the 'small' man in our society." He has lived in Brazil, Spain, and Mexico.

* * *

SHANE, Don G(raves) 1933-

PERSONAL: Born November 11, 1933, in Henryetta, Okla.; son of George Arthur and Catherine (a nurse) Shane; married Janis R. Smith (a preschool teacher), June 22, 1956. *Education:* Oklahoma Baptist University, B.A., 1955; Central Oklahoma State College, master of teaching, 1963; University of North Carolina, Ph.D., 1969. *Religion:* Protestant. *Home:* 2605 Northwest 110th, Oklahoma City, Okla. 73120. *Office:* Department of Special Education, Central State University, Edmond, Okla. 73034.

CAREER: Probation counselor, Oklahoma County Children's Court, 1959-61; high school teacher of mentally retarded students in Oklahoma City, Okla., 1961-63; coordinator of high school work-study program in Oklahoma City, 1963-65; instructor, University of North Carolina, 1965-67; Texas Tech University, Lubbock, assistant professor of special education, 1969-71; Central Oklahoma State University, Edmond, associate professor of special education, 1971—. *Military service:* U.S. Marine Corps, 1955-59; became first lieutenant. *Member:* National Education Association, Council for Exceptional Children, Oklahoma Education Association.

WRITINGS: (With William R. Van Osdol) *Exceptional Children: Psychology Survey,* Kendall-Hunt, 1972; (with William R. Van Osdol and Bob Van Osdol) *Learning Disabilities Manual: K-12,* Idaho Research Foundation, 1973; (with William R. Van Osdol) *Introduction to Exceptional Children,* W. C. Brown, 1974. Contributor to *Education and Training of the Mentally Retarded.*

* * *

SHANK, Alan 1936-

PERSONAL: Born May 12, 1936, in Philadelphia, Pa.; son of Nathan M. (a dentist) and Cecilia (a clerk in a business office; maiden name, Greenberg) Shank; married Bernice M. Spizer, March 6, 1960; children: Steven, Naomi. *Education:* Franklin & Marshall College, B.A., 1958; University of Pennsylvania, M.G.A., 1960; Rutgers University, Ph.D., 1967. *Home address:* Mohawk Ave., Geneseo, N.Y. 14454. *Office:* Department of Political Science, State University of New York College at Geneseo, Geneseo, N.Y. 14454.

CAREER: Boston University, Boston, Mass., assistant professor of political science, 1965-70; State University of New York College at Geneseo, associate professor of political science, 1970—, acting chairman of department, 1973-75. Candidate for Geneseo Village Board of Trustees, 1972; chairman of Geneseo Town Democratic Committee; press secretary to Democratic candidate for New York State Assembly Robert O'Mara, 1974. *Member:* American Political Science Association, American Society for Public Administration, Policy Studies Organization.

WRITINGS: *New Jersey Reapportionment Politics*, Fairleigh Dickinson University Press, 1969; *Political Power and the Urban Crisis*, Holbrook, 1969, 2nd edition, 1973; (editor with Melvin R. Levin) *Educational Investment in an Urban Society*, Teachers College Press, 1970; (contributor) Levin and Norman A. Abend, editors, *Bureaucrats in Collision*, M.I.T. Press, 1971; *American Politics, Policies, and Priorities*, Holbrook, 1974; (contributor) *Local Public Library Administration* (edited by American Library Association), International City Management Association, 1975; (with Ralph Conant) *Urban Perspectives*, Holbrook, 1975.

WORK IN PROGRESS: An integrated analysis of domestic, urban, national defense, and foreign policy issues of American government, with Neil George; preparing third edition of *Political Power and the Urban Crisis*.

* * *

SHANKS, Ann Zane (Kushner)

PERSONAL: Born in Brooklyn, N.Y.; daughter of Louis and Sadye (Rosenthal) Kushner; married Ira Zane (deceased); married Robert Horton Shanks (a television network vice-president), September 25, 1959; children: (first marriage) Jennifer, Anthony; (second marriage) John. *Education:* Attended Carnegie-Mellon University and Columbia University. *Home:* 201B East 82nd St., New York, N.Y. *Office:* Comco Productions, 850 Seventh Ave., New York, N.Y. 10019.

CAREER: Photographer, film maker, writer. Columbia Broadcasting Co., New York, N.Y., script editor, 1959; National Broadcasting Co., New York, producer of local television series, "Women on the Move," 1968; Comco Productions, New York, president, 1973-75. Producer and director of film shorts, "Central Park," Columbia Pictures, 1969, "Tivoli," 1972, and "Denmark: A Loving Embrace," Danish National Tourist Office, 1973; producer and director of syndicated television series, "American Life Style," 1972-75. Photographs have been exhibited at Museum of Modern Art, Museum of the City of New York, Metropolitan Museum of Art, Jewish Museum, Caravan Gallery, and others. Moderator of special symposia at Museum of Modern Art, Educational Alliance, and Village Camera Club, all New York.

MEMBER: American Society of Magazine Photographers (member of board of governors, 1969-71), Overseas Press Club. *Awards, honors:* Cine Golden Eagle Awards, 1969, 1973; Cambodia Film Festival Award, 1971, for "Central Park"; San Francisco Film Festival Award, 1971, and American Film Festival Award, 1972, both for "Tivoli"; International Film and Television Festival Gold Awards, 1972, 1973, 1974, for "American Life Style"; received four awards in *Photography* magazine international competitions, and three *National Housing Yearbook* competition awards.

WRITINGS—Self-illustrated: *About Garbage and Stuff* (juvenile), Viking, 1973.

Illustrator: Bob Shanks, *The Name's the Game*, Chilton, 1961.

Contributor of photographs to *Adolescent Development*, by E. B. Hurlock, McGraw, 3rd edition, 1967, and to textbooks published by Behrman House, Random House, Simon & Schuster, Lippincott, and other houses. Contributor to *New Jewish Encyclopedia*, and other yearbooks and encyclopedias, and to periodicals, including *Life, Look, Time, Esquire, New York, Camera 35, Cosmopolitan, Redbook, Woman's Day*, and *New York Times*.

WORK IN PROGRESS: A book of photographs and text, tentatively titled *On Growing Old*, for Viking.

* * *

SHANNON, Thomas A(nthony) 1940-

PERSONAL: Born September 28, 1940, in Indianapolis, Ind.; son of John E. (an industrial engineer) and Clara (an artist; maiden name, Schmalz) Shannon; married Catherine Haenn (a reading teacher), August 12, 1972; children: Ashley Elizabeth. *Education:* Quincy College, B.A., 1964; St. Joseph Seminary, Teutopolis, Ill., S.T.B., 1968; Boston University, S.T.M., 1970, Ph.D., 1973. *Politics:* Independent. *Religion:* Roman Catholic. *Home:* 132 Coolidge Rd,, Worcester, Mass. 01602. *Office:* Department of Humanities, Worcester Polytechnic Institute, Worcester, Mass. 01609.

CAREER: Quincy College, Quincy, Ill., instructor in theology, 1968-69; Worcester Polytechnic Institute, Worcester, Mass., assistant professor of social ethics, 1973—. *Member:* American Society of Christian Ethics, American Academy of Religion, Catholic Theology Society of America.

WRITINGS: *Render Unto God: A Theology of Selective Obedience*, Paulist Press, 1973. Contributor to *Insight* and *Medical-Moral Newsletter*.

WORK IN PROGRESS: Editing *Readings in Bioethics*; research in problems in medical ethics, specifically on the problem of informed consent.

* * *

SHARAT CHANDRA, G(ubbi) S(hankara Chetty) 1938- (Jean Parker)

PERSONAL: Born May 2, 1938, in Mysore, India; son of G. Shankara (attorney general of Mysore, India) and Lalithamma Chetty; married Jane Ronnermann, September 1, 1966; children: Bharat. *Education:* University of Mysore, A.B., 1956, LL.B., 1958; State University of New York at Oswego, M.S., 1964; Osgoode Hall Law School, LL.M., 1966; University of Iowa, M.F.A., 1968. *Home:* Southeast 330 Gladstone, Pullman, Wash. 99163. *Office:* Department of English, Washington State University, Pullman, Wash. 99163.

CAREER: Attorney in Mysore, India, 1958-60; Osgoode Hall Law School, Toronto, Ontario, fellow in law, 1966-67; Iowa Wesleyan College, Mount Pleasant, assistant professor of English, 1969-72; Washington State University, Pullman, assistant professor of English and poet-in-residence, 1972—. Officer of labor relations in Mysore, 1958-60. Translator for International P.E.N.

WRITINGS: *Bharata Natyam Dancer* (poems), W. W. Calcutta, 1968; *Will This Forest* (poems), Morgan Press, 1968; *Reasons for Staying* (poems), Coach House, 1970;

April in Nanjangud (poems), Alan Ross, 1971. Contributor of poems, occasionally under pseudonym Jean Parker, to American and foreign magazines. Editor for Carswell and Canada Law Publishers. Editor of *Kamadhenu Poetry Journal*, 1970—.

WORK IN PROGRESS: In the Third Country, a collection of poems; translations from Servagna, a sixteenth-century monk of India.

* * *

SHAVELSON, Melville 1917-

PERSONAL: Born April 1, 1917, in Brooklyn, N.Y..; son of Joseph and Hilda (Shalson) Shavelson; married Lucille T. Myers, November 2, 1938; children: Richard, Lynne. *Education:* Cornell University, A.B., 1937. *Politics:* Liberal Democrat. *Religion:* Jewish. *Home:* 11947 Sunshine Terrace, Studio City, Calif. 91604. *Agent:* Arthur Pine Associates, Inc., 1780 Broadway, New York, N.Y. 10019.

CAREER: Writer for "Bob Hope Pepsodent Show," NBC-Radio, 1938-43; screenwriter in Hollywood, Calif., 1943—; director of films, including "The Seven Little Foys," 1954, "Beau James," 1956, "Yours, Mine and Ours," 1968, "The War Between Men and Women," 1972; producer of films, including "The Pidgeon That Took Rome," 1962, "Cast a Giant Shadow," 1966, "Mixed Company," 1974; creator of television series, "Make Room for Daddy," ABC-TV, 1953, and "My World—And Welcome to It," NBC-TV, 1969. *Member:* Directors Guild of America, Writers Guild of America (member of executive board, 1960-73), Academy of Motion Picture Arts and Sciences, Writers Guild of America, West (president, 1969-70), Screenwriters Guild (past president), Writers Guild Foundation (president, 1975), Sigma Delta Chi. *Awards, honors:* Recipient of numerous television and film awards, including Sylvania Television Award, 1953, Emmy Award for best comedy series, 1953, and Christopher Award, 1959, all for television series, "Make Room for Daddy"; Academy Award nomination for original screenplay, "The Seven Little Foys," 1955, and for "Houseboat," 1958; *Fame* Magazine Award for directing, 1960, for "Champion of Champions"; Screenwriters Guild Award for best written American musical, 1959, for "The Five Pennies"; Emmy Award for best comedy series, 1969, for "My World—And Welcome to It"; United Jewish Appeal Award of Merit, 1966.

WRITINGS: How to Make a Jewish Movie, Prentice-Hall, 1971; *Lualda* (novel), Arbor House, 1975.

Screenplays: "The Princess and the Pirate," 1944; "Wonder Man," 1944; "Room for One More," 1951; "I'll See You in My Dreams," 1952; "The Seven Little Foys," 1954; "Beau James," 1956; "Houseboat," 1957; "The Five Pennies," 1958; "It Started in Naples," 1959; "On the Double," 1960; "The Pidgeon That Took Rome," 1962; "A New Kind of Love," 1963; "Cast a Giant Shadow," 1966; "Yours, Mine, and, Ours," 1968; "The War Between Men and Women," 1972; "Mixed Company," 1974.

Author of book for musical, "Jimmy" (based on novel *Beau James* by Gene Fowler), first produced in Philadelphia at Forrest Theatre, September 8, 1969, produced on Broadway at Winter Garden Theatre, October 23, 1969.

AVOCATIONAL INTERESTS: Tennis, swimming, gardening, photography, music, and amateur radio.

* * *

SHAW, Wayne E(ugene) 1932-

PERSONAL: Born May 23, 1932, in Covington Ind.; son of Charles A. (a farmer) and Mabel (Howard) Shaw; married Janet Broz (a college literature lecturer), December 21, 1957; children: Haydn Stewart, Scott Campbell, Barton Charles. *Education:* Lincoln Christian College, B.A., 1954; Christian Theological Seminary, B.D., 1960; Butler University, M.S., 1963; Indiana University, Ph.D., 1969. *Home:* Airport Rd., Lincoln, Ill. 62656. *Office:* Department of Preaching, Lincoln Christian Seminary, Lincoln, Ill. 62656.

CAREER: Ordained minister of Christian Church, 1954; Lincoln Christian Seminary, Lincoln, Ill., associate professor, 1966-71, professor of preaching, 1971—, dean, 1974—. Member of board of Chaplaincy Endorsement Commission of Christian Churches and Churches of Christ, 1971—.

WRITINGS: (With James D. Strauss) *Birth of a Revolution*, Standard Publishing, 1974.

* * *

SHAZAR, (Schneor) Zalman 1889-1974
(Schneor Zalman Rubashov)

October 6, 1889—October 5, 1974; Russian-born third President of Israel (1963-73), first Education Minister of Israel, scholar, poet, historian, translator, and former newspaper editor. Obituaries: *New York Times*, October 6, 1974; *Time*, October 14, 1974.

* * *

SHEAN, Glenn (Daniel) 1939-

PERSONAL: Born April 15, 1939, in New Orleans, La.; son of Walter (a cigar manufacturer) and Tes (a court reporter; maiden name, Sehrt) Shean; married, wife's name Chris; children: Kathleen Erin. *Education:* Louisiana State University, New Orleans Campus, B.A., 1962; University of Arizona, M.A., 1964, Ph.D., 1966. *Religion:* Taoist. *Agent:* Robert Earhardt, P.O. Box 7600, Skokie, Ill. *Office:* Department of Psychology, College of William and Mary, Williamsburg, Va. 23185.

CAREER: Veterans Administration Hospital, Palo Alto, Calif., psychology trainee, 1965-66; College of William and Mary, Williamsburg, Va., 1966—, now associate professor of psychology. Clinical psychologist at Psychiatric Research Institute of Eastern State Hospital, 1968—. *Member:* American Psychological Association.

WRITINGS: Study of Abnormal Behavior, Rand McNally, 1971. Contributor to *Journal of Behavior Therapy and Experimental Psychiatry, Journal of Psychosomatic Research*, and *Psychophysiology*.

WORK IN PROGRESS: Schizophrenia: Disease, Myth, or Misinterpretation of Reality?

* * *

SHELDON, Deyan

PERSONAL: Given name is pronounced Dee-Anne; born in New York, N.Y.; daughter of Kenneth Hogarth and Dorothy (Lyon) Sheldon. *Education:* Attended Columbia University, New York University, New School for Social Research, and Cooper Union. *Politics:* "Adaptable to time and situation but philosophically and economically conservative." *Religion:* "Infinite Way." *Home:* 878 Kingstown Rd., Wakefield, R.I. 02879. *Agent:* David Hull, James Brown Associates, 22 East 60th St., New York, N.Y. 10021.

CAREER: "Have done everything from swimming teacher to bike messenger to advertising copywriter."

WRITINGS: *Nail Hotel* (novel), Crowell, 1975.

WORK IN PROGRESS: Two novels, *The Dam* and *The Aegis Skyline*.

AVOCATIONAL INTERESTS: Travel, people, numerology.

* * *

SHEPHERD, L. P.

PERSONAL: Born in St. Louis, Mo.; son of Burton Osborne and Lucinda (Matlock) Shepherd; married Ruth Baehr, July 7, 1962; children: Rae Christina. *Education:* Kansas State Teachers College, B.S., 1961; Columbia University, A.M., 1962. *Home:* 198 Cedar, Fitchburg, Mass. 01420. *Office:* Department of English, Fitchburg State College, Fitchburg, Mass. 01420.

CAREER: Carnival spieler, sign hanger, salesman, comparison shopper, stevedore, janitor, stage electrician, busboy, counterman, and "artiste" with French Line; teacher of English and Spanish in the public high schools of Norwich, Kan., 1963; teacher in New York, N.Y., 1964; Oregon State College (now Oregon State University), Corvallis, instructor, 1965-66; Stanford University, Stanford, Calif., instructor, 1967-68; California State Polytechnic College, San Luis Obispo, instructor in English, 1969-73; Fitchburg State College, Fitchburg, Mass., instructor in English, 1973—. *Military service:* Kansas National Guard, 1960.

WRITINGS: *Cape House*, Dell, 1974. Contributor of poems, book reviews, and articles to *Boston Herald Traveler, Worcester Telegram*, and *Boston University Graduate Journal*.

WORK IN PROGRESS: Four novel manuscripts completed; a new novel.

AVOCATIONAL INTERESTS: Jogging, handgun shooting.

* * *

SHIELDS, Donald J(ames) 1937-

PERSONAL: Born October 28, 1937, in Paris, Ill.; son of John (a postal employee) and Harriet (Francis) Shields; married Donna Ruth Shields, June 17, 1962 (divorced July 2, 1974); children: Donald Gary, Christina Lynn. *Education:* Eastern Illinois University, B.S.Ed. (with honors), 1959; Purdue Univerisy, M.S., 1961, Ph.D., 1964. *Religion:* Presbyterian. *Home address:* R.R.1, Dennison, Ill, 62423. *Office:* Department of Speech, Indiana State University, Terre Haute, Ind. 47809.

CAREER: Indiana State University, Terre Haute, assistant professor, 1965-68, associate professor of speech, 1968—. Member of Indiana Young Democrats; president of Purdue Young Democrats, 1960-62. *Member:* International Communication Association, Speech Communication Association of America, Central States Speech Association, Indiana Speech Association, Indiana Intercollegiate Forensics Association (president, 1967-69), Delta Sigma Rho, Tau Kappa Alpha.

WRITINGS: (Editor) *History of Free Speech in Decision Making: Readings and Cases*, Kendall-Hunt, 1974.

WORK IN PROGRESS: *The Public Speech in Contemporary Politics*.

SIDELIGHTS: Shields writes: "I have always been concerned with political communication and the process of a free flow of communication in a free society. With the election of Nixon in 1968 I became increasingly aware of dangers to free communication and started research for a course and book on free speech in a free society."

* * *

SHORE, William B(urton) 1925-

PERSONAL: Born April 4, 1925, in Minneapolis, Minn.; son of Samuel Louis (an attorney) and Tessa (Woolpy) Shore; married Dorothy Fraser, December 30, 1949; children: Laura J. (Mrs. James C. Piccone), Sally Ann, Jeffrey Fraser, Melissa Beth. *Education:* University of Minnesota, B.A., 1948; University of Manchester, M.A., 1952; Syracuse University, further graduate study, 1953-55. *Politics:* Democrat. *Home:* 119 Cobb Lane, Tarrytown, N.Y. 10591. *Office:* Regional Plan Association, 235 East 45th St., New York, N.Y. 10017.

CAREER: Research director for Senator Hubert H. Humphrey, 1948-49; economist and writer, Office of International Labor Affairs, U.S. Department of Labor, 1949-50; supervisor of public administration projects, Community Service Department, University of Wyoming, 1955-56; American Society for Public Administration, Chicago, Ill., publications director, 1956-60, information director, 1964-69; Regional Plan Association, New York, N.Y., vice-president for public affairs, 1969—. Director of Westchester Housing Action Council, and Community Opportunity Center of Tarrytown; member of Arts Action Council of Westchester; vice-president, Water Resources Association of the Delaware River Basin. *Military service:* U.S. Army, Infantry, 1943-46.

WRITINGS: *Public Participation in Regional Planning*, Regional Plan Association, 1967; (with Boris Pushkariv) *How to Save Urban America*, edited by William Caldwell, New American Library, 1973; *Listening to the Metropolis*, Regional Plan Association, 1974; (contributor) Lowell Harriss, editor, *The Good Earth of America*, Prentice-Hall, 1974. Author of "How Fine a Place," a television script for series "Choices for '76," 1973. Managing editor of *Public Administration Review*, 1956-60.

WORK IN PROGRESS: A study of the implementation of regional planning.

* * *

SHORT, Jackson (pseudonym)

PERSONAL: Born September 7, 1939, in New York, N.Y. *Education:* Antioch College, A.B. *Agent:* Henry Morrison, Inc., 56 West Tenth St., New York, N.Y.

CAREER: Newspaper reporter and editor, 1960-63; advertising writer and supervisor, 1963—. *Military service:* U.S. Army Reserve National Guard, 1962-67.

WRITINGS—Novels: *Blue Alice*, Dell, 1972; *Getting Shafted*, Dell, 1973; *The Secret Sex Curse of Bertha T.*, Dell, 1973; *The Au Pair Girls*, Paperback Library, 1974.

WORK IN PROGRESS: A novel, *Fleeing Naked*.

* * *

SHOUMATOFF, Alex 1946-

PERSONAL: Born November 4, 1946, in Mount Kisco, N.Y.; son of Nicholas (an engineer) and Nina (Adamovich) Shoumatoff; married Leslie Moore (a production editor for a publishing house), February 16, 1974. *Education:* Harvard University, B.A., 1968. *Home and office:* Marsh Sanctuary, R.D.2, Mount Kisco, N.Y. 10649.

CAREER: *Washington Post*, Washington, D.C., reporter and book reviewer, 1968-69; variously employed as songwriter, freelance, and instructor in French at New England College, Henniker, N.H., 1969-73; natural history teacher in private school in Bedford, N.Y., 1973—. Executive director and resident naturalist at Marsh Sanctuary, 1973—. Minister of Universal Life Church. Member of board of trustees of Butler Sanctuary. *Military service:* U.S. Marine Corps, 1969-70. *Member:* Bedford Audubon Society (member of board of directors). *Awards, honors:* Woodrow Wilson fellowship, 1968.

WRITINGS: *Florida Ramble*, Harper, 1974; *A Social and Natural History of Westchester County, New York*, Harper, in press. Contributor to *Saturday Review of Science, Book World, Rolling Stone*, and *Village Voice*.

SIDELIGHTS: Shoumatoff writes that he spent his adolescence wandering in the summers in the Swiss Alps, and that he studied poetry with Robert Lowell and Robert Fitzgerald. He has an "abiding interest in the relationship of man and nature; in the type of writing that conveys the total picture of a place, both its natural and social history."

* * *

SHOWALTER, English, Jr. 1935-

PERSONAL: Born May 14, 1935, in Roanoke, Va.; son of English (a lawyer) and Jean (Staples) Showalter; married Elaine Cottler (a professor), June 8, 1962; children: Victoria, Michael. *Education:* Yale University, B.A., 1957, M.A., 1959, Ph.D., 1964. *Residence:* Princeton, N.J. *Office:* Department of French, Rutgers University, Camden, N.J. 08102.

CAREER: Haverford College, Haverford, Pa., assistant professor of French, 1961-64; University of California, Davis, assistant professor of French, 1964-66; Princeton University, Princeton, N.J., assistant professor of French, 1966-74; Rutgers University, Camden, N.J., associate professor of French and chairman of department, 1974—. *Member:* Modern Language Association of America, American Association of Teachers of French, American Society for Eighteenth Century Studies, American Association of University Professors. *Awards, honors:* American Council of Learned Societies grant, 1968.

WRITINGS: *The Evolution of the French Novel: 1641-1782*, Princeton University Press, 1972. Contributor to scholarly journals. Member of editorial board of *French Review*.

WORK IN PROGRESS: *Voltaire et ses amis d'apres la correspondance de Mme. de Graffigny* (title means "Voltaire and His Friends according to the Correspondence of Mme. de Graffigny"), Volume I: *1738-1739*; other books on the correspondence of Mme. de Graffigny; a study of Mme. de Graffigny.

* * *

SHOWERS, Victor 1910-

PERSONAL: Born March 24, 1910, in Altoona, Pa.; son of Victor (a printer) and Helen (Faraday) Showers; married Thelma Smeltzer, February 14, 1945. *Education:* University of Pittsburgh, B.A., 1931, M.A., 1943; Carnegie-Mellon University, B.S., 1938. *Home and office:* 1217 Shenandoah Rd., Alexandria, Va. 22308.

CAREER: Carnegie Library, Pittsburgh, Pa., reference assistant, 1938-45; University of Pittsburgh, Special Research Staff, Washington, D.C., writer, 1945-61, editor, 1961-62, editor-in-chief, 1962-68; Governmental Affairs Institute, Washington, D.C., senior research associate, 1968-70. *Member:* Sigma Delta Chi.

WRITINGS: *The World in Figures*, Wiley, 1973.

* * *

SHUKMAN, Harold 1931-

PERSONAL: Born March 23, 1931, in London, England; son of David (a tailor) and Masha (Ekinbert) Shukman; married Ann King-Farlow, December 22, 1956 (divorced, 1971); married Barbara King-Farlow (an artist), March 30, 1973; children: (first marriage) David, Henry, Clare; (stepchildren from second marriage) Ghislaine Jacobs, Amelia Jacobs, Adam Jacobs. *Education:* University of Nottingham, B.A. (first class honors), 1956; Oxford University, D.Phil., 1960. *Politics:* "Mildly reactionary/liberal." *Religion:* "Lapsed psychoanalysand." *Home:* 11 Cunliffe Close, Oxford, England. *Agent:* A. D. Peters, 10 Buckingham St., London S.W.1, England. *Office:* Russian Centre, St. Antony's College, Oxford University, Oxford, England.

CAREER: Standard Telephones, London, England, trainee radio engineer, 1947-51; Marconi Telecommunications, Chelmsford, Essex, England, executive, 1956-57; Oxford University, Oxford, England, fellow of St. Antony's College, 1961—, lecturer in modern Russian history, 1969—. Consultant to British Broadcasting Corp. *Military service:* Royal Air Force, Russian interpreter, 1951-53; became sergeant. *Member:* Jewellery and Silver Society of Oxford.

WRITINGS: (Translator and editor with Max Hayward and Michael Glenny) *Three Soviet Plays*, Penguin, 1965; (translator with Hayward) Valentin Kataev, *Holy Well*, Walker, 1967; *Lenin and the Russian Revolution*, Putnam, 1967; (translator with others) Yuli Daniel, *This Is Moscow Speaking*, Harvill, 1968; (with George Katkov) *Lenin's Path to Power*, Macdonald, 1971. Author of television script for "The Great War," a series for British Broadcasting Corp. Contributor to Slavic studies journals, including *Bulletin of Soviet and East European Jewish Affairs*.

WORK IN PROGRESS: A history of the Communist Party of the Soviet Union to 1917, with Leonard Schapiro.

SIDELIGHTS: Shukman writes: "The accident of having Yiddish-speaking Russian parents was responsible for my being propelled into Russian studies in general and aspects of Russian-Jewish history in particular. Otherwise I might have remained in a career with a future—electronics. However, the discovery of the French and Italian languages in 1950-51 coupled with eruption of late adolescent sensuality, diverted me into the vain search for a profession offering culture, luxury, wealth, and ego gratification. An Oxfordian enjoys only one of these all the time, and at most two some of the time." *Avocational interests:* Silversmithing.

* * *

SIEGEL, Robert (Harold) 1939-

PERSONAL: Born August 18, 1939, in Oak Park, Ill.; son of Frederick William (a personnel manager) and Lucille (Chance) Siegel; married Roberta Hill, August 19, 1961; children: Anne Lenaye, Lucy Blythe, Christine Elizabeth. *Education:* Attended Denison University, 1957-59;

Wheaton College, Wheaton, Ill., B.A., 1961; Johns Hopkins University, M.A., 1962; Harvard University, Ph.D., 1968. *Religion:* Christian. *Office:* Department of English, Dartmouth College, Hanover, N.H. 03755.

CAREER: Trinity College, Bannockburn, Ill., instructor in English, 1962-63; Dartmouth College, Hanover, N.H., assistant professor of English, 1967—. Visiting lecturer in creative writing, Princeton University, 1975-76. Resident poet at Greenlake (Wis.) Writers' Conference, 1974. *Member:* Modern Language Association of America. Conference on Christanity and Literature (director, 1969-72). *Awards, honors:* Fellowship from Breadloaf Writers' Conference, 1974; resident at Yaddo, 1974, 1975; Chicago Poetry Award from Society of Midland Authors and Illinois Council for the Arts, and Cliff Dwellers Arts Foundation Award, 1974, for *The Beasts and the Elders.*

WRITINGS: The Beasts and the Elders (poetry), University Press of New England, 1973. Contributor of poetry to *Atiantic Monthly, Poetry, Prairie Schooner, Granite, Georgia Review, Epoch*, and other magazines.

WORK IN PROGRESS: A book of poems based on folk rhymes; a sonnet cycle based on travels through Great Britain.

AVOCATIONAL INTERESTS: Cross-country walking, travel, "literate fantasy."

* * *

SILVER, Isidore 1934-

PERSONAL: Born April 16, 1934, in New York, N.Y.; son of Abraham (a tailor) and Anna (a tailor; maiden name, Levine) Silver; married Paula Frankl, June 20, 1960 (divorced June 14, 1968). *Education:* University of Wisconsin, B.S., 1955; New York University, J.D., 1959, M.A., 1965. *Home:* 16 West 16th St., New York, N.Y. 10011. *Office:* John Jay College of Criminal Justice, 445 West 59th St., New York, N.Y. 10019.

CAREER: Hunter College of the City University of New York, N.Y., lecturer in law, 1961-66; University of Massachusetts, Amherst, assistant professor, 1966-68, associate professor of law, 1968-70; John Jay College of Criminal Justice of the City University of New York, New York, N.Y., associate professor, 1970-73, professor of history, 1973—. Attorney in New York, N.Y. Member of executive committee and of board of directors of National Emergency Civil Liberties Committee, 1974—. *Military service:* U.S. Army, 1957. *Member:* National Humanities Faculty, New York State Bar Association.

WRITINGS: (Editor) *The Challenge of Crime in a Free Society*, Dutton, 1968; *The Crime-Control Establishment*, Prentice-Hall, 1974; (editor) *A National Strategy to Reduce Crime*, Avon, 1975. Contributor to law reviews and to *Commonweal*, *Congress Monthly*, and *New York Times Book Review*.

WORK IN PROGRESS: Research on constitutional history and on crime and society.

* * *

SIME, Mary 1911-

PERSONAL: Born March 28, 1911, in Tollesbury, Essex, England; daughter of Joseph Benjamin (a small businessman) and Emily Ada (a teacher; maiden name, Drake) Sime. *Education:* Bedford College, London, B.A. (with honors), 1933; Oxford University, teacher's diploma, 1934. *Politics:* "Active in attempts for international understanding." *Religion:* Quaker. *Home:* 105 Mell Rd., Tollesbury, Essex CM9 8SR, England. *Office:* Department of Education, Chorley College, Chorley, Lancashire, England.

CAREER: English Girls College (International), Alexandria, Egypt, teacher of geography and mathematics, 1939-45; teacher of geography, Werbcliff High School, Essex, England, 1947-49, and Camden School, London, England, 1953-55; United Nations Educational, Scientific, and Cultural Organization (UNESCO), specialist in geography and mathematics in Palestine, 1955-56; Maldon Secondary School, Essex, England, deputy headteacher, 1957-59; Government of North Nigeria, Kano, education officer, 1959-61; Chorley College, Chorley, England, principal lecturer in education, 1965—. Member of international reconciliation team of American Friends Service Committee and United Nations Relief and Works Agency in Palestine, 1949. *Member:* Comparative Education Society of Europe (founding member of United Kingdom branch), Froebel Society (London).

WRITINGS: (Contributor) A. G. Howson, editor, *Developments in Mathematical Education*, Cambridge University Press, 1973; *A Child's Eye View: Piaget for Young Parents and Teachers*, Thames & Hudson, 1973, Harper, 1974. Contributor to education and Quaker journals.

WORK IN PROGRESS: Research in teacher training.

SIDELIGHTS: Miss Sime has travelled in Europe, Africa, the Middle East, Russia, and the United States.

* * *

SIMON, Herbert 1898(?)-1974

1898(?)—November 13, 1974; English printing craftsman, former chairman and life-president of Curwen Press, and author of books on printing. Obituaries: *AB Bookman's Weekly*, December 16, 1974.

* * *

SIMPSON, Colin 1908-

PERSONAL: Born November 4, 1908, in Sydney, N.S.W., Australia; son of Henry F. V. (a tradesman) and Margaret (a nurse, maiden name, Langby) Simpson; married Claire Waterman (an artist), January 23, 1937; children: Julia Haden, Vivien Haden Simpson Ray. *Education:* Attended University of Sydney, 1926-27. *Religion:* Atheist. *Home and office:* 27 Glenview St., Gordon, N.S.W. 2072, Australia.

CAREER: Catts-Patterson Advertising Service, Sydney, Australia, copywriter and junior account executive, 1925-27; Daton Advertising Ltd., Sydney, copywriter, 1928; journalist for Sydney newspapers and periodicals, with posts including associate editor of *Pix Weekly*, supplement editor for *Australian Women's Weekly*, and magazine editor for *Sunday Telegraph* and *Sunday Sun*, all 1928-46; Australian Broadcasting Commission, Sydney, radio documentary writer, 1947-50; Hansen-Rubensohn (advertising agency), Sydney, Australia, account executive, 1957-58; creative group head for McCann-Erickson, 1959-60; full-time writer, 1960—. *Member:* P.E.N., Australian Society of Authors (vice-president, 1971—), Australian Journalist Association (honorary life member).

WRITINGS—All published by Angus & Robertson (Sydney), except as indicated: (with Kenneth Slessor and Harley Matthews) *Trio* (poems), Sunnybrook Press, 1931;

Adam in Ochre, 1951, Praeger, 1953; *Come Away Pearler*, 1952; *Adam with Arrows* (also see below), 1953; *Adam in Plumes* (also see below), 1954; *Islands of Men*, 1955; *Australian Image*, Legend Press, 1956; *The Country Upstairs* (also see below), 1956 (published in England as *Picture of Japan*, Angus & Robertson (London), 1957), published as *Japan: An Intimate View*, A. S. Barnes, 1962, revised edition, 1969; *Wake Up in Europe*, 1959, published as *Europe: An Intimate View*, A. S. Barnes, 1962; *Show Me a Mountain*, 1961; *Asia's Bright Balconies*, 1962; *Plumes and Arrows* (includes *Adam with Arrows* and *Adam in Plumes*), 1962; *Take Me to Spain*, 1963; *Take Me to Russia*, 1964 (published in England as *This Is Russia*, Hodder & Stoughton, 1965); *The Viking Circle*, 1966, Morrow, 1968; *Katmandu*, 1967, Taplinger, 1968; *Greece: The Unclouded Eye*, 1968, Morrow, 1969; *The New Australia*, 1971, Dutton, 1972; *Bali and Beyond*, 1971; *Off to Asia*, 1972; *This Is Japan* (incorporates *The Country Upstairs*), 1975. Contributor to numerous journals.

AVOCATIONAL INTERESTS: Reading and sunning.

BIOGRAPHICAL/CRITICAL SOURCES: Rohan Rivett, *Writing About Australia*, Angus & Robertson, 1969.

* * *

SINGER, Robert N.

EDUCATION: Brooklyn College of the City University of New York, B.S., 1961; Pennsylvania State University, M.S., 1962; Ohio State University, Ph.D., 1964. *Office:* Division of Human Performance, Florida State University, Tallahassee, Fla. 32306.

CAREER: Ohio State University, Columbus, 1963-65, began as instructor, became assistant professor; Illinois State University, Normal, 1965-68, began as assistant professor, became associate professor, assistant dean of College of Applied Science and Technology, 1968-69; Michigan State University, East Lansing, associate professor, 1969-70, professor, 1970-72; Florida State University, Tallahassee, professor and director of Motor Learning Research Laboratory, 1970-72, director of Division of Human Performance, 1972—. Consulting editor, Holt, Rinehart and Winston. *Member:* American Educational Research Association, American Psychological Association, American Association for Health, Physical Education, and Recreation, National College Physical Education Association for Men, North American Society for the Psychology of Sport and Physical Activity, Omicron Delta Kappa, Phi Epsilon Kappa.

WRITINGS: Motor Learning and Human Performance, Macmillan, 1968, 2nd edition, 1975; (editor) *Readings in Motor Learning*, Lea & Febiger, 1972; *Coaching, Athletics, and Psychology*, McGraw, 1972; (with others) *Physical Education: An Interdisciplinary Approach*, Macmillan, 1972; (editor) *The Psychomotor Domain: Movement Behavior*, Lea & Febiger, 1972; (with others) *Teaching Physical Education: A Systems Approach*, Houghton, 1974; *Myths and Truths in Sport Psychology*, Harper, 1975; (co-author) *Laboratory and Field Experiments in Motor Learning*, C. C Thomas, 1975; (editor) *Foundations of Physical Education*, Holt, 1975.

Contributor: W. P. Morgan, editor, *Ergogenic Aids and Muscular Performance*, Academic Press, 1972; *The Psychomotor Domain*, Gryphon Press, 1972; *Selecting Instructional Strategies and Media: A Place to Begin*, National Special Media Institutes, 1972; G. Lawrence Rarick, editor, *Physical Activity: Human Growth and Development*, Academic Press, 1973; *Research Methods*, American Association for Health, Physical Education, and Recreation, 1973; *Anthology of Sports Psychology*, Editura Stadian, in press.

Editor of series, "Issues in Contemporary Physical Education," published by Harper; co-editor of *Completed Research in Health, Physical Education, and Recreation*, American Association of Health, Physical Education, and Recreation, 1968-74. Contributor to *Encyclopedia of Sport Sciences and Medicine*; contributor of more than forty articles to professional journals. Member of editorial board of *Research Quarterly* and *Journal of Motor Behavior*; abstractor for *Psychological Reports*; special reader for *Perceptual and Motor Skills, Journal of Applied Psychology, Medicine and Science in Sports*, and *Educational Psychology.*

* * *

SITES, Paul 1926-

PERSONAL: Born July 22, 1926, in Indianapolis, Ind.; son of Edwin R. and Ione V. Sites; married Goldie Faris, July 6, 1946; children: Katherine, Danny, Mary (Mrs. Donald Johnson). *Education:* Indiana Central College, B.A., 1955; Purdue University, M.A., 1957, Ph.D., 1960. *Politics:* Democrat. *Home:* 5003 Rootstown Rd., Ravenna, Ohio 44266. *Office:* Department of Sociology, Kent State University, Kent, Ohio 44266.

CAREER: Indiana Central College, Indianapolis, instructor in sociology, 1956-57; Baldwin-Wallace College, Berea, Ohio, assistant professor, 1960-64, associate professor of sociology, 1964-65; Kent State University, Kent, Ohio, associate professor, 1965-70, professor of sociology, 1970—, director of graduate studies, 1967-70. Member of Portage County Community Action Council (member of board of trustees, 1969—; chairman of board of trustees, 1970-74). *Military service:* U.S. Army, 1944-47; became staff sergeant. *Member:* American Sociological Association, North Central Sociological Association.

WRITINGS: Lee Harvey Oswald and the American Dream, Pageant, 1967; *Control: The Basis of Order*, Dunellen, 1973; *Control and Constraint: An Introduction to Sociology*, Macmillan, in press.

WORK IN PROGRESS: A book *Control and Constraint: Toward an Integration of Sociological Theory*; a comprehensive study of a religious order, with a monograph or a series expected to result.

* * *

SKARDON, Alvin W(ilson, Jr.) 1912-

PERSONAL: Born December 4, 1912, in St. Francisville, La.; son of Alvin Wilson (a clergyman) and Genevieve (Hooper) Skardon; married Ruth Wahtola (an artist), June 26, 1971. *Education:* College of Charleston, A.B., 1933; University of Chicago, M.A., 1949, Ph.D., 1960. *Politics:* Democrat. *Religion:* Episcopalian. *Home:* 225 Outlook Ave., Youngstown, Ohio 44504. *Office:* Department of History, Youngstown State University, Youngstown, Ohio 44555.

CAREER: Hotel reservation clerk; Lafayette Hotel, Walterboro, S.C., manager, 1935-41; University of Chicago, Chicago, Ill., foreign student adviser, 1949-55; Youngstown State University (formerly Youngstown University), Youngstown, Ohio, 1957—, began as assistant professor, now professor of history. Visiting lecturer at Baldwin-Wallace College, 1956-57; visiting professor at Louisiana State University, New Orleans, summer, 1970. *Military service:* U.S. Army, 1941-45; served overseas; held prisoner of war by the Germans, 1944-45; became staff sergeant. *Member:* Organization of American Historians, American Historical Association, American Society of Church History, Urban History Group, Guild of Scholars (president, 1974-75), Southern Historical Association.

WRITINGS: Church Leader in the Cities: William Augustus Muhlenberg, University of Pennsylvania Press, 1971. Contributor to *Dictionary of the Western Church*.

WORK IN PROGRESS: A history of Youngstown University from its beginning about 1888 to state control in 1968.

* * *

SLATER, Eliot (Trevor Oakeshott) 1904-

PERSONAL: Born August 28, 1904, in London, England; son of Gilbert (a historian) and Violet (an artist; maiden name, Oakeshott) Slater; married Lydia Pasternak, 1935 (divorced, 1948); married Jean Foster (an artist), 1948; children: (first marriage) Michael, Nicolas, Catherine (Mrs. Peter Oppenheimer), Ann (Mrs. Craig Raine). *Education:* St. John's College, Cambridge, M.A., 1940, M.D., 1940; St. George's Hospital, University of London, F.R.C.P., 1945. *Politics:* Liberal. *Religion.* Pantheist. *Office:* Institute of Psychiatry, University of London, London SE5 8AF, England.

CAREER: St. George's Hospital, London, England, casualty officer, house surgeon and physician, and resident anaesthetist, 1927-30; West End Hospital for Nervous Diseases, London, house physician, 1930-31; Derby County Medical Hospital, Derby, England, assistant medical officer, 1931; Maudsley Hospital, London, assistant medical officer, 1932-39; Sutton Emergency Hospital, Sutton, Surrey, England, clinical director, 1939-45; Maudsley Hospital, London, physician, 1945-46; National Hospital, Queen Square, London, physician in psychological medicine, 1946-64; University of London, Institute of Psychiatry, London, honorary lecturer, 1964—. Honorary physician at Maudsley Hospital, 1946-69; director of Psychiatric Research Unit of Medical Research Council, 1959-69; member of Royal Commission on Capital Punishment, 1949-53.

MEMBER: World Federation of Neurology (founding member), Royal College of Psychiatrists (honorary fellow), Genetical Society, Eugenics Society, Voluntary Euthanasia Society (vice-president), Shakespearean Authorship Society (vice-president), American Psychiatric Association (distinguished fellow), Deutsche Gesellschaft fuer Psychiatrie and Nervenheilkunde (honorary member). *Awards, honors:* Named Commander of the Order of the British Empire, 1966; LL.D. from University of Dundee, 1971.

WRITINGS: (With William Sargant) *Introduction to Physical Methods of Treatment*, Livingstone, 1944, 4th edition, 1963; (with Moya Woodside) *Patterns of Marriage*, Cassell, 1951; *Psychotic and Neurotic Illnesses in Twins*, H.M.S.O., 1953; (with Willi Mayer-Gross and Martin Roth) *Clinical Psychiatry*, Cassell, 1954, 3rd edition, 1969; (with John Cowie and Valerie Cowie) *Delinquency in Girls*, Heinemann, 1968; *The Ebbless Sea* (poems), Outposts Publications, 1968; (with Valerie Cowie) *The Genetics of Mental Disorder*, Oxford University Press, 1971. Editor-in-chief of *British Journal of Psychiatry*, 1961-72.

WORK IN PROGRESS: Research on Shakespeare, concerning dating of plays and psychological issues.

BIOGRAPHICAL/CRITICAL SOURCES: James Shields and Irving I. Gottesman, editors, *Man, Mind and Heredity: Selected Papers of Eliot Slater on Psychiatry and Genetics*, Johns Hopkins Press, 1971.

* * *

SLOANE, R(obert) Bruce 1923-

PERSONAL: Born March 28, 1923, in Harrogate, Yorkshire, England; son of Robert and Violet (Kitson) Sloane; married Vera Taylor; children: Judith (Mrs. Thomas Lombardi), Joanna, Robert William, Polly, Thomas Robin, Eve. *Education:* University of London, M.B. and B.S., both 1945, M.D., 1950. *Office:* School of Medicine, Department of Psychiatry, University of Southern California, 2025 Zonal Ave., Los Angeles, Calif. 90033.

CAREER: Certified by American Board of Psychiatry and Neurology, 1963; Queen's University, Kingston, Ontario, professor of psychiatry, 1957-64, head of department, 1957-64; Temple University, Philadelphia, Pa., professor of psychiatry and chairman of department, 1964-72; University of Southern California, Los Angeles, professor of psychiatry and chairman of department, 1972—. *Military service:* Royal Air Force, medical specialist, 1946-48; became squadron leader.

MEMBER: American Academy of Psychoanalysts (fellow), American College of Neuropsychopharmacology (fellow), American Geriatric Society (fellow), American Psychiatric Association (fellow), Royal College of Psychiatrists (fellow), Royal Society of Medicine (fellow), Royal College of Physicians (fellow). *Awards, honors:* Fulbright scholarship, Harvard University, 1953-54; Nuffield visiting scientist, Great Britain, 1964; Commonwealth Fund book program grant, 1972.

WRITINGS: (Editor) *Abortion: Changing Views and Practice,* Grune, 1971; (with Diana F. Horvitz) *A General Guide to Abortion,* Nelson Hall, 1973; (with F. R. Staples, A. H. Cristol, N. J. Yorkston, and Katherine Whipple) *Psychotherapy versus Behavior Therapy,* Harvard University Press, 1974. Contributor to medical journals, including *Journal of Mental Science, American Practitioner and Digest of Treatment, Journal of Psychosomatic Research, Canadian Medical Association Journal, Journal of Neuropsychiatry, Internal Journal of Psychiatry,* and *Geriatrics.*

WORK IN PROGRESS: Research on the effect of chlorpromazine and thiothixene on process and reactive schizophrenia; continuing research on geriatrics, psychoses, schizophrenia, and comparisons of psychotherapy and behavior therapy.

* * *

SLOANE, William M. 1906-1974

August 15, 1906—September 15, 1974; American book publisher, founder of publishing firm William Sloane Associates, former editor or executive of several publishing houses, and author of science fiction novels and short stories. Obituaries: *New York Times*, September 26, 1974.

* * *

SLOCUM, William J(oseph Michael), Jr. 1912(?)-1974 (Bill Slocum, Michael Slocum)

1912(?)—November 26, 1974; American journalist, former radio reporter and producer, and author of several books on

Washington affairs. Obituaries: *New York Times*, November 27, 1974; *AB Bookman's Weekly*, December 16, 1974.

* * *

SLUNG, Louis Sheaffer 1912-
(Louis Sheaffer)

PERSONAL: Born October 18, 1912, in Louisville, Ky.; son of Abraham (a businessman) and Ida (Jacobson) Slung. *Education:* Attended University of North Carolina, 1930-31. *Politics:* Democrat. *Religion:* Jewish. *Agent:* John Schaffner, 425 East 51st St., New York, N.Y. 10022.

CAREER: *Brooklyn Eagle*, Brooklyn, N.Y., reporter, 1934-42, columnist, 1946-47, film critic, 1947-49, theater critic, 1949-55; Circle in the Square, New York, N.Y., theatrical press agent, 1955-56; journalist, 1956—. *Military service:* U.S. Army, 1942-46; became technical sergeant. *Member:* Authors Guild, Authors League of America. *Awards, honors:* Guggenheim fellowships, 1959, 1962, 1969; American Council of Learned Societies grants-in-aid, 1961, 1962; National Endowment for the Humanities grant, 1972; George Freedley Award from Theater Library Association, 1969, for *O'Neill: Son and Playwright*; Pulitzer prize in biography, 1974, for *O'Neill: Son and Artist*.

WRITINGS—Under pseudonym Louis Sheaffer: *O'Neill: Son and Playwright*, Little, Brown, 1968; *O'Neill: Son and Artist*, Little, Brown, 1973.

* * *

SMITH, Anthony 1938-

PERSONAL: Born March 14, 1938, in London, England. *Education:* Oxford University, B.A., 1960. *Home and office:* St. Antony's College, Oxford University, Oxford, England. *Agent:* Deborah Rogers Ltd., 29 Goodge St., London W.1, England.

CAREER: British Broadcasting Corporation (BBC), London, England, producer of political and current affairs television programs, 1960-71; Oxford University, Oxford, England, research fellow at St. Antony's College, 1971—. *Member:* International Broadcast Institute, European Cooperation Research Group, Royal Institute of International Affairs, Standing Conference on Broadcasting.

WRITINGS: *The Shadow in the Cave: The Broadcaster, the Audience and the State*, Allen & Unwin, 1973, University of Illinois Press, 1974; (editor) *British Broadcasting: A Book of Documents*, David & Charles, 1974; *The British Press Since the War*, David & Charles, 1974.

WORK IN PROGRESS: *A History of the British Journalist, 1620-1970*, for the Leverhulme Foundation and David & Charles.

* * *

SMITH, Cyril James 1909-1974

August 11, 1909—August 2, 1974; British concert pianist, Rachmaninoff specialist, judge of international piano competitions, teacher, and author of his autobiography. Obituaries: *New York Times*, August 3, 1974.

* * *

SMITH, David MacLeod 1920-
(David Mariner)

PERSONAL: Born July 15, 1920, in Strathpeffer, Ross and Cromarty, Scotland; son of A.E.D. (an army and excise officer) and Margaret (MacLeod) Smith; married Jean Armour Macinnes (a teacher), July 11, 1952. *Education:* Attended St. Andrews University, 1946-48, Ealing Technical College, 1951, and Manchester School of Technology, 1954. *Politics:* "Name one party, in any country, not motivated by self-interest. I'll join." *Religion:* Agnostic. *Home:* Ardcraig, by Dingwall, Ross and Cromarty IV 15 9TS, Scotland.

CAREER: Royal Navy, 1937-46; became chief petty officer. Participated in commando-type raids on French coast with naval battalion, Atlantic convoys, assault landings in North Africa, Sicily, Toe of Italy, also in East Indies, Indian Ocean, and South Atlantic; visited 51 countries during service in radar and gunnery. Worked as free-lance journalist and photographer, 1947-50; from 1950-64, worked variously as a salesman, export executive, sales manager, and marketing adviser. Novelist, 1964—. *Member:* Institute of Packaging (founding member, 1955).

WRITINGS—Novels; all under pseudonym David Mariner: *Devil's Bread*, R. Hale, 1969, published as *The Yaroslav Incident*, Zebra Publications, 1974; *The Chatham Rats*, R. Hale, 1969, published as *Operation Scorpio*, Pinnacle Books, 1975; *A Shackleton Called Sheila*, R. Hale, 1970, published as *Countdown 1000*, Pinnacle Books, 1974; *A White Lie and No Glory*, R. Hale, 1971, published as *The Last Bridge*, Pinnacle Books, 1974; *The Beaufort Dossier*, R. Hale, 1973, Zebra Publications, 1974; *Symbol of Vengeance*, R. Hale, 1975.

Contributor to *Newnes Children's Encyclopedia* and of over 250 articles and photographs to newspapers and magazines.

WORK IN PROGRESS: *Castle of the Dead*, a novel set on the west coast of Scotland.

SIDELIGHTS: Smith, who goes by the assumed name of David Mariner, told *CA*: "All men, and women too, possess the attributes of their parents and ancestors in some measure. This author claims to be the exception. His father's brother, a citizen of the U.S.A., was described in the 1950's as one of America's most versatile humorists, at which time he had his name in lights on Broadway. He was known as Fred Frazer of Syracuse. A cousin of the family was that intrepid Australian flier, Sir Charles Kingsford Smith, the author's boyhood hero who held the trans-Pacific and trans-Atlantic records in the late twenties, and the Australia to England record as well. A more distant relative was, however, the Scottish Jacobite Intriguer, beheaded in the Tower of London, charged with treason. David Mariner sadly admits that this is the only member of the family whom he takes after, which wholly explains the sinister quality in his books."

AVOCATIONAL INTERESTS: Music, study of wildlife, salmon net fishing, meditation, and conservation.

* * *

SMITH, David T. 1935-

PERSONAL: Born December 11, 1935, in Pawtucket, R.I.; son of Herbert J. (in textile sales) and Harriet (Thornton) Smith; married Sandra June Gustavson (in real estate sales), December 20, 1958; children: David, Jr., Douglas, Daniel. *Education:* Yale University, B.A., 1957; Boston University, J.D., 1960. *Politics:* Independent. *Religion:* Lutheran. *Home:* 6405 N.W. 18th Ave., Gainesville, Fla. 32605. *Office:* College of Law, University of Florida, Gainesville, Fla. 32611.

CAREER: Admitted to the Bar of Massachusetts; Indiana University, Bloomington, instructor in law, 1960-62; Duquesne University, Pittsburgh, Pa., assistant professor of law, 1962-63; Case Western Reserve University, Cleveland, Ohio, 1963-68, began as assistant professor, later associate professor of law; University of Florida, Gainesville, 1968—, began as associate professor, now professor of law. *Member:* American Law Institute, American Bar Association, American Association of University Professors, American Judicature Society, Massachusetts Bar Association, Phi Alpha Delta, Selden Society, Scribes. *Awards, honors:* Florida Blue Key Distinguished Faculty Award, 1974; Florida Student Government Outstanding Professor Award, 1974.

WRITINGS: (Editor with Oliver Schroeder) *De Facto Segregation and Civil Rights*, W. S. Hein, 1965; (editor) *Abortion and the Law*, Press of Case Western Reserve University, 1967; (with Marvin Sussman and J. Cates) *The Family and Inheritance*, Russell Sage, 1970; (reviser) Thomas, *Florida Estates Practice Guide*, Matthew Bender, revised edition, 1974.

* * *

SMITH, Jean Pajot 1945-

PERSONAL: Maiden name is pronounced *Pay*-zhoe; born November 14, 1945, in Saline, Mich.; daughter of Lawrence Joseph (a draftsman) and Dorothy May (Peckens) Pajot; married Pat Smith (director of Lansing's Community Design Center), August 19, 1967; children: Malcolm, Jason. *Education:* Michigan State University, B.F.A., 1968. *Politics:* Independent. *Home and office:* 1515 West Kalamazoo, Lansing, Mich. 48915.

CAREER: Michigan State University, East Lansing, medical illustrator for department of anatomy, 1965-68; writer, 1973—. Member of National Association for the Advancement of Colored People (NAACP) Emergency Schools Assistance Act Project advisory committee, 1973-74; member of Planning Committee for the Vivian Riddle Elementary School, Lansing.

WRITINGS: *Li'l Tuffy and His A.B.C.'s* (juvenile), Johnson Publishing Co. (Chicago), 1973; (contributor of medical illustrations) Daris R. Swindler and Charles D. Wood, *An Atlas of Primate Gross Anatomy: Baboons, Chimpanzee, and Man*, University of Washington Press, 1973.

WORK IN PROGRESS: *Li'l Tuffy and His Friends*, a book for preschool-age children, for Johnson Publishing Co.

SIDELIGHTS: Jean Smith writes: "Getting into the children's literature field came about through a request from a friend in the Minority book business and our own need to find relevant material to entertain our children. A marketplace research was established and conclusion drawn that a coloring book with a trendy ABC's would be viable and entertaining. Though the content may become dated due to the constant changes inherent in 'slang' languages, I still feel the total message of this particular coloring book will endure." *Avocational interests:* Sewing, crocheting, refinishing furniture, upholstering, baking bread.

* * *

SMITH, Pattie Sherwood 1909(?)-1974

1909(?)—December 27, 1974; American newspaper writer and author of a biography of Joseph Pulitzer. Obituaries: *New York Times*, December 29, 1974; *AB Bookman's Weekly*, January 27, 1975.

* * *

SMITH, Robert J(ohn) 1927-

PERSONAL: Born June 27, 1927, in Essex, Mo.; son of Will D. (an attorney) and Fern (Jones) Smith; married Kazuko Sasaki (a teacher), August 22, 1955. *Education:* University of Minnesota, B.A., 1949; Cornell University, M.A., 1951, Ph.D., 1953. *Home:* 107 Northview Rd., Ithaca, N.Y. 14850. *Office:* Department of Anthropology, Cornell University, Ithaca, N.Y. 14853.

CAREER: Cornell University, Ithaca, N.Y., instructor, 1953-55, assistant professor, 1955-61, associate professor, 1961-66, professor of anthropology, 1966-74, Goldwin Smith Professor of Anthropology, 1974—. *Military service:* U.S. Army, 1944-46. *Member:* American Anthropological Association (fellow), American Ethnological Society, Society for Applied Anthropology, Association for Asian Studies, Royal Anthropological Institute (fellow).

WRITINGS: (With John B. Cornell) *Two Japanese Villages*, University of Michigan Press, 1956; (editor with R. K. Beardsley) *Japanese Culture*, Aldine, 1962; (editor) *Social Organization and the Applications of Anthropology*, Cornell University Press, 1974; *Ancestor Worship in Contemporary Japan*, Stanford University Press, 1974. Editor of *Human Organization*, 1961-66.

* * *

SMITH, Rockwell Carter 1908-

PERSONAL: Born March 6, 1908, in Holyoke, Mass.; son of Stephen G. (in laundry) and Ethel (Carter) Smith; married Frances Dyer Eckardt (a psychologist), August 27, 1931. *Education:* DePauw University, B.A., 1928; Boston University, S.T.B., 1931; University of Wisconsin, Ph.D., 1942. *Politics:* Democrat. *Home:* 2801 North Montana, Roswell, N.M. 88201. *Office:* 417 Hinkle Bldg., 108 East Third St., Roswell, N.M. 88201.

CAREER: Ordained minister of United Methodist Church, 1927; pastor in Indiana, Massachusetts, Wisconsin, and Illinois, 1927-42; Garrett Theological Seminary, Evanston, Ill., assistant professor, 1940-43, associate professor, 1943-45, professor of rural sociology and sociology of religion, 1945-73, dean of students, 1957-69. *Member:* Rural Sociological Society, American Sociological Association, Society for the Scientific Study of Religion, European Society for Rural Sociology. *Awards, honors:* D.D., DePauw University, 1949; distinguished Alumnus, Boston University, 1966.

WRITINGS: *The Church in Our Town*, Abingdon, 1945, revised edition, 1955; *Rural Church Administration*, Abingdon, 1953; *People, Land, and Churches*, Friendship, 1959; *Rural Ministry and the Changing Community*, Abingdon, 1971.

WORK IN PROGRESS: Studying the regional social characteristics of the American Southwest; developing theoretical perspectives in sociology of religion.

* * *

**SMITH, Shirley M(ae) 1923-
(Ellis Ovesen)**

PERSONAL: Born July 18, 1923, in New Effington, S.D.; daughter of Einar W. and Augustine (Ovesen) Johnson;

married Thor Lowe Smith (a chemist), August 28, 1949; children: Theodore Lowe, Glen Everett. *Education:* University of Wisconsin, M.A. (cum laude), 1948. *Religion:* Christian. *Home:* 26885 Ortega Dr., Los Altos Hills, Calif. 94022.

CAREER: University of Wisconsin, Milwaukee, instructor in English, 1946-48; E. I. duPont Co., Wilmington, Del., advertising copywriter, 1948-49; San Jose State College (now California State University, San Jose), instructor in English, 1963; poet. Taught poetry course at Palo Alto, Calif. junior high school, 1970. *Member:* American Association of University Women, National Federation of State Poetry Societies (president of Peninsula Poets chapter, 1974—), American League of Penwomen, National Writers Club, California Federation of Chaparral Poets (president of Toyon branch, 1969-70), California Writers Club, San Francisco Poetry Center, Palo Alto Art Club. *Awards, honors:* Printing Industries of America second place award for beauty of content and design, 1974, for *Lives Touch*.

WRITINGS—All poetry under pseudonym Ellis Ovesen: *Gloried Grass*, West Coast Lithographers, 1970; *Haloed Paths*, American Poetry Fellowships, 1972; *Lives Touch*, St. Mary's College Press, 1973; (with Helen Carter King) *To Those Who Love*, Harlo, 1974; *The Last Hour*, American Poetry Fellowships, 1975.

WORK IN PROGRESS: A book of Haiku, *In Its Time*; a book of poems about birds, *Song Bars*; a book of poetry with Biblical quotations, *Beloved*; a book of religious inspirational poetry; a book of poems about growing up a woman.

AVOCATIONAL INTERESTS: Art, travel, golf, bowling, gardening, bird watching, collecting rocks.

* * *

SMITH, William Gardner 1927-1974

1927—November 5, 1974; American-born resident of France, journalist, editor, novelist, and author of books on the problems of black Americans. Obituaries: *New York Times*, November 8, 1974; *Washington Post*, November 8, 1974; *Publishers Weekly*, November 25, 1974; *AB Bookman's Weekly*, December 2, 1974; *Black World*, February, 1975.

* * *

SMITHSON, Peter (Denham) 1923-

PERSONAL: Born September 18, 1923, in Stockton on Tees, Durham, England; son of William Blenkiron (a commercial traveler) and Elizebeth (a teacher; maiden name, Denham) Smithson; married Alison Margaret Gill (an architect), August, 1949; children: Simon, Samantha, Soraya. *Education:* Studied at King's College, University of Durham, 1939-42, 1945-48, and Royal Academy Schools, 1948-49; Dip.Arch., 1947. *Home:* 24 Gilston Rd., London SW10 9SR, England.

CAREER: London County Council, Architects' Department, London, England, assistant in Schools Division, 1949-50; architect in private practice with his wife, London, England, 1950—. *Military service:* Queen Victoria's Own Madras Sappers and Miners, 1942-45; served in India and Burma; became lieutenant.

WRITINGS: Bath: Walks within the Walls, Adams & Dart, 1971.

With wife, Alison Smithson: *Uppercase 3* (monograph), edited by Theo Crosby, Architectural Design, 1960, expanded version published as *Urban Structuring*, edited by John Lewis, Reinhold, 1967; (contributor) Georgy Kepes, editor, *Structure in Art and in Sciences*, Braziller, 1965; *Ordinariness and Light: Urban Theories 1952-1960 and Their Application in a Building Project 1963-1970*, M.I.T. Press, 1970; *Without Rhetoric: An Architectural Aesthetic 1955-1972*, M.I.T. Press, 1973.

Films: (Narrator) "Haupstadt Berlin," National Film Archives (London), 1957; (with Alison Smithson) "Robin Hood Lane in Construction: Colour," British Broadcasting Corp. Television, 1970.

Contributor of articles, usually in collaboration with his wife, to architectural yearbooks and to journals in Europe, United States, Japan, and India; also has published poems and book reviews.

WORK IN PROGRESS: With wife, Alison Smithson, *The Charged Void*.

BIOGRAPHICAL/CRITICAL SOURCES: Architectural Association Journal, February, 1966.

* * *

SNOWMAN, Daniel 1938-

PERSONAL: Born November 4, 1938, in London, England; son of Arthur Mortimer (an insurance broker) and Bertha (Lazarus) Snowman. *Education:* Cambridge University, B.A., 1961; Cornell University, M.A., 1963. *Home:* 17A Langland Gardens, Hampstead, London N.W.3, England. *Agent:* Bolt & Watson Ltd., 8 Storeys Gate, London S.W.1, England. *Office:* British Broadcasting Corp., Broadcasting House, London W1A 1AA, England.

CAREER: University of Sussex, Brighton, England, lecturer in politics and American studies, 1963-67; British Broadcasting Corp., London, England, producer, 1967—.

WRITINGS: U.S.A.: The Twenties to Vietnam, Batsford, 1968, published as *America since 1920*, Harper, 1969; *Eleanor Roosevelt*, Heron Books, 1970.

WORK IN PROGRESS: A book comparing British and American society and social attitudes, especially since 1945.

* * *

SOBELL, Morton 1917-

PERSONAL: Born April 11, 1917, in New York, N.Y.; son of Louis (a pharmacist and engineer) and Rose (Pasternak) Sobell; married Helen Levitov (a computer programmer), March 10, 1945; children: Mark; (stepchildren) Sydney Clemens. *Education:* City College (now City College of the City University of New York), B.S.E.E., 1938; University of Michigan, M.S.E.E., 1942; attended Columbia University, 1969-70. *Politics:* "Radical." *Religion:* None. *Home:* 626 Riverside Dr., New York, N.Y. 10031. *Agent:* International Famous Agency, 1301 Ave. of the Americas, New York, N.Y. 10019. *Office:* 30 Virginia Rd., White Plains, N.Y. 10603.

CAREER: U.S. Department of the Navy, Bureau of Ordnance, Washington, D.C., electrical engineer, 1939-41; General Electric Co., Aeronautic and Marine Engineering Dept., Schenectady, N.Y., control engineer, 1942-47; Reeves Instrument Co., New York, N.Y., project engineer, 1947-50; Medical Electronics, White Plains, N.Y., project engineer, 1971—. Member of board of directors of Riverview Towers (housing cooperative), 1974—.

WRITINGS: On Doing Time, Scribner, 1974.

WORK IN PROGRESS: A continuation of *On Doing Time*.

SIDELIGHTS: In 1951 Sobell was brought to trial with Julius and Ethel Rosenberg, charged with conspiring to steal nuclear secrets. All three were found guilty. The Rosenbergs were executed at Sing Sing in 1953. Sobell was sentenced to thirty years in prison and served eighteen years (five of them in Alcatraz) before his release in 1969.

Sobell states that he and his wife falsely signed non-Communist affidavits in order to hold their jobs and fled to Mexico in 1951, fearing persecution for perjury; but he maintains that he and the Rosenbergs were completely innocent of the charges brought against them.

* * *

SOLE, Carlos A(lberto) 1938-

PERSONAL: Born September 9, 1938, in Panama, Republic of Panama; son of Carlos Sole Bosch (a newspaper editor) and Mercedes (Icaza) de Sole; married Yolanda Russinovich (a university professor), May 30, 1964; children: one. *Education:* Georgetown University, B.S., 1960, Ph.D., 1966. *Religion:* Roman Catholic. *Home:* 7304 Lamplight Lane, Austin, Tex. 78731. *Office:* Department of Spanish and Portuguese, University of Texas at Austin, Austin, Tex. 78712.

CAREER: Harvard University, Cambridge, Mass., assistant professor of Spanish, 1966-70; University of Texas at Austin, associate professor of Spanish, 1970—. *Member:* Modern Language Association of America, American Council on the Teaching of Foreign Languages, American Association of Teachers of Spanish and Portuguese, National Association of Modern Language Teachers, Asociacion de Linguistica y Filologia de America Latina, Programa Interamericano de Linguistica y Ensenanza de Idiomas.

WRITINGS: Los adjetivos espanoles terminados en -al, -ero, -ico, -oso, Georgetown University Press, 1966; *Bibliografia sobre el espanol en America: 1920-1967*, Georgetown University Press, 1970; (with wife, Yolanda Sole) *A Contrastive Grammar of Spanish*, Scribner, in press. General editor of Scribner "Spanish Series," 1973—.

WORK IN PROGRESS: Language maintenance among Spanish speaking communities in the United States.

* * *

SOLMSEN, Friedrich (Rudolf Heinrich) 1904-

PERSONAL: Born February 4, 1904, in Bonn, Germany; came to United States, 1937; naturalized citizen, 1944; son of Felix and Lily (Brach) Solmsen; married Lieselotte Salzer, March 12, 1932. *Education:* Attended University of Bonn, 1922; University of Berlin, Dr.phil., 1928; Cambridge University, Ph.D., 1936. *Home:* 810 Old Mill Rd., Chapel Hill, N.C. 27514. *Office:* Department of Classics, University of North Carolina, Chapel Hill, N.C.

CAREER: University of Berlin, Berlin, Germany, assistant professor of classics, 1929-33; Olivet College, Olivet, Mich., professor of philosophy, 1937-40; Cornell University, Ithaca, N.Y., assistant professor, 1940-44, associate professor, 1944-47, professor of classics, 1947-62, chairman of department, 1953-62; University of Wisconsin-Madison, professor of classics, 1962-74, Moses Slaughter Professor of Classical Studies, 1964-74, member of Institute for Research in the Humanities, 1962-74; University of North Carolina, Chapel Hill, visiting professor of classics, 1974—. Fulbright Professor, University of Frankfurt, 1958-59, University of Kiel, 1959, and University of St. Andrews, 1965; Herbert F. Johnson Visiting Professor, University of Wisconsin-Madison, 1960-61; visiting lecturer, University of Bonn, 1964, University of Heidelberg, 1968, 1973; visiting professor, Swarthmore College, 1970, Yale University, 1972.

MEMBER: American Philological Association, American Philosophical Association, Renaissance Society of America, Netherlands Academy of Letters and Sciences, American Philosophical Society, American Academy of Arts and Sciences, British Academy (corresponding fellow), Society for the Promotion of Hellenic Studies (honorary member). *Awards, honors:* Guggenheim fellowship, 1947-48; honorary Ph.D., University of Kiel, 1965, University of Bonn, 1968; Charles J. Goodwin Award of Merit from American Philological Association, 1972, for *Hesiodi Theogonia Opera et Dies Scutum*.

WRITINGS: Die Entwicklung der aristotelischen Logik und Rhetorik (title means "Development of Aristotle's Logic and Rhetoric"), Weidmann (Berlin), 1929; *Antiphonstudien: Untersuchungen zur entstehung der attischen gerichtsrede* (title means "Antiphon Studies on the Origin of Judicial Oratory in Athens"), Weidmann, 1931; *Plato's Theology*, Cornell University Press, 1942, reprinted, Johnson Reprint, 1967; *Hesiod and Aeschylus*, Cornell University Press, 1949, reprinted, Johnson Reprint, 1967; (editor and author of introduction) Aristotle, *Rhetoric*, Modern Library, 1954; *Aristotle's System of the Physical World: A Comparison with His Predecessors*, Cornell University Press, 1960; *Kleine Schriften* (title means "Shorter Works"), two volumes, Georg Olms, 1968; (editor with Reinhold Merkelbach and Martin L. West) *Hesiodi Theogonia Opera et Dies Scutum* (title means "Hesiod's *Theogony, Works and Days, Shield*"), Clarendon Press, 1970; *Methods and Intellectual Experiments of the Greek Enlightenment*, Princeton University Press, 1975.

* * *

SOLOMON, Samuel 1904-
(Britindian, Melusa Moolson)

PERSONAL: Born September 20, 1904, in Calcutta, India; son of Hillel Elias (a businessman) and Yochebeth (Duveck-Cohen) Solomon; married Moselle Solomon, September 16, 1937; children: Jonathan, Emma Berenice (Mrs. Chaim Klein), Celia (Mrs. Julio Ulanovsky). *Education:* King's College, Cambridge, B.A. (with honors), 1926, graduate study, 1927, M.A., 1971. *Politics:* Liberal Party. *Religion:* Jewish. *Home:* 51 Hollycroft Ave., London NW3 7QJ, England. *Agent:* Bertha Case, 42 West 53rd St., New York, N.Y. *Office:* c/o Grindlays Bank, 13 St. James's Sq., London S.W.1, England.

CAREER: Indian Civil Service, Bihar and Orissa, serving in various positions, including magistrate, judge, and district officer, 1927-47; full-time translator, author, and lecturer, 1947—. Parliamentary candidate in general elections of 1959 and 1964. Has lectured in Great Britain, Israel, and United States. *Member:* National Liberal Club.

WRITINGS: Poems from East and West, Erskine Macdonald (London), 1927; (under pseudonym Melusa Moolson) *The Saint and Satan*, Indian Publications (London), 1930; *Bihar and Orissa in 1934-35*, Government Press (Patna, Bihar, India), 1937; *The Dying Rajput and Other*

Poems, M. L. Cailingold (London), 1937; *Winning the Peace*, David Maximillian (Calcutta), 1942; *The Arch of Titus and Other Poems*, Himalaya Publications (Patna), 1945; (under pseudonym Britindian) *The Causes and Solution of India's Communal Problem*, Himalaya Publications, 1946; *Garden at Hazaribagh*, Himalaya Publications, 1947; (and translator) *The Jew in Heinrich Heine*, British Section, World Jewish Congress (London), 1972.

Translator and editor: Jean Racine, *The Complete Plays*, two volumes, Random House, 1967, revised edition, Modern Library, 1969; Pierre Corneille, *Seven Plays*, Random House, 1969; Franz Grillparzer, *Plays on Classic Themes*, Random House, 1970.

Contributor: P. W. Diebel and R. McBurney, editors, *A Parade of Poems*, Macmillan, 1965; E. R. Bentley, editor, *The Great Playwrights*, Doubleday, 1970; E. S. Neumann and Roger Johnson, Jr., editors, *Moliere and the Commonwealth of Letters*, University and College Press of Mississippi, 1975.

Author and co-narrator, "Racine: An Introduction," Sussex Tapes (London), 1971, Bailey Film Associates (Los Angeles), 1973; translator and author of introductory talk, "Mithridates" (from Racine), broadcast by BBC, 1973. Contributor to journals, including *Statesman* and *Capital* (both Calcutta), *Contemporary Review* and *London Magazine* (both London), *Tulane Drama Review*, and *Hudson Review*.

WORK IN PROGRESS: Translations of Louise Labe's *Complete Works* and Moliere's *Complete Theatre*; a critical appreciation of Racine's dramatic art; translation of selected poems of Heinrich Heine; a historical tragedy to be titled "The Fall of Hitler" or "Where Is Thy Peace?"

AVOCATIONAL INTERESTS: Instrumental and operatic music, gardens, travel.

* * *

SOMEKH, Emile 1915-

PERSONAL: Born November 3, 1915, in Bagdad, Iraq; son of Nissim and Farida (Sassoon) Somekh; married Evelyne Darwish, April, 1949; children: Ricky, Joseph, Lauraine. *Education:* Attended American University of Beirut, 1927-32, and Royal College of Medicine, Rome, Italy, 1932-37, 1948-50. *Home:* 310 Melbourne Rd., Great Neck, N.Y. *Office:* 131 Fulton Ave., Hempstead, N.Y. 11550.

CAREER: Licensed to practice medicine in New York, 1959; private practice of pediatric allergy medicine in Bagdad, Iraq, 1938-46, in Rome, Italy, 1946-48, in Tel-Aviv, Israel, 1950-56, and in Hempstead, N.Y., 1959—. Clinical teaching assistant in pediatric allergy at St. Vincents Hospital, New York, N.Y., Bellevue Hospital, New York, N.Y., New York University, and North Shore Hospital, New York, N.Y. *Member:* American Medical Association, American Academy of Allergy, American Clinical Allergy and Immunology Association, Royal Society of Health (honorary fellow), New York Allergy Society, Nassau County Medical Society.

WRITINGS: A Parent's Guide to Children's Allergies, C. C Thomas, 1972; *Allergy and Your Child*, Harper, 1974.

WORK IN PROGRESS: A book titled *The Allergy Pocketbook*.

SIDELIGHTS: In 1952, Somekh classified and discovered the molds that cause asthma in Israel. He speaks and writes Arabic, Hebrew, English, French, German, Italian and Spanish. *Avocational interests:* Swimming and gardening.

SOSA, Ernest 1940-

PERSONAL: Born June 17, 1940, in Cardenas, Cuba; spent 1948-49 in United States and returned to live permanently, 1954; naturalized citizen, 1959; son of Ernest S. and Maria (Garriga) Sosa; married December, 1961; children: E. David. *Education:* University of Miami, Coral Gables, Fla., B.A., 1961; University of Pittsburgh, M.S., 1962, Ph.D., 1964; Brown University, postdoctoral fellow, 1964-66. *Residence:* Providence, R.I. *Office:* Department of Philosophy, Brown University, Providence, R.I. 02912.

CAREER: University of Western Ontario, London, instructor, 1963-64, assistant professor of philosophy, 1966-67; Brown University, Providence, R.I., assistant professor, 1967-68, associate professor, 1968-74, professor of philosophy, 1974—, chairman of department, 1970—. Visiting professor at University of Miami, Coral Gables, winter, 1970, University of Western Ontario, summer, 1971, and University of Michigan, winter-spring, 1971-72. *Member:* American Philosophical Association (secretary-treasurer of Eastern Division, 1974—). *Awards, honors:* Carnegie postdoctoral interdisciplinary fellowship in philosophy and psychology, 1964-66; grants from Canada Council, 1964, National Endowment for the Humanities, 1968, American Council of Learned Societies, 1969, and National Science Foundation, 1970-72.

WRITINGS: (Editor with James M. Smith and contributor) *Mill's Utilitarianism*, Wadsworth, 1969; (editor and author of introduction) *Causation and Conditionals*, Oxford University Press, in press.

Contributor: J. J. Davis and others, editors, *Philosophical Logic*, Reidel, 1969, Humanities, 1970; Patrick Suppes, editor, *Logic, Methodology and the Philosophy of Science*, Humanities, 1973; *Modality, Morality and Other Problems of Sense and Nonsense*, Gleerup, 1973; Robert S. Cohen and Marx Wartofsky, editors, *Methodological and Historical Essays in the Natural and the Social Sciences*, Reidel, 1974. Contributor to *American Philosophical Quarterly*, *Journal of Philosophy*, *Mind*, *Philosophical Review*, and other philosophy journals. Member of board of editors, *American Philosophical Quarterly*, 1974—.

* * *

SOSA de QUESADA, Aristides V. 1908-

PERSONAL: Born January 22, 1908, in Matanzas, Cuba; son of Antonio (a businessman) and Manuela (de Quesada) Sosa; married Rafaela Vazquez, July 27, 1933; children: Aristides A., Rafael A. *Education:* University of Havana, LL.D., 1930, Ph.D.; Kansas State Teachers College, M.S., 1966. *Religion:* Roman Catholic. *Home:* 1752 Nebraska St., Blair, Neb. 68008. *Office:* Department of Spanish, Dana College, Blair, Neb. 68008.

CAREER: Cuban Army, officer, 1932-58, rising to major general and Advocate General of the Army; came to United States as exile, and taught in Nebraska public schools, 1964-66; Dana College, Blair, Neb., assistant professor of Spanish, 1967—. Cuban posts also included secretary to Secretary of Defense, 1942-44, professor of literature at Military Academy for High-Ranked Officers, 1944-52, president of Military Institute of Technology, 1953-58, mayor of Havana, and president of Military Supreme Court. President of Cuban National Council on Health, Education and Welfare, 1936-40, and National Organization of Public Libraries, 1954-58. *Member:* Cuban Bar Association (member in exile), American Association of Teachers of Spanish and Portuguese. *Awards, honors*—Military: Distinguished Service Medal, and other high Cuban decorations.

WRITINGS—Nonfiction; published by P. Fernandez (Havana), except as noted: *An International Army as a Guarantee for World Peace*, 1932, *El Consejo corporativo de educacion, sanidad y beneficencia y sus instituciones filiales*, Instituto Civico-Militar, 1937; *Motivaciones escolares*, 1939; *Tres Charlas en Mexico*, 1939; *Temas de Orientacion*, 1942; *Reliquias de Marti*, 1943; *Por la democracia . . . y por la libertad*, 1943; *Cuba esta presente*, 1944; *Marti, Maceo y Agramonte a traves de sus reliquias*, 1944; *Norteamericas al vuelo*, 1945.

Other books: *Tardes de Arisfael* (poems), P. Fernandez, 1948; *Wan-Pu* (novel), P. Fernandez, 1950; *Ayer sin fecha* (essays and poems), P. Fernandez, 1957; *Errante* (poems), Universal Press (Miami), 1967; *Brasas en la Nieve* (poems), New House Publishers (Miami), 1971.

Writer of series of articles, "Cuba escarnecida y sojuzgada," published in *Tiempo* (Bogota), 1962, and a play, "A Stranger at Home," first produced in 1964.

WORK IN PROGRESS: Bajo los alamos del parque, a novel; a collection of essays.

* * *

SPECHT, Harry 1929-

PERSONAL: Born August 1, 1929, in New York, N.Y.; son of Joseph (a gambler) and Helen (a pianist; maiden name, Frankele) Specht; married Riva Genfan (a social worker), June 5, 1954; children: Daniel Joseph, Eliot David. *Education:* City College (now of the City University of New York), B.A., 1951; Western Reserve University (now Case Western Reserve University), M.S.S.W., 1951; Brandeis University, Ph.D., 1962. *Politics:* Socialist. *Religion:* Jewish. *Home:* 807 Oxford, Berkeley, Calif. 94707. *Office:* School of Social Welfare, University of California, Berkeley, Calif. 94720.

CAREER: Mobilization for Youth, New York, N.Y., director of community organization, 1962-64; Contra Costa Council of Community Services, Walnut Creek, Calif., associate director, 1964-66; San Francisco State College (now University), San Francisco, Calif., associate professor, 1966-67; University of California, Berkeley, lecturer, 1967-69, associate professor, 1969-73, professor of social work, 1973—. *Awards, honors:* Senior Fulbright scholarship, London, England, 1973-74.

WRITINGS: Young Adults in Groups, National Jewish Welfare Board, 1964; (editor with Ralph Kramer) *Readings in Community Organization Practice*, Prentice-Hall, 1969; (with George Brager) *Community Organizing*, Columbia University Press, 1973; (with Neil Gilbert) *Dimensions of Social Welfare Policy*, Prentice-Hall, 1974; (with Gilbert) *The Model Cities Program*, U.S. Government Printing Office, 1974.

WORK IN PROGRESS: Practice in Social Planning; Social Welfare Perspectives.

* * *

SPEDDING, C(olin) R(aymond) W(illiam) 1925-

PERSONAL: Born March 22, 1925, in Cannock, England; son of Robert Kewley (a clergyman) and Ilynn (Bannister) Spedding; married Betty Noreen George, September 6, 1952; children: Geoffrey Robert, Lucilla Mary. *Education:* University of London, B.Sc., 1951, M.Sc., 1953, Ph.D., 1955, D.Sc., 1967. *Home:* Vine Cottage, Hurst, Reading, Berkshire, England. *Office:* Department of Agriculture and Horticulture, University of Reading, Reading, Berkshire RG6 2AH, England.

CAREER: Grassland Research Institute, member of staff, 1949—, head of ecology department, 1962—, assistant director, 1968-72, deputy director, 1972—; University of Reading, Reading, Berkshire, England, professor of agricultural systems, 1970—. *Military service:* Royal Naval Volunteer Reserve, 1943-46; became sub-lieutenant. *Member:* European Association of Animal Production, Farmer's Club, Institute of Biology (fellow), Nutrition Society, British Society for Animal Production, British Grassland Society, Zoological Society (scientific fellow), Society for the Study of Animal Behaviour, Association of Applied Biologists, British Society for Parasitology. *Awards, honors:* Recognition award from Canadian Institute of Agriculture, 1971; George Hedley Memorial Award, from National Sheep Association (England), 1971.

WRITINGS: Sheep Production and Grazing Management, Bailliere, Tindall & Cox, 1965, 2nd edition, Balliere, Tindall & Cassell, 1970; *Grassland Ecology*, Oxford University Press, 1971; (editor with E. C. Diekmahns) *Grasses and Legumes in British Agriculture*, Commonwealth Agriculture Bureau, 1972; *The Biology of Agricultural Systems*, Academic Press, 1975. Editor of *Agricultural Systems*, 1975—.

BIOGRAPHICAL/CRITICAL SOURCES: Farm, July/August, 1972.

* * *

SPILLMANN, Betty Evelyn 1920-

PERSONAL: Born July 5, 1920, in London, England; daughter of Walter Ernest (a press telegraphist) and Blanche (Curitt) Jackson; married Alain Spillmann (a doctor), July 5, 1952; children: Patrick, Claire. *Education:* Gregg Business College, student, 1936-38. *Politics:* Socialist. *Religion:* Christian. *Home and office:* Santa Marta, Mouans-Sartoux 06370, France.

CAREER: British Foreign Office, London, England, translator, 1943-46; United Nations, New York, N.Y., translator, 1948; World Health Organization, Geneva, Switzerland, translator, 1949-52; author, translator. *Wartime service:* W.J.A.C., 1941-45; became group commander.

WRITINGS: (Translator) Joseph Nuttin and others, *Experimental Psychology*, Volume V: *Motivation, Emotion, and Personality* (Spillmann was not associated with other volumes), Routledge & Kegan Paul, 1968; (translator) Francois Jacob, *Logic of Living Systems*, Penguin, 1974.

Contributor of translations to magazines, including *Inserm*.

WORK IN PROGRESS: Research for a novel set in a private hospital.

AVOCATIONAL INTERESTS: Oil painting (work has been shown in North and South America, and in Europe).

* * *

SPINK, Reginald (William) 1905-

PERSONAL: Born December 9, 1905, in York, England. *Education:* Educated in England. *Home and office:* 6 Deane Way, Eastcote, Ruislip, Middlesex HA4 8SU, England.

CAREER: Copenhagen correspondent for *Financial Times*, and for *Shipping World*, both London, England,

1946-49; writer. *Wartime service:* Special Operations Executive, senior member of Danish section, 1940-45, Political Warfare Executive, 1943-44. *Member:* Society of Authors, Translators Association (member of executive committee, 1965-67, 1972-74). *Awards, honors:* Freedom Medal from King Christian X, 1945; awarded Knight's Cross of the Order of the Dannebrog, 1966.

WRITINGS: (With Jens Otto Krag) *England bygger op* (title means "Britain Rebuilds"), Det danske Forlag, 1947; *The Land and People of Denmark*, Macmillan, 1953; *Fairy Tales of Denmark* (juvenile), Dutton, 1961; *The Young Hans Andersen* (juvenile), Roy, 1962; *Hans Christian Andersen and His World*, Thames & Hudson, 1972; *Hans Christian Andersen: The Man and His Work*, Hoest, 1972.

Translator: Carl Nielsen, *My Childhood*, Hutchinson, 1953; Nielsen, *Living Music*, Hutchinson, 1953; Palle Lauring, *The Roman*, Museum Press, 1956; Anton Bruun and others, *The Galathea Deep Sea Expedition*, Allen & Unwin, 1956; Lauring, *Land of the Tollund Man*, Lutterworth, 1957; Ludvig Holberg, *Three Comedies*, Theatre Arts, 1957; Poul Borchsenius, *Behind the Wall*, Simon & Schuster, 1957; Hans Christian Andersen, *Fairy Tales*, Dutton, 1958; Frank Wenzel, *The Buzzard*, Allen & Unwin, 1959.

Andersen, *Fairy Tales and Stories*, Dutton, 1960; Rolf Blomberg, *Chavante*, Allen & Unwin, 1960; Bengt Danielsson, *Terry in the South Seas*, Allen & Unwin, 1960; Danielsson, *Terry in Australia*, Allen & Unwin, 1961; Joergen Bisch, *Ulu: The World's End*, Dutton, 1961; Borchsenius, *And It Was Morning*, Simon & Schuster, 1962; Bisch, *Behind the Veil of Arabia*, Dutton, 1962; Bisch, *Mongolia: Unknown Land*, Dutton, 1963; Einar Rud, *Vasari's Life and Lives*, Thames & Hudson, 1963; Danielsson, *Gauguin in the South Seas*, Doubleday, 1965; Knud Soenderby, *The Blue Flashes*, Danish Ministry of Foreign Affairs, 1966; Poul Abrahamsen, *Royal Wedding*, Danish Ministry of Foreign Affairs, 1967.

Translator or editor of several editions of *Denmark: An Official Handbook*, Danish Ministry of Foreign Affairs, 1946—. Scandinavian correspondent for *New Leader*, 1935-39, 1945-50.

Contributor to American, British, Canadian, Australian, New Zealand, and Danish journals. Translator and English text editor of *Danish Foreign Office Journal* (now *Danish Journal*), 1946—; editor of *Denmark: A Quarterly Review of Anglo-Danish Relations*, 1961-74.

* * *

SPRENGEL, Donald P(hilip) 1938-

PERSONAL: Born August 5, 1938, in Chicago, Ill.; son of Andrew Cyril (a civil servant) and Margaret (Kirkpatrick) Sprengel; married Annette Rysiewski, June 13, 1964; children: Andrew, Jean. *Education:* Loyola University, Chicago, Ill., B.S., 1960; St. Louis University, A.M., 1962; University of North Carolina, Ph.D., 1966. *Politics:* Democrat. *Religion:* Roman Catholic. *Home:* 58 Sun Valley, St. Louis, Mo. 63141. *Office:* Department of Urban Affairs, St. Louis University, 221 North Grand, St. Louis, Mo. 63103.

CAREER: University of Iowa, Iowa City, assistant professor of political science, 1965-69; St. Louis University, St. Louis, Mo., assistant professor, 1969-70, associate professor, 1970-73, professor of Urban Affairs, 1973—. Member of Midwest American Assembly on State Legislatures and Mid-America American Assembly on States and Urban Crisis; staff director of Iowa Legislative Study Committee. *Member:* American Political Science Association, American Society for Public Administration, Midwest Political Science Association, Missouri Political Science Association, Pi Gamma Mu, Pi Sigma Alpha. *Awards, honors:* Grants from Iowa State Department of Public Instruction, 1967, U.S. Department of Housing and Urban Development, 1969-71, and U.S. Department of Labor, 1971-74.

WRITINGS: *Gubernatorial Staffs*, University of Iowa Press, 1969; *Comparative State Politics*, C. E. Merrill, 1971; (with Leonard E. Goodall) *American Metropolis*, C. E. Merrill, 1975.

* * *

SPRINGER, John 1916-

PERSONAL: Born April 25, 1916, in Rochester, N.Y.; son of W. A. (head of industrial relations for Eastman Kodak Co.) and Alice (Grosjean) Springer; married June Alicia Reimer (at time of marriage a television and Broadway singing star who used the name Monica Lane), June 3, 1953; children: Gary, Alicia, Cynthia. *Education:* Attended University of Toronto and Aquinas Institute; Marquette University, Ph.B., 1939. *Politics:* Democrat. *Religion:* Roman Catholic. *Home:* 130 East 67th St., New York, N.Y. 10021. *Office:* John Springer Associates, Inc., 667 Madison Ave., New York, N.Y. 10021.

CAREER: Radio-Keith-Orpheum Radio Pictures (RKO), New York, N.Y., magazine publicity director, 1946-57; Twentieth Century Fox, New York, magazine publicity director, 1957-60; Arthur Jacobs & John Springer Public Relations Co., New York, N.Y., partner, 1960-63; John Springer Associates, Inc. (public relations firm), New York, N.Y., president, 1963—. Has appeared in radio and television series on the major American media networks. *Military service:* U.S. Army Air Forces, 1942-45. *Awards, honors:* Byline Award from Marquette University, 1970, for distinctions in journalism career.

WRITINGS: *All Talking! All Singing! All Dancing!* (with introduction by actor Gene Kelly), Citadel, 1966; *Love for Sale*, Bartholomew Press, 1954; *The Fondas* (with introduction by John Steinbeck), Citadel, 1970; *They Had Faces Then*, Citadel, 1974. Contributor of articles on film and the theater to national publications, including *Cosmopolitan*, *Collier's*, *Coronet*, *Pageant*, *Photoplay*, and *Films in Review*.

WORK IN PROGRESS: *The Men Had Faces, Too* and *The Rest of the Faces*, sequels to *They Had Faces Then*.

SIDELIGHTS: John Springer originated the format of Tribute Evenings in a series of critically-acclaimed New York programs, opened by Bette Davis, and featuring other major film personalities. Clients of his public relations firm include Warren Beatty, Henry Fonda, Richard Burton, Mike Nichols, Hal Prince, Peggy Lee, Tony Randall, Elizabeth Taylor, and the New York Film Festival.

* * *

SPURRIER, William A(twell) 1916-

PERSONAL: Born June 19, 1916, in Newton, Mass.; son of William A. (a publisher) and Marian (Hunt) Spurrier; married Helene Messer, June 13, 1942; children: Anthony W., Robert D. *Education:* Williams College, B.A., 1939; Union Theological Seminary, New York, N.Y., B.D., 1942. *Politics:* Democrat. *Home:* 330 High St., Middletown, Conn. 06457. *Office:* Department of Religion, Wesleyan University, High St., Middletown, Conn. 06457.

CAREER: Ordained Episcopal clergyman, 1947. Amherst College, Amherst, Mass., instructor in religion and assistant chaplain, 1942-43; Wesleyan University, Middletown, Conn., instructor, 1946-49, assistant professor, 1949-54, associate professor, 1954-57, Hedding Foundation Professor of Religion, 1957—, chaplain of college, 1957-68. *Military service:* U.S. Army, infantry chaplain, 1944-46; served in European theater; became captain; received Bronze Star Medal. *Member:* Biblical Theologians (president, 1959-62), Church Society for College Work. *Awards, honors:* M.A. from Wesleyan University, 1957.

WRITINGS: Power for Action, Scribner, 1948; *Guide to the Christian Faith*, Scribner, 1952; *Guide to the Good Life*, Scribner, 1955; (contributor) James A. Pike, editor, *Modern Canterbury Pilgrims*, Morehouse, 1956; *Ethics and Business*, Scribner, 1962; *Natural Law and the Ethics of Love*, Westminster, 1974. Contributor of articles and reviews to *Christianity and Crisis, Virginia Quarterly, Episcopalian*, and *Virginia Seminary Review*. Editor of *Church Review*, 1961-63.

WORK IN PROGRESS: Christian Ethics and the Church in a Secular Society.

AVOCATIONAL INTERESTS: Sailing and cruising, golf, travel.

* * *

STAFFORD, William B(utler) 1931-

PERSONAL: Born February 6, 1931, in Pittsburgh, Pa.; son of Lee E. and Helen B. Stafford; married Barbara A. Svoboda (a teacher), August 11, 1956; children: Mark William, Debra Anne. *Education:* Ohio University, A.B., 1954, M.A., 1955; Indiana University, Ed.D., 1965. *Home:* 1415 Princeton Dr., Bethlehem, Pa. 18017. *Office:* School of Education, Lehigh University, Bethlehem, Pa. 18015.

CAREER: DePauw University, Greencastle, Ind., resident counselor, 1955-57; Indiana University, Laboratory School, Bloomington, counselor, 1957-65, assistant professor of education and director of pupil personnel services, 1965-67; Lehigh University, Bethlehem, Pa., assistant professor, 1967-72, associate professor of counselor education, 1972—. *Member:* American Personnel and Guidance Association, American College Personnel Association, Association of Counselor Educators and Supervisors, Pennsylvania Personnel and Guidance Association, Phi Delta Kappa.

WRITINGS: Schools Without Counselors: Guidance Practices for Teachers, Nelson-Hall, 1974. Contributor to *Elementary School Guidance and Counseling Journal.*

WORK IN PROGRESS: Psychological Foundations of Education.

* * *

STANCU, Zaharia 1902-1974

October 5, 1902—December 5, 1974; Rumanian poet, novelist, short story writer, journalist, editor, theater manager, president of the Rumanian Writers Union, deputy to the National Assembly, member of the central committee of the Communist Party, and member of the Council of State. Obituaries: *New York Times*, December 7, 1974; *AB Bookman's Weekly*, January 13, 1975.

STANFORD, Don(ald Kent) 1918-

PERSONAL: Born in 1918, in Chattanooga, Tenn.; son of Arthur Stanley Hannibal and Katherine (Rush) Stanford; married Frances Isabelle Schulman; children: two sons. *Education:* Attended Drexel Institute of Technology, Foreign Service Institute and University of Paris. *Home:* Wye Banks Farm, R.R. 3, Brantford, Ontario N3T 5L6, Canada. *Agent:* Lurton Blassingame, 60 East 42nd St., New York, N.Y. 10017; John Farquharson Ltd., 15 Red Lion Sq., London W.C.1, England; and H. N. Swanson Agency, 8523 Sunset Blvd., Los Angeles, Calif. 90069.

CAREER: Novelist, short story writer, author of scripts for films and television. *Member:* Writers Guild (West), Lambs Club and Metropolitan Club (both New York), Cercle interalliees (Paris).

WRITINGS: The Slaughtered Lovelies, Gold Medal Books, 1950; *Bargain in Blood*, Gold Medal Books, 1951; *The Red Car*, Funk, 1954; *Treasure of the Coral Reef*, Funk, 1956; *The Horsemasters*, Funk, 1957; *Ski Town!*, Funk, 1958; *Crash Landing*, Funk, 1959; *Ile de France*, Appleton, 1960; *Must Be Good Riders: Orphans Preferred*, Funk, 1962; *Mulligan's Pirates*, Simon & Schuster, 1966; *The Rice of Affection*, R. Hale, 1969.

Contributor of over eighty short stories and articles to magazines, including *Redbook, Argosy, Woman's Day, Cosmopolitan, This Week, Hitchcock, Coronet, Writer, True, Collier's, Saturday Evening Post, Reader's Digest*, and *Holiday.*

WORK IN PROGRESS: A novel; a nonfiction work, *The Face-Cards* (tentative title); a script for television pilot.

AVOCATIONAL INTERESTS: Gourmet food, wines, travel, horses, skiing, piloting airplanes.

* * *

STARK, John Olsen 1939-

PERSONAL: Born September 13, 1939, in Superior, Wis.; son of John and Phyllis (Olsen) Stark; married Faye Kaminski (an administrative secretary), June 8, 1968; children: Jeremy. *Education:* Attended University of Wisconsin, 1957-58; Northland College, B.A., 1961; Claremont Graduate School, M.A., 1963; graduate study at San Diego State College, 1963-64; University of Wisconsin, Ph.D., 1969. *Home:* 3631 Napoli Lane #4, Middleton, Wis. 53562.

CAREER: Wisconsin State University, Eau Claire, instructor in English, 1964-67; Kent State University, Kent, Ohio, assistant professor of English, 1969-73; free-lance writer and editor, 1974—.

WRITINGS: The Literature of Exhaustion: Borges, Nabokov, and Barth, Duke University Press, 1974. Contributor to English journals.

WORK IN PROGRESS: Thomas Pynchon and the Literature of Information.

* * *

STARK, Paul C. 1891(?)-1974

1891(?)—October 28, 1974; American horticulturalist credited with finding and developing the Golden Delicious apple, director of National Victory Garden Program during World War II, and author of books on horticulture. Obituaries: *New York Times*, November 1, 1974; *Washington Post*, November 2, 1974.

STARKE, Roland

PERSONAL: Born in Cape Town, South Africa; son of Alan and Margaret (Kennedy) Starke. *Education:* Attended University of Cape Town. *Residence:* London, England, and Los Angeles, Calif. *Agent:* Robin Dalton Assoc., 18 Elm Tree Rd., London N.W.8, England; Bart/Levy Assoc., 8601 Wilshire Blvd., Beverly Hills, Calif. 90211; Robbie Lanz, 114 East 55th St., New York, N.Y. 10022.

CAREER: Novelist and screenwriter. *Member:* Writers' Guild of Great Britain, Writers' Action Group, Travellers' Club, Pall Mall Club (both London). *Awards, honors:* Golden Plaque from International Writers' Guild, 1973, for best filmscript at twenty-third Berlin Film Festival.

WRITINGS: Freedom Ceremony, Triton, 1967; *Something Soft*, Faber & Faber, 1969, Doubleday, 1970; *I Never Touched You*, Hart-Davis, 1972. Author of screenplays, including "The Burning" and "The Fourteen" ("The Wild Little Bunch" in the United States).

WORK IN PROGRESS: Original screenplays, "A Mouth Full of Marbles," "Mirage," and "Candle in the Snow."

* * *

STARKLOFF, Carl F. 1933-

PERSONAL: Born July 3, 1933, in St. Louis, Mo.; son of Carl E. (a lawyer) and Hertha S. (Beck) Starkloff. *Education:* St. Louis University, B.A., 1958, M.A., 1962, S.T.L., 1967; University of Ottawa, Ph.D., 1968; St. Paul's University, S.T.D., 1969. *Politics:* Independent. *Home:* 5225 Troost Ave., Kansas City, Mo. 64110. *Office:* Department of Theology, Rockhurst College, 5225 Troost, Kansas City, Mo. 64110.

CAREER: Roman Catholic priest; formerly high school teacher and Indian missionary; Rockhurst College, Kansas City, Mo., associate professor of theology, 1972—, head of department, 1972—. Visiting research fellow at University of Aberdeen, 1974-75. Bishop's assistant for training of permanent deacons, 1971—. *Member:* College Theology Society, American Society of Missiology.

WRITINGS: The Office of Proclamation in the Theology of Karl Barth, University of Ottawa Press, 1969; *The People of the Center*, Seabury, 1974. Contributor to religion journals.

WORK IN PROGRESS: Researching U.S. Indian religion; a study of Karl Barth on religion.

* * *

STARR, Louis M(orris) 1917-

PERSONAL: Born November 1, 1917, in New York, N.Y.; son of Howard White (an electrical engineer) and Henrietta Delaplaine (Danforth) Starr; married Mary Belle Head (a literary agent), January 6, 1944; children: Jennifer (Mrs. Dennis Horning), Carolyn, Thomas, Theodore. *Education:* Yale University, A.B., 1940; Columbia University, M.A., 1953, Ph.D., 1954. *Home:* 461 Middlesex Rd., Darien, Conn. 06820. *Office address:* Box 20, Butler Library, Columbia University, New York, N.Y., 10027.

CAREER: Gallatin Examiner, Gallatin, Tenn., editor and publisher, 1942-44; *Chicago Sun*, Chicago, Ill., reporter and feature writer, 1944-47; Columbia University, New York, N.Y., staff member of Oral History Research Office, 1953-56, director, 1956—, assistant professor, 1957-59, associate professor of journalism, 1960—, director of International Division of Graduate School of Journalism, 1959-72. Member of Darien (Conn.) Board of Education, 1958-64; member of advisory board of Lyndon Johnson Oral History Project, 1968—; member of board of directors of Yale Alumni Fund, 1969-74. *Member:* American History Association, Organization of American Historians, Oral History Association (co-founder; first president, 1968), Yale Club of New York, Graduates Club (New Haven).

WRITINGS: Bohemian Brigade: Civil War Newsmen in Action, Knopf, 1954; (editor) *The Oral History Collection*, Oral History Office, Columbia University, 1960, 3rd edition, 1973; *The Second National Colloquium on Oral History*, Oral History Association, 1968; (editor) Gary L. Shumway, compiler, *Oral History in the United States*, Oral History Association, 1971. Contributor to *Dictionary of American Biography* and to "Advances in Librarianship" series; also contributor to *American Heritage, New York Times Sunday Book Review*, and other magazines. Book editor of *Columbia Journalism Review*, 1963-72.

* * *

STATEN, Patricia S. 1945-

PERSONAL: Born March 6, 1945, in Topeka, Kans.; daughter of Wilbur J. and Elnore B. (a secretary; maiden name, Hays) Staten. *Education:* Attended University of California, Berkeley, 1965; University of Colorado, Boulder, B.A., 1967; Columbia University, M.F.A., 1972. *Religion:* "Sometimes." *Home:* 336 East 59th St., New York, N.Y. 10022. *Agent:* Robert A. Freedman, Brandt & Brandt, 101 Park Ave., New York, N.Y. 10017.

CAREER: Playwright and author. Typist for University of California, Berkeley, 1967-68, Blue Shield, San Francisco, 1968, and in temporary positions in New York, N.Y., 1970-74; caseworker, Department of Social Services, New York, N.Y., 1969-70. *Member:* Dramatists' Guild, Authors League, Eugene O'Neill Memorial Theater Center. *Awards, honors:* Robert E. Sherwood Award of Dramatists' Guild, 1971; Eugene O'Neill Memorial Theater Center fellowship, 1972; Virginia Center for the Creative Arts fellowship, 1973; MacDowell Colony fellowship, 1973, 1975; Yaddo fellow, 1974; P.E.N. award, 1974.

WRITINGS—Plays: "A Disturbance of Mirrors," first produced in Waterford, Conn., at Eugene O'Neill Memorial Theater Center, 1972; "Iphigenia Again," first produced at Columbia University, 1973. Contributor of short fiction to *Aphra*.

WORK IN PROGRESS: Revision of "A Disturbance of Mirrors," completion expected in 1975; "Heartland," a television play for National Educational Television's "Visions" series, 1975; "Tornado," a full-length play about Kansas, 1975; a novel about Kansas, 1977; and another novel set in Berkeley, Haight-Ashbury, the East Village, and Kansas during the 1960's.

* * *

STECHOW, Wolfgang 1896(?)-1974

1896(?)—October 12, 1974; German-born American art historian, educator, museum curator, editor, and author of books on art. Obituaries: *New York Times*, October 14, 1974.

* * *

STEIGMAN, Benjamin 1889(?)-1974

1889(?)—July 20, 1974; American educator and author. Obituaries: *AB Bookman's Weekly*, October 21, 1974.

STEIN, Martha L(inda) 1942-

PERSONAL: Born February 27, 1942, in Montreal, Quebec, Canada; daughter of Bernard (a manufacturer) and Clare (Greenblatt) Stein. *Education:* McGill University, B.A., 1963; Simmons College, M.S.W., 1966; Hunter College of the City University of New York, doctoral candidate, 1972—. *Residence:* New York, N.Y. *Agent:* Carl Brandt, Brandt & Brandt, 101 Park Ave., New York, N.Y. 10017. *Office:* Psycho-Sexual Research Center, 663 Fifth Ave., New York, N.Y. 10022.

CAREER: Psycho-Sexual Research Center, New York, N.Y., director, 1968—. Member of board of directors of Community Sex Information, Inc., 1972-74. *Member:* Sex Information and Education Council of the United States, American Association of Sex Educators and Counselors, National Association of Social Workers, Society for the Scientific Study of Sex.

WRITINGS: Lovers, Friends, Slaves: The Nine Male Sexual Types, Their Psycho-Sexual Transactions with Call Girls, Putnam, 1974.

WORK IN PROGRESS: Romance and Life Fulfillment in the Middle Years; developing educational programs in the industrial setting as part of management development, and in the community for mid-life couples.

SIDELIGHTS: Martha Stein writes: "My research with clients of call girls made me acutely aware of how many men were struggling with mid-life crises, how little they understood what was happening to them, and how few were the opportunities for them to gain support and information."

* * *

STEINEM, Gloria 1934-

PERSONAL: Born March 25, 1934, in Toledo, Ohio; daughter of Leo and Ruth (Nuneviller) Steinem. *Education:* Smith College, B.A. (magna cum laude), 1956. *Agent:* Sterling Lord Agency, Inc., 660 Madison Ave., New York, N.Y. 10021. *Office: Ms.* Magazine, 370 Lexington Ave., New York, N.Y. 10017.

CAREER: Chester Bowles Asian Fellow at University of Delhi and University of Calcutta, 1956-58; Independent Research Service, Cambridge, Mass., director, 1959-60; free-lance writer, 1961—; founder and editor, *Ms.* Magazine, 1972—. Editorial consultant to Conde Nast Publications, 1962-69, Curtis Publishing, 1964-65, and McCall Publishing. *Member:* National Women's Political Caucus (founding member, 1971—), Women's Action Alliance (chairperson; member of board, 1971—), Student Non-Violent Coordinating Committee, Authors Guild of Authors League of America, Writers Guild, National Academy of Television Arts and Sciences, Society of Magazine Writers, Washington Press Club, Phi Beta Kappa. *Awards, honors:* Penney-Missouri journalism award, 1970, for a *New York* article on the women's movement; Dr. of Human Justice from Simmons College, 1973.

WRITINGS: The Thousand Indias, Government of India, 1957; *The Beach Book,* Viking, 1963; (contributor) Peter Manso, editor, *Running against the Machine,* Doubleday, 1969; (author of introductory note) Marlo Thomas and others, *Free to Be . . . You and Me,* McGraw, 1974. Writer for television, including series "That Was the Week that Was," NBC, 1964-65; has also written for films and political campaigns. Formerly author of column, "The City Politic," in *New York.* Contributor to periodicals, including *Esquire, Ms., Show, Vogue, Life,* and *Cosmopolitan.* Contributing editor, *Glamour,* 1962-69, *New York;* editorial consultant, *Seventeen,* 1969-70, *Show.*

SIDELIGHTS: Gloria Steinem, granddaughter of an early feminist, Pauline Steinem (president of a suffrage group and representative to the 1908 International Council of Women), dates her own involvement in the women's movement from a Redstockings meeting she attended in 1968 to get material on the group for her *New York* column. Steadily active in the movement since that time, she was one of the strategists for the Woman's Strike for Equality in 1970, one of the first demonstrations of strength on a national scale.

* * *

STEPHENS, Rockwell R(ittenhouse) 1900-

PERSONAL: Born February 16, 1900, in Portland, Ore.; son of John R. (a mechanical and mining engineer) and Cornelia (Rockwell) Stephens; married Isabella Campbell McLaughlin, May 12, 1927; children: Susanne, Margaret, David. *Education:* Attended University of Chicago, 1919-20. *Politics:* Independent liberal. *Residence:* South Woodstock, Vt. 05071.

CAREER: Chicago Daily News, Chicago, Ill., sports writer and auto and travel editor, 1921-26; Roche Advertising Co., Chicago, Ill., writer, 1927-29; Harvard University, Traffic Research-Study Foundation, Cambridge, Mass., executive secretary, 1929-32; Ski Sport Inc., Boston, Mass., president, 1933-43; Research Construction Co., Cambridge, Mass., assistant manager, 1943-45; member of the faculty of Putney School, Putney, Vt., 1952, and Woodstock Country School, Woodstock, Vt., 1953-62. *Member:* American Tree Farm System of American Forest Institute, Woodstock Rotary Club, Academy Historical Society (South Woodstock, Vt.), White Mountain Ski Runners (honorary member).

WRITINGS: (With Charles N. Proctor) *The Art of Skiing,* Harcourt, 1933; (with Proctor) *Skiing,* Harcourt, 1936; *One Man's Forest,* Greene, 1974. Contributor to *Vermont Life.*

WORK IN PROGRESS: A book on covered bridges and their construction.

AVOCATIONAL INTERESTS: Woodlot cultivation-conservation, cross-country skiing.

* * *

STERN, Alfred 1899-
(Fred Alstern)

PERSONAL: Born July 19, 1899, in Baden bei Wien (near Vienna), Austria; emigrated to the United States in 1944, naturalized citizen, 1949; son of Julius (a writer and critic) and Rose (Kohn) Stern; married Gloria Maria Pagan y Ferrer (a writer and poetess, under the pseudonym Marigloria Palma), November 15, 1946. *Education:* Piaristengymnasium, Vienna, Baccalaureus (Abiturientenpruefung), 1919; University of Vienna, Ph.D. (with honors), 1923. *Home:* Calle de la Luna 270, San Juan, Puerto Rico 00901.

CAREER: University of Paris, Sorbonne, lecturer in philosophy, 1934-39; Institut des Hautes Etudes de Belgique, Brussels, Belgium, professor of philosophy, 1935-40; Ecole Libre des Hautes Etudes, New York, N.Y., professor of philosophy, 1944-46; California Institute of Technology, Pasadena, professor of philosophy, 1947-68; University of Puerto Rico, Mayaguez, professor of philosophy, 1968-74, professor emeritus, 1974—. Part-time member of faculty at

University of Southern California, Los Angeles, 1946-60. *Military service:* Served in Austro-Hungarian Army, 1917-18; became lieutenant. Served as volunteer in French Army, 1939-40. *Member:* American Philosophical Association (president of Pacific division, 1964-65), Alliance Francaise (Los Angeles; vice-president, 1962-68), Alliance Francaise de Puerto Rico. *Awards, honors:* Officier of the Academy, France, 1950; Chevalier of the French Legion of Honor, 1954; Officer of the Order of Leopold II (Belgium), 1971; Honorary Academician of the Academia Tiberina (Italy), 1973; Ph.D. renewed by University of Vienna with laudatio, 1973; Austrian Honor-Cross for Science and Art, first class, 1975.

WRITINGS: Die philosophischen Grundlagen von Wahrheit, Wirklichkeit, Wert (title means "The Philosophical Foundations of Truth, Reality, Value"), Ernst Reinhardt (Munich), 1932; *La Philosophie des valeurs: Regard sur ses tendences actuelles en Allemagne* (title means "Philosophy of Values: A Glance at Its Present Tendencies in Germany"), Hermann & Co. (Paris), 1936, Spanish translation by Humberto Pinera Llera, revised and enlarged edition published as *Filosofia de los valores: Panorama de las tendencias actuales en Alemania*, Fabril (Buenos Aires), 1960; *La Filosofia de la politica y el sentido de la guerra actual* (title means "Philosophy of Politics and the Meaning of the Present War"), Minerva (Mexico), 1943; *Philosophie du rire et des pleurs* (title means "philosophy of Laughter and Tears"), Presses Universitaires (Paris), 1949, revised and enlarged edition of Spanish translation published as *Filosofia de la risa y del llanto* by Editorial Universitaria de Puerto Rico (Rio Piedras).

La Filosofia de Sartre y el psicoanalisis existencialista, Iman, 1951, published in English as *Sartre: His Philosophy and Psychoanalysis*, Liberal Arts Press, 1953, 2nd revised and enlarged edition published as *Sartre: His Philosophy and Existential Psychoanalysis*, Delacorte, 1967; *La Philosophie de l'histoire et le probleme des valeurs*, "Les Cours de Sorbonne," Centre de Documentation Universitaire (Paris), 1962, English translation by the author published as *Philosophy of History and the Problem of Values*, Mouton & Co., 1962, German translation by the author published as *Geschichtsphilosophie und Wertproblem*, Ernst Reinhardt, 1967; *The Search for Meaning: Philosophical Vistas*, Memphis State University Press, 1971; *Problemas filosoficos de la ciencia*, Editorial Universitaria Puerto Rico, c.1975.

Contributor to numerous learned journals in the United States and abroad; some articles published in Germany under pseudonym Fred Alstern, 1930-32. Adviser to *Folia Humanistica* (Barcelona) and *Atenea* (Mayaguez).

SIDELIGHTS: Stern writes that he lectures and writes with equal ease in German, French, English, and Spanish, and often translates his own works. His travels include Europe, North and South America, and North Africa ("Many of them were due to historical circumstances.").

BIOGRAPHICAL/CRITICAL SOURCES: Luis Carranza Siles, *Introduccion a la filosofia*, Libreria Editorial Juventud (La Paz, Bolivia), 1958; William Henry Werkmeister, *Historical Spectrum of Value Theories*, Volume II, Johnsen Publishing, 1973; "Festschrift en Honor a Alfred Stern," special double issue of *Atenea*, 1-2, 1974.

* * *

STERN, Edward Severin 1924-

PERSONAL: Born December 28, 1924, in Vienna, Austria; son of Paul (a lawyer) and Martha (Hoffmann) Stern; married Joy Pamela Aldridge (a scientist and teacher), 1947; children: David Paul, Vivienne Rachel. *Education:* Imperial College of Science and Technology, University of London, B.Sc., 1944, Ph.D., 1946. *Home:* 141 Sydenham Hill, London S.E. 23, England. *Office:* Gallaher Ltd., 65 Kingsway, London W.C.2, England.

CAREER: Distillers Co. Ltd., London, England, research scientist, 1946-50; J. F. Macfadan & Co. Ltd., London, research manager, 1960-62; Fisous Industrial Chemicals Ltd., London, research manager, 1963-74; Gallaher Ltd., London, general manager of research and development, 1974—. Senior executive, Imperial Chemical Industries, 1969. *Member:* Royal Institute of Chemistry, Chemical Society, Pharmacological Society, Research and Development Society (member of executive committee).

WRITINGS: (With A. E. Gillam) *Introduction to Electronic Absorption Spectrophotometry*, Edward Arnold, 1954, 3rd edition (with C. J. Timmons), 1970; (with J. A. D. Cropp and D. C. Harris) *Trade in Innovation*, Wiley, 1970; (with wife, Joy P. Stern) *Petrochemicals Today*, Edward Arnold, 1971; (editor) *The Chemist in Industry*, Clarendon Press (of Oxford University), Part I, 1973, Part II, 1974, Part III, 1975.

WORK IN PROGRESS: Editing *The Chemist in Industry*, Part IV.

* * *

STERNFIELD, Allen 1930-

PERSONAL: Born January 14, 1930, in Worcester, Mass.; son of Harry and Julia (Mintz) Sternfield; married wife, Vivian, March 15, 1964 (divorced February 20, 1975); children: Adam, Jason. *Education:* Attended high school in Boston, Mass. *Politics:* "Pessimistic." *Home:* 60 Bay State Rd., Boston, Mass. 02115.

CAREER: Professional trumpet player, 1950-68; playwright. Director and playwright in residence, Playwright's Platform; playwright in residence, University of North Carolina, 1973. *Military service:* U.S. Army, 1954-56. *Awards, honors: Holmes and Moriarity* was a selection of the O'Neill Conference, 1973.

WRITINGS: The Army of Various Defeats (novel), Windfall Press, 1972; *Holmes and Moriarty* (play), Fault, 1974; *Statement* (play), Dramatic Publishing, 1975; "Benito" (play), first produced by the American Conservatory Theatre, March, 1974. Also author of play, "Liberty Tree," produced in New York, N.Y. at Lincoln Center, 1974.

SIDELIGHTS: Sternfield told *CA* that he has "An overwhelming desire to write: in the last ten years I have written six novels and at least thirty plays. Especially interested in the aging process and in the emotional reflections of the elderly, a recurring theme in my plays."

* * *

STEVENS, (John) Austin

PERSONAL: Born in Stoke-on-Trent, Staffordshire, England; son of Samuel Clifford (an Anglican clergyman) and Margaret Jessie (Mackintosh) Stevens; married Eileen Power, June, 1951; children: Fiona Margaret, Paul John. *Education:* Attended Ellesmere College, 1934-37. *Agent:* Richard Scott Simon Ltd., 32 College Cross, London N.1 1 PR, England; and Georges Borchardt Inc., 45 East 52nd St., New York, N.Y. 10022.

CAREER: London Stock Exchange, London, England, authorized clerk, 1945-51; writer. *Military service:* British Army, 1939-43; served in Europe and North Africa.

WRITINGS: (With Charles Gifford) *Making Money on the Stock Exchange*, MacGibbon & Kee, 1955; *Time and Money*, Washburn, 1959; *On the Market*, J. Cape, 1960; *The Moon Turns Green*, J. Cape, 1961; *The Antagonists*, J. Cape, 1963; *The Dispossessed: German Jewish Refugees in Great Britain*, Barrie & Jenkins, 1975. Also author of scripts for BBC radio and television.

SIDELIGHTS: Stevens told *CA*: "Over the years my interests have shifted from the naturalistic novel that reflects a strata of financial or business activity—a *genre* once popular in America; never really accepted in Britain—towards the kind of writing that, if it is fiction, incorporates a good deal of fact; and, if it is called non-fiction, still seeks to achieve a novelist's empathy and insight. Thus my latest book *The Dispossessed*, which is wholly factual, still uses many of the novelist's methods to tell the story of the German Jewish refugees in Great Britain."

* * *

STEVENS, Michael 1919-

PERSONAL: Born September 27, 1919, in Winchester, England; son of James Howard and Hazel Mary St. John Stevens; married Marit Suul-Eriksson, July 31, 1948; children: Mary Christina. *Education:* Uppsala University, Ph.D., 1972. *Religion:* Church of England. *Home:* Valhallavaegen 48, 3 trappor, 114 22 Stockholm, Sweden. *Office:* Department of English, University of Stockholm, Fack, 104 05, Stockholm 50, Sweden.

CAREER: Teacher of English in state schools in England, 1947-68; University of Stockholm, Stockholm, Sweden, lecturer in English, 1968—. *Military service:* British Army, 1939-45; became major.

WRITINGS: (With Mats Ryden and Sverker Brorstroem) *Oevningar i engelsk grammatik och fraseologi foer universitetsstadiet* (title means "Exercises in English Grammar and Phraseology for University Studies"), Almquist & Wiksell (Stockholm), 1972; *V. Sackville-West: A Critical Biography*, Egnell (Stockholm), 1972, Scribner, 1974.

WORK IN PROGRESS: Research on emblemata.

AVOCATIONAL INTERESTS: Harpsichords, Renaissance music.

* * *

STEVENS, Patricia Bunning 1931-

PERSONAL: Born September 28, 1931, in Buenos Aires, Argentina; daughter of John William (an engineer) and Mary (a teacher) Bunning; married Eric T. Stevens (a college teacher), July 14, 1956 (divorced October 2, 1973); children: James, Patricia, John, Charles. *Education:* Loyola University, Chicago, Ill., B.S. (honors), 1953, M.A., 1960. *Religion:* Roman Catholic. *Home:* 110 North Catherine Ave., La Grange, Ill. 60525.

CAREER: Public school teacher in Chicago, Ill., 1953-55; Nazareth Academy, La Grange, Ill., teacher of history, 1955-56; Public Schools of Chicago, Ill., teacher, 1956—.

WRITINGS: God Save Ireland!: The Irish Conflict in the Twentieth Century, Macmillan, 1974. Contributor to *Britannica Junior Encyclopaedia.*

STEVENS, Peter S(mith) 1936-

PERSONAL: Born February 14, 1936, in Boston, Mass.; son of S. S. (a psychophysicist) and Maxine (Leonard) Stevens; married Joyce Sargent, December 2, 1961; children: David, Karl, Jean. *Education:* Harvard University, B.A. (with honors), 1958, M.Arch., 1962. *Home:* 24 Irving St., Arlington, Mass. 02174. *Office:* School of Medicine, Harvard University, Cambridge, Mass.

CAREER: Registered architect in State of Massachusetts. F. A. Stahl & Associates (architectural firm), Boston, Mass., designer, 1962-65; Peter F. McLaughlin (architect), Boston, Mass., job captain, 1964-65; Boston Architectural Center, Boston, Mass., instructor in architectural design, 1965-66; Bolt, Beranek & Newman, Inc. (acoustical consultants), Cambridge, Mass., consultant in architectural acoustics, 1966-68; Oceans General, Inc. (oceanographic firm), Miami, Fla., architectural principal, 1968-70; Harvard University, Cambridge, Mass., lecturer in visual and environmental studies, and research fellow at Carpenter Center, 1970-72, project architect at Harvard Medical School, 1972-73, director of Architectural Planning Office for the Harvard Medical Area, 1973—. *Member:* American Institute of Architects. *Awards, honors:* Guggenheim fellowship, 1970.

WRITINGS: Patterns in Nature, Little, Brown, 1974. Contributor to *Proceedings of the National Academy of Science* and *Systematic Zoology*.

WORK IN PROGRESS: Symmetry Groups, completion expected in 1976; *Visual Studies*, 1978; *Physical Implications of Euler's Formula*, 1980.

* * *

STIRLING, Matthew Williams 1896-1975

August 28, 1896—January 23, 1975; American anthropologist, archeologist, and author of several books in his field. Obituaries: *New York Times*, January 25, 1975; *Washington Post*, January 27, 1975.

* * *

STITES, Raymond S(omers) 1899-1974

June 19, 1899—December 6, 1974; American art historian, educator, expert on Leonardo da Vinci, first curator of education for the National Museum of Art, and author of art textbooks and studies of da Vinci. Obituaries: *New York Times*, December 7, 1974; *Washington Post*, December 8, 1974; *AB Bookman's Weekly*, January 13, 1975.

* * *

STOIL, Michael Jon 1950-
(Erich Augustine)

PERSONAL: Born in 1950, in Frankfurt-am-Main, Germany; son of Ted Stoil (a journalist) and Anita (a drama teacher; maiden name, Eastman) Stoil Wander. *Education:* George Washington University, M.A., 1972; also studied at University of Vienna, 1970, and Fordham University, 1974. *Home:* 824 New Hampshire Ave. N.W., Washington, D.C. 20037. *Office:* Department of Political Science, George Washington University, Washington, D.C. 20006.

CAREER: U.S. Department of State, Washington, D.C., writer for Bureau of Public Affairs, 1973-74; George Washington University, Washington, D.C., instructor in political science, 1974—. Consultant to American Film Institute. *Member:* International Studies Association, American Film Institute, Southern Political Science Associaton.

WRITINGS: (Translator) Andre Beaufre, *Military Problems of Modern Warfare*, Stamford Research, 1973; *Cinema Beyond the Danube*, Scarecrow, 1974. Author of children's play, "Chip Marbles," under pseudonym Erich Augustine; also wrote early fiction under pseudonym. Author of filmscript, "Leave It to Laurie," for American Cancer Society, 1971.

WORK IN PROGRESS: Cinema in the Balkans, a detailed political and social examination, completion expected in 1976.

SIDELIGHTS: Stoil told *CA*: "Although by training and preference I am a political scientist, specializing in foreign relations, the dearth of information on film as political communication has led me to conduct extensive research on cinema. . . . Outside of my specific interests in culture, I remain interested in all areas of comparative and international politics."

* * *

STONE, Christopher D(avid) 1937-

PERSONAL: Born October 2, 1937, in New York, N.Y.; son of I. F. and Esther M. (Roisman) Stone; married Ann Pope (an English instructor), July 26, 1962; children: Jessica Burr, Carey Brewster. *Education:* Harvard University, A.B., 1959; Yale University, LL.B., 1962. *Home:* 2337 Glendon Ave., Los Angeles, Calif. 90064. *Office:* School of Law, University of Southern California, Los Angeles, Calif. 90007.

CAREER: University of Chicago, Chicago, Ill., fellow in law and economics, 1962-63; University of Southern California, Los Angeles, assistant professor, 1965-66, associate professor, 1966-69, professor of law, 1969—.

WRITINGS: (With W. R. Bishin) *Law, Language, and Ethics*, Foundation Press, 1972; *Should Trees Have Standing?*, William Kaufmann, 1974, revised edition, Avon, 1975; *Where the Law Ends*, Harper, 1975. Contributor of articles and book reviews to *Los Angeles Times*, *New York Times*, *Nation*, and law journals.

* * *

STONE, Julius 1907-

PERSONAL: Born July 7, 1907, in Leeds, Yorkshire, England; son of Israel (a cabinet maker) and Ellen (Cohen) Stone; married Reca Lieberman (a company secretary), 1934; children: Michael Edward, Jonathan, Eleanor (Mrs. Roger Sebel). *Education:* Oxford University, B.A., 1928, B.C.L., 1929, D.C.L., 1934; University of Leeds, LL.M., 1930; Harvard University, S.J.D., 1933. *Politics:* "Not party affiliated but tend to vote social democratic-labour policies." *Religion:* Jewish. *Home:* 1 Holland Rd., Double Bay, Sydney, New South Wales 2028, Australia. *Agent:* Zena Sachs, 88 Brighton St., Petersham, Sydney, New South Wales, 2033, Australia. *Office:* School of Law, University of New South Wales, Sydney, New South Wales 2033, Australia.

CAREER: Harvard University, Cambridge, Mass., assistant professor of law, 1932-36; University of Leeds, Leeds, England, lecturer in law, 1936-38; University of New Zealand, Auckland, professor of law, and dean of faculty of law, 1938-41; University of Sydney, Sydney, Australia, Challis Professor of International Law and Jurisprudence, 1942-72, professor emeritus, 1972—. Visiting professor at Fletcher School of Law and Diplomacy, 1932-36, New York University, 1949, Columbia University, 1956, and University of Colorado, 1956; lecturer at Hague Academy of International Law, 1956; visiting Bemis Professor at Harvard University, 1956-57; Roscoe Pound Lecturer at University of Nebraska, 1957; Ford Foundation visiting professor in India, 1960; visiting professor at Stanford University, 1963-64; Pattee Lecturer at University of Minnesota, 1964; Coen Lecturer at University of Colorado, 1964; Johnson Lecturer at University of California, Berkeley, 1964; Roentgen Orator at Australian College of Radiologists, 1964; visiting distinguished professor at University of Washington, Seattle, 1967; Tagore Lecturer at University of Calcutta, 1972; Fullagar Lecturer at Monash University, 1972; distinguished professor at University of California, San Francisco, 1972—; Mooers Lecturer at American University, 1973; professor at University of New South Wales, 1973—. Fellow of Center for Advanced Study in the Behavioral Sciences, Stanford, Calif., 1963-64. Founding president of International Criminal Law Commission of World Peace Through Law Center; councillor of International Commission of Jurists, official observer at trial of Adolph Eichmann, 1961; sponsor of Amnesty International Fund for the Persecuted; honorary president of Foundation for the Establishment of an International Criminal Court. Founding member of Australian Social Sciences Research Council; chairman of Australian National UNESCO Committee on the Social Sciences, 1950-60. Radio broadcaster on international affairs. Originated the idea of a "hot line" between Washington, D.C. and Moscow in 1959.

MEMBER: International Law Association (first president of Australian branch), International League for the Rights of Man (member of advisory committee), International Association for Philosophy of Law and Social Philosophy, World Academy of Arts and Sciences (fellow), Institute of International Law (membre titulaire), American Society of International Law (honorary life member), Indian Society for International Law (honorary life member), Australian Universities Law School Association (founding member; former president; now honorary member), Australian Academy of Social Sciences (founding fellow).

AWARDS, HONORS: Award from American Society of International Law, 1956, for *Legal Controls of International Conflict*; prize from Netherlands Legatum Visserianum, 1956; Swiney Prize for Jurisprudence from Royal Society of Arts, 1964, for *The Province and Function of Law*; World Law Research Award from Washington Conference on World Peace Through Law, 1965; Torch of Learning Award from Hebrew University of Jerusalem, 1972; fellow of Woodrow Wilson International Center for Scholars, 1973; named Officer, Order of the British Empire, 1973; LL.D. from University of Leeds, 1973; International Criminal Law Award, from Foundation for the Establishment of an International Criminal Court, 1975.

WRITINGS: International Guarantees of Minority Rights, Oxford University Press, 1932; *Regional Guarantees of Minority Rights*, Macmillan, 1933.

The Atlantic Charter, Angus & Robertson, 1943; *Stand Up and Be Counted!*, Ponsford, Newman & Benson, 1944; *The Province and Function of Law*, Maitland Publications, 1946, Harvard University Press, 1950; (with S. P. Simpson) *Law and Society*, three volumes, West Publishing, 1949-50.

Legal Controls of International Conflict, Holt, 1954, revised edition, 1959; *Problems Confronting Sociological Inquiries Concerning International Law*, Hague Academy of International Law, 1956; *Aggression and World Order*, University of California Press, 1958.

Legal Education and Public Responsibility, Association of American Law Schools, 1961; *Quest for Survival*, Harvard University Press, 1961; *The Eichmann Trial and the Rule of Law*, International Law Association (Australian Section), 1961; *The International Court and World Crisis*, Carnegie Endowment for International Peace, 1962; *Legal System and Lawyers' Reasonings*, Stanford University Press, 1964; *Human Law and Human Justice*, Stanford University Press, 1965; *Social Dimensions of Law and Justice*, Stanford University Press, 1966; *Law and the Social Sciences*, University of Minnesota Press, 1966; *The Middle East under Cease-Fire*, Bridge Publications (Sydney), 1967; *Power Politics and Human Hopes*, Truman Center, Hebrew University of Jerusalem, 1968; *Research for the Advancement of Peace*, Truman Center, Hebrew University of Jerusalem, 1968; *No Peace—No War in the Middle East*, Maitland Publications, 1969.

(Editor with Robert K. Woetzel, and contributor) *Toward a Feasible International Criminal Court*, World Peace through Law Center, 1970; *Approaches to International Justice*, Truman Center, Hebrew University of Jerusalem, 1970; *Of Law and Nations: Between Power Politics and Human Hopes*, W. S. Hein, 1974.

Contributor: R. A. Falk, editor, *Espionage and International Law*, Ohio State University Press, 1962; Falk and Cyril E. Black, editors, *The Future of the International Legal Order*, Volume I: *Trends and Patterns*, Princeton University Press, 1969; V. Aubert, editor, *Sociology of Law*, Penguin Books, 1969.

Contributor to *International Encyclopedia of the Social Sciences* and *Encyclopaedia Britannica*, and to memorial volumes. Contributor of about eighty articles to European, Indian, and English language law journals, including *Syracuse Journal of International Law and Commerce*, *Quadrant*, *Hastings Law Journal*, *American University Law Review*, *Australian Law Journal*, and *Modern Law Review*. Member of editorial board of International Association for the Philosophy of Law and Social Philosophy; founder and general editor of *Sydney Law Review*, 1953-60.

WORK IN PROGRESS: Studies of law and social policy in contemporary Western societies, including studies of mass media and the first amendment, and current demands for a "law-free" society; research on the "problematics of equality and due process notions"; research on the limits of law among nations; studying the duties of scientists in the advancement of knowledge.

SIDELIGHTS: Stone writes: "I am the son of Jewish refugees who fled to England from Czarist Russia, raised in the industrial slums of Leeds. This background is relevant to a number of main drives of my interest and activity. (1) An over-riding re-examination of law for justice in operation and social honesty in exposition, exposing fiction, pretence and dysfunction; (2) A testing of orthodox international law doctrines against the realities of State practice especially in major conflicts of State interests; (3) A deep concern extending for half a century with the liberation of oppressed Jewish populations, and the mission of the State of Israel in this liberation, and in preserving and revitalising the millennial Jewish heritage."

Stone's books have been published in foreign languages, including German, Portuguese, and Arabic. *Avocational interests:* Landscape gardening.

STONER, Carol Hupping 1949-

PERSONAL: Born February 17, 1949, in Brooklyn, N.Y.; daughter of William F. (a personnel director) and Elizabeth (a teacher; maiden name, Fischer) Hupping; married George Michael Stoner, May 6, 1972. *Education:* Muhlenberg College, B.A., 1971; University of Vienna, further study, 1969-70. *Home address:* R.D. 1, Box 322, Kutztown, Pa. 19530. *Office:* Book Division, Rodale Press, 33 East Minor St., Emmaus, Pa. 18049.

CAREER: Rodale Press, Emmaus, Pa., associate editor of *Organic Gardening and Farming*, 1971-74, associate edition, *Environmental Action Bulletin*, 1971-73, co-editor, *Lehigh Valley Natural Foods Shopper*, 1972-73, senior editor of Book Division, 1973—. *Member:* National Organization for Women (Lehigh Valley chapter), Sigma Tau Delta.

WRITINGS: (Editor) *The Natural Breakfast Book*, Rodale Press, 1972; (editor) *Stocking Up: How to Preserve the Foods You Grow Naturally*, Rodale Press, 1973; (editor) *The Organic Directory*, Rodale Press, 1973; (editor) *Producing Your Own Power: How to Make Nature's Energy Sources Work for You*, Rodale Press, 1974. Contributor to *Organic Gardening and Farming*.

WORK IN PROGRESS: Editing *Managing Your Personal Food Supply*, for Rodale Press.

* * *

STOVER, Webster 1902-

PERSONAL: Born July 4, 1902, in Nazareth, Pa.; son of Mahlon Geisinger and Emma (Schultz) Stover; married Marion Allen, May 16, 1925; children: Marian (Mrs. John Paul Kelley), Frances. *Education:* Ursinus College, A.B., 1924; Union Theological Seminary, New York, N.Y., M.Div., 1927; Columbia University, M.A., 1929, Ph.D., 1930. *Home:* 365 Rye Beach Ave., Rye, N.Y. 10580.

CAREER: Ordained minister of United Church of Christ, 1925; College of William and Mary, Williamsburg, Va., assistant professor of Greek and English, 1927-28; Tusculum College, Greenville, Tenn., professor of psychology and education, 1930-31, head of department, 1930-31; Perkioman School, Pennsburg, Pa., headmaster, 1932-35; Arnold College, New Haven, Conn., president, 1935-39; Albert Teachers Agency, New York, N.Y., proprietor, 1940-71. Visiting professor at Bates College, summer, 1931.

WRITINGS: *Alumni Stimulation by the American College President*, Teachers College, Columbia University, 1930, reprinted, AMS Press, 1972; *How To Become a College President*, American Librarians' Agency, 1974.

WORK IN PROGRESS: Research in college administration.

* * *

STRAINCHAMPS, Ethel (Reed) 1912-

PERSONAL: Born December 21, 1912, in Bolivar, Mo.; daughter of John Allen (a farmer) and Emma (Williams) Reed; married Edmond Strainchamps, February 3, 1932; children: Edmond, Jr. *Education:* Southwest Missouri State University, B.S., 1952. *Politics:* Democrat. *Religion:* None. *Home:* 180 West End Ave., New York, N.Y. 10023. *Agent:* Gerard McCauley, P.O. Box 456, Cranbury, N.J.

CAREER: KTTS-Television and Radio, Springfield, Mo., radio commentator, 1950-51, radio-TV reporter, 1951-52; *Daily News Digest*, Springfield, Mo., editor, 1952-54; KTTS-TV, promotion manager, 1954-60; free-lance writer,

1960-66; Time-Life Books, New York, N.Y., editor, 1966-70; free-lance writer and editor, 1970—.

WRITINGS: Don't Never Say Cain't (autobiography), Doubleday, 1965; (contributor) Vivian Gornick and Barbara Moran, editors, *Woman in Sexist Society*, Basic Books, 1971; (editor) *Rooms with No View*, Harper, 1974; (with Porter G. Perrin) *Index to English*, Scott, Foresman, in press. Work is anthologized in *American Education Today*, edited by Paul Woodring and John Scanlon, McGraw, 1961, and *Dictionaries and That Dictionary*, edited by J. H. Sledd and W. R. Ebbitt, Scott, Foresman, 1962. Contributor to *Harper's*, *Saturday Review*, *College English*, *Coronet*, *Village Voice*, *Bookletter*, *More: A Journalism Review*, and *New York Times*. Reviewer and columnist for *St. Louis Post-Dispatch*, 1950-66.

WORK IN PROGRESS: Sensuous Words, tentative title, a book on sound semantics.

SIDELIGHTS: Ethel Strainchamps was born and raised in the Ozarks, and writes that "the Ozarks ambience is not exactly conducive to the early blossoming of lady book authors." Her first book was published when she was fifty-three years old. She writes: "I'm interested in changes in current English usage and in the status of women. I favor passivity in regard to the first and militancy in regard to the second."

* * *

STRAIT, Raymond 1924-
(Russell Ray)

PERSONAL: Born May 17, 1924, in Akron, Ohio; son of Charles Earl and Geraldine (Shirkey) Strait; married Angelle Logan, August 19, 1965; children: Mark Alan, Russell Ray. *Education:* Attended University of Wisconsin and Morris Harvey College. *Religion:* Christian. *Home and office address:* P.O. Box 624, Tarzana, Calif. 91356.

CAREER: Publicist and press secretary to film star Jayne Mansfield in Hollywood, Calif., 1957-67; free-lance writer in Tarzana, Calif., 1967—. Regional vice-president of California Democratic Council, 1973-74; chairman of San Fernando Valley Democratic Council, 1974-75. *Military service:* U.S. Navy, 1941. U.S. Army Air Forces, 1944-50; served in Germany and in Pacific theater; became technical sergeant. *Member:* Writers Guild of America, Press Club of Greater Los Angeles.

WRITINGS: Mrs. Howard Hughes, Holloway House, 1971; *The Tragic Secret Life of Jayne Mansfield*, Regnery, 1974. Author of "S.L.I.P." a feature film, for Tenth House Productions. Contributor to magazines, sometimes under pseudonym Russell Ray.

WORK IN PROGRESS: Working with Hollywood agent Al Rosen on his autobiography, tentatively titled *Miss Show Business*; *Judge of the Stars*, a biography.

* * *

STRASSER, Otto (Johann Maximilian) 1897-1974

September 10, 1897—August 27, 1974; German political leader, writer, editor, and early theoretician of the Nazi party who broke with Hitler in 1930 and founded the rival Black Front. Obituaries: *New York Times*, August 28, 1974; *Current Biography*, October, 1974.

* * *

STREANO, Vince(nt Catello) 1945-

PERSONAL: Born December 9, 1945, in Santa Barbara, Calif.; son of Ralph (a music teacher) and Francyl (Cowles) Streano; married Mary Jo Anne McMahon, August 17, 1969 (divorced, 1972). *Education:* San Jose State University, B.A., 1968. *Home and office address:* P.O. Box 662, Laguna Beach, Calif. 92652. *Agent:* Mike Hamilburg, 292 South La Cienega, Beverly Hills, Calif. 90211.

CAREER: San Jose Mercury, San Jose, Calif., photographer, 1967-68; *Los Angeles Times,* Los Angeles, Calif., photographer, 1968-73; writer and photographer, 1973—. *Member:* National Press Photographers Association, California Press Photographers Association (vice-president, 1972), Orange County Press Club. *Awards, honors:* National Cigar Institute's first prize in photography contest, 1970; named Orange County's photographer of the year, 1973.

WRITINGS: Touching America with Two Wheels (with photographs), Random House, 1974.

Illustrator: June Behrens, *Look at the Farm Animals,* Childrens Press, 1972; Behrens, *Look at the Desert Animals,* Childrens Press, 1973; Behrens, *How I Feel,* Childrens Press, 1973.

WORK IN PROGRESS: Illustrating two books for children by June Behrens, *Look at the Ocean Animals* and *Together.*

SIDELIGHTS: Streano writes: "I consider myself first and foremost a photojournalist, a writer second. I will write a story or a book only if I'm forced into it due to circumstances beyond my control. My motorcycle book came about more because of my desire to get some of the pictures I had taken into print rather than a burning desire to write the book. I may do a second motorcycle book on traveling through Mexico and . . . a book on an around-the-world trip by cycle.

"Since . . . June, 1973, I have traveled to fourteen foreign countries and have also visited most of the states, including Alaska and Hawaii, doing documentary photography. I am primarily interested in the many life styles and cultures that live within our country and would like to document photographically as many of them as possible."

* * *

STREET, James H(arry) 1915-

PERSONAL: Born November 17, 1915, in New Braunfels, Tex.; son of James William (a carpenter) and Kate (Goldenbagen) Street; married Mabel Carroll (a librarian), January 16, 1944; children: John William, Janet Pauline. *Education:* University of Texas, B.A., 1940, M.A., 1947; University of Pennsylvania, Ph.D., 1953. *Home:* 11 Lexington Dr., Metuchen, N.J. 08840. *Office:* Rutgers University, 192 College Ave., New Brunswick, N.J. 08903.

CAREER: New Braunfels Herald, New Braunfels, Tex., reporter and editor, 1933-36; U.S. Department of Agriculture, Washington, D.C., agricultural economist, 1941-43; U.S. Forest Service, Cooperstown, N.Y., statistician, 1943-46; University of Pennsylvania, Philadelphia, instructor in economics, 1946-48; Haverford College, Haverford, Pa., assistant professor of economics, 1948-52; Rutgers University, New Brunswick, N.J., assistant professor, 1952-55, associate professor, 1956-59, professor of economics, 1960—. Smith-Mundt Professor at National University of Asuncion, 1955; guest lecturer at Columbia University, 1967-70; lecturer for Foreign Service Institute, 1968-69; Fulbright-Hays lecturer in Mexico, 1970; lecturer at Argentine universities, 1957-58, and in Colombia, Costa Rica, El

Salvador, Guatemala, Honduras, Nicaragua, Panama, Peru, and Uruguay; lecturer on WABC-Television, 1964-65. Visiting fellow at Cambridge University, 1972-73; economic specialist for Central American Social Studies Seminars, summers, 1965-72; member of national screening committee for Fulbright-Hays awards, 1967; member of Council for International Exchange of Scholars, 1974-76. Member of board of directors of Metuchen Public Library, 1960-65.

MEMBER: American Economic Association, Association for Evolutionary Economics, Conference on Latin American History, Latin American Studies Association, Society for Latin American Studies (England), Royal Economic Society, Phi Beta Kappa (president of Alpha chapter of New Jersey, 1967-68). *Awards, honors:* Ec.Sc.D. and gold medal from National University of Asuncion, 1955; Ford Foundation study grant to South America, 1966; Latin American Studies Association research grant for Paraguay, 1968; M.A. from Cambridge University, 1972.

WRITINGS: Farmers' Attitudes toward the Use of Japanese Evacuees as Farm Labor, U.S. Bureau of Agricultural Economics, 1943; (editor) *Ideas and Issues in the Social Sciences,* Haverford College, Volume I: 1950, Volume II, 1951; *The New Revolution in the Cotton Economy: Mechanization and Its Consequences,* University of North Carolina Press, 1957; (with Diego Newbery) *La Argentina y las firmas norteamericanas* (title means "Argentina and the North American Firms"), Santiago Rueda, 1958; (with Guido G. Weigend) *Urban Planning and Development Centers in Latin America,* Rutgers University, 1967; (contributor) Richard N. Adams, editor, *Responsibilities of the Foreign Scholar to the Local Scholarly Community: Studies of U.S. Research in Guatemala, Chile, and Paraguay,* Education and World Affairs and Latin American Studies Association, 1969; (contributor) Samuel L. Baily and Ronald T. Hyman, editors, *Perspectives on Latin America,* Macmillan, 1974.

Contributor to *Encyclopedia Americana.* Contributor of more than forty articles and reviews to Latin American studies and economics journals, including *Journal of Economic Issues, Journal of Farm Economics, Atlantic, Reporter, American Economic Review,* and *El Trimestre Economico.*

WORK IN PROGRESS: The Economic Development of Argentina; research on the Latin American structuralist school of economic thought, inflation in Latin America, and educational reform in Argentina, Mexico, and Central America.

SIDELIGHTS: Street has traveled in Europe and the Soviet Union.

* * *

STYX, Marguerite (Salzer) 1908(?)-1975

1908(?)—January 10, 1975; Austrian-born American sculptress, ceramicist, jewelry designer, and author. Obituaries: *New York Times,* January 12, 1975; *Washington Post,* January 24, 1975.

* * *

SULLIVAN, Chester L(amar) 1939-

PERSONAL: Born September 2, 1939, in Hattiesburg, Miss.; son of Lamar Cornelius (a Navy career man) and Ethel Elisabeth Sullivan; married Peggy Joan Leuty, May 31, 1973. *Education:* Texas Christian University, B.A., 1961, Ph.D., 1974; East Texas State University, M.A., 1967. *Politics:* Liberal Democrat. *Office:* Department of English, University of Kansas, Lawrence, Kan. 66045.

CAREER: Austin College, Sherman, Tex., instructor in literature, 1967-68; Tarleton State University, Stephenville, Tex., assistant professor of English, 1972-73; University of Kansas, Lawrence, assistant professor of literature, 1974—. *Military service:* U.S. Army, infantry, 1962-66; served in Korea and West Germany; became captain. *Member:* Modern Language Association of America, National Audubon Society, Texas Institute of Letters. *Awards, honors:* Boswell Prize for Poetry from Texas Christian University, 1971, for "Matthew"; Jesse H. Jones Award from Texas Institute of Letters, 1973, for *Alligator Gar.*

WRITINGS: Alligator Gar (novel), Crown, 1973; *Transit Stakes* (novel), Crown, in press. Work in anthologized in *The Bicentennial Collection of Texas Short Stories,* edited by James P. White, Texas Center for Writers Press, 1974. Contributor of short stories and poems to *Descant, Forthcoming,* and *Pearl.*

WORK IN PROGRESS: Trotline Tales and Possum Stories; a monograph on the early poems of William Carlos Williams.

* * *

SULLIVAN, Judy 1936-

PERSONAL: Born October 6, 1936, in Abilene, Tex.; daughter of Jesse Harrison (an army officer) and Mary Lou (Sikes) Turner; married John B. Sullivan, July 1, 1955 (divorced, 1972); children: Mary Kathleen. *Education:* North Texas State University, B.A., 1960; Texas Woman's University, M.A., 1966; Southern University, further graduate study, 1968-69. *Politics:* "Feminist." *Religion:* "Feminist." *Residence:* New York, N.Y. *Agent:* Julia Cooper Smith, Curtis Brown Ltd., 60 East 56th St., New York, N.Y. 10022. *Office:* Webster Division, McGraw Hill Book Co., 1221 Avenue of the Americas, New York, N.Y. 10020.

CAREER: Washburn University, Topeka, Kan., instructor in art history, 1968-70; National Humanities Series, Princeton, N.J., professor/participant, 1970-73; McGraw Hill Book Co., New York, N.Y., marketing consultant to Webster Division, 1974—. Member of New York Textbook Committee of National Organization for Women. *Member:* New York Radical Feminists, Videowomen. *Awards, honors:* Ph.D. from Harriet Tubman University, 1974.

WRITINGS: Mama Doesn't Live Here Anymore, Arthur Field, 1974. Author of a column in *Emporia Gazette,* 1965-68. Contributor to *Majority Report.* Book editor for *Southern Voices,* 1973-74.

WORK IN PROGRESS: Editing a book by thirty female artists; a screenplay, with three other writers.

* * *

SULZBERGER, C(yrus) L(eo II) 1912-

PERSONAL: Born October 27, 1912, in New York, N.Y.; son of Leo Sulzberger and Beatrice (Josephi) Sulzberger Kahn; married Marina Tatiana Lada, January 21, 1942; children: Marina Beatrice (Mrs. Adrian Berry), David Alexis. *Education:* Harvard University, B.S. (magna cum laude), 1934. *Address:* c/o *New York Times,* 229 West 43rd St., New York, N.Y. 10036; and 184 rue de l'Universite, Paris 7eme, France.

CAREER: Pittsburgh Press, Pittsburgh, Pa., reporter and rewrite man, 1934-35; United Press, Washington, D.C., reporter, 1935-38; *London Evening Standard*, London, England, foreign correspondent, 1938-39; variously employed abroad by United Press, North American Newspaper Alliance, and British Broadcasting Corp., 1939-40; *New York Times*, New York, N.Y., correspondent with London bureau, covering the Balkans, Russia, and the Middle East, 1940-44, chief of foreign service, based in Paris, 1944-54, foreign affairs columnist, 1954—. *Member:* Phi Beta Kappa, Metropolitan Club (Washington, D.C.), Morfontaine (Paris). *Awards, honors:* Overseas Press Club award, 1941, for best reporting on the German-Russian front.

WRITINGS: Sit-Down with John L. Lewis, Random House, 1938; *The Big Thaw: A Personal Exploration of the "New" Russia and the Orbit Countries*, Harper, 1956; *What's Wrong with U.S. Foreign Policy*, Harcourt, 1959.

My Brother Death, Harper, 1961; *The Resistentialists*, Harper, 1962, published as *Unconquered Souls: The Resistentialists*, Overlook Press, 1973; *The Test: De Gaulle and Algeria*, Harcourt, 1962; *Unfinished Revolution: America and the Third World*, Atheneum, 1965; (with the editors of American Heritage) *The American Heritage Picture History of World War II*, American Heritage Publishing, 1966, abridged edition published as *World War II*, 1970; *A Long Row of Candles: Memoirs and Diaries, 1934-1954*, Macmillan, 1969.

The Last of the Giants (sequel to *A Long Row of Candles*), Macmillan, 1970; *The Tooth Merchant*, Quadrangle, 1973; *An Age of Mediocrity*, Macmillan, 1973; *The Coldest War: Russia's Game in China*, Harcourt, 1974.

SIDELIGHTS: In spite of his family ties in the newspaper business (his uncle, Arthur Hays Sulzberger, published the *New York Times*), C. L. Sulzberger chose to establish his career on an earned reputation as a journalist, rather than on his family name. When the *Times* eventually sought out his services in 1940, it was on the basis of his aggressive, objective reporting on the turmoil in Europe in 1938-40.

During World War II Sulzberger covered almost every major front in Europe, the Middle East, and in Russia. Millions of Americans followed the progress of the war through his front-page news stories and his feature articles in the *Times*. In his long and distinguished career as a foreign correspondent, Sulzberger has been witness to many of the major events of contemporary history, and has been close to most of the great and near-great figures of our time—Churchill, DeGaulle, and Eisenhower among many others.

Critics have been dismayed at times by the massive detail of people, places, and events in Sulzberger's memoirs, *A Long Row of Candles* and *The Last of the Giants*, both drawn from a vast file of working notes accumulated over the years. But as Christopher Lehmann-Haupt has observed, "*A Long Row of Candles* is not really about C. L. Sulzberger at all. It is more an autobiography of the world from 1938 to 1954 . . . not so much a book you read as it is a total historical environment through which you wander, pausing only to examine what catches your eye."

* * *

SUMMERHAYES, Victor Samuel 1897(?)-1974

1897(?)—December 27, 1974; international authority on the study and classification of orchids, and author of several books in his field. Obituaries: *AB Bookman's Weekly*, February 3, 1975.

* * *

SUNSTEIN, Emily W(eisberg) 1924-

PERSONAL: Born April 28, 1924, in Dallas, Tex.; daughter of Alex F. (an attorney) and Marie (Kahn) Weisberg; married Leon C. Sunstein, Jr. (a stockbroker), July 28, 1943; children: Paul, Kay (Mrs. Paul Hymowitz), Lauren. *Education:* Vassar College, B.A., 1944. *Politics:* Liberal. *Religion:* Jewish. *Address:* c/o Harper & Row Publishers, Inc., 49 East 33rd St., New York, N.Y. 10016.

CAREER: Writer. Chairman of Philadelphia chapter, American Jewish Committee, 1964-66, national secretary, 1973-75; commissioner of Pennsylvania State Human Relations Commission, 1970-74. Chairman of Philadelphia chapter, Americans for Democratic Action, 1966-68.

WRITINGS: A Different Face: The Life of Mary Wollstonecraft, Harper, 1975. Contributor to *Notes and Queries*, *Philadelphia Evening Bulletin*, and other publications.

* * *

SUSANN, Jacqueline 1921-1974

August 20, 1921—September 21, 1974; American author of three best-selling novels, and former actress. Obituaries: *New York Times*, September 23, 1974; *Washington Post*, September 23, 1974; *Newsweek*, September 30, 1974; *Time*, October 7, 1974; *AB Bookman's Weekly*, November 25, 1974; *Current Biography*, November, 1974. (*CLC* 3).

* * *

SUSSMAN, Barry 1934-

PERSONAL: Born July 10, 1934, in New York, N.Y.; son of Samuel and Esther (Rosen) Sussman; married Peggy Earhart, January 20, 1962; children: Seena, Shari. *Education:* Brooklyn College (now Brooklyn College of the City University of New York), B.A., 1956. *Religion:* Jewish. *Home:* 11016 Gainsborough Rd., Potomac, Md. *Office: Washington Post*, 1150 15th St. N.W., Washington, D.C.

CAREER: Bristol Herald Courier, Bristol, Va.-Tenn., reporter and editor, 1960-64, managing editor, 1962-64; *Washington Post*, Washington, D.C., editor, 1965—, city editor, 1971-73. *Awards, honors:* Drew Pearson Foundation award for investigative reporting, 1972; Washington Newspaper Guild prize for national reporting, 1973.

WRITINGS: The Great Coverup: Nixon and the Scandal of Watergate, Crowell, 1974.

* * *

SUSSMAN, Leonard R(ichard) 1920-

PERSONAL: Born November 26, 1920, in New York, N.Y.; son of Jacob (a dentist) and Carolyn (Marks) Sussman; married Frances Rukeyser, May 9, 1942 (divorced, 1958); married Marianne Rita Gutmann, May 28, 1958; children: (first marriage) Lynne, David William; (second marriage) Mark Jacob. *Education:* New York University, B.A., 1940; Columbia University, M.S., 1941. *Religion:* Jewish. *Home:* 215 East 73rd St., New York, N.Y. 10021. *Office:* 20 West 40th St., New York, N.Y. 10018.

CAREER: New York Morning Telegraph, New York, N.Y., copy editor, 1941; WQXR-Radio, New York, news editor, 1941; *San Juan World Journal*, San Juan, Puerto Rico, cable editor, 1942; Caribbean correspondent for *Busi-*

ness Week, and editor of Foreign Broadcast Intelligence Service, both 1942; press secretary to Governor of Puerto Rico, in San Juan, 1942-43; Government of Puerto Rico, San Juan, founder and director of information office in New York, N.Y., 1946-49; American Council for Judaism, New York, N.Y., regional director, 1949-56, national executive director, 1956-66; Freedom House, New York, N.Y., executive director, 1967—. Public affairs consultant for Nationwide Insurance Co. and industrial affiliates, 1953-56; accredited United Nations observer, 1961-66; executive director of Willkie Memorial Building, 1970—; trustee of International Council on the Future of the University, 1973—. *Military service:* U.S. Army, 1943-46; became technical sergeant; received Legion of Merit. *Member:* Overseas Press Club. *Awards, honors:* Black Cat Award from Press and Union Club of San Francisco, 1962.

WRITINGS: Puerto Rico Handbook, Office of Puerto Rico (Washington, D.C.), 1948; *Current Events Syllabus*, American Council for Judaism, 1956; (contributor) Lester Mondale, *Values in World Religions*, Beacon Press, 1958; *A Curriculum for the Reform Religious School*, American Council for Judaism, 1959; (contributor) Sidney Hook, Paul Kurtz, and Miro Todorovich, editors, *The Idea of a Modern University*, Prometheus, 1974.

Editor: (And contributor) David Goldberg, *Holidays for American Judaism*, Bookman Associates, 1954; (and contributor) Goldberg, *Stories about Judaism*, Books I and II, Bookman Associates, 1954; *Bible Story Color-In Book*, Bookman Associates, 1955; (and contributor) Goldberg, *Meet the Prophets*, Bookman Associates, 1956; Jacqueline Bregoff, *Holiday Time*, Bookman Associates, 1957; Goldberg, *The Leaven of Judaism*, Twayne, 1970.

Contributor to magazines and newspapers, including *Newsday, Christian Science Monitor, Journalism Quarterly, Mass Comm Review, American Library Association Bulletin*, and *Quadrant* (Australia). Originator and editor of *Growing Up*, a weekly magazine for children, 1953-60; editor of *Issues*, 1958-66, and of *Freedom at Issue*, 1970—. Member of editoral committee of Council of Liberal Churches, 1956-59.

WORK IN PROGRESS: Editing and contributing to *The Press at War* by Peter Braestrup and Burns W. Roper.

* * *

SUTTON, Denys 1917-

PERSONAL: Born August 10, 1917, in London, England; son of Edmund Miller and Dulcie Laura (a dancer; maiden name, Wheeler); married Sonja Kilbansky, 1940 (divorced); married Gertrud Koebke-Knudson, 1952 (divorced); married Cynthia Sassoon, 1960; children: one son, one daughter. *Education:* Exeter College, Oxford, B.A., B.Litt. *Politics:* Conservative. *Home:* 22 Chelsea Park Gardens, London S.W.3, England. *Office: Apollo*, 22 Davies St., London W.1, England.

CAREER: Employed in Foreign Office Research Department, London, England, 1940-46; International Commission for Restitution of Cultural Material, London, secretary, 1946; fine arts specialist, United Nations Educational, Scientific, and Cultural Organization (UNESCO), 1948; *Country Life*, London, art critic; *Apollo*, London, editor, 1962—; author. Organized Royal Academy art exhibitions, 1966, 1968. Visiting lecturer, Yale University, 1949. *Member:* Institut de France (corresponding member), Traveller's Club. *Awards, honors:* Decorated Chevalier of the Legion d'Honneur.

WRITINGS: Antoine Watteau: Les charmes de la vie, the Music Party, in the Wallace Collection, London, Lund, Humphries, 1946; (author of introduction) *Matisse: Paintings, 1939-1946*, Drummond, 1946; (compiler) *Some British Drawings from the Collection of Sir Robert Witt*, Arts Council of Great Britain, 1948; *American Painting*, Avalon Press, 1948; (translator) Jean Adhemar, *Goya*, House of Beric, 1948; *Picasso: Blue and Pink Periods*, Drummond, 1948; *French Drawings of the Eighteenth Century*, Pleiades Books, 1949.

Flemish Painting of the Royal Academy, Arts Plastique (Brussels), 1954; (author of foreword) *Suzanne Valadon, 1867-1938*, Lefevre Galleries (London), 1956; (author of biographical essay and notes) *Nicolas de Staeel, 1914-1955*, Whitechapel Art Gallery (London), 1956; (compiler) *Andre Derain, 1880-1954*, Wildenstein (London), 1957; (author of introduction and notes) *Bonnard (1867-1947)*, Faber, 1957; *Andre Derain*, Phaidon, 1959; *Christie's Since the War, 1945-1958: An Essay on Taste, Patronage, and Collecting*, Christie, Mason & Woods, 1959.

Nicolas de Staeel, Grove, 1960; (author of introduction) Maurice de Vlaminck, *Dangerous Corner*, Ryerson, 1961; *Lautrec*, Marboro Books, 1962; *Westwood Manor, Bradford on Avon: The History of the House and Its Inhabitants*, National Trust, 1962; (author of essay) R. A. M. Stevenson, *Velasquez*, G. Bell, 1962; *Nocturne: The Art of James McNeill Whistler*, Country Life Ltd., 1963, Lippincott, 1964; *Sergio de Castro*, Editions Fall (Paris), 1964; (author of essay) *Ker Xavier Roussel*, Wildenstein, 1964; *Titian*, Barnes & Noble, 1964; (author of essay) *Maurice Denis 1870-1943*, Wildenstein, 1964; (author of foreword) *Art Historians and Critics as Collectors*, Thomas Agnew & Sons, 1965; (editor with St. John Gore) *The Art of Painting in Florence and Siena from 1250 to 1500*, Wildenstein, 1965; (author of introduction) *Gauguin and the Pont-Aven Group*, Arts Council of Great Britain, 1966; (compiler) *James McNeill Whistler: Paintings, Etchings, Pastels & Watercolours*, Phaidon, 1966; (author of essay) *Gustave Caillebotte, 1848-1894*, Wildenstein, 1966; *Triumphant Satyr: The World and August Rodin*, Country Life Ltd., 1966, Hawthorn, 1967; *Diego Velasquez*, Barnes & Noble, 1967; (editor) *The Toledo Museum of Art*, Hillingdon Press, 1967; (compiler) *Drawings from the National Gallery of Ireland*, Wildenstein, 1967; (compiler) *France in the Eighteenth Century*, Royal Academy of Art, 1968, 2nd edition, 1968; (editor) *Richard Wilson: An Italian Sketchbook*, Paul Mellon Foundation, 1968; (compiler) *J.-F. Millet (1814-1875)*, Wildenstein, 1969.

(Compiler and author of essay) *Edgar Degas, 1834-1917*, Lefevre Galleries, 1970; (compiler and author of introduction) *Italian Drawings from the Ashmolean Museum, Oxford*, Wildenstein, 1970; (author of essay) *Pictures from Southampton*, Wildenstein, 1970; (author of essay) *Cornelis Theodorus Marie van Dongen, 1877-1968*, University of Arizona Museum of Art, 1971; (editor and author of introduction) *Letters of Roger Fry*, Random House, 1973.

Also author of *Artists in Seventeenth Century Rome* (with Denis Mahon), 1955; *Catalogue of French, Spanish, and German Schools in Fitzwilliam Museum, Cambridge* (with J. W. Goodison), 1960; and *Gaspard Dughet*, 1962. Contributor to journals in his field. Saleroom correspondent, *Daily Telegraph* (London); art critic, *Financial Times* (London).

WORK IN PROGRESS: Two books, *Life of W. R. Sickert* and *Study of Edith, Osbert and Sacheverell Sitwell*.

AVOCATIONAL INTERESTS: Theatre and swimming.

SWAIN, Frank G. 1893(?)-1975

1893(?)—January 18, 1975; American lawyer, judge, and author of verse. Obituaries: *New York Times*, January 20, 1975; *Washington Post*, January 22, 1975.

* * *

SWAIN, Margaret (Helen) 1909-

PERSONAL: Born May 13, 1909, in Lancashire, England; daughter of John (an iron and steel merchant) and Isabella (Johnston) Hart; married Richard H. A. Swain (a physician and Reader in virology at University of Edinburgh), November 27, 1937; children: John Richard, Christopher Paul, Catherine Fiona. *Education:* St. Bartholomew's Hospital, R.N., 1932; University of Edinburgh, student in fine arts, 1964-66. *Religion:* Presbyterian. *Home:* 8 South Gray St., Edinburgh EH9 1TE, Scotland.

CAREER: St. Bartholomew's Hospital, London, England, registered nurse and administrative officer, 1930-37; voluntary social worker for the disadvantaged and disturbed, 1954-74. Has organized festival exhibitions of historical needlework and costume in Edinburgh. Honorary consultant in textiles to Scottish museums. *Member:* Embroiderers Guild (member of council), Costume Society, Weavers' Workshop of Great Britain (associate member).

WRITINGS: The Flowerers: The Story of Ayrshire White Needlework, W. & R. Chambers, 1955; *A Devotional Miscellany* (facsimile of embroidered book of the 1660's), Museum of Fine Arts (Boston), 1964; *Historical Needlework*, Barrie & Rockliffe, 1970; *The Needlework of Mary Queen of Scots*, Van Nostrand, 1973. Contributor to museum journals and other magazines in Great Britain and the United States, including *Connoisseur*, *Antiques*, *Country Life*, *Embroidery*, *Times*, *Scottish Home and Country*, and *Scotsman*.

WORK IN PROGRESS: A catalogue of a collection of eighteenth-century manuscript needlework designs; research on textile furnishings of the seventeenth and eighteenth centuries.

SIDELIGHTS: "I regard myself as a research worker in the field of historical textiles," Margaret Swain wrote. "I am interested in establishing where workers in the past obtained materials, and why they used a given technique at a certain time. To me, textile history is a part of economic and social history; the people, amateur or professional, are as interesting as the product. I also study the engraved sources of textile design."

* * *

SWEIGARD, Lulu E. ?-1974

?—August 3, 1974; American dance teacher and author. Obituaries: *New York Times*, August 3, 1974.

* * *

SWENSON, Karen 1936-

PERSONAL: Born July 29, 1936, in New York, N.Y.; daughter of Howard (an architect) and Dorothy (Trautman) Swenson; married Michael Shuter, November, 1958 (divorced, 1970); children: Michael, Jr. *Education:* Barnard College, B.A., 1959; New York University, M.A., 1971, now in graduate study for Ph.D. *Home:* 430 State St., Brooklyn, N.Y. 11217. *Office:* Department of English, City College of the City University of New York, 135th St. and Convent Ave., New York, N.Y. 10033. *Agent:* Curtis Brown Ltd., 60 East 56th St., New York, N.Y.

CAREER: Has been employed in public relations, and worked as dishwasher, usher, and book saleswoman; City College of the City University of New York, New York, N.Y., lecturer in English, 1969—. *Member:* P.E.N., Barnard Alumni Association. *Awards, honors: Transatlantic Review* poetry fellowship at Bread Loaf Writers' Conference, 1973.

WRITINGS: An Attic of Ideals (poems), Doubleday, 1974. Contributor to *New Yorker*, *Nation*, *New York Quarterly*, and *Texas Quarterly*.

WORK IN PROGRESS: A new book of poems.

* * *

SWETMAN, Glenn R(obert) 1936-

PERSONAL: Born May 20, 1936, in Biloxi, Miss.; son of Glenn Lyle (a banker) and June (Read) Swetman; married Margarita Ortiz (a university professor and translator), February 8, 1964; children: Margot, Max, Glenda. *Education:* University of Southern Mississippi, B.S., 1957, M.A., 1959; Tulane University, Ph.D., 1966. *Religion:* Episcopalian. *Home:* 638 Fairway Dr., Thibodaux, La. 70301. *Office:* Department of English, Nicholls State University, Thibodaux, La. 70301.

CAREER: Arkansas State University, Jonesboro, instructor in English, 1958-59; McNeese State University, Lake Charles, La., instructor in English, 1959-61; Tulane University, New Orleans, La., instructor and special adviser in engineering, 1961-64; University of Southern Mississippi, Hattiesburg, assistant professor of English, 1964-66; Louisiana Technical University, Ruston, associate professor of English, 1966-67; Nicholls State University, Thibodaux, La., professor of English, 1967—. Special adviser in technical communication to Union Carbide. *Military service:* U.S. Army Reserve, 1957-63, active duty, 1957.

MEMBER: National Federation of State Poetry Societies (first vice-president, 1973—), Louisiana State Poetry Society (president, 1971-74), College Writers Society of Louisiana (vice-president, 1970-71; president, 1971-72), Japan Society of New Orleans, T. and A. Literary Society (president), Thibodaux Rifle Association, Nouma Terre-Bonne Rifle and Pistol Club, Country Club Civic Organization (chairman). *Awards, honors:* Haiku award from radio station KQUE, 1964; Black Ship Festival Haiku award, Yokosuka, Japan, 1967.

WRITINGS: (With Curtis Whittington and William Sullivan) *Poems from the McNeese Review*, McNeese University, 1960; *The Pagan Christians* (brochure), Examiner Press, 1962; *Tunel de Amor*, Xavier University (Bolivia), 1972, published as *Tunnel of Love*, Pterodactyl Press, 1974; *Deka I*, Paon Press, 1973. Contributor to literary magazines, including *Wisconsin Review*, *Kansas Quarterly*, *Midwest Quarterly*, and *International Surgery Bulletin*. Book reviewer and literary consultant for *Jackson State Times*.

* * *

SWICEGOOD, Thomas L. P. 1930-
(Charles K. Lowe, Jay Stierwell)

PERSONAL: Born October 15, 1930, in Key West, Fla.; son of Stephen P. (in U.S. Coast Guard) and Eola (Pinder) Swicegood. *Education:* University of Florida, B.A., 1951. *Religion:* Protestant. *Residence:* Los Angeles, Calif. *Agent:* Don Shepherd, 1680 Vine, Suite 1105, Hollywood, Calif. 90028. *Office address:* Eola Publishing Co., Box 42243, Los Angeles, Calif. 90042.

CAREER: American Trucking Association, Washington, D.C., in public relations and special assistant, 1956-57; WTOP-TV, Washington, D.C., floor director, 1957-58; KCOP-TV, Los Angeles, Calif., stage manager, 1960; writer. *Military service:* U.S. Coast Guard, 1951-55; became lieutenant senior grade. *Member:* Delta Chi.

WRITINGS: Other Side of the Wind, Eola Publishing, 1974; *Our God Too: Biography of a Church and a Temple*, Pyramid Publications, 1974. Author of television scripts, under pseudonym Charles K. Lowe or Jay Stierwell, for "The Untouchables," "Blue Angels," "U.S. Marshall," and "Sea Hunt." Author and producer of "Escape from Hell Island," and author and director of "The Undertaker and His Pals," both theatrical motion pictures.

WORK IN PROGRESS: A book, *Chattahoochee*.

SIDELIGHTS: Swicegood told *CA* that he is particularly interested in writing about homosexuals, "attempting to educate the general public to the fact that persecution of and discrimination against this large . . . and most misunderstood minority are humanly, legally, and scientifically unreasonable."

* * *

SWIFT, Marshall S(tefan) 1936-

PERSONAL: Born December 27, 1936, in Staten Island, N.Y.; married Naomi McLeod; children: Roderick, Randall. *Education:* State University of New York College at Oswego, B.S., 1957; Syracuse University, M.S., 1963, Ph.D., 1966. *Home:* 99 South Ivy Lane, Glen Mills, Pa. 19342. *Office:* Hahnemann Community Mental Health and Mental Retardation Center, 314 North Broad St., Philadelphia, Pa. 19102.

CAREER: Devereux Foundation, Devon, Pa., clinical psychologist, 1965-67; Hahnemann Community Mental Health and Mental Retardation Center, Philadelphia, Pa., instructor, 1967-69, assistant professor, 1969-71, associate professor of psychology, 1971—, associate director of research, 1967-74, director of consultation and education, and early intervention and prevention programs, 1974—. *Military service:* U.S. Army, Psychiatric Service, 1959-61. *Member:* American Psychological Association, American Board of Professional Psychologists, Pennsylvania Psychological Association, Philadelphia Society of Clinical Psychologists.

WRITINGS: (With Jerome J. Platt and George Spivack) *Interpersonal Problem-Solving Group Therapy* (monograph), Hahnemann Community Mental Health and Mental Retardation Center, 1974; (with Spivack) *Alternative Teaching Strategies: Helping Behaviorally Troubled Children Achieve*, Research Press, 1975. Contributor of more than twenty-five articles and reviews to psychology and education journals.

* * *

TABORI, Paul 1908-1974
(Peter Stafford, Christopher Stevens, Paul Tabor)

August 5, 1908—November 9, 1974; Hungarian-born British novelist, journalist, political writer, scriptwriter for radio, television, and films, and founder of the International Writers Guild. Obituaries: *New York Times*, November 17, 1974; *AB Bookman's Weekly*, December 2, 1974. (*CA*-5/6).

* * *

TAGESON, Carroll W(illiam) 1925-

PERSONAL: Born August 28, 1925, in Ludington, Mich.; son of George Herbert, Sr. (a crane operator) and Mabel (a bookkeeper; maiden name, Lonergan) Tageson; married Carol Ann Anticevich (a counselor), September 6, 1969. *Education:* San Luis Rey College, B.A., 1948; Catholic University of America, M.A., 1955, Ph.D., 1959. *Politics:* Democrat. *Religion:* Roman Catholic. *Residence:* South Bend, Ind. *Office:* Counseling Psychology Program, University of Notre Dame, P.O. Box 651, Notre Dame, Ind. 46556.

CAREER: San Luis Rey College, San Luis Rey, Calif., instructor, 1952-53, assistant professor, 1955-57, associate professor of psychology, 1959-68, president of college, 1955-57, acting president, 1959-61, dean of students, 1961-68; University of Notre Dame, Notre Dame, Ind., associate professor of education, 1969—, director of Counseling Psychology Program, 1970-72. Member of board of directors of National Catholic Guidance Conference, 1966-69. *Member:* American Psychological Association, American Personnel and Guidance Association.

WRITINGS: Relationship of Self-Perceptions to Realism of Vocational Choice, Catholic University of America Press, 1960; (translator with Virgilio Biasiol) Roberto Zavalloni, *Self-Determination: The Psychology of Personal Freedom*, Forum Books, 1962; (with John Koval and Willis Bartlett) *Study of Church Vocations*, National Center for Church Vocations, 1974. Contributor to psychology journals, including *Counseling and Values*, *Catholic Psychological Record*, and *Professional Psychology*.

WORK IN PROGRESS: The Self-Conscious Animal, a book on humanistic psychology, completion expected in 1976; research on social-psychological model of vocational involvement.

AVOCATIONAL INTERESTS: Travel, music, literature.

* * *

TALLMAN, Albert 1902-

PERSONAL: Born July 21, 1902, in Warsaw, Poland; son of Maurice Saul (an artisan) and Fay (Meyersdorf) Tallman; married Sue Ray Szternlicht, July 16, 1921; children: Irving, Gloria D. Tallman Norton. *Education:* Attended University of California, San Francisco. *Politics:* Democrat. *Religion:* Jewish. *Home:* 709 Nevada Ave., San Mateo, Calif. 94402.

CAREER: Employed in surgical and orthopedic appliances business, San Francisco, Calif., 1934-47; owner of embroidery business, San Francisco, Calif., 1947-74. Poet. *Member:* International Platform Association, Centro Studi e Scambi Internazionale (Rome), Avalon International, World Poetry Society, American Jewish Committee, South and West Literary Association, Commonwealth Club of California. *Awards, honors:* Hart Crane and Alice Crane Award, 1969, for poem "I Will Not Proselitize"; World Poetry Society award, 1970, for poem "Johann Sebastian Bach"; North American Mentor awards, 1972, for poem "Sysyphus," and 1973, for poem "Fear."

WRITINGS—Poetry: *The End of the Cycle*, Golden Quill Press, 1967; *Pebbles*, Centro Studi e Scambi Internazionale, 1968; *Kol Nidrei* (title means "All Vows"), Bitterroot Press, 1970; *Plus and Minus*, Branden Press, 1972.

Work is anthologized in *Wisconsin Poetry Magazine Poetry Collection*, edited by A. M. Stark, 1966. Contributor of articles to *Ocarina* and *Madras India*.

WORK IN PROGRESS: Plays.

TAMBS, Lewis Arthur 1927-

PERSONAL: Surname legally changed, 1948; born July 7, 1927, in San Diego, Calif.; son of Fred B. and Marguerite (Tambs) Jones; married Heather McEachern, 1959; children: Kari, Kristen, Jennifer, Heidi. *Education:* University of California, Berkeley, B.S.I.E., 1953; University of California, Santa Barbara, M.A., 1962, Ph.D., 1967. *Politics:* Republican. *Religion:* Roman Catholic. *Home:* 1317 East Steamboat Bend Dr., Tempe, Ariz. 85283. *Office:* Center for Latin American Studies, Arizona State University, Tempe, Ariz. 85281.

CAREER: Creighton University, Omaha, Neb., instructor, 1965-67, assistant professor of history, 1967-69; Arizona State University, Tempe, assistant professor, 1969-70, associate professor of Latin American history, 1970—, director of Center for Latin American Studies, 1972—. *Military service:* U.S. Army, 1945-47, 1950-51; became sergeant. *Member:* Catholic Historical Association, Pacific Coast Council for Latin American Studies (member of governing board, 1973—; vice-president, 1974-75), Southwest Alliance for Latin America (member of governing board, 1972—), Arizona Latin American Council, Arizona Mexico Commission, Council of Foreign Relations (Tucson branch).

WRITINGS: (Editor) *Latin American Government Leaders*, Center for Latin America Studies, Arizona State University, 1970; (with A. S. Birkos) *Academic Writer's Guide to Periodicals*, Kent State University Press, Volume I: *Latin American Studies*, 1971, Volume II: *Slavic and East European Studies*, 1973, Volume III: *African and Black American Studies*, Books for Libraries, 1975; (with Birkos) *Historiography, Method, History Teaching: A Bibliography of Books and Articles in English, 1965-73*, Shoe String, 1975; (with Birkos) *Bibliography of East European & Soviet Economic Affairs*, Books for Libraries, 1975.

WORK IN PROGRESS: March to the West: Six Centuries of Luso-Brazilian Expansion; *The Spanish Blue Division on the Russian Front: 1941-1945*; *The Amazon Rubber Boom of 1890-1912*.

* * *

TANNER, C(harles) Kenneth 1938-

PERSONAL: Born October 2, 1938, in Opp, Ala.; son of Charlie Tolbert (a farmer) and Clero (a textile worker; maiden name, Clark) Tanner; married Jacqueline Messer, June 8, 1962; children: Kipp, Todd, Mitzie Zanne. *Education:* Troy State University, B.S., 1961; Florida State University, M.S., 1966, Ed.D., 1968. *Office:* Department of Educational Administration, University of Tennessee, Knoxville, Tenn. 37916.

CAREER: Mathematics teacher in public high schools and junior high schools in Elba, Ala., 1961-62, Enterprise, Ala., 1962-63, and Niceville, Fla., 1963-65; administrative intern in public schools in Troy, Ala., 1965-66, Nassau County, Fla., 1966-67, and New Orleans, La., 1967-68; University of Tennessee, Knoxville, assistant professor, 1968-70, associate professor, 1971-74, professor of educational administration, 1974—. *Member:* International Society of Educational Planners, American Educational Research Association, University Council for Educational Administration, Phi Delta Kappa.

WRITINGS: (Contributor) D. H. Stollor, editor, *Analysis and Interpretation of Research for School Board Members*, Bureau of Research, U.S. Office of Education, 1971; *Designs for Educational Planning: A Systematic Approach*, Heath, 1971; (contributor) Kenneth Quindrey, editor, *State Financial Assistance to Local Governments*, State of Tennessee, 1973; (contributor) Stephen Hencley and James Yates, editors, *Futurism Education*, McCutchan, 1974. Contributor to *Church and State* and to education journals.

* * *

TANZI, Vito 1935-

PERSONAL: Born November 29, 1935, in Mola di Bari, Italy; naturalized U.S. citizen; son of Luigi and Maria (Tanzi) Tanzi; married Madeleine S. Gratet, 1965; children: Vito L., Alexandre B., Giancarlo O. *Education:* Attended University of Bari, 1954-56; George Washington University, B.A., 1959, M.A., 1961; Harvard University, M.A., 1963, Ph.D., 1966. *Home:* 5912 Walhonding Rd., Bethesda, Md. 20016. *Office:* Department of Economics, American University, Washington, D.C. 20016.

CAREER: George Washington University, Washington, D.C., assistant professor of economics, 1963-65; Organization of American States, Washington, D.C., senior economist in department of economics, 1965-67; American University, Washington, D.C., associate professor, 1967-70, professor of economics, 1970—, chairman of department, 1971-73. Consultant to Organization of American States, 1967—, Stanford Research Institute, 1969-70, and United Nations, 1970; economist on Organization of American States missions to Haiti, Ecuador, Colombia, Peru, Argentina, and Brazil between 1966-71, and on World Bank missions to Ecuador, 1971, and Haiti, 1973.

MEMBER: American Economic Association, Royal Economic Society, National Tax Association, Omicron Delta Epsilon. *Awards, honors:* Research grant from Ente Einaudi (Central Bank of Italy), 1974.

WRITINGS: The Individual Income Tax and Economic Growth, Johns Hopkins Press, 1969; (with J. B. Bracewell-Milnes and D. R. Myddelton) *Taxation: A Radical Approach*, Institute of Economic Affairs (London), 1970.

Contributor: John Due, editor, *The Role of Direct and Indirect Taxes in the Federal Revenue System*, Princeton University Press, 1964; *The Alliance for Progress and Latin American Development Prospects: A Five Year Review, 1961-1965*, Johns Hopkins Press, for Organization of American States, 1967; *Taxation as a Determinant of Economic Development*, Organization of American States, 1973; J. H. Weaver, editor, *Political Economy: Radical and Orthodox Approaches*, Allyn & Bacon, 1973; David Geithman, editor, *Fiscal Policy for Industrialization and Development in Latin America*, University of Florida Press, 1974. Contributor of more than thirty articles to professional journals in United States and Europe. Member of board of editors, *Akron Business and Economic Review*, 1972-74, *Public Finance Quarterly*, 1973-75.

* * *

TARRANT, John J(oseph) 1924-

PERSONAL: Surname is accented on first syllable; born July 5, 1924, in New York, N.Y.; son of John J. and Margaret Tarrant; married Dorothy Kuusela (executive director of Westport-Weston Community Council), November 8, 1948; children: Cathy, Patricia, John. *Education:* University of Missouri, B.J., 1948. *Politics:* Democrat. *Home:* 167 South Compo Rd., Westport, Conn. 06880. *Agent:* Arthur Pine Associates, Inc., 1780 Broadway, New York, N.Y. 10019.

CAREER: Free-lance writer and newspaperman, 1948-54; Research Institute of America, New York, N.Y., editorial director, 1954-64; Benton & Bowles (advertising agency), New York, N.Y., vice-president for training and development, 1964-67; free-lance writer, 1967—. Member of Westport Democratic Town Committee. *Military service:* U.S. Naval Reserve, 1943-45, 1950-52; became lieutenant senior grade.

WRITINGS: Tomorrow's Techniques for Today's Salesmen, Hawthorn, 1970; *The Corporate Eunuch*, Crowell, 1973; (with Auren Uris) *How to Win Your Boss's Love, Approval, and Job*, Van Nostrand, 1974; *Getting Fired*, Van Nostrand, 1974; *How to Negotiate for More Money*, Van Nostrand, 1975; (with Henry Voegeli) *Survival 2001*, Van Nostrand, 1975; (with Mortimer Feinberg and Robert Tanofsky) *New Psychology for Managing People*, Prentice-Hall, 1975. Contributor to professional journals.

WORK IN PROGRESS: Research for *The End of Exurbia*.

* * *

TASSIN, Ray(mond Jean) 1926-

PERSONAL: Born April 20, 1926, in Holdenville, Okla.; son of Bennie Raymond and Virginia (Lollis) Tassin; married Marthagrace Greer, March 26, 1948; children: Mark Alan. *Education:* Attended East Central State College, 1946-48; University of Oklahoma, B.A., 1950, M.A., 1957; University of Missouri, Ph.D., 1964. *Politics:* Democrat. *Religion:* Southern Baptist. *Home:* 600 Park Pl., Edmond, Okla. 73034. *Office:* Department of Journalism, Central State University, 100 North University Dr., Edmond, Okla. 73034.

CAREER: Oklahoma Daily, Norman, reporter and news editor, 1948-50; *Chickasha Daily Express*, Chickasha, Okla., reporter and sports editor, 1950-51; *Clinton Daily News*, Clinton, Okla., managing editor, 1951-53; *Konawa Leader*, Konawa, Okla., owner, publisher, and editor, 1953-56; *Oklahoman-Times*, Oklahoma City, Okla., reporter and rewriter, 1956-57; Baylor University, Waco, Tex., assistant professor of journalism, 1957-60; *Missourian*, Columbia, Mo., editor of editorial page, 1960-61; Central State University, Edmond, Okla., assistant professor, 1961-64, associate professor, 1964-68, professor of journalism, 1968—, chairman of department, 1965—. Laboratory teacher of reporting and typography at University of Oklahoma, 1956-57; director of public information program for Waco Naval Reserve Training Center, 1957-60; vice president of Southwest Journalism Congress, 1974-75. *Military service:* U.S. Naval Reserve, 1944—, gunner, active duty, 1944-45; served in Asiatic-Pacific theater; present rank in Reserve, commander; received Asiatic-Pacific campaign medal with twelve battle stars, Philippine Liberation campaign medal with two battle stars, Philippine Republic presidential unit citation.

MEMBER: Association for Education in Journalism, Medal of Honor History Roundtable (Oklahoma director, 1973—), Naval Reserve Association, Reserve Officers Association, Western Writers of America, Oklahoma Education Association, Oklahoma Press Association, Oklahoma Writers Federation, Kappa Tau Alpha, Pi Delta Epsilon, Sigma Delta Chi. *Awards, honors:* Okie Award for best non-fiction book of the year, from Oklahoma Writers Federation, 1973-74, and named Oklahoma professional writer of the year, by University of Oklahoma, 1974, both for *Stanley Vestal: Champion of the Old West*.

WRITINGS: Daily Newspaper Semi-Mergers, privately printed, 1957; *Red Men in Blue* (slightly fictionalized account of the Pawnee Battalion that protected construction of the Union Pacific Railroad), Avalon Books, 1960; *Steel Trails of Vengeance* (partly fictional account of a freight train that disappeared permanently in 1881), Avalon Books, 1961; *Stanley Vestal: Champion of the Old West* (biography of Walter S. Campbell), Arthur Clark, 1973; *Discount Homebuilding*, Drake Publishers, 1974.

Author of "East Central State College News," a weekly column in *Ada Times-Democrat*, 1946-48. Contributor to magazines. Copy editor of *Waco News-Tribune*, summer, 1959, and *Oklahoma City Times*, summer, 1962.

* * *

TAYLOR, Barbara J. 1927-

PERSONAL: Born June 27, 1927, in Provo, Utah; daughter of Theodore Marsden (a merchant) and Clara Mae (Orton) Taylor; married Dee Raymond Taylor (an architect), June 8, 1949; children: David Dee, Brad Lee. *Education:* Brigham Young University, B.S., 1957, M.S., 1960, Ph.D., 1971; Florida State University, graduate study, 1967-68. *Religion:* Church of Jesus Christ of Latter-Day Saints (Mormon). *Home:* 1385 East Oakcrest Lane, Provo, Utah 84601. *Office:* Department of Child Development and Family Relationships, Brigham Young University, Provo, Utah 84602.

CAREER: Brigham Young University, Provo, Utah, instructor, 1957-68, assistant professor of child development and family relationships, 1968—. *Member:* National Association for the Education of Young Children, Organisation Mondiale pour l'Education Prescolaire, British Association for Early Childhood Education, Utah Association for the Education of Young Children (past president).

WRITINGS: A Child Goes Forth, Brigham Young University Press, 1964, 2nd edition, 1975; *I Can Do* (juvenile), Brigham Young University Press, 1972; *When I Do, I Learn*, Brigham Young University Press, 1974.

WORK IN PROGRESS: A book on comparative preschool education in the United States and certain other countries; a book on administration and supervision in preschool.

* * *

TAYLOR, Robert R(atcliffe) 1939-

PERSONAL: Born July 10, 1939, in Victoria, British Columbia, Canada. *Education:* University of Victoria, student, 1957-60; University of British Columbia, B.A., 1961, M.A., 1964; University of Hamburg, further graduate study, 1962-63; Stanford University, Ph.D., 1970. *Office:* Department of History, Brock University, St. Catharines, Ontario, Canada.

CAREER: Brock University, St. Catharines, Ontario, lecturer, 1966-68, assistant professor, 1968-70, associate professor of history, 1970—.

WRITINGS: The Word in Stone: The Role of Architecture in the National Socialist Ideology, University of California Press, 1974.

WORK IN PROGRESS: Hohenzollern Architecture in Berlin: 1701-1918.

* * *

TAYLOR, Tim 1920-1974

May 5, 1920—October 1, 1974; American journalist, radio

and television writer, "ghost writer" of books and political speeches, and public relations adviser to political and theatrical figures. Obituaries: *New York Times*, October 3, 1974. (*CA*-45/48).

* * *

TEER, Frank 1934-

PERSONAL: Born September 9, 1934, in Manchester, England; son of Frank (a printer) and Patricia (Peck) Teer; married Constance May Turnbull, March 28, 1958; children: Catherine, John, Susan, Robert. *Education:* London School of Economics and Political Science, B.Sc. (honors), 1955. *Politics:* Liberal. *Home:* 13 Denbridge Rd., Bickley, Bromley, Kent, England. *Office:* Research Surveys of Great Britain, Broadway House, Broadway, London SW19 1RT, England.

CAREER: Board of Inland Revenue, Manchester, England, inspector of taxes, 1957-62 (qualified in accountancy and income tax, 1961); National Opinion Polls, London, England, senior research executive, 1962; Ford Motor Co., Dagenham, Essex, England, supervisor on business planning and finance staff, 1963; National Opinion Polls, director in charge of ad hoc research, 1963-66, joint managing director of research, 1966-72; Research Surveys of Great Britain, London, managing director, 1972—. *Military service:* British Army, 1955-57; became sergeant. *Member:* World Association for Public Opinion Research, European Society for Opinion Surveys and Market Research, Royal Statistical Society, Market Research Society (chairman, 1974-75).

WRITINGS: (Contributor) R. W. Worcester, editor, *Consumer Research Handbook*, McGraw, 1973; (with J. D. Spence) *Political Opinion Polls*, Hutchinson, 1974. Contributor to *Admap*.

* * *

TEMPLETON, Edith 1916-

PERSONAL: Born April 7, 1916, in Prague, Czechoslovakia; married William Stockwell Templeton, 1938 (divorced, 1947); married Edmund Ronald (a cardiologist), 1955; children: (second marriage) Edmund. *Education:* Attended French Lycee, Prague, 1931-35, and Medical University of Prague, 1936-37. *Religion:* Church of England. *Home:* Casa de Trez Arcos, rua Timor 7, Estoril, Portugal. *Agent:* Curtis Brown Ltd., 60 East 56th St., New York, N.Y. 10022.

CAREER: Worked as a medical coder in American War Office in the Office of the Surgeon General, Cheltenham and London, England, 1942-45; writer. *Military service:* British Army, 1945-46; conference and law court interpreter in Germany; became captain. *Member:* P.E.N.

WRITINGS: *Summer in the Country*, Eyre & Spottiswoode, 1950, published as *Proper Bohemians*, Houghton, 1952; *Living on Yesterday*, Eyre & Spottiswoode, 1951; *The Island of Desire*, Eyre & Spottiswoode, 1952; *The Surprise of Cremona* (Companion Book Club selection), Eyre & Spottiswoode, 1954, Harper, 1957; *This Charming Pastime*, Eyre & Spottiswoode, 1955; (with Arthur Gould and Calvin Kentfield) *Three: 1971*, Random House, 1971. Short stories represented in anthologies, including *Best New Yorker Short Stories of Decade, 1950-60*, Simon & Schuster, 1960; *Stories From the New Yorker*, Gollancz, 1961; *The Gourmets Companion*, edited by Cyril Ray, Eyre & Spottiswoode, 1963; *Abroad*, edited by Jon Evans, Gollancz, 1968. Contributor to *Vogue, Housewife, Holiday, Harpers, Atlantic Monthly, New Yorker*.

SIDELIGHTS: Miss Templeton speaks Bohemian, German, French, and "fluent bad Italian, unfluent bad Portuguese." *Avocational interests:* Travel.

* * *

TENNIES, Arthur C(ornelius) 1931-

PERSONAL: Born April 15, 1931, in Boston, Mass.; son of Raymond Ara (a clergyman) and Frances (a teacher; maiden name, Fiske) Tennies; married Janet Trowbridge, September 6, 1959; children: Diane, Linda, Susan, Philip. *Education:* Grove City College, B.S., 1953; Louisville Presbyterian Theological Seminary, B.D., 1956; Butler University, B.S., 1968. *Politics:* Republican. *Home:* 113 Green St., Fayetteville, N.Y. 13066. *Office:* New York State Council of Churches, 3049 East Genesee St., Syracuse, N.Y. 13224.

CAREER: Pastor of United Presbyterian churches in Vernon, Ind., 1956-58, Lewisville, Ind., 1958-64, and Burrows, Ind., 1965-66; New York State Council of Churches, Syracuse, researcher and planner, 1967—. Rural church specialist for United Presbyterian Program Agency, 1973—. *Member:* Religious Research Association, Presbyterian Historical Society, American Society of Planning Officials.

WRITINGS: *A Church for Sinners, Seekers, and Sundry Non-Saints*, Abingdon, 1974. Contributor to *National Observer* and to religious publications.

WORK IN PROGRESS: A sociological and historical survey of the first two-thirds of the twentieth century; research on the congregation as a unit of mission in the last part of the twentieth century.

* * *

THALMANN, Rita Renee Line 1926-

PERSONAL: Born June 13, 1926, in Nurnberg, Germany; daughter of Nathan and Helene (Hausmann) Thalmann. *Education:* Sorbonne, University of Paris, Agregee, 1968, Docteur d'Etat, 1973; College de France, further study, 1968-74. *Politics:* "Left and women movements." *Home:* 285 rue de Vaugirard, Paris 15, France. *Office:* Institute for German Studies, University of Tours, 3 rue des Tanneurs, Tours 37, France.

CAREER: Educator of orphans after World War Two; secondary school teacher in Blois and Paris, France, 1954-65; University of Tours, Tours, France, assistant professor, 1966-69, associate professor, 1969-73, professor of German civilization, 1973—, director of Institute for German Studies, 1969—. *Member:* Society for Ecclesiastical History, Comite d'Histoire de la Deuxieme Guerre Mondiale, Choisir (movement for women's emancipation; national secretary). *Awards, honors:* Decoration of the Republic of Poland, 1968; named Officier des palmes academiques, 1969.

WRITINGS: (With Emmanuel Feinermann) *La Nuit de Cristal*, Laffont, 1972, translation by Gilles Cremonesi published as *Crystal Night: 9-10 November, 1938*, Coward, 1974. Contributor to professional journals, including *Revue d'Histoire Moderne et Contemporaine*, *Revue d'Allemagne*, and *Revue d'Ethno-Psychologie*.

WORK IN PROGRESS: A biography of Jochen Klepper, a German Protestant writer; research on Protestantism and nationalism in Germany, 1900-1945.

SIDELIGHTS: Rita Thalmann writes: "Since the war (my parents were killed by Germans and I was in a camp) my interest goes to all problems involved with ideology and mentalities connected with the processes of oppression of minorities or groups."

* * *

THERIAULT, Albert A(ugustine), Jr. 1928-

PERSONAL: Surname is pronounced *Ter*-rio; born June 8, 1928, in New York, N.Y.; son of Albert A. (a salesman) and Mae Irene (a switchboard operator; maiden name, Gioe) Theriault; married Elizabeth A. Daly, June 15, 1957; children: Mary-Alice, John. *Education:* Stonehill College, student, 1947-48; Brandeis University, A.B., 1954; University of Rhode Island, M.A., 1961; further graduate study at Worcester State College, 1963-65, and Anna Maria College, 1964. *Home:* 98 Lincoln Ave., Holden, Mass. 01520. *Office:* Department of English, Quinsigamond Community College, Worcester, Mass. 01606.

CAREER: English and mathematics teacher in junior high school in Swansea, Mass., 1954-56 (coach of track, field, and cross country teams); high school English teacher in Holden, Mass., 1956-61 (track, field, and cross country coach); Casimir Lyceum and Gymentelyk Lyceum voor Meisjes, both in Amsterdam, Netherlands, Fulbright teacher of English, 1961-62; high school English teacher in Holden, Mass., 1962-69, track, field, and cross country coach, 1962, chairman of English department, 1963-69; Quinsigamond Community College, Worcester, Mass., associate professor, 1969-75, professor of English, 1975—. *Member:* National Council of Teachers of English, Massachusetts Council of Teachers of English, Phi Kappa Phi.

WRITINGS: Guide to Writing Term Papers, AMSCO, 1971.

WORK IN PROGRESS: Research on criteria and procedures for faculty evaluation in community colleges; experiments in group dynamics and games for English composition; research on a systems design approach to the teaching of English composition; development of a non-textbook humanities course.

AVOCATIONAL INTERESTS: Cross-country skiing, sailing, writing poems.

* * *

THISTLE, Mel(ville William) 1914-
(Theophilus Bohr)

PERSONAL: Born April 22, 1914, in St. John's, Newfoundland, Canada; son of William James (a mail officer) and Isabelle (Russell) Thistle; married Lauretta Jean Finlayson (a ballet critic), September 27, 1941; children: Paula Joanne (Mrs. Ronald Conlon), Diana Jean. *Education:* Mount Allison University, B.Sc., 1936, M.A., 1938. *Politics:* Liberal. *Home:* 1476 Farnsworth Ave., Ottawa, Ontario K1H 7C3, Canada. *Office:* School of Journalism, Carleton University, Ottawa, Ontario K1S 5B6, Canada.

CAREER: Royal Commission on Dominion-Provincial Relations, St. John, New Brunswick, statistical assistant, 1937; National Research Council, Ottawa, Ontario, biometrical assistant, 1938-40, biochemist, 1940-46, head of food engineering and divisional editor for biosciences, 1946-51, information officer, 1951-54, manager of public relations and historian, 1954-69; Carleton University, Ottawa, Ontario, professor of journalism, 1969—. Lecturer at Colorado State University, summers, 1962, 1965, and Carleton University, 1963-69; William V. Gordon Memorial Lecturer for Biological Photographers Association, Ottawa, 1971. Patentee in journalism, 1945. Member of board of directors of Allan Wargon Ltd., Pied Piper Films, and David Pictures Corp.

MEMBER: International Society for General Semantics, International Communication Association, Canadian Association of Science Writers, Institute of General Semantics, American Association for the Advancement of Science, Human Development Association (Montreal; member of board of directors). *Awards, honors:* Centennial Award for English Poetry from Centennial Commission of Canada, 1967, for *Time Touch Me Gently*; National Research Council grants, 1969, 1970, 1971, 1972, 1973.

WRITINGS: Peter the Sea Trout (juvenile), Bouregy & Curl, 1954; (editor) Roy Fraser, *Happy Journey*, Ryerson, 1958; *The Inner Ring: A History of the National Research Council of Canada*, University of Toronto Press, 1966; *Time Touch Me Gently* (poetry), Ryerson, 1970; (editor) *The Mackenzie-McNaughton Wartime Letters*, University of Toronto Press, 1975.

Contributor: H. C. Diehl and W. T. Pentzer, editors, *Refrigeration Applications*, American Society of Refrigerating Engineers, 1946; *Proceedings of the United Nations Scientific Conference on the Conservation and Utilization of Resources*, Department of Economic Affairs, United Nations, 1951; Diehl and Pentzer, editors, *Refrigerating Data Book: Applications Volume*, American Society of Refrigerating Engineers, 1952; *The Direction of Research Establishments*, H.M.S.O., 1957; J. T. Saywell, editor, *Canadian Annual Review for 1960*, University of Toronto Press, 1961; *Canadian Government Style Manual for Writers and Editors*, Queen's Printer (Ottawa), 1962; M. D. Blickle and M. E. Passe, editors, *Readings for Technical Writers*, Ronald, 1963; C. C. Lingard, editor, *Canada One Hundred: 1867-1967*, Queen's Printer (Ottawa), 1967; Lee Thayer, editor, *Communication Spectrum '7*, National Society for the Study of Communication, 1968; Thayer, editor, *Communication: General Semantics Perspectives*, Sparton, 1970. Also contributor to *Ethics of Communication: Practitioners' Volume*, edited by Thayer, 1974.

Author of a series of thirty articles under the pseudonym Theophilus Bohr, published in *Food in Canada*, 1945-56. Contributor to *Encyclopedia of Chemistry*. Contributor of more than fifty articles and reviews to technical and popular journals and newspapers, including *Canadian Food Industries*, *Saturday Night*, *Executive Decision*, *Canadian Author and Bookman*, *Canadian Finance*, and *Canadian Journal of Research*. Editorial writer for *Ottawa Citizen*, 1944-51; science editor for Royal Commission on Government Organization, 1961-62; contributing editor of *Communication*, 1972—.

WORK IN PROGRESS: Earth in Joy; editing, with Elwood Murray, *Humanizing the Information Sciences*.

AVOCATIONAL INTERESTS: Small spring bulbs (gardening), food, wine, exploration of general semantics.

* * *

THOMAS, Dante 1922-

PERSONAL: Born July 11, 1922, in Watertown, Mass.; son of Ralph Zaccagnini (a laborer) and Rosa (DiGregorio) Zaccagnini; married Constance North (a craftsman), October 28, 1948; children: Henry, Soeren. *Education:* State University of New York at Albany, B.A., 1948, M.A.,

1956, Ph.D., 1971. *Politics:* "Democrat leaning toward Philosophical Anarchy." *Religion:* "Comparative—Zen, German Mystics." *Home:* Wadsworth Homestead, Geneseo, N.Y. 14454. *Office:* Department of English, State University of New York, College at Geneseo, N.Y. 14454.

CAREER: Public school teacher of English in Cairo, N.Y., 1951-61; U.S. Information Agency, Bogota, Colombia, member of staff, 1961-62; State University of New York at Albany, instructor, 1963-66, College at Geneseo, 1967—, began as assistant professor, now associate professor of English. *Military service:* U.S. Air Force, 1941-45; became staff sergeant; served in Marianas.

WRITINGS: A Bibliography of John Cowper Powys, Appel, 1974. Contributor of poems to *Span, Western Review, La Huerta*, and *Quixote*.

WORK IN PROGRESS: Editing a book of John Cowper Powys' uncollected writings, publication by Appel expected in 1976.

* * *

THOMAS, Earl W(esley) 1915-

PERSONAL: Born January 22, 1915, in Sumner, Ill.; son of Lonnie W. (a farmer) and Mattie (Perrott) Thomas; married Ana Maria Sarmento, July 30, 1946 (divorced, 1952); married Marilyn Jean Tate, August 21, 1955; children: (first marriage) Marilyn (Mrs. Thomas Christopher); (second marriage) Brice, Leif, Beverly, Kevin. *Education:* University of Illinois, A.B., 1936, M.A., 1937; University of Michigan, Ph.D., 1947. *Politics:* Independent. *Home:* 6559 Brownlee Dr., Nashville, Tenn. 37205. *Office:* Department of Spanish and Portuguese, Vanderbilt University, Station B, Nashville, Tenn. 37235.

CAREER: Vanderbilt University, Nashville, Tenn., assistant professor, 1947-58, associate professor, 1958-64, professor of Spanish and Portuguese, 1964—. *Military service:* U.S. Coast Guard, 1943-45. *Member:* American Association of Teachers of Spanish and Portuguese, Southeastern Modern Language Association.

WRITINGS: The Syntax of Spoken Brazilian Portuguese, Vanderbilt University Press, 1969; *Grammar of Spoken Brazilian Portuguese*, Vanderbilt University Press, in press.

WORK IN PROGRESS: Recent Literature of the Brazilian Northeast.

AVOCATIONAL INTERESTS: Travel (Latin America, Europe).

* * *

THOMAS, J. James 1933-

PERSONAL: Born November 13, 1933, in Greenfield, Ind.; son of Jesse B. (a chemist) and Evalyn A. (a musician) Thomas; married Mary Alice Jennings (a teacher), September 6, 1954; children: Carla Suzanne, Claudia Louise, Lisa Marle, Jessica Adelle. *Education:* Taylor University, B.A., 1959; Northwestern University, Ph.D., 1967; Gestalt Institute of Cleveland, post-doctoral diploma, 1974. *Home:* 4309 Sherwood Court, Midland, Mich. 48640. *Office:* Saginaw Valley College, University Center, Mich. 48710.

CAREER: Northwestern University, Evanston, Ill., lecturer, 1964-67; Saginaw Valley College, University Center, Mich., assistant professor, 1967-70, associate professor, 1970—.

WRITINGS: The Revolutionary Hero: A Phenomenological Investigation (monograph), [University Center, Mich.], 1971.

WORK IN PROGRESS: The Youniverse.

* * *

THOMAS, Mary Martha Hosford 1927-

PERSONAL: Born November 11, 1927, in Dallas, Tex.; daughter of Hemphill Moffett (a university administrator) and Gladys (Garstang) Hosford; married Philip B. Thomas (a forester), April 2, 1949; children: Gordon, Jane, Stuart, Amy, Blair. *Education:* University of Arkansas, student, 1944-46; Southern Methodist University, B.A., 1948; University of Michigan, M.A., 1951; Emory University, Ph.D., 1971. *Politics:* Democrat. *Religion:* Episcopalian. *Home:* 904 Pine Dr., Jacksonville, Ala. 36265. *Office:* Department of History, Jacksonville State University, Jacksonville, Ala. 36265.

CAREER: Northern Michigan University, Iron Mountain, instructor in history, 1964-68; Jacksonville State University, Jacksonville, Ala., assistant professor, 1969-71, associate professor of history, 1971—. *Member:* Organization of American Historians, American Association of University Professors, Southern Historical Association.

WRITINGS: Southern Methodist University: Founding and Early Years, Southern Methodist University Press, 1974.

WORK IN PROGRESS: Research on the history of women.

* * *

THOMAS, T. M(athai) 1933-

PERSONAL: Born August 20, 1933, in Kerala, India; son of T. T. (a teacher) and Annamma Mathai; married Annamma Daniel, June 7, 1956; children: Mathews, Danny. *Education:* University College, Trivandrum, India, B.S., 1953; Meston College, M.Ed., 1962; Boston University, Ed.D., 1968. *Religion:* Mar Thoma Church. *Home:* 483 North Main St., Westport, Conn. 06880. *Office:* College of Education, University of Bridgeport, Bridgeport, Conn. 06602.

CAREER: High school teacher of science in Kerala, India, 1953-63; Springfield College, Springfield, Mass., assistant professor of philosophy of education, 1967-69; University of Bridgeport, Bridgeport, Conn., assistant professor of philosophy of education, 1969—. *Member:* Society for Educational Reconstruction (secretary-treasurer, 1969-73), Association of World Education, New England Philosophy of Education Society (president, 1973-74), Phi Delta Kappa.

WRITINGS: Indian Educational Reforms in Cultural Perspective, S. Chand, 1970; *Images of Man: Philosophic and Scientific Inquiry*, Dharmaram College Publications, 1974. Contributor of short stories to journals in India, and of articles to education journals.

* * *

THOMISON, Dennis 1937-

PERSONAL: Born March 31, 1937, in Rhinelander, Wis.; son of Bernard and Juanita (Anderson) Lapinski. *Education:* University of Wisconsin–Eau Claire, B.S., 1960; University of Denver, M.A., 1963; University of Southern California, Ph.D., 1972. *Politics:* Democrat. *Home:* 3234

Ellington Dr., Los Angeles, Calif. 90068. *Office:* School of Library Science, University of Southern California, Los Angeles, Calif. 90007.

CAREER: University of Wisconsin–Eau Claire, assistant professor of library science, 1963-68; University of Southern California, Los Angeles, assistant professor of library science, 1969—. Director of library education at University of California, Long Beach, 1967-68. *Member:* American Library Association, California Library Association.

WRITINGS: (Editor) *Readings about Adolescent Literature*, Scarecrow, 1970; (with Gail Schlachter) *Library Science Dissertations: 1925-1972*, Libraries Unlimited, 1973. Contributor to *Library Quarterly, Journal of Library History*, and *Wisconsin Library Bulletin*.

WORK IN PROGRESS: Black Artists in America; *A History of the American Library Association: 1876-1972*, completion expected in 1976.

* * *

THOMPSON, A(rthur) L(eonard) B(ell) 1917-
(Francis Clifford)

PERSONAL: Born December 1, 1917, in Bristol, England; son of George Bell (an oil executive) and Agnes Mary (Evans) Thompson; married Marjorie Bennett, February 4, 1944 (divorced, 1954); married Josephine Bridget Devereux (a company director), September 17, 1955; children: (first marriage) Peter Bell; (second marriage) Mark Bell. *Education:* Attended Christ's Hospital (boys' school), 1928-35. *Politics:* Liberal. *Religion:* Roman Catholic. *Home:* Grove Cottage, Grove Lodge, Old Ave., Weybridge, Surrey KT13 OPQ, England. *Agent:* David Higham Associates Ltd., 5-8 Lower John St., London W1R 4HA, England.

CAREER: Rice Merchant in Burma and in London, England, 1935-39; industrial journalist in England, 1946-59; full-time writer, 1960—. *Military service:* Indian Army, Burma Rifles, 1939-46; became major; awarded Distinguished Service Order. *Member:* Crime Writers Association, Mystery Writers of America, Detection Club. *Awards, honors:* Silver Dagger Award from Crime Writers' Association, 1970, for *Another Way of Dying*; Edgar Allan Poe Scroll from Mystery Writers of America, 1974, for *Amigo, Amigo*, and, 1975, for *Goodbye and Amen*; Silver Dagger Award from Crime Writers' Association, 1975, for *The Grosvenor Square Goodbye*.

WRITINGS—Novels; under pseudonym Francis Clifford: *Honour the Shrine*, J. Cape, 1953; *Trembling Earth*, Hamish Hamilton, 1955; *Something to Love*, Hamish Hamilton, 1958; *Overdue*, Dutton, 1958; *Act of Mercy*, Coward, 1960; *A Battle Is Fought to Be Won*, Coward, 1961; *Time Is an Ambush*, Hodder & Stoughton, 1962; *The Green Fields of Eden*, Coward, 1963; *The Hunting-Ground*, Coward, 1964; *The Third Side of the Coin*, Coward, 1965; *The Naked Runner*, Coward, 1966; *Spanish Duet*, Coward, 1966; *All Men Are Lonely Now*, Coward, 1967; *Another Way of Dying*, Coward, 1969; *The Blind Side*, Coward, 1971; *A Wild Justice*, Coward, 1972; *Amigo, Amigo*, Coward, 1973; *Goodbye and Amen*, Harcourt, 1974 (published in England as *The Grosvenor Square Goodbye*, Hodder & Stoughton, 1974).

WORK IN PROGRESS: A novel, *Drummer in the Dark*.

SIDELIGHTS: Thompson writes: "I write suspense novels because I believe that only when a character is at the end of his tether—be it physically, mentally, morally, spiritually or financially—is his (or her) true character revealed."

Act of Mercy was made into a film by Warner Brothers in 1962, and *The Naked Runner* by Warner Bros. in 1966.

* * *

THOMPSON, Dennis F(rank) 1940-

PERSONAL: Born May 12, 1940, in Hamilton, Ohio; son of Frank (an executive) and Florence (Downs) Thompson; married Carol Joslyn (a university administrator), June, 1963; children: Eric, David. *Education:* College of William and Mary, B.A., 1962; Balliol College, Oxford, B.A. (first class honors), 1964, M.A., 1968; Harvard University, Ph.D., 1968. *Home:* 182 Prospect, Princeton, N.J. 08540. *Office:* Department of Politics, Princeton University, Princeton, N.J. 08540.

CAREER: Harvard University, Cambridge, Mass., instructor in government, 1967-68; Princeton University, Princeton, N.J., assistant professor, 1968-72, associate professor of politics, 1972—. *Member:* Phi Beta Kappa. *Awards, honors:* Fulbright grant, 1962-64; Woodrow Wilson fellowship, 1964-66; Philip Frenau Bicentennial perceptorship, 1970-73.

WRITINGS: The Democratic Citizen: Social Science and Democratic Theory in the Twentieth Century, Cambridge University Press, 1970. Member of editorial board of *Philosophy and Public Affairs*; book review editor and member of editorial committee of *Political Theory*.

* * *

THOMPSON, Don(ald Arthur) 1935-
(Dick O'Donnell, joint pseudonym)

PERSONAL: Born October 30, 1935, in Warren, Pa.; son of Samuel Enos (a mailman) and Densie Ellen (Stroup) Thompson; married Margaret Curtis (a free-lance writer), June 23, 1962; children: Valerie Lee, Stephen Charles. *Education:* Pennsylvania State University, B.A., 1960. *Home:* 8786 Hendricks Rd., Mentor, Ohio 44060. *Agent:* Virginia Kidd, Box 278, Milford, Pa. 18337. *Office: Cleveland Press*, 901 Lakeside Ave., Cleveland, Ohio 44114.

CAREER: Worked as lifeguard, tree planter, farmhand; *Cleveland Press*, Cleveland, Ohio, copyboy, 1960-61, copy editor, 1961-62, financial reporter, 1962-66, police reporter, 1966-67, suburban reporter, 1967-71, Lake County editor, 1971—. *Military service:* U.S. Army, Signal Corps, 1954-56. *Member:* Science Fiction Writers of America (trustee of Nebula Awards, 1970-72), Rho Tau Sigma, Sigma Delta Chi.

WRITINGS: (Editor with Dick Lupoff) *All in Color for a Dime*, Arlington House, 1970; (editor with Lupoff) *The Comic-Book Book*, Arlington House, 1973. Has written occasionally with Dick Lupoff under joint pseudonym Dick O'Donnell. Contributor to popular magazines, including *Playboy*, *Venture Science Fiction*, *Dracula Lives*, *Unknown Worlds of Science Fiction*, *Monsters of the Movies*, and *Masters of Terror*.

WORK IN PROGRESS: Articles, short stories, book reviews, and comic-book adaptations of stories.

* * *

THOMPSON, Gerald E(verett) 1924-

PERSONAL: Born February 22, 1924, in Leland, Iowa; son of Gilbert T. (a farmer) and Clara (Charlson)

Thompson; married Betty Collman, August 26, 1950; children: David F. *Education:* University of Iowa, B.A., 1947, M.A., 1948, Ph.D., 1953; Harvard University, postdoctoral study, 1959-60. *Home:* 3333 South 30th St., Lincoln, Neb. 68502. *Office:* College of Business Administration, University of Nebraska, Lincoln, Neb. 68508.

CAREER: University of Toledo, Toledo, Ohio, assistant professor of economics, 1950-54; University of Nebraska, Lincoln, assistant professor, 1954-62, associate professor, 1962-69, professor of economics and management, 1969—. Associate professor at University of Michigan, 1965-66. *Military service:* U.S. Army Air Corps, B-17 bomber pilot, 1942-45; became first lieutenant; served in European theater; received Air Medal four times. *Member:* American Economic Association, American Statistical Association, American Institute for Decision Sciences. *Awards, honors:* Ford Foundation faculty fellowship for study at Harvard University's Institute of Basic Mathematics for Application to Business, 1959-60.

WRITINGS: *Linear Programming*, Macmillan, 1971; *Statistics for Decisions*, Little, Brown, 1972. Contributor to *American Economic Review* and *Review of Economics and Statistics*.

WORK IN PROGRESS: A book, *Management Science*, publication by McGraw expected in 1976.

* * *

THOMPSON, Laura (Maud) 1905-

PERSONAL: Born January 23, 1905, in Honolulu, Hawaii; daughter of William (a businessman) and Maud (Balch) Thompson; married Sam van H. Duker (a professor), June, 1963. *Education:* Mills College, Oakland, Calif., B.A., 1927; University of California, Berkeley, Ph.D., 1933; postdoctoral study at University of Chicago, 1941. *Home:* 1530 Palisade Ave., Fort Lee, N.J. 07024.

CAREER: Bishop Museum, Honolulu, Hawaii, assistant ethnologist, 1929-34; U.S. Naval Government, Guam, social scientist, 1938-40; Community Survey of Education, Hawaii, social scientist, 1940-41; U.S. Office of Indian Affairs, coordinator of Indian education research project, 1941-47; Institute of Ethnic Affairs, Washington, D.C., research consultant, 1946-54; City College (now City College of the City University of New York), New York, N.Y., professor of anthropology, 1954-56; University of North Carolina, Chapel Hill, visiting professor of anthropology, 1957-58; North Carolina State College, Raleigh, visiting professor of anthropology, 1958-60; Southern Illinois University, Urbana, professor of anthropology, 1961-62; San Francisco State College (now University), San Francisco, Calif., professor of anthropology, 1962-63; consulting anthropologist, 1963—. Representative of the U.S. National Indian Institute, Mexico, 1942; consultant to the U.S. Office of Indian Affairs, 1942-44; advisor to Policy Board of U.S. National Indian Institute, 1948; distinguished visiting professor of anthropology at Pennsylvania State University, 1961; consultant to Hutterite Socialization Project at Pennsylvania State University, 1962-65, and to Centennial Joint School System, Pennsylvania, 1964-66.

MEMBER: American Association for the Advancement of Science (fellow), American Anthropological Association (fellow), New York Academy of Sciences, Phi Beta Kappa. *Awards, honors:* Bernice P. Bishop fellowship, Yale University, 1933-34; Institute of Pacific Relations grant, 1934; Rosenwald fellowship, University of Hawaii, 1938; Social Sciences Research Council grant-in-aid, 1939; Viking Fund grant and Wenner-Gren fellowship, 1948 and 1951; Rockefeller Foundation grants, 1951 and 1952; LL.D., Mills College, 1973.

WRITINGS: *Southern Lau, Fiji: An Ethnography*, Bishop Museum (Honolulu), 1940; *Fijian Frontier*, Institute of Pacific Relations, 1940, new edition, Octagon Press, 1973; *Guam and Its People*, Institute of Pacific Relations, 1942, 3rd edition of 1947 reprinted, Greenwood Press, 1969; (with Alice Joseph) *The Hopi Way*, University of Chicago Press, 1945, reprinted, Russell & Russell, 1967; *Culture in Crisis: A Study of the Hopi Indians*, Harper, 1950, reprinted, Russell & Russell, 1973; *Personality and Government*, Institute of Ethnic Affairs (Washington, D.C.), 1951; *Toward a Science of Mankind*, McGraw, 1961; *The Secret of Culture: Nine Community Studies*, Random House, 1969. Contributor of more than one hundred articles to scientific journals.

SIDELIGHTS: In the course of anthropological expeditions and personal travel, Laura Thompson has visited Fiji, Guam, China, Japan, Germany, Iceland, the Andean Indians in South America, and the Hopi, Navaho, Papago, Zuni, and Sioux Indian tribes in North America.

* * *

THOMPSON, (William) Ralph 1910-

PERSONAL: Born May 23, 1910, in Toledo, Ill.; son of Joseph Samuel (a farmer) and Luella Mae (Olmstead) Thompson; married Claribel Martha Hessler (a teacher), November 26, 1936; children: Carl Ivan, Stanley Burton, William Frederick. *Education:* Greenville College, A.B., 1934, Th.B., 1935; Winona Lake School of Theology, B.D., 1940; Biblical Seminary in New York, S.T.B., 1950; Ball State University, M.A. in Ed., 1956; Northern Baptist Theological Seminary, Th.M., 1957, Th.D., 1960. *Home address:* Box 341, Concord, Mich. 49237. *Office:* Department of Religion, Spring Arbor College, Spring Arbor, Mich. 49283.

CAREER: Ordained minister of Free Methodist Church, 1937; pastor in Norwood, N.Y., 1936-37, and Saratoga Springs, N.Y., 1937-40; El Instituto Evangelico, Santiago, Dominican Republic, principal, 1941-45; Nogales Bible School, Nogales, Ariz., principal, 1947-49; Taylor University, Upland, Ind., assistant professor, 1953-55, associate professor, 1955-61, professor of religion, 1961-64, head of department, 1951-55; pastor in Harvey, Ill., 1955-59; Taylor University, Upland, Ind., professor of religion, 1959-64, head of department, 1959-64; Spring Arbor College, Spring Arbor, Mich., professor of religion, 1964—, head of department, 1964-71. Visiting professor at Free Methodist Seminary, Santiago, 1966, 1973, and Holy Light Theological Seminary, Taiwan, 1972. *Member:* American Academy of Religion, Christian Holiness Association, Wesleyan Theological Society (treasurer, 1965-67; secretary-treasurer, 1968-71), Evangelical Theological Society, Phi Delta Kappa.

WRITINGS: (Contributor) Kenneth E. Geiger, compiler, *Further Insights into Holiness*, Beacon Hill Press, 1963; (contributor) Geiger, compiler, *The Word and the Doctrine*, Beacon Hill Press, 1965; (Old Testament editor and contributor) Charles W. Carter, general editor, *The Wesleyan Bible Commentary*, Volumes I-III, Eerdmans, 1967-69.

WORK IN PROGRESS: A book on Old Testament theology and one on the Apocalypse.

THORBURN, David 1940-

PERSONAL: Born August 14, 1940, in New York, N.Y.; son of Frank (a health officer) and Claire (Feller) Thorburn; married Barbara Levitan, June 30, 1963; children: Daniel, Adam, Rachel. *Education:* Princeton University, A.B., 1962; Stanford University, M.A., 1965, Ph.D., 1968. *Home:* 9 Still Hill Rd., Hamden, Conn. 06518. *Office:* Department of English, Yale University, New Haven, Conn. 06520.

CAREER: Yale University, New Haven, Conn., instructor, 1966-68, assistant professor, 1968-72, associate professor of English, 1973—. Visiting associate professor, University of California, Santa Barbara, 1973-74. *Awards, honors:* Woodrow Wilson fellowship, 1962; Fulbright fellowship, 1965-66; Morse fellowship, 1970-71.

WRITINGS: (Editor) *Initiation: Stories and Short Novels on Three Themes*, Harcourt, 1971, 2nd edition, in press; (editor with Geoffrey Hartman) *Romanticism: Vistas, Instances, Continuities*, Cornell University Press, 1973; *Ronrad's Romanticism*, Yale University Press, 1974. Contributor of articles and reviews to literary periodicals, including *Partisan Review, Commentary*, and *Yale Review*.

WORK IN PROGRESS: A general introduction to modern fiction in English, for Yale University Press; studies of the novel as a genre and of American popular culture, especially American commercial television.

* * *

TILLEMAN, William Arthur 1932-

PERSONAL: Born February 6, 1932, in Chinook, Mont.; son of Arthur F. (a rancher) and Mary (Zich) Tilleman; married Jean Duke, December 31, 1953; children: Cherie Jean (Mrs. David W. Glenn), Sharon (Mrs. David B. Herbst), William Arthur II, John D., Karl Michael. *Education:* University of Utah, B.Sc., 1959, M.B.A., 1960, Ph.D., 1972. *Home:* 5536 Dalrymple Hill N.W., Calgary, Alberta T3A 1X1, Canada. *Office:* Department of Accounting and Finance, University of Calgary, Calgary, Alberta, Canada.

CAREER: Weber State College, Ogden, Utah, lecturer, 1960-64, instructor, 1965-68, assistant professor of finance, 1968-72; University of Wisconsin, La Crosse, associate professor of accounting and finance and chairman of department, 1972-74; University of Calgary, Calgary, Alberta, associate professor of accounting and finance, 1974—. Associate professor at Winona State College, 1973-74. Procurement staff specialist for Utah operations of Thiokol Chemical Corp., 1960-61; systems and procedures analyst for Utah operations of Hercules Power Co., 1961-62; supervisor of fixed asset accounting section of Thiokol Chemical Co., 1962-65; licensed agent for Occident Life Insurance Co., 1965-72; licensed securities agent, 1965-70; procurement officer for Hill Air Force Base, summers, 1967-69; vice-president of Dynamic Management Associates, 1968—. Director of executive development for University of Wisconsin—LaCrosse, 1972—. City magistrate for Justice Court in Washington Terrace, Utah, 1960-72. *Military service:* U.S. Air Force, 1951-55; became staff sergeant. *Member:* American Production and Inventory Control Society, Financial Management Association, Delta Sigma Pi, Beta Gamma Sigma, Phi Kappa Phi.

WRITINGS: *Money Matters in Your Marriage*, Deseret, 1971. Contributor to *Utah Economic and Business Review* and *Journal of Consumer Credit Management*.

WORK IN PROGRESS: Collecting viewpoints of third parties on auditors' independence.

* * *

TIMMEN, Fritz 1918-

PERSONAL: Born October 3, 1918, in Portland, Ore.; son of Horace Jacob (a laborer) and Margaret Gertrude (Davis) Timmen; children: Rick, Judy (Mrs. Ronald Starr), Terry, Kim, Peter, Catherine, Carrie. *Education:* Attended University of Oregon, 1940-42. *Politics:* Republican. *Religion:* Protestant. *Office address:* Port of Portland, P.O. Box 1050, Pasco, Wash. 99301.

CAREER: Worked in advertising and public relations in Portland, Ore., 1946-51; Inland Empire Waterways Association, Walla Walla, Wash., public relations director, 1951-56; Port of Portland, public relations director in Portland, Wash., 1956-74, manager of marketing office in Pasco, Wash., 1974—. Member of board of directors of World Affairs Council of Oregon, 1970-74. *Military service:* U.S. Army, Communications; served for two years during World War II. *Member:* Sons and Daughters of Oregon Pioneers (president, 1968), Propeller Club of Portland.

WRITINGS: *Blow for the Landing*, Caxton, 1973.

WORK IN PROGRESS: Articles on Pacific Northwest history expected to be compiled into book form; a regional novel based on Pacific Northwest Indian wars.

AVOCATIONAL INTERESTS: Prospecting, camping, hunting, hiking.

* * *

TOBIAS, J(ohn) J(acob) 1925-

PERSONAL: Born in 1925 in London, England. *Education:* London School of Economics and Political Science, University of London, B.Sc.Econ., 1958, Ph.D., 1965. *Address:* United Service Club, Pall Mall, London S.W.1, England.

CAREER: Served in Colonial Office, 1944-49, and in Department of Scientific and Industrial Research, 1958-59; National Police College, Hampshire, England, tutor in social studies, 1959-64, senior tutor of special courses, 1964-73; member of Civil Service Department, Whitehall, 1974—.

WRITINGS: *Crime and Industrial Society in the Nineteenth Century*, Schocken, 1967, 2nd edition published as *Urban Crime in Victorian England*, 1972; *Nineteenth-Century Crime: Prevention and Punishment*, Barnes & Noble, 1972; *In the Local Interest*, Ginn, 1972; *Prince of Fences: The Life and Crimes of Ikey Solomons*, Vallentine, Mitchell, 1975. Contributor to *British Journal of Criminology, Police Journal, Journal of Contemporary History*, and *Dickensian*.

WORK IN PROGRESS: Further research on crime and the police of the eighteenth and nineteenth centuries.

* * *

TOBIN, James 1918-

PERSONAL: Born March 5, 1918, in Champaign, Ill.; son of Louis Michael and Margaret (Edgerton) James; married Elizabeth Fay Ringo, September 14, 1946; children: Margaret Ringo, Louis Michael, Hugh Ringo, Roger Gill. *Education:* Harvard University, A.B. (summa cum laude), 1939, M.A., 1940, Ph.D., 1947. *Home:* 117 Alden Ave., New Haven, Conn. 06515. *Office:* Department of Economics, Yale University, Box 2125 Yale Station, New Haven, Conn. 06520.

CAREER: U.S. Government, Washington, D.C., economist with Office of Price Administration and other agencies, 1941-42; Harvard University, Cambridge, Mass., junior fellow, Society of Fellows, 1947-50 (1949-50 was spent in department of applied economics at Cambridge University); Yale University, New Haven, Conn., associate professor, 1950-55, professor of economics, 1955-57, Sterling Professor of Economics, 1957—, director of Cowles Foundation for Research in Economics, 1955-61, acting director, 1964-65, chairman of department of economics, 1968-69, 1974—. Noel Buxton lecturer at University of Essex, 1966; visiting professor at University of Nairobi, 1972-73; Janeway lecturer at Princeton University, 1972. Member of President's Council of Economic Advisers, 1961-62, consultant, 1962-68; consultant to Board of Governors of Federal Reserve System, 1955-57, 1963-66, 1967—, and U.S. Treasury, 1962-68, 1969—. Chairman of advisory committee for social sciences, National Science Foundation, 1967-68; senior adviser, Brookings Institution Panel on Economic Activity, 1970—; member of board of overseers, Harvard College, 1970—. *Military service:* U.S. Navy, line officer on destroyer, 1942-46; became lieutenant. U.S. Naval Reserve, 1946-55.

MEMBER: American Economic Association (member of executive committee, 1958-60, 1964-65; president, 1971), National Academy of Sciences (secretary of Class V, 1974—), American Academy of Arts and Sciences (fellow), American Statistical Association (fellow), Econometric Society (fellow; president, 1958; member of council, 1961-62, 1963-66, 1970-73), American Philosophical Society, American Association of University Professors, Council on Foreign Relations, Phi Beta Kappa.

AWARDS, HONORS: Social Science Research Council faculty research fellowship, 1952-55; John Bates Clark Bronze Medal of American Economic Association, 1955 (medal is given biennially to an American economist under forty judged to have made a significant contribution to economic thought and knowledge); LL.D. from Syracuse University, 1967, University of Illinois, 1969, and Dartmouth College, 1970.

WRITINGS: (With Seymour E. Harris, Carl Kaysen, and Francis X. Sutton) *The American Business Creed*, Harvard University Press, 1956; *National Economic Policy* (essays), Yale University Press, 1966; *The Intellectual Revolution in U.S. Economic Policy-Making* (Noel Buxton lecture at University of Essex), Longmans, Green, 1966; (with others) *Ten Economic Studies in the Tradition of Irving Fisher*, edited by William Fellner, Wiley, 1967; *Essays in Economics*, Volume I: *Macroeconomics*, North-Holland Publishing, 1971, Markham, 1972; *The New Economics One Decade Older*, Princeton University Press, 1974.

Monographs—Editor with Donald D. Hester and contributor: *Risk Aversion and Portfolio Choice*, Wiley, 1967; *Studies of Portfolio Behavior*, Wiley, 1967; *Financial Markets and Economic Activity*, Wiley, 1967.

Contributor: S. E. Harris, editor, *The New Economics*, Knopf, 1947; *Money, Trade, and Economic Growth: In Honor of John Henry Williams*, Macmillan, 1951; Arthur Smithies and J. Keith Butters, editors, *Readings in Fiscal Policy*, American Economic Association, 1955; Gerhard Colm, editor, *The Employment Act, Past and Future*, National Planning Association, 1956.

William Fellner and others, editors, *Fiscal and Debt Management Policies*, Prentice-Hall, for Commission on Money and Credit, 1963; Deane Carson, editor, *Banking and Monetary Studies*, Irwin, 1963; Bela Balassa, editor, *Changing Patterns in Foreign Trade and Payments*, Norton, 1964; Billy H. Wilkins and C. B. Friday, editors, *Economists of the New Frontier*, Random House, 1964; Warren L. Smith and Ronald L. Teigen, editors, *Readings in Money, National Income and Stabilization Policy*, Irwin, 1965; *Theory of Interest Rates*, Macmillan, for International Economic Association, 1965; M. G. Mueller, editor, *Readings in Macroeconomics*, Holt, 1966; Richard S. Thorn, editor, *Monetary Theory and Policy*, Random House, 1966; Edmund S. Phelps and others, editors, *Problems of the Modern Economy*, Norton, 1966; Richard A. Ward, editor, *Monetary Theory and Policy*, International Textbook Co., 1966; George L. Bach and Norton Seeber, editors, *Economic Analysis and Policy: Background Readings for Current Issues*, Prentice-Hall, 1966; Fritz Machlup, editor, *Maintaining and Restoring Balance in International Payments*, Princeton University Press, 1966; Lester C. Thurow, editor, *American Fiscal Policy: Experience for Prosperity*, Prentice-Hall, 1967; John R. Coleman, editor, *The Changing American Economy*, Basic Books, 1967; Almarin Phillips and O. E. Williamson, editors, *Price Issues in Theory, Practice and Public Policy*, University of Pennsylvania Press, 1967; *Agenda for the Nation*, Brookings Institution, 1968; Walter W. Heller, editor, *Perspectives on Economic Growth*, Random House, 1968; *Welfare Programs: An Economic Appraisal*, American Enterprise Institute for Public Policy Research, 1968; Karl Brunner, editor, *Targets and Indicators of Monetary Policy*, Chandler Publishing, 1969; Harold R. Williams and John D. Huffnagle, editors, *Macroeconomic Theory*, Appleton, 1969; Nancy D. Ruggles, editor, *Economics*, Prentice-Hall, 1970; Burkhard Strumpel, James N. Morgan, and Ernest Zahn, editors, *Human Behavior and Economic Affairs: Essays in Honor of George Katona*, Jossey-Bass, 1972.

Contributor to *International Encyclopedia of the Social Sciences*, 1968. Contributor of more than a hundred articles to journals and newspapers, including *Economia Internazionale*, *New Republic*, *Fortune*, *Yale Review*, *New York Times*, and *Washington Post*. Associate editor, *Econometrica*, 1951-53; American editor, *Review of Economic Studies*, 1952-54; member of editorial advisory board, *Journal of Money, Credit and Banking*, 1968—.

* * *

TOBIN, Terence 1938-

PERSONAL: Born September 24, 1938, in Chicago, Ill.; son of Harry Arthur (a brick retailer) and Helen (a teacher; maiden name, De Vaney) Tobin. *Education:* Our Lady of the Snows Scholasticate, B.A., 1961; Loyola University, Chicago, Ill., M.A., 1964, Ph.D., 1967; also studied at University of Chicago and University of Edinburgh. *Religion:* Roman Catholic. *Residence:* Valparaiso, Ind.

CAREER: Teacher of music and art in public schools in Chicago, Ill., 1962-66; Loyola University, Chicago, Ill., lecturer in English, 1966; Purdue University, Lafayette, Ind., assistant professor of English, 1966-70; Chicago City College, Chicago, Ill., associate professor of English, 1971-74; Instructional Dynamics, Inc., Chicago, Ill., writer and producer of filmstrips and audio cassette series, 1974—. Assistant manager of T. M. Tobin Co. (brick retailers), 1962-64; director and producer of radio series for Voice of America programs on WBAA and on WJOB, 1967-70; performs in one-man musical variety shows; member of board of trustees of Porter County Arts Commission. Consultant to Holt, Rinehart & Winston, Inc., 1972. *Awards, honors:* American Philosophical Society grants, 1969, 1971, 1973; grant from Purdue University, 1970.

WRITINGS: The Assembly by Archibald Pitcairne: A Critical Edition, Purdue University, 1972; (editor) *Letters of George Ade*, Purdue University, 1973; (editor) *Plays by Scots: 1660-1800*, University of Iowa Press, 1974.

Scripts for radio series: "Sound and Light: A Spectrum of the University Scene," 1967; "Chords on the Boards: A History of the American Musical Theater," 1968; "Pro Musica Britannia: Music of the London Stage, 1660-1900," 1969; "Black Ink," 1970.

Writer of filmstrips and audio cassette series; all for Instructional Dynamics: "Write Now," 1974, "Art for Today," 1974, and "Cheers for Ears: Adventures in Listening," 1975.

Foreign correspondent for *Drama Critique*, 1964. Writer of "Ye Olde Stuff," a column on antiques for Indiana newspapers, 1973—. Music and drama critic for *Gary Post Tribune*, 1967-69, 1973—. Contributor of about twenty-five articles and reviews to literature and music journals, including *Theatre Notebook, Seventeenth Century Studies, Music Journal, American Musical Digest, Notes and Queries*, and *Editor and Publisher*.

WORK IN PROGRESS: Editing *Plays by Scots: 1800-1850*, for University of Iowa Press; *James Bridie*, for Twayne; several novels.

SIDELIGHTS: "When in doubt, take it out. I have etched this rule on the formica typing table," Tobin told *CA*. "For writing that is easy and pleasurable to read, selectivity vies with condensation and wins. Creative products, in words, paint, or notes (I have tried them all) show others something they did not know before or give new perspective to familiar subjects. One of the most reassuring ways to determine whether you have achieved this in an endeavor is to sell it."

* * *

TODD, Edward N. 1931-

PERSONAL: Born August 4, 1931, in Winterhaven, Calif.; son of J. E. and Gertrude (Noel) Todd; married Cella Doss (a dietitian), November 22, 1950; children: Michael, Leslie, Elizabeth Catherine. *Education:* North Texas State College, B.A., 1953; Johns Hopkins University, M.A., 1958. *Home:* 403 West King's Highway, San Antonio, Tex. 78212.

CAREER: Denison University, Granville, Ohio, assistant professor of history, 1959-68; Dominican College, Houston, Tex., director of public information, 1968-69; Lutheran General Hospital, San Antonio, Tex., director of public relations, 1969-70; free-lance writer and photographer, 1970—. *Military service:* U.S. Army, Signal Corps, 1953-55.

WRITINGS: Copper Canyon, Doubleday, 1974.

* * *

TODD, Jerry D(ale) 1941-

PERSONAL: Born December 29, 1941, in Cincinnati, Ohio; son of Alfred B. (an accountant) and Jean (Kuntz) Todd; married Kay E. Ward, June 8, 1963; children: Deborah Jean, Diane Elaine. *Education:* Ohio State University, B.S., 1963, M.B.A., 1964; University of Wisconsin, Ph.D., 1968. *Religion:* Presbyterian. *Home:* 5802 Highland Hills Ter., Austin, Tex. 78731. *Office:* Department of Finance, University of Texas, Austin, Tex. 78712.

CAREER: Chartered Property and Casualty Underwriter, 1969; Chartered Life Underwriter, 1969. University of North Carolina, Chapel Hill, assistant professor of insurance, 1967-68; University of Texas, Austin, assistant professor, 1968-70, associate professor of insurance, 1970—. Deacon of Presbyterian Church. Consultant to Insurance Institute of America, Texas Trial Lawyers Association, and U.S. Federal Trade Commission. *Member:* American Risk and Insurance Association.

WRITINGS: Effective Risk and Insurance Management in Municipal Government, Bureau of Government Research, University of Texas, 1970; (with William T. Hold) *Foundations of Life and Health Insurance*, Bureau of Business Research, University of Texas, 1971; *Risk Management and Insurance: A Study Guide*, Bureau of Business Research, University of Texas, 1971; *Profits and Prices in the Title Insurance Business*, Texas Land Title Association, 1973; *NAIA Work/Study Manual*, National Association of Insurance Agents, 1974. Contributor to proceedings, and to journals in his field.

* * *

TOLL, Robert C(harles) 1938-

PERSONAL: Born September 10, 1938, in San Francisco, Calif.; son of Edward Charles and Helen Frances (Beale) Toll; married Judith Ann Dirks (a librarian), December 15, 1962. *Education:* California State University, San Jose, B.A., 1964; University of California, Berkeley, M.A., 1966, Ph.D., 1972. *Politics:* Liberal Democrat. *Religion:* None. *Home:* 3900 Harrison St., Apt. 301, Oakland, Calif. 94611.

CAREER: Writer. *Military service:* California National Guard, 1960-66. *Awards, honors:* Woodrow Wilson fellowship, 1965-66.

WRITINGS: (Co-editor) *Old Slack's Reminiscence and Pocket History of the Colored Profession from 1865 to 1891*, Popular Press, 1974; *Blacking Up: The Minstrel Show in Nineteenth Century America*, Oxford University Press, 1974; *Show Business in America: The First Century, 1830-1930*, Oxford University Press, in press. Contributor to *Journal of the Folklore Institute*.

AVOCATIONAL INTERESTS: Collecting Canadian Eskimo art.

* * *

TOLLEY, Howard B(oyd), Jr. 1943-

PERSONAL: Born October 30, 1943, in Montclair, N.J.; son of Howard B. (a research baker) and Dorothy (Jones) Tolley; married Nina Sutaria (a social worker), July 10, 1970; children: Mark, Naren. *Education:* Middlebury College, B.A. (cum laude), 1965; University of Lausanne, graduate study, 1967; Columbia University, M.A., 1968, Ph.D., 1971. *Home:* 626 Omar Circle, Yellow Springs, Ohio 45387. *Office:* Department of Political Science, Wilberforce University, Wilberforce, Ohio 45384.

CAREER: Peace Corps, Washington, D.C., teacher of African history and English in Nigeria, 1965-67; English teacher in public school in New York, N.Y., 1968-70; Wilberforce University, Wilberforce, Ohio, assistant professor of political science, 1971—. *Member:* American Political Science Association, American Association of University

Professors (president of Wilberforce chapter), Midwest Political Science Association. *Awards, honors: Children and War* was listed by *American Scholar* as one of the outstanding books from university presses in 1973-74; Danforth associate, 1974.

WRITINGS: Children and War: Political Socialization to International Conflict, Teachers College Press, 1973; (contributor) Stanley Renshon, editor, *Handbook of Political Socialization*, Free Press, in press. Contributor to *Intellect*. Associate editor of *Intellect*.

SIDELIGHTS: Tolley has traveled to India, Mexico, Greece, Switzerland, Africa, Italy, England, and Belgium.

* * *

TOMIKEL, John 1928-

PERSONAL: Born April 30, 1928, in Cuddy, Pa. *Education:* Clarion State College, B.S., 1950; University of Pittsburgh, M.Litt., 1956, Ph.D., 1972; graduate study at Allegheny College, 1958-61; Syracuse University, M.S., 1962. *Residence:* California, Pa. 15419. *Office:* Department of Earth Sciences, California State College, California, Pa. 15419.

CAREER: California State College, California, Pa., assistant professor, 1965-66, associate professor, 1966-72, professor of earth sciences, 1972—. *Military service:* U.S. Army, 1952-54. *Member:* Pennsylvania Earth Science Teachers Society (founder).

WRITINGS: (With V. K. Shepps) *Geology and Geography of Erie County*, Pennsylvania Geological Survey, 1969; *Where Sleeps My Love* (poetry), Mitre Press, 1970; *Teaching and Earth Science*, Allegheny Press, 1972; *American Geological Education*, Allegheny Press, 1972; *Edible Wild Plants*, Allegheny Press, 1973. Contributor to *Journal of Geological Education* and to poetry magazines.

* * *

TOPPING, Donald M(edley) 1929-

PERSONAL: Born November 1, 1929, in Huntington, W.Va.; son of Leroy B. (a decorator) and Thelma (White) Topping; married Linda Lambert, December, 1953 (divorced, 1962); married Annie Nguyen Ho Hong-Hai, August 28, 1966; children: (first marriage) Dee (Mrs. Thomas Johnson), Leslie; (second marriage) Miles, Minh. *Education:* University of Kentucky, B.A., 1954, M.A., 1956; Michigan State University, Ph.D., 1963. *Home:* 2514 Oahu Ave., Honolulu, Hawaii 96822. *Office:* Social Sciences and Linguistics Institute, University of Hawaii, 2424 Maile Way, Honolulu, Hawaii 96822.

CAREER: University of Hawaii, Honolulu, assistant professor, 1964-69, associate professor, 1969-73, professor of linguistics, 1973—, director of Pacific and Asian Linguistics Institute, 1969-74, and of Social Sciences and Linguistics Institute, 1974—. *Military service:* U.S. Army, 1948-51. *Member:* Linguistic Society of America. *Awards, honors:* Ancient Order of the Chamorri, 1974.

WRITINGS: Spoken Chamorro, University Press of Hawaii, 1969; *Chamorro Reference Grammar*, University Press of Hawaii, 1973; *Chamorro-English Dictionary*, University Press of Hawaii, in press.

* * *

TORGERSON, Dial 1928-

PERSONAL: Born April 18, 1928, in Southport, N.C.; son of Edwin Dial (a writer) and Leila (a writer; maiden name, Smith) Torgerson; married Ellen Heller, April 17, 1960; children: Christopher, Jordan Anne. *Education:* University of Southern California, B.A., 1951. *Home:* 1751 Silverwood Ter., Los Angeles, Calif. 90024. *Agent:* Mike Hamilburg, 10840 Lindbrook Dr., Los Angeles, Calif. 90024. *Office address: Los Angeles Times*, P.O. Box 49583, Nairobi, Kenya.

CAREER: Associated Press, Los Angeles, Calif., reporter, 1954-65; *Los Angeles Times*, Los Angeles, Calif., reporter, 1966-74, chief of bureau in Nairobi, Kenya, covering Sub-sahara Africa (including coup in Ethiopia, independence movement in Guinea-Bissau and Mozambique, and terrorist attacks in Rhodesia), 1974—. *Military service:* U.S. Army, 1952-54; became second lieutenant.

WRITINGS: Kerkorian: An American Success Story, Dial, 1974. Contributor to magazines.

* * *

TOWNSEND, Charles Bud 1929-

PERSONAL: Born November 5, 1929, in Nocona, Tex.; son of Claude Webster (an oilfield worker) and Dorothy (Keck) Townsend; married Mary L. Smith (a teacher), April 9, 1950; children: William, Mary Jane, Charles, Jr. *Education:* Midwestern University, B.A., 1960; Baylor University, M.A., 1961; University of Wisconsin, Ph.D., 1965. *Politics:* Democrat. *Religion:* Baptist. *Home:* 507 25th St., Canyon, Tex. 79015. *Office:* Department of History, West Texas State University, Canyon, Tex.

CAREER: Hardin-Simmons University, Abilene, Tex., associate professor of history, 1965-67; West Texas State University, Canyon, associate professor of history, 1967—. *Member:* American Historical Society, Organization of American Historians.

WRITINGS: Homecoming: Reflections on Bob Wills and His Texas Playboys, 1915-1973, United Artists, 1974; *San Antonio Rose: The Life and Music of Bob Wills*, University of Illinois Press, 1975.

* * *

TRACY, John A(lvin) 1934-

PERSONAL: Born November 8, 1934, in St. Joseph, Mo.; son of John S. (a businessman) and Verna (a practical nurse; maiden name, Pettigrew) Tracy; married Fay Jeffries, September 3, 1955; children: Mary, John, Christina, Jacquelynne, Tage. *Education:* Creighton University, B.S.C., 1956; University of Wisconsin, M.B.A., 1960, Ph.D., 1961. *Politics:* Democrat. *Religion:* Roman Catholic. *Home:* 2795 Vassar Dr., Boulder, Colo. 80303. *Office:* College of Business and Administration, University of Colorado, Boulder, Colo. 80302.

CAREER: University of Wisconsin, Madison, instructor, 1958-61, University of California, Berkeley, assistant professor, 1961-65, University of Colorado, Boulder, associate professor, 1965-71, professor of accounting, 1971—. *Member:* American Institute of Certified Public Accountants, Financial Executives Institute, American Accounting Association.

WRITINGS: Understanding Accounting, Prentice-Hall, 1971; *Fundamentals of Financial Accounting*, Wiley, 1974; *Fundamentals of Management Accounting*, Wiley, in press. Contributor to scholarly journals.

TRAPIER, Elizabeth du Gue 1893(?)-1974

1893(?)—October 15, 1974; American art historian, curator, expert on Spanish art, and author of books, articles, and catalogues on Spanish artists and their works. Obituaries: *New York Times*, October 16, 1974.

* * *

TRENDALL, Arthur Dale 1909-

PERSONAL: Born March 28, 1909, in Auckland, New Zealand; son of Arthur Dale (a teacher) and Iza (Uttley-Todd) Trendall. *Education:* University of Otago, M.A., 1929, Litt.D., 1936; Trinity College, Cambridge, B.A., 1933, M.A., 1937, Litt.D., 1968. *Office:* Menzies College, La Trobe University, Bundoora, Victoria 3083, Australia.

CAREER: Cambridge University, Trinity College, Cambridge, England, fellow, 1936-40; British School at Rome, librarian, 1936-38; University of Sydney, Sydney, Australia, professor of Greek and archeology, 1939-54, dean of the Faculty of Arts, 1947-50, chairman of professorial board, 1947-50, 1952, acting vice-chancellor, 1953; Australian National University, Canberra, master of University House, 1954-59, deputy vice-chancellor, 1958-64; La Trobe University, Menzies College, Bundoora, Australia, resident fellow, 1969—. Member of Australian National Capital Planning Committee, 1958-67; member of Australian Universities Commission, 1959-70; Geddes-Harrower Professor of Greek Art and Archaeology at University of Aberdeen, 1966-67.

MEMBER: Society of Antiquaries (fellow), British Academy (fellow), Australian Academy of the Humanities (foundation fellow), German Archaeological Institute, Accademia dei Lincei (Rome; foreign member), Pontifical Academy of Archaeology (Rome; corresponding member), Academy of Athens, Archaeological Society of Athens (honorary fellow). *Awards, honors:* Commendatore dell' Ordine di S. Gregorio Magno, 1956; Companion of the Order of St. Michael and St. George, 1961; Commendatore dell' Ordine al Merito della Repubblica Italiana, 1965; Cassano Gold Medal for Magna Graecia Studies, 1971; Galileo Galilei Prize, 1971; D.Litt. from University of Melbourne, 1956, University of Adelaide, 1960, Australian National University, 1970, University of Sydney, 1972.

WRITINGS: Paestan Pottery: A Study of the Red-Figured Vases of Paestum, Macmillan, for the British School at Rome, 1936; *The Shellal Mosaic* (booklet), Australian War Memorial (Canberra), 1942, 4th edition, 1973; (with J. R. Stewart) *Handbook to the Nicholson Museum*, University of Sydney, 2nd edition, 1948; *Vasi italioti ed etruschi a figure rosse*, [Vatican City], Volume I, 1953, Volume II, 1955; *The Felton Greek Vases* (booklet), International School Book Service, 1958; *Phlyax Vases*, Institute of Classical Studies, University of London, 1959, 2nd edition, revised and enlarged, 1967.

(With Alexander Cambitoglou) *Apulian Red-Figured Vase-Painters of the Plain Style*, Archaeological Institute of America, 1961; *South Italian Vase Painting*, British Museum, 1966; *The Red-Figured Vases of Lucania, Campania, and Sicily*, two volumes. Oxford University Press, 1967, first supplement, 1970, second supplement, 1973; *Greek Vases in the Felton Collection* (booklet), Oxford University Press, 1968; *Notes on Greek and Roman Art*, privately printed (Melbourne), 1969; *Greek Vases in the Logie Collection*, University of Canterbury (Christchurch, New Zealand), 1971; (with Thomas B. L. Webster) *Illustrations of Greek Drama*, Praeger, 1971; (editor) *Gli Indigeni nella pittura italiota*, [Taranto, Italy], 1971.

Author of papers published by the British School at Rome. Contributor to *Jahrbuch der Berliner Museen*, *Annual Bulletin of the National Gallery of Victoria*, to conference proceedings, and to encyclopedias of art and archeology; also contributor to journals, including *Journal of Hellenic Studies*, *Archaeological Reports*, *Art Bulletin of Victoria*, *American Journal of Archaeology*, *Scottish Art Review*, *Antiquaries Journal*, *Revue Archeologique*, and *Apollo*.

WORK IN PROGRESS: The History of the Red-Figured Vases of Apulia, completion expected in 1976, for Clarendon Press (of Oxford University).

* * *

TRIPP, Karen 1923-
(Karen Gershon)

PERSONAL: Born August 29, 1923, in Bielefeld, Germany; daughter of Paul (an architect) and Selma (Schoenfeld) Loewenthal; married Val Tripp (an art teacher), March 6, 1948; children: Christopher, Anthony, Stella, Naomi. *Address:* c/o Victor Gollancz Ltd., 14 Henrietta St., London WC2E 8QJ, England.

MEMBER: Society of Authors (England), Hebrew Writers' Association (Israel). *Awards, honors:* British Arts Council award for poetry, 1967; *Jewish Chronicle* book prize, 1967; Haim Greenberg Literary Award, 1968.

WRITINGS—Under pseudonym Karen Gershon: *The Relentless Year: New Poets, 1959*, Eyre & Spottiswoode, 1960; *Selected Poems*, Harcourt, 1966; (editor) *We Came as Children* (prose), Harcourt, 1966; (editor) *Postscript* (prose), Gollancz, 1969; *Legacies and Encounters* (poems), Gollancz, 1972; *My Daughters, My Sisters* (poems), Gollancz, 1975. Contributor to periodicals, including *Critical Quarterly, London Magazine, Encounter, Jewish Chronicle, Midstream,* and *Jerusalem Post* (Israel).

* * *

TRUBY, J(ohn) David 1938-

PERSONAL: Born April 17, 1938, in Bellefonte, Pa.; son of John H. (a bank executive) and Mable (Fiscus) Truby; married Nancy Berg (a teacher), June 11, 1962; children: Christopher Scott. *Education:* Pennsylvania State University, B.A., 1960, M.A., 1962, Ph.D., 1970. *Politics:* Republican. *Home:* 2587 Melloney Lane, Indiana, Pa. 15701. *Office:* Department of Journalism, Indiana University of Pennsylvania, Indiana, Pa. 15701.

CAREER: Centre Film Laboratory, State College, Pa., advertising director, 1959-60; WMAJ-Radio, State College, Pa., member of news staff, 1961-62; Clarion State College, Clarion, Pa., director of public relations, 1962-65; Barash Advertising, State College, Pa., senior copywriter, 1965-67; Indiana University of Pennsylvania, Indiana, associate professor, 1969-73, professor of journalism, 1973—. *Military service:* U.S. Army, Intelligence, 1960-61; became sergeant.

MEMBER: Alpha Delta Sigma, Alpha Phi Gamma, Sigma Delta Chi. *Awards, honors:* Pennsylvania Newspaper Publishers Association Press column award, 1971; *Fifth Estate* writing awards, 1971, 1974.

WRITINGS: Advertising for You, MacMurray Publishers, 1965; *Speech: Science/Art*, Bobbs-Merrill, 1969; *Silencers, Snipers, and Assassins*, Paladin Press, 1972; *The Quiet*

Killers, Paladin Press, 1972; *Improvised-Modified Firearms*, Paladin Press, 1974; *Lewis: The Name Known round the World*, Normount Armament Co., in press. Contributor of nearly two hundred articles to magazines.

WORK IN PROGRESS: Four books.

* * *

TRUMAN, Ruth 1931-
(Marty Trudix)

PERSONAL: Born October 5, 1931, in Ashland, Ky.; daughter of Rexford Maitland (a clergyman) and Allene G. (Barber) Dixon; married Wallace Lee Truman (a clergyman), June 5, 1952; children: Mark Leroy, Rebecca Joy, Timothy Wallace, Nathan Lee. *Education:* Asbury College, student, 1948; Taylor University, B.S., 1952; California State University, Los Angeles, M.S., 1967; University of California, Los Angeles, doctoral study, 1974—. *Politics:* Democrat. *Religion:* United Methodist. *Residence:* Westlake Village, Calif. *Office:* Counseling Center, California Lutheran College, Thousand Oaks, Calif. 91360.

CAREER: Elementary school teacher in Atco, N.J., 1954-55; high school home economics teacher in Chatham, N.J., 1955-56; Citrus College, Azusa, Calif., counselor, 1966-67, instructor in marriage and the family, 1967-69; California Lutheran College, Thousand Oaks, director of counseling, 1970-74. Member of executive committee of Ventura County Drug Abuse Council. *Member:* American College Personnel Association, American Personnel and Guidance Association, California Women Administrators and Counselors.

WRITINGS: Underground Manual for Ministers' Wives, Abingdon, 1974.

WORK IN PROGRESS: No Safe Place, a novel about college life, under pseudonym Marty Trudix.

SIDELIGHTS: Ruth Truman traveled with youth teams to work in Israel, 1964, Australia, 1970, and Naples, 1973. *Avocational interests:* Music, drama, the role of women in society, parapsychology.

* * *

TSCHICHOLD, Jan 1902(?)-1974

1902(?)—1974; German-born Swiss typographer, book designer, authority on Chinese woodcut printing, and author of several books in his field. Obituaries: *AB Bookman's Weekly*, October 21, 1974.

* * *

TUCKER, Robin 1950-
(Kay Nibor)

PERSONAL: Born November 20, 1950, in Glendale, Calif.; daughter of Forrest Robert (a transportation manager) and Dorothy (Kowalski) Tucker. *Education:* University of California, Los Angeles, B.A., 1972. *Politics:* Democrat. *Religion:* Protestant. *Home:* 9828½ Vidor Dr., Los Angeles, Calif. 90035. *Office: Playgirl*, 1801 Century Park E., Los Angeles, Calif. 90067.

CAREER: Ward Ritchie Press, Los Angeles, Calif., editor, 1973; *Playgirl*, Los Angeles, Calif., managing editor, 1974—.

WRITINGS: Feet First: Cityside and Countryside Walking Tours in Los Angeles, Ward Ritchie Press, 1973.

Editor; all published by Ward Ritchie Press in 1973: *Guidebook to the Mojave Desert*, two volumes; *Where to Take Your Children in Nevada; Backyard Treasure Hunting; Exploring Big Sur, Carmel, Monterey; Exploring Small Towns; Guidebook to the Delta Country of Central California; Guidebook to Southern California Fossil Hunting; Guidebook to Vancouver Island; Moussaka, Baklava & Love; Crossroads of Cooking.*

Contributor to magazines, sometimes under pseudonym Kay Nibor.

WORK IN PROGRESS: Children's stories.

AVOCATIONAL INTERESTS: Reading, music, singing, art, gourmet cooking, tennis, travel.

* * *

TUNSTALL, Velma 1914-
(Shana Barrett Tunstall)

PERSONAL: Born August 11, 1914, in Vidette, Ark.; daughter of Sterling Isam (a barber and farmer) and Cecil Anna (a teacher; maiden name, Jack) Barrett; married Earl Archer Tunstall (a butcher), October 30, 1934; children: Patricia Gail, Deanna Mae. *Education:* Attended public schools in Fulton County, Ark. *Home:* 928 Third Pl., Upland, Calif. 91786.

CAREER: Poetess. *Member:* International Platform Association, California State Poetry Society, California Federation of Chaparral Poets. *Awards, honors:* Certificate from Hall of Fame, West Plains, Mo., for literary achievements; certificate of merit, 1971, and plaque and certificate of honor, 1974-75, from *International Who's Who in Poetry*; certificates from International Platform Association, 1973, 1974.

WRITINGS: (Under pseudonym Shana Barrett Tunstall) *Shadows on My Soul* (poetry), Royal Publishers, 1971.

WORK IN PROGRESS: Other volumes of poetry.

* * *

TURNER, Alice K. 1940-

PERSONAL: Born May 29, 1940, in China; daughter of William T. (a diplomatic officer) and Florence B. (Green) Turner. *Education:* Bryn Mawr College, B.A., 1962. *Home:* 184 West Tenth St., New York, N.Y. 10014. *Office: Publishers Weekly*, 1180 Avenue of the Americas, New York, N.Y. 10036.

CAREER: Has been employed as editorial assistant for *New York Post*, features editor for *Charlie* magazine, and contributing editor for *Eye* magazine; David Frost Show, (television), New York, N.Y., associate producer, 1969; *Holiday*, New York, N.Y., senior editor, 1969-70; currently paperback editor with *Publishers Weekly*, New York.

WRITINGS: Yoga for Beginners, F. Watts, 1973.

* * *

TURNER, Bessye Tobias 1917-

PERSONAL: Born October 10, 1917, in Liberty, Miss.; daughter of Aaron (a railroad employee) and Bessie (Smith) Tobias. *Education:* Rust College, A.B., 1939; Columbia University, M.A., 1954, M.A., 1964, graduate study, 1964, 1968. *Home:* 829 Wall St., McComb, Miss. 39648.

CAREER: High school teacher of English in McComb, Miss., 1939-44, and in Brookhaven, Miss., 1950-55; Bureau of Internal Revenue Service, Bronx, N.Y., clerk, 1945-49;

Alcorn A. & M. College, Lorman, Miss., assistant professor of English and speech, and director of theatre, 1955-62; Southern University, Baton Rouge, La., assistant professor of English and speech, 1962-63; Texas Southern University, Houston, assistant professor of English and speech, 1964-66; Mississippi Valley State College, Itta Bena, assistant professor of English and speech, 1968-71. Director of Communication Workshop at Natchez Separate School District, 1961, 1962.

MEMBER: Centro Studi e Scambi Internazionali (permanent representative, 1971—), International Clover Poetry Association, International Poetry Association, Intercontinental Biographical Association, National Council of Teachers of English, Speech Communication Association, United Methodist Women, Order of Eastern Star, New York Poetry Forum, Alpha Kappa Alpha, Kappa Delta Pi. *Awards, honors:* Certificates of merit from Centro Studi e Scambi Internazionali and Leonardo Da Vinci International Exhibition, 1971, 1972, for poetry displays, and from Danae International Clover Poetry Association, 1974; honorable mention from New York Poetry Forum, 1974, for "Lets Plant a Rose America!"

WRITINGS: La Librae: An Anthology of Poetry for Living, Harlo, 1969; *Peace and Love* (poems), Centro Studi e Scambi Internazionali, 1972.

WORK IN PROGRESS: Three books of poetry including *Crowns for My King* and *Petals from a Rose*; United States publication of *Peace and Love* with addition of unpublished poems; short stories on local color and regionalism; a documentary treatise on perils of teaching based on accurate accounts of hostilities and deprivations.

AVOCATIONAL INTERESTS: Fashion designing, directing plays.

* * *

TURNER, George E(ugene) 1925-
(Tex Lowell, Lloyd Scott)

PERSONAL: Born September 30, 1925, in Burk Burnett, Tex.; son of George A. and Lula (Orr) Turner; married Leona McLendon, June 26, 1954 (divorced, 1969); children: Lowell G., David A., Douglas S., James L. *Education:* West Texas State University, B.S., 1950; also studied at Art Institute of Chicago, 1948-49, and American Academy of Art, 1949-50. *Home:* 116 North LaSalle St., Amarillo, Tex. 79106. *Office:* Globe-News Co., P.O. Box 2091, Amarillo, Tex. 79105.

CAREER: U.S. Air Force, Amarillo, Tex., civilian illustrator, 1950-51; Globe-News Co., Amarillo, Tex., staff artist, 1951-54; Russell Printing & Publishing, Amarillo, Tex., art director, 1955-60; U.S. Air Force, civilian illustrator, 1960-65; Globe-News Co., Amarillo, Tex., art director, 1965—. Instructor at Amarillo College, 1960-62. *Military service:* U.S. Naval Reserve, active duty, 1943-46; served in Asiatic campaign; became sonarman first class.

WRITINGS: George Turner's Book of Gunfighters (self-illustrated), Baxter Lane, 1972, revised edition, 1974; *George Turner's Book of American Indians* (self-illustrated), Baxter Lane, 1973; (with Baxter Lane) *Chuckwagon Cookin'* (self-illustrated), Baxter Lane, 1973; (with Stefan Kramar) *Panhandle Portrait,* Pemberton, 1974; *Murder in the Palo Duro* (self-illustrated), Nortex, 1974; *Secrets of Billy the Kid* (self-illustrated), Baxter Lane, 1974; *Fisherman's Laugh Book* (self-illustrated), Baxter Lane, 1974; *Land of the Comanche* (self-illustrated), Nortex, in press; (with Orville Goldner) *The King Kong Book,* A. S. Barnes, in press; (contributor) Irving Wallace, editor, *The People's Almanac,* Doubleday, in press.

Illustrator: J. A. Hill, *More Than Brick and Mortar,* West Texas State University Press, 1959; Glenn Zulauf and Ray Franks, *Palo Duro,* Franks, 1965; Dulcie Sullivan, *The LX Brand,* University of Texas Press, 1971; Jerry Sinise, *The Reluctant Gunfighter,* Nortex, 1974. Also illustrator of textbook, *Working Hands,* by John Miller, 1970.

Illustrator of U.S. Air Force Jet Training Schools textbooks, 1950's and 1960's. Author of cartoon series, "The Ancient Southwest," 1951-54, and "Sodbuster Sam," 1960's. Wrote and illustrated scientific features for Copley Newsfeatures in the 1960's. Wrote publicity material for major motion picture studios, 1960's. Author of "Flashbacks," a daily column in the Amarillo *Globe-Times,* 1974—.

Contributor of illustrations, photographs, scientific and historical articles (sometimes under pseudonyms Tex Lowell and Lloyd Scott) to magazines, including *Popular Photography, Art and Camera, Fate, Science Digest, Quarter Horse Journal,* and *Punch.* Co-publisher and co-editor of *Southwest Heritage,* 1966-69.

WORK IN PROGRESS: Secrets of Jesse James; with Orville Goldner, *Of Gods and Monsters,* on the development of Universal Pictures, 1913-1936; with Jean Wade, *Panhandle Murders,* a collection of detective stories; a book on special effects work in motion pictures, with Orville Goldner.

SIDELIGHTS: Turner writes that his material tends to be apolitical, that he is more interested in facts than opinions. He is appalled by the great body of misinformation found in most factual books on his favorite subjects, which he feels is repeated until it is blindly accepted as fact. His ambition is to "set the record straight" in matters of history and especially film history, and he "blushingly admits" that he has perpetrated his share of bloopers in the course of his work.

His original ambition was to be museum sculptor and painter. This led to a study of natural sciences. Turner's four sons share this interest and together have made some unusual finds, particularly involving Triassic fauna.

AVOCATIONAL INTERESTS: Paleontology, archaeology, and other areas of natural history; swimming; hiking; painting (drawings, oils, and watercolors in private and public collections); collecting original art by illustrators and cartoonists; travel, especially jungle and undersea exploration in the South Pacific.

* * *

UDOLF, Roy 1926-

PERSONAL: Born August 7, 1926, in New York, N.Y.; son of Barney (an executive) and Ester (Kadis) Udolf; married Marcelle Temkin, June 1, 1950; children: Bruce Lee, Penny Jill, Bradley Robert, David William. *Education:* New York University, B.E.E., 1950, graduate study in law; Brooklyn Law School, LL.B. (cum laude), 1954, J.D. (cum laude), 1967; Hofstra University, M.A., 1963; Adelphi University, Ph.D., 1971. *Home:* 2777 Granz Ct., East Meadow, N.Y. 11554. *Office:* Department of Psychology, Hofstra University, Hempstead, N.Y. 11554.

CAREER: Admitted to New York State Bar and Bar of U.S. Supreme Court; certified psychologist by State of New York. Electronic Products Co., Mt. Vernon, N.Y., engineer, 1950-51; Radio Marine Corp. of America, New York, N.Y., engineer, 1951-52; Mackay Radio & Telegraph Co., New York, N.Y., project engineer, 1952-54; Sperry Rand Corp., Great Neck, N.Y., associate engineer, 1955-56; American Bosch Arma Corp., Garden City, N.Y., test engineer, 1956-63; Gyrodyne Co. of America, St. James, N.Y., assistant head of Ground Support Equipment department, 1963-67; Hofstra University, Hempstead, N.Y., part-time member of faculty, 1964-67, associate professor of psychology, 1967—. Private practice of law, 1954-60. Principal human factors engineer for Litcom Division of Litton Industries, 1971-73. *Military service:* U.S. Marine Corps, 1944-46.

MEMBER: American Psychological Association, American Psychology-Law Society, American Institute of Aeronautics and Astronautics, New York State Bar Association, New York County Lawyers' Association, Nassau County Bar Association, Sigma Xi, Sigma Kappa Alpha, Psi Chi.

WRITINGS: Logic Design for Behavioral Scientists, Nelson Hall, 1973. Contributor to *American Psychologist*, *Psychological Reports*, *Electronics*, *Spectrum*, *Psychonomic Science*, and *Arma Engineer*.

WORK IN PROGRESS: The College Teacher's Guide to Teaching and Academia, for Nelson Hall.

AVOCATIONAL INTERESTS: Ham radio, horses, archery.

* * *

UNDERWOOD, Norman 1878(?)-1974

1878(?)—December 8, 1974; American chemical engineer, pioneer in working with emulsion types of printing ink, amateur genealogist and historian of Washington (D.C.), and author of books on related subjects. Obituaries: *Washington Post*, December 10, 1974.

* * *

UNRUH, Adolph 1908-

PERSONAL: Born September 14, 1908, in Dolton, S.D.; son of John C. D. (a carpenter) and Matilda (Ortman) Unruh; married Glenys Grace (an educator), May 24, 1932; children: Marla Unruh Lee, Shirley (Mrs. Charles Herrick), Janet Lynn. *Education:* Wichita State University, A.B., 1933; University of Wisconsin, M.A., 1937; University of Colorado, Ph.D., 1948. *Politics:* Independent. *Religion:* Protestant. *Home:* 151 North Bemiston Ave., Clayton, Mo. 63105. *Office:* School of Education, St. Louis University, 221 North Grand, St. Louis, Mo. 63103.

CAREER: Rural school teacher in Harvey County, Kan., 1929-32; high school teacher, later superintendent of public schools in Burr Oak, Kan., 1933, 1936-43, and in Downs, Kan., 1943-44; supervising principal in Planeview, Kan., 1944-45; junior college dean in Chanute, Kan., 1945-47; Washington University, St. Louis, Mo., 1948-64, became professor of education and dean of summer school, 1957-64, director of Bureau of Consultants, 1956-62; University of Missouri, St. Louis, dean of the school of education, 1964-68; St. Louis University, St. Louis, Mo., professor of education, 1968—. Visiting lecturer at Cornell University, 1948, University of Colorado, 1953, College of the Pacific, 1955 and 1957.

MEMBER: American Educational Research Association, National Society for the Study of Education, National School Public Relations Association, Association for Supervision and Curriculum Development, National Association of Secondary School Principals, American Association of School Administrators, North Central Association of Secondary Schools and Colleges, Missouri School Board Association, Missouri Association of Secondary School Principals, Missouri State Teachers Association, Missouri Association for Supervision and Curriculum Development, Phi Delta Kappa, Kappa Delta Pi. *Awards, honors:* Scholarship from Kappa Delta Pi, 1972, to study comparative education in Russia.

WRITINGS: (With Sidney Rollins) *Introduction to Secondary Education*, Rand McNally, 1964; (with Rudyard K. Bent) *Secondary School Curriculum*, Heath, 1969; (with Harold E. Turner) *Supervision for Change and Innovation*, Houghton, 1970; (with Robert A. Willier) *Public Relations for Schools*, Fearon, 1974. Contributor of more than forty articles and reviews to education journals, including *School and Community, School Activities, Educational Administration and Supervision, National Education Association Journal, Progressive Education*, and *Educational Forum*.

WORK IN PROGRESS: Editing *Administration from the Inside*.

* * *

URETSKY, Myron 1940-

PERSONAL: Born May 28, 1940; married; children: four. *Education:* City College of the City University of New York, B.B.A., 1961; Ohio State University, M.B.A., 1962, Ph.D., 1965. *Home:* 434 Elm St., West Hempstead, N.Y. 11552. *Office:* Graduate School of Business Administration, New York University, New York, N.Y. 10003.

CAREER: Certified public accountant in Ohio, 1962, and Illinois, 1967. Senior accountant for Samuel Uretsky (certified public accountant), 1958-61; Ohio State University, Columbus, assistant instructor in accounting, 1962-64; University of Illinois, Champaign-Urbana, assistant professor of accounting, 1964-67; Columbia University, New York, N.Y., associate professor of business administration, 1967-70, director of computer resources for Graduate School of Business, 1969-70; New York University, New York, N.Y., associate professor, 1970-73, professor of business administration, 1973—, director of Management Game, 1971—, chairman of computer applications and information systems area, 1972—. Guest lecturer at Karl Marx University and at Central Management Training Institute (Warsaw).

MEMBER: American Accounting Association, American Institute of Certified Public Accountants, Association for Computing Machinery, Institute of Management Sciences, New York State Society of Certified Public Accountants. *Awards, honors:* Ford Foundation grant to develop management game for use in Hungarian universities; grant from U.S. State Department and Ford Foundation to develop a centralized planning simulation for Polish Management Institute; grant from U.S. Army, U.S. Navy, and U.S. Air Force for Fortran teaching experiment at Coordinated Science Laboratories.

WRITINGS: (Contributor) Enoch Haga, editor, *Automated Education Systems*, Business Press, 1968; (contributor) *Empirical Research in Accounting: Selected Studies, 1969*, Institute of Professional Accounting, University of Chicago, 1969; (with Neill C. Churchill and J. Kempster) *Computer-Based Information Systems for Management: A Survey*, National Association of Accountants, 1969. Contributor of about twenty articles to business and computer science journals, including *Computer Decisions, Columbia Journal of World Business, Simulation and Gaming, Journal of Systems, College and University Business*, and *Management Accounting*.

* * *

UTTLEY, Alice Jane (Taylor) 1884-
(Alison Uttley)

PERSONAL: Born December 17, 1884, in Derbyshire, England; daughter of Henry (a farmer) and Hannah (Dickens) Taylor; married James A. Uttley, August 10, 1911 (deceased); children: John Uttley. *Education:* Manchester University, B.Sc. Hons. Physics, 1906; attended Cambridge University, 1907. *Politics:* Conservative. *Religion:* Church of England. *Home:* Thackers, Beaconsfield, Buckinghamshire, England.

CAREER: Fulham Secondary for Girls, London, England, science mistress, 1908-11; full-time professional writer, 1929—. *Awards, honors:* D.Litt., Manchester University, 1970.

WRITINGS—All under name Alison Uttley: *The Squirrel, the Hare and the Little Grey Rabbit*, Heinemann, 1929, new edition illustrated by Jennie Corbett, 1968; *How Little Grey Rabbit Got Back Her Tail*, Heinemann, 1930, new illustrated edition, 1966; *The Great Adventure of Hare*, Heinemann, 1931, new illustrated edition, 1968; *The Country Child*, Faber, 1931, new edition, 1945; *Moonshine and Magic*, Faber, 1932; *The Story of Fuzzypeg, the Hedgehog*, Heinemann, 1932; *Squirrel Goes Skating*, Collins, 1934; *Wise Owl's Story*, Collins, 1935; *Candlelight Tales*, Faber, 1936; *Little Grey Rabbit's Party*, Collins, 1936; *The Adventures of No Ordinary Rabbit*, Faber, 1937; *Ambush of Young Days* (autobiographical reminiscences), Faber, 1937, new edition, 1951; *Squirrel Goes Skating*, Collins, 1937; *The Knot Squirrel Tied*, Collins, 1937; *Fuzzypeg Goes to School*, Collins, 1938; *High Meadows*, Faber, 1938, new edition, 1966; *Mustard, Pepper and Salt*, Faber, 1938; *A Traveller in Time*, Faber, 1939, Putnam, 1940, new edition, Viking, 1964; *Tales of the Four Pigs and Brock the Badger*, Faber, 1939; *Little Grey Rabbit's Christmas*, Collins, 1939.

Moldy Warp the Mole, Collins, 1940; *Adventures of Sam Pig*, Faber, 1940; *Six Tales of the Four Pigs*, Faber, 1941; *Sam Pig Goes to Market*, Faber, 1941; *Ten Tales of Tim Rabbit*, Faber, 1941; *The Farm on the Hill*, Faber, 1941, new edition, 1949; *Six Tales of Brock the Badger*, Faber, 1941; *Six Tales of Sam Pig*, Faber, 1941; *Ten Candlelight Tales*, Faber, 1942; *Nine Starlight Tales*, Faber, 1942; *Little Grey Rabbit's Washing-Day*, Collins, 1942; *Sam Pig and Sally*, Faber, 1942; *Hare Joins the Home Guard*, Collins, 1942; *Water-Rat's Picnic*, Collins, 1943; *Country Hoard*, Faber, 1943; *Cuckoo Cherry-Tree*, Faber, 1943; *Sam Pig at the Circus*, Faber, 1943; *The Spice-Woman's Basket, and Other Tales*, Faber, 1944; *Little Grey Rabbit's Birthday*, Collins, 1944; *When All is Done* (novel), Faber, 1945; *The Weather Cock, and Other Stories*, Faber, 1945; *The Speckledy Hen*, Collins, 1945; *Some Moonshine Tales*, Faber, 1945; *Little Grey Rabbit to the Rescue* (play), Collins, 1945; *Adventures of Tim Rabbit*, Faber, 1945; *Mrs. Nimble and Mr. Bumble*, Barmerlea, 1945; *Country Things*, Faber, 1946; *The Washerwoman's Child: A Play on the Life and Stories of Hans Christian Andersen*, Faber, 1946; *Little Grey Rabbit and the Weasels*, Collins, 1947; *Grey Rabbit and the Wandering Hedgehog*, Collins, 1948; *Sam Pig in Trouble*, Faber, 1948; *Carts and Candlesticks*, Faber, 1948; *John Barleycorn: Twelve Tales of Fairy and Magic*, Faber, 1948; (editor) *In Praise of Country Life* (anthology), Muller, 1949.

Macduff, Faber, 1950; *Little Brown Mouse Books*, Heinemann, 1950; *Little Grey Rabbit Makes Lace*, Collins, 1950; *Snug and Serena Pick Cowslips*, Heinemann, 1950; *Buckinghamshire*, R. Hale, 1950; *The Cobbler's Shop, and Other Tales*, Faber, 1950; *Snug and Serena Meet a Queen*, Heinemann, 1950; *Going to the Fair*, Heinemann, 1951; *Toad's Castle*, Heinemann, 1951; *Yours Ever, Sam Pig*, Faber, 1951; *Mrs. Mouse Spring-Cleans*, Heinemann, 1952; *Hare and the Easter Eggs*, Collins, 1952; *Plowmen's Clocks*, Faber, 1952; *Christmas at the Rose and Crown*, Heinemann, 1952; *Magic in My Pocket*, Penguin, 1957; *The Gypsy Hedgehogs*, Heinemann, 1953; *Snug and Chimney-Sweeper*, Heinemann, 1953; *The Stuff of Dreams*, Faber, 1953; *Little Red Fox and the Wicked Uncle*, Heinemann, 1954, Bobbs-Merrill, 1963; *Little Grey Rabbit Goes to the Sea*, Collins, 1954; *Sam Pig and the Singing Gate*, Faber, 1955; *Here's a New Day*, Faber, 1956; *Hare and Guy Fawkes*, Collins, 1956; *Little Red Fox and Cinderella*, Heinemann, 1956; *A Year in the Country*, Faber 1957; *Little Red Fox and the Magic Moon*, Heinemann, 1958; *Little Grey Rabbit's Paint-Box*, Collins, 1958; *Snug and Serena Count Twelve*, Heinemann, 1959, Bobbs-Merrill, 1962; *The Swans Fly Over*, Faber, 1959; *Tim Rabbit and Company*, Faber, 1959.

Grey Rabbit Finds a Shoe, Collins, 1960; *John at the Old Farm*, Heinemann, 1960; *Sam Pig Goes to the Seaside: Sixteen Stories of Sam Pig*, Faber, 1960; *Something for Nothing*, Faber, 1960; *Three Little Grey Rabbit Plays* (includes "Grey Rabbit's Hospital," "The Robber," and "A Christmas Story"), Heinemann, 1961; *Grey Rabbit and the Circus*, Collins, 1961; *The Little Knife Who Did All the Work: Twelve Tales of Magic*, Faber, 1962; *Little Red Fox and the Unicorn*, Heinemann, 1962; *Wild Honey*, Faber, 1962; *Grey Rabbit's May Day*, Collins, 1963; *Snug and Serena Go to Town*, Bobbs-Merrill, 1963; *Tim Rabbit's Dozen*, Faber, 1964; *Cuckoo in June*, Faber, 1964; *Hare Goes Shopping*, Collins, 1965; *Sam Pig Storybook*, Faber, 1965; *A Peck of Gold*, Faber, 1966; *Enchantment*, Heinemann, 1966; *Recipes from an Old Farmhouse*, Faber, 1966; *Little Grey Rabbit's Pancake Day*, Collins, 1967; *The Button-Box, and Other Essays*, Faber, 1968; *Little Red Fox and the Great Big Tree*, Heinemann, 1968; *Lavender Shoes: Eight Tales of Enchantment*, Faber, 1970; *The Sam Pig Storybook*, Faber, 1970; *Ten O'Clock Scholar* (essays), Faber, 1970; *Fuzzypeg's Brother*, Collins, 1971; *Secret Places* (essays), Faber, 1972; *Grey Rabbit's Spring Cleaning Party*, Collins, 1972; *The Little Red Fox Book*, Heinemann, 1972.

WORK IN PROGRESS: Books of essays and tales for children; fairy tales; Grey Rabbit, Sam Pig, and Tim Rabbit tales.

SIDELIGHTS: Mrs. Uttley writes: "I was born and brought up on a hill farm in Derbyshire. The house was built on a plateau on a hill, with wide views of hills and valleys. My family had lived there for over 200 years, but the house itself had been rebuilt on the old foundations of rock only a hundred years before, when the family lived for some months in a barn during the work. I was devoted to my home, and most of my books have taken this house for the scene of the action. . . .

"The writers of children's books have to exercise care in the presentation of their subjects. A feeling of security should be built up, for who knows what terrors already lurk in a child's mind? When I was told that the earth moves round the sun, that the world is a globe, upon which we live, I had an awful vision of myself falling off the spinning globe and dropping into an abyss without bottom. Childhood fears are far worse than adult fears, as the joys are perhaps more intense than later in life. So I take the children, or anyone who reads the books, into a land without real fear—although there are small fears which are surmounted.

"I heard of children during the air-raids in London who carried my books to the underground shelters and clutched them for safety. I know of many who have gone to hospitals with the little books. Tales for the very young should be secure, comforting, but not sentimental. A little boy in a Nottinghamshire school said to his teacher, after hearing that Hare [one of Mrs. Uttley's characters] had joined the Home Guard: 'If the Germans come I bet Hare would turn them out.'"

AVOCATIONAL INTERESTS: Music, gardening, birds, and art (specifically seventeenth-century Dutch painting).

BIOGRAPHICAL/CRITICAL SOURCES: Roger Lancelyn Green, *Tellers of Tales*, Watts, 1965; Eleanor Cameron, *The Green and Burning Tree*, Atlantic-Little, Brown, 1969.

* * *

UTZ, Robert T(homas) 1934-

PERSONAL: Born August 6, 1934, in Madison, Wis.; son of Irwin C. (an athletic coach) and Genevieve (Johnson) Utz; married Sharon Kay Williams (a nursing educator), June 26, 1965; children: Kristine, Thomas. *Education:* Washington University, St. Louis, Mo., A.B., 1956, M.A.Ed., 1959, Ph.D., 1968. *Politics:* Democrat. *Home:* 3405 Deepwood, Lambertville, Mich. 48144. *Office:* College of Education, University of Toledo, Toledo, Ohio 43606.

CAREER: High school teacher of social studies and journalism in the public schools of Webster Groves, Mo., 1959-63, and Fremont, Calif., 1964-65; University of Toledo, Toledo, Ohio, assistant professor, 1968-72, associate professor of education, 1972—. Evaluator for education programs, Toledo Model Cities Project, 1970-72. *Military service:* U.S. Army Reserve, 1957-63. *Member:* American Educational Research Association, American Educational Studies Association, Association on American Indian Affairs, National Parks Association, Common Cause, Zero Population Growth, Friends of the Earth, Phi Delta Kappa.

WRITINGS: (With Leo Leonard) *A Competency Based Curriculum: A Model for Teachers*, Kendall-Hunt, 1971; (with Leonard) *Building Skills for Competency Based Teaching*, Harper, 1974. Author of articles, book reviews, research papers, and book abstracts. Member of editorial review board of *Journal of Abstracts in International Education*, 1971—.

WORK IN PROGRESS: A book with Leo Leonard, *Educational Foundations and Competency Based Education* (tentative title).

AVOCATIONAL INTERESTS: Travel, twentieth-century history, gardening, sports.

* * *

VACULIK, Ludvik 1926-

PERSONAL: Surname is pronounced Vaht-*soo*-leek; born July 23, 1926, in Brumov, Czechoslovakia; son of Martin (a carpenter) and Anna (Lysackova) Vaculik; married Marie Komarkova (a clerk), June 4, 1949; children: Martin, Ondrej, Jan. *Education:* High School for Social and Political Sciences, Prague, Czechoslovakia, B.Soc. and Pol. Sci., 1951. *Politics:* Member of Communist Party, 1946-69. *Residence:* Prague, Czechoslovakia.

CAREER: Ceskoslovenska Kolben-Danek (machine works), Prague, Czechoslovakia, educator, 1950-51; Rude pravo (publishing house), Prague, Czechoslovakia, editor, 1953-57; *Beseda venkovske rodiny* (weekly illustrated), Prague, Czechoslovakia, editor, 1957-59; Czechoslovak Radio, Prague, Czechoslovakia, editor, 1959-66; *Literarni noviny* (weekly publication of Writers Union), Prague, Czechoslovakia, editor, 1966-69; writer, 1969—. *Military service:* Czechoslovakian Armed Forces, 1951-53. *Awards, honors:* State award for activities in the radio youth program, 1964; prize from Ceskoslovensky Spisovatel, 1967, for *Sekyra*.

WRITINGS: *Rusny dum*, Ceskoslovenky Spisovatel (Prague), 1963; *Sekyra*, Ceskoslovensky Spisovatel, 1966, translation by Marian Sling published as *The Axe*, Harper, 1973; *The Guinea Pigs* (translation from the original manuscript, "Morcata," by Kaca Polackova), Third Press, 1973.

SIDELIGHTS: Vaculik told *CA*, "I find writing harder than digging in the garden." He also noted that since 1969 he has been a "private writer, without employment."

Vaculik's books have been published in German, French, Norwegian, and Yugoslavian editions.

* * *

VALERIANO, Napoleon D(iestro) 1917(?)-1975 (Napoleon Diestro Valeriano Serrano)

1917(?)—January 20, 1975; Philippine-born American expert on counterinsurgency, former colonel in the United States and Philippine Armies, lecturer, and author. Obituaries: *New York Times*, January 22, 1975; *Washington Post*, January 22, 1975.

* * *

VALES, Robert L(ee) 1933-

PERSONAL: Born June 23, 1933, in Cleveland, Ohio. *Education:* Case Western Reserve University, B.A., 1960, M.A., 1961, Ph.D., 1964. *Office:* Department of English, Gannon College, Erie, Pa. 16501.

CAREER: Ohio State University, Columbus, instructor in English, 1963-64; University of Illinois, Chicago, assistant professor of English, 1964-70; Gannon College, Erie, Pa., associate professor of English, 1970—. *Member:* Modern Language Association of America, American Society for Eighteenth-Century Studies.

WRITINGS: *Peter Pindar: John Wolcot*, Twayne, 1974. Editor of *Genre*.

WORK IN PROGRESS: A book on James Macpherson.

SIDELIGHTS: Vales is host of "Movie Log," a film criticism program on WERG-FM Radio.

* * *

VALLENTINE, John F(illmore) 1931-

PERSONAL: Born August 1, 1931, in Clark County, Kan.; son of John Fillmore (a rancher) and Venna Irene (Wilson) Vallentine; married Bonnie Blanche Clawson, August 10,

1950; children: Dixie Lee (Mrs. Michael Davis), Cinda Grace, John Michael. *Education:* Kansas State University, B.S., 1952; Utah State University, M.S., 1953; Texas A & M University, Ph.D., 1959. *Religion:* Church of Jesus Christ of Latter-Day Saints (Mormon). *Home:* 1081 South 700 E., Springville, Utah 84663. *Office:* Department of Botany and Range Science, Brigham Young University, 114 B-49, Provo, Utah 84602.

CAREER: Utah State University, Logan, assistant professor of range science, 1958-62; University of Nebraska, North Platte, associate professor of range science, 1962-68; Brigham Young University, Provo, professor of range science, 1968—. Certified genealogist in Utah, 1969. *Military service:* U.S. Air Force, 1953-55; became first lieutenant. *Member:* Society for Range Management, American Society of Animal science, Utah Genealogical Association (member of board of directors, 1972—), Alpha Zeta, Sigma Xi, Xi Sigma Pi.

WRITINGS: (Editor) *Handbook for Genealogical Correspondence*, Book Craft, 1962, 2nd edition, Everton, 1974; *Range Development and Improvements*, Brigham Young University Press, 1971; *Livelys of America*, National Association of Lively Families, 1971; *Locality Finding Aids for U.S. Surnames*, Everton, 1975. Contributor to *Journal of Range Management, American Genealogist, Ecology, Genealogical Society of Pennsylvania Publications, American Hereford Journal*, and *Nebraska Quarterly*. Editor of *Genealogical Journal*, 1972—.

WORK IN PROGRESS: A ranch planning manual.

* * *

VANDERBILT, Amy 1908-1974

July 22, 1908—December 27, 1974; American expert on etiquette, syndicated columnist, hostess of radio and television programs, and author of several books on etiquette. Obituaries: *New York Times*, December 28, 1974, and December 29, 1974; *Newsweek*, January 6, 1975; *Time*, January 6, 1975; *AB Bookman's Weekly*, January 20, 1975; *Current Biography*, February, 1975. (*CA*-4).

* * *

VanDERHOOF, Jack W(arner) 1921-

PERSONAL: Born June 10, 1921, in Boonton, N.J.; son of Raymond and Elizabeth (Warner) VanDerhoof; married Evelyn Roberts, 1944; children: Lynne, Douglas, Susan. *Education:* Drew University, A.B., 1942; Columbia University, M.A., 1947, Ph.D., 1951. *Residence:* Troy, N.Y. *Office:* Department of History, Russell Sage College, Troy, N.Y. 12150.

CAREER: Kansas Wesleyan University, Salina, associate professor, 1951-55, professor of history, 1955-63; Russell Sage College, Troy, N.Y., associate professor, 1963-66, professor of history, 1966—. *Military service:* U.S. Army Air Forces, 1942-46.

WRITINGS: The Time Now Past, Kansas Wesleyan University, 1962; *Bibliography of Novels Related to American Colonial and Frontier History,* Whitston Publishers, 1971. Contributor of articles and reviews to journals.

WORK IN PROGRESS: Three volumes of bibliographies: *Novels and Colonial History, Novels and Frontier, Novels and American Revolution.*

van der POEL, Cornelius J(ohannes) 1921-

PERSONAL: Born September 19, 1921, in the Netherlands; son of Jacobus (a farmer) and Laurentia (van der Geest) van der Poel. *Education:* Paters van de H. Geest, B.A., 1940; Scholasticaat Paters van de H. Geest, M.A., 1948; Iona College, M.S.Ed., 1969. *Home:* 646 Monroe Ave., Detroit, Mich. 48226. *Office:* Detroit Archdiocese, 305 Michigan Ave., Detroit, Mich. 48226.

CAREER: Member of the Congregation of the Holy Ghost Fathers, ordained Roman Catholic priest, 1947; St. Thomas Aquinas Seminary, Morogoro, Tanzania, assistant professor, 1948-51, professor of moral theology, 1951-55; St. Peter's Seminary, Bagamoyo, Tanzania, instructor in religious sciences, 1955-59; pastoral ministry in Morogoro, Tanzania, 1959-62; St. Mary's Seminary, Norwalk, Conn., associate professor, 1962-64, professor of moral theology, 1964-67; teacher and lecturer in New England and Pennsylvania, 1967-69; Clergy Development Center, La Crosse, Wis., codirector, 1970-74; Detroit Roman Catholic Archdiocese, Detroit, Mich., director of Family Life Bureau, 1974—. Visiting research professor at University of Guam, 1973; visiting professor at St. John's Provincial Seminary (Plymouth, Mich.), 1974—. *Member:* National Association of Social Workers, Academy of Pastoral Counselors, Canon Law Society of America.

WRITINGS: Utangulizi kwa Kitabu cha Kilegio (title means "Introduction to the Handbook of the Legion of Mary"), Tanganyika Mission Press, 1961; *Hotuba kwa Walegio* (title means "Instructions to Members of the Legion of Mary"), Tanganyika Mission Press, 1962; (contributor) Charles E. Curran, editor, *Absolutes in Moral Theology?*, World Publishing, 1968; *God's Love in Human Language: A Study of the Meaning of Marriage and Conjugal Responsibility*, Duquesne University Press, 1969.

(Contributor) *A Religious Leader's Guide for Intimacy: A Program for Marriage Enrichment*, Human Development Institute, Bell & Howell, 1971; *The Search for Human Values: Moral Growth in an Evolving World*, Paulist-Newman, 1971; *Religious Life: A Risk of Love*, Dimension Books, 1972; *Guam in Search of Its Own Identity: A Research Report on Human and Cultural Values in a Time of Rapid Change*, Volume I: *Analysis and Interpretation*, Volume II: *Approximations of Factor Analysis*, University of Guam, 1973, also published as condensed edition in single volume, 1973.

Contributor of about twenty articles to theology journals, including *Homiletic and Pastoral Review, Jurist, Journal of Pastoral Counseling, Living Light, Pacific Voice,* and *Chicago Studies.*

WORK IN PROGRESS: "Inquiry for the Assessment of Spirituality," a spirituality assessment test, with manual for interpretation.

* * *

VANDERPOOL, Harold Y(oung) 1936-

PERSONAL: Born June 28, 1936, in Port Arthur, Tex.; son of Guy Gibson (an atomic engineer) and Hallye Claire (a drama teacher; maiden name, Young) Vanderpool; married Nathalie Akin (a psychological counselor), June, 10, 1960; children: Jonathan Young, Katherine Claire, James Harold. *Education:* Harding College, B.A. (summa cum laude), 1958; Abilene Christian College, M.A. (cum laude), 1960; Harvard University, B.D. (cum laude), 1963, Ph.D., 1971. *Politics:* Democrat. *Home:* 756 Washington St.,

Wellesley, Mass. 02181. *Office:* American Studies Program, Wellesley College, Wellesley, Mass. 02181.

CAREER: Wellesley College, Wellesley, Mass., instructor, 1965-66, assistant professor of religion, 1966—, director of American studies, 1973—. *Member:* American Historical Association, American Studies Association, American Society of Church History, American Academy of Religion, Alpha Chi. *Awards, honors:* Ford Foundation fellowships, summers, 1971, 1974.

WRITINGS: (Editor with Roger A. Johnson, Ernest Wallwork, Clifford Green, and H. Paul Santmire, and contributor) *Critical Issues in Modern Religion*, Prentice-Hall, 1973; *Darwin and Darwinism: Revolutionary Ideas Concerning Man, Nature, Religion, and Society*, Heath, 1973. Contributor of articles and reviews to *Mission*, *New England Quarterly*, *Church History*, *Restoration Quarterly*, and *Journal of the Academy of Religion*.

WORK IN PROGRESS: The Trinitarian Intellect in New England, a study of the "non-unitarian" New England mind from 1800 to 1880; editing and writing introduction for a volume of Jonathan Edwards' *Works*, for Yale University Press.

SIDELIGHTS: Vanderpool writes: "I am increasingly fascinated by problems involving ethical issues and modern medicine, and have also done extensive work on the social roles and functions of religion in America." *Avocational interests:* Tennis, guitar, gardening, poetry.

* * *

VAN HORN, Richard L. 1932-

PERSONAL: Born November 2, 1932, in Chicago, Ill.; son of Richard L. (an executive) and Mildred (Wright) Van Horn; married Susan Householder (an historian), May 29, 1954; children: Susan Elizabeth, Patricia Suzanne, Lynda Sue. *Education:* Yale University, B.S., 1954; Massachusetts Institute of Technology, M.S., 1956. *Politics:* Democrat. *Home:* 2048 Beechwood Blvd., Pittsburgh, Pa. 15217. *Office:* Carnegie-Mellon University, 5000 Forbes, Pittsburgh, Pa. 15213.

CAREER: Carnegie-Mellon University, Pittsburgh, Pa., associate dean of Graduate School of Industrial Administration, 1967-71; European Institute for Advanced Studies in Management, Brussels, Belgium, director and professor, 1971-73; Carnegie-Mellon University, vice-president, 1973—. *Member:* Operations Research Society, Association for Computing Machinery, Institute of Management Sciences (secretary-treasurer, 1962-65).

WRITINGS: (With R. H. Gregory) *Automatic Data-Processing Systems*, Wadsworth, 1960; (with Gregory) *Business Data Processing and Programming*, Wadsworth, 1963; (editor with C. Kriebel and T. Heames) *Management Information Systems*, Carnegie Press, 1971. Department editor of *Management Science*, 1960-74; member of editorial board of *European Business*.

* * *

VAN KLEEK, Peter Eric 1929-

PERSONAL: Born March 15, 1929, in St. Petersburg, Fla.; son of John R. (a golf course designer) and Joan Miller (a restaurant owner; maiden name, Hill) Van Kleek; married Barbara Jane King, June 12, 1954; children: Laura, Jennifer, Erica. *Education:* Cornell University, B.S., 1955. *Politics:* Republican. *Religion:* Episcopal. *Address:* Route 2, Wellsville, N.Y. 14895. *Office:* Vocational Division of State University of New York at Alfred, Wellsville, N.Y. 14895.

CAREER: Baringe Hotels, Charlotte, N.C., vice-president and general manager, 1959-63; general manager of Jack Tar Hotels in Asheville and Winston Salem, N.C., and Baton Rouge, La., 1963-65; Mimosa Inn, Tryon, N.C., owner and manager, 1964-66; State University of New York at Alfred, assistant professor of food service, 1966—. *Military service:* U.S. Army, 1950-52; served in Italy; became sergeant. *Member:* Food Service Executives Association, Council on Hotel, Restaurant, and Institutional Education, Cornell Society of Hotel Management, Rotary Club.

WRITINGS: Anthology of Vegetable Cooking, Community Colleges of North Carolina, 1964; *Menu Planning*, McGraw, 1973; *Cooking with Pride*, MSS Educational Publishing, 1973.

WORK IN PROGRESS: Gourmet Planning for a Profit.

AVOCATIONAL INTERESTS: Farming.

* * *

VAN OSDOL, William R(ay) 1927-

PERSONAL: Born December 22, 1927, in Oklahoma; son of Ralph R. and Lovest H. (Stover) Van Osdol; married Beverly D. Davies, March 8, 1950; children: Kelly, Scott, Chris. *Education:* North Oklahoma Junior College, A.A., 1950; Cumberland University, student, 1950; Central Oklahoma State College, B.A., 1952; Wichita State University, student, 1955-56; University of Oklahoma, M.Ed., 1961, Ph.D., 1964. *Religion:* Protestant. *Home:* 2017 Edgewood, Edmond, Okla. 73034. *Office:* Department of Special Education, Central State University, Edmond, Okla. 73034.

CAREER: General and special education teacher in public schools of Oklahoma, California, and Kansas, 1952-54, 1956-61; employed by Boeing Airplane Co., 1954-56; commercial pilot and flight instructor, 1962-63; Central State University, Edmond, Okla., assistant professor, 1964-67, associate professor, 1967-72, professor of special education, 1972—. Consultant to private schools for the emotionally disturbed. *Military service:* U.S. Navy, 1945-47. *Member:* American Psychological Association, Council for Exceptional Children, Association for Learning Disabilities, Southwestern Psychological Association, Oklahoma Education Association, Oklahoma Psychological Association.

WRITINGS: Putting Your Newspaper to Work, Burgess, 1970; (with Don G. Shane) *Exceptional Children: Psychology Survey,* Kendall-Hunt, 1972; (with Shane and brother, Bob Van Osdol) *Learning Disabilities Manual K-12,* Idaho Research Foundation, 1973; (with Shane) *Introduction to Exceptional Children,* W. C. Brown, 1974; *P.T.K.: Parents, Teachers, Kids,* MSS Information Corp., 1974. Also author of *Categorization of Normal and Subnormal Boys Using Visual Cues,* Montpellier University (France), 1967, and *Teaching Adolescent Schizophrenics in a Hospital Setting,* REDEPSI, Psicologia Clinics (Republic of Panama), 1973.

* * *

van PEURSEN, Cornelius Anthonie 1920-

PERSONAL: Surname rhymes with "person"; born July 8, 1920, in Rotterdam, Netherlands; son of Dirk and Areke Cornelia (Deenik) van Peursen; married Jeanne Marguerite Ueltschi, June 17, 1950; children: Anthonie, Albertine, Jacqueline, Genevieve. *Education:* University of Leiden, D.Phil., 1948. *Religion:* Reformed (Protestant). *Home:*

Witte Singel 34, Leiden, Netherlands. *Office:* Department of Philosophy, University of Leiden, Leiden, Netherlands.

CAREER: Netherlands UNESCO Commission, The Hague, Netherlands, secretary, 1948-50; University of Utrecht, Utrecht, Netherlands, reader in philosophy, 1950-53; University of Groningen, Groningen, Netherlands, professor of philosophy, 1953-60; University of Leiden, Leiden, Netherlands, professor of philosophy, 1960—. Extraordinary professor at Free University of Amsterdam, 1963—; member of Netherlands UNESCO Commission.

WRITINGS: Body, Soul, Spirit: A Survey of the Body-Mind Problem, translation by Hubert H. Hoskins, Oxford University Press, 1966; *Leibniz: A Guide to His Philosophy*, translation by Hoskins, Faber, 1969, Dutton, 1970; *Wirklichkeit als Ereignis* (title means "Reality as Event"), Alber Verlag, 1969; *Ludwig Wittgenstein*, Faber, 1969, Dutton, 1970; *Phenomenology and Analytical Philosophy*, Duquesne University Press, 1972; *Phenomenology and Reality*, translation by Henry J. Koren, Duquesne University Press, 1972; *The Strategy of Culture*, North-Holland Publishing, 1974.

WORK IN PROGRESS: Research on philosophy as a clarification of the position of man in contemporary culture, and on the structure of the sciences related to cultural diversity.

SIDELIGHTS: Van Peursen has lectured in Tokyo, Kyoto, Manila, Delhi, Jakarta, Yogyakarta, Yaounde, Johannesburg, and throughout Europe. His books have been published in German, Indonesian, Spanish, and Polish.

* * *

VAN TINE, Warren R(ussell) 1942-

PERSONAL: Born August 28, 1942, in Philadelphia, Pa.; son of John R. and Jeanne (Cope) Van Tine; married Anne Darling (a researcher in labor relations), August 20, 1966. *Education:* Baldwin-Wallace College, B.A., 1965; Northern Illinois University, M.A., 1967; University of Massachusetts, Ph.D., 1972. *Home:* 1499 Kohr Pl., Columbus, Ohio 43211. *Office:* Department of History, Ohio State University, Columbus, Ohio 43210.

CAREER: Ohio State University, Columbus, assistant professor of history, 1970—.

WRITINGS: The Making of the Labor Bureaucrat, University of Massachusetts Press, 1973.

WORK IN PROGRESS: With Melvyn Dubofsky, *John L. Lewis: A Biography.*

* * *

VAN TUYL, Barbara 1940-

PERSONAL: Surname rhymes with "style"; born November 26, 1940, in Brooklyn, N.Y.; daughter of Edgar Everett (a stockbroker) and Alexandra (a musician; maiden name, Tolkoff) Van Tuyl. *Education:* Attended public schools of Scarsdale, N.Y. *Home address:* P.O. Box 145, Clintondale, N.Y. 12515. *Agent:* Paul R. Reynolds, Inc., 12 East 41st St., New York, N.Y. 10017.

CAREER: Scarsdale National Bank, Scarsdale, N.Y., teller, 1958-59; Lucky Leaf Stable, Port Chester, N.Y., working partner, 1959-62; International Business Machines (IBM), White Plains, N.Y., secretary, 1962-65; Kling Employment Agency, White Plains, N.Y., placement manager, 1965-66; Scarsdale Medical Center, Scarsdale, N.Y., secretary-assistant to doctors, 1966-67; Banbury Cross Riding Club, Rye, N.Y., working partner, 1969-71; writer, 1971—; breeding, training, schooling, showing, and racing horses.

WRITINGS: Select, Buy, Train, and Care For Your Own Horse, Grosset, 1969; (with Patricia H. Johnson) *The Sweet Running Filly* (juvenile), New American Library, 1971; (with Johnson) *A Horse Called Bonnie* (juvenile), New American Library, 1971; (contributor) Richard Glyn, editor, *The World's Finest Horses and Ponies*, Harrap, 1971; *How To Ride and Jump Your Best*, Grosset, 1973; *The Horseman's Handbook*, Prentice-Hall, 1973; *Sunbonnet: Filly of the Year* (juvenile), New American Library, 1973; *Bonnie and the Haunted Farm* (juvenile), New American Library, 1974; *Winning Ways at Horse Shows*, Grosset, 1975; *The Betrayal of Bonnie* (juvenile), New American Library, 1975. Contributor to *American Horseman*. Contributing editor of *Practical Horseman*, 1973—.

WORK IN PROGRESS: Four books with tentative titles, *How To Buy and Sell a Horse* for Scribner, *No Fence Too High: The Story of Good Twist* (biography), *Correcting Horse Problems*, and *Sisters*, fox and hound fiction, completion expected in 1976.

SIDELIGHTS: Barbara Van Tuyl told *CA*: "My life has been dedicated to the extension of my knowledge of horses and to this end I have spent many years working with instructors, trainers, farm managers, veterinarians, farriers, grooms and the like in an effort to learn as much as I could about horses—thoroughbreds in particular. I was fortunate enough to own an American Horse Shows Association high score champion in 1958. This was my first horse and she was purchased by me with my life savings at the time which amounted to $425.00, and in gaining the annual championship in the Green Working Hunter division she had to beat horses worth anywhere from ten to thirty times her own purchase price. Her success story was in part the inspiration for my fiction series for NAL, although another mare I bought from a despicable junk dealer caused me to dream up the final plot for the first of the series. . . . I am on the verge of racing my first home-bred—a filly out of the junk dealer mare—and her training has been a wonderful education for me."

AVOCATIONAL INTERESTS: Dogs, music.

* * *

VAN VLECK, L(loyd) Dale 1933-

PERSONAL: Born June 11, 1933, in Clearwater, Neb.; son of Harold F. (a farmer) and Patricia (Scott) Van Vleck; married Dee O'Connor (a librarian), June 28, 1958; children: Elizabeth Scott, John Patrick. *Education:* University of Nebraska, B.S., 1954, M.S., 1955; Cornell University, Ph.D., 1960. *Home:* 322 Winthrop Dr., Ithaca, N.Y. 14850. *Office:* Department of Animal Science, Cornell University, B-22 Morrison Hall, Ithaca, N.Y. 14850.

CAREER: Cornell University, Ithaca, N.Y., research geneticist, 1960-62, assistant professor, 1962-66, associate professor, 1966-73, professor of animal genetics, 1973—. Visiting professor at University of Nebraska, 1973. *Military service;* U.S. Army, chemical corps, 1955-57; became first lieutenant. *Member:* American Dairy Science Association, American Society of Animal Science, Biometrics Society, Genetics Association of America, American Association for the Advancement of Science, American Institute of Biological Sciences, Sigma Xi, Phi Kappa Phi, Gamma Sigma Delta, Alpha Zeta. *Awards, honors:* American Society of Animal Science breeding and genetics award, 1972; National Association of Animal Breeders award, 1974.

WRITINGS: Notes on Theory and Application of Selection Principles for the Genetic Improvement of Animals, Department of Animal Science, Cornell University, 1972, revised edition, 1974; *Summary of Methods of Estimating Genetic Parameters,* Department of Animal Science, Cornell University, 1972, revised edition, 1973; (with G. H. Schmidt) *Principles of Dairy Science,* W. H. Freeman, 1974; (with H. F. Hintz, J. Warren Evans, and A. Burton) *The Horse* (textbook), W. H. Freeman, 1975; (with Elizabeth Oltenacu) *Introductory Animal Genetics,* W. H. Freeman, in press. Contributor to *Biometrics, Genetics, Journal of Dairy Science, Journal of Animal Science, Animal Production,* and *Genetical Research.* Member of editorial board of American Dairy Science Association, 1966-71, *Theoretical and Applied Genetics,* 1973—, and Springer Verlag, 1973—.

* * *

VARDY, Steven Bela 1936-

PERSONAL: Born July 3, 1936, in Bercel, Hungary; naturalized U.S. citizen; son of Alexander (an architect) and Elizabeth (Kiss) Vardy; married Agnes M. Huszar (an assistant professor of literature), July 14, 1962; children: Attila Nicholas, Zoltan Alexander. *Education:* Western Reserve University, student, 1953-55; John Carroll University, B.S., 1959; Indiana University, M.A., 1961, Ph.D., 1967; graduate study at Kent State University, 1961, and University of Vienna, 1962-63. *Politics:* Independent. *Religion:* Roman Catholic. *Home:* 2617 Beechwood Blvd., Pittsburgh, Pa. 15217. *Office:* Department of History, Duquesne University, Pittsburgh, Pa. 15219.

CAREER: Washburn University, Topeka, Kan., instructor in history, 1963-64; Duquesne University, Pittsburgh, Pa., assistant professor, 1964-67, associate professor, 1967-71, professor of East European and Near Eastern history, 1971—. Visiting scholar at Hungarian Academy of Sciences and University of Budapest, 1969-70. Member of planning committee, ethnic heritage studies of western Pennsylvania, 1971—; vice-president of Hungarian Cultural Foundation, 1973—. *Military service:* Ohio National Guard, 1953-56. U.S. Army Reserve, 1956-61. *Member:* American Historical Association, American Association for the Advancement of Slavic Studies, American Association for the Study of Hungarian History, Hungarian Professional Association (president, 1973—), Arpad Academy of Arts and Sciences (corresponding member). *Awards, honors:* Carnegie Foundation institutional grant, 1967-70; International Research and Exchanges Board faculty fellowship, 1969-70; research grant, American Hungarian Studies Foundation, 1973-74.

WRITINGS: (With D. G. Kosary) *History of the Hungarian Nation*, Danubian Press, 1969; *Magyarsagtudomany az eszak-amerikai egyetemeken es foiskolakon* (title means "Hungarian Studies at North American Colleges and Universities"), Arpad Publishers (Cleveland), 1973; *Hungarian Historiography and the "Geistesgeschichte" School*, Arpad Academy (Cleveland), 1974. Contributor to *Encyclopedia of World Biography*, of articles to professional journals and Hungarian newspapers in Europe and North America, and of poems and fiction to Hungarian periodicals. Member of editorial board, *Hungarian Historical Review*, 1970—, and *Turkish Review*, 1972—.

WORK IN PROGRESS: History and Historians in Hungary; Joseph Eotvos: Political Profile of a Liberal Hungarian Statesman and Thinker; a volume of lyrical poetry in Hungarian; research for a book, *Ottoman Turkish Impact on European Civilization.*

SIDELIGHTS: Vardy speaks German, in addition to Hungarian and English, and has reading competence in French, Turkish, Russian, and Latin.

* * *

VARNALIS, Costas 1884-1974

1884—December 16, 1974; Greek poet, teacher, and holder of the Lenin Peace Prize. Obituaries: *Washington Post*, December 21, 1974; *AB Bookman's Weekly*, February 3, 1975.

* * *

VERNER, Coolie 1917-

PERSONAL: Born April 25, 1917, in Ohio, *Education:* College of William and Mary, A.B. 1937, A.M., 1950; Columbia University, M.A., 1951, Ed.D., 1952. *Office:* Adult Education Research Centre, University of British Columbia, Vancouver, British Columbia V6T 1W5, Canada.

CAREER: Florida State University, Tallahassee, associate professor, 1953-57, professor of adult education, 1957-61; University of British Columbia, Vancouver, professor of adult education, 1961—. *Military service:* U.S. Army, bomb disposal specialist, 1942-47; served in European and Pacific theaters; became captain; received Purple Heart Medal and five battle stars. *Member:* American Sociological Association, Rural Sociological Society, Society for Applied Anthropology, Southern Sociological Society. *Awards, honors:* Fulbright fellowship, 1952-53; award from *Imago Mundi*, 1959; British Council fellowship, 1964; Canada Council fellowships, 1968-69, 1975-76.

WRITINGS: A Further Checklist of the Separate Editions of Jefferson's Notes on the State of Virginia, Bibliographical Society, University of Virginia, 1950; *Recreation for Virginians: A Study of Municipal Recreation*, Virginia Recreation Society, 1950; *Mr. Jefferson Distributes His Notes: A Preliminary Checklist of the First Edition*, New York Public Library, 1952.

(With Lowry Nelson and Charles E. Ramsey) *Community Structure and Change*, Macmillan, 1960; *A Carto-Bibliographical Study of the English Pilot: The Fourth Book with Special Reference to the Charts of Virginia*, University Press of Virginia, 1960; *Adult Education Theory and Method: A Conceptual Scheme for the Identification and Classification of Processes for Adult Education*, Adult Education Association, 1962; (with Alan Booth) *Adult Education*, Center for Applied Research in Education, 1964; *Maps of the Yorktown Campaign, 1780-1781: A Preliminary Checklist of Printed and Manuscript Maps Prior to 1800*, Map Collectors Circle, 1965; (with Frank W. Millerd) *Adult Education and the Adoption of Innovations in the Okanagan Valley*, Department of Agricultural Economics, University of British Columbia, 1966; (with Peter M. Gubbels) *The Adoption or Rejection of Innovations by Dairy Farm Operators in the Lower Fraser Valley*, Agricultural Economics Research Council of Canada, 1967; *Planning and Conducting a Survey: A Case Study, Rural Development Branch*, Department of Forestry and Rural Development (of Canada), 1967; *Smith's Virginia and Its Derivatives: A Carto-Bibliographical Study of the Diffusion of Geographical Knowledge*, Map Collectors Circle, 1968;

(with E. Patrick Alleyne) *The Adoption and Rejection of Innovations by Strawberry Growers in the Lower Fraser Valley* (monograph), Department of Agricultural Economics, University of British Columbia, 1969; (with Alleyne) *Personal Contacts and the Adoption of Innovations* (monograph), Department of Agricultural Economics, University of British Columbia, 1969; *Captain Collins' Coasting Pilot: A Carto-Bibliographical Analysis*, Map Collectors Circle, 1969.

(With Gary Dickinson, Walter Leirman, and Helen Niskala) *The Preparation of Adult Educators: A Selected Review of the Literature Produced in North America*, Adult Education Association (U.S.), 1970; (with Dickinson) *Community Structure and Participation in Adult Education* (monograph), Information Canada, 1971; (with Catherine V. Davison) *Psychological Factors in Adult Learning and Instruction*, Department of Adult Education, Florida State University, 1971; (with Davison) *Physiological Factors in Adult Learning and Instruction*, Department of Adult Education, Florida State University, 1971; *Maps by John Arrowsmith in the Publications of the Royal Geographical Society*, May Collectors Circle, 1971; (with Frances Woodward) *Explorer's Maps of the Canadian Arctic: 1818-1860*, Canadian Cartographer, 1972; (with June Nakamoto) *Continuing Education in the Health Professions*, Capitol Publications, 1973; (with Dickinson) *Education within the Canadian Labour Congress*, Adult Education Research Centre, University of British Columbia, 1973; (with Alexander McGechaen) *Maps in the Parliamentary Papers by the Arrowsmiths: A Finding List*, two volumes, Carta Press, 1973.

Author of bibliographical notes: *Pole's History of Adult Schools: A Facsimile of the 1816 Edition with an Introduction and Bibiographical Notes*, Adult Education Association (of the United States), 1967; *The English Pilot: The Fourth Book*, Theatrum Orbis Terrarum, 1967; (with R. A. Skelton) *The English Pilot: The Third Book*, Theatrum Orbis Terrarum, 1970; *The English Pilot: The Fifth Book*, Theatrum Orbis Terrarum, 1973.

WORK IN PROGRESS: Theory and Method in Adult Education; *An Introduction to Carto-Bibliographical Description.*

* * *

VERNON, (Elda) Louise A(nderson) 1914-

PERSONAL: Born March 6, 1914, in Coquille, Ore.; daughter of Herman Oscar (a teacher and miller) and Elda (Farlow) Anderson; married Cecil Charles Vernon, May 24, 1957 (died April 27, 1972). *Education:* Willamette University, A.B., 1936. *Home:* 4262 Haines Ave., San Jose, Calif. 95123. *Agent:* Georgia Nicholas, Nicholas Literary Agency, 161 Madison Ave., New York, N.Y. 10016.

CAREER: High school English teacher in Cove, Ore., 1936-37, Culver, Ore., 1937-38, Camas Valley, Ore., 1939-40, and Junction City, Ore., 1940-48; Rosicrucian Order (Ancient Mystical Order Rosae Crucis), San Jose, Calif., editorial assistant, 1949-52; employed as secretary, 1954-72. Teacher in Metropolitan Adult Education Program, 1963—. *Awards, honors:* First award for children's book with a Christian message, from National Association of Christian Schools, 1972, for *Ink on His Fingers*.

WRITINGS—Historical fiction for children: *Peter and the Pilgrims*, Review & Herald, 1963; *Strangers in the Land*, Review & Herald, 1964; *The Bible Smuggler*, Herald Press, 1967; *Ink on His Fingers*, Herald Press, 1967; *The Secret Church*, Herald Press, 1967; *Key to the Prison*, Herald Press, 1968; *Night Preacher*, Herald Press, 1969; *The Beggars' Bible*, Herald Press, 1971; *Doctor in Rags*, Herald Press, 1973; *Thunderstorm in Church*, Herald Press, 1974; *A Heart Strangely Warmed*, Herald Press, 1975.

WORK IN PROGRESS: The Man Who Laid an Egg, historical fiction for children, on the life of Erasmus.

AVOCATIONAL INTERESTS: European travel.

* * *

VESENYI, Paul E. 1911-
(Peter Bod)

PERSONAL: Born August 16, 1911, in Budapest, Hungary; son of Eugen (a ministerial counselor) and Clara (Horvath) Vesenyi; married Catherine Farago (an executive secretary), July 14, 1949. *Education:* Pazmany Peter University, Ph.D., 1934; Columbia University, M.S., 1961. *Religion:* Roman Catholic. *Home:* 177 East Hartsdale Ave., Hartsdale, N.Y. 10530. *Office:* Library, Herbert H. Lehman College of the City University of New York, Bronx, N.Y. 10468.

CAREER: City of Budapest, Department of Culture, Budapest, Hungary, executive, 1935-49; Herbert H. Lehman College of the City University of New York, Bronx, N.Y., assistant professor and librarian, 1961—.

WRITINGS: Parlaix Ur Meghivasa (short stories; title means "The Invitation of Mr. Parlaix"), Konyvek, 1944; *European Periodical Literature in the Social Sciences and the Humanities*, Scarecrow, 1969; *An Introduction to Periodical Bibliography*, Pierian, 1974. Author of radio plays. Contributor of a serialized novel, articles, short stories, and reviews to magazines.

WORK IN PROGRESS: Research on methods of bi-lingual subject approach in libraries serving bi-lingual communities.

* * *

VICKERY, Tom Rusk 1935-

PERSONAL: Born December 14, 1935, in Dallas, Tex.; son of Tom R. (a welder) and Lillian (Smith) Vickery; married Sandra Stone (a teacher), June 6, 1959. *Education:* Attended University of Texas, 1953-55; Baylor University, B.A., 1957; Southern Baptist Theological Seminary, B.D., 1960; North Texas State University, M.Ed., 1965; University of Florida, Ed.D., 1967. *Home:* 111 Berkeley Dr., Syracuse, N.Y. 13210. *Office:* School of Education, Syracuse University, 150 Marshall St., Syracuse, N.Y. 13210.

CAREER: High school English teacher in Wichita Falls, Tex., 1961-65; Northwestern University, Evanston, Ill., assistant professor of education and director of research, 1967-69; Syracuse University, Syracuse, N.Y., associate professor of education and chairman of curriculum, 1965—. *Member:* American Educational Research Association, Association for Supervision and Curriculum Development, National Council on Measurement in Education, American Educational Studies Association, Philosophy of Education Society.

WRITINGS: (Editor) *Man and His Environment: The Effects of Pollution on Man*, Syracuse University Press, 1970; (with Robert Diamond and Ed Kelly) *Instructional Development in Higher Education*, Educational Technology Press, in press.

WORK IN PROGRESS: Exploring the reasons for curriculum failure, especially those failures resulting from organizational, conceptual, and training characteristics.

* * *

VIERECK, Ellen K. 1928-

PERSONAL: Born May 4, 1928 in Brookline, Mass.; daughter of Frederick Stillman (an architect) and Felicia (an architect; maiden name, Doughty) Viereck; married Phillip Viereck (an elementary school principal and children's book author), December 28, 1948; children: Jennifer Olaranna, Timothy Doughty, Pamela Neagus, Margaret Ann. *Education:* Vassar College, B.A., 1949; Plymouth State College, M.Ed., 1957. *Politics:* Democrat-Independent. *Religion:* Unitarian-Universalist. *Home address:* RFD 2, North Bennington, Vt. 05257. *Office:* Molly Stark School, Willow Rd., North Bennington, Vt. 05201.

CAREER: Has held positions as teacher at Bennington College Nursery School, Bennington, Vt., and with Alaska Native Service, King Island, Alaska, and as activity director at Pine Cobble School, Williamstown, Mass.; Bennington School District, Bennington, Vt., teacher of disabled children, 1969—. *Member:* National Education Association (life member), Vermont Education Association, Vermont Council on Reading, Elementary-Kindergarten-Nursery Educators Association, Vermont Association for Learning Disabled, Common Cause, United States Combined Training Association, United States Pony Club. *Awards, honors:* Honorable mention for illustrations, 1968, for *The New Land.*

WRITINGS—Illustrator of children's books by husband, Phillip Viereck; all published by John Day: *Eskimo Island*, 1962; *Independence Must Be Won*, 1964; *The Summer I Was Lost*, 1965; *The New Land*, 1967; *Let Me Tell You about My Dad*, 1971.

Illustrator: Irving Adler, *Groups in the New Mathematics*, John Day, 1967; Olive W. Burt, *The National Road*, John Day, 1968; Irving Adler and Ruth Adler, *Directions and Angles*, John Day, 1969; Irving Adler and Ruth Adler, *Energy*, John Day, 1970.

SIDELIGHTS: Ellen Viereck writes: "Teaching Eskimos led to the writing of our first book, written for them and still in use in some Alaskan schools (it also fulfilled project requirements for M.Ed. degree)." *Avocational interests:* New England and U.S. history, horses, and cross-country skiing.

* * *

VIERTEL, Janet 1915-

PERSONAL: Surname is pronounced *Veer*-tell; born August 4, 1915, in Newark, N.J.; daughter of Albert Eugene (a physician) and Hilda (a real estate broker; maiden name, Isaacs) Man; married Joseph Maurice Viertel (in real estate and a novelist), September 13, 1939; children: Thomas, Alice Viertel Krieger, John. *Education:* Attended New York University, 1932-37. *Home address:* Box 3081, Christiansted, St. Croix, Virgin Islands 00820. *Alternate address:* 275 Dogwood Lane, Stamford, Conn. 06903.

CAREER: R. H. Macy, New York, N.Y., saleswoman and model, 1937-38; Limited Editions Book Club, New York, general office work, 1938-39; photographer and writer. *Member:* American Society of Photographers in Communication, Connecticut League of Women Voters (director), Stamford League of Women Voters (president).

WRITINGS: Undersea Garden of the Virgin Islands, Dukane Press, 1969; (photographer and author) *Blue Planet: Man's Hopes for Life in the Sea*, edited by Alice Beaton Thompson (for high school students), Grosset, 1973.

WORK IN PROGRESS: Underwater Holidays (tentative title) for Grosset.

AVOCATIONAL INTERESTS: Travel (Africa, Europe, including Russia, the Caribbean).

* * *

VIESSMAN, Warren, Jr. 1930-

PERSONAL: Surname is pronounced *Vees*-man; born November 9, 1930, in Baltimore, Md.; son of Warren (an engineer) and Helen B. (a teacher; maiden name, Berlincke) Viessman; children: Wendy, Stephen, Suzanne, Michael, Thomas, Sandra. *Education:* Johns Hopkins University, B.E., 1952, M.S.E., 1958, D. Eng., 1961. *Home:* 2620 South 70th St., Apt. 107, Lincoln, Neb. 68506. *Office:* Nebraska Water Resources Research Institute, University of Nebraska, Lincoln, Neb. 68503.

CAREER: University of Nebraska, Water Resources Research Institute, Lincoln, director, 1968—. Executive secretary of Universities Council on Water Resources. *Military service:* U.S. Army, 1952-54; became first lieutenant. *Member:* Society of Civil Engineers, American Water Works Association, American Water Resources Association, American Geophysical Union, Water Pollution Control Federation, American Society of Agricultural Engineers, National Society of Professional Engineers, Society of Xi.

WRITINGS: Water Supply and Pollution Control, Intext, 1965; *Introduction to Hydrology*, Intext, 1972. Contributor to proceedings; contributor to *Water Resources Bulletin*, *Water Resources Research*, and *Public Works*.

WORK IN PROGRESS: A text book on environmental systems; research on analysis of complex water resources systems.

* * *

VIKIS-FREIBERGS, Vaira 1937-

PERSONAL: Maiden name is pronounced *Vee*-kiss; born December 1, 1937, in Riga, Latvia; naturalized Canadian citizen; daughter of Karlis (a seaman) and Annemarie (Rankis) Vikis; married Imants F. Freibergs (a professor of computer science), July 16, 1960; children: Karl, Indra. *Education:* University of Toronto, B.A., 1958, M.A., 1960; McGill University, Ph.D., 1965. *Religion:* Evangelical Lutheran. *Office:* Department of Psychology, University of Montreal, C.P. 6128, Montreal, Quebec, Canada.

CAREER: Toronto Psychiatric Hospital, Toronto, Ontario, clinical psychologist in Outpatients Clinic, 1960-61; University of Montreal, Montreal, Quebec, assistant professor, 1965-72, associate professor of psychology, 1972—. Has conducted educational work in Latvian communities in Canada and the United States. *Member:* Canadian Psychological Association, Association Canadienne-Francaise pour l'Avancement des Sciences, American Psychological Association, Association for the Advancement of Baltic Studies, Sigma Xi. *Awards, honors:* Fellowship from Canadian Council of Arts, 1974-75.

WRITINGS: Frequence d'usage des mots au Quebec: Etude psycholinguistique d'un echantillon de la region montrealaise (title means "Word Frequency in Quebec French: Analysis of a Sample from the Montreal Area"), Presses de l'Universite de Montreal, 1974. Contributor to professional journals, including *Canadian Journal of Psychology*, *Psychopharmacologia*, *Journal of Abnormal Psychology*, and *Psychological Review*. Associate editor of folklore for *Journal of Baltic Studies*.

WORK IN PROGRESS: The Prodigal Sun: An Analysis of Semantic and Metaphorical Structure, a structural analysis of poetic imagery and associative networks in a computer-accessible corpus of Latvian folk-songs about the Sun.

SIDELIGHTS: Vaira Vikis-Freibergs writes: "The work on the sun-songs will allow me to combine interests in poetry, linguistics and experimental psychology. It will hopefully give English-speaking readers some idea about the richness of Latvian folklore, and provide new translated material to students of Indo-European mythology."

* * *

VILLIARD, Paul 1910-1974
(J. H. deGros)

January 16, 1910—August 18, 1974; American photographer and author of several books of nonfiction and books for children. Obituaries: *New York Times*, August 24, 1974. (*CA*-25/28).

* * *

VOGEL, Steven 1940-

PERSONAL: Born April 7, 1940, in Beacon, N.Y.; son of Max (a pharmacist) and Jeanette (Zucker) Vogel; married Mariette Booth, June 3, 1963 (divorced, January, 1974); married Jane G. McKean, December 13, 1974; children: (first marriage) Roger Booth. *Education:* Tufts University, B.S., 1961; Harvard University, A.M., 1963, Ph.D., 1966. *Politics:* Non-doctrinaire liberal. *Religion:* Jewish. *Home:* 1212 Woodburn Rd., Durham, N.C. 27705. *Office:* Department of Zoology, Duke University, Durham, N.C. 27706.

CAREER: Tufts University, Medford, Mass., instructor in biology, 1962; Duke University, Durham, N.C., assistant professor, 1966-71, associate professor of zoology, 1971—. Instructor at Marine Biological Laboratory, Woods Hole, Mass., 1972. *Awards, honors:* Woodrow Wilson fellow, 1961.

WRITINGS: (With S. A. Wainwright) *A Functional Bestiary: Laboratory Studies about Living Systems*, Addison-Wesley, 1969; (with K. C. Ewel) *A Model Menagerie: Laboratory Studies about Living Systems*, Addison-Wesley, 1972. Contributor to biological journals.

WORK IN PROGRESS: A book concerning bases and applications of fluid mechanics in biology; research on ways in which organisms utilize environmental velocity gradients.

* * *

VOLKER, Roger 1934-

PERSONAL: Born November 3, 1934, in Chicago, Ill.; son of Paul and Clarabel (Rinehimer) Volker; married Carol Bennett, 1957; children: Paul, Christopher, Timothy. *Education:* Iowa State University, B.S., 1956, M.S., 1963, Ph.D., 1970. *Religion:* Methodist. *Home:* 215 Ninth St., Ames, Iowa 50010. *Office:* Instructional Resources Center, 321 Curtiss Hall, Iowa State University, Ames, Iowa 50010.

CAREER: Iowa State University, Ames, assistant professor, 1967-71, associate professor of education, 1971—, director of Instructional Resources Center, 1967—. *Military service:* U.S. Army National Guard, 1956-62. *Member:* Association for Educational Communications and Technology, Phi Delta Kappa, Phi Mu Alpha, Pi Kappa Alpha, Kiwanis.

WRITINGS: Creative Biology Teaching, Iowa State University Press, 1969; *Foundations of Life Science*, Holt, 1972; *Media for Teachers*, Kendall-Hunt, 1972.

AVOCATIONAL INTERESTS: Music, woodworking, restoring antique automobiles.

* * *

von BLOCK, Sylvia 1931-
(Beverly Beaumont, Theodore Clifford, Caroline Hennessey, Gordon Randolph, W. D. Sprague; Ilya Chambertin, joint pseudonym)

PERSONAL: Born July 20, 1931, in Brooklyn, N.Y.; daughter of Jacob and Golda (Gertzis) Guttenplan; married Bela W. von Block (a writer), December 31, 1952. *Education:* Attended public schools in Brooklyn, N.Y. *Home and office:* San Severo 5013, Venice, Italy.

CAREER: American Museum of Natural History, New York, N.Y., assistant in department of archaeology, 1946-48; dental assistant in New York, N.Y., 1949-50; American Can Co., New York, N.Y., assistant in purchasing department, 1951-53. Free-lance writer and editor.

WRITINGS: (With husband, Bela von Block) *Super-Detective*, Playboy Press, 1973.

Under pseudonym Beverly Beaumont: *Young Stallions*, Midwood, 1969.

Under pseudonym Theodore Clifford: *Crash and the Cannibal*, Lancer Books, 1970.

Under pseudonym Caroline Hennessey: *I, Bitch*, Lancer Books, 1970; *Strategy of Sexual Struggle*, Lancer Books, 1971.

Under pseudonym Gordon Randolph: *Beyond Yoga*, Lancer Books, 1973.

Under pseudonym W. D. Sprague: *Case Histories from the Communes*, Lancer Books, 1972.

With Bela von Block, under joint pseudonym Ilya Chambertin; all published by Lancer Books: *Astro-Analysis*, 1970; *How to Get What You Want Out of Life Through Astrology*, 1970; *How to Meet and Keep Your Man Through Astrology*, 1971; *Personal Astrology: Your Star Guide to Love and Romance*, 1971; *Encyclopedia of Astrology*, 1972.

SIDELIGHTS: Mrs. von Block told *CA*: "I speak Italian and Yiddish fluently; some German and a modicum of Hungarian. . . .I am a strong advocate of Fem Lib (and was, long before it became a popular issue)." *Avocational interests:* Travel, amateur archaeology, Italian Renaissance literature, sexual behavior and aberrations, cooking, breeding French poodles.

* * *

WADDELL, Evelyn Margaret 1918-
(Lyn Cook)

PERSONAL: Born May 4, 1918, in Weston, Ontario, Canada; daughter of Edward Frank and Emma (Crawford) Cook; married Robb John Waddell, September 19, 1949;

children: Christopher Robb, Deborah Lyn. *Education:* University of Toronto, B.A. (honors), 1940, B.L.S., 1941. *Home:* 72 Cedarbrae Blvd., Scarborough, Ontario M1J 2K5, Canada. *Agent:* Scargall of Markham, 1 Talisman Cres., Markham, Ontario L3P 2C8, Canada.

CAREER: Librarian in public libraries in Toronto, Ontario, 1941-42; Sudbury Public Library, Sudbury, Ontario, children's librarian, 1946-47; Canadian Broadcasting Corp. (CBC), Toronto, Ontario, script writer, director, and narrator of children's show "A Doorway in Fairyland," 1947-52. Teacher of creative drama to children for New Play Society Theatre School, 1956-65. Conducts story-telling and creative drama group for pre-school children in a branch of Scarborough Public Libraries. *Military service:* Royal Canadian Air Force, Women's Division, meteorological observer, 1942-46; received Canada Service Medal.

WRITINGS—Books for nine-to-twelve-year-old children, all under name Lyn Cook: *The Bells on Finland Street*, Macmillan, 1950; *The Little Magic Fiddler*, Macmillan, 1951; *Rebel on the Trail*, Macmillan, 1953; *Jady and the General*, Macmillan (Toronto), 1955, St. Martin's, 1956; *Pegeen and the Pilgrim*, St. Martin's, 1957; *The Road to Kip's Cove*, Macmillan (Toronto), 1961, St. Martin's, 1962; *Samantha's Secret Room*, Macmillan (Toronto), 1963, St. Martin's, 1964; *The Brownie Handbook for Canada*, Girl Guide Association of Canada, 1965; *The Secret of Willow Castle*, Macmillan, 1966; *The Magical Miss Mittens*, Macmillan, 1974.

Picture-story books; under name Lyn Cook: *Toys from the Sky*, Clarke, Irwin, 1972; *Jolly Jean-Pierre*, Burns & MacEachern, 1973; *If I Were All These*, Burns & MacEachern, 1974. Writer for "Sounds Fun," a radio series for Canadian Broadcasting Corp., and "The Mystery Makers Makers," a television series for Canadian Broadcasting Corp., 1967.

WORK IN PROGRESS: Two novels for ten- to twelve-year-old readers, one set in the French River area of Ontario, and the other set in the Ottawa Valley; several picture-story books.

SIDELIGHTS: Lyn Waddell writes: "I feel strongly that novels have a great role to play in a child's development, helping him to adventure freely in the realm of emotions, and exercising and strengthening the imaginative faculty with which he was endowed and which can, as the years go by, illumine every area of his life."

All of Mrs. Waddell's books were published in Canada before they were published elsewhere. *The Bells on Finland Street* has also been published in a German edition in Switzerland.

BIOGRAPHICAL/CRITICAL SOURCES: In Review, spring, 1967; *Quill and Quire*, October 24, 1969; *Index*, May, 1970; Irma McDonough, editor, *Profiles*, Canadian Library Association, 1971; Virginia Davis, editor, *Connections, Writers and the Land*, Manitoba School Library Audio-Visual Association (Winnipeg), 1974.

* * *

WADDINGTON, Raymond B(ruce) 1935-

PERSONAL: Born September 27, 1935, in Santa Barbara, Calif.; son of Raymond Bruce, Sr. and Marjorie (Waddell) Waddington; married Linda Jones (a social worker), September 7, 1957; children: Raymond Bruce III, Edward Jackson. *Education:* Stanford University, B.A., 1957; Rice University, Ph.D., 1963; Johns Hopkins University, postdoctoral study, 1965-66. *Home:* 4010 Paunack Ave., Madison, Wis. 53711. *Office:* Department of English, University of Wisconsin, 600 North Park St., Madison, Wis. 53706.

CAREER: University of Houston, Houston, Tex., instructor in English, 1961-62; University of Kansas, Lawrence, assistant professor of English, 1962-65; University of Wisconsin-Madison, 1966—, began as assistant professor, now professor of English. *Member:* Modern Language Association of America, Milton Society of America, Logos, Friends of Bemerton. *Awards, honors:* American Philosophical Society grant, 1965; Samuel S. Fels postdoctoral fellowship in humanities, at Johns Hopkins University, 1965-66; Huntington Library summer fellowship, 1967; fellowship from Institute for Research in the Humanities at University of Wisconsin, 1971-72; Guggenheim fellowship, 1972-73.

WRITINGS: (Contributor) J. A. Wittreich, editor, *Calm of Mind*, Press of Case Western Reserve University, 1971; (editor with Thomas O. Sloan) *The Rhetoric of Renaissance Poetry from Wyatt to Milton*, University of California Press, 1974; *The Mind's Empire: Myth and Form in George Chapman's Narrative Poems*, Johns Hopkins Press, 1974. Contributor to language and literature journals, including *Modern Philology*, *Journal of Medieval and Renaissance Studies*, *Journal of the Warburg and Courtauld Institutes*, *PMLA*, *Review of English Studies*, *Shakespeare Studies*, *New Mexico Quarterly*, and *Texas Studies in Language and Literature*. Member of editorial board of *Literary Monographs* and *Sixteenth Century Journal*.

WORK IN PROGRESS: A book on Shakespeare's sonnets; editing a book on the contexts of Milton's thought, with C. A. Patrides; further research on Shakespeare, Milton, and George Herbert.

AVOCATIONAL INTERESTS: Renaissance art and iconography, history of ideas, travel (England, France, Italy, Spain).

* * *

WADE, Jerry L(ee) 1941-

PERSONAL: Born January 29, 1941, in Mason City, Iowa; son of Joe Anderson (a factory worker and farmer) and Ruth (Liptrap) Wade; married Mary Kay Edgington (an environmental education planner), May 13, 1965; children: Kimberly Sue. *Education:* University of South Dakota, student, 1958-63; University of Missouri, B.A., 1964, M.A., 1967, further graduate study, 1968-72. *Home:* 22 Downing Dr., Chatham, Ill. 62629. *Office:* Environments and People Program, Sangamon State University, Springfield, Ill. 62708.

CAREER: Ironworker in Kansas City, Mo., 1961-70; Howard County Human Development Corp., Fayette, Mo., executive director, 1966-67; Sangamon State University, Springfield, Ill., assistant professor of sociology, 1972—. *Member:* American Sociological Association, Rural Sociological Society, National Association for Environmental Education, American Associaton for the Advancement of Science, Midwest Sociological Society, Illinois Association for Environmental Education.

WRITINGS: (With Rex R. Campbell) *Society and Environment: The Coming Collision*, Allyn & Bacon, 1972.

WORK IN PROGRESS: Research on interdisciplinary environmental education with emphasis on the meaning of human society as integral part of the on-going dynamics of ecosystems; research on political, social, economic, ethical, philosophical, and social change implications of society within ecosystems as ways of addressing environmental concerns, with a book expected to result.

SIDELIGHTS: Wade writes: "The human experiment is probably in a major transition stage. The patterns and forms of our social, political, and economic responses to the major questions facing the world society (human dignity and decency, population, natural resource use, and nature of warfare) will be the crucial factors determining what the transition is toward. The challenge is the creative development of adequate responses, since many of the patterns and forms of the present are out-moded for today's world, as, for example, the nation-state as the dominant form of international political organization."

* * *

WAEHRER, Helen (Youngelson) 1938-

PERSONAL: Surname rhymes with "bearer"; born February 23, 1938, in New York, N.Y.; daughter of Alex (a taxicab driver) and Lillian (Wiseman) Youngelson; married Edgar Waehrer (an architect), November 25, 1962; children: Keith, Christopher. *Education:* City College (now City College of the City University of New York), B.A., 1958; Columbia University, Ph.D., 1966. *Home:* 3480 Northwest Raleigh St., Portland, Ore. 97210. *Office:* Department of Economics, Portland State University, P.O. Box 751, Portland, Ore. 97207

CAREER: City College of the City University of New York, New York, N.Y., lecturer in economics, 1959-63, 1966; New York University, New York, N.Y., lecturer in economics, 1966; Portland State University, Portland, Ore., assistant professor, 1967-72, associate professor of economics, 1972—. Lecturer at Reed College, 1973. Member of Oregon Council for Women's Equality; member of board of directors of Portland Young Women's Christian Association (YWCA), 1972—. *Member:* American Economic Association, Association of Evolutionary Economists, Western Economic Association, League of Women Voters (Portland), Phi Beta Kappa.

WRITINGS: (Contributor) Peter B. Kenen and Roger Laurence, editors, *The Open Economy*, Columbia University Press, 1968; (editor with Nona Glazer-Malbin) *Women in a Man-Made World*, Rand McNally, 1972; (author of student exercise book) Kevin Lancaster, *Modern Economics*, Rand McNally, 1973.

* * *

WAGNER, Helmut R(udolf) 1904-

PERSONAL: Born August 5, 1904, in Dresden, Germany; naturalized U.S. citizen; son of Rudolf Richard and Olga (Fischer) Wagner; married Hannelore Joseph, July 16, 1951; children: Claire Marianne. *Education:* New School for Social Research, Ph.D., 1955. *Home:* 401 West High St., Geneva, N.Y. 14456. *Office:* Department of Anthropology and Sociology, Hobart and William Smith Colleges, Geneva, N.Y. 14456.

CAREER: Adult Education System, Thuringia Region, Germany, lecturer, 1925-33; has held various technical positions in Switzerland, 1934-41, and in the United States, 1941-49; New School for Social Research, New York, N.Y., lecturer in sociology, 1952-56; Bucknell University, Lewisburg, Pa., assistant professor, 1956-58, associate professor, 1958-62, professor of sociology, 1962-64; Hobart and William Smith Colleges, Geneva, N.Y., professor of sociology, 1964—, chairman of department of anthropology and sociology. Research sociologist for Institute for World Affairs, 1953-56. *Member:* American Sociological Association, Society for the Scientific Study of Religion, Society for Phenomenology and Existential Philosophy, Eastern Sociological Society, Central Sociological Association, Pennsylvania Sociological Society (president, 1963-64).

WRITINGS: (Contributor) Milton L. Barron, editor, *Contemporary Sociology*, Dodd, 1964; (editor) *Alfred Schutz on Phenomenology and Social Relations*, University of Chicago Press, 1970, revised edition, 1973; (contributor) George Psathas, editor, *Phenomenological Sociology: Issues and Applications*, Wiley, 1973; (contributor) R. Serge Denisoff and others, editors, *Theories and Paradigms in Contemporary Sociology*, F. E. Peacock, 1974. Contributor of more than twenty-five articles to sociological journals.

WORK IN PROGRESS: *Alfred Schutz: An Intellectual Biography*, for University of Chicago Press, completion expected in 1975; *German Phenomenology and American Sociology: A Cross-Cultural Synthesis*; *Phenomenology and History: Edmund Husserl and the Historicity of Philosophy*.

SIDELIGHTS: Wagner writes: "Having studied with Professor Carl Mayer, a foremost expert on Max Weber, and with Professor Alfred Schutz, who worked out a synthesis between Weberian sociology and phenomenology, my own orientation and active field of inquiry is that of a sociology of understanding and, in particular, that of the development of what during the last six years has become known and recognized as phenomenological sociology.

"Such substantive areas as the sociology of religion and the sociology of knowledge, which continue to fascinate me, present opportunities for the further testing and expansion of the basic conceptions developed in the areas of Weberian and Schutzean sociology, that is, a sociology utilizing the subjective approach to social phenomena". *Avocational interests:* Long-distance running, watching track and field events.

* * *

WAGNER, Joseph Frederick 1900(?)-1974

1900(?)—October 12, 1974; American composer, conductor, teacher, and author of books on music. Obituaries: *New York Times*, October 25, 1974.

* * *

WAGNER, Kenneth A. 1919-

PERSONAL: Born November 30, 1919, in Union City, Ind.; son of Guy R. (a farmer) and Rose L. (Anderson) Wagner; married Ruth E. Saltsgaver, September 1, 1945; children: Cynthia Zoe. *Education:* DePauw University, A.B., 1941, A.M., 1946; University of Michigan, Ph.D., 1951. *Home:* 1010 Vincent, Big Rapids, Mich. 49307. *Office:* Department of Biology, Ferris State College, Big Rapids, Mich. 49307.

CAREER: Machinist in Union City, Ind., 1941-42; Air Service Command, Dayton, Ohio, junior aircraft maintenance engineer, 1942-44; University of Tennessee, Knoxville, instructor in botany, 1947-49; Florida State University, Tallahassee, assistant professor of botany, 1949-54; Old Dominion College, Norfolk, Va., professor of biology, 1954-59, head of department, 1954-59; Powell Laboratories (of Canadian Biological Supply Co.), Gladstone, Ore., science coordinator, 1959-66; North Carolina Wesleyan College, Rocky Mount, professor of biology, 1966-69; Ferris State College, Big Rapids, Mich., professor of biology, 1969—. Conducted botanical field research in Honduras, summer, 1938, and archaeological studies in Santa Clara, Cuba, summer, 1953; participated in a camping ecology field trip, 1969.

MEMBER: National Wildlife Federation, Smithsonian Institution, Michigan Natural Areas Council. *Awards, honors:* Grant from Office of Naval Research, 1952-53; National Philosophical Society grant, 1953; grant from University of Georgia, 1955; National Science Foundation grants, 1959, 1968, and 1969.

WRITINGS: (With Herman Kurz) *Saltmarshes of the Southeast*, Florida State University, 1957; (with P. C. Bailey) *Introduction to Modern Biology*, Intext Educational Publishing, 1973; (with Bailey and Glenn Campbell) *Under Siege*, Intext Educational Publishing, 1974. Contributor of about twenty-five articles to scientific and popular journals, including *American Photography*, *Mechanix Illustrated*, *Bryologist*, *Ecology*, *American Midland Naturalist*, and *Southwestern Naturalist*.

WORK IN PROGRESS: Revising *Under Siege*; research on salt marshes, desert ecology, and slime molds.

SIDELIGHTS: Wagner feels that "Students must see the error of 'politics for the present'—feeding the starving without population controls can only lead to a much greater suffering in the near future."

* * *

WALDE, Ralph E(ldon) 1943-

PERSONAL: Born March 8, 1943, in Perham, Minn.; son of Robert Frank (a farmer) and Augusta (Berger) Walde; married Constance Ann Johnson, March 7, 1970; children: Emily, Jason. *Education:* University of Minnesota, B.A., 1964; University of California, Berkeley, Ph.D., 1967. *Home:* 132 Newbury, Hartford, Conn. 06114. *Office:* Department of Mathematics, Trinity College, Hartford, Conn. 06106.

CAREER: University of Minnesota, Minneapolis, assistant professor of mathematics, 1967-72; Trinity College, Hartford, Conn., assistant professor of mathametics, 1972—. *Member:* American Mathematical Society, Mathematical Association of America.

WRITINGS: (With Arthur A. Sagle) *Introduction to Lie Groups and Lie Algebras*, Academic Press, 1973.

* * *

WALDEN, John C(layton) 1928-

PERSONAL: Born September 15, 1928, in Clinton, Ill.; son of Carter B. (a welder) and Bernice (a secretary; maiden name, Bell) Walden; married Shirley Butterfield, February 1, 1952; children: Deanne C., Kirk A. *Education:* University of California, Los Angeles, B.A., 1952; California State University, Los Angeles, M.A., 1957; Claremont Graduate School, Ph.D., 1966. *Home:* 132 Carter St., Auburn, Ala. 36830. *Office:* School of Education, Auburn University, Auburn, Ala. 36830.

CAREER: Public school teacher in Redlands, Calif., 1952-53, and Monrovia, Calif., 1953-56, assistant principal in Monrovia, 1956-57, principal of junior high school, 1957-66; Auburn University, Auburn, Ala., assistant professor, 1966-69, associate professor, 1969-73, professor of education, 1973—, chairman of department of educational administration, 1970—. *Military service:* U.S. Navy, 1946-48. *Member:* American Educational Research Association, National Organization on Legal Problems of Education, National Conference on Professors of Educational Administration, American Association of School Administrators, Southern Regional Council on Educational Administration (chairman, 1972-73), Phi Delta Kappa.

WRITINGS: (With W. L. Pharis and L. E. Robison) *Decision Making and Schools for the Seventies*, National Education Association, 1970; (with E. M. Blue) *Desegregation and Superintendent Turnover* (monograph), Auburn University Press, 1970. Author of "Law and the School Principal," a column on school law in *National Elementary Principal*, 1972—. Contributor to *Phi Delta Kappan, Today's Education*, and *Administrator's Notebook*.

WORK IN PROGRESS: A book on governance of school children, with E. T. Ladd, for National Association of Elementary School Principals.

* * *

WALDRON, Ingrid 1939-

PERSONAL: Born December 8, 1939, in Nyack, N.Y.; daughter of Paul Henry (a manager) and Esther (Zachs) Waldron; married Joseph Eyer (a teacher), July 15, 1972; children: Jessie. *Education:* Radcliffe College, A.B., 1961; University of California, Berkeley, Ph.D., 1967. *Office:* Leidy Laboratory, University of Pennsylvania, Philadelphia, Pa. 19174.

CAREER: University of Pennsylvania, Philadelphia, assistant professor, 1968-72, associate professor of biology, 1972—. *Member:* American Association for the Advancement of Science.

WRITINGS: (With Robert E. Ricklefs) *Environment and Population: Problems and Solutions*, Holt, 1973. Contributor to scientific journals.

WORK IN PROGRESS: Research on why death rates are rising for young adults, and on why women live longer than men.

* * *

WALGENBACH, Paul H(enry) 1923-

PERSONAL: Born May 3, 1923, in Peru, Ill.; son of Martin F. and Marie (Haas) Walgenbach. *Education:* Northwestern University, B.B.A., 1948, M.B.A., 1952; University of Illinois, Ph.D., 1958. *Home:* 5010 Milward Dr., Madison, Wis. 53711. *Office:* Graduate School of Business, University of Wisconsin, 1155 Observatory Dr., Madison, Wis. 53706.

CAREER: Martin, Johnson & Bolton (certified public accountants), Chicago, Ill., staff accountant, 1948-50; Butler University, Indianapolis, Ind., assistant professor of business, 1950-53; University of Wisconsin, Madison, assistant professor, 1953-58, associate professor, 1958-67, professor of business, 1967—. *Military service:* U.S. Army Air Forces, 1943-46; became first lieutenant. *Member:* American Institute of Certified Public Accountants, American Accounting Association (secretary-treasurer, 1960-63), Wisconsin Institute of Certified Public Accountants, Delta Mu Delta, Beta Alpha Psi.

WRITINGS: *Retail Credit and Collection*, University of Wisconsin Extension, 1959; (with N. E. Dittrich) *Accounting: An Introduction*, Harcourt, 1973; *Financial and Managerial Accounting*, Harcourt, in press.

WALKER, Charles R(umford) 1893-1974

July 31, 1893—November 26, 1974; American editor, university official, and author of novels, short stories, and nonfiction. Obituaries: *New York Times*, November 28, 1974; *AB Bookman's Weekly*, December 16, 1974. (*CA*-17/18).

* * *

WALKER, Ethel Valerie 1944-

PERSONAL: Born March 16, 1944, in Liverpool, England; daughter of Reginald John (a schoolmaster) and Ethel (a teacher; maiden name, Glover) Walker; married Elfed Morgan (a dairyman), September 8, 1971; children: Gareth Clynnog, Hefin James. *Education:* University of Nottingham, B.A. (honors), 1966; University of Essex, M.A., 1967. *Religion:* Congregational. *Home:* 7 Maes Henllan, Llandre, Bow St., Dyfed, Wales. *Office:* Department of Political Science, University College of Wales, Aberystwyth, Wales.

CAREER: London Transport, London, England, management trainee, 1967-68; University College of Wales, Aberystwyth, research officer, 1968-71. *Member:* Conservation Society.

WRITINGS: (With P. J. Madgwick and Non Griffiths) *Politics of Rural Wales: A Study of Cardiganshire*, Hutchinson Educational, 1973.

* * *

WALKER, Laurence C(olton) 1924-

PERSONAL: Born September 8, 1924, in Washington, D.C.; son of Hobart Theodore (a printer) and Laura (Johnson) Walker; married Anne Sinclair, June 17, 1948; children: Janet (Mrs. Steven Rhenda), Stephen, Wendy, Jean. *Education:* Pennsylvania State University, B.S.F., 1948; Yale University, M.F., 1949; State University of New York College of Forestry at Syracuse University, Ph.D., 1953. *Politics:* "Ford—man for the present." *Religion:* Presbyterian. *Home:* 514 Millard Dr., Nacogdoches, Tex. 75961. *Office:* School of Forestry, Stephen F. Austin State University, Nacogdoches, Tex. 75961.

CAREER: U.S. Forest Service, San Augustine, Tex., assistant district ranger, 1948-51; U.S. Forest Service, Brewton, Ala., research forester and project leader, 1953-54; University of Georgia, Athens, assistant professor, 1954-56, associate professor of forestry, 1956-63; Stephen F. Austin State University, Nacogdoches, Tex., professor of forestry and dean of School of Forestry, 1963—. *Military service:* U.S. Army, Signal Corps, 1943-46.

MEMBER: Society of American Foresters, Soil Science Society of America, American Forestry Association, American Association for the Advancement of Science (member of council, 1972-73), Texas Forestry Association (director), Deep East Texas Development Association (president, 1974, 1975), Deep East Texas Council of Governments (director), Chamber of Commerce (director), Rotary International, Gideons. *Awards, honors:* Distinguished service award from Society of American Foresters, 1968.

WRITINGS: (Contributor) John Clover Monsma, editor, *The Evidence of God in an Expanding Universe*, Putnam, 1958; (contributor) John W. Barrett, editor, *Regional Silviculture*, Ronald, 1962; (contributor) W. G. Wahlenberg, editor, *Slash and Loblolly Pine Plantation Management in the Southeastern U.S.A.*, Georgia Forestry Research Council, 1965; (contributor) Monsma, editor, *Beyond the Dim Unknown*, Putnam, 1966; *Ecology and Our Forests*, A. S. Barnes, 1972; *Reporting Technical Information*, Kendall-Hunt, 1973.

Contributor of about a hundred fifty articles to technical and popular journals, including *Texas Farmer-Stockman*, *American Forests*, *Journal of Forestry*, *Consultant*, *Forest Science*, and *Presbyterian Journal*.

WORK IN PROGRESS: Axes, Oxen, and Men: A Pictorial Account of the Early Days of the Southern Pine Lumber Company; *The Southern Forest*.

SIDELIGHTS: Walker writes: "I'm a practical forester, because I was reared in the tar and mortar in the middle of a big city. I'm still running from the city, though the trail took me through a research detour with government on the way to academia. Too long from the laboratory, my writing is now mostly to tell laymen what professionals tell professionals. I do a little philosophic writing about Christian theology. Although all my schooling is Yankee, all my professional employment as a forester has been [in the] South."

* * *

WALKER, Lawrence David 1931-

PERSONAL: Born October 4, 1931, in Las Animas, Colo.; son of Edward Robert (an electrician and realtor) and Annie Frances (Leonard) Walker; married Billie Barlow (a registered nurse), December 18, 1954; children: Lawrence Arthur, Gregory Anthony. *Education:* Pueblo Junior College, A.A., 1950; Stanford University, A.B. (with great distinction), 1953, M.A., 1957; graduate study at San Diego State College (now University), 1955-56; University of California, Berkeley, Ph.D., 1964. *Home:* 407 South Linden, Normal, Ill. 61761. *Office:* Department of History, Illinois State University, Normal, Ill. 61761.

CAREER: Stanford University, Stanford, Calif., instructor in western civilization, 1961-63; University of Southern Calif., Los Angeles, assistant professor of history, 1964-69; Illinois State University, Normal, associate professor of history, 1969—. *Member:* American Historical Association. *Awards, honors:* Younger Humanist fellowship in Munster, Germany, from National Endowment for the Humanities, 1971-72.

WRITINGS: Hitler Youth and Catholic Youth, 1933-36: A Study in Totalitarian Conquest, Catholic University of America Press, 1971. Contributor to *Revue d'histoire de la deuxieme guerre mondiale*.

WORK IN PROGRESS: Research on the German and Austrian youth movements.

AVOCATIONAL INTERESTS: Psychology.

* * *

WALKER, Robert Newton 1911-

PERSONAL: Born November 2, 1911, in Johnstown, Pa.; son of Charles E. (a clerk) and Minnie (Woy) Walker; married Dorothy E. Schultz, 1934; children: Marilyn, Virginia, Thomas. *Education:* University of Pittsburgh, student, 1929-31, M.Ed., 1937; University of Virginia, B.S.Ed., 1933, Ph.D., 1939. *Politics:* Republican. *Religion:* Lutheran. *Home:* 2605 Chimney Rock, Huntsville, Tex. 77340. *Office:* Sam Houston State University, Huntsville, Tex. 77340.

CAREER: High school teacher of English and government

in Johnstown, Pa., 1933-37; Wilson College, Chambersburg, Pa., assistant professor of education, 1939-41; West Chester State College, West Chester, Pa., professor of education, 1946-51; American University, Washington, D.C., adjunct professor of education, 1951-68; Eastern Kentucky State University, Richmond, professor of psychology, 1968-69; American University, adjunct professor of criminal justice, 1969-70; Sam Houston State University, Huntsville, Tex., professor of sociology, 1970-72, professor of criminal justice, 1972—. Research analyst for U.S. Department of the Army, Medical Department, 1951-63; research consultant to International Association of Chiefs of Police, 1966-68. *Military service:* U.S. Army, Intelligence Corps and Medical Corps, 1941-46; served as liaison officer between Generals Eisenhower and DeGaulle, 1942-43; received Medaille de la Reconnaisance Francaise. U.S. Army Reserve, 1931-72; became lieutenant colonel. *Member:* American Psychological Association, American Correctional Association, Masons.

WRITINGS: (With Nelson A. Watson) *Police Work with Juveniles* (booklet), International Association of Chiefs of Police, 1966; *Psychology of the Youthful Offender*, C. C Thomas, 1972, 2nd edition, 1973. Author of classified material for U.S. Army, published by U.S. Government Printing Office, 1951-63. Contributor to *Police Chief*. Book reviewer for *Army* (magazine), 1950-64.

WORK IN PROGRESS: Psychology for Law Enforcement and Corrections Officers.

SIDELIGHTS: Walker knows French, German, Russian, and Spanish, and has traveled widely throughout the world.

* * *

WALL, Michael Morris 1942-
(Mike Wall)

PERSONAL: Born October 20, 1942, in Slaton, Tex.; son of Guy Pascal (an employee on a cattle feed lot) and Berniece Julia (a cook in a cafeteria; maiden name, Behlen) Wall; married Karen McKenzie, August 28, 1965 (divorced April 25, 1970); children: David Michael, Patrick Lawrence. *Education:* Texas Tech University, student, 1961-65. *Politics:* Democrat. *Home:* 1604 Milwaukee St., Plainview, Tex. 79072. *Office:* Office of J. E. Laney, State Capitol Building, Austin, Tex. 78767.

CAREER: Olton Enterprise, Olton, Tex., and *Hart Beat*, Hart, Tex., news editor, 1965-66, editor-publisher, 1966-67; *Levelland Daily Sun-News*, Levelland, Tex., editor, 1966; *Plainview Daily Herald*, Plainview, Tex., reporter and photographer, 1967-72, news editor, 1972-74; administrative aide to Texas State Representative J. E. Laney in Austin, 1974—. Member of boards of directors of Olton Chamber of Commerce, 1966-67, and of American Red Cross, Hale County (Tex.) chapter. *Awards, honors:* Writing award from Texas Railroad Association, 1967, for feature story and photographs in *Olton Enterprise* and *Hart Beat*.

WRITINGS: (Under name Mike Wall) *Wooden Sails: A Collection of Poetry and Photography*, Nortex Press, 1974.

WORK IN PROGRESS: Bittersweet Echoes, a collection of poems; a novel on neurological social change.

AVOCATIONAL INTERESTS: Playing the guitar.

* * *

WALTERS, Stanley D(avid) 1931-

PERSONAL: Born July 30, 1931, in Lawrence, Kan.; son of Orville S. (a psychiatrist) and Geneva F. (Faley) Walters; married Adrienne R. Swallow (a teacher), August 13, 1955; children: David Stewart, Constance Ruth. *Education:* Greenville College, A.B., 1952; Asbury Theological Seminary, B.D., 1955; Princeton Theological Seminary, Th.M., 1960; Yale University, Ph.D., 1962. *Politics:* Independent. *Religion:* Christian. *Home:* 1321 East Chippewa St., Mt. Pleasant, Mich. 48858. *Office:* Anspach Hall 103, Central Michigan University, Mt. Pleasant, Mich. 48859.

CAREER: Greenville College, Greenville, Ill., assistant professor, 1961-63, associate professor, 1963-67, professor of religion, 1967-68; Central Michigan University, Mt. Pleasant, professor of religion, 1970—. Research fellow of Institute for Advanced Christian Studies, 1968-70. *Member:* Society of Biblical Literature.

WRITINGS: Exodus-Numbers: A Study Guide, Light and Life Press, 1961; *Water for Larsa*, Yale University Press, 1970.

WORK IN PROGRESS: Critical commentary on the Hebrew books of Samuel; a study of religion in the ancient Near East.

* * *

WALTON, H(enry) J(ohn) 1924-

PERSONAL: Born February 2, 1924, in South Africa; married Sula Wolff. *Education:* University of Capetown, M.B., Ch.B., 1946, M.D., 1954; University of London, diploma in psychological medicine, 1956; Royal College of Physicians, London, diploma in psychological medicine, 1956; University of Edinburgh, Ph.D., 1966; Royal College of Physicians, Edinburgh, F.R.C.P., 1968. *Office:* Department of Psychiatry, Royal Edinburgh Hospital, Morningside Park, Edinburgh EH10 5HF, Scotland.

CAREER: Groote Schuur Hospital, Capetown, South Africa, resident physician, 1946-48; Maudsley Hospital, London, England, registrar, 1955-57, senior registrar, 1957; Groote Schuur Hospital, head of department of phychiatry, 1957-60; Columbia University, New York, N.Y., research fellow, 1960-61; University of Edinburgh, Edinburgh, Scotland, 1962—, began as senior lecturer, now professor of psychiatry, head of department, and consultant psychiatrist at Royal Edinburgh Hospital. Senior lecturer, University of Capetown; consultant to department of psychiatry at Western General Hospital, Edinburgh. *Member:* Association for Medical Education in Europe (president), Association for the Study of Medical Education (chairman), Association of University Teachers of Psychiatry (chairman).

WRITINGS: Alcoholism, Penguin, 1974; *Small Group Therapy*, Penguin, 1974. Contributor to medical journals.

* * *

WANKOWICZ, Melchior 1892(?)-1974

1892(?)—September 10, 1974; Polish-American author of works on wartime subjects and on the condition of the Polish minority in eastern Germany. Obituaries: *AB Bookman's Weekly*, November 25, 1974.

* * *

WARD, Maisie 1889-1975
(Mary Josephine Ward)

1889—January 28, 1975; English-born publisher, biographer, social activist, and founder, with husband Frank Sheed, of the publishing house of Sheed & Ward. Obituaries: *New York Times*, January 29, 1975; *AB Bookman's Weekly*, February 17, 1975; *Publishers Weekly*, February 17, 1975.

* * *

WARD, Ronald A(rthur) 1908-

PERSONAL: Born August 24, 1908, in Croxley Green, Rickmansworth, Hertfordshire, England; son of Benjamin Horace (a businessman) and Caroline (Newman) Ward; married Evelyn Annie Powell (a writer), July 15, 1933; children: Philip Paul Ben, John Powell, Timothy Ronald. *Education:* University of London, B.D., 1934, B.A., 1937, M.A., 1947, Ph.D., 1949. *Home:* 58 Union St., P.O. Box 519, St. Stephen, New Brunswick, Canada.

CAREER: Ordained clergyman of Church of England, 1949; University of London, St. John's Hall, London, England, lecturer in Biblical studies, 1949-51; University of Toronto, Wycliffe College, Toronto, Ontario, professor of New Testament, 1952-63; rector of Kirby Cane and Ellingham, England, 1963-67; Stone Church, St. John, New Brunswick, rector, 1967-75. Examining chaplain to Bishop of Toronto, 1955-63, and to Bishop of Fredericton, 1968—; rural dean of St. John, 1969-75; canon of Christ Church Cathedral, Fredericton, 1971—. *Member:* Studiorum Novi Testamenti Societas, Canadian Authors Association, Tyndale Fellowship for Biblical Research.

WRITINGS: *Royal Sacrament*, Marshall, Morgan & Scott, 1958; *Proclaiming the New Testament: The Gospel of John*, Baker Book, 1961; *Royal Theology*, Marshall, Morgan & Scott, 1964; *Epistles of John and Jude*, Baker Book, 1965; *Mind and Heart*, Baker Book, 1966; *Hidden Meaning in the New Testament*, Marshall, Morgan & Scott, 1969; (contributor) *New Bible Commentary Revised*, Inter-Varsity Press, 1970; *Commentary on 1 & 2 Thessalonians*, Word Books, 1973; *Commentary on 1 & 2 Timothy and Titus*, Word Books, 1974. Contributor to *Baker's Dictionary of Practical Theology* and *The New Testament from Twenty-six Translations*. Editor of *Evangelical Christian*, 1959-63.

WORK IN PROGRESS: *God's Call to His People Today: Unity in Diversity in the New Testament*; *The Theological Relevance of Charles Haddon Spurgeon*; *The Practical Relevance of Charles Haddon Spurgeon*; *Commentary on the Epistle to the Ephesians*.

* * *

WARD, Theodora 1890-1974

November 13, 1890—August 16, 1974; American artist, scholar, authority on Emily Dickinson, and author or editor of several books concerning the poetess. Obituaries: *New York Times*, August 18, 1974. (*CA*-33/36).

* * *

WARNER, Francis (Robert le Plastrier) 1937-

PERSONAL: Born October 21, 1937, in Bishopthorpe, Yorkshire, England; son of Hugh Compton (an Anglican priest) and Nancy le Plastrier (Owen) Warner; married Mary Hall, August 8, 1958; children: Georgina Claire, Lucy Robine. *Education:* Attended Christ's Hospital and London College of Music; St. Catharine's College, Cambridge, B.A., 1958, M.A., 1965. *Religion:* Church of England. *Agent:* Margaret Kelley, 14 Pond View Rd., Canton, Mass.; and Patricia Macnaughton, P. L. Representation, 33 Sloane St., London S.W.1, England. *Office:* St. Peter's College, Oxford University, Oxford, England.

CAREER: Cambridge University, St. Catharine's College, Cambridge, England, teacher, 1958-65; Oxford University, St. Peter's College, Oxford, England, fellow and tutor in English literature, 1965—. Founder of Pilgrim's Way Players, 1954; founder of Cambridge University Elgar Centenary Choir and Orchestra, 1957; director of first James Joyce Symposium in Dublin, 1967; assistant director of Yeats International Summer School, 1961-67; founder of Samuel Beckett Theatre, 1967. *Member:* Athenaeum Club. *Awards, honors:* Messing International Award, 1972, for distinguished contributions to literature.

WRITINGS—Poems: *Perennia*, Golden Head Press, 1962; *Early Poems*, Fortune Press, 1964; *Experimental Sonnets*, Fortune Press, 1965; *Madrigals*, Fortune Press, 1967; *Poetry of Francis Warner*, Pilgrim Press, 1970.

Plays: *Maquettes* (a trilogy of one-act plays), Oxford Theatre Texts, 1972; *Requiem*, Oxford Theatre Texts, Part I: *Lying Figures*, 1972, Part II: *Killing Time*, 1975, Part III: *Meeting Ends*, 1974.

Contributor: R. O'Driscoll, editor, *Theatre and Nationalism in Twentieth Century Ireland*, University of Toronto Press, 1971. Contributor to *Antios*.

WORK IN PROGRESS: A bibliographical edition of the Latin text of *De Occulta Philosophia*, by H. Cornelius Agrippa, with a revised edition of the 1651 translation.

* * *

WARNER, Robert 1905-
(Bob Warner)

PERSONAL: Born July 23, 1905, in Brookline, Mass.; son of Robert Lyon (a public utility owner) and Anne (Pearson) Warner; married Anne Marie Homer, June, 1932 (divorced, 1950); married Sylvia Beckman (a painter), August 24, 1950; children: (first marriage) Jonathan Robert, William B. *Education:* Attended Hamilton College and Columbia University. *Politics:* Democrat. *Religion:* Protestant. *Home and office:* Four Steeples Rd., Washington Depot, Conn. 06794. *Agent:* Lurton Blassingame, 60 East 42nd St., New York, N.Y. 10017.

CAREER: Has held positions as manager of the scrap metals program for the National Production Authority, chairman of the Vermont Post-War Recreation and Development Committee, vice-president of the National Foremen's Institute, 1948-52, director of International Trade Fair Program for the Middle East and Far East, 1955, 1956, and coordinator of exhibits for the U.S. Pavilion at the Brussels World's Fair, 1958-59. Secretary of civil and military affairs for the State of Vermont; member of Vermont State Planning Board. *Wartime service:* Civilian service in Southeast Asia Command with Office of Strategic Services during World War II. *Member:* Housatonic Valley Association (member of executive committee and director), Century Association, Anglers' Club of New York.

WRITINGS: (Under name Bob Warner) *Don't Blame the Fish*, Winchester Press, 1974. Contributor to *Esquire, True, True Hunting Annual, True Fishing Annual, Outdoor Life, Field & Stream, Sports Afield, American Sportsman, Saga, Fishing World, Sport Fisherman, Connecticut Magazine, Garcia Fishing Annual*, and *Orvis News*.

WORK IN PROGRESS: Another book on fishing humor; a novel.

* * *

WARNER, Seth 1927-

PERSONAL: Born July 11, 1927, in Muskegon, Mich.; son

of Seth Lemoine and Agnes (Brustad) Warner; married Emily Rose, June 16, 1962; children: Susan Emily, Sarah Southall, Seth Lawrence. *Education:* Yale University, B.S., 1950; Harvard University, M.A., 1951, Ph.D., 1955. *Religion:* Episcopalian. *Home:* 2433 Wrightwood Ave., Durham, N.C. 27705. *Office:* Department of Mathematics, Duke University, Durham, N.C. 27706.

CAREER: Duke University, Durham, N.C., instructor, 1955-57, assistant professor, 1957-61, associate professor, 1961-65, professor of mathematics, 1965—. *Military service:* U.S. Army, 1946-48. *Member:* American Mathematical Society, Mathematical Association of America, Phi Beta Kappa (president of Duke University chapter, 1973-74), Sigma Xi.

WRITINGS: *Modern Algebra*, two volumes, Prentice-Hall, 1965; *Classical Modern Algebra*, Prentice-Hall, 1971.

AVOCATIONAL INTERESTS: Organ.

* * *

WARREN, Mary Phraner 1929-

PERSONAL: Born March 27, 1929, in New York; daughter of Wilson W. (a warehouse executive) and Mary (Arthur) Warren; married Lindsay Dune Warren (a free-lance calligrapher), May 5, 1956; children: Rose Ann, Bernadine, Roy, Mike, Fred, Mary Belle, Linda Marie. *Education:* Attended Mount Holyoke College, 1948-49; University of Colorado, B.A., 1951; Union Theological Seminary, New York, N.Y., M.A., 1954. *Religion:* Quaker. *Home:* 2607 Northeast 14th Ave., Portland, Ore. 97212. *Agent:* Lenniger Literary Agency, Inc., 11 West 42nd St., New York, N.Y. 10036.

CAREER: St. Luke's Hospital, New York, N.Y., play director in pediatrics, 1955-56; free-lance writer, 1956—. Teacher of weekly writing workshop sponsored by Portland Community College.

WRITINGS—Juvenile: *Walk In My Moccasins*, Westminster, 1966; *Shadow on the Valley*, Westminster, 1967; *Eight Bells for Wendy*, Westminster, 1968; *A Snake Named Sam*, Westminster, 1969; *Ghost town for Sale*, Westminster, 1973; (with Don Kirkendall) *Bottom High to the Crowd*, Walker & Co., 1973; *The River School Detectives*, Westminster, 1974.

WORK IN PROGRESS: A juvenile mystery, *The Haunted Kitchen.*

* * *

WARREN, Peter Whitson 1941-
(Whitson)

PERSONAL: Born September 7, 1941, in Concord, Mass.; son of Richard (a professor) and Dorothy (Brown) Warren; married Sandi Twomey, July 7, 1972 (divorced July 30, 1973). *Education:* University of New Hampshire, B.A., 1963; University of Iowa, M.A. and M.F.A., both 1967. *Home:* 315 South 34th St., Billings, Mont. 59101. *Office:* Department of Art, Eastern Montana College, Billings, Mont. 59101.

CAREER: Eastern Montana College, Billings, instructor, 1967-69, assistant professor of art, 1969—. *Member:* American Association of University Professors, Yellowstone Art Center.

WRITINGS: (Contributor) Martin Farren, Joan Benjamin Farren, and Clarence Hall, compilers, *Storefront*, Aware Press, 1972; *Al's Ham-'n'-Egger and Body Shop Again* (poetry and drawings), Basilisk, 1974. Contributor of poems, collages, drawings to little magazines, usually under name Whitson, including *Vile*, *491*, *Riverside Quarterly*, *Nimrod*, *Davinci*, *Clown War*, and *West Bay Dadaist*.

SIDELIGHTS: Warren's Correspondence Art has been shown at American and Canadian universities, museums, and galleries. *Avocational interests:* Transcendental meditation, bicycling.

* * *

WASHTON, Nathan S(eymour) 1916-

PERSONAL: Born November 9, 1916, in New York, N.Y.; son of Max and Lena (Winer) Washton; married Sylvia Salitsky, December 24, 1944; children: Gale (Mrs. Edward DuBrow), Ruth (Mrs. Roger Katz), Laura. *Education:* New York University, B.S., 1939, Ed.D., 1949; Columbia University, M.A., 1941. *Home:* 30 Oaktree Lane, Manhasset, N.Y. 11030. *Office:* Department of Education, Queens College of the City University of New York, 65-30 Kissena Blvd., Flushing, N.Y. 11367.

CAREER: Newark (N.J.) public schools, chairman of department of science and director of guidance at Newark Junior College and substitute teacher at other schools, 1939-42; Dwight School, New York, N.Y., head of science and mathematics department, 1945-46; Rutgers University, Newark Campus, Newark, N.J., chairman of department of general science and director of guidance, 1946-50; Queens College of the City University of New York, Flushing, N.Y., assistant professor, 1950-57, associate professor, 1957-63, professor of education, 1963—, coordinator of science education, 1950—. Visiting professor at Upsala College, 1946-50, University of Puerto Rico, summer, 1948, Yeshiva University, 1958-59, and University of Hawaii, 1962-63. *Military service:* U.S. Army Air Forces, 1942-45; became captain.

MEMBER: National Association for Research in Science Teaching (member of executive committee, 1955-56; vice-president, 1956-57; president, 1957-58), American Educational Research Association, National Science Teachers Association, American Association for the Advancement of Science (fellow), American Association of University Professors, Central Association of Science and Mathematics Teachers. *Awards, honors:* Distinguished Service Award of National Association for Research in Science Teaching, 1958.

WRITINGS: *Science Teaching in the Secondary School*, Harper, 1961; *Teaching Science Creatively in Secondary Schools*, Saunders, 1967; *Teaching Science in Elementary and Middle Schools*, McKay, 1974. Author of teacher's guide to *The Sea*, Silver Burdett, 1964, and co-author of Educational Testing Service science test for college students. Editor, "Man and His World," science teaching series published by Saunders, 1966-68, and "Web of Life" series published by Benziger, 1971. Contributor of more than fifty articles to journals in his field.

WORK IN PROGRESS: *Meaning of Science.*

* * *

WASSERMAN, Aaron O(sias) 1927-

PERSONAL: Born October 15, 1927, in New York, N.Y.; son of Isador (in rubber garment industry) and Ray (Gelernter) Wasserman; married Solange Lurie, March 29, 1969; children: Gilbert. *Education:* City College (now of the City University of New York), B.S., 1951; University of Texas, Ph.D., 1956. *Religion:* Jewish. *Home:* 5 Westdale Ave., Hillsdale, N.J. 07642. *Office:* Department of Biology, City College of the City University of New York, Convent Ave. and 138th St., New York, N.Y. 10031.

CAREER: City College of the City University of New York, New York, N.Y., instructor, 1956-63, assistant professor, 1963-67, associate professor, 1968-73, professor of biology, 1974—. Member of advisory board of Negative Population Growth, Inc. *Military service:* U.S. Army, 1946-47; became sergeant. *Member:* Society for the Study of Evolution, American Society of Zoologists, American Society of Ichthyologists and Herpetologists, Zero Population Growth, Southwestern Association of Naturalists, Sigma Xi.

WRITINGS: Biology, Appleton, 1973. Contributor to *Cytogenics*, *Copeia*, and *Southwestern Naturalist*.

WORK IN PROGRESS: Anuran Cytogenetics, comparative cytotaxonomy of frogs.

* * *

WASSERMAN, Burton 1929-

PERSONAL: Born March 10, 1929, in Brooklyn, N.Y.; son of Louis (a tailor) and Matilda (Kravitz) Wasserman; married Sarah Francis Masher (a high school teacher of business education), November 2, 1950; children: Marc. *Education:* Brooklyn College (now Brooklyn College of the City University of New York), A.B., 1950; Columbia University, M.A., 1954, Ed.D., 1958. *Politics:* "Open-minded independent." *Home and studio:* 204 DuBois Rd., Glassboro, N.J. 08028. *Office:* Department of Art, Glassboro State College, Glassboro, N.J. 08028.

CAREER: Artist and teacher of art. Teacher in secondary schools of Mineola and Roslyn, N.Y., and in several adult education programs, 1954-59; Glassboro State College, Glassboro, N.J., associate professor, 1960-66, professor of art, 1966—. Has had more than twenty solo shows of paintings and graphics at galleries, art centers, and colleges in four states and Canada since 1959; work included in group exhibitions at Silvermine Guild of Artists, Smithsonian Museum, Newark Museum, Brooklyn Museum, Philadelphia Museum of Art, Pennsylvania Academy of Fine Arts, among others; represented in private collections, and in permanent collections of Philadelphia Museum of Art, Montreal Museum of Fine Arts, Norfolk Museum of Arts and Sciences, New Jersey State Museum, Philadelphia Civic Center Museum, and college and university collections; four private galleries handle his original silk screen prints. *Military service:* U.S. Army, 1951-53; served in western Europe.

MEMBER: American Color Print Society (member of executive council, 1967—), Artists Equity Association (national president, 1971-73). *Awards, honors:* Brickhouse Prize at XXI American Drawing Biennial, Norfolk Museum of Arts and Sciences, 1965; Kelsey Purchase Prize, 1966, and Ryan Purchase Prize, 1967, at Annual Art from New Jersey Exhibition; U.S. Information Agency purchase for American Pavilion at International Exposition in Osaka, Japan, 1970; Esther and Philip Klein Award at Color Prints of the Americas Exhibition, New Jersey State Museum, 1970; other prizes for graphics and oils.

WRITINGS: Bridges of Vision: The Art of Prints and the Craft of Printmaking, New Jersey State Museum, 1970; *Modern Painting: The Movements, the Artists, Their Work*, Davis Publications (Worcester, Mass.), 1970; (with Sarita Rainey) *Basic Silkscreen Printmaking*, Davis Publications, 1971; (with Rainey) *Crayon Resist Techniques*, Davis Publications, 1972.

WORK IN PROGRESS: An art appreciation text, for Davis Publications (Worcester, Mass.).

* * *

WASWO, Richard 1939-

PERSONAL: Born October 26, 1939, in Washington, D.C.; son of Arthur and Mildred (Slaybaugh) Waswo; married Ann Lardner (an assistant professor of history), August 22, 1964. *Education:* Stanford University, A.B., 1961; Harvard University, A.M., 1962, Ph.D., 1970. *Office:* Department of English, University of Virginia, Charlottesville, Va. 22901.

CAREER: Houghton Library, Cambridge, Mass., assistant to curator of manuscripts, 1963; San Francisco State College (now University), San Francisco, Calif., instructor in humanities, 1964-65; San Jose State College, San Jose, Calif., assistant professor of English, 1967-70; University of Virginia, Charlottesville, assistant professor of English, 1970—. *Member:* Modern Language Association of America, Renaissance Society of America, Southeastern Renaissance Conference, South Atlantic Modern Language Association, Phi Beta Kappa. *Awards, honors:* Woodrow Wilson fellow, 1961-62; University of Virginia Sesquicentennial research associate, 1974-75.

WRITINGS: The Fatal Mirror: Themes and Techniques in the Poetry of Fulke Greville, University Press of Virginia, 1972. Contributor to *Journal of Medieval and Renaissance Studies* and *Genre*.

WORK IN PROGRESS: An investigation of the changing relationship between language and meaning in the Renaissance.

* * *

WATERS, Harold A(rthur) 1926-
(Chris Waters)

PERSONAL: Born November 8, 1926, in Wilmington, N.C.; son of Harold C. (a writer) and Theo (a secretary; maiden name, Baring-Gould) Waters; married Lenore Paley, June 26, 1952; children: Gwyneth, Jennifer. *Education:* Harvard University, A.B., 1949; University of Paris, graduate study, 1950-51; University of Washington, Seattle, A.M., 1954, Ph.D., 1956. *Home address:* Church Way, Saunderstown, R.I. 02874. *Office:* Department of Languages, University of Rhode Island, Kingston, R.I. 02881.

CAREER: College of William and Mary, Williamsburg, Va., instructor, 1955-57, assistant professor of French and Spanish, 1957-60; Carleton College, Northfield, Minn., assistant professor of French, 1960-62; University of Rhode Island, Kingston, assistant professor, 1962-65, associate professor, 1965-69, professor of French, 1969—. *Military service:* U.S. Army, 1945-46. *Member:* American Association of Teachers of French, Modern Language Association of America, American Association of University Professors, Paul Claudel Society, Societe Paul Claudel, Les Amis de Celef, Northeast Modern Language Association (member of board of directors, 1971-74), Rhode Island Foreign Language Association, Phi Sigma Iota.

WRITINGS: Paul Claudel, Twayne, 1970. Contributor of poems and translations (under pseudonym Chris Waters), articles, and reviews to literary journals. Editor of *Claudel Newsletter*, *Claudel Studies*, and *University of Rhode Island French Newsletter*.

WORK IN PROGRESS: Guide to Black Theater in French, completion expected in 1976.

AVOCATIONAL INTERESTS: Tennis, biking, skin-diving.

* * *

WATKINS, (Arthur) Ronald (Dare) 1904-

PERSONAL: Born August 29, 1904, in Kingston Hill, Surrey, England; son of George Henry and Florence Mary (Snowden) Watkins; married Margaret Watson Brown, December 30, 1948. *Education:* King's College, Cambridge, M.A., 1927; University of Basel, graduate study, 1928. *Home:* Lobswood, South Hill Ave., Harrow-on-the-Hill, Middlesex HA1 3NX, England.

CAREER: Gave readings of poetry and prose on radio in England, 1928-32; Harrow School, Middlesex, England, teacher of classics and English, 1932-64, director of annual Shakespeare production, 1941-64; full-time lecturer and writer, 1964—. Has directed productions of Shakespeare in England and Scotland, and at University of Colorado, 1967; has lectured on Shakespeare in United Kingdom, Europe, and United States; member of advisory board, St. George's Elizabethan Theatre, 1973; Regents' Lecturer, University of California at Riverside, 1965; George Fullmer Reynolds Lecturer, University of Colorado, 1965, visiting professor, 1967 and 1974. *Member:* Garrick Club.

WRITINGS: Moonlight at the Globe, M. Joseph, 1946; *On Producing Shakespeare*, M. Joseph, 1950, Benjamin Blom, 1964; (editor with Jeremy Lemmon) *The Harrow Shakespeare: Macbeth*, Oxford University Press, 1964.

Author with Jeremy Lemmon, "Shakespeare's Playhouse" series, published by Rowman & Littlefield, Volume I: *The Poet's Method*, Volume II: *Hamlet*, Volume III: *Macbeth*, Volume IV: *A Midsummer Night's Dream*, all 1974.

Contributor to drama journals, including *Theatre, Drama, Sur* (Buenos Aires).

WORK IN PROGRESS: Lectures on Shakespeare.

SIDELIGHTS: Watkins told *CA*: "The theme of my lectures and books is the importance of presenting or imagining Shakespeare's plays as they were performed in his own life-time and in his own playhouse."

* * *

WATSON, James 1936-

PERSONAL: Born November 8, 1936, in Darwen, Lancashire, England; son of James (a wages clerk) and Miriam (a clerk; maiden name, Arnold) Watson; married Catherine Rose Downey (a nurse), July 6, 1963; children: Rosalind, Miranda, Francesca. *Education:* University of Nottingham, B.A. (honors), 1958. *Home:* Vale Towers, Flat B, 58 London Rd., Tunbridge Wells, Kent, England. *Agent:* A. D. Peters & Co., 10 Buckingham St., London W.C.2, England. *Office:* West Kent College, Tunbridge Wells, Kent, England.

CAREER: British Council, Milan, Italy, teacher of English, 1960-61; *North East Evening Gazette*, Middlesbrough, Yorkshire, England, journalist and art critic, 1961-63; Dunlop Co., London, England, education officer and editor of educational literature, 1963-65; West Kent College, Tunbridge Wells, Kent, England, lecturer in English and liberal studies, 1965—. Founder of local arts cooperative; member of Tunbridge Wells No-Censorship Committee. *Military service:* British Army, Royal Army Educational Corps, National Service Officer, 1958-60. *Member:* Association for Liberal Education, Tunbridge Wells and West Kent College Film Society (treasurer), Teesside Film Club (founder-secretary), Purcell Recorder Consort (amateur recorder and early music enthusiasts).

WRITINGS: Sign of the Swallow (juvenile), Thomas Nelson, 1967; *The Bull Leapers* (juvenile), Coward, 1970; *Legion of the White Tiger* (juvenile), Gollancz, 1973; *Liberal Studies in Further Education*, National Foundation for Educational Research, 1973. Author of "Gilbert Makepeace Lives!," a radio play for British Broadcasting Corp., 1972. Contributor to *London Times*, *Guardian*, *Studio*, and *Arts Review*.

WORK IN PROGRESS: Miscellaneous works of fiction, including a novel for children, set in Europe in the 1930's and during the Spanish Civil War.

AVOCATIONAL INTERESTS: The arts, archeology, exploring old castles and churches, soccer, cricket, and camping.

* * *

WATSON, Peter L(eslie) 1944-

PERSONAL: Born December 30, 1944, in Forfar, Scotland; son of Alec (a chemist) and Helen (a bookkeeper; maiden name, Stewart) Watson; married Evelyn Anne Pollock (a social worker), August 21,1969; children: Melissa Anne Margaret. *Education:* University of Edinburgh, M.A. (honors), 1967, Ph.D., 1973. *Office:* Transportation and Urban Projects Department, International Bank for Reconstruction Development, 1818 H St. N.W., Washington, D.C. 20433.

CAREER: Northwestern University, Evanston, Ill., assistant professor of economics and research associate at Transportation Center, 1970—. Transport economist at International Bank for Reconstruction and Development, Washington, D.C., 1974-75. Consultant to Wilbur Smith & Associates (on transportation study for Kuala Lumpur, Malaya), U.S. Army Corps of Engineers, and other agencies. Secretary of traveler behavior and values committee, Highway Research Board, 1973—. *Awards, honors:* Fred Burger Award of Transportation Research Board, 1973, for best paper by an analyst under thirty years of age.

WRITINGS: (With Richard M. Michaels) *Social and Psychological Factors in Urban Transport Mode Choices* (monograph), Transportation Center, Northwestern University, 1972; *The Value of Time: Behavioral Models of Mode Choice*, Heath, 1973; (with R. W. Adams, R. M. Michaels, and J. L. Schofer) *Public Transportation in the Chicago Region: Present Performance and Future Potential* (monograph), Transportation Center, Northwestern University, 1973; (contributor) J. N. Wolfe, editor, *Cost Benefit and Cost Effectiveness: Studies and Analysis*, Unwin University Books, 1973; *Urban Goods Movement: A Disaggregate Approach*, Heath, in press. Contributor to transportation and regional economics journals.

WORK IN PROGRESS: Research on road pricing.

AVOCATIONAL INTERESTS: Skiing, sailing, playing squash.

* * *

WATTS, Ann Chalmers 1938-

PERSONAL: Born April 14, 1938, in Evanston, Ill.; daughter of Gordon Keith (a college president) and Roberta

T. (Swartz) Chalmers; married Terence Leslie Watts (a university professor), June 30, 1962; children: Gordon, Vivien. *Education:* Radcliffe College, B.A., 1959; Yale University, M.A., 1962, Ph.D., 1965. *Residence:* Metuchen, N.J. *Office:* Department of English, Rutgers University, 360 High St., Newark, N.J. 07102.

CAREER: Tufts University, Medford, Mass., instructor, 1964-65, assistant professor, 1965-70, associate professor of English, 1970; Rutgers University, Newark, N.J., associate professor of English, 1971—. *Member:* Mediaeval Academy of America, Modern Language Association of America.

WRITINGS: The Lyre and the Harp, Yale University Press, 1969. Contributor to journals in her field.

WORK IN PROGRESS: Studies in Old and Middle English literature.

* * *

WATTS, David 1935-

PERSONAL: Born June 14, 1935, in Chapel-on-le-Frith, England; son of John Mark (a farmer and postman) and Eva Jane (Waterhouse) Watts. *Education:* University College, London, B.A. (honors), 1956; University of California, Berkeley, M.A., 1959; McGill University, Ph.D., 1963. *Home:* 21 Hall Walk, Walkington, Beverley, East Yorkshire, England. *Office:* Department of Geography, University of Hull, Hull, East Yorkshire, England.

CAREER: University of Hull, Hull, East Yorkshire, England, lecturer, 1963-73, senior lecturer in geography, 1973—. *Member:* Institute of British Geographers, Association of American Geographers.

WRITINGS: Man's Influence on the Vegetation of Barbados, University of Hull, 1966; *Principles of Biogeography*, McGraw, 1971. Editor of *Journal of Biogeography*, 1973—.

WORK IN PROGRESS: The Eastern Caribbean in Maps, completion expected in 1976; *Economic Development of the Caribbean*, 1976.

AVOCATIONAL INTERESTS: Theatre, music, painting, walking, fishing, good food, excellent wine.

* * *

WAYNE, Stephen J(ay) 1939-

PERSONAL: Born March 22, 1939, in New York, N.Y.; son of Arthur G. and Muriel (Marks) Wayne. *Education:* University of Rochester, A.B., 1961; Columbia University, M.A., 1963, Ph.D., 1968. *Home:* 2408 39th St. N.W., Washington, D.C. 20007. *Office:* Department of Political Science, George Washington University, Washington, D.C. 20052.

CAREER: Ohio Wesleyan University, Delaware, instructor in political science, 1966-68; George Washington University, Washington, D.C., assistant professor, 1968-73, associate professor of political science, 1973—. *Military service:* U.S. Navy, 1963-65; became lieutenant. *Member:* American Political Science Association, Academy of Political Science, Southern Political Science Association.

WRITINGS: (Editor and contributor) *Investigating the American Political System: Problems, Methods, and Projects*, Schenkman, 1974. Contributor of articles and book reviews to *George Washington Law Review, American Political Science Review*, and *Political Science Quarterly*.

WORK IN PROGRESS: Presidential Policy-Making, for Dodd.

WEATHERFORD, Richard M(orris) 1939-

PERSONAL: Born May 14, 1939, in Seattle, Wash.; son of Morris Lee and Emily Sutherland (Reed) Weatherford; married Harriet Minna Pistor, August 5, 1967; children: Matthew Bradley, Stephen Morris. *Education:* Pacific University, Forest Grove, Ore., B.A., 1961; University of Washington, Seattle, M.A., 1962; University of California, Los Angeles, Ph.D., 1970. *Home:* 1836 Upper Chelsea Rd., Columbus, Ohio 43212. *Office:* Department of English, Ohio State University, Columbus, Ohio 43210.

CAREER: Ohio State University, Columbus, assistant professor of English, 1970—. Owner of R. M. Weatherford Fine and Rare Books, dealing in rare anthropology and ethnology books on the Indians of the Northwest coast of North America. Editorial consultant for Ohio State University Press. *Member:* Modern Language Association of America. *Awards, honors:* American Philosophical Society grants, 1971, 1973.

WRITINGS: Stephen Crane: The Critical Heritage, Routledge & Kegan Paul, 1973.

WORK IN PROGRESS: Calendar of American Literary Manuscripts: Stephen Crane.

AVOCATIONAL INTERESTS: Making stained-glass windows.

* * *

WEBBER, (Edwin) Ronald 1915-

PERSONAL: Born January 20, 1915, in Somerset, England; son of Edwin Arthur and Maud (Caswell) Webber; married Mabel Edith Porter, June 20, 1942; children: Christine (Mrs. Cliff Fane). *Education:* Attended Wellington School and Somerset Farm Institute in Somerset, England. *Politics:* Variable. *Religion:* Church of England. *Home:* 57 The Wells House, Well Walk, London NW3 ILU, England.

CAREER: Worked in a plant nursery, with a commercial fruit, vegetable, and flower firm in London's Covent Garden, and as a free-lance journalist; *The Grower*, London, England, staff journalist, 1955-67. *Military service:* British Army, 1940-46; served in North Africa and Italy. *Member:* National Union of Journalists.

WRITINGS: The Early Horticulturists, A. S. Barnes, 1968; *Covent Garden: Mud Salad Market*, Dent, 1969; *The Village Blacksmith*, David & Charles, 1971; *Market Gardening: A History*, David & Charles, 1972; (contributor) Brice Alexander, editor, *Crafts and Craftsmen*, Croom Helm, 1974; *Percy Cane—Garden Designer*, Bartholomew, in press. Contributor to periodicals.

WORK IN PROGRESS: Research on market gardens of the Old and New World, on the Peasant's Revolt of 1381, and on Nell Gwyn; a novel based on life in the British Army in World War II.

* * *

WEBER, Robert L(emmerman) 1913-

PERSONAL: Born March 1, 1913, in Dayton, Ohio; son of William A. (a professor of religious education) and Justina A. (a teacher; maiden name, Lemmerman) Weber; married Marion Louise Fleming (assistant to dean of College of Human Development at Pennsylvania State University), August 19, 1949; children: Robert F., Karen L., Meredith A., Ruth E. *Education:* Yale University, B.A., 1934, M.A., 1936; Pennsylvania State University, Ph.D., 1938.

Religion: Presbyterian. *Home:* 625 West Ridge Ave., State College, Pa. 16801. *Office:* Department of Physics, Pennsylvania State University, 205 Davey Building, University Park, Pa. 16802.

CAREER: Pennsylvania State University, University Park, instructor, 1938-42, assistant professor, 1942-47, associate professor of physics, 1947—. *Member:* American Association of University Professors (member of executive committee), Electron Microscope Society of America, American Association for the Advancement of Science, American Association of Physics Teachers, American Society for Engineering Education, Institute of Physics (London), Sigma Xi (past vice-president of Pennsylvania State University chapter), Gamma Alpha. *Awards, honors:* National Science Foundation grant, 1966-68, for developing instructional scientific equipment; National Book League citation, 1974, for *A Random Walk in Science*.

WRITINGS: Temperature Measurement and Control, Blakiston, 1941; (with M. W. White and K. V. Manning) *Practical Physics*, McGraw, 1943, 2nd edition, 1955; (with White and Manning) *College Technical Physics*, McGraw, 1947, 2nd edition published as *College Physics*, McGraw, 1952, 5th edition, 1975; *Heat and Temperature Measurement*, Prentice-Hall, 1950; (with White and Manning) *Physics for Science and Engineering*, McGraw, 1957, revised edition, 1959; (with C. H. Blanchard, C. R. Burnett, and R. G. Stoner) *Introduction to Modern Physics*, Prentice-Hall, 1958, 2nd edition, 1969; (contributor) T. B. Brown, editor, *Lloyd William Taylor Manual of Advanced Undergraduate Experiments in Physics*, Addison-Wesley, 1959; *Physics for Teachers: A Modern Review*, McGraw, 1964; (with White and Manning) *Basic Physics*, McGraw, 1968; (compiler) Eric Mendoza, honorary editor, *A Random Walk in Science: An Anthology*, Institute of Physics (London), 1973, Crane Russack & Co., 1974.

Collaborator in "College Physics," a series of films, McGraw, 1952. Contributor of about a dozen articles to *Physical Review*, *Journal of the Optical Society of America*, and *American Journal of Physics*. Member of editorial board of *Review of Scientific Instruments*, 1952-54.

WORK IN PROGRESS: Life Science Physics, with G. K. Strother, for Houghton.

* * *

WEBSTER, Brenda S. 1936-

PERSONAL: Born November 17, 1936, in New York, N.Y.; daughter of Wolfgang Simon (a lawyer) and Ethel (an artist; maiden name, Kremer) Schwabacher; married Richard Allen (a professor of history), March 3, 1961; children: Lisa Anna, Michael Wolf, Rebecca Gabrielle. *Education:* Swarthmore College, student, 1954-56; Barnard College, B.A., 1958; Columbia University, M.A., 1960; University of California, Berkeley, Ph.D., 1967.

CAREER: Writer.

WRITINGS: Yeats: A Psychoanalytic Study, Stanford University Press, 1973.

WORK IN PROGRESS: Research on a psychoanalytic study of William Blake.

* * *

WEIDHORN, Manfred 1931-

PERSONAL: Born October 10, 1931, in Vienna, Austria; naturalized U.S. citizen in 1947; son of Aron (a merchant) and Anne (a diamond cutter; maiden name, Gelber) Weidhorn; married Phyllis Greenstein, January 12, 1969; children: Aron Homer, Eric Winston. *Education:* Columbia University, B.A., 1954, Ph.D., 1963; University of Wisconsin, M.A., 1957. *Politics:* "I'm against whoever and whatever is in." *Religion:* "Still waiting for the facts." *Office:* Department of English, Yeshiva University, 500 West 185th St., New York, N.Y. 10033.

CAREER: Self-employed diamond cutter in New York, N.Y., 1948-54; University of Alabama, Tuscaloosa, instructor in English, 1957-58; Brooklyn College, City University of New York, Brooklyn, N.Y., instructor in English, 1960-63; Yeshiva University, New York, N.Y., assistant professor, 1963-68, associate professor, 1968-73, professor of English, 1973—. *Military service:* U.S. Army, Artillery, 1954-56. *Awards, honors:* Danforth associate, 1969—.

WRITINGS: Dreams in Seventeenth-Century English Literature, Mouton & Co., 1970; *Richard Lovelace*, Twayne, 1970; *Sword and Pen: A Survey of the Writings of Sir Winston Churchill*, University of New Mexico Press, 1974. Contributor of more than twenty articles to scholarly journals.

WORK IN PROGRESS: Chapters and essays on Churchill's writings; studies of the juncture of literature, history, psychology, and political science, of Shakespeare and miscellaneous matters, and of European views of America in the eighteenth and nineteeth centuries.

AVOCATIONAL INTERESTS: Travel, chess.

* * *

WEILL, Gus 1933-

PERSONAL: Born March 12, 1933, in Lafayette, La.; son of Leopold, Sr. (a mule dealer) and Bernice (Weill) Weill; married Ann Harris, September 14, 1954; children: Gus II. *Education:* Louisiana State University, B.A., 1955. *Politics:* Democrat. *Religion:* Jewish. *Agent:* Betty Ann Clarke, International Famous Agency, 1301 Avenue of the Americas, New York, N.Y. 10019. *Office address:* P.O. Box 645, Baton Rouge, La. 70821.

CAREER: Executive secretary to governor of Louisiana, 1964-68; Louisiana State University, Baton Rouge, visiting professor of playwriting, 1970; now president of an advertising and public relations agency in New Orleans and Baton Rouge, La. *Military service:* U.S. Army, special agent for Counter Intelligence, 1956-58; became first lieutenant. *Member:* Dramatists Guild, Authors League of America. *Awards, honors:* Finalist for Stanley Drama Award, 1974, for "Son of the Last Mule Dealer."

WRITINGS: Paradiddle, Citadel, 1974; *A Woman's Eyes*, Dial, 1975. Author of plays, "To Bury a Cousin," first produced Off-Broadway, 1968, and "Geese," first produced Off-Broadway, 1969.

WORK IN PROGRESS: The Bonnet Man, a novel; *Yesterday and Maybe Tomorrow*, a political novel.

* * *

WEINBERG, Steven 1933-

PERSONAL: Born May 3, 1933, in New York, N.Y.; son of Fred and Eva (Israel) Weinberg; married Louise Goldwasser (a professor of law), July 6, 1954; children: Elizabeth. *Education:* Cornell University, A.B., 1954; Institute for Theoretical Physics, Copenhagen, Denmark, graduate study, 1954-55; Princeton University, Ph.D., 1957. *Home:* 1 Berkeley Pl., Cambridge, Mass. 02138. *Office:* Department of Physics, Harvard University, Cambridge, Mass. 02138.

CAREER: Columbia University, New York, N.Y., instructor in physics, 1957-59; University of California, Berkeley, research associate of Lawrence Radiation Laboratory, 1959-60, assistant professor, 1960-62, associate professor, 1962-64, professor of physics, 1964-69; Massachusetts Institute of Technology, Cambridge, professor of physics, 1969-73; Harvard University, Cambridge, Mass., Higgins Professor of Physics, 1973—. Senior scientist at Smithsonian Astrophysical Observatory, 1973—. Morris Loeb Lecturer at Harvard University, 1966-67; visiting professor at Massachusetts Institute of Technology, 1967-68; Richtmeyer Memorial Lecturer of American Association of Physics Teachers, 1974. Councillor of American Physical Society, 1971-75; consultant to Stanford Research Institute.

MEMBER: National Academy of Sciences, American Academy of Arts and Sciences, Council for Foreign Relations, American Physical Society, American Astronomical Society, American Mediaeval Academy. *Awards, honors:* Oppenheimer Prize from University of Miami, 1972.

WRITINGS: *Gravitation and Cosmology*, Wiley, 1972. Contributor of more than ninety articles to scientific journals, including *Scientific American* and *Science*; also to *New York Times Book Review* and *Daedalus*.

* * *

WEISS, Francis Joseph 1899(?)-1975

1899(?)—January 21, 1975; Austrian-born American scientist, economist, researcher, and author. Obituaries: *Washington Post*, January 23, 1975.

* * *

WEISS, Melford Stephen 1937-

PERSONAL: Born July 25, 1937, in Brooklyn, N.Y.; son of Matthew (an engineer) and Rose (a teacher; maiden name, Rivlin) Weiss; married Paula Helene Weinstein (a teacher), August 30, 1964; children: Nicole Daveen, Stacey Meredith. *Education:* State University of New York at Binghamton, B.A., 1963; Michigan State University, M.A., 1969, Ph.D., 1971. *Politics:* "Flexible." *Religion:* Independent. *Home:* 122 Harber Ct., Sacramento, Calif. 95825. *Office:* Department of Anthropology, California State University, Sacramento, Calif. 95819.

CAREER: Ball State University, Muncie, Ind., assistant professor of anthropology, 1966-67; California State University, Sacramento, assistant professor, 1967-72, associate professor of anthropology, 1972—. *Military service:* U.S. Army, 1958-60. *Member:* American Anthropological Association (fellow), Asian Studies Association, Southwestern Anthropological Association.

WRITINGS: (Contributor) Stanley Sue and Nathaniel Wagner, editors, *Asian Americans: Psychological Perspectives*, Science & Behavior Books, 1973; *Valley City: A Chinese Community in America*, Schenkman, 1974. Contributor of articles and reviews to academic journals, including *Transaction, Society, Social Issues, Journal of Marriage and the Family*, and *Urban Anthropology*.

WORK IN PROGRESS: A study of life-styles and social structure of "swinging-single" community life.

SIDELIGHTS: Weiss writes: "I dig fieldwork research which is as much, if not more exciting, than the completed writing. My works are about social life, excitement, offbeat concerns and the characteristics that make people human. I am interested in everything and anything." *Avocational interests:* Tennis, skiing, bridge, swimming.

* * *

WEITZMAN, Arthur J(oshua) 1933-

PERSONAL: Born September 13, 1933, in Newark, N.J.; son of Louis I. (a merchant) and Cecle Weitzman; married Judith Finman (a college administrator), June 5, 1963; children: Peter, Anne. *Education:* University of Chicago, B.A., 1956, M.A., 1957; New York University, Ph.D., 1964. *Politics:* Democrat. *Religion:* Jewish. *Home:* 58 Channing Rd., Newton Centre, Mass. 02159. *Office:* Department of English, Northeastern University, Boston, Mass. 02115.

CAREER: Brooklyn College of the City University of New York, Brooklyn, N.Y., instructor in English, 1960-63; Temple University, Philadelphia, Pa., assistant professor of English, 1963-69; Northeastern University, Boston, Mass., associate professor, 1969-72, professor of English, 1972—. *Member:* Modern Language Association of America, American Society of Eighteenth-Century Studies. *Awards, honors:* Fellowship from National Endowment for the Humanities, 1972-73.

WRITINGS: (Editor) G. P. Marana, *Letters Writ by a Turkish Spy*, Columbia University Press, 1970. Contributor of about a dozen articles to literary journals, including *Essays in Criticism*, *Papers of the Bibliographical Society of America*, *Journal of the History of Ideas*, *Notes and Queries*, *Milton Newsletter*, and *Philological Quarterly*. Founder and co-editor of *Scriblerian*, 1968—.

WORK IN PROGRESS: Research on literature and urban life in the eighteenth century.

AVOCATIONAL INTERESTS: Travel, bookbinding, tennis.

* * *

WELCH, Mary Ross 1918-

PERSONAL: Born May 30, 1918, in Newburgh, N.Y.; daughter of John Henry and Clara (a factory worker; maiden name, Buttjer) Miller; married second husband, John Welch (an assembler technician), December 28, 1963; children: Margaret (Mrs. Thomas Kidder). *Education:* Attended public schools in Poughkeepsie, N.Y. *Religion:* Baptist. *Address:* P.O. Box 898, Poughkeepsie, N.Y. 12602.

CAREER: Former clerical worker; writer. *Military service:* Women's Army Auxiliary Corps, 1943. Women's Army Corps, 1943-44. *Member:* St. David's Christian Writers Association, Writers Guild of the Mid-Hudson Valley (past president).

WRITINGS: *Bury Me Deep* (poems), Story Book Press, 1948; *Trying for Purple* (poems), Story Book Press, 1953; *The Color of Loneliness* (novel), Dorrance, 1958; *Prouder Than Wine* (poems), Royal Publishers, 1965; *The Cross Will Splinter* (poems), Prairie Press, 1970.

WORK IN PROGRESS: A book of poems selected from previously published books; a collection of short poems.

* * *

WELKOWITZ, Joan 1929-

PERSONAL: Born April 17, 1929, in New York, N.Y.;

daughter of Abraham (a small businessman) and Ray (Young) Horowitz; married Walter Welkowitz (a professor), June 17, 1951; children: David, Lawrence, Julie. *Education:* Queens College (now of the City University of New York), B.A., 1949; University of Illinois, M.A., 1954; Columbia University, Ph.D., 1960. *Home:* 138 Highland Ave., Metuchen, N.J. 08840. *Office:* Department of Psychology, New York University, 4 Washington Pl., New York, N.Y. 10003.

CAREER: Veteran's Administration, East Orange, N.J., social psychology trainee, 1956-58; chief research psychologist, Department of Child Psychiatry, Mt. Sinai Hospital, 1959-62; lecturer, Mt. Sinai School of Nursing, 1960-62; Bleuhler Psychotherapy Center, New York, N.Y., research psychologist, 1962-64; Rutgers University, University College, New Brunswick, N.J., adjunct assistant professor in department of psychology, 1963-64; New York University, New York, N.Y., associate professor of psychology, 1969—. *Member:* American Psychological Association, Society for Psychotherapy Research, Harry Stack Sullivan Society.

WRITINGS: Introductory Statistics for the Behavioral Sciences, Academic Press, 1971. Contributor to *Journal of Consulting and Clinical Psychology*.

WORK IN PROGRESS: Research in rhythms of dialogue and patterns of communication between therapist and patient.

* * *

WELLESZ, Egon Joseph 1885-1974

October 21, 1885—November 9, 1974; Austrian musician, composer, musicologist, music historian, authority on Byzantine music, and author. Obituaries: *New York Times*, November 11, 1974; *Washington Post*, November 13, 1974; *AB Bookman's Weekly*, December 16, 1974.

* * *

WELLS, Evelyn

AGENT: Harold Matson, 22 East 40th St., New York, N.Y. 10016.

CAREER: Has worked as a newspaper writer, syndicated columnist, speechwriter, and has lectured and taught creative writing; free-lance writer and editor. *Awards, honors:* Christopher Award, State of Washington's Governor's Award, and Bookseller's Award, all 1968; MacDowell Colony fellowship; Huntington Hartford Foundation fellowship.

WRITINGS: Fremont Older (biography), Appleton, 1936, reprinted, Arno, 1970; *Champagne Days of San Francisco*, Appleton, 1939; (with Leo L. Stanley) *Men at Their Worst*, Appleton, 1940; *A Treasury of Names*, Duell, Sloan, & Pearce, 1946, reissued as *What to Name the Baby*, Doubleday, 1953; *Jed Blaine's Woman* (novel), Doubleday, 1947; (with Harry Peterson) *The Forty Niners*, Doubleday, 1949; *Life Starts Today*, Doubleday, 1951; *Gentle Kingdom of Giacomo* (novel), Doubleday, 1953; *Nefertiti* (biography), Doubleday, 1964; *Carlos P. Romulo: Voice of Freedom* (biography), Funk, 1964; *City for St. Francis* (novel; Literary Guild selection), Doubleday, 1968; *Hatshepsut* (biography), Doubleday, 1969; *I Am Thinking of Kelda* (novel), Doubleday, 1974. Has worked as a ghost-writer, collaborator, or editorial consultant on numerous books.

Screenplays: "I Am Joachin," "Loves of Lola Montez," "Men at Their Worst," "Jed Blaine's Woman," "Kit Carson."

SIDELIGHTS: Jed Blaine's Woman was filmed by Paramount, and *Men at Their Worst* by Metro-Goldwyn-Mayer.

* * *

WELSH, James Michael 1938-

PERSONAL: Born July 15, 1938, in Logansport, Ind.; son of James Vincent (a hospital attendant) and Ione Louise (a registered nurse; maiden name, Williams) Welsh; married Anne Robison, August 12, 1960; children: Katherine Elizabeth, Emily Ione. *Education:* Indiana University, B.A., 1963; University of Kansas, M.A., 1965, further graduate study, 1966—. *Politics:* Democrat. *Religion:* Roman Catholic. *Home:* 723 North Somerset Ave., Princess Anne, Md. 21853. *Office:* Department of English, Salisbury State College, Salisbury, Md. 21801.

CAREER: University of Kansas, Lawrence, assistant instructor in English, 1963-64, 1966-70, research assistant in bibliography, 1966-71; Salisbury State College, Sallisbury, Md., instructor, 1971-74, assistant professor of English and film, 1974—. Host and interviewer on "Films of the Gatsby Era," a series produced by Maryland Center for Public Broadcasting, 1973. *Member:* Modern Language Association of America, Shakespeare Association of America, Society for Cinema Studies, American Film Institute, South Atlantic Modern Language Association, Bibliographical Society of the University of Virginia, Bibliographical Society (London, England).

WRITINGS: (With D. Heyward Brook) *Ben Jonson: A Quadricentennial Bibliography, 1947-1972*, Scarecrow, 1974. Co-author of television scripts for "Films of the Gatsby Era." Contributor of articles and reviews to literature journals, including *Film Comment, Comparative Drama, Film Society Review, American Speech, Arts in Society*, and *Cinema Journal*. Associate editor of *Literature-Film Quarterly*.

WORK IN PROGRESS: Abel Gance and the Seventh Art, with Steven Kramer; *His Majesty the American: The Films of Douglas Fairbanks, Sr.*, with John Tibbetts; biblio-textual research on the plays of Shakespeare.

AVOCATIONAL INTERESTS: Film history, popular culture.

* * *

WENDEL, Thomas H(arold) 1924-

PERSONAL: Born October 3, 1924, in Portland, Ore.; son of Harold Fox and Elise (Fleischner) Wendel; married Charlotte Alexander, August 4, 1956; children: Harold, David. *Education:* Yale University, B.A., 1949; University of Washington, Seattle, M.A., 1962, Ph.D., 1964. *Home:* 285 Manchester Ave., Campbell, Calif. 95008. *Office:* Department of History, San Jose State University, San Jose, Calif. 95192.

CAREER: Putney School, Putney, Vt., teacher of history, 1949-54; Lakeside School, Seattle, Wash., teacher of history and admissions director, 1956-64; San Jose State University, San Jose, Calif., assistant professor, 1964-68, associate professor, 1968-72, professor of history, 1972—. *Military service:* U.S. Army Air Forces, Meteorology, 1943-46. *Member:* American Association of University Professors, American Historical Association, Organization of American Historians, California Historical Society (member of board of trustees, 1973—), San Jose Symphony Association (member of board of trustees, 1971—).

WRITINGS: Benjamin Franklin and the Politics of Liberty, Barron's, 1974. Contributor to *Pennsylvania Magazine of History and Biography*, *Pennsylvania History*, *Social Studies*, and *Reviews in American History*. Contributor of abstracts of articles to *Historical Abstracts*, American Bibliographical Center, 1974—.

WORK IN PROGRESS: Research on the speaker of the Lower House of Assembly in colonial America.

AVOCATIONAL INTERESTS: Music.

* * *

WENK, Edward, Jr. 1920-

PERSONAL: Born January 24, 1920, in Baltimore, Md.; son of Edward and Lillie (Heller) Wenk; married Carolyn Frances Lyford, December 21, 1941; children: Lawrence Shelley, Robin Edward Alexander, Terry Allan. *Education:* Johns Hopkins University, B.E. (with honors), 1940, Dr.Engr., 1950; Harvard University, M.Sc., 1947. *Home:* 15142 Beach Dr. N.E., Seattle, Wash. 98155. *Office:* Program in Social Management of Technology, University of Washington, Seattle, Wash. 98195.

CAREER: Registered professional engineer. U.S. Navy, David Taylor Model Basin, Washington, D.C., specialist on submarine strength, 1942-50, head of Structures Division, 1950-56; Southwest Research Institute, San Antonio, Tex., chairman of department of engineering mechanics, 1956-59; Library of Congress, Washington, D.C., senior specialist in science and technology in Legislative Reference Service, 1959-61; White House Federal Council on Science and Technology, Washington, D.C., executive secretary of council and technical assistant to President's science adviser, 1961-64; Library of Congress, chief of Science Policy Research Division in Legislative Reference Service, 1964-66; Executive Office of the President, Washington, D.C., executive secretary of National Council on Marine Resources and Engineering Development, 1966-70; University of Washington, Seattle, professor of engineering and public affairs, 1970—, director of program in social management of technology, 1973—. Sigma Xi national lecturer, 1966, 1975; lecturer at University of Maryland; William M. Murray Lecturer at National Academy of Engineering, 1969. Visiting scholar at Woodrow Wilson International Center for Scholars, 1970-72. Member of board of directors of U.R.S. Corp. Chairman of committee on public engineering policy of National Academy of Engineering and chairman of study of priorities for National Science Foundation; member of President's national advisory committee on ocean and atmosphere, 1971-72; member of Congressional Office of Technology Assessment Advisory Council, 1973—; member of executive committee of Assembly of Engineering of National Research Council, 1974—. Adviser to United Nations Secretariat; consultant to National Science Foundation and Congressional Research Service. *Military service:* U.S. Naval Reserve, active duty, 1944-45.

MEMBER: Society for Experimental Stress Analysis (national President, 1957), American Society of Civil Engineers, American Society of Mechanical Engineers (fellow), National Society of Professional Engineers, National Oceanography Association (vice-president in public affairs, 1970-72), American Association for the Advancement of Science, National Academy of Engineering, American Society for Public Administration, Sigma Xi, Tau Beta Pi, Chi Epsilon, Everett Yacht Club, Cosmos Club. *Awards, honors:* Meritorious civilian service award from U.S. Navy, 1946; Dr.Sc. from University of Rhode Island, 1968; fellowship from Ford Foundation, 1970; governor's award to Washington State authors, 1973.

WRITINGS: The Politics of the Ocean, University of Washington Press, 1972. Contributor of articles on engineering mechanics, submarine analysis and design, science policy, government organization for science policy, roles of the engineering profession, marine affairs, environmental affairs, and technology assessment to professional journals. Reviewing editor of *Experimental Mechanics*, 1953-56, and *Engineering Mechanics*, 1956-58; member of editorial board of *Ocean Management*, 1973.

WORK IN PROGRESS: Margins for Survival, on coping with the impact of technology on society.

SIDELIGHTS: Wenk is the designer of the "Aluminaut" submarine, 1959, and of concepts for deep diving submarines. *Avocational interests:* Boating, photography, archaeology, futures research, and citizen participation in democratic government.

* * *

WENKAM, Robert 1920-

PERSONAL: Born January 1, 1920, in Oakland, Calif. *Education:* Attended Lassen Junior College, Modesto Junior College, and University of Hawaii. *Office:* 1319 Kalakava #2, Honolulu, Hawaii 96814.

CAREER: Civil engineer in Honolulu, Hawaii, 1941-46; U.S. Army Corps of Engineers, Honolulu, Hawaii, civil engineer (civilian), 1946-48; architectural designer with various firms in Honolulu, Hawaii, 1948-50; free-lance advertising photographer, 1950-70; writer and photographer in Hawaii, 1970—. State land use commissioner in Hawaii, 1962-66. *Member:* Friends of the Earth (Pacific representative), Sierra Club (organizer and first chairman of Hawaii chapter, 1967), Federation of Western Outdoor Clubs (president). *Awards, honors:* Worlds Best Travel Poster award from American Society of Travel Agents, 1967; numerous awards for advertising photography, including Best of Show award from Honolulu Art Directors Club, 1968.

WRITINGS—With photographs by author: *Kauai and the Park Country of Hawaii*, Sierra Club, 1967; *Maui: The Last Hawaiian Place*, Friends of the Earth, 1970; *Hawaii*, Rand McNally, 1972; *New England*, Rand McNally, 1974; *The Great Pacific Rip-Off*, Follett, 1974; *Hawaii, the Big Island*, Rand McNally, 1975; *How to Photograph Hawaii*, Rand McNally, 1975.

Contributor of photographic illustrations: Lorraine Kuch, *The Modern Tropical Garden*, Tongg Publishing, 1955; *A Guide to Architecture in Honolulu*, Hawaii Chapter, American Institute of Architects, 1956; John M. Kelly, Jr., *Folk Music Festival in Hawaii*, Boston Music Co., 1959; Harland Bartholomew and others, *Tourist Destination Areas in Hawaii*, State of Hawaii, 1960; *The General Plan of the State of Hawaii*, State of Hawaii, 1961; *State of Hawaii*, Bank of America, 1963; *Plan for the Metropolitan Area of Hilo*, County of Hawaii, 1964; *Hawaii's Shoreline*, State of Hawaii, 1965; Alma E. Thoene, *The First Book of Hawaii*, F. Watts, 1967; Ruth Tabrah, *Hawaii Nei*, Follett, 1967; *The Kohala Coast Resort Region*, Olohana Corporation, 1967; John C. Caldwell, *Let's Visit Micronesia*, John Day, 1969; John S. Kay, *Land Development Plan and Program*, C. Brewer, 1969; *Hawaii's Treasures*, Planning Division, State of Hawaii, 1971; *Princeville at Hanalei: The Origin*,

Eagle County Development Corp., 1971; Byron Baker, *Micronesia: Breadfruit Revolution*, University Press of Hawaii, 1971; Ken Brower, *Micronesia: Pacific Wilderness*, Friends of the Earth, 1975.

* * *

WERNER, Peter Howard 1944-

PERSONAL: Born June 26, 1944, in Appleton, Wis.; son of Francis E. (a factory worker) and Marguerite T. Werner; married Mary Engsberg, June 10, 1967; children: Amy Lea. *Education:* La Crosse State University (now University of Wisconsin–La Crosse), B.S. (with honors), 1966; Indiana University, M.S. (with honors), 1967, P.E.D., 1971. *Home:* 311 West Chestnut, Oxford, Ohio 45056. *Office:* Department of Physical Education, Miami University, Phillips Hall, Oxford, Ohio 45056.

CAREER: Elementary school teacher in Indianapolis, Ind., 1967-69; Miami University, Oxford, Ohio, assistant professor, 1971-74, associate professor of physical education, 1974—, director of Perceptual-Motor Learning Laboratory, 1971-74. *Member:* American Alliance for Health, Physical Education and Recreation, Midwest Association for Health, Physical Education and Recreation, Ohio Association for Health, Physical Education and Recreation, Phi Epsilon Kappa.

WRITINGS: (with Richard A. Simmons) *Do It Yourself: Creative Movement Experiences with Innovative Physical Education Equipment*, Kendall-Hunt, 1973; (with David L. Gallahue and George C. Luedke) *A Conceptual Approach to Moving and Learning*, Wiley, 1975; (editor) *Selected Readings in Elementary School Physical Education*, American Alliance for Health, Physical Education and Recreation, 1975; (with Lisa Rini) *Inexpensive Equipment Ideas and Activities for Use in Perceptual-Motor Development*, Wiley, 1976; (editor) *How We Do It Game Book*, American Alliance for Health, Physical Education and Recreation, in press.

Contributor of more than fifteen articles to education and physical education journals, including *Journal of Health, Physical Education and Recreation, Ohio High School Athlete, Perceptual and Motor Skills, Physical Educator*, and *Research Quarterly*.

SIDELIGHTS: Werner holds a patent for his invention of a spring-mounted balance beam. He also made "Urban Folk Dance," a sound recording, with Vivian Lewis and Herb Drummond, for Educational Activities, Inc., 1975. *Avocational interests:* Outdoor education, camping, canoeing.

* * *

WEST, Earle H(uddleston) 1925-

PERSONAL: Born August 3, 1925, in Asheville, N.C.; son of Earle H. (a lawyer) and Irene H. (a teacher; maiden name, Sowell) West; married Tommie Ann Hickox (a teacher), June 11, 1951; children: Mary Ann (Mrs. Byron Sudbury), Earle H., Jr., Elizabeth N., Paul S. *Education:* Freed-Hardeman College, junior college certificate, 1944; Vanderbilt University, B.A., 1946, M.S., 1951; George Peabody College for Teachers, Ph.D., 1961. *Religion:* Church of Christ. *Home:* 10016 Reddick Dr., Silver Spring, Md. 20901. *Office:* School of Education, Howard University, Washington, D.C. 20001.

CAREER: David Lipscomb College, Nashville, Tenn., instructor in chemistry, 1946-56; Oklahoma Christian College, Bartlesville, dean, 1957-58; minister, West Side Church of Christ, Cleveland, Ohio, 1958-62; Howard University, Washington, D.C., assistant professor, 1962-65, associate professor, 1965-70, professor of education, 1970—. *Member:* American Educational Research Association, History of Education Society, John Dewey Society.

WRITINGS: (Editor) *Bibliography of Doctoral Research Related to the Negro, 1933-1966*, Xerox Corp., 1969; (editor) *The Black American and Education*, C. E. Merrill, 1972. Acting editor of *Journal of Negro Education*, 1970-73.

WORK IN PROGRESS: A history of Black education.

* * *

WEST, Herbert B(uell) 1916-

PERSONAL: Born April 19, 1916, in Birmingham, Ala.; son of Edward Hamilton (a realtor) and Clarine (Buell) West; married Maria Selden McDonald, November 29, 1946; children: Newill, Herbert Buell, William McDonald, Maria Selden, Jane Hamilton. *Education:* Birmingham-Southern College, A.B., 1936. *Religion:* Episcopalian. *Home:* 28 Driftway Lane, Darien, Conn. 06820. *Office:* New York Community Trust, 415 Madison Ave., New York, N.Y. 10017.

CAREER: Batten, Barton, Durstine & Osborn (advertising agency), New York, N.Y., writer, 1936-50, vice-president and account supervisor, 1950-66; New York Community Trust (community foundation for New York City), New York, N.Y., director, 1967—, member of distribution committee, 1967—; Community Funds, Inc. (corporate affiliate of New York Community Trust), New York, N.Y., president, 1967—; James Foundation, New York, N.Y., president, 1968—. Chairman of board of American Branch, International Social Service, 1966-72; member of board of trustees, United Community Funds and Council of America, 1968-71, and Fay School, 1970—; member of board of directors and vice-president, Travellers Aid-International Social Service, 1972—; member of board of trustees, New York University Medical Center, 1973—. *Military service:* U.S. Army, Adjutant Generals' Corps, 1941-46; became major; received Legion of Merit. *Member:* Century Association, Tokeneke Club.

WRITINGS: *Stay With Me, Lord*, Seabury, 1974.

* * *

WEST, Herbert Faulkner 1898-1974

January 6, 1898—November 9, 1974; American educator, book collector, and author of several books on book collecting. Obituaries: *New York Times*, November 11, 1974; *AB Bookman's Weekly*, December 2, 1974. (*CA*-19/20).

* * *

WHEELER, Burton K(endall) 1882-1975

February 27, 1882—January 6, 1975; American lawyer, politician, former U.S. Senator from Montana (1923-47), and author. Obituaries: *New York Times*, January 8, 1975; *Washington Post*, January 8, 1975; *Time*, January 20, 1975.

* * *

WHEELER, Charles (Thomas) 1892-1974

March 14, 1892—August 22, 1974; British sculptor, painter, and author. Obituaries: *New York Times*, August 23, 1974. (*CA*-29/32).

WHIPKEY, Kenneth Lee 1932-

PERSONAL: Born June 5, 1932, in Cortland, Ohio; son of Charles Leigh and Marjorie (Hefner) Whipkey; married Mary Nell Glaser (a mathematics professor), March 2, 1962. *Education:* Attended Youngstown University, 1950-52; Kent State University, A.B., 1953, M.A., 1958; summer graduate study at French Ministry of Education, 1954, and University of Colorado, 1955, 1959; graduate study at Michigan State University, 1960; Case Western Reserve University, Ph.D., 1969. *Home:* 456 Bradley Lane, Youngstown, Ohio 44504. *Office:* Department of Mathematics, Westminster College, New Wilmington, Pa. 16142.

CAREER: High school teacher of mathematics and physics, and assistant principal in the public schools of Kinsman, Ohio, 1954-57; Youngstown University, Youngstown, Ohio, instructor, 1957-60, assistant professor of mathematics, 1960-67; Westminster College, New Wilmington, Pa., assistant professor, 1968-69, associate professor of mathematics, 1969—. Assistant statistician, Mallory Sharon Titanium Corp, summer, 1955; workshop instructor, Holt, Rinehart & Winston, 1961; instructor, National Science Foundation-In-Service Year Institute, 1964-67; trustee, Mountain View Club, 1973—. *Member:* National Council of Teachers of Mathematics, American Numismatic Association, Kappa Mu Epsilon, Pi Mu Epsilon. *Awards, honors:* Danforth associate, 1961—.

WRITINGS: The Power of Calculus, Wiley, 1972, 2nd edition, 1975.

WORK IN PROGRESS: Linear Mathematics on Finite Domain for Wiley; *Power of Basic Mathematics* for Prentice-Hall.

* * *

WHITAKER, Ben(jamin Charles George) 1934-

PERSONAL: Born September 15, 1934, in London, England; son of Sir John and Lady Pamela (Snowden) Whitaker; married Janet Alison Stewart, December 18, 1964. *Education:* New College, Oxford, B.A., 1957. *Home:* 13 Elsworthy Rd., London N.W.3, England. *Agent:* A. D. Peters, 10 Buckingham, London W.C.2, England.

CAREER: Called to the Bar, Inner Temple, 1959. Private practice as barrister, 1959-67; Labor member of Parliament for Hampstead, 1966-70; British Government, junior minister for Overseas Development, 1969-70; Minority Rights Group, London, England, deputy director, 1970-71, director, 1971—. Vice-chairman of Danilo Dolci Trust, 1960-69; lecturer in law at University of London, 1963-64; member of council, University College, London. *Military service:* Served in British Army, Coldstream Guards, 1952-54; became lieutenant.

WRITINGS—All nonfiction: *The Police*, Eyre & Spottiswoode, 1964; (editor) *A Radical Future*, J. Cape, 1967; *Crime and Society*, Anthony Blond, 1967; (with Kenneth Browne) *Parks for People*, Winchester Press, 1971; (editor) *The Fourth World: Victims of Group Oppression*, Shocken, 1973; *The Philanthropoids: Foundations and Society*, Morrow, 1974 (published as *The Foundations: An Anatomy of Philanthropy and Society*, Eyre Methuen, 1974). General editor of "Sources for Contemporary Issues" series, David & Charles, 1974—. Contributor of articles and reviews to periodicals and newspapers, including *New Statesman, London Times, Times Literary Supplement, Observer*, and *New Society*.

WORK IN PROGRESS: Editing a book titled *On Censorship*; a book on the police.

* * *

WHITAKER, T(ommy) J(ames) 1949-

PERSONAL: Born January 5, 1949, in Vicksburg, Miss.; son of Tommy James, Sr. (a laborer) and Mary Helen Whitaker; married Verna Lenora Wilson, May 26, 1973; children: Kenneth Raymond Wheatley (stepson), Cherisse Yvonne. *Education:* Hinds Junior College, student, 1973—. *Religion:* Baptist. *Home and office:* 2316 Grove St., Vicksburg, Miss. 39180.

CAREER: Free-lance photographer. Photographic laboratory technician at Waterways Experiment Station, Vicksburg, Miss., 1972—. *Military service:* U.S. Air Force, 1968-72; became sergeant. *Member:* International Black Writers Conference, Black Arts Music Society of Jackson, Umojo Creative Workshop. *Awards, honors:* Second prize in poetry from International Black Writers Conference, 1972.

WRITINGS: (Contributor) Beatrice M. Murphy, editor, *Today's Negro Voices*, Messner, 1970; *The Empty Road* (poems), Ja Vekcher, 1971; (with Barbara Townley and Harrison Havard) *Black Love's Black Wealth*, Ja Vekcher, 1974. Author of "The Grassroot Woman," one-act play, first performed in Vicksburg, Miss., at Baltes Gym, April 27, 1973. Contributor to *Black Writers News*, *Black Expressions*, *Wisconsin Poetry*, and *Nkombo*.

WORK IN PROGRESS: The Real War, a novel; "Ain't Nothin' Real but Laughter," a one-act play; "The Blues Ain't Nothin' but a Good Man Feelin' Bad," a play; a novel set in Vicksburg during the 1950's.

* * *

WHITE, Howard B. 1912(?)-1974

1912(?)—November 4, 1974; American educator, political philosopher, editor, and author. Obituaries: *New York Times*, November 6, 1974.

* * *

WHITE, James 1928-

PERSONAL: Born April 7, 1928, in Belfast, Northern Ireland; married Margaret Sarah Martin, May 17, 1955; children: Patricia, Martin, Peter. *Education:* Educated in Northern Ireland. *Politics:* None. *Religion:* Roman Catholic. *Home:* 10 Riverdale Gardens, Belfast BT11 9DG, Northern Ireland. *Agent:* Leslie Flood, E. J. Carnell Agency, 17 Burwash Rd., London SE 18, England. *Office:* Shorts Aviation, Airport Rd., Belfast BT3 9DZ, Northern Ireland.

CAREER: Ladies' & Gents' Tailoring Co., Belfast, Northern Ireland, apprentice, 1943-48, salesman, 1948-61, manager, 1961-65; Shorts Aviation, Belfast, technical clerk, 1965-66, publicity assistant, 1966-68, publicity officer, 1968—; novelist. *Member:* Science Fiction Writers of America, Knights of St. Fantony. *Awards, honors:* Europa Special Science Fiction Award, 1972, for *All Judgment Fled*.

WRITINGS—Novels: *The Secret Visitors*, Ace Books, 1957; *Hospital Station*, Ballantine, 1962; *Star Surgeon*, Ballantine, 1962; *Second Ending*, Ace Books, 1963; *Deadly Litter*, Ballantine, 1964; *Open Prison*, Ace Books, 1965; *The Watch Below*, Whiting & Wheaton, 1966; *All Judg-*

ment Fled, Rapp & Whiting, 1968; *The Aliens among Us*, Ballantine, 1969; *Tomorrow Is Too Far*, M. Joseph, 1971; *Major Operation*, Ballantine, 1971; *Dark Inferno*, M. Joseph, 1973; *The Dream Millennium*, M. Joseph, 1974.

WORK IN PROGRESS: An untitled science fiction novel.

SIDELIGHTS: White told *CA*: "I am non-racist, non-sectarian, non-violent and an optimist despite living in Belfast's Andersonstown district, and I hope I am too old or too stubborn to change these sentiments. I believe that the best stories are those which face ordinary characters (not necessarily human characters) with extraordinary situations, which is why I prefer to write science fiction."

* * *

WHITE, Jo Ann 1941-

PERSONAL: Born September 7, 1941, in Fredericksburg, Va.; daughter of Lloyd (a U.S. Navy career officer) and Josephine (Kosinski) White; married Edgar E. Coons, Jr. (a college professor), January 3, 1969. *Education:* Duke University, B.A., 1959; University of Pennsylvania, graduate study, 1963; New York University, M.A., 1970. *Home:* 650 Ocean Ave., #D-7, Brooklyn, N.Y. 11226. *Office:* Simon & Schuster, Inc., 1 West 39th St., New York, N.Y. 10018.

CAREER: Greystone Press, New York, N.Y., writer, 1964-65; Crowell-Collier & Macmillan Co., New York, N.Y., writer, 1965-67; Holt, Rinehart & Winston, Inc., editor, 1967-68; Simon & Schuster, Inc., New York, N.Y., editor, 1968-74.

WRITINGS: Impact!: African Views of the West, Messner, 1971; *African Views of the West*, Messner, 1972; *The Complete Shih Tzu*, Howell Book, in press. Member of editorial board of *Shih Tzu Bulletin*.

AVOCATIONAL INTERESTS: Breeding and showing Shih Tzu, long-haired Chinese toy dogs (Ms. White is an A.K.C. licensed handler).

* * *

WHITE, Orion F(orrest), Jr. 1938-

PERSONAL: Born January 24, 1938, in Wharton, Tex.; son of Orion F. and Bernice (Martin) White; married Patricia Louise Oliver, August 22, 1958; children: Phyllis Suzanne, Orion Paige. *Education:* University of Texas, A.B., 1960; Indiana University, Ph.D., 1964. *Home address:* Shady Lawn Ct., Chapel Hill, N.C. 27514. *Office:* Department of Political Science, University of North Carolina, Chapel Hill, N.C. 27514.

CAREER: University of Texas, Austin, assistant professor, 1964-67, associate professor of political science, 1967-69; Syracuse University, Syracuse, N.Y., associate professor of political science, 1969-72; University of North Carolina, Chapel Hill, associate professor of political science, 1972—. Visiting associate professor at University of California (Berkeley), 1969. *Member:* American Political Science Association, American Society for Public Administration.

WRITINGS: (Editor with John S. Waggaman and C. Richard Hofstetter, and contributor) *Rush County Indiana: Voting in General Elections, 1890-1965*, Indiana Historical Society, 1967; (with Gideon Sjoberg and H. Donald Hancock) *Politics in the Post-Welfare States: A Comparison of the United States and Sweden*, Indiana University, 1968; (with E. S. Redford) *What Manned Space Program after Reaching the Moon: Government Attempts to Decide, 1962-1968*, Inter-University Case Program, Syracuse University, 1971; *Psychic Energy and Organizational Change*, Sage Publications, 1973.

Contributor: Frank Marin, editor, *Toward a New Public Administration*, Chandler Publishing, 1970; Dwight Waldo, editor, *Public Administration in a Time of Turbulence*, Chandler Publishing, 1971; George Frederickson, editor, *Neighborhood Control in the 1970's*, Chandler Publishing, 1973; Hancock and Sjoberg, editors, *Politics in the Post-Industrial State: Responses to the New Individualism*, Columbia University Press, 1971.

Contributor to *Public Affairs Comment*, *Public Administration Review*, *Southwestern Social Science Quarterly*, *Journal of Comparative Administration*, *Maxwell Review*, and *Policy Studies Journal*.

WORK IN PROGRESS: A book presenting a theory of public administration based on the idea of individualism.

* * *

WHITESIDE, Robert L(eo) 1907-

PERSONAL: Born November 24, 1907, in Madera, Calif.; son of Leonard Grenzil (a chef) and Mable Adele (Busby) Whiteside; married Adeline Elizabeth Holt (a personologist), March 17, 1928; children: David (deceased), Daniel, Margot (Mrs. Warren E. Massey). *Education:* University of California, Berkeley, B.A., 1950. *Home:* 2 Palm Ave., Larkspur, Calif. 94939. *Office:* Interstate College of Personology, 1209 Burlingame Ave., Burlingame, Calif. 94010.

CAREER: Tulare Advance-Register, Tulare, Calif., news editor, 1929-45; certified teacher and counselor, Personology Foundation, Los Angeles, Calif., 1942; San Francisco Personology Foundation, San Francisco, Calif., director, 1946-57; Interstate College of Personology, Burlingame, Calif., founder and president, 1957-75. Member of board of advisers of Institute for Humane Studies. *Member:* American Academy of Personology Counselors and Teachers, Lions (president, 1920-30), Bi-County Tennis League, Tulare Chamber of Commerce (past member of board of directors).

WRITINGS: You: The Most Important Person in the World, Tulare Times Press, 1944; *This Is Personology*, Personology College Press, 1961, 2nd edition, 1963; *Personology: The Dynamics of Success*, Fell, 1969; *Face Language*, Fell, 1974. Editor of *Personology Journal*, 1946-75.

WORK IN PROGRESS: A sequel to *Face Language*.

* * *

WHITMAN, Howard 1915(?)-1975

1915(?)—January 29, 1975; American writer, syndicated radio and television commentator, and editor. Obituaries: *New York Times*, January 31, 1975; *Washington Post*, February 1, 1975.

* * *

WHITNEY, Alex(andra) 1922-

PERSONAL: Born October 8, 1922, in Flushing, N.Y.; daughter of John (president of American Spice Exchange) and Fanita (Moll) Clarke; married Roger Whitney (an industrial lighting designer), March 31, 1942; children: Susan A. (Mrs. George W. Lewis III). *Education:* Attended David Mannes College of Music, 1938-41. *Office:* Henry Z. Walck, Inc., 750 Third Ave., New York, N.Y. 10017.

CAREER: Henry Z. Walck, Inc. (children's book division of David McKay Co.), New York, N.Y., promotion director, 1963—. *Member:* Publishers' Library Promotion Group (president, 1968-71), Publishers Ad Club, Children's Book Council.

WRITINGS—Books for children: *Once a Bright Red Tiger*, Walck, 1973; *Stiff Ears: Animal Folktales of the North American Indian*, Walck, 1974.

WORK IN PROGRESS: A study of pre-Columbian Central and South America.

* * *

WIARDA, Howard J(ohn) 1939-

PERSONAL: Born November 30, 1939, in Grosse Pointe, Mich.; son of John R. and Cornelia (Drooger) Wiarda; married Ieda Siqueira (a researcher in political science), 1964; children: Kristy, Howard, Jonathan. *Education:* University of Michigan, B.A., 1961; University of Florida, M.A., 1962, Ph.D., 1965. *Home:* 85 Mechanic St., Amherst, Mass. 01002. *Office:* Department of Political Science, University of Massachusetts, Amherst, Mass. 01002.

CAREER: University of Florida, Gainesville, lecturer in political science, 1963; Florida Atlantic University, Boca Raton, instructor in political science, 1965; University of Massachusetts, Amherst, assistant professor, 1965-69, associate professor, 1969-73, professor of political science, 1973—. Member of Amherst Town Meeting. Consultant to Peace Corps, Institute for the Comparative Study of Political Systems, and U.S. Department of State.

MEMBER: American Political Science Association, Latin American Studies Association, Iberian Social Studies Association, Northeast Political Science Association, Northeast Latin American Studies Association, Phi Kappa Phi, Pi Sigma Alpha. *Awards, honors:* Fulbright-Hays fellowship, 1964-65; National Endowment for the Humanities post-doctoral fellowship, summer, 1968; award from *Choice*, 1968, for *Dictatorship and Development*; senior fellowship from Mershon Center of Ohio State University, 1969-70; foreign area fellowship from Social Science Research Council and American Council of Learned Societies, 1972-73; research grant from Center for Population Research of National Institutes of Health, 1972-74.

WRITINGS: (Editor) *Dominican Republic: Election Factbook*, Institute for the Comparative Study of Political Systems, 1966; (editor) *Materials for the Study of Politics and Government in the Dominican Republic: 1930-1966*, Universidad Catolica Madre y Maestra, 1968; *Dictatorship and Development: The Methods of Control in Trujillo's Dominican Republic*, University of Florida Press, 1968; *The Dominican Republic: Nation in Transition*, Praeger, 1969; *The Brazilian Catholic Labor Movement: The Dilemmas of National Development*, Labor Relations and Research Center, University of Massachusetts, 1969; (editor and contributor) *Politics and Social Change in Latin America*, University of Massachusetts Press, 1974.

Contributor: Gary J. Mounce and Anne H. Sutherland, editors, *After Santo Domingo, What?: United States Intervention in Latin America, An Inquiry*, Colloquy on Public Issues, University of Texas, 1966; *Caribbean Area Studies Seminar: Readings*, Center for Advanced International Studies, University of Miami (Coral Gables, Fla.), 1968; Ben G. Burnett and Kenneth Johnson, editors, *Political Forces in Latin America: Dimensions of the Quest for Political Stability*, Wadsworth, 1968; Eugenio Chang-Rodriguez, editor, *The Lingering Crisis*, Las Americas, 1969; Richard R. Fagen and Wayne A. Cornelius, editors, *Political Power in Latin America*, Prentice-Hall, 1970; Martin Needler, editor, *Political Systems of Latin America*, Van Nostrand, 1970; William Tyler and H. Jon Rosenbaum, editors, *Contemporary Brazil: Issues in Economic and Political Development*, Praeger, 1972; Lewis Hanke, editor, *History of Latin American Civilization*, Volume II, Little, Brown, 1973; Terry McCoy, editor, *The Politics of Population in Latin America*, Ballinger, 1974; Frederick Pike and Thomas Stritch, editors, *The New Corporatism: Social and Political Structures in the Iberian World*, University of Notre Dame Press, 1974; Jack M. Hopkins, editor, *Studies of Latin American Elites*, Dunnellen, in press.

Contributor to *Encyclopaedia Britannica* and *Encyclopedia of Latin America*. Contributor of more than thirty articles and reviews on Latin America to journals, including *Dissent*, *American Political Science Review*, *New Republic*, *Polymagma*, *Caribbean Monthly Bulletin*, *Review of Politics*, *Iberian Studies*, *World Politics*, and *Western Political Quarterly*. Editorial assistant of *Hispanic American Historical Review*, 1962; advisory editor of *Social Science Quarterly*, 1968—, and *Western Political Quarterly*, 1973—. Manuscript reviewer for *Polity*, *Western Political Quarterly*, *American Journal of Political Science*, *Comparative Politics*, *Journal of Politics*, and for Wadsworth, Duxbury, Scott, Foresman, Lexington Publishing, University of Texas Press, University of Massachusetts Press, Rutgers University Press, and University of Chicago Press.

WORK IN PROGRESS: Dictatorship, Development, and Disintegration: The Political System of the Dominican Republic; *The Politics of Population Policy in Latin America*, with wife, Ieda Siqueira Wiarda; *The Other Great "Ism": Corporatism and Development in Modern Portugal*; *Politics and Development in Modern Portugal*; research on development in Iberia and Latin America.

SIDELIGHTS: Wiarda has traveled in Latin America and Western Europe.

* * *

WIDERBERG, Siv 1931-

PERSONAL: Born June 12, 1931, in Bromma, Sweden; daughter of Nils (an art critic) and Gertrud (a midwife) Palmgren; married Bertil Widerberg (an editor); children: Gertrud. *Education:* Educated in Sweden. *Politics:* Communist. *Religion:* None. *Home:* Hagagatan 16, 113 48 Stockholm, Sweden.

CAREER: Teacher in Sweden, 1951-55; journalist, 1955—, and full-time writer, 1966—. Member of board of directors of Swedish Authors Fund, 1972-74. *Member:* Society of the Swedish Union of Authors (member of board of directors, 1971-72), Writers' Centre.

WRITINGS—Children's books: *Gertrud paa daghem* (title means "Gertrud in kindergarten"), Raben & Sjoegren, 1966; *Snart sjutton* (title means "Soon Sixteen"), Raben & Sjoegren, 1966; *Apropaa mej* (title means "About Me"), Raben & Sjoegren, 1967; *Aakes trafikskola* (title means "Aakes Traffic School"), Raben & Sjoegren, 1967; *Mamma pappa barn*, Zindermans, 1967, translation by Irene D. Morris published as *The Kid's Own XYZ of Love and Sex*, Stein & Day, 1972; *Alldeles vanliga Hjalmar och Hedvig* (title means "Not Unusual Hjalmar and Hedvig"), Raben & Sjoegren, 1968; *Se upp moln* (title means "Look! The Sky"), Gebers, 1968; *Min baesta vaen*, Raben & Sjoegren, 1969, translated and published as *My Best Friend*,

Putnam, 1970; *Agneta och Bjoern* (title means "Agneta and Bjoern"), Raben & Sjoegren, 1969; *En syl i vaedret* (title means "Please Talk"), Gebers, 1969; *Ett enda stort ljug* (title means "A Big Lie"), Raben & Sjoegren, 1970; (with Goeran Palm) *Graeddvargen* (play; title means "The Cream Wolf"), Foerfattarfoerlaget, 1970; *Jag heter Siv* (title means "My Name Is Siv"), Foerfattarfoerlaget, 1971; *Nya byxor och gamla* (title means "New and Old Trousers"), Gebers, 1972; *Ingrid och Soeren* (title means "Ingrid and Soeren"), Raben & Sjoegren, 1973; *I'm Like Me*, translated from the Swedish by Verne Moberg, Feminist Press, 1973; *Sitt inte paa mej* (title means "Don't Sit on Me"), Gebers, 1973; *Vi aer maanga* (title means "We Are Many"), Gebers, 1974.

Also author of plays for children, (with others) "Haall mej haart" (title means "Come Close to Me"); "Klara, faerdiga, spring" (title means "Let's Run"); "Killarna" (title means "The Guys"); "Hjaelp tjyven" (title means "Help the Thief"); "Den nya staden" (title means "The New Village"); (with Ylva Maartens) "Soerens far" (title means "Soeren's Daddy").

WORK IN PROGRESS: Five TV programs about China for children; editing a children's page in a weekly, *Folket i Bild*; a children's book with poetry about China; political (socialistic) books and plays for children; television and radio plays.

* * *

WIDICUS, Wilbur W(ilson), Jr. 1932-

PERSONAL: Born March 31, 1932, in Edwardsville, Ill.; son of Wilbur Wilson and Agnes (Closterman) Widicus; married Isabel Kemp Thornton (a teacher), December 23, 1963; children: Shona Agnes, Maura Anna Kemp. *Education:* Southern Illinois University, B.S., 1958; Indiana University, M.B.A., 1959; Columbia University, Ph.D., 1964. *Home:* 2985 Northwest Princess St., Corvallis, Ore. 97330. *Office:* School of Business, Oregon State University, Corvallis, Ore. 97331.

CAREER: University of Vermont, Burlington, instructor in business, 1959-61, 1962-63; Pace College, New York, N.Y., assistant professor of finance, 1964; Oregon State University, Corvallis, assistant professor, 1964-67, associate professor of finance, 1967—, chairman of department of marketing, finance and production, 1968-71, associate dean, 1971—. *Military service:* U.S. Coast Guard, 1951-54. *Member:* American Finance Association, Financial Management Association, Western Finance Association.

WRITINGS: (With T. E. Stitzel) *Personnel Investments* (textbook), Irwin, 1971; (with Stitzel) *Today's Investments for Tomorrow's Security* (textbook), Dow Jones/Irwin, 1971.

WORK IN PROGRESS: Revising *Personnel Investments* and *Today's Investments for Tomorrow's Security*.

* * *

WIGGINS, Arthur W. 1938-

PERSONAL: Born March 5, 1938, in South Bend, Ind.; son of Donald A. (a skilled tradesman) and Miriam (Zurbuch) Wiggins; married Regina Ritter (an administrative assistant), February 4, 1961; children: Ann Marie, John Patrick. *Education:* University of Notre Dame, B.S., 1960; University of Michigan, M.S., 1965, further graduate study. *Office:* Department of Physics, Oakland Community College, Farmington Hills, Mich.

CAREER: Bendix Corp., Ann Arbor, Mich., research physicist in electronics research, 1960-64; Conductron Corp., Ann Arbor, Mich., section head in electronics research, 1964-68; University of Michigan, Ann Arbor, research associate, 1968-69; Oakland Community College, Farmington Hills, Mich., associate professor of physics, 1969—. *Member:* American Association of Physics Teachers.

WRITINGS: Physical Science with Environmental Applications, Houghton, 1974.

WORK IN PROGRESS: Physics: From the Simple to the Elegant, completion expected in 1976; science fiction stories with educational or environmental overtones.

SIDELIGHTS: Wiggins writes: "The immensely difficult job of learning to live in harmony with nature and with each other must involve some knowledge of science. My goal is to teach science to college students with humanity and humor so that they can get on with the more difficult sociological problems."

* * *

WILCOX, Daniel 1941-

PERSONAL: Born April 17, 1941, in New York, N.Y.; son of Philip Emerson (in advertising) and Mildred (a writer; maiden name, Harris) Wilcox. *Education:* Cornell University, B.A., 1963. *Home and office:* 749 West End Ave., New York, N.Y. 10025.

CAREER: Robert Keeshan Associates, New York, N.Y., staff writer for "Captain Kangaroo" series, 1965-68; Children's TV Workshop, New York, staff writer for "Sesame Street" series, 1970-73; ETC Theatre Co., New York, managing director and producer, 1973-74; Chamber Theatre, New York, program director, 1973; full-time, freelance writer, 1974—. Consultant to Western Publishing and to City University of New York. *Member:* American Society of Composers, Authors and Publishers; Writers Guild of America, East. *Awards, honors:* Emmy Award from National Academy of Television Arts and Sciences, 1969-70, for "Sesame Street."

WRITINGS—All children's books: (With Emily Kingsley, Jeffrey Moss, and Norman Stiles) *The Sesame Street 1,2,3 Story Book*, Random House, 1973; (with Stiles) *The Perils of Penelope*, Random House, 1973; (with Stiles) *Grover and the Everything in the Whole Wide World Museum*, Random House, 1974; (with Moss and Stiles) *The Sesame Street A,B,C Story Book*, Random House, 1974. Head writer of script for "Come to Florida—Before It's Gone," broadcast by PBS, 1971, and an episode for "That's My Mama," ABC, 1975.

WORK IN PROGRESS: Ernie the Cave King and Sherlock the Smart Person in "The Invention of Paper," and *I'm My Mommy/I'm My Daddy*, "Sesame Street" books for Western; *The Great Sesame Street A,B,C Hunt*, for Me-Books.

* * *

WILDER, Robert (Ingersoll) 1901-1974

January 25, 1901—August 22, 1974; American novelist, journalist, playwright, author of screenplays, and publicist. Obituaries: *New York Times*, August 23, 1974; *Washington Post*, August 23, 1974; *Publishers Weekly*, September 16, 1974. (*CA*-13/14).

WILES, David K(imball) 1942-

PERSONAL: Born February 23, 1942, in Tuscaloosa, Ala.; son of Kimball (a professor of education) and Hilda (a teacher; maiden name, Long) Wiles; married Marilyn McCall (a professor of education), December 31, 1964; children: Corey, Matthew. *Education:* Florida State University, B.S., 1964; University of Florida, M.Ed., 1967, Ed.D., 1969. *Home:* 1337 Dana Dr., Oxford, Ohio 45056. *Office:* School of Education, Miami University, Oxford, Ohio 45056.

CAREER: University of Toronto, Toronto, Ontario, assistant professor of education, 1969-72; Virginia Polytechnic Institute and State University, Blacksburg, associate professor of education, 1972-74; Miami University, Oxford, Ohio, associate professor of educational administration, 1974—. *Military service:* U.S. Army, 1965-66; became first lieutenant. *Member:* American Educational Research Association, Association for Supervision and Curriculum Development, Phi Delta Kappa.

WRITINGS Changing Perspectives in Educational Research, Charles A. Jones, 1972. Contributor to education journals, including *Teachers College Record, Behavioral Science, Educational Forum, Educational Administration Quarterly, Midwest Journal of Public Administration,* and *Education and Urban Society*. Abstractor for *Educational Administration Abstracts*.

WORK IN PROGRESS: Political Perspectives of Educational Administration (tentative title).

SIDELIGHTS: Wiles writes: "Writing is a means by which existing myths of schooling governance and prescriptive methodologies for its analysis can be challenged through institutional channels of reward and legitimacy. The dilemma of becoming a corporate 'radical' or personal 'institution' is mediated by realization of the incremental muddling called organizational change, the instrumental nature of policy rationality, and the inadequacy of communication by legitimized channels of the institution."

* * *

WILK, David 1951-

PERSONAL: Born March 17, 1951, in New York, N.Y.; son of Max (a writer) and Barbara (a writer, artist, and teacher; maiden name, Balensweig) Wilk. *Education:* Yale University, B.A. (magna cum laude), 1972; attended Antioch Graduate School of Education, 1972. *Politics:* Radical/anarchist. *Religion:* Pantheo-Buddhism. *Office address:* Box 86, Carrboro, N.C. 27510.

CAREER: Truck (magazine), Carrboro, N.C., editor, 1970-74; Common Ground Cooperative, Inc., Brattleboro, Vt., manager, 1973; Atlantis Sound Inc., Chapel Hill, N.C., salesman, 1974; South Carolina Arts Commission, Columbia, S.C., poet-in-residence, 1974-75; free-lance writer, 1975—. Member of the board of directors of Middle Earth, Inc., 1970-71. *Member:* Coordinating Council of Literary Magazines, Committee of Small Magazine Editors and Presses, Southern Committee of Small Magazine Editors and Presses (chair-one, 1974-75), New England Small Press Association.

WRITINGS: Sassafras (poems), Tansy Press, 1973; *Road Man* (poems and prose), Magenta Press, 1974; *Bullets* (poems), Magenta Press, 1975. Contributor of poems and essays to small magazines, including *Io* and *Man/Root*. Contributing editor of North Atlantic Books, 1973-74.

WORK IN PROGRESS: Poems and exploratory prose, *The Phenomenology of Landscape*; a book of poems, *Can I Get a Witness*; continuing research toward the revival of the spirit world.

SIDELIGHTS: Wilk told *CA* he is interested in "mammalian studies, floral geographies, history of the American continent, distant beginnings of living with the world as it presents itself as house and HOME, and the continuation of those beginnings in the present."

* * *

WILKINS, Ernest J. 1918-

PERSONAL: Born November 10, 1918, in Franklin, Ariz. *Education:* Brigham Young University, B.A., 1947; Stanford University, M.A., 1949, Ph.D., 1953. *Religion:* Church of Jesus Christ of Latter-Day Saints. *Home:* 351 East Center, Provo, Utah 84601. *Office:* Olympus Research Corp., One Olympus Plaza, Salt Lake City, Utah 84105.

CAREER: Research analyst on Howard Hughes staff in Los Angeles, Calif., 1951-53; Brigham Young University, Provo, Utah, professor of Spanish and Latin American literature, 1953-61, director and president of Language Training Mission, 1961-70, director of Language Research Center, 1971-74. Director of Institutes for Language Teaching training, summers, 1956-60; project director of Defense Language Institute, 1970-71, and Olympus Research Corp., 1974-75. *Military service:* U.S. Army, Counter-Intelligence Corps. *Member:* Latin American Studies Association (charter member, 1956), Rocky Mountain Latin American Studies Association (vice-president, 1956-57), Utah Council of Foreign Language Teachers (past president).

WRITINGS: (With Terrence L. Hansen) *Espanol Para Misioneros*, Deseret, 1964; (with Hansen) *Espanol Para Jovenes*, Brigham Young University Press, 1964; (with Hansen) *Portugues Para Missionarios*, Deseret, 1964; *Espanol A Lo Vivo*, Level I, Blaisdell Publishing, 1964, 3rd edition (with workbook and instructor's manual), Xerox College Publishing, 1974, Level II, Blaisdell Publishing, 1966, 2nd edition (with workbook and instructor's manual), Xerox College Publishing, 1972; *Deutsch fuer Missionare*, Deseret, 1965; (with Anita Jarvis) *Por los Senderos de lo Hispanico*, Xerox College Publishing, 1971; (editor with Donald B. Holsinger) *Brasil Para Principiantes*, Brigham Young University Press, 1971; (with Jon Enos) *Le Francais Vivant* (with workbook and instructor's manual), Xerox College Publishing, Level I, 1972, 2nd edition, 1975, Level II, 1975; (with Barry Nielsen) *Beginning German: A Practical Approach* (with workbook and instructor's manual), Xerox College Publishing, 1972; *Individualized Conversational Spanish for Education Executives*, Link Enterprises, in press; *Individualized Conversational Spanish for Supervisors and Teachers of Migrant Education*, Olympus Publishing, in press. Contributor to *Enciclopedia Proliber S.A.* and *Brigham Young University Studies*.

SIDELIGHTS: Wilkins was a director of residence study tour programs in Mexico City.

* * *

WILLIAMS, Harold R(oger) 1935-

PERSONAL: Born August 22, 1935, in Arcade, N.Y.; son of Harry A. (a laborer) and Gertrude Anna (Sharf) Williams; married Lucia Dorothy Preuschoff (a teacher), 1955; children: Theresa, Mark. *Education:* Harpur College,

B.A., 1961; Pennsylvania State University, M.A., 1962; University of Nebraska, Ph.D., 1966; Harvard University, postdoctoral study, 1969-70. *Home:* 415 Suzanne Dr., Kent, Ohio 44240. *Office:* Department of Economics, Kent State University, Kent, Ohio 44242.

CAREER: Pennsylvania State University, University Park, instructor in economics, 1962-63; University of Nebraska, Lincoln, instructor in economics, 1965-66; Kent State University, Kent, Ohio, assistant professor, 1966-68, associate professor, 1968-72, professor of economics, 1972—. *Military service:* U.S. Army, Intelligence, 1954-57; served in Far East. *Member:* American Economic Association, Econometric Society, International Economic Association, Midwest Economic Association (vice-president, 1969-70), Midwest Finance Association, Southern Economic Association, Omicron Delta Epsilon, Beta Gamma Sigma, Pi Gamma Mu. *Awards, honors:* National Science Foundation faculty fellowship, 1969-70.

WRITINGS: Macroeconomics: Problems, Concepts and Self-Tests (workbook to accompany Wallace Peterson's *Income Employment and Economic Growth*), Norton, 1967, revised edition, 1974; (editor with John D. Huffnagle) *Macroeconomic Theory: Selected Readings*, Appleton, 1969; (with Henry Woudenberg) *Money, Banking, and Monetary Theory: Problems and Concepts*, Harper, 1969, revised edition, 1973; *Money and Banking Manual* (to accompany Lester V. Chandler's *The Economics of Money and Banking*), Harper, 1969, revised edition, 1973; (editor with Woudenberg) *Money, Banking, and Monetary Policy: Readings in Domestic and International Policy*, Harper, 1970. Contributor to journals in his field.

AVOCATIONAL INTERESTS: Bicycling, tennis, table tennis, walking through woods.

* * *

WILLIAMS, Hermann Warner, Jr. 1908-1974

November 2, 1908—November 3, 1974; American art historian, a pioneer in the history of American art, art museum director, and author of books on art. Obituaries: *New York Times*, November 4, 1974; *Washington Post*, November 4, 1974; *AB Bookman's Weekly*, November 25, 1974. (*CA*-7/8).

* * *

WILLIAMS, Ira E., Jr. 1926-

PERSONAL: Born October 14, 1926, in Wimauma, Fla.; son of Ira E. (a clergyman) and Oroll (McLeod) Williams; married Marilyn Lee Towers, August 26, 1952; children: Mary, Jeanie, Shelley, Wesley. *Education:* Oklahoma City University, B.A., 1949; Southern Methodist University, B.D., 1952. *Home:* 1418 Woodridge Dr., Abilene, Tex. 79605. *Office:* St. Paul Methodist Church, 525 Beech, Abilene, Tex. 79601.

CAREER: Ordained United Methodist minister; pastor in Santa Rosa, Calif., 1953-55, El Paso, Tex., 1955-58, Clinton, Okla., 1958-62, and Albuquerque, N.M., 1962-74; St. Paul Methodist Church, Abilene, Tex., pastor, 1974—. Treasurer of board of directors of Bataan Memorial Hospital, 1966-70; member of board of trustees of McMurry College. *Member:* Rotary. *Awards, honors:* D.D., McMurry College, 1967.

WRITINGS: God in Unexpected Places, Abingdon, 1974. Contributor to *Pulpit Digest* and *Texas Methodist*.

WORK IN PROGRESS: A book on theology for lay persons that will be "as easy to read as the sports page."

AVOCATIONAL INTERESTS: Snow-skiing, water sports, camping, travel.

* * *

WILLIAMS, John A(lfred) 1925-

PERSONAL: Born December 5, 1925, in Jackson, Miss.; son of John Henry (a laborer) and Ola Mae Williams; married Carolyn Clopton (divorced); married Lorrain Isaac, October 5, 1965; children: (first marriage) Gregory D., Dennis A.; (second marriage) Adam J. *Education:* Syracuse University, A.B., 1950, graduate study, 1950-51. *Residence:* New York, N.Y.

CAREER: Public relations man with Doug Johnson Associates, Syracuse, N.Y., 1952-54, and later with Arthur P. Jacobs Co.; Columbia Broadcasting System, Hollywood, Calif. and New York, N.Y., staff member for radio and television special events programs, 1954-55; Comet Press Books, New York, N.Y., publicity director, 1955-56; *Negro Market Newsletter*, New York, N.Y., publisher and editor, 1956-57; Abelard-Schuman Ltd., New York, N.Y., assistant to the publisher, 1957-58; American Committee on Africa, New York, N.Y., director of information, 1958; European correspondent for *Ebony* and *Jet* (magazines), New York, N.Y., 1958-59; Station WOV, New York, special events announcer, 1959; *Newsweek*, New York, N.Y., correspondent in Africa, 1964-65; City College of the City University of New York, New York, N.Y., lecturer in writing, 1968; College of the Virgin Islands, St. Thomas, lecturer in Afro-American literature, summer, 1968; guest writer at Sarah Lawrence College, Bronxville, N.Y.; University of California, Santa Barbara, regents lecturer, 1972; La Guardia Community College, Long Island City, N.Y., distinguished professor of English, 1973-74. Member of boards of directors of Black Academy of Arts and Letters, Rabinowitz Foundation, and New York State Council on the Arts. Work for National Educational Television includes narrating and writing "The History of the Negro People: Omwale—The Child Returns Home" (Nigeria), 1965; narrating, writing, and co-producing "The Creative Person: Henry Roth" (Spain), 1966; interviewer for "Newsfront" program, 1968. Has given lectures or readings at more than twenty major colleges and universities in the United States. *Military service:* U.S. Naval Reserve, pharmacist's mate, active duty, 1943-46; served in the Pacific. *Member:* Authors Guild. *Awards, honors:* Award from National Institute of Arts and Letters, 1962; centennial medal for outstanding achievement from Syracuse University, 1970.

WRITINGS: The Angry Ones (novel), Ace Books, 1960; *Night Song* (novel), Farrar, Straus, 1961; (editor) *The Angry Black* (anthology), Lancer Books, 1962; *Sissie* (novel), Farrar, Straus, 1963; *Africa: Her History, Lands, and People* (nonfiction), Cooper Square, 1963; *The Protectors* (nonfiction), Farrar, Straus, 1964; *This Is My Country Too* (nonfiction), New American Library, 1965; *The Man Who Cried I Am* (novel), Little, Brown, 1967; (cditor) *Beyond the Angry Black* (anthology), Cooper Square, 1967; *Sons of Darkness, Sons of Light* (novel), Little, Brown, 1969.

The Most Native of Sons (nonfiction), Doubleday, 1970; *The King God Didn't Save: Reflections on the Life and Death of Martin Luther King, Jr.* (nonfiction), Coward, 1970; *Captain Blackman* (novel), Doubleday, 1972; *Flashbacks* (nonfiction), Doubleday, 1973; *Mothersill and the Foxes* (novel), Doubleday, in press; *Minorities in the City* (nonfiction), Harper, in press.

Work is represented in anthologies, including *Harlem: A Community in Transition*, Citadel, 1964; *Best Short Stories of Negro Writers*, Little, Brown, 1967; *Black on Black*, Macmillan, 1968; *Thirty-Four by Schwartze Lieb*, Barmier & Nickel, 1968; *How We Live*, Macmillan, 1968; *Dark Symphony*, Free Press, 1968; *Nat Turner: Ten Black Writers Respond*, edited by John Henrik Clarke, Beacon Press, 1968; *The Now Reader*, Scott, Foresman, 1969; *The New Black Poetry*, International, 1969; *Black Literature in America*, Crowell, 1970; *The Black Novelist*, C. E. Merrill, 1970; *Black Identity*, Holt, 1970; *A Native Sons Reader*, Lippincott, 1970; *The New Lively Rhetoric*, Holt, 1970; *Brothers and Sisters*, Macmillan, 1970; *Nineteen Necromancers from Now*, Doubleday, 1970; *Black Insights*, Ginn, 1971; *The Immigrant Experience*, Dial, 1971; *Cavalcade*, Houghton, 1971; *Racism*, Crowell, 1971; *An Introduction to Poetry*, St. Martin's, 1972; *Different Drummers*, Random House, 1973.

Has worked for about fifteen American newspapers as writer of special assignments, stringer, or contributor. Contributor of more than thirty stories and articles to magazines, including *Negro Digest, Yardbird, Holiday, Saturday Review, Ebony*, and *New York*. Member of editorial board of *Audience*, 1970-72; contributing editor of *American Journal*, 1972—; co-editor of *Amistad: Writings on Black History and Culture*, 1970.

SIDELIGHTS: Williams was awarded a grant to American Academy in Rome, in 1961, on the basis of his work in *Night Song*, but the grant was rescinded by the awarding panel. Williams felt that this happened because he was black, and because of rumors that he was about to marry a white woman, which he later did. He has said: "The plain, unspoken fact is that the Negro is superfluous in American society as it is now constructed. Society must undergo a restructuring to make a place for him, or it will be called upon to get rid of him." Williams is an angry man, but some of his critics feel there is a bitter-sweet trace of hope intertwined with his anger. He is attempting to bridge the racial gap by telling the truth about both sides, but his theme is one of white exploitation and black survival. He also describes a need for middle class blacks to rediscover their roots among the black poor. Williams' books have had editions in Holland, England, and Sweden. *Avocational interests:* Travel (Belgium, Cameroun, the Caribbean, Congo, Cyprus, Denmark, Egypt, Ethiopia, France, Germany, Ghana, Great Britain, Greece, Israel, Italy, Mexico, the Netherlands, Nigeria, Portugal, Senegal, Spain, the Sudan, Sweden).

BIOGRAPHICAL/CRITICAL SOURCES: New York Times, October 19, 1967, June 2, 1968; *Book World*, June 2, 1968.

* * *

WILLNER, Dorothy 1927-

PERSONAL: Born August 26, 1927, in New York, N.Y.; daughter of Norbert and Bella (Richman) Willner. *Education:* University of Chicago, Ph.B., 1947, M.A., 1953, Ph.D., 1961; graduate study at Johns Hopkins School of Advanced International Studies, summer, 1952, and University of Paris, 1953-54. *Residence:* Lawrence, Kan. *Office:* Department of Anthropology, University of Kansas, Lawrence, Kan. 66045.

CAREER: New York University, New York, N.Y., instructor in sociology and anthropology, spring, 1953; Jewish Agency, Jerusalem, Israel, anthropologist for department of land settlement, 1955-58; United Nations, New York, N.Y., technical assistance administration expert in community development in Mexico, 1958; University of Iowa, Iowa City, assistant professor of sociology and anthropology, 1959-60; University of Chicago, Chicago, Ill., research associate at Research Center in Economic Development and Cultural Change, 1961-62; University of North Carolina, Chapel Hill, assistant professor of sociology and anthropology, 1962-63; Hunter College of the City University of New York, New York, N.Y., assistant professor of anthropology, 1964-65; University of Kansas, Lawrence, associate professor, 1966-70, professor of anthropology, 1970—. Has conducted field work in Israel, 1955-58, Mexico, 1958, and Washington, D.C., 1964.

MEMBER: American Anthropological Association (fellow), Society for Applied Anthropology (fellow), American Ethnological Society, Current Anthropology (associate). *Awards, honors:* Wenner-Gren Foundation grant, 1950-51, for ethnographic research in Ecuador on technology and social organization of highland Indians, under auspices of Heye Foundation of Museum of the American Indian; National Institute of Mental Health special fellowship at University of Rochester, 1968-69.

WRITINGS: Community Leadership, United Nations, 1960; (contributor) H. H. Kebschull, editor, *Politics in Transitional Societies*, Appleton, 1968; *Nation-Building and Community in Israel*, Princeton University Press, 1969; (contributor) E. A. Nordlinger, editor, *Politics and Society: Studies in Comparative Political Sociology*, Prentice-Hall, 1970; (contributor) A. R. Davis, editor, *Traditional Attitudes and Modern Styles in Political Leadership*, Angus & Robertson, 1973; (contributor) Ronald Ye-Lin Cheng, editor, *The Sociology of Revolution*, Regnery, 1973.

Contributor to *International Encyclopedia of the Social Sciences*. Contributor of more than a dozen articles and reviews to sociology and anthropology journals, including *Current Anthropology, Human Organization, Annals of the American Academy of Political and Social Science, Jewish Journal of Sociology, International Community Development Review*, and *Megamoth*.

WORK IN PROGRESS: A Theory of Directed Change; research on incest prohibitions; research on the anthropology of extreme situations, related to survival and adaptation.

* * *

WILSON, Erica

PERSONAL: Born in England; came to United States, 1952; married Vladimir Kagan (a furniture designer). *Education:* Attended Royal School of Needlework. *Office:* Erica Wilson Needle Works, 717 Madison Ave., New York, N.Y. 10021.

CAREER: Teacher of needlework at home and at Cooper Union Museum, New York, N.Y.; owner of Erica Wilson Creative Needlework Society (mail order firm), New York, N.Y., and of Erica Wilson Needle Works, retail stores in New York City, Southampton, N.Y., and Nantucket, Mass.; author and lecturer on needlework. Organizer of needlework seminars, 1974—; has appeared on her own Public Broadcasting System television series, "Erica."

WRITINGS—All published by Scribner: *Crewel Embroidery*, 1962, abridged edition published as *Craft of Crewel Embroidery*, 1971; *Fun with Crewel Embroidery*, 1965;

Erica Wilson's Embroidery Book, 1973; "*Needleplay*," in press.

* * *

WILSON, Forrest 1918-

PERSONAL: Born April 21, 1918, in San Francisco, Calif.; son of Royal and Josephine (Paine) Wilson; married Elizabeth Cherubino, 1960; children: Jonathan, Robert, Paul. *Education:* Diplomas from California School of Fine Arts, San Francisco, 1939, and Atelier of Modern Sculpture; also studied Art in Paris, 1951-52, and at Pratt Institute. *Politics:* "Dissident." *Religion:* None. *Home:* 5815 Bryn Mawr Rd., College Park, Md. 20740. *Office:* School of Architecture, Catholic University of America, Washington, D.C. 20017.

CAREER: Worked as carpenter, draftsman, construction superintendent, designer, and sculptor, 1947-60, working in French Morocco, 1952; Pratt Institute, New York, N.Y., instructor, 1960-61, assistant professor of architecture and interior design, 1961-65; *Progressive Architecture*, New York, N.Y., and Stamford, Conn., associate editor, 1965-69, editor, 1969-71; Ohio University, Athens, professor of architecture and director of School of Architecture, 1971-74; Catholic University of America, Washington, D.C., professor of architecture and chairman of School of Architecture, 1974—. Teacher of evening courses at Pratt Institute and Parsons School of Design, 1965-69; has also held positions of adjunct professor at State University of New York and University of California, Berkeley. Member of Athens Planning Commission. *Military service:* U.S. Merchant Marine, 1941-47; served in North Atlantic and the Mediterranean. *Member:* American Institute of Architects (corporate member), Construction Specifications Institute (corporate member), American Association of University Professors, Royal Society of the Arts (fellow).

WRITINGS: Architecture: A Book of Projects for Young Adults, Van Nostrand, 1968; *What It Feels Like to Be a Building* (juvenile), Doubleday, 1969; (with Arnold Friedmann and John F. Pile) *Interior Design: An Introduction to Architectural Interiors*, American Elsevier, 1970; *Structure: The Essense of Architecture*, Studio Vista, 1971; *Architecture and Interior Environment*, Van Nostrand, 1972; *What It Feels Like to Be a CIDOC*, Centro Intercultural de Documentacion, 1972; *Early American Village* (juvenile), Pantheon, 1973; *Moon Settlement* (juvenile), Pantheon, 1973; (editor) Richard Bender, *A Crack in the Rear-View Mirror: A View of Industrialized Building*, Van Nostrand, 1973; *A History of Architecture on the Disparitive Method*, Van Nostrand, 1974; *Conversations with Lev Zetlin*, Cahners, in press; *City Planning: A Book of Games*, Van Nostrand, in press.

WORK IN PROGRESS: Children's books on architecture and design, and a children's book on fantasy; examination of the design process in relation to the industrial revolution.

* * *

WILSON, (James) Harold 1916-

PERSONAL: Born March 11, 1916, in Huddersfield, Yorkshire, England; son of James Herbert (an industrial chemist) and Ethel Wilson; married Gladys Mary Baldwin, 1940; children: Giles Daniel John, Robin James. *Education:* Jesus College, Oxford, graduate with first class honors, 1937. *Office:* 10 Downing St., Whitehall, London S.W.1, England.

CAREER: Oxford University, Oxford, England, lecturer in economics at New College, 1937-38, fellow of University College, 1938-39, praelector in economics and domestic bursar of University College, 1945; economic assistant, War Cabinet Secretariat, 1940-41; member of staff, Ministry of Fuel and Power, 1941-43, director of economics and statistics, 1943-44; member of Parliament representing Ormskirk Division of Lancashire, 1945-50, representing Huyton Division, 1950—; became member of Privy Council, 1947; leader of the Labor Party, 1963—; leader of the opposition, 1963-64, 1970-74; Prime Minister and Lord of the Treasury, 1964-70, 1974—. Parliamentary secretary, Ministry of Works, 1945-47; secretary for overseas trade, Board of Trade, 1947, president of Board, 1947-51; member of Labor Party national executive committee, 1952—, chairman of national executive committee, 1961-62, member of parliamentary committee, 1954—, chairman of public accounts committee, 1959-63; principal opposition spokesman on economic affairs, 1956, on foreign affairs, 1961. Leader of British delegations to food and trade conferences, 1946-49. Honorary fellow, Jesus College and University College, both Oxford University, 1963; chancellor, University of Bradford, 1966—; elder brother, Trinity House, London, 1968. Chairman, Fabian Society, 1954-55.

MEMBER: Royal Society (fellow), Royal Statistical Society (president, 1972—). *Awards, honors:* Officer, Order of the British Empire, 1945; LL.D. from University of Lancaster, 1964, University of Liverpool, 1965, University of Nottingham, 1966, University of Sussex, 1966; D.C.L., Oxford University, 1965; D.Tech., University of Bradford, 1966; doctorate from University of Essex, 1967.

WRITINGS: New Deal for Coal, Contact, 1945; *The War on World Poverty: An Appeal to the Conscience of Mankind*, Bond Street Publications, 1953; *The New Britain: Labour's Plan* (selected speeches), Penguin, 1964; *Purpose in Politics: Selected Speeches*, Houghton, 1964; *The Relevance of British Socialism*, Weidenfeld & Nicolson, 1964; *The New Britain*, Penguin, 1964; *Purpose in Power: Selected Speeches*, Weidenfeld & Nicolson, 1966, published with new foreword by Wilson as *Purpose and Power: Selected Speeches*, Houghton, 1966; *A Personal Record: The Labour Government, 1964-1970*, Little, Brown, 1971 (published in England as *The Labour Government, 1964-1970: A Personal Record*, Weidenfeld & Nicolson, 1971). Contributor to periodicals.

AVOCATIONAL INTERESTS: Golf.

BIOGRAPHICAL/CRITICAL SOURCES: Michael M. Foot, *Harold Wilson: A Pictorial Biography*, Pergamon, 1964; Gerard E. Noel, *Harold Wilson and the New Britain*, Gollancz, 1964; Dudley G. Smith, *Harold Wilson: A Critical Biography*, R. Hale, 1964; Leslie G. D. Smith, *Harold Wilson: The Authentic Portrait*, Hodder & Stoughton, 1964; Anthony Howard and Richard West, *The Road to Number 10*, Macmillan, 1965 (published in England as *The Making of the Prime Minister*, J. Cape, 1965); Anthony Shrimsley, *The First Hundred Days of Harold Wilson*, Praeger, 1965.

* * *

WILSON, Marie B(eatrice) 1922-
(Jeanne Marie)

PERSONAL: Born April 9, 1922, in Portland, Ore.; daughter of Floyd Foster (a clerk) and Muriel (Carter) Fuller; married Helmut E. Wilson (a carpenter supervisor), April 9, 1944; children: Richard L., Ronald D., Krystyna

A. *Education:* Attended Everett Business College, 1955-56. *Politics:* Democrat. *Religion:* Protestant. *Home and office:* 5615 80th N.E., Marysville, Wash. 98270.

CAREER: Waitress, secretary, and writer. *Member:* Pacific Northwest Writers Conference.

WRITINGS—Under pseudonym Jeanne Marie: *Black for a Bride*, Lenox Hill, 1973; *Arrow of Terror*, Lenox Hill, 1974; *Wait for Me, Wendy*, Lenox Hill, in press. Contributor to confession magazines and other periodicals.

WORK IN PROGRESS: Shadows on the Tide, a Gothic novel.

SIDELIGHTS: Marie Wilson believes in reincarnation and is studying parapsychology and related subjects. *Avocational interests:* Travel.

* * *

WILSON, Samuel, Jr. 1911-

PERSONAL: Born August 6, 1911, in New Orleans, La.; son of Samuel (a businessman) and Stella (Poupeney) Wilson; married Ellen Elizabeth Latrobe, October 20, 1951. *Education:* Tulane University, B.Arch., 1931. *Home:* 1121 Washington St., New Orleans, La. 70130. *Office:* Koch & Wilson, Architects, 914 Masonic Temple Building, New Orleans, La. 70130.

CAREER: Office of Moise H. Goldstein, New Orleans, La., draftsman, 1930-33; Historic American Buildings Survey in Louisiana, New Orleans, researcher, 1934-35; Richard Koch, Architect, New Orleans, La., architect, 1935-42, associate, 1945-55; Koch & Wilson, Architects, New Orleans, La., partner, 1955—. Lecturer on Louisiana architecture at Tulane University, 1945—; visiting lecturer at Cornell University, Columbia University, University of Illinois, and other universities and museums; presented television series, "New Orleans Houses," 1953. Member of board of curators, Louisiana State Museum, 1953-56; state preservation coordinator in Louisiana, 1968-72. Member of board of Vieux Carrer Property Owners and Associates, 1953-68, Maison Hospitaliere, 1963—, Friends of the Cabildo, 1964—, and New Orleans Area Council of Boy Scouts of America, 1972. Adviser to General Services Administration and to board of Historic Natchez Foundation. *Military service:* U.S. Coast Guard Reserve, active duty, 1942-45.

MEMBER: American Institute of Architects (fellow; chairman of committee on historic buildings, 1960—), Association for Preservation Technology, National Trust for Historic Preservation, Society of Architectural Historians (former member of board; member of bicentennial commission, 1971—), National Council of Architectural Registration Boards, Louisiana Landmarks Society (member of board, 1950—; president, 1950-56), Louisiana Historical Society, Louisiana Architects Association, New Orleans Book Collectors Club, Boston Club. *Awards, honors:* Edward Langley scholarship of American Institute of Architects, 1938, for travel and study in Europe; Silver Beaver Award of Boy Scouts of America, 1939; Award of Excellence of New Orleans Chamber of Commerce for restorations, 1972, and for urban design landscaping, 1973; Louisiana Council for Music and the Performing Business and Arts Award, 1974.

WRITINGS: (Editor and author of introduction and notes) Benjamin Henry Boneral Latrobe, *Impressions Respecting New Orleans: Diary and Sketches, 1818-1820*, Columbia University Press, 1951; (with Garland Taylor and Leonard V. Huber) *Louisiana Purchase*, Louisiana Landmarks Society, 1953; (chairman of guide book committee) *A Guide to Architecture of New Orleans, 1699-1959*, Reinhold, for Louisiana Landmarks Society, 1959; (with Huber) *Baroness Pontalba's Buildings, Their Site and the Remarkable Woman Who Built Them*, Louisiana Landmarks Society, 1964, 2nd edition, 1966; (with Huber) *The Basilica on Jackson Square and Predecessors, Dedicated to St. Louis King of France, 1727-1965*, [New Orleans], 1965, 3rd edition, 1969; (contributor) John F. McDermott, editor, *The French in the Mississippi Valley*, University of Illinois Press, 1965; *Bienville's New Orleans: A French Colonial Capital, 1718-1768*, Friends of the Cabildo, 1968; *The Vieux Carre, New Orleans: Its Plan, Its Growth, Its Architecture* (historic district demonstration study), Bureau of Governmental Research (New Orleans), 1968; (with Huber) *The Cabildo on Jackson Square*, Friends of the Cabildo, 1970, revised edition, 1973; (author with Bernard Lemann of text in Volume I and author with others of text in Volume II) *New Orleans Architecture*, Pelican, for Friends of the Cabildo, Volume I: *The Lower Garden District*, 1971, Volume II: *The American Sector*, 1972; (contributor) Ian M. Quimby, editor, *Winterthur Portfolio 8*, University Press of Virginia, 1973; (author of introduction) *The Autobiography of James Gallier, Architect* (reprint of 1864 edition), DeCapo, 1973.

Contributor to other historical symposia. Author or co-author of booklets on historical sites and architecture of New Orleans. Contributor to *Proceedings* of U.S. Naval Institute, *Magazine of Art, Antiques*, and other journals; reviewer for *Louisiana History* and *Times Picayune*. Member of editorial board, Louisiana Historical Society, 1974.

* * *

WILSON, Trevor (Gordon) 1928-

PERSONAL: Born December 24, 1928, in New Zealand; son of Andrew Gordon (a commercial traveler) and Winifred (Banyard) Wilson; married Jane Verney (a musician), September 7, 1957; children: Jennifer, Sara. *Education:* University of Auckland, B.A., 1948, M.A., 1951; Oxford University, D.Phil., 1959. *Office:* Department of History, University of Adelaide, Adelaide 5001, South Australia.

CAREER: University of Canterbury, Christchurch, New Zealand, assistant lecturer in history, 1952; University of Auckland, Auckland, New Zealand, assistant lecturer in history, 1953-55; University of Manchester, Manchester, England, research assistant in government, 1957-59; University of Adelaide, Adelaide, South Australia, lecturer, 1960-65, senior lecturer, 1965-68, professor of history, 1968—. Commonwealth fellow at St. John's College, Cambridge, 1972. *Member:* Australian Academy of Humanities (fellow), Royal Historical Society (fellow). *Awards, honors:* New Zealand overseas traveling scholarship, 1953; Gilbert Campion Prize from Hansard Society, 1960; Nuffield dominion traveling fellowship, 1964; Higby Prize from American Historical Association, 1965.

WRITINGS: The Downfall of the Liberal Party: 1914-1935, Cornell University Press, 1966; (editor) *The Political Diaries of C. P. Scott: 1911-1928*, Cornell University Press, 1970.

WORK IN PROGRESS: A history of Great Britain and World War One.

WINANT, Fran 1943-

PERSONAL: Born October 28, 1943, in New York, N.Y. *Education:* Fordham University, B.A., 1975. *Address:* P.O. Box 398, New York, N.Y. 10009.

MEMBER: Poetry Society of America. *Awards, honors:* Isaacson Poetry Award from New School for Social Research, 1968.

WRITINGS: Looking at Women, Violet Press, 1971.

Plays: "Closer Since the Shooting" (one-act), first produced in New York at Judson Poets' Theatre, February 8, 1969; "Play 1, 2, 3, 4" (one-act), first produced in New York at Cubiculo Theatre, June 13, 1969.

WORK IN PROGRESS: A novel tentatively titled *Search the Room.*

SIDELIGHTS: Fran Winant has been influenced by the women's and gay liberation movements.

* * *

WINCHELL, Wallace 1914-

PERSONAL: Born March 8, 1914, in Jersey City, N.J.; son of Wallace William (a lieutenant colonel in the Salvation Army) and Ida May (a leader and pioneer in the Salvation Army; maiden name, Harris) Winchell; married Margaret R. Wallace, June 17, 1942; children: Faith (Mrs. Richard Pickering), Joy (Mrs. Michael Herman), Deborah. *Education:* Montclair State Teachers College, B.A., 1936; Union Theological Seminary, New York, N.Y., M.Div., 1944; Wayne State University, M.A., 1954. *Politics:* Republican. *Residence:* Manchester, Conn. *Office:* Humanities Division, Manchester Community College, 60 Bidwell St., Manchester, Conn. 06040.

CAREER: Salvation Army field officer in Elizabeth, N.J., 1936-37, Jersey City, N.J., 1937-40, and Hackensack, N.J., 1940-43; pastor of United Churches of Christ in Milford, N.J., 1943-47, Royal Oak, Mich., 1947-53, Methuen, Mass., 1954-59, and Broad Brook, Conn., 1960-69; University of Hartford, Hartford, Conn., adjunct lecturer in speech, 1962-65; Manchester Community College, Manchester, Conn., part-time lecturer, 1966-71, full-time instructor in English, 1972—. American Association of University Professors, Poetry Society of America, Spiritual Frontiers. *Awards, honors:* Brotherhood Award from Detroit Round Table of Catholics, Jews, and Protestants, 1949; George Washington Honor Award from Freedoms Foundation, 1959; DiCastagnola Award from Poetry Society of America, 1970.

WRITINGS: Poet's Voice in Babylon (monograph), Antioch Press, 1968; *The Poetry of the Shakers* (monograph), Abingdon, 1970; *The House of Bethlehem*, Dragon's Teeth Press, 1972; *Century-Spanning Significance*, Manchester Community College Press, 1974. Contributor to literary journals, including *Literary Review*, *Lyric*, *Antioch Review*, and *Chicago Tribune Magazine*.

WORK IN PROGRESS: The Seer; The Poetry of Spiritual Communities, completion expected in 1976.

SIDELIGHTS: Winchell writes: "As a teacher, writer, and full-time minister for many years, closely associated with the youth of a new age, I am convinced of the necessity of balancing the Scientific-Technological culture with a new humanity by entering through our consciousness into spaces and dimensions contiguous to Spacetime. By knowing more of the darkness and light, the terror and glory, we shall emerge with a new worldview. Our sense of God and humankind so united, so harmonious, shall put to flight these twentieth-century barbarisms so we can face the new millenium without fear. My hope is to contribute to such awarenesses."

* * *

WINGERT, Paul S. 1900(?)-1974

1900(?)—December 22, 1974; American art historian, anthropologist, educator, and author. Obituaries: *New York Times*, December 24, 1974; *AB Bookman's Weekly*, January 20, 1975.

* * *

WINNER, Viola Hopkins 1928-

PERSONAL: Born March 13, 1928, in Cleveland, Ohio; daughter of Jerry (a baker) and Marie (a store manager; maiden name, Lopata) Polanka; married Terence K. Hopkins, December 20, 1950 (divorced, 1960); married Anthony Winner (a college professor), February 2, 1964; children: (second marriage) David Dario. *Education:* Oberlin College, B.A., 1949; New York University, M.A., 1953, Ph.D., 1960. *Residence:* Charlottesville, Va. *Office:* Department of English, Sweet Briar College, Sweet Briar, Va. 24595.

CAREER: Adelphi College, Garden City, N.Y., instructor in English, 1954-57; Hunter College of the City University of New York, New York, N.Y., instructor in English, 1960-64; University of Virginia, Charlottesville, assistant professor of English, 1965-72; Sweet Briar College, Sweet Briar, Va., professor of English, 1973—. *Member:* Phi Beta Kappa. *Awards, honors:* National Endowment for the Humanities senior fellowship, 1972-73.

WRITINGS: (Contributor) Tony Tanner, editor, *Henry James: Modern Judgments*, Macmillan, 1968; *Henry James and the Visual Arts*, University Press of Virginia, 1970. Contributor of articles and reviews, sometimes under name Viola Hopkins, to *Accent*, *American Literature*, *Nineteenth-Century Fiction*, *Criticism*, and *P.M.L.A.*

WORK IN PROGRESS: A critical study of British caricaturist and illustrator Richard Doyle; editing *Fast and Loose*, a juvenile novelette by Edith Wharton.

* * *

WINTON, Kate Barber 1882(?)-1974

1882(?)—December 21, 1974; American author of scientific books. Obituaries: *AB Bookman's Weekly*, January 27, 1975.

* * *

WITT, Shirley Hill 1934-
(Katherine Thundercloud)

PERSONAL: Born April 17, 1934, in Whittier, Calif.; daughter of Melvin Ward and Cordelia (Bertiome) Hill; children: Randall Jacobs Witt, Hilary Witt. *Education:* University of Michigan, B.A., 1965, M.A., 1966; University of New Mexico, Ph.D., 1969. *Politics:* Independent. *Religion:* Iroquois Longhouse. *Home:* 460 South Marion Parkway, Denver, Colo. 80209. *Agent:* Elizabeth McKee, Harold Matson Co., Inc., 22 East 40th St., New York, N.Y. 10016. *Office:* U.S. Commission on Civil Rights, 1726 Champa, Denver, Colo. 80202.

CAREER: University of North Carolina, Chapel Hill, visiting assistant professor of anthropology, 1970-72; Colorado

College, Colorado Springs, associate professor of anthropology, 1972-74; U.S. Commission on Civil Rights, Denver, Colo., director of Mountain States Regional Office, 1975—. Member of board of directors of Highlander Center, 1968-70; member of Colorado Springs Human Relations Commission, 1972-74; member of steering committee of National Women's Political Caucus, 1972—; member of college committee of Colorado Commission on the Status of Women, 1973—; consultant to U.S. Commission on Civil Rights, American Indian Task Force, Office of Civil Rights, Department of Health, Education and Welfare, and Task Force for Spanish-Speaking Education.

MEMBER: American Anthropological Association (fellow), American Association for the Advancement of Science, American Association of Physical Anthropologists, American Civil Liberties Union, National Association of Human Rights Workers (vice-president of Colorado chapter, 1973—). *Awards, honors:* Anisfield-Wolf Award for Race Relations, 1968, for *The American Indian Today*.

WRITINGS: The Saginaw Band of Chippewa Indians, U.S. Government Printing Office, 1967; (contributor) Stuart Levine and Nancy O. Lurie, editors, *The American Indian Today*, Everett-Edwards, 1968; *The Tuscaroras*, Crowell, 1972; (editor with Stan Steiner) *The Way: An Anthology of American Indian Life and Literature*, Knopf, 1972; (contributor) William C. Sturtevant, editor, *Handbook of North American Indians*, Volume III: *Environment, Origins, and Population*, Smithsonian Institution, in press.

Author of scripts for "Silent Heritage: The American Indian," an eleven-part series for University of Michigan Television Center, produced by National Educational Television, 1966-67. Contributor to *Civil Rights Digest* and *Midcontinent American Studies Journal*; contributor to newspapers, under pseudonym Katherine Thundercloud.

WORK IN PROGRESS: Editing *Costa Rica: Studies in Nutrition and Human Biology*; writing articles to be included in *The Encyclopedia of the American Indians*.

SIDELIGHTS: Shirley Witt is a member of the Akwesasne Mohawk Nation, Wolf Clan. She has done research among American Indians, Chicanos, and people living in Appalachia; she has also studied people in Costa Rica and Canada. She writes: "The path of my life has taken me through human situations which have left me with an undeniable need to participate in matters concerning civil—human—rights. This is seen in my writings. . . ."

* * *

WODEHOUSE, Lawrence 1934-

PERSONAL: Surname is pronounced *Wood*-house; born June 14, 1934, in Norwich, England; son of Walter G. and Flora (Parsons) Wodehouse. *Education:* University of Durham, diploma in architecture, 1959; University of London, diploma in town planning, 1962; Cornell University, M.Arch., 1963; Royal Institute of British Architects, A.R.I.B.A. [meaning Associate of the Royal Institute of British Architects].

CAREER: North Carolina State University, Raleigh, assistant professor of architectural history, 1964-69; Pratt Institute, Brooklyn, N.Y., associate professor, 1969-73, professor of architectural history, 1973-74; University of Dundee, Jordanstone College, Dundee, Scotland, lecturer in architecture, 1974—.

WRITINGS: (Editor) *American Architecture from the Civil War to the First World War*, Gale, 1975; (editor) *American Architecture from the First World War to the Present*, Gale, 1975. Contributor of more than two dozen articles to professional journals, including *Art Journal, Antiques, Historic Preservation, Journal of the Society of Architectural Historians*, and *Old Time New England*.

WORK IN PROGRESS: Research on the work of architect Stanford White.

* * *

WOLF, Marguerite Hurrey 1914-

PERSONAL: Born April 23, 1914, in Montclair, N.J.; daughter of Charles D. (with International Y.M.C.A.) and Daisy (a teacher; maiden name, Girton) Hurrey; married George A. Wolf, Jr. (a medical college professor), August 2, 1939; children: Patty (Mrs. Tage Stroem), Debbie. *Education:* Mount Holyoke College, B.A., 1936; graduate study at Bank Street College of Education, 1936-37. *Home address:* Box 96, Jericho, Vt. 05465.

CAREER: Elementary school teacher in New York, N.Y., 1937-42; Sarah Lawrence College, Bronxville, N.Y., teacher of nursery school, 1942-44; writer. *Member:* Association of American Pen Women, League of Vermont Writers.

WRITINGS: Anything Can Happen in Vermont, Wake-Brook, 1965; *How To Be a Doctor's Wife without Really Dying*, Wake-Brook, 1967; *Vermont Is Always with You*, Greene, 1969; *I'll Take the Poack Road*, Greene, 1975. Contributor to *Saturday Evening Post, Parents' Magazine, Vermont Life, Medical Times, M.D.'s Wife, Massachusetts Audubon*, and *Christian Home*. Contributing editor of *Resident and Staff Physicians*, 1965—.

WORK IN PROGRESS: A book on a doctor's wife.

* * *

WOLF, Peter (Michael) 1935-

PERSONAL: Born December 6, 1935, in New Orleans, La.; son of Morris (a cotton broker) and Ruth (New) Wolf; married Alessandra Cantey (a counselor); children: Phelan Godchaux, Alexis Ambler. *Education:* Yale University, B.A., 1957; Tulane University, M.A., 1963; New York University (Institute of Fine Arts), Ph.D., 1968. *Home:* 325 West End Ave., New York, N.Y. 10023. *Office:* Institute for Architecture and Urban Studies, 8 West 40th St., New York, N.Y. 10018.

CAREER: Wolf & Co. (cotton brokers), New Orleans, La., partner, 1958-62; Wilbur Smith & Associates, New York, N.Y., associate, 1968-70; Pratt Institute, Brooklyn, N.Y., instructor in history of architecture and planning, 1968-70; Cooper Union, New York, N.Y., associate professor, 1971-74, professor of architectural history and planning, 1974—; Institute for Architecture and Urban Studies, New York, chairman, 1972—. Planning consultant, 1968—. Has had exhibitions at Museum of Modern Art and Whitney Museum of American Art, both New York. Trustee, Wexham Foundation. *Member:* International Federation of Housing and Planning, American Society of Planning Officials, American Institute of Planners, Society of Architectural Historians, New York State Council on the Arts, Architectural League of New York (member of executive committee, 1972—), New York Cultural Council. *Awards, honors:* Fulbright fellow in Paris, 1965-66; grants from Ford Foundation and American Federation of Arts, 1969, for preparation of *The Future of the City*.

WRITINGS: Eugene Henard and the Beginning of Urbanism in France, 1900-1914, International Federation of Housing and Planning (The Hague) and Centre de Recherche de Urbanisme (Paris), 1969; *Another Chance for Cities* (exhibition catalog), Whitney Museum of American Art (New York), 1970; *The Future of the City: New Directions in Urban Planning*, Watson, 1974; *The Evolving City: Urban Design Proposals by Ulrich Franzen and Paul Rudolph*, American Federation of Arts, 1974. Contributor to *Art in America, Perspecta, Traffic Engineering*, and *Architectural Forum*.

* * *

WOLFE, John N. 1910(?)-1974

1910(?)—December 16, 1974; American ecologist, educator, and author. Obituaries: *Washington Post*, December 21, 1974.

* * *

WOLFMAN, Augustus 1908(?)-1974

1908(?)—October 21, 1974; American photography expert, magazine editor and publisher, former pharmacist, and writer on photography. Obituaries: *New York Times*, October 23, 1974.

* * *

WOLFSON, Harry Austryn 1887-1974

November 2, 1887—September 19, 1974; Russian-born American philosopher, scholar in comparative religion, educator, and author of books on philosophy and religion. Obituaries: *New York Times*, September 21, 1974; *Washington Post*, September 21, 1974; *AB Bookmen's Weekly*, October 28, 1974. (*CA*-19/20).

* * *

WOMACK, David A(lfred) 1933-
(David Buchan)

PERSONAL: Born June 14, 1933, in Vancouver, British Columbia, Canada; son of Alfred R. (a minister and laborer) and Jean M. (Buchan) Womack; married L. Barbara Voltz (a clerk typist), June 26, 1954; children: Joyce Barbara, Carol Jean. *Education:* Northwest College, Kirkland, Wash., B.A., 1956, M.A., 1960. *Office:* Assemblies of God, 1445 Boonville Ave., Springfield, Mo. 65802.

CAREER: Ordained minister of the Assembly of God Church, 1958; associate pastor and pastor in Washington State, 1955-60; Assemblies of God Headquarters, Springfield, Mo., foreign missionary in Columbia, South America, 1960-65, foreign missions editor, 1965-69, foreign missions home secretary, 1970—. *Member:* Kansas City Business Mail Association.

WRITINGS: The Wellsprings of the Pentecostal Movement, Gospel Publishing, 1968; *Breaking the Stained-Glass Barrier*, Harper, 1973; *The Pyramid Principle*, Harper, in press. Contributor of more than five hundred articles to *Writer* and other magazines.

WORK IN PROGRESS: A novel on Columbia; a religious book on human communication with the spirit world, for Harper; research for a book on the creation of the world and the origin of man, completion expected in 1978; several novels under pseudonym David Buchan.

SIDELIGHTS: Womack told *CA:* "I felt 'called' to three vocations—to preach, to be a missionary, and to write—and I now have the only job in my church that effectively combines my interests. I preach about 120 times a year, I am on the committee that leads the work of 1,100 missionaries in 92 countries, and I am writing for major publishers."

* * *

WOOD, R(ichard) Coke 1905-

PERSONAL: Born December 20, 1905, in Clement, Okla.; son of Nathan Alexander (a Methodist minister) and Lenora (Gilmore) Wood; married Ethelyn Edson (a teacher), August 28, 1936; children: Colyn (Mrs. Daryl Lambert). *Education:* Attended University of Nevada, 1926, and University of Hawaii, 1930-31; College of the Pacific (now University of the Pacific), A.B., 1932, M.A., 1934; University of Southern California, Ph.D., 1950. *Religion:* Congregational. *Home:* 120 West Elm St., Stockton, Calif. 95204. *Office:* Pacific Center for Western Studies, University of the Pacific, Stockton, Calif. 95211.

CAREER: Bishop High School, Bishop, Calif., teacher of social studies, 1932-34; teacher of Social Studies at Bret Harte Sanatorium in Murphys, Calif., 1942-50; San Joaquin Delta College, Stockton, Calif., instructor, 1951-56, assistant professor, 1956-60, associate professor, 1960-65, professor of history, 1965-70; University of the Pacific, Stockton, Calif., part-time professor, 1952-70, professor of history, 1970—, occupant of Rockwell D. Hunt Chair in California History, 1966—, director of Pacific Center for Western Studies, 1970—. Executive secretary, Conference of California Historical Societies, 1953-71; member of California Historical Landmarks Advisory Commission, 1965—, chairman, 1969-71; member of American Revolution Bicentennial Commission of California, 1970—; has conducted university courses on television and historical series on radio and television in California.

MEMBER: California Heritage Council (member of board of directors, 1971—), Stockton Heritage Council (member of board of directors, 1969—), Calaveras County Historical Society (co-founder, 1952; vice-president, 1953-63), San Joaquin Pioneer and Historical Society (member of board of directors, 1963), Phi Beta Kappa, Phi Delta Kappa. *Awards, honors:* Award of merit from American Association for State and Local History, 1958, for television series, "History of California"; named "Mr. California" by joint resolution of California Legislature, 1969, for work in preserving the history of California.

WRITINGS: Calaveras, Land of Skulls, Mother Lode Press, 1955; (with Leon George Bush) *The California Story: Its History, Problems, and Government*, Fearon, 1957, 3rd edition with Bush and Delmar M. McComb, 1970; (with Bush) *California Government and Problems*, Fearon, 1958; (with V. Covert Martin) *Stockton Album Through the Years*, Rosicrucian Press, 1959; (with Bush) *California History and Government*, Fearon, 1962, abridged edition published as *California History*, 1963; (with Frances E. Bishop) *Big Tree–Carson Valley Turnpike, Ebbetts Pass and Highway Four*, Old Timers Museum, 1968; (editor and author of introduction) Emmett Joy, *Annals of Mokelumne Hill*, Old Timers Museum, 1968; *Owens Valley As I Knew It*, Pacific Center for Western Studies, 1972; (editor and author of introduction) Joy, *Chronicles of Mokelumne Hill*, Old Timers Museum, 1972; (editor and author of introduction) Elizabeth Kaler, *Untold Tales of Murphys*, Old Timers Museum, 1972; (compiler with others) *California Colonial History Time Line*, California Bicentennial Commission, 1974.

Also author of *Murphys, Queen of the Sierra*, 1948, and *Tales of Old Calaveras*, 1949. Author of introduction to *Tamsen Donner, Heroine of Donner Party*, by Mary Anderson. Author and editor of numerous historical pamphlets. Author of historical column in *Calaveras Prospect*, 1965-66; California editor, *Merit Student Encyclopedia*, 1967; editor, *Las Calaveras*, 1952-64, and *The Clamper*, 1960-63.

SIDELIGHTS: Wood's interest in California history led him and his wife to restore the oldest stone building in Murphys, Calif. in 1949. The building in which they maintain the "Old Timers Museum" was declared a historical landmark by the State of California in 1953.

* * *

WOOD, Robin 1931-

PERSONAL: Born February 23, 1931, in London, England; son of Robert (an artist) and Florence (Earthy) Wood; married Aline Macdonald, May 17, 1960 (divorced September, 1974); children: Carin, Fiona, Simon. *Education:* Jesus College, Cambridge, B.A., 1953, diploma in education, 1954. *Politics:* "Leftish." *Religion:* Atheist. *Home:* 21 Ralph Rd., Coventry, Warwickshire, England. *Office:* Department of Film Studies, University of Warwick, Coventry, Warwickshire, England.

CAREER: Teacher of English in schools in England and Sweden, 1954-58, 1959-69; University of Lille, Lille, France, lecturer in English, 1958-59; Queen's University, Kingston, Ontario, lecturer in film, 1969-72; University of Warwick, Coventry, England, lecturer in film studies, 1973—. *Member:* Campaign for Homosexual Equality.

WRITINGS: Hitchcock's Films, Tantivy, 1965, revised edition, 1969; *Howard Hawks*, Secker & Warburg, 1967; *Arthur Penn*, Studio Vista, 1967; *Ingmar Bergman*, Studio Vista, 1968; (with Ian Cameron) *Antonioni*, Studio Vista, 1968; (with Michael Walker) *Claude Chabrol*, Studio Vista, 1970; *The Apu Trilogy*, Studio Vista, 1971; *Personal Views: Explorations in Film*, Gordon Fraser Gallery, in press. Contributor to *Movie*, *Film Comment*, *Times Educational Supplement*, *Motion*, *Definition*, *Oxford Opinion*, *New Left Review*, *Cahiers du Cinema* (France), *Positif* (France), and *Chaplin* (Sweden).

WORK IN PROGRESS: Murnau's Night and Sunrise, for Gordon Fraser Gallery.

* * *

WOODFORD, Arthur M(acKinnon) 1940-

PERSONAL: Born November 23, 1940, in Detroit, Mich.; son of Frank Bury (a writer) and Mary-Kirk (MacKinnon) Woodford; married Margaret Holmes, August 29, 1964; children: Mark, Amy. *Education:* University of Wisconsin, student, 1958-60; Wayne State University, B.A., 1963; University of Michigan, A.M.L.S., 1964. *Politics:* Independent. *Religion:* Methodist. *Home:* 1167 Audubon Rd., Grosse Pointe Park, Mich. 48230. *Office:* Grosse Pointe Public Library, 10 Kercheval, Grosse Pointe, Mich. 48236.

CAREER: Detroit Public Library, Detroit, Mich., librarian, 1964-68, assistant director of personnel, 1968-72, director of personnel, 1972-74; Grosse Pointe Public Library, Grosse Pointe, Mich., first assistant and chief of central library, 1974—. Military service: *U.S. Naval Reserve, 1958-64*. Member: *American Library Association, U.S. Naval Institute, Great Lakes Maritime Institute, Michigan Library Association, Algonquin Club of Detroit and Windsor, Prismatic Club of Detroit.*

WRITINGS: (With father, Frank B. Woodford) *All Our Yesterdays*, Wayne State University Press, 1969; *Detroit and Its Banks: The Story of Detroit Bank and Trust*, Wayne State University Press, 1974.

WORK IN PROGRESS: Research on the battle of Lake Erie in 1813; research on Johnsons Island, a military prison in Sandusky, Ohio, 1861-1864.

AVOCATIONAL INTERESTS: Reading, bridge, tennis, model shipbuilding.

* * *

WOODS, Richard (John) 1941-

PERSONAL: Born July 30, 1941, in Albuquerque, N.M.; son of James Edward (an engineer) and Margaret Louise (Corcoran) Woods. *Education:* Aquinas Institute of Philosophy, B.A., 1964, M.A., 1966; Aquinas Institute of Theology, M.A., 1969; Loyola University of Chicago, Ph.D. candidate, 1974—. *Home:* 1143 West North Shore Ave., Chicago, Ill. 60626. *Office:* Institute of Pastoral Studies, Loyola University, 6525 North Sheridan Rd., Chicago, Ill. 60626.

CAREER: Entered Order of Preachers (Dominicans), 1962, ordained Roman Catholic priest, 1969; teacher at Loyola University, Institute of Pastoral Studies, Chicago, Ill., 1970—, and at Northeastern Illinois University, Chicago, 1974—. Lecturer at Thomas More Association, 1972-74. Research at Oxford University, Religious Experience Research Unit, 1974-75. *Member:* Academy of Religion and Psychical Research (treasurer, 1973-74), American Society for Psychical Research, Society for Scientific Study of Religion, American Academy of Religion, Common Cause, Association of Chicago Priests.

WRITINGS: The Media Maze, Pflaum, 1969; *The Occult Revolution*, Seabury, 1971; *The Devil*, Thomas More Press, 1973. Contributor to *Listening, Sign, Cross and Crown, Soundings in Satanism, Catholic Library World, Critic, Spiritual Frontiers, Chicago Studies, Catholic Mind, Progressive*, and *Chicago Tribune*. Special editor of *Listening*, fall, 1974.

AVOCATIONAL INTERESTS: Travel, photography, painting.

* * *

WOOLNER, Frank 1916-

PERSONAL: Born October 8, 1916, in Worcester, Mass.; son of Fred L. (an automobile painter) and Martha M. (Matthews) Woolner; married Joanne E. Dunn, 1950 (divorced, 1953); children: Leslie Elizabeth. *Education:* Educated in Worcester, Mass. *Politics:* Independent. *Religion:* Agnostic. *Home:* 92 Green St., Shrewsbury, Mass. 01545. *Office: Salt Water Sportsman*, 10 High St., Boston, Mass. 02110.

CAREER: Worked as auto painter, 1937-40; free-lance writer and outdoor photographer, 1940—; *Salt Water Sportsman*, Boston, Mass., editor, 1950—. Appeared on "Woolner Brothers Outdoors," on WSMW-Television, 1971-73. *Military service:* U.S. Army, 1942-45; served in Europe; became sergeant; received Bronze Star, Belgian Fouragere Croix de Guerre, and Army Commendation Medal.

MEMBER: International Game and Fish Association, Outdoor Writers Association of America, National Rifle Association (life member), Ducks Unlimited, Salt Water

Fly Rodders of America, Third Armored Division Association (life member), New England Outdoor Writers Association (past president). *Awards, honors:* Outstanding achievement award from New England Outdoor Writers Association, 1970; excellence in craft award from Outdoor Writers Association of America, 1974; Al Reinfelder Memorial Award from Striped Bass Fund, 1974.

WRITINGS: (With Murray Fowler and others) *Spearhead in the West*, U.S. Armed Forces, 1945; (with Henry Lyman) *The Complete Book of Striped Bass Fishing*, A. S. Barnes, 1954; (with Lyman) *The Complete Book of Weakfishing*, A. S. Barnes, 1959; *Grouse and Grouse Hunting*, Crown, 1970; (with Lyman) *Tackle Talk*, A. S. Barnes, 1971; *My New England*, Stone Wall Press, 1972; *Modern Saltwater Sport Fishing*, Crown, 1972; *Timberdoodle*, Crown, 1974.

Author of a column, "All Outdoors," in *Worcester Evening Gazette*, 1946-61. Contributor to outdoor magazines, including *Field and Stream*, *Outdoor Life*, *Sports Afield*, *American Sportsman*, and *Salt Water Sportsman*.

WORK IN PROGRESS: *Trout Hunting* (tentative title), for Winchester Press.

AVOCATIONAL INTERESTS: Angling, salt water angling, upland hunting, big game hunting, recreational boating, recreational vehicles, woodcraft, natural history, target and skeet shooting, international bicycle racing (held New England States Amateur Bicycle League of American track and road championship from 1936-40, retiring undefeated), military history (especially aerial and armored warfare), figure skating.

BIOGRAPHICAL/CRITICAL SOURCES: George Reiger, *Profiles in Salt Water Angling*, Prentice-Hall, 1973.

* * *

WRAGG, David William 1946-

PERSONAL: Born August 13, 1946, in Winchester, England; son of Simpson Herbert (a Royal Navy career officer) and Mary Anna (Brennan) Wragg. *Education:* Attended Royal Naval School (Tal Handak, Malta), 1957-59. *Politics:* "Traditionalist Monarchist Conservative." *Religion:* Anglican. *Home and office:* 8 Downview Close, Wood Rd., Beacon Hill, Hindhead, Surrey GU26 6PY, England.

CAREER: In the service of the British Government, 1963-73; free-lance journalist, 1967—. *Member:* Authors Club, Society of Authors, United Service and Royal Agro Club, National Viewers and Listeners Association, Monday Club.

WRITINGS: *World's Air Fleets*, Ian Allen, 1967; *World's Air Forces*, Osprey, 1971; *A Dictionary of Aviation*, Osprey, 1973, Fell, 1974; *Flight before Flying*, Fell, 1974; *Speed in the Air*, Fell, 1974. Financial aviation stringer for *Sunday Telegraph*, 1968-73; political correspondent for *International Freighting Weekly*, 1971-72. Contributor to *Spectator, Field, Flight International*, and *Scotsman*.

WORK IN PROGRESS: *Flight with Power: The First Ten Years.*

SIDELIGHTS: Wragg writes that he is ". . . very much a traditionalist, of Anglo-Northern Irish descent. A firm believer in the need to oppose Communism, Liberalism, and Petty Nationalism, while maintaining a distinct British National Identity in the face of creeping Europeanism and and excessive 'new' Commonwealth immigration. The West must re-arm, re-affirm its beliefs, support South Africa and Rhodesia, and the Ulster Loyalists!"

* * *

WRIGHT, G(eorge) Ernest 1909-1974

September 5, 1909—August 29, 1974; American Biblical scholar, educator, archeologist, museum curator, author of numerous books on religion and archeology, and Presbyterian minister. Obituaries: *New York Times*, August 31, 1974. (*CA*-2).

* * *

WRIGHT, William 1930-

PERSONAL: Born October 22, 1930, in Philadelphia, Pa.; son of William Connor and Josephine (Hartshorne) Wright. *Education:* Yale University, B.A., 1952. *Residence:* New York, N.Y. 10028. *Agent:* Helen Brann, 14 Sutton Pl. S., New York, N.Y. 10022.

CAREER: *Holiday*, New York, N.Y., associate editor, 1960-65; *Venture*, New York, articles editor, 1968-70; *Chicagoan Magazine*, Chicago, editor, 1969-70; *Leisureguide*, Chicago, editor, 1971-74; *Chicago Magazine*, Chicago, interim editor, 1974; full-time writer, 1974. General manager of Gian Carlo Menotti's Spoleto Festival, 1965. *Military service:* U.S. Army, Chinese translator, 1952-55.

WRITINGS—Nonfiction: *Ball: A Year in the Life of the April in Paris Extravaganza*, Saturday Review Press, 1972; *The Washington Game*, Dutton, 1974. Contributor to *Oui*, *Travel, Leisure, Town & Country*, and *Diversions*.

WORK IN PROGRESS: A novel.

* * *

WUELLNER, Flora Slosson 1928-

PERSONAL: Born June 21, 1928, in Richmond, Va.; daughter of Preston W. (a professor and author) and Lucy (a teacher and writer; maiden name, Denny) Slosson; married Wilhelm Wuellner (a professor), May 28, 1954; children: Christine, Virginia, Lucy. *Education:* University of Michigan, B.A., 1949, M.A., 1950; Chicago Theological Seminary, B.D., 1954. *Politics:* Independent. *Home:* 1870 Capistrano, Berkeley, Calif. 94707.

CAREER: Ordained United Church of Christ minister, 1954; pastor in Chicago, Ill., 1955-58. *Member:* Order of St. Luke, Spiritual Frontiers Fellowship, Northern California Conference of United Church of Christ.

WRITINGS: *Prayer and the Living Christ*, Abingdon, 1969; *To Pray and to Grow*, Abingdon, 1970; *Release for Trapped Christians*, Abingdon, 1974.

WORK IN PROGRESS: Research on theological theory as it relates to practical life and to spiritual growth.

AVOCATIONAL INTERESTS: History, travel.

* * *

WULF, Helen Harlan 1913-

PERSONAL: Born August 15, 1913, in Chicago, Ill.; daughter of N. Robert (a physician) and Helen (a dietitian; maiden name, Hammel) Harlan; married Hans H. Wulf (a manufacturers sales representative), September 4, 1936; children: Robert, Karin (Mrs. James W. Benson), John, Janet. *Education:* Northwestern University, B.A., 1935; graduate study at University of Chicago, 1935, 1936, and University of Michigan, 1936, 1937; Southern Methodist

University, M.A., 1958. *Politics:* Independent. *Religion:* Episcopalian. *Home:* 9305 Waterview Rd., Dallas, Tex. 75218.

CAREER: Cook County Welfare Department, Chicago, Ill., social worker, 1935-36; J. L. Hudson Co. (department store), Detroit, Mich., in training department, 1937-38; H. H. Wulf Associates, Dallas, Tex., manager of showroom, 1948-70, bookkeeper, 1970—. *Member:* P.E.O. Sisterhood (president of Dallas chapter, 1953-54), Phi Beta Kappa.

WRITINGS: Aphasia: My World Alone, Wayne State University Press, 1973.

WORK IN PROGRESS: Continuing research on aphasia from the viewpoint of the aphasic.

SIDELIGHTS: "My ability to communicate in writing was not affected by aphasia," Helen Wulf told *CA*. "I felt the need to plead for more understanding of all aphasics; I knew it was important for professionals to read the unedited work of one who had had brain damage by stroke . . ."

* * *

WYLLIE, Peter J(ohn) 1930-

PERSONAL: Surname is pronounced like "Wiley"; born February 8, 1930, in London, England; son of George W. and Beatrice (Weaver) Wyllie; married Frances R. Blair (an interior designer), June 9, 1956; children: Andrew, Jean (deceased), Lisa, John. *Education:* University of St. Andrews, B.Sc. (geology and physics), 1952, B.Sc. (geology; first class honors), 1955, Ph.D., 1958. *Residence:* Chicago, Ill. *Office:* Department of Geophysical Sciences, University of Chicago, Chicago, Ill. 60637.

CAREER: British West Greenland Expedition, glaciologist, summer, 1950; British North Greenland Expedition, geologist, 1952-54; University of St. Andrews, St. Andrews, Scotland, assistant lecturer in geology, 1955-56; Pennsylvania State University, University Park, research assistant, 1956-58, assistant professor of geochemistry, 1958-59; University of Leeds, Leeds, England, research fellow in chemistry, 1959-60, lecturer in experimental petrology, 1960-61; Pennsylvania State University, associate professor of petrology, 1961-65, acting head of department of geochemistry and mineralogy, 1962-63; University of Chicago, Chicago, Ill., professor of petrology and geochemistry, 1965—, associate dean of college and of Physical Sciences Division, 1972-73, master of physical sciences in Collegiate Division, 1972-73. Member of International Commission on Experimental Petrology at High Pressures and Temperatures, 1970—.

MEMBER: American Association for the Advancement of Science, American Geophysical Union, Geological Society of America, Mineralogical Society of America (councillor, 1970-72), National Association of Geology Teachers, Association of Earth Science Editors, Geochemical Society (councillor, 1973-76), Mineralogical Society (London). *Awards, honors:* Polar Medal from Queen of England, 1954; award from Mineralogical Society of America, 1965; D.Sc. from University of St. Andrews, 1974.

WRITINGS: (Editor) *Ultramatic and Related Rocks*, Wiley, 1967; *The Dynamic Earth*, Wiley, 1971; *The Way the Earth Works*, Wiley, in press. Editor of "Minerals, Rocks, and Inorganic Materials," a monograph series, Springer-Verlag, 1967—. Managing editor of *Journal of Petrology*, 1965-67; editor of *Journal of Geology*, 1967—.

WORK IN PROGRESS: Introduction to Petrology, for Wiley.

YEZZO, Dominick 1947-

PERSONAL: Born June 21, 1947, in Manhattan, N.Y.; son of Frank and Josephine (Gasparo) Yezzo; married Margaret Winfield Shirk, January 23, 1971. *Education:* Attended Academy of Aeronautics, 1966, and Queens College of the City University of New York, 1969-75. *Home:* 34-45 Murray St., Flushing, N.Y. 11354.

CAREER: Writer. *Military service:* U.S. Army, 1967-69; received Army Commendation, Air Medal, and Vietnamese citation with two overseas stars.

WRITINGS: A G.I.'s Vietnam Diary, F. Watts, 1974. Contributor to *Focus*.

WORK IN PROGRESS: A novel.

SIDELIGHTS: Yezzo's aim is "to bring the written word to an audience who would ordinarily not consider reading."

BIOGRAPHICAL/CRITICAL SOURCES: Focus, December, 1974.

* * *

YORK, Helen 1918-

PERSONAL: Born October 27, 1918, in Braddock, Pa.; daughter of Andrew and Mary (Parish) York. *Education:* Carlow College, B.A., 1941; Los Angeles State College (now California State University), M.A., 1962. *Religion:* Roman Catholic. *Home:* 311 Churchill Rd., Pittsburgh, Pa. 15235. *Agent:* Ann Elmo, 52 Vanderbilt Ave., New York, N.Y. 10017.

CAREER: Public school teacher of English in Pasadena, Calif., 1957-68.

WRITINGS: Malverne Manor (novel), Doubleday, 1974.

WORK IN PROGRESS: Temorra Towers, a suspense novel.

AVOCATIONAL INTERESTS: Travel, particularly in Europe.

* * *

YOUNG, Alison 1922-

PERSONAL: Born June 8, 1922, in Hove, England; daughter of Andrew John (a clergyman and poet) and Janet (Green) Young; married Edward Lowbury (a physician and poet), June 12, 1954; children: Ruth, Pauline, Miriam. *Education:* University of Edinburgh, Mus.Bac., 1943; Royal College of Music, London, G.R.S.M., A.R.C.M., 1944. *Politics:* Moderate Labour. *Religion:* Agnostic. *Home:* 79 Vernon Rd., Birmingham B16 9SQ, England.

CAREER: Edgbaston High School for Girls, Birmingham, England, music teacher, 1967—; pianist, free-lance musician.

WRITINGS: (With husband, Edward Lowbury, and Timothy Salter) *Thomas Campion: Poet, Composer, Physician*, Barnes & Noble, 1970.

WORK IN PROGRESS: A book on pianoforte teaching or technique.

* * *

YOUNG, Billie 1936-
(Penelope Ashe; a joint pseudonym)

PERSONAL: Born June 27, 1936, in Brooklyn, N.Y.; daughter of Albert (a president of a chemical company) and Reda (an artist) Young; married Simeon Paget (a publisher), January 2, 1959; children: Bruce, Richard, Dana,

Laurie, Leif, Kristie. *Education:* Attended Brooklyn College (now of the City University of New York), 1949-51, and New School for Social Research, 1953-54. *Residence:* Port Washington, N.Y. *Office:* Ashley Books, Inc., P.O. Box 768, Port Washington, N.Y. 11050.

CAREER: Have-a-Maid Agency, Inc., Great Neck, N.Y., president, 1957-65; *Suffolk Sun*, Deer Park, N.Y., reporter, 1967-68; Ashley Books, Port Washington, N.Y., president, 1971—. Vice-president of Hampton Agencies Ltd. (employment agency), 1960-65; secretary and treasurer of On Call Telephone Answering Service, 1964-66; newspaper reporter for Cowles Communications, 1967-68; treasurer of Born Blessed Publications, 1973. Public relations director for American Repertory Theatre, 1968; an organizer of North Shore Community Arts Center, 1953; has worked as lecturer, interviewer, and advertising copywriter. *Member:* American Booksellers Association, American Library Association, Publishers Ad Club.

WRITINGS: (Under pseudonym Penelope Ashe, with others *Naked Came the Stranger*, Lyle Stuart, 1969; *The Naked Chef*, Ashley Books, 1971; *Viva la Difference*, Ballantine, 1975. Author of two plays, as yet unproduced.

Work is anthologized in *Extension: An Anthology of Modern Poetry*, edited by H. M. Rosenberg, Idlewild Publishing, 1969. Contributor to *McCall's, Viva, Forum*, and *Penthouse*.

WORK IN PROGRESS: a novel.

SIDELIGHTS: Naked Came the Stranger was revealed, shortly after its publication, to be a hoax, written by twenty-five newspaper reporters, including Billie Young, each of whom contributed a chapter. Engineered by her brother-in-law, Mike McGrady, it was intended to disgust even the people who normally read the racy pulp-style bestsellers being written today. Not surprisingly, despite the tongue-in-cheek style of the authors, the book was a great success. Young has since made a successful writing career in her own name.

She writes: "I love children and animals, live with . . . an afghan hound and a siamese cat. Love to cook, on a gourmet level, consider it a waste of time to cook for less than six, and always prepare enough for eight. I am an avid reader, read anything and everything. . . . Love pretty clothes, the theatre, poetry. I am a romanticist, moody, am married to the only man left in an emasculated world, love people, parties, friends. I love to decorate homes, could probably make a living as a decorator. Have travelled extensively in Jamaica, Mexico, and Cuba (before Castro)."

BIOGRAPHICAL/CRITICAL SOURCES: Library Journal, June 1, 1969; *New York Post*, August 14, 1969; *Newsweek*, August 18, 1969; *Life*, August 22, 1969; *Detroit Free Press*, September 7, 1969.

* * *

YOUNG, Miriam 1913-1974

February 26, 1913—September 12, 1974; American novelist, author of numerous books for children, and a biography of her vaudevillian-parents. Obituaries: *New York Times*, September 13, 1974; *Washington Post*, September 14, 1974; *Time*, September 23, 1974; *Library Journal*, November 15, 1974. (*CA*-37/40).

* * *

YOUNG, Otis E., Jr. 1925-

PERSONAL: Born October 10, 1925, in South Bend, Ind.; son of Otis E. (a professor) and Madge (a teacher; maiden name, Oliver) Young; married Ruth K. Thomas (a music teacher), June 10, 1950; children: Otis E. III, Benjamin T. *Education:* Indiana University, A.B., 1948, M.A., 1949, Ph.D., 1952; State University of Iowa, graduate study, 1949-50; Ohio State University, postdoctoral study, 1959-60. *Agent:* Mrs. Robert Morris, 1332 Denison Circle, Norman, Okla. 73069. *Office:* Department of History, Arizona State University, Tempe, Ariz. 85281.

CAREER: Alpena Community College, Alpena, Mich., instructor in history, 1952-54; Bradley University, Peoria, Ill., assistant professor of history, 1954-59, 1960-63; Arizona State University, Tempe, associate professor, 1963-69, professor of history, 1969—. *Military service:* U.S. Army, 1943-46; became sergeant. U.S. Air Force Reserve, 1948-62; became first lieutenant. *Member:* Council on Abandoned Military Posts (past president of Arizona unit), Phi Alpha Theta, Pi Sigma Alpha, Acacia Fraternity.

WRITINGS: The First Military Escort on the Santa Fe Trail, Arthur Clark, 1952; *The West of Philip St. George Cooke*, Arthur Clark, 1955; *How They Dug the Gold*, Arizona Historical Society, 1967; *Western Mining*, University of Oklahoma Press, 1970; *The Mining Men*, Lowell, 1974. Contributor of about a dozen aritcles to scholarly journals.

WORK IN PROGRESS: Black Powder and Hand Steel: Miners and Machines on the Mineral Frontier, for University of Oklahoma Press; research on American mineral frontiers.

* * *

ZAGORIN, Perez 1920-

PERSONAL: Born May 29, 1920, in Chicago, Ill.; son of Solomon Novitz and Mildred (Ginsburg) Zagorin; married Honore Desmond Sharrer, May 29, 1947; children: Adam. *Education:* University of Chicago, A.B., 1941; Harvard University, A.M., 1947, Ph.D., 1952. *Home:* 4927 River Rd., Scottsville, N.Y. 14546. *Office:* Department of History, University of Rochester, Rochester, N.Y. 14627.

CAREER: Amherst College, Amherst, Mass., instructor in history, 1947-49; Vassar College, Poughkeepsie, N.Y., lecturer, 1951-53; McGill University, Montreal, Quebec, assistant professor, 1955-61, associate professor, 1961-63, professor of history, 1963-65; University of Rochester, Rochester, N.Y., professor of history, 1965—, chairman of department, 1968-69. Senior fellow, Canada Council, 1958-59; faculty research fellow, Social Science Research Council, 1959-60, and 1963; senior research fellow, Folger Shakespeare Library, 1964-65; Amundsen Visiting Professor, University of Pittsburgh, 1964; visiting professor, Johns Hopkins University, 1964-65; member of advisory council of Center for the Study of Parliamentary History, Yale University, 1967—; member of Institute for Advanced Study, 1972-73; William Andrews Clark Memorial Library Professor, University of California, Los Angeles, 1975-76. *Member:* American Historical Association, Royal Historical Association (fellow), Renaissance Society of America, Economic History Society, Conference on British Studies.

WRITINGS: A History of Political Thought in the English Revolution, Routledge & Kegan Paul, 1954, 2nd edition, 1966; *The Court and the Country: The Beginning of the English Revolution*, Atheneum, 1970.

WORK IN PROGRESS: Studies in sixteenth and seventeenth-century history; studies of revolution.

SIDELIGHTS: Lawrence Stone commented that *The*

Court and the Country "is a most erudite work, sparkling with brand-new and telling quotations taken from an extremely wide range of sources; it is well written; and it shows great insight into the workings of revolutionary politics. As a political narrative of the events leading up to the war . . . it is the best we have. . . ." Arnold Beichman further observed that the book "is an important contribution not alone to English history but also to a further understanding of 'revolution.'"

* * *

ZAVIN, Theodora 1922-

PERSONAL: Born January 29, 1922, in New York, N.Y.; daughter of Irving and Lillian (Meyers) Itkowitz; married Benjamin Zavin (a writer), June 17, 1945; children: Jonathan, Daniel. *Education:* Hunter College (now Hunter College of the City University of New York), A.B., 1941; Columbia University, LL.B., 1943. *Home:* 79 West Twelfth St., New York, N.Y. 10011. *Office:* Broadcast Music, Inc., 40 West 57th St., New York, N.Y. 10019.

CAREER: Admitted to the Bar of the City of New York, 1944; Greenbaum, Wolff & Ernst (law firm), New York, N.Y., staff attorney, 1944-50; Boradcast Music, Inc., New York, N.Y., house counsel, 1952-57, assistant vice-president, 1957-63, vice-president, 1964-68, senior vice-president, 1968—. *Member:* American Bar Association, Association of the Bar of the City of New York.

WRITINGS: (With Harriet F. Pilpel) *Your Marriage and the Law*, Rinehart, 1952, revised edition, 1964; (with Pilpel) *Rights and Writers*, Dutton, 1960; (with Freda Stuart) *The Working Wives Cookbook*, Crown, 1963; *Around the World in Twenty Meals*, Aurora Publications, 1972; *The Everybody Bring a Dish Cookbook*, Quadrangle, 1974.

WORK IN PROGRESS: Revised and enlarged edition of *The Working Wives Cookbook*, publication expected in 1975.

* * *

ZAYAS-BAZAN, Eduardo 1935-

PERSONAL: Born November 17, 1935, in Camaguey, Cuba; son of Manuel Eduardo (a longshoreman) and Aida Loret (de Mola) de Zayas-Bazan; married Elena Pedroso (a teacher), December 12, 1959; children: Eddy, Elena. *Education:* University of Havana, student, 1953-56; Universidad Nacional Jose Marti, J.D., 1958; Kansas State Teachers College, M.S., 1966. *Religion:* Roman Catholic. *Home:* 1419 Meadowbrook Dr., Johnson City, Tenn. 37601. *Office:* Department of Languages, East Tennessee State University, Johnson City, Tenn. 37601.

CAREER: Swimming instructor in Camaguey, Cuba, 1958-59; insurance broker and attorney in Camaguey, 1959-60; prisoner in Cuba, 1961-62; U.S. Cuban Refugee Assistance Program, Miami, Fla., social worker, 1962-64; high school Spanish teacher in Plattsmouth, Neb., 1964-65, and Topeka, Kan., 1965-66; Appalachian State University, Boone, N.C., instructor in Spanish, 1966-68; East Tennessee State University, Johnson City, assistant professor, 1968-73, associate professor of Spanish and chairman of department of languages, 1973—, director of three summer-abroad programs in Spain and Mexico. President of People-to-People in Johnson City, 1972—. *Military service:* Cuban Exile Brigade, frogman in "Bay of Pigs" invasion, 1961.

MEMBER: American Association of Teachers of Spanish and Portuguese, Association of Departments of Foreign Languages, National Association for Bilingual Education, National Association of Cuban Lawyers, Southeastern Conference on Latin-American Studies, Sigma Delta Pi.

WRITINGS: (Editor with Anthony G. Lozano) *Del amor a la revolucion: An Intermediate Spanish American Reader* (title means "From Love to Revolution"), Norton, 1975. Contributor to *Hispania, Paris Review, Fitzgerald-Hemingway Annual*, and *Tennessee Teacher*.

WORK IN PROGRESS: A beginner's Spanish reader; research on bilingual education in Dade County, Fla.

* * *

ZELDITCH, Morris, Jr. 1928-

PERSONAL: Born February 29, 1928, in Pittsburgh, Pa.; son of Morris (a social worker) and Anne (a social worker; maiden name, Hankin) Zelditch; married Bernice Osmola (a teacher), June 12, 1950; children: Miriam (Mrs. John Kingman Walter), Steven Morris. *Education:* Oberlin College, B.A., 1951; Harvard University, Ph.D., 1955. *Religion:* Jewish. *Home:* 936 Lathrop Pl., Stanford, Calif. 94305. *Office:* Department of Sociology, Stanford University, Stanford, Calif. 94305.

CAREER: Columbia University, New York, N.Y., assistant professor of sociology, 1955-60, sociologist for College of Physicians and Surgeons, 1958-61; Stanford University, Stanford, Calif., associate professor, 1960-66, professor of sociology, 1966—. Fellow of Center for Advanced Study in the Behavioral Science (Stanford, Calif.), 1968-69. *Military service:* U.S. Army, 1945-47. *Member:* American Sociological Association, Pacific Sociological Association (vice-president, 1967), Phi Beta Kappa. *Awards, honors:* Woodrow Wilson fellow, 1951-52.

WRITINGS: A Basic Course in Sociological Statistics, Holt-Dryden, 1958, 2nd edition (with T. R. Anderson) published as *A Basic Course in Statistics: With Sociological Applications*, Holt, 1968, 3rd edition, 1975; *Types of Formalization in Small Groups Research*, Houghton, 1962; (with Joseph Berger and B. Anderson) *Sociological Theories in Progress*, Houghton, Volume I, 1966, Volume II, 1972. Editor of *American Sociological Review*, 1975—.

WORK IN PROGRESS: An experimental investigation of power, authority, and status.

SIDELIGHTS: Zelditch began as a sculptor, attending art school for eight years. He taught in Italy, 1963, France, 1968, and Great Britain, 1974.

* * *

ZILAHY, Lajos 1891(?)-1974

1891(?)—December 1, 1974; Hungarian-born American novelist and playwright. Obituaries: *New York Times*, December 3, 1974; *AB Bookman's Weekly*, December 16, 1974.

* * *

ZIMMERMAN, Toni Ortner 1941-

PERSONAL: Born March 11, 1941, in Brooklyn, N.Y.; daughter of Melvin (owner of a machine corporation) and Sylvia (a teacher) Ortner; married Stephen Michael Zimmerman (a college professor), May 27, 1962; children: Lisa Michelle. *Education:* Hofstra University, B.A., 1963. *Office:* Department of English, Bronx Community College of the City University of New York, 120 East 184th St., Bronx, N.Y. 10468.

CAREER: Formerly executive secretary at Columbia University, in Graduate School of Journalism, and for Dean of Admissions of Columbia College; Bronx Community College of the City University of New York, Bronx, N.Y., adjunct professor of English, 1971—.

WRITINGS—All poetry: *Woman in Search of Herself*, Know, Inc., 1974; *To an Imaginary Lover*, Morgan Press, 1974; *Entering Another Country*, Basilisk Press, in press; *Stones*, South & West, in press.

WORK IN PROGRESS: Terminal Company, Inc., a collection of short stories about women; three books of poems, *Traveling: A Perspective, Rising from a Fast Embrace*, and *The Day My Mother Caught Me Flying*.

* * *

ZIMMERMAN, William 1936-

PERSONAL: Born in 1936, in Washington, D.C. *Education:* Swarthmore College, B.A. (with honors), 1958; George Washington University, M.A., 1959; Columbia University, Ph.D., 1965. *Home:* 1925 Lorraine Pl., Ann Arbor, Mich. 48104. *Office:* Center for Russian and East European Studies, University of Michigan, Ann Arbor, Mich. 48104.

CAREER: University of Michigan, Ann Arbor, lecturer, 1963-64, assistant professor, 1964-69, associate professor, 1969-74, professor of political science, 1974—, director of Center for Russian and East European Studies, 1972—. Visiting assistant professor at Columbia University, summer, 1966.

MEMBER: Phi Kappa Phi. *Awards, honors:* William Bayard Cutting traveling fellowship, from Columbia University, 1962-63, for study in the Soviet Union and Eastern Europe; research grant from Institute for War and Peace Studies and Russian Institute of Columbia University, summer, 1965; fellowship from Inter-University Committee on Travel Grants, 1966, for study in the Soviet Union; Helen Dwight Reed Award from American Political Science Association, 1966; research grant from Program on International Organization of University of Michigan, summer, 1967, 1968, summer, 1972; Fulbright-Hays grant, 1970, for research in Yugoslavia; Ford Foundation grant, 1972-76, for research on industrialization, mobilization, and mass attitude change in Eastern Europe; Pi Sigma Alpha Award from American Political Science Association, 1974.

WRITINGS: (Contributor) Alexander Dallin and Thomas Larson, editors, *Soviet Politics Since Khrushchev*, Spectrum, 1968; (editor with Harold Jacobson) *The Shaping of Foreign Policy*, Atherton, 1969; *Soviet Perspectives on International Relations: 1956-1967*, Princeton University Press, 1969; (contributor) Erik P. Hoffmann and Frederic J. Fleron, Jr., editors, *The Conduct of Soviet Foreign Policy*, Atherton, 1971; Steven Spiegel and Kenneth N. Waltz, editors, *Conflict in World Politics*, Winthrop, 1971; (contributor) Charles Gati, editor, *Caging the Bear: Containment and the Cold War*, Bobbs-Merrill, 1974. Contributor of about fifteen articles to political science journals, including *Survey*, *American Political Science Review*, *Journal of Conflict Resolution*, *International Organization*, *Journal of International Affairs*, and *Problems of Communism*.

* * *

ZIVKOVIC, Peter D(ragi) 1929-

PERSONAL: Surname is accented on first syllable; born July 10, 1929, in Turtle Creek, Pa.; son of Dragi (a laboratory technician) and Kathryn (Stubrich) Zivkovic; married Dorinda June Stanis (a ceramic artist), June 10, 1955; children: Jeffrey Vaughan, Anthony Joseph, Cassandra Lea. *Education:* Attended Geneva College; University of Illinois, B.S., 1957, M.A., 1959; University of Iowa, M.F.A., 1960. *Politics:* "Anti-Republican." *Religion:* Orthodox. *Home address:* Route 4, Box 577, Fairmont, W.Va. 26554. *Office:* Fairmont State College, Locust Ave., Fairmont, W.Va. 26554.

CAREER: Auburn University, Auburn, Ala., assistant professor of English, 1960-66; Georgia Institute of Technology, Atlanta, assistant professor of English, 1967-69; Fairmont State College, Fairmont, W.Va., associate professor of English, 1969—. Former professional baseball player. *Military service:* U.S. Army, Security Agency, 1951-53; became staff sergeant. *Member:* Modern Language Association of America, South Atlantic Modern Language Association, West Virginia Poetry Society, Georgia Writers Association. *Awards, honors:* West Virginia Poetry Society's Oscar Dubois Award, 1970, for "December Midnights"; Georgia Writers Association first prize for short-short fiction, 1971, for "Henhouse by the Tracks"; and other poetry awards.

WRITINGS: Bezich (novella), New College Press, 1969; *Little Book, Little Book* (poems), Windfall Press, 1974. Contributor of more than two hundred fifty stories, poems, and reviews to more than ninety literary journals.

WORK IN PROGRESS: No Wine of This World, a novel; *Swimming in Condemned Waters*, poems; *The Other Side of Nothing*, poems.

SIDELIGHTS: Zivkovic writes: "I farm on a part-time basis and observe nature full time, on my hundred seventy-two acre property in West Virginia, where there are no 'no anything' signs posted. I ride horses often and believe in pest and photography hunting, but especially in woods-walking, trespassing, etc. I thrive on conversation, reading, picnics, and watching the leaves grow and fall."

* * *

ZUCKERMAN, George 1916-

PERSONAL: Born August 10, 1916, in Brooklyn, N.Y.; son of David (a businessman) and Sarah (Miller) Zuckerman; married Blanche Kleid (a medical secretary), April 13, 1946; children: Gregg, Laurie. *Education:* University of South Carolina, A.B., 1940. *Home:* 853 18th St., Santa Monica, Calif. 90403. *Agent:* Arthur Pine Associates, Inc., 1780 Broadway, New York, N.Y. 10019.

CAREER: Has held various positions as newspaperman, magazine writer, and screenwriter. *Military service:* U.S. Army and U.S. Army Air Forces, 1941-45. *Member:* Writers Guild of America, West (member of council), Authors League.

WRITINGS: The Last Flapper, Little, Brown, 1969; *Farewell, Frank Merriwell*, Dutton, 1973; *The Potato Peelers*, Dodd, 1974. Also author of sixteen screenplays. Contributor of novelettes, short stories, and articles to *Cosmopolitan*, *Collier's*, and numerous other periodicals.

WORK IN PROGRESS: An untitled novel about the lost Eldorado of Hollywood.

SIDELIGHTS: Zuckerman writes: "*The Last Flapper* was based on my friendship with Zelda Fitzgerald in Montgomery, Ala. during the war. My two best films were "The Tarnished Angels" (based on William Faulkner's *Py-*

lon—which he highly praised) and "Written on the Wind" (Robert Wilder's novel) which won an Academy Award for Dorothy Malone."

BIOGRAPHICAL/CRITICAL SOURCES: Richard Corliss, editor, *The Hollywood Screenwriter*, Avon, 1972.

* * *

ZWART, Pieter (Hendrik) 1938-

PERSONAL: Surname rhymes with "naught"; born September 8, 1938, in Cape Town, South Africa; son of Wiebe Jilling (a Dutch consul) and Mieke (a journalist; maiden name, Siegers) Zwart; married Christine Lee (a journalist), July 14, 1962; children: Christiaan, Ophelia, Miranda. *Education:* University of Natal, B.A., 1958; Oxford University, M.A., 1961. *Home:* 11 Northchurch Rd., London N14EB, England. *Agent:* Murray Pollinger, 11 Longacre, London W.C.2, England. *Office: Times*, New Printing House Sq., London WC1X 8E2, England.

CAREER: Daily Mirror, Manchester, England, reporter, 1962-64; *Evening Standard*, London, England, leader writer, 1964-65; *Times*, London, England, obituarist and writer of special reports, 1966—.

WRITINGS: Islington: A History and Guide, Sidgwick & Jackson, 1973.

CONTEMPORARY AUTHORS

INDEX (Volumes 1—56)

Includes references to Contemporary Literary Criticism, Volumes 1—4.

A

C

E

F

G

I

K

L

M

N

O

P

Q

R

S

U

V

W

X

Y

Z